W9-BIM-834

1984

BRITANNICA
BOOK OF THE YEAR

1984

BRITANNICA BOOK OF THE YEAR

ENCYCLOPÆDIA BRITANNICA, INC.

CHICAGO

AUCKLAND, GENEVA, LONDON, MANILA, PARIS, ROME, SEOUL, SYDNEY, TOKYO, TORONTO

Library of Congress Catalog Card Number: 38-12082
International Standard Book Number: 0-85229-417-4
International Standard Serial Number: 0068-1156

Printed in U.S.A.

THE UNIVERSITY OF CHICAGO

The Britannica Book of the Year is published with the editorial advice of the faculties of the University of Chicago.

CONTENTS

Number-and-letter combinations appearing in brackets at the end of some articles refer to the *Propædia* volume of *Encyclopædia Britannica*; e.g., after Health and Disease: Dentistry, [422.E.1.a.ii] refers to Propædia Part Four, Division II, Section 2 (422), Topic E, subtopic 1.a.ii (Teeth and gums). There the reader finds references to relevant material in various Macropædia volumes.

Frontispiece photo credits (page 149): (left, from top to bottom) UPI; Hoagland—Gamma/Liaison; Wide World; (right, from top to bottom) Francis Dias—Sygma; National Magazine—Sygma; Azar—Gamma/Liaison

AT THE CORE OF THE PROBLEM OF PEACE— ISRAEL AND THE WEST BANK: TWO VIEWS

by Shlomo Avineri and Shmuel Schnitzer

Don't Annex:

Shlomo Avineri

Israel should be ready to give up control of the West Bank and Gaza and limit its demands to adequate security arrangements. *For an opposite view, see Shmuel Schnitzer on page 14.*

The political debate in Israel about the future of the West Bank and Gaza has been going on since 1967, when Israel gained control of these areas during the Six-Day War. With the return of the much larger area of Sinai to Egypt following the Camp David accords of 1978, the debate about the West Bank and Gaza became even more heated. These regions, being part of the historical Land of Israel, raise not only strategic and security issues but also deeply felt questions of historical identity, religious associations, and traditional symbolism.

Two Schools of Thought. To characterize this debate as one between "hawks" and "doves" greatly oversimplifies the issue, nor does it do justice to the complexity of the problems involved. While there are many nuances in the articulation of the political views expressed in connection with the debate about the West Bank and Gaza, one may roughly classify them under two headings. The one school, roughly representing the position of parties comprising the Likud bloc and its partners, I would like to call the "territorial" school; the opposite view, mainly represented by the Labour Party, I would call the "sociological" school.

Both schools view the issue of the future of the West Bank and Gaza on a much broader canvas than that of the future of an area or its population. For both schools of thought, the debate is about the very nature of Israel—the kind of society it will become, its principal goals, the hierarchical order of its value system. In short, it is a debate about the soul of the nation and is justly viewed as the most important issue faced by the Jewish state since its inception in 1948.

Eretz Israel. The *territorial* school argues that the most important criterion for Israeli decision making should be the maximization of Jewish control over as much territory of historical Eretz Israel as possible. According to this school, the whole Land of Israel is—and should be—the homeland of the Jewish people. If the Zionist movement accepted the 1947 UN resolution calling for partition of the British Mandate of Palestine, this acceptance should be

DAVID RUBINGER/TIME MAGAZINE

viewed as a temporary measure only, to be revised if and when conditions permit.

According to the territorial school, such an occasion presented itself to Israel in 1967. The West Bank—Judaea and Samaria in Hebrew—as well as Gaza are an inseparable part of the historic Jewish homeland. Zionism, and the State of Israel, should do their utmost to guarantee that these areas will never again come under another sovereignty or jurisdiction. In this interpretation of Zionism, the more territory of historical Eretz Israel is being controlled by the Jewish state, the more Jewish and the more Zionist that state is going to be. Therefore, Jewish settlements should be put up in these areas, both to demonstrate their inseparability from Israel within its pre-1967 borders and to make a reversion to those pre-1967 borders either impossible or extremely difficult.

It should be added that this "territorial" view did not prevent Prime Minister Menachem Begin from giving up all of Sinai to Egypt at Camp David, nor did it prevent his government from uprooting the Jewish settlers from Yamit and other settlements in northeastern Sinai in the course of implementing the peace treaty. The reason for this was that Sinai—unlike Judaea and Samaria—is not considered part of the historical Land of Israel and hence could be traded off for the benefits of a peace treaty. The relationship to the West Bank and Gaza, on the other hand, is viewed by the territorial school as absolute and Jewish rights with regard to it as inalienable.

Quantity and Quality. The other school of thought, the *sociological* school, views the decision to be taken by Israel against a different set of criteria. It does not deny Israel's historical links to Judaea and Samaria; after all, these areas were the historical cradle of the Israelite nation. But the main argument of the sociological school is that, when Israel comes to decide on and negotiate about its borders, it should focus not on the quantity of territory under its control but on the quality of the society Israel would become.

According to the sociological school, if Israel ultimately absorbs the West Bank and Gaza, it will add 1.2 million Arab Palestinians to its population. Including the Arabs already living in Israel proper, this means that the population of Israel in its expanded borders would consist of 60% Jews and 40% Arabs. Such a country would be less Jewish, and less Zionist, than an Israel with more limited territory but with a clear 85% Jewish majority. More territory means upsetting the demographic and ethnic balance of the Jewish state and thus spells catastrophe for the Zionist dream of a Jewish commonwealth.

In an Israel 40% of whose population was Arab, the sociological school sees an utter perversion of the Zionist dream. In such a society, the large Arab minority would tend to become the proletarian class of a predominantly Jewish middle-class majority; the whole social vision of Zionism as a social revolution would disappear. Moreover, ultimately Israel would be faced with the problem of political rights for such a large Arab minority. If—as a democratic country, committed to equal rights—it were to grant this Arab minority equal political rights, Israel would become virtually a binational state, with 40% of its electorate, parliament, civil service, and army consisting of Arabs. This would be a far cry from the Zionist vision. Alternatively, if such an Arab minority were denied equal rights, Israel would become another South Africa. If one considers that the Arab birthrate is higher than the Jewish one, the large Arab minority could even become a majority in the not too distant future.

It is because of these considerations that the sociological school prefers a smaller Israel, roughly within the 1967 borders (yet preserving the unity of Jerusalem), to a larger Israel that could easily become the undoing of the Jewish state through overextension and overreaching.

SVEN NACKSTRAND—GAMMA/LIAISON

Israeli settlements on the West Bank are not huts but rather modern urban developments. Shown on opposite page is Maʿale Adumim, east of Jerusalem. At left, some 2,000 members of Israel's Peace Now movement demonstrated in Hebron in July to protest the Israeli government's policy of settlements on the West Bank.

KENNETH NEBENZAHL, INC.

Confusion and disputes about boundaries in the Middle East are as old as the human imprint on the land. This map and the one on page 11 are a pair drawn in Paris in 1646. This one shows the "Modern Holy Land" at that date, when it was part of the Ottoman Empire. It includes, from north to south, Galilee, Samaria (Samarie), and Judaea (Iudee). Administrative divisions were principalities of one emir (*Hemir*) or another and the Sanjak (*Sangiac*) of Jerusalem. To the east lies part of the Royaume des Arabes (Kingdom of the Arabs).

Finding a Partner. The following remarks are intended to spell out some of the options that follow from acceptance of the sociological argument. I personally believe that the territorial philosophy of the Likud bloc poses grave dangers to Israel and to Zionism. It not only denies the right of 1.2 million Palestinians not to be ruled by a government alien to them, it also threatens the Zionist achievements and undermines the ideas of social and national justice inherent in Zionism. Israel should be ready to give up control of the West Bank and Gaza and limit its demands to adequate security arrangements in providing some measure of assurance that these areas would not be used as a springboard for military or terroristic attacks. These security considerations could be met without staking a claim for sovereignty or control over the West Bank and Gaza and without depriving their Arab Palestinian population of the right to rule themselves.

The main question facing anyone ready to consider an Israeli withdrawal from the West Bank hinges, ultimately, on the question of finding an adequate partner for negotiations and peacemaking. This is not a mere abstract question of rights; it is a concrete question of politics and diplomacy as a means of realizing claims of such rights. Discussions of the Middle East sometimes overlook the fact that the main problems are not territorial issues but questions of legitimacy. While the present Israeli occupation of the West Bank and Gaza certainly exacerbates the Arab-Israeli conflict, that is not its origin or primary cause. Its cause lies in the Arab refusal to accept any form of Jewish sovereignty over any part of Palestine. Until 1977 this Arab refusal was universal and total. In 1977 Anwar as-Sadat of Egypt dramatically changed the whole political climate in the Middle East by signifying his readiness to accept the legitimacy of Israel, provided it retreated to pre-1967 lines. Sadat and Egypt were ostracized by the rest of the Arab world not because of Arab unhappiness about any particular detail of Camp David but because of Sadat's very acceptance of Israel's existence and legitimacy. Once its legitimacy was accepted by Egypt, Israel was able and willing to make the territorial concessions that led to Camp David and to the evacuation of Sinai and its return to Egyptian sovereignty.

The same problems arise over the West Bank and Gaza: With whom should Israel negotiate? Who should be seen as a legitimate spokesman for the Palestinians? What should be the political organization of the West Bank and Gaza after Israel leaves?

To these questions there are basically two sets of answers. One would have the West Bank and Gaza constitute an independent Palestinian state, either headed by the Palestine Liberation Organization (PLO) or under a more moderate leadership. The other would look to Jordan and would prefer a solution linking the West Bank and the East Bank of the Jordan into some sort of political entity. Such an entity might be federal, confederal, or unitary, but the main argument of the second school is that the two banks of the Jordan are inseparable, economically as well as politically.

KENNETH NEBENZAHL, INC.

This 1646 French map (*see* also page 10) depicts Israel in 1016 BC, in its golden age, during the reign of King Solomon. It is divided into 12 eparchies or provinces reflecting Solomon's total administrative reorganization of the land. Many of the place-names reflect the 12 Tribes of Israel—Reuben, Simeon, Judah, Issachar, Zebulun, Gad, Asher, Dan, Naphtali, Benjamin, Manasseh, and Ephraim; the 10 northernmost were variously assimilated and dispersed after their conquest by the Assyrians in c. 721 BC.

A Destabilizing Influence. I would like to argue in favour of the second set of answers, the so-called Jordanian option. The reason I think the establishment of an independent Palestinian state on the West Bank and in Gaza is the least satisfactory solution does not stem from any fear for the future of Israel. A West Bank and Gaza state, even if it were unfriendly to Israel, would not be a "mortal danger to Israel," as former prime minister Begin sometimes called it. But it would not be an adequate solution to the Palestinian problem; it would be a basically destabilizing element in the Middle East, and it would not become a foundation for a lasting peace between Israel and the Palestinians. The reasons why a West Bank and Gaza state is viewed as unsatisfactory by myself—and by many in Israel who would like to see an Israeli withdrawal—are many and complex. Let me enumerate a few of them.

First, the 1.2 million Palestinians in the West Bank and Gaza are less than one-third of the Palestinian people. There are about 600,000 Palestinians who still live in refugee camps in Lebanon, Syria, and Jordan east of the river. If a true solution to the problem is to be found, these people must be settled on a permanent basis somewhere within the historical boundaries of Palestine. A West Bank/Gaza state would be so small, overpopulated, and basically poor that these refugees could not settle within its boundaries. The West Bank has been an area of emigration for the last four decades, and it could hardly absorb a significant number of refugees for resettlement. It has neither the arable land nor the resources to support such a massive settlement effort. The consequence would be that the refugees would continue to vegetate in the festering camps in Lebanon and Syria, a continuous focus for the growth of resentment and terrorism, an unabated source for destabilization. The refugees have a right to be resettled, for both political and humanitarian reasons. A West Bank/Gaza state would be unable to do anything for them, and their problem would continue to exist, together with the problems of human misery and political instability associated with it.

If, on the other hand, a joint West Bank-East Bank solution were sought, the East Bank—which is ten times as large as the West Bank—could become the area of refugee resettlement. Because it is also part of historical Palestine, the East Bank is not alien country for the Palestinian refugees, nor is its population, since 60% of the people on the East Bank of the Jordan are of Palestinian origin.

This leads us to the second consideration suggesting that a West Bank/Gaza state would not solve the Palestinian issue. Of the population of the East Bank, about one million are Palestinians, and they too have a right to be part and parcel of a Palestinian homeland. A West Bank/Gaza Palestinian state would leave them outside such a Palestinian entity and would create deep friction between the two "Palestinian" states, one on the West Bank and another in Jordan. Family connections, and the common historical past of the two banks of the Jordan, would further exacerbate the problem.

Last but not least, even those Israelis who are

ALAIN MINGAM—GAMMA/LIAISON

On April 25, 1982, Israel formally returned the Sinai Peninsula to Egypt. The Egyptians present broke out their flag and celebratory banners and posters.

ready to give up the West Bank and Gaza realize that these areas could become bases for anti-Israel operations and insist on some guarantees that this would not happen. One way of taking care of such legitimate Israeli concerns would be demilitarization of the West Bank and Gaza. Now, if the West Bank and Gaza were to become a separate, independent state, this would mean insisting that the whole territory of this new state, the symbol and epitome of Palestinian sovereignty and self-determination, become demilitarized. This is a demand that no state would find acceptable, and it may justifiably be viewed as oppressive and even obscene. If, however, a joint West Bank-East Bank solution were to be contemplated, demilitarization of its western province, bordering on Israel and comprising less than 10% of its overall territory, might be far more acceptable. After all, the Camp David accords stipulate a similar demilitarization of an area a few dozen miles deep, running all along the Israeli border in Sinai.

While an independent Palestinian West Bank/Gaza state would not automatically become a Soviet satellite or immediately join the camp of the Arab radicals, the dangers that it could be subverted relatively easily should be taken seriously. Unable to solve the refugee problem, landlocked between Israel and Jordan, lacking administrative and political machinery, and saddled with a history of rival terrorist factions within the Palestinian organizations abroad, such a state would not have a rosy chance for peaceful development. An association with Jordan, with its relatively well-ordered political structure and—given Arab realities—not too-oppressive bureaucracy, with its economic base and outlet to the sea and other Arab countries—such a joint West Bank-East Bank entity would have a much better chance for stable and peaceful development.

The Jordanian Option. In short, the Jordanian solution seems to meet Israel's minimal legitimate security claims as well as to provide the Palestinians with a decent and honorable solution. They would again be ruled by themselves and could offer their refugee brethren a constructive solution within a Palestinian entity, thus laying the foundation for a relationship of mutual respect with Israel.

The present Jordanian administration is certainly interested in reasserting its rights on the West Bank, given the right conditions. Even after more than 15 years of Israeli occupation, Jordan continues to maintain the Jordanian citizenship of Arab West Bank residents and even selectively grants it to Gaza residents (who before 1967 were under Egyptian military administration). It continues to pay the salaries of public servants and teachers on the West Bank, even if they draw another salary from the Israeli military authorities. It continues to subsidize the Arab municipalities on the West Bank and offers loans and grants to various organizations there. And after the defeat of the PLO in Beirut, it tried in the spring of 1983 to get a green light from Yasir Arafat, the head of the PLO, to join the Reagan Plan, which is basically premised on lines similar to those advocated here from an Israeli perspective.

The PLO, whether riding high as it did before the Lebanon war or splintered and harassed as it is now, cannot become a viable partner for negotiations. Supported by a broad spectrum of Arab countries, from Saudi Arabia to Libya, from Iraq to Egypt, it has to operate on the basis of a broad consensus, and in the Arab world such a consensus, unfortunately, can be only a negative one. When such a consensus breaks down—as it did during the recent Palestinian bloody fratricide in Tripoli in Lebanon—the PLO ceases to be an effective and coherent organization.

In either case it does not represent an adequate vehicle for meaningful negotiations with Israel.

Israel should reach out to those Palestinians who would be ready to negotiate their future through Jordan. The present government in Israel is not ready to negotiate sovereignty over Judaea, Samaria, and Gaza; its version of autonomy is premised on Israeli control, massive Jewish settlement in the area, and ultimate incorporation into Israel. But another government in Israel is possible, and this should be the policy it follows.

Such a Jordanian option still leaves a number of difficult issues to resolve. The most intractable is Jerusalem. No Israeli government can be imagined that would give up the unification of Jerusalem, and no Jordanian-Palestinian coalition can be expected to cede East Jerusalem explicitly to Israeli sovereignty. So Jerusalem—like Berlin in the negotiations that led to the normalization of relations between East and West Germany—should be the last item on the agenda, and agreements should be found on the other issues while an agreement to disagree about Jerusalem prevailed for the time being. Once the other outstanding issues between Israel and a Jordanian-Palestinian entity were worked out and had proved practicable, there is a reasonable chance that positions on Jerusalem might eventually soften on both sides. A more reasonable attitude on the part of all concerned could then lead to a more constructive and acceptable solution.

Another issue is that of the Jewish settlements on the West Bank, where about 30,000 Jews now reside. This is certainly not an easy problem. But for all the differences between the West Bank situation—with its holy sites and historical associations—and that of the Sinai settlements, it is a fact that the settlements were not, ultimately, an insurmountable obstacle to the Camp David agreement.

Some of the settlers would certainly leave once it became clear that the area would not remain under Israeli control. Others might have to be lured away from their newly acquired homes by adequate—and sometimes more than adequate—compensation, as was the case in Yamit. Still others might decide to stay, even under Arab sovereignty, and though their number might not be large, it should be emphasized that there is no reason why, under conditions of peace, a number of Jews should not live in an Arab-controlled West Bank. There are about half a million Arabs in Israel proper, so why does it have to be assumed that a small number of Jews would not be allowed to live in an Arab country, if they so wish? Finally, some of the settlers would have to be forcibly evacuated. Again, this happened in Yamit, under a Begin-Sharon government. We deal here with a difficult problem, but the settlers present a far from

In accordance with the agreement with Egypt that no Israeli settlers would remain in the Sinai, the Israeli Army leveled the town of Yamit. Those residents who refused to leave were sprayed with carbonic foam (left), and those who still refused were caged until the bulldozers had completed their work.

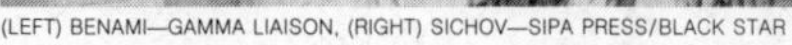

(LEFT) BENAMI—GAMMA LIAISON, (RIGHT) SICHOV—SIPA PRESS/BLACK STAR

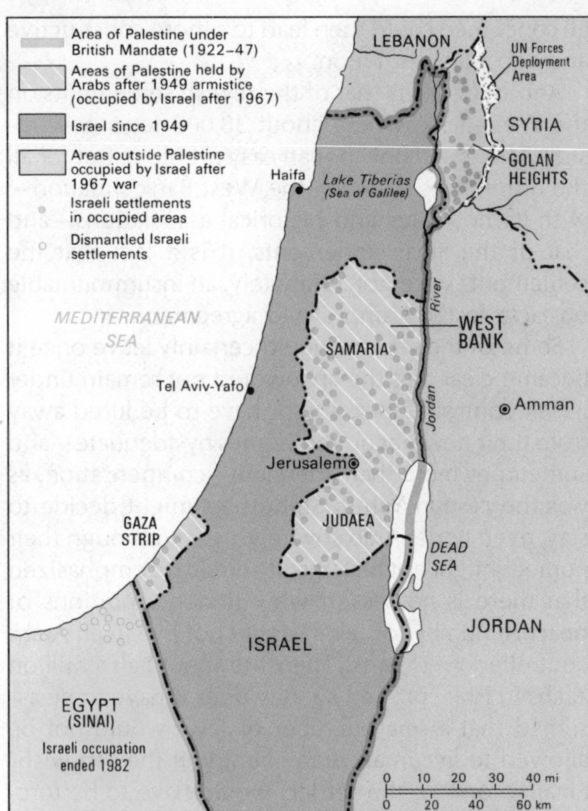

Location of Israeli settlements in occupied territories are shown above. Those in the Sinai were razed and the peninsula was returned to Egypt in 1982. There are settlements in the West Bank and Gaza Strip and in Syria's Golan Heights.

uniform population, and certainly the very existence of these settlements, difficult as they may make the negotiations, should not prevent an honest effort by both sides to try and reach an agreement.

Only the United States, with the influence it possesses vis-à-vis Israelis and Arabs alike (and its relative dependence, in internal politics as well as international economics, on groups friendly to both sides), can help to move both parties to an eventual understanding. As in the case of the Israeli-Egyptian negotiations, the decision has to be taken by the local powers themselves, but the U.S. should be ready to make itself, its diplomacy, and its resources available in the search for a solution that provides freedom and justice for both sides, without satisfying the maximum claims of either. Only such a solution, based on mutual compromise, can prove both acceptable and workable.

Shlomo Avineri is professor of political science at Hebrew University of Jerusalem and is presently on leave as a fellow at the Woodrow Wilson Center in Washington, D.C. He is the author of (among others) The Social and Political Thought of Karl Marx *and* The Making of Modern Zionism *and a member of Israel's Labour Party; in 1976–77 he was director general of Israel's Ministry of Foreign Affairs.*

Annex:

Shmuel Schnitzer

The same Arab incentive to wipe Israel off the map would exist in the future should Israel return to its previous borders. *For an opposite view, see Shlomo Avineri on page 8.*

Armed conflicts have been terminated by a variety of temporary agreements, including separation of forces, truces, cease-fires, and similar arrangements, that—while never superseded by peace treaties—proved as effective as the most formal and binding instruments of peace. The elaborate system of treaties that concluded World War I did not prevent—and perhaps even triggered—the renewed outbreak of hostilities in Europe 21 years later, while the lack of similar conventional arrangements to terminate World War II has not endangered peace in Europe over a period almost twice as long. Obviously, it is the intention that counts, not the form and contents of the official documents.

In the conflict between Israel and the Arab nations that, formally at least, has been going on since 1948, every known instrument of pacification has been tried, ranging from local truces negotiated through the good offices of UN observers to a peace treaty countersigned by a U.S. president. Since all these measures have failed to lay firm foundations for comprehensive peace and genuine coexistence in the Middle East, there is a tendency to pass judgment on the warring parties; more often than not Israel is blamed for refusing to reestablish the pre-1967 situation and boundaries. To the half-informed onlooker, the Arab claim for the return of the territories lost in the war of 1967 seems more reasonable than the Israeli assertion that the pre-1967 borderlines caused the war and that an aggressor is not entitled to reimbursement. But the question needs further investigation. The intentions of the warring nations should be scrutinized carefully and their behaviour examined before apportioning blame or rushing the adversaries into precipitate agreements that will not stand the test of time.

The Right to Exist. Observers in the West do not always realize that the Arab-Israeli war differs in many ways from the conventional pattern of warfare between nations. Most wars are triggered by territorial or economic conflicts of interest, actual or alleged infringements of minority rights, competing religions or ideologies, or similar causes. Consequently, they can be settled by redressing wrongs or compromising on trade controversies or overthrowing the offending regime and establishing a more acceptable government. Among contemporary wars, few instances can be cited in which a nation contested the very right of its opponent to exist as a sovereign entity. One must go back to World War II to find cases of warring powers trying to obliterate established states.

The Arab war against Israel, initiated on the day the Jewish state proclaimed its independence, was motivated by refusal to recognize the young state's right of existence. The principal war aim was to wipe out this newly established geopolitical unit. To many Arabs this still is the goal. Assurances to the contrary are habitually given by Western statesmen who interpret Arab intentions. The Arab leaders tend to be more cautious. Arab spokesmen considered to be paragons of moderation painstakingly avoid any explicit reference to Israel's right of existence. Most Arab leaders still turn down any suggestion that they meet Israeli statesmen face to face, the notable exceptions being Egypt, Lebanon, and Jordan (the latter consents to secret meetings only). Many Israelis do not trust vague hints emitted by peace protagonists who ostentatiously walk out of any international meeting hall where an Israeli representative is about to speak.

Roadblocks to Peace. Most wars are declared, waged, and terminated by governments. While popular resistance may occasionally continue for a while, the power of the government to conclude peace is taken for granted. The Israeli-Arab war has been unique from this aspect as well. Since the Israeli War of Independence (1948–49), hostilities that involved Arab governments have been of short duration. The Sinai campaign of 1956 lasted 3 or 4 days; the 1967 war was over in 6 days; the October war of 1973 went on for 19 days. In addition, there were periods of intermittent shelling and border skirmishes and Israeli reprisal raids involving regular forces. Between the outbursts of official warfare, however, Arab irregulars maintained constant harassment, causing extensive damage and many casualties. UN observers have habitually absolved the Arab governments of any blame or responsibility for the behaviour of irregular forces operating from their territories. Israel's claim that these governments not only tolerated hostile operations by these forces but actually assisted them and often even organized them has been rejected repeatedly by the UN Security Council.

The question of whether these governments will have authority over irregular forces and, particularly, over the Palestine Liberation Organization once a peace treaty is signed looms large in Israeli doubts and anxieties. It is a gnawing worry based on experience, as well as the knowledge that the PLO is diversified enough to produce splinter groups for all purposes, ready to disavow any agreement and undermine it by the use of terror.

An additional factor tends to make peace efforts risky. In the West a continuous binding commitment to international treaties and obligations is more or less taken for granted, even after dramatic changes of governments and policies. The Arab countries take a different view. Political upheavals in the Middle East are frequent and violent. In most Arab countries they are the only practical way of changing governments and deposing leaders, since free elections are nonexistent. When a more radical regime takes over, it often denounces or inactivates treaties that were signed by its predecessors, particularly when a change in foreign policy and big-power orientation is involved. It is easy to imagine the fate of an American-made Arab-Israeli peace if power on the Arab side shifted to pro-Soviet radicals, and the countries that are most often mentioned as possibilities, as far as peace with Israel is concerned, happen to be pro-Western monarchies threatened by radical subversion.

Finally, it should be remembered that armed conflicts having a religious background and motivation are sometimes irreconcilable. Hindus and Muslims in India, Roman Catholics and Protestants in Northern Ireland, and Iraqi Sunnis and Irani Shiʿah have been fighting each other with ferocious fanaticism. The Arab-Israeli war is over territory but also over shrines and a holy city. All the classic accusations against Jews have been mustered in the battle of words that accompanies the battle of guns. Occasionally the Arabs have threatened to proclaim jihad or holy war against the unbelievers, making it the duty of every Muslim in the world to join the fight against Israel and its supporters.

It is a deep popular hatred, goaded by the Muslim clergy, that peacemakers will have to face and overcome. So intense is this animosity that two Arab leaders who favoured peace with Israel, King Abdullah of Jordan and President Sadat of Egypt, paid for their moderation with their lives.

The Territorial Dilemma. The conclusions are obvious. The basic conditions for a genuine, durable peace are popular recognition of Israel as a fact of life and universal Arab acceptance of the necessity of maintaining normal relations with it. Official willingness to conclude peace would be most welcome, of course, but it would constitute a rather shaky foundation for peace as long as popular intransigence remained.

In any case, Israel would have to insist that, even after the signing of a peace treaty, it remain as strong

---

Shmuel Schnitzer is editor and a founder of Israel's largest-circulation newspaper, the evening daily Maʿariv *of Tel Aviv. He is the author of* African Adventures *and* Aliyah Picturebook *and the translator of many books from English, French, Dutch, and German into Hebrew.*

militarily as it is today. Any weakening of its military posture would encourage the Arab extremists to try to reverse the process. Two generally accepted assumptions would seem to be fraught with danger: one is that after making peace Israel would not have to spend the huge amounts of money it now earmarks for the acquisition of modern military equipment; the other is that it would be able to give up the territories it now occupies as a protection against sudden attack. Peace is not a magic formula making war impossible. It must be backed up by measures making war a risky and costly undertaking.

Israel's pre-1967 frontiers were delineated in battle. They followed, with minor changes, the frontlines of 1948–49. The war for independence, forced on an Jewish population of 650,000 by the regular armies of six Arab nations, left the greater part of the hilly regions of the country in Arab hands. It also created Israel's narrow waist, an area some 30 km (20 mi) north of Tel Aviv where the width of the country does not exceed 16 km (10 mi). The fact that even short-range artillery shells could reach Israel's largest city and the seeming possibility that tanks could roll down the hills and reach the shore in minutes constituted a mighty incentive for bellicose Arabs. I believe that this probably was the decisive reason for King Hussein's decision, in 1967, to join Egypt in its attempt to wipe Israel off the map. The same kind of incentive would exist in the future should Israel agree on a return to its previous borders.

This, then, is Israel's dilemma. If it withdraws to its former borders in order to allay Arab suspicions, it may revive the old Arab dream of driving the Jews into the sea. If it sticks to its present borders, it may lend credibility to the Arab contention that Israel wants expansion, not peace. In the eyes of many Israelis, the second option entails the lesser risk.

Arab suspicions are not the result of Israel's occupation of the so-called West Bank. Long before the 1967 war, Arab spokesmen used to cite as proof of Israel's territorial ambitions a map allegedly displayed in the Israeli Knesset building, showing a Jewish state extending from the Nile to the Euphrates. Needless to say, the map never existed, but such suspicions cannot be laid to rest by facts. The Arabs must be shown that, come what may, they will never be able to wipe Israel off the map. Israel must be strong in peace as in war if it wants to survive.

The Palestinian Problem. There is a growing realization in Israel that no enduring peace can be achieved without a radical solution of the Palestinian problem. Furthermore, the Palestinian problem concerns not only the political future of the areas commonly designated the West Bank (or, to Israelis, Judaea and Samaria) and the Gaza Strip but also the fate of the Palestinian diaspora. According to claims put forward by the PLO (they may be somewhat exaggerated), there are close to four million Palestinians living today. Fewer than one-third, or 1.2 million, live in Judaea, Samaria, and Gaza. Some

At left, an Israeli soldier oversees a column of Egyptian prisoners during the Yom Kippur war of 1973. Below, one of eight Palestinian terrorists appears on the balcony of the Israeli quarters in Munich, West Germany, during the Olympic Games in 1972. Eleven members of the Israeli Olympic team were killed and five terrorists were slain by police.

LAURENT MAOUS—GAMMA/LIAISON

Thousands of Palestinians are sheltered in refugee camps in Jordan like this one, known as the Schneiler camp.

690,000 are Israeli Arabs. The remainder are scattered through various Middle Eastern countries, some in refugee camps, others as temporary residents and foreign workers in Saudi Arabia, Kuwait, and the Gulf emirates. Permanent homes must be found for hundreds of thousands of them, and the Palestinians in Lebanon, who are unwanted there and live in constant fear, are in urgent need of resettlement. The idea of trying to absorb them in Judaea and Samaria is absurd.

Most people do not realize how small the disputed area is. Israel within its pre-1967 borders comprises about 20,700 sq km (8,000 sq mi). The West Bank and the Gaza Strip have an area of 6,257 sq km (2,416 sq mi). With a population of 1.2 million, it is already one of the most densely populated areas of the world. Considering that there is little or no industry, that the country is hilly and partly arid, and that there is very little scope for large-scale agricultural development, one should consider the West Bank overpopulated even now. As a matter of fact, a sizable part of its labour force is migrant. Some 80,000 are employed in Israel, thousands work in Jordan, and additional thousands leave their homes for months or years to find jobs in the rich oil-producing states. The money they send home is the mainstay of the West Bank's economy.

The diaspora comprises the more militant elements of the Palestinian population. In their political program, the idea of the Return plays a very important part. It is the dream of the refugees and the central motive of Palestinian education. When they speak of returning, the refugees do not have in mind the hills of Judaea and Samaria. They think of Jaffa, Haifa, Ramla, and the clusters of villages they left in 1948, hoping that within days or weeks they would be able to return with the victorious Arab armies. The dream of destroying Israel and scattering its Jewish population still survives. But suppose the refugees could be persuaded to relinquish their dream of returning to Jaffa and Haifa, where could they go? Surely not to the tiny, overpopulated area of the West Bank and the Gaza Strip, which can hardly support the present population.

Anyone who thinks realistically must realize that granting some form of self-determination to the population of Judaea, Samaria, and Gaza leaves the crux of the problem unsolved. The plight of the refugees will not go away; their bitterness and pent-up hate will not dissolve; their effect on the world's conscience will not decrease. Are we then to witness a second phase of the Palestinian struggle, in which the hundreds of thousands to whom the establishment of a Palestinian homeland will bring no relief resume the fight against Israel? And will they then be able to use the territory of the Palestinian homeland as a base for their operations? This is the reasoning behind Israel's almost unanimous refusal to consider the establishment of a Palestinian state.

Labour's Plan. To forestall such a possibility, the Israeli Labour Party conceived a plan that has become known as the Jordanian option. It provides for a substantial Israeli withdrawal, with the condition that the ceded territory be returned to the Hashemite Kingdom of Jordan, which exercised control over the West Bank prior to 1967. The returned areas would be demilitarized. The Israeli Army would remain in its present positions along the Jordan Valley, where Labour governments established a string of Jewish settlements.

The idea is that Jordan would then be saddled with the Palestinian problem. U.S. Pres. Ronald Reagan endorsed the concept in his speech of Sept. 1, 1982, including it in his so-called peace plan. Nevertheless, its chances of ever being put to the test are rather slim. Hussein has yet to agree to the contin-

ED GAMBLE © THE FLORIDA TIMES-UNION

"You know, of course, the penalty for mutiny?"

ued presence of Israeli troops in the Jordan Valley. He would also have to undertake never to grant the Palestinians the complete sovereignty they crave. He would have to agree to crush any attempt by Palestinian terrorists to continue their war against Israel from territory under his control. In carrying out these provisions, he would have to withstand international pressure, and he would be drawn into conflict with most of the Arab states. What benefits could he reap in return for such a commitment?

The Israeli Labour Party expects Jordan not only to carry the burden of the Palestinians but also to relinquish Jerusalem. Ever since the city was reunited in 1967, all major political parties in Israel have opposed any thought of dividing it again or agreeing to Arab participation in ruling it. Supporters of the Jordanian option avoid the issue, knowing quite well that Israeli public opinion will reject any compromise on this highly emotional issue. But can Hussein really be expected to waive a claim that has been foremost among Arab demands? Would he not be reviled by Arab moderates and extremists alike and become an object of scorn to all Muslims.

Evidently the Jordanian option involves a lot of wishful thinking. The bitter truth is that between 1967 and 1977, when the Israeli Labour Party still held power, it did not make much headway in its efforts to convince Hussein. The issue of Jerusalem is almost insoluble, and the problem of the Palestinian refugees will not go away as soon as the West Bank is returned to Jordan. On the contrary, it may erupt in the faces of the contracting parties.

Jordan's Role. There is only one country that can satisfy the pressing needs of the Palestinians, and that country is Jordan. Its area is nearly 95,000 sq km (37,000 sq mi). Its Palestinian inhabitants—refugees who were granted Jordanian citizenship and migrants who were attracted by better economic opportunities on the East Bank—outnumber the indigenous population.

Transjordan (as the East Bank used to be called) was originally part of the mandated territory of Palestine entrusted to Great Britain by the League of Nations in 1920. Separated from western Palestine by the British, it was handed over to a Hejazi prince who had won the loyalty of its predominantly Bedouin population of 300,000. The influx of Palestinian refugees in 1948 changed the character of the country. The newcomers had been in contact with Western education and ideas. Many of them were literate, resourceful, and energetic. They made Jordan into what it is today: an accessible, progressing part of the Arab East, in which the Bedouin component of the population, while receding demographically, still is the most powerful because of its predominance in the Army and its special relationship with the king. A large-scale Palestinian immigration coupled with bold development projects would only deepen and accelerate the process of change.

Bringing the Palestinian problem into true focus, by concentrating on a feasible solution of the refugee problem while simultaneously responding to the need for full expression of the Palestinian national identity, will probably ease the tension that has built up around the West Bank. Israel's security needs will more easily be reconciled with the aspirations of the Arab population if their paramount needs have been provided for elsewhere.

Jews in the Arab World. One final point should be made. Peace generally presupposes the creation or existence of a full range of normal relations between the parties, including the free movement of citizens of both countries across the border dividing them. As part of a durable peace, one would expect a certain amount of intermigration between neighbouring states. The well-being of minorities might be considered one of the touchstones of normality in the relationship of such nations. That Jews would be particularly sensitive on the subject is only to be expected. They would consider behaviour toward their fellow Jews in any given country a true test of its decency and moral calibre.

The relationship between Muslims and Jews during the centuries of their coexistence has not always been a happy one. Fundamentalist Islam does not consider Jews (or Christians, for that matter) equal citizens. Separate quarters and distinct clothes or headgear for Jews have been as common in Islamic countries as they were in medieval Christian societies, and discrimination, pogroms, and forced conversions were as familiar to Oriental Jews as to their brethren living in the West. It is therefore only to be expected that Israel would regard the opportunity for Jews to reside in Arab countries as respected minorities as a test of Arab goodwill.

Unfortunately, most if not all of the Arab countries have failed that test. At the time the State of Israel came into being, in 1948, there were over 800,000 Jews living in Arab countries. The greater part of these Jews, having found that they were hostages in the hands of governments and mobs alike, decided to immigrate to Israel. Most Iraqi and Yemenite Jews, and hundreds of thousands living in Morocco, Libya, Algeria, and Tunisia, joined the exodus. Some went illegally; others had to buy their way out. For generations there had been no Jews residing in Saudi Arabia and Jordan (ironically, the two Arab countries universally regarded as solidly pro-West and therefore moderate). Even today, both refuse entry to Jews intending to settle there, and foreign firms employing Jews in executive positions may be barred from doing business.

There are some 690,000 Arabs living in Israel. On the other hand, there are only 20,000 or 30,000 Jews left in the Arab world. To Israelis it is clear that if peace with Damascus is ever achieved, provision should be made for the remnants of Syrian Jewry, now virtual prisoners of Hafez al-Assad's regime, to make their way out. But should peace really be based on the assumption that no Jew can be welcome, or safe, in an Arab country? And should peace-loving Israelis accept Arab aversion to Jews as an irremediable reality? Or, to confront an actual situation, are the Jews settling in Judaea and Samaria really an obstacle to peace? And is peace credible and trustworthy if its premise is that the presence of Jews amid the Arabs is unbearable to the latter?

What is it that the advocates of barring Jews from the scene of the ancient biblical traditions are after—peace and coexistence between Israel and its neighbours, or the perpetuation of the existing abyss of prejudice and hatred?

DON SMETZER—CLICK/CHICAGO

Many sites in the Holy Land are sacred to more than one people. The Dome of the Rock in the Old City of Jerusalem is a late 7th-century Muslim shrine housing the rock from which according to Muslim tradition the Prophet Muhammad ascended to Heaven. To Jews it is the rock where the patriarch Abraham prepared to sacrifice his son Isaac. The Wailing Wall (foreground) is all that remains of the Second Temple of Jerusalem; it is a major pilgrimage site for religious Jews. Under Jordanian rule (1949–67), Jews were forbidden to visit the Wall.

(TOP) GILLES PERESS—MAGNUM; (BOTTOM) LAVON H. BAIR

Above, Simone de Beauvoir in 1975 with Jean-Paul Sartre. She holds a copy of the frequently banned paper *The Cause of the People*, which he edited. At left, Beauvoir being interviewed by Deirdre Bair.

WOMEN'S RIGHTS IN TODAY'S WORLD

A Provocative Interview with Simone de Beauvoir

by Deirdre Bair

Simone de Beauvoir (*see* BIOGRAPHIES) is one of France's preeminent intellectuals, an influential, controversial, often stormy figure of the left. She is something of a doyenne of Existentialism, having shared her life for many years with the founder of that school of philosophy, Jean-Paul Sartre, until his death in 1980.

When the editors of the *Britannica Book of the Year* undertook to examine, for this issue, the state of women's rights in the world of 1984 (*see* chart, pages 26 and 27), they quickly discovered that in country after country of Africa and Asia, as well as Europe and the Americas, scholars in this field trace the beginnings of the modern women's movement to one event and one woman: the publication in local languages of *The Second Sex* by Simone de Beauvoir.

First published in France in 1949 as *Le Deuxième Sexe*, it has been translated into 20 or more languages and is still in print in most of them. When it was written, Beauvoir did not count herself a feminist, but in the generation that has elapsed since she has become—as you will see—a most passionate one. As private citizen or official government observer, she has visited countries such as Japan, China, Cuba, Brazil, the Soviet Union, Egypt and other African countries, as well as the United States in the summer of 1983. She wrote books and articles about her travels at the time and has stayed informed through continuing friendships with resident writers, educators, and intellectuals of the left.

Today Beauvoir no longer writes at lengths greater than introductions or appreciations of the works of other feminists. However, she was willing to be interviewed, and we invited Deirdre Bair, associate professor of English at the University of Pennsylvania and an authority on the life, works, and influence of Simone de Beauvoir, to conduct the interview. Professor Bair, whose *Samuel Beckett: A Biography* won the 1981 American Book Award, is at work on a critical biography of Beauvoir. The two women discussed the interview in New York City in August 1983 and conducted it in several sessions the following month in Beauvoir's Paris apartment. As we hoped, Professor Bair has elicited views that are stimulating, startling, and controversial, and statements that some readers may find infuriating. Such views, of course, are those of Simone de Beauvoir and not of the publishers of the *Britannica Book of the Year*.

Your writings have been both influential and inspirational in advancing women's rights. They have served as models not only in Western societies but also throughout the world. I wonder if you would comment upon what you perceive both your influence and these changes to have been during the past 20 or so years.

I think *The Second Sex* has had the most influence of all my writings. I received many, many letters after it was published in French in 1949 and then translated into many languages. I still get letters about it, and to this day I am deeply moved by them. I know how that book is cited so often as the moving force behind the current women's movement. Sometimes I agree with the way in which it is interpreted, but many times I don't. I see how parts are quoted either correctly, as I intended it to be interpreted, or else according to whatever point of view the writer wishes to further. So I have to say that although I am pleased, even at times surprised, by the way in which *The Second Sex* is regarded, I sometimes find it difficult to comprehend exactly what the influence of the book really is, what it really means to people.

When I wrote it, I thought all the information it contained was something everyone already knew, that I was simply collecting it and writing it all down. I thought everything was already so obvious, so self-explanatory, that my role was largely [that of] collector and organizer, and that all I needed to do was to arrange it and make it available to all women. It was not until the book was published that I realized my role had been more visionary, more discerning. In a larger sense, that made me sad, because I realized how much women had to learn about their condition before they could even begin to think about changing it.

But as for the changes in the 34 years since that book was published, or more particularly, in the last 20 or so years, I don't know how to answer except to give my personal impressions, to comment only from my personal observations, readings, correspondence, and conversations with people throughout the world.

I think everything connected with changes in the condition of women depends on the society in which they live. I link the words progress and regression because they seem to follow each other, to

ALAIN NOGUES—SYGMA

"The wearing of veils has once again become the major issue. . . ." Muslim women wear the veil on their way to work in Jidda, Saudi Arabia.

go in cycles. For instance, the situation in Iran is worse than ever before, and in all the Muslim countries, repression seems dominant now. The wearing of veils has once again become the major issue, and it serves as a convenient excuse for avoiding the larger issues of the right of women to education, to the control of their bodies. I am not speaking specifically about contraception or abortion here, although those are included. I am referring to simple decisions such as whether to marry or not, and if so, the freedom to choose the mate. One of the most dreadful acts of all, the genital mutilation of little girls, is still widespread. About 30 million undergo clitoridectomy every year, so I can't see much progress in Muslim societies.

I'd like to be able to say that I see great change in the condition of women in China, but I can't. I wrote a not-very-important book about China some years ago, and I spoke of being sorry for the condition of women, from those who could not work because of such things as bound feet to those who were doomed to early death because they were so overworked. I was glad to see changes effected after the revolution there, but I ask myself, how much has been gained when I read that girl babies are still being drowned at birth and women are still dying young because they are not given enough food for the amount of work they are expected to do. In Japan I think it is the Communists who try to hasten emancipation, but I don't think they are too successful. They supposedly have laws to protect women in India, but there are too many women being burned, tortured, or even murdered because they did not bring a satisfactory dowry to their marriage, so I don't think local custom has too much respect for national law. In Greece they expect praise because the right to inherit property when the husband dies has recently been given to widows rather than to the next male heir, but that is only one small change in women's lot in that country.

In Western countries the struggle takes a more blatant political form. The repression in the United States since Ronald Reagan was elected is very frightening to me. The right-wing political elements seem to have organized themselves so they have power and influence. The failure of the Equal Rights Amendment is a good example of their power. There is a very active and exciting women's movement in the United States today, but regressive behaviour emanating from the Reagan government has eaten into any gains it has made. What is especially frightening to me is the way right-wing propaganda has influenced so many women to become antifeminist. This is disappointing because the rest of the world looks to the United States to take the lead in social justice and reform.

I can't speak about England or its dependent nations because, generally speaking, the English don't like French intellectuals very much. With very few exceptions, they did not like Sartre as a philosopher, and they don't really like me very much either as a writer or as a feminist thinker, and so I don't take much interest in the situation there. It is different in Italy. They have movements and they struggle, but they have to withstand the power and influence of the Roman Catholic Church there. There are strong groups in Milan, Bologna, and other industrial cities. You notice, I think, that feminist action generally happens in the north of Italy, even though I think women throughout the country are in agreement with the struggle. Now they have the right to divorce in Italy, and they are fighting for legal abortion. They are fighting for many basic human rights in that country, and I think they should be applauded and supported in their efforts.

I know there is a rather strong feminist movement in West Germany just now but, just as in France, the movement has become divided into factions. That kind of dissension directed against itself, against the common goal, makes me very sad because it dissipates energies and wastes time. I get occasional letters from people in Spain, Portugal, and even French Canada, so I know that some women there want change, but whether they can do so will remain to be seen.

Let's talk about the situation in France today:

I think we have made small but real progress in France. This has happened because the Socialist government is in favour of equality under the law for women.

President François Mitterrand has stated that he is very grateful for your support in the last election. Why did you support him?

I decided to support him because I felt that despite all the mistakes his government would probably make, it would still be better for more people than [former president Valéry] Giscard d'Estaing's. I have always believed that socialism was a more enlightened form of government than the so-called liberalism of earlier [post-World War II] French governments. I knew very well that Mitterrand would not be able to conduct a real, genuine socialist revolution because he thinks too much like a capitalist and because a real, genuine socialist revolution would bring too much violence and nobody wants that. I didn't expect him to perform miracles, but I thought that with his election all the people in France would have to be aware of the policies of socialism whether they accepted to believe in it or not.

It is not possible to have a genuine revolution which would redistribute goods and services, and we had violence enough when Mitterrand's ministries tried to help the underprivileged. The privileged classes became furious: they took their money out of the country, and many of them left with it. Thus they create a self-fulfilling prophecy: they say things are going badly, and they make this happen by investing their capital elsewhere. They call this behaviour "capitalist," or "Giscard's democracy," but it is not really democracy to think more of selfish profit than the common good. It is this powerful segment of French society that is against Mitterrand, and thus his progress toward a better distribution of the benefits of life for all social classes is greatly slowed. Nevertheless, I have no regrets about having supported Mitterrand, and I'd do it again, of course.

Let's talk specifically about the condition of women in France today under the Mitterrand government. Also, let's go back a few years, begin with [Charles] de Gaulle, and talk about some of the changes which have affected women in France since then:

My opinions of de Gaulle are well known to anyone who has read my memoirs. To put it quite simply here: de Gaulle never made a public comment about women to my knowledge, and I don't think he thought about them either. I suppose it was Giscard who first gave public voice to the situation of women. He created something called "the Ministry of the Feminine Condition," or something like that, but he neglected one very important fact: he gave no money, no budget at all. I don't think the women in charge were feminist in the truest sense of wanting to work for the betterment of women, because their first goal was to work to better the image of the government under which they served.

Of contraception and abortion: French women demonstrated in 1972 for the right to have "A baby—if I wish, when I wish." Beauvoir says of abortion, . . ."under Giscard, women got this very important right in France, just as in 1944 women got the first very important right, which was to vote."

ALAIN NOGUES—SYGMA

Under the Giscard government, we did win the victory to legalize abortion, a fight led by Simone Weil, but this was primarily because of the strong feminist movement which began in France in the early 1970s and not because of any social enlightenment on the part of that government. Giscard was, however, what we might call a modernist, a political figure who wanted France to become an advanced liberal society, and therefore he had to permit advanced liberal legislation, which is how abortion came to be legal in France. We must be careful not to equate the abortion issue with leftist beliefs because there are many reactionary societies—Japan, for example—in which abortion is permitted. In the case of Japan, abortion serves governmental policy because it restricts population. If the right-wing elements in the United States were to have their way, abortion would be outlawed to serve fundamentalist religious beliefs. The absolute rejection of the right to legal abortion is, however, absolutely reactionary.

So, under Giscard, women got this very important right in France, just as in 1944 women got the first very important right, which was to vote. And now, under Mitterrand, we have a lot more, thanks essentially to his recognition of the need for women to have not only a ministry but also a budget that enables it to get things done. I don't think Mitterrand is personally a feminist in his thinking, but he is perceptive enough to recognize that women play a key role in political elections in France, and so he supports them.

Let's talk about the Ministry for the Rights of Women:

Mitterrand was very wise to appoint Yvette Roudy to this position. She has been a committed feminist for many years. She is a translator, a scholar, a perceptive political woman. Happily, Mitterrand has given her enough of a budget so that, in combination with her energy and intelligence, she can effect change. She has passed a very important law which forbids antisexist exploitation of women and their bodies in the media. She works to obtain equal salaries, the opportunity for women to enter jobs and professions that have been closed to them, and of course she supports the right of women to make their own decisions about their bodies.

Yvette Roudy has formed a commission within her ministry to study the role of women in French society and to write a report on the subject. She has named you honorary chairperson. Can you talk a little about this?

Oh yes, it is an honour for me to be on this "Commission Beauvoir," as we call it. Yvette Roudy asked a certain number of intellectuals to do some work to see what kind of proposals we could make to the government about the question of women and culture, which is actually the formal name of this group, the Commission Femme et Culture. We do research on various aspects of the role women play within their culture so that we can then make concrete proposals to the government. We believe that we must examine the entire culture in order to understand the feminine condition.

Let me explain: we begin with the proposition that women are excluded from most parts of culture. They have little or no money of their own, therefore they have no real economic control. They are excluded from education or they are given inferior education or less training than men, thus fewer professions are open to them and they are generally inferior. Even in intellectual and creative pursuits like writing and painting, women must still suffer from the restrictions that require them to tend first to household and family needs before they try to fit their work into whatever free time they can manage. A society evolves in which parents feel it is not necessary to educate the daughter well because she can always get married. If she does marry, even if she marries well, she finds herself responsible for all the aspects of life because the husband must be free to follow his business, his profession. The woman is overwhelmed by daily life, and there is no leisure to read or think. She does not control enough money to do any good with it, and so the endless cycle continues.

I like very much Virginia Woolf's thoughts about William Shakespeare's imaginary sister in that excellent book *A Room of One's Own:* even if Shakespeare's sister were as gifted as her brother, the world would not have known it because she would have been too busy with daily life to have done anything creative.

These are some of the issues the Commission Beauvoir is charged to address because until we change the culture and society so that women are admitted to all parts of it with equal status, we won't have solved the problem of the feminine condition. The importance of this commission lies in the fact that it was created by an official arm of the government in power, which charges it to come up with recommendations for action. As such, it makes legitimate the issue of woman's place within society, and it shows that the Mitterrand government is in favour of positive change.

How did your personal feminist activity begin?

There is a very direct response to that question: my direct, active feminism began in 1970, when a number of militant feminists asked me to sign a declaration on abortion. The declaration, which became known as the "Manifeste des 343," was signed by famous French women as well as those who were unknown. In it, all declared that they had

FRILET—SIPA PRESS/BLACK STAR

NICOLAS TIKOMIROFF—MAGNUM

"The promises in Algeria were not kept. Women who fought for the FLN (right; 1961) were very disappointed to find after the war for liberation ended that they were sent right back into their homes to be dependent on their fathers or their husbands." At left, women in Algiers, veiled in white, in 1979 celebrated the 25th anniversary of the beginning of the anticolonial struggle against France.

had abortions. It was illegal to be aborted in France, and if discovered, women were tried and sentenced to jail. We made this declaration to force the government to act, because we knew that they would not put 343 women on trial and sentence us to jail. So that's how I really started.

From then on, I was involved in militant action with these women, all of whom were much younger than I and who were fighting seriously for the rights of women. After the fight for legal abortion, there were countless meetings for other issues. They held a meeting in 1972 when they denounced crimes against women. They published journals and magazines, and I wrote articles, reviews, and prefaces for them. I went to meetings, I took part in demonstrations, I helped whenever I could, but my actions always arose from my commitment to women's issues. By that I mean causes separate from masculine causes or movements because I discovered that whenever men were involved, the causes and needs of women were minimized.

I believe that militant feminism grew directly from the '68 demonstrations [by students and workers in France], that properly feminist attitudes arose when women discovered that the men of '68 did not treat them as equals. Men made the speeches, but women typed them. Men were on the soapboxes and the podiums, but women were in the kitchen making coffee. So they got fed up with this because they were intelligent women. They realized that they would have to take their fate into their own hands and separate their battles from the larger revolutionary rhetoric of the men. I agreed with them because I understood that women could not expect their emancipation to come from general revolution but would have to create their own. Men were always telling them that the needs of the revolution came first and their turn as women came later—it was this way in Algeria and Cuba—and so I realized that women would have to take care of their problems in ways that were personal, direct, and immediate. They could no longer sit waiting patiently for men to change the society for them because it would never happen unless they did it themselves.

Let me ask you about Algeria and some of the other countries that have gained their independence in the last 20 or so years: do you think the commitments to women made at the time of independence have been honoured or dishonoured?

The promises in Algeria were not kept. Women who fought for the FLN [National Liberation Front] were very disappointed to find after the war for liberation ended that they were sent right back into their homes to be dependent on their fathers or their husbands. These women were very disappointed. But then, so were the women who fought alongside men in Cuba. You never even hear of women, let alone of programs for women or prominent women leaders in that country. I have to conclude that political revolution is made by men for their own benefit, without consideration of the needs of women.

You have spoken of politics in regard to the condition of women: what role do you think religion plays in this matter?

All religions are just as bad as possible for women because religions have been created by and for men

Status of Women in Selected Countries[1]

Country	POLITICAL PARTICIPATION: Year of women's suffrage[2]	Women in national legislature (%)[3]	EDUCATION: Adult illiteracy (%)[4] M	Adult illiteracy (%)[4] F	Female enrollment (%) in:[5] Primary	Secondary	Higher	MARRIAGE AND REPRODUCTIVE FREEDOM: Mean age at first marriage[6] M	Mean age at first marriage[6] F	Births/woman (total fertility rate)[7]	Women using contraception (%)[8]	Government's policy toward contraception[9]	Date of abortion law
AFRICA													
Algeria	1958	3.4 (1977)	58.2	87.4	42	38	24	NA	NA	7.3	NA	direct support	1966–76
Egypt	1956	7.6 (1979)	46.4	77.6	40	37	31	NA	NA	4.8	17	direct support	1937
Kenya	1963	NA	40.0	65.2	47	41	NA	NA	NA	8.0	9	direct support	1972
Nigeria	NA	NA	54.4	77.0	NA	NA	NA	NA	NA	6.9	NA	indirect support	1958
South Africa	1930	1 (1981)	43.0	43.0	50	NA	NA	25.1	22.4	5.1	NA	direct support	1975
Tunisia	1959	4 (1973)	48.9	75.2	42	37	30	27.9	23.3	5.1	21	direct support	1973
AMERICA													
Argentina	1947	2 (1975)	6.5	8.3	49	53	50	26.4	23.1	2.8	NA	no support	1921, 1967
Brazil	1932	1 (1975)	22.0	25.7	49	54	38	26.2	23.0	4.0	NA	direct support	1940, 1941
Canada	1948	6.2 (1980)	0.5	0.5	49	NA	50	NA	NA	1.9	NA	direct support	1955, 1970
Cuba	1934	NA	4.3	4.9	47	51	46	23.3	19.4	2.2	NA	direct support	1979
Mexico	1953	NA	13.8	20.2	49	47	32	24.4	21.2	5.0	56	direct support	1931
Nicaragua	1955	NA	NA	NA	51	53	35	NA	NA	6.1	NA	direct support	1949
United States	1920	4.5 (1982)	1.1	1.0	NA	50	51	23.5	21.5	1.8	83	direct support	1973
ASIA													
China	1947	14 (1975)	8.0	24.4	45	39	24	NA	NA	2.9	74	direct support	1979
India	1949	5 (1975)	52.3	80.6	38	30	25	22.7	17.7	4.8	23	direct support	1971/72, 1975
Iran	1963	1 (1980)	52.4	75.7	39	36	31	25.0	18.5	6.0	23	direct support	1974, 1976
Israel	1948	7 (1973)	7.4	16.7	49	52	47	25.4	22.8	3.3	NA	direct support	NA
Japan	1945	2 (1970)	0.7	0.8	49	49	33	27.6	24.5	1.7	67	direct support	1907, 1948
Philippines	1947	NA	15.7	19.1	49	53	53	25.4	22.8	4.6	48	direct support	1930
Saudi Arabia	—	—	65.5	87.8	39	38	29	NA	NA	7.3	NA	access limited	NA
Syria	1949	4 (1973)	40.4	80.0	43	37	29	25.9	20.7	7.4	NA	direct support	1949, 1970
Thailand	1932	NA	7.5	17.1	48	45	43	24.7	22.0	3.9	59	direct support	1956
Turkey	1934	NA	22.8	56.9	45	33	25	23.6	20.5	4.6	38	direct support	1965
EUROPE													
France	1944	NA	1.1	1.3	49	52	46	26.0	23.1	1.9	88	direct support	1979
Germany, East	NA	NA	NA	NA	50	NA	57	24.7	20.8	1.4	NA	direct support	1972
Germany, West	1919	7 (1975)	0.5	0.5	48	52	41	26.2	23.3	1.4	NA	indirect support	1974–76
Greece	1952	2 (1975)	6.0	17.1	48	44	39	28.4	23.8	2.3	NA	NA	1950, 1978
Ireland	1922	NA	0.5	0.5	49	52	40	25.8	23.5	3.2	NA	no support	1861
Italy	1945	NA	3.6	5.4	49	47	42	27.2	22.6	1.9	NA	indirect support	1977, 1978
Poland	1919	15 (1975)	.7	1.7	49	50	56	25.6	21.5	2.2	57	direct support	1956, 1969
Sweden	1919	21 (1975)	0.5	0.5	49	51	46	28.0	25.7	1.7	NA	direct support	1974
United Kingdom	1928	4 (1975)	0.5	0.5	49	49	36	24.8	21.4	1.7	81	direct support	1967
Yugoslavia	1946	NA	6.6	19.4	48	47	40	24.9	21.3	2.2	59	direct support	1974
OCEANIA													
Australia	1902	NA	0.5	0.5	49	50	45	24.4	22.0	1.9	66	indirect support	NA
Papua New Guinea	NA	NA	52.4	70.2	42	28	11	NA	NA	5.2	NA	direct support	1899, 1902
U.S.S.R.	1917	13 (1975)	1.0	1.9	NA	NA	51	NA	NA	2.4	NA	direct support	1965, 1969

Note: (—) indicates data are nil or do not apply. (NA) indicates data are not available. [1]For latest year available after 1970. [2]Exercise of right may involve discriminatory age, racial, or status requirements. [3]Female composition as percentage of whole from election year noted. [4]1982 data for population 15 years and older (Papua New Guinea 10 years and older); some estimates included. [5]As percentage of student body at each level. [6]Among those ever marrying. [7]Total number of children an average woman will bear in her lifetime, assuming no premature mortality. [8]Percentage of married or "exposed" women (married or in a recognized union) using method at time of survey (late 1970s). [9]"Access limited" applies where the government prohibits access to modern contraceptive methods (about 7% of all countries); where access is authorized, 16% provide no support, 13% provide indirect support such as contraceptive education and publicity, and 64% provide direct support, including free or subsidized distribution.
Sources: Elise Boulding *et al.*, *Handbook of International Data on Women* (1976); European Communities, *Eurostat* 1-1983; International Labour Organization, *Yearbook of Labour Statistics* (1982); United Nations, *Demographic Yearbook* 1981, *World Population Trends and Policies, 1981 Monitoring Report;* UNESCO, *Statistical Digest* 1981 and 1982, *Statistical Yearbook* (1982); U.S. Department of Commerce, *Country Demographic Profiles;* U.S. Department of Health and Human Services, *Social Security Programs Throughout the World* (1981); World Bank, *World Development Report* (1983); Worldwatch Institute, *Worldwatch Paper 3: Women in Politics: A Global Review;* various country sources.

and are consequently against women. I have met feminists in Egypt who have studied the Koran in order to refute the men who tell them that it says they must be secluded behind the veil because they are not equal to men, that their brains are smaller, or the feminine nature is inferior and must be protected. These women say that the Koran does not insist upon seclusion and that their refusal to wear the chador is in keeping with the democratic spirit of Islam. But I also know of Iranian women who insist upon wearing the chador voluntarily because they believe they are making both feminist and political statements by doing so. Another example: The pope tells the Catholic bishops and priests in Latin America who engage in social reform to stay out of politics, to stay inside the church and help the women to pray, but the pope himself makes no secret of his political activity on behalf of Poland. This just goes to show how religion can be interpreted in both progressive and regressive ways.

There are those, particularly in Muslim countries, who would have you believe that Zionism is the worst enemy of women, but I believe it is the Muslim religion that is the worst. I am not saying that the Jews are guiltless or that they treat women as equals of men, but Judaism represses a much smaller segment of humanity than Islam. Islam accepts, among other atrocities, genital mutilation, which is the worst possible crime against women.

Do you think the progressive male leaders of Muslim nations have done much for women? Perhaps we could speak of Habib Bourguiba or, from an earlier time, Kemal Ataturk, as examples.

The fact that one hears nothing about conditions in Turkey makes me think that little lasting good has come from Ataturk's time. In Tunisia I believe that Bourguiba has had good intentions to do something for women, to protect them against rape, to give them an education, to allow them to consider working outside the home. But we have to understand the nuances of all this and interpret it correctly. I have seen articles and statistics which show that conditions for women in Tunisia are better now than they were 50 years ago, but that doesn't mean much. The changes have not been far-reaching and are effective only up to a minor point. I must conclude

Legal grounds for abortion[10]	Penalties for woman undergoing illegal abortion[11]	EMPLOYMENT Female participation in labour force (%)[12]	Ratio of women's to men's average wages (%)[13]	Women in professional positions (%)[14]	Sex segregation in jobs[15]	Maternity leave and benefits under social security system[16]	Country
							AFRICA
Med.	I, 6 months–2 years	8.9	NA	NA	13	100%, 14 weeks	Algeria
Med., Eug.	I, NA	7.6	62.8	NA	16	75%, 100 days	Egypt
Med. (life only)	I, up to 7 years	33.3	79.6	NA	NA	100%, 2 months	Kenya
Med. (life only)	I, 7–14 years	40.2	NA	NA	NA	50%, 12 weeks	Nigeria
Med., Eug., Jur.	I, up to 5 years; F	34.0	NA	NA	NA	45%, 26 weeks	South Africa
Req.: Med., Eug.	NA	20.1	NA	14	NA	66 2/3%, 30 days	Tunisia
							AMERICA
Med., Jur.	I, 1–4 years	28.6	NA	NA	12	100%, 90 days; M	Argentina
Med. (life), Jur.	I, from 4 years	21.6	NA	33	12	100%, 12 weeks; M	Brazil
Med.	I, 2 years	40.1	67–89	44	9	60%, 15 weeks	Canada
Req.	NA	19.5	NA	NA	18	100%, 18–20 weeks	Cuba
Med. (life), Jur.	I, up to 5 years	18.5	NA	28	10	100%, 84 days; M	Mexico
Med. (life only)	I, 2–4 years	21.2	NA	NA	7	60%, 12 weeks	Nicaragua
Req.: Med.	NA	42.8	60.0	38	6	provided by some states	United States
							ASIA
Req.	—	34.0	NA	30	NA	100%, 56–70 days	China
Sec., Med., Eug., Jur.	I, 3–7 years; F	32.2	NA	15	21	100%, 12–16 weeks	India
Sec., Med., Eug.	NA	14.8	NA	32	22	66 2/3%, 24 weeks; M	Iran
Med., Eug., Jur.	NA	36.8	NA	46	12	75%, 6–12 weeks; M	Israel
Sec., Med., Eug., Jur.	I, up to 1 year	37.7	53.3	35	30	60%, 12 weeks; M	Japan
Med. (life only)	I, 6 months–6 years	37.0	NA	54	18	100%, 45 days	Philippines
Med. (life only)	NA	4.8	NA	NA	NA	NA	Saudi Arabia
Med. (life only)	I, up to 3 years	5.8	68.8	25	71	NA	Syria
Med., Jur.	I, up to 3 years, or F	47.3	NA	37	47	100%, 30–90 days	Thailand
Med. (life), Eug., Jur.	I, 1–5 years	33.7	NA	25	70	66 2/3%, 12 weeks; M	Turkey
							EUROPE
Req.: Med., Eug.	NA	38.9	80.4	NA	13	90%, 16–26 weeks; M	France
Req.: Sec., Med., Eug., Jur.	NA	NA	NA	NA	NA	100%, 26 weeks	Germany, East
Sec., Med., Eug., Jur.	I, up to 1 year	38.2	72.5	35	13	100%, 30 weeks; M	Germany, West
Med., Eug., Jur.	I, up to 3 years	30.1	67.2	NA	37	50%+, 84 days; M	Greece
Med. (life only)	I, from 2 years to life	27.0	68.4	40	22	fixed benefit, 12 weeks; M	Ireland
Req.: Sec., Med., Eug.	NA	33.3	84.7	NA	15	80%, up to 31 weeks	Italy
Sec., Med., Eug., Jur.	—	46.1	NA	NA	22	100%, 16–26 weeks; M	Poland
Req.: Sec., Med., Eug., Jur.	NA	45.2	90.1	51	9	90%, 180–270 days	Sweden
Sec., Med., Eug.	NA	39.1	69.4	NA	4	fixed benefit, 18 weeks; M	United Kingdom
Req.: Med., Eug.	NA	35.9	NA	NA	35	100%, 105 days; M	Yugoslavia
							OCEANIA
Req.: Sec., Med., Eug., Jur.	NA	36.7	86.2	35	6	NA	Australia
Med.	NA	41.1	NA	NA	NA	NA	Papua New Guinea
Req.: Med., Eug.	—	51	NA	59	NA	100%, 16–18 weeks; M	U.S.S.R.

[10]Abortion available on request (Req.) in some countries; medical (Med.) grounds include risk to mother's health and/or life; socioeconomic (Sec.) grounds include economic hardship; eugenic (Eug.) grounds include danger of serious congenital disorder or other damage to fetus; juridical (Jur.) grounds may include rape, incest, and other criminal acts. [11]Permissible duration of incarceration (I) and/or fine (F), according to law; in 1980 China was the only country to have completely decriminalized abortion. [12]Percentage of women in labour force as a whole; includes those unemployed and looking for work but excludes full-time homemakers. [13]For all nonagricultural activities, except in the case of Canada, where only selected office occupations are included. [14]Percentage of women among all professional, technical and related, administrative and managerial workers; in South Africa, among managers only; in the U.S.S.R., among intellectual (*v.* physical) workers. [15]Shown as the percentage of females (or males) who would have to change job status in order that sex distribution be equal: The four status levels include employer, own-account worker, employee, and unpaid family worker. [16]Cash benefits for insured worker, given as % of previous earnings and duration of coverage; maternity grants (M) may cover layette and/or nursing expenses; in both Kenya and Thailand the employer is responsible for providing benefits; in some countries maternity benefits are not part of social security system, while others (*e.g.*, East Germany, Ireland, Italy, the U.S.S.R.) offer extended leave at no or reduced earnings.

(BRENDA E. BERMAN)

that the actions of well-meaning men are better than those of men with ill intentions, but it will take more than one or a few to make real change.

Then let us talk about women who are heads of government and what, if anything, they have done or are doing for women:

I would be really surprised if a woman were to become the head of state in either France or the United States for a very long time. I know that more women are being elected to public office in both countries today, but they are always in low positions. For example, in your government, you have quite a few representatives but how many senators do you have? It's the same in France. Anyway, to elect women would not effect very much change because the moment a woman gets power, she takes on all the attitudes, behaviour, and consequently the faults of men. These women become just as greedy for power because it goes to their heads, too. If you have a little power, you want a lot. Look at Indira Gandhi, and especially at Margaret Thatcher—she can make war as well as any man. No, I don't believe that women as heads of state will make any significant change in society because, as I said, the moment a woman gets power, she loses the solidarity she had with other women. She will want to be equal in a man's world and will become ambitious for her own sake.

Are you saying that because these women are not true feminists men do not object to sharing power with them?

Of course. In a sense, by giving women power, men are buying their loyalty. They know full well that any woman who is operating in a man's world is behaving as a man and will not betray men because it would mean losing her power.

What do you think has resulted from the International Women's Year, 1975, and the Women's Decade, 1975–85?

I want to comment specifically on the International Conference in Mexico City as an example of what we have just been discussing. All the women there were appointed by their male governments, and so they spoke in the name of that power. If they did not represent their governments, then they represented their husbands. They were terribly antifemi-

ATLAN—SYGMA

"If the right-wing elements in the United States were to have their way, abortion would be outlawed to serve fundamentalist religious beliefs. The absolute rejection of the right to legal abortion is, however, absolutely reactionary."

nist because they were all supporting their national interests. What good could come of that? The conference in Copenhagen which took place later also had women representatives of masculine power. They were not there to speak as women among women. Nationalism is terrible for feminism.

How do you feel about how far women have come in the past 20 years? Could you describe your thoughts about the condition of women today?

There has been progress in the last few years especially, and I am optimistic for the future—but a far distant future—50 to 100 years from now. I think the distinctions we have presently between men and women will come to seem barbaric in the future, but I think much time will have to pass first because men are not ready to be dispossessed of their power, both religious and political.

Do you have an opinion of what women should be doing now?

Well, first I have to say that I disagree entirely with Betty Friedan and her "second stage." Women will have to continue to fight to change their lives radically, not just to learn, as Friedan believes, how to manage a career and a home at the same time. I believe that one of the great battlefronts for women today concerns home life and especially housework. We have to fight that situation all over the world, not just in the United States and France. I have said many times that if I were to write *The Second Sex* today, I would stress more the economic foundations rather than the philosophical. It is a shame to make women do this housework without reward; billions of hours every year without earning a cent, and it is laughed at by men who don't take it seriously. Now housekeeping help has become so expensive most women can't afford it and must do the work themselves. If women do not break this pattern, it will mean real economic and professional paralysis for them.

This sounds like a very negative view of the possibility for change to me, and I thought you said you were optimistic:

I hope. I really hope, because it seems irrational to believe that things will not change. Men try more and more to dominate all of nature, especially women, under the pretext that a woman is an extension of their natural world. This is why I don't believe the situation can continue, because women in greater numbers refuse to allow themselves to be considered any longer as natural property to be controlled or dominated. Women will turn to feminism for their self-education, and the fight will begin. It will be a hard struggle because men will not easily surrender their freedom from housework and family responsibility and all other burdens that typify women's lot today.

Are you saying then that women will become radical, or more active politically in the future?

I think that when women really begin to consider liberating themselves seriously, they will take more of an interest in politics. And since liberation is a democratic concept, they will become more democratic and thus more radical. Men must be made to understand that, in the final analysis, feminist behaviour is not gratuitous but serious. Feminists are not useless and silly hysterics. They have studied and thought, and they want to make changes that will benefit all of society. Throughout the world, women are still being sold, beaten, raped, and killed, so this is a struggle that must be in the minds of all women and be the basis of all female behaviour. We can no longer tolerate antifeminist behaviour, from other women or from men.

STRUCTURAL UNEMPLOYMENT:

The Reality Behind the Myth

by Joe Rogaly

Three current myths blur any straightforward analysis of modern unemployment. First, it is widely asserted that the rapid growth of jobless lines experienced in many countries since the early 1970s is an economic phenomenon with adverse social consequences. In fact the reverse is closer to the truth: the causes of contemporary mass unemployment are more social than economic, and the consequences are at least as adverse for economic policy-making as for the affected societies. Second, terms like structural unemployment, loosely used, imply that it is fundamentally changes in technology that are to blame. It is probable that this is no more correct today than it has been at any time since the start of the Industrial Revolution in the 18th century. Third, traditional economists will explain all unemployment by the absence of a sufficient level of demand for goods and services. Again, while there is some truth in this explanation, it alone does not suffice.

Basic Statistics. If the true picture is to emerge from the muddle of mythology, we must start with some statistics. The broad numbers present a dispiriting beginning, especially for those to whom the very word unemployment conjures up a gray picture of a starving line of workers outside a 1930s soup kitchen. In most developed countries of the world, the reality is quite different from that, in the direction of lesser impoverishment; in the developing and underdeveloped nations the picture is considerably worse. Yet most of the reliable statistics pertain to the industrial nations, and it is in most cases these that must be used. The consequences for the others must usually be inferred rather than measured in precise terms.

The statistical side of the story is best summed up in a remarkable statement of position published by the Organization for Economic Cooperation and Development (OECD) in September 1983. The OECD analyses cover its member countries, which are the nations of Western Europe, plus Canada and the U.S., Iceland, Turkey, Australia, New Zealand, and Japan. The September 1983 analysis opens thus:

> The general magnitude of the task of dealing with unemployment can be illustrated by the following simple calculation: 20,000 extra jobs will be required every day during

Structural unemployment: are changes in technology to blame? No. "It is probable that this is no more correct today than it has been at any time since the start of the Industrial Revolution in the 18th century."

ANDREW SACKS—BLACK STAR

Joe Rogaly is executive director of the Financial Times, *London. He has written extensively on socioeconomic issues and is the author of* Grunwick *(about a notorious British industrial dispute of the 1970s) and* Parliament for the People.

WIDE WORLD

The word unemployment conjures up echoes of the impoverishment visible in this Great Depression soup kitchen. But "In most developed countries of the world, the reality is quite different from that."

the last five years of this decade if OECD unemployment is to be cut to its 1979 level of 19 million. The labour force is likely to grow by some 18 to 20 million people over the five years 1984–89 and 1984 unemployment is projected to be 34¾ million—so up to 20 million jobs need to be created just to keep unemployment from rising and over 15 million extra jobs are needed to get unemployment down to 19 million. This rate at which new jobs would need to be created is significantly larger than the figure of 11,500 jobs a day which was achieved during the period of recovery after the first (1973) oil shock.

If that is the outlook in the wealthy industrial countries, it can only be far worse in Latin America, most of Africa, and nearly all of Asia other than the islands of exception, such as Hong Kong, Singapore, and regions of South Korea—industrial magnets to which workers are drawn from rural or across-the-border sources of supply. Some idea of the orders of magnitude involved can be derived from World Bank figures.

World Labour Force

	Average annual growth (%)		
	1960–70	1970–80	1980–2000
Poor countries	1.6	2.2	1.9
Middle-income countries	2.0	2.3	2.6
Capitalist industrial countries	1.2	1.3	0.7
Communist industrial countries	0.7	1.2	0.6

The social causes of high unemployment can be deduced from these and similar extrapolations. In all countries the high birthrates following the end of World War II led to a wave of new entrants to the labour force in the 1970s (although this was not the only factor, as shall be seen). In the wealthier countries, capitalist or Communist, this wave is expected to lose impetus during the last two decades of the century. In the very poor countries there may be some loss of impetus, especially where mass birth-control campaigns take effect, but there will clearly still be a very high growth in the number of job seekers. In the "middle-income" group—developing and rapidly developing countries among them—there will actually be an increase in the rate of growth of the labour force, partly exacerbated, perhaps, by inward migration. The latter may to some extent match the pace of more rapid economic growth and hence job creation, but there is no indication, in any of these countries, of a close concurrence between, on the one hand, the economic cycle and the consequent fluctuation in the demand for labour and, on the other hand, the social cycle, and its consequent fluctuation in supply.

It is this social cycle that will be more closely described in the rest of this article, since it goes a long way toward explaining both the primary causes of high unemployment and some of its social and economic effects. The principal causes of an increase in the supply of labour at a pace greater than can be absorbed by increases in demand, especially at a time of low or zero economic growth, are: the growth in the population size, the entry of women into the labour force, and changes in working hours and other employment practices. These are mitigated by other factors, such as migration and changes in employment between sectors, not to mention rapid technological change. (The sources of most of the facts, figures, and arguments contained in the following exposition are OECD publications, World Bank statistics, and publications from the International Labour Organization [ILO] in Geneva.)

Demographic Factors. The Malthusian proposition that the economy of a given nation or indeed of the world can sustain no more than a fixed or finite number of people carried little weight during the years of seemingly infinite growth experienced by most of the industrial countries and some of the poorer ones in the years prior to 1973 (although, paradoxically, the fear that the world may run short of natural resources was most fervently expressed during this period). As a long-term proposition Malthusianism is still widely considered to be of little consequence, partly because birthrates do decline as countries become wealthier and partly because the world's ability to feed itself has been regarded as an ever improving characteristic. Yet in terms of employment the consequences of rapid population growth cannot be denied. During the 1970s, for example, the working-age population in the OECD area expanded at about 1.1% annually, the same pace as in the 1960s, in spite of sharp falls in the birthrate in most member countries.

Since the working age is taken as between 15 and 64 years in the majority of standard texts, the "baby boom" of the 1950s and early 1960s is depicted in this instance as the primary moving force. This spread among the OECD countries following the end of World War II. In many Asian and African countries the postcolonial era has led to an even greater population explosion as the standard of natal and prenatal care has advanced while average life spans have become longer. The growth pattern has been seen in other poor and undeveloped nations as well, most dramatically in Latin America, although in the wealthier countries the birthrate began to fall at the end of the 1960s and continued to do so during the 1970s, with a small pickup during the first years of the present decade. The effect of this downturn in the population cycle will not be felt in a slackening of demand for jobs until the next decade. It should be stressed that there is no attempt here to imply that an increase in population leads to a directly proportionate or permanent increase in unemployment: clearly, the extra people will demand extra goods and services and thus stimulate the creation of extra employment. The difficulty lies in the time lag between the arrival on the labour market of extra numbers of people and the consequent generation of higher demand in the economy.

In any event, the raw numbers of people of working age do not tell the full story. The worldwide increase in the rate of divorce and in the social acceptance of illegitimate births has resulted, in some countries, in a rapid growth in the number of one-parent families. This has increased the number of actual or potential breadwinners in society, since the missing parent—usually the father—will be an active member of the labour force, while the single mother will also need to work to support herself and her child. Other apparently "minor" factors can have a disproportionate effect on the total size of the labour force: the propensity of young people to combine higher education with some form of work, or at least some form of official registration that will provide unemployment benefits, varies from country to country; early retirement in, say, the older industrial towns of northern England (forced, perhaps, by the closure of large plants) may be matched, in global terms, by the drive to win employment rights for the over-60s in the U.S.

Women and the Labour Market. Significant as many of these demographic and behavioural phenomena may be, the social factor that has had the most marked effect on the demand for employment, and hence on the records of unemployment, has been the entry of women into the labour market. There are many ways of measuring this. Two fundamental measures are the relative shares of men and women of prime working age—25 to 54—in the total labour force and the "participation rate"—the degree to which people of active working age actually go out to seek work.

Between 1960 and 1980 the shares as between men and women of prime working age changed, in favour of women, in almost every member country of the OECD. For example, in the U.S. the proportion of males in the prime age category fell from 44.2% of the work force in 1960 to 35.5% in 1980, while the figures for women rose from 20.4 to 25.4%. There was a similar change in Britain, a more dramatic one in Canada, and so on; only in a very few OECD countries, such as Greece, was the change in favour of male workers of prime age.

The other measure—the "participation rate"—tells the same story. In the OECD area as a whole, the male participation rate (the number in the labour force divided by the number in the working-age population) fell from 87.1% in 1975 to 84.7% in 1982, while the rate for females rose from 49.3 to 54.1%. Taken over a short seven-year span—very short indeed by the time standards of such a major sea change in social behaviour—these alterations in the balance between males and females are of major importance to any understanding of the contemporary state of the labour market.

What is happening appears to be that males aged 25–54 more often than not retain their jobs longer than other groups during downturns in the cycle, while other groups enter and leave employment according to the condition of the economy. So *young* men and women will be jobless longer in a period of low demand for workers. (In the richer countries the educational system acts as a buffer, retaining people longer in full-time higher schooling.) Since young women are now more likely to aspire to employment and register as unemployed, the female factor swells the ranks of the officially recognized unemployed. At the other end of the age scale, older workers, predominantly male, take advantage of better pensions and early retirement schemes, or are forced out by closures, and leave the work force; this reduces the male participation rate but not the female one since women are low in numbers in this category.

In the prime age group the growth in jobs previously dominated by men—heavy industry, mining, hard factory labour—has either slowed down or been replaced by sharp declines. Over the years there is a net outflow from these jobs as the jobs themselves disappear. There is, however, a net inflow, not necessarily balancing, into new jobs. Much of this inflow consists of women, and a great many of the jobs are in the service sector of the economy—banking, insurance, administration, social services, and the like.

The Changing Pattern of Employment. In the OECD countries an extra 19 million people found jobs in the period 1975–79, some 17.3 million of them in service industries and only 3.6 million in traditional industry. As for agriculture, around two million jobs disappeared during that period. The same trends continued in the years 1980–81, at a far slower pace; a fall of a million jobs in agriculture and 1.3 million in traditional industry was barely exceeded by a rise of 2.7 million in service jobs.

It might be thought that this tendency for industry to replace agriculture and services, in their turn, to replace traditional industry is a luxury affordable only by rich countries. Surely it is not happening in the third world? Apparently, it is. According to a study by an ILO economist, Michael Hopkins, the developing countries are experiencing much the same phenomenon. He has analyzed data from 92 developing countries (almost all of them, excluding China) and concludes that between 1960 and 1980 the share of the labour force accounted for by agriculture dropped from 72.6 to 59.1%. The proportion of the labour forces engaged in industry in those countries rose from 13 to 20%, although most of the growth took place in the first of the two decades under scrutiny. The most dramatic growth came in services, which by 1980 accounted for some 44% of the third world's gross domestic production and 21% of its work force, as compared with only 14.5% in 1960.

This similarity of tendency between the developed world and the poor countries should not be confused with any more direct similarity. For example, Hopkins points out that in most regions of the developing world (places such as Hong Kong and Singapore apart) population growth is now outstripping economic growth, which could lead eventually, perhaps, to a doubling of present rates of unemployment in those countries. He also postulates that underemployment—work in jobs of less value than the available skills imply—rose from 421 million to 448 million in the period from 1974 to 1982. The situation was worst in the poorest parts of tropical Africa, where, according to Hopkins, underemployment rose from 55 million to some 76 million in the same eight-year period. Thus the concern expressed by the OECD analysts against the background of their relatively precise statistical data base is necessarily addressed to a phenomenon of a quite different order from that facing the developing or underdeveloped nations of the world, even if in the latter case the analysis must, of necessity, be rougher and the conclusions that are drawn must be somewhat more impressionistic.

The nub of the matter remains constant, however:

Rapid growth in the number of one-parent families has also increased the number of working women. "The missing parent—usually the father—will be an active member of the labour force, while the single mother will also need to work to support herself and her child."

CHRISTOPHER KEAN/BUSINESS WEEK

PETER YATES/THE NEW YORK TIMES

Workers fear displacement by machines such as the welding robots being operated by this General Motors Corp. assembly plant worker. But the author finds it "highly likely that the number of jobs created by the microchip" and other technological advances "will eventually exceed the number displaced."

over and above cyclical changes in demand, social factors, such as the entry of women into the labour force, have a strong impact on the level of total unemployment. This social change, in its turn, either is influenced by or influences what might truly be called a structural change: the onward flow of job opportunities away from the fields and into the factories, then away from the factories and into shops, offices, and public service institutions. Set against this, the change to automated or computerized methods of manufacture of certain goods is of relatively low significance.

It is not, of course, of no significance at all. In an ILO publication entitled *Industries in Trouble,* Robert Plant sketches the course of the argument since wheelwrights, coach builders, harness makers, hostlers, stagecoach drivers, and others saw their jobs swept out of existence by the advent of the steam locomotive. Some of the displaced workers could easily turn to other jobs: the old coach bodies were fixed to railway bogies. Other craftsmen's jobs disappeared forever. In the end, many more workers were employed on railways than had ever worked on the stagecoaches. There was, however, a painful period of adjustment.

The same sequence of events is expected by some economists to apply today as the microchip-driven devices replace the old machines. Many thousands of workers are being displaced from old mechanical telephone switching equipment manufacture, for example, and it is widely believed, though rarely demonstrated, that the number of white-collar jobs in the new offices and administrative buildings will fall as microelectronics takes its toll. It is, however, highly likely that the number of jobs created by the microchip will eventually exceed the number displaced, for it offers a great many opportunities to devise and provide new services—but that is hardly much consolation for those caught in the time lag between the 1980s, perhaps the decade of displacement, and the 1990s, perhaps the decade of blossoming new opportunities. Robert Plant, in addressing himself to mass production and technological change in general, concludes that a high sustained rate of economic growth is required to maintain employment in modern technologically progressive societies. It does seem self-evident that if growth is low, as it has been after both oil shocks, the social and technological factors together can have a devastating effect.

Political and Social Consequences. The effect of this on the people who lose their jobs, or fail to find employment when entering the job market after a spell of voluntary absence, is mitigated by a number of particularly modern circumstances. In many Western societies it is now accepted that a relatively short spell—say six months or less—out of work can be endured but that the move into long-term unemployment can cause great psychological and other damage to both families and individuals. In 12 major OECD countries the average proportion of long-term unemployed (defined as out of work for a year or more) rose from one-eighth of the total unemployed in 1979 to one-sixth in 1982. In specific areas the picture is worse: in 1984 it is possible that 45% of the unemployed in France will have been out of work for a year or more; in the U.S. this proportion, while traditionally far lower, is in danger of exceeding 10% in 1984.

Perhaps surprisingly, this sharp rise in unemployment, even of the most distressing kind, has not so far led to the kind of political extremism associated with the Great Depression of the 1930s. One reason is that many of the long-term unemployed are older men, effectively retired early, dispirited and often cruelly treated by the changes around them, but not ready to take organized revenge on society. There is also high youth unemployment; here, perhaps, the relatively large amounts of unemployment compensation available help to mitigate the sense of frustration that led to the events of half a century ago. This has yet to be conclusively demonstrated, however, since youth unemployment, according to the OECD, may rise to alarming heights in the next few years—perhaps 30% in Italy and 40% in Spain, for example. Long-term unemployment among the young is also growing.

Many devices have been tried in an effort to cushion the shock. Working hours in all OECD countries continue to fall, while holiday entitlements continue to lengthen. The rate of growth of part-time jobs, a form of work sharing, is between two and four times as rapid as the rate of growth of jobs in general, at least in OECD countries. In some countries, including the U.K., governments have invented a variety of "job creation" schemes; these do not quite amount to digging holes and filling them up again, although to some of the clients they may not, perhaps, seem so very different. Expenditure on training in new skills continues to rise, and this is almost certainly beneficial, since many of the long-term unemployed, of whatever age, have no hope of obtaining jobs unless they can match their skills to the new demands of the labour market.

The worst affected in the present worldwide tidal wave of unemployment are undoubtedly the unskilled; the most fortunate, those in possession of newly desirable skills. In spite of the greater participation rate of women in the work force, this hits them perhaps harder than men in general since, as new entrants, many women come to the job marketplace with low or underdeveloped skills. For such, the chances of getting a job are considerably poorer and the chances of losing a job are considerably greater.

It seems likely that further social changes will arise out of the very tensions created by the present ones. Some observers have noted an apparent correlation between a swing of the pendulum toward conservatism, in both the political and the social and behavioural senses, and the rapid growth in joblessness and its attendant insecurity. High unemployment by its very nature weakens trade unions, as has been clear in Britain. The rapid emergence of a new, comparatively wealthy, technologically able "information industry" class in society is proceeding at the same pace as the far sadder phenomenon of the emergence of an older, grayer, "discarded" class of displaced workers.

The "disgrace" of collecting welfare in the 1930s is being replaced by an apparent general acceptance, in many countries, that for young people this is a natural thing to do when jobs are not available. Whether this leads to a greater general acceptance of individual dependence upon the state for income support is an open question. In some countries, notably the U.S., high unemployment can lead to a greater propensity for individuals to try their luck as private entrepreneurs, small businessmen, and self-employed professional or craft workers. These do not swell the ranks of the technically employed but could, if successful, become the new yeast of growth for the 1990s.

The notion that leisure, whether financed by state dependence, a part-time job, or a full-time job, is of itself a good is spreading; paradoxically this is leading to particularly rapid growth in industries aimed at filling leisure hours, such as entertainment and tourism. These new industries, in cable television, personal computers, active sports equipment, and the like, are of course themselves the source of new employment opportunities.

Equal Opportunity. Other social changes are having yet other effects. It is arguable that women are traditionally part of the labour force, as they have been in agricultural work or in domestic service, and that their present greater participation is a return to the "natural order" rather than something new. Perhaps; what is clear is that in the advanced industrial countries women are demanding, and beginning to receive, opportunities to share equally in the more desirable jobs and jobs with higher skills—as is evident in Deirdre Bair's accompanying feature interview with Simone de Beauvoir.

The social consequences of this movement will certainly be profound. And it is having reverberative effects, at least on the fringes of higher-income white-collar society, as the sharing of job opportunities leads to sharing of domestic responsibilities, or the subdivision into one-parent families. What is not yet known is how widespread this movement will become. At its strongest in the United States, it has yet to spread itself through all classes of society in Britain, or to all countries in continental Western Europe—where West Germany, for example, still retains a strong penchant for regarding women as best placed in the home. The myths that shape our view of the causes of unemployment need not be replaced by myths about the eventual outcome of the great social upheavals whose shape we can discern with limited clarity for the very reason that we are in their midst.

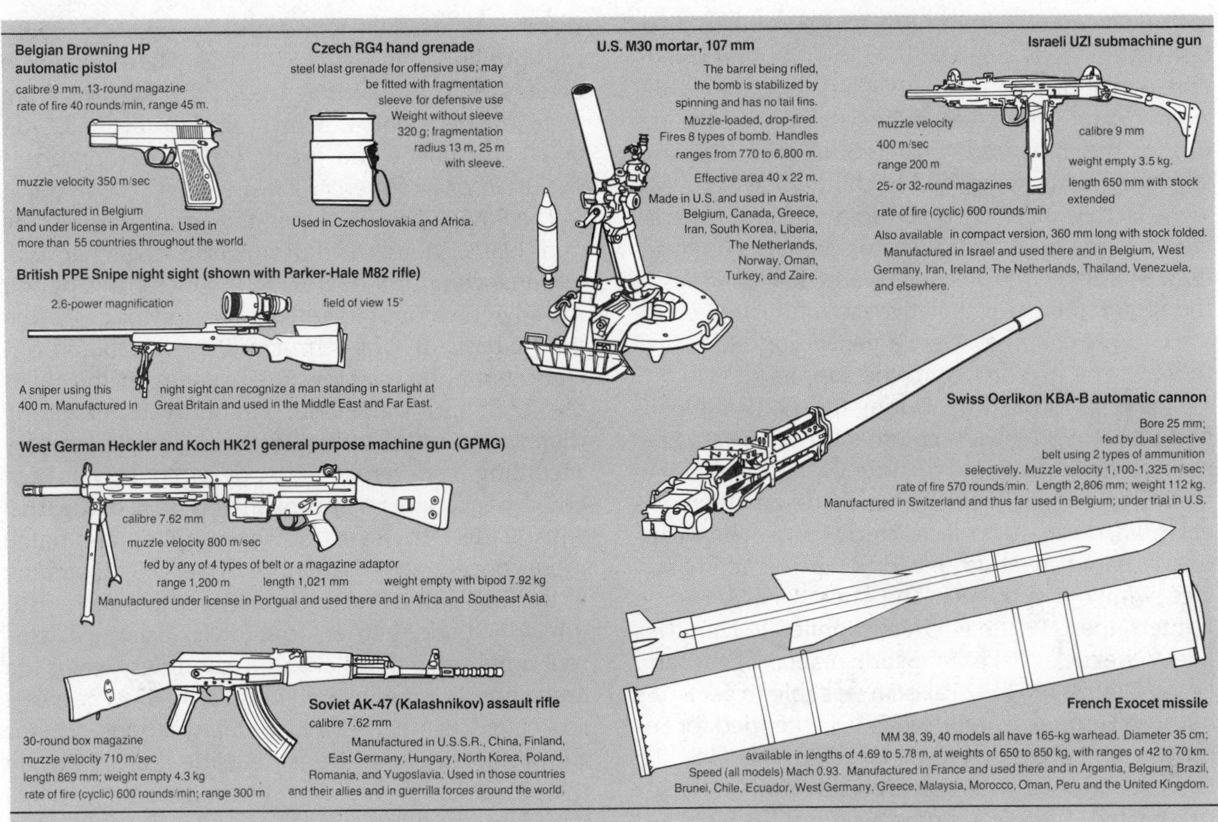

FLOURISHING, WORLDWIDE, DEADLY

The Open Market in Arms

by Mary Kaldor

In recent years the debate about disarmament has focused largely on the nuclear arms race and the possibility of war in Europe. Yet increasingly the third world intrudes on the debate. The U.S. invasion of Grenada, the worsening situation in Lebanon, the Falklands war, and the seemingly endless conflict between Iran and Iraq are insistently drawing attention to other aspects of the arms race and other "theatres" of war. It is estimated that 25 million people have died in wars since 1945, almost exclusively in the third world. At least eight million people are refugees, many as a consequence of wars in places like Afghanistan and Indochina. Countless others have died or are dying from hunger, disease, or exposure caused, at least in part, by the massive diversion of resources to arms procurement.

In 1980, the last year for which figures were available, international arms deliveries amounted to $26 billion, with over 70% of total arms exports going to less developed countries. Many third world countries have begun to develop their own domestic armaments industries. However, even in countries as developed as Israel and South Africa, such industries are heavily dependent on imports of subsystems, components, and capital equipment and on license agreements and other forms of technological assistance. Thus it appears that such production results in little if any foreign exchange saving.

Mary Kaldor, senior fellow at the Science Policy Research Unit, University of Sussex, previously worked at the Stockholm International Peace Research Institute. She is a leading figure in the antinuclear movement in Great Britain and a writer on defense policy and international affairs; her publications include The Arms Trade with the Third World, The Disintegrating West, *and* The Baroque Arsenal.

In the ten years from 1971 to 1980, the international arms trade doubled in real terms, and the increase in arms sold to less developed countries was even greater. Moreover, during this period the nature of the arms trade changed. In the 1950s and 1960s the arms transferred to third world countries were largely given away or sold cheaply on easy credit terms or in exchange for primary commodities. Moreover, the weapons were usually surplus to the requirements of the advanced industrial countries. In general, they were a generation older than those in the inventories of the suppliers.

This is no longer true. During the 1970s the arms trade became a heady commercial business. Payment is normally in hard currency, although some countries, especially the United States and the Soviet Union, do arrange special credit terms. The weapons supplied are as advanced as those entering service with the suppliers. The latest U.S. Air Force fighters, the F-16 and F-15, are supplied to countries like Venezuela, Pakistan, Saudi Arabia, Egypt, and Israel. During 1981–82 Pakistan was able to get F-16s because European-produced F-16s, intended for European air forces, were diverted to the U.S. Air Force. Saudi Arabia has ordered the immensely sophisticated AWACS (airborne warning and control systems) plane, at a cost of $128 million. Similarly, Syria received the new Soviet T-72 tank in 1979, before it was delivered to the Warsaw Pact countries, and it is thought that the slow introduction of the tank into Europe is due to heavy export demand. The advanced Soviet MiG-25 fighter has been sold to Algeria, India, Libya, and Syria, though no deliveries to Warsaw Pact countries have yet been reported. The Western European countries also compete to provide the latest equipment. French Mirage and Super Étendard aircraft are sold all over the world. The British destroyer HMS "Sheffield" was sunk during the Falklands war by a French-made Exocet missile.

"Military Assistance." Starting with the Truman Doctrine in 1947, which provided for military assistance to help Greece and Turkey combat Communist threats, the United States after World War II began to build a global collective security system. This consisted of mutual defense treaties with individual countries and a chain of regional alliances—SEATO in Southeast Asia (now dissolved), ANZUS with Australia and New Zealand, CENTO (of which the U.S. was not formally a member; disbanded in 1979) in the Middle East, NATO, and the Rio Treaty in Latin America. Military assistance—the provision of arms, advice, and training—was considered essential to implement these treaties.

In addition to these so-called forward defense areas, the United States sold or gave arms to what were known as free world orientation areas, countries not linked to the U.S. by treaty but thought to be amenable to its influence. In the 32 years from 1946 to 1977, the U.S. provided some $78,718,000,000 in loans and grants for military purposes exclusive of commercial sales.

The Soviet Union entered the arms market in the mid-1950s, though it did not really challenge U.S. dominance until the late 1960s. During this period the Soviet Union sold arms at very low prices, often on the basis of long-term credits, repayable in primary commodities at low interest rates. By the 1980s the U.S. and the Soviet Union were exporting roughly similar quantities of arms (the figures vary according to different methods of counting). Each country accounts for approximately 30% of the total arms trade. However, Soviet supplies are much more concentrated than those of the U.S. According to the Stockholm International Peace Research Institute arms trade registers, the Soviet Union has current arms trade deals with 28 countries, while the corresponding figure for the U.S. is 67. The same source reports that 61 major U.S. weapons systems are produced under license outside the U.S., while the Soviet Union has only 11 similar arrangements with four countries—Czechoslovakia, Poland, India, and North Korea.

During the 1950s and 1960s the chief purpose of military assistance was considered to be political. It was a way of building political support throughout the world. For the U.S. the aim was to "contain Communism." For the Soviet Union arms supplies were seen largely as a mechanism for penetrating the chain of military alliances that encircled it and for countering U.S. influence. Whether or not these aims were successful—U.S. military assistance did not prevent revolutions, and recipients of Soviet aid on occasion turned against their supplier—the massive transfer of arms did succeed in bringing the third world into the global East-West conflict. This was not simply because it created pro-West or pro-East regimes. Rather, it was because ideas about military power, based on the East-West conflict, were transferred to the third world.

Through the provision of arms, training, and advice, the U.S. and the Soviet Union were able to fashion third world armies in their own image, based on the vision of an East-West conflict in Europe: F-16s, Mirages, AWACS aircraft, and Type-42 destroyers were all designed for war in Europe or the Atlantic. Because they were considered important in Europe, they came to be viewed as necessary attributes of military power, regardless of the actual situation on the ground. But sophisticated weapons systems may actually be a handicap to a nation that lacks the skills and infrastructure (roads, airfields, communications) needed to exploit them effectively. In the wars between India and Pakistan in 1965 and 1971, Pakistan could not make use of the sophisticated equipment provided by the U.S., and India found that older weapons, like the Gnat aircraft and the Centurion tank, were more effective, given available skills. In fighting between Iran and Iraq, both sides have had considerable difficulty operating and maintaining advanced military equipment, particularly aircraft and missiles.

Yet third world governments continue to devote considerable resources to the acquisition of up-to-date weapons systems. Pakistan is still anxious to buy the F-16. India is acquiring the French Mirage and Anglo-French Jaguar aircraft. Thirty years of arms acquisition have established a set of criteria for military power—and hence perceptions of political power—that appear to be almost impervious to actual military experience. In this sense the provision of military assistance did serve an important political purpose, for it imposed a kind of world military order, a common acceptance of a military hierarchy of nations with the superpowers on top.

The Economics of Arms Sales. In the 1970s balance of payments difficulties, stemming largely from the oil price "shocks" and the rising cost of military equipment, increased the economic importance of the arms trade. For the Soviets balance of payments considerations appear to have been paramount in their push to sell arms. Increased imports of grain and foreign technology necessitated a search for new sources of foreign currency. Together with oil and gold, arms are one of the U.S.S.R.'s most important ways of earning foreign exchange. In 1980 arms accounted for 12% of total Soviet exports, and the percentage has been higher in previous years, amounting to as much as 25% of exports in 1973. The Soviet government has also had to bear the cost (in payments never made) of failed relationships with client states: $5 billion in the case of Egypt and $3 billion in the case of Indonesia.

Arms are a less important component of trade for Western countries, although the balance of payments is widely used to justify arms exports. In particular, arms exports are often treated as a form of compensation for overseas military spending. The foreign exchange costs of keeping troops abroad or of arms imports are set against the earnings from arms exports. In fact, for most Western countries, arms exports amount to less than 3% of total exports and, in general, the defense industry is less export-intensive than most manufacturing sectors. In the early 1970s arms exports may have been important for the United States; in 1972, the year after the U.S.

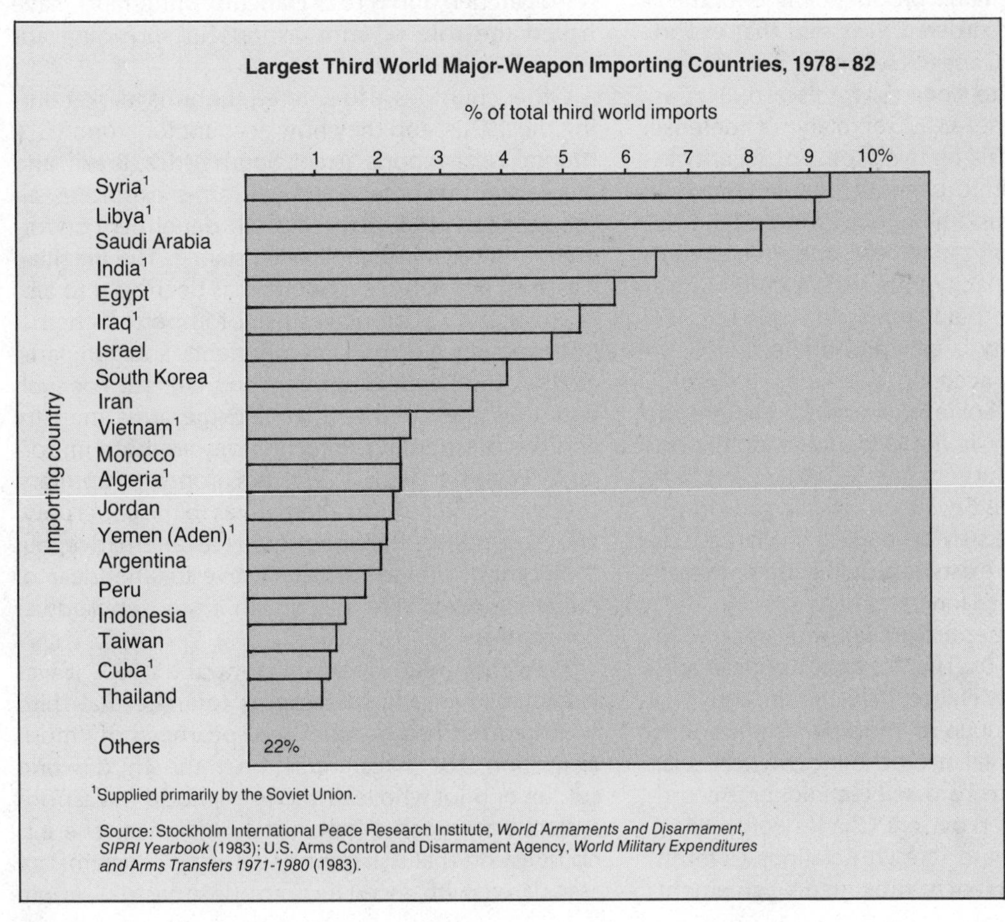

[1]Supplied primarily by the Soviet Union.

Source: Stockholm International Peace Research Institute, *World Armaments and Disarmament, SIPRI Yearbook* (1983); U.S. Arms Control and Disarmament Agency, *World Military Expenditures and Arms Transfers 1971-1980* (1983).

trade balance went into deficit for the first time since 1936, they accounted for more than 8% of total exports.

More important has been the contribution of arms exports to the survival of domestic arms industries. As the cost of weapons systems has risen, it has become harder and harder for governments to maintain capacity in the arms industry. Arms exports lower production costs and, to a limited extent, help to recoup research and development expenditures. Above all, they help to keep production lines open between government orders. This has been especially important for European governments, whose military budgets are small in relation to the size of their defense industries. For the major Western European suppliers, arms exports account for between 20 and 30% of total production. For some companies the dependence is even greater. The French manufacturer of Mirage aircraft, Dassault-Breguet, exports over 70% of its output. The recently closed Vickers tank factory at Elswick, England, was almost entirely dependent on exports.

This factor has become increasingly important for the U.S. as well, especially with the decline in domestic procurement following the end of the Vietnam war. The Grumman Corp. was saved from bankruptcy by a $200 million loan from the shah of Iran in order to maintain a production line for the F-14 fighters Iran had ordered. It is said that exports "saved" Northrop, General Dynamics, and Vought. In his annual report to Congress for fiscal 1984, Caspar Weinberger, the U.S. secretary of defense, placed great emphasis on this aspect of security assistance. Its economic benefits, he said, include "production line smoothing, expansion of the defense industrial mobilization base, and . . . maintaining a production capacity-in-being for current front line systems that are being replaced while the new production capability is coming on line."

Although exports account for a surprisingly high proportion of total Soviet military production, the Soviet arms industry is not dependent on exports because of the nature of the U.S.S.R.'s centrally planned system. The Soviet Union fills gaps in domestic military orders by producing civilian goods. Excess capacity, if it exists, is a deliberate or mistaken consequence of planning.

Commercial competition to sell arms became intense during the 1970s. The Western European arms suppliers, particularly France, Italy, Britain, and West Germany, became much more important, accounting for 30% of the total market. France, in particular, became famous for its hard-sell techniques. According to figures released by Sen. Charles Percy, chairman of the U.S. Senate Foreign Relations Committee, the value of French arms trade agreements signed in 1980 exceeded the value of U.S. arms trade agreements. For both Britain and France, the export of military technology appears almost to have become an end in itself. Prime Minister Margaret Thatcher and Pres. François Mitterrand have hailed the role of arms exports in spreading advanced technology.

Arms Exports, 1980/Shares by Suppliers

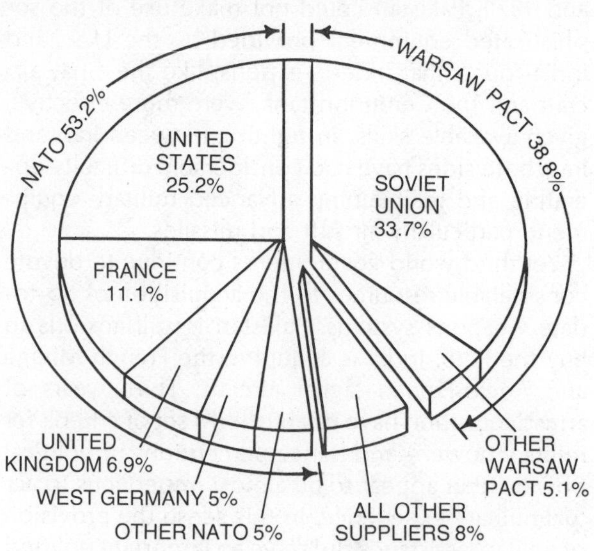

Source: U.S. Arms Control and Disarmament Agency, *World Military Expenditures and Arms Transfers 1971-1980* (1983).

Other countries also entered the arms market during the 1970s, and they now account for around 5% of total arms exports. Israel, South Africa, Brazil, and India have become significant arms exporters, although their products are heavily dependent on foreign imports and technical assistance. The Brazilian Cascavel armoured car, which has been sold to Libya, Iraq, and Qatar, makes use of imported engine, transmission, electronic components, and gun parts, as does the Bandeirante transport aircraft. For such countries the need to maintain the arms industry and the prestige of the technology are both important. Together with Western European suppliers, they stress their role as alternatives to the superpowers. As suppliers they do provide an alternative, but they cannot provide an alternative for the ideas of military power that are drawn from superpower conceptions.

Skewed Modernization. During the 1960s it was fashionable among sociologists to argue that third world armies had become the spearhead of "modernization" or "westernization": the third world soldier or pilot who learns to use a modern weapons system becomes a Western industrial man. There is no question that weapons-acquisition programs are associated with a certain form of industrialization.

The acquisition of major weapons systems directly influences the process of industrialization and, at the same time, contributes to the formation of states with a vested interest in guaranteeing that process. However, the benefits are far from evident.

The acquisition of a major weapons system creates demands for airfields, roads, telephones, radar systems, repair shops, special skills, spare parts, and special types of steel and petroleum products. In an underdeveloped country like Saudi Arabia, a large proportion of military spending goes toward infrastructure, especially construction. It has been argued that these infrastructural demands, particularly where domestic arms manufacture is undertaken, can represent the main impetus behind industrialization, although that industrialization is biased toward the types of industry that are characteristic of arms production in rich countries. In countries like Argentina and Brazil, the establishment of a diversified arms industry—shipbuilding, aerospace, and armoured cars—has played a central role in industrial development. Many commentators have noted the profound influence of arms imports and production on the formation of heavy industry and national research and development centres, as well as transport and communications.

But this form of industrialization is very expensive. It is highly capital-intensive, import-intensive, and skill-intensive. Arms imports average between one-fifth and one-half of the total capital imports of third world countries. The investment required to create one job in the arms industry or related industries is much greater, especially in terms of foreign exchange, than investment in civilian industry or agriculture. Moreover, the job is likely to require the kind of skill that is scarce in less developed countries. Nor is it clear that such industrialization has a positive effect on growth. With very rare exceptions, third world countries can never learn enough to compete in the world market for advanced technology products. Nor does the technology seem to be appropriate for solving some of the basic problems that afflict third world societies, such as hunger and disease.

To pay for this type of industrialization, third world countries must either obtain foreign assistance, through grants or loans, or increase their exports of primary products. The consequent impoverishment of the countryside is a common phenomenon. Rural producers are drawn into the money economy (resulting in a fictitious statistical increase in agricultural income) as more and more commodities are produced for urban and world markets instead of subsistence. Cheap labour is drawn into the towns as poor farmers are squeezed out by the introduction of more efficient production methods, by worsening terms of trade between manufactured and primary commodities, or by imports of cheap food from industrialized countries. Yet jobs are scarce in the towns because industrial investment is so capital-intensive. The result is a characteristic pattern of uneven development, with extremes of wealth and poverty and immense social and cultural dislocation. In case after case this turbulent process is "managed" by means of militarism and war. The weapons sustain the legitimacy of third world regimes, often dominated by the military, and they are used in the wars that result from the pattern of uneven development.

Restraining the Arms Trade. Some arms suppliers do exercise restraint. Countries like Sweden, Austria, and Japan that have a greater interest in stability than in arms exports refuse to supply arms to countries in conflict or to those deemed to violate human rights. Both the West German and British governments also claim to exercise restraint, and they attempt to distance themselves from the commercial "hurly-burly" of arms transfers. And because a political policy implies discrimination among recipients, it can be argued that during the 1950s and 1960s both the U.S. and the Soviet Union exercised a form of implicit restraint. More sophisticated and/or offensive types of equipment were often withheld.

Restraint seems to wither away, however, in the face of commercial or political pressure to sell arms. In practice, neither West Germany nor Britain seems to exercise restraint effectively. West Germany uses co-production with Britain and France, among other methods, to circumvent its own legal guidelines.

World Arms Exporters, 1980

Country	Total arms exports ($000,000)	Arms exports as % of total exports	% of total world arms exports
U.S.S.R.	8,800	11.5	33.7
United States	6,600	3.0	25.2
France	2,900	2.5	11.1
United Kingdom	1,800	1.6	6.9
West Germany	1,300	0.7	5.0
Czechoslovakia	700	4.4	2.7
Italy	650	0.8	2.5
Yugoslavia	340	2.8[1]	1.3
Poland	320	1.9	1.2
Switzerland	290	1.0	1.1
South Korea	250	1.4	1.0
China	220	1.1	0.8
North Korea	190	6.1[1]	0.7
Netherlands, The	180	0.2	0.7
Saudi Arabia	170	0.2	0.7
Turkey	150	5.4	0.6
Belgium	140	0.2	0.5
Israel	140	2.5	0.5
Romania	130	0.7	0.5
Brazil	110	0.5	0.4

[1]1979.
Source: U.S. Arms Control and Disarmament Agency, *World Military Expenditures and Arms Transfers 1971–1980* (1983).

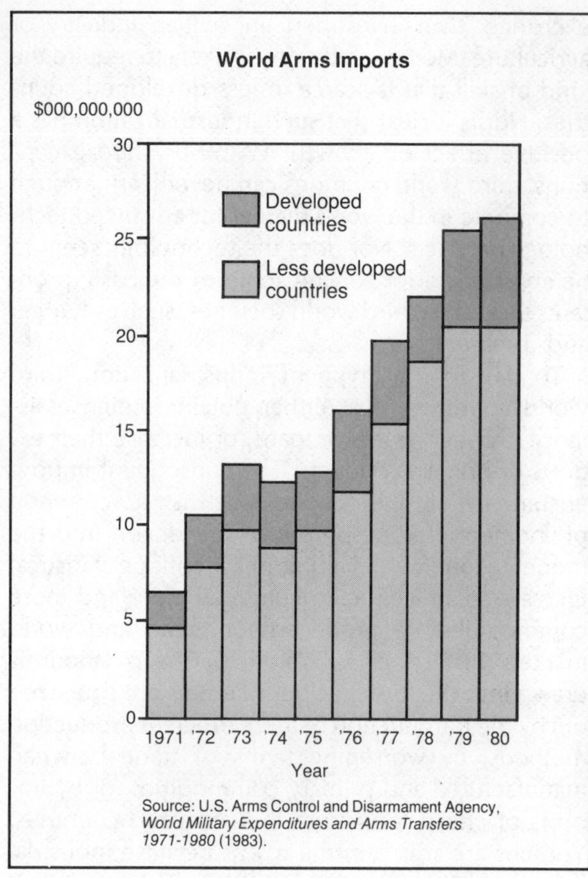

Source: U.S. Arms Control and Disarmament Agency, *World Military Expenditures and Arms Transfers 1971-1980* (1983).

Britain's more "pragmatic" forms of restraint do not appear to have prevented the sale of arms to both belligerents in the Iran-Iraq war or to violators of human rights such as Indonesia or Turkey. Despite the embargo on South Africa, U.K. defense products get through. Sometimes restraint is inoperable because of the zeal of the salesman. According to Frederic S. Pearson ("The Question of Control in British Defence Sales Policy," *International Affairs*, Spring 1983), "Some in the Foreign Office still recall with dismay 'excesses' of the Defence Sales Organisation during the multifarious and lucrative deals with Iran during the mid to late 1970s. Evidently, for instance, the Foreign Office was not consulted when Sir Ronald Ellis, then the Head of Defence Sales, concluded an approximately £1 billion deal for an Iranian military installation during a personal meeting with the Shah, agreeing to accept payment . . . in oil."

During Jimmy Carter's administration, the U.S. government tried to introduce restraint, but several important exceptions were made and, in any case, Carter's policy was reversed by Ronald Reagan. U.S. arms trade agreements reached record levels in 1981, and military assistance—now called security assistance—was substantially increased. Major efforts have been made to support pro-U.S. regimes in areas of tension, especially the Middle East. Israel and Egypt are primary U.S. recipients, and both have been "forgiven" substantial debts. Other favoured recipients include Pakistan, Turkey, Tunisia, Sudan, Morocco, and Venezuela.

Also during the Carter administration, attempts were made to restrain the arms trade on a multilateral basis. Between December 1977 and December 1978, conventional arms transfer talks were held between the Soviet Union and the U.S. Both sides expressed clear interest, but the talks died when the U.S. vetoed discussions of "Soviet-proposed" regions in East and West Asia. On the side of the recipients, proposals for multilateral restraint on a regional basis have been put forward. In 1974, in the Declaration of Ayacucho, eight Andean states committed themselves "to create conditions which permit effective limitations of armaments and put an end to their acquisition for offensive warlike purposes in order to dedicate all possible resources to economic and social development." However, the declaration did not include Brazil, and it did not prevent sizable arms purchases by Chile, Peru, and Ecuador.

The problem with all these proposals is that they are based on the same assumptions that underlie the arms trade itself. Third world governments complain that they are discriminatory, and within the framework of the world military order, this is true. The acquisition of arms gives third world nations a place in the international military hierarchy, and according to the logic of the world military order, a third world nation would descend in the hierarchy if arms transfers to it were restrained.

The alternative for third world countries is to opt out of the hierarchy entirely. Quite apart from the fact that the East-West conflict is not necessarily the appropriate model for third world countries, and that sophisticated equipment is not much use without a sophisticated technological base, third world countries are condemned to a permanent subordinate position. What difference does it make if India has an aircraft carrier if the U.S. has several and Soviet cruisers sail freely around the Indian Ocean? Would it not be just as effective, in international political terms, to use tugs?

But the prospects for this do not seem bright as long as the superpower rivalry continues. Political pressures to obtain arms could be reduced only by questioning the East-West conflict and the utility of the nuclear arms race. The arms trade and the resulting combination of war, militarism, and underdevelopment in the third world can be described as the underside of the arms race among advanced industrial countries. If the arms trade were to be restrained, the arms race itself would have to be challenged.

CALENDAR OF EVENTS OF 1984

JANUARY

1 *New Year's Day; Canadian anniversary celebrations*

3 *25th anniversary of Alaska's admission to the Union*

4 *175th anniversary of Louis Braille's birth; Independence Day in Burma (1948)*

6 *Feast of Epiphany*

14 *Opening of the International Olympic Games for the Disabled*

15 *Birthday of the Rev. Martin Luther King, Jr.*

19 *175th anniversary of Edgar Allan Poe's birth*

26 *Australia Day (1788); Proclamation of the Republic Day in India (1950)*

28 *100th anniversary of the births of the Piccard twins*

1 **Canadian anniversary celebrations.** Several Canadian provinces and cities celebrate important anniversaries during 1984. The province of Quebec commemorates the 450th anniversary of Jacques Cartier's explorations, and Trois-Rivières, Que., observes its 350th anniversary. The provinces of New Brunswick and Ontario both celebrate bicentennials. Toronto marks its 150th year and Calgary its 100th.

4 **175th anniversary of Louis Braille's birth.** Louis Braille was blinded by an accident at the age of three. Seven years later he entered the National Institute for Blind Youth in Paris, where he distinguished himself in the fields of science and music. In 1824 the young Frenchman devised his own system of embossed dots that blind persons could read with their fingers. The raised-dot codes represented letters, numerals, and punctuation marks. Braille, an accomplished organist and cellist, also developed a system of musical notation for the blind. He was born on Jan. 4, 1809, and died of tuberculosis on Jan. 6, 1852.

28 **100th anniversary of the births of the Piccard twins.** Jean-Félix and Auguste Piccard, identical twins, achieved celebrity as scientists and adventurers. In 1932 Auguste, a physicist, attached an airtight gondola that he had invented to a large hydrogen-filled balloon and ascended some 16,000 m (53,000 ft) into the stratosphere to gather information on cosmic rays and radioactivity. In 1953 he and his son Jacques descended more than 3,000 m (10,000 ft) below the surface of the Mediterranean in a bathyscaphe that the elder Piccard had designed. From 1922 to 1954 Auguste taught physics at the University of Brussels. Jean-Félix was a chemist and aeronautical engineer. In 1934 he and his pilot wife, Jeannette, ascended about 17,000 m (57,000 ft) in a balloon to study cosmic rays. He made another ascent in 1937, using an open gondola and 98 balloons, each measuring 2 m (6 ft) in diameter. The record-setting flight was the first manned ascent using multiple balloons. Jean-Félix became a U.S. citizen in 1931 and taught aeronautical engineering at the University of Minnesota from 1936 to 1952. Auguste and Jean-Félix were born on Jan. 28, 1884, in Basel, Switz. Auguste died in Lausanne, Switz., on March 24, 1962; Jean-Félix died in Minneapolis, Minn., on his 79th birthday.

FEBRUARY

2 *Chinese New Year; Candlemas Day*

4 *Independence Day in Sri Lanka (1948)*

6 *Waitangi Day in New Zealand (1840)*

8 *Winter Olympic Games open in Sarajevo, Yugos.*

12 *175th anniversary of the births of Charles Darwin and Abraham Lincoln*

14 *St. Valentine's Day*

18 *Independence Day in The Gambia (1965)*

27 *Independence Day in Dominican Republic (1844)*

29 *Intercalary, or Leap Year, Day*

8 **Winter Olympic Games open in Sarajevo, Yugos.** Unlike the Summer Olympic Games, which have antecedents in antiquity, the Winter Olympic Games were first held in 1924 in Chamonix, France. Sarajevo, the site of the 1984 Winter Games, is the capital of Yugoslavia's Socialist Republic of Bosnia and Hercegovina. Situated at the foot of Mt. Trebevic in the Miljacka River valley, Sarajevo has preserved many physical reminders of its colourful past. Attractions include ancient mosques, a 16th-century clock tower, museums, and the famed coppersmith's bazaar. In 1914 the assassinations in Sarajevo of Austro-Hungarian Archduke Francis Ferdinand and his wife triggered World War I.

29 **Intercalary Day.** Julius Caesar's astronomers are credited with introducing the first Leap Year after calculating that it took the Earth 365.25 days to complete its orbit around the Sun. Beginning in 46 BC, an intercalary day was added to the Julian calendar to keep the date of the equinox the same year after year. Caesar's astronomers had the right idea, but their calculations needed further refinement. Because the Earth's orbit around the Sun is actually 365.242 days, the Julian calendar was about ten days off when Pope Gregory XIII ordered a revision. In 1582 Gregory abolished the Julian calendar (along with the ten extra days) and substituted the Gregorian, or New Style, calendar. To keep the discrepancy between the calendar and Sun time from widening again, Gregory ordered that Leap Year be skipped in all centenary years except those divisible by 400. Thus 1600 was a Leap Year, but not 1700, 1800, and 1900. However, even Gregory's solution was not quite on the mark. It turns out that the year is still 26 seconds too long. If no further modifications are made before the year 4905, astronomers will have to get rid of an entire day.

MARCH

3 *Hina Matsuri, Japan's Doll Festival*

7 *Ash Wednesday*

8 *International Women's Day*

12 *Commonwealth Day*

15 *Ides of March (Julius Caesar assassinated in 44 BC)*

17 *St. Patrick's Day*

18 *Jewish Feast of Purim*

20 *Vernal equinox in the Northern Hemisphere; autumnal equinox in the Southern Hemisphere*

24 *150th anniversary of John Wesley Powell's birth*

25 *Independence Day in Greece (1821)*

18 **Jewish Feast of Purim.** The background of the Jewish Feast of Purim is contained in the Megillah (story) of Esther in the Bible. Haman, chief minister of the Persian king Ahasuerus, was incensed that Mordecai, a Jew, held him in disdain, so he planned to have all the Jews in the kingdom massacred after informing the king that they were rebellious. Esther, the beautiful Jewish queen of Ahasuerus, got wind of the plot and begged her husband to intervene. The king, who was led to believe that Haman had attacked the queen, ordered his minister to be hanged. Jews celebrate their deliverance on the Feast of Purim, which occurs on the 14th day of the Hebrew month of Adar. Purim is also called the Feast of Lots because the day of the intended slaughter had been determined by casting lots (Hebrew *purim*).

24 **150th anniversary of John Wesley Powell's birth.** The famed explorer had originally intended to become a minister like his father, but he drifted toward botany, natural history, and the life of an adventurer. As a young man he made solitary trips down the Mississippi, Illinois, and Ohio rivers. When the Civil War broke out, he enlisted in the Union Army and quickly became an officer and a member of Gen. Ulysses S. Grant's staff. Though he lost his right arm during the Battle of Shiloh in 1862, he returned to active duty and was honourably discharged in January 1865. Powell then taught geology and served as a museum curator in Illinois. He was still

working as a curator in 1868 when he developed a plan to lead a flotilla down the unexplored canyons of the Green and Colorado rivers. Powell made two trips between 1869 and 1872. The first made him a national hero. On the second (1871–72) he was accompanied by several prominent geologists. Powell, who was also a talented administrator, later headed up both the Bureau of Ethnology for the Smithsonian Institution and the U.S. Geological Survey. The highly detailed geologic and topographic maps produced by the survey are a legacy of his administration. Powell was born on March 24, 1834, and died on Sept. 23, 1902.

APRIL

1 *April Fools' Day*

4 *35th anniversary of the signing of the North Atlantic Treaty; anniversary of the liberation of Hungary (1945)*

9 *U.S. Civil War ends with the surrender of Gen. Robert E. Lee (1865); Academy Awards presentations*

15 *Palm Sunday*

17 *Jewish feast of Passover begins*

20 *Good Friday*

22 *Easter Sunday in both Western and Orthodox churches*

27 *Union Day in Tanzania (1964); Arbor Day in the U.S.*

29 *Emperor's birthday in Japan*

30 *Queen's Day in The Netherlands*

1 **April Fools' Day.** Playing practical jokes on friends on April 1 is a folk tradition that has been observed in several countries for many centuries, though no one is quite sure how April Fools' Day began. It has similarities to Hilaria, an ancient Roman festival, and to the Holi festival in India. One aspect of this spring celebration is the throwing of coloured water or powder on others. Bonfires lit in the streets are said to be cremation fires of the flame-breathing Holika, who was consumed by a pyre she had prepared for her brother. The date of April Fools' Day also seems to tie it to the vernal equinox, which occurs about ten days earlier. At that time of year nature "fools" mankind with abrupt changes in the weather.

4 **35th anniversary of the signing of the North Atlantic Treaty.** The U.S., Canada, and ten European nations signed the North Atlantic Treaty in Washington, D.C., on April 4, 1949. The European signatories were Belgium, Denmark, France, Great Britain, Iceland, Italy, Luxembourg, The Netherlands, Norway, and Portugal. Article 5, the key provision of the treaty, stipulated that an attack against any one country would be considered an attack against all of them. The nations that signed the treaty feared the spread of Soviet imperialism, which was seen as a growing threat after the Communists seized Czechoslovakia and the Soviets blockaded Berlin in 1948. The treaty led to the formation of the North Atlantic Treaty Organization (NATO) in 1950. Greece and Turkey signed in 1951 and West Germany in 1954. After France reduced its NATO commitments in later years, the Supreme Headquarters Allied Powers Europe (SHAPE) was moved (1967) from Paris to Casteau, Belgium.

MAY

1 *May Day*

5 *Kentucky Derby*

6 *Mozart music festival in Augsburg, West Germany*

8 *100th anniversary of Harry S. Truman's birth; Germany surrenders to the Allies (1945)*

12 *Native American Day; Louisiana World Exposition begins*

13 *Mother's Day in the U.S.*

17 *Constitution Day in Norway (1814)*

21 *350th anniversary of the Oberammergau Passion Play*

28 *Memorial Day in the U.S.*

30 *Annular eclipse of the Sun, visible in parts of North America, Africa, and Europe*

31 *Republic Day in South Africa (1961)*

8 **100th anniversary of Harry S. Truman's birth.** Pres. Franklin D. Roosevelt had completed less than three months of his fourth term when he died suddenly of a cerebral hemorrhage on April 12, 1945. That same day Vice-Pres. Harry S. Truman took the oath of office as president. He was quoted as saying to reporters: "Boys, if you ever pray, pray for me now." Truman's successes as president included the Truman Doctrine (economic and military aid to Greece and Turkey); the Marshall Plan; desegregation of the armed forces; and the signing of the North Atlantic Treaty. Two of his most controversial decisions were the dropping of atomic bombs on Hiroshima and Nagasaki and the removal of Gen. Douglas MacArthur from his command during the Korean War. Truman was born on May 8, 1884, in Lamar, Mo. He attained the rank of captain during World War I and married Bess Wallace in 1919. He studied law at night but never graduated from law school or college. After serving out Roosevelt's unexpired term, Truman defeated Thomas E. Dewey in the 1948 presidential election. His two-million-vote margin stunned political pundits who had predicted his defeat. Truman died in Kansas City, Mo., on Dec. 26, 1972, at the age of 88.

21 **350th anniversary of the Oberammergau Passion Play.** The Bavarian village of Oberammergau is situated about 65 km (40 mi) from Munich, West Germany. When a plague struck the town in 1633, the villagers vowed to reenact the passion of Christ every ten years if they were spared further casualties. The first production was accordingly staged in 1634. After 1674 the schedule was changed so that performances fell on decimal years; *e.g.*, 1680, 1690, 1700. With few exceptions the play has been faithfully performed every ten years since that time. The 1984 off-year production commemorates the 350th anniversary of the play. It attracts a worldwide audience, lasts for eight hours, and employs hundreds of actors, 124 of whom have speaking parts. Most of the actors reside in the village or its immediate environs.

JUNE

2 *Republic Day in Italy (1946)*

5 *Constitution Day in Denmark (1849)*

6 *40th anniversary of D-Day*

9 *Queen Elizabeth II's official birthday*

10 *Pentecost*

11 *Kamehameha Day in Hawaii*

12 *Independence Day in Philippines (1898)*

14 *100th anniversary of John McCormack's birth*

17 *Father's Day in the U.S.*

21 *Summer solstice in the Northern Hemisphere; winter solstice in the Southern Hemisphere*

25 *All England Lawn Tennis Championships begin at Wimbledon*

26 *25th anniversary of the dedication of the St. Lawrence Seaway*

30 *Islamic feast of Id al-Fitr (All Islamic feasts depend on visual sighting of the new Moon and may, therefore, occur later than the projected date)*

6 **40th anniversary of D-Day.** Operation Overlord, better known as D-Day, took place on June 6, 1944. The daring landing on the beaches of Normandy during World War II involved 4,000 ships, several thousand smaller craft, more than 1,000 planes and gliders, and included 150,000 U.S., Canadian, and British soldiers. The combined forces, under the command of Gen. Dwight D. Eisenhower, hit the French coast between Cherbourg and Le Havre and suffered 10,000 casualties. The worst losses were sustained by U.S. forces at Omaha Beach, where casualties in some sections ran as high as 66%. On May 8, 1945, less than a year later, Germany surrendered and the war in Europe was over.

14 **100th anniversary of John McCormack's birth.** The great Irish tenor was born in 1884 at Athlone, County Westmeath. After studying in Italy, he made his operatic debut at Covent Garden in London, singing in *Cavalleria rusticana*, and later appeared in productions of the Chicago, Boston, and New York Metropolitan opera companies. He also toured Australia with Nellie Melba, the popular Australian coloratura soprano. In 1913 McCormack turned

to the concert stage, where he enjoyed great success singing German lieder. He similarly delighted recital audiences with his renditions of Irish folk songs. McCormack's popularity was sustained by the marketing of phonograph recordings of songs spontaneously associated with his name. He became a U.S. citizen in 1919 and died near Dublin in 1945.

JULY

1 *Canada Day (1867)*
4 *Independence Day in the U.S. (1776)*
6 *Calgary Stampede begins*
10 *Independence Day in The Bahamas (1973)*
13 *400th anniversary of the arrival of English settlers in the New World*
14 *Bastille Day in France (1789)*
20 *15th anniversary of man's first landing on the Moon*
23 *National Day in Egypt (1952)*
25 *Constitution Day in Puerto Rico (1952)*
28 *Summer Olympic Games open in Los Angeles*

13 **400th anniversary of the arrival of English settlers in New World.** In 1584 Philip Amadas and Arthur Barlowe landed on the coast of what is now North Carolina and selected the site for the first English colony in the New World. They were emissaries of Sir Walter Raleigh, who had received a patent to colonize the area from Queen Elizabeth I. The colonists departed England in 1585 in seven small ships commanded by Sir Richard Grenville and established a settlement at the north end of Roanoke Island. The following year, threatened by famine and hostile Indians, the colonists returned to England. Several other attempts were made to colonize the territory, but for one reason or another all early efforts failed.

28 **Summer Olympic Games open in Los Angeles.** The first Olympic Games were held in 776 BC in a sacred grove at Olympia, Greece. The only competitive event was a foot race, called a *stade* because it covered a distance more or less equal to the length of the stadium. Over the years many other events were added, including the pentathlon in 708 BC. The ancient Games reached their highest point of prestige and influence during the 5th century BC; they then began a slow decline as the emphasis on winning encouraged cities to hire professional athletes. About AD 393, after Greece had lost its independence, the Roman emperor Theodosius abolished the Games. During the centuries that followed, the Games belonged solely to history, but in 1894 a revival was under way. Baron Pierre de Coubertin, a French scholar and educator, convened a conference in Paris and persuaded delegates from 12 nations to support a modern version of the Olympic Games. The event took place in Athens in 1896. Since that time, except during World Wars I and II, the Games have been held every four years. The sports calendar of events has undergone modification, and political developments have led to boycotts and even terrorist murders, but the Games seem destined to thrive for the indefinite future. The 1984 Summer Games in Los Angeles will close on August 12.

AUGUST

2 *Signing of the U.S. Declaration of Independence*
6 *Hiroshima Peace Festival; Independence Day in Jamaica (1962)*
7 *25th anniversary of the first pictures of Earth taken from space*
9 *Moment of Silence in Nagasaki*
10 *Independence Day in Ecuador (1809)*
14 *Japan surrenders to the Allies (1945)*
21 *25th anniversary of Hawaii's admission to the Union*
26 *100th anniversary of Mergenthaler's patent on the Linotype machine*

6 **Hiroshima Peace Festival.** Each year since 1952 Japanese have paid homage to those who died when an atomic bomb was dropped on Hiroshima on Aug. 6, 1945. Though the number of fatalities is unknown (estimates range from 80,000 to three times that number), the effects were far worse than those experienced in Nagasaki when it was bombed three days later. In 1947 the Atomic Bomb Casualty Commission was established in Hiroshima to conduct medical and biological research on the effects of radiation on man. Five public hospitals and dozens of private clinics still provide free treatment to victims of the bombing. The annual ceremony in Hiroshima is held in Peace Memorial Park, which contains a museum and the remains of the only building not leveled by the blast; it has been named the Atomic Bomb Memorial Dome.

26 **100th anniversary of Mergenthaler's patent on the Linotype machine.** Ottmar Mergenthaler was born on May 11, 1854, in Hachtel, now in West Germany. He immigrated to the U.S. in 1872 and became a citizen in 1878. While working in the Baltimore, Md., machine shop of a relative, he dedicated himself to mechanizing the tedious task of typesetting. Composing words letter by letter was a laborious and time-consuming undertaking. When Mergenthaler devised a keyboard method of setting type that produced a whole line of words cast as a single unit, he had made a contribution that revolutionized the printing and publishing industries. Because printing became faster and cheaper, there was a dramatic expansion in all fields of publishing. Mergenthaler contracted tuberculosis and died on Oct. 28, 1899.

SEPTEMBER

3 *Labor Day in the U.S. and Canada*
6 *Islamic Feast of Id al-Adha*
7 *Independence Day in Brazil (1822)*
15 *Independence Day in Costa Rica (1821)*
16 *Independence Day in Mexico (1810)*
18 *Independence Day in Chile (1810)*
21 *Independence Day in Belize (1981)*
22 *Autumnal equinox in the Northern Hemisphere; vernal equinox in the Southern Hemisphere*
26 *Islamic New Year*
27 *Rosh Hashana, Jewish New Year*
28 *Birthday of Confucius*

16 **Independence Day in Mexico.** Mexicans look back to Sept. 16, 1810, as the pivotal date in their struggle for independence even though their fight to be free was no more assured or complete on that day than it was for the United States on July 4, 1776. Political developments in Mexico were closely tied to political events taking place at that time in far-off Europe. Napoleon Bonaparte had occupied Spain in 1808 and imprisoned King Ferdinand VII. Bonaparte then tried to place his brother Joseph on the throne. Spain, which controlled Mexico, countered Napoleon by assembling its Cortes (parliament) to rule in the place of the absent king. Mexicans were consequently confused and divided over conflicting orders coming from Spain. Miguel Hidalgo y Costilla, the parish priest of Dolores, Michoacán, was especially fearful of what these events portended for Mexico. He therefore urged his countrymen to fight and die under the aegis of Our Lady of Guadalupe to prevent the "godless French" from taking over Mexico. It was on Sept. 16, 1810, that Hidalgo issued his historic "Cry of Dolores," demanding independence for Mexico, equitable treatment of all races, and redistribution of land. Tens of thousands followed him to Guanajuato, a major colonial mining town. The elite among the resident Spaniards and Creoles turned a warehouse into a makeshift fort but they were overwhelmed by Hidalgo's forces. The town was pillaged, and many of the Creoles were massacred. These acts bolstered the viceroy's position when he moved against the rebels. Hidalgo's forces were defeated at the Bridge of Calderón on Jan. 17, 1811, and two months later the parish priest of Dolores was captured. His execution on July 31 appeared to end the civil unrest. But José María Morelos y Pavón, a parish priest closely associated with Hidalgo, took charge of the crusade for freedom and established control over large sections of southern Mexico. In 1814 the constituent congresses he had convened issued a formal declaration of independence at Apatzingán. Though fighting would continue for decades, Mexico had already won its battle for independence.

OCTOBER

1 *Founding of the People's Republic of China (1949)*

6 *Yom Kippur, Jewish Day of Atonement*

8 *Thanksgiving Day in Canada*

11 *100th anniversary of Eleanor Roosevelt's birth*

12 *Columbus sights Guanahaní (1492)*

24 *United Nations Day*

26 *150th anniversary of the patent on the Hansom Safety cab*

29 *Republic Day in Turkey (1923)*

31 *Halloween*

11 **100th anniversary of Eleanor Roosevelt's birth.** Anna Eleanor Roosevelt was born on Oct. 11, 1884, to Elliott and Anna Hall Roosevelt, both of whom came from wealthy and socially prominent families. Her uncle was Pres. Theodore Roosevelt; her husband, whom she married in 1905, was Pres. Franklin D. Roosevelt. Throughout her life Eleanor was known as a humanitarian and reformer. During World War I she did relief work for the Red Cross in Washington, D.C. Later she helped plan work camps for girls and in 1935 had a hand in establishing the National Youth Administration. Among other causes to which she lent her prestige were civil rights, equal wages for women, and preservation of Native American cultures. Pres. Harry Truman named Eleanor a delegate to the United Nations, where she became chairman of the Commission on Human Rights and helped compose the Universal Declaration of Human Rights. After leaving the UN in 1952, she lectured, wrote books and magazine articles, and worked on behalf of Democratic presidential candidates. She was reappointed to the UN in 1961 by Pres. John F. Kennedy and died in New York City on Nov. 7, 1962, at the age of 78.

12 **Columbus sights Guanahaní.** When Christopher Columbus set sail from Spain on his first voyage he was prepared to meet an old civilization or new savages—he knew not which. He personally commanded the "Santa María," a ship some 36 m (118 ft) long. The "Pinta," about 15 m (50 ft) in length, was under the command of Martín Alonso Pinzón, a pilot and shipowner who became Columbus's partner in the expedition. The "Niña" sailed under the command of Pinzón's brother, who later became one of the great sailors of his time. As the ships sailed westward and days turned into weeks, uncertainty increased and murmurs of mutiny grew louder. On October 7 Columbus reluctantly accepted Pinzón's advice and pointed his fleet in a southwesterly direction. Two hours after midnight on October 12 a sailor aboard the "Pinta" spotted land. At dawn Columbus led an expedition ashore and claimed the land in the name of Spain. He had discovered the New World. The place was Guanahaní, one of the Bahama Islands, which the Spaniards renamed San Salvador.

NOVEMBER

1 *All Saints Day*

2 *250th anniversary of Daniel Boone's birth*

3 *Independence Day in Panama (1903)*

5 *Guy Fawkes Day (1605)*

6 *Election day in the U.S.*

7 *Anniversary of the Bolshevik Revolution (1917)*

11 *Veterans Day in the U.S.*

22 *Total eclipse of the Sun, visible mainly from locations in the equatorial and southern Pacific; Thanksgiving Day in the U.S.*

24 *200th anniversary of Zachary Taylor's birth*

29 *Proclamation of the republic of Yugoslavia (1945)*

2 **250th anniversary of Daniel Boone's birth.** The famed frontiersman, hunter, and Indian fighter Daniel Boone was born on Nov. 2, 1734, near present-day Reading, Pa., and died in St. Charles, Mo., on or about Sept. 26, 1820. The hero of American folklore helped blaze a trail through Cumberland Gap, a notch in the Appalachian Mountains that opened up Kentucky to permanent settlement. Though Boone has often been credited with discovering and founding Kentucky, many whites had traversed the area before him. He did, however, attempt to lead his own family and others to Kentucky in 1773, but the party was attacked by Cherokee Indians who captured, tortured, and murdered Boone's son. Boone, who was twice captured by Indians, is properly credited with establishing the first permanent white settlement in Kentucky, in August 1775.

24 **200th anniversary of Zachary Taylor's birth.** Zachary Taylor, the third of nine children, was born on Nov. 24, 1784, to a family of prominent Virginians. They moved to what is now northern Kentucky shortly after Zachary was born. Though keenly interested in farming, he received a military commission in 1808 and embarked on an army career that lasted 40 years. Taylor fought in the War of 1812, in various Indian wars, and in the Mexican War. Abraham Lincoln served under him in the Black Hawk War as did Ulysses S. Grant and Jefferson Davis in the Mexican War. Taylor won his greatest distinction as a military commander in 1847 when he defeated a superior force of Mexicans led by Antonio López de Santa Anna. The victory ended the war in northern Mexico and made Taylor a national hero. Though he had never held political office, his military fame was viewed as a great political asset by the Whigs, who made him their presidential candidate. Taylor won the 1848 election by a margin of 163 electoral votes to 127 for the Democratic candidate, Lewis Cass. Taylor laid the cornerstone for the Washington Monument on July 4, 1850. That same evening he became ill with cholera and died five days later.

DECEMBER

2 *First Sunday of Advent*

5 *Birthday of the king of Thailand; Islamic feast Mawlid an-Nabi, Muhammad's birthday*

6 *Independence Day in Finland (1917)*

10 *Human Rights Day*

19 *First day of Hanukka*

21 *Winter solstice in the Northern Hemisphere; summer solstice in the Southern Hemisphere*

25 *Christmas Day*

26 *Boxing Day*

29 *Murder of Thomas Becket (1170)*

26 **Boxing Day.** In Great Britain and certain Commonwealth nations the day after Christmas is designated as the time to show special appreciation to those who have performed personal public services during the year. The day after Christmas came to be known as Boxing Day from the boxed gifts that were traditionally given to mail carriers, garbage collectors, and the like. In modern times gifts of money have become acceptable substitutes for boxed merchandise.

29 **Murder of Thomas Becket.** Thomas Becket, one of Britain's most fascinating and enigmatic public figures, was born in London about 1118. After working in secular jobs he joined the household of Archbishop Theobold, who, after recognizing Thomas's considerable talents, persuaded King Henry II to appoint Thomas chancellor of England. Henry appreciated Thomas's accomplishments and his unswerving loyalty, especially when the interests of state and church came into conflict. A profound and somewhat mysterious transformation, however, occurred when Thomas was made archbishop of Canterbury. Opulence gave way to austerity, and loyalty to the church replaced loyalty to the throne. When Thomas rejected the king's pleas and resigned the chancellorship, the close relationship that had existed between the two men quickly deteriorated. Matters finally reached a crisis over the Constitutions of Clarendon. The king laid claim to such traditional royal privileges as the right to punish "criminous clerks" (clerics), receive the revenues of vacant sees, and intervene in episcopal elections. Thomas insisted that such practices were incompatible with church law. When the exasperated monarch finally ordered Thomas to stand trial on a point of feudal obligations, the archbishop fled to France. Animosities intensified during the six years Thomas remained in exile, but eventually both Henry and Thomas agreed that the archbishop should return. Hope of a lasting reconciliation quickly vanished when Thomas not only refused to lift excommunications he had imposed but pronounced still others on hostile royal servants. On Dec. 29, 1170, four knights followed Thomas into Canterbury Cathedral and cut him down with their swords. Thomas was canonized in 1173.

JANUARY

3 *Poland forms new labour unions*

New government-sanctioned labour unions came into existence in Poland, but only for individual workplaces. The government clearly hoped such unions would deal a death blow to Solidarity, the national federation of labour unions, and to other independent unions, all of which had been outlawed. Poland's official news agency reported that workers welcomed the news with a "mood of reserve."

Fernando Schwalb takes office in Peru

Fernando Schwalb López Aldaña, a former ambassador to the U.S., was sworn in as prime minister of Peru. He had taken over the duties of the office on Dec. 9, 1982, after Manuel Ulloa Elías resigned. The country was in financial difficulties and was still trying to suppress terrorist violence, which began in 1980 when democracy was restored under Pres. Fernando Belaúnde Terry.

5 *UN reviews economic status of Latin-American countries*

The UN Economic Commission for Latin America reported that in 1982 the region posted its worst record in 40 years. In many nations inflation was rampant, and the region had cumulative foreign debts amounting to almost $275 billion. These debts more than offset the gains made by an overall 19% decline in imports.

France bans Corsican group

The French government declared that the Corsican National Liberation Front was a private armed organization and as such was illegal. Participation in such an organization was made punishable by a prison sentence of six months to two years. To show its resolve to combat violence against the government, France also created a special police commissioner's post for the island. During 1982 the Front, a separatist group, took credit for several hundred bombings in France and Corsica and for other acts of violence.

6 *Warsaw Pact arms proposals*

The Warsaw Pact nations, after a two-day meeting in Prague, Czech., proposed radical reductions of medium-range nuclear weapons in Europe. The Soviet-bloc nations also proposed a mutual reduction of conventional arms and suggested, among other actions, a nonaggression pact with NATO based on a mutual renunciation of the first use of military force. Representatives of the Western nations promised to give the proposals serious consideration, but some officials publicly doubted that the offer differed substantively from others made in the past. On January 31 U.S. Pres. Ronald Reagan offered to meet with Yury V. Andropov, the general secretary of the Soviet Communist Party, to sign an agreement "banning U.S. and Soviet intermediate-range land-based nuclear missile weapons from the face of the Earth." The following day Andropov brushed the offer aside as "nothing new."

El Salvador commander rebels

Lieut. Col. Sigifredo Ochoa Pérez, reputedly one of El Salvador's most effective leaders in its war against leftist guerrillas, refused Defense Minister José Guillermo García Merino's order to step down as commander of some 1,000 troops in Cabañas Province and become military attaché in Uruguay. Ochoa, who had the support of extreme rightists who wanted García replaced, surrendered his command on January 12 at the request of Pres. Alvaro Alfredo Magaña. García resigned under heavy pressure on April 18.

India to hold Assam elections

The Indian government announced that elections would be held in the state of Assam in February, despite fierce opposition from native Hindus, who claimed they were being overwhelmed by illegal Muslim immigrants coming mostly from neighbouring Bangladesh.

7 *Guatemala to get U.S. arms*

The U.S. government terminated the total arms embargo it had imposed on Guatemala in 1980. A spokesman for the U.S. State Department asserted that the change was justified because Guatemala's human rights record had improved significantly. Some international human rights groups disagreed. Gen. Efraín Ríos Montt, who proclaimed himself head of a military government in June 1982, had a few weeks earlier contended that subversives no longer posed a major threat to his regime, but he was nonetheless anxious to purchase spare parts for the Air Force.

12 *Japan to aid South Korea*

Japan agreed to provide South Korea with $4 billion in aid over a period of seven years. The agreement was formalized during Japanese Prime Minister Yasuhiro Nakasone's visit to Seoul. Somewhat less than half the total would take the form of low-interest loans for development projects; the rest would consist of credits with the Japanese Export-Import Bank. South Korea had originally asked for $6 billion, arguing that its heavy defense spending negatively affected its own economy while indirectly enhancing Japan's national security. During a banquet, Nakasone declared that the continued development of a "dynamic and mutually beneficial relationship of absolute equality" between the two countries was a common task of great importance.

13 *China angry over limits placed on textile exports to U.S.*

After a week of unsuccessful negotiations, the U.S. unilaterally announced that China's 1983 textile exports to the U.S. could not exceed those of 1982. China had argued for a 6% increase because its trade balance with the U.S. for the first

Nigeria's expulsion of illegal aliens (January 17) set off a rush for Ghana, through Togo and Benin. The border between these two countries and Ghana was not opened until January 29, triggering fights between and among soldiers and Ghanaian refugees.

MICHEL SETBOUN—SIPA PRESS/BLACK STAR

ten months of 1982 showed a deficit of more than $650 million. On January 19 China manifested its displeasure by banning the importation of U.S. cotton, soybeans, and chemical fibres for the rest of the year.

Saudi Arabia and Libya restore diplomatic ties

Saudi Arabia announced the successful conclusion of talks with Libya on the restoration of diplomatic relations between the two countries. Saudi Arabia had severed those ties in October 1980 after Libyan leader Col. Muammar al-Qaddafi called for a holy war to liberate Mecca, Islam's and Saudi Arabia's holiest shrine.

17 *Nigeria expels illegal aliens*

Nigeria's minister of internal affairs ordered all illegal aliens to leave the country by the end of the month. The edict affected an estimated two million people, including tens of thousands of teachers and skilled workers, but many observers believed the move would help diffuse civil and religious strife and make the country's economic problems more manageable. Nigeria's financial difficulties were rooted in its heavy dependence on oil revenues, which had fallen off sharply because of the huge oil surplus on world markets. The departing aliens, for the most part Ghanaians, also included illegal immigrants from such countries as Benin and Togo, whose leaders initially feared that Ghanaians traveling across their territories might not be allowed to reenter their native country. That fear was laid to rest on January 29 when Ghana opened its border.

Zhao Ziyang ends African tour

Chinese Premier Zhao Ziyang (Chao Tzu-yang) concluded a month-long visit to Africa that included stops in 11 third world nations. The trip was undertaken principally to strengthen China's economic and political ties with that part of the world.

18 *Nakasone and Reagan confer*

Japanese Prime Minister Yasuhiro Nakasone arrived in Washington for talks with President Reagan and other government officials. The U.S. was especially anxious to increase food exports to Japan and have Japan accelerate its program for national defense. Nakasone explained that increased imports of U.S. beef and citrus products—the main U.S. concern—created serious problems for Japan, but he promised to review the matter when the present trade agreement expired in March 1984. The prime minister also expressed a desire to build up Japan's air force to inhibit Soviet bombers from flying over Japanese territory. When news of this reached Japan, whose constitution outlaws war but permits self-defense, there was a storm of protest. In his farewell remarks, Reagan said that trade still "weighed heavily" on Japan-U.S. relations.

Gromyko visits West Germany

Soviet Foreign Minister Andrey Gromyko ended a three-day visit to West Germany during which he tried to dissuade the country's leaders from deploying Pershing II and cruise missiles on West German soil. In talks with Chancellor Helmut Kohl and others, Gromyko reviewed the entire arms debate and the Soviet position on disarmament, but neither side indicated a willingness to depart from its basic policies. A few days later French Pres. François Mitterrand arrived in Bonn to emphasize the importance of Western unity if the Geneva arms-control talks with the U.S.S.R. were to succeed.

South Africa reasserts direct control over Namibia

South Africa announced the dissolution of South West Africa/Namibia's National Assembly shortly after the Council of Ministers resigned. South Africa then declared it would resume direct control of the territory with the assistance of local citizens who would act as advisers. The multiracial council had been headed by Dirk Mudge, who reportedly resented South Africa's treatment of Namibia. Only recently P. W. Botha's government had refused to sanction the nonobservance in Namibia of several South African holidays. The resignation of Mudge and other council members was generally viewed as a blow to UN efforts to negotiate independence for Namibia.

IMF fund increased for emergencies

Representatives of the so-called Group of Ten—Belgium, Canada, France, Great Britain, Italy, Japan, The Netherlands, Sweden, the U.S., and West Germany—agreed in Paris that the General Arrangements to Borrow unit of the International Monetary Fund (IMF) should be increased to $19 billion from $7.1 billion. The emergency fund was also opened to other IMF members besides the Group of Ten, specifically those nations facing defaults of such magnitude that their collapse would jeopardize the world's monetary system. During the meeting the group also agreed that steps could now be taken to stimulate the world economy because significant progress had been made in controlling inflation.

19 *Trudeau ends visit to Asia*

Canadian Prime Minister Pierre Trudeau ended a 17-day visit to Asia, during which he sought to promote Canadian exports. From Hong Kong he traveled to Thailand, Singapore, Malaysia, Indonesia, Brunei, the Philippines, and Japan. While in Manila he urged the Asian Development Bank (ADB) to follow a more equitable policy. According to Trudeau, Canada had thus far received contracts worth only one-third of the relative value of its contributions to the ADB.

21 *El Salvador to get more U.S. aid*

The Reagan administration certified to Congress that El Salvador had made perceptible progress in safeguarding human rights and thus qualified for U.S. military aid for six more months. Progress in other specific areas was also affirmed to meet the requirements of a law passed by Congress in 1981. Several human rights organizations opposed the aid.

23 *More Thai rebels surrender*

Thailand announced that 466 Communist guerrillas had taken advantage of the government's offer of amnesty by surrendering en masse during a ceremony in the northern part of the country. A government spokesman claimed that more than 1,800 insurgents had turned themselves in since the government made its offer on Dec. 1, 1982. The defections were generally seen as proof that the Communists had become demoralized and that their organization now faced a crisis of survival.

25 *Jiang Qing gets life sentence*

The Supreme People's Court of China commuted to life imprisonment the death sentence imposed on Jiang Qing (Chiang Ch'ing) in 1981. Jiang, the widow of Communist Party chairman Mao Zedong (Mao Tse-tung), was considered the most vicious of the "gang of four," who had been convicted of ruthlessly persecuting their enemies during the Cultural Revolution and creating chaos in the country. Jiang's close associate Zhang Chunqiao (Chang Ch'un-ch'iao) also had his death sentence commuted to life imprisonment. No mention was made of the other two members of the gang. Wang Hongwen (Wang Hung-wen) had already received a life sentence during the trial and Yao Wenyuan (Yao Wen-yuan) a 20-year prison term.

Barbie arrested in Bolivia

Klaus Barbie, a notorious Nazi war criminal, was arrested in Bolivia and then extradited to France on February 5. The French government had tried Barbie in absentia in 1954 and sentenced him to death for crimes he committed while serving as head of the Gestapo in Lyon during World War II. Barbie was also wanted in West Germany (*see* BIOGRAPHIES).

27 *Arms talks resume in Geneva*

After a two-month recess, the U.S. and the Soviet Union resumed negotiations on the reduction of intermediate-range nuclear missiles in Europe. The U.S. offered to cancel the deployment of its missiles if the Soviets dismantled the missiles it had in Europe.

FEBRUARY

2 *START talks resume in Geneva*

Soviet and U.S. negotiators resumed strategic arms reduction talks (START) in Geneva. Edward L. Rowny, the chief U.S. negotiator, once again called on the U.S.S.R. to accept a limit of 850 intercontinental ballistic missiles for both sides—a reduction from 2,350 for the Soviet Union and 1,700 for the U.S. In addition, missile warheads would be limited to 5,000 for each of the two superpowers, half of which could be mounted on land-based missiles. The Soviet negotiators re-presented a proposal that called for a 25% reduction in all existing strategic delivery systems and an end to the development of new strategic weapons.

4 *Portuguese Parliament dissolved*

Portuguese Pres. António Ramalho Eanes dissolved Parliament and called for new elections on April 25, the ninth anniversary of the revolution that restored democracy after half a century of dictatorship. Before Parliament was dissolved, it passed a provisional budget that curbed government spending, increased taxes, and kept the 1983 deficit at the 1982 level of $1.6 billion.

6 *Paraguayan president reelected*

Gen. Alfredo Stroessner, who seized control of Paraguay in a 1954 military coup, was elected president for the seventh straight time. He faced only token opposition from two government-approved candidates whose campaigning had been severely restricted.

8 *Israeli commission issues final report on Beirut massacre*

The three-man Israeli commission investigating the September 1982 massacre of Palestinians in the Sabra and Shatila refugee camps in West Beirut issued its final report. Though no evidence was found implicating any Israeli directly in the killings, Defense Minister Ariel Sharon was criticized for "blunders" and "nonfulfillment of duty." The commission recommended he resign or be dismissed. The panel also concluded that three generals were indirectly responsible for what happened and Prime Minister Menachem Begin was marginally responsible inasmuch as he seemed unconcerned about a situation replete with danger. The Cabinet, except for Sharon, voted February 10 to accept the report's recommendations. According to the chief justice of the Supreme Court and his two colleagues, the Christian Phalangists bore sole responsibility for the indiscriminate slaughter of the unarmed Palestinians.

Hitachi pleads guilty

Hitachi Ltd., one of Japan's leading electronics firms, pleaded guilty in a U.S. federal court to charges of conspiracy to obtain classified information about IBM computers. The company's lawyer contended that Hitachi's top officers were unaware of the plan. Two of Hitachi's employees also pleaded guilty and, like the company itself, were fined.

10 *Anglican Church speaks out against unilateral disarmament*

The General Synod of the Church of England voted 338–100 against calling upon Great Britain to divest itself of all nuclear weapons. Robert Runcie, the archbishop of Canterbury and head of the church, said he could not "accept unilateralism as the best expression of a Christian's prime moral duty to be a peacemaker." On the contrary, the Synod urged Britain to "maintain adequate forces to guard against nuclear blackmail and to deter nuclear and non-nuclear aggressors." At the same time, it called upon Britain to renounce the first use of nuclear weapons even though the conventional armaments of the Warsaw Pact were greater than those of NATO.

Bush ends trip to Western Europe

U.S. Vice-Pres. George Bush completed a 12-day visit to Europe that included stops in West Germany, The Netherlands, Belgium, Switzerland, Italy, France, Great Britain, and the Vatican. Bush later told reporters that the Western allies spoke with one voice when they urged the U.S. to be flexible during negotiations with the Soviet Union on arms reductions. Prime Minister Ruud Lubbers of The Netherlands told Bush that although he supported President Reagan's "zero option" proposal, The Netherlands was not committed to accepting cruise missiles.

George Shultz concludes Asian trip

U.S. Secretary of State George Shultz returned to Washington after visiting Japan, China, South Korea, and Hong Kong. In Japan he tried to allay Japanese fears that in U.S.-U.S.S.R. arms talks the Soviets might agree to limit weapons threatening Europe but not others threatening Japan. In China Shultz addressed such issues as U.S. arms sales to Taiwan, the defection of Chinese tennis star Hu Na, and the restriction of Chinese textile exports to the U.S. He told South Korean officials they could continue to rely on U.S. support. In Hong Kong, Shultz held discussions with the heads of various U.S. missions in Asia.

12 *Esmat Sadat sentenced to prison*

Esmat Sadat, the half brother of the late Egyptian president Anwar as-Sadat, was convicted of corruption by a court of ethics and sentenced to one year in prison. Sadat had been accused of amassing a huge fortune through black marketeering, fraud, and influence peddling. During the trial he vigorously denied the charges and offered to turn the money over to the government the moment anyone produced evidence that it existed.

13 *Greek Cypriots reelect Kyprianou*

Spyros Kyprianou, a member of the Democratic Party, was reelected president of Cyprus with 57% of the vote. Turkish Cypriots did not participate in the voting. Kyprianou, a Greek Cypriot, had cam-

Indian Red Cross workers improvised field hospitals to treat victims of the ethnic and political violence in Assam state during February.

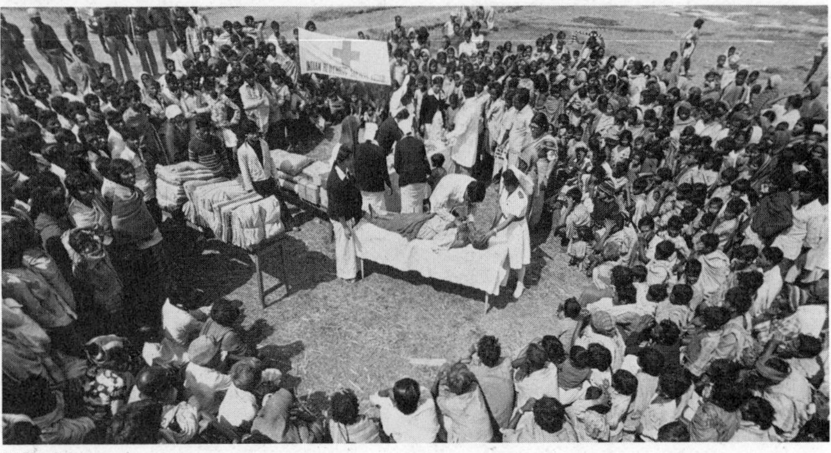

BALDEV—SYGMA

paigned under two political banners because he had entered into an alliance with the Communists in 1982 after they outpolled his own party in parliamentary elections in 1981.

15 *Beirut finally reunited*

After months of negotiations with the Lebanese government, the Christian Phalangist militia and their supporters withdrew from East Beirut and took up positions outside the city. Their departure gave the government control of the entire capital for the first time since the mid-1970s. Its ultimate goal was the withdrawal of all foreign troops from Lebanon. An estimated 25,000 Israeli troops still occupied a large area in the south, and an equal number of Syrians, backed up by 7,000 Palestinians, held the Bekaa Valley and territory in the north.

16 *Libya said to threaten Sudan*

At the request of Egyptian Pres. Hosni Mubarak, the U.S. sent four airborne warning and control systems surveillance planes to Egypt and dispatched the nuclear aircraft carrier "Nimitz" to waters off Egypt's coast. Mubarak feared that Sudan, Egypt's neighbour and close ally, was about to be attacked by Libya, which had moved fighter planes to the border. On February 22 Sudanese Pres. Gaafar Nimeiry claimed that an intercepted telex provided proof of Libya's intentions. It reportedly ordered the operation delayed for one or two months.

18 *Ex-CIA agent Wilson sentenced*

Edwin P. Wilson, an agent of the U.S. Central Intelligence Agency from 1954 to 1970, was sentenced to 17 years in prison and fined $145,000 for illegally exporting explosives to Libya. Though Wilson was also under indictment for reportedly seeking to have two federal prosecutors and several witnesses assassinated, Federal District Court Judge Ross Sterling declined to classify Wilson as a "dangerous special offender" worthy of an additional eight years in prison. On Nov. 17, 1982, a federal jury had convicted Wilson on seven other counts of illegally transporting arms to Libya. For those offenses he was given a 15-year prison term.

19 *Brushfires ravage Australia*

Brushfires that had been devastating southeastern Australia since February 16 were finally brought under control. Prime Minister Malcolm Fraser described the holocaust as one of the great disasters in Australian history. Seventy-one persons were reported killed and 2,000 homes destroyed. Total damage in the states of Victoria and South Australia was estimated to run into hundreds of millions of dollars. (*See* AUSTRALIA: *Special Report.*)

21 *Soviet premier visits Greece*

Soviet Premier Nikolay A. Tikhonov arrived in Athens to discuss a wide range of topics with Greek Prime Minister Andreas Papandreou. The meeting occurred at a time when Greece and the U.S. were still negotiating the future of U.S. military bases in Greece. Besides signing a ten-year agreement on trade, Tikhonov and Papandreou issued a joint communiqué in which they called for nuclear-free zones as a contribution to disarmament, the lowest possible levels of both conventional and nuclear weapons, participation of the Palestine Liberation Organization in Middle East peace talks, and the reunification of Cyprus. It also urged the withdrawal of all foreign troops from Cyprus. However, Turkey was not directly condemned for its occupation of the northern part of the island.

22 *U.S. to buy contaminated town*

The U.S. government offered to buy all the homes and businesses in Times Beach, Mo., because the level of dioxin in the soil posed an imminent hazard to the health of the 2,400 residents. The cost of the purchase and the subsequent demolition of the buildings was estimated at $33 million. Tests conducted by the Centers for Disease Control showed some patches of soil contained as much as 300 parts per 1,000,000,000. A concentration exceeding one part per 1,000,000,000 was considered hazardous over the long term to humans.

24 *Hundreds killed in Assam*

The Indian government revealed that more than 1,300 persons had been killed in Assam state during a three-week period of ethnic and political violence. Unofficial estimates of the fatalities ran as high as 3,000. Prime Minister Indira Gandhi had insisted on holding elections despite repeated threats from several Hindu groups that they would never permit the millions of illegal Muslim immigrants in the state to usurp the land, jobs, and political rights that, they said, rightfully belonged to Hindus. Aware of the potential danger, Gandhi dispatched 90,000 special police and paramilitary forces to Assam to keep order, but they could not control the populace. The worst single incident occurred on February 18, when Hindus raided 17 settlements near Nellie and killed at least 600 people. On February 27 Hiteswar Saikia, a member of Gandhi's Congress (I) party, was sworn in as chief minister of Assam, thereby ending the central government's direct role in governing the state.

Mexico and Brazil get loans

Mexico announced that more than 500 Western banks had underwritten a $5 billion loan that would be used to help faltering Mexican banks meet their foreign debt obligations. Mexico also received a $433 million short-term loan that was urgently needed until the first part of the $5 billion was made available. On February 28 the International Monetary Fund granted Brazil a $5.4 billion loan. Because both countries had huge foreign debts they could not repay on schedule, special efforts were being made to help them regain financial stability.

25 *Ban on Korean politicians lifted*

South Korean Pres. Chun Doo Hwan lifted a ban that had been imposed on 250 politicians in 1980. Though they had been forbidden to take part in political activities until June 1988, they had, the government said, shown repentance and, in any case, "had had relatively little responsibility for the irregularities and confusion of the old days."

MARCH

1 *China and U.S.S.R. resume talks*

China and the Soviet Union, after a three-year interval, resumed talks in Moscow on ways to improve relations between their two countries. China indicated it was looking for concrete proof that the U.S.S.R. was sincere in wanting a better relationship. China wanted the Soviet Union to end its military support of Vietnamese troops occupying Cambodia so that free elections could be held there under UN supervision. China also cited the Soviet Union's refusal to discuss its military presence in Afghanistan and elsewhere as an obstacle to normalization.

2 *Pope visits Central America*

Pope John Paul II arrived in Costa Rica, the first stop on an eight-nation tour that included visits to Nicaragua, Panama, El Salvador, Guatemala, Honduras, Belize, and the Caribbean nation of Haiti. Though the Vatican emphasized the religious nature of the trip, the pope's frequent references to human rights, poverty, oppression, and injustice had strong political implications. In Nicaragua, where the church was sharply divided in its view of the Sandinista government, crowds repeatedly drowned out the pontiff's words by shouting slogans. In El Salvador John Paul called on both sides to engage in dialogue to end the civil war ravaging that country.

PATRICK RIVIERE—GAMMA/LIAISON

Robert Hawke savoured the fruits of victory when his Australian Labor Party won the March 5 general election, making him the next prime minister.

3 *Greeks protest U.S. military bases*

An estimated 80,000 Greeks attended a protest rally in Athens to demand the closing down of all U.S. military bases in the country. The demonstration was jointly organized by an independent leftist organization, by the Greek Communist Party, and, most notably, by the Panhellenic Socialist Movement (Pasok), the party of Prime Minister Andreas Papandreou.

5 *Australians vote for change*

The Australian Labor Party (ALP), under the leadership of Robert Hawke, won an absolute majority in elections to the 125-seat House of Representatives. Prime Minister Malcolm Fraser and his Liberal-National Country Party coalition lost control of the government even though Fraser claimed the ALP would adopt expensive government programs that would bankrupt the country. During the campaign the ALP focused attention on economic problems.

6 *West Germany holds elections*

The Christian Democratic Union, the party of West German Chancellor Helmut Kohl, and its Bavarian wing, the Christian Social Union, won a total of 244 seats in the 498-seat Bundestag (lower house of parliament). Because the two parties fell 5 seats short of having an absolute majority, they would continue to run the government with the help of the Free Democratic Party, which captured 34 seats (a loss of 19). A major issue in the campaign was Kohl's backing of NATO's decision to deploy Pershing II and cruise missiles in Europe if the U.S.-Soviet arms-control talks did not succeed by the end of the year. Though the Social Democratic Party lost 25 seats in the election, it remained a potent force with 193 seats in the Bundestag. For the first time, the ecology-oriented "Greens" received at least 5% of the vote, thereby qualifying for representation in the Bundestag, where they won 27 seats.

7 *Nonaligned nations meet in India*

Indian Prime Minister Indira Gandhi welcomed leaders of third world nations to a conference in New Delhi. The Palestine Liberation Organization and the South-West Africa People's Organization were also full members of the group that represented itself as politically nonaligned. In her opening address, Gandhi pleaded for more financial aid for less developed countries and urged conciliation on political issues. She also appealed to the superpowers to renounce all use of nuclear weapons. Cuban Pres. Fidel Castro, who preceded Gandhi as chairman of the organization, turned his speech into a tirade against the U.S. As the conference progressed, pro-Soviet elements seemed to have lost ground to those favouring more balanced nonalignment.

9 *Joshua Nkomo flees Zimbabwe*

Joshua Nkomo, a longtime political rival of Prime Minister Robert Mugabe, fled Zimbabwe and took refuge in neighbouring Botswana. From there he flew to South Africa, then on to London. Nkomo claimed that Mugabe was planning to have him killed. Government troops had in fact raided Nkomo's home a few days earlier and killed his driver.

Burford resigns as EPA administrator

Anne M. Burford resigned as head of the U.S. Environmental Protection Agency (EPA) after a series of unresolved conflicts with Congress. Burford, who had been cited for contempt of Congress by the House of Representatives in December 1982, insisted she was simply following President Reagan's orders when she refused to turn over files on the agency's enforcement of toxic waste regulations. Before the president accepted Burford's resignation "with deep regret," the White House agreed to make the disputed documents available to all congressional committees investigating the EPA. On March 21 Reagan appointed William D. Ruckelshaus head of the EPA. As the agency's first administrator, Ruckelshaus had won wide approval.

10 *President of Indonesia reelected*

Indonesian President Suharto, who came to power in 1966, was elected to a fourth five-year term by the People's Consultative Assembly. The voting was a formality because Suharto ran unopposed. The Assembly also gave him special powers to provide for the nation's security, and it endorsed Suharto's choice for vice-president, Gen. Umar Wirahadikusumah.

14 *OPEC forced to cut oil prices*

The 13 members of the Organization of Petroleum Exporting Countries (OPEC) agreed on the need to cut prices for the first time since the group was formed in 1961. By lowering the benchmark cost of Saudi light crude oil to $29 a barrel from $34, OPEC hoped to put an end to cutthroat pricing and restore equilibrium to world markets. Non-OPEC countries, however, were not involved in the agreement and could, if they so chose, continue to undercut OPEC prices.

17 *Chad wants UN help in border dispute with Libya*

Chad asked the UN Security Council for help in settling a long-standing border dispute with Libya. The desert area in question was presently occupied by Libya, which claimed it under terms of a World War II treaty. The problem was complicated by the fact that Libya did not recognize the government of Hissen Habré, who in June 1982 overthrew Goukouni Oueddei. The former president had gained power in 1980 with the help of Libyan soldiers and tanks.

19 *Australia resumes trade with U.S.S.R.*

Australian Prime Minister Robert Hawke announced that he was renewing trade and cultural ties with the Soviet Union that had been interrupted after Soviet troops invaded Afghanistan in 1979.

21 *EC countries realign currencies*

The eight European Communities (EC) nations belonging to the European Monetary System (EMS) realigned their currencies after difficult negotiations. At one point France threatened to withdraw from the EMS rather than devalue the franc to a level needed to bring it into line with other currencies. France, which had recently spent nearly $3.4 billion to support the battered franc, finally accepted a compromise that had the approval of the other finance ministers: the value of the West German mark would be increased by 5.5% and the French franc would be devalued by 2.5%. The Dutch guilder, the Danish krone, and the Belgian and Luxembourg francs were all revalued upward by 1.5 to 3.5%. The Italian lira and the

Irish pound were devalued, respectively, by 2.5 and 3.5%.

Socialists win Finnish election

Finland's Social Democrats increased their plurality in Parliament in national elections that lasted two days. Many had predicted that voters would give the Conservatives massive support, but this failed to materialize. Whereas the Social Democrats won 57 of the 200 seats, an increase of 5, the Conservatives captured only 44 seats, a loss of 3.

Recipient of artificial heart dies

Barney Clark, the first recipient of a permanent artificial heart, died at the University of Utah Medical Center. The 62-year-old retired dentist lived 112 days after the historic operation, but he finally expired from circulatory collapse and multiorgan failure. The heart continued to function normally to the end. Clark had faced certain death from a degenerative disease of the heart muscle when he was rushed into surgery for what he knew was an experimental procedure.

Ríos Montt lifts state of siege

Guatemalan Pres. Efraín Ríos Montt lifted the state of siege he had imposed in July 1982, but he also forbade all political activities, public meetings, strikes, labour organizing, and publication of news about guerrilla activities that did not come from government sources. He also promised free elections but set no date. Many characterized the announcements as a charade.

Denmark ends Soviet sanctions

The Danish Parliament voted 78–68 to end the trade sanctions that had been imposed on the Soviet Union for its role in having martial law declared in Poland. The minority centre-right government wanted the sanctions to remain but was overruled by the Social Democrats and their allies.

UN discusses Nicaragua's charges

The UN Security Council convened an emergency session to discuss Nicaragua's charges that U.S.-backed rebels had invaded the country from Honduras. During the heated debate, the language was often acrimonious. Mexico, Colombia, Panama, and Ecuador were among those who supported Nicaragua, but Jeane Kirkpatrick, the U.S. ambassador, repeatedly insisted that the Nicaraguan people had spontaneously turned against the Sandinista leaders, "whom they originally believed to be their liberators." Honduras denied it had sent troops across the border into Nicaragua and called for a peaceful resolution of disputes in the region. The U.S. was training insurgents in Honduras, but the Reagan administration insisted it was interested only in interdicting the alleged shipment of arms to El Salvador. The UN special session ended on March 29 with a recommendation from Great Britain that a regional conference seek solutions to the problems.

25 *Reagan signs jobs bill*

President Reagan signed legislation that would provide about 350,000 new jobs and financial assistance to the unemployed. The two houses of Congress had held different views on how the money should be allocated, but they finally agreed that more than one-third of the $4,650,000,000 would go to financially strapped states for mass transit and a wide variety of other projects. Some $1.7 billion was provided for public works altogether, and $500 million was earmarked for public service jobs, which included day-care and home health services, usually provided by women.

31 *Teamsters boss sentenced to prison*

Roy L. Williams, president of the International Brotherhood of Teamsters, was sentenced to 55 years in prison on 11 counts of fraud and conspiracy. Among other things, he had been found guilty of attempting to bribe a U.S. senator. U.S. Federal District Court Judge Prentice Marshall indicated he would substantially reduce the sentence after Williams's medical condition was evaluated. On April 15 Williams resigned as head of the labour union. In exchange, he was allowed to remain out of prison until his appeal had been heard.

Sale of F-16s to Israel halted

President Reagan said he would not approve the shipment of F-16 fighter planes to Israel until it had withdrawn its troops from Lebanon. He implied that U.S. law forbade such sales because the U.S. arms agreement with Israel stipulated that such weapons be used only for defensive purposes. Israeli Foreign Minister Yitzhak Shamir called the announcement regrettable. He said Israel had crossed the border into Lebanon only to destroy the power of the Palestine Liberation Organization (PLO). Even though the PLO had been routed, Israel said it felt compelled to remain in Lebanon because the PLO and Syrian forces that remained in the Bekaa Valley refused to leave Lebanon and thus still posed a threat to Israel's national security. President Reagan lifted the ban on May 20 on the grounds that Israel had signed an agreement to withdraw its troops from Lebanon if Syria did the same. The highly sophisticated planes were due for delivery in 1986.

APRIL

1 *Europeans protest nuclear weapons*

Britons by the tens of thousands formed a 22-km (14-mi)-long human chain to protest NATO's planned deployment of Pershing II and cruise missiles in Europe. The line stretched from an air base at Greenham Common, on past a nuclear weapons research laboratory, to an armaments factory at Burghfield. The next day about 4,000 people staged a "die-in" in Glasgow, Scotland.

4 *U.S. grants asylum to Hu Na*

The U.S. announced it was granting political asylum to one of China's top-ranking female tennis players, Hu Na. Her request for asylum was granted on the basis of her "well-founded fear of persecution" because she steadfastly refused to join the Communist Party. Chinese authorities were so upset by the U.S. decision that they canceled nine cultural exchange programs and Chinese participation in ten international sports programs to be held in the U.S. during 1983.

5 *King Hussein and Yasir Arafat confer*

Yasir Arafat, the leader of the Palestine Liberation Organization, and King Hussein of Jordan ended several days of talks in Amman after failing to work out a basis for cooperating in President Reagan's peace plan for the Middle East.

France expels 47 Soviets as spies

The French government, in an unprecedented move, expelled 47 Soviet citizens because they were "engaged in a systematic search on French territory for technological and scientific information, particularly in the military area." The Soviet embassy in Paris called the expulsion order a "totally unfounded and arbitrary decision."

10 *Jordan will not pursue peace talks*

Jordan announced that it would no longer participate in peace talks on the basis of President Reagan's Middle East peace plan, despite U.S. assurances that it would try to stop Israel from establishing more settlements in the West Bank.

11 *MX panel makes recommendations*

A special panel appointed by President Reagan and headed by retired air force

WIDE WORLD

U.S. Representative Harold Washington (right) was sworn in as Chicago's mayor on April 29. He became the first black to win that office.

general Brent Scowcroft reported on its study of deployment methods for the multiple-warhead MX missiles. The panel recommended the use of existing Minuteman silos in the states of Nebraska and Wyoming. The group also proposed the development of single-warhead intercontinental ballistic missiles that would be land-based but mobile.

12 *Vietnam claims a victory over rebels in Kampuchea*

Vietnam claimed its two-week offensive against various rebel factions in Kampuchea had ended in victory. The fighting occurred along the Thai border and, according to the Thai government and Kampuchean witnesses, involved hundreds of civilian fatalities at the hands of the Vietnamese.

Chicago gets first black mayor

U.S. Rep. Harold Washington (Dem., Ill.) was elected the first black mayor of Chicago in a very close race. His Republican opponent was Bernard Epton, a lawyer and former state legislator. The often bitter campaign was marred by frequent references to race despite a plea by both candidates to the voters to consider only their qualifications for office. Mayor Jane Byrne, who had lost the primary election to Washington in March, launched a last-minute write-in campaign that quickly collapsed when fellow Democrats refused to support her.

13 *Japan-U.S.S.R. talks fail*

High-ranking Japanese and Soviet government officials ended two days of talks in Tokyo without reconciling their major differences. The U.S.S.R., dismissing complaints that Soviet SS-20 missiles stationed in Siberia posed a threat to Japan's security, insisted that the missiles were meant to counter U.S. missiles carried aboard submarines. During the talks Japan turned down Soviet offers of a nonaggression pact and long-term economic cooperation.

16 *Brazil holds Libyan planes loaded with arms for Nicaragua*

The Brazilian government detained four Libyan planes that were suspected of carrying arms to Nicaragua. The Libyan crews initially insisted the cargo was medical supplies for Colombia, but on April 22 Nicaragua admitted the planes carried a "military donation" from Libya. An international convention permitted such undeclared cargo to be detained. On June 8 Brazil allowed the planes to fly their cargo back to Libya.

18 *U.S. embassy in Beirut bombed*

The U.S. embassy in Beirut, Lebanon, was virtually destroyed by what was believed to have been a car bomb. The 63 confirmed fatalities included 17 Americans. Shortly after the explosion an anonymous phone caller said the Islamic Jihad Organization, a pro-Iranian group, had carried out the terrorist attack. On April 23 the bodies of the dead Americans were flown home for burial.

19 *U.S. and Mexican officials confer*

U.S. Secretary of State George Shultz and several other top U.S. government officials concluded two days of talks with members of the Cabinet of Mexico's Pres. Miguel de la Madrid Hurtado. Shultz remarked that there were few voices the U.S. respected more than Mexico's and promised to pay attention to Mexico's views on Central America, but he cautioned that the U.S. was committed to playing an active role in the region. Shultz also told his hosts that the U.S. would stand by Mexico during its time of financial difficulties and expressed a hope that bilateral trade could be revived.

20 *Reagan signs Social Security bill*

President Reagan signed legislation that would reform the U.S. Social Security system and help to ensure its short- and long-term solvency. Basically, the new law would balance income and expenditures by increasing Social Security taxes and trimming benefits. The current 6.7% payroll tax, for example, would gradually rise to 7.65% by 1990. A major innovation was the inclusion of all new federal employees in the Social Security system. Eventually, the retirement age would also be raised, thereby conserving additional millions of dollars. Additional revenues would be provided by raising payroll taxes for the self-employed.

22 *"Hitler diaries" discovered*

The West German magazine *Stern* announced that it had acquired 60 volumes of handwritten documents, purportedly the personal diaries of Adolf Hitler covering the years 1932–45. On May 6, however, the West German government said chemical tests had proved conclusively that the documents were forgeries. (*See* PUBLISHING: *Sidebar.*)

U.S. to offer grain to U.S.S.R.

President Reagan announced that the U.S. was ready to negotiate long-term grain sales to the Soviet Union. Since 1981, when the last five-year deal expired, sales had been negotiated year by year to protest the Soviet Union's role in having martial law imposed on Poland. Bill Brock, the U.S. special trade representative, said the political point had been made and it was now time for the U.S. to reestablish itself as a reliable supplier.

24 *Austrian Socialists suffer defeat*

The Socialist Party of Austria (SPÖ) lost its absolute majority in Parliament when it managed to win only 90 of 183 seats in national elections. The loss of 5 seats was termed a "decisive defeat" by Chancellor Bruno Kreisky, who announced he would step down. The conservative Austrian People's Party captured 81 seats, an increase of 4, and the Freedom Party of Austria (FPÖ) won 12. One month later Fred Sinowatz, a member of the SPÖ, became chancellor and head of a coalition government that included the FPÖ.

Turkey restores political parties

Turkey's military government moved the country a step closer to democracy by announcing its intention to permit the formation of political parties. A ban remained in force, however, for 150 politicians who had gained prominence before the 1980 military coup. Included in that number were Bulent Ecevit and Suleyman Demirel, both former prime ministers. New political parties could come into being on May 16, but no pre-coup party that had been outlawed could be revived.

In addition, no party advocating Communism, fascism, or theocracy would be permitted; and no student, university professor, civil servant, or member of the military could join a political party. Elections to the new 400-seat National Assembly would be held on November 6.

27 *Reagan tells Congress more aid needed for Central America*

President Reagan, addressing a rare joint session of Congress, urged the nation's legislators to provide more military and economic aid to Central America to avert an impending crisis in that part of the world. A setback in Central America, Reagan said, not only would represent a threat to all the Americas but would call into question the ability and willingness of the U.S. to deal with threats to more distant nations. The president placed special emphasis on El Salvador. He conceded that the country still had major problems in such areas as "human rights, the criminal justice system and violence against noncombatants," but the president noted that some progress had been made in these matters. Sen. Christopher Dodd, replying on behalf of fellow Democrats, contended that too much emphasis was being placed on military solutions.

28 *Argentina closes book on missing*

The Argentine government, in a nationally televised address, said that the thousands of people who had disappeared during the "dirty war" against terrorism in the 1970s were now officially considered dead. Pres. Reynaldo Bignone called the actions by the police and military during that time "acts of service," even though there had admittedly been excesses and indefensible violations of human rights.

29 *Swiss close Soviet news office*

The Swiss ordered Novosti, the Soviet news agency, to close its office in Bern because of "repeated and increasingly grave interventions in Swiss internal affairs." Novosti was accused of using two of its Swiss employees to try to infiltrate antinuclear and dissident youth movements. The Novosti news office in Geneva was not affected by the order.

30 *Prem retains post in Thailand*

Gen. Prem Tinsulanond, who had no political affiliation, was renamed prime minister of Thailand by King Bhumibol Adulyadej, following elections in which no party won a majority. Prem had headed the previous coalition government. The old coalition, with the National Democratic Party replacing the Thai Nationalist Party, then returned to power.

MAY

1 *Poles protest against government*

Tens of thousands of Poles observed May Day by demonstrating against the government and martial law. Police used tear gas to disperse about 20,000 marchers in Gdansk, the birthplace of Solidarity, the outlawed federation of labour unions. In Warsaw, the nation's capital, a crowd of about 10,000 marched to express displeasure with the government. Another 10,000 people were scattered by tear gas and water cannons in Nowa Huta, where one demonstrator was reported killed. The crowd fought police with rocks and bottles. All told, demonstrators took to the streets in at least 20 cities despite the government's show of force and official celebrations that were meant to undermine unauthorized rallies. The government clearly hoped that popular support of the official parades would demonstrate that Solidarity had lost its vitality and that underground supporters of Solidarity were fighting for a hopeless cause.

3 *U.S. Catholic bishops oppose nuclear weapons*

The National Conference of (Roman) Catholic Bishops, during a meeting in Chicago, approved a 150-page pastoral letter on nuclear weapons. The vote was 238–9. The document, which was an amended version of a third draft, called for a halt to the development, production, and deployment of nuclear weapons. The letter stated that nuclear war was immoral and stressed the bishops' resistance to the notion that a nuclear war could even be survived, let alone won. One section of the letter read: "We do not perceive any situation in which the deliberate initiation of nuclear warfare, on however a restricted scale, can be morally justified."

House committee bars covert aid to rebels in Nicaragua

The U.S. House Permanent Select Committee on Intelligence voted 9–5 to cut off funds for all covert operations against Nicaragua. All five Republicans supported the Reagan administration's policy by opposing the ban. Though the bill went beyond the Boland amendment, which made allowances for covert efforts to interdict the flow of arms from Nicaragua to leftist guerrillas in El Salvador, it did authorize $80 million in overt aid for operations undertaken by friendly Central American nations to stop the arms shipments.

4 *El Salvador makes offer of amnesty*

El Salvador's Constituent Assembly unanimously passed a law offering amnesty to an estimated 250 political prisoners and to leftist guerrillas who surrendered to the authorities within 60 days. Those who accepted amnesty would be given help to leave the country if they so desired. During the assembly debate Mauricio Mazzier Andino criticized fellow legislators for doing nothing to abolish right-wing death squads and end violations of human rights.

Iran outlaws Communist Party

The Iranian government outlawed Tudeh, the Iranian Communist Party organization, and ordered 18 Soviet diplomats to leave the country within 48 hours. On April 30 Nureddin Kianuri, the head of Tudeh, confessed on television that the Iranian Communist Party had engaged in espionage and treason by sending political and military reports to the Soviet Union. Six other Tudeh officials made similar admissions. All had been in police custody for several months.

5 *GATT members report on foreign debts*

Representatives of the 88 nations that had signed the General Agreement on Tariffs and Trade (GATT) issued a report on six of the world's most debt-ridden countries. The study showed that the six ran combined deficits of $22 billion in 1982, a substantial improvement compared with the $36 billion combined deficit they had posted the previous year. The difference was mainly due to restrictions that the nations in question had placed on imports. The six nations mentioned in the report were Brazil (with a foreign debt of $87 billion), Mexico ($85 billion), South Korea ($39 billion), Argentina ($38 billion), Poland ($25 billion), and Yugoslavia ($20 billion).

6 *Israel accepts troop plan*

The Israeli government approved a U.S.-sponsored plan for the simultaneous withdrawal of Israeli and Syrian troops from Lebanon. On May 13, however, Syria officially rejected the proposal. Lebanon formally approved the plan on May 14. Israel and Syria both had approximately 30,000–40,000 troops inside Lebanon, and the Palestine Liberation Organization had about 8,000 troops in Lebanese areas controlled by Syria. Though eventual implementation of the plan was by no means guaranteed, the partial agreement was viewed as an important step toward restoring the authority of the Lebanese government of Pres. Amin Gemayel over its own territory. Internecine warfare resumed when Syria demanded that Lebanon renounce the agreement.

7 *China to get back hijacked plane*

The director general of China's Civil Aviation Administration arrived in Seoul, South Korea, to negotiate the return of a Chinese plane that had been hijacked on May 5 while on a domestic flight from Manchuria to Shanghai. It was the first official contact between the two countries since the Chinese Communists came to power in 1949. After two days of negotiations it was agreed that the plane, its crew, and its passengers would all return to China but that the six hijackers would remain in South Korea to stand trial.

9 *Nicaragua's sugar quota cut*

The Reagan administration informed the Nicaraguan government that its sugar exports to the U.S. during the next fiscal year would be limited to about 10% of its present quota. Central American nations friendly to the U.S. would have their quotas correspondingly increased. By cutting Nicaragua's U.S. trade earnings by about 16%, the U.S. hoped to pressure Nicaragua into halting its alleged arms shipments to leftist rebels fighting in El Salvador.

10 *Nakasone visits ASEAN nations*

Japanese Prime Minister Yasuhiro Nakasone ended a trip that included visits to the five nations that comprise the Association of Southeast Asian Nations (ASEAN). He also stopped briefly in Brunei. Nakasone promised Japan would continue to buy 15% of its oil from Indonesia and would provide aid to Thailand, which felt itself threatened by Vietnam's attempts to subdue rebels in occupied Kampuchea. While in Singapore, Malaysia, and the Philippines, Nakasone assured his hosts that Japan would defend its vital sea-lanes without posing any threat to friendly nations.

11 *Chile suppresses demonstrations*

Chilean police shot and killed two persons while trying to quell antigovernment demonstrations organized by six labour unions. Union officials claimed that millions of Chileans took to the streets to vent their anger and frustration over the high cost of living and the severe economic depression currently affecting their country. The protest was the first such action since Gen. Augusto Pinochet Ugarte seized power in 1973. Three days later soldiers and police rounded up an estimated 1,000 people in predawn raids in Santiago. Many were released after being taken to sports fields and police stations to be searched and interrogated. Further demonstrations were held in mid-June.

15 *Hu Yaobang ends visit to Eastern Europe*

Hu Yaobang (Hu Yao-pang), general secretary of the Chinese Communist Party, ended visits to Romania and Yugoslavia. The purpose of the trip was to "convey friendship, study experience, exchange views, and enhance unity." Hu praised Romania for defending its right to follow a path independent of the Soviet Union and told Yugoslavian officials that both governments would continue to "think with our own heads, walk with our own feet, resolute in our respect for independence, equality, and noninterference."

17 *Upper Volta premier ousted*

Jean-Baptiste Ouedraogo, president of the African republic of Upper Volta, announced a purge of government officials that included the arrests of Premier Thomas Sankara and other members of the People's Salvation Council. All were accused of plotting to overthrow the government. Ouedraogo, who had led a successful coup against Col. Saye Zerbo in November 1982, also expelled the Libyan chargé d'affairs on suspicion of involvement in the alleged coup attempt.

20 *Car bomb exploded in South Africa*

A car bomb detonated in South Africa's capital city of Pretoria killed 18 persons and injured almost 200. A government minister called the bombing of the Air Force headquarters an ugly act of sabotage. The next day the outlawed African National Congress (ANC), in a statement issued from its headquarters in Zambia, said that "the escalating armed struggle, which was imposed on us as a result of the apartheid regime, will make itself felt among an increasing number of those who have chosen to serve in the enemy's forces of repression." Previous attacks had been mostly confined to empty buildings to minimize casualties.

22 *Reagan asks Iran to spare Baha'is*

President Reagan urged the Iranian government not to carry out the planned executions of 22 members of the Baha'i faith. The president pleaded for clemency because the Baha'is appeared to be completely innocent of the political charges against them. On May 28 Iran in effect rejected Reagan's plea by calling the Baha'is "spies whose activities were dictated by their Zionist masters." An estimated 150 Baha'is had already been executed since the Islamic Iranian republic was established in 1979. The Baha'i faith, an offshoot of Islam that began in Iran in the mid-19th century, had long displeased Iran's fundamentalist clergy because it teaches that no one religion should dominate any other religion.

24 *AIDS made top health priority*

The U.S. government named acquired immune deficiency syndrome (AIDS) the government's top medical priority. A spokesman for the U.S. Department of Health and Human Services stated that a nonstop effort was already under way to identify the disease so that effective treatment could be developed. Though the mysterious and usually fatal disease seemed to be largely confined to quite different but clearly identified groups, there was deep concern that AIDS might eventually spread to the general public, though there was no medical evidence that normal social contact was responsible for spreading the disease.

Youths battle police in Paris

Several protest marches organized by students opposed to planned reforms in the structure of higher education in France turned to violence when a small group of so-called uncontrollables brawled with Paris police. The student demonstrations began in April, but efforts to keep them peaceful were frustrated by left- and right-wing extremists and by apolitical youths who apparently found excitement in battling police.

Parisian students' opposition to educational reforms led to protest marches and angry confrontations with the police; some encounters gave way to violence in April and May.

IMAPRESS/PICTORIAL PARADE

25 *U.S. to export high-technology items to China*

During the first meeting of the China-United States Joint Commission on Commerce and Trade in Beijing (Peking), U.S. Commerce Secretary Malcolm Baldrige remarked that the U.S. would soon facilitate the sale of high-technology items to China. Some of the industrial items could also have military applications. Among such items that China had already requested were computers and a ground satellite-tracking system.

26 *Iceland gets new government*

Steingrímur Hermannsson replaced Gunnar Thoroddsen as prime minister of Iceland and became the head of a coalition government that included the conservative Independent Party as well as his own Progressive Party. Together the two parties controlled 37 of the 60 seats in the Althing (parliament).

28 *World leaders discuss economy*

The government leaders of Canada, France, Great Britain, Italy, Japan, the U.S., and West Germany met in Williamsburg, Va., for their annual review of the world's economies. The president of the Commission of the European Communities was also present. In a joint statement issued on May 30 the heads of the world's seven major industrial democracies agreed that the worldwide economic recession showed clear signs of abating. They called for an end to burgeoning protectionism, a greater emphasis on new technologies, more stringent efforts to control structural budget deficits, and a review of the world's monetary system.

30 *Peru in state of emergency*

Protracted civil unrest and occasional violence in Peru led Pres. Fernando Belaúnde Terry to declare a state of emergency for 60 days, suspend some civil rights, and authorize the detention of suspected terrorists for up to 15 days without charges being filed. The next day the government activated a secret national security plan to combat terrorism by the left-wing Sendero Luminoso ("Shining Path") guerrillas. They had recently dynamited two electrical power stations in Ayacucho Department and almost destroyed the Bayer chemical plant in Lima. Numerous other terrorist attacks were also launched in other parts of the country. An undetermined number of people had been killed or injured and hundreds arrested by police searching for explosives and trying to identify insurgents and their supporters.

JUNE

1 *Arafat leadership challenged*

Musa Awad (Abu Akram), a leading civilian member of Al Fatah, announced that he and about two dozen other prominent members of Yasir Arafat's group were joining those who opposed Arafat's continued leadership of the Palestine Liberation Organization (PLO). The news was significant because it indicated that some of Arafat's closest allies were taking sides against him and joining hard-line extremists backed by Syrian Pres. Hafez al-Assad. On June 23 Arafat accused Syria of actively aiding PLO guerrillas who had mutinied against Arafat in Lebanon. The next day Arafat was accused of slandering Syria and was expelled from the country. He was then put on a plane bound for Tunis, Tunisia, where he maintained his headquarters.

6 *China convenes National Congress*

Delegates to China's National People's Congress convened in Beijing (Peking) to hear Premier Zhao Ziyang (Chao Tzu-yang) report on the state of the nation. Zhao reiterated the need to control government spending, and he deplored the fact that losses from poorly managed industrial enterprises in 1982 amounted to $2.1 billion. Other speakers concurred in Zhao's analysis. On June 18 the delegates named Li Xiannian (Li Hsien-nien) president; the post had been revived during the previous People's Congress in September 1982.

7 *U.S. closes Nicaraguan consulates*

The U.S. ordered Nicaragua to close all six of its consulates and informed 21 Nicaraguan consular officials they could no longer remain in the country. The orders followed by one day Nicaragua's expulsion of three U.S. diplomats on charges of plotting to poison Nicaragua's defense minister. During a news conference Nicaraguan officials introduced a woman said to be a double agent. Paraphernalia that could be used by spies was exhibited as material given to her by CIA agents. On June 10 the U.S. Civil Aeronautics Board, at the request of the State Department, revoked Nicaragua's right to operate charter flights between Managua and Miami, Fla. Relations between the U.S. and Nicaragua deteriorated further on June 29 when the U.S. vetoed a $2.2 million loan to Nicaragua from the Inter-American Development Bank.

8 *OAU holds meeting in Ethiopia*

The Organization of African Unity (OAU) met in Addis Ababa, Eth., to discuss problems confronting the region and the world. Earlier attempts to convene the organization had failed because about 20 nations refused to attend as long as the Saharan Arab Democratic Republic (SADR) insisted on being present. SADR represented the Polisario Front, which had long fought Morocco for control of the Western Sahara. SADR in effect made it possible for the OAU to meet by announcing that it was "voluntarily and temporarily" relinquishing its seat. During the conference the delegates called for direct negotiations between Morocco and the Polisario Front so that a referendum could be held to decide the question of sovereignty.

Norway forms new government

Kåre Willoch returned to power as head of a coalition government in Norway. His Conservative Party, which won 53 seats in the 155-seat Storting (parliament), was supported by the Christian People's Party (15 seats) and the Centre Party (11). Willoch pledged that the new government would continue to pursue its previous defense, foreign, and social policies.

9 *Thatcher remains prime minister*

In parliamentary elections, the Conservative Party led by British Prime Minister Margaret Thatcher captured 397 of the 650 seats in the House of Commons. The Labour Party won only 209 seats, its worst showing since before World War II. The Social Democratic-Liberal Alliance attracted votes that would normally have gone to the Labour Party, but the Alliance won only 23 seats: 17 by the Liberals and 6 by the Social Democrats. Despite the Conservatives' overwhelming victory, they won only 43% of the popular vote, slightly less than they did in 1979. Labour won 28% and the Alliance about 25%. The major parties presented voters with a clear choice. The Conservatives had promised to increase Britain's nuclear defense capabilities, remain in the European Communities, and promote private enterprise. Labour had promised just the opposite.

Soares named Portuguese premier

Mário Soares, leader of Portugal's Socialist Party, was sworn in as head of a coalition government that included the Social Democratic Party. The two parties controlled 176 seats in the 250-seat National Assembly. In his inaugural address, Soares said the country's severe economic problems could be solved only through austerity. He was prepared to follow that course, he said, even if it undermined his popularity. Strong opposition was expected from Communist-led labour unions, which struck the bus and subway systems in Lisbon.

STUART FRANKLIN—SYGMA

Prime Minister Margaret Thatcher, returned to office in parliamentary elections that routed the Labour Party, greeted cheering supporters.

13 *Pioneer 10 leaves solar system*

The unmanned spacecraft Pioneer 10 crossed the orbit of Neptune and thus became the first man-made vehicle ever to travel beyond the solar system. As it began its voyage into interstellar space, Pioneer 10 continued to radio information back to Earth. The space probe was launched in 1972 at the Kennedy Space Center in Florida, and the following year Pioneer 10 completed a fly-by of the planet Jupiter, one of its principal missions. It was the first spacecraft equipped with an atomic battery because its flight would take it far beyond the Sun, making solar power unfeasible.

15 *Supreme Court rules on abortion*

The U.S. Supreme Court issued three decisions that limited the power of state and local governments to restrict access to legal abortions. The rulings reaffirmed the landmark decision handed down in 1973 in *Roe* v. *Wade,* which established the unrestricted right to abortions during the first trimester of pregnancy. On June 28 the Senate rejected a proposed constitutional amendment that read: "A right to abortion is not secured by this Constitution."

Cuba imprisons plane hijackers

The U.S. State Department chided Cuba for failing to return plane hijackers to their country of origin and for failing to publicize the punishment given to those who were put on trial and convicted. That same day Cuba turned over to the U.S. a report on what had happened to such hijackers between 1980 and 1982. Initially, offenders received sentences that averaged about three years, but later the prison terms ranged from 12 to 20 years.

16 *Japanese-Americans to get recompense*

The federal Commission on Wartime Relocation and Internment of Civilians recommended after a two-year study that the U.S. government pay $20,000 to each of the estimated 60,000 surviving Japanese-Americans who had been placed in detention camps during World War II. The payments would serve as an "act of national apology" for the "grave injustice" that had been done to 120,000 Japanese-Americans. The commission estimated that the internees may have cumulatively lost the present equivalent of $2 billion in property and income.

Pope again visits his Polish homeland

Pope John Paul II returned to his native Poland for a second visit that had profound political as well as religious implications. The pontiff met twice with Gen. Wojciech Jaruzelski, Poland's premier, and once with Lech Walesa, who had headed Solidarity, the independent federation of labour unions that had been outlawed by the government. During his visit the pope openly called for a return to the agreements of August 1980 that had led to the establishment of Solidarity. He also sought to instill hope and confidence in the minds of the millions who listened to his words.

Andropov elected Soviet president

Yury Andropov, general secretary of the Soviet Communist Party, was elected chairman of the Presidium of the Supreme Soviet, a position equivalent to president. The only other Soviet leader to be both head of state and leader of the Communist Party was the late Leonid Brezhnev.

17 *Heads of EC nations meet*

Representatives of the ten European Communities nations convened in Stuttgart, West Germany, to discuss financial problems and other issues. Great Britain had long complained that the EC budget was unjust because it subsidized inefficient farmers and cost food-importing nations such as Great Britain huge sums of money they could never recover. The EC met this complaint by tentatively pledging to give Britain a $670 million rebate on its 1983 contribution.

23 *Supreme Court restrains Congress*

The U.S. Supreme Court, in settling a case involving a Kenyan student and the U.S. Immigration and Naturalization Service, ruled that the so-called legislative veto used by Congress to stem the powers of the president and federal regulatory agencies was unconstitutional. Chief Justice Warren Burger, speaking for the majority, said the veto was in clear conflict with the Constitution because it gave the legislative branch of government powers that belonged to the executive branch. The court's ruling could invalidate nearly 200 statutes that incorporated the legislative veto.

24 *"Challenger" makes second flight*

The U.S. space shuttle "Challenger" landed at Edwards Air Force Base in California after completing a near perfect mission that began on June 18. The plan to land on a runway at Cape Canaveral in Florida had to be scrubbed because of bad weather. The crew of five included Sally K. Ride, the first U.S. woman astronaut launched into space.

25 *Shultz heads for Asia and Middle East*

U.S. Secretary of State George Shultz left the U.S. for a visit to Asia that included stops in the Philippines, Thailand, India, and Pakistan. He then continued on to the Middle East at the behest of President Reagan. While in Thailand, Shultz promised to continue pushing for the withdrawal of Vietnamese troops from Kampuchea. In India he announced that the U.S. was prepared to lift a ban on the export of nuclear reactor components even though India refused to allow inspection of its nuclear facilities. The secretary encouraged Pakistani leaders to continue to promote a peaceful solution to the problems created by the Soviet occupation of Afghanistan. Shultz's visit to the Middle East failed to produce a breakthrough that would have hastened the withdrawal of foreign troops from Lebanon. There had been reports that Syrian Pres. Hafez al-Assad might be ready to negotiate terms for withdrawing his country's troops, but a five-hour meeting with Assad brought no results.

30 *Alberta and Ottawa agree on fuel*

The Canadian federal government and the province of Alberta reached an agreement on energy that canceled planned increases in oil and natural gas prices during the next year and a half. The pact meant that oil discovered before 1974 would be sold at Can$29.75 per barrel, about 83% of the world price. However, any oil discovered after 1974, as well as "new" oil extracted from pre-1974 wells that had subsequently been redrilled, could be sold at world prices. Natural gas prices would rise twice before 1985, but the increase would be offset by government reductions in the gas excise tax. The new price structure was expected to increase supplies and improve the producers' cash flow.

JULY

4 *Helmut Kohl visits U.S.S.R.*

West German Chancellor Helmut Kohl arrived in Moscow to discuss military issues with top Soviet officials. There was reportedly a blunt exchange of views, with Kohl holding fast to his position that West Germany would deploy Pershing II and cruise missiles on its soil if the U.S.-Soviet talks in Geneva on limitation of intermediate nuclear forces failed to produce an agreement before the end of the year. Tass, the Soviet news agency, reported that Soviet Pres. Yury V. Andropov warned Chancellor Kohl that the U.S.S.R. would take countermeasures if new medium-range nuclear missiles were deployed in West Germany.

Talks on new Uruguayan charter stalled

Uruguay's three opposition political parties withdrew from discussions with the military government of Gen. Gregorio Conrado Álvarez Armelino over a new constitution when the government insisted it should reserve significant powers to the military. The Blanco Party instigated the action and was supported by the Colorado and Civic Union parties. The Por la Patria faction of the Blanco Party had already withdrawn from the talks after its weekly magazine was closed on May 27. The new constitution was to have been prepared before presidential elections scheduled for November 1984. A revised version of the constitution prepared by the military government was rejected by the voters in 1980.

7 *Brazilians protest austerity*

Some 60,000 Brazilian metalworkers in São Paulo State joined a strike begun the day before by oil refinery workers protesting the government's plan to curb spending in state-owned companies in order to meet conditions for a loan from the International Monetary Fund (IMF). Among other changes, workers would no longer share profits or receive loans at subsidized interest rates. The companies were also ordered to cut expenditures by 5% during the latter half of the year and by an additional 5% during the first half of 1984. The year's inflation rate was expected to be about 130%. Government-run enterprises employed about 1.4 million people and accounted for nearly half of the nation's goods and services. On July 11 the Bank for International Settlements refused to grant Brazil a third extension on repayment of a $400 million loan. This increased pressure on Brazil to meet the requirements of the IMF. A general strike on July 21 failed to get wide support except in the city of São Paulo, where some 300 persons were arrested.

8 *Caricom wants fighting to end*

The 12-nation Caribbean Community (Caricom) ended its conference in Trinidad after welcoming The Bahamas into the organization and debating a broad range of issues. The Caricom nations went on record as opposing foreign involvement in Central America and endorsed efforts initiated by the Contadora Group (Mexico, Colombia, Venezuela, Panama) to find a peaceful solution to the military upheaval in the region. Caricom also expressed a hope that the U.S. Congress would soon pass the tax and trade provisions of the Reagan administration's Caribbean Basin Initiative.

Pope's assailant implicates Soviets

Mehmet Ali Agca, a Turk convicted in Italy of attempting to assassinate Pope John Paul II in May 1981, told inquiring reporters in Rome that Soviet and Bulgarian agents were involved in his act of terrorism. Italian police had in fact earlier arrested a Bulgarian suspect who had been an airline employee in Rome and was still being held in custody. Agca claimed to have been trained in terrorism by the KGB, the Soviet Union's security and intelligence agency. The official Soviet press called Agca's statement "threadbare propaganda."

11 *Peruvian terrorists stage raid in Lima*

Terrorists, presumed to be members of the organization called Sendero Luminoso (Shining Path), broke into the Lima headquarters of Peru's ruling Popular Action Party and killed two persons. Some 30 others were injured when the building came under attack from machine-gun fire and bombs. The Communists joined other political parties in denouncing the latest in a long series of guerrilla attacks on a wide variety of targets throughout the country.

12 *China and U.K. discuss Hong Kong*

Representatives of China and the U.K. met in Beijing (Peking) to continue discussions on Hong Kong's future after Britain's lease expired in 1997. Though details of this and previous meetings had not been made public, China was reportedly considering a proposal to designate the territory a special administrative zone so that it could continue to operate for a considerable period of time under its present economic, legal, and social systems. Many Hong Kong Chinese, however, continued to be apprehensive about the future and some had begun moving their money out of the colony.

13 *Britain again rejects death penalty*

The British House of Commons voted 361–245 not to revive the death penalty, which had been abolished in 1964. Prime Minister Margaret Thatcher and other prominent Conservatives had urged its reinstatement for such crimes as acts of terrorism and the murder of policemen and prison guards, but Conservative members of Parliament were left free to vote according to their consciences.

15 *Armenians bomb Paris airport*

Five persons were instantly killed and more than 50 others injured when a bomb, enclosed in a suitcase, exploded at the Turkish Airlines counter at Orly Airport outside Paris. The Armenian Secret Army for the Liberation of Armenia (ASALA) claimed responsibility. On July 20 the French government announced that a 29-year-old Syrian citizen of Armenian extraction had confessed to planting

West German Chancellor Helmut Kohl (centre) was welcomed to Moscow in July for a four-day visit by Soviet Foreign Minister Andrey Gromyko (far left). Between them is West German Foreign Minister Hans-Dietrich Genscher.

A.P.N./GAMMA/LIAISON

UPI

The Contadora Group met in Cancún, Mexico, in July seeking peace in Central America. The members are (from left) Presidents Belisario Betancur Cuartas (Colombia), Luis Herrera Campins (Venezuela), Miguel de la Madrid Hurtado (Mexico), and Ricardo de la Espriella (Panama).

the bomb. He said he headed the French branch of the ASALA. One day before the Orly attack several different Armenian groups took responsibility for shooting a Turkish diplomat to death in Brussels. The violence continued on July 27 when four Armenian terrorists shot their way into the residence of the Turkish ambassador to Portugal, then blew themselves up. Four gunmen, a policeman, and a woman were killed. A fifth gunman was shot and killed before the explosion. During the 12 months preceding the attack in Lisbon, Armenians were blamed for ten other acts of terrorism in various parts of the world. Their principal motive was revenge for the deaths of hundreds of thousands of Armenians at the hands of Turkish soldiers between 1894 and World War I. Turkey had never admitted that it systematically killed the Armenians.

U.S. to retain Greek military bases

Representatives of Greece approved an agreement that would permit the U.S. to retain its Greek military facilities for an additional five years. The bases could be used for defensive purposes only and not, therefore, to support U.S. involvement in Middle Eastern countries friendly to Greece. Greek Prime Minister Andreas Papandreou stated that the U.S. had agreed during the sometimes difficult negotiations not to upset the current balance of military power between Greece and Turkey.

16 *OAU speaks out on war in Chad*

A nine-nation committee of the Organization of African Unity (OAU) recommended that all foreign nations cease their involvement in Chad so that its local warring factions could resolve their conflicts through negotiations. Chadian Pres. Hissen Habré's troops had already lost about one-third of the country to rebel forces loyal to Goukouni Oueddei, who had been overthrown by Habré in June 1982. Libya's interference on the side of Goukouni had prompted France to step up its military commitment to Habré and led to U.S. shipments of food, clothing, vehicles, and fuel to Habré's government. Zaire, fearful of Libya, had also sent troops to defend Habré's regime.

17 *Contadora Group urges peace talks*

The presidents of Mexico, Venezuela, Colombia, and Panama, during a meeting in Cancún, Mexico, called upon all nations with an interest in Central America to commit themselves unreservedly to settlement of disputes through negotiations rather than through war. The so-called Contadora Group's proposals included a freeze on the shipment of military items to the region, the withdrawal of all foreign troops and advisers, and the establishment of international border patrols. On July 19 the foreign ministers of Guatemala, Costa Rica, Honduras, and El Salvador issued an eight-point peace plan that included the basic tenets of the Contadora communiqué.

18 *Kissinger named to head panel*

President Reagan announced he would appoint Henry Kissinger, a former U.S. secretary of state, head of a new 12-member National Bipartisan Commission on Central America. Its task would be to examine basic problems in the area and then make recommendations on what long-term policies the U.S. should follow. The commission would be asked to report to the president by December 1. Kissinger, whose appointment delighted some and dismayed others, had earlier expressed approval of U.S. support for Nicaraguan rebels and of efforts to prevent Communists from taking control of Central American countries.

19 *Report criticizes U.S. education*

An extensive report on U.S. education indicated that the public school system needed far-reaching restructuring to address its "deeply entrenched and virtually chronic" problems. John I. Goodlad, former dean of the Graduate School of Education at the University of California at Los Angeles, directed the eight-year study. Basic data were obtained by 43 researchers who attended classes in 13 communities and evaluated tens of thousands of interviews and questionnaires. Among Goodlad's recommendations were: earlier schooling, smaller schools, a core of general education for all high school students, and the abolition of "tracking"—the assignment of students of like ability to the same classrooms.

20 *Israel to redeploy troops in Lebanon*

The Israeli Cabinet approved a proposal to withdraw its troops from the suburbs of Beirut and from the Shuf Mountains of Lebanon and redeploy them to the south along the Awali River. Both the Lebanese and U.S. governments, whose shared goal was to restore Lebanese authority over the entire country, opposed the Israeli pullback because it had the potential to divide Lebanon permanently into areas dominated by Israel and Syria.

21 *Poland ends martial law*

Poland announced that martial law, which had been in effect since December 1981, would be lifted at midnight. Before the announcement, Poland's constitution had been modified to permit the government to declare a state of emergency in the event of unrest and then assume extraordinary powers. Wojciech Jaruzelski, who held the post of premier and also headed the Polish Communist Party and the Defense Ministry, warned that any antisocialist activity would be dealt with severely. The Sejm (parliament) then granted a partial amnesty to most political prisoners and to those serving time for violations of martial law. On July 28 the Sejm, ignoring strong opposition from the Roman Catholic Church, gave the government new powers to control a wide range of activities.

Shake-up reported in Burma

The *New York Times* reported that U Ne Win, chairman of the ruling Burma Socialist Program Party, seemed to be continuing an apparent shake-up of the government that had begun some two months earlier. Several prominent figures from the Cabinet, the military, the diplomatic corps, and the intelligence agencies had been replaced. Brig. Gen. Tin Oo, long considered a probable successor to 72-year-old Ne Win, was reported to have resigned and some of his closest friends were said to have been removed from seats of power. Since Ne Win remained in full control of the nation, there was speculation that the shake-up may have been triggered by evidence of smuggling on the part of high-ranking officials. Another factor was thought to be Ne Win's desire to be succeeded by a collective leadership along Yugoslavian lines rather than by a single individual.

David Dodge released in Middle East

The U.S. government verified that David Dodge, the former acting president of the American University in Beirut, Lebanon, had finally been released more than one year after he was abducted on a street in Beirut. Though few details were made public, Dodge had reportedly been taken to Syria and then to Iran, probably by Shi'ah Muslims. The U.S. expressed special thanks to Syrian Pres. Hafez al-Assad and his brother, the Syrian chief of security, for their humanitarian efforts in helping secure Dodge's release.

26 *U.S.S.R. to try economic reforms*

The Soviet Union announced its intention to experiment with limited economic reforms that would give certain factory managers greater control over such things as wages, bonuses, and technical innovations. It was hoped that the program would stimulate productivity, encourage personal initiative, and hasten technical progress while heightening each factory's responsibility for the quality and quantity of the goods it produced.

Italy sentences terrorists

A mass trial in Turin, Italy, ended when 12 defendants, all alleged members of the Red Brigades, were sentenced to life imprisonment and 48 others to lesser terms; one was acquitted. The accused had been charged with committing ten murders and numerous other acts of violence in the Turin area between 1973 and 1980. One week later a similar trial ended in Sardinia. Two of the terrorists received life sentences and 37 others terms ranging up to 18 years; 21 were acquitted. Two terrorists who were arrested in 1982 when U.S. Gen. James Dozier was rescued from his kidnappers reportedly provided evidence used in convicting the Sardinians.

27 *Pershing II again fails test*

A Pershing II missile malfunctioned shortly after it was test fired from Cape Canaveral, Fla. It was the 3rd failure in the last 4 tests and the 5th failure during a series of 16 tests. The U.S. Defense Department, however, seemed satisfied that the problems with the medium-range missile were minor and would not delay the scheduled deployment of the nuclear weapons in Europe at the end of the year if U.S.-Soviet arms-control talks proved unsuccessful.

31 *Stone meets Salvadoran rebel leader*

Richard B. Stone, the U.S. special envoy to Central America, had his first face-to-face meeting with Ruben Zamora, the leader of one of the five leftist guerrilla organizations fighting the central government in El Salvador. The meeting in Bogotá, which was arranged by Colombian Pres. Belisario Betancur Cuartas, increased hopes that in time the government of Salvadoran Pres. Álvaro Magaña Borjo might enter into direct peace negotiations with the rebels.

U.S. and China sign textile pact

President Reagan's special trade representative, Bill Brock, confirmed that China and the U.S. had reached agreement in Geneva on Chinese textile exports to the U.S. Brock estimated that China's quota would increase by 2 to 3% a year over the next five years. U.S. textile executives had vigorously fought any increase and had insisted that the new pact, which they interpreted as permitting an annual increase of 3 to 4%, would be disastrous for U.S. manufacturers because they could not match the lower cost of most Chinese goods. Brock said he expected that the textile agreement would improve overall trade relations between China and the U.S. and would encourage China to buy more U.S. grain and other agricultural products. Two-way trade between China and the U.S. totaled approximately $5.2 billion in 1982.

AUGUST

4 *Italy chooses Socialist premier*

Bettino Craxi was sworn in as Italy's first Socialist premier. The new five-party coalition government (Italy's 44th government since World War II) included Socialists, Christian Democrats, Republicans, Social Democrats, and Liberals. Craxi gave the Christian Democrats, Italy's largest political party, 16 of the 30 posts in his Cabinet. The new premier supported Italy's present ties to the U.S. and Western Europe and said he favoured the deployment of medium-range missiles in Europe if the Geneva arms talks failed. His top domestic priorities would include reducing unemployment, cutting the nation's current 16% inflation rate by one-third, and reducing the government's deficit spending by $20 billion. Craxi was sure to face strong opposition from the Communist Party, which had the second largest representation in Parliament but was excluded from the ruling coalition.

5 *Sri Lanka bans separatist groups*

The predominantly Sinhalese Sri Lankan Parliament approved a constitutional amendment that effectively outlawed any group advocating a separate state for the minority Tamil population. The move followed a new period of rioting, looting, burning, and killing that began on July 23 when Tamil guerrillas ambushed and killed 13 soldiers in Jaffna. Two days later 37 Tamils were murdered by fellow prisoners in a Colombo prison. Before the violence subsided, nearly 400 persons in various parts of the country had been killed. For almost two decades Tamil separatists had been demanding with ever greater insistence that they be given independence.

Leader of Upper Volta ousted

Capt. Thomas Sankara, a former premier, announced the successful overthrow of Maj. Jean-Baptiste Ouedraogo, who had ruled Upper Volta since seizing power in November 1982. Sankara, a paratrooper who had supported Ouedraogo's own coup, claimed the government had served "the interests of foreign domination and neocolonialism." Though Sankara openly admired Libyan leader Col. Muammar al-Qaddafi and had reportedly received military support from him, Sankara insisted that his country would never become a Libyan pawn.

Bomb kills 19 at Lebanese mosque

A powerful car bomb that exploded in front of the Bakkar Mosque in Tripoli, Lebanon, killed at least 19 persons and injured 43. No group claimed responsibility for the incident, but a Sunni Muslim group accused Christian supporters of Pres. Amin Gemayel of committing the atrocity. After the bombing anti-Syrian Sunni Muslims and pro-Syrian Alawite Muslims exchanged sniper fire in the streets.

6 *Shagari reelected in Nigeria*

Nigerian Pres. Alhaji Shehu Shagari, a member of the National Party of Nigeria, was elected to a second four-year term. Shagari received about 12 million votes in the six-candidate race; his closest rival, Chief Obafemi Awolowo of the Unity Party of Nigeria, was selected on about 8 million ballots. Shagari also met an additional requirement for election when he captured at least 25% of the vote in each of at least 13 of Nigeria's 19 states.

8 *Guatemalan leader overthrown*

The president of Guatemala, Gen. Efraín Ríos Montt, was overthrown in a military coup and replaced by Brig. Gen. Oscar Humberto Mejía Victores, the minister of defense. Prospects for an elected civilian president increased when Mejía restored civil liberties and top military leaders reaffirmed their commitment to constitutional democracy. The coup was justified on the grounds that a "fanatic and aggressive religious group"—Ríos Montt, an evangelical fundamentalist, belonged to the California-based Church of the Word—had used the government for its own benefit. The vast majority of Guatemalans were Roman Catholic.

10 *Rebels take northern Chad town*

Chadian rebels loyal to former president Goukouni Oueddei captured the key northern town of Faya-Largeau with the substantial help of Libyan soldiers, planes, armoured vehicles, and artillery. The previous day France had responded to a plea for military assistance from Pres. Hissen Habré by increasing to 500 the number of paratroopers it was sending as instructors to its former colony. On August 13 an additional 180 French paratroopers and three helicopters arrived in the eastern city of Abéché. The French troops had orders to return fire if attacked and thus constituted an implicit warning to antigovernment forces not to attack Abéché or the capital, N'Djamena.

13 *More die in Chilean protests*

The Chilean government announced that the 7 persons killed that day during protests against the regime of Pres. Augusto Pinochet Ugarte raised the two-day death total to 24. Some residents living in the areas where deaths had occurred accused the police and soldiers of firing randomly into crowds and of shooting demonstrators who were merely taunting them or throwing rocks. The violence was reportedly the worst since Pinochet came to power in 1973.

14 *Thousands clash in Pakistan*

Thousands of supporters of Pakistani Pres. Mohammad Zia-ul-Haq challenged thousands of antigovernment demonstrators during a protest march in Karachi. Both groups had organized to commemorate the 36th anniversary of Pakistan's independence. Police fired tear gas into the rock-throwing crowds and arrested two leaders of the Movement for the Restoration of Democracy; the men were charged with violating martial law by holding a political rally. Police also made arrests in Peshawar after breaking up an antigovernment rally. Present and former provincial leaders were among those arrested.

Reagan meets with de la Madrid

President Reagan arrived in La Paz, Mexico, for a brief visit with Pres. Miguel de la Madrid Hurtado. Reagan defended certain of his foreign policy decisions, saying: "We believe that people should be able to determine their own solutions, and that is why we've responded to calls for help from certain of our Latin American neighbors." De la Madrid had on several occasions called for the withdrawal of all foreign troops from the region in the hope that local and regional problems could be solved through negotiations. The president of Mexico remarked that the meeting with Reagan, despite differences of opinion, had expanded "the climate of cordiality and good faith that characterized our relations."

16 *Nkomo returns to Zimbabwe*

Joshua Nkomo, the leader of the Zimbabwe African People's Union and the chief political opponent of Prime Minister Robert Mugabe, returned to Zimbabwe from self-imposed exile in London. Nkomo had fled to Britain in early March because, he said, he feared for his life. On August 17 Nkomo resumed his seat in Parliament, but there was little hope that the two men who had fought together for Zimbabwe's independence would be able to reconcile their present differences in the foreseeable future.

U.S. admits protecting Barbie

The U.S. Justice Department publicly acknowledged that Klaus Barbie, who headed Nazi Germany's Gestapo unit in Lyon, France, from 1942 to 1944, was employed as a paid spy by the U.S. Army's Counter Intelligence Corps (CIC) beginning in 1947. The CIC later realized that Barbie might be subject to prosecution as a war criminal but feigned ignorance of his whereabouts when French authorities sought to locate him. The CIC also helped Barbie and his family escape to South America. The events of the past assumed new importance after Barbie was arrested in Bolivia on January 25 and extradited to France, where he was charged with crimes against humanity. The U.S. government sent a formal note of apology to France for having actively impeded the lawful search for the man known in France as the "Butcher of Lyon."

WIDE WORLD

Bettino Craxi (left) was congratulated after being sworn in as Italy's first Socialist premier by Pres. Alessandro Pertini.

18 *South Korea sentences hijackers*

A judge in Seoul, South Korea, sentenced six Chinese citizens to prison terms ranging from four to six years for hijacking a Chinese civilian airliner to South Korea in May. The plane was commandeered during a domestic flight to Shanghai. It seemed likely that the six would be allowed to settle in Taiwan, as they had requested. Officials in Beijing (Peking) had initially insisted that the hijackers be returned to China to stand trial, but the South Korean government, which returned the plane, rejected the demand.

19 *Argentines protest amnesty*

Some 40,000 Argentines marched in Buenos Aires to protest a proposed amnesty that would protect military personnel from prosecution for human rights violations committed during the 1970s. If approved by the present military government, the amnesty could prevent a future civilian government from punishing members of the armed forces for such crimes as wanton killings, torture, and kidnapping.

20 *Reagan lifts pipeline curbs*

President Reagan lifted controls that had been placed on the export of certain pipelaying equipment to the Soviet Union. The change in U.S. policy was backed by Secretary of State George Shultz and Secretary of Commerce Malcolm Baldrige but opposed by Secretary of Defense Caspar Weinberger and William P. Clark, the president's national security adviser, even though the equipment had no military significance.

21 *Benigno Aquino is slain in Manila*

Benigno S. Aquino, Jr., a severe critic of Philippine Pres. Ferdinand Marcos and a former senator, was shot and killed just minutes after he returned to Manila. He had been released from prison to undergo heart surgery in the U.S. and had remained there for about three years. Aquino's alleged assassin was instantly shot and killed on the tarmac by soldiers, but circumstances surrounding the shooting were so unusual that anti-Marcos factions said they were convinced the government had been involved. Though reporters were not allowed to follow

BALDEV—SYGMA

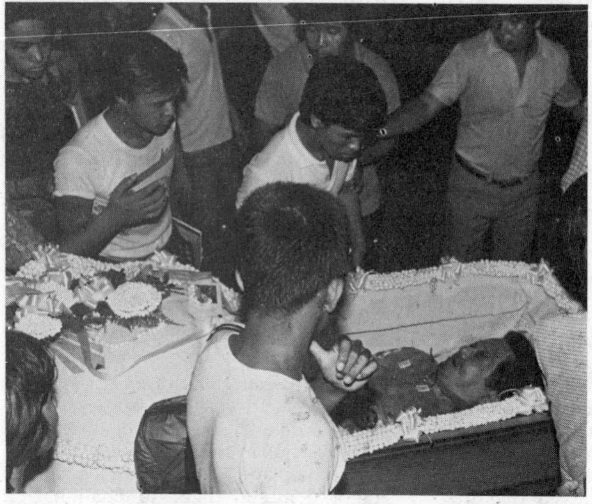

Benigno Aquino, slain on landing in Manila after three years in exile, was mourned by thousands.

Aquino as he was escorted off the plane by security guards and directed through an exit that led directly to the tarmac rather than into the airport building, a Japanese reporter claimed to have seen a soldier shoot Aquino. Other witnesses later made similar statements, but there were still conflicting reports about what had actually happened. Hundreds of thousands later viewed Aquino's blood-splattered body as it lay in a glass-enclosed coffin. An estimated one million or more Filipinos accompanied Aquino's body to the cemetery on August 31. The murder triggered numerous antigovernment demonstrations, some violent. Marcos refused to heed calls for his resignation and threatened to reimpose martial law if there was no other way to restore order.

Apartheid foes organize movement

A new multiracial antigovernment movement called the United Democratic Front formally took shape in South Africa during a sizable rally in Cape Town. Members of the group opposed government efforts to modify the constitution so that Indians and Coloureds (those of mixed blood), but not blacks, could actively participate in the white-dominated government. The movement could have been easily stifled, but observers believed the government was uncharacteristically tolerant because it hoped to induce the participants to accept the new proposals.

24 *Swiss select German tanks*

Switzerland announced that it would buy 420 West German Leopard II tanks rather than M-1 Abrams tanks manufactured in the U.S. The Swiss reportedly viewed the Leopard II as a superior weapon and would be allowed to produce about 70% of the tanks in their own factories. The contract called for an initial procurement of 210 tanks at a cost of $1.2 billion.

27 *Huge crowd commemorates 1963 march*

A crowd of at least 250,000 gathered in Washington, D.C., to commemorate the 1963 march on the nation's capital that was highlighted by the Rev. Martin Luther King, Jr.'s memorable "I have a dream" speech. The theme of the 1983 event was "Jobs, Peace and Freedom." Benjamin Hooks, the executive director of the National Association for the Advancement of Colored People, led the crowd in chanting anti-Reagan slogans.

28 *Menachem Begin to resign*

Menachem Begin, who had become increasingly withdrawn from public life in recent weeks, informed the Israeli Cabinet that he would formally resign within a few days as prime minister and as leader of the Herut Party. His decision, he said, was based on personal, not political, considerations. Yitzhak Shamir, the 68-year-old foreign minister, was considered Begin's most likely successor. With Shamir heading the government, no major changes were expected in Israel's domestic and foreign policies in the near future.

29 *Two U.S. Marines die in Lebanon*

Two U.S. Marines serving with the international peacekeeping force in Lebanon were killed when a mortar struck their positions near Beirut's international airport. They were the first U.S. servicemen to die in Lebanon. On August 30 the French contingent of the peacekeeping force suffered its first fatalities when four of its soldiers were killed in Beirut.

Salvadoran officials meet rebels

Two representatives of the government and two persons representing the opposition in El Salvador's civil war met in Bogotá, Colombia, for the first time. Though no significant developments were reported and no date was set for any subsequent meeting, the coming together was in itself noteworthy. The government repeated its desire to have the rebels participate in a national election next year, but the rebels continued to insist that elections should follow the establishment of a new provisional government.

31 *Poles commemorate Solidarity*

Poles in various parts of the country commemorated the third anniversary of the accords that led to the establishment of Solidarity, the now outlawed national federation of labour unions. The day was marked by clashes with police, especially in Nowa Huta, as well as by marches, religious services, peaceful boycotts, and wreath-laying ceremonies.

SEPTEMBER

1 *Soviets shoot down unarmed South Korean commercial airliner*

An unarmed South Korean commercial airliner that had been flying off course over sensitive Soviet military installations was shot down near Sakhalin Island by a Soviet fighter pilot. All 269 persons aboard the plane were killed. Important details about the disaster would probably never be known with certainty because efforts to locate the flight recorder in the Sea of Japan were unsuccessful. The Soviet Union insisted from the start that the plane had not responded to signals and warnings from the Soviet fighters and was on a spy mission for the U.S. as it flew from Alaska to Seoul. President Reagan vigorously denied the charge even though the U.S. later admitted that one of its spy planes had been in the area earlier. The Soviet action was denounced in many parts of the world as totally unjustified. On September 6 the U.S.S.R. admitted for the first time that one of its pilots had shot the plane down. During a dramatic session of the UN Security Council that day, the pilot's recorded words were played back for the benefit of the delegates. The pilot was reporting to ground control the step by step procedures he was following. Leaders of the international pilots' association, representing most of the world's commercial airline pilots, expressed outrage over the incident and called upon its members to boycott flights to the Soviet

Union for 60 days. On September 12 the Soviet Union vetoed a UN Security Council resolution deploring the destruction of the airliner and "the tragic loss of civilian life therein." On September 21 a Soviet delegate attending a conference in Edinburgh, Scotland, told an interviewer from the British Broadcasting Corporation that the pilot had wrongly identified the airliner as a military reconnaissance plane and made a mistake when he destroyed it. This was the first Soviet admission of error concerning the destruction of the airliner.

5 *Space shuttle lands in darkness*

The U.S. space shuttle program reached another milestone when the "Challenger" landed at Edwards Air Force Base in California in early morning darkness. The nighttime launch on August 30 was also the first such ever attempted. The five-man crew of the "Challenger" included three navy officers; one air force officer, who attracted special attention as the first U.S. black astronaut in space; and a 54-year-old civilian physician (the oldest person to fly in space), who was an expert on space sickness. On August 31 the crew launched an Insat-1B satellite for India; it was to be used to gather weather data and for telecommunications.

10 *Peru lifts state of emergency*

Peru lifted the state of emergency that had been decreed in May after guerrillas attacked the capital city of Lima. Civil rights, however, were not restored in Apurimac, Ayacucho, and Huancavelica, three Andean departments that still harboured numerous leftist guerrillas.

11 *Violence in Chile continues*

At least ten persons were reported to have been killed in recent days as antigovernment protesters in Chile continued to demand the resignation of Pres. Augusto Pinochet Ugarte. On September 8 in some areas of Santiago bonfires were lit on street corners and demonstrators carried pictures of Salvador Allende, the leftist former president who was killed in the 1973 military coup that paved the way for Pinochet's rise to power.

12 *Shamir asked to form government*

Israeli Foreign Minister Yitzhak Shamir, who succeeded Menachem Begin as leader of the Herut Party on September 2, was asked by all six parties in the ruling coalition to form a new government. The Herut Party held only 23 of the 120 seats in the Knesset (parliament), and the Likud bloc, to which Herut belonged, controlled a total of only 46 seats. Shamir, however, was finally able to satisfy the demands of other members of the coalition and was sworn in as prime minister on October 10. The new administration immediately devalued the shekel and cut government subsidies on basic goods and services by an average of 50% in an attempt to head off an economic crisis.

16 *Syrian positions in Lebanon shelled*

Two U.S. naval vessels off the coast of Lebanon began a bombardment of antigovernment military units "deep inside Syrian-controlled" territory. It was the first use of U.S. naval power against Syrian-held positions and was a response to rocket and artillery attacks that were "endangering American lives." France actively entered the combat on September 22, when it ordered air strikes against rebel forces after French soldiers in the peacekeeping force were heavily shelled.

Yasir Arafat returns to Lebanon

Yasir Arafat, leader of the Palestine Liberation Organization (PLO), was reported to be in Tripoli, Lebanon, where he conferred with his military commanders and exhorted his supporters by reaffirming that Palestinian guerrillas would fight alongside others attempting to overthrow the government of Lebanese Pres. Amin Gemayel. Arafat had been forced to leave Lebanon in August 1982, some three months after Israel launched an offensive to destroy PLO strongholds.

20 *UN convenes amid controversy*

The UN General Assembly opened its 38th annual meeting in New York while emotions still ran high over the shooting down of a South Korean commercial airliner by a Soviet pilot on September 1. Three days before the UN was scheduled to convene, the U.S.S.R. announced that Foreign Minister Andrey A. Gromyko would not attend. The U.S. had banned Aeroflot flights to the U.S. in 1981 following the imposition of martial law in Poland, and special permission was required to allow Soviet planes to land at commercial airports. To protest the destruction of the Korean plane, permission was not granted, but Soviet officials were notified that their delegation would be welcome aboard a Soviet military plane that could land at a military airfield or on an aircraft of another country. Gromyko refused, but 61 other Soviet delegates landed in New York on September 17 aboard a Belgian airliner.

21 *Manila demonstration turns violent*

A peaceful anti-Marcos demonstration that attracted an estimated 500,000 people in Manila turned violent after nightfall. The government reported that by the next morning 11 persons had been killed and about 200 injured. The rally, which had been organized to coincide with the anniversary of the imposition of martial law in 1972, was held to demand the resignation of Pres. Ferdinand Marcos. The date also kept alive the memory of Benigno Aquino, Jr., who had been assassinated just one month earlier moments after his plane landed in Manila. Jaime Cardinal Sin, the Roman Catholic archbishop of Manila and an outspoken critic of the Marcos regime, said on September 22 that the government's policies revived "memories of Mr. Goebbels of Nazi Germany" and did not inspire faith and confidence in the government.

25 *Weinberger visits China*

U.S. Secretary of Defense Caspar W. Weinberger arrived in China to discuss increased military cooperation between

Five thousand South Korean Christians rallied before a Seoul church to protest the shooting down of a Korean Air Lines jumbo jet by Soviet fighter aircraft over Sakhalin Island on September 1.

WIDE WORLD

SEPTEMBER

China and the U.S. During talks with Chinese Defense Minister Zhang Aiping (Chang Ai-p'ing), Weinberger emphasized the danger of the Soviet Union's global military might and offered to provide China with a variety of U.S. weapons. Certain additional items would also be available if China pledged not to pass them on to any other country. On September 27 Premier Zhao Ziyang (Chao Tzu-yang) admitted that China was anxious to modernize its armed forces and could not achieve that goal without foreign purchases. But he also made it clear that the U.S. offer of mainly defensive weapons would not satisfy China's needs. Weinberger was also told that China was not at all disposed to become attached to any one power or bloc.

Irish prisoners escape from Maze

Thirty-eight members of the Provisional Irish Republican Army escaped from the Maze maximum security prison in Belfast, Northern Ireland, after killing one guard and injuring others. Four days later 19 were still at large. The group managed to escape in a van that had entered the prison compound to deliver food. Garret FitzGerald, the prime minister of Ireland, said he would not permit his country to become "a haven for terrorists" and would, therefore, cooperate in tracking down the prisoners.

Margaret Thatcher visits Canada

British Prime Minister Margaret Thatcher arrived in Canada, where the following day she addressed a rare joint session of Parliament. She told her audience that it was "time for freedom to take the offensive" in the "battle of ideas" with the Soviet Union, which, she said, had been waging a relentless propaganda campaign to sap the morale of the democracies. She also called the downing of the South Korean commercial airliner by a Soviet military plane on September 1 a terrible and tragic reminder of the Soviet Union's willingness to resort to force without regard for the human consequences.

26 *Reagan addresses UN on arms control*

President Reagan told members of the UN General Assembly that he had authorized the chief U.S. negotiator at the Geneva arms talks to present new proposals to the Soviet delegation. Reagan said the U.S. plan called for reductions and limits on arms "on a global basis," for a limit on aircraft as well as missiles, and for reconsideration of "the mix of missiles." The president explained that the U.S. was prepared to reduce the number of its Pershing II ballistic missiles and ground-launched cruise missiles if this was necessary to reduce arms to equal levels with the Soviet Union. He also pledged to seek and accept "any equitable, verifiable agreement that stabilizes forces at lower levels than currently exist." Soviet Pres. Yury V. Andropov replied on September 28 that Reagan's words were "mere declarations that can convince no one."

YVES SMET—PHOTO NEWS/GAMMA/LIAISON

Uncollected garbage in Brussels was one symptom of a nationwide strike by Belgian state employees angered by yet another austerity budget adopted for 1984.

Cease-fire takes hold in Lebanon

A cease-fire formally took effect in Lebanon following negotiations between Lebanon and Syria. Saudi Arabia had acted as mediator. The leaders of the two countries agreed to initiate talks that, it was hoped, would reconcile differences among the various political and religious factions involved in the civil war.

U.S. reveals new refugee quotas

U.S. Attorney General William French Smith submitted the Reagan administration's 1984 refugee program to Congress, which, according to law, had the right to review it and make nonbinding recommendations. The refugee quotas were set at 50,000 for East Asia, 12,000 for Eastern Europe and the Soviet Union, 6,000 for South Asia and the Near East, 3,000 for Africa, and 1,000 for the Caribbean and Latin America. The total fell 18,000 short of the 90,000 that had been authorized for fiscal year 1983. In actual fact, however, the number of refugees admitted during fiscal 1983 was expected to be about 60,000. The U.S. Border Patrol announced in late September that it had caught more than one million Mexican aliens trying to cross the U.S. border illegally during the previous 12 months.

Belgian workers end strike

Some 900,000 public sector workers returned to their jobs in Belgium after accepting terms for settling a strike that had lasted half a month and had shut down all forms of public transportation, closed down government-operated schools, disrupted mail service, and halted garbage pickups. The workers went on strike to protest cuts in their salaries and benefits, which were part of the government's austerity plan to trim the nation's budget deficit. The strikers claimed that the government measures placed a disproportionate share of the burden on their backs. The strike was settled when both sides made concessions.

27 *Argentina passes antiterrorist law*

Argentina's military government passed a law that, it said, would protect democracy against terrorist activities. Under the new law the military could, among other things, search homes and make arrests without warrants and detain suspected terrorists without filing charges for ten days or informing a judge of the arrest for two days. In addition, accused terrorists would be tried before the Federal Court of Appeals and have no further recourse if found guilty.

29 *Reagan cancels trip to Manila*

President Reagan decided to cancel his planned early November trip to the Philippines, Thailand, and Indonesia because Congress would be debating "contentious issues" during that period. The president would, however, visit Japan and South Korea at the originally scheduled time. U.S. government officials reportedly admitted to newsmen that cancellation of the Philippine trip was prompted by fears of anti-Reagan demonstrations in Manila and concern for the president's safety should he appear to support Pres. Ferdinand Marcos so soon after the assassination of Benigno Aquino, Jr., Marcos's political foe. A few days before Reagan made his decision, Marcos warned protesting business executives that they would not "find sanctuary in the tall buildings of Makati," Manila's business district. Nonetheless, on September 30 Makati once again became the scene of antigovernment demonstrations. Shredded paper floated into the streets as drivers honked their horns despite warnings that they would be arrested.

OCTOBER

2 *U.K. Labourites choose Kinnock*

Neil Kinnock, a 41-year-old Welshman, was elected head of Britain's Labour Party with 71.3% of the votes cast during the party's annual conference in Brighton. Labour members of Parliament and representatives of trade unions and local party organizations picked him to succeed Michael Foot. On October 5 the conference adopted a resolution that committed the Labour Party "unconditionally" to nuclear disarmament and the scrapping of "all nuclear weapons systems." A small minority of delegates deplored the policy, saying such statements during Foot's tenure as party leader had contributed heavily to Labour's devastating defeat in June.

4 *Swedes protest new business taxes*

At least 75,000 Swedish industrialists, bankers, businessmen, and white-collar workers marched on the Riksdag (parliament) to protest legislation that would exact additional taxes from businesses and give the money to trade unions to buy stocks. It was the largest demonstration by conservatives in the nation's history.

5 *Walesa awarded Nobel Peace Prize*

Lech Walesa, the 40-year-old Pole who founded Solidarity, the outlawed national federation of trade unions, was awarded the 1983 Nobel Peace Prize for his defense of human rights and his determined efforts "to solve his country's problems through negotiation and cooperation without resorting to violence." Egil Aarvik, chairman of the Nobel Prize committee, remarked: "I don't expect any thanks or gratitude from the Polish authorities, but I can imagine that the attitude of the Polish people will be very different."

6 *Army units foil coup in Niger*

Army forces loyal to Pres. Seyni Kountché of Niger suppressed a coup by "a few ambitious people" while the country's leader was visiting France. There was no official report on the number of casualties. The revolt was the second attempted coup against Kountché since he seized control of the West African nation in April 1974.

India's Punjab state to be ruled by central government

The government of Indian Prime Minister Indira Gandhi took over direct control of Punjab state after deciding that the local government was unable to control the growing violence there. Punjab was one of the country's most prosperous regions and the home of millions of Sikhs, whose religious differences with Hindus and economic differences with the central government had led to clamour for an autonomous Sikh state. In recent weeks tensions had mounted after Sikhs reportedly killed about 20 persons, some apparently after they had simply acknowledged they were Hindus.

Brazil to get new $12 billion loan

Sixty major banks, negotiating for more than 800 other banks around the world, agreed to grant Brazil $6.5 billion in new loans so it could pay the interest due on its huge foreign debt. An additional $5.5 billion loan would be used to repay the principal on debts that came due in 1984. Repayment of the entire $12 billion would begin in 1988 and extend over four years. The deal, entered into to save Brazil from possible bankruptcy, required the consent of the 800 lending banks and was contingent on Brazil's compliance with an austerity program that had been drawn up by the International Monetary Fund. One item stipulated that wage increases not exceed 80% of the inflation rate.

IBM and Hitachi settle court case

A U.S. federal judge in San Francisco announced that IBM, the world leader in computer technology, and Hitachi Ltd. of Japan had reached agreement on settling a civil suit involving the theft of industrial secrets from IBM. Hitachi, which assured IBM it had not used any of the information it had illegally obtained, promised to return the stolen industrial secrets. The company also agreed to pay the cost of IBM's investigation and prosecution and to identify all individuals who had offered to sell IBM secrets to Hitachi. As part of the settlement, IBM agreed to drop its suit against two Hitachi employees.

9 *Top South Korean officials slain in Burma by terrorist bomb*

Twenty-one persons, including four members of South Korean Pres. Chun Doo Hwan's Cabinet, were killed by a terrorist bomb that was prematurely detonated moments before the beginning of a wreath-laying ceremony at the Martyr's Mausoleum in Rangoon, Burma. Chun's top economic advisers and the South Korean ambassador to Burma were also killed. Four of the dead were Burmese. President Chun, who escaped death because his car had been delayed in traffic, immediately canceled the 18-day trip he had planned to make to six Asian and Pacific countries. On November 4 Burma announced that two captured North Korean commandos had confessed to the crime. A third North Korean terrorist had been killed in a gun battle with police. Burma

ALAIN MINGAM—GAMMA/LIAISON

Thousands of West Germans demonstrated against nuclear weapons in Bonn in late October. The protests focused on the scheduled deployment of U.S. Pershing II and cruise intermediate-range nuclear missiles but also criticized Soviet weapons. This banner reads: "Neither NATO nor Warsaw [Pact]—Down with imperialist warmongering."

also announced it was breaking off diplomatic relations with North Korea even though the two countries had had a very amicable relationship.

French warplanes arrive in Iraq

Five French Super Étendard jet planes were reportedly delivered to Iraq, but French officials refused to affirm or deny that the aircraft had arrived in Baghdad. The U.S., Britain, West Germany, and certain Persian Gulf nations had urged France not to turn over the jets because Iraq could then arm the planes with Exocet missiles already in its possession and attack Iranian oil installations and tankers with relative impunity. Iran in turn warned that if such an attack occurred, it would cut off much of the world's oil supplies by making the vital Strait of Hormuz—the entrance to the Persian Gulf—impassable. According to unconfirmed reports, French officials privately expressed the belief that Iraq's increased military potential might move Iran to begin negotiating an end to its inconclusive war with Iraq.

UPI

The death toll reached 241 after a truck loaded with explosives crashed into the U.S. Marine headquarters at the Beirut airport on October 23. Here Marines, Lebanese soldiers, and civilian rescue workers seek survivors.

11 *China announces consolidation of its Communist Party*

The second plenary session of the Chinese Communist Party's 12th Central Committee approved a "necessary and urgent" program to "rectify Party style" and "consolidate Party organizations" over a period of three years, beginning in the winter of 1983. In effect, the qualifications of some 40 million party members would be reviewed to ferret out those with lingering leftist tendencies, those with records of violence against others during the Cultural Revolution (1966–76), and those who belonged to political factions resisting the policies of China's current leaders. Because the Central Committee presented the rectification campaign as one of great importance, it seemed certain that some prominent officials would be among those denied membership in the Communist Party. Persons who joined the party during the Cultural Revolution would be among those most carefully scrutinized.

12 *Tanaka convicted of bribery*

Kakuei Tanaka, who had served as prime minister of Japan from July 1972 to December 1974, was convicted of bribery by a three-judge panel of the Tokyo District Court and sentenced to four years in prison. The nation's most powerful politician was also fined 500 million yen ($2.1 million), the sum he received for having illegally arranged the purchase of Lockheed aircraft by All Nippon Airways, a privately owned company. Immediately after the trial, which had lasted more than seven years, Tanaka's lawyers filed an appeal; a final ruling in the case was not expected for many years. There were nationwide demands that 65-year-old Tanaka resign from the Diet (parliament), where he controlled the largest faction within the ruling Liberal Democratic Party. Tanaka, however, indicated that he had no intention of giving up the seat he had occupied for 36 years.

15 *FBI arrests technician as spy*

The FBI arrested James D. Harper, Jr., a technician working in California's Silicon Valley, on charges of selling "extremely sensitive" military research data to a Polish spy for $250,000. The material was subsequently turned over to the U.S.S.R. When Harper appeared before a federal magistrate on October 17, he promised full cooperation with the government. Access to the documents reportedly had been provided by Harper's late wife.

19 *U.S. honours Martin Luther King with federal holiday*

The U.S. Senate voted 78–22 to honour slain black civil rights leader Martin Luther King, Jr., with an annual federal holiday. Beginning in 1986, the third Monday in January would commemorate the birth of the Rev. Dr. King on Jan. 15, 1929. The only other American so honoured was George Washington. The House of Representatives had passed similar legislation in August. Opposition to the holiday was led by Republican Sen. Jesse Helms of North Carolina. As with all other federal holidays, individual states, local governments, and nonfederal organizations were free to decide if and how they would observe the day. President Reagan signed the legislation in a White House ceremony on November 2.

22 *Marcos names new panel to probe assassination of Aquino*

Philippine Pres. Ferdinand Marcos named five private citizens to a new commission to investigate the assassination of his chief political opponent, Benigno S. Aquino, Jr., on August 21. Members of an earlier panel had resigned amid accusations that they could not be impartial. Corazon J. Agrava, a 68-year-old former justice of the Court of Appeal, was chosen head of the new group.

Europeans protest nuclear weapons

An estimated two million people took part in various demonstrations across Europe to protest the planned deployment of U.S. Pershing II and cruise missiles. Protesters in West Germany, where Pershing II missiles were to be located, gathered in large numbers in Bonn, Hamburg, West Berlin, Stuttgart, and Neu Ulm to conclude ten days of relatively peaceful demonstrations. A London rally attracted an estimated 250,000 people, and an even larger crowd took to the streets in Rome. On October 23 some 300,000 turned out in Brussels and about one-third that number in Madrid. Antinuclear rallies in the U.S. resulted in more than one thousand arrests, mainly for trespassing. On October 29 Princess Irene, the younger sister of Queen Beatrix of The Netherlands, endorsed the protest at a rally attended by about 500,000 people in The Hague. That same day about 200,000 people marched in Denmark.

23 *Car bombs kill hundreds of U.S. and French soldiers in Lebanon*

A suicidal terrorist drove a truckload of high explosives through a series of barricades and into the U.S. Marine Corps headquarters at the Beirut airport in Lebanon. The subsequent explosion demolished the four-story building and killed 239 U.S. servicemen. Numerous others were injured, and two died later. In an

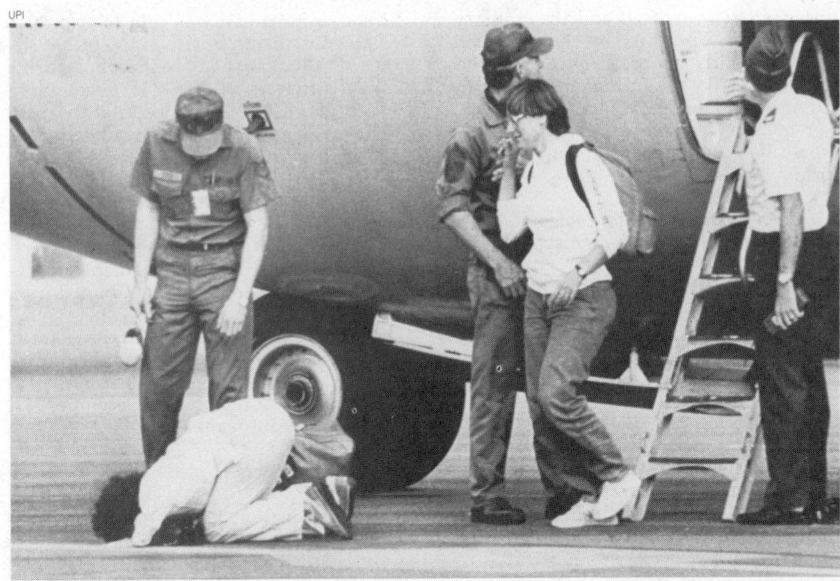

American medical students enrolled at St. George's University School of Medicine were the first to leave Grenada after the U.S. invasion. Here one of them, upon arriving at Charleston Air Force Base in South Carolina, kisses the ground.

almost simultaneous early morning attack about 3.2 km (2 mi) to the north, another bomb-laden truck smashed into an eight-story building used as a barracks by French paratroopers; 58 were killed when the structure collapsed. It was not immediately clear who was responsible for the attacks, but U.S. Secretary of Defense Caspar W. Weinberger said circumstantial evidence "points in the direction of Iran." Iran and Syria, however, both denied they had been involved.

25 *U.S. leads invasion of Grenada*

A seven-nation assault force, spearheaded by U.S. Marines and Army Rangers, began a predawn invasion of the Caribbean nation of Grenada. The troops quickly seized the country's two airfields and occupied the island's power and broadcast stations and St. George's University School of Medicine, where more than 600 American students were enrolled. The heaviest initial resistance came from Cuban soldiers and construction workers at the Point Salines airstrip. The expeditionary force included nearly 2,000 U.S. troops and 300 soldiers from Antigua, Barbados, Dominica, Jamaica, St. Lucia, and St. Vincent. The head of the Organization of Eastern Caribbean States said the U.S. had been asked to intervene because the military buildup in Grenada posed a serious threat to the entire region. The governor-general of Grenada, it was later revealed, had also requested help after Prime Minister Maurice Bishop was overthrown on October 13 and then killed. British Prime Minister Margaret Thatcher, however, vigorously opposed U.S. intervention in the former British colony, but she failed to dissuade President Reagan from taking military action. Many members of the Organization of American States also protested the invasion. On October 27 Reagan said the invasion took place just in time to prevent Grenada from becoming a "Soviet-Cuban colony." Some Soviet advisers, in fact, were among those rounded up and deported. On October 28 the U.S. vetoed, as expected, a UN Security Council resolution condemning the invasion as a "flagrant violation of international law." On October 31 the U.S. Department of Defense confirmed that a U.S. Navy plane had bombed an unmarked hospital during the first stage of the invasion and had killed at least 12 persons. Unconfirmed reports suggested that several times that number may have been killed. All U.S. military personnel were expected to be out of Grenada by the end of the year, but an OECS security force would probably remain until a new government was elected, perhaps within six months.

29 *Sino-Soviet talks still at impasse*

Soviet officials left Beijing (Peking) after the third round in a series of ongoing talks with Chinese officials aimed at the eventual restoration of normal relations between the two countries. No progress was reported on China's demands that the U.S.S.R. withdraw its troops from Afghanistan, stop supporting the Vietnamese occupation of Kampuchea, and reduce its military forces along the Sino-Soviet border.

30 *Argentina elects civilian president*

Raúl Alfonsín, candidate of the Radical Civic Union, was elected Argentina's first civilian president in nearly eight years. His victory over Itako Luder ended the Peronists' decades-long domination of Argentine politics. Alfonsín asked that his inauguration, slated for January 30, be advanced to early December so he could begin work on some of the country's staggering economic problems, including an annual inflation rate approaching 1,000%. Alfonsín, a co-founder of the Argentine Permanent Assembly for Human Rights, promised he would annul the amnesty the military had granted itself to avoid prosecution for often flagrant violations of human rights.

31 *Talks to end Lebanon's civil war get under way in Geneva*

Representatives of Lebanon's principal religious and political factions convened in Geneva for talks that, it was hoped, would lead to an end to the civil war that had been ravaging the country for almost a decade. During his opening remarks Lebanese Pres. Amin Gemayel told the gathering that all parties shared blame for the tragedy that had befallen Lebanon. Though all parties acknowledged the gravity of the situation, there were serious doubts that the participants' profound differences could be resolved during the conference.

NOVEMBER

1 *India reports arrests in Punjab*

All-India Radio reported that more than 1,400 people had been taken into custody in violence-racked Punjab state during the previous two weeks. A large quantity of ammunition and illegal firearms had also been confiscated during the police raids. The arrests came in the wake of the central government's takeover of the region on October 6. On October 7 Punjab had been proclaimed a "disturbed area."

2 *South African whites to share some political power*

South African white voters approved by a two-to-one margin a new constitution that for the first time accorded Coloureds and Asians a limited voice in government. Each racial group would elect representatives to decide matters affecting its "own affairs." This was understood to mean such things as local government, housing, social welfare, health, and education. The representatives would meet in a new tricameral legislature. Whites would be represented by the House of Assembly (178 members), Coloureds by the House of Representatives (85), and Asians by the House of Delegates (45). An 88-member electoral college that reflected the proportional representation of the three legislatures would choose the president. Blacks, who comprised 70% of South Africa's population, would still be excluded from participation in the nation's political process.

3 *Arafat's troops face critical defeat*

Members of the Palestine Liberation Organization (PLO) who remained loyal to Yasir Arafat came under heavy artillery and rocket fire near Tripoli, Lebanon. Arafat's survival in Lebanon and his fate as chairman of the PLO appeared to hinge on the final outcome of the fighting. Arafat claimed that Syrian and Libyan soldiers were fighting alongside PLO rebels, some of whom came from his own al-Fatah faction. By November 8 Arafat's troops had retreated to Beddawi, a Palestinian refugee camp that had served as Arafat's headquarters for nearly two months. After its defenses were breached on November 16, Arafat's last hope was to take refuge in Tripoli, a city of 600,000 on the Mediterranean Sea. A cease-fire and the evacuation of Arafat's troops then seemed a likely prospect because both sides wanted to spare the civilian population further suffering.

4 *Israel retaliates after car bombing in Lebanon*

Israeli jets attacked Palestinian positions along the Beirut-Damascus highway in Lebanon just hours after a car bomb exploded inside the Israeli military compound in Tyre. At least 60 persons were killed; some were suspected Palestinian guerrillas being held for questioning. According to unconfirmed reports, Israeli planes also attacked Sofar, a Syrian stronghold, and destroyed 16 Soviet-made T-54 tanks. On November 7 Syria began a general military mobilization, even though the U.S. and Israel had declared they had no intention of attacking Syria directly to avenge the car bombings of their respective headquarters in Lebanon. On November 17 French planes attacked pro-Iranian Shi'ah Muslim troops near Baalbek in the Bekaa Valley. French forces had also been victims of a car bombing in October.

6 *Turkey elects new Parliament*

In the first parliamentary elections since Turkey's military government came to power in 1980, voters gave candidates of the Motherland Party (MP) 212 of the 400 seats in the national legislature. The left-of-centre Populist Party finished second with 117 seats. The Nationalist Democracy Party (NDP), the only other party allowed to field candidates, won the remaining 71 seats. Before the election the MP seemed to have placed the greatest distance between itself and the military government. The NDP, by contrast, had been implicitly endorsed by Kenan Evren, the head of the ruling military council. After the election results were known, Evren expressed satisfaction that the MP would be strong enough to rule without forming a coalition.

8 *French bishops accept nuclear weapons as legitimate deterrents*

The Roman Catholic bishops of France, in a nearly unanimous vote, approved the development of nuclear weapons as a necessary and legitimate defense against Marxist-Leninist aggression. The prelates remarked that unqualified condemnation of war places peace-loving peoples at the mercy of those seeking domination of others, and unilateral disarmament can even provoke aggression because an unarmed nation is an easy and tempting prey. The bishops, however, noted that morally acceptable nuclear deterrents must involve only defense and remain within reasonable limits. In addition, every precaution must be taken to ensure that such weapons are never used through miscalculations. The document they issued, called "Win the Peace," contrasted sharply with the pastoral letter "The Challenge of Peace" issued by U.S. Catholic bishops in May. The U.S. prelates had called for a halt to the development, production, and deployment of nuclear weapons.

9 *China to act on Hong Kong*

China's Foreign Ministry announced that its government would unilaterally announce its future policy toward Hong Kong in September 1984 if no agreement had been reached with Great Britain by that time. Britain's lease over most of the colony's territory was due to expire in 1997, but no agreement on the future status of the colony had been reached during the two years of periodic negotiations with China. Continued uncertainty about Hong Kong's future had already adversely affected its economy.

Grenada gets interim government

Sir Paul Scoon, governor-general of Grenada, appointed nine Grenadians to serve on a nonpartisan Advisory Council until voters could choose a new permanent government. Meredith McIntyre, a UN employee, was chosen to head the council but was unable to serve because of ill health. He was replaced on December 9 by Nicholas Braithwaite.

10 *Turkey tightens press controls*

Turkey's National Security Council approved a new law that authorized severe punishment for publishers, editors, and writers who published articles considered a threat to national security or an offense against public morality. Publishers could temporarily lose their right to publish or in more serious cases lose their presses; writers and editors could receive long prison sentences after being tried in a criminal court. The military government's action came a few days before the new civilian Parliament was to assume legislative powers for the "transition to democracy." The International Press Institute denounced the law as "an outright violation of press freedom and freedom of expression."

14 *Reagan ends visit to Asia*

President Reagan returned to Washington, D.C., after state visits to Japan and

One more coffin from Lebanon is carried to burial on Jerusalem's Mt. Herzl. At least 60 persons were killed in the November 4 terrorist bombing of Israeli military headquarters in Tyre, Lebanon.

UPI

South Korea. He summed up the trip by saying, "Prospects for a more secure peace and prosperity are better today than a week ago." In Tokyo Reagan lauded Japan's cultural values and its economic progress and urged Japan to join the U.S. in "a powerful partnership for good." Reagan also promised to continue working for an arms agreement with the Soviet Union, but he assured Japan that he would never sanction a pact that jeopardized Asian security. While in Seoul, Reagan reaffirmed the U.S. commitment to its mutual defense treaty with South Korea after publicly recognizing "the need for vigilance and strength to deter aggression and preserve peace and economic progress." He also encouraged the continued expansion of political freedoms in South Korea because, he said, true security is based on a national consensus.

15 *Turkish Cypriots divide country*

Rauf Raif Denktash, leader of the Turks in Cyprus, informed a waiting crowd that the Turkish Cypriot Assembly had voted unanimously for independence. Spyros Kyprianou, the Greek Cypriot president of the country, quickly announced that his government would use every peaceful means available to reverse the Turkish decision. Turkish troops had occupied the northern section of the island republic in 1974 when it appeared that Greece and Cyprus might be united. Since that time a "green line" had divided the capital city of Nicosia and separated the minority Turkish population in the northern third of the island from the ethnic Greeks in the south. Though Turkey immediately recognized the Turkish Republic of Northern Cyprus, it appeared that most countries would continue to recognize the Greek Cypriot government as the sole legitimate authority. On November 16 a spokesman for the Turkish Cypriots said his people had acted to focus world attention on the region and increase the possibility of establishing an island federation based on equality.

Contadora Group proposes treaty

The foreign minister of Venezuela revealed that Colombia, Mexico, Panama, and Venezuela—known collectively as the Contadora Group—had drafted a treaty of peace and reconciliation to help end the conflicts in Central America. The head of Nicaragua's ruling junta was reported to have been favourably impressed with the basic principles of the draft. Among other things, clandestine traffic in arms would be forbidden in the region, rebel groups would be denied support, and democratic reforms would be initiated. Panama's representative to the Organization of American States (OAS) sought to persuade other members of the OAS to support a resolution urging Costa Rica, El Salvador, Guatemala, Honduras, and Nicaragua to sign the accords immediately. On November 16 the foreign ministers of these five nations agreed to begin negotiations in December with the Contadora group serving as mediator.

WIDE WORLD

The declaration of a Turkish republic in northern Cyprus in mid-November by Turkish Cypriot leaders was protested before the presidential palace in Nicosia, Cyprus, by Greek Cypriot students. Turkey was the only country that recognized the declaration.

21 *Polish Parliament gives military vast emergency powers*

The Polish Sejm (parliament) established a National Defense Committee with powers to decide when the country faced a state of emergency. In that eventuality, the committee would rule the country unhampered by normal procedures. The committee appeared to have unusual powers even in ordinary circumstances because it had the responsibility to "review all the issues of national defense in connection with the whole complex of socioeconomic issues." The government was reportedly already uneasy about possible protests when food prices were to be increased in January 1984.

23 *Soviets discontinue arms talks*

The Soviet Union discontinued talks with the U.S. on limiting medium-range nuclear weapons in Europe. The walkout was not unexpected because the Soviets had warned that positioning U.S. Pershing II and cruise missiles in Western Europe would jeopardize the arms talks. NATO, however, had long insisted that deployment of the weapons would start by the end of the year unless an arms agreement had been reached by that time. Despite numerous proposals and counterproposals, no agreement was in sight. The first cruise missiles had accordingly arrived in Great Britain on November 14 and the first Pershing II's in West Germany on November 23. Eventually Belgium, Italy, The Netherlands, and West Germany were all expected to deploy cruise missiles. The Soviet Union did not indicate when it might resume the arms negotiations, which had begun in Geneva on Dec. 1, 1981.

Cosmonauts end 150-day flight

Two Soviet cosmonauts returned to Earth in their Soyuz T-9 module after spending 150 days in the Salyut 7 orbiting laboratory. There was no public admission of difficulties encountered during the long mission, but three cosmonauts reportedly had to return to Earth in April after failing to dock with the Salyut, and two other cosmonauts had been involved in a dangerous launch pad explosion in late September. Among other tasks, the crew undertook geophysical studies of the Earth, studied crystal formation and the production of pure protein, and tested new methods and instruments for guiding vehicles orbiting in space. They also installed new solar batteries on the outside of the Salyut during two prolonged space walks.

24 *Israel and PLO swap prisoners*

The Palestine Liberation Organization (PLO) and Israel, after months of negotiations, exchanged prisoners captured during the war in Lebanon. Though only six Israeli soldiers were involved in the exchange, about 4,500 Arabs were released in Lebanon or flown to Algeria. Some had been sentenced to life imprisonment for terrorist attacks against Israeli civilians. Israeli Prime Minister Yitzhak Shamir accepted the unequal exchange, he said, because the Israeli soldiers were in grave danger in Tripoli, where PLO chairman Yasir Arafat's forces were under fierce attack from rebels seeking to seize control of the organization.

25 *British printers walk off jobs*

A British labour dispute involving printers at some of the country's leading newspapers reached a flash point when a High Court judge in Manchester fined the National Graphical Association £100,000 ($147,000) and ordered the seizure of the union's assets after it refused to halt illegal picketing and pay a recently imposed £50,000 fine for contempt of court. The printers then walked off the job. The trouble began when the owner of a small printing plant in Cheshire refused to rehire six men who had been fired for illegal picketing. By November 28 seven of the country's nine struck newspapers were being published even though union workers had not given management definite assurances there would not be another walkout.

26 *UNESCO compromises on press issue*

UNESCO concluded its five-week conference in Paris after approving a two-year study on the influence of news organizations on less developed countries and international relations. The U.S. had successfully argued against an international code for journalists, saying it would limit freedom of the press. Third world countries, supported by the Soviet Union, had wanted to draw up such a code because, they said, Western journalists ignored or downplayed positive developments in their countries.

27 *Uruguayans hold huge protest*

Some 300,000 Uruguayans staged a government-sanctioned demonstration in the capital city of Montevideo to demand that the military junta headed by Gen. Gregorio Álvarez Armelino advance the 1985 date it had set for the restoration of democracy. The protest, which was organized by three officially recognized political parties, was said to be the largest in the nation's history.

29 *Commonwealth meets in India*

The heads of government of the Commonwealth of Nations, after a week-long meeting in New Delhi, India, issued an official statement offering to support a peacekeeping force in Grenada, but it did not condemn the U.S. invasion because members of the Organization of Eastern Caribbean States had requested such intervention. The Commonwealth leaders also called on all nations to withhold assistance from the newly declared Turkish Republic of Northern Cyprus. On the issue of South West Africa/Namibia, the conference condemned the U.S. for insisting that the withdrawal of South Africa from the region had to be accompanied by the withdrawal of Cuban forces from Angola. The conference viewed this demand as interference in matters to be settled by the UN. Strong disagreement was reflected in the conference's compromise statement that "many heads of government" wanted the "withdrawal of all foreign armed forces from Lebanon, other than those present at the express request of the Government of Lebanon."

West German Cabinet minister faces bribery charge

Otto Lambsdorff, the economics minister in the Cabinet of West German Chancellor Helmut Kohl, was named a defendant in a $50,000 payoff scandal said to involve the write-off of some $175 million owed by a holding company. Formal indictment could not be undertaken until the Bundestag voted to lift Lambsdorff's immunity. Since the Federal Republic of Germany came into existence in September 1949, no incumbent Cabinet minister had ever been indicted.

30 *Reagan's inaction kills rights bill*

President Reagan in effect vetoed legislation dealing with human rights and social reforms in El Salvador by refusing to sign a bill within ten legislative days after it was received from Congress. As a consequence, the Reagan administration was no longer obliged to certify to Congress every six months that El Salvador had improved its record on human rights and social reforms in order to qualify for continued U.S. financial aid. A White House spokesman explained that although the administration supported the goals of the legislation, it did not feel that the certification process would "serve to support these endeavors." It appeared certain, however, that new legislation on El Salvador would be introduced in Congress shortly after it reconvened in January.

DECEMBER

1 *Druze religious leader slain*

Sheikh Halim Takieddin, president of the Supreme Druze Religious Court in Lebanon, was shot and killed by an unidentified gunman in West Beirut. The shooting occurred after two days of intense fighting between Druze forces and forces of the Lebanese Army and Christian militiamen. Takieddin had advocated that all religious groups live together in peace, but he had publicly voiced support for the political leader of the Druze, Walid Jumblatt. Jumblatt accused "criminals belonging to fascist gangs" of Christian Phalange militia for the shooting.

2 *Caribbean leaders predict progress*

After a four-day meeting in Miami, Fla., representatives of Caribbean-area nations expressed confidence that President Reagan's soon-to-be-implemented Caribbean Basin Initiative would produce significant benefits for that part of the world. Among other things, the program would give 28 Caribbean and Central American nations duty-free access to U.S. markets for 12 years. Some adjustment in the local economies would have to occur to take advantage of the new opportunities.

4 *Venezuelans choose president*

Jaime Lusinchi, the 59-year-old candidate of the Democratic Action (AD) party, easily defeated Rafael Caldera and ten other candidates in an election for the presidency of Venezuela. Caldera had been the first former president to seek reelection after a legally mandated ten-year waiting period. Venezuela's economic crisis (which was partly attributable to declining oil prices), a rising crime rate, and government corruption were important issues during the campaign. Incomplete election returns indicated that voters were turning away from the ruling Social Christians in such numbers that the AD would probably also win control of Congress and many state legislatures.

Sandinistas offer amnesty

The Sandinista National Liberation Front government of Nicaragua officially announced that almost all citizens who had left the country in recent years could return without fear of punishment. Those who had held positions of responsibility during Somoza's dictatorship were excluded from the amnesty. On December 1 the leaders of four antigovernment guerrilla groups had asked President Reagan's special envoy to Central America to try to arrange peace talks with the Sandinistas. In the final analysis, one leader noted, a conflict among Nicaraguans had to be resolved by Nicaraguans.

6 *EEC ends meeting in Greece*

Leaders of the ten-nation European Communities (EC) ended a meeting in Athens, Greece, without reaching agreement on a single important issue. The main points of controversy centred on proposed cuts in agricultural subsidies and Great Britain's insistence that it be given a $1 billion refund on its budget contributions. Britain had long argued that, as a food-importing nation, it had to bear a disproportionate share of the budget. Because the EC could not resolve its most pressing problems, it postponed indefinitely a decision on admitting Spain and Portugal into the organization.

Scotland Yard charges suspect in record gold heist

Anthony J. Black, a 31-year-old employee of Brinks-Mat Ltd., was formally charged with involvement in the theft of three tons of gold bullion from his company's London airport warehouse on November 26. The stolen 6,800 bars of gold, together with diamonds, platinum, and traveler's checks, were valued at £26,369,777 (about $38 million); it was the largest theft in British history. On December 7 seven more suspects were reportedly arrested, but Scotland Yard refused to comment on the case.

12 *Five sites in Kuwait bombed*

Six persons were killed and 63 injured when the U.S. and French embassies and four other sites in Kuwait were bombed by Muslim extremists having close ties to Iran. The U.S. embassy was hit by a truck loaded with explosives; the other places were damaged by car bombs detonated by remote control devices. On December 18 the Kuwaiti government accused nine Iraqi and three Lebanese Shi'ah Muslims of involvement in the attacks. Ten had reportedly confessed after being arrested. On December 27 seven more suspects were taken into custody, but their nationalities were not mentioned in the report.

13 *Members of Argentina's junta to face criminal charges*

Raúl Alfonsín, who was sworn in as civilian president of Argentina on December 10, announced that nine generals and admirals would be tried in a military court for the "terror, pain, and death" they had caused while serving in turn as members of the three-man junta that had ruled the country since 1976. The president also announced that seven leftist terrorists would stand trial in civilian courts. On December 24 Alfonsín signed a bill that revoked the amnesty the military had given itself before relinquishing power. On December 29 and 30 court-martial proceedings began for the nine military officers, who were formally arraigned and charged with illegally kidnapping, torturing, and killing thousands of people during an antiterrorist campaign. The fates of more than 6,000 Argentines who had disappeared were of special concern to their relatives and the new civilian authorities.

Turkey gets new government

Turkish Prime Minister Turkut Ozal and his 22-member Cabinet assumed office after Gen. Kenan Evren, the president, gave his approval as required by the constitution. Evren had seized power in 1980 but sanctioned parliamentary elections on November 6 so that the country could revert to civilian rule. Before Ozal was forced to resign as deputy prime minister in 1982, he earned high praise for reducing the country's runaway inflation rate from 120 to 30%. Ozal was expected to give priority to combating resurgent inflation, reducing the bureaucracy, and modernizing the economy, but those who opposed the stringent measures he was expected to adopt would be freer to protest than they had been under military rule.

15 *U.S. revises policy on arms sales*

The Reagan administration decided that friendly nations in need of U.S. arms could procure them in the future "without draining their reserves." In accordance with the new policy, Israel was expected to receive some $1.4 billion worth of U.S. arms free of cost during the next fiscal year, and Egypt would get military equipment worth $1.1 billion. Other friendly nations might also receive outright grants or, depending on their situations, be asked to pay only a portion of the actual cost of the weapons. In the past, U.S. weapons were usually purchased by friendly nations with money loaned by the U.S. government at prevailing market rates of interest.

18 *Japanese voters rebuff government*

In national elections, Japan's ruling Liberal-Democratic Party (LDP) lost its majority in the 511-seat lower house of the Diet (parliament) and was forced to form a coalition with a small group of conservatives. The LDP's loss of 36 seats gave it a new total of only 250, but with the support of the conservatives it was able to elect Prime Minister Yasuhiro Nakasone to a second term on December 26. The prime minister had been forced to call early elections after Kakuei Tanaka, a former prime minister and a leading member of the LDP, refused to resign from the Diet after being convicted in October of bribery and foreign currency violations. Nakasone's reputation had also been sullied by the scandal because he had become prime minister with Tanaka's help. To mute widespread criticism of the government, Nakasone pledged to eliminate Tanaka's influence in government affairs. Despite his conviction, Tanaka retained his seat in the Diet and remained free on bond while his conviction and four-year prison sentence were under appeal.

WIDE WORLD

Egyptian Pres. Hosni Mubarak (right) welcomed PLO leader Yasir Arafat to Cairo for meetings in late December. It was the first time Arafat had visited Egypt since its 1979 peace treaty with Israel.

IRA admits bombing in London

The Irish Republican Army (IRA) acknowledged that the car bomb exploded the previous day outside Harrods, a London department store, was the work of IRA terrorists. Five persons were killed and 91 injured. The IRA leaders. however, claimed the attack had not been authorized and promised that such attacks would not be repeated.

20 *Yasir Arafat departs Lebanon*

Yasir Arafat, chairman of the Palestine Liberation Organization (PLO), departed Tripoli, Lebanon, aboard a Greek ferry flying the United Nations and Palestinian flags and escorted by French naval vessels. Some 4,000 Palestinian guerrillas loyal to Arafat were also evacuated by Greek ships. It was the second time in 16 months that Arafat's forces had been driven out of Lebanon, but this time the military pressure came not from Israel but from dissident PLO troops supported by Syria. The chairman of the Palestine National Council, speaking in Syria, called for an emergency meeting of all factions within the PLO to prevent a disintegration of the organization. On December 22 Arafat met with Egyptian Pres. Hosni Mubarak in Cairo. Because Egypt had signed a peace treaty with Israel, the meeting was vehemently condemned by hard-line Arabs, but it was praised in other quarters as a possible step toward peace in the Middle East. On December 24 Arafat arrived with 1,000 followers in Yemen (San'a'). There he was expected to discuss the Cairo meeting with other PLO leaders.

22 *Thai Communists surrender*

More than 5,000 Thai Communist guerrillas and their supporters formally surrendered to government officials in Nan Province near Thailand's border with Laos. It was the largest formal ceremony of surrender since the government began offering amnesty to rebels willing to lay

DECEMBER

WIDE WORLD

Nigerian Maj. Gen. Mohammed Buhari, a Cabinet minister in the last military government, was made chief of state in Nigeria's December 31 coup that toppled the government of Pres. Alhaji Shehu Shagari, who had been recently reelected.

down their arms. The surrender terminated serious fighting in the north but an estimated 1,200 Communists were still armed and fighting in the south.

25 *Jordan and Egypt sign accord*

Egypt and Jordan signed a new protocol that, according to Egypt's economy and trade minister, signified the resumption of trade and of economic and financial relations between the two countries. Jordan and most other Arab countries had imposed an economic and political boycott on Egypt after Pres. Anwar as-Sadat signed a peace treaty with Israel in 1979. Jordan's King Hussein was expected to urge other Arab leaders to follow his lead in renewing their relations with Egypt.

26 *Andropov's absence sparks rumours of serious illness*

Soviet Pres. Yury V. Andropov's failure to appear at a meeting of the Communist Party's Central Committee increased suspicions that, contrary to official pronouncements, he was seriously ill. His last public appearance had been on August 18. Andropov's absence, without a creditable explanation, was unprecedented, as was also his nonappearance in Red Square on November 7 for the traditional Revolution Day parade. The Central Committee conducted business without Andropov but listened to a speech he had prepared for the occasion. The president acknowledged that economic progress had been made during the past year but he severely condemned inexcusable errors in economic planning and called attention to huge quantities of consumer goods that were so shoddy that thousands of potential buyers shunned them at a recent sales fair. Despite Andropov's protracted absence from public functions, his political power appeared to be intact because four of his close associates were promoted by the Central Committee.

28 *Witness contradicts story of Aquino's assassination*

Ramon Balang, a 28-year-old ground engineer for the Philippines Airlines, told a five-member committee investigating the August 21 assassination of Benigno Aquino, Jr., that Roland Galman, the alleged assassin, "did not have the opportunity to fire a shot." Galman had been shot dead by soldiers moments after Aquino was slain. Balang, who had been assigned to inspect the aircraft on which Aquino returned to Manila, said he saw two soldiers flanking Aquino as the trio descended a movable stairway placed next to the plane. A third soldier was close behind. The engineer testified that he then heard a shot and saw Aquino falling and Galman standing with his palms extended. An autopsy showed that Aquino had been shot at close range in the back of the head. Another alleged witness, who fled the country, gave a similar statement to U.S. reporters who then passed on the information to the board of inquiry.

Report says bombing of U.S. Marine headquarters was preventable

The U.S. Defense Department released a censored report on the car-bombing of the U.S. Marine headquarters in Lebanon on October 23; the explosion killed 241 U.S. servicemen. The five-man commission that studied the incident criticized the policy of increasing U.S. involvement in Lebanon and called U.S. military intelligence and security precautions at the headquarters inadequate. The commission did not recommend that any military officers be disciplined even though some failed to carry out their responsibilities. President Reagan had attempted to blunt the negative effect of the report before it was made public by saying that any blame "properly rests here in this office and with the president."

29 *U.S. to quit UNESCO*

The U.S. government gave formal notice that it intended to terminate its membership in the United Nations Educational, Scientific and Cultural Organization (UNESCO) by the end of 1984. U.S. disenchantment with the UN agency did not extend to the UN itself or to its other specialized agencies. Alan D. Romberg, a spokesman for the U.S. State Department, remarked: "UNESCO has extraneously politicized virtually every subject it deals with, has exhibited hostility toward the basic institutions of a free society, especially a free market and a free press, and has demonstrated unrestrained budgetary expansion." The U.S., which paid 25% of UNESCO's budget, had frequently advised the agency's executives that failure to respond to U.S. complaints would force the U.S. to reconsider its participation in the organization.

30 *Salvadoran rebels capture army base*

Leftist guerrillas captured a Salvadoran army base 65 km (40 mi) north of San Salvador, then withdrew after six hours. It was the first time in the four-year-old civil war that insurgents had taken an installation of such importance. A report broadcast over a rebel-controlled radio station said the attack had been carried out by the Farabundo Martí Liberation Front, which represented five guerrilla groups seeking to overthrow the government. Government troops had just launched a massive military campaign against the guerrillas in 11 of the country's 14 provinces. In mid-December the Reagan administration had warned the Salvadoran government that the U.S. would cease giving active support unless specific steps were taken to curb right-wing death squads, which continued to operate with disregard for human rights.

31 *Nigerian government overthrown*

Brig. Saleh Abacha announced that the armed forces had deposed Nigerian Pres. Alhaji Shehu Shagari and taken over the government. Shagari, who was accused of inept and corrupt leadership, had been elected to a second four-year term in August. Two days before the coup, Shagari had sanctioned stern economic measures to combat the nation's critical financial problems. Nigeria, with a population of nearly 90 million, had been the world's fourth largest democracy.

DISASTERS OF 1983

The loss of life and property from disasters in 1983 included the following:

AVIATION

January 16, Ankara, Turkey. A Turkish jetliner carrying 67 persons made a crash landing during heavy snow and high winds that caused the aircraft to plunge off the runway; the plane then broke in two and caught fire. At least 40 persons were killed in the wreckage and 22 others were injured.

June 2, Cincinnati, Ohio. A DC-9 jetliner flying from Dallas-Fort Worth, Texas, to Toronto, Ont., made an emergency landing at the Greater Cincinnati International Airport when a fire broke out aboard the aircraft; 23 persons lost their lives in the blaze.

June 16, Kauai Island, Hawaii. A U.S. Navy P-3 Orion patrol plane buffeted by high winds crashed on a remote mountain ridge while participating in maneuvers; all 14 aboard were killed.

July 1, Near Labé, Guinea. A Soviet-built Il-62 airplane carrying 23 North Korean construction workers crashed in a remote region of Guinea; there were no survivors.

July 11, Cuenca, Ecuador. A Boeing 737 traveling from Quito to Cuenca slammed into the side of a mountain while attempting to land; all 119 persons aboard were killed in the fiery crash.

July 11, Philippines. A helicopter crashed in the southern part of the country, and 12 persons lost their lives.

July 16, English Channel. An S-61 helicopter shuttling passengers from Penzance to the Scilly Isles crashed and sank in the English Channel; 20 of the 26 persons aboard were killed.

August 17, Arizona. A Las Vegas, Nev., sight-seeing plane crashed into a mountain in a remote area of the Grand Canyon; all ten persons aboard were killed.

August 21, Near Silvana, Wash. A twin-engine Lockheed Learstar carrying 18 skydivers stalled at an altitude of some 3,800 m (12,500 ft), went into a spinning nosedive, and crashed into a highway embankment; 11 persons were killed.

August 28, Near Adavale, Queensland, Australia. A chartered airplane carrying 12 persons crashed; all aboard were killed.

September 1, Sea of Japan. A South Korean commercial airliner traveling from New York to Seoul was shot from the sky by a Soviet jet fighter after the airliner apparently strayed into Soviet airspace; all 269 persons aboard were killed.

September 14, Guilin (Kuei-lin), China. A domestic airliner carrying 100 passengers collided with a military plane on the runway moments before takeoff; 10 persons were killed and 21 injured.

September 23, Near Abu Dhabi, United Arab Emirates. A Gulf Air Boeing 737 jetliner carrying 111 persons crashed in desert mountains and burst into flames; there were no survivors.

November 8, Lubango, Angola. A Boeing 737 jetliner carrying 126 persons crashed shortly after takeoff; there were no survivors.

November 27, Near Madrid, Spain. A Colombian Boeing 747 jetliner, carrying 194 persons, crashed and exploded some 8 km (5 mi) from Madrid's Barajas airport; 183 persons were killed in the fiery crash, making it one of the ten worst accidents in aviation history.

November 28, Near Enugu, Nigeria. A Fokker F-28 airliner carrying 74 persons from Lagos crashed some 3 km (2 mi) short of its destination at Enugu Airport; at least 53 persons were known dead, 3 were missing, and 18 others survived.

December 7, Madrid, Spain. A Boeing 727 jetliner carrying 93 persons crashed into a DC-9 airplane carrying 42 persons when it was making its takeoff down the runway in heavy fog; there were no survivors from the DC-9 airplane, which had apparently followed the wrong route to position itself for departure. Of the 45 survivors from the 727 jetliner, 30 were injured.

December 14, Medellín, Colombia. A Boeing 707 airliner dropped an engine into a factory following takeoff and crashed nearby; some 53 persons, most of them factory workers, were killed and 19 others were injured.

FIRES AND EXPLOSIONS

February 13, Turin, Italy. A fire that swept through a movie theatre claimed the lives of 64 persons and injured dozens of others.

February 16–20, South Australia and Victoria, Australia. Fifty brushfires fanned by gale-force winds incinerated some 6,700 sq km (2,600 sq mi) of farmland, forest, and scrub along the southern coast of the country and killed at least 72 persons.

April 18, Taegu, South Korea. A fire broke out at a disco club packed with some 400 teenagers and trapped stampeding patrons near the only exit; the blaze claimed the lives of 25 persons.

May 7, Istanbul, Turkey. A raging fire consumed a hotel filled with sleeping foreign tourists; at least 42 persons were killed and 60 others were injured.

May 8, Tlapacoya, Mexico. A fireworks explosion gutted a church filled with worshipers who had congregated to honour the patron saint of the town; 19 persons were killed and at least 350 others were injured in the blast.

May 27, Benton, Tenn. An explosion in an illegal fireworks factory on a worm farm claimed the lives of 11 persons.

August 31, Pojuca, Brazil. Two fuel tanker cars from a derailed train exploded in flames as hundreds of people, ignoring police orders to disperse, attempted to collect gasoline and diesel fuel from the train; at least 42 persons were killed.

October 23, Beirut, Lebanon. A suicide terrorist drove a pickup truck packed with explosives into a building where sleeping U.S. Marines were housed; the death toll ultimately reached 241. Some 3 km (2 mi) away a building used by French paratroopers was blown apart in the same manner; 58 were killed and 12 wounded.

November 22, Kakegawa, Japan. A propane gas cylinder exploded in a crowded recreation centre and ripped through the building; at least 12 persons were killed and 20 others were injured.

December 14, Kwangmyung, South Korea. A three-story bathhouse some 24 km (15 mi) south of Seoul was engulfed in flames when fire swept through the building; some of the customers panicked and jumped from the windows, resulting in the deaths of 10 persons and injuries to 15 others.

December 16, Amsterdam, Neth. A sex and gambling club in the city's red-light district was set afire by a disgruntled former employee who poured gasoline on the floor and then fired a gun into the pool to ignite the blaze; at least 13 persons were killed.

December 17, Madrid, Spain. A fire erupted in a basement discothèque when an electrical short circuit apparently set heavy curtains on fire; at least 81 persons died in the blaze.

A Colombian Boeing 747 jetliner crashed and burned near Madrid on November 27, killing 183 of the 194 persons aboard.

AGENCIA EFE/PHOTO TRENDS

MARINE

February 12, Off the coast of Chincoteague, Va. A 185-m (605-ft) coal freighter carrying 27,000 tons of coal and 147,000 gal of fuel capsized and sank in storm-battered seas; only 3 of the 36 crewmen aboard survived.

March 1, Guangdong (Kwangtung) Province, China. A ferry carrying some 232 persons from Canton to Zhaoqing (Chao-ch'ing), a popular tourist area, capsized on a river during a thunderstorm; 147 persons were missing and presumed dead.

May 25, South of Abu Simbel, Egypt. A passenger steamer tugging two barges and carrying over 600 persons was enveloped in flames when a butane gas cylinder exploded. The boat sank in Lake Nasser's crocodile-infested waters, and at least 300 persons were feared dead.

June, Off the coast of Kamchatka, U.S.S.R. A Soviet submarine sank in the Pacific Ocean; the 90 crewmen aboard were believed dead.

June 5, Ulyanovsk, U.S.S.R. A cruise ship traveling on the Volga River hit a railway bridge and, according to reports, the crowded upper deck was severed from the ship. It was further reported that a freight train on the bridge had tumbled onto the boat; at least 400 persons were feared dead.

June 17, Near Sulawesi, Indon. An interisland ferry with schoolchildren aboard was reported sunk in the Banda Sea; at least 80 persons were believed dead.

August 4, Off the coast of Masalembo Island, Indonesia. An overcrowded passenger boat, authorized to carry as many as 100 passengers, sprang a leak and sank in the Java Sea with 200 persons aboard; 104 persons were missing and presumed drowned.

August 5, Bangladesh. A boat capsized and sank during a storm; 60 persons were feared drowned.

September 28, Lake Nicaragua, Nicaragua. A wooden passenger boat carrying 127 persons caught fire and sank between Zapatera and Ometepe islands; 26 persons were rescued.

October 26, Off the coast of Hainan, China. A U.S. oil ship, the "Glomar Java Sea," sank in the South China Sea near its drill site after Tropical Storm Lex ripped the ship from its offshore mooring; all 81 persons aboard were presumed drowned.

November 21, Off the coast of Mindanao Island, Philippines. A ferryboat carrying 388 passengers and crew members sank in a typhoon; more than 200 persons were missing and feared dead.

MINING

February 6, Cebu Island, Philippines. An explosion in a coal mine, touched off by a cigarette, was claimed to have killed 15 workers and injured 9 others.

March 7, Near Eregli, Turkey. A gas explosion and rockfalls claimed the lives of 98 miners at the Armutcuk mine; the accident was the country's worst mining disaster to date.

Early June, Serbia, Yugoslavia. A powerful gas explosion ripped through a coal mine and claimed the lives of 12 miners; 74 others were initially trapped underground but were later rescued.

June 22, Oroszlany, Hung. An explosion in a coal mine claimed the lives of 36 miners.

August, Near Yengema, Sierra Leone. A boulder caved in on a mining site and claimed the lives of 50 miners.

September 12, Natal Province, South Africa. A methane gas explosion ripped through a coal mine where 80 miners were working two sections of a horizontal seam cut 6 km (4 mi) into a mountainside; 64 miners were burned to death.

MISCELLANEOUS

January 3, Diyarbakir, Turkey. A newly completed seven-story apartment building that had been certified as unfit for occupancy collapsed after the owner had disregarded the order and allowed families to live there; 39 persons were killed.

January–February, Mozambique. A prolonged drought resulted in a cholera epidemic in the drought-affected districts of Maputo, Gaza, Inhambane, Manica, Sofala, and Zambesi; at least 189 persons succumbed to the disease.

February 13, Champoluc, Italy. Three cable cars plunged to the ground after high winds blew the first car off the cable, producing a chain reaction that knocked two other cars down; ten persons, including two children, were killed in the crash.

March, Sumatra, Indonesia. An outbreak of malaria claimed the lives of at least 120 persons in remote villages in Lampung Province during a five-month period.

Early June, Ghana. An outbreak of cholera was reported to have taken the lives of 43 persons.

Late June, Swaziland. A protein deficiency disease called kwashiorkor, an effect of a prolonged drought, claimed the lives of 500 children.

August 13, Himachal Pradesh, India. Some 7,000 pilgrims, who were making their way up a slope to the shrine of the goddess Naina Devi, stampeded in panic after a hillside market collapsed; 53 persons were trampled to death and 30 others were injured.

August 20, Cairo and Alexandria, Egypt. A four-story apartment building in Cairo collapsed when the weight of an illegally added fifth-floor penthouse proved too heavy for the foundation; at least 15 persons were feared dead. In Alexandria, a seven-story building collapsed after additional stories were added to the structure; nine persons were known dead and six others were missing and presumed dead.

August 24, Fengyuan, Taiwan. The roof of a high school building collapsed on some 635 students in a meeting hall during a heavy rainstorm; 26 teenagers were killed and 6 others were missing.

Late November–Early December, Bangladesh. Three separate outbreaks of cholera killed at least 500 persons in six weeks.

Mid-December, Kalangan, Phil. A stomach ailment that affected more than 1,200 persons claimed the lives of 21 preschool children.

NATURAL

January, India. A three-week cold wave in the northern part of the country led to the deaths of more than 400 persons.

January, Ecuador. Extensive flooding precipitated by torrential rains caused some $90 million in damage and led to the deaths of 30 persons.

January 3, Belo Horizonte, Brazil. Heavy rains forced the Arrudas River to overflow its banks and send water rushing through the centre of the city; 40 persons were killed.

January 21–29, California. Four storms during a one-week period lashed the counties of Marin, San Mateo, Los Angeles, and San Diego, and high tides caused extensive damage to exclusive oceanfront homes in Malibu; there were 11 storm-related deaths.

January–February, Northern Peru. Forty days of severe rains left at least 70 persons known dead; 20 others were missing.

February 1–2, Northern Europe. Deadly storms lashed northern Europe with some of the highest tides in 30 years; hardest hit was Britain, where the steel gates of the River Thames flood barrier were raised to prevent a tidal surge from inundating London; ten deaths were reported in Britain, East Germany, West Germany, and Sweden, and eight crewmen of the Danish merchant navy schooner "Activ" drowned off the northern Dutch coast.

February 11–12, Northeastern U.S. A blizzard buried every major city in the Northeast with up to 600 mm (2 ft) of snow and was responsible for the deaths of at least 11 persons; Baltimore, Md., accumulated 500 mm (20 in) of snow, Washington, D.C., nearly 600 mm, and New York City up to 560 mm (22 in).

February 18–22, Near Alayh, Lebanon. A succession of blizzards paralyzed traffic on the Beirut-to-Damascus highway and claimed the lives of at least 47 persons, many of whom were found frozen to death in their cars.

February 27–March 5, California. A weeklong avalanche of punishing Pacific storms accompanied by two rare tornadoes and two earthquakes caused the deaths of at least 17 persons. Eight counties in the Los Angeles area were declared disaster areas; storm damage was estimated at $160 million.

March, Santa Cruz, Bolivia. Torrential rains throughout the month precipitated flash floods and caused the Pirai River to overflow its banks; 96 persons were dead or missing.

Early March, Guangdong (Kwangtung) Province, China. Heavy rains precipitated widespread flooding that damaged more than 900 houses and killed at least 27 persons.

March 6, Papua New Guinea. Torrential rains touched off a landslide that buried a village in the Jimi River region; 45 persons were killed.

March 7, Central China. A landslide of rocks swept down on a commune in Dongxiang (Tung-hsiang) County, Gansu (Kansu) Province; 270 persons were killed and 22 others were injured.

Mid-March, Northern Peru. Heavy rains triggered mudslides that buried at least two towns in Casma Province; 50 persons were known dead and some 500 others were missing and presumed to be dead.

March 20–21, Peru and Bolivia. Two days of relentless rain caused floods and mudslides that left at least 260 people dead and hundreds of others missing.

March 23, Near Tornamesa, Peru. A landslide of mud and rocks hurtled down on a central highway, forcing two passenger buses off the road and into a river; of the 96 persons aboard the two vehicles, only 6 survived.

March 26, Between Amol and Teheran, Iran. A spate of 15 earthquake tremors rumbled through 11 villages in the mountainous region between Amol and Teheran; 30 persons were killed and 61 others were injured.

March 31, Popayán, Colombia. A devastating earthquake measuring 5.5 on the Richter scale demolished 3,000 buildings, left 150,000 persons homeless, and killed at least 264 persons.

Early April, Near Kabul, Afghanistan. An avalanche near Awlang Bridge, some 100 km (60 mi) north of Kabul, destroyed a bridge and swept away four Soviet military outposts; an undisclosed number of soldiers were killed.

Early April, Louisiana, Mississippi, Alabama. More than 300 mm (12 in) of rain inundated three southern U.S. states, claiming the lives of at least 15 persons and forcing some 25,000 others from their homes; in New Orleans, La., telephone communication with the rest of the nation was knocked out.

Early April, Near Dacca, Bangladesh. A hailstorm pelted the areas around the capital and flattened crops; 41 deaths were attributed to the storm.

Early April, West Bengal, India. A fierce cyclone ripped through 21 villages and killed 76 persons, injured some 1,500 others, and left 6,000 people homeless.

April 2, Costa Rica. An earthquake measuring 7.1 on the Richter scale killed ten persons and injured hundreds of others.

April 11, Fujian (Fukien) Province, China. A tornado ripped through two communes in Jianyang (Chien-yang) County and killed 54 persons.

April 12, Near Calcutta, India. A cyclone battered some 21 coastal villages near Calcutta, claimed the lives of at least 50 persons, injured 1,500 others, and left 6,000 persons homeless.

April 14, Chimbote, Peru. An earthquake measuring 5.2 on the Richter scale destroyed several buildings and killed ten persons.

April 14, Peru. Flooding precipitated landslides in Piura and Tumbes departments; 37 persons were known dead.

April 19, Near Bandung, Indon. A landslide in central Java claimed the lives of 19 persons.

April 26, Khulna, Bangladesh. A tornado struck the Ganges delta town of Khulna and killed 12 persons; 200 others were injured.

April 27, Cunchi, Ecuador. A thunderous landslide that occurred on the Pan-American Highway buried four cars and three buses under tons of rock and mud; at least 100 persons were feared dead.

April 30, Near Chepén, Peru. A flash flood swept over a bridge on the Pan-American Highway and knocked at least eight vehicles, including a bus, into the Chaman River; at least 50 persons were feared drowned.

Late April–Early May, Hunan Province, China. Tornadoes, hail, and rainstorms killed at least 275 persons.

Early May, Bangladesh. Brutal storms lashed areas of Bangladesh, causing severe flooding; 75 persons lost their lives.

May, France, West Germany. Severe flooding resulted when major rivers in northern France and southern Germany overflowed; 18 persons were drowned in northwestern and northeastern France, and 7 persons were killed in the Cologne, Bonn, and Koblenz areas in Germany.

May, Argentina, Brazil, Paraguay. A driving rain led to extensive flooding in the Paraguay and Paraná river basins; 23 persons died in southern Brazil and 27,000 were left homeless; 134,000 people were driven from their homes in Argentina, and property damage in the three countries was estimated at $338 million.

Mid-May, Himachal Pradesh, India. Relentless rain coupled with snow killed 26 persons in the state.

Mid-May, Central Vietnam. Whirlwinds killed more than 76 persons and injured many others.

May 18–20, Texas, Tennessee, Missouri, Georgia, Louisiana, Mississippi, Kentucky. At least 59 tornadoes and hail the size of baseballs, compounded by storms that produced flash floods, battered the Southern states and claimed the lives of at least 24 persons; hardest hit was the Houston, Texas, area, where 350 homes were destroyed, trailer parks were annihilated, power was interrupted, and at least 10 persons were killed.

May 22, Tressenda, Italy. A huge landslide killed 17 persons and injured several others.

May 26, Northern Honshu, Japan. An earthquake measuring 7.7 on the Richter scale, accompanied by a tsunami (seismic sea wave) that swept 46 children playing on the Oga Peninsula out to sea, toppled buildings and touched off fires. Forty construction workers were also swept into the Sea of Japan after boarding small boats. At least 58 persons were known dead.

Early June, Turkey. Two days of heavy rain flooded cities along the country's western and Black Sea coasts; 15 persons were killed when they were struck by lightning.

June, Ecuador. Several months of unusually heavy rain caused widespread sporadic flooding, landslides, and disruption in communications; at least 300 persons were killed.

June 5, Central Taiwan. Floods and landslides triggered by three days of torrential rain killed 24 persons.

June 11, Bikramganj, India. A windstorm caused the tin roof of a movie theatre to collapse on some 600 patrons; at least 80 persons were killed and some 100 others were injured.

Late June, Gujarat State, India. Four days of relentless rain caused severe flooding that left at least 935 persons dead or missing; some 130,000 others were marooned in the Saurashtra region.

Late June–Early July, China. Major flood tides precipitated by torrential rains surged down the Changjiang (Yangtze) River and flooded seven provinces; at least 90 persons were drowned in Anhui Province and hundreds of others were feared drowned in the six other provinces.

Mid-July, Nepal. Thunderous landslides touched off by torrential rains killed at least 21 persons on Himalayan slopes in central and eastern Nepal.

July 15, Philippines. A brutal storm that caused some $1.2 million in property damage claimed at least 45 lives; most of the fatalities were from the coastal areas of Bataan Province.

July 23, Masuda, Japan. A 500-mm (20-in) downpour inundated highways, destroyed 450 homes, swept away 47 bridges, and washed out roads; 82 persons were killed in the floods and the resulting landslides.

Late July, United States. A two-week heat wave with temperatures soaring into the upper 90s and low 100s claimed the lives of 80 persons nationwide; hardest hit was St. Louis, Mo., where 38 persons died from heat-related causes.

July–August, Middle West and East, U.S. A blistering heat wave, with temperatures soaring as high as 107° F in Augusta, Ga., led to the deaths of at least 188 persons.

July 17–25, France. Gale-force winds pummeled central and southwestern France; 13 persons were killed.

July 22, Northern Greece. Fierce gales accompanied by hailstones overturned small boats and swept 16 persons out to sea; the storm also ignited a forest fire that destroyed 502 ha (1,240 ac) of woodland north of Athens.

July 28, Gachalá, Colombia. Two mudslides that occurred 70 minutes apart at a hydroelectric dam under construction killed some 41 persons and injured 33 others.

Late July, Indonesia. Intense flooding swept across the Banggai regency and inundated 34 villages; 11 persons were drowned and 2,000 others were left homeless.

Early August, Bangladesh. Week-long flooding caused the deaths of 41 persons.

August 4–5, Northern Pakistan. Severe rains led to the deaths of 19 persons in Mansahra district.

August 11, Xicola, Mexico. A thunderous avalanche unleashed tons of rock onto the valley of Xicola; 50 persons were killed.

August 17, Philippines. An earthquake measuring 6.2 on the Richter scale struck the industrial and farming centre of Laoag on Luzon Island and prompted tidal waves to pummel the coastal areas of Ilocos Norte Province; at least 21 persons were known dead and property damage was estimated at $2,270,000.

August 18, Southern Texas. Deadly Hurricane Alicia, packing winds of up to 115 mph, roared through the island city of Galveston ripping walls from buildings and smashing cars before blasting Houston with 97-mph wind gusts that sent missiles of glass and stone from downtown skyscrapers crashing to the ground; at least 17 deaths were attributed to the hurricane, and property damage was expected to reach $1.6 billion.

August 26, France and Spain. Torrential rains precipitated the worst flooding in the Spanish-French Basque region in 30 years; at least 33 persons were killed and 13 others were missing.

September, India. Monsoon rains precipitated flooding that submerged hundreds of villages and killed more than 400 persons.

September, Papua New Guinea. Severe floods caused extensive property damage estimated at $11.9 million; 11 persons were reported killed.

September 29, Honshu, Kyushu, and Shikoku, Japan. Devastating Typhoon Forest battered three islands with as much as 48 cm (19 in) of rain; 16 persons were known dead, 22 others were missing, and 30,000 homes were flooded.

Late September, Northern and northwestern Bangladesh. Intense flooding in nine districts led to the deaths of at least 61 persons, including 23 who were washed away by floodwaters from the Brahmaputra River and 6 others who died of snakebites they received while climbing into trees to escape the floodwaters.

Late September–Early October, Southern Arizona. A week of desert rainstorms caused widespread flooding when swollen rivers ravaged the towns of Clifton, Marana, Morenci, Tucson, Safford, and Nogales and left many of them under several feet of water; the state's worst natural disaster in memory claimed 13 lives.

WIDE WORLD

Nearly half the population of this small Turkish village died in an earthquake in October.

October 14, Uttar Pradesh, India. A new wave of torrential rains flooded 871 villages; 42 persons were killed.

October 15, Bangladesh. A cyclone slashed the country's southern coast with heavy rains and high winds, sweeping across the port city of Chittagong and destroying 1,000 homes; at least 25 persons were drowned, and the fate of some 200 fishing boats with several hundred people aboard was not known.

Mid-October, Thailand. Widespread flooding affected 16 of the country's 73 provinces and devastated the city of Bangkok; at least 18 persons were known dead.

October 20, Off the coast of Mazatlán, Mexico. Fierce Hurricane Tico claimed the lives of 105 fishermen who were lost at sea in their shrimp boats during the intense storm.

October 30, Eastern Turkey. A major earthquake measuring 7.1 on the Richter scale devastated 44 villages in eastern Turkey; more than 1,300 persons were known dead, more than 500 others were injured, and thousands were left homeless.

November 6, Shandong (Shantung), Hebei (Hopeh), and Henan (Honan) provinces, China. A strong earthquake measuring 5.9 on the Richter scale jarred agricultural communities in eastern China; at least 30 persons were killed and heavy property damage was reported.

November 28, Wyoming, Colorado, South Dakota, Nebraska, Kansas, Minnesota, and Iowa. A deadly blizzard that produced back-to-back snowstorms set a record for the month of November with drifts that were up to 2.7 m (9 ft) high; at least 56 deaths were attributed to the storms.

December, Malaysia. Heavy monsoon rains prompted the evacuation of some 15,000 people from the inundated east coast states; at least 10 persons drowned.

December 8, Bar Elias, Lebanon. A landslide, caused by a leaking water tank that eroded part of the hill on which it was positioned, descended upon the village before dawn, crushing 10 houses and killing at least 20 persons.

December 17–31, United States. A record-breaking Arctic cold wave that invaded much of the U.S. sent temperatures plummeting to record-breaking lows across the country and at least 500 deaths were blamed on the two-week freeze; crop losses, especially of citrus fruit, were expected to top $500 million. Southern states including Texas and Florida were especially hard hit and were paralyzed with temperatures in the low teens; thousands of water pipes froze and burst there and across the nation.

December 22, Near Gaoual, Guinea. An earthquake measuring 6.3 on the Richter scale annihilated 16 villages in northwestern Guinea and killed at least 300 persons; a severe tremor two days later claimed at least 143 more lives in the town of Koumbia.

December 23, Tamil Nadu, India. A downpour that resulted in 380 mm (15 in) of rain in some areas claimed the lives of at least 26 persons, many of whom were killed when the saturated mud walls of houses and huts collapsed on them.

December 31, Pakistan. An early morning earthquake measuring 6.5 on the Richter scale jolted northern Pakistan along its border with Afghanistan; at least 12 persons were killed.

Torrential rains caused flooding and mudslides in Shimane Prefecture, southwestern Japan, in July. The municipal offices of the town of Misumi—and cars and debris driven by the raging waters—reflect the disaster.

UPI

RAILROADS

February 1, Qalama, Egypt. An express train slammed into the rear of a stationary military train after running a stop signal; 19 persons were killed and 77 others were injured in the crash.

February 19, Near Empalme, Mexico. A freight train rammed into a stopped passenger train experiencing mechanical problems, and 16 cars derailed, some igniting; at least 100 persons were killed and 69 others were injured.

March 16, Calcutta, India. A suburban commuter train slammed into the rear of another commuter train at Howrah station; at least 15 persons were killed and more than 200 others were injured.

March 21, Near Dacca, Bangladesh. A train, derailed by a storm-uprooted tree, caused a bridge to collapse some 240 km (150 mi) northwest of the capital. The engine and two cars plunged into a river; at least 60 persons were killed.

May 31, Egypt. An express train traveling from Cairo to Alexandria smashed into five cars of a derailed train that had been advancing from the opposite direction; 10 persons were killed and 40 others were injured.

June 10, Near Cairo, Egypt. A passenger train slammed into a stopped train in the village of Kafr Ammar and upended the last car of the latter; 26 persons were killed and 47 others were injured.

September 28, Near Gospic, Yugos. A commuter train slammed into a bus loaded with schoolchildren and factory workers at an unprotected crossing; the accident, which occurred in thick fog, claimed the lives of 25 persons and injured 25 others.

October 21, Punjab, India. Twelve of 17 cars of a train derailed after terrorists ripped out some 60 m (20 ft) of tracks near Ludhiana; at least 16 persons were killed in the incident.

November 3, Dhulwari, India. Two railroad cars filled with gasoline exploded at a train station; 36 persons were killed and more than 100 others were injured.

December 11, Tanzania. A train packed with schoolchildren was derailed by vandals who placed an iron bar across the tracks; at least 20 persons were killed and 79 others were seriously injured.

December 24, Near Hwange, Zimbabwe. After a train derailed, the locomotive and 13 coaches plunged down a ravine; as many as 30 persons were believed dead and 60 others were injured.

TRAFFIC

February 4, Near Agra, India. A traffic accident claimed the lives of 12 members of a wedding party.

February 4, Gujarat, India. A truck overturned, and 13 persons lost their lives in the accident.

February 8, Bandhani, India. A head-on collision between two trucks killed 20 passengers and injured 24 others.

February 11, Near Thebes, Greece. A head-on collision between a car-carrier truck and a bus resulted in the deaths of 15 persons.

March 13, Near Missão Velha, Brazil. A flatbed truck, loaded with more than 70 persons returning from a political rally, lost its brakes on a hill, overturned into a ravine, and exploded in flames; 30 persons were killed and 39 others were injured.

April 16, Chungchong Namdo, South Korea. An intercity bus, which made a sharp turn while attempting to pass a bicycle, ran over and killed 12 pedestrians who were either crossing the street or walking on sidewalks; the bus proceeded a short distance before falling from an embankment and turning over.

April 21, India. A crowded passenger bus traveling from Kottayam to Kerala State lost its brakes in hill country, hurtled down a ravine, and burst into flames; 35 persons were killed.

April 26, Florence, Italy. A school bus carrying 43 teenagers and 3 teachers slammed head-on into a truck in a tunnel on the Autostrada del Sole, killing 12 schoolchildren and injuring 35 others.

May 5, Java, Indonesia. A traffic pileup occurred after the driver of a military truck carrying 38 soldiers lost control of the vehicle on a narrow road near Semarang and plowed into two buses and a motorbike; 10 persons were killed in the accident.

May 27, Madhya Pradesh, India. A bus experiencing brake failure plummeted into a gorge; at least 60 persons were feared dead.

July 7, Near Kozakli, Turkey. A truck transporting farm workers ran off the road and crashed; at least 40 persons were killed and 20 others were injured.

August 1, Bhaluka, Bangladesh. A passenger bus traveling to the town of Mymensingh collided head-on with a truck; 20 persons were killed and some 50 others were injured.

August 10, Near Coachella, Calif. A car carrying 11 Mexican illegal aliens ran a stop sign while being pursued by the border patrol and was hit broadside by a truck; all the occupants of the car were killed.

September 12, Ecuador. A bus plummeted down a ravine in the Andes Mountains south of Quito; 50 persons were killed.

December 18, Italy. A bus carrying Italian sailors from Genoa to a soccer game in Turin skidded into a guard rail, bounced across a rain-slick highway, and crashed through a guard rail; of the 38 persons aboard only 4 survived.

December 23, Near Devers, Texas. A head-on collision between a church bus and a tractor-trailer truck during a cold, misty rain claimed the lives of 10 persons, including both drivers.

PEOPLE OF THE YEAR

BIOGRAPHIES

The following is a selected list of men and women who influenced events significantly in 1983.

Agca, Mehmet Ali

On May 13, 1981, during an open-air general audience in St. Peter's Square in Vatican City, Mehmet Ali Agca, a Turkish terrorist, tried to assassinate Pope John Paul II. He failed to accomplish his mission and was arrested on the spot. Tried in an Italian court, he was convicted of attempted murder and sentenced on July 22 to life imprisonment. During the trial he claimed that he had no accomplices and had acted alone, but in prison he recanted and said he had been paid to kill the pope by Bulgarians acting for the KGB.

Mehmet Ali Agca was born in 1958 at Guzelyurt, a village north of Malatya, Turkey, the son of a miner. After his primary education at Malatya he entered the local teacher training college. Graduating in 1976, he left economically depressed eastern Anatolia and moved to Ankara, where in 1977 he registered at the university's faculty of history and geography. He showed little interest in studying and the following year left Ankara to register at the Istanbul School of Economics, but again he soon dropped out.

By now Agca was a member of the "Gray Wolves," a commando under the orders of Alparslan Turkes, a former army officer and now leader of the extreme right-wing National Action Party. On Feb. 1, 1979, in Istanbul, Agca shot Abdi Ipekci, editor of the liberal newspaper *Milliyet*. A few weeks later he was recognized by an informer, and he was arrested on June 25 and charged with the murder. Agca first confessed but later claimed to be innocent. On November 25 he escaped from the maximum security military prison at Maltepe.

According to Agca, his controllers had other plans for him. Supplied with a false Indian passport made out for "Yoginder Singh," Agca was ordered to Iran. After a stay in Teheran he returned to Turkey, went underground, and in July 1980 landed in Bulgaria. In Sofia a Turk named Omer Mersan provided him with a Turkish passport in the name of Faruk Orgun. Another Turk, Bekir Celenk, an arms trafficker living in Sofia, promised Agca $1,250,000 if he should kill the pope. At the same Sofia hotel he also met three Bulgarians who introduced themselves as "Kolev," "Petrov," and "Bayramik." Later Agca identified two of his Sofia acquaintances as Bulgarian embassy employees and the third as a Bulgarian airline official at Rome airport named Sergey Antonov, who Agca said drove him to the pope's audience. Antonov was arrested but denied knowing Agca, whose account of the "Bulgarian connection" was believed by Italian jurists and police, denied by Bulgaria, and widely doubted elsewhere. At year's end he was visited in prison by his intended victim, Pope John Paul II, to whom he voiced repentance and who forgave Agca in private as he had done in public. (*See* BULGARIA.)

(K.M. SMOGORZEWSKI)

Alfonsín, Raúl

In winning the Argentine presidential election of Oct. 30, 1983, Raúl Alfonsín, leader of the Unión Cívica Radical (Radical Civic Union), was not only presiding over the country's return to democracy after more than seven years of military rule but was also signaling the end of the dominance of Argentine politics by the Peronist Party, maintained since its creation in 1945 by Juan Domingo Perón. Peronist rivalries helped, but Alfonsín's victory was attributable mainly to his campaign for permanent change in the administration of Argentina, which he began as soon as the military government had announced in 1982 that there would be elections in 1983. His inauguration as president, for a six-year term, took place on December 10.

Alfonsín was born on March 13, 1926, in Chascomus, Buenos Aires Province, where his father was a shopkeeper. He attended a military academy for five years and then in 1950 obtained a law degree at the University of Buenos Aires. He practiced law in Chascomus and dedicated himself to the Radical Party, spurning the military regimes and the populism of Peronism. After becoming a town councillor at the age of 24, he went on to win election to the National Congress. He became provincial president of the actually moderate Radical Party in 1965 but was opposed to the conciliatory attitude toward the military and the Peronists that was adopted by the party leader, Ricardo Balbín. In 1972 Alfonsín formed a left-of-centre faction within the party, called Renovation and Change. Alfonsín was a harsh critic of the military repression of the 1970s, and when Balbín died in 1982 the Radicals united behind him and his ideals of civil liberty, human rights, and parliamentary government free from corruption and inefficiency.

President Alfonsín's government faced an enormous task in tackling the military's legacy of economic crisis and in restoring confidence. Strong public support greeted his forceful early actions to curb the military's power in all sectors. He quickly won repeal of the military regime's amnesty of its secret killers and torturers and began prosecutions. The public also supported his policies of trade union reform, freezing prices, and gradually restoring real wages. Equally important to the new president was the normalization of foreign relations: seeking a diplomatic solution to the Falklands/Islas Malvinas dispute with Britain, repairing relations with Chile, and forging new, independent links with the U.S. Brutal problems remained, however, notably Argentina's rampant inflation and massive foreign debt.

(BEN BOX)

Aoki, Isao

In October 1978 35-year-old Isao Aoki became a national hero in Japan when he won the world match-play golf tournament at Virginia Water, England. Since that moment Aoki has been a top contender in every tournament he has entered. Perhaps his most thrilling moment to date came in June 1980 when he finished second to Jack Nicklaus in the U.S. Open. Playing together in all four rounds, they pushed each other to a new record. Nicklaus's eight-under-par 272 was two strokes better than Aoki's score, but each won a $50,000 bonus for breaking the old mark of 275. Aoki got revenge of sorts in 1982 at Liphook, England, where he defeated Nicklaus by two strokes and earned $50,000—the largest one-day purse in British golfing history.

In February 1983 Aoki, who five consecutive times was named Japan's golfer of the year, won the Hawaiian Open with what sports writers called one of the greatest shots of all time. Standing 128 yd from the cup, he hoped for a birdie to tie Jack Renner and go into a play-off. But the wedge shot he hoisted over a bunker rolled in for an eagle three, one stroke better than Renner's total. It was the first time a Japanese golfer had won a major U.S. title. The following September Aoki won the European Open with a six-under-par 274.

Isao Aoki was born in Abiko City, Chiba Prefecture, on August 31, 1942, the fourth child of a farm family. He was 15 when the golf craze hit Japan in 1957 and learned on a local course with small greens and many bunkers. His style on the greens is unusual, influenced by playing at one period with a borrowed putter too long for him. Instead of placing his centre-shafted putter flat on the grass, he tilts it at an angle and then bats the ball—which somehow consistently drops into the cup. Crowds seem to love his go-for-broke attitude and his personal enthusiasm. One moment of special exhilaration came in October 1979 when Aoki teed off at the second hole at Virginia Water. The ball sailed exactly 155 yd through the air and across the green for a hole in one. It was one of the most rewarding shots in golf history because for it Aoki received a $120,000 luxury home overlooking the Gleneagles golf course. (JOHN RODERICK)

Arafat, Yasir

In 1983 Yasir Arafat, chairman of the Palestine Liberation Organization (PLO), faced the eclipse of his long-held, undisputed leadership of the Palestinian resistance to Israel. In early November units of the Palestine Liberation Army supported by Syrian troops had his 5,000 supporters trapped in the northern Lebanese city of Tripoli. Although retaining the support of moderate Arab leaders, including the influential moderate Arab nations of the Gulf Cooperation Council (GCC), Arafat and 4,000 of his loyalists were forced to evacuate the city in late December. His diplomatic importance had declined greatly since his refusal in early 1983 to work with King Hussein of Jordan toward a Middle East settlement based on the so-called Jordanian option, by which Palestinians would have autonomy on the West Bank under Jordan. Criticism of Arafat had mounted in Palestinian circles after his retreat from Beirut at the end of August 1982. Nevertheless, after leaving Tripoli he began a round of visits to Arab capitals, including a dramatic meeting with Pres. Hosni Mubarak of Egypt.

Muhammad Abed Ar'ouf Arafat (also known as Abu Ammar—"the builder") was born in 1929 in Jerusalem, one of seven children of a well-to-do merchant whose wife was related to the anti-Zionist grand mufti of Jerusalem. He spent his childhood in Gaza, where a teacher first gave him the name Yasir. At an early age he became leader of the Gaza youth section of Al Faoutouwa, a Palestinian guerrilla organization. Arafat attended Cairo University, where he graduated in engineering. There he joined the Muslim Brotherhood and the Union of Palestinian Students, of which he was president during 1952–56. He joined the Egyptian Army and served in the 1956 Suez war with a demolition unit. At this time, with his friends Salah Khalaf and Khaled al-Wazir, known later as Abu Ayad and Abu Jihad, he began to form the idea of an independent Palestinian movement.

After Suez, Arafat went to Kuwait, where he worked as an engineer. While there, he was a co-founder of al-Fatah, which was to become the leading military component of the PLO. He became chairman of the PLO in 1969 and commander in chief of the Palestinian Revolutionary Forces in 1971. Subsequently, he directed his efforts to rehabilitating the PLO's image as an organization pledged to political persuasion rather than terrorism. In November 1974 Arafat's finest hour came when he was the first representative of a nongovernmental organization (the PLO) to address a plenary session of the UN General Assembly.

(JOHN WHELAN)

Attenborough, Sir Richard Samuel

Richard Attenborough's film *Gandhi* won eight Oscars—including recognition as the best film of 1982—in the April 1983 awards ceremony of the Academy of Motion Picture Arts and Sciences, and it was to prove one of the most profitable films in the history of the British cinema (it was in fact a coproduction with India). This was a gratifying and somewhat unexpected culmination to Attenborough's distinguished but not markedly spectacular 40-year career in British films.

Gandhi itself, a dramatized biography of the great Indian political and spiritual leader, did not seem in advance to be destined for that kind of success. Indeed, it had taken Attenborough 20 years to find financial backing for the project, and throughout its production there were forebodings within the film industry about its chances. Its eventual success was probably due in large part to Attenborough's tenacious dedication, sincerity, and deep personal admiration for his subject.

Richard Attenborough was born in Cambridge, England, on Aug. 29, 1923, the son of a teacher and historian who became principal of University College, Leicester. After grammar school in Leicester he won a scholarship to the Royal Academy of Dramatic Art and made his first stage appearance in 1941 as Richard Miller in Eugene O'Neill's *Ah, Wilderness!* His film debut took place the following year, while still a student, in Noel Coward's *In Which We Serve.* Attenborough's first starring film role was as Pinkie in *Brighton Rock* (1947), a part he had created on stage in 1943, just before joining the Royal Air Force.

After World War II Attenborough was for a time equally active in both theatre and motion pictures, but he rarely appeared on the stage after 1957, when he played Theseus in *The Rape of the Belt*. In 1959 he moved into film production, in partnership with Bryan Forbes. Their company, Beaver Films, scored a success with its first production, *The Angry Silence* (1959), at the time highly controversial for its story of trade-union victimization.

Attenborough made an ambitious directorial debut in 1968 with an adaptation of *Oh! What a Lovely War*, which won 16 international awards. The same antiwar theme was to recur in *A Bridge Too Far* (1976) and *Gandhi*. Those films, as well as *Young Winston* (1972), which won a Hollywood Golden Globe, confirmed his preference for historical themes and epic scale. Attenborough was knighted in 1976.

(DAVID ROBINSON)

Barbie, Klaus

The former Nazi Gestapo official known as the "Butcher of Lyon" was finally brought back to France in February 1983 to be put on trial for "crimes against humanity" committed during World War II. Both the French and West German governments had been maneuvering since the early 1970s—after he was discovered—to extradite Klaus Barbie from La Paz, Bolivia, where he lived and maintained close and, for many years, secure connections with various Bolivian military juntas. However, the opportunity the two Western European governments had been waiting for came in January with Barbie's arrest by Bolivian police for fraud involving a debt. The civilian government of Hernán Siles Zuazo, which came to power in 1982, turned on Barbie, ruling his citizenship invalid, and he was flown out of the country, first to French Guiana and then to France. He was officially charged with crimes against humanity, including murder, torture, and arbitrary arrests and jailings, and specifically with the execution or deportation of some 950 people, mostly Jews. Barbie could not be tried for any offenses against members of the French Resistance, including the death in 1943 of the renowned Resistance leader Jean Moulin; crimes against humanity, by definition, involve only acts committed against civilians.

Klaus Barbie was born in Bad Godensberg, near Bonn, on Oct. 15, 1913. An indifferent student, he finished high school two years later than the rest of his class. He then joined the SS (Schutzstaffel, the black-shirted elite guard of the Nazi Party) and rose steadily in its ranks. He was sent to The Hague, Neth., promoted to full lieutenant, and eventually moved to Amsterdam, where he allegedly helped deport some 300 Dutch Jews to the Mauthausen concentration camp in Austria. He was next transferred to Lyon, where he served as the SS commander from November 1942 to November 1944.

Barbie's reputation was that of a sadist, a savage torturer. Surviving witnesses recalled the pleasure he took in administering fatal beatings. Including people he killed personally, he was reported to have been responsible for sending over 4,000 people to their deaths and deporting more than 7,500 French men, women, and children to Nazi concentration camps.

After the war Barbie burned off his SS identification tattoo and, after being captured briefly by the British, he was employed by certain members of the U.S.

Army's Counter Intelligence Corps (CIC) as an intelligence source about Communist activities. In 1951 he was helped by CIC officers to escape to South America as Klaus Altmann, mechanic. He settled in Bolivia, a country that was already harbouring other Nazis on the run. Before his extradition, Barbie had already been tried for war crimes and sentenced to death twice in absentia in Lyon. (BONNIE OBERMAN)

Beauvoir, Simone de

"You are not born a woman, you become one," Simone de Beauvoir wrote in her 1949 classic *Le Deuxième sexe (The Second Sex)*, a work that laid down the agenda for the women's liberation movement and which, with its emphasis on the individual in relation to the Other, gave a new and highly productive direction to the existentialist philosophy of Jean-Paul Sartre. Until Sartre's death in 1980, he and Beauvoir were the "dream ticket" in anyone's election for the century's preeminent left-wing intellectual couple. The reminiscences she later published, starting with *La Cérémonie des adieux* (1982), shocked some of Sartre's admirers by their frank revelations of his final years. However, uncompromising honesty was the hallmark of her work, and there had never been any likelihood that she would retire into the role of the idolizing "widow" of the man who had been her closest personal and literary associate for more than 50 years.

Born in Paris on Jan. 9, 1908, Simone Lucie Ernestine Marie Bertrand de Beauvoir had a conventional middle-class upbringing against which she rebelled while studying at the École Normale Supérieure to become a teacher. There it was that she met Sartre, and she ranked second behind him in their graduating class. She then became a teacher in Marseille, Rouen, and Paris before publishing her first novel, *L'Invitée*, in 1943. Through Sartre, she was introduced to the existentialist intellectual circles she depicted in *Les Mandarins*, the novel that won the 1954 Prix Goncourt. Meanwhile, her essays, in particular *The Second Sex*, had established her as a leading figure in French intellectual life.

Increasingly, Beauvoir's search for the origins of women's alienation in a male-dominated society took her back to her own experience, and her account of this in her memoirs, starting with *Mémoires d'une jeune fille rangée (Memoirs of a Dutiful Daughter)* in 1958, is highly personal and at the same time a penetrating analysis of French society. *Une Mort très douce (A Very Easy Death*; 1964), the devastating story of her mother's last illness and death, is a moving tribute from one woman to another across the barriers of generation and belief.

It was perhaps inevitable that Beauvoir's feminine awareness should make her thought diverge from Sartre's. Hailed as one of the country's greatest writers, she was no longer seen (or saw herself) as merely the companion of his intellectual adventure. And, by the time of his death, while his work seemed somewhat outmoded, hers had gained in relevance. *The Second Sex*, translated and read around the world, became one of the principal engines of the modern women's movement everywhere. (*See* Feature Article: *Women's Rights in Today's World.*) (ROBIN BUSS)

Bernardin, Joseph Cardinal

In May 1983 the Roman Catholic bishops in the U.S. voted overwhelmingly in favour of a controversial pastoral letter entitled "The Challenge of Peace: God's Promise and Our Response." It urged a halt to the testing, production, and development of new nuclear weapons systems and expressed opposition to the first use of nuclear weapons or their use in a limited war. The principal architect of that letter, the head of the committee that drafted it, was Chicago's Joseph Cardinal Bernardin. Over the past two years, Bernardin had shepherded the document through three drafts and numerous amendments. The pastoral letter was intended as a teaching instrument for American Catholics on what the bishops viewed as a moral as well as a political and military issue.

Joseph L. Bernardin was named archbishop of Chicago in July 1982, succeeding John Patrick Cardinal Cody; in February 1983 he was elevated to the Sacred College of Cardinals by Pope John Paul II. In Chicago Bernardin confronted a legacy of problems, including an alienated priesthood and lay population, racial tension, and ethnic divisions. He began by implementing an increased collegiality, listening to the views of local priests on such matters as the church's financial accountability and its social mission.

Bernardin was born on April 2, 1928, in Columbia, S.C., into a family of Italian immigrants. He received his B.A. in philosophy from St. Mary's Seminary in Baltimore, Md., in 1948 and his master's in education from Catholic University in 1952, when he was ordained a priest. He served in Charleston, gradually rising to the position of administrator in 1964. Two years later he was consecrated a bishop and assigned to Atlanta, Ga.

Bernardin moved to Washington, D.C., in 1968 as general secretary of the National Conference of Catholic Bishops (NCCB) and its social action agency, the United States Catholic Conference. Four years later he was appointed archbishop of Cincinnati, Ohio, where he became known for paying attention to the views of the local clergy. In 1974 he was elected president of the NCCB and a member of the international Synod of Bishops. Though considered a liberal on many social issues, such as opposition to capital punishment, Bernardin adhered to the church's more conservative stance against abortion and the ordination of women. (JOAN N. BOTHELL)

Bhindranwale, Jarnail Singh

Referred to by many in India as the "Khomeini of the Sikhs," a "militant" or a "crusader," Sant (holy man or priest) Jarnail Singh Bhindranwale emerged in 1983 as the most powerful leader of India's 16 million Sikhs in their campaign for greater political autonomy in the rich farming state of Punjab in northwestern India, where they constituted more than half the population. Bhindranwale's aim was to "liberate the Sikh nation from the yoke of the Hindu." In support of his cause, in May 1983, 35,000 Sikhs resident in the U.K. marched through London to demonstrate outside the Indian High Commission.

Jarnail Singh was born in 1946 in the village of Rode, Faridkot district, Punjab. His father, Joginder Singh, was a local Sikh leader. Jarnail Singh was the seventh of eight brothers, each of whom, according to a family friend, was a devout Sikh. At the age of five Jarnail Singh was sent to Bhindranwale *taxal* for his schooling. (A *taxal*—literally, "mint"—is where young Sikhs are inculcated with the tenets of their religion.) Singh gave up his studies before completing them in order to serve his teacher, Kartar Singh Bhindranwale, with whom he remained for the next 27 years. In 1977 Kartar Singh died in a road accident. Jarnail Singh, his favourite disciple, took his place and came to be known as Sant Jarnail Singh Bhindranwale—one of the youngest of the 35 Sikh priests in India.

Jarnail Singh Bhindranwale first attracted nationwide attention in April 1980 when he led a group of armed Sikhs to attack a meeting of the Nirankaris—regarded by mainstream Sikhs as heretics. Seventeen people, including 13 of Bhindranwale's raiding party, were killed, and he was arrested, jailed, and later returned to his headquarters. From there he announced the date, time, and place for his surrender to the authorities. That took place in September 1981, when a force of several thousand police came to arrest him, provoking rioting in which more than a dozen people were killed.

As the Sikh campaign gained ground, with further violent confrontations, its leadership passed for all practical purposes to Bhindranwale. He directed operations from his retreat in the Golden Temple in Amritsar, the Sikhs' foremost shrine and place of pilgrimage. Although the police had registered a number of charges against him, including one of sedition, they held back from moving to rearrest him. (DILIP GANGULY)

Bieber, Owen

For nearly 40 years a veritable dynasty led the automobile workers of the United States: first Walter Reuther, then his long-time aide Leonard Woodcock, and finally Douglas Fraser, who had been handpicked by Woodcock. But in 1983, with no obvious successor to Fraser, an energetically contested three-way race ensued for the presidency of the 1.1 million-member union, formally known as the United Automobile, Aerospace and Agricultural Implement Workers of America. As one business journal observed, "The election of a UAW president is important because he negotiates contracts that set the tone for settlements in rubber, steel, aerospace and farm equipment" as well as in cars.

The winner was a quiet giant of a negotiator and a second-generation UAW member, Owen Bieber. Born Dec. 28, 1929, in North Dorr, Mich., he followed his father at the age of 18 to work at the McInerney Spring and Wire Co. in Grand Rapids making seats for Cadillacs and Hudsons. A year later, in 1949, he became a shop steward and soon started climbing the union ladder. In short order he was named to his local's executive board and then became its president in 1956. After serving as a regional organizer and international representative, he became director of the region comprising two-thirds of Michigan. Elected a vice-president of the UAW in 1980, he was appointed director of the union's General Motors Department. In that job during tough economic times, he negotiated contracts notable for union concessions to hard-pressed GM, though he later warned, "Don't confuse the UAW's position when you're losing millions with our approach when you're earning millions."

Not expected to lead the union in radical or new directions, Bieber is regarded as capable if unspectacular. Called "forthright, gentle, and tolerant" but also a hardworking "country boy," he is widely respected for spotless integrity.

The challenges facing the UAW loom as large as Bieber's 6-ft 5-in frame. Having lost 400,000 members during recent years because of automation and recession, the union plans to rebuild its ranks, especially outside the automobile industry. Among Bieber's aims are to negotiate stronger job security for his members, to organize workers in Japanese car plants in the U.S., and to push legislation requiring progressively more U.S.-made components in imported vehicles. (PHILIP KOPPER)

Biya, Paul

Following Ahmadou Ahidjo's voluntary retirement on Nov. 6, 1982, after 22 years as Cameroon's president, he was succeeded by Paul Biya, his prime minister. On Sept. 14, 1983, Biya also succeeded Ahidjo as chairman of the republic's sole political party, the Cameroonian National Union (CNU). The seemingly smooth transfer of power was disrupted when Ahidjo, while still CNU president, realized that he would not be able to retain effective control as the "power behind the throne," as he had apparently intended. Biya was clearly his own man, with his own ideas on how the country should be run, and his election as CNU president enabled him to plan for a more democratic political system.

Paul Biya was born in the Sangmelima district of southern Cameroon (then part of French Equatorial Africa), on Feb. 13, 1933. A Roman Catholic by upbringing (Ahidjo was a Muslim from the north), he attended mission school at Ndem, seminaries at Edea and Akono, and finished his secondary education at the Lycée Leclerc in Yaoundé. After studying law and political science at the University of Paris, where he was also a pupil at the Institut des Hautes Études d'Outre-Mer—the former "Colonial School"—he decided to pursue a political career instead of the priesthood as originally intended.

Returning to Cameroon in 1962, Biya was at first head of the Department of Development Aid for a year before becoming director of the Cabinet of the Ministry of National Education, Youth, and Culture. In 1967 he was appointed director of the Cabinet of President Ahidjo and the following year was named minister of state and secretary-general of the presidency. When the post of prime minister was created in July 1975, Biya was appointed to it and remained in that office until he became president. He was thus one of Ahidjo's closest collaborators during a period of 15 years.

Considered to be tolerant and moderate in his outlook, Biya nevertheless possessed determination, as was shown during the brief crisis in his relations with his predecessor in the summer of 1983. He also had a reputation for integrity and a capacity for hard work. Most popular in the south of the country, where his roots were, he was nonetheless respected in the north, where support for Ahidjo had been strongest. (PHILIPPE DECRAENE)

Block, John R(usling)

When John Block became U.S. secretary of agriculture in 1981, his major goals were to give the nation a healthy farm economy by expanding exports and to get the government out of the farmer's business by cutting the number and size of costly federal farm support programs. But events combined to frustrate most of Secretary Block's intentions. After three years in office he was confronted with a sickly farm economy, the continuation of most government support programs, angry farmers, and hostile farm-belt politicians.

Recession, drought, foreign competition, crop surpluses, and large equipment loans resulted in an economic disaster for many farmers. While the 1983 growing season produced some bumper crops, drought in the South and Midwest destroyed corn, rice, and soybeans. Farm income declined, and agriculture lagged behind the rest of the country's economic recovery.

The power of the farm lobby in Congress thwarted Block's efforts to reduce the estimated $23 billion annual cost of farm support programs, and budget cuts hampered the delivery of disaster relief on the scale demanded by political leaders in regions hit hardest by the drought and depressed agricultural conditions.

Democrats and some Republicans criticized Block for tightening the eligibility rules covering the controversial food stamp program. In a highly publicized demonstration, Block and his family lived for a week on a $58 food-stamp allotment to show that with careful shopping it could provide proper nutrition. Congress responded with a resolution against any further cuts in the food-stamp level.

Block was born on Feb. 15, 1935, in Galesburg, Ill., near his father's farm. He studied agriculture in high school but then attended the U.S. Military Academy, where he was graduated in 1957. After three years' service in the 101st Airborne Division he returned to the family farm as his father's partner. By 1980 his management had increased the size of the farm from 300 ac to 3,000 (120 to 1,200 ha) and its annual production from 200 pigs to 6,000. From 1977 to 1981 he served as the director of the Illinois Department of Agriculture. (HAL BRUNO)

Bolkiah Mu'izzadin Waddaulah, Sir Muda Hassanal

For Sir Muda Hassanal Bolkiah, sultan of Brunei, 1983 marked above all the achievement of political independence after Brunei's 95 years as a British protectorate. The British formally pulled out of the tiny, oil-rich territory on December 31, but the sultan declared February 23 as official independence day. Though he expressed a wish for continued friendly relations with Britain, there were some bumps in 1983. Hassanal Bolkiah wanted to keep Britain's 900-strong Gurkha force in Brunei under his control after independence, but London was hesitant. After inconclusive talks, Brunei transferred the management of its massive £3,000 million investment portfolio from Britain's crown agents to the independent Brunei Investment Agency under U.S. advice. By September, however, word was out that London would permit one battalion of Gurkhas to stay on under British control in Brunei for an unspecified period, and the sultan was reportedly reconsidering the question of the investment portfolio.

Muda Hassanal Bolkiah was born on July 15, 1946, the eldest son of Sultan Sir Muda Omar Ali Saifuddin. His early education was private; later, he attended the Victoria Institute in Kuala Lumpur, Malaysia, and the Royal Military Academy at Sandhurst, England. He was named crown prince and heir apparent by his father in 1961 and in 1967, at the age of 21, he became sultan when Sir Omar abdicated. For the next decade, however, Hassanal's father remained the power behind the throne as the young ruler occupied himself less with affairs of state than with polo, fast cars, and pleasure trips overseas, predilections that raised eyebrows in conservative circles in mostly Muslim Brunei. After the death in 1979 of Hassanal's influential mother, however, his father withdrew into the background and the sultan quickly took a dominant role in Brunei's administration. In recent years, Hassanal made frequent trips into the kampongs (villages) to listen to his subjects as well as to fortify his own image as their ruler. In preparation for political independence, he initiated priority programs aimed at creating a viable bureaucracy, phasing out British expatriates in the civil service and replacing them with capable Bruneians, and cracking down on corruption. (THOMAS HON WING POLIN)

Borge Martínez, Tomás

As the oldest member of the Sandinista National Liberation Front (FSLN) National Directorate and the only surviving founder of the FSLN, Tomás Borge, minister of the interior in Nicaragua's Government of National Reconstruction, undoubtedly enjoyed the widest popular support of all the Sandinista leaders. He had, however, always resisted the creation of a personality cult, emphasizing instead the joint nature of the nine-member leadership. For 17 years he had fought to overthrow Anastasio Somoza Debayle's dictatorship. He suffered long periods of imprisonment and torture, and his wife was murdered by Somoza's National Guardsmen only months before the Sandinistas' final victory in July 1979.

Immediately after the overthrow of Somoza, the FSLN began to implement its program for Nicaragua's reconstruction. Borge played a prominent part in restructuring the Nicaraguan Army from the heterogeneous FSLN forces that existed at the time of the final insurrection in 1979. As minister for the interior he was quick to dismiss Sandinista police for any reported abuses of authority, being keenly aware of the damage that any such abuses could do to relations between the FSLN and the Nicaraguan people. Borge believed that the Sandinistas won an important moral victory when they decided not to execute any prisoners in 1979; it was part of their desire to create a humanist revolution. However, by 1983 the Nicaraguans were paying dearly as a consequence of that policy. Since 1979 former National Guardsmen had been mounting attacks from the Honduran border. In 1983 these raids escalated.

Following the U.S. invasion of Grenada in October, Borge's gravest worry was that Nicaragua might be next on Pres. Ronald Reagan's hit list. Hopes of defusing the Reagan administration's antagonism to the Sandinista regime faded when Borge's intended visit to the U.S. at the end of November was blocked by the U.S. Department of State's refusal of a visa.

Borge was born in 1931 in Matagalpa and was educated at the National University, Léon. In July 1961 he, together with Carlos Fonseca Amador and Silvio Mayorga—all veterans of the student struggle of the 1950s—met in Tegucigalpa, capital of Honduras, to found a national liberation movement. They drew their inspiration from Fidel Castro's revolution in Cuba and from a Nicaraguan folk hero, Gen. César Augusto Sandino, who in 1927 had organized an army of workers and peasants to drive out the U.S. Marines then occupying the country. (LESLIE CRAWFORD)

Bowie, David

If 1981 and 1982 had been the years of the Rolling Stones, with their triumphant tours of the U.S. and Britain, then 1983 was the year of the live comeback of David Bowie, a performer who might not be able quite to match Mick Jagger on stage but who could claim to have had an even greater influence on the rock scene. His triumph was all the greater when it was recalled that he had also been the outstanding artist of 1973, at which time he had apparently committed artistic suicide by announcing his retirement, breaking up his band, and killing off his stage persona, Ziggy Stardust.

In 1983 Bowie returned to the stage for his first live rock shows in five years, with a world tour that took him from Europe and Britain to the U.S. and then Japan and Australia. The tour followed the release of his most commercial album, *Let's Dance*, a confident collection of partly crooned white funk dance songs, and his appearance in the film *Merry Christmas, Mr. Lawrence.* Though not his first venture into acting, this role was unlike anything Bowie had done before, but this was what his audiences expected of him. For Bowie's contribution to pop music was his belief in style and change. While the performers of the 1960s had believed in honest self-expression and individualism, Bowie saw himself as the "cracked actor," taking on different roles, personas, and looks and discarding them when they were no longer needed.

Born David Jones in Brixton, London, Jan. 8, 1947, Bowie first started performing in the 1960s with songs that showed his theatrical bias. His first hit, "Space Oddity," in 1969, was a bizarre, haunting tale of a doomed spaceman. In the early 1970s Bowie took over from Marc Bolan as leader of the so-called glam-rock or glitter movement, wearing makeup and extraordinary clothes and leading his band, The Spiders from Mars, under the persona of Ziggy Stardust.

Leaving Ziggy and the band at the height of their success, he began another rapid series of changes, pioneering white Philadelphia soul with *Young Americans* (1975) and moving into more experimental blends of funk, crooned ballads, and electronics for albums like *Station to Station* (1976) and *Low* (1977). By now he had adopted a new persona, *The Thin White Duke.* There followed excellent and varied albums such as *Heroes* (1977) and the more direct *Scary Monsters* (1980). (ROBIN DENSELOW)

Brittan, Leon

The youngest member of the British Cabinet formed by Margaret Thatcher after the June 1983 election was Leon Brittan. Appointed home secretary at the age of 43, he was the youngest to hold that office since Winston Churchill in 1910–11. In the previous government Brittan had taken a Cabinet seat at the age of 41 as chief secretary to the Treasury. The Home Office is generally reckoned to be one of the pinnacles of power in the British system of government. It is also a destroyer of reputations, embracing as it does a wide range of responsibilities for law, police, crime prevention, immigration, community relations, and a dozen other aspects of internal affairs.

Brittan had risen fast, perhaps dangerously so. He won a reputation as a brilliant lawyer and as a capable, diligent Treasury minister who could be relied upon to master his brief. But he was not at his best in the rough and tumble of House of Commons debate on sensitive and emotional issues such as crime and punishment and race relations.

Brittan also found himself somewhat uneasily poised between the reformist tradition of the old Conservative Party and the monetarists of the new right. In economics he was a convinced monetarist; as home secretary his instincts were for humane and rational reforms, which set him apart from the simplistic prejudices of some of the Tory right wing. Nevertheless, when the Commons debated (and rejected) restoration of capital punishment, favoured by Margaret Thatcher among other Conservatives, his equivocal stance disappointed abolitionists.

Leon Brittan was born in London on Sept. 25, 1939, into an Orthodox Jewish family of Lithuanian origin; his father had come to England in 1927 after studying medicine in Berlin. Brittan was active in Conservative politics from his student days at the University of Cambridge, where he graduated in English and law at Trinity College; he was also a Henry fellow at Yale University. At Cambridge he became president of the university debating society—a route to a political career taken by many British politicians. He was called to the bar and in 1962 went into practice as a libel lawyer. After two unsuccessful attempts to enter Parliament he became member for Cleveland and Whitby in 1974. (HARFORD THOMAS)

Broderick, Matthew

Matthew Broderick's world might be considered somewhat topsy-turvy, a place where the realms of reality and fantasy have been juggled in various ways. For example, his father, the late James Broderick, made his living portraying other people—as an actor on screen and television. When Matthew himself became an actor, his first Broadway success was in portraying the boy who grew up to be the play's living author. In his second film and first major triumph, *WarGames*, he played a youth who unlocks the U.S. Defense Department's electronic codes and makes contact with the computer that is programmed to perform in place of human beings should war break out. No sooner had the film been released nationally, with successful results at the box office, than reports of actual computer break-ins began to snowball.

Born (March 21, 1963) and raised in New York City, Broderick decided to spend one year after high school trying to determine whether he had any future in acting. He studied with actress Uta Hagen at the celebrated Berghof Studio and beat his own self-imposed deadline. He won his first professional stage part as the adopted homosexual son of a drag queen in *Torch Song Trilogy*, which moved from off-off-Broadway to off-Broadway and eventually to Broadway itself (though Broderick had left the show by then).

Making the rounds of casting calls one day, he auditioned for starring roles in a movie and a play. He won both parts. The film was *Max Dugan Returns*, in which Broderick played the 15-year-old son of a widowed teacher. The play, which opened in March 1983, was *Brighton Beach Memoirs* by Neil Simon. Broderick played the adolescent Simon in the autobiographical drama. Simon later signed an autograph for Broderick that read, "I never knew I was so cute and so talented."

The young actor, praised for being able to look 15 yet bring mature acting skills to bear, told interviewers he tried not to mimic Simon. Instead, he crafted the role from the script and won a Tony award nomination for his effort. (PHILIP KOPPER)

Burgess, Anthony

The son of Joseph Wilson and Elizabeth Burgess, Anthony Burgess wrote stories and essays most frequently under his mother's maiden name. However, he wrote a book about literature under the name John Burgess Wilson, and *The End of the World News* (1983), a novel by Anthony Burgess, had a foreword attributed to John B. Wilson B.A. He also wrote music: A and B (or A and B flat) sometimes appeared on his books' covers, in musical notation. He wrote other novels under the pseudonym of Joseph Kell and once wrote, under another name, a newspaper review of a book he had written. This led to the suspicion that he was not wholly "serious." He had something in common with Graham Greene and other British writers in the Roman Catholic tradition: literary critics could not take their religion seriously and found their sense of humour and entertainment disturbingly foreign.

His book of essays, *This Man and Music* (1982), contained a long list of his musical compositions and also a chapter of autobiography, called "Biographia Musicalis."

According to this he was born in Lancashire during World War I (Feb. 25, 1917), and when his father came home from the Army he found his wife and daughter dead and the baby boy chuckling in a cot. Three years later Burgess acquired a stepmother, an Irish widow who kept a pub in Manchester. His father was a semiprofessional pianist as well as a cashier. Burgess hoped to study music at the local university; frustrated in this plan, he studied English literature instead. His books, however, were strongly influenced by musical forms.

When Burgess was 22, World War II broke out and he joined the Royal Army Medical Corps. Nine years after the war he became an education officer in Malaya and subsequently published his popular novel *Time for a Tiger* (1956), the first volume of his Malayan trilogy. Extremely prolific, he wrote a score of novels and seemed always ready to write newspaper articles and appear on television.

One of Burgess's more experimental stories, *A Clockwork Orange* (1962), was written in an imaginary language and was largely concerned with the effect of music on behaviour. His way of bringing "great men" (Beethoven, Shakespeare, Napoleon) into his fiction, while retaining a sort of working-class playfulness, made many of his literary critics uncomfortable—especially when his cleverness and knowledge were blatantly displayed, in an almost "un-English" manner. (D. A. N. JONES)

Cram, Steve

While the British public cheered on their current stars, Sebastian Coe and Steve Ovett, in the 1,500 m at the 1980 Olympic Games in Moscow, those with an eye to the future noted that a third Briton had reached that exclusive final. Steve Cram, only 19 at the time, finished eighth of the nine runners. However, he was soon to cast off the "also-ran" status. In 1982 he collected the European and Commonwealth 1,500-m titles, and he crowned his achievements in 1983 by winning the same event at the world championships in Helsinki, Fin., beating a field that included Steve Scott of the U.S., Sayid Aouita of Morocco, and Ovett.

In the tradition of many British athletes, Stephen Cram came from the northeast of England. Born Oct. 14, 1960, in Hebburn, County Durham (now Tyne and Wear), he ran for the Jarrow and Hebburn athletic club, where he was coached by Jimmy Hedley. He won the English Schools 1,500-m title in 1978 and 1979 and the European Junior 3,000-m title in 1979. While still a student in Newcastle, he won the U.K. Amateur Athletic Association 1,500-m event in three successive years (1981–83).

Cram's attitude to the sport emerged as refreshingly different. He admitted that he hated training and regretted that fear of injury restricted his participation in other sports. Comparisons with Ovett and Coe were inevitably drawn; while they had concentrated on setting world records, Cram had quietly collected many of the major titles. He claimed to shun world records, maintaining that, for him, winning the race was all-important. He did have one world-best time to his name at year's end. Set at Crystal Palace, London, in August 1982, it was for the 4 x 800-m relay, in which his co-runners were Peter Elliott, Garry Cook, and Coe.

The depth of Cram's talent was clearly evidenced by the fact that he recorded the fastest time in the world at 800 m in both 1982 and 1983, while his fastest 1,500 m, run at Brussels in August 1983, was, at 3 min 31.66 sec, just 0.3 sec slower than the world record. Toward the end of the 1983 season Cram defeated Ovett at Crystal Palace in a thrilling race that held promise of the contest that might come in the following, Olympic year. (LOUISE WATSON)

Craxi, Bettino

Sworn in on Aug. 4, 1983, as Italy's first Socialist premier, Bettino Craxi, an instinctively combative but highly professional politician, had emerged as a coming man in July 1976, when he became leader of the Socialist Party after its weak performance in general elections the previous month. Craxi took over a party divided between libertarian, Marxist, and Social Democrat factions. It was a measure of his determination that he succeeded in gradually uniting the party on a clear Social Democrat and Atlanticist platform, winning overwhelming support at the party congress in Palermo in May 1981. Craxi's policy was to present a clear message to the electorate and to give the Socialists an identity wholly distinct from that of the much larger Communist Party.

Dismissed by sections of the press as an arrogant apparatchik when he became party leader, Craxi soon managed to highlight issues and often set the terms of political debate. The Socialists' membership in four of the six coalition governments between 1979 and 1983 enabled the party to share power as a frank and critical ally. Craxi realized that the Socialists, though they obtained just under 10% of the vote for the Chamber of Deputies in the 1979 general elections, were still the third largest party in Italy. As a vital element in coalition building, they had a voice three or four times greater than their electoral weight.

CAMERA PRESS, LONDON

Craxi's decision to pull out of the Christian Democrat-led coalition in April 1983 provoked premature general elections in June, leading, in turn, to his being invited to form a government.

Bettino (christened Benedetto) Craxi was born on Feb. 24, 1934, in Milan, where his father, a Sicilian lawyer, had settled. He joined the Socialist Party in his late teens and by the age of 25 had been given the task of keeping the Socialist flag flying in the Communist stronghold of Sesto San Giovanni. He won a seat in the national Chamber of Deputies in 1968 and became one of three deputy secretaries of the Socialist Party in 1970. In private life Craxi was an admirer of Garibaldi and a collector of Garibaldiana. He found time to open a Garibaldi museum in New York City during an official visit to the U.S. as premier. (CAMPBELL PAGE)

Davis, Steve

In May 1983 Steve Davis regained the world professional snooker title that he had first held two years previously. The apparent ease with which he dispatched two former champions—Alex "Hurricane" Higgins by 16 frames to 5 in the semifinal and Cliff Thorburn (*q.v.*) by 18 to 6 in the final—left commentators asserting, once again, that Davis was in a class apart. At 25 years of age, and perhaps the U.K.'s highest paid sporting personality, he had met practically every challenge that the snooker world had to offer. During the year he widened his activities to include appearances at a Conservative Party pre-election rally and on television as a talk-show host.

Born on Aug. 22, 1957, in Plumstead, London, Davis served his snooker apprenticeship in south London and Essex workingmen's clubs. From his father he inherited an enthusiasm for the game and a perfectionist's dedication and technique, and from his mother, it was said, the "ice-cool" temperament that was to serve him so well in competition. In 1971, the year he made his first century break, his interest in snooker began to turn to commitment. When he left school at 18, his family gave him what he needed—a year to prove himself on the amateur circuit. Within months Davis had met Barry Hearn, manager of the Romford Lucania snooker halls, who was to direct his career. Hearn was later able to devote all his energies to managing a "stable" of players that included Davis, Tony Meo, and Terry Griffiths.

By 1978 Davis was competing for the England amateur team, and in midyear he turned professional. While the professional circuit took note of his play, the TV public soon became aware of this elegantly dressed young redhead, first of a new wave of young snooker stars. In just over a year, in 1981–82, he won, besides the world professional title, the Benson and Hedges Masters, the Jameson International Masters, and the Coral U.K. professional championship. Davis's image as a single-minded, nonsmoking, nondrinking professional who relaxed by playing mental chess was in many respects true, but his unsuccessful defense of the world title in 1982 added a human quality. (LOUISE WATSON)

Dean, Christopher

See TORVILL, JAYNE.

Deukmejian, (Courken) George, Jr.

Bucking the 1982 Democratic electoral tide and winning still another surprising victory in his 20-year political career, Republican George Deukmejian was inaugurated as governor of California on Jan. 3, 1983. With the odds consistently against him, Deukmejian had eked out pluralities that landed him in both state legislative houses, the attorney general's office, and, ultimately, the governor's office.

Courken George Deukmejian, Jr., was born June 6, 1928, in Menands, N.Y., to immigrant Armenian parents who stressed high morality and a serious work ethic. Deukmejian forgot neither as he worked his way through high school in Watervliet, N.Y.; Siena College in upstate New York; and St. John's University in New York City, where he received his law degree in 1952. After two years in the U.S. Army's Judge Advocate Corps in Paris he moved to California, where he began to practice law.

First elected to the California Assembly in 1962, Deukmejian moved to the state senate in 1966 and was named majority leader in 1969. Having early established himself as a Republican conservative, he campaigned against crime, the evils of big government, and collective bargaining for state employees. He was a staunch supporter of capital punishment and indeed once vainly sought to add armed robbery to the list of capital offenses. He drafted a widely praised capital punishment law to replace one invalidated by the U.S. Supreme Court.

In the 1970 Republican primary election Deukmejian ran for attorney general and lost. But in 1978 he was nominated for that office and won the general election with about 53% of the vote, again stressing anti-crime legislation and support for the death penalty. Once elected, he scrutinized subordinates' cases to be certain his policies were not being violated. He created a special division to investigate and prosecute organized crime and narcotics dealers. He successfully urged on the legislature a bill to lengthen criminal sentences, and he sharply criticized members of the judiciary whom he considered soft on crime, notably including the state's chief justice, Rose Bird.

Deukmejian announced his decision to run for governor in December 1981. He defeated another conservative, Lieut. Gov. Mike Curb, in the June 1982 primary and in the general election went on to defeat, by a slim margin, Los Angeles Mayor Tom Bradley. Restoration of fiscal solvency through cuts in spending rather than tax increases was promised in his inaugural address. Most of this was accomplished in the first major piece of legislation he pushed through the Democrat-controlled legislature. (BONNIE OBERMAN)

Dole, Elizabeth Hanford

The appointment in early 1983 of Elizabeth Dole as secretary of transportation continued her steady rise in important and influential U.S. government positions. The first female head of a Cabinet department in the administration of Pres. Ronald Reagan, Mrs. Dole enjoyed an admirable reputation in Washington, where she had served under five presidents, beginning with Lyndon Johnson. Her interests and expertise

WIDE WORLD

range from education issues and trade regulation to consumer affairs.

Elizabeth Hanford was born July 29, 1936, in Salisbury, N.C. A diligent student throughout her school career, she graduated from Duke University with honours in political science and a Phi Beta Kappa key. She did postgraduate work at the University of Oxford in 1959 and the following year received a master's degree in education at Harvard University. Realizing she wanted a government career, she went on to study law at Harvard, one of 15 women in a class of 550. After obtaining her degree in 1965, she moved to Washington, D.C.

Her first government appointment came in 1966 when she was made a staff assistant to the secretary of the former Department of Health, Education, and Welfare. From 1969 to 1971 she served as executive director of the President's Commission on Consumer Interests. In 1973 Pres. Richard Nixon appointed her to a seven-year term on the five-member Federal Trade Commission. One year earlier, when advocating inclusion of a consumer plank in the Republican Party platform, she presented her arguments to Sen. Robert Dole of Kansas, then chairman of the Republican National Committee. They began seeing each other regularly in 1974 and were married one year later.

In 1976 Mrs. Dole took a leave of absence from her FTC post to campaign for her husband, who was Pres. Gerald Ford's vice-presidential running mate. Three years later, when Senator Dole was seeking the presidency, she resigned from the commission. After her husband withdrew, she went to work in Ronald Reagan's campaign organization. On Dec. 20, 1980, President-elect Reagan appointed her to a key White House post, assistant to the president for public liaison. Although her eventual Cabinet appointment came amid criticism from women's groups that she was not vocal enough regarding women's rights, she was loudly praised by Congress and the press and was confirmed by the Senate on February 1. (BONNIE OBERMAN)

Fielding, Joy

When Joy Fielding wrote her first novel, her ambition was to write a book that would be listed as number one on the *New York Times* best-seller list. Although *The Best of Friends* (1972) did not earn that honour for her, *Kiss Mommy Goodbye* (1981) did appear on the Canadian best-seller list of the *Toronto Star*. *Kiss Mommy Goodbye* launched Fielding's career; it was a Doubleday Book Club alternate and a Literary Guild alternate. Sam Goldwyn bought the film rights and asked Fielding to write the script. While one reviewer declared that in her work Joy Fielding was "skillful in portraying the human psyche," others asserted that she specialized in domestic drama and wrote "potboilers" and "beauty-parlour books." Fielding herself considered her books to be novels for today's women, well written and, in general, "good reads." Her novels dealt with contemporary issues and events. *Kiss Mommy Goodbye* was a novel about kidnapping children; *The Other Woman* (1983) concerned divorce. Her two suspense novels had plots based on recent events: *The Transformation* (1976) was based on the Charles Manson slayings, and *Trance* (1978), on the Patty Hearst ordeal.

Fielding was born Joy Tepperman on March 18, 1945, in Toronto. She obtained a B.A. in English from the University of Toronto in 1966. While a university student, she acted in campus productions and gained minor roles in Shakespeare Festival productions at Stratford, Ont. After graduation she went to Hollywood to make a career in acting. In her two years there, however, her credits included only an appearance on the television series "Gunsmoke." Returning to Toronto, she taught school and acted in television commercials.

Fielding then decided to write. From a list of authors, she chose the pen name of Fielding, after Henry Fielding. She wrote two plays that were produced by the Canadian Broadcasting Corporation: *Drifters* and *Open House* (1970–71). Because she found that she could be in control of characters and could manipulate people and events in novels, Fielding found satisfaction in writing fiction. Her first novel was written at her parents' kitchen table in five weeks. As the wife of a Toronto corporation lawyer (whom she married on Jan. 11, 1974), Fielding wrote her subsequent novels at her own kitchen table. (DIANE LOIS WAY)

Foster, Norman Robert

In 1983 Foster, at age 47, became the youngest recipient in 135 years of the Royal Gold Medal awarded by the Royal Institute of British Architects (RIBA). Foster was one of the two leading British exponents of "high tech," a style of architecture that draws on aerospace and electronics for its aesthetic inspiration, valuing the precise detail and hard-edge functionalism of the aircraft hangar and factory. Yet Foster's architecture relied equally on a classical, traditional proportion and harmony. His buildings were sleek, cool, and neat, with uncluttered exteriors, often of aluminum or glass, and clearly modulated interiors. He paid meticulous attention to detail and was considered an acute and skillful businessman, able to adhere to budgets and schedules, as well as being a brilliant designer.

Foster was born in Reddish, England, on June 1, 1935, and studied architecture and town planning at the University of Manchester. In 1962 he won a scholarship to Yale University School of Architecture, where he was to become friends with another leading high tech architect of his generation, Richard Rogers. In 1963 Foster and his wife along with Rogers and George Wolton formed Team 4 Architects in England. Their Reliance Controls factory in Swindon won the first (1967) *Financial Times* award for industrial buildings and was one of the first to draw upon the aesthetic of the factory shed. Foster and Rogers parted in 1967; subsequently Foster and his wife practiced as Foster Associates, establishing a reputation for efficiency and design excellence and collaborating on various projects with Buckminster Fuller (*see* OBITUARIES).

Important commercial commissions followed, including an office for IBM at Cosham, near Portsmouth (1970), the Sainsbury Centre for the Visual Arts at the University of East Anglia, Norwich (1977), and a new headquarters at Ipswich for insurance brokers Willis, Faber and Dumas (1979). The Willis Faber building featured a sleekly curved bronzed glass facade, making imaginative use of a tricky site. The Sainsbury Centre allowed works of art to be displayed and stored without air-conditioning by making clever use of natural ventilation. Important works in progress included the skyscraper headquarters in Hong Kong for the Hong Kong and Shanghai Banking Corporation and the new Radio Centre for the British Broadcasting Corporation on a prominent London site.

(SANDRA MILLIKIN)

Gardner, David Pierpont

"Our nation is at risk," the National Commission on Excellence in Education told the U.S. in April 1983. "For the first time in the history of our country, the educational skills of one generation will not surpass, will not equal, will not even approach those of the parents. . . . The educational foundations of our society are presently being eroded by a rising tide of mediocrity. If an unfriendly foreign power had attempted to impose on America the mediocre educational performance that exists today, we might well have viewed it as an act of war. We have, in effect, been committing an act of unthinking unilateral educational disarmament."

Americans had long had qualms about their educational system, but the commission's report, titled *A Nation at Risk*, touched off a frenzy of breast-beating unmatched since the Soviets beat the U.S. into space in 1957 and called U.S. technological superiority into question. (*See* EDUCATION.) The scathing indictment was given added weight by the commission's prestige. Appointed by Secretary of Education Terrel Bell, the 18-members included a chairman emeritus of Bell Labs, a Nobel laureate, a "teacher of the year," and the president of Yale. Chairing the group was the president of the University of Utah, David Gardner.

That Gardner was willing to take on difficult tasks was indicated earlier in the year, when he accepted a bid to become president of the nine-campus University of California, considered by many to be the best public university system in the U.S. but beset by declining state aid and a need to modernize, especially in the areas of science and technology. He was no stranger to California, having been born in Berkeley on March 24, 1933. A Mormon, he did his undergraduate work at Brigham Young University before returning to Berkeley for his master's and doctor's degrees. He was assistant chancellor (1966–69) and vice-chancellor (1969–71) of the University of California at Santa Barbara during a period of student unrest and served as vice-president of the University of California System before taking on the presidency of the University of Utah in 1973. His accomplishments in improving that institution, both academically and financially, were among the credentials he brought to the National Commission.

(PHILIP KOPPER)

Gielgud, Sir (Arthur) John

The year began auspiciously for one of Britain's premier theatrical knights when Sir John Gielgud, at a public dinner in January 1983, received the *Standard* Special Drama Award—the fourth member of his profession to be so honoured—for services to the British theatre. It was handed to him by his friend and fellow actor Sir Ralph Richardson (*see* OBITUARIES), whom he had first met in 1930 on the stage of the Old Vic Theatre, where he himself had made his London debut in 1921 as the Herald in *Henry V*. In 1983, too, the famous 165-year-old Old Vic on London's South Bank was reopened after two years of refurbishing. It was there that Gielgud had cut his teeth on the works of Shakespeare, Congreve, and Chekhov, among many others, and acted the role of Hamlet that he was to play in one version or another over 500 times.

Ironically, Gielgud had said goodbye to the living theatre after appearing for the last time on the stage in the flesh in *Half-Life*, first at the National Theatre, then in the West End, and finally in Canada, in 1977. After 60 years as an internationally applauded theatre director and stage star—his one-man show *The Ages of Man* toured the world several times in the 20 years before his retirement—he devoted the years after 1977 to films, television, and radio.

Gielgud won an Oscar for best supporting actor as Dudley Moore's butler in *Arthur* (1981), and his most recent film appearance was as an elderly punk in *Scandalous*. On television he appeared in the series "Brideshead Revisited." In October 1983 he unveiled the BBC's new "Val Gielgud" Radio Drama Studio, named after his late brother Val, head of the BBC radio drama section from 1929 to 1963, and himself starred in a recording of Rhys Adrian's *Passing Time* there.

The scion of two notable acting families, one of them of Lithuanian descent, Gielgud was born in London on April 14, 1904, to a stockbroker father and the actress Kate Terry-Lewis. After attending Westminster School, he studied at the Royal Academy of Dramatic Art. In 1932 he made his film debut (in *The Good Companions*) and his stage directing debut (*Richard of Bordeaux*, in which he played the title role). Gielgud was knighted in 1953 and made a Companion of Honour in 1977. He wrote several books on the theatre and an autobiography, *An Actor and His Time* (1979; with John Miller and John Powell).

(OSSIA TRILLING)

Gowrie, Alexander Patric Greysteil Hore-Ruthven, 2nd Earl of

Like many British aristocrats who inherited a seat in Parliament in the House of Lords, Lord Gowrie chose to make politics his profession. After ten years as a politically active member of the Conservative Party in the Lords, he was at the age of 43 appointed minister for the arts in Margaret Thatcher's second government, formed in June 1983. The appointment fitted his interests and his style of life. He could be variously described as an aesthete, intellectual, poet, university lecturer in literature (at Harvard, among other places, where he was a friend of the poet Robert Lowell), London art dealer, and authority on modern painting. It was at Harvard in the late 1960s that he became seriously interested in politics, and in the early 1970s he began to take up some junior political posts in the Lords.

Gowrie shared the Thatcherite monetarist view of economics, and for that reason rather than his knowledge of the arts he qualified in Margaret Thatcher's terms as "one of us." He took over his post as minister of the arts at a time when the budget for support of the arts was under pressure as a target for spending cuts. Gowrie was ready to be critical of wasteful expenditure. But by the end of 1983 he had secured a rise in the Arts Council budget with the aid of a report that pointed out that several of the U.K.'s major arts companies were seriously underfunded. Gowrie was anxious not to be thought a political dilettante interested only in the arts, and for this reason he took on responsibilities as head of the Management and Personnel office charged with promoting economy and efficiency in the civil service. On this he was to report directly to the prime minister.

Born on Nov. 26, 1939, Lord Gowrie grew up in an Anglo-Irish Protestant family in the far west of Ireland in County Donegal. His education was typically English upper class: Eton and Balliol College, Oxford. After graduation he served as visiting lecturer (1963–64) at the State University of New York, Buffalo, then as a tutor (1965–68) at Harvard and lecturer in English and American literature (1969–72) at University College, London. In 1971–72 he was a Conservative whip in the House of Lords, then a lord in waiting, or government whip (1972–74), opposition spokesman on economic affairs (1974–79), and minister of state in the Department of Employment (1979–81).

(HARFORD THOMAS)

Hart, Evelyn

Lyricism, liquidity of movement, musicality, and polished ease described the artistry of prima ballerina Evelyn Hart of the Royal Winnipeg Ballet. A principal dancer since 1979 in Canada's oldest classical ballet company, Hart performed her first major classical role in 1981 in a new production of *Romeo and Juliet*, staged by choreographer Rudi van Dantzig for the Royal Winnipeg Ballet. Lean and long-limbed at 5 ft 4 in and 98 lb, Hart had the ability to draw out her movements to fill the music. She was compared to the great Soviet ballerina Galina Ulanova.

Hart first came to international attention in 1980 when she and her partner David Peregrine (also of the Royal Winnipeg Ballet) won the bronze medal at the World Ballet Concours in Osaka, Japan. Later in 1980 Hart and Peregrine competed at the tenth International Ballet Competition in Varna, Bulg. There Hart won both the gold medal for best female dancer and the Exceptional Artistic Achievement Award for her exquisite dancing in the pas de deux from *Giselle* and in the premiere of Norbert Vesak's pas de deux *Belong*. *Belong*, which won the choreographic award for Vesak, became Hart's trademark.

Born in Toronto on April 4, 1956, Hart spent her early life in Peterborough, Ont. When she was ten years old, she saw the National Ballet of Canada's production of *Romeo and Juliet* on television and soon afterward decided to become a dancer. She began regular ballet lessons when she was 14 and won a scholarship to the National Ballet School in Toronto. Lacking confidence to compete with her more experienced classmates, she quit after three months. At age 17 she was accepted by the Royal Winnipeg Ballet's Professional School, where she was coached by David Moroni. At this school Hart earned the nickname "the Wild One" because of her impatience to make up for her lost years. She joined the ballet company in 1976, was promoted to soloist in 1978, and became principal dancer in 1979.

Hart wanted to become a highly accomplished dancer like Marcia Haydee of Stuttgart or the Royal Ballet's Dame Margot Fonteyn and, like them, to be known as the best interpreter of one or two roles.

(DIANE LOIS WAY)

Hawke, Robert James Lee

In 1983 Bob Hawke achieved his life's ambition: to be prime minister of Australia. That came about after the Australian Labor Party (ALP) defeated the Liberal-National Party government in the March federal election. The ALP's victory was the result of miscalculations by the incumbent prime minister, Malcolm Fraser, who expected, when he sought an early election, to run against his old adversary Bill Hayden, parliamentary leader of the ALP from 1977. However, as soon as the ALP knew that an election was in the wind, Hayden was dropped as leader and replaced by the more charismatic Hawke, whose flamboyant, distinctively "Australian" personality exerted a powerful appeal.

CAMERA PRESS, LONDON

Hawke fought a brilliant campaign, projecting an image of peacemaker in a divided society. After the election he called a conference of business, labour, political, and sectional interests in order to draft a new economic policy based on consensus. The conference was an immediate success and formed the basis for a smooth transition to power for the ALP. Meanwhile, Hawke made his mark on the international scene with an overseas tour that took him to London and Washington.

Hawke was not so lucky on all occasions, however. He drew criticism for his handling of a breach of national security involving the expulsion of a Soviet diplomat, a royal commission inquiry concerning a former ALP federal secretary, and the resignation of a minister. Hawke's pro-development stand on uranium mining was criticized from within his party, though it was eventually approved by a comfortable majority. Any damage to his image from the security scandal was quickly repaired by his televised appearance at celebrations of Australia's winning of the America's Cup.

Born in Bordertown, South Australia, on Dec. 9, 1929, Hawke was the son of a Congregationalist minister and his schoolteacher wife. After graduating in law and economics at the University of Western Australia, two years as a Rhodes scholar at the University of Oxford, and a period of research at the Australian National University, Canberra, he seemed set for an academic career. Instead, he joined the Australian Council of Trade Unions (ACTU), gained a reputation as a negotiator of wage settlements, and eventually became president (1970–80) of the ACTU. He also became president (1973–78) of the ALP, which he had joined as a student. In 1980 he was elected to the federal Parliament.

(A. R. G. GRIFFITHS)

Henning, Doug

At the age of seven Doug Henning began making magic after being captivated by a television magician. His parents encouraged these parlour tricks as a cure for Henning's excessive shyness. Soon he was performing at birthday parties in his hometown of Fort Garry, Man., and by his 17th year he was featured in a Barbados nightclub. His pilot father died in a plane crash when Henning was in college; he worked the rest of his way through McMaster University, Hamilton, Ont., doing "illusions" and then decided "to give magic a whirl" before entering medical school. The whirl went on longer than knotted scarfs pulled out of a silk hat. Now 35, he was still at it in 1983 with a mesmerizing television special once a year and occasional appearances on Broadway. One, *The Magic Show*, ran for nearly five years in the 1970s.

Recently and most spectacularly, Henning starred in 1983 in a Broadway extravaganza called *Merlin*, which cost $4 million to produce and had to bring in $275,000 a week to break even. Embellished with song and dance, the thin plot involved the discovery of young King Arthur despite the carryings-on of a wicked queen played by Chita Rivera. But she was no more the star of the show than was the ballerina who played a unicorn or Henning in the title role. The stars were Henning's spectacular illusions. Critics reported that many of them had not been seen since the days of Houdini and Blackstone. Even fellow magicians gasped at Merlin's entrance in a five-inch bubble that mysteriously expanded to life-size before the wizard emerged. Other illusions were no less astonishing. On centre stage, Debby (Henning's wife and supporting performer) instantaneously vanished. Henning, as Merlin, flew through the air, turned upside down and sideways, and floated under an arch. As the audience watched, Merlin disappeared, leaving only his costume behind.

Eschewing the term tricks, Henning describes his performances as "illusions" or "illusory magic," for which he prepares with the mind-centring techniques of Transcendental Meditation. Aided by a deepening ability to concentrate, he envisions going beyond illusion into what he calls "real magic," a brew of telepathy, psychokinesis, and clairvoyance. "My goal is to be enlightened so that my mind can ultimately control the laws of nature. I hope to do real magic; I believe I'm very close to it."

(PHILIP KOPPER)

Hermannsson, Steingrímur

When Iceland's right-of-centre government coalition of the Independence Party and the Progressive Party came into office on May 27, 1983, the larger Independence Party demanded and got six out of ten ministries in the Cabinet. The office of prime minister was accorded to the Progressives in compensation and was filled by their party leader, Steingrímur Hermannsson. An electrical engineer by training, Hermannsson had been a politician for a number of years and the chairman of the Progressive Party since 1979.

The new prime minister was considered to be a middle-of-the-road politician. This had enabled him and his party to form coalitions both with the leftist anti-U.S. Peoples' Alliance at one time and with the right-of-centre and pro-U.S. Independence Party at other times, with equal ideological ease. The Progressive Party had its main support in rural areas and confined its interests mostly to farmer-related issues, such as agricultural subsidies and farmers' cooperatives. In international affairs Hermannsson and his party had for years been pro-NATO, but they had at times made moves to go along with left-wing parties to press for the withdrawal of the U.S. base in Iceland. In recent years they had abandoned this position and instead sided with the Independence Party as firm supporters of NATO and the U.S. military presence in the country.

Born June 22, 1928, Hermannsson studied electrical engineering at the Illinois Institute of Technology in Chicago and at the California Institute of Technology in Pasadena, where he gained his master's degree. After some years in industry, he became director in 1957 of Iceland's National Research Council, retaining that post until 1978, when he entered the government. He then served successively as minister of justice, ecclesiastical affairs, and agriculture (1978–79) and of fisheries and communications (1980–83). Hermannsson benefited politically from a dynamic personality and boyish good looks. He was a keen skier who liked to get away every year to continental Europe for a short skiing holiday.

(BJÖRN MATTHÍASSON)

Herzog, Chaim

Elected president of Israel on March 22, 1983, and sworn in on May 5, Chaim Herzog (Vivian to his friends) was a man of varied talents and experience—a soldier, diplomat, writer, and broadcaster. The son of a former chief rabbi of Ireland and of Israel, he was also a man of considerable personal charm, highly articulate in Hebrew and in English (with an Irish brogue). More could scarcely be asked of any presidential candidate, and in the election Herzog, candidate of the opposition Labour Alignment, easily defeated the government coalition's choice.

Herzog was born in Belfast on Sept. 17, 1918, in the midst of the Irish turmoil that led to civil war. After spending some time at the yeshiva at Hebron in Palestine in 1935, he graduated in law at the University of Cambridge and was called to the bar by Lincoln's Inn, London. He served with the British Army in northwestern Europe in World War II before returning to Palestine. In 1948 he was appointed director of military intelligence, a post that later qualified him for the task of defense attaché at Israel's embassy in the U.S. and later in Canada. In 1954 Herzog was posted as military commander of the Jerusalem district. He remained there until 1959 and after holding a variety of other staff appointments was again named director of military intelligence (1959–62).

Herzog's broadcasts as military commentator during the Six-Day War in 1967 achieved world renown, and he was appointed as the first Israeli military governor of the West Bank after the conquest of Jerusalem. Like his brother-in-law, former foreign minister Abba Eban, he became an outstanding and popular ambassador at the UN, where he remained from 1975 until 1978. These were difficult years for an Israeli representative at a time when Arab, third world, and Soviet bloc attacks on Israel occurred frequently.

Herzog returned to Israel in 1978 to resume his law practice and his broadcasts, which showed again, during the war in Lebanon, that he made his own judgments and did not accept the opposition's criticism of the war. As president his diplomatic skill helped him to gauge how far he could go without offending either the government or the constituency that elected him. On his official visit to the U.S., in his meeting with Pres. Ronald Reagan and in his address to the UN General Assembly, he demonstrated that his independence of mind was not confined by the trappings of officialdom.

(JON KIMCHE)

Hope, Bob

For his 80th birthday *Time* magazine devoted its entire "People" page to him, and NBC televised a three-hour "party" staged at the Kennedy Center in Washington, D.C. They were honouring Bob Hope, a man who could well be described as "America's national comedian."

He had long since won four special motion-picture Oscars, a television Emmy, and distinguished service awards from every branch of the armed forces for his more than 40 USO-sponsored Christmas tours to entertain U.S. troops. An honorary Commander of the Order of the British Empire, Hope had received a People to People Award from Pres. Dwight Eisenhower, the Congressional Gold Medal from Pres. John F. Kennedy, and the Medal of Freedom from Pres. Lyndon Johnson. Pres. Ronald Reagan was his straight man at the Kennedy Center event, which doubled as a benefit for the USO. "I love it when you call me kid," quipped Reagan. "Can I call you Pops?"

"Only in America," said Hope, "can an ex-hoofer from Cleveland be sitting next to an ex-disc jockey from Iowa—in the Presidential box." He was born Leslie Townes Hope on May 29, 1903, in Eltham, England. His father, a stonemason, and his mother, a Welsh choral singer, immigrated to the U.S. four years later, settling in Cleveland, Ohio. Young Hope won prizes for his Charlie Chaplin imitation and gave tap dancing lessons after the regular teacher moved to Hollywood. As "Packy East" he tried semiprofessional boxing but gave it up after finishing fourth in a tournament. He entered vaudeville as part of a two-man curtain raiser when Roscoe ("Fatty") Arbuckle's tour reached Cleveland, then went on the road to share billing with a Siamese-twin act. Auditioned in New York City by Kate Smith and Ruby Keeler, Hope made his Broadway debut in *The Sidewalks of New York* in 1927. During the next decade on stage he appeared with Fay Templeton, Sydney Greenstreet, Ethel Merman, Jimmy Durante, and Fanny Brice. A radio star as well, he went to Hollywood in 1938 to film a pastiche of radio shows called *The Big Broadcast of 1938*. It was in this movie that he sang "Thanks for the Memory," which became his theme song.

Two years later, with Bing Crosby and Dorothy Lamour, he made *The Road to Singapore*, the first of the famous six-film "Road" series. As of 1983 Hope admitted to having starred in 53 movies and to having won 42 honorary degrees (including a Doctor of Humane Humor) along with one high-school diploma. He also has eight books of light memoirs to his credit, and the list of his television appearances and benefit shows could fill another volume.

(PHILIP KOPPER)

Howe, Sir (Richard Edward) Geoffrey

In Margaret Thatcher's first government, Britain's chancellor of the Exchequer was Sir Geoffrey Howe. When the government was reorganized after the election of June 1983, Howe became secretary of state for foreign affairs. The switch was in effect a promotion as well as a change. As chancellor of the Exchequer he had been one of Thatcher's closest supporters in pressing through the readjustment of the British economy in accordance with monetarist policies.

Howe had been a Conservative spokesman on financial and economic affairs while in opposition for four years during the 1974–79 period of Labour government. Before that he had been one of the principal law ministers and then one of the trade ministers. This path might not have been expected to lead him to the Foreign Office, but as chancellor he found himself increasingly involved in international negotiations on economic affairs, at economic summits of the world's leading finance ministers, at the International Monetary Fund, and in the European Communities.

Howe therefore brought to British foreign policy a strong and to some extent new economic perspective at a time when the unsettled state of the world economy was a major cause of international disagreement and even a threat to peace. In his early months at the Foreign Office he stressed the urgency of finding more stable financial systems to enable world recovery to get under way. A testing time for Howe came in the aftermath of the U.S. invasion of Grenada, which many Conservative backbenchers thought Britain should have supported. It fell to him to support Thatcher's condemnation of the U.S. action and propose a role for Britain in the restoration of democracy in Grenada.

Born on Dec. 20, 1926, at Port Talbot, Glamorgan, Wales, Howe attended Winchester College, then took a law degree at Trinity Hall, University of Cambridge, and was called to the bar in 1952. During his 20s he was one of the founders of the Bow Group, an unofficial think tank of young liberal-minded Conservatives that became influential in the party's political debates. Not so ideological as some of the monetarist zealots, he chose to deliver a lecture to a Conservative audience in 1982 under the title "Agenda for Liberal Conservatism." Howe was in character during his first months as foreign secretary when he did not join in the East-West exchange of accusations and counteraccusations that was labeled "megaphone diplomacy."

(HARFORD THOMAS)

Hoxha, Enver

In 1983 Enver Hoxha, leader of Europe's poorest and most politically isolated country, celebrated his 75th birthday and the 40th anniversary of his election as first secretary of the Albanian (Communist) Party of Labour. It was Hoxha's boast that under his leadership Albania had become the only authentic Marxist-Leninist and atheist nation; he denounced the Soviet Union, China, and Yugoslavia for their deviations from Marxism. Ironically, this skillful and cynical politician, who had maintained his supremacy by the ruthless elimination of rivals, had closer educational links with the West than any other Communist leader.

Enver Hoxha was born on Oct. 16, 1908, at Gjirokastër near the Greek border, the son of middle-class Muslim parents. After secondary education at the French school at Korce, in 1930 he went on a state scholarship to the University of Montpellier, France. When the scholarship was discontinued, he went to Paris, where he came into contact with French Communists. He was then employed in a secretarial capacity by the Albanian consul in Brussels and at the same time studied law at Brussels University. Returning to Albania in 1936, he became a teacher at his old school in Korce. In 1939, when Italy invaded Albania, he was dismissed for refusing to join the newly formed Albanian Fascist Party and opened a retail tobacco store at Tirana which became a Communist cell. After Germany and Italy partitioned Yugoslavia in April 1941, Hoxha on November 8 formed the Albanian Party of Labour. In 1943 he was elected secretary-general of its Central Committee by the first party congress.

After World War II Albania became a Communist republic under Yugoslav protection. Resenting this tutelage, Hoxha exploited the enmity between Joseph Stalin and Tito to break with Yugoslavia in 1948. A visit by Soviet leader Nikita Khrushchev to Albania in 1959 resulted in a reaffirmation of Albania's allegiance to the Soviet bloc. But after 1960 Albanian-Soviet relations deteriorated, and by December 1961 all contacts had ceased. Meanwhile, ties with Maoist China were strengthened.

For Hoxha, the bond with China was an effective economic aid and a means of irritating Moscow. But the alliance was not to last. On July 7, 1977, Hoxha castigated the "three-worlds" theory invoked by the new Chinese leaders to justify better relations with the U.S. The following year China severed all economic and military ties with Albania. (K. M. SMOGORZEWSKI)

Imamura, Shohei

Shohei Imamura's film *The Ballad of Narayama* won the Golden Palm award at the 1983 Cannes Film Festival. The theme of the dark film, according to the Japanese director, is this: "To live is to die, and to die is to live." Enigmatic as it sounds, the message is not all that obscure once the story unfolds. The film is set in a mountain village whose inhabitants, when they reach the age of 70, must by tradition ascend the slopes of Narayama to die so that scarce food can be conserved for younger people in the impoverished village. An elderly woman does not want to make the journey but her son, despite intense anguish, must carry her to certain death. During the film's final 35 minutes there is no dialogue, for what after all is there to say? Imamura concedes that because he himself does not fully understand the underlying truths, non-Japanese may find the film difficult to comprehend. Even so, all viewers will sense Imamura's love of life that somehow emerges from the tragic tale.

Shohei Imamura was born in Tokyo on Sept. 15, 1926. After graduating from Waseda University in 1951 he followed an ancient Japanese custom and "consulted" his deceased grandfather on the choice of a career. Deciding to work in the film industry, he began as an assistant director at Ofuna studios. There he worked with Yasujiro Ozu, a prolific director whose realistic depiction of Japanese family life has perhaps never been surpassed. After three years Imamura entered Nikkatsu studios, the oldest film company in Japan, and produced his first films in 1958. He has a reputation for working slowly and carefully to capture on film what he has learned from long hours of research. When it came time to select a site for Narayama, he chose a deserted mountain in Nagano Prefecture, even though all the equipment had to be carried up the mountain on foot.

Imamura professes to see two main currents in traditional Japanese culture. One manifests itself in the tea ceremony, Kabuki, and other arts derived from the lives of the samurai. The other is revealed in the lives of ordinary people. His interest is clearly with the latter whether his subject is gangsters, a traveling group of actors, or children of poverty-stricken parents. Imamura says he plans to make three more films; then he will head for Narayama. (JOHN RODERICK)

Jackson, The Rev. Jesse

Throughout 1983 the Rev. Jesse Jackson traveled across the United States, working for black candidates and spearheading a successful campaign to increase voter registration of blacks. His appearances increasingly drew the call to "Run, Jesse, Run," so it came as no surprise when Jackson announced his intention to seek the Democratic nomination for president in 1984. Jackson's declaration was yet another step in an often controversial career. At year's end he was in Syria seeking the release of a captured black U.S. airman.

Jesse Louis Jackson was born in poverty on Oct. 8, 1941, in Greenville, N.C. He received a football scholarship to the University of Illinois, but he soon returned to the South and obtained his degree (1964) at Agricultural and Technical College of North Carolina, where he became active in the emerging civil rights movement. He studied at the Chicago Theological Seminary for two years, during which time he joined Martin Luther King, Jr.'s Southern Christian Leadership Conference (SCLC). He was later ordained a Baptist minister. Jackson's loyalty and eloquence led King to name him (1966) to head a new Chicago branch of the Atlanta-based Operation Breadbasket.

After King's assassination in 1968 Jackson gained national prominence as "mayor" of Resurrection City during the 1968 Poor People's Campaign in Washington, D.C. His flamboyant style, however, soon brought him into conflict with the SCLC leadership, and in 1971 he reorganized his Chicago office as People United to Save (later Serve) Humanity (Operation PUSH). As director of PUSH and its offshoots, Jackson developed social and economic programs in Chicago and elsewhere and campaigned for "parity" for blacks. After thousands of newly registered blacks in Chicago elected Harold Washington (*q.v.*) mayor in April 1983, Jackson focused his attention on politics.

Jackson frequently drew criticism for his tactics, his abrasive style, and his lack of follow-through; even Jackson admitted that he was more of a motivator than an administrator. While few observers believed that he could win the Democratic nomination in 1984, many feared that he would draw support away from white candidates sympathetic to black aspirations. His supporters, however, felt that his participation would raise issues of importance to minorities and influence the party's platform. It was widely agreed that as a result of his campaign for the nomination the eventual winner could hardly afford to ignore the growing political activism among U.S. blacks. (MELINDA SHEPHERD)

Jayawardene, J(unius) R(ichard)

In 1983 Sri Lanka's Pres. J. R. Jayawardene faced the most serious internal crisis since he assumed the presidency in February 1978. During the summer the long-simmering and at times violent hostility between Sri Lanka's Sinhalese and Tamil communities erupted into bloody riots in which, according to official sources, some 375 Tamils were killed – though the Tamil United Liberation Front (TULF) claimed that more than 2,000 Tamils fell victim to Sinhalese terrorism. At issue was the republic's territorial unity, for the TULF demanded a separate Tamil state within a federal framework. Jayawardene rejected this, but following talks with Indian Prime Minister Indira Gandhi in New Delhi he announced that an all-party roundtable conference would be held to seek a solution to the island's ethnic problems. (India had a special interest because of its own large Tamil community.)

As leader of the United National Party (UNP), which won a sweeping victory in the 1977 general elections, Jayawardene became prime minister in July that year. Within weeks of taking office he had to contend with an outbreak of communal conflict similar to that of 1983, though more limited in extent. Jayawardene's plan for a French-style presidential form of government was approved by Parliament in September 1977, and on Feb. 4, 1978, he became president. A new constitution promulgated in September that year maintained Sinhalese as the only official language of the Democratic Socialist Republic of Sri Lanka, although Tamil was spoken by more than one-fifth of the Sri Lankan population.

Junius Richard Jayawardene was born in Colombo on Sept. 17, 1906, the son of a Supreme Court judge. A Buddhist by religion, he took a law degree at the University of Ceylon and practiced as a barrister until 1943. In 1938 he joined the Ceylon National Congress (forerunner of the UNP), formed in 1918 to agitate for political reforms and freedom from British rule. In 1943 he was elected to the State Council. In 1948 he became minister of finance in Stephen Senanayake's UNP government, and in 1950 he was co-author of the Commonwealth aid and development scheme known as the Colombo Plan. During the next years he held several high government positions and in 1973 became party leader on the death of Dudley Senanayake, the son of Stephen. (K. M. SMOGORZEWSKI)

Jumblatt, Walid

In 1983 a prominent figure on the bloodied checkerboard of Lebanese factional conflict was Walid Jumblatt, traditional leader of the Druze people in Lebanon's Shuf Mountains. Born Aug. 7, 1947, he inherited the leadership when his father, Kamal Jumblatt, was assassinated in 1977. He also inherited his father's position as head of the Progressive Socialist Party (PSP), a mildly left-wing party founded by Kamal Jumblatt in the late 1940s. The Jumblatt residence

STEPHEN SHAMES—BLACK STAR

was at Mukhtara, where "Walid Bey" held court in traditional fashion. He was also a substantial businessman and had invested heavily in real estate in Beirut and also in development projects, including a cement plant, in the Shuf.

Before his father's death Jumblatt was best known as a playboy, constantly to be seen in nightclubs in Beirut and Paris. His interest in politics was marginal. He afterward developed into a rather remote political leader who was uneasily in alliance with the Syrians. Jumblatt's own political beliefs were moderately reformist. He favoured, as did his father, greater secularization of Lebanon. But he was also conscious of his duty to the Druze, whose control over the Shuf, once uncontested, came under increasing pressure from Maronite Christian immigrants in the 19th century.

Walid Jumblatt was also one of the leaders of the National Salvation Front, which included his PSP along with Muslim and Christian antigovernment groups in northern Lebanon. During the Lebanese peace talks in Geneva in the fall of 1983, Jumblatt achieved a degree of reconciliation with Lebanon's Pres. Amin Gemayel, but continued shelling between Druze and Lebanese Army and rightist forces after the peace conference indicated that there had been no real rapprochement.

Jumblatt's power base among his own people was strengthened immeasurably in September when his forces asserted their mastery over almost all the Shuf Mountains, mainly at the expense of their arch-rivals, the predominantly Maronite and right-wing Phalange. Although much of the weaponry for his estimated 5,000 warriors came from Syria, there were increasing contacts with Israel after Moshe Arens became the Israeli defense minister in March. (JOHN ROBERTS)

Kent, Msgr. Bruce

Msgr. Bruce Kent first hit the headlines in April 1983, when battle was joined in Britain on whether a priest should "engage in politics." General secretary of the Campaign for Nuclear Disarmament (CND) since February 1980, Kent had revived the fortunes of CND as a mass movement. His own approach to the problem of nuclear weapons was, he said, moral rather than political. But as Britain's June 1983 election approached and Kent debated with Member of Parliament Winston Churchill and Minister of Defense Michael Heseltine, it became more difficult to draw a clear distinction. Right-wing Catholics bombarded Basil Cardinal Hume of Westminster and Archbishop Bruno Heim, the papal pronuncio in London, with protests against this troublesome priest. They claimed to have Pope John Paul II on their side.

Heim agreed and remarked that the unilateralists were the unconscious dupes and "useful idiots" of the Communist Party. Hume, though a convinced multilateralist himself, took a more tolerant view, declaring that Kent had not yet overstepped the bounds. But another storm broke in November when Kent told the British Communist Party congress that "during the lean years of disarmament . . . the Society of Friends and the Communist Party were two groups who did an enormous amount to keep the flag flying." Once again, Cardinal Hume warded off right-wing criticism and repeated Kent's right to state his views, provided it was recognized that he did not express the official Roman Catholic position and CND stayed within the law.

With his rubicund cheeks and half-lenses poised on the end of his nose, Bruce Kent looked like a friendly, comfortable, cricket-playing country vicar. Born in Blackheath, London, on June 22, 1929, son of a Canadian businessman, he went to school at the Jesuit Stonyhurst College, did his military service in a tank regiment, took a law degree at Brasenose College, Oxford, and then spent six years at St. Edmund's, Ware, the Westminster seminary. Ordained in 1958, he was briefly secretary to John Cardinal Heenan—when he picked up the domestic prelature that gave him the title monsignor—and was chaplain (1967–74) to the University of London. There he was "radicalized" by his students, who involved him in various projects, including a spell as field director for War on Want in Bangladesh. This led him naturally into Pax Christi, the Roman Catholic international peace movement, and thence to CND.

(PETER HEBBLETHWAITE)

Kidder, Margot

Although Margot Kidder had performed with such leading men as Robert Redford in *The Great Waldo Pepper* (1975) and Michael Sarrazin in *The Reincarnation of Peter Proud* (1975), she became best known to motion-picture audiences as Superman's girlfriend Lois Lane in *Superman* (1978) and Superman II (1981). Her Hollywood film debut was in *Gaily, Gaily* (1969), a film based on Ben Hecht's early life as a Chicago newspaper reporter, and she followed this with *Quackser Fortune Has a Cousin in the Bronx* (1970) with Gene Wilder. After those two films Kidder went to New York City to take acting lessons, and she then used her earnings from *Quackser Fortune* to retire to a peach farm in British Columbia. Retirement did not last long, however. She was soon in Vancouver helping Robert Altman to edit *Brewster McCloud*. In 1972 she starred in "Nichols," a television series. After her marriage to novelist Tom McGuane, Kidder retired again—this time to McGuane's ranch in Montana. By 1976, however, she was working in the role of Lois Lane in *Superman*. She then starred in such films as *Willie and Phil* (1980) and *Trenchcoat* (1983).

Because her father was a mining engineer, Kidder spent her childhood in small mining communities in Canada. She was born Margaret Kidder in Yellowknife, N.W.T., on Oct. 17, 1948, and grew up in Labrador City, Que. She read widely and at age 13 received a scholarship to a private girls' school in Toronto. In school productions there she gained her first acting experience. She moved from Toronto to Vancouver, where she appeared on television in 1964. In 1965 Kidder entered a drama course at the University of British Columbia but dropped out after one year to join the touring cast of *Oliver!* For her role in the Canadian Broadcasting Corporation drama "Does Anybody Here Know Denny?" she won an Etrog Award for the most promising new acting talent.

Kidder later became interested in directing. She joined the Women's Directing Workshop of the American Film Institute in 1978. With a grant from the Institute she made her own film, *And Again*, based on Robert Penn Warren's story "A Place to Come To." (DIANE LOIS WAY)

Kim Dae Jung

For Kim Dae Jung, South Korea's best-known critic of the government, 1983 marked a new phase in his long and eventful political career. In a surprise move, South Korean Pres. Chun Doo Hwan suspended Kim's 20-year jail sentence in December 1982 and allowed him and his immediate family to go into exile in the U.S., ostensibly for medical treatment. Kim took a post as visiting fellow at Harvard University's Center for International Affairs at the start of the 1983–84 academic year.

Kim Dae Jung was born in 1924 in Korea's southwestern port of Mokpo, where his father was a shipping operator of modest means. Kim's involvement in politics began in the early 1950s, during the Korean War. When Communist troops from the North seized Mokpo, he was jailed and sentenced to death as a "reactionary." He escaped and joined the resistance, but because many of his fellow prisoners had been executed by the Communists, his survival was later attributed by some to "collaboration" with his captors. Accused of being a Communist sympathizer, Kim said many years afterward: "In my youth, I dabbled in leftist party politics but quit immediately after I found out what it was."

Before he was 40, Kim had carved out a reputation as one of South Korea's most gifted orators and charismatic politicians. A year after his surprise election as president of the Korean Democratic Party, Kim narrowly lost the 1971 national presidential election to Park Chung Hee after a vigorous campaign against corruption in Park's incumbent administration. It was during this campaign that Kim suffered a chronic hip injury in a road accident that he later described as "a clear assassination attempt."

In 1973, while Kim was in self-exile in Tokyo, he was kidnapped back to Korea by South Korean intelligence personnel. The affair, which nearly ruptured Japanese-South Korean relations, brought Kim substantial international attention for the first time. For further strident attacks on the Park government he was jailed from March 1976 to December 1978. Kim immediately became a top contender for the presidency when Park was assassinated in October 1979. But all moves toward an election were abruptly halted when Gen. Chun Doo Hwan came to power after a military coup in 1980. Kim and his supporters were arrested, and four months later he was sentenced to death, a penalty that was later commuted to life imprisonment and then to 20 years. (THOMAS HON WING POLIN)

Kinnock, Neil Gordon

After a disastrous defeat in the general election in June 1983, the British Labour Party turned to a new generation for a new leader. By a three-to-one majority, the party conference in October picked Neil Kinnock, a 41-year-old Welshman from the coal-mining valleys of South Wales, a traditional stronghold of British socialism. Kinnock took over the leadership of the official opposition in Parliament without ever having held any office in government. Whether this would prove a handicap time would show, but there was no doubt that he had prepared himself for the job.

Born on March 28, 1942, in Tredegar, Kinnock was brought up in a highly political working-class family. Married to a politically active wife whom he had met at University College, Cardiff, where he took a degree in industrial relations and history, he had made his way into the House of Commons with a safe South Wales seat by the age of 28. Turning down the chance of a junior minister's job in the Labour government of 1974–79 gave him greater freedom. In 1978 he secured a seat on the party's national executive committee, where the key policy battles then dividing the party were fought out. Meanwhile, he was establishing himself as an articulate television performer with wit and charisma and as an eloquent platform speaker in the Welsh tradition of impassioned political oratory. During the years of Margaret Thatcher's first government, he took a place in Labour's front bench team as opposition spokesman on education. Kinnock was the author of *Wales and the Common Market* (1971) and *As Nye Said* (1980) and in private life nourished a suitably Welsh addiction to male choral music and rugby football.

Kinnock stood on the left of the Labour Party, but he kept clear of the ideological feuding between left and right. This enabled him to team up with a much more experienced right-of-centre contender for the leadership, Roy Hattersley, on the so-called dream ticket, with Hattersley as deputy leader. That helped to identify him as the kind of flexible, pragmatic leader the party needed if it was to recover its unity. Opinion polls soon after Kinnock was elected recorded a substantial swing back to Labour. (HARFORD THOMAS)

Kissinger, Henry Alfred

After a hiatus of more than six years, Henry Kissinger, who had served as U.S. national security adviser and secretary of state under Presidents Richard Nixon and Gerald Ford, returned to public life when Pres. Ronald Reagan appointed him in July 1983 to head a national commission on Central America. The stated purpose of the bipartisan 12-member commission was to advise the president on a long-term U.S. policy in Central America that could win broad public support. Kissinger's admirers hailed the appointment, citing the diplomatic skills evidenced in his previous posts. His critics, however, attacked from both left and right, the former assailing his role in the Vietnam War and his inexperience in Latin America, and the latter his advocacy of East-West détente.

Kissinger's foreign policy accomplishments under Nixon were appraised harshly in Seymour Hersh's controversial book *The Price of Power*, published earlier in 1983. Hersh, an investigative reporter, marshaled evidence to depict the man popularly perceived as a great statesman as a duplicitous seeker after power. He recited Kissinger's role in the secret bombing of Cambodia (Kampuchea), the escalation of the Vietnam War, interference in Chilean affairs, and the wiretapping of his own associates. The book elicited both heated condemnation and defense of its subject.

Kissinger was born May 27, 1923, in Fürth, Germany, and was brought to the U.S. by his parents in 1938. He attended high school in New York and served in the U.S. Army in World War II. A graduate of Harvard (B.A. 1950, Ph.D. 1954), he directed studies for the Council on Foreign Relations and the Rockefeller Brothers Fund before returning to Harvard to teach in 1957. He was a consultant to defense-related government agencies under every president from Truman to Nixon, and in 1969 Nixon named Kissinger head of the National Security Council and special assistant for national security affairs. His major efforts included the development of a policy of détente with the Soviet Union, which led to the strategic arms limitation talks; resolving the Vietnam conflict; establishing contacts with China (1972); and using "shuttle diplomacy" to end the Arab-Israeli war of 1973.

Kissinger was named secretary of state in 1973, a post he continued to hold under Nixon's successor, Gerald Ford. After the election of Jimmy Carter, Kissinger became an international consultant, writer, and lecturer. (JOAN N. BOTHELL)

Kolvenbach, Peter-Hans

On Sept. 13, 1983, the 33rd General Congregation, representing the world's 26,000 Jesuits, elected Father Peter-Hans Kolvenbach as superior general and thus brought to an end a period of crisis and uncertainty. Two years earlier Pope John Paul II had blocked the attempted resignation of Kolvenbach's predecessor, Father Pedro Arrupe, and imposed on the Jesuits a "personal delegate of the pope"; his task was to restore order and discipline and, in particular, to reduce the level of political commitment of Jesuits in Latin America.

Though the media expressed surprise at Kolvenbach's election, some Jesuits had long recognized that he had the right mix of qualities. A Dutchman, he had led an international team in Beirut, Lebanon, as provincial superior (1974–81) of the vice-province of the Near East. One of his men was killed when a shell sliced through his apartment. In 1981 Father Arrupe brought Kolvenbach to Rome as rector of the Pontifical Oriental Institute, which specializes in study of the Orthodox tradition. He became a member of the official Vatican Commission for dialogue with the Orthodox churches and was put in charge of the Oriental colleges in Rome belonging to the Uniate churches—those in communion with Rome. This combination of international and Roman experience, as well as formidable linguistic skills—he spoke at least eight languages—made him a likely candidate to succeed Arrupe. But it was some more undefinable quality that led to his election on the first ballot. St. Ignatius, founder of the Jesuits, said that the general should be characterized by a "quick intelligence and a great heart."

WIDE WORLD

Kolvenbach was born near Nijmegen, Neth., on Nov. 30, 1928. He entered a Jesuit seminary 20 years later and transferred to the Near East vice-province in 1959. Ordained a priest in Beirut in 1961, he continued his linguistic studies in Paris and The Hague, Neth., before returning to Beirut to teach. Kolvenbach was the first Jesuit general belonging to an Oriental rite, the Armenian Rite (hence his beard), and the first to be elected while his predecessor was still alive (Arrupe, tactfully, did not vote). His style was low-key. After his election he renewed the team in the Jesuit curia, not because he wanted to repudiate Arrupe's policies but to have fresh minds at the top.

Kolvenbach considered that the 33rd General Congregation not only elected him but gave him his mandate. It accepted some of the papal criticisms, denouncing "one-sided secular activism" and urging greater collaboration with pope and bishops. At the same time, the Jesuits renewed their commitment to Vatican II, to social justice, and to renewal. (PETER HEBBLETHWAITE)

Koppel, Ted

The intellectual content of late evening hours in the "vast wasteland" called U.S. commercial television used to rival only the Saturday morning cartoon marathons. NBC-TV offered the long-running "Tonight" show, which made Jack Paar and then Johnny Carson famous for chitchat, while other networks typically ran old movies and local stations even older ones. In 1980 ABC-TV, traditionally the weakest network for news and cultural programming, started changing all that with an almost accidental program called "News Nightline."

It began as a brief nightly update, after the local news, on the seemingly endless story of the U.S. hostages in Iran. Soon expanding to a well-watched half hour, it threatened to remake national viewing habits as the hostage crisis reached its finale. As one wag put it, "The man most responsible for the success of 'Nightline' is the Ayatollah Khomeini. The man second most responsible is Ted Koppel."

After the hostages' release, "Nightline" remained on the air and broadened its scope to embrace virtually any subject of public interest or concern. Koppel came to be regarded as one of the best interviewers in television news. Like the "MacNeil-Lehrer Report" on public TV, "Nightline" focused on a single issue each night, but with the advantage of ABC's news organization and satellite communications. In the fall of 1983 it was expanded to an hour, but the result was sometimes thin, especially on a quiet news day. The ratings fell, and ABC announced plans to return to the half-hour format.

Born in Lancashire, England, of German parents in 1940, Koppel moved to the United States at the age of 13 and later earned degrees at Syracuse and Stanford universities. He then worked briefly for a New York City radio station and joined ABC as a general assignment reporter in 1963, the year he became a naturalized citizen of the U.S. Two years later he covered civil rights demonstrations in the South, and in 1967 he was assigned to the war in Vietnam. He served as ABC bureau chief in Miami and in Hong Kong before becoming the network's chief diplomatic correspondent throughout the 1970s. He was prominently mentioned as a successor to Frank Reynolds (*see* OBITUARIES) on the ABC evening news, the most prestigious anchor position the network could offer. But "Nightline" had become so completely his own that in the end he was considered irreplaceable in that spot.

(PHILIP KOPPER)

Kratochvilova, Jarmila

After years of finishing in silver-medal position, Jarmila Kratochvilova produced a remarkable series of winning performances at 400 m and 800 m in 1983. In Munich, West Germany, on July 26 the Czechoslovak runner backed out of a scheduled 200-m race after feeling a twinge of leg cramp and, in order to avoid the punishment of a short sprint, entered the 800 m instead. In only her third race at that distance, she set a world record of 1 min 53.28 sec. A particularly impressive aspect of this run was its even pacing; her two laps were timed at 56.28 sec and 57 sec. Just two weeks later Kratochvilova won both the 400 m and 800 m at the world championships in Helsinki. In the process she set another world-record time, 47.99 sec in the 400 m, and she went on to finish the meet with a spectacular anchor run that brought the Czechoslovak team the silver medal in the 4 x 400-m relay.

The headlines that followed her successes were less concerned with her times than with her appearance. Her extreme muscular development raised questions about her sexual identity and caused some commentators to suggest that she should not be competing in women's races. Two years earlier a West German athlete had called for a boycott of Kratochvilova's races on the grounds that she resembled a man too much. But she had the results of a chromosome test to prove that she was a woman. Her coach, Miroslav Kvac, pointed out that her muscles were due to a progressive weight-training program that was part of her punishing training schedule.

What was more unusual about Kratochvilova's career was her relatively late development as a runner. Born in Golcuv Jenikov, Czech., on Jan. 26, 1951, she did not begin running seriously until she was 16. She first became a name to be reckoned with ten years later, in 1977, when she won the 400-m European indoor title, one that she held again in 1981 and 1982. In the major outdoor contests, however, she consistently finished second to East Germany's Marita Koch. She was in that position again in the 400-m final at the 1980 Olympic Games in Moscow. Her first major victory over Koch came in 1981 in the World Cup 400 m. Koch, unable to compete because of an injury, was among the first to congratulate Kratochvilova on her successes at Helsinki.

(LOUISE WATSON)

Lang, Jack

In a country that prides itself on its civilized values, French ministers of culture have tended to project an image of polish and distinction—to seem, in a word, cultured. This was not a word, however, that entirely described the present minister, Jack Lang. Though an intellectual and something of a dandy, he was inclined to ignore protocol in matters of dress and to prefer pop music, movies, and avant-garde theatre to the monuments of French tradition. With a style closer to that of the Latin Quarter than the Louvre, he was the most visible symbol of the Socialist administration that took power in May 1981.

His predecessors may have shunned controversy in a field supposedly above politics, but Lang denounced their culture as elitist and set out to steer it in a popular and Socialist direction. From his appointment to the Cabinet on May 22, 1981, he attacked France's staid cultural institutions, relaxed the government hold on radio and television, and brought cultural life into the workplaces and the provinces.

At the same time Lang hoped to restore his country's role as a leader in world cultural life. A report commissioned by his ministry called for measures against the influx of foreign records and deplored U.S. influence on French film, television, and popular music. In December 1983 he toured Brazil as part of an attempt to revive links with Latin America. He stepped up French involvement in third-world cinema, was host to an international conference on "culture and development," and denounced U.S. "intellectual imperialism."

Born at Mirecourt (Vosges) on Sept. 2, 1939, Lang studied at the University of Nancy, where he later taught international law and wrote a thesis on the legal problems of the North Sea continental shelf. Involved in theatre from his student days, he took a leading part in launching the Nancy International Festival of Student Theatre in 1963 and directed it for the next nine years. He went on to administer the Théâtre de Chaillot, mounting a highly successful season in 1973, though he was subsequently dismissed for exceeding his budget and, allegedly, for his radical views. In 1977 he was elected a municipal councillor in Paris and dean of the faculty of law and economics at Nancy. Although he lost his Cabinet seat in March 1983, Lang remained in the government as minister-delegate for culture.

(ROBIN BUSS)

Lawson, Nigel

Prime Minister Margaret Thatcher picked Nigel Lawson, the most absolutist of the monetarists in her inner circle of favoured ministers, to take over the Treasury as chancellor of the Exchequer in the reconstruction of the Conservative government that followed the British general election of June 1983. Lawson had been in the middle ranking post of financial secretary to the Treasury for two years (1979–81), and his keen financial mind impressed those who worked with him. He then moved on to become minister of energy, giving him a place in the Cabinet. His approach to energy policy was focused mainly on plans for the selling of energy undertakings in the public sector to private enterprise.

On returning to the Treasury, Lawson took over the monetarist stance of his predecessor, Sir Geoffrey Howe (*q.v.*). It was the recipe as before—to bring down inflation by cutting back government spending and limiting public borrowing, and to reduce taxation in order to stimulate private enterprise. But Lawson, like Howe before him, found himself trapped in the contradictions of this policy. Economic recession was prolonged by monetarist constraints. This, in turn, led to persistent unemployment that increased government expenditure on unemployment relief. At the same time defense spending was rising in response to the arms race. The cumulative effect was to leave little or no room for cuts in taxation. Industrialists, usually the core of Conservative Party support, were increasingly restive at such a prospect.

The son of a London tea merchant, born on March 11, 1932, Nigel Lawson was educated at Westminster School and the University of Oxford and did his military service (1954–56) in the Royal Navy. He came into politics after making a notable reputation for himself as a financial journalist and, while still in his 30s, as editor (1966–70) of the weekly *Spectator*. But it was not until 1974, at the age of 41, that he was able to find a seat in Parliament. By 1977, however, he had won his way into Margaret Thatcher's circle of economic advisers.

(HARFORD THOMAS)

Le Carré, John

From late March of 1983 through the fall, *The Little Drummer Girl* marched at the top of the best-seller lists for hardcover fiction. Like the previous successes of author John Le Carré, *Drummer Girl* is a gripping, realistic spy novel set in a world where love and trust are warped or shattered by the struggle for advantage or revenge. It is, however, a radical departure for Le Carré in that it involves a battle between the Israeli secret service and a Palestinian terrorist instead of the usual fencing between the British and Soviet espionage establishments. It also differs in using a politically naive young woman instead of an experienced male spy as the central character.

For *Drummer Girl*, Le Carré made four trips to the Middle East, spent time in the Palestine Liberation Organization's Beirut, Lebanon, headquarters, and interviewed PLO leader Yasir Arafat and members of the Israeli intelligence community.

John Le Carré is the pseudonym of David Cornwell, born in Poole, Dorset, England, on Oct. 19, 1931, the second son of Ronnie Cornwell, a confidence man who made several fortunes, marriages, and trips to jail. David attended the Sherborne School, St. Andrew's Preparatory School, the University of Bern, Switz., and Lincoln College, Oxford, from which he was graduated in 1956 with honours in modern languages. He taught at Eton for a few years, then entered the British Foreign Service in Germany in 1959, in time for what he calls "a worm's eye view of the cold war." He was second secretary in Bonn (1960–63) and consul in Hamburg (1963–64).

He began writing to relieve the alienation he felt in his work. His first two novels, murder mysteries with spymaster George Smiley as detective, were well received by critics, but it was not until *The Spy Who Came in from the Cold* (1963) that he achieved the success that allowed him to become a full-time writer. His novels include *The Looking-Glass War* (1965), *A Small Town in Germany* (1968), *The Naive and Sentimental Lover* (1971), *Tinker, Tailor, Soldier, Spy* (1974), *The Honourable Schoolboy* (1977), and *Smiley's People* (1980). Most feature Smiley, the antithesis of Ian Fleming's dashing spy, James Bond—bookish, portly, rumpled, vague, unlucky in love. Le Carré has won numerous awards for his work, and *Tinker, Tailor* and *Smiley's People* were made into popular TV programs starring Sir Alec Guinness. (DAVID A. OATES)

Levine, James

Often described as the most powerful opera conductor in the United States, James Levine is the music director and principal conductor of the Metropolitan Opera in New York City. Having already achieved great prestige at age 39, he sought in 1983 to enhance his astonishing career by attempting to take complete artistic control of the Met. Although his current contract would not expire until 1986, he was jockeying for much of the power held by Anthony Bliss, the general manager, who would retire July 31, 1985. It was Levine's desire to have the final say on repertory, casting, conductors, and directors—indeed all that is involved in the artistic creation of the Metropolitan's operatic presentations.

Levine was born in Cincinnati, Ohio, on June 23, 1943. He was picking out tunes on the family piano before his second birthday. He began piano lessons at four and performed in recitals at age six. He made his debut with the Cincinnati Symphony Orchestra in 1953, performing Mendelssohn's Piano Concerto No. 2. Following this, and at the recommendation of the Juilliard School, he began his formal musical education with Walter Levin, the principal violinist of the LaSalle Quartet.

As much as Levine loved the piano, he was becoming enthralled with opera. He would listen incessantly, conducting and singing parts from scores. His mother bought him a miniature stage, and he put on his own productions.

In 1956, at the age of 13, Levine got his first taste of conducting, at the Marlboro Festival in Vermont. At age 18 he enrolled at Juilliard to study conducting. In 1964 Levine met George Szell, a conductor who had made his own debut at age 17 and who had made the Cleveland Symphony Orchestra into one of the nation's fine ensembles. Szell offered Levine a job, and the two men worked together for six years until Szell died in 1970.

Levine made his debut at the Metropolitan in 1971 and with the help of an agent began a swift career rise. The next year, following the retirement of the Met's general manager, Sir Rudolf Bing, and the tragic death of his successor, Göran Gentele, he became the principal conductor of the renowned company and in 1976 its music director. In 1983, in the midst of negotiating his next contract, Levine wanted all the power and was willing to take the blame for any failures or misjudgments. (BONNIE OBERMAN)

Lewis, Carl

People had compared Carl Lewis to Jesse Owens even before he seized the Athletics Congress (TAC) 1983 national track and field championship meet and ran with it. Then the figures spoke for themselves. Lewis became the first man since 1886 to win the 100-m and 200-m dashes and the long jump in a national outdoor championship, and he won them spectacularly. It was the same triple crown in individual events that Owens had won in the 1936 Olympic Games.

Lewis established two personal records at the TAC meet, held June 17–19 in Indianapolis, Ind. His long jump of 8.79 m (28 ft 10¼ in) was just short of Bob Beamon's 15-year-old record. It was the longest low-altitude jump ever made, although Lewis had to shorten his steps at the end of the runway to avoid fouling. He passed up four more allotted jumps to save energy for the 200-m, which he won in a U.S. record time of 19.75 sec, just 0.03 sec over Pietro Mennea's world record.

The 200 m was a new event for Lewis in 1983. He wanted a new challenge after winning the national 100 m and long jump two straight years. Lewis would have broken the world 200-m record at Indianapolis if he had not spread his arms aloft 10 m before the finish, a celebratory gesture of showmanship that antagonized other runners. "I have no regrets. I have fun competing," Lewis said.

Before the TAC meet Lewis had run a best 100-m time of 9.96 sec, just 0.01 sec behind Jim Hines's world record. He had set indoor records of 6.02 sec in the 60-yd dash and 8.56 m (28 ft 1 in) for the long jump. Within two months of the TAC meet and his 22nd birthday, Lewis helped set a world record of 37.86 sec in the 4 x 100-m relay at the first world track and field championships at Helsinki, Fin., where he also won the long jump and 100 m. Lewis opened his team's lead from one metre to five in an anchor leg estimated at 8.9 sec, possibly the fastest 100 m ever run.

Lewis was born on July 1, 1961, in Birmingham, Ala., the third of four athletic children of Bill and Evelyn Lewis, both professional track coaches. His sister Carol, two years younger, has been the best female long jumper in the U.S. The Lewises moved from Birmingham to the Philadelphia suburb of Willingboro, N.J., when Carl was two. He attended college at the University of Houston, where he developed his method of performing the long jump. (KEVIN M. LAMB)

Lexcen, Ben

Abandoned by his soldier-father during World War II, the child who became Ben Lexcen was left with grandparents near Sydney, Australia, and took "to going down to the dock and playing in the water. The sea became my parent." He was born Bob Miller in 1936 in Newcastle, New South Wales. As a boy he raced model boats in wading pools and then graduated to full-sized yachts. He did not attend school until he was 11 and quit at 14 to be an apprentice locomotive mechanic, racing yachts the while. He eventually abandoned railroading to become Australia's master sailmaker, designer, and builder. He found the name Lexcen by computer scan in the 1970s after leaving his name with his design firm after a fallout with his partner. Almost inevitably, perhaps, Lexcen joined forces with fellow countryman Alan Bond, who had begun his working career as a sign painter and had become a millionaire several times over.

Visiting Long Island Sound in 1970, the two Australians learned about one of the most exclusive competitions in the sporting world, the roughly quadrennial quest for the America's Cup. They had stumbled on "Valiant," a 12-m sloop under construction, and were threatened with bodily

ADAM STOLTMAN—DUOMO

harm by a crewman for going aboard uninvited. Bond took offense and told Lexcen, "I want you to design me a boat like that. I'm going to win that cup."

The America's Cup was named for a New York-built yacht that won a match race around the Isle of Wight in 1851. Subsequently it was dedicated to international competition but became the virtual property of the New York Yacht Club as U.S. entries won every competition. In an effort to change this situation, Bond spent $16 million to launch four challengers from Lexcen's drawing board, each one of them faster than the last. Finally, his "Australia II" was so different that when it was hoisted from the water after each day's practice, its hull was veiled. The yacht's secret was a radically new keel shape that enabled the boat to turn in half the normal distance and to resist heeling when sailing into the wind, thus reducing the hull's "wetted surface" and frictional drag. The keel slanted forward rather than aft and had horizontal fins like jet fighter wings.

In a thrilling series of seven races against the U.S. yacht "Liberty," skippered by Dennis Conner, "Australia II" was the winner. Though Conner won three of the first four races and needed only one more, "Australia II" prevailed and the America's Cup was surrendered. Taken to Perth's Royal Yacht Club, it was to be put up for nautical grabs in the Indian Ocean by 1987. In sum, self-taught Ben Lexcen, 47, had rethought the principles of yacht design and in so doing had taken the America's Cup away from America at last.

(PHILIP KOPPER)

Li Xiannian

UPI

Li Xiannian (Li Hsien-nien) became China's president in 1983, the first chief of state since Mao Zedong (Mao Tse-tung) purged Liu Shaoqi (Liu Shao-ch'i) in the 1960s. The choice was made by the National People's Congress, China's nominal parliament, with the blessing of Deng Xiaoping (Teng Hsiao-p'ing), China's paramount leader. The appointment appeared to be a concession to the still powerful and influential conservatives in order to foster political stability. Li, a member of the Standing Committee of the Politburo, had managed the national economy in the 1970s, but the old revolutionary warrior later showed little enthusiasm for the political and economic reforms initiated by Deng.

Li was born in 1905 to a peasant family in Hongan (Huang-an) County, Hubei (Hupeh) Province. He worked as a carpenter in his early years, joined the Communist Party in 1927, and began organizing peasants in the late 1920s. A veteran of the Long March (1934–35), he served in various party and army posts in the late 1930s and '40s. After the establishment of the People's Republic in 1949 he became governor of Hubei and mayor of Wuhan. In 1954 he was named finance minister and vice-premier. During the next two decades Li was a leading figure in China's economic and financial affairs under the leadership of Premier Zhou Enlai (Chou En-lai). When, however, it became clear that Li's continued insistence on capital construction and his emphasis on heavy industry were incompatible with Deng's pragmatic approach to economic development, his economic responsibilities were turned over to younger men.

In the largely ceremonial post of president, Li was expected to continue his role as spokesman for the old guard. Still, the restoration of the presidency after nearly 15 years and the selection of Li to fill the post demonstrated Deng's desire to give China political stability and substitute formal institutions for the cult of personality that flourished until Mao died in 1976.

(WINSTON L. Y. YANG)

Lloyd Webber, Andrew

For 35-year-old Andrew Lloyd Webber ("the most important writer of musicals since Sir Arthur Sullivan") 1983 was only slightly more successful than any year since he launched the ever popular *Jesus Christ Superstar*. His annual income from all sources was rated at more than £1 million, and his record-breaking musical *Cats*, based on T. S. Eliot's *Old Possum's Book of Practical Cats*, gained a Drama Desk Award and seven Tony awards on Broadway and achieved productions on three continents.

In August 1983, after two failed bids to buy the Aldwych and the Old Vic theatres, Lloyd Webber acquired his own theatre, the 92-year-old Palace, where *Jesus Christ Superstar* had been the world's longest running musical (topping eight years) in the 1970s and for which he paid £1.3 million. Before that he formed "The Really Useful Company Limited," which put on the successful *Daisy Pulls It Off* at the Globe Theatre.

At the end of 1982 Lloyd Webber became the first composer to have three musicals running simultaneously in New York and London, and while *Evita*, *Jesus Christ Superstar*, and *Song and Dance* were selling out in London in 1983, he composed and privately tried out his *Starlight Express*, with lyrics by Richard Stilgoe and a cast of singing roller skaters who impersonate U.S. railroad trains competing for supremacy. It was scheduled for a London opening in March 1984, later to be followed by *Aspects of Love*, "the first musical to treat sexual love in an adult way," based on a David Garnett novel with lyrics by Trevor Nunn, the director of *Cats*.

Born into a musical family in London on March 22, 1948 (his father, the late William Lloyd Webber, had been director of the London College of Music), Andrew was nine when he began writing music for the toy theatre that he and his cellist brother Julian ran at home. After attending Westminster School and spending a single term at the University of Oxford, he teamed up with Tim Rice in 1967. Together they wrote *Joseph and the Amazing Technicolor Dreamcoat* (1968), a 25-minute pop-oratorio for children, still performed worldwide in its later full-length version. There followed six more musicals or "operas," the last four without Rice as collaborator, three scores for motion pictures, the theme music for the 1978 soccer World Cup and for the London Weekend Television "South Bank Show," and *Theme and Variations for Cello and Rock Band*, his first solo album.

(OSSIA TRILLING)

Louganis, Greg

Greg Louganis had not won an Olympic gold medal for his diving at the end of 1983, but the United States boycotted the only Olympic Games held since he was 16. In all the other diving meets throughout the world Louganis had twisted and spun for more gold than Rumpelstiltskin.

In 1983 alone, competing in both the 10-m platform and 3-m springboard in five international competitions, he had nine of a possible ten first-place finishes and one second. He won gold medals in both events in the World Cup and the quadrennial Pan American Games, where he also had triumphed in both in 1979.

By the end of 1983 Louganis had won 24 U.S. national championships, more than any man in history. He regularly won the platform and the 3-m and 1-m springboard competitions in both indoor and outdoor national meets, although he finished second in the 1-m outdoors in 1983.

If there had been any question about Louganis's prominence in diving history, he splashed cold water on it by winning the platform and 3-m events in the 1982 world championships, the first time anyone had won gold medals for both in either a world championships or an Olympics. In that competition he gained the highest score ever awarded for a single springboard dive and became the second person in history to receive seven perfect 10s from the nine judges on one dive. And he did it soon after sitting out ten months with shoulder injuries that might have kept him inactive the rest of the year.

Gregory Louganis was born Jan. 29, 1960, to Samoan and Scotch-English parents and was adopted nine months later by Frances and Peter Louganis, who raised him in the San Diego, Calif., suburb of El Cajon. He was dancing and tumbling before his second birthday. Growing up, Louganis danced in stage shows, competed in acrobatics, and ultimately graduated with a degree in drama from the University of California at Irvine. This training, along with his ability to make a vertical jump of more than one metre and his compact build, helped make him uncommonly smooth and graceful. He soars higher than most divers, makes demanding gymnastics look as natural as climbing out of bed, and lands with barely a splash.

Louganis's father asked a former Olympic platform champion, Sammy Lee, to coach Greg in 1975. The next year, at 16, Louganis won a silver medal in the Olympic platform competition, nearly upsetting Klaus DiBiasi, who won his third gold medal. In the 1978 world championships and the 1979 World Cup, Louganis won gold medals in the platform.

(KEVIN M. LAMB)

McFarlane, Robert Carl

Although he had held successively more important government posts in three Republican administrations since 1971, Robert McFarlane's name was virtually unknown to the public in July 1983, when, ten days after his 46th birthday, he was appointed the chief United States negotiator in the Middle East. "Bud" McFarlane's studied invisibility was an asset for Pres. Ronald Reagan, who was determined to occupy centre stage in a preelection year dominated by foreign policy concerns. Three months later, in October, Reagan made McFarlane his national security adviser.

The son of a Democratic congressman from Texas, McFarlane was graduated from the U.S. Naval Academy at Annapolis, Md. As a promising young officer in the Marines, he was sent to study international relations at the prestigious Institut de Hautes Études in Geneva. That was a springboard to a White House fellowship in 1971–72, and he soon caught the eye of two important mentors, Henry Kissinger (*q.v.*) and Lieut. Gen. Brent Scowcroft, who served successively as national security advisers to Presidents Richard Nixon and Gerald Ford.

Kissinger, impressed by McFarlane's capacity for long working hours and quiet but adroit dealings with Congress, kept him on until 1975 as his military assistant. But after two more years in Washington as special assistant to Scowcroft, McFarlane's career came momentarily unstuck; he was thought to have strayed too far from strictly military concerns, and the Marines reassigned him to Okinawa.

Bored, and unhappy with Pres. Jimmy Carter's foreign policies, he resigned his commission. By then, however, he was a firmly established figure in the power network, and he soon joined the staff of the Senate Armed Services Committee. In 1981, with the Republicans back in the White House, McFarlane reentered the mainstream, serving as counselor at the State Department and then as Reagan's deputy assistant for national security affairs until he was named envoy to the Middle East. As national security adviser McFarlane immediately set about resolving arguments among various government agencies over the conduct of international policy.

(JAMES L. YUENGER)

Magaña Borjo, Alvaro Alfredo

A 58-year-old lawyer and economist, Alvaro Magaña became El Salvador's provisional president in May 1982, following elections for the Constituent Assembly held in March of the same year. Although not a politician, Magaña had advised previous governments over the past 17 years in his capacity as president of the country's largest mortgage bank, the Banco Hipotecario. During El Salvador's recent turbulent years he established himself as a respected public figure without becoming attached to any political faction. This, as well as his acknowledged good relations with the military, convinced the Constituent Assembly to break its three-week deadlock over the nomination of the provisional president.

Magaña described himself as a reluctant candidate, which was hardly surprising, given the near-impossible task he was expected to fulfill. The U.S.-sponsored elections failed to create any focus of political authority independent of the armed forces, and the military remained the effective rulers of the country. Their war against insurgent guerrilla forces entered its fourth year in 1983.

As a man with liberal political leanings, Magaña was expected to provide a counterweight to the rightist coalition led by Roberto d'Aubuisson, which dominated the Constituent Assembly. However, his numerous attempts at securing a working relationship between d'Aubuisson's group and the Christian Democrats (the largest single party in the Assembly) were unsuccessful. By November the Constituent Assembly had failed three times to meet its self-imposed deadline to approve El Salvador's new constitution. As a result, general elections scheduled for the end of 1983 had to be postponed. Magaña was expected to hold the office of provisional president until such time as the elections were held.

Alvaro Magaña was born on Oct. 8, 1925, in Ahuachapán, in the westernmost province of El Salvador. His family moved to the capital, San Salvador, when he was ten. He studied law at the University of El Salvador, received his master's degree from the University of Chicago, and did postgraduate work in public administration at the University of Rome. On his return to El Salvador in 1956, he worked for the Ministry of Finance and taught at the University of El Salvador. In 1965 he was appointed president of the Banco Hipotecario, a post he held until being nominated provisional president in 1982. (LESLIE CRAWFORD)

Mahre, Phil

Two years after he became the first U.S. skier to win a World Cup championship, Phil Mahre became the third skier from any nation to win three of them. He clinched his 1983 title March 7 at Aspen, Colo., when he skied the fastest times in both giant slalom runs. As the season ended, Aspen was one of 18 World Cup races that Mahre had won in blazing a trail to prominence for the United States ski team.

Going into 1984, Mahre had the realistic goal of becoming the first U.S. man to win an Olympic gold medal in Alpine skiing, especially since the co-favourite in the slalom and giant slalom, Sweden's Ingemar Stenmark, the World Cup champion in 1976–78 and defending Olympic gold medalist in both slalom competitions, was barred from the Olympics for professionalism. Mahre also had a chance to become the first skier to win four consecutive World Cups.

Phillip Mahre was born May 10, 1957, four minutes before his twin brother, Steven, the second-best U.S. male Alpine skier. The twins grew up with two brothers and five sisters in White Pass, Wash., where from 1962 his father managed a ski area. Mahre began skiing at the age of six and finished fifth in the giant slalom at the 1976 Olympics when he was 18. His overall World Cup points ranked second in 1978 and third in 1979 and 1980. To many, he is best remembered for his gutsy slalom race in the 1980 Olympics. He won a silver medal on a still-mending ankle that had been broken in three places, not quite a year earlier, on the same Whiteface Mountain in Lake Placid, N.Y. He had been unable to ski for more than five months after doctors patched his leg with a three-inch metal plate and seven screws.

When a rule change in 1979 favoured versatility, Mahre began training for the more reckless downhill in addition to the more technical slaloms. That edge helped him gain the combined victory (for times in slalom, giant slalom, and downhill) that clinched his first World Cup in 1981.

Mahre's twin has never been far behind. In fact, it was Steve whose giant slalom victory in 1982 won the first gold medal for the U.S. in the world championships, and when Steve beat Phil by 0.08 sec once that year, it was the first time that two Americans ever finished one-two in a World Cup race. (KEVIN M. LAMB)

Mansour, Agnes Mary

Sister Agnes Mary Mansour abandoned a 30-year vocation in 1983 after becoming Michigan's social services director. The step did not represent a change of heart—"In my heart I'm still a nun," she said—but a new wrinkle in the long controversy over separation of state from church.

Born to Lebanese Christian immigrants in Detroit on April 10, 1931, she attended Mercy College there and on graduation in 1953 joined the religious order that operates it (and numerous hospitals, schools, and other social agencies), the Sisters of Mercy of the Union. She went on to earn, with honours, a Ph.D. in biochemistry (1963), and she taught, was a consultant to the U.S. Department of Health, Education, and Welfare (among others), and served as president of her alma mater for a decade.

WIDE WORLD

She also won political experience by losing a congressional primary election.

She also possessed a certain liberality of mind, or at least a lack of doctrinaire rigidity. At her confirmation hearing on being appointed Michigan's social services director, she testified, "I recognize that we live in a morally pluralistic society that government must be respectful of, and that my morality may not be someone else's morality." At ultimate issue was the matter of abortion, which she personally opposes in concert with the Roman Catholic Church. But abortion is legal in Michigan, and the state's Social Services Department channels some $5.7 million a year in Medicaid funds to pay for the abortions of needy women. Sister Agnes's faith and morality notwithstanding, she acknowledged that the poor were entitled to public aid under the law.

Pope John Paul II had discouraged nuns and priests from holding political office and ordered those who do to obtain permission from their bishops. Archbishop Edmund Szoka, whose Detroit see includes the Sisters of Mercy convent, granted the necessary permission, but on the condition that Sister Agnes state her unequivocal opposition to the state's funding of abortion. Sister Agnes refused to speak out. Archbishop Szoka then ordered her to resign the state job. When she refused, he appealed to Rome, and the Vatican dispatched a canon law expert who told Sister Agnes she must obey her archbishop. Instead she left the sisterhood, with the order's consent. It was this order's national superior who, during the pope's 1979 visit to Washington, D.C., politely but firmly criticized the church for prohibiting women's ordination.

(PHILIP KOPPER)

Martins, Peter

The world-renowned New York City Ballet gained a new ballet master-in-chief in 1983: the 36-year-old Danish dancer Peter Martins, who joined the company 13 years earlier. The former illustrious head of the troupe, George Balanchine (*see* OBITUARIES), had become ill late in 1982. Martins was one of a small group to oversee the company during that time and, as its new head, had responsibility for its day-to-day operations as well as artistic decision making.

Martins was born in Copenhagen on Oct. 27, 1946. His exposure to ballet came early. His uncle, a member of the Royal Danish Ballet, was the first Dane to dance the title role in Balanchine's *Apollo,* a role that is also considered one of Martins's triumphs. Peter was accepted at age eight at the Royal Danish Ballet School but was uncooperative until he became an enthusiastic student of Stanley Williams, now a faculty member at the New York City Ballet's official school. Under the guidance of Williams the young dancer progressed rapidly and made his Danish debut in 1964.

In 1967 Martins filled in as an emergency replacement in *Apollo* with the New York City Ballet at the Edinburgh Festival. He loved the speed and energy of American dancing and continued to be a guest artist with the troupe until he joined it permanently during the 1969–70 season.

Martins was considered one of the greatest living male dancers, known for his classic dignity and magnificence of movement. But though critics considered him to be at the height of his powers, he retired from performing in 1983 to devote himself to the NYCB and choreography. His last appearance was in the 1,000th performance of Balanchine's *The Nutcracker*.

Martins acknowledges a great debt to Balanchine, not only for what he learned from him about dancing but also for Balanchine's continued tutoring in the art of choreography. Martins's first choreographic effort, *Calcium Light Night* (1977) to music by Charles Ives, was highly praised and eventually became a part of the company's repertoire. As of 1983, 14 of Martins's works had been presented by the company. In 1981 he was appointed by Balanchine to be one of the New York City Ballet's four ballet masters.

(BONNIE OBERMAN)

Mejía Victores, Oscar Humberto

In a palace coup on Aug. 8, 1983, Gen. Oscar Mejía Victores overthrew the regime of Brig. Gen. Efraín Ríos Montt and declared himself chief of state of Guatemala. The new chief was known to be a hard-liner and was described by local politicians as a "pure" military man, politically unsophisticated and clumsy at public relations. Unlike his predecessor, he was a fervent Roman Catholic and a member of the "old guard"—a supporter of former president Fernando Romeo Lucas García, whose government had been toppled in March 1982.

Born in 1930, Oscar Mejía joined the Army at age 18, took special courses in the U.S.-ruled Canal Zone within Panama in 1955, and attended the Superior Military School in Mexico in 1960. By June 1980 he had reached the rank of brigadier general and was posted to the headquarters of the General Justo Rafino Barrios military zone in Guatemala City. Subsequently, he was appointed inspector general of the Army and was made first vice-minister of defense and, later, minister of defense under Ríos Montt's administration.

Mejía had little experience in politics. He was a strong anti-Communist, highly critical of the Nicaraguan government, and spoke out on several occasions against the Contadora peace-seeking proposals. Relations with the U.S. remained uneasy after a brief honeymoon period. In November the U.S. suspended $10,250,000 of arms sales to Guatemala as well as $13 million in development aid and $40 million in economic aid that had been scheduled for fiscal 1984. Concern over the violation of human rights mounted, and General Mejía appeared hard-pressed in retaining control of a divided and corrupt Army.

Mejía's promises to fulfill the election timetable outlined by his predecessor (to start campaigning for a Constituent Assembly in March 1984, followed by balloting in July) could well be preempted by another coup. His internal power base was weak, and opposition mounted because he did not abolish an unpopular value-added tax but merely reduced it from 10 to 7%.

(LUCY BLACKBURN)

Mintoff, Dom(inic)

Prime minister of Malta since 1971, in 1983 Dom Mintoff could justly claim that, following the resignation of Austria's Bruno Kreisky, no other Western European head of government had remained in office as long as he. Something of a maverick in his conduct of Malta's external relations, he had more than once attracted international attention. The last occasion was during the closing stages of the 1983 session of the Helsinki Accords review conference in Madrid, when Malta delayed for two months consensual agreement on the conference's final document. (*See* SPAIN: *Sidebar.*)

A fiery public speaker and a skillful political operator, Mintoff has been described as a Maltese Machiavelli. Born at Cospicua, Malta, on Aug. 6, 1916, the son of a former Royal Navy cook, he studied engineering at the University of Malta and English, as a Rhodes scholar, at Oxford. He worked in Britain as a civil engineer during 1941–43 and then returned to Malta to practice as an architect. In 1944 he joined the Maltese Labour Party and helped to reorganize it. In 1945 he was elected to the Council of Government and in 1947 was appointed deputy prime minister of works.

In 1949 Mintoff became leader of the Maltese Labour Party. At that time his aim was Malta's political integration with the U.K. He failed to achieve that during his first prime ministership (1955–58) when the British government rejected his proposal. When self-government, revoked by Britain in 1959, was restored in 1962, Mintoff led the opposition against the Nationalist government of George Borg Olivier, who on Sept. 21, 1964, proclaimed Malta's independence within the Commonwealth of Nations.

When Olivier lost the general election in June 1971, Mintoff returned to power. Under his leadership Malta's relations with Britain fell to a low ebb, especially when he declared that the use of Malta as a "NATO aircraft carrier" was humiliating and must be ended. The withdrawal of British forces began in January 1972, but on March 26 the U.K. government undertook to pay Malta £14 million annually for the next seven years for the use of Malta as a naval base. When this agreement expired in 1979 and was not renewed, the British base was finally closed down on March 31.

Early in his term of office Mintoff developed close relations with Libya, and in 1976 he played host to Libyan leader Col. Muammar al-Qaddafi. However, Maltese-Libyan relations suffered a setback in 1980, and Mintoff then entered into an agreement with Italy guaranteeing Malta's neutrality.

(K. M. SMOGORZEWSKI)

Mulroney, Brian

On June 11, 1983, Brian Mulroney won his first election. He became leader of the Progressive Conservative Party of Canada, defeating former leader Joe Clark. Clark had defeated Mulroney for the post in the 1976 leadership race and then had gone on to become prime minister of Canada (though his tenure had been shortlived). Mulroney believed that he could do the same. Charming, clever, and bilingual in French and English, he was perceived by the delegates as the man who could win a federal election for the Tories and in addition make gains for the party in the province of Quebec, a Liberal Party stronghold.

Born on March 20, 1939, in Baie Comeau,

CANAPRESS PHOTO SERVICE

Que., Martin Brian Mulroney was sent to boarding school in New Brunswick at the age of 14 because his parents believed that education was the road to success. He received a B.A. from St. Francis Xavier University in Antigonish, Nova Scotia, and a law degree from Laval University in Quebec city. During a successful career as a labour lawyer in Montreal, Mulroney prided himself on being a skillful negotiator and a deft conciliator. In 1974 he was named a commissioner of the Quebec Royal Commission into Violence in the Construction Industry in Quebec (the Cliche Commission). Because the hearings were televised, he received wide public exposure. He launched his unsuccessful attempt to win the leadership of the Progressive Conservative Party in 1976, basing his campaign upon the publicity and popularity he had achieved in the course of the hearings. He finished a close second to Joe Clark in the balloting.

William Bennett, one of Mulroney's legal clients, recruited Mulroney as his successor as president of the Iron Ore Co. of Canada, an office he held from 1977 to 1983. During Mulroney's tenure he ended labour troubles, and the company made a profit. He resigned his position in March 1983 to run for the leadership of the Progressive Conservative Party.

Although he had been active in politics since his days at Laval University, Mulroney had not held any elected office. Once he became leader of the Tories, his first priority was to win a seat in the Canadian House of Commons. One of his supporters, Elmer MacKay, a member of Parliament from Nova Scotia, obliged Mulroney by resigning his seat in the House. Mulroney ran in a by-election and won the riding of Central Nova on August 29. Thus he could lead his party from the floor of the House rather than from the visitors' gallery.

(DIANE LOIS WAY)

Murphy, Eddie

In 1983 almost everything Eddie Murphy touched turned to gold. He made his first two films, *48 Hrs.* and *Trading Places,* both of which were major hits largely because of his performances; his first two record albums were big successes; he signed a television contract for $30,000 per show with "Saturday Night Live"; and his face appeared on the cover of *Rolling Stone* magazine, managing to look sexy and charming with the tip of one diamond-ringed finger in his nose.

In the film *48 Hrs.* Murphy played a convict released for two days to help cop Nick Nolte find a killer. His scene as the lone black facing down the crowd in a tough cowboy bar was one of the most memorable of the year. When *The New Yorker* film critic Pauline Kael reviewed *48 Hrs.*, she said, "Eddie Murphy is a whiz of a performer; he has concentration and intensity, and he's so young there's an engaging spirit in what he's doing."

Murphy was born in 1961 in the Bushwick section of Brooklyn, and his parents separated when he was three. When he was nine, his mother married Vernon Lynch, and they moved to Roosevelt on Long Island. Murphy became a class comedian early, and when he was graduated from high school his wit had won him the title of "most popular" in his class.

When he was 13, Murphy would lock himself in his room, listen to Elvis Presley, and write comedy. He told people when he was in junior high school that he would be bigger than Bob Hope and a millionaire at 22, and he worked hard toward that goal, performing in nightclubs on Long Island at 15 and graduating at 19 to being one of the few bright spots in the dismal season just after the original cast left "Saturday Night Live."

Murphy made his name on the television show with his imitations of Stevie Wonder and Bill Cosby and with a host of character creations ranging from Little Richard Simmons, a combination of Little Richard and Richard Simmons, to art-world-pet convict-poet Tyrone Greene ("C-I-L-L my landlord"). Also hilarious and full of energy was his Mr. Robinson, a black Mr. Rogers, who, after his landlord cuts off the heat, croons: "Mr. Landlord is not very nice, is he children?"

(DAVID A. OATES)

Nakasone, Yasuhiro

When Yasuhiro Nakasone was elected prime minister of Japan in November 1982, he ended a 28-year climb up the political ladder. He had already earned himself the nickname "Weathervane" for his propensity to swing with the political winds. He was first elected to the Diet (parliament) in 1947 and learned how to deal with government bureaucracies as minister of trade and industry and director general of the defense agency. Less self-effacing and more direct than most of his postwar predecessors, Nakasone set himself apart from fellow Liberal-Democratic Party (LDP) politicians who generally preferred behind-the-scenes deals to public discussions.

Nakasone's first year in office was relatively successful. He visited South Korea, which received $4 billion in aid, and traveled to Washington, where he established close relations with Pres. Ronald Reagan. During a visit to Southeast Asia, Nakasone promised that Japan would play a larger role in the development of Asia. Diplomatic successes abroad, however, were sometimes viewed in a different light at home. Nakasone's remark in Washington that Japan should become an "unsinkable aircraft carrier" caused a political commotion at home. Though Nakasone subsequently toned down his remarks, no one doubted that the prime minister fully intended to strengthen the nation's defense forces if he remained in office.

Yasuhiro Nakasone was born in Gumma Prefecture on May 27, 1918, the son of a well-to-do lumber dealer. He graduated from Tokyo University School of Law in 1941 and served in the Navy during World War II before entering politics. When Nakasone became head of government, it was with the indispensable support of Kakuei Tanaka (*q.v.*), a powerful member of the Liberal-Democratic Party and a longtime friend. That relationship would soon threaten Nakasone's political future. In October Tanaka was convicted of bribery and violations of the foreign exchange law. The uproar was so intense that Nakasone was forced to call elections for mid-December. The LDP lost 35 seats and its majority in the lower house of the Diet. It was only after a small conservative party agreed to form a coalition with the LDP that Nakasone was reelected to a second term on December 26. But he first had to pledge that Tanaka's influence in the LDP would come to an end.

(FRANK GIBNEY, JR.)

Nelligan, Kate

Veteran actress Kate Nelligan became well known to a broad U.S. audience in 1983 in the film *Without a Trace,* in which she played a woman whose child has disappeared in an apparent kidnapping. Though the film itself received less than enthusiastic reviews, Nelligan generally won praise for her performance.

Even stronger praise greeted her first stage appearance in the U.S.—in David Hare's play *Plenty,* which opened off-Broadway in October 1982 and moved to Broadway in January 1983. Her portrayal of the postwar life of a woman who had fought with the French Resistance in World War II was described by *Time* magazine as "unique, mesmerizing and shattering at the same time." It earned her a nomination for a Tony award for best actress.

Nelligan's acclaim in the U.S. followed nearly a decade of similar approbation in Great Britain. Patricia Colleen Nelligan was born in London, Ont., on March 16, 1951, into a millwright's family. She had four sisters and a brother, but it was Patricia who was pushed by her mother to excel at ballet and tap dancing and at tennis. She entered York University's Glendon College on a scholarship at age 16, and there she discovered theatre. After two years she won an audition for one of two North American places in the Central School of Speech and Drama in London, England. Upon graduation she adopted the name Kate and joined the Bristol Old Vic company, giving her first professional performance in 1972. Her first television role was in the BBC series "The Onedin Line."

Nelligan's London debut in David Hare's *Knuckle* in 1974 was a triumph and marked the start of her successful professional association with that playwright. She began appearing regularly with the National

Theatre and the Royal Shakespeare Company (her first professional Shakespearean role was in *As You Like It* in 1977). Motion pictures, such as *The Count of Monte Cristo* (1976), *Bethune* (1976), *Dracula* (1979), and *Eye of the Needle* (1981), followed; although the films generally were not widely praised, Nelligan herself usually garnered critical accolades. The theatre was more rewarding, and her performance in the London production of *Plenty* earned her the London *Evening Standard*'s award as best actress in Great Britain in 1978.

(JOAN N. BOTHELL)

Neuharth, Allen Harold

On Sept. 15, 1983, Allen H. Neuharth celebrated the first birthday of a brainchild that few of his competitors thought would survive so long. *USA Today* had already achieved the status of a legitimate national newspaper, a weekday journal available to half the nation's residents in some 2,000 cities and towns. Born at a cost of perhaps $25 million, it might take five years to turn a profit for its owners, the Gannett Co., of which Neuharth is chairman and president. Yet circulation had inched past projections to 1,165,000, compared with 960,000 daily for the *New York Times* and 2 million for the *Wall Street Journal.*

USA Today was unique in using satellite technology from the outset. Written, designed, and laid out by a 300-strong editorial staff in Washington, D.C., the paper was beamed page by page via satellite to regional production centres. Neuharth tailored his national daily to an "audience of gypsies," people who travel on business regularly and move often. Four copies out of five sold through newsstands and streetcorner vending machines. Brightened by colour photographs, charts, and graphics, the paper featured capsule reports of international, national, and state news. It devoted one of its 40 pages (later 48) to weather from coast to coast and offered perhaps the most comprehensive sports coverage of any widely circulated daily.

Sports journalism held special meaning for Neuharth, who had founded a statewide sports weekly in his native South Dakota 30 years earlier, one of his few failures. Born March 22, 1924, in Eureka, he took his first job—as a newsboy—at 11. In high school he edited the student paper, then spent four years in the armed forces during World War II. Back at the University of South Dakota, he was graduated with honours and went to work for Associated Press before founding the short-lived weekly. After its demise he joined the *Miami* (Fla.) *Herald* and swiftly scaled the editorial ladder. In 1963 he moved to Gannett as general manager of that chain's two Rochester, N.Y., papers and became president of the company seven years later. He served as president of the American Newspaper Publishers Association and was named a fellow of the Society of Professional Journalists, Sigma Delta Chi.

(PHILIP KOPPER)

Peng Zhen

Peng Zhen (P'eng Chen) was elected chairman of China's nominal parliament, the National People's Congress, in 1983, replacing the aging and frail Ye Jianying (Yeh Chien-ying). Even though ultimate power resided with the Politburo of the Chinese Communist Party, which Deng Xiaoping (Teng Hsiao-p'ing) dominated, Peng's selection made him the most influential figure in China's highest legislative body, which had become increasingly more important since Deng began stressing the need for formal institutions and collective leadership.

Peng, who was born in 1902 in Quwo (Ch'ü-wo) County, Shanxi (Shansi) Province, joined the Communist Youth League and party in 1923. During the 1930s he worked in the underground Communist labour movement in northern China and eventually became the chief of the Communist Party's Organization Department and vice-president of its Central Academy. During the 1940s he was a key figure in the Northeast Bureau of the party. After the establishment of the People's Republic in 1949, he became a member of the Politburo and mayor of Beijing (Peking), where a number of major construction projects were completed under his leadership. Purged by Mao Zedong (Mao Tse-tung) during the Cultural Revolution that began in 1966, Peng regained his seat in the Politburo in 1979 and became vice-chairman of the National People's Congress. As a member of the party's old guard, Peng advocated relatively harsh policies against criminals, dissidents, and those acknowledging that alienation can exist in a socialist society. Nonetheless, he remained a strong supporter of Deng's pragmatic programs.

(WINSTON L. Y. YANG)

Pepper, Claude Denson

He rises at 6:30 AM and starts the day with a breakfast of soup and crackers (his most notable eccentricity). Then, armed with trifocals, twin hearing aids, a pacemaker, and an artificial heart valve, 82-year-old Rep. Claude Pepper (Dem., Fla.) sets out on another day as premier spokesman for the 26 million senior citizens in the U.S.

Following the example of John Quincy Adams, who made his most lasting mark on national affairs in the House of Representatives after retiring from the White House, Pepper—having served 15 years in the upper house—returned to Washington as a representative in 1962, after a 12-year hiatus. Over the next two decades he became a power in Congress. As chairman of the House Select Committee on Aging, he was instrumental in reorganizing the nearly bankrupt Social Security System and in forcing another senior citizen, Pres. Ronald Reagan, to back down on reducing benefits. In 1983 he became chairman of the crucial Rules Committee, but he intended to continue focusing on matters affecting the elderly.

Born Sept. 8, 1900, in rural Alabama, Pepper was graduated with honours from the state university at 20 and went on to Harvard Law School. After teaching in Arkansas (future senator J. William Fulbright was his student), he moved to Florida. As a first-term Florida legislator, he sponsored his first bill for the elderly, exempting older anglers from buying fishing licenses. He then lost a reelection bid after opposing a resolution to censure Mrs. Herbert Hoover for inviting a Negro to the White House. Elected to fill a U.S. Senate vacancy in 1936, he was called a "fighting liberal" by Pres. Franklin D. Roosevelt. In the 1950 election, at the height of the McCarthy period, Pepper was defeated after a campaign notorious for smears and innuendo. He returned to practicing law in Florida, but when the state gained an additional congressional seat as a result of reapportionment, he ran for it and won.

Among his accomplishments were sponsorship of the bills that established the National Cancer Institute and raised mandatory retirement ages. He was one of the first to fear Hitler's rise in the 1930s and helped pass the program that became Lend-Lease. A childless widower after 43 years of marriage, the oldest member of the Congress, and the second most senior in terms of Capitol service, he continued to maintain a heavy work load. A year before the 1984 elections, he admitted to flirting with the idea of running for vice-president.

(PHILIP KOPPER)

Presser, Jackie

Promising that his union would present a new face to the world, Jackie Presser, soon after becoming its president, did something no Teamster boss had ever done before: he appeared voluntarily before a U.S. congressional committee. Bringing new energies to bear on public relations, he also stressed the fact that he had never been so much as indicted for a major felony. (Three of the last four Teamster presidents had criminal records.)

Born in Cleveland, Ohio, on Aug. 6, 1926, Presser quit school after the eighth grade and drove a truck delivering pinball machines until he joined the U.S. Navy. After serving in World War II, he joined the staff of a restaurant workers' union in Cleveland and then became an organizer for the Ohio Teamsters. Observers maintain that his rise through union ranks was helped by his father's influence; William Presser was president of the Ohio state branch of the Teamsters and vice-president of the international union (formally known as the International Brotherhood of Teamsters, Chauffeurs, Warehousemen and Helpers of America).

With his father's help, Jackie Presser set up Local 507, which grew from a dozen paint company workers to some 6,000 warehousemen, though the U.S. Department of Labor accused him of raiding other locals to do it. But while serving as vice-president of the Ohio Coalition of Teamsters, Presser supported housing projects for the elderly, retraining programs for the jobless, sports and summer jobs for youngsters, and a circus for the handicapped.

Having succeeded his father as international vice-president, Presser in 1980 spurred Teamster support for Ronald Reagan as U.S. president. After Reagan's victory, Presser was named an adviser to the president-elect's transition team and labour co-chairman of the Reagan inauguration. Meanwhile, allegations continued to reach the public—sometimes in the form of sworn testimony—that Presser had variously misused union funds, accepted kickbacks, and padded payrolls.

In April Roy Williams stepped down from the Teamster presidency as a condition of remaining out of jail pending appeal of a federal fraud conviction. The union's executive board elected Presser to succeed him on April 21, 1983, at an annual salary of $225,000. One of Presser's major goals for the union was increased representation among white-collar workers in the public sector and in high-technology enterprises. (PHILIP KOPPER)

Qaddafi, Muammar Muhammad al-

Libyan leader Col. Muammar al-Qaddafi's erratic conduct of his country's foreign relations, through which he had acquired something of the character of an international pariah during his tenure of power since 1969, was toned down somewhat in 1983, when he made conciliatory advances to a number of Arab nations with whose leaders he had previously been at loggerheads. However, his reputation for military adventurism was maintained by the renewed intervention of Libyan forces in the civil war in Chad on the side of former Chadian president Goukouni Oueddei. (*See* CHAD.)

Qaddafi's first years in power since the 1969 coup that deposed King Idris had been characterized by moves against Western interests, banks, and oil companies and by persistent and unsuccessful attempts to unify Libya with other Arab countries. At the same time he began to strengthen relations with the Soviet Union. Libya was implicated in coup attempts in Egypt and Sudan in 1974 and later gave support to liberation movements as diverse as the Black Panthers in the U.S. and the Irish Republican Army. From 1974 onward Qaddafi began to espouse a form of Islamic socialism to which he gave expression in his *Green Book*, published in 1976. He emphasized the move toward decentralization of power by giving the General People's Congress the legislative powers previously held by the Revolutionary Command Council. In March 1979 Qaddafi claimed he had abandoned all official posts, remaining only "the leader, theoretician, and symbol" of the revolution and that from then on the people would "exercise and consolidate all power."

Qaddafi was born near Surt in Libya to a family of nomads in 1942. His father had taken part in an abortive rebellion against Italian rule in 1931. Educated at Koranic elementary school and high school in Fezzan, Qaddafi formed at school his first teenage revolutionary group with Abdul Salam Jalloud, later his deputy. At Benghazi military college in 1963 Qaddafi founded his Free Officers Movement, which espoused the political ideas of Egypt's Pres. Gamal Abdel Nasser. He underwent signals training as a soldier in England. On Sept. 1, 1969, the Free Officers led by Qaddafi staged a successful coup against King Idris and proclaimed a Libyan Arab Republic. On September 13 Qaddafi became chairman of the Revolutionary Command Council. (JOHN WHELAN)

Rama Rao, Nandamuri Taraka

In a truly epic contest with Indian Prime Minister Indira Gandhi's Congress (I) party, the newly born Telegu Desam ("Land of the Telegues") party emerged victorious in the January 1983 legislative assembly election in Andhra Pradesh state. Telegu Desam's founder and leader, film-star-turned-politician N. T. Rama Rao, popularly known to his fans and supporters as NTR, thus became chief minister of the state.

Rama Rao was born on May 28, 1923, in the village of Nimmakuru, Pammaru, in the Krishna district of Andhra Pradesh. He attended college in Vijayawada and later Guntur, where he was graduated. Keenly interested in acting, he performed with college drama groups. After college he entered government service in 1948 as a subregistrar but soon gave this up when he was offered a film part. His first film, *Mana Desam* ("My Country"), was released in 1949. Since then he had appeared in more than 300 films—some with mythological, historical, social, or folklore themes, others just simple love stories.

At the time he gave up his film career in May 1982, Rama Rao was the highest paid actor in the Telegu film industry. He appeared in about a dozen films every year, for each of which he reportedly received Rs 2 million ($200,000). He also produced and directed films himself. An enthusiastic and successful campaigner for worthy causes, during India's border conflict with China in 1962 and the war with Pakistan in 1965, Rama Rao was active in raising money for national defense funds. In 1968 Pres. Zakir Husain conferred on him the Badmashri (Lotus) order.

In March 1982 Rama Rao launched Telegu Desam to bring back, in his own words, "the 3,000-year-old heritage of the Telegu people." For voters, 70% of whom lacked formal education, the real-life Rama Rao and his film personality blended into a potent political mixture. For them, he personified the virtues extolled by his scriptwriters—honesty, morality, fearlessness, and altruism. Victory came after a nine-month-long campaign in which Rama Rao traveled more than 35,000 km (21,735 mi) and was seen and heard by 30 million people. (DILIP GANGULY)

Reagan, Ronald

Historically, a U.S. president's third year in the White House is a crucial period during which he consolidates the programs that characterize his administration. For Pres. Ronald Reagan, 1983 was a third year in which he compromised on domestic affairs, lost control of federal spending, and launched a series of controversial foreign policy actions. He began the year at a low point in the public opinion polls but ended it with the highest approval rating since his inauguration.

After two years of dealing with a docile Republican Senate and an undisciplined Democratic House of Representatives, Reagan was confronted in 1983 with a 98th Congress less willing to go along with his economic programs. A recession and the 1982 midterm election ended the coalition of Republicans and conservative Democrats who had passed the budget and tax cuts known collectively as "Reaganomics." In 1983 Reagan was forced to compromise in order to save the financially strapped Social Security system (*see* SOCIAL SECURITY AND WELFARE SERVICES) as Congress passed a $4.6 billion antirecession jobs bill and refused to accept further cuts in domestic spending.

In foreign policy the president's special envoys in the Middle East and Central America were unable to implement his peace plans. Tension increased with the Soviet Union, and there was little progress at the nuclear disarmament talks in Geneva. A new generation of missiles was deployed in England and West Germany despite bitter opposition from the European peace movement and nuclear-freeze proponents in the United States. The murder in August of Philippine opposition leader Benigno Aquino, Jr., caused the cancellation of a visit by Reagan to Manila and other Southeast Asian capitals. By late summer the president's foreign policy appeared to be in trouble all over the world.

Then came a series of startling events, beginning in September when a Soviet jet fighter shot down a South Korean passenger plane over the Sea of Japan. President Reagan's angry but restrained reaction brought support from world leaders and the U.S. public. Then, in Lebanon, 239 U.S. servicemen were killed in October (2 died later) when a terrorist truck loaded with explosives rammed into their barracks. Two days later U.S. military forces invaded Grenada at the request of neighbouring island countries after a radical coup ousted a Marxist government and allegedly threatened the safety of U.S. medical students on the island. In one of his most effective television speeches, Reagan explained his actions in Grenada and his determination to keep the Marines in Lebanon. His critics were overwhelmed as the U.S. people rallied to support him. (HAL BRUNO)

Reich, Robert

"America has a choice," wrote Robert Reich in his controversial book *The Next American Frontier* (1983). "It can adapt itself to the new economic realities by altering its organizations, or it can fail to adapt and thereby continue its present decline." Reich, a lawyer who teaches courses on public policy, public management, and business strategy at Harvard University's John F. Kennedy School of Government, argued that the United States was not turning away quickly enough from the high-volume, standardized production that had characterized its economy in recent times but that was now moving increasingly to the third world. Reich maintained that the U.S. must direct itself toward a more flexible system of specialized production of high-value products, particularly high-technology items such as specialized metals and semiconductors. The new system would require extensive retraining of workers, a less hierarchical organization in the workplace, and other social and economic changes that would better use what Reich considered the unique resource of the U.S.: Americans themselves.

A leading proponent of a federal industrial policy, Reich advocated a strong government role in advancing such changes, urging a coherent policy to replace the current hodgepodge of price supports, subsidized loans, and tax expenditures that affect the economy. He was particularly critical of what he called "paper entrepreneurialism," management techniques of mergers, acquisitions, and tax avoidance that create short-term profits by rearranging industrial assets but rarely create real productive activity. In Reich's view, "in the emerging era of productivity, social justice is not incompatible with economic growth, but essential to it."

Reich was born on June 24, 1946, in Scranton, Pa., and grew up in the family of a well-to-do Connecticut businessman. He attended Dartmouth College, where he was active in liberal causes. As a Rhodes scholar, he went on to receive a master's degree in economics from the University of Oxford. He also received a law degree from Yale University. He became assistant to the U.S. solicitor general in 1974 and was the director of policy planning at the Federal Trade Commission from 1976 to 1981. Reich's abiding interest has been institutional economics: how people organize themselves for work. He expounded his views on a national industrial policy in an earlier book entitled *Minding America's Business* (1982), written with Ira C. Magaziner. (JOAN N. BOTHELL)

Ride, Sally

On June 18, 1983, astronaut Sally Ride became the first U.S. woman to fly in space. Only two other women preceded her, both from the Soviet Union. A mission specialist aboard the space shuttle "Challenger" or the seventh shuttle flight, Ride performed various scientific tasks and served as flight engineer. During the six-day flight she and her colleagues deployed two communications satellites and for the first time released and retrieved a satellite using the shuttle's mechanical arm, in the development of which she had participated.

The 32-year-old Ride, who was hailed as a heroine and role model by feminists, acknowledged that the women's movement paved the way for her chance in space. Nonetheless, she deplored the attention that her gender alone attracted, stating that it was "no big deal" and regretting that American society was not sufficiently advanced to accept her participation as a matter of course.

WIDE WORLD

Sally Kristen Ride was born on May 26, 1951, in Encino, Calif., where as a growing girl she often played baseball and football with the boys of her neighbourhood. She became highly proficient at tennis and thereby won a partial scholarship to a girls' preparatory school in Los Angeles, where she became interested in science. She majored in physics at Swarthmore (Pa.) College, but dropped out as a sophomore to concentrate on tennis. However, she rejected strong recommendations that she turn professional and returned to school at Stanford University, where she earned a bachelor of science degree in physics and a bachelor of arts degree in English. She pursued physics in graduate school and received a doctorate in astrophysics in 1978. She had learned that the National Aeronautics and Space Administration (NASA) was recruiting young scientists and filed an application in 1977. The next year she found herself one of 6 women and 29 men selected from more than 8,000 applicants.

Like other candidates, Ride received training at the Lyndon B. Johnson Space Center in Houston, Texas. On the second and third shuttle flights Ride was capsule communicator, the person on the ground who talks to the astronauts in flight, a job that demands not only detailed knowledge of the flight but also a calm and articulate manner. (JOAN N. BOTHELL)

Ripken, Cal, Jr.

While some U.S. athletes were dragging battered hero images through courtrooms, Cal Ripken, Jr., was making milk commercials. The polite, unassuming shortstop for the Baltimore Orioles was aware of the boy-next-door standard for an all-American idol and meant to meet it. If the third-base coach of the Orioles said that the batting cage had too many baseballs around it, Ripken was likely to be the first to stoop for them.

The coach happened to be his father, Calvin Edwin, Sr., which was another element in Ripken's storybook life that proceeded from American League rookie of the year in 1982 to most valuable player in 1983, when the Orioles won the World Series. He had literally been around baseball all his life, leaving his Aberdeen, Md., home when school let out to follow his father's career as minor league manager.

Ripken, born Aug. 24, 1960, was a junior at Aberdeen High School when he took batting practice at the Orioles' stadium and littered the seats with baseballs. That was when his father, impressed with the boy's strength and bat speed, first suspected that his son had a chance for major league stardom. The scouts concurred the next year, when Ripken batted .492 with 29 runs batted in (RBI's) in 20 games and pitched for a 7–2 won-lost record, a 0.70 earned-run average, and 100 strikeouts in 60 innings.

The Orioles drafted Ripken and, after he made all-league teams in three consecutive minor-league seasons, they traded all-star third baseman Doug DeCinces to make room for him in their 1982 lineup. The season started poorly, though; Ripken had a .117 average through 18 games before a chance conversation with slugger Reggie Jackson turned him around.

Jackson sympathized with Ripken, un-

FOCUS ON SPORTS

derstanding how frustrating it was to have well-meaning advice about snapping his slump. As Ripken recalled, Jackson told him, "'Do what Cal Ripken can do, not what others think you can do.' My father had been telling me that all along, but it didn't register. When Reggie said it, it sort of jolted something in there and brought me back to earth." The rest of the season Ripken batted .281 to finish with an average of .264. He also hit 28 home runs and had 93 RBI's. During the year he moved to shortstop because it was the Orioles' more pressing need.

Ripken played every inning of every game in 1983, when he batted .318 with 27 home runs and 102 RBI's. He led the league with 211 hits, 121 runs, 47 doubles, and 78 extra-base hits, and he led shortstops in assists, total chances, and double plays.

(KEVIN M. LAMB)

Ruckelshaus, William

When he returned to Washington in 1983 to take over leadership of the Environmental Protection Agency, William Ruckelshaus was back in familiar surroundings. Thirteen years earlier Pres. Richard Nixon had appointed him to be the new agency's first administrator, and at that time he won the respect of environmentalists as well as the industries he regulated.

For that reason Pres. Ronald Reagan turned to Ruckelshaus to replace Anne Gorsuch Burford, forced out as head of the EPA in March 1983 amid charges of inefficiency, weak enforcement of EPA regulations, and favouring business interests over environmental considerations.

There was some question about Ruckelshaus because he had been employed as vice-president of a major timber and wood products firm and had represented business clients in environmental cases while engaged in private law practice. But Congress quickly and unanimously approved his appointment.

EPA employees cheered when Ruckelshaus arrived at headquarters to fire the Burford team and set about the task of restoring the agency's morale and reputation. Despite the Reagan administration's commitment to deregulation, the president had given him a mandate to "launch a new beginning" in cleaning up the nation's air and water pollution. Ruckelshaus found an EPA that in recent years had become more politicized in its efforts to deal with complex and controversial problems.

Ruckelshaus was born July 24, 1932, in Indianapolis, Ind., the son of a lawyer active in county, state, and national Republican politics. He was educated at Princeton University and Harvard Law School and practiced law in the family firm from 1960 to 1968. He won a seat in the Indiana legislature in 1966, and after losing a U.S. Senate bid two years later he went to Washington to serve as head of the civil division of the U.S. Department of Justice. He was named EPA administrator in 1970 and then in 1973 became acting director of the FBI and deputy attorney general. Ruckelshaus was fired during the notorious "Saturday Night Massacre" of Oct. 20, 1973, when he disobeyed President Nixon's order that he dismiss Archibald Cox as the special prosecutor investigating the Watergate scandal.

(HAL BRUNO)

Rushdie, Salman

The words "Indian" and "Western" have many meanings. Salman Rushdie's first novel, *Grimus* (1975), was a fantastic, surrealist tale about an Indian called "Flapping Eagle" trying to make his way in a mysterious Western land. The region is something like a nightmare vision of America's "Wild West," with Indians in danger of being lynched by white settlers, but it is also like a British "public" school or college, a wonderland where a newcomer from the East may learn classical and local traditions, puns, riddles, anagrams, and schoolboy jokes. The Indian is guided by an eccentric scholar called V. B. C. Jones. "Virgil" is the first of Mr. Jones's names—and the reader is meant to think of the Roman Virgil who guided the poet Dante.

This dreamlike book made some reference to the circumstances of the author's life. Salman Rushdie was himself an Indian—but not of the same tribe as Flapping Eagle, the American "Redskin." Rushdie was born in Bombay on June 19, 1947, the child of prosperous Indian parents of the Muslim faith. He was brought up to speak both English and Urdu, which is one of the official languages of Pakistan but is also spoken by 23 million citizens of India. There was very little reference to Rushdie's Asian background in his novel *Grimus,* but his next two, *Midnight's Children* (1981) and *Shame* (1983), made full use of his knowledge of India and Pakistan, still in a dreamlike manner but with a closer reference to historical facts.

Rushdie's father sent him to England to be educated in the most exclusive and traditional way, at Rugby and then at King's College, Cambridge. In the 1960s his surrealistic tendency was encouraged by work with a multimedia theatre company in the London borough of Lambeth. His skill with English wordplay was expressed in his work as an advertising copywriter.

Grimus won no prizes, but *Midnight's Children* won the Booker McConnell Prize for Fiction in 1981, partly because there was a serious theme in the fantasy—the story of the partition of the Indian subcontinent into India and Pakistan. Two years later *Shame,* a fantasy about the recent history of Pakistan, very nearly won the same prize.

(D. A. N. JONES)

Sankara, Thomas

Upper Volta's fifth head of state since independence in 1960, Capt. Thomas Sankara, took over on Aug. 4, 1983, as president of a National Revolutionary Council (CNR). A captain of paratroops, Sankara was believed to have set up the coup that had ousted Col. Saye Zerbo on Nov. 7, 1982, and brought Maj. Jean-Baptiste Ouedraogo to power. Sankara served as premier under Ouedraogo during January–May 1983 and then was purged from the ruling People's Salvation Council on suspicion of subversive activity, including the cultivation of close links with Libya. He was held in custody for two weeks and afterward placed under house arrest. His takeover from Ouedraogo on August 4 was achieved with the support of a company of paratroopers and cost some 15 lives.

The 35-year-old Sankara belonged to a new generation of army officers in black Africa, fervently nationalistic in outlook and guarded in their attitude toward the former colonial power (France in the case of Upper Volta); a typical example was Jerry Rawlings of Ghana, with whom Sankara had much in common and whose system of "people's defense committees" he imitated in Upper Volta. Interviewed by the French press while attending the Franco-African summit in October, Sankara played down Libyan influence, claiming that the Voltaic revolution was a purely domestic product—and not one for export. On the subject of Franco-Voltaic relations, he remarked, not without irony, that French arms supplied to the previous regime had proved most useful on August 4.

Sankara's undoubted popularity, especially among the young and in the capital, Ouagadougou, owed not a little to a talent probably possessed by few other heads of state: the ability to accompany his own songs—on revolutionary themes—on the electric guitar. He had first become a well-known figure as a result of his exploits during border skirmishes with Mali in 1974. His resignation from the post of secretary of state for information under Colonel Zerbo, following a dispute with the latter, also won him respect. It was thought that in 1980 Sankara had himself planned to overthrow Zerbo's predecessor, Maj. Gen. Sangoulé Lamizana, who had ruled Upper Volta since 1966, but had been preempted by Zerbo.

(PHILIPPE DECRAENE)

Shamir, Yitzhak

On Sept. 2, 1983, Yitzhak Shamir, then Israel's foreign minister, was elected leader of the Herut Party and, therefore, its candidate to succeed Menachem Begin as prime minister. On October 10 Israel's Knesset (parliament) approved the coalition government put together by Shamir after his attempt to form a government of national consensus had broken down. On the way he had defeated a challenge from the much younger deputy prime minister, David Levy, and an attempt by the opposition leader Shimon Peres to form a Labour-based coalition government.

Shamir was born Yitzhak Jazernicki in Bialystok, a traditional centre of Jewish life in Poland, in 1915. He studied law at the University of Warsaw and immigrated to Palestine in 1935, where he was a construc-

UPI

tion worker for a time and then continued his studies at the Hebrew University, graduating with a law degree. In 1937 he joined the Irgun Zvai Leumi. At the outbreak of World War II the Irgun split. The majority at first supported the British war effort, while a minority under Abraham Stern formed the Freedom Fighters for Israel, known as Lehi or, by the British, as the "Stern Gang." In 1942 Stern was shot, and Shamir and two others took over the leadership of Lehi. Meanwhile, he had been arrested by the British in 1941 and escaped from the Mizra prison camp in 1942. In 1946 he was again arrested and sent to a prison camp in Eritrea, but once more he escaped and was given asylum in France.

Shamir returned to Israel in 1948 after the establishment of the Jewish state but did not join the newly formed Israel Defense Forces; instead he maintained the Jerusalem unit of Lehi. Following UN mediator Count Folke Bernadotte's assassination in Jerusalem in 1948, the Israeli government ordered the dissolution of Lehi. Shamir then withdrew from political activity and engaged in private business. In 1955 he was recruited into the Mossad (secret intelligence service) and served mainly in Europe until 1965, when he returned to private business. After joining the Herut Party in 1970, he became a member of the Knesset in 1973. When Begin formed his first government in 1977, Shamir was elected speaker, remaining in that office until his appointment as foreign minister in March 1980.

A man of extraordinary reserve, Shamir used words sparingly and without revealing more than was necessary; he abstained in the vote on the Camp David agreement but let it be known that he was opposed to returning the Sinai Peninsula to Egypt. On the question of a Palestinian state and the future of the West Bank, he held the same views as Begin, but if anything more strongly.

(JON KIMCHE)

Simmonds, Kennedy

After 3½ years as premier of St. Christopher and Nevis (St. Kitts), the last of the six associated states established by Britain in the Caribbean in 1967, Kennedy Simmonds led his country to full independence on Sept. 19, 1983. As prime minister of the new nation, Simmonds took office in the face of hostility from the opposition Labour Party; he headed a coalition government made up of his own People's Action Movement (PAM) and the smaller Nevis Reformation Party (NRP), led by Finance Minister Simeon Daniel. The opposition, which had claimed that Simmonds had no right to proceed to independence without holding new elections, also complained that the independence constitution gave too much power to Nevis, the lesser of the two islands in the new federation. Simmonds replied that the draft constitution, which gave Nevisians "autonomy over certain of their affairs," had been thoroughly discussed throughout the country.

A founding member of the PAM in 1965, Simmonds made three unsuccessful attempts to enter the House of Assembly before winning a by-election in the Central Basseterre constituency in January 1979. The seat had become vacant on the death of the sitting member, Premier Robert Bradshaw. Simmonds was reelected in the general election of Feb. 18, 1980, when the PAM-NRP coalition defeated the Labour Party, which had held power for 30 years. In St. Kitts, Simmonds was in the minority, Labour winning 58% of the votes and four of the seven seats, but the NRP's two Nevis seats gave the coalition a single-seat majority.

When he became prime minister of the newly independent nation, Simmonds did so against a background of economic depression, a declining sugar industry, and a tense labour situation. His pro-business administration intended to diversify agriculture, strengthen light industry and tourism, and seek more aid from the U.S.

Kennedy Simmonds was born on April 12, 1936, in Basseterre, St. Kitts. A scholarship student at St. Kitts-Nevis Grammar School, in 1954 he won the coveted Leeward Islands Scholarship to study medicine at the University College of the West Indies at Mona, Jamaica. He graduated in 1962 and did his medical internship at Kingston Public Hospital in Jamaica in 1963, returning to enter medical practice in St. Kitts and Anguilla in 1964. He gave up his practice in 1980 on assuming the premiership.

(ROD PRINCE)

Sinclair, Sir Clive Marles

When Sinclair Research launched its first personal computer, the Sinclair ZX80, in February 1980, its inventor and the chairman of the company, Clive Sinclair, correctly predicted that its introduction would dramatically expand the personal computer market. It was the first computer in the world to retail for under £100. (£1 in 1982 equaled $1.71.) The Sinclair ZX81 and ZX Spectrum advanced the model and confirmed their maker's name as a household word. Their success, deriving from Sinclair's policy of manufacturing smaller and cheaper computers than anyone else, brought him a knighthood in June 1983.

Born in London on July 30, 1940, Sinclair attended more than a dozen schools before completing his education at the age of 17. The fact that he did not attend a university was, he considered, an advantage in the rapidly expanding field of electronics. Four years as a technical journalist provided the grounding for a business career that began in 1962 when he founded Sinclair Radionics, a mail-order firm that sold radio and amplifier kits from a base in Islington, north London. Rapid expansion took the firm to Cambridge and later St. Ives, just outside Cambridge, and earned Sinclair a growing reputation as an electronics pioneer with a particular gift for miniaturization. However, throughout the 1970s his innovations, including an early pocket calculator and digital watch, were rapidly overtaken by U.S. and Japanese advances. By 1979 policy differences had emerged within the company: Sinclair wanted to concentrate exclusively on research into and development of consumer electronics, and in July 1979 he resigned all executive responsibility in Sinclair Radionics in order to pursue this aim.

By early 1983 Sinclair Research was laying claim to the title of the world's largest volume manufacturer of personal computers. Sinclair himself, with direct responsibility for the advanced products division, was already channeling his energies into other projects. In September he unveiled a flat-screen pocket television, the size of a paperback book; its price of under £80 ($120) once again undercut all competition. His aim for the future was to develop an electric vehicle for urban driving.

(LOUISE WATSON)

Sinowatz, Fred

On May 24, 1983, Fred Sinowatz was sworn in as Austria's federal chancellor at the head of a coalition government consisting of the Austrian Socialist Party (SPÖ) and the Austrian Freedom Party (FPÖ). Five months later, at a national convention of the SPÖ, Sinowatz was elected party chairman in succession to Bruno Kreisky, federal chancellor since 1970. Kreisky had resigned as chancellor after the SPÖ lost its absolute majority in the April election to the Nationalrat (lower house of Parliament) but had remained as SPÖ leader during the coalition negotiations with the FPÖ.

Sinowatz, who had been vice-chancellor since 1981, succeeded a statesman who had gained a considerable reputation in the field of foreign relations. He himself was not well known internationally but had a varied and successful career in provincial and federal politics behind him. Since 1971 he had been federal minister of education and the arts and as such had presided over far-reaching reforms of the Austrian school system, aimed at achieving equality of opportunity for the nation's youth. A convinced social democrat, he was considered to be a moderate and a conciliator—useful qualities for the leader of a party in some internal disarray after the election setback. Asked how he felt about succeeding Kreisky, Sinowatz said that he would not try to copy him. "I shall always seek advice from him, but I will remain Fred Sinowatz," he declared. The new chancellor's first exercise in foreign relations was a state visit to neighbouring Hungary on November 15–17.

Fred Sinowatz was born on Feb. 5, 1929, at Neufeld an der Leitha in the eastern Austrian province of Burgenland. His working-class parents belonged to the Croatian national minority, and he grew up speaking Croatian and German. After graduating with a doctorate in philosophy from Vienna University in 1953, he entered the Burgenland provincial government service, became an active SPÖ member, and was elected to the provincial Landtag in 1961. The same year he became party secretary to the provincial SPÖ organization. When the SPÖ won the 1964 provincial election, Sinowatz became first president of the Burgenland legislature. From 1966 until his appointment to the federal government in 1971 he was provincial spokesman on cultural affairs.

(K. M. SMOGORZEWSKI)

Smith, Billy

As he went into the 1983 Stanley Cup series, Billy Smith brought along reputations as both the National Hockey League's (NHL's) best play-off goaltender and as a battler who would cheerfully bite off the nose of anyone who might be caught sniffing around too close to his net. He came out of the series with both reputations fortified and also with the Conn Smythe Trophy as the tournament's most valuable player. In body and in spirit Smith had led the New York Islanders to their fourth consecutive NHL championship.

Smith always has been aggressive, actually intimidating players free to fire pucks toward him at more than 100 mph. A friendly father of two off the ice, on it he defends the goal with the fervour of a mother bear whose cubs are threatened. Most of all, he would not stand for someone circling his net at close range.

That is what Wayne Gretzky, the Edmonton Oilers' sensational scorer, was doing when Smith stabbed Gretzky's leg with his stick late in the second game of the Stanley Cup finals. An Edmonton newspaper called Smith "Public Enemy No. 1" on its front page the next day. By the time he accepted the Smythe Trophy, Smith had incited such an uproar that he said, "There's probably people rolling over in their graves with me getting this award." The Oilers had not been shut out in 199 games until Smith beat them 2–0 in the first contest of the finals.

Smith's father, Joe, was a railway worker who had emigrated from Belfast, Northern Ireland, at 16 and had two other sons before William John Smith was born Dec. 12, 1950. Joe flooded and lit his backyard in Perth, Ont., so that his three boys could play hockey at night. At 21 Billy played only five games for Los Angeles in his first NHL season, but his combative play in a hopeless game attracted the attention of general manager Bill Torrey, who was preparing to start up the Islanders team the next season.

Smith shared time in the Islanders' net until the 1980 play-offs, when he was not only spectacular but also inspired the Islanders to play with the aggressiveness they had lacked when they were upset in the previous two play-offs. Their Stanley Cup streak then began. Smith's best regular season was 1981–82, when he led the NHL with 32 wins in 46 games, ranked third with a goals-against average of 2.97, and won the Vezina Trophy for the NHL's best goaltending.

(KEVIN M. LAMB)

Soares, Mário

Leader and co-founder of the Portuguese Socialist Party (PSP), Mário Soares in 1983 became Portugal's premier for a second time after his party's qualified success in the April general election and its establishment with the Social Democrats (PSD) of a governing coalition. Following arguments with party dissidents over PSP support for the 1980 reelection of Pres. António Ramalho Eanes, Soares had been rebuilding his power base and standing within the party. His renewed popularity and influence ensured his reelection for the fifth time in a row as secretary-general of the PSP at the party's congress in October.

More important perhaps in the long term, Soares's list of candidates for the PSP national executive won 63.47% of the vote, for a total of 97 members against 37 for the anti-Soares faction and 6 for the left wing. Additionally, all but 2% of the 1,041 delegates approved a motion that recognized the shift of the PSP from revolutionary socialism to a position where the quest for social justice remained relevant but talk of socialization of the means of production was expunged from the party's manifesto. Another indication of Soares's renewed standing in the PSP was a motion that he be adopted as candidate for president of the republic from 1985. Soares, however, argued against the motion as likely to create political instability and threaten the coalition agreement with the PSD. He maintained that it was essential to concentrate in the near term on Portugal's grave economic problems.

Born Dec. 7, 1924, in Lisbon, Soares graduated in arts from the University of Lisbon and in law from the Sorbonne in Paris. He was a founder of the United Democratic Youth Movement and a member of its central executive from 1946 to 1948. Under the authoritarian regimes of António de Oliveira Salazar and his successor, Marcello Caetano, Soares was imprisoned on 13 occasions for his political activity and in 1970 went into exile in France. He returned to Portugal after the 1974 military coup and was foreign minister (1974–75) in the subsequent provisional governments. After the 1976 election he headed a minority Socialist government until 1978 and while in office negotiated Portugal's first agreement with the International Monetary Fund.

(MICHAEL WOOLLER)

Strout, Richard Lee

As he prepared to celebrate his 85th birthday on March 14, 1983, Richard Strout decided it was time to hold just one job. Therefore, although he retired after 40 years as the *New Republic*'s Washington columnist, he continued, as he had for the last 62 years, to be a reporter for the *Christian Science Monitor*. Among the most remarkable people in U.S. journalism, he was described as "irreplaceable" by the *New Republic*.

Strout was born in 1898 in Cohoes, N.Y. He had been a newspaper reporter since 1919, first in Sheffield, England, on the *Sheffield Independent*, and then, recrossing the Atlantic, briefly on the *Boston Post* in 1921. From 1921 to 1925 he was a reporter for the *Christian Science Monitor*, joining its Washington bureau in 1925. He served as a war correspondent during World War II, covering, among other major events, the Allied invasion of Normandy, France, in 1944.

Strout was asked to take over the *New Republic*'s anonymous Washington column in 1943. Called TRB (the initials were the inspiration of an earlier columnist who finished each contribution on New York City's BRT subway line; from inside the car the initials painted on the window read TRB), the column had had a series of authors and was a kind of weekly summary of opinionated inside information. Strout, partly because he was a veteran correspondent by this time and partly because he was a thoughtful journalist, brought to the column a broader view, but one that was finely tuned, and a point of view that could be called balanced liberal. It was said that he wrote, week to week, a moral history of the times.

The length of his career has allowed Strout to scrutinize carefully one-third of all U.S. presidents, although he modestly denies knowing any of them very well. He has not been taken in by fads and indeed regretted the onset of television coverage of presidential press conferences because of its effect on the behaviour of members of the media. He has expressed the wish that the U.S. governmental system were a parliamentary one, which, he believes, would train future leaders well.

Strout's columns were lucid accounts of inside Washington. His research was thorough, his opinions were thoughtful, and his integrity was unquestioned. He brought an intellectual panache to TRB that seemed certain to be sorely missed.

(BONNIE OBERMAN)

Tanaka, Kakuei

Kakuei Tanaka would long remember 1983 as one of his roughest years. After a trial that lasted nearly seven years, the former prime minister of Japan was convicted of bribery and a violation of the foreign exchange law. He was then sentenced to four years in prison and fined the equivalent of $2.1 million—the amount he received from the Lockheed Corp. in 1972 for helping the company sell its airplanes in Japan. Although Tanaka immediately appealed the verdict and remained free on bond, he might well have reached the beginning of the end of his spectacular political career. The ruling of the Tokyo District Court touched off demands by politicians and the news media that Tanaka resign from politics, but Tanaka simply refused to discuss the issue. The conviction also sparked a six-week boycott of Diet (parliament) proceedings that was resolved only when Prime Minister Yasuhiro Nakasone (*q.v.*) promised to hold new elections in December.

In many ways Tanaka's case was a modern Japanese political tragedy. He was born in Niigata Prefecture on May 4, 1918, the only boy among seven children of a poor cattle dealer who could not afford to send him to school. Young Tanaka went to Tokyo and worked as a construction clerk, attending technical school at night. He set up a construction business which thrived during World War II. He was first elected to public office in 1947 at the age of 28. During his 36 years in politics he received extraordinary popular support. Although he was the only modern Japanese prime minister not to have finished high school or to have graduated from an established Japanese university, Tanaka was more successful than any of his contemporaries at pushing through government projects. That talent earned him the nickname "Computerized Bulldozer." He was also responsible for revitalizing much of western Japan. Among his major accomplishments as prime minister was the restoration of diplomatic relations with China.

Despite the political cloud that enveloped Tanaka after his indictment in 1976, he continued to rule over the largest faction of the ruling Liberal-Democratic Party and thus had a major say in the selection of the past four prime ministers. He might no longer wield such influence because Prime Minister Nakasone distanced himself from Tanaka by moving some of the latter's key supporters out of the reorganized Nakasone Cabinet. But Tanaka could be counted on to continue brokering behind the scenes for as long as he could win support.

(FRANK GIBNEY, JR.)

Te Kanawa, Dame Kiri

Among her many engagements in a typically busy year for one of the great operatic stars of the past decade, soprano Kiri Te Kanawa appeared at the Metropolitan Opera, New York City, in Richard Strauss's *Arabella* and *Der Rosenkavalier* and sang with the Chicago Symphony Orchestra during the early months of 1983. At the Royal Opera House, Covent Garden, in the spring and summer she sang the title role in Puccini's *Manon Lescaut* and that of Donna Elvira in Mozart's *Don Giovanni.* Back at the Met in the fall she was Violetta in Verdi's *La Traviata,* then finished the year as Rosalinde in the Royal Opera's production of Johann Strauss's *Die Fledermaus.* In June she visited the University of Oxford to receive an honorary doctorate of music.

Te Kanawa had shot to stardom in the 1970s with a series of appearances at Covent Garden and the enthusiastic support of conductors such as Sir Colin Davis and Sir Georg Solti. Her first big success was as the Countess in Mozart's *Marriage of Figaro* in 1971. That was followed by a run of Mozart operas and, among others, a production of Puccini's *La Bohème* in which she sang Mimi to Luciano Pavarotti's Rudolfo. Her debut at the Met in 1974 as Desdemona in Verdi's *Otello* was acclaimed by both critics and public. In 1981 the prince of Wales—"one of her greatest fans"—asked her to sing at his marriage to Lady Diana Spencer, and her rendering of Handel's "Let the Bright Seraphim" reached a worldwide television audience of more than 600 million. In Queen Elizabeth II's 1982 birthday honours Te Kanawa was created a Dame Commander of the Order of the British Empire.

Kiri Te Kanawa was born on March 6, 1944, at Gisborne, North Island, New Zealand. Her parents were unmarried and in poor circumstances, and when Kiri was five weeks old she was adopted by Tom and Nell Te Kanawa; Tom, like her true father, was a Maori, and his wife, like Kiri's true mother, was of British descent—a great-niece of composer Sir Arthur Sullivan. Kiri attended a Roman Catholic girls' college in Auckland, where one of the sisters was a well-known teacher of singing. After leaving school she won various singing competitions in New Zealand and Australia and in 1966, after a period as a popular singer and recording artist, became a student at the London Opera Centre.

(MOZELLE A. MOSHANSKY)

Thatcher, Margaret Hilda

In a landslide victory in the British general election on June 9, 1983, Margaret Thatcher was returned to power to head a Conservative government for a second term, with an overall majority of 144 in the House of Commons. This confirmed her in her determination to pursue policies that would shift the balance of power in a mixed economy decisively back into the hands of the private sector. A program of monetarist financial policies, the selling off of state-owned enterprise, legislation to curb trade union power, and the cutting back of welfare-state expenditure had by now come to be identified in one word: "Thatcherism."

Thatcher had frequently said that this program would take two terms of government to complete. In post-World War II British history, however, second terms had proved hazardous to prime ministers. This had been the experience of Clement Attlee, Harold Macmillan, and Harold Wilson. Some disenchantment with Thatcher set in soon after her general election triumph. Committed as she was to "conviction politics," she placed the most loyal Thatcherites in key positions in her Cabinet and sacked or shunted onto the sidelines those she distrusted. Her suspicion of the civil service "mandarins" led her to import more personal advisers from outside government. This, combined with her presidential style, caused resentment.

A measure of bad luck contributed to this change of mood. She had a worrying few weeks when the sight of one eye was threatened by a partly detached retina. This was successfully corrected, but the supposedly inexhaustible Thatcher looked tired and strained. A September visit to the U.S., where she received the Winston Churchill Award, led some critics to complain that she was too unquestioningly Reaganite. Yet when she rebuked Pres. Ronald Reagan for the U.S. invasion of Grenada she infuriated the right-wing Tories.

UPI

Margaret Thatcher, born in the provincial market town of Grantham on Oct. 13, 1925, epitomized the upwardly mobile middle class from which her new-style conservatism drew its strength. A science graduate of the University of Oxford, she entered Parliament in 1959 and was a Cabinet minister in the Edward Heath government of 1970–74. She was elected party leader in 1975, becoming prime minister after winning the general election of 1979. She soon came to be nicknamed "the iron lady," a reputation that was confirmed by her unflinching leadership during the Falkland Islands conflict in 1982.

(HARFORD THOMAS)

Theismann, Joe

In ten seasons Joe Theismann went from a brash, irritating third-string quarterback to the most valuable player in the National Football League. He led the Washington Redskins to a 14–2 regular-season record in 1983, the most victories ever achieved in one season by a National Football Conference (NFC) team. The Redskins set an NFL single-season record with 541 points, never scoring fewer than 23, and became the first defending NFL champion in four years to return to the play-offs.

Theismann ranked second among NFL passers in 1983 with a 97.0 rating. His ratio of touchdown passes to interceptions was a remarkable 29–11, anything better than 1–1 being considered very good. Theismann's dashing, gambling style made him unlikely to throw so few interceptions, but he also was known for his quick thinking. Hall of Fame coach Sid Gillman called him the best NFL quarterback at operating on the run, and many pass rushers called him the hardest quarterback to tackle.

His success, style, and gregarious charm made Theismann an endearing sports hero and walking conglomerate. During the 1983 season, he owned a newspaper and two restaurants and had his own shows on radio and television. He had appeared in several movies, made countless television commercials, was in heavy demand as a banquet speaker and talk-show guest, and even dined occasionally at the White House.

The solid Theismann empire did not seem likely to begin crumbling even after the Redskins' embarrassing 38–9 defeat to the Los Angeles Raiders in the Super Bowl on Jan. 22, 1984. He was still remembered as the quarterback who led them to their 27–17 Super Bowl victory over Miami a year earlier and to 36 triumphs in their last 42 games. A week after the 1984 Super Bowl he was back in form, leading the NFC to a 45–3 victory over the American Football Conference in the Pro Bowl and setting Pro Bowl records for completions (21 of 27) and touchdown passes (3).

Joseph Robert Theismann, born on Sept. 9, 1949, in New Brunswick, N.J., attracted professional baseball scouts when he played at South River (N.J.) High School. But he chose instead to play football at Notre Dame, where in his senior year he finished second in the voting for college football's most outstanding player. After earning a B.A. in sociology (1971), Theismann played three seasons in the Canadian Football League, where he led the Toronto Argonauts to the championship game as a rookie. He joined the Redskins in 1974 and became a permanent starter in 1978.

(KEVIN M. LAMB)

Thorburn, Cliff

Snooker was described by Cliff Thorburn as a one-to-one game in which a player need not apologize to anyone but himself for his mistakes. However, Thorburn—considered one of the world's most feared players—rarely needed to apologize even to himself. During the 1983 world professional snooker championships in Sheffield, England, he sank all 21 snooker balls in sequence for a perfect score of 147, the first "maximum break" game in the history of the tournament. Thorburn lost in the finals to Steve Davis (*q.v.*), but he was the Benson and Hedges snooker champion and the Australian Masters' snooker champion. In 1982 he was captain of the Canadian team that won the world team snooker championship in England. When Thorburn played in the world professional snooker championship in Sheffield in 1977, he became the first non-British player to reach the finals. Three years later, in 1980, he became the first non-British player to win the championship.

Born Clifford Charles Devlin Thorburn on Jan. 16, 1948, in Victoria, B.C., he was always a sports enthusiast, but team sports did not interest him as much as snooker. Played on a green-covered 6- by 12-ft table with 15 red balls, 6 balls of other colours, and a white cue ball, the game fascinated him as a child because of the many colours involved. He excelled in eye-to-hand coordination and was described as methodical, measured, and calm as a competitor. Thorburn won his first North American snooker championship in 1971 and his first Canadian snooker championship in 1974. In all, he was North American champion two times and Canadian champion ten times. In 1975 he became the first Canadian to be seeded in world snooker play. His stamina was tested in 1983 when he played and won a seven-hour frame, the longest in the history of the world professional championship. Normally a frame lasts 20 minutes.

In 1979 Thorburn moved to England, where most of his games were played. He returned to live in Canada in 1982, making his home near Toronto with his wife, Barbara, but he still had to spend six months of the year in England. While in Canada, he devoted much of his time to promoting the sport, particularly at the university level.

(DIANE LOIS WAY)

Torvill, Jayne, and Dean, Christopher

A British skating couple who set unprecedented standards in ice dancing, Jayne Torvill and Christopher Dean of Nottingham, England, won their third consecutive world title in Helsinki, Fin., in 1983 with a free-dance performance that received maximum marks for presentation from each of the nine judges—a feat implying perfection and never before achieved in that or any other branch of figure skating.

Torvill, born on Oct. 7, 1957, and Dean, born on July 27, 1958 (both in Nottingham), first teamed together in 1975 and became British champions three years later, a title they successfully defended each following year. European champions in 1981 and 1982, they could not defend that title in 1983 because of an injury to Torvill's shoulder, but the quality of their subsequent third world championship victory made them favourites for an Olympic Games gold medal in 1984. Made members of the Order of the British Empire by Queen Elizabeth II in 1980 and granted the freedom of Nottingham in 1983, they were also voted team of the year in various national polls, in competition with the stars of all other sports.

Their dramatic rise to the top was a reward for exceptional dedication to training, with consequent social sacrifices. Their early successes, until 1980, were accomplished while each was employed full-time, Dean as a police constable and Torvill as an insurance clerk; they had to compete against many who had no such restrictions on their hours of preparation. When international success seemed possible, the solution to this problem and soaring training costs came with generous sponsorship from the Nottingham City Council.

Their superiority over their contemporaries—and, indeed, their predecessors—owed much to painstaking attention to details of finesse that helped to provide the extra gloss. Their rapport was almost uncanny, with actions totally in alignment and always with smooth, flowing grace. Some of their innovative movements proved too intricate for others to imitate. Their above-waist actions of heads, arms, hands, and even fingers synchronized with seemingly telepathic understanding. Their facial expressions and precise interpretation of mood and intelligently chosen music added a unique charismatic appeal.

(HOWARD BASS)

Vogel, Hans-Jochen

After the breakup of the coalition of Social Democrats and Free Democrats in September 1982, Hans-Jochen Vogel was chosen as the Social Democrats' chancellor candidate in the West German federal election of March 6, 1983. The decision of the former chancellor, Helmut Schmidt, not to stand again caused many centrist voters to withdraw their support from the Social Democratic Party (SPD). This was one of the main reasons why the SPD suffered such a heavy defeat. Vogel was an able and intelligent politician, but his efforts to attract the far left cost his party many votes. This strategy, recommended by the SPD's chairman, former chancellor Willy Brandt, ill befitted Vogel, traditionally a firm centrist if not slightly to the right of centre.

Vogel, a Roman Catholic, was born on Feb. 3, 1926, in Göttingen, where his father was a university lecturer. After military service he studied law at the universities of Munich and Marburg and subsequently became an official in the Munich city legal department. He joined the SPD in 1950. Ten years later, after an impressive performance in municipal and regional politics, he was elected mayor of Munich. He supervised many major developments, which helped bring the Olympic Games to Munich in 1972.

SAHM DOHERTY/TIME MAGAZINE

A few months before the Games took place, Vogel, weary of battles with the left, withdrew from office and opened a law practice. This interlude was short. He accepted Chancellor Brandt's invitation to become federal minister of housing and town planning in August 1972, and four years later, under Chancellor Schmidt, he was appointed federal minister of justice.

In 1981 Vogel was sent to West Berlin as mayor, replacing Dietrich Stobbe, who had resigned in the wake of a series of scandals in the city's SPD. Vogel coped well, but the malaise in the party had gone too deep, and in June 1981, after the SPD's poor showing in a city election, he resigned to make way for a Christian Democrat mayor. After the 1983 federal election, Vogel remained in Bonn as opposition leader in the Bundestag (parliament). (NORMAN CROSSLAND)

Walker, Herschel

Herschel Walker left the University of Georgia and its football team on Feb. 23, 1983, with a rich professional contract in a new football league. There he resumed breaking records, as he had done regularly in three seasons at Georgia.

Walker left the Bulldogs team with one year of unused college football eligibility and 14 major college football records, including most yards rushing for a freshman and a sophomore. The 6 ft 2 in, 220-lb running back wound up third on the all-time rushing list with 5,259 yd, a record for three seasons. He averaged 5.3 yd per carry and 159.3 yd per game. He had nine games with at least 200 yd and 162 carries for at least 10 yd. His 1,891 yd rushing as a sophomore in 1981 was the third highest total in college football history.

In Heisman Trophy voting for the country's most outstanding college football player Walker finished third as a freshman, second as a sophomore, and first as a junior. His teams won 32 of 33 regular-season games, 3 Southeast Conference championships, and the 1980 national championship, which Walker helped clinch by running for 150 yd and scoring two touchdowns as most valuable player in that season's Sugar Bowl.

Walker was born on March 3, 1962, in Wrightsville, Ga. He was a natural football player who had considered turning professional since he was a college freshman. A Canadian Football League team wooed him as a freshman, and when he went professional it sent the state of Georgia into public displays of mourning. His attorney, Jack Manton, approached the new United States Football League (USFL) as it prepared for its inaugural March-to-July season in 1983. Although the USFL, along with the National Football League, prohibited signing underclassmen, both parties agreed that signing Walker could give the new league instant credibility and make Walker an instant millionaire. His three-year contract with the New Jersey Generals was estimated at $3.9 million to $5.4 million. The Generals announced that they sold nearly 6,000 season tickets in the three days after Walker joined them.

The Generals won just 6 of 12 games in 1983, but Walker led USFL rushers with 1,812 yd and 18 touchdowns. With 489 yd on pass receptions, he became the sixth professional football player to gain 2,000 total yards in a season. Against Washington on May 29 he had the new league's best rushing game (194 yd) and longest run (83 yd). After the season he returned to the University of Georgia, where he continued studies toward a degree in criminology.

(KEVIN M. LAMB)

Washington, Harold

In a year when black politicians in the U.S. scored several major victories, no one faced a greater challenge or more frustration than Harold Washington of Chicago, who on April 12, 1983, was elected that city's first black mayor in a race-dominated battle that drew national attention. A native Chicagoan, Washington was born April 15, 1922, the son of a Democratic precinct captain. He was graduated (1949) from Chicago's Roosevelt University, obtained his law degree (1952) from nearby Northwestern University, and practiced law in Chicago until he entered the state legislature in 1965. In the early 1970s he ran afoul of the law himself,

GEORGE MARS CASSIDY—GLOBE PHOTOS/STOCKPHOTOS, INC.

serving a month in jail for failure to file federal income tax forms for four years. His law license also was suspended for a time when he failed to perform paid legal work. He was serving his second term in the U.S. House of Representatives when black leaders in Chicago convinced him to run for mayor.

In the February 22 primary Washington faced incumbent Mayor Jane M. Byrne and Cook County State's Attorney Richard M. Daley, son of the late mayor and party boss Richard J. Daley. Byrne and Daley, who represented rival factions of the Democratic machine, rejected race as an issue, but their campaigns, particularly Byrne's, exploited the racial fears of white ethnic voters. Washington further polarized the election by campaigning almost entirely among blacks, promising sweeping reforms in City Hall and an end to the patronage hiring system. Byrne and Daley split the white vote, while blacks, who made up 40% of Chicago's population, voted overwhelmingly for Washington, giving him a narrow victory with slightly more than 36% of the total.

In the general election Washington faced Republican businessman and former state legislator Bernard Epton. Washington made a greater effort to attract white voters, but racial tensions, fear of his planned changes, and concern over his past drove thousands of Democrats to vote for Epton. Washington won in a record turnout with almost 52% of the vote (including almost 20% of the white and Hispanic vote).

After his inauguration the new mayor struggled with labour unrest, severe financial strains, and a rebellious City Council where regular Democrats who opposed him formed a majority coalition of 29 aldermen under party chief Edward Vrdolyak and blocked his attempts at reform. The stalemate was not broken until late December, when Washington's forces reached a last-minute budget compromise with the Vrdolyak 29. (MELINDA SHEPHERD)

Watt, James

From the moment he was nominated to be U.S. secretary of the interior, James Watt was embroiled in controversy with environmentalists, liberal members of Congress, and anyone else who opposed his crusade to "change America, to match his own vision for it." Eventually, even Republican Party leaders came to believe that Watt's policies favouring economic development over conservation and his abrasive personal style were making him a political liability. But for 2½ years he had the support of Pres. Ronald Reagan and survived one turbulent incident after another, determined to stay on the job until he no longer could serve the president in a useful way.

That day finally came on Oct. 9, 1983, when Reagan "reluctantly" accepted Watt's resignation. The final storm was touched off by Watt's flippant description of the balance reflected in a coal-leasing advisory panel he had appointed: "... a black ... a woman, two Jews and a cripple." In his resignation letter Watt concluded that his "usefulness ... had come to an end." The man had become as much of an issue as his policies, and many of those responsible for Reagan's reelection wanted Watt out before the 1984 campaign got under way.

MARK SENNET—SHOOTING STAR

A career change for U.S. Secretary of the Interior James Watt was triggered by public reaction to his description of this coal-leasing advisory panel: "... a black [Andrew F. Brimmer], ... a woman [Julia M. Walsh], two Jews [David F. Linowes, centre rear, and Richard L. Gordon, right front], and a cripple [Gordon, who has a paralyzed arm]." Watt did not include the other member of the group, Donald C. Alexander, a WASP (right rear).

A self-described fundamentalist in religion, politics, and economics, Watt believed in using, not merely reserving, public lands. But in one coal-leasing deal, a General Accounting Office report claimed that the government settled for $100 million less than fair-market value from western energy interests. In Congress the Republican-controlled Senate joined the Democratic House in measures to restrict several of Watt's Interior Department programs, including the development of offshore oil and gas reserves.

Born in Lusk, Wyo., on Jan. 31, 1938, Watt was a studious youth, active in athletics and student affairs. He earned a bachelor's degree with honours at the University of Wyoming. He was elected to Phi Kappa Phi and went on to take a law degree at the university. He served as a middle-level bureaucrat at the Department of the Interior from 1969 to 1972 and was chief counsel from 1977 to 1980 for a Denver legal foundation that specialized in fighting against environmental protection programs. As secretary of the interior he embarked on a conservative crusade to open vast federal landholdings to mineral exploration, timber exploitation, and multiple uses by recreation and commercial interests. He sought to ease restrictions against environmental pollution and stopped acquiring new national park land, shifting funds to rehabilitation of run-down existing facilities. (HAL BRUNO)

Yamani, Ahmad Zaki

Saudi Arabia's petroleum minister, Ahmad Zaki Yamani, was typical of the group of highly qualified commoners, mostly trained in the West, who held senior technical posts in the Saudi government. Gregarious, urbane, and intelligent, he ran by far the best ministry in the Saudi establishment. He supported the current ambitious Saudi development plan and hoped to see a rapid modernization of the kingdom. A honey-tongued spokesman for Saudi policy abroad, he chaired the final press conference of the key March 1983 meeting of the Organization of Petroleum Exporting Countries (OPEC) in London. (*See* ENERGY: *Petroleum.*)

Yamani was born in the holy city of Mecca in 1930 and was educated in Cairo and at Harvard University, where he obtained a doctorate. A lawyer by training, he first entered government in Saudi Arabia as legal adviser to the Council of Ministers in 1958–60. On the dismissal of Abdullah Tariki, the kingdom's first oil minister, Yamani became King Faisal's chief spokesman on oil policy and a director of the national oil company, Aramco. In the climactic talks in Teheran in January–February 1971 that broke the power of the oil industry, Yamani emerged as the most subtle and persuasive tactician of the OPEC camp. Wrapped in his gold-threaded black bishla, he symbolized the popular image of the Arab oil sheikh, although in fact he was more of a servant to King Faisal than a policy maker, as he was also to be to King Khalid and his successor, King Fahd.

Yamani was the first to suggest that the Arabs might use oil as a weapon against countries supporting Israel. By contrast with his stand during 1971–74, he later became a voice for moderation on oil price increases by OPEC. He was aware at an early stage, when an oil revenue surplus began to pile up after 1974, that the health of the Saudi government depended on maintaining the strength of the U.S. economy. Yamani was present at the assassination of King Faisal in March 1975 and was briefly kidnapped by international terrorists in December of that year during the OPEC ministers' meeting in Vienna. He later recalled that he was so frightened that he began reciting verses from the Koran.

(JOHN WHELAN)

The seven 1983 Nobel laureates ranged in age from 40 to 81, but the group as a whole was much older than usual. Only Lech Walesa, the Polish electrician who was awarded the Prize for Peace, was less than 60 years of age. The oldest of the group, cytogeneticist Barbara McClintock, became only the third woman in Nobel history to receive an unshared prize for scientific work. In winning the Prize for Physiology or Medicine she thus joined the illustrious company of Marie Curie and Dorothy Hodgkin. The Prize for Economics went to French-born Gerard Debreu, a professor at the University of California at Berkeley. Henry Taube of Stanford (Calif.) University was given the Prize for Chemistry, while astrophysicists Subrahmanyan Chandrasekhar and William A. Fowler shared the Prize for Physics. The Prize for Literature was the most controversial. One Swedish Academy juror publicly repudiated the choice of Englishman William Golding and was in turn denounced by the secretary of the Academy for possessing "the soul of a magpie." The outbursts were as unprecedented as they were unseemly, but the controversy partially lifted the veil on Nobel committee proceedings. Two names that reportedly remained year after year on a list of potential recipients were those of Graham Greene and Jorge Luis Borges. The latter, it appeared, had been repeatedly passed over because some members of the committee objected to his politics.

Each 1983 prize carried an honorarium of 1.5 million kronor, or about $192,000.

Prize for Peace

Lech Walesa, founder of Solidarity, the now outlawed Polish federation of labour unions, was hunting mushrooms with friends when Western reporters brought word that he had been awarded the Nobel Peace Prize. Later, at a news conference in a Gdansk church, the 40-year-old electrician remarked that many lesser-known people deserved the award. Walesa, who pledged that the money would be put into a fund administered by the Roman Catholic Church for the benefit of Polish farmers, was honoured for his defense of human rights and his determined efforts "to solve his country's problems through negotiations and cooperation without resorting to violence." Egil Aarvik, chairman of the Nobel Prize committee, remarked: "I don't expect any thanks or gratitude from the Polish authorities, but I can imagine that the attitude of the Polish people will be very different."

Lech Walesa was born in the village of Popowo, north of Warsaw, on Sept. 29, 1943. After moving to Gdansk, he began working as an electrician in the gigantic Lenin shipyard. He was in Gdansk during the 1970 food riots when police killed a number of demonstrators. When new protests erupted six years later, Walesa was a member of the strike committee. He then began to edit an underground paper and established contact with the Workers Self-Defense Committee. Tensions increased in 1980 when an elderly female crane operator was fired and the government announced another increase in prices. Though Walesa had been fired several years earlier for trying to organize the workers, he scaled the shipyard fence and joined the workers inside because he feared they might capitulate in the face of intense government pressure. It was a decision with far-reaching consequences. Walesa took charge of an interfactory strike committee that in time issued a set of bold political demands that included the right to strike and to form free unions. The iron gates at the Lenin shipyard—festooned with Polish flags, flowers, and pictures of Pope John Paul II—came to symbolize the hopes of the workers for a new life under the Communist regime. The world watched in wonder and feared for the worst, but Soviet tanks did not intervene. To reduce the risk of violent confrontation in such a charged atmosphere, Walesa insisted on strict discipline and banned the consumption of alcohol. His plucky courage and good humour helped sustain the spirit of his fellow workers.

Fearing a national revolt, the Communist authorities yielded to the workers' principal demands. When some ten million people joined semiautonomous unions, Walesa was suddenly the chief spokesman for a national federation, called Solidarity, that united the individual unions. Walesa then showed remarkable political skills in dealing with the government. He seemed to know instinctively just how far he could go in challenging the authorities without inviting disaster. But more radical factions did not share this caution. When less pragmatic workers called for a referendum on Poland's Communist government and the country's alliance with the Soviet Union, authorities imposed martial law. Solidarity was outlawed and Walesa interned for 11 months. When he emerged, his constituency was in disarray. Walesa did not go to Oslo to receive the prize because he feared that he would not be permitted to reenter Poland. His wife, Danuta, read his speech of thanks, in which he said that, despite all that had been going on in Poland, there was no alternative to agreement between the state authorities and the people.

Prize for Economics

In 1776 Adam Smith asserted that an "invisible hand" controlled supply and demand. In 1959 Gerard Debreu mathematically dissected that hand and analyzed its anatomy in *The Theory of Value: An Axiomatic Analysis of Economic Equilibrium*. The 114-page monograph, immediately praised by the *American Economics Review* as an incipient classic, was the keystone of an oeuvre for which Debreu was awarded the Nobel Memorial Prize for Economics.

The Royal Swedish Academy of Sciences cited Debreu for designing "a mathematical model of a market economy where different producers planned the output of goods and services and thus also their demand for factors of production [*e.g.*, labour, capital, resources] in such a way that their profit was maximized." The *Washington Post* applauded Debreu's "elegant mathematical proof that in a competitive capitalist economy the forces of supply and demand can be balanced at the point of maximum efficiency."

The laureate himself, who teaches both economics and mathematics at the University of California at Berkeley, said: "I seek to set up abstract models, couched in mathematical terms, to give an account of the way the many agents of which an economy is composed make decisions, and how those decisions are consistent with each other." He also remarked: "I am doubly pleased, for myself and for the type of work I am doing, which is the application of mathematical theory to economics."

Born in Calais, France, on July 4, 1921, Debreu studied at the École Normale Supérieure in Paris and the University of Paris, where he earned a doctorate in economics in 1956. After serving with French occupation forces in Germany, he joined the Cowles Commission at the University of Chicago in 1950. The study group, later relocated at Yale University, is remarkable for having employed seven of the dozen

Nobel laureates for 1983 assembled in the library of the Royal Academy at Stockholm. They are (standing, from left) Henry Taube (Chemistry), Barbara McClintock (Physiology), William Fowler (Physics), Gerard Debreu (Economics), Subrahmanyan Chandrasekhar (Physics), all of the U.S.; and (seated) William Golding (Literature) of the United Kingdom.

SVENSKT PRESSFOTO/PICTORIAL PARADE

Americans who have won the Nobel Prize for Economics since its inception in 1969. The selection of Debreu was somewhat unusual for the Swedish Academy's five-man nomination committee and 262-member electorate. Most previous winners had been noted for their involvement with macroeconomics and particular political schools of thought. Debreu was a "carefully nonpolitical" scholar, in the view of the *Wall Street Journal*, and "provided the foundation for modern microeconomic theory." He is so involved with describing the bricks others use to build huge constructs that, unlike many in his field, he declines to accept offers to act as a corporate consultant. The Academy may have intentionally underscored the importance of pure research in selecting Debreu because his analyses have such universal application that they are used by every school of applied macroeconomic thought.

Prize for Literature

As a Royal Navy officer during World War II, William Golding witnessed the sinking of the German battleship "Bismarck" and the invasion of Normandy. The war, he later acknowledged, was a turning point in his life. "I began to see what people are capable of doing.... Anyone who moved through those years without understanding that man produces evil as a bee produces honey must have been blind or wrong in the head." It was this vision that inspired his novels and led to a Nobel Prize.

Golding was born in Cornwall, England, on Sept. 19, 1911. His mother was a suffragette and his father, scion of a long line of schoolmasters, an "incandescent omniscience" who "inhabited a world of sanity, and logic, and fascination." Golding was sent to Marlborough Grammar School and then to Brasenose College, Oxford, to study science. Rebelling against the course his father had set for him, he turned to literature and published a volume of poems. After graduation Golding tried settlement house work and provincial theatre, then became a teacher at Bishop Wordsworth's School in Salisbury. He wrote reviews and essays on the side and, after the war, produced three novels. When none found a publisher, Golding gave up trying to suit commercial tastes. His days were occupied by English schoolboys whose resemblance to the hero of *Treasure Island* was slight at best. "I said to Ann [his wife], wouldn't it be a good idea to write a book about real boys on an island, showing what a mess they'd make?" The result was *Lord of the Flies* (1954). Though the book was a near-failure in hardcover, one North American paperback edition sold 7.5 million copies. The book focuses on a troop of boys placed on a tropical island for their own safety at the outset of World War III. They gradually devolve into tribes of idol-worshiping savages and murder two of their own. But, in typical Golding fashion, a few boys hold onto their humanity. That spark of human decency gleams in all of Golding's works. In *The Inheritors* (1955) it shines as the spirit of sylvan Neanderthals who are vanquished by a new breed of rapacious *Homo sapiens* armed with weapons. Golding's other novels include *The Spire, Darkness Visible, Pincher Martin, Free Fall, The Pyramid, The Scorpion God,* and *Rites of Passage.* The latter won the 1980 Booker McConnell Prize, Britain's most honoured literary award. All these works feature dark situations and some dour characters but, as the Swedish Academy noted, the books "are not only somber moralities and dark myths about evil and treacherous, destructive forces. They are also colourful tales of adventure which can be read as such, full of narrative joy, inventiveness and excitement."

In its official citation, the Academy honoured Golding "for his novels which, with the perspicuity of realistic narrative art and the diversity and universality of myth, illuminate the human condition in the world of today." An unusually wide circle of scholars and critics have been attracted to his "strata of ambiguity and complication ... in which odd people are tempted to reach beyond their limits, thereby being bared to the very marrow." Indeed, the author takes wry delight in noting that books about his books outnumber his works themselves. After confessing that he had read only about 10% of what others have written about his novels, Golding observed: "But it gives employment, doesn't it? Academic light industry."

Bearded and gnomelike at 72, Golding comments: "In all these books, I have suggested a shape in the universe that may, as it were, account for things. The greatest pleasure is not, say, sex or geometry. It is just understanding.... If you can just get people to understand their own humanity." (PHILIP KOPPER)

Prize for Physiology or Medicine

The Prize for Physiology or Medicine was awarded to Barbara McClintock of the Cold Spring Harbor (N.Y.) Laboratory, a cytogeneticist who first explained some of the cellular mechanisms that account for the mutability of the hereditary traits of living things. She made her discoveries in the course of a lifelong study of the maize plant (Indian corn), correlating the variations in outwardly visible properties, such as the pigmentation patterns of the kernels and leaves, with changes in the genetic elements of the cell nuclei. These elements, the chromosomes, can be seen with the aid of a microscope, using methods that McClintock perfected.

Her mastery of the details of the development of the corn plant so far surpassed the knowledge of other investigators that when she presented her complicated findings in 1951 there was scarcely anyone else in the world who could comprehend what she had accomplished. Eventually, during the 1960s and 1970s, other geneticists became familiar with the behaviour of chromosomes and found that McClintock's analysis applied to many organisms besides maize. In recent years, widening recognition of the fundamental importance of her research has brought her several significant awards.

Barbara McClintock was born on June 16, 1902, in Hartford, Conn., and, despite her mother's opposition, entered Cornell University, Ithaca, N.Y., in 1919. She had intended to study plant breeding, but that curriculum was deemed unsuitable for women at the time, so she earned her bachelor's, master's, and doctor's degrees as a botany major. Again she overrode convention by electing to wear a pair of blue jeans, instead of a less practical skirt, while working in the cornfield tended by the members of Rollins Emerson's small plant-breeding group, which was studying the genetics of maize in a program like that carried out earlier by Thomas Hunt Morgan on the fruit fly. (Morgan's research earned him the Nobel Prize in 1933.)

Emerson's investigation proceeded more slowly than Morgan's; one reason was that the maize plant takes a year to reproduce (the fruit fly is sexually mature ten days after it hatches). A second reason was the lack of a technique for characterizing the chromosomes of the maize cells. The life cycle of the corn plant is beyond human intervention, but McClintock made a major contribution to the study of its genetic mechanisms by developing the cytological procedures needed for visualizing and classifying the ten pairs of chromosomes in the somatic cells of the plant or the ten unpaired chromosomes in its germ cells.

After receiving her doctorate in 1927, McClintock remained at Cornell until 1931 as an instructor. During that period she capitalized on her method of observing the maize chromosomes by carrying out field and laboratory experiments showing that trait-determining (genetic) information is transferred in the crossing-over stage of meiotic cell division. In this process the paired chromosomes—one from each parent—intertwine and exchange segments; when the pairs later separate, each chromosome, now containing elements from both parent cells, becomes part of a male or female germ cell, or gamete.

For the rest of the 1930s McClintock continued her research on maize while holding brief appointments at the California Institute of Technology, Pasadena; the University of Freiburg, Germany; Cornell; and the University of Missouri, Columbia. She had long since made a commitment to plant genetics, but the academic establishment of that era extended scant hospitality to a female scientist working in any field, least of all to one whose reputation as a maverick and a loner was just as firmly established as were her credentials as a skilled, imaginative, and diligent investigator.

In 1942 McClintock accepted an appointment to the staff of the Cold Spring Harbor Laboratory, which was then operated by the Carnegie Institution of Washington. (It is now a self-governing organization supported by Carnegie funds and those of a group of universities and other sponsors; its director is James D. Watson, whose research on the structure of the genetic material DNA brought him a share of the Nobel Prize in 1962.) Soon after joining the laboratory, McClintock observed the distinctive pattern of mutations in the pigmentation of the maize plant that revealed—to her practiced eye—a genetic anomaly waiting to be explained. For six years she spent the summers tending her crossbred corn crops and the winters analyzing the chromosomes and planning the next season's experiments. The mass of data built up in this solitary campaign satisfied her that the variations in the leaves and kernels resulted from a previously unsuspected instability of the chromosomes. She realized that two kinds of mobile elements in the chromosomes (nicknamed "jumping genes" by a later generation of geneticists) participate in causing the changes.

One of McClintock's mobile elements, which she designated *Ac*, can spontaneously migrate within the chromosomes of maize. Its movement can cause the second element, *Ds*, to relocate; if *Ds* thereby becomes the neighbour of a pigment-forming gene, that gene's activity is suppressed. If *Ac* causes *Ds* to move again, the pigment formation resumes, and a characteristically speckled kernel develops. Transposition of *Ds* or *Ac* can also cause breaks in the chromosomes, changes that can be detected by microscopic examination.

The validity and generality of McClintock's conclusions did not receive their due recognition until after the revolution in molecular biology that was initiated by the discovery by Watson and Francis Crick of the chemical structure of DNA. The extension of their research led inevitably to the rediscovery of mobile elements in the chromosomes of many plants and animals and has finally resulted in universal acknowledgment of McClintock's insight.

Prize for Chemistry

The Prize for Chemistry was presented to Henry Taube of Stanford (Calif.) University, who had devoted more than three decades to investigations of the structures and reactions of dissolved inorganic compounds, particularly oxidation-reduction reactions, in which electrons are transferred from one atom to another. His interpretations of these phenomena have been widely adopted by other scientists as guides in selecting metallic compounds for use as catalysts, pigments, and superconductors and in understanding the essential functions of metal ions that are present in the molecules of many substances that are involved in biological processes.

Metals differ from the rest of the elements in that one or more of the electrons present in their atoms are only weakly attracted to the nucleus. In the compounds of metals, some or all of these loosely bound electrons have been removed, and the originally neutral atom has been converted to a positively charged ion. The number of electrons lost is commonly designated the oxidation state of the element; several metals form series of compounds in which the oxidation state has different values, corresponding to the loss of varying numbers of electrons.

When metallic compounds are dissolved in water, many of the positive ions form stable chemical bonds with surrounding neutral molecules, such as ammonia, or negative ions, such as chloride. In combinations of this kind, called coordination compounds, the molecules or ions attached to the central metal ion are called ligands. The Swiss chemist Alfred Werner won the Nobel Prize for Chemistry in 1913 for his investigations of coordination compounds, which provided the first orderly and comprehensive theory of their structure.

For a long time chemists suspected that water molecules could act as ligands in the same fashion as ammonia or chloride ions, but direct proof was lacking because there was no way to distinguish the bonded water molecules from those making up the bulk of the solution. In the later 1940s Taube carried out experiments with isotopes, showing that in water solution the ions of metals do indeed form chemical bonds with several molecules of water and that the rates at which one ligand replaces another vary greatly, depending on the identity and the oxidation state of the metal. Additionally he helped to develop other techniques for studying coordination compounds and interpreted their properties in terms of the known distribution of the least tightly bound electrons among the possible ways that they can interact with the nucleus.

In the oxidation or reduction of one metal ion by another, one or more electrons are exchanged between the two ions. Many such reactions occur rapidly in aqueous solution, even though a layer of water molecules or other ligands should keep the metal ions from getting close enough for the electrons to be transferred directly. Taube's research showed that, in an intermediate stage of the reaction, a chemical bond forms between one of the ions and a ligand that is still bonded to the other. This ligand acts as a temporary bridge between the ions, and its bond to the original metal ion later breaks in such a way as to bring about the movement of the electrons.

Taube, who was born on Nov. 30, 1915, in Neudorf, Sask., earned bachelor's and master's degrees in chemistry at the University of Saskatchewan, Saskatoon, and, in 1940, a doctorate at the University of California at Berkeley. He taught at Berkeley, at Cornell University, and at the University of Chicago before joining the faculty of Stanford in 1961. He became a U.S. citizen in 1942.

Prize for Physics

The Prize for Physics was divided equally between two astrophysicists, Subrahmanyan Chandrasekhar of the University of Chicago and William A. Fowler of the California Institute of Technology, Pasadena, for complementary—rather than collaborative—careers of research on the processes that take place during the evolution of stars. Chandrasekhar has concentrated on the large-scale phenomena, those that affect entire stars during the successive periods of their existence; he has accurately predicted how the mass of a star determines its ultimate transformation into a white dwarf, a neutron star, or a black hole. At the other extreme, Fowler has devoted his attention to the nuclear reactions that account for the release of energy and the changes in chemical composition of different classes of stars at various stages of their history. He has outlined processes by which all of the naturally occurring elements are formed in the interiors of stars; the results of his calculations are in good agreement with the best experimental data on the abundance of the elements in the universe.

During a long sea voyage from India to England in 1930, Chandrasekhar began considering the alternatives that lay in store for large stars, which shine for billions of years as their initial supply of hydrogen is converted to helium and heavier elements by nuclear fusion. Most stars are not much more massive than the Sun, and earlier scientists had concluded that as they burn out, gravity causes them to contract to white dwarf stars about the size of the Earth. In such an object, the mass of the Sun would be squeezed into the volume of the Earth, and the electrons and nuclei of the atoms in its core would be compressed to a state of extremely high density.

Chandrasekhar calculated that a star having a mass more than 1.4 times that of the Sun could not collapse in this way. Its gravitational contraction would generate so much kinetic energy that the star would explode as a supernova; the excess matter would be blown out into space, and the remnant would finally shrink into an object even denser than a white dwarf star. Later research has confirmed Chandrasekhar's ideas. In particular, no white dwarf has been found to have a mass greater than 1.4 times that of the Sun, a value now called the Chandrasekhar limit.

Since the 1940s Fowler has directed his attention to nuclear reactions by which the chemical elements could be formed in stars. In the earliest stars the conversion of hydrogen to helium would be the principal process, and as these stars aged, the helium would be returned to space, either gradually or—in the case of big stars—suddenly in supernova explosions. Successive generations of stars, condensing from matter containing growing proportions of helium, would be the sites of more and more complex reactions leading to still heavier nuclei, such as those of carbon, nitrogen, and oxygen. After several cycles, all the elements through iron would evolve. The iron nucleus is composed of 56 particles, either protons (hydrogen nuclei) or neutrons. The formation of nuclei beyond iron takes place under the most drastic cosmic conditions—those of supernovas.

Fowler collaborated with Margaret and Geoffrey Burbidge and Sir Fred Hoyle in formulating a comprehensive theory that summarizes the nuclear reactions leading to the synthesis of all the naturally occurring elements in the proportions that have been observed by astronomers. Their celebrated article, referred to by their initials, BBFH, was published in 1957.

Chandrasekhar was born on Oct. 19, 1910, in Lahore, which was then in India and is now in Pakistan. He is the nephew of Sir Chandrasekhara Venkata Raman, who won the Nobel Prize for Physics in 1930 for the discovery of the characteristic changes in the wavelength of light as it passes through transparent materials. Chandrasekhar graduated from Presidency College of Madras University, India, and received a doctorate from the University of Cambridge, England, in 1933. He remained at Cambridge as a fellow of Trinity College until 1937, and then accepted the position of research associate at the University of Chicago. He was named Morton D. Hull distinguished service professor of astrophysics in 1952.

Fowler was born on Aug. 9, 1911, in Pittsburgh. He graduated from Ohio State University and earned a doctorate in physics at the California Institute of Technology in 1936. He stayed at Caltech as a member of the faculty and in 1970 was designated the first Institute professor of physics.

(JOHN V. KILLHEFFER)

OBITUARIES

The following is a selected list of prominent men and women who died during 1983.

Albright, Ivan (Le Lorraine), U.S. painter (b. Feb. 20, 1897, North Harvey, Ill.—d. Nov. 18, 1983, Woodstock, Vt.), was dubbed "the painter of horrors" by critics who recognized the haunting quality of his meticulously detailed portraits and still lifes, which focused on the signs of decay and corruption. Albright, who created paintings of scars, varicose veins, and blisters, was a Chicago painter in the magic realism style. After serving in World War I, he studied at the Art Institute of Chicago, the Pennsylvania Academy of Fine Arts, and the National Academy of Design. During the 1920s Albright concentrated on portraits, including "Woman" (1928), a study of a bloated, cracked woman of indeterminate age who seems to be rotting before the viewer's eyes, and "Into the World Came a Soul Called Ida" (1930), a repulsive depiction of a flabby prostitute. In 1927 Albright, his twin brother, Malvin, and his father bought an abandoned church in Warrenville, Ill., where they painted side by side into the 1940s. During the 1930s Albright turned to still lifes and won recognition with such paintings as "The Door" and "The Window"; he worked on the latter intermittently for some 21 years to perfect what is viewed as possibly his finest work. In 1943 he returned to portraiture and with Malvin created a series of horrifying portraits depicting the moral degeneration of the title character in MGM's screen version of Oscar Wilde's *The Picture of Dorian Gray.* Because Albright's family was wealthy, he was able to spend years completing a single painting, and his works commanded high prices. His 43 paintings and several lithographs were featured in a 1964–65 retrospective exhibition organized by the Art Institute of Chicago and shown by the Whitney Museum of American Art in New York City. After 1980 Albright immersed himself in a series of self-portraits.

Aldrich, Robert, U.S. film director (b. Aug. 9, 1918, Cranston, R.I.—d. Dec. 5, 1983, Los Angeles, Calif.), was a maverick filmmaker who scorned his family's banking empire to immortalize the misfits and derelicts who appeared in such motion pictures as *The Dirty Dozen* (1967), *The Longest Yard* (1974), and *The Choirboys* (1977). Aldrich, who launched his career in 1941 as a production clerk for RKO studios, later served (1945–52) as assistant director to such directorial giants as Jean Renoir, Orson Welles, and Charlie Chaplin. Aldrich, however, developed an individual style that was characterized by gritty realism often punctuated with brutal violence. After making his debut as a director with *The Big Leaguer* in 1953, he founded his own production company and released *Apache* (1954), *Vera Cruz* (1954), *The Big Knife* (1955), and *The Angry Hills* (1959). In 1962 he turned to melodrama and coaxed Bette Davis out of retirement to star in *What Ever Happened to Baby Jane?* and then in *Hush . . . Hush, Sweet Charlotte* (1964). Some of his other film credits included *The Flight of the Phoenix* (1965), *The Killing of Sister George* (1968; the first X-rated film in the U.S.), *Twilight's Last Gleaming* (1977), and his last, *All the Marbles* (1981).

Alemán, Miguel, Mexican politician (b. Sept. 29, 1903, Sayula, Mexico—d. May 14, 1983, Mexico City, Mexico), as president of Mexico from 1946 to 1952 helped increase the self-sufficiency of the country by promoting industrialization and improvements in agriculture and by increasing the efficiency of Pemex, Mexico's government-owned oil-production monopoly. Alemán, the son of a revolutionary general who in 1911 helped depose the dictator Porfirio Díaz, was a prominent labour lawyer before he was appointed a senator from Veracruz. In 1936 Alemán became governor of the state but resigned in 1940 to manage the successful presidential campaign of Gen. Manuel Avila Camacho, who in gratitude named Alemán minister of the interior. Six years later Alemán, who ran for office on the ticket of the Partido Revolucionario Institucional, became the first nonmilitary candidate ever to be elected to the presidency. During his tenure in office Alemán also oversaw the construction of major highways and of the University City complex. After Alemán left office, his regime was charged with widespread graft and corruption, but in the early 1960s he was nonetheless chosen to serve as president of a national tourist council, a post he held until his death.

Anderson, Maxie Leroy, U.S. balloonist (b. Sept. 10, 1934, Sayre, Okla.—d. June 27, 1983, near Bad Brückenau, West Germany), was a venturesome entrepreneur who captured the imagination of the world when on Aug. 17, 1978, together with Ben Abruzzo and Larry Newman, he completed the first crossing of the Atlantic Ocean in a balloon after piloting the "Double Eagle II" 5,000 km (3,000 mi) in six days from a clover field in Presque Isle, Maine, to a barley field in Miserey, France. Anderson, a prosperous mining executive from Albuquerque, N.M., sported a trademark black eye patch and used his wealth to pay for his ballooning feats. He made his first transatlantic flight attempt in September 1977 with Abruzzo, but the pair were rescued from the sea off the coast of Iceland four days after taking off from Massachusetts. Despite their brush with death, they enlisted Newman as their navigator and the following year conquered the Atlantic in their helium-filled balloon. Anderson also held the record for flying the longest distance across the North American continent, though he fell short of the Atlantic coast. After making his third unsuccessful attempt to balloon around the world in 45 days, Anderson abandoned this quest. He and veteran balloonist Don Ida were killed when the gondola of their balloon crashed in a Bavarian forest some 40 km (25 mi) from the East German border. A subsequent investigation revealed that a mechanical device used to sever lines holding the gondola to the helium-filled balloon failed to operate properly during a landing maneuver, causing the men to plunge to their deaths. The two were among 18 teams competing in the Gordon Bennett International Balloon Race.

Andrzejewski, Jerzy, Polish writer (b. Aug. 19, 1909, Warsaw, Poland—d. April 19, 1983, Warsaw), was the author of the novel *Popiol i diament* (1948; *Ashes and Diamonds,* 1962), the 1958 film adaptation of which, by Andrzej Wajda, was widely shown in the West. In 1976 he became a member of the Workers' Defense Committee (KOR), which was instrumental in the founding of Solidarity. Andrzejewski studied Polish literature at the University of Warsaw and became a contributor to a right-wing literary weekly, *Prosto z Mostu* ("Straight from the Shoulder"). He admired the French Catholic writers François Mauriac and Georges Bernanos, and his novel *Lad serca* (1938; "Harmony of the Heart") showed their influence. During World War II Andrzejewski remained in Warsaw and was active in the resistance. After the war he joined the Communist Party. Elected president of the Polish Writers' Union in 1949, he wrote a few books in "socialist realist" vein but gradually became disillusioned with Marxism and in 1957 left the party. His increasingly dissident attitude became clear with the publication of *Ciemnosci kryja ziemie* (1957; *The Inquisitors,* 1960), a story of the Spanish Inquisition. *Apelacja* (1968; *The Appeal,* 1971) overtly attacked the Marxist system.

Aquino, Benigno Simeon, Jr. ("NINOY"), Philippine politician (b. Nov. 27, 1932, Tarlac, Phil.—d. Aug. 21, 1983, Manila, Phil.), was a charismatic senator who became the chief political opposition leader

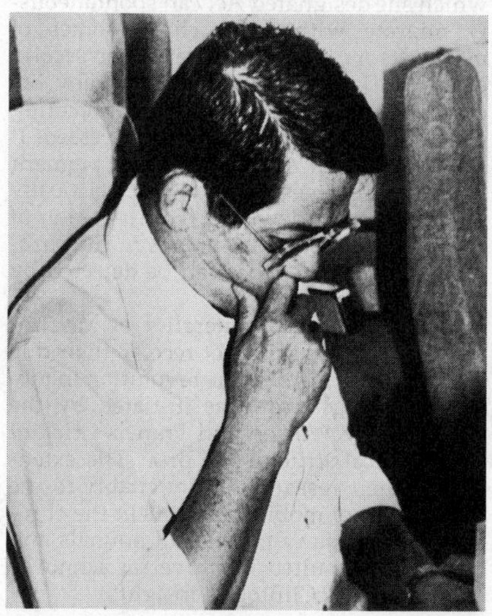
UPI

after Ferdinand E. Marcos was elected president of the country in 1965. Aquino, who served as a journalist before embarking on a political career in 1955, was elected mayor of Concepcion at age 22, becoming the youngest mayor in the entire archipelago. In 1961, after having served for two years as vice-governor of Tarlac Province, he succeeded to the governorship; he was the youngest official in the country to serve in that capacity. He was elected governor in his own right in 1963 and shortly thereafter married the daughter of one of the largest landowners in the Philippines. A self-described "radical rich guy," Aquino became secretary-general of the Liberal Party in 1966, one year after Marcos had resigned from the Liberal Party and had been elected president of the Philippines as leader of the Nationalist Party. In 1967 Aquino was the only Liberal Party member to win a Senate seat and made such an impression with his silvery oratory that he was viewed as a potential presidential candidate in the 1973 elections. However, when Marcos declared martial law on Sept. 23, 1972, Aquino was immediately jailed on charges of murder and subversion. He was sentenced to death and had served eight years in prison before he was granted permission by Marcos in 1980 to travel to the U.S. for open-heart surgery. Aquino resided in the U.S. during the following three years but purportedly made trips to the Middle East to meet with and gain the support of Philippine Muslim leaders. In 1983 Aquino, who had learned that Marcos was ailing, decided to end his self-imposed exile and return to his homeland to try to persuade Marcos to return the country to democracy. Having been warned at least three times about assassination plots against him, Aquino donned a bulletproof vest, but while disembarking from the plane in Manila escorted by three security guards, he was shot in the back of the head. The alleged assassin was instantly slain on the heavily guarded tarmac. (*See* PHILIPPINES.)

Aron, Raymond-Claude-Ferdinand, French philosopher (b. March 14, 1905, Paris, France—d. Oct. 17, 1983, Paris), upheld a rationalist humanism that was often contrasted with the Marxist existentialism of Jean-Paul Sartre. Though his range was slightly narrower than Sartre's and his international reputation less, the two men were often associated, both because of the parallels between their lives and because, within France, Aron enjoyed intellectual authority on the centre-right comparable to that of Sartre on the left. The son of a Jewish jurist, he met Sartre at the École Normale Supérieure where they both studied from 1924 and, like

Sartre, went to Berlin before teaching in Le Havre. Aron obtained a Ph.D. in 1930 with a thesis on the philosophy of history and was professor of social philosophy at the University of Toulouse when World War II broke out. He joined Charles de Gaulle in London and edited the paper *La France Libre* from 1940 to 1944. On his return to France he became professor at the École Nationale d'Administration and from 1955 to 1968 professor of sociology at the Sorbonne. He also taught at the Institut d'Études Politiques and the École Pratique des Hautes Études and from 1970 was professor at the College de France. Throughout his life he was active as a journalist, on *Le Figaro*, then *L'Express*, having contributed to *Combat* immediately after the war. Among his most influential works were *L'Opium des Intellectuels* (1955), in which he attacked left-wing conformism and the totalitarian tendencies of Marxist regimes; *La Tragédie algérienne* (1957), which voiced his support for Algerian independence; and *La République impériale* (1973), an attack on the unthinking hostility aimed at the U.S. by the left. A continuing theme throughout his works was the subject of violence and war, as evidenced in *Histoire et dialectique de la violence* (1973), a reply to Sartre, and in his works on Clausewitz. *De Gaulle, Israël et les Juifs* (1968) reaffirmed Aron's support for the state of Israel, though he saw himself as an "assimilated" Jew, closer to France than to Oriental Judaism despite his strong feeling for the Jewish state. Notwithstanding their political differences, he retained an affectionate feeling for Sartre and in 1979 the two men found themselves sharing a platform in support of the Vietnamese "boat people." In 1983 Aron published his *Mémoires*.

Auric, Georges, French composer (b. Feb. 15, 1899, Lodève, France—d. July 23, 1983, Paris, France), was a member of the group Les Six, which included Francis Poulenc and Darius Milhaud. He studied at the Paris Conservatoire and with Vincent d'Indy at the Schola Cantorum before making his debut in 1914 with a song cycle. In 1924 he wrote *Les Fâcheux* for Diaghilev's Ballets Russes. His association with the company also produced *Les Matelots* (1925) which, with *Phèdre* (1950), represents his most important ballet music. His work, iconoclastic, irreverent, and sometimes humorous, ranged from chamber works to film scores. The poet Jean Cocteau was a close friend and Auric contributed to several of Cocteau's films, including *Le Sang d'un poète* (1931) and *La Belle et la bête* (1945). Auric also wrote the scores for *Hue and Cry, Bonjour Tristesse,* and some 40 other films. From 1954 to 1977 he composed a series of chamber works, *Les Imaginées,* and it was on these ambitious, experimental pieces that he felt his reputation would rest. He was many times president of SACEM, the French society for authors and composers of music, a member of the Légion d'Honneur, and from 1962 to 1968 administrator of the Paris Opéra and Opéra-Comique.

Bagley, Desmond, British thriller writer (b. Oct. 29, 1923, Kendal, Westmorland, England—d. April 12, 1983, Southampton, England), achieved instant success with his first novel, *The Golden Keel* (1963), which was followed by many highly popular tales set in exotic locations. Bagley left school at 14 and during World War II was a worker in aircraft production. After the war he traveled extensively in Africa, Australia, Europe, and the U.S., gathering material for his books. Bagley then served as a critic with the South African *Rand Daily Mail* before becoming a full-time writer and settling in the Channel Islands, where he produced a new book almost every year. His novel *Running Blind* (1970) also became a best-seller, and by this time he had acquired a faithful readership both in the English-speaking world and in the many countries where his work was translated. Though Bagley made no literary claims for his books, his adventurous plots were noted for their authentic details. His books, which also included *High Citadel* (1965), *The Tightrope Men* (1973), and *The Snow Tiger* (1975), sold nearly ten million copies.

Baillie, Dame Isobel, British soprano (b. March 9, 1895, Hawick, Scotland—d. Sept. 24, 1983, Manchester, England), was a concert singer whose performances of works by Elgar and Howells were greatly admired by the composers. She also appeared in opera, in *Orphée* in 1937 and *Faust* in 1941, though she always felt more at home on the concert platform than on stage. Baillie studied with Guglielmo Somma in Milan and made her London debut in 1923. Ten years later she appeared at the Hollywood Bowl. Her singing was remarkable for its pure tone and lack of affectation, apparent in such works as *Elijah, The Creation,* and *The Messiah.* She helped create Ralph Vaughan Williams's *Serenade to Music* when it was first performed in 1938, and her other performances of modern works included Elgar's *The Kingdom* and Howells's *Hymnus Paradisi.* In 1960–61 she was professor of singing at Cornell University, Ithaca, N.Y. She published an autobiography, *Never Sing Louder than Lovely* (1982), and was made a Dame of the Order of the British Empire in 1978.

Bakaric, Vladimir, Yugoslav politician (b. March 8, 1912, Zagreb, Yugos.—d. Jan. 16, 1983, Zagreb), was a member of the Presidium of the League of Communists of Yugoslavia and vice-president of the federal republic's collective Presidency. He was the last survivor of Marshal Tito's World War II compatriots to retain high office within the party hierarchy. Under the system of rotation of offices instituted by Tito, Bakaric would have succeeded Petar Stambolic as head of state in May 1983. A lawyer by training, Bakaric was a member of the Communist Party from 1933. During the war he helped organize partisan resistance in his native Croatia, and in 1945 he headed the first postwar government of the Croatian national republic within the Yugoslav federation. In 1971–72 he supported Tito's moves to suppress Croatian nationalism. A Marxist theoretician who was, nevertheless, strongly opposed to the Soviet system, Bakaric helped frame the 1974 federal constitution designed to promote decentralization.

Balanchine, George (GEORGY MELITONOVICH BALANCHIVADZE), Russian-born choreographer and dancer (b. Jan. 9 [Jan. 22, old style], 1904, St. Petersburg, Russia—d. April 30, 1983, New York, N.Y.), was an artistic genius whose plotless, streamlined, neoclassical ballets ushered in 20th-century dance in the U.S. Balanchine, who studied at the Imperial School of Ballet at the Maryinsky Theatre (later the Soviet State School of Ballet), danced with the Soviet State Dancers before joining Sergey Diaghilev's Ballets Russes in Paris in 1924 as ballet master. During his tenure with the Ballets Russes he created ten ballets, most notably *Apollo* (1928), his first neoclassical ballet, and *The Prodigal Son* (1929). During his brief sojourn in 1932 with the Ballets Russes de Monte Carlo, Balanchine enhanced his reputation with *La Concurrence* (1932) and *Cotillon* (1932). In 1933 Balanchine founded his own company, Les Ballets, and its productions so impressed U.S. balletomane Lincoln Kirstein that he invited Balanchine to the U.S. to help him found the School of American Ballet (1934) and the American Ballet Company (1935). Balanchine worked in the classical dance idiom and staged the masterpiece *Serenade* in 1935; the ballet epitomized his artistic philosophy: a themeless, continuous flow of movement, steps, and combinations of steps, with each dancer gliding in and out of the ensemble to play an individual role. In 1936 the American Ballet became the resident ballet company at the Metropolitan Opera in New York, but the association ended in 1938 and Balanchine was again bereft of a ballet company. He began a remarkable eight-year collaboration with Hollywood and Broadway and was deemed a pioneer with his celebrated *Slaughter on Tenth Avenue* ballet in *On Your Toes* (1936), the first Broadway musical to integrate dance sequences with the plot. During this period he also created ballets for the American Ballet Caravan, including *Concerto Barocco* and *Ballet Imperial,* and for the Ballets Russes de Monte Carlo.

MARTHA SWOPE

In 1946 Kirstein, who was determined to launch a U.S. ballet company under the artistic direction of Balanchine, founded Ballet Society, for which Balanchine produced *The Four Temperaments* and *Orpheus.* In 1948 Balanchine and Kirstein founded the New York City Ballet, which served as a showcase for some of Balanchine's greatest works, including *The Nutcracker, Don Quixote, La Valse, Scotch Symphony, Ivesiana, Stars and Stripes,* and *A Midsummer Night's Dream.* Balanchine created more than 170 ballets, some 50 of them considered masterpieces, and the New York City Ballet's beloved "Mr. B" established the company as one of the most respected in the world. His longtime musical collaboration with Igor Stravinsky began in 1928 with the landmark *Apollo,* which became a turning point in his career. During the next half century the two produced such outstanding works as *Agon, Danses Concertantes, Firebird, Symphony in Three Movements,* and *Violin Concerto,* the latter two for the dazzling 1972 Stravinsky Festival. Balanchine also introduced a new version of *Noah and the Flood* for the New York City Ballet's 1982 Stravinsky Centennial Celebration. Balanchine was perhaps the century's greatest choreographer; he composed rapidly and inspired his dancers to perform with unfathomable speed. Balanchine, who fervently believed that "ballet is woman" and that man creates for his ideal woman, married five ballerinas (one by common law) whom he had made stars: Tamara Geva, Alexandra Danilova, Vera Zorina, Maria Tallchief, and Tanaquil LeClerq.

Bee, Clair, U.S. basketball coach (b. March 2, 1896, Grafton, W.Va.—d. May 20, 1983, Cleveland, Ohio), as the dynamic basketball coach of Long Island University (LIU) from 1931 to 1952, sparked his teams to some of the longest winning streaks in the nation, with 43, 38, 28, and 26 consecutive wins, and ended his career with an astonishing record of 357 wins and 79 losses. In 1935–36 and 1938–39 LIU was undefeated, and in 1939 and 1941 the Blackbirds were crowned National Invitational Tournament (NIT) champions. Bee, who was a master at taking advantage of his opponents' weaknesses, originated the popular 1–3–1 zone defense and the three-second-rule violation, which prohibits a player from standing in the lane in front of the team's defensive basket for more than that time. One of Bee's greatest disappointments, however, was associated with the sport he loved best. In the early 1950s three of his LIU players were involved in a point shaving scandal, and Bee felt that he had somehow failed them. After LIU dropped basketball from its program, Bee served as the coach of the Baltimore Bullets professional basketball team from 1952 to 1954 and helped institute the 24-second shot clock. From 1954 to 1967 he served as athletic director of the New York Military Academy, and in 1967 Bee was elected to the Basketball Hall of Fame.

CAMERA PRESS, LONDON

Bidault, Georges Augustin, French politician (b. Oct. 5, 1899, Moulins, Allier, France—d. Jan 26, 1983, Cambo-les Bains, France), was foreign minister (1944–48), premier (1946; 1949–50), and leader of the Mouvement Républicain Populaire. He played a leading role in the foreign policy of successive governments under the Fourth Republic, but his opposition to Charles de Gaulle's Algerian policy after 1958 led to his exile and subsequent exclusion from politics. A history teacher and journalist on a Catholic paper before World War II, he became president of the National Council of the Resistance after the death of Jean Moulin in 1943. Bidault shared de Gaulle's ambitions for postwar French independence, although he steadfastly believed that Europe could not survive unless it cooperated with the U.S. Bidault represented France at negotiations for the North Atlantic Treaty, worked for reconciliation with Germany, and engineered France's entry into the European Coal and Steel Community. Bidault never accepted decolonization in Indochina or Algeria and fell out with his own party over the Algerian war. When de Gaulle came to power, Bidault, like other supporters of French Algeria, was dismayed by what he viewed as a reversal of the general's policy and virtually allied himself with the extreme right-wing Secret Army Organization (OAS). In 1962, charged with plotting against the state, he went into exile, only returning to France six years later when the charges were dropped. For the remainder of his life he lived in seclusion. Bidault published two books, *D'une Résistance à l'autre* (1965) and *Le Point* (1968).

Birla, Ghanshyamdas, Indian industrialist (b. 1894, Pilani, Jaipur, India—d. June 11, 1983, London, England), with his three younger brothers founded the industrial firm Birla Brothers Ltd. and became a prominent figure in India. A friend of Mahatma Gandhi, Birla helped to finance the movement for independence and took part in the negotiations with Britain. It was in the garden of the Birla house in Delhi that Gandhi was assassinated. Birla's book *In the Shadow of the Mahatma* (1953) recounted his role in the struggle for independence and his friendship with Gandhi. The son of a businessman, Birla headed one of India's major industrial empires, producing sugar, cotton, steel, and automobiles, and directed engineering, banking, and insurance firms as well. He was a member of the Bengal Legislative Council and the Indian Legislative Assembly until 1930 and continued to play a political role through the Indian Chamber of Commerce and as owner of such newspapers as the *Eastern Economist* and the *Hindustan Times.*

Bishop, Maurice, Grenadian politician (b. May 29, 1944, Grenada—d. Oct. 19, 1983, St. George's, Grenada), was a lawyer by profession who in 1972 became a prominent leader in the New Jewel Movement (an acronym for Joint Endeavour for Welfare, Education, and Liberation) and in March 1979 became prime minister after engineering a bloodless coup against the repressive regime of Sir Eric Gairy. Bishop attended Grenada's Roman Catholic Presentation College before earning a law degree from London University. He was called to the bar in 1969, and while practicing law in London he was influenced by the black civil rights movement of the 1960s and became more radical, in part through his association with Black Power militants and through viewing the plight of poor blacks. He returned to Grenada in 1970 and set up a law practice with Bernard Coard, who later became Bishop's deputy prime minister. During the 1970s Gairy's parapolice aides, the Mongoose Gang, made brutal physical attacks on members of the People's Revolutionary Government movement. In 1973 Bishop was so badly beaten that he had to go to Barbados for treatment, and in the following year his father, Rupert Bishop, was murdered "by persons unknown." Bishop was henceforth determined to oust Gairy. He became a champion of the poor and organized strikes just before Grenada became independent in February 1974. In 1976 he was elected to Parliament, and in 1979, when Gairy was out of the country, Bishop seized the radio station and proclaimed a revolutionary government. A Marxist, Bishop promised to return the country to democracy, but he failed to hold elections, stifled the press, and limited political opposition. Nevertheless, many citizens were pleased with social tranquillity, rising exports, and some 72 km (45 mi) of new roads. Though many of the country's projects were sponsored by Soviet bloc assistance, including a new Cuban-built airport, Bishop made an attempt to thaw icy relations with the U.S. His more moderate stance was felt to have enraged Coard, who toppled Bishop in a power struggle in October 1983, though the Army led by Gen. Hudson Austin quickly took control and Coard disappeared. Bishop was being held under an Army-imposed house arrest when throngs of his supporters pushed past the guards and carried him outdoors, after which they proceeded to Market Square and then to Ft. Rupert, a Grenadian Army compound. Eyewitness reports revealed that Army troops opened fire on the crowd and forced Bishop and his Cabinet ministers inside the fort where they were executed.

Blake, Eubie (James Hubert Blake), U.S. jazz musician (b. Feb. 7, 1883, Baltimore, Md.—d. Feb. 12, 1983, Brooklyn, N.Y.), was an enduring ragtime composer and pianist who even at the age of 90 electrified audiences with energetic performances highlighted by such all-time favourite songs as "I'm Just Wild About Harry," "Memories of You," and "You Were Meant for Me." Blake, who displayed his extraordinary musical talent at age six when he spontaneously began playing an organ in a store, had found work as a pianist in a brothel by the time he was 15. The following year he wrote his first rag, "Sounds of Africa," but because he could not write scores the piece was not published until after 1919 as "Charleston Rag." After publishing his first piano composition, "Chevy Chase," in 1914, Blake teamed up in 1915 with the lyricist Noble Sissle, and the two wrote their first song, "It's All Your Fault." Their careers were launched when Sophie Tucker incorporated the tune into her vaudeville act. In 1916 the duo joined James Reese Europe's Society Orchestra, and besides working as a piano-vocal team, they began composing songs in the musical-comedy genre. After World War I Blake and Sissle went into vaudeville as the Dixie Duo and became showstoppers when they played at New York City's top vaudeville house, the Palace. In 1921 the duo joined another black vaudeville team, Aubrey Lyles and Flournoy Miller, who had prepared the book for a musical comedy. Blake wrote the music and Sissle supplied the lyrics for the all-black Broadway hit *Shuffle Along,* which broke the colour barrier at white theatres and introduced such hit songs as "Love Will Find a Way" and "I'm Just Wild About Harry" (which later became Pres. Harry S. Truman's 1948 campaign song). Blake and Sissle then wrote the score for the black musical *Chocolate Dandies* and composed a dozen songs for the white musical *Elsie.* In 1925 Blake and Sissle broke up, and Blake teamed up with Andy Razaf to write the score for *Blackbirds of 1930,* which featured the well-known song "Memories of You." In 1946 Blake retired from performing to attend New York University and study the Schillinger system of composition. During the following 23 years he spent most of his time composing and transcribing songs he had memorized. But during the 1960s ragtime enjoyed a revival, and when the two-record album *The Eighty-Six Years of Eubie Blake* was released by Columbia in 1969, Blake reemerged as a vivacious octogenarian, making appearances, giving concerts, and becoming a jazz raconteur. Blake, who made his last professional appearance at the age of 99, was awarded the U.S. Medal of Freedom in 1981. He died five days after celebrating his centennial.

Bloch, Felix, U.S. physicist (b. Oct. 23, 1905, Zürich, Switz.—d. Sept. 10, 1983, Zürich), shared the 1952 Nobel Prize for Physics with Edward Mills Purcell for the discovery of nuclear magnetic resonance (NMR) and its development into a powerful technique for studying the atoms and molecules of solids and liquids by measuring the magnetic behaviour of their atomic nuclei. In the mid-1940s Bloch found that a strong stationary magnetic field applied to certain kinds of atomic nuclei caused them to align with the field like tiny bar magnets; when probed with weak, carefully tuned external radio waves, the nuclei could be made to resonate, or vibrate, absorbing and reemitting characteristic amounts of energy that could be used to evaluate the immediate chemical environment. In the early 1980s NMR emerged as a promising tool for medical diagnosis in the form of a device that produces cross-sections of the human body similar to those made by computerized axial tomographic (CAT) scanners. During his scientific career Bloch also made many contributions to solid-state physics and devised a method for polarizing neutrons, separating them according to the clockwise or counterclockwise direction of their intrinsic spins. Bloch, who earned a Ph.D. from the University of Leipzig in Germany, immigrated to the U.S. when the Nazis came to power in 1933 and in 1934 joined the faculty of Stanford University. There he held the post of Max H. Stern professor of physics until his retirement in 1971. Bloch had also served (1954–55) as the first director general of the European Commission for Nuclear Research, a project set up in Geneva by 12 European governments for large-scale nuclear research.

Blunt, Anthony Frederick, British art historian (b. Sept. 26, 1907, Bournemouth, England—d. March 26, 1983, London, England), was surveyor of the queen's pictures from 1945 to 1972 and director of the Courtauld Institute from 1947 to 1974. He appeared to enjoy an unassailable reputation as one of the most distinguished contemporary historians of Renaissance art until the public revelation in 1979 that he had spied for the Soviet Union while serving during World War II with British military intelligence (MI5). Blunt developed an early enthusiasm for art while studying modern languages at Trinity College, Cambridge. In the early 1930s he traveled abroad on study visits and, in addition to sharpening his understanding of art history, he made the acquaintance of Marxist scholar Friedrich Antal, who influenced his political views. His study of the French painter Nicholas Poussin, his volume on French Renaissance art for the Pelican "History of Art" series, and his writings on Blake, Picasso, and Baroque architecture were acknowledged as authoritative and scholarly contributions to art history. Blunt's many honours included a knighthood in 1956 and the Légion d'Honneur in 1958. While at Cambridge, however, he had met Guy Burgess, whose influence seems to have been decisive in translating Blunt's Marxist sympathies and disillusionment with British society into active work for the Soviet Union. Blunt began to sound out other possible recruits to the Soviet cause and, when the opportunity arose to do war service with MI5, he began passing information to the Soviets. His career as an active intelligence agent ended in 1945, but he maintained contact with his friends, including Burgess, who by this time was a member of the British diplomatic service. In 1951 Blunt helped Burgess and Donald Maclean (*q.v.*) defect. Though under suspicion, Blunt avoided prosecution through lack of evidence. After Kim Philby defected in 1964, Blunt confessed his activities to the security services, but because there was not enough evidence to ensure a conviction, Blunt was granted immunity in exchange for his full confession. Blunt's secret was kept for 15 years until a book by Andrew Boyle, *The Climate of Treason* (1979; rev. ed., 1980), revealed the story. Blunt attributed his actions to misguided political sympathies and loyalty to friends. His knighthood was annulled, but he was allowed to live the rest of his life in seclusion.

Bobet, Louis (LOUISON), French cyclist (b. March 12, 1925, Saint-Méen-le-Grand, Ille-et-Vilaine, France—d. March 13, 1983, Biarritz, France), won the French amateur championship in 1946 and, during his professional career, demonstrated his mastery as a sprinter, distance racer, and hill climber—skills that secured his place as one of the leading all-around cyclists in post-World War II France. His dedication to cycling gained him his first professional championship in 1950, and the following year he emerged on the international scene with victories in the Milan–San Remo and Lombardy races. After winning the Grand Prix des Nations and Paris–Nice in 1952, he gained the first of three successive team victories in the Tour de France in 1953 and the world championship in 1954. By the time of his retirement in 1962, he had added other triumphs such as the 1956 Paris–Roubaix and the 1959 Bordeaux–Paris.

Boult, Sir Adrian Cedric, British conductor (b. April 8, 1889, Chester, England—d. Feb. 23, 1983, Farnham, Surrey, England), founded the BBC Symphony Orchestra and, as director of music at the BBC from 1930 to 1950, displayed both his versatility and his interpretive gifts. Temperamentally different from some of his more flamboyant contemporaries, he made a lasting contribution to music in Britain—in particular to English music, championing the works of Elgar, Holst, Vaughan Williams, and other English composers. Boult studied at Oxford and then under Arthur Nikisch in Leipzig before embarking on his career as a conductor with the Royal Philharmonic Society in 1918. In 1924 he was appointed conductor of the City of Birmingham Orchestra and during the 1920s was involved in the competition festival movement in Winchester and Petersfield. In 1927 he succeeded Vaughan Williams as conductor of the London Bach Choir and in the following decade established an international reputation with foreign tours. By 1939 he had built the BBC Symphony Orchestra into a highly respected instrument, attracting many celebrated guest conductors. When the orchestra was revived after World War II, he resumed his work with it but, failing to achieve his earlier success, retired in 1950. For the next ten years his recordings gained a wide audience in Britain and the U.S. Despite his age, he continued to conduct, and he served as maestro at the 1969 Oxfam concert at the Royal Albert Hall on his 80th birthday. Boult, who conducted at the coronations of King George VI and Queen Elizabeth II, was knighted in 1937. His autobiography, *My Own Trumpet,* was published in 1973.

Box, Sydney, British film producer (b. April 26, 1907, Beckenham, Kent, England—d. May 25, 1983, Perth, Western Australia), established his motion-picture reputation with *The Seventh Veil* (1945) after a successful career in writing for the stage. He trained as a journalist, eventually editing the *Christian Herald,* and in collaboration with his wife, Muriel, wrote numerous one-act plays. His first major venture in films was in the field of advertising shorts with his own company, Verity Films. After Box produced *The Seventh Veil* for Gainsborough Films, he joined the company as managing director. The screenplay won an Oscar, and Box produced and wrote several other films for Gainsborough, including *The Man Within* (1947) and such costume melodramas as *Jassy* (1947) and *So Long at the Fair* (1950). During the 1950s he served as a director of Tyne Tees Television. In 1963, following a serious illness, Box made an unsuccessful bid for British Lion Films. His last film was *Rattle of a Simple Man* (1964). During the late 1960s illness forced Box to retire to Australia, where he remained active as a novelist and as a member of the Western Australia Arts Council.

Boyd of Merton, Alan Tindall Lennox-Boyd, 1ST VISCOUNT, British politician (b. Nov. 18, 1904, Merton-in-Penninghame, Scotland—d. March 8, 1983, London, England), as secretary of state for the colonies from 1954 to 1959 played a central role in relations with colonial territories at a time of rapid change in Britain's stature in world affairs. He brought intelligence, moderation, and, at 6 ft 5½ in, a considerable physical presence to the task of supervising the movement toward independence, although he ultimately favoured less rapid progress than was in fact achieved. Lennox-Boyd studied at Christ Church, Oxford, then read for the bar, entering Parliament in 1931 as Conservative member for Mid-Bedfordshire. Although he held his first ministerial appointment at the Ministry of Labour and was, after war service, a junior minister in the Ministry of Aircraft Production, his main interest had always been in colonial affairs. After the Conservative victory in 1951, he spent two years as minister of state at the Colonial Office. As colonial secretary he steered a middle course between demands for the granting of immediate independence to the colonial territories and right-wing pressures to resist any change. During his tenure the Gold Coast achieved independence as Ghana, and Lennox-Boyd laid the foundations for the emergence of the Federation of Nigeria. By 1959, however, Prime Minister Harold Macmillan had bowed to the "wind of change" and accelerated Britain's policy of disengagement. Lennox-Boyd was criticized for British repressive actions during disturbances in Nyasaland (now Malawi) and Kenya and retired after the 1959 election. In 1960 he was made viscount and Companion of Honour. In 1979 he led a Conservative mission to oversee the Zimbabwe elections.

Boyer, Lucienne, French cabaret singer (b. 1903, Paris, France—d. Dec. 6, 1983, Paris), achieved national and international success in 1930 with the song "Parlez-moi d'amour," delivered in an intimate and sensual style that inspired such singers as Juliette Gréco. Boyer started as a cabaret singer at the age of 16 and made her first recording in 1928. After "Parlez-moi d'amour," written by Jean Lenoir, established her career, Boyer became a well-known figure in the cabarets of Montparnasse and Montmartre during the 1930s. She later ran several of her own establishments, including Chez les Clochards and Chez Lucienne. Some of her other songs of the 1930s, including "Un Amour comme le nôtre" and "Mon P'tit Kaki," were successful, but her main achievement remained the creation of a deep-throated, vibrant style of crooning in her best-known song which outlived her own reputation.

Bradley, Caroline, British horsewoman (b. April 1946—d. June 1, 1983, Ipswich, England), was for 15 years one of the world's leading show jumpers and the most outstanding woman rider of her generation. Besides winning the Canadian championship in 1968, she was a member of the British teams that won the world championship in 1978 and the European championship in 1979. Bradley also won the Queen Elizabeth II Cup in 1978 and 1980. She began her career as an enthusiastic pony club member and, after two seasons' training near Oxford with Lars Sederholm, was chosen for the British team in Dublin in 1966. She captured two events and subsequently, on the Olympic horse Franco, established her reputation as a competitor of world class. Her greatest success came with the gray Tigre, which she jointly owned from 1976 to 1981; not only did she manage a horse considered by others to be unridable but she showed that women riders were fully the equal of men in the sport. Her stunning performance, which led to victory as a member of the 1982 women's team in Dublin, confirmed the point. Bradley was voted *Daily Express* "Sportswoman of the Year" in 1979 and was made a Member of the Order of the British Empire in 1980. She died at the height of her career while competing in the Suffolk Show.

Brandt, Bill, British photographer (b. 1905, London, England—d. Dec. 20, 1983, London), was one of the first British photographers to have his work taken seriously by the public as an art form. The Brandt style, which often utilized the light of dusk to give a "haunted" effect to the scene and heavy contrasts between black and white, first became known through his work for *Picture Post* during the 1930s and in his book *The English at Home* (1936), which depicted the gap between lower-class and upper-class life-styles. During World War II he worked for the Ministry of Information and took many moving photographs of Londoners in the Blitz. After the war his work became more and more abstract, suggesting the influence of Man Ray and the Surrealists, with whom he studied in Paris during the late 1920s. Brandt did an extensive series of nudes in landscapes, the bodies elongated or distorted so as to be virtually unrecognizable and blending with the rocks or pebbled beaches around them. Nudes also appeared in his later work, sometimes masked, in interior settings; these were illustrated in Steve Dwoskin's film portrait, *Shadows from Light,* shown at the 1983 London Film Festival. From his first one-man exhibition in Paris in 1938 to the major retrospective being prepared by the Victoria and Albert Museum at the time of his death, he exhibited frequently and, whether as reporter, portrait photographer (his studies of Francis Bacon and Dylan Thomas were probably the definitive images of these personalities), or experimental artist, he was recognized as the outstanding British photographer of his time.

Brewin, (Francis) Andrew, Canadian lawyer and politician (b. Sept. 3, 1907, Brighton, England—d. Sept. 21, 1983, British Columbia, Canada), was an influential civil liberties lawyer who championed the labour movement and minority groups before helping to found the New Democratic Party (NDP) in 1961 and serving (1962–77) as an MP representing the Toronto riding of Greenwood. Brewin, who was called to the Ontario bar in 1930, drafted the landmark Saskatchewan Trade Labour Act, which was considered the most sophisticated labour legislation in North America at that time. After World War II he represented Japanese Canadians before the Supreme Court of Canada when the government threatened a mass deportation of Canadian residents of Japanese origin. He also sought damages for the internment and confiscation of their property during the war. Though Brewin served as president of the Ontario Co-operative Commonwealth Federation (CCF) from 1946 to 1948 and served as the national treasurer of the party, he lost six federal elections. In 1961, however, the CCF was merged into the NDP, and Brewin was elected an MP the following year. He retired from Parliament in 1977.

Bryant, Paul ("BEAR"), U.S. college football coach (b. Sept. 11, 1913, Moro Bottom, Ark.—d. Jan. 26, 1983, Tuscaloosa, Ala.), was the much-beloved and respected football coach at the University of Alabama from 1958 to 1982 and became the winningest coach in college football history when the Crimson Tide defeated Auburn, 28–17, on Nov. 28, 1981, for Bryant's 315th victory, surpassing the record held by Amos Alonzo Stagg. An awesome figure at 6 ft 4 in, Bryant acquired his nickname in high school when he wrestled a scrawny bear to the ground at a theatre promotion. He was an aggressive tackle on the Fordyce High School football team, and at the University of Alabama he played end on teams that compiled a record of 23–3–2 in 1933–35. After graduation he served as an assistant coach at various universities before joining the Navy in 1941. In 1945 Bryant accepted the head coaching job at the University of Maryland, but he moved to the University of Kentucky the following year and later to Texas A & M before returning to his alma mater as head coach. At Alabama he sparked fire in players who had won only four football games in three years, and he later produced six top-ranked teams (1961, 1964, 1965, 1973, 1978, 1979). Bryant, who supervised the team practices from a tower, became a godlike figure to his players, who feared the wrath of the "Bear." He was a stickler for training rules and a strict disciplinarian who instilled in his players the same obsession for winning that he possessed. Bryant became a legendary figure in the South,

UPI

standing along the sidelines with his craggy face intent and with his ever present houndstooth hat. During his career at Alabama, Bryant's teams averaged 8.5 victories a year and never had a losing season. His players regarded him as a helpful coach, and he was instrumental in developing the careers of such superstar quarterbacks as Joe Namath, Ken Stabler, and Richard Todd. In 1971 Bryant recruited the first black player on the Alabama team and was credited with helping to spur integration of college football at predominantly white Southern schools. When he announced his retirement on Dec. 29, 1982, Bryant had chalked up 323 victories, 85 losses, and 17 ties. The giant of intercollegiate athletics died of a massive heart attack five weeks after his retirement.

Buñuel, Luis, Spanish-born film director (b. Feb. 22, 1900, Calanda, Spain—d. July 29, 1983, Mexico), caused a riot in Paris in 1930 with his first full-length feature, *L'Age d'or;* its Surrealist humour and its anarchistic contempt for conventional morality were a declaration of intent to which he remained faithful throughout his career. He studied philosophy before going to Paris where Surrealists turned him against the values instilled in him by his middle-class parents and Roman Catholic Jesuit teachers. His short film *Un Chien andalou* (1928) set out merely to shock with images drawn from the subconscious. *L'Age d'or* combined these in a direct attack on society. But for the next 20 years, apart from *Las Hurdes* (1932), a documentary made in Spain, his career faltered; he worked for the Republican government during the Civil War, represented it in France and the U.S., then settled, from 1947, in Mexico, apparently forgotten except as the creator of two outstanding Surrealist masterpieces. He returned triumphantly in 1950 with *Los Olvidados,* a semidocumentary account of life in the slums of Mexico City, which won the best director prize at the Cannes Film Festival. During the next eight years he made a series of films (*Robinson Crusoe, El, Wuthering Heights*) all bearing the hallmarks of his style but more commercially oriented. The last in the series, *Nazarin* (1958), was a sympathetic study of a priest which, though it was recommended for an award from the Office Catholique du Cinéma, was only apparently a softening of its creator's contempt for organized religion. Impressed by his reputation, the Franco government invited him back to Spain and no doubt regretted it when he made *Viridiana* (1961); the eroticism, anticlericalism, and savage humour of the film caused a scandal almost equal to that provoked by *L'Age d'or.* Condemned by the Vatican and awarded the Cannes Palme d'Or, it was perhaps his most characteristic work. He returned to France to make an astonishing series of masterpieces, less overtly violent than some of his earlier work but no less savage in their attack on the hypocrisy and fundamental immorality of bourgeois life. They included *Diary of a Chambermaid* (1964), *Belle de jour* (1966), *The Discreet Charm of the Bourgeoisie* (1972), and his last film, *This Obscure Object of Desire* (1977). Another major work of this period was *Tristana* (1970), made in Mexico.

Burchett, Wilfred, Australian journalist (b. Sept. 16, 1911, Melbourne, Australia—d. Sept. 27, 1983, Sofia, Bulg.), was the first Western journalist to visit Hiroshima after its destruction by the atomic bomb in 1945 and later reported on the wars in Korea and Vietnam from the Communist side. His left-wing opinions gave him a unique access to Communist leaders, and his sympathy for radical causes and for the downtrodden made him one of the most controversial and committed journalists in the West. Burchett suffered during the Depression and during the 1930s went to Europe. He visited Germany before World War II, helped to get Jews out of the country, and during the war worked for the London *Daily Express.* His report from Hiroshima was at first denied by the U.S. authorities and his later reports from North Korea led to the confiscation of his Australian passport. There and in North Vietnam his inside knowledge gave a valuable picture of the "other side." He was a friend of Ho Chi Minh, and his meeting with Henry Kissinger in 1971 may have helped spur moves toward peace. He wrote many books and also collaborated on Prince Norodom Sihanouk's *My War with the CIA* (1973). From 1968 he lived in Paris and in 1982 he went to Bulgaria.

Byrne, Muriel St. Clare, British writer and historian (b. May 31, 1895, Hoylake, Cheshire, England—d. Dec. 2, 1983, London, England), was a lecturer at the Royal Academy of Dramatic Art (RADA) and a popular historian of the Elizabethan period who devoted nearly 50 years to editing *The Lisle Letters.* This correspondence of Arthur Plantagenet, Lord Lisle, and his family, written while Lisle was lord deputy of Calais from 1533 to 1540, was a unique record of Tudor court and domestic life that survived in the Public Records Office after Lord Lisle's arrest. Byrne studied at Oxford and lectured at RADA from 1923 to 1955 and was an extramural lecturer at London and Oxford universities. She published studies of Elizabethan life and was conducting research for a collection of letters by Henry VIII when, in 1932, she came across the 3,000 letters in the Lisle correspondence. Eventually published in six volumes in 1981 by the University of Chicago Press, her edition included about two-thirds of the total and was hailed as one of the most important historical documents from the Tudor period. A smaller compilation from her massive edition appeared in 1982. She was made an Officer of the Order of the British Empire in 1955.

Canova, Judy (JULIETTE CANOVA), U.S. comedian (b. Nov. 20, 1916, Starke, Fla.—d. Aug. 5, 1983, Hollywood, Calif.), possessed a knack for high-decibel yodeling and hillbilly humour that became her trademark for 12 years on the "Judy Canova Show," one of the most popular radio programs of the 1940s. Canova, who appeared in braids and a straw hat and carried a battered suitcase to enhance her image as a country bumpkin, made her Broadway debut in *Ziegfeld Follies of 1936.* She also appeared on Broadway in *Calling All Stars* and *Yokel Boy* and in such motion pictures as *Going Highbrow* (1935), *Puddin' Head* (1941), *Chatterbox* (1943), and *The Adventures of Huckleberry Finn* (1960). In 1976 she returned to the screen in *Cannonball* but was more visible on such television shows as "Police Woman," "Love American Style," and "Love Boat."

Cardew, Michael Ambrose, British potter (b. May 26, 1901, Truro, Cornwall, England—d. Feb. 11, 1983, Truro), was a leading figure in the 20th-century revival of pottery as an art and an inspiring teacher of his craft. Though he was apprenticed for three years to Bernard Leach and Shoji Hamada, the main influence on his work after World War II came from Africa rather than the Far East. Cardew taught in the Gold Coast (Ghana) from 1942, founded the Volta Pottery there in 1945 and spent 15 years in Nigeria until forced to return to Britain in 1965 because of ill health. His first pottery, during the 1920s, had been the Winchcombe Pottery in Gloucestershire; then in 1939 he moved to Cornwall and set up the Wenford Bridge Pottery. When Cardew returned from Nigeria, he settled once more at Wenford Bridge, though he made lecture tours in the U.S. and Australia. Many exhibitions of his work were held in Britain, and he was the author of *Pioneer Pottery* (1969; U.S. edition, 1971). Recognized, with Bernard Leach, as an outstanding British exponent of studio pottery, Cardew was appointed Member of the Order of the British Empire in 1965 and Commander of the Order of the British Empire in 1981.

Carpenter, Karen, U.S. singer (b. March 2, 1950, New Haven, Conn.—d. Feb. 4, 1983, Downey, Calif.), with her brother Richard formed the Carpenters, a major 1970s pop instrumental duo that sold 30 million albums, won three Grammy awards, and recorded such golden ballads as "Close to You" and "We've Only Just Begun." Carpenter, who originally played the drums with the Carpenter Trio, later abandoned the instrument to concentrate on vocals. Though she and her brother briefly performed with a six-piece band called Spectrum, it was as the soft-sounding Carpenters that they became an instant hit. Carpenter's dulcet voice became their trademark, and Richard became known for his musical arrangements, receiving his inspiration from the Beatles, the Beach Boys, and Burt Bacharach. Other records that climbed to the top of the charts included "Goodbye to Love," "A Song for You," "Yesterday Once More," and such gold records as "Rainy Days and Mondays," "Superstar," "Hurting Each Other," and "Top of the World." Carpenter, who had been suffering from bouts of anorexia nervosa since 1975, died of cardiac arrest.

Carter, Lillian, mother of former U.S. president Jimmy Carter (b. Aug. 15, 1898, Richland, Ga.—d. Oct. 30, 1983, Americus, Ga.), was propelled into the limelight when her son Jimmy became the 39th president of the U.S. in 1976. "Miss Lillian," as she was known to neighbours and millions of Americans, reveled in her unorthodox life-style. She was trained as a nurse, and even after her marriage in 1923 to James Earl Carter and the birth of her children (Jimmy, Ruth, Billy, and Gloria) she raised eyebrows when she continued to work and voice her liberal opinions. An early champion of civil rights, she served in 1964 as co-chairman of Pres. Lyndon B. Johnson's campaign in Sumter County. Two years later the unflappable Miss Lillian joined the Peace Corps at the age of 67 and served a tour of duty in India for two years. When her son Jimmy received the Democratic nomination for president she made hundreds of campaign speeches that were usually punctuated by her candid views. Her many interviews revealed that she was a supporter of women's causes, a Christian who was not averse to indulging in an occasional cigarette or some bourbon, an avid reader of mysteries, a Brooklyn Dodger fan, and a soap opera addict. After Jimmy was elected president Miss Lillian served as an unofficial ambassador by representing him on a number of foreign trips. In 1977 she became the first woman to receive the Covenant of Peace Prize of the Synagogue Council of America, and in 1978 she received the Ceres Medal of the UN Food and Agriculture Organization. In 1981 the plucky Miss Lillian underwent a modified radical mastectomy after a tumour was discovered in her left breast. She died of cancer.

Cary, William Lucius, U.S. lawyer (b. Nov. 27, 1910, Columbus, Ohio—d. Feb. 7, 1983, New York, N.Y.), as the resolute chairman of the Securities and Exchange Commission (SEC) from 1961 to 1964, initiated a major reorganization of the American Stock Exchange, increased the enforcement powers of the SEC, and tightened trading rules that prohibited "insiders" from using confidential securities information for private gain. Cary, who graduated from Yale University Law School in 1934, was a noted authority on tax and corporation law and taught for 24 years at Columbia University. After joining the SEC in 1938, he served as special assistant to the head of the tax division of the Justice Department before serving in the Marine Corps during World War II. He later became lecturer at Northwestern University Law School before joining the faculty at Columbia in 1955. After being named chairman of the SEC by Pres. John F. Kennedy, Cary instigated the 1963 Special Study of the Securities Markets, the first extensive examination into the markets in 25 years. This study precipitated the 1964 Securities Acts Amendments, which led to sweeping changes on Wall Street during the following 15 years, including the eventual elimination of fixed brokerage commissions. After his stint at the SEC, Cary returned to Columbia, where he was named Dwight professor in 1964. Some of his writings include *Politics and Regulatory Agencies, Effects of Taxation on Corporate Mergers,* and *the Law and Lore of Endowment Funds.*

Casariego, Mario Cardinal, Spanish-born prelate of the Roman Catholic Church (b. Feb. 13, 1909, Figueras de Castropol, Spain—d. June 15, 1983, Guatemala), was the outspoken archbishop of Guatemala who on April 28, 1969, became the first Central American cleric to be named to the College of Cardinals. Casariego, who had a reputation for bluntness, was a liberal in church matters and was known to appeal for peace to both right- and left-wing militant groups in Guatemala. In 1968 a right-wing terrorist group kidnapped Casariego, threatened to kill him, and demanded the resignation of the country's president, who in turn declared a "state of siege." Several days later, however, Casariego was released unharmed. Casariego, who was orphaned in Spain at an early age, lived with an uncle in Mexico, moved to Guatemala and then to El Salvador, and finally returned to Guatemala. He was ordained a priest in 1936 and held various posts before being named archbishop of Guatemala in 1963. Cardinal Casariego accompanied Pope John Paul II during his March 1983 visit to Guatemala, but he was hospitalized as a result of heart problems shortly after the pope departed.

Casey, James E., U.S. businessman (b. March 29, 1888, Candelaria, Nev.—d. June 6, 1983, Seattle, Wash.), was just a teenager in Seattle when he and a friend with a $100 stake founded (1907) American Messenger Co. (later renamed United Parcel Service [UPS]). Casey, who began working as a delivery boy at the age of 11, started a messenger service at the age of 15 but sold his share two years later. When he was 19 Casey co-founded what was later known as UPS. Shortly after the company's inception, Casey expanded his services to include package delivery, and by 1922 the brown UPS trucks had become familiar sights in Oakland and Los Angeles, Calif. In 1930 Casey introduced UPS in New York, and after World War II the company boomed when Casey developed more efficient package-sorting machinery. As an officer and president of the company, Casey was an innovator; he instituted one of the first employee profit-sharing programs in the United States. Casey, who remained active in the company through his 95th birthday, saw his concern prosper; UPS delivered more than six million packages daily in the United States in 1982.

Catledge, Turner, U.S. newspaper reporter and editor (b. March 17, 1901, near New Prospect, Miss.—d. April 27, 1983, New Orleans, La.), as the refined managing editor (1951–64) and executive editor (1964–68) of the *New York Times,* expanded that paper's coverage of domestic and foreign news and instructed reporters to sharpen their stories and shorten their sentences. Before joining the *Times,* Catledge was a resourceful reporter for a string of Southern newspapers, impressing his superiors with his touch typing and repertory of hymns. In 1927 he gained the respect of Herbert Hoover, then secretary of commerce, with his incisive knowledge of the devastating 1927 Mississippi River floods. Hoover had been sent to Memphis, Tenn., by Pres. Calvin Coolidge to oversee the flood relief effort and was so impressed with Catledge's detailed account of the disaster that he contacted Adolph Ochs, publisher of the *New York Times,* and suggested that he hire Catledge. From 1927 to 1929, though, Catledge worked for the *Baltimore Sun,* but when Hoover became president of the U.S. and reiterated his request to Ochs, Catledge joined the staff of the *Times.* Catledge steadily rose through the ranks and during his tenure as editor gained a reputation for evenhandedness. His most controversial decision was the publication of a story ten days before the abortive Bay of Pigs invasion disclosing that counterrevolutionaries were training in the U.S. and in Central America for a Cuban invasion in 1961, though references to the CIA and to the imminence of the invasion were deleted. From 1968 until his retirement in 1970 Catledge served as a vice-president of The New York Times Co.

Chamson, André, French writer (b. June 6, 1900, Nîmes, France—d. Nov. 9, 1983, Paris, France), was an art historian and novelist whose fictional works were particularly concerned with the life of the peasants in his native Cévennes. The independent spirit of this largely Protestant region in a Catholic country, evoked in his first novel, *Roux le bandit* (1925), influenced Chamson's own outlook on life. He studied geography in Montpellier and Paris, then wrote a thesis on the Cévennes for the École des Chartes before working at the Bibliothèque Nationale and the Palace of Versailles as a curator. During the 1930s, after publishing *L'Homme contre l'histoire* (1927), he turned to history, politics, and journalism, showing an early appreciation of the Fascist threat. He wrote *Rien qu'un témoignage* after a visit to Spain during the Civil War and served with the French Army and the Resistance during World War II. He was the curator of the national museums in Paris until 1959. His later novels mainly adopted the regional settings of his earlier work, often with a historical background, to describe peasant resistance to persecution. He used experiences from his own childhood as a source for *Le Chiffre de nos jours* (1954). An international president of the worldwide writers' association PEN, Chamson was elected to the Académie Française in 1956.

Chang Ta-ch'ien, Chinese artist (b. May 10, 1899, Sichuan [Szechwan] Province, China—d. April 2, 1983, Taipei, Taiwan), produced such masterful landscapes, birds, and lotus flowers that critics considered him one of Asia's finest 20th-century painters. Chang, who received painting lessons from his mother at the age of nine, later studied seal-style calligraphy under Li Jui-ch'ing. But the greatest influence on Chang's work came from his own examination of the artistic works of two 17th-century monks, Shih T'ao and Chu Ta. During Chang's travels through China, he visited, in 1940, the Tun-huang caves in Gansu (Kansu) Province. He was so mesmerized by the Buddhist frescoes adorning the caves that he and a group of helpers spent two years copying the paintings. His reproductions gave the general public their first glimpse of the Buddhist masterpieces. After the Communists took power in 1949, Chang resided in various countries, including India, Argentina, Brazil, and the United States.

Charles, Prince of Belgium (CHARLES THEODORE HENRI ANTOINE MEINRAD), former regent of Belgium (b. Oct. 10, 1903, Brussels, Belgium—d. June 1, 1983, Ostend, Belgium), spent World War II in seclusion and in hiding with the Belgian resistance before serving as acting head of state from 1944 to 1950. He was unanimously elected to the regency during this transitional period because of the accusations of collaboration leveled against his brother, King Leopold III (*q.v.*); the latter abdicated in favour of his son Baudouin in 1951, thus ending the constitutional crisis. Charles, a retiring man who had nevertheless made an important contribution to the successful resumption of national affairs after the war, was happy to withdraw to his home near Ostend. His support for his brother's abdication, however, may have helped to cause some bitterness in his relations with the rest of the family. He was trained at the Royal Naval College, Dartmouth, England, and retained a love of the sea throughout his life. His other great enthusiasm was painting; under the name Karel van Vlaanderen (reflecting his preferred title of the count of Flanders), he held a number of successful exhibitions of his work. In his later years Prince Charles gained notoriety as a result of disputes with his entourage and mismanagement of his financial affairs.

Citrine, Walter McLennan Citrine, 1ST BARON, British trade unionist (b. Aug. 22, 1887, Liverpool, England—d. Jan. 22, 1983, Brixham, England), as general secretary of the Trades Union Congress (TUC) from 1926 until 1946, greatly increased the prestige and influence of the TUC as the central body of British unionism. His career spanned the General Strike of 1926 and the rise of the post-World War II Labour government in 1945. An electrician by trade, Citrine served as district secretary (1914–20) of the Electrical Trades Union and later as its assistant general secretary (1920–23). In 1917–18 he was also president of the Merseyside branch of the Federated Engineering and Shipbuilding Trades. In 1924 he moved to London as assistant secretary at the TUC, became acting secretary in 1925, and was elected general secretary the following year. From 1928 until 1945 he was president of the International Federation of Trade Unions. After leaving the TUC in 1946, Citrine was first a member of the National Coal Board and then the first chairman (1947–57) of the Central Electricity Authority, which grouped private and municipal utilities under national control. Later, he was a part-time member (1958–62) of the Electricity Council and of the U.K. Atomic Energy Authority. He was knighted in 1935 and raised to the peerage in 1946.

Clark, Kenneth Mackenzie Clark, BARON, British art historian (b. July 13, 1903, London, England—d. May 21, 1983, Hythe, Kent, England), was a leading authority on Italian Renaissance art who held many posts in art administration and enjoyed a distinguished reputation as a writer on art before becoming internationally known for his television series "Civilisation," first broadcast by the British Broadcasting Corporation in 1969. This sweeping panorama of European art from the Dark Ages to the 20th century illustrated his scholarship, his enthusiasm, his talent as an urbane communicator, and also the limitations of his middle-of-the-road approach to the subject. The series, which made him a television personality, did little for his standing with fellow art historians and was sometimes criticized for its very success in presenting the "establishment" view of art. Clark's brilliant career, helped by inherited wealth, began after he left the University of Oxford and went to study with Bernard Berenson in Florence. Clark published *The Gothic Revival* (1928) and helped to organize the Royal Academy exhibition of Italian art in 1930. In the following year he was appointed keeper of fine art at the Ashmolean Museum in Oxford, and in 1934 he became one of the youngest-ever directors of the National Gallery and surveyor of the King's Pictures, a post that led to his scholarly catalog of the Leonardo drawings in the royal collection. When World War II broke out, the National Gallery collections were evacuated to safe storage in Wales, and Clark demonstrated his flair for publicity with the gallery's lunchtime concerts and "Picture of the Month" scheme. He also worked for the Ministry of Information and on the War Artists' scheme. After resigning as director of the National Gallery in 1945, he served as chairman of the Arts Council from 1953 to 1960 and chairman of the Independent Television Authority from 1954 to 1957. His works *Leonardo da Vinci* (1939), *Landscape into Art* (1949), and *The Nude* (1956) reached a wide public, did much to encourage popular appreciation of painting, and were viewed as probably his most notable achievements. He also published books on Rembrandt and Piero della Francesca, as well as two volumes of autobiography, *Another Part of the Wood* (1974) and *The Other Half* (1977). Clark was knighted in 1938, made a Companion of Honour in 1959, a life peer in 1969, and was awarded the Order of Merit in 1976.

Claude, Albert, Belgian-born scientist (b. Aug. 24, 1898, Longlier, Belgium—d. May 22, 1983, Brussels, Belgium), shared the 1974 Nobel Prize for Physiology or Medicine with Christian René de Duve and George Emil Palade for their research on structural and functional organization of cells. Claude, who never graduated from high school, was given special dispensation by the Belgian government to begin university studies in 1922 after his valorous service during World War I. In 1928 Claude earned his medical degree at Liège University and pioneered the use of the electron microscope and the centrifuge as essential tools in the study of cell structure. In 1933 he became the first to isolate and chemically analyze a cancer virus and to identify it as a ribonucleic acid virus. After he became a U.S. citizen in 1941, Claude revolutionized modern cell biology with the publication in 1945 of the first detailed view of cell anatomy. While working at the Rockefeller University in New York City, Claude and his colleagues not only found that cells contain a variety of specialized internal organs but also discovered the function of such cell constituents as ribosomes and lysosomes. Claude also discovered the presence of mitochondria, which store the cell's energy. In 1950 he left the U.S. to become head of the cytology department at the Free University of Brussels. He later served as director of the Institut Jules Bordet and founded a cancer research laboratory in Brussels.

Clegg, Hugh Anthony, British physician (b. June 19, 1900, East Anglia, England—d. July 6, 1983, London, England), as editor of the *British Medical Journal* (*BMJ*) from 1947 to 1965, enhanced the journal's layout and contents and guided its course during the controversies that arose during the formative years of Britain's National Health Service. He also played an active and influential role in international relations in the medical field. Clegg, the son of a country parson, was educated at Westminster School and at the University of Cambridge. After qualifying at St. Bartholomew's Hospital, London, in 1925, he served as house physician there and at the Brompton Hospital for Diseases of the Chest and later as medical registrar at Charing Cross Hospital. Lacking the funds then needed to become a consultant, in 1931 he became a subeditor on the *BMJ*, the journal of the British Medical Association (BMA), advancing to deputy editor in 1934 and editor in 1947. In 1953 Clegg organized the World Medical Association's (WMA's) First World Conference on Medical Education in London. As a member of the WMA council and chairman of its Committee on Medical Ethics, he drafted the code of ethics on human experimentation adopted in modified form as the Declaration of Helsinki (1964; revised 1975). Clegg later set up the Royal Society of Medicine's Office for International Relations in Medicine and was its first director (1967–72). He also founded and edited (1971–72) *Tropical Doctor*. He was awarded the BMA's Gold Medal in 1966 and the same year was made Commander of the Order of the British Empire.

Coates, Edith Mary, British singer (b. May 31, 1908, Lincoln, England—d. Jan. 7, 1983, Worthing, England), was for many years principal mezzo-soprano with the Sadler's Wells opera company and later with the Royal Opera, Covent Garden. She displayed her versatility and impressive stagecraft in more than 60 operatic roles, including Carmen, Azucena, Amneris, Delilah, and Ortrud. Her first Carmen was at Sadler's Wells in 1931, and she created several roles, including that of Auntie in Benjamin Britten's *Peter Grimes* at Sadler's Wells (1945) and Grandma in Grace Williams's *The Parlour* with the Welsh National Opera (1966). Also notable was her title role in Tchaikovsky's *The Queen of Spades* at Covent Garden (1950–51 and 1961). Coates, who also sang with the English Opera Group during the 1960s, was made an Officer of the Order of the British Empire in 1977.

Colley, George Joseph, Irish politician (b. Oct. 18, 1925, Dublin, Ireland—d. Sept. 17, 1983, London, England), was *tanaiste* (deputy prime minister) of Ireland from 1977 to 1981 and held office in the Ministries of Finance and Education. Within the Fianna Fail Party he was the focus for opposition to Charles Haughey, and their rivalry in some ways blighted Colley's political career. The two men were at school together, Colley becoming a solicitor before his first election to the Dail (parliament) in 1961. Four years later he was appointed minister of education and in 1966, when he stood unsuccessfully for the party leadership, he became minister for industry and commerce. In 1970, when Haughey was dismissed from the post of minister of finance after a scandal over illegal arms imports, Colley succeeded him; but Haughey returned to beat him in the leadership contest in 1977.

Cooke, Terence (James) Cardinal, U.S. prelate (b. March 1, 1921, New York, N.Y.—d. Oct. 6, 1983, New York), as archbishop of New York (1968–83) was the spiritual leader of the 1.8 million Roman Catholics in the archdiocese, titular head of New York State's bishops, and, by canon law, military vicar. Cooke, who was ordained a priest on Dec. 1, 1945, served as a parish priest at St. Athanasius in the South Bronx before entering the Catholic University in Washington, D.C., to earn a master's degree in social work. After completing graduate work at the University of Chicago, he returned to New York and from 1949 to 1954 served as a youth worker for Catholic Charities. His remarkable fund-raising abilities were soon recognized by Francis Cardinal Spellman, who named Cooke treasurer of St. Joseph's Seminary in 1954. After becoming Cardinal Spellman's secretary in 1956, Cooke rose rapidly in the church hierarchy, successively serving as vice-chancellor, chancellor, auxiliary bishop, and vicar general. As Cardinal Spellman's protégé Cooke gained valuable experience by supervising all the construction in the archdiocese. When Cardinal Spellman died, Pope Paul VI installed Cooke as archbishop of the nation's fourth largest archdiocese on April 4, 1968, the same day that Martin Luther King, Jr., was assassinated. One year later, at the age of 48, Cooke was elevated to cardinal. He guided his flock through the transformation in the church precipitated by Vatican II, and though he was theologically a traditionalist he favoured a more collegial decision-making process. Cardinal Cooke, who was known for his humility and patience, was also a shrewd financial manager; he taxed wealthy suburban parishes so that inner-city churches could keep their parochial schools open. A bitter foe of abortion, Cardinal Cooke was also conservative in his views on the military. In 1982 he stated that nuclear weapons were "tolerable" and that a limited nuclear war could be fought, but many priests and nuns rejected his stance and called for a total renunciation of nuclear weapons. Cardinal Cooke, who was less of a commanding figure than his predecessor and mentor, worked quietly behind the scenes to achieve a more democratic process in running the church.

WIDE WORLD

Cowles, John, U.S. newspaper publisher (b. Dec. 14, 1898, Algona, Iowa—d. Feb. 25, 1983, Minneapolis, Minn.), was the scion of a newspaper dynasty headed by his father in Des Moines, Iowa, but in 1935 he began building his own newspaper empire in Minneapolis when he purchased the *Star*, a flagging afternoon daily, and then bought out the two local competitors, the *Journal* in 1939 and the *Tribune* in 1941. Cowles, a tough-minded publisher who took his editors to task by circling their errors in red, was a staunch advocate of internationalism and an influential Republican who urged both Wendell L. Willkie in 1940 and Dwight D. Eisenhower in 1952 to run for president. As publisher of the *Star* and the *Tribune*, Cowles was dedicated to educating readers on civic and political matters and to delivering "all the news, without bias or slant or distortion or suppression, in the news columns." While Cowles was at the helm the Minneapolis Star & Tribune Co. flourished and the *Tribune* became one of the most respected newspapers in the country, but after his retirement in 1968 and the installation of his son, John Jr., as publisher, the company began a steady decline that culminated in his son's ouster in January 1983.

Crabbe, Buster (CLARENCE LINDEN CRABBE), U.S. swimmer and actor (b. Feb. 7, 1908, Oakland, Calif.—d. April 23, 1983, Scottsdale, Ariz.), was a superb athlete who won the gold medal in the 400-m freestyle swim in the 1932 Olympics but gained even greater fame for his 1930s and '40s starring roles as the original Flash Gordon and Buck Rogers. Though Crabbe appeared as a Tarzan-like Lion Man in *King of the Jungle* (1933) and then as Tarzan in *Tarzan the Fearless* (1933), it was as the science-fiction hero Flash Gordon that he became a star. Crabbe, who referred to himself as the "King of the Serials," also portrayed Captain Gallant of the French Foreign Legion on television in 1955. In later years he swam two miles a day, amassed a small fortune by endorsing Buster Crabbe swimming pools, and devoted much of his time to lecturing on physical fitness for the elderly. He was also the author of a book on calisthenics, *Energistics*. Some of Crabbe's film credits include *Nevada* (1935), *Flash Gordon's Trip to Mars* (1938), *Buck Rogers* (1939), and *Arizona Raiders* (1965).

Crowther, J. G., British science journalist (b. 1899?—d. March 30, 1983, Bridlington, England), in effect created his own profession when, in 1929, he applied for a post as science writer on the *Manchester Guardian* and was told by the editor, C. P. Scott, that no such branch of journalism existed. Scott, however, hired him, and over the next 25 years Crowther pioneered the treatment of topical scientific developments in the daily press, with special attention to their social and political repercussions. He traveled to Germany, the Soviet Union, and the U.S. and was able to report such significant developments as the state of scientific research in Germany during the 1930s and the impact of nuclear physics. During World War II, while still on the staff of the *Manchester Guardian*, he served as director of the science department of the British Council. In later years he published biographies and an autobiography and was a contributor to *Encyclopædia Britannica.*

Cukor, George (Dewey), U.S. motion picture director (b. July 7, 1899, New York, N.Y.—d. Jan. 24, 1983, Los Angeles, Calif.), was hailed for his witty and sophisticated yet sensitive films that served as showcases for the acting talents of a legion of topnotch performers. Cukor, who was adept at eliciting Academy Award-winning performances, directed such Oscar winners as Ingrid Bergman in *Gaslight* (1944), Judy Holliday in *Born Yesterday* (1950), James Stewart in *The Philadelphia Story* (1940), Ronald Colman in *A Double Life* (1947), and Rex Harrison in *My Fair Lady* (1964). For the last-named, Cukor received the Academy Award for best director. Because he unwittingly built a reputation as a women's director, Cukor was fired from *Gone with the Wind* because Clark Gable feared that Cukor might let the female characters dominate the film. Cukor began working in 1918 as a stage manager on Broadway, but when the talkies emerged in 1929 he went to Hollywood. He made his directorial debut with *Tarnished Lady* (1931) but scored his first major success in 1933 with *Little Women.* His other critical and artistic achievements included *Dinner at Eight* (1933), *David Copperfield* (1935), *Camille* (1936), *Romeo and Juliet* (1936), *The Women* (1939), *Keeper of the Flame* (1943), *A Star Is Born* (1954), and such Katharine Hepburn-Spencer Tracy vehicles as *Adam's Rib* (1949) and *Pat and Mike* (1952). In 1975 Cukor received an Emmy award for the television film *Love Among the Ruins.* Cukor directed his last film, *Rich and Famous,* in 1981.

Cunningham, Sir Alan Gordon, British army officer (b. May 1, 1887, Dublin, Ireland—d. Jan. 30, 1983, Tunbridge Wells, England), as general officer commanding British forces in East Africa (Kenya), played a leading role in the World War II campaign that resulted in the surrender of Italian forces in Abyssinia (Ethiopia) in May 1941. He then commanded the British 8th Army in the opening phase of the Libyan Desert offensive against the German Afrikakorps under Gen. Erwin Rommel. Cunningham was commissioned into the Royal Artillery in 1906 and served with distinction throughout World War I. Between the wars he held staff appointments and at the beginning of World War II was a divisional commander in the U.K. In the Abyssinian campaign Cunningham's forces, comprising South, East, and West African troops, covered some 2,700 km (1,700 mi) in 57 days and took 50,000 prisoners. In Libya, Rommel's early successes put Cunningham on the defensive, and on Nov. 25, 1941, he was replaced as 8th Army commander by Gen. Neil Ritchie. During the remainder of the war Cunningham held commands in the U.K. He was promoted to full general in 1945, and in that year he was appointed high commissioner and commander in chief, Palestine, where he remained until the withdrawal of British troops in 1948. Cunningham was knighted in 1941 in recognition of his contribution to the successful Abyssinian campaign.

Dalio, Marcel, French film actor (b. Sept. 23, 1899, Paris, France—d. Nov. 20, 1983, Paris), played many minor parts in film and television throughout his career but would be remembered especially for his work in three important films of the 1930s, *Pépé le Moko, La Grande illusion,* and *La Règle du jeu.* He studied at the Conservatoire, then acted on stage before playing opposite Jean Gabin in *Pépé le Moko* (1936) and again as his fellow prisoner in Jean Renoir's *La Grande illusion* (1937). This was followed by his portrayal of the decadent aristocrat in *La Règle du jeu* (1939)—perhaps his finest role—and a host of smaller parts. After the German occupation in 1940, Dalio (whose real name was Israel Blauschild) left France to avoid persecution as a Jew and went to the U.S., where he played a croupier in *Casablanca* and small parts in other films including *The Song of Bernadette, Donovan's Reef,* and *Catch-22.* After France was liberated, he returned to Paris and resumed his career in films and from time to time in the theatre, increasingly typecast as a comic old man. Dalio published his memoirs, *Mes Années folles,* in 1976, and during the later part of his career he appeared on television.

D'Arcy, Jean, BARON, French television administrator and company director (b. June 10, 1913, Versailles, France—d. Jan. 19, 1983, Paris, France), as television programs director (1952–59) of Radiodiffusion-Télévision Française (RTF), France's state-run broadcasting service, was instrumental in setting up, in 1954, the Eurovision system linking Western Europe's national television networks. A graduate of the École des Hautes Études Commerciales and of the Law Faculty of the University of Paris, Baron d'Arcy became a career army officer and was decorated for his service in the Resistance during World War II. After the war he held various posts in government service, attended conferences on Indochina (1946), and was technical adviser to the minister of information from 1948 until joining RTF. In 1959 the new Gaullist government's desire for greater control over broadcasting did not accord with d'Arcy's liberal views on freedom of expression, and he was transferred to head RTF's department of international relations. In 1961 he moved to New York City as director of the UN radio and visual services division but returned to France in 1971 to set up Multivision, a company promoting cable television. From 1975 until his death he was president of the London-based International Institute of Communications (formerly the International Broadcast Institute). D'Arcy was a member of the Moinot Commission appointed by Pres. François Mitterrand's government in 1981 to prepare the way for the following year's reform of French broadcasting.

Del Rio, Dolores (DOLORES ASUNSOLO), Mexican actress (b. Aug. 3, 1905, Durango, Mexico—d. April 11, 1983, Newport Beach, Calif.), was a strikingly beautiful leading lady who because of her heritage was typecast in the roles of Indian maidens, peasant girls, and Latin enchantresses. After Del Rio made her motion-picture debut in the silent film *Joanna* (1925), she established herself as an important actress in the landmark film *What Price Glory?* (1926), in which she portrayed a French peasant. Del Rio then turned in a superb performance in *The Loves of Carmen* (1927) and gained top billing in *Resurrection* (1927) as a Russian peasant and in *Ramona* (1928) as a Spanish-Indian beauty. Because of her accent, Del Rio's roles were limited even further with the advent of the talkies, yet she starred in *Flying Down to Rio* (1933) and *Madame Du Barry* (1934) before leaving Hollywood for Mexico. While there, she helped launch the Mexican film industry with *Maria Candelaria* (1943) and *The Fugitive* (1947) and won four Ariels, the Mexican equivalent of an Academy Award. In the 1960s Del Rio returned to Hollywood, where she appeared in *Flaming Star, Cheyenne Autumn,* and *The Children of Sanchez.*

Demarest, William, U.S. actor (b. Feb. 27, 1892, St. Paul, Minn.—d. Dec. 28, 1983, Palm Springs, Calif.), was a vaudevillian for some 20 years before embarking on a highly successful motion picture and television career appearing in comic supporting roles as tough guys, smart alecks, and most memorably as softhearted curmudgeons. He probably gained his greatest visibility as the gruff but lovable Uncle Charley O'Casey on the television sitcom "My Three Sons" from 1965 to 1972. Demarest won an Emmy nomination for the role. Earlier he made his motion picture debut in *Fingerprints* (1927) and appeared in the first talkie, *The Jazz Singer,* with Al Jolson the same year. Some of Demarest's other film credits included *Wedding Present, Mr. Smith Goes to Washington, Miracle of Morgan's Creek, Hail the Conquering Hero,* and *The Great McGinty.* Besides his seven-year stint on "My Three Sons," Demarest also appeared on the television series "Tales of Wells Fargo" and "Love and Marriage." During his last 15 years he was active in various charity organizations.

Demaret, Jimmy, U.S. golfer (b. May 24, 1910, Houston, Texas—d. Dec. 28, 1983, Houston), who captured the prestigious Masters championship three times (1940, 1947, 1950) and became one of the sport's most engaging personalities with his wardrobe of brightly coloured slacks and shirts. A supreme showman, Demaret not only excited spectators with his golfing expertise but gained a following when he became the first golfer to shun the traditional golfing attire. He became a professional golfer at the age of 17 and in 1935 won the Texas PGA before triumphing in the Masters in 1940. Service in the military during World War II interrupted his golfing career, but he returned to the tour in 1945. Demaret captured two more Masters but was probably better remembered for his outlandish costumes. With Jack Burke, Jr., Demaret built the Champions Golf Club, north of Houston, Texas; its layout was considered one of the best in the world and served as a testimonial to one of the best-loved golfers of all time. He was also a member of the PGA Hall of Fame.

Dempsey, Jack (WILLIAM HARRISON DEMPSEY; "MANASSA MAULER"), U.S. prizefighter (b. June 24, 1895, Manassa, Colo.—d. May 31, 1983, New York, N.Y.), reigned as world heavyweight boxing champion from 1919 to 1926 during the "Golden Age" of sports and, because of his endurance, powerful punches, and ability to sustain punishment, was regarded as one of the greatest boxers of all time. Dempsey, who first started fighting under the name Kid Blackie, later adopted the name Jack Dempsey when he substituted in a fight for his brother, who was boxing under that name. Dempsey quickly proved his prowess by scoring 21 first-round knockouts before he methodically destroyed heavyweight champion Jess Willard and knocked him out in the third round to capture the heavyweight championship in 1919. In 1920 Dempsey twice defended his title by knocking out both Billy Miske and Bill Brennan, and in 1921 he stopped Georges Carpentier in the fourth round. The bout was the first prizefight for which ticket sales exceeded $1 million. In 1923 Dempsey beat Tommy Gibbons and went on to meet the Wild Bull of the Pampas, Argentina's Luis Angel Firpo, in one of the most thrilling prizefights in ring history. Seconds after the starting bell, Firpo dazed Dempsey with a right to the jaw, and Dempsey, who was only half-conscious, felled Firpo four times before Firpo knocked the champion out of the ring into the press row. With an instinctive shove from the reporters, Dempsey was returned to the ring and knocked out Firpo in the second round. On Sept. 23, 1926, Dempsey lost the heavyweight crown to Gene Tunney, but the following year the two staged a rematch before a record

UPI

crowd at Soldier Field in Chicago. Though Dempsey floored Tunney in the seventh round, he failed to move to a neutral corner, and the referee was impelled to delay the count until Dempsey retreated. At the "long count" of 9, Tunney staggered to his feet, knocked down Dempsey in the eighth round, and retained the championship by winning a ten-round decision. The "long count" fight became one of the most enduring controversies in sports history, and Dempsey, who was long reviled as a slacker during World War I, became a folk hero after Tunney had punched him nearly blind. During the 1930s and early 1940s Dempsey appeared in exhibition bouts before becoming the renowned proprietor of Jack Dempsey's Restaurant in New York City. His willingness to pose for thousands of photos and to sign countless autographs convinced many that Dempsey was a champion both in and out of the ring.

Denby, Edwin, U.S. dance critic and poet (b. Feb. 4, 1903, Tientsin, China—d. July 12, 1983, Searsport, Maine), as one of the foremost dance critics in the country, had a decided influence on young writers and dancers with the publication of *Looking at the Dance* (1949) and *Dancers, Buildings and People in the Street* (1965), which together constitute the most important and profound dance criticism of modern times. Denby, who preferred to be known as a poet, was the author of four volumes of verse: *In Public, In Private* (1948), *Mediterranean Cities* (1956), *Snoring in New York* (1974), and *Collected Poems* (1975). His dance reviews were marked by a witty and vivid poetic imagery that conjured up the beauty, rhythm, and movement of dance. Denby's analytical prose was also distinguished by his lavish use of metaphors, especially when he praised the works of Jerome Robbins, Martha Graham, and George Balanchine. Though Denby originally contemplated becoming a psychoanalyst, he embarked on a dancing career after studying modern dance at the Hellerau-Laxenburg School in Vienna. From 1929 to 1935 he performed with dance troupes in Germany and Switzerland before immigrating to the U.S. in 1936 and serving (1936–42) as dance critic for *Modern Music* magazine. During World War II Denby was dance critic for the *New York Herald Tribune,* but in 1945 he began to free-lance for such publications as *Dance Magazine, The Nation,* and *Saturday Review.* Denby, who was viewed as the preeminent critic of classical ballet in the U.S., took his own life.

Denham, Reginald, British-born actor, director, and writer (b. Jan. 10, 1894, London, England—d. Feb. 4, 1983, Englewood, N.J.), had an unremarkable career as an actor with Sir Frank Benson's Shakespearean company before finding his niche as the director of more than 100 Broadway plays, most notably such suspense dramas as *The Two Mrs. Carrolls, Duet for Two, Obsession, Dial M for Murder, Temper the Wind,* and *The Bad Seed.* After Denham made his U.S. directing debut with *Rope's End,* he compiled an impressive list of Broadway directing successes before returning to Britain to join Paramount British Pictures in 1931. Two years later he became a film director and during the following three years directed 15 motion pictures, including *Called Back, The Primrose Path,* and *The Village Square.* In 1938 Denham embarked on a playwriting career and produced such works as *Give Me Yesterday, Suspect, Dark Hammock,* and *Be Your Age.* During the 1950s and 1960s Denham and his wife composed more than 100 dramatic scripts for television.

Dietz, Howard, U.S. lyricist (b. Sept. 9, 1896, New York, N.Y.—d. July 30, 1983, New York), was a prolific songwriter who wrote the words to more than 500 songs and the effervescent director of advertising and publicity for Goldwyn Pictures (later [1924] Metro-Goldwyn-Mayer) from 1919 to 1957. After attending Columbia University, Dietz joined the Philip Goodman Advertising Agency, where he was given the task of developing a trademark for Goldwyn Pictures. He used his alma mater's mascot lion as an inspiration for the roaring MGM "Leo the Lion" and added the accompanying motto, "Ars Gratia Artis"—"Art for Art's Sake." After joining Goldwyn Pictures in 1919, Dietz began writing lyrics in his spare time, but it was not until he teamed up with Arthur Schwartz in 1929 and the duo established their reputation with *The Little Show* that his talents were recognized. The two collaborated on such classics as "Dancing in the Dark," "You and the Night and the Music," "I Guess I'll Have to Change My Plan," "Moanin' Low," and "Something to Remember You By." In addition Dietz wrote the lyrics for such shows as *Three's a Crowd, Sadie Thompson,* and *The Gay Life* and collaborated with such leading composers as Jerome Kern and George Gershwin. The multitalented Dietz also translated the librettos of the operas *La Bohème* and *Die Fledermaus* into English and devised a two-handed bridge game that was named after him.

Dike, Kenneth Onwuka, Nigerian historian (b. Dec. 17, 1917, Awka, eastern Nigeria—d. Oct. 26, 1983, Nigeria), was internationally renowned as a historian and leading figure in Nigerian academic life. He studied in Nigeria, England, and Scotland, receiving a doctorate for his thesis on *Trade and Politics in the Niger Delta, 1830–1885.* He taught in Ibadan, then at the West African Institute of Social and Economic Research, where he laid the foundations of the Nigerian National Archives, of which he was the first director. From 1956 he was professor at the University College, Ibadan, and from 1958 principal, then vice-chancellor of the University of Ibadan when it was granted full university status. Dike played a major role in the creation in 1963 of the International Congress of Africanists and in 1965 was chairman of the Association of Commonwealth Universities. By this time, he was credited with playing a leading role in the creation of a generation of African historians who could interpret their own history without being influenced by a European outlook. But the secession in 1967 of Nigeria's Eastern Region as independent Biafra divided the country, and Dike cast his lot with the secessionists. He began to work on establishing a Biafran university at Port Harcourt, but the defeat of the rebel state put an end to this project and he left for Harvard to become Andrew W. Mellon professor of African history. At the end of his life, he returned to Nigeria as president of the Anambra State University.

Dlimi, Ahmed, Moroccan army officer (b. July 1931, Sidi-Kacem, Morocco—d. Jan. 25, 1983, Marrakesh, Morocco), as chief aide-de-camp to King Hassan II, was head of counterespionage and responsible for operations in the Western Sahara against the Popular Front for the Liberation of Saguia el Hamra and Río de Oro (Polisario Front). In 1965 Dlimi and Moroccan Defense Minister Gen. Muhammad Oufkir were suspected by the French authorities of having engineered the disappearance (in October 1965) of the leader of the Moroccan opposition, Mehdi ben Barka. Dlimi voluntarily gave himself up and stood trial in Paris, apparently to avoid damaging Franco-Moroccan relations. In June 1967 he was acquitted, though Oufkir (d. 1972) was sentenced in absentia to life imprisonment. At the time of his death, Dlimi, who trained as an army officer in Morocco and France, had largely succeeded in defeating the Polisario Front guerrilla forces. His death, in a collision between his car and a truck, aroused speculation that he might have been assassinated while plotting against the regime, although he had previously been one of the king's most loyal supporters.

Docker, Norah (LADY DOCKER), British society figure (b. June 23, 1906, Derby, England—d. Dec. 11, 1983, London, England), delighted gossip columnists and some of their readers with her extravagant parties and flamboyant antics in the otherwise austere 1950s. Her story, told in her autobiography *Norah,* was that of a penniless dancing girl who married three millionaires: the first, Clement Callingham, died in 1945; the second, Sir William Collins, died after only a year of marriage in 1947; and two years later she married Sir Bernard Docker, chairman of the BSA and Daimler group of companies, with whom she was to make newspaper headlines throughout the following decade. While Sir Bernard appealed for cuts in government spending, she paraded her gold-plated Daimler limousine and expensive furs, entertained King Farouk of Egypt on her Mediterranean yacht, and was involved in a costly lawsuit over an infringement of the foreign travel allowance. She delighted in the publicity but it was less welcome to Sir Bernard's business associates, and in 1956 he lost his seat on the BSA board. The Dockers lived in Italy and Monaco, were expelled from Monaco after a trivial nightclub incident, and retired to Jersey. After Sir Bernard's death in 1978, Lady Docker lived in seclusion.

Dolin, Sir Anton (PATRICK HEALEY-KAY), British ballet dancer and choreographer (b. July 27, 1904, Slinfold, Sussex, England—d. Nov. 26, 1983, Paris, France), presided over the entire development of modern British ballet as a dancer for 30 years and then as a teacher and choreographer. He joined Diaghilev's company in 1921, as the only British male dancer to achieve any prominence at a time when British ballet was virtually nonexistent. He danced in *Daphnis and Chloe, Les Biches,* and *Les Facheux,* and in *Le Train Bleu,* which Cocteau wrote as a showcase for Dolin's extraordinary technical and acrobatic skills. He also appeared in revue and music hall, exhibiting his talents as a theatrical personality as well as a dancer, while at the same time working for the creation of a British national ballet. He danced during the 1930s with various companies, including the Vic-Wells and the Markova-Dolin, which he founded with Alicia Markova. During World War II he was in Australia and the U.S., where he helped to found the American Ballet Theatre, before returning to join the Sadler's Wells Ballet in 1948. From there he went to the Festival Ballet, which he directed until 1961. In later years, after two seasons with the Rome Opera, he became a free-lance producer. He also performed a one-man show and appeared in the film *Nijinsky* (1980). Dolin published a book on partnering, studies of Markova and Spessivtseva, and volumes of autobiography. He was knighted in 1981.

Dorticós Torrado, Osvaldo, Cuban lawyer and politician (b. April 17?, 1919, Cienfuegos, Cuba—d. June 23, 1983, Havana, Cuba), was a prominent lawyer who became a member of Fidel Castro's clandestine revolutionary movement to overthrow the regime of Fulgencio Batista and was installed as Cuba's president shortly after Castro ousted Batista in 1959. Though Dorticós was viewed as a figurehead president, he had a commanding knowledge of law and economics. In 1963 Dorticós seized control of the Ministry of Economy and the Central Planning Board and by 1965 was recognized as the country's undisputed economic planner. Dorticós, who earned a law degree from the University of Havana in 1941, became a leader of the underground revolutionary cause in 1957 but, because of his dignified and conservative appearance, was regarded as somewhat of a bourgeois Communist. When Castro first seized power, Dorticós was appointed minister of laws and decrees with responsibility for creating laws for the new government, but in July Castro forced Manuel Urrutia Lleo to resign as president and appointed Dorticós his successor. Dorticós, who served as president until 1976, was deeply depressed and took his own life.

Drummond, (James) Roscoe, U.S. journalist (b. Jan. 13, 1902, Theresa, N.Y.—d. Sept. 30, 1983, Princeton, N.J.), served as a reporter and editor for the *Christian Science Monitor* before heading the paper's Washington bureau from 1940 to 1953 and rising to prominence with his front-page column "State of the Nation," a succinct and penetrating analysis of national affairs. When Drummond joined the *New York Herald Tribune* in 1953, his column was syndicated in 150 newspapers and, at its peak, it appeared three times a week. When he left the *Herald Tribune* in 1955, he began writing the "State of the Nation" for the Los Angeles Times Syndicate. During his 50-year career "Bulldog" Drummond tenaciously recorded the pulse of Washington power and politics under 11 presidents. From 1949 to 1951 he also served as European director of information for the Marshall Plan, a U.S.-sponsored European recovery program designed to rehabilitate the economies of post-World War II European nations. From 1962 to 1967 he served as a member of the board of trustees of Freedom House, an organization of liberal, moderate, and conservative leaders in public affairs. During his later years and even up to his death Drummond remained active, compiling a book of reminiscences of his dealings with notable public figures including the U.S. presidents from Franklin D. Roosevelt to Jimmy Carter.

Du Plat Taylor, (Frederica Mabel) Joan, British archaeologist (b. 1906, Glasgow, Scotland—d. May 21, 1983, Cambridge, England), was librarian at the Institute of Archaeology of the University of London from 1945 to 1970 and played a leading role in encouraging the development of underwater archaeology. During the 1930s she was assistant curator at the Cyprus Museum, Nicosia, and excavated several sites on the island. Du Plat later directed the excavation of Iron Age sites in Italy. In 1960 she helped in the excavation of a Bronze Age vessel wrecked off Cape Gelidonya in Turkey and further promoted this branch of archaeology by making amateur divers aware of underwater opportunities. For eight years she edited the *International Journal of Nautical Archaeology,* published by the Council for Nautical Archaeology, which she helped to found. She was also first president of the Nautical Archaeology Society, a fellow of the Society of Antiquaries, and editor of *Marine Archaeology.* She lived to see the successful raising, in 1982, of Henry VIII's ship "Mary Rose," a symbolic tribute to her pioneering work in directing attention to the importance of underwater sites.

Egk, Werner, German composer (b. May 17, 1901, Auchsesheim, Bavaria, Germany—d. July 10, 1983, Inning, Bavaria, West Germany), established his reputation with *Die Zäubergeige,* an opera first performed in 1935. He continued to work mainly for the theatre, producing popular operas and ballets that were accessible to a wide public but did not always survive the test of time. He composed an orchestral work for the Berlin Olympic Games in 1936 and was conductor (1936–40) at the Berlin State Opera. His opera *Peer Gynt* was performed in 1938. During World War II he was attached to the German Institute in Paris and was responsible for helping many Jewish musicians to escape deportation by the Nazis. His ballets included *Abraxas* (1948), a version of the Faust legend, and *Casanova in London* (1969). *Irische Legende* (1955) and *Der Revisor* (1957) were the most notable of his later operas. He also wrote a piano sonata, songs, and orchestral works.

Eisner, Lotte H., German-born film critic and historian (b. March 5, 1896, Berlin, Germany—d. Nov. 25, 1983, Paris, France), was Germany's first woman film critic, a leading authority on German expressionist cinema, and one of those who helped to create and establish the Cinémathèque Française. She studied art history before entering journalism with the *Berliner Tageblatt* and, from 1927 to 1933, the *Film Kurier.* When Hitler came to power, she was denounced as a "Jewish Bolshevik" and joined her sister in Paris, where she met Henri Langlois and Georges Franju. She assisted them in building up the French film archive, the basis for the Cinémathèque Française, while at the same time continuing her research into the German cinema of the 1920s. Eisner drew on her own friendship with Fritz Lang and other leading figures, as well as her recollections of cultural life during the period, for *L'Écran démoniaque* (1952; *The Haunted Screen,* 1969), a classic study of German expressionism. She also wrote a biography of Lang and a study of F. W. Murnau that helped to revive the reputation of a neglected figure. Briefly imprisoned during the German occupation of France, she was protected by Langlois and in 1945 became a curator at the Cinémathèque. The new German cinema of the 1960s and 1970s aroused her enthusiasm: she admired Werner Herzog, who reciprocated her feeling by making a journey on foot from West Germany to Paris to visit her. In 1982 she was admitted into the Légion d'Honneur.

Emerson, Faye, U.S. actress and television personality (b. July 8, 1917, Elizabeth, La.—d. March 9, 1983, Deya, Majorca), was a congenial, blond-chignoned actress who appeared in some 20 films before finding her niche on television, first as a panelist on quiz shows and later as the classy pioneer of the late-night interview show. Emerson, who attracted viewers with her plunging V-necked evening gowns, emceed two 15-minute programs, "Paris Cavalcade of Fashion" and "The Faye Emerson Show," before becoming host of the highly popular 30-minute variety show "Faye Emerson's Wonderful Town" in 1951. For five years (1944–49) she was married to Elliot Roosevelt, son of Franklin D. Roosevelt, and she later (1950–58) was married to the musician Skitch Henderson. In 1948 Emerson made her Broadway debut in *The Play's the Thing,* but after her divorce from Henderson a decade later, she retreated from the public eye. Among her films were *Nurse's Street, Bad Men of Missouri, The Desert Song,* and *Her Kind of Man.*

Emery, Dick (Richard Gilbert Emery), British comedian (b. Feb. 7, 1917, London, England—d. Jan. 2, 1983, London), owed his greatest success to television and to the format of his own "Dick Emery Show," which allowed him to display the range of his talents as an impersonator. Emery also created a variety of male and female comic characters for the program, including Mandy, with her catchphrase "Ooh, you are awful . . . but I like you," and the engaging Lampwick, who tottered on the brink of senility and was always in danger of losing his false teeth. His impersonations, with their variety and attention to details of dress and mannerism, were the product of hard work and a lifetime in entertainment. As a child Emery joined his parents in their stage act, graduating from pantomime and "The Gang Show" to variety and radio comedy. On television he appeared in "Two's Company" and "It's a Square World" before the first "Dick Emery Show" was broadcast in 1963. In 1972 Emery won the BBC-TV Personality award from the Variety Club of Great Britain, and he remained one of Britain's most popular television personalities until his death.

Erlich, Simcha, Israeli politician (b. Dec. 15, 1915, Lublin, Poland—d. June 19, 1983, Jerusalem, Israel), was leader of the Liberal Party and deputy prime minister from 1979 after serving two years as a controversial minister of finance. Erlich immigrated to Israel in 1934 and worked on a farm before setting up a factory to manufacture optical instruments. He entered politics in 1969 as a Liberal member of the Knesset (parliament). Erlich was a personal friend of Menachem Begin and, after the Likud victory in 1977, was appointed to the Finance Ministry. Erlich implemented policies to encourage private enterprise and reduce government subsidies, but he was blamed for failing to control inflation. In 1981 he became minister of agriculture as well as deputy prime minister and took over responsibility for settlement on the West Bank. But in most respects he was considered a moderate, and it was Erlich who led the attacks on former defense minister Ariel Sharon over the latter's conduct of the invasion of Lebanon in 1982.

Euler (-Chelpin), Ulf Svante von, Swedish physiologist (b. Feb. 7, 1905, Stockholm, Sweden—d. March 9, 1983, Stockholm), shared the 1970 Nobel Prize for Physiology or Medicine with Julius Axelrod and Bernard Katz for discoveries concerning the chemistry of nerve transmission. Von Euler was honoured for his discovery in 1946 of the compound noradrenaline, the key neurotransmitter (or impulse carrier) in the sympathetic nervous system. He also confirmed that noradrenaline was stored within nerve fibres themselves. These discoveries laid the groundwork for Axelrod's determination of the role of enzymes in nerve activity and led to the development of drugs for treatment of Parkinson's disease and mental illness. Von Euler's father, Karl von Euler-Chelpin, was the Nobel laureate in chemistry in 1929, and in the following year von Euler earned his M.D. from the Karolinska Institute. He served as professor of physiology at his alma mater from 1939 to 1971 and from 1966 to 1975 was president of the prestigious Nobel Foundation. Von Euler also conducted research on prostaglandins, hypertension, and arteriosclerosis. Besides his Nobel Prize, von Euler was recipient of the Swedish Order of the North Star and the Stouffer Prize.

Fabre-Luce, Alfred, French writer (b. May 16, 1899, Paris, France—d. May 17, 1983, Paris), was a maverick right-wing intellectual whose support for Marshal Philippe Pétain during World War II did not prevent his imprisonment by the Germans for hostility to their anti-Semitic policies. Fabre-Luce was later known for his opposition to Gen. Charles de Gaulle. Fabre-Luce joined the diplomatic service before embarking on a career in journalism that made him one of the country's best known and most controversial figures. After the Liberation he was imprisoned for collaboration, and when de Gaulle returned to power in 1958, he revived his wartime hatred of the general and firmly opposed granting independence to Algeria. His novel *Haute-Cour* (1962) was proscribed for insulting the head of state, and he was fined a token sum, but the ban on the book remained. Despite his rightist stance, at the time of the 1968 "events," when student demonstrations were at their peak, he expressed support for another anti-Gaullist, the Socialist Pierre Mendès-France. Fabre-Luce later rallied to Pres. Valéry Giscard d'Estaing, a relative. An individualist and a defender of individual freedoms, he wrote many books, including *La Victoire* (1924), *Journal de la France* (1939–44), *Demain en Algérie* (1957), and biographies of Talleyrand, Benjamin Constant, and D. H. Lawrence.

Firyubin, Nikolay Pavlovich, Soviet diplomat (b. April 4, 1908, Simbirsk [now Ulyanovsk], Russia—d. Feb. 14?, 1983, Moscow, U.S.S.R.), was a Soviet deputy foreign minister from 1957 and former ambassador to Czechoslovakia (1954–55) and Yugoslavia (1955–57). He graduated from the Moscow Aviation Institute and served in various posts in the Communist Party before starting his diplomatic career in 1953. Firyubin was general secretary of the Political Consultative Committee of the Warsaw Pact; in 1961 he announced the severing of Soviet relations with Albania. As deputy foreign minister he was in charge of relations with South Asia and made visits to India and Pakistan as well as taking responsibility for diplomatic relations with Afghanistan following the Soviet invasion in December 1979.

Fitzgibbon, (Robert Louis) Constantine Lee-Dillon, Irish-American historian and writer (b. June 8, 1919, Lenox, Mass.—d. March 23, 1983, Dublin, Ireland), recorded his disillusionment with Marxism in the political fiction *When the Kissing Had to Stop* (1960) and published historical works, including *The Shirt of Nessus* (1955), on resistance in Germany to Nazism. Because Fitzgibbon was raised in the U.S. and France and educated in England, France, and Germany, he gained an international outlook and a knowledge of languages that he was able to exploit as the translator of more than 30 books. During World War II he served with both the British and U.S. armies but attempted to resign his commission in the latter to protest the use of the atomic bomb. He achieved some success with his third novel, *Cousin Emily* (1952; also published as *Dear Emily*), and notoriety with *When the Kissing Had to Stop.* After a television adaptation of the latter was shown in 1962, a viewer's description of the author provided him with the title for the essays in *Random Thoughts of a Fascist Hyena* (1963). His political views were often eccentric, but his best historical works were the result of careful research. One of his most lasting achievements was his biography of Dylan Thomas, published in 1965; it was inspired by his friendship with the Welsh poet, whom he met in the 1930s. Fitzgibbon recounted one of their shared interests, and a lifelong addiction, in *Drink* (1979). He also edited a selection from Thomas's letters and was the author of the article on Thomas in the *Encyclopædia Britannica.* Fitzgibbon's autobiography, *Through the Minefield,* appeared in 1967.

Fix, Paul, U.S. actor (b. March 13, 1901, Dobbs Ferry, N.Y.—d. Oct. 14, 1983, Santa Monica, Calif.), was a commanding character actor who appeared in some 300 films, especially in Westerns with Tom Mix and John Wayne and in crime movies portraying both criminals and lawmen. Fix, however, was probably best remembered for his television role as Marshal Micah Torrance in "The Rifleman." Fix, who began his career on the stage, made his film debut in silent Westerns and comedies in the 1920s. His film credits include *The First Kiss* (1928), *After the Thin Man* (1936), *Back to Bataan* (1945), *Giant* (1956), *To Kill a Mockingbird* (1962), *The Undefeated* (1969), and *Grayeagle* (1977). Fix also wrote the screenplays for such films as *Tall in the Saddle, Back to Bataan,* and *Wake of the Red Witch.*

Follows, Sir Denis, British sports administrator (b. April 13, 1908—d. Sept. 17, 1983, London, England), was secretary of the Football Association from 1962 to 1973 and chairman of the British Olympic Association from 1977. An ardent defender of sport against interference by politicians, he aroused controversy by his support for links with South Africa and for British participation in the 1980 Moscow Olympic Games. Never an outstanding sportsman himself, he was secretary of his school football club. As a teacher in the 1930s, he began a lifelong participation in the Universities Athletics Union, becoming its chairman in 1948 and president in 1972. During World War II he served with the Royal Air Force. As secretary of the Football Association he took a leading role in organizing the 1966 World Cup. His defense of links with South Africa led to his defeat in 1981 for the presidency of the Association of National Olympic Committees. Knighted in 1978, in 1980 he gained the silver medal of the Olympic Order and an award from the British Sports Writers' Association.

Fontanne, Lynn (Lillie Louise Fontanne), British-born actress (b. Dec. 6, 1887, Woodford, England—d. July 30, 1983, Genessee Depot, Wis.), was a seemingly ageless star on Broadway for 40 years and together with her husband, Alfred Lunt, gained a reputation as the greatest husband-and-wife team in the history of the theatre. Fontanne's mentor, the British actress Ellen Terry, secured her debut as a chorus girl in *Cinderella* (1905). Fontanne made her U.S. debut in New York City in *The Harp of Life* (1916). After scoring a major success in *Dulcy* (1921), Fontanne married Lunt in 1922, and the two captivated audiences as co-stars in 27 plays, including *The Guardsman* (1924), *Arms and the Man* (1925), *The Doctor's Dilemma* (1927), *Design for Living* (1933), and *The Pirate* (1942). Their superlative performances, especially in comedies focusing on marital infidelity, brought many triumphs for the Theatre Guild, under whose auspices they appeared from 1924 to 1929. Their biggest hit, however, was *O Mistress Mine,* which opened in 1946 and ran for 451 performances. The couple constantly strove for perfection and rehearsed almost continuously to attain the effortless rapport that was their hallmark. Though they were considered at their best in comedies by Shaw, Coward, and Rattigan, Fontanne and Lunt appeared in two dramas, *There Shall Be No Night* (1943) and *The Visit,* which opened in London and then in the U.S. in 1958 at the newly dedicated Lunt-Fontanne Theatre on Broadway. Fontanne, who appeared in several films with Lunt, including *Second Youth, The Guardsman,* and *Stage Door Canteen,* soloed in *The Man Who Found Himself.* The two, who were almost inseparable both on and off stage during their 55-year marriage (Lunt died in 1977), received the U.S. Medal of Freedom in 1964.

Foy, Eddie, Jr., U.S. vaudevillian and actor (b. 1905, New Rochelle, N.Y.—d. July 15, 1983, Woodland Hills, Calif.), was only five when he launched his show business career performing with his siblings in his father's celebrated vaudeville act "Eddie Foy and the Seven Little Foys"; later he captured the limelight as a nimble, comic song-and-dance man and irrepressible mugger. In 1929 Foy made his Broadway debut in *Show Girl* and in the same year began accepting supporting roles in motion pictures. Foy, who often stole the show with his rubbery face and loose-jointed limbs, was probably best remembered for his performances in both the musical and motion picture versions of *The Pajama Game* (1957). Foy also appeared in *Queen of the Night Clubs* (1929), *The Farmer Takes a Wife* (1953), and *Bells Are Ringing* (1960), but his top screen credits were those in which he portrayed his father, including *Frontier Marshall* (1939), *Lillian Russell* (1940), *Yankee Doodle Dandy* (1942), and *Wilson* (1944). In 1968 Foy made his last screen appearance in *30 Is a Dangerous Age Cynthia,* a British film.

Friendly, Alfred, U.S. journalist (b. Dec. 30, 1911, Salt Lake City, Utah—d. Nov. 7, 1983, Washington, D.C.), as managing editor of the *Washington Post* from 1955 to 1965 increased the newspaper's international coverage and science reporting and as a roving correspondent for the *Post* from 1966 to 1971 won the 1968 Pulitzer Prize for international reporting for his frontline dispatches during the 1967 Arab-Israeli war. Friendly, who worked as a reporter for the *Washington Daily News* from 1936 to 1939, joined the *Post* in 1939, serving as a reporter until 1952 when he became associate managing editor. After his stint as managing editor of the newspaper he was an associate editor and correspondent (1966–71). He retired in 1971. Friendly, the author of such books as *The Guys on the Ground* (1944), *Crime and Publicity: The Impact of News on the Administration of Justice* (1967; with Ronald Goldfarb), and *The Dreadful Day: The Battle of Manzikert* (1981), died of a self-inflicted gunshot wound after a long battle with cancer.

Fulford, Sir Roger Thomas Baldwin, British writer (b. Nov. 24, 1902, Carnforth, Lancashire, England—d. May 18, 1983, Carnforth), composed historical works on the political life and notable figures of the 19th century and was particularly known for his works on the British monarchy. His historical knowledge, scholarship, and literary abilities were illustrated in his biographies *George IV* (1935), *The Prince Consort* (1949), *Queen Victoria* (1951), and *Samuel Whitbread* (1967); in his editions of royal letters; and in his study *Votes for Women* (1957). After Fulford attended the University of Oxford, he was called to the bar in 1931 and made an unsuccessful bid to enter Parliament as a member of the Liberal Party. Meanwhile, he joined *The Times,* spent a period as lecturer at King's College, London, and was assistant private secretary at the Air Ministry during World War II. His first book, *Royal Dukes* (1933), was followed by *The Greville Memoirs* (1937; co-edited with Lytton Strachey), *A History of Glynn's* (1953), and *The Right Honourable Gentleman* (1945), a political satire. Fulford also defined his lifelong Liberal convictions in *The Liberal Case,* published in conjunction with the 1959 election. He was knighted in 1980.

Fuller, R(ichard) Buckminster, U.S. inventor (b. July 12, 1895, Milton, Mass.—d. July 1, 1983, Los Angeles, Calif.), was a visionary Renaissance man who was best known as the designer of the geodesic dome and as a tireless advocate of innovative methods of seeking solutions to mankind's problems. Fuller, who was a self-described engineer, mathematician, architect, cartographer, comprehensive designer, and choreographer, was twice expelled from Harvard University by his own design. He was then dispatched to Canada by his family to work in a machinery factory, but Fuller was fascinated by the experience. He held a variety of jobs before joining the Navy and marrying Anne Hewlett during World War I. After his naval discharge in 1919, Fuller worked for a meat packer and as a sales manager for a trucking company before starting a business with his father-in-law in 1922. In the same year, Fuller's life was shattered when his daughter died on her fourth birthday. He went on a five-year drinking binge, was forced out of business, and contemplated suicide in 1927. He rejected the idea, however, and decided to dedicate his life to discovering the principles operative in the universe and turning them over to his fellow men. His determination to prove that technology could "save the world from itself, provided it is properly used," led him to turn to building, the industry for which he was best suited. In his early career Fuller was viewed as a lovable crackpot, as the creator of a prefabricated Dymaxion House that had rooms hung from a central mast and outer walls of continuous glass and of a Dymaxion three-wheeled automobile that used a standard 90-hp engine and could reach a speed of 120 mph. Both inventions were commercial failures. In 1943, however, he captured the serious attention of scientists when he designed the Dymaxion Airocean World Map, which showed the Earth's entire surface in a single flat view without a visible distortion. In 1947 he patented his geodesic dome, constructed of light, straight structural elements in

TOM MUNK—R. BUCKMINSTER FULLER ARCHIVES

tension, arranged in a framework of triangles to reduce stress and weight. The dome was innovative because, unlike other large domes, the geodesic dome could be placed directly on the ground as a complete structure. Eventually more than 200,000 geodesic domes were built; some of the finest examples of his own domes include the Union Tank Car Co. maintenance shop in Baton Rouge, La., and the U.S. exhibition dome at Expo 67 in Montreal. Fuller was also the author of some 25 books, including *Operating Manual for Spaceship Earth* (1969). Though he never formally studied architecture, he was awarded the prestigious Gold Medal of the American Institute of Architects in 1970, and in 1983 he was presented with the Presidential Medal of Freedom in recognition of his many innovations.

Funès, Louis de, French actor (b. July 31, 1914, Courbevoie, Seine, France—d. Jan. 27, 1983, Nantes, France), reached the height of a successful screen career in the 1960s with films that exploited his talent for visual comedy and quirky characterization. They included *Le Gendarme de Saint-Tropez* (1964), *La Grande Vadrouille* (1966), and *Oscar* (1967). He was voted France's most popular actor in 1968. The son of Spanish parents, Funès held a variety of jobs, including that of piano player in a cabaret, before his acting career began in 1945. In the early 1950s he had parts in films by Sacha Guitry and in stage reviews, and during the next decade he appeared in more than 100 films. His title role in *Le Gendarme de Saint-Tropez* gave rise to a series that included *Le Gendarme à New York* (1965). *Fantômas* (1965) also had sequels, including *Fantômas contre Scotland Yard* (1967). Later films included *La Folie des Grandeurs* (1971, with Yves Montand), *Les Aventures de Rabbi Jacob* (1973), and *La Soupe aux choux* (1981). On the stage he appeared in plays by Maxwell Anderson, Tennessee Williams, and Jean Anouilh.

Fury, Billy (RONALD WYCHERLEY), British rock star (b. 1941, Liverpool, England—d. Jan. 28, 1983, London, England), rose to prominence in the late 1950s as Britain's answer to Elvis Presley, but ill health and the public's declining interest in rock music hampered his career so that by 1978 he was bankrupt. In 1959, however, with "Maybe Tomorrow," he had launched a series of 26 hit records that kept him on the charts longer than any other singer apart from Presley and the Beatles. His hit songs, which included "Halfway to Paradise" and "Like I've Never Been Gone," led to a film career in the 1960s and '70s with *Play It Cool, I've Got a Horse,* and *That'll Be the Day.* As an adolescent he suffered from rheumatic fever and, in reaction, cultivated a lifestyle that was in keeping with his stage name. In reality, however, he was a somewhat withdrawn man, interested in his childhood hobby of bird watching and the racehorses that he bred with the earnings from his work. Fury wrote many of his own songs and struggled to rebuild his career after his bankruptcy, though aware, from the time of his first heart attack in 1972, that he was living on borrowed time.

Gates, Thomas Sovereign, Jr., U.S. banker and government official (b. April 10, 1906, Germantown, Pa.—d. March 25, 1983, Philadelphia, Pa.), was a banker by profession who was better known for his short but influential stints as secretary of the navy (1957–59) and defense (1959–61) during Dwight D. Eisenhower's administration. As navy secretary Gates was instrumental in retiring battleships in favour of nuclear-powered submarines and in promoting nuclear missile experimentation. During his year as secretary of defense, he overhauled Pentagon management procedures and helped propel the Defense Department into the age of modern tactics and nuclear weaponry. Gates was also remembered for authorizing the ill-fated U-2 reconnaissance flight of Francis Gary Powers. When the latter was shot down (May 1, 1960) deep inside the Soviet Union, Gates advised Eisenhower to accept responsibility for the mission. After government service Gates became chairman of the executive committee of the Morgan Guaranty Trust Co., the nation's fifth largest bank, in 1961; he was its president from 1962 to 1965 and served (1965–69) as chairman of the bank. In 1976 Pres. Gerald Ford called Gates out of retirement to act as chief of the U.S. liaison mission in Beijing (Peking).

Géraldy, Paul (PAUL LEFÈVRE-GÉRALDY), French writer (b. March 6, 1885, Paris, France—d. March 10, 1983, Paris), built his reputation during the 1920s and '30s with dramas of love and marriage. His work had the delicacy, even the frivolity, of boulevard comedy but belied its origins in its almost classical concern for form and near-tragic themes. Géraldy's first erotic poems, *Toi et moi* (1913), were followed four years later by his successful drama *Les Noces d'argent.* Over the next 30 years he wrote nearly 20 plays, including *Aimer* (1922), *Si je voulais* (1924), *Robert et Marianne* (1925), *Duo* (1938; from Colette's novel), and *Ainsi soit-il* (1946). In 1955 he adapted Noël Coward's *Quadrille* for the French stage. His other works include a novel, *Le Prélude* (1923), and the memoirs *Souvenirs d'un auteur dramatique* (1923). After World War II Géraldy's reputation declined, but his best work showed psychological insight and is remembered, at least, as an acute and entertaining study of social behaviour.

Gershwin, Ira, U.S. lyricist (b. Dec. 6, 1896, New York, N.Y.—d. Aug. 17, 1983, Beverly Hills, Calif.), with his younger brother George helped shape modern popular music and reigned as one of the major song-writing teams in the history of the Broadway theatre with such hit songs as "The Man I Love," "'S Wonderful," "I Got Rhythm," "Embraceable You," and "Somebody Loves Me." After disappointing literary endeavours, Ira began writing lyrics for George's songs under the pseudonym Arthur Francis. Their first song, "Waiting for the Sun to Come Out" in 1920, was followed by a string of stage successes including *Lady Be Good* (1924), their first collaboration in which Ira's name appeared as lyricist; *Tip Toes* (1925); *Oh Kay!* (1926); *Strike Up the Band* (1929); *Funny Face* (1927); and *Girl Crazy* (1930). *Of Thee I Sing* (1931) won Ira the first Pulitzer Prize for a lyricist and was also the first musical to win a Pulitzer Prize for drama. After Ira and DuBose Heyward wrote the libretto for George's operatic masterpiece *Porgy and Bess* (1935), the Gershwins went to Hollywood, where they wrote such hit songs as "They All Laughed," "Let's Call the Whole Thing Off," "They Can't Take That Away from Me," and "A Foggy Day" for a succession of Fred Astaire motion pictures. The Gershwin brothers' collaboration was suddenly shattered in 1937, however, when George died of a brain tumour at the age of 38. Ira completed the score for *The Goldwyn Follies* with Vernon Duke, but it was not until 1940 that he began working again. He later teamed up with composer Kurt Weill for the songs for *Lady in the Dark,* with Jerome Kern for *Cover Girl* (1944), and with Harold Arlen for the musical remake of the motion picture *A Star Is Born*

J. R. EYERMAN/TIME MAGAZINE

(1954). After his retirement in 1954, Ira published *Lyrics on Several Occasions* (1959; reissued 1973), a collection of his cleverly crafted lyrics. In 1983 the hit Broadway musical *My One and Only* featured scores that relied entirely on Gershwin songs from other shows.

Gilpin, John, British ballet dancer (b. Feb. 10, 1930, Southsea, England—d. Sept. 5, 1983, Monte Carlo, Monaco), was a leading dancer with the Festival Ballet from 1950, after a successful career as soloist with the Ballet Rambert and the Ballets de Paris. A prodigious talent, he won the gold medal of the Royal Academy of Dancing at the age of 13, having already made his debut as a child actor in films and on stage. After choosing in 1945 to devote himself to dance rather than acting, he joined the Ballet Rambert and made an immediate reputation with his performances in works by Sir Frederick Ashton and Antony Tudor. He spent a year in Paris with the companies of Roland Petit and the marquis de Cuevas before joining the Festival Ballet on its formation in 1950. Among his outstanding roles were those in Lander's *Études,* Charnley's *Alice in Wonderland,* Anton Dolin's (*q.v.*) *Variations for Four,* and Carter's *The Witch Boy.* He also appeared as guest dancer with the Royal Ballet and in 1965 with American Ballet Theatre. From 1962 he was artistic director of the Festival Ballet, but ill health forced him to resign and in 1970 he left, devoting his time to teaching and production. Gilpin successfully overcame his addiction to alcohol and in 1983 married Princess Antoinette of Monaco, but he died of a heart attack just when he seemed on the brink of a new career. He wrote an autobiography, *A Dance with Life.*

Ginastera, Alberto (Evaristo), Argentine composer (b. April 11, 1916, Buenos Aires, Arg.—d. June 25, 1983, Geneva, Switz.), was an internationally acclaimed Latin-American composer renowned for his use of local and national idioms in rhythmic compositions that boasted a contemporary, eclectic style. Ginastera, who showed a musical talent at an early age, entered the Williams Conservatory at 12, and from 1936 to 1938 he studied at the National Conservatory. Though he began composing in 1930, Ginastera destroyed most of his early endeavours. He classified his artistic evolution into three segments: objective nationalism (1936–48), subjective nationalism (1948–54), and neoexpressionism (1958–83). His first recognized work, the ballet *Panambi* (1936), was an imaginary re-creation of primitive Indian rites and established his reputation as a nationalistic composer. Later compositions characterized by objective nationalism dealt with the symbolism of the pampas and the Argentine "gauchesco tradition." Ginastera's subjective nationalism emerged with the String Quartet No. 1 (1948), and though he still used the rhythms and motifs of the music of the pampas, he used allusions rather than explicit statements. Ginastera's progression to neoexpressionism was marked by his String Quartet No. 2 (1958). During this period he used a variety of techniques, including the integration of microtones, serial procedures, and chance music, as well as older, established forms. Ginastera was a traditionalist who adhered to a strict construction. Though his celebrated opera *Don Rodrigo* (1964) was unsuccessful in its premiere in Buenos Aires, it was critically acclaimed in New York City in 1966. But his chamber opera, *Bomarzo* (1967), was hailed as a masterpiece and established him as one of the leading opera composers of the 20th century. The latter and his third opera, *Beatrix Cenci,* reinforced Ginastera's contention that "sex, violence, and hallucination are three of the basic elements from which grand opera can be constructed." Ginastera also composed concerti, vocal and chamber music, and film scores. Though he lived most of his life in Argentina, he resided in the U.S. from 1946 to 1947 after receiving a Guggenheim award. In Argentina he organized the Latin American Centre for Advanced Musical Studies at the Instituto Torcuato di Tella in Buenos Aires and served as its director from 1962 to 1970. He later made his home in Switzerland.

Godfrey, Arthur (Morton), U.S. radio and television personality (b. Aug. 31, 1903, New York, N.Y.—d. March 16, 1983, New York), during the 1940s and '50s was an enduring radio and television star who enthralled an audience of some 40 million listeners with his folksy chitchat, irreverent ad-libs during commercials, and his unremarkable skills on the ukelele. The "Ole Redhead," as Godfrey referred to himself, launched his radio career while in the Coast Guard. He performed as an amateur banjo and ukelele player on a Baltimore, Md., radio program before he became an announcer on WFBR. But it was not until Godfrey was hospitalized after a serious automobile accident that he spent long hours listening to the radio; he then decided to adopt an informal approach for his listeners. His homespun humour made him an overnight sensation, and some remarked that his fans would soon drop the last syllable from his name and simply refer to him as "God." With the advent of television, Godfrey became a pioneer in the medium, and his popularity was enormous and virtually immediate. Godfrey's television programs included "Arthur Godfrey's Talent Scouts," "Arthur Godfrey and His Friends," and the "Arthur Godfrey Show." Though Godfrey's style was unorthodox and sponsors sometimes winced at his wisecracks, he nonetheless vigorously sold such products as Lipton's tea and chicken soup and brought in as much as 12% of the revenue for the CBS network. He momentarily raised the ire of his fans in 1953

UPI

when he told crooner Julius La Rosa, during a live broadcast, that he was singing his swan song. But Godfrey's detractors grew silent when he was stricken with lung cancer in 1959; his operation made national headlines. After his recovery from the removal of a cancerous lung, Godfrey returned to the airwaves on radio until 1972 but never made a successful comeback on television. Godfrey once quipped, "That little screen is merciless, and if you aren't constantly . . . intriguing, the public will drop you ruthlessly."

Gramm, Donald, U.S. opera singer (b. Feb. 26, 1927, Milwaukee, Wis.—d. June 2, 1983, New York, N.Y.), was a critically acclaimed bass-baritone who used his sonorous voice, instinctive acting ability, and finely honed musicianship to create a wealth of masterful characterizations. Gramm, who had a long association with the Opera Company of Boston, made his New York City debut in Berlioz's *Enfance du Christ* with the Little Orchestra Society in 1951, and in 1952 he made his New York City Opera debut as Colline in Puccini's *La Bohème.* A gifted dramatic as well as comic actor, Gramm demonstrated his versatility in such roles as Figaro in *The Marriage of Figaro,* Orlovsky in *Die Fledermaus,* Dandini in *Cenerentola,* and in the title role in *Falstaff.* In 1964 Gramm made his debut at the Metropolitan as Truffaldino in *Ariadne auf Naxos,* but it was not until later that he was offered major roles with the Met. In 1982 Gramm secured the roles of Alfonso in *Così fan tutte* and Waldner in *Arabella.*

Grimm, Charles John ("Jolly Cholly"), U.S. baseball player and manager (b. Aug. 29, 1898, St. Louis, Mo.—d. Nov. 15, 1983, Scottsdale, Ariz.), as a first baseman for the Philadelphia Athletics and the Chicago Cubs professional baseball teams, appeared in 2,164 games, had 2,229 hits, 1,078 runs batted in, and accumulated a career batting average of .290 but was better known as the effervescent manager of the Cubs, who won their most recent pennant (1945) under Grimm's leadership. Grimm, who was a major-league manager for 19 seasons, most of them with the Cubs, led the latter to three pennant victories, in 1932, 1935, and 1945. In 1949 he was replaced by Frankie Frisch but was briefly recalled to manage the team in 1960 before Lou Boudreau was hired. Grimm remained in the Cub organization and was a special assistant to general manager Dallas Green.

Gruenther, Alfred Maximilian, general (ret.), U.S. Army (b. May 23, 1899, Platte Center, Neb.—d. May 30, 1983, Washington, D.C.), demonstrated remarkable ability to absorb and analyze huge amounts of data, while highlighting the important points, as deputy chief of staff to Generals Dwight D. Eisenhower and Mark W. Clark during World War II. Because of his keen analytical powers, he was dubbed "the brain." Gruenther, a West Point graduate, had a staid military career teaching mathematics at his alma mater before he was promoted to deputy chief of staff of the 3rd Army under Eisenhower. After the U.S. entered World War II, he was stationed in London as chief U.S. planner of the Allied invasion of French North Africa. He later served as chief of staff of the 5th Army under General Clark and helped plan the invasion of Italy. In 1951, when Gruenther became chief of staff at NATO headquarters, he received his fourth star, thus becoming at the age of 53 the youngest four-star general in army history. From 1953 until his retirement from the military in 1956, he served as head of NATO forces and kept the Allied forces in such a high state of preparedness that some NATO members, believing this was sufficient for defense, reneged on their own original commitment and reduced their own forces. Gruenther later became known as the much traveled and outspoken president of the American Red Cross (1957–64).

Guardia, Ernesto de la, Jr., Panamanian politician (b. May 30, 1904, Panama City, Panama—d. May 2, 1983, Panama City), served in the diplomatic corps before becoming president of Panama in 1956. De la Guardia, who assumed the presidency during a turbulent period in Panamanian politics, became embroiled in controversies with the U.S. over interpretations of the 1955 Canal Zone treaty. He also faced an attack in 1959 by a band of invaders, sponsored by Fidel Castro, who were attempting to overthrow the government. The alleged conspiracy was led by Roberto Arias, son of a former president, and his wife, Dame Margot Fonteyn, a well-known British ballerina. De la Guardia invoked the Rio Treaty and, with help from the U.S. and 19 other American republics, the coup was squelched. Arias escaped, but Fonteyn and three others who were captured named Cuba as their point of departure, though Castro denied any complicity. The mercenaries were taken into custody and returned to Cuba for trial. In 1960 de la Guardia vacated the presidential office.

Halas, George (Stanley), U.S. football player and coach and sports executive (b. Feb. 2, 1895, Chicago, Ill.—d. Oct. 31, 1983, Chicago), was the coach, owner, and founder of the Chicago Bears professional football team and one of the founding fathers in 1920 of the American Professional Football Association (APFA), which became the National Football League (NFL) in 1922. Halas, who graduated from the University of Illinois in 1918 with letters in football, baseball, and basketball, was a gifted all-around athlete who played 12 baseball games as a New York Yankee right fielder before a hip injury forced him to retire in 1919. The following year he organized the Bears (originally the Decatur [Ill.] Staleys and then the Chicago Staleys) and became one of the visionary founders of the NFL. In 1921 Halas moved the team to Chicago. As a player from 1920 to 1929 Halas was a scrappy defensive end, and in 1923 he set a league record that stood for more than 40 years when he ran 98 yd after recovering a Jim Thorpe fumble. Under Halas's 40-year reign as coach (1920–30, 1933–42, 1946–55, 1958–68), the "Monsters of the Midway" captured eight divisional titles and six NFL championships (1932, 1933, 1940, 1941, 1946, 1963), and "Papa Bear" Halas recorded 326 NFL victories, more than any other coach. Though the Bears also won the NFL championship in 1943, Halas was serving in the Navy at the time. After Halas signed the legendary Red Grange ("the Galloping Ghost") in 1925, the first huge crowds were attracted to the stadium and pro football was established as a national sport. The following year the Bears went on an 18-game coast-to-coast tour and cleared a quarter of a million dollars. In 1931 Halas revolutionized pro football when he revived the "T" formation and added a man in motion to the basic T. The Chicago Bears became such a powerful team that in the 1940 NFL championship game they routed the Washington Redskins 73–0. When Halas returned to coaching (1946) after World War II, the Bears captured another NFL championship. As an owner, Halas was considered tough and aggressive and was sometimes accused of being tightfisted. In 1965 he took George Allen to court when Allen tried to leave the Bears coaching staff to become head coach of the Los Angeles Rams. After Halas won his court case, however, he let Allen go. In 1968 Halas retired as coach but in 1970 he was elected president of the NFL's National Conference. "Papa Bear" continued to exert influence over the handling of the Bears. His death marked the passing of the last of the group of men who had organized professional football in Canton, Ohio, in 1920. Halas was a charter member of the National Professional Football Hall of Fame.

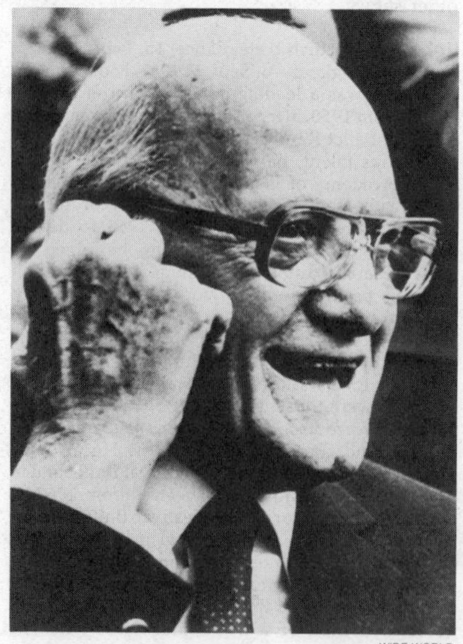

WIDE WORLD

Hartline, H(aldan) Keffer, U.S. biophysicist (b. Dec. 22, 1903, Bloomsburg, Pa.—d. March 17, 1983, Fallston, Md.), shared the 1967 Nobel Prize for Physiology or Medicine with George Wald and Ragnar Granit for discoveries about chemical and physiological visual processes in the eye. Hartline, who earned an M.D. from Johns Hopkins University in 1927, conducted research at the universities of Leipzig, Munich, and Pennsylvania before serving as professor of physiology at Cornell University Medical College and as professor of biophysics at his alma mater. In 1953 Hartline joined the Rockefeller University, where he did research in the electrophysiology of the retina. By studying the optic nerve of the horseshoe crab and other marine animals, Hartline came to understand the integrative action of the retina. His basic research laid the foundation for nearly every advance in the neurophysiology of vision. Hartline retired from the Rockefeller University in 1974.

Hergé (Georges Remi), Belgian cartoonist (b. May 22, 1907, Brussels, Belgium—d. March 3, 1983, Brussels), created the comic strip hero Tintin in 1929. Over the next 50 years the teenaged reporter's adventures filled 23 albums and sold 70 million copies in some 30 languages, though Tintin himself remained recognizably the same, with his quiff of hair and his plus fours. Hergé, whose pen name derived from the pronunciation of his transposed initials, began to publish his cartoons at the age of 19 and created Tintin for the children's supplement of the daily newspaper *Le Vingtième Siècle.* The first adventure was later published as the album *Tintin in the Land of the Soviets,* but it was not until 1958 that *The Black Island* became the first Tintin album in English translation. It was followed, with growing success, by others taking Tintin and his friends on adventures in many different countries (though Hergé himself traveled little, preferring to live quietly in Brussels). The stories, which appealed to children because of their gentle humour and eventful plots, were never violent; the villains might be menacing and the plots were filled with action, but in almost every case heroes and villains emerged largely unscathed. The drawings, especially in the later albums, lovingly created the details of Tintin's world, but their charm did not translate well to the screen in the animated feature films and television cartoons made from them.

Hibberd, (Andrew) Stuart, British radio announcer (b. Sept. 5, 1893, Canford Magna, Dorset, England—d. Nov. 1, 1983, Budleigh Salterton, Devon, England), was an announcer on British Broadcasting Corporation (BBC) radio from 1924 to 1951 and during the 1930s probably the best known voice in British broadcasting. He studied at St. John's College, University of Cambridge, before joining the Army in 1914, serving in Gallipoli, Mesopotamia, and Waziristan, and only leaving the military in 1922 when his regiment, the Dorsets, was disbanded. He nearly took up a professional singing career but went instead into broadcasting where the quality of his voice, both authoritative and friendly, projected the BBC image into millions of homes. He took his work seriously (he was famous for his belief that announcers should wear evening dress to read the radio news) and described his career in a book of memoirs, *This Is London* (1951). He was created a Member of the Order of the British Empire and made a Fellow of the Royal Society of Arts.

Hillier, Tristram Paul, British painter (b. April 11, 1905, Beijing [Peking], China—d. Jan. 18, 1983, Bristol, England), was best known for the representational landscapes of his later years, though as a young man he painted abstract and Surrealist compositions. The son of a diplomat, he went to school in England but returned to China in the early 1920s to study the language before completing his education at the University of Cambridge and the Slade School in London. He then went to Paris to study under André Lhôte and was influenced by the Surrealists. Hillier remained in France until the outbreak of World War II and served in the Royal Navy and Free French Naval Forces. He held his first one-man exhibition in 1929 in Paris and also exhibited frequently in London. His representational work, from the late 1930s, was remarkable for its qualities of clarity and serenity and its technical skill. He settled in Somerset during the postwar years but traveled frequently, continuing to work in his own individual style, which was relatively distinct from any contemporary school. Hillier's autobiography, *Leda and the Goose,* appeared in 1954.

Hines, Earl Kenneth ("FATHA"), U.S. jazz pianist (b. Dec. 28, 1905, Duquesne, Pa.—d. April 22, 1983, Oakland, Calif.), was a seminal figure in the development of jazz piano with his "trumpet style" playing (so called because he emulated the single-note instruments, such as the trumpet, by producing hornlike solo lines in octaves with his right hand and stating the harmony with his left hand), which established the piano as a solo jazz instrument and influenced a generation of musical giants, including Charlie Parker and Dizzy Gillespie. Hines, who was influenced by the great Louis Armstrong, played in Armstrong's band in 1927, and the two made such classic recordings as *Louis Armstrong/Earl Hines,* which is a part of the Smithsonian Collection, and *Weather Bird* (V.S.O.P. [Very Special Old Phonography, 1927–28], vol. 3 and 4), which contains some of Hines's finest solo pieces. From 1928 to 1947 Hines led his own band, though its membership was constantly fluctuating. Hines recorded solo hits including "My Monday Date," "Caution Blues," and "Fifty-Seven Varieties," establishing his reputation as a virtuoso, but his best-known composition is "Rosetta." Hines's band played at Chicago's Grand Terrace Ballroom for more than a decade and featured singers Sarah Vaughan and Billy Eckstine, who popularized "Jelly Jelly" and "Stormy Monday Blues." In 1948 Hines rejoined Armstrong as a member of the latter's All Stars, but in 1951 he formed his own sextet. During the 1950s Hines's popularity waned, but in the '60s he made a triumphant comeback; he continued to perform through the early 1980s, touring Europe, Japan, and the U.S.

Hinton of Bankside, Christopher Hinton, BARON, British engineer (b. May 12, 1901, Tisbury, Wiltshire, England—d. June 22, 1983, London, England), as chairman of the Central Electricity Generating Board (CEGB) from 1957 to 1964 strongly influenced the British nuclear power industry at a crucial stage in its development. Trained as an engineer, Hinton designed and oversaw the construction of the first generation of nuclear power plants in Britain, notably Calder Hall (opened 1956), the world's first large-scale nuclear power station. He also supervised the construction of a second generation of reactors under the Dounreay program, which made Britain one of the leading exploiters of nuclear power for peaceful purposes. Hinton studied at Trinity College, Cambridge, before joining Imperial Chemical Industries Ltd. (ICI). During World War II he was on loan from ICI to the Ministry of Supply, and in 1946 he was appointed the ministry's deputy controller for atomic energy production. He continued to work on the design problems associated with nuclear reactors as managing director (1954–57) of the industrial group of the U.K. Atomic Energy Authority at Harwell. Hinton's abilities both as an engineer and as an administrator led to his appointment as chairman of the CEGB when it was formed in 1957. Knighted in 1951, he was made Knight Commander of the Order of the British Empire in 1957 and a life peer in 1965.

Hoffer, Eric, U.S. longshoreman and author-philosopher (b. July 25, 1902, New York, N.Y.—d. May 21, 1983, San Francisco, Calif.), was an itinerant farm worker for 23 years and later a longshoreman whose piquant epigrams on life, power, and social order established him as a remarkably cogent philosopher. Hoffer, who intimated that he had no formal schooling, demonstrated his insights into the nature of mass movements and the people who compose them with his first work, *The True Believer* (1951). The book received critical acclaim from both scholars and laymen and catapulted Hoffer into the limelight. His second work, *The Passionate State of Mind* (1955), a collection of some 300 aphorisms, was followed by *The Ordeal of Change* (1963), *Temper of Our Time* (1967), *Reflections on the Human Condition* (1972), and *Before the Sabbath* (1979). Besides lecturing at the University of California at Berkeley, Hoffer also wrote a column in the *San Francisco Examiner* and was a guest of Pres. Lyndon B. Johnson at the White House in 1967. That year he left the docks, and in 1970 he retired to private life. Hoffer quipped, "I'm going to crawl back into my hole where I started. I don't want to be a public person or anybody's spokesman. I am not the type for it and I dislike it." In 1983 Pres. Ronald Reagan awarded him the Presidential Medal of Freedom.

Hoffman, Julius J(ennings), U.S. judge (b. July 7, 1895, Chicago, Ill.—d. July 1, 1983, Chicago), was a tireless jurist who presided over the sensational 1969–70 trial of the "Chicago 7," a group of prominent radicals including Lee Weiner, David Dellinger, Jerry Rubin, Tom Hayden, John Froines, Rennie Davis, and Abbie Hoffman, who were charged with crossing state lines with intent to incite riots at the 1968 national Democratic convention in Chicago. When the defendants, notably Abbie Hoffman, converted their defense into a guerrilla theatre trial of the judicial system, Judge Hoffman resorted to drastic measures to restore courtroom decorum. He ordered an eighth defendant, Black Panther leader Bobby Seale, bound and gagged after a bitter exchange, later separating Seale's case; it was never tried. During the six-month trial, the diminutive judge (5 ft $4^1/_2$ in) repeatedly snapped "You'll learn I don't frighten very easily" in response to various provocations, and issued more than 170 contempt citations, even sentencing defense counsel William M. Kunstler to four years in prison and co-counsel Leonard Weinglass to 20 months. All but 13 of the contempt citations were vacated on appeal, and none resulted in prison terms. In 1970 the jury found Davis, Dellinger, Hayden, Rubin, and Hoffman guilty of crossing state lines with intent to incite a riot. However, an appeals court overturned those sentences, criticizing Judge Hoffman's "deprecatory and often antagonistic attitude" toward the defendants. Hoffman was an Illinois superior court judge for six years and a U.S. district court judge for 20 before he became a senior federal judge in 1972. He compiled a distinguished record on the federal bench until the Chicago 7 defendants succeeded in baiting him into overreacting at their provocations. From 1982, when he was 87 years old, he was assigned no further cases but he continued to occupy his chambers each day and two days before his death performed naturalization ceremonies for 150 new citizens.

Holyoake, Sir Keith Jacka, New Zealand politician (b. Feb. 11, 1904, Pahiatua, North Island, N.Z.—d. Dec. 8, 1983, Wellington, N.Z.), was prime minister of New Zealand from 1960 to 1972 and governor-general from 1977 to 1980. His long period in office as prime minister was marked, toward its end, by his success in dealing with British entry to the European Economic Community (EEC) and the resulting decline in New Zealand's traditional market, both by negotiating favourable terms for New Zealand and by diversifying the economy. Holyoake came from a family of small farmers, left school at 12, but made a name as a local sportsman and was elected to Parliament in 1932. A man of considerable political skills and a good debater, he was appointed deputy prime minister and minister of agriculture in 1949 after the National Party victory in that year. He took over as prime minister for a brief period in 1957 but lost the election a few months later. After 1960 his main problems as leader concerned the enforced changes in the country's traditional agricultural economy and the maintenance of regional security after the withdrawal of British forces from Southeast Asia. Holyoake decided to support the U.S. in Vietnam, despite criticism. In 1972 he resigned and from then on, notably during his period as governor-general, played a subdued and statesmanlike role in the country's affairs.

Howells, Herbert Norman, British composer (b. Oct. 17, 1892, Lydney, Gloucestershire, England—d. Feb. 23, 1983, London, England), made an outstanding contribution to modern church music and was a noted teacher of composition at the Royal College of Music for more than 50 years. Howells studied at the Royal College of Music and worked briefly as a cathedral organist, but he devoted most of his life to teaching. His own work was influenced by his friend Ralph Vaughan Williams and by Edward Elgar; it combined classical and modern influences in a recognizable personal style. Howells was best known for his choral works, *Hymnus Paradisi* and *Missa Sabrinensis,* but his chamber works and especially his clavichord music successfully embodied a modern yet essentially English idiom. He supervised music at St. Paul's Girls School (1936–62) and was King Edward professor of music at the University of London (1954–64). He was president of the Incorporated Society of Musicians and of the Royal College of Organists during the 1950s and master of the Worshipful Company of Musicians in 1959. He was appointed Commander of the Order of the British Empire in 1953 and Companion of Honour in 1972.

Humphreys, (Travers) Christmas, British lawyer (b. Feb. 15, 1901, London, England—d. April 13, 1983, London), was senior crown prosecutor from 1950 to 1959 and later a controversial judge. He was also noted for his eccentricities and his interests outside the law as a leading British Buddhist, a Shakespearean scholar, and a poet. His father was a judge, his mother a justice of the peace, and, after studying at Trinity Hall, Cambridge, he was called to the bar in 1924. Humphreys was converted to Buddhism after the death of his brother in World War I; he wrote many books on the faith and in 1924 became president of the London Buddhist Lodge (now Buddhist Society). As a lawyer Humphreys was personally opposed to capital punishment, yet he preferred to act for the prosecution and was the counsel in hundreds of murder cases. He was prosecutor at two of the most controversial British trials of the 1950s: that of Timothy Evans, who was posthumously pardoned for the crime for which he was convicted and hanged, and that of Ruth Ellis, the last woman to be executed in Britain. In 1975 his leniency, coupled with his liberal opinions, led to public outrage when Humphreys passed a suspended sentence on a man convicted of two cases of rape. A motion in the House of Commons was called for his dismissal, but some defended the judge's right to use his own discretion in sentencing, and the motion was dropped. Made queen's counsel in 1959, Humphreys was a judge from 1968 until his retirement in 1976.

Hutcheson, Maurice A., U.S. labour leader (b. May 7, 1897, Saginaw, Mich.—d. Jan. 9, 1983, Lakeland, Fla.), for two decades (1952–72) served as president of the United Brotherhood of Carpenters and Joiners of America, an 800,000-member union. "Maurice the Silent," who succeeded his father, William L. ("Big Bill") Hutcheson, as president, had a style that contrasted dramatically with that of his autocratic predecessor. During his tenure Hutcheson became notable for ending a 40-year jurisdictional feud with the rival International Association of Machinists in 1954 and three years later, despite his friendship with George Meany, for voting against the ouster from the AFL-CIO of the International Brotherhood of Teamsters, headed by Jimmy Hoffa. In 1958 Hutcheson was brought up on charges of bribing an Indiana state official for the advance siting of new highways. Though he was convicted and sentenced in 1960, the Indiana Supreme Court voided the conviction three years later. Meanwhile, two U.S. Senate committees were investigating Hutcheson's operations. He refused to answer questions and was convicted in 1960 for contempt of Congress. When the AFL-CIO leadership demanded that Hutcheson reveal his activities and he remained close-mouthed, Meany intervened and blocked Hutcheson's ouster from the executive council of the AFL-CIO. At the age of 75 Hutcheson retired as president.

Idris I (SIDI MUHAMMAD IDRIS AL-MAHDI AS-SANUSI), former king of Libya (b. March 13, 1890, Cyrenaica [now in Libya]—d. May 25, 1983, Cairo, Egypt), began ruling the country in 1951, the same year that the three provinces of Tripolitania, Cyrenaica, and the Fezzan were united to form modern Libya, but was deposed in a 1969 coup led by Col. Muammar al-Qaddafi. His subsequent exile in Egypt meant that more that one-third of his long life was spent outside his country. The son of a Sanusi leader who died opposing French colonial rule in 1902, Idris formally succeeded his father as leader of the sect in 1920. The Italians recognized him as emir in Cyrenaica, but the more aggressive colonial policies of the Fascist government drove him into exile in Egypt. With the outbreak of World War II, he and the Sanusi allied themselves with the British forces in exchange for a promise of liberation from Italian rule. During the postwar years he negotiated for the independence and federation of the three provinces into a united Libya, which was finally achieved in December 1951. Under his rule the country maintained close relations with the West, accepting economic aid in exchange for British and U.S. military bases, but this policy made Idris the object of attack from Arab nationalists, particularly after the 1956 Suez crisis. Though the rapid development of the Libyan oil fields, starting in 1959, revolutionized the economy, the king, by now old and suffering from increasing ill health, was unable to deal adequately with the social and political tensions that were intensified by the 1967 Arab-Israeli war. In 1969, while on a visit to Greece for medical treatment, he announced his abdication, but before it could be put into effect, the regime was overthrown by a group of army officers under the leadership of Colonel Qaddafi. Idris, who had lived without ostentation and never transferred his private wealth abroad, went into exile in Egypt. He was buried in Saudi Arabia, in the holy city of Medina.

Ignatiev, Semyon, Soviet politician (b. 1903—d. November 1983), was minister of state security in the U.S.S.R. from 1951 to 1953 and responsible for investigating the "Doctors' Plot." As Nikita Khrushchev revealed at the 20th Communist Party Congress in 1956, Ignatiev had been ordered to obtain confessions from a group of Kremlin doctors, most of whom were Jews, under threats from Stalin that his own life would be taken if he failed. The doctors were alleged to have murdered Stalin's henchman Andrey Zhdanov in 1948 and to have tried to destroy the health of other leading figures. Two of the doctors died during interrogation and the others were released after Stalin's death. Ignatiev himself, who was reported to have suffered a heart attack, was dismissed for his part in the affair by Lavrenty Beria and then rehabilitated by Khrushchev. He became a regional party secretary until his retirement in 1960.

Illia, Arturo Umberto, Argentine politician (b. Aug. 4, 1900, Pergamino, Arg.—d. Jan. 18, 1983, Córdoba City, Arg.), was elected president of Argentina on July 7, 1963, and served in that office until he was ousted in a bloodless military coup on June 28, 1966. Illia, who was a country doctor by profession, was propelled into politics after the democratic government of Pres. Hipólito Irigoyen was overthrown in a 1930 military coup. In 1935 Illia was elected to the Córdoban provincial Senate, and from 1940 to 1943 he served as vice-governor of Córdoba. In 1948, during the reign of Juan Perón, Illia, one of the rare non-Peronists, was elected to the National Assembly. Illia used his seat to speak out against Perón's dictatorship, and even though he lost his assembly seat in the 1952 election, he had gained a national reputation for daring to oppose Perón. In 1963 Illia was chosen by the People's Radical Civic Party as their presidential candidate. Illia's defeat of Oscar Alende marked a return to a constitutional government. As president, Illia ended foreign control of Argentina's oil industry, but his administration was weakened by the Peronist General Confederation of Labour, the scarcity of beef after a two-year drought, and the drop in oil production during negotiations with the U.S. over the petroleum companies. In 1966 a disgruntled military ousted Illia as president.

Illyes, Gyula, Hungarian poet, novelist, and dramatist (b. Nov. 2, 1902, Racegres, Hung.—d. April 14, 1983, Budapest, Hung.), was a prominent dissident who nevertheless remained in Hungary all his life. After his student days he occupied a preeminent position on the Hungarian literary scene. As a youth Illyes supported the short-lived Soviet Republic of Bela Kun. After being sought by the police, he left for Vienna, then went to Berlin and to Paris, where he completed his education at the Sorbonne. He returned to Hungary in 1926 and contributed to the literary review *Nyugat* ("The West"), which was edited by his friend and mentor Mihaly Babits. When the latter died in 1941 Illyes took over the editorship. His major novel, *Pusztak nepe* (1936; *People from the Puszta,* 1967), described the miserable condition of the Hungarian peasantry. During the Nazi occupation of Hungary (1944–45) Illyes went underground, but in November 1945 he was elected to Parliament as a member and cofounder of the Hungarian Smallholders' Party. When Stalin's agent Matyas Rakosi took over the government of Hungary in the late 1940s, Illyes, though not a Marxist, was nevertheless tolerated. In 1951 he wrote a poem entitled "Egy mandat a zsarnoksagrol," an indictment of the Rakosi regime which was published during the October 1956 uprising; an English translation, "One Sentence on Tyranny," appeared in 1957. Among other works to appear in English were his *Selected Poems* (1971) and his 1936 biography of the 19th-century Hungarian poet Sandor Petofi (trans. 1974). Vice-president of PEN International from 1970, Illyes was a three-time winner of the Kossuth Prize (1948, 1953, and 1970).

Jackson, Henry Martin ("SCOOP"), U.S. politician (b. May 31, 1912, Everett, Wash.—d. Sept. 1, 1983, Everett), was a powerful and influential Democratic senator from Washington who, while serving in Congress for over 40 years, became an outspoken supporter of military preparedness, organized labour, and civil rights. A titan in the Senate, Jackson won six elections decisively and was regarded as the nucleus of those Democrats who viewed themselves as neoconservatives (liberals in domestic policy but hawkish in foreign policy). Because he persisted in trying to win military contracts for Boeing (his state's largest employer), Jackson was dubbed "the senator from Boeing." Despite two unsuccessful bids for the presidency, first in 1972 and again in 1976, Jackson's political strength was great and undisputed. He served as a senator under seven presidents. He took part in the Army-McCarthy hearings in 1954, and sharply criticized the "witch hunts" of that era. He was selected by Pres. John F. Kennedy to head the Democratic National Committee in 1960, forced the Nixon administration to alter the SALT I agreement, forced through legislation in 1974 that pressured the Soviet Union into allowing Jews to emigrate, and was one of the major architects of the landmark 1969 National Environmental Policy Act. Jackson, who was the ranking Democrat on the Senate Armed Services Committee, was perhaps best known as the most vocal Democratic skeptic with regard to the Soviet Union. Hours before his death from a massive heart attack, Jackson had denounced the Soviet Union for downing a commercial Korean airliner carrying 269 civilians.

James, Harry Haag, U.S. trumpeter and bandleader (b. March 15, 1916, Albany, Ga.—d. July 5, 1983, Las Vegas, Nev.), was a flamboyant trumpet virtuoso who from 1937 to 1939 ignited the Benny Goodman Orchestra with his sizzling jazz trumpet solos, became a major swing-era figure, and was an enduring bandleader who delighted audiences for over 40 years with a repertory of popular hit songs. James, who was the son of circus performers, learned to play the drums at the age of 4 and the trumpet at 8; when he was 12 he led one of the circus bands. After traveling with the circus for several years as a contortionist, James settled with his family in Beaumont, Texas. He played with various bands operating within the state, but his break came when he joined the Ben Pollack Orchestra in 1935. Two years later, as a member of Goodman's orchestra, James joined trumpeters Ziggy Elman and Chris Griffen to comprise the "powerhouse" trio, one of the most celebrated big-band trumpet sections in jazz history. James, however, remained a major soloist with the Goodman orchestra and soared to fame with his interpretations of such songs as "Sing Sing Sing," "One O'Clock Jump," and "Life Goes to a Party." James formed his own band in 1939, but it was not until 1941, when he introduced a trumpet version of the song "You Made Me Love You," that he became an overnight sensation. That success prompted James to introduce a string of sorrowful ballads, including "I Cried for You" and "I Don't Want to Walk Without You," while such hit songs as "I Had the Craziest Dream" and "Ciribiribin" (his theme song) helped propel the band to fame. At the height of his popularity, in 1943, James married the actress Betty Grable, the most famous World War II "pin-up girl." He then appeared in a string of films including *Do You Love Me?* and *Springtime in the Rockies* and also played all the trumpet parts in the Kirk Douglas motion picture *Young Man with a Horn.* When the big-band era ended in the early 1950s, James went into semiretirement, but he reemerged in 1955 with a new band that adopted the style of Count Basie's orchestra. James led bands based mostly in Nevada for the remainder of his life and last performed just a few weeks before succumbing to lymphatic cancer.

Jones, Carolyn, U.S. actress (b. April 28, 1929, Amarillo, Texas—d. Aug. 3, 1983, Los Angeles, Calif.), received an Academy Award nomination for best supporting actress for her portrayal of a love-starved beatnik in the film *The Bachelor Party* (1957) but was better remembered for her television role as Morticia, the ghoulish matriarch of "The Addams Family" (1964–66). After Jones made her motion-picture debut in *The Turning Point* (1952), she appeared in such films as *The Big Heat* (1953),

The Seven Year Itch (1955), *Marjorie Morningstar* (1958), *Ice Palace* (1960), and *Eaten Alive* (1977), but none of her film roles could compete with her success as Morticia Addams.

Kadosa, Pal, Hungarian composer and pianist (b. Sept. 6, 1903, Leva, Hung. [now Levice, Czech.]—d. March 30, 1983, Budapest, Hung.), exercised a major influence on the development of modern music in Hungary both as professor at the Budapest Academy of Music from 1945 and as a composer in his own right. He studied under Zoltan Kodaly at the Budapest Academy and was among those who in 1928 founded the Society of Modern Hungarian Musicians. After World War II he found the political climate hostile to the more demanding forms of contemporary music and composed works such as the cantata *The Oath of Stalin.* But starting with the fourth of his eight symphonies, he reverted to the greater technical complexity of his prewar compositions, ultimately developing a style of considerable restraint and craftsmanship. Kadosa wrote four piano concerti, two violin concerti, an opera, as well as many shorter works.

Kahn, Herman, U.S. social and political theorist (b. Feb. 15, 1922, Bayonne, N.J.—d. July 7, 1983, Chappaqua, N.Y.), was recognized as a brilliant and influential thinker, but he provoked controversy with his distinctive ideas on nuclear war. Kahn attracted national attention in 1960 with the publication of *On Thermonuclear Warfare.* In his book he claimed that thermonuclear war was not only a possibility but a probability, that the U.S. should be prepared to defend itself against a nuclear onslaught, and that a nuclear war would not necessarily mean the annihilation of civilization. He was severely criticized by those who felt that by minimizing the dangers of nuclear war, Kahn made such a war more likely. After receiving an M.S. degree from the California Institute of Technology in 1948, Kahn worked as a mathematician and physicist for the Rand Corp., a research organization that worked on contract for the U.S. Air Force. In 1961, however, Kahn founded his own think tank, the Hudson Institute, at Croton-on-Hudson, N.Y., where he meditated on problems dealing with national security and international order. He spouted predictions on a wide range of subjects and advocated thinking "unthinkable" thoughts. A zealous optimist, Kahn stated his views on nuclear war in *Thinking About the Unthinkable* (1962), and in *The Coming Boom* (1982) he prophesied a bright future for the U.S., with median family income reaching $65,000 by the year 2033, an attractive public education system, a rise in productivity, and an abundance of resources. He foresaw a bright future for the world's long-term prospects in *The Next Two Hundred Years*, but tempered his original projection, set forth in *The Emerging Japanese Superstate* (1970), of Japanese economic ascendancy over the U.S. by the end of the century. In *The Japanese Challenge* (1979) Kahn warned that Japan could achieve economic superiority only if it strengthened its domestic economy and curbed its exports. Though his unequivocal pronouncements raised the ire of unbelievers, his influence was substantial and far-reaching. At the time of his death Kahn was contemplating such diverse issues as the prospects for electronic transmission of mail, strategies for winning a war in El Salvador, alternatives to the U.S. federal income tax, and the future of Australia.

Kaplan, Mordecai Menahem, U.S. rabbi (b. June 11, 1881, Svencionys, Lithuania—d. Nov. 8, 1983, New York, N.Y.), was the founder of the Jewish Reconstructionist movement and the author of *Judaism as a Civilization* (1934), which defined the principles of Reconstructionism. Kaplan, who immigrated to the U.S. with his family at the age of nine, received a master's degree (1902) from Columbia University and was ordained (1902) at the Jewish Theological Seminary of America in New York City. Although Kaplan's views on Judaism diverged from the beliefs held by the conservative seminary, he nonetheless became principal of its teachers' institute in 1909, dean in 1931, and served as professor there until his retirement in 1963. Though Kaplan was raised as an Orthodox Jew, he defined Judaism as a "civilization" embracing language, custom, and culture beyond the conventional limitations of religious belief. He designated the State of Israel as the cradle of Jewish civilization and thus a spiritual centre for the Jewish people. In 1916 Kaplan organized the Jewish Center in New York, a secular community organization with a synagogue as its nucleus. He served as the centre's rabbi until 1922, and in the same year he was credited with instituting the bat mitzvah ceremony for 13-year-old girls to mark their passage to Jewish adulthood. He also founded the Society for the Advancement of Judaism in 1922, which became the cornerstone of the Reconstructionist movement. In 1935 the *Reconstructionist,* a biweekly periodical edited by Kaplan, appeared and subsequently served as the voice of the movement. His many books expounding on the goals of the movement included *Judaism Without Supernaturalism* (1958) and *The Religion of Ethical Nationhood* (1970). As co-author of the Reconstructionist *Sabbath Prayer Book* (1945), Kaplan outraged Orthodox rabbis who banned the book because Kaplan rejected the Orthodox precepts that Jews were the chosen people and that the Torah was the inspired word of God. A towering figure in modern Judaism, Kaplan died at the age of 102.

Karandash (Mikhail Nikolayevich Rumyantsev), Soviet circus clown (b. Dec. 10, 1901, St. Petersburg, Russia—d. April 1, 1983, Moscow, U.S.S.R.), was a star of the Moscow State Circus and a master at poking fun at postwar life in the Soviet Union. Though his satirical themes at times displeased the Soviet authorities, his popularity with his audiences probably helped to protect him from serious punishment. Karandash made his debut in Leningrad in 1934 after working as a commercial artist and training at the School of Circus Arts. With his baggy trousers and huge boots, he developed a routine of stunts that were often preposterous and daring; during World War II he satirized leading Nazis and later extended his satire to life in the Soviet Union. Karandash was arrested on several occasions and was banished to Stalinabad in 1954, but he later rejoined the circus on its Soviet and foreign tours. Karandash, who also appeared in films, was made a Hero of Soviet Labour in 1979.

Kleffens, Eelco Nicolaas van, Dutch diplomat (b. Nov. 17, 1894, Heerenveen, Neth.—d. June 17, 1983, Portugal), was foreign minister in the Dutch government-in-exile in London during World War II and president of the UN General Assembly in 1954. A career diplomat, he joined the Dutch Foreign Ministry in 1922 after studying for a doctorate in law at the University of Leiden and working with the League of Nations. He was appointed foreign minister in August 1939 and retained the post after escaping to Britain following the German invasion of The Netherlands in May 1940. During this time, though a strong advocate of the Atlantic alliance, he defended the rights of European nations to order their own affairs under any postwar settlement. In 1947 he was appointed ambassador to Washington and also served as The Netherlands' representative at the UN. He served as ambassador to Portugal (1950–56), representative (1956–58) at NATO and the Organization for Economic Cooperation and Development, and then as representative (1958–67) in London of the European Coal and Steel Community. After his retirement he went to live in Portugal. Van Kleffens was the author of several books on historical and legal topics.

Koestler, Arthur, Hungarian-born writer (b. Sept. 5, 1905, Budapest, Hung.—d. March 3, 1983, London, England), testified to the sufferings and triumphs of the human spirit in the 20th century in novels and essays. His nonfiction dealt with science and the paranormal. *Darkness at Noon* (1940), his finest novel, was a classic analysis of the Soviet mentality by a man who had left the Communist Party in 1938, at the time of the Moscow trials. Koestler, who spoke both Hungarian and German, attended the University of Vienna before entering journalism and traveling extensively. Four years after visiting the Soviet Union in 1932, he was assigned to Spain to report on the Civil War for the British newspaper the *News Chronicle.* Koestler was imprisoned by Loyalists and spent more than three

HORST TAPPE—PICTORIAL PARADE

months under sentence of death, an experience that he recounted in *Spanish Testament* (1938). His first novel, *The Gladiators* (1939), dealt allegorically with Stalinism, a theme that was more fully and directly explored in *Darkness at Noon.* Another novel, *Thieves in the Night* (1946), described the creation of the state of Israel. From 1940 Koestler wrote in English, and he became a naturalized British citizen eight years later. His writings on science, and, more particularly, on the history of science and the scientific community, included *The Yogi and the Commissar* (1945), *The Sleepwalkers* (1959), and *The Case of the Midwife Toad* (1971). From the 1950s he turned increasingly to the study of mysticism, then to the investigation of paranormal phenomena. He was made a Commander of the Order of the British Empire in 1972 and a Companion of Literature in 1974. He was a believer in voluntary euthanasia, and he and his wife, Cynthia, took their own lives when his health started to fail.

Lanoux, Armand Louis, French novelist (b. Oct. 24, 1913, Paris, France—d. March 23, 1983, Paris), was a realist in the tradition of the 19th-century novelist Émile Zola and is best remembered for his trilogy of World War II, *Le Commandant Watrin* (1956; Prix Interallié), *Le Rendezvous de Bruges* (1958), and *Quand la mer se retire* (1963). The last of these won the Prix Goncourt. Lanoux, who started his career as an illustrator and journalist, was taken prisoner during World War II. When he was released in 1942, he worked for the information service of the Vichy government. His first novel, *La Nef des fous,* won the Prix Populiste in 1948, the first of many awards. He also wrote biographies of Zola and Maupassant, poetry (a collection, *Le Colporteur,* won the Prix Apollinaire in 1953), and a much-acclaimed history of the 1871 Commune of Paris. His last book, a biography of Madame Steinheil, mistress of Pres. Félix Faure, appeared in 1983. Lanoux was president of the Société des Auteurs et Compositeurs Dramatiques from 1978 to 1981, of the French PEN Club from 1972 to 1975, and of the Conseil Permanent des Écrivains from 1979.

Lansky, Meyer (Maier Suchowljansky), Russian-born organized crime figure (b. July 4?, 1902, Grodno, Belorussia—d. Jan. 15, 1983, Miami Beach, Fla.), as the financial wizard of the underworld and its leading banker, was responsible for laundering, investing, and concealing the Mafia's cache of funds. After becoming a U.S. citizen in 1928, Lansky, whose associates included such hoodlums as Lucky Luciano, Frank Costello, Bugsy Siegel, Dutch Schultz, and Albert Anastasia, formed his own gang known as the Bugs and Meyer Mob. The gang's foremost enterprise was boot-

BOOK OF THE YEAR

NEWS PHOT—PICTORIAL PARADE

legging rum, but after the repeal of Prohibition in 1933, Lansky and Costello opened illegal gambling casinos in New York, New Orleans, La., and southern Florida. In 1935, after Schultz, the top New York crime figure, was slain, Lansky and five others gained control of all rackets in Manhattan, Brooklyn, and Newark. Lansky, who persuaded Cuba's dictator, Fulgencio Batista, to legalize gambling, accumulated a fortune as the holder of the franchise for gambling in Havana. After World War II organized crime burgeoned; Lansky became involved in gambling operations in The Bahamas and acquired major interests in the Flamingo Hotel in Las Vegas and in prime Miami Beach real estate. After he served a brief jail term in 1953 for running a gambling operation in Saratoga Springs, N.Y., he moved to Florida, where he handled his investments. In 1970 Lansky intended to retire in Israel, but he was denied permission to stay. Several other countries rejected his $1 million offer for sanctuary, and he was forced to return to Miami, where he was placed under arrest for tax evasion, conspiracy, and skimming profits. Lansky was adjudged too ill to stand trial, was cleared of the charges against him, and lived in seclusion in Miami for the rest of his life. At the time of his death his personal fortune was estimated at between $100 million and $300 million.

Lawson, Frederick Henry, British jurist (b. July 14, 1897, Leeds, England—d. May 15, 1983, Cleveland, England), was professor of comparative law at the University of Oxford from 1948 to 1964 and a leading academic lawyer who edited legal journals, participated in the work of international organizations in his field, and lectured in Europe and the U.S. He studied at Oxford and obtained degrees in both history and law before being called to the bar in 1923. When Lawson returned to Oxford, he held posts as a research fellow in Byzantine, and then constitutional and Roman, law. After publishing (with D. L. Keir) *Cases in Constitutional Law* (1928; 6th ed., 1979), Lawson became reader in Roman law at All Souls College in 1931. Besides becoming the first holder of the chair in comparative law at Oxford, he demonstrated his acute analytical approach to the principles of legal theory in such works as *The Rational Structure of English Law* (1951) and *An Introduction to the Law of Property* (1958). After his retirement from Oxford, he became part-time lecturer at the University of Lancaster and published *The Remedies of English Law* (1972).

Lederer, Jiri, Czech journalist (b. 1922—d. Oct. 12, 1983, Bad Reichenhall, Bavaria, West Germany), was a leading dissident whose name was associated with the reforms of the "Prague Spring" of 1968 and with the subsequent human rights movement, Charter 77. Both of his parents died in Nazi concentration camps and he spent World War II in hiding in Poland. On his return to Czechoslovakia he joined the Social Democratic Party, and then in 1948 the Communist Party. Three years later he was expelled from the Writers' Union, and until 1968 he worked in factories and as a free-lance journalist, with brief periods on the staff of *Literarny Noviny*. In 1968 he joined *Literarny Listy,* and a series of articles on anti-Semitism in Poland led to his imprisonment in 1972. In 1977 Lederer was sentenced to a three-year term in prison as one of the signatories of the Charter 77 document. On his release he was allowed to emigrate to West Germany with his family.

Leigh, Carolyn, U.S. lyricist (b. April 21, 1926, New York, N.Y.—d. Nov. 19, 1983, New York), whose songs highlighted Broadway shows and served as vehicles for Frank Sinatra, who scored hits with such numbers as "Hey Look Me Over," "The Best Is Yet to Come," and "Young at Heart." Leigh worked briefly as an advertising copywriter before a musical publisher recognized her knack for composing lyrics. By age 25 she had completed more than 200 unpublished song lyrics. In 1954 she made her Broadway debut with *Peter Pan,* for which she co-wrote the songs "I've Gotta Crow," "I Can Fly," and "I Won't Grow Up." Her hit songs, which expressed a persistent optimism, also included "Witchcraft," "When in Rome," "A Real Live Girl," and "I've Got Your Number." During her career she collaborated with such composers as Elmer Bernstein, Jule Styne, and Cy Coleman, and at the time of her death she was working with Marvin Hamlisch on a musical adaptation of *Smiles.*

Le Mesurier, John, British actor (b. April 5, 1912, Bedford, England—d. Nov. 15, 1983, Ramsgate, England), was a character actor best known for his roles in film and television comedy, though he was capable of performances of considerable depth as he showed in his role as Sergeant Wilson in the popular television series "Dad's Army" and in his award-winning portrayal of the spy Kim Philby in the 1971 television play "Traitor." His success in this "straight" role was no surprise: even in comedy he wore the sombre air of a haunted man and used it to achieve some of his best effects as the nervous psychiatrist in *Private's Progress* or the bemused time-and-motion man in *I'm All Right, Jack.* It was with these films that he established his reputation during the 1950s, though he had made his first appearance on television in 1938 and played in repertory before serving with the Royal Armoured Corps during World War II. His other films included *The Pink Panther* and *The Wrong Box.* "Dad's Army" started in 1968 and his Sergeant Wilson, upper-class, vague, and slightly stammering, was the perfect foil to Arthur Lowe's portrayal of his superior officer, but social inferior, in the Home Guard platoon. His last television role was in "A Married Man," and he was a frequent performer on radio, as in the adaptation of Tolkien's *Lord of the Rings* in 1981.

Leopold III, former king of the Belgians (b. Nov. 3, 1901, Brussels, Belgium—d. Sept. 25, 1983, Brussels), was the son of King Albert I and his consort, Elisabeth, duchess of Bavaria. Educated in England, at Eton College, he served as a private soldier during the latter part of World War I. In 1926 he married Princess Astrid of Sweden by whom he had three children, including the future king Baudouin (b. 1930). Leopold succeeded his father as king in February 1934 after the latter's death in a rock-climbing accident. On Aug. 28, 1935, when King Leopold and his wife were touring Switzerland, Astrid was killed in a motor accident near Lucerne. Leopold became king as a dramatic sequence of events was about to unfold in Europe. On March 7, 1936, the German Army marched into the Rhineland, though its demilitarization was stipulated by the Treaty of Versailles and confirmed by the Pact of Locarno of 1926. As neither France nor Great Britain was willing to act in the face of that aggression, which posed a direct threat to Belgium, Leopold withdrew from the Locarno Pact, declaring that his country would henceforth pursue "a policy exclusively and completely Belgian." The hope of avoiding invasion was a vain one, and on May 10, 1940, German forces crossed the frontier. The Belgian Army under King Leopold fought well, but after capitulation of the Dutch Army, and with the French and British in retreat, Leopold surrendered on May 28. He was taken to the palace of Laeken and held prisoner there. On Sept. 11, 1941, he married morganatically Liliane Baels. In June 1944 Leopold and his wife and infant son were removed to a fort in Saxony, then in March 1945 to Strobl, near Salzburg, Austria, where in May they were liberated by U.S. forces. The king's role during the war and his eventual return to the throne were intensely controversial in Belgium. His brother Prince Charles (*q.v.*) was appointed regent in 1944 while Leopold remained in Switzerland (1945–50). In a referendum held on March 12, 1950, nearly 58% of the votes were in his favour, and on July 22 he returned to Brussels. Opposition to him, mainly from the Walloon community, remained fierce, and on July 16, 1951, he abdicated in favour of Baudouin.

Liberman, Yevsey Grigoryevich, Soviet economist (b. Oct. 2, 1897, Slavuta, Ukraine—d. March 12, 1983, Moscow, U.S.S.R.), attracted interest in the West during the 1960s as a critic of Soviet economic processes. The son of a Jewish shopkeeper, he studied law at Kiev University, earned a Ph.D. in economics, and was professor at Kharkov University from 1957 until his retirement. In an article in the *Voprosy Ekonomiki* ("Problems of Economics") in August 1962 he insisted that profitability was the criterion of efficiency. The article, though controversial, was reproduced in *Pravda* on September 9. Nikita Khrushchev, who authorized the reprint, announced two months later that the Soviet Union had something to learn from the capitalist countries when it came to industrial efficiency. After Khrushchev's downfall, Liberman explained his views in a letter to the editor of *The Economist* (London) of Oct. 31, 1964. Central planning, he insisted, did not mean that every detail of production had to be dictated from above. Embarrassed by Western praise of his ideas, he declared in an interview with a TASS agency representative that "Libermanism is a myth" and that his ideas were the outcome of collective work. When his key book was published in English (*Economic Methods and the Effectiveness of Production,* 1971), he wrote in the preface that "profit is not the goal of planned socialist production nor the only yardstick for assessing its effectiveness."

Lichty, George (GEORGE MAURICE LICHTENSTEIN), U.S. cartoonist (b. May 16, 1905, Chicago, Ill.—d. July 18, 1983, Santa Rosa, Calif.), was the creator (1932) and longtime artist (1932–74) of the satirical newspaper panel series "Grin and Bear It," a comical exposé that poked fun at politicians, taxes, marriage, love, and even death. Lichty studied at the Art Institute of Chicago from 1924 to 1925 but was dismissed when his interest in studying declined and when he reportedly drew mustaches on some of the portraits adorning the school's gallery. After graduating from the University of Michigan in 1929, he joined the staff of the *Chicago Times* newspaper and began sketching a short-lived gag strip about a soda jerk, "Sammy Squirt." In 1932 he introduced "Grin and Bear It" and a cast of contemporary characters, most notably the bombastic Senator Snort, who became a favourite of Pres. Harry S. Truman. At the height of its popularity the series was syndicated in 300 newspapers, and his original drawings became collector's items. Lichty retired in 1974 and turned over his creation to Fred Wagner.

Liley, Sir (Albert) William, New Zealand obstetrician (b. March 12, 1929, Auckland, N.Z.—d. June 15, 1983, Auckland), was professor in perinatal physiology at the University of Auckland and a pioneer in the treatment of erythroblastosis fetalis (hemolytic disease of the newborn). Liley's experimental work concentrated on rhesus factor incompatibility (incompatibility of blood group between mother and fetus). By use of amniocentesis he was able to diagnose and treat afflicted fetuses who might otherwise have been stillborn. He administered blood transfusions to the fetus in utero—an innovative step because transfusions were heretofore given postnatally. His findings also provided an invaluable first step toward the diagnosis and treatment of a variety of other conditions in the unborn child. Liley studied at the University of Auckland, at the Australian National University, and at Columbia University in New York City before joining the New Zealand Medical Research Council Postgraduate School of Obstetrics and Gynaecology in Auckland. His accomplishments were recognized by his appointment as Companion (1967) and Knight Commander (1973) of St. Michael and St. George. Other honours included fellowship of the Royal Society of New Zealand and of the Royal College of Obstetricians and Gynaecologists.

Livingstone, Mary (Mrs. Jack Benny), U.S. radio comedian (b. 1906?, Seattle, Wash.—d. June 30, 1983, Holmby Hills, Calif.), the inimitable partner of the comedian Jack Benny, was his wife of 47 years and appeared as his comic foil in the character of Mary Livingstone of Plainfield, N.J., on "The Jack Benny Program" (1932–55). Livingstone, who was born Sadie Marks, met Benny while working as a hosiery clerk at the May Co. store in Los Angeles. In 1927 they were married, and in 1935 she joined a cast that included Dennis Day, Eddie Anderson, Don Wilson, and Phil Harris, who adroitly deflated Benny's ego to the delight of radio listeners. Livingstone adapted so well to the brash, peppery role of Mary that her real identity was forgotten, and she legally changed her name to that of her radio character. During their heyday, Livingstone and Benny reigned as one of the first families of radio comedy, alongside the team of George Burns and Gracie Allen, but during the early 1950s Livingstone retired from show business. After Benny's death in 1974 she wrote a number of reminiscences of him for magazines, and in 1978 she published an affectionate biography of him.

Llewellyn, Richard (Richard Dafydd Vivian Llewellyn Lloyd), British novelist and dramatist (b. Dec. 8, 1906, St. David's, Pembrokeshire, Wales—d. Nov. 30, 1983, Dublin, Ireland), wrote the best-selling novel of the South Wales coalfields, *How Green Was My Valley*. Published in 1939, it was an immediate success, not only for its convincing portrayal of the hardships of the miner's life and its vein of nostalgia for the warmth of the valley communities but because it found a language in which to convey a rich working-class tradition. It was filmed and followed many years later by two sequels, *Up, Into the Singing Mountain* (1960) and *And I Shall Sleep . . . Down Where the Moon Is Small* (1966). But none of Llewellyn's later work equaled the success of his first novel. He started his career in the Army, then suffered considerable hardship before finding work as a journalist and making a name with his play *Poison Pen* (1938). His later novels, including *None But the Lonely Heart* (1943) and *A Flame for Doubting Thomas* (1954), achieved some critical success and showed a maturing of his technique but failed to repeat the popular triumph of *How Green Was My Valley*. Having moved to the U.S., he greatly broadened his range, perhaps at the expense of immediacy and personal involvement. His later novels of life in Wales suggested that his long absence had clouded his vision of the country and its people. He also wrote books for children and plays, including *The Scarlet Suit* (1962) and *Ecce!* (1972).

Lofts, Norah, British popular novelist (b. Aug. 27, 1904—d. Sept. 10, 1983, Bury St. Edmunds, Suffolk, England), wrote more than 50 novels, the majority historical tales which sold well in Britain and the U.S. A history teacher who began writing in 1935, she wrote such best-sellers as *Bless This House* (1954), *Queen in Waiting* (1955), and *The King's Pleasure* (1970). Sales of her books ran into millions and she gained a faithful readership, but Lofts never won critical acclaim. *Jassy* (1944) was made into a motion picture. *The Claw* (1981), based on a series of rapes in the university town of Cambridge during the 1970s, attracted wider attention to a work that escaped from her usual themes and historical approach. She also took part in local politics.

Lutyens, (Agnes) Elisabeth, British composer (b. July 9, 1906, London, England—d. April 1983, London), was one of the leading British exponents of serial music and the author of works ranging from chamber music to radio scores and opera. A daughter of the architect Sir Edwin Lutyens, she studied at the Royal College of Music and at the Paris Conservatoire. By the late 1930s she had abandoned her early style of composition in favour of serial music and had produced some notable chamber works, in particular her chamber concerti. After World War II she continued to write for the concert hall and also composed many radio and film scores and choral and operatic works. *Time Off? Not a Ghost of a Chance* was performed at Sadler's Wells in 1972. Among her choral works was a setting of texts by the philosopher Ludwig Wittgenstein. Her music was uncompromising and sometimes difficult; despite the range of her achievement, she never enjoyed wide popularity. Lutyens's autobiography, *A Goldfish Bowl*, appeared in 1972.

McBride, Lloyd, U.S. labour leader (b. March 16, 1916, Farmington, Mo.—d. Nov. 6, 1983, Whitehall, Pa.), started working in the steel industry at the age of 14 and steadily rose through the union ranks to become president of the United Steelworkers of America (USW) in 1977, in one of the most bitter and highly publicized political campaigns in labour history. In 1936 McBride was one of the first to join the Steel Workers Organizing Committee, the forerunner of the USW. McBride, who had a flair for organizing workers, engineered a sitdown strike in the plant when his Local 1295 was trying to negotiate a better contract. After the dispute was settled, McBride was chosen president of the local by acclamation at the age of 22. He continued to recruit workers for the growing steel union and in 1940 was made president of the St. Louis Industrial Union Council. In 1942 he was named president of the CIO's Council for Missouri. Though he interrupted his union activities to serve in the Navy during World War II, he returned after the war and made steady advancements. In 1965, the same year that I. W. Abel became president of the USW, McBride became district director of Missouri, Kansas, Nebraska, and part of Illinois. During the next decade the union prospered with steady contractual gains, but when McBride became president of the USW after beating Ed Sadlowski by a 3–2 margin in a heated contest, the steel industry was depressed and the union began losing strength. Its membership dropped from 1.4 million members to 750,000, and negotiations with steel managements became more difficult. McBride tried to steer a moderate course, but he was plagued with health problems and was unable to take part in the 1980 and 1983 contract negotiations. He died a few weeks after undergoing multiple bypass heart surgery.

Macdonald, Ross (Kenneth Millar), U.S. novelist (b. Dec. 13, 1915, Los Gatos, Calif.—d. July 11, 1983, Santa Barbara, Calif.), was a first-rate mystery writer who was credited with elevating the detective novel to the level of literature with his compactly written tales of murder and despair. Macdonald, who adopted a wide array of pseudonyms, wrote his first novels under his real name, Kenneth Millar; these included *The Dark Tunnel* (1944), *Trouble Follows Me* (1946), and *The Three Roads* (1948). He penned *The Moving Target* (1949; reissued as *Harper* [1966]) under the name John Macdonald and introduced the shrewd private investigator Lew Archer, unabashedly modeled after such fictional sleuths as Sam Spade and Philip Marlowe. Macdonald then assumed the pen name John Ross Macdonald for such Archer mysteries as *The Way Some People Die* (1951), *The Ivory Grin* (1952), *Find a Victim* (1954), and *The Name Is Archer* (1955). A writer of intricate and ingenious plots, he was especially adept at twisting new plots around a few central themes. He used a seedy section of southern California as his backdrop to convey "a vision of hopeless pessimism." Under the name Ross Macdonald he wrote such Archer works as *The Barbarous Coast* (1956), *The Doomsters* (1958), and *The Galton Case* (1959). Such later novels as *Sleeping Beauty* and *The Underground Man* had environmentalist themes and reflected Macdonald's abiding interest in conservation. His last work, *The Blue Hammer*, was published in 1976.

McKay, Sir Alick Benson, Australian-born publishing executive (b. Aug. 5, 1909, Adelaide, Australia—d. Jan. 15, 1983, Australia), was a dynamic figure in Fleet Street advertising who served as deputy chairman (1969–78) and group managing director (1976–77) of Rupert Murdoch's News International Ltd. McKay's wife was kidnapped from their London home in 1969, and the conviction of two men for her murder attracted attention to McKay, who had for many years been an influential personality behind the scenes. He started his career in Adelaide before transferring to Melbourne and then Sydney as manager of News Ltd. In 1952 he became director of Argus and Australasian Ltd. Invited to England to take over the advertising of the Daily Mirror Group in 1957, McKay made an impact by his tough approach and energetic methods. He was a director of the International Publishing Corp. from 1963 until 1969 before joining News International, where he remained until his retirement in 1978. McKay was knighted in 1977.

Maclean, Donald Duart, British-born diplomat (b. May 25, 1913—d. March 6, 1983, Moscow, U.S.S.R.), was at the centre of Britain's most notorious post-World War II spy scandal when he defected to the Soviet Union with Guy Burgess in 1951. Both men, who had met at the University of Cambridge during the 1930s, where they belonged to a circle that included future Soviet agents Anthony Blunt (*q.v.*) and Kim Philby, passed information to the Soviet intelligence services while working with the Foreign Office. Their defection was a serious blow to the confidence and credibility of British intelligence services. Maclean, the son of a former Liberal Cabinet minister, seemed an unlikely traitor. While serving at the British embassy in Washington and as head of the Foreign Office American Department in 1950, he had an outwardly successful career that gave him access to much vital classified information, notably in the sphere of Anglo-U.S. relations. Close colleagues were aware, however, of his instability and alcoholism, and his defection caused a tightening up of vetting procedures. He and Burgess did not reappear publicly until 1956. Maclean subsequently worked for the Soviet Foreign Ministry, then as head of the British desk at the Institute of World Economic and International Relations in Moscow. He published a book on British foreign policy, *British Policy Since Suez, 1956–68* (1970), learned Russian, and took Soviet citizenship. After his death his ashes were returned to Britain.

Markevitch, Igor, Russian-born composer and conductor (b. July 27, 1912, Kiev, Russia—d. March 7, 1983, Antibes, France), wrote some 20 musical works between 1928 and 1941 but then abandoned composing and established an international reputation as a conductor, particularly in the field of modern music. A child prodigy whose parents left Russia when he was two, he showed great promise as a pianist and composer and attracted the attention of Alfred Cortot, who accepted him at the École Normale de Musique. Markevitch then studied composition under Nadia Boulanger and wrote a piano concerto and a ballet for Sergey Diaghilev. Another ballet, *Icare* (1932), was considered his most important work. Markevitch's compositions, on the borderline between traditionalism and the avant-garde, attracted renewed attention in the late 1970s after long neglect, but it was as a conductor that he achieved fame after World War II, first with the Salzburg Festival orchestra, then as guest conductor for orchestras in Stockholm, Montreal, Havana, and Paris. Markevitch, who was also recognized as an outstanding teacher and theorist, published some critical writings, including a critical edition of Beethoven's symphonies, and an autobiography, *Être et avoir été.*

Massey, Sir Harrie Stewart Wilson, Australian nuclear physicist (b. 1908, near Melbourne, Australia—d. Nov. 27, 1983), was a world authority on the theory of atomic collisions and the joint author of a standard work on the subject, published in 1933. He was Quaim professor of physics at University College, London, from 1950 to 1975 (afterward emeritus) and first chairman of the British National Committee for Space Research from 1959. He studied at the University of Melbourne, writing a dissertation on the field of wave mechanics, and went to the Cavendish Laboratory in Cambridge where he contributed to the understanding of the wave nature of electrons. In 1933 he was appointed lecturer at Queen's University, Belfast, and in 1938 professor of applied mathematics at University College, London. During World War II he was chief scientist at the naval Mine Design Department and made a substantial contribution to the field. During 1943–45 he worked in Berkeley, Calif., on the development of the fission bomb. On his return to Britain he continued his research into atomic theory and at the same time established his reputation as a leading expert in other fields, including space physics and astronomy. His publications include *Negative Ions* (1938), *Electronic and Ionic Impact Phenomena* (with E. H. S. Burhop, 1952), *Atomic and Molecular Collisions* (1979), and numerous research articles. He was elected to the Royal Society in 1940 and served as its vice-president and physical secretary. His other honours included the Royal Society's Hughes Medal and Royal Medal, and he was knighted in 1960.

Massey, Raymond, Canadian-born actor (b. Aug. 30, 1896, Toronto, Ont.—d. July 29, 1983, Los Angeles, Calif.), was a hollow-cheeked, lanky character actor who was credited with "taking Abraham Lincoln off the penny" after his brilliant portrayal in *Abe Lincoln in Illinois* (1939, stage; 1940, screen). He later became identified with the gruff but lovable Dr. Gillespie on the television series "Dr. Kildare" (1961–66). While serving with the Canadian Army during World War I, Massey organized a minstrel show; the experience whetted his desire to become an actor. He made his professional debut in London in 1922 in Eugene O'Neill's *In the Zone* and appeared in scores of English productions before making his Broadway debut in 1931 in an unorthodox production of *Hamlet.* However, it was his poignant portrayal of Lincoln that propelled him to prominence and earned him an Academy Award nomination for best actor in 1940. Massey's versatility was manifested in roles in which he played villains, moralists, and fanatics. His powerful presence and forceful portrayals were best evidenced in such films as *The Scarlet Pimpernel* (1935), *The Prisoner of Zenda* (1937), *Reap the Wild Wind* (1942), *East of Eden* (1955), and *Seven Angry Men* (1955). After his retirement in 1970, Massey wrote two volumes about his career, *When I Was Young* (1976) and *A Hundred Different Lives* (1979).

UPI

Masters, John, British-born novelist (b. Oct. 26, 1914, Calcutta, India—d. May 7, 1983, Albuquerque, N.M.), established a literary reputation with the best-selling novel *Bhowani Junction* (1954), which described life in India under the British raj. Masters's family had been established in India for several generations and, like his father, he chose a career in the Indian Army after training at the Royal Military Academy, Sandhurst. He was on active service in the North-West Frontier region of India during the 1930s and in the Middle East in 1941 before serving as a major with the Chindits in Burma. Masters was twice decorated for his war service. In 1948 he left the Army and went to live in the U.S., where he wrote *Nightrunners of Bengal* (1951) and *The Deceivers* (1952) as part of a projected series chronicling the history of British rule in India. *Bhowani Junction,* which was successfully filmed, was set on the eve of independence.

Medeiros, Humberto Cardinal, U.S. prelate (b. Oct. 6, 1915, Arrifes, São Miguel Island, Azores—d. Sept. 17, 1983, Boston, Mass.), was spiritual leader of two million Roman Catholics as head (1970–83) of the archdiocese of Boston, the third largest archdiocese in the U.S. Medeiros came to the U.S. at age 15 and swept floors in a textile plant until he learned to speak English. He later studied for the priesthood at Catholic University in Washington, D.C., and after his ordination in 1946 served as assistant pastor in parishes in Fall River, New Bedford, and Sommerset, Mass. In 1966 Medeiros was named bishop of Brownsville, Texas, where he became a champion of Mexican-American migrant workers and an advocate of church-sponsored housing for the needy. In the aftermath of Hurricane Beulah, which devastated Brownsville in 1967, Medeiros welcomed at least 11 needy families into the bishop's mansion. When Richard Cardinal Cushing retired in 1970 because of illness, Medeiros was appointed to succeed him as Boston's archbishop, the first cleric not of Irish heritage to occupy that position. In 1973 he was elevated to cardinal. Though Medeiros was known for his commitment to social issues (especially his longtime support of labour unions), he was slow to involve himself in Boston's racial problems and was criticized for foot-dragging until he organized (1979) an ecumenical coalition that drafted a "covenant of justice, equity, and harmony" for Bostonians to sign. Medeiros, who was regarded as an ecclesiastical conservative, staunchly defended Vatican policies. He was adamantly opposed to liberalized abortion laws and in 1980 created a stir by opposing proabortion political candidates.

Mennin, Peter, U.S. composer and educator (b. May 17, 1923, Erie, Pa.—d. June 17, 1983, New York, N.Y.), fostered the growth in prestige of the Juilliard School of Music in New York while serving as its exacting president from 1962 to 1983 and was the accomplished composer of nine symphonies, eight of which were established in the repertoire of the New York Philharmonic Orchestra. Mennin was a child prodigy who started his first symphony at age 11, produced it at 19, and then studied at the Oberlin Conservatory of Music during the 1940s. After earning a Ph.D. from the Eastman School of Music in 1947, he joined the faculty of Juilliard but resigned his post to become director of the Peabody Conservatory in Baltimore, Md. In 1962 Mennin was named president of Juilliard, and under his vigilant oversight students were challenged to compete with one another and to perfect their performance technique. Mennin not only strengthened the faculty with well-known virtuosos but established the Juilliard Theatre Center in 1968 and the American Opera Center in 1970; he also founded Juilliard's Contemporary Music Festival, which became a showcase for new works. But it was for his own sonorous musical compositions that Mennin wished to be recognized, and he produced a wealth of concerti, music for chorus and orchestra, and chamber and choral music. His last symphony, which was commissioned by the National Symphony in Washington, D.C., was first performed at the celebration of the symphony's 50th anniversary in 1983.

Messmer, Otto, U.S. cartoonist and film animator (b. 1894, Union City, N.J.—d. Oct. 28, 1983, Teaneck, N.J.), as the ingenious creator of Felix the Cat, developed the character of the distinctive black feline in more than 300 short films during the 1920s and '30s and from 1924 to 1951 drew a "Felix the Cat" cartoon strip for the daily and Sunday editions of the *New York Journal-American.* Messmer, who joined the Pat Sullivan Studios in 1916, created a black cat character named Tom in the same year. In 1917 the *Tail of Thomas Kat* (considered by some to be the first Felix the Cat film because Thomas exhibited the same mannerisms as Felix) was released after Messmer left to fight with the American Expeditionary Force in Europe. After Messmer returned to Sullivan Studios in 1919 he revitalized the cat character in the series "Feline Follies" (1920; though the cat was still named Tom). Eventually the cat in the series was identified as Felix, and he became a huge success in both the U.S. and Europe with a profusion of stuffed toys, phonograph records, and sheet music bearing his name. After Sullivan died in 1933 Messmer continued to draw the cartoon strip until 1951 but the silent animated films featuring Felix disappeared because they could not compete with sound. Messmer, who was considered a master in the art of silent animation, turned the strip over to Joe Oriolo in 1954 and went into advertising. He retired at age 80.

Micombero, Michel, former president of Burundi (b. 1940—d. July 16, 1983, Mogadishu, Somalia), overthrew the monarchy in an army coup in 1966 and held power for ten years before being driven into exile in Somalia. He studied at the Catholic school in Bujumbura, then at the Military Academy in Brussels, returning to Burundi after the country achieved independence in 1962. A member of the politically dominant Tutsi tribe, he helped foil a coup by members of the more numerous Hutu after his appointment as minister of defense in 1965, then became involved in moves to replace the king, Mwambutsa IV, by his son. When the new king took power, he made Micombero prime minister, but Micombero deposed him in November 1966. Micombero made himself president and pursued a conciliatory policy up to 1969, releasing political prisoners and trying to gain support from the Hutu. In October 1969, however, he announced the discovery of a plot led by Hutu officers, many of whom were executed. In 1972 the Hutu rebelled, killing some 2,000 Tutsi. The Tutsi reacted with a savage repression of the Hutu, in which an estimated 100,000 died. The government's role in this, and that of the Army, remained obscure, but the division between the two peoples was now irreconcilable. In 1976 Micombero was overthrown by Col. Jean-Baptiste Bagaza and remained quietly in exile, working for international relief agencies.

Mikhailov, Aleksandr Aleksandrovich, Soviet astronomer (b. April 26, 1888, Morshansk [now Tambov], Russia—d. October 1983, Leningrad, U.S.S.R.), was director of the Pulkovo Observatory from 1947 to 1964 and enjoyed an international reputation for his work in the classical fields of positional astronomy and eclipses. He was educated at Moscow University, where he taught from 1918 to 1948. The Pulkovo Observatory was completely destroyed during World War II, and he played an important role in the rebuilding and reequipping that allowed it to open again in 1954. His knowledge of telescope design helped to make Pulkovo one of the most advanced observatories from a technical point of view. Mikhailov was vice-president of the International Astronomical Union in 1947 and 1967, an associate of the Royal Astronomical Society, and a corresponding member of the Bureau des Longitudes. His many awards included four Orders of Lenin and the Polish Order of Merit.

Miller, William Edward, U.S. lawyer (b. March 22, 1914, Lockport, N.Y.—d. June 24, 1983, Buffalo, N.Y.), was a seven-term conservative Republican congressman from upstate New York who achieved fleeting fame when, in 1964, he became the vice-presidential running mate on Barry Goldwater's unsuccessful presidential ticket. From 1961 to 1963 Miller served as Republican national chairman and in this office gained a reputation for stinging partisan commentary. After his loss in the 1964 election, Miller retired from politics, but in 1975 he reemerged briefly in an American Express credit-card commercial posing the question, "Do you know me?"

Miró, Joan, Spanish painter (b. April 20, 1893, Barcelona, Spain—d. Dec. 25, 1983, Palma, Majorca), was the last survivor of the group of writers and painters whose work in Paris during the early part of the century revolutionized Western literature and art. He might ultimately be seen as the greatest of the Surrealists, and he was an important influence in the development of American art during the 1940s. Miro first visited Paris in 1919 after studying at the La Lonja Academy of Fine Art and with Francisco Galí in Barcelona. He met Picasso and came to spend half the year in France and half in Spain, having studios in both countries. His early naive works were influenced by Cubism, but the ideas of André Breton and the Surrealists introduced a new element in his work; this combined with his study of Dutch painting (source of his

BOUCHARD

Dutch interiors of the late 1920s) to establish his best-known style, with its suggestion of meticulously painted, hallucinatory forms deriving from microscopic studies of creatures such as amoebas. They clearly derived from an understanding of both Freudian and Surrealist writings on the subconscious but were remarkable for their decorative qualities and for the poetic vision that Miró brought to them. He took part in the Surrealist exhibitions and contributed to *Minotaure* but was never a doctrinaire member of the group. He returned to Spain after 1940 but was opposed to the Franco government and later went to live on Majorca rather than the mainland. He began to work in ceramics, sculpture, and murals, examples of which can be seen at Harvard University, the UNESCO building in Paris, and the Foundation Maeght at Saint-Paul de Vence. His graphic work won the Grand Prix at the 1954 Venice Biennale and the Guggenheim Prize in 1958. He was the subject of numerous exhibitions, including a major retrospective in Paris in 1974 at which his later works aroused some critical controversy.

Moorehead, Alan McCrae, Australian-born journalist and author (b. July 22, 1910, Croydon, Victoria, Australia—d. Sept. 29, 1983, London, England), was a highly successful war correspondent who later established his reputation as a popular but substantial historian with such works as *Gallipoli* (1956) and *The Fatal Impact* (1966). He studied at the University of Melbourne and worked as a journalist in Australia before reporting World War II for the London *Daily Express* and *The Manchester Guardian.* His first book, *Mediterranean Front* (1941), was built on his experience as a correspondent, and he published a number of works of biography and fiction before *Gallipoli.* An immediate success, this vivid reconstruction of the World War I battles combined solid historical research with a novelist's skill in storytelling. It won several prizes and showed the popularity of a literary genre that Moorehead was to make peculiarly his own. *The White Nile* (1960) and *The Blue Nile* (1962) told the story of African exploration, and *Cooper's Creek* (1963) recounted the explorations of Robert Burke and William Willis in Australia. Like *Gallipoli,* these were stories illustrating the futility of human endeavour rather than man's triumphs, told with a vein of lyrical sadness. This was also evident in *No Room in the Ark* (1959), examining the destruction of wildlife, and in *The Fatal Impact* (1966), which showed the destructive power of Western civilization in contact with the cultures of the South Pacific. His other books included *Darwin and the Beagle* (1969) and an autobiography, *A Late Education* (1970). Moorehead was made a Commander of the Order of the British Empire in 1968 and an Officer of the Order of Australia in 1978.

Mozzoni, Umberto Cardinal, Italian prelate of the Roman Catholic Church (b. 1904?, Buenos Aires, Arg.—d. Nov. 7, 1983, Rome, Italy), was a leading Vatican expert on Latin America. Ordained in 1927, he worked as a parish priest in Italy where he had gone as a child, then served with the Vatican diplomatic service in Canada and London. He was first secretary of the apostolic delegation in Portugal, then, from 1954, papal nuncio in Bolivia, where he undertook important work to improve the security of foreign missionaries in the region. He continued his work after 1969 in Brazil, having earlier served for 11 years in Argentina. In 1973 he was made cardinal and returned to Italy. He was president of the sanctuaries of Pompeii and Loreto.

Murray, Stephen, British actor (b. Sept. 6, 1912, Partney, Lincolnshire, England—d. March 31, 1983), was a fine and versatile performer in the theatre and on radio. His work in radio drama made his voice one of the best known in the medium. Murray, who studied at the Royal Academy of Dramatic Art, made his debut at Stratford-upon-Avon in *Much Ado About Nothing* before joining the Birmingham Repertory Company. There and at the Westminster Theatre and the Old Vic he established a reputation as a sensitive interpreter of Shakespeare and Shaw. His career was interrupted by army service during World War II, but after he was demobilized, he acted in films and on radio, tried his hand at directing, and made the first of many television appearances. Murray's radio work illustrated the range of his talent, involving him in classical drama and modern plays as well as light situation comedy. In all, he contributed several thousand performances to the medium. He continued to appear on the stage, notably in *Shadow of Heroes* in 1958, *Who's Afraid of Virginia Woolf?* at Edinburgh in 1965, and *School for Scandal* at Stratford, Ont., in 1970.

Nakagawa, Ichiro, Japanese politician (b. March 9, 1925, Hokkaido, Japan—d. Jan. 9, 1983, Sapporo, Japan), was a fiercely ambitious politician who became an outspoken right-wing member of the Liberal-Democratic Party (LDP) and in 1982 a prime-ministerial aspirant. Nakagawa emerged as one of the country's most colourful figures and became a member of the lower house of the Diet (parliament) in 1963. A decade later, intent on furthering his career, he formed a secretive ultraconservative group called the *Seirankai* (Blue Storm Society), whose 31 members helped one another advance in the ruling LDP. During the late 1970s the club disbanded, but Nakagawa had already established a foothold in the party and in 1982 was the youngest of four candidates for the presidency of the LDP. Nakagawa, who placed last in the election, became deeply depressed and took his own life by hanging himself with his kimono sash.

Navarre, Henri, French army officer (b. July 31, 1898, Villefranche-de-Rouergue, Aveyron, France—d. June 21, 1983, Paris, France), succeeded Gen. Raoul Salan in March 1953 as commander in chief of French forces in Indochina. Navarre's troops captured and consolidated the fortress of Dien Bien Phu, well behind enemy lines, strategy based on Navarre's belief that the stronghold was beyond the reach of the Vietnamese artillery. The outpost was taken in November 1953 by French paratroopers and heavily fortified. But it had to be supplied entirely by air and, to Navarre's surprise, the Vietnamese besieged it, succeeded in moving up their artillery, and in March 1954 opened an attack that eventually overran the base and signaled the defeat of the French expeditionary force. Navarre, who retired in 1956, defended his actions in *Agonie de l'Indochine* and other writings that reflected his austere temperament and his dislike of politicians. His military career began in World War I, and he earned a degree in German before becoming head of the German section in the army intelligence services. His mistrust of politicians dated from 1939, when, despite his warnings, the government was unprepared for the German advance that led to the French defeat in the following year. Navarre rebuilt the intelligence service in the occupied zone during World War II and was deputy commander in chief, French forces in Germany, from 1952 until his appointment to Indochina.

Nichols, Beverley, British author and journalist (b. Sept. 9, 1898, Bristol, England—d. Sept. 15, 1983, Kingston-upon-Thames, England), was a prolific writer who never completely fulfilled his early promise and whose work ranged from the wistful sentimentality of *Down the Garden Path* (1932) to the savagery of his biography of Somerset Maugham, *A Case of Human Bondage* (1966). Nichols, the son of a solicitor, revealed in his autobiography, *Father Figure* (1972), a personality deeply scarred by his father's brutality and drunkenness; he was denied his first ambition to be a pianist and claimed that he had tried to kill his father on three occasions. None of this, however, was evident in his brilliant early career. He published his first novel, *Prelude* (1920), on public school life, just after starting at Balliol College, Oxford, followed it with another on life at university (*Patchwork,* 1921), and was president of the Oxford Union and editor of the university magazine, *Isis.* A great social success, he entered journalism and produced a stream of novels, plays, travelogues, and essays that made him one of the literary stars of the interwar period. *Cry Havoc!* (1933), with its hints of admiration for fascism, showed the superficiality of his political opinions. Nichols was more at home when describing his delight in cats or gardens or gossip; the last of these, rather than a profound analysis of personality, made up a good portion of his Maugham biography, written to defend Maugham's wife, Syrie. To some, Nichols himself seemed to have opted for superficial notoriety rather than an exploitation of his very real literary gifts; but his autobiographies, which also included *The Unforgiving Minute* (1978), suggested the roots of his complex personality and his need for approbation.

Niven, (James) David Graham, British film actor (b. March 1, 1910, Kirriemuir, Scotland—d. July 29, 1983, near Lake Geneva, Switz.), created the character of a debonair English gentleman which he played in most of his 90 films and became a bestselling author with two autobiographies that confirmed the charm and polish of his screen personality and revealed his genius as a raconteur. His books evoked the extraordinary world of Hollywood where he arrived in the 1930s after an unhappy childhood (his father was killed in World War I), three years as an army officer, and a succession of casual jobs. He appeared in *The Charge of the Light Brigade* (1936), *The Prisoner of Zenda* (1937), *Dawn Patrol* (1938), and *Wuthering Heights* (1939), giving apparently effortless performances that seemed only marginally to have impinged on his social life in a circle that included Errol Flynn, Tyrone Power, Clark Gable, and other figures of that legendary era in Hollywood. On the outbreak of World War II he returned to Britain, joined the Rifle Brigade, and served in France, The Netherlands, and Germany, rising to the rank of colonel. He also made two films, *The First of the Few* (1942) and *The Way Ahead* (1944). On his return to Hollywood he tried to resume his career, but it was not until 1956, with Mike Todd's *Around the World in 80 Days*, that he found a part worthy of his abilities. Two years later he won an Oscar for *Separate Tables*, in which he played a bogus army officer; it was one of the few undoubtedly testing roles in the career of an actor who seemed too often content to achieve adequate performances or to rise above clearly inadequate scripts. However, his natural charm, the hint of mischief behind the immaculate exterior, and his refusal to take himself seriously ensured the affection of a wide public for films like *The Pink Panther* (1964). In 1971 he published *The Moon's a Balloon* which, with its sequel, *Bring on the Empty Horses* (1975), sold more than 10 million copies and ensured that he would be remembered as a delightful man and affectionate friend.

Nkumbula, Harry, Zambian politician (b. 1916, Northern Rhodesia [now Zambia]—d. Oct. 8, 1983, Lusaka, Zambia), was president of the Northern Rhodesian (later African) National Congress during the 1950s and later minister of education in a coalition government from 1962 to 1964. A dominant figure in the movement for African independence, he saw his influence wane and apparently lost his sense of direction at the very moment when this goal was being achieved. A teacher, he entered politics as a member of the Kitwe African Society and, in London after World War II with a scholarship to study at the London School of Economics, joined Jomo Kenyatta and Kwame Nkrumah in the African Committee. On his return to Africa he joined the Northern Rhodesian National Congress and became its president with Kenneth Kaunda as his deputy. In 1958, however, Kaunda left the now-renamed African National Congress to form the Zambia National Congress. Kaunda had no overall majority in the 1962 elections and invited Nkumbula's party to form a coalition. But Nkumbula was already showing signs of a weakening political will, and when independence came in 1964 he found his party in opposition. It was banned eight years later. By that time, though he joined the ruling United National Independence Party under Kaunda, he was a spent force in Zambian politics.

O'Brien, Pat (WILLIAM JOSEPH PATRICK O'BRIEN), U.S. actor (b. Nov. 11, 1899, Milwaukee, Wis.—d. Oct. 15, 1983, Santa Monica, Calif.), as Hollywood's quintessential Irishman in some 100 films, portrayed sensitive and fair-minded priests and policemen but was best remembered as the inspirational Notre Dame football coach in the title role of *Knute Rockne—All American* (1940). As a boy, O'Brien met Spencer Tracy at a military academy and the two became fast friends. They dropped out of school and enlisted in the Navy together. After World War I O'Brien attended Marquette University in Milwaukee to study law, but he then rejoined Tracy to study acting at the American Academy of Dramatic Art in New York. O'Brien made his debut on Broadway as a chorus boy in *Adrienne* (1923), but he did not receive a substantial role until he appeared in *A Man's Man* in 1925. During the 1930s he was variously cast in the roles of priest, soldier, and policeman and created a motion-picture mold for newspapermen as the cynical, hard-boiled reporter Hildy Johnson in *The Front Page* (1931). He also portrayed a gruff male journalist in such films as *The Final Edition, Scandal for Sale,* and *Off the Record.* O'Brien's other memorable roles featured him as the foil for bad guy James Cagney in such films as *Here Comes the Navy* (1934), *Devil Dogs of the Air* (1935), *Torrid Zone* (1940), and the classic *Angels with Dirty Faces* (1938). His portrayals of priests included Father Duffy in *The Fighting 69th,* Father O'Hara in *The Fireball*, Father Connolly in *Angels with Dirty Faces*, and Father Dunne in *Fighting Father Dunne*. His motion-picture career was climaxed, however, by his gripping portrayal of Knute Rockne who inspired his team to "go out and win one for the Gipper," played by Ronald Reagan. In 1959 O'Brien appeared in *Some Like It Hot*, but during the 1960s he left films to perform in nightclubs and summer stock. During his last years O'Brien appeared in *The End* (1978) and with Cagney in *Ragtime* (1981).

Pascal, Pierre, French historian (b. July 22, 1890, Paris, France—d. July 1, 1983, Neuilly, Paris), was professor at the University of Paris from 1950 to 1960 and a scholar who, after 17 years in Russia before, during, and after the Revolution, made an outstanding contribution to Russian studies in France. He studied at the École Normale Supérieure, made his first visit to Russia in 1911, and was wounded during World War I before being sent with the French military mission to the Russian general staff in 1916. A Christian Socialist, he witnessed the Bolshevik Revolution in 1917 and ignored the order to return to France. He met Lenin (and later compiled an anthology of his works) but fell out with the regime, and gained a precarious living as a researcher at the Marx-Engels Institute. He returned to France in 1933, spent four years sorting out his position with the French authorities, and wrote a remarkable thesis on Avvakum and 17th-century religion, concentrating on the relationship between Christianity and the state. Pascal published other works on the Russian "Old Believers," made some fine translations of Russian writers including Dostoyevsky (he also wrote a book on Dostoyevsky's religious beliefs), and taught in Lille and at the École des Langues Orientales before taking the chair of Russian history and civilization at the Sorbonne. His other works included a masterly summary, *Les Grands courants de la pensée russe contemporaine,* and his personal journal, an eyewitness account of the Revolution and a testimony to his love of Russian culture and the Russian people.

Pelshe, Arvid Yanovich, Latvian Communist leader (b. Feb. 7, 1899, Grunwald [now Bauska], Latvia—d. May 29, 1983, Moscow, U.S.S.R.), was a member of the Politburo of the Communist Party of the Soviet Union (CPSU), chairman of the party control commission from 1966, and a member of the CPSU Central Committee from 1956. The son of a farmer, in 1914 he entered the Riga School of Engineering, then during World War I worked in Russian factories. A member of the Russian Communist Party from 1915, he was elected a deputy of the Petrograd Workers' and Soldiers' Soviet and took part in the Bolshevik Revolution of October 1917 led by Lenin. In 1919 he was attached to the Red Army and was a participant in the unsuccessful attempt to establish Soviet power in Latvia. Pelshe graduated from the Institute of Red Professors in 1931, became a member of the party organization in Kazakhstan in 1933, then served (1937–40) as a lecturer at the Moscow Higher Educational Institute. In June 1940 he played a leading role in the armed sovietization of Latvia. The following year he became a secretary of the Central Committee of the Latvian Communist Party and from 1959 was its first secretary. As the oldest ethnically non-Russian member of the Communist summit, he was honoured by having his ashes placed in the Kremlin wall in Moscow.

Pevsner, Sir Nikolaus Bernhard Leon, German-born art historian (b. Jan. 30, 1902, Leipzig, Germany—d. Aug. 18, 1983, London, England), was a distinguished scholar and writer acclaimed for his studies and interpretation of English architecture and design. His learned and meticulous approach was evidenced by his monumental 46-volume *The Buildings of England* (1951–74), in which he recorded, county by county, England's noteworthy architecture. Pevsner studied at the universities of Leipzig, Munich, Berlin, and Frankfurt before fleeing Nazi Germany in 1934 and settling in England. He served as Slade professor of fine art at the Universities of Cambridge (1949–55) and Oxford (1968–69), but his longest academic association was with Birkbeck College, University of London, where he was appointed professor of the history of art in 1959. His output was prolific, and in it he brought a fresh approach to the evaluation of English art. His *Pioneers of the Modern Movement, from William Morris to Walter Gropius* (1936) proposed that Morris originated some of the concepts of modern European architecture, while in his series of Reith Lectures delivered in 1955 he discussed "The Englishness of English Art." *An Outline of European Architecture* (1942) became a standard work. Honoured by many societies and universities, Pevsner was one of the very few nonarchitects to receive the Royal Gold Medal (in 1967) from the Royal Institute of British Architects. He was appointed Commander of the British Empire in 1953 and knighted in 1969 for services to art and architecture.

Pickens, Slim (LOUIS BERT LINDLEY, JR.), U.S. actor (b. June 29, 1919, Kingsberg, Calif.—d. Dec. 8, 1983, Modesto, Calif.), for some 20 years was a top-notch broncobuster, bull rider, and rodeo clown whose gravelly, twangy voice, grizzled features, and rodeo expertise made him a natural for low-budget Westerns. He adopted the name Slim Pickens as a teenager to hide his rodeo work from his father. The name, he added, was indicative of the prize money he earned. After making his motion picture debut in *Rocky Mountain* (1950), he appeared in scores of "B" Westerns including *Old Overland Trail* (1953), *The Outcast* (1954), *One-Eyed Jacks* (1961), and the Western spoof *Blazing Saddles* (1974). His most notable role, however, was as the wild-eyed Texan who exuberantly straddled a nuclear bomb as it was being dropped on the Russkies in *Dr. Strangelove* (1964). Some of his later films included *The Apple Dumpling Gang* (1975), *The Swarm* (1979), and *Beyond the Poseidon Adventure* (1979).

Pilkington, William Henry Pilkington, BARON, British industrialist (b. April 19, 1905, St. Helens, Lancashire, England—d. Dec. 22, 1983, St. Helens), was chairman of Pilkington Brothers Ltd. from 1949 to 1973 and helped to make the company into one of the world's leading glass manufacturers, building on the revolutionary float-glass process devised by his cousin, Sir Alastair Pilkington. He was also a notable figure in British public life, serving as president (1953–55) of the Federation of British Industries, a director (1955–72) of the Bank of England, and chairman of many government commissions. These last included investigations into the condition of school buildings, doctors' and dentists' pay, and a controversial committee on broadcasting that advised a reorganization of independent television in 1962. Pilkington was educated at Magdalene College, Cambridge, and joined the glass industry in 1927, becoming a member of the Pilkington Brothers board in 1934. The growth that he inspired in the company during his chairmanship was partly responsible for a strike in 1970, but he reviewed the company's industrial relations, and when he was succeeded by Sir Alastair Pilkington three years later the firm had successfully made the transition from family firm to public company. He was knighted in 1953 and made a life peer in 1968.

Pinheiro de Azevedo, José Batista, Portuguese naval officer and politician (b. June 5, 1917, Luanda, Angola—d. Aug. 10, 1983, Lisbon, Port.), was a major figure in Portugal's 1974 revolution and for a short time held the post of premier. The son of a Portuguese official in Angola, he entered the naval academy in Lisbon at 17, starting a long career in the Navy. He returned to Angola years later as commander of the sea defenses (1963–65) at the mouth of the Congo River. In 1972 Pinheiro de Azevedo took command of the Marine Corps and mobilized support within the Navy for the coming revolution. Immediately after the coup of April 25, 1974, he was promoted to the rank of admiral; he was also the third most powerful member of the ruling junta. Widespread anti-Communist riots preceded his appointment as premier in August 1975. While Pinheiro de Azevedo's revolutionary socialist leanings made him acceptable to the Communists, his political program nevertheless allayed fears of a Communist takeover. Within months, however, his government faced a Communist-led revolt. The crisis was averted, and in its aftermath the administration became more moderate. The following year Pinheiro de Azevedo unsuccessfully ran for the presidency; lacking the support of any one political party and suffering from ill health during the campaign, he received only 14% of the vote.

Pittermann, Bruno, Austrian politician (b. Sept. 3, 1905, Vienna, Austria—d. Sept. 19, 1983, Vienna), was leader of the Austrian Socialist Party from 1957 to 1967 and served as federal vice-chancellor in coalition governments with the Conservative leaders Julius Raab, Alfons Gorbach, and Josef Klaus. Pittermann was first elected to Parliament in 1945. When the Socialist leader Adolf Scharf became federal president in 1957, Pittermann succeeded him as party chairman and served as vice-chancellor. In 1964 he became president of the Socialist International. In 1966 the Conservatives won a majority in Parliament, the Socialists were forced out of the coalition, and Pittermann lost his place in the government. Pittermann retired in the following year and was succeeded as party leader by Bruno Kreisky.

Podgorny, Nikolay Viktorovich, former Soviet head of state (b. Feb. 18, 1903, Karlovka, Poltava Province, Ukraine—d. Jan. 11, 1983, Moscow, U.S.S.R.), was the son of a foundry worker. An apprentice metalworker at age 14, he became an engineer and worked in the Ukrainian sugar industry from 1931 to 1939. A member of the Communist Party from 1930, he survived Stalin's great purges and in 1940 was appointed deputy people's commissar of the Soviet food industry. During 1942–44 he was director of the Moscow technological institute for the food industry. His first important post in the party apparatus was as first secretary (1950–53) of the Kharkov regional party committee. After Nikita Khrushchev secured the party leadership in 1953, Podgorny became second secretary of the Ukrainian party. The 20th all-union party congress (1956) elected him a member of the Central Committee. He became a candidate Politburo member two years later and a full member in 1960. In 1963 he joined the secretariat of the Central Committee in Moscow. Although a Khrushchev protégé, Podgorny was not immediately dismissed by Leonid Brezhnev when the latter became party leader in 1964. However, a year later he lost his secretaryship of the Central Committee and was given the less influential post of chairman of the Presidium of the Supreme Soviet, or titular head of state. When in 1972 Podgorny's protégé Pyotr Shelest was replaced by Vladimir Shcherbitsky, a Brezhnev supporter, as first secretary of the Ukrainian party, Podgorny's influence was further reduced. Podgorny resisted Brezhnev's idea of combining the party secretaryship with the state chairmanship; in May 1977 he was removed from the Politburo and in June from his position of chairman of the Presidium. Podgorny did not disappear completely from public life, as he remained a deputy of the Supreme Soviet.

ROBERT COHEN—PICTORIAL PARADE

Price, T. Rowe, U.S. money-market pioneer (b. March 16, 1898, Glyndon, Md.—d. Oct. 20, 1983, Baltimore, Md.), as the pioneering founder in 1937 of the Baltimore investment counseling company T. Rowe Price, was credited with popularizing the "growth stock" concept of investment after World War II. Price's strategy included identifying companies for which he could project faster than average growth in both earnings and dividends and then to make long-term investments during the early stages of growth. Price, who had a knack for recognizing a growth stock, made the initial investment for the T. Rowe Price Growth Stock Fund in shares of IBM stock. In 1960 Price established the New Horizons Fund, which sought long-term growth of capital through investment in smaller companies. His first choice was the Xerox Corp. Price, who always remained flexible in his investment strategies, started the New Era Fund in 1969, an early buyer of gold and energy stocks. In 1970 he sold out all holdings in his company and concentrated on handling portfolios for his family and friends. His 1980 book, *The Money Masters,* analyzed the successful strategies of nine prominent investors.

Pridi Phanomyong, Thai politician (b. May 11, 1900, Ayutthaya, Siam—d. May 2, 1983, Paris, France), was an instigator of the June 24, 1932, coup d'etat that forced King Prajadhipok (Rama VII) to relinquish the absolute monarchy in favour of a constitution and later served as prime minister for five months in 1946. After King Ananda Mahidol was found dead of gunshot wounds on June 9, 1946, public support for Pridi's government was shattered. He left the country the following year and became an influential focus of radical opposition during his exile in China and, from 1970, in France. Pridi studied in Paris and taught law at Chulalongkorn University before becoming the main ideologist of the 1932 constitutional regime. A counterrevolutionary coup drove him into exile, but he returned and, as minister of the interior, foreign affairs, and finance, introduced social and economic measures meant to modernize the country. During the Japanese occupation from 1941, he was a member of the Regency Council, using his position to organize resistance and establish contact with the Allied forces. When the war ended, Pridi negotiated a settlement with the Allied forces, an accomplishment that was viewed as one of his most important achievements for Thailand. Pridi was branded a Communist by his opponents but, though he was certainly influenced by nationalist and Communist movements that shared his ideals of modernization, he was essentially a radical democrat and a skilled politician. The opposition of successive Thai regimes to his return after his exile in 1947 testified to his ability to influence public opinion in Thailand.

Qiao Guanhua (CH'IAO KUAN-HUA), Chinese political leader (b. 1914?, Jiangsu [Kiangsu] Province, China—d. Sept. 22, 1983, Beijing [Peking], China), established a reputation as a leftist journalist writing under the pen name Qiao Mu (Ch'iao Mu) before becoming a protégé of Prime Minister Zhou Enlai (Chou En-lai), who named Qiao foreign minister in 1974. Two years later, however, after Zhou and Mao Zedong (Mao Tse-tung) died, Qiao fell from prominence when he was discredited by his connection (through his second wife's friendship with Mao's widow, Jiang Qing [Chian Ch'ing]) with the notorious radical faction known as the gang of four. Qiao, who had earned a Ph.D. from the University of Tubingen in Germany, was fluent in both German and English and had a command of Japanese, Russian, and French. He reportedly joined the Communist Party in 1940 and from 1946 to 1949 was bureau chief of the New China News Agency in Hong Kong, but when the Communists took power in 1949 he returned to the mainland. In 1954 Qiao began his career as a diplomat, accompanying Zhou on his many travels abroad; he was instrumental in developing the first cautious contacts with the U.S. as a drafter (with Henry Kissinger) of the 1972 Shanghai communiqué, which paved the way for normalization of relations between China and the U.S. Qiao served as foreign minister from 1974 to 1976 but lived under house arrest after his dismissal from that position. In 1982 he reappeared and was given a minor foreign affairs post.

Rankovic, Aleksandr, Yugoslav politician (b. Nov. 28, 1909, Dazevac, Serbia—d. Aug. 19, 1983, Dubrovnik, Yugos.), headed Yugoslavia's security forces and was regarded at one time as a likely successor to Marshal Tito until he fell from favour in 1966. An active Communist while still a teenager, Rankovic was imprisoned for six years (1929–35) because of his political activities. During this time he came into contact with others who, like himself, became leaders of the Yugoslav resistance movement in World War II. After the war, his close association with Tito already established, he was appointed head of state security. Unrest among Albanian nationalists in the Kosovo region during the postwar period was quelled with ruthless efficiency. After Tito's break with Moscow in 1948, Rankovic played a major role in ousting Soviet sympathizers. His appointment as vice-president in 1963 appeared to signal that the way was clear for him to succeed Tito, but only three years later, when Tito carried out a sudden and dramatic purge of the security forces, Rankovic lost not only his job but also his membership in the League of Communists. Various accusations—that he had obstructed the party line on economic and social reform, that he had encouraged secret police activity beyond its proper domain, and that he had arranged to have Tito's home bugged—were never answered by Rankovic and never proved against him. The charges were later dropped. He enjoyed a peaceful retirement after having promised not to reveal any state secrets to which he had been privy during his time in power.

Rashidov, Sharas Rashidovich, Soviet politician (b. Nov. 6, 1917, Turkistan [now Uzbek S.S.R.]—d. Oct. 31, 1983), was a leading figure in the Uzbek Soviet Socialist Republic from the time of his appointment in 1959 as first secretary of the Communist Party of Uzbekistan until his death. Having risen to power under Stalin, he thus survived the regimes of both Nikita Khrushchev and Leonid Brezhnev without loss of political influence. The son of a peasant, he attended teacher training college and taught in a school before working as a journalist and serving with the Soviet Army. He edited the newspaper *Kzyl Uzbekistan* during 1947–49 and was president of the Uzbek writers' union before becoming president of the Presidium of the Supreme Soviet of Uzbekistan in 1950. He played a leading part in organizing the Afro-Asian Solidarity Committee meeting in Cairo in 1959, but his influence in Soviet politics was mainly confined to Central Asia despite his membership from 1970 in the Presidium of the Supreme Soviet and other party or national bodies. He did, however, do much to encourage the industrial and agricultural development of the region. Among his many decorations were seven awards of the Order of Lenin.

BOOK OF THE YEAR

Reeve, Ted (EDWARD HENRY REEVE), Canadian athlete and sportswriter (b. 1902, Toronto, Ont.—d. Aug. 27, 1983, Toronto), was a gifted all-around athlete who played in two national junior rugby championships, three Mann Cup senior lacrosse championships, and two Grey Cup football championships before serving as a witty sportswriter for the *Toronto Telegram* from 1928 to 1971. His column, "Reeve's Sporting Extras," was made distinctive by the humorous anecdotes of such characters as Moaner McGruffy (a chronic sports pessimist) and Alice Snippersnapper (a clever sports poet). Reeve, who was affectionately referred to as "The Moaner," gained a wide audience with his straightforward prose. When the *Toronto Telegram* folded in 1971, he joined the staff of the newly created *Toronto Sun* as sports columnist and continued in this capacity until the time of his death. During the 1930s Reeve was also a successful football coach with Balmy Beach and Queen's University. In 1958 he was elected to Canada's Sports Hall of Fame.

Reichelderfer, Francis Wilton, U.S. meteorologist (b. Aug. 6, 1895, Harlan, Ind.—d. Jan. 26, 1983, Washington, D.C.), as chief (1938–63) of the U.S. Weather Bureau (now the National Weather Service), built the agency into one of the most effective and sophisticated national meteorological services in the world. After graduating from Northwestern University, Evanston, Ill., in 1917, Reichelderfer studied advanced meteorology at the Blue Hill Observatory of Harvard University before joining the U.S. Navy in 1918 and earning his aviator's wings. His expertise in the field of meteorology was recognized when he was assigned to Lisbon to provide weather information for the first transatlantic flight (by the Navy's flying boat NC-4). In 1921 he was promoted to lieutenant and served (1922–28) as director of the Naval Meteorological Organization at the Bureau of Aeronautics in Washington. Reichelderfer then studied at the Geophysical Institute in Bergen, Norway, and, while serving (1935–36) as executive officer at the naval air station in Lakehurst, N.J., made four transatlantic flights on the German dirigible "Hindenburg." In 1938, after the death of Willis Gregg, Reichelderfer was named acting chief of the U.S. Weather Bureau, and in the following year the appointment was made permanent. During his tenure he introduced frontal analysis and forecasting, 5- and 30-day forecasts, and the Earth-orbiting weather satellite program, which was probably his crowning achievement. He also helped develop the bureau's own advanced meteorological radar system. For many years he wrote the article "Meteorology" for the *Britannica Book of the Year.*

Reisch, Walter, U.S. screenwriter (b. May 23, 1903, Vienna, Austria—d. March 28, 1983, Los Angeles, Calif.), was a talented writer and director who wrote scripts for such blockbuster films as *Ninotchka* (1939), *Gaslight* (1944), and *That Hamilton Woman* (1941) before winning the Academy Award in 1953 for the disaster epic *Titanic.* Reisch, who was a journalist in Berlin before finding his niche as writer or director of more than 25 films in Austria and Germany, fled Nazi Germany for England, where he wrote and directed *Men Are Not Gods* (1936). In 1937 he arrived in the U.S. and garnered an impressive list of credits. Other films include *The Great Waltz, Comrade X, The Heavenly Body, The Girl on the Red Velvet Swing,* and *Journey to the Center of the Earth.*

Renault, Mary (MARY CHALLANS), British-born historical novelist (b. Sept. 4, 1905, London, England—d. Dec. 13, 1983, Cape Town, South Africa), wrote imaginative re-creations of life in ancient Greece. Three of her novels, *The Last of the Wine* (1956), *The King Must Die* (1958), and *The Bull from the Sea* (1962), established her popular reputation and remained her most enduring work; they combined elements of history and mythology, propounding a matriarchal interpretation of early history and revealing her interest in sexual and particularly in homosexual relationships. But her uneven style and her lack of classical scholarship meant that her reputation with critics lagged behind her popular success; they praised her abilities as a storyteller and entertainer but seldom took her seriously as either a novelist or a historian. She studied in Bristol and at the University of Oxford, worked as a nurse, and in 1948 immigrated to South Africa where she was a member of the Progressive Party and opposed to apartheid. Her first novel had been published in 1939 and she was to publish several on contemporary themes before *The Last of the Wine,* inspired partly by her reading of Robert Graves. Her later books included two novels about Alexander the Great.

Rey, Jean, Belgian politician (b. July 15, 1902, Liège, Belgium—d. May 19, 1983, Liège), was president of the European Commission from 1967 to 1970 and a firm believer in the European ideal. His support for a federal Europe brought him into conflict with French Pres. Charles de Gaulle, whose policies were opposed to closer integration on the political level. Rey studied law at the University of Liège before entering local, then national, politics. Commissioned in the army reserve during World War II, he spent five years as a prisoner of war. After his return, as a leading member of the Liberal Party he was minister for reconstruction and later minister for economic affairs before joining the European Commission in 1958. He attacked the French veto of British entry into the European Economic Community in 1963 but was recognized as a moderate by the French, who did not oppose his presidential candidacy in 1967. After retiring from the Commission, he went into industry but continued his work for Europe as president of the International European Movement (1974–78) and a member of the European Parliament (1979–80).

Reynolds, Frank, U.S. news correspondent (b. Nov. 29, 1923, East Chicago, Ind.—d. July 20, 1983, Washington, D.C.), was an uncompromising newscaster who was universally admired for his exacting standards, honesty, fairness, and commitment to his work. Reynolds, a seasoned Chicago reporter, became correspondent in Washington for ABC in 1965 and covered a number of beats, including the White House. In 1968 Reynolds moved to New York to anchor the ABC "Evening News" with Howard K. Smith but was replaced by Harry Reasoner in 1970, apparently because the network felt his commentaries were too liberal. For the following eight years he provided coverage of national political conventions, space flights, and other major stories before he was reinstated in 1978 as chief anchor on ABC's evening news program, "World News Tonight." Armed with a wealth of knowledge and experience, Reynolds also conveyed a deep sense of caring. He showed his pain at the assassination of Egyptian Pres. Anwar as-Sadat and was visibly angry when conflicting reports emerged about the condition of presidential press secretary James Brady after the attempted assassination of Pres. Ronald Reagan. In 1983 the "World News Tonight" moved into the second slot in the ratings ahead of NBC's news program but, when Reynolds was forced to resign in April owing to his poor health, the show tumbled back to third. A World War II army veteran and recipient of the Purple Heart, Reynolds was buried at Arlington National Cemetery.

Richardson, Sir Ralph David, British actor (b. Dec. 19, 1902, Cheltenham, Gloucestershire, England—d. Oct. 10, 1983, London, England), was an outstanding actor in both classical and modern parts whose performances in the theatre and on the screen conveyed an unforgettable impression of warmth, humour, and humanity. With Sir John Gielgud and Lord Olivier, he was one of the three greatest actors of his generation and of the three it was Richardson who was the most approachable and the most immediately appealing to any kind of audience. Yet he brought to his work an intelligence and dedication that were no less than theirs and he imbued it with a poetry that was uniquely his own. He made his debut in 1921 with a semi-amateur company and later toured with Charles Doran in Shakespeare. After touring in repertory, he made his London debut in *Yellow Sands* in 1926. He joined the Old Vic and during the early 1930s found increasing popularity with London audiences in a series of West End productions of modern works, triumphing at the Haymarket in *The Amazing Doctor Clitterhouse* in 1936. He appeared again at the Old Vic with Olivier before serving in the Fleet Air Arm during World War II. With the Old Vic company immediately after the war he played Peer Gynt, Uncle Vanya, Falstaff, and Cyrano, with Olivier dominating the company in its most memorable seasons. But this success was followed by mediocre performances in Stratford during the early 1950s, and it was not until his return from touring in Australia in the later part of the decade that the London stage again found him at the peak of his form. In *Flowering Cherry* (1958) and *Six Characters in Search of an Author* (1963) he gained critical acclaim and during the late 1960s appeared again at the Haymarket. He toured South America, Europe, and Australia before one of his best performances, as John Gabriel Borkman, in 1975 at the National Theatre. He played opposite Gielgud in *Home* in 1970 and *No Man's Land* in 1975, the contrasting styles and personalities of the two friends admirably matched in these plays by David Storey and Harold Pinter. From his creation during the 1930s of parts in plays by J. B. Priestly to his last stage role in *Inner Voices* (1983), he projected a personality unique in the British theatre, charming, mischievous, yet capable of hinting at sinister or tragic depths in the characters he played. He made more than 40 films, appearing as the butler in *The Fallen Idol* (1949), with Olivier in *Richard III* (1956), and in *Oh Lucky Man!* (1973) and *Rollerball* (1975).

Ritchie, Sir Neil Methuen, British army officer (b. July 29, 1897, Liss, Hampshire, England—d. Dec. 11, 1983, Toronto, Canada), was a junior officer when, in 1941, he was given command of the British 8th Army in North Africa and succeeded in reversing previous British losses, driving Erwin Rommel back to El Agheila. But through inexperience he allowed his forces to become overextended and during subsequent German counterattacks the 8th Army was forced to retreat to El Alamein and lost 30,000 men taken prisoner in Tobruk. Ritchie was sent back to England, but it was felt that he deserved another chance and he led the 12th Army Corps with great success during the invasion of Europe. After World War II he confirmed this recovered reputation, particularly as commander in chief, East Asia Land Forces, and served in Washington, D.C., from then until his retirement in 1951. He studied at the Royal Military College, Sandhurst, and served with the Black Watch during World War I, winning the DSO and Military Cross. He was then posted to the War Office and India before taking command of a battalion of the King's Own Royal Regiment. In 1940, as brigadier, general staff, to Sir Alan Brooke, he played an important part in the withdrawal from Dunkirk. After his retirement Ritchie lived in Canada where he was president of the Mercantile and General Insurance Co. He was knighted in 1945.

Rizzoli, Andrea, Italian publisher (b. Sept. 16, 1914, Milan, Italy—d. May 31, 1983, Nice, France), was chairman of a leading Italian publishing group and owner of the newspaper *Corriere della Sera.* His purchase of the paper proved financially disastrous, and both he and his family were involved in scandals concerning Masonic activities among leading figures in Italian public life. His two sons were arrested in 1983, and his own affairs were under police investigation. He inherited the Rizzoli publishing empire from his father, Andrea senior, in 1970 after having worked with the firm since 1933. In 1978 Rizzoli retired and named his son Angelo as chairman of the group. By the time of Rizzoli's death, the firm's financial situation had seriously deteriorated as a result of losses by the *Corriere della Sera* and the charges pending against his sons and the group's managing director.

Robinson, Joan Violet, British economist (b. Oct. 31, 1903, Camberley, Surrey, England—d. Aug. 5, 1983, Cambridge, England), made a major contribution to the study of economics during a lifetime's academic association with the University of Cambridge. Educated at St. Paul's Girls' School, London, and Girton College, Cambridge, she returned to that university as a lecturer in 1931. She was professor of economics from 1965 until her retirement in 1971. Robinson collaborated with John Maynard Keynes as he prepared *The General Theory of Employment, Interest and Money* (1935). In her own book, *Introduction to the Theory of Employment* (1937), she produced the first simplified account of the ideas contained in that complex work. In the post-World War II period, Robinson helped to push the Keynesian model beyond its theoretical framework. The dynamic theory of the overall growth of the economy was the thesis for *The Accumulation of Capital* (1956). Her travels to India and China led to an understanding of and sympathetic approach to economic systems other than capitalism, and as an academic she won great respect for her ability to simplify any concept. This incisive quality was evidenced in such classic studies as *Economic Philosophy* (1962) and *An Introduction to Modern Economics* (1973).

Robinson, The Right Rev. John Arthur Thomas, British Anglican clergyman (b. June 15, 1919, Canterbury, England—d. Dec. 5, 1983, Yorkshire, England), was bishop of Woolwich from 1959 to 1969 and achieved notoriety as the author of *Honest to God* (1963), in which he questioned some aspects of faith then considered central to Anglican (and Christian) belief. He had already created a stir by his appearance for the defense at the trial of Penguin Books over the unexpurgated edition of D. H. Lawrence's novel *Lady Chatterley's Lover,* claiming that Lawrence's view of sex was not incompatible with a Christian approach to human relationships. Educated at the University of Cambridge, he was ordained in 1945 and in the following year gained his Ph.D. A considerable scholar, he published works on New Testament theology, was dean of Clare College, Cambridge, from 1951 to 1959, and was considered by some to have sacrificed an outstanding academic career by his involvement in the controversies that made him, for a time, a household name. Robinson's later writings showed that he was, in fact, conservative in his approach to New Testament history, and he wrote in defense of the authenticity of the Turin Shroud. His other works included *Liturgy Coming to Life* (1960), *The Human Face of God* (1973), and a study of the relationship of Christianity to Indian religion. On leaving Woolwich he became fellow and dean of chapel at Trinity College, Cambridge.

Rochet, Waldeck Émile, French Communist Party leader (b. April 5, 1905, Sainte-Croix, Saône-et-Loire, France—d. Feb. 15, 1983, Nanterre, France), was secretary-general (1964–72) of the French Communist Party when the party lent its support to other left-wing parties to form the Federation of the Democratic and Socialist Left, which succeeded in keeping Charles de Gaulle from an absolute majority in the first round of the 1965 presidential election. Rochet joined the Communist Party at the age of 19 and trained in Moscow before becoming a prominent member of the Lyon branch. In 1936, after the French Communist Party affiliated with Léon Blum's leftist Popular Front coalition government, Rochet became a deputy in the National Assembly. During World War II Rochet was imprisoned in North Africa until the Allied landings. From 1945 to 1958 he served the party as deputy for Saône-et-Loire, later rose to third secretary, and in 1961 was named deputy to Secretary-General Maurice Thorez, whom he succeeded three years later. A loyal party member, Rochet took a cautious view of destalinization yet played an important role in developing the policy of a "French road" to power by collaboration with other leftist parties. In 1968 the Federation of the Democratic and Socialist Left disbanded, and in the following year illness forced Rochet to hand over effective power to Georges Marchais, who formally replaced him three years later.

Ronet, Maurice, French film actor (b. April 13, 1927, Nice, France—d. March 14, 1983, Paris, France), made his film debut in Jacques Becker's *Rendezvous de Juillet* in 1949 and went on to play leading roles for such directors as Louis Malle, René Clément, Marcel Carné, and Claude Chabrol. Ronet's career started in the theatre, but it was as the star of Malle's films *Ascenseur pour l'échafaud* (1958) and *Le Feu follet* (1963) that he demonstrated the range of his talent and achieved the maturity that made his collaboration with Chabrol so productive. In all, Ronet played in more than 60 films, and he also gained a considerable reputation as a television director with such productions as "Bartleby" (1976) and "Folie Douce" (1979). He wrote a book, *Le Métier de comédien* (1977), on his craft. His last film part was in Bob Swain's *La Balance* (1982), which won an award as best French film for that year.

Rosenberg, Anna M(arie) (Mrs. Paul G. Hoffman), U.S. government official and labour and public relations consultant (b. June 19, 1902, Budapest, Hung.—d. May 9, 1983, New York, N.Y.), held literally dozens of public positions in the U.S. and New York City and state from the 1930s through the 1960s, often as the first or only woman appointed to a particular position. At the time of her death no other woman had been so highly placed in the U.S. defense establishment as she when serving as assistant secretary of defense (1950–53). Born Anna Marie Lederer, she was brought to the U.S. at age ten by her parents. As a high school student in Manhattan she organized a political club and was active in student affairs until she dropped out to marry Julius Rosenberg. Her mother later persuaded her to return to school.

Immediately upon her naturalization in 1919 Rosenberg became active in Democratic politics and came to the attention of Al Smith's mentor, Belle Moskowitz. This connection prompted her to set up shop as a consultant in labour and public relations. Rosenberg excelled as a mediator, and her petite stature was no bar to commanding respect from both parties during a dispute. Once she donned hip boots to examine the underground site of a machine that figured in a grievance; she was also capable of directing a stream of waterfront profanity at a local union leader if necessary to get his attention.

Through her political contacts she began advising New York Gov. Franklin D. Roosevelt about labour matters, and after he became president of the U.S. she was appointed regional director of the National Recovery Administration (NRA). Meanwhile, her consulting business flourished, numbering among its clientele at various times R. H. Macy & Co., Nelson A. Rockefeller, and Encyclopædia Britannica, Inc. When the U.S. entered World War II she was named regional director of the War Manpower Commission. She undertook observation missions to the European Theater of Operations for President Roosevelt in 1944 and the following year for Pres. Harry Truman. At war's end she returned to her own business. In 1950 President Truman appointed her assistant secretary of defense, and in that role she applied her expertise in manpower utilization to military recruitment and training during the Korean War.

After leaving the Defense Department she returned to her consulting firm. In 1962 she was divorced and married Paul G. Hoffman. He was a director of Encyclopædia Britannica, Inc., and after his death in 1974 she succeeded him as a director, remaining active in its affairs until her death.

Rossi, Tino, French popular singer and film actor (b. April 29, 1907, Ajaccio, Corsica, France—d. Sept. 27, 1983, Paris, France), sold more than 200 million records, with one song alone, "Petit Papa Noël," accounting for some 18 million sales. He was blessed with an immense Corsican charm (his main asset in an otherwise unremarkable acting career) and a voice that covered three octaves. His success as a singer was enhanced by his willingness to confine himself to the repetition of the same sentimental themes. Even the majority of his films retold the same story of a singer's rise to fame. His Parisian debut at the Casino de Paris in 1934, with his great success "Veni, veni," coincided with the heyday of radio and 78-rpm phonograph records. Rossi offered both media a remarkable voice and simple emotional appeal, rivaling the popularity in France of American crooners like Bing Crosby. His audience forgot the Depression and the threat of war as they took up the simple refrains of love and romance, carried away by Rossi's sleek good looks and honeyed tones. The films, with few exceptions, were vehicles for the songs; he made some 25 of them between 1936 and 1954, introducing "Petit Papa Noël" in *Destins* (1946). Rossi hinted at the possibility of a real acting talent only in *Fièvres* (1941). He continued throughout his life to produce regular recordings, an institution whose popularity never failed. In 1982, at the Casino de Paris, he celebrated 50 years as a singer.

Roy, Gabrielle, Canadian novelist (b. March 22, 1909, St. Boniface, Man.—d. July 13, 1983, Quebec City, Que.), carved a niche in French-Canadian literature with social novels that authentically depicted the lifelong struggles of poverty-stricken working-class people in the cities of Canada. She wrote other works that chronicled isolated rural life in Manitoba. Her first novel, *Bonheur d'occasion* (1945; *The Tin Flute,* 1947), a gloomy view of a working-class neighbourhood in Montreal, became a classic in Canadian literature. Roy also penned such novels as *La Petite Poule d'eau* (1950; *Where Nests the Water Hen,* 1951), *Alexandre Chenevert, caissier* (1954; *The Cashier,* 1955), and *Rue Deschambault* (1955; *Street of Riches,* 1957), a semiautobiographical story of childhood spent on the prairie. Roy, who won international acclaim for her sensitive, realistic novels, was a three-time winner of the Governor General's Award, Canada's highest prize for literature. In 1977 Roy published her last novel, *Les Enfants de ma vie* (*Children of My Heart*), but in 1979 delighted young and old alike with the children's story *Cliptail,* for which she was awarded the Canada Council's prize for the best children's book in French for that year. At the time of her death Roy was working on her memoirs, and on the day of her death the film version of her most famous novel, *Bonheur d'occasion,* had its world premiere at the Moscow Film Festival.

Samorè, Antonio Cardinal, Italian prelate of the Roman Catholic Church (b. Dec. 4, 1905, Bardi, near Piacenza, Italy—d. Feb. 3, 1983, Rome, Italy), was a leading member of the Vatican diplomatic service and, as president (1967–71) of the Pontifical Commission for Latin America, had a special role in Latin-American affairs. In 1978 Samorè was sent to South America to prevent a war between Chile and Argentina over three islands in the Beagle Channel. He led negotiations on this dispute in the hope of achieving a long-term resolution, but ill health forced him to relinquish his responsibilities. After his ordination in 1928, Samorè was appointed bishop in 1950 and cardinal in 1967. He served as nuncio in Bogotá, Colombia, and in leading posts in Vatican departments before being appointed librarian and archivist of the Holy Roman Church in 1974.

Sartawi, Issam, Palestinian nationalist (b. 1935, Acre, Palestine [now Akko, Israel]—d. April 10, 1983, Albufeira, Port.), became one of the moderate leaders in the Palestine Liberation Organization (PLO) but attracted much hostility because he advocated coexistence with Israel. Trained as a doctor, he was engaged in research in the U.S. as a heart surgeon at the time of the 1967 Arab-Israeli war. He returned to the Middle East to join al-Fatah, the guerrilla wing of the PLO, and accepted its view that the Palestine problem could be solved only through armed struggle. Later his attitude changed, and he began to pursue a dialogue with moderate Israelis in the hope of achieving a reconciliation between the two sides. There was little sympathy within the PLO for his views, however, and official Israeli policy was uncompromising. In April 1983 he attended a meeting of the Socialist International in Portugal and was shot dead in the lobby of the hotel where the conference was being held. An Arab was detained after the shooting, and an organization that had previously split from the PLO took credit for killing Sartawi, officially denouncing him as a traitor to his country and his people.

Savitch, Jessica Beth, U.S. television news correspondent (b. 1947, Kennett Square, Pa.—d. Oct. 24, 1983, near New Hope, Pa.), was visible to millions of Americans as the vibrant Washington news correspondent, anchor, and reporter on NBC and as the anchor of the controversial PBS news magazine "Front Line." Savitch, who joined NBC in 1977 after serving two years as weekend anchor and correspondent for KHOU-TV in Houston, Texas, and five years in a similar position at KYW-TV in Philadelphia, had recently signed a six-figure contract with NBC. She and Martin Fischbein, an executive of the *New York Post,* were killed when their car skidded on a rain-slick highway, plunged into a Delaware River canal, and sank upside down in $1^1/_2$ m (5 ft) of mud.

UPI

Schapiro, Leonard Bertram, British historian and political scientist (b. April 22, 1908, Glasgow, Scotland—d. Nov. 2, 1983, London, England), was professor of political science at the London School of Economics (LSE) from 1963 to 1975 and one of the best-known writers on Soviet affairs. His own childhood was spent mainly in Russia, where his family originated, and he witnessed the 1917 Revolution. He studied in London and was called to the bar in 1932, practicing as a barrister until the outbreak of World War II. He spent the war years with the BBC Monitoring Service and with army intelligence before returning to legal practice, at the same time pursuing research into contemporary political history. In 1955 he published *The Origins of the Autocracy,* a study of opposition in Russia during the years after the Revolution, and in the same year joined the staff at the LSE. He based his opposition to the Soviet state partly on the arbitrary nature of its rule and the absence of constitutional controls and sanctions. *The Communist Party of the Soviet Union* (1960; 7th edition, 1977), his major work, was recognized as the most scholarly and authoritative treatment of the subject and was followed by studies of Soviet government and politics and of 19th-century Russian political thought that showed the same gift for analysis and scholarship. He also wrote a book on Turgenev.

Scott, The Rev. (Guthrie) Michael, British Anglican clergyman (b. July 30, 1907, Lowfield Heath, Sussex, England—d. Sept. 14, 1983, London, England), was a courageous campaigner on behalf of political causes ranging from the movement against apartheid in South Africa to the Campaign for Nuclear Disarmament. Imprisoned, attacked, often ridiculed, assailed by doubts and never far from controversy, he was tireless whenever he found a cause to believe in. His father was also a clergyman, and he was brought up in a slum parish in Southampton, early contracting the tuberculosis that was the start of a lifetime of ill health. He was ordained in 1930 and worked in Sussex and London before going to India as chaplain in Calcutta. He had been attracted by Marxism, though he broke with the Communists over the Nazi-Soviet Pact and, despite his sympathy for Gandhi's policy of nonviolence, joined the Royal Air Force. Invalided out, he went to South Africa for his health, campaigned against racial discrimination, and spent three months in jail. His next cause, that of South West Africa/Namibia, attracted worldwide attention and gained little sympathy from his fellow clergymen; he left South Africa, was declared a prohibited immigrant, and had his license to preach revoked. In 1952 he helped found the Africa Bureau in London where he worked in the field of African affairs. In 1958 Scott joined the antinuclear movement, was again imprisoned for civil disobedience, and in 1960 was a founder-member of Bertrand Russell's Committee of 100. In 1966 he was expelled from India because of his support for the Nagaland rebels. His evident integrity, his courage, and his gentle manner were powerful weapons; he was not awed by the hatred of governments or the frequent embarrassment of his church. In the end he compelled respect. In 1975 he was made honorary canon of St. George's Cathedral, Windhoek, Namibia, and he was honoured by the government of Zambia for his work in African causes. His autobiography, *A Time to Speak,* was published in 1958. Other books included *Shadow over Africa* (1950), *Bertrand Russell: Philosopher of the Century* (1967), and *A Search for Peace and Justice* (1980).

Scullard, Howard Hayes, British historian (b. Feb. 9, 1903, Bedford, England—d. March 31, 1983, London, England), was professor of ancient history at King's College, University of London, from 1959 until his retirement in 1970 and a noted scholar of Roman history. In addition to his own major works, he played an important role in the development of the discipline by encouraging others to contribute to such publications as the *Oxford Classical Dictionary* and the series *Aspects of Greek and Roman Life,* which he edited. Scullard also devoted considerable time and effort to revising Cary's *History of Rome.* After studying at St. John's College, Cambridge, Scullard taught at New College, London, before moving to King's College, where he remained for the rest of his career. He published *History of the Roman World from 753 to 146 BC* in 1935, *Roman Politics 220–150 BC* in 1951, and *From the Gracchi to Nero* in 1959. Besides maintaining a constant output of scholarly articles, including some for *Encyclopædia Britannica,* he was active as vice-president of the Society for the Promotion of Roman Studies.

Seghers, Anna (NETTI RADVANYI), German writer (b. Nov. 19, 1900, Mainz, Germany—d. June 1, 1983, East Berlin), was a leading figure in the literary life of East Germany but always managed to avoid becoming a party "hack." She was universally admired as the author of such novels as *Das siebte Kreuz* (1942; *The Seventh Cross,* 1943), set in prewar Nazi Germany and later filmed by Fred Zimmerman with Spencer Tracy. Seghers studied in Cologne and Heidelberg and earned her Ph.D. for a thesis on Rembrandt. During the 1920s she published her first stories and a novel, *Der Aufstand der Fischer von Sankt Barbara* (1928; *The Revolt of the Fishermen,* 1929), which won the Kleist Prize. Other novels followed, including *Die Gefährten* (1932; *The Companions*), with themes that reflected her adherence, from 1928, to the Communist Party. After 1933, as a Communist and a Jew, she was arrrested but managed to escape with her husband, Laszlo Radvanyi, to Paris. When World War II broke out, Radvanyi was interned, but eventually, with the help of the League of American Writers, the family managed to escape to Mexico. In 1947, however, they returned to East Germany. There Seghers was hailed as a major socialist writer, gaining the National Prize in 1951, 1959, and 1971 and the Stalin Peace Prize in 1951. Her realistic narrative style adapted well to the demands of "socialist realism," and her later novels included *Die Toten bleiben jung* (1949; *The Dead Stay Young,* 1950) and *Die Entscheidung* (1959; *The Decision*). Seghers also wrote short stories and essays that expressed her humanist beliefs with power and conviction.

Sereni, Vittorio, Italian poet and novelist (b. July 27, 1913, Luino, Varese, Italy—d. Feb. 10, 1983, Milan, Italy), developed a highly personal elegiac voice in his poetry, though he was influenced by the allusive manner of "hermeticism." After studying at the University of Milan, Sereni taught until the outbreak of World War II, which he ended as a prisoner in North Africa. His first collection, *Frontiere* (1941), was followed by *Diario d'Algeria* (1947), which added a note of tragic lyricism to the rather nostalgic mood of his earlier work. His humanism, as well as his love for his native Lombardy, was reflected in *Gli strumenti umani* (1965; revised 1975) and in his prose diary, *Gli immediati dintorni* (1962). During the 1950s he joined the publishing house of his friend Oscar Mondadori and made a wry commentary on international publishing with his satirical novel *L'opzione e allegati* (1964). Sereni, who was highly respected as one of Italy's most original modern poets, was also a noted translator of French and American literature, including the poetry of Ezra Pound and William Carlos Williams.

Sert, José Luis (JOSEP LLUIS SERT), Spanish-born architect (b. July 1, 1902, Barcelona, Spain—d. March 15, 1983, Barcelona), was a disciple of Le Corbusier and under his tutelage became a leading proponent of modernism in architecture. Sert was celebrated for his accomplishments in city planning and urban development and for softening the edges of modernism's austere cement-and-glass structures. He frequently added colourful Mediterranean touches to his structures and in his designs of large buildings was famous for his trademark semicircular light scoops, which made maximum use of natural light. After graduating from the Escuela Superior de Arquitectura, Barcelona, in 1929, Sert formed his own architectural firm and was primarily devoted to town planning. Two years after he designed the Spanish pavilion at the 1937 Paris World's Fair, Sert immigrated to the U.S. and in 1941 joined Town Planning Associates, an organization that provided planning and urban design for South American cities. Sert's experience in town planning was utilized in his work for the campuses of Harvard and Boston universities (1959–65 and 1950–65) and was evident in his designs for the Fondation Maeght at Saint-Paul-de-Vence, France (1968), and for the Fundacíon Joan Miró at Barcelona. Sert, who was president of CIAM (Congrès Internationaux d'Architectue Moderne) from 1947 to 1956, served as dean of the Graduate School of Design at Harvard University from 1953 to 1969 and in 1980 was awarded the coveted Gold Medal of the American Institute of Architects, one of the highest awards given to an architect.

Seznec, Jean, French-born scholar and critic (b. March 18, 1905, Morlaix, France—d. Nov. 21, 1983, Oxford, England), was professor of French literature at the University of Oxford from 1950 to 1972. He was perhaps better known as an art historian. His first major appointment after leaving the École Normale Supérieure was as a fellow at the École Française de Rome to study under Émile Mâle. Seznec then taught at Cambridge, Marseille, at the French Institute in Florence, and (after a brief period of military service in World War II) at Harvard (1941–50). He returned frequently to the U.S. as a visiting lecturer after his appointment at Oxford. At Harvard he helped to establish the subject of a group of unpublished drawings by Fragonard, and in 1940 he published his major work on Renaissance art and literature, *La Survivance des dieux antiques,* which received the Prix Fould in 1948. His other major undertaking was the publication of his edition of Diderot's *Salons* (1957–66), which demonstrated his profound knowledge of 18th-century art and culture. Diderot was also the subject of *Essais sur Diderot et l'antiquité* (1958).

Shearer, Norma (EDITH NORMA SHEARER), Canadian-born actress (b. Aug. 10, 1900?, Montreal, Que.—d. June 12, 1983, Woodland Hills, Calif.), was a charismatic beauty who was considered the epitome of chic and glamour during her heyday with MGM studios during the 1920s and '30s. She was one of the few stars to make a successful transition from the silent movies to the talkies. After making her motion-picture debut in 1920, Shearer appeared in such classic silent films as *He Who Gets Slapped* (1924), as a bareback rider, and *The Student Prince* (1927), as the barmaid Kathi. In 1927 Shearer, who was promoted by MGM as the "First Lady of the Screen," married MGM production chief Irving Thalberg, who substantially advanced her career. Shearer was cast in romantic and daring roles and won an Academy Award for best actress for her leading role in *The Divorcee* (1930). The following year she sent shock waves through audiences when she was manhandled by Clark Gable in *A Free Soul*. She received five other Academy Award nominations for best actress for her performances in *Their Own Desire* (1929), *A Free Soul* (1931), *The Barretts of Wimpole Street* (1934), *Romeo and Juliet* (1936), and *Marie Antoinette* (1938), her first film after the death of Thalberg. Shearer, who also received rave reviews for *Idiot's Delight* (1939) and *The Women* (1939), retired permanently from the screen after the failures of *We Were Dancing* and *Her Cardboard Lover*, both released in 1942.

Slade, Humphrey, British-born Kenyan lawyer and politician (b. 1905, London, England—d. Aug. 10, 1983, Nairobi, Kenya), was an influential figure in Kenyan politics both before and after independence. Although he had been an outspoken critic of majority rule, and had been partly responsible for the arrest of Jomo Kenyatta at the outbreak of the Mau Mau rebellion in the early 1950s, he was nevertheless requested by Kenyatta to stay on as speaker in the first government following independence in 1963. In this role he did much to assist the country's transition from a British colony to an independent nation. Slade first went to Kenya in the early 1930s to join a firm of lawyers. His legal career flourished; in 1946 he was called to the bar. Soon after he turned his attention to politics and was first elected to the Legislative Council in 1952. He retired from Parliament to return to his law practice in 1969, one year after being awarded the Order of the Burning Spear by Kenyatta.

Slezak, Walter, Austrian-born actor (b. May 3, 1902, Vienna, Austria—d. April 22, 1983, Flower Hill, N.Y.), was an accomplished character actor whose expanding girth typecast him in roles of portly, menacing villains or sentimental, cherubic vagabonds. Slezak, who was a matinee idol in German plays and motion pictures during the 1920s and '30s, launched his career in the U.S. on Broadway in the operetta *Meet My Sister* (1930). His performance was so impressive that he was given leading roles in scores of major musicals and dramas. His most memorable screen role was as a deceitful German submarine commander in the Alfred Hitchcock thriller *Lifeboat* (1944); on Broadway he delighted audiences as a Marseille shopkeeper in *Fanny* (1954), for which he won a Tony award. Some of his screen credits include *Once Upon a Honeymoon* (1942), *Sinbad the Sailor* (1947), *The Inspector General* (1949), *Bedtime for Bonzo* (1951), and *Dr. Coppelius* (1966). His book of reminiscences, *What Time's the Next Swan?,* was published in 1962. Deeply despondent over his failing health, Slezak took his own life.

Smith, Hermon Dunlap ("DUTCH"), U.S. business executive (b. May 1, 1900, Chicago, Ill.—d. May 11, 1983, Lake Forest, Ill.), was instrumental in expanding the offices and increasing the clientele of the international insurance brokerage firm Marsh & McLennan Inc. He served as the company's dynamic president and chief executive officer (1955–63) and chairman (1963–66) and was a prominent community leader who used his inherent leadership qualities on behalf of such organizations and institutions as the Field Foundation, the Newberry Library, the Chicago Historical Society, and the Adler Planetarium, all in Illinois. After earning a B.A. from Harvard University in 1921, Smith worked for Chicago's Northern Trust Co. before joining Marsh & McLennan in 1934. Smith quickly ascended the corporate ladder, and even after his retirement in 1966 he remained a director of the company. From 1969 to 1971 he also served as director of Marlennan, the holding company for Marsh & McLennan. Smith, who donated his services to innumerable community and philanthropic organizations, also served as chairman of the National Merit Scholarship Corp., as a member of the board of directors of Encyclopædia Britannica, Inc., and as a member of the board of directors of Encyclopædia Britannica Educational Corp. As testimony to his many valued contributions, the University of Chicago awarded Smith the William Benton Medal for Distinguished Public Service in 1976.

Spry, Graham, Canadian broadcasting pioneer (b. Feb. 20, 1900, St. Thomas, Ont.—d. Nov. 23, 1983, Ottawa, Ont.), with Alan B. Plaunt formed the Canadian Radio League in Ottawa in 1930, which inspired the formation of the Canadian Broadcasting Corporation (CBC), established in 1936. Spry, a long-time radio enthusiast who promoted the medium as an instrument of national unity, culture, and entertainment, was regarded by many as the "father of the CBC." In 1946 he was appointed agent general for Saskatchewan in London, a post he held until his retirement in 1968. In 1972 the Association of Canadian Radio and Television Artists bestowed on Spry the John Drainie Award for "distinguished contribution to broadcasting."

Sraffa, Piero, Italian economist (b. Aug. 5, 1898, Turin, Italy—d. Sept. 3, 1983, Cambridge, England), was emeritus reader in economics and fellow of Trinity College, Cambridge, and one of the most influential modern figures in a relatively esoteric field of theoretical economics. His theories, reviving those of the 19th-century economist David Ricardo, greatly influenced Marxist thinking and were based on a critique of the orthodox marginal theory of value and distribution. He studied in Turin and became professor at the University of Cagliari. During a visit to the English economist John Maynard Keynes in 1921, he wrote a series of articles that offended Benito Mussolini and decided to leave Italy. Sraffa eventually settled in Cambridge with Keynes's help in 1927. Made a fellow of Trinity College in 1939, Sraffa was never a keen university lecturer or a prolific writer, but his few publications had effects quite disproportionate to their length. They included his 1925 article on marginal theory (published in the *Economic Journal* in 1926), his edition of *The Works and Correspondence of David Ricardo* (11 vol., 1951–73), and his *Production of Commodities by Means of Commodities* (1960). The last, far-reaching in its implications, opened a debate that revised both Marxist and liberal theories. He was elected a fellow of the British Academy in 1954.

Stankiewicz, Richard Peter, U.S. sculptor (b. Oct. 18, 1922, Philadelphia, Pa.—d. March 27, 1983, Worthington, Mass.), welded discarded scrap metal and rusty machine parts including pipes, nuts, bolts, screws, clockworks, springs, wheels, and boilers into imaginative sculptured figures that expressed elegance and wit. Stankiewicz's sculptures were often anthropomorphic or zoological constructions, and after an exhibition of his work in 1958 he was dubbed the "Audubon of the junkyard." He was originally interested in painting and studied with the painters Hans Hofmann in New York City (1948–49) and Fernand Léger in Europe (1950) before coming under the influence of the sculptor Ossip Zadkine (1951–52). After returning to the U.S., Stankiewicz began assembling his sculptures and, unlike other junk-art sculptors, used objects without transforming them from their original state. Stankiewicz, who was a pioneer in the field, was especially noted for his humanistic approach. His sculptures include "Kabuki Dancer," "The Warrior," and "The Bride," which features a veil made out of bedsprings. His works are in the Museum of Modern Art, the Whitney Museum of American Art, and the Beaubourg (Pompidou Centre) in Paris.

Stead, Christina Ellen, Australian novelist (b. July 17, 1902, Sydney, Australia—d. March 31, 1983, Sydney), was a writer of great power and originality, though it was not until the last decade of her life that she enjoyed full recognition of her talent. Her novels, which include *House of All Nations* (1938), *The Man Who Loved Children* (1940), and *The Dark Places of the Heart* (1966), are remarkable for their simple narrative style and character development. Stead trained as a teacher but abandoned this career for business. From 1928 she lived in London, then Paris, where she was influenced by such French writers as Émile Zola and Louis Guilloux. She published *The Salzburg Tales* in 1934 and followed this with her first novel, *Seven Poor Men of Sydney* (1935). She traveled to Spain and the U.S., worked for a time as a writer with Metro-Goldwyn-Mayer in Hollywood, and returned to Europe in 1947, settling near London after 1953. After the death of her husband, William J. Blake, in 1968, she accepted a post as fellow at the Australian National University. When *The Man Who Loved Children* was reissued in 1965, it was hailed as a masterpiece, and Stead was nominated for the Nobel Prize for Literature. She also benefited during the 1970s from a climate that was more sympathetic to women writers with a forceful feminine viewpoint. Her other works include *The Puzzleheaded Girl* (1967), *The Little Hotel* (1974), and *A Christina Stead Reader* (1979), which contains excerpts from 11 of her novels.

Stevens, Bernard George, British composer (b. March 2, 1916, London, England—d. Jan. 2, 1983, Halstead, Essex, England), was professor of composition at the Royal College of Music from 1948 to 1981 and a versatile composer whose works include orchestral and chamber music as well as film scores. Though Stevens left the Communist Party in 1956 at the time of the Hungarian uprising, his work was profoundly influenced by Marxism. He nonetheless showed an almost mystical spirituality in works that he composed to mark the 100th anniversary of the birth of Teilhard de Chardin. His *Symphony of Liberation,* first performed in 1946, was widely acclaimed, and his mature style was exhibited in his *Variations for Orchestra,* his Violin Concerto, and his Second String Quartet. Stevens also wrote a mass and a liturgical cantata. At the time of his death, a piano concerto and an opera, *The Shadow of the Glen,* were scheduled to have their first performances. A founding member of the Campaign for Nuclear Disarmament, Stevens was an inspiring teacher and a well-known writer on music.

Stout, Alan Ker, British philosopher (b. May 9, 1900, Oxford, England—d. July 20, 1983, Hobart, Tasmania), was professor of moral and political philosophy at the University of Sydney from 1939 until 1965. Son of the distinguished psychologist and philosopher G. F. Stout, Alan Stout studied at the University of Oxford and was a lecturer at the University College of North Wales (1924–34) and at the University of Edinburgh (1934–39) before being appointed professor in Sydney. A neoplatonist, Stout edited the *Australasian Journal of Philosophy* from 1950 to 1967. His published works included articles and papers on Cartesian philosophy and moral theory, and he edited his father's Gifford lectures under the title *God and Nature* (1952). In his capacity as a practical moral philosopher, Stout was much consulted, by the government and the media, for his views on the day's leading issues. He was president (1964–67) of the Council for Civil Liberties and a council member (1963–79) of the Australian Consumers' Association. Besides philosophy, his abiding interest was in the theatre and films. He was active in the development of Australia's film industry through his founding membership (1945–47) of the Australian National Film Board and as governor (1960–75) of the Australian Film Institute. He was also a director (1972–77) of the Tasmanian Theatre Company.

Surkov, Aleksey Aleksandrovich, Soviet poet and novelist (b. Oct. 13, 1899, Serednevo, Yaroslavl region, Russia—d. June 1983, Moscow, U.S.S.R.), was first secretary of the Soviet Writers' Union from 1954 to 1959 and was notorious for his role in the campaign against Boris Pasternak, who was prevented from accepting the 1958 Nobel Prize for Literature and expelled from the Writers' Union. Surkov served in the Red Army from 1918 to 1922 and made his name as a poet. His work, orthodox in style, became especially popular during World War II because of its patriotic themes. He reported for various newspapers, including *Krasnaya Zvezda* ("Red Star"), the organ of the Red Army, and, as secretary of the Writers' Union, was chief editor of its paper, *Literaturnaya Gazeta.* He led the attack on Pasternak and, when *Doctor Zhivago* was banned in the U.S.S.R., Surkov tried to prevent its publication in Italy. In 1962, however, he appeared to adopt a more liberal attitude and signed an appeal in favour of writers and artists criticized by the Soviet leader Nikita Khrushchev. Surkov later recanted and for the rest of his life remained a pillar of literary orthodoxy, defending the party line in his criticism of dissidence and as editor of the *Shorter Encyclopaedia of Soviet Literature* from 1962. His *Collected Works* were published during 1978–79.

Svestka, Oldrich, Czechoslovak journalist (b. March 24, 1922, Pozorka, Czech.—d. June 8, 1983, Prague, Czech.), was editor of the Czechoslovak Communist Party newspaper *Rude Pravo* from 1958 to 1968 and editor in chief from 1975 until his death. An orthodox Communist, he was a member of the party Central Committee from 1962 and appeared sympathetic to the reform movement as it began to gather strength during the decade. After the Soviet invasion in 1968, he lost his post as candidate member of the party Presidium and was ousted from *Rude Pravo.* Later Svestka submitted to the new party line and was appointed editor of the official weekly *Tribuna;* from this position he supported the post-Dubcek regime. In 1970 he became a member of the secretariat of the Central Committee.

Swanson, Gloria (GLORIA MAY JOSEPHINE SVENSSON), U.S. actress (b. March 17, 1899, Chicago, Ill.—d. April 4, 1983, New York, N.Y.), reigned as Hollywood's glittering glamour queen during the "Golden Age" of silent motion pictures, accomplished a successful transition to the talkies, and probably made the most spectacular comeback of any star as Norma Desmond, a faded, jaded, silent-movie actress in the film *Sunset Boulevard* (1950). Swanson launched her career at the Essanay studios in Chicago playing small parts in such Wallace Beery films as *Sweedie Goes to College.* She married Beery (the first of six husbands) and went to Hollywood, where she appeared in a string of Mack Sennett comedies. Swanson was featured in eight Triangle domestic melodramas before she worked for Cecil B. De Mille, who starred her in such sexual romps as *Male and Female* (1919), *Don't Change Your Husband* (1919), and *Why Change Your Wife?* (1920). Though her well-defined features were in sharp contrast to the sweet faces of other ingenues, they were admirably suited to De Mille's masquerades of sexual intrigue among the rich and sophisticated. These films, in which Swanson was enveloped in genuine jewels and furs, encouraged her lifelong penchant for extravagance and established her as a symbol of American female chic. After six films with De Mille, Swanson's contract was taken over by Paramount, and she had an even greater opportunity to exhibit her versatility. She starred opposite Rudolph Valentino in *Beyond the Rocks* (1922) and showed her talents as a spirited comedian in such varied roles as a pickpocket (*The Humming Bird,* 1924), a gum-cracking salesclerk (*Manhandled,* 1924), and a foolish kitchen maid who boxes with a female giant during a vaudeville show's amateur night (*Stage Struck,* 1925). After making *Madame Sans-Gêne* (1925) in France, Swanson turned down a $1 million-a-year contract with Paramount and founded her own production company, which received backing from Joseph P. Kennedy. During this period she gave two of her best dramatic performances; for *Sadie Thomson* (1928) she received an Academy Award nomination for best actress, and though the sexually charged *Queen Kelly* was never released in the U.S., it was considered a masterpiece. In 1929 she made her first talkie, *The Trespasser,* but during the 1930s her star waned. Although Swanson made several comeback attempts, it was not until 1950, when the semiautobiographical *Sunset Boulevard* was released, that critics acknowledged the magnitude of her skills. Her triumphant comeback was epitomized in a classic exchange in the film. After being told, "You used to be big," Norma retorts, "I *am* big—it's the pictures that got small." In her last film, *Airport 1975,* Swanson played herself. Her autobiography, *Swanson on Swanson* (1980), gave credence to her affair with Joseph Kennedy but discounted the rumours that her son Joseph (named after her father) was Kennedy's son.

UPI

Tailleferre, Germaine, French composer (b. April 19, 1892, Saint-Maur-des-Fossés, France—d. Nov. 6, 1983, Paris, France), was the last surviving member of Les Six (the group also included Darius Milhaud, Georges Auric, Francis Poulenc, Arthur Honegger, and Louis Durey), which revitalized French music in the 1920s; she was one of those who best typified the group's desire to bring spontaneity and even humour into musical compositions. Tailleferre studied at the Conservatoire and published her *String Quartet* in 1919 before collaborating with Jean Cocteau on *Les Mariés de la tour Eiffel* (1921), the ballet-drama that was a key work of the period. She also wrote other works for the theatre (including the ballet *Le Marchand d'oiseaux*) and for films, as well as numerous chamber pieces. Although Tailleferre experimented with serial music, she never took either to this or to electronic music, despite her willingness to use elements of jazz and popular music in her work. In later years she suffered from neglect, though her *Concerto de la fidélité* was produced at the Paris Opéra in 1982. After World War II she lived for a time in the U.S. and in 1968 joined the Communist Party. She received many awards, including grand prix from the Académie des Beaux-arts and the City of Paris.

Tambimuttu, Meary James Thurairajah, Ceylonese-born editor (b. 1915, Ceylon [Sri Lanka]—d. June 22, 1983, London, England), edited *Poetry London* from 1939 to 1947, during which time he published work by virtually every British poet of any note and left an indelible mark on the British cultural scene. He immigrated to Britain in 1937 and founded *Poetry London* less than two years later as a showcase for new talent, including such gifted individuals as Dylan Thomas, Kathleen Raine, Stephen Spender, and George Barker. "Tambi," who preferred energy and enthusiasm to intellectualism, held court in the pubs of London's Fitzrovia rather than in university common rooms. In spite of the paper shortages during World War II and his own eccentricities, he kept the magazine going. Tambimuttu displayed a genius for spotting genuine poetry and encouraging then-unknown writers. In 1947 he went to the U.S., founded *Poetry London-New York,* and immersed himself in such other projects as Dr. Timothy Leary's League for Spiritual Discovery. He planned a new poetry review with the Beatles, but it was not unil 1979, more than ten years after his return to Europe, that *Poetry London/Apple Magazine* appeared. His final project was the founding of an Indian Arts Council in London, which opened in 1983. He is remembered as a man of great charm and generosity and as a unique figure on the English literary scene.

Tank, Kurt, German aircraft designer (b. Feb. 24, 1898, Bromberg, Germany [now Bydgoszcz, Poland]—d. June 5, 1983, Munich, West Germany), was technical director of the Focke-Wulf company and designer of some of the most successful German planes used during the 1930s and World War II. His aircraft included the Fw 200 Condor, which established a record in 1938 for the first nonstop transatlantic crossing by a passenger aircraft in both directions, and the Fw 190 and Ta 152 fighters, which scored notable successes against British planes. The Ta 152 had a top speed of 760 km/h (472 mph) and was a night fighter of outstanding potential. But by the time it was in full production, the German economy was unable to produce sufficient planes to challenge Allied bombers. Tank also designed a jet aircraft, the plans for which may have been captured by the Soviets and used as a prototype for the MiG 15. After the war Tank lived in Argentina and India before returning to West Germany in the late 1960s.

Tarsis, Valery Yakovlevich, Russian-born writer (b. Sept. 23, 1906, Kiev, Russia—d. March 3, 1983, Bern, Switz.), spent eight months in a Soviet psychiatric hospital, an experience that he chronicled in his book *Ward 7* (1965). This indictment of the regime that had persecuted him for publishing his work abroad made him one of the best known Soviet dissident writers and led, in 1966, to the withdrawal of his Soviet citizenship. After graduating from the university in Rostov-on-Don in 1929, he worked as a translator at the State Fiction Publishing House and started to publish his own stories. But after World War II, facing an apparent ban on his work in the Soviet Union, Tarsis sent two novels abroad. One of them, *The Bluebottle* (1962), expressed his own disillusionment with Communism. His experiences in the psychiatric hospital, however, left him a broken man. As an exile in Switzerland he wrote such works as *The Pleasure Factory* (1967) and *Russia and the Russians* (1970).

Terayama, Shuji, Japanese playwright (b. Dec. 10, 1935, Aomori Prefecture, Japan—d. May 4, 1983, Tokyo, Japan), was a prolific avant-garde artist whose plays and films were characterized by their shocking effect on audiences. Terayama, who was partial to using puppets, dwarfs, hunchbacks, and fat women in his Surrealist productions, founded Tenjosajiki theatre in 1967 (translated as Peanut Gallery). There he created a sensation with such works as *La Marie Vision* and *Knock.* The latter created such a stir that members of its cast were arrested. Terayama, the winner of several prizes for his creations, produced such films as *Festival Hide and Seek,* the official Japanese entry at the 1975 Cannes Film Festival, and *Emperor Tomatocatsup,* a parody of revolution pitting children against adults. In 1980 Terayama staged one of his most spectacular plays, *Directions to Servants,* a combination of dazzling stage effects and hard rock music set to a sardonic essay by Jonathan Swift.

Thériault, Yves, French-Canadian novelist (b. Nov. 28, 1916, Quebec City, Que.—d. Oct. 20, 1983, Montreal?), was one of the most prolific writers in Canada with some 1,300 radio and television scripts and some 50 books to his credit. He was hailed as a literary genius after the publication of *Agaguk* (1958; trans., 1967), a poignant tale about an Eskimo family faced with the white man's code of law. Thériault, who dropped out of school at the age of 15, held a variety of jobs before becoming a writer for the National Film Board (1943–45) and Radio Canada (1945–50). Some of his other works include *Aaron* (1954), which explored the problems faced by a Jewish family in a Gentile world; *Ashini* (1960), a lyrical tale of the last chief of the Montagnais to live by ancestral customs; and *N'Tsuk* (1968), the life story of a 100-year-old Eskimo woman. Thériault's works, which were translated into German, Italian, Portuguese, Japanese, and Spanish, earned him numerous awards and secured his position as a giant in French-Canadian literature.

Thoroddsen, Gunnar, Icelandic politician (b. Dec. 29, 1910, Reykjavik, Iceland—d. Sept. 25, 1983, Reykjavik), was prime minister of Iceland from 1980 to 1983 and leader of a splinter group of the Independence Party in a coalition government that included the People's Alliance (Communist) and Progressive (Farmers') parties. A lawyer who took up politics at the age of 24, he was also professor at the University of Iceland (1940–47) and in 1970 a judge of the Supreme Court. He became minister of finance in 1959 and served as ambassador to Denmark (1965–69) and minister of energy and social affairs (1974–78). He was also vice-president of the Independence Party until 1981.

Travis, Merle, U.S. country singer (b. Nov. 29, 1917, Muhlenberg County, Ky.—d. Oct. 20, 1983, Tahlequah, Okla.), was a versatile and influential music man who earned top honours as a guitarist, as a singer, and as the writer of the song "Sixteen Tons" (1947), which became a hit for Tennessee Ernie Ford in 1955. Travis, who learned the basics of his guitar style from Mose Rager, developed a complex finger style that had a profound influence on other guitarists, especially Chet Atkins. Travis's other hits included "Smoke! Smoke! Smoke! (That Cigarette)," "Divorce Me C.O.D.," "So Round, So Firm, So Fully Packed," "Dark as a Dungeon," and "Double Talking Baby." After serving with the U.S. Marines during World War II, Travis appeared at barn dances before becoming famous in the 1950s on such television shows as "Hometown Jamboree" and "Town Hall Party" and as a guitar-playing sailor in the 1953 Academy Award-winning motion picture *From Here to Eternity*. The multitalented Travis was voted into the Songwriters Hall of Fame in 1970, was awarded the Pioneer of Country Music Award in 1974, and was inducted into the Country Music Association's Hall of Fame in 1977. Three years earlier he had garnered a Grammy award for the duet guitar record "The Atkins-Travis Traveling Show." In 1982 he made an appearance in the Clint Eastwood motion picture *Honky Tonk Man*.

Troisgros, Jean, French chef and restaurateur (b. Dec. 2, 1926, Chalon-sur-Saône, France—d. Aug. 8, 1983, Vittel, France), in partnership with his brother Pierre greatly influenced the development of modern French cuisine. After training in some of the top Paris kitchens, he earned an apprenticeship with Fernand Point. The latter originated what became known as "nouvelle cuisine," a dramatic departure from traditional, rich dishes. During the 1960s and '70s the Troisgros brothers were leading innovators in this new cuisine, which minimizes the use of flour and fat and favours light sauces and the use of fresh, seasonal produce. Their restaurant, Les Frères Troisgros, was established in 1954 in their father's hotel in Roanne. Despite its great success (including a three-star rating in the *Guide Michelin* from 1968), it remained unostentatious and was a favourite venue for local celebrations as well as a must for gourmets from far and wide. Escalope of salmon with sorrel sauce—perhaps the most famous of the many dishes invented by the brothers—was created for a luncheon held in 1975 by French Pres. Valéry Giscard d'Estaing in honour of the Troisgros brothers and other chefs of their generation.

Tunner, William Henry, general (ret.), U.S. Air Force (b. July 14, 1906, Elizabeth, N.J.—d. April 6, 1983, Gloucester, Va.), masterminded three of the 20th century's most extraordinary airlifts, including the 1948–49 Berlin operation, which provided the two million people of West Berlin with 2.3 million tons of food, fuel, and machinery during an 11-month Soviet blockade of the city. Tunner, a 1928 graduate of the U.S. Military Academy, was a brilliant tactician who was adept at facilitating the movement of large quantities of men and matériel by air; for this reason he spent a greater portion of his career in executive posts than in the air. Tunner also commanded the 1943 cargo transport over the Himalayan "Hump" from India to China during World War II and headed the Combat Cargo Command, which in 1950 airlifted supplies to U.S. troops trapped in North Korea by the Chinese. In 1951 he was named deputy commander of Air Material Command, and from 1953 to 1957 he was commander in chief of the U.S. Air Force in Europe. Following these posts he served (1957–58) as deputy chief of staff for operations at U.S. Air Force headquarters in Washington, D.C., and as commander of the Military Air Transport Service (1958–60) before his retirement. Tunner, who was a four-time recipient of the Distinguished Service Medal, was again honoured when Gen. Douglas MacArthur personally awarded him the Distinguished Service Cross for his service during the Korean War.

Tupper, Earl S., U.S. businessman (b. July 28, 1907, Berlin, N.H.—d. Oct. 3, 1983, San José, Costa Rica), was a chemist by profession who became a millionaire as the inventor of an array of plastic food-and-drink containers known as Tupperware. Tupper, who opened a small factory in Massachusetts in 1937, began producing Tupperware in 1942. Five years later his company had grossed more than $5 million and his Tupperware Home Parties had become an American institution. Though Tupper was not the first to hold sales parties in customers' homes, he did use his imagination to add a sense of excitement to the concept. His products, which included cups, canisters, and vegetable storage bins, were revolutionary because they had airtight lids. By 1983 the line of products, which had been expanded to include toys and indoor garden equipment, was being distributed by more than 250,000 Tupperware dealers. In 1958, after making his fortune, Tupper sold his company to the Rexall Drug Co. for more than $9 million. In 1973 he moved to Costa Rica and later became a citizen of that country. In 1982 the 40-year-old company had sales in excess of $800 million.

Ullman, Walter, Austrian-born medieval historian (b. Nov. 29, 1910, Palkau, Austria—d. Jan. 18, 1983, Cambridge, England), was a fellow of Trinity College, University of Cambridge, from 1959 and a professor of medieval history at the university from 1965 to 1978. A man of immense physical and intellectual energy, he made outstanding contributions to the study of ecclesiastical and political history and the relationship between law and government during the Middle Ages. Ullman studied at the Universities of Vienna and Innsbruck and taught for three years at the University of Vienna until the Nazi Anschluss forced his departure for England in 1938. There he joined Ratcliffe College, Leicester, and the University of Leeds before becoming a lecturer at Cambridge in 1949. His doctoral thesis, published as *The Medieval Idea of Law as Represented by Lucas de Penna* (1946), prompted him to investigate medieval political thought and the role of the papacy. His findings were published in *Principles of Government and Politics in the Middle Ages* (1961), *A Short History of the Papacy in the Middle Ages* (1972), and, in what was probably Ullman's most original work, *The Individual and Society in the Middle Ages* (1967). His tireless research efforts produced a stream of books, articles, reviews, and editions of medieval texts.

Umberto II, former king of Italy (b. Sept. 15, 1904, Racconigi, Italy—d. March 18, 1983, Geneva, Switz.), succeeded his father, Victor Emmanuel III, who abdicated the throne in his son's favour on May 9, 1946. However, 12 days after a June 2 referendum in which a narrow majority of Italians (some 54%) voted for a republic, Umberto went into permanent exile in Portugal. Though he enjoyed popularity as a young prince, his career and education, both strictly military, did little to prepare him for the throne. He was a lieutenant in the 1st Regiment of Sardinian Grenadiers, rose to become a general under the Mussolini regime, and enjoyed a reputation as a sportsman rather than as a potential head of state. He was also manipulated by Mussolini, who used Umberto's exalted military position to demonstrate royal support for the alliance with Germany. After the Allies captured Rome in June 1944, Victor Emmanuel appointed Umberto lieutenant general of the realm, but when the opportunity arose in 1946 to distance himself from the Fascist cause, Umberto verbally dissociated the monarchy from the Mussolini regime but, at the same time, did nothing to demonstrate his sympathy for the anti-Fascist resistance. Before the referendum Umberto campaigned for retention of the monarchy, but he failed to win support from the Roman Catholic Church, which declared its neutrality. Under the republican constitution, neither Umberto nor his male descendants were permitted to return to Italy, though at the time of his death the Italian Parliament apparently favoured a revision of the constitutional article concerned.

Van Brocklin, Norm(an) ("DUTCHMAN"), U.S. football player and coach (b. March 15, 1926, Eagle Butte, S.D.—d. May 2, 1983, Atlanta, Ga.), as a feisty quarterback for the Los Angeles Rams (1949–57) and the Philadelphia Eagles (1958–60) professional football teams, played in five NFL championship games (1949, '50, '51, '55, '60), nine Pro Bowls, and climaxed his career in 1960 when he was named the NFL's most valuable player after leading the Eagles in a 17–6 victory over the Green Bay Packers in the NFL championship game. Though Van Brocklin alternated with Bob Waterfield and Billy Wade when he quarterbacked the Rams, he led the NFL three times in passing and in 1951 established a one-game passing record of 554 yd. During his career as a professional player, Van Brocklin completed 1,553 of 2,895 passes (53.6%) for 23,611 yd and 173 touchdowns. After retiring as an active player in 1960, Van Brocklin coached the Minnesota Vikings (1961–67) and the Atlanta Falcons (1968–73) football teams. He was inducted into the Professional Football Hall of Fame in 1971.

Vangsaae, Mona, Danish ballerina (b. April 29, 1920, Copenhagen, Den.—d. May 16, 1983, Copenhagen), became a member of the Royal Danish Ballet in 1938 and was one of its principal dancers from 1942 until her retirement in 1963. She triumphed in the Bournonville ballets presented at Covent Garden in 1953 and in Frederick Ashton's *Romeo and Juliet* (Prokofiev) in Copenhagen and Edinburgh in 1955. Some of her other most successful performances were in *Serenade,* choreographed by George Balanchine (*q.v.*), Léonide Massine's *Old and New,* and Birgit Cullberg's *Moon Reindeer.* After Vangsaae retired as a dancer, she founded a ballet school and in 1971 started a career as a producer for the London Festival Ballet. She collaborated in her teaching with her former husband, Frank Schaufuss, and in production with their son, Peter. Her many contributions to Danish ballet were recognized when she was made a member of the Order of the Dannebrog.

Vorster, Balthazar Johannes, South African politician (b. Dec. 13, 1915, Jamestown, South Africa—d. Sept. 10, 1983, Cape Town, South Africa), was prime minister of South Africa from 1966 to 1978, then president until 1979. He had previously

UPI

earned a reputation for championing tough policies as minister of justice from 1961. As a member of the extreme Nationalist organization Ossewabrandwag, he was expected to prove a repressive and reactionary leader, committed to racialist policies and apartheid. In fact, Vorster was above all a politician and a pragmatist, whose chief aim was the survival of his country, even though he interpreted that term as meaning the white-dominated society from which he came. He achieved a notable improvement in South Africa's relations with other African countries and laid the foundations for a degree of power-sharing with the Coloured community, though he never wavered in his belief in the concept of "separate development" of the races. Vorster studied at Stellenbosch University and practiced law. He was interned during World War II because of his sympathies for the Ossewabrandwag, an Afrikaner movement with Fascist tendencies. Elected to Parliament in 1953, he was a junior education minister before becoming minister of justice. When Hendrick Verwoerd was assassinated in 1966, Vorster succeeded him as prime minister and set about calming the fears of more moderate whites while keeping the support of extreme nationalists. He created the Bureau of State Security in 1969, as a demonstration of his continuing hard line against opposition, and this may have lost him some votes in the 1970 elections, but by 1974 he felt confident enough to open talks with black African leaders. During the next few years Vorster was occupied with the question of Rhodesia (Zimbabwe), and he made clear his position that he would not support a last-ditch stand by the white minority. In South West Africa/Namibia, too, he declared support in principle for Namibian independence. Though some African leaders responded to his overtures, South Africa continued to face international hostility, and the 1976 Soweto riots showed the desperation of the country's blacks. In 1978 Vorster resigned on the grounds of ill health shortly before the revelation of irregularities involving his information minister, Connie Mulder. What became known as the "Muldergate affair" eventually forced his resignation from the presidency and overshadowed his final years. He also expressed increasing opposition to his successor's plans for power-sharing with the Asian community, which went further than he had intended.

Wallenstein, Alfred Franz, U.S. conductor (b. Oct. 7, 1898, Chicago, Ill.—d. Feb. 8, 1983, New York, N.Y.), was principal cellist with the Chicago Symphony Orchestra (1922–29) and with the New York Philharmonic (1929–36) before becoming the first U.S.-born and U.S.-trained musician to conduct major symphony orchestras. As music director of the Mutual Network's radio station WOR from 1935 to 1945, Wallenstein was instrumental in bringing classical music to the airwaves. In 1943 he was appointed director of the Los Angeles Philharmonic, and during his 13-year tenure he built the orchestra into one of the nation's leading ensembles. After he left the Los Angeles Philharmonic, Wallenstein served as music director of the Caramoor Festival from 1958 to 1961, conductor of the Symphony of the Air, and guest conductor of major orchestras in Europe and the U.S. In 1968 he joined the faculty of the Juilliard School and in 1979 made his last conducting appearance with the Juilliard Orchestra.

Walton, Sir William Turner, British composer (b. March 29, 1902, Oldham, England—d. March 8, 1983, Ischia, Italy), developed an individual style in the manner of the late-19th-century composers that nonetheless betrayed an essentially English temperament. Walton wrote two well-known coronation marches, but it was for his First Symphony (1935) and his choral work *Belshazzar's Feast* (1931) that he became known as one of the most dominant figures in British music. His formal training was as a choirboy and later as an undergraduate at Christ Church, Oxford. Though he never graduated, Walton nonetheless achieved success with the music for Edith Sitwell's poems in *Façade,* first performed in 1923. Three years later his overture *Portsmouth Point* was performed in Zürich, and he began to establish an international reputation. Walton acknowledged few foreign influences, however, and composed sparingly, refining his style and his technique. His one ballet, *The Quest,* was written in 1943, and in 1954 he composed the opera *Troilus and Cressida,* one of his major works, performed first at Covent Garden in London, then at La Scala, Milan. Meanwhile, he achieved wider popular fame as the composer of stirring music for the film *First of the Few* (1942) and then of scores for Laurence Olivier's three Shakespearean films, *Henry V* (1944), *Hamlet* (1948), and *Richard III* (1955). His Second Symphony was completed in 1960, and his other works included song sequences and concerti for viola, violin, and piano. From the early 1950s he lived on the Italian island of Ischia, which he rarely left, but in 1982 he visited London for the celebration of his 80th birthday.

Ward, Theodore, U.S. playwright (b. Sept 15, 1902, Thibodaux, La.—d. May 8, 1983, Chicago, Ill.), as the distinguished author of such critically acclaimed works as *Big White Fog* (1940) and *Our Lan'* (1947), made important contributions to Afro-American literature with his poignant portrayals of black families striving to overcome racial oppression during Reconstruction in the U.S. Ward, who launched his writing career with *Sick and Tired,* worked for one of the "Negro Units" of the Works Progress Administration's Federal Theater projects in Chicago. He was a recipient of both a Rockefeller and a Guggenheim fellowship. Finding that there was little support for black theatre in New York City, he helped to found the Negro Playwrights Company there. Although many of his 31 plays were never produced, his works were highly successful in establishing American heroes for blacks.

Waterfield, Robert S. ("RIFLE"), U.S. football player (b. 1920, New York, N.Y.—d. March 25, 1983, Burbank, Calif.), was a phenomenal quarterback for UCLA (1941, 1942, 1944) and for the Cleveland (later Los Angeles) Rams professional football team (1945–52). A consummate all-around player, he also served as placekicker, punter, and defensive back. In 1945 Waterfield became the first rookie in National Football League history to lead his team to a world championship; he was also voted most valuable player that year. The following year Waterfield led the NFL passers with 127 completions in 251 attempts for 1,747 yd and 18 touchdowns, and in 1951 he regained his crown as NFL passing leader with 88 completions in 176 attempts for 1,566 yd and 13 touchdowns. Waterfield also became the 1947, 1949, and 1951 field goal leader and in 1965 was inducted into the Professional Football Hall of Fame. He was married to actress Jane Russell from 1943 to 1968.

Waters, Muddy (MCKINLEY MORGANFIELD), U.S. blues guitarist (b. April 4, 1915, Rolling Fork, Miss.—d. April 30, 1983, Westmont, Ill.), as the undisputed king of the "Chicago sound," influenced a generation of U.S. and British rock bands with his raw yet vibrant Mississippi Delta blues. Waters, a seminal figure in the development of blues, was inspired by Son House and Robert Johnson, two masters of bottleneck-guitar playing. Waters was a self-taught harmonica player, a compelling guitarist, and a legendary singer of such blues favourites as "Hoochie Coochie Man" and "Got My Mojo Working," a blues-rock standard. Early in the 1940s Alan Lomax and John Work traveled throughout the South recording traditional musicians for the Library of Congress. They taped Waters's rough, unamplified style of country blues, but after he went to Chicago in 1943, he electrically amplified his blues and started making recordings for Chess Records. During the 1950s Waters led the first electric blues-rock band; it served as an impetus to Jimi Hendrix and the Rolling Stones, who derived their name from Waters's hit song "Rollin' Stone." Though Waters never achieved the riches that flowed to the bands he inspired, he was nonetheless revered for his contributions to contemporary music. Some of his other hit songs include "You're Gonna Miss Me When I'm Dead," "I Feel Like Going Home," and "I Can't Be Satisfied."

West, Dame Rebecca (CICILY ISABEL ANDREWS, née FAIRFIELD), British journalist (b. Dec. 21, 1892, London, England—d. March 15, 1983, London), used her sharp wit and astute mind to capture the cultural and political climate of the times in her novels but was probably best known for her reports on the Nuremberg trials of war criminals (1945–46), notably the trial for treason of the Nazi propagandist William Joyce ("Lord Haw-Haw") for *The New Yorker* magazine. Though West was trained for the stage, she abandoned acting and became a leading suffragette. At the age of 19 she worked for *Freewoman,* contributing political commentary and literary criticism to other periodicals as well. It was at this time that she assumed the name of the heroine of Ibsen's *Rosmersholm.* Shortly after West was sent to interview H. G. Wells, they began an affair that had a profound influence on her outlook and resulted in the birth (1914) of a son, Anthony (who later became an author and critic). In 1918 she published her first novel, *The Return of the Soldier.* This and other works of fiction, though not of the very highest rank, were marked by considerable craftsmanship and intellectual penetration. While devoting most of her time to reporting in the 1930s, she continued to write novels. Her best, *The Fountain Overflows* (1957), appeared after a long gap between

WIDE WORLD

works. Her journeys to Serbia with her husband produced the masterly two-volume *Black Lamb and Grey Falcon* (1942), an examination of Balkan politics, culture, and history. Her reports on the Nuremberg trials led to the publication of *The Meaning of Treason* (1949), the first of a series of works that analyzed the motives for disloyalty, the character of traitors, and their relationship to the state. This subject held a lasting fascination for West, who later published *The New Meaning of Treason* (1964). Her other works include *The Court and the Castle* (1958) and a final novel, *The Birds Fall Down* (1966). She was made Chevalier of the Legion of Honour in 1957, Dame Commander of the Order of the British Empire in 1959, and Companion of Literature in 1968. The collection *Rebecca West: A Celebration; Selections from Her Writings by Her Publishers with Her Help* appeared in 1977.

Wigg, George Edward Cecil Wigg, Baron, British politician (b. Nov. 28, 1900, London, England—d. Aug. 11, 1983, London), reached the height of his parliamentary career in the mid-1960s when he acted as close adviser to Harold Wilson during Wilson's first Labour Party government. It was Wigg who in 1963 brought details of the liaison between John Profumo, then secretary of state for war, and Christine Keeler to the notice of Labour Party chiefs and to the world, thus breaking a scandal that almost destroyed Harold Macmillan's Conservative government. When, the following year, a Labour Party government came to power, Wigg was appointed paymaster general, a position that left his powers undefined. In this post he acted as confidential aide to Wilson on matters of security and defense and shared Wilson's extreme concern about leaks to the press, particularly those that involved military information. Wigg's commitment to army affairs was longstanding; born the son of an army officer, he joined the Tank Corps in 1919 after four years spent working in a factory and remained in the Army with only one short break until the end of World War II. When he began his parliamentary career in 1945, he brought with him a passion for the services and a barracks-room approach to Westminster debating. He was a Labour Party whip during the years 1951–54 and a tireless worrier of the Conservative government from the opposition benches. An early supporter of Wilson, he managed his campaign for the party leadership in 1963. Wigg retired from the government in 1967 when he was appointed chairman of the Horserace Betting Levy Board; the turf had been another of his great interests for many years. In the same year he was created a life peer. His autobiography, *George Wigg*, was published in 1972.

Williams, Tennessee (Thomas Lanier Williams), U.S. playwright (b. March 26, 1911, Columbus, Miss.—d. Feb. 25, 1983, New York, N.Y.), was a penetrating dramatist whose best plays reveal tortured human relationships set against a backdrop of sex and violence, yet tempered by an atmosphere of romantic gentility. Williams, who was acknowledged as the greatest American playwright after Eugene O'Neill, was the poet laureate of the outcast. His most important plays, which delve into such taboo subjects as homosexuality, nymphomania, castration, and cannibalism, include *The Glass Menagerie, A Streetcar Named Desire, Summer and Smoke, The Rose Tattoo, Cat on a Hot Tin Roof, Sweet Bird of Youth,* and *The Night of the Iguana.*

Williams, who was brought up by an overprotective, puritanical mother, was also the son of a gruff shoe salesman whom the young Williams despised. His older sister, Rose, underwent a prefrontal lobotomy after being diagnosed schizophrenic; he also had a younger brother, Dakin. Williams began writing plays while attending the University of Missouri at Columbia and Washington University, St. Louis, Mo. The Depression forced him to leave school and work in a shoe factory, a two-year stint that ended when he suffered a nervous breakdown. A year after graduating (1938) from the University of Iowa, Williams left home at age 28 and adopted the name Tennessee. In 1939 his career as a playwright was launched when he won a Group Theatre award for

JESSE A. FERNANDEZ—KEYSTONE

American Blues, a collection of one-act plays, but it was not until 1944, when the highly autobiographical *The Glass Menagerie* opened in Chicago and later on Broadway, that Williams established his reputation. *The Glass Menagerie,* which won the New York Drama Critics' Circle Award for the 1944–45 season, concerns the inability of the domineering mother, Amanda, and her cynical son, Tom, to secure a proper suitor for Tom's crippled sister, Laura, who lives in a fantasy world of glass animals. Williams's next hit was *A Streetcar Named Desire* (1947), the Pulitzer Prize-winning play about Blanche DuBois, a Southern belle driven mad and destroyed by her brutish brother-in-law, Stanley Kowalski. Williams's controversial fantasy play *Camino Real* (1953) was followed by *Cat on a Hot Tin Roof* (1955), which explores the explosive relationship between Big Daddy and his son Brick. The play earned Williams a second Pulitzer Prize and another Critics' Circle Award. In his writing Williams, who was brought up in a puritanical environment, tried to outrage that puritanism and effectively did so in such plays as *Suddenly Last Summer* (1958), dealing with lobotomy, pederasty, and cannibalism, and *Sweet Bird of Youth* (1959), which culminates in the castration of a gigolo who has infected a Southern belle with a venereal disease. Williams's last major hit was *The Night of the Iguana* (1961), for which he won a Critics' Circle Award. His later works were regarded as repetitious by critics, and for the remainder of his life Williams was plagued by alcohol and drug addiction. In 1969 he suffered a serious mental and physical breakdown, but his genius was preserved in the revival of his plays and the adaptation of his plays to motion pictures. His last play to appear on Broadway, *Clothes for a Summer Hotel,* was a failure, and his last play, *A House Not Meant to Stand,* was presented at the Goodman Theatre in Chicago in 1982. Williams, who was a hypochondriac obsessed with sickness, failure, and death, choked to death on a plastic bottle cap from either a nasal spray or container of eye solution.

Wilson, Dennis, U.S. drummer and singer (b. Dec. 4, 1944, Hawthorne, Calif.—d. Dec. 28, 1983, Marina del Rey, Calif.), together with his brothers Brian and Carl, cousin Mike Love, and Al Jardine, comprised the rock and roll band the Beach Boys, who rode the wave of success for 20 years with upbeat songs that glorified the utopia of suburban California and the joys of surfing and cars. Dennis, who was the only member of the group actually to surf, formed the group (originally known as Carl and the Passions and later as Kenny and the Cadets) with his brothers, Love, and Jardine when he was 17. The Beach Boys became an international sensation in 1961 when they emerged with "Surfin'," followed by "Surfin' Safari," "Surfin' U.S.A.," and an album, "Surfer Girl," all of which ushered in the surfing culture. The Beach Boys, who released 35 albums (15 of which sold more than one million copies), later produced more sophisticated songs including "Good Vibrations" and "I Can Hear Music" but were best remembered for their early 1960s hits. Dennis was the only member of the group to produce a solo album, and he also made a cameo appearance in the motion picture *Two-Lane Blacktop.* He drowned after diving off a slip at Marina del Rey.

Wincott, Leonard, British-born Soviet writer and translator (b. 1906?, Leicester, England—d. Jan 18, 1983, Moscow, U.S.S.R.), played a leading role in the 1931 Invergordon mutiny, a rebellion against a 25% pay cut by naval ratings (enlisted men) in the Royal Navy's Atlantic fleet. In his book *Invergordon Mutineer* (1974), Wincott described his role in inspiring the uprising, which caused a crisis in the Royal Navy and the British government and led to the discharge of 997 men, including Wincott. He then joined the Communist Party and went to the Soviet Union. There he worked in a seamen's club, in a factory, and as a teacher until the outbreak of World War II. He was in air defense in Leningrad during the German siege and gained the Leningrad Defense Medal in recognition of his services. However, he was charged with spying for Britain before receiving the award and was sent for ten years to a labour camp. After Stalin's death Wincott was released, became a Soviet citizen, and worked as a translator and writer. He returned to Britain in 1974 on a temporary visa.

Yang Yong (Yang Yung), Chinese military leader (b. 1906, Liuyang County, Hunan Province, China—d. Jan. 6, 1983, Beijing [Peking], China), established his credentials as a dedicated Communist by joining Mao Zedong (Mao Tse-tung) and others in the arduous 10,000-km (6,000-mi) Long March (1934–35) from southern China to a sanctuary in the northwest. Relatively few survived the hardships of the trek and the relentless attacks by Chiang Kai-shek's Kuomintang (KMT) army. Following Japan's defeat in World War II, Yang's troops engaged the KMT army in southern China until Chiang Kai-shek was decisively defeated and the People's Republic formally established in 1949. Yang then became governor of Guizhou (Kweichow) Province. In the early 1950s he successively headed the Second Senior Infantry School and the 20th Army Corps before becoming deputy commander of the so-called Chinese People's Volunteers, who joined North Koreans in their battle against UN forces defending South Korea. In 1959 Yang was named commander of the Beijing Military Region and Beijing-Tianjin (Tientsin) Garrison; not long after that he became deputy chief of staff of the People's Liberation Army (PLA). In 1967, during the Cultural Revolution, he was purged along with other top military leaders, but by 1973 he was deemed politically fit to command the Xinjiang (Sinkiang) Military Region. He later became senior deputy chief of staff of the PLA and in 1979, as a member of the Military Commission, headed a delegation to Great Britain.

Young, Claude ("Buddy"), U.S. football player (b. Jan. 5, 1926, Chicago, Ill.—d. Sept. 4, 1983, near Terrell, Texas), was a star running back with the New York Yankees, the Dallas Texans, and the Baltimore Colts professional football teams. His success seemed even more spectacular because Young was 5 ft 4 in tall and weighed 172 lb. During his professional career (1947–55) Young rushed for 2,727 yd on 597 carries and scored 17 touchdowns; he also caught 179 passes for 2,711 yd and 21 touchdowns. Earlier Young was an all-American running back at the University of Illinois, where in 1944 he tied the school record (held by Red Grange) for touchdowns in a season with 13. In 1964 Young was named director of player relations for the National Football League and in 1968 was elected to the Professional Football Hall of Fame. He was killed in an automobile accident while en route to the airport in Dallas. The previous day Young had been the league's representative at a memorial service for Joe Delaney, a star running back with the Kansas City Chiefs.

ARTICLES FROM THE 1984 PRINTING OF THE BRITANNICA

Two of the Macropaedia articles presented here, Cancer *and* Solar System, *were entirely rewritten for the 1984 printing of* Encyclopædia Britannica, *and one,* Instrumentation, *was substantially revised and updated; its new material appears in excerpt form. Together, they reflect the unceasing pressure of science and technology against new boundaries of knowledge. New knowledge about cancer and about our solar system have demanded new kinds of medical and astronomical instrumentation, and the resulting progress in instrumentation has opened still new discoveries in both fields. The articles appear in alphabetical order.*

Cancer

Cancer in humans is a complex of diseases characterized by uncontrolled multiplication and disorganized growth of the affected cells; it may arise in any of the body's tissues. Cancer cells infiltrate and destroy adjacent tissues, eventually gain access to the circulatory system, are transported to distant parts of the body, and ultimately destroy the host. Concomitant with their capacity for unrestrained growth, cancer cells and the tissues they constitute lose their normal appearance, as viewed through a microscope, and assume aberrant functions.

Not all abnormal growths are malignant; those that are not are referred to as benign tumours. In contrast to malignant growths, benign tumours consist of an orderly growth of cells that often are identical to or very closely resemble their normal counterparts. They are not aggressive and do not invade surrounding tissues, spread to distant sites, or kill the host.

Cancer was known in antiquity. Malignant tumours have been found in Egyptian and Pre-Columbian mummies, about 5,000 and 2,400 years old, respectively. They are documented in ancient medical writings, such as the Edwin Smith and Ebers papyruses, both written about 3,500 years ago. Cancer is also seen in other species, such as domestic animals, birds, reptiles, and fishes.

Incidence and mortality

Statistics of cancer incidence and mortality show striking geographic differences, varying significantly from country to country; and within countries differences occur between the sexes, various ethnic groups, and various occupations. Epidemiologic analysis of such statistics continues to provide valuable clues and insights into the myriad factors that appear to be involved in the causation of cancer.

CAUSES

It is now known that cancer can be caused by a variety of factors acting either singly or in concert. These include a wide variety of chemical substances, various types of ionizing radiation, and various classes of viruses. This knowledge has accrued from a composite of epidemiologic studies of cancer in humans and from experimental studies in the laboratory. Although much is known about how cancer is caused, the precise mechanism or group of mechanisms involved continues to elude researchers.

Chemicals. Chemicals numbering in the hundreds are known to induce cancer in laboratory animals, and some of these have also been shown to be carcinogenic for humans. While it is well established that long exposure to certain chemicals gives rise to cancer in humans, it is most difficult to determine accurately what proportion of human cancer is due to such exposure. The difficulty arises from the fact that the length of time between exposure and the appearance of cancer is usually prolonged, lasting some 20–30 years; that exposure is more often than not to a variety of chemicals, so that identifying the carcinogen may be difficult, if not impossible; and that carcinogenesis, *i.e.*, the induction and development of cancer, is a process that involves many factors and many phases.

Experiments on laboratory animals have established that the majority of carcinogenic chemicals are not capable of inducing cancer in their original form. Chemical carcinogens are toxic compounds that are foreign to the host. Once they gain entrance into the body by ingestion, inhalation, or absorption, they are modified by metabolic processes in the host's tissues to forms that are less toxic and water-soluble. The modification is an attempt by the host to detoxify the foreign chemicals and eliminate them. As in most cases, however, this protective property is not foolproof, and in the process of detoxification certain forms of the carcinogen may arise that are even more toxic than the parent compound. In this instance the host renders a less toxic compound into one that causes injury to its cells and may eventually cause them to become cancerous. Highly reactive forms of such chemicals interact with vital macromolecules in the host's cells, causing them to be chemically altered. It is believed that when deoxyribonucleic acid (DNA), the genetic material of cells, is so altered that its expression is accompanied by uncontrolled growth, the cell undergoes a transformation that eventually leads to the development of cancer.

DNA appears to be the most probable macromolecule whose alteration leads to cancer, because once cells become malignant their transformed behaviour is passed on to subsequent cell generations, indicating that it is a heritable change. There is evidence, however, that alterations of nongenetic macromolecules capable of regulating cell growth may also be involved.

The alteration of DNA is one phase of carcinogenesis. The second phase is a prolonged one during which the genetically altered cell loses its ability to grow in a regulated fashion. During this phase the altered cell, not yet expressing its malignant potential, apparently is influenced by other factors, including noncarcinogenic chemicals; dietary components, such as fat; or substances produced by the host, such as hormones. Since this phase is prolonged and subject to manipulation, it is a major focus of contemporary cancer research; it is hoped that persons at high risk of developing cancer (presumably with cells genetically altered by a chemical, but not yet cancerous) may be treated to prevent overt cancer from developing. Certain chemical substances, such as antioxidants and vitamin A, are particularly promising in this regard.

Despite the fact that cancer is a prevalent disease in modern society, quantitative experimental evidence in animals suggests that, following the exposure of cells to a carcinogenic chemical, the ultimate development of cancer is a relatively rare event. This is no doubt due to the fact that some genetic mutations lead to the death of the affected cells, so that no cancer can develop. A second, more important, reason is due to the ability of cells to "repair" altered or damaged DNA. In this process the segments of damaged DNA are excised, and identical single strands of the required segments are synthesized; these are then spliced into the defect, reestablishing its continuity. If the synthesis has accurately copied the DNA segment as it was prior to damage, there will be no adverse effects. If, on the other hand, the repair process is defective, so that cell replication occurs before the damage is repaired, the altered DNA is copied and the damage is amplified. When such cells undergo division the genetic defect is passed on to their descendants.

Occupational chemicals. Numerous carcinogenic chemical hazards have been identified in a variety of industries. These include polycyclic hydrocarbons present in coal tar and its derivatives, such as pitch, tar oils, and creosote, and in products of the combustion and distillation of coal, oil, shale, lignite, and petroleum. In the past skin cancer took the lives of many long-time workers in these industries. Fumes inhaled by workers during coke-oven operations and in the fogs, mists, and sprays of various oils encountered in refineries have been associated with high incidences of lung cancer. Benzene, a product of coal-tar distillation, may affect blood-forming tissues and is suspected of being a carcinogen capable of inducing leukemia. Various metals have been implicated as carcinogens for the lung and several other body sites among copper-ore miners and smelters of nickel and cobalt ores. Beta-naphthylamine, a chemical once widely used in the manufacture of aniline dyes, has been shown to be a carcinogen for the urinary bladder.

Asbestos and lung cancer

Asbestos has been established as a carcinogen for the lung and for the mesothelium (membrane) that lines body cavities. Workers chronically exposed to dust containing asbestos fibres have an incidence of lung cancer 10 times the normal rate. (It is noteworthy that the risk of cancer is increased 90-fold in asbestos workers if they also smoke. This is an excellent example of two agents acting synergistically to induce cancer at a higher incidence and often in a shorter time than either agent does alone.) Although a serious and sustained effort has been made to monitor and reduce industrial exposure to asbestos in many countries, in some parts of the world occupational pollution remains a serious problem.

Environmental chemicals and pollution. The environment, which includes the atmosphere, land, seas, lakes, and rivers, reflects the activities of society. Environmental pollutants include the myriad effluents of daily living, industrial as well as naturally occurring. Among the greatest atmospheric pollutants are the gaseous and particulate emissions that range from the massive outputs of industry and motor transport, measuring millions of tons annually, to individual puffs of cigarette smoke.

Smoking and cancer

Cigarette smoke has been shown to contain numerous compounds that are known to cause cancer in experimental animals and that appear to be strongly linked to human cancer, especially lung cancer. In addition, tobacco smoke has been implicated in the causation of cancer of the mouth, and to a lesser extent the esophagus, pancreas, biliary system, and urinary bladder. Cigarette smoke also has been shown to contain a number of cocarcinogens, substances that appear to enhance the effect of carcinogens when administered concomitantly.

Increasing evidence has accrued to suggest that the release of polychlorinated hydrocarbons and certain insecticides into the environment may pose a carcinogenic hazard. Some of these compounds have enjoyed such widespread use that significant areas of land and bodies of water have been contaminated.

The effect of environmental pollution can best be illustrated by describing the phenomenon of bioconcentration and its impact on the food chain. Widely used chemical substances, such as certain classes of insecticides, which metabolically degrade very slowly and are highly soluble in fat, are a case in point. After being applied on land for agricultural uses, such compounds are washed by rains into streams, rivers, and lakes, where they are ingested by microscopic life forms, which serve as food for fish that are, in turn, the major food source for larger fish and aquatic birds. Since these compounds are soluble in fat, after being ingested by an animal they are stored and concentrated in the animal's body fat. Repeated feeding eventually leads to high concentrations of the compounds in the animal's body, so that its subsequent ingestion by a larger predator, perhaps by humans, presents the predator with a significant level of the compound.

Food additives and cancer

Food additives are another source of environmental chemicals that has caused concern. Although these have been the object of dispute and have given rise to the "natural food" fad, there is no evidence that food additives cause human cancer. In fact, some food additives, especially those that protect foods from becoming rancid, have been shown to prevent chemically induced cancer in experimental animals. An additive that remains a matter of concern, however, is sodium nitrite, which is widely used to preserve processed meats. It has been shown that nitrite can react in the stomach with amines, which arise from the digestion of meat, to form nitrosamines, which are potent carcinogens for certain laboratory animals. These compounds are formed in such minute amounts in the stomach that some researchers doubt that they pose a significant carcinogenic hazard for humans. Similarly, the demonstration that certain compounds formed by the burning of meat are carcinogenic for animals must be placed in proper perspective. Carcinogenesis experiments in animals usually require continuous exposure to high levels of chemicals to obtain statistically valid results in their relatively short life span of a year or two; extrapolation of these results to the effect on human health should be approached most carefully.

Problems of greater importance are the naturally occurring carcinogens, which constitute an important hazard in certain environments. One of these, aflatoxin, is formed by *Aspergillus flavus*, a mold that is widely distributed and is a frequent contaminant of improperly stored nuts, grains, meals, and certain other foods. In certain areas of Africa, for example, the high incidence of liver cancer in humans appears to coincide with their ingestion of foods highly contaminated with aflatoxin. Such correlations must be interpreted conservatively, however, since these populations are also often plagued by viral hepatitis B, which also has been linked to liver cancer.

Radiation. The carcinogenic effects of ionizing radiation first became apparent at the turn of the 20th century with reports of cancer of the skin in physicians who pioneered the application of X-rays and radium to medicine. Since then it has been well established that ionizing radiations of all forms, including ultraviolet light, are carcinogenic.

Occupational radiation. Numerous examples of radiation carcinogenesis have been documented in occupational settings. Well known among these were women who developed bone cancer as a consequence of the chronic ingestion of radium salts that resulted from licking brushes to a fine point while painting luminous watch dials. Following ingestion, radium is deposited in the mineral component of bones. Another notable example is uranium mine workers, who develop lung cancer to a significantly higher degree than the general population. The cause has been traced to the inhalation of the radioactive gas radon, released from trace amounts of radium in uranium ore.

Sunlight and cancer

Environmental radiation. The environment contains three major natural sources of radiation: radioactive elements in mineral deposits, ultraviolet light from the Sun, and cosmic rays. The carcinogenic potential of radioactive elements and ultraviolet light has been established, while that of highly energetic cosmic radiation remains to be documented. Clearly, chronic exposure to intense sunlight is a major cause of skin cancer in humans; incidence is high in farmers, sailors, and habitual sunbathers. Since the most effective natural screen for ultraviolet light is the natural skin pigment, melanin, individuals with large amounts of melanin—blacks, for example—are resistant to the carcinogenic effects of ultraviolet light. Fair-complexioned people, on the other hand, are quite susceptible. It is important to point out that the term skin cancer, as it is generally used, includes not only malignant tumours of the nonpigmented cells of the skin but also tumours of the pigmented cells (melanoma).

The environment also contains dangerous ionizing radiation from artificial sources. These include X-rays used for medical diagnosis and therapy, radioactive chemicals, radioactive elements used in atomic reactors, and radioactive fallout arising from the testing of nuclear devices. Home appliances have been known to emit potentially harmful X-rays under certain circumstances, as was the case with some colour television sets made during the 1950s. Radiation leaks from improperly constructed or operated microwave ovens can also occur, but the health hazards from such exposures have yet to be established.

Certain medical applications of X-rays, such as those used to establish the size and position of a fetus before birth and to control acne, have been largely abandoned because of the increased risk of cancer. Modern technology has greatly reduced the risk of diagnostic X-rays, however. During therapeutic X-irradiation for the treatment of cancer, great care is taken to focus radiation on the tumour and to shield the adjacent normal body tissues from undue exposure. Laboratory workers who use radioactive chemicals are careful to prevent undue exposure by contamination and to dispose of radioactive wastes properly. The cancer risk from radioactive fallout resulting from the testing of atomic devices is virtually impossible to establish with certainty because of the large geographic areas affected. In general, such exposure is low, and immediate effects are probably not of high significance. The absorption by growing crops and farm animals of long-lived radioactive isotopes, such as strontium, from fallout may pose a threat to humans, however.

Viruses. Numerous viruses have been identified that can induce cancer in every major class of vertebrates, including lower vertebrates such as fish. The evidence for the viral causation of cancer in humans long remained strong but only circumstantial; it is now clear, however, that Burkitt's lymphoma, nasopharyngeal cancer, and T-cell leukemia are almost surely caused by viruses.

Oncogenic (cancer-causing) viruses are classified according to the type of nucleic acid they contain. A common feature of oncogenic viruses is that they induce malignant transformation of target cells, which, upon transplantation into suitable animal hosts, exhibit true autonomous growth, local invasion, and metastases to distant sites. Another common feature is physical integration of virus-specific genetic material in the DNA of the host cells. In the case of DNA tumour viruses, the viral genes are integrated directly, whereas with ribonucleic acid (RNA) viruses the RNA is first transcribed into DNA, which is then integrated. Furthermore, RNA tumour viruses are frequently replicated by the cells they transform, while DNA tumour viruses are not. The complexities of tumour viruses are such that progress to establish cause and effect has been quite difficult. The following viruses are strongly suspected of being oncogenic for humans.

Herpes-type viruses. A herpesvirus has been found to be closely associated with two cancers in humans: Burkitt's lymphoma, a malignant tumour of lymphatic tissue first described in children in East and Central Africa; and nasopharyngeal carcinoma, a squamous-cell carcinoma of the posterior part of the nasal cavity, which occurs in high incidence in Chinese originating from South China. Biopsies from both tumours grown in culture gave rise to cell lines in which a DNA virus of the herpes class was identified; it was named the Epstein-Barr (EB) virus. Patients with either type of cancer have high levels of antibody directed against EB virus, indicating that they have encountered the virus and responded to it. Human blood lymphocytes also can be transformed in culture by EB virus.

Burkitt's lymphoma

A second herpesvirus that is becoming increasingly suspect as a human oncogen is the herpes simplex virus type 2 (HSV-2), a close relative of the virus that causes the common fever blister. The epidemiology of squamous-cell cancer of the uterine cervix is entirely consistent with the possibility that it may be caused by an agent that is transmitted during sexual intercourse. Evidence has shown that a woman who develops a herpes infection of the cervix is at an increased risk to develop cervical cancer, and women with cervical cancer often have high levels of HSV-2 antibody. The experimental application of radioactive probes of antibodies to specific viral proteins and to components of the viral genome have localized either the integrated genome or the viral antigens of HSV-2 in the cells of cervical cancer in women. Although this cannot be taken as unequivocal evidence that the virus is indeed a causal agent, it does strengthen the suspicion.

Herpes simplex virus type 2 and cancer

Although the implication of virus as a cause of human cancer has been largely circumstantial, it appears that in one human cancer, thymus-derived (T-cell) leukemia–lymphoma, the evidence is quite impressive. These tumours, which appear to be localized to the southernmost island of Japan and the West Indian population in the Caribbean, have been shown by seroepidemiologic studies possibly to have an infectious basis. Furthermore, an RNA virus, human T-cell leukemia virus (HTLV), appears to be present in patients with T-cell leukemia and can be isolated from their tumours with reasonable reproducibility. Finally, infection of normal blood T lymphocytes in culture by HTLV leads to their uncontrolled growth.

Infection with hepatitis B virus (HBV) is endemic in populations that also have a high incidence of liver cancer. This has led some researchers to conclude that the virus is the cause of liver cancer. As noted earlier, however, cancer is a multifactorial disease, and liver cell cancer is an excellent example. HBV infection invariably leads to the augmented growth of liver cells, which renders them exquisitely sensitive to the effects of carcinogens. Since populations plagued by a high incidence of liver cancer are also chronically exposed to numerous toxic substances, some of which are carcinogenic for the liver, it is difficult to dissect the interactions of virus and carcinogen with sufficient precision to either indict or exonerate HBV.

Oncogenes. Progress in tumour genetics and molecular biology may lead to a clearer understanding of how cells undergo malignant transformation. As stated earlier, RNA tumour viruses invariably integrate their DNA into the host's DNA. Cells of numerous vertebrate species, including humans, have such integrated DNA in their genes. The conservation of such genes throughout so many diverse species suggests that they probably serve an important role in cells, perhaps in growth regulation. The fact that such genes are almost ubiquitous in their distribution and apparently are simply not expressed in normal cells led to the oncogene hypothesis, which suggests that silent (unexpressed) oncogenes, or genes capable of inducing cancer, can, upon proper stimulation, become expressed and thus cause a previously normal cell to become malignant. Oncogenes have been found in chromosome 8 in Burkitt's lymphoma cells and in a variety of other human tumours. Introduction of such oncogenes in DNA from human tumours into normal cells in culture causes the normal cells to become transformed and behave like cancer cells. Activation of an oncogene in a human tumour has been shown to be accompanied by a minor change in its chemical structure. This suggests that silent oncogenes may be activated by chemicals, radiation, and viruses, all of which are known to alter DNA and to cause cancer. The oncogene may be the common denominator through which such diverse agents act.

Genetic factors. The common cancers of humans are not generally inherited, although some families show an incidence of a particular cancer beyond expectations. When leukemia develops in one of a pair of identical twins, the other twin also develops leukemia in about 15 percent of the cases. Among fraternal twins this happens less than 1 percent of the time. Some familial tendencies have also been observed for cancer of the breast, uterus, prostate, stomach, colon–rectum, lung, and other organs and tissues, although the hereditary effect is not strong. It is possible that familial tendencies reflect common environmental relationships or an environmental factor superimposed on a genetic one.

Leukemia in twins

Pheochromocytoma, a rare cancer of the adrenal gland, and carcinoma of the thyroid medulla (the inner portion of the thyroid) sometimes occur in various members of the same family. Either both tumours or only one may occur. Xeroderma pigmentosum, an inherited, abnormal sensitivity of the skin to ultraviolet radiation, almost always leads to skin cancers. The sensitivity is due to an inherited defect in the ability of cells to repair DNA that has been damaged by ultraviolet light.

Children with Down's syndrome, or mongolism, a disorder associated with an extra chromosome in each cell, have a much increased likelihood of developing leukemia. Persons with Fanconi's aplastic anemia (in which all types of blood cells are abnormally few and the bone marrow is not fully developed) and some other rare syndromes characterized by greatly increased chromosome breakages also have an increased risk of leukemia.

There is increasing evidence that genetic alterations are involved in the causation of cancer, and that these can be either inherited or induced and involve either a minute point in a strand of DNA or a major rearrangement of a chromosome.

Trauma and infection. Repeated trauma (injury) or irritation has been associated with some cancers. Ill-fitting dentures associated with cancer of the mouth and chronic infection of the uterine cervix associated with cervical cancer are examples. In each instance it must be remembered that injury and infection are invariably followed by healing, which involves increased local growth of host cells in the affected tissues, and such cells are quite sensitive to carcinogenic factors. There is no scientific basis to support the notion that trauma alone is a carcinogenic stimulus.

THE SPREAD OF CANCER

The ability of certain cancers to spread from their sites of origin, rendering their treatment and eradication difficult, is the major reason for the sense of hopelessness that is closely associated with them. If it were not for this ability to spread, most cancer could be successfully treated.

The spread of cancer results from either or both of two processes: cancer cells may spread by direct extension from the primary site as a consequence of growth and tumour cell movement invading the surrounding normal tissues, or they may enter the vascular system by invading lymphatics or blood vessels and be transported to sites distant from the primary site.

Direct extension. The ability of a localized focus of cancer to spread into adjacent tissues is dependent upon its interaction with surrounding adjacent tissue. Research has shown that experimental and some human cancers with a high incidence of spread contain enzymes capable of digesting elements of the surrounding normal connective tissues. This allows cancer cells to migrate through the connective tissues, which normally serve as a barrier. Once invasion by local extension has occurred, the opportunity for successful therapy is diminished.

Metastasis. Metastasis is the process by which cancer cells are spread to sites distant from the primary tumour. The process requires that the cancer cells enter the vascular system, which includes lymphatics, veins, and arteries. Once they are within the system, the cancer cells are transported passively to distant sites. In lymphatics they are trapped in lymph nodes, which may serve as temporary barriers. They may enter the blood vessels by extension from lymph nodes or, more rarely, by passing directly through the connective tissue sheath surrounding lymph nodes. The cancer cells are eventually entrapped in the smallest branches of blood vessels, the capillaries, and become the "seeds" from which larger colonies of tumour cells grow into secondary sites, called metastases.

It was once thought that the pattern of metastasis was a random process. Within certain limits, however, the patterns of metastases now appear to be tumour-specific. For example, cancer of the breast and prostate have a predilection for spreading to bone, in contrast to melanoma and kidney cancer, which lodge preferentially in the lung. It appears that the process of lodgement of cancer cells in a distant organ may be related to specific interactions (perhaps to mutual attraction) between the cancer cells and those of the organ in which they ultimately settle and resume their growth. Basic research on the nature and mechanism of such interactions may eventually lead to a better understanding of the metastatic process and may result in therapeutic strategies to either limit or totally prevent metastasis. Since the capacity for distant metastasis appears to be a property of a small subpopulation of cancer cells within the primary tumour, prevention or control of metastases may prove to be both feasible and effective in the future.

Spread of cancer and survival. Clinical experience with the relation of the spread of cancer to patient survival is dramatically emphasized by the statistics of cancer of the colon and rectum and of the female breast. In both the colon and the rectum, cancer begins in the cells that line the inner surface of the thin-walled, sausage-like connective tissue structure of the organ. If the cancer cells are localized to and within the wall, 94 percent of patients survive five years after surgical removal of the cancer; when the cancer has spread through the wall, but has not entered the adjacent lymph nodes, five-year survival is 88 percent. On the other hand, once cancer has involved the lymph nodes, the five-year survival decreases to 55 percent. Similarly, in breast cancer in women the 10-year survival rate in the absence of nodal involvement is 72 percent, and when lymph nodes closest to the tumour are involved, 10-year survival is 66 percent. When the tumour has spread to more distant nodes, however, five-year survival decreases to only 31 percent. It is important, therefore, to diagnose cancer and begin treatment before cancer cells begin to spread.

Effects of metastasis on survival

TYPES OF CANCER

Cancers are classified by pathologists based on the type of tissue in which they arise and the cell type that constitutes the tumour. This time-honoured system of classification recognizes in humans more than 150 types of cancer with different biological behaviours.

Types of tissue. The organs of the body consist of a variety of tissues, including those that line their inner surfaces (epithelia) and those that render structural support and contain their blood supply (the connective tissues). Tumours (from Latin *tumēre*, "to swell") of a given type of tissue differ from those of the normal tissues in that and other organs but may closely resemble tumours of the similar tissue in other organs or regions of the body.

Classification of cancers according to the tissue from which they evolve is by two major types: carcinoma (from Greek *korkinos*, "crab") and sarcoma (from Greek *sarkōma*, "fleshy growth"). Carcinoma, the larger category, refers to cancers of epithelial tissues, which cover the external body (the skin) and line the inner cavitary structures of organs such as the breast; the respiratory and gastrointestinal tracts; the endocrine glands, such as the pituitary, thyroid, and adrenals; and the genitourinary system, which includes the prostate, testes, ovaries, fallopian tubes, uterus, kidneys, and urinary bladder. Sarcoma refers to cancers of the various elements that constitute the connective tissues, such as fibrous tissues, muscle, blood vessels, bone, and cartilage. Rarely, a cancer is composed of both epithelial and connective tissue simultaneously and is referred to as carcinosarcoma. Leukemias, lymphomas, and other cancers of the blood-forming tissues are classified separately, although strictly speaking they can be regarded as a subset of the connective tissues. Tumours of nerve tissues, including the brain, and melanoma, a cancer of the pigmented cells of the skin, are also classified separately.

Carcinoma and sarcoma

A carcinoma of the intestine has more in common with a carcinoma of the stomach, lung, or breast than with a sarcoma of lymphoid cells of the intestine. It is on the tissue and cells of origin, not the organ of origin, that the peculiar and characteristic properties of a tumour more usually depend.

Types of cells. Tumours are also classified according to the type of cell from which they are derived. For example, skin cancer includes tumours composed of the major cellular component, squamous cells, giving rise to squamous-cell carcinoma; of the less frequent basal cells found at the base of the skin, whose tumours are referred to as basal-cell carcinomas; and of the still more rare cells that produce melanin pigment, whose malignant tumours are classified as melanomas. Cancers in different organs and individual carcinomas of the same cell type may have different doubling times (*i.e.*, the time it takes for the tumour mass to double in the number of cells or in size). Doubling times observed for lung cancer, for instance, may vary widely from case to case, with ranges from eight days for very rapidly growing tumours to more than 700 days for the more slowly growing.

Squamous-cell and basal-cell carcinomas

In addition to the obvious problems associated with the local mechanical effects of tumours, as well as their distant spread to vital organs such as the lungs, brain, and liver, where their subsequent growth may interfere with function, tumours may also exert other potent biological effects. These tumour-associated phenomena are referred to collectively as paraneoplastic syndromes and may include a wide and bewildering variety of adverse effects, such as loss of appetite, body wasting, fatigue, stupour, coma, excessive thirst, inappropriate flushing of the skin, anemia, spontaneous bleeding, clotting, loss of motor function, dementia, and paralysis. Some of these

Paraneoplastic syndromes

effects have been linked to the inappropriate production and release of certain hormones by tumours, while other effects remain unexplained. The fact that some effects appear before cancer is diagnosed and disappear as soon as the tumour is removed suggests that many of the unexplained effects are probably also caused by substances released by the tumours. Such effects can be so severe and debilitating that they present a more acute clinical problem than the underlying cancers.

Death in patients with cancer is more often than not due to a superimposed systemic complication, such as an overwhelming infection or uncontrollable hemorrhage. In certain instances death is the result of tumour invasion of contiguous tissues, leading to kidney obstruction or perforation of the gastrointestinal tract.

Sites of origin. Cancers of organs such as the brain, lung, esophagus, stomach, liver, gallbladder, pancreas, kidney, prostate, ovary, and testis grow to form firm masses and hence are referred to as solid tumours. These are contrasted with those tumours involving cells of the blood-forming organs and lymphatic systems, which are normally free and circulating and remain so when they become malignant. Some of the more common forms of cancer are discussed below.

The skin. Cancers of the skin are relatively common; they occur in highest incidence on the exposed skin of the head and neck of persons chronically exposed to sunlight. The most common form, about 82 percent of all cases, is that arising from basal cells in the deepest layer of the skin. The initial lesion is a small pimple-like elevation, which enlarges very slowly and after a few months forms a shiny, somewhat translucent lesion that eventually develops a small central ulcer. When the scablike surface is denuded it tends to bleed and then appears to "heal" by forming another shiny covering. Although basal-cell carcinomas grow slowly and only very rarely metastasize, they do invade locally and cause considerable destruction of adjacent tissues, which can result in disfigurement. Either ample surgical excision or radiation therapy are curative.

Squamous-cell carcinoma arises from the platelike flat cells that constitute the major cellular component of skin. The early lesion is less localized and elevated than that of basal-cell cancer. It is red and scaly and may be confused with eczema or infection. Eventually, the lesion becomes larger, elevated, and ulcerated. The behaviour of squamous-cell carcinoma differs somewhat from that of basal-cell cancer, in that the cells are not only capable of local invasion but also may metastasize to regional lymph nodes and, rarely, to more distant sites. Treatment is identical to that for basal-cell cancer.

Mortality for the Six Most Frequent Sites of Cancer (1976–77)*
(crude death rates per 100,000 population)

men		women	
site	rate	site	rate
lung	60.4	breast	26.4
colon and rectum	27.4	colon and rectum	21.2
stomach	26.8	stomach	13.7
prostate	21.2	lung	11.3
leukemia	7.3	uterus (including cervix)	10.8
oral	4.9	leukemia	4.7
all sites	223.8	all sites	144.4

*The countries on which the data are based are Australia, Austria, Canada, Chile, Denmark, France, Ireland, Israel, Japan, The Netherlands, New Zealand, Norway, Scotland, Sweden, Switzerland, the United Kingdom, the United States, and West Germany.
Source: World Health Organization, *World Health Statistics Annual,* 1979–80.

The lung. Lung cancers arise in the epithelium lining the bronchi (the branching complex of air passages), by which air passes to the lungs, or in the fine air sacs at the periphery. The most common forms arise in bronchial glandular epithelium that has been altered by long exposure to cigarette smoke to form less specialized squamous cells, which eventually evolve into squamous-cell carcinomas. Structurally, unaltered glandular epithelia of bronchi may also undergo malignant transformation to give rise to adenocarcinomas, but these tumours do not appear to be related to cigarette smoking.

Cancers of the lung tend to metastasize widely to lymph nodes in the neck and chest, to the pleura (membrane) lining the chest and lungs, and to the liver, adrenals, and bone. The average survival of persons with untreated lung cancer is about nine months after diagnosis. By the time a sign or symptom appears, spread to regional or distant lymph or to distant sites has usually occurred. In operable cases removal of the tumour may prolong life for a number of months. Five-year survival of patients affected with squamous-cell carcinoma of the lung is about 25 percent and for adenocarcinoma 12 percent.

The breast. Cancer of the breast is the leading cause of death from cancer in women. The incidence of and death from cancer of the breast is significantly higher in North America and northern Europe than in Asian and African countries, indicating that different populations have different risks for breast cancer. Major risk factors include menstrual and reproductive history, family history, and history of benign disease of the breast. For example, women who begin menstruation at an early age are at greater risk than those who begin later, and women who have their ovaries removed surgically before age 35 appear to be at significantly less risk than women who undergo natural menopause. Women who bear their first child before age 18 have one-third the risk of developing breast cancer of those who have their first full-term pregnancy between ages 18 and 30. Treatment is reasonably successful when it is guided by and based on knowledge of the degree of sensitivity of the tumour cells to the female hormone estrogen.

Risk factors for breast cancer

Esophagus. Cancer of the esophagus may arise at any point along the passage through which food is conveyed to the stomach, although the most frequent site is the middle third. The tumours are bulky, fungus-like growths that rapidly close the esophagus. More rarely they may spread superficially without causing obstruction. Esophageal cancers are usually poorly differentiated squamous-cell carcinomas that invade locally and metastasize rapidly to organs in the chest as well as to more distant sites. Even with the best therapy available, the cure rate is quite low. Chronic smoking and use of alcohol are considered to be major risk factors, and diet and certain environmental factors may also be involved.

Stomach. Cancer of the stomach is a major cause of death from cancer worldwide. In some countries, such as the United States, the death rate from stomach cancer has decreased dramatically since the 1930s, for reasons that remain unknown. Risk factors are poorly understood. The cancers are almost exclusively of the glandular epithelium lining the stomach and are adenocarcinomas. The tumours infiltrate and invade the wall of the stomach or form masses that protrude from the surface and ulcerate. These tumours tend to metastasize early and widely. Surgery is the treatment of choice but is curative only when the tumour is diagnosed and removed early.

Liver. Cancer of the liver is a disease whose incidence varies widely; in African countries such as Nigeria and Benin and among Chinese in Singapore, Taiwan, and Hawaii the incidence is high, while in the continental United States and in western Europe primary cancer of the liver is relatively rare. Environmental factors appear to play an important role; the disease is linked to infectious hepatitis B virus, to malnutrition, and to natural chemical carcinogens such as aflatoxin B_1, toxic alkaloids from plants used to brew certain native teas, and nitrosamines. Chronic alcohol abuse, which leads to cirrhosis (scarring) of the liver, is a significant risk factor, especially in the Western world, since it appears to predispose a person to the development of liver cancer. Primary cancers of the liver are carcinomas arising from liver cells, the major cellular component of liver (hepatocellular carcinomas), or, more rarely, from a minor cellular component of liver, bile duct cells (cholangiocarcinomas). Both types of carcinoma tend to spread extensively within the liver; and the hepatocellular carcinomas also grow into the veins of the liver, from which they may spread to more distant sites, such as the lungs. Cancer of the liver may be successfully treated surgically if the tumour has not spread widely within the liver or beyond it.

Pancreas. Pancreatic cancer arising from the epithelium lining the duct system is the most frequent malignant tumour of this organ. In the United States, England, Israel, and several Scandinavian countries the incidence of the disease is high; in other western and eastern European countries and Japan it is intermediate; and in southern Europe and Southeast Asia it is low. Risk factors include cigarette smoking, diabetes mellitus, and perhaps the typical Western diet, consisting of a high intake of meat and fat. Onset of the disease is insidious, so that by the time symptoms and signs such as loss of appetite and weight, jaundice, and painless enlargement of the gallbladder due to obstruction are apparent, the tumour has often already involved contiguous tissues and organs. The cancers are adenocarcinomas that metastasize early and often widely. These characteristics are responsible for the lethality of this disease, which has less than a 2-percent five-year survival rate. Despite considerable clinical research aimed at the development of new diagnostic techniques, surgical resection has succeeded only in a relatively small percentage of patients who have an early diagnosis.

Risk factors of pancreatic cancer

Colon and rectum. Colorectal cancer is very common in the Western world, with nearly equal incidence in males and females. By contrast, its incidence in Japan, many South American countries, and sub-Saharan African countries is very low. Epidemiologic studies suggest that a major risk factor may be the low fibre content and high meat protein and fat content of the Western diet. It has been observed that Japanese immigrants to the United States within a generation acquire a much higher incidence of colorectal cancer than their counterparts in Japan. Similarly, their children, and the children of other immigrant ethnic groups from countries with low incidence, have incidences for colon and rectal cancer equal to those of other Americans. This is an excellent example of the role of the environment in the causation of cancer. Numerous studies seem to indicate that the majority of cases arise from certain types of preexisting polyps and that these may remain benign for many months before becoming malignant. The tumours are adenocarcinomas, and some apparently also grow very slowly, taking as long as six to eight years to reach a size of about 2.4 inches (six centimetres). Once the tumour has grown through the wall of the bowel, successful treatment becomes more difficult. The tumours metastasize to the liver, lung, and other sites. Surgery is the most favoured treatment, although chemotherapy and radiation therapy may also be used when warranted by the extent of the disease.

Kidney and bladder. Adenocarcinoma of the kidney, which arises in the epithelium lining the renal tubules, is the most common primary malignancy affecting this organ. It is more common in men than in women and appears during the fifth and sixth decades of life. Although its causes remain to be determined, a number of retrospective epidemiologic studies implicate an association with cigarette smoking. An important manifestation is blood in the urine (hematuria), which may be painless or accompanied with flank pain. Tumours are large and bulky and may occupy a large portion of the kidney. Renal adenocarcinoma spreads by direct extension to adjacent tissues, and metastasis occurs to lung and bone. Some tumours may become quite large, however, without any evidence of metastasis. The mean survival rate following surgical removal is about 35 percent. A special type of kidney cancer occurs in infancy and early childhood. Called nephroblastoma, or Wilms' tumour, it arises from abnormal embryonic tissue and involves both connective tissue and epithelial cells. It can spread both by direct invasion and by the lymphatics and the bloodstream. Early diagnosis and combined surgical removal and radiation therapy give favourable results, with a cure rate of about 80 percent.

Wilms' tumour in children

Incidence of epithelial tumour of the urinary bladder varies significantly from country to country. In the United States bladder tumours account for about 6 percent of all cancers, while in Zimbabwe, Egypt, and Iraq bladder cancer constitutes about 40 percent of all cancers. The disease is three times more frequent in men than in women. Naphthylamine and other chemicals used in the production of dyes are known to cause bladder cancer. A metabolite of the amino acid trypthophan, present in meat proteins, is also carcinogenic and may represent one of the means by which bladder cancer appears in people having no contact with the chemical industry. Chronic conditions of the bladder, such as infestation by the parasite *Schistosoma*, found in the Middle East and Africa, and developmental defects that predispose a person to the formation of bladder stones and infection are also considered high risk factors. Hematuria is the most important symptom associated with this disease. Tumours often begin as benign lesions (papillomas), which become progressively more aggressive and finally malignant. The majority are carcinomas of transitional-cell epithelium, which lines the bladder. The tumours can be treated successfully with early diagnosis and vigorous treatment. Once they invade the bladder wall and enter adjoining structures, the prognosis is poor.

Prostate. Cancer of the prostate is a common disease, but markedly low incidences are seen in Oriental populations, especially in Japan. As with other tumours, immigration from low-incidence to high-incidence countries is followed by an increased incidence in the migrant population. Although no definite etiologic factors have been established, research has suggested that viruses might be involved. The fact that prostatic carcinoma is rare before the age of 50, increases in incidence in subsequent years, is not seen in castrates, and regresses following castration implicates aging and the presence of male hormone as significant factors. Cancer arises in the epithelium lining the prostatic acini and small ducts, and, more rarely, in the main ducts. The majority are adenocarcinomas that tend to spread to the rectum, the base of the bladder, and eventually to more distant sites. Metastases to the bones are quite common and, together with involvement of nerves in the pelvis, are often the cause of considerable pain. Treatments include castration, administration of the female hormone estrogen, and, as the extent of involvement may require, surgical removal, radiation therapy, and chemotherapy.

Uterus. Cancers of the uterus are relatively common and represent about 19 percent of all malignant diseases in women in the United States, compared with, for example, Thailand, countries of the Far East such as Japan, and African countries, where they are relatively rare. The two major types of uterine cancer are adenocarcinoma of the lining of the uterus (endometrium) and squamous-cell carcinoma of the womb or cervix. Endometrial carcinoma has its highest incidence late in the sixth decade. The disease is associated with obesity, diabetes, hypertension, and late menopause. Etiology has not been established, but the hormone estrogen probably plays a significant role. Endometrial cancer spreads both superficially and by invasion of the muscular wall of the uterus. Lymphatic spread occurs late. Inappropriate bleeding from the fifth decade of life onward is an important symptom that must be heeded early if treatment is to be effective. Treatment of choice is radiation therapy followed by surgical removal, and the cure rate is good. Treatment for disease that spreads beyond the uterus includes hormonal therapy with progesterone and, less frequently, chemotherapy.

Major types of uterine cancer

Squamous-cell carcinoma of the uterine cervix is a somewhat more common disease than endometrial cancer and tends to occur at a younger age, beginning as early as the third decade. A viral etiology is strongly implicated and is supported by a higher incidence of the disease in women who have had an early and active sexual history, including multiple pregnancies. Such cancers are infrequent in women who have not been pregnant and are very rare in celibate women. An early symptom of the disease is abnormal bleeding. The cancers arise in the squamous epithelium of the womb and tend to remain confined to the lining for a number of years in the in situ stage before becoming invasive. Women who have an annual examination, including a Papanicolaou (Pap) test, a painless sampling of cells from the cervix, have an improved chance of early diagnosis. Once the tumour becomes invasive, involving both direct extension and lymphatic metastasis, the prognosis becomes grave.

Incidence of cancer of the ovary

Ovary. Cancer of the ovary is the fourth most frequent cause of death from cancer in women of the highly industrialized countries of the Western world. It is relatively uncommon in Far Eastern countries, especially Japan, and in less developed countries. Immigrants to Western countries show higher incidences about 20 years after their immigration, suggesting the possible role of environmental factors; no firm associations have been established, however. Many different types of ovarian cancer have been identified; the most common forms are adenocarcinomas arising in the epithelium. The tumours may be treated successfully through surgery if they are diagnosed early. Extension of the disease beyond the ovary requires more radical treatment, such as radiation therapy and chemotherapy.

Lymphoid tissue. Malignant diseases of lymphoid tissue (lymphomas) are the seventh most common cause of cancer death in the United States, and certain forms are common throughout many countries of the world. In African countries and on New Guinea, Burkitt's lymphoma is common, while in the Western countries it is relatively rare. Certain lymphomas in humans have been closely linked with viruses; other established lymphomas are linked to significant chronic exposure to ionizing radiation and to inherited immunologic deficiency or to such deficiency induced to prevent rejection of organ transplants or resulting from treatment for certain diseases. Malignancies of lymphoid tissue may arise in one or more of the organs rich in such tissue, including the lymph nodes, spleen, bone marrow, and thymus. More rarely they can arise in organs containing small amounts of such tissue, including the stomach, intestines, testis, and breast. Lymphomas are aggressive malignancies that tend to spread to distant organs and become systemic in their distribution. As with other malignant tumours, early diagnosis and aggressive treatment by radiation therapy, chemotherapy, or both have resulted in an increasing number of cures.

Blood-forming tissues. Leukemias are a heterogeneous group of malignancies of the blood-forming (hematopoietic) tissues, which include the bone marrow, lymph nodes, and spleen. The acute form of the disease in adults is rapidly fatal, with infiltration of bone marrow and other hematopoietic tissues by the malignant cells, while the acute form in children has yielded to treatment and a number of cures are documented. The disease has a worldwide distribution, and the best established etiologic factor involves chronic exposure to ionizing radiation. Other factors that have been implicated include congenital disorders associated with increased chromosomal fragility and instability, such as Down's syndrome, Bloom's syndrome, and Fanconi's anemia; viruses; and certain chemicals and drugs. Leukemic cells tend to disseminate through the bloodstream, lodging in blood-forming and other tissues and organs. The cells proliferate to the extent that they often crowd out normal elements of the blood, so that patients afflicted with leukemia are rendered anemic by an interference with red blood cell production or from bleeding because of abnormalities of the blood-clotting mechanisms. They are rendered susceptible to infection by a diminution of the various types of white blood cells, which comprise a major defense system of the body. Treatment involves attempts to correct these complications by transfusion of normal blood and blood products, as well as the use of antibiotics to combat infection and of chemotherapeutic agents to destroy the malignant cells. Chronic, more slow-growing, and less aggressive forms of leukemia may continue for years and may respond favourably to radiation therapy, surgical removal of the spleen, and chemotherapy.

TREATMENT

Successful treatment of cancer requires the complete removal or destruction of all cancerous tissue. If therapy fails to remove all of the cancer cells, the disease recurs. Surgery and radiation are the most effective forms of treatment. Chemotherapy—treatment with drugs and hormones—is helpful in some forms of cancer. Choice of therapy is governed by the type, location, size, and extent of invasion and metastases of the cancer at the time of diagnosis, and by the general condition of the patient.

Surgery. For surgery to be curative, it must be performed before the cancer has spread into organs and tissues that cannot be safely removed. Since the late 19th century increasingly radical operations for cancer have become standard. Despite the increasing extent of these procedures, risk has been reduced by improvements in surgical techniques, anesthesiology, and preoperative and postoperative care, especially in the control of infection.

Reconstructive techniques

Major advances have been made in the restoration of structures altered by cancer surgery and in rehabilitation following radical surgery. Patients undergoing certain surgical procedures for cancer of the colon or rectum, for instance, can be equipped with simple devices for the elimination of solid waste. For patients with cancer of the head and neck, the use of grafting methods and of tissue flaps make it possible to apply reconstructive techniques at the time the cancer is removed.

Rehabilitation of the patient also plays an important role. Women who have extensive surgery for breast cancer are given treatment for restoration of muscle tone needed for movement of the arms. Progress has also been made in teaching new mechanisms of speech to people who have undergone surgical removal of the larynx.

In addition to saving lives by eradicating cancer, surgery also may improve the remaining months or years of life for persons whose cancers cannot be eradicated, restoring comfort and a sense of usefulness. When severe pain accompanies cancer, surgery may bring relief by severing the nerve pathways that carry the painful sensations. In addition, surgery is sometimes necessary to treat abscesses resulting from either the tumour or infection and to relieve intestinal obstructions.

Surgery is also valuable as a preventive measure in controlling cancer. It may be used to eliminate precancerous conditions in the mouth, chronic ulcers (ulcerative colitis) that may lead to cancer of the colon, and certain precancerous polyps in the colon and rectum. It may be used to remove burn scars that may lead to cancer, precancerous nodules in the thyroid gland, and certain precancerous pigmented moles.

Radiation therapy. Radiation therapy makes use of ionizing radiations—X-rays, gamma rays, particles (electrons, neutrons, and pi-mesons)—to destroy cells by impairing their capacity to divide. Although some normal cells are also killed during radiation therapy, this is minimized by careful shielding of adjacent areas.

Some cancers do not respond to radiation therapy. The differing sensitivities of various malignant tumours to irradiation are due primarily to the variations in the cells of origin of the tumours. In addition, individual cells within a tumour may have a widely different susceptibility to irradiation. Poor circulation within some tumours decreases their oxygen supply, further diminishing their sensitivity to radiation.

Development of instruments that produce energy in the range of millions of electron volts has permitted extensive use of radiation therapy. Such instruments can deliver a greater radiation dose to deep-seated tumours without the serious skin reactions and discomfort often associated with lower energy X-ray beams. Large areas can be irradiated more precisely and therefore with more protection of adjacent vital structures. The greater versatility of such equipment has made possible the development of treatment techniques involving multiple intersecting radiation beams, rotation of the patient or the radiation source, large fields of radiation shaped to the contours of particular organs, and the pinpointing of beams for cancers of the eye and the larynx. Because of their increased usefulness, instruments (linear accelerators, betatrons, and radioactive cobalt-60 teletherapy apparatus) have become standard instruments for radiation therapy of deep-seated cancers.

Chemotherapy. Chemotherapy can cure certain forms of cancer. Cancers frequently cured by drugs include choriocarcinoma, a rare, highly malignant tumour that originates in the placenta; acute leukemia of childhood; and Burkitt's lymphoma. Treatments with combinations of drugs have produced long-term, disease-free remissions in many children with acute leukemia and in persons with advanced stages of Hodgkin's disease. Multiple carcinomas of the superficial layers of the skin have been eradicated after the application of certain cancer-drug ointments to the skin. Many other forms of cancer benefit temporarily or partially by chemotherapy.

Problems with chemotherapy

Most cancer drugs are limited in their usefulness. One problem is that only a certain proportion of cells is dividing at any one time, and most cancer drugs can destroy only that part of the cell population undergoing division. Another problem is that cancer drugs damage normal, as well as malignant, cells and tissues. In addition, some cancer cells eventually become resistant to drugs. To help overcome these difficulties, combinations of chemotherapeutic agents that act on cells in different ways have been used in various treatment programs simultaneously or in sequence.

Special measures have been developed to protect persons undergoing cancer chemotherapy from the combined effects of the drugs and the disease. Refinements in the transfusion of blood platelets permit multiple transfusions in leukemia patients with critical platelet deficiencies caused either by leukemia or drug toxicity. During periods when a patient's white blood cells are depleted, administration of antibiotics offers protection from many infections. Relatively germ-free environments, such as specially designed hospital rooms, provide sterile atmospheres to protect against fatal infection. Transfusion of type-matched white blood cells, and, more recently, transplantation of bone marrow cells from carefully matched donors, have also been of value in protecting persons with nonfunctioning bone marrows against infections.

Experimental treatments. Since the 1970s considerable effort has been expended toward the development, control, and elimination of cancer by immunotherapy. Methods have involved the use of immunotherapeutic agents such as bacille Calmette-Guérin (BCG), a vaccine against human tuberculosis; killed suspensions of several types of bacteria; chemical products isolated from certain bacteria; and interferon, a family of proteins that inhibit the growth of viruses. All of these substances appear to stimulate the immunologic defense system. It may someday prove possible to cure cancer by manipulating the complex immunologic mechanisms of the host.

Hyperthermia

A second experimental approach involves the use of hyperthermia (high temperature). Research indicates that cancer cells are more sensitive to the killing effects of high temperature than are their normal counterparts. The success of treatment by hyperthermia appears to depend on the development of instrumentation that will allow application of highly localized heat to a tumour.

Two developments in radiation therapy that may add significantly to its effectiveness include the use of chemicals that greatly sensitize tumour cells to the damaging effects of ionizing radiation, while not affecting normal cells, and the application of particle-beam radiation therapy, using beams of protons, helium ions, and heavy ions. Such beams have sufficiently high energy to penetrate deeply into tissues; they do more damage to malignant cells than do the less energetic forms of ionizing radiation administered at the same dosages. Such developments may allow treatment of deep-seated tumours without significantly damaging overlying normal tissues.

BIBLIOGRAPHY

Books: MARTIN D. ABELOFF (ed.), *Complications of Cancer* (1979), a text for physicians; *Cancer Risk, Assessing and Reducing the Dangers in Our Society* (1982), a report to the Office of Science and Technology by an advisory panel; NATIONAL INSTITUTES OF HEALTH, *Coping with Cancer: An Annotated Bibliography of Public, Patient and Professional Information and Education Materials* (1980); RICHARD DOLL and RICHARD PETO, *The Causes of Cancer* (1981), an epidemiologic approach toward the identification of major risk factors involved in human cancer; MARILEE I. DONOVAN (ed.), *Cancer Care: A Guide for Patient Education* (1981), written by a nurse to assist nurses; G. GIRALDO and E. BETH (eds.), *The Role of Viruses in Human Cancer*, vol. 1 (1980); I.I. KESSLER (ed.), *Cancer Control: Contemporary Views on Screening, Diagnosis and Therapy* (1980); THOMAS H. MAUGH II and JEAN L. MARX, *Seeds of Destruction: The Science Report on Cancer Research* (1975), a popular presentation; GUY R. NEWELL and NEIL M. ELLISON (eds.), *Nutrition and Cancer: Etiology and Treatment* (1981); MARVIN A. RICH and PHILIP FURMANSKI (eds.), *Biological Carcinogenesis* (1982), a general consideration of viral and chemical carcinogenesis; MICHAEL B. SHIMKEN, *Science and Cancer*, 3rd revision (1980), a general review for the layman; THOMAS SYMINGTON and R.L. CARTER (eds.), *Scientific Foundations of Oncology* (1976), an authoritative text; H.VAINIO, M. SORSA, and K. HEMMIMKI (eds.), *Occupational Cancer and Carcinogenesis* (1981); MORRIS S. ZEDECK and MARTIN LIPIN (eds.), *Inhibition of Tumor Induction and Development* (1981), a consideration of various chemical substances that inhibit cancer.

Journals: Journal of the National Cancer Institute (monthly), published by the U.S. National Cancer Institute; *Cancer Research* (monthly), published by the American Association for Cancer Research; *Cancer* (semimonthly), published by the American Cancer Society, primarily reporting clinical research; *British Journal of Cancer* (monthly), published by the British Empire Cancer Campaign for Research; *Carcinogenesis* (monthly), a research journal; *European Journal of Cancer and Clinical Oncology* (monthly), published by the Ministry of Education of Belgium, with articles in French and English; *International Journal of Cancer* (monthly), published primarily in English by the International Union Against Cancer.

(CARL G. BAKER; DANTE G. SCARPELLI)

Instrumentation

The modern level of technology would not have been attained without the development and use of precise measuring instrumentation. Every advance in mankind's technological capabilities from the earliest times was necessarily preceded by the development of instrumentation that enabled people to see, measure, and gain access to the unknown they were probing. . . .

III. Nonmanufacturing applications

BIOMEDICAL INSTRUMENTATION

Laboratory analysis. As knowledge in medical science increases, the need grows for instrumentation in laboratory analysis. In wide use is a device capable of providing 40 to 60 analyses an hour; it consists of a long fine tube through which are drawn samples of such substances as blood serum or urine, separated by quantities of neutral solution (distilled water in most cases). The samples and stretches of water between them are separated by air bubbles. A proportioning pump, by way of a manifold, introduces the air bubbles into the sample streams and advances precise quantities of all solutions and diluents into the system. For specific analyses, reactions are initiated in the samples with reagents that cause a noticeable colour change. These are monitored in a colorimeter, which measures the degree of absorption of this colour by the sample; this measurement is displayed as a peak on a moving graph paper. The degree of absorption is related to the composition of the sample, and the concentration of many constituents, such as albumen and uric acid, can be determined. This type of instrument is especially versatile if a small computer is used to control and record its functions. From each patient a blood sample is sent to a multi-channel analyzer, which provides information to a small computer. The computer not only sets up calibration curves and checks periodically for errors but also provides a tabulation of each patient's results, indicating those surpassing safe levels. About 1,100 tests can be run each hour with such computerized instrumentation.

Few instrumental methods are available to analyze compounds of high molecular weight in the human body, such as proteins in blood plasma and muscle. The white cells (leukocytes) in blood continuously synthesize about 2,000 proteins, which originate by a complex series of biochemical processes using genes (deoxyribonucleic acid; DNA) as a template. These proteins can now be separated and studied by a two-dimensional electrophoresis technique (see Figure 3). In this technique the proteins extracted from blood are first separated according to their isoelectric point by focussing them through a tube filled with a gel. The gel is then extruded and becomes the sample, which is separated in the second dimension by using a voltage applied across a rectangular gel slab. This causes

By courtesy of the Institute of Clinical Biochemistry, University of Oslo

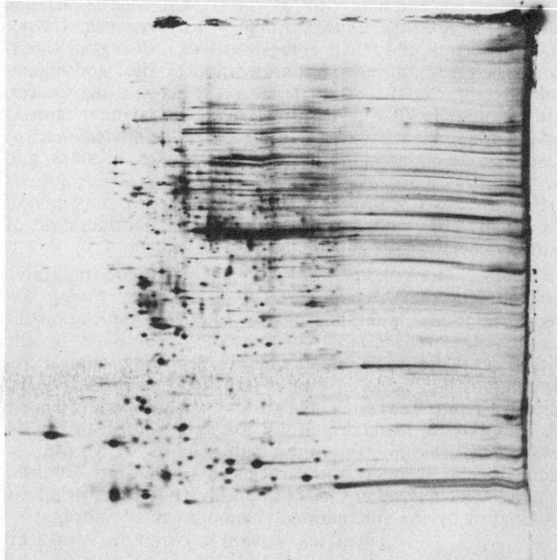

Figure 3: Two-dimensional electrophoresis separation of proteins from human leukocytes. Each spot corresponds to a separated protein.

the proteins to migrate down the gel slab and separate according to their molecular weight.

Computer use. The use of computers in the biomedical field is continually growing, most obviously in processing the output of biomedical measuring devices. Computers can record and store the electrical analogue of a physiological event, and play it back later, at a different speed if desired. They can also be programmed to recognize certain patterns in the data and to signal this recognition.

Computer-assisted measuring instruments

An example of a computer–measuring-instrument combination using the special abilities of the computer is a system to scan and analyze cell images. The computer is used in conjunction with a vidicon scanner and a high-resolution microscope. A stained blood smear is illuminated with monochromatic light and scanned with a vidicon. The information from some 4,000 points is stored in the computer, which is programmed to analyze it into the five categories of white blood cells.

Computerized axial tomography (CAT) combines the technologies of X-ray, scintillation counting, computer processing, and cathode-ray tube (CRT) display. The result is a picture of a transverse section of a body part that looks like an anatomic section. It is a reconstructed image of the area, formed by the computer's ability to calculate small differences in attenuation of a narrow beam of X-rays sweeping through the tissues. These differences cannot be seen by ordinary X-ray techniques. The images formed can show a transverse section of the brain, for example, in which eight slices—each 1.3 centimetres (0.5 inch) thick—will clearly define the condition of the structure. This noninvasive technique can show lesions of the brain, such as tumours, hematomas, cysts, and metastatic diseases. Diagnosis of tumours is about 99 percent accurate. Abnormalities of the liver, pancreas, bladder, and related structures can also be evaluated with CAT.

Another noninvasive instrument, which produces images similar to CAT, is based on nuclear magnetic resonance (NMR). NMR has been used by analytical chemists since the 1950s as a tool to determine molecular structures because it produces a spectrum that uniquely defines protons within atomic nuclei in a molecule. In the human body proton densities vary from tissue to tissue, and images can be formed that can detect cancerous tissue and outline structures within the body. The NMR image is formed by superimposing a linear magnetic field gradient on the uniform magnetic field gradient applied to the object being studied. The NMR signal is a one-dimensional projection of a three-dimensional object. By taking a series of these projections at different gradient orientations, a two- or even three-dimensional image can be produced and displayed by a computer and CRT, just as in the CAT technique. Images based on proton densities in the body provide medical information quite different from that of the CAT, which is primarily based on electron densities.

A third noninvasive method of imaging interior portions of the body is based on ultrasonics. In this technique a beam of high-frequency sound energy between one and 15 megahertz is pulsed into the body and its echoes—which occur when the beam strikes a tissue or fluid interface—are converted to electrical impulses and displayed on a CRT. The outline of structures is thereby produced. Images can be produced to follow the course of pregnancies, to show organs, and to outline the presence of tumours. A distinct advantage of this instrumentation is that it is inexpensive, portable, and simple to operate. . . .

SPACE INSTRUMENTATION

During the 1970s many successful uses of instrumentation in space were developed. These were centred on miniaturization of existing instruments and their adaptation for special uses and remote control, rather than the creation of entirely new instruments. The accomplishments of the 1970s were embodied in the Viking missions to Mars, the Pioneer Venus missions, and the Voyager missions that flew by Jupiter and Saturn and their satellites on their way to Uranus and Neptune and the limits of the solar system. In all these space experiments, computers played a key role in control of the instruments and transmission of their data back to Earth.

The Viking missions. Two identical Viking spacecraft, launched 30 days apart in 1975, successfully landed on Mars after almost a year in space flight (see Figure 5). Each carried an impressive array of instrumentation primarily concerned with the detection of life, although other conditions were studied. Each spacecraft had an orbiter section that delivered a lander module to a selected point for descent to the surface and then acted as a relay station to control the lander's functions and transmit data back to Earth. Radio transmission over the 321,860,000-kilometre (200,000,000-mile) distance required 40 minutes round-trip. The orbiter carried television cameras, an infrared thermal mapper, and an infrared spectrometer for water-vapour mapping. By the end of the orbiter mission in August 1980, almost 55,000 pictures of the planet had been taken.

The landers operated for several years and, although no evidence of biological life was detected, a huge amount of information on soil chemistry and meteorological conditions was obtained. Three types of instrumentation systems were mounted on the lander: an X-ray fluorescence spectrometer to analyze surface materials, a module to perform biological experiments, and a molecular analysis module to identify atmospheric constituents and organic molecules in the Martian soil. The lander had a long mechanical arm to scoop up soil from the surface and deliver a sample to the instruments. Surface dust was introduced to the X-ray fluorescence spectrometer. The X-ray spectra produced were matched by computer to known spectra for elements of atomic number greater than 11.

The biological module performed three experiments on portions of a common soil sample collected from the Martian surface. The pyrolytic release experiment measured the assimilation of a mixture of radioactive carbon dioxide and carbon monoxide from the atmosphere by living matter after incubation under the Martian atmosphere. The degree of assimilation could be determined by analyzing the gases and pyrolysis products of organic matter that might be present with a gas chromatographic procedure. The labelled release experiment detected assimilation of organic material and its conversion to carbon dioxide by living matter. Martian soil was moistened with a nutrient mixture of simple, radioactively labelled organic compounds, and the headspace gas over the mixture was monitored for an increase of radioactivity with time. The gas exchange experiment was similar; a gas chromatographic analysis was conducted on the headspace gas.

Detection of carbon compounds

The module containing the gas chromatograph/mass spectrometer (GC/MS) unit was designed not only to analyze for atmospheric gases but primarily to detect organic carbon compounds—a necessary condition for the presence of life. The organic compounds were investigated by pyrolyzing a sample of soil to decompose it into compounds easily identifiable by the GC/MS technique. A total of 14 organic analyses were performed on four soil samples and 57 atmospheric samples. The GC/MS analyses showed the soil contained no organic molecules, despite detection sensitivities in the parts-per-1,000,000,000 range. Having successfully completed their mission, the GC/MS instruments were turned off during March–April 1977.

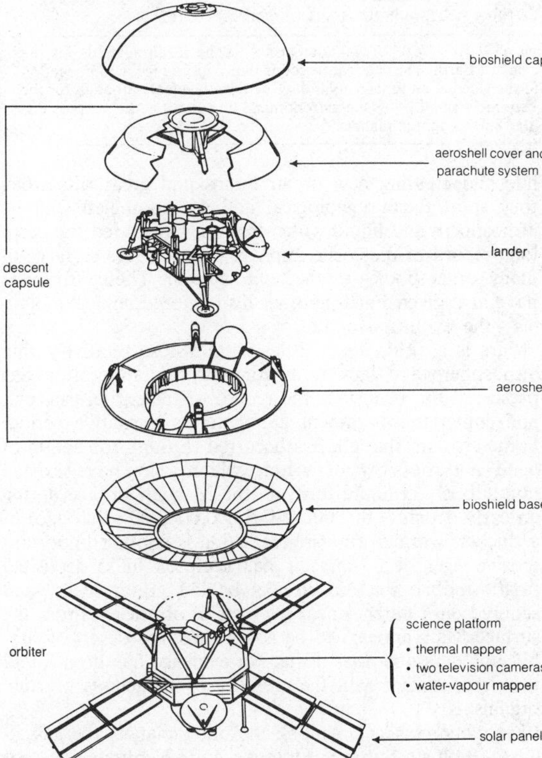

Figure 5: Sections of the Viking spacecraft sent to Mars.
By courtesy of Martin Marietta Corporation

The Pioneer Venus missions. In 1978 two Pioneer Venus spacecraft were launched, requiring six months to reach the planet. The spacecraft, one consisting of an orbiter and the other essentially comprising four probes that descended to the surface, carried numerous instruments. The orbiter used a Bennett-type mass spectrometer to directly measure the ions present in the Venusian ionosphere. Electrons and their temperature were measured electronically. A quadrupole mass spectrometer operating for 243 Earth days measured the neutral gas composition of the upper atmosphere. An ultraviolet spectrometer produced valuable information about the sulfur oxide content of the atmosphere and its photochemical changes. A radiometer mapped thermal emission data, providing large-scale meteorological information.

Of the four probes, the main probe entered the Venusian atmosphere in December 1979 and descended slowly to the surface (part of the way by parachute), producing data for nearly one hour below an altitude of 62 kilometres (38 miles). A magnetic mass spectrometer measured the composition of gases relative to carbon monoxide, the dominant gas, producing 51 mass spectra before impact. A gas chromatograph provided an alternate method to measure atmospheric gas composition. A solar flux radiometer measured solar radiation as a function of altitude to increase knowledge of the extraordinary surface temperature of Venus.

The Voyager missions. Launched in 1977, each of the two Voyager spacecraft carried sophisticated infrared and ultraviolet spectrometers to explore the outer reaches of the solar system. The infrared spectrometer used was a Fourier transform infrared (FTIR) interferometer type, which extracts the infrared spectrum from an interferogram rather than producing it from an optical scan. It operates from thermal emission of the sample. In this application, the solar bodies being studied are the samples whose emissions are gathered by a telescope.

RESEARCH IN INSTRUMENTATION

In the evolution of instruments for use in research, spectroscopy is increasing in importance; the instruments tend to be of greater complexity and capability, with more automatic operations and more assistance from computers. Among the newer methods of spectroscopy, the emphasis is on the electron and the ion. Photochemical dissociation spectroscopy, a type of chemical spectroscopy, is the product of pulsed high-power lasers, molecular beams, and time-of-flight mass spectrometry. The ion microanalyzer, which combines the functions of a mass spectrometer and an ion emission microscope, provides a visual display of the complete composition of a minute section of a solid surface.

Plasma chromatography

Ion-mobility spectrometry (IMS) originated in 1970 as plasma chromatography. The simple technique is based on ions reacting with trace molecules at atmospheric pressure. The capabilities of IMS are many: it has uncomplicated instrumentation giving femtogram (10^{-15} gram) sensitivities; it is capable of operating as a five-mode gas chromatographic detector; it can be used to make basic studies on ion-molecule reactions; and it has an ability to selectively monitor ultra-trace components in air. Major advances have been made in development and use of IMS instrumentation in defensive military applications as a detector of chemical warfare agents, principally the deadly nerve gases.

(FRANCIS W. KARASEK)

Solar System

The solar system consists of the Sun and all matter under the gravitational control of the Sun in its 225,000,000-year period of revolution around its galaxy. Any body not having sufficient velocity to escape from the Sun remains in a closed path (orbit) around it and is a part of its system.

The Sun

Plan of the solar system. More than 99 percent of the mass of the solar system is in the Sun, whose mass is 1.989×10^{30} kilograms (4.385×10^{30} pounds)—333,000 times that of the Earth. The Sun is a gas (predominantly hydrogen) throughout its nearly 700,000-kilometre (435,000-mile) radius because it is heated by continuous nuclear fusion of the hydrogen in its core, where temperatures are near 15,000,000 K (27,000,000° F). As a result, the visible surface of the Sun has a temperature of about 5,780 K (or nearly 9,950° F) and continuously radiates a power of 3.85×10^{26} watts into space. Earth intercepts less than half of one-billionth of that power, but it is sufficient to make Earth a warm, habitable planet.

Of the remaining mass in the solar system more than 99 percent is found in the nine known planets, and more than 90 percent in Jupiter and Saturn alone. Most of the planets follow nearly circular paths around the Sun, with most of the circles nearly in the same plane. Only Mercury and Pluto, the innermost and outermost planets, and also the smallest, have orbital eccentricities greater then 0.2 and inclinations greater than 5°. (Eccentricity measures the amount by which an orbit departs from circularity, being zero for a circle and one for a parabola. Inclination is the angle between the plane of a planet's orbit and that of Earth's orbit.) These and other basic figures for all of the planets are given in the table.

The planets can be divided physically into two groups—an inner group of small, rocky, high-density bodies (Mercury, Venus, Earth, and Mars), called the terrestrial planets, and an outer group of large, gassy, low-density objects (Jupiter, Saturn, Uranus, and Neptune), called the giant planets. This leaves Pluto as a curious anomaly—small, icy, of low density, and in its makeup more like a

Comparative Data for Solar System Bodies

	mass (Earth = 1)*	equatorial Earth radius (Earth = 1)†	mean density (gm/cm³)	rotation period‡ (h = hours, d = days) mean solar	side-real	inclin-ation of axis	mean distance from Sun (a.u.)§	orbital eccen-tricity	orbital inclin-ation	number of known satellites
Mercury	0.055	0.383	5.44	175.97^{d}	58.65^{d}	near 0°	0.387	0.206	7°004′	0
Venus	0.8150	0.9488	5.245	116.75^{d}	243.02^{d}	177°2′	0.723	0.007	3°394′	0
Earth	1.0000*	1.0000†	5.517	24^{h}	23.934^{h}	23°45′	1.000	0.017	0° by definition	1
Mars	0.1074	0.5326	3.945	24.660^{h}	24.623^{h}	25°2′	1.524	0.093	1°850′	2
Jupiter	317.9	11.19	1.33	9.926^{h}	9.925^{h}	3°1′	5.203	0.048	1°305′	16
Saturn	95.26	9.46	0.70	10.657^{h}	same	26°7′	9.539	0.056	2°489′	20+
Uranus	14.6	4.11	1.17	~16^{h}	same	97°9′	19.182	0.047	0°773′	5
Neptune	17.2	3.88	1.66	~18^{h}	same	28°8′	30.058	0.009	1°773′	2
Pluto	0.0025	~0.3	0.5–0.9	6.387^{d}(?)	same	unknown	39.785	0.254	17°137′	1
Ceres‖	0.0002	0.078	~2.3	9.080^{h}	9.078^{h}	direct rotation	2.768	0.077	10°60′	0
Halley's Comet	$\sim 2\times10^{-11}$	4.7×10^{-4}	~1(?)	—	~10^{h}	20–40°(?)	17.94	0.967	162°24′	—

*The mass of Earth is 5.9733×10^{24} kilograms. †The equatorial radius of Earth is 6,378.137 kilometres. ‡The mean solar day is the length of the day as measured by the average motion of the Sun, the clock day of Earth. The sidereal period is that required for a 360° rotation relative to the stars. Only if a planet did not move relative to the Sun could the sidereal and mean solar days be *exactly* equal, although for the outer planets, where the orbital motion is very slow, the differences are extremely small. §One astronomical unit (a.u.) is the average distance of Earth from the Sun, or 149,598,000 kilometres. ‖Largest of the known minor planets.

satellite than a planet. Discussion of a possible 10th planet is heard from time to time, but there is not strong evidence of any solar system member beyond Pluto except the long-period comets (see below).

Planetary surfaces. *The inner planets.* The inner, or terrestrial, planets are bodies made of refractory materials. They are composed mainly of outer shells of silicates with inner metallic cores, yet their surfaces show strongly differing morphologies because of their vastly different surface environments that evolved over their 4,500,000,000-year histories. Despite similar gross compositions, the terrestrial planets differ in their volatile inventories—*i.e.*, substances such as CO_2 (carbon dioxide) and H_2O (water). The relatively slight difference among them has given Mercury a hellishly hot, crater-pocked surface; has turned the surface of Venus into a gaseous, suffocating inferno; has given Mars a history of megafloods and Arctic-like permafrost; and has allowed Earth's surface to be mainly oceans of liquid water.

Mercury

Mercury is a planet of craters, fantastic temperature extremes, no water, and utter desolation. Because of its proximity to the Sun, early in the history of its formation much of its original supply of volatile substances must have been driven off into space. It is mainly a thin silicate crust covering a large nickel-iron core. Its surface shows the result of eons of cratering from meteorite impacts, with craters packed even more closely together than on the surface of Earth's Moon. Volcanic activity on Mercury has filled in many of the craters, and shrinkage stresses in the thin silicate crust during cooling have crinkled the surface much like the skin on a cooled baked apple. While much of the surface of Mercury is heated strongly by the Sun, the dark side of the planet at any given time is plunged into frigid darkness and reaches temperatures as low as 80 K (−315° F).

Venus

Venus, being slightly closer to the Sun than Earth, had more surface heating, which eventually forced its surface volatiles, in particular CO_2, into a thick atmosphere. Surface atmospheric pressures are nearly 100 times those of Earth, and surface temperatures are hundreds of degrees Celsius, even on the side facing away from the Sun, because of atmospheric heat transport. Information on the surface morphology of Venus is sparse, but featureless rubble-strewn plains, continent-sized plateaus, and ocean-sized basins are known.

Earth

Earth has one of the least explored planetary surfaces in the solar system. Three-quarters of Earth's surface is under water and therefore inaccessible to conventional visual exploration. Only recently have methods been developed to view the great rift valleys and basins, undersea mountains, and canyons and landslides that comprise the ocean floors. The occurrence of massive liquid water oceans is just one of the factors that make Earth an anomaly. Another is the presence of ocean- and continent-sized plates of crust that move relentlessly over geological time, pushing up mountains and volcanoes when they collide and creating new ocean basins and great rifts when they split. Earth's geological activity, combined with its atmosphere and liquid water erosion, has erased the eons-long record of meteorite impacts that scar the surfaces of many other bodies in the solar system. These attributes have also given Earth another distinction among the planets—the evolution of life.

Mars

Mars is a cold, dusty little world whose relatively thin atmosphere and lack of continuous rainfall erosion has preserved on its surface the record of meteorite, asteroid, and comet bombardment dating to its formative period. Some erosion, though, has occurred through the action of wind and possibly of water, which may have existed ubiquitously in liquid form on the Martian surface during an early epoch (4,000,000,000–3,000,000,000 years ago) of a thicker, warmer atmosphere. Wind is another important erosive agent on Mars; it has sculpted hills, deposited bright mobile dust in streaks behind crater walls, and scoured dark patches near all sorts of obstacles. From the surface Mars appears to be a wind-scoured desert of rubbly boulders and dust drifts. No evidence has been found that is consistent with the presence of indigenous Martian organisms.

The outer planets. Among the outer planets the gas giants—Jupiter, Saturn, Uranus, and Neptune—do not have accessible surfaces. Their rocky cores are submerged beneath massive atmospheres. Pluto is so small and distant that is is equally unknown.

Planetary atmospheres. Atmospheres are the parts of planets and other solar-system bodies that are mostly gaseous. Mercury, closest to the Sun, has no appreciable atmosphere. Venus, Earth, and Mars all have thin atmospheric layers surrounding the solid portions comprising the bulk of their masses. Jupiter, Saturn, Uranus, and Neptune all have atmospheres that are so substantial that no detection of solid surfaces had been made by the early 1980s, although theoretical models predict solid cores deep in their interiors. A thin atmosphere of CH_4 (methane) has been detected above the surface of Pluto.

Surface temperatures and pressures

For the inner planets with atmospheres, their increasing distance from the Sun results in a progressive drop of surface temperatures and is partially the cause of a like drop in surface atmospheric pressures. For Venus the surface temperature is about 730 K (855° F), and the surface pressure is 90 atmospheres (*i.e.*, 90 times the pressure at Earth's sea level). The average surface temperature of Earth is about 289 K (60° F). For Mars the average surface temperature is 218 K (−67° F), and the average surface pressure is 0.007 atmosphere. The temperatures of the atmospheres of both Earth and Mars vary widely with changes in season. Further, Mars shows large seasonal changes in surface pressure because it gets cold enough for part of its atmosphere to freeze.

The temperature differences among the giant planets are due to differences in solar heating and to the amount of energy coming independently from the interiors of the planets. At the level where the total pressure is equal to one atmosphere, the temperature of Jupiter is about 166 K (−160° F), and the temperature of Saturn is about 91 K (−295° F). Uranus and Neptune are both roughly 72 K (−330° F) at the same pressure level. The temperatures of both Jupiter and Saturn are known to change with position on the planet and with season. The surface temperature of Pluto is estimated at 55 K (−360° F), and its surface pressure is at least 0.0001 atmosphere.

Chemical composition

The chemical composition of the atmospheres of Venus and Mars are similar. The atmosphere of Venus is 96 percent CO_2 and 3.5 percent N_2 (molecular nitrogen); Mars is 95 percent CO_2 and 2.7 percent N_2 with another 1.6 percent Ar (argon). In contrast, Earth's atmosphere is 77 percent N_2, 21 percent O_2 (molecular oxygen), 1 percent H_2O, and 0.93 percent Ar. The remainder of the composition of each atmosphere is shared by several species of chemicals. For Venus the most abundant of these are SO_2 (sulfur dioxide), H_2O, Ar, and CO (carbon monoxide); for Earth they are CO_2, Ne (neon), and He (helium); and for Mars they are O_2, CO, and H_2O.

The bulk of the outer-planet atmospheres is H_2 (molecular hydrogen), with mixtures of smaller amounts of He. Jupiter is known to be about 89 percent H_2 and 11 percent He, with minor abundances of CH_4 and NH_3 (ammonia). Measurements of Saturn show 94 percent H_2 and 6 percent He, but the He content is expected to be greater in the interior of the planets; its atmosphere also contains minor and trace chemicals similar to those of Jupiter. CH_4 is estimated to comprise from 0.2 to 4 percent of the total volumes of the atmospheres of Uranus and Neptune, which are otherwise mostly H_2 and He. The only known constituent of the atmosphere of Pluto is CH_4.

Visible clouds

All of the atmospheres contain some liquid droplets and solid particles in suspension. In the case of Venus concentrations of H_2SO_4 (sulfuric acid) droplets form the bright clouds that completely obscure the surface of the planet. Earth's atmosphere is usually 50 percent covered by H_2O liquid and ice clouds, often clustered in storm patterns over the surface. Clouds of H_2O and CO_2 are sometimes visible in the Martian atmosphere, which is always filled with dust particles carried from the surface by strong winds; at certain seasons almost none of the surface is visible because of global dust storms.

The visible clouds of the giant planets generally form bands that surround the planets and are parallel to their equators. Jupiter's bands are the most striking in colour and duration; they are accompanied by smaller regions of local clouds, one of the most observed and long-lasting of which is the Great Red Spot. Saturn's clouds are more subdued in colour and contrast. The uppermost clouds of Jupiter and Saturn are probably NH_3 ice particles; at deeper levels clouds of NH_4HS (ammonium hydrogen sulfide) and H_2O may exist. The colours of the clouds may be due mostly to the presence of elemental sulfur or complex hydrocarbons. Cloud patterns have been detected in the atmospheres of Uranus and Neptune; above NH_3 clouds there may be CH_4 ice clouds in the atmospheres of both planets. The absorption of visible red light by gaseous CH_4 above the cloud tops makes both Uranus and Neptune appear bluish-green in colour.

Satellites. A satellite is a body in orbit around a planet or other body that, in turn, is in orbit around the Sun or, in principle, another star. When a satellite reaches half the size of the planet it circles, as seems to be the case with Pluto and its satellite, Charon, the system might better be called a double planet. At the other extreme, the planetary rings around Jupiter, Saturn, and Uranus are made up of innumerable tiny satellites, typically a few metres in diameter in the main rings of Saturn and probably much smaller in Jupiter's rings. Evidence has been put forth for satellites of minor planets in one or two cases, but it is not totally convincing.

The number of verified satellites in the solar system in the early 1980s was at least 44. Their diversity in size, morphology, and composition is at least as great as that among the planets themselves. In size they range from Jupiter's Ganymede and Saturn's Titan—which are larger than the planet Mercury—to tiny, irregular bodies such as Mars's Deimos. As might be expected, the inner planets have silicate satellites. Earth's Moon has a composition very much like that of Earth's own upper layers, mostly iron-magnesium silicates, but has no water. Phobos and Deimos, the small satellites of Mars, have a predominately silicate composition (based on considerations of density and spectra); they are probably captured asteroids.

Jovian satellites

The satellites of Jupiter present a somewhat more complex situation. Of the planet's Galilean satellites Io, which is mainly silicate, has been well differentiated—since it shows no spectral signature of water—and is the most geologically active body in the solar system. Io is being constantly pushed and pulled, as it orbits close to Jupiter, by the gravity fields of Jupiter and of Europa, the next satellite out. Europa is also mostly silicate but exhibits the spectral signature of water ice and is very bright. Ganymede has substantially more water than the inner two Galilean satellites and exhibits huge, rifted icy plates that, earlier in its history, were probably mobile over a plastic or partially molten water interior. Callisto has even more water than Ganymede and a relatively stable crust with little mobility over geologic time. Amalthea, a small inner satellite, could be a captured asteroid and is probably mainly silicate. The outer satellites are all small. Some are in retrograde orbits and may be captured minor planets or condensed remnants of a circumjovian cloud.

The major satellites of Saturn, with the exception of Titan, all have bulk densities within 40 percent of water, and that substance is undoubtedly a major constituent of all of them. The remarkable trait common to the major Saturnian satellites is that they appear to have had episodes of geologic activity, indicating internal heat sources with mobilization of surface materials. How such small icy bodies (all less than about 750 kilometres in radius), with little silicate material to generate internal heat through radioactive decay, could exhibit episodes of geological activity is still a mystery.

Titan

Titan is one of the most interesting objects in the solar system. It is the only satellite to possess a substantial atmosphere. The pressure at the surface of Titan is 1.6 atmospheres. Its atmosphere is probably composed of 82 percent N_2, 12 percent Ar, and 6 percent CH_4, with minor amounts of H_2. Complex hydrocarbons and nitriles (molecules with hydrogen, carbon, and nitrogen atoms) also exist in Titan's atmosphere. Clouds of CH_4 liquid droplets and other unidentified chemicals completely obscure its surface and give it a reddish-orange colour. It is possible that methane plays a role on Titan much like water does on Earth, with liquid methane seas and solid methane polar caps. Liquid hydrocarbons are probably raining down from the upper atmosphere, enough to produce a tar-like layer 100 metres thick. Its complex organic chemistry may hold clues to the beginnings of chemical evolution of life on Earth.

Little is known about the surfaces of the satellites of Uranus and Neptune. Triton, the largest satellite of Neptune, has a measurable amount of CH_4 gas, the surface pressure of which is roughly 0.0001 atmosphere.

Minor planets (asteroids). The innumerable bodies orbiting the Sun—other than the nine major planets and their satellites—that can in principle be studied individually are officially called either minor planets or comets, although the former are more commonly called asteroids. The first minor planet was discovered in 1801 and named Ceres. Ceres proved to be in a nearly circular orbit 2.77 astronomical units (a.u.) from the Sun, and modern observations give its diameter as about 1,000 kilometres, the largest of the minor planets. (One astronomical unit is the average distance of Earth from the Sun, or 149,598,000 kilometres.) Once a minor planet has a well-determined orbit, it is given a number and a name. By the end of 1982 there were 2,818 numbered minor planets, more than 95 percent of them fitting the original criteria. Statistical studies indicate that there are more than 1,000,000 minor planets between Mars and Jupiter with a diameter greater than one kilometre, but the total mass of all these is roughly equal to that of Ceres, and the total mass of all "main-belt" minor planets, including Ceres, is certainly less than a thousandth of Earth.

Ceres

Most minor planets are small objects of somewhat irregular shape. Broadly speaking, they show properties similar to Earth's Moon—probably cratered and overlain with rocky, dusty debris. Certain differences in colorimetric properties of the minor planets suggest different compositional families. Those of the C-type, with very low albedo (surface reflective power) are probably similar to carbonaceous chondrite meteorites, which are probably brittle, dark bodies with fine opaque material throughout and with hydrated (water-rich) mineral phases. Those of the S-type are thought to be similar to stony-iron meteorites in composition. Another, rarer group is the M-type, which is probably similar to nickel-iron meteorites.

The five percent of minor planets that, because of their orbits, do not fit the classical criteria include the Amor-class objects, which come nearer to the Sun than the perihelion distance of Mars (1.38 a.u.); the Apollo-class objects, which come nearer the Sun than Earth's mean distance (1 a.u.); and the Aten-class objects, whose average distance from the Sun is less than Earth's. There are at least 1,000 Trojan minor planets in the same orbit as Jupiter, but preceding or following it by roughly 60°. In 1977 a body a few hundred kilometres in diameter was discovered in an orbit extending inside Saturn's (to 8.5 a.u.) and outward nearly to that of Uranus (to 18.9 a.u.); it has been named Chiron.

Comets. Comets are believed to be "snowballs" of frozen gases and dust a few hundred metres to a few tens of kilometres in diameter. They move in very elongated orbits, and only when they approach near enough to the Sun for the ices to begin vaporizing rapidly do they become obvious and clearly identifiable. Yet the very process that makes them visible destroys them. After 1,000 passages near the Sun, there should be little left except, possibly, a small inert core. A typical short-period comet makes a revolution in 10 years or less, giving it a total lifetime of less than 10,000 years. A large body, especially Jupiter, can make major alterations (perturbations) in the orbit of any comet passing near it, sometimes shortening the period of revolution, sometimes lengthening it. Statistical studies of this process and others affecting cometary orbits and lifetimes indicate that the total number of comets may be as many as 3×10^{12}. Their combined mass would be nearly two Earth masses.

The Oort Cloud

Most comets are believed to be resident in the "Oort Cloud," with average distances from the Sun of 20,000 a.u. and periods of revolution about the Sun of several million years. Few of these ever come near enough to the Sun to become visible, but occasional orbital changes are brought about by passing stars, and a few of the comets so affected then come into the inner solar system as visible, long-period comets. A tiny fraction of these and other comets, which never become visible but still pass near the giant planets, are captured into short-period orbits. The major consequence of this behaviour is that nearly all comets that have been seen before and have well-determined orbits are old, faint, small, and nearly "worn-out." Among comets with periods of less than 100 years, only Halley's Comet is large enough (diameter about six kilometres) and bright enough to be seen with the naked eye at every appearance and to show all of the features common to the typically brighter long-period comets.

Every few years an unknown, large, long-period comet appears that comes close enough to the Sun and Earth to be spectacular. Examples are the comets Ikeya-Seki (1965), Bennett (1970), and West (1976). Because such objects are discovered only a few weeks before their closest approach to the Sun, it is nearly impossible to plan coordinated worldwide scientific study of them.

Meteoroids. Any body too small to be studied individually and moving in or through the solar system is called a meteoroid. Upon impact with an atmosphere it becomes a meteor. If some part survives and reaches the surface, it is a meteorite.

The smallest minor planets that have been studied individually are a few near one kilometre in diameter that have approached close to Earth, in some cases barely more than the distance of the Moon. There is also direct evidence of meteoroids in the solar system. Meteorites weighing from a few grams up to more than 50 metric tons (55 short tons) and roughly 3 × 3 × 1 metres in size have been found after impact on Earth. Craters, such as Arizona's Meteor Crater, give evidence of yet larger impacts. Every clear night, meteors ("shooting stars") are visible streaking across the sky, most of them particles only a few millimetres in diameter that burn up from atmospheric friction without ever reaching the ground.

The interplanetary medium also contains even lighter components than the smallest meteoroids, namely individual molecules, atoms, ions, and electrons from many sources. Most neutral molecules and atoms lost from comets or planets are fairly rapidly ionized by solar ultraviolet radiation, while the Sun itself is the largest source of interplanetary charged particles, which escape from the solar chromosphere. This "solar wind" has sufficient velocity to escape from the solar system, so although it is always present as a component of the interplanetary medium, individual ions, protons, and electrons are not in closed paths around the Sun. Solar activity, such as flares, triggers sporadic outbursts of charged particles that move much more rapidly across the solar system than the solar wind and also escape the system.

Theories of origin. It is generally thought that the solar system evolved from a nebular cloud associated with the proto-Sun. As that rotating cloud cooled and condensed, it formed a disk in which compositional and thermal gradients evolved. That early nebular differentiation is reflected in the systematic change in planetary composition, physical properties, correlated surface morphological properties, and composition of planetary atmospheres from the Sun outward through the solar system. The inner planets are silicate and metal-rich, while proportionately more and more volatiles such as water and methane are incorporated in planets and satellites that presumably had a cooler formation environment. The Jupiter system is an interesting analogue to the entire solar system from the standpoint of composition and physical properties—of the Galilean satellites Io is the closest and has the highest density and the least water, while Callisto is the farthest from Jupiter and possesses the most water.

Increasing evidence suggests that most of the original gases in the inner solar system were blown away during its early history. All the lighter gases, such as H_2 and He, exist only in the colder and gravitationally more powerful giant planets. The atmospheres of Venus, Earth, and Mars are considered to have evolved substantially over the course of time by extrusion of materials from their interiors in tectonic processes and volcanism. The differences between them are probably due to the effect of different amounts of sunlight and also to the extent to which their interiors were heated. The abundance of O_2 on Earth is almost certainly due to the presence of photosynthetic life, which converts CO_2 to O_2. The massive gravity of Jupiter probably allowed it to retain the same chemical constituents that existed at its distance from the Sun in the early solar nebula. This should also be true to some extent for the other giant planets, and their compositions, and those of comets, should provide the best clues to the distribution of chemicals in the outer solar system at the time of its formation.

BIBLIOGRAPHY. Popular accounts include: FRED L. WHIPPLE, *Orbiting the Sun: Planets and Satellites of the Solar System* (1981); J. KELLY BEATTY, BRIAN O'LEARY, and ANDREW CHAIKIN (eds.), *The New Solar System*, 2nd ed. (1982), a comprehensive account; and DAVID MORRISON, *Voyages to Saturn* (1982), and, with JANE SAMZ, *Voyages to Jupiter* (1980), discussions of the Voyager spacecraft studies. See also issues in the University of Arizona Space Science series, including: TOM GEHRELS (ed.), *Jupiter* (1976), *Protostars and Planets* (1978), and *Asteroids* (1979); JOSEPH A. BURNS (ed.), *Planetary Satellites* (1977); LAUREL L. WILKENING (ed.), *Comets* (1982); and DAVID MORRISON (ed.), *The Satellites of Jupiter* (1981). Authoritative reviews are found in *Annual Review of Earth and Planetary Sciences* and in *Annual Review of Astronomy and Astrophysics*. Most original work on the solar system is published in technical journals, the most prominent being: *Icarus* (monthly); *JGR: Journal of Geophysical Research* (monthly), containing a section on solid planets; *Astronomical Journal* (monthly); and *Science* (weekly).

(RAY L. NEWBURN, JR.; GLENN S. ORTON; DAVID C. PIERI)

February in Assam

November in El Salvador

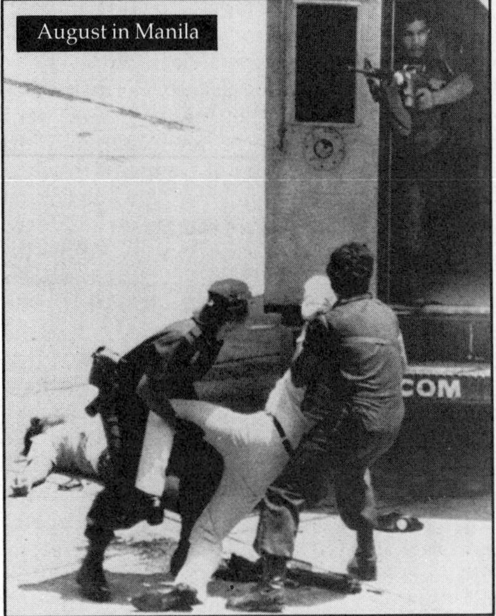

August in Manila

Christmas in London

May in Pretoria

October in Beirut

events of 1983

An experiment on a more enlarged ſcale was now projected; and a new machine, containing about 650 cubic feet, was made, which broke the cords that confined it, and roſe to the height of about 600 feet. Another of 35 feet in diameter roſe about 1000 feet high, and fell to the ground three quarters of a mile from the place where it aſcended. A public exhibition was next made on the 5th of June 1783, at Annonay, where a vaſt number of ſpectators aſſembled. An immenſe bag of linen, lined with paper, and containing upwards of 23,000 cubic feet, was found to have a power of lifting about 500 pounds, including its own weight. The operation was begun by burning chopped ſtraw and wool under the aperture of the machine, which immediately began to ſwell: and after being ſet at liberty aſcended into the atmoſphere. In ten minutes it had aſcended 6000 feet; and when its force was exhauſted, it fell to the ground at the diſtance of 7668 feet from the place from whence it ſet out.

Soon after this, one of the brothers arrived at Paris, where he was invited by the academy of ſciences to repeat his experiments at their expence...

...Along with this machine was ſent a wicker cage, containing a ſheep, a cock, and a duck, which were the firſt animals ever ſent through the atmoſphere. The full ſucceſs of the experiment was prevented by a violent guſt of wind which tore the cloth in two places near the top before it aſcended; However, it roſe to the height of 1440 feet; and after remaining in the air about eight minutes, fell to the ground at the diſtance of 10,200 feet from the place of its ſetting out. The animals were not in the leaſt hurt.

FROM THE THIRD EDITION OF *ENCYCLOPAEDIA BRITANNICA*, EDINBURGH, 1797

Aerial Sports

Extraordinary weather conditions in the California mountains led to the toppling of four world hang-gliding records on a single day in an aerial sports year that also featured the largest free-fall parachute formation in history and a world sailplane competition honoured as "the championship of champions." On July 13, flying from Horseshoe Meadows, Calif., Larry Tudor of the United States flew a 1-65 Comet II for 354.4 km (221.5 mi) to claim the world straight-distance record for hang gliding, breaking the 225-km (139.8-mi) record set by Robert Thompson of the U.S. in 1982. Flying the same day in the same location, Klaus Kohmstedt of Monaco logged an out-and-return distance world record of 272 km (170 mi), as well as a distance-to-goal flight of 224.7 km (140.44 mi) and an open-distance flight of 243 km (151.9 mi). Steve Moyes of Australia turned in a 305-km (190-mi) distance flight and John Pendry of the United Kingdom one of 299.2 km (187 mi).

Also at Horseshoe Meadows on July 13, Judy Leden of the U.K. claimed a straight-distance women's world record of 234.9 km (146.8 mi), flying a Wills Wing Duck. Two days later, again at Horseshoe Meadows, Lori Judy of the U.S. logged a women's out-and-return record of 123.7 km (77.3 mi).

At the world hang-gliding championship at Tegelberg, West Germany, from June 5 to 19, Steve Moyes won first place with 14,074 points in a Missile GT. Stu Smith of the U.S. was second with 13,315 points in a Sensor S-10, and Graham Hobson of the U.K. finished third with 13,130 points in a Magic-3.

The world soaring championship, held from June 21 to July 11 at Hobbs, N.M., attracted 109 entries from 25 countries, including such celebrated world champions as George Lee of the U.K., George Moffat of the U.S., Sweden's Goran Ax, Australia's Ingo Renner, and Marc Schroeder and François-Louis Henry of France. Turning in spectacular performances in excellent weather, Renner won first place in the open class with 11,784 points. Bruno Gantenbrink of West Germany was second with 11,295 points, and Henry placed third with 10,955 points. All three flew Nimbus 3s. In the standard class, Oye Stig of Denmark finished first with 10,780 points in an LS-4. Tom Beltz of the U.S. placed second with 10,771 points in an LS-4a, and John Buchanan of Australia was third with 10,714 points in an LS-4. The 15-m class was won by Kees Musters of The Netherlands with 11,259 points in a Ventus A, while Karl Striedieck of the U.S. was second with 11,145 points in an AS-W 20B, and Laurens Goudriaan of South Africa took third with 10,709 points in an AS-W 20.

On April 4 Thomas Knauff of the U.S. set the world absolute out-and-return distance record for gliders, flying 1,646.7 km (1,022.6 mi) from Ridge Soaring Gliderport, Julian, Pa., to Williamsport, Pa., and back in a Nimbus 3. This broke the record of 1,634.7 km (1,015.8 mi) set by Striedieck in 1977.

The Fédération Aéronautique Internationale

(FAI), world governing body for sport aviation, also certified the Dec. 14, 1982, world record claim of 195.3 km/h (121.4 mph) made by Ingo Renner for speed around a 100-km (62-mi) course in a Nimbus 3 at Tocumwal, Australia. Also confirmed was the Oct. 31, 1982, claim by S. H. and Helen Georgeson of New Zealand for the multiplace world record of 993.8 km (617.5 mi) straight-line distance set in a Janus C from Alexandra to Gisborne, N.Z.

The world parachute record for largest free-fall formation was achieved on April 3 by a 72-member male and female U.S. team, jumping from five aircraft at about 4,400 m (14,500 ft) over Deland, Fla. The previous official record was a 40-person free fall by a U.S. team achieved in 1980 over Yolo, Calif. The world women's record for biggest free-fall formation was set on August 14 by 32 U.S. women jumping over Freeport, Ill. An eight-canopy speed formation world record of 56.8 seconds was achieved by a U.S. team on June 22 at Muskogee, Okla.

The fifth annual World Relative Work Parachute Championship took place December 9–19 in the black South African state of Bophuthatswana. In the eight-way event the U.S. won first place with 102 points; Switzerland finished second with 72; and South Africa was third with 53. Switzerland won the four-way event with 115 points, followed by the U.S. with 108 and South Africa with 101. More than half the nations that usually participate in the tournament did not do so as a protest against South Africa's racial policies.

The year was the 200th anniversary of manned flight, celebrating the 1783 hot-air balloon voyage of the Montgolfier brothers of France. For balloonists it was also a year of tragedy and controversy. Maxie Anderson of the U.S., one of the three balloon pilots who thrilled the world with the first balloon crossing of the Atlantic in 1978, was killed in a crash on June 27 during a race in West Germany (*see* OBITUARIES). The tragedy was blamed on a gondola release mechanism that malfunctioned when Anderson and co-pilot Don Ida attempted an emergency landing to avoid crossing into East Germany.

As a gesture to France, the world hot-air balloon championship was held in Nantes from August 29 to September 5, but U.S. and Canadian teams withdrew over what they charged were numerous violations of FAI rules by French contest authorities. Peter Vizzard of Australia won the competition with 7,726 points, Olivier Roux-Devillas of France was second with 7,184 points, and David Bareford of the U.K. was third with 7,036 points.

A world record for duration with balloons of 600–900 cu m was set by John Burk of the U.S. with a time of 5 hours 44 minutes at Carlisle, Pa. Edward Chapman of the U.S. had his Dec. 12, 1982, altitude mark of 10,084.3 m (33,085 ft) over Prior Lake, Minn., established as the record for balloons of 1,200–1,600 cu m. A duration record of 8 hours 12 minutes was set on May 30 for balloons of less than 250 cu m by Coy Foster of the U.S. at Plano, Texas. He also set a distance record of 274.4 km (171.5 mi). Josef Starkbaum of Austria reached 13,670 m (45,111 ft) at Lole, Austria, on August 6 to establish a new world's altitude record for balloons of 2,200–3,000 cu m.

WIDE WORLD

A combination of airplane and parachute is the paraplane, flown here by Ray Hill, outdoor editor of *Popular Mechanics*. He flew the twin-engined craft at 42 kilometres per hour (26 miles per hour) after 15 minutes of ground instruction. If the engine fails, the plane settles to the ground with its parachute.

On a flight that ended on February 18, Brooke Knapp, who became a pilot in 1978 to overcome a fear of flying, set a round-the-world speed record for business jets of 50 hours 22 minutes 49 seconds in a Gates Learjet 35A. It was her 14th world record. (MICHAEL D. KILIAN)

Afghanistan

Afghanistan

A people's republic in central Asia, Afghanistan is bordered by the U.S.S.R., China, Pakistan, and Iran. Area: 652,090 sq km (251,773 sq mi). Pop. (1982 est.): 16,786,000, including (1978 est.) Pashtun 53%; Tadzhik 20%; Uzbek 9%; Hazara 9%; other 9% (though estimates vary, by 1983 the exodus to Pakistan and Iran accounted for approximately 4.5 million). Cap. and largest city: Kabul (pop., 1979 prelim., 749,000). Language: Pashto and Persian. Religion: Muslim 99% (including 80% Sunni; 20% Shi'ah); Hindu, Sikh, and Jewish 1%. President of the Revolutionary Council in 1983, Babrak Karmal; prime minister, Sultan Ali Keshtmand.

During 1983 the Muslim insurgency against the Soviet-backed government of Pres. Babrak Karmal remained locked in military stalemate against Soviet and Afghan troops. The government controlled the cities, while the guerrillas controlled the countryside. There were conflicting reports on the success of the regime in either neutralizing the insurgency movement or crushing it with the aid of some 110,000 Soviet troops. Reports on the war were sketchy and probably biased, since they were based on accounts given either by Pakistan-based rebel groups or by journalists taken on conducted tours by the government.

Predictions of a change in Soviet policy toward Afghanistan had gained credence in some Western

Aden:
see Yemen, People's Democratic Republic of

Advertising:
see Industrial Review

Aerospace Industry:
see Defense; Industrial Review; Space Exploration; Transportation

PIERRE ISSOT-SERGENT—GAMMA/LIAISON

More than three years after their invasion of Afghanistan, Soviet troops and troops of the Soviet-backed Afghan government had failed to eradicate resistance forces such as this band of guerrillas.

capitals after the death of Soviet Pres. Leonid I. Brezhnev in November 1982 and the appointment of Yury Andropov as his successor. Western analysts claimed that Andropov, in his previous post as head of the Soviet State Security Committee (KGB), had consistently opposed Soviet military intervention in Afghanistan. But in a statement issued on Dec. 31, 1982, the Soviet news agency TASS declared that Soviet troops would remain in Afghanistan until long-standing Soviet conditions for their withdrawal were met. These conditions included an assurance of noninterference by Pakistan, Iran, and other nations in the internal affairs of Afghanistan.

Nevertheless, Andropov, Soviet Foreign Minister Andrey Gromyko, and UN Secretary-General Javier Pérez de Cuéllar held talks in Moscow on March 28 on ways of normalizing the situation in Afghanistan. No definite results emerged from the discussions, but the UN continued its efforts to find a political solution to the Afghan issue.

Diego Cordovez, UN special representative for Afghanistan, held consultations in Pakistan, Afghanistan, and Iran from January 21 to February 7. He reported that the consultations centred on "substantive contents of a comprehensive settlement" and maintained that it was possible to widen the understanding reached at Geneva in June 1982. The interrelated elements of a comprehensive settlement were the withdrawal of foreign troops, international guarantees of noninterference and nonintervention, and arrangements for the return of Afghan refugees to Afghanistan.

Seven days of talks sponsored by the UN on the withdrawal of Soviet troops ended in Geneva on June 24 with no sign of major progress on the issue. The talks were conducted by a UN negotiator who met separately and alternately with delegates from Pakistan and Afghanistan. Pakistan was involved in the talks because an estimated three million Afghan refugees had crossed into its territory and because the Soviet Union asserted that Pakistan was the main supporter of the *mujaheddin* (Islamic guerrillas) and the major channel through which arms reached them. Iran, which by its own estimate housed 1.5 million Afghan refugees, was boycotting the talks because it believed that no negotiations should be undertaken without the participation of the guerrillas.

At home President Karmal was firmly in command of the ruling People's Democratic Party. Infighting between the Parcham and Khalq factions of the party was less evident in 1983 than in previous years, and it appeared that the Soviets had succeeded in bringing them under control.

Afghanistan continued to depend on the Soviet Union for economic aid and food assistance. The turnover of trade between the two countries in 1982 reached a record figure of 700 million rubles, 40 million higher than in 1981. A Soviet spokesman reported that a considerable portion of Afghan exports consisted of products from some 170 projects that had been set up with Soviet assistance. As many as 12 new Soviet-assisted projects

AFGHANISTAN

Education. (1980–81) Primary, pupils 1,044,969, teachers (1979–80) 32,937; secondary, pupils 123,126, teachers (1979–80) 4,903; vocational (1979–80), pupils 16,784, teachers 1,211; higher, students (1979–80) 22,974, teaching staff 1,448.

Finance. Monetary unit: afghani, with (Sept. 20, 1983) an official rate of 50.60 afghanis to U.S. $1 (free rate of 76 afghanis = £1 sterling). Gold and other reserves (June 1983) U.S. $260 million. Budget (1980–81 est.): revenue 23,478,000,000 afghanis; expenditure 19,213,000,000 afghanis. Money supply (March 1982) 48,509,000,000 afghanis.

Foreign Trade. Imports (1980–81) 38,491,000,000 afghanis; exports (1981–82) 35,130,000,000 afghanis. Import sources (1979–80): U.S.S.R. 54%; Japan 12%. Export destinations (1979–80): U.S.S.R. 52%; Pakistan 11%; India 9%; U.K. 7%; West Germany 7%. Main exports: natural gas 39%; fruits and nuts 32%; carpets 10%.

Transport and Communications. Roads (1978) 18,752 km. Motor vehicles in use (1980): passenger c. 34,100; commercial (including buses) c. 29,000. Air traffic (1981): c. 129 million passenger-km; freight c. 19.4 million net ton-km. Telephones (1980) 32,000. Radio receivers (1980) 1.2 million. Television receivers (1980) 45,000.

Agriculture. Production (in 000; metric tons; 1982): wheat c. 3,100; corn c. 805; rice c. 483; barley c. 353; grapes c. 450; cotton, lint c. 22; wool, clean c. 14. Livestock (in 000; 1981): cattle c. 3,800; karakul sheep c. 4,500; other sheep c. 15,500; goats c. 3,000; horses c. 410; asses c. 1,300; camels c. 270.

Industry. Production (in 000; metric tons; 1980–81): coal 119; natural gas (cu m) 2,790,000; cotton fabrics (m) 43,300; rayon fabrics (m) 14,800; nitrogenous fertilizers (nutrient content; 1981–82) c. 49; cement 87; electricity (kw-hr; 1981) 1,035,000.

went into production in 1983, thus contributing to the overall rise of 3.7% in industrial production and the 5% growth in the gross national product. In 1983 the Soviet Union imported increased quantities of natural gas, cotton, wool, dried fruits, and carpets from Afghanistan and supplied it with more machinery and equipment, petroleum products, fertilizer, timber, and newsprint.

(DILIP GANGULY)

African Affairs

Africa's major concerns during 1983 were the deepening economic crisis, exacerbated by one of the worst droughts ever experienced over such a large part of the continent; the future of the Organization of African Unity; the failure to settle the conflict over South West Africa/Namibia; the resumption of civil war in Chad; and the continuing conflict in the Western Sahara. However, there were also some encouraging developments, especially a reduction of tension in the Maghrib.

The Organization of African Unity. The damaging conflict within the 50-nation Organization of African Unity (OAU), whose future existence had seemed to be threatened by two successive failures during 1982 to muster quorums for the 19th annual summit meeting scheduled for Tripoli, Libya, was finally resolved in June 1983 when members agreed to move the site of the meeting to the OAU's headquarters in Addis Ababa, Eth. As it was customary for the host country to assume the chair for the ensuing year, this change of venue meant that Ethiopia's head of state, Col. Mengistu Haile Mariam, became chairman instead of Libya's Col. Muammar al-Qaddafi (*see* BIOGRAPHIES).

One of the issues that had aborted the Tripoli summit was the acceptance by the Saharan Arab Democratic Republic (SADR), Western Sahara's government-in-exile, of OAU membership. This issue was temporarily resolved when the movement behind SADR, the Popular Front for the Liberation of Saguia el Hamra and Río de Oro (Polisario Front), was persuaded to leave the SADR seat vacant at the Addis Ababa summit. This opened the way for Morocco to accept a new formula for resolving the long-standing dispute; the agreement provided for an early referendum under international supervision to allow Saharans to choose between complete independence or Moroccan sovereignty.

The search for agreement over the Chad conflict proved equally elusive. Following the OAU refusal to recognize the claims of the ousted president Goukouni Oueddei over those of Pres. Hissen Habré, Libya again became militarily involved in support of the former. This led to a new round of fighting which caused Zaire's Pres. Mobutu Sese Seko to dispatch several thousand troops to assist Habré; more important, though, was France's decision to provide strong air support and arms for Habré. This external support made it possible for Habré to repel the attackers, but not to defeat them entirely, so that the country remained divided and in a state of continuing civil war. The OAU failed to get both rival leaders to a conference because Habré refused to sit down with Goukouni.

Southern Africa. UN Secretary-General Javier Pérez de Cuéllar visited South Africa in August in a new initiative to break the deadlock over Namibia. Pérez de Cuéllar reported encouraging progress in persuading the South African government to accept all the necessary conditions in fulfillment of the UN Security Council's Resolution 435, which established the machinery for achievement of the territory's independence; however, implementation of the agreement continued to be blocked by South Africa's insistence that the estimated 17,000 Cuban combat troops in Angola should be withdrawn first. This precondition was supported by the U.S. but not by the other members of the Western contact group (Britain, France, West Germany, and Canada). The Angola regime continued to resist any proposal to link the two issues, and in December France pulled out of the contact group, in large measure because of its disagreement with the South Africa/U.S. position.

Meanwhile, the situation in Angola itself grew more difficult because of the growing military challenge presented by Jonas Savimbi's Union for the Total Independence of Angola (UNITA). The security situation inside South Africa and around its borders also steadily worsened. The South African Defense Forces (SADF) no longer restricted themselves to transborder attacks to strike at the

Pres. Ahmed Kerekou (in white) of Benin and Pres. Gnassingbe Eyadema of Togo jointly announced the opening of their common border to allow the passage of thousands of Ghanaians to their homeland following their ouster from Nigeria.

MICHEL SETBOUN—BLACK STAR

AFRICAPIX/SIPA PRESS—BLACK STAR

Not since the mid-1960s has a high-ranking Chinese official visited Africa. Premier Zhao Ziyang (Chao Tzu-yang) made the trip in 1983; he is shown (foreground) with Pres. Daniel arap Moi of Kenya.

guerrilla forces of the South West Africa People's Organization (SWAPO) of Namibia but maintained permanent garrisons in southern Angola.

Guerrilla insurgents of the externally based African National Congress (ANC) succeeded in making a number of damaging attacks on targets inside South Africa; after each major attack the SADF made retaliatory attacks into Lesotho and Mozambique to strike at ANC positions and, as South Africa insisted, to show that support for the guerrillas would not go unpunished. South Africa also continued to support opposition movements in Angola, Mozambique, and Lesotho but strongly denied involvement in the sabotaging of a substantial part of the Zimbabwe Air Force or in the flare-up of dissident activities in the Matabeleland region of Zimbabwe. Zimbabwe's Prime Minister Robert Mugabe, however, continued to insist that his government had evidence to prove South Africa's military involvement.

The Horn of Africa. The Ethiopian military regime continued to pursue its goal of deepening the Marxist-Leninist revolution in its country and had several high-level discussions with Soviet-bloc leaders to promote this aim. The revolutionary momentum was held back by armed resistance, particularly in Eritrea and Tigre. While the security situation in the Ogaden no longer posed a serious threat, relations with Somalia continued to be troubled.

A serious new development in the region was the renewal of violence in the southern Sudan with the rebirth of the Anya Nya movement, named after a particularly poisonous insect, which had led a bitter armed struggle during the years 1956–72. The resurgence of violence from elements of the non-Muslim population coincided with the decision of Pres. Gaafar Nimeiry's regime to split Sudan's southern region into three provinces for reasons of administrative convenience; some southerners saw this as a move by the government to divide and rule over them. Resentment was sharpened by the president's decree in September applying Shariʿah (Islamic law) to the entire country.

Coups and Inter-African Affairs. There were two successful military coups during 1983. In Upper Volta's second coup in as many years, Capt. Thomas Sankara (*see* BIOGRAPHIES) seized power in August. He denied suggestions of Libyan involvement. More disquieting was the situation in Nigeria, where, on the last day of the year, the civilian government of Pres. Alhaji Shehu Shagari was overthrown and a military government was installed under Maj. Gen. Mohammed Buhari. Only a few months earlier, Shagari's ruling party had received a convincing mandate in the country's first general election under civilian rule in almost 20 years.

While Qaddafi's speeches and his avowedly military role in Chad helped fan the suspicions of a number of African governments that Libya was a centre of subversion, he pursued a much more accommodating policy toward Morocco, Tunisia, and Algeria. At the same time, there was a major thaw in relations between Algeria and Morocco. These various changes provided greater promise for a settlement to the Sahara conflict, which had acutely divided the Maghrib countries.

Although the Economic Community of West African States (ECOWAS), which linked 14 French-speaking and English-speaking nations, had not yet lived up to expectations of bringing about closer integration in the region, the Community nevertheless survived the painful episode of the mass expulsion of an estimated two million West Africans from Nigeria. In East Africa there was a significant improvement in relations between Kenya and Tanzania, and with Uganda friendly to both its neighbours, there was fresh hope of final agreement in the long dispute over apportionment of the assets of the former East African Community and a new form of economic association.

Political Systems. Growing political pressures for democratic government and the need felt by a number of regimes to legitimize their rule led to the holding of a number of national elections. Elections in Mauritius caused the defeat of the Mauritius Militant Movement, which had swept to power in the 1982 polls. In Seychelles Pres. France-Albert René showed that his ruling party could mobilize a sizable measure of popular support, but in Madagascar Pres. Didier Ratsiraka's party was returned to office less convincingly. Equatorial Guinea held its first elections in 19 years. Zambia's Pres. Kenneth Kaunda had little difficulty in retaining a position he had held since 1964.

External Relations. Although one consequence of the deepening economic crisis was to strengthen the ambivalence underlying much of Africa's relations with the Western community, it also compelled the continent's leaders to accept, however reluctantly, that there was little alternative to their relying on the markets and financial systems of Europe and North America, as well as on such institutions as the International Monetary Fund (IMF) and the World Bank. Recognition of these realities was shown in the steady flow of visits by African leaders to Western capitals and a reduced number of such visits to the Soviet bloc. Even the leaders of such self-proclaimed Marxist regimes as Angola, Mozambique, Cape Verde, and Benin found it necessary to go with this tide.

The U.S. remained a major donor of economic and military aid to those governments that it especially favoured, in particular Egypt, Morocco, Tunisia, Sudan, Kenya, and Somalia. Its militant opposition to Qaddafi's regime proved controversial, as did its policy of insisting on the Cuban withdrawal from Angola. While most African governments voted in favour of the U.S.-sponsored resolution in the UN Security Council denouncing the U.S.S.R. over the shooting down of a South Korean civil aircraft, virtually no support was to be had for the U.S. decision to invade Grenada.

Contrary to expectations, French Pres. François Mitterrand's Socialist government kept up an activist policy in regard to Africa. Its decision to provide military aid to Habré's regime in Chad was a complete reversal of the stand previously taken by Mitterrand. The annual summit meeting of the Franco-African community in France in October attracted a larger number of delegates than any previous meeting.

Soviet-bloc countries made only a small contribution toward alleviating the continent's acute financial needs; even their support of governments sympathetic to them was relatively unimportant. Soviet interests focused mainly on helping to promote the Ethiopian revolution, providing military and technical support to Marxist-oriented countries as well as Libya, and backing two liberation movements, the ANC and SWAPO. However, there was no real evidence that the Soviets wished to become seriously involved in any of the inter-African conflicts.

China's premier and other government leaders undertook visits to a number of African countries. While not significantly increasing its economic aid, China did make some major new contributions, particularly to Tanzania and Zambia. Liberia became the second OAU member, after Zaire, to breach the OAU boycott by establishing diplomatic ties with Israel. However, Israel's hopes of substantially breaching the boycott remained unfulfilled.

Economic and Social Affairs. The deterioration in Africa's economy, which began in the 1970s, showed signs of worsening, partly because of the continuing world economic recession and also because of an exceptionally prolonged period of drought. The UN Economic Commission for Africa warned that current trends could lead to poverty of "unimaginable dimensions." The World Bank and the IMF pointed out that all the main economic indicators—growth rates, export levels, agricultural growth rates, and food imports—gave rise to extreme concern. The situation was worst in sub-Saharan Africa, where, excluding Nigeria, economic growth in 1981 and 1982 was only 1.2%, less than half the rate of population growth. While the IMF noted promising signs in a few countries, notably Uganda, Sudan, Ivory Coast, the Congo, and Nigeria, it warned that per capita income was continuing to fall.

The UN Food and Agriculture Organization gave details in July of 18 African countries that faced famine through drought, disease, and war. Calling for an urgent international rescue operation, it reported that, of the 120 million inhabitants in drought-stricken territories, more than 4 million were in urgent need of grain to avert actual starvation. Worst affected were southern Africa and the Sahel area, covering a band of countries from Cape Verde and Mauritania eastward to Chad and Sudan. In October the FAO lengthened the list of countries facing catastrophic food shortages to 22. (COLIN LEGUM)

See also Dependent States; articles on the various political units.

Agriculture and Food Supplies

The year 1983 was a mediocre one overall for agricultural and food production. Food shortages were rampant in large parts of Africa, while at the same time expensive agricultural surpluses burdened the governments of major agricultural countries in the developed world. The existence of these surpluses and the measures adopted to control them intensified the skirmishing between those nations in the realm of agricultural trade policy. For the longer term a tentative consensus appeared to be developing in the scientific community that the global climate was warming and would require important adaptations in agriculture.

Production. World agricultural and food production was likely to have declined in 1983 because of the effects of drought and supply restraint programs in the United States and smaller crops in Western Europe. As a result, per capita food production fell in 1983 according to preliminary estimates (in December 1983) of the U.S. Department of Agriculture's (USDA's) Economic Research Service. Two areas that experienced sharp production reverses in 1982, Asia and Oceania, had strong increases in output in 1983, and the performance of the Soviet Union was better than it had been for some time. China fell considerably short of the large gains that it registered in 1982. Aggregate food production probably increased a little more slowly than did population growth in the less developed countries, although per capita food production rose in the less developed countries of Asia. As of September 1983 the United Nations Food and Agriculture Organization (FAO) reported 33 countries to be suffering from abnormal food shortages.

These food emergencies were increasingly concentrated in sub-Saharan Africa. The western and southern parts of that continent were hardest hit. The south experienced the worst drought of the century; some seven million people there faced the threat of severe hunger and, possibly, starvation. Many areas suffered the effects of drought for the second year in a row, and food supplies were short in 20 or more countries. Political strife and long-term economic problems were the causes of, or contributed to, food crises in other nations.

Most of these African countries were among the poorest and were dependent upon food aid to meet their increased needs. Only Ivory Coast and South Africa appeared able to afford sufficient commercial imports to cover shortages. The USDA estimated that 18 of the poorest sub-Saharan countries would need nearly three million tons of food aid in 1983–84 in addition to projected commercial purchases of close to five million tons. The FAO estimated that food aid to some 22 African countries would have to be increased from 1.5 million tons of cereal in 1982–83 to 3.2 million tons in 1983–84.

In the fall the secretary-general of FAO called upon donors to increase their food aid to Africa, and the U.S. proposed to increase its emergency food assistance from $25 million to $50 million; total U.S. food aid to southern Africa totaled about $200 million in fiscal 1984.

GRAINS. After two years of large increases, world grain production was expected to decline in 1983–84 because of a sharp drop in the output of coarse grains, those other than wheat and rice. World trade in grains was expected to show little growth in 1983–84, largely because of slow economic growth that continued to depress the demand for coarse grains. Although world stocks of coarse grains were expected to be drawn down sharply by the end of 1983–84, those of wheat remained ample. As a result, world prices of coarse grains strengthened, while those for wheat remained depressed.

Another bumper world wheat crop was harvested in 1983–84 despite an estimated 5% reduction in harvested area from 239 million ha (1 ha = 2.47 ac) in 1982–83. Government programs in the United States operated to reduce the harvested area for wheat by nearly 23% from 1982–83, but U.S. wheat output declined only 14% from the 76 million metric tons harvested at that time because farmers tended to set aside their least productive land and the drought that devastated corn production came too late to affect wheat.

The availability of large wheat supplies in all of the major wheat-exporting countries led to intensified price and credit competition for shares of an import market that had shown little growth over the past four years. Among the other major wheat exporters, Australia harvested 10 million tons more wheat than its 9 million-ton, drought-reduced crop in 1982–83; Canada very nearly matched the 1982–83 record output of almost 27 million tons; and the production of the European Economic Community (EEC) almost equaled the 1982–83 total of 60 million tons. Of the major wheat-importing countries, both China and India had large wheat harvests.

Total world production of wheat was likely to exceed the total use of wheat for the third year in a row, contributing to a further buildup in the already ample wheat stocks. The U.S. by the end of 1982–83 was holding nearly 43% of the total, and its share was expected to decline to a little under 40% by the end of 1983–84. A large Soviet harvest of coarse grains in 1983–84 was making possible the substitution of coarse grains for wheat in that country's animal feed rations. The U.S.S.R. was

Table I. Selected Indexes of World Agricultural and Food Production

1969–71 = 100

Region or country	Total agricultural production						Total food production						Per capita food production					
	1978	1979	1980	1981	1982	1983[1]	1978	1979	1980	1981	1982	1983[1]	1978	1979	1980	1981	1982	1983[1]
Developed countries	116	120	118	123	125	115	117	120	119	124	126	116	109	112	110	113	115	105
United States	118	124	117	131	131	106	119	125	118	131	132	109	110	114	107	117	117	95
Canada	119	116	118	129	135	130	122	118	121	132	140	134	110	106	107	115	121	114
Western Europe	115	119	124	121	126	123	116	119	124	121	126	123	111	114	119	116	120	117
EEC	114	118	123	122	125	122	114	118	123	122	125	122	111	114	119	117	120	117
Japan	105	105	94	96	98	99	105	105	94	96	98	99	95	94	84	85	87	87
Oceania	122	117	108	115	108	120	132	124	113	121	113	127	117	110	99	104	96	107
South Africa	133	129	137	153	135	115	136	131	142	160	140	118	112	106	111	122	104	86
Centrally planned economies	126	126	125	126	134	138	127	127	125	126	134	138	111	109	107	106	111	113
U.S.S.R.	123	115	113	109	116	123	123	114	112	108	115	123	115	105	102	98	104	109
Eastern Europe	126	124	121	124	128	125	127	125	122	125	129	125	120	117	115	116	119	116
China[2]	132	147	148	156	172	179	133	149	149	155	170	176	113	125	124	127	136	139
Less developed countries	129	129	132	139	139	142	131	131	134	141	142	145	108	105	106	108	106	106
East Asia[3]	143	143	147	156	158	160	147	146	150	160	162	165	122	119	120	125	125	124
Indonesia	134	139	150	165	161	167	139	143	155	171	168	173	117	118	126	136	130	132
South Korea	164	161	143	152	158	161	163	160	142	152	158	161	139	135	118	125	127	128
Malaysia	147	158	165	168	179	174	161	180	192	199	216	208	132	143	149	151	161	151
Philippines	138	136	142	151	148	147	140	137	143	152	149	147	112	107	109	112	107	103
Thailand	162	145	165	173	166	174	175	150	176	180	177	187	142	119	137	137	132	136
South Asia	124	118	121	130	127	138	125	119	121	131	128	141	105	97	97	102	98	105
Bangladesh	114	114	121	120	125	129	115	115	124	124	129	133	93	91	95	91	93	92
India	127	118	121	132	128	142	127	118	121	132	127	143	106	97	97	104	98	108
Pakistan	113	128	129	140	143	141	123	132	134	145	148	151	100	104	102	106	105	104
West Asia	140	138	141	140	146	147	142	140	143	141	147	147	112	108	107	103	105	102
Iran	160	149	135	127	129	132	165	152	139	130	133	136	130	118	104	94	93	92
Turkey	132	132	135	139	146	143	132	133	136	141	149	145	107	106	105	107	110	105
Sub-Saharan Africa[4]	110	114	117	121	122	119	112	116	119	124	124	121	90	90	90	91	88	84
Ethiopia	93	99	101	104	107	109	91	97	99	103	106	107	77	82	84	86	87	86
Nigeria	111	121	127	127	131	122	112	122	128	128	131	123	92	93	90	90	90	81
North Africa	118	120	127	123	128	124	122	123	130	126	132	128	99	97	100	94	95	90
Morocco	121	119	121	98	123	109	120	119	122	98	123	109	96	92	92	72	88	75
Egypt	113	117	122	123	126	127	120	123	127	130	135	138	100	100	99	99	100	100
Latin America	134	138	142	150	149	148	137	141	145	153	154	151	112	113	114	117	115	111
Argentina	134	139	127	138	144	132	135	141	128	141	146	134	118	121	108	117	120	108
Brazil	136	144	161	169	163	176	143	150	171	172	175	182	117	120	133	131	130	132
Colombia	141	150	158	161	165	162	144	152	161	161	168	167	122	127	132	130	132	129
Mexico	143	145	146	160	148	146	148	151	152	168	157	154	117	116	114	123	112	107
Venezuela	146	146	153	154	160	158	148	149	156	158	165	163	108	104	105	102	104	99
World	123	124	124	128	132	130	124	125	125	129	133	131	107	106	104	105	107	103

[1] Preliminary. [2] Represents about two-thirds of all field crops (includes all major field crops), but excludes livestock products. [3] Excludes Japan. [4] Excludes South Africa.
Source: USDA, Economic Research Service, International Economic Division, January 1984.

UPI

Iowa farmers rallied at Des Moines, calling for a moratorium—later granted at least temporarily—on foreclosures on farms with delinquent mortgages.

also thought to be in a position to add to its wheat stocks for the first time since 1978–79 despite a third straight year of disappointing wheat harvests. In several of the world's market economies, large global wheat stocks translated into low market prices for wheat, which, together with rapidly climbing prices for coarse grains, encouraged the substitution of wheat for feed grains in animal rations.

World rice production was expected to rise in 1983–84, although rice consumption probably exceeded output. As a result, stocks of rice were expected to continue at somewhat below normal levels. Favourable monsoon rainfall permitted India to harvest a record rice crop, 20% larger than the previous year's drought-damaged harvest, and to build up its stocks. China's rice harvest was smaller than in 1982–83, but even so a bumper

Table II. World Cereal Supply and Distribution
In 000,000 metric tons

	1980–81	1981–82	1982–83	1983–84[1]
Production				
Wheat	442	449	480	485
Coarse grains	731	767	783	686
Rice, milled	270	280	286	293
Total	1,443	1,496	1,549	1,464
Utilization				
Wheat	442	445	468	479
Coarse grains	740	736	760	760
Rice, milled	272	281	290	294
Total	1,454	1,461	1,519	1,533
Exports				
Wheat	94	101	98	101
Coarse grains	108	98	91	91
Rice, milled	13	12	12	12
Total	215	212	201	203
Ending stocks[2]				
Wheat	81	85	97	103
Coarse grains	85	115	138	60
Rice, milled	22	21	16	16
Total	188	221	251	178
Stocks as % of utilization				
Wheat	18.2%	19.2%	20.6%	21.4%
Coarse grains	11.5%	15.6%	18.1%	7.9%
Rice, milled	8.1%	7.5%	5.7%	5.3%
Total	12.9%	15.2%	16.5%	11.6%
Stocks held by U.S. in %				
Wheat	33.3%	37.1%	43.3%	37.7%
Coarse grains	40.7%	62.0%	71.4%	37.8%
Rice, milled	2.3%	7.6%	14.0%	8.3%
Total	33.0%	47.2%	56.8%	35.2%

[1] Forecast.
[2] Does not include estimates of total Chinese or Soviet stocks but is adjusted for estimated changes in Soviet stocks.
Source: USDA, Foreign Agricultural Service, December 1983.

wheat crop reduced that country's need for food grain imports in 1983–84. Indonesia continued to make substantial rice imports, despite an increased rice crop, in order to avoid further depletion in stocks.

World output of coarse grains was forecast to decline nearly 13%, primarily because of a 53% reduction in U.S. production of coarse grains. U.S. corn (maize) production plummeted 51% from the 213 million tons harvested in 1982–83 because of the effects of both controls on supply and a severe drought. Soviet coarse grain output rose an estimated 22 million tons from 86 million tons in 1982–83. Among other major coarse grain importers, production was down substantially in both Western and Eastern Europe. Among the other exporters, Canadian coarse grain production declined, while harvests in early 1985 by both Australia and South Africa were expected to recover from the effects of drought in 1982–83.

Coarse grain utilization was expected to increase in 1983–84 despite the sharp drop in coarse grain output because of the large stocks carried in after the 1982–83 season. However, rising coarse grain prices, low prices for feed wheat, and the small growth in consumption of livestock products in many countries because of slow economic recovery were slowing demand for coarse grains. An 18 million-ton decline in U.S. coarse grain consumption was expected to be offset by a nearly identical increase in Soviet utilization. The factors dampening the demand for feed grains were also likely to contribute in 1983–84 to a reduction in world trade in coarse grains for the second year in a row.

Global utilization of coarse grains was expected to exceed production by about 78 million tons in 1983–84 and to result in an equivalent reduction in world grain stocks. The U.S. share of those stocks had grown to nearly 75% of the total by the end of 1982–83, but it was likely to decline to under 40% in 1983–84. Prices of the major coarse grains rose dramatically.

CASSAVA. World cassava production was forecast (in July) by the FAO to decline about 4% in 1983, largely because of drought and pests in Afri-

Table III. World Cassava Production
In 000,000 metric tons (root equivalent)

Region	1981	1982[1]	1983[2]
Far East	47.1	48.8	46.8
China	3.3	3.3	3.3
India	5.8	5.6	5.6
Indonesia	13.7	13.0	13.0
Philippines	2.3	2.3	2.3
Thailand	16.5	16.8	14.8
Vietnam	3.4	3.0	3.0
Africa	47.5	48.8	46.8
Angola	1.9	2.0	2.1
Ghana	1.9	1.9	1.5
Mozambique	2.9	2.9	1.9
Nigeria	11.8	11.7	11.7
Tanzania	4.7	4.7	4.4
Zaire	13.0	13.2	13.0
Latin America	31.3	31.2	31.0
Brazil	24.8	24.5	24.5
Colombia	2.2	2.0	2.0
Total	125.9	128.8	124.6

[1] Preliminary.
[2] Forecast.
Source: FAO, *Food Outlook* (July 1983).

ca and reduced plantings in Thailand. Losses were particularly severe in Mozambique and Ghana. Thailand began a major crop diversification program in cassava-producing areas in 1982; it was partly financed by the EEC to compensate for its restrictions on cassava imports. The development of a new variety of cassava in Thailand with a greater starch content than the standard variety—about 23% compared with 18%—was favouring its substitution for rice starch in several countries, especially for the production of alcohol.

The FAO warned that the cassava mealybug represented a serious threat to cassava production and, thus, to the many Africans who relied upon cassava as an important staple food. The pest was indigenous to South America and apparently was introduced into Africa in 1973. The International Institute of Tropical Agriculture proposed a large-scale project for its biological control.

OILSEEDS. Global oilseed production was forecast late in the year to decline sharply in 1983–84. The 9% decline mostly reflected the impact of events in the U.S., where drought and the effects of programs designed to restrain grain production cut soybean output by nearly one-third. However, because of the very large carryover of soybean stocks from the bountiful 1982–83 harvest, oilseed demand, as measured by the global oilseed crush, was expected to fall less than 3% from the 145 million tons in 1982–83. As a result, oilseed stocks, which had risen 20% to 16.4 million tons during 1982–83, were expected to be cut more than half by the end of 1983–84.

World stocks of soybeans rose about one-third in 1982–83 to about 12.8 million tons, and prices responded by falling by October 1982 to the lowest point since 1975, an average of $212 per ton (cost, insurance, freight [c.i.f.], Rotterdam). The very sharp drop in 1983–84 soybean output was expected to drive down stocks by more than 50%, and soybean prices climbed steadily to $350 by September 1983 before easing somewhat.

Smaller supplies and rising prices of soybeans were expected to reduce their crushing in both the U.S. and the EEC in 1983–84. Some increase in soybean output and crushings was expected from the Southern Hemisphere harvest in early 1984. Nevertheless, world crushings of soybeans, which had increased 2.4% in 1982–83 to a total of 76.6 million tons, were expected to fall about 5% in 1983–84. Thus, output of soybean meal was forecast to decline 6% in 1983–84 after reaching 60.9 million tons in 1982–83.

Prices of soybean meal bottomed out at an average of $192 per ton (c.i.f., Rotterdam) in October 1982 but recovered to $277 by September 1983 before receding a little. The increased spread between soybean meal prices and lower priced protein sources for animal feeds such as corn, but also wheat and nonfat dry milk from record or near-record EEC stocks, was reducing the EEC's demand for imports of both soybeans and soybean meal. Shortages of foreign exchange and credit in Eastern Europe were limiting that region's importation and consumption of soybean meal and oil.

Sluggish demand for livestock products throughout much of the world resulting from slow economic growth also acted to limit demand for protein meals. The only substantial anticipated increase in soybean meal consumption and imports was in the Soviet Union. A provision allowing the substitution of 500,000 tons of soybeans (or soybean meal equivalent) for grain was included in the 1983 U.S.-U.S.S.R. grain agreement.

World exports of soybeans and soybean meal (28.7 million and 21.8 million tons, respectively, in 1982–83) were expected to decline about 18% and 4%, respectively, in 1983–84. U.S. exports of both soybeans and soybean products were expected to account for nearly all of the decline.

Table IV. World Production of Oilseeds and Selected Crops and Products
In 000,000 metric tons

	1981–82	1982–83[1]	1983–84[2]
World oilseed production	170.3	179.2	162.3
Soybeans	86.3	94.0	77.5
Cottonseed	28.2	27.3	26.2
Peanuts	19.9	17.6	19.3
Sunflower seed	14.7	16.4	16.3
Rapeseed	12.4	15.1	14.5
Flaxseed	2.1	2.6	2.2
Copra	4.8	4.4	4.2
Palm kernels	1.9	1.8	2.1
Selected Northern Hemisphere crops			
U.S. soybeans	54.4	60.7	41.8
Chinese soybeans	9.3	9.0	9.3
U.S. sunflower seed	2.1	2.4	1.4
U.S.S.R. sunflower seed	4.7	5.3	5.4
U.S. cottonseed	5.8	4.3	2.7
U.S.S.R. cottonseed	5.2	5.0	5.1
Chinese cottonseed	5.9	7.2	7.4
Canadian rapeseed	1.8	2.2	2.7
Chinese rapeseed	4.1	5.7	4.4
Indian rapeseed	2.4	2.5	2.5
U.S. peanuts	1.8	1.6	1.4
Chinese peanuts	3.8	3.9	3.9
Indian peanuts	7.2	5.6	7.3
Selected Southern Hemisphere crops			
Argentine soybeans	4.0	3.6	4.7
Brazilian soybeans	12.8	14.8	15.3
Argentine sunflower seed	1.8	2.2	2.5
World production[3]			
Total fats and oils	55.1	57.4	56.8
Edible vegetable oils	40.6	42.4	41.8
Animal fats	12.5	13.1	13.2
Industrial and marine oils	2.0	1.9	1.8
High-protein meals[4]	93.5	95.1	91.2

[1] Preliminary.
[2] Forecast.
[3] Processing potential from crops in year indicated.
[4] Converted, based on product's protein content, to weight equivalent to soybeans of 44% protein content.
Source: USDA, Foreign Agricultural Service, May and November 1983.

MEAT AND LIVESTOCK. World meat output in the major producing countries was estimated to have edged upward in 1983, led by a modest increase in

Table V. Livestock Numbers and Meat Production in Major Producing Countries[1]
In 000,000 head and 000,000 metric tons (carcass weight)

Region and country	1982	1983	1982	1983
	Cattle		Beef and veal	
World total	935.8	938.3	40.34	40.15
Canada	11.6	11.3	1.03	1.04
United States	115.2	115.0	10.43	10.71
Mexico	30.0	28.9	1.20	0.98
Argentina	58.9	60.5	2.58	2.30
Brazil	93.0	93.5	2.40	2.50
Uruguay	10.3	9.4	0.38	0.42
Western Europe	92.2	92.4	8.32	7.94
Eastern Europe	37.3	37.3	2.48	2.31
U.S.S.R.	117.1	119.0	6.60	6.80
Australia	22.5	22.0	1.68	1.39
India	247.7	248.7	...	...
	Hogs		Pork	
World total	404.5	411.1	36.12	37.13
Canada	9.9	9.8	0.83	0.85
United States	53.9	56.5	6.45	6.84
Mexico	16.0	14.0	1.20	1.08
Western Europe	106.8	107.5	11.88	12.14
U.S.S.R.	76.5	79.5	5.20	5.60
Japan	10.3	10.4	1.43	1.45
	Poultry		Poultry meat	
World total	...	...	22.20	22.51
United States	...	...	7.05	7.23
Brazil	...	...	1.59	1.60
EEC	...	...	4.37	4.30
U.S.S.R.	...	...	2.40	2.60
Japan	...	...	1.21	1.28
	Sheep and goats		Sheep, goat meat	
World total	658.0	659.8	4.49	4.52
			All meat	
Total	...	...	103.15	104.31

[1] Preliminary livestock numbers at year's end. Consists of 47 countries for beef and veal, 35 for pork and poultry meat, and 29 for sheep and goat meat, and roughly the same coverage for cattle and hog numbers, but 21 for sheep and goat numbers. Includes nearly all European producers, the most significant in the Western Hemisphere, and scattered countries elsewhere.
Source: USDA, Foreign Agricultural Service, November 1983.

the production of pork. The decline in cattle numbers continued, however, influenced by persistent soft demand for meat attributable to the slow growth in much of the world economy, but the decline in hog numbers was arrested. Stronger world prices for feedstuffs in 1983 were beginning to have a depressing effect on livestock and poultry production, and this was considered likely to continue into 1984.

Drought in Australia that continued into early 1983 resulted in a further decline in cattle herds and contributed to a strong buildup in sheep flocks that accounted for nearly all the world increase in sheep numbers in 1983. Consequently, 13% less Australian beef and veal was available for export in 1983, and it was expected that considerably less would be shipped in 1984 by this world's leading beef exporter.

Argentine cattle inventories increased in 1983 as ranchers, aided by favourable pasture conditions, held back cattle from export markets. They did this in part because of the disincentive of export taxes but also because of loss of the British market during the conflict over the Falkland Islands. Brazil showed signs of joining the EEC as a competitor with Argentina in export markets, particularly in the Middle East. Brazil benefited from the reduced availability of Australian and New Zealand meat exports in 1983.

In the Soviet Union good weather resulted in larger feed and forage crops that helped increase beef production in 1983 and sustain the second year of a substantial expansion in cattle herds after several years of stagnant growth. Slow demand for beef resulting from the sluggish performance of the Mexican economy made it likely that cattle numbers would continue to decline there through 1983 and into 1984.

The expansion of hog inventories and pork production was most rapid in the United States and the U.S.S.R. in 1983. Low feed prices relative to pork prices in the U.S. during 1982 and early 1983 contributed to that nation's buildup, but rising feed grain prices in 1983 resulted in a reduction of hog breeding herds and increased pork production. The effects of the rising feed grain prices were expected to continue to be experienced by both U.S. and foreign pork producers in 1984.

World production of poultry continued to expand in 1983, but expansion had proceeded at a slower rate during the past few years than it had in the 1970s. Broiler production increased substantially and in 1983 accounted for more than two-thirds of poultry production in the major producing countries. The poultry industry also was adversely affected by rising grain prices. The EEC, the world's largest exporter of poultry meat, was meeting stiff competition from Brazil, especially in Middle Eastern markets.

DAIRY PRODUCTS. World milk production continued to accelerate in 1983, leading to a sharp expansion in output of manufactured dairy products. Some of the largest increases in production were stimulated by dairy price support programs in the EEC and the United States, where the consumption of dairy products continued to lag far behind production. Low prices for feed grains and oilseed meal early in 1983 and rising productivity also aided the increase. The result was an additional substantial buildup in government-financed stocks of dairy products in those regions and a weakening of prices for dairy products in international trade. India was achieving rapid advances in milk output, and the Soviet Union's production

Table VI. World Production and Stocks of Dairy Products[1]
In 000,000 metric tons

Region		1981	1982	1983[2]
		Production of cow milk		
North America		75.2	76.8	77.6
United States		60.3	61.6	63.0
South America		19.0	19.0	19.4
Brazil		10.5	10.0	10.7
Western Europe		127.4	131.0	135.3
EEC		104.9	108.2	112.2
France		26.8	27.4	28.1
West Germany		24.9	25.5	26.6
Italy		10.6	10.8	11.1
Netherlands, The		12.1	12.7	13.1
United Kingdom		15.9	16.7	17.6
Other Western Europe		22.5	22.8	23.1
Eastern Europe		40.2	39.4	40.8
Poland		15.3	15.2	15.9
U.S.S.R.		88.9	91.0	96.8
India		14.0	14.7	15.2
Australia/New Zealand[3]		12.0	12.2	12.4
Japan/South Africa		9.1	9.2	9.4
Total		385.8	393.4	406.9
	Production		Year-end stocks	
Product/Region	1982	1983	1982	1983
Butter	6,388	6,918	834	1,280
EEC	2,056	2,277	392	819
U.S.	570	598	212	250
Cheese	8,803	8,964	1,428	1,552
EEC	3,550	3,573	581	589
U.S.	2,059	2,165	483	590
Nonfat dry milk	4,503	4,942	1,660	2,031
EEC	2,154	2,478	688	1,019
U.S.	635	690	582	660

[1] Based on 37 major producing countries.
[2] Preliminary.
[3] Year ending June 30 for Australia and May 31 for New Zealand.
Source: USDA, Foreign Agricultural Service, December 1983.

World Production and Trade of Principal Grains (in 000 metric tons)

	Wheat			Barley			Oats			Rye			Corn (Maize)			Rice		
	Production 1961–65 average	Production 1982	Imports− Exports+ 1979–82 average	Production 1961–65 average	Production 1982	Imports− Exports+ 1979–82 average	Production 1961–65 average	Production 1982	Imports− Exports+ 1979–82 average	Production 1961–65 average	Production 1982	Imports− Exports+ 1979–82 average	Production 1961–65 average	Production 1982	Imports− Exports+ 1979–82 average	Production 1961–65 average	Production 1982	Imports− Exports+ 1979–82 average
World total	254576	487570	−89264 +88870	98474	160446	−16450 +17592	47775	45288	−1168 +1370	33849	29924	−957 +954	216429	450843	−78758 +76901	254711	421573	−12417 +12695
Algeria	1254	c1200	−c1707	476	c650	−c280	28	c80	−c16[1]	—	—	—	4	c1	−c192	7	c1	−c17[1]
Argentina	7541	11256	+4451	679	c108	+28	676	524	+81	422	244	+31	4984	c9600	+5954	193	413	−c6[1] +96
Australia	8222	8600	+11088	978	1740	+1902	1172	840	+262	11	c9	−1[1]	176	212	−4[1] +20	136	783	−1[1] +387
Austria	704	c1200	−1[1] +202	563	c1382	−14 +52	322	322	−5	393	355	+42[1]	197	c1400	−27 +1[1]	—	—	−46
Bangladesh	37	800	−c1150	15	c12[2]	−c1[1]	—	—	—	—	—	—	4	c1[2]	—	15048	21853	−c170
Belgium	826	c930	−1369[3] +701[3]	485	c760	−1320[3] +700[3]	389	c130	−59[3] +6[3]	120	c30	−12[3] +8[3]	2	c25[2]	−2677[3] +c1380[3]	—	—	−186[3] +113[3]
Brazil	574	2250	−4248	26	101[2]	−89	20	68	−21	17	38	—	10112	21711	−1005 +141	6123	9681	−315 +18
Bulgaria	2213	c4400	−117 +560	694	c1500	−100[1] +11	141	50	—	58	34	—	1601	c3000	−555 +43	37	71[2]	−4[1] +1[1]
Burma	38	c80[2]	—	—	—	—	—	—	—	—	—	—	58	232	+c16[1]	7786	14146	+c673
Canada	15364	26866	+15853	3860	13598	+4293	6075	3671	+203	319	879	+404	1073	5928	−1012 +716	—	—	−97
Chile	1082	c650	−904	74	c115	−28 +4	89	145	−c1[1] +c1[1]	7	6	—	204	c425	−316	85	100	−24 +6[1]
China	22200	68420	−c12460	c5700	c3500	−c470 +c1[1]	c1600	c800	−c2[1]	c1500	c1000	—	c22500	c61000	−c4330 +c109	c86000	161240	−c180 +c960
Colombia	118	62[2]	−c468	106	c55	−c71	—	c5[2]	−c10	—	—	—	826	895	−c106	576	1954	−6[1] +23
Czechoslovakia	1779	c5000	−398 +103	1556	c3600	−55 +c16	792	c500	−c1[1] +c9[1]	897	c600	−c13 +c1[1]	474	c850	−1031 +c6[1]	—	—	−c76 +c3[1]
Denmark	535	c1050	−41 +166	3506	c6380	−88 +625	713	c180	−13 +5	380	c200	−11[1] +57	—	—	−229	—	—	−12[1] +2
Egypt	1459	c2016	−c4120	137	c122	−c11[1]	—	—	—	—	—	—	1913	c2709	−c1055	1845	c2287	+c67
Ethiopia	540	c590	−c246	628	c1100	−c8[1]	5	c12	—	—	—	—	743	c950	−c13[1]	—	—	−3[1]
Finland	488	435	−326 +3[1]	400	1599	−90 +25	828	c1320	−8[1] +4[1]	141	35	−66	—	—	−42	—	—	−16
France	12495	25342	−738 +10133	6594	10026	−133 +3890	2583	1804	−2[1] +c262	367	320	−3[1] +c67	2760	9833	−635 +3247	120	c21[2]	−256 +14
Germany, East	1357	c2947	−c720 +c64	1291	c4049	−c730 +c160	850	c846	−c87 +c122	1741	c2500	+c20	3	c2[2]	−c1920	—	—	−c42
Germany, West	4607	8632	−1331 +676	3462	9460	−1064 +364	2185	3113	−98 +9	3031	c1700	−41 +199	55	1054	−2205 +152	—	—	−173 +33
Greece	1765	2983	−1[1] +c170	248	853	−c56 +c12	143	81	—	19	6	—	239	1448	−c866 +11[1]	88	83	−1[1] +14[1]
Hungary	2020	c6200	−26 +950	970	c980	−104 +18	108	c80	−3 +1[1]	271	c120	−8	3350	c7400	−10 +183	36	c35[2]	−20
India	11191	37833	−c1260 +119	2590	2012	−c2[1] +c16[1]	—	—	—	—	—	—	4593	c6500	−c9[1]	52733	c68000	−c54 +c710
Indonesia	—	—	−1289	—	—	—	—	—	—	—	—	—	2804	3207	−49 +7	12396	34104	−1195 +3[1]
Iran	2873	c6500	−c1570	792	c1200	−c280	—	—	—	—	—	—	24	c50[2]	−c510	851	c1400	−c470
Iraq	849	c900	−c1540	851	c550	−c180	—	—	—	—	—	—	2	c90[2]	−c170	142	c250	−c350
Ireland	343	c320	−c251 +43	575	c1450	−c20 +138	357	c90	−9	1	c1	—	—	—	−c193 +4[1]	—	—	−4[1]
Italy	8857	8998	−3125 +58	276	1020	−1309 +52	545	360	−96 +1[1]	87	33	−2	3633	6820	−2562 +74	612	915	−175 +600
Japan	1332	742	−5738	1380	c393	−1458	145	c7	−c156	2	c1	−38	96	c3[2]	−c12850	16444	12838	−c43 +c616
Kenya	122	250	−c92	15	c80[2]	+1[1]	2	c7	—	—	—	—	1110	2300	−c220 +40[1]	14	40[2]	−c8[1]
Korea, South	170	57[2]	−1862	1148	749	−1[1] +1[1]	—	—	—	18	5	−1[1]	26	145[2]	−c2746	4809	7308	−1010
Malaysia	—	—	−c482	—	—	c1[1]	—	—	−c4[1]	—	—	—	8	8[2]	−c460	1140	2062	−c288
Mexico	1672	4468	−871 +c21	175	495	−82	76	c80	−c1[1]	—	—	−c1[1]	7369	12215	−1884	314	600	−c52 +1[1]
Morocco	1516	2183	−c1702	1514	2334	−c58[1]	18	74	—	2	c2	—	405	247	−c130	20	c17[2]	—
Netherlands, The	606	967	−1484 +542	390	247	−456 +127	421	136	−21 +41	312	27	−51 +9	—	c2[2]	−2770 +411	—	—	−187 +126
New Zealand	248	320	−c51	98	407	+c40	34	57	—	—	c1	—	16	177[2]	+c26	—	—	−7[1]
Nigeria	16	c21[2]	−c1200	—	—	—	—	—	—	—	—	—	997	c1650	−c216	207	c1400	−c620
Norway	19	c61[2]	−367 +2[1]	440	607	−30	126	501	−1[1]	3	2	−37	—	—	−64	—	—	−8
Pakistan	4153	11570	−856	118	c135	+30	—	—	—	—	—	—	514	950	−3[1]	1824	5053	+976
Peru	150	c117[2]	−c826	185	c155	−c36	4	c1	−c7[1]	1	c1	—	490	625	−c307 +c2[1]	324	765	−c148
Philippines	—	—	−803	—	—	—	—	—	−c3[1]	—	—	—	1305	3475	−220	3957	8346	+129
Poland	2988	4476	−3361 +20	1368	3647	−912 +12	2641	2608	−75	7466	7245	−277 +21[1]	20	79[2]	−1890	—	—	−93
Portugal	562	445	−c730	61	53	−c42	87	83	−1[1]	177	c110	−c12	617	464	−c2430	167	143	−c84 +4[1]
Romania	4321	6460	−c730 +c320	415	c3000	−c75[1]	154	c59	−c28[1]	95	c45	−c16[1]	5853	c12600	−c1310 +c1040	40	c65	−c56 +c5[1]
South Africa	834	2296	−74 +c91	40	97[2]	−c10[1] +20	107	92	−c5[1] +c1[1]	10	7	−1[1]	5248	8344	−c4[1] +c3470	2	c3	−c141 +1[1]
Spain	4365	4368	−c260 +c171	1959	5280	−c510 +c240	447	474	+3[1]	385	170	—	1101	2284	−c4660 +1[1]	386	409	−1[1] +c62
Sweden	909	1377	−47 +357	1167	2103	−26[1] +206	1304	1559	+294	142	207	−5[1] +40	—	—	−40	—	—	−22
Switzerland	355	c423	−338	102	c211	−397	40	c61	−129	52	c31	−21	14	c117[2]	−253	—	—	−30
Syria	1093	1556	−25 +3	649	661	−63 +171	2	1	—	—	—	—	7	89[2]	−201	1	—	−c80
Thailand	—	—	−155	—	—	—	—	—	—	—	—	—	816	c3004	+2426	11267	c17500	+3137
Turkey	8585	c17650	−199 +409	3447	c6000	−1[1] +234	495	c330	—	734	c480	+7[1]	950	c1400	+3[1]	222	290[2]	−19
U.S.S.R.	64220	c87000	−c14200 +c1770	20318	c41000	−c2639 +c40	6052	c14000	−c230 +c11[1]	15093	c10000	−c324 +c7[1]	13122	c12000	−c13400 +c150	390	c2500	−c980 +c17
United Kingdom	3520	10258	−c2030 +c1250	6670	10884	−c170 +c2640	1541	587	−c25 +c4	21	24	−c17	—	c1	−c2590 +c11	—	—	−c170 +c19[1]
United States	33040	76443	−4 +38456	8676	11374	−155 +1406	13848	8955	−16 +56	828	506	+76	95561	213302	−28 +56548	3084	6995	−3[1] +2757
Uruguay	465	316	−c57 +c60	28	c100	−c18 +c14	66	34	−8[1] +1[1]	—	—	—	148	196[2]	−c23[1] +2[1]	67	419	+c191 +c191
Venezuela	1	c1	−c820	—	—	—	—	—	−c4	—	—	—	477	501	−c916	136	670	+c44
Yugoslavia	3599	5218	−c744 +c30	557	669	−c24 +c18	343	269	−1[1] +6[1]	169	84	—	5618	11137	−365[1] +c178	23	c40[2]	−23[1] +2[1]

Note: (—) indicates quantity nil or negligible. (*c*) indicates provisional or estimated. [1]1979–81 average. [2]1981. [3]Belgium-Luxembourg economic union.
Sources: *FAO Monthly Bulletin of Statistics; FAO Production Yearbook 1981; FAO Trade Yearbook 1981.*

(M. C. MacDONALD)

continued to rebound, reducing that country's dairy imports.

The production of butter and butter oil in 37 major producing countries was expected to increase about 8% in 1983 to 6.9 million tons. Butter stocks were estimated to have expanded more than 50% to 1,280,000 tons, with government-financed EEC intervention stocks at year's end more than double the 392,000 tons at the end of 1982. The rise in U.S. butter stocks to 250,000 tons was held to 18% by increases in domestic and foreign food aid programs.

Production of nonfat dry milk (NFDM) was estimated to have increased about 10% in 1983 to 4,942,000 tons, and NFDM stocks were expected to grow 22% to about two million tons. The growth in EEC intervention stocks—48%, to about one-half of the total—was beginning to slow down because larger subsidies were being paid for use of NFDM in livestock feed. U.S. stocks of NFDM held by the government increased an estimated 13% to 660,000 tons.

Cheese production increased about 2% in 1983 to nearly nine million tons. EEC stocks stabilized at about 589,000 tons by year's end, but U.S. stocks grew 22% to match them.

In the United States new dairy legislation enacted late in 1983 aimed at reducing milk production. Beginning Dec. 1, 1983, the support price for manufacturing milk was reduced 50 cents per hundredweight (cwt). Although the $1-per-cwt deduction from prices received by producers for all milk sold was eliminated, a 50-cents-per-cwt deduction to help fund a milk-diversion program was introduced, along with the requirement that producers, to be eligible for program benefits, had to agree to cut milk sales by 5 to 30% of their historical marketings. The deduction under the 15-month diversion program beginning Jan. 1, 1984, might be increased later in 1984.

SUGAR. World sugar production in 1982–83 was much greater than forecast early in the season because of better-than-expected performance in Western Europe and India. Global production of sugar exceeded consumption by an estimated nine million tons, with the result that world sugar stocks continued their rapid buildup while sugar prices plunged. World sugar output was forecast to decline about 6% in 1983–84, primarily because of widespread unfavourable weather, but still was expected to exceed global consumption of sugar by about 800,000 tons. Output of beet sugar (typically 37% of all centrifugal sugar) was expected to fall, largely because of bad weather in Western Europe, and a sharp reduction in cane sugar was anticipated in part because of a shift to other crops in India.

World sugar consumption grew about 2.9% in 1982–83 to about 92 million tons, compared with an increase of 1.1% in 1980–81. Growth of about 2% was forecast for 1983–84. The less developed countries—particularly those of Asia, Africa, and the Middle East—were the source of most of the variation in sugar use as they adjusted to changes in domestic production or foreign exchange resources needed to finance imports. Those countries, with their low levels of per capita use, were also responsible for most of the growth in sugar consumption. China's sugar consumption increased 20% from 1980–81, and growth was also rapid in India and Pakistan. Growth of sugar consumption in the industrialized countries was slower and more stable. Most of the sugar consumed in those nations was contained in prepared foods and beverages, the demand for which was depressed by the recent economic recession. Sugar consumption continued to decline in the United States, influenced by the substitution of high fructose corn syrup and noncaloric sweeteners.

Table VII. World Production of Centrifugal (Freed from Liquid) Sugar
In 000,000 metric tons raw value

Region	1981–82	1982–83	1983–84[1]
North and Central America	10.3	10.3	10.0
United States	5.6	5.3	5.2
Mexico	2.8	3.1	2.9
Caribbean	10.1	9.0	9.3
Cuba	8.2	7.2	7.5
South America	13.4	14.3	14.4
Argentina	1.6	1.6	1.6
Brazil	8.4	9.3	9.4
Europe	24.0	23.4	19.4
Western Europe	18.2	17.3	13.6
EEC	16.0	14.8	11.4
France	5.6	4.8	3.4
West Germany	3.7	3.6	2.9
Italy	2.2	1.3	1.4
Eastern Europe	5.9	6.1	5.8
U.S.S.R.	6.4	7.4	8.5
Africa and the Middle East	8.8	9.5	8.5
South Africa	2.2	2.3	1.5
Asia	23.6	23.2	21.3
China	3.4	3.9	3.9
India	9.7	9.6	8.5
Indonesia	1.7	1.6	1.6
Philippines	2.5	2.5	2.3
Thailand	2.8	2.3	1.7
Oceania	4.1	4.0	3.3
Australia	3.6	3.4	3.0
Total	100.6	101.0	94.7

[1] Preliminary.
Source: USDA, Foreign Agricultural Service, November 1983.

World trade in sugar increased 2% in 1982–83 to approximately 28.1 million tons, but it was forecast to fall by about 6% in 1983–84. The Soviet Union, the world's largest importer of sugar, was expected to account for most of the decline because it had a good sugar-beet harvest after a series of poor crops.

Global sugar stocks totaled 45.4 million tons—49% of consumption—at the end of 1982–83 after two years of record large sugar harvests, and they were likely to grow more in 1983–84. The indicator price of the International Sugar Agreement (ISA) had been below the floor price of the ISA (11 cents per pound) since March 1982, rising from about 6.5 cents per pound in mid-1982 to approximately 10 cents per pound in the fall of 1983.

Two negotiating conferences for a new ISA were conducted under the auspices of the United Nations Conference on Trade and Development (UNCTAD) in Geneva in 1983. Reconciling the differences between exporting and importing nations was proving to be difficult, and a third conference was scheduled for March 1984.

COFFEE. Early-season estimates of world coffee production indicated a substantial recovery from 1982–83, when the effects of the 1975 Brazilian drought were experienced as a 17% decline in world coffee output. Exportable coffee production (total production less domestic consumption in exporting countries) was estimated to have increased almost 18% to 72.2 million bags. Heavy rains in

May and June 1983 in major coffee regions of Brazil inhibited the recovery.

Coffee exports by members of the International Coffee Organization (ICO)—which produced over 99% of the world's coffee—were forecast to rise less than 1% above the 65.9 million bags shipped in 1982–83. About 95% of coffee exports were unprocessed green beans; almost all of the remainder was soluble coffee, of which Brazil accounted for about 75% of sales.

The stocks of coffee held in exporting countries fell about 4.6 million bags during 1982–83 to about 41.2 million bags, but they were forecast to rise about 15% by the end of 1983–84 to the highest level in more than a decade. Some countries held the equivalent of a whole year's production in stocks. Shifts in Brazil's stockholdings accounted for the bulk of the change in world stocks. But even with a trend toward increased stocks, coffee prices, as measured by the ICO indicator average price, remained relatively stable through October 1983, fluctuating around $1.25 per pound. Production trends suggested that world coffee stocks might grow seven million to ten million bags annually over the next several years.

A new International Coffee Agreement (ICA), to remain in force for six years from October 1983, was established in September 1982. It included a system for adjusting export quotas of shipments of green coffee to members, a system that was designed to maintain prices within a $1.15- to $1.45-per-pound price range. A new formula, to take effect on Oct. 1, 1984, would allocate at least 70% of an individual country's export quota on the basis of its export record in recent years, with the balance calculated from the level of carryover stocks. Quotas totaling 56 million bags were negotiated on an ad hoc basis for the 1982–83 year.

Table VIII. World Green Coffee Production
In 000 60-kg bags

Region	1981–82	1982–83	1983–84
North America	15,501	16,829	15,876
Costa Rica	1,609	2,300	2,070
El Salvador	2,887	2,855	2,600
Guatemala	2,653	2,420	2,625
Honduras	1,230	1,456	1,350
Mexico	4,050	4,100	4,000
South America	51,785	35,323	48,215
Brazil	33,000	17,750	30,750
Colombia	14,343	13,300	13,000
Ecuador	1,792	1,835	1,650
Africa	20,249	19,695	19,617
Cameroon	1,953	1,867	1,900
Ethiopia	3,212	3,350	3,350
Ivory Coast	4,050	3,900	3,650
Kenya	1,489	1,460	1,530
Uganda	2,885	3,200	3,100
Zaire	1,425	1,450	1,400
Asia and Oceania	10,807	9,637	9,865
India	2,540	2,100	2,450
Indonesia	5,785	5,250	5,000
Total	98,342	81,484	93,573

Source: USDA, Foreign Agricultural Service, September 1983.

A two-tier price system had grown up under which members of the ICO shipped about 10% of their total exports to nonmembers. These sales, motivated by financial pressures or large stocks threatening to become unmanageable, were usually made at lower prices than were charged to member countries. In recent years such exports—particularly to the Middle East and Eastern Europe—had grown more rapidly than those to members.

Table IX. World Cocoa Bean Production
In 000 metric tons

Region	1981–82	1982–83	1983–84[1]
North and Central America	106	105	101
South America	468	466	495
Brazil	315	339	350
Ecuador	88	62	77
Africa	1,035	843	899
Cameroon	120	106	117
Ghana	225	178	160
Ivory Coast[2]	456	351	400
Nigeria[3]	182	160	170
Asia and Oceania	114	121	149
Malaysia	62	69	95
Total	1,723	1,535	1,644

[1] Forecast.
[2] Includes some cocoa marketed from Ghana.
[3] Includes cocoa marketed through Benin.
Source: USDA, Foreign Agricultural Service, October 1983.

Some coffee traders in member countries complained that much of this coffee circumvented the ICA and found its way back into their nations, where its cheaper price competed unfairly with coffee that they purchased under ICA rules. They claimed that such practices threatened the continued existence of the ICA. Hungary, Israel, and Hong Kong were reported to have quit the ICA to take advantage of lower prices to nonmembers. In January 1983 various measures to control such trade through documentation were adopted, and others were proposed.

COCOA. World output of cocoa was expected to recover in 1983–84 after dry weather late in the season in Ivory Coast and other major producing countries resulted in an 11% decline in production in 1982–83. Cocoa grindings increased almost 1% in 1983 to 1,618,000 tons, exceeding gross production for the first time since 1976–77, and a similar rise was forecast for 1984.

The resulting estimated 98,000-ton reduction in cocoa stocks caused cocoa prices to bottom out at about 66 cents per pound (New York futures, nearest three-month average) and to climb to almost $1 per pound in the summer of 1983 before declining a little on forecasts of a larger 1983–84 harvest. The existence of excess cocoa stocks, the increased use of cocoa substitutes and extenders, and competition from nonchocolate confections had kept cocoa prices well below the International Cocoa Agreement's (ICCA's) price range of $1.06 to $1.46 per pound since July 1980.

Table X. World Cotton Production
In 000,000 480-lb bales

Region	1981	1982	1983
Western Hemisphere	23.0	17.9	14.0
United States	15.6	12.0	7.5
Mexico	1.4	0.8	0.9
Brazil	3.0	3.0	2.8
Europe	0.9	0.7	0.8
U.S.S.R.	13.3	11.9	13.0
Africa	5.1	5.5	5.5
Egypt	2.3	2.1	2.0
Sudan	0.7	0.9	1.0
Asia and Oceania[1]	28.5	31.6	32.0
China	13.6	16.5	17.0
India	6.4	6.3	6.6
Pakistan	3.5	3.8	3.1
Turkey	2.2	2.2	2.3
Total	70.7	67.7	65.3

[1] Includes Middle East.
Source: USDA, Foreign Agricultural Service, May and November 1983.

SACK/MINNEAPOLIS STAR AND TRIBUNE

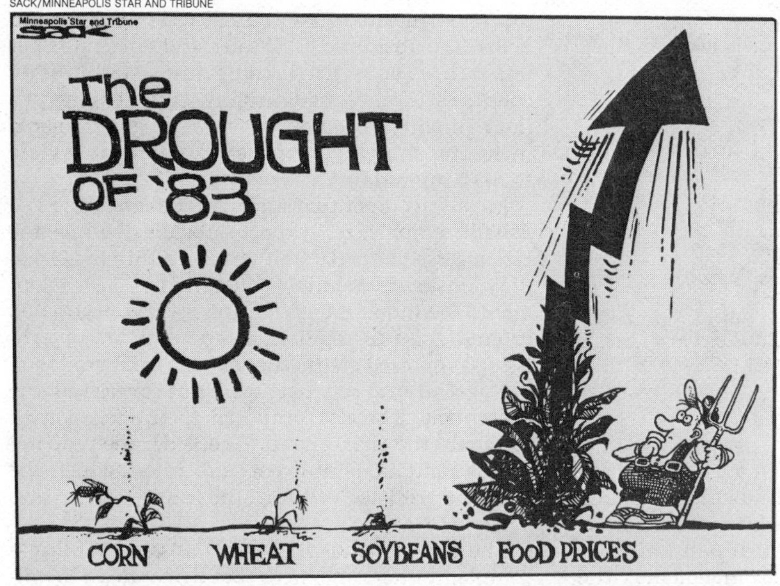

Weather problems beset farmers in many parts of the world and elicited this editorial cartoon commentary and forecast in the U.S. upper Midwest.

Work was under way to draft a new ICCA by March 1984 to replace the current one, which was to expire on Sept. 30, 1984. Operation of the ICCA was hindered by the fact that neither the largest exporter of cocoa (Ivory Coast) nor the largest importer (United States) had signed the agreement.

COTTON. World cotton production was expected to decline for the second year in a row in 1983–84. The drastic reduction in U.S. output, resulting from the effects of area reduction programs and drought, was responsible for nearly all the decline. Cotton production outside the U.S. was expected to grow nearly 4%, mostly in the U.S.S.R. and China, although insect infestations cut output in Pakistan.

Global consumption of cotton, which grew 3% in 1982–83 to 67.7 million bales, was expected to expand about 2.5% and to exceed cotton production in 1983–84. Most of the gains were in cotton-importing nations, particularly in China, which was rapidly expanding its textile industry. Consumption also rose, however, in the major exporting nations, the United States and the Soviet Union.

World stocks of cotton changed little during 1982–83, reaching 28.9 million bales by the end of the year, but they were expected to decline about 14% during 1983–84. Most of the drawdown was in U.S. stocks. Cotton prices, which averaged 76.7 cents per pound in 1982–83, fluctuated near 90 cents per pound in the fall of 1983. World trade in cotton totaled 18.4 million bales in 1982–83, down about 9% from 1981–82, and it was not expected to expand much in 1983–84.

Trade Maneuvers. The 1983 report of the General Agreement on Tariffs and Trade (GATT) concluded that the bitterest commercial conflicts among the large industrial countries originated in agricultural trade and grew out of widespread government interference with the market mechanism in agriculture. Such large-scale interventions, which had a long history, implied quantitative planning by such countries of both exports and imports. The report estimated that considerably

Floods and snows wrought havoc in many parts of the U.S. during the spring and drought plagued much of the world during the summer months. In McCamey, Texas, farmhands used butane torches (left) to burn the spines off cactus plants so cattle could safely feed on them.

PHOTOGRAPHS, FRED R. CONRAD/THE NEW YORK TIMES

Table XI. Shipments of Food Aid in Cereals
In 000 metric ton grain equivalent

	Average 1978–79, 1980–81	1981–82	1982–83[1]	1983–84[2]
Australia	338	485	348	400
Canada	688	600	805	850
EEC	1,214	1,579	1,561	1,580
By members	573	733	...	...
By organization	641	846	842	...
Japan	651	507	408	450
Sweden	99	119	74	40
United States	5,596	5,341	5,400	5,200
Others	525	508	458	382
Total[3]	9,110	9,139	9,054	8,902

[1]Partly estimated.
[2]Allocations, some estimated.
[3]Includes Argentina, Austria, China, Finland, India, Norway, OPEC Special Fund, Saudi Arabia, Spain, Switzerland, Turkey, and World Food Program, but not necessarily for all years.
Source: FAO, *Food Outlook* (Nov. 29, 1983).

more than half of world trade in agriculture was dependent on government subsidies and credits and was either transacted in the form of state trading or was conducted within similar politically negotiated arrangements. Such arrangements, the report argued, were mutually incompatible unless there were extensive individual or multilateral agreements among countries to determine the volume of trade flows. The obvious difficulties of reaching such extensive agreements inevitably generated uncertainty and conflict among governments.

This reasoning appeared to explain the continuing skirmishing between the U.S. and the EEC that continued to dominate agricultural trade issues in 1983. Both were attempting to adjust their agricultural policies in order to offset the undesired consequences of policy interventions in their domestic markets, but the adjustments were proving difficult and were themselves frequently the source of conflict.

The U.S. in January 1983 concluded a sale of wheat flour to Egypt that was openly characterized as a direct challenge to the EEC practice of subsidizing agricultural exports at prices below world and U.S. export prices. The one million-ton deal was supported by direct export subsidies and "blended" credits (a combination of credit guarantees and a subsidized below-market interest rate). These measures resulted in a price at least $140 per ton below unsubsidized U.S. sales and about $25 per ton below subsidized competition from other countries. France had usually supplied Egypt's flour imports. The cost to the U.S. government, including shipping subsidies, was probably close to $175 million.

In their competition for market shares, the EEC usually emphasized export subsidies, while the U.S. stressed liberal credit terms. Within the Organization for Economic Cooperation and Development, the industrialized countries had negotiated ground rules to regulate competition in government-supported credit sales of industrial products, but agricultural products were not covered by the agreement. The EEC proposed their inclusion in 1983, but the U.S. refused to consider the proposal unless limitations of export subsidies, which the EEC had resisted within the GATT, were also covered.

The EEC responded to the U.S. sale by filing a complaint under the GATT that demanded $30 million in compensation by the United States. In March a GATT panel reacted ambiguously to a similar earlier U.S. complaint that the EEC had displaced the United States as the world's largest flour exporter through use of export subsidies. The panel acknowledged the EEC's use of subsidies but said that the U.S. had not proved its case and avoided ruling upon the critical legal question of whether the EEC had gained a "more than equitable share" of the flour market—a finding considered necessary to establish a violation of the GATT code regarding subsidies.

The United States kept the pressure on by selling 28,000 tons of surplus butter and cheese to Egypt. The EEC claimed that the price was under the minimum established by the 1979 GATT dairy agreement and objected to the low interest rate. The EEC was especially sensitive because it regularly subsidized the export of surplus dairy products to cut down the expenses of the most costly EEC support program, while the U.S. had not ordinarily disposed of its large dairy surpluses in commercial markets.

The U.S. and the Soviet Union concluded a new

After many years of deficient harvests, Soviet agriculture enjoyed a good year. Here workers in the Kirgiz Soviet Socialist Republic take in the bounty.

JOHN F. BURNS/THE NEW YORK TIMES

UPI

In January some 10,000 farmers thronged the U.S. embassy in Tokyo to protest any increase in Japanese imports of U.S. farm products, including beef, pork, and oranges.

grain supply agreement under which the Soviets agreed to purchase eight million to nine million tons of wheat and corn each year for five years, beginning Oct. 1, 1983. This constituted a two million-ton increase, as compared with the previous agreement, in the minimum required purchase by the Soviet Union.

Suggesting a link between the level of U.S. import restrictions applied to its textile exports, the Chinese government announced that it would be unable to import the roughly two million-ton balance of wheat in 1983 under its sales agreement with the U.S. Later it said that it would buy that amount from the U.S. crop harvested in 1983 for shipment in 1984.

EEC Reform of the CAP. Independent of trade policy considerations, the EEC was beginning to find the budgetary cost of its common agricultural policy (CAP) to be prohibitively expensive. EEC expenditures on agriculture—about $14 billion in 1983—grew at an annual average of 23% between 1974 and 1979 and in 1983 accounted for about two-thirds of the entire EEC budget. Total EEC budgetary obligations almost exceeded total revenues in 1983. EEC rules forbade incurring a deficit, and so politically painful decisions in regard to choosing which expenditures to eliminate would have been required had a budgetary supplement not been approved.

The source of these expenditures—and of the trade disputes with the United States—was illustrated by the CAP for wheat. Similar programs were in operation for dairy products, sugar, certain oilseeds, and most other farm products. The CAP guaranteed the purchase of whatever quantities of domestic wheat were necessary from EEC producers to boost the domestic price to an administratively determined level that had been set far in excess of world market prices. To avoid the full budgetary cost of acquiring and storing an ever increasing stock of costly wheat, the EEC paid subsidies (export restitutions) to its exporters that were roughly equal to the difference between the high EEC domestic price of wheat and the much lower world price charged by such competing exporters as the U.S. The CAP also included a variable levy on imported wheat to keep EEC consumers and livestock feeders from buying lower priced foreign wheat, which would force the EEC also to purchase the domestic wheat displaced by those imports.

To reduce these expenditures, the European Communities (EC) Commission in July 1983 proposed a series of measures to the European Council (composed of EC heads of government) for reforming the CAP. A fundamental objective of the reform was gradually—over five to eight years—to reduce domestic grain prices to the level prevailing in international markets by reducing its guarantees to purchase excess production and by accepting "a growing measure of market discipline."

However, the specific reforms proposed further intensified the trade dispute with the U.S. One of them revived a 1982 proposal to restrict the importation of nongrain feed substitutes by imposing a tariff quota on the importation of corn gluten feed from the United States above the three million tons currently imported annually. The U.S. had refused to negotiate modification of the duty-free treatment agreed to by the EEC in an earlier GATT trade accord. The EEC argued that unrestricted imports of cheap feed grain substitutes would defeat its efforts to reduce its grain prices. Since the U.S. advocated such reductions, the EEC maintained that it was in its interest to share in the cost of the new policy.

The EEC made a similar argument in support of its proposed internal tax on sales of nondairy fats and oils. The tax, designed in part to make EEC butter—currently in large surplus—more competitive with margarine and vegetable oils, would make the importation of U.S. soybeans less attractive.

Although the impact of the proposed tax upon U.S. trade was thought to be small, the United States feared that it was a possible "first move in a concerted attack" threatening imports of oilseeds and oilseed products currently worth about $4 billion annually. The U.S. claimed that the use of import levies and export subsidies to maintain the CAP already cost the U.S. some $6 billion a year in lost trade, resulting in the loss of net farm income to U.S. farmers of $2 billion–$3 billion and an increase in U.S. government payments of $1 billion–$2 billion.

The heads of government of the EEC met in Athens in December 1983 to act on an interrelated group of issues that included budgetary reform, national shares of expenditures, limitations on EEC agricultural expenditures, and reform of the CAP. Their failure to reach agreement on any issue increased the prospect that the EEC budget would be exhausted sometime after the first half of 1984. That would threaten the very existence of the EEC, but most commentators thought that the danger of such an event would force EEC leaders to reach a difficult political compromise.

U.S. Farm Problems. The United States tried to offset the effects of two years of bumper harvests that had resulted in vast grain stocks, depressed commodity prices, and increased farm bankruptcies with an emergency Payment in Kind program (PIK) in early 1983. U.S. expenditures on farm programs, which had averaged $3 billion to $4 billion annually in the 1970s, climbed to $12 billion in 1982. One aim of the program was to support farm income by raising commodity prices, thus also reducing costly government deficiency payments to farmers. It aimed also at reducing government payments to acquire and store farm surpluses by distributing wheat, corn, cotton, and other grains to farmers from government stocks as an inducement to hold land out of production.

Sheep ate the last dry scraps of grass on the drought-devastated plains of eastern Australia; when it was gone, the sheep died and the earth cracked wide beneath parched trees.

DAVID AUSTEN—BLACK STAR

PIK and the severe drought in the summer of 1983 resulted in a much larger reduction in corn and oilseed stocks than was anticipated, leading to sharply rising feed grain prices and the potential for far higher prices should production be low again in 1983–84. U.S. stocks of wheat remained high and wheat prices low, leaving the United States sensitive to the actions of such competitors as the EEC. In addition, the cost of farm support programs jumped to more than $20 billion in 1983.

The higher world prices for grains, oilseeds, and sugar in the second half of 1983 actually eased somewhat the budgetary pressures on the EEC for reform of the CAP and demonstrated the increasing interdependence of agricultural policies among nations. Higher prices allowed the EEC to reduce its payments for export subsidies on wheat and sugar, which, together with smaller EEC grain and sugar harvests, resulted in reduced storage expenditures. At the same time, higher oilseed prices resulted in smaller direct subsidies to oilseed and olive-oil producers.

The Reagan administration, reacting to ballooning farm expenditures and large projected budget deficits, concluded that U.S. domestic farm legislation worked against U.S. farm exports. It claimed that the 1981 farm bill set support levels for U.S. agriculture too high, giving farmers incentives to produce more but also tending to price some U.S. commodities out of foreign markets and give other countries an incentive to produce more.

International Actions. The Agriculture Committee established after the GATT ministerial meeting in November 1982 began work on a two-year program "to bring agriculture more fully into the multilateral trading system by improving the effectiveness of GATT rules . . . to seek to improve terms of access to markets, and to bring export competition under greater discipline." The committee was asked to determine whether subsidies to promote agricultural exports violated GATT trade rules or were "seriously prejudicial to the trade or interests of GATT members." The committee was to complete an inventory of the agricultural trade policies of the GATT's 88 members before presenting a list of recommendations in support of agricultural trade liberalization to the GATT ministers in September 1984.

A new International Natural Rubber Agreement became operational in 1983. An agreement on jute and jute products, concluded late in 1982, was designed to promote more efficient production, use, and marketing of jute, but it contained no mechanism for stabilizing markets. The headquarters of the new International Jute Organization was Dacca, Bangladesh.

Total food aid in the form of cereals did not increase in 1982–83 despite the buildup in world wheat stocks. However, more dairy products appeared to have been made available from surplus dairy stocks. The ten million-ton cereals goal set by the World Food Conference in 1974 for food aid had been approached but never achieved.

Pledges to the International Emergency Food Reserve (IEFR) in 1983 were a little under the 500,000-ton target. The World Food Program (WFP) was designated to distribute 86% of the total. Emergency operations by the WFP, through November 1983, totaled $144 million, 77% from the IEFR. About 62% of such emergency commitments were used to help refugees, displaced persons, and victims of war and civil disturbances, while the remainder helped relieve sufferers from natural disasters. Of the 52 operations, 28 were in Africa, 10 in Asia, 3 in the Middle East, and 11 in Latin America.

At the end of October 1983, pledges to the regular resources of the WFP totaled 80% of the $1.2 billion target for 1983–84. The goal for 1985–86 was $1,350,000,000.

Climate and Agriculture. Research and speculation on the future of the Earth's climate attracted considerable attention in 1983. Some was generated by concern over rising political tensions between the United States and the Soviet Union and predictions that large-scale use of nuclear weapons would lead not just to widespread carnage and destruction but to the end of all life on Earth. This, it was claimed, would follow from supercooling of the atmosphere caused by airborne debris blocking the Earth's absorption of heat from the Sun.

Global warming, however, was the focus of two research reports issued in October by the U.S. Environmental Protection Agency (EPA) and by the U.S. National Research Council (NRC), the latter an organ of the U.S. National Academy of Sciences. Both studied the consequences of the "greenhouse" effect produced by the increase of carbon dioxide and various trace gases in the atmosphere that results from the burning of fossil fuels; the carbon dioxide inhibits the reflection of the Sun's heat from the Earth back into space. Both reports emphasized the uncertainties connected with predictions of a complex physical system for which historical data were sparse and expressed their results within ranges of probability and time span. Nevertheless, a consensus appeared to be growing in the scientific community that global warming was likely to occur and would do so earlier than had previously been expected.

The EPA midrange estimate included a doubling of preindustrial carbon-dioxide levels by the middle of the next century, leading to a rise in average temperature of 2° C (3.6° F) and an increase of 5° C (9° F) by 2100. It predicted that this temperature increase would be accompanied by dramatic changes in precipitation and storm patterns that would significantly alter agricultural conditions. Both reports emphasized that impacts upon agriculture would vary greatly from region to region, depending upon geographic location and the character of agriculture in each region.

The NRC report predicted similar results but with the long-run effects delayed about 25 years. U.S. agriculture might be little affected in 2000 by an expected 1° C (1.8° F) rise in average temperature because of the offsetting effects of more rain and a perhaps ten-day-longer growing season in the North and drier conditions in the South. However, a 4° C (7.6° F) rise over the next century could devastate agricultural areas of the Southwest now dependent upon irrigation. The EPA study concluded that the increased use of fossil fuels because of population and economic growth could only be slowed, not halted, even by employing extremely severe measures that were unlikely to be politically feasible. However, both reports—especially that by the NRC—indicated that, on a global basis, agriculture had considerable capacity for adaptation through geographic shifts in crops and improved technologies. (RICHARD M. KENNEDY)

See also Environment; Fisheries; Food Processing; Gardening; Industrial Review: *Alcoholic Beverages; Textiles; Tobacco.*
[451.B.1.c; 534.E; 731; 10/37.C]

Agricultural gases: Robert Foster (left), of Middlebury, Vermont, uses a methane generator to produce electricity from cow manure; John W. Cary (right), a U.S. Agricultural Research Service scientist, uses a testing device to measure oxygen and carbon dioxide concentrations in the soil, both of which are important to crop growth.

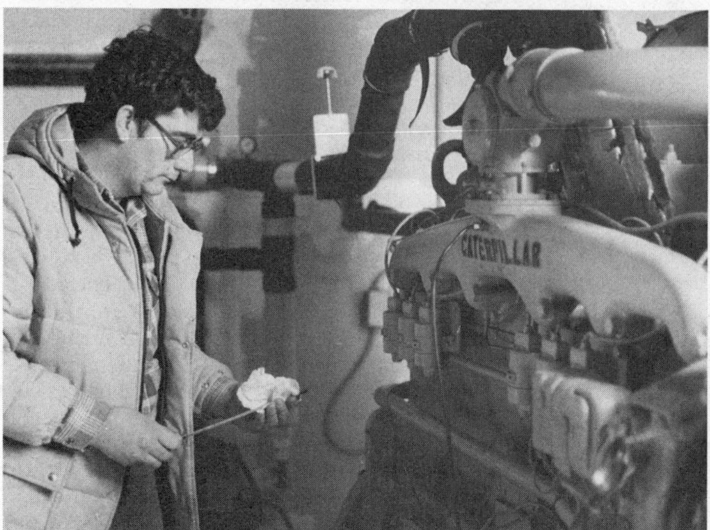

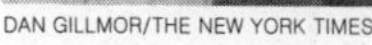
DAN GILLMOR/THE NEW YORK TIMES

USDA SCIENCE AND EDUCATION ADMINISTRATION

Albania

A people's republic in the western Balkan Peninsula, Albania is on the Adriatic Sea, bordered by Greece and Yugoslavia. Area: 28,748 sq km (11,100 sq mi). Pop. (1983 est.): 2,846,000. Cap. and largest city: Tirana (pop., 1980 est., 194,000). Language: Albanian. Religion: officially atheist; historically Muslim, Orthodox, and Roman Catholic communities. First secretary of the Albanian (Communist) Party of Labour in 1983, Enver Hoxha; chairman of the Presidium of the People's Assembly (president), Ramiz Alia; chairman of the Council of Ministers (premier), Adil Carcani.

In 1983 there was no improvement in the strained relations between Albania and the Soviet Union. On Nov. 29, 1982, the Soviet newspaper *Pravda* had marked Albania's national day and signaled the U.S.S.R.'s readiness to reestablish diplomatic links. However, Pres. Enver Hoxha (*see* BIOGRAPHIES), who had broken with Moscow in 1961, once again slammed the door on the Soviet initiative. Indeed, Hoxha described the U.S.S.R. and the U.S. as the main enemies of Albania, which he declared "the only true socialist country in the world."

China, Albania's chief ally and a major source of economic aid during the years 1961–78, had become ideologically unsound under the successors of Mao Zedong (Mao Tse-tung), according to Hoxha. In April 1983, however, a Chinese trade delegation arrived in Tirana to discuss the possibility of renewing trade between the two countries; China was to purchase chromium from Albania in exchange for industrial spare parts and agricultural products. (K. M. SMOGORZEWZKI)

CAMERA PRESS/PHOTO TRENDS

Pres. Enver Hoxha voted in the Tirana local elections. The only slate permitted won 99.9% of the vote.

Albania

ALBANIA

Education. (1979–80) Primary, pupils 555,910, teachers 25,900; secondary, pupils 30,455, teachers 957; vocational, pupils 125,965, teachers (1973–74) 3,990; higher (1977–78), students 14,695, teaching staff 1,015.

Finance. Monetary unit: lek, with (Sept. 20, 1983) a free exchange rate of 6.71 leks to U.S. $1 (10.10 leks = £1 sterling). Budget (1982 est.): revenue 8,550,000,000 leks; expenditure 8.5 billion leks.

Foreign Trade. (1979) Imports c. 900 million leks; exports c. 1 billion leks. Import sources: Czechoslovakia c. 12%; Yugoslavia c. 12%; China c. 10%; Italy c. 8%; Poland 8%; West Germany c. 7%. Export destinations: Czechoslovakia c. 11 %; Yugoslavia c. 10%; Italy c. 10%; China c. 9%; Poland c. 7%; West Germany c. 7%. Main exports (1964; latest available): fuels, minerals, and metals (including crude oil, bitumen, chrome ore, iron ore, and copper) 54%; foodstuffs (including vegetables and fruit) 23%; raw materials (including tobacco and wool) 17%.

Transport and Communications. Roads (1971) 5,500 km. Motor vehicles in use (1970): passenger c. 3,500; commercial (including buses) c. 11,200. Railways: (1979) c. 330 km; traffic (1971) 291 million passenger-km, freight (1978) c. 127 million net ton-km. Shipping (1982): merchant vessels 100 gross tons and over 20; gross tonnage 56,127. Shipping traffic (1975): goods loaded c. 2.8 million metric tons, unloaded c. 760,000 metric tons. Telephones (Dec. 1965) 13,991. Radio receivers (Dec. 1980) 202,000. Television receivers (Dec. 1980) 10,000.

Agriculture. Production (in 000; metric tons; 1981): corn c. 250; wheat c. 510; oats c. 30; potatoes c. 140; sugar, raw value c. 40; sunflower seed c. 38; olives c. 50; grapes c. 93; tobacco c. 15; cotton, lint c. 9. Livestock (in 000; 1981): sheep c. 1,170; cattle c. 476; pigs c. 125; goats c. 670; poultry c. 2,480.

Industry. Production (in 000; metric tons; 1981): crude oil c. 2,200; lignite c. 1,600; petroleum products c. 2,140; chrome ore (oxide content; 1980) c. 454; copper ore (metal content; 1980) c. 10; nickel ore (metal content; 1980) c. 8; fertilizers (nutrient content) c. 79; cement (1980) c. 1,000; electricity (kw-hr) c. 2,650,000.

Aircraft:
see Aerial Sports; Defense; Industrial Review; Transportation

Air Forces:
see Defense

Alcoholic Beverages:
see Industrial Review

American Literature:
see Literature

Algeria

A republic on the north coast of Africa, Algeria is bounded by Morocco, Western Sahara, Mauritania, Mali, Niger, Libya, and Tunisia. Area: 2,381,741 sq km (919,595 sq mi). Pop. (1983 est.): 20,695,000. Cap. and largest city: Algiers (pop., 1981 est., 2.2 million). Language: Arabic (official), Berber, and French. Religion (1980): Muslim 99.1%; Christian 0.8%; none 0.1%. President in 1983, Col. Chadli Bendjedid; premier, Mohamed Ben Ahmed Abdelghani.

During 1983 Algeria began a new drive for unity within northern Africa. Pres. Chadli Bendjedid met with King Hassan II of Morocco on February 26, thus initiating a cautious return to normal relations despite the continuing major disagreement over the Western Sahara. Border settlements were made with Niger on January 5 and Mali on May 8, and Algeria signed a 20-year treaty of concord with Tunisia in March as a step toward unity in the region. The process culminated in a three-day visit by Pres. Habib Bourguiba of Tunisia to Algiers in June. There remained, however, disagreements with Libya over the border with Algeria and over Libya's intervention in Chad. These matters were discussed during a visit by Col. Muammar al-Qaddafi of Libya to Algiers on July 27.

The Algerian government continued to improve relations with France. Visits by the French agriculture minister in January, the foreign minister in March, and the education minister in September were capped by Premier Pierre Mauroy's visit in early September. President Bendjedid visited France in November. Relations with the U.S. also

THIERRY CAMPION—GAMMA/LIAISON

Tunisian Pres. Habib Bourguiba (right) was welcomed to Algiers by Pres. Chadli Bendjedid (left). Hundreds of thousands of Algerians lined the streets to greet the visiting statesman.

improved after a visit on September 13 by Vice-Pres. George Bush.

Algeria's economic position was little affected by the oil glut, mainly because of an emphasis on refined petroleum products and natural-gas sales. Crude oil represented only 20% of petroleum-related foreign-currency earnings, and revenue declined by only 12%, to $12.7 billion in 1982 from a 1981 high of $14.1 billion. Algeria's foreign debt was reduced from $24 billion in 1980 to $20 billion by 1983.

As a result of these factors, the 1983 budget, approved by the National Assembly on January 13, was increased by one-third to more than $20 billion, split evenly between current expenditure and development. Imports in 1983 were to be reduced by 5%, and exports were to be held steady. The dispute with Italy over the price of gas supplied via the new trans-Mediterranean pipeline was finally settled in April.

The National Liberation Front congress in December confirmed Bendjedid as sole candidate for the January 1984 presidential elections and dropped several prominent members of the government from the party Central Committee.

The government continued its cleanup campaign in major cities. Attempts were also made to root out corruption, both past and present. Several people, including Muhammad Zeghar, a prominent businessman, and Laid Anane, a senior official in the Ministry of Planning, were arrested on charges of endangering the national economy. On August 11 former foreign minister Abdel Aziz Bouteflika was accused of embezzling some $20 million, and another former minister, Ben Cherif, was ordered to reimburse over $100,000. Moves against Muslim fundamentalists continued with the arrest of a group in February for involvement in arms smuggling. Former president Ahmed Ben Bella, in exile in France, was accused of being involved in these affairs. (GEORGE JOFFÉ)

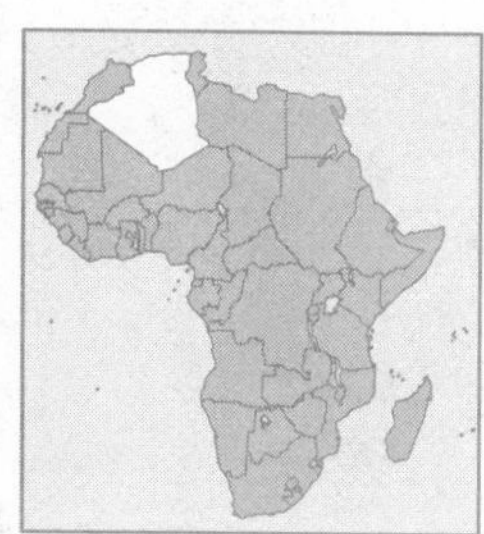
Algeria

ALGERIA

Education. (1981–82) Primary, pupils 4,250,000, teachers 104,500; secondary, pupils 1,350,000, teachers (1980–81) 38,845; vocational (1980–81), pupils 12,903, teachers 1,168; teacher training (1980–81), students 13,315, teachers 1,124; higher, students 100,000, teaching staff 8,573.

Finance. Monetary unit: dinar, with (Sept. 20, 1983) a free rate of 4.93 dinars to U.S. $1 (7.43 dinars = £1 sterling). Gold and other reserves (June 1983) U.S. $2,101,000,000. Budget (1981 est.): revenue 68,305,000,000 dinars; expenditure 36,195,000,000 dinars (excludes 31,593,000,000 dinars development expenditure). Money supply (Sept. 1982) 112,801,000,000 dinars.

Foreign Trade. Imports (1981) c. 47.5 billion dinars; exports (1982) 42,138,000,000 dinars. Import sources (1980): France 23%; West Germany 14%; Italy 12%; U.S. 7%; Belgium-Luxembourg 6%; Spain 5%. Export destinations (1980): U.S. 48%; France 13%; West Germany 12%; Italy 6%; The Netherlands 5%. Main exports (1980): crude oil 82%; petroleum products 9%; natural gas 7%.

Transport and Communications. Roads (1981) c. 72,091 km. Motor vehicles in use (1981): passenger 574,000; commercial 248,300. Railways: (1980) 3,890 km; traffic (1979) 1,875,000,000 passenger-km, freight 2,529,000,000 net ton-km. Air traffic (1981): c. 2,400,000,000 passenger-km; freight c. 16 million net ton-km. Shipping (1982): merchant vessels 100 gross tons and over 130; gross tonnage 1,364,709. Shipping traffic (1979): goods loaded 58,045,000 metric tons, unloaded 13,038,000 metric tons. Telephones (Jan. 1981) 484,973. Radio receivers (Dec. 1980) 3,230,000. Television receivers (Dec. 1980) 975,000.

Agriculture. Production (in 000; metric tons; 1982): wheat c. 1,200; barley c. 650; oats c. 80; potatoes c. 610; tomatoes c. 190; onions c. 123; dates c. 207; oranges c. 250; mandarin oranges and tangerines c. 130; watermelons c. 180; olives c. 120; wine c. 230. Livestock (in 000; 1981): sheep c. 13,600; goats c. 2,723; cattle c. 1,370; asses c. 521; horses c. 134; camels c. 149; chickens c. 18,554.

Industry. Production (in 000; metric tons; 1981): iron ore (53–55% metal content) 3,350; phosphate rock (1980) 1,025; crude oil (1982) 36,400; natural gas (cu m) c. 25,500,000; petroleum products 10,506; fertilizers (nutrient content; 1981–82) nitrogenous 24, phosphate 23; cement c. 4,450; crude steel (1980) 345; electricity (kw-hr) 7,170,000.

Andorra

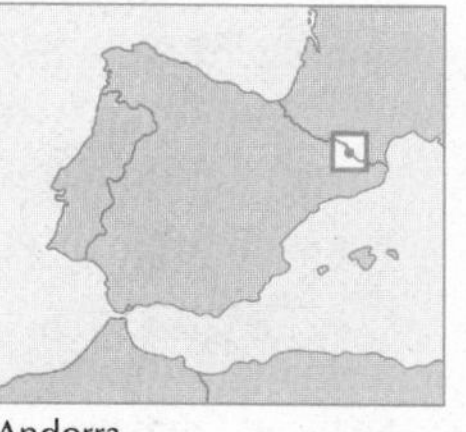
Andorra

An independent co-principality of Europe, Andorra is in the Pyrenees Mountains between Spain and France. Area: 468 sq km (181 sq mi). Pop. (1982): 38,050. Cap.: Andorra la Vella (commune pop., 1982, 14,900). Language: Catalan (official), French, Spanish. Religion: predominantly Roman Catholic. Co-princes: the president of the French

ANDORRA

Education. (1979–80) Primary, pupils 4,711, teachers 207; secondary, pupils 2,134, teachers 98.

Finance and Trade. Monetary units: French franc and Spanish peseta. Budget (1981 est.): revenue 3,364,000,000 pesetas; expenditure 4,213,000,000 pesetas. Foreign trade: imports from France (1981) Fr 1,007,021,000 (U.S. $185.3 million), from Spain (1980) 10,924,000,000 pesetas (U.S. $152.4 million); exports to France (1981) Fr 25,308,000 (U.S. $4.7 million), to Spain (1980) 788,850,000 pesetas (U.S. $11 million). Tourism (1982) c. 6 million visitors.

Communications. Telephones (Jan. 1981) 15,800. Radio receivers (Dec. 1980) 7,000. Television receivers (Dec. 1980) 4,000.

Agriculture. Production: cereals, potatoes, tobacco, wool. Livestock (in 000; 1981): sheep c. 12; cattle c. 4.

Republic and the bishop of Urgel, Spain, represented by their *veguers* (provosts) and *batlles* (prosecutors). An elected Council General of 28 members elects the first syndic, in 1983 Francesc Cerqueda Pascuet; chief executive, Oscar Ribas Reig.

After the formation of Andorra's first Executive Council (Cabinet) in January 1982, relations between the government and the Council General remained harmonious for over a year and a half. On Aug. 18, 1983, the latter passed a unanimous vote of confidence in the former. Within days of this vote, however, the Council General was in uproar when the chief executive, Oscar Ribas Reig, submitted to its members his government's proposal that an income tax be levied in Andorra. The chief executive threatened to resign before the innovation was finally approved. Twelve members voted in favour of the motion, while eight voted against and the remainder abstained.

Previously, Andorra's budget had been financed by indirect taxes, which were often passed on to tourists. The economy, however, was suffering from the effects of the world recession, and it had been further weakened by severe flood damage in November 1982. The new tax, which was to be paid to the two co-princes of Andorra, was expected to have the most effect on banks and hotels.

(K. M. SMOGORZEWSKI)

Angola

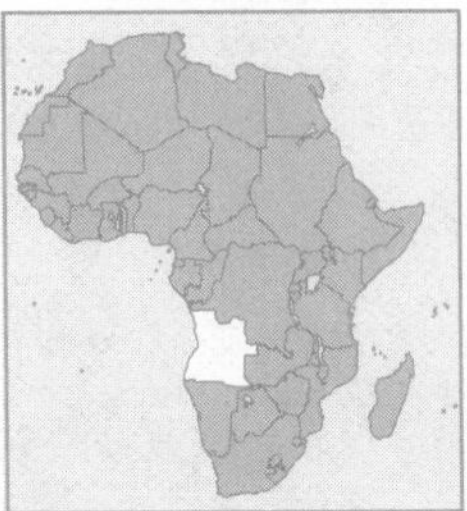

Angola

Located on the west coast of southern Africa, Angola is bounded by Zaire, Zambia, South West Africa/Namibia, and the Atlantic Ocean. The small exclave of Cabinda, a province of Angola, is bounded by Congo and Zaire. Area: 1,246,700 sq km (481,353 sq mi). Pop. (1982 est.): 6,943,700, including (1978 est.) Ovimbundu 35.7%; Mbundu 22.3%; Kongo 12.6%; Lunda-Chokwe 9.1%; Nganguela 8.6%; Nuaneka-Humbe 6.7%; other 5%. Cap. and largest city: Luanda (pop., 1979 est., 475,300). Language: Bantu languages (predominant), Portuguese (official), and some Khoisan dialects. Religion (1980): Roman Catholic 68.7%; Protestant 19.8; tribal 9.5%; other Christian 1.5%; none 0.5%. President in 1983, José Eduardo dos Santos.

In January 1983 divisions within the ruling Popular Movement for the Liberation of Angola (MPLA) resulted in a purge of some of the party's more radical elements. Three leading members, Costa Andrade, Vantagen Lara, and Lucio Lara, were imprisoned, together with one other person, while another 32 party activists were suspended from membership. This was the culmination of a long struggle between those who wished to remove Cuban troops from the country because they were an obstacle to any settlement between the government and the guerrilla forces of the National Union for the Total Independence of Angola (UNITA) and those who followed the Moscow line that to get rid of the Cubans would be a concession to U.S. pressure. (The U.S. had insisted that no further progress could be made toward the independence of South West Africa/Namibia until the Cubans had left Angola.) More than half the suspended members were reinstated in February because Pres. José Eduardo dos Santos was anxious to restore unity within the party.

Coinciding with the struggle within the ranks of the MPLA came a marked increase in guerrilla activity in the southeast. On January 31 the Lomaum Dam in Benguela Province was severely damaged by South African troops, causing a loss of power in three provinces and flooding considerable areas of agricultural land. The fighting also hindered discussions between representatives of the Angolan and South African governments who met in Cape Verde in February in an attempt to bring an end to the war along Angola's southern border.

The troubled political and military situation was cited as the reason for the People's Assembly's decision in March to postpone elections, originally scheduled for late 1983, until 1986. It was claimed that it would have been impossible to provide the information needed for the construction of electoral registers.

The worsening food supply, particularly on the central plateau, where bad weather and guerrilla activity had brought severe hardship, was one of the factors leading to the dispatch of a trade mission to Argentina in the hope of purchasing grain and wheat. In April France agreed to assist in rehabilitating Angola's coffee plantations and to cooperate in the fields of transportation, energy, water supply, ocean fishing, and vocational training. In May, however, tension developed between the two countries because of criticisms leveled against the Angolan government by the Luanda correspondent of the French news agency, Agence France-Presse, and by a French television and radio team that had entered the country illegally with the cooperation of UNITA and South Africa.

In May President dos Santos visited Moscow for official talks. Soviet Pres. Yury Andropov accepted his invitation to pay a reciprocal visit to Angola at a later date. The Soviet Union reaffirmed its solidarity with Angola and other nations of the region in their struggle for the liberation of southern Africa from white domination.

The offer of Soviet support came at an appropriate moment; just before the president's departure for Moscow, his government received a severe shock from a report that alleged extensive diamond smuggling and implicated several senior officials. Western powers seemed undisturbed by the news. Spain entered into an economic and trade agree-

Anglican Communion: see Religion

ANGOLA

Education. (1978–79) Primary, pupils 1,388,110, teachers (1977–78) 25,000; secondary and vocational, pupils 153,000, teachers (1972–73) 4,393; teacher training (1972–73), students 3,388, teachers 330; higher (1980–81), students 3,146, teaching staff 225.

Finance and Trade. Monetary unit: kwanza, with a free rate (Sept. 20, 1983) of 30.21 kwanzas to U.S. $1 (45.50 kwanzas = £1 sterling). Budget (1981 est.) balanced at 108,874,000,000 kwanzas. Foreign trade (1982): imports c. U.S. $1.1 billion; exports c. U.S. $1.7 billion. Import sources: U.S. c. 16%; France c. 12%; Brazil c. 9%; Soviet Union c. 8%; Portugal c. 7%; Italy c. 6%; West Germany c. 6%; Japan c. 5%. Export destinations: U.S. c. 38%; The Bahamas c. 18%; The Netherlands c. 9%; Spain c. 9%; Belgium-Luxembourg c. 8%; Algeria c. 6%; Brazil c. 5%. Main exports (1979): crude oil 68%; coffee 14%; diamonds 11%; petroleum products 6%.

Transport and Communications. Roads (1974) 72,323 km. Motor vehicles in use (1980): passenger 142,000; commercial (including buses) 43,000. Railways: (1982) c. 2,800 km; traffic (1974) 418 million passenger-km, freight 5,461,000,000 net ton-km. Air traffic (1981): c. 692 million passenger-km; freight c. 34 million net ton-km. Shipping (1982): merchant vessels 100 gross tons and over 56; gross tonnage 90,428. Shipping traffic (1977): goods loaded c. 9.4 million metric tons, unloaded c. 1.9 million metric tons. Telephones (Dec. 1980) 40,000. Radio receivers (Dec. 1980) 125,000. Television receivers (Dec. 1980) 30,000.

Agriculture. Production (in 000; metric tons; 1982): corn c. 250; cassava c. 1,900; sweet potatoes c. 180; dry beans c. 40; bananas c. 280; citrus fruit c. 81; palm kernels c. 12; palm oil c. 40; coffee c. 35; cotton, lint c. 11; sisal c. 20; fish catch (1981) 123; timber (cu m; 1981) c. 8,969. Livestock (in 000; 1981): cattle c. 3,200; sheep c. 230; goats c. 940; pigs c. 420.

Industry. Production (in 000; metric tons; 1980): cement c. 400; diamonds (metric carats) c. 1,000; crude oil (1982) c. 6,403; petroleum products (1981) 941; electricity (kw-hr; 1981) c. 1.5 million.

ment with Angola in May, and a conference held in London in June concluded that the time was ripe for investment in Angola.

In July the government announced an amnesty for all UNITA and National Front for the Liberation of Angola (FNLA) rebels inside and outside the country, but in August Minister of Foreign Affairs Paulo Jorge reaffirmed his government's uncompromising hostility toward those who persisted in their rebellion as virtual agents of South Africa. This did not rule out direct talks with South Africa itself as the principal in the struggle.

(KENNETH INGHAM)

Antarctica

The number of nations sending expeditions to Antarctica continued to grow during the 1982–83 summer research season. After several years of planning, Brazil sent a two-ship expedition to the Antarctic Peninsula in a major reconnaissance effort. Spain sent a sloop into the same waters, turning an originally private voyage into a government-sponsored expedition. Both Spain and Brazil had acceded to the Antarctic Treaty.

India finally acceded to the treaty in August 1983 and made another visit to the Dakshin Gangotri coastal weather station, which had been established in 1981. Twenty-eight scientists participated in the expedition. Chinese scientists worked with expeditions from Australia and New Zealand in 1982–83. China acceded to the treaty in June 1983, signaling its intention to become a full participant in modern Antarctic exploration.

The treaty nations continued their discussions of a possible regime for mineral exploitation during meetings in Wellington, N.Z., Bonn, West Germany, and Canberra, Australia. Progress was reported, but details were not yet available. (*See* ENVIRONMENT.) The nonaligned nations, meeting in New Delhi, India, in March, decided to call on the UN General Assembly to begin a comprehensive study of Antarctica. The 12th Consultative Meeting of the treaty nations was held in Canberra in September. For the first time all nations that had acceded to the treaty were invited to send observers. India and Brazil were approved for full consultative status, expanding the group to 16.

National Programs. ARGENTINA. A full program of research was conducted at 11 permanent and temporary bases in the Antarctic Peninsula. Shipboard programs emphasized meteorology, krill and seal biology, and sea-ice studies. Geologic research concentrated on resource-exploration programs.

AUSTRALIA. Research continued at three mainland bases, with major efforts directed at krill research in Prydz Bay and a resumption of the glaciologic traverse from Casey Station. The krill work was part of the international BIOMASS (Biological Investigation of Marine Antarctic Systems and Stocks) program. Preliminary results indicated that krill concentrate in the top few metres of water when heavy ice is present but disperse to depths of 100 m (330 ft) when the seas are ice-free. The glaciologic party extended the network of snow-accumulation and ice-movement markers another 450 km (1,475 ft). Traveling along the 2,000-m (6,560-ft) contour line, the six Australians used ice radar to determine a maximum ice thickness of about 3,400 m (11,150 ft). The Australian government announced plans to build permanent runways for long-range aircraft at Casey, Davis, and Mawson stations. All three would allow wheeled long-range aircraft to operate between Antarctica and Australia. In addition, the government committed itself to building an icebreaking marine research ship.

CHILE. Three permanent and several temporary bases were used by more than 60 scientists. The Chilean Air Force continued its support operations by building several small airstrips along the Antarctic Peninsula where meteorologic and other observations were being made.

FRANCE. Katabatic (downslope) wind studies were the primary research emphasis of a traverse that traveled some 400 km (250 mi) from Dumont d'Urville station into East Antarctica. Construction began on a permanent all-weather runway at the station, which was expected to take three to five years to complete. It would allow direct flights between Antarctica and Tasmania.

JAPAN. Glaciologic work was emphasized in East Antarctica. A traverse along the 2,000-m contour line southeast of Syowa Station to the Sor Rondane Mountains was conducted. Marine geophysical and geologic surveys were carried out for the third consecutive summer, this time in the Wilkes Basin and the Ross Sea. The icebreaker "Fuji" made its

LONDON EXPRESS/PICTORIAL PARADE

Mirnyy ("Peaceful") station is the oldest of seven permanent Antarctic stations operated by the Soviet Union. During the summer the permanent stations were augmented by a number of seasonal stations where geologists and other researchers were based. Over 300 scientists and technicians remained for the winter.

last voyage to the Antarctic before being replaced by the new "Shirase."

NEW ZEALAND. The New Zealand Antarctic Research Program again concentrated its efforts near McMurdo Sound and in the dry valleys of South Victoria Land. Other parties worked along the coast of North Victoria Land at Terra Nova Bay and conducted a penguin census along the coast to Cape Hallett. Sediment cores were taken in Taylor Valley for analysis of the region's history during the Cenozoic Era (65 million years ago to the present).

SOUTH AFRICA. Grunehogna, an 18-man base, was built in the Ahlmann Ridge. Field parties working from Grunehogna would extend the geologic mapping program some 250 km (155 mi) from SANAE base. Automatic weather stations were installed on Bouvet Island, and South Africa joined a multination study of the upper atmosphere.

UNITED KINGDOM. Major funding increases following the 1982 Falkland Islands war allowed the British Antarctic Survey to reverse the decline in the level of its work in the Antarctic. Two new aircraft were purchased; high-speed satellite communications equipment was installed at Antarctic bases; and a new geophysical observatory was built at Halley Station. Geologists began a comprehensive geophysics program on the Ronne Ice Shelf, while paleontologists worked in the rich fossil deposits on James Ross Island.

UNITED STATES. More than 285 scientists worked on 84 projects during 1982–83. The seismic network on Mt. Erebus recorded thousands of small earthquakes, as many as 650 in one day. Mt. Melbourne, a second active volcano near the Ross Sea, was also visited. Drillers recovered more than 200 m (650 ft) of ice core at the South Pole. New concentrations of meteorites were discovered in the Thiel Mountains. After extensive laboratory analysis, National Aeronautical and Space Administration (NASA) scientists confirmed that a meteorite discovered near the Allan Hills originated on the Moon. The U.S. Coast Guard cutter "Polar Star" became the seventh ship to circumnavigate Antarctica when it carried an Antarctic Treaty inspection team to 12 bases of various countries. Extensive surveys of a possible uranium deposit at Szabo Bluff were disappointing; only low-level radiation was found.

U.S.S.R. Rescuers reached the 20 men wintering at Vostok Station during the 1982 winter some eight months after their power plant was destroyed by fire. The men survived by using diesel fuel candles and an ice drill generator for power. The intense cold caused severe damage to the station. In spite of the hardships, the Soviet crew continued scientific observations and extended the deep ice core hole an additional 82 m (269 ft) to almost 2,220 m (8,270 ft). During the summer the largest Soviet expedition ever worked at seven permanent and several seasonal stations. Two major glaciologic traverses were conducted in East Antarctica. Geologic work was concentrated in the Prince Charles Mountains in East Antarctica and in Coates Land in West Antarctica. Almost 350 scientists and technicians remained to winter over. A new record for the lowest temperature on the Earth's surface—−89.2° C (−128.6° F)—was recorded at Vostok Station on July 21, 1983.

WEST GERMANY. Two expeditions worked in Antarctica. Ganovex III went to North Victoria Land to continue the geologic work interrupted in 1981–82 when the supply ship "Gotland II" was crushed by the ice. A second expedition resupplied Georg von Neumayer Station and put ashore personnel and equipment to establish a geologic field camp in New Schwabenland.

OTHER NATIONS. Cuba and East Germany sent scientists to work with the Soviet Antarctic Expedition. Peru and Italy had observers traveling in Antarctica: two Peruvians worked with the Chileans and one with the Australians. Italy again had observers with the New Zealand expedition. Poland continued its low-level biological programs at Arctowski Station on King George Island.

(PETER J. ANDERSON)

Anthropology

Intense public interest in the creation science versus evolutionary theory debate and Derek Freeman's highly publicized critique of Margaret Mead and "cultural determinism" thrust anthropologists into the media limelight in 1983. Within the profession, anthropologists faced declining student enrollments, shrinking research funds, the highest unemployment rate among academic professions (40.5% of all doctorate recipients at the time of graduation, according to a National Academy of Sciences survey), and a major reorganization of the American Anthropological Association. These events, however, had little effect on the high level of scholarly activity in the field. Scientific meetings, new organizations and journals, and scholarly publications all testified to the continuing vitality of the discipline.

Anthropology in 1983 stood at the threshold of a new synthesis of theory and information. Recent advances in symbolic, structural, ecological, and Marxist anthropology provided new ways of understanding human behaviour. Ethnographers, for their part, increasingly turned their attention toward the study of complex modern cultures in response to dramatic changes in economic, political, and social life throughout the world. Interdisciplinary and international cooperation between anthropologists, especially women, and scholars in other fields was increasing. Most important, growing numbers of ethnologists were accepting private or government employment as applied or practicing anthropologists. These and other developments promised to redirect anthropological inquiry into new and exciting areas of research.

STEVEN MOSHER

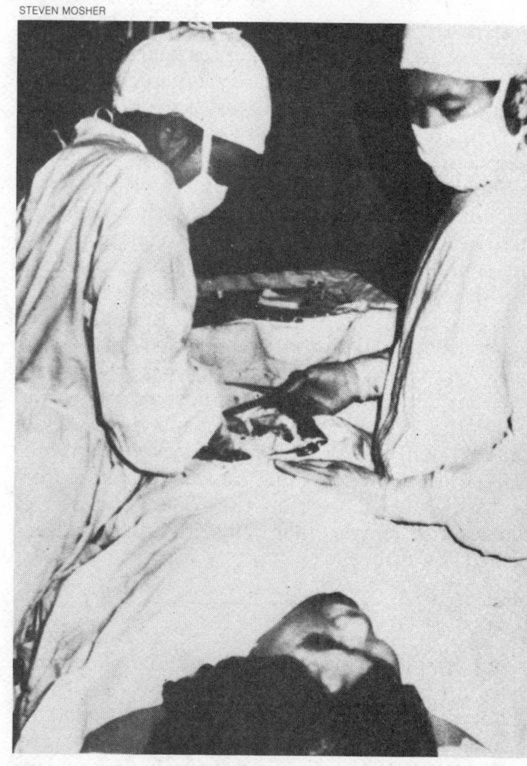

Steven Mosher was expelled from Stanford University's department of anthropology because of his controversial study of Chinese birth control practices.

Various religious groups continued to press for teaching of the biblical version of creation as scientific fact in American schools, despite the overturning of an Arkansas statute requiring balanced treatment of "creation-science" and evolution by a

Anthropologist Derek Freeman (top right) stirred controversy with his attack on the early work in Samoa of Margaret Mead (bottom right). Mead is shown at left with the daughter of a Samoan chief during her 1925 trip to the islands. (*See* Sidebar.)

(LEFT) INSTITUTE FOR INTERCULTURAL STUDIES; (TOP RIGHT) MICHAEL JENSEN/TIME MAGAZINE; (BOTTOM RIGHT) MAGGI CASTELLOE/PEOPLE WEEKLY © 1977 TIME INC.

U.S. district court in January 1982. Anthropologists had testified at the Arkansas trial and continued to oppose creationists by organizing public symposia and publishing books and articles. Among the more useful publications were Ashley Montagu's *Science and Creationism* and a selected bibliography prepared by Patrick McKim.

The expulsion of Steven W. Mosher from the graduate program of Stanford University following completion of his dissertation also caused a stir in the anthropological community. Both the Stanford anthropology faculty and a specially convened grievance committee concluded that Mosher acted unethically during his fieldwork in China by disregarding the laws of the host country, manipulating his informants and displaying a lack of candour with his professors and government officials. Mosher charged that he was terminated because of his writings on the forced abortion of fetuses and female infanticide in China and appealed the ruling.

By far the most prominent dispute centred around the critique by Derek Freeman, professor emeritus at the Australian National University, of Margaret Mead's Samoan research in particular and the discipline of cultural anthropology in general. (*See* Sidebar.) As much a media event as a scholarly controversy, the furor over this latest salvo in the ongoing nature-nurture debate promised to intensify in the immediate future.

The drop in student enrollment, which approached 10% per year during the late 1970s, leveled off in 1983. Research funding and unemployment, however, continued to present major problems. Increases in National Science Foundation funding for fiscal year 1984 were offset by decreased appropriations to other agencies that traditionally supported anthropological research. Pressed by budgetary restrictions and restrained by existing hiring policies, anthropologists were unable to reverse the trend of rising unemployment.

Bombing Margaret Mead

A bombshell burst in the anthropological community on Jan. 31, 1983, when the *New York Times* reported that Harvard University Press planned publication of a scathing indictment of Margaret Mead's 1928 book *Coming of Age in Samoa*—the best-selling anthropological work of all time—by an eminent colleague. The book, entitled *Margaret Mead and Samoa: The Making and Unmaking of an Anthropological Myth*, was written by Derek Freeman, professor emeritus at the Australian National University, who had conducted fieldwork on Samoa at various times since 1940. In it he asserted that Mead's romantic vision of South Seas life, inadequate command of the Samoan language, overreliance on playful adolescent girls as informants, and ambition to prove that cultural rather than biological factors determine human behaviour caused her to commit serious errors of fact and interpretation. Freeman acknowledged Mead's position as one of the most prominent women scientists of the century. Thus, by attacking her, he indirectly challenged the viewpoints she supported.

Press releases stated that Freeman's book promised to "intensify the often bitterly contested nature versus nurture controversy" between scholars supporting the view that heredity determines behaviour and those who favour cultural causes. The controversy had surfaced most recently in the sociobiology debate, in which scholars such as E. O. Wilson (*Sociobiology: The New Synthesis*) attempted to establish the biological origins of such phenomena as human aggression and male dominance.

As the Mead-Freeman uproar intensified, many laymen assumed it was a scandal, though the *Times* put the matter in perspective by stating, in an editorial on Feb. 3, 1983, that "the clangorous exchange of insult merely announces that a vigorous discipline is in full health."

Was the uproar justified? Other anthropologists had recognized the deficiencies of Mead's work while building on the strengths of her field techniques, but Freeman asserted that such improvements were negated by ethnology's refusal to recognize the biology of human behaviour and inferred that the emphasis on cultural variables at the expense of biology made cultural anthropology "unscientific." Freeman, however, did not use biological data to refute Mead's findings. Using his own cultural field data and materials drawn from the High Court of American Samoa in the 1920s, Freeman claimed that Mead's portrayal of Samoans as mild, gentle, egalitarian, cooperative, and sexually free was erroneous. He replaced it with a vision of a rank-obsessed, puritanical, competitive society with the highest rates of rape and assault in the known world. While it remained to be seen if the Samoans would be pleased by Freeman's reappraisal of their culture, it should be noted that his methods were in many ways less methodical than those used by Mead. It was difficult to see, for instance, how Freeman's data on the high incidence of virginity gathered from high-ranking men could be more accurate than Mead's data to the contrary gathered from adolescent girls. Freeman used historical sources to place Samoan culture in a historical framework; Mead did not. Freeman, however, discounted the effects of colonialism as causes for high rates of crime.

Many biological anthropologists hailed Freeman's work. Ethnologists, on the other hand, found much to criticize. No one doubts that a rapprochement between biological and cultural anthropologists has long been needed, but Freeman's contentious attempt at giant-killing did little to bring the two disciplines together. Mead's *Coming of Age in Samoa*, deficiencies and all, played a significant role in exposing people to the possibilities and importance of anthropological research. As such, it would be remembered for what it is, an early classic attempt to understand another culture, long after the controversy Freeman set in motion was forgotten.

An Internal Revenue Service ruling jeopardizing the tax exempt status of the American Anthropological Association compelled the executive board to recommend the merger of its constituent societies into a more centrally organized association. Several affiliated societies within the AAA, such as the Society for American Archaeology, the American Association of Physical Anthropologists, and the Society for Applied Anthropology, rejected the reorganization. Fully 86% of the AAA membership, however, voted in favour of the change in an election held during the fall. Special sessions were planned for the AAA annual meeting to facilitate future participation by members of the dissident societies.

More than 200 meetings of societies as diverse as the Association for the Anthropological Study of Play and the American Society for Ethnohistory were organized or heavily attended by anthropologists. The annual meeting of the AAA and the International Congress of Anthropological and Ethnological Sciences (ICAES) also drew large numbers of participants. The AAA and ICAES meetings were heavily weighted toward women's studies and such applied fields as medical, urban, and development anthropology and the anthropology of law, aging, and education.

Several new societies, such as the Society of Practicing Anthropologists, the Association for Anthropological Diplomacy, Politics, and Society, and the Society for Economic Anthropology, had been organized during the past few years. New journals and monograph series such as *Culture*, the journal of the Canadian Ethnology Society, *Anthro-Tech*, a journal of speculative anthropology,and a monograph series entitled *History of Anthropology* had also begun publication. The Consortium of Social Science Associations (COSSA) held its first annual meeting in November 1982. COSSA was established to enable officers of social science disciplinary associations to cooperate on issues of mutual concern.

Joined by common political and social agendas, women in anthropology also established interdisciplinary and international academic organizations, such as the International Women's Anthropology Conference.

A number of significant studies have been published in recent years. Among the more important structural-symbolic volumes were James A. Boon's *Other Tribes, Other Scribes*, Michael Jackson's *Allegories of the Wilderness: Ethics and Ambiguities in Kuranko Narratives*, and Stanley Walens's *Feasting with Cannibals: An Essay on Kwakiutl Cosmology*. Evidence that anthropologists had rediscovered history could be found in Loretta Fowler's *Arapahoe Politics, 1851–1978* and Marshall Sahlins's *Historical Metaphors and Mythical Realities*. A political economic perspective of history appeared in Eric Wolf's *Europe and the People Without History*, and a fine interdisciplinary approach characterized *Politics and History in Band Societies*, edited by Eleanor Leacock and Richard Lee. Other noteworthy titles included Jean Jackson's provocative *The Fish People: Linguistic Exogamy and Tukanoan Identity in Northwest Amazonia*, Henry F. Dobyns's *"Their Number Became Thinned": Native American Population Dynamics in Eastern North America*, and a festschrift in honour of Walter Goldschmidt, *Culture and Ecology: Eclectic Perspectives*, edited by John Kennedy and Robert Edgerton. Among the many studies on women were Sherry Ortner and Harriet Whitehead's edited volume on *Sexual Meanings* and Peggy Reeves Sanday's *Female Power and Male Dominance*. (ROBERT S. GRUMET)

See also Archaeology.

Antigua and Barbuda

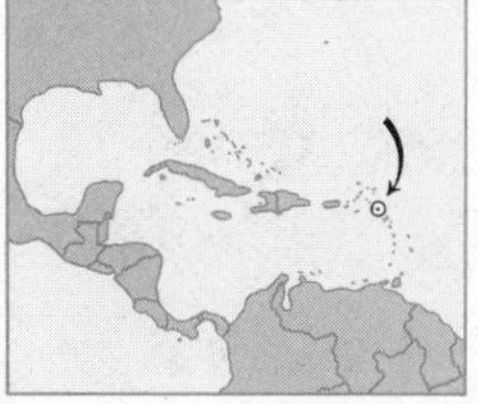
Antigua and Barbuda

An independent state and a member of the Commonwealth, Antigua and Barbuda comprises the islands of Antigua (280 sq km), Barbuda (161 sq km), and Redonda (uninhabited, 1 sq km) and lies in the eastern Caribbean approximately 60 km north of Guadeloupe. Total area: 442 sq km (171 sq mi). Pop. (1983 est.): 78,000. Cap.: Saint John's (pop., 1979 est., 25,000). Language: English. Religion: Church of England (predominant), other Protestant sects, and Roman Catholic. Queen, Elizabeth II; governor-general in 1983, Sir Wilfred E. Jacobs; prime minister, Vere Cornwall Bird.

Economic problems continued to preoccupy the government of Antigua and Barbuda during 1983. Despite a streamlined budget in April, designed to trim the annual deficit to ECar$17 million from the 1982 figure of ECar$24 million, an application to the International Monetary Fund for assistance appeared inevitable by September. Deputy Prime Minister Lester Bird, who was also minister of economic development, announced that the government was hoping to obtain about ECar$3 million from the IMF.

The economy suffered a severe blow when it was decided to close the West Indies Oil Company's refinery, reopened in April 1982 after an eight-year shutdown. The refinery lost ECar$16 million during the first half of 1983.

Prime Minister Vere Bird continued his efforts to strengthen overseas links, visiting China, Hong Kong, and South Korea in July and August. At home, talks opened between two opposition parties, the Antigua Caribbean Liberation Movement and the United People's Movement, on the formation of an electoral alliance. Antigua and Barbuda participated with the U.S. and with other Eastern Caribbean countries in the invasion of Grenada in October. (ROD PRINCE)

ANTIGUA AND BARBUDA

Education. (1980–81) Primary, pupils 10,660, teachers 431; secondary, pupils 4,526, teachers 318; vocational (1976–77), pupils 153, teachers 18; teacher training (1976–77), students 89, teachers 9.

Finance and Trade. Monetary unit: East Caribbean dollar, with (Sept. 20, 1983) a par value of ECar$2.70 to U.S. $1 (free rate of ECar$4.07 = £1 sterling). Budget (1981): revenue ECar$77 million; expenditure ECar$86 million. Foreign trade (1978 est.): imports ECar$111 million; exports ECar$34 million. Import sources: U.S. 31%; U.K. 28%; Canada 9%; Iran 7%. Export destinations: U.S. 35%; Trinidad and Tobago 21%; Saint Lucia 11%; U.K. 8%; Saint Christopher and Nevis and Anguilla 6%. Main exports: aircraft parts and engines 12%; clothing 8%; stoves, furnaces, ranges, etc. 5%; rum 5%. Tourism (1981) 96,084 visitors.

Archaeology

Eastern Hemisphere. The year 1983 brought no detailed report of any singularly spectacular find in the Eastern Hemisphere. The half life-size bronze chariots found in China or the large human figurines found in ʿAin al-Ghazal (Jordan) might yet prove to be such, but few details concerning them were available. The most fascinating laboratory-based archaeological news depended on the completion of new radioactive-carbon age-determination laboratories at Oxford and the University of Arizona. Heretofore, the practical reliable backward reach of radiocarbon dating had been 10,000 years. With the new mass spectrometry techniques at Arizona and Oxford, however, the anticipated backward reach was up to 100,000 years, and the assaying of much smaller samples than previously required was also anticipated.

As usual, archaeology was affected by various political factors. Along with renewed pressure by Greece for the return, from various Western museums, of such artifacts as the Elgin Marbles, Iraq sought the return of the stela bearing the 3,700-year-old Code of Hammurabi. The work of Israeli archaeologists continued to suffer from attacks by religious zealots who did not want the bones of ancestors disturbed.

Certainly one of the most impressive and important archaeological exhibits of the year was the Council of Europe's 18th exhibition, "The Anatolian Civilizations," in Istanbul. In New York City the Metropolitan Museum of Art's large and newly arranged Egyptian galleries were reopened.

PLEISTOCENE PREHISTORY. Several new studies strengthened the probability that changes in the orbit and in the axial tilt of the Earth had affected climate during the past million years, thus influencing the sequence of glacial activities and the environments within which human cultures evolved. It was reported that radar images, made from the U.S. space shuttle "Columbia," revealed features in the Egyptian desert that might aid in studies of past climatic and human activity as far back as 100,000 years.

In Western Europe interest centred on the opening to the public of a full-sized replica of the famous Lascaux cave in southwestern France. The actual cave, with its magnificent series of wall paintings of 14,000 years ago, was closed to public inspection in 1963 because the paintings were deteriorating. It was announced that the equally magnificent cave art at Altamira, Spain, was suffering deterioration.

EGYPT. Archaeologists from Canada, France, Poland, Switzerland, and the U.S., as well as from Egypt, were at work along the Nile River and in the adjoining desert. The activity around Luxor included the 60th campaign of the Oriental Institute at "Chicago House," which concentrated during the season on the overall architectural and decorative history of the Luxor temple itself. Teams from the Royal Ontario Museum continued work at Tell el-Maskhuta in the north and in the Dakhileh oasis. At Maskhuta the remains of an early 2nd-millennium BC farm village with pottery usually associated with the Hyksos (invaders from Asia) was exposed.

Near Cairo repairs were proceeding on the Sphinx, and some five tons of silica gel had been shipped to Egypt for use in the preservation of the wood of the royal ship of the pharaoh Khufu (Cheops; about 2600 BC). The ship, some 48 m (158 ft) long, was in a special museum near Khufu's pyramid, but the wood needed to be artificially moisturized by the gel.

SOUTHWESTERN ASIA. In Iraq, Jordan, and Turkey considerable attention was being given to salvage excavations on sites that soon would be covered by water above new dams on the Tigris, Euphrates, and Yarmuk rivers. Because not much time was left before flooding would occur, salvage work, as in most such situations, demanded a fair degree of selectivity and ruthlessness in excavation techniques if information about the past was to be saved. Unfortunately, many archaeologists had been carefully trained *not* to be selective and ruthless and so were finding it difficult to adapt their field techniques to salvage situations.

In Israel a joint U.S.-Israeli expedition under Trude Dothan continued work at the site of Tel Miqne, once a large Philistine city. In Jordan the important excavations at the early village site of Beidha were resumed under Diana Kirkbride-Helbaek's direction. At ʿAin al-Ghazal, near Amman, a group of half life-size human figures of sun-dried clay or plaster, with traces of red ochre paint, were found in an early village context said to date from about 6000 BC. These figures appeared to belong to the same complex of traits that had appeared in both pre- and post-World War II excavations at Tell es-Sultan (Jericho). It was reported that the laboratory cleaning of a silver amulet, found near Mt. Zion in Jerusalem and dated to the 6th century BC, revealed the inscription "Yud-heh-vav-heh" (YHVH). It was the first time that excavations in Jerusalem had yielded an object bearing the Hebrew form of the name of God.

THE GRECO-ROMAN WORLD. Having already worked for several seasons at the late Egyptian Red Sea port town of Quseir, Donald Whitcomb of the Oriental Institute undertook an archaeological survey along the Red Sea coast of the Sinai Peninsula. Roman, early Islamic, Ottoman, and even Chinese artifacts were located; they complemented finds at Quseir and hinted at the Red Sea trade of the time. Various Hellenistic and Roman sites were investigated in Israel and Jordan; work at the port town of Caesarea in northern Israel continued, and in Jordan the Roman frontier forts (on the Limes Arabicus of about AD 300) were surveyed.

There was considerable activity regarding Greek, Roman, and Byzantine sites in Turkey. At Perge, Jale Inan recovered statues of Athena and of Aphrodite. Martin Harrison of Newcastle University described the remains of a large and sumptuous Byzantine church recently discovered in Istanbul. It appeared to have been modeled on biblical descriptions of Solomon's temple.

In Greece, along with the campaign for the return of the Elgin Marbles from the British Museum, attention was concentrated on the restoration

PHOTOGRAPHS, WIDE WORLD

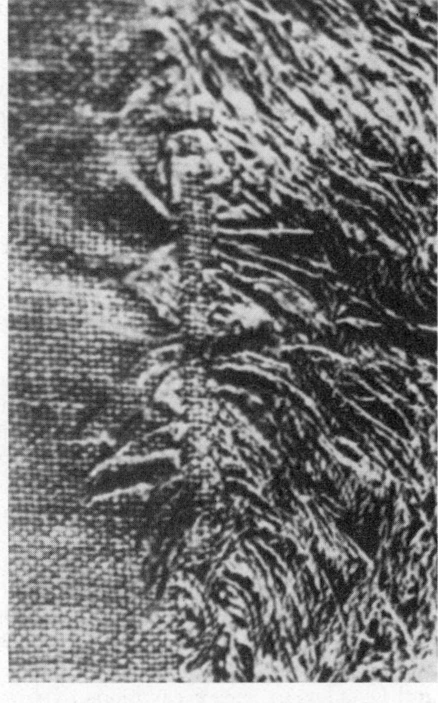

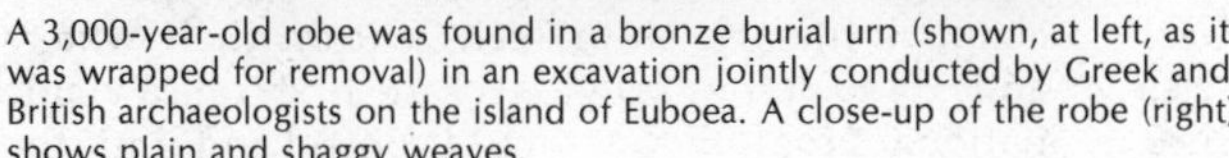

A 3,000-year-old robe was found in a bronze burial urn (shown, at left, as it was wrapped for removal) in an excavation jointly conducted by Greek and British archaeologists on the island of Euboea. A close-up of the robe (right) shows plain and shaggy weaves.

and preservation of those monuments that draw the most tourist interest. The buildings on the Acropolis in Athens were of particular concern because of deterioration caused by acid rain; the Erechtheum had been swathed in scaffolding for four years. For the Parthenon, whose deterioration in the early 1800s had prompted Lord Elgin to remove the marbles, preservation work was beginning; a special crane was developed to fit between the columns so that overall scaffolding would not be needed for restoration work.

In Rome the city government had announced a master plan to excavate and restore the forums and much of the centre of ancient Rome. The main efforts concerned the markets of Trajan, the forum of Nerva, and the reinforcement of now-standing ruins such as the Arch of Constantine.

Considerable archaeological activity was taking place at Herculaneum and Pompeii. At Herculaneum almost 100 human skeletons of victims of the ancient eruption of Vesuvius were cleared, and there were undoubtedly many more to uncover (skeletons were not preserved at Pompeii). They were in good condition and would yield useful information if given laboratory study, but they would disintegrate if left exposed on the site. In preliminary studies the bones yielded important information concerning Roman diet and the prevalence of lead poisoning among Romans.

SOUTHERN AND EASTERN ASIA, AFRICA, AND OCEANIA. At Bhagor in Madhya Pradesh, northern India, a triangular stone suggesting a female form was found in the centre of a stone platform. It could well be a shrine, dating from about 10,000 years ago. The Chinese Academy of Social Sciences resumed work near the "Ch'in tombs," a great tumulus that contains some 6,000 life-size terra-cotta soldiers of about 200 BC. One of the most recent finds was reported to be a pair of half life-size bronze two-wheeled chariots, each with four horses and with drivers in the chariots holding the reins. Laboratory study of the surface of a Chinese sword blade of the Shang dynasty (about 1800–1100 BC) revealed the earliest known traces of silk thread.

For Africa, where the volcanic glass obsidian was often used for chipped stone tools, the Pennsylvania State University's obsidian dating laboratory issued an impressive list of dates for the later Pleistocene and early historic ranges of East Africa. They included dates from about 120,000 to 2,000 years ago for archaeological sites in Kenya.

The magnificent series of metal castings of life-size human heads and of vessels and other artifacts from Benin City, Nigeria, now in the British Museum, was receiving new study in the museum's research laboratory. The new research also included pieces recovered by the Nigerian Antiquities Department at Igbo Ukwu around 1960, for which there were radiocarbon dates to the 9th century AD. Two different alloys of copper were utilized in the castings, but smithing as well as casting techniques were used. Also, the presence of silver in the Igbo Ukwu castings strongly suggested that the copper was made by very primitive procedures; European or Arab metallurgists of the period would certainly have extracted the silver from the original copper ore. This was taken as a good indication that the whole complex of metallurgical procedures involved was independently achieved in Africa.

During the year there was a marked increase in news concerning archaeology in Oceania. The High Court of Australia effectively halted a hydroelectric project in Tasmania that would have flooded significant ecological and archaeological resources. Cave sites in Tasmania had yielded evidence that prehistoric hunters had already penetrated that far south of the Equator by 20,000 years ago. (ROBERT J. BRAIDWOOD)

Western Hemisphere. Trends and events within archaeology in the Americas during 1983 continued to reflect larger political and economic currents throughout the hemisphere. Whole areas remained unavailable for study and field research. Financial or political constraints throughout much of the Caribbean and Latin America limited the number of foreign research teams in Latin countries. The 1983 financial crisis in South America constricted and, in many places, stopped programs of archaeological research and preservation. The inflationary crisis in Mexico resulted in zero funding and no new field excavation projects by National Institute of Culture archaeologists in 1983. At the same time, and as reported in *American Antiquity*, a scarcity of funding and the aforementioned political realities brought major shifts in U.S. funding priorities. Instead of support for new field projects, money was allocated for data analysis and the laboratory study of already excavated collections by U.S. scholars.

South and Central America. Within the Andean countries, continued military activities in the highlands of Peru all but stopped high-altitude archaeological research. Instead, recent discoveries had been made in the desert coastal areas of Peru and Ecuador. In Peru excavations by Christopher Donnan at the deeply stratified 1st millennium AD sites of Chotune and Chonancap in the Lambayeque valley revealed a large architectural complex containing a long, six-colour mural that shows a procession of figures, many carrying trophy heads. Along the northern Ecuadorian coast of Manabi, James Zeidler reported the discovery of an elaborate and previously unrecognized northern manifestation of the 3rd millennium BC Valdivia culture. This rich northern Valdivia culture area was revealed at the site of San Isidro, a large ceremonial centre that was distinguished by elaborate ceramics and ornately decorated plaques.

To the north, in the isthmus region of central Honduras, intensive survey and excavation field projects by U.S. and Honduran scholars documented 141 new Early and Late Classic Mayan sites, ranging from scatters of stone tools to large ceremonial and residential centres with hundreds of structures. Sponsored by the Instituto Hondureño de Antropologia e Historia and the Empreas Nacional de Energia Electrica and directed by Kenneth Hirth and Gloria Lara Pinto, this systematic regional study was conducted as a first step in the large-scale salvage excavation of the sites threatened by the planned El Cajon reservoir.

WIDE WORLD

The figurehead of the U.S. armed schooner "Hamilton" still graces her bow after 171 years at the bottom of Lake Ontario, where she was sent by a sudden squall during the War of 1812. Underwater archaeologists photographed her thus by remote control at a depth of 92 metres (300 feet) in February 1983.

Underwater Archaeology. The year was notable for major trends and discoveries in maritime archaeology. In terms of policy, funding, and effort, the concern with underwater wrecks was until recently dominated by privately financed treasure hunters more interested in profit than in scientific control. New discoveries of historic ships commonly disappeared as archaeological sites in a matter of days or weeks, with their contents going to private collectors and the international antiquities market. During the year, however, after a decade of conflict between salvage divers and archaeologists, protective legislation was introduced in the U.S. Congress. The Historic Shipwreck Preservation Act would allow states to lay claim to historic shipwrecks within their waters and, by so doing, provide for the first time a viable national program that would control and limit the number and scope of salvage permits granted. At the same time, it would allow each state to develop preservation and funding programs.

This development came about just as recent discoveries were highlighting the range and historical significance of shipwrecks, not only for the information they yielded on important maritime technologies and undocumented trade routes but also for their value as archaeological time capsules of critical importance for the dating of previously ill-defined historic artifacts. Furthermore, through the use of new techniques and the increasing ability to explore deeper and previously less accessible underwater locations, underwater archaeologists were discovering a variety of exceptionally well-preserved remains that document the material traces of everyday activities not generally found preserved in contemporary historic terrestrial sites. For example, a recently completed underwater survey of the Cayman Islands by underwater archaeologists for the Institute of Nautical Archaeology in College Station, Texas, provided the Cayman government with an inventory of 70 recently identified shipwreck sites dating from the 16th to the 20th century. A variety of wrecks dating to the 16th and 17th centuries reflected repeated hostile encounters between Spanish and British fishing and raiding vessels. The results of this government-sponsored survey transformed this little-studied group of Caribbean islands into a major new data centre of colonial economic trade patterns.

Marine technology was also providing archaeologists with new access to unlooted, deep-water wrecks. Using underwater robot systems and spacesuit-like diving equipment, underwater archaeologists obtained clear close-up views and made manual contact with well-preserved shipwrecks in two deep-water Canadian sites. Joseph B. MacInnes, a Canadian underwater scientist, reached the 19th-century British ship "Breadal-

UPI

A female skeleton estimated to be almost 10,000 years old was found in Texas. It is one of the three oldest ever found in North America.

bane," the northernmost shipwreck discovered on the seafloor, under approximately 100 m (350 ft) of Arctic ice and water.

North America and the Caribbean. Working with the Bahamian government, U.S. archaeologists announced the discovery of concrete evidence of Columbus's 1492 landing at San Salvador Island, one of the smallest of the Bahamian archipelago, located 565 km (350 mi) southeast of Miami. After a 12-year joint effort between the Bahamian government and the New York Center of Finger Lakes, archaeologists under the field direction of Charles Hoffman of Northern Arizona University announced the discovery of four green and yellow glass beads (datable to between 1490 and 1560), metal spikes, two brass buckles, and Spanish pottery together with native Arawak shards, all found at a depth of 20 cm (8 in) below the modern surface. Based on his journals, it is known that Columbus traded beads, buckles, and rings with the Indians. Given that the native population was wiped out by disease and slavery by 1520 and that the beads and European pottery predate their demise, the investigators believe it is possible that these finds belong to the site of Columbus's first landing in the New World.

Deep underground on the Tennessee-Kentucky border, archaeologists discovered seldom-found traces of prehistoric daily life. The discovery was suppressed for several years for fear that vandals might loot the fragile traces, but in 1983 archaeologists Patty Jo Watson, Louise Robbins, and Ronald Wilson reported the discovery of some 269 male and female footprints dating to at least 4,500 years ago, perfectly preserved deep in the moist clay of a 13-km (8-mi) labyrinth of the caverns of Blowing Cave in Pall Mall, Tenn.

Finally, as a modern demonstration of the potential utility of ancient techniques and tools, 39-year-old L. Adrian Hannus, a U.S. archaeologist, underwent two hours of abdominal surgery with a modern replica of a razor-sharp ancient prismatic stone blade. Not only did the patient do well, but the experiment demonstrated that those stone blades could work as well as modern surgical instruments. This experiment also augmented previous archaeological evidence (in the form of healed bone incisions found in burials throughout the Americas) that the ancient Mexicans, Peruvians, and other New World groups performed major surgery on organs and bones thousands of years ago. (Joel W. Grossman)

See also Anthropology.
[723.G.8c; 10/41.B.2.a.ii]

Architecture

The mode of architectural design or "style" christened "postmodernism" in the late 1970s had certainly come of age in 1983. The work of U.S. architect Michael Graves, in particular his Portland (Ore.) Building, attracted wide comment and strong emotions. Could this style now be said to be the dominant preferred clothing for new buildings in the United States?

In January John M. Dixon, editor of *Progressive Architecture*, reviewed the magazine's 1983 awards and attempted to trace and tabulate trends in design of the winning projects over the past five years. Postmodernism remained the style chosen by a majority of winners of the past two years, though overall there was no one dominant trend in a period characterized by randomness and variety. Dixon's stylistic categories included modern, postmodern, classical, vernacular, historical ornament, contextual, and energy-conscious. Modern was defined as having "functionally determined form, nonbearing walls, exposed structure, and fluid interiors." This would appear to include many of the buildings described as "high tech," which are distinguished by their brightly coloured exposed service ducts and structural members, often enclosing a "glass box" space and usually having industrial or technological references. "Postmodern," by contrast, is historical in form, if not detail, and is characterized by traditional loadbearing walls, pierced window openings, defined interior rooms rather than interconnecting flowing spaces, complexity, and perhaps irony, ambi-

Archery:
see Target Sports

CERVIN ROBINSON

The original design for the Portland (Oregon) Building was modified when the client objected to some of the exterior embellishments. The result was the building at right.

guity, and wit. Subcategories of postmodern might include the historical, classical, and vernacular. Postmodern is a method of design that relies on past tradition and adapts and rephrases elements of the classical or vernacular architectural language. For example, pediments, columns, swags, and moldings appear in abstracted or rearranged compositions and in new relationships to one another. Ornament and texture are important. In many examples there is more than a hint of the streamlined "moderne" or "Art Deco" mode of the 1920s and '30s. Renderings in pale washes and flat planes are reminiscent of architects' drawings of 50 years earlier.

It was noteworthy that two firms had won five *Progressive Architecture* awards over the past five years. These were Michael Graves & Associates and Skidmore, Owings & Merrill. A closer look at some of their recent work provides a lesson in current architectural fashion. Michael Graves's Portland Building was certainly the most hotly debated new structure. Hated by some and seen by others as a pointer to the new architecture to come, it was completed late in 1982. It was the first postmodernist building of major importance in terms of civic prominence and of sheer size. The commission was awarded to Graves in 1980 as a result of a competition held by the city of Portland for a new municipal office building. The design provides office space for 900 city employees, four floors of rental space, and 540 sq m (6,000 sq ft) of commercial space. The site is bounded on two sides by neoclassical civic buildings—the city hall and the county courthouse—with a park on the third side and glass-skinned towers on the fourth.

Graves's design makes a symbolic statement as to the nature of democracy and civic character. It is an urban monument of both classical grandeur and whimsy with an almost "pop" use of colour, pattern, detail, and abstraction. The composition defers to the traditional Portland City Center grid pattern, being regular in shape and of traditional construction with pierced window openings. The tripartite division of the structure into base, body, and head is traditional, but the decorative treatment is not. Columns support a gigantic flat abstracted keystone on the front, and the different functions are given separate exterior expressions. Sculpture is used decoratively, and broad ribbons in relief (swags in the original winning design) decorate the facade. It is a building that fits into its street pattern and yet at the same time proclaims newness and modernity.

Similarly whimsical, but perhaps less serious, were the new studios in Camden Town, London, for TV-AM, a new company producing television shows. The studios were designed by Terry Farrell Partnership. The project consisted of a low-cost conversion of a garage into studios and offices, and the eclectic influences discernible include Art Deco, Hollywood, and modern furniture design. Coloured pipes applied to the metal-clad box, together with a sunrise motif and a series of finials decorated with blue and yellow fibreglass egg cups, were some of the decorative features. The slick composition was described as "throwaway" and might be as ephemeral as a television program. Yet it was all slick and professional with imaginative use of inexpensive materials in a form that could be completed within a tight time scale.

A review of architectural periodicals made it clear that far more interest than ever before was being shown in architectural history, especially of classical architecture, and also in the traditional architecture of the Orient and India. In March a ten-day conference on interior design was held in Beijing (Peking), notable as the first such meeting to be held in China since 1949, when that country was cut off from Western traditions. During the Cultural Revolution beginning in 1966, architects had virtually ceased to exist, and engineering was decreed the only necessary discipline for erecting buildings. The Architectural Society of China had recently begun a program of activities designed to reinstate architectural schools and to encourage contact between foreign and Chinese architects. The few foreign architects who had worked in China in recent years had been largely financed by foreign groups with Chinese interests rather than by the government of China, but it was hoped that the situation would now change.

One recent notable building financed by the Chinese government was I. M. Pei's Fragrant Hill Hotel in Beijing. Pei, a Chinese-born architect who immigrated to the U.S. in 1935, received the fifth annual Pritzker Architecture Prize in 1983, consisting of $100,000 and a Henry Moore sculpture. It was the third time that the award had gone to a U.S.-based architect. Among Pei's other notable recent works was the East Building of the National Gallery of Art in Washington, D.C.

Other Awards. The Royal Institute of British Architects (RIBA) Royal Gold Medal for 1983 was awarded to Norman Foster (*see* BIOGRAPHIES) of Foster Associates, whose work included the Hong

Kong and Shanghai Commercial Banking Corporation headquarters in Hong Kong and the new British Broadcasting Corporation's Radio Centre in Langham Place, London. Six additional RIBA awards were made for "outstanding examples of current architecture." The winners, selected by regional juries, were: Robinson College, Cambridge, by the Scottish firm Gillespie, Kidd, and Coia; a candy factory for Trebor Ltd. at Colchester, by Arup Associates; the City Art Centre, Edinburgh, by the city architect; galleries for the Ulster Folk Museum, Northern Ireland, by Ferguson and McIbreen; a swimming pool at Newcastle upon Tyne, by Napper Collerton Partnership; and a primary school in Hampshire, comprising an interior garden and aviary, by the county architect. Among 25 commended projects was the reconstruction by Robert Hurd and Partners of Aboyne Castle in Aberdeenshire.

The American Institute of Architects (AIA) Gold Medal for 1983 was awarded to Nathaniel Alexander Owings, co-founder in 1936 of Skidmore, Owings & Merrill, long among the leading U.S. architectural firms. From 1952 to 1983 the firm received more AIA Honour Awards for design (16 in all) than any of its competitors. Recent projects included a railroad station in Providence, R.I., and a triangular office building for San Francisco. The Providence station was to be resited and rebuilt as part of a major civic redevelopment plan near the city's historic State House. Skidmore, Owings & Merrill's design was for a neoclassical structure with a domed central rotunda and colonnaded facades reminiscent of the formal grandeur of the early-20th-century railroad stations.

By contrast, the San Francisco building, a high-rise mixed-use project at 388 Market Street, is in a more modern idiom. Its triangular shape with a circular end, like a flatiron, was dictated by the unusual and prominent site. The structure is of steel, clad with polished red granite, and there is a formal "base" 12 m (40 ft) high from which the bulk of the building soars.

Educational and Cultural Buildings. Architect Richard Meier's Clifty Creek Elementary School in Columbus, Ind., was dedicated in November 1982. Designed to accommodate 700 pupils, the building was criticized for its austerity and clinical gray and white colour scheme. Neo-International Style motifs, including metal railings, smooth surfaces, flat roofs, and ramps, contributed to the austerity, as did the chosen material of gray blocks above and glazed white tiles below.

I. M. Pei's Indiana University Art Museum at Bloomington, Ind., was dedicated late in 1982. The $10 million structure of poured concrete features two interlocking wings surrounding an atrium, reminiscent of Pei's East Building of the National Gallery. The stark, sculptural composition provided facilities for a teaching museum, library, offices, and conservation laboratories.

Construction of a College of Architecture for the University of Houston, Texas, designed by John Burgee Associates with Philip Johnson and Morris/Aubry Architects, was scheduled to begin in the autumn of 1983. The design, in complete contrast to the modern context created by surrounding buildings, was for a blatantly historicist brick cross-shaped box, derived from the "House of Education" published by French neoclassicist Claude-Nicolas Ledoux in the late 18th century.

RICHARD BRYANT, LONDON

A low-cost conversion of garage space to offices and studios for London's new TV-AM was designed with airiness and whimsy by Terry Farrell Partnership.

Also in Houston, Morris/Aubry was architect for the Wortham Theater Center, which was to be part of a large performing arts complex. The project, at the design stage only, featured an entranceway in the form of a vast glass greenhouse dome filled with plants.

Public, Commercial, and Industrial Buildings. An exhibition at the Museum of Modern Art in New York City featured "Three New Skyscrapers," showing three distinct approaches to the architectural problems posed by the urban office building. Foster Associates' Hong Kong and Shanghai Commercial Banking Corporation building, Hong Kong, featured three bays with prefabricated service modules and exposed structural elements, described as "technomania." Skidmore, Owings & Merrill's National Commercial Bank of Jidda, Saudi Arabia, was a 28-story monolith of triangular plan broken only by three vast pierced openings. Johnson/Burgee was represented by International Place at Fort Hill Square in Boston, a design for two tall towers with crenellated historicist detail and various low connecting buildings costumed in Palladian windows.

Skidmore, Owings & Merrill's Lever House, one of the most influential skyscrapers of the 20th century and the prototype for glass towers with steel structures throughout the U.S. and elsewhere, was threatened with demolition. However, the future of the 24-story tower, built in 1952 in New York City, was assured by the Landmarks Preservation Commission, which designated it a city landmark even though it was only barely over 30 years old.

One of the most notable industrial buildings of

1983 was Foster Associates' Renault Centre in Swindon, England. Though it was superficially very different from the classicism of Graves's Portland Building, both had in common one element—fun. The Renault Centre was essentially a huge glass box suspended from yellow steel tentlike poles and wires like a giant circus marquee. Tubular steel rods pierce the roof and carry tension rods from which the internal structure is suspended. The detailing is of high quality, decorative yet functional, with the yellow external structure dominating the landscape.

Similar in style was the Inmos Factory in Newport, South Wales, by Richard Rogers & Partners. This single-story steel structure again featured an exposed brightly painted (blue this time) structural framework over a glass box and provided office and factory facilities for a high-technology microchip company. The design was said to have evolved logically from the central functional requirement to provide a clean, dust-free space for microchip assembly.

Work was in progress for the Patcenter International Technology and Science Center, Princeton, N.J., by Richard Rogers & Partners in collaboration with Kelbaugh & Lee of Princeton. This single-story research centre for a British firm's U.S. headquarters also featured a tentlike suspended steel structure composed of prefabricated elements.

A competition for an expanded civic centre for Beverly Hills, Calif., was won by architects Charles Moore/UIG. The project would include a new police headquarters, fire station, cultural resources centre, and parking facilities. Moore's scheme, in sympathy with the existing Spanish-style buildings, featured connected precast concrete structures linked by a series of complex open spaces including arcaded oval courtyards.

Pres. François Mitterrand of France chose the winning scheme for the Tête de la Défense, a new monumental western gateway for Paris. The successful design, by Danish architect Johan Otto von Spreckelsen, featured a cubic interpretation of a triumphal arch, a sort of open cube with accommodation in the main piers. The project had been the subject of several competitions since the 1960s.

Extensive renovation of the Statue of Liberty in New York Harbor was scheduled to begin late in 1983 and be completed by July 1986 in time for the statue's 100th birthday. The interior was to be cleaned by sandblasting and all structural elements examined for weakness. The copper exterior skin would be cleaned and repaired.

Two major figures in modern architecture and one of the century's leading architectural historians died in 1983. Buckminster Fuller (*see* OBITUARIES) was a pioneering architect, engineer, and philosopher whose early projects foresaw many of the theories that would become commonplace 50 years later. His Dymaxion house and geodesic dome were forerunners of later prefabrication and evolved out of his early concern with mass housing. He received the AIA and RIBA gold medals and was awarded the Presidential Medal of Freedom in 1983. José Luis Sert (*see* OBITUARIES), an early follower of Le Corbusier and an influential educator, was dean of the Harvard Graduate School of Design from 1953. His buildings include two well-known museums: the Fondation Maeght at Saint-Paul-de-Vence, France, and the Miró Museum in Barcelona, Spain. Sir Nikolaus Pevsner (*see* OBITUARIES) was a pioneer historian of the modern movement in architecture and author and editor of *The Buildings of England*, a comprehensive survey of the architectural treasures of England, county by county. (SANDRA MILLIKIN)

PHOTOGRAPHS, C. C. PEI

I. M. Pei's design for Beijing's Fragrant Hill Hotel was influenced by his visit to China in 1978. He shunned the skyscraper approach in favour of more Asian lines and adapted classic Chinese lines for large windows flanking main entries (top photo) and centred on long walls, as in interior photo below.

See also Engineering Projects; Historic Preservation; Industrial Review.
[626.A.1–5; 626.C]

Arctic Regions

Alaska. In March it was reported that most of the $2.5 billion in taxes collected by Alaska in 1982 came from the oil industry. The taxes collected were about $225 million higher than the year before. According to a report published in July, the oil industry planned to spend $3 billion in ongoing development at the Prudhoe Bay and Kuparuk River oil fields in 1983. In connection with this development work, the Atlantic Richfield Co. and the Standard Oil Co. of Ohio planned to drill just over 100 development wells.

The discovery of a massive oil field off the coast of California might cause Alaska crude oil from Prudhoe Bay to become less attractive to the states on the West Coast and lead to the loss of up to $200 million in Alaskan oil revenues. The Alaska Division of Petroleum Revenues reported in April that the only other markets for Alaska crude were U.S. states on the Gulf of Mexico and other nations. However, according to an August report in the *Anchorage Times*, the mere mention of lifting the export ban on Alaska crude would produce serious opposition from the U.S. Congress, which in 1979 had established it by a vote of 340–61. Both Alaska and Japan were in favour of lifting the ban. Alaska would benefit from an estimated $400 million per year in severance and royalty taxes if it were able to export its crude oil.

In January a $300 million pipeline across the Isthmus of Panama began operating at full capacity to allow Alaskan oil to be transported from the Pacific to the Atlantic Ocean for the use of the states on the Gulf of Mexico. Previously, supertankers had to transfer their cargoes to smaller vessels that could pass through the Panama Canal.

According to a March report by the U.S. Geological Survey, massive geologic structures with potential for oil and gas lie beneath the Bering Sea. However, it was expected to take years before the technology was developed to drill in such deep waters, which reach depths of 3,000 m (10,000 ft) in some places.

The *Anchorage Daily News* reported that industrial pollution from the Soviet Union, the Eastern European countries, and possibly from the northeastern United States might be fouling the Arctic air. The gray-blue "arctic haze," first discovered in Alaska, is composed of pollutants from heavy industry and is apparently a phenomenon that has been building up since the 1950s. Some scientists warned that a continuation of the pollution could result in a warming of the Arctic atmosphere that could trigger global flooding.

In July *Alaska* magazine reported on autopsies performed on a family of Eskimos that had been found frozen, killed by an accident estimated by radiocarbon dating to have occurred about AD 1500. The findings showed that they had suffered from serious health problems, including hardened arteries and trichinosis. These problems were probably caused by poor living conditions and periods of malnutrition during the winter months. In a second reported case the 1,600-year-old skeleton of a middle-aged Eskimo woman found near Homer showed the ravages of cancer. These remains were said to be further proof in a growing body of scientific knowledge indicating that Eskimos did suffer from cancer and other serious diseases long before contact with Western man.

Canada. In midyear the Canadian financial backers of the $2.5 billion Arctic Pilot Project were reported to be turning toward the British market in order to get the stalled enterprise moving again. An attempt was made to persuade the U.K. to buy natural gas from the eastern Arctic and then ship it to Britain in two giant supertankers. Because of a glut of gas on the international market that was expected to last until 1990, and because it would require about four years to complete building the ships and other production facilities, construction of the project would normally not start until 1986. The British were thought to have an interest in developing it earlier provided they were given the opportunity to build the two 65,000-ton supertankers.

In August it was announced by Canada's Department of Indian and Northern Affairs that agreements had been negotiated with six oil and gas companies for exploration on lands in the Mackenzie Valley. These agreements marked a resumption of industrial activity in the area. More than 9 million ha (22.5 million ac) of land were involved in the negotiations, which called for 24 wells to be drilled at a total estimated cost of $175 million. The announcement noted that more than $3.6 billion committed to oil and gas exploration in

CANADIAN PRESS

Ice Station Cesar was built by Canada on ice of the Arctic Ocean for the scientists and technicians of the Canadian Expedition to Study the Alpha Ridge (CESAR). The ridge is one of the world's last great uncharted geologic features.

PETER B. KAPLAN—PHOTO RESEARCHERS

Alaska continues to be the focus of conflict between those who would restrict public access (with the exception of subsistence hunters) to such wildly beautiful areas as Lake Kathleen (above), those who would give recreational hunters and fishermen ready access, and those who would open certain federally protected areas to commercial exploration.

the north during the next three to five years had been negotiated under various agreements.

In July the Canadian federal government provided funding of $1.5 million to assist the Dene Indians and Métis of the Northwest Territories to enter an equal partnership with Esso Resources Canada, Ltd., in a joint-venture drilling company. In making the announcement at Norman Wells, N.W.T., Minister of Indian and Northern Affairs John Munro stated that he hoped the unique venture would "blaze the trail for similar partnerships between other native groups and companies."

Continued progress was reported toward the settlement of native land claims in Canada. A process for approving a land-claim settlement involving every Yukon Indian community was adopted by the Council of Yukon Indians in July. The financial part of the settlement involved $600 million over 20 years.

During the summer some progress was made in land claims negotiations in the Northwest Territories. The Dene Nation and the Métis Association reached a joint agreement covering those people who would be eligible to participate. In addition a new joint-claims negotiating structure with a mandate to develop single negotiating positions on the different aspects of the agreement was established.

The Inuit Circumpolar Conference (ICC) met in Frobisher Bay, N.W.T., in July. More than 100,000 Inuit (Eskimos) from Canada, Greenland, and the U.S. were represented by just over 50 delegates. A circumpolar "policy in principle" was adopted for discussion. The policy included resolutions that would restrict the military use of the Arctic; establish mechanisms for the protection of the Arctic environment and renewable resources; promote recognition of Inuit economic, political, and judicial rights in their homeland; and require ICC representation in national and international organizations and agencies vital to Inuit interests. A "ghost" chair was established to represent Inuit of the U.S.S.R., who were not permitted by their government to attend.

Unseasonable temperatures and northerly winds, which pushed grinding Arctic ice floes ahead of them, trapped some 30 Soviet freighters in the Chukchi Sea, off the northeastern coast of Siberia. Many ships were damaged and one sank.

PONOMAREFF—GAMMA/LIAISON

The *Christian Science Monitor* reported in February that the sealskin boycott aimed at halting the Canadian seal pup harvest had damaged Greenland's sealskin trade. According to an official of Greenpeace in Denmark, the Greenland seals were not an endangered group, and only adult seals were harvested by the Greenland Inuit hunters.

The Soviet North. In July the Soviet news agency *Tass* reported that workers had finished laying the Siberia-to-Europe natural-gas pipeline, the cause of a U.S. trade embargo that had strained relations between the U.S. and its European allies in 1982. The 4,450-km (2,750-mi) pipeline stretches from Siberia to the western border of the Soviet Union and was laid in a record 14 months.

In August *Pravda* reported that oil output in western Siberia, which accounts for more than half of Soviet production, would continue to rise until the end of the century. The head of the Siberia Institute in Novosibirsk indicated that production was increasing by 20 million metric tons a year. (KENNETH DE LA BARRE)

Argentina

The federal republic of Argentina occupies the southeastern section of South America and is bounded by Chile, Bolivia, Paraguay, Brazil, Uruguay, and the Atlantic Ocean. It is the second-largest Latin-American country, after Brazil, with an area of 2,780,091 sq km (1,073,399 sq mi). Pop. (1983 est.): 29,627,000. Cap. and largest city: Buenos Aires (pop., 1983 est., 2,910,000). Language: Spanish. Religion: Roman Catholic 92%. Presidents in 1983, Maj. Gen. Reynaldo Bignone and, from December 10, Raúl Alfonsín.

Domestic Affairs. In general elections held in Argentina on Oct. 30, 1983, the Radical Civic Union, a democratic and essentially middle-class party led by Raúl Alfonsín (*see* BIOGRAPHIES), gained an absolute majority in the presidential electoral college and Congress, returning democratic rule to the country after a succession of military and Peronist regimes. The Peronists, led by Italo Luder, lost surprisingly heavily and even failed to hold their traditional power base of Buenos Aires Province. The results gave the Radicals 318 and the Peronists 258 of the 600 deputies in the national electoral college that formally ratified Alfonsín as president at the end of November. In Congress the Radicals won 129 to the Peronists' 111 and the Intransigent Party's 3 seats. (For tabulated results, *see* POLITICAL PARTIES.)

The Peronists' campaign was hampered by internal rivalries that prevented the early nomination of its candidate, thereby giving Alfonsín a campaign advantage of almost two months. Luder did not align himself with any particular party faction, a fact that assisted his selection, and he emphasized his position as a compromise candidate. The Peronists had delayed their choice as they waited in vain for former president María Estela ("Isabel") Martínez de Perón to announce when she would return from Spain. She had been granted a partial pardon in September but did not return until Alfonsín's inauguration.

The military government, in office since the coup of March 1976, was scheduled to hand over power at the end of January 1984, but Alfonsín requested that the date be brought forward to Dec. 10, 1983. During the junta's final months in power there was no respite from the problems that had accumulated in the previous years. Human-rights groups continued to press for the release of political prisoners and to demand information on those who had vanished during the "dirty war" against terrorists in the 1970s. At the end of April the junta issued a document that, while failing to clarify the armed forces' antisubversion operations, declared that the *desaparecidos* ("disappeared persons") should be considered dead. The report was met with outrage, both at home and abroad, in particular from Pres. Alessandro Pertini of Italy. In response the junta condemned Pertini's stance, but later retracted the condemnation.

On September 23 a law was passed granting amnesty to military security personnel who had committed crimes in antiguerrilla campaigns during the years 1973–82, as well as to people accused of certain subversive activities. (Most of the people held without trial since the 1970s were released before the elections.) Again, the amnesty for members of the security forces was roundly condemned, and in his campaign Alfonsín swore to repeal the law if he was elected. A second law giving the military special powers to search for and detain suspected terrorists was met with similar rejection and promises of repeal since it was seen as a legalization of the methods employed in the "dirty war."

Argentina

Pressure for reform and for an investigation of human-rights violations combined with damning statements by former military leaders and with the dire state of the economy put great strain on the armed forces and their civilian advisers during the final months of their regime. The strain was evidenced by the fact that the actions of many past and current members of the administration were called into question.

In keeping with his campaign promises, Alfonsín announced on December 13 that he planned to prosecute nine members of the military junta including three former presidents, Lieut. Gen. Jorge Videla, Gen. Roberto Viola, and Lieut. Gen. Leopoldo Galtieri. Alfonsín also moved to repeal the amnesty law and decreed that seven left-wing terrorists active in the 1970s be tried by civilian courts.

Foreign Relations. A military commission's report on the Falkland Islands/Islas Malvinas war of 1982 recommended that certain key figures in the conflict should stand trial. Among those named were Lieutenant General Galtieri, who was president at the time; Gen. Mario Menéndez, governor of the islands during their occupation; and former foreign minister Nicanor Costa Méndez. The report found fault with Argentina's military strategy and operations, its analysis as to how Britain and the U.S. would react to an invasion, and its economic measures during the conflict. Both main parties were adamant that the U.K. should negotiate promptly the transfer of the islands to a civilian Argentine government, adding that there was no

Areas:
see Demography; *see also the individual country articles*

Raúl Alfonsín, of the Radical Civic Union, was elected president of Argentina in October 1983, restoring democratic government to the country and marking the end of nearly eight years of military rule.

question of formally ending hostilities in the meantime.

Relations between Britain and Argentina did not improve significantly during 1983. The U.K. did not respond to a UN resolution proposing direct negotiations on the islands' future; Argentina did not declare a formal end to hostilities; and, although Argentina released the U.K.'s frozen assets in order to prevent the U.K. from blocking a commercial bank loan, trade restrictions between the two countries remained in force.

Relations between Argentina and Chile remained tense in 1983. This was partly because a resolution was not found to their dispute over the sovereignty of three islands in the Beagle Channel and also because Argentina was greatly displeased by Chile's close ties with the U.K. during and after the Falklands conflict.

The Economy. The military government's attempts to deal with Argentina's economic crisis received scant praise. One-day general strikes were called in protest against its policies in March and October as the real value of wages continued to fall. The cost of living rose by 168% during the first eight months of 1983, representing a rise of 335.3% in the 12 months to August.

Production stagnated during the year; overall gross domestic product registered a fall of 5.7% in 1982, compared with a decline of 5.9% in 1981. The performance of industry, which registered a fall of 4.5% in 1982, was limited by high interest rates and the depressed domestic demand that resulted from an erosion of purchasing power. Since the agricultural sector showed positive growth in 1982, it was hoped that grain and beef exports would increase foreign-exchange earnings to service the foreign debt. However, despite a record grain and oilseed harvest, estimated at 38.3 million metric tons, exports did not match expectations, and beef sales were well below forecast. Nevertheless, owing to greatly reduced imports, Argentina was expected to have a trade surplus in 1983 of $2 billion–$2.5 billion.

The foreign debt was officially put at $39 billion. In view of the constraints imposed by the debt, the International Monetary Fund (IMF) granted Argentina a credit of 2,180,000,000 Special Drawing Rights in January and a commercial-bank short-term loan of $1.1 billion for the payment of overdue interest. Subsequently, a syndicate of 300 banks, including several in Britain, raised a $1.5 billion medium-term loan, the terms of which were agreed upon in September. However, the first $500 million installment of this loan was de-

ARGENTINA

Education. (1982–83) Primary, pupils 4,197,372, teachers 206,535; secondary, pupils 594,167, teachers 81,026; vocational, pupils 831,481, teachers 110,703; higher, students 550,556, teaching staff 53,166.

Finance. Monetary unit: new peso, introduced June 1, 1983, at the rate of 1 new peso = 10,000 old pesos, with (Sept. 20, 1983) a free rate of 11.95 pesos to U.S. $1 (18 pesos = £1 sterling). Gold and other reserves (May 1983) U.S. $2,989,000,000. Budget (1981 est.): revenue 6,314,000,000 new pesos; expenditure 9,163,000,000 new pesos. Gross national product (1981) 54,290,000,000 new pesos. Money supply (Feb. 1983) 17,469,000,000 new pesos. Cost of living (Buenos Aires; 1975 = 100; June 1983) 403,919.

Foreign Trade. (1982) Imports 10,811,400,000 new pesos; exports 14,628,500,000 new pesos. Import sources (1981): U.S. 22%; Japan 10%; West Germany 10%; Brazil 9%; Italy 5%. Export destinations (1981): U.S.S.R. 32%; U.S. 9%; The Netherlands 8%; Brazil 7%. Main exports (1980): meat 12%; wheat 10%; soybeans 8%; corn 6%; animal and vegetable oils 6%; animal fodder 5%; textile fibres 5%; chemicals 5%; leather 5%; machinery 5%.

Transport and Communications. Roads (1978) 207,630 km. Motor vehicles in use (1978): passenger 2,866,000; commercial (including buses) 1,244,000. Railways: (1981) c. 34,459 km; traffic (1982) 10,152,000,000 passenger-km, freight 11,475,000,000 net ton-km. Air traffic (1982): 5,150,000,000 passenger-km; freight 175.9 million net ton-km. Shipping (1982): merchant vessels 100 gross tons and over 523; gross tonnage 2,255,758. Shipping traffic: goods loaded (1981) 30,160,000 metric tons, unloaded (1980) 10,540,000 metric tons. Telephones (Jan. 1981) 2,880,754. Radio receivers (Dec. 1978) 10.2 million. Television receivers (Dec. 1980) 5,140,000.

Agriculture. Production (in 000; metric tons; 1982): wheat 11,256; corn c. 9,600; sorghum c. 8,000; millet 154; barley c. 108; oats c. 244; rice 413; potatoes 1,817; sugar, raw value 1,615; linseed 720; soybeans c. 4,000; sunflower seed 1,780; tomatoes 573; oranges c. 600; lemons c. 390; apples 828; wine c. 2,780; tobacco 69; cotton, lint 162; cheese c. 233; wool, clean 80; beef and veal c. 2,600; fish catch (1981) 360; quebracho extract (1981) 92. Livestock (in 000; 1982): cattle 57,882; sheep 30,000; pigs 3,900; goats 3,000; horses 3,000; chickens 40,000.

Industry. Fuel and power (in 000; metric tons; 1982): crude oil 25,236; natural gas (cu m) 9,600,000; coal 520; electricity (excluding most industrial production; kw-hr) 36,282,000. Production (in 000; metric tons; 1982): cement c. 5,800; crude steel 2,995; cotton yarn (1981) 58; man-made fibres (1981) 28; petroleum products (1981) 24,782; plastics and resins (1981) 119; sulfuric acid (1981) 233; newsprint 107; other paper (1980) 695; passenger cars (including assembly; units; 1981) 143; commercial vehicles (including assembly; units; 1981) 29. Merchant vessels launched (100 gross tons and over; 1982) 161,900 gross tons.

layed for a number of reasons, principal among them being that Argentina's much-reduced currency reserves had forced the government into an undeclared cessation of payments.

The IMF also delayed the third portion of its loan. This was because the government had failed to keep the balance of payments deficit and the inflation rate within targets, had introduced import controls, and had imposed restrictions on the sale of foreign exchange, with the result that quotations for the U.S. dollar on the black market were forced up to 96,000 pesos while the official rate remained at 80,000 pesos. (The new "peso Argentino" was introduced on June 1 at 1 to 10,000 old pesos.) Alfonsín stated that he would respect rescheduling agreements made by the military government, though he questioned the legitimacy of some of the junta's liabilities.

Despite the deterioration in diplomatic relations between Argentina and Italy, the Italian-French consortium of Impregilo and Dumez was awarded the contract for the construction of the $10 billion Yacyretá hydroelectric project on the Río Paraná, a joint Argentine-Paraguayan effort. The World Bank and the Inter-American Development Bank each agreed to lend $210 million to help finance it.

In May a state of emergency was declared in the provinces of Formosa, Chaco, Corrientes, Entre Ríos, and Santa Fé after flooding from the Río Paraná destroyed many homes. (BEN BOX)

Art Exhibitions

New York City was host to a series of art exhibitions and other cultural events in the spring and summer of 1983 as part of a festival entitled "Britain Salutes New York." Hailed by *The Times* of London as "the greatest outpouring of British culture ever to go abroad," it was the most extensive foreign cultural and arts festival ever staged in the U.S. The shows mounted during the festival, in more than 20 separate locations, featured various aspects of British art and culture, past and present.

One of the most spectacular of the art exhibitions was "Constable's England," the first major exhibition of that artist's work in the U.S in more than 30 years. It featured 64 paintings and sketches lent by collections in the U.S. and Britain, showing (at the Metropolitan Museum of Art) the full range of Constable's artistic output. The Metropolitan Museum also held a major retrospective devoted to the work of the English sculptor Henry Moore, marking his 85th birthday with the first such show to be seen in New York since 1946.

"Holbein and the Court of St. James's" featured 70 drawings lent by Queen Elizabeth II from her great collection at Windsor, together with a single painted miniature by Hans Holbein the Younger. Another exhibition, including works by Henry Moore, Ben Nicholson, and Francis Bacon, focused on British art from 1930 to the present. "The Best in British Graphic Art and Photography" featured over 3,000 posters produced by London Transport from 1908 to the present. A fine show of silver by English silversmiths was also on view, while the American Museum of Natural History

AUTHENTICATED NEWS INTERNATIONAL

Holbein's portrait of Sir Thomas More was lent by Queen Elizabeth II to New York City for one show in the "Britain Salutes New York" festival.

had an exhibition devoted to the different types of plants taken back to England by Capt. James Cook from his voyages between 1768 and 1771. British architectural drawings from the Royal Institute of British Architects collection formed another show, and Sir Winston Churchill's paintings received their first "one man" show in the U.S. Also exhibited were works by British artists now domiciled in New York.

A major loan exhibition of drawings by the English 18th-century painter Thomas Gainsborough opened in October at the National Gallery of Art, Washington, D.C. Later it traveled to the Kimbell Art Museum in Fort Worth, Texas, and early in 1984 it was to be shown at the Yale Center for British Art at New Haven, Conn. A show at the San Antonio (Texas) Museum of Art brought together, for the first time, preparatory drawings and oil sketches for an unexecuted cycle of paintings by Benjamin West entitled "Revealed Religion." The series had been intended to decorate George III's private chapel at Windsor Castle. The exhibition also displayed other religious works by West, made for St. George's Chapel, Windsor, and Fonthill Abbey, Wiltshire.

The J. Paul Getty Museum of Art, Malibu, Calif., was host to a fine selection of Italian, French, and Flemish manuscripts lent by the British Library in London. The 45 manuscripts on show ranged from works by Fouquet to examples by Perugino, and the show itself was called "Renaissance Manuscript Painting from the British Library." In early 1984 it would travel to the Pierpont Morgan Library in New York City and subsequently would be on view at the British Library.

There were two important exhibitions devoted to the work of the American architect Frank Lloyd Wright in New York City. At the Cooper-Hewitt Museum, "Frank Lloyd Wright and the Prairie

Armies:
see Defense

Art:
see Architecture; Art Exhibitions; Art Sales; Dance; Literature; Museums; Theatre

JOSLYN ART MUSEUM, OMAHA

New York City's Whitney Museum presented the first major show of the works of Grant Wood since the 1940s in its exhibition "Grant Wood: The Regionalist Vision." Among the works displayed was the painter's "Stone City."

School" examined the development of that early 20th-century style of building by means of drawings, photographs, furniture, glass, and silverware. The Max Protetch Gallery showed architectural drawings by Wright from 1893 to 1959. One hundred of these were on sale, an unusual opportunity for the collector to purchase drawings rarely available on the art market. The drawings were offered for sale by the Frank Lloyd Wright Foundation to raise money for the preservation of Taliesin, the architect's former home and studio in Wisconsin.

The Guggenheim Museum in New York City held a show assembled from the Peggy Guggenheim collection. The 60 works were lent by the Palazzo Venier dei Leoni in Venice, the former home of Mrs. Guggenheim, whose uncle founded the museum bearing his name. The collection was particularly strong in Surrealist works. New York's Museum of Modern Art and the Art Institute of Chicago housed an exhibition organized by the National Gallery of Art, Washington, entitled "Alfred Stieglitz." It was the first exhibition in some 50 years to be devoted to the work of Stieglitz, one of the pioneers of 20th-century photography. The show was taken from the National Gallery's collection of 1,600 photographic plates, presented by Stieglitz's widow, the artist Georgia O'Keefe, in 1949.

A show devoted to the well-known American

A major retrospective show of the works of Édouard Manet opened in the U.S. at the Metropolitan Museum of Art in New York City in September, under the simple title "Manet, 1832–1883." Among the 95 paintings was his "A Bar at the Folies-Bergère" (1881–82).

COURTLAND INSTITUTE GALLERIES, LONDON

artist Grant Wood (1892–1942) and organized by the Minneapolis (Minn.) Institute of Arts was mounted at the Whitney Museum in New York City. Wood, a major exponent of the Midwestern regionalist movement of the 1930s, is best known for his "American Gothic," showing a stern farmer and his severe wife (or sister). This picture, widely reproduced and widely parodied, is one of the most famous paintings ever produced. However, the show illustrated Wood's wide range and great mastery of various subjects. It was later shown in Minneapolis. Another exhibition at the Whitney during the summer was "An Aesthetic in the Making: American Art 1958–1963." It explored the transition period between Abstract Expressionism and the various art movements of the 1960s such as Pop and Minimal Art. Included were canvases by Andy Warhol and Frank Stella.

Several major anniversaries were marked by art exhibitions. The centenary of the death of Édouard Manet was commemorated by a show at the Grand Palais in Paris that attracted very large audiences in the spring and summer. The international loan exhibition, which included paintings, drawings, and prints, moved later in the year to the Metropolitan Museum in New York. One hundred works illustrating "Manet and Modern Paris" were shown at the National Gallery in Washington.

A number of shows were devoted to the Italian Renaissance artist Raphael, including two in the autumn at the Pitti Palace and one at the Uffizi in Florence. "Raphael et la France" was shown in the autumn at the Grand Palais in Paris and "Raphael and American Art," illustrating the artist's influence on American painters and collectors, at the National Gallery in Washington. A large exhibition devoted to Raphael as architect would open in Rome early in 1984.

Several important exhibitions held late in 1982 and into 1983 commemorated the 300th anniversary of the death in 1682 of the landscapist Claude Lorrain. A show at the National Gallery in Washington, on view in Paris at the Grand Palais in the spring of 1983, included the largest number of Lorrain's works ever brought together, with 53 paintings, 76 drawings, and 51 etchings. Paintings were borrowed from a wide range of sources, including many private collections. Another Lorrain show was seen at the Haus der Kunst in Munich, West Germany, in the spring.

"The Vatican Collections: The Papacy and Art" toured the U.S., traveling from the Metropolitan Museum in New York City to Chicago and San Francisco. Among the items shown were several important works by Raphael, Leonardo, and Poussin. It was remarkable that such valuable works were allowed to leave Italy, and the *Burlington Magazine* criticized the lending policy. In its view, the missionary values of the traveling treasures were being given a higher priority than their conservation and safety. The exhibition attracted large crowds of visitors.

A show at the Frick Collection in New York City in the winter was the first major exhibition devoted to French clocks ever held in the U.S. "French Clocks from North American Collections" included nearly 100 items, dating from about 1532 to 1824, that were as much objects of decorative art as of horology. Many clocks were actually functioning, and there were some sumptuous examples.

ART RESOURCE

"The Miraculous Draught of Fishes" was one of the many works of art included in "The Vatican Collections: The Papacy and Art," which traveled to New York City, Chicago, and San Francisco.

The Japan House Gallery in New York City was the first stop for an unusual show, organized by the Japan Society and the American Federation of Arts, entitled "Kanban: Shop Signs of Japan." The show was also seen at the Peabody Museum in Salem, Mass. The Kanban symbolize the function of the shop by depicting relevant objects, and many are still in use in Japan. Featured Kanban included a wooden carved vinegar cask from Nara, a wooden paddle from an inn near a ferry, and a giant brush. A ball of cedar twigs denoted a shop selling sake. Also with a Japanese theme, "Reflections of Reality in Japanese Art" was the last exhibition to be organized by Sherman Lee of the Cleveland (Ohio) Museum of Art on the eve of his retirement. Among the 125 works of art were 9 items designated by the Japanese government as National Treasures and more than 50 Important Cultural Properties, lent by Japan. The works were selected to show realism in the Japanese tradition, from the earliest ceramics to the paintings of the late 19th century.

Morris Graves, the visionary American artist known for his delicate renderings of birds, was the subject of an exhibition organized by the Phillips

Collection, Washington, D.C., and also seen at Greenville, N.C., the Whitney Museum of American Art in New York City, and at Seattle, Wash., and Oakland and San Diego, Calif. Entitled "Morris Graves: Vision of the Inner Eye," it was the largest retrospective ever devoted to that artist and the first since 1956. The show was widely praised for its many lyrical, haunting, and poetic images, symbolic of man's fate.

"Vienna 1900" at the National Museum of Antiquities of Scotland was organized as part of the 1983 Edinburgh International Festival. The show displayed photographs, documents, drawings, paintings, furniture, costume, and examples of applied arts. Also in Edinburgh, the room designed by the Scottish architect Charles Rennie Mackintosh for the 1900 Secession Exhibition in Vienna was re-created at the Fine Art Society, complementing the show at the National Museum of Antiquities. "Masquerade" at the Museum of London in the summer re-created the fanciful 18th-century ambience of the pleasure garden and costume ball with paintings by Longhi, Guardi, and Canaletto and portraits by Zoffany, Reynolds, and Thomas Hudson. A show devoted to the work of Matthew Smith, held in the autumn at the Barbican Art Gallery, centred around the studio collection given to the Corporation of London in 1974. The first major exhibition of Smith's work since 1960 (When a memorial exhibition was held), it contained some 90 paintings supplemented by drawings, watercolours, sketchbooks, and photographs.

The Arts Council mounted a large survey of sculpture in Britain for 1983, divided between the Hayward Gallery and the Serpentine Gallery. Fifty artists were represented, including many of the younger generation whose names were not well known. The variety of media and themes was notable, but no one dominant sculptural trend emerged. The Courtauld Institute of Art marked its 50th anniversary in the academic year 1982–83 with several exhibitions at the Courtauld Institute Galleries and elsewhere. "A Private Collection of the late 19th and 20th Century Paintings and Sculpture" exhibited works from the collection of the art dealer and historian Lilian Browse. It was announced that this collection would ultimately be given to the institute. It is especially strong in works by Degas, Rodin, Sickert, and contemporary artists. "Mantegna to Cézanne: Master Drawings from the Courtauld" was mounted at the British Museum, and "Paintings from the Courtauld" was at the National Gallery of Art in London.

A show at the Fitzwilliam Museum in Cambridge, England, displayed principal acquisitions made by that museum in recent years. The centrepiece was George Stubbs's "Gimcrack," acquired by the museum to prevent its export. A large show in the autumn at the Royal College of Art in London took as its theme the life and work of Prince Albert, consort to Queen Victoria, and included items illustrative of his wide range of patronage and interests.

At Lugano, Switz., 40 major French Impressionist paintings, drawn from the Hermitage, Leningrad, and the Pushkin Museum, Moscow, and lent by the Soviet government, were on view at the Thyssen-Bornemisza Collection at the Villa Favorita. An equal number of Old Masters from that collection would go to the Soviet Union as part of an exchange. Works on show in Switzerland included canvases by Van Gogh, Cézanne, Renoir, Gauguin, Picasso, and Matisse, works rarely seen in the West and of exceptional quality. In Geneva at the Petit Palais, 100 Russian paintings from the period 1900 to 1930 were temporarily on loan from the Tratiakov Gallery in exchange for 100 canvases by Nicholas Tarkhoff, lent to the Pushkin Museum in Moscow by the Petit Palais, home of most of Tarkhoff's works. The works from Switzerland would also be seen at the Museum of Russian Art in Leningrad.

In Paris 150 watercolours by French 19th-century artists from the drawings collection of the Louvre were on show at the Pavillon de Flore. Drawings were selected depicting subjects of historical interest as well as the more usual landscapes and portraits. The influence of English draftsmen on French artists of the period was well illustrated by a selection of works by the English watercolourist R. P. Bonnington and his French followers. "On the Trader's Route—Chinese Influences on Islamic Pottery" at the Israel Museum in Jerusalem was drawn from the museum's own collection. The theme was the influence of Chinese ceramics on western Asian pottery which occurred as a result of communication via the trade routes.

The Cleveland Museum in Ohio mounted a fine exhibition composed of 90 etchings, engravings, and woodcuts by Albrecht Dürer, the second in a series of exhibitions devoted to Old Master prints from the museum's own collection. The first of these was a survey of 15th-century prints and the third would be on Rembrandt prints. Two exhibitions devoted to Dutch art were on view at the Art Institute of Chicago in the spring. "Mauritshuis: 17th Century Dutch Painting from the Royal Picture Palace" included 40 masterpieces from the Dutch museum by major 17th-century artists. "Dutch Prints and Drawings from the Permanent Collection" included many works by Rembrandt drawn from the Art Institute's own rich resources.

An exhibition devoted to the work of James Ensor, one of Belgium's greatest modern artists, known for his disturbing Expressionistic canvases painted in the late 19th century, was organized for the Kunsthaus, Zürich, Switz., and later shown at the Musée Royal des Beaux-Arts in Antwerp, Belgium. Ensor's 1888 masterpiece "The Entry of Christ into Brussels," a huge canvas in the style of Bosch or Breughel, was included. Ferdinand Hodler, also an Expressionist and the leading Swiss artist of the turn of the century, was the subject of a major retrospective at the Nationalgalerie in Berlin. It was the largest Hodler retrospective ever held and was likely to increase interest in this somewhat underrated and little-known artist.

In Lisbon the 17th Council of Europe exhibition, "Portuguese Discoveries and Renaissance Europe," opened in May at several different sites. It focused on aspects of 15th- and 16th-century Portuguese culture, including crosscurrents between

America and Portugal and between Portugal and the rest of Europe. At about the same time, the 18th Council of Europe exhibition, "The Anatolian Civilizations," opened in Istanbul. Major parts of the show were at the St. Irene Museum, where the exhibits were devoted to the prehistoric and Byzantine periods, and at the Topkapi Palace Museum, which housed items from the Seljuk and Ottoman periods. Loans from Turkish museums were supplemented by items from museums belonging to member states of the Council of Europe.

Finally, the Dog Museum of America in New York City, operated by the American Kennel Club Foundation, organized a show called "Fidos and Heroes in Bronze." It consisted of 50 sculptures depicting canine subjects, dating from the 5th century BC to the present day. (SANDRA MILLIKIN)

[613.D.1.b]

WIDE WORLD

Degas's pastel "L'Attente" ("Waiting") was auctioned for $3,740,000, the highest price recorded for the work of an Impressionist.

Art Sales

Market Trends. The battle for possession of Sotheby's, the world's leading art auctioneer, was a disrupting factor in the market during 1982–83. The company had experienced losses during the previous season, and its draconian cost-cutting measures were so clear an indication of trouble that art owners were frightened of using its services. This was particularly true in New York City, where Sotheby's autumn 1982 turnover was down by 40%. Most of the business went to Christie's, whose turnover in New York rose 26% for the same period.

The financial opportunities involved in helping put the company to rights attracted the attention of two New York businessmen, Marshall Cogan and Stephen Swid. In December 1982 they acquired 14.2% of Sotheby's shares and approached the board offering to collaborate in management. Sotheby's board was quick to dub them unsuitable and refused collaboration. In April 1983 Cogan and Swid made a formal bid for Sotheby's at 520 pence a share. By political lobbying, Sotheby's ensured that the British secretary of state for trade referred the bid for investigation by the Monopolies and Mergers Commission. It also found a rival bidder in Alfred Taubman, reputedly one of the richest men in the U.S. Taubman revealed his interest in June and secured the agreement of Cogan and Swid to sell him their holding, then totaling 29.9%, at 700 pence a share. In September the trade secretary announced, on the advice of the Monopolies and Mergers Commission, that the Taubman takeover could go ahead. The bid was made through Taubman Holdings.

By July Sotheby's profitability and turnover had picked up dramatically, and they were forecasting profits of £4 million for the year to August 1983. This reflected both their cost-cutting achievements and the strong improvement in the market. The art market had entered 1982–83 in recession, with owners of artworks holding back until prices rose. The market began to improve in the spring of 1983 with a new influx of U.S. buyers following advances on Wall Street. The new strength was concentrated at the top of the market and revealed itself most dramatically in the Havemeyer sale in New York on May 18.

To restore their fortunes, Sotheby's had offered a better deal than either Christie's or a consortium of leading dealers for the right to sell a group of 16 paintings from the collection of the sugar magnate H. O. Havemeyer and his wife. The Havemeyers were the first serious collectors of the Impressionists' work, buying with the advice of the artist Mary Cassatt. The cachet that attached to works from this collection was enormous, and consignors strove to get their pictures into the same sale. The result was a 90-lot sale that totaled $37.2 million, a resounding record for any art auction. The 16 Havemeyer paintings totaled $16.8 million. Seven auction records for individual artists were broken,

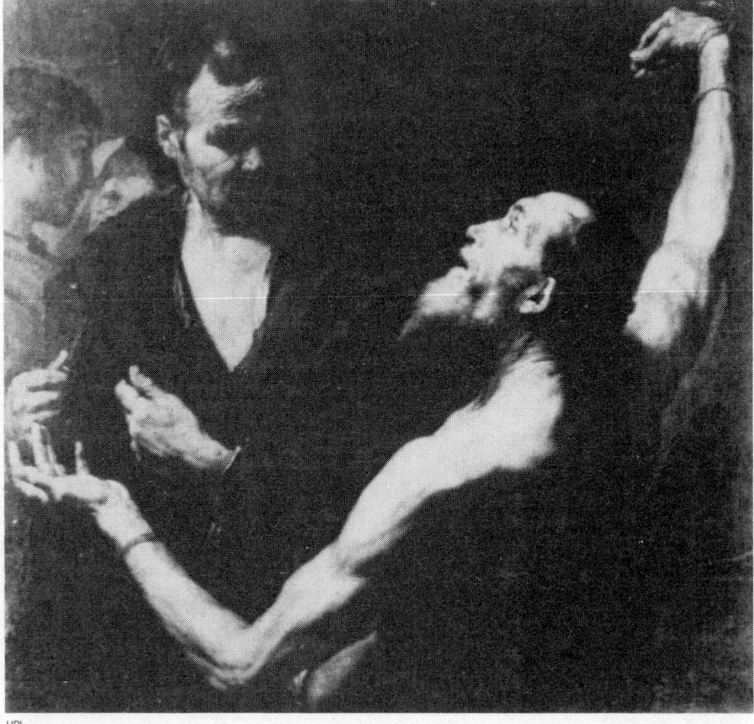

UPI

José de Ribera's work "The Martyrdom of St. Bartholomew" fetched £660,000 at Sotheby's. It was bought by a London dealer.

COURTESY, SOTHEBY PARKE BERNET

An 18th-century Rhode Island Chippendale dressing table was sold for $687,500, the highest price ever paid at auction for a piece of American furniture.

including Degas's "L'Attente," bought jointly by Norton Simon and the J. Paul Getty Museum at $3,740,000, a Renoir "Baigneuse" at $2,750,000, and a Monet "Nymphéas" at $2,640,000.

Works of Art. The funds of the J. Paul Getty Museum, Malibu, Calif., were unscrambled from family lawsuits during 1982, leaving the museum with a requirement under California law to spend around $60 million a year in order to retain its charitable status. The museum bought extensively in 1982–83, mainly through dealers. It paid a reputed $3.5 million for a marble sculpture of "Bathsheba" by Giovanni da Bologna, paid a reputed $4 million for a full-length Goya portrait of "The Marquesa de Santiago," and purchased a large painting of "Pan and Echo" by Dosso Dossi from Lord Northampton for £1.8 million. A red marble sculpture of a "Centaur," excavated at Castel Gandolfo, near Rome, in the mid-19th century, was another sensational acquisition.

Competition between a group of U.S. collectors drove prices for the best furniture to new levels. At Sotheby's in July 1983 a new auction price record for any piece of furniture was set with £990,000 paid for a black lacquer cabinet made for Louis XVI at Versailles, probably by Adam Weisweiler. Christie's sale of the contents of Godmersham Park in June attracted the U.S. collectors to Kent, and the superb 18th-century furnishings made unlooked-for prices, including a record for an English 18th-century chair at £81,000 and a Régence giltwood table at £91,800.

The strength of the U.S. market was reflected in new auction records for American art and artifacts. A Rhode Island Chippendale dressing table from the Goddard-Townsend workshop set a new auction record for American furniture at $687,500 in January, and a Philadelphia Chippendale chair set a record for a chair at $275,000 in October 1982. Two albums of crayon portraits of North American Indians by George Catlin, which had passed through Christie's at £1,300 in 1953, were resold for £194,400 in October 1982, while a Mary Cassatt portrait of her mother, "Reading *Le Figaro*," set a new price record for the artist at $1.1 million in May 1983.

The collections of historic arms and armour, ivories, and other works of art formed by William Waldorf Astor, later Viscount Astor, at Hever Castle in Kent provided the highlight of Sotheby's summer season in London. A suit of 16th-century Milanese armour made for Henry II of France topped all price records for works of art at £1.9 million, paid by U.S. investment banker B. H. Trupin. A Gothic ivory casket fetched £418,000.

Christie's sold the collection of 16 abstract paintings formed by Armand Bartos, a New York architect, in London in June for £4,079,808; a new auction record for any abstract painting was set when Mondrian's "Composition with Red, Blue, and Yellow" sold for £1,512,000 to a Japanese collector. The auction price record for a Victorian painting was broken twice during 1983, first when Sotheby's sold Richard Dadd's "Oberon and Titania" for £550,000 in March and then when Christie's sold a portrait of Kathleen Newton by James Joseph Tissot for £561,600 in June.

Books. Exceptional books brought exceptional prices during the 1982–83 season, but run-of-the-mill items proved hard to sell. At the beginning of the season Sotheby's, the world's largest book auctioneer, radically altered its policy, cutting the number of sales by turning away books worth less than £100 and losing staff—three of whom set up a new firm, Bloomsbury Book Auctions, aimed at servicing the lower end of the market.

The most sensational single deal of the year was the sale of the collection of illuminated manuscripts formed by West German millionaire Daniel K. Ludwig to the J. Paul Getty Museum for a reputed £50 million. Ludwig had previously promised the collection to the city of Cologne, which had already published catalogs and was preparing an exhibition centre. Another outstanding privately negotiated deal was the single vellum sheet copy of Magna Carta, dated 1297 and endorsed with the seal of Edward I, valued at £1,250,000. A copy of a 1776 printed broadsheet of the Declaration of Independence was sold by Christie's for $412,500 in April 1983.

Musical manuscripts made some exceptional prices. An archive of Igor Stravinsky's manuscripts and letters was bought from the trustees of his estate by the Paul Sacher Foundation of Basel, Switz., for $5.2 million. A lost manuscript of Stravinsky's *The Rite of Spring* sold for £330,000 at Sotheby's in November 1982 in a sale that also included two manuscript scores of Bach cantatas at £209,000 and £165,000. Mme. Jean Voilier sold the love letters she had received from the poet Paul Valéry for Fr 1,470,000 through Ader et Picard in Monte Carlo in October 1982. A Psalter written and illuminated in France around 1530 for Anne Boleyn, the second wife of King Henry VIII of England, made £154,000 at Sotheby's in December 1982. In May 1983 the complete set of books printed on vellum by the Kelmscott Press, assembled by the U.S. collector John A. Saks, was sold by Christie's for $660,000. A sensation of the young 1983–84 season was the sale of a 12th-century illuminated manuscript, the Gospel Book of Henry the Lion, at Sotheby's in London for a record $14.6 million. (GERALDINE NORMAN)

Astronomy

A year for many notable achievements in astronomy, 1983 was capped by spectacular discoveries made by the Infrared Astronomical Satellite (IRAS) and by the award of the Nobel Prize for Physics to two American astrophysicists, William A. Fowler of the California Institute of Technology and Subrahmanyan Chandrasekhar of the University of Chicago, for their research on the physics of stellar evolution (*see* NOBEL PRIZES).

Solar System. On January 25 IRAS, a joint Dutch/U.S./British project, was launched into Earth orbit from Vandenberg Air Force Base in California. From the start it performed perfectly. Containing an array of detectors sensitive to wavelengths of 8–120 micrometres in the infrared region of the electromagnetic spectrum, the satellite was the first real infrared observatory in space. The importance of these particular wavelengths is that they allow observations of cool material (often not detectable at optical wavelengths) ranging from planets, asteroids, and comets in the solar system to interstellar molecules and cold gas and dust throughout our own Galaxy as well as other galaxies. During its ten months of operation it made two complete surveys of the sky as well as selected extended observations of specific objects previously known to be infrared sources and of ones discovered during the mission itself.

One of the earliest discoveries announced by the IRAS team, which comprised more than 500 scientists, was the first detection of a new comet by a satellite. On April 25, while routinely scanning the sky, IRAS observed a fast-moving object. Meanwhile on May 3 (before any formal announcement of the discovery had been made) Genichi Araki in Japan and George Alcock in Great Britain each independently made the same find. In keeping with tradition the comet was named after its discoverers: Comet IRAS-Araki-Alcock. Remarkably, on May 11 it passed within 4.7 million km of the Earth, thus making the closest cometary approach since Comet Lexell in 1770 (1 km = 0.62 mi).

On May 13 IRAS discovered a second comet, this time without human co-discoverers. At the time it was some 145 million km from the Earth and very dim (about 17th magnitude). Having been made aware of the existence of such dim comets, which might never have been seen from Earth, scientists needed to revise their estimates of the number of comets in the solar system. By November IRAS had discovered a total of five new comets. It also found a long, thin (optically invisible) tail of cometary debris behind the well-known comet Tempel 2. Finally IRAS discovered an object that appeared to be a burned-out comet. Designated minor planet 1983 TB, it is probably the parent body that gave rise to the Geminid stream of meteors. The object also passes closer to the Sun (some 24 million km) than any planet or known asteroid.

Perhaps the most startling discovery made within the solar system by IRAS was what appeared to be three narrow bands of dust lying at the same distance from the Sun as the asteroid belt, which

NASA

The Infrared Astronomical Satellite (IRAS), shown in an artist's impression in Earth orbit, surveyed the entire sky in a joint project for the United States, The Netherlands, and the United Kingdom.

resides between Mars and Jupiter at some 300 million to 500 million km from the Sun. The central band is contained within the asteroid belt itself, wheras the other two bands seemed to lie some 9° above and below the ecliptic plane (the plane in which the planets move). The IRAS team speculated that a collision between a comet and an asteroid produced the dusty material, which eventually settled into the orbits observed.

While IRAS discovered rings in the outer solar system, a Japanese group found evidence for one or possibly two dust shells or rings surrounding the Sun at a distance of only three to four solar radii, far inside the orbit of Mercury. Shizo Isobe of Tokyo University and Toshinori Maihara of Kyoto University observed the Sun with an infrared detector flown on a high-altitude balloon during the total eclipse of the Sun that was visible from Indonesia in June. The observed shells presumably arise from dust that spirals into the Sun, heating up and radiating in the infrared to produce the appearance of the rings.

As infrared astronomers were studying dust and rocky material in the solar system indirectly, a number of meteorite experts reported the probable discovery of a Moon rock—and perhaps even a Mars rock—on Earth. A small meteorite fragment called ALHA 81005, found in Antarctica in January 1982, was analyzed in succeeding months by some 20 separate groups. In March 1983, experts meeting at the annual Lunar and Planetary Science Conference in Houston, Texas, came to almost unanimous agreement that certain isotope anomalies, similar to those found in some of the lunar rock samples brought back to Earth during the Apollo missions, indicated a lunar origin for this meteorite. The rock was probably thrown toward the Earth by a meteoritic impact on the Moon. Some months earlier Donald Bogard and Pratt Johnson of the National Aeronautics and Space Administration's Johnson Space Center in Houston had made an even more startling announcement: that another Antarctic meteorite, EETA 79001, showed isotopic ratios of such rare gases as argon and xenon thought to be more in keeping with a Martian, rather than an asteroidal, origin. These suggestions, that Moon and Mars rocks

Association Football: *see* Football

Astronautics: *see* Space Exploration

(TOP) JET PROPULSION LABORATORY; (BOTTOM) AUTHENTICATED NEWS INTERNATIONAL

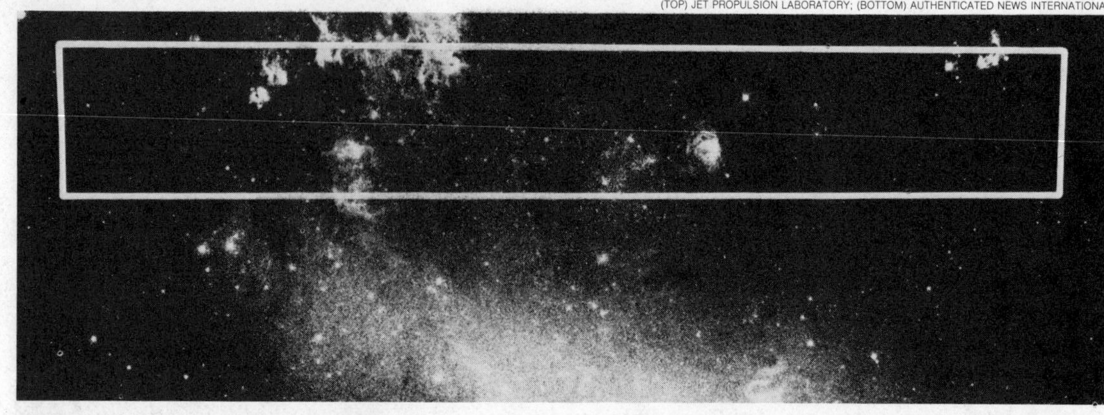

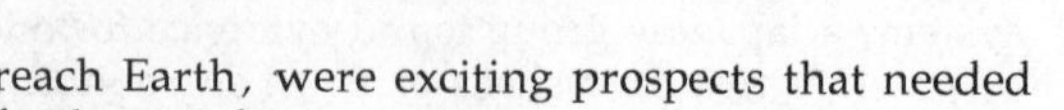

Boxed region of the Large Magellanic Cloud (top), a nearby satellite galaxy of the Milky Way, was examined in infrared light by IRAS early in the year. Astronomers believed that the complex of signal-strength peaks appearing in the left portion of a three-scan mosaic of the region (bottom) represents the birth of a massive cluster of stars never before observed.

Earth Perihelion and Aphelion, 1984

Jan. 3	Perihelion, 147,008,000 km (91,347,000 mi) from the Sun
July 3	Aphelion, 152,014,000 km (94,457,000 mi) from the Sun

Equinoxes and Solstices, 1984

March 20	Vernal equinox, 10:24[1]
June 21	Summer solstice, 05:02[1]
Sept. 22	Autumnal equinox, 20:33[1]
Dec. 21	Winter solstice, 16:23[1]

Eclipses, 1984

May 15	Moon, penumbral (begins 15:02[1]), visible in S. America, Antarctica, Africa except extreme E, Madagascar, Europe except the NE, N. America except the NW, S Greenland, the Atlantic O., and the E Pacific O.
May 30	Sun, annular (begins 13:54[1]), visible in N. America except NW, Arctic regions, Greenland, Iceland, extreme NW of S. America, W Africa, and Europe.
June 13	Moon, penumbral (begins 13:42[1]), visible in Australia, Antarctica, Asia except NW, New Zealand, the Indian O., and the Pacific O.
Nov. 8	Moon, penumbral (begins 15:39[1]), visible in Asia, Australia, New Zealand, extreme NW N. America, Arctic regions, W Africa, E Europe, Greenland, Pacific O., the Indian O., and E Atlantic O.
Nov. 22–23	Sun, total (begins 20:13[1]), visible in Indonesia, Australia, S Philippines, Papua New Guinea, Antarctica, New Zealand, and extreme S S. America.

[1] Universal time.
Source: *The Astronomical Almanac for the Year 1984* (1983).

reach Earth, were exciting prospects that needed further study.

Stars. Perhaps the most exciting development in stellar astronomy concerned the ongoing studies of an extemely fast pulsar discovered in 1982 by Donald C. Backer and colleagues at the University of California at Berkeley. While studying the peculiar radio source 4C 21.53 they detected a pulsar that emits flashes of radio waves at 642 times per second. Shortly thereafter R. N. Manchester and collaborators of Siding Spring Observatory in Australia detected optical pulsations from the object at about 25th magnitude, making it one of the two dimmest objects ever detected optically.

This so-called millisecond pulsar excited astrophysicists for three reasons. First, since a pulsar is thought to be a rotating magnetized neutron star whose beaconlike radio beam flashes past the Earth with each rotation, this one must be rotating so rapidly that it is on the verge of flying apart. Second, the pulsar seemed to be "spinning down" exceedingly slowly; that is, its period is a constant to an accuracy of 10^{-19} seconds per second. This feature implied that it has a relatively weak magnetic field (for a pulsar) of some 100 million gauss (one gauss being about the strength of the Earth's field). Moreover, its small spin-down rate apparently made it the most precise clock known in the entire Milky Way. Third, the pulsar did not appear to lie within an observable remnant of a supernova, the presumed origin of pulsars. Thus it may be fairly old, although the fast pulsation normally would be the sign of a rather young age. This contradiction led to the suspicion that the object was formed in a manner different from most of the 300 or so other pulsars so far studied.

Within six months of the discovery of the first fast pulsar Valentin Boriakoff and colleagues from Cornell University in Ithaca, N.Y., reported a second fast pulsar, one with a pulse rate of 163 times per second. This object is in a very widely separated binary star system whose components revolve around each other in a period of 120 days. The quick discovery of this second fast pulsar supported the notion that there is another class of rapidly pulsing, very weak (and presumably weakly magnetized) neutron stars filling our Galaxy.

During the year the discovery of the first pulsar lying outside the Galaxy was announced by an Australian group headed by P. M. McCulloch. It lies in the Large Magellanic Cloud, one of the Milky Way's satellite galaxies. All of these discoveries injected new life into studies of pulsars 15 years after they were first reported, in 1968.

Among the tens of thousands of stars surveyed by the IRAS satellite, one stands out as particularly intriguing. The bright star Vega, which with Deneb and Altair forms a prominent triangle in the summer sky, is often used as a calibration source by astronomers because of its presumed "normality." The IRAS team, however, found that this source is surrounded by a large shell of dusty, asteroidal, or possibly even planetary material. The shell extends to a distance around the star of about 11,900,000,000 km (twice the Sun–Pluto distance). In view of the fact that Vega is a relatively young star (1,000,000,000 years old or less, compared with the Sun's age of about 4,600,000,000 years), the surrounding debris must be left over from Vega's initial formation, much as the Sun's planetary system consists of initial star-formation residue. IRAS found perhaps another 50 such sys-

UPI

Newly discovered comet IRAS-Araki-Alcock, shown head-on throwing off dust and gas, came within 4.7 million kilometres (2.9 million miles) of Earth.

tems, lending support to the notion that the solar system to which the Earth belongs is not unique.

Another object studied by IRAS, a dark molecular cloud in the Milky Way called Barnard 5, contains an object much like the early Sun. The source, about ten times more luminous than the Sun, radiates at a temperature between −243° and 227° C (−405° and 440° F), compared with the Sun's present surface temperature of 6,000° C (10,800° F). This observation agreed with some theories of star birth which suggest that the Sun went through a brief luminous (but cool) phase prior to thermonuclear ignition as a normal star.

At the other end of stellar evolution the red-giant star Betelgeuse was found by IRAS to be surrounded by three giant dust shells. Since this star is already at the end of its evolutionary history and will remain a red giant for only about 100,000 years, these shells must have been ejected in the recent past and represent the material out of which new stars (and presumably their planets) will form in subsequent generations.

Galaxies. The nearest galaxies to the Milky Way have long been thought to be the Large and Small Magellanic Clouds. During the past year Donald S. Mathewson of Mount Stromlo Observatory in Australia announced that the Small Magellanic Cloud is not one galaxy but two, and he dubbed the new neighbour the Mini-Magellanic Cloud. This galaxy, not recognized previously because it overlaps the Small Cloud as viewed from the Earth, was probably formed only 200 million years ago by a collision or a near encounter between the Large and Small Clouds.

Computer-enhanced image reveals a ring of microscopic dust particles around the Sun, as photographed by video camera from a balloon over Indonesia during June's solar eclipse.

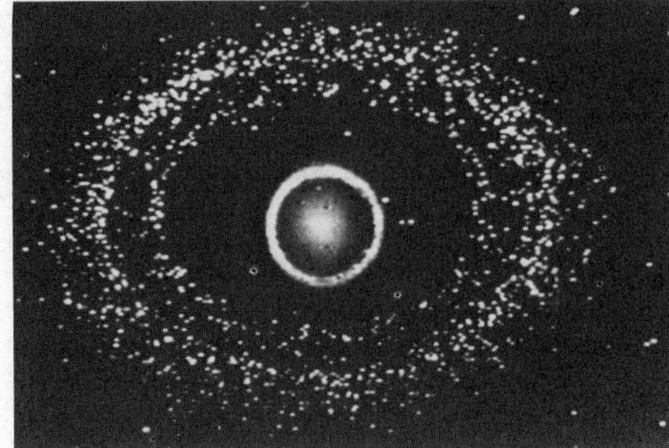

WIDE WORLD

Although optical visibility is the usual criterion necessary for the detection of a galaxy, a team of scientists from Cornell University working with the Arecibo radio telescope in Puerto Rico reported for the first time the detection at radio wavelengths of an intergalactic cloud of neutral hydrogen. Presumably the progenitor of a future galaxy, the cloud appeared to contain about 1,000,000,000 solar masses of radiating hydrogen and to rotate at about 80 km per second at its periphery. In order for it to spin that rapidly, however, it must contain about 100 times more matter than is revealed by its radio emissions. This raised anew the question of how much "dark" or "missing" matter (matter not detectable by any direct means) exists in the universe. (KENNETH BRECHER)

See also Space Exploration.
[131.A.3.d; 131.E.2.a.i; 131.E.2.b.i; 132.B.5.e; 133.A.4.a–d]

Australia

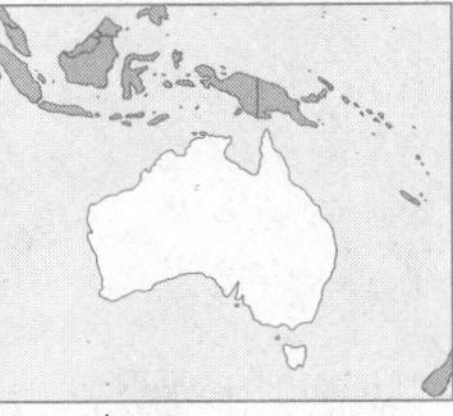

Australia

A federal parliamentary state and a member of the Commonwealth, Australia occupies the smallest continent and, with the island state of Tasmania, is the sixth largest country in the world. Area: 7,682,300 sq km (2,966,200 sq mi). Pop. (1983 est.): 15,265,000. Cap.: Canberra (statistical district pop., 1982 est., 225,000). Largest city: Sydney (metro. pop., 1981, 3,280,900). Language: English. Religion (1981): Roman Catholic 29.6%; Church of England 27.7%; Methodist 7.3%; Presbyterian 6.6%; Lutheran 1.4%; Baptist 1.3%; other Christian 8.6%; Jewish 0.5%. Queen, Elizabeth II; governor-general in 1983, Sir Ninian Martin Stephen; prime ministers, Malcolm Fraser and, from March 11, Robert J. Hawke.

Domestic Affairs. The Liberal Party-National Party coalition, which had ruled Australia since the fall of Gough Whitlam's Labor government in 1975, lost office in 1983. On February 3 Prime Minister Malcolm Fraser, misjudging the mood of the electorate, called an election for March 5, nine months before the government's term of office was due to expire. Fraser had anticipated an undignified and divisive battle for the leadership of the opposition Australian Labor Party (ALP). However, even as Fraser visited the governor-general to request an early election, the ALP ended its internecine fighting. William (Bill) Hayden stood aside, and the party elected Robert J. Hawke (*see* BIOGRAPHIES) as its leader. Under Bob Hawke, the ALP presented a unified front to the electorate, which returned it with a handsome majority and a mandate to carry out a new economic policy.

The Liberal Party's election manifesto was concerned with measures to curb the power of the trade unions, who were blamed for worsening the economic effects of the recession by their excessive wage demands. In contrast, the ALP campaign promoted the idea that reconciliation would form the basis for recovery. Days before the election, the Australian Council of Trade Unions (ACTU) agreed to cooperate with a Labor government on a prices and incomes policy.

In the event, the ALP increased its share of seats in the House of Representatives to 75. This result

Athletics:
see articles on the various sports

UPI

Robert J. Hawke succeeded in "stopping Fraser" in Australia's March 5 election. The new prime minister is at the microphone.

gave it a commanding lead over the combined forces of the Liberal Party (33 seats) and the National Party (17 seats). In elections to the Senate, held on the same day, the ALP gained 3 seats to bring its total to 30, but it failed to win an overall majority. Of the remaining seats in the 64-seat Senate, 24 were won by the Liberal Party, 4 by the National Party, and 1 by an independent; the Australian Democratic Party retained 5 seats, thus emerging once again as holder of the balance of power in the Senate.

Immediately after the election, Fraser resigned the leadership of his party, and the Liberals elected Andrew Peacock in his place. In a two-way contest, Peacock defeated John Howard, the deputy leader of the Liberal Party and former federal treasurer, by 36 votes to 20. At the end of March Fraser also resigned his parliamentary seat.

The ALP, anxious to avoid the excesses of reformist zeal that had characterized the first days of the Whitlam era a decade earlier, moved cautiously. Among its earliest initiatives were a devaluation of the currency and the summoning of a summit conference to discuss a proposed wages and prices policy. Within three months, however, the ALP was confronted with a number of awkward problems, two of which were the subject of royal commissions.

First, the Australian Broadcasting Commission forced an inquiry into the role of the Labor premier of New South Wales, Neville Wran, in a court case six years earlier involving misappropriation of funds. He was forced to stand down as premier in May while a royal commission inquired into whether a chief stipendiary magistrate in New South Wales, Murray Farquhar, had attempted to influence the outcome of proceedings against Kevin Humphreys. Accused of misappropriating A$52,000 from the Balmain Rugby Leagues Club, Humphreys had had his case dismissed in August 1977. At the heart of the royal commission's inquiry was the question of whether Farquhar had tried to influence the case at the request or on the instruction of Wran. Wran, who was not only the senior ALP state premier but also party president, was eventually judged blameless by the royal commission.

Second, a royal commission was appointed on May 17 to investigate the expulsion of a Soviet diplomat, Valery Ivanov, from Canberra, and also to investigate the role played in the matter by David Combe, a former national secretary of the ALP. Combe, having failed to obtain endorsement for a safe parliamentary seat, had taken up a career as a lobbyist, using his influence and inside knowledge of ALP matters to assist special-interest groups in their relations with the new government. In the aftermath of the decision to expel Ivanov in April, it emerged that one of the reasons the government had taken action was its knowledge of the existence of an association between Ivanov and Combe.

Since the royal commission, under Justice Robert Hope, was concerned with national security and was largely conducted in camera, at first neither the public nor, indeed, Combe himself knew precisely what Combe was thought to have done, or what had caused the Hawke government to place him outside the pale of acceptable lobbyists. However, when sections of the royal commission transcript were later released by Hope, they showed that Harvey Barnett, the director general of the Australian Security Intelligence Organization, believed Combe was a "potential KGB agent in the political field." Combe strenuously denied the suggestion.

The Hawke government did gain some satisfaction from the courts. In July the High Court, in a majority judgment of 4 to 3, accepted the federal government's right to stop construction of the Gordon-below-Franklin hydroelectric dam in Tasmania. The ALP had included, as part of its election program, a promise to halt the building of the dam, thus preserving one of the last remaining areas of temperate wilderness in the world. However, the new government had encountered strong opposition from the Tasmanian state government when it attempted to implement the ban. (*See* ENVIRONMENT.)

In considering the problem, Chief Justice Sir Harry Gibbs commented, the High Court did not concern itself with the question of whether or not building the dam was desirable on environmental grounds. The only questions considered had been strictly legal ones. Prime Minister Hawke gave his unequivocal assurances that the federal government would not rush to extend its activities into new areas as a result of the High Court's decision. He also said that he intended to cooperate fully with Tasmania in conserving and managing the wilderness area and in developing an alternative strategy for Tasmania's economic advancement.

During the third week of February, the election

campaign was suspended temporarily when bushfires swept across southeastern Australia, leaving a trail of destruction. (*See* Special Report.)

Foreign Affairs. The change in government from Conservative to Socialist led to alterations in Australian foreign policy, although not to the extent wished by the left wing of the ALP. While former leader Bill Hayden took up the foreign affairs portfolio and made some interesting new initiatives in Australia's relations with the Association of Southeast Asian Nations (ASEAN), Prime Minister Hawke took a leaf from Malcolm Fraser's book and conducted foreign policy debates in person with heads of state. During the winter parliamentary recess, Hawke traveled to Indonesia, Paris, and Washington, where he made important observations about the direction of Australia's foreign policy in the future.

The Hawke government gave a high priority to improving relations with Indonesia, Australia's closest Asian neighbour and a country whose security and foreign policy ambitions were perceived as inextricably entwined with those of Australia. Hawke trod carefully in two highly sensitive areas. The first involved Indonesia's strained relations with Papua New Guinea, with which it had a common border. Papua New Guinea, a former Australian external territory, was the biggest recipient of Australian overseas aid.

The second area of contention, where some diplomatic progress was made, concerned the Indonesian administration of East Timor, which had been annexed by Indonesia after it ceased to be a Portuguese colony. Abandoning previous ALP policy, Hawke announced in Jakarta that Indonesia's role in East Timor was a fait accompli that Australia, in the interest of harmony with a great and powerful Asian nation, would have to recognize and support. Hawke's acceptance of Indonesian hegemony in East Timor, while solving a thorny problem in international relations for the new government, led to bitter criticism from those within the ALP ranks who favoured self-determination for East Timor.

In contrast to his statements on East Timor, which broke new ground, Hawke stuck to party orthodoxy where France was concerned. As a result, Australian-French relations took a backward step. During his visit to Paris on June 9, Hawke informed his fellow socialist, French Pres. François Mitterrand, that Australia wished to see self-determination for France's Pacific territories and an end to nuclear-weapons testing in Australia's region. To underline his point, Hawke told President Mitterrand that Australia would hold up shipments of uranium to France. The French government described as an "unfriendly act" Hawke's decision to delay uranium shipments in retaliation for nuclear-weapons testing. President Mitterrand dispatched a special envoy, Régis Debray, to Australia to try to dispel what France considered to be "numerous misconceptions" about the welfare of the people on the test area of Mururoa Atoll. Debray delivered an invitation to the Australian government, offering to allow an Australian scientist to visit the French nuclear-weapons test site in the Pacific.

While Prime Minister Hawke dealt with Indonesia and France, Foreign Minister Hayden concentrated his efforts on an ambitious program of bridge-building between Vietnam and Australia's ASEAN neighbours. Hayden hoped that Australia could act as a go-between in negotiations between ASEAN and Vietnam. Neither party seriously welcomed Hayden's overtures, however; ASEAN was too affronted by Vietnam's foreign policy, and Vietnam was annoyed by Australia's failure to grant it foreign aid. To make matters worse, U.S. Secretary of State George Shultz, at an ASEAN summit meeting in Bangkok, Thailand, in June, was reported to have described the Australian initiative as "stupid." Shultz made it clear that the U.S. was not expecting much from Hayden's visit to Hanoi, which took place at the end of June, and deplored the possibility that Australia might try approaches outside the ASEAN strategy, thereby ending Vietnam's isolation.

Despite the expulsion of a Soviet diplomat for being a KGB spy and the Soviet Union's criticism of Hawke's pro-U.S. stance during his visit to Washington, in June, the new Labor government tried to improve Soviet-Australian relations. Cultural and scientific interchange, dropped by Fraser as a protest against the Soviet presence in Afghanistan, was reestablished, and Soviet cruise ships were again admitted to Australian ports. In common with most of its allies, Australia condemned the destruction of a Korean civil airliner by the Soviet Union in September. The Soviet ambassador was left in no doubt about the government's unequivocal abhorrence of what had occurred.

The Economy. There were some significant alterations in Australian economic policy in 1983. The first act of the Hawke administration involved economic matters. On March 8 the currency was devalued by 10%, despite the Labor Party's preelection undertaking to maintain the Australian dollar's value. The government then called an economic summit conference to which representatives of the various interest groups were invited. Delegates representing trade unions, company directors, taxpayers, and the government met in Canberra in April in an atmosphere of harmony and goodwill and forged a wages policy that envisioned a return to centralized wage fixing. The mood of optimism soon proved misplaced, however. The new government was no more able to combat unemployment and inflation than its conservative predecessor. Hawke placed much of the blame for his government's failure to implement some of its election promises on the huge concealed budget deficit of A$9.6 billion; he claimed that the Fraser government knew of the existence of this deficit but did not reveal its full extent during the election campaign.

In May the government introduced new financial measures that were designed to dismantle the previous administration's policies and to lay the foundation for even tougher measures expected in the August budget. These tougher measures did not, in fact, materialize.

The government's attempt to alter the superannuation (retirement pension) laws governing lump-sum payments proved overwhelmingly un-

CAMERA PRESS/PHOTO TRENDS

As promised, Prime Minister Bob Hawke convened an "economic summit" of business and labour leaders seeking a consensus to solve the nation's economic problems. The group met in the House of Representatives in Canberra.

popular with many of the members of pension programs. While the loudest opposition came from some trade-union quarters, including the dockworkers, it was the airline pilots who had the most leverage on the government. Minister of Finance Sydney Dawkins claimed that the new policies were an attempt to spread the benefits of superannuation further in the community, and he believed that he could best do this by heavily taxing lump-sum payments as an inducement to pensioners to convert their lump sums into annuities. The pilots rejected the government's decision and threatened to strike.

Relations with New Zealand in the economic field became less than cordial when the Australian government refused to allow the British-owned National Bank of New Zealand to set up branches in Australia or to give New Zealand favourable investment access to Australia. Though Hawke described the breakdown in trans-Tasman trade relations as "hiccups," New Zealand Prime Minister Robert Muldoon took the matter so seriously that he threatened to drop the tariff advantages that applied in New Zealand to Australian-made automobiles. From May 25 Muldoon placed a ban on Australian companies wishing to invest in New Zealand.

A key to economic success for the Hawke government was the decision taken by the Commonwealth Conciliation and Arbitration Commission in the national wage case. The ACTU advocate, Jan Marsh, described the first national wage case of the Hawke era as "the most significant in years." Pointing out that a consensus for a prices and incomes policy had emerged from the national economic summit, Marsh argued that a new environment existed in which a centralized wage-fixing system could work effectively. On September 23 the commission ordered a 4.3% wage increase, which took effect on October 6. Until 1985, when the system would be reviewed, the commission planned to hold hearings in February and August, following publication of the quarterly consumer price index.

Australians received a welcome surprise in August when Treasurer Paul Keating delivered the first Labor budget since the Whitlam years. The government decided not to increase personal income tax but to rely on traditional means of raising revenue by increasing the excise tax on beer, petrol (gasoline), and tobacco. The treasurer announced that for the first time excise taxes would automatically be increased in line with inflation. Keating anticipated that during 1983–84 the inflation rate would be reduced to about 7.5% from the current 11.2%.

At the same time, the treasurer was gloomy about prospects for reducing the number of unemployed. Keating believed that the average level of employment would remain static, but he observed that, because the working-age population was continuing to grow, it would take time for the upward trend in unemployment to be reversed. Keating summed up his budget by claiming that it was about fairness and equity, "a re-ordering of priorities." The chief victims of the budget, apart from beer drinkers, smokers, and petrol users, were avaricious old-age pensioners, on whom the government fixed its sights. Keating said that tax burdens were to be spread throughout the community on the basis of capacity to pay. Accordingly, a means test for pensioners would be reintroduced on both assets and incomes, along lines similar to the test that applied in 1976.

(A. R. G. GRIFFITHS)

See also Dependent States.

AUSTRALIA

Education. (1981–82) Primary, pupils 1,871,617, teachers 91,386; secondary and vocational, pupils 1,115,782, teachers 86,364; teacher training, students 25,219, teachers 939; higher (1982–83), students 335,988, teaching staff 32,289.

Finance. Monetary unit: Australian dollar, with (Sept. 20, 1983) a free rate of A$1.12 to U.S. $1 (A$1.69 = £1 sterling). Gold and other reserves (June 1983) U.S. $6,422,000,000. Budget (1982 actual): revenue A$43,558,000,000; expenditure A$44,545,000,000. Gross national product (1982) A$152.7 billion. Money supply (May 1983) A$17,566,000,000. Cost of living (1975 = 100; Jan.–March 1983) 215.2.

Foreign Trade. (1981–82) Imports A$23,003,000,000; exports A$19,586,000,000. Import sources: U.S. 23%; Japan 20%; U.K. 7%; West Germany 6%; Saudi Arabia 5%. Export destinations: Japan 27%; U.S. 11%; New Zealand 5%. Main exports: coal 12%; wool 9%; wheat 9%; meat 7%; iron ore 6%; alumina 6%; nonferrous metals 5%. Tourism (1981): visitors 936,727; gross receipts U.S. $1,255,000,000.

Transport and Communications. Roads (1980) 810,918 km. Motor vehicles in use (1981): passenger 6,911,000; commercial 399,000. Railways: (government; 1979) 39,388 km; freight traffic (1978–79) 32,056,000,000 net ton-km. Air traffic (1981): 24,522,000,000 passenger-km; freight 608.7 million net ton-km. Shipping (1982): merchant vessels 100 gross tons and over 558; gross tonnage 1,875,316. Shipping traffic (1980–81): goods loaded 175.2 million metric tons, unloaded 31.2 million metric tons. Telephones (June 1980) 7,396,000. Radio receivers (Dec. 1980) 15 million. Television receivers (Dec. 1980) 5,525,000.

Agriculture. Production (in 000; metric tons; 1982): wheat 8,600; barley 1,740; oats 840; corn 212; rice 783; sorghum 1,310; potatoes 919; sugar, raw value 3,560; tomatoes *c.* 200; apples 294; oranges *c.* 360; pineapples 115; wine *c.* 400; sunflower seed 180; wool, clean 436; milk 5,199; butter 76; cheese 153; beef and veal 1,573; mutton and lamb 506. Livestock (in 000; March 1982): sheep 137,412; cattle 24,490; pigs 2,354; horses (1981) 489; chickens 44,761.

Industry. Fuel and power (in 000; metric tons; 1982): coal 107,538; lignite 37,813; crude oil 17,510; natural gas (cu m) *c.* 11,600,000; manufactured gas (including some natural gas; cu m) *c.* 22,000,000; electricity (kw-hr) 106,119,000. Production (in 000; metric tons; 1982): iron ore (64% metal content) 87,660; bauxite 23,622; pig iron 5,956; crude steel 6,371; aluminum 362; copper 165; lead 219; tin 3; zinc 291; nickel concentrates (metal content; 1980–81) 73; uranium (1981) 2.6; gold (troy oz) 881; silver (troy oz) 25,100; sulfuric acid 1,927; fertilizers (nutrient content; 1981–82) nitrogenous *c.* 206, phosphate *c.* 745; plastics and resins (1980) 709; cement 5,757; newsprint 364; other paper (1979–80) 1,209; cotton yarn 22; wool yarn 20; passenger cars (including assembly; units) 379; commercial vehicles (including assembly; units) 37. Dwelling units completed (1982) 130,200.

AGAIN THE SUMMER AGONY: Australia's Great 1983 Bushfires

by A. R. G. Griffiths

The bushfires that swept across southeastern Australia on Feb. 16, 1983, were the worst natural disaster to hit the continent since the city of Darwin was destroyed by Cyclone Tracy in December 1974. Natural disasters are part of the Australian way of life and a constant reminder of the need to keep alive a pioneering spirit. Bushfires are annual events: southeastern Australia shares with parts of California and the mountains above the French Riviera the distinction of being one of the most fire-prone regions in the world. On Jan. 13, 1939 (as a subsequent royal commission put it), the whole state of Victoria was alight; 71 people died and millions of hectares were destroyed. In 1967, 62 people were burned to death in a bushfire near Hobart. The disasters of February 1983, which caused 72 deaths, were part of a pattern that was bound to be repeated.

Tinder-Dry Bush. The bushfires followed a prolonged period of extemely hot weather. With strong winds and drought conditions in the countryside, a catastrophe was almost inevitable. Before the fires broke out, it was unpleasant and difficult to walk in the streets of Melbourne and Adelaide. A wind of over 30 knots was blowing from the north, and the temperature was above 40° C (104° F). The winds brought dust storms that reduced visibility and closed the airports, thus making the usual aerial fire-spotting detection system useless. Arsonists, some of them members of the volunteer Country Fire Authority who turned out to fight the fires, began to strike. Their efforts added to the developing crisis. Electric power lines began to fray in the high winds and, as they touched, sent showers of sparks down onto the grass by the roadside. The scrub and bush were soon alight.

Reports of the unfolding disaster began to reach Adelaide and Melbourne in the early afternoon. The first areas to be burned were small towns where people seeking a village atmosphere went to live close to nature amid the eucalyptus forests. Aireys

A. R. G. Griffiths is a senior lecturer in history at the Flinders University of South Australia.

CAMERA PRESS, LONDON

Australia's disastrous drought left livestock and vegetation dead and watercourses cracked and arid expanses of land.

Inlet, on a coastal road, and the foothills of the Dandenongs were places where suburbia met the bush. In the Dandenongs, where the town of Cockatoo was engulfed in flames, 120 children hiding in a kindergarten survived as if by a miracle when the town burned. At the Upper Yarra Dam 83 people fled into a tunnel carrying water pipes in an effort to escape the fire near Warburton.

It is an odd but often remarked coincidence that natural disasters in Australia seem to occur on days of religious or occult significance: Friday the 13th for the 1939 bushfire disaster, Christmas Day for Cyclone Tracy. Ash Wednesday is a movable feast, but two major bushfires have broken out near Adelaide on Ash Wednesday: one in 1980, the second and more catastrophic in 1983. The 1983 fire near Adelaide was first reported from McLaren Flat. By midday fires were blazing in the Clare Valley and in the state pine forests in the southeast. The fires spread at rates that equaled or exceeded known records for sustained fire runs, moving in forests at between 8 and 16 km/h (5–10 mph) and through grasslands at 18 km/h (11 mph). It was soon clear that this was more than an "average bad" bushfire—that is to say, one in which, although lives and property are lost, a measure of control of the moving fire can be achieved and the potential damage reduced. On Ash Wednesday of 1983 "conflagration" conditions existed. The fire intensity was so great, and the rate of spread so rapid, that there was little that could be done until the weather changed or until the fire burned itself out.

Counting the Cost. The fires burned through the bush until stopped by fire fighters, changes in the wind, or the lack of combustible material, continuing until February 20 in some areas. In Victoria 20,000 fire fighters were gathered from Country Fire Authority volunteers, the national parks, police, and the Army. Since 8,000 people had lost their homes, emergency relief stations had to be set up. The Red Cross coordinated the distribution of welfare aid from the state and federal governments.

When the dust and ash settled, the survivors gathered to face their immediate future. Emily Bickerton, who as a child had lived through the inferno of the World War II London blitz and remembered a circle of flames round the River Thames, said she had been just as terrified in Cockatoo. "We didn't think we'd survive. I don't think I should go through it twice. It's unfair." Others, who had seen all three landscapes, likened the devastation to Hiroshima after the atomic bomb or war-torn Beirut, Lebanon. The Australian opera singer Dame Joan Hammond was one of those who lost everything. After the fire she sat in the ruins of her house. A torn sheet of music fluttered in the rubble, her Steinway piano was just a heap of wire, and all she had left were her memories. The burns unit at the Alfred Hospital in Melbourne had its busiest day on record.

In South Australia the State Government Insurance Commission (SGIC) calculated the total monetary value of losses at A$200 million. Apart from the dead, 1,500 people were treated by the St. John's Ambulance brigades during the fires, and 85 were hospitalized as a result of their injuries. Property losses included 312 homes damaged or destroyed, 564 vehicles destroyed, 247,000 sheep and 9,700 head of cattle lost. They were only part of the damage: 973 privately owned rural properties were affected by fires, and 10,000 km (6,000 mi) of fencing was destroyed. The Woods and Forests Department lost 25,000 ha (62,000 ac) of commercial forest, and many national park areas were burned. Under natural disaster relief arrangements, the state government contributed A$9 million, the Commonwealth A$26.6 million, and public appeals raised A$8,850,000 for the victims.

Prolonged drought, then high winds: a prescription for catastrophe. The fields were consumed in another great Australian bushfire.

PATRICK RIVIERE—GAMMA/LIAISON

Continuing Risk. In the wake of the fires, governments and organizations involved in the disaster carried out a postmortem and tried to work out ways to avoid such catastrophes in the future. In South Australia, for example, the SGIC recognized that, since southeastern Australia was a bushfire-prone zone and since a large and still increasing population wished to live in a "natural" environment, the chances of future bushfires were high. To some extent the damage could be minimized by a new approach. Since there were no more than two or three days each summer when the inevitability of bushfire could be predicted, the SGIC advised that "Red Alert" days be proclaimed at such times.

On those days conservation and recreation parks would be closed and work in the open in rural industries would be stopped. Many farms and forests had been burned in the past when machinery and vehicles had been working on unpaved areas. The SGIC recommended that schoolchildren in the hills and in country districts be kept home and that members of volunteer fire-fighting units be paid by their employers to be on standby. The SGIC also proposed that able-bodied persons wishing to protect their homes be allowed to stay within disaster areas and that storage dumps be established to hold fire-retardant chemicals. It was suggested that the electricity supply be disconnected on Red Alert days in those areas of the state at greatest risk and that house design and landscaping be required to meet minimum standards, involving, for example, the planting of fire-resistant trees and shelterbelts, the clearing of combustible materials, and the provision of safety screening against sparks.

Whether the postmortem recommendations were accepted or not, the fact remained, as one journalist put it, that Australia is not a bland rock that can be tamed by building three-bedroom bungalows and bitumen roads on it. Bushfires are as much a part of the country as redgum and kangaroos. As long as the sun blazes and cruel winds blow hot, and as long as Australians live among their delectable eucalyptus trees, they will be threatened by fire.

Austria

A republic of central Europe, Austria is bounded by West Germany, Czechoslovakia, Hungary, Yugoslavia, Italy, Switzerland, and Liechtenstein. Area: 83,853 sq km (32,376 sq mi). Pop. (1983 est.): 7,574,000. Cap. and largest city: Vienna (pop., 1981, 1,515,700). Language: German. Religion (1982): Roman Catholic 87.9%. President in 1983, Rudolf Kirchschläger; chancellors, Bruno Kreisky and, from May 24, Fred Sinowatz.

In the general election of April 24, 1983, the Socialist Party of Austria (SPÖ) lost the overall parliamentary majority it had held continuously since 1971. The makeup of the 183-seat Nationalrat (National Council; the lower house) after the election was: SPÖ 90 (−5); Austrian People's Party (ÖVP) 81 (+4); Freedom Party of Austria (FPÖ) 12 (+1). The new environmentalist Alternative List of Austria and United Greens of Austria both attracted considerable numbers of voters, but neither they nor the Communists won any seats. (For tabulated results, *see* POLITICAL PARTIES.)

Bruno Kreisky, SPÖ chairman since 1967 and chancellor since 1970, acknowledged his party's defeat and announced his impending withdrawal from active politics. He recommended that Vice-Chancellor Fred Sinowatz (*see* BIOGRAPHIES) be nominated as SPÖ candidate to head a "little coalition" of the SPÖ and FPÖ. The two parties concluded a four-year pact, and the new coalition government was sworn in on May 24, with Sinowatz as chancellor and Norbert Steger (FPÖ) as vice-chancellor and minister of trade, commerce, and industry. The FPÖ also supplied the ministers of justice and national defense, Harald Ofner and Friedhelm Frischenschlager, respectively. A newly created portfolio of family policy went to Elfriede Karl (SPÖ)—the only woman in the Cabinet. The remaining ten Cabinet members all belonged to the SPÖ. The government also included eight state secretaries, five (including two women) from the SPÖ and three from the FPÖ.

So ended the 13-year-long "Kreisky era," dominated by a politician whose international stature owed much to his initiatives in the Middle East conflict. The increasing incompatibility of the Austrian welfare state with a worsening economic situation and the erosion of Kreisky's charisma as a result of advancing age and sickness were considered to be the chief reasons for the Socialists' poor showing at the polls.

The coalition government continued its predecessor's employment policy, with state-supported programs and subsidization of nationalized industries. Also under discussion were the creation of more jobs through such measures as extended vacations, reduced working hours, lowering of the pensionable age, and a ban on overtime. The 1984 budget deficit was partially offset by increases in the value-added tax, rail fares, and postal charges, by a new tax on interest from savings accounts, and by various economy measures in the public sector. Inflation and unemployment rates of 5.3–5.5% and 5.5–5.7%, respectively, were forecast for 1984, together with a 1–2% increase in gross domestic product. Real wages fell by 1%.

Gerulf Stix (FPÖ) was nominated deputy president of the Nationalrat after Friedrich Peter's candidacy was withdrawn following revelations of his Nazi past. The election to the Nationalrat of Josef Cap, former chairman of the Socialist youth organization, attracted particular attention. In October 1982, as a result of adverse criticism within the party, he had been obliged to withdraw from the SPÖ committee and appeared to have little prospect of election in 1983. However, he was returned as an independent by Socialist voters in Vienna and became a symbol of rank-and-file opposition to the "neo-feudalism" of party functionaries.

In April two ÖVP deputies implicated in the previous year's financial scandal involving a housing cooperative received prison sentences. Also in April, a new Vienna city council was elected; the SPÖ lost one seat but retained overall control. In elections to the Salzburg (October 1982) and Graz (January 1983) city councils, candidates representing environmentalist and citizens' rights interests attracted many voters away from the established parties.

WIDE WORLD

Bruno Kreisky, bowing to the applause of his colleagues, resigned after 13 years as Austria's chancellor when his Socialist Party lost its majority in Parliament.

Foremost among official visitors to Austria in 1983 was Pope John Paul II. His September visit marked the 300th anniversary of the Christian victory over the Turks at Vienna and coincided with the largest assembly in the history of the Austrian Catholic Church. (*See* RELIGION: *Roman Catholic Church.*) (ELFRIEDE DIRNBACHER)

AUSTRIA

Education. (1982–83) Primary, pupils 378,956, teachers 27,731; secondary, pupils 562,606, teachers 57,735; vocational, pupils 380,376, teachers 20,772; teacher training, students 9,124, teachers 864; higher, students 134,339, teaching staff 10,870.

Finance. Monetary unit: schilling, with (Sept. 20, 1983) a free rate of 18.74 schillings to U.S. $1 (28.22 schillings = £1 sterling). Gold and other reserves (June 1983) U.S. $5,487,000,000. Budget (1981 actual): revenue 230,130,000,000 schillings; expenditure 257,840,000,000 schillings. Gross national product (1982) 1,134,490,000,000 schillings. Money supply (June 1983) 167.8 billion schillings. Cost of living (1975 = 100; June 1983) 149.6

Foreign Trade. (1982) Imports 332,550,000,000 schillings; exports 266,860,000,000 schillings. Import sources: EEC 61% (West Germany 41%, Italy 9%); U.S.S.R. 5%; Switzerland 5%. Export destinations: EEC 53% (West Germany 29%, Italy 9%); Switzerland 7%. Main exports: machinery 24%; iron and steel 9%; chemicals 9%; textile yarn and fabrics 7%; metal manufactures 5%; paper and board 5%; motor vehicles 5%. Tourism (1981): visitors 14,241,392; gross receipts U.S. $5,716,000,000.

Transport and Communications. Roads (1981) 106,865 km (including 955 km expressways). Motor vehicles in use (1981): passenger 2,312,900; commercial 190,300. Railways (1981): 6,409 km; traffic 7,246,000,000 passenger-km, freight 10,805,000,000 net ton-km. Air traffic (1982): 1,235,000,000 passenger-km; freight 20.3 million net ton-km. Navigable inland waterways in regular use (1981) 358 km. Shipping (1982): merchant vessels 100 gross tons and over 12; gross tonnage 101,020. Telephones (Jan. 1981) 3,010,100. Radio licenses (Dec. 1980) 3,322,000. Television licenses (Dec. 1980) 2,225,000.

Agriculture. Production (in 000; metric tons; 1982): wheat c. 1,200; barley c. 1,382; rye 355; oats 322; corn c. 1,400; potatoes 1,121; sugar, raw value c. 600; apples 429; wine c. 500; meat c. 768; timber (cu m; 1981) 14,256. Livestock (in 000; Dec. 1981): cattle 2,530; sheep 194; pigs 4,010; chickens 15,656.

Industry. Fuel and power (in 000; metric tons; 1982): lignite 3,297; crude oil 1,291; natural gas (cu m) c. 1,200,000; manufactured gas (cu m) 670,000; electricity (kw-hr) 44,414,000 (72% hydroelectric in 1981). Production (in 000; metric tons; 1982): iron ore (31% metal content) 3,330; pig iron 3,113; crude steel 4,688; magnesite (1981) 1,159; aluminum 133; copper 41; zinc 23; cement 5,012; newsprint 182; other paper (1981) 1,671; petroleum products (1981) 8,321; plastics and resins 410; fertilizers (nutrient content; 1981–82) nitrogenous c. 239, phosphate c. 95; man-made fibres (1979) 140.

Bahamas, The

The Bahamas

A member of the Commonwealth, The Bahamas comprises an archipelago of about 700 islands in the North Atlantic Ocean just southeast of the United States. Area: 13,864 sq km (5,353 sq mi). Pop. (1983 est.): 223,000. Cap. and largest city: Nassau (urban area pop., 1980 prelim., 135,400). Language: English (official). Religion (1970): Baptist 28.8%; Anglican 22.7%; Roman Catholic 22.5%; Methodist 7.3%; Saints of God and Church of God 6%; others and no religion 12.7%. Queen, Elizabeth II; governor-general in 1983, Sir Gerald Cash; prime minister, Sir Lynden O. Pindling.

Increased tourist business and a falling inflation rate were expected to produce an improvement in the economic position of The Bahamas during 1983. The tourist industry accounted for approximately 70% of gross domestic product. The government increased the Ministry of Tourism's budget by almost 40% and planned to make investments in infrastructure, agriculture, fisheries, and industry.

BAHAMAS, THE

Education. (1980–81) Primary, pupils 37,399, teachers (1981–82) 1,768; secondary, pupils 23,761, teachers 1,276; vocational (1975–76), pupils 1,823, teachers 92; teacher training (1975–76), students 731, teachers 21; higher (College of the Bahamas), students 4,093, teaching staff 127.

Finance and Trade. Monetary unit: Bahamian dollar, with (Sept. 20, 1983) a par value of B$1 to U.S. $1 (free rate of B$1.51 = £1 sterling). Budget (1982 actual): revenue B$273.6 million; expenditure B$288.2 million. Cost of living (1975 = 100; May 1983) 170.3. Foreign trade (1981): imports B$4,203,000,000; exports B$3,519,000,000. Import sources (1977): U.S. 35%; Saudi Arabia 24%; Iran 10%; Nigeria 9%; Libya 7%; Angola 5%. Export destinations (1977): U.S. 81%; Saudi Arabia 10%. Main exports: crude oil and petroleum products 95%. Tourism: visitors (excludes cruise passengers; 1981) 1,022,000; gross receipts (1980) U.S. $650 million.

Transport and Communications. Shipping (1982): merchant vessels 100 gross tons and over 96; gross tonnage 432,502. Telephones (Jan. 1981) 71,880. Radio receivers (Dec. 1980) 110,000. Television receivers (Dec. 1980) 31,000.

Prime Minister Sir Lynden O. Pindling repeated complaints that the U.S. was putting pressure on his government to water down its bank secrecy law. Provision of information to the U.S. tax authorities, he maintained, was being made a condition of assistance under the Caribbean Basin Initiative.

There was rising concern in government and business circles about the effects of the country's 25% unemployment rate. Employers and government ministers drew attention to the declining work ethic, which they said was leading to lower standards of service in tourism and other industries. Crime, drug trafficking, and an increasingly vocal militancy among youths also gave rise to anxiety on the part of the authorities.

At its summit meeting in Trinidad and Tobago in July, the Caribbean Community (Caricom) admitted The Bahamas as a full member. (ROD PRINCE)

Bahrain

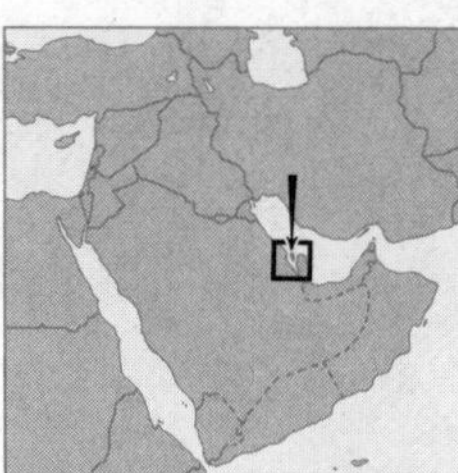

Bahrain

An independent monarchy (emirate), Bahrain consists of a group of islands in the Persian Gulf, lying between the Qatar Peninsula and Saudi Arabia. Total area: 668 sq km (257 sq mi). Pop. (1983 est.): 393,000. Cap. and largest city: Manama (pop., 1981, 109,000). Language: Arabic (official), Persian. Religion (1981): Muslim 85%, of which 50% are Shi'ah Muslim; Christian 7.3%; others 7.7%. Emir in 1983, Isa ibn Sulman al-Khalifah; prime minister, Khalifah ibn Sulman al-Khalifah.

The fall in oil revenue experienced by its neighbours in the Gulf adversely affected Bahrain in 1983. Its attractions as a financial and services centre were accordingly somewhat diminished. The Bahrain Petroleum Company announced plans to

Automobile Industry: *see* Industrial Review; Transportation

Automobile Racing: *see* Motor Sports

Aviation: *see* Defense; Transportation

Badminton: *see* Racket Games

WIDE WORLD

War damage to an Iranian oil well threatened the coastline of Bahrain with an encroaching oil slick; an inflatable boom was placed to protect the main harbour and desalination plants.

cut its work force by one-fourth, arousing fears of new social tensions among the laid-off workers. Bahrain's delicate sectarian balance, in a community equally divided between Sunni and Shi'ah Muslims, had been upset in the past, notably in December 1981 when an attempted coup was mounted by radicals against the monarchist government.

Attempts to strengthen Bahrain's ties with the other states in the Gulf Cooperation Council continued. Work was in progress on the causeway link with the Saudi Arabian mainland. A joint Saudi-Bahraini bank, licensed in August, emphasized the close relations existing between the business communities of the two countries. Despite the Kuwaiti stock market crash of 1982, Bahrain was pushing ahead with plans for its own stock exchange; initially, this was to be limited to the local market. The total assets of the offshore banks based in Bahrain reached $60 billion during the year. Although growth had slowed, Bahrain remained the most active money centre between Europe and Singapore.

A huge oil slick from a war-damaged Iranian oil well polluted 30 km (20 mi) of Bahrain's coastline in late May. (JOHN WHELAN)

BAHRAIN

Education. (1980–81) Primary, pupils 48,406, teachers 2,963; secondary, pupils 23,727, teachers 951; vocational, pupils 2,749, teachers 213; teacher training, students 97, teachers 20; higher, students 3,650, teaching staff 159.

Finance and Trade. Monetary unit: Bahrain dinar, with (Sept. 20, 1983) an official rate of 0.376 dinar to U.S. $1 (0.566 dinar = £1 sterling). Gold and other reserves (June 1983) U.S. $1,481,000,000. Budget (1981 actual): revenue 477 million dinars; expenditure 378 million dinars. Foreign trade (1982): imports 1,402,300,000 dinars; exports 1,424,600,000 dinars. Import sources (1981): Saudi Arabia 60%; U.S. 9%; Japan 6%; U.K. 6%. Export destinations (1981): United Arab Emirates 18%; Singapore 10%; Japan 8%; U.S. 6%. Main exports: crude oil and petroleum products 83%; aluminum 5%.

Industry. Production (in 000; metric tons; 1981): petroleum products 12,620; crude oil (1982) 2,187; natural gas (cu m) 4,619,000; aluminum 141; electricity (kw-hr) 1,830,000.

Bangladesh

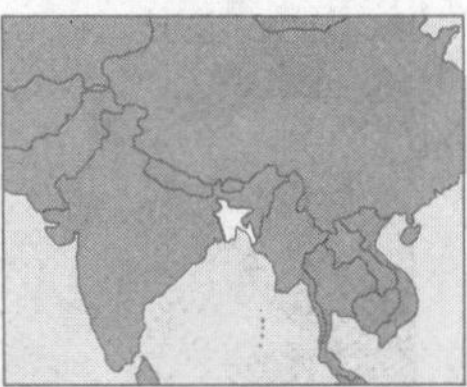

Bangladesh

An independent republic and member of the Commonwealth, Bangladesh is bordered by India on the west, north, and east, by Burma in the southeast, and by the Bay of Bengal in the south. Area: 143,998 sq km (55,598 sq mi). Pop. (1983 est.): 94,651,000. Cap. and largest city: Dhaka (1981 prelim., city pop. 2,244,000; metro. pop. 3,459,000). Language: Bengali. Religion (1980): Muslim 85.9%, Hindu 12.7%, with Christian and Buddhist minorities. President to Dec. 11, 1983, Abul Fazal Mohammad Ahsanuddin Choudhury; chief martial law administrator and president from December 11, Lieut. Gen. Hossain Mohammad Ershad.

The most important development of 1983 was Lieut. Gen. Hossain Mohammad Ershad's promise to return the country to a new form of democracy. Ershad announced in July that general elections would be held in March 1985. In a surprise announcement on November 14, made shortly before the arrival of Queen Elizabeth II during a tour of the Indian subcontinent, this date was moved up to Nov. 25, 1984, while presidential elections were scheduled for May 1984. Ershad also announced that free political activity would be permitted. As a first step toward a return to democracy, local elections were scheduled to take place from December 1983 through March 1984.

The freeze on political activity was reimposed after antigovernment riots in Dhaka and Chittagong on November 28 and 30, in which six people were killed. On December 11 Ershad announced that he was taking over the presidency, while the former president, Abul Fazal Mohammad Ahsanuddin Choudhury, became convenor of the Army-based People's Party, which was expected to support Ershad in the presidential election.

On December 14 Ershad released some 200 political prisoners who had been detained in the wake of the November riots, among them Begum Khalida Zia, widow of the late president Ziaur Rahman, and Sheikh Hasina Wajad, daughter of the late president Mujibur Rahman. Ershad called for a dialogue with the opposition to help pave the way for the return to democracy. Twenty-two of the nation's largest parties had formed into two groupings, a 15-party alliance and a 7-party forum. All had insisted that parliamentary elections be held before a new president was chosen.

Throughout 1983 Ershad ruled Bangladesh with a strong hand. He sacked corrupt officials, arrested student leaders, and removed two stalwarts of his martial law regime from sensitive posts. Maj. Gen. V. M. K. Choudhury was relieved of his position as home affairs minister, and Maj. Gen. Abdur Rahman, commander of the army division in charge of the capital, was offered an ambassadorial post. In February students in Dhaka protested against the continuing military rule. Clashes between students and police resulted in a number of deaths; news reports put the total at five.

The most urgent problem facing Bangladesh concerned population. With some 8,000 babies be-

Balance of Payments: *see* Economy, World

Ballet: *see* Dance

Ballooning: *see* Aerial Sports

Students at Dhaka University protested Lieut. Gen. Hossain Mohammad Ershad's continuing military rule and a suggestion (later abandoned) that Arabic be a required language; police dispersed demonstrators with a water cannon.

ing born each day, the country's population rose to an estimated 94,650,000. Despite adverse weather conditions, total food production in 1982 rose by 5% to a record 15 million metric tons of grain. It was estimated that if a 6% growth rate were maintained for two to three years, Bangladesh would become self-reliant in food. A new government policy for industry was implemented during the year. Some 600 industrial ventures, including about 60 jute and textile mills, were transferred to the private sector.

BANGLADESH

Education. (1981) Primary, pupils 8,236,526, teachers 188,234; secondary, pupils 2,055,897, teachers 85,067; vocational, pupils 345,166, teachers (1980) 17,540; teacher training, students 6,825, teachers 734; higher (1979), students 232,780, teaching staff 12,329.

Finance. Monetary unit: taka, with (Sept. 20, 1983) a free rate of 24.40 taka to U.S. $1 (36.75 taka = £1 sterling). Gold and other reserves (June 1983) U.S. $343 million. Budget (1982–83 est.): revenue 27,678,000,000 taka; expenditure 20,376,000,000 taka (excludes development budget 33 billion taka). Gross domestic product (1981–82) 213,680,000,000 taka. Money supply (April 1983) 24,901,000,000 taka. Cost of living (1975 = 100; May 1983) 189.6.

Foreign Trade. (1982) Imports 50,640,000,000 taka; exports 17,049,000,000 taka. Import sources: Japan 13%; Saudi Arabia 9%; U.S. 8%; China 5%. Export destinations: Singapore 11%; U.S. 10%; Japan 6%; Pakistan 5%; U.S.S.R. 5%; U.K. 5%; Mozambique 5%. Main exports (1981–82): jute manufactures 54%; jute 17%; hides, skins, and leather 11%; fish 7%; tea 6%.

Transport and Communications. Roads (state maintained; 1980) 5,691 km. Motor vehicles in use (1979): passenger 29,400; commercial 11,900. Railways: (1981) 2,884 km; traffic (1981–82) 5,631,000,000 passenger-km, freight 806 million net ton-km. Navigable waterways (1977) 8,430 km. Air traffic (1981): 1,308,000,000 passenger-km; freight c. 22.8 million net ton-km. Shipping (1982): merchant vessels 100 gross tons and over 223; gross tonnage 411,282. Shipping traffic (1981–82): goods loaded 1,240,000 metric tons, unloaded 5,930,000 metric tons. Telephones (Dec. 1980) 116,500. Radio licenses (Dec. 1980) 706,400. Television licenses (Dec. 1980) 78,100.

Agriculture. Production (in 000; metric tons; 1981): rice 21,853; wheat 800; potatoes 1,084; sweet potatoes c. 800; sugar, raw value c. 550; onions 132; mangoes c. 203; bananas c. 663; pineapples c. 159; rapeseed 123; tea c. 42; tobacco 51; jute 879; meat c. 324; fish catch (1981) 687; timber (cu m; 1981) c. 10,929. Livestock (in 000; 1982): cattle c. 35,070; buffalo c. 1,640; sheep c. 1,150; goats c. 11,800; chickens c. 73,000.

Industry. Production (in 000; metric tons; 1980–81): cement 345; crude steel 139; natural gas (cu m) 1,390,000; petroleum products 1,208; fertilizers (nutrient content; 1981–82) nitrogenous 192, phosphate 30; jute fabrics 590; cotton yarn 46; newsprint 31; other paper 34; electricity (kw-hr; 1981) 2,962,000.

In general, Ershad's government enjoyed the support of major Western countries as well as China and India. However, relations with the latter were strained in August when India announced its intention to construct a fence along their common border to stop the illegal infiltration of Bangladeshi nationals into northeastern India. The move drew an angry reaction from Ershad, who said that no country had the right to encircle a neighbour with barbed wire. Two other major issues—the sharing of the Ganges River waters and ownership of tiny New Moore Island in the Bay of Bengal—continued to elude solution.

In March Ershad attended the seventh meeting of nonaligned nations, which was held in New Delhi, India. (DILIP GANGULY)

Barbados

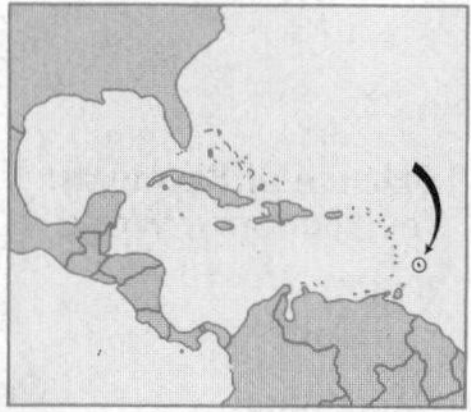

Barbados

The parliamentary state of Barbados is a member of the Commonwealth and occupies the most easterly island in the southern Caribbean Sea. Area: 430 sq km (166 sq mi). Pop. (1983 est.): 251,000; 91% black, 4% white, 4% mixed. Cap. and largest city: Bridgetown (pop., 1980, 7,500). Language: English. Religion: Anglican 53%; Methodist 9%; Roman Catholic 4%; Moravian 2%. Queen, Elizabeth II; governor-general in 1983, Sir Deighton Lisle Ward; prime minister, J. M. G. Adams.

Despite a modest recovery in the tourism sector during the first half of 1983, when tourist arrivals rose slightly compared with the same period in 1982, the general economic outlook for Barbados was one of further stringency. The central bank warned in May that "severe pressures" on the balance of payments would persist. The sugar harvest was again disappointing; production, at 85,000 metric tons, was the lowest since 1948.

Manufacturing also remained depressed. During the first months of 1983, a further problem arose for export manufacturers in the shape of a trade dispute among members of the Caribbean Community (Caricom); this was instigated by Jamaica's decision to adopt a two-tier exchange rate. The dispute was resolved in May, when Jamaica agreed to introduce a special favourable exchange rate for Caricom imports, but in the meantime a

BARBADOS

Education. (1980–81) Primary, pupils 31,147, teachers (1978–79) 1,261; secondary and vocational, pupils 28,818, teachers (1978–79) 1,453; higher, students (1979–80) 1,380, teaching staff (1978–79) 135.

Finance and Trade. Monetary unit: Barbados dollar, with (Sept. 20, 1983) an official rate of Bar$2.01 to U.S. $1 (free rate of Bar$3.03 = £1 sterling). Budget (1981–82 actual): revenue Bar$454 million; expenditure Bar$648 million. Cost of living (1975 = 100; May 1983) 219.9. Foreign trade (1982): imports Bar$1,106,100,000; exports Bar$528,610,000. Import sources (1981): U.S. 35%; U.K. 12%; Trinidad and Tobago 12%; Canada 9%; Venezuela 5%; Japan 5%. Export destinations (1981): U.S. 37%; Trinidad and Tobago 15%; U.K. 7%; Jamaica 6%; Canada 5%. Main exports (1980): sugar 23%; electrical equipment c. 20%; clothing c. 16%; petroleum products 12%; chemicals 7%. Tourism (1981): visitors 352,600; gross receipts U.S. $260 million.

Agriculture. Production (in 000; metric tons; 1981): corn c. 2; sweet potatoes c. 4; sugar, raw value c. 96.

WIDE WORLD

Barbados participated in requesting the U.S. invasion of Grenada and sent troops to take part in the multinational force. Their departure was watched by Prime Minister J. M. G. Adams (right).

freeze on trade had led to factory closings and layoffs in Barbados.

Relations between the government and the opposition became strained early in the year during a wrangle over the conditions under which Barbados had obtained assistance from the International Monetary Fund in October 1982. Donald Blackman, minister of health and community services, was dismissed in September.

With the U.S. and five other Caribbean countries, Barbados participated in the invasion of Grenada on October 25. (ROD PRINCE)

Baseball

The 1983 major league baseball season was rife with off-field colour and controversy, but the sport enjoyed another successful summer, nevertheless. Paid attendance exceeded 45 million customers for the first time, and team owners signed a record $1.1 billion television contract with two networks.

World Series. The Baltimore Orioles, one of baseball's most admired franchises, won the 1983 World Series by defeating the Philadelphia Phillies four games to one. It was the first Series conquest since 1970 for the Orioles, who owned the best overall won-lost record in the major leagues during the last 25 years.

In the 1983 Series opener at Baltimore on October 11, Joe Morgan and Garry Maddox hit home runs to lead the Phillies to a 2–1 victory. The Orioles were limited to five hits by Philadelphia's John Denny and Al Holland.

However, the next evening, Baltimore's brilliant rookie pitcher, Mike Boddicker, surrendered just three singles as the Orioles rebounded with a 4–1 triumph. That evened the Series at one victory each.

When the best-of-seven set moved to Philadelphia on October 14, the Phillies hoped to benefit from their home crowd and an artificial turf surface. But the Orioles, who play their home games on natural grass, took a liking to the surroundings and won three straight games.

In the third game the Orioles rallied from a 2–0 deficit to prevail 3–2. They defeated Philadelphia's veteran left-handed pitcher, Steve Carlton; many baseball experts viewed that event as the turning point of the Series.

In the fourth contest, on October 15, the Orioles won 5–4 after employing four straight pinch hitters (a World Series record) to score two runs in their sixth inning. Baltimore beat Denny, who had been so impressive in the Series opener.

The Orioles then stunned the Phillies again on October 16 with a 5–0 triumph before 67,064 fans in Philadelphia's hushed Veterans Stadium. Scott McGregor, loser in the first game, pitched all nine innings, and Eddie Murray, the Baltimore slugger who had had only two singles in 16 previous at bats, clubbed two home runs.

Rick Dempsey, the Oriole's fiery catcher, was selected as most valuable player for the World Series. He had a record five extra-base hits (one home run, four doubles) in 13 at bats and was credited with much of the success enjoyed by the Baltimore pitching staff. In nine post-season games, including four play-off contests, Oriole pitchers allowed just 12 runs, 2 of which were unearned. In the Series they limited Philadelphia slugger Mike Schmidt to one single in 20 times at bat.

The Orioles thus became only the fourth team in baseball annals to lose a Series opener and then rebound with four consecutive victories. During the Series they were not allowed to use the designated hitter on offense as they had done during the regular season. Nonetheless, the Orioles became the first American League team to win the World Series since 1978 and the sixth different team to capture the "fall classic" in as many years.

Play-offs. The Orioles also lost the first game of the American League championship series when LaMarr Hoyt of the Chicago White Sox handcuffed them in Baltimore 2–1 on October 5. But on October 6 Boddicker struck out 14 White Sox as the Orioles won 4–0. In Chicago the next evening Baltimore cruised to an 11–1 rout. On October 8 in Chicago the Orioles clinched their sixth American League pennant with a 3–0 conquest over the White Sox in 10 innings. Tito Landrum snapped a

Banking:
see Economy, World

Baptist Churches:
see Religion

WIDE WORLD

Rick Dempsey, the fiery catcher of the Baltimore Orioles, was voted most valuable player in the World Series.

scoreless tie with a home run in the top of the tenth inning.

In the National League championship series, the Phillies downed the Los Angeles Dodgers by three games to one for their second pennant in four years. Carlton pitched brilliantly to win the opener at Los Angeles on October 4 by 1–0. The Dodgers captured the next game 4–1, but lost 7–2 at Philadelphia on October 7 and again by the same score the next evening. The play-off result reversed a trend between the two teams, for the Dodgers had won 11 of 12 games from Philadelphia during the regular season.

Regular Season. It was a year of transition for the Orioles, who had been managed by Earl Weaver since mid-1968. Joe Altobelli took over in 1983, and the Orioles struggled for a spell as injuries depleted their pitching staff. But the team—kept afloat by first baseman Murray and shortstop Cal Ripken, Jr. (*see* BIOGRAPHIES)—promoted pitchers such as Boddicker from its bountiful farm system. From mid-August through September the Orioles surged and won the American League East by six games over the Detroit Tigers.

In late May the White Sox were six games under .500 and 7½ games out of first place in the American League West. But they then went on a tear, winning 83 and losing 39 to complete the schedule with a 99–63 record, the best in the major leagues. The White Sox finished in first place by 20 games over Kansas City. They boasted two 20-game winners on a deep pitching staff—Hoyt (24–10) and Richard Dotson (22–7)—plus rookie slugger Ron Kittle, who had 35 home runs and 100 runs batted in. The White Sox won three of the four postseason awards for the American League. Hoyt gained the Cy Young award as the league's outstanding pitcher; Kittle was named rookie of the year; and Tony LaRussa was voted manager of the year. The fourth prize, most valuable player, was won by the Orioles' Ripken.

The Phillies endured some trials before they won the National League East. In mid-July they were in first place "but not playing well," according to general manager Paul Owens. He fired manager Pat Corrales and took over that job himself. With Denny, Carlton, and Holland leading the pitching staff and with Schmidt contributing 40 home runs, the Phillies outdistanced the second-place Pittsburgh Pirates by six games. The Phillies' roster contained several veterans, such as Pete Rose, 42, Tony Perez, 41, and Morgan, 40.

Conversely, the Dodgers were in a rebuilding process for much of 1983. They had parted with two standbys—Steve Garvey, the first baseman, who signed with San Diego, and Ron Cey, the third baseman, who joined the Chicago Cubs. The transition period was difficult for a while. At one time the Dodgers were 6½ games in back of the Atlanta Braves. But, under the vocal direction of manager Tom Lasorda, the Dodgers finished ahead of the Braves by three games in the National League West. Lasorda was voted the National League manager of the year. Other post-season award winners were Dale Murphy of the Braves as most valuable player and Darryl Strawberry of the New York Mets as rookie of the year. The Cy Young award went to Denny.

Bill Madlock of the Pittsburgh Pirates won his fourth batting crown with a .323 average; Wade Boggs of the Boston Red Sox took the honour in the American League with a .361 average. Mike Schmidt won his sixth National League home run title with 40, while Boston's Jim Rice was the American League's best with 39. Rice and Milwaukee's Cecil Cooper each amassed 126 runs batted in, while Murphy topped the National League with 121. Hoyt was the American League's top winner, while Denny (19–6) led the National League in victories. Kansas City Royals relief star Dan Quisenberry established a major league mark for most saves, 45.

Other Developments. The 1983 baseball season would be remembered for many other events, not the least of which occurred in New York City on July 24. Kansas City's George Brett hit a two-run homer, only to have it taken away by umpires. They ruled that Brett had breached the 18-in limit for use of pine tar, a sticky substance that, when applied to a bat, affords the hitter a better grip. The umpires were subsequently overruled by American League president Lee MacPhail. After the season the rule was changed; a bat with too much pine tar would be removed from the game, but a play made before the pine tar was detected would stand.

The American League had a happier moment two weeks earlier when it trounced the National League 13–3 in the 50th anniversary All-Star Game at Comiskey Park in Chicago. The American League—losers of 11 consecutive midsummer All-Star Games—were paced by California Angel Fred Lynn, who smashed the first grand-slam home run in All-Star history.

In an off-field development Bowie Kuhn, the embattled commissioner of baseball, resigned in early August but agreed to stay on until the owners could find a replacement. Three of the sport's playing legends, meanwhile, retired. Johnny Bench, arguably the finest catcher in baseball history, quit the Cincinnati Reds at age 35. Carl

UPI

Bowie Kuhn resigned as commissioner of baseball when it became clear that U.S. major league owners would not support a second term.

Yastrzemski, who performed for the Boston Red Sox for 23 seasons until the age of 44, played his last game. Gaylord Perry, the 44-year-old pitcher often accused of throwing a spitball or greaseball, also retired. His 314 career victories were the second-highest total in the major leagues since World War I. (ROBERT WILLIAM VERDI)

Latin America. None of the winter national Caribbean champions of 1981–82 won a pennant race in 1982–83. The Licey Tigers defeated the Cibao Eagles in the final series in the Dominican Republic. In Puerto Rico the Arecibo Wolfs upset the Ponce Lions' bid for a repeat championship. The Tomato Growers of Culiacán won the Mexican Pacific League pennant by defeating the former champions, the Orange Growers of Hermosillo. In Venezuela the La Guaira Sharks surprisingly gained the title; as a consequence, the Caracas Lions did not have the opportunity to defend their Caribbean title.

All of the national winners met in February in Caracas for the Caribbean Series. Culiacán, playing with an all-Mexican team that relied heavily on the pitching of Vicente Romo and Salomé Barojas, lost six games in a row. The Dominicans, favoured by some to win the Series, ended up with an even record of three wins and three losses. La Guaira had the support of a partisan crowd but suffered two defeats and had to be content with second place. The Arecibo Wolfs won the Series for Puerto Rico after a consistent performance that earned them five victories against only one loss. Glen Walker, left fielder for the champion team, was designated most valuable player of the Series.

In Cuba, a country with a solid baseball tradition, Las Villas won the national championship. As in the past, Cuba did not participate in the professional Caribbean circuit.

The Campeche Pirates won their first Mexican League championship, which is played during the spring and summer, defeating the defending champion Ciudad Juárez Indians in a best-of-seven series. In Mexico's National Baseball League, also played during the spring and summer, the Torreón Falcons won the pennant after defeating the Zacatecas Gophers. (SERGIO SARMIENTO)

Japan. The Seibu Lions of Tokorozawa, the Pacific League pennant winners, beat the Yomiuri Giants, winners of the Central League, four games to three in the best-of-seven Japan Series. A combination of effective pitching and powerful batting by Koji Ota, Terry Whitfield, and Steve Ontiveros gained the Lions their championship. Ota, an outfielder, was chosen the most valuable player of the Series. In the Central League the Giants won the pennant for the first time in two years and the 32nd time in all. Leading the Giants were pitcher Suguru Egawa and batters Reggie Smith and Tatsunori Hara.

Akinobu Mayumi of the Hanshin Tigers of Osaka won the Central League batting title with .353, while the home-run title was shared by Koji Yamamoto of the Hiroshima Toyo Carp and Yasunori Oshima of the Chunichi Dragons of Nagoya with 36. The runs-batted-in championship was captured by Hara, who collected 103. Hara also batted .302, hit 32 home runs, and was chosen for the first time as the league's most valuable player.

The Pacific League adopted a new rule under which a play-off is held only if the second-place team is within five games of the leader after the regular 130-game season ends. The Lions, led by manager Tatsuro Hirooka, demonstrated unrivaled strength in both pitching and batting to win the pennant by a wide margin of 17 games over the Hankyu Braves of Nishinomiya. Contributing to the victory were pitchers Osanu Higashio, Masayuki Matsunuma, Tadashi Sugimoto, and reliever Shigekatsu Mori and batters Koichi Tabuchi, Whitfield, and Ontiveros.

Final Major League Standings, 1983

AMERICAN LEAGUE

East Division

Club	W.	L.	Pct.	G.B.
Baltimore	98	64	.605	—
Detroit	92	70	.568	6
New York	91	71	.562	7
Toronto	89	73	.549	9
Milwaukee	87	75	.537	11
Boston	78	84	.481	20
Cleveland	70	92	.432	28

West Division

Club	W.	L.	Pct.	G.B.
Chicago	99	63	.611	—
Kansas City	79	83	.488	20
Texas	77	85	.475	22
Oakland	74	88	.457	25
Minnesota	70	92	.432	29
California	70	92	.432	29
Seattle	60	102	.370	39

NATIONAL LEAGUE

East Division

Club	W.	L.	Pct.	G.B.
Philadelphia	90	72	.556	—
Pittsburgh	84	78	.519	6
Montreal	82	80	.506	8
St. Louis	79	83	.488	11
Chicago	71	91	.438	19
New York	68	94	.420	22

West Division

Club	W.	L.	Pct.	G.B.
Los Angeles	91	71	.562	—
Atlanta	88	74	.543	3
Houston	85	77	.525	6
San Diego	81	81	.500	10
San Francisco	79	83	.488	12
Cincinnati	74	88	.457	17

Hiromitsu Ochiai of the Lotte Orions of Kawasaki won the league's batting title with .332, his third consecutive win. The home-run championship was captured by Hiromitsu Kadota of the Nankai Hawks of Osaka, and Jitsuo Mizutani of the Braves won the runs-batted-in crown with 114. The most valuable player award was won by pitcher Higashio of the Lions, who had the league's most wins with 18 and the best earned-run average at 2.92. (RYUSAKU HASEGAWA)

Basketball

United States. COLLEGE. The University of Houston's Cougars were supposed to be invincible. And they were, right up to the final second of a tense National Collegiate Athletic Association (NCAA) championship game in Albuquerque, N.M. Then the miracle happened, just as it had all through the tournament for North Carolina State and its ebullient coach, Jim Valvano. With the score tied, North Carolina State's Dereck Whittenburg heaved a 30-ft shot toward the basket. It bounced off the rim, and the desperate struggle seemed destined for an overtime period. Unaccountably, however, Houston's 2.13-m (7-ft) centre, Akeem Olajuwon, had left the lane unprotected, enabling Lorenzo Charles to flash underneath and tip in the rebound for a stunning 54–52 North Carolina State triumph. It was the only mistake in a flawless performance by Olajuwon. The 19-year-old Houston sophomore was named most valuable player of the tournament, only the second time since 1966 that this honour had been awarded to a member of a losing team.

When Olajuwon and his Cougar teammates defeated Louisville 94–81 in the NCAA semifinal, the 1983 college crown was all but conceded to them. A total of 13 dunk shots demoralized the losers, 7 of them stuffed through the hoop by the Nigerian star. The "Phi Slamma Jamma" label, hung on the Cougars by Houston columnist Tommy Bonk in salute to their crowd-pleasing stuffs, made them seem unbeatable.

But not to Valvano, the canny coach who had come from Brooklyn to lead North Carolina State to the basketball summit. He devised a game plan with emphasis on clipping the Cougars' deadly fang, the dunk shot. It worked splendidly, limiting the losers to a lone stuff, by Olajuwon.

The Wolfpack slowed the tempo most of the way, getting excellent rebounding and defensive work from its tallest players, Thurl Bailey and Cozell McQueen, both 2.12 m (6 ft 11 in). They frustrated the running offense ignited by Clyde ("the Glide") Drexler, prevented Olajuwon from dominating the middle completely, and hit crucial long-range shots.

But even with their most potent weapon muzzled, the Cougars still seemed to be wearing down their smaller opponents midway through the second half. A 17–2 explosion put Houston in front by seven points with ten minutes remaining, and another blowout appeared to be in the making.

Then Houston coach Guy Lewis made a controversial coaching decision, leashing his greyhounds by calling for a more deliberate offense. It opened the door just a crack for the Wolfpack shooters, who responded with amazing accuracy. Beset by a storm of criticism after the game, Lewis defended his move, admitting it had backfired on Houston.

WIDE WORLD

In women's basketball, the U.S. beat Romania in the World University Games. Tresa Spaulding of Brigham Young University, held up by teammates, helped cut down the net as a souvenir.

"I'm a lot better coach than the ones who are second-guessing me," he said. "We slowed things down to pull the N.C. State defense out and get some lay-ups."

Missed free throws in the closing minutes gave North Carolina State a chance to hit six straight long-range baskets, three by Sidney Lowe. Alvin Franklin's errant foul shot with 1:05 to go enabled the Wolfpack to freeze the ball until Charles saw Whittenburg's rebound fall into his hands and made the tip-in. Thus, Phi Slamma Jamma, after living by the dunk all season, swiftly died by it. The defeat was just the third in 34 games for Houston, while the Wolfpack finished with a 25–10 mark.

In the National Invitation Tournament (NIT) the sentimental favourite, DePaul and its long-time coach Ray Meyer, also lost in the final. Fresno State's relentless defense wore down the Blue Demons 69–60 in Madison Square Garden to win the NIT in its first appearance.

In women's basketball, freshman Cheryl Miller sparked the University of Southern California to a 69–67 victory over Louisiana Tech, the defending champion. The All-America forward scored 27 points, grabbed nine rebounds, and blocked four shots.

PROFESSIONAL. After signing a $15 million contract, Moses was supposed to lead the Philadelphia

Beer:
see Industrial Review

76ers to the promised land. He did. Perhaps the best offensive rebounder in history, Moses Malone rose to new heights during the National Basketball Association (NBA) championship sweep of the frustrated Los Angeles Lakers. He polished off the Lakers on their home court to wrap up the championship with a businesslike 115–108 victory.

That gave the 76ers four straight victories over the defending champions in the best-of-seven final play-off, and they made it look easy. Malone contributed 24 points and 23 rebounds in the final game, making his choice as most valuable player in the series a foregone conclusion.

Also outstanding for the 76ers was Julius ("Dr. J") Erving. After losing three previous final play-offs, Erving savoured his first NBA title. With off-court grace rivaled only by his offensive ballet, he had no trouble finding players, reporters, and fans to share his pleasure.

The beginning of a potential 76er dynasty was overshadowed by a landmark labour agreement between the 23 team owners and the NBA Players Association. In effect, it locked them into a partnership, with the players guaranteed 53% of the league's gross income. The players also were to tap NBA radio and television revenue, a breakthrough greeted with interest by players' unions in professional football and baseball. The football players' demand for a percentage of revenue was resisted by the owners until a 1982 strike crumbled.

Minimum and maximum salary levels were imposed on NBA teams by the settlement, an attempt to equalize talent and competition among the league's rich and poor franchises. By the 1986–87 season each team would be required to spend at least $4 million on players' salaries.

Also during the year, the NBA and its players' union agreed to bar permanently from the league any player convicted of or pleading guilty to the use or distribution of cocaine or heroin. Any player found to have used those drugs illegally would also be barred.

After eight and a half years as commissioner of the NBA, Larry O'Brien announced his resignation, effective in February 1984. To succeed him, the owners picked David J. Stern, the league's executive vice-president. (ROBERT G. LOGAN)

World Amateur. The ninth Asian Games were played in New Delhi, India, Nov. 30–Dec. 3, 1982. In the women's tournament India and Japan were no match for South Korea, North Korea, and China. In the final, between China and South Korea, Chen Yue Tang, the giant of the Chinese women's team at 2.05 m (6 ft 6 in), scored 16 points and took possession of eight loose balls, leading her team to a 75–67 victory for the gold medal. In the men's tournament the final again was between China and South Korea, but this time it was South Korea that triumphed. The final men's standings were: (1) South Korea, (2) China, (3) Japan, (4) Philippines, (5) North Korea, (6) Kuwait.

The outstanding teams of the ninth Basketball Championship for Women in Africa, held in Luanda, Angola, in April 1983, were Zaire and Senegal. In the match between them Zaire scored an exciting 72–68 victory.

The 23rd European Championship for Men took place in France, May–June 1983. In this remarkable tournament two of the giants of European basketball, the Soviet Union and Yugoslavia, finished third and seventh, respectively. In Caen the Soviet team defeated Israel by a slender margin 92–87, while in Limoges the Yugoslavs defeated France by a mere four points and later demonstrated their poor form when Italy defeated them 91–74. This Italian victory put Yugoslavia out of the running and made Italy the favourite to win the gold, which it achieved with a dazzling display of athletic ability and basketball skills. In the final, Spain, which had beaten the Soviet Union 95–94, played with flair and brilliance but could not match the triumphant and confident play of the Italian team, which won 105–96. In the contest to decide the bronze medal, the Soviet Union defeated The Netherlands 105–70. France finished fifth and Israel sixth.

The second Commonwealth Championship for Men and the first Championship for Women took place in New Zealand during August 1983. In the women's competition Australia defeated England in the final 85–51. In the men's tournament England triumphed over Canada 88–86. The latter, however, recovered to defeat the favourite, Australia, 83–82 in the cross-over semifinals, while England beat New Zealand 79–78. In the final, England, putting on its finest performance ever, managed to keep ahead of Canada to win 86–80.

The ninth World Championship for Women was held July–August in Brazil. The championship provided, as expected, some of the finest women's basketball ever seen. China provided stiff competition for the U.S., which eventually won 101–91. The Soviet Union had been dominant in women's basketball for many years, but the threat posed by the U.S., South Korea, and China teams was an increasing one. Nevertheless, after winning their pool match against the U.S. 84–82, the Soviets went on to beat them 85–84 in a spectacular final game in São Paulo, thus clinching the gold medal. China finished third, followed by South Korea and Bulgaria. (K. K. MITCHELL)

NBA Final Standings, 1982–83

Team	Won	Lost
EASTERN CONFERENCE		
Atlantic Division		
Philadelphia	65	17
Boston	56	26
New Jersey	49	33
New York	44	38
Washington	42	40
Central Division		
Milwaukee	51	31
Atlanta	43	39
Detroit	37	45
Chicago	28	54
Cleveland	23	59
Indiana	20	62
WESTERN CONFERENCE		
Midwest Division		
San Antonio	53	29
Denver	45	37
Kansas City	45	37
Dallas	38	44
Utah	30	52
Houston	14	68
Pacific Division		
Los Angeles	58	24
Phoenix	53	29
Seattle	48	34
Portland	46	36
Golden State	30	52
San Diego	25	57

The Philadelphia 76ers won the NBA championship, besting the Los Angeles Lakers in four straight games. The trophy is held by Julius Erving (left) and Moses Malone; behind it is coach Billy Cunningham.

WIDE WORLD

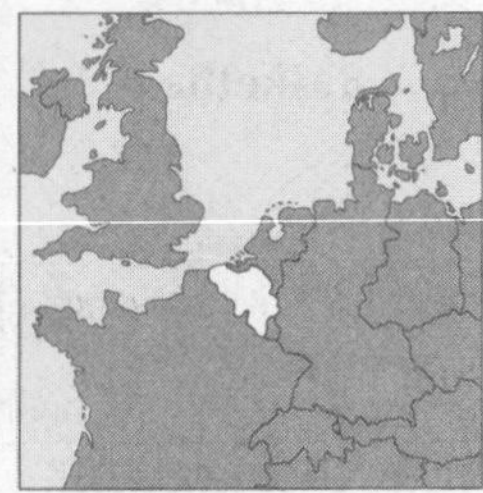

Belgium

Belgium

A constitutional monarchy on the North Sea coast of Europe, the Benelux country of Belgium is bordered by The Netherlands, West Germany, Luxembourg, and France. Area: 30,519 sq km (11,783 sq mi). Pop. (1982 est.): 9,854,600. Cap. and largest urban area: Brussels (pop., 1982 est., metro. area 994,800, commune 138,900). Language: Dutch, French, and German. Religion: predominantly Roman Catholic. King, Baudouin I; prime minister in 1983, Wilfried Martens.

Throughout 1983 the Social Christian-Liberal government in Belgium stuck to its austerity policy. Two of its four major objectives were achieved: Belgian industries recovered their competitiveness, and the balance of payments was greatly improved. Attempts to provide more jobs and reduce the government deficit were less successful. In order to regain control of public expenditure, on June 12 the government obtained additional special powers from Parliament that were to last until the end of 1983. Despite severe pruning and a series of harsh measures, the deficit for the proposed 1984 budget stood at BFr 500 billion, or 11.5% of gross national product. The budget proposals led in mid-September to spontaneous strikes by railway workers, followed by a general strike in the public services that lasted 14 days. Unemployment continued to increase but at a slower pace. Minister of Employment and Labour Michel Hansenne submitted a scheme designed to redistribute the available labour by means of a 5% reduction of working time coupled with new hirings and wage reductions.

Debate raged throughout the year over the future of the state-controlled Cockerill-Sambre steel conglomerate in French-speaking Wallonia. Friction arose between the French and Flemish language communities over financing of the company's losses, which amounted to BFr 11.9 billion in 1982. Flemish politicians pushed the idea of regionalizing the five remaining so-called national industrial sectors, among them steel. A bill to this effect introduced by a Flemish Social Christian representative led to weeks of political tension, until the government produced a solution that placed financial responsibility for Cockerill-Sambre on Wallonia.

On May 13 Jean Gandois, a French steel consultant, was asked to present a plan to secure the future of Cockerill-Sambre beyond 1985 and to put the company back on a sound financial basis. He suggested that by 1985 capital investment worth BFr 95 billion should be injected, BFr 78 billion of it in 1983; some 8,000 workers should be laid off; and production should be lowered to 4.5 million metric tons. Two out of the four steel mills would be closed down. The European Communities' decision to reduce Belgium's total production quota by a further 1.4 million metric tons to 12.9 million metric tons, in line with a five-year plan begun in 1980, struck a severe blow to the industry.

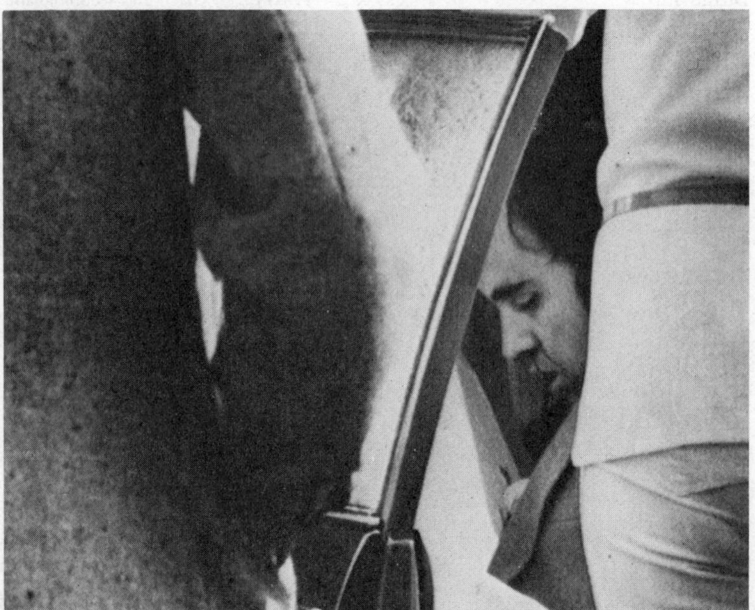

WIDE WORLD

A secret army for the liberation of Armenian terrorists shot and killed an attaché of the Turkish Embassy in Brussels on July 14. A single assassin fired twice with a 9-mm revolver, then fled into a nearby woods.

BELGIUM

Education. (1980–81) Primary, pupils 857,418, teachers 46,430; secondary and vocational, pupils 848,717, teachers (1976–77) 71,170; higher, pupils 196,153, teaching staff (university level; 1979–80) *c.* 9,000.

Finance. Monetary unit: Belgian franc, with (Sept. 20, 1983) a free commercial rate of BFr 53.82 to U.S. $1 (BFr 81.05 = £1 sterling) and a free financial rate of BFr 54.68 to U.S. $1 (BFr 82.35 = £1 sterling). Gold and other reserves (June 1983) U.S. $6,626,000,000. Budget (1982 actual): revenue BFr 1,193,700,000,000; expenditure BFr 1,736,600,000,000. Gross national product (1981) BFr 3,589,000,000,000. Money supply (March 1983) BFr 874 billion. Cost of living (1975 = 100; June 1983) 170.4.

Foreign Trade. (Belgium-Luxembourg economic union; 1982) Imports BFr 2,642,300,000,000; exports BFr 2,394,500,000,000. Import sources: EEC 63% (West Germany 20%, The Netherlands 18%, France 14%, U.K. 7%); U.S. 7%. Export destinations: EEC 71% (West Germany 20%, France 19%, The Netherlands 14%, U.K. 10%, Italy 5%). Main exports (1981): chemicals 12%; machinery 11%; motor vehicles 11%; food 9%; iron and steel 9%; petroleum products 8%; precious stones 6%; textile yarn and fabrics 6%. Tourism (1981) gross receipts (Belgium-Luxembourg) U.S. $1,585,000,000.

Transport and Communications. Roads (1980) 126,800 km (including 1,192 km expressways). Motor vehicles in use (1981): passenger 3,206,500; commercial 284,600. Railways: (1981) 3,930 km; traffic (1982) 6,879,000,000 passenger-km, freight 6,773,000,000 net ton-km. Air traffic (1982): 5,276,000,000 passenger-km; freight 492.2 million net ton-km. Navigable inland waterways in regular use (1981) 1,509 km. Shipping (1982): merchant vessels 100 gross tons and over 316; gross tonnage 2,271,096. Shipping traffic (1982): goods loaded 39,885,000 metric tons, unloaded 70,921,000 metric tons. Telephones (Jan. 1981) 3,636,100. Radio licenses (Dec. 1980) 4.5 million. Television licenses (Dec. 1980) 3.5 million.

Agriculture. Production (in 000; metric tons; 1982): wheat *c.* 930; barley *c.* 760; oats *c.* 130; potatoes *c.* 1,400; tomatoes *c.* 95; apples *c.* 250; sugar, raw value *c.* 1,040; milk *c.* 3,780; pork *c.* 680; beef and veal *c.* 290; fish catch (1981) 49. Livestock (in 000; Dec. 1981): cattle 2,859; pigs 5,076; sheep 79; horses 31; chickens 27,695.

Industry. Fuel and power (in 000; 1982): coal (metric tons) 6,538; manufactured gas (cu m) 530,000; electricity (kw-hr) 50,696,000. Production (in 000; metric tons; 1982): pig iron 7,830; crude steel 9,900; copper 502; lead 84; tin 2.2; zinc 241; sulfuric acid 1,720; plastics and resins 2,023; fertilizers (nutrient content; 1981–82) nitrogenous *c.* 735, phosphate *c.* 440; cement 6,337; newsprint 100; other paper (1981) 828; cotton yarn 46; cotton fabrics 53; wool yarn 71; woolen fabrics 34; man-made fibres (1979) 64. Merchant vessels launched (100 gross tons and over; 1982) 263,000 gross tons.

UPI

Thousands of demonstrators protested Belgian unemployment in Brussels. Police countered thrown rocks and bottles with tear gas, water cannons, and arrests.

Despite King Baudouin's warning against the trend toward further regionalization and federalization of the country, and Prime Minister Wilfried Martens's admission that the 1980 constitutional changes in the state structures did not function properly, regional and communal executives were repeatedly at odds with the national government over their powers and authority. On July 8 the official gazette published a law creating a Court of Arbitration that would deal with such conflicts in the future. Many municipalities were confronted with serious financial problems following a government decision that they should balance their budgets by 1986.

The presence of large numbers of North African and Turkish immigrants in certain communes and the arrival of many destitute political refugees from countries such as Pakistan, Poland, and Vietnam put a severe strain on local finances. Jean Gol, minister of justice and institutional reform, introduced a bill to limit the flow of new immigrants, despite objections by a number of organizations. In August Gol, who was also senior deputy prime minister, took over as acting prime minister when Martens underwent open-heart surgery. Martens resumed his activities in mid-October.

Preparations were begun for the installation of 48 intermediate nuclear missiles at the Florennes air force base, despite active opposition by members of peace movements. (JAN R. ENGELS)

Belize

A constitutional monarchy on the eastern coast of Central America and a member of the Commonwealth, Belize is bounded on the north by Mexico, west and south by Guatemala, and east by the Caribbean Sea. Area: 22,965 sq km (8,867 sq mi). Pop. (1983 est.): 154,000. Cap.: Belmopan (pop., 1980, 2,900). Largest city: Belize City (pop., 1980, 39,800). Language: English (official); Spanish, Creole, Maya, and Garifuna. Religion (1980): Roman Catholic 61.7%; Anglican 11.8%; Methodist 6%; other 20.5%. Queen, Elizabeth II; governor-general in 1983, Minita Gordon; prime minister, George Cadle Price.

BELIZE

Education. (1982) Primary, pupils 35,081, teachers 1,468; secondary, pupils 6,289, teachers 352; vocational, pupils 619, teachers 33; teacher training (1979–80), pupils 144; higher, students (1978–79) 580, teaching staff (1977–78) 20.

Finance and Trade. Monetary unit: Belize dollar, with (Sept. 20, 1983) a par value of Bel$2 = U.S. $1 (free rate of Bel$3.01 = £1 sterling). Budget (1980–81 actual): revenue Bel$80.6 million; expenditure Bel$89.1 million. Foreign trade (1982): imports Bel$263 million; exports Bel$187 million. Import sources (1978): U.S. 39%; U.K. 17%; Netherlands Antilles 9%; Mexico 6%. Export destinations (1978): Mexico 32%; U.S. 28%; U.K. 22%; Colombia 10%. Main exports (1978): sugar 30%; machinery 13%; dairy produce 11%; clothing 9%; watches 7%.

Belize

Belize continued to face problems that, at least in part, stemmed from the fact that it was geographically small, politically weak, and economically dependent on other countries and their fluctuating currencies. Nonetheless, the nation continued on a relatively even course during the year and was, generally speaking, better off than most of its neighbours.

In May Prime Minister George Price traveled to Washington to encourage U.S. investment in his country. Belize's foreign earnings had decreased because of a reduced demand for sugar, its principal export. Other major exports, notably citrus fruits and bananas, also brought lower prices on world markets.

Several U.S. oil companies began drilling operations at various sites throughout the country even though no previously discovered deposit had produced enough oil to be commercially significant.

On March 9, during an eight-day tour of Central America and the Caribbean, Pope John Paul II stopped in Belize, a largely Roman Catholic country, and celebrated mass at the international airport. (INES T. BAPTIST)

Benin

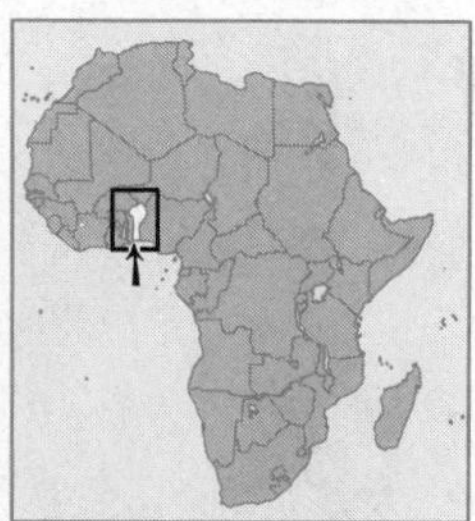

Benin

A republic of West Africa, Benin is located north of the Gulf of Guinea and is bounded by Togo, Upper Volta, Niger, and Nigeria. Area: 112,600 sq km (43,475 sq mi). Pop. (1982 est.): 3,620,900, including Fon 25.9%, Yoruba 14%, Bariba 12.3%, Goun 12.3%, Adja 11.1%, Somba and related tribes 7.3%, Fulani and Dogon 6.9%, Aizo 4.6%, Mina 3%, Dendi 2.1%, other 0.5%. Cap.: Porto-Novo (pop., 1982 est., 208,258). Largest city: Cotonou (pop., 1982 est., 487,020). Language: French, Fon and other local dialects. Religion: animist 65%; Christian 15%; Muslim 13%; other 7%. President in 1983, Brig. Gen. Ahmed Kerekou.

The visit to Benin in January 1983 of French Pres. François Mitterrand marked a reconciliation after a long period of coolness between Benin and the former colonial power; it was the first visit by a French president since Benin (then called Dahomey) achieved independence in 1960.

Also in January, there was a reshuffle of portfolios within the National Executive Council, and three new ministers were appointed. In February the three-year mandates of the Revolutionary Na-

BENIN

Education. (1980) Primary, pupils 379,926, teachers 7,994; secondary, pupils (1979) 64,275, teachers (1978) 1,215; vocational, pupils 7,129, teachers (1975) 150; teacher training, students (1977) 172, teachers (1975) 10; higher (1979), students 3,003, teaching staff (universities only) 234.

Finance. Monetary unit: CFA franc, with (Sept. 20, 1983) a parity of CFA Fr 50 to the French franc and a free rate of CFA Fr 403 to U.S. $1 (CFA Fr 607 = £1 sterling). Budget (1982 est.) balanced at CFA Fr 47,863,000,000.

Foreign Trade. (1978) Imports CFA Fr 70,197,000,000; exports CFA Fr 6,140,000,000. Import sources: France 27%; U.K. 13%; India 10%; The Netherlands 6%; China 6%; West Germany 6%; Japan 5%. Export destinations: The Netherlands 28%; Japan 27%; France 24%. Main exports: cotton 36%; cocoa 30%; palm kernel oil 12%.

Agriculture. Production (in 000; metric tons; 1982): sorghum c. 60; corn c. 350; cassava c. 1,000; yams c. 800; dry beans c. 50; peanuts c. 65; palm kernels c. 75; palm oil c. 36; coffee c. 2; cotton, lint c. 8; fish catch (1981) c. 26. Livestock (in 000; 1981): cattle c. 770; sheep c. 965; goats c. 930; pigs c. 460.

tional Assembly (elected November 1979) and of Pres. Ahmed Kerekou (reelected February 1980) were extended by 18 months. Despite international pressure for their release, large numbers of political detainees remained in prison.

Benin was the first of several West African states to feel the effects of Nigeria's expulsion of illegal immigrants in January. It was also among those countries whose 1983 crops were most affected by drought. (PHILIPPE DECRAENE)

Bhutan

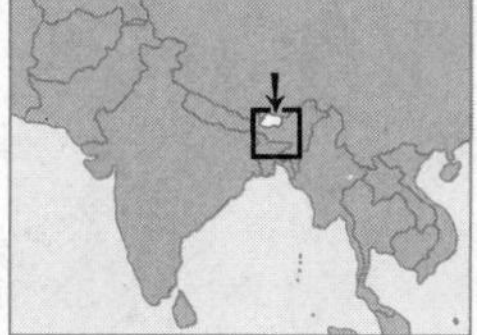
Bhutan

A monarchy situated in the eastern Himalayas, Bhutan is bounded by China and India. Area: 46,100 sq km (17,800 sq mi). Pop. (1982 est.): 1 million, including (1978 est.) Bhutia 60.7%; Gurung 15.8%; Assamese 13.5%; other 10%. Official cap.: Thimphu (pop., 1982 est., 15,000). Administrative cap.: Paro (population unavailable). Language: Dzongkha (official), Lhasa and various Tibetan and Nepalese dialects, and English. Religion (1980): Buddhist 69.3%; Hindu 24.8%; Muslim 5%; tribal 0.9%. Druk gyalpo (king) in 1983, Jigme Singye Wangchuk.

During 1983 Jigme Singye Wangchuk of Bhutan continued to maintain close relations with neighbouring India. He met Indian Prime Minister Indira Gandhi when he traveled to New Delhi to attend the summit meeting of the nonaligned movement in March. Bhutan established formal diplomatic relations with Nepal in July, but India remained the dominant force in Bhutanese foreign relations.

Loan, grant, and other financial assistance from India amounted to Rs 500 million, an increase of Rs 20 million over 1982. India confirmed that it would provide a total of Rs 1,390,000,000 during the course of Bhutan's fifth development plan (1981–87). It was agreed that 1,500 Tibetan refugees living in Bhutan would be settled in India.

On February 11 Bhutan's first airline, Druk-Air, made its inaugural flight to Calcutta. The airline's sole aircraft covered the distance of 585 km (373 mi) in 90 minutes. (DILIP GANGULY)

BHUTAN

Education. (1981–82) Primary, pupils 22,288, teachers 797; secondary, pupils 14,546, teachers 520; vocational, pupils 401, teachers 49; teacher training, pupils 121, teachers 17; higher, pupils 204, teaching staff 16.

Finance and Trade. Monetary unit: ngultrum, at par with the Indian rupee (which is also in use), with (Sept. 20, 1983) a free rate of 10.21 ngultrums to U.S. $1 (15.38 ngultrums = £1 sterling). Budget (1979–80): revenue 97 million ngultrums; expenditure 90 million ngultrums. Foreign trade (1980): imports c. U.S. $2 million; exports c. U.S. $1.5 million. Most external trade is with India. Main exports: timber, fruit and vegetables, cardamom. Tourism (1979–80): visitors 1,500; gross receipts U.S. $1 million.

Bicycling: see Cycling

Billiard Games

Billiards. The 38th world three-cushion billiard championship began May 3 in Aix-les-Bains, France. The international field of 12 men consisted of defending champion Rini Van Bracht of The Netherlands; former champion Raymond Ceulemans of Belgium, who had not participated in 1982; Nobuaki Kobayashi and Satoomi Horike of Japan; Muhammad Mustapha Diab of Egypt; José Viteri of Ecuador; Luis Doyharzabal of Argentina; Torbjorn Blomdahl of Sweden; Richard Bitalis and Egidio Vierat of France; and present and former U.S. champions Harry Sims and Frank Torres.

Although nine of the players came to the tournament with averages in excess of 1,000 balls per inning, none equaled that average in the first session. In the second set both Ceulemans and Kobayashi began to show championship form, and they were joined by Bitalis, who took the lead with a 1.500 average. In the next three days the contestants settled into true form. In the most exciting game, Blomdahl made a series of stunning plays against Ceulemans, only to lose 60 to 56 in 39 innings.

On the fifth and final day Bitalis won a bitterly contested match with Kobayashi. Thus the scene was set for the finale between Bitalis, now averaging 1.350, and Ceulemans with a 1.500. At 49 innings the score was 52–50 in favour of the latter. The tournament ended when Bitalis ran a series of 8, and then 2, to reach 60. Ironically, this made Ceulemans the winner and world champion because of his higher tournament average.

Pocket Billiards. Detroit was the scene of all three Billiard Congress of America (BCA) championship tournaments in 1983. The fifth, and largest, All-American League championships in June brought together 44 women's and 66 men's teams, representing eight-ball leagues from all sections of the U.S. and Canada. Playing on 24 tables, the men's division was reduced to 12 surviving teams at the end of the third day and did not include the perennial defending champions, The Wizards from Colorado Springs, Colo. In the final match it was the Cabaret II team from Lansing, Mich., playing against Mike's Lounge of Pittsburgh, Pa. In the "race to thirteen" for the title the two groups battled evenly to 12 games apiece. In the final game the Cabarets appeared to be certain winners with only the 15 and 8-ball remaining to be sunk. What

WIDE WORLD

A ballroom at New York City's Roosevelt Hotel became a poolroom for championship matches played in September. Attire was formal.

appeared to be an easy shot turned into a heartbreaker when the 15 was pocketed, only to be followed by the cue ball for a "scratch" and loss of game, tournament, and championship to Mike's Lounge. The winning team was manned by John Marcolini, Joe Starr, Bill Greenhow, Bill Falcachio, Paul Mottey, Gary Wrobleski, and Bob Wiggins. Third place went to Cabaret I of Lansing.

In the women's division the championship match took place between the Bank Shots from Colorado Springs and Richard's Pigeon Inn from Lansing, Mich., the same finalists as in 1982. The defending champions, the Pigeons, were not surprised when, like the men, they also found themselves tied 12–12 with one game remaining. Following the men's script, a straight-in shot was all that remained for the Bank Shots to win the title. But it was not to be. Under pressure Margie Justice missed the pocket, and the Pigeons' team captain, Chi Zeeb, cheered on by teammates Carla Johnson, DeeDee Bailey, Vicki Frechen, Julie Hunter, Kim Foreman, Eva Mataya, and Roxy Carpenter, sunk the elusive eight-ball to take the crown home for another year.

In the BCA National eight-ball singles championships the 1982 champion, Joe Sposit, was hoping to defend his title against a strong field of 64 contestants, including such nationally known players as Buddy Hall, "Cornbread Red" Burge, Richie Ambrose, and Dick Spitzer. To everyone's surprise none of those top-ranked contenders made the finals. Delmar Smether defeated Hall, Tom Chapman put away Sposit, and Steve Maniccia dispatched both Ambrose and Spitzer. Bob Rezi, Bruce Goodwin, Jerry Priest, and Bob Garz made up the remaining finalists. Only one man, Mike Sardelli of Warren, Mich., went undefeated through the entire tournament as he bested Chapman in the final match to take the BCA crown.

The women's singles tournament began with eight brackets of 44 players and produced a number of hotly contested matches. One, between Jeri Engh of Wisconsin and Brenda Humble of California, lasted almost 6½ hours before Engh established herself as a finalist. Other finalists included Sher Lively, Peg Ledman, Jo Benson, Kathy Legal, Linda Moore, Mary Beth Ogburn, and Georgana Casteel. At the conclusion Casteel captured the 1983 women's title by staving off Lively in a well-played showdown.

World-class straight pool received a boost during the year when the BCA revived the most prestigious tournament of them all, the U.S. Open 14.1 championships. Reigning champions Tom Jennings and Jean Balukas were on hand to defend their titles in Detroit's Cobo Hall after a five-year hiatus. Opposing them were former BCA champions Dallas West, Irving Crane, Nick Varner, and Steve Mizerack. In the women's division Balukas went undefeated through a small but strong field with a high run of 50 against second-place winner Loree Jon Ogonowsky. It was her seventh consecutive U.S. Open title.

The men's division was not so easily decided. The 28-man field was divided into two flights. In the first grouping former BCA national eight-ball champion Varner defeated Crane, Scott Kitto, Frank McGowan, and Jennings (twice) to earn a place in the finals. In the second flight West took a loss from Danny DiLiberto and was forced to fight his way through the losers' bracket to make the finals. In the process he defeated, in order, George Fixx, Mike Massey, DiLiberto, Lou ("Machine Gun") Butera, Don Edwards, and four-time open champion Steve Mizerack, who had just won the Professional Pool Players straight pool title in New York City. In the finals West handily defeated Varner 200–90.

Snooker. The 1983 world professional snooker title was won by Steve Davis (*see* BIOGRAPHIES), the young British player who first won the championships two years previously. Cliff Thorburn (*see* BIOGRAPHIES) failed to retain the Canadian professional title: he was defeated in the semifinals by Frank Jonik, who went on to lose the finals to Kirk Stevens. (ROBERT E. GOODWIN)

Biographies: *see* People of the Year

Biological Sciences: *see* Life Sciences

Birth Statistics: *see* Demography

Boating: *see* Rowing; Sailing; Water Sports

Bobsledding: *see* Winter Sports

Bolivia

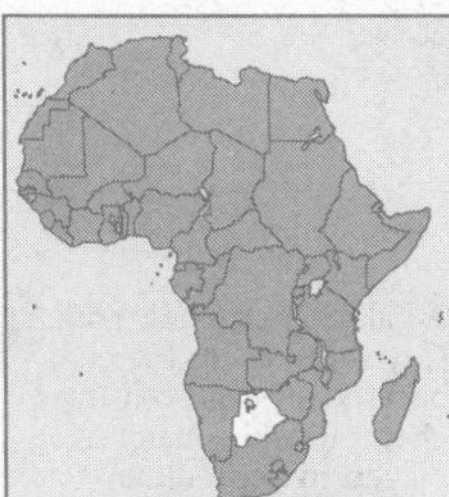
Botswana

Bolivia

A landlocked republic in central South America, Bolivia is bordered by Brazil, Paraguay, Argentina, Chile, and Peru. Area: 1,098,581 sq km (424,165 sq mi). Pop. (1983 est.): 6,081,800, of whom more than 50% are Indian. Judicial cap.: Sucre (pop., 1983 est., 82,500). Administrative cap. and largest city: La Paz (pop., 1983 est., 916,300). Language (1978): Spanish 46%; Quechua 33%; Aymara 21%. Religion (1982 est.): Roman Catholic 94%. President in 1983, Hernán Siles Zuazo.

Pres. Hernán Siles Zuazo, who had returned from exile to take office in Bolivia in October 1982, had to deal with three crises simultaneously during 1983. First was the arrival of El Niño, the warm ocean current that occurs occasionally off the western coast of South America. El Niño brought with it climatic upsets that in turn caused widespread crop failure. The effects bore heavily on Bolivia's peasant and cattle farmers, while the loss of the potato crop led to riots.

Second, the government had to face the effects of the austerity program it introduced in response to the country's severe foreign-debt problems and in the wake of prolonged negotiations with the International Monetary Fund for a standby loan. Third, the Cabinet was reshuffled three times in its first ten months in office and finally resigned. In January the Movimiento Izquierda Revolucionaria (the Movement of the Revolutionary Left), which had held six Cabinet posts, left the coalition. The upshot was that the government found itself in a minority in Congress, though it retained a majority in the Senate. At the same time, the government had to preserve its authority against challenges from the left-wing trade union movement, especially the miners' union, which took over installations belonging to Comibol, the state mining agency, in April. The union abandoned its occupation only when it gained co-management status in the company. A 48-hour general strike was called in December to enforce wage demands. On December 14 the Cabinet collectively resigned but remained in office pending appointment of a Cabinet of national unity.

At the end of 1982 the government carried out a purge of the armed forces. Former president Gen. Luis García Meza Tejada was among those dismissed from their posts. Nevertheless, rumours of a military coup continued to threaten the nascent democracy during 1983, and the government's efforts to combat the conspiracy between the military and the drug runners that had financed the 1980 coup met with little success. Antidrug pressures from the U.S. remained strong. On February 4 Bolivia expelled Klaus Barbie (*see* BIOGRAPHIES), who returned to France to face charges resulting from his activities as head of the Nazi Gestapo in Lyon during World War II.

On September 6 Bolivia advised its international creditors that it was unable to pay the final installment of $30 million on its renegotiated 1980–81 foreign debts. The government stated in explanation that Argentina had delayed payments for gas imports. (Argentina, in turn, was owed money by Brazil.) The Bolivians also stated that they did not have the funds to import the most elementary products. (MICHAEL WOOLLER)

BOLIVIA

Education. (1981) Primary, pupils 904,874, teachers 53,044; secondary and vocational, pupils 210,385, teachers 9,974; teacher training, pupils (1976) 17,000, teachers (1970) 344; higher, students 178,217, teaching staff 6,179.

Finance. Monetary unit: peso boliviano, with (Sept. 20, 1983), following the devaluation of Nov. 8, 1982, a par value of 196 pesos to U.S. $1 (free rate of 295 pesos = £1 sterling). Gold and other reserves (June 1983) U.S. $229 million. Budget (1981 actual): revenue 14,069,000,000 pesos; expenditure 24,285,000,000 pesos. Gross domestic product (1980) 134,987,000,000 pesos. Money supply (Nov. 1982) 47,088,000,000 pesos. Cost of living (La Paz; 1975 = 100; May 1983) 1,767.

Foreign Trade. (1982) Imports U.S. $522.1 million; exports U.S. $832 million. Import sources (1981): U.S. 28%; Argentina 11%; Japan 10%; West Germany 10%; Brazil 7%; Peru 5%. Export destinations (1981): Argentina 36%; U.S. 27%; The Netherlands 7%. Main exports: natural gas 46%; tin 33%; zinc 5%.

Transport and Communications. Roads (1978) 38,866 km. Motor vehicles in use (1980): passenger 48,300; commercial 53,700. Railways (1980): 3,929 km; traffic 529 million passenger-km, freight 646 million net ton-km. Air traffic (1982): 780 million passenger-km; freight 28.3 million net ton-km. Telephones (Jan. 1981) 135,100. Radio receivers (Dec. 1980) 500,000. Television receivers (Dec. 1980) 300,000.

Agriculture. Production (in 000; metric tons; 1982): barley c. 50; corn c. 250; rice c. 100; cassava c. 230; potatoes c. 730; sugar, raw value c. 270; bananas c. 220; oranges c. 87; coffee c. 19; cotton, lint c. 10; rubber c. 5. Livestock (in 000; 1981): cattle c. 4,100; sheep c. 8,900; goats c. 3,050; pigs c. 1,500; horses c. 410; asses c. 780.

Industry. Production (in 000; metric tons; 1981): tin 20; lead ore (metal content) 17; antimony 15; tungsten (oxide content) 3.4; zinc 47; copper 2.6; silver (troy oz) 6,400; gold (troy oz) 64; cement (1980) 318; crude oil (1982) 1,165; natural gas (cu m) 2,800,000; petroleum products 935; electricity (kw-hr) 1,677,000.

Botswana

A landlocked republic of southern Africa and a member of the Commonwealth, Botswana is bounded by South Africa, a part of Bophuthatswana, South West Africa/Namibia, Zambia, and Zimbabwe. Area: 581,700 sq km (224,600 sq mi). Pop. (1983 est.): 1,000,400, almost 99% African. Cap. and largest city: Gaborone (pop., 1983 est., 72,200). Language: English (official) and Setswana. Religion: Christian 60%; animist. President in 1983, Quett Masire.

Addressing the opening of Parliament in November 1982, Pres. Quett Masire had noted that the world recession and a decline in the diamond market had adversely affected the economy. When Vice-Pres. Peter Mmusi presented the 1983 budget in February, however, he managed to strike a note of cautious optimism: there was to be no further devaluation of the pula and personal income taxes were to be reduced.

Meat production had reached record levels in 1982, but mining had not fared as well. Bamangwato Concessions (copper) recorded a loss, and Mmusi described the future of its Selebi-Pikwe mine as grim. Unemployment was causing growing concern. Botswana required an additional

Bonds:
see Stock Exchanges

Books:
see Art Sales; Literature; Publishing

Bophuthatswana:
see South Africa

Botanical Gardens:
see Zoos and Botanical Gardens

Botany:
see Life Sciences

BOTSWANA

Education. (1982–83) Primary, pupils 195,000, teachers 6,930; secondary, pupils 21,420, teachers 979; vocational, pupils 1,741, teachers 227; teacher training, students 1,020, teachers 58; higher, students 1,022, teaching staff 144.

Finance and Trade. Monetary unit: pula, with (Sept. 20, 1983) a free rate of 1.10 pula to U.S. $1 (1.66 pula = £1 sterling). Budget (1982–83 actual): revenue 293 million pula; expenditure 380 million pula. Foreign trade (1982): imports 655.3 million pula (87% from South Africa in 1980); exports 442.3 million pula (63% to Europe, 21% to U.S., 7% to South Africa in 1980). Main exports: diamonds 55%; meat 18%; copper-nickel ore 13%.

Agriculture. Production (in 000; metric tons; 1981): corn c. 15; sorghum c. 45; peanuts c. 2; beef and veal c. 47. Livestock (in 000; 1981): cattle c. 2,950; sheep c. 180; goats c. 700; chickens c. 870.

Industry. Production (in 000; metric tons; 1981): copper ore (metal content) 18; nickel ore (metal content) 15; coal 381; diamonds (metric carats; 1980) 5,146; electricity (kw-hr) 540,000.

17,000 jobs a year but was creating only 10,000. The National Employment Incomes Council was authorized to develop a job-creating strategy.

Botswana was badly affected by the drought in southern Africa. The Gaborone reservoir, designed to supply enough water for 25,000 persons, had to meet the needs of three times that number. The crisis continued throughout 1983.

Relations with Zimbabwe reached a low point in March when Joshua Nkomo, the Zimbabwean opposition leader, left Zimbabwe and stopped for a short period in Botswana, to the government's embarrassment. (GUY ARNOLD)

Bowling

Tenpin Bowling. WORLD. The 1982–83 Europe Cup for national teams, held in October 1982 at Scheveningen, Neth., comprised 12 women's and 16 men's quintets in round-robin one-game matches. After the final ball had been rolled, women from The Netherlands were on the top of the prize list, with Finland as runner-up. Sweden won the men's division, with France placing second.

The 18th annual Bowling World Cup also took place in Scheveningen. Arne Strøm of Norway became the second bowler to win the World Cup twice, triumphing over Thailand's Krua Somsak 223–195 in the title match. A new champion, Jeanette Baker from Australia, was crowned in the women's division. She outpinned Sweden's Inger Levhorn 212–166 in the title match. Baker was fresh from victories in the South Pacific classic and the singles division of the Asian amateur championships in Manila in November 1982.

One of the highest scoring title matches ever achieved in a championship tournament occurred in April 1983 in the European Singles Cup in Ålborg, Den.; Martti Koskela from Finland outclassed Sweden's Ronny Hanson with superb games of 289 and 277, totaling 566 against Hanson's 396. The winner of the women's cup was Birgitte Jensen from Denmark.

Major international events of the season were the Southeast Asian Games, held in Singapore in June 1983, and the Pan American Games, staged in August in Caracas, Venezuela. In Singapore the hosts won all the individual and team events with the exception of the men's doubles (Thailand), the women's team of five (Philippines), and the women's masters (Bec Watanabe, Philippines). In Caracas, bowlers from 12 American nations competed for a week for the titles. Venezuela's Luis Cedeño gave the hometown fans plenty to cheer about when he won the six-game men's singles with 1,181. In the women's six-game event, Isabel de Makino brought Peru its first bowling gold medal even when she scored 1,143. Jean Hammond and Mary Lou Vining won a gold medal for the U.S. in the women's doubles with 2,171, and Puerto Rico won the men's event with 2,338; Puerto Rico also captured the mixed-team event with 4,322. Hammond gained her second gold medal when she won the singles title match from Puerto Rico's Ashie González, the 1971 world amateur champion, 346–302. Pedro Carreyo of Venezuela defeated Rich Wonders (U.S.) 212–170 in the men's final. (YRJÖ SARAHETE)

UNITED STATES. Professional bowlers attract most of the media attention in the U.S., but by far the largest bowling tournaments each year are the events conducted for amateurs by the American Bowling Congress (ABC) and the Women's International Bowling Congress. The WIBC meet, staged in Las Vegas, Nev., over an 83-day period in mid-1983, attracted a record 73,360 entrants competing in three divisions according to their talents.

In Division II doubles, for example, the $2,900 first prize went to a pair of sisters who seldom bowl together, Dorothy Croxton of Philadelphia and Elizabeth Richardson of Richmond, Va. Richardson rolled 565, well over her 150 league average. Croxton, who had a 145 average, used a 9-lb ball—compared with the 15- or 16-lb balls used by professionals—to total 588. Their combined 1,153 was the highest Division II score in the tournament's history. Other Division II champions included: singles, Linda Anderson, Spanish Forks,

COURTESY, WOMEN'S INTERNATIONAL BOWLING CONGRESS

Sisters who seldom bowl together, Dorothy Croxton (left) of Philadelphia, Pa., and Elizabeth Richardson of Richmond, Va., won first prize in Division II of the Women's International Bowling Congress.

Utah, 631; team, Scat's Brats No. 1, Simi Valley, Calif., 2,523; all-events, Peg Borer, Albion, Neb., 1,689.

In the Open Division of the WIBC tournament, the winners were: doubles, Jeanne Maiden, Sue Robb, Cleveland, Ohio, 1,312; singles, Aleta Rzepecki-Sill, Detroit, 726; team, Teletronic Systems, Manila, 2,868; all-events, Virginia Norton, South Gate, Calif., 1,922. Division I champions included: doubles, Bea Hatfield, Shawnee, Kan., Rose Swain, Lenexa, Kan., 1,233; singles, Doylie Seibel, Angleton, Texas, 652; team, Production Plating, Lexington, Ky., 2,814; all-events, Michelle Casella, Sun Valley, Calif., 1,827. In addition, Rzepecki won the $26,000 first prize in the Avon/WIBC Queens Tournament in Las Vegas.

On the opening day of the ABC tournament in Niagara Falls, N.Y., the Niagara Frontier Bowling Supply team posted a 3,286 total in Regular Division play to take the lead. When the meet ended 100 days later, the Niagara Falls team still had the highest score, and it received the $10,000 prize. Other Regular Division champions were: doubles, Rick McCardy and Tony Loiacano, Detroit, 1,382; singles, Rickey Kenrick, Springfield, Ill., 735; all-events, Tony Cariello, Chicago, 2,059. In the ABC Masters event Mike Lastowski of Havre de Grace, Md., a schoolteacher and part-time professional bowler, defeated Pete Weber of St. Louis, Mo., 202–189, in the title match to win $40,500.

Brazil

In Professional Bowlers Association (PBA) competition, Earl Anthony, the 1982 bowler of the year, appeared to be headed for a sixth such honour with two championships (for a career total of 41) and $135,000 in earnings with several tournaments remaining. Leading challengers appeared to be Tom Milton of St. Petersburg, Fla., with three PBA victories and $88,000, and Marshall Holman of Jacksonville, Ore., two victories and $94,000. On October 16 Anthony announced his retirement from the PBA tour. (JOHN J. ARCHIBALD)

Lawn Bowls. Late in 1983 the Yorkshire Bowling Association, England, passed a resolution that promised to bring English bowlers into conflict with British government policy. The resolution stated that the boycotting of South African sports events and the barring of South Africans from events elsewhere constituted a limitation of human rights. (Hilton Armstrong, while president of the English Bowling Association in 1982, had taken a party of bowlers on a tour of South Africa against the wishes of the British Ministry of Sports and had subsequently resigned his presidency.) The English Bowling Association was expected to approve the Yorkshire resolution.

In February Bob Sutherland, aged 40, of the West Lothian club, Scotland, won the world indoor singles championship at Coatbridge, Scotland, beating Burnie Gill, 28, of Port Elgin, Ont., 21–10 in the final and winning a purse of £4,500. Sutherland had defeated David Bryant of England 21–20 in a semifinal. In March Sutherland won the British Isles indoor singles championship, and Bryant won the English indoor championship. At Worthing, Sussex, in June, George Souza of Hong Kong beat Bryant 21–18 in the final of the Kodak Masters tournament. (C. M. JONES)

Boxing:
see Combat Sports

Brazil

A federal republic in eastern South America, Brazil is bounded by the Atlantic Ocean and all the countries of South America except Ecuador and Chile. Area: 8,512,000 sq km (3,286,500 sq mi). Pop. (1983 est.): 129,660,000. Principal cities (pop., 1980 prelim.): Brasília (cap.; city proper) 411,300; São Paulo 7,033,500; Rio de Janeiro 5,093,200. Language: Portuguese. Religion (1980): Roman Catholic 89.2%. President in 1983, Gen. João Baptista de Oliveira Figueiredo.

Domestic Affairs. In Brazil the political year began in March 1983 with the investiture of the state governors and the new Congress, who had been elected in November 1982. Candidates for governor from opposition parties won in 10 of Brazil's 23 states, including the country's 3 most economically significant: São Paulo, Rio de Janeiro,

BRAZIL

Education. (1981) Primary, pupils 22,598,254, teachers 884,257; secondary, vocational, and teacher training, students 2,819,182, teachers 198,087; higher (1980), students 1,352,807, teaching staff 116,827.

Finance. Monetary unit: cruzeiro, with a free rate (Sept. 20, 1983) of 700 cruzeiros to U.S. $1 (1,054 cruzeiros = £1 sterling). Gold and other reserves (June 1983) U.S. $3,934,000,000. Budget (1982 actual): revenue 4,617,800,000,000 cruzeiros; expenditure 4,611,200,000,000 cruzeiros. Gross national product (1981) 25,816,000,000,000 cruzeiros. Money supply (Feb. 1983) 3,961,100,000,000 cruzeiros. Cost of living (São Paulo; 1975 = 100; June 1983) 7,014.

Foreign Trade. (1982) Imports 3,924,000,000,000 cruzeiros; exports 3,537,000,000,000 cruzeiros. Import sources: Saudi Arabia 15%; U.S. 15%; Iraq 13%; Venezuela 5%; Japan 5%. Export destinations: U.S. 20%; Japan 7%; West Germany 6%; The Netherlands 6%; Italy 5%. Main exports (1981): machinery 10%; animal fodder 10%; coffee 8%; iron ore 8%; motor vehicles 6%; sugar 5%; soybeans and oil 5%.

Transport and Communications. Roads (1981) 1,399,443 km. Motor vehicles in use (1981): passenger 9,565,900; commercial 954,800. Railways (1980): 31,127 km; traffic 12,429,000,000 passenger-km, freight 86,131,000,000 net ton-km. Air traffic (1981): 16,304,000,000 passenger-km; freight c. 670 million net ton-km. Shipping (1982): merchant vessels 100 gross tons and over 666; gross tonnage 5,678,111. Shipping traffic (1981): goods loaded 123,990,000 metric tons, unloaded 64,066,000 metric tons. Telephones (Jan. 1981) 7,496,000. Radio receivers (Dec. 1980) 35 million. Television receivers (Dec. 1980) 15 million.

Agriculture. Production (in 000; metric tons; 1982): wheat 2,250; corn 21,711; rice 9,681; cassava (1981) 25,050; potatoes 2,095; sugar, raw value c. 9,420; tomatoes 1,772; dry beans 2,951; soybeans 12,810; bananas 7,088; oranges 9,587; coffee 1,003; cocoa 318; cotton, lint 640; sisal 253; tobacco 422; rubber c. 32; beef and veal c. 2,300; pork c. 970; fish catch (1981) c. 900; timber (cu m; 1981) c. 235,662. Livestock (in 000; 1982): cattle c. 93,000; pigs c. 33,500; sheep c. 17,500; goats c. 8,500; horses c. 6,300; chickens c. 448,000.

Industry. Fuel and power (in 000; metric tons; 1982): crude oil 12,998; coal (1981) c. 5,500; natural gas (cu m) 3,029,000; manufactured gas (cu m; 1979) c. 730,000; electricity (kw-hr; 1981) 142,430,000 (92% hydroelectric). Production (in 000; metric tons; 1982): cement 25,444; pig iron 11,399; crude steel 12,898; iron ore (exports; 68% metal content) 65,645; bauxite (1981) c. 6,700; manganese ore (1980) 3,044; gold (troy oz) c. 1,120; wood pulp (1980) 3,300; paper (1981) 3,298; fertilizers (nutrient content; 1981–82) nitrogenous c. 349, phosphate c. 1,181; passenger cars (including assembly; units) 659; commercial vehicles (units) 143. Merchant vessels launched (100 gross tons and over; 1982) 469,000 gross tons.

and Minas Gerais. This prompted the military government to remove control of the military and police from the state governors. The formal majority held by the four opposition parties in the Chamber of Deputies was temporarily broken when the ruling Social Democratic Party (PDS), with 234 seats, reached a cooperation arrangement with the Brazilian Labour Party (PTB), a small populist opposition party with 13 deputies. However, the arrangement broke down when the government decided not to tie wage increases to the cost-of-living index.

The new governor of São Paulo, André Franco Montoro of the Brazilian Democratic Movement Party (PMDB), faced his first serious challenge after barely three weeks in office, when serious rioting erupted in the city of São Paulo in early April. Thousands of jobless looted stores and broke into the grounds of the governor's palace demanding food and work. In September disturbances of a similar nature took place in Rio de Janeiro.

Unemployment and the high level of inflation were at the root of the violent outbreaks, and the economic adjustment program that followed Brazil's accord with the International Monetary Fund (IMF) in February placed almost intolerable strains on the population. The widespread unpopularity of the austerity measures introduced by the government, which included sharp reductions in government spending and foreign borrowing, triggered a wave of strikes in midyear, culminating in a general strike called for July 21. Although the strikes received only a limited response, they were instrumental in bringing together "official" and "radical" wings of the labour union movement.

Pres. João Baptista de Oliveira Figueiredo was away from office for six weeks in July and August in order to undergo heart bypass surgery in the U.S. The question of presidential succession began to dominate the political agenda. Among the favourites for the presidency were Mário Andreazza, minister of the interior and close associate of Planning Minister Antônio Delfim Netto, and Paulo Maluf, the former governor of São Paulo, who now sat in the Chamber of Deputies. The government's modifications to the structure of the electoral college were expected to ensure a majority for the PDS candidate. However, because of factional disputes within the party, the PDS had not made its choice by the end of the year.

The Economy. The economic recession deepened markedly in 1983. Gross domestic product was expected to decline by about 3% following a modest 1.4% growth in 1982. Agricultural production suffered serious losses as a result of the worst flooding of the century in the fertile southern states, where thousands of people were made homeless. In the northeast the drought entered its fifth year. Some six million metric tons of crops were lost, and concern was expressed over the possibility of food shortages occurring near the end of the year.

The scarcity and high cost of credit continued to afflict the industrial sector, where productive output decreased. In the industrial heartland of São Paulo, production fell by 1.8% in the first half of the year, and it was expected to decline 4% by the end of 1983. Business confidence was severely shaken in July by the bankruptcy of the Matarazzo conglomerate, one of the oldest and most established industrial groups in the country. By 1983 the number of industrial workers in the state of São Paulo had fallen to the level of ten years earlier. Unemployment and underemployment were thought to be affecting about one-third of the work force, and the absence of unemployment benefits aggravated social tensions.

The rate of inflation accelerated sharply as a result of the removal of subsidies for wheat and petroleum. Inflation overtook the balance of payments as the government's primary preoccupation since it seemed likely that the annual rate for 1983 would exceed 150%, compared with the 1982 figure of 99.7%.

In February the central bank devalued the cruzeiro by 23%. The trade balance improved dramatically from a modest $778 million in 1982 to an accumulated surplus of $3,637,000,000 in the first seven months of 1983, leaving little doubt that the desired surplus of $6 billion for the year would be achieved. In addition to the all-out export drive, imports were severely restricted.

O GLOBO

Workers protested unemployment in Brazil, and in São Paulo an organized demonstration turned into a mob of looters.

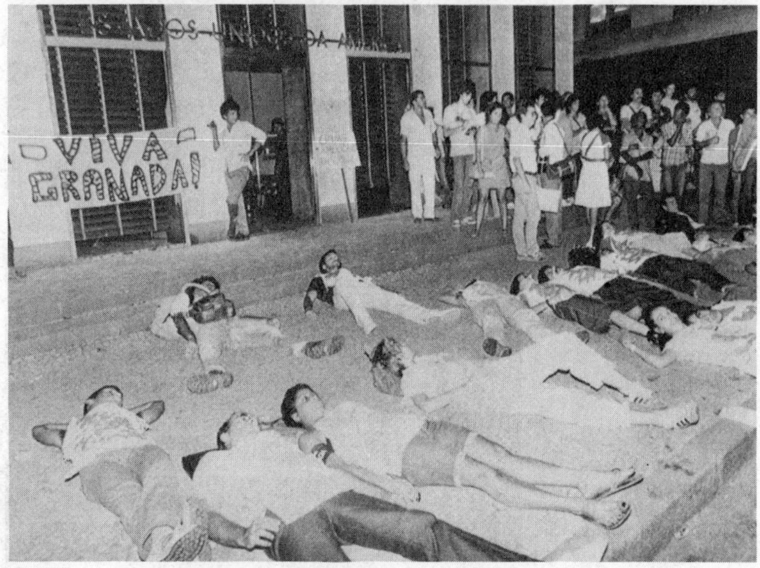

WIDE WORLD

Some 400 Brazilians demonstrated before the U.S. consulate in Rio de Janeiro to protest the U.S. invasion of Grenada. Among them were 18 with mock bloodstains on their clothing who lay before the consulate.

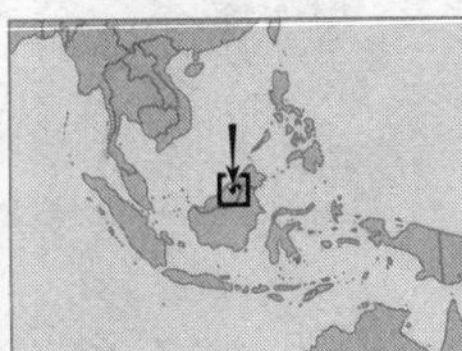
Brunei

Bulgaria

The Brazilian economic team came under growing pressure from political, business, and academic circles to declare some form of debt moratorium. Increasing difficulties were experienced in servicing the $90 billion foreign debt, the largest in the world, and by August the government was already $2 billion in arrears with its interest payments. Brazil's difficulties were compounded by the IMF's refusal to disburse portions of its loan after May, when it became clear that Brazil had failed to meet any of the agreed domestic targets. By early September a new technical understanding between the IMF and the Brazilian government had been reached. However, the conditions set by the IMF led to the resignation of Carlos Langoni, president of the central bank. He was replaced by Afonso Pastore, a professor of economics, and within days the Brazilian letter of intent had been signed and delivered to the IMF. In early November Congress finally approved a measure limiting wage increases. Some weeks earlier, a group of major foreign banks that were coordinating negotiations with Brazil had agreed to $6.5 billion in new loans plus postponement of $5.5 billion repayment on principal due in 1984. It was expected that approval of the wage measure would speed commitments to the new loans by the 800 banks with loans to Brazil outstanding. (LESLIE CRAWFORD)

Brunei

An independent sultanate, Brunei is located on the north coast of the island of Borneo; it is surrounded on its landward side by the Malaysian state of Sarawak. Area: 5,765 sq km (2,226 sq mi). Pop. (1983 est.): 209,000, including (1982) Malay 65.2%; Chinese 20.5%; Indian 3.1%; other 11.2%. Cap. and largest city: Bandar Seri Begawan (pop., 1982 est., 51,600). Language: Malay and English. Religion (1982): Muslim 63.4%; Buddhist 14%; Christian 9.7%; other 12.9%. Sultan, Sir Muda Hassanal Bolkiah Muʿizzadin Waddaulah.

As Brunei approached independence after nearly a century of British rule, the sultan reviewed the troops of his small, wealthy land.

TUCCI—GAMMA/LIAISON

BRUNEI

Education. (1980–81) Primary, pupils 31,677, teachers 1,800; secondary, pupils 16,805, teachers 1,326; vocational, pupils 570, teachers 127; teacher training, students 714, teachers 85; teacher's college, students 143, teaching staff 57.

Finance. Monetary unit: Brunei dollar, with (Sept. 20, 1983) a free rate of Br$2.14 to U.S. $1 (Br$3.22 = £1 sterling). Budget (1982 est.): revenue Br$7.1 billion; expenditure Br$1.9 billion.

Foreign Trade. (1981) Imports Br$1,264,700,000; exports Br$8,591,730,000. Import sources: Singapore 24%; Japan 22%; U.S. 19%; U.K. 9%; Malaysia 5%. Export destinations: Japan 70%; U.S. 11%; Singapore 7%. Main exports: crude oil 56%; natural gas 40%.

Agriculture. Production (in 000 metric tons; 1981): rice c. 10; cassava c. 3; bananas c. 3; pineapples c. 3. Livestock (in 000; 1981): buffalo c. 14; cattle c. 4; pigs c. 14; chickens c. 1,159.

Industry. Production (in 000; 1981): crude oil (metric tons) 7,933; petroleum products (metric tons) 115; electricity (kw-hr) 405,000.

At the end of 1983 the U.K. transferred sovereignty to its last protectorate in Southeast Asia, the oil-rich sultanate of Brunei. Although January 1 was a date of rejoicing, the government announced that henceforth February 23 would be observed as Independence Day.

For a generation Britain had sought to terminate its 1888 treaty with Brunei, but the sultans of Brunei, afraid that their state was too small to survive on its own, resisted. In 1962 a revolt by left-wing groups tried to overthrow the reigning sultan, Sir Muda Omar Ali Saifuddin. The revolt was led by A. M. Azahari, whose principal backer was President Sukarno's Communist-oriented regime in Indonesia. British troops were called in, and the revolt was suppressed.

One of the first steps independent Brunei was expected to carry out in foreign affairs was to join ASEAN, the Association of Southeast Asian Nations. Led by its young sultan, Sir Muda Hassanal Bolkiah (son of Omar Ali Saifuddin), Brunei was also expected to become a member of the Commonwealth.

Brunei produced about $3 billion in oil revenue annually and was estimated to have the highest per capita income of any country in Asia, about $12,000. More than 90% of its revenue was derived from oil exports, largely to Japan. About 80% of its food was imported from ASEAN.

Since the 1962 revolt the U.K. had deployed a battalion of Gurkhas (part of the British Army) to protect the oil fields. The sultan wanted to retain them with pay, but the U.K. feared they would be used as an internal security force. In September it was agreed that Brunei would pay for the troops but Britain would retain control over them.

(ARNOLD C. BRACKMAN)

Bulgaria

A people's republic of Europe, Bulgaria is situated on the eastern Balkan Peninsula along the Black Sea, bordered by Romania, Yugoslavia, Greece, and Turkey. Area: 110,912 sq km (42,823 sq mi).

Brazilian Literature: see Literature

Bridge: see Contract Bridge

Bridges: see Engineering Projects

Buddhism: see Religion

Building and Construction Industry: see Engineering Projects; Industrial Review

Pop. (1982 est.): 8,905,000, including 87% Bulgarians, 8.5% Turks, 2.5% Macedonians, and 2% Gypsies. Cap. and largest city: Sofia (pop., 1981 est., 1,070,300). Language: chiefly Bulgarian. Religion: official sources classify 35.5% of the population as religious, although this figure is suspect since the regime promotes atheism. Of those who practice religion, it is estimated that 26.7% are Bulgarian Orthodox, 7.5% Muslim, 0.7% Protestant, 0.5% Roman Catholic, and 0.1% Jewish. General secretary of the Bulgarian Communist Party and chairman of the State Council in 1983, Todor Zhivkov; chairman of the Council of Ministers (premier), Grisha Filipov.

During 1983 controversy continued to rage over assertions that Bulgaria was involved in the assassination attempt on Pope John Paul II in May 1981. After being sentenced by the Italian courts to life imprisonment in July 1981, Mehmet Ali Agca (*see* BIOGRAPHIES), the Turkish terrorist who shot the pope, claimed that he had been in contact with three Bulgarians when he first arrived in Rome from Sofia. One of these—Sergey Antonov, an official of the Bulgarian airline—was arrested by the Italians in November 1982. Bulgaria's official news agency described his arrest as part of a slander campaign being conducted by the U.S. The Italians, in reply, called the shooting of the pope an act of war in peacetime. During an emergency debate in the Italian Parliament, an accusing finger was pointed at both the Soviet security force (KGB) and the Bulgarian state security system. In July 1983 the KGB denied any involvement.

CAMERA PRESS/PHOTO TRENDS

Electric trucks for the Soviet Union are assembled at the Drouzhba factory in Lom, Bulgaria, on the Romanian border.

In February General Secretary Todor Zhivkov met Romanian Pres. Nicolae Ceausescu in Burgas. They discussed, among other things, the Giurgiu-Ruse industrial development, a joint enterprise between the two countries. In June Zhivkov visited East Germany. In July the West German and Polish foreign ministers, Hans-Dietrich Genscher and Stefan Olszowski, visited Sofia.

On May 30 prices of basic foodstuffs were increased by 21%. Imported spirits went up 70% in price, and imported beer 28%. In order to ensure Bulgaria's self-sufficiency in meat by 1985, a plan to produce 12,000 metric tons of rabbit meat annually was announced. (K. M. SMOGORZEWSKI)

BULGARIA

Education. (1981–82) Primary, pupils 1,030,698, teachers 57,682; secondary, pupils 103,810, teachers 7,986; vocational, pupils 207,011, teachers 17,976; teacher training, pupils 7,260, teachers 680; higher, students 95,820, teaching staff 13,910.

Finance. Monetary unit: lev, with (Sept. 20, 1983) a free exchange rate of 0.98 lev to U.S. $1 (1.48 leva = £1 sterling). Budget (1982 est.): revenue 15,824,000,000 leva; expenditure 15,809,000,000 leva.

Foreign Trade. (1982) Imports U.S. $10,868,000,000; exports U.S. $10,746,000,000. Main import sources (1981): U.S.S.R. 55%; East Germany 6%; West Germany 5%. Main export destinations (1981): U.S.S.R. 48%; East Germany 6%; Libya 5%. Main exports (1981): machinery 35%; transport equipment 11%; tobacco and cigarettes 9%; chemicals 7%; fruit and vegetables 5%. Tourism: visitors (1981) 6,045,600; gross receipts (1980) *c.* U.S. $260 million.

Transport and Communications. Roads (1981) 35,978 km (including 112 km expressways). Motor vehicles in use (1980): passenger 815,549; commercial (including buses) *c.* 130,000. Railways: (1981) 4,267 km; traffic (1982) *c.* 7,100,000,000 passenger-km, freight 18,276,000,000 net ton-km. Air traffic (1981): *c.* 780 million passenger-km; freight *c.* 9.9 million net ton-km. Navigable inland waterways (1973) 471 km. Shipping (1982): merchant vessels 100 gross tons and over 193; gross tonnage 1,248,210. Telephones (Dec. 1981) 1,382,100. Radio licenses (Dec. 1981) 2,115,000. Television licenses (Dec. 1981) 1,659,000.

Agriculture. Production (in 000; metric tons; 1982): wheat *c.* 4,400; corn *c.* 3,000; barley *c.* 1,500; potatoes 466; sunflower seed *c.* 360; tomatoes 865; grapes 1,219; apples 392; tobacco 149; meat 729. Livestock (in 000; Jan. 1982): sheep 10,726; cattle 1,807; goats 490; pigs 3,844; horses *c.* 120; asses *c.* 340; chickens 38,765.

Industry. Fuel and power (in 000; metric tons; 1982): lignite 31,800; coal 240; crude oil (1981) *c.* 246; natural gas (cu m; 1981) 137,000; electricity (kw-hr) 40,438,000. Production (in 000; metric tons; 1982): cement 5,614; iron ore (33% metal content) 1,554; manganese ore (metal content; 1980) 14; copper ore (metal content; 1980) 62; lead ore (metal content; 1981) 96; zinc ore (1980) *c.* 78; pig iron 1,600; crude steel 2,586; sulfuric acid 891; nitric acid (1980) 931; soda ash (1980) 1,449; fertilizers (nutrient content; 1981) nitrogenous 753, phosphate 258; cotton yarn 85; cotton fabrics (m) 365,000; wool yarn (1981) 34; woolen fabrics (m) 40,000. Merchant vessels launched (100 gross tons and over; 1982) 171,000 gross tons.

Burma

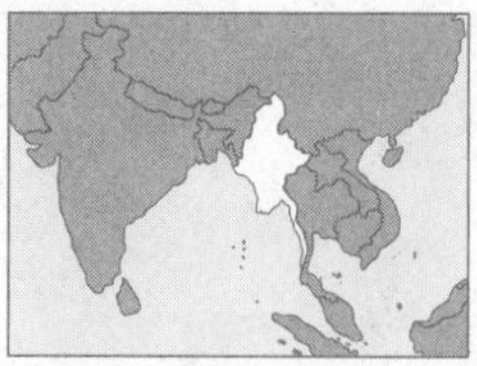

Burma

A republic of Southeast Asia, Burma is bordered by Bangladesh, India, China, Laos, Thailand, the Bay of Bengal, and the Andaman Sea. Area: 676,577 sq km (261,228 sq mi). Pop. (1983 est.): 37,982,000. Cap. and largest city: Rangoon (pop., 1980 est., 2,186,000). Ethnolinguistic groups: Burmese (including Arakanese) 75.2%; Shan 8.9%; Karen 6.6%; Mon 2.3%; Chin 2.3%; other 4.7%. Religion: Buddhist 88.2%. Chairman of the State Council in 1983, U San Yu; prime minister, U Maung Maung Kha.

During 1983 there was a major political shake-up in Burma. In May government newspapers announced the resignation of the powerful Brig. Gen. Tin Oo from the State Council and the suspension of Col. Bo Ni, the home and religious affairs minister. Tin Oo had been considered one of the country's strongmen; for many years he had been a close associate of U Ne Win, chairman of the Burma Socialist Program Party and former chairman of the State Council, and he was widely regarded as Ne Win's probable successor. After his resignation from the council, Tin Oo was arrested and charged with corruption and with attempting to cover up an alleged misappropriation of funds by

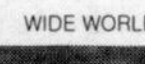

Burmese officials probed the wreckage at Rangoon's Martyr's Mausoleum after a terrorist bomb killed 17 Koreans, 4 Cabinet ministers among them. The verdict: North Korea ordered the blast.

Bo Ni's wife; in November Tin Oo was sentenced to life imprisonment.

Insurgency groups were fairly inactive during the year. Burmese troops shelled a stronghold of the Karen separatists near the Thai border in July and a further attack was launched in November. Other rebel groups remained dormant. The year was the first of the fourth five-year plan. The total investment target for 1983 was 10,491,900,000 kyats. Loans and aid accounted for 3,065,600,000 kyats. Gross domestic product in 1981–82 increased by 5.9%. On October 9, during a visit to Burma by South Korean Pres. Chun Doo Hwan, a bomb exploded at the Martyr's Mausoleum in Rangoon, where members of Chun's entourage were awaiting his arrival for a wreath-laying ceremony; 21 persons were killed, including 4 members of the South Korean Cabinet. In November Burma severed relations with North Korea after two North Korean Army officers had confessed to the bombing. They were sentenced to death in December.

(DILIP GANGULY)

BURMA

Education. (1981–82) Primary, pupils 4,242,697, teachers 86,354; secondary, pupils 1,027,411, teachers 35,725; vocational, pupils 12,088, teachers 974; teacher training, students 5,400, teachers 388; higher, students 146,461, teaching staff 5,147.

Finance. Monetary unit: kyat, with (Sept. 20, 1983) a free rate of 8.09 kyats to U.S. $1 (12.18 kyats = £1 sterling). Gold and other reserves (June 1983) U.S. $57 million. Budget (1981–82 est.): revenue 38,750,000,000 kyats; expenditure 48,493,000,000 kyats.

Foreign Trade. Imports (1982) 3,178,000,000 kyats; exports 2,957,000,000 kyats. Import sources (1979): Japan 34%; U.S. 12%; West Germany 9%; U.K. 8%; China 5%. Export destinations (1978): Switzerland 12%; Singapore 10%; Hong Kong 10%; Sri Lanka 10%; U.S. 9%; Japan 9%; Indonesia 9%. Main exports: rice 42%; teak 25%; pulses 8%; nonferrous metals and ores c. 6%.

Transport and Communications. Roads (1978) 22,471 km. Motor vehicles in use (1980): passenger 43,300; commercial (including buses) 44,700. Railways: (1978) 4,473 km; traffic (1980–81) c. 3,490,000,000 passenger-km, freight c. 670 million net ton-km. Air traffic (1981): c. 229 million passenger-km; freight c. 1.5 million net ton-km. Shipping (1982): merchant vessels 100 gross tons and over 109; gross tonnage 87,972. Telephones (March 1982) 49,096. Radio receivers (Dec. 1980) 700,000.

Agriculture. Production (in 000; metric tons; 1982): rice 14,146; corn 232; dry beans 216; onions c. 109; plantains c. 400; sesame seed 170; peanuts 567; cotton, lint c. 36; jute 33; tobacco 87; rubber 16; fish catch (1981) 625; timber (cu m; 1981) 27,194. Livestock (in 000; 1982): cattle c. 8,698; buffalo c. 1,979; pigs c. 2,225; goats c. 625; sheep c. 235; chickens c. 24,372.

Industry. Production (in 000; metric tons; 1981–82): cement 372; crude oil 1,697; natural gas (cu m) 665; electricity (public supply only; kw-hr) 1,405,000; lead 7.6; zinc concentrates (metal content) 9; tin concentrates (metal content) 1.6; tungsten concentrates (oxide content) 0.7; nitrogenous fertilizers (nutrient content) 60; cotton yarn 15.

Burundi

A republic of eastern Africa, Burundi is bordered by Zaire, Rwanda, and Tanzania. Area 27,834 sq km (10,747 sq mi). Pop. (1983 est.): 4,561,000, mainly Hutu, Tutsi, and Twa. Cap. and largest city: Bujumbura (pop., 1979, 141,000). Language: Rundi and French. Religion (1980): Roman Catholic 78%; Protestant 5%; Muslim 1%; most of the remainder are animist. President in 1983, Col. Jean-Baptiste Bagaza.

Population growth was the most important problem facing Burundi in 1983. Overuse of land and consequent erosion presented a growing hazard. A project was begun to move 3,475 families to Mpanda in the east, where irrigation was expected to make farming easier. The project, costing $42.5 million, was aided by the International Fund for Agricultural Development.

Burundi faced chronic communications problems. Since the route to the coast through Tanzania had not improved, the government was looking more to the longer route through Uganda to Mombasa, Kenya. As a member of the Kagera Basin development group, Burundi would benefit from the proposed construction of a railway linking Burundi and Rwanda into the Tanzanian and Ugandan railway systems.

Spending on the fourth five-year development plan (1983–87) was put at $1.2 billion. Bankers saw Burundi as underborrowed, although foreign debt had risen sharply. Diversification away from the main crop, coffee, was planned, and long-term prospects for mineral development looked bright.

In July Michel Micombero (*see* OBITUARIES), former president of Burundi, died in exile in Somalia.

(GUY ARNOLD)

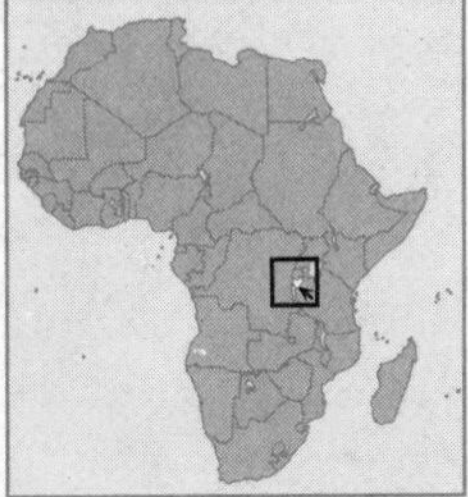

Burundi

BURUNDI

Education. (1979–80) Primary, pupils 159,729, teachers 4,623; secondary, pupils 7,967, teachers 501; vocational, pupils 1,918, teachers (1978–79) 131; teacher training, students 6,525, teachers 370; higher, students 1,784, teaching staff 231.

Finance. Monetary unit: Burundi franc, with (Sept. 20, 1983) a par rate of BurFr 90 to U.S. $1 (free rate of BurFr 136 = £1 sterling). Gold and other reserves (June 1983) U.S. $29 million. Budget (1982 actual): revenue BurFr 13,851,000,000; expenditure BurFr 15,061,600,000.

Foreign Trade. (1982) Imports BurFr 19,280,000,000; exports BurFr 7,883,000,000. Import sources: Belgium-Luxembourg 16%; Iran 14%; France 12%; West Germany 8%; Japan 8%; U.S. 5%. Export destinations: U.S. 32%; West Germany 24%; Belgium-Luxembourg c. 10%; Algeria 7%; Finland 5%. Main export: coffee 89%.

Agriculture. Production (in 000; metric tons; 1982): sorghum c. 98; corn c. 140; cassava c. 1,200; sweet potatoes c. 930; peanuts c. 42; dry beans c. 181; bananas c. 960; coffee c. 24; tea c. 2; cotton, lint c. 3. Livestock (in 000; 1981): cattle c. 872; sheep c. 332; goats c. 686; pigs c. 37.

Cameroon

A republic of west Africa on the Gulf of Guinea, Cameroon borders on Nigeria, Chad, the Central African Republic, Congo, Gabon, and Equatorial Guinea. Area: 465,458 sq km (179,714 sq mi). Pop. (1983 est.): 9,065,000, including Fang 20%; Bamileke 18.6%; Duala 14.9%; Fulani 8.7%; Tikar 7.4%; Massa and related groups 6%; Mandara 5.7%; Maka 4.9%; Mbum 3.7%; other 10.1%. Cap.: Yaoundé (pop., 1981 est., 435,900). Largest city: Douala (pop., 1981 est., 637,000). Language: English and French (official), Fang, Duala, and other Benue-Congo languages. Religion (1980): Roman Catholic 35%; animist 25%; Muslim 22%; Protestant 18%. President in 1983, Paul Biya; prime ministers, Bello Bouba Maigari and, from August 22, Luc Ayang.

Relations between Pres. Paul Biya (*see* BIOGRAPHIES) and his predecessor, Ahmadou Ahidjo, deteriorated in 1983. In August Biya announced the unmasking of a plot allegedly involving supporters of Ahidjo. The situation eased after Biya took over from Ahidjo as president of the Cameroonian National Union, the sole political party. Prime Minister Bello Bouba Maigari was dismissed after the revelation of the plot, and Luc Ayang was appointed interim prime minister. In June French Pres. François Mitterrand visited Cameroon.

French aid for Chad was routed through Cameroon, which took in large numbers of Chadian refugees. Cameroon also had to take back some 120,000 of its own nationals in the exodus of illegal immigrants from Nigeria in January.

(PHILIPPE DECRAENE)

CAMEROON

Education. (1979–80) Primary, pupils 1,302,974, teachers 25,289; secondary, pupils 153,618, teachers 5,602; vocational, pupils 57,316, teachers 2,596; teacher training, students 1,926, teachers 176; higher, students 11,901, teaching staff 439.

Finance. Monetary unit: CFA franc, with (Sept. 20, 1983) a parity of CFA Fr 50 to the French franc and a free rate of CFA Fr 403 to U.S. $1 (CFA Fr 607 = £1 sterling). Budget (total; 1982–83 est.) balanced at CFA Fr 410 billion.

Foreign Trade. (1982) Imports CFA Fr 392.6 billion; exports CFA Fr 326.9 billion. Import sources (1981): France 41%; U.S. 6%; Japan 6%; West Germany 5%; Italy 5%. Export destinations (1981): U.S. 38%; France 19%; The Netherlands 15%; West Germany 6%; Italy 5%. Main exports (1980): crude oil 31%; coffee 23%; cocoa and products 21%; timber 11%.

Transport and Communications. Roads (1980) 32,226 km. Motor vehicles in use (1980): passenger *c.* 66,800; commercial (including buses) *c.* 47,100. Railways (1981): *c.* 1,320 km; traffic 280 million passenger-km, freight 710 million net ton-km. Air traffic (1981): *c.* 485 million passenger-km; freight *c.* 33 million net ton-km. Shipping (1982): merchant vessels 100 gross tons and over 43; gross tonnage 37,987. Telephones (June 1973) 22,000. Radio receivers (Dec. 1980) 760,000.

Agriculture. Production (in 000; metric tons; 1982): corn *c.* 526; millet *c.* 408; sweet potatoes *c.* 140; cassava *c.* 1,020; bananas *c.* 100; plantains *c.* 1,030; peanuts *c.* 120; coffee *c.* 105; cocoa *c.* 120; palm kernels *c.* 47; palm oil *c.* 81; rubber *c.* 17; cotton, lint *c.* 34; timber (cu m; 1981) 10,275. Livestock (in 000; 1981): cattle *c.* 3,284; pigs *c.* 1,257; sheep *c.* 2,174; goats *c.* 2,434; chickens *c.* 10,712.

Industry. Production (in 000; metric tons; 1981): crude oil 6,008; cement (1980) 227; aluminum (1980) 43; electricity (kw-hr) *c.* 1,660,000.

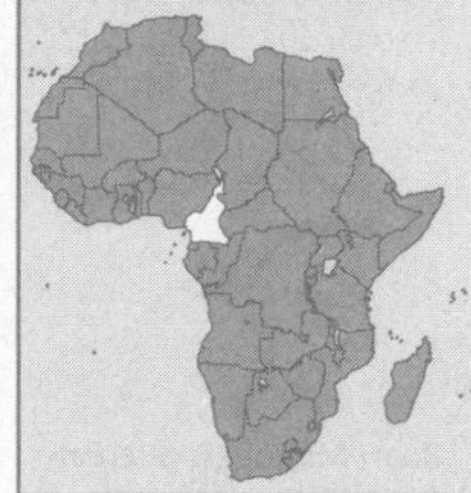
Cameroon

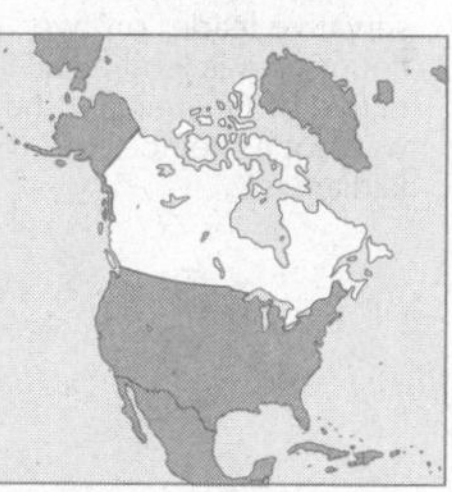
Canada

Canada

Canada is a federal parliamentary state and member of the Commonwealth covering North America north of conterminous United States and east of Alaska. Area: 9,976,139 sq km (3,851,809 sq mi). Pop. (1983 est.): 24,907,100. Cap.: Ottawa (metro pop., 1982 est., 726,100). Largest cities: Toronto (metro pop., 1982 est., 3,029,300); Montreal (metro pop., 1982 est., 2,850,900). Ethnic origin (1981): British 40.1%; French 26.7%; Indian and Inuit 1.7%; other 31.5%. Language (mother tongue, 1981): English 61%; French 26%; other 13%. Religion (1981): Roman Catholic 46%; Protestant 41%. Queen, Elizabeth II; governor-general in 1983, Edward R. Schreyer; prime minister, Pierre Elliott Trudeau.

Domestic Affairs. Canada's political mood in 1983 reflected the anticipation of change. For all but nine months over the last 20 years, the Liberal Party had been in power, since 1968 under Pierre Trudeau. Now 64, Trudeau was well on his way to becoming the longest-serving French-speaking prime minister in Canada's history. But across the country his personal standing and that of his party were at a low ebb. He was seen as high-handed, prone to confrontation, absorbed in constitutional matters when Canada's real problems were economic. His cherished policy of bilingualism, gradually gaining acceptance in central Canada and the Maritimes, was still a cause of controversy, especially among those living in the west.

When Trudeau returned to office in 1980, after nine months in opposition, he had stated that he would not lead his party into another election. Three years later, having easily put down party grumblings over his leadership, he defiantly stated, "I'm no quitter." While the country speculated about his possible retirement, the enigmatic Trudeau gave no hint of his personal plans. (*See* Special Report.)

A possible reason for Trudeau's hesitation about leaving politics was the emergence of a new leader of the opposition Progressive Conservative Party. Joe Clark had led the party for almost seven years, but many Canadians saw him as ineffectual. Members of his party blamed him when his nine-month government lost a general election in February 1980. At a convention in Winnipeg, Man., held to review his leadership, a vote on January 28 gave Clark the support of only 66% of the delegates. Believing that a more substantial vote of confidence was required to sustain his leadership, the 44-year-old Clark recommended that the party hold a formal leadership-selection meeting. This took place in Ottawa in June, when 3,000 delegates assembled to choose among Clark and seven challengers. Three had been ministers in the Clark government of 1979–80; another was a man Clark had defeated for the party leadership in 1976.

Clark's earlier rival was Brian Mulroney (*see* BIOGRAPHIES), a 44-year-old Montreal lawyer and business executive who had made his name as a bilingual labour lawyer before moving to the presidency of the Iron Ore Co. of Canada. Handsome

Business:
see Economy, World; Industrial Review

Cambodia:
see Kampuchea

UPI

Brian Mulroney celebrated with his wife, Mila, his election as leader of Canada's Conservative Party; he was a rare Conservative leader on two counts: he is a bilingual native of Quebec and he was not a member of Parliament.

and articulate, he captured the Conservative leadership on the fourth ballot, winning 54% of the delegates' votes in a straight contest with Clark. For many Conservatives, Mulroney's appeal lay in his claim that, as a native son, he could capture the votes in Quebec so necessary for a future Conservative victory. Others admired his emphasis on private enterprise, his commitment to strengthen defense, and his promise to reduce the size and waste of the federal bureaucracy.

Mulroney had never been a member of Parliament, and it was important for him to secure a seat. This he did handily in a Nova Scotia by-election on August 29. On September 7–8, after being sworn in as an MP, Mulroney announced a shadow cabinet of 35 Conservative members to keep watch on the various ministerial departments. The new leader's concern for party solidarity was revealed by the fact that 20 of his appointees had supported Joe Clark in the June convention. Thus when Parliament resumed on September 12 after the summer recess, the Liberals faced a united and reinvigorated opposition. The Conservatives were heartened by the opinion polls; one taken in early September showed that 62% of decided voters would vote for them in the next election. Some 23% indicated support for the Liberals. Translated into votes and seats, the opinion results would mean a large parliamentary majority for the Tories in the next election, which many observers felt would be called in 1984.

Trudeau shuffled almost half his Cabinet on August 12, hoping to regain popularity for his government. Five ministers seen as weak performers were dropped, and five backbenchers (MP's not in the government) were given office. Three of the new junior ministers were from constituencies in Toronto, Canada's largest metropolitan area and a region of crucial importance for Liberal electoral fortunes. Trudeau was embarrassed when, ten days after his appointment, one of the new ministers tendered his resignation. Roger Simmons, an MP from Newfoundland who had been named minister of state for mines, at first refused to give reasons for his withdrawal but later announced that he faced charges of evading income tax.

The ghost of an old controversy rose to provoke a new round of debate in 1983. The issue lay in the contentious area of minority language rights, this time for the French-speakers of Manitoba. In 1870 Manitoba had entered the confederation as a bilingual province, but in 1890 the language rights of the minority in education and government had been swept away by the English-speaking majority. A Supreme Court decision in 1979 declared that these rights would have to be restored. The Manitoba government began the process of adding government services in French and took up the task of translating the province's important statutes into that language. Opposition soon developed, with Manitoba's former premier, Sterling Lyon, taking a strong stand on behalf of the Conservatives.

When it seemed possible that the provincial government might back away from its promise to restore language rights to the 6% of Manitobans who were French-speaking, Prime Minister Trudeau entered the controversy. On October 6 he proposed a resolution in the House of Commons supporting the restoration of bilingualism in Manitoba. In a rare show of unity, he gained the backing of both Mulroney and the New Democratic Party leader, Edward Broadbent. Mulroney brought the full weight of the federal Conservatives behind the resolution, which was considered to have been approved unanimously without the necessity of a vote. The focus of the controversy then returned to Manitoba, where the government's bilingual measures were being considered by the legislature.

An agreement to continue discussion on the rights of native people emerged from a historic conference of federal and provincial ministers and the leaders of four aboriginal rights groups held in Ottawa, March 15–16. Convened under the terms of the 1981 constitutional accord, the meeting ended with a commitment to hold three more meetings on aboriginal rights over the next four years. Although the leaders of the Indian, Inuit (Eskimo), and Métis (half-bloods) groups did not gain the veto they desired over constitutional amendments affecting their rights, they received assurances of full consultation.

Only one province held an election in 1983. British Columbia went to the polls on May 5, giving Premier Bill Bennett and his Social Credit government a sweeping victory. In spite of high unemployment, the Bennett government won its third consecutive term in office, taking 35 of the 57 seats in the legislature, a gain of 4. The opposition New Democratic Party captured the remainder, a disappointing result after a campaign in which party leader David Barrett had emphasized the need for job-creating policies. Barrett later announced he would step down as leader. Following the election, the Bennett government introduced a controversial package of bills intended to reduce the size and cost of the province's public service.

The Economy. Starting from a disastrous performance in 1982, the worst in almost 50 years, the Canadian economy in 1983 recouped most of its losses and showed signs of moving ahead. In April Finance Minister Marc Lalonde predicted 2.3%

PONOMAREFF—GAMMA/LIAISON

Thousands of Canadians marched against nuclear weapons in Montreal in October. The demonstration was part of an international week of protests against the deployment of cruise and Pershing II missiles in Europe. The Canadians were also protesting the Canadian government's agreement with the United States permitting the cruise missile to be tested at Canada's Cold Lake test range.

real growth over the year ahead. This would result in a seasonally adjusted gross national product of $374.5 billion. Consumer confidence was a prime cause of the improvement. Manufacturing production was up, as was forestry output. Exports were strong, especially those of large cars to the U.S. Housing construction rebounded, and inventories were built up following their decline in 1982.

The economic future was cloudy, however, as real interest rates remained high, a consequence of large government deficits. The Bank of Canada lending rate stood at 9.48% in October, well above the level of inflation. The inflation rate began to fall in January for the first time in four years. It continued to do so throughout the following months, reaching a low of 5% in September. This represented the smallest year-to-year increase in prices in more than ten years. Unemployment remained distressingly high: 11.1% of the labour force in October. Among young people 15–24 years old, the jobless rate ran around 20%, with little prospect that it could be reduced in the short run. The government claimed, however, that it was creating new jobs at a faster rate than any other industrial country in the world.

The prospect of stability for energy prices was raised by the signing of an agreement on June 30 between Ottawa and Alberta that froze conventional oil prices at the current level of $29.75 (Canadian) a barrel until the end of 1984, barring unforeseen sizable fluctuations in world prices. The agreement priced Canadian oil at about 83% of the world rate, somewhat higher than the 75% level the two governments had endorsed in a 1981 pricing arrangement. That agreement had been based on the mistaken assumption that world prices would increase steadily. In April the federal government cut the export price of natural gas to the U.S. by 11% in the hope of marketing additional volumes.

Finance Minister Lalonde acknowledged the problem of closing the gap between revenues and spending when he introduced the 1983 budget on April 19. He announced a $6 billion boost in the deficit to $31.3 billion for the 1983–84 fiscal year. A reduction in the deficit, he stated, would have to await a better economic climate. There were two themes in the finance minister's message: a determination to create jobs that would be both satisfying and permanent and the conviction that private investment would have to lead the way to recovery. Lalonde declared his intention to spend $1.7 billion on capital projects over the next four years, most of it in 1983 and 1984. The budget contained many tax concessions to private business. The individual taxpayer was not so fortunate, since personal income tax changes introduced in the budget were expected to produce $290 million in additional revenue over the next two years.

Foreign Affairs. Canada reacted angrily to the Soviet destruction of a South Korean airliner on August 31 by suspending all flights into Montreal by the Soviet airline Aeroflot for 60 days. The ban shut the only remaining North American gateway for the Soviet carrier. Plans to sign an agreement allowing more Soviet planes to refuel at Gander, Newfoundland, were also frozen. For the moment Soviet aircraft flying south to Cuba used the airport at Shannon, Ireland. There had been only three Soviet landings at Gander during the year and none since the Korean plane was shot down. On September 12 the Canadian House of Commons unanimously condemned the Soviet Union for using force against a civilian aircraft. The Trudeau government also gave formal notice that it expected compensation from the Soviets for the loss of 10 Canadians who were among the 269 victims of the crash. Later, Prime Minister Trudeau seemed to tone down his condemnation of the Korean airliner incident. In an exchange in the House of Commons on October 4, he referred to it as "an accident of war" brought about by a "reckless pilot and a misguided commander on the ground."

Canada expressed reservations over the reasons for the decision of the U.S. and six Caribbean states to invade the island of Grenada on October 25. The Trudeau government was not consulted before the event, and difficulties were created when some of the island-states blocked Canada's efforts to evacuate its citizens from Grenada before the landings. Canada declared its willingness to participate in a Commonwealth force to be established to guarantee a peaceful transition to democratic rule.

Prime Minister Margaret Thatcher of Great Britain addressed a joint sitting of the Canadian Commons and Senate on September 26, during the course of a three-day visit to Canada. In a strongly worded speech, she told Parliament it was time for the Western democracies to take the offensive for freedom. Prime Minister Trudeau, speaking later the same day at a banquet in Toronto in Mrs. Thatcher's honour, took issue with what he termed "megaphone diplomacy." This appeared to be a reference to the British leader's vigorously expressed anti-Soviet position. Trudeau emphasized that, "because all of us live under the mushroom cloud," it was vital for all nations to work for disarmament. Mrs. Thatcher later went to Alberta, where the cruise missile was to be tested early in 1984.

Prime Minister Trudeau attended the ninth annual economic summit conference at Williamsburg, Va., May 29–30. There the seven leaders of the West and Japan backed the U.S. position in nuclear arms talks with the Soviet Union, although Trudeau objected to a part of the final communiqué on the grounds that a negotiating position in the arms talks should not be set down in a public statement. At a news conference he urged the Soviets to make concessions in the deadlocked arms talks.

Prime Minister Trudeau set off on a self-styled "pilgrimage of peace" in early November, hoping to promote a suitable climate for the political management of the arms race. On November 8 he flew to Europe, where he met the leaders of six Western states, and later he took his message to Japan and to the Commonwealth heads-of-government meeting in New Delhi, India. He also consulted with the governments of the U.S., the Soviet Union, and China on his proposal for an early conference of the world's five nuclear powers.

A U.S. proposal to test the cruise missile over Canada's northern wilderness evoked sharp controversy. On February 10 an exchange of notes in Washington spelled out conditions for the testing of a range of weapons in Canada during the next ten years. In announcing the agreement, External Affairs Minister Allan MacEachen stated that Canada would make a specific decision on cruise missile testing in light of progress in the arms-reduction talks in Geneva. Opposition broke out immediately, the argument being that the cruise missile was a new and dangerous weapon and that its use would end any lingering hopes of nuclear disarmament. Trudeau defended his government's stance in an "open letter" sent to newspapers across the country. The demonstrators, he stated, were blind in failing to protest the arms buildup by the Soviet Union. Canada, as a member of NATO, had a duty to show solidarity with its allies in the agreed policy of placing cruise and Pershing missiles in Europe.

A formal request from the U.S. to test the cruise missile came on June 13, and on the following day the New Democratic Party forced a debate on the subject in Parliament. The NDP motion to reject the request was defeated by the Liberals and Conservatives 213–34. The government deliberated for a month before announcing, on July 15, that it would permit testing of the cruise guidance system early in 1984. The missiles would be launched from B-52 bombers high over the Beaufort Sea and would not possess nuclear warheads.

Opponents again swung into action, and a coalition of 25 groups and labour unions petitioned the Federal Court for an injunction to stop the testing. Their argument was that the testing would threaten the guarantees of life, liberty, and security set out in Canada's new Charter of Rights. In opposition, the federal government claimed that Cabinet decisions touching on questions of defense and security could not be challenged in the courts. On September 15 a Federal Court judge decided that the hearing could go ahead, a ruling that was promptly appealed by federal lawyers in a second court session on October 11. After two days of argument, the Federal Court of Appeal announced that it was withholding its decision. Provided the court challenges were overcome, testing of the cruise was scheduled to begin in March 1984.

(D. M. L. FARR)

CANADA

Education. (1983–84 prelim.) Primary, pupils 2,888,055; secondary, pupils 1,462,315; primary and secondary, teachers 271,820; higher, students 736,020, teaching staff 58,930.

Finance. Monetary unit: Canadian dollar, with (Sept. 20, 1983) a free rate of Can$1.23 to U.S. $1 (Can$1.86 = £1 sterling). Gold and other reserves (June 1983) U.S. $4,376,000,000. Budget (1982–83 actual): revenue Can$72.3 billion; expenditure Can$91.3 billion. Gross national product (1982) Can$348.9 billion. Money supply (Feb. 1983) Can$37,630,000,000. Cost of living (1975 = 100; June 1983) 200.8.

Foreign Trade. (1982) Imports Can$72,063,000,000; exports Can$87,915,000,000. Import sources: U.S. 71%; Japan 5%. Export destinations: U.S. 68%; Japan 5%. Main exports (1981): motor vehicles 16%; machinery 11%; cereals 7%; natural gas 6%; chemicals 6%; newsprint 5%; crude oil and products 5%; metal ores 5%; nonferrous metals 5%; wood pulp 5%. Tourism (1981): visitors 12,860,000; gross receipts U.S. $2,545,000,000.

Transport and Communications. Roads (1976) 882,071 km. Motor vehicles in use (1980): passenger 10,255,500; commercial 2,902,700. Railways: (1980) 67,066 km; traffic (1982) 1,610,000,000 passenger-km, freight 200,840,000,000 net ton-km. Air traffic (1981): 35,608,000,000 passenger-km; freight c. 848 million net ton-km. Shipping (1982): merchant vessels 100 gross tons and over 1,299; gross tonnage 3,212,562. Shipping traffic (includes Great Lakes and St. Lawrence traffic; 1979): goods loaded 134,639,000 metric tons, unloaded 67,414,000 metric tons. Telephones (Dec. 1980) c. 16.5 million. Radio receivers (Dec. 1980) 26,551,000. Television receivers (Dec. 1980) 11,280,000.

Agriculture. Production (in 000; metric tons; 1982): wheat 26,866; barley 13,598; oats 3,671; rye 879; corn 5,928; potatoes 2,750; tomatoes c. 550; apples 464; rapeseed 2,073; linseed 714; soybeans 833; tobacco 101; beef and veal c. 1,040; fish catch (1981) 1,362; timber (cu m; 1981) 136,741. Livestock (in 000; Dec. 1981): cattle c. 12,520; sheep 505; pigs 9,261; horses c. 350; chickens 82,811.

Industry. Labour force (April 1982) 11,665,000. Unemployment (Dec. 1982) 12.7%. Index of industrial production (1975 = 100; 1982) 106. Fuel and power (in 000; metric tons; 1982): coal 32,294; lignite (including subbituminous coal) 20,420; crude oil 62,163; natural gas (cu m) 70,000,000; petroleum products (1981) 85,768; electricity (kw-hr) 375,067,000 (70% hydroelectric and 10% nuclear in 1981). Metal and mineral production (in 000; metric tons; 1982): iron ore (shipments; 61% metal content) 33,046; crude steel 11,963; copper ore (metal content) 643; nickel ore (metal content; 1981) 155; zinc ore (metal content) 1,183; lead ore (metal content) 341; aluminum (exports; 1981) 1,118; uranium ore (metal content; 1981) 8.4; asbestos (1981) 1,133; gold (troy oz) c. 2,010; silver (troy oz) c. 44,000. Other production (in 000; metric tons; 1982): cement 8,049; wood pulp (1980) 19,432; newsprint 8,118; other paper and paperboard (1980) 4,794; sulfuric acid (1981) 4,117; plastics and resins (1980) c. 1,300; synthetic rubber 182; fertilizers (nutrient value; 1981–82) nitrogenous c. 1,750, phosphate c. 676, potash c. 6,043; passenger cars (units) 814; commercial vehicles (units) 470. Dwelling units completed (1982) 176,000. Merchant vessels launched (100 gross tons and over; 1982) 98,000 gross tons.

WINDS OF CHANGE: CANADA AFTER TRUDEAU

by Peter Ward

The winds of political change were sweeping across Canada in 1983. By midyear it was apparent that, barring a political miracle, the days of Pierre Elliott Trudeau as prime minister and Liberal Party leader were numbered. With the Gallup Poll indicating almost certain defeat for the Liberals in the next general election if he continued as leader, pressure on Trudeau to resign mounted within his party. The man who had dominated the Canadian political scene for 15 years and changed the face of Canada—perhaps more than any other national leader in the 20th century—was confronted by the narrow choice of resignation or defeat at the polls. Almost certainly, an era was coming to an end.

Liberals in Decline. Unquestionably, Canada's suffering during the worldwide economic recession had much to do with public disenchantment over Trudeau. His government's lack of action in the face of the gathering economic storm and its continued high spending and patronage displeased an increasing number of Canadians. English-speaking Canada, particularly, had grown impatient over Trudeau's preoccupation with the new Canadian constitution while small business, farm, and personal bankruptcies hit record rates, interest rates soared to over 21%, and unemployment topped 12%.

In 1979, after Trudeau's 11 years in office, the Liberals had lost a general election, and Trudeau had resigned as party leader. But before a date could be set for a convention to select his replacement, the short-lived Progressive Conservative government of Joe Clark was brought down on a no confidence vote in Parliament. Trudeau decided to stay on as leader of the Liberals, and he led them to victory in the election of February 1980. Elections must be held at least every five years in Canada, but they can come sooner at the discretion of the prime minister or if the government is defeated in Parliament. Four years is the usual period between elections, indicating that Canada could expect a general election sometime in 1984.

In June 1983 Clark was replaced as Conservative leader by a Montreal labour lawyer, Brian Mulroney (*see* BIOGRAPHIES). Mulroney was elected to Parliament for a Nova Scotia constituency on August 29 and assumed the role of leader of the official opposition in Parliament. The Gallup Poll had shown the Conservatives under Clark enjoying wide support. With Mulroney at the helm, their lead over the Liberals increased slightly, varying from 20 to 28 percentage points in the monthly popularity sweepstakes. Even in the Liberal stronghold of Quebec, the polls showed that the Conservatives could elect a substantial number of candidates. In Ontario, western Canada, and the Atlantic provinces, Liberal fortunes were at their lowest ebb ever, and most party members blamed the prime minister. Canada's love-hate affair with Pierre Elliott Trudeau seemed to be stuck in the hate phase.

As an indication of Liberal slippage, when Trudeau came to power in 1968 there were Liberal provincial governments in Newfoundland, New Brunswick, Prince Edward Island, and Saskatchewan. Two more provinces followed suit within two years. At the federal level, Parliament included Liberal members from every province. As of late 1983 there were no Liberal provincial governments, and the only Liberal MP's from the four western provinces were two from Manitoba.

Big Government, Big Problems. Trudeau, who brought such colour into Canadian politics, also polarized the country: between French and English speakers and between east and west. At 64 he was still colourful, still a regular on ski slopes that daunt all but the most proficient amateurs, still cutting a spectacular figure on a trampoline, and still keeping his impressive diving skills honed in the prime ministerial swimming pool. But much had soured. His relations with the Ottawa press corps, never good, had deteriorated to icy silences and exchanged profanities.

Under Trudeau, Canada had asserted itself in foreign policy as never before, but it failed to achieve Trudeau's goal of balancing U.S. influence on Canada by cultivating deeper relations with Europe and the Soviet Union. At first Trudeau's governments deliberately reduced Canada's armed forces and froze the weapons budget. Then, under prodding from West Germany and other NATO allies, it began attempting to rebuild the armed forces, but by that time it was also encountering severe financial difficulties.

Also on Trudeau's agenda were increased social welfare programs, including the world's most generous system of unemployment insurance. A growing bureaucracy and major social programs, undertaken in conjunction with the provinces, sent government spending virtually out of control and led to in-

---

Peter Ward operates Ward News Services Canada in the Parliamentary Press Gallery, Ottawa.

creased borrowing. When Trudeau came to power, some 10% of the federal budget went for interest on the national debt. By 1983–84 the budget was ten times larger, and 21.7% of the total was earmarked for debt interest. Canada's 1983–84 deficit was expected to reach $31.2 billion, about one-third larger than the projected federal deficit of the United States on a per capita basis.

French Power. The greatest accomplishments of Trudeau's 15 years in power were, without doubt, his successful push for a new Canadian constitution and the improvements he made in rights for French-speaking Canadians. These would remain no matter which party came to power in Ottawa.

Before Trudeau, French-speaking members of the governing party filled such Cabinet posts as Justice, External Affairs, and Culture and Citizenship. Economic portfolios were the exclusive preserve of English-speaking ministers, who consequently wielded most of the real power. That tradition was broken when Trudeau appointed Jean Chrétien as minister of national revenue, then minister of industry, trade and commerce, president of the Treasury Board, and finally, in 1977, minister of finance. Chrétien was the first French-speaking minister of finance in Canada's history.

In 1983 French-speaking ministers dominated the federal Cabinet—Marc Lalonde at Finance, Chrétien at Energy, and 11 other French-speaking ministers held most of the reins of power. Influential English-speaking ministers like John Turner and Donald Macdonald had left the Cabinet and had been replaced by lightweights. There were few strong English-speaking ministers left. Though the balance might shift somewhat in the future, it was unlikely that French Canada would ever again be without an equitable share of power at the federal level.

Achieving power for French-speaking politicians was one of Trudeau's stated aims when he entered federal politics in 1965. He was convinced that the only way to keep Quebec within the Canadian confederation was to give French-speaking Canadians a fair share of influence. That meant a new constitution guaranteeing language rights and a truly bilingual senior civil service. The latter would automatically produce a heavy representation of French speakers, who were more likely to be bilingual than English speakers. It was the French-speaking Canadians, after all, who had the most to gain by learning English, the dominant language of North America.

Though the number of French-speaking civil servants in senior jobs may have risen too rapidly for some English-Canadian tastes, as of 1983 the proportions were still slightly less than one might expect from total population figures. However, several divisions of federal departments had been designated as French-speaking, enabling French-speaking Canadians within the federal government to work in their mother tongue for the first time. The French presence had impressed itself on Ottawa to such a degree that no politician of any party would be able to aspire to high office without some knowledge of both the nation's official languages. It was unlikely that Canada would ever again have a prime minister who spoke only one of them.

UPI

Pierre Elliott Trudeau: public disenchantment helped end an era.

The Trudeau Legacy. To some Canadians the arrival of French power was a shock. If powerful English-speaking ministers of the past had failed to understand the aspirations and problems of French Canada, the French ministers in Trudeau's Cabinet proved equally insensitive to the needs of English Canada, particularly western Canada. Problems of culture and language between the two groups were aggravated by Trudeau's organizational, structural approach to problems that western Canadians were used to handling pragmatically. To a Jesuit-trained lawyer like Trudeau, the letter of the law is important. A western entrepreneur will do what works.

In part, those differences in attitude accounted for the problems with western Canada that Trudeau encountered in the struggle over the constitution. Provincial governments were also afraid that Trudeau's centralism would strip them of long-held powers. Critics of the constitution, with its charter of human rights (including language rights), predicted that the new law would create mass confusion and chiefly benefit the nation's lawyers. That was proving to be largely correct.

Nevertheless, the constitution, severing the last symbolic ties of authority between Britain and Canada, would be counted as Trudeau's major historic achievement. He would also be credited with making a place for French-speaking Canadians that would assure them a voice in the future affairs of their country. Controversial himself, Trudeau might have to fade from the scene before tempers could cool, but in the long term it was likely that history would attribute to him the forging of a new understanding between French and English Canadians.

Cape Verde

An independent African republic, Cape Verde is located in the Atlantic Ocean about 620 km (385 mi) off the west coast of Africa. Area: 4,033 sq km (1,557 sq mi). Pop. (1983 est.): 306,400. Cap. and largest city: Praia (pop., 1980 prelim., 37,500). Language: Portuguese. Religion (1982): 95% Roman Catholic. President in 1983, Aristide Pereira; premier, Pedro Pires.

After acting as host to a number of international summit meetings during 1982, Cape Verde in 1983 increased its reputation as an important centre for conferences. A major reason for this was the nation's policy of nonalignment. Pres. Aristide Pereira, an old-style nationalist, was trusted by moderates in Africa as well as in the West. It was significant that in November 1982 U.S. Vice-Pres. George Bush had made the first stop of his African tour in Cape Verde, while in March 1983 the U.S. appointed its first resident ambassador to the nation. President Pereira in 1983 visited a number of countries during the year, while Minister of Foreign Affairs Silvino Manuel da Luz traveled to Britain.

Premier Pedro Pires used the tenth anniversary of the assassination of Amílcar Cabral, founder of the African Party for the Independence of Guinea-Bissau and Cape Verde, as an occasion to praise Guinea-Bissau's independence struggles. Despite the presence in Cape Verde of Luis Cabral (Amílcar's brother), exiled former leader of Guinea-Bissau, relations between the two countries were normalized in July.

A new law on agrarian reform came into operation. Peasant farmers who had previously rented land and shared the produce with the owner were given the right in certain cases to own the land that they farmed. (GUY ARNOLD)

CAPE VERDE

Education. (1980–81) Primary, pupils 50,778, teachers 1,436; secondary, pupils 8,716, teachers 348; vocational, pupils 679, teachers 40; teacher training, pupils (1977–78) 198, teachers (1976–77) 32.

Finance and Trade. Monetary unit: Cape Verde escudo, with (Sept. 20, 1983) a free rate of 72.67 escudos to U.S. $1 (109.44 escudos = £1 sterling). Budget (1981 est.): revenue 944 million escudos; expenditure 1,082,000,000 escudos. Foreign trade (1980): imports 2,742,900,000 escudos; exports 170 million escudos. Import sources (1978): Portugal 33%; The Netherlands 8%; West Germany 7%; U.S. 6%; U.K. 5%; France 5%. Export destinations (1978): Portugal 42%; Angola 18%; U.K. 11%; Zaire 7%. Main exports (1978): fish 32%; salt 17%; machinery 10%; bananas 10%.

Transport. Shipping (1982): merchant vessels 100 gross tons and over 20; gross tonnage 10,793. Shipping traffic (1980): goods loaded 12,000 metric tons, unloaded 149,000 metric tons.

Central African Republic

The landlocked Central African Republic is bounded by Chad, the Sudan, the Congo, Zaire, and Cameroon. Area: 622,436 sq km (240,324 sq mi). Pop. (1983 est.): 2,512,000. Cap. and largest city: Bangui (pop., 1982 est., 387,100). Language: French (official), local dialects. Religion (1980): Protestant 50%; Roman Catholic 33.1%; tribal 12%; Muslim 3.2%; Baha'i 0.3%. Head of state and chairman of the Military Committee of National Recovery in 1983, Gen. André Kolingba.

Opposition to Gen. André Kolingba's military regime continued, supported by sympathizers in France and elsewhere. Abel Goumba, former rector of the University of Bangui, was convicted of conspiring to set up a clandestine revolutionary organization and sentenced to five years' imprisonment and ten years' loss of civil rights. On August 31, however, to mark the second anniversary of his takeover, General Kolingba pronounced an amnesty for 64 political prisoners, including Goumba.

Relations with Libya deteriorated, and the Libyan military mission was asked to leave in May, when Gervil Yambala, instrumental in effecting the rapprochement with Libya, was replaced as foreign minister by Lieut. Salle Michel. In November France warned that former emperor Jean-Bédel Bokassa planned to return from exile in Ivory Coast.

The economy continued to stagnate, and the country remained heavily dependent on foreign, mainly French, aid. (PHILIPPE DECRAENE)

CENTRAL AFRICAN REPUBLIC

Education. (1979–80) Primary, pupils 247,782, teachers (1977–78) 3,690; secondary, pupils (1980–81) 33,189, teachers (1977–78) 462; vocational, pupils 2,898, teachers (1977–78) 156; teacher training, students (1980–81) 923, teachers (1977–78) 67; higher, students 2,094, teaching staff 279.

Finance. Monetary unit: CFA franc, with (Sept. 20, 1983) a parity of CFA Fr 50 to the French franc and a free rate of CFA Fr 403 to U.S. $1 (CFA Fr 607 = £1 sterling). Budget (total; 1982 est.): revenue CFA Fr 29,995,000,000; expenditure CFA Fr 38,203,000,000.

Foreign Trade. (1981) Imports CFA Fr 40.1 billion; exports CFA Fr 31.9 billion. Import sources (1980): France 61%; Japan 7%. Export destinations (1980): France 52%; Belgium-Luxembourg 14%; Israel 8%; U.S. 5%. Main exports: timber 26%; diamonds 26%; coffee 20%; cotton 15%.

Agriculture. Production (in 000; metric tons; 1982): millet *c.* 51; corn *c.* 40; cassava *c.* 1,040; peanuts *c.* 128; bananas *c.* 84; plantains *c.* 63; coffee *c.* 18; cotton, lint *c.* 13. Livestock (in 000; 1981): cattle *c.* 1,272; pigs *c.* 135; sheep *c.* 86; goats *c.* 951; chickens *c.* 1,600.

Industry. Production (in 000): electricity (kw-hr; 1981) 65,000; diamonds (metric carats; 1980) *c.* 279; cotton fabrics (m; 1978) 2,619.

Chad

A landlocked republic of central Africa, Chad is bounded by Libya, the Sudan, the Central African Republic, Cameroon, Nigeria, and Niger. Area: 1,284,000 sq km (495,755 sq mi). Pop. (1983 est.): 4,990,000, including Africans (Saras, Tebu, Tama, Masalit) and Arabs. Cap. and largest city: N'Djamena (pop., 1979 est., 303,000). Language: French (official). Religion (1980): Muslim 44%; Christian 33%; animist 23%. President in 1983, Hissen Habré.

In 1983 the civil war in Chad took on a new, international dimension after an uneasy respite fol-

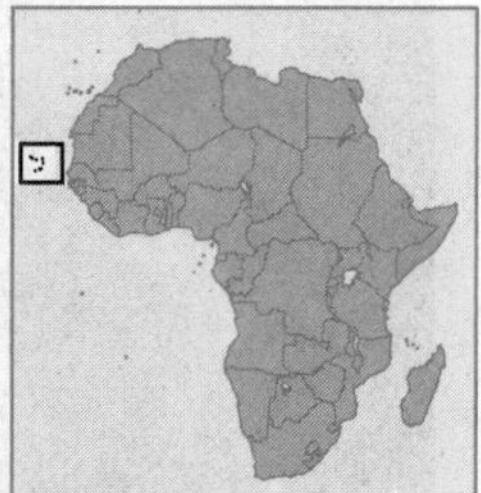
Cape Verde

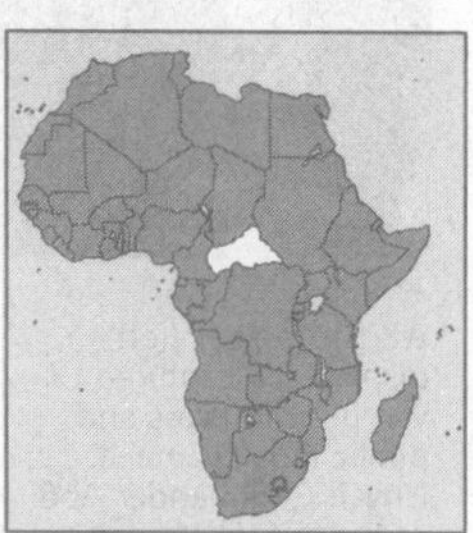
Central African Republic

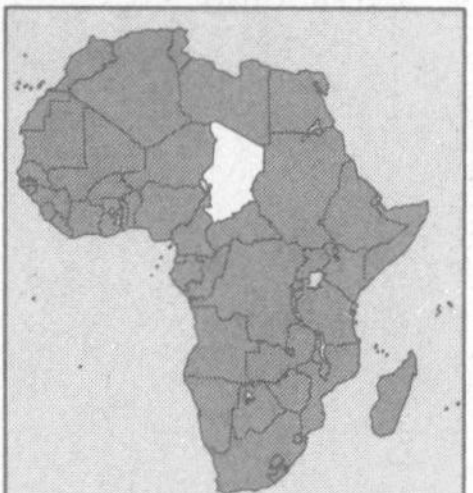
Chad

Canadian Literature: *see* Literature

Canoeing: *see* Water Sports

Catholic Church: *see* Religion

Cave Exploration: *see* Speleology

Census Data: *see* Demography; *see also the individual country articles*

Central America: *see* Latin-American Affairs; *articles on the various countries*

Ceramics: *see* Materials Sciences

P. HABANS—SYGMA

A Chad officer (left) displayed a captured Libyan pilot to press and public at N'Djamena. Libyan Commander Abd as-Salam Muhammad Charfadine was shot down in a Soviet-built Sukhoi 22 over Faya-Largeau, Chad.

lowing the June 1982 victory of Pres. Hissen Habré's forces over those of former president Goukouni Oueddei. At the end of 1983 the country was virtually partitioned; the Franco-African summit in October found no solution, and a roundtable conference of the various factions, which the Organization of African Unity proposed should be held in Addis Ababa, Eth., on December 21, was postponed until 1984.

After the strategically important northern town of Faya-Largeau fell to Goukouni's Libyan-backed forces in June, international involvement escalated rapidly. In July the U.S. began to airlift $10 million worth of military supplies to N'Djamena for Habré's forces. Meanwhile, Zaire, at U.S. Pres. Ronald Reagan's behest, dispatched a company of paratroopers—later reinforced—along with supporting aircraft. On July 30 Habré's government forces retook Faya-Largeau, but 11 days later, after intensive bombardment by Libyan aircraft, it was again in rebel hands. On August 6 the U.S. sent two AWACS (airborne warning and control systems) aircraft to Sudan for surveillance of Chadian airspace.

France, which had maintained that the conflict was a domestic affair with only indirect Libyan intervention, came under increasing U.S. pressure to intervene militarily in Chad—a French "sphere of influence." However, Pres. François Mitterrand was reluctant to do so. Nevertheless, on August 9 French Defense Minister Charles Hernu, accusing Libya of responsibility for internationalizing the conflict, announced that a contingent of "military instructors" had been ordered to Chad. By the end of August more than 3,000 French troops, with air support, had been deployed to the north and east of N'Djamena; they and the Zairian troops were faced by a Libyan-controlled "Islamic Legion" of 5,000–6,000 in the Faya-Largeau region. There was no significant military action during the remainder of the year. (PHILIPPE DECRAENE)

CHAD

Education. (1976–77) Primary, pupils 221,191, teachers 2,610; secondary, pupils 18,382, teachers 590; vocational, pupils 649, teachers (1968–69) 150; teacher training, students 549, teachers 30; higher, students (1980–81) 800, teaching staff 62.

Finance. Monetary unit: CFA franc, with (Sept. 20, 1983) a parity of CFA Fr 50 to the French franc and a free rate of CFA Fr 403 to U.S. $1 (CFA Fr 607 = £1 sterling). Budget (total; 1978 est.) balanced at CFA Fr 17,084,000,000.

Foreign Trade. (1977) Imports CFA Fr 11,255,000,000; exports CFA Fr 6,862,000,000. Import sources (1975): France 41%; Nigeria 11%; The Netherlands 7%; Cameroon 6%; U.S. 6%. Export destinations (1975): Nigeria 20%; Japan c. 14%; France 6%; Congo 5%. Main exports (1975): cotton 66%; petroleum products 8%; beef and veal 7%.

Agriculture. Production (in 000; metric tons; 1982): millet c. 580; sweet potatoes c. 37; cassava c. 190; peanuts c. 118; beans, dry c. 41; dates c. 27; mangoes c. 31; cotton, lint c. 43; meat c. 55; fish catch (1981) c. 115. Livestock (in 000; 1981): horses c. 150; asses c. 255; camels c. 420; cattle c. 3,800; sheep c. 2,300; goats c. 2,300.

Chemical Industry: *see* Industrial Review

Chemistry

Organic Chemistry. In 1983 developments in synthesis techniques continued apace while reflecting increased emphasis on chemoselectivity and new reagents, particularly organic compounds of lithium, boron, and silicon. Culminating more than a decade of work by several research groups in Japan and the U.S., Harvard University chemist Yoshito Kishi and his colleagues determined the structure of palytoxin, an extremely complicated molecule first found in species of marine coral and one of the most poisonous substances known. Palytoxin's natural origin, complex mode of action, and toxicity against malignant cells made it of considerable interest to pharmacologists. Another potential antitumour drug was synthesized by a team of 14 chemists from Colorado State University. Called (−)-maysine, the ingenious preparation of a mere three milligrams (a ten-thousandth of an ounce) was hailed as a milestone in preparative chemistry. Other medically important compounds to be synthesized were bleomycin A_2, an antitumour antibiotic; new members of the penems, a class of β-lactam antibiotics (which include the penicillins and cephalosporins); and qinghaosu, an antimalarial drug and active constituent in an ancient Chinese herbal medicine.

Among structurally interesting new compounds were [4]peristylane (1), a basket-shaped hydrocarbon, and sexipyridine (2), a ring of six pyridine molecules that had evaded construction for more than 50 years. Sexipyridine is structurally related to the crown ethers, a class of ring compounds with linked ether groups. One of the most stable, 18-crown-6 (18 atoms in the crown, of which 6 are oxygen), has an electron-rich cavity (hence the general name cavitand) in which "guest" atoms, ions, or molecules can be trapped. Synthesis of the sulfur analogue hexathia-18-crown-6 was also announced in midyear. Host-guest compounds like these can be tailored to achieve highly specific chemical interactions. Donald Cram and co-workers at the University of California at Los Angeles, in trying to copy the action of the enzyme chymotrypsin, one of nature's best catalysts, designed a model host-guest catalyst that speeded up the rate of a particular reaction more than 100,000,000,000 times.

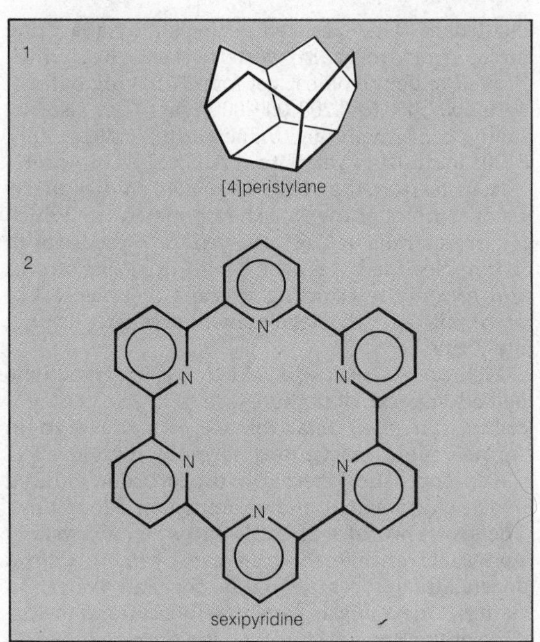

Polymer science continued to expand as a major branch of organic chemistry. Applications for electrically conducting polymers looked more promising as chemists found ways of increasing performance and stability. Interest remained high in polymers that lose all electrical resistance and become superconducting at low temperatures. Workers at the IBM Research Laboratory in San Jose, Calif., made a new kind of polymer called *bis*(ethylenedithiolo)tetrathiafulvaline, which becomes a superconductor within two degrees of absolute zero and pressures above 4,000 times atmospheric pressure. Greater attention was given to developing conducting polymer films for lightweight plastic batteries. In related work at Northwestern University, Evanston, Ill., Tobin Marks and his group combined a silicon-based conducting polymer with superstrong Kevlar aramid polymer to give flexible, conductive fibres that might eventually replace wires in electrical circuits.

Industrial production of polymers looked set for a shake-up with an announcement by Owen Webster of Du Pont of a fundamentally new process, called group transfer polymerization (GTP), for building up long molecular chains step-by-step from smaller identical subunits. Claimed as the first major advance in polymer technology since the 1950s, GTP allows an unusual degree of control over the length and nature of the final product. Applications to car finishes, protective coatings, biopolymers, and electronics were envisaged.

Inorganic Chemistry. Metal clusters—small groups of metal atoms bonded together—and their compounds remained the focus for much experimental and theoretical study, particularly in view of their potential in industrial catalysis. Richard Smalley at Rice University, Houston, Texas, experimented with a pulsed laser beam to generate a hot ionized gas of metal atoms (a metal plasma). Carried along by helium gas, the metal atoms combined to form small clusters that, on expanding into a vacuum chamber, were cooled to near absolute zero, ready for study by molecular spectroscopy. Condensation of metal clusters in an inert gas at extremely cold temperatures was expected to improve the understanding of interactions between metals and catalyst supports, thus hastening the arrival of a new breed of catalysts.

Work on organometallic clusters, which have metal atoms at the kernel of an organic shell, continued to centre on carbonyls. One of the largest metal carbonyls prepared to date, containing 38 platinum atoms, was $[Pt_{38}(CO)_{44}H_x]^{2-}$. The metal-atom framework often represents a portion of the structure of pure bulk metal and can aid understanding of bulk-metal properties.

Related work in the U.S. and West Germany uncovered processes that one day might compete with conventional technologies. M. J. Chen and coworkers at Argonne National Laboratory in Illinois developed a method, based on a variety of metal carbonyls, for converting methanol and synthesis gas (carbon monoxide and hydrogen) to ethanol. Binding an iron carbonyl cluster, $HFeCo_3(CO)_{12}$, to a silica support was Michael Röper's trick for converting synthesis gas to short-chain, mainly six-carbon, hydrocarbons. The technique, developed at Aachen Technical College in West Germany, avoided aggregation of the catalyst and loss of selectivity yet provided an alternative to the Fischer-Tropsch method, which yields a broad range of long-chain hydrocarbons requiring extensive separation.

Synthetic and natural zeolites, which are crystalline aluminosilicates having an extremely fine porous structure, found increasing applications during the year. In addition to their use as molecular sieves, ion-exchange media, and shape-selective catalysts, so helpful in the chemical industry, they had important roles in the paper and detergent industries, as feed supplements for farm animals, and as soil conditioners. In view of the importance of these aluminosilicates, it was no surprise that the chemical industry welcomed the news of a completely new class of microporous solids based on an aluminophosphate framework. Developed by Edith Flanigen, Stephen Wilson, and Brent Lok at Union Carbide Corp., this family included some 20 members by late 1982, and potential applications looked extensive.

Physical Chemistry. In October physical inorganic chemist Henry Taube of Stanford University received the 1983 Nobel Prize for Chemistry for his work on the mechanisms of electron-transfer reactions in complexes of the transition metals. Much of Taube's work relied on such methods as ultraviolet-visible spectroscopy for monitoring reaction rates. (*See* NOBEL PRIZES.)

Other techniques helped in the study of extremely rapid reactions, such as electron transfer, as well as very short-lived intermediate compounds that are produced during reactions. A method that received much attention in the past year was picosecond spectroscopy. This technique monitors the events that occur when an ultrashort pulse of laser light is absorbed by a molecule. The time scale is 10^{-12} seconds, or a millionth of a millionth of a second. Such methods were permitting

COURTESY, DR. KENNETH R. MILLER,
DIVISION OF BIOLOGY AND MEDICINE, BROWN UNIVERSITY

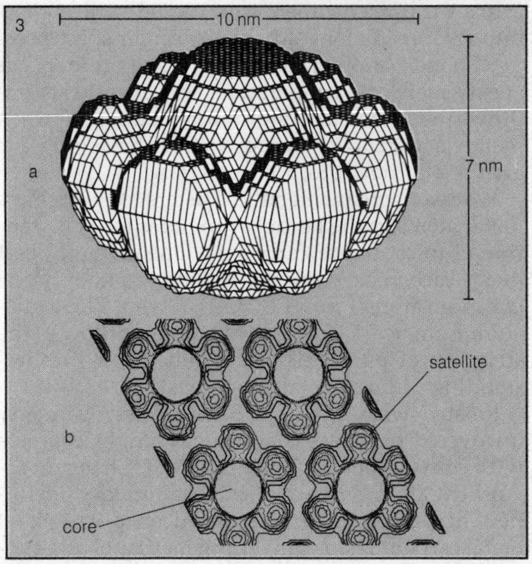

chemists to study some of the most fundamental molecular changes and to look at electronic processes in semiconductors and the mechanisms of photosynthesis and human vision.

Photosynthesis was also under study by researchers Kenneth Miller at Brown University in Rhode Island and H. Ti Tien and co-workers at Michigan State University. Miller used electron microscopy and computer graphics to reveal the fascinating three-dimensional structure of the subunits making up the photosynthetic membrane of the bacterium *Rhodopseudomonas viridis.* He suggested that the light-collecting proteins of each subunit are sited in six "satellite" groups surrounding a central core (3a), which carries out the functions of electron transport and other subsequent reactions of photosynthesis (packing of the subunits in the membrane is modeled in 3b). Tien's group synthesized a molecular complex containing both an electron-donor group resembling chlorophyll and a quinone, an electron acceptor of the type present in natural photosynthesis. When incorporated in a lipid-bilayer membrane, the complex responded to sunlight by transferring electrons from donor to acceptor in much the same way as a photosynthetic membrane. Detailed study of this model photosynthetic system could help chemists understand the primary events of an essential life process.

Analytical Chemistry. Interest in analytical chemistry remained high, as evidenced by the more than 21,700 people who visited the field's most prestigious event of the year, the Pittsburgh Conference and Exposition on Analytical Chemistry and Applied Spectroscopy, held in Atlantic City, N.J., in March. Few real innovations were offered to analysts; many were useful but largely cosmetic. Of particular interest was an X-ray fluorescence spectrometer that, because of the need to work in the dark, could be programmed to accept as many as 100 voice commands in any language, thereby improving efficiency and accuracy over keyboard typing.

Armed with a growing array of advanced techniques, chemists coped with a range of analytical challenges. They assisted geologists by analyzing zircon from rocks in western Australia, which proved to be the oldest yet found, having dates of 4,100,000,000 to 4,200,000,000 years; they also virtually confirmed that a meteorite, called ALHA 81005 for its discovery site at Allan Hills in Antarctica, came from the Moon. In related studies analysis of samples of the Murcheson meteorite, which fell in Australia in 1969, showed the presence of all five nucleotide bases, the building blocks of DNA and RNA and, according to some theories, a key prerequisite for the development of self-replicating life-forms.

Medical science was aided by analysts who helped suggest that the cause of weak calf syndrome, an often fatal disease of cattle born in spring, might be due to abnormally high levels of the adrenocortical steroid hydrocortisone induced by the cold weather and sustained for a long time. The sports world was badly hit when analysts in Venezuela uncovered drug use by more than a dozen athletes competing in the Pan American Games. One analysis gave possible clues to the decline of the Roman Empire: wine prepared in lead-lined vessels according to an ancient Roman recipe yielded a mixture with 240 to 1,000 mg of lead per litre, more than enough to cause chronic lead poisoning with its symptoms of gout and brain damage. Perhaps the analysis that could have saved the most money was that of the purported diaries of Adolf Hitler covering the years 1932 to 1945, for which the West German magazine *Stern* paid $4 million. These were shown to be fakes by scientists at the West German Federal Criminal Office, who found that the pages contained substances not used in papermaking and bookbinding until after World War II. (GORDON WILKINSON)

See also Materials Sciences; Nobel Prizes.
[122.A.6; 122.E.1.c,u; 123.C.1.d; 123.H; 214.A.4.a.x.; 312.A.2; 321.B.7; 321.C.6; 322.A; 732.D.1.a; 732.D.5.b]

Chess

World champion Anatoly Karpov (U.S.S.R.) won the World Cup television tournament at Hamburg, West Germany, in September 1982, beating Boris Spassky (U.S.S.R.) in the final. In December Viktor Korchnoi (Switz.) and Jan Timman (Neth.) tied 3–3 in a match at Hilversum, Neth. The annual tournament at Sochi, U.S.S.R., was won by Mikhail Tal (U.S.S.R.). Rafael Vaganian, who won the First League of the U.S.S.R. championship in December, also won the Hastings, England, tournament (Dec. 28, 1982–Jan. 12, 1983). The 1982 Chess Oscar went to Garry Kasparov (U.S.S.R.) with 1,021 points, ahead of Karpov 943, and Ulf Andersson (Sweden) 594; in the women's section Nona Gaprindashvili (U.S.S.R.) finished first with 793 points, followed by the current world champion, Maya Chiburdinadze (U.S.S.R.), with 683 and Pia Cramling (Sweden) with 632.

In January 1983 the Hoogoven (Neth.) tournament was won by Andersson. A tournament at Linares, Spain, in February was taken by Spassky. First prize in the Banco di Roma tournament went to Josef Pinter (Hung.). The Keres Memorial Tournament, held in Tallinn, Estonia, in February and March, ended in a tie between Tal and Vaganian.

The quarterfinals and semifinals of the candidates series of matches were played in 1983. The quarterfinals took place in March and April; Kasparov beat Aleksandr Beljavsky (U.S.S.R.) 5½–2½, Korchnoi beat Lajos Portisch (Hung.) 6–3, and Zoltan Ribli (Hung.) beat Eugenio Torre (Phil.) 6–4. The match between Vassily Smyslov (U.S.S.R.) and Robert Hübner (West Germany) ended in a 7–7 draw and was decided by a spin of the roulette wheel in favour of Smyslov. In the semifinals, played in London during November and December, Kasparov beat Korchnoi 7–4 and Smyslov beat Ribli 6½–4½. Kasparov and Smyslov were due to meet in the final in the spring of 1984, and the winner would play Karpov in the autumn of that year.

In the women's quarterfinals Nana Joseliani (U.S.S.R.) beat Liu Shilan (China) 6–3; Lidia Semyonova (U.S.S.R.) beat Margareta Muresan (Romania) 5½–4½; Irina Levitina (U.S.S.R.) beat Gaprindashvili 6–4; and Nana Alexandrija (U.S.S.R.) beat Tatiana Lemachko (Switz.) 5½–4½.

In March Bent Larsen (Den.) won the P. Frydman Memorial Tournament at Buenos Aires, Arg. The 50th Soviet championship, which had been deferred from 1982, was won by Karpov, with 9½ out of 15. Mikhai Suba (Romania) came first in a tournament at Dortmund, West Germany, in April. Predrag Nikolic (Yugos.) won a tournament at Sarajevo, Yugos., with 10½ out of 15, a point ahead of Andreas Adorjan (Hung.) and Jan Smejkal (Czech.).

In official international ratings issued in July, Karpov again led with 2,710 points, followed by Kasparov with 2,690. The next eight players were Ljubomir Ljubojevic (Yugos.) 2,645, Andersson 2,640, Hübner, Vaganian, Tal, and Lev Polugayevsky (U.S.S.R.) 2,620, Ribli 2,615, and Korchnoi 2,610.

The European team championship, held at Plovdiv, Bulg., in June, was won by the U.S.S.R. with 38 points. Yugoslavia finished second with 33 and Hungary third with 31, followed by England with 30 and The Netherlands with 29½. Jonathan Mestel won the British championship for the second time, ahead of Murray Chandler. The U.S. championship, held in Greenville, Pa., ended in a triple tie between Walter Browne, Larry Christiansen, and Roman Dzindzihasvili. The world under-16 championship, held at Bucaramanga, Colombia, in August, was won by the Soviet player Aleksey Dreyev. Also held in August, the junior world championship tournament at Belfort, France, was won by Kiril Georgiyev (Bulg.). The world youth team championship (under 26 years), held in Chicago from August 21 to September 3, was won with some ease by the powerful Soviet side with a score of 34 points out of 44. West Germany and Iceland tied for second with 28, and the U.S. finished fourth with 26½.

The strongest tournament of the year was held at Niksic, Yugos., in August and September. With the exception of Karpov, almost all the world's leading players competed; the event was a triumph for the 20-year-old Kasparov, who finished first with 11 points, ahead of Larsen with 9, Portisch and Spassky 8, Andersson and Tony Miles (U.K.) 7½, and Tal and Timman 7. (Kasparov scored 2–0 against Korchnoi.) Two days later the second "world blitz championship" was staged at Herceg Novi, Yugos. The first had been won by Bobby Fischer (U.S.); this time it was won just as decisively by Kasparov, who scored 13½ in a double-round event, ahead of Korchnoi 10½, Tal 9½, Ljubojevic 8½, and Timman 8. Karpov won the strong Tilburg (Neth.) tournament in October with a score of 7 points, half a point ahead of Ljubojevic and Portisch. (HARRY GOLOMBEK)

Played in Round Four of the Niksic International Tournament 1983

Q. P. Queen's Indian Defense

White G. Kasparov	Black L. Portisch	White G. Kasparov	Black L. Portisch
1 P–Q4	N–KB3	19 BxP ch	KxB
2 P–QB4	P–K3	20 RxB	K–N1 (c)
3 N–KB3	P–QN3	21 BxP	KxB
4 N–B3	B–N2	22 N–K5	KR–Q1
5 P–QR3 (a)	P–Q4	23 Q–N4 ch	K–B1
6 PxP	NxP	24 Q–B5 (d)	P–B3 (e)
7 P–K3	NxN	25 N–Q7 ch	RxN
8 PxN	B–K2	26 RxR	Q–B4
9 B–N5 ch	P–B3	27 Q–R7	R–B2
10 B–Q3	P–QB4	28 Q–R8 ch	K–B2
11 0–0	N–B3	29 R–Q3	N–B5
12 B–N2	R–QB1	30 KR–Q1	N–K4 (f)
13 Q–K2	0–0	31 Q–R7 ch	K–K3 (g)
14 QR–Q1	Q–B2	32 Q–N8 ch	K–B4
15 P–B4	PxP (b)	33 P–N4 ch	K–B5
16 PxP	N–R4	34–R–Q4 ch	K–B6
17 P–Q5	PxP	35 Q–N3 ch	resigns (h)
18 PxP	BxQP		

(a) Played to prevent Black from pinning his N with the KB, this is a favourite maneuver with Kasparov, which he used with effect in his match against Korchnoi in London in 1983. (b) White wins a pawn after 15 . . . , B–B3; 16.P–Q5, N–K4; 17.NxN, BxN; 18 BxP ch. (c) If 20 . . . , Q–B7; 21.R–Q2, Q–B4; 22.N–K5 cutting off the Black Queen from the Kingside defenses. (d) Better than 24.N–Q7 ch, RxN; 25 RxR, Q–K4 when Black's King is safe. (e) After 24 . . . , B–Q3; 25.Q–B6, K–N1; 26.Q–N5 ch, K–B1; 27.Q–R6 ch. K–N1; 28.N–N4, Black cannot meet the threats of N–B6 ch and R–N5 ch. (f) Obvious and bad; he should have tried 30 . . . , B–Q3 though White could then still continue the attack with 31.R–Q5. (g) Or 31 . . . K–B1; 32.R–Q8 ch, BxR; 33.RxB mate. (h) If 35 . . . , Q–B6; 36.Q–Q5 ch, K–K7; 37.Q–K4 ch.

WIDE WORLD

Pawn to Queen 4 proved the winning move in the world chess semifinal. Viktor Korchnoi (Switz.; at left) played it to open. When Garry Kasparov (U.S.S.R.) did not appear, referee George Koltanowski (right) stopped the clock and declared the match forfeited to Korchnoi. Later Kasparov agreed to play; the decision was reversed, and the semifinal was rescheduled.

Chile

Chile

A republic extending along the southern Pacific coast of South America, Chile has an area of 756,626 sq km (292,135 sq mi), not including its Antarctic claim. It is bounded by Argentina, Bolivia, and Peru. Pop. (1983 est.): 11,584,300. Cap. and largest city: Santiago (metro. pop., 1983 est., 4,085,500). Language: Spanish. Religion: predominantly Roman Catholic. President in 1983, Maj. Gen. Augusto Pinochet Ugarte.

Domestic Affairs. In 1983 Pres. Augusto Pinochet Ugarte's authority, once considered solid, was undermined by the severest economic crisis experienced since he came to power in 1973. Opposition to the regime mounted during the year, and demands for an acceleration in the timetable for a return to democracy became widespread. From May 11 a series of monthly "days of action" were held. The nature of these protests, in particular the *caceroleo*—banging of pots and pans and honking of horns—bore an uncanny resemblance to those that had preceded the downfall of Pres. Salvador Allende in 1973. Few commentators believed that President Pinochet would complete his full term of office and remain in power until 1989.

Opposition to the regime came not only from the workers, who attempted a general strike in mid-June 1983, but also from large sections of the middle class, who felt betrayed by the collapse of their country's economy. Many industrialists and farmers who previously had backed the regime wholeheartedly switched their allegiances and became eager for change. Even within the ranks of the Army discontent was alleged to be rife. In July a group of army officers issued a document calling upon soldiers "in the interests of our fatherland and with honour and responsibility . . . to make imperative a change in the helm of the government and in the supreme command of the armed forces." Certain officials in the Air Force and Navy, such as Maj. Gen. Fernando Matthei and Adm. Toribio Merino, also distanced themselves from the regime.

The government's reaction to the wave of demonstrations varied from outright repression to attempts at reconciliation. The initial hard-line approach, in which the Army was put on the streets, a curfew was imposed, and many arrests were made (including that of Rodolfo Seguel, president of the copper workers' union), served only to aggravate the conflict and to antagonize moderate elements at home and abroad. Later a more conciliatory policy was adopted; three Christian Democratic leaders who had been arrested were released, and certain minor concessions were offered in the hope of dividing the opposition. A Cabinet reshuffle on August 10 increased the number of civilian ministers from 9 to 12. Among more dramatic gestures, Pinochet announced his decision to allow more than 1,000 exiles to return and on August 26 lifted the controversial state of emergency. However, such signs of an opening, in Chilean politics produced few early results. By October talks held by the new interior minister, Sergio Onofre Jarpa Reyes, with the church and Alianza Democrática (a group of five parties including the Christian Democrats) had made little progress, and demands for a return to democracy within 18 months, reform of the constitution, and a plebiscite had not been met. Moreover, the Public Disturbance Law, which restricted public demonstrations and was due to expire in August, was extended for a further six months.

Foreign Relations. Chile's relations with the West deteriorated as a result of the continued and conspicuous violation of human rights. French Foreign Minister Claude Cheysson was the most

Student protesters were dragged away by riot police when some 2,000 demonstrators gathered in downtown Santiago.

UPI

CHILE

Education. (1981) Primary, pupils 2,139,319, teachers (1979) 66,354; secondary, pupils 392,940, teachers (1980) 24,387; vocational, pupils 161,809, teachers (1980) 4,176; higher, students 152,682, teaching staff (full time; 1975) 11,419.

Finance. Monetary unit: peso, with (Sept. 20, 1983) a free rate of 81 pesos to U.S. $1 (122 pesos = £1 sterling). Gold and other reserves (June 1983) U.S. $1,325,000,000. Budget (1980 actual): revenue 352,406,000,000 pesos; expenditure 299,175,000,000 pesos. Gross national product (1982) 1,123,110,000,000 pesos. Money supply (Dec. 1982) 81,118,000,000 pesos. Cost of living (Santiago; 1975 = 100; June 1983) 2,486.

Foreign Trade. (1982) Imports U.S. $3,528,000,000; exports U.S. $3,822,000,000. Import sources: U.S. 26%; Venezuela 7%; Brazil 7%; Japan 6%; West Germany 6%. Export destinations: U.S. 21%; Japan 11%; West Germany 11%; Brazil 8%; U.K. 5%; Italy 5%. Main exports (1980): copper 46%; chemicals 9%; timber 6%; meat and fish meal fodder 5%; wood pulp 5%; vanadium and molybdenum ores 5%.

Transport and Communications. Roads (1981) 78,025 km. Motor vehicles in use (1981): passenger c. 505,000; commercial c. 210,000. Railways: (1979) c. 10,100 km; traffic (1982) 1,537,000,000 passenger-km, freight 1,780,000,000 net ton-km. Air traffic (1982): 1,794,000,000 passenger-km; freight 139.7 million net ton-km. Shipping (1982): merchant vessels 100 gross tons and over 192; gross tonnage 494,939. Telephones (Jan. 1981) 570,000. Radio receivers (Dec. 1980) 3,250,000. Television receivers (Dec. 1980) 1,225,000.

Agriculture. Production (in 000; metric tons; 1982): wheat c. 650; barley c. 115; oats 145; corn c. 425; rice 100; potatoes 842; rapeseed c. 13; dry beans 162; tomatoes c. 158; sugar, raw value (1981) c. 250; apples c. 350; wine c. 574; wool, clean c. 12; beef and veal 178; fish catch (1981) 3,393; timber (cu m; 1981) c. 16,097. Livestock (in 000; 1982): cattle 3,800; sheep (1981) 6,185; goats c. 600; pigs 1,190; horses c. 450; poultry (1981) c. 25,000.

Industry. Production (in 000; metric tons; 1982): coal 756; crude oil (1981) 1,871; natural gas (cu m) 3,100,000; petroleum products (1981) 4,392; electricity (kw-hr) 11,822,000; iron ore (61% metal content) 6,472; pig iron 455; crude steel (ingots) 481; copper ore (metal content; 1981) 1,079; copper (1981) 762; nitrate of soda (1981) 624; manganese ore (metal content; 1981) 8.8; iodine (1981) 2.7; molybdenum concentrates (metal content; 1981) 15.4; gold (troy oz) c. 608; silver (troy oz; 1981) 11,610; cement (1981) 1,863; nitrogenous fertilizers (1981–82) 108; newsprint 123; other paper (1980) 230; fish meal (1978) 379.

WIDE WORLD

Gabriel Valdes (centre), leader of Chile's Christian Democratic Party, was released after being held incommunicado for several days in July on suspicion of organizing antiregime protests.

outspoken critic of the regime, describing President Pinochet as a curse upon the country. A petition signed by seven European countries (France, West Germany, The Netherlands, Italy, Denmark, Belgium, and the U.K.) was sent to Foreign Minister Miguel Schweitzer, expressing "live concern" at the current situation.

The U.S. also appeared to have changed its attitude toward the regime. U.S. Ambassador James Theberge held meetings with union leaders and, in a press interview in mid-July, stated that "we are convinced that democracy is the system of government wished by the great majority of Chileans and the one that best satisfies U.S. interests in the region."

The Economy. In January 1983 particular difficulties in the banking sector led to the Superintendency of Banks taking control of five banks and liquidating two others. The former laissez-faire economic policy was temporarily abandoned, and state intervention increased, as exemplified in the launching of public sector programs, domestic debt refinancing, and the adoption of an exchange rate adjusted since March on the basis of Chilean inflation. In the external sector the government had to resort to an International Monetary Fund loan of $882.5 million and the rescheduling of $3.4 billion due in 1983 and 1984.

The Chilean economic model, previously described by its advocates as a "miracle of monetarism," collapsed, taking with it several ministers of finance and economy. On Feb. 14, 1983, barely six months after his appointment and in the midst of debt renegotiation talks, Rolf Lüders was dismissed as a convenient scapegoat for the country's disastrous economic performance. His place in the Finance Ministry was taken by Carlos Cáceres, former president of the central bank. In June, in an attempt to unify the differing views within the Cabinet, Cáceres was also granted overall responsibility for the financial aspects of the ministries of economy, agriculture, public works, transport, housing, and social services.

Official forecasts for gross domestic product growth in 1983 were revised downward from 4% to a rate of between −0.5% and 1%. The rapid depreciation of the peso appeared to have had little effect in stimulating exports. By July exports were only $2.2 billion, the same level as 12 months earlier, and imports had contracted to $1.5 billion. International reserves stood at only $1.5 billion in July, down from $2.5 billion in December 1982. Bankruptcies continued to be widespread, and no real sign of industrial growth was apparent. Inflation, fueled by the rapid depreciation of the peso, had risen to 31.6% in the 12 months prior to August 1983, exceeding the government's forecast of 20% by the end of the year. Official unemployment levels for the Santiago metropolitan region stood at an average 18.6% of the work force in the period May to July and would have been far higher if the public works schemes had been included. Despite an expected rise in copper prices, the overall outlook for the Chilean economy remained gloomy, promising further unrest.

(LUCY BLACKBURN)

China

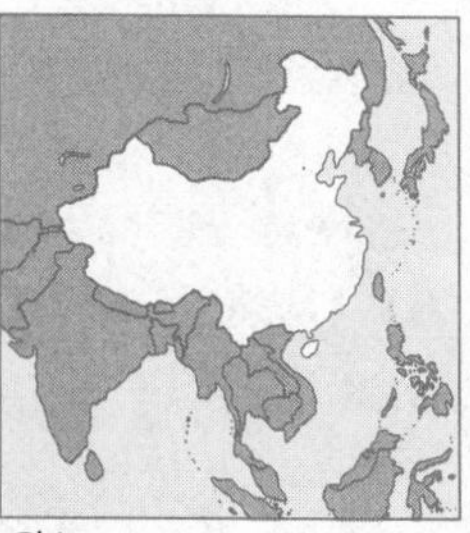

China

The most populous country in the world and the third largest in area, China is bounded by the U.S.S.R., Mongolia, North Korea, Vietnam, Laos, Burma, India, Bhutan, Nepal, Pakistan, and Afghanistan and also by the Yellow Sea and the East and South China seas. From 1949 the country has been divided into the People's Republic of China (Communist) on the mainland and on Hainan and other islands, and the Republic of China (Nationalist) on Taiwan. (*See* TAIWAN.) Area: 9,561,000 sq km (3,691,521 sq mi), including Tibet and excluding Taiwan. Population of the People's Republic (1983 est.): 1,015,410,000. Capital: Beijing (Peking; metro. pop., 1982, 9,230,700). Largest city: Shanghai (metro. pop., 1982, 11,859,700). Language: Chinese (varieties of the Beijing dialect predominate). President from June 18, 1983, Li Xiannian (Li Hsien-nien); general secretary of the Communist Party, Hu Yaobang (Hu Yao-pang); premier, Zhao Ziyang (Chao Tzu-yang).

During 1983 China continued its movement away from the radical, convulsive policies of the Maoist era and toward policies favouring economic growth and political stability. In domestic affairs, China's leadership, effectively headed by Deng Xiaoping (Teng Hsiao-p'ing), emphasized consolidation, institutionalization, and a wide-ranging agenda of political and administrative reform. In the economic sphere, efforts continued to devise a strategy favouring agricultural and light industrial production. In foreign policy, the leadership reinvigorated its efforts to achieve a stable, nonconfrontational external environment that would facilitate China's economic development objectives.

Domestic Affairs. Chinese internal politics revealed a continuing concern with institutionalizing the succession to Deng Xiaoping (now approaching 80) and guaranteeing the continuity of his policies. Deng redoubled his efforts to weed out incompetent or aged officials opposed to meaningful reform, to recruit younger, technically

UPI

China's Premier Zhao Ziyang (left) delivered the opening address to China's sixth National People's Congress. Beside him sat Li Xiannian, who was named to the long-vacant office of president.

skilled cadres committed to his reformist course, and to scrutinize the political credentials of the 40 million-strong Chinese Communist Party. The July 1 publication of Deng's *Selected Works* provided a comprehensive statement of his reformist initiatives. Deng's writings were intended to serve as the official policy guidelines for China's continuing movement away from the policies of Mao Zedong (Mao Tse-tung), who had led the CCP for more than 40 years until his death in 1976.

In mid-October the CCP Central Committee initiated a major rectification campaign directed against "serious impurities in ideology, work style, and organization" within the party. The campaign, scheduled to culminate in three years with the reregistration of all party members, was intended in part to expel those who had risen to prominence during the Cultural Revolution of the late 1960s and early 1970s, when radical leaders dominated Chinese internal politics. Many of these officials remained entrenched in their local power bases.

The rectification campaign, however, was also aimed at liberal critics of Deng's policies. In Deng's view, various intellectual and literary figures were far too critical of Chinese socialism and much too enamoured of Western forms of artistic expression. In late October, the official media launched harsh attacks on those susceptible to Western "spiritual pollutants," which quickly reached high leadership levels. Zhou Yang (Chou Yang), a long-time leading party official responsible for literary and artistic matters, admitted his ideological error in arguing that alienation was possible under socialism as well as capitalism. In mid-November the dismissal of two ranking officials of *People's Daily*, the CCP's official newspaper, portended a major clampdown on political and intellectual expression when it diverged from officially sanctioned viewpoints.

The Chinese leadership insisted that these developments did not presage widespread purges or renewed political instability, but the rectification campaign indicated that Deng's political agenda was still encountering substantial opposition. On the left and within the armed forces, there were complaints that Deng and his allies had moved too quickly in dismantling Mao's political legacy and in displacing aged leaders. The creation of a party advisory commission, however, enabled senior leadership figures to make a graceful exit from the political scene. In early March Ye Jianying (Yeh Chien-ying), at 85 one of the few surviving marshals of the Chinese Army and an intermittent critic of Deng's efforts, stepped down from the chairmanship of the Standing Committee of the National People's Congress, thereby removing a potential source of resistance within the politically powerful military establishment. Li Xiannian (Li Hsien-nien; *see* BIOGRAPHIES), a veteran economic planner, was appointed to the long-vacant position of president, providing China with its first chief of state since the late 1960s. Though the position remained largely ceremonial, Li's appoint-

China's de facto leader, Deng Xiaoping, and U.S. Secretary of State George Shultz were flanked by interpreters as they conversed in Beijing during a Shultz visit; one result of the discussion has been called a de facto, temporary coexistence with Taiwan.

UPI

WIDE WORLD

A landslide in China's Gansu Province killed more than 270 people; army troops combed the debris in search of survivors.

ment was expected to dampen his past opposition to the full range of Deng's reforms.

The Economy. Chinese economic planners continued to grapple with the extremely complicated tasks of restructuring China's economic system and defining an effective, politically acceptable strategy for economic development. The overall goal of quadrupling China's agricultural and industrial output between 1980 and the year 2000 remained the subject of substantial leadership debate. Even more important, concentration on high growth targets threatened to undermine efforts at structural reform of the economic system. At the meeting of the sixth National People's Congress in early June, Premier Zhao Ziyang (Chao Tzu-yang), one of the leading advocates of economic reform, reiterated the leadership's commitment to China's new economic strategy; for the remainder of the period of China's sixth five-year (1981–85) plan, China should adhere to a strategy of moderate economic growth (approximately 4–5% a year) and continue to maintain strict limits on capital expenditure. Zhao had to fend off pressures from advocates of higher levels of investment in major development projects, who favoured China's heavy industrial sector at the expense of agriculture and light industry, as well as from supporters of greatly increased autonomy for individual enterprises and factories.

These competing pressures were discussed extensively in October by Bo Yibo (Po Yi-po), a senior economic planner and vice-chairman of the Party Advisory Commission. According to Bo, consumption and capital construction had both "gone out of control" during 1982, outstripping the state's available resources. Most of these increases were attributable to projects undertaken by localities, provinces, departments, and enterprises, outside the scope of the five-year plan. Some industries and localities had grown at an unexpectedly rapid rate, leading to further economic imbalances and prompting fears of excessive inflation, since approximately 85% of the increases in national income had been allocated to higher wages, worker bonuses, and higher prices for agricultural and consumer products. In Bo's view, the Chinese economy needed to achieve real growth (*i.e.,* increases in productivity) rather than production for production's sake.

At the same time, the leadership's commitment to improving living standards and enhancing local autonomy were not blank checks to circumvent the central planning apparatus. Careful controls had to be maintained on both consumption and capital expenditure, lest the state lose too much of its authority over economic decision making. The policies of economic reform had contributed to significant new opportunities for individual initiative and had begun to permit the operation of market forces, especially in the countryside. The greatest challenge was to continue these new policies without undermining China's adherence to a socialist system and the central planning process. These dilemmas were most pronounced in agriculture, where the peasantry had assumed increased responsibility for production. Upon completion of their output quotas, peasants could retain any additional earnings rather than returning them to the state. These policies had resulted in dramatic increases in agricultural production and in the income of numerous peasant households. Yet some officials voiced concern that the new system was too close to capitalism.

In view of the extraordinary success of the "responsibility system" in agriculture, major efforts were undertaken during the year to introduce similar arrangements in industry and commerce. In June all state-owned industrial enterprises officially assumed responsibility for their own profits and losses. Rather than simply returning any profits to the state, factories would now be required to pay taxes on their profits, with the individual enterprises free to use their residual earnings for worker bonuses and investment decisions. In addition, enterprises were granted significant new powers to hire and fire workers on the basis of job perfor-

XINHUA NEWS AGENCY/UPI

Armand Hammer, U.S. industrialist and early trader with the Soviet Union, was welcomed to China by Qin Wencai, president of the China National Offshore Oil Corporation. Hammer's Occidental Petroleum heads a consortium to conduct oil exploration.

mance. Despite the boldness of such experiments, it remained to be seen how workable they might prove. Some advocates of reform felt that the new system would never approach its full potential unless the state also allowed significant price reforms.

Over the longer run, China still had to devote vast resources to infrastructure. The largest constraints impeding Chinese economic development included severe energy shortages in industry, a woefully underdeveloped transportation network, outmoded industrial facilities, an inefficient research and development process, and acute shortages of skilled manpower. These requirements made imperative the curtailing of nonessential capital construction. Infrastructural needs also helped assure China's continued commitment to acquiring technological assistance from abroad, especially from the U.S. and Japan. Chinese planners announced that they intended to import approximately 3,000 items of advanced technology between 1983 and 1985. To pay for increased purchases of machinery and finished industrial products from abroad (for example, high-grade steel), China had to step up its exports of petroleum, petroleum by-products, and textiles. Agreements with a number of foreign oil companies for joint exploration of China's promising offshore oil reserves underscored Beijing's long-term stake in technological and economic cooperation with the advanced capitalist states.

Foreign Affairs. China continued to define its international role as an independent major power that stood apart from alignment with any other major power. It sought simultaneous improvement of both Sino-U.S. and Sino-Soviet relations, even though Beijing continued to castigate both superpowers for their "hegemonist policies." At the same time, Chinese diplomacy was highly active among the third world nations. The Chinese recognized that a long-term peaceful international environment was essential to their plans for economic development.

Sino-U.S. relations experienced a marked upswing during 1983. During the first two years of the Reagan administration, they had deteriorated sharply, as differences over the Taiwan issue and other bilateral disputes clouded the relationship. The two sides weathered disputes over the U.S. imposition of limits on Chinese textile exports to the U.S. and over Washington's granting political asylum to a young Chinese tennis star. Both countries also maintained a lower profile on the Taiwan

Family planning centres are part of China's effort to hold down population. A typical centre in Chengdu declares state policy (growth rate below 13 per 1,000 per year) and displays contraceptive devices.

WIDE WORLD

question and continued limited U.S. military sales to the island.

Perhaps most important, the U.S. undertook a major effort to meet China's increasingly explicit requests for sophisticated technology (for example, advanced computers) with both civilian and military applications. In June the U.S. announced that China had been placed in a different category (Category V) for export of various sensitive technologies, confirming its status in U.S. eyes as a "friendly, modernizing, non-aligned country." This gave China access to a much wider range of advanced equipment. Many of the terms of technology transfer, however, remained to be resolved. In particular, the U.S. continued to insist that China not transfer any sensitive technologies to third parties. Substantial progress was also achieved on Sino-U.S. cooperation in the civilian uses of nuclear energy, potentially including sales of U.S. commercial nuclear reactors.

The improvement in U.S.-Chinese relations was amply demonstrated by a major increase in high-level leadership visits. Three members of the Cabinet visited China during 1983: Secretary of State George Shultz in February, Secretary of Commerce Malcolm Baldrige in May, and Secretary of Defense Caspar Weinberger in September. Foreign Minister Wu Xueqian (Wu Hsüeh-ch'ien) visited Washington during October. In addition, the two sides reached agreement on two major trips to occur in 1984: the long-delayed visit of Premier Zhao Ziyang to the U.S., scheduled for January, and a visit to China by Pres. Ronald Reagan in April. Minister of National Defense Zhang Aiping (Chang Ai-p'ing) also planned a visit to the U.S. during early 1984.

Irritants nevertheless continued to exist. In mid-November China complained that a Senate Foreign Relations Committee resolution calling for peaceful settlement of the Taiwan issue infringed on Chinese sovereignty and posed renewed risks to improved relations. Beijing also took issue with U.S. insistence that China's proposed entry into the Asian Development Bank not lead to the expulsion of Taiwan, one of the bank's founding members. But both states acknowledged that deteriorating relations ran the risk of damaging prospects for stability and cooperation in East Asia.

Similar concerns were reflected in Sino-Japanese relations. During the latter half of 1982 and early 1983, the Chinese had accused some Japanese leaders of promoting the return of "Japanese militarism." Despite China's reservations about the prospect of an expanded Japanese security role in East Asia, the need for close economic and political relations remained paramount. After a 30% drop in Japanese exports to China in 1982, trade accelerated again in 1983, and Japan seemed certain to remain central to China's foreign trade calculations. The November visit of party General Secretary Hu Yaobang (Hu Yao-pang) to Japan further underscored Japan's importance to China.

Sino-Soviet relations also evidenced some improvement in 1983, although no major breakthrough occurred. During March and October, the Soviet and Chinese vice-foreign ministers exchanged visits to one another's capitals. In addition, M. S. Kapitsa, the Soviet Foreign Ministry's ranking Asian expert, traveled to China in September and held discussions with Foreign Minister Wu. These consultations and discussions resulted in plans to increase Sino-Soviet trade in 1984 to more than $1.6 billion, double the 1983 figure and more than five times the figure for 1982. In comparison with China's economic ties with the West, however, this trade remained minuscule: two-way trade in 1982 between China and Japan amounted to more than $8.8 billion, and U.S.-China trade in 1982 totaled approximately $5.2 billion. The Soviet Union offered to refurbish some of China's aging industrial facilities built by the U.S.S.R. during the 1950s. Sino-Soviet cultural, scientific, and athletic exchanges also increased appreciably.

Both publicly and privately, however, the Chinese made clear that Sino-Soviet political relations would not improve significantly unless Moscow began to address what Beijing termed the "obstacles" impeding better relations: the Soviet occupa-

CHINA

Education. (1980–81) Primary, pupils 146,270,000, teachers 5,499,400; secondary, pupils 55,080,800, teachers 3,019,700; vocational, pupils 1,214,900, teachers 114,200; teacher training, students 482,100, teachers 37,600; higher, students 1,280,000, teaching staff 236,637.

Finance. Monetary unit: yuan, with (Sept. 20, 1983) a market rate of 1.99 yuan to U.S. $1 (2.99 yuan = £1 sterling). Gold and other reserves (May 1983) U.S. $13,848,000,000. Budget (1982 actual): revenue 112.4 billion yuan; expenditure 115.3 billion yuan. National income (1982) 425 billion yuan. Money supply (March 1983) 113.1 billion yuan. Cost of living (1975 = 100; 1982) 118.7.

Foreign Trade. (1982) Imports 35,770,000,000 yuan; exports 41,430,000,000 yuan. Import sources: Japan 22%; U.S. 18%; Hong Kong 12%; Canada 6%; Australia 5%. Export destinations: Hong Kong 24%; Japan 23%; U.S. 10%. Main exports: crude oil and products 22%; food 16%; textile yarn and fabrics 14%; clothing 11%; chemicals 6%.

Transport and Communications. Roads (1981) 897,000 km. Motor vehicles in use (1980): passenger c. 60,000; commercial (including buses) c. 870,000. Railways: (1981) 50,000 km; traffic (1982) 157,500,000,000 passenger-km, freight 612,000,000,000 net ton-km. Air traffic (1982): 6,000,000,000 passenger-km; freight 200 million net ton-km. Inland waterways (1981) 109,000 km. Shipping (1982): merchant vessels 100 gross tons and over 1,108; gross tonnage 8,056,849. Telephones (Dec. 1977) c. 5 million. Radio receivers (Dec. 1980) c. 55 million. Television receivers (Dec. 1980) c. 4 million.

Agriculture. Production (in 000; metric tons; 1982): rice 161,240; corn c. 61,000; wheat 68,420; barley c. 3,500; millet c. 6,500; sorghum c. 8,000; potatoes 15,000; sweet potatoes c. 120,000; soybeans 9,030; peanuts 3,916; rapeseed 5,656; sugar, raw value c. 4,500; tobacco c. 1,500; tea 397; cotton, lint c. 3,300; jute 1,060; cow's milk 1,618; beef 266; pork 12,718; mutton 524; fish catch (1981) 4,605; timber (cu m; 1981) c. 224,600. Livestock (in 000; Dec. 1982): horses c. 11,000; asses c. 7,400; cattle 76,070; buffalo c. 18,000; sheep c. 106,000; goats c. 76,000; pigs 300,780; chickens c. 870,000.

Industry. Fuel and power (in 000; metric tons; 1982): coal (including lignite) 666,000; crude oil 102,120; natural gas (cu m) 11,930,000; electricity (kw-hr) 327,700,000. Production (in 000; metric tons; 1982): iron ore (metal content) c. 37,000; pig iron 35,510; crude steel 37,160; bauxite (1981) c. 1,500; aluminum (1980) c. 360; copper (1980) c. 280; lead (1980) c. 175; zinc (1980) c. 160; magnesite (1980) c. 2,000; manganese ore (metal content; 1980) c. 300; tungsten concentrates (oxide content; 1980) c. 15; cement 95,200; sulfuric acid 8,170; plastics 1,003; fertilizers (nutrient content) nitrogenous 10,219, phosphate 2,537; soda ash 1,735; caustic soda 2,073; cotton yarn 3,354; cotton fabrics (m) 15,350,000; man-made fibres 517; paper 5,890; motor vehicles (units) 196.

tion of Afghanistan, Soviet backing for the Vietnamese occupation of Kampuchea, and the Soviet military presence in Outer Mongolia and along the Sino-Soviet border, including the deployment of more than 100 SS-20 intermediate-range missiles east of the Urals. According to Chinese officials, unless the Soviet Union seriously addressed these concerns, China would not consider a wider range of Soviet political initiatives, including elevating the consultations to the ministerial level and the signing of a document on the principles governing interstate relations.

China also was engaged in sensitive, difficult negotiations with Britain over the future of the British colony of Hong Kong. This vibrant capitalist enclave along China's southeastern coast is home to 5.1 million people, more than 98% ethnically Chinese, many of whom had fled China's Communist system. The expiration of the British lease on Hong Kong in 1997 and British expressions of concern over Hong Kong's future led to a series of high-level negotiations between London and Beijing during 1983. China repeatedly made clear its intention to recover sovereignty over the island, while also stressing that China would demonstrate due regard for the prosperity of its citizens. The prospect of China asserting political control over Hong Kong—even by indirect means—led to mounting anxieties about the island's future, reflected in the flight of capital and declining stock market and real estate values. China reiterated that, without an agreement with Britain before the fall of 1984, it would unilaterally announce its policy stand on the Hong Kong issue. (*See* DEPENDENT STATES.)

A different sort of negotiating challenge confronted Chinese officials during early May, when a Chinese airliner on a domestic flight was hijacked to South Korea. Despite the fact that China and South Korea maintain no official relations and that China is closely aligned with South Korea's long-term enemies in North Korea, the Civil Aviation Administration of China (CAAC) almost immediately proposed direct negotiations with Seoul. For the first time in more than 30 years, representatives of the two governments negotiated on an official, bilateral basis, with Shen Tu (Shen T'u), director general of the CAAC, signing a document in which both states' official names were used. As a result, the aircraft, crew, and passengers (except the hijackers) were all returned to China within a matter of days. Although China subsequently denied that the episode had any political significance, it had clearly demonstrated its concern for stability in East Asia, even if this required actions that contravened its long-standing ideological and political convictions. (JONATHAN D. POLLACK)

Colombia

Colombia

A republic in northwestern South America, Colombia is bordered by Panama, Venezuela, Brazil, Peru, and Ecuador and has coasts on both the Caribbean Sea and the Pacific Ocean. Area: 1,141,748 sq km (440,831 sq mi). Pop. (1983 est.): 27,663,000. Cap. and largest city: Bogotá (pop., 1981 est., 4,486,200). Language: Spanish. Religion: Roman Catholic (97%). President in 1983, Belisario Betancur Cuartas.

FRANCOIS LOCHON—GAMMA/LIAISON

A severe earthquake devastated much of Popayán and two neighbouring villages in southern Colombia, killing more than 250 people and collapsing the cathedral at Popayán.

In August 1983 Pres. Belisario Betancur Cuartas reshuffled his Cabinet. The changes were seen as an attempt to increase his political support for domestic economic and social measures. Six new appointments were made, among them Rodrigo Lara Bonilla as minister of justice; he was the first New Liberal to be given a Cabinet post and was renowned as a defender of human rights and a critic of right-wing murder groups.

An amnesty offered by the government to guerrillas in November 1982 met with mixed success. More than 1,000 fighters surrendered, and the leadership of the two main guerrilla movements, the Colombian Revolutionary Armed Forces (FARC) and M-19, expressed approval of the amnesty and of subsequent efforts to start peace negotiations. Nevertheless, these and other groups continued to carry out kidnappings, bank robberies, and armed actions during 1983. They were met with military counterinsurgency action and with reprisals from right-wing paramilitary groups such as MAS ("Death to Kidnappers"). The amnesty did not receive wholehearted support from the Army. During the year Otto Morales Benítez resigned as president of the Peace Commission because, he claimed, opponents of peace were attempting to undermine conciliation efforts from within the government.

M-19 suffered a major setback in April when the group's leader, Jaime Bateman Cayón, was killed in an airplane crash near the Panama border. He was replaced by Iván Marino Ospina, a lawyer.

Running parallel to President Betancur's domestic peace efforts was his prominent role in the Contadora Group, the joint initiative of Colombia, Venezuela, Panama, and Mexico to achieve peace in Central America. His positive steps in this regard, which included bringing together Richard Stone, U.S. special envoy to Central America, and Rubén Zamora of the Salvadoran Frente Democrático Revolucionario, were lauded abroad, but they prompted criticism at home that domestic issues should have priority.

On March 31 a severe earthquake struck Popayán, one of Colombia's most beautiful colonial cities. More than 150 people died in Popayán itself, while in nearby villages more died and many thousands were left homeless. Many fine historic buildings were destroyed, including the cathedral, which collapsed on top of worshipers at Holy Thursday celebrations. A second tragedy occurred in July when landslides killed 120 workers at the Guavio hydroelectric project east of Bogotá.

Growth in the gross domestic product was expected to be similar to the 1.4% rate in 1982 (2.5% in 1981). The peso appreciated against the currencies of Venezuela and Ecuador when the latter

UPI

Colombia's Pres. Belisario Betancur Cuartas (centre) provided auspices for a first meeting between Salvadoran rebels and government spokesmen, which occurred in Bogotá in August. Flanking Betancur are (from left) rebels Carlos Molina and Oscar Bonilla, and Francisco Quiñones and Bishop Marco René Revelo Contreras, representing El Salvador's government.

were devalued, and the resultant loss of competitiveness contributed to a fall in industrial production and a rise in the trade deficit. The government was unwilling to change its policy of gradual devaluation; however, the rate was speeded up to 25% against the U.S. dollar by the end of 1983 (19% in 1982). Measures were taken to stem the inflow of cheap imports and to halt the dwindling of foreign exchange reserves. Coffee exports were affected by a low quota granted by the International Coffee Organization as well as by low prices, and efforts were made to find buyers in countries that were not members of the organization in order to reduce the record level of coffee stocks. Despite difficulties in managing its current account deficit, Colombia was one of only two Latin-American countries—the other was Paraguay—not to reschedule its foreign debt. (BEN BOX)

COLOMBIA

Education. (1980) Primary, pupils 4,168,200, teachers 136,381; secondary, vocational, and teacher training, pupils 1,811,003, teachers 88,905; higher (1981), students 306,269, teaching staff 31,474.

Finance. Monetary unit: peso, with (Sept. 20, 1983) a free rate of 82.60 pesos to U.S. $1 (124.40 pesos = £1 sterling). Gold and other reserves (June 1983) U.S. $2,924,000,000. Budget (1981 est.): revenue 212,374,000,000 pesos; expenditure 247,577,000,000 pesos. Gross national product (1981) 2,011,300,000,000 pesos. Money supply (Dec. 1982) 321,710,000,000 pesos. Cost of living (Bogotá; 1975 = 100; June 1983) 570.9.

Foreign Trade. (1982) Imports U.S. $5,480,000,000; exports U.S. $3,097,000,000. Import sources (1981): U.S. 34%; Japan 10%; Venezuela 8%; West Germany 6%. Export destinations (1981): U.S. 23%; West Germany 20%; Venezuela 12%; The Netherlands 5%. Main exports (1981): coffee 49%; textiles and clothing 8%; fruit and vegetables 5%. Tourism: visitors (1981) 1,285,000; gross receipts (1980) U.S. $357 million.

Transport and Communications. Roads (1980) 74,735 km. Motor vehicles in use (1981): passenger 672,385; commercial 110,943. Railways: (1979) 2,912 km; traffic (1980) 312 million passenger-km, freight 888 million net ton-km. Air traffic (1982): 4,196,000,000 passenger-km; freight 240.8 million net ton-km. Shipping (1982): merchant vessels 100 gross tons and over 74; gross tonnage 313,904. Telephones (Jan. 1981) 1,623,100. Radio receivers (Dec. 1980) 3,010,000. Television receivers (Dec. 1980) 2,250,000.

Agriculture. Production (in 000; metric tons; 1982): corn 895; rice 1,954; sorghum 665; potatoes *c.* 2,000; cassava (1981) 2,150; soybeans 94; cabbages (1981) *c.* 462; onions *c.* 270; tomatoes *c.* 251; bananas *c.* 1,274; plantains (1981) 2,400; sugar, raw value *c.* 1,317; palm oil *c.* 95; coffee 840; tobacco 35; cotton, lint *c.* 33; beef and veal 627; timber (cu m; 1981) 43,596. Livestock (in 000; 1982): cattle 24,499; sheep 2,749; pigs *c.* 2,179; goats 657; horses (1981) *c.* 1,710; chickens 33,000.

Industry. Production (in 000; metric tons; 1982): crude oil 7,326; natural gas (cu m; 1981) 2,820,000; coal (1981) *c.* 5,300; electricity (kw-hr; 1981) 23,690,000; iron ore (metal content) 445; crude steel 215; gold (troy oz) 500; emeralds (carats; 1979) 1,228; salt (1980) 617; cement 4,573; caustic soda 15; fertilizers (nutrient content; 1981–82) nitrogenous *c.* 42, phosphate *c.* 49; paper (1980) 330.

Combat Sports

Boxing. World Boxing Council (WBC) champion Larry Holmes (U.S.) dominated the heavyweight scene in 1983, bringing his total title defenses to 17 with points wins against Lucien Rodriguez (France) and Tim Witherspoon (U.S.), a five-round knockout victory against Scott Frank (U.S.), and a first-round knockout against Marvis Frazier (U.S.). In December Holmes announced that he was giving up his WBC crown because of a dispute over the money offered him for his next title defense; in the future, he said, he would fight as champion of the newly organized International Boxing Federation. The World Boxing Association (WBA) heavyweight title changed hands. Michael Dokes (U.S.) retained the crown in a bout with former holder Mike Weaver (U.S.), but Dokes was later knocked out in ten rounds by Gerrie Coetzee (South Africa). Coetzee became the first white heavyweight to win a world championship since Ingemar Johansson (Sweden) defeated Floyd Patterson in 1959. He was only the sixth fighter not from the U.S. to win a world heavyweight title.

At cruiserweight Carlos de León (P.R.) regained the WBC championship from S. T. Gordon (U.S.) and then retained it by stopping Alvaro ("Yaqui") López in four rounds. WBA champion Ossie Ocasio

Chinese Literature: *see* Literature

Christian Church (Disciples of Christ): *see* Religion

Christianity: *see* Religion

Churches of Christ: *see* Religion

Cinema: *see* Motion Pictures

Ciskei: *see* South Africa

Clothing: *see* Fashion and Dress

Coal: *see* Energy

Coins: *see* Philately and Numismatics

Colleges: *see* Education

Colonies: *see* Dependent States

WIDE WORLD

Alberto Dávila succeeded in his fourth attempt to win the vacant bantamweight title of the World Boxing Council by knocking out Francisco (Kiko) Bejines in the 12th round at Los Angeles in September. Bejines died three days later as a result of brain injuries received in the bout.

(P.R.) remained champion by outpointing Randy Stephens (U.S.). Michael Spinks (U.S.), WBA light-heavyweight titleholder, became undisputed champion after outpointing WBC champion Dwight Muhammad Qawi (Dwight Braxton; U.S.).

The only other undisputed world champion, Marvin Hagler (U.S.), retained the middleweight championship, stopping Tony Sibson (England) in six rounds, Wilford Scypion (U.S.) in four, and outpointing Roberto Durán (Panama) over 15 rounds. Durán, the WBA junior middleweight champion and previous holder of world lightweight and welterweight titles, was bidding for an all-time record of four titles at different weights. He remained one of only seven boxers ever to have held three championships in different divisions.

Thomas Hearns (U.S.) remained unchallenged WBC junior middleweight champion. However, an upset took place when WBA champion Davey Moore (U.S.), having stopped Gary Guiden (U.S.) in four rounds, was halted in eight rounds by Durán.

Milton McCrory (U.S.) and Colin Jones (Wales), matched by the WBC to find a successor to Sugar Ray Leonard, who had retired in 1982 as undisputed welterweight champion, boxed to a draw and were rematched six months later. In the second contest McCrory received a split decision from the judges to become WBC titleholder. The WBA nominated Donald Curry (U.S.) and Jun Sok Hwang (South Korea) to decide who succeeded Leonard; Curry took the crown on points and then retained the title by knocking out Roger Stafford (U.S.) in one round. Leonard in December boxed several rounds in an exhibition fight and indicated his intention to come out of retirement.

Bruce Curry (U.S.) became WBC junior welterweight champion, outpointing Leroy Haley (U.S.) after Haley had successfully defended the title against Saoul Mamby (U.S.). Curry retained the crown with victories against Hidekazu Akai (Japan) and again over Haley. Bruce was the brother of WBA welterweight champion Donald Curry, and so for the first time brothers held world titles simultaneously. Aaron Pryor (U.S.) continued to dominate the WBA version of the championship, knocking out Kim Sang Hyun (South Korea) in three rounds and Alexis Argüello (Nicaragua) in ten. At the end of the year Pryor notified the WBA through his lawyer that he intended to retire as undefeated champion. His record stood at 33 wins in 33 contests with 31 opponents knocked out. Pryor, however, said he would remain in training and would consider offers of fights.

Argüello, loser to Pryor but winner of three world titles, announced his retirement as WBC lightweight champion. The WBC then matched Edwin Rosario (P.R.) with José Luis Ramírez (Mexi-

Table I. Boxing Champions

as of Dec. 31, 1983

Division	World	Europe	Commonwealth	Britain
Heavyweight	Larry Holmes, U.S.* Gerrie Coetzee, South Africa†	Lucien Rodriguez, France	Trevor Berbick, Canada	Dave Pearce, Wales
Cruiserweight	Carlos de León, Puerto Rico* Osvaldo Ocasio, Puerto Rico†	...	...	...
Light heavyweight	Michael Spinks, U.S.*†	Rudi Koopmans, Neth.	Lottie Mwale, Zambia	Tom Collins, England
Middleweight	Marvin Hagler, U.S.*†	Louis Acaries, France	Mark Kaylor, England	Mark Kaylor, England
Junior middleweight	Thomas Hearns, U.S.* Roberto Durán, Panama†	Herol Graham, England	Herol Graham, England	Prince Rodney, England
Welterweight	Milton McCrory, U.S.* Donald Curry, U.S.†	Gilles Elbilia, France	Colin Jones, Wales	Lloyd Honeyghan, England
Junior welterweight	Bruce Curry, U.S.* vacant†	Patrizio Oliva, Italy	Billy Famous, Nigeria	Clinton McKenzie, England
Lightweight	Edwin Rosario, Puerto Rico* Ray Mancini, U.S.†	Lucio Cusma, Italy	Claude Noel, Trinidad	George Feeney, England
Junior lightweight	Hector Camacho, U.S.* Roger Mayweather, U.S.†	Alfredo Raininger, Italy	Langton Tinago, Zimbabwe	...
Featherweight	Juan LaPorte, Puerto Rico* Eusebio Pedroza, Panama†	Barry McGuigan, N.Ire.	Azumah Nelson, Ghana	Barry McGuigan, N.Ire.
Junior featherweight	Jaime Garza, U.S.* Leonardo Cruz, Dominican Republic†	...	...	...
Bantamweight	Alberto Dávila, U.S.* Jeff Chandler, U.S.†	Walter Giorgetti, Italy	Paul Ferreri, Australia	John Feeney, England
Super flyweight	Payo Pooltarat, Thailand* Jiro Watanabe, Japan†	...	...	...
Flyweight	Frank Cedeno, Philippines* Santos Laciar, Argentina†	Antoine Montero, France	Keith Wallace, England	Kelvin Smart, Wales
Junior flyweight	Chang Jung Koo, South Korea* Lupe Madera, Mexico†	...	...	...

*World Boxing Council champion; in December Holmes relinquished his title. †World Boxing Association champion.

co) to succeed Argüello as champion. Rosario won on points. Ray Mancini (U.S.) remained WBA champion, knocking out Orlando Romero (Peru) in nine rounds.

WBC junior lightweight champion Bobby Chacon (U.S.) outpointed Cornelius Boza-Edwards (Uganda), but the WBC refused to recognize the fight as a championship contest and stripped Chacon of the title for refusing to meet Hector Camacho (U.S.). Though Chacon took the WBC to court, Camacho stopped Rafael Limón (Mexico) in five rounds and was accepted as champion. Roger Mayweather (U.S.) captured the WBA junior lightweight championship from Sam Serrano (P.R.) with an eighth-round knockout and retained it by knocking out Jorge Alvarado (Panama), also in eight, and Benedicto Villablanca (Chile) in one.

New York-based WBC featherweight champion Juan LaPorte (P.R.) held off the challenges of Rubén Castillo (U.S.) and Johnny de la Rosa (Dominican Republic) with points victories. Eusebio Pedroza (Panama) beat José Caba (Panama) and Rocky Lockridge (U.S.) to record his 17th defense of the WBA crown.

Another long-reigning champion, Wilfredo Gómez (P.R.), also defended the WBC junior featherweight title for the 17th time in six years, stopping Lupe Pintor (Mexico) in 14 rounds, and then relinquished the title to move up to the featherweight division. Jaime Garza (U.S.) and Bobby Berna (Phil.) met to decide the vacant title, and Garza succeeded Gómez as champion with a second-round knockout. Leonardo Cruz (Dominican Republic) continued as WBA titleholder with points wins against Soon Hyun Chung (South Korea) and Cleo García (Nicaragua).

Juan Pintor (Mexico), not having defended the WBC bantamweight crown since June 1982, was stripped of the title, and U.S.-based Alberto Dávila (Mexico) became official champion after knocking out Francisco Bejines (Mexico) in 12 rounds. Tragically, Bejines died in the hospital from injuries received in the fight. Jeff Chandler (U.S.) continued as WBA bantamweight champion, outpointing Gaby Canizales (U.S.) and stopping Eijiro Murata (Japan) in ten. Payo Pooltarat (Thailand) became WBC super flyweight champion by outpointing defending titleholder Rafael Orono (Venezuela). Jiro Watanabe (Japan) kept the WBA title, knocking out Luis Ibáñez (Peru), outpointing Roberto Ramírez (Mexico), and beating Kwon Soon Chung (South Korea). The WBC flyweight title changed hands three times. Eleoncio Mercedes (Dominican Republic) won it from Freddie Castillo (Mexico) and then lost it to Charlie Magri (England) in seven rounds. Magri was then knocked out in six rounds by Frank Cedeno (Phil.). Santos Laciar (Arg.) retained the WBA flyweight title with knockouts against Ramón Neri (Dominican Republic) in nine rounds, Shuichi Hozumi (Japan) in two rounds, and Shin Hee Sup (South Korea) in one round. Chang Jung Koo (South Korea) took the WBC junior flyweight crown from Hilario Zapata (Panama) in three rounds and successfully defended it, knocking out Masahura Iha (Japan) in two rounds and outpointing Germán Torres (Mexico). Lupe Madera (Mexico), having failed to take the WBA championship from Katsuo Tokashiki (Japan) with a drawn decision, captured the crown from Tokashiki in a controversial contest when awarded a technical points win after only four rounds. Madera was leading on all three judges' scorecards when the boxers' heads clashed in the fourth round and Madera was unable to continue because of injury. WBA rules state that if a contest ends with an accidental stoppage after more than three rounds, the fighter leading on points is declared the winner. Madera later settled any possible argument by outpointing the Japanese fighter in their third title clash.

In Europe Lucien Rodriguez (France) was not called upon to defend his heavyweight title, and Rudi Koopmans (Neth.) made only one light-heavyweight defense, knocking out Manfred Jazzman (West Germany) in eight rounds. Middleweight champion Louis Acaries (France) beat Pierre-Frank Winsterstein (France). There were eight new champions at lower divisions. Herol Graham (England) took over the junior middleweight title relinquished by Luigi Minchillo (Italy), stopping Luxembourg-based Clemente Tsinza (Zaire). Gilles Elbilia (France) beat Frankie Decaestecker (Belgium) to succeed Colin Jones (Wales), who had given up the welterweight title to challenge for the world crown. Patrizio Oliva (Italy) captured the junior welterweight championship from Roberto Gambini (France) and retained it against Giovanni Gimenez (Italy). Lucio Cusma (Italy) took the lightweight title from Joey Gibilisco (Italy) and held it, drawing with René Weller (West Germany) and beating Aldo Benedetto (Italy). Alfredo Raininger (Italy) won the junior lightweight crown from Roberto Castañón (Spain). The featherweight title, relinquished by Pat Cowdell (England), went to Loris Stecca (Italy), who stopped Steve Sims (Wales). Stecca then gave up the title, which was claimed by Barry McGuigan (Northern Ireland). McGuigan knocked out former champion Valerio Nati (Italy). Walter Giorgetti (Italy) took the bantamweight crown from Giuseppe Fossati (Italy). Charlie Magri (England) gave up the flyweight crown, which was taken over by Antoine Montero (France) when he stopped Mariano García (Spain).

(FRANK BUTLER)

Wrestling. The 1983 amateur wrestling world championships were held in Kiev, U.S.S.R., in the fall. Placing third or better in 19 of the 20 weights, the Soviet Union again dominated both the freestyle and Greco-Roman tournaments and established itself as the team to beat in the upcoming 1984 Olympic Games.

Table II. World Wrestling Champions, 1983

Weight class	Freestyle	Greco-Roman
48 kg (105.5 lb)	Hwan Cher Kim, N. Korea	B. Tsenov, Bulgaria
52 kg (114.5 lb)	V. Jordanov, Bulgaria	B. Pachaian, U.S.S.R.
57 kg (125.5 lb)	S. Beloglasov, U.S.S.R.	M. Ito, Japan
62 kg (136.5 lb)	V. Alekseev, U.S.S.R.	H. Lahtinen, Finland
68 kg (149.5 lb)	A. Fadzaev, U.S.S.R.	T. Sipila, Finland
74 kg (163 lb)	D. Schultz, U.S.	M. Mamiachvili, U.S.S.R.
82 kg (180.5 lb)	T. Dzgoev, U.S.S.R.	T. Aphasava, U.S.S.R.
90 kg (198 lb)	P. Naniev, U.S.S.R.	I. Kanygin, U.S.S.R.
100 kg (220 lb)	A. Khadartzev, U.S.S.R.	A. Dimitrov, Bulgaria
100+ kg	S. Khasimikov, U.S.S.R.	E. Arthuine, U.S.S.R.

STEVE POWELL/SPORTS ILLUSTRATED

Dave Schultz, of Oklahoma, was the only American winner in the 74-kilogram class at the 1983 amateur wrestling world championships, fought in Kiev, U.S.S.R. Schultz bested Taram Magomadov 11–6.

In team scoring the U.S.S.R. placed first with 56 points, followed by Bulgaria with 34, the U.S. with 22, and Japan with 16. The Soviets again showed their superiority in Greco-Roman by placing first with 56 points, followed by Mongolia with 47, Bulgaria with 39, and Spain with 28.

The University of Iowa continued its domination of the U.S. National Collegiate Athletic Association wrestling championships with its sixth straight win. Scoring 155 points, Iowa set a new NCAA scoring record, breaking its own one-year-old record of 131.75 points. Oklahoma State University finished second with 102 points, and Iowa State University was third with 94.25 points.

(MARVIN G. HESS)

Fencing. A repeat victory by Aleksandr Romankov of the Soviet Union in men's foil and the unexpected emergence of Bulgaria as a power in individual sabre were among the noteworthy developments in the world championships held in July in Vienna. The success by Romankov represented his fifth individual triumph with that weapon in ten years. Matthias Gey of West Germany and Marion Sypniewski, Poland, placed second and third in the foil.

The outcome in individual sabre provided the biggest surprise of the tournament when the Bulgarians won two medals. The achievement was registered by twin brothers, Vassil and Khristo Etropolski, who finished first and third, respectively. Sandwiched between them was Gianfranco Dallabarba of Italy. In team sabre the Soviet Union was the winner, followed by Hungary and Italy.

A significant result of the world championships was the fine overall effort by the Italians and West Germans. The Italians captured 7 of the 24 medals, while West Germany gained 5.

Elmar Borrmann, with a gold medal, led the West Germans with a triumph in individual épée. This occurred a few days after his colleagues had taken the gold in team foil. Second in the latter event was East Germany and third was Cuba. Trailing Borrmann in individual épée were Daniel Giger of Switzerland and Italy's Angelo Mazzoni. France won team épée, followed by West Germany and Italy.

Italy provided the big news in women's foil, Dorina Vaccaroni and Carola Cicconetti providing a one-two finish. Luan Juji of China placed third. In the team event—women compete only with the foil—Italy again dominated, West Germany and Hungary finishing second and third in that order.

(MICHAEL STRAUSS)

Judo. Yasuhiro Yamashita continued his dominance of judo in 1983, both inside and outside Japan, by capturing the heavyweight title of the world championships in Moscow, October 13–16, and winning the All-Japan championships on April 29 for the seventh consecutive year. His victory over Willi Wilhelm (Neth.) in the world championship was Yamashita's 189th consecutive triumph. The Japanese won three other gold medals at the world tournament: Hitoshi Saito in the open weights, Nobutoshi Hikage in the light-middleweight class, and Hidetoshi Nakanishi in the lightweight. East Germany took two gold medals, Andreas Preschel in the light-heavyweight class and Detlef Ultschin in the middleweight. The seventh gold medal went to Nikolay Solodukhin of the U.S.S.R. in the featherweight category; of the six competing 1980 Olympic champions he was the only winner. Yamashita also won the over-95-kg division of the All-Japan weight class championships for the sixth time, decisioning Saito, whom he also beat in the All-Japan championships. Japan also took six of the eight weight-class titles as well as the team championship in the International University Judo Tournament, with Saito winning the open-weights competition. France and the Soviet Union won the other two titles.

The U.S.S.R. won five gold medals at the 32nd European men's judo championships in Paris, while France took two titles and Britain one. French women won three of the four championships at stake in the women's competition in Paris, with a West German taking the fourth. Japanese men and U.S. women dominated the third Pacific Rim judo championships in Hong Kong.

Karate. Yuichi Suzuki avenged his early-round loss in 1982 to Hisao Murase by defeating Murase in the semifinals and then going on to win the 1983 All-Japan All-Styles karate championships in December at Tokyo's Nippon Budokan. Suzuki, of Kanagawa Prefecture, beat fellow *Wado-kai* specialist Seiji Nishimura in the finals with two *chudan-zuki* (middle straight punches). Takako Imamatsu, a Tokyo office worker, completely overwhelmed her opponent in the finals of the women's individual *kumite* (free-fighting) competition to capture the title.

Nishimura won the 1983 *Wado-kai* Japanese national title, while Noriko Kande won the women's *kumite* event and Meiji University took the team title. Nishimura also won the 70-kg event at the French international championships held on April 15–16 in Paris. Other winners at that 13-nation meet were Kathirim of France in the 60-kg event; R. Malone of Sweden, 65 kg; A. Spataro of Belgium, 75 kg; and T. Hill of the U.S., 80 kg.

At the fourth world amateur karate championships, held on November 15–16 in Cairo, the Japanese team won every team and individual event. Hideo Yamamoto took the men's individual *kumite* title; Yoshihara Osaka won the men's *kata* (prescribed forms) crown; and C. Moria took the women's *kata* event. Yamamoto and Osaka also won their respective specialties in the Japanese Karate Association's National Shotokan Tourney in Tokyo on September 22–23. Yasuto Onishi won the All-Japan Kokushin-kai championships on November 12–13 at the Tokyo Municipal Gymnasium in the year's only contact-karate tournament. Onishi won when the judges penalized the other finalist, Kazuhiko Ogasawara, for illegal blows to the head. Yorihisa Uchida of Kyoto Industrial University emerged victorious in the All-Japan college championships on July 3.

Sumo. The outstanding development in sumo in 1983 was the emergence of a new *yokozuna* (grand champion) in Takanosato and his challenge to the supremacy of *yokozuna* Chiyonofuji. Both won the championships of two of the six 15-day *basho* (tournaments) and both finished those events with perfect 15-0 performances. However, Takanosato won Rikishi (Sumo Wrestler) of the Year honours because his annual win-loss record of 78–12 was better than the 68–22 record chalked up by Chiyonofuji, who sat out the May tournament with a shoulder dislocation. The other two tourney titles were won by *ozeki* (champion) Kotokaze and *sekiwake* (junior champion) Hokutenyu.

Also noteworthy during the year were the premature retirement of 29-year-old *yokozuna* Wakanohana II and the lengthy inactivity of the injury-plagued third *yokozuna*, 30-year-old Kitanoumi. The latter fought in only one complete tournament during the year, tying for third with an 11–4 record in November in Fukuoka. Former college star Asashio and 23-year-old Hokutenyu were elevated to the second-highest rank of *ozeki*.

Ozeki Kotokaze took the *yusho* championship of the Hatsu *basho* in January by defeating *sekiwake* Asashio in an exciting play-off after both finished regular tournament action with identical 14–1 records. *Yokozuna* Chiyonofuji came roaring back in the Haru *basho* in March at Osaka with a perfect 15–0 victory. With his teammate Kitanoumi sidelined from March until September with a series of injuries, Hokutenyu captured the Natsu *basho* in Tokyo in May with a spectacular 14–1 mark to ensure his promotion as the fifth active *ozeki*. Both Chiyonofuji and Kitanoumi sat that one out, marking the first time in 11 years that a tournament had been held without a *yokozuna* competing. In the Nagoya *basho* in July *ozeki* Takanosato defeated *yokozuna* Chiyonofuji on the final day to capture the championship with a 14–1 record and ensure his promotion as the 59th *yokozuna*. Then in the Aki *basho* Takanosato racked up a maximum total of 15 in September, again defeating fellow-*yokozuna* Chiyonofuji on the final day in a bout that pitted two undefeated grand champions against each other for the first time since the mid-1960s. Takanosato's achievement was also the first time a *rikishi* had scored a perfect record in his *yokozuna* debut since Futabayama in 1938. In November in the Kyushu *basho*, the final tournament of the year, Chiyonofuji beat Takanosato to rack up his ninth career title.

Kendo. With the 1982 world championships behind them, Japanese kendoists settled down to their normal tournament routine in 1983, highlighted by the 31st All-Japan Men's Individual Championships in November at Tokyo's Nippon Budokan. Two policemen fought it out in the finals, with 33-year-old Kazuyoshi Higashi of the Aichi prefectural police edging 31-year-old Koji Kitamura of the Kumamoto prefectural police by a

SOVFOTO

ASAHI-SHINBUN, TOKYO

(Far left) Japan's Hitoshi Saito (left) won a gold medal in open-weights judo over Angelo Parisi of France in the world championship matches in Moscow. (Left) two *yokozuna* (grand champions) at sumo vied; Takanosato (facing camera) won top honours. During the year, he won 78 matches and lost 12 while Chiyonofuji won 68 and lost 22.

WIDE WORLD

In November Commonwealth prime ministers took a two-day break from their meetings in New Delhi, India, and went to Goa on the Arabian Sea, where Indian Prime Minister Indira Gandhi (right) greeted them.

men (helmet) strike. The All-Japan Women's Individual Championships was virtually a repeat of the 1981 tournament, as Mizue Morita of Tokyo defeated Nagako Kawazoe in the final match by a *kote* (forearm guard) strike. In the All-Japan Team Championships at the Osaka Central Gymnasium, Miyazaki Prefecture beat Osaka 3–2. Masaaki Endo won the National Police Championship on May 24 at the Budokan with *do* (side) and *men* strikes against Kenichi Ishida, the All-Japan individual champion in 1982. (ANDREW M. ADAMS)

Commonwealth of Nations

For much of 1983 member states of the Commonwealth were brought closer together by the continuing effects of their united condemnation of the Argentine invasion of the Falkland Islands/Islas Malvinas in 1982. The "Falklands factor" strengthened mutual support for self-determination and sovereign integrity. Various political upheavals, including riots in Sri Lanka, Swaziland's succession problems, and violent outbreaks in Ghana and Nigeria, were steadied under the Commonwealth umbrella.

However, events in Grenada, the Commonwealth's only Marxist state in the Caribbean, brought division. The coup by extreme left-wing elements in the government, during which Prime Minister Maurice Bishop (*see* OBITUARIES) was killed, resulted in a regime that was unacceptable to certain other nations of the Caribbean. Though under house arrest at the time, Governor-General Sir Paul Scoon, the representative of Queen Elizabeth II on Grenada, requested military aid from the Organization of Eastern Caribbean States (OECS). The six countries that supported the U.S. military intervention on October 25 were all members of the Commonwealth; Jamaica and Barbados joined four OECS members, Antigua and Barbuda, Dominica, St. Lucia, and St. Vincent and the Grenadines. The U.K., which was also approached for help, did not feel that its own military intervention was justified; it sent police and technical advisers when hostilities ended in early November. At the Commonwealth heads of government meeting in New Delhi, India (November 23–29), angry words, from some African leaders in particular, were directed toward those who had taken part in the invasion. However, the phrasing of the final communiqué was tempered by a resolve to look forward rather than make recriminations.

The New Delhi conference discussed the South West Africa/Namibia issue, deteriorating economic conditions in the third world, and the urgent problem of making the world safe for small nations without breaching the principle of nonintervention in the affairs of sovereign states. The Commonwealth considered the problems of Belize and Guyana, toward whom Guatemala and Venezuela, respectively, harboured territorial ambitions.

In September the U.K. associated state of St. Kitts-Nevis achieved independence and became the 48th member of the Commonwealth. The sultanate of Brunei, which became independent at midnight on December 31, announced its intention to take up full Commonwealth membership.

Several important regional conferences took place during the year. The South Pacific Forum held its 14th meeting in Australia in August. The Caribbean Community celebrated its tenth anniversary in July.

The effects of the 1981 Melbourne Declaration continued to be felt in terms of mutual economic support. The U.K. remained the fifth-largest aid donor in the world and the second-largest overseas investor. British overseas aid, over 70% of which went to Commonwealth countries, was officially set at a record £1,057 million for 1983–84. More than two-thirds of Britain's bilateral aid went to the Commonwealth, with India the largest recipient at £168 million. The U.K. concentrated over 40% of its aid on the poorest countries. During 1982 the Commonwealth Development Corporation made new commitments worth £103 million in 20 countries to bring total investment to £704 million in 50 countries. (MOLLY MORTIMER)

See also articles on the various political units.
[972.A.1.a]

Comecon:
see Economy, World

Commerce:
see Economy, World

Commodity Futures:
see Stock Exchanges

Common Market:
see Economy, World; European Unity

Communications:
see Industrial Review; Television and Radio

Comoros

An island state lying in the Indian Ocean off the east coast of Africa between Mozambique and Madagascar, the Comoros administratively comprise three main islands, Grande Comore (Ngazídja), Moheli (Mohali), and Anjouan (Dzouani); the fourth island of the archipelago, Mayotte, continued to be a de facto dependency of France. Area: 1,862 sq km (719 sq mi). Pop. (1982 est., excluding Mayotte): 372,000. Cap. and largest city: Moroni (pop., 1980 prelim., 20,100), on Grande Comore. Language: Comorian (which is allied to Swahili), Arabic, and French. Religion: Islam (official). President in 1983, Ahmed Abdallah; premier, Ali Mroudjae.

On May 13, 1983, the fifth anniversary of the coup that restored Pres. Ahmed Abdallah to power following his ouster in 1975, the president proclaimed an amnesty under which all those serving prison terms of less than ten years for political and criminal offenses would be released. On the same occasion, he said that he hoped to see the island of Mayotte, still under French administration, reunited with the Comoros.

In July the Democratic Front opposition movement announced through its Paris office that some 40 of its members had been arrested during elections to the three island councils on July 24. Also in July, it was reported that the Australian attorney general was to prosecute a group of alleged mercenaries on charges of plotting to overthrow a lawful government recognized by Australia, namely, that of the Comoros.

In January Anjouan, one of the three main islands of the Comoros, was devastated by a cyclone, with the loss of many lives.

(PHILIPPE DECRAENE)

COMOROS

Education. (1980–81) Primary, pupils 59,709, teachers 1,292; secondary, pupils 13,528, teachers 432; vocational, students 151, teachers 9; teacher training, students 119, teachers 8.

Finance and Trade. Monetary unit: CFA franc, with (Sept. 20, 1983) a parity of CFA Fr 50 to the French franc and a free rate of CFA Fr 403 to U.S. $1 (CFA Fr 607 = £1 sterling). Budget (1982 est.): revenue CFA Fr 1,898,000,000; expenditure CFA Fr 3,208,000,000. Foreign trade (1980): imports CFA Fr 6,147,000,000; exports CFA Fr 2,712,000,000. Import sources (1977): France 41%; Madagascar 20%; Pakistan 8%; Kenya c. 5%; China 5%. Export destinations (1977): France 65%; U.S. 21%; Madagascar 5%. Main exports (1979): vanilla 61%; essential oils 18%; cloves 12%; copra 8%.

Computers

Following a year of economic doldrums, the computer industry rebounded strongly in 1983, scoring particularly impressive gains in the sale of personal computers and semiconductors—the fingernail-sized silicon chips that process and store information in a computer system. Computers, which a decade earlier had become fixtures in the workplace, found their way into five million more U.S. homes during the year. Taking advantage of new federal tax regulations, computer makers donated to universities twice the value of computer equipment and services that they had provided in 1982; among the major donations was a $50 million gift to the Massachusetts Institute of Technology by IBM and Digital Equipment Corp.

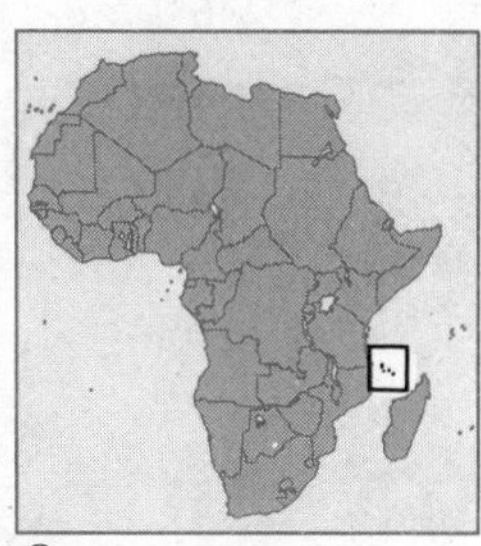

Comoros

Business. Semiconductor manufacturers such as Intel Corp., Texas Instruments, Inc., and National Semiconductor Corp., all of which had implemented severe cost-saving measures in 1982, operated at full capacity in 1983, struggling to meet the demands of chip-hungry computer makers. So great was the demand for semiconductors that temporary shortages of silicon developed by midyear. Much of the increased demand for semiconductors came from makers of personal computers, the sales of which grew nearly 50% compared with 1982. But the healthy sales figures belied serious problems within the personal computer market. Several manufacturers of home computers, including Texas Instruments, Mattel, Inc., and Atari, Inc., posted staggering quarterly losses as price competition destroyed the once-lofty profit margins. In a frenzied three-day period during the summer, Texas Instruments' stock lost one-third of its paper value while bad news on the home computer front mounted. Later, Texas Instruments withdrew entirely from the home computer market, while at the same time IBM entered the fray with its relatively expensive and powerful PCjr.

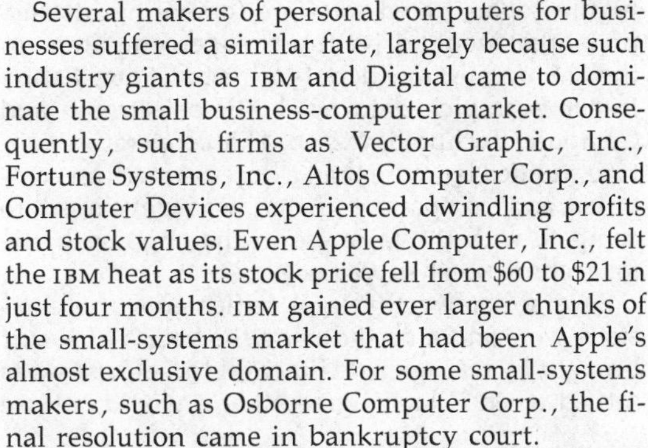

Several makers of personal computers for businesses suffered a similar fate, largely because such industry giants as IBM and Digital came to dominate the small business-computer market. Consequently, such firms as Vector Graphic, Inc., Fortune Systems, Inc., Altos Computer Corp., and Computer Devices experienced dwindling profits and stock values. Even Apple Computer, Inc., felt the IBM heat as its stock price fell from $60 to $21 in just four months. IBM gained ever larger chunks of the small-systems market that had been Apple's almost exclusive domain. For some small-systems makers, such as Osborne Computer Corp., the final resolution came in bankruptcy court.

The year was also a difficult one for Digital Equipment, the second-largest computer company, which posted its first profit decline in 13 years. Like other major manufacturers, Digital began the arduous process of internal reorganization in order to become better attuned to the demands of the marketplace. In September the firm introduced a more powerful version of its Rainbow 100 personal computer. By year's end virtually all the traditional mainframe (large computer) companies, such as NCR Corp. and Hewlett-Packard Co., had introduced personal computers to take advantage of that rapidly growing market. Coleco Industries, previously known for its video games, unveiled the Adam, which featured 80,000 bytes (one byte equals eight bits of internal memory), a high-speed tape drive for permanent storage of data, and a ten-character-per-second letter-quality printer. Production of the Adam fell short of expectations, however, and it was in short supply at Christmas.

The computer technology race between the U.S.

WIDE WORLD

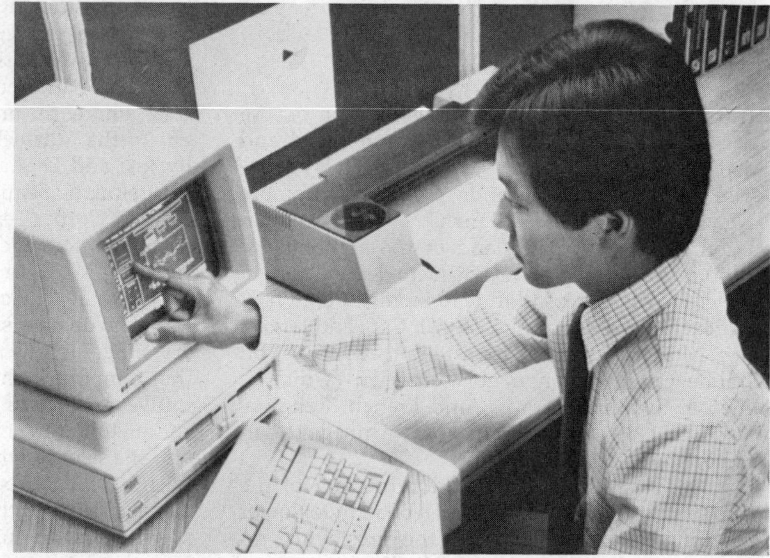

One innovation in the personal computer field allows the operator to move images from one part of the screen to another merely by touching the screen at various points.

and Japan attracted more attention than ever before in 1983 as the spirit of nationalism boosted cooperative research and development efforts in both countries. Japan's Ministry of International Trade and Industry gave its blessing to that country's fifth-generation project, the development of a supercomputer capable of processing an almost unthinkable 1,000,000,000 computations per second. Parallel efforts were under way to develop the highly sophisticated software (operating instructions) that would drive future supercomputers. In the U.S. former CIA deputy director Adm. Bobby Inman was picked to head Microelectronic and Computer Technology Corp. This cooperative venture, funded by more than a dozen American computer and component firms, was developed to compete with the Japanese in the ongoing battle for technological supremacy.

Several noteworthy legal settlements and decisions were announced during the year. A lawsuit brought by IBM against Hitachi, Ltd., of Japan was settled when Hitachi agreed that it would not use any trade secrets stolen from IBM, that it would return those secrets to IBM, and that the names, addresses, and business affiliations of all those who offered to sell IBM secrets to Hitachi would be disclosed. In a related case Mitsubishi Electric Corp. of Japan pleaded no contest to charges that it had conspired to transport trade secrets from IBM to Japan; Mitsubishi was fined $10,000. In September a U.S. federal appeals court ruled that all computer programs can be copyrighted, even when they are an integral part of a computer's circuitry.

Technology. The rapid pace of technological advances in microcircuitry continued to shrink both the size and price of computer equipment. These advances helped the personal computer to become a feature in many homes and most businesses. Meanwhile, the giant of the industry, IBM, introduced a barrage of new products that helped strengthen its position in virtually every segment of the computer market. Even IBM's strongest competitors had to rethink technology and marketing strategies as the "Armonk Giant" sought to repeat

"I did it! I broke into the Fitzsimmons' computer and got Edith's recipe for lasagna!"

the performance that made it the most profitable industrial company in the U.S. in 1983.

As computers entered the lives of increasing numbers of relatively unsophisticated users, several computer makers introduced various devices, called user-friendly interfaces, that were designed to break down the psychological barriers between man and machine. Apple Computer, Inc., unveiled its Lisa business computer, which allows users to gain access to and manipulate data files not with a keyboard but with a hand-held device called a "mouse." The HP 150, Hewlett-Packard Co.'s entry into the commercial personal computer market, included a touch-sensitive display screen that also circumvented the keyboard for many functions. And several companies, led by Texas Instruments, Inc., announced advances in voice recognition, a harbinger of the day when users would be able to interact with computers by speaking simple English-language commands.

Major advances in software technology had a definite personal computer flavour in 1983. The number of software packages written solely for personal computers grew tremendously, with more than 1,000 different commercially available programs written for the IBM personal computer alone. Also, several vendors of programs for mainframe computers announced products that would give personal computers access to a mainframe's data files, manipulate the data on the personal computer, and then return it to the mainframe or host system. However, as mainframe files became accessible to increased numbers of computer users, the existence of these kinds of software raised serious questions of data security. Security concerns were highlighted when a group of Milwaukee teenagers used their personal computers to "break into" the computer system of the Memorial Sloan-Kettering Cancer Center in New York City and more than 60 other systems, including some belonging to the U.S. Department of Defense. (*See* CRIME AND LAW ENFORCEMENT.)

The portable cordless computer made its commercial debut in 1983, fueled by a growing market for computing on demand, anywhere and everywhere. The cordless portables of Radio Shack, Nippon Electric Co., Xerox Corp., and Epson America, Inc., were variations on the theme, each one containing its own small display screen and weighing under 2½ kg (5 lb). All were designed to be carried in a briefcase and to fit conveniently on the fold-down tray of an airplane. The cordless portables run on penlight batteries or household current, have enough expandable memory capacity to store about 20 typewritten pages of text, and generally cost under $1,000. They also have varying capabilities to communicate over telephone lines with large mainframe systems.

The Japanese began test marketing versions of a 256-kilobit memory chip. (A kilobit equals 1,024 bits, a bit to a computer being the smallest increment of usable data.) The new chip, which could store four times the data of the 64-kilobit chip it would replace, was expected to intensify the already stiff competition between Japanese and U.S. semiconductor companies. In September IBM announced that it had developed an experimental version of a 512-kilobit chip. The ability to pack such tremendous memory capabilities into a box the size of a personal computer (a 256-kilobit chip can store the equivalent of about 80 double-spaced typewritten pages of text) would allow more user-friendly computer programs that respond to simple English-language commands to be operated on personal computers, because these kinds of programs require large amounts of computer memory. Trilogy, Ltd., a U.S.-based company incorporated for tax purposes in Bermuda, also unveiled a promising new chip technology that could be the heart of the next generation of large computers. The Trilogy technology would allow one silicon wafer 6 cm (2½ in) in diameter to replace as many as 100 conventional circuit chips, pointing the way to further shrinking the size of computers while increasing processing power.

Wang Laboratories, Inc., introduced a major breakthrough in office automation technology, unveiling an imaging processor that is capable of storing the contents of paper documents within a computer's memory and then re-creating precise copies of those documents. This new technology promised to take the "office of the future" a giant step closer to becoming a more paper-free environment, devoid of the now ubiquitous rows of cabinets containing paper files.

(WILLIAM E. LABERIS)

[735.D; 10/23.A.6–7]

Congo

A people's republic of equatorial Africa, the Congo is bounded by Gabon, Cameroon, the Central African Republic, Zaire, Angola, and the Atlantic Ocean. Area: 342,000 sq km (132,047 sq mi). Pop.

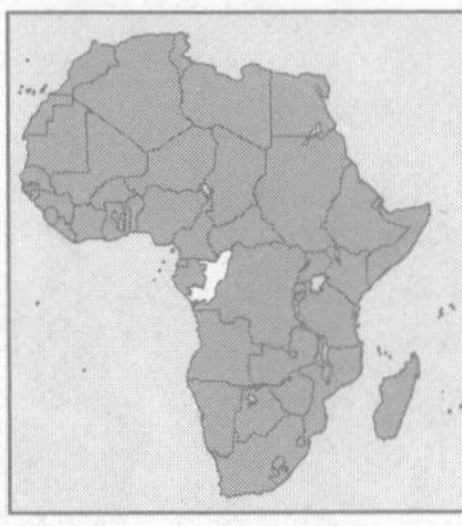

Congo

CONGO

Education. (1980–81) Primary, pupils 390,676, teachers 7,186; secondary, pupils 168,718, teachers 3,649; vocational, pupils 16,933, teachers 1,239; teacher training, students 1,934, teachers 229; higher, students (1979–80) 6,848, teaching staff 681.

Finance. Monetary unit: CFA franc, with (Sept. 20, 1983) a parity of CFA Fr 50 to the French franc and a free rate of CFA Fr 403 to U.S. $1 (CFA Fr 607 = £1 sterling). Budget (1982 est.) balanced at CFA Fr 279.9 billion.

Foreign Trade. (1982) Imports CFA Fr 265,250,000,000; exports CFA Fr 321,030,000,000. Import sources (1978): France 52%; Italy 6%; West Germany 6%; U.S. 5%. Export destinations (1978): Italy 32%; Brazil 17%; Spain 10%; France 10%; U.S. 7%; The Netherlands 5%. Main export: crude oil 97%.

Transport and Communications. Roads (all-weather; 1977) 8,246 km. Motor vehicles in use (1980): passenger c. 20,000; commercial c. 14,000. Railways (1980): c. 800 km; traffic 337 million passenger-km, freight 538 million net ton-km. Air traffic (including apportionment of Air Afrique; 1981): c. 229 million passenger-km; freight c. 22.3 million net ton-km. Telephones (Dec. 1979) 14,000. Radio receivers (Dec. 1980) 92,000. Television receivers (Dec. 1980) 3,500.

Agriculture. Production (in 000; metric tons; 1982): cassava c. 530; sweet potatoes c. 26; peanuts c. 14; sugar, raw value c. 22; bananas c. 32; plantains c. 34; coffee c. 5; cocoa c. 4; palm oil c. 9; tobacco c. 1. Livestock (in 000; 1981): cattle c. 75; sheep c. 69; goats c. 133; pigs c. 53; chickens c. 1,150.

Industry. Production (in 000; metric tons; 1980): cement 34; crude oil (1982) c. 3,980; petroleum products (1979) c. 300; lead concentrates (metal content) 0.9; zinc ore (metal content) 1.8; electricity (kw-hr; 1981) 165,000.

(1983 est.): 1,694,000, including Kongo 52%; Teke 24%; Kota 5%; Mboshi 4%; other 15%. Cap. and largest city: Brazzaville (pop., 1980 est., 422,400). Language: French (official), Kikongo, Lingala, Monokutuba, Sanga, and local Bantu dialects. Religion (1977 est.): Roman Catholic 40.5%; Protestant 9.6%; Muslim 2.9%; animist 47%. President in 1983, Col. Denis Sassou-Nguesso; premier, Col. Louis Sylvain Ngoma.

In August 1983 Congo was host to a meeting of statesmen from other African countries for the purpose of finding a solution to the conflict in Chad. In September Pres. Denis Sassou-Nguesso visited Tripoli for talks with Libyan leader Col. Muammar al-Qaddafi, with the same object in view. At the Franco-African summit at Vittel, France, in October, the president was among those who opposed any form of foreign intervention in Chad.

On the domestic political scene, despite less frequent use of Marxist terminology, there was little sign of liberalization. In April Lieut. Col. Florent Ntsiba, minister of information and telecommunications, was dismissed from his post and from the central committee of the Congolese Labour Party because of "ideological inconsistencies." Crude oil production, the mainstay of Congo's five-year (1982–86) development plan, was expected to reach 100,500 bbl a day in 1983.

(PHILIPPE DECRAENE)

Consumerism

During 1983 the UN Economic and Social Council (Ecosoc) drafted a set of "guidelines for consumer protection." Considerable interest in the document was expressed in both consumer and business circles. The International Chamber of Commerce, while insisting it was sympathetic to consumer protection, also expressed a number of reservations, particularly because no clear distinction was made between the needs of developed and less developed countries and because the pharmaceutical and food industries had been singled out for special mention. On the other hand, the International Organization of Consumers Unions (IOCU) welcomed the draft and called on its members to urge their governments to support it. The July 1983 session of Ecosoc, during which the document was first presented, did not take a ratification vote.

In December 1982 the UN General Assembly adopted a resolution to check the international trade in hazardous products. Among other things, it called for compilation of a list of goods that had been banned by member states. The vote was 132 to 1, with only the U.S. opposed.

International Cooperation. For the international networks of nongovernmental organizations (NGO's)—Health Action International (HAI), Pesticide Action Network (PAN), and the International Baby Food Action Network (IBFAN)—1983 was a year of consolidation and expansion. HAI established more contacts in Africa and in Latin America. A meeting in Lima, Peru, in April was attended by consumer and health groups and professionals from ten Latin-American countries. In its efforts to promote rational health policies, HAI presented a draft international code on pharmaceuticals at a meeting of the UN Conference on Trade and Development Committee on the Transfer of Technology in November 1982. The document contained proposals on standards for drug promotion, pricing, sales, distribution, trade, technologies, and research. Partly as a result of HAI's continued campaign against dangerous drugs, Ciba Geigy, the main manufacturer of clioquinol, which causes a crippling and blinding disease, announced withdrawal of the drug from 65 countries by the end of 1983.

PAN, founded in Malaysia in 1982, began to widen its base by holding regional seminars in the U.S., Europe, Latin America, and Africa. PAN also started to make its voice heard in the international community. At a meeting of the European Environmental Bureau in Schneverdingen, West Germany, representatives of 35 NGO's from 15 countries recommended a number of measures regarding pesticides to governments of the European Communities (EC). Meanwhile, Friends of the Earth representatives toured Europe to organize a collective response to a proposed UN Food and

Discount stores offering bargains on brand-name merchandise are proving to be serious competition for department stores.

DARRYL HEIKES/U.S. NEWS AND WORLD REPORT

Congregational Churches: see Religion

Conservation: see Environment

Construction Industry: see Engineering Projects; Industrial Review

Agriculture Organization voluntary code, which PAN felt was ineffective.

IBFAN continued to focus on monitoring violations of the World Health Organization code for the marketing of breast milk substitutes. With UNICEF support, regional meetings were held in the Philippines, India, and Peru. Although disappointed that the World Health Assembly in May 1983 postponed a scheduled review of the infant formula code, IBFAN nevertheless continued to prepare material to support its claims of violations.

IOCU increased the effectiveness of its Consumer Interpol, which existed to share information on and campaign against the trade in hazardous products. The network, linking over 50 consumer groups, sent out more than 30 alerts during its first year of operation. Consumer Interpol also produced a press pack of materials, sent to over 1,600 media outlets worldwide, that included a list of more than 100 products banned or restricted in one or more countries. It also contained information on lead in gasoline, the pesticide Galecron (which Ciba Geigy admitted to testing on Egyptian children), and the promotion of anabolic steroids as a supplementary treatment for malnutrition. In the view of medical experts, use of steroids for malnourished children could cause irreversible masculinization of girls and retard bone growth.

Regional Developments. The Bureau Européen des Unions de Consommateurs (BEUC) was pressing for a formal hazard-notification system within the EC structure while actively operating its chapter of Consumer Interpol. In a related field, it published dossiers on the use of antibiotics in animal husbandry, the herbicide 2,4,5-T (dioxin), and irradiation of food. A major priority was a campaign to urge the introduction of lead-free gasoline by 1985. (*See* ENVIRONMENT.)

In Australia greater interest in a broad spectrum of consumer protection issues was reflected in consumer publications, particularly of the Sydney-based Australian Consumers' Association. This group spearheaded formation of the Australian chapter of Consumer Interpol, incorporating HAI, PAN, and IBFAN members in the country.

Consumer education through various means remained a cornerstone of the activities of third world groups. The emphasis, however, was more on basic needs such as clean water and proper sanitation, rational health policies, housing, transport, and nutrition. Some groups, like the Consumers' Association of Penang, Malaysia, and the Citizens' Alliance for Consumer Protection in the Philippines, put much of their effort into commenting on state policies and resource management. Their rationale was that the government, as the biggest single provider of funds, could also accomplish the most if its policies served the consumer interest. (LIM SIANG JIN)

On Oct. 1, 1983, the U.S. banking industry moved another step toward deregulation when banks and savings and loan associations were allowed to set their own rates on consumer certificates of deposit longer than 31 days and on the minimum balance requirements for deposits. At the same time, penalties for early withdrawal were reduced. The new rules were designed to make the banking industry more competitive with other financial institutions.

A study conducted at the University of California and published in the *New England Journal of Medicine* found that cigarette smokers who switched to brands low in nicotine could be inhaling as much nicotine as users of regular brands. This was the latest round in the continuing debate over whether the measurements used by the Federal Trade Commission (FTC) to evaluate the amount of tar and nicotine in cigarettes were misleading. In a written comment, the FTC claimed its testing methods were meant to provide consumers with information based on laboratory tests, not the amount of tar and nicotine actually absorbed by a smoker.

A U.S. Supreme Court decision reconsidering resale price maintenance legislation was expected by mid-1984. In 1975 consumer pressure led Congress to force states to abide by a 1911 Supreme Court ruling that, under the Sherman Act, resale price maintenance was illegal. Prior to 1975, many states had legislation giving manufacturers the right to dictate retail prices. The aim was to protect traditional retail stores from being undersold by discount houses. "Lemon laws," giving consumers the right to return new automobiles that required excessive repairs, became popular in 1983. Connecticut was the first state to pass such legislation. By the end of 1983 ten other states had enacted similar laws, and ten more were considering them.

In response to the 1982 poisonings of seven persons who took cyanide-laced Tylenol capsules purchased off the shelf in retail stores, the Food and Drug Administration issued regulations requiring all over-the-counter drugs to be packaged in tamper-resistant containers by February 1983. Warning statements were also required cautioning consumers not to use the product if a problem was suspected. All over-the-counter drugs not in compliance were to be removed from the shelves by February 1984. Imported products also had to abide by the regulations, but cosmetics and food products, including vitamins, were exempt.

A unanimous appeals court decision overturned a ban imposed by the Consumer Product Safety Commission (CPSC) on urea-formaldehyde foam insulation on the grounds that the CPSC did not present sufficient evidence to support the existence of either an acute or a chronic hazard from the substance. Consumer groups claimed it caused headaches, dizziness, respiratory problems, nausea, and ear, eye, nose, and throat irritation. In early 1983 the CPSC conducted a crackdown on apparel resembling children's sleepwear that did not meet federal flammability standards. To avoid the standards, some companies had promoted and sold children's playwear as sleepwear at half the sleepwear price. The CPSC also conducted burn tests of interior furnishings, upholstery, carpets, and appliance housings. Approximately 70% of the deaths resulting from residential fires in the U.S. were caused by inhalation of toxic gases.

(EDWARD MARK MAZZE)

See also Economy, World; Industrial Review: *Advertising.*
[532.B.3; 534.H.5; 534.K]

BUYING BY MAIL

by Donald Morrison

Mail order is a mode of business familiar everywhere in the Western world. Its peaks of development have occurred more often than not in the United States. Opulence by mail is one of the latest of these. For $299 The Sharper Image in San Francisco offers a folding bicycle. For $114 Huntington Clothiers of Columbus, Ohio, advertises a men's wool sports coat in the Black Watch tartan. Land's End Direct Merchants of Dodgeville, Wis., has a hand-held wind meter ("a must for small boat sailors") for $39, and Orvis Co. of Manchester, Vt., presents a four-ounce container of belúga caviar for $115. In no case does a customer have to visit San Francisco, Columbus, Dodgeville, or Manchester to take advantage of such bonanzas.

Rapid Growth. Mail-order buying, a practice nearly as old as the mail itself, has become one of the fastest growing trends in consumer spending. Customers in the U.S. ordered an estimated $40 billion worth of clothing, food, toys, records, seed, household gadgets, and other goods through the mail in 1982, or about 7% of all consumer merchandise sold that year. Half of the books and 15% of the gardening products purchased in the U.S. are ordered through the mail. Retailing industry experts are confident that mail-order buying in the U.S. topped the $45 billion mark in 1983. It has been growing in recent years at an annual rate of 15%, some five times as fast as in-store sales.

The U.S. Postal Service estimates that the average U.S. household receives about 15 pieces of mail a week, of which 3 are third-class commercial mailings. These typically include sales pitches for magazine subscriptions, book clubs, and insurance policies, but the odds are that one of the three is a merchandise catalog. More than 5,000,000,000 copies of 4,000 different catalogs were mailed to U.S. households in 1982. That works out to an average of 40 or so per family, a number that may well have reached 50 in 1983. According to at least one study, Americans have become addicted to mail-order buying. A 1978 survey by Ogilvy & Mather Direct Response found that nearly two-thirds of all adults had bought something through the mail in the past year and that four-fifths had done so at least once in their lives.

Working Women and Gasoline Prices. The reasons behind the popularity of catalog shopping are nearly as numerous as the catalogs. Perhaps most significant is the rise of the working woman. Of the 18 million jobs added to the U.S. economy in the decade ending in 1981, two-thirds went to women. With less time left in the day for making the rounds of retail stores, working women have found it more convenient to do their shopping from catalogs. That precludes bargain hunting and other satisfactions of visiting a shopping centre or downtown commercial district. For many wage earners, however, time has become as important a consideration as money, especially in the growing number of two-income families. "Working women particularly find it's faster and easier to flip through five to ten catalogs than go to five to ten stores," said Roger Horchow, whose Horchow Collection of Dallas, Texas, mails its catalogs to some two million households a year.

In addition, the sharp rise in gasoline prices in the 1970s helped convince many people that there were better ways to buy things than by cruising the landscape in their automobiles. Some shoppers also believe that stores have lost ground to mail-order firms because of a decline in the quality of over-the-counter service; salesclerks, they complain, are not as helpful, well-informed, or even available as they once were. Many store owners would ruefully agree, pointing out that rising costs for labour and other overhead—and sharper competition from the mail-order business—have forced them to reduce their sales staffs, even as the variety and complexity of their merchandise increase.

Origins. It was a shortage not of sales staffs but of stores themselves that helped launch the mail-order business. The practice of buying goods through the mail can probably be traced to the golden age of empire, when far-flung colonists would write to London or Paris or Madrid for items not available locally. Tiffany & Co., the New York City jewelry store, claims to have the oldest continuing U.S. mail-order catalog; it was first issued in 1845.

The man generally considered to be the pioneer of the mail-order business in the U.S. is Aaron Mont-

Donald Morrison is Senior Editor of Time *magazine.*

gomery Ward, a Chicago entrepreneur who produced a catalog in 1872 that offered everything from kitchen utensils to underwear for a nation that was then mostly rural. Montgomery Ward's was followed in 1886 by Sears, Roebuck & Co., and both firms are today among the nation's leading catalog merchandisers.

Recent Developments. The growth of their businesses (Sears alone sold goods worth nearly $4 billion from its catalogs in 1982) was for years based on the relatively cheap and reliable parcel service provided by the U.S. That and much else about mail-order buying have changed dramatically. To start with, the term mail order is a bit of a misnomer, since about 90% of all goods ordered from catalogs in the U.S. are delivered by a commercial firm, United Parcel Service. In addition, more and more catalog orders are not even placed by mail but by telephone. Nearly all major catalog houses maintain toll-free numbers (area code 800), many with operators available 24 hours a day to take customer orders. Many callers now pay for their merchandise by credit card. Indeed, the rapid growth of card ownership and the expansion of toll-free telephone service are two of the major factors fueling the explosion in mail-order buying.

Perhaps the most important development for the catalog business has been the introduction of the computer. It has allowed mail-order firms to process a large volume of orders with unprecedented speed and economy. More than that, computers are now being used to keep track of a customer's buying habits, allowing a firm to produce smaller, more specialized catalogs and to send them to targeted buyers. For example, a man who buys work clothes from J. C. Penney Co. may well find a smaller, work-clothes-only catalog in his mailbox eventually. American Express Co., which sold about $30 million in catalog merchandise in 1981, uses computers to sort its customers into four categories, according to their past purchases. In 1982 the company was able to prepare four versions of its Christmas gift catalog, one for each group.

Such selective marketing has made the mail-order business much more profitable. On average, only about 2% of the people who receive a catalog actually buy something from it. By making sure that customers receive a catalog filled with just the sort of merchandise that they have purchased in the past, a firm may be able to double or triple the rate of return. In addition, specialized catalogs are cheaper to produce. Sears spent about $4 per copy to compile and mail its 1,351-page 1983 Spring-Summer book, but not much more than 50 cents for each of its 20 or so specialty catalogs.

Mail-order retailers have developed several psychological techniques to enhance sales. One is to omit any index or table of contents from a catalog; that forces even customers who know what they want to leaf through pages bursting with tantalizing photographs of other merchandise. Another, somewhat less manipulative, strategy is to allow customers to return unwanted items without restriction; that helps ease the natural reluctance to buy something that cannot be examined in person. Nearly all major catalog houses have adopted a liberal return policy. Nevertheless, Better Business Bureaus across the U.S. handled 83,691 mail-order complaints in 1982, and the U.S. Postal Service received 200,000 gripes. In many cases customers had not received the items that they ordered. The Federal Trade Commission requires that mail-order merchandise be shipped within 30 days after the order is received, unless the offer states otherwise.

"This is Grace Fairlawn, and these are her gift catalogues."

For those too timid to risk buying something they cannot see, merely looking at the catalogs can be satisfying. Top name photographers and fashion models are hired for many of the books. Some have become so lavishly illustrated that they are desirable merchandise in themselves. Regular customers of Dallas-based Neiman-Marcus Co. receive its catalog free; others pay $3 a copy.

Technology continues to transform the shape of mail-order buying. Two-way cable television already allows some customers to make purchases from their homes without benefit of catalogs. That is the case in a few towns in Ohio, New Jersey, and Florida, where such interactive systems have been introduced. In the meantime, consumers can expect to find a rising tide of glossy paper in their mailboxes, bringing them visions of a wider world that they can savour, and even buy, without leaving their living rooms.

Contract Bridge

A political cloud that hovered over the bridge world was temporarily dispersed on the eve of the major event of the year, the Bermuda Bowl contest, the official world championship, played in Stockholm in late September and October 1983. The American Contract Bridge League (ACBL) had previously awarded the 1984 Olympiad to Mexico City, a member of the ACBL. But in March 1983 it was realized that South African players would not be granted entry visas to Mexico, and therefore the ACBL moved the event to Seattle, Wash. But the question remained as to the effect South African participation might have upon other member countries. The World Bridge Federation (WBF) conducted a poll among its members on South African participation: 54 voted against, 11 for, and 15 did not reply. A second poll was more specific. "Would you play if South Africa was in the field?" To this 34 replied that they would play in Seattle, a neutral venue; 5 that they would come if it could be guaranteed that they would not have to play directly against South Africa; 21 that they would not be able to come; and, again, 15 did not reply. On the eve of a meeting of the Executive Council of the WBF the president of the South African Bridge Federation, Julius Butkow, informed the WBF that in the interests of world bridge South Africa would not play in Seattle.

The 25th Bermuda Bowl contest was in many ways the most dramatic in its history. For the first time ten teams competed. France, the European champion, and U.S. I were exempted until the semifinal stage, while the remaining eight teams played a week-long tournament to decide the other two semifinalists. Before the end U.S. II had qualified for one place. With only 16 boards remaining to play in this 448-board test, four teams were still in close contention for the other place—New Zealand, Italy, Pakistan, and Sweden. On the very last board Italy qualified by virtue of bidding a slam which their opponents had failed to reach.

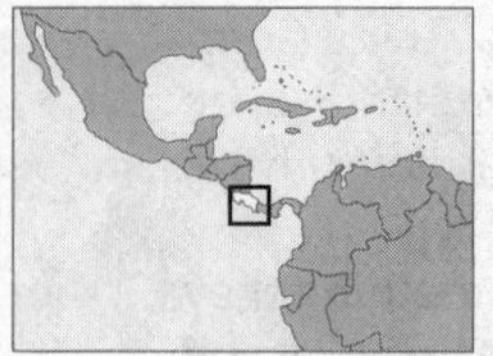
Costa Rica

The semifinal match between U.S. I and U.S. II was won by the first team of Bob Wolff and Bob Hamman, Alan Sontag and Peter Weichsel, Mike Becker and Ron Rubin, with Joe Musumeci as non-playing captain (npc). The other semifinal was a desperately close affair between France (Michel Lebel and Philippe Soulet, Henri Szwarc and Hervé Mouiel, Michel Corn and Philippe Cronier, with Pierre Schemeil as npc) and Italy (Giorgio Belladonna and Benito Garozzo, Soldano De Falco and Arturo Franco, Lorenzo Lauria and Carlo Mosca, with Filippo Palma as npc). Eventually, four boards from the end, the French bid six clubs, the Italians bid four clubs, and both made four clubs. Italy won 346–335.

In the final the lead changed hands throughout with neither team ever assuming a clear ascendancy. With three boards to play the U.S. led by two points. Board 174 is illustrated.

The last two boards, already played in the closed room, were apparently flat with safe games on both of them. On the first of them Belladonna and

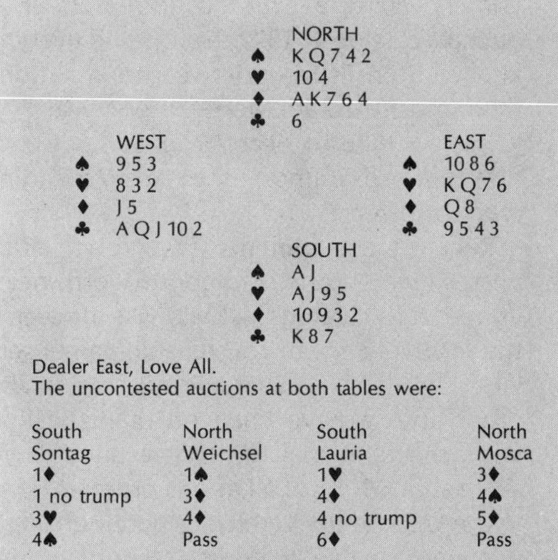
NORTH
♠ K Q 7 4 2
♥ 10 4
♦ A K 7 6 4
♣ 6

WEST
♠ 9 5 3
♥ 8 3 2
♦ J 5
♣ A Q J 10 2

EAST
♠ 10 8 6
♥ K Q 7 6
♦ Q 8
♣ 9 5 4 3

SOUTH
♠ A J
♥ A J 9 5
♦ 10 9 3 2
♣ K 8 7

Dealer East, Love All.
The uncontested auctions at both tables were:

South Sontag	North Weichsel	South Lauria	North Mosca
1♦	1♠	1♥	3♦
1 no trump	3♦	4♦	4♠
3♥	4♦	4 no trump	5♦
4♠	Pass	6♦	Pass

Sontag and Weichsel were playing Precision Club, and the opening bid of one diamond did not promise more than two cards in the suit. North did show at least 5–5 in spades and diamonds, and his partner's decision not to support diamonds directly was a close one. Mosca's response of three diamonds showed a good hand with five spades and five diamonds. The decision to support diamonds was a clear one. The slam needed a fair diamond break, and when the diamonds broke the Italians led by eight points.

Garozzo had a misunderstanding about a bid of four no trump and ended in a slam bid with two aces missing. The U.S. cashed the two aces to move three points ahead, and there were no further mishaps on the last board. The final score was the U.S. 413, Italy 408. A huge crowd was vastly entertained by the best visual presentation ever mounted at a WBF event, for which credit was due to the Swedish organizers.

(HAROLD FRANKLIN)

Costa Rica

A Central American republic, Costa Rica lies between Nicaragua and Panama and has coastlines on the Caribbean Sea and the Pacific Ocean. Area: 51,100 sq km (19,730 sq mi). Pop. (1982 est.): 2,371,500, including white and mestizo 98%. Cap. and largest city: San José (metro. pop., 1982 est., 653,400). Language: Spanish. Religion: predominantly Roman Catholic. President in 1983, Luis Alberto Monge Álvarez.

In 1983, its first full year in office, the social democratic Partido de Liberación Nacional government of Pres. Luis Alberto Monge Álvarez maintained its program of economic austerity in an attempt to combat the economic chaos that it had inherited from the previous administration. The 1982 figures revealed a 5.9% decline in gross domestic product and an inflation rate of 100%. Static growth and lower inflation were predicted for 1983.

The foreign debt totaled more than $4 billion, $1.2 billion of which was rescheduled in September. The terms included a three-year grace period during which only interest was to be paid. Also in September, the International Monetary Fund

Cost of Living: *see* Economy, World

Council for Mutual Economic Assistance: *see* Economy, World cleared a $19.5 million payment to compensate for the fall in export earnings to the end of February. The World Bank granted a structural adjustment loan worth $80 million, which was conditional on an economic policy package.

Relations with the U.S. strengthened in the face of growing political turmoil in Central America, though Costa Rica reaffirmed its stance of strict neutrality in military conflicts. Costa Rica voted in favour of the UN resolution condemning the U.S. invasion of Grenada in October. The foreign minister, Fernando Volio, resigned in protest against the vote. Volio was a strong opponent of accommodation with the Sandinista government of Nicaragua and a supporter of U.S. policy regarding that country. Costa Rica remained the only country in the region without a national army, and later in the year its civil police were confronted with increasing activity, often lethal, by rival factions from neighbouring states. Relations with Nicaragua, in particular, deteriorated in 1983.

(FIONA B. MERRY)

COSTA RICA

Education. (1981) Primary, pupils 347,708, teachers 10,536; secondary, pupils 103,579, teachers 4,263; vocational, pupils 30,229, teachers 2,056; higher, students 60,990, teaching staff (universities only) 4,382.

Finance. Monetary unit: colón, with (Sept. 20, 1983) a free rate of 43.35 colones to U.S. $1 (65.29 colones = £1 sterling). Gold and other reserves (June 1983) U.S. $328 million. Budget (1982 actual) revenue 12,948,000,000 colones; expenditure 13,884,000,000 colones. Gross national product (1981) 50,988,000,000 colones. Money supply (Nov. 1981) 10,643,000,000 colones. Cost of living (San José; 1975 = 100; April 1983) 504.6.

Foreign Trade. (1982) Imports 32,574,000,000 colones; exports 32,815,000,000 colones. Import sources (1981): U.S. 33%; Japan 10%; Mexico 9%; Venezuela 8%; Guatemala 5%; West Germany 5%. Export destinations (1980): U.S. 33%; Nicaragua 12%; West Germany 11%; Guatemala 6%; El Salvador 5%. Main exports: bananas 27%; coffee 27%; chemicals c. 7%; beef 6%. Tourism (1980): visitors 345,000; gross receipts U.S. $87 million.

Transport and Communications. Roads (1981) 28,525 km. Motor vehicles in use (1981): passenger 48,188; commercial 13,863. Railways: (1978) c. 1,003 km; traffic (main only; 1976) 99 million passenger-km, freight 16 million net ton-km. Air traffic (1981): 578 million passenger-km; freight c. 21.5 million net ton-km. Telephones (Jan. 1981) 236,100. Radio receivers (Dec. 1980) 180,000. Television receivers (Dec. 1980) 162,000.

Agriculture. Production (in 000; metric tons; 1982): sorghum c. 45; corn (1981) 88; rice (1981) 210; potatoes c. 29; bananas c. 1,150; oranges c. 77; sugar, raw value (1981) 195; coffee c. 113; cocoa c. 6; palm oil c. 24. Livestock (in 000; 1981): cattle 2,275; horses 113; pigs c. 240; chickens 5,300.

Industry. Production (in 000; metric tons; 1981): petroleum products 457; cement c. 440; nitrogenous fertilizers (1981–82) c. 42; electricity (kw-hr) 2,300,000 (93% hydroelectric).

Court Games

Handball. Naty Alvarado of Los Angeles won his fifth U.S. National Open handball title in 1983 by defeating Fred Lewis of Tucson, Ariz., 21–5, 15–21, 11–5, at the Houston (Texas) YMCA. Alvarado then teamed with Tucson's Vern Roberts to win the national doubles title, the second year in a row that Alvarado had achieved handball's version of the "Grand Slam" by winning both singles and doubles titles in the same year. Alvarado and Roberts defeated Jaime Paredes and Dennis Haynes of San Diego, Calif., 21–8, 21–20 in the finals.

In women's play Diane Harmon of Newport Beach, Calif., upset defending champion Rosemary Bellini of New York City in the finals 21–18, 21–13 to win her first U.S. National Open singles title. Allison Roberts of Cincinnati, Ohio, and Gloria Motal from Austin, Texas, won their second straight national doubles title, defeating Susan Oakleaf and LeeAnn Tyson of Austin 21–2, 21–10.

Lake Forest (Ill.) College won the national intercollegiate title at the Charlie Club, Palatine, Ill. Chris Roberts, a Lake Forest senior, won the singles championship, defeating teammate Jon Kendler in the finals 21–18, 21–14. Roberts then teamed with Steve Kiser to win the doubles title for Lake Forest. Steve Stapleton of Memphis State University won the B singles title by defeating Eric Bedard of Laval University in Quebec. Allison Roberts of Memphis State defeated Susan Oakleaf of Texas A&M 21–13, 21–17 for the women's singles crown.

Alfonso Monreal of Los Angeles gained a victory in the U.S. National Junior championship held at Fort Lauderdale, Fla. He defeated Jon Kendler of Chicago in the finals 21–8, 21–18.

(TERRY CHARLES MUCK)

Volleyball. The major emphasis in volleyball competition in 1983 was on qualifying teams for the 1984 Olympic Games. The Soviet Union men and women, as the 1980 Olympic champions, and the U.S. men and women, as the host country, were already qualified. Also already qualified were the Brazilian men, second to the Soviets in the 1982 world championship, the Cuban men, second to the Soviet men in the 1981 World Cup, and the Chinese women, the 1982 world champions. The Canadian men and the Cuban women qualified by each finishing second to the U.S. men and women in the 1983 North Central America and Caribbean Volleyball Championships. This

WIDE WORLD

In volleyball at the Pan American Games, Brazil's Fernanda Silva slammed the ball past U.S. team members Paula Weishoff (1) and Rita Crokett (3). The American women lost in the finals to Cuba.

tournament took place in Indianapolis, Ind., in July and was the first one in which the U.S. won two gold medals.

In the European Championships the Polish men qualified for the Olympics by finishing second to the Soviet Union, while the women of East Germany qualified by winning the championship. In South America already-qualified Brazil was the men's champion, followed by Argentina, with the latter thereby qualifying for the Olympics. On the women's side, Peru captured the title, followed by Brazil, but both teams gained entrance to the Olympics as the result of a decision earlier in the year by the Executive Committee of the Federation Internationale de Volleyball (FIVB). Apparently the African continent notified the FIVB that its women's champion would not participate in the 1984 Games.

Other significant world-level volleyball competitions in 1983 included the Pan American Games, played in Caracas, Venezuela, and the World University Games, played in Edmonton, Alta. In the Pan American finals the Cuban women narrowly edged the U.S. women for the gold medal while Brazil was capturing the men's gold over Cuba. At the University Games the Cuban men narrowly defeated the Canadian men for the championship, with the Brazilian women edging China.

(ALBERT M. MONACO, JR.)

Jai-Alai. Amateur jai-alai continued its tradition of holding a major tournament every four years. The next such event was scheduled for 1986, in Spain. Traditional competing countries include the United States, France, Italy, Mexico, Spain, and the Philippines.

Professional jai-alai is a major pari-mutuel betting sport in the states of Connecticut, Florida, and Rhode Island. Two of the three professional frontons in Connecticut, Berensons' Hartford Jai-Alai and Milford Jai-Alai, completed their second tournament in 1983. Remen of Hartford won the singles championship, and Zulaica-Boniquen of Milford captured the doubles award.

Other nations in which professional jai-alai continued to be played included Mexico, Indonesia, the Philippines, and Italy. There were more than a dozen professional frontons in Spain, the majority being in the Basque region. Southern France, specifically in the Basque area, sported half a dozen frontons.

Jai-alai had gone through little change in the last 50 years as to the ball and basket used. Recently, a basket made of plastic rather than reed was introduced, but acceptance was minimal. The jai-alai ball remained handmade of Virgin de Para rubber, and top professional balls cost in excess of $100.

(LOUIS S. BERENSON)

Cricket

International cricket continued to proliferate in 1982–83, culminating in the third World Cup one-day matches in England in June 1983. In the closing rounds Australia, England, West Indies, Pakistan, India, and New Zealand were joined by Sri Lanka and Zimbabwe, and in the final unfancied India beat the defending champions and favourites, West Indies, at Lord's, London, by 43 runs. The surprise of the competition was Zimbabwe's win over Australia at Trent Bridge by 13 runs, and the best individual feat was performed by K. Dev, the Indian captain and all-rounder, who made 175 not out out of a total of 266 to beat Zimbabwe at Tunbridge Wells by 31 runs.

In a short tour of India, Sri Lanka gained a draw in the only test. The captain, L. R. D. Mendis, made a century in each innings, and the Indian captain, S. M. Gavaskar (155), and S. M. Patel (114 not out) were the main contributors to India's huge first innings; in their second innings A. F. de Mel took 5 for 68.

During the early season there was a remarkable win by Pakistan under Imran Khan at home over Australia, which suffered three humiliating defeats under K. J. Hughes. For Pakistan, Zaheer Abbas, Mohsin Khan, Mansoor Akhtar, and Javed Miandad all made centuries, and leg-spinner Abdul Qadir (22 wickets) was the rear match-winner. G. M. Ritchie was the only Australian centurion, and G. F. Lawson took the most wickets.

Disappointing England under R. G. D. Willis was convincingly beaten by Australia at home 2–1. D. W. Randall and D. I. Gower were England's century-makers, with A. J. Lamb in close support, and Willis and I. T. Botham took 18 wickets each. For Australia, captained for the last time by G. S. Chappell, Hughes, Chappell, and K. C. Wessels made centuries, and fast-bowlers Lawson and J. R. Thomson and offspinner B. Young were their best bowlers. England's one win was by three runs, the last Australian pair, A. R. Border (62 not out) and Thomson (21), adding 70 for the last wicket amid intense excitement. In a concurrent series of one-day matches between Australia, England, and New Zealand, Australia beat New Zealand in the two finals by six wickets and 149 runs. England went from Australia to New Zealand and lost all three one-day games by big margins. G. M. Turner (New Zealand), with scores of 88, 94, and 34, was rivaled only by England's Gower—84, 2, and 53.

In Pakistan the home team beat India 3–0 with three draws. Zaheer, Mudassar Nazar, and Javed all averaged 100 in the six tests. Twelve centuries were made, including one from the captain, Imran, whose fast-bowling gave him 40 wickets. For India M. Amarnath and Gavaskar were in a class of their own with the bat, as was the captain, Dev, with the ball (24 wickets). Imran's superb all-round performance made the difference.

West Indies under C. H. Lloyd defeated India under Dev 2–0 with three draws. Lloyd won all five tosses and made 407 runs, including two centuries. Six others made a century each, with C. G. Greenidge, D. L. Haynes, and wicketkeeper P. L. Dujon joining Lloyd in the high-scoring draw that ended the series. Fast-bowlers A. M. E. Roberts (24) and M. D. Marshall (20) took most wickets. India's Amarnath was the outstanding batsman of the series with 598 runs, including two centuries. Dev, R. J. Shastri, and Gavaskar also reached the century mark, and Dev was a great all-rounder in taking 17 wickets, but with little support.

At home against Sri Lanka, New Zealand, un-

THE TIMES, LONDON

Batsman R. J. Hadlee of New Zealand hit 84 runs to add to his 6 wickets of July 14 in the first test of England versus New Zealand.

der G. P. Wowarth, won both tests and three one-day games. Their seam bowlers, R. J. Hadlee, B. L. Cairns, E. J. Chatfield, and M. C. Snedden, were too accurate for a Sri Lanka side short of its two best batsmen, R. Dyas and Mendis. But R. S. Madugalee showed promise, and others who played well were S. Wettimuny and the captain, D. S. de Silva. Top scorers for New Zealand were J. V. Coney and wicketkeeper W. K. Lees.

The first-ever test between Sri Lanka and Australia was won by Australia, for whom D. W. Hookes and Wessels (centuries) and G. M. Yallop (98) were main scorers. For Sri Lanka, Wettimuny, A. Ranatunge, and Mendis made 96, 90, and 74, respectively. Sri Lanka won two one-day games by two wickets and four wickets (the other two matches were rain-spoiled draws).

At home England, again under Willis, beat New Zealand, again under Howarth, 3–1. New Zealand celebrated its first win ever in England, by five wickets, thanks mainly to a superb bowling feat by medium-paced Cairns (7 for 74), fine batting by the team openers, J. G. Wright (93) and B. A. Edgar (84), and a skillful 75 by fast-bowler Hadlee. England's success was based on superior batting strength with Lamb, Gower, Botham, C. J.

Test Series Results, September 1982–August 1983

Test	Host country	and its scores	Visiting country	and its scores	Result
	India	566 for 6 wkt dec and 135 for 7 wkt	Sri Lanka	346 and 394	India won by 3 wkt
1st	Pakistan	419 for 9 wkt dec and 47 for 1 wkt	Australia	284 and 179	Pakistan won by 9 wkt
2nd	Pakistan	501 for 6 wkt dec	Australia	168 and 330	Pakistan won by an innings and 3 runs
3rd	Pakistan	467 for 7 wkt dec and 64 for 1 wkt	Australia	316 and 214	Pakistan won by 9 wkt
1st	Australia	424 for 9 wkt dec and 73 for 2 wkt	England	411 and 358	Match drawn
2nd	Australia	341 and 190 for 3 wkt	England	219 and 309	Australia won by 7 wkt
3rd	Australia	438 and 83 for 2 wkt	England	216 and 304	Australia won by 8 wkt
4th	Australia	287 and 288	England	284 and 294	England won by 3 runs
5th	Australia	314 and 382	England	237 and 314 for 7 wkt	Match drawn
1st	Pakistan	485 and 135 for 1 wkt	India	379	Match drawn
2nd	Pakistan	452	India	169 and 197	Pakistan won by an innings and 86 runs
3rd	Pakistan	652 and 10 for 0 wkt	India	372 and 286	Pakistan won by 10 wkt
4th	Pakistan	581 for 3 wkt dec	India	189 and 273	Pakistan won by an innings and 119 runs
5th	Pakistan	323	India	235 for 3 wkt	Match drawn
6th	Pakistan	420 for 6 wkt dec	India	393 for 8 wkt dec and 224 for 2 wkt	Match drawn
1st	West Indies	254 and 173 for 6 wkt	India	251 and 174	West Indies won by 4 wkt
2nd	West Indies	394	India	175 and 469 for 7 wkt	Match drawn
3rd	West Indies	470	India	284 for 3 wkt	Match drawn
4th	West Indies	486 and 1 for 0 wkt	India	209 and 277	West Indies won by 10 wkt
5th	West Indies	550	India	457 and 247 for 5 wkt dec	Match drawn
1st	New Zealand	344	Sri Lanka	144 and 175	New Zealand won by an innings and 25 runs
2nd	New Zealand	201 and 134 for 4 wkt	Sri Lanka	240 and 93	New Zealand won by 6 wkt
	Sri Lanka	271 and 205	Australia	514 for 7 wkt dec	Australia won by an innings and 38 runs
1st	England	209 and 446 for 6 dec	New Zealand	196 and 270	England won by 189 runs
2nd	England	225 and 252	New Zealand	377 and 103 for 5 wkt	New Zealand won by 5 wkt
3rd	England	326 and 211	New Zealand	191 and 219	England won by 127 runs
4th	England	420 and 297	New Zealand	207 and 345	England won by 165 runs

Tavare, and G. Fowler all making centuries, on the fast-bowling of Willis (20 wickets), and on the arrival of slow left-arm N. G. B. Cook, who in his only two tests took 17 wickets. Hadlee, 301 runs and 21 wickets, once again proved New Zealand's mainstay, with Cairns his chief bowling support.

Essex emerged as narrow winners of the English county championship after Middlesex had appeared to be the best team for most of the season. Hampshire placed third. In the one-day competitions Middlesex defeated Essex by four runs to win the Benson and Hedges final, and Somerset beat Kent by 24 runs to win the NatWest Trophy. The John Player League was won by Yorkshire. The two brilliant West Indians, V. Richards (Somerset) and Greenidge (Hampshire), were first and second in the first-class averages, and South African K. McEwan (Essex) scored the most runs, 2,176; M. W. Gatting (Middlesex) was the leading Englishman.

In Australia New South Wales won the Sheffield Shield. In South Africa Transvaal won the Currie Cup, and in the West Indies Guyana won the Shell Shield. In New Zealand Wellington won the Shell Trophy. In India, Rest of India won the Irani Trophy, North Zone the Duleep Trophy, and Karnataka the Ranji Trophy. In Pakistan Habib Bank won the Paco Pentagular (the senior trophy played for by the top teams in the Qaid-i-Azam) and Central Bank the Qaid-i-Azam Trophy.

(REX ALSTON)

Crime and Law Enforcement

Violent Crime. TERRORISM. Throughout 1983 a grim series of terrorist assaults and assassinations threatened the search for peaceful solutions to long-standing political conflicts. On April 18 a massive car bomb explosion ripped through the U.S. embassy in Beirut, Lebanon, killing at least 63 persons and injuring more than 100. Responsibility for the attack was claimed by several terrorist organizations, but it was believed to be the work of an obscure pro-Iranian group, the Islamic Jihad Organization. Iranian-backed terrorists were also suspected in the October 23 car bombings of barracks where members of the multinational peacekeeping force in Lebanon were billeted; 241 U.S. servicemen and 58 French soldiers were killed.

Another blow against moderation in the Middle East was the assassination on April 10 of Issam Sartawi (*see* OBITUARIES), a prominent official of the Palestine Liberation Organization (PLO). Sartawi and an aide were gunned down in the lobby of a hotel in Albufeira, Port., where they were attending the congress of the Socialist International. A close associate of PLO leader Yasir Arafat (*see* BIOGRAPHIES), Sartawi was one of the few PLO members who openly advocated Palestinian coexistence with the State of Israel. The Revolutionary Council of the Fatah (or Black June Group), an extremist splinter faction of the PLO led by the secretive Iraqi-based PLO renegade Abu Nidal, claimed responsibility.

Portugal was the site of a second major terrorist attack on July 27 when members of a group calling itself the Armenian Revolutionary Army stormed the Turkish embassy in Lisbon and seized the wife of the Turkish chargé d'affaires and her son. Surrounded by police, four of the terrorists detonated a bomb that killed them as well as the diplomat's wife and a policeman. The attack, the third incident of its type in Europe in less than a month, was part of a continuing campaign of revenge for massacres of Armenians earlier in the century, which the Turks refused to admit. On July 14 a Turkish diplomat was killed in Brussels, and on July 15 a

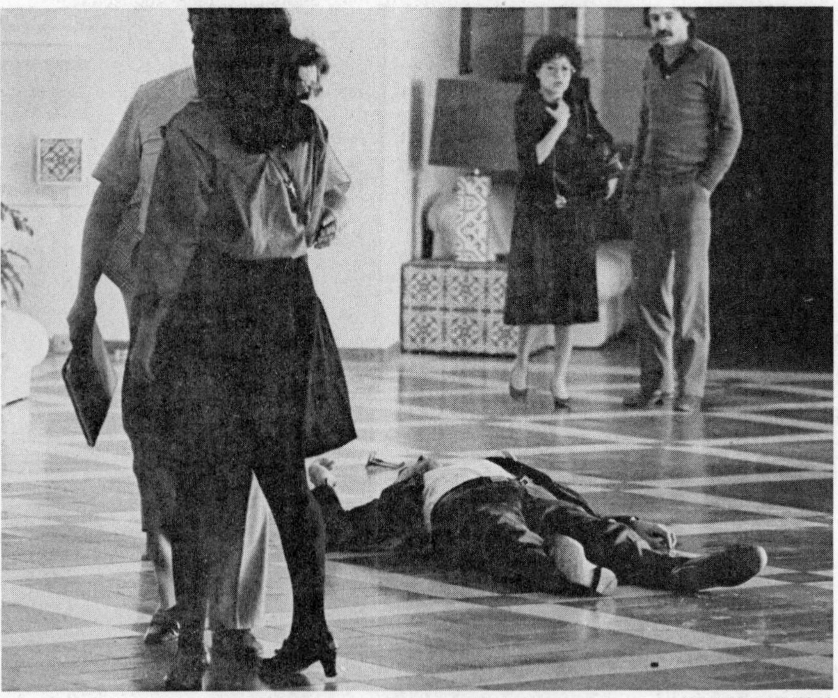

The fate of moderates befell Issam Sartawi of the PLO. A close associate of Yasir Arafat, Sartawi advocated Palestinian coexistence with Israel. He was assassinated in a Portuguese hotel lobby in April by PLO hard-liners.

AGENCIA EFE/PHOTO TRENDS

WIDE WORLD

EDITORIAL ATLANTIDA/GAMMA/LIAISON

Bolivian authorities jailed Klaus Barbie, the "Butcher of Lyon" (in his cell, at right), and extradited him (at left, under blanket) to France for trial.

bomb blast at a Turkish Airlines ticket counter at Orly Airport near Paris killed 7 and injured more than 60. A Syrian-born Armenian, Varadjian Garbidjian, was subsequently charged by French authorities with planting the bomb.

Politically motivated violence was not confined to Europe and the Middle East. On August 21 Benigno Aquino, chief political rival of Philippine Pres. Ferdinand Marcos, was shot dead moments after he stepped from a plane at Manila Airport following three years of exile in the U.S. (*See* PHILIPPINES.) On October 9 a bomb explosion in a cemetery in Rangoon, Burma, killed 4 Burmese and 17 visiting South Koreans, including 4 Cabinet ministers, who were attending a wreath-laying ceremony. South Korean Pres. Chun Doo Hwan, who escaped only because his car was delayed in traffic, blamed North Korea. (*See* KOREA.) A powerful car bomb explosion outside the headquarters of the South African Air Force in Pretoria killed at least 18 people and injured more than 200 on May 20. Responsibility for South Africa's worst terrorist incident was claimed by the banned African National Congress. (*See* SOUTH AFRICA.)

In early February Klaus Barbie (*see* BIOGRAPHIES), a long-hunted Nazi war criminal, was returned to Lyon, France, to face trial on charges of crimes against humanity. Known as the "Butcher of Lyon" for atrocities committed while he was serving as a Gestapo officer during the German occupation of France in World War II, Barbie had been living for more than 30 years in Bolivia under an assumed name.

MURDER AND OTHER VIOLENCE. In the U.S. FBI preliminary Crime Index figures for 1982 revealed a modest but encouraging decline of 4% in the number of serious crimes known to police. Of the offenses measured, only aggravated assault showed an increase, and that of only 1%. Murder and robbery each fell by 7%, and forcible rape was down 5%. A report issued by the U.S. Justice Department's Bureau of Justice Statistics, based on regular interviews with 50,000 Americans, showed that in 1982 nearly 25 million households were touched by violent crime or theft, 1% fewer than in 1981. FBI Director William H. Webster attributed this at least partially to local crime prevention programs, but criminologists had been predicting a drop in the crime rate in the mid- to late 1980s, when there would be fewer people in the crime-prone young adult age group.

Growing public concern over the incidence of family-related violence led U.S. Attorney General William French Smith to establish a special task force to study such crimes as child molestation and wife beating. It was difficult to determine the dimensions of the problem because many victims did not report the incidents to the police. Justice Department figures suggested that about 17% of all of the murders in the U.S. involved family relationships.

In June police in Montague, Texas, began a search for bodies in a number of states after Henry Lee Lucas, a former mental patient convicted of killing his mother, claimed that since 1975 he had slain as many as 100 women across the country. The Lucas case, as well as other highly publicized mass murders in recent years, pointed up the poor record of police in apprehending repetitive killers. In an attempt to improve police performance in this area of criminal investigation, a Justice Department-funded study began in August with the aim of developing a national centre for the collection and analysis of information about repetitive killers and other serious violent offenders. Between 1966 and 1981, so-called serial murders had risen from 6% to about 18% of all known homicides in the U.S.

A royal commission convened by the provincial government of Ontario began an inquiry in April

STEVE POWELL/SPORTS ILLUSTRATED

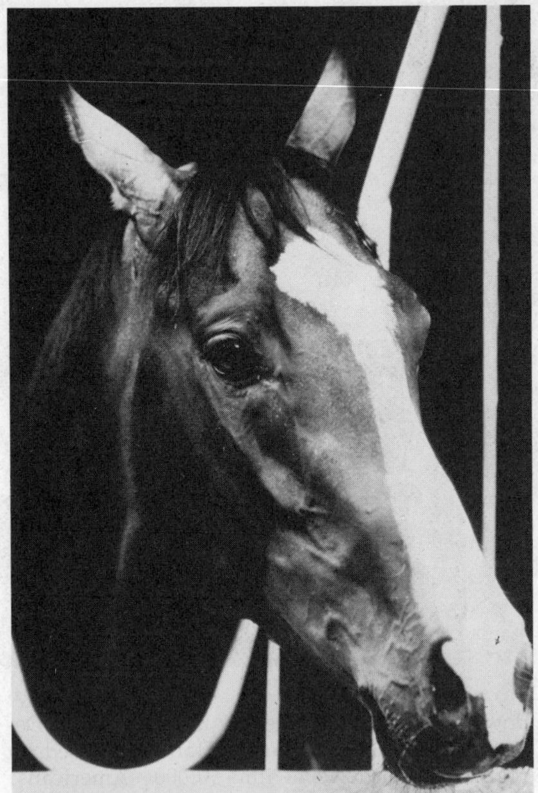

One of Ireland's most famed kidnap victims was the five-year-old stallion Shergar. The hunt for this valuable racehorse was called off in May; authorities believed him to be dead.

into the suspicious death of 36 babies on the cardiac ward of the Toronto Hospital for Sick Children in 1980 and 1981, possibly caused by fatal overdoses of a powerful heart drug. Murder charges brought against a nurse at the hospital were dismissed at a preliminary court hearing in May 1982, and no new suspects had been identified. Law enforcement agencies probing the deaths of seven Chicago area residents who swallowed cyanide-laced capsules of Extra-Strength Tylenol in 1982 reported no success in their investigations.

In April the British-based insurance company Lloyd's offered a £500,000 reward for information leading to the capture of armed robbers who stole at least £7 million in cash from a London security firm over the Easter holiday. The theft was the largest cash robbery in British history, far exceeding the previous record of £2.6 million set in the so-called Great Train Robbery of 1963. However, Britain's biggest theft—and perhaps the largest in history—took place in the early morning of November 26, when six masked robbers stole £26 million in gold and two boxes of diamonds from a warehouse near Heathrow Airport. Insurance companies offered a reward of £2 million, but Scotland Yard speculated that the gold had been melted down almost immediately. In June Lloyd's underwriters announced that they would pay out £7 million for the loss of the racehorse Shergar, winner of the 1981 Epsom Derby and Irish Sweeps Derby, which was kidnapped from a stud farm in Ireland in February and held for a ransom of £7 million. Police on both sides of the Irish border called off their hunt for the stallion in May, believing him to be dead, although the search for the kidnappers continued.

Also in June, Scotland Yard announced that an armed gang, wearing rubber masks, had robbed a London jewelry store of gems valued at up to £10 million, one of the biggest jewel thefts ever. The increasing use of firearms in British robberies prompted calls for the U.K. government to introduce mandatory minimum sentences for crimes in which guns were carried or used. In London during the first five months of 1983, 193 robberies were committed in which guns were fired, compared with 59 in all of 1982.

Canadians were also concerned about the rising use of handguns in robberies. Although a federal government study, published in September, revealed that more stringent gun control laws introduced in Canada in 1976 were helping to keep the national rate of gun-related homicides relatively stable, Canadian police claimed that many handguns were being smuggled across the virtually

British police are usually not armed, but they were during the pursuit of an armed fugitive charged with the attempted murder of a policeman. The car shown received 14 bullets when the police mistakenly thought they had found the suspect. The victim, badly wounded, survived. Three policemen were suspended.

PRESS ASSOCIATION

SUZUKI—SYGMA

Former prime minister Kakuei Tanaka of Japan, shown arriving by car at court, was convicted in the Lockheed bribery scandal and sentenced to four years in prison.

open U.S. border. In the U.S., where the debate over gun control continued to rage, the Supreme Court refused to review an appellate court decision upholding the right of Morton Grove, Ill., a Chicago suburb, to outlaw handguns. The full implications of the ruling remained unclear, although proponents of gun control hailed it as a "stunning victory."

Nonviolent Crime. POLITICAL CRIME. On October 12 the Tokyo District Court found former Japanese prime minister Kakuei Tanaka (*see* BIOGRAPHIES) guilty of accepting 500 million yen (about $2 million) from the Lockheed Aircraft Corp. to promote the sale of its planes in Japan during his tenure as premier. The court sentenced Tanaka to four years' imprisonment and imposed a fine equivalent to the amount of the bribe. The verdict was immediately appealed.

Repercussions of Italy's biggest postwar scandal continued with the August escape from a Swiss jail of Licio Gelli, former grand master of the secret Propaganda Due (P2) Masonic lodge. Revelation of the existence of the lodge in 1981 had brought down the government of Arnaldo Forlani. It was widely believed that members of the lodge, including prominent government, business, and military figures, were involved in a series of right-wing terrorist attacks, political crises, and financial frauds that culminated in the 1982 collapse of the Banco Ambrosiano, Italy's largest private bank. At the time of his escape, Italian authorities were seeking extradition of Gelli in order to interrogate him about the activities of P2.

Gelli's case was linked to the mysterious death of the president of the Banco Ambrosiano, Roberto Calvi, whose body was found hanging from London's Blackfriars Bridge in June 1982. In March Calvi's family, who believed the banker was murdered, won the right to a new inquest when Britain's High Court quashed a verdict of suicide by a coroner's jury. In June a second jury returned an open verdict in regard to the cause of death.

In the U.S. corruption and violence continued to plague the giant Teamsters union. In March its president, Roy Williams, was sentenced to prison for attempting to bribe a U.S. senator. Williams, the third Teamster leader convicted of crime in 25 years, stepped down as a condition of remaining free while appealing the case. In January a co-defendant, Teamster consultant Allen Dorfman, had been killed gangland-style in the parking lot of a suburban Chicago hotel.

WHITE COLLAR CRIME AND THEFT. In April the West German magazine *Stern* announced it had achieved "the journalistic scoop of the post-World War II period" by acquiring Adolf Hitler's secret diaries, said to have been purchased for *Stern* by its correspondent Gerd Heidemann. Following several weeks of controversy, however, West German government experts announced that the diaries were a forgery. By the end of May, West German police had arrested and charged Heidemann and Konrad Kujau, a Stuttgart dealer in Nazi memorabilia, in connection with the case. (*See* PUBLISHING: *Sidebar*.) Attempts to curtail the burgeoning $3 billion-a-year international trade in smuggled art were bolstered in June when the U.S. began implementing a UNESCO convention banning the importation of artifacts lacking proper export papers.

The suicide in September of Alan David Saxon, chairman of Bullion Reserve of North America, brought to light the possibility of a major fraud. Auditors indicated they could not find some $60 million in gold, silver, and platinum supposedly purchased as an investment by Bullion Reserve customers and stored in vaults.

The rapid growth of computer literacy and the spread of personal computers produced what one expert described as an "epidemic" of computer tampering across the U.S. In August, for example, an FBI report revealed that a group of young Milwaukee area computer enthusiasts or "hackers," called the 414s, had been linked to computer system break-ins at the Los Alamos (N.M.) National Laboratory, New York City's Memorial Sloan-Kettering Cancer Center, a major West Coast bank, a

Dallas, Texas, consulting firm, and a Canadian cement company. Most of these incidents, like the one dramatized in the popular movie *WarGames*, seemed to be pranks, but the potential for harm prompted a major search for new methods of ensuring computer security.

The use of illegal drugs such as cocaine by athletes continued to cause concern. A number of sports figures were involved in drug-related cases during the year, among them former Miami Dolphin running back Eugene ("Mercury") Morris and Cy Young award pitcher Vida Blue. Cocaine was allegedly becoming more plentiful and cheaper as the output of increased plantings in South America flooded the market.

Law Enforcement. Security planning by U.S. law enforcement agencies for the 1984 Olympic Games to be held in Los Angeles continued amid some controversy. A federal government study warned that security for the Games could be compromised because of the number of law enforcement jurisdictions involved. Local officials appeared particularly resentful of any attempts by the FBI to assume a leading role in the handling of any major terrorist incident.

In Northern Ireland the Royal Ulster Constabulary claimed to have inflicted severe damage on the Irish Republican Army (IRA) and its Protestant paramilitary adversaries through the use of a network of informers, or "supergrasses." Reportedly, almost 300 reputed terrorists had been arrested or convicted on the strength of information from about 30 supergrasses, all of whom were given new identities to protect them against retaliation. The Canadian government introduced legislation to establish a new domestic civilian Security Intelligence Service with sweeping powers to investigate a wide range of subversive groups and activities. The new agency was intended to replace the Royal Canadian Mounted Police Security Service. The move had been recommended in a 1981 royal commission report that reviewed a long list of alleged wrongdoings by RCMP Security Service officers in the early 1970s.

In Rio de Janeiro, Brazil, in April, a court sentenced ten military police to extended prison terms for their involvement in death squads that were believed to have assassinated some 60 citizens in Nova Iguaçu. More trials were anticipated as the newly elected governor of Rio de Janeiro state, Leonel Brizola, pledged to end corruption and the arbitrary use of violence by law enforcement officers. As part of a major campaign against corruption among public officials in Mexico, Pres. Miguel de la Madrid Hurtado named an army general, Raymon Mota Sánchez, as the new police chief of Mexico City. Sánchez was ordered to clean up the city's notoriously corrupt department. President de la Madrid also moved to dismantle Mexico City's Division of Investigations to Prevent Delinquency, said to be responsible for crimes ranging from extortion to murder.

Public outrage against police was expressed in London in January when a squad of armed officers, without prior warning, shot and gravely injured an unarmed man whom they mistakenly believed to be a dangerous escapee. Scotland Yard formally apologized, and criminal charges were subsequently brought against several of the officers involved. The case raised questions about the apparently increasing practice of issuing guns to the normally unarmed British police. Police in South Africa were also criticized for their "speed on the trigger" following a number of shootings, including those of an innocent white man mistaken for a car thief and a black community leader killed during an illegal protest meeting. Research at the University of Cape Town revealed that in

A wave of executions of convicted criminals was reported from China. Pictures of the condemned with records of their crimes were posted outside court chambers at the intermediate court in Beijing (Peking).

WIDE WORLD

WIDE WORLD

Geriatric crime: these two "drug grannies," as the Australian press dubbed them, were apprehended with nearly two tons of hashish in their camper. Unexpectedly released from prison, Vera Todd Hayes (top) and Florice Bessire returned to San Francisco.

1981, the latest year for which figures were available, South African police shot a total of 175 people—141 blacks, 32 of mixed race, and 2 whites.

Reports from China indicated that the government was carrying out a major campaign against crime. Diplomats in Beijing (Peking) estimated that hundreds of common criminals had been executed and many more "hooligans" had been arrested and sent to labour camps. China had long claimed that crime had been virtually eradicated under the Communist regime, but increasing concern with a rise in violent crime had been evident in recent years. (DUNCAN CHAPPELL)

See also Prisons and Penology.
[522.C.6; 543.A.5; 552.C and F; 737.B; 10/36.C.5.a]

Cuba

The socialist republic of Cuba occupies the largest island in the Greater Antilles of the West Indies. Area: 110,922 sq km (42,827 sq mi), including several thousand small islands and cays. Pop. (1983 est.): 9,858,000, including (1953) white 72.8%; mestizo 14.5%; Negro 12.4%. Cap. and largest city: Havana (pop., 1983 est., 1,952,300). Language: Spanish. Religion (1980): Roman Catholic 42.1%; atheist 6.4%; other 2.8%; none 48.7%. President of the Councils of State and Ministers in 1983, Fidel Castro Ruz.

Cuba's relations with the United States remained hostile during 1983, and in September the U.S. Congress approved the creation of Radio Martí, a Spanish-language station that was to broadcast to Cuba from Florida under the authority of the Voice of America. Cuba's military presence in Africa and its growing involvement in Central America and the Caribbean, especially Nicaragua, further affected relations within the region. At a rally in July, however, Pres. Fidel Castro voiced support for a negotiated settlement to the Central American conflict and expressed willingness to withdraw military advisers from Nicaragua as part of any comprehensive peace agreement. He backed the initiative of the Contadora group of four Latin-American countries—Colombia, Mexico, Panama, and Venezuela—in its efforts to promote peace in the region.

Castro expressed shock over the October 19 murder of Pres. Maurice Bishop of Grenada (*see* OBITUARIES), with whom he had had close relations, but he denounced in the strongest terms the subsequent U.S. invasion of the island. Speaking before burial services for 24 Cubans killed in the invasion, he said the leaders of the coup against Bishop "had opened the doors to imperialist aggression." Castro denied U.S. claims that most of the Cubans on Grenada were military rather than civilian personnel and that they had opened fire on U.S. forces. Some 700–750 Cubans taken prisoner on Grenada had been repatriated by the end of November.

Cuba's relations with certain of its neighbours in Latin America and the Caribbean continued to strengthen as a result of its anti-British stance during the South Atlantic conflict between the U.K. and Argentina in 1982. In August 1983 Venezuela and the Soviet Union renewed a lapsed agreement whereby, in order to save transportation costs, Venezuela supplied crude oil to Cuba in exchange for Soviet oil supplied to West Germany.

CUBA

Education. (1981–82) Primary, pupils 1,409,765, teachers 83,113; secondary, pupils 918,629, teachers 87,703; vocational, pupils 263,981, teachers 16,154; teacher training, students 92,152, teachers 6,461; higher, students 165,496, teaching staff (1980–81) 10,860.

Finance. Monetary unit: peso, with (Sept. 20, 1983) a free rate of 0.87 peso to U.S. $1 (1.31 pesos = £1 sterling). Budget (1981 est.): revenue 11,201,000,000 pesos; expenditure 11,197,000,000 pesos. Net material product (1980 est.) 9,684,000,000 pesos.

Foreign Trade. (1980) Imports 4,509,000,000 pesos (62% from U.S.S.R.); exports 3,967,000,000 pesos (54% to U.S.S.R.). Main exports: sugar 83%; nickel ore 5%.

Transport and Communications. Roads (main, 1980) 14,847 km. Motor vehicles in use: passenger (1979) 152,600; commercial (including buses; 1976) c. 40,000. Railways: (main; 1980) 13,685 km; traffic (1981) 1,835,000,000 passenger-km, freight 2,626,000,000 net ton-km. Air traffic (1981): c. 1,242,000,000 passenger-km; freight c. 14.5 million net ton-km. Shipping (1982): merchant vessels 100 gross tons and over 414; gross tonnage 949,216. Telephones (Dec. 1979) 362,000. Radio receivers (Dec. 1980) 2,914,000. Television receivers (Dec. 1980) 1,273,000.

Agriculture. Production (in 000; metric tons; 1982): rice c. 480; cassava c. 330; sweet potatoes c. 330; tomatoes c. 226; sugar, raw value 8,207; bananas c. 169; oranges c. 400; coffee c. 21; tobacco c. 45; jute c. 11; beef and veal c. 153; fish catch (1981) 165. Livestock (in 000; 1982): cattle c. 6,200; pigs c. 2,000; sheep c. 375; goats c. 101; horses (1981) c. 829; chickens c. 26,173.

Industry. Production (in 000; metric tons; 1982): crude oil 540; natural gas (cu m) c. 10,700; petroleum products (1981) 6,288; electricity (kw-hr) 10,782,000; copper ore (metal content) 2.6; chrome ore (oxide content; 1980) 10; nickel ore (metal content; 1980) 38; salt (1980) 131; paper (1980) 73; sulfuric acid 335; fertilizers (nutrient content; 1981–82) nitrogenous 142, phosphate 6; cement 3,164; crude steel (1980) 304; cotton yarn 24; cotton fabrics (sq m) 110,000.

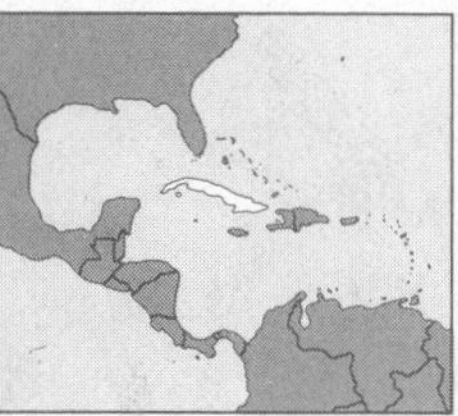

Cuba

Crops:
see Agriculture and Food Supplies

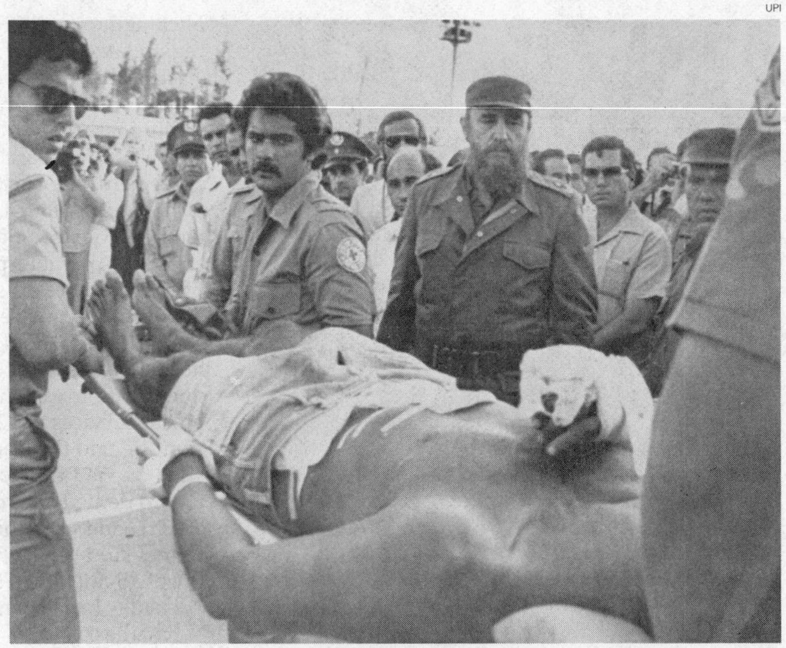
UPI

Cubans wounded in the U.S. invasion of Grenada were carried from a Red Cross airplane at Havana as Cuban Pres. Fidel Castro watched.

Economic pressure from the U.S. continued. The 21-year-old trade embargo was estimated to have cost Cuba about $9 billion. Pressure was exerted on Japan to stop importing nickel from Cuba for stainless steel production, though Cuban nickel represented only 0.3% of the total imported for that purpose. The U.S. threatened to stop importing from Japan certain goods—such as automobiles and motorcycles—in which stainless steel was used. In June the U.S. Supreme Court upheld Citibank's refusal to honour a $193,000 claim by a former Cuban bank because international law had been violated when Cuba seized Citibank's assets in 1960.

In midyear a U.S. circuit court in Boston overturned regulations introduced in April 1982 limiting travel to Cuba by U.S. citizens. However, the Supreme Court maintained a temporary stay of injunction in order to consider an appeal from the administration. The U.S. government asked Cuba to take back "several thousand undesirable refugees" who had arrived in Florida in 1980. However, the Cuban government refused to grant the request unless it was included in wider negotiations on the normalization of migration between the two countries. The "undesirables" made up a small unspecified percentage of the 125,000 who had arrived by boat from the port of Mariel.

The U.S. called on Western creditors not to "go soft" on the renegotiation of Cuba's debts. In September 1982 Cuba asked to reschedule $1.2 billion of its hard-currency external debt out of a total of $3.2 billion. By March 1983 one-third of this had been rescheduled, and an agreement on economic targets was signed as a precondition to rescheduling an additional $250 million due in 1984.

Cuba was to start repaying its debts to the Soviet Union in 1986. They were thought to total $5 billion in interest-free loans, repayable over 25 years. Apart from military aid, Soviet economic assistance took two forms: balance of payments support through subsidized trade, under which sugar and nickel exports were priced in excess of world levels and oil and other imports priced well below world levels; and assistance for development projects. However, there appeared to be a shift away from trade subsidies and toward trade credits, which were repayable.

Official figures indicated that real growth of the Cuban economy was about 2.5% in 1982; the forecast for 1983 was about 2%. In 1982 sugar prices fell to their lowest level since 1979, averaging three cents per kilogram (seven cents per pound), well below production costs. Sugar sales to the world market provided almost 80% of Cuba's hard-currency exports. Future prospects in this market would depend on the outcome of negotiations over a new International Sugar Agreement.

Early predictions for 1982–83 were that sugar production would equal or slightly exceed the excellent 1981–82 figure of 8.2 million metric tons. However, record rain and wind between January and April 1983, during the harvest, caused severe losses, and the final output was put at 6.7 million metric tons. Tobacco production was also affected by the weather, which destroyed or badly damaged 8,000 ha of plantation out of a total of 33,500 ha (1 ha = 2.47 ac). Hopes of equaling the 1980–81 record output of 52,000 metric tons were dashed, and preliminary estimates placed production at nearer 40,000 metric tons.

Foreign partners were being sought for joint ventures in tourism, oil exploration, food processing, milling, steel, and petrochemical projects. This was the result of a new law published in February 1982 that encouraged foreign investment. (FIONA B. MERRY)

Cycling

The dominant feature of the 1983 world cycling championships, held in Switzerland, was the overall performance of the U.S., which, for the

Curling:
see Winter Sports

first time ever, was the most successful nation. Greg Lemond, a 22-year-old Californian, became the first U.S. rider to win the world professional road race, which took place at Altenrhein on the shores of Lake Constance. The track program in Zürich produced victories for Connie Paraskevin, in the women's sprint, and Connie Carpenter, who beat compatriot Cynthia Olavarri in the women's individual pursuit final. The team's success highlighted the rapid growth of cycling in the U.S. during a year marked by the first professional Tour of America, which ran from Virginia Beach, Va., to Washington, D.C., and attracted several European teams, and a first U.S. winner of the Tour of Britain "Milk Race," Matt Eaton.

Koichi Nakano of Japan won the world professional sprint title for a record-equaling seventh time as the competition in Zürich witnessed four nonaltitude outdoor world-best performances. These were set by Carpenter (women's pursuit, 3 min 49.53 sec), West Germany (team pursuit, 4 min 16.62 sec), and Soviet riders Sergey Kopylov (1,000-m time trial, 1 min 3.94 sec) and Viktor Koupovets (individual pursuit, 4 min 37.31 sec).

Injury denied Bernard Hinault the chance of a record-equaling fifth overall victory in the professional Tour de France. The Frenchman won his preparation race, the Tour of Spain, but aggravated an old tendon problem in the right knee, which required surgery and kept him on the sidelines for the rest of the year. France instead hailed a new hero in 22-year-old Laurent Fignon, who became the first Parisian to win his national tour since Georges Speicher in 1923. Fignon took over as leader when another Frenchman, Pascal Simon, was forced to retire with a fractured shoulder. Scotland recorded a first-ever success when Robert Millar won the mountainous 198-km tenth stage between Pau and Bagnères de Luchon.

Three West German riders were stripped of their world championship medals after failing post-event dope tests. Claudia Lommatzsch, second in the women's sprint, and bronze medal tandem pair Fredy Schmidtke and Dieter Giebken were all disqualified. (JOHN R. WILKINSON)

1983 Cycling Champions

Event	Winner	Country
WORLD AMATEUR CHAMPIONS—TRACK		
Men		
Sprint	L. Hesslich	East Germany
Tandem sprint	F. Dêpine, P. Vernet	France
Individual pursuit	V. Koupovets	U.S.S.R.
Team pursuit	R. Golz, G. Strittmatter M. Marx, R. Günther	West Germany
1,000-m time trial	S. Kopylov	U.S.S.R.
50-km points	M. Marcussen	Denmark
50-km motor paced	R. Podlesch	West Germany
Women		
Sprint	C. Paraskevin	U.S.
Individual pursuit	C. Carpenter	U.S.
WORLD PROFESSIONAL CHAMPIONS—TRACK		
Sprint	K. Nakano	Japan
Individual pursuit	S. Bishop	Australia
50-km points	U. Freuler	Switzerland
One-hour motor paced	B. Vicino	Italy
Keirin	U. Freuler	Switzerland
WORLD AMATEUR CHAMPIONS—ROAD		
Men		
Individual road race	U. Raab	East Germany
100-km team time trial	Y. Kashirin, A. Zinoviev, S. Novolokin, O. Szougeda	U.S.S.R.
Women		
Individual road race	M. Berglund	Sweden
WORLD PROFESSIONAL CHAMPION—ROAD		
Individual road race	G. Lemond	U.S.
WORLD CHAMPIONS—CYCLO-CROSS		
Amateur	R. Simunek	Czechoslovakia
Professional	R. Liboton	Belgium
MAJOR PROFESSIONAL ROAD-RACE WINNERS		
Tour de France	L. Fignon	France
Tour of Italy	G. Saronni	Italy
Tour of Spain	B. Hinault	France
Paris–Nice	S. Kelly	Ireland
Milan–San Remo	G. Saronni	Italy
Tour of Flanders	J. Raas	The Netherlands
Paris–Roubaix	H. Kuiper	The Netherlands
Flèche Wallonne	B. Hinault	France
Liège–Bastogne–Liège	S. Rooks	The Netherlands
Bordeaux–Paris	G. Duclos-Lassalle	France
Dauphiné Libéré	G. Lemond	U.S.
G.P. de Midi Libre	J. R. Bernaudeau	France
Tour of Switzerland	S. Kelly	Ireland
Tour of America	B. Oosterbosch	The Netherlands
Tour de l'Avenir*	O. Ludwig	East Germany
Tour of Britain	M. Eaton	U.S.
Warsaw–Berlin–Prague†	F. Boden	East Germany

*Mixed professional/amateur.
†Amateur.

WIDE WORLD

Sergio Scremin of Italy won the gold medal in the men's individual cycling road race at the World University Games at Edmonton, Alberta. As they approached the line Greg Mercer (6) of the U.S. and Rafael Gonzdiez (147) of Mexico crashed behind him.

Cyprus

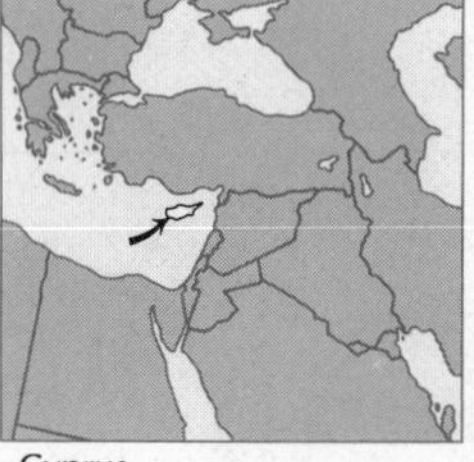

Cyprus

An island republic and a member of the Commonwealth, Cyprus is in the eastern Mediterranean. Area: 9,251 sq km (3,572 sq mi). Pop. (1983 est.): 650,700, including (1980 est.) Greeks 80.7%; Turks 18.7%; others 0.6%. Cap. and largest city: Nicosia (pop., 1982 est., 161,000). Official population estimates may not take into account the extensive internal migration or the recent and reportedly extensive Turkish immigration and Greek emigration. Language: Greek and Turkish. Religion (1980 est.): Greek Orthodox 76.2%; Muslim 18.7%; other Christian 2.7%; other 0.6%; none 1.8%. President in 1983, Spyros Kyprianou.

In a year marked by a high level of political activity, the unilateral declaration of independence (UDI) by Turkish-Cypriot leader Rauf Denktash on Nov. 15, 1983, dominated all other events and plunged the island into its worst political crisis since Turkey invaded it in 1974. The declaration, recognized only by Turkey and condemned by the world community, ended the already tenuous contact between the two peoples on the divided island and left the future of the 23-year-old republic in doubt. Denktash named his new state the Turkish Republic of Northern Cyprus.

Denktash had threatened to declare independence in May after a UN General Assembly resolution, which he considered to be pro-Greek, called for the immediate withdrawal of Turkish troops from Cyprus. At the same time, Denktash abandoned the intercommunal talks that had been aimed at setting up a federal republic.

A major new initiative launched by UN Secretary-General Javier Pérez de Cuéllar in August in an attempt to break the deadlock soon fizzled out. Pérez de Cuéllar proposed basic negotiating positions to both sides; these concentrated on the main constitutional requirements for a federation. Pres. Spyros Kyprianou accepted the UN approach to the problem but stopped short of agreeing to the negotiating positions. Denktash sidestepped the UN proposals and demanded instead a summit meeting with Kyprianou.

While moves toward a summit appeared to be in progress, Denktash, apparently taking advantage of a government changeover in Turkey, declared UDI. Despite his earlier threats, the proclamation shocked and surprised the government and the entire diplomatic community in Cyprus. Kyprianou quickly gained the backing of a UN Security Council resolution that condemned the UDI and called for its cancellation. Denktash failed in an early drive to gain recognition from some sympathetic Islamic nations; he also faced a virtual ban on Turkish-Cypriot produce entering the European Communities as a result of an agreement between the EC and Kyprianou's government.

In presidential elections held in February, Kyprianou, whose Democratic Party had formed an alliance with the Communists, was returned for a second five-year term. He won 57% of the vote in a three-way contest. Turkish Cypriots took no part in the election.

Cyprus continued to maintain a healthy economy, with inflation at 5% and unemployment at 3.5%. But budget plans for 1984 incorporated a credit squeeze and strong indirect taxation measures in order to reduce a budget deficit of $247 million and to curb consumer spending on imported goods.

In December the UN Security Council extended the life of the UN peacekeeping force in Cyprus for another six months. (THOMAS O'DWYER)

CYPRUS

Education. (1982–83) Greek schools: primary, pupils 46,317, teachers 2,212; secondary, pupils 43,000, teachers 2,549; vocational, pupils 5,527, teachers 510; teacher training (1981–82), students 102, teachers 13; higher, students 1,629, teaching staff 192. Turkish schools: primary, pupils 18,179, teachers 670; secondary, pupils 10,868, teachers 570; vocational, pupils 1,824, teachers 246; teacher training, students 135, teachers 7; higher, students 266, teaching staff 25.

Finance. Monetary unit: Cyprus pound, with (Sept. 20, 1983) a free rate of C£0.55 to U.S. $1 (C£0.82 = £1 sterling). The Turkish lira is also in use in North Cyprus (Turkish Federated State). Gold and other reserves (June 1983) U.S. $495 million. Budget (1981 actual): revenue C£191.2 million; expenditure C£258.6 million. Excludes budget of Turkish Federated State (total; 1982–83 est.) balanced at 10,918,000,000 Turkish liras.

Foreign Trade. (South only; 1982) Imports C£582 million; exports C£259 million. Import sources: U.K. 13%; Italy 10%; Iraq 9%; Japan 9%; West Germany 9%; Greece 7%; U.S. 7%; France 5%. Export destinations: U.K. 20%; Lebanon 12%; ships' stores 10%; Saudi Arabia 9%; Iraq 7%; U.S.S.R. 5%. Main exports: fruit and vegetables 26%; clothing 15%; footwear 8%; cement 6%; wine and spirits 5%. Tourism (1981): South, visitors 429,000, gross receipts U.S. $244 million; North, visitors 78,000.

Transport and Communications. Roads (1981) 10,778 km. Motor vehicles in use (1981): passenger 96,100; commercial 26,054. Air traffic (1982): 854 million passenger-km; freight 19.9 million net ton-km. Shipping (1982): merchant vessels 100 gross tons and over 557; gross tonnage 2,149,869. Telephones (Jan. 1981) 113,400. Radio receivers (Dec. 1980) 313,000. Television licenses (Dec. 1980) 150,000.

Agriculture. Production (in 000; metric tons; 1982): barley *c.* 80; wheat *c.* 21; potatoes (1981) *c.* 216; grapes *c.* 222; oranges *c.* 123; grapefruit *c.* 90; lemons *c.* 41; olives *c.* 35. Livestock (in 000; 1981): sheep *c.* 525; cattle *c.* 41; pigs *c.* 183; goats *c.* 360.

Industry. Production (South only; in 000; metric tons; 1981): asbestos 29; iron pyrites 36; chromium ore (oxide content; 1980) 7.8; petroleum products 513; cement (1982) 1,068; electricity (kw-hr; 1982) 1,141,000.

Czechoslovakia

A federal socialist republic of central Europe, Czechoslovakia lies between Poland, the U.S.S.R., Hungary, Austria, and East and West Germany. Area: 127,889 sq km (49,378 sq mi). Pop. (1983 est.): 15.4 million, including (1980) Czech 64.1%, Slovak 30.6%, other 5.3%. Cap. and largest city: Prague (pop., 1981 est., 1,182,400). Language: Czech and Slovak (official). General secretary of the Communist Party of Czechoslovakia and president in 1983, Gustav Husak; federal premier, Lubomir Strougal.

The state of the economy continued to be the central concern of the Czechoslovak leadership during 1983. The figures for 1982 were less than encouraging. Overall, the Czechoslovak economy grew by 0.6% over 1981, which had itself been a rather indifferent year. Estimates put the real inflation rate at about 8% at the end of 1982. Official spokesmen, outlining the 1983 plans, were nevertheless guardedly optimistic and were looking forward to a growth target of over 2%. The half-yearly figures for January–June 1983 went part of the way toward justifying their optimism, with some improvement over the rather low 1982 output being recorded.

However, the broad structural problems with which Czechoslovak planners had been grappling remained untouched for all practical purposes. One good illustration of this was the evolution of the agro-industrial complex, the food production and processing sector. In the mid-1970s Czechoslovakia had been close to self-sufficiency in food, supplying some 85% of its needs from its domestic resources. By the early 1980s, however, this picture had changed. Agricultural output had begun to decline, and observers believed that this was part of a long-term trend rather than something attributable to, for instance, adverse weather conditions. Planners were, therefore, faced with the

CZECHOSLOVAKIA

Education. (1981–82) Primary, pupils 1,930,634, teachers 90,282; secondary, pupils 149,210, teachers 8,918; vocational, pupils 229,543, teachers 16,391; teacher training, pupils 14,590, teachers 962; higher, students 198,362, teaching staff 18,560.

Finance. Monetary unit: koruna, with (Sept. 20, 1983) a commercial rate of 6.45 koruny to U.S. $1 (9.71 koruny = £1 sterling) and a noncommercial rate of 11.30 koruny to U.S. $1 (17.02 koruny = £1 sterling). Budget (1981 est.): revenue 311.6 billion koruny; expenditure 310.9 billion koruny. Net material product (1981) 469.6 billion koruny.

Foreign Trade. (1982) Imports 94,217,000,000 koruny; exports 95,562,000,000 koruny. Import sources: U.S.S.R. 43%; East Germany 9%; Poland 6%; Hungary 5%; West Germany 5%; Yugoslavia 5%. Export destinations: U.S.S.R. 41%; East Germany 9%; Poland 6%; Hungary 5%; West Germany 5%. Main exports (1981): machinery 40%; motor vehicles 8%; iron and steel 8%; textiles and clothing 6%; chemicals 6%.

Transport and Communications. Roads (1974) 145,455 km (373 km expressways in 1981). Motor vehicles in use (1981): passenger 2,475,774; commercial 298,324. Railways: (1981) 13,130 km (including 3,081 km electrified); traffic (1980) 18,050,000,000 passenger-km, freight (1982) 71,583,000,000 net ton-km. Air traffic (1982): 1,590,000,000 passenger-km; freight 17.1 million net ton-km. Navigable inland waterways (1980) c. 480 km. Shipping (1982): merchant vessels 100 gross tons and over 21; gross tonnage 184,798. Telephones (Dec. 1981) 3,226,000. Radio licenses (Dec. 1981) 4,099,700. Television licenses (Dec. 1981) 4,296,000.

Agriculture. Production (in 000; metric tons; 1982): wheat c. 5,000; barley c. 3,600; oats c. 500; rye c. 600; corn c. 850; potatoes 3,608; sugar, raw value c. 890; grapes 275; apples 504; beef and veal c. 373; pork c. 750; timber (cu m; 1981) 18,879. Livestock (in 000; Dec. 1981): cattle 5,103; pigs 7,302; sheep 959; chickens 45,295.

Industry. Index of industrial production (1975 = 100; 1982) 127. Fuel and power (in 000; metric tons; 1982): coal c. 27,500; brown coal c. 99,000; crude oil 90; petroleum products (1981) 17,203; natural gas (cu m; 1981) c. 640,000; manufactured gas (cu m; 1981) 7,700,000; electricity (kw-hr) 75,000,000. Production (in 000; metric tons; 1982): iron ore (26% metal content) 1,862; pig iron 9,690; crude steel 14,993; cement 10,324; sulfuric acid 1,252; caustic soda (1981) 331; plastics and resins (1981) 913; fertilizers (nutrient content; 1981) nitrogenous c. 674, phosphate 340; cotton yarn 144; cotton fabrics (m; 1981) 636,000; woolen fabrics (m; 1981) 60,200; man-made fibres (1981) 151; paper (1981) 1,183; passenger cars (units) 173; commercial vehicles (units) 90. Dwelling units completed (1982) 107,000.

problem of raising the volume of imports, particularly feed grains, required to sustain high levels of meat consumption.

The reasons for the slow decline in agricultural output were many, but they included a poor strategy of chemical fertilizer use, overcentralization, and the stagnation of investment in agriculture. In all, the picture presented by the agro-industrial complex was one of slow, inexorable deterioration rather than catastrophe. Much the same could be said of the rest of the economy.

Energy was another serious problem, for two interconnected reasons. Czechoslovakia was rather poor in domestic energy resources. Therefore, the nation had evolved a strategy of relying on imports of Soviet oil. During the 1960s this was delivered at advantageous prices, with the consequence that a highly wasteful attitude toward energy use developed. Indeed, Czechoslovakia's per capita energy use was one of the highest in the world. But in recent years oil prices had risen, and the Soviet Union made it clear that it was no longer willing to subsidize Czechoslovakia's needs at the same rate as before. It was estimated that in 1982 the cost of Soviet oil had risen by 23% over 1981, and in 1983 by 17% over 1982. A major jump in prices was expected to occur in 1985, when the Soviet-Czechoslovak agreement was scheduled to come up for renegotiation.

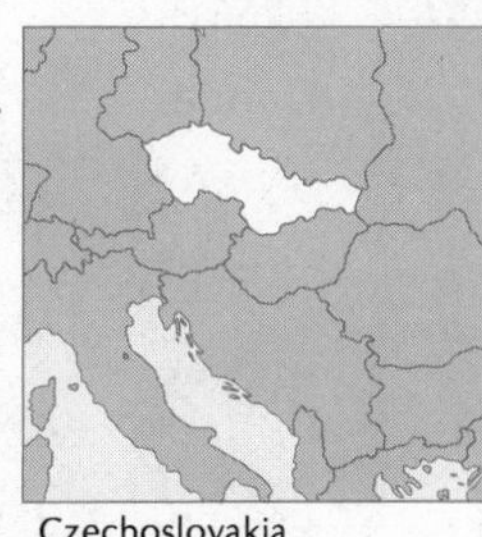
Czechoslovakia

The political life of the country remained in a relatively low key, and no major changes within the Communist Party of Czechoslovakia (CPC) were registered, although there was an air of expectancy that changes might be imminent. This derived from a number of sources. The pressure from the economic constraint was the most obvious. A section of the party leadership was ready to accept the probability that genuine structural changes, with potentially political implications for the distribution of power between the party and the managers, could not be delayed much longer. Some decentralization of power would, therefore, mark the first move away from strict central control in a decade and a half. The death in April of Vaclav Hula, one of the most important advocates of centralized planning, was a significant development in this area. The succession of Pres. Yury Andropov in the Soviet Union and its concomitant changes was another, given the close connections between the Czechoslovak leaders and the various currents in the Kremlin. One suggested direction for change was toward a Soviet-type strategy of reform based on an alliance between the technocrats and the secret police. Finally, the illness of Prime Minister Lubomir Strougal was noteworthy, inasmuch as it weakened the strength of the pragmatists in the leadership.

In regard to the Communist Party, the apathy of many years' standing remained the order of the day. Membership held steady at about 1.6 million, but there was virtually no net increase. One phenomenon reported was the reluctance of the younger generation and of manual workers to obtain CPC membership, somewhat to the dismay of ideologists. There were complaints too of opportunism and careerism, of slack party discipline, and of "mechanical" patterns of recruitment; the latter re-

UPI

Shortly after his accession to power in the U.S.S.R., Yury Andropov (left) was welcomed to Czechoslovakia by Pres. Gustav Husak.

ferred to the practice of recruiting people for membership because they came from a particular social category, such as "worker" or "intellectual," rather than because they were convinced by the ideas of the party.

Corruption remained a problem, despite the launching of campaigns against it. Alarm was expressed over the spread of drug abuse, including glue sniffing, among young people. But the most visible means of popular dissent and dissatisfaction was adherence to religion. There were a number of instances of this, notably the signing of a letter in March protesting against police harassment of believers. In August Frantisek Cardinal Tomasek, archbishop of Prague, sent a letter to the authorities protesting against acts of persecution and the hard-line policies of discrimination against believers. For their part, the authorities were clearly worried about the continuing popularity of religion among young people and the evidence of surprisingly high levels of religiousness in the population as a whole. According to surveys, approximately one-third of the people of Czechoslovakia were defined as religious.

The Charter 77 opposition group published a number of documents during the year, notably one on the moral damage wrought upon Czechoslovak society by the current regime and another on the ecological catastrophe facing northern Bohemia, the result of excessive industrial exploitation. One of the group's founders, the writer Jiri Lederer, died in October (*see* OBITUARIES).

(GEORGE SCHÖPFLIN)

Dance

North America. The death of George Balanchine (*see* OBITUARIES) on April 30 marked the end of a golden age of choreographic innovation. Balanchine had renewed the soul of classical ballet and brought it to preeminence among 20th-century arts. This tragic loss in the midst of economic and aesthetic doldrums prompted gloomy thoughts about the art's future. No choreographer of major dimension was emerging on the horizon and, despite unremitting activity, the much-touted dance boom appeared to be waning.

Balanchine's choreography, influence, and protégés were spread worldwide, but nowhere was the force of his conception more clearly etched than on the company and academy he and Lincoln Kirstein began in 1933 (1983 marked the 50th anniversary of their School of American Ballet—SAB). As Balanchine's life ebbed, he was proclaimed ballet master emeritus of the New York City Ballet (NYCB); Peter Martins (*see* BIOGRAPHIES) and Jerome Robbins were appointed ballet masters in chief (co-directors), with Martins assuming day-to-day direction of the company. After Balanchine's death, Martins announced he would retire from dancing at year's end to devote himself wholly to company affairs and choreography. Rosemary Dunleavy, who with ballet masters John Taras, Robbins, and Martins had kept dancers and repertory vibrant during Balanchine's illness, was named ballet mistress.

NYCB's repertory, lacking a new Balanchine ballet for the first time, was enlarged by two works from Jerome Robbins, *I'm Old Fashioned* (homage to Fred Astaire) and *Glass Pieces* (music by Philip Glass). Martins added his *Delibes Divertissements,* made for SAB students, along with his new *Rossini Quartets.* Helgi Tomasson's *Ballet d'Isoline* marked his promising choreographic debut with the company, but Jacques d'Amboise's *Celebration* was less favourably received. Former Bolshoi dancers Valentina and Leonid Kozlov joined NYCB as soloists. The Balanchine legacy was documented on television in two programs of Stravinsky-Balanchine ballets and a posthumous company tribute. Institutional solidity and the unsurpassed brilliance of company performances allayed concerns, at least for the time being, over the welfare of Balanchine's choreography and the company's ability to survive creatively without him.

Shock tremors of other sorts shook American Ballet Theatre's foundations. The season began belatedly but in good form, following settlement of a bitter labour dispute, with a week's engagement at the Kennedy Center in Washington, D.C., launching a national tour. It ended with a financially disastrous 11-week Metropolitan Opera House season. By September the board was being asked to guarantee a $2 million loan to keep the company afloat. Departures by executive director Herman Krawitz, chairman Donald Kendall, and three other board members left artistic director Mikhail Baryshnikov vulnerable to board pressures. He announced he would remain until the end of the 1983–84 season (though the board had voted to renew his contract through 1986, it had never been executed). The loan was secured, and the company began rehearsals for a full-length *Cinderella,* co-choreographed by Baryshnikov and Peter Anastos, replacing Baryshnikov's 1976 *Nutcracker* as Kennedy Center's holiday fare.

Baryshnikov restated his goal of upgrading the company's dancing so that it would be "the real star," while the board reportedly sought a successor. A no-stars policy, excessive ticket prices, an elongated New York season, the recession, a dearth of exciting new ballets, board intrigues, and failure to act swiftly to offset losses had nearly scuttled the company. Highlights of the embattled 1983 season were a revelatory restoration from notation of Balanchine's 1947 *Symphonie Concertante,* Erik Bruhn's grand opera-scale restaging of *La Sylphide,* a taut revival of Robbins's *N.Y. Export: Opus Jazz,* and Twyla Tharp's romantic mini-ballet *Once Upon a Time.* John McFall's *Follow the Feet* and *Interludes,* Lynne Taylor-Corbett's *Estuary,* and Jiri Kylian's *Torso* were notably less successful.

Opening its first bicoastal season at the Los Angeles Music Center, the Joffrey Ballet presented Laura Dean's *Fire* (with discordant decor by post-modern architect Michael Graves), Gerald Arpino's sombre *Round of Angels,* company premieres of William Forsythe's *Love Songs* and Sir Frederick Ashton's *Five Brahms Variations in the Manner of Isadora Duncan,* and revivals of 20th-century classics by John Cranko, Antony Tudor, Ashton, and Vaslav Nijinsky. Paul Taylor's and Jiri Kylian's modern dances became de rigueur in 1983 ballet

Dams:
see Engineering Projects

repertories. In New York the Joffrey danced Taylor's *Cloven Kingdom* and Kylian's *Dream Dances,* along with world premieres by expatriate Joffrey dancer Forsythe (*Square Deal*) and by Arpino (*Quarter-Tones for Mr. B.* and *Italian Suite*).

Dance Theatre of Harlem began its touring year in New York with Bronislava Nijinska's exotic *Les Biches,* David Lichine's *Graduation Ball,* Balanchine's *Square Dance,* and Agnes de Mille's *Fall River Legend* but no commissioned works. San Francisco Ballet's gala 50th anniversary season boasted Kylian's *Forgotten Land* and such novelties as *Pixellage* by Betsy Erickson (with computer graphics decor) and *Romanze* by director Michael Smuin with film producer Francis Ford Coppola. Under Robert Weiss's leadership, Pennsylvania Ballet's refurbished repertory included Richard Tanner's *XVIII Symphonic Etudes* (Schumann), Peter Martins's *Calcium Light Night,* Lynne Taylor-Corbett's *Ordinary Rhythms,* Paul Taylor's *Arden Court* and *Musette,* and a revised *Coppélia.*

Boston Ballet founder E. Virginia Williams resigned as artistic director, leaving Violette Verdy alone at the helm. Houston Ballet mounted the first U.S. production of Ashton's *The Two Pigeons.* Ballet West and Houston Ballet in their Washington, D.C., debuts showed more technical than choreographic strength. Frederic Franklin restaged Ruth Page's *Billy Sunday* for Cincinnati Ballet, which took up dual-city residence in New Orleans, La. (as New Orleans City Ballet). Paul Taylor (*Sunset,* music by Edward Elgar) and Merce Cunningham (*Quartet*) exhibited unflagging creative brilliance in major company seasons. Cunningham marked his 40th year with collaborator John Cage and his 30th with his company by making a world tour. Martha Graham postponed a New York season and presented her 172nd dance, *Phaedra's Dream,* fittingly enough in Athens. Alvin Ailey's company won praise for Talley Beatty's *The Stack-Up* and Bill T. Jones's *Fever Swamp* and celebrated its 25th anniversary year with an alumni-studded gala. Twyla Tharp dazzled audiences with her TV version of *The Catherine Wheel.*

Interest in black dance peaked with a historic conference/festival (Dance Black America) at the Brooklyn Academy of Music (BAM); the first Festival Africa south of the Mason-Dixon Line at the American Dance Festival in Durham, N.C.; and an 81st birthday gala honouring John Bubbles, father of rhythm tap dance, in Los Angeles. Such popular forms as "breaking," "electric boogie," and "popping" moved from city streets to Hollywood (*Flashdance*), trendy clubs, and the concert and theatre stage. BAM mounted a two-part festival of vanguard artists in collaboration (Next Wave) featuring choreographers Dana Reitz, Bill T. Jones and Arnie Zane, David Gordon, Trisha Brown, Lucinda Childs, Molissa Fenley, and Nina Wiener. The Palm Beach Festival paid tribute to Ashton with the first U.S. performance of *Soupirs* by Antoinette Sibley and Anthony Dowell.

Major awards went to Katherine Dunham (Kennedy Center Honors), George Balanchine (Presidential Medal of Freedom), and Paul Taylor (Samuel H. Scripps $25,000 award). Dancers swept Broadway's Tony awards: Natalia Makarova for *On Your Toes* and Tommy Tune, Thommie Walsh, and Charles ("Honi") Coles for *My One and Only.*

In Canada Erik Bruhn took the reins from Alexander Grant as artistic director of National Ballet of Canada following a season that featured James Ku-

JOHAN ELBERS/BEATRIZ SCHOLLER

Israel's Bat-Dor Dance Company was well received in New York City; one of the works performed there was *And After.*

delka's *Hedda*, Michael Peters's *Quartet*, and Constantin Patsalas's *Canciones*. Grant's parting performance was in Peter Schaufuss's production of *Napoli*. The Royal Winnipeg Ballet mounted Peter Wright's staging of *Giselle* (danced by Evelyn Hart; *see* BIOGRAPHIES), while in Montreal Les Grands Ballets Canadiens feted its 25th anniversary and Les Ballets Jazz marked its 10th.

In addition to Balanchine, the dance world mourned the loss of critic-poet Edwin Denby, Judson Dance Theater pioneer Judith Dunn, and Balanchine's costume designer, Barbara Karinska.

(SALI ANN KRIEGSMAN)

Europe. More than 100 new works, large and small, were currently being made and performed each year in Britain alone, reflecting a continuing growth in public interest in most European countries. Television had become a contributory factor, to the extent that the BBC in Britain devoted 35 minutes of prime time on six consecutive Sundays in 1983 to a multistyled dance revue ("The Hot Shoe Show"). The first videocassettes of classic Royal Ballet productions were successfully marketed.

The Royal Ballet from Covent Garden went round the world in May, making its first visit to China. London Festival Ballet visited Caracas, Venezuela, as Britain's main contribution to the Simon Bolívar bicentennial. These and other British companies engaged in an unprecedented degree of foreign touring, almost all in association with the British Council, the public agency for supporting cultural and educational projects overseas, which expected to spend more than £800,000 on dance touring alone during the year.

Kenneth MacMillan, the Royal Ballet's principal choreographer, received a knighthood in Queen Elizabeth's birthday honours. His *Valley of Shadows*, premiered in March, proved a melodramatic treatment of Giorgio Bassani's novel *The Garden of the Finzi-Continis*, but it revealed Alessandra Ferri, then 19, Italian-born and Royal Ballet trained, as an upcoming ballerina of major talent. She was later cast for the lead in MacMillan's new TV version of Brecht and Weill's *Seven Deadly Sins*.

Sadler's Wells Royal Ballet dancer David Bintley, 25, was named company choreographer. His latest work, *Choros*, his first to specially composed music (by Aubrey Meyer), was premiered to general acclaim. The company continued to foster young creative talent with new works by Jonathan Burrows (*The Winter Play*, based on an old tradition of English street theatre; music by Dudley Simpson) and Michael Corder (*St. Anthony Variations*, to music by Brahms).

Ballet Rambert visited the Edinburgh Festival for the first time. The festival theme, "Vienna 1900," was reflected in the commissioned premiere of *Murderer, Hope of Women* by the American-born Glen Tetley. Derived from the 1907 Expressionist play by Oskar Kokoschka, it required the dancers to speak the fragmentary text (in English translation) while dancing, with no music except percussion support. The device was not thought to be successful, despite committed performances by the dancers, led by Lucy Burge and Albert van Nierop. The same company at Edinburgh provided the first involvement with dance by the distinguished artist Bridget Riley. Her experiments on canvas with the active properties of one colour laid directly beside another were transmuted into five varied drop cloths for *Colour Moves*. The effects were heightened by Robert North's choreography as the dancers moved in front of the designs, to music by Christopher Benstead.

In July, after 15 years as artistic director of London Contemporary Dance Theatre, Robert Cohan gave up day-to-day control of the leading European outpost of American modern dance. He remained an artistic adviser to the Contemporary Dance Trust, which oversees the work of the company and its associated vocational school, and he hoped to continue choreographing.

New York City Ballet made its first tour following the death of Balanchine with visits to Covent Garden (London), Copenhagen, and Paris. It brought thoroughbred dancing of impeccable classical style and musicality in a repertory of works more than half of which were new to European audiences. Other visitors to London included the

Under Mikhail Baryshnikov, the American Ballet Theatre broadened its range somewhat. In *Once Upon a Time* by Twyla Tharp are (from left) Amanda McKerrow, Baryshnikov, Deirdre Carberry, Elaine Kudo, and Nancy Raffa.

MARTHA SWOPE

Houston and Boston ballets; a Brazilian company, Grupo Corpo; Sweden's Cramér Dance Company, with an intriguing mixture of folklore, mask, and mime as well as dance; and the Caracalla Dance Company of Lebanon, which had miraculously kept together in strife-torn Beirut and was touring with a somewhat cabaret-style dance entertainment in an oriental *Taming of the Shrew.*

The Irish National Ballet was a new title conferred officially from June 1, 1983, on the Irish Ballet, first formed in 1974. It continued to be directed by Joan-Denise Moriarty and to be based at Cork. France acquired a new company in the Ballet du Nord, directed by the Cuban-born Alfonso Catà, formerly director at Frankfurt am Main and Geneva. The company had a regular base at the National Choreographic Centre of Roubaix, northeast France, and performed a repertory of new and classic ballets in conjunction with other theatres in nearby Lille and Tourcoing. Some West German opera houses, including those of Hamburg and Munich, responded to audience demand by increasing the number of dance performances in relation to opera (as also occurred in Vienna).

Changes in ballet directors affected more than a dozen German houses, but at Stuttgart Marcia Haydée, artistic director since 1976, accepted a further five-year extension, giving an unusual degree of continuity to a major German company.

Elsewhere, Rudolf Nureyev began his first season in charge of the Paris Opêra Ballet, Maina Gielgud left Britain to direct the Australian Ballet, and Maris Liepa, a teacher at the Bolshoi School, took over the State Opera Ballet at Sofia, Bulg. Another distinguished Soviet artist, Maya Plisetskaya (who staged and danced in her Chekhov-based *The Seagull* with the Florence Maggio Musicale company), was to assume directorship of the Rome Opera Ballet in 1984.

The full Bolshoi Ballet went to the Vienna Festival and to Wiesbaden, West Germany, and a smaller group, Stars of the Bolshoi, to Paris. The latter performed an oddly assorted triple bill under the title "Hommage à Ulanova." Galina Ulanova herself, at 73, staged *Giselle* at Hamburg for the American director there, John Neumeier, and the current Bolshoi director, Yury Grigorovich, produced his version of the classic *Don Quixote* for the Royal Danish Ballet at Copenhagen. Other activity in Scandinavia included a new summer ballet festival at Malmö, Sweden; an updated, modern-dress version of *Giselle* by Mats Ek for Sweden's Cullberg Ballet; and, at Göteborg, Sweden, no less a project than Wagner's *Ring of the Nibelungs* transcribed into a four-hour dance form by Ulf Gadd and Svenerik Goude. Britain's Ballet Rambert was among the companies taking part in Finland's Kuopio Dance Festival.

Gluck's opera *Orpheus and Euridice* was produced as a full-scale ballet at Basel, Switz., with choreography by Heinz Spoerli; the singers performed with the orchestra in the pit. Spoerli also designed the set, which showed Hell as an industrial maze with a treadmill as the ultimate frustration for Orpheus and his beloved. The Netherlands Dance Theatre maintained its reputation for enterprise with various new works, including three by its Czechoslovak-born artistic director, Jiri Kylian. One of these, *Curses and Blessings,* involved double choreography by Kylian and the British choreographer Christopher Bruce, to music for chorus and for orchestra by Peter Eben. Each choreographer had nine dancers, and the toss of a coin decided who should work with which music. A common theme of oppression and competition was treated as a naturalistic pantomime fable by Bruce to the orchestral music, and more abstractly by Kylian to the choral music, but their combination as a single entity was found to be excessively lopsided.

Deaths during the year included those of Donald Britton, former Royal Ballet principal dancer and teacher; John Gilpin, former principal dancer and teacher; Alan Hooper, director of the London Royal Academy of Dancing; Valeria Kratina, an outstanding exponent of German Expressionist dance; and Mona Vangsaae, former ballerina of the Royal Danish Ballet (*see* OBITUARIES).

(NOËL GOODWIN)

See also Music; Theatre.
[652]

AGIP/PICTORIAL PARADE

Stars of the Bolshoi, a ballet spectacle presented in Paris under the direction of the Moscow Opera's Vladimir Vassiliev, included *Fragments of a Biography* on its program.

Defense

Five developments that had emerged over the last decade continued in 1983. These were, first, the Soviet military buildup; second, the reemergence in the third world of traditional, often bitter rivalries previously contained by the now-defunct European empires; third, the Soviets' exploitation of these rivalries to their own advantage; fourth, Soviet development of proxy forces, including those of Eastern Europe (especially East Germany), Cuba, Libya, and Vietnam; and fifth—in large measure a response to the other four—the Reagan administration's reestablishment, since 1980, of the U.S. policy of containing Soviet expansion by economic, political, and military means.

These trends had led to greater instability. The Soviet conviction that the correlation of forces, military and political, was moving in their favour led them to take actions previously regarded as too risky, such as intervention in the Caribbean and Central America. Such interventions, plus U.S. counterinterventions, were involving the superpowers in local conflicts that neither could wholly control, as in the Middle East. Adding to the instability was the growing quantity of sophisticated weapons being transferred by gift or sale to third world governments and revolutionary groups. (*See* Feature Article: *Flourishing, Worldwide, Deadly: The Open Market in Arms.*) Examples included Soviet arms transfers to Cuba, Nicaragua, and Syria and French sales of Super Étendard strike aircraft armed with Exocet air-to-surface (antiship) missiles (ASM) to Iraq. The enhanced accuracy of weapons systems, both conventional and nuclear, was increasing the advantages accruing to the side striking first, and the Soviets were more and more willing to exploit this advantage at the risk of escalating regional conflicts and forcing U.S. counterintervention.

Two major defense issues reemerged. The first was the U.S.-U.S.S.R. nuclear balance of strategic and intermediate-range nuclear forces. Attempts to achieve effective arms control via the strategic arms limitation (now reduction) talks (SALT/START) and those on limiting intermediate nuclear forces (INF) had been frustrated, and the U.S. had begun to rebuild strategic nuclear forces (SNF) and, with NATO-Europe, NATO's INF. But these moves had triggered opposition from politically important antinuclear movements in both the U.S. and Europe. The second issue was the NATO-Warsaw Pact balance of military forces, nuclear, chemical, and conventional. The upheavals in Poland, especially, intensified the Soviets' fears concerning their control over Eastern Europe and the threat to that control posed by a democratic, prosperous Western Europe.

Three events in the fall dramatized these disturbing defense developments. On September 1 the Soviet Air Defense Command shot down Korean Air Lines flight 007 with the loss of 269 lives. Though the evidence indicated that the plane had accidentally strayed into Soviet airspace, quite possibly because of a computer error, the Soviets refused to apologize and insisted that KAL 007 was on a spy mission. On October 23 a suicide bombing attack on the U.S. contingent of the international peacekeeping force in Lebanon killed 241 U.S. servicemen. Similar attacks were made on the French contingent, Israeli forces in southern Lebanon, and installations (including the U.S. embassy) in Kuwait. Responsibility was claimed by a fundamentalist Shi'ah group with ties to Iran and Syria. On October 25 U.S. and Caribbean forces landed on the tiny Caribbean island of Grenada, which had come under increasing Cuban domination. The action underlined the U.S. administration's determination to roll back Soviet control of countries outside Eastern Europe.

Danish Literature: *see* Literature

Deaths: *see* Demography; *see also obituaries of prominent persons who died in 1983 listed under* People of the Year

UNITED STATES

Defense was becoming a major political issue as the 1984 presidential election campaign began. Support for a freeze on superpower nuclear weapons was sharply reduced by the shooting down of KAL flight 007 and by evidence that the Soviets were violating existing arms control agreements. It was also apparent that a freeze would work to the Soviets' advantage because U.S. S/INF were so much older than the Soviet counterparts. (*See* TABLE I.) However, controversy over the size of the defense budget and how it was being spent grew more acrimonious.

U.S. defense expenditure for 1982–83 of $215.9 billion, for armed forces totaling 2,136,400 personnel, amounted to 7.2% of the gross domestic product (GDP). Comparatively, this was below the 25-year (1950–75) average of 10% of GDP but above President Carter's record low 5.1% in 1978. In 1982 defense took 15% of public spending or 29.2% of federal spending, suggesting that defense expenditures need not require socially unacceptable cuts in other government programs.

The question of a basing mode for the MX Peacekeeper intercontinental ballistic missile (ICBM), which had bedeviled two administrations, was referred early in the year to a bipartisan presidential commission headed by Brent Scowcroft, a retired Air Force general and national security adviser to Pres. Gerald Ford. Reporting in April, the commission recommended production of 100 Peacekeepers, to be deployed in existing Minuteman ICBM silos. Since this basing mode could not survive a Soviet attack, it was likely to be changed. However, the commission viewed this as an interim measure, pending the recommended development of a small, single-warhead mobile ICBM for deployment in the 1990s. Production of the first 26 Peacekeepers was approved by Congress. These, together with the planned 100 B-1B bombers carrying air-launched cruise missiles (ALCM), would be deployed from 1986 onward. Until then, the Air Force would retain 1,000 fixed-silo land-based Minuteman II and III ICBM but would retire all 45 Titan II ICBM. The strategic bomber force had been reduced to 191 B-52G/H's, being converted to carry up to 20 ALCM each, and 56 FB-111A medium-range bombers. Pres. Ronald Reagan's March 23 "Star Wars" speech committed the U.S. to a 20-year program to develop effective defenses against ballistic missiles.

The Navy planned to continue deployment of the Ohio-class ballistic missile submarines (SSBN), each carrying 24 Trident I submarine-launched ballistic missiles (SLBM) and, from 1989 onward, the longer-range (6,400 nautical miles) and more accurate Trident II. Three Ohio-class SSBN were deployed and seven more were on order. Of the 31 older SSBN, the 12 Franklin class had been converted to carry 16 Trident I's each, while the 19 Lafayette class each retained 16 Poseidon C-3 SLBM. Some 3,000 SLBM were being deployed on nuclear attack submarines and major surface combatants, with some allocated to tactical and some to strategic missions.

U.S. general purpose forces continued their rebuilding, emphasizing high technology and mobility. The Grenada operation was a model in terms of the successful deployment of an appropriate mix of forces. The newly formed Central Command (Centcom) replaced the Rapid Deployment Joint Task Force to control deployments in Southeast Asia and the Indian Ocean, including the Persian Gulf. It could muster about 300,000 personnel on mobilization, drawing on U.S. forces assigned to Central Europe.

The 569,000-strong Navy, with 95 nuclear submarines and 187 major surface combatants, provided 13 carrier battle groups with 2 more planned. Each battle group comprised an attack carrier with an air wing of 70–95 aircraft and escorting surface vessels and submarines. Of the 11 modern (post-1955) carriers, four were nuclear powered. Naval aircraft included 240 F-14A Tomcat fighters, replacing the last 48 F-4 Phantoms. The recommissioned World War II battleship "New Jersey" combined a 16-in. main battery for fire support with multiple Tomahawk surface-to-surface missile (SSM) launchers. The 9 nuclear and 19 conventionally powered guided weapons (GW) cruisers included the first Ticonderoga-class ships with the Aegis fleet air defense missile/radar system. Other major surface combatants included 37 GW (4 new Kidd class) and 31 gun/antisubmarine warfare (ASW) Spruance-class destroyers and 37 GW (31 Perry class) and 53 gun (40 Knox class) frigates.

The Marine Corps with 194,600 personnel, still the principal U.S. power projection force, was organized into three divisions, each with its integral air wing for close support. F-18 Hornet fighters were replacing the 108 F-4N/S Phantoms, and the 50 A-6E Intruder strike aircraft and 95 A-4M Skyhawks were being retired. The 45 AV-8A/C Harrier vertical/short takeoff and landing (V/STOL) fighter/ground-attack aircraft were U.S. versions of the British Harrier that had proved so effective in the 1982 Falklands war. The key role of the Corps was shown by its casualties in 1983: more than 220 killed, the worst since the Vietnam war.

The 592,000-strong Air Force had some 3,700 combat aircraft. Modern types included 376 F-15 Eagle interceptors, 360 Falcon fighter-bombers, and 29 E-3A Sentry airborne warning and control systems (AWACS). Among older types were 528 F-4 Phantom fighter-bombers, 252 F-111A/D/E/F medium-range bombers, and 288 A-10A Thunderbolt ground-support aircraft. The Army of 780,000 personnel provided 16 divisions (18,500 men each): 4 armoured, 6 mechanized, 4 infantry, 1 air assault, and 1 airborne. New equipment included 1,229 M-1 Abrams main battle tanks and 45 M-3 Bradley mechanized infantry combat vehicles (MICV). Also new were 63 multiple launch rocket systems and the first 14 Patriot surface-to-air missile (SAM) battalions (60 missiles each).

JAMES LONG—JAMES L. LONG ASSOCIATES

The strategic arms reduction talks included discussion of the MX Peacekeeper intercontinental ballistic missile. Here, hoisted out of its canister by steam, the missile ignited in the air and sped 4,100 nautical miles to its target. This launch, in June, was its first flight.

Overseas force deployments remained concentrated in NATO-Europe (some 404,000 personnel) and the Pacific (approximately 150,000, including 40,000 in South Korea and some 2,000 in Japan). U.S. forces in Latin America totaled about 15,500. The combination of the Lebanon and Grenada operations stretched U.S forces very thinly. This underlined the elementary but vital point that the adequacy of U.S. defense forces and defense budgets could be properly assessed only in relation to the U.S. interests they were expected to protect and the threats posed by hostile powers.

U.S.S.R.

The Soviet military machine was the most powerful in the world in 1983. Its 5.5 million personnel included 1.5 million command and general support personnel and 450,000 paramilitary security forces. There were indications that the military and the security services, especially the State Security Committee (KGB), were increasing their political power at the expense of the Communist Party. These forces represented a heavy burden on the Soviet people, however, especially as defense spending was growing faster (4–8.5% per year) than the economy (2–3%). For 1981, the Soviet

UPI

The U.S. battleship "New Jersey" launched its first test of the Tomahawk surface-to-surface missile a distance of some 500 nautical miles into a test target area in Nevada.

defense budget was estimated at $267 billion, representing 14–20% of GDP.

The Strategic Rocket Forces, with 325,000 troops, increased their superiority over U.S. and NATO S/INF in terms of missile and warhead numbers and warhead numbers and yields. They were functionally equivalent in terms of accuracy for strikes against hardened targets. The figures shown in Table I are low because the Soviets deployed multiple reload missiles for their ICBM/intermediate range ballistic missile (IRBM) and SLBM launchers. The Soviets were testing two new ICBM, the PL-4 and PL-5 (one a mobile ICBM); three new cruise missiles, an ALCM, a ground-launched cruise missile (GLCM)—the SSC-X-4 with a 3,000-km range (1 km=0.62 mi)—and a sea-launched cruise missile (SLCM), the SS-NX-21; and a new strategic bomber, the Blackjack-A. The first Typhoon-class SSBN, larger than the U.S. Ohio class and carrying the new SS-NX-20 SLBM, was operational.

The Soviet National Air Defense Troops (Voyska-PVO) formed a separate service, with over 500,000 personnel and 1,250 aircraft. It was a Voyska-PVO Su-15 Flagon E that shot down KAL flight 007 on orders from its ground control station. The incident highlighted the Soviets' rigid command and control procedures and their extreme sensitivity about incursions into their airspace. At the same time, significant weaknesses were indicated by their difficulty in intercepting a 747 jumbo jet. Other defense forces included 32 antiballistic missile (ABM) launchers around Moscow. A nationwide ABM system was under construction, including 10 radar/battle management stations.

The 1.8 million-strong Army was organized into 50 tank, 134 motor rifle (mechanized), 15 artillery, and 7 airborne divisions (11,000–14,000 men each). Organizational changes included the establishment of three theatre commands, Western, Southern, and Far Eastern, plus a Central Strategic Reserve area that included the Moscow, Volga, and Ural military districts. The Western Theatre was subdivided into theatres of military operations controlling S/INF and naval as well as air and ground forces. There were reports of plans to form operational maneuver groups under wartime conditions; these would be all-arms, mobile forces comprising several divisions, intended to penetrate NATO rear areas, disrupt supply lines, and destroy nuclear weapons in their storage areas. Current equipment included 50,000 tanks (with 7,500 new T-72/-80 and 35,000 older T-54/-55/-62 main battle tanks) and 62,000 armoured fighting vehicles (AFV).

Deployment remained concentrated against NATO-Europe, with 30 divisions (16 tank, 14 motor rifle) and 1 artillery unit in Central and Eastern Europe and 65 divisions (23 tank, 37 motor rifle, 5 airborne) and 8 artillery units in the European U.S.S.R. The Central Reserve area held 16 divisions, the Southern Theatre 28 divisions, mainly motor rifle, and the Far Eastern Theatre 7 tank and 45 motor rifle divisions, plus 4 artillery units. Outside Eastern Europe, the major force deployment abroad (100,000–120,000 troops) was in Afghanistan, where guerrilla fighters continued to resist the Soviet occupation. (*See* AFGHANISTAN.) Soviet casualties there were uncertain but significant. The next three largest overseas deployments were in Syria (7,000–10,000), Vietnam (7,000), and Cuba (5,000), and there were smaller deployments of 1,000–2,500 troops each in Algeria, Ethiopia, Iraq, Libya, and Yemen (Aden).

The Navy (460,000 personnel) was a significant power projection force, with 288 major surface combatants and more than 200 attack and 69 cruise-missile submarines. Major surface combatants included three Kiev helicopter/V/STOL fighter carriers (a fourth nearing completion), two Moskva-class ASW helicopter carriers, and one Kirov-class nuclear-powered GW battle cruiser, displacing 20,000 tons (a second nearing completion). The first Black-Com I-class GW cruiser, the "Krasina," now operational, carried 16 SSM, 6–8 SAM, and 4 ASW missiles. The 40 GW destroyers included 2 of the new Sovremenny class with SSM and SAM and 2 of the new Udaloy class with SAM and ASW missiles. Of the 69 cruise-missile submarines, 49 were nuclear; the 2 new Oscar class each carried 24 SS-N-19 SLCM (460-km range, 200–350-kiloton warhead). The nine Yankee-I class SSBN the Soviets were required to scrap under SALT I had apparently been retained or converted. Soviet naval deployment was in four fleets. The two largest were the Northern Fleet in the Kola Peninsula, with 46 SSBN, 135 submarines (all types), and 76 surface combatants, and the Pacific Fleet with 28 SSBN, 92 other submarines, and 89 major surface combatants. The Baltic and the Black Sea fleets had, respectively, 30 and 25 submarines and 40 and 83 major surface combatants.

The 365,000-strong Air Force was equipped with some 6,000 combat aircraft and 2,300 helicopters. There were about 2,500 fighter-bombers, with modern types including 650 MiG-27 Flogger D/J's, 650 Su-17 Fitter D/H's, 800 Su-24 Fencer A/C's, and 75 of the Su-25 Frogfoot. Of the 3,000 fighters, newer types included 1,750 MiG-23 Flogger B/G's and 60 MiG-25 B/D/M Foxhounds. The new MiG-29 Fulcrum and Su-27 Flanker fighters were being deployed. Reconnaissance aircraft totaled 640, including 150 MiG-25 B/D's.

WARSAW PACT

Events in Poland in recent years had intensified the political uncertainties over whether non-Soviet Warsaw Pact forces would support a Soviet attack on NATO-Europe or whether they might turn on the Soviet forces stationed on their territory. These included 20 divisions in East Germany, 2–3 in Poland, 4 in Hungary, and 5 in Czechoslovakia. Of these four Eastern European nations, Poland had the largest forces, totaling 340,000 personnel and including a 230,000-strong Army with 3,400 T-54/-55 main battle tanks and an 88,000-strong Air Force with 705 combat aircraft (430 MiG-17/-21 interceptors). Czechoslovakia's 204,500-strong forces, the second largest, comprised an army of 148,000 with 3,500 T-54/-55/-72 tanks and an air force of 56,500 with 470 combat aircraft (252 MiG-21/-23 interceptors).

The East German armed forces totaled 167,000 personnel. The 116,000-strong Army had 1,500 T-54/-55/-72 tanks plus 1,600 in storage, and the Air Force of 37,000 had 360 combat aircraft, including 300 MiG-21/-23 interceptors. Hungary's armed forces, with 105,000 personnel, comprised an army of 84,000 with 1,200 T-54/-55 tanks and an air force of 21,000 with 120 MiG-21 and 20 MiG-23 interceptors. All four countries allocated a much lower proportion of GDP to defense than the U.S.S.R.: 6.5% for East Germany, 5.2% for Czechoslovakia, about 3% for Poland, and 2.4% for Hungary.

Table I. U.S./NATO–Soviet Strategic and Intermediate Nuclear Force Balance, July 1983

Weapons systems	Range (km)	Payload[1] (000 lb)	Warheads, yield[2]	CEP[3]	Speed (Mach)	Number deployed
UNITED STATES Strategic Forces						
Intercontinental ballistic missiles (ICBM)						1,000
Titan II	15,000	8.3	1 × 9 mt	1,300	...	45–0[4]
Minuteman II	11,300	1.6	1 × 1–2 kt	370	...	450
Minuteman III Mod 1	13,000	2.4	3 × 170 kt	280	...	250
Mod 2	...	...	3 × 335 kt	220	...	300
Submarine-launched ballistic missiles (SLBM; in 36 nuclear submarines)						520
Poseidon C-3	4,600	3.3	10 × 50 kt or 14 × 50 kt	450	...	304
Trident I/C-4	7,400	2.9	8 × 100 kt or 14 × 50 kt	450	...	264
Manned bombers and air-launched cruise missiles (ALCM)						
B-52G	12,000	70	...	...	0.95	90
B-52H	16,000	70	...	...	0.95	90
FB-111A	4,700	37.5	...	...	2.5	56
AGM-86B ALCM	2,400	0.2	200 kt	100	0.7	200
U.S./NATO Intermediate Nuclear Forces[5] (Total: 341 weapons, 191 delivery systems)						
Intermediate-range ballistic missiles (IRBM)						
U.S. Pershing II	1,800	...	5 × 50+ kt	30	...	9
Manned bombers and ground-launched cruise missiles (GLCM)						
U.S. F-111A/E	4,700	28	2	...	2.5	252[6]
Tomahawk	2,250	0.2	200 kt	100	0.7	32
BRITAIN (Strategic Nuclear Forces only)[7]						
Submarine-launched ballistic missiles (SLBM; in 4 nuclear submarines)						
Polaris A-3	4,600	1	3–6 × 200 kt	900	...	64
Strike aircraft						
Buccaneer	3,700	12	2	...	0.95	45[4]
Tornado	2,800	16	2	...	.95	32
FRANCE (Strategic and INF)[7]						
Submarine-launched ballistic missiles (SLBM; in 5 nuclear submarines)						
MSBS M-20	3,000	...	1 × 1 mt	...	...	80
Intermediate-range ballistic missiles (IRBM)						
SSBS S-3	3,500	...	1 × 1 mt	...	...	18
Strike aircraft						
Mirage IVA	3,200	16	1 × 60 kt	...	2.2	34
Mirage IIIE	2,400	19	2 × 15 kt	...	1.8	30
Super Etendard	1,500	2	2 × 15 kt	...	1.0	36
SOVIET UNION Strategic Forces						
Intercontinental ballistic missiles (ICBM)						1,700+
SS-11 Mod 1	10,500	2	1 × 1 mt	1,400	...	550
Mod 3	8,800	2.5	3 × 100–300 kt	1,100		
SS-13 Savage	10,000	1	750 kt	2,000	...	60
SS-16	9-10,000	...	3 × 150 kt	...	...	200[8]
SS-17 Mod 1	10,000	6	4 × 750 kt	450	...	150
Mod 2	11,000	3.6	6 mt	450		
Mod 3	10,000	...	4 ×2 kt	...		
SS-18 Mod 1	12,000	16.5	20 mt	450	...	308
Mod 2	11,000	16.7	8 × 900 kt	450		
Mod 3	10,500	16	20 mt	350		
Mod 4	11,000	16.7	10 ×500 kt	300		
SS-19 Mod 2	10,000	7.5	5 mt	300	...	330
Mod 3	10,000	8	6 × 550 kt	300	...	
Submarine-launched ballistic missiles (in 70 nuclear plus 14 diesel submarines)						c. 1,000
SS-N-5 Serb	1,400	...	1 × 1–2 mt	2,800	...	48
SS-N-6 Mod 1, 2	3,000	1.5	1 × 1 mt	900	...	384
Mod 3	3,000	1.5	2 × 200 kt	1,400	...	
SS-N-8 Mod 1	7,800	1.5	1 × 1 mt	1,300	...	292
Mod 2	9,100	8	1 × 800 kt	900		
SS-N-17	3,900	2.5	1 × 1 mt	1,500	...	12
SS-N-18 Mod 1	6,500	5	3 × 200 kt	1,400	...	224
Mod 2	8,000	...	1 × 450 kt	600	...	
Mod 3	6,500	...	7 × 200 kt	600	...	
SS-N-20	8,300	...	9-12 × 200 kt	...	...	20
Manned bombers						140
Tu-95 Bear	12,800	40	...	...	0.78	100
Mya-4 Bison	11,200	20	...	...	0.87	43
Tu-26 Backfire B	8,000	17.5	4	...	2.5	210
Soviet INF (Total: 4,500–4,700 warheads, 2,145–2,445 delivery systems)						
Variable/intermediate/medium-range ballistic missiles (V/I/MRBM)[9]						
SS-4 Sandal	2,000	3	1 × 1 mt	2,300	...	223
SS-5 Skean	4,100	3.5	1 × 1 mt	1,100	...	16
SS-20 Mod 1	5,000	1.2	1 × 1.5 mt	...	...	...
Mod 2	5,000	...	3 × 150 kt	400	...	1,200
Mod 3	7,400	...	1 × 50 kt	...	...	...
Medium/short-range ballistic missiles and sea-launched cruise missiles[10]						
SS-22 MRBM	1,000	...	1 ×500 kt	300	...	c. 100
SS-N-12 G/SLCM	1,000	...	1 × 350 kt	2.2	...	c. 100
Manned bombers[11]						745
Tu-16 Badger	4,800	20	2	...	0.8	440
Tu-22 Blinder	4,000	12	2	...	1.5	165

[1] Payload refers to a missile's throw weight or a bomber's weapons load.
[2] For MIRV and MRV the figure to the left of the multiplication sign gives the number of warheads and the figure to the right is the yield per warhead. For bombers, weapons per bomber are given.
[3] Circular Error Probable: the radius (in metres) of a circle within which at least half of the missile warheads aimed at a specific target will fall.
[4] Obsolete systems being withdrawn; excluded from number deployed.
[5] INF systems are missiles with ranges or aircraft with unrefueled combat radii of 1,000 km or more; combat radii are about one third or less of the range.
[6] Total deployed worldwide, including FB-111A; 150 is the inventory normally based in Europe, or within striking range of Europe.
[7] British nuclear forces are under national control, but may be assigned to NATO. French nuclear forces are controlled and targeted independently of NATO.
[8] Mobile SS-16 ICBM reported deployed, based on SS-20 V/IRBM.
[9] Total deployed against both NATO and China theatres; two-thirds are thought to be deployed against NATO. Two missiles per launcher.
[10] Although not classified as Soviet INF, Soviet M/SRBM and G/SLCM could hit targets in Western Europe and are therefore shown for illustrative purposes.
[11] Total deployed worldwide. Of these, about half are allocated to Soviet Naval Aviation (some 220 Tu-16, 40 Tu-22, and 100 Tu-26). Two-thirds of the remaining strike bombers and ASM carriers are considered deployed against NATO. Tu-26 Backfire is now counted as strategic.

Sources: International Institute for Strategic Studies, *The Military Balance 1983–1984;* and *Aviation Week and Space Technology.* Figures for Soviet forces, especially INF, can only be estimates.

Table II. Approximate Strengths of Regular Armed Forces of the World

Country	Military personnel in 000s			Warships[1]			Jet aircraft[3]			
	Army	Navy	Air Force	Aircraft carriers/ cruisers	Submarines[2]	Destroyers/ frigates	Bombers and fighter-bombers	Fighters/ recon-naissance	Tanks[4]	Defense expenditure as % of GNP
I. NATO										
Belgium	69.7	4.6	20.5	—	—	4 FFG	90 FB	36, 18 R	334	3.3
Canada	13.0	5.5	15.3	—	3	23 DDG	76 FB	38, 18 MR	114	2.0
Denmark	17.5	5.8	7.4	—	5 C	5 FFG, 5FF	52 FB	40, 16 R	208	2.0
France[5]	311.2	68.0	100.4	2 CV, 1 CVH, 1 CG	17, 1 SSN, 5 SSBN	20 DDG, 25 FFG	34 SB, 250 FB	165, 45 R, 42 MR	1,240	4.1
Germany, West	335.5	36.4	106.0	—	24 C	7 DDG, 3 FFG, 4 FF	450 FB	60, 60 R, 19 MR	4,254	4.3
Greece	142.0	19.5	23.5	—	10	14 DD, 2 FFG, 5 FF	232 FB	89, 28 R, 8 MR	1,463	6.7
Italy	258.0	44.5	70.6	1 CVH, 2 CAH	10	4 DDG, 7 FFG, 4 FF	162 FB	72, 24 R, 14 MR	1,770	2.6
Luxembourg	0.7	—	—	—	—	—	—	—	—	1.2
Netherlands, The	67.0	17.4	17.5	—	4 C	2 DDG, 15 FFG	126 FB	18 R, 9 MR	916	3.3
Norway	24.2	8.9	9.9	—	14 C	5 FFG	70 FB	15, 6 R, 7 MR	116	3.0
Portugal	41.0	13.0	9.5	—	3 C	17 FF	63 FB	4 R	55	3.3
Spain	260.0	54.0	33.0	1 CVH	5 C	9 DD, 11 FFG, 4 FF	35 FB	116, 17 R, 6 MR	760	2.6
Turkey	470.0	46.0	53.0	—	14 C	15 DD, 2 FF	305 FB	36, 43 R	3,577	5.2
United Kingdom	159.0	71.7[6]	89.8	3 CVH	15, 12 SSN, 4 SSBN	13 DDG, 45 FFG	44 B, 143 FB	135, 27 R, 28 MR	1,030	5.1
United States	780.8	763.6[6]	592.0	1 BBG, 4 CVN, 10 CV, 9 CGN, 19 CG, 5 LHA, 7 LPH, 13 LPD, 31 LSD/T	5, 90 SSN, 34 SSBN	37 DDG, 31 DD, 37 FFG, 53 FF	236 SB, 252 B, 1,550 FB	770, 180 R, 330 MR	11,769	7.2
II. WARSAW PACT										
Bulgaria	120.0	8.5	33.8	—	2	2 FFG	64 FB	140, 24 R	1,360	2.9
Czechoslovakia	148.0	—	56.5	—	—	—	164 FB	252, 55 R	3,500	5.2
Germany, East	116.0	14.0	37.0	—	—	2 FFG	47 FB	300, 12 R	1,500	6.5
Hungary	84.0	—	21.0	—	—	—	—	140	1,260	2.4
Poland	230.0	22.0	88.0	—	4	1 DDG	220 FB	430, 55 R	3,450	3.0
Romania	150.0	7.5	32.0	—	—	—	70 FB	224, 18 R	1,380	1.6
U.S.S.R.	1,825.0+ 1,500.0[7]	460.0[6]	1,190.0[8]	3 CV, 2 CVH, 1 CGN, 26 CG, 8 CA	137, 70 SSN, 70 SSBN, 13 SSB, 49 SSGN, 20 SSG	40 DDG, 25 DD, 32 FFG, 151 FF	353 SB, 605 B, 2,700 FB	4,200, 900 R, 290 MR	50,000	14–20
III. OTHER EUROPEAN										
Albania	30.0	3.2	7.2	—	3	—	—	100	100	...
Austria	45.0	—	4.6	—	—	—	32 FB	—	170	1.2
Finland	34.9	2.5	3.0	—	—	—	—	33	—	1.7
Ireland	13.4	1.0	0.8	—	—	—	—	—	—	1.8
Sweden[9]	48.5/700.0	10.0	9.5	—	12 C	—	117 FB	216, 54 R	670	3.1
Switzerland[9]	10.5/580.0	—	8.0/45.0	—	—	—	150 FB	101, 16 R	815	2.1
Yugoslavia	191.0	12.0	36.7	—	7 C	2 FFG	185 FB	150, 35 R	1,300	...
IV. MIDDLE EAST AND MEDITERRANEAN; SUB-SAHARAN AFRICA; LATIN AMERICA[10]										
Algeria	120.0	8.0	12.0	—	—	2 FFG	12 B, 140 FB	113, 17 R	630	1.9
Egypt	315.0	20.0	27.0	—	12	5 DD, 2 FF	14 B, 203 FB	152, 38 R	1,910	7.4
Iran[11]	150.0	20.0	35.0	—	—	3 DDG, 3 DD, 4 FFG	62 FB	50, 13 R	940	...
Iraq[11]	475.0	4.2	38.0	—	—	—	12 B, 140 FB	150	2,360	...
Israel[9]	135.0/450.0	9.0/10.0	28.0/37.0	—	3 C	—	510 FB	20 R	3,600	37.9
Jordan	65.0	0.3	7.5	—	—	—	60 FB	23	580	11.3
Kuwait	10.0	0.5	1.9	—	—	—	30 FB	20	240	...
Lebanon[12]	22.3	0.3	1.3	—	—	—	6 FB	—	54	...
Libya	58.0	6.5	8.5	—	6	1 FFG	7 B, 200 FB	270, 13 R	2,900	...
Morocco	125.0	6.0	13.0	—	—	1 FFG	80 FB	—	135	...
Oman	20.0	2.0	2.0	—	—	—	20 FB	—	18	...
Qatar	5.0	0.7	0.3	—	—	—	—	8	24	...
Saudi Arabia	35.0	2.5	14.0	—	—	—	65 FB	65	450	...
Sudan	53.0	2.0	3.0	—	—	—	30 FB	—	160	...
Syria	170.0	2.5	50.0	—	—	2 FF	205 FB	244, 2 R	4,200	...
Tunisia	23.0	3.5	2.0	—	—	1 FF	—	—	14	...
United Arab Emirates	46.0	1.5	1.5	—	—	—	3 FB	30	118	...
Yemen, North	20.0	0.6	1.0	—	—	—	—	75	714	18.6
Yemen, South	22.0	1.0	2.5	—	—	—	10 B, 60 FB	36	450	...
Angola[13]	35.0	1.0	1.5	—	—	—	67 FB	—	325	...
Ethiopia[14]	244.5	2.5	3.5	—	—	—	100 FB	—	890	...

NATO

Since 1949, when the alliance was founded, the basic objective of NATO had remained constant: to deter a Soviet/Warsaw Pact attack on Western Europe. The dilemmas this created also remained constant. Soviet military superiority could be countered only if NATO-Europe governments spent much more on defense than their electorates wished to spend. So to compensate for weaknesses in conventional and chemical forces, NATO relied on theatre nuclear forces (TNF). But this alarmed most NATO-Europe electorates and some governments because, if deterrence failed and TNF had to be used, Europe could become a nuclear battleground and hence suffer severe damage.

Three panaceas were proposed in 1983, but all were seriously flawed. The first, a NATO doctrine of no first use of nuclear weapons, was proposed by, among others, former U.S. secretary of defense Robert S. McNamara. But such a doctrine could, in fact, encourage a Soviet attack because it would leave NATO conventional forces vulnerable, while the Soviets would not believe it. The second was the 4% solution put forward by Gen. William Rogers, the supreme Allied commander, Europe. It called for a 1% addition to the NATO members' 1978 Long-Term Defense Program commitment to increase defense spending by 3% per year in real terms (after inflation). This would provide a credible NATO conventional defense. However, most NATO members, other than the U.S. and the U.K., had failed to meet even the 3% goal by wide margins. U.S. defense spending, at 7.2% of GDP, was half again as large, proportionately, as that of France and West Germany (4.1 and 4.3%, respec-

	Military personnel in 000s			Warships[1]			Jet aircraft[3]			
Country	Army	Navy	Air Force	Aircraft carriers/ cruisers	Submarines[2]	Detroyers/ frigates	Bombers and fighter-bombers	Fighters/ recon-nais-sance	Tanks[4]	Defense expenditure as % of GNP
Kenya	13.0	0.7	2.4	—	—	—	12 FB	—	72	...
Madagascar	20.0	0.6	0.5	—	—	—	12 FB	—	—	...
Mozambique[15]	11.0	0.7	1.0	—	—	—	35 FB	—	200	...
Nigeria	120.0	4.0	9.0	—	—	2 FF	30 FB	—	65	2.8
Somalia	60.0	0.6	2.0	—	—	—	9 FB	37	140	...
South Africa	67.4/404.5	5.0	10.0	—	3 C	1 FF	15 B, 114 FB	30, 11 R, 25 MR	250	3.9
Tanzania	38.5	0.9	1.0	—	—	—	—	30	30	...
Zaire	22.0	1.5	2.5	—	—	—	—	7	—	...
Zimbabwe	40.0	—	1.3	—	—	—	5 B, 7 FB	—	28	...
Argentina	100.0	36.0	17.0	1 CV	2 C	5 DDG, 4 DD	7 B, 65 FB	80, 5 MR	255	...
Brazil	182.8	49.0	45.3	1 CV	8	3 DDG, 7 DD, 6 FFG	36 FB	15, 28 MR	75	...
Chile	53.0	28.0	15.0	1 CG, 2 CA	2	2 DDG, 2 DD, 2 FFG	65 FB	13, 8 MR	171	...
Colombia	57.0	9.0	4.2	—	2	2 DD, 1 FF	—	16	—	...
Cuba	125.0	12.0	16.0	—	2	—	50 FB	290	660	...
El Salvador	22.0	0.3	2.4	—	—	—	10 FB	—	—	3.8
Mexico	94.5	20.0	5.5	—	—	4 DD, 6 FF	8	7	—	...
Nicaragua	47.0	0.3	1.5	—	—	—	...	...	48	...
Peru	75.0	20.5	40.0	1 CG, 1 CA	6, 6C	2 DDG, 8 DD, 2 FFG	12 B, 66 FB	—	375	2.0
Venezuela	27.5	8.5	4.5	—	3 C	6 FFG	20 B, 12 FB	36, 2 R	75	1.6
V. FAR EAST AND OCEANIA[10]										
Afghanistan[16]	40.0	—	7.0	—	—	—	20 B, 54 FB	25	650	...
Australia	32.9	17.1	22.5	—	6	3 DDG, 8 FFG	24 FB	53, 14 R, 20 MR	103	3.1
Bangladesh	73.0	5.3	3.0	—	—	3 FF	20 FB	6	50	...
Burma	163.0	7.0	9.0	—	—	1 FF	—	—	25	...
China	3,250.0	360.0	490.0	—	100, 2 SSN, 1 SSBN	14 DDG, 16 FFG, 5 FF	90 SB, 700 B, 500 FB	4,600, 130 R	11,450	...
India	960.0	47.0	113.0	1 CV	8	2 DDG, 8 FFG	45 B, 172 FB	400, 8 R, 13 MR	2,100	...
Indonesia	210.0	42.0	29.0	—	3	10 FF	14 FB	16, 24 MR	—	...
Japan	156.0	42.0	43.0	—	14	18 DDG, 13 DD, 13 FFG, 4 FF	60 FB	240, 16 R, 120 MR	950	1.0
Korea, North	700.0	33.5	51.0	—	21	4 FF	70 B, 332 FB	240	2,675	10.2
Korea, South	540.0	49.0	33.0	—	—	11 DD, 8 FF	320 FB	60, 10 R, 20 MR	1,200	7.6
Laos	50.0	1.0	2.0	—	—	—	—	20	—	...
Malaysia	80.0	8.7	11.0	—	—	2 FFG	19 FB	3 MR	—	8.0
Mongolia	25.0	—	0.1	—	—	—	—	12	—	...
New Zealand	5.7	2.8	4.4	—	—	3 FFG	11 FB	5 MR	—	...
Pakistan	450.0	11.0	17.6	—	11 C	1 DDG, 6 DD	11 B, 51 FB	144, 13 R, 3 MR	1,321	7.0
Philippines	60.0	28.0	16.8	—	—	7 FF	24 FB	22, 1 MR	—	2.2
Singapore	45.0	4.5	6.0	—	—	—	72 FB	21, 8 R	—	5.6
Taiwan	310.0	38.0	77.0	—	2 C	17 DDG, 7 DD, 9 FF	422 FB	18, 4 R, 39 MR	310	...
Thailand	160.0	32.2	43.1	—	—	6 FF	15 FB	36, 7 R, 22 MR	55	3.9
Vietnam	1,200.0	8.0	12.5	—	—	4 FF	10 B, 295 FB	210	1,900	...

Note: Data exclude paramilitary, security, and irregular forces. Naval data exclude vessels of less than 100 tons standard displacement. Figures are for July 1983.

1 Aircraft carrier (CV); helicopter carrier (CVH); general purpose amphibious assault ship (LHA); amphibious transport dock (LPD); amphibious assault ship (helicopter) (LPH); dock/tank landing ship (LSD/T); battleship (BBG); heavy cruiser (CA); guided missile cruiser (CG); helicopter cruiser (CAH); destroyer (DD); guided missile destroyer (DDG); frigate (FF); guided missile frigate (FFG); N denotes nuclear powered.

2 Nuclear powered attack submarine (SSN); ballistic missile submarine (SSB); guided (cruise) missile submarine (SSG); coastal (C); N denotes nuclear powered.

3 Bombers (B), fighter-bombers (FB), strategic bombers (SB), reconnaissance fighters (R); maritime reconnaissance (MR) data include jet combat aircraft from all services including naval and air defense. MR also includes propeller driver ASW and ECM aircraft; data exclude light strike/counter-insurgency (COIN) aircraft.

4 Main battle tanks (MBT), medium and heavy, 31 tons and over.

5 French forces were withdrawn from NATO command structure in 1966, but France remains a member of NATO.

6 Includes marines.

7 Soviet forces total 5,500,000, including, under Army, 1,500,000 command and support troops and 450,000 para-military KGB/MVD troops.

8 Figure includes the Strategic Rocket Forces (SRF; 325,000) and the National Air Defense Troops (500,000), both separate services.

9 Second figure is fully mobilized strength.

10 Sections IV and V list only those states with significant military forces.

11 Losses in Iran-Iraq war made remaining force estimates uncertain.

12 Lebanese Army re-forming and expanding. Excludes sectarian militia, totalling perhaps 20,000, and forces deployed by Syria (20,000–25,000) and the Soviet Union (7,000–10,000).

13 Plus 19,000 Cubans and 2,500 East Germans serving with Angolan forces.

14 Ethiopia also has 14,000 Cuban plus other Soviet bloc troops.

15 Plus Soviet, Cuban, Warsaw Pact, and Chinese advisers and technicians in Mozambique.

16 Figures approximate, given Soviet occupation of Afghanistan. Excludes 100,000+ Soviet occupation troops.

Sources: International Institute for Strategic Studies, 23 Tavistock Street, London, *The Military Balance 1983–1984, Strategic Survey 1982–1983.*

tively) and up to three times that of Belgium, Canada, Denmark, The Netherlands, and Norway (2 to 3.3%).

The third panacea involved improved conventional weapons, including the so-called smart munitions, to be used especially for interdiction of a Soviet second-echelon attack. NATO could defeat the first wave of a Soviet/Warsaw Pact attack and so offer a prolonged conventional defense, provided the second and third waves of Soviet/Pact troops could be stopped from reaching the battlefield. Smart precision-guided munitions could also nullify Soviet armoured forces, tanks, MICV, armoured personnel carriers (APC), and self-propelled artillery. However, it was not at all clear that the existing smart munitions could interdict enough of the Soviet second and third echelon attacks to serve the purpose. Such weapons were also expensive, and large numbers of them would be needed.

Meanwhile, the Soviet/Warsaw Pact's quantitative advantage in qualitatively comparable equipment was increasing: 4 million versus 2.6 million men; 173 versus 84 divisions; 42,500 versus 13,000 main battle tanks; 24,300 versus 8,100 antitank guided weapon launchers; 31,500 versus 10,750 MICV/APC; 78,800 versus 30,000 artillery/mortar tanks; 700 versus 400 attack helicopters; and 7,240 versus 3,000 aircraft. (For a discussion of the controversy over missile deployment in NATO-Europe, *see* Special Report.)

UNITED KINGDOM

Defense expenditure for 1983–84, at $25,168,000,000 (5.1% of GDP in 1982), included replacements for losses in the Falklands war. The resounding victory of Prime Minister Margaret Thatcher's Conservative Party in the June elections meant that Britain's national nuclear force modernization program would continue. This involved construction of four or five SSBN carrying U.S.-built Trident II SLBM. Meanwhile, the four Resolution-class SSBN, each carrying 16 Polaris A-3 SLBM, were being upgraded by refitting the missiles with new Chevaline warheads, probably doubling the number of warheads per missile.

The Royal Navy, with 71,730 personnel, was the third largest in the world and the only one with experience in guided weapons combat. As a result of the Falklands war, increased emphasis was being placed on defense against missile attack, especially on terminal (point) defense systems like the U.S. Phalanx 20-mm cannon firing depleted uranium bullets. The Royal Navy had 27 attack submarines and 64 major surface combatants, including 3 ASW carriers (each with five Sea Harrier V/STOL ground-attack fighters and nine Sea King helicopters) and 13 GW destroyers. Royal Marines personnel totaled 7,754.

The Royal Air Force (RAF) had 89,827 personnel and some 620 combat aircraft. The new Tornado multirole combat aircraft was being deployed in ground-attack/reconnaissance, ground-attack/fighter, and air defense models; 20 were operational. Other modern types included 44 Harrier GR-3/T-4 V/STOL, 72 Jaguar GR-1 ground-attack fighters, 24 Jaguar GR-1 reconnaissance planes, and 28 Nimrod MR-1/-1A-2 maritime reconnaissance aircraft.

The 159,000-strong Army was replacing 900 Chieftain main battle tanks with the Challenger. The major overseas deployment remained the British Army of the Rhine, with 55,000 Army and 10,300 RAF personnel. Some 5,000 personnel were in the Falkland Islands, where a major military base was being constructed to accommodate modern fighter-bombers and transport aircraft.

FRANCE

Pres. François Mitterrand's Socialist government continued to emphasize France's national nuclear force at the cost of conventional forces. Defense spending, at $17,929,000,000, represented 4.1% of GDP. Modern French nuclear forces included five SSBN, with a sixth building and a seventh authorized. The M-20 SLBM was being replaced by the M-4, with a greater range and probably 3 x 200-kiloton multiple independently targetable reentry vehicles (MIRV), and the 18 S-3 IRBM were to be replaced by the Hades IRBM, probably mobile. Medium-range and tactical forces included 30 Mirage II's and 45 Jaguars; the 36 carrier-borne Super Étendard fighter-bombers each carried one or two 15-kiloton bombs. French enhanced radiation weapons (neutron bombs) were being developed.

Army personnel dropped to 311,200, comprising eight armoured, four motor rifle, and one alpine division, plus a Quick Reaction Force composed of one air-portable and one parachute division. The five SSM regiments had 42 Pluton SSM (120-km range, 15–25-kiloton warhead). The Air Force of 100,400 personnel had 520 combat aircraft. The Mirage 5F and Jaguar ground-attack fighters were replacing older Mirage III's. The 68,000-strong Navy's 46 major surface combatants included 2 Clemenceau-class light carriers, one with 24 Super Étendards.

The French intervention in Chad in September, with some 3,000 troops, demonstrated once again that major political gains can be achieved in the third world with relatively minor military forces. (*See* CHAD.) Under strong pressure from both President Reagan and French public opinion, President Mitterrand used French forces to block the advance of Libyan troops, which had invaded Chad in support of one of its numerous factions. This left the desolate country divided between Libyan- and French-controlled sectors.

Erich Honecker, general secretary of East Germany's Socialist Unity (Communist) Party, signed a joint communiqué of the Warsaw Pact at its 18th summit meeting in January.

SIPA PRESS/BLACK STAR

WEST GERMANY

Even under its new conservative government, West German defense spending remained relatively low: 4.3% of GNP, though this still amounted to $18,934,000,000. Standing armed forces totaled 495,000, 60% of them volunteers, rising to 1,250,000 on mobilization. The 335,500-strong Army was organized around the 5,000-man brigade (17 armoured, 15 armoured infantry, 1 mountain, 3 airborne). Armour included 585 new Leopard 2 and 2,400 Leopard 1 tanks.

Combat aircraft for the 106,000-strong Air Force included 30 new Tornado multirole combat aircraft, replacing the 108 obsolete F-104G ground-attack fighters. The 36,400-strong Navy was designed to deny the Baltic and North seas to Soviet/Warsaw Pact forces, using 33 fast attack craft armed with Exocet SSM and 123 naval combat aircraft; 34 Tornados were replacing 43 F-104G and 27 RF-104G strike and reconnaissance planes.

ARMS CONTROL AND DISARMAMENT

On November 23 the Soviets walked out of the negotiations with the U.S. on INF reduction, as they had threatened to do if NATO went ahead with deployment of cruise and Pershing II missiles in Europe. (*See* Special Report.) Later, though less ostentatiously, they also withdrew from the START negotiations and from the long-standing talks between NATO and the Warsaw Pact on mutual and balanced force reductions in Europe. U.S. officials expressed the belief that the Soviets would eventually resume negotiations, but for the time being efforts toward arms control were clearly in disarray. The remaining arena for negotiations, the 45-nation UN Conference on Disarmament, continued to be deadlocked.

Although the first strategic arms limitation talks agreement (SALT I) had expired (except for the ABM treaty) and SALT II had never been ratified by the U.S. Senate, the two superpowers had both said they would abide by the agreed provisions pending further negotiations. However, evidence continued to mount that the Soviets were in violation or in substantive noncompliance. The agreements were often so loosely worded, and U.S. national technical means of verification (mainly satellite surveillance) was so limited, that this was frequently difficult to prove, but two clear-cut violations were detected in 1983. The Soviets tested two types of ICBM, the PL-4 and PL-5, instead of the one allowed under SALT II, and U.S. reconnaissance satellites detected a massive ABM battle-management radar at Abalakovo, Mongolia, an unambiguous violation of the ABM treaty. There was also evidence that the Soviets continued to violate the 1974 treaty limiting underground nuclear weapons testing to 150 kilotons, as well as the various international agreements banning use of chemical and biological weapons.

Nevertheless, public and political interest in obtaining effective arms control remained high, as was shown, among other events, by the controversy in the spring over the qualifications of Kenneth Adelman to be director of the U.S. Arms Control and Disarmament Agency. Arms control emerged as a major foreign policy issue as the U.S. presidential campaign got under way, and there was a revival of interest in a ban on antisatellite weapons, under development by both superpowers.

THE MIDDLE EAST

Both superpowers were involved in regional conflicts in the Middle East, a situation that became increasingly dangerous since neither was firmly in control of events. Both had ground forces committed in Lebanon, the U.S. as part of the symbolic international peacekeeping force introduced following the 1982 Lebanon war between Israel and Palestine Liberation Organization (PLO)-Syrian forces (2,000 U.S., 2,000 Italian, 1,100 French, and 100 British troops). The U.S. contingent, stationed in an exposed position at the Beirut airport where it was subject to hostile shelling, was being supported by a U.S. naval contingent offshore, including 2,000–4,000 Marines afloat. The U.S. also retaliated for attacks on U.S. reconnaissance planes from Syrian-held territory.

The Syrians, who had originally entered Lebanon as a "peacekeeping" force, now controlled much of the northern part of the country, with Soviet support. Massive supplies of Soviet equipment had replaced Syrian losses in the 1982 war, and Soviet air defense troops were deployed in the Bekaa Valley, manning 48 fixed SA-5 and mobile SA-6 SAM batteries, antiaircraft batteries, and radars. Syria was also behind the rebellion of dissident PLO elements against chairman Yasir Arafat (*see* BIOGRAPHIES). Arafat's last stand in Tripoli, which ended with his evacuation by ship in December, resulted in some 5,000 Palestinian and Lebanese casualties. Israeli forces, meanwhile, had withdrawn to the more defensible line of the Awali River. By the year's end, the situation in Lebanon had become extremely unstable. (*See* LEBANON.)

Against Syria alone, Israel was militarily superior, with armed forces of 172,000 that could rise to about 500,000 on mobilization. The Army of 135,000 (450,000 on mobilization) was equipped with 3,600 main battle tanks, including 250 new Israeli-built Merkava I/II's. Armour was a mixture of Israeli, U.S., and captured Soviet equipment, the last modified to Israeli standards. The Air Force (28,000; 37,000 on mobilization) had 550 combat aircraft, with newer types including 40 F/TF-15 Eagles and 72 F-16A/B Falcons, plus 150 Israeli Kfir-C1/-C2 fighter-bombers. The burden of defense spending was heavy—37.9% of GDP, or roughly $6,461,000,000, plus 1982 war costs of $1.5 billion–$2 billion.

The strength and effectiveness of Syria's forces were difficult to assess because not all the new equipment could be absorbed, especially given losses in trained personnel and internal political considerations. Nonetheless, even before their November mobilization, Syrian forces totaled 222,500, including an army of 170,000 personnel and an Air Force of 50,000. The approximately 4,200 Soviet-made tanks included 900 modern T-72 and 1,100 T-62 main battle tanks, while the Air Force had perhaps 450 combat aircraft, notably 20

MiG-23 and 230 MiG-21PF/MF interceptors and 70 MiG-23BM Flogger F and 40 Su-20 fighter-bombers. The 24 MiG-25 Foxbat A interceptors were Soviet-manned. The Soviet deployment of the SS-21 SSM (120-km range) added a new element of instability since these systems were nuclear capable, although they were probably conventionally armed for use against Israeli airfields.

Egypt had been removed from the Arab-Israeli confrontation by the 1978 Camp David agreements, but these showed some signs of breaking down. Egypt's armed forces remained weakened by their conversion from Soviet to Western equipment; only a third of the Soviet equipment was operational. Personnel totaled 447,000, including an army of 315,000 with 1,460 Soviet (500 effective) and 250 U.S. main battle tanks. Of the 27,000-strong Air Force's 500 combat aircraft, effective types were 20 F-16 Falcons, 53 Mirage 5SDE2s, and 44 Chinese F-6s (MiG-19), while the 85,000-strong Air Defense Command had 40 F-16A and 54 Mirage 5SDE1 interceptors and 142 (47 effective) MiG-21s. Jordan's Army (65,000 personnel) had 550 main battle tanks and the Air Force (7,500) had 103 aircraft.

The Iran-Iraq war was in its fourth year, with no end in sight. Losses on both sides had been heavy in terms of both lives and equipment, making the figures in Table II very rough estimates. Only a small percentage of the modern armour and artillery was operational, and perhaps only 10% of the aircraft. The war had thus become a World War I-type stalemate between entrenched infantry forces, supported by artillery and small quantities of armour.

Libya remained a volatile element in the region. Until France intervened, Libya's incursion into Chad was laughably one-sided. The Libyan forces totaled 73,000 with 2,900 main battle tanks and 533 combat aircraft, while Chad's basically paramilitary forces totaled 4,200, and included neither aircraft nor armour.

SOUTH, EAST, AND SOUTHEAST ASIA

Iran's military weakness and the continued Soviet occupation of Afghanistan raised the possibility of a Soviet military move against Iran's oil fields and the Baluchistan area of Pakistan. Pakistan's armed forces totaled 478,600 personnel, including an army of 450,000 with 1,300 main battle tanks and an air force of 17,600 with 260 combat aircraft. The defense budget of $1,801,000,000 represented 7% of GDP. Pakistan's regional enemy, India, had armed forces totaling 1,120,000 personnel. The Army of 960,000, mostly infantry, had 2,100 tanks, including 800 T-54/-55, 200 T-72, and 1,100 Vijayanta (Indian Centurion) main battle tanks. Combat aircraft for the 113,000-strong Air Force totaled 727. Defense spending, at about 3.5% of GDP, amounted to approximately $5,560,000,000.

China's military forces remained strong in manpower (4,750,000) but weak in equipment. Manpower was reduced, as was defense spending—to perhaps 8–10% of GDP. Despite the prospect of U.S. sales of arms and military technology, it appeared that China's forces would retain only a limited defense capability for the foreseeable future. China's nuclear and thermonuclear weapons stockpile amounted to several hundred, but delivery systems were inadequate. These included China's first Xia- (Hsia-) class SSBN, with 12 SLBM, 4 T-5 ICBM (13,000-km range, 1 x 5-megaton warhead), 110 intermediate- and medium-range ballistic missiles, and 90 medium bombers. The Army (3,250,000 personnel) had only 11,500 main battle tanks, all older Soviet models or Chinese adaptations, and the Air Force (490,000) had 5,300 combat aircraft, all older types.

The major active military power in Southeast Asia was Vietnam, with armed forces totaling 1,220,500. The Army of 1.2 million personnel was organized in 58 infantry divisions averaging 10,000 men, with integral armoured support from 1,500 Soviet and 400 captured U.S. main battle

Britain's Royal Artillery modified its Rapier missile system by mounting it on a self-propelled vehicle. The earlier version, which was used effectively in the Falklands war, was towed into position.

UPI

AGIP/PICTORIAL PARADE

France's Mirage 2000N aircraft, which was designed for nuclear attack missions, flew at a top speed of Mach 1.5 in its first test flight in February.

tanks. The Air Force, with 12,500 personnel, had 287 combat aircraft, including 68 MiG-17 and 43 Su-7 fighter-bombers. Deployment included 45,000 troops in Laos and 170,000 in Kampuchea. Accusations that Vietnam was using Soviet-supplied chemical weapons, especially against the Hmong tribes in Laos, continued.

Tensions between North and South Korea were exacerbated by the assassination of 17 South Koreans, including 4 Cabinet members, in Burma in October. (*See* KOREA.) However, North Korea still seemed to lack sufficient armed strength to repeat its 1950 invasion of the South, although its forces were much the larger of the two: 784,500 personnel, 2,700 main battle tanks, 1,000 APC, and 740 combat aircraft (mostly older types) for the North, compared with 622,000 personnel, 1,200 main battle tanks, 500 APC, and 450 combat aircraft for the South. During President Reagan's visit to South Korea in November he reaffirmed the U.S. commitment to defend the country from attack by the North.

President Reagan's earlier stop in Japan had failed to persuade the Japanese to spend more than 1% of GDP ($10,360,000,000) on defense. (*See* JAPAN.) Japan's armed forces totaled 241,000 personnel, including an army of 156,000 with only 950 main battle tanks. The Air Force and Navy each had 43,000 personnel. Equipment included 56 Japanese-made F-1 fighter-bombers; 20 F-15J, 112 F-4EJ Phantom, and 61 F-104J Starfighter ground-attack fighters; 31 destroyers (23 GW); 17 frigates; and 14 submarines. Taiwan had 464,000 personnel under arms. The Army, with 310,000 personnel, had 310 main battle tanks, and the 77,000-strong Air Force had 474 combat aircraft, including 330 F-5A-F fighter-bombers. Defense spending, at about $3,323,000,000, represented 8% of GDP.

AFRICA SOUTH OF THE SAHARA

The ouster of Cubans from Grenada revived speculation concerning the stability of various African governments being bolstered by Cuban or Eastern bloc forces. In Angola the Luanda government, with a poor quality infantry force of 37,500, relied on 25,000 Cuban troops, under 2,000–3,000 Soviet and East German military directors, to retain control of its territory. The antigovernment forces of the National Union for the Total Independence of Angola (UNITA), with perhaps 15,000 troops but aided by South Africa, had made important gains in the south. Antigovernment forces in Mozambique, numbering about 10,000, were also active. Opposing them were 11,000 government troops and perhaps 3,000 Soviet, East German, and Cuban forces. Some 2,400 Soviets and 11,000 Cubans, as well as East German and Yemen (Aden) troops, were in Ethiopia operating 850 main battle tanks, 800 MICV/AFV/APC, and 100 ground-attack fighters. Ethiopian forces totaled 250,000, less losses in the smoldering conflicts in Eritrea and elsewhere.

South African forces, the strongest in the region, totaled 82,400, rising to 404,500 on mobilization. Another 135,000 were in paramilitary forces. Equipment included 250 main battle tanks, 2,100 AFV, and 313 combat aircraft (45 Mirage F-1AZ/CZ's and 28 Mirage III's). These forces had proved much more effective than the indigenous African and Cuban forces with whom they had been in combat. South Africa might have manufactured some nuclear weapons, with Israeli help.

LATIN AMERICA

Since entering office, the Reagan administration had repeatedly warned that the extension of Soviet power into Central America and the Caribbean was posing a major threat to the interests of the U.S. and of the indigenous governments in the region. Thus, in Grenada (1979) and Suriname (1982), coups by pro-Soviet/Cuban groups had overthrown elected governments, while in Nicaragua a broadly based revolutionary government had been taken over by the Marxist Sandinista faction. Geopolitically, as the map shows, this raised the possibility that bases in territories controlled by pro-Soviet governments could be used in wartime to cut U.S. oil supply lines and tie down U.S. forces.

In this context, Grenada was seen as a test case of U.S. willingness to enforce the Monroe Doctrine. Although the Grenadian government insisted it was being built to accommodate tourist flights, the 3,000-m (10,000-ft) runway nearing completion at the Point Salines airfield would take the largest Soviet transport aircraft and hence could provide a staging point for Soviet/Cuban military personnel

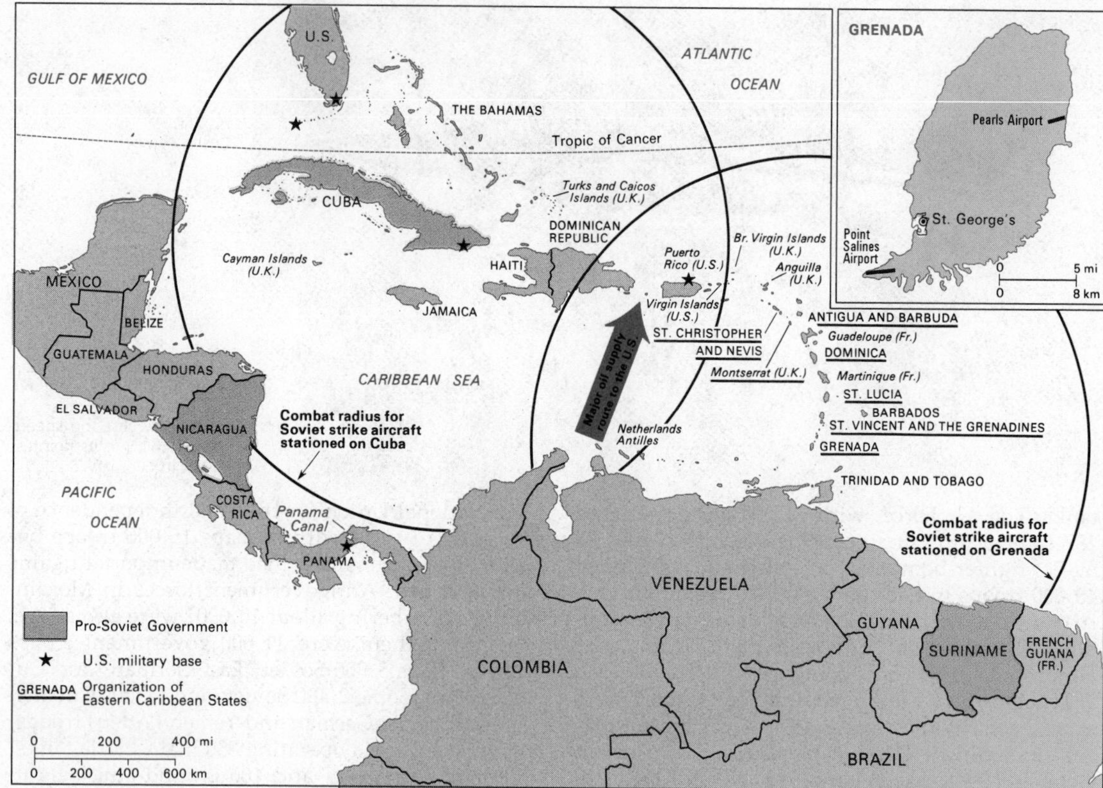

The potential interruption of strategic oil routes to the U.S. in case of war concerned the U.S. before the invasion of Grenada.

and supplies being shipped to Africa and Central America. It could also handle strategic bombers and the nuclear-capable MiG-23 ground-attack fighter. The U.S. decision to intervene militarily in Grenada was triggered by two interrelated developments. One was the murder of Prime Minister Maurice Bishop and the leadership of his New Jewel Movement, which had seized power in 1979, by an even more hard-line Marxist group of military officers. The other was intelligence information of the imminent reinforcement of the existing 800–1,000-strong Cuban contingent on Grenada with 4,000—and later 12,000—Cuban troops. This would have tranformed Grenada into a major military base.

These considerations led the Organization of Eastern Caribbean States (OECS) to request U.S. assistance in restoring democracy to Grenada. The OECS members had become increasingly concerned over their vulnerability to subversive influences emanating from Cuba and Grenada. Their poverty bred unrest, while their armed forces were too small to protect them against outside intervention. Bishop's murder meant the complete collapse of order in Grenada, and the U.S. medical students at St. George's Hospital Medical School could easily be taken hostage. Sir Paul Scoon, the Grenadian governor-general who had been under house arrest, also asked for help.

Militarily, the U.S.-OECS operation on Grenada was extremely successful. Strategic surprise was achieved by keeping the decision to intervene secret, diverting to the Caribbean a carrier task force destined for Lebanon, and only mobilizing U.S.-based forces the day before. While tactical warning of the attack was received on Grenada, no move was made to send reinforcements, presumably because of overwhelming U.S. strength in the area. The initial landings were by 200 U.S. Army Ranger paratroopers, who jumped at 150 m (500 ft) to avoid Cuban antiaircraft guns protecting the Point Salines airport. The airport was seized, and 500 more Rangers were flown in, followed by 5,000 men of the 82nd Airborne Division, airlifted from U.S. bases. Simultaneously, U.S. Navy Seal Special Forces secured beach landings, preparing the way for 2,000 Marine Corps amphibious and helicopter forces, and released the governor-general.

Initial resistance was sharp, since most of the Cubans who were helping to build the runway proved to be army construction engineers, equipped for combat. They were outnumbered, however, and most surrendered after two days. Comparatively few of the Grenadian forces resisted, while most of the Grenadian population assisted the U.S. forces. A force of some 300 from the OECS countries accompanied the U.S. troops. Casualties were relatively light: U.S., 18 killed and 116 wounded; Cubans, perhaps 24 killed and 59 wounded; the Grenadian People's Army, 21 killed; Grenadian civilian casualties, 24 dead and 337 wounded.

By mid-December all U.S. combat troops had been withdrawn, leaving some 300 noncombat U.S. servicemen to assist the OECS's peacekeeping force. A few Cubans and Grenadian revolutionaries remained at large in the island's rugged interior, posing a security threat. An interim government was set up by Sir Paul Scoon, and massive U.S. aid was expected. (ROBIN RANGER)

See also Space Exploration.
[535.B.5.c.ii; 544.B.5–6; 736]

NATO MISSILES IN EUROPE
Failure of a Six-Year Soviet Campaign
by Robin Ranger

In December 1983 the first modernized NATO intermediate nuclear forces (INF) were deployed in Europe: 16 ground-launched cruise missiles (GLCM) in Britain and 9 Pershing II intermediate-range ballistic missiles (IRBM) in West Germany. This marked the defeat of a six-year Soviet campaign to prevent the planned NATO deployment of 572 modernized INF (464 GLCM and 108 Pershing II's) by 1988 and a victory for those who believed that upgraded INF were needed to restore the balance of deterrence, destabilized by the massive, Soviet INF buildup. Yet politically the decision had proved the hardest and most divisive since the alliance was formed in 1949.

Within NATO, opposition groups claimed the missiles were not needed, while their deployment would prevent arms control agreements and erode East-West détente in Europe. Among the most vocal groups were the West German Green Party, the British Campaign for Nuclear Disarmament (CND), European Nuclear Disarmament (END), and the nuclear freeze movements in the U.S. By the fall of 1983 the debate had become polarized, with opponents of deployment staging mass demonstrations and at times resorting to violence, while the Soviet Union attempted to exploit the situation.

The Soviet Buildup. The Soviets' geographic position made nuclear weapons delivery systems with INF ranges (1,000–5,500 km; 1 km = 0.62 mi) much more useful to them than to the U.S. From Soviet territory, INF can cover targets in Western Europe, the Middle East, the Far East, and parts of the U.S. (*See* MAP.) Accordingly, in the 1950s the Soviets built up an INF of some 800 medium/intermediate-range ballistic missiles (M/IRBM) and 800 medium-range bombers. In contrast, the U.S., relying on its strategic (long-range intercontinental) forces for deterrence, retired its INF in NATO-Europe in the 1960s.

The Soviets exploited this INF gap with the deployment, in the mid-1970s, of replacement INF, chiefly the SS-20 and the Backfire bomber. The SS-20 was a variable (intermediate and intercontinental)-range (5,000–7,400 km) missile with varying warhead yields, deployed on mobile launchers. Each of the nearly 400 launchers had two reload missiles, for a total of three per launcher (to be increased to four), and each missile had an average of three warheads. The Backfire bomber's range was intercontinental (8,000 km), but it was more effective over intermediate ranges. Current deployment was about 200 Backfires carrying 800 warheads. Two-thirds of this INF force was deployed against NATO and one-third against the Far East.

By 1983 these forces were more than sufficient to destroy all major NATO targets, including NATO nuclear weapons storage sites, in a first strike. The Soviets could thus threaten to decouple the U.S. from the defense of NATO-Europe by disabling NATO defenses, including U.S. forces, without touching U.S. territory. This aggravated European fears that the U.S. would not risk Soviet strategic retaliation to defend Europe. At the same time it raised the spectre of "finlandization," with the Soviets using their military advantage to secure economic and political concessions from NATO-Europe.

Proposed NATO Deployment. By 1977 NATO-Europe governments had become concerned about the situation, and West Germany's then Chancellor Helmut Schmidt raised the issue publicly. In 1979 the U.K. Labour government joined West Germany in persuading a reluctant U.S. Pres. Jimmy Carter and other NATO-Europe countries to agree to INF modernization, but their so-called two-track decision was an uneasy compromise. The NATO members agreed, in principle, to deploy 572 missiles beginning in December 1983 (the deployment track) and, meanwhile, to enter into INF limitation negotiations with the Soviets, aimed at reducing or eliminating the need for deployment (the arms control track).

Militarily, the 572 missiles were too few to cover the targets in Eastern Europe and the Soviet Union that would have to be destroyed to halt a Soviet/Warsaw Pact invasion. The cruise missiles and Pershing II's carried only one warhead each, and no reload missiles were provided. The cruise missiles were to be deployed in groups of four, on transporter-erector launchers, while the Pershings were to be deployed on single launchers. These could move only on roads (the SS-20 launcher could travel cross-country) and required large convoys of support vehicles, making them vulnerable to Soviet strikes.

Robin Ranger is associate professor, Defense and Strategic Studies Program, School of International Relations, at the University of Southern California.

Basing the missiles on land, rather than at sea, was dictated by NATO's need to recouple the U.S. to the defense of NATO-Europe and to join all the NATO-Europe members in their mutual defense. NATO INF were thus to be based in five countries: Belgium, Britain, The Netherlands, Italy, and West Germany. This also met Schmidt's nonsingularity principle: the political burden of deployment must be shared by NATO members other than West Germany and Britain. To avoid future Soviet charges of West German fingers on the nuclear trigger, it was agreed that the new systems would be U.S. owned and manned—not two-key systems, manned by the host NATO-Europe country but with U.S.-controlled warheads.

The Arms Control Track. Liberal groups in NATO-Europe, especially The Netherlands and West Germany, expected that the arms control track would make deployment unnecessary. It was assumed that the 1979 SALT II strategic arms limitation treaty would be ratified by the U.S. Senate and negotiations would be started on both SALT III and INF agreements. The Soviets fed these hopes with a brilliant propaganda campaign. Its main points were, first, that there was a balance in INF that NATO deployment would upset, and, second, that the Soviets (despite their continuing INF buildup) were establishing a moratorium on INF deployment. The Soviets also threatened unspecified, but dire, retaliation if NATO deployment proceeded. In some cases they attempted to manipulate the European peace movements directly.

The deterioration in superpower relations, especially after the Soviet invasion of Afghanistan at the end of 1979, had a paradoxical effect. On the one hand, it made chances of any agreement on INF less likely and INF modernization more necessary. On the other, it increased public pressure for arms control. In response to Afghanistan, President Carter shelved SALT II, and it was 1981 before INF negotiations began in Geneva. Leading the U.S. delegation was Paul Nitze, who in 1949–50 had written a notable National Security Council memorandum (NSC-68) laying out an integrated military, political, and economic strategy for U.S. containment of Soviet

Intermediate range nuclear missiles based in Europe by Soviet and NATO forces. Published data, derived from Western intelligence sources, give only a general location of Soviet bases and the areas of deployment are only illustrative.

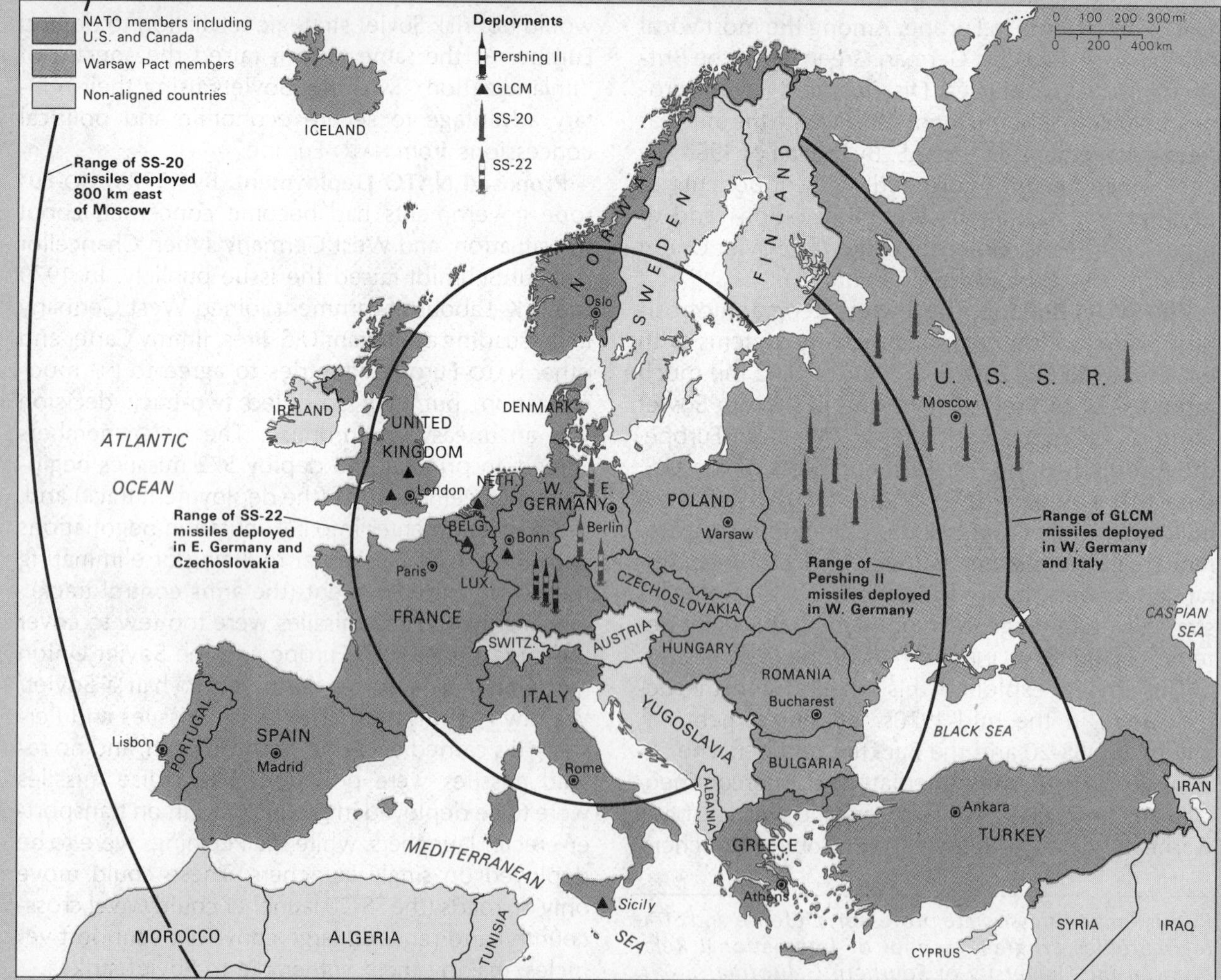

expansion. But despite his experience and expertise, an INF agreement could not be reached.

The Soviets rejected all U.S. proposals, on behalf of NATO, for verifiable, balanced limits on INF, including the so-called zero option put forward by Pres. Ronald Reagan in November 1981. Under this proposal, the Soviets would undertake the verified destruction of all SS-4/-5/-20 M/IRBM missiles and launchers, while NATO would refrain from its planned deployment. Also rejected was the proposal that, as an interim step, the Soviets and NATO reduce their INF deployment to an agreed number of warheads.

The Soviets, meanwhile, based their negotiating stance on the assumption that a balance of INF in Europe already existed. They included in their totals exaggerated numbers of U.S. and NATO medium-range strike aircraft (which they called forward-based systems) while excluding similar Soviet aircraft. But medium-range strike aircraft are dual capable, able to carry either nuclear or conventional weapons, and are deployed in large numbers by both NATO and the Warsaw Pact. (*See* DEFENSE: *Table II*.) It would be impossible to determine how many of these aircraft could be counted as nuclear armed, to devise effective limits on them, or to verify such limits. The Soviets also tried to count the British and French national nuclear forces as part of the NATO nuclear force, although both are under the command of their respective governments. This was a new problem. The U.S. could not include these forces in either the START (strategic arms reduction) or INF negotiations without British and French permission, and this they refused to give. Both national nuclear forces were too small to be reduced but were being modernized. The Soviets wanted to prevent this modernization or to obtain compensation in the form of more Soviet INF.

The Soviet Gamble. Behind the propaganda, the Soviet aim was simple: no reduction of Soviet INF but no deployment of NATO INF. The Soviets particularly opposed the Pershing II, claiming that it was a first-strike weapon, that it threatened their command, control, and communications systems, and that it could reach Moscow. The Pershing II could do none of these things, but it did set a precedent for NATO deployment of modern IRBM systems. The Soviets gambled that their propaganda campaign, by exploiting Western European fears, could stop the NATO deployment without an INF agreement.

The gamble failed. The Soviets' heavy-handed attempts to interfere in domestic European politics may well have helped to return governments committed to INF deployment in Britain and West Germany. Of the other NATO-Europe governments that were to have INF, Italy supported deployment publicly and Belgium privately. Only the Dutch remained reluctant but would probably go along. Even France's Socialist Pres. François Mitterrand was a strong supporter of INF modernization. The major NATO-Europe governments and the U.S. administration were thus in basic agreement. When arms control negotiations failed, deployment had to begin. To have done otherwise would have given the Soviets a veto over NATO defense programs.

Future Prospects. Soviet retaliation for INF deployment was expected to take four forms. The first occurred on November 23, when the Soviets walked out of the INF talks (later they also withdrew from START. The second could involve publicizing the long-standing Soviet deployment of short- and medium-range missiles in Eastern Europe. Third could be deployment of long-range submarine-launched ballistic missiles on nuclear and conventional submarines stationed close to the U.S., and fourth, the forward deployment of SS-20s at Siberian bases, from which they could hit Alaska and parts of the U.S. West Coast. Other possibilities included Soviet abrogation of the 1972 antiballistic missile treaty, an announcement that the SS-20 is a mobile ICBM, or an attempt to deploy SS-20s in Cuba or elsewhere in the Central America-Caribbean region. Certainly East-West relations would deteriorate further.

In the longer run, however, the outlook was not necessarily pessimistic. By stabilizing the NATO-Warsaw Pact balance of deterrence, NATO deployment of INF could well make effective arms control more possible. Soviet retention of a one-sided advantage in INF would have been militarily destabilizing, and Soviet prevention of NATO deployment would have been politically destabilizing. NATO's INF deployment can thus enhance stability and give the Soviets an incentive to negotiate seriously.

Renewed negotiations might combine the INF and START talks. The distinction between strategic nuclear forces (SNF) and INF based on range has always been relatively arbitrary. It made less and less sense as more and more weapons systems were deployed with ranges making them capable of both strategic and theatre missions. Such gray-area systems include the SS-20, the Backfire bomber, and long-range (over 600 km) air-, ground-, and sea-launched cruise missiles. Moreover, some Soviet and some U.S. ICBM and submarine-launched ballistic missiles have been allocated to theatre missions in Europe and the Pacific. Combining SNF and INF limitations would be logical, and it would prevent the circumvention of limits on SNF by deployment of INF and vice versa. Also, since the military capabilities of national nuclear forces were increasing, they would have to be considered in arms control talks, requiring British and French participation.

Demography

According to the world population report issued by the Center for International Research of the U.S. Bureau of the Census, the number of people on Earth at mid-1983 was estimated to be 4,721,886,000. Since mid-1982 the annual growth rate of 1.8% had resulted in the addition of a record 82 million persons, equal to the combined populations of the U.K., Ireland, and the rest of northern Europe. Almost one-quarter of the world population resided in China, and about half lived in the four most populous nations: China, India, the Soviet Union, and the U.S.

Future significant increases were indicated for the less developed countries, particularly the nations of Africa (3% average annual growth rate) and Latin America (2.3%). The growth rate of the more developed countries was only 0.6%. According to estimates prepared by the Population Reference Bureau, Europe's low annual growth (0.4%) reflected a balance of births and deaths in Austria, East Germany, Hungary, and Sweden and a near balance in Belgium, Italy, Luxembourg, and the U.K. There was an excess of deaths over births in Denmark and West Germany. Negative growth rates indicated the effects of war and devastation in Afghanistan (−0.3%), Lebanon (−0.8%), and El Salvador (−0.2%).

One measure of the effect of growth rates is the "population doubling time," the time it could take for any population to double in size. With a growth rate of 3.3%, Nigeria's population could double to 170 million in just 21 years. Mexico's population of 76 million could become 151 million in 27 years, and India's could rise to 1,500,000,000 in 33 years. In contrast, at current rates it would take Austria and Sweden 3,000 years to double their populations. Doubling could take 95 years for the U.S. and 83 years for the Soviet Union.

At current growth levels, the world population was expected to exceed 6,000,000,000 in the year 2000 and to approach 8,000,000,000 in 2020. By then, the less developed countries, which contained about 75% of the total population in 1983, could include over 80%.

Table I. World's 25 Most Populous Urban Areas[1]

Rank	City and Country	City proper		Metropolitan area	
		Population	Year	Population	Year
1	Tokyo, Japan	8,363,000	1983 estimate	30,000,000	1983 estimate
2	Osaka, Japan	2,625,000	1983 estimate	16,224,000	1981 estimate
3	New York City, U.S.	7,096,600	1982 census	16,121,297	1980 census
4	Mexico City, Mexico	9,373,400	1980 census[2]	15,668,800	1982 estimate
5	São Paulo, Brazil	7,033,529	1980 census[2]	12,588,439	1980 census[2]
6	London, U.K.	6,765,100	1982 estimate	12,225,400	1982 estimate
7	Cairo, Egypt	5,650,000	1981 estimate	12,001,000	1983 estimate
8	Shanghai, China	6,320,872	1982 census[2]	11,859,748	1982 census[2]
9	Los Angeles, U.S.	3,102,000	1982 estimate	11,497,568	1980 census
10	Rhine-Ruhr, West Germany	[3]	[3]	10,984,900	1982 estimate
11	Buenos Aires, Argentina	2,910,000	1983 estimate	9,677,200	1981 estimate
12	Beijing, China	5,597,972	1982 census[2]	9,230,687	1982 census[2]
13	Calcutta, India	3,291,655	1981 census[2]	9,165,650	1981 census[2]
14	Rio de Janeiro, Brazil	5,093,232	1980 census[2]	9,018,637	1980 census[2]
15	Seoul, South Korea	[4]	[4]	8,961,500	1982 estimate
16	Paris, France	2,176,243	1982 census	8,823,751	1982 census
17	Moscow, U.S.S.R.	8,111,000	1982 estimate	8,302,000	1982 estimate
18	Bombay, India	[4]	[4]	8,227,332	1981 census[2]
19	Nagoya, Japan	2,095,000	1983 estimate	7,968,000	1981 estimate
20	Chicago, U.S.	3,010,900	1982 estimate	7,869,542	1980 census
21	Tianjin, China	5,142,565	1982 census[2]	7,764,141	1982 census[2]
22	Chongqing, China	2,702,000	1980 estimate	7,030,400	1982 estimate
23	Jakarta, Indonesia	[4]	[4]	6,556,000	1981 estimate
24	Manila, Philippines	1,725,500	1983 estimate	6,406,300	1983 estimate
25	Delhi, India	4,865,077	1981 census[2]	5,713,581	1981 census[2]

[1]Ranked by population of metropolitan area.
[2]Preliminary figures.
[3]An industrial conurbation within which no single central city is identified.
[4]City proper not identified by reporting countries.

Birth Statistics. The National Center for Health Statistics reported that an estimated 3,704,000 births occurred in the U.S. in 1982, some 2% more than in 1981. This was the largest number of births since the peak year of 1970, when 3,731,000 were recorded. The birthrate was 16 live births per 1,000 population, higher than at any time since 1971. The fertility rate was 67.8 births per 1,000 women 15–44 years of age, up slightly from 67.6 in 1981. During the first half of 1983, the birthrate declined somewhat to 15.3 live births per 1,000 population, compared with 15.6 for the corresponding period of 1982.

In recent years the greatest increases in birthrates had been observed for women 30–34 years, and there had been a substantial increase in the number of women in their 30s having a first child. Final data for 1980, by race, showed that the white birthrate was 14.9 live births per 1,000 white population and the black birthrate was 22.1. The total fertility rate, which estimates the number of babies that would be born to each woman through her lifetime under current conditions, was 1.8 children for all races, 1.7 for white mothers, and 2.3 for black mothers. There were 665,747 births to unmarried mothers in the U.S. in 1980, an increase of about 8% over 1979. More than one-tenth of all white births and more than half of all black births were to unmarried mothers.

The world birthrate for 1983, as reported by the Population Reference Bureau, was 29 births per 1,000 population. In the more developed countries it averaged 15 and in the less developed, 33. Africa had the highest average rate (46), followed by Latin America (31) and Asia (30). A total fertility rate of between 2.1 and 2.5 children born to each woman through her childbearing years indicates birth levels at which populations may be replaced, not taking into account migration or mortality factors. The highest total fertility rates were found in Africa (western Africa 6.8, eastern Africa 6.6, northern Africa 6.4, and middle Africa 6). High levels also characterized rates in certain Asian and Latin-American regions (Southwest Asia 5.5, Middle America 4.9). Most European countries were well below replacement level.

The high levels of fertility in less developed countries resulted in younger populations. In about half of the African countries, over 45% of the population was below 15 years of age, and similar conditions prevailed in many Asian countries. In Latin America, Central America had the highest proportion under 15 (*e.g.*, Nicaragua 48%). By contrast, in Europe, North America, and Japan less than one-quarter of the population was under 15 (U.S. 23%). The developed countries were characterized by larger dependent populations in the older age groups.

Death Statistics. The number of deaths in the U.S. in 1982 was estimated at 1,986,000, slightly less than in 1981. The provisional death rate was

continued on page 288

Table II. World Populations and Areas[1]

Country	AREA AND POPULATION: MIDYEAR 1982 Area in sq km	Total population	Persons per sq km	POPULATION AT MOST RECENT CENSUS Date of census	Total population	% Male	% Female	% Urban	Age distribution (%)[2] 0–14	15–29	30–44	45–59	60–74	75+
AFRICA														
Algeria	2,381,741	19,954,000	8.4	1977	17,422,000	49.7	50.3	40.6	47.9	25.4	12.7	8.2	4.5	1.3
Angola	1,246,700	6,944,000	5.6	1970	5,620,001	52.1	47.9	14.2	41.7	23.2	17.0	7.4	3.8	1.0
Benin	112,600	3,621,000	32.2	1979	3,338,240	47.9	52.1	14.2	49.0		—39.4—		—11.6—	
Botswana	581,700	966,000	1.7	1981	941,027	47.1	52.9	15.9	...	...	...	...	...	...
British Indian Ocean Territory	60	...	...	...	...	...	...	...	...	...	...	...	...	...
Burundi	27,834	4,778,000	171.7	1979	4,111,310	48.4	51.6	...	...	...	...	...	...	...
Cameroon	465,458	8,853,000	19.0	1976	7,663,246	49.9	50.1	28.5	42.2	26.4	16.5	9.7	—5.2—	
Cape Verde	4,033	335,000	83.1	1980	296,093	46.3	53.7	26.2	...	...	...	...	...	...
Central African Republic	622,436	2,456,000	3.9	1975	2,054,610	48.0	52.0	34.6	43.5	23.5	17.1	12.4	2.7	0.8
Chad	1,284,000	4,643,000	3.6	1975	4,029,917	47.7	52.3	16.0	40.6	28.3	17.2	9.5	—4.4—	
Comoros[3]	1,862	372,000	199.8	1980	346,992	50.1	49.9	33.4	...	...	...	...	...	...
Congo	342,000	1,619,000	4.7	1974	1,300,120	48.5	51.5	37.8	45.6	22.2	15.5	11.3	4.7	0.7
Djibouti	23,200	306,000	13.2	1961	81,200	...	...	57.4	...	...	...	...	...	...
Egypt	997,667	45,000,000	45.1	1976	38,198,204	48.8	51.2	42.0	38.3	25.6	15.9	10.2	5.0	1.0
Equatorial Guinea	28,051	380,000	13.5	1965	254,684	50.0	50.0	47.6	...	...	...	...	...	...
Ethiopia	1,223,600	32,580,000	26.6	1970	24,068,800	50.7	49.3	9.7	43.5	27.0	16.3	8.8	3.7	0.7
French Southern and Antarctic Lands	7,366	...	...	...	...	...	...	...	...	...	...	...	...	...
Gabon	267,667	1,335,000	5.0	1970	950,009	47.9	52.1	31.8	35.4	19.1	22.3	16.4	—6.5—	
Gambia, The	10,690	635,000	59.4	1973	493,499	50.7	49.3	15.9	41.4	28.3	17.5	9.1	3.3	0.4
Ghana	238,533	12,244,000	51.3	1970	8,559,313	49.6	50.4	28.9	46.9	24.4	15.8	7.5	3.8	1.6
Guinea	245,857	5,285,000	21.5	1972	5,124,284	47.6	52.3	...	43.1		—49.5—		—7.4—	
Guinea-Bissau	36,125	812,000	22.5	1979	767,739	48.2	51.8	...	44.3	25.5	15.1	8.2	4.7	2.2
Ivory Coast	322,463	8,938,000	27.7	1975	6,702,866	51.9	48.1	32.4	44.6	27.4	16.8	7.7	2.7	0.7
Kenya	580,367	17,142,000	29.5	1979	15,327,061	49.6	50.4	15.1	48.4	26.9	12.9	7.1	3.5	1.1
Lesotho	30,355	1,407,000	46.4	1976	1,216,815	48.3	51.7	...	39.1	25.5	15.5	10.4	3.9	5.6
Liberia	99,067	1,990,000	20.1	1974	1,503,368	50.5	49.5	29.1	40.9	26.7	17.7	8.8	4.6	1.3
Libya	1,749,000	3,425,000	2.0	1973	2,249,237	53.0	47.0	59.8	44.3	22.2	15.4	8.2	4.0	1.6
Madagascar	587,041	9,400,000	16.0	1975	7,603,790	50.0	50.0	16.3	44.4	25.7	14.2	10.0	4.6	1.1
Malawi	118,484	6,507,000	54.9	1977	5,547,460	48.2	51.8	8.5	44.6	25.7	14.2	9.0	1.5	4.6
Mali	1,240,192	7,342,000	5.9	1976	6,394,918	48.8	51.2	16.8	44.0	24.9	16.1	8.7	4.8	1.5
Mauritania	1,030,700	1,731,000	1.7	1976	1,419,939	50.1	49.9	21.9	...	...	...	...	...	...
Mauritius	2,040	964,000	472.5	1983	960,000	...	...	...	...	...	...	...	...	...
Mayotte	374	53,000	141.7	1978	47,246	49.9	50.1	53.3	50.2	23.4	13.9	7.0	3.8	1.7
Morocco	458,730	20,420,000	44.5	1982	20,419,555	...	...	42.7	...	...	...	...	...	...
Mozambique	799,380	12,615,000	15.8	1980	12,130,000	48.7	51.3	...	...	...	...	...	...	...
Niger	1,189,000	5,634,000	4.7	1977	5,098,427	49.3	50.7	11.8	...	...	...	...	...	...
Nigeria	923,768	89,118,000	96.5	1963[4]	55,670,055	50.5	49.5	16.1	43.0	31.9	16.5	5.1	2.5	1.0
Réunion	2,512	516,000	205.4	1982	515,814	...	...	...	...	...	...	...	...	...
Rwanda	26,338	5,276,000	200.3	1978	4,819,317	48.8	51.2	4.3	—60.0—			—40.0—		
St. Helena & Ascension Islands	412	5,000	12.1	1976	5,866	52.0	48.0	29.4	34.2	27.7	16.3	10.8	8.4	2.6
São Tomé & Príncipe	964	86,000	89.2	1981	95,000	...	...	...	...	...	...	...	...	...
Senegal	196,722	5,991,000	30.5	1976	4,907,507	49.2	50.8	29.6	42.5	27.3	17.2	8.6	3.7	0.1
Seychelles	444	68,000	153.2	1977	61,898	50.4	49.6	37.1	39.7	26.3	14.0	10.8	6.9	2.2
Sierra Leone	71,740	3,672,000	51.2	1974	2,729,479	54.1	45.9	...	36.7	27.2	19.4	9.0	—7.6—	
Somalia	638,000	5,116,000	8.0	1975	3,253,024	52.0	48.0	15.0	45.0			—55.0—		
South Africa	1,123,226	25,687,000	22.9	1980	23,771,970	...	...	53.5	51.8		—43.2—		—5.3—	
Bophuthatswana[5]	40,000	1,347,000	33.7	1980	1,328,637	46.8	53.2	15.7	50.7	22.8	11.4	10.1	3.1	2.0
Ciskei[5]	5,386	645,000	119.8	1980	635,631	46.2	53.8	36.3	49.5		—43.2—		—7.3—	
Transkei[5]	43,553	2,400,000	55.1	1970	1,745,992	41.2	58.8	3.2	46.4	22.8	14.1	—15.3—		1.2
Venda[5]	6,198	374,000	60.3	1970	265,129	38.8	61.2	0.2	48.1	22.7	13.7	6.4	7.6	1.5
South West Africa/Namibia	824,292	1,051,000	1.3	1970	761,562	50.8	49.2	24.9	...	...	...	...	...	...
Sudan	2,503,890	19,435,000	7.8	1973	14,819,000[6]	50.4	49.6	18.5	45.9	25.3	17.4	7.8	2.6	1.2
Swaziland	17,364	585,000	33.7	1976	494,534	45.6	54.4	15.2	47.7	25.2	13.7	7.9	3.7	1.7
Tanzania	945,050	19,111,000	20.2	1978	17,551,925	49.2	50.8	13.8	46.2	—39.3—			—14.5—	
Togo	56,785	2,747,000	48.4	1981	2,703,000	48.2	51.8	15.2	...	...	...	...	...	...
Tunisia	154,530	6,630,000	43.2	1975	5,588,209	50.8	49.2	49.0	43.7	25.6	14.7	10.0	4.9	0.9
Uganda	241,139	13,651,000	56.6	1980	12,630,076	49.5	50.5	8.1	...	...	...	...	...	...
Upper Volta	274,200	6,360,000	23.2	1975	5,638,203	50.2	49.8	9.0	47.4	21.1	16.1	9.3	—6.1—	
Western Sahara	266,769	86,000	0.3	1970	76,425	57.5	42.5	45.3	42.9	27.2	16.3	7.4	4.4	1.8
Zaire	2,344,885	30,369,000	13.0	1976	25,568,640	48.5	51.5	18.2	—52.8—			—47.2—		
Zambia	752,614	6,330,000	8.4	1980	5,679,808	49.0	51.0	43.0	...	...	...	...	...	...
Zimbabwe	390,759	7,540,000	19.3	1982	7,539,000	...	...	...	...	...	...	...	...	...
Total AFRICA	30,207,913	504,882,000	16.7											
ANTARCTICA total	14,294,900	[7]												
ASIA														
Afghanistan	652,090	16,786,000	25.7	1979	13,051,358[8]	51.4	48.6	15.1	44.5	26.9	15.8	8.6	3.6	0.6
Bahrain	668	371,000	555.4	1981	350,798	58.4	41.6	80.7	32.9	34.5	20.1	8.8	3.0	0.7
Bangladesh	143,998	92,619,000	643.2	1981	87,052,024	51.5	48.5	...	...	...	...	...	...	...
Bhutan	46,100	1,200,000	26.0	1969	931,514	...	...	...	...	...	...	...	...	...
Brunei	5,765	200,000	34.7	1981	192,832	53.4	46.6	59.4	38.5	32.7	16.4	7.9	—4.5—	
Burma	676,577	37,065,000	54.8	1973	28,885,867	49.7	50.3	...	40.5		—53.4—		—6.0—	
China	9,561,000	1,008,175,000	105.4	1982	1,008,175,288	51.5	48.5	21.2	...	...	...	...	...	...
Cyprus	9,251	645,000	69.7	1976	612,851	50.0	50.0	...	25.4	29.0	17.9	13.4	10.8	3.5
Hong Kong	1,068	5,233,000	4,899.8	1981	4,986,560	53.2	48.7	...	24.8	32.7	17.7	14.6	—10.2—	
India	3,287,782	698,000,000	212.3	1981	683,810,051	51.7	48.3	23.7	...	...	...	...	...	...
Indonesia	1,919,443	151,720,000	79.0	1980	147,490,298	49.7	50.3	22.3	40.8	27.0	16.4	10.2	4.5	1.1
Iran	1,648,000	40,476,000	24.6	1976	33,708,744	51.5	48.5	47.0	44.5	25.2	14.8	10.1	3.8	1.0
Iraq	438,317	14,014,000	32.0	1977	12,000,497	51.5	48.5	63.7	48.9	24.5	12.3	8.2	4.2	1.9
Israel	20,700	4,064,000	196.3	1972	3,147,683	50.3	49.7	85.3	32.6	26.9	15.6	13.6	9.2	2.0
Japan	377,727	118,460,000	313.6	1980	117,060,396	49.2	50.8	76.2	23.5	21.5	24.2	17.9	9.8	3.1
Jordan	94,946	2,415,000	25.4	1979	2,147,594	52.3	47.7	59.5	51.8	23.3	13.4	7.3	—4.2—	
Kampuchea	181,035	5,882,000	32.5	1962	5,728,771	50.0	50.0	10.3	43.8	24.9	16.8	9.8	4.1	0.6
Korea, North	121,929	18,789,000	154.1	—	—	—	—	—	—	—	—	—	—	—
Korea, South	98,992	39,331,000	397.3	1980	37,448,836	50.1	49.9	57.3	34.0	30.0	18.4	11.5	5.1	1.0
Kuwait	17,818	1,562,000	87.7	1980	1,357,952	57.2	42.8	100.0	40.2	28.2	21.7	7.7	1.9	0.4

Table II. World Populations and Areas[1] *(Continued)*

Country	AREA AND POPULATION: MIDYEAR 1982 Area in sq km	Total population	Persons per sq km	POPULATION AT MOST RECENT CENSUS Date of census	Total population	% Male	% Female	% Urban	Age distribution (%)[2] 0–14	15–29	30–44	45–59	60–74	75+
Laos	236,800	3,901,000	16.5	—	—	—	—	—	—	—	—	—	—	—
Lebanon	10,230	3,314,000	323.9	1970	2,126,325	50.8	49.2	60.1	42.6	23.8	16.7	9.1	7.7	
Macau	16	298,000	18,625.0	1981	276,673	...	...	...	...	...	...	...	...	...
Malaysia	329,747	14,344,000	43.5	1980	13,136,109	50.2	49.8	34.2	39.6	29.0	16.5	9.2	4.6	1.1
Maldives	298	155,000	520.1	1978	142,832	52.6	47.4	20.7	...	...	...	...	...	...
Mongolia	1,566,500	1,732,000	1.1	1979	1,594,800	50.1	49.9	51.2	...	...	...	...	...	...
Nepal	145,391	15,769,000	108.4	1981	15,020,451	...	...	...	...	...	...	...	...	...
Oman	300,000	948,000	3.2	—	—	—	—	—	—	—	—	—	—	—
Pakistan	796,095	87,125,000	109.4	1981	83,782,000	...	...	...	...	...	...	...	...	...
Philippines	300,000	50,740,000	169.1	1980	48,098,460	50.2	49.8	...	...	...	...	...	...	...
Qatar	11,400	258,000	22.6	—	—	—	—	—	—	—	—	—	—	—
Saudi Arabia	2,240,000	8,905,000	4.0	1974	7,012,642	...	...	...	...	...	...	...	...	...
Singapore	618	2,472,000	4,000.0	1980	2,413,945	51.0	49.0	100.0	27.0	34.7	19.8	11.3	5.9	1.3
Sri Lanka	65,610	15,189,000	231.5	1981	14,850,001	50.8	49.2	21.5	35.3	29.6	17.9	10.6	5.2	1.4
Syria	185,179	9,413,000	50.8	1981	9,172,000	51.1	48.9	47.9	47.9	27.3	12.4	7.9	3.5	1.0
Taiwan	36,002	18,271,000	507.5	1980	18,031,825	...	...	...	...	...	...	...	...	...
Thailand	513,115	48,450,000	94.4	1980	44,278,000	49.7	50.3	17.3	38.2	29.8	16.3	10.2	5.5	
Turkey	779,452	46,312,000	59.4	1980	45,217,556	51.6	48.4	...	38.5	27.7	16.0	11.2	6.6	
United Arab Emirates	77,700	1,122,000	14.4	1981	1,043,225	69.0	31.0	80.9	...	...	...	...	...	...
Vietnam	329,465	55,503,000	168.5	1979	52,741,766	48.5	51.5	19.2	...	...	...	...	...	...
Yemen (Aden)	338,100	1,990,000	5.9	1973	1,590,275	49.5	50.4	33.3	47.3	20.8	15.8	8.6	6.6	
Yemen (San'a')	200,000	7,341,000	36.7	1981	8,556,974	...	...	...	...	...	...	...	...	...
Total ASIA[9,10]	44,614,154	2,718,251,000	60.9											
EUROPE														
Albania	28,748	2,862,000	99.6	1979	2,591,000	...	...	35.3	37.0		55.6		7.4	
Andorra	468	38,000	81.2	1982	38,051	53.7	46.3	66.8	...	...	...	...	...	...
Austria	83,853	7,571,000	90.3	1981	7,555,338	...	...	55.1	...	...	...	...	...	...
Belgium	30,519	9,855,000	322.9	1981	9,848,647	48.8	51.2	...	20.0	23.7	19.1	18.6	12.8	5.8
Bulgaria	110,912	9,108,000	82.1	1975	8,727,771	49.9	50.1	58.0	21.8	22.4	20.6	18.6	13.0	3.4
Channel Islands	194	130,000	670.1	1981	133,000	48.1	51.9	...	...	...	...	...	...	...
Czechoslovakia	127,889	15,375,000	120.2	1980	15,283,095	48.7	51.3	65.5	24.3	22.9	19.8	17.2	11.5	4.3
Denmark	43,080	5,125,000	119.0	1982[11]	5,119,115	49.3	50.7	...	19.5	22.6	21.6	16.0	14.0	5.8
Faeroe Islands	1,399	44,000	31.4	1977	41,969	52.4	47.6	...	27.6		58.4		14.0	
Finland	338,145	4,818,000	14.2	1980	4,787,778	48.3	51.7	59.8	20.2	24.3	22.2	16.9	12.4	4.1
France	544,000	54,257,000	99.7	1982	54,257,300	49.0	51.0	...	22.0	...	...	...	17.6	
Germany, East	108,333	16,732,000	154.4	1981	16,732,500	47.0	53.0	76.4	...	...	...	...	...	...
Germany, West	248,687	61,713,000	248.2	1981[11]	61,654,300	47.8	52.2	...	17.2	23.7	21.1	18.4	13.5	6.1
Gibraltar	6	30,000	5,000.0	1981	29,648	...	...	...	...	...	...	...	...	...
Greece	131,990	9,793,000	74.2	1981	9,740,151	...	...	58.1	...	...	...	...	...	...
Hungary	93,036	10,702,000	115.0	1980	10,709,536	48.5	51.5	53.2	21.7		61.4		16.9	
Iceland	103,000	232,000	2.2	1982[11]	235,537	50.4	49.6	88.9	26.7	27.4	18.6	13.6	9.5	4.3
Ireland	70,285	3,483,000	49.6	1981	3,443,405	50.2	49.8	...	...	...	...	...	...	...
Isle of Man	588	67,000	113.9	1981	64,679	...	...	...	...	...	...	...	...	...
Italy	301,268	56,224,000	186.6	1981	56,243,935	48.7	51.3	...	...	...	...	...	...	...
Jan Mayen	380	—	—	1973	37	...	...	—	...	...	...	...	...	...
Liechtenstein	160	26,000	162.5	1980	25,215	50.0	50.0	...	23.0	26.5	24.1	14.1	9.2	3.1
Luxembourg	2,586	365,000	141.1	1981	364,602	48.8	51.2	...	18.5	23.7	21.2	18.8	12.8	5.0
Malta	320	360,000	1,125.0	1967	314,216	47.9	52.1	94.3	29.8	25.9	17.6	13.8	10.2	2.7
Monaco	1.9	27,000	14,210.5	1982	27,063	...	...	...	...	...	...	...	...	...
Netherlands, The	41,548	14,286,000	343.8	1982[11]	14,285,829	49.6	50.4	...	21.5	46.9		31.6		
Norway	323,895	4,113,000	12.7	1980	4,091,132	49.5	50.5	...	44.5		34.9		20.6	
Poland	312,683	36,062,000	115.3	1978	35,061,000	51.3	48.7	57.5	23.8	27.5	35.6		13.2	
Portugal	91,985	10,056,000	109.3	1981	9,784,201	...	...	...	...	...	...	...	...	...
Romania	237,500	22,638,000	95.3	1977	21,559,400	49.3	50.7	47.8	27.2	24.6	22.7	13.5	9.8	2.2
San Marino	61	22,000	360.6	1976	20,284	50.4	49.8	...	24.4	23.0	19.9	17.4	11.4	3.9
Spain	504,750	37,935,000	75.2	1981	37,746,260	49.1	50.9	...	...	...	...	...	...	...
Svalbard	62,050	3,000	0.05	1974	3,472	...	...	...	...	...	...	...	...	...
Sweden	486,661	8,327,000	17.1	1980	8,320,582	49.5	50.5	...	19.4	20.6	21.2	16.7	15.7	6.4
Switzerland	41,293	6,384,000	154.6	1980	6,365,960	48.7	51.3	50.9	19.8	23.2	21.6	17.3	12.8	5.4
United Kingdom	244,035	55,782,000	228.6	1981	55,618,374	48.6	51.4	...	21.1	22.5	19.2	17.3	14.3	5.6
Vatican City	.44	1,000	2,272.7	—	—	—	—	—	—	—	—	—	—	—
Yugoslavia	255,804	22,646,000	88.5	1981	22,418,331	49.4	50.6	...	24.7	25.3	20.0	18.4	8.7	2.9
Total EUROPE[10]	10,543,213	689,500,000	65.4											
NORTH AMERICA														
Anguilla	96	7,000	72.9	1974	6,519	...	...	...	...	...	...	...	...	...
Antigua and Barbuda	442	77,000	174.2	1970	64,794	47.2	52.8	33.7	44.0	24.2	12.0	11.7	8.0	
Bahamas, The	13,864	240,000	17.3	1980	209,505	48.6	51.4	69.2	43.6	24.3	16.8	9.8	2.6	1.1
Barbados	430	254,000	590.7	1980	248,983	47.6	52.4	...	28.9	32.3	14.2	11.2	13.3	
Belize	22,965	150,000	6.5	1980	144,857	...	...	...	...	...	...	...	...	...
Bermuda	53	55,000	1,037.7	1980	54,050	48.8	51.2	100.0	22.7	27.5	22.2	15.7	9.0	2.9
British Virgin Islands	153	14,000	91.5	1980	12,034	...	...	...	...	...	...	...	...	...
Canada	9,976,139	24,625,000	2.5	1981	24,343,181	49.6	50.4	...	22.5	28.1	20.6	28.8		
Cayman Islands	264	18,000	68.2	1979	16,677	48.6	51.4	54.3	29.1	25.8	22.1	13.1	7.3	2.6
Costa Rica	51,100	2,372,000	46.4	1973	1,871,780	50.1	49.9	40.6	43.3	27.0	14.2	8.4	4.4	2.7
Cuba	110,922	9,799,000	88.3	1981	9,706,364	50.6	49.2	69.0	25.4		17.0	12.1	9.0	
Dominica	750	81,000	108.0	1970	69,549	47.4	52.6	46.2	49.1	21.2	11.2	10.0	6.3	2.2
Dominican Republic	48,442	5,813,000	120.0	1981	5,647,977	50.1	49.9	52.0	...	...	...	...	...	...
El Salvador	21,041	5,087,000	241.8	1971	3,544,648	49.6	50.4	39.4	46.2	25.1	15.2	8.2	4.3	1.0
Greenland	2,175,600	51,000	0.02	1981[11]	50,643	54.4	45.6	...	28.6	32.5	21.9	11.4	4.5	1.0

Table II. World Populations and Areas[1] *(Continued)*

Country	AREA AND POPULATION: MIDYEAR 1982 Area in sq km	Total population	Persons per sq km	POPULATION AT MOST RECENT CENSUS Date of census	Total population	% Male	% Female	% Urban	Age distribution (%)[2] 0–14	15–29	30–44	45–59	60–74	75+
Grenada	345	113,000	327.5	1970	92,775	46.2	53.8	25.3	47.1	23.0	11.6	9.4	6.6	2.2
Guadeloupe	1,780	315,000	177.0	1982	328,400	...	...	...	...	...	...	...	...	...
Guatemala	108,889	7,699,000	70.7	1981	6,043,559	49.9	50.1	...	...	...	...	...	...	...
Haiti	27,750	5,195,000	187.2	1971	4,329,991	48.2	51.8	20.4	41.5	25.8	16.5	9.5	5.0	1.7
Honduras	112,088	3,955,000	35.3	1974	2,656,948	49.5	50.5	37.5	48.1	25.8	13.9	7.8	3.6	0.9
Jamaica	10,991	2,222,000	202.2	1980	2,176,762	49.4	50.6	...	36.7	29.8	12.9	10.1	3.0	7.5
Martinique	1,100	326,000	296.4	1982	326,717	48.5	51.5	56.9	28.4	30.4	16.2	13.2	8.6	3.3
Mexico	1,958,201	73,011,000	37.3	1980	67,382,581	49.4	50.6	...	42.9	27.6	14.9	8.5	5.9	
Montserrat	102	12,000	117.6	1980	11,606	48.1	51.9	54.1	31.5	68.5				
Netherlands Antilles	993	267,000	268.9	1972	223.196	48.8	51.2	...	38.0	26.7	16.7	10.3	6.4	1.8
Nicaragua	127,662	2,643,000	20.7	1971	1,877,972	48.3	51.7	48.0	48.1	25.6	14.1	7.4	3.8	1.1
Panama	77,082	1,922,000	24.9	1980	1,824,796	50.7	49.3	49.3	39.1	27.9	16.4	9.6	5.1	1.8
Puerto Rico	8,958	3,952,000	441.2	1980	3,196,520	48.7	51.3	66.8	31.6	26.4	18.5	12.3	8.3	2.9
St. Christopher-Nevis	261	45,000	172.4	1980	43,309	48.1	51.9	37.1	37.2	30.4	9.5	9.4	10.0	3.6
St. Lucia	622	122,000	196.1	1970	99,806	47.2	52.8	36.9	49.6	21.3	11.6	9.8	5.5	2.2
St. Pierre & Miquelon	242	5,000	20.7	1982	6,041	...	...	...	...	...	...	...	...	...
St. Vincent & the Grenadines	388	122.000	314.4	1970	86,314	47.3	52.7	...	51.2	21.7	11.0	8.8	7.2	
Trinidad and Tobago	5,128	1,185,000	231.1	1980	1,059,825	49.8	50.2	...	...	...	...	...	...	...
Turks and Caicos Islands	500	6,000	12.0	1980	7,436	...	...	...	...	...	...	...	...	...
United States	9,363,123	231,990,000	24.8	1980	226,504,825	48.6	51.4	73.7	22.6	27.4	19.1	15.2	11.3	4.4
Virgin Islands (U.S.)	345	116,000	336.2	1980	96,569	47.8	52.2	29.6	36.0	24.2	21.5	11.1	5.7	1.4
Total NORTH AMERICA	24,288,811	383,866,000	15.8											
OCEANIA														
American Samoa	199	33,000	165.8	1980	32,297	50.7	49.3	17.5	40.9	28.8	16.0	9.4	4.0	0.9
Australia	7,682,300	15,054,000	2.0	1981	15,053,600	...	...	...	25.0	46.1		28.9		
Canton and Enderbury Islands	70	—	—	—	—	—	—	—	—	—	—	—	—	—
Christmas Island	135	3,000	22.2	1981	2,871	66.8	33.2	...	25.9	26.4	35.8	10.8	1.1	
Cocos Island	14	600	42.8	1981	555	53.7	46.3	...	27.4	28.3	27.2	11.2	5.9	
Cook Islands	236	17,000	72.0	1981	17,754	51.7	48.3	...	42.7	26.6	13.7	10.4	5.2	1.3
Fiji	18,273	650,000	35.6	1976	588,068	50.5	49.5	37.2	41.1	29.8	16.2	8.8	3.3	0.8
French Polynesia	4,182	153,000	36.6	1977	137,382	52.5	47.5	39.7	42.0	27.2	17.0	8.9	4.9	
Guam	541	106,000	195.9	1980	105,979	52.2	47.8	39.5	34.9	30.6	19.4	10.5	3.9	0.5
Johnston Island	3	1,000	333.3	1970	1,007	...	...	0	...	...	...	...	...	...
Kiribati	712	60,000	84.3	1978	55,835	49.3	50.7	...	41.2	28.2	14.9	10.0	4.8	1.0
Midway Islands	5	2,000	400.0	1970	2,220	...	...	...	...	...	...	...	...	...
Nauru	21	8,000	381.0	1977	7,254	54.2	45.8	0	...	...	...	...	...	...
New Caledonia	19,103	146,000	7.6	1976	133,233	52.0	48.0	42.1	38.6	26.3	18.6	10.4	4.9	1.2
New Zealand	269,057	3,190,000	11.8	1981	3,175,737	49.7	50.3	83.6	26.7	25.9	19.0	14.3	10.5	3.5
Niue	259	3,000	11.6	1976	3,843	50.2	49.8	...	46.1	23.8	13.7	7.9	5.8	2.3
Norfolk Island	35	2,000	57.1	1981	2,175	49.1	50.9	...	22.2	21.2	21.7	19.3	15.7	
Pacific Islands, Trust Territory of the	1,858	143,000	77.0	1980	133,019	51.4	48.6	28.4	46.0	26.7	13.3	8.4	4.5	1.1
Papua New Guinea	462,840	3,126,000	6.8	1980	3,006,799	52.3	47.7	13.1	...	...	...	...	...	...
Pitcairn Island	4	53	13.2	1981	54	...	...	0	...	...	...	...	...	...
Solomon Islands	27,556	244,000	8.8	1976	196,823	52.2	47.8	...	47.9	24.1	14.5	8.4	3.6	1.5
Tokelau	12	2,000	166.7	1981	1,575	49.4	50.6	...	...	...	...	...	...	...
Tonga	747	99,000	132.5	1976	90,085	51.1	48.9	...	44.4	26.2	14.8	9.5	5.1	
Tuvalu	26	9,000	346.2	1979	7,349	46.8	53.2	...	33.4	31.1	14.7	13.0	7.7	
Vanuatu	12,190	126,000	10.3	1979	111,251	53.1	46.9	17.8	45.4	27.5	15.0	7.7	3.4	1.1
Wake Island	8	2,000	250.0	1970	1,647	...	...	...	...	...	...	...	...	...
Wallis and Futuna	274	11,000	40.1	1976	9,192	50.0	50.0	...	46.6	23.6	14.0	9.9	5.1	0.8
Western Samoa	2,831	158,000	55.8	1976	151,938	51.7	48.3	21.1	48.2	26.0	12.6	8.7	3.5	1.0
Total OCEANIA	8,503,491	23,402,000	2.8											
SOUTH AMERICA														
Argentina	2,780,091	28,438,000	10.2	1980	27,862,771	49.2	50.8	86.3	...	...	...	...	...	...
Bolivia	1,098,581	5,916,000	5.4	1976	4,613,486	49.1	50.9	41.7	41.5	27.0	15.4	9.8	4.6	1.7
Brazil	8,512,000	124,343,000	14.6	1980	119,098,992	49.7	50.3	67.6	39.1	28.6	16.4	10.0	5.9	
Chile	756,627	11,275,000	14.9	1982	11,275,440	49.0	51.0	81.0	32.2	29.1	18.9	11.7	6.3	1.8
Colombia	1,141,748	27,098,000	23.7	1973	22,915,229	48.6	51.4	63.6	44.1	27.3	14.9	8.5	4.1	1.0
Ecuador	281,341	8,073,000	28.7	1982	8,072,702	...	...	...	...	...	...	...	...	...
Falkland Islands	16,265	2,000	0.1	1980	1,957	55.2	44.8	55.1	26.7	22.4	50.8			
French Guiana	83,533	73,000	0.9	1982	73,022	...	...	...	...	...	...	...	...	...
Guyana	215,000	944,000	4.4	1970	699,848	49.7	50.3	33.3	47.1	25.1	13.4	9.0	4.4	1.0
Paraguay	406,752	3,251,000	8.0	1982	3,015,670	50.3	49.7	42.2	41.0	27.8	14.2	10.3	5.9	1.2
Peru	1,285,215	17,401,000	13.5	1981	17,005,210	49.7	50.3	64.6	41.4	27.7	15.5	9.3	4.2	
Suriname	163,820	356,000	2.2	1980	352,041	49.2	50.8	...	39.1	60.9				
Uruguay	176,215	2,967,000	16.8	1975	2,788,429	49.0	51.0	83.0	27.0	22.6	19.2	16.9	10.8	3.5
Venezuela	912,050	14,714,000	16.1	1971	10,721,522	49.9	50.1	73.1	45.0	26.9	14.9	8.5	3.7	1.0
Total SOUTH AMERICA	17,829,238	244,851,000	13.7											
U.S.S.R.[10]	22,402,200	270,000,000	12.0	1979	262,436,200	46.6	53.4	62.0	...	...	...	...	...	...
in Asia[10]	16,831,100	67,692,000	4.0											
in Europe[10]	5,571,100	202,308,000	36.3											
TOTAL WORLD[12]	150,281,720	4,564,752,000	33.6											

[1]Any presentation of population data must include data of varying reliability. This table provides published and unpublished data about the latest census (or comparable demographic survey) and the most recent or reliable midyear 1982 population estimates for the countries of the world. Census figures are only a body of estimates and samples of varying reliability whose quality depends on the completeness of the enumeration. Some countries tabulate only persons actually present, while others include those legally resident, but actually outside the country, on census day. Population estimates are subject to continual correction and revision; their reliability depends on: number of years elapsed since a census control was established, completeness of birth and death registration, international migration data, etc. The symbol . . . means figures not available; — means not applicable.

[2]Data for persons of unknown age excluded, so percentages may not add to 100.0.

[3]Excludes Mayotte, shown separately.

[4]A census was taken in Nigeria in 1973, but the results were officially repudiated.

[5]Transkei received its independence from South Africa on Oct. 26, 1976; Bophuthatswana on Dec. 6, 1977; Venda on Sept. 13, 1979; Ciskei on Dec. 4, 1981. All are Black homeland states whose independence is not internationally recognized.

[6]Sudan census excludes three southern autonomous provinces.

[7]May reach a total of 2,000 persons of all nationalities during the summer.

[8]Excludes nomadic population.

[9]Includes 18,130 sq km of Iraq-Saudi Arabia neutral zone.

[10]Asia and Europe continent totals include corresponding portions of U.S.S.R.

[11]Yearly register figures; not an official census.

[12]Area of Antarctica excluded in calculating world density.

continued from page 284

also lower, 8.6 deaths per 1,000 population. The primary causes of death in 1982 were:

Cause of death	Estimated rate per 100,000 population
1. Diseases of the heart	327.8
2. Malignant neoplasms	188.1
3. Cerebrovascular diseases	68.9
4. Accidents and adverse effects	41.3
5. Chronic obstructive pulmonary diseases and allied conditions	25.9
6. Pneumonia and influenza	21.8
7. Diabetes mellitus	14.3
8. Suicide	12.0
9. Chronic liver disease and cirrhosis	11.8
10. Atherosclerosis	11.5
11. Homicide and legal intervention	9.6
12. Conditions of the perinatal period	9.0
13. Nephritis, nephrotic syndrome, and nephrosis	7.9
14. Congenital anomalies	5.7
15. Septicemia	4.9

Table III. Birthrates and Death Rates per 1,000 Population and Infant Mortality per 1,000 Live Births in Selected Countries, 1982*

	Registered			Estimated		
Country	Birth-rate	Death rate	Infant mortality	Birth-rate	Death rate	Infant mortality
Africa						
Algeria	40.6[1]	7.8[1]	70.8[1]	47.4[2]	14.2[2]	125.3[2]
Egypt	36.9	10.3	74.2[1]	...	...	...
Guinea-Bissau	10.8[3]	1.9[3]	112.7[3]	40.0[2]	23.0[2]	154.3[2]
Madagascar	45.0[4]	18.0[4]	53.2[4]	45.0[2]	19.0[2]	75.7[2]
Mauritius	22.8	6.7	30.2	...	...	...
Nigeria[2]	...	...	...	49.8	17.8	140.5
Rwanda	19.5[3]	5.2[3]	50.4[3]	51.5[5]	22.0[5]	127.0[5]
Seychelles	24.0	7.5	19.4	...	...	...
South Africa[2]	...	...	...	37.9	10.3	100.6
Tunisia	32.9	7.3	14.9	...	11.1[2]	106.5[2]
Zaire[2]	...	...	...	46.2	18.7	116.6
Asia						
Bangladesh[2]	...	...	...	47.0	17.6	139.6
China	20.9[3]	6.4[3]	21.3[2]	21.3[2]	7.4[2]	48.7[2]
Cyprus	20.8[4]	8.3[4]	17.7[4]	19.6[2]	9.1[2]	19.5[2]
Hong Kong	16.5	4.8	9.8	...	...	...
India	...	...	...	33.2[1]	12.8[1]	130.0[1]
Indonesia	...	...	...	33.6[2]	16.2[2]	98.7[2]
Israel	24.0	6.8	13.0	...	...	...
Japan	12.9	6.1	6.6	...	...	...
Korea, South	17.7[4]	5.1[4]	37.0[3]	25.3[2]	8.1[2]	36.7[2]
Kuwait[3]	35.5	3.2	24.1	...	...	...
Pakistan	...	...	...	42.0	12.0	90.0
Singapore	17.2	5.2	10.7	...	...	...
Vietnam	31.3[1]	6.4[1]	...	40.1[2]	14.3[2]	106.4[2]
Europe						
Austria	12.5	12.0	12.8	...	...	...
Czechoslovakia	15.2	11.7	16.2	...	...	...
Denmark	10.3	10.8	7.9	...	...	...
France	12.8	7.1	9.3	...	...	...
Germany, East[4]	14.2	13.9	12.3	...	...	...
Germany, West	10.1	11.6	11.6	...	...	...
Hungary	12.5	13.5	20.0	...	...	...
Italy	11.7	9.5	12.6	...	...	...
Netherlands, The	12.0	8.2	8.1	...	...	...
Poland	19.4	9.2	20.2	...	...	...
Spain	13.6	7.3	10.3	...	...	...
Sweden	11.1	10.9	6.8	...	...	...
United Kingdom[4]	13.1	11.8	11.2	...	...	...
North America						
Canada	15.1	6.9	9.6	...	...	...
Cuba	16.3	5.8	17.3	...	...	...
El Salvador[4]	33.5	7.7	44.0	...	...	...
Greenland	20.5	8.5	32.4	...	...	...
Guatemala[3]	41.8	7.1	65.9	...	...	...
Martinique[4]	17.5[4]	6.6[4]	12.6[4]	...	...	23.0[2]
Mexico	33.6[4]	5.3[4]	38.5[4]	38.3[2]	...	59.8[2]
Panama	28.5[4]	4.3[4]	21.7[3]	...	6.0[2]	36.2[2]
United States	16.0	8.6	11.2	...	...	...
Oceania						
Australia[4]	15.4	7.4	10.0	...	...	...
Guam[4]	28.9	3.9	16.3	...	...	...
New Zealand	15.8	8.1	11.8	...	...	...
Papua New Guinea[2]	...	...	...	42.5	15.7	110.9
Tokelau	27.7	16.0	...	...	...	...
South America						
Argentina[1]	24.2	8.8	38.5	...	...	...
Brazil	23.3[3]	6.8[3]	68.1[3]	33.3[2]	9.1[2]	82.4[2]
Chile[4]	23.4	6.2	27.0	...	...	...
Guyana	29.4	7.0	45.0	...	...	...
Paraguay	36.0	7.2	63.2	36.7[2]	7.6[2]	48.6[2]
Peru	35.4	10.8	95.2	39.6[2]	11.6[2]	93.5[2]
Uruguay	18.3[4]	9.0	34.1[4]	...	...	...
Venezuela	35.5[3]	5.5[3]	31.6[3]	36.9[2]	6.1[2]	44.8[2]
U.S.S.R.[3]	18.5	10.2	27.7	...	...	...

*Both registered and estimated rates are shown only for countries with incomplete registered rates.
[1]1979. [2]1975–80. [3]1980. [4]1981. [5]1976.
Sources: United Nations, *Population and Vital Statistics Report;* various national publications.

Heart disease, cancer, and stroke accounted for over two-thirds of all deaths. Significant declines from the previous year were noted for infections of the kidney (−18%), pneumonia and influenza (−11%), motor vehicle accidents (−11%), chronic liver disease and cirrhosis (−8%), atherosclerosis (−8%), homicide and legal intervention (−6%), and diabetes mellitus (−5%). Increases were particularly noted for septicemia (11%) and leukemia (9%).

The estimated crude death rate for the world was 11 per 1,000 population. Despite high mortality in some countries, the overall death rate for less developed regions remained relatively low, as indicated by the averages for middle Africa (19), middle South Asia (15), and tropical South America (9). Lower mortality rates prevailed in Europe, the lowest being estimated for Albania (7), Iceland (7), Spain (7.3), and The Netherlands (8.2).

Expectation of Life. Life expectancy had improved in many areas of the world in the last decade, but there remained a gap of 15 years between the average for the less developed countries (58 years) and that for the developed countries (73 years). African countries generally had the lowest life expectancy; of 51 countries for which data were available, 38 had average life expectancies of 50 years or less at birth. Asia as a whole had higher averages, but in 11 Asian countries (out of 44) the average length of life was 50 years or less. In Latin America the overall average was 64 years, ranging from 50 years in Bolivia to 73 years in Puerto Rico. The Scandinavian countries and Switzerland reported high rates of about 75 years.

Average life expectancy at birth in the U.S. for 1982 was estimated at 74.5 years, 78.2 years for women and 70.8 years for men. These averages were the highest ever reported for the U.S. New high levels were also recorded by race and sex: 78.7 years for white women, 73.8 years for black women, 71.4 years for white men, and 64.8 years for black men.

Infant Mortality. The total world infant mortality rate remained high, around 85 deaths to infants under one year of age per 1,000 live births. The highest estimates were for African countries (Sierra Leone 206, Upper Volta 210, The Gambia 197). Rates for middle South Asia were over 100, and for tropical South America the average was 73. Low rates were characteristic of the Scandinavian countries (Sweden 6.8), other European nations (The Netherlands 8.1, Switzerland 9.1, France 9.3), and Japan (6.6).

There were an estimated 41,700 infant deaths in the U.S. in 1982, a 2% decrease from 1981. The infant mortality rate was 11.2 deaths per 1,000 live births, the lowest ever estimated for the U.S. The downtrend continued into 1983. During the first six months the rate was 11.1, compared with 11.7 for the corresponding period of 1982. Detailed data for 1980 show that the infant mortality rate for black infants was about twice that for white infants.

Marriage and Divorce Statistics. An estimated 2,495,000 marriages took place in the U.S. in 1982, the highest number on record. The marriage rate was 10.8 per 1,000 population, higher than in any year since 1973. According to final figures for 1980, the median age at first marriage was 21.8 years for brides and 23.6 years for grooms; in 1963 it had averaged 20.3 years for brides and 22.5 years for grooms. Median age at remarriage in 1980 was 32 years for brides and 35.2 years for grooms.

The proportion of marriages that were first marriages for both bride and groom declined from 69% in 1970 to 56% in 1980, while the proportion where both were remarrying rose from 17 to 23%.

In 1982 the number of divorces in the U.S. dropped for the first time in 20 years. According to provisional data, there were 1,180,000 divorces in 1982, a decline of 3% from 1981. The divorce rate also dropped, from 5.3 per 1,000 population in 1981 to 5.1 in 1982. Details on divorce, available for 1980, show that the number of children involved fell from 1,181,000 in 1979 to 1,174,000 in 1980. The number of children involved in divorce each year had almost quadrupled between 1950 and 1979. The median duration of marriage was 6.8 years in 1980, a figure that had not changed significantly for many years.

Table IV. Life Expectancy at Birth in Years, for Selected Countries

Country	Period	Male	Female
Africa			
Burundi	1980–85[1]	45.3	48.6
Egypt	1980–85[1]	55.9	58.4
Ivory Coast	1980–85[1]	46.9	50.2
Kenya	1980–85[1]	56.3	60.0
Nigeria	1980–85[1]	48.3	51.7
Swaziland	1980–85[1]	46.8	50.0
Asia			
China	1980	66.0	69.0
Hong Kong	1982	71.9	77.6
India	1981	53.9	52.9
Indonesia	1980–85[1]	51.2	53.9
Israel	1980	72.1	75.7
Japan	1982	74.2	79.7
Kuwait	1980–85[1]	68.1	72.9
Pakistan	1980–85[1]	54.4	54.2
Taiwan	1981	69.7	74.6
Thailand	1980–85[1]	59.5	65.1
Europe			
Albania	1978–79	66.8	71.4
Austria	1981	69.3	76.4
Belgium	1980	69.0	75.0
Bulgaria	1980	69.0	75.0
Czechoslovakia	1980	66.8	74.0
Denmark	1980–81	71.1	77.2
Finland	1980	69.2	77.6
France	1981	70.2	78.5
Germany, East	1980	68.7	74.6
Germany, West	1979–81	69.9	76.6
Greece	1980	71.0	75.0
Hungary	1981	66.0	73.4
Iceland	1979–80	73.7	79.7
Ireland	1980	70.0	75.0
Italy	1980	70.0	76.0
Netherlands, The	1980	72.4	79.2
Norway	1980–81	72.5	79.2
Poland	1981	67.1	75.2
Portugal	1980	66.0	74.0
Romania	1980	68.0	73.0
Spain	1980	70.0	76.0
Sweden	1981	73.1	79.1
Switzerland	1980	72.0	78.0
United Kingdom	1978–80	70.2	76.2
Yugoslavia	1979	67.5	72.9
North America			
Canada	1980	70.0	77.0
Costa Rica	1980	68.0	72.0
Cuba	1980	71.0	74.0
Martinique	1980–85[1]	67.8	73.0
Mexico	1980	62.0	67.0
Panama	1980	68.0	72.0
Puerto Rico	1979	69.6	76.1
Trinidad and Tobago	1980	66.0	72.0
United States	1982	70.8	78.2
Oceania			
Australia	1980	70.0	76.0
New Zealand	1980	70.0	76.0
South America			
Argentina	1980–85[1]	66.8	73.2
Brazil	1980	60.0	64.0
Chile	1980–85[1]	63.8	70.4
Peru	1980–85[1]	56.7	59.7
Suriname	1980–85[1]	66.3	71.5
Uruguay	1980–85[1]	67.1	73.7
Venezuela	1980	64.0	69.0
U.S.S.R.	1981	65.0	74.0

[1]Projection.
Sources: United Nations, *World Statistics in Brief*, statistical pocketbook, 6th edition (1981), *World Population Trends and Prospects by Country, 1950–2000*, summary report of the 1978 assessment; official country sources.

Censuses and Surveys. The UN Statistical Office reported that many countries had achieved their goals during the 1975–84 Census Decade. Of 212 countries or areas, 174 had taken censuses, the largest being the China census of 1982. Another 18 countries would complete census taking in 1984. Of the remaining 20 countries, several planned to take a census in 1985–86. Of 54 African countries, 50 would have taken censuses during the period, many for the first time. The UN estimated that by the end of the 1975–84 Census Decade, 95% of the world's population would have been enumerated.

(ANDERS S. LUNDE)

[338.F.5.b; 525.A; 10/36.c.5.d]

Denmark

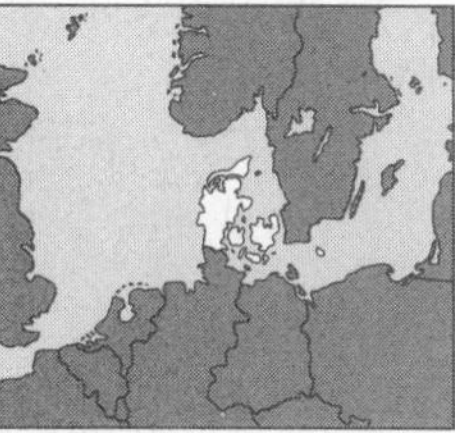
Denmark

A constitutional monarchy of north central Europe lying between the North and Baltic seas, Denmark includes the Jutland Peninsula and 100 inhabited islands in the Kattegat and Skagerrak straits. Area (excluding Faeroe Islands and Greenland): 43,080 sq km (16,633 sq mi). Pop. (1982 est.): 5,124,700. Cap. and largest city: Copenhagen (pop., 1982 est., 645,200). Language: Danish. Religion: predominantly Lutheran. Queen, Margrethe II; prime minister in 1983, Poul Schlüter.

In 1983 Denmark's minority government, comprising the Conservative, Liberal Democratic (Venstre), Centre Democratic, and Christian People's parties, continued to lead a dangerous life, based as it was on only 66 of the 179 seats in the Folketing (parliament). During the year it survived several crises with the help of two other parties, the Radical Liberals and the Progress Party, but in December, after the proposed budget was defeated 93–77, the Folketing was dissolved and elections were called for Jan. 10, 1984—Denmark's eighth election in 15 years.

The biggest threat to the government's stability during much of the year stemmed from the disarray within the antitaxation Progress Party. After several years of litigation, Mogens Glistrup, its founder and leader, was sentenced in June to three years in prison for tax fraud. Subsequently, he was expelled from the Folketing, and he began to urge Progress Party members to vote against the government. Three members left the party so they could continue to vote with the government.

The government aimed to cut expenditure by 10 billion kroner and to reduce the balance of payments deficit by a similar amount. At the same time, it acknowledged that unemployment figures would continue to rise, possibly reaching 300,000 in 1984. Specific proposals in the 1984 budget included an increase in personal income-tax allowances from 20,000 kroner to 22,200 kroner; an increase in tax allowances for families with young children; introduction of new taxes on mineral water; and the abolition of subsidies on milk.

At the same time, a program of wide-ranging public-expenditure cuts was proposed. Prime Minister Poul Schlüter announced that the savings program would not result in downgrading of the welfare state. The government also proposed that wealthier citizens make an extra "health service" payment of about 1,000 kroner a year, which would go toward offsetting hospital bills. The central government was attempting to control local-government spending by reducing its grant to the municipalities and by requesting that they keep local taxes down. These savings would hit locally supplied services, such as kindergartens and sports centres. There were a number of protests against public-expenditure cuts during the year. At the same time, opinion-poll findings showed Schlüter's government to be the most popular since such polls were first used some 40 years earlier. In October over 80% of those questioned judged the government's performance to be "good" or "quite good."

The government was negotiating with 30 or so oil companies that had expressed an interest in prospecting for petroleum in the Danish sector of the North Sea and at certain onshore sites. After voting to leave the European Communities (EC) in 1982, Greenland was in the process of negotiating the terms of its departure. During the year the Danish Foreign Office protested that West German, and possibly British, vessels were fishing illegally in Greenland's water. Under pressure from Denmark in particular, the EC reached agreement on a common fisheries policy in late January, though disputes continued. (*See* FISHERIES.)

A Social Democrat-sponsored resolution, supported by the Socialist People's Party and the Left Socialists, was introduced calling on the government to convene an extraordinary meeting of the NATO ministerial council, at which it should call for a review of progress made at the intermediate nuclear force (INF) negotiations, an extension of these talks, and a delay in deployment of new INF missiles in Europe while the discussions continued. With the government parties abstaining, the resolution won a majority in the Folketing in November. In December the Folketing voted to reject the deployment of cruise and Pershing II missiles in Europe. (STENER AARSDAL)

DENMARK

Education. (1980–81) Primary, pupils 505,116; secondary, pupils 205,036; primary and secondary, teachers 72,308; vocational, pupils 150,971; higher, students 96,056, teaching staff (universities only; 1978–79) 6,702.

Finance. Monetary unit: Danish krone, with (Sept. 20, 1983) a free rate of 9.57 kroner to U.S. $1 (14.41 kroner = £1 sterling). Gold and other reserves (June 1983) U.S. $3,159,000,000. Budget (1982 est.): revenue 124,359,000,000 kroner; expenditure 164,250,000,000 kroner. Gross national product (1982) 452.4 billion kroner. Money supply (Jan. 1983) 95,120,000,000 kroner. Cost of living (1975 = 100; June 1983) 215.3.

Foreign Trade. (1982) Imports 140,299,000,000 kroner; exports 127,473,000,000 kroner. Import sources: EEC 49% (West Germany 20%, U.K. 11%, The Netherlands 7%); Sweden 12%; U.S. 7%. Export destinations: EEC 49% (West Germany 17%, U.K. 14%, France 6%, Italy 5%); Sweden 11%; Norway 6%; U.S. 6%. Main exports: machinery 19%; meat 14%; chemicals 8%; dairy products 6%; fish 5%. Tourism: visitors (1980) c. 3.5 million; gross receipts (1981) U.S. $1,239,000,000.

Transport and Communications. Roads (1981) 69,428 km (including 525 km expressways). Motor vehicles in use (1981): passenger 1,366,900; commercial 242,800. Railways: (1979) 2,944 km; traffic (1979–80) 3,353,000,000 passenger-km, freight (1980–81) 1,570,000,000 net ton-km. Air traffic (including apportionment of international operations of Scandinavian Airlines System; 1982): 2,940,000,000 passenger-km; freight 128.6 million net ton-km. Shipping (1982): merchant vessels 100 gross tons and over 1,152; gross tonnage 5,214,063. Shipping traffic (1982): goods loaded 7,990,000 metric tons, unloaded 29,511,000 metric tons. Telephones (including Faeroe Islands and Greenland; Jan. 1981) 3,316,709. Radio licenses (Dec. 1981) 1,949,300. Television licenses (Dec. 1981) 1,861,200.

Agriculture. Production (in 000; metric tons; 1982): wheat c. 1,050; barley c. 6,380; oats c. 180; rye c. 200; potatoes 1,236; rutabagas (swedes) 727; sugar, raw value c. 576; apples c. 120; rapeseed c. 334; butter 121; cheese 246; pork 991; beef and veal 231; fish catch (1981) 1,814. Livestock (in 000; July 1982): cattle 2,873; pigs 9,319; sheep 58; chickens 15,185.

Industry. Production (in 000; metric tons; 1982): crude steel 560; cement 1,770; fertilizers (nutrient content; 1981–82) nitrogenous 131, phosphate 108; plastics and resins (1976) 145; crude oil 1,686; petroleum products (1981) 5,969; manufactured gas (cu m; 1981) c. 300,000; electricity (kw-hr) 22,017,000. Merchant vessels launched (100 gross tons and over; 1982) 419,000 gross tons.

Dentistry:
see Health and Disease

Dependent States

Two U.K. dependencies achieved full independence during 1983: the associated state of St. Kitts-Nevis in September and the protected sultanate of Brunei at midnight, December 31. (*See* BRUNEI; SAINT CHRISTOPHER AND NEVIS.)

One of St. Kitts-Nevis's first actions as a sovereign state was to vote against the resolution of the Organization of Eastern Caribbean States to intervene in Grenada in October; Montserrat also did not support the plan. Nevertheless, the U.S.-led intervention took place, and Grenada's own status as an independent country was called into question. (*See* GRENADA; LAW: *International.*)

Europe and the Atlantic. U.K. Prime Minister Margaret Thatcher received a warm welcome when she paid a surprise visit to the Falkland Islands in January. In April the families of the British servicemen who had died in the 1982 conflict traveled to the islands to be present at the dedication of a war memorial. Both the British and Argentine governments reported on the events of the previous year. The Franks Report commented that the British government could neither have prevented nor foreseen Argentina's invasion. In Argentina, on the other hand, a government report recommended that several leading figures in the action, including Gen. Leopoldo Galtieri, president at the time, stand trial for failing to assess the consequences of their decision to invade.

During the year the UN General Assembly and the movement of nonaligned nations urged the two parties to discuss the sovereignty issue. The elected civilian government that assumed power in Argentina at the end of 1983 reasserted its view that Argentina possessed an "unconditional right" to the islands; while it would pursue the same objectives as the military junta, it would do so in

WIDE WORLD

Strikers took an occasional break during a November hotel strike in Papeete, Tahiti. They established this encampment for the duration of the strike in a downtown Papeete park.

"democratic fashion" and would accord to the people of the Falklands the same democratic right that the people of Argentina had just exercised.

The Spanish government further relaxed its border controls with Gibraltar, a territory that it disputed with the U.K. It announced in January that Gibraltarians resident in Spain would be allowed to cross the border. However, the arrival in Gibraltar of several ships of the Royal Navy—including the aircraft carrier HMS "Invincible," which had served in the Falklands campaign—prompted a strong protest from Spain in April. Spain claimed that the presence of the ships indicated a breakdown of trust, but the U.K. replied that they were simply taking part in routine maneuvers. The new administration in Spain was eager to reopen discussions on the question of sovereignty for Gibraltar, and the foreign ministers of Spain and the U.K. met in September and held exploratory talks.

Greenland's decision to leave the European Communities (EC) by Jan. 1, 1984, was a subject for negotiation during the year, as the government tried to establish satisfactory terms with other members. In June the European Parliament voted to respect the islanders' wish to leave the EC. After elections in April, the ruling anti-EC Siumut ("Forward" Party) continued in power, though it held a minority of seats in Parliament. The small Inuit Ataqatigiit ("Eskimo Movement"), which won seats for the first time, called for increased links with the Eskimo of North America.

Caribbean. The U.K.'s only remaining associated state, St. Kitts-Nevis, attained independence on September 19. Of the U.K.'s remaining Caribbean dependencies, only Bermuda experienced any discussion of independence; the others—Anguilla, the Cayman Islands, Montserrat, the Turks and Caicos Islands, and the British Virgin Islands—indicated that independence was not on their agendas for the foreseeable future.

Premier John Swan of Bermuda said in May that his government was preparing a White Paper on independence, but he added that, as a matter of principle, the island should not become independent "until it is the will of the Bermudian people." He pointed out that no time frame for the matter had been established. Swan's United Bermuda Party was returned to power with 26 out of 40 seats in the House of Assembly in general elections on February 3, the opposition Progressive Labour Party taking the remaining 14. In March the island's governor, Sir Richard Posnett, resigned over allegations of irregularities in his expense account, which he strongly denied; he was replaced by Viscount Dunrossil.

Elections also took place in February in Montserrat. The People's Liberation Movement headed by Chief Minister John Osborne retained power, though it lost two of the seven seats in the Legislative Council to the opposition Progressive Democratic Party led by Austin Bramble. Osborne had said he was seeking a "mandate against socialism." After his reelection he said that he had no intention of thrusting independence on the island.

The Cayman Islands continued to show a rising volume of financial and tourist business. Tourist arrivals increased from 121,214 in 1981 to 279,499 in 1982, mainly because the number of passenger cruise ships calling there doubled. The total number of companies registered in the islands at the end of 1982 was 16,712, compared with 14,391 at the end of 1981.

The Turks and Caicos Islands announced a

continued on page 295

ANTARCTIC

Claims on the continent of Antarctica and all islands south of 60° S remain in status quo according to the Antarctic Treaty, to which 19 nations are signatory. Formal claims within the treaty area include the following: Australian Antarctic Territory, the mainland portion of French Southern and Antarctic Lands (Terre Adélie), Ross Dependency claimed by New Zealand, Queen Maud Land and Peter I Island claimed by Norway, and British Antarctic Territory, some parts of which are claimed by Argentina and Chile. No claims have been recognized as final under international law.

AUSTRALIA

CHRISTMAS ISLAND

Christmas Island, an external territory, is situated in the Indian Ocean 1,410 km NW of Australia. Area: 135 sq km (52 sq mi). Pop. (1981 est.): 3,300. Main settlement: Flying Fish Cove and the Settlement (pop., 1978 est., 1,400).

COCOS (KEELING) ISLANDS

Cocos (Keeling) Islands is an external territory located in the Indian Ocean 3,685 km W of Darwin, Australia. Area: 14 sq km (5.5 sq mi). Pop. (1981 est.): 569.

NORFOLK ISLAND

Norfolk Island, an external territory, is located in the Pacific Ocean 1,720 km NE of Sydney, Australia. Area: 35 sq km (13 sq mi). Pop. (1981): 2,200. Cap. (de facto): Kingston.

DENMARK

FAEROE ISLANDS

The Faeroes, an integral part of the Danish realm, are a self-governing group of islands in the North Atlantic about 580 km W of Norway. Area: 1,399 sq km (540 sq mi). Pop. (1982 est.): 44,100. Cap.: Thorshavn (pop., 1982 est., 14,000).

Education. (1982–83) Primary, pupils 5,558; secondary, pupils 3,119; primary and secondary, teachers 505; vocational, pupils (1981–82) 1,527, teachers (1976–77) 79; teacher training, students 98, teachers (1976–77) 30; higher, students 26.

Finance and Trade. Monetary unit: Faeroese krone, at par with the Danish krone, with (Sept. 20, 1983) a free rate of 9.57 kroner to U.S. $1 (14.41 kroner = £1 sterling). Budget (1980–81 est.): revenue 661,761,000 kroner; expenditure 684,727,000 kroner. Foreign trade (1981): imports 1,481,000,000 kroner; exports 1,186,000,000 kroner. Import sources: Denmark 64%; Norway 19%. Export destinations: U.K. 17%; Denmark 16%; West Germany 13%; U.S. 12 %; Italy 8%; France 8%; Spain 6%; Norway 6%. Main exports: fish 81%; fish meal 7%; fishing vessels 6%.

Transport. Shipping (1982): merchant vessels 100 gross tons and over 178; gross tonnage 67,952.

Agriculture and Industry. Fish catch (1981) 242,000 metric tons. Livestock (in 000; 1981): sheep c. 71; cattle c. 2. Electricity production (1981) 165 million kw-hr.

GREENLAND (Kalâtdlit-Nunât)

An integral part of the Danish realm, Greenland, the largest island in the world, lies mostly within the Arctic Circle. Area: 2,175,600 sq km (840,000 sq mi), 84% of which is covered by ice cap. Pop. (1982 est.): 51,400. Cap.: Godthaab (Nûk; pop., 1982 est., 10,200).

Education. (1982–83) Primary, pupils 7,985; secondary, pupils 2,439; primary and secondary, teachers 1,092; vocational, pupils 1,257, teachers (1979–80) 53; teacher training, students 242, teachers (1979–80) 27.

Finance and Trade. Monetary unit: Danish krone. Budget (1980 est.): revenue 643 million kroner; expenditure 568 million kroner. Foreign trade (1981): imports 2,129,000,000 kroner; exports 1,480,000,000 kroner. Import sources: Denmark 72%; Norway 7%; U.S. 6%; U.K. 5%. Export destinations: Denmark 51%; France 12%; West Germany 7%; U.S. 7%; Finland 7%; U.K. 5%. Main exports: fish 70%; zinc ore 14%; lead ore 6%; aircraft 5%.

Agriculture. Fish catch (1981) 103,400 metric tons. Livestock (in 000; 1981): sheep 17; reindeer 2.

Industry. Production (in 000; metric tons; 1981): lead ore (metal content) 38; zinc ore (metal content) 140; silver (troy oz; 1980) 547; electricity (kw-hr) 170,000.

FRANCE

FRENCH GUIANA

French Guiana is an overseas département situated between Brazil and Suriname on the northeast coast of South America. Area: 83,533 sq km (32,252 sq mi). Pop. (1982 prelim.): 73,000. Cap.: Cayenne (pop., 1982 prelim., 38,100).

Education. (1979–80) Primary, pupils 12,290, teachers 613; secondary, pupils 5,660, teachers 341; vocational, pupils 1,532, teachers 142.

Finance and Trade. Monetary unit: French (metropolitan) franc, with (Sept. 20, 1983) a free rate of Fr 8.06 to U.S. $1 (Fr 12.14 = £1 sterling). Budget (total; 1982 est.) balanced at Fr 578 million. Foreign trade (1981): imports Fr 1,355,390,000; exports Fr 192,080,000. Import sources: France 53%; Trinidad and Tobago 15%; U.S. 10%; Japan 5%. Export destinations: U.S. 54%; Japan 17%; France 15%. Main exports: shrimp 73%; timber 11%.

FRENCH POLYNESIA

An overseas territory, French Polynesia consists of islands scattered over a large area of the south central Pacific Ocean. Area of inhabited islands: 4,182 sq km (1,615 sq mi). Pop. (1982 est.): 153,400. Cap.: Papeete, Tahiti (pop., 1981 est., 23,400).

Education. (1981–82) Primary, pupils 29,371, teachers 1,544; secondary, pupils 11,258; vocational, pupils 3,050; secondary and vocational, teachers 998; higher, students 124, teaching staff 10.

Finance and Trade. Monetary unit: CFP franc, with (Sept. 20, 1983) a parity of CFP Fr 18.18 to the French franc and a free rate of CFP Fr 147 to U.S. $1 (CFP Fr 221 = £1 sterling). Budget (1982) balanced at CFP Fr 28.1 billion. Foreign trade (1982): imports CFP Fr 62,307,000,000; exports CFP Fr 3,349,000,000. Import sources (1981): France 47%; U.S. 21%; New Zealand 5%; Singapore 5%. Export destinations (1981): France 64%; Italy 12%; Japan 7%; U.S. 5%. Main exports (1981): war matériel 37%; coconut oil 18%; pearls 14%; precision instruments 8%; aircraft 6%; machinery 5%. Tourism (1981): visitors 96,800; gross receipts U.S. $85 million.

GUADELOUPE

The overseas département of Guadeloupe, together with its dependencies, is in the eastern Caribbean between Antigua to the north and Dominica to the south. Area: 1,780 sq km (687 sq mi). Pop. (1982 prelim.): 328,400. Cap.: Basse-Terre (pop., 1982 prelim., 13,700).

Education. (1981–82) Primary, pupils 62,303, teachers (1979–80) 2,744; secondary, pupils 45,843; vocational (1979–80), pupils 10,059; secondary and vocational (1978–79), teachers 2,602; higher (1980–81), students 3,800.

Finance and Trade. Monetary unit: French (metropolitan) franc. Budget (total; 1981 est.) balanced at Fr 1,257,000,000. Cost of living (Basse-Terre; 1975 = 100; March 1983) 218.9. Foreign trade (1981): imports Fr 3,192,020,000 (69% from France, 5% from U.S.); exports Fr 509.3 million (65% to France, 19% to Martinique, 7% to U.S.S.R.). Main exports: bananas 36%; sugar 29%; rum c. 8%; wheat meal and flour 8%.

MARTINIQUE

The Caribbean island of Martinique, an overseas département, lies 39 km N of St. Lucia and about 50 km SE of Dominica. Area: 1,100 sq km (425 sq mi). Pop. (1982 prelim.): 326,500. Cap.: Fort-de-France (pop., 1982 prelim., 97,800).

Education. (1979–80) Primary, pupils 50,142, teachers 2,751; secondary, pupils 38,778; vocational, pupils 9,854; secondary and vocational (1978–79), teachers 3,040; higher, students 1,475, teaching staff 77.

Finance and Trade. Monetary unit: French (metropolitan) franc. Budget (1981 est.) balanced at Fr 936 million. Cost of living (Fort-de-France; 1975 = 100; Jan. 1983) 226.9. Foreign trade (1981): imports Fr 4,010,000,000; exports Fr 704.6 million. Import sources: France 58%; Venezuela 17%; U.S. 5%. Export destinations: Guadeloupe 50%; France 32%; Greece 9%. Main exports: petroleum products 43%; bananas 22%; ships and boats 9%; rum c. 6%. Tourism (1981) 141,100 visitors.

MAYOTTE

An African island dependency of France that was formerly a part of the Comoros, Mayotte lies in the Indian Ocean off the east coast of Africa. Area: 374 sq km (144 sq mi). Pop. (1982 est.): 53,000. Cap.: Dzaoudzi (pop., 1978, 4,300).

Education. (1981–82) Primary, pupils 12,800, teachers 355; secondary, pupils 1,011, teachers 49.

Finance and Trade. Monetary unit: French (metropolitan) franc. Budget (1982 est.) balanced at Fr 144 million. Foreign trade (1982): imports Fr 116 million; exports Fr 5 million. Import sources: France 57%; Kenya 16%; South Africa 11%; Pakistan 8%. Export destinations: France 79%; Réunion 10%; Comoros 10%. Main exports: ylang-ylang 67%; vanilla 9%.

NEW CALEDONIA

The overseas territory of New Caledonia, together with its dependencies, is in the South Pacific 1,210 km E of Australia. Area: 19,103 sq km (7,375 sq mi). Pop. (1981 est.): 142,500. Cap.: Nouméa (pop., 1976, 56,100).

Education. (1981) Primary, pupils 26,779, teachers 1,518; secondary, pupils 10,137, teachers 602; vocational, pupils 3,386, teachers 352; higher, students 476, teaching staff 60.

Finance and Trade. Monetary unit: CFP franc. Budget (1981 est.): revenue CFP Fr 23,766,000,000; expenditure CFP Fr 21,386,000,000. Foreign trade (1982): imports CFP Fr 43,735,000,000; exports CFP Fr 32,055,000,000. Import sources (1981): France 32%; Bahrain 13%; Australia 12%; U.S. 7%; Japan 5%; New Zealand 5%. Export destinations (1981): France 54%; Japan 29%; U.S. 13%. Main exports: ferroalloys 50%; nickel 26%; nickel ores 19%.

RÉUNION

The overseas département of Réunion is located in the Indian Ocean about 720 km E of Madagascar and 180 km SW of Mauritius. Area: 2,512 sq km (970 sq mi). Pop. (1982 prelim.): 515,800. Cap.: Saint-Denis (pop., 1982 prelim., 109,100).

Education. (1980–81) Primary, pupils 125,305, teachers 4,392; secondary and vocational, pupils 63,889, teachers 3,111; higher (university only), students 2,108, teaching staff 62.

Finance and Trade. Monetary unit: French (metropolitan) franc. Budget (1981 est.) balanced at Fr 5,341,000,000. Cost of living (Saint-Denis; 1975 = 100; March 1983) 209.2. Foreign trade (1981): imports Fr 4,281,460,000; exports Fr 571,620,000. Import sources: France 62%; Bahrain 6%; South Africa 5%. Export destinations: France 76%; U.S.S.R. 7%; Algeria 5%. Main exports: sugar 76%; essential oils 4%.

SAINT PIERRE AND MIQUELON

The self-governing overseas département of Saint Pierre and Miquelon is located about 20 km off the south coast of Newfoundland. Area: 242 sq km (93 sq mi). Pop. (1982 prelim.): 6,000. Cap.: Saint Pierre, Saint Pierre (pop., 1982 prelim., 5,400).

Education. (1981–82) Primary, pupils 703, teachers 58; secondary, pupils 530; vocational, pupils 199; secondary and vocational, teachers 61.

Finance and Trade. Monetary unit: French (metropolitan) franc. Budget (1981 est.) balanced at Fr 42.1 million. Foreign trade (1981): imports Fr 220.9 million; exports Fr 38.7 million. Import sources: Canada 66%; France 28%. Export destinations: U.S. 58%; France 18%. Main exports: fish 88%; shellfish 6%; fish-meal fodder 5%.

WALLIS AND FUTUNA

Wallis and Futuna, an overseas territory, lies in the South Pacific west of Western Samoa. Area: 274 sq km (106 sq mi). Pop. (1982 est.): 11,000. Cap.: Mata Utu, Uvea (pop., 1976, 558).

Education. (1982) Primary and secondary, pupils 3,600.

NETHERLANDS, THE

NETHERLANDS ANTILLES

The Netherlands Antilles, a self-governing integral part of the Netherlands realm, consists of an island ɹp near the Venezuelan coast and another group he north near St. Kitts-Nevis-Anguilla. Area: 993 :m (383 sq mi). Pop. (1981 est.): 253,300. Cap.: lemstad, Curaçao (pop., 1970 est., 50,000).

ducation. (1976–77) Primary, pupils 36,365, :hers 1,458; secondary, pupils 10,685, teachers ; vocational, pupils 7,825, teachers 619; teacher ning, pupils 358, teachers 46; higher (university y), students c. 95, teaching staff c. 22.

inance. Monetary unit: Netherlands Antilles guil- or florin, with (Sept. 20, 1983) a par value of 1.80 herlands Antilles guilders to U.S. $1 (free rate of 1 Netherlands Antilles guilders = £1 sterling). lget (1979 actual): revenue 213 million Nether- ds Antilles guilders; expenditure 256 million herlands Antilles guilders. Cost of living (Aruba, aire, and Curaçao; 1975 = 100; 1982) 181.2.

oreign Trade. (1980) Imports 12,187,000,000 herlands Antilles guilders; exports 10,897,- ,000 Netherlands Antilles guilders. Import rces: Venezuela c. 68%; United Arab Emirates c. %; U.S. c. 7%. Export destinations: U.S. c. 55%; aica c. 5%. Main export: crude oil and petroleum ducts 98%. Tourism (1980): visitors c. 500,000; ss receipts U.S. $410 million.

ransport and Communications. Roads (1972) 50 km. Motor vehicles in use (1980): passenger c. 100; commercial (including buses) c. 8,800. Ship- g traffic (1977): goods loaded c. 24.8 million met- tons, unloaded c. 31.1 million metric tons. ephones (1980) 56,000. Radio receivers (1980) ,000. Television receivers (1980) 43,000.

ndustry. Production (in 000; metric tons; 1981): roleum products 25,175; phosphate rock (1980) salt (1980) c. 250; electricity (kw-hr) 2,275,000.

W ZEALAND

OOK ISLANDS

e self-governing territory of the Cook Islands con- s of several islands in the southern Pacific scat- ed over about 2.2 million sq km. Area: 236 sq km sq mi). Pop. (1983 est.): 16,900. Seat of govern- nt: Rarotonga Island (pop., 1981, 9,500).

ducation. (1982) Primary, pupils 2,909, teachers ; secondary, pupils 1,833, teachers 137; teacher ning (1977), students 48; higher (1980–81), pupils , teachers 41.

inance and Trade. Monetary unit: Cook Islands lar, at par with the New Zealand dollar, with (Sept. 1983) a free rate of CI$1.53 to U.S. $1 $2.30 = £1 sterling). Budget (1981–82 actual): enue CI$21.1 million; expenditure CI$21.4 mil- . Foreign trade: imports (1981) CI$26,616,000; orts (1982) CI$4,980,000. Import sources (1978): w Zealand 62%; Japan 11%; Australia 6%; U.S. . Export destinations (1977): New Zealand 99%. in exports: clothing 39%; pawpaws 14%; bananas %; copra 9%. Tourism (1982) 17,464 visitors.

UE

e self-governing territory of Niue is situated in the ific Ocean about 2,400 km NE of New Zealand. a: 259 sq km (100 sq mi). Pop. (1981 prelim.): 00. Capital: Alofi (pop., 1979, 960).

ducation. (1982) Primary, pupils 537, teachers secondary, pupils 401, teachers 29.

inance and Trade. Monetary unit: New Zealand lar. Budget (1981–82): revenue NZ$2,613,000 (ex- ding New Zealand subsidy of NZ$2,370,000); ex- nditure NZ$4,983,000. Foreign trade (1981): orts NZ$3,838,000 (80% from New Zealand in 79); exports NZ$590,000 (98% to New Zealand in 79). Main exports (1978): passion fruit 36%; copra %; plaited ware 12%; limes, fresh and juice 9%; ney 9%.

KELAU

e territory of Tokelau lies in the South Pacific ean about 1,130 km N of Niue and 3,380 km NE of w Zealand. Area: 12 sq km (4.6 sq mi). Pop. 81): 1,600.

ducation. Primary, pupils (1981–82) 434, teach- (1982–83) 30.

RWAY

N MAYEN

e island of Jan Mayen, a Norwegian dependency, lies within the Arctic Circle between Greenland and northern Norway. Area: 380 sq km (147 sq mi).

SVALBARD

A group of islands and a Norwegian dependency, Svalbard is located within the Arctic Circle to the north of Norway. Area: 62,050 sq km (23,957 sq mi). Pop. (1981 est.): 3,000.

PORTUGAL

MACAU

The overseas territory of Macau is situated on the mainland coast of China 60 km W of Hong Kong. Area: 16 sq km (6 sq mi). Pop. (1981 prelim.): 320,000.

Education. (1980–81) Primary, pupils 27,687, teachers 1,032; secondary, pupils 9,878, teachers 583; vocational, pupils 2,917, teachers 221.

Finance and Trade. Monetary unit: patacá, with (Sept. 20, 1983) a free rate of 8.52 patacás to U.S. $1 (12.84 patacás = £1 sterling). Budget (1981 est.) balanced at 486 million patacás. Foreign trade (1981): imports 4,132,900,000 patacás; exports 4,012,-900,000 patacás. Import sources: Hong Kong 36%; China 33%; Japan 10%; U.S. 6%. Export destinations: Hong Kong 22%; U.S. 21%; West Germany 13%; France 11%; U.K. 7%; Italy 5%. Main exports (1980): clothing 78%; textile yarns and fabrics 9%. Tourism (1980) 601,000 visitors.

Transport. Shipping traffic (1980): goods loaded 647,000 metric tons, unloaded 456,000 metric tons.

SOUTH WEST AFRICA/NAMIBIA

South West Africa has been a UN territory since 1966, when the General Assembly terminated South Africa's mandate over the country, renamed Namibia by the UN. South Africa considers the UN resolution illegal. Area: 824,292 sq km (318,261 sq mi). Pop. (1982 est.): 1,050,600. National cap.: Windhoek (pop., 1978 est., 75,100). Summer cap.: Swakopmund (pop., 1978 est., 16,800).

Education. (1980) Primary, secondary, and vocational, pupils 228,287, teachers 7,741.

Finance and Trade. Monetary unit: South African rand, with (Sept. 20, 1983) a free rate of R 1.11 to U.S. $1 (R 1.67 = £1 sterling). Budget (total; 1982–83 est.): revenue R 460 million; expenditure R 840 million. Foreign trade (included in the South African customs union; 1980 estimate): imports c. R 800 million (c. 80% from South Africa in 1972); exports c. R 1 billion (about 50% to South Africa in 1972). Main exports: diamonds c. 50%; uranium c. 30%; karakul c. 6%; livestock c. 6%.

Agriculture. Production (in 000; metric tons; 1981): corn c. 30; millet c. 15; beef and veal c. 74; sheep and goat meat c. 27; fish catch 249. Livestock (in 000; 1981): cattle c. 1,700; sheep c. 4,500; goats c. 2,000; horses c. 45; asses c. 67.

Industry. Production (in 000; metric tons; 1981): copper ore (metal content) 39; lead ore (metal content) c. 50; zinc ore (metal content; 1980) 25; tin concentrates (metal content) 0.9; uranium 3.9; diamonds (metric carats; 1980) c. 1,560; salt c. 230; electricity (kw-hr; 1963) 188,000.

UNITED KINGDOM

ANGUILLA

The island of Anguilla is a non-self-governing dependency. It was a part of the associated state of St. Kitts-Nevis-Anguilla until Dec. 19, 1980. It received a constitution separating its government from that of St. Kitts-Nevis-Anguilla in 1976. Area: 96 sq km (37 sq mi). Pop. (1982 est.): 7,000.

Education. (1979) Primary, pupils 1,610, teachers 68; secondary, pupils 450, teachers 20.

Finance and Trade. Monetary unit: East Caribbean dollar, with (Sept. 20, 1983) a par value of ECar$2.70 to U.S. $1 (free rate of ECar$4.07 = £1 sterling). Budget (1982 est.): revenue ECar$9.9 million (excluding U.K. grant of ECar$1.1 million); expenditure ECar$10.8 million. Foreign trade (1979 est.) exports c. ECar$1.6 million. Main export destinations: Trinidad and Tobago c. 40%; Puerto Rico c. 30%; Guadeloupe c. 10%; U.S. Virgin Islands c. 10%. Main exports: salt c. 40%; lobster c. 38%; livestock c. 13%.

BERMUDA

The colony of Bermuda lies in the western Atlantic about 920 km E of Cape Hatteras, North Carolina. Area: 53 sq km (20.5 sq mi). Pop. (1980): 54,700. Cap.: Hamilton, Great Bermuda (pop., 1980, 1,600).

Education. (1981–82) Primary, pupils 5,878, teachers 320; secondary, pupils 4,215, teachers 362; higher (university only), pupils 575, teachers 63.

Finance and Trade. Monetary unit: Bermuda dollar, at par with the U.S. dollar (free rate, at Sept. 20, 1983, of Ber$1.51 = £1 sterling). Budget (1982–83 est.): revenue Ber$155.1 million; expenditure Ber$154.9 million. Foreign trade (1982): imports Ber$351 million; exports Ber$17.3 million. Import sources: U.S. 56%; Netherlands Antilles 10%; U.K. 9%; Canada 8%. Export destinations: U.S. 32%; Australia 14%; The Netherlands 9%; Brazil 8%; Italy 7%; U.K. 6%; New Zealand 5%. Main exports: drugs and medicines 57%; electronic supplies 10%. Tourism: visitors (1981) 429,800; gross receipts (1980) U.S. $258 million.

Transport. Roads (1981) 400 km. Motor vehicles in use (1981): passenger 14,400; commercial 3,180. Shipping (1982): merchant vessels 100 gross tons and over 68; gross tonnage 474,402.

BRITISH INDIAN OCEAN TERRITORY

Located in the western Indian Ocean, this colony consists of the islands of the Chagos Archipelago. Area: 60 sq km (23 sq mi). No permanent civilian population remains. Administrative headquarters: Victoria, Seychelles.

BRITISH VIRGIN ISLANDS

The colony of the British Virgin Islands is located in the Caribbean to the east of the U.S. Virgin Islands. Area: 153 sq km (59 sq mi). Pop. (1981 est.): 12,200. Cap.: Road Town, Tortola (pop., 1980, 9,300).

Education. (1980–81) Primary, pupils 1,974, teachers 109; secondary, pupils 510; vocational, pupils 281; secondary and vocational, teachers 55.

Finance and Trade. Monetary unit: U.S. dollar. Budget (1982 est.): revenue $14,750,000; expenditure $14,536,000. Foreign trade (1980): imports $36 million; exports $1,087,000. Import sources (1976): U.S. 28%; Puerto Rico 24%; U.K. 15%; U.S. Virgin Islands 12%; Trinidad and Tobago 11%. Export destinations (1974): U.S. Virgin Islands 53%; Anguilla 22%; St. Martin (Guadeloupe) 9%; U.K. 5%. Main exports (domestic): fresh fish, sand and gravel, fruit and vegetables. Tourism: visitors (1980) 172,700; gross receipts (1978) U.S. $24 million.

CAYMAN ISLANDS

The colony of the Cayman Islands lies in the Caribbean about 270 km NW of Jamaica. Area: 264 sq km (102 sq mi). Pop. (1982 est.): 18,300. Cap.: George Town, Grand Cayman (pop., 1979, 2,700).

Education. (1982–83) Primary, pupils 1,922, teachers 129; secondary, pupils 986, teachers (1980–81) 207; vocational, pupils 475; higher (1981–82), pupils 267, teachers 22.

Finance and Trade. Monetary unit: Cayman Islands dollar, with (Sept. 20, 1983) a par value of CayI$0.83 to U.S. $1 (free rate of CayI$1.25 = £1 sterling). Budget (1982 est.): revenue CayI$47.9 million; expenditure CayI$46 million. Foreign trade (1980): imports CayI$85.8 million; exports CayI$2,227,000. Import sources: U.S. 72%; Trinidad and Tobago 7%. Export destinations: West Germany 34%; U.S. 28%; U.K. 12%; Japan 11%; Jamaica 7%. Main exports: turtle meat 31%; chemicals 25%; turtle fat 12%; pearls and precious stones 11%; turtle shell 5%.

Shipping. (1982) Merchant vessels 100 gross tons and over 242; gross tonnage 311,396.

FALKLAND ISLANDS

The colony of the Falkland Islands and dependencies is situated in the South Atlantic about 800 km NE of Cape Horn. Area: 12,173 sq km (4,700 sq mi). Pop. (1980): 1,800. Cap.: Stanley (pop., 1980, 1,050).

Education. (1980) Primary, pupils 223, teachers 15; secondary, pupils 90, teachers 11.

Finance and Trade. Monetary unit: Falkland Island pound, at par with the pound sterling, with (Sept. 20, 1983) a free rate of U.S. $1.51 = FI£1. Budget (1981–82 est.): revenue FI£2,892,000; expenditure Fl£2,565,000. Foreign trade (1980): imports Fl£2,590,000 (86% from U.K. in 1975); exports c. Fl£3.3 million (100% to U.K. in 1975). Main exports: wool c. 81%; postage stamps c. 18%.

GIBRALTAR

Gibraltar, a self-governing colony, is a small peninsula that juts into the Mediterranean from southwestern Spain. Area: 5.80 sq km (2.25 sq mi). Pop. (1982 est.): 30,000.

Education. (1981–82) Primary, pupils 2,194, teachers 152; secondary, pupils 1,794, teachers 130; vocational, pupils 50, teachers 22.

Finance and Trade. Monetary unit: Gibraltar pound, at par with the pound sterling. Budget (1981–82 est.): revenue Gib£44,265,000; expenditure Gib£42,594,000. Foreign trade (1981): imports Gib£65,826,000 (65% from U.K.); reexports Gib£25,556,000 (mainly bunkers and ships' supplies). Main reexports: petroleum products 78%; tobacco and manufactures 20%. Tourism (1981) 132,400 visitors.

Transport. Shipping traffic (1979): goods loaded 9,000 metric tons, unloaded 307,000 metric tons.

GUERNSEY

Located 50 km W of Normandy, France, Guernsey, together with its small island dependencies, is a crown dependency. Area: 78 sq km (30 sq mi). Pop. (1982 est.): 56,400. Cap.: St. Peter Port (pop., 1976, 17,000).

Education. (1979–80) Primary and secondary, pupils 9,400, teachers 524.

Finance and Trade. Monetary unit: Guernsey pound, at par with the pound sterling. Budget (1981): revenue £54,513,000; expenditure £44,319,000. Foreign trade (1979): imports £150 million; exports £110 million. Main source and destination: U.K. Main exports (1979): manufactures c. 62%; tomatoes c. 21%; flowers and ferns c. 11%. Tourism: visitors (1981) 329,000; gross receipts (1979) U.S. $85 million.

HONG KONG

The colony of Hong Kong lies on the southeastern coast of China about 60 km E of Macau and 130 km SE of Canton. Area: 1,060 sq km (409 sq mi). Pop. (1983 est.): 5,287,800. Cap.: Victoria (pop., 1981, 590,800).

Education. (1981–82) Primary, pupils 539,545, teachers 17,972; secondary, pupils 444,718; vocational, pupils 11,485; secondary and vocational, teachers 15,927; teacher training, students 1,632, teachers 215; higher, students 39,695, teaching staff 2,810.

Finance. Monetary unit: Hong Kong dollar, with (Sept. 20, 1983) a free rate of HK$8.20 to U.S. $1 (HK$12.35 = £1 sterling). Budget (1982–83 est.): revenue HK$25.2 billion; expenditure HK$20.8 billion.

Foreign Trade. (1982) Imports HK$151,086,000,000; exports HK$129,669,000,000. Import sources: China 23%; Japan 22%; U.S. 11%; Singapore 7%; Taiwan 7%; U.K. 5%. Export destinations: U.S. 29%; China 9%; U.K. 7%; West Germany 6%; Japan 5%. Main exports: clothing 25%; machinery (except telecommunications) 12%; textile yarns and fabrics 9%; plastic toys and dolls, etc. 6%; watches and clocks 7%; telecommunications apparatus 6%. Tourism (1981): visitors 2,535,200; gross receipts U.S. $1,590,000,000.

Transport and Communications. Roads (1982) 1,227 km. Motor vehicles in use (1981): passenger 227,700; commercial 64,200. Railways (1982): 94 km; traffic 406 million passenger-km, freight 55 million net ton-km. Shipping (1982): merchant vessels 100 gross tons and over 255; gross tonnage 3,498,512. Shipping traffic (1982): goods loaded 9,127,000 metric tons, unloaded 28,021,000 metric tons. Telephones (Dec. 1982) 1,947,000. Radio receivers (Dec. 1980) 2,550,000. Television receivers (Dec. 1980) 1,114,000.

ISLE OF MAN

The Isle of Man, a crown dependency, lies in the Irish Sea approximately 55 km from both Northern Ireland and the coast of northwestern England. Area: 588 sq km (227 sq mi). Pop. (1981): 64,700. Cap.: Douglas (pop., 1981, 19,900).

Education. (1982–83) Primary, pupils 5,532, teachers (state only; 1981–82) 250; secondary, pupils 5,267, teachers (state only; 1981–82) 265; vocational and higher, pupils 3,656.

Finance and Trade. Monetary unit: Isle of Man pound, at par with the pound sterling. Budget (1982–83 est.): revenue £73.3 million; expenditure £74.3 million. Foreign trade included with the United Kingdom. Main exports: herring, barley, coal, scrap metal. Tourism (1982) 413,000 visitors.

JERSEY

The island of Jersey, a crown dependency, is located about 30 km W of Normandy, France. Area: 116 sq km (45 sq mi). Pop. (1982 est.): 74,000. Cap.: St. Helier (pop., 1981, 24,900).

Education. (1981–82) Primary, pupils 5,686; secondary, pupils 5,350; primary and secondary (1976–77), teachers 670.

Finance. Monetary unit: Jersey pound, at par with the pound sterling. Budget (1981): revenue £118,519,000; expenditure £94,323,000.

Foreign Trade. (1980) Imports £230,895,000 (85% from U.K.); exports £89,930,000 (67% to U.K.). Main exports: fruit and vegetables 16%; motor vehicles 11%; telecommunications apparatus 10%; works of art 6%; knitted fabrics 6%; jewelry 6%; tea 5%; musical instruments 5%; clothing 5%. Tourism (1981): visitors 1,198,900; gross receipts U.S. $240 million.

MONTSERRAT

The colony of Montserrat is located in the Caribbean between Antigua, 43 km northeast, and Guadeloupe, 60 km southeast. Area: 102 sq km (40 sq mi). Pop. (1982 est.): 11,700. Cap.: Plymouth (pop., 1980, 1,590).

Education. (1981–82) Primary, pupils 1,943, teachers (1979–80) 87; secondary, pupils 872, teachers (1979–80) 68; vocational, pupils 49, teachers (1979–80) 8.

Finance and Trade. Monetary unit: East Caribbean dollar. Budget (1982 est.): revenue ECar$20,894,000; expenditure ECar$20,232,000. Foreign trade (1981): imports ECar$51 million; exports ECar$6 million. Import sources (1978): U.K. 33%; U.S. 23%; Trinidad and Tobago 9%; Canada 5%. Export destinations (1978): U.S. 54%; Trinidad and Tobago 7%; Antigua 5%. Main exports (domestic only): packaging 50%; clothing 12%; live plants 10%; electrical equipment 10%; fruit and vegetables 8%. Tourism: visitors (1981) 21,400; gross receipts (1980) U.S. $4.3 million.

PITCAIRN ISLAND

The colony of Pitcairn Island is in the central South Pacific, 5,150 km NE of New Zealand and 2,170 km SE of Tahiti. Area: 4.53 sq km (1.75 sq mi). Pop. (1983 est.): 61, all of whom live in the de facto capital, Adamstown.

ST. HELENA

The colony of St. Helena, including its dependencies of Ascension Island and the Tristan da Cunha island group, is spread over a wide area of the Atlantic off the southwestern coast of Africa. Area: 412 sq km (159 sq mi). Pop. (1982 est.): 5,300. Cap.: Jamestown (pop., 1978 est., 1,500).

Education. (1982–83) Primary, pupils 697; secondary, pupils 602, teachers, primary and secondary, 71; vocational (1981–82), pupils 32, teachers 1; teacher training (1981–82), students 6, teachers 2.

Finance and Trade. Monetary unit: St. Helena pound, at par with the pound sterling which is also used. Budget (1980–81 est.): revenue St.H£4,488,000; expenditure St.H£4,552,000. Foreign trade (1981–82): imports St.H£2,485,800 (50% from U.K., 44% from South Africa); exports St.H£32,700 (78% to U.K., 22% to South Africa in 1967–68). Main exports: fish 80%; handicrafts 20%.

TURKS AND CAICOS ISLANDS

The colony of the Turks and Caicos Islands is situated in the Atlantic southeast of The Bahamas. Area: 500 sq km (193 sq mi). Pop. (1980 est.): 7,400. Seat of government: Grand Turk Island (pop., 1980 est., 3,100).

Education. (1981–82) Primary, pupils 1,518, teachers (1978–79) 90; secondary, pupils 606, teachers (1978–79) 38.

Finance and Trade. Monetary unit: U.S. dollar. Budget (1981–82 est.): revenue $5,912,000; expenditure $7,186,000. Foreign trade (1981–82): imports $15,234,000; exports $2,668,000. Main exports: crayfish 60%; conch meat 38%. Tourism (1981) 12,348 visitors.

UNITED STATES

AMERICAN SAMOA

Located to the east of Western Samoa in the South Pacific, the unincorporated territory of American Samoa is approximately 2,600 km NE of the northern tip of New Zealand. Area: 199 sq km (77 sq mi). Pop. (1981 est.): 33,000. Cap.: Pago Pago (pop., 1980, 3,100).

Education. (1981–82) Primary, pupils 5,596, teachers (1980–81) 313; secondary and vocational, pupils 2,473, teachers (1980–81) 130; higher (1980–81), students 3,217, teaching staff (1979–80) 60.

Finance and Trade. Monetary unit: U.S. dollar. Budget (1980 est.) balanced at $59 million (including U.S. grants of $34.3 million). Foreign trade (1979–80): imports (excluding fish for canneries) $95.1 million (73% from U.S., 12% from Japan, 6% from New Zealand in 1977–78); exports $127.1 million (99% to U.S. in 1976–77). Main exports (1977–78): canned tuna 93%; pet food 5%. Tourism (1981) 89,565 visitors.

GUAM

Guam, an organized unincorporated territory, is located in the Pacific Ocean about 9,700 km SW of San Francisco and 2,400 km E of Manila. Area: 541 sq km (209 sq mi). Pop. (1981 est.): 109,900. Cap.: Agana (pop., 1980, 900).

Education. (1981–82) Primary, pupils 17,784, teachers 772; secondary and vocational, pupils 13,183, teachers 587; higher (university), students 2,496, teaching staff 162.

Finance and Trade. Monetary unit: U.S. dollar. Budget (1979–80 est.): revenue $128.7 million; expenditure $140.1 million. Foreign trade (1979–80): imports $544 million (32% from U.S., 7% from Japan in 1978–79); exports $61 million (49% to U.S. Trust Territories, 26% to U.S., 16% to Taiwan in 1978–79). Main exports (1978–79): petroleum products 38%; copra, watches, clothing. Tourism (1981): visitors 312,900; gross receipts U.S. $190 million.

Agriculture and Industry. Production (in 000; metric tons; 1981): copra c. 1; eggs 1; fish catch 0.13; petroleum products 1,564; electricity (kw-hr) 1,115,000.

PUERTO RICO

Puerto Rico, a self-governing associated commonwealth, lies about 1,400 km SE of the Florida coast. Area: 8,958 sq km (3,459 sq mi). Pop. (1981 est.): 3,251,000. Cap.: San Juan (pop., 1980 mun., 433,000).

Education. (1981–82) Primary, pupils 492,908, teachers (1980–81) 23,154; secondary (1980–81), pupils 337,187, teachers 13,297; vocational (1980–81), pupils 148,859, teachers 1,522; higher, students 131,184, teaching staff (1979–80) 3,300.

Finance. Monetary unit: U.S dollar. Budget (1980–81 actual): revenue $4,420,000,000; expenditure $3,919,000,000. Gross domestic product (1981–82) $16,157,000,000. Cost of living (1975 = 100; Feb. 1983) 149.4.

Foreign Trade. (1981–82) Imports $8,491,000,000 (64% from U.S., 7% from Venezuela); exports $8,795,000,000 (84% to U.S.). Main exports (1979–80): chemicals 32%; petroleum products 14%; machinery 11%; clothing 9%; fish 5%; instruments 5%. Tourism (1981–82): visitors 1,564,000; gross receipts U.S. $682 million.

Transport and Communications. Roads (maintained paved; 1981) 11,137 km. Motor vehicles in use (1981): passenger 929,600; commercial 163,400. Railways (1980) 96 km. Telephones (Jan. 1981) 631,500. Radio receivers (Dec. 1980) 2 million. Television receivers (Dec. 1980) 800,000.

Agriculture. Production (in 000; metric tons; 1982): sugar, raw value c. 137; pineapples c. 38; bananas c. 109; oranges c. 29; coffee 14; tobacco 1; milk c. 424; meat (1981) 70. Livestock (in 000; Jan. 1981): cattle 489; pigs 241; chickens 7,455.

Industry. Production (in 000; metric tons; 1982): cement 1,044; beer (hl) 551; rum (hl; 1981) c. 680;

petroleum products (1981) 9,394; electricity (kw-hr) c. 12,404,000.

TRUST TERRITORY OF THE PACIFIC ISLANDS

The Trust Territory islands, numbering more than 2,000, are scattered over 7,750,000 sq km in the Pacific Ocean from 720 km E of the Philippines to just west of the International Date Line. Separate administrative actions within the Trust Territory have, since 1978, created four new administrative entities that are to form the framework for local government upon cessation of the UN trusteeship: the Commonwealth of the Northern Mariana Islands (1978); the Federated States of Micronesia (Yap, Ponape, Kosrae, and Truk; 1979); the Marshall Islands (1979); and the Republic of Palau (early 1981). The government of the Trust Territory will not, however, cease to exist until the UN permits its dissolution, subject to referenda. Area: 1,858 sq km (717 sq mi). Pop. (1981 est.): 135,600 (including the Northern Mariana Islands, 17,300). Seat of government: Saipan municipality (pop., 1980, 14,500).

Education. (1981–82) Primary, pupils 28,300, teachers (1978–79) 1,578; secondary, pupils 6,100, teachers (1978–79) 520; higher, students (1980–81) 224, teaching staff (1978–79) 155.

Finance and Trade. Monetary unit: U.S. dollar. Budget (1981–82 est.): revenue $125.1 million (including U.S. grant of $98.6 million); expenditure $118.9 million. Foreign trade (1977–78): imports $39 million (35% from U.S., 25% from Japan, 6% from Australia in 1976–77); exports $19 million (54% to Japan in 1972). Main exports: coconut oil 57%; fish 27%; copra 11%.

VIRGIN ISLANDS

The Virgin Islands of the United States is an organized unincorporated territory located about 60 km E of Puerto Rico. Area: 342 sq km (132 sq mi). Pop. (1981 est.): 99,400. Cap.: Charlotte Amalie, St. Thomas (pop., 1980, 11,800).

Education. (1981–82) Primary, pupils 19,489, teachers 782; secondary, pupils 13,346, teachers 459; vocational (1980–81), pupils 2,500, teachers 56; higher (1980–81), students 593, teaching staff 98.

Finance. Monetary unit: U.S. dollar. Budget (1981–82 est.): revenue $225.6 million; expenditure $225.3 million.

Foreign Trade. (1981) Imports $5,014,000,000; exports $5,068,000,000. Import sources (1978): Iran 46%; U.S. c. 12%; Libya 11%; Nigeria 9%; United Arab Emirates 8%; Angola 6%. Export destinations (1978): U.S. 92%. Main exports (1978): petroleum products 91%; chemicals 6%. Tourism (1981): visitors 1,316,000; gross receipts U.S. $317 million.

continued from page 291

sharply increased trade deficit for 1982, totaling $18.3 million, which was caused by a surge in imports and a slight fall in exports. It was announced that Club Méditerannée was starting work on a £5 million tourist resort on the island of Providenciales, for which the British government had already built an airport and roads. The decision to go ahead followed a threat of legal action against Club Méditerannée by the U.K. Foreign Office. In the British Virgin Islands Chief Minister Lavity Stoutt presented a balanced, tax-free budget for 1983, following what he said was a relatively good economic performance in 1982.

Puerto Rico experienced further intense political controversy during 1983. It surrounded the governing Partido Nuevo Progresista, whose leader, Gov. Carlos Romero Barceló, was seeking nomination for reelection in 1984. Romero was opposed within the party by Hernán Padilla, mayor of San Juan, who in August was reportedly trying to form a new party. It was predicted that the split might bring victory in the elections to the opposition Partido Popular Democrático, which controlled the two chambers of Congress.

In the Netherlands Antilles a constitutional conference reached agreement on separate status for Aruba, to be granted in 1986, with a target date of 1996 for independence. Aruba's pro-independence leader, Betico Croes, was shot in the stomach by a policeman during the April election campaign; his party slightly increased its majority in the island council. Left-wing parties increased their vote in Curaçao and Bonaire. In February Luis Herrera Campíns became the first president of Venezuela to visit the islands.

A series of bomb explosions occurred in the French overseas départements of French Guiana, Guadeloupe, and Martinique in May. The Caribbean Revolutionary Army (ARC) claimed responsibility for the attacks. After a further outbreak of bombings in Guadeloupe in November, 100 riot police were sent from France to help restore order. The authorities in Guadeloupe suspected the Movement for the Independence of Guadeloupe of involvement in the troubles.

Africa. UN Secretary-General Javier Pérez de Cuéllar visited South Africa in August in an attempt to break the deadlock in negotiations over independence for South West Africa/Namibia. He secured South Africa's agreement concerning the composition of a UN multinational peacekeeping force for the area, but one obstacle still remained—the South African and U.S. demand that Cuban troops must leave Angola before the UN's plan for independence could be implemented.

In regard to Namibia's internal politics, there was an increase in tension between Danie Hough, South Africa's administrator general of Namibia, and the Democratic Turnhalle Alliance; the DTA had won the 1978 elections that were boycotted by the South West Africa People's Organization. In January Dirk Mudge, head of the DTA, submitted his resignation as chairman of the Council of Ministers (head of the interim government), and the members of the council resigned with him. Hough then dissolved the National Assembly and assumed responsibility for government. In February South Africa appointed a new administrator general, Willie van Niekerk.

Indian Ocean. In Mayotte Christian Pellerin succeeded Yves Bonnet as commissioner in January. The nonaligned movement meeting in New Delhi, India, in March denounced France's "occupation" of the island and reaffirmed its view that Mayotte was an integral part of the Comoros. After the defeat of the left wing in Mauritius's general elections in August, there was less pressure on the U.K. to return the island of Diego Garcia, in the Chagos Archipelago, to that nation.

The Cocos Islands, one of Australia's last remaining dependencies, had been bought by the government from John Clunies-Ross in 1978. The islanders began to press for a decision to be made about their future. The government was still involved in a court battle to gain possession of certain property that Clunies-Ross retained on the islands, but the inhabitants asked Australia to organize an act of self-determination under UN auspices. Australia was expected to present three options to the islanders: integration with Australia, free association, or independence.

Pacific. In general elections held in March, Sir Thomas Davis, premier of the Cook Islands, lost his seat, and his Democratic Party lost office to the Cook Islands Party led by Geoffrey Henry, cousin of the late Albert Henry, a former premier. Henry was appointed premier, but under the Cook Islands constitution the premier had to be elected by Parliament. By the time this point had been established by a court challenge, by-elections and the defection of Albert Henry's son, Tupui, had creat-

DON HOGAN CHARLES/THE NEW YORK TIMES

The UN Security Council voted unanimously in May to call on Secretary-General Javier Pérez de Cuéllar to seek a cease-fire in South West Africa/Namibia, leading to its eventual independence from South Africa.

ed a deadlock between the parties. A further election was, therefore, necessary, and Geoffrey Henry acted as head of an interim caretaker government. The new elections, held in early November, returned Davis and his party to power; Tupui Henry lost his seat.

Despite a troubled year, there were signs of a new willingness to compromise in New Caledonian politics. The Union Calédonienne, which sought a Kanak (indigenous Melanesian) and socialist independent state by 1984, walked out of constitutional talks in Paris in November 1982 because the discussions assumed a movement toward increased self-government instead of immediate independence. Political demonstrations in Nouméa followed. In January two policemen were killed and others wounded in a riot near La Foa. The trouble was sparked by the opening of a new sawmill but reflected deeper tensions over land ownership. The French high commissioner placed an indefinite ban on the sale and use of firearms. In local government elections factions for and against independence had about equal success in regional centres and rural areas, but the inherent divisions in New Caledonia were again highlighted by the winning of all 45 Nouméa seats by French-dominated anti-independence factions and parties. After a visit in May by Georges Lemoine, French secretary of state for overseas départements and territories, further constitutional talks were held in July; all factions agreed to work toward the formulation of a new development plan. This new conciliatory mood was subsequently threatened when a new tourist hotel on Ouvea, in the Loyalty Islands, was burned down and the car of a pro-independence leader was bombed. The motive for the sabotage of the hotel was thought to be a grievance over land.

In April Tahiti and other islands of French Polynesia were badly damaged by Hurricane Veena, one of a series of six such storms that struck the area in as many months; major relief programs were initiated. Development proposals included new tourist facilities, plans to build a garbage-fired power station, and the construction of a major seawall to protect Mururoa Atoll, the site of French nuclear tests, from storm damage. In response to continuing protests against nuclear testing at Mururoa, the French government invited a scientific team from Australia, New Zealand, and other South Pacific Forum countries to make an inspection of the atoll. In November, after violent clashes between striking hotel workers and police, reinforcement troops were flown in from New Caledonia.

In 1983 the Trust Territory of the Pacific Islands moved closer toward the termination of UN trusteeship status. In a referendum on the draft compact reached between the U.S. and Micronesian negotiators, 62% of the voters of the Republic of Palau (Belau) endorsed the proposals for a form of self-government that would give the U.S. control over foreign affairs and defense and the right of strategic denial. However, only a bare majority, and not the required 75%, voted to amend Belau's "non-nuclear" constitution, which was incompatible with the proposed compact. This deadlock was resolved in July when negotiators signed a treaty allowing the U.S. to transport nuclear materials through, but not to store or test them in, the island republic.

Any such incompatibility was removed prior to the referendum in the Marshall Islands when the legislature passed an act specifying that the draft compact, once endorsed by a majority, would prevail over the constitution. Despite some opposition from Bikini Islanders, the compact received a 60% endorsement in the referendum. In the Federated

Disasters:
see page 71

Disciples of Christ:
see Religion

Diseases:
see Health and Disease

Divorce:
see Demography

States of Micronesia, Yap, Kosrae, and Truk all endorsed the draft compact; the fourth district, Ponape, rejected it in the referendum but was committed to an acceptance of the overall majority. The referenda had all been delayed by controversies over funding and a political education program.

During the year the U.S. and the Marshall Islands government agreed that compensation worth $180 million would be provided for Marshallese affected by nuclear testing in the islands in the 1940s and 1950s. The Bikini Atoll Rehabilitation Committee reported to the U.S. Department of the Interior that the area would remain contaminated with high-level radiation for another century unless its topsoil was replaced. The U.S. announced plans for the construction of a chemical disposal plant at Johnston Atoll, 1,200 km (750 mi) southwest of Hawaii. For some years the atoll had been used for the storage of nerve gas and other poisonous chemicals.

East Asia. As Brunei prepared for independence in the last days of 1983, final discussions with the U.K. to settle its future defense arrangements proved surprisingly complex. Sultan Muda Hassanal Bolkiah (*see* BIOGRAPHIES) of Brunei finally agreed in September to finance a battalion of Gurkha troops—part of the British Army—after independence, while letting it remain under British command.

Talks between the U.K. and China over the future of Hong Kong entered a more detailed phase during the year. The U.K.'s lease on the New Territories, forming the bulk of Hong Kong's land mass, was due to expire in 1997. China was anxious to resume sovereignty over the entire colony, including Hong Kong Island and Kowloon Peninsula, which had in fact been leased to the U.K. in perpetuity. While the British delegation seemed prepared to make concessions on the sovereignty issue, the question of the future administration of the colony proved much more of a stumbling block to progress.

As the sixth round of talks ended in Beijing (Peking) in November, there were indications that the two parties were no closer to a solution. The Chinese reminded the U.K. that Prime Minister Margaret Thatcher had agreed that progress should be made within two years when she visited China in the fall of 1982; if an agreement was not reached by September 1984, therefore, the Chinese said that they would make a unilateral declaration of policies and guidelines for Hong Kong's future.

Hong Kong and Macao were seriously affected by Typhoon Ellen. The storm struck in September, killing 18 people in the two territories.

(PHILIPPE DECRAENE; BARRIE MACDONALD; ROD PRINCE; LOUISE WATSON)

See also African Affairs; Commonwealth of Nations; United Nations.

Djibouti

An independent republic in northeastern Africa, Djibouti is bordered by Ethiopia, Somalia, and the Gulf of Aden. Area: 23,200 sq km (8,900 sq mi). Pop. (1982 est., excluding refugees): 306,000, including (1978 est.) Cushitic Afar 38%; Somali Issa 28%; Issachar and Gad 20%; European 9%; Arab 5%. Capital: Djibouti (pop., 1980 est., 200,000). Language: Arabic and French (official); Saho-Afar and Somali are spoken in their respective communities. Religion (1980 est.): Muslim 90.6%; Christian 8.7%; other 0.7%. President in 1983, Hassan Gouled Aptidon; premier, Barkat Gourad Hamadou.

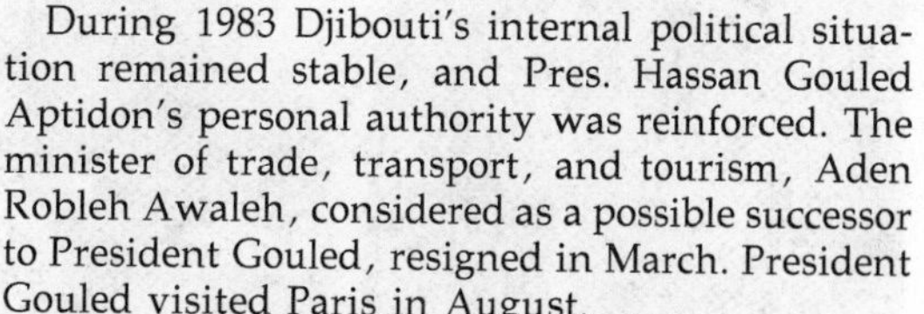

DJIBOUTI

Education. (1980–81) Primary, pupils 16,841, teachers 375; secondary, pupils 3,812, teachers 174; vocational, pupils 1,279, teachers 88; teacher training, students 65, teachers 11; higher, students 150.

Finance. Monetary unit: Djibouti franc, with (Sept. 20, 1983) a par value of DjFr 177.72 to U.S. $1 (free rate of DjFr 268 = £1 sterling). Budget (total; 1981 est.): revenue DjFr 28,450,000,000; expenditure DjFr 25,190,000,000.

Foreign Trade. (1979) Imports DjFr 31,477,000,000; exports DjFr 2,023,000,000. Import sources: France 47%; U.K. 8%; Japan 8%; Belgium-Luxembourg 5%. Export destination: France 87%. Main export (most trade is transit; 1977): cattle c. 7%.

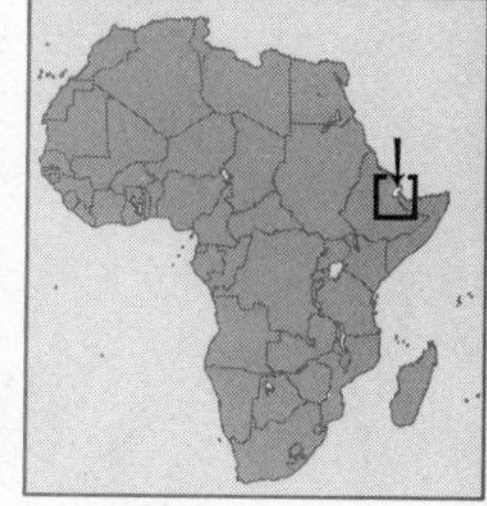

Djibouti

During 1983 Djibouti's internal political situation remained stable, and Pres. Hassan Gouled Aptidon's personal authority was reinforced. The minister of trade, transport, and tourism, Aden Robleh Awaleh, considered as a possible successor to President Gouled, resigned in March. President Gouled visited Paris in August.

Relations with Ethiopia and Somalia were a dominant concern. An offer by Djibouti to mediate in those nations' dispute over the Ogaden region was made by Foreign Minister Moumin Bahdon Farah during a visit to Somalia in July. In September a start was made, under the auspices of the UN High Commissioner for Refugees, on the repatriation of some of the 30,000 or more Ethiopians who had taken refuge in Djibouti during the Ogaden war of the late 1970s.

Djibouti's almost total dependence on external aid was underlined by a conference of donor countries and international organizations held there in November. Aid of $400 million was agreed upon to finance development during 1984–89.

(PHILIPPE DECRAENE)

Dominica

A republic within the Commonwealth, Dominica, an island of the Lesser Antilles in the Caribbean Sea, lies between Guadeloupe to the north and Martinique to the south. Area: 750 sq km (290 sq mi). Pop. (1983 est.): 74,000. Cap.: Roseau (pop., 1981, 8,300). Language: English (official), French patois. Religion: Roman Catholic. President in 1983, Aurelius Marie; prime minister, Eugenia Charles.

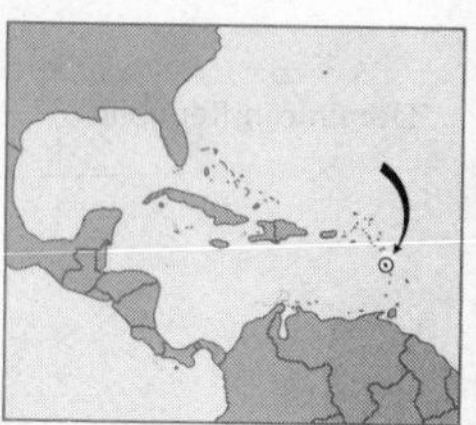

Dominica

In July 1983, against a background of modest economic growth in 1982, Prime Minister and Finance Minister Eugenia Charles presented a budget for 1983–84 that allowed for a slight increase in current expenditure but made a 30% cut in capital spending. Earlier in the year, however, plans had been announced for the restructuring and rehabilitation of the banana and lime industries, with

WIDE WORLD

Prime Minister Eugenia Charles of Dominica (at microphone) stood with Pres. Ronald Reagan at the White House to brief reporters on the U.S. invasion of Grenada at the behest of several of its Caribbean neighbours.

funding from the U.S. Agency for International Development and the Caribbean Food Corporation.

The political climate turned less favourable for Charles and her Freedom Party during the year. The reunited Dominica Labour Party, under the leadership of former prime minister Oliver Seraphin, performed unexpectedly well in a municipal by-election in the capital in June. Subsequently, the Labour Party began talks with other opposition groups with a view to presenting a united front in the 1985 general election. Internal divisions within the government came to light in August, when Minister of Communications and Works Henry Dyer was dismissed.

Charles took a leading role in the instigation of the invasion of Grenada in October. As head of the Organization of Eastern Caribbean States, she was responsible for issuing the invitation to the U.S. to intervene, and she accompanied U.S. Pres. Ronald Reagan when he announced the invasion.

(ROD PRINCE)

DOMINICA

Education. (1978–79) Primary, pupils 15,220, teachers 423; secondary, pupils 9,814, teachers 299; vocational, pupils 400, teachers 21; teacher training, students 49, teachers 6; higher, students 154, teachers 8.

Finance and Trade. Monetary unit: East Caribbean dollar, with (Sept. 20, 1983) a par value of ECar$2.70 to U.S. $1 (free rate of ECar$4.07 = £1 sterling). Budget (1981–82 est.): revenue ECar$59.2 million; expenditure ECar$64.3 million. Foreign trade: imports (1980) ECar$143.6 million; exports (1981) ECar$52.1 million. Import sources (1978): U.K. 27%; U.S. 15%; St. Lucia 7%; Trinidad and Tobago 7%; Canada 5%. Export destinations (1978): U.K. 67%; Barbados 5%. Main exports (1978): bananas 59%; soap 12%; coconut oil 5%; grapefruit 5%.

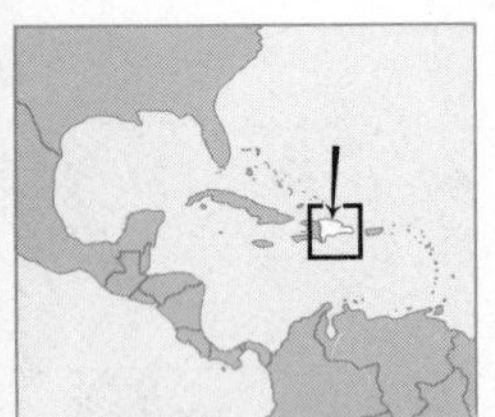

Dominican Republic

Drama:
see Motion Pictures; Theatre

Dress:
see Fashion and Dress

Earthquakes:
see Earth Sciences

Dominican Republic

Covering the eastern two-thirds of the Caribbean island of Hispaniola, the Dominican Republic is separated from Haiti, which occupies the western third, by a rugged mountain range. Area: 48,442 sq km (18,704 sq mi). Pop. (1982 est.): 5,812,900, including mulatto 75%; white 15%; black 10%. Cap. and largest city: Santo Domingo (pop., 1981, 1,313,200). Language: Spanish. Religion: mainly Roman Catholic (98%), with Protestant and Jewish minorities. President in 1983, Salvador Jorge Blanco.

During 1983 Pres. Salvador Jorge Blanco struggled to heal divisions within the ruling Partido Revolucionario Dominicano as two factions began early electioneering for the 1986 polls. The president also had to cope with a split in the top ranks of the Army, having to do with a reshuffle of the high command. In August rumours of the existence of a secret left-wing training school for guerrillas provoked a wave of repression by police; nearly 100 people were arrested in a two-week-long search for subversives.

The government faced balance of payments shortfalls caused by low world prices for sugar, nickel, and other exports. In August pressure on the peso pushed the parallel exchange rate 62.5% higher than the official rate, the highest ever recorded. In September creditor banks agreed to convert $560 million of 1982–83 maturities into a six-year loan. Earlier in the year, the government signed a three-year, $455 million extended-facility program with the International Monetary Fund.

(SARAH CAMERON)

DOMINICAN REPUBLIC

Education. (1980–81) Primary, pupils 1,105,730, teachers 22,672; secondary and vocational, pupils 331,471, teachers 11,716; teacher training, students (1978–79) 1,392, teachers (1975–76) c. 49; higher (universities only), students (1978–79) 42,412, teaching staff (1975–76) 1,435.

Finance. Monetary unit: peso, at parity with the U.S. dollar, with a free rate (Sept. 20, 1983) of 1.51 pesos to £1 sterling. Gold and other reserves (June 1983) U.S. $209 million. Budget (1982 actual): revenue 752.8 million pesos; expenditure 988.8 million pesos. Gross domestic product (1981) 7,227,000,000 pesos. Money supply (June 1983) 662.5 million pesos. Cost of living (Santo Domingo; 1975 = 100; March 1983) 190.3.

Foreign Trade. (1982) Imports 1,444,200,000 pesos; exports 767.7 million pesos. Import sources: U.S. 39%; Venezuela 18%; Mexico 14%; Japan 5%. Export destinations: U.S. 54%; Switzerland 12%; U.S.S.R. 8%. Main exports: sugar 37%; gold and alloys 21%; coffee 12%; cocoa 8%.

Transport and Communications. Roads (1982) 17,362 km. Motor vehicles in use (1981): passenger 102,100; commercial 56,830. Railways (1981) 588 km. Telephones (Jan. 1981) 165,300. Radio receivers (Dec. 1980) 220,000. Television receivers (Dec. 1980) 385,000.

Agriculture. Production (in 000; metric tons; 1982): rice c. 384; sweet potatoes (1981) c. 85; cassava (1981) c. 180; sugar, raw value c. 1,220; dry beans c. 50; tomatoes c. 160; peanuts c. 36; oranges c. 72; avocados (1981) c. 134; mangoes c. 182; bananas c. 330; plantains (1981) c. 625; cocoa c. 32; coffee c. 57; tobacco c. 31. Livestock (in 000; June 1981): cattle c. 2,155; sheep c. 55; goats c. 385; horses c. 204; chickens c. 8,300.

Industry. Production (in 000; metric tons; 1981): cement 960; bauxite (1982) 139; nickel ore 19; gold (troy oz) 412; silver (troy oz) 2,062; petroleum products 1,256; electricity (kw-hr) 3,350,000.

Earth Sciences

GEOLOGY AND GEOCHEMISTRY

Geology and geochemistry are global disciplines, and in 1983 international programs directed to their study continued to provide stimulus for many research developments. The International Lithosphere Program, emphasizing the evolution of the continental lithosphere (crust), provided the integrating theme for the 1980s. Progress to date and plans for the rest of the decade were to be discussed during the 27th International Geological Congress to be held in Moscow in August 1984.

During the past year planning meetings were already under way for formulating a new program for the 1990s, tentatively called the International Geosphere-Biosphere Program (IGBP). Its planners were framing scientific programs of global character in solar-terrestrial relationships, lithosphere dynamics, oceans and atmospheres, and the biosphere. Biogeochemical cycles including the transfer of carbon, nitrogen, and sulfur across land, sea, and air boundaries were central issues and served as examples of the integrating themes envisaged for the IGBP. Some aspects of the planning paralleled recent reports addressing the feasibility of a major research initiative of the National Aeronautics and Space Administration in the U.S. to document, understand, and predict 5–50-year global changes that can affect the habitability of the Earth. These efforts would involve coordination of global measurements from space platforms, exploit new technologies for observation, and use improved computational facilities for data management and mathematical modeling.

The biogeochemistry of carbon dioxide (CO_2) and its atmospheric role in changing global temperatures—and thus climates—through the "greenhouse effect" is an excellent example of the need for interdisciplinary approaches. Fluctuations in atmospheric carbon dioxide may be caused by many factors still unrecognized or poorly understood. The content of carbon in various parts of the global system needed better definition—in the biosphere, the soils, the atmosphere, the ocean, and sediments. In the past few years much scientific attention has been focused on fluctuations in oceanic biological production of CO_2 and its exchange between atmosphere and ocean, the area and character of forests and their role as sources or sinks for carbon, and CO_2 emission from volcanoes and from combustion of fossil fuels.

A recently published computer model by R. A. Berner of Yale University, A. C. Lasaga of Pennsylvania State University, and R. M. Garrels indicated that the carbon dioxide content of the atmosphere is highly sensitive to changes in the rate of seafloor spreading and continental area and that plate tectonics is therefore a major control of world climate. Over the long term the effect of plate tectonics on the release of CO_2 by way of metamorphism, igneous activity, and alterations the land area available for rock weathering appeared to be more influential than the factors listed in the preceding paragraph, which have been commonly considered to provide the major controls for atmospheric carbon dioxide over the comparatively short span of 50–100 years. Their results suggested that mean annual air temperatures at the Earth's surface through the Cretaceous, particularly 60 million to 100 million years ago, were 5°–10° C (9°–18° F) higher than the present value and were consistent with independent results from oxygen-isotope studies of marine plankton fossils.

Ancient climates were also being studied as part of a monumental project by A. M. Ziegler and his associates at the University of Chicago. Nearly

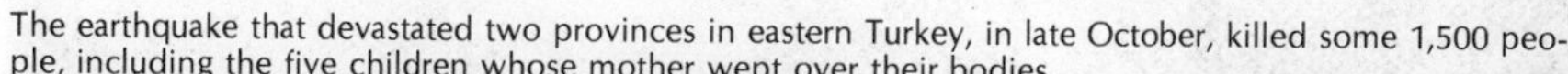

The earthquake that devastated two provinces in eastern Turkey, in late October, killed some 1,500 people, including the five children whose mother wept over their bodies.

WIDE WORLD

ready for publication was their *Atlas of Paleogeographic Maps,* comprising computer-generated colour maps that traced the positions of drifting continents, at intervals of about 20 million years, back to 580 million years ago. The project used information based on the residual magnetism found in rocks to locate past latitudes of continents, as had earlier efforts at mapping the Paleozoic (about 580 million to 225 million years ago). What made this set of maps distinctive was the compilation of paleontological and geological information from more than 30,000 localities along with determination of the geological and climatic environment. Cross-checking among data derived from paleogeography, paleobiology, and paleoclimatology (studies of the geography, life, and climates of the ancient past) yielded increasingly precise reconstructions.

Although there were at least 2,000 geological points for each map, there also remained large unknown areas. As continents migrate, the oceans change in size, shape, and distribution. These changes influence wind patterns, ocean currents, and biogeography. Application of the principles of modern oceanography and meteorology to the ancient map configurations and the distributions of mountain ranges permitted deductions about climatic conditions and provided an integrated picture yielding information about the unknown parts of each map. These approaches were making it possible to predict ancient sites of ocean upwelling where consequent high biological productivity would have produced sediments including phosphorites and deposits rich in organic material. Where the subsequent geological history has been suitable, these deposits could be exploited as sources of fertilizer and petroleum. In similar fashion the locations of potentially ore-bearing volcanic rocks could be located or predicted. This comprehensive approach to the reconstruction of paleogeography could prove to be a valuable prospecting tool for geological resources.

The drill ship "Glomar Challenger," which had been such a brilliant success in the Deep Sea Drilling Project (DSDP; see *Geophysics,* below) and the International Program of Ocean Drilling (IPOD), was phased out of action in late 1983. Despite the collapse of plans in 1981 for the Ocean Margin Drilling Program (OMDP), which involved a larger vessel, the "Glomar Explorer," the U.S. National Science Board in 1982 had strongly endorsed continuation of a scientific ocean-drilling program and conversion of the "Glomar Explorer" for use as a scientific drill ship. In 1983, however, the depressed condition of the world oil business made available several commercial drill ships, which could be chartered at day rates comparable with "Challenger" rates. The latest plans were to lease such a vessel, with Texas A&M University replacing Scripps Institution of Oceanography in La Jolla, Calif., as the ship operator. Drilling would resume sometime in 1985.

The great success of DSDP and IPOD contributed to recommendations from the Continental Scientific Drilling Committee of the U.S. National Academy of Sciences for funding of deep drilling of the

Kilauea Volcano, on the island of Hawaii, sent out some warning rumbles in January 1983 but exploded in earnest early in March, sending fingers of molten lava in and near Hawaii Volcanoes National Park.

WIDE WORLD

continents for scientific purposes. As of 1983 results had been obtained only from add-on experiments using some of the many holes drilled for purposes other than scientific research. Regional consortia were established to plan for the dedicated drilling projects, which it was believed would soon be funded.

There was an excellent prospect for extending a planned commercial steam-production well 3.7 km (2.3 mi) deep in the Salton Sea geothermal field in California to 5.5 km (3.4 mi) for scientific study prior to the well's commercial use. Republic Geothermal, Inc., which expected to begin drilling by the end of 1983, responded favorably to the proposal from William A. Elders and Lewis H. Cohen at the University of California at Riverside to drill the deepest geothermal well in the world.

Recent studies of the brines from a geothermal power station in the Salton Sea by A. Maimoni of the Lawrence Livermore National Laboratory in Livermore, Calif., indicated a high potential for recovery of minerals. If new recovery techniques under investigation could be developed, revenue from the minerals could exceed that from the power station.

One of the challenges commonly cited for the 1980s was to develop better methods of using computers to evaluate mineral resources. Hypotheses for the occurrence of various types of mineral deposits were converging into generally accepted models, which in turn were becoming basic tools of the mining industry. These mineral-occurrence models fostered the use of "intelligent" computer systems to evaluate geophysical, geochemical, and geological data and theory in order to locate ore deposits. There was great promise that such computer systems would become refined into diagnostic tools.

Remote sensing from satellites showed increasing promise for resource exploration. The multispectral scanner on Landsat satellites, for example, yielded data in digital form, which could be manipulated by computer before the final images were formed. Important advances were made in interpreting images produced from the spectral properties of rocks and of images of vegetation responding to geochemically induced soil anomalies. Recent results showed that the thematic mapper scanner aboard Landsat 4, which had been launched in July 1982, would provide an improved mapping tool for porphyry copper deposits and in exploration for deposits of base and precious metals. (PETER JOHN WYLLIE)

[212.B.4; 214.A.4.c; 214.B.2.f.ix; 214.C.4.b; 224.D.2.c.iii; 241.F–G]

GEOPHYSICS

The largest earthquake of 1983, registering a magnitude of 7.9, occurred on March 28 at latitude 4.9° S, longitude 153.4° E near the coast of New Britain Island in the southwestern Pacific. Fortunately there were no population centres or major construction in the vicinity; only minor damage resulted on eastern New Britain and the southeast coast of New Ireland. A second shock, only slightly smaller (magnitude 7.8) but much more destructive, struck on May 26 in the Sea of Japan at latitude 40.4° N, longitude 139.2° E. It and the giant sea wave, or tsunami, that it created killed more than 100 persons and extensively damaged dwellings, roads, and vessels from southern Hokkaido to Niigata on Honshu. Tsunamis reached heights of 14 m at Minehama, Honshu, 8 m along the Soviet coast, and 3 m at points along the coast of South Korea (1 m = 3.3 ft). On October 30 an earthquake of magnitude 7.1 flattened 44 villages in eastern Turkey. At least 1,500 lives were lost and thousands left homeless.

Seismic activity between late 1982 and late 1983 was unique in the unusually large number (near 20) of small or moderate earthquakes that caused fatalities. One of the most catastrophic of these occurred on Dec. 13, 1982, on the western Arabian Peninsula in a region where no earthquake had ever before been detected with instruments. This shock had a magnitude of only 6.0 but resulted in 2,800 fatalities and left 700,000 homeless, destroying or severely damaging 350 villages. On March 31 a comparatively small shock (magnitude 5.5) in Colombia resulted in at least 260 deaths, destroyed 3,000 buildings, and left 150,000 homeless.

Although volcanic activity during the year was widespread, involving more than two dozen volcanoes, it was mostly minor. Activity of special interest, however, was closely monitored and continued to cause some concern. One such scene of activity was the Long Valley Caldera near the town of Mammoth Lakes, Calif. This 480-sq-km (185-sq-mi) depression, created by a gigantic volcanic blast 700,000 years ago, experienced 200–300 small earthquakes in a one-hour interval on Dec. 14, 1982. Two earthquakes of magnitude 3.3 were recorded on December 21, and the next day a swarm of 100 events occurred in the space of 20 minutes. These were followed on January 6 by the largest swarm ever encountered in the 2½ years since the Long Valley disturbances were first noted. The series began with two earthquakes, of magnitude 5.5 and 5.6, followed by many hours of spasmodic tremor, a succession of events so close together in time that they could not be individually identified. The depth of identifiable shocks ranged from very shallow to ten kilometres (1 km = 0.62 mi). Activity dropped off sharply after January 9 but continued at an abnormally high level for several months thereafter. Since many scientists believed that these swarms could presage a renewal of volcanism in this ancient caldera, their study was considered extremely important in attempting to discover if or when such a renewal could be expected.

In Mexico El Chichón, which erupted violently in March and April 1982 and produced a pervasive volcanic cloud having a high sulfur dioxide content in the upper atmosphere, experienced only minor activity in 1983. The cloud persisted during the year, however, causing Bishop's rings (reddish-brown coronas around the Sun) and spectacular sunsets worldwide. Recent studies by scientists at the University of Wyoming discovered one of its by-products, a continent-sized cloud of sulfuric acid droplets. This secondary cloud was higher than the main cloud, ranging from 29 to 35 km in altitude. It contained 40 times the amount of acid produced by the eruption of Mt. St. Helens in 1980 and was circling the globe at about 80 km/hr.

Satellite measurements by the U.S. National Oceanic and Atmospheric Administration (NOAA) of sea-surface temperatures were disrupted by the sulfuric acid cloud, resulting in readings that were about 3.3° C (6° F) too low. This effect permitted a determination of the horizontal extent of the cloud. At last report it encircled the globe, covering the area between latitude 10° and 30° N. NOAA scientists believed that the cloud was growing, fueled by the photochemical conversion of sulfur dioxide from the main cloud to sulfuric acid droplets, and that it would remain a feature of the stratosphere for several years.

The Deep Sea Drilling Project (DSDP) being carried out aboard the research ship "Glomar Challenger" continued in the Pacific Ocean. Leg 85 comprised five drilling sites, two at the eastern end and three in the central portion of the equatorial sediment bulge, located west of Ecuador and south of the Clipperton Fracture Zone. A notable finding at the eastern end was a sedimentation rate of 70 metres per million years, nearly twice the usual rate in the region. Sedimentation rates as well as their variations and hiatuses (periods of little sedimentation) are significant because they can help establish geologic age and evolutionary sequences.

Leg 86 traversed the Pacific from Honolulu to Yokohama, Japan, for the purpose of investigating the oceanography of the northwest Pacific's ancient past. The Nankai Trough southwest of Japan and the Japan Trench off the coast of northern Honshu were explored on Leg 87 to obtain more detailed information on the subduction process in which the Pacific crustal plate dips sharply under the Asian continent. As expected, sedimentation rates were found to be much higher than those found in the central Pacific: nearly 900 metres per million years prior to 400,000 years ago and 300 metres per million years thereafter. Although evidence of the subduction zone was inconclusive, interpretation of certain cores indicated that the drill did penetrate through the hanging continental layer into the subducted plate.

An ocean sub-bottom seismometer, designed to operate beneath the seafloor, was successfully deployed on Leg 88 just south of the Hokkaido Fracture Zone. Land-based instruments positioned close enough to plate boundaries to record small earthquakes were invariably subjected to a high level of seismic noise due to geologic factors and meteorologic and oceanic disturbances, while ocean-bottom seismometers were limited by ocean currents and inefficient coupling with the crust. On the other hand, theory and logic predicted that sub-bottom seismometers situated near the boundary on the relatively stable oceanic plate would be as quiet seismically as the best mid-continent sites. Attempts to install a sophisticated seismograph developed for the U.S. Department of Defense and requiring an oversized borehole were unsuccessful. However, an ocean sub-bottom seismometer developed by the Hawaii Institute of Geophysics was available. Designed to fit a standard drill pipe and borehole, it was clamped 23 m below the ocean bottom, where it operated successfully for 65 days.

Subsequently the "Glomar Challenger" departed for New Caledonia on Leg 89, occupying sites in the Mariana and Nauru basins, off the Marshall Islands, and on the Ontong Java Plateau. This last borehole was combined with those of Leg 90 in one of the most extensive cruises to date, a latitude traverse beginning at the Equator north of New Britain Island, south between Australia and New Caledonia, then west of New Zealand along the Lord Howe Rise, and finally off the southeast coast of South Island, N.Z., at latitude 45° S. Nine sites were occupied, and more than 30,000 samples were obtained, amounting to 22 tons. Three notable achievements during this cruise were the recovery of a 315-m continuous core, the longest so far obtained; two complete cores across the major boundary between the Eocene and the Oligocene corresponding to 38 million years ago; and the very close correlation at one site between a layer of detritus indicative of high volcanic activity and the extinction of several forms of marine animals.

(RUTLAGE J. BRAZEE)

[212.D.4; 213.B; 231.D; 241.F–G]

HYDROLOGY

Streamflow was normal or above normal in most of the U.S. in 1983. The combined flow of that country's three largest rivers—the Mississippi, St. Lawrence, and Columbia—was 26% above the long-term average, 13% more than in 1982, and the greatest flow since 1974. Severe flooding during the year caused extensive property damage in the Gulf Coast and the West. Among the states hit hardest were Nevada, Utah, Arizona, New Mexico, Colorado, Oklahoma, Texas, and the coastal and desert areas of southern California. Damage from landslides was extensive in Nevada and Utah during the spring as water-saturated soils became unstable. In June rapid runoff occurred in the mountainous western states when a record accumulation of snow, containing the equivalent of as much as 1,000 mm (40 in) of rainfall, began melting because of warm temperatures and late spring rains. The Colorado River, swollen by one of the heaviest runoffs on record, crested in late July, and flows below Hoover Dam and Lake Powell were highest since these reservoirs were constructed. The Great Salt Lake in Utah rose to its highest level since 1924. In January and again in April, record-breaking floods inundated parts of Louisiana and Mississippi along the Pearl and Amite rivers.

In contrast to this abundance of water, several areas in the Midwest and Southwest experienced severe drought. The drought in these regions in August was primarily agricultural and the result of a lingering heat wave and precipitation much below normal.

Water use in the U.S. increased about 2½ times between 1950 and 1980—to a record high of 450,000,000,000 gal per day—largely because of irrigation, growing urban use, and water for energy production, according to a report recently published by the U.S. Geological Survey. The report, *Estimated Use of Water in the United States in 1980,* noted that 80% of the water came from surface

WIDE WORLD

The worst flooding in almost 20 years hit West Germany and nearby Europe in April. In the little Moselle River valley town of Zell, a volunteer worker wades in hip-deep water.

water and the remainder from groundwater. California withdrew more water than any other state, about 54,000,000,000 gal per day, which was more than twice as much as Florida or Texas, the next largest water users. Groundwater use increased steadily during the 30 years under study but exceeded surface-water withdrawals only in Arizona, Kansas, Nebraska, and Oklahoma. Although the largest single use of groundwater was for irrigation, about one out of two Americans relied on groundwater for domestic supplies.

The outcome of two recent court cases could have a major effect on future water-resource development. In 1982, in the case *Sporhase* v. *Nebraska*, the U.S. Supreme Court determined that water was an article of interstate commerce under the commerce clause of the U.S. Constitution. This decision placed limits on the ability of a state to restrict the export of water beyond state boundaries. In 1983 a federal court held in the case *El Paso* v. *Reynolds (New Mexico)* that New Mexico's ban on water exports to the city of El Paso, Texas, was discriminatory because it treated in-state and out-of-state water users differently.

Acid rain and the leaching of toxic chemicals from land disposal sites into rivers and lakes posed problems for Canadians during 1983, chemical landfill sites along the Niagara River being of particular concern. In October a Canadian-U.S. high-level meeting failed to achieve agreement on how to deal with the acid-rain issue, but it did make a major step toward improving the quality of the Great Lakes. A phosphorus-control supplement to the Great Lakes Water Quality Agreement was signed, thereby committing the two nations to a further reduction of phosphorus entering the lakes, primarily from nonsewage sources.

(JOHN E. MOORE)

[222.A.2.b; 223.D.6.a and c; 355.D.5.a.ii]

METEOROLOGY

During the year a spectacular interaction between the ocean and the atmosphere—a massive warming of the surface waters of the tropical eastern Pacific Ocean—was linked to extraordinary weather conditions over the entire globe. Called El Niño, it triggered extreme weather events beginning in late 1982 and continuing into much of 1983.

Although El Niño recurs intermittently, the

UPI

Streams in the Black Forest evaporated under West Germany's record-breaking summer heat. A family of four was able to walk the bottom of the Dreisam without getting their feet wet.

A February blizzard disrupted New York City's major arteries, as reflected in this scene along Grand Central Parkway in the borough of Queens. Motorists, unable to continue, pulled off the road, and police rescued hundreds before they froze or succumbed to exhaust gases while trying to keep their cars warm.

1982–83 event was the strongest ever recorded and might well be the most extensive climatic phenomenon of the century. It built up over a long period of time and released enormous amounts of heat and energy into the atmosphere, influencing the entire global circulation. Abnormally warm waters extended west from the South American coast along the Equator to more than one-fourth of the distance around the Earth. Across the equatorial Pacific, patterns of wind, pressure, and large-scale rainfall shifted eastward. Regions of low pressure and high pressure weakened. Ordinarily dry areas in the central eastern equatorial Pacific got heavy rainfall, while in the west much of Australia and Indonesia were deprived of their normal rains. Changes in the atmosphere and ocean south of the Equator affected the northern Pacific. Abnormally strong jet streams appeared in both hemispheres and varied from their usual courses. In the Northern Hemisphere the jet stream was diverted southward in a great arc down the U.S. West Coast, across the Gulf of Mexico, and then back up the East Coast.

Meteorologists disagreed somewhat over the relationship between the 1982–83 El Niño and several meteorological anomalies, particularly the warm winter weather east of the Rocky Mountains in 1983, the huge snowstorms in the northeastern U.S. in January and February, and the heat wave and drought from July to September over much of the U.S. Nevertheless, most meteorologists linked El Niño's effects to a number of other extreme events: high winds and excess rains in California, Oregon, and Washington, which caused extensive damage during the winter months; excessive rainfall leading to heavy flooding and erosion in the Gulf Coast states and Cuba between December 1982 and April 1983; a prolonged dry spell over the Hawaiian Islands in early 1983 following a rare, extremely destructive hurricane, Iwa, in November 1982; record-breaking rainfall in Ecuador, northern Peru, and Bolivia between October 1982 and June 1983, causing Ecuador's worst flooding disaster of the century; widespread and devastating droughts in Australia, the Philippines, South Africa, Indonesia, southern India, and Sri Lanka, in which hundreds of people perished from starvation and heat and crop losses amounted to several billion dollars; and an eastward shift in the region of the South Pacific Ocean that is normally hit by tropical storms, thus giving French Polynesia five hurricanes and Tahiti its worst hurricane in modern times, on April 12. Other major weather events that might have been influenced by El Niño include record high temperatures in Siberia, cold and snow in the Middle East, wet weather in southern China, and flooding in western Europe.

Hurricane forecasters in the U.S. were also studying a connection between the strong El Niño and depressed Atlantic hurricane activity. The 1982 hurricane season (June to November) was the lightest in more than half a century. The 1983 hurricane season was also relatively inactive, but the first hurricane of the year, Alicia, was a major one. It struck the Galveston-Houston area of Texas on August 17 and 18 with winds of 185 km/hr (115 mph) and a storm surge that was 3–3½ m (10–12 ft) high. It took 22 lives and caused $1.5 billion in damages.

An understanding of El Niño and its consequences was important to all nations of the world and required a comprehensive scientific program dealing with the entire global atmosphere. Such a program was needed to understand the climate of planet Earth and its sensitivity to various natural forces and human activities. At the ninth Congress of the World Meteorological Organization, which was held in Geneva in May 1983, delegates of 138 member countries agreed to press forward with the World Climate Program, a unified worldwide thrust to develop the capability to predict climatic fluctuations with emphasis on variations ranging from weeks to decades. A major international research program focused on El Niño would be one part of this effort. (See *Oceanography*, below, and Special Report.) (RICHARD E. HALLGREN)

[221.B.1–3,5; 224.D]

OCEANOGRAPHY

The term El Niño originally signified a warming of ocean surface waters off the coasts of Peru and Ecuador, often occurring around Christmastime. This warming has taken place irregularly (six times in the past 83 years), and with it has come drastic changes in marine life. Usually abundant microscopic plants and animals become scarce, the creatures which feed upon them starve, and ultimately the stock of fish available for human harvesting and consumption drops. Such an event occurred in 1972. It was at least in part responsible for the subsequent collapse of the Peruvian anchovy fishery (from a peak of 12.3 million tons in 1970 to less than 2 million tons in 1973). As catastrophic as are such events locally, it has become clear that they are but a small part of a global change in the climate of both the atmosphere and the upper ocean. During 1982–83 the world experienced the most intense El Niño ever recorded. Modern observing techniques together with a heightened sense of the possible effects of this event also made this El Niño the most thoroughly described one ever.

In early 1982 Earth-orbiting weather satellites and drifting buoys monitoring ocean surface temperature began to show abnormally warm temperatures in the eastern tropical Pacific. Far to the west across the Pacific, atmospheric pressure at sea level at Tahiti began to fall, while even farther to the west at Darwin, Australia, atmospheric pressure at sea level began to rise. These seemingly unrelated events signaled the beginning of El Niño.

Atmospheric pressure at sea level at Tahiti usually is higher than at Darwin. When this pattern began to reverse, the resulting difference in pressure opposed the normally westward trade winds, which commonly dominate the tropics. They began to weaken and even to reverse, first in the western tropical Pacific (autumn 1982) and then in the eastern tropical Pacific (spring 1983). By March 1983 surface winds over the equatorial Pacific were eastward from Australia to South America. In effect, there were no trade winds over the equatorial Pacific. The surface flow of the ocean, normally westward under the trades in this region, also reversed and became primarily eastward. Normally the trades also drive water away from the Equator (owing to the Earth's rotation) and thus cause deeper, cooler, nutrient-rich water to upwell there. In the absence of the trades the layer of surface water warmer than 25° C (77° F) deepened steadily throughout 1982 by more than 150 m (490 ft) in the eastern tropical Pacific. Warm surface water appeared off Peru in late 1982 and by the end of the year was 4°–7° C (7.2°–12.6° F) warmer than normal.

In early 1983, by the time it was clear that a full-fledged El Niño was in progress, some signs suggested that the event was fading. The near-surface layer of warm water in the eastern tropical Pacific became shallower by almost 100 m (330 ft), and the Darwin-Tahiti pressure difference began to decrease. But sea-surface temperatures off Peru and Ecuador continued to rise, reaching values 9°–12° C (16.2°–21.6° F) above normal in May. Only in July, as sea-surface temperatures off Peru fell toward normal values, did it appear fairly certain that El Niño was coming to an end. Even so, offshore in the eastern tropical Pacific there was still unusually warm water at the surface, and eastward surface flow was recorded as late as the end of July.

All these events resulted in drastic changes in the weather of the tropical Pacific. Peru and Ecuador were struck by heavy damaging rains. Five hurricanes and a sixth storm of near-hurricane proportions passed through French Polynesia,

In early March the rain and windstorms that had plagued California in January and February came roaring back, sending pounding waves up and down the coast and damaging residential areas, including this community near San Francisco.

UPI

HYDRO PRODUCTS

Robotics at the bottom of the sea: in submarine exploration, the smallest of the remotely operated vehicles are virtually swimming cameras that can observe and inspect, then relay findings to computers for evaluation and analysis. Beside this one is its source of illumination.

whereas previously the chance of a hurricane there, estimated from past occurrences, had been once in 50 years. At Christmas Island (directly south of Hawaii and about 320 km, or 200 mi, north of the Equator) the usual trade winds were replaced by eastward winds, and monthly mean rainfalls exceeded all previous records, sometimes being five to ten times normal values. The normal population of some 14 million sooty terns literally vanished (observers saw none at all in November 1982), and four individuals were all that remained of a normal population of several thousand blue-faced boobies. Intense abnormal rainfall was the rule over the entire tropical Pacific while, at the same time, Australia and Indonesia suffered from prolonged drought.

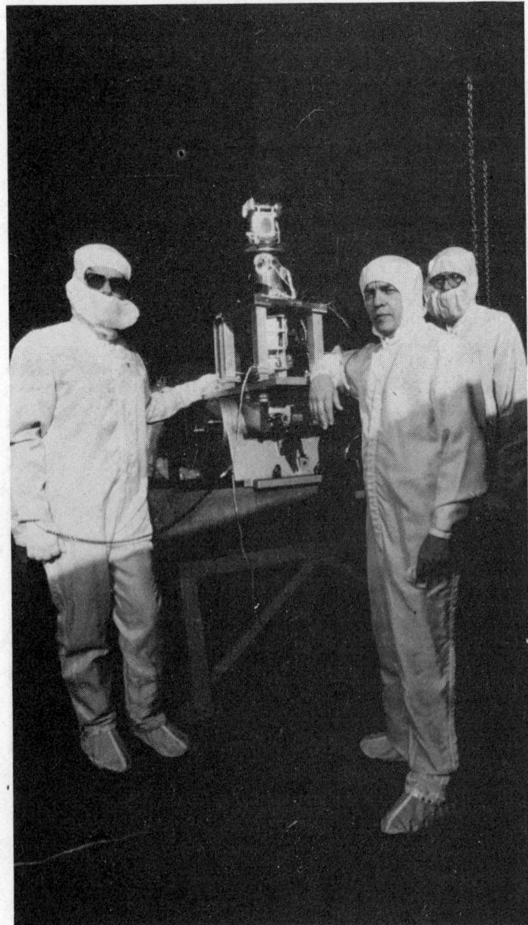
BRIAN R. WOLFF

The instrumentation in SAGE II, slated for launching in 1984, will keep track of spreading clouds of dust and debris after a volcanic eruption. It is prepared for flight in a clean room.

Nor were the effects of El Niño restricted to the tropics. Unusually warm surface waters were observed as far north as California. These warm waters brought species of marine life that normally are found much farther south to the ocean off California. The beaches of southern California were covered with small lobsterlike crabs, and sardines again appeared at Monterey Bay. Birds that normally breed on the Farallon Islands near San Francisco found their normal supply of anchovies and krill disrupted by the warm water and disappeared from the islands.

By starting in the spring instead of the fall, by first appearing in the western Pacific rather than in the eastern Pacific, and by peaking well into the following spring, the most recent El Niño differed from all previous ones. Its unusual time and place of appearance kept scientists from recognizing it until it was well under way. It caused scientists to discard a hypothesis which had been proposed as a predictor of El Niño—that the trades intensify before El Niño and then collapse—because it appeared without any prior buildup of the trades.

There was evidence that these events in the tropics also affected weather in higher latitudes (see *Meteorology*, above, and Special Report). A great deal of further study was needed before El Niño and its effects would be understood and predicted with useful skill. (MYRL C. HENDERSHOTT)

[221.B.1–3,5; 223.A; 224.D]

See also Disasters; Energy; Life Sciences; Mining and Quarrying; Space Exploration; Speleology.

Eastern European Literature:
see Literature

Eastern Non-Chalcedonian Churches:
see Religion

Eastern Orthodox Churches:
see Religion

Ecology:
see Environment; Life Sciences

THE WORLD'S CRAZY WEATHER

by Stephen H. Schneider

In 1816 farmers in New England complained of the "year without a summer." Historians have pointed to that same year as the "last great subsistence crisis" in Europe. Frosts in June and July helped wreak havoc with food crops, causing already economically distressed segments of societies grave difficulties. J. M. W. Turner, the renowned English painter, put on canvas what people often call "Turner sunsets," richly luminous skies now believed to have been partly inspired by the vast stratospheric cloud created by the 1815 eruption of Mt. Tambora in Indonesia. That violent explosion spread volcanic debris worldwide and was sufficient not only to create Turner sunsets but also to block out enough sunlight for the Earth's temperature to have dropped a few degrees over the next year or two.

But did the eruption cause the "great subsistence crisis" of 1816 in Europe or the "year without a summer" in New England? Clearly, these events were related to temperature drops of more than just a few degrees, and thus something else had to be implicated. Recent evidence suggests that the jet stream, the upper atmospheric river of air that steers the storm systems, was strongly misdirected that year, plunging cold Arctic air deep into New England and perhaps Europe as well. This condition in the upper level westerly winds—"blocking," as meteorologists call it—could have combined with the volcanic cooling to help create those catastrophic events. Then again, one may wonder if the eruption could have created both the abnormal wind conditions and the temperature drop, which seem to have occurred simultaneously.

Two Modern-Day Suspects. Although there have been other significant volcanic eruptions in the past century and a half, few seem to have been of the magnitude of the scientific "gift" that nature gave to climatologists in the spring of 1982 when El Chichón erupted in Mexico. Its enormous dust veil spent its first six months circling the globe primarily between the Equator and latitude 30° N, screening out some 5–10% of the sunlight that normally falls on the tropics (roughly comparable to an average smoggy day in Los Angeles). The volcanic cloud then spread north and south, covering most of the Northern Hemisphere and moving into the Southern Hemisphere as well. Modern climatologists had an advantage over their few colleagues from Mt. Tambora's day, for this time aircraft, satellites, and worldwide instrumentation networks were prepared to monitor not just the effect of the volcanic dust on the sunlight striking the Earth but also the climatic conditions in its aftermath.

The atmospheric scientists involved with El Chichón found themselves unable to give it their undivided attention for long, for soon thereafter another phenomenon of major interest to both oceanographers and meteorologists began to develop. It had been known for some time that every few years the surface temperature of the eastern equatorial Pacific Ocean rises, eliminating the cool waters that normally lie off Peru and Ecuador. As a result the catch of the anchovy fishery in the region declines, and both rainfall and temperature along western South America increase dramatically. Since there is a tendency for this oceanic warming to occur around January, it has come to be known as El Niño, "The Child," a reference to the date of the celebration of the birth of Christ. El Niño, however, is hardly confined to December or January—or to the offshore waters of South America. Associated with the El Niño warming is a large chain of events stretching across the entire Pacific Ocean and involving the atmosphere as well—effects that appear to be truly global. Not only does precipitation increase in the eastern Pacific, but it seems to decrease in the western Pacific at the same time. Pressure changes occur between the eastern and western Pacific, and wind patterns literally flip-flop during such El Niño periods. Hence, drought in Australia has been blamed on this phenomenon, along with torrential rains and heat in South America.

Trouble Up North. Among the more intriguing aspects of El Niño (and its associated atmospheric effects, known as the Southern Oscillation) is a scientific question of fundamental importance to people in most of the developed countries: Does this tropical phenomenon also affect weather in northern temperate latitudes? Evidence gathered during the past several years seems to give a strong but qualified "yes." Empirical studies as well as computer-modeling analyses suggest that the temperature of the tropical ocean, the principal source of moisture and energy that drive the entire atmospheric

Stephen H. Schneider is head of the Visitors Program and deputy director of the Advanced Study Program at the National Center for Atmospheric Research, Boulder, Colo. He is the primary author of The Coevolution of Climate and Life.

circulation, does influence the climate of the mid-latitudes, primarily by modulating the position and intensity of the jet stream. Since the jet stream both steers storm systems and helps to divide warm from cold regions of the Northern Hemisphere, any phenomenon that can cause anomalies in the position of the jet is an important subject for study.

Under the close watch of several groups of scientists, the El Niño that began in early 1982 across the mid-Pacific developed during 1983 into what was the largest and longest lasting ever recorded. Although interest in this phenomenon had long triggered both scientific and popular speculation about its potential effects on the weather, El Niño watchers this time had fleets of ships, aircraft, and satellites waiting for the next big event in order to document its effect. They were not disappointed. By mid-1983 surface temperatures in the ocean had risen to unprecedented heights, and major climatic anomalies were becoming obvious.

In 1983 many unusual weather events occurred outside of the equatorial Pacific region. The jet stream crossed the U.S. Pacific coast far to the south of its normal position in winter and spring, bringing extremely heavy rainfall to California. Although winter temperatures across the U.S. were generally mild, spring rains were excessive and spring temperatures ranked among the coldest on record in parts of the central U.S. On the other hand, summer brought persistent hot and dry conditions across the corn belt and southeastern states, causing billions of dollars in damage to corn, soybeans, and other summer crops. The summer of 1983 also produced record heat in much of western Europe. These anomalous climatic conditions were consistent with the altered patterns of the jet stream observed that year.

Too Much of a Good Thing. Unfortunately—and there almost always is an "unfortunately" in the long-range weather prediction business—nature had played a trick on the atmospheric scientists. It gave them what might well be the largest volcanic eruption and the largest El Niño event of the century—but both at the same time! To be sure, 1983 brought massive amounts of precipitation to the U.S. West Coast in the winter, undoubtedly related to the southward position of the jet relative to normal. But was the anomalous jet an El Niño effect? And springtime temperatures were well below normal. Could the cold spring have been an El Chichón effect? There are advocates of both of these positions. In truth, it is simply too soon to be certain of the extent to which either or both of these events contributed to the unusual patterns of 1983. Again, some scientists have suggested a causal connection between the two events, but there seems to be little evidence at present to support the proposition. Because of their large magnitudes, had either event occurred by itself it would have been a particularly convincing case study of the effect of some of nature's extremes on climate. Such knowledge might have aided markedly our ability to forecast future events, providing the warnings to producers of food, water, and energy and to consumers that are so badly needed to mitigate the effect of sudden, extreme weather fluctuations. But, by bad luck, the simultaneous occurrence confounded the interpretation of cause and effect and required scientists to be more cautious in their pronouncements.

In early 1982 changes in patterns of atmospheric pressure over the Pacific Ocean caused a weakening of the trade winds that influence the strength and timing of the El Niño effect (an eastern extension of warm equatorial currents that displaces the colder Peru Current and its fisheries). Its magnitude became apparent when sea-surface temperatures increased more than 6° C (11° F) and sea levels rose by 15 to 20 centimetres (6 to 8 inches) in the eastern Pacific. The 1982–83 event began earlier and lasted longer than usual, was particularly strong, and triggered weather disturbances worldwide.

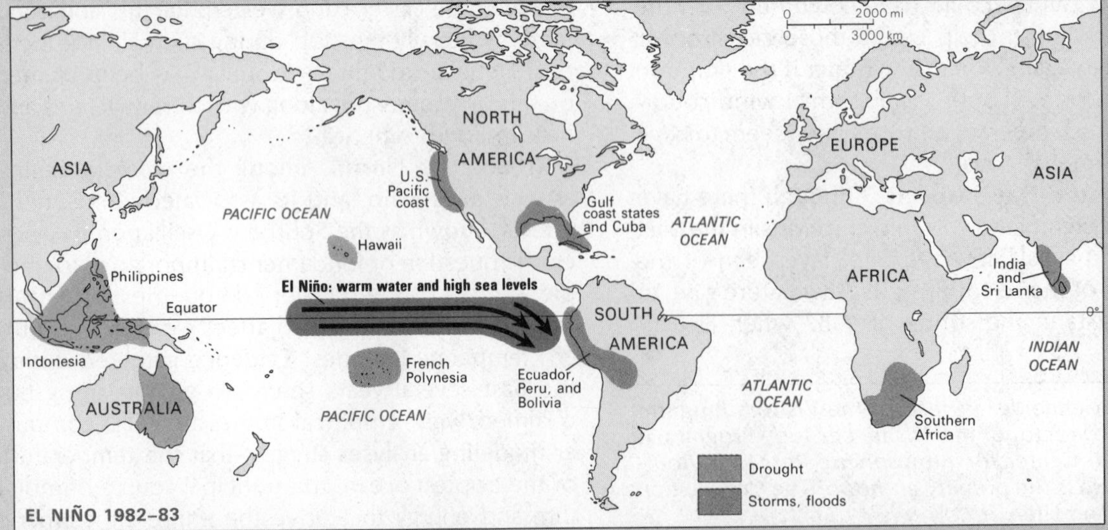

(LEFT) DAVID AUSTEN—BLACK STAR; (RIGHT) SAN JOSE MERCURY NEWS/BLACK STAR

El Niño scattered trouble around the globe. Drought that killed cattle in Australia (left) was paired with storms that drove the Pacific into California homes (right).

One additional aspect should be considered. Nature is not the only polluter on the planet, of course, as daily headlines remind us. One reason that volcano watchers were so excited about El Chichón was the opportunity that it gave them to measure the climatic effect of its natural smog in order to gain a better idea of the speed and seriousness with which certain man-made pollutants might be affecting climate. Over the next several years the information being gathered should help in that regard, but the simultaneity of El Niño and El Chichón could once again reduce confidence in any conclusions.

The Wondrous Weather Machine. It is becoming increasingly clear that events like El Niño and exploding volcanoes, despite their pervasiveness, do not operate on climate in isolation. Each is but part of a system of interlocking influences—some no doubt still waiting to be discovered—that include variations in the energy output of the Sun, abnormal patterns of sea ice, and human activities. One year's pattern of weather is characteristically different from the next for a variety of causes, and whenever there exists this variety it is rash to look to one cause as clearly paramount. Through field studies, data analyses, and computer modeling, atmospheric scientists are making slow but real progress in understanding each of these causal factors and their cumulative potential influence on climate. At a very minimum we may soon gain some idea of what indeed can be predicted. At the very best we will have some actual additional predictive skill that may be of significant value to society. Thanks to El Niño and El Chichón this skill may come a little easier and sooner than it would otherwise.

BRIAN R. WOLFF

The eruption of El Chichón in Mexico in 1982 sent up a dust veil that circled a narrow band of the Earth for six months before it dispersed. The cloud then spread over most of the Northern and part of the Southern hemispheres.

Economy, World

The long-awaited economic recovery in the developed world began in 1983. Contrary to some fears, this was not accompanied by an acceleration in the rate of inflation or a potentially dangerous relaxation of fiscal and monetary policies. Although the position varied greatly from country to country, the year ended on a note of general optimism in regard to both the achievements to date and the outlook for the months ahead. In late 1983 it seemed that member countries of the Organization for Economic Cooperation and Development (OECD) would record an economic growth of just over 3%, compared with a decline of 0.3% in 1982 and gains of only 1.6 and 1.2% in the two previous years.

Important reasons for this unexpectedly good growth were the cautious but generally accommodating fiscal and monetary policies pursued in the large countries. In the United States, which acted as the engine of the world recovery with a growth in gross national product (GNP) of about 3.5% (as compared with a fall of 1.9% in 1982), business activity was stimulated by tax cuts implemented in July and by a relatively relaxed approach to the continuing budget deficit. Similarly, although in the United Kingdom the control of public borrowing remained an important part of official policy, signs that the fiscal and monetary budgets might be exceeded did not lead to a deflationary squeeze. As a result, the year-end indications implied for Britain a gross domestic product (GDP) gain of 3% for 1983, as against an increase of 1.8% in the preceding year.

CHART 1

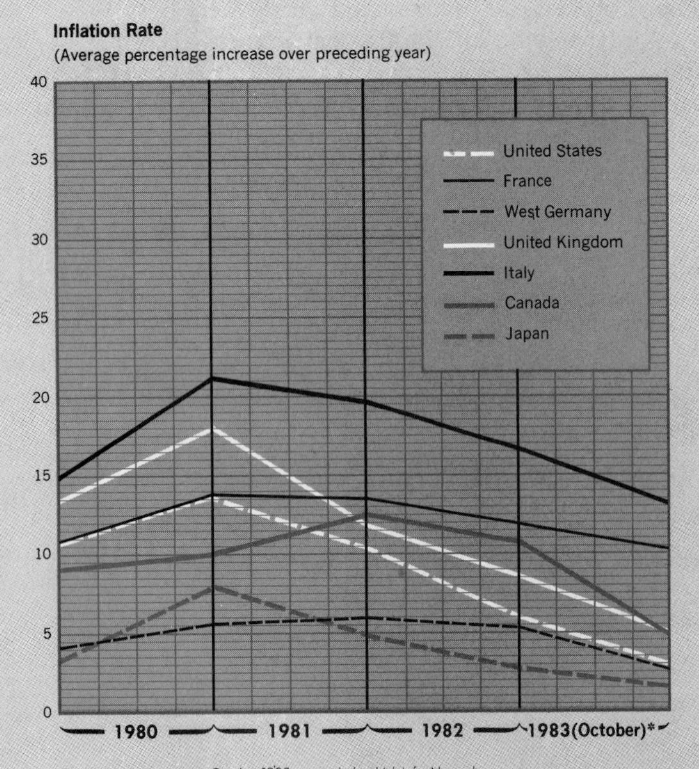

*Percentage increase over October 1982, except Italy which is for November.
Sources: OECD, *Economic Outlook, Main Economic Indicators; the Economist, Economic and Financial Indicators.*

West Germany, too, followed a relatively relaxed policy that helped to bring about a growth of 1% in GDP as against a decline of 1.1% in 1982. Japan, however, maintained a marginally restrictive approach until late 1983 and was not expected to improve on the economic growth rate of 3% that it achieved in 1982.

As in 1982, the greatest contrast to the general trend was provided by France. Even as early as 1982, Pres. François Mitterrand's inflationary dash for growth lay in ruins as inflation accelerated, the external payments position deteriorated, and the currency came under pressure. But the deflationary measures forced upon the government by those developments in 1982 were not enough; in March 1983 a further bout of deflation and currency devaluation was engineered, and—partly as a result of this—there was expected to be no growth in France in 1983 as against a rise of 1.8% in 1982. Another of the year's outstanding failures was Italy, which increased its negative growth of 0.3% in 1982 into one of 1.8% in 1983.

Most other advanced countries experienced some increase (but not necessarily an acceleration of growth) in their GNP; the most spectacular performance, outshining even that of the U.S., was achieved by Canada, where a GDP decline of 4.4% in 1982 was transformed into a gain of 3.3%.

One reason why most governments felt able to pursue gently accommodating fiscal and monetary policies was the favourable trend of prices. The rate of inflation fell nearly everywhere, partly in response to falling oil and weak commodity prices, to the effects of earlier anti-inflationary measures, and to a general moderation in the level of wage settlements. Wages were influenced, as in 1982, by the high rate of unemployment.

The effect of these anti-inflationary factors varied from country to country. However, the average fall in OPEC (Organization of Petroleum Exporting Countries) crude oil prices of some 12%, following the 4% drop in 1982, was a powerful factor throughout the advanced world that was only partially offset by a hardening in prices of food and agricultural raw materials. All in all, consumer prices in the OECD area probably rose by 5% in 1983, a significant improvement over the figure of 7.8% during the previous year. Among the larger countries the star performer was Japan with an inflation rate of less than 2%, followed by West Germany with around 3%. At the end of the year it seemed that, despite the rapid acceleration in the tempo of economic activity, U.S. consumer price inflation would decline from over 6% in 1982 to about 3.5%—an improvement that was partly due to the relative strength of the dollar against most other major currencies. The U.K. also experienced a good fall in the inflation rate (from 8.6% to some 4.6%); France managed only a small improvement, from 12 to 9.5%, while Italian prices were still rising at nearly three times the OECD average. As was the case with overall economic growth, Western Europe's performance in the fight against inflation was distinctly less spectacular than that of other developed countries. Thus, the annual rate of inflation in Western Europe as a whole was still about 8%, as against a figure of only about 4% for non-European OECD members.

In broad economic terms the most predictable and least satisfactory feature of the year was the high level of unemployment. As 1982 drew to a close, just over 8% of the OECD labour force—equivalent to approximately 30 million people—was on the unemployment register. Twelve months later, despite a better than expected economic performance, the total number of those without a job was calculated to have risen to as much as 33 million–34 million, accounting for more than 9% of the labour force. Nor were there any realistic expectations of a significant decline in the near future, although in the case of a few countries there were hopes of a modest improvement in the situation. Once again the best news came from North America. In the U.S. the unemployment rate declined from 10.8% in December 1982 to 8.1% in December 1983, and the indications pointed to a further improvement in the months ahead. In Canada the 1983 result was likely to have been a modest decrease, but in most other countries more people were unemployed at the end of 1983 than at the end of the previous year. One exception was the U.K., where the year-end position was broadly comparable with the situation 12 months earlier.

During 1983 much of the stimulus to the faster growing national economies came from private consumption. The most important underlying factors were falling inflation rates (and in some cases rising real incomes), a general improvement in consumer expectations, and a reduction in savings. In the U.K. the proportion of personal income saved fell from 10.8 to 8.5% between 1982 and 1983, and the rise in consumer expenditure accelerated from 1.3 to over 3%. U.S. consumers, greatly assisted by Pres. Ronald Reagan's July tax cuts, followed a similar path, increasing their volume spending during 1983 by approximately 6–7% from 1% in 1982. Other countries, such as Canada

Table I. Real Gross Domestic Products of Selected OECD Countries

% change, seasonally adjusted at annual rates

Country	Average 1971–81	Change from previous year 1981	1982	1983*
United States	2.8	2.3	−1.7†	3.0†
Japan	4.8	4.0	3.0†	3.25†
West Germany	2.5	0.2	−1.1†	0.5†
France	3.1	0.2	1.7	−0.5
United Kingdom	1.4	−2.0	1.2	1.75
Canada	3.7	3.8	−4.8†	2.0†
Italy	2.9	−0.2	−0.3	−0.5
Total major countries	3.1	1.8	−0.3	2.0
Australia	2.9	4.1	0.1	−0.5
Austria	3.2	0	1.1	1.0
Belgium	2.7	−1.8	−0.1	0.25
Denmark	2.1	0.1	3.1	1.0
Finland	3.5	1.3	1.8	2.0
Greece	3.9	−0.4	0	0.5
Ireland	3.8	1.1	1.4	−0.25
Netherlands, The	2.4	−1.2	−1.4	−0.25
New Zealand	2.2	4.0	−0.7	−0.5
Norway	4.3	0.8	−0.6	0.25
Spain	3.3	0.3	1.1	1.50
Sweden	1.8	−0.6	−0.1	1.75
Switzerland	1.0	1.9	−2.0	−0.5
Total OECD countries	3.0	1.6	−0.2	2.0

*OECD projection. †GNP.
Sources: Adapted from OECD, *Economic Outlook,* July 1983; National Institute of Economic Review; EIU estimates.

WIDE WORLD

Talks intended to realign the currencies of European Community countries belonging to the European Monetary System almost came to naught in March. At a later meeting the finance ministers agreed to an adjustment of the values of their currencies. For a short time only foreign exchange rates were fixed, leaving traders on their own at the telephone.

and West Germany, also did well in this regard, but France, where personal incomes were squeezed by the March austerity measures, and some smaller European OECD members experienced a weakening in private consumption demand.

Of the other major components of domestic demand, public current and investment expenditures were generally weak as governments everywhere tried (but frequently failed) to reduce their deficits. Private investment activities varied greatly from country to country; although most governments provided incentives to such investment, growth was generally disappointing.

Together with the acceleration in the overall tempo of economic activity, industrial production also was recovering. Manufacturing output rose strongly in the U.S. for the greater part of the year in response to consumer demand and a desire to rebuild inventory. The same two factors also resulted in a better performance in the U.K., but in Japan the bulk of the modest gain in industrial output was attributed to a rapid growth in exports. All in all, it was estimated that the year as a whole would yield a 1.5–2% increase.

As would be expected in times of accelerating economic growth, the level of world trade increased. On the basis of incomplete statistics, it was estimated that the volume of world trade rose 1% in 1983, representing a sharp turnaround from the 2% decline recorded in 1982. The trade of the developed world was thought to have increased a little faster, perhaps 1.2–1.5%. The overall figures, however, hid some major variations in the performance of individual countries in terms of total growth and the balance between exports and imports. OECD volume exports rose by about 1%, but the great bulk of the increase was provided by Japan, France, and Italy, where the combination of weak domestic demand and weak exchange rates resulted in strong growth. By contrast, with the exception of Canada, most countries registering a strong acceleration in GNP growth did relatively poorly in this area. For example, in the U.S., where the relative international strength of the dollar provided an additional hindrance, export volume actually fell for the year, as it also did in the U.K.

Most OECD countries (except Japan and France) recorded an increase in the volume of their imports, with the result that total imports rose faster than exports. Overall, the effect of this on the balance of payments was largely offset by the relative fall in import prices. Nevertheless, the external payments position of the U.S. deteriorated significantly and was headed for a current account deficit in 1983 of $35 billion, some four times as large as in 1982. This deficit was a source of considerable concern to other OECD members, who believed that, except for the imbalance, the U.S. authorities would have been able to allow interest rates to drop, thereby further stimulating the world economy. The U.K. also experienced weakening in its external payments position but still managed to achieve a current account surplus. At the other extreme was Japan, which, through a determined export drive and a reduction in demand for imports, was in danger of producing an annual current account surplus of $20 billion, some 3½ times larger than during the previous year. Again, this was greeted by strong criticism from Japan's trading partners and produced fresh fears of a rise in protectionist sentiment.

The degree of volatility in the foreign-exchange markets was not as marked as in 1982. The major feature of exchange rates during the year was the growing strength of the U.S. dollar. It gained ground in most major countries, with the result that its weighted average rate against a representative basket of other currencies was some 8% higher in the third quarter of 1983 than the average for 1982. The Japanese yen also did well (third quarter figure 9.5% above 1982) against most currencies except the dollar, while the French franc lost further ground and was devalued in March. The U.K. started the year off rather badly with a significant weakening in the effective rate in the opening quarter of 1983, but by the third quarter about half of the early decline had been recovered. One of the factors having an adverse effect on the international strength of sterling was the weakness of oil prices. The Deutsche Mark was relatively stable, with a modest improvement in the first half of the year being followed by a marginal weakening in subsequent months.

Table II. Percentage Changes in Consumer Prices in Selected OECD Countries

Country	1978	1979	1980	1981	1982	1983*
United States	7.7	11.3	13.5	10.4	6.1	2.9
Japan	3.8	3.6	8.0	4.9	2.7	0.7
West Germany	2.7	4.1	5.5	5.9	5.3	2.9
France	9.1	10.8	13.6	13.4	11.8	10.1
United Kingdom	8.3	13.4	18.0	11.9	8.6	5.1
Canada	8.9	9.2	10.2	12.5	10.8	5.0
Italy	12.1	14.8	21.2	19.5	16.6	13.3
Australia	7.9	9.1	10.2	9.7	11.2	9.2
Austria	3.6	3.7	6.4	6.8	5.4	3.3
Belgium	4.5	4.5	6.6	7.6	8.7	7.3
Denmark	10.0	9.6	12.3	11.7	10.1	6.0
Finland	7.8	7.5	11.6	12.0	9.3	9.4
Greece	12.6	19.0	24.9	24.5	21.0	21.3
Iceland	44.9	44.1	57.5	51.6	49.1	n.a.
Ireland	7.6	13.3	18.2	20.4	17.1	10.0
Luxembourg	3.1	4.5	6.3	8.1	9.4	8.6
Netherlands, The	4.1	4.2	6.5	6.7	5.9	2.3
New Zealand	12.0	13.8	17.1	15.4	16.1	5.4
Norway	8.1	4.8	10.9	13.6	11.3	7.8
Portugal	22.5	23.9	16.6	20.0	22.4	28.5
Spain	19.8	15.7	15.5	14.6	14.4	11.8
Sweden	10.0	7.2	13.7	12.1	8.6	9.5
Switzerland	1.1	3.6	4.0	6.5	5.6	1.4
Turkey	61.9	63.5	94.3	37.6	32.7	29.0
Total OECD countries	7.9	9.8	12.8	10.5	7.8	5.1

*Twelve-month rate of change (not directly comparable with annual changes).
Sources: OECD, *Economic Outlook*, July 1983; OECD, *Main Economic Indicators*.

In 1982 there had been a heavy strain on the world's banking system arising out of the inability of some large debtor countries to meet their obligations. During 1983, however, there was some improvement in the situation and, although it would be an exaggeration to suggest that the debt problem was overcome, there was no talk at the end of 1983 about a possible world financial collapse. Contributing to the improvement were the reduction in the current account deficits of some less developed countries and the greater control of credit to large debtors, which had the effect of reducing the rate of increase in bank lending to the less developed world.

High-grade Nigerian crude oil was aggressively priced after Britain and Norway cut the price of their crude oil in February. Nigeria's wells kept pumping, as excess gas, lacking a market, was burned off.

WILLIAM CAMPBELL/TIME MAGAZINE

NATIONAL ECONOMIC POLICIES

Developed Market Economies. UNITED STATES. Economic recovery arrived with a vengeance during 1983. Although the advance indicators had been signaling an upswing since the latter part of 1982, and official forecasts pointed confidently to a growth rate of 1.5%, the pace of economic activity turned out to be more rapid than expected and resulted in an estimated annual growth of 3.5%. This compared very favourably with the decline of 1.9% registered in 1982. The recovery was largely due to a revival in consumer spending, which in turn was encouraged by a low inflation rate and fueled by an accommodating monetary policy and an expansionary fiscal stance.

The turn of the year was also a turning point for the U.S. economy. Compared with a 1.9% decline in the GNP during the final quarter of 1982, the new year opened with a respectable 2.5% growth rate. It was accompanied by a strong upswing in personal consumption and residential investment, together with buoyant conditions in industrial production, automobile manufacturing in particular. All of this pointed to a bright prospect for the remainder of the year, soon confirmed by the second quarter's economic statistics. A frenzied growth rate of not less than 9.7% was realized, the strongest annualized quarterly growth rate since 1978. It would have been unrealistic to expect the economy to grow at the same rate during the second half, and indeed a modest deceleration to 7.7% was greeted with relief. During the final quarter the economy was expected to continue to cool off slightly, reducing the growth rate to about 6%.

Housing starts were particularly strong during the first half of the year and were nearly 80% above the corresponding period of 1982. Despite a noticeable softening in the housing market from July onward, both housing starts and new home sales activity remained comparatively buoyant. Industrial production rose strongly, too, in response to higher final demand. By October it had risen by nearly 12% from its November low, while capacity utilization in manufacturing had reached 77% (66% in December 1982). One of the main reasons for large gains in industrial production was the inability of business to restock in the face of a surge in consumer demand.

The main impetus to the upswing in personal consumption came from a strong rise in real incomes and from a reduction in savings. Personal incomes rose at an average rate of 0.5% per month during the first half of the year but shot up to 1.7% in July when the third and final installment of the Reagan administration's tax cut took effect on July 1. The tax cut injected $29 billion, at an annual rate, into the economy. Although most of the additional incomes were channeled into savings, in overall terms the ratio of savings to total income during 1983, at 4.5%, was at the lowest rate for more than a decade. Economists interpreted this decline as a sure sign that consumers had perceived that the recession was over as employment prospects improved and inflationary expectations stabilized. Personal spending (a broader measure of consumer activity than retail sales) rose 7% during the first ten months of 1983 and was expected to remain buoyant for the remainder of the year. An analysis of consumer expenditure showed that expenditures on durable goods led the way—a major beneficiary being sales of automobiles—but that in the latter part of the year spending on services and nondurable goods was also strong.

Capital spending by the business sector, a major casualty of the recession, continued to lag during 1983 despite an improvement in capacity utilization and improving corporate profitability. However, as the year drew to a close, it appeared that capital spending was set to take over from residential construction and consumer spending as the main engine of economic recovery.

The decline in unemployment was quite remarkable. The rate of unemployment hit a peak of 10.8% in December 1982, and the official projections, thought to be optimistic at the time, pointed to a level of 8.5% by the end of 1985. After an erratic improvement during the first half, which resulted in the unemployment rate's falling to 9.5% in August, it gathered momentum and by October stood at 8.8%, within a whisper of the 1985 target. By that time some 2.8 million more Americans were employed than had been in December 1982.

Despite the rapid economic growth, inflation, which had been brought under control during 1982, did not show the usual tendency to surge ahead at the first sign of economic improvement. True, the annual rate of inflation, having dropped to 2.4% in July, the lowest since 1966, rose mildly thereafter. The underlying long-term trend ap-

CHART 2

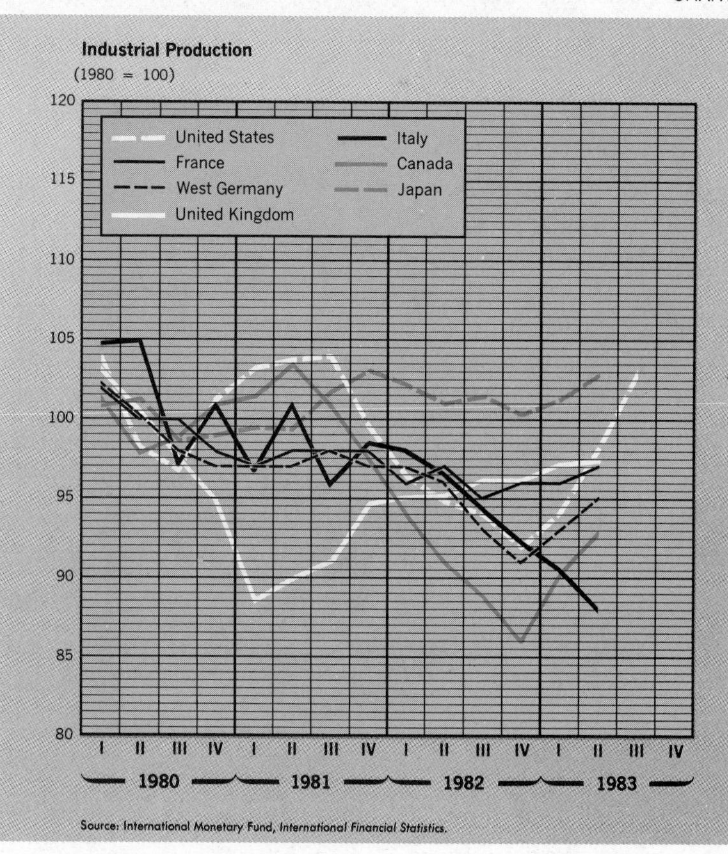

peared to be stable, in the 4–4.5% per annum range. Stable oil prices, a strong dollar, and a modest rise in wages (up by 3.9% in the 12 months to September 1983) all contributed to keeping the lid on inflation.

One worrisome feature of the U.S. economy during the year was the widening trade deficit. In response to the vigorous recovery and the strength of the dollar, the trade deficit widened to $63 billion for the first eleven months of 1983, and a current account deficit of about $35 billion seemed highly likely.

In contrast to the previous year, during 1983 the Federal Reserve Board (Fed) followed a tolerant and pragmatic monetary policy despite a rapid expansion in the monetary aggregates (M1 and M2). This was in keeping with its announcement during the previous October that it was modifying the monetary policy techniques in use since 1979. That policy, introduced in the midst of a U.S. currency and inflation crisis, focused on controlling money supply through managing bank reserves directly rather than through the Federal Funds Rate (overnight interbank interest rates). Soaring and widely fluctuating interest rates (over 20%) and a deep recession were some of the fruits of that new monetary stringency. Taking advantage of a strong dollar and success in halving the inflation rate to 6%, the Fed decided that in the future it would be placing less emphasis on short-term monetary aggregates (M1). Broader measures of money supply (M2) and the state of the real economy were to assume a greater role.

CHART 3

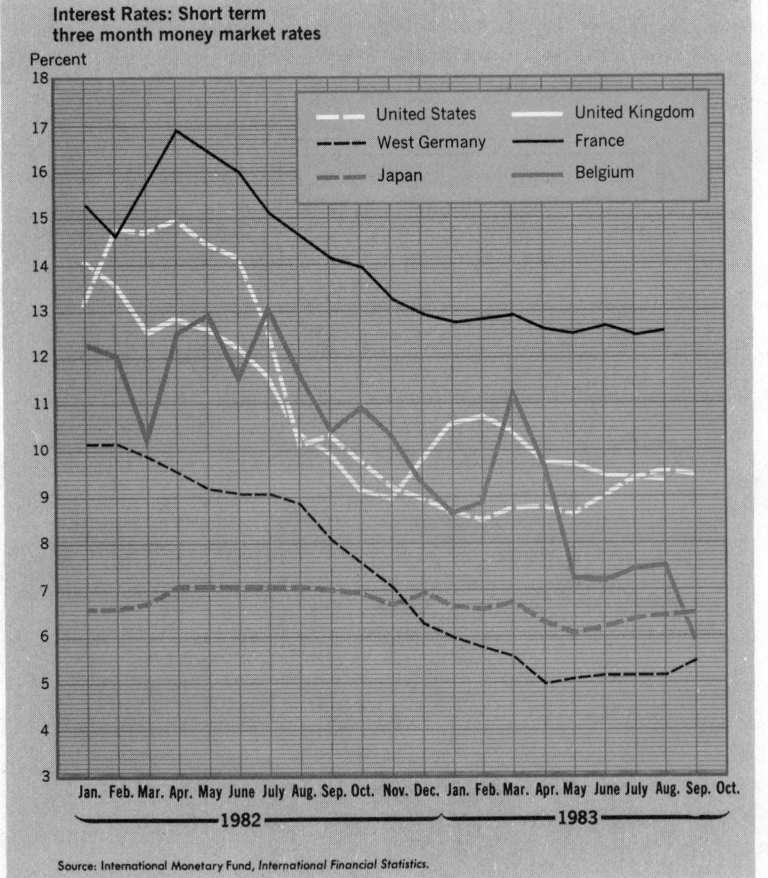

Table III. Standardized Unemployment Rates in Selected OECD Countries

% of total labour force, seasonally adjusted

Country	1978	1979	1980	1981	1982	1983*
Australia	6.2	6.2	6.0	5.7	7.1	10.0
Canada	8.3	7.4	7.5	7.5	10.9	11.0
France	5.2	5.9	6.3	7.3	8.0	8.2
West Germany	3.5	3.2	3.0	4.4	6.1	8.2
Italy	7.1	7.5	7.4	8.3	8.9	9.5
Japan	2.2	2.1	2.0	2.2	2.4	2.8
Sweden	2.2	2.1	2.0	2.5	3.1	3.9
United Kingdom	6.3	5.6	7.0	10.7	12.5	13.0
United States	5.9	5.7	7.0	7.5	9.5	9.0

*Partially estimated.
Source: OECD, *Main Economic Indicators.*

This flexible monetary stance enabled interest rates, which had begun falling swiftly in the latter part of 1982, to remain soft during the first half of 1983 against a backdrop of an economic upswing and a rapid acceleration in the monetary aggregates. However, during the summer the Fed cautiously tightened the financial reins in order to moderate possible inflationary pressures arising from the second quarter's torrid economic growth. Tnis immediately gave rise to fears of a monetary squeeze and pushed up the yields on a wide range of securities by nearly two percentage points. In the autumn, as the money supply slowed (but still remained outside the upper end of the range), coupled with evidence that the economy was cooling off without further restrictive measures from the Fed, short-term rates returned to the spring levels. One disappointing feature of U.S. interest rates was that, in comparison with progress made on the inflation front, nominal interest rates remained sticky, giving rise to a historically high real interest rate of between 6 and 7%.

The Reagan administration's continuing budget deficits explain in part why interest rates did not come down further. The budget deficit for fiscal 1983 (ended on Sept. 30, 1983) was officially estimated at $195,350,000,000, some $20 billion higher than the revised amount expected at the beginning of the fiscal year. A budget deficit of about 7% of the GNP with little or no real improvement in prospect for the foreseeable future worried many economists. They feared that as private-sector borrowing gathered pace in the wake of the economic upturn – and given the low level of savings in the economy – the budget deficit would lead to higher interest rates unless the government took urgent steps to raise taxes and introduce other measures to reduce it. They feared that this, in turn, would curtail investment, damage exports, and probably lead the economy into another recession.

The administration took a more sanguine view, no doubt influenced by the forthcoming presidential election in 1984, though it did concede that deficits did matter. It pointed to the 1984 budget, which envisioned a sweeping reduction in government expenditures (except defense) and increased taxes on payroll, energy, and medical benefits over the next five years. Given the strength of the economic recovery and a stable inflation rate,

President Reagan judged that on balance there was probably sufficient slack in the economy and that the risk of an overheated economy was more acceptable than a stagnation caused by restrictive measures.

JAPAN. Although Japan recorded a respectable growth by international standards during 1983, it was one of the few major advanced countries that failed to achieve a significant improvement over the previous year. In fact, as the year drew to a close, there were some fears that the final result would be real GNP growth of no more than 2.8–2.9%, compared with a 3% advance recorded in 1982. This comparatively poor performance was due to two major factors: the government's inability to provide any worthwhile fiscal stimulus owing to the already high degree of deficit financing, and the Bank of Japan's reluctance—maintained until October 1983—to reduce the official discount rate for fear of weakening the already weak yen/dollar exchange rate. As a result domestic demand was left largely to its own devices and became increasingly sluggish as the year went on, although a considerable part of this weakness was offset by stronger exports. As a result unemployment rose somewhat, although the rate of 2.51% (registered in July) remained extremely low by international standards. The relative weakness of demand and weak oil prices secured a further deceleration in inflation with the result that the average consumer price level for the first three quarters of the year was only 0.2% over 1982, a year in which the rate of consumer price inflation was 2.7%.

During the last few months of 1982 there was a sudden and unexpected weakening in the tempo of economic activity. This confirmed earlier fears that domestic demand was running out of steam and resulted in considerable doubt and skepticism over the chances of achieving the official growth target of 3.4% for the 1983–84 fiscal year (ending in March 1984). The government, however, refused to take any action, pinning its hopes on the delayed effects of the modest package of measures announced during the previous October. The most important element of this package was an increase in public works spending; however, because of the need to contain the growing deficit, a substantial part of the effect of this increase was offset by the December supplementary budget, which provided for a reduction in public expenditure in the first quarter of 1983.

Not surprisingly, the year opened with an annualized quarterly GDP growth of only 0.9%, brought about by a fall in the level of both private and public investments and by a sharp slowdown in the growth of consumer expenditure. Industrial production recorded a 1% decline from the corresponding period of 1982, and the capacity utilization ratio index fell by some 2%. Business expectations were further depressed by a fairly cautious budget, which, by providing for an increase of only 1.4% in general expenditure and a rise of 2% in the Treasury's loan and investment program, was expected to have an overall deflationary effect. Even this, however, implied a heavy reliance on the issue of national bonds (accounting for 27.6% of the general accounts budget), which was seen as putting a serious strain on domestic financial markets.

Faced with this weakening outlook, in April the authorities brought forward yet another "business supporting package." However, as with previous such efforts, it was drawn up under the constraints of a weak yen and the need to prevent a rapid expansion in the scope of deficit financing. Consequently, the package did not amount to much; its principal feature was a concentration of public works expenditure into the first half of the year, a measure that had been a standard feature of economic policy for several years and had not proved to be particularly effective. Nevertheless, during the April–June quarter it provided a boost to public investment outlays, which, together with a sharp improvement in the country's export performance, provided some stimulus to demand. The growth of consumer expenditure, however, fell back, largely because of the modest 4.4% wage increase received during the spring labour offensive and because of the government's failure to include a reduction in personal taxation in its April package. This was all the more disappointing because there was widespread agreement on the need for tax reform; it was generally accepted that consumer expenditure was unlikely to grow without a reduction in the burden of personal taxation. During the April–June quarter there was also a staggering 44% reduction in housing investment. All in all, therefore, the growth of domestic demand was relatively weak, contributing only about one-third of the overall annualized increase in GNP of 3.6%.

The idea of exports taking over as the engine of economic growth was regarded with some concern, largely because of the adverse international consequences (in particular the growth of protectionism) associated with a sharp improvement in Japan's trade and current account balances. During the first half of the year the current account surplus was some five times as large as it had been in the same period of 1982, and the signs were that

DAN WASSERMAN/LOS ANGELES TIMES SYNDICATE

without an upturn in domestic demand the gap would become even wider.

In the third quarter there appeared to be a better balance between the domestic and external components of demand. However, the underlying trend of the former was still judged to be too weak, while that of the latter continued to be regarded as inconsistent with the country's desired international image. It was largely because of these considerations that the authorities decided to bring in yet another package of economic measures in October. This time, however, the package was expected to provide an effective stimulus to growth in the medium term. Its key feature was an income-tax cut of some one trillion yen to stimulate private consumption (and thereby increase demand for imported products). There was also an increase in public works outlays of 1,880,000,000,000 yen, as well as the long-awaited reduction (the first for 22 months) in the Bank of Japan's discount rate from 5.5 to 5%. In an attempt to ensure that this did not weaken the yen, a number of measures were taken to encourage the inflow of capital. At the same time, in order to reinforce the import-boosting effect of stronger private consumption as well as to placate foreign critics of Japanese trading practices, some import duties were reduced.

UNITED KINGDOM. In common with most other advanced countries, the United Kingdom experienced an improvement in its economic fortunes during 1983. In part this was the result of a cautious and largely successful balancing act by the government between a determined anti-inflationary stance and a comparatively relaxed fiscal and monetary policy. More important, however, was the stimulating effect of the recovery in other major countries, notably the United States. By the end of 1983 the advance indicators pointed to a real growth in GDP of nearly 3%, compared with a gain of 1.8% in 1982 and a decline of 2.6% in 1981. Particularly encouraging was the fact that this upturn was achieved without a corresponding acceleration in the rate of inflation: the index of retail prices, which recorded an increase of 8.9% for 1982, was expected to rise only about 5%.

Toward the end of the year the recovery in output was also beginning to have a small but highly welcome effect on unemployment. Although the percentage of the labour force without a job rose between the final quarter of 1982 and the opening months of 1983, by the spring there were signs that the increase was leveling off, and by late autumn there were indications of a modest downward movement. Thus, by December the rate of unemployment was 12.9% (equivalent to 3,080,000). This was a modest improvement from the peak of 13.8% registered in January. Therefore, whereas 1982 closed on a note of uncertainty and doubt about the government's ability to engineer a substantial upturn in the economy, 1983 ended with a general feeling of confidence that the recovery was in full swing.

As in 1982 the authorities followed a policy of "pragmatic monetarism," a policy that maintained the fight against inflation and the control of public spending and borrowing as the basic objectives but that also recognized the need to encourage the tender signs of the recovery. During the first half of the year economic decision making was largely overshadowed by widespread speculation about the date of the general election and by Prime Minister Margaret Thatcher's subsequent decision to seek a new five-year mandate from the country in June. In order to preserve its options with regard to the date of the election, the government brought in a relatively early budget in March. By providing for a reduction in personal income taxation and some other tax concessions not fully offset by higher duties on gasoline, cigarettes, and alcohol, this was seen to be mildly reflationary, especially as far as personal disposable incomes were concerned. At the same time, the principal monetary targets were left unchanged (money supply growth 7–11%, public-sector borrowing requirement 2.75% of GDP); because of the reduced rate of inflation this implied a relaxation in official policy.

Following its resounding election victory in June, the government announced steps to cut back public expenditure. However, because these were prompted by a faster than expected growth in previous months, they were regarded as a corrective move to get back to the budget strategy rather than as a tightening in the underlying fiscal stance of the authorities. In fact, the chancellor of the Exchequer was not wholly successful in getting back to the original projections, and by October it was publicly conceded that the public-sector borrowing requirement for the year would exceed the target of £8,000 million by as much as £2,000 million.

Reflecting the comparatively relaxed conditions, interest rates, which had showed some

Table IV. Changes in Output in the Less Developed Countries, 1968–82

% changes

Area	Annual average 1968–72	Change from preceding year 1978	1979	1980	1981	1982
All less developed countries	6.0*	5.2	5.2	4.6	2.0	1.9
Major oil-exporting countries†	9.0	2.0	3.1	−2.3	−4.3	−4.8
Non-oil less developed countries‡	5.9	6.3	5.0	4.8	2.5	1.7
Median	4.9	5.6	4.5	3.5	3.0	2.2
Africa‡	4.8	2.2	2.3	4.4	2.9	1.1
Asia‡	4.5	7.9	3.3	3.4	5.8	3.7
Europe‡	6.0	5.4	3.9	1.5	2.2	2.0
Middle East‡	7.5	7.4	4.3	7.3	4.7	2.7
Western Hemisphere	7.6	4.5	6.7	6.0	−0.1	−1.5

*1960–73 average.
†Comprises Algeria, Indonesia, Iran, Iraq, Kuwait, Libya, Nigeria, Oman, Qatar, Saudi Arabia, United Arab Emirates, and Venezuela.
‡Weighted average.
Source: Adapted from IMF, *Annual Report 1983;* World Bank, *Annual Report 1983.*

Table V. Changes in Consumer Prices in the Less Developed Countries, 1968–82

% changes

Area	Annual average 1968–72	Change from preceding year 1978	1979	1980	1981	1982
Major oil-exporting countries*†	8.0	9.8	10.9	12.7	12.9	9.8
Non-oil less developed countries†‡	9.1	23.4	28.8	36.5	36.5	38.3
Africa	4.6	15.9	19.3	20.1	22.0	15.8
Asia‡	6.5	5.6	9.8	15.9	14.8	9.9
Europe	6.1	19.7	25.9	37.8	24.3	23.8
Middle East	4.3	21.7	26.0	43.4	35.3	37.6
Western Hemisphere	15.3	42.4	49.6	58.2	65.4	78.0

*Comprises Algeria, Indonesia, Iran, Iraq, Kuwait, Libya, Nigeria, Oman, Qatar, Saudi Arabia, United Arab Emirates, and Venezuela.
†Weighted average.
‡Excluding China.
Source: Adapted from IMF, *Annual Report 1983.*

signs of hardening at the beginning of the year, were allowed to fall in subsequent months. In part this reflected the trend of interest rates in the U.S., but it was also symptomatic of the government's determination not to risk slowing down the recovery. As a result there was a fairly steady downward trend in the base rate of the London clearing banks; by November this was down to 9%, as against 11% at the start of the year. In real terms, however, there was no decrease; on the contrary, given the fall in the rate of inflation, the real cost of borrowing money increased.

During 1983 the most buoyant area of demand was consumer expenditure, which was expected to register an annual real increase of some 3–3.5% as against an advance of only 1.3% in 1982. This was the result of easier credit, declining inflation, tax concessions in the budget, and a reduction in the amounts saved; the savings ratio, which stood at 10.8% in 1982, was estimated to be 8.5% at the end of 1983. Despite the continuing emphasis on restraining the growth of public spending, current government expenditure rose faster than in the previous year; toward the end of 1983 the estimated increase was about 2.5%, compared with a gain of 1.4% in 1982. Fixed investment, however, was weaker than expected; although there was a good recovery in both public and private residential construction, capital spending by industry was thought to have fallen by 2%. This was the result of continuing overcapacity in many key areas of manufacturing as well as a sharp contraction in investment in oil exploration and production activities. All in all, therefore, fixed investments for the year as a whole were expected to rise by approximately 2.5%, only about half the rate chalked up in 1982.

The greatest disappointment of the year was the failure of exports to take full advantage of the upturn in world economic activity. Export performance was generally sluggish throughout the year, and the indications in late 1983 were pointing to an annual volume growth of only some 0.5%, compared with an increase of over 2% in 1982. The reasons for the poor outcome were regarded as something of a mystery, especially as the beneficial effects of the world recovery should have been boosted by the improvement in the competitiveness of U.K. exporters arising out of the weakening in the sterling exchange rate. Partly in response to weak oil prices and the government's refusal to prop up interest rates, sterling lost considerable ground against the U.S. dollar, starting with £1 = $1.57 in January 1983 and falling back to about £1 = $1.48 by late November. The movement against other major currencies, however, was in the opposite direction, with the result that sterling's effective exchange rate against a representative basket of currencies remained largely unchanged between the end of 1982 and November 1983. Unlike exports, imports recorded a relatively rapid growth of 4.6% in volume terms. Partly as a result of these developments, the surplus on the current account of the balance of payments was estimated to have fallen from £5,428 million in 1982 to about £1,600 million, the worst performance since 1979.

An encouraging feature of the year was the sharp decline in the rate of wage increases and a reduction in the number of days lost through strikes and other industrial action. This was largely the consequence of the large-scale unemployment, which reduced the bargaining power of organized labour, and also the strong stance adopted by most public employers in wage negotiations. The effect of these could be seen in the fall in the rate of wage increases during the first nine months of the year to 8.3% from 10.3% in the same period of 1982 and a reduction of 37% in the number of working days lost. One consequence of this (and of the high level of unemployment) was a significant improvement in labour productivity; in the first half of 1983 manufacturing output per head was 5.6% higher than it had been 12 months previously. Thus, although 1983 was a year of uneven achievement, it produced a better all-round performance than any other since 1975.

West Germany. After two years of decline, the West German economy stabilized during 1983 and was estimated to have expanded by about 1% in real terms. Progress was also made in further reducing the inflation rate, and gains made in the current account of the balance of payments were consolidated. Yet 1983 was regarded generally as a difficult year in economic terms. Owing to a number of unfavourable external developments, including high interest rates in the U.S. and realignment within the European Monetary System, the West German economy had to run fast to stand still.

For the first time since World War II the economic recovery was led by domestic demand rather than by exports. Spurred by lower interest and inflation rates, as well as by the change in government the previous autumn, domestic consumption forged ahead. Retail sales during the first nine months of the year expanded by nearly 5.5%. Sales

JEAN-CLAUDE FRANCOLON—GAMMA/LIAISON

A Gallic approach to slowing imports: the French government ruled in November 1982 that all Japanese and other foreign-made video tape recorders must enter the country through the small, sparsely staffed customs depot at Poitiers.

of consumer durables were particularly strong, enabling retailers to reduce inventories and swell the manufacturers' order books. Demand for investment goods, which got off to a poor start, staged a slight recovery later in the year, leading to hopes that it would take over from consumption in fostering economic upturn. The construction industry, benefiting from special government aid, experienced considerable buoyancy; steel, shipbuilding, and heavy engineering remained dull.

As in most other countries, inflationary pressures continued to abate. This improvement was all the more satisfactory because it was from a low base of 5%. Thanks to encouraging modest wage settlements, in the 2.5–3.2% range, and to lower interest rates, inflation during the first ten months dropped to an annual rate of 2.5%. Although there was a gentle upward shift in the curve in the autumn, this did not amount to much, and the annual increase from 1982 was likely to be about 3%. Unemployment, however, continued to lag behind the economic upswing. In October the seasonally unadjusted number of unemployed stood at just below 3.2 million, representing 9.3% of the work force, compared with just under 2 million a year earlier. One encouraging aspect of the unemployment figure was that in the second half of the year the average monthly rise slowed consistently. However, there was only limited improvement in the total labour market, underlining the grim fact that it would take a number of years of fast economic growth—at least 4% per year—to achieve a sustained fall in unemployment.

While an export boom was never considered to be a likely outcome during the year, the decline of about 2% in nominal terms was disappointing. West German exporters failed to benefit from the buoyant U.S. economy despite a 10% weakening in the Deutsche Mark against the dollar, partly because traditionally they were not geared to exporting to the dollar area. Imports, on the other hand, reflecting the strong domestic demand and the adverse currency movements, were on a gently rising trend. The result was a smaller (DM 5 billion) trade surplus for the year as a whole compared with the previous year. At the same time, there was a smaller deficit on invisibles, enabling the nation's current account to achieve a slightly better surplus than 1982.

The fiscal policy of the government remained broadly unchanged after the March election. Its goal of reducing public spending and borrowing and, in the longer term, switching the focus of government spending away from current to capital outlays was reaffirmed. The goal of the 1983 budget was to maintain the federal deficit at about the 1982 level, and the authorities seemed to have met with considerable success in accomplishing this (DM 41.5 billion, or 2½% of GNP). A lower than expected deficit was achieved in total public-sector deficit (which includes federal government, local authorities, and state governments). To gain these favourable results a number of unpleasant measures, such as higher value-added tax rates, compulsory interest-free savings from high earners, and higher social security contributions, had to be introduced. Budget cuts and revenue-raising measures were partly counterbalanced by investment incentives in the form of corporate tax relief, tax allowances, and interest subsidies for housing construction.

Table VI. Balances of Payments on Current Account, 1979–83

In $000,000,000

Area	1979	1980	1981	1982	1983*
Industrial countries	−5.5	−40.2	−0.3	−3.6	16.0
Less developed countries					
Oil-exporting countries	68.6	114.3	65.0	−2.2	−27.0
Non-oil countries	−61.0	−89.0	−107.7	−86.8	−68.0
Africa	−9.9	−12.9	−14.0	−13.2	−13.5
Asia	−14.8	−24.3	−22.2	−15.6	−17.5
Europe	−9.9	−12.5	−10.5	−7.1	−4.0
Middle East	−8.5	−9.4	−11.1	−12.9	−12.0
Western Hemisphere	−21.4	−33.4	−45.4	−34.9	−21.5
Total	2.1	−14.9	−43.0	−92.6	−79.0

*IMF projection.
Source: Adapted from IMF, *Annual Report 1983*.

In the second half of 1982, as inflationary pressures eased and the current account returned to surplus, the Bundesbank eased the monetary restrictions and thereby enabled interest rates to fall. The same mildly expansionary policy continued during 1983. In the spring the discount and the Lombard rates were lowered by 1% to 4 and 5%, respectively. The Bundesbank's 1983 monetary target was set within the 4–7% range, and to encourage economic recovery it was intended to allow money supply to expand at the upper end of the range. For nearly nine months the Bundesbank tolerated an annualized money expansion of nearly 10%, partly because the figures were distorted by speculative inflows arising from changes in the European Monetary System in March. The weakness of the Deutsche Mark against the dollar and the continuing outflow of capital lured by higher interest rates available elsewhere finally forced the Bundesbank's hand. In September the Lombard rate was raised by 0.5%, signaling a slight tightening in the monetary policy. The authorities then were faced with the difficult problem of balancing the risks of higher interest rates that might choke off the fledgling recovery with rapid expansion in money supply that might rekindle inflation. As the year drew to a close, it appeared that the Bundesbank had learned to walk the tightrope.

France. The French economy was once again out of step with the other major countries and registered a zero growth rate during 1983. This was hardly surprising given the additional deflation imposed in March on top of the restrictive measures adopted in 1982. Thus, little of the original social aims of the government of Pres. François Mitterrand remained, while the improvements in the trade deficit and the rate of inflation continued to be somewhat disappointing. The austerity program seemed likely to continue well into 1984, dashing hopes of an early upswing.

Even before the March measures were felt, overall economic activity during the first half of the year was stagnant, with GDP showing virtually zero growth. Partial data for the next two quarters indicated a fairly steep decline of nearly 0.6% before it bottomed out in the final quarter. The main reason for the stagnation in GDP growth was the rapid deceleration in demand, particularly private consumption. Retail sales in the first ten months declined by more than 2%, and at the year's end the trend was still pointing sharply downward. Other components of domestic demand were also weak; gross fixed investment was expected to decline by nearly 3% after a 5% decline in 1982.

Despite the overall weakness of the economy, industrial output fared better, with an estimated increase of 3%. Part of the increase was due to an upturn in car production, which was hit by strikes in 1982; an involuntary building of inventories was also evident as demand collapsed. A slight improvement in the chemical and rubber sectors took place in response to an encouraging trend for industrial exports. The combination of depressed demand and a weak currency was reflected in lower imports, which in volume terms declined by almost 2%. By contrast, the successive devaluations of the French franc, coupled with buoyant economic conditions among France's major trade partners, produced a minor export boom (volume growth of nearly 8%). Both the trade deficit and the current account deficit improved, taking some of the pressure off the balance of payments and, for the time being, the franc. A trade deficit of Fr 50 billion, well within the government's target of Fr 60 billion, was widely predicted.

Progress on the inflation front was slow. Despite widespread skepticism, France's inflation rate was reduced to just under 10% by December 1982. The prices and incomes policy introduced in November 1982 to succeed the earlier price freeze remained in force during 1983. The official target called for a reduction in the inflation rate to 8%. During the first four months of the year, however, the inflation rate rose to 12%, reflecting the weakness of the franc and higher unit labour costs. After that, the inflationary pressures subsided somewhat, enabling inflation to return to single-digit levels. Although the government drew some comfort from this improvement, the inflation rate remained above the official target and was still rising at over twice the average rate of neighbouring European countries.

Table VII. Industrial Production in Eastern Europe

1975 = 100

Country	1978	1979	1980	1981	1982
Bulgaria	122	128	134	142	147
Czechoslovakia	117	121	125	128	127
East Germany	116	121	127	133	137
Hungary	117	120	118	121	124
Poland	122	126	125	111	108
Romania	...	...	...	...	...
U.S.S.R.	116	120	124	129	132

Source: UN, *Monthly Bulletin of Statistics.*

Table VIII. Foreign Trade of Eastern Europe

In $000,000

	Exports			Imports		
Country	1980	1981	1982	1980	1981	1982
Bulgaria	10,372	10,685	...	9,650	10,800	...
Czechoslovakia	14,891	14,887	18,443	15,148	14,650	18,724
East Germany	17,312	...	...	19,082	...	...
Hungary	8,677	8,712	8,795	9,285	9,128	8,825
Poland	16,998	13,249	10,552	18,871	15,475	9,655
Romania	12,230	12,610	...	13,201	12,458	...
U.S.S.R.	76,481	...	...	65,523	...	...

Source: UN, *Monthly Bulletin of Statistics.*

The French policymakers intended to continue with the restrictive fiscal policies introduced the year before so as to reduce the budget and trade account deficits. However, additional deflationary measures had to be introduced in March, accompanied by a devaluation of the franc within the European Monetary System. This was the third devaluation since Mitterrand's Socialist government came to power. While the main objective of the austerity measures introduced in June 1982 was to contain and reduce the inflationary pressures in the economy, the main objective of the spring 1983 measures was to reduce the unstable trade and balance of payments deficits. By the year's end reasonable progress had been made toward reaching the main goal of reducing the central government deficit to about 3% of GDP.

By and large, monetary policy was in tune with the restrictive fiscal stance. The target for the M2 growth rate was initially set at 10%, compared with 12.5–13.5% in 1982, but it was reduced to 9% in March to take account of the expected reduction in government borrowing. Despite the abundance of credit controls, total bank lending for the year as a whole was likely to have expanded by around 13%. This was a substantial deceleration from the previous year's 17%. The weakness of the franc, coupled with high interest rates in the U.S., prevented interest rates from declining noticeably. Although long-term interest rates fell by nearly 1% during 1983, prime lending rates declined by less than 0.5%. Despite the short-term success of the restrictive fiscal and monetary policies, as 1983 came to an end there was as yet no measurable headroom for an economic recovery.

Less Developed Countries. Economic growth in the less developed countries was hampered by the continuing recession among the industrialized nations. Two major problems were weak demand from the developed world, which led to lower prices and reduced purchases for primary commodities, and high interest rates. These two adverse factors led to severe balance of payments problems, forcing many countries to follow deflationary economic policies.

OUTPUT. According to World Bank estimates, during 1982 (the latest year available) economic growth in all less developed countries taken as a group deteriorated slightly to about 1.9% from the already poor performance of 2.09% registered the year before. Thus, for the second straight year the actual growth rate was less than half the medium-term average (1973–80) of 4.8% per annum. However, the preliminary indications were that there was a noticeable improvement in 1983. A gentle upswing in the world economy led by the U.S., a moderation in the high interest rates, and steady oil prices created a more favourable external environment. However, it remained doubtful whether growth equaled or exceeded the medium/long-term averages.

With the exception of high-income oil-exporting countries of the Middle East, there was little variation in the economic performance of the oil-importing and oil-exporting less developed countries. All experienced a slight decrease in the level of economic activity. The high-income oil-exporting group suffered a severe setback as economic growth during 1982 declined by nearly 12%, compared with a relatively small decline of 1.8% in 1981. This was a direct result of reduced world demand for oil and consequent cuts in price. Predictably, the impact was greatest in the oil sectors of the economies of those nations. The International Monetary Fund (IMF) estimated a fall in output of 16.5%. But the non-oil sectors were also adversely influenced, with growth in output slowing down to 3.6% from 5% in 1981. Thanks to considerable diversification in the economies of those countries, the overall impact was cushioned.

Among the oil-importing group, East Asian countries went against the trend and achieved high economic growth rates. The World Bank attributed this to their more flexible economies, which enabled them to cope better with the adverse international conditions. However, even in those countries growth during 1982 was well below the historical trend.

CONSUMER PRICES. The average annual rate of inflation among the non-oil less developed countries remained above 30% for the third year in a row. In contrast to the industrialized world, the trend during 1982 and the early part of 1983 was distinctly upward. The IMF attributed this poor performance to a small number of large countries in the Western Hemisphere with unusually high inflation rates exerting a pronounced adverse effect on the average. The movements in median inflation rates, on the other hand, show that the improvement in the inflation rate that started in 1980 (when it stood at 15%) continued and that in 1982 it dropped to 11.5%. Best progress was in the Asian region, where the median inflation rate fell to 7.9% in 1982 from 13.4% the year before. According to the IMF the continuing high rates of inflation in the non-oil countries resulted from the need to accommodate fiscal and monetary policies of the previous few years, which resulted in rapid expansion in money supply. The resulting upward pressure on domestic prices was reinforced by currency depreciations that were necessitated by the balance of payments problems.

The oil-exporting group also experienced a moderation in the inflation rate. The weighted average rate declined to 9.8% in 1982, compared with 12.9% in 1981. Cautious financial policies and the strength of those nations' currencies were the main stabilizing factors.

TRADE POSITION. The current account surplus of the oil-exporting countries disappeared during 1982, and a deficit was likely during 1983. Only three years earlier, in 1980, their current account surplus had stood at a record $114 billion, thanks to the second major hike in the oil price. The rapid turnaround was a direct result of lower demand for oil, leading to greatly reduced export earnings. Although there was an across-the-board reduction in imports in response to declining export revenues, there was considerable variation among the individual countries. Small countries with strong reserve positions were able to ride it out without significant adjustment to import programs.

The lot of the non-oil-exporting countries was much harder. They experienced lower export revenues as well as diminished opportunities for borrowing from international capital markets. As their level of economic activity stagnated, a slight improvement in their current account position emerged. During 1982 the current account deficit of this group declined to $86.8 billion, compared with the previous year's record deficit of $107.7 billion. A further improvement to about $68 billion during 1983 was expected by the IMF.

Confronted by the continuing decline in their export revenues, both oil-exporting and non-oil-exporting countries had to adopt restrictive financial policies. Those countries that relied heavily on international borrowings had to adjust even more quickly so as to give their creditors greater confidence that they would be able to stay within the terms of their debt agreements. This was no easy task, given the high interest rates and heavy repayment obligations arising from the short-term nature of many of the commercial loan agreements concluded over the past three to five years.

Centrally Planned Economies. The 37th plenary session of the Council for Mutual Economic Assistance (CMEA or Comecon) was held in East Berlin on Oct. 18–20, 1983. This council session, in which premiers of the member countries partici-

CHART 4

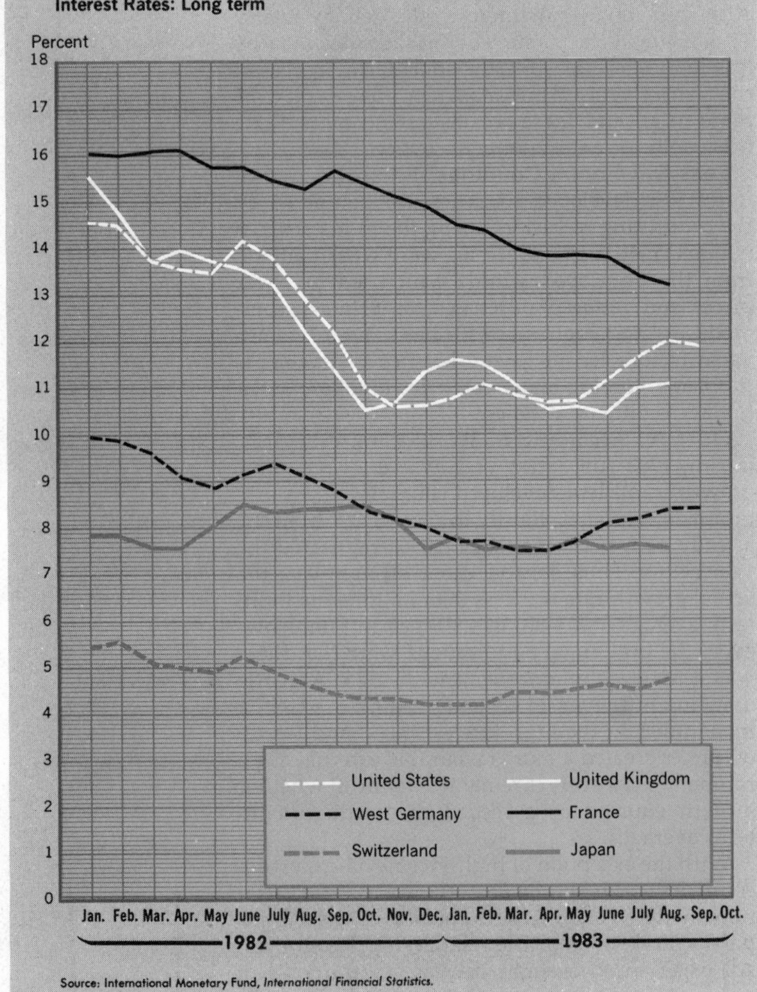

Source: International Monetary Fund, *International Financial Statistics.*

Table IX. Output of Basic Industrial Products in Eastern Europe, 1982

In 000 metric tons except for natural gas and electric power

Country	Anthracite (hard coal)	Lignite (brown coal)	Natural gas (000,000 cu m)	Crude petroleum	Electric power (000,000 kw-hr)	Steel	Sulfuric acid	Cement
Bulgaria	240	31,994	...	...	40,440	2,592	891.6	5,616
Czechoslovakia	...	...	...	...	...	14,988	1,252.8	10,320
East Germany	...	...	...	...	...	7,164	948.0	11,724
Hungary	3,036	23,040	250,908	2,028	24,528	3,708	568.8	4,368
Poland	189,360	37,644	191,796	...	117,564	14,472	2,682.0	16,032
Romania	...	...	...	...	...	...	...	...
U.S.S.R.	...	...	...	...	...	...	...	...

Source: UN, *Monthly Bulletin of Statistics.*

pate, is the most important annual event for the CMEA, although its main powers are largely undefined. The council makes recommendations and defines the main directions of the organization's activities. It is up to the governments of the member countries to implement them. As of 1983 the CMEA comprised ten full members: the U.S.S.R., Bulgaria, Cuba, Czechoslovakia, East Germany, Hungary, Mongolia, Poland, Romania, and Vietnam. Yugoslavia had a "limited participation status," while Angola, Afghanistan, Ethiopia, Mozambique, and Yemen (Aden) had observer status. In 1983 for the first time a Nicaraguan delegation took part in the session.

At the end of the session a final communiqué was announced. It stated that, in spite of worsening external conditions, additional growth of national income was achieved and the welfare of the working people was improving.

One important multilateral agreement was signed. It involved a joint project in the building of the Krivoi Rog iron-ore processing plant in the U.S.S.R. The signatories to the agreement were the Soviet Union, Czechoslovakia, East Germany, and Hungary. The CMEA premiers deplored the renewed escalation of the arms race, claiming that it would adversely affect the people's standard of living. In spite of the fairly optimistic tone of the final communiqué, it was clear that the CMEA countries had entered a difficult period both politically and economically.

The postponement of the plenary session from its usual time in June to October was caused by basic disagreements as to the joint policy that should be adopted in solving mutual problems, as well as by the lack of clear guidance from the U.S.S.R. For a few years many member countries, including the U.S.S.R., had been demanding a summit meeting at which not only the premiers but also top Communist Party leaders, who hold the real power in those nations, would take part. It was argued that only in this way could major problems be resolved. Various preparations for such a meeting were undertaken, but at the end of 1983 no date had been agreed on.

The 37th plenary session took place in a more frank atmosphere than many previous ones. The most outspoken in his criticism of CMEA practices was Romanian Premier Constantin Dascalescu. He claimed that the main task of the CMEA was to provide member countries with enough fuels, energy, and raw materials to meet their basic requirements and that this should be done on the basis of rational norms and levels of consumption per inhabitant that should not differ much from one country to another. Soviet Premier Nikolay A. Tikhonov answered this statement by saying, "It is understandable that our possibilities in many ways are dependent on the amounts of products essential for the Soviet economy which are delivered by other CMEA countries."

The problem of oil deliveries from the Soviet Union to other CMEA countries was probably the most difficult to resolve. In spite of recent price increases the U.S.S.R. continued to sell its oil to CMEA countries at prices below world market rates. But the deliveries were based on strict quotas that recently had been cut. Tikhonov's speech contained a clear warning that these deliveries would not be increased in the foreseeable future and could be cut even further if the U.S.S.R.'s Eastern European partners did not fulfill the deliveries of their industrial products to the Soviet Union.

It was also clear from various speeches delivered at the session that no agreement on a joint economic policy was achieved. There also were notable differences in the assessment of relations with the West. Both Tikhonov and Czechoslovakia's Premier Lubomir Strougal spoke about discriminatory practices by the West in regard to trade and economic cooperation, while Hungarian Premier Gyorgy Lazar and Dascalescu mentioned only a complex situation in world trade. The latter also emphasized their willingness to keep their markets open to Western countries while at the same time continuing the CMEA program of self-reliance.

Poland's Premier Wojciech Jaruzelski understandably kept a low profile at the session. Poland's economic and political problems were far from being resolved, and no joint CMEA rescue package was envisioned. Nevertheless, the consequences of the Polish crisis continued to be felt severely by other CMEA countries, and Poland was constantly getting various forms of credits and subsidies, mostly from the U.S.S.R. Generally, the terms of trade within CMEA were not favourable for the U.S.S.R. The main causes for this were the artificially low price for Soviet oil and the poor quality of Eastern European goods exported to the U.S.S.R. On the other hand, the U.S.S.R., as the main supplier of fuels and raw materials to its Eastern European partners, had a powerful leverage over them and used this to its own political advantage.

While most of the European members of the CMEA made some progress in reducing their indebtedness to the West, the overall economic picture was one of stagnation. There was no joint approach to solving the problem on a regional basis. The whole structure of the CMEA was based on bilateral agreements in which the U.S.S.R. played by far the most dominant role.

In 1983 emphasis was once again placed on increasing internal trade within the CMEA, but some of the speakers at the last plenary session stressed that this should lead to a greater measure of "self-reliance." This belief was caused not only by the general political deterioration of relations between East and West but also by the fact that the Polish crisis made many Western creditors reluctant to lend money to Communist countries. The repayment of debts had been only partially successful, although on the whole in 1983 most Eastern European countries improved their trade balance in convertible currency. This was achieved mostly by drastic cuts of imports rather than by an increase of exports. Thus a new problem was created, namely, a severe curtailment of investments, especially those requiring modern technology.

INTERNATIONAL TRADE

World trade stagnated in 1983 for the second year in succession. In 1982 the relatively poor markets in the U.S. and some other industrialized countries had caused overall trade volumes to falter. In 1983 the U.S. economy recovered and with it the U.S. demand for imports. There were also improvements in some other major importing nations. But these were outweighed by the weakness in the economies of other industrial countries and by the restrictions (some self-imposed, others unwillingly accepted) on the demand for imports in the less developed nations, both oil-producing and nonoil. Therefore, after the 1982 decline in world trade volumes, all that was achieved in 1983 was a maintenance of that low level. World trade in manufactured goods remained constant too, while oil volumes traded internationally remained weak. World trade in agricultural products recovered a little, as did trade in metals and other raw materials.

The threat to world trade in 1982 had been from the widespread restrictions on free trade. The possibility of wholesale protectionism had undoubtedly influenced investment decisions; businessmen had to judge whether the markets that an investment was to serve would still be open to them by the time the output from that investment was ready. That threat still existed throughout 1983 but seemed to be in the background. Japan's agreement to limit "voluntarily" its exports to the European Economic Community (EEC) or the U.S. in sensitive categories of goods removed much of the pressure for formal protectionist measures. The Japanese agreement with the EEC on video tape recorders, for example, allowed the Japanese the chance to maintain their large share in this market, probably at enhanced prices.

The threat to trade in 1983 was the collapse of the financing arrangements for trade with the less developed countries. After the debt crises of 1982 (and especially those with Mexico, Brazil, and Argentina), banks were reluctant to lend any more than was absolutely necessary to many less developed countries. To the nations already heavily in debt, this meant receiving loans of only that amount necessary to avert the possibility of default by the borrowing country. Even to those not in heavy debt, the general increase in caution resulted in trade credit's being more difficult to obtain. It was, after all, the accumulation of excessive short-term credits that had led to Mexico's downfall.

This denial of trade credit left less developed countries with severe financial problems, especially as the continued high level of interest rates on Eurocurrency credits caused a high proportion of their export earnings to be used to service previous debts. This shortage forced many nations to seek IMF help, and in turn the IMF had to seek agreement for an $8.4 billion increase in its resources. This increase was granted late in 1983 after being held up for months in the U.S. Congress. It was clear by then that the problems of less developed countries would necessitate another increase in IMF resources in 1984.

Demand by the oil-producing countries also declined, as their revenues fell by 10%. Many oil producers with previously high credit ratings found themselves caught up in the same general nervousness about finance. They were, therefore, forced to reduce their demand for imports by the cancellation or postponement of projects. This, in turn, damaged the export markets of West Germany, France, the U.S., Japan, and other major industrial exporters of plant and equipment. It also highlighted the basic problem of the withholding of finance, which was that the cutbacks were generally in investment projects; it was the exports of plant and equipment that suffered most rather than those of consumption goods. Thus, the economic infrastructure, necessary for producing the goods that would eventually repay the loans now being made, was not being constructed.

One proposed solution to these difficulties was for world interest rates to fall. But this required that U.S. rates fall, and the market sentiment was that this was unlikely while the U.S. budget deficit was high. The reduction of the deficit would re-

Table XI. Soviet Crude Petroleum and Products Supplied to Eastern Europe
In 000 rubles

Country	1981	1982
Bulgaria	1,310,920	1,546,132
Czechoslovakia	1,617,945	2,067,504
East Germany	1,744,515	2,414,248
Hungary	913,503	1,120,233
Poland	1,613,405	1,889,191
Romania	523,641	...

Source: U.S.S.R. Foreign Trade Statistics/Moscow.

Table X. Soviet Trade with Eastern European Countries
In 000,000 rubles, current prices

	Exports			Imports		
Country	1980	1981	1982	1980	1981	1982
Bulgaria	3,660.2	4,374.5	4,884.6	3,438.9	3,696.9	4,288.1
Czechoslovakia	3,648.1	4,382.3	5,047.5	3,535.9	4,104.8	4,731.9
East Germany	4,873.4	5,526.1	6,419.6	4,326.6	5,154.6	5,776.2
Hungary	2,981.6	3,306.7	3,707.2	2,756.6	3,300.4	3,746.4
Poland	4,405.9	4,931.3	4,812.9	3,596.1	3,220.8	4,097.0
Romania	1,350.3	1,779.1	1,423.6	1,441.2	1,673.1	1,683.4

Source: U.S.S.R. Foreign Trade Statistics/Moscow.

quire tax increases, which would, in turn, weaken the strong growth in the U.S. economy. Other countries were reluctant to reduce interest rates while those in the U.S. remained high, for fear of a fall in the value of their currency and renewed inflation. World trade remained in the doldrums, therefore, as the world economy tried to drag itself out of a difficult and still potentially destabilizing situation.

Industrialized Nations. For 1983 the picture was generally one of depressed economies either reaching the trough of the recession or starting to move slowly into an upward phase. The depressed level of economic activity reduced the ability of countries to absorb imports, often through deliberate policies on the part of governments to undermine consumers' ability to pay. But in other nations the lower levels of inflation generated a move to lower savings ratios and to greater consumer spending. This generally benefited importers, as did a rebuilding of inventory levels in some countries. Overall, therefore, the current account deficit of the industrialized nations changed little from its 1982 level. But the division in 1983 should be drawn not between the seven major economies and the other OECD countries but between the U.S. and the rest. The U.S. current deficit ballooned by nearly $20 billion, while there was an improvement of $22 billion in the combined current accounts of the other industrialized nations. This latter improvement could be divided between the other six major economies (better by nearly $17 billion) and the lesser industrial nations (better by about $5 billion).

While the world was recovering slowly from a deep recession, the U.S. economy was bouncing back at top speed. A rapid upsurge in GNP took place there in the middle of 1983, and overall growth for the year was more than 6%. Industrial production rose even faster and, not surprisingly, the trade account went severely into deficit. The government's budget deficit did not help; heavy borrowing from the rest of the world helped to keep the dollar's value strong. The high level of interest rates also boosted the dollar and thus reduced competitiveness of U.S. exports in world markets and domestic goods in the home market. This reduced competitiveness occurred even though domestic inflation was back to 1960s levels (helped, it must be said, by the dollar's strength causing reduced import prices). Thus export volumes declined in 1983, while import volumes rose rapidly. Both trade and current account deficits reached new record levels, and the overall trade deficit was approximately $70 billion for the year as a whole. Even after deducting the perennial huge surplus of the U.S. on invisibles, the deficit on current account for the year was about $30 billion.

In many ways the Japanese economy had the same problems as did that of the U.S. It too had a large public-sector deficit (at least by Japanese standards). There was considerable pressure to reduce that deficit by either tax increases or public spending cuts. Such action would help to reduce the level of interest rates and thus boost private investment, which in general was weak. But it would also have reduced consumption expenditures, and they were even weaker. Indeed the only strong part of the Japanese economy was the export sector, and this continued to fuel the by now familiar tension between Japan and its major trading partners, the U.S. and the European Community. Despite high levels of real interest rates (Japanese inflation was nearly zero by the end of the year), the yen remained undervalued; an upsurge in its trade-weighted effective exchange rate through 1983 did not satisfy the critics in the U.S. or Europe. Japanese domestic demand was not strong enough to pull in imports, and the export sector continued its relentless push into world markets. So while the U.S. fell deeper into deficit, Japan rose higher into surplus; its trade account was some $28 billion to the good in 1983. After deduction of the deficit on invisibles, this still left a surplus of $19 billion on current account.

West Germany's exports suffered from the difficulties in its traditionally important markets. With investment spending weak in most major economies, West German machinery manufacturers found it difficult to maintain sales. In France and Italy economic growth was either slow or negative, and this caused them to import fewer West German consumer goods. The sluggish oil market had mixed blessings for West Germany; it reduced the oil bill but also meant that demand from the oil producers was depressed. So despite a slight reduction in the effective exchange rate of the Deutsche Mark through the year, exports were unable to maintain momentum. The only area of the West German economy to strengthen after a poor 1982 was the consumer sector. As price inflation fell, savings ratios also were reduced and consumer spending rose. This helped maintain a high level of imports, and the overall trade surplus seemed likely to be about $18 billion. While second only to Japan among the industrialized nations, this surplus was all but offset by the invisibles deficit, so the current account surplus was around $4 billion.

After a substantial deficit in 1982, the French government set itself the task of reducing the trade shortfall in 1983. After the March European Monetary System realignment, it introduced austerity measures to cut back domestic demand and thus spending on imports. Cuts in the budget deficit, increased taxes on petroleum, and increased utility prices were all introduced. More important, there were currency restrictions for French travelers abroad, together with tightening of exchange controls. These appeared to have had their effect, with substantial reductions in the French trade deficit through the year. Indeed after the trade surplus in September, the government relaxed the restrictions on spending by travelers overseas.

With the franc's improved exchange rate against the Deutsche Mark and the recovery in consumer spending in West Germany, French exporters were doing better in their major markets, and exports were up some 2% in volume. The trade deficit, therefore, declined to $8 billion, and the government's restrictions meant that the invisibles account attained virtual balance. The current account was thus in deficit at $8 billion also.

The British economy climbed slowly out of recession in 1983, with the only growth sector being personal consumption. Consumer spending rose in spite of stagnant real disposable incomes because of a fall in savings ratios as inflation stabilized at 5%. Spending on durables was particularly strong, and this helped the growth of imports. The lack of competitiveness also helped import growth; despite a fall in the effective exchange rate through the year, the pound was still relatively overvalued compared with the yen and the Deutsche Mark.

With the major markets in the European Community fairly weak, British exports found it difficult to make headway, and export volumes were virtually identical to those of 1982. Manufacturing exports were particularly weak, and export shares fell while import penetration rose. Only the large balance of payments benefit of North Sea oil kept the external account in surplus. The non-oil trade deficit was large enough to outweigh the surplus on oil trade, so that the U.K. was marginally in deficit overall. The usual invisible surplus was down slightly, but even so the current account surplus for the year was about $4 billion.

The Italian economy remained in serious difficulties through 1983. Gross national product fell, but wages continued to outstrip prices, and both were at levels that were extremely high by the standards prevailing in most industrialized countries. Therefore, despite a substantial decline in the value of the lira, both against the dollar and against all other currencies, Italian exporters found it difficult to remain competitive. But importers into Italy also found life difficult; domestic demand was weak, and the falling lira kept import competitiveness down. Thus the combination of falling import volumes and weakly rising export volumes reduced the trade deficit to about $10 billion. With the invisibles account performing well (from high tourism revenue and reduced interest payments on Italy's foreign debt), the deficit on current account had been virtually eradicated by the end of the year.

With the U.S. providing the bulk of Canada's imports but also providing a market for two-thirds of Canadian exports, the U.S. upsurge provided a boost to the Canadian economy. Therefore, the rise of the Canadian dollar (in line with that of its U.S. counterpart) did not affect competitiveness in its major market. The trade account thus remained heavily in surplus, to the tune of $11 billion; despite the usual deficit on invisibles, the current account was also in surplus, by $2 billion.

Other smaller industrial nations were not so fortunate. With generally depressed markets in the big four European economies, the smaller Western European countries were not able to improve their trade positions as much as they might have hoped. Elsewhere, Australia remained in current account deficit despite a decline in GNP that caused a reduction in import demand.

Less Developed Countries. Less developed countries had a difficult time in 1983, although it was likely that their overall deficit had fallen considerably from its 1982 levels. Oil-exporting countries suffered from the decline in the price of petroleum, which directly affected their ability to buy imports. Non-oil less developed countries benefited from the fall in oil prices, and commodity prices recovered substantially in almost all cases (metals being the general exception). But several factors combined to hold back both import and export growth in those nations. Lack of banking finance following the crises in Latin America in 1982 reduced those countries' ability to pay for imports. Even where such finance was available, it was often given under IMF-approved economic plans, which seemed invariably to require cuts in living standards and thus in the ability to purchase imports. With interest rates remaining high, a substantial portion of that funding was used to finance debt service.

Recession in many of the major industrial economies continued to restrict the demand for exports from the less developed countries. In addition, protectionist pressures were increasing as unemployment continued to rise or remain high in most industrial nations. Thus it was little wonder that many countries turned to barter trade, agreeing to accept imports from industrialized nations only if an equivalent quantity of exports were accepted in exchange.

Centrally Planned Economies. The centrally planned economies, especially the Eastern European nations, had problems similar to those of the less developed countries. But this had the effect of boosting the level of trade surplus that Eastern Europe had with Western Europe. After Poland's payment problems, trade finance was much more difficult for the Eastern bloc to obtain, and this limited their ability to purchase imports. Meanwhile, cuts in prices of Eastern European exports helped to maintain the volume levels of those exports, even in the distinctly sluggish European market. Thanks to a good wheat crop, the U.S.S.R. required fewer grain imports from the U.S., Canada, France, and other sources in the West. Given the weak prices for wheat, this meant that its need for foreign exchange was considerably reduced. China too did not import as much grain as in previous years and, together with its much more restrained development program, this held back import growth. Overall, therefore, the current account surplus of the centrally planned economies probably increased.

INTERNATIONAL EXCHANGE AND PAYMENTS

In the course of everyday economic life, the news media tend to concentrate attention on the current account of the balance of payments. They neglect in general the capital side of the payments account, forgetting that in the end the balance of payments must balance. This is understandable, given that the public can understand more easily the concepts of flows of goods and services into and out of a particular country. It becomes more difficult to consider the shifts in capital account items, such as direct investment in physical assets, portfolio investment in stocks and bonds, or transactions by governments with other governments or with supranational organizations such as the IMF. But events in 1983 demonstrated sharply how movements on the capital account can be influential on the current account. For in that year the major influences on the current account included the difficulties that many less developed economies had in financing their imports, and also the capital inflows that helped to maintain the overvalued dollar and keep the U.S. current balance in deficit.

Among the major industrial countries, the U.S. experienced rapid growth and fell into massive current account deficit. Canada grew rapidly on the back of the U.S. upsurge but avoided a deterioration of the current account, while Japan improved its current surplus dramatically, with this external success offset by weak domestic demand. West Germany also improved its current balance, though that resulted from a domestic recession. Other industrialized countries suffered a mixed response, depending on whether their import requirements fell further as a result of poor home demand than their export trade fell as a result of weak export markets.

One crucial market that weakened considerably in 1983 was that of the OPEC nations, where the March oil-price cut forced most countries to cut back planned spending. The position might have been worse but for the fact that oil demand stayed reasonably stable; conservation measures lowered the energy required per unit of output, but overall OECD economies recorded significant if not substantial growth. Nevertheless, the OPEC market was much more difficult for exporters, and even the lower level of activity was sustained only by disinvestment by many oil exporters of some of the assets they had acquired previously.

But it was in the less developed economies that the most marked change occurred. The current balance of the less developed countries improved, mainly because of reduced import demand. Export markets for those economies were in the OECD countries, and they had still not recovered sufficiently from the recession to provide significant growth. The centrally planned economies managed to carve out a larger market share, even in the depressed European market, but problems with trade credit forced them to cut back imports. They were, therefore, able to improve their current account balance.

The centrally planned economies faced difficulties with trade credit primarily because of a loss of confidence following Poland's restructuring of its debts. The embargoes of 1982 did not help the confidence of potential consumers either. Western banks were reluctant to lend at previous levels to the centrally planned economies, and this loss of hard currency forced the cutback of imports. To make sure it has sufficient hard currency to meet its import bill, a centrally planned economy must either increase exports to the West, borrow from Western banks, sell physical assets and real estate to Western purchasers (an unlikely prospect), or cut back imports to meet resources.

The less developed economies had the same problem but to a more substantial degree. The problems with debt servicing that occurred in 1982 with economies such as Mexico, Brazil, and Argentina brought home at last the serious problem that commercial banks faced. Many less developed countries had taken out long-term debts over the previous decade to sustain domestic activity and promote growth despite the burden of heavily increased oil payments. During the 1980s many banks had grown wary of lending further to certain less developed economies whose debt service payments had grown too large relative to export earnings. This had forced several of those economies to resort to more short-term funding, of the sort normally used for trade credit. Ultimately many had to declare these short-term loans unpayable, thus requiring the banks to renegotiate these short-term credits over longer periods (up to eight years in some cases).

This misuse of short-term funding quickly produced repercussions. Many banks already faced renegotiation of substantial long-term loans (or else faced writing off the loans; in many cases this would have totally eliminated the bank's equity capital). They were, therefore, much more wary of granting even short-term credits to the major debtor countries for fear these credits would then have to be renegotiated/rescheduled to long-term loans. Even where the countries involved were not considered to be in long-term debt difficulties, several (Venezuela, Colombia, South Korea) had short-term debt positions considerably above those needed for trade purposes only. Therefore, banks cut back short-term lending, expecially to the Latin-American countries. In the six months to March 1983, the change in outstanding claims on less developed nations by banks reporting to the Bank for International Settlements was only 4% at an annual rate. Latin America did even worse, with only a 1% increase. Chile, Peru, Venezuela, and others actually faced decreases in bank credit over this period.

But the situation improved through the rest of 1983 as the immediate crisis was passed. New credit needs from the Western banks were estimated at about $25 billion, and it appeared that this level was reached. Latin America was still not in favour, however; while Asian less developed countries in general got what they wanted from the banks, Latin America received less than the target 7% increase. This lack of bank credit forced the Latin-American economies to cut back their imports; decreases of 10, 20, or even 30% were commonplace.

Many less developed countries turned to IMF aid during this period, and the policies imposed as conditions for the Fund's aid also served to cut imports. The Fund was successful in all cases; the harsh domestic restraint required to restore economic equilibrium could not be sustained successfully in many countries (Argentina, Brazil, and Peru, for example). The Fund's activities, however, served to maintain progress toward a solution of the immediate difficulties. The Fund itself was contained by a shortage of resources, as a much needed quota increase was held up in the U.S. Congress till late in the year. Even this $8.4 billion of additional resources was already preempted by the demands of the less developed countries under the wing of the IMF, and its commitments for further loans required it to seek further resources in 1984.

As the less developed countries experienced a shortage (however temporary) of capital inflows, many turned to controls on trade or capital flows. This, in turn, led to a cutback in investment

CHART 5

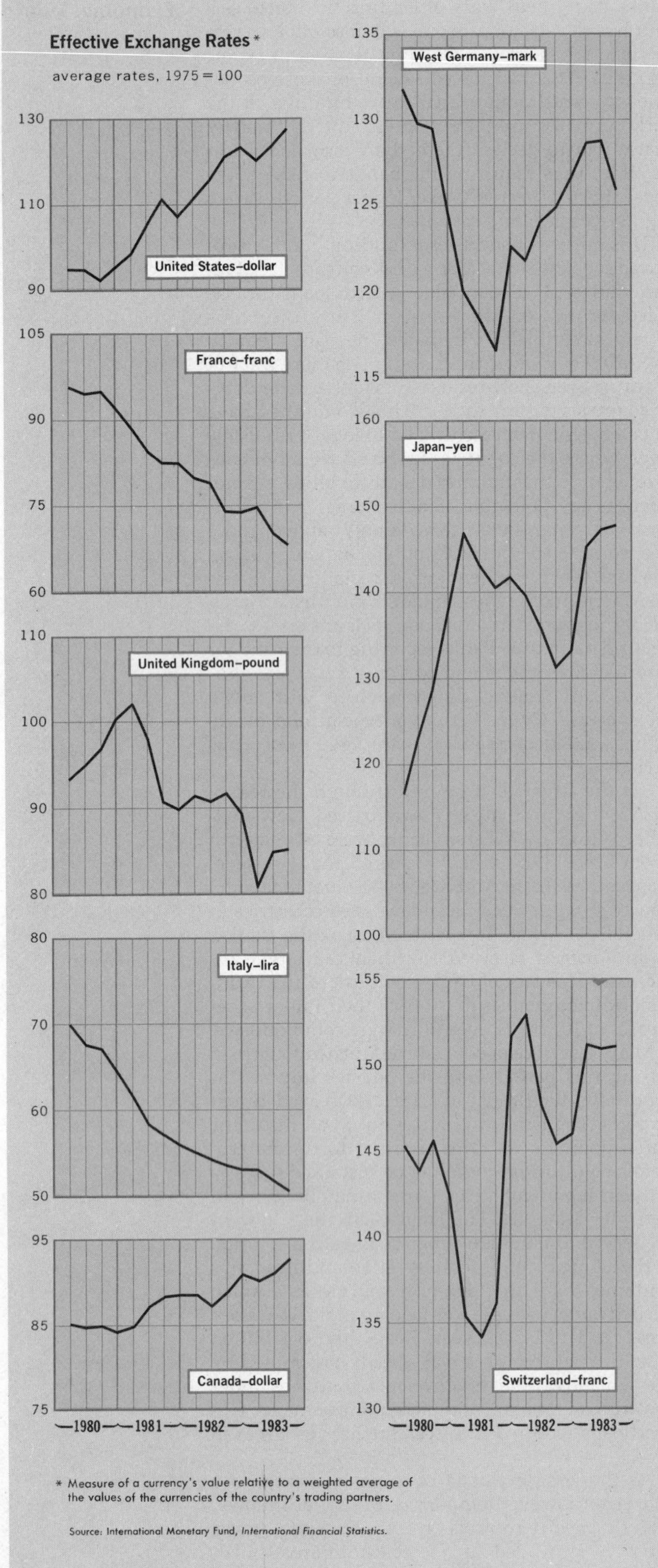

* Measure of a currency's value relative to a weighted average of the values of the currencies of the country's trading partners.

Source: International Monetary Fund, *International Financial Statistics.*

spending by multinational companies in those countries, since those firms could not be sure that they would be able to repatriate their investments or the dividends and profits flowing from them.

The very factors that drew capital away from the less developed economies drove it toward the U.S. After the 1982 recession the U.S. economy was showing tremendous growth, and the annual rate of inflation had declined down to 2–3%, levels not seen since the 1960s. The growth was fed by a substantial public-sector deficit, and the domestic savings ratio fell to low levels as inflation tumbled. The consequence was that domestic savings were insufficient to fund both the government's demand for funds and the corporate sector's requirement for additional finance. In 1983 the corporate sector was recovering from the recession, and its demand for funds was not as large as it might have been. But worries in the financial community that the government's demand for funds would "crowd out" the private sector led to the continuation of high interest rates.

Taken together with the large and very accessible markets for financial securities, land, bank deposits, and other assets, the prospect of high interest rates in the immediate future prompted a sizable inflow of foreign investment into the U.S. This helped to ease somewhat the pressure on funds available for the financing of domestic investment. It also helped to maintain the strong value of the dollar; without the inflow, the rest of the world would have been accumulating dollars at a rate similar (in relative terms) to the rate that prompted the crisis in the dollar in the early 1970s. Such a situation could still occur, but in 1983 the U.S. was a profitable place for foreign funds.

As a result of these circumstances, during the course of the year the effective exchange rate increased in the case of the dollar by about 5%. This led it to levels at which most commentators considered it overvalued.

Conversely, other currencies fell in value over the year. The French franc was forced to readjust its European Monetary System parities in March, a move followed by severe internal and external financial controls to curb domestic demand and preserve the new parities. The Japanese discussed ways of relaxing controls in the financial markets that could help the yen to rise further, though it had made sizable gains during the year in the wake of Japan's substantial current account surplus. The Deutsche Mark, on the other hand, failed to make much progress, its popularity suffering as that of the dollar increased.

There remained the problem that in the late 1980s there would be another bunching of interest and principal repayments, at about the time when the world economy might be in the depths of recession again. Also it was not clear whether the debtor countries would accept the situation (likely to arise in the near future) where net inflows of capital into the less developed countries were exceeded by net outflows of interest and principal repayments. At that point the ultimate sanction against those countries repudiating their foreign debt—that they would receive no further inflows of capital—would be useless. (EIU)

U.S. ECONOMY: ERODING POLITICAL AND TECHNOLOGICAL CLOUT

by Brijesh Khindaria

The U.S. remained the world's dominant economic power in 1983, although rising competition from Europe and Japan had eroded its political and technological clout. A U.S. economic recession still sent shock waves around the world, while recovery, if handled properly, could serve to lead other countries to better times.

At first glance the U.S. did not seem to be preponderant. It accounted for only 12.5% of world exports and about 15% of primary product imports while producing one-quarter of total world output. But that impression was quickly dispelled by its overwhelming dominance in finance, the essential prerequisite for trade and economic growth. Every country, including Communist countries, measures its currency against the dollar. Dollars make up three-quarters of all central bank reserves, 80% of all international bank loans, and 55% of all international trade invoices. Consequently, movements in dollar interest and foreign exchange rates, as well as in U.S. budget and trade deficits, can significantly help or hinder the economic policies of other nations. The 1980–82 recession in the U.S. not only worsened unemployment in Western Europe but also precipitated the third world debt crisis, jeopardizing the solvency of many Western banks.

The U.S. Budget Deficit. The strong U.S. recovery of 1983 brought some solace to both developed and less developed countries. Europeans saw a tapering off in unemployment growth, although the average rate remained a high 8–10%. Non-oil-exporting less developed countries benefited from a 30% increase in nominal commodity prices following a 45% drop in real prices (after adjusting for inflation) in the last decade. Fears soon arose, however, that the U.S. recovery might not last beyond the end of 1984 unless Pres. Ronald Reagan could control the burgeoning budget deficit, estimated at $225 billion, or 6% of gross domestic product, in 1983. It was forecast that the deficit would hit $315 billion in 1988, even if the economy grew at an average 4% yearly—a rate many economists thought could not be sustained beyond 1984 without radical policy changes. The deficit, financed by government borrowing, hurt other nations by bidding up dollar interest rates and raising the cost of investments needed to sustain economic recovery.

Throughout 1983 the Reagan administration fought a solitary battle against critics at international meetings. It stubbornly insisted that U.S. recovery would be enough to bring the rest of the world out of recession, regardless of whether the budget deficit was reduced. But other governments and many economists argued that U.S. recovery would itself peter out without a general revival of world economic activity. They therefore called for separate but simultaneous U.S. measures to promote economic recovery in Europe and economic development in the third world.

Third World Resignation; European Disillusion. Less developed countries sank into a mood of resignation after the most acrimonious North-South confrontation in two decades. At the sixth UN Conference on Trade and Development (UNCTAD) in June-July 1983, the 123 third world governments failed to get a hoped-for package of emergency financial measures to increase their purchasing power by $100 billion within two years, a package that would have eased the burden of heavy indebtedness and falling export earnings.

Less developed countries feared that without fresh aid and loans they would not be able to take sufficient advantage of the increased demand for their exports during the U.S. upturn. Their nightmare was that the U.S. would have entered a new recession by the time they exported enough to have some cash left over after debt service (interest and administration) payments and repatriation of profits. Nor did the U.S. respond to a call by the March summit of nonaligned nations for a new international monetary conference to give them more say in the work of such financial institutions as the World Bank and the International Monetary Fund (IMF).

European leaders repeatedly accused President Reagan of dragging his feet in implementing pledges made at the Williamsburg (Va.) summit of the seven major non-Communist industrial powers in May 1983 to control climbing dollar interest and exchange rates and to reduce protectionism. Just days after the Williamsburg pledges, the U.S. slapped tight import controls on specialty steels, creating a crisis in U.S.-European Communities (EC)

Brijesh Khindaria is financial correspondent of the International Herald Tribune *in Geneva, specializing in the role of private enterprise in economic growth.*

U.S. Pres. Ronald Reagan addressed a summit meeting of industrialized nations in May at Williamsburg, Virginia. From left: Sir Geoffrey Howe (Exchequer, U.K.), Amintore Fanfani (Italy), Helmut Kohl (West Germany), François Mitterrand (France), Pierre Elliott Trudeau (Canada), Yasuhiro Nakasone (Japan).

trade and nearly wrecking domestic EC measures to save its collapsing steel industry. Interest rates climbed again after a temporary drop, while the dollar reached its highest level in two years.

The Europeans were convinced that the opportunity for sustained economic recovery through the 1980s afforded by the unexpectedly strong U.S. recovery in 1983 would be lost if interest rates and dollar values remained high. Therefore, they wanted to see a sharp cut in the U.S. budget deficit, accompanied by low inflation levels in the 3–5% range. The U.S. attained a 3.9% inflation rate in 1983, but no solution was in sight for the rising budget deficit, caused in large measure by heavy defense spending.

The Debt Crisis. Consensus emerged among a large body of economists that, without help, many less developed countries might be forced to default on large sections of their medium- and long-term debt, estimated at $637 billion in 1983, and short-term borrowings of at least $100 billion. The consequences would be disastrous for many Western banks, some of which had lent up to 400% of their reserves. Since less developed countries buy about 40% of U.S. exports, U.S. producers would also be seriously hurt. The heaviest debtors—Mexico and Brazil—nearly halved their imports from the U.S. between 1980 and 1983. The total debt of less developed countries was expected to reach 128% of their export earnings in 1984.

Fearing widespread default, commercial banks, the main source of credit, were likely to cut lending to $7.4 billion in 1984 from $23 billion in 1981. Direct foreign investment was also expected to drop, to $11 billion from $15.4 billion in 1981. The World Bank and IMF might supply another $15 billion, provided the U.S. raised its contributions to both agencies.

Opposing Views. U.S. Treasury Secretary Donald Regan summarized administration views at the joint annual meeting of the IMF and the World Bank in Washington, D.C., in September 1983: "Rather than another traditional cycle of recession to recovery, I think we are witnessing a more fundamental change." In his view, governments were now preferring long-term goals to short-term expediency, inflation was at low levels, and less developed countries were accepting painful economic readjustment to overcome their financial problems. Dollar interest rates were at half their 1981 levels despite a larger U.S. deficit, and private investment was growing. Cutting the deficit through more taxation would stifle rather than promote recovery.

This view failed to win many converts among international economists. The main suggestions made by such economists were the following:

1. The U.S. should take measures to reduce both dollar exchange and interest rates. No easy solutions were available, however. As long as the demand for dollars exceeded the supply because of borrowing by both governments and business investors, interest and exchange rates were likely to remain high. Increasing the supply of dollars would only feed inflation and undermine economic growth.

2. The U.S. should allow the IMF and World Bank to expand their lending to allow insolvent countries to take advantage of the U.S. upturn by strengthening their capacity to meet higher demand for their exports. Failure to do so would make debt defaults inevitable. The expectation that enough financial resources would be available worldwide to keep demand for goods and services at higher levels would also persuade businessmen to invest in new production capacity rather than short-term instruments.

3. The U.S. should end protectionism to allow other countries to earn more, both to repay loans and to buy more U.S. exports. The resulting increase in world trade volume would boost world output and demand for both finance and services. That would not only fuel economic recovery but also prevent wastage of investment funds on inefficient protected industries.

4. Perhaps the most useful suggestion was that one or several conferences should be called to work out international approaches to monetary and trade problems. But conferences are of little use if their results are not implemented. That requires a political determination that had not yet emerged in a sufficient number of either developed or less developed country governments.

Ecuador

A republic on the west coast of South America, Ecuador is bounded by Colombia, Peru, and the Pacific Ocean. Area: 281,341 sq km (108,627 sq mi), including the Galápagos Islands (7,976 sq km), which is an insular province. Pop. (1982 prelim.): 8,072,700. Cap.: Quito (pop., 1982 prelim., 881,400). Largest city: Guayaquil (pop., 1982 prelim., 1,181,200). Language: Spanish, but Indians speak Quechuan and Jivaroan. Religion: predominantly Roman Catholic. President in 1983, Osvaldo Hurtado Larrea.

Ecuador's economic and financial position continued to deteriorate in 1983. Pres. Osvaldo Hurtado Larrea faced strikes by labour unions, severe criticism from the business sector, and the alienation of the political parties. A slight lull in congressional opposition was noticeable, however, as the parties prepared for presidential elections scheduled for January 1984. Eight candidates were to contest the presidential elections; since no single party could expect to attract enough support, alliances among them had to be negotiated.

Heavy rain at the beginning of the year affected most of the country and caused death and devastation in some regions, particularly in the Guayaquil area. Crops were destroyed, with the result that sugar and other foodstuffs had to be imported and exports of bananas and cocoa were expected to be halved. Gross domestic product was forecast to decline by about 2%.

Against this background, the authorities negotiated with the International Monetary Fund for a standby facility of 157.5 million Special Drawing Rights and agreed to implement an austerity program to strengthen the balance of payments. Ecuador also agreed with creditor governments to defer payment of about $200 million in loans. In October it signed agreements with international commercial banks for refinancing public- and private-sector external debt maturing in 1983, for a new loan of $431 million over six years, and for the maintenance of trade credit lines worth $700 million. The sucre was devalued progressively during the year. Inflation reached an unusually high annual rate of 56.5% at the end of July, compared with 14.5% in the year ended July 1982. (SARAH CAMERON)

UPI

In early March students clashed with police in Quito, Ecuador. The confrontation was touched off by rumours of gasoline price increases and a possible currency devaluation.

ECUADOR

Education. (1981–82) Primary, pupils 1,572,556, teachers 44,905; secondary, pupils 626,833, teachers 37,052; vocational, pupils 164,089, teachers 8,487; higher, students 267,900, teaching staff 11,186.

Finance. Monetary unit: sucre, with (Sept. 20, 1983) an official market rate of 48.73 sucres to U.S. $1 (73.39 sucres = £1 sterling), and a free market rate of 89.35 sucres to U.S. $1 (134.56 sucres = £1 sterling). Gold and other reserves (June 1983) U.S. $309 million. Budget (1981 actual): revenue 35,493,000,000 sucres; expenditure 50,846,000,000 sucres. Gross national product (1982) 377,840,000,000 sucres. Money supply (April 1983) 77,989,000,000 sucres. Cost of living (Quito; 1975 = 100; June 1983) 323.7.

Foreign Trade. (1982) Imports U.S. $1,988,500,000; exports U.S. $2,138,800,000. Import sources (1981): U.S. 34%; Japan 12%; West Germany 7%. Export destinations (1981): U.S. 39%; Japan 12%; Taiwan 7%. Main exports: crude oil 55%; bananas 10%; coffee 6%.

Transport and Communications. Roads (1982) 32,185 km. Motor vehicles in use (1981): passenger 232,600; commercial 23,900. Railways: (1980) 965 km; traffic (1979) 69 million passenger-km, freight 29 million net ton-km. Air traffic (1982): 862 million passenger-km; freight c. 39.4 million net ton-km. Shipping (1982): merchant vessels 100 gross tons and over 110; gross tonnage 354,443. Telephones (Jan. 1981) 272,000. Radio receivers (Dec. 1980) 2,650,000. Television receivers (Dec. 1980) 500,000.

Agriculture. Production (in 000; metric tons; 1982): rice 405; corn (1981) c. 246; potatoes c. 349; cassava (1981) c. 236; sugar, raw value c. 270; bananas c. 2,265; pineapples c. 140; oranges c. 520; coffee 75; cocoa c. 85; fish catch (1981) 686. Livestock (in 000; 1981): cattle 3,032; sheep 3,034; pigs 3,721; horses c. 299; chickens c. 23,479.

Industry. Production (in 000; metric tons; 1981): cement 1,450; crude oil (1982) 11,404; natural gas (cu m) 55,000; petroleum products 4,321; electricity (kw-hr) 2,950,000; gold (troy oz) 3.7; silver (troy oz) 44.

Education

In the industrialized countries, the burning issue of 1983 concerned the poor employment prospects of school-leavers aged 16 to 18. Within the countries of the European Communities (EC), one of every four unemployed persons was under 25. In the U.S. the unemployment rate for teenagers decreased somewhat as the economy began to recover, but it remained above 20%, about two and a half times the rate for adults.

Ecuador

Programs offering training to young people, originally viewed as temporary expedients, were now described as permanent. In the U.K., for example, the Youth Training Scheme provided for some 460,000 training slots for 16-year-olds who did not go into full-time higher education or into jobs. Similar plans were put into operation elsewhere in Western Europe. In West Germany Chancellor Helmut Kohl promised training to every youngster "capable and willing." In both the U.K. and West Germany there was some relaxation of the labour laws in order to widen the scope for youth employment, although this led to accusations by the unions that the government was creating cheap labour. Similar union objections greeted U.S. Pres. Ronald Reagan's suggestion that the minimum wage be lowered for young workers.

A meeting of EC education and employment ministers was held in Luxembourg in the spring to thrash out a common policy on education and training for 16- to 19-year-olds. The European Commission tried to get agreement on a two-stage guarantee: 12 months' training and then further training at any time up to age 25. In the event, however, the member states would accept only a six-month training period.

In strife-torn areas of the world, the issues facing educational systems were much more stark. The war in Lebanon, for example, had led to widespread demoralization, all the more tragic because the UN Relief and Works Agency (UNRWA) had built up an impressive educational system for the Palestinian community. The fighting closed 40 of the 86 UNRWA schools. Besides the problems of interrupted education, the Palestinians, in particular, faced deteriorating job prospects in the Middle East. Over the years, many well-educated Palestinians had found employment as high-level managers and technicians in oil-rich Arab countries such as Saudi Arabia and Kuwait, but now these countries were beginning to produce highly qualified personnel from among their own nationals. In beleaguered Chad the effects of war and famine were compounded by an inappropriate curriculum, based on the French colonial model. With support from UNICEF, the government was attempting to introduce "pilot" schools that had more relevance to the nation's run-down economy.

The outlook was brighter in Zimbabwe, now emerging from many years of civil disorder. The government reported that, in the three years since independence, the number of children in primary schools had more than doubled and the number in secondary education had tripled, from 74,000 in 1980 to 218,000 in 1982. As in many less developed countries, school-leavers tended to seek civil service jobs in the towns. To combat this trend, the government was encouraging "education with production." Most schools were involved in projects that contributed toward their budgets, and many had become self-sufficient in food, grown by the pupils as part of their agricultural training. In the Falkland Islands the effects of the 1982 war proved minor. During the Argentine occupation, an attempt was made to introduce more Spanish into the school in Port Stanley, but there was no attempt to cut back the teaching of English in Argentina. The two best-known English schools, St. George's and St. Hilda's in Buenos Aires, continued to experience a rising demand for places by middle-class Argentine families.

Most Western governments, faced with economic recession and declining enrollments, continued their efforts to contain or reduce educational expenditures. There were some important exceptions. The new Socialist government in Spain determined to increase spending on schools, as did the Labor government in Australia. A more common situation, however, was that in West Germany, where fewer pupils and the resultant teacher surplus led inevitably to clashes with the teachers' unions. The West German teachers' union estimated that 30,000 teachers were unemployed and that by 1990 the figure could rise to at least 70,000 or even 150,000. The union pressed for a 35-hour week and more part-time work for teachers. In Sweden it was estimated that 10,000 fewer primary school teachers would be needed by 1988, and the Finnish teachers' union projected that 6,000 of the country's 45,000 teachers would be out of a job by 1987.

As U.S. schools opened for the 1983–84 school year, spending for education was expected to reach $230 billion, $15 billion more than in 1982–83. This included $141 billion for elementary and secondary schools and $89 billion for colleges and universities. Public schools and colleges were expected to spend $184 billion, while private institutions at all

A golden apple for the 1983 Teacher of the Year was presented by U.S. First Lady Nancy Reagan to LeRoy E. Hay, a 38-year-old teacher of English from Manchester, Connecticut, at the White House in April. The national event is sponsored by the Encyclopaedia Britannica Companies, *Good Housekeeping* magazine, and the Council of Chief State School Officers.

WIDE WORLD

levels anticipated spending $46 billion. Nine percent of these moneys came from the federal government, 39% from state governments, 24% from local governments, and 28% from other sources such as tuition and fees, endowment earnings, and private gifts and grants.

Meanwhile, the number of students fell by 1% or 400,000, putting expected enrollments for 1983–84 at 56.7 million. Rising birthrates in the early 1980s pointed toward a reversal of the long-term decline in school enrollments as these children reached school age. The U.S. Census Bureau estimated that there would be some four million more children in elementary school in 1995 than in 1988. However, the Census Bureau expected the current "baby boom" to peak in 1988, after which the nation would move toward equilibrium between births and deaths, projected to occur around the mid-21st century.

In 1983 education was the primary activity for three out of every ten Americans, or some 70 million people. This figure included students, faculty, administrators, and support personnel. There were 3.3 million teachers and 300,000 superintendents, principals, supervisors, and other instructional staff. Relatively few teachers' strikes occurred at the start of the 1983–84 school year, although several hundred thousand students were affected. The largest was in the financially troubled Chicago public schools, where the teachers, who had not received a raise since 1980, struck for 15 school days—the longest such action in the system's history. Other strikes took place in California, Illinois (outside Chicago), Michigan, Missouri, Ohio, Pennsylvania, Rhode Island, and Washington State.

Primary and Secondary Education. The deficiencies of public education in the U.S. became the focus of public attention in 1983 to a degree not seen since the late 1950s, when the orbiting of the first Soviet Sputnik had sparked fears that the U.S. educational system was not producing the scientists and engineers needed to maintain the nation's technological lead. In 1983 the precipitating factor was the release of several national studies that were strongly critical of the public schools.

The most alarmist was *A Nation at Risk: The Imperative for Educational Reform,* issued by the National Commission on Excellence in Education. Appointed by Secretary of Education Terrel Bell early in the Reagan administration and chaired by David Gardner (*see* BIOGRAPHIES), president of the University of Utah, the commission claimed, in a much-quoted passage, that "If an unfriendly foreign power had attempted to impose on America the mediocre educational performance that exists today, we might well have viewed it as an act of war." It called for several specific reforms, including more required core courses such as mathematics, science, and computer science, better use of classroom time, tougher discipline, higher expectations for students, and better pay for teachers. Other recommendations were for a lengthened school year, more requirements for high school graduation, higher college entrance requirements, more homework, more fiscal support, and greater parental demands on their children. The report criticized what it called the "smorgasbord" of high school electives.

Other reports, while making many recommendations comparable to those of the National Commission, provided additional criticisms, suggestions, and insights on the origins of the school "crisis." The Carnegie Foundation for the Advancement of Teaching, in its *High School: A Report on Secondary Education in America,* expressed concern that the brightest high school graduates were not opting for teaching careers. The report advocated a federal scholarship program for good students interested in teaching. While other reports focused on mathematics and science, the Carnegie report urged greater stress on English, writing, and critical thinking. In *Making the Grade,* the Twentieth Century Fund Task Force on Federal Elementary and Secondary Education Policy called for a stronger federal role, including the provision of financial rewards for professional improvement. The Education Commission of the States, in *Action for Excellence,* joined the National Commission in urging a return to basics, as well as "reskilling" students for a technological age. It also recommended developing higher regard for teachers and improving school leadership and funding. The National Science Foundation board report called for upgrading of mathematics, science, and technology instruction and suggested the use of talented uncertified citizens to supplement teaching staffs.

Late in the year these warnings were underlined by the results of an academic achievement test, developed for the *Dallas* (Texas) *Times Herald* and given to children in eight cities in industrialized countries around the world. The American children—from two Dallas schools chosen because their scores on the widely used Iowa Test of Basic Skills were close to the national average—scored last in math and well down in science and geography. Japanese children did best in math, with scores twice as high as those of the Americans, while Swedish children scored highest in science and geography. More than a fifth of the children at one of the Dallas schools could not locate the U.S. on a world map.

Predictably, as the 1984 presidential election ap-

HARRIET GANS/THE NEW YORK TIMES

Enrollment in computer classes grew rapidly throughout the year. In many schools the number of students enrolled in elective computer courses doubled or tripled.

World Education

Most recent official data

Country	1st level (primary)			General 2nd level (secondary)[1]			Vocational 2nd level			3rd level (higher)			Literacy	
	Students (full-time)	Teachers (full-time)	Total schools	Students (full-time)	Teachers (full-time)	Total schools	Students (full-time)	Teachers (full-time)	Total schools	Students (full-time)	Teachers (full-time)	Total schools	% of population	Over age
Afghanistan	1,044,969	32,937	2,166	123,126	4,903	318	16,784	1,211	27	22,974	1,448	29	16.2	15
Algeria	4,250,000	104,500	9,263[2]	1,363,315	39,969	1,174	12,903	1,168	25	100,000	8,573	...	26.4	15
Angola	1,388,110	25,000	5,585	156,388[3]	4,723[3]	182	—	—	68	3,146	225	1	15.0	15
Argentina	4,197,372	206,535	20,201	594,167	81,026	1,942	831,481	110,703	2,954	550,556	53,166	1,041	94.9	15
Australia	1,871,617	91,386	8,180	1,115,782[3]	86,364[3]	1,553[3]	—	—	—	335,988	32,289	91	99.5	...
Austria	378,956	27,731	3,434	571,730	58,599	2,107	380,376	20,772	1,170	134,339	10,870	43	81.0	15
Bahrain	48,406	2,963	114	23,824	971	22	2,749	213	4	3,650	159	2	63.4	15
Bangladesh	8,236,526	188,234	40,313	2,062,722	85,801	8,841	345,166	17,540	49	232,780	12,329	396	25.8	15
Bermuda	5,878	320	22	4,215[3]	362[3]	13	—	—	...	575	63	1	97.5	15
Bolivia	904,874	53,044	7,890	227,385[3]	10,318[3]	2,881[3]	—	—	—	178,217	6,179	10	63.2	15
Botswana	195,000	6,930	515	22,440	1,037	45	1,741	227	23	1,022	144	1	52.0	15
Brazil	22,598,254	884,257	201,926	2,819,182[3]	198,087[3]	7,443	—	—	...	1,352,807	116,827	882	77.2	15
Brunei	31,677	1,800	175	14,846	1,230	29	570	127	4	143	57	1	77.8	15
Bulgaria	1,030,698	57,682	776	103,810	7,986	2,774	207,011	17,976	524	95,820	13,910	44	95.0	8
Burma	4,242,697	86,354	23,099	1,032,811	36,113	1,898	12,088	974	68[4]	146,461	5,147	35	69.7	15
Cameroon	1,302,974	25,289	4,721	155,544	5,778	318	57,316	2,596	147	11,901	439	10	47.4	10
Canada	2,888,055	271,820[5]	15,392[5]	1,462,315[3]	—	—	—	—	—	736,020	58,930	66	95.6	14
Chile	2,139,319	66,354	8,220	392,940	24,387	700	161,809	4,176	277	152,682	11,419	15	90.8	15
China	146,270,000	5,499,400	1,002,623	55,562,900	3,056,700	107,892	1,214,900	114,200	...	1,280,000	236,637	715	34.0	15
Colombia	4,168,200	136,381	32,230	1,811,003[3]	88,905[3]	3,252	—	—	—	306,269	31,474	70	56.0	15
Congo	390,676	7,186	1,310	170,652	3,878	122	16,933	1,239	36[4]	6,848	681	1	28.0	...
Costa Rica	347,708	10,536	3,509	103,579	4,263	242	30,229	2,254	74	60,990	4,382	4	8.0	15
Cuba	1,409,765	83,113	13,115	1,010,781	94,164	1,313	263,981	16,154	337	165,496	10,860	28	72.0	15
Cyprus	64,496	2,882	439	54,105	3,139	88	7,351	756	11	1,895	217	13	93.0	15
Czechoslovakia	1,930,634	90,282	6,612	163,800	9,880	366	229,543	16,391	524	198,362	18,560	42	99.5	15
Denmark	505,116	72,308[5]	2,263	205,036	—	2,516	150,971	...	271	96,056	6,702	358	100.0	15
Ecuador	1,572,566	44,905	12,823	626,835	37,052	1,565	164,089	8,487	374	267,900	11,186	17	79.0	18
Egypt	4,662,816	167,821	10,604	2,295,259	87,512	2,519	633,909	34,487	397	502,884	21,680	11	43.0	10
El Salvador	754,897	17,364	3,103	28,153	1,870	164	9,064	1,210	98	35,268	2,757	2	57.1	15
Fiji	116,190	4,146	656	46,211	2,514	141	2,386	235	37	667	180	1	77.5	15
Finland	373,347	25,959	4,853	341,926	20,010	1,056	103,111	14,136	541	86,026	6,471	21	100.0	15
France	4,621,000	169,416	51,440	5,014,000	280,972	11,378	799,209	45,364	...	1,017,775	40,585	82	100.0	7
Germany, East	2,212,715[5]	170,115[5]	12,179	—	—	5,906	448,386	16,553	1,214	277,938	37,789	290	100.0	15
Germany, West	4,820,200	286,500	23,766[5]	3,615,796	215,400	...	2,701,300	84,600	5,350	1,203,121[4]	129,781	3,147	99.0	15
Greece	910,576	33,466	9,593	613,720	28,515	2,162	125,039	...	1,991	117,407	7,932	157	86.0	15
Guatemala	803,404	23,770	7,708	126,844	9,613[3]	753	29,768	—	...	54,284	4,017	...	36.7	15
Honduras	704,612	19,270	6,264	123,245[3]	3,406[3]	296	—	—	11	27,925	1,606	3	59.5	10
Hong Kong	540,022	19,285	769	139,830	16,925[3]	402	11,598	—	19	32,697	3,222	23	80.9	15
Hungary	1,213,465	78,053	3,800	209,300	15,966	531	157,400	10,700	328[4]	102,564	13,843	57	98.2	15
India	72,687,840	1,345,376	484,165	29,352,019[3]	1,731,978[3]	156,055	—	—	1,704	4,296,242	244,448	6,784	36.2	15
Indonesia	23,862,488	713,222	110,050	5,256,117	307,376	15,721	576,791	2,049	2,049	248,524[2]	22,789[2]	43[2]	72.0	10
Iran	4,403,106	154,577	40,197	2,428,173	94,948	7,913	256,303	10,041	704	175,675	15,453	244	36.1	15
Iraq	2,615,910	94,000	10,560	976,494	29,366	1,625	56,924	4,148	109	102,430	6,515	62	52.0	15
Ireland	568,364	20,068	3,494	287,017	18,255	822	6,792	202	47	41,928	3,983	58	100.0	15
Israel	573,280	41,888	1,808	193,516	31,570[3]	651	84,919	—	376	88,258	13,981	51	93.3	14
Italy	4,335,911	285,908	29,785	3,723,671	290,376	31,524	1,575,791	135,614	5,334[4]	719,449	48,118	67	93.6	15
Ivory Coast	954,190	24,441	2,697	174,366	4,113	127	22,437	620	...	12,470	580	2	41.2	15
Japan	11,739,466	474,018	25,044	10,421,973[3]	526,388[3]	16,318	—	—	...	2,261,167	130,109	1,052	100.0	15
Jordan	454,391	14,303	1,095	238,763	11,267	1,333	9,880	641	44	18,906	816	31	60.0	15
Korea, South	5,465,848	124,572	6,501	3,672,565	92,191	3,024	879,550	28,347	745	879,335	26,529	236	94.3	15
Kuwait	148,983	8,035	180	181,461	15,257	206	421	85	34[4]	12,435	1,143	1	59.6	15
Laos	463,098	14,983	2,125	80,769	3,487	46	1,849	218	18	1,157	118	3	41.0	15
Lebanon	405,402	22,646	2,144	256,107	21,736	257	31,203	2,956	...	85,087	2,313	15	88.0	15
Lesotho	244,838	4,782	1,081	23,355	940	96	1,140	121	12[4]	1,682	162	9	60.0	15
Liberia	227,431	9,099	1,151	52,301	1,146	275	2,322	63	6[4]	3,789	190	3	25.4	15
Libya	674,960	34,557	2,539	299,939	22,812	1,156	16,900	1,004	129[4]	25,700	1,340	19	52.4	15
Luxembourg	27,927	1,449	541	9,232	1,801[3]	...	16,443	—	...	404	168	2	100.0	15
Malawi	809,802	12,540	2,371	19,760	942	71	1,077	91	6	2,000	190	2	16.5	15
Malaysia	2,120,050	81,664	6,518	1,191,588	54,702	1,071	19,916	1,611	34	56,521	5,131	35	75.0	10
Mali	298,831	7,214	1,263	73,136	3,125	15	2,609	540	3	5,281	489	6	2.2	15
Mauritius	131,594	6,420	262	76,308	3,144	149	508	69	7	436	79	2	84.6	15
Mexico	14,981,028	400,417	76,266	3,970,721	218,986	15,110	1,361,410	82,953	2,912	875,600	69,553	941	78.8	15
Morocco	2,418,385	63,157	2,498	900,694	39,035	644	10,300	...	...	98,513	2,558	19	22.2	...
Mozambique	1,376,865	18,751	5,709	135,956	3,789	138	...	...	...	1,852	224	...	27.5	15
Nepal	1,142,900	29,139	10,340	558,996[3]	17,154[3]	4,253	—	—	...	38,450	2,918	10	12.5	15
Netherlands, The	1,368,176	66,359	9,710	828,221	56,101	1,552	582,199	52,000	1,863	251,293	26,000	373	100.0	15
New Zealand	493,856	21,300	2,808	230,827	15,232	396	140,706	2,506	29[4]	31,549	3,043	15	100.0	15
Nicaragua	509,240	14,105	4,976	118,647	1,801	333	17,982	1,066	52	34,710	1,299	4	87.0	15
Nigeria	12,554,222	309,597	36,287	1,840,063	67,392	3,182	57,492	2,619	126	115,166	5,748	77	29.9	15
Norway	383,599	30,124	3,526[5]	282,231	13,517	—	86,393[4]	14,992[4]	967	71,789	6,695	199	100.0	15
Pakistan	6,451,000	147,000	58,398	2,080,000[3]	129,035[3]	8,989	—	—	...	384,181	19,878	554	26.7	10
Panama	336,740	12,853	2,347	130,427	6,545	198	44,364	2,379	115	45,361	3,456	3	84.6	15
Papua New Guinea	300,536	9,935	2,077	41,350	1,790	108	7,984	499	88	2,224	413	3	30.4	10
Paraguay	530,083	19,748	3,425	124,481[3]	9,830[3]	745	—	—	10	27,138	2,017	4	3.4	15
Peru	3,161,400	80,331	20,776	1,362,600	37,383	2,456	...	...	682[4]	249,800	13,468	33	82.3	15
Philippines	8,033,642	264,241	33,180	2,928,525[3]	85,779[3]	2,445[2]	—	—	...	1,182,103	40,022	...	76.4	15
Poland	4,341,800	224,500	13,926	429,900	22,500	1,201	1,692,000	82,300	6,310	386,500	55,450[4]	91	98.0	15
Puerto Rico	470,089	23,154	1,618	337,153	13,297	619	60,045	2,600	68	130,105	3,300	27	90.5	14
Romania	3,285,073	157,709	14,381	1,027,106	48,468	971	148,040	2,060	903[4]	190,903	14,354	44	100.0	8
Rwanda	704,924	11,912	1,606	8,602	887[3]	80	2,065	—	38	1,266	229	4	22.9	15
Saudi Arabia	926,531	50,511	4,983	343,890	25,966	1,617	5,106	822	88	56,252	6,598	17	25.0	...
Senegal	419,748	9,842	1,493	80,076	3,574	89	7,679	578	124[4]	12,373	638	130	45.6	14
Singapore	289,092	9,452	342	177,845	8,515	151	14,990	1,199	17	25,736	2,586	4	84.8	10
South Africa	4,391,089	—	2,511[5]	1,633,092	182,953[3,6]	...	29,591	—	153	251,723	16,673	106	89.0	...
Soviet Union	34,800,000	—	71,400	9,949,000	2,831,300[3,6]	57,000	3,713,000	—	4,500	5,284,000	345,000	891	100.0	15
Spain	6,778,877	228,307	216,653	1,091,197	66,160	2,445	558,808	36,556	2,142	649,098	40,321	120	90.1	15
Sri Lanka	2,081,391	—	3,846	1,267,323	142,689[6]	5,973	4,778	1,239	...	36,628	2,017	...	86.5	10
Sudan	1,464,227	43,451	5,729	368,649	18,148	1,496	15,545	684	41	26,996	6,497	17	68.6	10
Suriname	75,139	2,803	285	31,065	2,002	100	4,394	249	...	2,353	155	2	65.0	15
Swaziland	119,913	3,586	470	25,450	1,592	88	538	65	1	979	108	1	22.0	15
Sweden	662,581	40,747	4,922	606,152	82,393[3]	...	103,485	—	526	205,431	...	...	100.0	15
Syria	1,523,339	54,519	7,750	575,940	31,669	1,345	25,148	3,194	60	110,823	1,332	8	61.5	15
Taiwan	2,226,699	70,055	2,428	1,269,373	58,713	1,023[3]	394,258	14,442	—	364,162	17,292	104	85.9	15
Thailand	7,370,846	304,400	32,956	1,610,286	71,446	2,249	297,114	12,680	309	472,995	25,045	12	81.8	10
Togo	506,356	9,193	2,000	128,475	2,877	113	7,973	326	22	3,638	291	2	54.9	14
Tunisia	1,045,011	26,989	2,613	214,996	12,777[3]	237	80,190	—	1	31,887	3,647	...	45.0	10
Turkey	5,691,066	215,073	44,098	1,697,454	78,208	5,062	503,205	33,840	1,718[4]	271,138	15,502	331	54.7	6
Uganda	1,223,850	36,442	4,294	74,003	3,501	227	3,926	274	15	6,192	677	4	47.9	15
United Kingdom	5,133,710	270,346	...	5,116,354	333,515[3]	...	243,743	—	...	799,462	42,840	...	100.0	15
United States	30,780,000[7]	1,359,000[7]	...	13,495,000[3]	1,035,000[3]	...	—	—	...	12,400,000[1]	870,000[4]	...	100.0	15
Uruguay	331,247	14,768	2,307	130,203	14,321	284	45,663	4,200	80	36,296	3,847	1	93.9	15
Venezuela	2,456,815	88,493	12,753	780,396	45,888[3]	1,447	40,264	—	...	299,773	27,025	68	84.9	15
Western Samoa	40,475	1,460	162	12,082	512	39	211	38	3	85	6	6	98.3	10
Yugoslavia	1,431,582	59,391	13,119	1,838,269	131,348[3]	5,905	587,895	—	1,630[4]	448,755	24,171	349	83.5	15
Zaire	3,919,395	80,481	5,924	749,519	14,483[3]	2,511	70,342	—	...	28,430	2,782	36	57.9	15
Zambia	1,068,314	23,100	2,809	103,347	5,056	139	5,487	515	12	3,603	334	1	40.7	15
Zimbabwe	1,934,614	36,734	2,548	224,609	6,112	177	640	36	...	2,525	483	...	70.8	15

Note: ... indicates figures not available; — indicates not applicable.
[1]Unless otherwise specified, secondary includes teacher training where available. [2]Public schools only. [3]Includes vocational. [4]Includes teacher training. [5]Includes secondary. [6]Includes primary.
[7]Includes preprimary.

proached, the issue of "excellence in education" was taken up by the politicians. Both President Reagan and the numerous contenders for the Democratic nomination emphasized their support for the concept, although Reagan continued to insist that primary responsibility for improving the schools lay with the states and local districts. One remedy espoused by Reagan, among others, was merit pay for teachers, with salaries based on proficiency rather than length of service or number of degrees. Teachers and their unions remained generally fearful that the decision as to who was most proficient would become politicized. They stressed that the first step was to raise salaries for all teachers; once teaching had been one of the few occupations open to women, but with the lowering of sex barriers in higher paying and more prestigious professions, the best female students were entering other fields.

Contrasting with the findings of the various task forces and commissions, a Gallup Poll indicated that most Americans believed lack of discipline was the public schools' biggest problem. Lack of discipline in the home was pinpointed by 72% of the adults surveyed. Fifty-four percent said lack of respect for law and authority was the second most important cause of discipline problems. The survey found large declines in the number of persons who would like their children to be teachers and of those who thought school taxes should be raised. Most respondents opposed lengthening the school year, and only 35% thought teacher salaries were too low.

The educational ferment in the U.S. was partly reflected and partly stimulated by an educational historian's critical evaluation of modern U.S. education. In *The Troubled Crusade: American Education, 1945–1980,* Diane Ravitch traced the shift from the Progressive goal of creating useful citizens to the personal fulfillment of the 1970s. In the process she demonstrated that U.S. schools, far from confining their mission to education, have often been the arena where political struggles—e.g., the civil rights movement—are first worked out. But she was ultimately optimistic, believing that present concerns and the resiliency of U.S. education could bring useful reformation.

The president continued to support tuition tax credits for parents who preferred to send their children to private schools, but no legislative action was taken during the year. Meanwhile, a national study carried out by Ohio State University indicated that public school students are as well prepared for college as students from Roman Catholic schools and slightly better prepared than those from other private schools. These findings contradicted a study made in 1981 by James Coleman for the U.S. National Center for Education Statistics. The new study did find that students graduating from private schools were more likely to go to college. It concluded that parental educational level and income were the determining factors.

Earlier findings were also contradicted in a study funded by the Department of Education, which reported that children of single and working parents score lower than other children on achievement tests. A National Institute of Education study had found no difference between the scores of children with working mothers and those with mothers in the home.

BILL PIERCE/TIME MAGAZINE

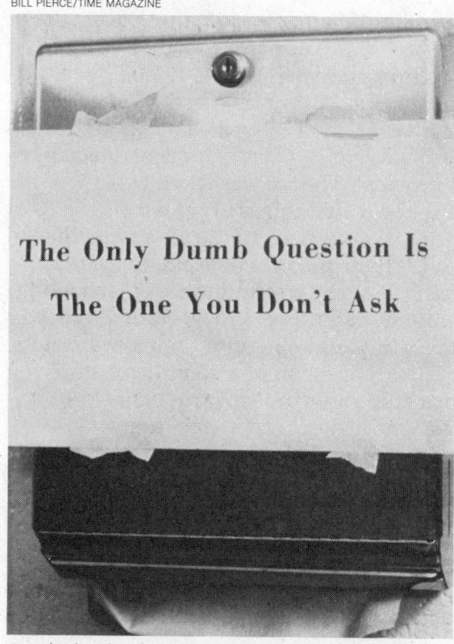

One high school science laboratory featured a sign designed to elicit questions—any questions.

Continuing the trend of the previous year, mathematics scores on the Scholastic Aptitude Test, used to help determine college admission, rose slightly. The increase of about 1% in mathematics scores was balanced by a similar decline in the verbal section. (*See* Sidebar.)

In China Premier Zhao Ziyang (Chao Tzuyang), speaking at the sixth People's National Congress in June, spelled out China's commitment to education as a "prerequisite for invigorating [the] national economy." The main complaint was a familiar one in expanding educational systems: too many people were opting for higher education and not enough were learning technical and vocational skills. China, it was argued, must lose no time in setting up "vocational and technical schools in a planned way." The intention was that senior "middle" vocational school students should account for more than 40% of the total over the next five years. Concern with vocational education also surfaced in the West, notably in the U.K., where a Technical and Vocational Educational Initiative was introduced by the Conservative government. This trend toward "vocationalism" in the secondary schools was not altogether favourably received, partly because it was felt that it might distort the curriculum and partly because it smacked of too much interference from the central government. However, since, it represented the only new money being injected into the system, local authorities were willing to embrace it.

Several newly elected socialist regimes experienced ideological struggles during the year. The French government's proposals to bring about a measure of integration between the public and private sectors—mainly the highly subsidized Roman Catholic schools—met fierce opposition. A public opinion poll in June showed that 48% opposed any change, while 42% supported the government. The hard fact was that many Socialist voters sent their own children to parochial schools. The much criticized *baccalauréat* examination, used to determine whether 18- and 19-year-old school-leavers would gain university admission, remained an intractable problem. The *bac* was taken by 40% of the age group, about two-thirds of whom (*i.e.*, 28% of the age group) succeeded. To the distress of the Socialists, with their theories of equal education for all, the *bac* had a perverse influence on schooling, since ambitious parents were desperate to get their children into schools known for their good results. Antoine Prost, chairman of a committee studying *lycée* reforms, recommended introducing continuous assessment instead of a single exam.

In Spain, too, relations between the Roman Catholic Church and the state were deteriorating. A major controversy arose in June when the church distributed 200,000 catechisms for fifth- and sixth-year students in private and public schools and the government ordered their withdrawal. The church controlled some 30% of Spain's school system.

The Labor government in Australia determined to cut assistance to private schools, as promised in its election manifesto. In practice only some 40 private schools would be affected, and they were in no way designed for the needy. The new minister of education, Susan Ryan, managed to increase educational spending by £30 million in real terms. Her measures included a grant for improving schools in disadvantaged areas and an allocation for schools serving the Aboriginal community. In Austria, where elections reduced the lead of the Social Democrats, the comprehensive (general secondary) school experiment was more or less abandoned.

Proper provision for the education of ethnic minorities was a growing concern. In England the Inner London Education Authority proposed a number of measures to ensure greater black participation in school government. There was some difference of opinion in Western countries, however, especially where immigrant communities were concerned. At an international conference in Würzburg, West Germany, the federal education minister, Dorothee Wilms, said that immigrants should either integrate or return home since genuine multicultural development, in her view, was not an option. In the U.S. critics of the Reagan administration noted that the Department of Justice had ceased to intervene actively in desegregation cases and had supported congressional action to ban the use of busing as a solution to school segregation. In its first two and a half years, the administration had undertaken only one new desegregation lawsuit.

The military regime in Turkey imposed a National Education Law that lowered the starting age from seven to six and provided for eight years of compulsory education, including compulsory

A Hysteria of Wastern Sybilization

Learned treatises have deplored the state of North American education in the past year, but perhaps more eloquent testimony comes from the students themselves. The following brief sketch of Western civilization was culled from freshman history essays handed in at the University of Alberta and at McMaster University. This article is abridged from the original published in the *Wilson Quarterly* for Spring 1983. Copyright 1983 by the Woodrow Wilson International Center for Scholars; used by permission.

Compiled by Anders Henriksson

History is always bias, because human beings have to be studied by other human beings, not by independent observers of another species.

During the Middle Ages everbody was middle aged. Middle Evil society was made up of monks, lords and surfs. After a revival of infantile commerce slowly creeped into Europe, merchants appeared. They roamed from town to town exposing themselves and organized big fairies in the countryside. Murder during this period was nothing. Finally, Europe caught the Black Death. It was spread from port to port by inflected rats.

The Middle Ages slimpered to a halt. The renasence bolted in from the blue. Life reeked with joy. Man was determined to civilise himself and his brothers, even if heads had to roll! Europe was full of incredable churches with great art bulging out their doors.

The Reformnation happened when German nobles resented the idea that tithes were going to Papal France or the Pope thus enriching Catholic coiffures. An angry Martin Luther nailed 95 theocrats to a church door. Theologically, Luther was into reorientation mutation. Calvinism was the most convenient religion since the days of the ancients. The Popes, of course, were usually Catholic.

Louis XIV became King of the Sun. He gave the people food and artillery. If he didn't like someone, he sent them to the gallows to row for the rest of their lives. The enlightenment was a reasonable time. Philosophers were unknown yet. The French revolution was accomplished before it happened. History, a record of things left behind by past generations, started in 1815.

Great Brittian, the USA and other European countrys had demicratic leanings. Among the goals of the chartists were universal suferage and an anal parliment. Voting was to be done by ballad. Founder of the new Italy was Cavour, an intelligent Sardine from the north.

World War I broke out around 1912–1914. Germany was on one side of France and Russia on the other. Peace was proclaimed at Versigh, which was attended by George Loid, Primal Minister of England, and President Wilson with 14 pointers. In 1937 Lenin revolted Russia.

Germany was displaced after WWI. This gave rise to Hitler. A huge anti-semantic movement arose. Moosealini invaded Hi Lee Salasy. Germany invaded Poland. France invaded Belgium, and Russia invaded everybody. War screeched to an end when a nukuleer explosion was dropped on Heroshima. The last stage is us.

moral and religious teaching. Private schools intended to prepare for university entrance were to cease from the summer of 1984, but there was strong opposition, and it was said that most private schools would go underground. Fines were also introduced for illiterates who failed to go to literacy classes, though it was unclear how the law would be enforced. In Czechoslovakia, where the 1976 reform of secondary education had made its way through the schools, fresh emphasis was being placed on science. Emphasis on science in the new examinations for university entrance in Hungary caused widespread resentment, but the point of the reform was to make the universities more accessible to students from vocational schools and reduce the input from grammar schools, where less time was spent on science and technology.

A report of the South African government's Human Sciences Research Council, issued in September, claimed that 50 to 60% of blacks in South Africa were literate, compared with an average for the third world of 30%. Nonetheless, the literacy rate was too low for a largely industrial society. The report blamed the high dropout rate from black schools. In a sense, Japan faced the opposite problem, an excessive addiction to education with a high rate of suicides among would-be university students who failed their examinations and an increasing incidence of delinquency. High pressure in the schools and cramming for examinations were blamed, together with the growing influence of the individualistic values of the West and the beginnings of a tendency to rebel against a system characterized by uniformity and rote learning.

Higher Education. The relationship between universities and politics was apparent in many countries. In Sri Lanka student protests preceded the turbulence that wracked the nation during the summer. (*See* SRI LANKA.) Pres. J. R. Jayawardene strengthened central control over all higher education. In Ghana all three universities, with a student body of 8,000, were closed in May following serious disturbances. Iran began cautiously reopening the universities closed following the 1978–79 revolution. Of the 5 universities and 11 higher education colleges in Teheran, 12 were partially opened, though the student body totaled only 4,500–5,000, compared with 17,000 before the shah was overthrown. In Poland the government and the universities remained at odds, despite the 1982 Education Act, which guaranteed faculty tenure and self-government to the universities. The death of a student in May, after a police beating, led to strong protests and a national student boycott of the traditional matriculation festivities. Sporadic protests continued to be reported from black universities in South Africa. In particular, there was student unrest at the two large universities in the Lebowa homeland and at the University of Fort Hare in Ciskei.

Financial restrictions on universities were widely reported. In Israel, where the Lebanon campaign had drained the treasury, university budgets were reduced by 10% as part of a major budget slash in August. The education minister, Zevulun Hammer, announced that he would fight the cuts. Shlomo Gazed, the president of Ben-Gurion University in Beersheba, said that cuts at such a level would have very serious effects and could mean that Israel would lose its qualitative edge over the Arab states in science and technology. He claimed that 90,000 students in the Arab states were studying computers, compared with 20,000 Israelis.

ART SHAY/TIME MAGAZINE

Drab lab: not only was the ceiling paint peeling at this University of Illinois chemistry laboratory, but some equipment worked only part of the time and some not at all. Similar problems surfaced across the country, as public colleges and universities faced stiff competition for the allocation of scarce resources.

In Canada draconian proposals to abolish faculty tenure were made by the new Social Credit legislature elected in British Columbia. In other provinces relatively small increases in expenditures for universities were proposed, with the exception of Manitoba, which agreed to an increase of 10.3%. The universities decided to hold a National Universities Week in October to "enhance national awareness" of their importance. In the U.K. budgetary retrenchment continued to bear hard on the universities. The vice-chancellors predicted that the cuts would amount to about 1.5% per annum over the next few years.

In France, by contrast, there was the promise of more spending for technology and electronics graduate students and for the in-service training of teachers in the use of information technology. More controversially, a University Reform Bill was presented by the Socialist government which attempted to restructure higher education, notably by bringing the elite *grandes écoles* under the same policy umbrella as the universities and by linking universities more closely with their own regions. The proposals led to violent demonstrations, especially in the Law Faculty of the University of Paris, well known for its right-wing associations. In Spain the new government continued its attempts to open up the universities to outside influences, but with only modest results. Against fierce opposition, a law was passed opening university posts to Spanish speakers from Latin America and the U.S.

The Australian Labor government gave a boost to the flagging Australian universities by promising 25,000 more university places over three years and an 11% increase in university budgets. There was also some expansion in Malaysia, partly because fewer students were going to universities abroad. The Malaysians especially resented the fact that the U.K. government had increased fees for overseas students. In addition to the five universities already in Malaysia, a Saudi-financed Islamic university was promised for Kuala Lumpur.

Proposals to increase the number of states in Nigeria—possibly to 45 from the current 19—raised the prospect of a corresponding increase in the number of university institutions. The policy hitherto had been that there should be at least one university for each state. The proposal was not viewed uncritically, however, since it seemed apparent that there were not enough secondary-school-leavers with adequate qualifications to justify that many new establishments. In terms of comparative populations, however, the biggest expansion was proposed in Greenland, where it was decided to open a mini university in January 1984. The new institution would provide a two-year course in preparation for further higher education in Denmark. The emphasis was to be on the study of Greenland's heritage.

Although the number of university students in India increased, it was becoming evident that standards were on the decline. In 1951 India had 27 universities with 360,000 students; by 1983 the figures had grown to 120 universities with over 3 million students. In the same period, the number of affiliated colleges had risen from 524 to 33,000, at least 1,500 of which had been declared "nonviable" by the University Grants Commission. Despite this, private institutions continued to grow. Indicating the difficulties with standards, the vice-chancellor of Bombay University was eased out and replaced by a senior civil servant with sweeping powers in order to forestall problems over the holding of examinations and the announcement of examination results.

REBOURS—SIPA PRESS/BLACK STAR

Paris in springtime: students protested education reforms proposed by the Socialist government's Savary Commission. Certain proposals were aimed at linking higher education institutions more closely with their regions. Many of the protesters were rightists, but the group in the foreground proclaimed "Neither right nor left, (but) together against the reform."

In the U.S. college graduates were told to expect bleak job prospects as the number of high-level jobs increased at a rate lower than the number of persons graduating. The outlook was brightest for graduates with degrees in electrical engineering, computer science, and accounting, but even in these fields the number of openings was decreasing. Geologists, in great demand a few years earlier, found the field overcrowded as oil companies cut back on exploration. The College Placement Council reported that starting salaries for liberal arts majors had fallen 7% between 1982 and 1983, to an average of slightly over $14,000, and many graduates were being forced to accept low-prestige jobs far removed from their fields of study.

The poor outlook for graduates of traditional colleges brought a boom in private vocational and technical schools. It also rekindled the debate about the worth of a college education. Some educators feared that the U.S.—like many less developed countries—was producing a class of highly educated unemployables, and they called for colleges and universities to align their courses more closely to the needs of the job market. Others insisted that the monetary returns of college training had always been oversold and that the true purpose of higher education was to produce cultured and thinking citizens, fitted for an economy in which two or three career changes over the course of a person's working life might well become the norm. Meanwhile, the colleges themselves continued to wrestle with decreased or inflation-pinched spending levels and declining enrollments. Competition to attract outstanding high school graduates was especially keen, and some prestigious institutions were offering merit scholarships to bright students regardless of need.

But finance was not the only embarrassment for universities. In England the bequest left by Arthur Koestler and his wife—both of whom died in a suicide pact—was to found a chair in parapsychology. This was a "discipline" with few supporters in England. Nonetheless, £400,000 was £400,000 and, moreover, professors of parapsychology were not unknown. They existed in the U.S. and in Utrecht, Neth., and Freiburg, West Germany. In the event, several university contenders emerged, though some suspected it was all a Koestlerian joke to embarrass English academics, who had been so hostile to him during his lifetime.

(JOEL L. BURDIN; TUDOR DAVID)

See also Libraries; Motion Pictures.

Egypt

A republic of northeast Africa, Egypt is bounded by Israel, Sudan, Libya, the Mediterranean Sea, and the Red Sea. Area: 997,667 sq km (385,201 sq mi). Pop. (1983 est.): 45,851,000. Cap. and largest city: Cairo (pop., 1981 est., 5,650,000). Language: Arabic. Religion (1980 est.): Muslim 81.8%; Christian 17.8%; atheist 0.4%. President in 1983, Hosni Mubarak; prime minister, Ahmad Fuad Mohieddin.

Pres. Hosni Mubarak's taciturn and cautious style still had its critics, but his tough line on corruption and his ability to placate religious factions helped him to consolidate his power base in Egypt during 1983. Although relations with Arab countries had not improved as quickly as expected, Arab private investment remained steady. Friendship with Western countries, particularly the U.S., remained warm, but relations with Israel deteriorated.

On October 6 Egypt celebrated the tenth anniversary of the crossing of the Suez Canal that launched the 1973 war with Israel. It was also the second anniversary of the assassination of Pres. Anwar as-Sadat. Four days before the anniversary, Parliament agreed on a further extension of the state of emergency declared after Sadat's death. This legalized arbitrary arrest and detention without trial, as well as restricting freedom of assembly. The extension was justified in a statement listing 13 attempts to overthrow the government during the previous 12 months.

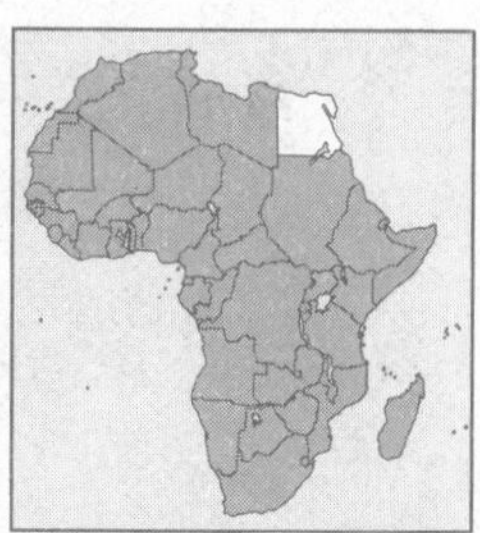
Egypt

Among those held in detention was the Coptic leader Shenuda III, who was under house arrest, accused of inciting religious hatred. In October the president stated that he could make no promises about when Shenuda would be released. Coptic leaders expressed fears that Egypt might follow Sudan's decision in September to introduce Islamic law and punishments. On May 25 the president attended the opening of the Nile Valley Parliament, an Egyptian-Sudanese political forum, and presided at a meeting of the Higher Council for Integration between Egypt and Sudan.

President Mubarak's campaign to clean up public life resulted in the sacking of two ministers following the trial on corruption charges of Esmat as-Sadat, brother of the late president. On March 11 the Court of Ethics alleged that three ministers and other officials had failed to prevent the crimes committed by Sadat and three of his sons. Two of the ministers named, Minister of Supply and Internal Trade Ahmad Nouh and Industry and Mineral Resources Minister Fuad Abu Zaghla, were dismissed from the Cabinet; they were replaced by Muhammad Sayed Al-Gharouri and Muhammad Nagui Shatla, respectively. The third man accused in the case, Soleiman Metwali, kept his position as minister of transport and communications. Sadat and his sons received one-year jail sentences in February and were ordered to forfeit family assets totaling $148 million.

As part of his antiluxury drive, President Mubarak imposed restrictions on the importation of television sets and other electrical appliances. Subsidies were removed from some items, and a ban was imposed on the importation of medicines and

EGYPT

Education. (1980–81) Primary, pupils 4,662,816, teachers 167,821; secondary, pupils 2,238,882, teachers 83,364; vocational, pupils 633,909, teachers 34,487; teacher training, students 56,377, teachers 4,148; higher (universities only), students (1979–80) 502,884, teaching staff (1978–79) 21,680.

Finance. Monetary unit: Egyptian pound, with (Sept. 20, 1983) an official rate of E£0.70 to U.S. $1 (free rate of E£1.05 = £1 sterling) and a special transactions rate of E£0.82 to U.S. $1 (E£1.24 = £1 sterling). Gold and other reserves (June 1983) U.S. $762 million. Budget (1980–81 est.): revenue E£5,925 million; expenditure E£5,707 million. Gross national product (1982-83) E£23,126 million. Money supply (May 1983) E£8,386 million. Cost of living (1975 = 100; May 1983) 297.4

Foreign Trade. (1982) Imports E£6,354 million; exports E£2,184 million. Import sources: U.S. 19%; West Germany 10%; Italy 8%; France 8%; Japan 5%. Export destinations: Italy 22%; Israel 14%; France 7%; Romania 6%; The Netherlands 5%; United States 5%. Main exports (1981): crude oil 54%; cotton 15%; petroleum products 10%; cotton yarn 5%.

Transport and Communications. Roads (1982) 28,010 km. Motor vehicles in use (1982): passenger 461,300; commercial 176,600. Railways (1980): 4,667 km; traffic 10,995,000,000 passenger-km, freight (1979) 2,472,000,000 net ton-km. Air traffic (1982): 3,643,000,000 passenger-km; freight c. 56 million net ton-km. Shipping (1982): merchant vessels 100 gross tons and over 341; gross tonnage 635,801. Telephones (Jan. 1981) 534,000. Radio receivers (Dec. 1980) 6 million. Television receivers (Dec. 1980) 1.4 million.

Agriculture. Production (in 000; metric tons; 1982): wheat c. 2,016; millet c. 633; corn c. 2,709; rice c. 2,287; potatoes c. 1,100; sugar, raw value c. 758; tomatoes c. 2,500; onions c. 657; dry broad beans (1981) c. 262; watermelons (1981) c. 1,267; dates c. 393; oranges c. 916; grapes c. 309; cotton, lint 452; cheese 259; beef and buffalo meat c. 278. Livestock (in 000; 1981): cattle 1,912; buffalo 2,347; sheep c. 1,700; goats c. 1,500; asses c. 1,746; camels 84; chickens c. 27,903.

Industry. Production (in 000; metric tons; 1982): crude oil 35,100; natural gas (cu m) 2,670,000; petroleum products (1981) 13,575; cement (1981) 3,432; iron ore (metal content; 1981) 900; sulfuric acid (1981) 47; fertilizers (nutrient content; 1981–82) nitrogenous c. 482, phosphate c. 117; salt (1981) 837; cotton yarn 238; cotton fabrics (m) 834,000; electricity (kw-hr; 1981) 18,590,000.

UPI

Egypt's Pres. Hosni Mubarak (left) and Sudan's Pres. Gaafar Nimeiry discussed closer cooperation between their countries in the first meeting of the Higher Council for Integration at Khartoum in February.

cosmetics that were locally produced. The clampdown on dissidents, begun after Sadat's death, continued. More than 300 had been put on trial since December 1982. Among them were 176 members of the Jihad movement of Muslim fundamentalists, who were accused of plotting to overthrow the government.

On October 11 a group of 52 U.S. senators demanded that President Mubarak restore his ambassador to Tel Aviv, withdrawn following the massacre of hundreds of Palestinian refugees in Lebanon in September 1982. The senators said that Egypt was mounting a "cold war" against Israel in contravention of the 1978 Camp David accords. Indeed, in a first comment on the new Israeli government of Prime Minister Yitzhak Shamir (*see* BIOGRAPHIES), Minister of Foreign Affairs Kamal Hassan Ali "regretted" that Shamir had pledged to build more Jewish settlements in occupied Arab territory. In response to U.S. complaints, President Mubarak was reported to have made the return of Egypt's ambassador contingent on an end to the building of settlements on the West Bank and a total withdrawal of Israel's forces from Lebanon. He was also reported to have demanded progress in talks on the return of Taba, a small strip of land on the Gulf of Aqaba, which Egypt claimed should have been returned with the rest of Sinai in 1982. Israel was quick to condemn Mubarak's warm meeting with Yasir Arafat (*see* BIOGRAPHIES) on December 22. The Palestine Liberation Organization (PLO) chairman visited Cairo after his evacuation from Tripoli, Lebanon, where he and his followers had been besieged by PLO dissidents.

The bleak tone of these events contrasted sharply with the atmosphere earlier in 1983, when Egyptian and Israeli officials held talks on trade and commerce in Giza during March 14–16. Egypt said that Israel could expect normal, but not special, trade links.

The main effect of Sadat's foreign policy had been to alienate Egypt from Arab countries opposed to Camp David. Aid had ceased, and the Saudi Arabian government had declined to go ahead with the financing of F-5E fighter aircraft for the Egyptian Air Force. The loss of Arab aid, however, was more than offset by economic and military assistance from the U.S. In the 1983–84 fiscal year Egypt was expected to receive up to $2.3 billion in economic and military aid, compared with $2,075,000,000 in 1982–83. Egyptian officials expressed concern over the U.S.-Israeli agreement on "strategic cooperation," worked out during Shamir's trip to Washington in late November, although the U.S. offered assurances that the agreement had not changed its attitude toward peace in the Middle East.

Trade between Egypt and Arab countries had slowed after 1978, but necessity dictated a cautious resumption of relations. Iraq and Jordan led the way at a semiofficial level. The war with Iran forced Iraq to turn to Egypt for spare parts, weapons, and ammunition. Jordan agreed to resume trade relations in April, and an end to the Jordanian embargo was announced in December. Algeria, Morocco, and Iraq reopened airline offices in Cairo and resumed flights.

The year was a difficult one for the economy, but there were some encouraging signs. Earnings from oil sales were projected at $2.3 billion for 1983–84, while tolls from the Suez Canal were expected to reach $1 billion. Tourism had recovered from the shock of Sadat's assassination. Remittances from Egyptians working abroad were steady at about $3 billion a year. Nevertheless, the planned budget deficit for 1983–84 was $6 billion, external debt stood at $22 billion, and the estimated current account deficit for 1983–84 was approaching $3 billion.

A five-year (1983–87) plan gave special priority to the rehabilitation of water and waste-water networks throughout the country, particularly in Cairo and Alexandria. Another priority was housing. Demand for new homes had been established at some 200,000 a year, but only about 80,000 were being built. Adding urgency to these problems were Egypt's rapid population growth and the long-term loss of prime farmland to urban and village sprawl. Self-sufficient in food less than ten years earlier, Egypt now had to import half of its food, at an estimated cost in 1983 of almost $4 billion. Food shortages had become common.

Military spending continued at a high level. The equipment of the armed forces was still largely Soviet in origin, but closer relations with Washington had brought increasing amounts of U.S. military hardware. On September 14 the U.S. Defense Department told Congress that it intended to supply 16 Harpoon tactical antiship cruise missiles to Egypt. The U.S. also contracted to provide 94 tanks and other military equipment worth $145 million, while F-16 fighter aircraft, battle tanks, and Sidewinder air-to-air missiles were to be supplied in separate arrangements. Egypt's own armaments industry had become more sophisticated and was earning the country some $1 billion a year. The first locally made surface-to-air missile, known as Hawkeye, was launched for the first time in October.

On November 1 talks resumed with the International Monetary Fund (IMF) over the terms for a new standby credit. Reports from Cairo suggested that the payments deficit might first be eased by the World Bank, which was contemplating increasing its loans from $350 million to $650 million annually over a five-year period. Wagih Shindy, the investment and international cooperation minister, said that negotiations with the IMF could result in a standby credit of $700 million–$800 million over three years. In return it was expected that Egypt would have to implement IMF austerity measures, including gasoline price increases and adjustments in the value of the Egyptian pound.

President Mubarak received a warm welcome during a state visit to China in April. He was the first Egyptian head of state to visit Beijing (Peking). The visit had considerable significance as an indication of the distance Egypt had traveled from the pro-Moscow line it followed during the years of Pres. Gamal Abdel Nasser. Another sign of the eclipse of Soviet influence was the decision to call in U.S. engineers to repair faults in the Soviet-built Aswan High Dam, opened in 1964.

(JOHN WHELAN)

Electrical Industries: *see* Energy; Industrial Review

Electronics: *see* Computers; Industrial Review

PETER R. McCORMICK/THE NEW YORK TIMES

Salvadoran guerrilla leader Salvador Cayetano Carpio (centre) attended the funeral of his comrade Mélida Anaya Montes at Managua, Nicaragua, and posed between Sandinista leaders Interior Minister Tomás Borge Martínez (left) and Daniel Ortega Saavedra, coordinator of the Nicaraguan junta. A few days later Carpio killed himself, it was said because he learned that Anaya Montes had been betrayed by a comrade.

El Salvador

A republic on the Pacific coast of Central America and the smallest country on the isthmus, El Salvador is bounded on the west by Guatemala and on the north and east by Honduras. Area: 21,041 sq km (8,124 sq mi). Pop. (1983 est.): 4,998,600. Cap. and largest city: San Salvador (pop., 1982 est., 440,000). Language: Spanish. Religion: Roman Catholic (1980) 96.2%. President of the civilian-military junta in 1983, Álvaro Alfredo Magaña Borjo.

El Salvador's violent civil war entered its fourth consecutive year in 1983 without any end to the conflict in sight. The conflict was characterized by an unusually high number of civilian deaths as the military forces tried to eliminate all potential support for the guerrilla forces, which were organized into the Farabundo Martí National Liberation Front (FMLN). The Ministry of Defense estimated that more than 30,000 people had died since the beginning of hostilities in 1979. Among the victims in 1983 were Marianella García Villas, one of the founders of the Salvadoran Commission for Human Rights, and three teachers from a UNESCO-sponsored literacy campaign. In addition, hundreds of thousands of people were displaced from their homes and were living in refugee camps either inside El Salvador or in other countries.

A U.S. embassy report said that war damage had caused overall losses to the economy of some $600 million since 1979. Gross domestic product fell 25% in three years (1979–82) as a result of factory closings, farms left idle, and increased spending on defense. Export earnings dropped by 33%, and per capita income declined from $670 to $470. Guerrilla sabotage caused some $40 million worth of damage to the electricity grid and an additional $100 million in damage to bridges and power plants. The economy maintained its level of economic activity only by large injections of foreign funds from the International Monetary Fund, the Inter-American Development Bank, and the U.S. government. The latter provided a total of $165 million in economic and $76 million in military aid during the 1982–83 fiscal year. The administration of U.S. Pres. Ronald Reagan would have liked to increase military aid to $86 million in 1984, reflecting its hardening attitude toward the conflict in El Salvador. However, both Congress and the U.S. Department of Defense, which was opposed to direct U.S. intervention, were pressing for a political solution. U.S. Secretary of State George Shultz gave Congress the required semiannual report that the government of Pres. Álvaro Alfredo Magaña Borjo (*see* BIOGRAPHIES) was making progress on human rights, although the American Civil Liberties Union and other voluntary organizations cited continuing right-wing death squad activity and

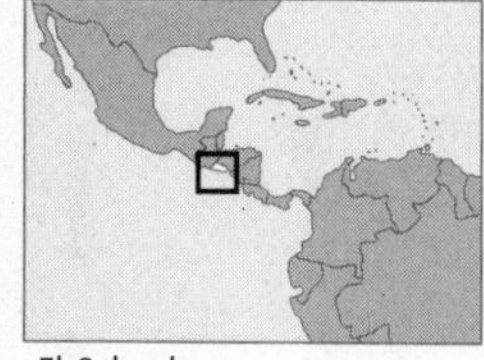

El Salvador

EL SALVADOR

Education. (1981) Primary, pupils 754,897, teachers (1980)17,364; secondary, pupils 24,702, teachers (1980) 1,805; vocational, pupils 9,064, teachers (1980) 1,210; teacher training (1980), students 3,451, teachers 65; higher (1979), students 35,268, teaching staff 2,757.

Finance. Monetary unit: colón, with (Sept. 20, 1983) a par value of 2.50 colones to U.S. $1 (free rate of 3.76 colones = £1 sterling). Gold and other reserves (June 1983) U.S. $143 million. Budget (1982 actual): revenue 1,091,300,000 colones; expenditure 1,694,600,000 colones. Gross national product (1982) 8,954,000,000 colones. Money supply (April 1983) 1,268,500,000 colones. Cost of living (1975 = 100; June 1983) 263.9.

Foreign Trade. (1982) Imports 2,207,200,000 colones; exports 1,760,000,000 colones. Import sources (1981): U.S. 25%; Guatemala 25%; Mexico 5%; Costa Rica 5%. Export destinations (1981): West Germany 22%; Guatemala 18%; U.S. 17%; Japan 5%. Main exports: coffee 58%; textile yarns and fabrics (1980) 9%; cotton 6%; chemicals (1980) 6%.

Transport and Communications. Roads (1982) 12,270 km. Motor vehicles in use (1981): passenger 77,300; commercial 63,000. Railways: (1980) 602 km; traffic (1981) 14 million passenger-km, freight 31 million net ton-km. Air traffic (1982): 335 million passenger-km; freight 10.4 million net ton-km. Telephones (Jan. 1981) 75,900. Radio receivers (Dec. 1980) 1,550,000. Television receivers (Dec. 1980) 300,000.

Agriculture. Production (in 000; metric tons; 1982): corn *c*. 479; sorghum *c*. 137; dry beans *c*. 37; sugar, raw value *c*. 185; bananas (1981) *c*. 53; oranges *c*. 100; coffee *c*. 143; cotton, lint *c*. 42. Livestock (in 000; 1981): cattle 1,211; pigs 386; horses *c*. 88; chickens *c*. 5,050.

Industry. Production (in 000; metric tons; 1981): cement *c*. 500; petroleum products 657; fertilizers (nutrient content; 1979–80) nitrogenous *c*. 15, phosphate *c*. 2; cotton yarn (1977) 6.4; electricity (kw-hr) 1,565,000.

finally at the end of the year the U.S. government seriously and repeatedly pressed the Salvadoran regime to put a stop to the murder squads—which Vice Pres. George Bush pointedly characterized in a toast in San Salvador as the best possible recruiting propaganda for the guerrillas. The number of civilian deaths recorded by the embassy in the first half of 1983 rose to 1,054, about 9% above the total for the corresponding period of 1982, but did not approach the huge total of 1981. The massacre of possibly more than 100 men, women, and children by a U.S.-trained Army battalion was reported in November.

Gen. José Guillermo García, widely criticized for his incompetence, was replaced by Gen. Eugenio Vides Casanova as minister of defense in April. Since 1979 Vides Casanova had been head of the National Guard, the largest and most feared of the three security organizations.

The guerrillas retained their strongholds in the provinces of Chalatenango, Morazán, and La Unión. For two days in January they held the industrial city of Berlín, while in September they temporarily occupied San Miguel, the third largest city in the country. Following the deaths in April of two of their leaders—Mélida Anaya Montes ("Ana María") and Salvador Cayetano Carpio—the guerrillas moved closer to a position that favoured talks with the government. However, international attempts to mediate between the two sides met with no more success than in the past. On December 30 guerrillas overran a major army installation near El Paraíso.

The visit to El Salvador by Pope John Paul II in March prompted the government to announce plans for a political amnesty and to bring forward the date for presidential elections from March 1984 to December 1983. Later in the year, however, the elections were postponed until the Constituent Assembly, elected in March 1982, was able to reach agreement on the proposed constitution. Approval of the constitution was delayed because of disagreement between a right-wing coalition of parties led by Roberto d'Aubuisson and the Christian Democrats over the content of provisions in the charter relating to land reform. The much publicized amnesty, which took effect on May 4, was generally recognized to have been a political failure. Although 1,137 political prisoners benefited from the reprieve, the cells were soon filled with new detainees and the number of disappearances rose again. (LESLIE CRAWFORD)

Energy

During 1983 a highly significant event took place in international oil markets. For the first time in its 22-year history, the Organization of Petroleum Exporting Countries (OPEC) announced a decrease in its benchmark price for oil. The year began with weakness in the oil markets and widespread discounting from official prices. So strong was the pressure to cut those prices that a price war and total collapse of the market seemed imminent. An OPEC meeting in January failed to produce any agreement among the members.

Employment:
see Economy, World

In February the pressure intensified. Nigeria formally lowered its price by $5.50 per barrel, and the U.K. and Norway lowered their prices for North Sea oil by $3 per barrel. In the United States the cheapest grade of gasoline was sold at the pump in some localities for less than $1 a gallon for the first time in four years. (This happy state of affairs for consumers was short-lived, however; on April 1 the federal excise tax on gasoline was raised from four cents to nine cents a gallon.)

At a protracted and acrimonious meeting in March, OPEC finally reached agreement. The official "marker" price of $34 per barrel for Saudi Arabian light crude oil was reduced to $29 per barrel, and production quotas were set for individual members that reduced total OPEC output to 17.5 million bbl a day (compared with peak OPEC production of 31.3 million bbl a day in 1977). Non-OPEC producers fell in line, and the crisis for OPEC was over.

Some strengthening in demand during the summer led to speculation that OPEC would once again announce a price increase, but at the September and December meetings it was decided to hold the line on both price and quotas. At the same time, nervousness in oil-importing countries developed, as Iran threatened to close the Strait of Hormuz at the outlet of the Persian Gulf (and thus stop Persian Gulf exports) in response to threats by Iraq on the main Iranian oil export facilities. Demand, however, did not remain strong in the fourth quarter, and oil stocks rose as some OPEC countries exceeded their production quotas.

In the largest municipal default in U.S. history, the Washington Public Power Supply System (WPPSS, known as Whoops to its luckless bondholders) defaulted on bonds raised to build two of its five nuclear power plants and halted work on two others.

DOUG WILSON—BLACK STAR

THOM STATER/BUSINESS WEEK

Coal showed signs of reviving as a fuel for U.S. ships, but coal transportation cost nearly as much as the coal itself.

The Iran-Iraq hostilities had already caused another problem. In February a tanker accidentally rammed an Iranian producing platform in the Persian Gulf, causing the wells to spew 1,000–2,000 bbl of oil per day into the water. Iraq refused to guarantee the safety of the foreign experts called in to stop the leakage and, with additional shelling of the installations, caused several more wells to leak. By midsummer more than 10,000 bbl per day were spewing into the waters of the Gulf, creating one of the worst oil spills in history. Later in the year Iranian technicians succeeded in reducing the leakage to 2,000 bbl a day, but as the war dragged on there was no prospect of any early end to the polluting flow of oil.

The low level of world demand for OPEC oil throughout the year caused great difficulties for the OPEC countries. In addition to coping with lower total revenues, which affected the budgets of all of them, the Persian Gulf nations, especially Saudi Arabia, faced problems due to the lower output of natural gas that is produced along with the oil. The Gulf countries relied on this gas for power production and water desalination and were forced to rely on makeshift arrangements to maintain the fuel supply to such facilities. The lower gas production also reduced the world supply of the liquids that are processed from it, such as ethane, butane, and propane, and resulted in abnormal increases in the prices of those products.

As part of their reaction to the changed circumstances in the world oil markets, some OPEC countries began to move into "downstream" activities. Kuwait bought European refining and marketing operations from a major oil company; Saudi Arabia announced its intention to do the same; Venezuela arranged a joint refining venture in West Germany with the state-owned oil company.

In oil exploration, drilling in the Santa Barbara Channel off the coast of southern California resulted in the largest discovery in the United States outside Alaska in many years. The record for deep-water drilling was twice broken: a French oil company drilled a well in water 1,595 m (5,264 ft) deep in the Mediterranean Sea some 95 km (60 mi) off the French coast, and a U.S. oil firm began drilling a well in 1,894 m (6,448 ft) of water in the Baltimore Canyon area off the U.S. East Coast. Meanwhile, drilling continued on two superdeep wells in the Soviet Union, both intended to reach a total depth of 15,000 m (49,500 ft). After protracted negotiations, exploration began in waters off the China coast with the awarding of contracts to foreign oil companies by the Chinese government.

Among other oil events of the year, in March trading in crude oil futures began for the first time on commodity exchanges in New York City and Chicago. In June the U.S. Supreme Court ruled that the windfall profits tax on crude oil, passed by the U.S. Congress in 1980, was constitutional.

Like the oil industry, the natural gas industry throughout the world struggled to cope with slack demand. In a rare reversal of the normal trend, the price of new gas supplies in the United States fell. The average price of all gas to the user continued to rise, however, and pipelines and distributors found themselves with gas that could not be marketed. Burdened with contracts that committed them to pay for gas whether or not they took it, many balked and there was a flurry of litigation over breach of contract. State utility commissions and the Federal Energy Regulatory Commission, charged by law with regulating pipeline and distributor activities, also wrestled with the price and market glut problem throughout the year. The same problem faced Canada and Mexico, traditional suppliers to the U.S. natural gas market. The dispute over import quantities and appropriate prices for those imports led to some friction in U.S.-Canadian relations.

Elsewhere, a pipeline for the transport of Algerian gas to Italy across the Mediterranean seafloor became operational in June. The Soviet Union also declared finished the large pipeline it had constructed to take natural gas from western Siberia to Western European countries. This was, however, true only in a technical sense. The compressor stations needed to move the gas through the pipeline had not been completed. This reflected an earlier United States decision to prohibit the export of U.S. compressor technology and equipment for use in the pipeline. The ultimate effect of this action was only to delay the pipeline's completion, not to prevent it.

The depressing effects of worldwide recession, which had made 1982 a bad year for the U.S. coal industry, continued into 1983 and were intensified during the first half of the year by a mild winter. By midyear coal stocks at electric utility generating plants were well above normal, and coal production was down correspondingly. A prolonged, record-breaking heat wave in most of the country during the summer, however, helped draw down the excessive stocks as the use of air conditioners reached new peaks.

The coal industry also took some comfort from the first signs of a possible revival of the use of coal as fuel for ships. In March the first modern U.S. vessel to use coal, an ocean freighter, sailed on its maiden voyage from the U.S. West Coast to the Middle East. In June the first coal-fired steamship built in the United States since 1929 was christened. The vessel was built to carry coal from mid-Atlantic ports to power plants along the Massachusetts coast.

Coal transportation was also the subject of a bitter contest in the U.S. Congress. After several years of struggle, proponents succeeded in bringing to a vote in the Senate a bill that would give the right of eminent domain to pipelines that would carry coal as "slurry," suspended in water. The bill was necessary in order to give slurry pipelines the right to cross railroad rights of way. The railroads, naturally, opposed this competition to their transport of coal and succeeded in convincing senators from Western states that it would also place heavy demands on scarce water supplies. The result was a defeat for slurry pipeline backers, who vowed that they would be back again.

A U.S. commercial synthetic fuel plant based on coal began operations at Kingsport, Tenn., converting 900 tons of coal a day into gas equivalent to 1,300 bbl of oil. The gas, in turn, was processed to produce cellulose acetate for such uses as textiles and cigarette filters. China signed a tentative agreement with a U.S. coal company to develop and operate one of the world's largest coal mines, about 480 km (300 mi) west of Beijing (Peking).

The summer heat wave was a boom to the electric utility industry. August was the hottest on record, and the summer as a whole was the 17th hottest in history for the entire U.S. Electricity use, as a result, also established a record. There were several developments in the application of new technology to electricity production and use. Electricity was produced for the first time with a superconducting generator. Such a generator uses wire of a special alloy, which when cooled to −273° C (−460° F) has no resistance. The result is extremely high efficiency. In another application of superconductivity, the Bonneville Power Administration installed the world's first superconducting magnetic storage system. With almost no loss a coil of superconducting alloy holds a charge of electricity until it is tapped for use.

Advanced technology and declining costs made solar power development for commercial use more attractive. Test equipment like that below was used to evaluate the performance of photovoltaic solar cells.

BART BARTHOLOMEW

Still another technological milestone was the opening of a section of rapid transit line in Vancouver, B.C., constituting the first commercial application of the linear induction motor in transportation. The motor employs no moving parts. The equivalent of the rotor in a conventional motor is actually a third rail between the rails that carry the train; the equivalent of the stator is a flat metal strip attached to the bottom of each car. Application of an electric current creates magnetic fields in the stator and rotor which produce a force that propels the train.

In Brazil the first generating unit of what was eventually to be the world's largest hydroelectric plant began operating. Located on the Paraná River, which forms the border between Paraguay and Brazil, the plant was designed to have a capacity of 12,600 MW.

Nuclear power continued to be beset with problems in the United States but to increase in use elsewhere in the world. In April the U.S. Supreme Court upheld a California law banning the construction of new nuclear plants until an acceptable method of disposal of high-level radioactive wastes was found. In October the Senate rejected a bill to continue funding the Clinch River demonstration breeder reactor, thus killing that project. The reactor had been approved originally in 1972, when it appeared that uranium supplies would become increasingly scarce as nuclear plants continued to be built in many countries and nuclear fuel requirements grew ever larger. Plutonium created in breeder reactors would satisfy that need. With the demise of the Clinch River project, the U.S. had no program to develop a commercial breeder reactor.

With the beginning of power production by the Kalpakkam nuclear plant, India joined the few countries capable of designing and building as well as operating such plants. The nuclear fuel and heavy water used by the plant were also produced in India.

In the area of renewable energy resources, construction began on the first commercial power plant in the United States to use geothermal hot water rather than steam. Located in the Imperial Valley in California, the plant was scheduled for completion in 1985. Nicaragua inaugurated its first geothermal power plant, which was designed to supply 12% of the country's needs. The plant was situated at the foot of Momotombo, the country's most famous volcano. In Europe a 300-kw photovoltaic facility, the continent's largest solar power station, began operations on the West German island of Pellworm in the North Sea. And in Brazil a plant began converting the shells of babassu (a tropical fruit) into fuel gas as part of that country's program of biomass gasification.

(BRUCE C. NETSCHERT)

COAL

"When will the coal market take off again?" was the headline over a mid-1983 survey of the complex coal scene with its many conflicting signals. Yet, despite the continuation of the world recession and the 9.2% decline in world steel production in 1982, world coal production increased in that year. World production of petroleum fell, and the increase in coal output appeared to be related partly to a switch by consumers from oil to coal but also to increases in coal stocks by both producers and consumers. In fact, suppliers were overoptimistic, and the coal markets came under pressure from buyers because supply considerably exceeded demand.

According to UN reports, world production of hard coal in 1982 amounted to 2,918,000,000 metric tons (all absolute figures given below are in metric tons). This was an increase of 107 million tons or 4.1% over 1981. Largest producers were the U.S. with 24.2% of world production, China (21.9%), the U.S.S.R. (19%), and Poland (6.5%). These, with South Africa, India, the U.K., Australia, West Germany, and North Korea, together yielded 93.2% of the world's hard coal. As a proportion of the increased world production, the most striking advances were in Asia, where—starting from a base of existing large output in both cases—production rose 6.9% in China (to 640 million tons) and 9% in India (to 134 million tons). Other areas that reported increases included Eastern Europe (notably Poland, up 16.1% to 189 million tons), Western Europe, Canada, and Australia. Brazil, Colombia, and Mexico had big relative increases but they were based on small absolute outputs of about 5 million to 7 million tons. A few countries had decreases, including the U.K.

World production of brown coal also increased. Output in 1982 was 1,061,000,000 tons, an increase of 3.5% over 1981. Again the world picture was dominated by East Germany, which accounted for 26% of world production. Europe, including the U.S.S.R., yielded 86.4% of the world total.

TRADE. Although in 1982 Poland reentered the market with substantial supplies at competitive prices, demand was sufficient only to keep international trade at about the same level as in 1981, and there were high stocks in major consuming areas so that prices tended to be reduced. The excess of supply over demand continued into 1983. In 1982 the U.S. remained the world's largest exporter with 97.9 million tons (down from the previous year), followed by Australia (48.5 million tons) and Poland and South Africa (both 28.5 million tons). Other major exporters were the U.S.S.R., Canada, and West Germany. Japan continued to be the world's largest importing country, taking 78.5 million tons. Western Europe imported a total of 111.3 million tons; France (22.9 million tons) and Italy (19.1 million tons) were the largest individual country importers in the region. The coal trade forecasts by Chase Manhattan Bank—quoted by the UN Economic Commission for Europe (ECE)—expected a drop in coal trade in 1983 even assuming a strong world economic recovery. Furthermore, the proportion of coking coal in world trade would also fall, reflecting the worldwide decline in steelmaking.

Synthetic fuels development lost some of its lustre and plans for commercial plants were abandoned or set back in several countries. The owners of this plant, now being built in Beulah, North Dakota, have reported to the Department of Defense that the plant may no longer be economically feasible.

JEFF BLUME/THE NEW YORK TIMES

INVESTMENT. Several energy policy commentators during 1982 and 1983 castigated companies and governments for their reluctance to invest in energy conservation and in conversion from oil to coal, a result of the surpluses of coal and oil and the tendency of prices to fall. In its 1982 review of energy policies, the International Energy Agency (IEA) listed major energy projects canceled or postponed in its member countries. The agency's major conference in June 1982 on implementing earlier recommendations for expanding the use of coal concluded that low economic activity was preventing rapid conversion to coal; also, industry was short of cash for self-financing, and high interest rates discouraged borrowing. The conference endorsed the view that it was dangerous to relax efforts toward efficiency and conversion.

COAL-LIQUID MIXTURES. The uncertain early prospects for the energy market also had a dampening effect on enthusiasm for developing coal-liquid dispersions that could be handled and burned in equipment originally designed for oil. Mixtures of coal with oil had been considered for many years since they are cheaper than fuel oil per unit of energy content and are more convenient to use than coal alone. But in the current situation British Petroleum in the U.K. shut down its project after building a plant to process 100,000 tons a year of mixed fuel for industrial trials. The U.K. National Coal Board confirmed in its economic studies that a market for the coal-oil mixtures existed at 1983 fuel prices in only a narrow range of conditions. Nevertheless, many organizations continued research and development in the expectation of opportunities in the future. A European conference held in October reviewed ways of preparing and stabilizing the mixed fuel, and of designing demonstration projects, as well as discussing the economic conditions suitable for their introduction.

ENVIRONMENT. Coal producers and users from the U.S., Austria, Canada, West Germany, and Sweden studied environmental problems in projects in ten countries. Their aim was to increase the use of coal in industry and electricity generation. In their report *Coal Use and the Environment*, published by the Organization for Economic Cooperation and Development (OECD), they confirmed that these concerns were perceived by industry as one of the major constraints in expanding the use of coal. They made detailed recommendations, based on 31 case studies, for reducing net pollution levels by nations that were developing balanced energy and environmental policies; taken together, these would achieve the national goals in a cost-effective manner. Specific problems examined included dust emission, sulfur dioxide, oxides of nitrogen, noise, and the transfer of pollution across national boundaries. Responding to widespread public concern, the leading scientific bodies of three countries—the Royal Society of London, the Norwegian Academy of Science and Letters, and the Royal Swedish Academy of Sciences—initiated a long-term collaborative program on causes of acidification of surface waters in Norway and Sweden and the implications for fisheries. The Commission of the European Communities also sponsored a symposium in September 1983 on origins of acid deposition and methods for its abatement; the aim was to set air quality standards within its area of authority. This was of course not only a question affecting the use of coal but also involved all fuels in all contexts, including emissions from cars. (*See* ENVIRONMENT.)

COAL CONVERSION. Although work was well advanced on the Great Plains plant in Beulah, N.D.—the first U.S. commercial synthetic gas facility—which was designed to gasify some 5 million tons of lignite yearly, in general the price uncertainties led to cancellations and postponements of projects throughout the world. West Germany continued with two major coal gasification projects, but a new Japanese method for liquefying coal by partial solution, proved successful in pilot-plant tests, was being delayed. Meanwhile, the IEA carried out economic studies (*Coal as a Petroleum Substitute*) to establish the effects of various price relationships on the prospects for the Exxon Donor Solvent, the H-Coal, the German Kohleöl, the U.K. Liquid Solvent Extraction processes, and others. One important conclusion was that methanol plants in Australia that were using low-cost subbituminous coal could economically supply such coal to plants in Japan for further conversion to ethylene.

FORECASTS. The ECE Coal Committee examined several projections concerning world coal prospects and concluded that demand, production, and trade were all likely to grow considerably to the end of the century. The accompanying table is based on government replies to a questionnaire from countries supplying 86% of global coal. With the addition of Japan, the same countries represent the largest coal consumers.

(ISRAEL BERKOVITCH)

National Coal Production, Current and Projected

(in million metric tons oil equivalent; % share of global production in parentheses)

Nation	1980	Nation	1990	Nation	2000
United States	673 (25.3)	United States	927 (24.0)	United States	1,430 (27.8)
U.S.S.R.	486 (18.2)	U.S.S.R.	679 (17.6)	China	856 (16.6)
China	434 (16.3)	China	643 (16.6)	U.S.S.R.	745 (14.5)
Poland	164 (6.2)	Australia	205 (5.3)	Australia	300 (5.8)
West Germany	128 (4.8)	Poland	192 (5.0)	India	285 (5.5)
United Kingdom	107 (4.0)	India	168 (4.4)	South Africa	264 (5.1)
South Africa	92 (3.5)	South Africa	162 (4.2)	Poland	200 (3.9)
India	79 (3.0)	West Germany	127 (3.3)	West Germany	131 (2.5)
East Germany	78 (2.9)	United Kingdom	110 (2.8)	United Kingdom	121 (2.3)
Australia	71 (2.7)	East Germany	93 (2.4)	East Germany	97 (1.9)
Total	2,312 (86.9)		3,306 (85.6)		4,429 (85.9)

Source: UN ECE Coal Committee, *World Coal Trade up to the Year 2000.*

ELECTRICITY

There was confirmation during 1983 of the view that in the developed industrial countries coal and uranium would be the fuels for the foreseeable future for the large-scale generation of electricity. No new oil-fired utilities in those countries were projected. Two examples sufficed to support this view: the conversion of oil-fired to coal-fired utilities in the U.S. and the decision in France to shut down a score of aging power stations in the next two years, almost all of them oil-fired.

The story was different in the less developed countries, especially those within OPEC, where oil was cheap. Diesel-powered small electric generators would still have a place in sparsely populated areas, though they were now strongly challenged by renewable sources of energy.

It also became evident that electricity, once an indicator of economic growth, might cease to be so in the future. In the period 1971–72, for example, electricity generated in the U.S. increased by 8% and in the European member countries of the OECD by 6%. Then came the devastating oil crisis, and in the years 1973–75 generation decreased, after which recovery was slow. During 1983 there was continued contraction in Italy, The Netherlands, and Portugal, while average growth in the European OECD countries stood at about 1%. The U.S. increase was somewhat higher but still did not approach the growth registered a decade earlier, when generating authorities and companies could plan ahead with confidence.

The world economic recession accounted for most of the slowdown, but another factor, so far unquantified in general terms, was publicized by prophets of both doom and boom during the past year. This was the elimination or reduction of the waste on which civilization had so thoughtlessly been based. There were national energy conservation campaigns in many developed countries, and though much of the sought-for saving would be in heat energy, much was also being done—and remained to be done—that affected the generation of electricity. There was, for example, the use of the waste heat from electricity generation to supply heat for a neighbourhood, resulting in less use of electricity for heat by local commercial, industrial, and domestic consumers. Such schemes, initially small scale, were started in the U.K. during the year. In

Electrical Power Production of Selected Countries, 1982

By source

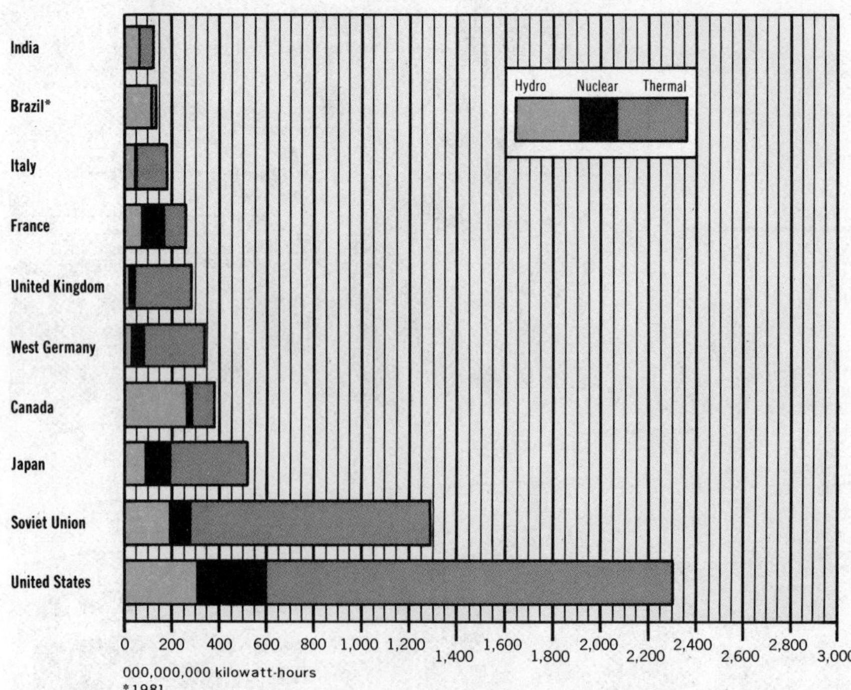

*1981.

Sources: U.S. Department of Energy, *1982 International Energy Annual;* United Nations, *Monthly Bulletin of Statistics.*

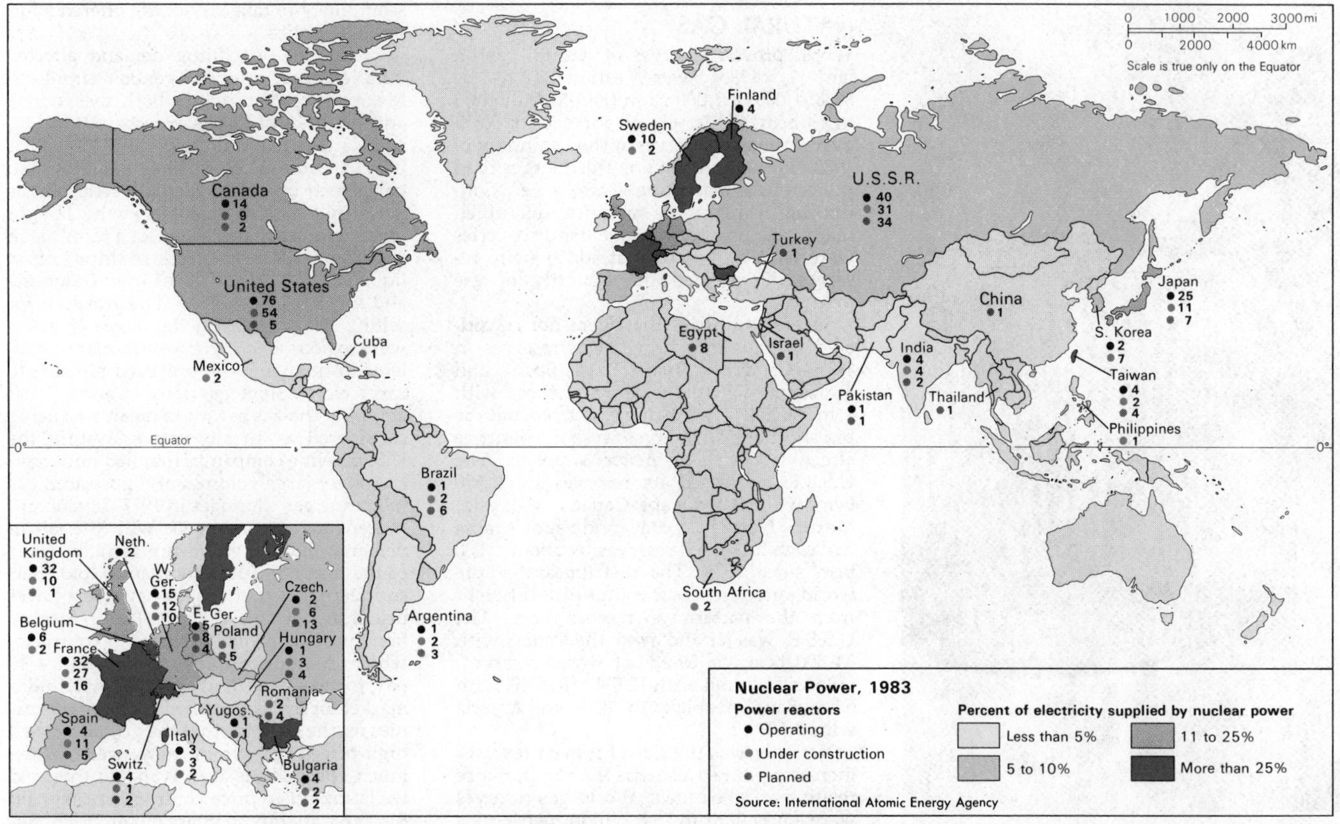

World reliance on nuclear energy in terms of power reactors in service, under construction, and planned; and proportion of electricity produced by reactors.

the U.S. a comprehensive study by the Energy Center of Washington State University showed that in the residential sector conservation programs could save 19 million megawatt-hours of electricity in the years up to 2000 and would cost less than new coal-fired generating stations.

In the U.K. official statements did not seem to support any large savings from conservation, but this view was criticized. In France engineers reported on an attempt to quantify conservation by establishing a "gamma coefficient," the number of therms of gas or oil that would do the same task as one kilowatt-hour of electricity. They provided examples of gamma coefficients ranging from 1.3 for heating furnaces to 13.1 for cookers used in starch and flour processing. (Savings, if any, would depend, of course, on the cost of electricity as compared with that of oil or gas.) A lengthy British report produced by Earth Resources Research, Ltd., based on work instigated by the chief scientist at the Department of Energy and carried out by the Energy Technology Support Unit with the help of the University of Aberdeen, suggested that current improvements in the efficiency of lighting sources, refrigerators, and other domestic devices; motor drives (in which there were considerable developments during the year); transportation equipment; and other areas would lead to a great reduction in the demand for electricity so that by the year 2025 electricity would provide only 6% of all delivered energy, half of the figure in 1976. There were thus strong indications that the electricity industry was likely to experience considerable change as a result of conservation policies. The more saved, the less the demand, with consequences to the supply industry in manpower and money. None of this applied to the less developed countries, which were racing to emulate the prosperous industrial countries in their existing state.

Meanwhile, the fuels for large-scale generation remained coal and uranium and perhaps some plutonium. Coal was under some critical pressure because of the harmful effects of "acid rain"—sulfur compounds emitted in the atmospheric discharges from power stations and factories—on lakes and forests, particularly in Scandinavia, West Germany, and North America. To remove the problem by installing gear that would reduce the sulfur emissions would, in the U.K., cost some £4,000 million and thereby increase the price of electricity to the British people by perhaps 15%. Therefore, during the year the Central Electricity Generating Board and the National Coal Board agreed to fund a joint research program to be carried out by the Royal Society of London, the Norwegian Academy of Science and Letters, and the Royal Swedish Academy of Sciences to examine the problem of acid rain, which was now seen to be more complex than was first thought. (*See* ENVIRONMENT.)

Nuclear fission as a source of energy in reactors to create the steam for generators had its ups and downs during the year. Owing to surplus capacity in the continuing economic recession, some countries announced cutbacks in nuclear projects, notably the U.S., France, and Spain. In general, however, progress continued, despite protests by antinuclear organizations in some countries, particularly West Germany. In the OECD countries production of electricity in nuclear power stations increased by 8.2% overall. Nuclear production in France accounted for some 41% of total national electric power generation and, despite projected cutbacks, could reach 50% within a few years; a figure as high as 80% of total electricity produced was forecast for the year 2000. In Britain the figure stood at about 16%, but three new stations were on stream at half production and a fourth was half completed. South Africa's nuclear-energy commissioner forecast more large nuclear power stations there in the future. The less developed countries still showed great interest in nuclear power stations; during the year South Korea inaugurated its third nuclear power plant.

The fast breeder reactor, too, was in the news, with an announcement that negotiations had been started toward a collaborative agreement among six Western European nations on the design of a commercial fast breeder reactor power station that would not only extract more energy from uranium but would create new plutonium. This would make the economics of nuclear power look even better than at present, with stockpiles of uranium ample for many years. Small nuclear power stations using natural uranium, such as the Magnox stations now in action in Britain, were currently projected as useful exports to less developed countries. In the U.S., however, Congress voted to discontinue funding for the nation's only breeder reactor project.

The first experiments in the world's largest nuclear fusion project, the Joint European Torus at Culham in the U.K., took place during the year. However, a power station

UPI

Conventional electric utility transformers waste great quantities of electric energy as heat. This prototype, expected to cut such loss by two-thirds, was tested at Morristown, New Jersey, by Allied Corporation in a joint program with Osaka Transformer, Ltd., of Japan.

based on fusion was still many years off.

During 1983 there was increased and strengthened interest in the so-called renewable sources of energy that could be used to generate electricity—for all foreseeable uses, the Sun and the wind. The U.K. entered the wind field, previously pioneered and dominated by the U.S. Three prototypes came on stream, and larger plants were planned. Most of them used horizontal-axis devices, making use of lessons learned from U.S. experience. One under construction was based on an original vertical-axis design by British engineer Peter Musgrove. There were problems regarding really large-scale wind generation, but many had already been solved. The Netherlands—with its long tradition of windmills—was among the leading developers, along with Sweden. Europe's largest wind generator, with an output of 3 MW, was inaugurated in West Germany during the year. Wind generation was considered promising for remote sites, and enormous markets were forecast.

For the first time there was a considerable reduction in the cost of solar power with the first production in bulk, in Japan, of photovoltaic cells of amorphous silicon. The International Electrotechnical Commission set up a committee to develop standards for the evolving photovoltaic technology. Wind versus Sun seemed to be the future contest between renewable sources for electricity in large areas of the less developed world. (C. L. BOLTZ)

NATURAL GAS

World proven reserves of natural gas on Jan. 1, 1983, were estimated to be 88,054,000,000,000 cu m (88,054 billion cu m or bcm). This was an increase of 3.6% over estimated reserves at the beginning of 1982 and was almost one-third larger than the estimate made five years earlier. Continuing exploration activity identified many new prospects, and older discoveries were reevaluated, so that additions to reserves outweighed the quantity of gas produced.

Several countries that were not considered to have any proven gas reserves in 1978—Cameroon, Ivory Coast, Spain, and Tanzania—joined the ranks of those with commercially interesting resources, but the big additions to reserves were in countries already possessing major supplies. The U.S.S.R. increased its reserves by 8,500 bcm, while Abu Dhabi, Canada, Malaysia, Mexico, Norway, Qatar, and Saudi Arabia had each increased reserves by about 1,000 bcm since 1978. The distribution of the world's gas reserves was thus little different from the pattern of recent years. The U.S.S.R. was far and away the leader, with 34,500 bcm, or 39.2% of world reserves, followed by Iran with 12.9%, the U.S. with 6.5%, Saudi Arabia with 3.8%, and Algeria with 3.6%.

Not only was the size of proven reserves increasing but so also was their importance relative to other fuels. World gas reserves were equivalent to 78.8 billion metric tons of oil, or 86% of world oil reserves. In 1960 the ratio of gas to oil reserves was only 39%, and in 1970 it was 45%. Discoveries of gas were being made faster than those of oil, while oil was being used faster than gas.

Gas production declined in 1982, from 1,549 bcm to 1,525 bcm. Falling oil prices not only made gas less attractive but also reduced the production of oil and hence of associated gas, particularly in Saudi Arabia. The combination of energy conservation and economic recession in the industrialized countries produced a marked reduction in demand. The European Community countries, for instance, used 6% less gas than they had a year earlier, and U.S. consumption fell by 8%. The U.S. continued to be the largest consuming nation, but it was overtaken by the U.S.S.R. as the largest producer. In 1982 the U.S.S.R. produced 501 bcm and the U.S. 497 bcm. Other producers were far behind: Canada, 70 bcm; The Netherlands, 68 bcm; Romania, 39 bcm; and the U.K., 38 bcm.

Declining gas demand in 1982–83 tended to reduce forecasts of demand in the major gas-importing countries and slowed progress in the international gas trade. Only about 12% of all the gas produced was traded internationally, but such trade was expected to grow considerably, with major contracts for supplies from Algeria and the U.S.S.R. having been agreed to by several nations in 1981–82. It seemed possible that Western Europe might face a surplus of imported gas; Belgium was trying to reduce the amount of gas it had contracted to buy from Algeria.

The controversial Soviet pipelines to the West were being completed ahead of schedule, but France and West Germany did not seem likely to take any of the offered additional supplies.

In the U.S. declining demand affected both external and indigenous suppliers. Mexico agreed to reduce both the volume and the price of its gas exports to the U.S., and Canada reduced the price of its exports by 11% from $4.94 to $4.40 per thousand cubic feet; on July 6 Canada reduced the price to $3.40 for customers who bought large volumes of gas. Plans for a terminal in southern California to receive shipments of liquefied natural gas (LNG) from Indonesia and Alaska were shelved. The prospects for selling Alaskan gas in the lower 48 states were so poor, and there were so many problems in financing the proposed pipeline to carry North Slope gas across Canada, that shipping the gas as LNG to Japan was being considered as an alternative. Within the U.S. pipeline companies that had undertaken to buy large volumes of high-priced gas following gas shortages in 1977–78 took unprecedented steps to cope with the fall in demand. Suddenly and unilaterally, some of the major pipeline companies told their suppliers that they would pay much lower prices or not take the gas. This refusal to honour "take or pay" clauses in contracts, which committed pipeline companies to pay for gas even if they could not find a market for it, was justified by those companies on the grounds that they could not sell high-priced gas from new wells when much cheaper gas was available from old wells subject to price control. Pres. Ronald Reagan's attempt to phase out all price controls by 1986 became enmeshed in legislative delays, with supporters and opponents making widely varying claims about the effect of decontrol on the prices consumers would have to pay. In November the Senate defeated a bill that would have rolled back prices on "new" gas to August 1982 levels and an amendment that would have removed all federal controls over gas prices within a 44-month period.

In Japan demand for gas was still increasing, and the first shipment of LNG from Malaysia arrived in February 1983. Japan could also provide a market for LNG from Qatar, which decided to develop its giant North Dome field. Two other LNG projects that made progress during 1983 were the development of Cameroon's gas, in which France, West Germany, and Italy expressed interest, and the sale of LNG from Indonesia to South Korea, which was to begin in 1986.

Iran abandoned the ambitious prerevolution plans to sell gas to the U.S.S.R. and Europe; its massive reserves would be dedicated to the domestic market, and the pipelines that had already been built to carry gas to the Soviet border would form the basis of an internal gas network.

After long delays the first gas flowed through the pipeline from Algeria, through Tunisia, and across the Mediterranean to Italy in June 1983. This link across the Mediterranean revived interest in the proposal for a pipeline to carry Algerian gas to Spain; it also gave added impetus to a more ambitious project put forward by the Spanish government, for a pipeline to carry gas from Nigeria across the Sahara and then across the Mediterranean to Spain, where it would be linked with the European gas network. (RICHARD J. CASSIDY)

PETROLEUM

In 1983 the oil spotlight was firmly focused upon OPEC. During the early part of the year demand for OPEC oil was insufficient to enable the various members to cover their revenue needs, a situation exacerbated by the financial requirements of the two warring member states, Iran and Iraq. In this predicament there were pressures to offer rebates, thus undermining the strength of the $34-per-barrel marker price of Saudi Arabian light crude oil. Because the impact of the continuing economic recession was accompanied by a mild winter, depletion of stocks on a large scale, and more efficient energy conservation measures by consumers, there was no significant upturn in demand for oil. Instead, consumption continued to decline in the industrialized countries.

This situation caused problems for the unity of OPEC members as political and economic questions jostled for prominence and the international banking system braced itself for financial strains resulting from a possible collapse of oil prices and defaults on obligations already incurred—for example, in Mexico or Nigeria. In December 1982 at Vienna and in January 1983 at Geneva, OPEC members failed to reach agreement on price differentials and production quotas as pressure increased for lower prices. Part of their difficulty was the significant amount of non-OPEC oil in the markets.

Preparatory OPEC meetings were followed by a crucial conference in London in March at which the extent and seriousness of the problems were realized and the role of such non-OPEC producers as Mexico, the U.K., and Norway was recognized. A spirit of economic compromise helped to dissipate some political rivalry in the interest of oil price stability. An agreement was reached that included: (1) a new marker price of $29; (2) new differentials over Nigerian and African crude oils; (3) an overall production ceiling of 17.5 million bbl a day; (4) an output quota system; and (5) definition of Saudi Arabia's role as a supplier.

By and large, helped by some increased trading as stocks were built up again and consumption generally steadied, the March agreement proved acceptable and tenable. The Helsinki conference in July confirmed the arrangements without any certainty of how far the recovery would be sustained.

In the first half of 1983 world oil production generally increased over the same period in the previous year, apart from the Middle East, where it continued to fall, by 19%. There was a strong recovery of 14% in Western Europe and 8% in Africa. Offshore production that began in The Netherlands in October 1982 rose to 25,000 bbl a day. There were similar production increases from recent offshore fields in Denmark, Italy, and Spain during the first half of 1983. Production from the North Sea for the U.K. increased by 10% and for Norway by 21%. In September Magnus, the 23rd U.K. offshore oil field, officially came on stream; it was the most northerly, the deepest-water, and, at £1,300 million, the most costly development in Europe.

RESERVES. For the last decade or so the absolute level of world recoverable "published proved" reserves had changed little. The same was generally true for the end of 1982, with a minor fall of 800 million bbl, to 677,400,000,000 from 678,200,000,000 at the end of 1981. Within that total, Western Hemisphere reserves, mostly from Latin America, dropped by 1% to 122,400,000,000 bbl; this was 18.1% of the world total. Conversely, Middle Eastern reserves increased by 1%, from 362,600,000,000 bbl in 1981 to 369,000,000,000 bbl in 1982; this was 54.4% of the world total. Reserves for Africa increased by 1.6% (8.5% of the world total) to 57,800,000,000 bbl, whereas those for Western Europe fell by 1.7% to 23,500,000,000 bbl. The share of the world reserves of the U.S.S.R. at 9.3%, 63,000,000,000 bbl, remained the same, as did those of the U.S. at 5.5%, 36,900,000,000 bbl. China and Eastern Europe were marginally lower, at 2.9%, 19,500,000,000 bbl, and 0.4%, 2,400,000,000 bbl, respectively.

PRODUCTION. World oil production decreased in 1982 from 1981 by 4.9%. The Middle East registered the greatest regional fall, down 20% from 15,995,000 bbl a day to 12,780,000 bbl, but within that overall total there were some significant variations. Thus, the share of the major producer, Saudi Arabia, 12% of the world total and more than half of the regional share of 22.9%, fell by 33%, from 9,985,000 bbl a day to 6,690,000 bbl. Its share of the world total fell below that of the U.S.S.R., with 22.3% at 12,430,000 bbl, and the U.S., with 15.7% at 8,670,000 bbl. Elsewhere in the Middle East there were major decreases in Kuwait, down 28.2% to 695,000 bbl, Abu Dhabi, 22.8% to 875,000 bbl, and Qatar, 18.4% to 340,000 bbl. Iran and Iraq, though locked in war with each other, raised their production by 49.4 and 9.1%, respectively, to 1,975,000 bbl and 980,000 bbl, against previous five-year declining trends of 19.1 and 17.7%.

Indonesian production, 2.4% of the world total, also fell, by 16.8% to 1,335,000 bbl per day; Australasia dropped by 5.3% to 390,000 bbl. Africa as a whole decreased by 5.1% to 4,585,000 bbl with falling production in Algeria, 17.1% to 835,000 bbl, Nigeria, 10.1% to 1,295,000 bbl, and Gabon, 7.5% to 140,000 bbl, whereas there were minor increases in Libya, 3.7% to 1,150,000 bbl, and Egypt, 3% to 710,000 bbl. In Western Europe U.K. production increased by 15.6% to 2,120,000 bbl per day, 3.8% of the world total. This accounted for the major part of the regional share, as production in Austria, France, Norway, and West Germany fell.

Although production in Latin America was up slightly, by 2.7% to 6,485,000 bbl per day, there were wide variations. Brazil and Mexico were up by 23.5 and 16.4%, respectively, to 275,000 bbl and 3,005,000 bbl, but production in Venezuela, Trinidad, Ecuador, and Argentina fell by, respectively, 12.8% to 1,895,000 bbl, 11.9%

WIDE WORLD

In February utility customers protested electric bills and heating gas prices in many cities, including Buffalo, New York.

Energy

KATZ—BLACK STAR

Falling oil prices have discouraged exploration, and oil-well equipment, formerly at a premium, began to pile up unsold.

to 175,000 bbl, 4.1% to 210,000 bbl, and 1.6% to 480,000 bbl. Total North American production was steady at 11,755,000 bbl per day, compared with 11,725,000 bbl in 1981, as was that of China at 2,045,000 bbl (2,035,000 bbl in 1981). Eastern European production, against the trend, was up by 16.5% to 410,000 bbl. World production, excluding the U.S.S.R., Eastern Europe, and China, was down by 6.9% to 41,325,000 bbl. For members of OPEC, which produced 34.2% of the world total, there was a 17.6% decline, almost double that of the previous five-year average of 9.7%, and production was almost half that of the peak year of 1980.

CONSUMPTION. World oil consumption, after peaking in 1979 at 64,145,000 bbl a day, totaled 58,510,000 bbl in 1982, a drop of 3% from 1981 against an average growth in the decade 1972–82 of 0.8%. The fall in consumption in Western Europe was most marked, 4.9%, for a world total share of 21.4% (12,455,000 bbl), the lowest since 1969. Only Turkey (6.9%), Norway (4.3%), Portugal (3.1%), and the U.K. (1.3%) showed increases. The Netherlands had the largest decline, 14.7%, followed by Ireland with 11.6%. West Germany was the greatest consumer, with 4% of the world total at 2,360,000 bbl a day, followed by France with 3.3% at 1,935,000 bbl, Italy with 3.2% at 1,845,000 bbl, the U.K. with 2.7% at 1,580,000 bbl, and Spain with 1.7% at 970,000 bbl.

Consumption in North America declined by 6.2%; at 16,485,000 bbl a day it was 27.5% of the world total. Canada had the greatest fall, 10.6%, to 1,580,000 bbl. The U.S. remained the highest consumer, with 24.9% of the world total, at 14,905,000 bbl. However, this was a 5.8% decrease from 1981.

Consumption rose in Latin America by 3.6% to 8.3% of the world total at 4.9 million bbl, in the Middle East by 2.4% for a world share of 3.1% at 1,720,000 bbl, in Africa by 4.1% to 2.8% of the world total at 1,635,000 bbl, and in South Asia by 4% to 1.6% of the world total at 925,000 bbl. There was a significant 7.6% decrease in consumption in Japan, the third-largest consumer, which totaled 4,380,000 bbl for 7.3% of the world total. China, with 2.9% of the world share, had a drop of 2.8% to 1,660,000 bbl; Southeast Asia, at 4.3%, fell by 1.8% to 2,435,000 bbl; and Eastern Europe, at 3.6%, dropped by 1.3% to 2,085,000 bbl. The U.S.S.R., the world's second-largest consumer, with 15.9% of the world total, had a modest increase of 1% to 9,075,000 bbl per day.

REFINING. Although overall world refining capacity fell by 2.8% in 1982 to 79,395,000 bbl a day, its lowest since 1978, most of the decline occurred in the industrial countries, corresponding to their drop in consumption. Thus, Western Europe, with 22.7% of the world capacity, fell by 9.9% to 18,035,000 bbl a day, compared with a previous five-year average fall of 2.5%. Some countries experienced large reductions; *e.g.*, Belgium 31.5% to 660,000 bbl, France 15.1% to 2,745,000 bbl, West Germany 14.7% to 2,520,000 bbl, Italy 12.3% to 3.5 million bbl, The Netherlands 10.5% to 1,590,000 bbl, and the U.K. 9.7% to 2,135,000 bbl. Spain remained unchanged at 1,550,000 bbl.

U.S. capacity, at 17,390,000 bbl, slightly less than that of Western Europe and 21.9% of the world total, fell by 4.9% and thus reversed an average 0.5% increase over the previous five years. Canada was also down, 3.5% to 2,080,000 bbl, as was Venezuela, 3.2% to 1,360,000 bbl. The rest of the world was increasing its refinery capacity or continuing at the same level. Saudi Arabia increased by 31.1% to 865,000 bbl, and in the Middle East as a whole capacity rose 9.7% to 3,570,000 bbl, 4.5% of the world total. Africa increased 15.5% to 2,375,000 bbl, South Asia increased 13% to 1 million bbl, and Southeast Asia maintained its capacity of 3,515,000 bbl, 4.4% of the total. The capacity of the U.S.S.R., Eastern Europe, and China together rose by 2.1%, half of the previous five-year average increase, to 16,330,000 bbl a day, 20.6% of the world total. Japanese capacity fell by 30% to 5.5 million bbl, 6.9% of the world total.

Refinery yields by volume in 1982 for gasolines, middle distillates, fuel oil, and others were 50, 30, 9, and 11% in North America, 27, 36, 21, and 16% in Western Europe, and 24, 33, 33, and 10% in Japan. World refining in 1982 at 55,445,000 bbl per day was the lowest since 1975.

TANKERS. The size of the world tanker fleet continued to decline from its 1977 peak and in 1982 fell by 9.5% to 303.7 million tons deadweight (dw), the lowest since 1975. Fewer tankers were on order in 1982 than had been the case in many years; the total was 155 vessels at 6 million tons dw. Scrappings of tankers in 1982 were the greatest ever, nearly doubling the 1981 figure; the total rose from 12 million tons dw in 1981 to 22 million tons dw, 7% of the world tanker fleet. Liberia owned the largest share of world tonnage, 27.8%, followed by Japan (9.4%), Norway (7%), the U.K. (5.8%), and the U.S. (5.5%).

Tankers of 205,000–285,000 tons dw constituted 39% of the world tanker fleet by size, followed by 17% for those of 65,000–125,000 tons dw. Supertankers of 285,000 tons dw and over, at 46.6 million tons dw, were at their highest total to date. Some 25.5 million bbl a day of oil were transported in tankers. Western Europe imported the most, 9,350,000 bbl per day, of which half came from the Middle East; the U.S. followed with 5,040,000 bbl of imports, of which 2,050,000 bbl came from Latin America, 770,000 bbl from the Middle East, and 605,000 bbl from West Africa. Japan imported 4,155,000 bbl, of which 2,755,000 bbl came from the Middle East and 890,000 bbl from Southeast Asia. (R. W. FERRIER)

See also Engineering Projects; Industrial Review; Mining and Quarrying; Transportation.

[214.C4; 721; 724.B2; 724.C1–2; 737.A.5]

Engineering Projects

Bridges. For the past 30 years reinforced and prestressed concrete had largely superseded steel for smaller bridges. In Britain a report by the government's Constructional Steelwork Economic Development Committee recommended that in cases where cost estimates for a concrete and steel bridge were within 7% of one another it should be standard policy to allow alternative plans to proceed to the bidding stage. It was also believed that there had been an unwarranted assumption that concrete structures endured longer than steel. Only when the duration of good service had been as well established for concrete as it had for steel bridges would it be possible to make a fair comparison of the full costs of constructing and maintaining bridges of both materials.

Bigger and bigger concrete bridges continued to be built. In 1983 the American Consulting Engineers gave their prestigious Grand Conceptor Award for the $175 million Columbia River bridge carrying Interstate Highway 205 between Washington and Oregon. Called the Glenn L. Jackson Memorial Bridge, it was used by 40,000 vehicles daily within a year of its opening. It had eight traffic lanes and separate lanes for cyclists and pedestrians. The main span was 183 m (1 m=3.3 ft) long, the adjacent spans were each 146 m; and the total length was 3.6 km (2.225 mi). It was the first major bridge in the U.S. to be built by free cantilever erection, although the principle had been used in Europe for 25 years or more. After each pier is built, a pair of traveling forms are erected and used to cast-in-place the concrete segments. Successive balancing segments are then added in each arm and strengthened by post-tensioned tendons. The bridge boasted the biggest concrete segments ever cast—21.6 m wide, an average 9.8 m deep, and 4.9 m long. The approach spans were built more conventionally by precasting the segments on the ground and then lifting them into place.

By far the most ambitious bridge projects under construction in 1983 were in Japan, in particular the two road and rail crossings between the main islands of Honshu and Shikoku and the intervening smaller islands. Construction, now well advanced, had been hampered by the very deep water of the Seto Inland Sea as well as by fast sea currents, typhoons, and congested marine traffic. Both crossings were designed to have double-deck bridges to carry two six-lane highways and twin tracks for the high-speed Shinkansen railway. The central crossing, between Hayashim on Honshu and Sakaide on Shikoku, called for three suspension bridges, a three-span truss bridge, and two stayed-girder bridges, each with main spans of 420 m. The most easterly route consisted of two parts: the Ohnaruto suspension bridge, 1,629 m long with a main span of 870 m, and the Tozaki Viaduct on the Shikoku side, both of which were nearly complete, and the Akashi Kaikyo suspension bridge with a main span of 1,780 m on the Honshu side. Because of the difficulties of coping with the severe winds, designs for the Akashi Kaikyo bridge, which would have the longest bridge span in the world, were still being considered. All the bridges had been designed to withstand earthquakes up to 8.5 on the Richter scale. In case of typhoons all had been designed for basic wind speeds of 50 m per sec (112 mph); and gusts as high as 83 m per sec (186 mph) had been allowed for at the top of the towers of the Ohnaruto bridge.

Another interesting Japanese project was the recently completed Usagawa Bridge, built to carry the Chugoku Motorway at an altitude of 1,000 m.

Fireworks illuminated New York City's famous Brooklyn Bridge to mark its 100th anniversary on May 24.

UPI

COURTESY, ARCHITECTS & ENGINEERS—FOSTER ASSOCIATES. PHOTOGRAPH, KEN KIRKWOOD

Cables from high tubular steel columns supported the roof of the new Renault Centre at Swindon, England.

It had a concrete arch with a main span of 204 m, which carried spandrel columns to support the road deck. During the construction of the arch a temporary steel girder was inserted between the cantilevered concrete segments, thus enabling the arch to be completed without imposing excessive loads on the temporary ties to the anchorage columns.

Preliminary studies for a bridge or tunnel crossing of the Strait of Gibraltar between Spain and Morocco were completed. Although the strait at the narrowest point was only 14 km (8.7 mi) wide, in places the water was approximately 1,000 m deep and the currents were fast. A tunnel below the strait could be used only by electric trains (ventilation for internal-combustion road traffic being out of the question), but a bridge crossing able to carry both road and rail was found to be technically possible.

May 24 marked the centenary of the opening of New York City's Brooklyn Bridge. In Britain the much younger Severn Bridge, opened in 1966 and at that time the world's seventh longest suspension bridge, was found likely to be carrying a traffic load (12 million vehicles yearly) far in excess of that for which it was designed. Pending consideration of proposals to strengthen the structure at a possible cost of £25 million ($38 million) or to introduce a system of traffic monitoring and control, the government imposed severe traffic restrictions in October. (DAVID FISHER)

Buildings. Work started in 1983 on what was believed would be the tallest building outside North America. At 280 m high, the Overseas Bank Centre in Singapore would have a 63-story tower surrounded by a 6-story podium around the base. Below ground level would be a four-story basement. The superstructure of the tower block was to be framed in structural steelwork, with standard column sections but with less conventional steel truss beams. This led to a much greater height between floors than was usual for that type of building. Because of the unsatisfactory foundation material at shallow depths, the main tower was to be carried on seven large concrete caissons sunk some 100 m into the ground. These would have a shaft diameter of 5 to 6 m, belled out to nearly 12 m at the base. The building was scheduled for completion in 1986.

During the year the Aga Khan awards for architecture were made. (These are made triennially for buildings of Muslim character that have been completed and in use for at least three years.) Of particular engineering interest among the winning projects was the Haj Terminal at the new Jidda Airport in Saudi Arabia. This consisted of a central spine flanked on each side by 105 bays of tentlike tension structures. The individual bays were 45 m square and set in a grid of 15 by 7 bays.

On Oct. 15, 1983, the first sporting event took place in the newly completed 19,000-seat Olympic Saddledome in Calgary, Alta. This 134 by 128 m indoor stadium was to form the centrepiece of the 1988 Winter Olympic Games. As its name implied, the roof of the building was in the form of a saddle-shaped shell acting as a compressive arch in one direction and a tension catenary arch in the other direction. A novel feature was the use of roof cables as a tension structure during construction to support coffered precast lightweight concrete units that were then jointed with in situ concrete to form a continuous shell structure. The edge beam, which carried the tensions and compressions from the shell, was buttressed at the lowest points of the saddle and supported on columns around the remainder of the perimeter. The connections between the columns and the edge beam used elastomeric bearings to allow unrestrained thermal and load-induced horizontal movements while at the same time providing vertical support.

Advanced energy management was a key feature of the new State of Illinois Center in Chicago. Illinois Gov. James Thompson required a building for the year 2000, and this was reflected in its sophisticated energy specification. When completed, it would be the largest mixed-use government building in the U.S., containing 110,000 sq m (1,184,029 sq ft) of floor area and having both retail and commercial space on its first three floors. Eight large ice tanks would store ice produced in off-peak times to offset a part of the high cooling costs incurred during the summer.

The architectural press continued to emphasize what was termed "high tech" building construction. The main feature attributable to this type of building was the large proportion of specially designed factory fabricated components that were used, often coupled with some nontraditional engineering concepts. This approach to building went back to the cast-iron prefabricated component constructions of Joseph Paxton in his design for London's Crystal Palace in the last century. In reality the level of technology was not significantly different from that of buildings constructed by traditional methods. An interesting example of this type of construction was the new Renault Centre in Swindon, England. The main part of this building consisted of 25-m-square bays, each with a 16-m-high tubular steel column at the centre. The roof beams were of light steel I-beam sections having pierced webs. These were borne by the steel columns but were, in addition, supported by tension members above the roof that sloped down from the top of the columns to intermediate points along the beams. (*See also* ARCHITECTURE.)

Houston, Texas, is situated in the hurricane zone bordering the northern shores of the Gulf of Mexico. In 1983 the city was hit by Hurricane Alicia, the first major storm to affect the city since before the construction boom of the last decade. Although no major structural collapses were reported, there was widespread damage to building exteriors. Many of the new buildings were clad in glass, and about 165 streets had to be sealed off because of the danger of flying glass.

(GEOFFREY M. PINFOLD)

Dams. An exceptional amount of flooding took place in 1983, and many dams could not hold back the floodwaters. Hoover Dam, on the Colorado River, with its huge reservoir of 29.3 million ac-ft that had not been full since 1941, overflowed. Glen Canyon Dam, also on the Colorado River and located upstream from the Hoover, could not stop the flow. Heavy snows in the mountains combined with a May heat wave to produce the floods. Many small dams were overtopped and washed out. Rains in many other parts of the world caused similar damage.

As a consequence of the destruction, the safety of dams continued to be a major topic of confer-

ADAM WOOLFITT—WOODFIN CAMP

The Netherlands is at work on one of the most massive engineering undertakings in history in the Delta Project. In fair weather the dikes will remain open, permitting normal current flow and marine life. During violent North Sea storms, the gates will close to protect the coast and the Rhine River estuary.

ences and discussions, as well as legislative actions, during the year. Technical developments and new construction methods to ensure safety were featured topics. Dam safety continued to stimulate the development of various instruments designed to monitor dam behaviour after construction and to provide performance data for the analysis of predicted design behaviour. On large dams the data are recorded automatically, whereas on small ones they are collected manually throughout a period of two or three reservoir fillings and drawdowns.

The pace of dam construction slowed somewhat. The largest construction activity in 1983 involved the building of the Oosterschelde 9.6-km (5.6-mi) flood barrier, a key part of the massive Delta Project to protect the coastal areas of The Netherlands from North Sea storms. It is a sea dam with 66 concrete piers to be linked by huge gates. The piers were towed out to sea and sunk in place in water 25 m deep. Each pier weighs about 18,000 metric tons, is 45 m high. The total cost of the Oosterschelde barrier was expected to exceed $2 billion.

In India construction began on a project that included the Sardar Sarovar Dam. It was expected to take 20 years to complete, at a cost of $5 billion. The dam itself was to be similar in size to the Grand Coulee Dam in the U.S.

China was completing one of its largest dams, the Panjiakou (P'an-chia-k'ou) on the Luan River. It was designed to provide 450 MW of capacity and supply water to Tianjin (Tientsin), China's second largest industrial city. Construction began in 1975.

The second powerhouse at the Bonneville Dam on the Columbia River went into operation during the summer. It furnished 558 MW of power, more

Major World Dams Under Construction in 1983[1]

Name of dam	River	Country	Type[2]	Height (m)	Length of crest (m)	Volume content (000 cu m)	Gross reservoir capacity (000 cu m)
Altinkaya	Kizilirmak	Turkey	E, R	195	604	15,310	5,763,000
Atatürk	Euphrates	Turkey	E, R	179	1,700	84,500	48,700,000
Boruca	Terraba	Costa Rica	E, R	267	700	43,000	14,960,000
Canales	Genil	Spain	E, R	156	340	4,733	7,070,000
Casa de Piedra	Rio Colorado	Argentina	E	25	11,000	16,000	3,600,000
Chapeton	Paraná	Argentina	E, G	34	6,554	37,910	53,750,000
Dabaklamm	Dorferbach	Austria	A	220	332	1,000	235,000
Dongjiang	Lei Shui	China	A	157	438	1,389	8,120,000
El Cajon	Humuya	Honduras	A	226	382	1,480	5,650,000
El M'Jara	Ouergha	Morocco	E	87	1,600	25,000	4,000,000
Grand Maison	Eau d'Olle	France	E, R	160	550	18,450	140,000
Guavio	Orinoco	Colombia	E, R	250	461	17,000	10,000,000
Guri (Raúl Leoni)	Caroní	Venezuela	E, R, G	162	11,409	75,700	136,335,000
Ihla Grande	Paraná	Brazil	E, G	29	7,060	11,573	30,000,000
Inguri	Inguri	U.S.S.R.	A	272	680	3,960	2,500,000
Itaipú	Paraná	Brazil/Paraguay	E, R, G	185	7,900	27,000	29,000,000
Itaparica	São Francisco	Brazil	E, R	105	4,150	16,530	10,700,000
Karakaya	Euphrates	Turkey	A, G	180	420	2,000	9,580,000
Kenyir	Trengganu	Malaysia	E, R	155	900	18,350	13,600,000
Khudoni	Inguri	U.S.S.R.	A	197	545	1,475	365,000
Kishau	Tons	India	E, R	253	360	N.A.	2,400,000
La Grande No. 4	La Grande	Canada	E, R	125	7,243	20,000	19,390,000
Lakhwar	Yamuna	India	G	192	440	2,000	580,000
Longyangxia	Huang He	China	G	172	342	1,300	24,700,000
Lower Tunguska	Lower Tunguska	U.S.S.R.	E, G	200	6,200	23,000	45,000,000
Maqarin	Yarmuk	Jordan	E, R	164	700	21,000	486,000
Mazar	Mazar	Ecuador	G	175	400	1,600	500,000
Menzelet	Ceyhan	Turkey	E, R	150	420	7,000	19,500,000
Mihoesti	Aries	Romania	E, R	242	242	180	6,000
Mosul	Tigris	Iraq	E	100	3,600	36,000	11,100,000
Naramata	Naramata	Japan	E, R	158	520	12,000	90,000
Nurek	Vakhsh	U.S.S.R.	E	300	704	42,670	10,500,000
Oosterschelde	Vense Gat Oosterschelde	The Netherlands	E, G	45	8,400	35,000	2,000,000
Oymapinar	Manavgat	Turkey	A	185	360	575	310,000
Özköy	Gediz	Turkey	E, R	180	420	11,251	940,000
Porto Primavera	Paraná	Brazil	E, G	38	11,385	8,441	18,500,000
Revelstoke	Columbia	Canada	E, R, G	175	1,615	13,000	5,310,000
Rogun	Vakhsh	U.S.S.R.	E	335	612	71,100	13,300,000
Roncador	Uruguay	Brazil/Argentina	E, R	78	1,600	6,500	33,580,000
Salvajina	Cauca	Colombia	E, R	154	368	4,000	773,000
San Rouge	Agno	Philippines	E	210	930	43,000	990,000
São Felix	Tocantins	Brazil	E, R	160	1,950	34,000	55,200,000
Sardar Sarovar	Narmada	India	G	155	1,210	6,100	9,492,000
Sterkfontein	Nuwejaarspruit	South Africa	E	93	3,060	19,800	2,656,000
Tehri	Bhagirathi	India	E, R	261	570	25,200	3,539,000
Thein	Ravi	India	E, R	47	878	21,920	3,670,000
Thomson	Thomson	Australia	E, R	165	1,275	13,200	1,100,000
Tianshengqiao	Hongshui He	China	G	185	993	420	354,000
Tres Irmaos	Tiete	Brazil	E, G	90	3,700	15,000	14,200,000
Tucurui	Tocantins	Brazil	E, G	106	10,677	68,000	43,000,000
Upper Wainganga	Wainganga	India	E	43	181	N.A.	50,700,000
Yacyreta-Apipe	Paraná	Paraguay/Argentina	E, G	41	72,000	81,000	21,000,000
Zillergründl	Ziller	Austria	A	180	505	980	90,000
Major World Dams Completed in 1982 and 1983[1]							
Amaluza	Paute	Ecuador	A	170	410	1,157	120,000
Baishan	Songhua Jiang	China	G	150	677	1,663	900,000
Dry Creek	Dry Creek	U.S.	E	110	915	23,000	310,000
Emborcacao	Paranaiba	Brazil	E, R	158	1,607	25,000	17,600,000
Gura Apelor Retezat	Riul Mare	Romania	E, R	168	460	9,000	225,000
La Grande No. 2	La Grande	Canada	E, R	160	2,835	22,937	61,720,000
La Grande No. 3	La Grande	Canada	E, R	100	3,855	22,187	60,020,000
La Honda	Uribante	Venezuela	E	150	600	10,500	775,000
Los Leones	Los Leones	Chile	E	179	510	9,200	106,000
Tokuyama	Ibi	Japan	E, R	161	420	10,600	660,000
Yacambu	Yacambu	Venezuela	E, R	158	110	3,400	427,000

[1] Having a height exceeding 150 m (492 ft); or having a volume content exceeding 15 million cu m (19.6 million cu yd); or forming a reservoir exceeding 14,800 x 10^6 cu m capacity (12 million ac-ft).
[2] Type of dam: E = earth; R = rockfill; A = arch; G = gravity.
NA = not available.

(T. W. MERMEL)

than doubling the existing 518-MW plant built in 1938.

Norway's highest dam, Storvatin, with a reservoir capacity of 8 million ac-ft, began to fill in 1983. In South Korea the 97-m-high Chungju Dam now under construction was designed to provide 400 MW of power and supply water to Seoul. The 60-m-high rockfill Kalavosos Dam under construction in Cyprus was being built to provide water for irrigation and municipal purposes.

A proposal was made in Australia to reverse the flow of rivers in Queensland and New South Wales. Among the benefits would be the irrigation of approximately 29,000 ha (72,000 ac) in Queensland. In England the River Thames barrier to protect London from costly floods was completed.

Because of environmental issues some dams faced delays or abandonment. The Nan Chuan Dam in Thailand and the Tembeling Dam in Malaysia were involved in such action. The Silent Valley Dam in India raised the classic question of which should be given higher priority, protection of the environment or improvement of living standards. Progress on that dam was halted until the issue was resolved.

Egypt was planning to develop hydroelectric energy at the Qattara depression in the Sahara. The depression is 130 m below the level of the Mediterranean Sea, from which water would be diverted by a 56-km (35-mi) canal. Once the depression was filled to a predetermined level, solar evaporation would be enough to permit continual diversion of Mediterranean water to produce 3,000 gigawatt hours of energy per year, equivalent to saving 50 million bbl of oil annually. The project was estimated to cost $2 billion. (T. W. MERMEL)

Roads. Innovative financing methods made headlines in the highway industry throughout the world in 1983, as decreased revenues and increased construction costs caused highway administrators to examine ways to provide a sustained level of highway service with fewer financial resources. A five-cent increase in highway user taxes in the United States revived a moribund highway construction industry, while in other countries ranging from the United Kingdom to Pakistan and Thailand, road agencies were inviting private firms and consortiums to build and maintain roads and then collect their profits from tolls.

In the United Kingdom the government invited bids from contractors to build and operate an $86 million toll highway in the Midlands. In Pakistan the 1,542-km (1 km = 0.62 mi) four-lane motorway from Karachi on the Arabian Sea to Peshawar near the Afghanistan border was to be built and operated privately, under license from the government. In Thailand two toll highways with a total length of 430 km (from Nakhon Ratchasima to Sara Buri, and from Nakhon Sawan to Pathum Thani) were to be built with private funds instead of public revenues.

Conventional highway financing strengthened in at least two major countries. The British government increased its highway funding for 1983–84 by $90 million, 40% higher than in 1982–83 and 16% higher than in 1981–82. In the United States the federal user charge on motor fuel rose from four cents per gallon to nine cents per gallon. Four cents of the increase was dedicated to highways. The resulting boom in highway construction and maintenance included creation of 90,000 more jobs in the road industry than there had been a year earlier. As of 1983 the U.S. Interstate System was 95.9% complete. Total cost of the system to date was estimated at $112.8 billion. The remaining 4.1% was expected to cost $35.8 billion. One of the most expensive and controversial segments of the Interstate System, the $2 billion, 6.8-km Westway in New York City, under discussion for 12 years, was delayed at least another 2 years to permit evaluation of the impact of the project on the striped bass in the Hudson River.

In Brazil a 1,438-km highway neared completion in the states of Rondonia and Mato Grosso, part of Brazil's program to settle its sparsely populated northwest region. Also in South America the first road to link Bolivia, Peru, Ecuador, Colombia, and Venezuela, 1,450 km in length, was under construction.

The Philippines was proceeding with the second stage of construction of the 1,712-km Daang Maharlika (Pan-Philippine) Highway, spanning the entire archipelago and passing through 21 provinces and 11 cities. In Singapore the $110 million Pan Island Expressway, part of an ambitious program to reduce traffic congestion in the island nation, was opened. Isolated areas of Burma were to be opened up by a 700-km highway under construction along the banks of the Irrawaddy River, from Bassein to Monywa, near Mandalay.

Australia implemented a special $1,736,000,000 surcharge on motor fuels to finance construction of national, regional, and local roads in time for the nation's 200th birthday in 1988. Construction of the four-lane motorway from Melbourne to Sydney was proceeding on schedule. Asphalt sealing of Australia's main north-south highway from Darwin to Adelaide was in progress and was expected to be completed by 1986.

In the United Kingdom the most important current road project was the M-25 Motorway, the 193-km ring road around London, scheduled for completion in 1986. Italy was reactivating its motorway construction program after a six-year ban on new construction. The $5 billion program was to include a new bypass for Rome, completion of the link between Rome and Genoa, and completion of the Sicilian motorway network. Belgium's Ardennes E-9 Motorway, opened in 1983, included a 60-m-high, 370-m-long viaduct over the Ourthe Valley, the largest structure of its kind in Belgium. Also during the year the first section of the A42 Autoroute between Neyron, a suburb of Lyon, France, and Chazey, near Geneva, was opened to traffic. (HUGH M. GILLESPIE)

Tunnels. The year's most notable event in tunneling was the completion, after 19 years, of the Seikan Pilot Tunnel. This 23-km section of the 54-km rail tunnel between the Japanese islands of Hokkaido and Honshu was driven by drill and blast methods some 100 m beneath the seabed of the Tsugaru Strait. The maximum depth of the water was 140 m, and at times water entered the tunnel at a rate of 11 tons (2,400 gal) a minute.

During the work some 69 km of advance-probe drilling were carried out and 67,000 tons of grout were injected. The tunnel would eventually become a section of the national railway system.

Work began near Geneva on the LEP (large electron-positron) project at the European Laboratory for Particle Physics (CERN). Described as the world's biggest machine, it would include 24 km of 3.7-m-diameter tunnels. Driven to form the outer rim of an 8.5-km-diameter circle, the tunnels would house electron-positron beam generation, transmission, and measurement equipment for experiments in particle physics. Access shafts and a complex arrangement of huge halls and galleries were to be constructed at depths of up to 140 m below ground. CERN specified that full-face tunnel boring machines (TBM's) would be used to cut through the fine-grained sandstone stratum. The constant-radius curved tunnels were to be driven to tight tolerances and at guaranteed weekly advance rates. The tunnels would be lined with concrete segmental rings erected behind the TBM's and later lined with in situ concrete in an unusual design capable of preventing radiation contamination of any natural groundwater springs.

Three world records were claimed during the year, all by hard-rock tunneling machines. In Norway a 3.5-m-diameter Robbins TBM drove 240.5 m through hard granite in one week. A second, 4.1-m-diameter, Robbins TBM completed the world's longest inclined shaft, the Pitzaler Glacier railroad tunnel in Austria, which involved 3.7 km of tunnel through granitic gneiss at inclines of 26°–37.5°. In South Africa, at the Vaal Reef Mines, a record raisebore (a rock shaft bored upwards from tunnel to surface) of 580 m in 85 days was achieved. A 2.13-m-diameter Reed machine bored through lava with compressive strengths of 40,000 psi.

Traditional drill and blast tunneling, now using advanced hydraulic drilling equipment, began to take advantage of the rapid growth of applied computer technology. Face drilling was beginning to be carried out under programmed robotic control, providing accurate predetermination of blast hole depth and spacing for a wide range of rock types. Atlas Copco of Sweden developed a novel hollow-tube rock bolt, expanded and tensioned by water, injected at 4,500 psi. Engineers in the U.S. produced a 7.4-m-diameter TBM capable of 3 million lb of thrust to drive a 6.5-km tunnel through the granite mountains of the Sierra Nevada. Japan and West Germany maintained their world domination of slurry shield construction, with both countries actively pursuing overseas opportunities for their equipment and expertise.

Pipe jacking continued to enjoy popularity with engineers as tunneled lengths of more than one kilometre from a single shaft became commonplace. In more and more countries public authorities and consultants made the method their first choice for the construction of water-supply and sewerage pipelines of up to four metres in diameter.

Mass transit subway systems offered the best market for international and national contractors able to construct large-diameter tunnels. Major cities constructing or about to start substantial lengths of subway included Antwerp, Belgium; Baghdad, Iraq; Caracas, Venezuela; Singapore; Taipei, Taiwan; Lyon, France; Atlanta, Ga.; and Pittsburgh, Pa. Another field of tunneling that began to emerge involved the long-term storage of nuclear or toxic wastes in deep underground caverns. (*See* ENVIRONMENT: *Special Report.*)

(GEOFFREY J. NOBLETT)

[733; 734.A]

Japanese workers have completed the world's longest tunnel, a 54-kilometre (33-mile) link under Tsugaru Strait, between the main island of Honshu and the northernmost island, Hokkaido.

RENE BURRI—MAGNUM

Environment

In political terms, 1983 was marked by the environmentalists' achievement, for the first time, of national representation: in the West German federal elections in March, the "Greens" won 28 seats in the Bundestag (including one awarded to them by the Berlin senate, which nominates 22 Bundestag members). Elsewhere, the movement was less successful politically, though in Austria the "Green" vote contributed to the loss of the Social Democrats' overall parliamentary majority.

Greenpeace, the environmental protest group, maintained its intense pressure on governments. It received worldwide publicity for its "invasion" of the U.S.S.R. in July, when a party was landed on Soviet soil to photograph what was alleged to be an installation using whale meat to feed livestock raised for fur. The story made front-page news just as the International Whaling Commission was meeting in Brighton, England. (See *Wildlife Conservation,* below.) A more significant victory for environmentalists was gained in Australia, where the state Hydro-Electric Commission in Tasmania wished to dam the Gordon and Franklin rivers. This would have flooded some 140 sq km (54 sq mi) of land supporting temperate rain forest in what had been declared a World Heritage Area. The new federal government elected in March overruled the state government, and the scheme was abandoned.

A June decision by three major British trade unions to refuse to handle nuclear waste scheduled for dumping at sea prevented dumping by Britain. It also caused the Belgian authorities to abandon their dumping plans, since the unions denied them the British vessels they intended to use. Japan also abandoned its dumping plans in June.

"Acid rain" pollution continued to be a major cause for concern in Europe and North America. Similar pollution was reported from China.

INTERNATIONAL COOPERATION

United Nations. At the annual meeting of the UN Environment Program (UNEP) governing council, held in Nairobi, Kenya, May 11–24, it was decided that UNEP would produce a document describing the global environment for the coming half century. At the same time, it would recommend goals that member governments might work toward and would establish a commission of eminent people who would concentrate world attention on environmental issues. The organization remained underfunded. It had anticipated an income of $85 million for 1984–85 but predicted that actual subscriptions would yield no more than $65 million. The meeting agreed on a budget of $70 million.

On March 24, at Cartagena de Indias, Colombia, 27 nations signed the Cartagena Convention to protect the marine environment of the Caribbean. This marked the culmination of negotiations that began in 1976, under the auspices of UNEP. The convention was permissive rather than restrictive and did not deal with pollution from land-based sources—although work had begun on a protocol to achieve that end. It did include a protocol dealing with oil spills at sea. Implementation of the $1.5 million Caribbean Action Plan, for which UNEP was seeking funds, was expected to begin with the protection of coastal waters, especially mangrove swamps.

Protection of the Mediterranean advanced another step in August, when the 1980 Athens Treaty on Land-Based Sources of Pollution came into force with ratification by 6 of the original 16 signatories: Algeria, Tunisia, Egypt, Turkey, Monaco, and France. The remaining signatories were expected to ratify the treaty shortly. The (UN) Geneva Convention on Long-Range Transboundary Air Pollution came into force on March 15. The convention called for collaboration in research and for the exchange of information regarding pollutants, especially new pollutants. At a meeting of signatories held in Geneva in June, an appeal by West Germany to reduce sulfur dioxide emissions 30% by 1993 was rejected.

By August the Law of the Sea Convention, drafted by the third UN Conference on the Law of the Sea, which ended in December 1982, had been ratified by 6 of the signatories (60 ratifications were required for it to come into force). The Soviet Union and Japan, both of which had originally abstained, added their signatures to the convention. The first meeting of the International Seabed Authority was held in Jamaica on March 15. The U.S. continued its attempts to persuade Britain, West Germany, and France to join it in a new, alternative treaty, and on January 5 UN Secretary-General Javier Pérez de Cuéllar rebuked the U.S. government for saying that it would withhold its contributions to the committee drafting rules for seabed exploration and mining. When Pres. Ronald Reagan proclaimed a 200-mi exclusive economic zone for the U.S. on March 10, diplomats feared it might be an attempt to unravel the Law of the Sea treaty. (*See* LAW: *Sidebar.*)

European Communities. At the end of January the EC Commission proposed to form two environment funds, with a total budget of $1.5 million rising to $6 million by 1987. One fund would promote conservation and the other clean technologies, and both would become operational in 1984. The proposal awaited the approval of the Council of Ministers.

Following publication of the interim report of the Turin Project on environmental lead, the European Parliament began to urge the elimination of lead in gasoline (petrol) throughout the EC. On June 6 the Parliament approved a report calling for a reduction from 0.4 grams of lead per litre of gasoline to 0.15 grams per litre by 1985, and for the introduction of lead-free gasoline "as soon as possible." This proposal was modified on June 16, when environment ministers from West Germany, Denmark, The Netherlands, and Luxembourg spoke against the dangers of lead in the environment but agreed to a ban on lead in gasoline only "if need be." At the same meeting, a directive calling for the introduction of environmental impact assessments was rejected.

A draft directive issued by the Commission at the end of February dealt with the movement of

England:
see United Kingdom

English Literature:
see Literature

Entertainment:
see Dance; Motion Pictures; Music; Television and Radio; Theatre

Entomology:
see Life Sciences

WIDE WORLD

When the supertanker "Castillo de Bellver" burned and broke apart off Cape Town, South Africa, its 260,000 tons of crude oil threatened the coast with a slick more than 40 kilometres (25 miles) long.

toxic wastes across frontiers. It proposed that the countries of origin, transit, and destination be notified of each shipment and that no waste be moved unless a suitable disposal facility had agreed to accept it. Each member state would have to report annually the amount and type of waste moved. The drafting of toxic waste regulations was delayed by the failure of seven member states to submit reports on their methods of handling such wastes to the Commission. The reports should have been available by the end of 1981, but by early August 1983 only the U.K., West Germany, and Luxembourg had submitted them, and the Commission threatened to take the defaulting members to court. (*See* Special Report.)

Antarctica. Signatories of the Antarctic Treaty held two weeks of talks in Wellington, N.Z., in January, where they considered the establishment of an authority to regulate commercial activity on the continent. This was the second round of talks on the subject, the first having been held in June 1982. The third round was held in Bonn, West Germany, on July 11–12, 1983. The aim was to form a scientific, environmental, and technical organization—followed by a commission when interest in mining increased—to ensure that the development of mineral resources caused the least possible environmental damage. More than 100 environmental groups opposed the proposals.

THE MARINE ENVIRONMENT

The war between Iran and Iraq caused oil pollution in the Persian Gulf, complicated measures taken to deal with it, and finally led to considerable confusion concerning the extent of the problem. Pollution came from two Iranian wells in the Nowruz area close to the main Iranian export terminal on Kharg Island. One well was damaged in February when a ship collided with it, the other in an Iraqi attack on March 2, which caused a fire. On March 28 an oil slick containing more than 100,000 bbl and covering about 36 sq km (14 sq mi) was said to be about two weeks' drifting time from the northern coast of Bahrain, traveling at approximately 9.5 km (6 mi) a day. Reportedly, the wells were continuing to release about 5,000 bbl a day.

By early April, as a team of 35 experts from the British Petroleum (BP) Environmental Control Centre were standing by ready to fly to the area to help, the slick was said to cover thousands of square kilometres and to be about to strike the coast between Qatar and Bahrain. There was fear that it would clog pumps and filters in the nearby desalination plants on which several countries depended for potable water. Talks to devise ways of dealing with the leak were postponed on April 14, as Iranian and Iraqi delegates accused one another of responsibility for the incident.

When the coastal pollution from the slick failed to appear by the end of April, experts began to suspect that the size of the leak had been exaggerated. Investigation showed that the well that had been set on fire, and that continued to burn, was releasing no oil, but the well whose platform had collapsed following the collision with a ship was leaking probably 1,200 bbl a day. Iran and Iraq had both inflated the problem, and tanker captains had used it as a cover for cleaning out their tanks at sea, so some pollution did occur. In mid-July the World Wildlife Fund reported sightings of dead birds, turtles, sea snakes, fish, dolphins, and dugongs.

Early on August 6 fire broke out on the Spanish tanker "Castillo de Bellver" as it was rounding the Cape of Good Hope with a cargo of 260,000 tons of Gulf crude on its way to Spain. The weather was stormy, but 29 crew members and two wives were rescued quickly by a fishing boat, and two more crew members were rescued later by helicopter; three people were lost. The wind was moving the ship and the oil it was spilling to the northeast. In midmorning, about 112 km (70 mi) northwest of Cape Town, the ship broke in two. The stern sank, reappeared briefly two hours later, then disappeared finally in about 300 m (1,000 ft) of water, 32 km (20 mi) from the coast. The bow section remained afloat with much of its cargo trapped inside it. A 32-km slick drifted toward the coast, soon growing to 43 km (27 mi) long and 11 km (7 mi) wide. Soot from the fire fell ashore, covering farm crops and sheep. On August 7 the tug "John Ross" got a line to the bow section and towed it out to sea. The weather changed, and the slick was caught by the Benguela Current and carried southeastward, away from the coast. No coastal pollution was reported.

The 218,000-ton Irano-British Shipping Services tanker "Sivand" was damaged on September 17 while trying to moor at Immingham in the Humber Estuary, on England's eastern coast. The ship reached the mouth of the estuary in the evening, made rendezvous with six tugs, and took on two Humber pilots. Caught by the ebb tide, "Sivand" overshot the jetty. The tugs lost control, and the ship collided with a mooring point and several other objects. A 20-m (66-ft) horizontal hole was torn in its side, affecting two of its tanks. About 6,000 tons of crude oil were released, polluting mud flats and sandbanks. The estuary is of considerable ornithological importance, but few birds were affected, and the slick dispersed. On October 3 the emergency operation to clear it was halted.

THE FRESHWATER ENVIRONMENT

Heavy pollution of the Rhine waters caused growing concern, particularly in The Netherlands. Alsatian Potash Mines, a French state-owned company said to be dumping 130 kg (287 lb) of chloride a second into the river, was taken to court in Strasbourg, France, by ten Dutch towns whose water was contaminated by salt. Despite the court's decision that it had been breaking the law for three years, the company told its 5,800 employees in August that it would not cut potash production. It planned to appeal the ruling.

An International Water Tribunal composed of experts on environmental pollution and related matters began hearings in Rotterdam, Neth., on October 3. The governments of the five member states of the International Commission for the Protection of the Rhine Against Pollution (France, West Germany, Luxembourg, Switzerland, and The Netherlands, which subsidized the tribunal), together with the East German government and 45 international firms, were charged by Dutch and other European environmental organizations with causing or permitting serious pollution of the river. None of the governments or firms so charged chose to be represented before the tribunal. Environmentalists held that the governments concerned had failed in their duty to take legal action against firms causing pollution.

In the U.K. a report by the nitrates subcommittee of the Standing Technical Advisory Committee on Water Quality, a joint committee of the Department of the Environment and the National Water Council, was leaked to the press on February 27. It suggested that nitrate levels in some British rivers were above the EC recommended limit of 50 parts per million, due to be implemented in 1985. The rising nitrate level was attributed to increased use of nitrogen fertilizer on farmland. At the beginning of September the Thames Water Authority (TWA) awarded a prize of £250 to Russell Doig for catching the first salmon from the river in 150 years. The TWA began restocking the river with salmon in 1979.

On May 10 it was announced that Switzerland would ban phosphates from all washing compounds over the next two to three years in order to protect the fish in its lakes. The ban would reduce the amount of phosphate entering Swiss lakes by two-thirds. In early August cyanide in the Meuse River, which supplies drinking water to five million people, killed thousands of birds near Liège, Belgium.

LAND CONSERVATION

In Australia controversy over the Tasmanian Hydro-Electric Commission's projected Gordon-below-Franklin dam continued during the first half of 1983. The area of southwestern Tasmania affected by the project lies in a temperate rain forest and includes major archaeological sites. In particular, it includes caves occupied by humans between 16,000 and 20,000 years ago, providing evidence of a late Pleistocene settlement with a hunting economy based on the large wallaby. In mid-December 1982 southwestern Tasmania was designated a World Heritage Area by UNESCO, on the recommendation of the federal government.

The argument became heated. At a World Conservation Strategy meeting in Wales, the prince of Wales said the destruction of natural timber in wilderness areas provided a poor example for less

WIDE WORLD

The National Film Board of Canada circulated two films about the causes and effects of acid rain. For a time a sensitive Reagan administration classified the movies in the U.S. as "political propaganda," requiring that they be registered and carry a disclaimer stating that their contents had not been approved by the U.S. government. The classification was later withdrawn.

developed countries, and the duke of Edinburgh said the economic case for the dam was "not frightfully convincing." Both were denounced by John Ashton of the Tasmanian Hydro-Electric Commission. On Jan. 12, 1983, David Bellamy, a botanist and television personality, flew from Britain to join the protest. He was arrested on January 17 for trespass, together with 27 other protesters, and was released on bail on January 21. He agreed not to return to the site, but he did return to Britain and to a stream of radio, TV, and press interviews.

The issue figured in the federal election, and the help of environmental groups in marginal constituencies may have contributed to the Australian Labor Party victory. Robert Hawke, the new prime minister, announced over the weekend of March 5–6 that he would halt construction of the dam as soon as the World Heritage (Properties Protection) Bill, already passed by the Senate, had been passed by the House of Representatives. At the end of March, before the bill had been passed, the federal government issued the World Heritage (Western Tasmania Wilderness) Regulation, forbidding construction of the dam without federal approval. The regulation was challenged in the High Court but was sustained, and the project was abandoned. (*See* AUSTRALIA.)

In February the Mediterranean Dead Sea Company announced that the scheme to link the Dead Sea and the Mediterranean had reached the detailed planning stage and might be completed by 1990. This would allow water to enter the Dead Sea, which is drying up and has split into two parts. Jordan opposed the plan because of tourist facilities and a potash works built close to the edge of the Dead Sea, which would be lost if the water rose beyond its present level.

Early in March the Soviet newspaper *Pravda* admitted to a problem with the dam built in 1980 across the neck of the Kara-Bogaz-Gol, a gulf 160 km (100 mi) long and 140 km (87 mi) wide but only 2 to 3 m (6 to 10 ft) deep, on the eastern side of the Caspian Sea. The gulf once formed a natural evaporation pan through which the Caspian was losing water, and the dam was intended to block it off and allow it to dry. By the time of the *Pravda* report it had dwindled from 18,000 to 6,000 sq km (7,000 to 2,300 sq mi) and to a depth of 50 cm (20 in). This was causing difficulties for the Karabogazsulfat Trust, which extracts chemicals from the subterranean brines, but the main fear was that, if the gulf dried completely, salt deposits from it would blow inland, contaminating fertile soils and fish farms over a wide area. *Pravda* said the State Committee for Science and Technology had recommended immediate construction of a sluice in the dam that would allow sufficient water to enter to prevent such contamination.

The Malaysian government announced in February that it had abandoned plans to flood the Taman Negara national park. However, it planned to remove the protected status of the Klias Peninsula national park in order to permit construction of a pulp and paper mill. The mill would be supplied by 8,000 ha (200,000 ac) of softwood trees planted on land cleared of forest just outside the park boundary.

TOXIC WASTES AND POLLUTANTS

In mid-May the U.S. Center for Disease Control (CDC) and the Brookhaven (Upton, N.Y.) and Oak Ridge (Tenn.) national laboratories published the report of a survey conducted among residents of the Love Canal area at Niagara Falls, N.Y., which had been contaminated by toxic chemical wastes. No chromosomal abnormalities were found, and there was no evidence of illness that might be linked to such abnormalities.

In July it was revealed that leakage of toxic wastes from electronics companies in the 200-sq km (77-sq mi) "Silicon Valley" area in California had contaminated wells. In December the Justice Department sued the Shell Oil Co. for almost $1.9 billion in damage to the environment allegedly caused by the company's pesticide factory near Denver, Colo., the largest such suit in U.S. history.

Dioxin. Waste weighing 75 kg (165 lb) and contaminated with 250–300 g (9–10 oz) of dioxin from Seveso, northern Italy (where the Icmesa chemical plant explosion in 1976 caused widespread dioxin poisoning), packed in 41 metal drums, left Italy on Sept. 10, 1982, and for some time vanished completely. The waste itself consisted of dioxin mixed with sodium chloride and tars that had formed a hard cake on the sides of the vessel in which the explosion had occurred, and some soil. Rumours that it was headed for East Germany were denied by authorities there. At the end of March 1983, Hoffmann-La Roche, owners of the Seveso plant, admitted that the drums had crossed into France, transported by an Italian company.

The French authorities traced the drums as far as Saint-Quentin, Picardy, where they had spent several months in a warehouse owned by a French waste-disposal firm. West German, Belgian, and Dutch authorities joined the search, and on April 22 British ports were warned to look out for the drums, since fresh rumours suggested they might be headed for Britain. Finally, they were discovered on May 19, still in France, in an abandoned abattoir at Anguilcourt-le-Sart, near Saint-Quentin. The next day they were removed by the French Army, and over the weekend of June 4–5 they were taken to the Hoffmann-La Roche establishment in Basel, Switz., presumably for disposal in the Ciba Geigy incinerator nearby. The trial at Monza of five senior officials from the Icmesa plant ended on September 24 with the conviction of all the defendants. They were sentenced to prison terms ranging from two and a half to five years.

In May the West German chemical company Boehringer announced it would close the only factory in the country producing the herbicide 2,4,5-T, of which dioxin is a by-product. New laws forbidding the transport of substances contaminated with dioxin made further production impractical. This was followed in July by the decision of Chemie Linz of Austria to cease manufacture of 2,4,5-T because of pressure from environmentalists. No other factories in Western Europe were now making the herbicide.

During severe flooding on Dec. 12, 1982, the CDC discovered that inhabitants of Times Beach, near St. Louis, Mo., were exposed to high levels of

WIDE WORLD

The extent of dioxin pollution in Times Beach (near St. Louis), Missouri, was assessed by technicians from the EPA. Here they drill for soil samples near the home of Ben and Rosemary Essen.

dioxin. In the 1970s chemical wastes had been mixed with used oil and spread on dirt and gravel roads to control dust. The CDC advised that the evacuation of the area, necessitated initially by the flooding, be made permanent. As the investigation continued, more extensive contamination was discovered, and in February 1983 the federal government took the unprecedented step of buying the town in its entirety and declaring it unfit for human habitation. The government planned to spend $33 million to buy 800 homes and 50 businesses and to compensate 2,500 residents.

Another dioxin scare emerged in June at Newark, N.J., when soil samples from the site of a factory that had manufactured Agent Orange (the 2,4,5-T defoliant used in the Vietnam war) in the 1960s were found to contain dioxin. The contamination appeared to be confined to a small area and to be less severe than that at Times Beach. (*See* Special Report.)

Lead. On April 18 Tom King, the U.K. secretary of state for the environment, announced that beginning in 1990 all cars in Britain would have to run on lead-free gasoline. There was disagreement on how this might be achieved, however. The oil industry preferred to market a 92-octane, lead-free gasoline, which automobile manufacturers were unwilling to accept. In March it was learned that British canned-food firms were phasing out the use of lead-based solder for sealing cans. Leaded gasoline would be banned in West Germany from Jan. 1, 1986, when all cars would have to be fitted with catalytic converters.

Asbestos. The policy of selling obsolete power stations to private demolition contractors had to be reconsidered after work was halted at the Fulham power station, London, in July. The Health and Safety Executive ordered the halt following protests by local residents. The contractor, Barlborough Metal Deptford, was required to demonstrate to the executive that it could remove 500 tons of asbestos insulation safely.

At its meeting on August 23, the Health and Safety Commission considered two reports on asbestos and recommended a government ban on the import of blue (crocidolite) and brown (amosite) asbestos. The commission issued new regulations, believed to be the strictest in the world. From August 1984 employers might not permit employees to be exposed to more than 0.5 fibres per millilitre (f/ml) of white (chrysotile) asbestos, or 0.2 f/ml of blue or brown. The controls applied only in the workplace, and the commission planned to discuss with other government departments ways to introduce comparable measures for the general environment.

Air Pollution. Following the previous year's introduction of pollution controls in Athens, a meeting of international experts in September 1983 discussed the damage air pollution was causing to the west frieze of the Parthenon. Steps were proposed to afford temporary protection until the frieze could be removed and stored indoors. (*See* HISTORIC PRESERVATION.)

Ozone, mainly from vehicle exhausts, might be reducing U.S. crop yields by 10 to 25%, according to a report from the Boyce Thompson Institute for Plant Research at Cornell University, Ithaca, N.Y., published in September. The ozone encourages plants to mature faster, thus reducing the period during which photosynthesis takes place. Reports issued in October by the U.S. Environmental Protection Agency (EPA) and the National Academy of Sciences both warned that the "greenhouse effect," in which heat is trapped in the Earth's atmosphere as a result of carbon dioxide buildup (resulting mostly from burning of fossil fuels), could raise temperatures on the Earth by several degrees during the next century. However, while the EPA predicted catastrophic consequences and called for immediate action, the National Academy opposed hasty steps and recommended further research.

Acid Rain. The report of a survey presented to the Welsh Water Authority in May showed that fish stocks in many Welsh rivers were being reduced severely by acid rain pollution. The Authority confirmed the findings in its own study, conducted later. On September 6 it was announced that the U.K. Central Electricity Generating Board and the National Coal Board would each contribute £2.5 million to a five-year study of the acid rain problem in northwestern Europe. The British government planned to take no action to reduce sulfur dioxide emissions from power stations until the report of the study became available.

The dispute between the U.S. and Canada moved closer to resolution late in the year with agreement on a joint study. In February, however, the U.S. administration ordered that two Canadian National Film Board films portraying the effects of acid rain pollution on forests and lakes (as well as a film on nuclear war) should include a disclaimer stating that they represented the opinion of a foreign agency and did not reflect the official U.S. view. The order was later ruled unconstitutional by a federal judge. In December 1982 U.S. funding of research into acid rain had been cut from $650,000 to $150,000. In September 1983 the EPA completed a review of the problem and recommended that the U.S. reduce its sulfur dioxide emissions 15 to 17% by 1990.

The state of West Germany's forests was the subject of some controversy. It was estimated that one-third of the country's total woodland area might be affected in varying degrees by acid rain. In December 1982 the Pollution Control Establishment of North Rhine-Westphalia published a report stating that most of the damage was being caused not by sulfur dioxide but by ozone, formed by the action of sunlight on oxides of nitrogen. In June Hubert Ziegler of the Technical University of Munich supported this view, having found that in the Black Forest dying trees supported lichens, usually sensitive indicators of sulfur pollution.

At a conference on the subject held in Lindau on June 7–9, scientists confirmed that sulfur dioxide levels in the Black Forest were low and lichens abundant. Nevertheless, new laws came into effect in July aimed at reducing sulfur dioxide emissions. Within ten years power stations with a capacity of more than 400 MW must emit no more than 400 mg per cu m, a reduction of 95%, and those with a capacity of 200 to 400 MW must emit no more than 2,000 mg per cu m, a reduction of 60%. However, the limits did not apply to 90% of West German power stations, since they had less than five years of life left and were exempt, and the law permitted an increase in the sulfur content of the coal being burned.

The Czechoslovak Communist Party newspaper *Rude Pravo* reported in April that in some parts of the country 10 to 70% of forest trees were being affected by acid rain. Lignite-fueled power stations were blamed. The forestry industry was told late in 1982 that it would have to reduce its cull substantially to allow for the estimated pollution loss of 600,000 to 800,000 sq m (700,000 to 950,000 sq yd) of timber a year. In China the newspaper *Guangming Daily* reported early in May 1983 that, of 2,400 sites examined, 44.5% had unusually high acid rain and that rice planted on 1,320 ha (3,300 ac) near Chongqing (Chungking) had wilted and died suddenly. The affected area seemed to be confined to the region south of the Chiang Jiang (Yangtze River).

UPI

William Ruckelshaus won applause from Pres. Ronald Reagan, who picked him to take over the controversy-ridden Environmental Protection Agency. Ruckelshaus had compiled an excellent record as the agency's first administrator and was easily confirmed by the U.S. Senate.

GREENPEACE—SYGMA

Protesters from Greenpeace landed on Soviet soil from their converted British trawler "Rainbow Warrior" to take photographs and distribute leaflets charging that U.S.S.R. whalers were making illegal use of whale meat. The boat was chased away by two Soviet gunboats, while seven people were seized and held for a week.

Nuclear Waste. On January 6, French military police seized the Greenpeace cutter "Sirius" after bombarding it with tear-gas grenades. The cutter was trying to dock in Cherbourg to protest the imminent arrival of a ship carrying Japanese nuclear waste for reprocessing. The French action led to protests in Denmark and in Sweden, where a police guard was mounted on the waste carrier "Sigyn." On January 6 the "Sigyn" sailed for Cherbourg with a cargo of waste, pursued by Greenpeace demonstrators who later abandoned their attempt to interrupt its journey.

In the U.K. the dumping of low-level radioactive wastes at sea was a focus of protest. The London Dumping Convention, meeting on February 17, voted for a two-year moratorium on dumping. On June 18 the National Union of Seamen, the Associated Society of Locomotive Engineers and Firemen, and the Transport and General Workers' Union urged the government to respect the moratorium and to store on land waste that was scheduled for dumping about 300 km (500 mi) off Land's End. At the same time, they said their members would not handle the waste, thus making the dumping impossible and leaving the authorities no choice but to find a storage site on land.

The public inquiry into the building of a reactor at Sizewell, Suffolk, opened January 11 and continued through the year.

"GREEN" POLITICS

In the Austrian general election held on April 24, "Green" candidates won 1.89% of the votes cast. This gained them no parliamentary seats, but it did take votes from the ruling Social Democrats, who lost their overall majority, leading to the resignation of Chancellor Bruno Kreisky.

In elections to the West German Bundestag on March 6, the "Greens" (Grün-Alternative-Liste) took 5.6% of the vote and won 27 parliamentary seats; an additional seat was awarded by the Berlin senate. On March 29, as they went to take their seats, they staged a symbolic march on the Bundestag building.

Early in the year President Reagan made radical changes in the staff of the EPA. In February Matthew Novick, the agency's inspector general, and John Horton, its assistant administrator, were dismissed, following the earlier dismissal of Rita Lavelle, who had been in charge of the $1.6 billion fund created to pay for cleaning up toxic waste dumps. It was alleged that Lavelle had collaborated too closely with polluting industries and that the fund was being allotted to states in ways that might influence the outcome of congressional elections. She was tried for contempt of Congress in July and was acquitted, but later she was convicted of perjury and obstructing a congressional inquiry. On March 9 Anne Burford (formerly Gorsuch), the administrator, resigned. Further resignations followed, including those of Louis Cordia, alleged to have prepared a list of employees and scientific advisers with notes on their political leanings, and Deputy Administrator John Hernandez. On March 21 President Reagan nominated William Ruckelshaus (*see* BIOGRAPHIES), who had been the agency's first head, as the new EPA administrator.

In January the Wilderness Society, the Audubon Society, the Sierra Club, and three other conservation groups said they would sue Secretary of the Interior James Watt (*see* BIOGRAPHIES) over his decision to remove protection from 156 sites, comprising 300,000 ha (740,000 ac) of land under consideration as federal wilderness areas. The removal of protection meant the areas could be licensed for mineral exploration and development, and conservationists maintained that Watt had exceeded his powers. However, Watt was losing support even among Republican senators, largely because of his politically disastrous public statements, and on October 11 his resignation was announced. His successor, former national security adviser William Clark, was less abrasive but was thought to share Watt's views on land management.

In May the Polish government established a Main Office for Environmental Protection and Water Resource Management to deal with environmental problems, which were said to be serious. (MICHAEL ALLABY)

WILDLIFE CONSERVATION

On Nov. 19, 1982, the European Parliament had voted by 52 to 10, with four abstentions, in favour of a total Community ban on the import of the skins of pups of harp and hooded seals. There were some fears that the ban might lead to retaliation by Canada and Norway, especially over fishing rights, but the vote was meant to influence the decision to be made by the Council of Ministers on December 3. Between the two meetings, however, a report by scientists of the International Council for the Exploration of the Seas, commissioned jointly by the EC and Canada, failed to support the ban. The ministers were unable to reach agreement and deferred the matter to the meeting of environment ministers on December 17. The environment ministers agreed to a temporary ban, but on Feb. 28, 1983, they failed to agree to ban the sale of baby seal products. Uncertainty over the Community's attitude affected the market in seal products. Canadian hunters decided to cull only adult seals, and the price for their skins was halved.

The International Whaling Commission (IWC), meeting in July 1983 in Brighton, England, confirmed that commercial whaling would be phased out before January 1986, in accordance with the 1982 meeting's resolution. Peru withdrew its previous objection, and Chile announced that it had already given up whaling. Norway, the U.S.S.R., and Japan, the last three unrepentant whaling nations, had to face worldwide disapproval and, in the case of Japan and Norway, economic sanctions. The meeting agreed that quotas should be cut by 18%. There was concern over stocks of minke whales, hunted in the North Atlantic by Norway and in the Antarctic by Japan and the U.S.S.R., and Bryde's whales, hunted off the Peruvian coast by Peru, largely on behalf of Japan. The U.S. agreed to accept a quota of 18 bowhead whales hit but not necessarily landed; in 1982 the quota had been set at 45 over three years. It was believed that

The Siberian crane is near extinction, in part, it is believed, because of the skill of Pakistani hunters with this ancient weapon. A cord, weighted with lead, is whirled and then let go into the night sky to entangle the migrating cranes, flying at low levels.

PHOTOGRAPHS, STEVEN E. LANDFRIED

the prospect of a ban on commercial whaling was leading whaling nations to prepare plans for "coastal subsistence" whaling, which would allow them to continue.

The most publicized event while the meeting was in session was the landing by Greenpeace protesters at Lorino, U.S.S.R. On July 16 "Rainbow Warrior," their converted trawler, crossed from Alaska and landed a party of six people to take photographs and distribute leaflets. They were arrested, as was Jim Henry, photographing the scene from an inflatable craft offshore. "Rainbow Warrior" was chased by several vessels, including a gunboat, but escaped to Nome, Alaska. On July 24 the prisoners were returned at the International Date Line, at sea. Greenpeace claimed that, contrary to an international agreement that whale meat may be used only for human consumption, the U.S.S.R. was using meat from gray whales to feed livestock being raised for fur. Pictures that had not been seized by the Soviets were rushed to Brighton and presented to the IWC.

Countries signatory to the Convention on International Trade in Endangered Species of Wild Fauna and Flora (CITES) held their biennial meeting in Gaborone, Botswana, during April and May under UNEP auspices. Some 300 delegates from 81 countries discussed possible additions to, or removals from, the CITES list of protected species.

Conservation of the world's endangered birds achieved some successes. There were now 80 breeding pairs of the noisy scrub bird (*Atrichornis clamosus*) of Western Australia; its numbers were dangerously low when it was rediscovered in 1961, after having been believed extinct for 70 years. The Lord Howe wood rail (*Tricholimnas sylvestris*) had been brought back from the brink of extinction. In May 1980 only 15 birds were left, but by April 1983 captive breeding had produced 120, and 57 of these had been released at Lord Howe Island (New South Wales), where they were rearing their own chicks. A less spectacular increase was achieved by foster incubation of eggs of the Chatham Island black robin (*Petroica traversi*). The population had risen to 11 from 5 in 1977.

The California condor (*Gymnogyps californianus*) recovery program received a boost when one captive-hatched chick proved to be a female—the only one in captivity. If all went well, it could breed in six to ten years. In addition, two chicks hatched in the wild in 1983. (*See* ZOOS AND BOTANICAL GARDENS: *Zoos*.) Crane numbers gave cause for concern at the International Crane Workshop in India in March. The worst news was that fewer than 500 black-necked cranes (*Grus nigricollis*) remained. The ancient sport of catching migrating cranes by throwing weighted cords into the air, still practiced in some villages of northern Pakistan, was threatening the endangered Siberian crane (*Grus leucogeranus*). Two probable bird extinctions were reported: the Santa Barbara song sparrow (*Zonotrichia melodia graminea*), which had not been seen since 1952, and the Colombian grebe (*Podiceps andinus*), last seen ten years earlier.

I. S. C. Parker and Esmond Bradley Martin, writing in *Oryx*, the journal of the Fauna and Flora Preservation Society (FFPS), estimated that 51,571 elephants died for the 700 metric tons of ivory exported from Africa in 1982. The Sudan was now the largest single exporter of ivory, and there were reports of highly organized illegal elephant hunting there. The war in Chad probably resulted in wildlife as well as human casualties. The endangered scimitar-horned oryx (*Oryx dammah*) and addax (*Addax nasomaculatus*) were not seen in a survey of their last stronghold near the Chad-Niger border. In another war-torn zone, near the Cambodian border in northeast Thailand, five kouprey (*Bos sauveli*), a species of wild cow feared to be extinct, were sighted.

Most of the arrow bamboo in China's Wolong (Wo-lung) and Baoxing (Pao-hsing) reserves flowered, threatening 300 pandas with starvation. The Chinese government and the World Wildlife Fund, which were cooperating on the panda project, were trying to find alternative food sources, planting bamboo seeds in deforested areas and providing supplementary food. If absolutely essential, pandas would be taken into captivity and released when the bamboo had regenerated. In the past, when mass flowering of bamboos occurred in one area, pandas were able to move to another area. Now, however, suitable habitat existed only in the country's 11 isolated panda reserves.

Wolves had less public appeal than pandas, and it was often difficult to gain support for their conservation. The gray wolf (*Canis lupus pallipes*) in India was often killed despite legal protection, and its numbers were down to perhaps 500–800. In Minnesota, where most of the remaining 1,200 wolves in the conterminous U.S. live, it was decided to allow ranchers and hunters to kill 50–160 wolves a year, but in Italy, where wolves numbered fewer than 200, their protection was backed up by compensation payments to farmers for losses of livestock. In Norway, with a wolf population of perhaps less than 20, conservationists were outraged by the offer of a $3,000 bounty by the Directorate of Game and Freshwater Fish for a wolf believed to have taken a large number of sheep. The government upheld the directorate's action but stated that in the future such wolves would be trapped alive and not shot.

A baby aye-aye (*Daubentonia madagascariensis*) was seen in the nature reserve on Nosy Mangabé Island. The aye-aye, thought to have been extinct since 1933, was rediscovered on mainland Madagascar in 1956, and nine of these rare lemurs were transferred to the island reserve in 1965. The 1983 baby was the first sign that the aye-aye were breeding in their new home.

Invertebrates, a vast group of often neglected animals, claimed attention with the publication of the *Invertebrate Red Data Book* by the International Union for Conservation of Nature. Many people learned for the first time of the plight of the giant triton (*Charonia tritonis*), threatened by collecting and coral reef destruction, and of the depletion of queen conch (*Strombus gigas*) populations around the Caribbean islands.

(MICHAEL ALLABY; JACQUI M. MORRIS)

See also Agriculture and Food Supplies; Energy; Fisheries; Historic Preservation; Life Sciences; Transportation.
[355.D; 525.A.3.g and B.4.f.i; 534.E.2.a; 724.A; 737.C.1]

POISONS TO BURN—OR BURY

by John Elkington

The disposal of hazardous industrial wastes has once again become a highly charged political issue, both in the U.S. and in Europe. Early in 1983, for example, the Reagan administration was shaken by a scandal that centred on "sweetheart deals" between industrial waste disposers and the U.S. Environmental Protection Agency. Critics argued that the EPA, in pursuing consensus rather than confrontation, had ended up in industry's pocket.

In Europe, meanwhile, the Swiss multinational combine Hoffmann-La Roche found itself embroiled in an equally fierce controversy. In May 1983, 41 bbl of dioxin-contaminated waste from the ill-fated Icmesa (Industrie Chemiche Meda Societa, Anonima) plant in Seveso, Italy, where an explosion had led to contamination of a wide area in 1976, were traced to a disused slaughterhouse in the northern French village of Anguilcourt-le-Sart. Givaudan, the Hoffmann-La Roche subsidiary that owned Icmesa, had signed an agreement with Mannesmann AG of West Germany under which Mannesmann undertook to dispose of the waste safely. Clearly, it had failed to do so.

Dioxin, which was also involved in controversies in Britain and the U.S., is at least 10,000 times as dangerous as cyanide, causes acute skin disease, and is suspected of causing cancer. The best (albeit expensive) disposal option was to burn the waste, although this requires a specialized incinerator able to reach and maintain temperatures as high as 1,300° C (2,372° F). Country after country refused to accept the Icmesa waste for disposal. The task was ultimately undertaken by Switzerland's Ciba-Geigy AG.

Who Disposes . . . and How? A similar reaction greeted plans to incinerate, in Britain, some 60 metric tons of waste contaminated with the pesticide Kepone. The waste had been inherited by Allied Chemical Co. of the U.S. from its now-defunct subsidiary Life Science Products Co. Leo Abse, member of Parliament for Pontypool, stated that "no-one, certainly not one of my constituents, doubts the compelling necessity to have controlled waste disposal centres." But why, he asked, had all the U.S. states turned down the wastes? Pontypool might have a suitable incinerator, run by Re-Chem International, but should Wales allow itself to become a "receptacle for the excreta of American capitalism?"

Despite such problems, toxic waste disposal was becoming big business, though the U.S. industry, in particular, had an appalling public image. The U.S. Office of Technology Assessment (OTA) estimated that by 1990 at least $12 billion would be spent each year in the U.S. on toxic waste disposal, compared with less than $5 billion in 1983. As of 1983, EPA regulations covered only about 35 million metric tons of the 275 million metric tons of hazardous waste produced annually, but the proportion was increasing in the wake of such disasters as Times Beach, Mo., and Love Canal at Niagara Falls, N.Y., where residential areas became contaminated. As the volume of regulation grew, so would the waste-disposal industry's markets.

These markets are not recession-proof, however. As industrial production fell in the economic downturn of the early 1980s, the amount of toxic waste being generated declined along with it. Another effect of recession was to put the illegal "cowboy" waste contractors or "midnight dumpers" back on the road. Re-Chem International, for example, said it had lost 15% of its waste chemical treatment business in one year.

It is difficult to compare the performance of different countries in the toxic-waste-disposal field. Many countries are lax about collecting the relevant information, and even when they do collect it, they use different definitions of what constitutes "toxic waste." Among European Community (EC) nations, only Britain, Luxembourg, and West Germany supplied the reports on toxic waste disposal required by the European Commission by the end of 1981. But, accepting that the figures are far from reliable, indications are that the amount of hazardous waste generated in Western Europe as a whole is of the order of 40 million tons a year.

There are six main disposal methods available to those who produce such wastes: disposal at sea, which is increasingly regulated; landfill; long-term storage (those Kepone-contaminated wastes ended up in a West German salt mine); physical, chemical, or biological treatment, with any residues landfilled; incineration, either on land or in incinerator ships; and reclamation and recycling.

John Elkington has worked as environmental consultant for such agencies as the U.K. Department of the Environment, the Hudson Institute, the Nature Conservancy Council, the Organization for Economic Co-operation and Development, the UN Development Program, the World Bank, and the World Wildlife Fund. He is the author of Pollution 1990, The Ecology of Tomorrow's World *and* Seven Bridges to the Future *and editor of* Biotechnology Bulletin.

The Dnestr was known as the cleanest river in Soviet Europe until a calamitous spill of toxic waste salts burst out of a fertilizer plant and poisoned some 480 kilometres (300 miles) of it above the Novodnestrovsk Dam.

National Policies. Almost all the developed countries have become conscious of the toxic waste issue within the last ten years, and some have made major strides. France, for example, has moved rapidly toward its goal of a national network of special waste-disposal facilities. West Germany, which produces more toxic waste than any other European country, has established over 60 facilities of various types. Since the early 1970s, West Germany has closed approximately 50,000 unregulated dumps and has moved away from landfill. On the other hand, Britain, with about 500 sites licensed for hazardous waste disposal, uses landfill for over three-quarters of such wastes; 40% of them go into in-house sites operated by industry, while more than 90% of the remainder goes to some 50 contractual sites.

Landfill is still by far the most important option in most countries. Britain stresses controlled co-disposal of hazardous wastes with domestic waste. This approach, it is argued, exploits natural mechanisms of degradation, attenuation, and dispersal. Britain points out that it has suffered none of the problems that have plagued, say, The Netherlands, where Dutch counterparts of Love Canal have emerged at Lekkerkerk, near Rotterdam, and De Staart, near Dordrecht.

The OTA estimates that, while it might have cost $2 million to dispose of the Love Canal wastes properly, cleaning up the site will cost at least $100 million—in addition to the cost of settling some $2 billion in lawsuits. Yet many of the smaller industrial countries still have no modern toxic-waste-disposal facilities, other than in-house facilities operated by companies. Belgium, The Netherlands, and Ireland, for example, have tended to export a considerable proportion of their wastes.

The problem is much worse in the less developed countries. While Japan, which industrialized rapidly after World War II, is coming to grips with its toxic waste problem, countries like Taiwan are encountering severe environmental problems. In some cases, less developed countries have accepted waste from other countries in order to earn foreign currency, even though they have no suitable facilities. Some companies, like the Nedlog Technology Group, have been thinking of setting up waste-disposal operations in the third world to avoid regulations imposed in the U.S. or elsewhere.

Future Prospects. New waste-treatment technologies emerge almost daily. The field of biotechnology, in particular, is generating many new options. Ananda Chakrabarty, who patented the first genetically engineered microorganism (designed to degrade oil spills), has been working with organisms found at Love Canal that have a remarkable ability to degrade dioxin and other persistent chemicals. In the U.K., Imperial Chemical Industries Ltd. and the University of Kent, having worked out how fungi cope with the cyanide released as a defense by plant cells, have developed an immobilized enzyme system that detoxifies industrial cyanide.

Whether or not such systems are used will depend on the speed with which legislation is introduced and the rigour with which it is enforced. Meanwhile, the evidence from around the world suggests that the environmental effects of waste disposal may not be quite as serious as was believed ten years earlier—although the Mediterranean, for example, still receives annually 5,000 tons of zinc, 1,400 tons of lead, 950 tons of chromium, and 10 tons of mercury from coastal industries alone.

From an environmental point of view, the most hopeful trend is probably the decline of the more polluting, heavy industries, a trend speeded by the recession. Many companies are also introducing much cleaner production processes. And many of the new industries are intrinsically cleaner, although even the "ultraclean" microchip industries of Silicon Valley in California produce toxic wastes that have caused some major pollution problems. Clearly, national and international government agencies will need to keep up the pressure, with new legislation such as the 1978 European Commission directive that controls chemicals from production to ultimate disposal. Worldwide, the long-term prospects of the toxic-waste-disposal industry seem assured.

Equatorial Guinea

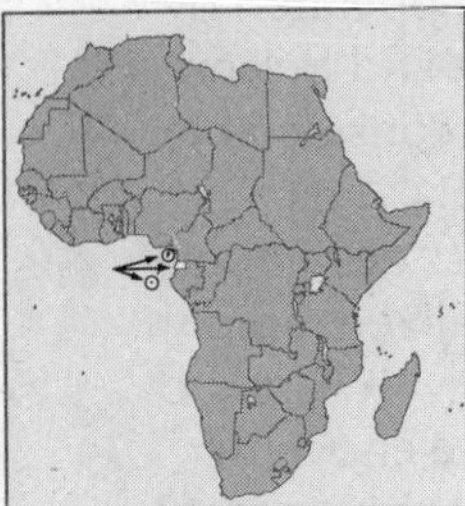
Equatorial Guinea

The African republic of Equatorial Guinea consists of Río Muni, which is bordered by Cameroon on the north, Gabon on the east and south, and the Atlantic Ocean on the west; and the offshore islands of Bioko and Annobon. Area: 28,051 sq km (10,831 sq mi). Pop. (1983 est.): 389,000, including (1978 est.) Fang 71.5%; Bubi 14.3%; other African 13.3%; European 0.9%. Cap. and largest city: Malabo, on Bioko (pop., 1974 est., 25,000). Language: Spanish (official), Fang, Bubi. Religion (1980): Christian 88.8%; tribal 4.6%; atheist 1.4%; Muslim 0.5%; other 0.2%; none 4.5%. President of the Supreme Military Council in 1983, Lieut. Col. Teodoro Obiang Nguema Mbasogo.

Equatorial Guinea's application to become a member of the Central African Customs and Economic Union (UDEAC) was accepted in principle by UDEAC members in January 1983.

Relations with Spain were strained during the year. In April the Spanish government considered halting aid to Equatorial Guinea and concentrating only on small-scale projects. Spain reacted adversely to Equatorial Guinea's application to join the UDEAC, interpreting it as a move by the nation to ally itself with the French-speaking group of countries. In May an attempt by junior officers in the military to overthrow the government failed, and one of the leaders, Sgt. Venancio Mikó Obiang, took refuge in the Spanish embassy. The Spanish finally handed him over to the government on condition that he receive a fair trial. Following the attempted coup, Spain's foreign minister flew to Malabo to clarify the situation and ensure that the 300 Spanish nationals in the country were safe. Relations eventually improved when Pres. Teodoro Obiang Nguema Mbasogo visited Spain in July and persuaded his hosts to reschedule the country's debts. (GUY ARNOLD)

EQUATORIAL GUINEA

Education. (1980–81) Primary, pupils 40,110, teachers 647; secondary, vocational, and teacher-training, pupils 3,013, teachers 288.

Finance and Trade. Monetary unit: ekwele (bikwele for more than one), with (Sept. 20, 1983) a par value of 2 bikwele to 1 Spanish peseta (free rate of 304 bikwele = U.S. $1; 458 bikwele = £1 sterling). Budget (1982 est.): revenue 2,980,000,000 bikwele; expenditure 4,038,000,000 bikwele. Foreign trade (1981): imports 7,982,000,000 bikwele; exports 2,502,000,000 bikwele. Import sources: Spain 80%; Cameroon 7%. Export destination: Spain 87%. Main exports: cocoa 71%; timber 24%.

Agriculture. Production (in 000; metric tons; 1982): sweet potatoes c. 34; cassava c. 55; bananas c. 16; cocoa c. 8; coffee c. 7; palm kernels c. 3; palm oil c. 5; timber (cu m; 1981) c. 465. Livestock (in 000; 1981): sheep c. 34; cattle c. 4; pigs c. 4; goats c. 7; chickens c. 134.

Epidemics: see Health and Disease

Episcopal Church: see Religion

Equestrian Sports

Thoroughbred Racing and Steeplechasing. UNITED STATES AND CANADA. In her first three starts of the year in her native France, All Along finished third in a Grade Three stakes, seventh in a Grade One race, and second in another Grade Three. The four-year-old daughter of Targowice-Agujita, by Vieux Manoir, owned by Daniel Wildenstein, was then undefeated the remainder of the season. Competing against males as she had in her three previous starts, All Along won four of the most prestigious and richest stakes in the world: the Trusthouse Forte Prix de l'Arc de Triomphe at Longchamp, Paris; the Rothmans International at Woodbine in Toronto; the Turf Classic at Aqueduct in New York City; and the Washington, D.C., International at Laurel, Md.

She was a decisive winner in each of the North American classics, an unprecedented accomplishment that earned her owner a bonus of $1 million and for All Along an Eclipse Award as champion female turf horse of 1983. She established a single-season earnings record of $2,138,963.

Other Eclipse Award winners, in the voting conducted by the National Turf Writers Association, *Daily Racing Form,* and the Thoroughbred Racing Associations, were: two-year-old colt, Devil's Bag; two-year-old filly, Althea; three-year-old colt, Slew o' Gold; three-year-old filly, Heartlight No. One; older male horse, Bates Motel; older filly or mare, Ambassador of Luck; male turf horse, John Henry, for a record third time; sprinter, Chinook Pass; and steeplechaser, Flatterer.

Woodford C. ("Woody") Stephens, who trained Devil's Bag, won his first Eclipse Award. Other Eclipse winners were: jockey, Angel Cordero, Jr., for the second consecutive year; apprentice jockey, D. J. Murphy; owner, John Franks; and breeder, Edward P. Taylor (Winfields Farm). Cordero's mounts earned $10,116,697, breaking the single-season mark he had set the previous year with $9,702,520. Cordero's 48 stakes victories established another standard, surpassing Willie Shoemaker's previous high of 46 set in 1971. Horses owned by Franks earned approximately $2.5 million. Pat Day took the riding title for the second consecutive year with 455 winning mounts.

Hickory Tree Stable's Devil's Bag (Halo-Ballade, by Herbager) was undefeated in five starts, winning easily each time. Highly regarded from the beginning of his career, he won the Cowdin, Champagne, and Laurel Futurity. At season's end he was syndicated for $36 million, comprising 36 shares. He would race as a three-year-old.

Althea (Alydar-Courtly Dee, by Never Bend), owned by David Aykroyd, Helen Alexander, and Helen Groves, won four stakes, but none ranked as a Grade One. She was first in the Juvenile Championship and Starlet at Hollywood Park and in the Debutante and Futurity at Del Mar. Althea earned $692,625, the most ever won by a two-year-old filly.

Equusequity Stable's Slew o' Gold (Seattle Slew-Alluvial, by Buckpasser) won his first test in a Grade One race for three-year-olds, taking a division of the Wood Memorial. He finished fourth in the Kentucky Derby and second in the Belmont and Travers. He did not compete in the Preakness. Slew o' Gold earned Eclipse honours by defeating older horses in the Woodward and Jockey Club Gold Cup. Between those races he lost the Marlboro Cup by a neck to Highland Blade, a defeat that cost his owner a $1 million bonus. In the Triple Crown races for three-year-olds, Sunny's Halo won the Kentucky Derby, Deputed Testamony the Preakness, and Caveat the Belmont.

Burt Bacharach's Maryland-bred Heartlight No. One (Rock Talk-Icantell, by Tell) finished first in five consecutive races, including the Hollywood Oaks by 12 lengths, the Del Mar Oaks, and the Ruffian Handicap. Another lightly raced Thoroughbred was Michael Riordan's Bates Motel (Sir Ivor-Sunday Purchase, by T V Lark). He made eight appearances, won five times, and earned $783,000. He captured four consecutive stakes—the San Antonio, Santa Anita, San Diego, and Monmouth—and ended his campaign by losing a decision by a nose to Slew o' Gold in the Woodward and finishing a close third to Highland Blade and Slew o' Gold in the Marlboro Cup.

Dotsam Stable's John Henry (Ole Bob Bowers-Once Double, by Double Jay) won two stakes in five starts, earned $675,875, and increased his world-record earnings total to $4,281,297. The eight-year-old gelding launched his 1983 campaign with a victory in the American Handicap. He lost by a neck to Tolomeo in the Budweiser Million, was fifth in the Jockey Club Gold Cup, ran a close second to Zalataia in the Oak Tree Invitational, and won the Hollywood Turf Cup.

Ambassador of Luck (What Luck-Detente, by Dark Ruler), a four-year-old Pennsylvania-bred filly owned by the Envoy Stable, was six-for-six in 1983. She won two overnight handicaps and an allowance race in New York and then scored in the Molly Pitcher, the Ballerina, and the Maskette.

The four-year-old gelding Chinook Pass (Native Born-Yu Turn, by Turn-to), owned and bred by the Hi Yu Stable in Washington state, raced only on the West Coast. His five stakes victories included the Sierra Madre, Potrero Grande, and San Simeon at Santa Anita, the Bing Crosby at Del Mar, and the Longacres Mile at Longacres.

Kinghaven Farm won two of the Triple Crown events for Canadian-foaled three-year-olds—the Prince of Wales with Archdeacon and the Breeders' Stakes with Kingsbridge. Bompago took the third classic, the Queen's Plate. The Canadian Oaks went to First Summer Day. Travelling Victor was voted Canada's horse of the year.

(JOSEPH C. AGRELLA)

EUROPE AND AUSTRALIA. Fillies dominated major weight-for-age events in the second half of the 1983 European season so completely that the three-pound sex allowance during the closing months of the year seemed certain to be removed in the near future. As noted, Daniel Wildenstein's four-year-old filly All Along won the Trusthouse Forte Prix de l'Arc de Triomphe at Paris, by one length over the English challenger, Sun Princess. Two more fillies, Luth Enchantée and Time Charter, finished inches behind in third and fourth, and in eastern North America All Along went on to beat the best of both sexes during a four-week period in October and November.

Her victims at Paris had already built their reputations. Sun Princess had won the Oaks, Yorkshire Oaks, and St. Leger and also ran a close third to Time Charter and Diamond Shoal in the King George VI and Queen Elizabeth Diamond Stakes. Luth Enchantée had established herself as Europe's top miler with impressive victories in the Prix Jacques le Marois and Prix du Moulin de Longchamp, while Time Charter, in addition to her Ascot success, had defeated All Along in the Prix Foy, run over the Arc course in September.

The Irish-trained mare Stanerra, winner of two races in four days at Royal Ascot, ran sixth in the Arc and then recovered from a bad bout of coughing to take the Japan Cup at Fuchu, Tokyo, at the end of November. Zalataia, winner of three races in France, beat the U.S. champion, John Henry, in the Oak Tree Invitational at Santa Anita in California.

These feminine triumphs were due partly to the commercial pressures that encouraged the early retirement of top-class colts. Such colts were quite likely not to be seen again after a significant triumph, as Shareef Dancer was not seen after apparently establishing himself as the best colt in Europe by beating the Prix du Jockey Club win-

WIDE WORLD

Deputed Testamony appeared to literally fly through the air in winning the Preakness Stakes at Baltimore's Pimlico Race Track in May.

ner, Caerleon, and the Epsom Derby winner, Teenoso, in the Irish Sweeps Derby. The spring of 1983 was particularly wet, and the Epsom Derby was almost postponed because of heavy overnight rain. In the race Teenoso gave jockey Lester Piggott a record ninth triumph in the slowest time since 1891.

L'Émigrant, the leading three-year-old colt in France in the wet first half of the season, held his form better than Lomond, Shareef Dancer, Solford, and Wassl, each of which enjoyed a brief moment of glory. Tolomeo, which finished second or third in five of the top mile and ten-furlong events in Britain, showed that the general standard of competition in Europe was high when he defeated John Henry in the Budweiser Million at Arlington Park near Chicago. On his only subsequent outing Tolomeo was beaten by a head by Cormorant Wood, yet another filly, in the Dubai Champion Stakes but was relegated to fourth for causing interference.

A disappointment was the failure of the three outstanding juvenile colts of 1982, English-trained Gorytus and Diesis and the French-trained Saint-Cyrien, to win a race in 1983. El Gran Señor, which came from Ireland to beat Rainbow Quest in the William Hill Dewhurst Stakes at Newmarket, and the English-trained Lear Fan both appeared to be top-class juveniles, but the earlier disappointments made people reluctant to hail them as future champions.

Habibti, yet another filly, whose successes included the William Hill July Cup, the Sprint Championship, and the Prix de l'Abbaye de Longchamp, completed the female domination by being chosen horse of the year in Britain. Her only serious challenger for the title was Sun Princess. Willie Carson was champion jockey.

Jumping in Britain was dominated by the Yorkshire trainer Michael Dickinson, who saddled the first five in the Cheltenham Gold Cup, won by Bregawn, and in France by André Fabre, who was also responsible for Zalataia and other good horses on the flat. The Champion Hurdle was won by Gaye Brief, trained by Mercy Rimell, the first woman to train a winner of that race. Corbière was the first Grand National Winner to be trained by a woman, Jenny Pitman. John Francome was champion National Hunt jockey.

Kiwi, from New Zealand, was the appropriately named winner of Australia's most famous race, the Melbourne Cup, an event that recently had been dominated by New Zealand-bred stayers. This six-year-old, which had won the Wellington Cup at home, was trained by his owner-breeder, Ewen Lupton. Significant for the future was the continued success of Strawberry Road, champion three-year-old and horse of the year in Australia for the 1982–83 season, when he won both the AJC and Queensland Derbys. U.S.-bred stallions reached Australasia later than most other parts of the racing world but were making their presence felt; both Kiwi and Strawberry Road were sons of such horses. (ROBERT W. CARTER)

Harness Racing. In the U.S. the pacer It's Fritz, son of Keystone Ore, broke all previous race records on half-mile, five-eighths-mile, and one-mile tracks with a best mile of 1 min $51\frac{4}{5}$ sec. Winkie's Gill (Bonefish) became the fastest female race-winning trotter ever with a 1-min $55\frac{2}{5}$-sec win in the Review Futurity at Springfield, Ill., and French gelding Iris de Vandel set a record as the fastest aged trotter with 1 min $55\frac{2}{5}$ sec at the Meadowlands in New Jersey. The Pacing Triple Crown (Little Brown Jug, Messenger, and Cane) went to the Meadow Skipper colt Ralph Hanover, who also took the $1,251,000 Meadowlands three-year-old pace. Power Seat won the trotters' Kentucky Futu-

All Along (14) pressed ahead out of the back stretch to win the Trusthouse Forte Prix de l'Arc de Triomphe at Paris in October. The purse was Fr 2.5 million ($312,000).

WIDE WORLD

UPI

Stanley Dancer drove the three-year-old filly Duenna to win the third division of the 58th running of the Hambletonian Trot in August at the Meadowlands Race Track at East Rutherford, New Jersey. The purse was $1,080,000, the time 1:57.2.

rity final; he also won the $580,090 World Trotting Derby final at Du Quoin, Ill. Turn the Tide was the season's fastest filly. Shannon's Fancy captured the $1,062,000 Stake for two-year-old fillies at the Meadowlands. Fastest two-year-old was Panorama with a 1-min 54⅗-sec mark in a heat of the Fox Stake, while Hit Parade became the fastest two-year-old filly, winning the Almahurst Farm Stake in 1 min 54⅗ sec. In the $1,080,000 Hambletonian Trot, the Green Speed filly Duenna beat the colts in the final. Carl's Bird beat Truetone Lobell by a nose at the $1.7 million Woodrow Wilson Pace for two-year-olds. The filly Laught A Day (Most Happy Fella-Tarport Cheer) fetched a record $625,000 at Tattersalls sale at Lexington, Ky.

In Australia 1983 was the year of the first million-dollar locally bred harness horse; Gammalite, by Thor Hanover, reached that mark when he won the $20,000 City Tattersalls Golden Mile at Harold Park, Sydney, on October 28. At the new Brisbane raceway Popular Alm recorded 1 min 55.8 sec in winning the $100,000 Craven Filter Sprint and later won at the same track in Australian record time of 1 min 54.5 sec. Trotter of 1983 was Scotch Notch, which won the Inter-Dominion Trotters Championship in New Zealand. Star of the three-year-old fillies was Karamea Duplicity, winner of the Simpson Sprint and declared Sires Stakes Grand Champion. The New Zealand juvenile championship for two-year-olds at Auckland was won by Slugger, and the $60,000 New Zealand Derby at Christchurch went to Mighty Me. The Rowe Cut for trotters at Auckland was won by Sir Castleton, son of Game Pride. The Auckland Cup for pacers went to Armalight in a record time of 1 min 59.7 sec for 2,700 m. Champion mare Bonnie Chance was voted New Zealand horse of the year after winning the $60,000 New Zealand Cup and the New Zealand Free For All.

The Kriterium, richest Swedish race of the year with $60,000 going to the winner, was taken by Lass Quick. A world record was claimed for The Onion, winner of the Swedish sprint championship (one mile) in 1 min 55.9 sec. The Danish Derby ($330,000; over 3,000 m) was won by For Ever Vicki, while the Derby Mare Stake went to Frøken Tempo.

At Vincennes, France, Idéal du Gazeau won the Prix d'Amérique ($122,000) for the second time. This plus his later win in the Roosevelt International (for the third time) made him the world's richest and probably greatest trotter. In The Netherlands the Criterium was won by White Power, White Shadow won the Derby, and Filli Hanover took the Derby Consolation. At the St. Michel Stake in Finland, Busy Randy won the final in 1 min 58.1 sec. In the Norway Grand Prix, Flora T. won the final. At Gelsenkirchen in West Germany, the Eliterennen Trot was won by the French Lutin D'Isigny with Darster F. second.

The magnificent Macau racing complex lacked only good attendance. Sub-two-minute miles were recorded, and the Caesar's Palace Gold Cup went for approximately $250,000. At an international driving championship there in April 1983 the Macau team was victorious over Australia, New Zealand, and the U.S. (NOEL SIMPSON)

Show Jumping. The Swiss team of Walther Gabathuler (on Beethoven II), Heidi Robbiani (Jessica V), Willi Melliger (Van Gogh), and Thomas Fuchs (Willora Swiss) won the European team championship at Hickstead, England, in July 1983; they had earlier won the Nations' Cup at Aachen, West Germany. At Hickstead they beat the British and the defending champions from West Germany. Final scores were: Switzerland 12.19 penalty points, Britain 21.89, and West Germany 24.32, followed by (4) The Netherlands, (5) France, and (6) Austria. On the Hanoverian Deister, now 12 years old, Paul Schockemöhle of West Germany retained the European individual championship with just 2.49 points. John Whitaker and Ryan's Son (9.27) were runners-up for Britain.

The European three-day event championship was held at Frauenfeld, Switz. Fielding an all-girl team, Sweden (239.6 points) defeated Britain, defending team champion and world champion, by 11.4 points. This was Sweden's first major victory

Major Thoroughbred Race Winners, 1983

Race	Won by	Jockey	Owner
United States			
Acorn	Ski Goggie	C. McCarron	Zenya Yoshida
American Derby	Play Fellow	P. Day	Nancy Vanier, Carl Lauer, and Robert Victor
Arkansas Derby	Sunny's Halo	E. Delahoussaye	David J. Foster
Arlington Classic	Play Fellow	P. Day	Nancy Vanier, Carl Lauer, and Robert Victor
Arlington Handicap	Palikaraki	W. Shoemaker	Sidney L. Port
Arlington-Washington Futurity	All Fired Up	R. Evans	Muckler Stables
Belmont	Caveat	L. Pincay, Jr.	August Belmont IV, Robert Kirkham, and Jim P. Ryan
Blue Grass	Play Fellow	J. Cruguet	Nancy Vanier, Carl Lauer, and Robert Victor
Brooklyn	Highland Blade	J. Vasquez	Pen-Y-Bryn Farm
Budweiser Million	Tolomeo	P. Eddery	Carlo d'Alessio
Champagne	Devil's Bag	E. Maple	Hickory Tree Stable
Charles H. Strub	Swing Till Dawn	P. Valenzuela	Paniolo Ranch
Coaching Club American Oaks	High Schemes	J. L. Samyn	Joseph O. Morrissey, Jr.
Delaware	May Day Eighty	J. Vasquez	Calumet Farm
Flamingo	Current Hope	A. Solis	Robert Baker, Howard Kaskel, and Robert Levey
Florida Derby	Croeso	F. Olivares	Cardiff Stud and Roy Fowler
Futurity	Swale	E. Maple	Claiborne Farm
Gulfstream Park	Christmas Past	J. Velasquez	Cynthia Phipps
Hialeah Turf Cup	Nijinsky's Secret	J. A. Velez, Jr.	Mrs. John A. McDougald
Hollywood Derby	Royal Heroine	F. Toro	Robert Sangster
(2 divisions)	Ginger Brink	F. Toro	David Sofro
Hollywood Gold Cup	Island Whirl	E. Delahoussaye	Elcee-H Stable
Hollywood Turf Cup	John Henry	C. McCarron	Dotsam Stable
Hopeful	Capitol South	J. Bailey	Darby Dan Farm
Jockey Club Gold Cup	Slew o' Gold	A. Cordero, Jr.	Equusequity Stable
Kentucky Derby	Sunny's Halo	E. Delahoussaye	David J. Foster
Kentucky Oaks	Princess Rooney	J. Vasquez	Mrs. Paula Tucker
Laurel Futurity	Devil's Bag	E. Maple	Hickory Tree Stable
Man o' War	Majesty's Prince	E. Maple	John D. Marsh
Marlboro Cup Invitational	Highland Blade	J. Vasquez	Pen-Y-Bryn Farm
Matron	Lucky Lucky Lucky	A. Cordero, Jr.	Leslie Combs II
Metropolitan	Star Choice	J. Velasquez	Frances A. Genter
Monmouth	Bates Motel	T. Lipham	Mrs. Jacqueline Getty Phillips, Michael Riordan, and John R. Gaines
Oak Tree Invitational	Zalataia	F. Head	Edith de Gil
Preakness	Deputed Testamony	D. A. Miller, Jr.	Francis P. Sears
Ruffian	Heartlight No. One	L. Pincay, Jr.	Burt Bacharach
Santa Anita Derby	Marfa	J. Velasquez	L. R. French, Barry Beal, and D. Wayne Lucas
Santa Anita	Bates Motel	T. Lipham	Mrs. Jacqueline Getty Phillips, Michael Riordan, and John R. Gaines
Santa Susana	Fabulous Notion	D. Pierce	Pine Meadows Thoroughbreds
Sapling	Smart N Slick	D. A. Miller, Jr.	Arthur Hock
Sorority	Officer's Ball	C. Perret	Peter M. Brant
Spinaway	Buzz My Bell	J. Velasquez	Caesar P. Kimmel
Suburban	Winter's Tale	J. Fell	Rokeby Stable
Super Derby Invitational	Sunny's Halo	L. Pincay, Jr.	David J. Foster
Swaps	Hyperborean	F. Toro	Craig Singer
Travers	Play Fellow	P. Day	Nancy Vanier, Carl Lauer, and Robert Victor
Turf Classic	All Along	W. Swinburn	Daniel Wildenstein
United Nations	Acaroid	A. Cordero, Jr.	Tartan Stable
Washington, D.C., International	All Along	W. Swinburn	Daniel Wildenstein
Widener	Swing Till Dawn	C. Perret	Doug McClure, Frank DeMarco, Richard Dick, Robert Primm, and Paniolo Ranch
Wood Memorial	Bounding Basque	G. McCarron	Jacques D. Wimpfheimer
(2 divisions)	Slew o' Gold	E. Maple	Equusequity Stable
Woodward	Slew o' Gold	A. Cordero, Jr.	Equusequity Stable
England			
One Thousand Guineas	Ma Biche	F. Head	Maktoum al-Maktoum
Two Thousand Guineas	Lomond	P. Eddery	R. Sangster
Derby	Teenoso	L. Piggott	E. B. Moller
Oaks	Sun Princess	W. Carson	Sir M. Sobell
St. Leger	Sun Princess	W. Carson	Sir M. Sobell
Coronation Cup	Be My Native	L. Piggott	K. Hsu
Ascot Gold Cup	Little Wolf	W. Carson	Lord Porchester
Coral Eclipse Stakes	Solfort	P. Eddery	R. Sangster
King George VI and Queen Elizabeth Diamond Stakes	Time Charter	J. Mercer	R. Barnett
Sussex Stakes	Noalcoholic	G. Duffield	W. Du Pont III
Benson & Hedges Gold Cup	Caerleon	P. Eddery	R. Sangster
Dubai Champion Stakes	Cormorant Wood	S. Cauthen	R. J. McAlpine
France			
Poule d'Essai des Poulains	L'Émigrant	C. Asmussen	S. Niarchos
Poule d'Essai des Pouliches	L'Attrayante	A. Badel	Mme. C.-H. Thieriot
Prix du Jockey Club	Caerleon	P. Eddery	R. Sangster
Prix de Diane Hermès	Escaline	G. W. Moore	Mme. J. Fellows
Prix Royal-Oak	Old Country	P. Eddery	Mme. O. Abegg
Prix Ganay	Lancastrian	A. Lequeux	Sir M. Sobell
Prix Lupin	L'Émigrant	C. Asmussen	S. Niarchos
Grand Prix de Paris	Yawa	P. Waldron	Elisha Holding
rand Prix de Saint-Cloud	Diamond Shoal	S. Cauthen	P. Mellon
Trusthouse Forte Prix Vermeille	Sharaya	Y. Saint Martin	H. H. Aga Khan
Trusthouse Forte Prix de l'Arc de Triomphe	All Along	W. R. Swinburn	D. Wildenstein
Grand Critérium	Treizième	G. Dubroeucq	T. Tatham
Ireland			
Irish Two Thousand Guineas	Wassl	A. Murray	Ahmed al-Maktoum
Irish One Thousand Guineas	L'Attrayante	A. Badel	Mme. C.-H. Thieriot
Irish Sweeps Derby	Shareef Dancer	W. R. Swinburn	Maktoum al-Maktoum
Irish Guinness Oaks	Give Thanks	D. Gillespie	Mrs. O. White
Irish St. Leger	Mountain Lodge	D. Gillespie	Lord Halifax
Italy			
Derby Italiano	My Top	P. Perlanti	Scuderia Siba
Gran Premio del Jockey-Club	Awaasif	L. Piggott	Sheikh Mohammed
West Germany			
Deutsches Derby	Ordos	P. Alafi	Gestüt Zoppenbroich
Grosser Preis von Baden	Diamond Shoal	S. Cauthen	P. Mellon
Grosser Preis von Berlin	Abary	A. Tylicki	Gestüt Fährhof
Preis von Europa	Esprit du Nord	L. Piggott	R. F. Scully

in 31 years. The individual title went to Britain's Rachel Bayliss, on Mystic Minstrel, who won over the reigning world champion combination of Lucinda Green on the Australian-bred Regal Realm. (PAMELA MACGREGOR-MORRIS)

Polo. In the Piaget-sponsored World Cup championship at Palm Beach, Fla., victory went to Nigerian-backed Anadariya by 10–8 over White Birch-A&K. White Birch took the United States Polo Association's Gold Cup by beating Glenlivet 15–11. The Royal Palm Club's $100,000 Gold Cup went to Brookfield, which beat Ampak 12–11. In Australia Wirragulla avenged its previous year's defeat in the Countess of Dudley Cup with an 8–7 victory over defending champion Goulbourn. In England's high-goal season, Cowdray Park led all the way to take the coveted Queen's Cup by 8–7 over the 1982 champion Centaurs. The British Open championship, for the Cowdray Park Gold Cup, brought together the Centaurs and Falcons in an epic struggle, with the Falcons the victors by 8–7.

The Argentine Open, arguably the most important domestic tournament in the sport, was won by Santa Ana 16–13 over Coronel Suarez. In the biggest international contest of the year, the Ceresit-sponsored Coronation Cup, England I beat New Zealand 8–6. In the Silver Jubilee Cup, England II lost to France 7–6. (COLIN J. CROSS)

Ethiopia

A socialist state in northeastern Africa, Ethiopia is bordered by Somalia, Djibouti, Kenya, the Sudan, and the Red Sea. Area: 1,223,600 sq km (472,400 sq mi). Pop. (1983 est.): 33,679,600. Cap. and largest city: Addis Ababa (pop., 1982 est., 1,408,100). Language: Amharic (official) and other tongues. Religion (1980 est.): Ethiopian Orthodox 57%; Muslim 31%; tribal 11%; other 1%. Head of state and chairman of the Provisional Military Administrative Council in 1983, Lieut. Col. Mengistu Haile Mariam.

The year began with a major speech delivered by the head of state, Lieut. Col. Mengistu Haile Mariam, in January 1983 to the second national congress of the Commission for Organizing the Party of the Working People of Ethiopia (COPWE). The congress declared that the party would be formed by the time the next congress convened. In the interim COPWE was performing the functions of a national political party.

Mengistu's comprehensive speech, which was more than four hours in length, took a critical view of the performance of the economy in recent years. It identified poor organization, ineffective management, and the persistence of outdated practices as being responsible for low rates of output and productivity. Other problems were the run-down capital equipment taken over from private enterprise in the early years of the revolution and the impact of the disturbed international economy.

Commenting on agricultural production, Mengistu noted that the corn (maize) crop yield of the state farms was little more than that of the peasant

INGE LIPPMAN/TIME MAGAZINE

Ethiopian Marxists build strong ties with the Soviet bloc, and billboards feature slogans and heroic portraits of Marx, Engels, and Lenin. But other billboards feature capitalist symbols, reflecting the maintenance of strong ties with the West, a source of non-arms aid.

farmers. He attributed this to widespread inefficiency in management. For the nationalized industries and smaller scale private industries, the problem was one of stimulating investment so that they could expand. Subsequently, a proclamation on joint ventures between the government and foreign investors was issued. The system of distribution and exchange, where the private sector predominated, was identified as having a particularly low level of performance.

It was not surprising that this forthright review was followed in April and May by a significant reshuffle of ministers. New ministers were appointed for finance, agriculture, and industry, the latter being Ato Hailu Yemanu, who also held the posts of senior minister and secretary-general of the National Revolutionary Development Campaign. Lieut. Col. Berhanu Bayih, a senior member of the Provisional Military Administrative Council (PMAC), became minister of labour and social affairs. PMAC Secretary-General Fikre-Selassie Wogderess became deputy chairman of the Council of Ministers. A number of posts were created within the Council of Ministers for coordination of the major sectors, with the effect of transferring all but the strictly planning functions at the national level from the Central Planning Supreme Council.

These significant changes set the stage for the formation of the political party and the launching of the ten-year development plan in 1984. The year 1984 was anticipated, therefore, as one of multiple celebration, as it also marked the tenth anniversary of the revolution and the 100th anniversary of the founding of the capital, Addis Ababa.

The year 1983 marked the 25th anniversary of the UN Economic Commission for Africa and the 20th anniversary of the Organization of African Unity (OAU). The first was celebrated in April in Africa Hall, Addis Ababa, and was attended by UN Secretary-General Javier Pérez de Cuéllar. The second, which took place in May, was somewhat obscured by continuing efforts to convene the 19th OAU summit meeting originally scheduled for August and then November 1982 in Tripoli, Libya. This finally took place in Addis Ababa in early June, when the chairmanship was transferred from Pres. Daniel arap Moi of Kenya to Mengistu.

In May the government announced plans for national military service, plans that had been anticipated for some time in view of the continued problems in the north and southeast of the country. This required the registration of all citizens between the ages of 16 and 30 and a continued liability for active service until the age of 50.

Ethiopia continued to develop close ties with the Soviet bloc. Romanian Pres. Nicolae Ceausescu visited in July, while Soviet Chairman of State Planning Nikolay Baibakov, on a visit in March, pledged assistance in the implementation of the

ETHIOPIA

Education. (1980–81) Primary, pupils 2,130,716, teachers 33,329; secondary, pupils 427,597, teachers 9,962; teacher training, students 4,610, teachers 240; higher, students (1979–80) 14,949, teaching staff 1,085.

Finance. Monetary unit: birr, with (Sept. 20, 1983) a par value of 2.07 birr to U.S. $1 (free rate of 3.12 birr = £1 sterling). Gold and other reserves (June 1983) U.S. $203 million. Budget (total; 1980–81 est.): revenue 2,184,800,000 birr; expenditure 2,678,000,000 birr. Gross national product (1981–82) 9,134,000,000 birr. Money supply (April 1983) 2,105,000,000 birr. Cost of living (Addis Ababa; 1975 = 100; Dec. 1982) 232.9.

Foreign Trade. (1982) Imports 1,627,800,000 birr; exports 835.5 million birr. Import sources (1981): U.S.S.R. 20%; Italy 17%; West Germany 9%; U.S. 8%; Japan 7%; U.K. 6%. Export destinations (1981): U.S. 21%; West Germany 10%; Saudi Arabia 9%; Japan 7%; France 7%; Italy 7%; Yemen (Aden) 6%. Main exports: coffee 61%; hides and skins 10%; petroleum products (1980) 7%.

Transport and Communications. Roads (1982) 36,391 km. Motor vehicles in use (1982): passenger 43,100; commercial 13,000. Railways: (1981) c. 987 km; traffic (including Djibouti traffic of Djibouti–Addis Ababa line; excluding Eritrea; 1978–79) 171 million passenger-km, freight 148 million net ton-km. Air traffic (1982): c. 762 million passenger-km; freight c. 26.2 million net ton-km. Telephones (Jan. 1981) 87,800. Radio receivers (Dec. 1980) 250,000. Television receivers (Dec. 1980) 30,000.

Agriculture. Production (in 000; metric tons; 1982): barley c. 1,100; wheat c. 590; corn c. 950; millet c. 200; sorghum c. 1,150; potatoes (1981) c. 240; sugar, raw value (1981) c. 165; sesame seed c. 36; chick-peas c. 150; dry peas c. 190; dry broad beans (1981) c. 277; bananas (1981) c. 73; coffee 202; cotton c. 27. Livestock (in 000; 1982): cattle c. 26,200; sheep c. 23,350; goats c. 17,220; horses c. 1,540; mules c. 1,455; asses c. 3,900; camels c. 1,000; poultry c. 54,000.

Industry. Production (in 000; metric tons; 1980–81): cement c. 180; petroleum products c. 534; cotton yarn (1979–80) 9.3; cotton fabrics (sq m; 1979–80) 86,000; electricity (kw-hr) 677,000.

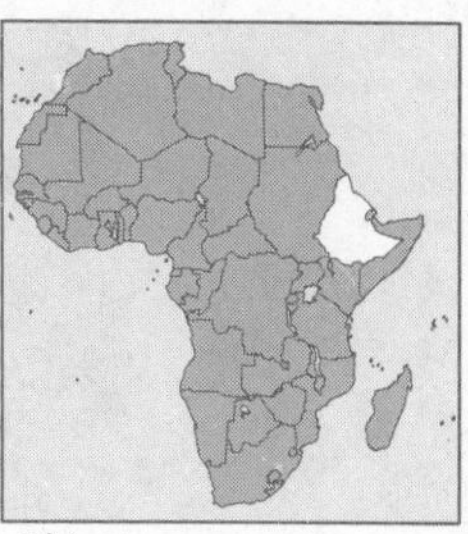

Ethiopia

ten-year plan. Nevertheless, equally strong links were maintained with the West and with international organizations that provided significant development assistance. The UN Development Program was to provide 220 million birr during the period 1982–86, and UNICEF 165 million birr during 1983–86, while a number of development programs were financed by the International Development Association, the African Development Bank, and the European Communities. Bilateral assistance included the provision of equipment for technical education from the U.S.S.R. and a Fr 90 million grant from France for the rehabilitation and development of the Djibouti-Addis Ababa railway system.

The Ethiopian economy showed a reasonably consistent movement forward. In particular, the economy was not plagued by the problems of overwhelming external debt that had restricted the options of other less developed countries. Insurgent activity in Eritrea and Tigre continued, as did antigovernment activity supported by Somalia in the Ogaden. These exceptions apart, Ethiopia demonstrated a high level of stability.

However, there remained the problem of devastating drought conditions, which put between two million and three million people at direct or potential risk. International concern was reflected in visits from the senior officials of almost all the international food and emergency aid organizations. An important outcome of these visits, apart from promises of increased assistance, was the denial of reports in the international press about the misuse of emergency food aid.

European Unity

At the outset of 1983 the dark cloud of world economic recession hung over the countries of the European Communities (EC; the European Economic Community [EEC], the European Coal and Steel Community [ECSC], and Euratom). There were widespread fears that the recession would precipitate some major crisis in international monetary and trade flows, leading to an irreversible lurch into national protectionism that could threaten the Community's existence. The bleak economic situation also exacerbated the other long-term internal crises facing the EC governments. In particular, it aggravated the tortuous and increasingly strident arguments over future financing of the Community budget and the reform both of its spending policies and of the unequal burden carried by the various contributing governments.

At a meeting of European Community finance ministers, Gerhard Stoltenberg (left) of West Germany and Jacques Delors of France worked out a revaluation of the Deutsche Mark and a devaluation of the French franc.

WIDE WORLD

There was an uneasy truce in foreign trade conflicts between the EC and the U.S. at the start of the year, but transatlantic trade tensions rose again in January when the U.S. negotiated a heavily subsidized contract to sell wheat to Egypt, a traditional EC market. At the same time, the U.S. authorities moved to restrict European imports of certain specialty steels, and in July the EC took the matter to the General Agreement on Tariffs and Trade, the world trade regulatory body. Nevertheless, intense diplomatic activity on both sides of the Atlantic ensured that an all-out trade war did not break out. The authorities were assisted in this by the first signs, evident in early summer, of a recovery in the U.S. economy. In addition, the high exchange rate of the U.S. dollar, a matter for European concern on other grounds, made exporting to the U.S. somewhat easier.

At the same time, trade tensions between the EC and Japan remained unresolved. Despite Japanese concessions on import tariffs and access to Japan's internal markets, announced in January, the Community began to monitor electronics imports from Japan in March. France imposed unilateral import controls on Japanese video tape recorders, only lifting them in April in return for Japanese guarantees on voluntary export restraint.

Despite mounting unemployment, the predominantly centre-right governments of the EC countries refused to change course from their economic strategies of austerity. The French Socialist government, supported only by the Greek government, found itself increasingly isolated as it tried to follow policies aimed at growth. This dislocation between the economic policies of France and those of most other EC member countries contributed to a major crisis within the European Monetary System (EMS) in March. After a weekend of negotiations in Brussels, EC finance ministers eventually agreed on a series of currency realignments within the EMS, including devaluation of the French franc and accompanying deflationary measures by the government in Paris.

The emergency meeting of finance ministers overshadowed the meeting of EC heads of government, which took place in Brussels immediately afterward. The summit conference failed to find any long-term answers to the urgent internal problems faced by the Community, including budget reform, control of agricultural spending, and the planned enlargement of the EC to include Portugal and Spain. These difficult questions dominated ministerial meetings throughout much of the year.

It became increasingly clear that the increase in farm spending was again threatening to exceed the rate of growth in the fixed sources of EC budget revenue. The May decision by EC agriculture min-

REGIS BOSSU—SYGMA

Participants in the European Community summit at Stuttgart, West Germany, encountered a disarmament demonstration outside the conference.

isters to raise prices paid to farmers by an average of around 7% was followed by revelations in September that butter and milk powder surplus stocks were again increasing dramatically. Nevertheless, no consensus was reached among the governments of the ten member countries about the precise reforms needed to bring the cost of the common agricultural policy (CAP) under control. Although most governments realized that changes would have to be made, there was little support for the more radical overhaul of the CAP demanded by Britain and West Germany. Other governments were all too aware of the potential political influence of their domestic farm lobbies. There was also growing pressure from France, Greece, and Italy to extend more of the benefits of the CAP—hitherto restricted to northern European dairy and meat farmers—to Mediterranean farmers in the south. A first breakthrough was achieved at a meeting of agriculture ministers in Luxembourg in October, when agreement was reached on a common marketing policy for agricultural products from the Mediterranean area.

At the EC summit held in Stuttgart, West Germany, in June, the central issue of agricultural reform was seen as intimately linked with the timing of Community enlargement and with overall budget reform, including the specific questions of whether to reduce the excessive net contributions to the budget by Britain and West Germany and whether and by how much overall future budget revenue should be increased. The West German presidency of the EC Council of Ministers, in office for the first half of 1983, was unable to obtain political agreement on even the outlines of reform. The Greek presidency in the second half of the year fared no better.

At the Stuttgart summit, delayed temporarily because of the British general election, British Prime Minister Margaret Thatcher hinted that, unless a firm long-term agreement to reduce Britain's net budget payments was reached by the end of the year, Britain might take unilateral action to cut its payments. However, a majority of the other EC governments appeared ready to consider such a concession, provided that Britain lifted its objection to increasing the ceiling on transfers of up to 1% of national value-added tax payments to the EC budget. At a series of joint meetings of EC finance and foreign ministers in September and October, there was bitter disagreement over the wisdom of raising the budget ceiling. Britain, backed by West Germany, wanted an agreement on drastic cuts in agricultural spending before this was even considered.

The summit meeting in Athens in December ended in deadlock, with no agreement on the CAP, on Britain's budgetary complaints, on financial reform, or on a timetable for Spanish and Portuguese entry. The disagreement was so deep that, for the first time, no joint communiqué was issued, and there was no statement on foreign policy positions. The failure of the summit raised the possibility of an EC cash crisis before the next meeting, scheduled for March 1984.

Despite these conflicts, there was a general consensus that the EC needed to take radical and concerted action to improve the international competitiveness of its industry. The European Commission proposed a series of policies to increase industrial self-sufficiency in research and investment in the new technologies.

The problem of budget reform was further complicated by the involvement of the European Parliament. On several occasions during 1983, the directly elected body used its restricted powers to delay endorsing the decision taken by the Council of Ministers to give Britain and West Germany specific rebates on their annual budget payments. (The refunds were blocked again in December.) This was just one issue where the assembly attempted to assert its rights as elections to the Parliament (scheduled for June 1984) drew nearer. In January the European Parliament had taken the Council of Ministers to the European Court for failure to meet the objectives of the Treaty of Rome for a common transport policy. The following month the European Court of Justice upheld the Parliament's right to decide where it should meet. The Parliament had decided in July 1981 that it wished to hold all its plenary sessions in Strasbourg, France, and thus discontinue the practice of holding one-third of its sessions in Luxembourg. The decision had been contested by the government of Luxembourg, but the court decided that the Parliament was entitled to take any measures that would ensure its efficiency.

Progress was made on a number of complaints by Greece on the terms of its accession, which had been negotiated by a previous Greek government. The EC governments were pleased that Greece, for its part, pushed ahead with overdue commitments to integrate its internal regulations with those of the Community. However, in the second half of the year serious differences arose over foreign policy. The Greek government made known its opposition to the deployment by NATO of new U.S. medium-range nuclear missiles in Western Europe at the end of 1983, and it was less ready than others to condemn Soviet policy on such matters as the shooting down of a South Korean civil airliner in September.

There were also some differences among governments on how far cooperation on foreign policy should be extended into the area of security policy. The Italian and West German governments proposed a new "European Act" that would allow EC foreign ministers to review security issues, as well as committing the ten to move toward greater use of majority voting in the Council and faster economic integration. However, the proposal was effectively shelved at the Stuttgart summit. The whole issue of institutional reform continued to preoccupy the Community in view of the proposed enlargement to 12 member states. By the closing months of 1983 the enlargement negotiations had made progress only on peripheral issues, leaving the central question of agriculture unresolved. Despite the achievement of members in agreeing on a common fisheries policy in January, this issue continued to divide the EC fishing nations. Successive attempts to get an agreement on the distribution of catch allocations, particularly of the more scarce species, failed. (*See* FISHERIES.)

There were intensified efforts to secure greater observance of EC competition rules. This proved a particularly sensitive matter in steel and other industries that were receiving increased government support to tide them over the slump. A series of Community directives in March aimed at making free movement of peoples and goods within the EC easier. Later in the year, however, fears arose that a variety of open and hidden protection measures were threatening the internal unity of the EC market.

With the increasing focus on the role of the EC, other European institutions necessarily took a back seat during the year. The wider Council of Europe held meetings on a variety of political and human rights issues. The Council also debated the issue of Turkey's continued membership. Although Turkey was not formally expelled from the Council, most governments expressed their opposition to continued military rule, alleged violations of human rights, and the unsatisfactory arrangements for an eventual return to democratic government. The European Court of Human Rights at Strasbourg also heard cases involving appeals against a variety of national laws and government regulations.

Relations between the EC and the European Free Trade Association (EFTA) became closer. There was discussion about widening the area of cooperation between the two organizations, and some EFTA members, notably Norway, expressed interest in being kept more closely informed about the major foreign-policy discussions and decisions of the EC governments.

At a meeting of foreign ministers in Paris in June, European members of NATO reaffirmed their commitment to the NATO nuclear modernization program and reviewed the state of East-West disarmament negotiations. Demonstrations calling for nuclear disarmament were held in many countries as the date for deployment of U.S. cruise and Pershing II missiles approached. During the weekend of October 22–23, an estimated two million people attended rallies throughout Europe.

(JOHN PALMER)

See also Defense; Economy, World.

Fashion and Dress

More packaged than dressed, women slogged through the winter months of 1982–83 as if bent on guerrilla warfare. The only relief to the dreariness of this tough look was provided by bright-coloured leg warmers rippling down in heavy folds, like the skin of the newly fashionable Shar-Pei dog (now being reared in the U.S. after centuries of near extinction in China, its country of origin). But from these frequently shapeless bundles, where huge drifting shawls were added to ponchos and brimmed hats concealed the face, a redefined woman emerged in the spring. Gone also was the seedy look of "distressed leather" and patch-pocketed, stone-washed buffalo bush jackets, products of London's King's Road or the Paris flea market. Now it was a case of Tender over Tough, and Super Woman made her exit.

In London the princess of Wales became a fashion leader for the young set. She wore hats and she wore low heels, and both items were picked up by her followers. In the evening she was dazzling, and her jewels were superb. London's young fashionables became more and more fashion conscious and eager to follow in her elegant footsteps. The "genteel look" made its appearance with well-mannered, well-fitted suits—even classic gray flannel was revived for spring. Shoulders were squared off, jackets were shortened, skirts were slim, and blouses had plunging necklines instead of high necklines closed with bows.

The pantsuit was on the wane. Skirts gained over pants, with the average length just below the knee for town wear. For casual wear, the previously popular "ra-ra" skirt, well above the knee and flared, tennis-playing style, was replaced by one that was equally short but tight and flat, front and

Evangelical Churches:
see Religion

Exhibitions:
see Art Exhibitions; Museums; Photography

Faeroe Islands:
see Dependent States

Falkland Islands:
see Dependent States

Farming:
see Agriculture and Food Supplies

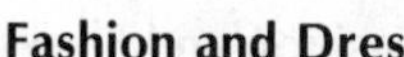

WIDE WORLD

WIDE WORLD

Japan's Kansai Yamamoto offered (far left) a white and gray woolen suit crossed with a belt and with gray woolen pants as part of his spring and summer collection for 1984. The fall and winter haute couture collection of Lanvin featured an asymmetrical split skirt in black velvet with a bow at the hip.

back, all very snug and nifty. For town the prevailing style was the Grace Kelly, "High Society" look, full of the spirit of the 1950s. There was, for example, a near replica of the famous Balenciaga line: voluminous sleeves on seven-eighths-length coats, square cut, straight sleeves on dresses, and combinations of coffee and brown and black in insets or prints. Also straight from the '50s were the jersey tunic, the chemise dress or "sack" tapered to the knees, even the bib front descending to a point from a high, rounded neckline. The overall effect was indeed "genteel."

The first colours of spring were delicate sweet-pea shades, principally light mauve and pink, appearing in soft dresses and casual, open jackets. Shoes, in colours to match, were mostly plain pumps with stumpy medium or fine high heels or classical ballerinas. Even the traditional ghillie shoe was seen in pastels. A neutral "string" colour was chosen for see-through knits—including batwing sweaters—for webbing belts, and for net handbags, the last sometimes banded with coloured stripes.

Pure white made a breakthrough in the summer. The frothy blouse of all-white cotton or fine linen, with full, breezy sleeves and deep, plunging neckline, was teamed indifferently with jeans for daytime or a dressy silk skirt for evening—an all-purpose standby that replaced the familiar shirt-blouse. Also in pure white were tapered cotton trousers, rounded at the top and cut off well above the ankle, seen in town or on holiday and worn with very wide boat-necked, long-sleeved tops. Some slipped to bare one shoulder, in the style popularized by the movie *Flashdance*, or were cut in a deep V in the back. Pure white eyelet embroidery and Irish lace were used for see-through tops and gathered skirts or for side-wrapped cover-ups seen on the beaches. Pure white transparencies worn over swimsuits were cut high at the neck, with long sleeves and deep armholes.

Another reprise from the 1950s was the *guêpière* or wasp-waisted corset, introduced to the haute couture of the time by Marcel Rochas. The little white corset baring the shoulders was the latest evening look at Saint-Tropez, worn over a flaring miniskirt in bright coloured tulle with an uneven hemline. The same skirt could accompany a one-piece swimsuit with V's cut to the waist in front and back, crossed in the back by narrow straps.

Fighting the notion of women as "sex objects," Japanese designers had come out with their own "pure line" in the spring. Shapeless and often shredded, the clothes were purposely torn and irregular at the hemline, with two layers of different lengths cut on the diagonal. At Saint-Tropez T-shirts were ripped with scissors on the spur of the moment to make a low V at the front or back, enlarge armholes, suppress the hem, or to decorate shoulders and back with fancy cutouts. Bandana headbands worn straight over the eyebrows topped rather messy and disheveled heads of hair for which "After the Fight" would have been an appropriate name. But, generally speaking, punk hairdos had little effect on more sophisticated heads. This trendy look remained strictly for summer holiday wear. Young people used the Japanese influence in their own way, layering various fabrics and colours to express themselves. They also adopted the Japanese paddy boots, in soft, quilted leather with above-the-ankle cuffs and low wedge soles.

Oldtime Hollywood glamour provided the inspiration for another fashion trend, a body-clinging form with hips draped, wrapped, and bowed. Sleeves gathered at the shoulders for extra width were puffed to the elbow; necklines were slit in a deep V; and chunky jewelry circled the base of the neck. For evening wear, wrapped hips often sported ruffles, cascading in double or triple tiers down to uneven hemlines in a dashing, Spanish manner. One could almost hear the rattling of castanets at every step.

The black and white "penguin" look appeared in the autumn: white blouse, black skirt; white collar, lapels, belt, or bow on black dress; black and white asymmetrical banding and insets trimming dresses, hats, bags, and shoes. The daytime scene became very sombre, with all black or clerical gray predominating. There was glossy black leather for miniskirts and dull black jersey for sweater dresses. Relieving the all-black look for evening, bands of imitation gems gleamed down the front or back of a dress or along one side of above-the-elbow black gloves. But basically it was black—black lace, black silk, black jet for earrings, black stockings, and black shoes.

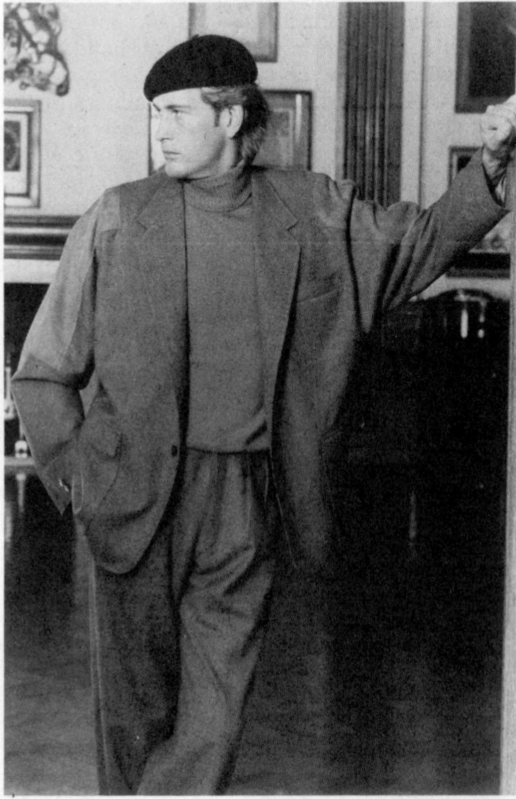

Loose-fitting, comfortable, two-piece leisure outfits in simple colours were a feature of men's fashion showings.

REID & TAYLOR, LONDON

Then, as if struck by fire, the all-black look was toppled by the appearance of pimento red, in lively knitted jackets and open kimono coats worn over black dresses and black stockings. The Japanese influence was evident in short quilted jackets with wide kimono sleeves and bulky shoulders, in black and white but flashing a pimento red lining. Some kimono-cut winter coats, ample at the top and tapered to the hem, were casually wrapped in front and belted like a bathrobe. Pimento red accents were provided by accessories—hats, gauntlet gloves, belts, and envelope handbags.

The emphasis on hats, whether mannish felt, sombreros, fedoras with curled brims, boaters, or berets, demanded a neat haircut, eliminating excessive fuzziness and curls at the nape of the neck. The side-brushed fringe cut was followed by the straight cut, slightly shorter at the back and sides and with a slight slant toward the front. The purpose was to give a new volume to hair and lighten its mass. In makeup, the look for summer was fresh and healthy. A "Cool Beige Liquid Make-up" from Estée Lauder, with a "Candle-Lit Rose" for cheeks and a "Claret Glaze" on lips, was perfect to set off pastels and grays. To balance the all-black look of the winter, Saint Laurent's line of 20 luminous reds for lips, Chanel's "Sparkling Red," and Helena Rubinstein's "China" were among the many choices. (THELMA SWEETINBURGH)

Men's Fashions. The sweltering summer in Europe—Britain experienced its hottest July in 300 years—brought about two fashion changes in 1983. Fewer jackets and ties were worn in offices, and short-sleeved shirts became acceptable for business wear, as they had been for some time in the U.S. and Australia. There was also growing acceptance of the redesigned cotton string vest or T-shirt, worn not as underwear but as an outer garment. This latter change could be attributed to the teams of designers whose innovations were responsible for 1983 being designated the Year of the Designer.

Their original creations, introduced at menswear trade fairs in Amsterdam, Cologne, West Germany, Florence, Italy, Paris, and London, typified the perhaps more significant shift from the conventional to the unconventional in both fabric and fashion. Leisure outfits, mostly featuring blazers, jackets, or shirt-jackets rather than blousons, and jeans (rather than traditional sports trousers) were designed primarily for younger men. They were loose-fitting and comfortable.

Simple colours, including basic blacks and whites with some grays, were used for these two-piece ensembles in cotton, linen, and what the International Wool Secretariat called "cool wool." Cotton denims were stone-washed, and some cottons were splash-dyed to give a marbled effect. Special jackets, some with quilted linings, were designed for cyclists, and coveralls (boilersuits) were popular for leisure wear. Many were in printed stretch denim. Track suits were still fashionable, and military-style outfits added such terms as Jungle Patrol, Jeep, and Urban Guerrilla to the fashion vocabulary.

"Establishment" suits—those worn for business and formal occasions—were much lighter in weight, for both winter and summer. Vertical patterns such as pin and chalk stripes were favoured at the expense of the traditional glen plaids and gun club checks, although these continued to be fashionable for sports suits. (STANLEY H. COSTIN)

See also Industrial Review: *Furs.*
[451.B.2.b and d.i; 629.C.1]

Field Hockey and Lacrosse

Field Hockey. At Melbourne in December 1982 Australia won the ten nations' tournament, beating India 6–1 in the final. The Netherlands finished third, followed in order by New Zealand, West Germany, and Pakistan. Earlier, Pakistan had retained the gold medal for Asian Games hockey in New Delhi with a 7–1 victory over India; the gold medal for women was won by India. In April 1983 against Wales on artificial turf at Swansea, The Netherlands' men's team won 4–0 and 4–1. At Cardiff England achieved the triple crown among the home countries, beating Scotland 3–1, Wales 2–0, and Ireland 4–0. Indoors, Scotland recovered the home countries title from England at Belfast.

The fourth European championship (outdoors) was played on artificial turf in August at Amstelveen, Neth. The Netherlands won the title for the first time by defeating the U.S.S.R. in the final on penalty strokes, the score, after extra time, having been tied at 4–4. West Germany placed third, followed by Spain, England, and France. At about the same time Australia won a five-nations tournament in Kuala Lumpur, Malaysia, by beating Pakistan 1–0 in the final. Australia won the Champions Trophy in Karachi, finishing ahead of host Pakistan.

In women's hockey England gained the triple crown among the home countries for the fourth year in succession by beating Wales 4–0, Ireland 6–1, and Scotland 3–0. In the annual match at Wembley in March, England defeated West Germany 3–2. Twenty-three nations took part in two tournaments in Kuala Lumpur, April 9–23. The Netherlands won the World Cup, beating Canada 4–2 in the final; other placings were (3) Australia, (4) West Germany, (5) England, and (6) the U.S. Ireland won the Intercontinental Cup, defeating Spain 2–1 in the final. (SYDNEY E. FRISKIN)

Lacrosse. MEN. In the U.S. National Collegiate Athletic Association final, played at Rutgers University Stadium in Piscataway, N.J., the winner was Syracuse (N.Y.) University, which defeated Johns Hopkins University of Baltimore, Md., 17–16. The North Collegiate All Stars defeated the South Collegiate All Stars 14–9 at Baltimore. In club lacrosse, Maryland defeated Long Island 13–12. The Lieut. Raymond Enners Memorial Award (for top player in the First Division) went to Brad Kotz (midfielder) from Syracuse University. At a lacrosse international festival at Baltimore in June, a Canadian team defeated Hobart College of Geneva, N.Y., 21–10. Syracuse University beat an American Native Team 28–5 and a Canadian National Team 14–13.

In Canada the Mann Cup was won by "Victoria Pay Less" of British Columbia, with the Minto Cup going to Peterborough, Ont. The Kelly Trophy, awarded to the player who was most valuable to his team, was won by John Crowther of the Mann Cup winners. At the junior level the First Division winner was Brampton, Ont.

In England the South of England Men's Lacrosse Association celebrated its centenary with a festival held at the Oval cricket ground, London. The Iroquois Cup (the English club championship) was won by Sheffield University, which easily defeated Kenton. Kenton, however, won the South of England Senior Flags. Sheffield University also won the University Cup for the second successive

COURTESY, SYRACUSE UNIVERSITY

Syracuse University defeated Johns Hopkins University to win the U.S. National Collegiate Athletic Association lacrosse championship. Here Travis Solomon (2), Jeff McCormick (rear), and Mark Wenham (31) fight off a Johns Hopkins assault.

year. Cheadle was the North of England league champion, and Cheshire won the county championship.

In Australia the champion state was South Australia; Williamstown was the champion team in Victoria, East Torrens in South Australia, and East Fremantle in Western Australia.

(CHARLES DENNIS COPPOCK)

WOMEN. The exciting inaugural world tournament of September 1982, dominated by the eventual winners and runners-up, the U.S. and Australia, was followed by a period of reconstruction and rethinking for the six participating countries—England, Wales, Scotland, Australia, Canada, and the U.S. The retirement of several senior players and the need to develop new strategies and skills resulted in new patterns of selection, training, and coaching.

The main international event of 1983 was Scotland's tour to Australia. Scotland defeated Tasmania, Western Australia, and two combined-clubs sides but narrowly lost to South Australia and Victoria. The three matches between Scotland and the Australian national team were hard-fought, fast, dramatic games that resulted in three victories for Australia, 11–5 in Melbourne, 11–3 in Adelaide, and 9–3 in Perth.

In Britain the All-England Counties Tournament resulted in the first tie in years, and so the title was shared by the defending champion, Middlesex, and the combined Hampshire-Wiltshire team. The South held onto the territorial championship, defeating the North 5–4, but the North won the Territorial Reserves Tournament. The All-England Clubs and Colleges Tournament was again won by Bedford College of Physical Education, which survived several close games, including the final against Putney. In the home internationals England, revitalized after the humiliation of finishing second to last in the world tournament, trounced Wales 15–4 and Scotland 15–7 and also devastated its Reserves 25–2 in a brilliant display at Crystal Palace, London.

(MARGARET-LOUISE O'KEEFFE)

Fiji

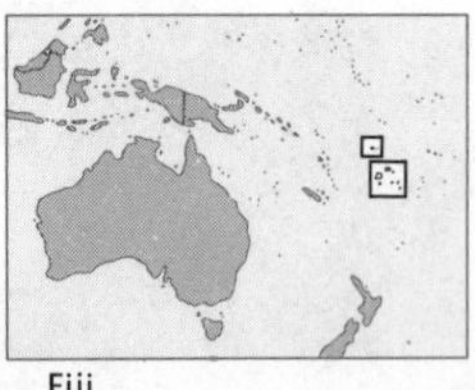

Fiji

An independent parliamentary state and member of the Commonwealth, Fiji is an island group in the South Pacific Ocean, about 3,200 km E of Australia and 5,200 km S of Hawaii. Area: 18,273 sq km (7,055 sq mi), with two major islands, Viti Levu (10,388 sq km) and Vanua Levu (5,535 sq km), and several hundred smaller islands. Pop. (1982 est.): 650,000, including 50% Indian, 45% Fijian. Cap. and largest city: Suva (pop., 1980 est., 68,200). Language: English, Fijian, and Hindi. Religion (1980): Christian 49.7%; Hindu 40.9%; Muslim 7.8%; other 1.6%. Queen, Elizabeth II; governors-general in 1983, Ratu Sir George Cakobau and, from February 12, Ratu Sir Penaia Ganilau; prime minister, Ratu Sir Kamisese Mara.

In March 1983 a royal commission began to investigate allegations of irregularities in the 1982 election campaign in Fiji. The opposition National Federation Party (NFP) accused the Alliance Party government of having exploited racial tensions between the Fijian and Indian communities. The government, in turn, claimed that the NFP had accepted funds from Soviet sources and had promised, should it gain power, to grant favours to the U.S.S.R.

Sugar production suffered from the effects of drought and two hurricanes that struck in March. In London in April, Prime Minister Ratu Sir Kamisese Mara sought assurances that third world producers would not be required to sell sugar at subsidized rates on the world market but would continue to have access to the countries of the European Communities under the Lomé Convention. He emphasized that less developed countries preferred trade to aid. In an attempt to boost agricultural production, the budget for 1983 removed export taxes from sugar, molasses, and copra.

(BARRIE MACDONALD)

FIJI

Education. (1981) Primary, pupils 116,190, teachers 4,146; secondary, pupils 45,844, teachers 2,442; vocational, pupils 2,386, teachers 235; teacher training, students 367, teachers 72; higher, students 667, teaching staff 180.

Finance and Trade. Monetary unit: Fiji dollar, with (Sept. 20, 1983) a free rate of F$1.04 to U.S. $1 (F$1.57 = £1 sterling). Budget (1981 actual): revenue F$257.1 million; expenditure F$292.8 million. Foreign trade (1982): imports F$475,720,000; exports F$266,550,000. Import sources: Australia 39%; New Zealand 16%; Japan 14%; Singapore 9%. Export destinations: U.K. 22%; Australia 11%; New Zealand 10%; U.S. 10%; Malaysia 5%. Main exports (1981): sugar 49%; petroleum products 19%; fish 6%. Tourism (1981): visitors 206,000; gross receipts U.S. $143 million.

Transport and Communications. Roads (1982) 4,295 km. Motor vehicles in use (1982): passenger 26,000; commercial 16,700. Railways (1980) 1,062 km. Air traffic (1982): 397 million passenger-km; freight c. 4.3 million net ton-km. Shipping traffic (1982): goods loaded 850,000 metric tons, unloaded 710,000 metric tons. Telephones (Jan. 1981) 45,300. Radio receivers (Dec. 1980) 300,000.

Agriculture. Production (in 000; metric tons; 1982): sugar, raw value 487; rice c. 18; cassava (1981) c. 95; copra 21. Livestock (in 000; 1981): cattle c. 155; pigs c. 28; goats c. 55; horses c. 39; chickens c. 957.

Industry. Production (in 000; 1981): cement (metric tons) 92; gold (troy oz) 31; electricity (kw-hr) 311,000.

Finland

The republic of Finland is bordered on the north by Norway, on the west by Sweden and the Gulf of Bothnia, on the south by the Gulf of Finland, and on the east by the U.S.S.R. Area: 338,145 sq km (130,559 sq mi). Pop. (1983 est.): 4,841,500. Cap. and largest city: Helsinki (pop., 1982 est., 482,900). Language: Finnish, Swedish. Religion (1982): Lutheran 90%; Orthodox 1.1%; other 8.9%. President in 1983, Mauno Koivisto; prime minister, Kalevi Sorsa.

Pres. Mauno Koivisto, in his second year in office, underlined the continuity of Finland's neutrality policy by extending, in unamended form, the 1948 treaty of friendship, cooperation, and mutual assistance with the Soviet Union from 1990 to 2003. The signing, in Moscow on June 6, 1983, climaxed Koivisto's first state visit to the U.S.S.R. During an official visit to the U.S. from September 24 to October 5, Koivisto received assurances that

Fencing:
see Combat Sports

the Western component in Finland's delicate balancing act was in order. Pres. Ronald Reagan reaffirmed U.S. support for "Finland's internationally recognized neutrality."

The dilemma posed by Finland's geography was illustrated in September following the downing of a Korean airliner by a Soviet military plane. A boycott of flights to Moscow by Finnair pilots contrasted with government pressure on ground staff not to act against the Soviet airline Aeroflot. On the other hand, the country's bridge-building potential between East and West, even when tensions were high, was demonstrated by the holding in Helsinki, from October 25, of preparations for the 1984 Stockholm Disarmament Conference.

Some observers maintained that Koivisto's "low-profile" presidency was encouraging a change in the style, if not the substance, of foreign policy and opening the floodgates to much "freer" debate. On March 3, however, Koivisto went before Parliament to quash speculation aroused by a growing wave of unorthodox views, expounded, in particular, by academics.

A general election on March 20–21 produced an upheaval in the composition of Parliament. Among the four large parties, only the Social Democrats gained ground. The National Coalition (Conservatives) was expected to advance strongly, but instead it lost seats. The Communist-dominated People's Democratic League, which had dramatically withdrawn from the government coalition in the last week of 1982, suffered heavy losses. The most sensational electoral outcome, however, was the resurgence of the Rural Party, buoyed by widespread public disenchantment with perceived abuses of power and scandals involving the political establishment. Almost tripling their vote, the Rurals finished one seat short of their record in 1970, when they had mobilized the "forgotten people" of the backwoods with a populist campaign. Finland was second only to West Germany in gaining two Green members of Parliament. (For tabulated results, *see* POLITICAL PARTIES.)

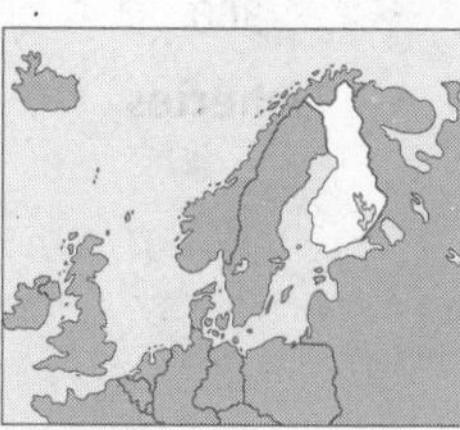

Finland

FINLAND

Education. (1980–81) Primary, pupils 373,347, teachers 25,959; secondary, pupils 341,054, teachers 19,822; vocational, pupils 103,111, teachers 14,136; teacher training, students 872, teachers 188; higher (1981–82), students 86,026, teaching staff 6,471.

Finance. Monetary unit: markka, with (Sept. 20, 1983) a free rate of 5.69 markkaa to U.S. $1 (8.57 markkaa = £1 sterling). Gold and other reserves (June 1983) U.S. $1,059,000,000. Budget (1981 actual): revenue 51,699,000,000 markkaa; expenditure 51.4 billion markkaa. Gross national product (1982) 229,320,000,000 markkaa. Money supply (June 1983) 21,362,000,000 markkaa. Cost of living (1975 = 100; June 1983) 222.7.

Foreign Trade. (1982) Imports 64,710,000,000 markkaa; exports 63,003,000,000 markkaa. Import sources: U.S.S.R. 25%; West Germany 13%; Sweden 12%; U.K. 7%; U.S. 6%. Export destinations: U.S.S.R. 27%; Sweden 12%; U.K. 11%; West Germany 9%; Norway 5%. Main exports: paper 22%; machinery 15%; ships 8%; timber 6%; chemicals 5%; clothing 5%; wood pulp 5%.

Transport and Communications. Roads (1982) 75,448 km (including 205 km expressways). Motor vehicles in use (1982): passenger 1,352,100; commercial 161,700. Railways: (1981) 6,089 km; traffic (1982) 3,326,000,000 passenger-km, freight 8,000,000,000 net ton-km. Air traffic (1982): 2,589,000,000 passenger-km; freight 66.8 million net ton-km. Navigable inland waterways (1981) 6,057 km. Shipping (1982): merchant vessels 100 gross tons and over 354; gross tonnage 2,376,995. Telephones (Jan. 1981) 2,374,500. Radio receivers (Dec. 1980) *c.* 4 million. Television licenses (Dec. 1980) 1,530,000.

Agriculture. Production (in 000; metric tons; 1982): wheat 435; barley 1,599; oats *c.* 1,320; potatoes 601; sugar, raw value (1981) 89; rapeseed 96; butter 70; cheese 74; eggs 77; meat (1981) 328; fish catch (1981) 133; timber (cu m; 1981) 43,859. Livestock (in 000; June 1982): cattle 1,705; sheep 104; pigs 1,475; reindeer 245; horses 20; poultry 7,763.

Industry. Production (in 000; metric tons; 1982): pig iron 1,944; crude steel 2,426; iron ore (66% metal content) 886; cement 1,794; sulfuric acid 1,225; petroleum products (1981) 10,595; plywood (cu m; 1981) 509; cellulose (1981) 4,549; wood pulp (1980) mechanical 2,346, chemical 4,885; newsprint 1,297; other paper and board (1980) 4,353; electricity (kw-hr) 39,360,000; manufactured gas (cu m) 20,000.

To general consternation, Social Democratic Prime Minister Kalevi Sorsa brought the Rurals, previously political outcasts, into his fourth centre-left coalition Cabinet, which assumed office on May 6. For the first time since 1977 the Communists were excluded from the government, and the

WIDE WORLD

Finland's Pres. Mauno Koivisto (left) visited Moscow in June. He is shown here bidding farewell to Soviet leader Yury Andropov.

Conservatives remained in opposition, as they had been since 1966. With portfolios split between the Social Democratic Party (eight), Centre Party (five), Rural Party (two), and Swedish People's Party (two), the Sorsa team survived 1983 with less trouble than had been foreseen. However, the seamy side of power that disillusioned so many voters was exemplified by a number of corruption trials.

Reasons for a sluggish economic performance included the erosion of the competitive advantage gained from the previous October's devaluation and fewer export openings in the Soviet market. The budget, submitted on September 21, predicted a growth in gross domestic product of 2.5% for 1983 and 3% for 1984. The target of cutting inflation from 9 to 6% in 1984 was made conditional on a 3% ceiling on increases in pay, prompting rumblings on the industrial relations front.

(DONALD FIELDS)

Fisheries

The problems and crises that had plagued the world's fisheries in 1982 showed no signs of resolution in 1983. There was little indication that adoption of the 200-mi Exclusive Economic Zone (EEZ) by coastal nations had brought prosperity to anyone other than the shipyards lucky enough to be building fishing fleets for the newly fish-rich countries. Neither Canada nor the U.S. appeared to have gained much from the greater exclusivity. The U.S. east coast fleet found itself serving a somewhat depressed market, and some processing plants had to close. Alaskan pollack was living up to expectations, however, and large quantities were being transshipped to Japanese and Eastern-bloc vessels. Thousands of tons were also being processed into crab-flavoured "ocean sticks," based on Japanese-style fish mince, and sales of this product were one of the year's success stories.

Early in the year it had become apparent that all was not well with the Canadian Maritime Provinces fish industry. Several large processing companies were acutely short of cash and threatened with closure unless new capital could be found. A committee was appointed to diagnose the malaise and find solutions, backed if necessary by public money. Among its 57 recommendations were $410 million in state aid, shared between the east and west coasts; greater state control of the ailing industries; a reduction in the number of fishing vessels; and improvement in the quality of fish products. In July the federal government decided to form a new processing and marketing company, which would be the second largest of its type in the world, injecting $75 million in state aid and securing 1,600 jobs in the Maritimes.

On the U.S. east coast, the haddock catch on Georges Bank was down 500,000 tons—said to be equivalent to a $450 million loss. However, the Alaskan pollack catch was expected to reach 100,000 tons, while the Bristol Bay salmon fishery reported a 30 million-fish season. Not so good was the southern shrimp fishery, where the Oregon fleet had shrunk from 94 to 67 vessels and the catch had almost halved. Bad times also afflicted the Pacific tuna fishery; Star Kist and Van Camp put 19 tuna boats up for sale, despite new estimates of a potential ten million-ton tuna harvest in the western Pacific.

Mexico was still taking delivery of tuna boats, ordered in a spirit of optimism a few years earlier. Now they had no U.S. market, catches had fallen, and the Japanese had more than doubled their purse seine fleet in the Pacific, despite internationally low prices and poor demand. Surprisingly, the

Advances in fisheries technology included the "controlled atmosphere pack," which was expected to enhance sales.

COURTESY, H. S. NOEL

Table I. Whaling: 1981–82 Season (Antarctic); 1981 Season (Outside the Antarctic)
Number of whales caught

Area and country	Fin whale	Sei/ Bryde's whale	Hump-back whale	Minke whale	Sperm whale	Killer whale	Total	Percentage assigned under quota agree-ment[1]
Antarctic pelagic (open sea)								
Japan	—	—	—	3,577	—	—	3,577	44.15
U.S.S.R.	—	—	—	3,577	—	—	3,577	44.15
Brazil	—	—	—	—	—	—	—	11.70
Total	—	—	—	7,154	—	—	7,154	100.00
Outside the Antarctic								
Japan	—	485	—	374	869	5	1,733	
U.S.S.R.	—	—	—	—	—	—	135[2]	
Brazil	—	—	—	749	—	—	749	
Peru	—	250	—	—	264	—	514	
Iceland	254	100	—	201	43	3	601	
Spain	146	—	—	—	—	—	146	
Norway	—	—	—	1,877	—	13	1,890	
Korea, South	—	1	—	760	—	2	763	
Others	9	—	—	191	280	—	480	
Total	409	836	—	4,152	1,456	23	7,011	

[1]Minke; Southern Hemisphere only.
[2]Represents gray whales; figure is included in both vertical and horizontal totals.
Source: The Committee for Whaling Statistics, *International Whaling Statistics*.

Seattle (Wash.)-based Marco group announced the establishment of a tuna-boat-building facility in Taiwan to serve "an expanding market." A major shellfish conference in Dublin was warned that the maximum level of shrimp exploitation worldwide had been reached. Delegates were told that the solution was to step up shrimp farming. This had been done in Ecuador, but the risks inherent in aquaculture had been highlighted by damage from unexpected rains, which had affected growing ponds and resulted in losses estimated at $10 million. The cause was said to be the change in the warm water current known as El Niño. (*See* EARTH SCIENCES: *Special Report*.) This current had been moving northward up the Pacific coast, cutting Peru's anchoveta catch almost in half and adversely affecting that country's developing pilchard fishery. Also threatened by the warmer northern waters were the U.S. shrimp and squid fisheries.

Peru's fishing industry was still in trouble. National economic strictures forced the government to call in loans to 12 canneries, and the Pescaperu company asked for a $4 million handout to keep going. With only 57 food-fish boats at sea, compared with 240 in 1982, the government decided to put in its own team to manage the company. Yet, overall, Latin America boosted its catch to a new high of 13 million tons, an increase of 22% for which Chile and Mexico were mainly responsible.

On the other side of the Atlantic, on January 25 the European Economic Community (EEC) at last agreed on a common fisheries policy (CFP) after overcoming a veto by Denmark. Kent Kirk, a Danish member of the European Parliament and a fishing skipper, briefly made headlines when he took his boat into Britain's coastal fishing zone to challenge the EEC's right to declare which country was entitled to net the largest quota of commercially valuable fish. However, he failed to receive the support that he had expected from other Danish skippers. While no one doubted that the EEC fleet was too large by some 30–40% and too efficient for the fish stocks available, no one seemed eager to be the first to cut back. Feelings ran especially high over the division of herring and mackerel stocks—both now limited—and there were accusations of quota jumping, particularly against Denmark. In the autumn funds were allocated for an EEC policing team of 18 inspectors, but little concrete action seemed to follow.

The Netherlands appeared to be rising above these problems. It continued to build large freezer trawlers and to operate "vacuum cleaner" beam trawlers in the North Sea. Denmark complained that these ships were ruining the fishing grounds, but there was now hope that less destructive and fuel-hungry beam trawlers would alleviate the problem. Britain's Sea Fish Industry Authority carried out successful trials on an electric trawl that "shocked" fish out of the seabed instead of digging them out with chains. The search for fuel economy continued. Meters that gave the skipper a continuous reading of fuel consumption were widely fitted. France, Britain, and the U.S. were among a number of countries applying modern technology to sail propulsion, and fuel savings of up to 25% were recorded. Britain tested "aerofoil" sails, and a French shipyard, in collaboration with marine scientist Jacques Cousteau, experimented with an updated Magnus effect cylindrical "mast-sail." Fortunately, fuel prices remained steady while fish prices overall turned upward.

Greenland, which had opted to leave the European Communities in 1982, was buying up big trawlers and building a fleet that was causing some concern in Europe. It was felt that so much catching power could upset the delicate balance in Community waters; there were rumblings already over fish quotas allocated to Norway. Iceland, outside the Community and with an exclusive 200-mi fishing zone, had experienced a poor year in 1982. However, no alarm was expressed in Reykjavik, despite some falloff in sales of fish to the U.S.

Spain and Portugal moved a little closer toward European Community membership, with a possible target date of 1986. Fears of a Spanish fleet allowed to range freely in EEC waters were widely expressed, particularly by France. The provisional terms set by the Community were tough, and it was said in Spain that the intention must be to render its fleet harmless before allowing entry. Feelings still ran high in Britain and France over Spanish trawlers fishing under the British flag in EEC waters, and the British skipper of one such vessel was injured by a rifle shot in the Bay of Biscay. New crewing regulations were introduced by Britain, requiring the employment of British crewmen, and new havens were sought by the vessels' owners. In Ireland the Irish-Spanish joint venture was accused of transshipping Spanish fish and of failing to live up to its promises of local prosperity.

After months of exclusion from the sardine-rich waters of Morocco, Spain signed a new agreement in September allowing limited access for its Mediterranean fleet. Heavy and increasing license fees would be required over a four-year phaseout period, while Morocco rebuilt its own fleet and infrastructure, using Spanish credit and suppliers. Farther down the African west coast, the 200-mi zone had brought no overnight miracles. Fisheries

COURTESY, H. S. NOEL

The drive for fuel economy sparked new interest in wind power. The "Cameleon" is a motor trawler assisted by two modern "aerofoil" sails. The result is a 25% reduction in fuel costs.

were still dominated by foreign fleets and joint ventures. In South West Africa/Namibia, awaiting independence from South African administration, there was bitterness over the poor state of pilchard and anchovy stocks. It was said that these had been grossly overfished with the tacit approval of South Africa, though the official reason given was "weather anomalies."

The potential of Southeast Asia received considerable attention, with an international "Asiafish" conference in Singapore and the success of the Infofish service, set up earlier in Malaysia by Wolfgang Krone of the UN Food and Agriculture Organization. India enjoyed a record year for shrimp exports, and seafood exports rose 50% to $342 million for 1981–82. N. P. Singh, president of the Indian Fishing Industry, urged expansion of the deep-sea fisheries to stimulate home markets and ancillary industries. Like many other nations, Australia found that the 200-mi zone was no panacea, and 51% of fish supplies were still imported. A $A4 million company was formed with Thailand. New Zealand inshore fishermen protested new fish quotas that gave most of the deepwater catch to nine large companies at the expense of small operators and cooperatives.

Poland, West Germany, and the U.S.S.R. were still taking limited quantities of krill in the Antarctic, though the value hardly justified the high cost. However, Danish technologists developed a method of peeling shrimp and krill that could drastically change the economics of this fishery, said to have a catch potential running into six figures. Other more subtle marketing developments also heralded changes in the fisheries. New packaging and preserving methods, such as the "controlled

Floods:
see Earth Sciences; Engineering Projects

Table II. World Fisheries, 1981[1]
In 000 metric tons

Country	Catch		Trade	
	Total	Freshwater	Imports	Exports
Japan	10,656.5	316.7	1,038.0	683.1
U.S.S.R.	9,545.9	964.0	57.2	419.0
China	4,605.0	1,304.5	...	101.3
United States	3,767.4	362.1	1,043.5	454.3
Chile	3,393.4	[2]	1.8	594.0
Peru	2,750.5	15.4	0.2	294.6
Norway	2,551.5	14.6	74.4	726.7
India	2,415.4	996.1	...	70.9
South Korea	2,366.0	44.8	50.3	400.0
Indonesia	1,862.7	451.2	63.0	65.2
Denmark	1,813.9	24.3	267.5	736.8
Philippines	1,650.9	273.4	39.7	89.4
Thailand	1,650.0	146.2	43.5	269.0
Mexico	1,564.8	89.1	34.6	57.4
North Korea	1,500.0	80.0	...	...
Iceland	1,441.2	0.4	0.2	489.3
Canada	1,362.2	132.0	100.6	520.7
Spain	1,263.6	36.5	271.0	256.1
Vietnam	1,013.5	176.3	...	...
Brazil	900.0	170.8	49.0	47.9
United Kingdom	825.7	3.2	732.6	376.0
Malaysia	796.0	6.3	163.0	99.7
France	768.0	2.0	500.8	140.6
Bangladesh	686.6	556.0	...	5.5
Ecuador	685.7	...	0.4	149.3
Poland	629.6	28.0	98.8	82.0
Burma	624.5	156.3	[2]	1.1
South Africa	611.8	0.1	89.7	125.0
Nigeria	496.2	183.2	155.0	0.8
Turkey	470.2	17.3	[2]	15.3
Italy	449.3	38.5	341.9	97.3
Netherlands, The	434.4	2.2	352.2	436.7
Morocco	381.9	0.7	[2]	132.9
Argentina	359.6	9.6	15.5	168.5
Pakistan	317.8	62.1	0.3	20.5
West Germany	313.3	15.7	764.9	233.1
Sweden	262.8	12.9	175.6	137.6
Portugal	254.6	0.1	81.3	47.4
South West Africa/ Namibia	249.4	[2]	...	...
Faeroe Islands	242.0	1.0	6.3	106.6
East Germany	241.2	16.2	38.6	...
Ghana	240.4	44.0	28.9	3.3
Tanzania	226.0	190.0	1.5	0.2
Sri Lanka	206.8	29.6	7.5	2.7
Senegal	206.7	13.5	20.6	66.8
Other	5,705.5	...	...	...
World	74,760.4	8,053.7[3]	9,129.3[3]	9,946.1[3]

[1]Excludes whaling.
[2]Less than 100 metric tons.
[3]Includes unspecified amounts in Other category.
Source: United Nations Food and Agriculture Organization, *Yearbook of Fishery Statistics*, vol. 52 and 53.

atmosphere pack," and better utilization of less popular species by reprocessing fish mince into more easily marketed products could upgrade values and perhaps ease the economic pressures on fishermen.

The International Whaling Commission (IWC) agreed at its 1983 meeting that commercial whaling should end by January 1986. However, whaling and nonwhaling nations continued their altercation, and Japan, which together with Norway and the U.S.S.R. objected to the IWC resolution, was warned that it might lose fishing rights in U.S. waters unless its objections were withdrawn. (*See* ENVIRONMENT.) (H. S. NOEL)

See also Food Processing.
[731.D.2.a]

Food Processing

In a stagnant market, the food-processing industry continued to struggle with legislative problems, health controversies, and rising costs. Many countries suffered from overproduction, and the European Economic Community (EEC) faced financial disaster as a result of growing surpluses of butter, powdered milk, wheat, sugar, beef, sultana grapes, olive oil, and wine. A report prepared for the U.K. National Advisory Committee on Nutrition Education recommended drastic reductions in the consumption of fats (including reductions in the fat content of milk, cheese, and meat), sugar, and salt with compensatory increases in bread, potatoes, and dietary fibre. Such diet and health controversies caused problems for food processors, heated debate in medical and nutritional circles, and a mixture of alarm and cynical indifference among consumers.

Processing Technology. Economic pressures hastened the introduction of highly sophisticated computerized control and maintenance systems by many food manufacturers. New systems were developed to control batch processes that required close monitoring of recipes and the continuous determination of such factors as viscosity, meat fat content, and the carbon dioxide content of beverages. Robots developed in Britain and Japan could cope with size and shape variations and identify different products by means of visual and tactile sensing. Automatic optical sensing systems capable of screening single rice grains or judging the colour of cookies were introduced. Enzymes were being widely used to improve product quality, though in Britain their introduction was being hampered by legislative impediments.

Fruits, Vegetables, and Cereals. Using a technique for assessing the pleasure value of sounds made while eating, U.S. researchers established that fresh vegetables had higher scores than processed ones. In New Zealand scientists developed a cryogenic process that reduced freezing times to seconds while preserving the crispness, flavour, and nutritional value of fruits and vegetables. Special lightweight cartons developed in West Germany were introduced for the aseptic packaging of fruit juices in Iraq, soy milk in South Korea, and coconut milk in Singapore. French technologists developed a process for vacuum packing precleaned new potatoes that extended their shelf life to 2½ months without refrigeration. A soybean cultivar produced in Japan was devoid of lipoxygenase, which causes the "grassy" flavour unacceptable to many Western consumers.

For U.S. soft drinks saccharin as a sweetener could go the way of long-banned cyclamates. A replacement is aspartame, here poured by workers at G. D. Searle & Co., which markets it as NutraSweet.

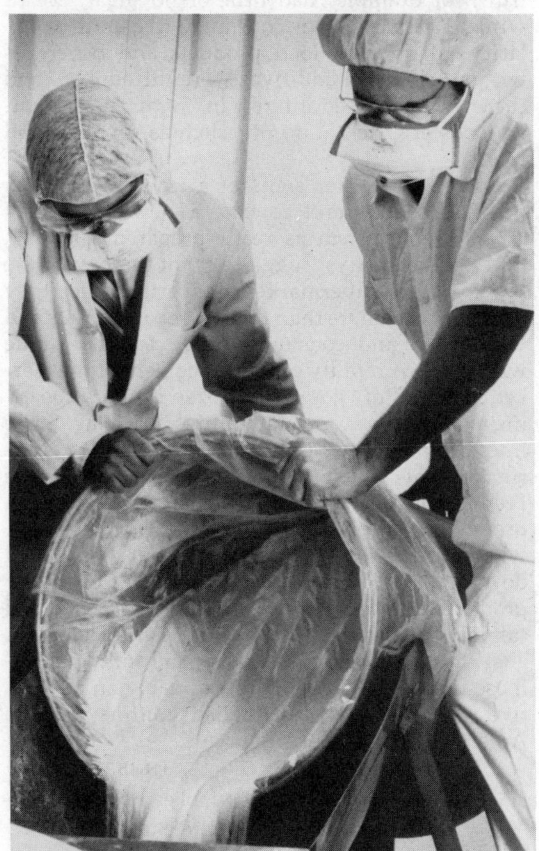

STEVE KRONGARD/TIME MAGAZINE

U.S. Department of Agriculture scientists developed an ultrasonic technique that greatly increased the rate of hydrogenation of edible oils, to the point where continuous hydrogenation became practical. The successful introduction of a soy-oats infant formula to fight malnutrition, developed jointly by the Mexican Nutrition Institute and a manufacturing company, received an award from the U.S. Institute of Food Technologists.

Dairy Products. The results of milking cows three times a day instead of the usual two were being studied in several countries. More frequent milking appeared to eliminate variations in milk composition and to increase milk yield, although feed intake remained the same. Also under study was the possibility of reducing the number of milk collections from farms by extending storage life, either through the use of natural enzyme systems or by heat-treating milk on the farm. The increased use of dairy products in various manufactured foods aroused interest when a U.K. research survey revealed that 85% of housewives thought dairy ingredients improved both flavour and nutritional quality. Trials showed that skimmed milk and whey proteins enhanced the texture of many meat products.

Enzymes were being used to hasten cheese ripening and to sharpen flavour, enabling the introduction of strong-flavoured cheese varieties for use in manufactured products. Australian scientists developed a continuous cheese-making process that retained the whey proteins; it was faster than conventional methods, gave better yields, and resulted in a superior product. Fruit-flavoured milk with fluoride added was introduced in Scotland after extensive clinical trials in the U.S. and Hungary, where a 74% reduction in dental caries was claimed. A British company invested £34 million in a yogurt factory said to be the largest in Europe. Yogurt became popular as an ingredient in other foods; a natural yogurt powder for commercial use was introduced in Britain.

Meat and Seafood. The regulatory problems that had plagued the U.K. meat-processing industry in 1982 were not resolved by the issuance of new draft regulations, described as "sadly lacking" by one county authority. It was estimated that the mechanical recovery of meat from bones could add two million metric tons of red meat, one million tons of poultry meat, and two million tons of fish meat to the world's food supply annually. Lack of texture made the resulting product difficult to use in processed foods, however, and this problem was the subject of considerable research. Health concerns increased the demand for lean meat. Consumers visiting the Royal Smithfield Show in London showed a strong preference for lean beef, and the leanest joint, with an average fat content of 30%, was favoured by 59.9%. In 1955, 61.6% of the consumers had preferred a fat content of 40%. The Danish Meat Research Institute was investigating rapid physical methods to replace the slower chemical procedures for determining water and meat content and evaluating the collagen in comminuted meat. Such assessments were required by law in a number of countries. A New Zealand company developed a meat-grading probe for classifying carcasses automatically. It measured subcutaneous fat, intramuscular fat, and carcass section thickness and displayed carcass class and lean meat yield.

The UN Food and Agriculture Organization reported that there was little prospect of increasing the fish catch to meet the world's future protein requirements, especially since fish farming in less developed countries was inhibited by cost. It recommended that the culture of mollusks, which have a very high productivity rate, be investigated. British fishery scientists made some potentially important advances in fish culture. Turbot cultivation had been hampered by the need to feed the fry on live food. Prolific brackish-water rotifers and brine shrimps proved nutritionally inadequate because they lack certain fatty acids, but their nutritional value was enhanced by feeding them certain unicellular algae. Optimum growth of the turbot was obtained by raising the fry in warm water effluents. Research was also undertaken to improve the survival of rainbow trout eggs and to increase growth and feed conversion. Sexual maturation decreases the growth rate of trout. To capitalize on the fact that females have a lower mortality rate than males and mature later, a commercially practicable method of producing entirely female stock was developed.

Dutch scientists developed a technique for supplying catfish fry throughout the year. Mexican scientists, assisted by the U.K. Tropical Development and Research Institute, were working on a project to utilize as food the large quantities of small edible fish normally discarded from the shrimp catch. U.S. Food and Drug Administration proposals to reduce the sodium (salt) content of foods alarmed the fishing industry. Catches must be brine-frozen for transport from distant waters, and this increases the salt content substantially. However, the FDA delayed taking action in the matter. (*See* FISHERIES.)

New Products. Numerous new products were introduced during the year, and some established ones were given a new look. Some were elevated to the "gourmet" category (enabling higher prices to be charged), while others were new in the sense that they were home-produced simulations of products that previously had been imported. A U.K. company was reported to have spent £24 million on the development of new cheeses in order to combat foreign imports. A number of recent research reports had emphasized the unhealthful properties of caffeine, a standard ingredient in many soft drinks, especially those with a cola base. Soft-drink manufacturers, who for some years had promoted sugar-free "diet" beverages, scrambled during the year to introduce new products that were free of caffeine and, in some cases, of both caffeine and sugar. A "tea" made from the South African rooi plant (*Aspalathus linearus*), said to have no caffeine and little tannin, joined the various "herbal teas" that had gained popularity in recent years.

There were many new permutations and combinations of milk beverages containing fruit juices and purees, exotic fruits, peppermint, nut, and other flavours, and with or without milk fat. New yogurt varieties also multiplied, including baby yogurts (U.K. market worth £3.5 million), children's and picnic yogurts, and yogurt confectionery, dips, and beverages. Practically all these products were offered in "natural," full-fat to very low-fat, sweetened or sugar-free varieties, and with whole or pureed fruit.

Salt-free or low-sodium foods constituted a growing market, especially in the U.S. New salt-free yeast-derived flavourings were introduced for use in sauces, soups, sausages, and Oriental foods, which traditionally had a very high sodium content. Salt-free canned vegetables, cereals, condiments, and cheeses also proliferated. The designation "light," originally used to promote low-calorie beer, began to be used for a wide variety of products. Like "natural," it had no exact definition, and some authorities feared that it might be subject to abuse. Generally, it was meant to imply a lower-calorie product. "Light" canned fruit, for example, had little or no sugar. Meanwhile, "natural" foods continued to gain in popularity. Many new food products and beverages without chemical additives were introduced, and there was increased interest in "natural" fermented foods of Oriental origin, such as soy milk and tofu.

There were other signs of a trend away from processed foods and toward a new concept of "fresh" foods, such as ready-prepared salads. A U.K. market analyst suggested that these were the key to future supermarket prosperity, since they tended to cost more than the unprepared fruits and vegetables, and consumers often equated value with price. A rapidly growing segment of the market consisted of "gourmet" frozen dinners, boasting exotic recipes and with a high price tag. Some lines combined the "gourmet" label with low calorie content, often drawing heavily from the French nouvelle cuisine. The chief target for such products was considered to be the working wife, who had little time to prepare food but who looked down on the traditional frozen dinner. Other new products introduced during the year included salmon cured in malt whiskey (Farne Islands), goat cheese with truffles (U.K.), and simulated adipose tissue (U.S. patent), presumably an alternative to lean meat. Real English muffins, new to America, proved a great success.

(H. B. HAWLEY)

See also Agriculture and Food Supplies; Health and Disease; Industrial Review: *Alcoholic Beverages*.
[451.B.1.c.ii; 731.E–H]

Football

Association Football (Soccer). The year after the World Cup finals is inevitably somewhat less exciting, but the various competitions were disputed with undiminished fervour in 1983. The site of the 1986 World Cup finals was switched from Colombia to Mexico after the former withdrew because of financial difficulties. Andrei Radulescu, president, and Florian Dumitrescu, secretary, of the Romanian Federation were dismissed because of a bungle that led to that country's missing a place in the European Cup-Winners' Cup; Romania's national cup final was set for July 6, whereas the deadline set by the Union of European Football Associations (UEFA) for entry was a week earlier.

Off-field problems continued to be present, with hooliganism still uppermost in many people's thoughts—notably in Greece, where fans rioted and caused severe damage in Athens after the cup final at the Olympic Stadium. There were also scandals connected with bribery and gambling. In Hungary the Football Association suspended nearly 200 players for alleged implication in "fixing" matches, while Yugoslavia, The Netherlands, and Italy suffered similar scandals. On the lighter side, there were charges in some central African countries that attempts had been made to affect the outcome of games with the use of black magic, dead chickens' heads having been placed between the goalposts overnight.

EUROPEAN CHAMPIONS' CUP. SV Hamburg of West Germany broke the six-year English monopoly of this trophy when it defeated Juventus of Turin at the Olympic Stadium in Athens on May 25 with a single goal by Felix Magath. The former German international carried the ball to the edge of the penalty area before loosing off a left-foot curling shot that beat the ageless Dino Zoff between the Juventus posts. Thus ended the expensive dream of the northern Italian club, which had paid some $3 million for World Cup players Michel Platini (France) and Zbigniew Boniek (Poland) in quest of the prestigious trophy.

It was the clinical efficiency of the northern German side and the somewhat inflexible tactics of Juventus that determined the destination of the trophy and the passport to the Inter-Continental Cup, a clash with the South American champions Gremio of Brazil. The Juventus defenders forgot some of the basic principles, and Magath and Jurgen Milewski exploited the gaps left by usually reliable defenders.

EUROPEAN CUP-WINNERS' CUP. Aberdeen brought the trophy back to Scotland after a gap of 11 years by defeating the pride of Spain, Real Madrid, in a rain-swept Göteborg (Sweden) stadium in extra time on May 11. The conditions, with the field sporting pools of water, undoubtedly gave the Scots a distinct edge over their Spanish opponents as the weather was more familiar to them. Nevertheless, full credit had to be given to the men from Aberdeen, who swept ahead with a seventh-minute goal from Eric Black. Fullback Juan José turned Willie Miller's header into Black's path for him to slot the ball home. Yet within ten minutes the Scots were pegged back. A back pass stopped in a pool of water, and goalkeeper Jim Leighton brought down Real's Carlos Santillana in a desperate dive for the ball. Juan Juanito scored from the penalty spot. Black hit the crossbar and headed over the top as the Scots went for goals, but not in an unbridled fashion. With eight minutes remaining in extra time, Aberdeen gained its reward: Mark McGhee dispossessed Juanito of the ball in midfield, broke down the left flank, and pulled the ball across for John Hewitt—he had replaced Black after 87 minutes—to head home the winner.

UEFA CUP. Anderlecht, coached by the legendary Paul Van Himst who graced many a Belgian international side, narrowly beat Benfica by two goals to one over two legs of this final during May, but the score did not do real justice to the Brussels team's superior tactics. In the first leg at the Heysel stadium on May 4, Anderlecht gained the all-important one-goal advantage when Danish striker Ken Brylle put into tangible form the midfield edge gained by Ludo Coeck, Frankie Vercauteren, and Juan Lozano. Coeck engineered the goal with almost half an hour of the game gone. He turned

Table I. Association Football Major Tournaments

Event	Winner	Country
Inter-Continental Cup	Gremio	Brazil
European Super Cup	Aberdeen	Scotland
European Champions' Cup	SV Hamburg	West Germany
European Cup-Winners' Cup	Aberdeen	Scotland
UEFA Cup	Anderlecht	Belgium
Libertadores Cup (South American Champions' Cup)	Gremio	Brazil
World Youth Cup	Brazil	
European Youth Cup	France	

Table II. Association Football National Champions

Nation	League winners	Cup winners
Albania	Vllazania	Nendori
Argentina	Estudiantes de la Plata	
Austria	Rapid Vienna	Rapid Vienna
Belgium	Standard Liège	Beveren
Bolivia	Bolívar	
Brazil	Flamengo	
Bulgaria	CSKA Sofia	CSKA Sofia
Colombia	América	
Cyprus	Omonia Nicosia	Omonia Nicosia
Czechoslovakia	Bohemians	Dukla Prague
Denmark	Odense Boldklub	B93 Copenhagen
Ecuador	Nacional	
England	Liverpool	Manchester United
Finland	Kuuysi	Haka
France	Nantes	Paris Saint-Germain
Germany, East	Dynamo Berlin	Magdeburg
Germany, West	SV Hamburg	Cologne
Greece	Olympiakos	AEK
Hungary	Raba Gyor	Ujpest Dozsa
Iceland	Vikingur	IB Akranes
Ireland	Athlone	Sligo
Italy	Roma	Juventus
Luxembourg	Jeunesse	Avenir Beggen
Malta	Hamrun	Hamrun
Mexico	Puebla	
Netherlands, The	Ajax	Ajax
Northern Ireland	Linfield	Glentoran
Norway	Viking Stavangar	Brann
Paraguay	Olimpia	
Poland	Lech Poznan	Lech Poznan
Portugal	Benfica	Benfica
Romania	Dinamo Bucharest	Univ. Craiova
Scotland	Dundee United	Aberdeen
Spain	Athletico Bilbao	Barcelona
Sweden	IFK Göteborg	IFK Göteborg
Switzerland	Grasshoppers	Grasshoppers
Turkey	Fenerbahce	Fenerbahce
U.S.S.R.	Dynamo Minsk	Dynamo Kiev
U.S.	Tulsa Roughnecks	
Uruguay	Peñarol	
Wales		Swansea
Venezuela	Atlético San Cristóbal	
Yugoslavia	Partizan Belgrade	Dynamo Zagreb

two Benfica defenders and swept the ball in from near the corner flag for the waiting Brylle to stab home.

In the return leg in Lisbon a fortnight later, nearly 80,000 spectators packed into the Stadium of Light to see if Benfica could erase that one-goal deficit. Certainly they were on the attack from the opening whistle, but they were without striker Zoran Filipovic (ir ˈured) and José Luis Silva, following his dismissal in the first leg. Yet, as so often happens to a side going all out on attack, they were caught by a rapid counterattack. Erwin Vandenbergh had the ball in the net for Anderlecht, but Dutch referee Charles Corver disallowed the point for offside. However, Benfica defender Humberto Coelho redressed the balance when he chested the ball down for Han Sheu to drive into the net after 36 minutes. Benfica then lost concentration, and Anderlecht tied the score within three minutes. In the second half Anderlecht brought on an extra defender, Hugo Broos, and, operating with a sweeper behind the back four, managed to contain the Portuguese side's attacks; when Benfica did break through, Jacques Munaton was there to produce some smart saves. Thus, Van Himst, who was on the losing side in the 1972 final, saw his team reap its reward a decade later.

U.K. Home International Tournament. England again triumphed in what proved to be the penultimate occasion of this century-old event when they defeated Scotland decisively at Wembley, London, on June 1 by two goals to none. It was the 34th time since the competition began in 1884 that England finished as outright victors. Declining attendances and other harsh economic factors forced the English to scrap the event in the season beginning August 1984.

North American Soccer League. The nasl in 1983 remained beset with problems of staying alive and in financial health. After the close of the summer outdoor season, two teams, the Seattle Sounders and the Montreal Manic, folded because of declining attendance, and a question mark hung over the survival of some of the ten remaining members of the competition. The reason was partly that soccer was not really a game played in almost all schools and colleges, as it was in Europe and South America. Yet in 1983 there were more "home grown" North American players competing in the league than before, and this augured well for the future, as did the limiting of imported players to two new signings per season.

There was no lack of enthusiasm among the 53,326 spectators who saw the Tulsa Roughnecks, coached by Welshman Terry Hennessey, win their first league title by beating the Toronto Blizzard 2–0 in the Soccer Bowl final in Vancouver, B.C., on October 1. Key to their triumph was their superiority at set-piece play and also the Blizzard's dependence on a containing game and attempts to exploit the rapid counterattack. The two goalkeepers, the Blizzard's Jan Moller and the Roughnecks' Winston DuBose, did little more than watch the action in the first half. Blizzard midfielder Ace Ntsoelengoe almost broke the deadlock when he sent a diving header in the 12th minute against the goal frame, and a few minutes later he had the ball in the net but was offside. Njego Pesa opened the scoring with a free kick, drilling the ball home off a defender (56 minutes), and five minutes later Ron Futcher added the second goal following a corner. (trevor williamson)

Latin America. Uruguay, a small country with a brilliant football tradition, defeated the powerful Brazilian national team in November to win the Americas Cup. The superiority of the underdog Uruguayans was particularly manifest in the first game, played in Montevideo, where they achieved a 2–0 victory. Later, in Salvador, Brazil, they held their rivals to a 1–1 tie.

Earlier in the year, however, Uruguay's Peñarol was defeated by Gremio of Brazil in the final series of the Libertadores de América Cup. Peñarol, the surprise club of 1982, played to a tie in the first game in Montevideo but then went on to lose 2–1 in a tense game in Pôrto Alegre, Brazil. Gremio

Japan's Yoshinori Ishigami of the Yamaha Football Club captures the ball with a leaping kick in the second half of a match with Brazil's Botafago F.R. team held at Omiya, Japan. The match in the Japan Cup Kirin world soccer 1983 meet ended in a 1–1 draw.

WIDE WORLD

WIDE WORLD

Members of a soccer team formed to represent the United States in international competition met with President Reagan in the White House rose garden in May.

went on to repeat Peñarol's 1982 feat of winning the Libertadores de América trophy and the Inter-Continental Cup, the unofficial world clubs' championship. The disappointment for Peñarol was sweetened somewhat by the fact that the club won Uruguay's national title again in 1983.

The Argentine national championship was, as usual, a charged affair. There were serious incidents in a number of games—on and off the field—and the final matches of the competition were even temporarily suspended after two small bombs were detonated in the dressing room of Estudiantes de la Plata during a game against Vélez-Sarsfield. Eventually, Estudiantes won the title.

In Brazil the final series for the national title was a throwback to older times. Santos F.C., Pelé's old club, reached the finals after a long hiatus, and for a time it seemed as if it would win the national championship again. But it was not to be. A star-studded but aging Flamengo, which was defeated 2–1 in the first game in São Paulo, rallied to win the decisive match 3–0 before 180,000 spectators in Rio de Janeiro's Maracaná Stadium.

Bolívar of La Paz gained the national title in Bolivia. In Colombia, América of Cali took its second championship ever (the first one was in 1979). Cobreloa was an easy winner in Chile. In Ecuador, Nacional of Quito and Barcelona of Guayaquil were tied in points at the end of the Professional League Division A final round, but a three-game play-off resulted in the victory of Nacional.

Puebla won its first Mexican League championship in 44 years of competition after defeating Guadalajara. The victory was, however, far from convincing. Guadalajara had undergone a traumatic semifinal series against its traditional rival, América of Mexico City, losing seven players through suspension and three more from injuries. Still, Guadalajara made a valiant effort and managed to remain tied after two games and the overtime periods. The winner was decided, for the second year in a row, by a series of penalties.

Olimpia won the Paraguayan championship, while in Peru competition was suspended after a dispute between the clubs and the Football Association. In Venezuela, Atlético San Cristóbal achieved a considerable feat when it gained the professional league title in its first season.

(SERGIO SARMIENTO)

Rugby. RUGBY UNION. The chief event of 1982–83 was the tour by the British Isles team, the Lions, to New Zealand in May, June, and July 1983. The Lions played 18 games in New Zealand, winning 12 and losing 4 with a points record of 478 for and 276 against.

While the Lions, managed by W. J. McBride and captained by Ciaran Fitzgerald, lost only two provincial matches (to Auckland and Canterbury), they were defeated in all four tests. For the All Blacks of New Zealand, therefore, the test series was a triumph. The first test, at Christchurch, was close, the All Blacks winning by 16–12. In the second, at Wellington, the All Blacks showed remarkable forward control and won 9–0. The third, at Dunedin, saw the Lions give probably their best display of the tour, but the All Blacks eventually won 15–8.

In the fourth test, at Auckland, the All Blacks played forceful and brilliant attacking rugby and won 38–6, the widest margin of defeat ever suffered by a Lions team. Stu Wilson, the All Blacks' right-wing threequarter, scored three tries and thus became the most prolific try scorer in New Zealand test history; but the man of the match and of the series was Dave Loveridge, the All Blacks' scrum half. The All Blacks' success in the tests owed much to the captaincy of Andy Dalton, their hooker, and to the coaching of Bryce Rope.

The Maoris of New Zealand made a seven-match tour of Wales in October and November 1982. They won three of their seven games, lost three, and drew one, scoring 119 points for with 91 against. In the only international match of the tour, they were beaten 25–19 by Wales. In September and October 1982 the Fijians toured England and Scotland and failed to win any of their ten games. In the two internationals of the tour they were defeated 32–12 by Scotland at Murrayfield and 60–19 by England at Twickenham. The Pumas of Argentina toured France and Spain in October and November 1982, winning four and losing four of their eight games. They played France twice, losing 25–12 at Toulouse and 13–6 in Paris. They then went to Spain and defeated the national team 28–19 in Madrid.

The home international championship, played in January, February, and March 1983, ended with France and Ireland as joint champions. France lost only to Ireland, and Ireland lost only to Wales. Third place was taken by Wales, with Scotland fourth and England last. England achieved only one championship point. This came from its draw of 13–13 at Cardiff, where it had not won since 1963.

RUGBY LEAGUE. On their tour of Britain and France late in 1982, the Australians proved one of the outstanding teams of all time. They played 15 games in Britain and 7 in France and won them all, scoring 714 points for with 100 against; this included the scoring of 166 tries with only 9 against. In their six tests they defeated Wales 37–7 at Cardiff; Great Britain 40–4 at Hull, 27–6 at Wigan, and 32–8 at Headingley; and France 15–4 at Avignon and 23–9 at Narbonne. (DAVID FROST)

U.S. Football. PROFESSIONAL. In an unexpectedly one-sided game, the Los Angeles Raiders defeated the defending National Football League (NFL) champion Washington Redskins 38–9 in the 18th Super Bowl in Tampa, Fla., on Jan. 22, 1984. The Raiders' 38 points were the most ever scored in a Super Bowl game, and their margin of victory was the largest.

Raider running back Marcus Allen gained a Super Bowl record of 191 yd and scored two touchdowns, one on a run of 74 yd. He was voted the game's most valuable player. Also outstanding was the Raider defense, which held the Redskins to 90 yd gained rushing, intercepted two passes by Washington quarterback Joe Theismann (*see* BIOGRAPHIES), and scored a touchdown on a blocked Washington punt.

The ball got away from Allan Harvin of the Philadelphia Stars when he was hit by Ronnie Paggett of the Michigan Panthers in the first USFL championship game at Mile High Stadium, Denver. The Michigan Panthers won the game with a score of 24–22.

WIDE WORLD

The Raiders were impressive throughout the play-offs, defeating Pittsburgh 38–10 and then winning the championship of the American Football Conference (AFC) by beating Seattle 30–14. In the first round of National Football Conference (NFC) play, Washington crushed the Los Angeles Rams 51–7. The Redskins later won the NFC title 24–21 over San Francisco with a last-minute field goal by Mark Moseley.

During the regular season Washington became the first NFC team ever to win 14 games. The Redskins, in winning the NFC Eastern Division, set a league record with 541 points, scoring at least 30 in 11 of their 16 games and never fewer than 23. Their innovative offensive alignments, with one running back and two tight ends, were widely imitated, and their defense allowed the fewest rushing yards in the league.

Individually for Washington, Mark Moseley's 161 points by a kicker and John Riggins's 24 rushing touchdowns also set records. Quarterback Joe Theismann was the NFL's most valuable player and ranked second in passing efficiency. Safety Mark Murphy led the league with nine interceptions.

Miami and the Raiders had the best won-lost records in the AFC, each finishing 12–4 and winning the Eastern and Western divisions, respectively. Pittsburgh won the AFC Central, and Denver and Seattle made the play-offs as wild-card teams. In the NFC San Francisco won the Western Division, Detroit the Central, and Dallas and the Los Angeles Rams were wild-card teams. Detroit's division championship was its first since 1957.

San Francisco, Denver, and the Rams all reached the play-offs by improving their won-lost records by 3½ games. The only bigger improvement was by Baltimore, which went from 0–8–1 to 7–9 and led the AFC in rushing.

Dan Marino of Miami became the first rookie quarterback to earn a Pro Bowl start. Miami won nine of its last ten games, its defense allowing the fewest points in the NFL and Marino leading the AFC in passing efficiency with a .020 interception percentage that ranked second in the league.

Rookies also led both conferences in rushing. Eric Dickerson of the Rams set a rookie record with 1,808 rushing yards and a league record with 390 carries. Seattle's Curt Warner led the AFC with 1,449 rushing yards. Seattle's new coach, Chuck Knox, gave the eight-year-old franchise its first play-off appearance and became the first man to guide three different teams to the play-offs. The Rams also had a new coach, John Robinson, but none of the six other teams with new coaches had a winning record.

George Halas (*see* OBITUARIES), the all-time leader in NFL coaching victories, died October 31 at 88. He was the owner of the Chicago Bears and the last surviving NFL founder.

Green Bay's Lynn Dickey and Kansas City's Bill Kenney became the fourth and fifth NFL players ever to pass for more than 4,000 yd in one season. Dickey led the league with 4,458 yd passing, 9.2 yd per attempt, 32 touchdown passes, and 29 interceptions. Green Bay led the NFC in total yards

WIDE WORLD

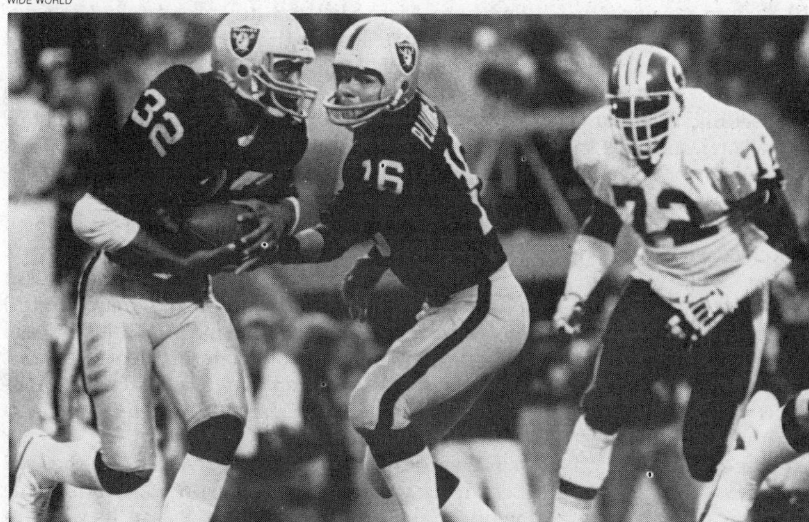

The Super Bowl's most valuable player Marcus Allen (32) takes a hand-off from Los Angeles Raiders quarterback Jim Plunkett as Dexter Manley of the Washington Redskins charges. The Raiders' victory, 38–9, was the most lopsided in Super Bowl history.

and passing yards. Atlanta's Steve Bartkowski had the NFL's best passing efficiency and interception percentage (.012). Ken Anderson's .667 completion percentage for Cincinnati led the league.

Todd Christensen of the Raiders led the NFL with 92 catches, a record for a tight end. Other league leaders were St. Louis's Roy Green with 14 touchdown catches and Philadelphia's Mike Quick with 1,409 yd on receptions.

The league's field-goal accuracy of 71.7% was more than 5% better than ever before. Ali Haji-Sheikh kicked 35 in one season for the New York Giants, and Jan Stenerud extended his career total to 338, both new records.

The NFL's most hallowed record, Jim Brown's career rushing total of 12,312 yd, was under siege by both Pittsburgh's Franco Harris and Chicago's Walter Payton. Harris moved to within 362 yd with his record-setting eighth 1,000-yd season. Payton moved to within 687 yd and helped Chicago lead the league in yards gained by rushing. Brown, at 47, threatened a comeback to extend his record.

Tampa Bay's record fell the furthest, from 5–4 to 2–14, but San Diego's collapse was the most surprising. San Diego's record dropped from 6–3 to 6–10, even though it led the AFC in total yards and passing yards. Other disappointing teams were the Giants, falling from 4–5 to 3–12–1, and Cincinnati, which tumbled from 7–2 to 7–9 despite allowing the fewest yards in the NFL and leading the AFC in both rush and pass defense. New Orleans led the entire league in pass defense and the NFC in total defense but extended the NFL's longest play-off absence to 17 years.

Cincinnati lost six of its first seven games after two of its best players were suspended for four games when they admitted they had bought cocaine. They were among four players suspended the same day in the NFL's counterattack against increasing revelations of illegal drug use by players.

The NFL had a different kind of problem with the emergence of the rival United States Football League (USFL). The USFL, playing from March to July, bid up players' salaries and wooed several players and prime draft prospects away from the established league. One of the USFL's prize rookies, Anthony Carter, caught nine passes for 179 yd and the decisive touchdown when the Michigan Panthers defeated the Philadelphia Stars 24–22 in the league championship game on July 17 at Denver.

The USFL's other star rookies included most valuable player Kelvin Bryant of Philadelphia; New Jersey's Herschel Walker (*see* BIOGRAPHIES), who led the league with 1,812 rushing yards and 18 touchdowns; and Chicago's Trumaine Johnson, who led with 81 catches and 1,322 yd on receptions. Oakland quarterback Fred Besana led the league with a .627 pass completion percentage and 2,980 passing yards; Chicago safety Luther Bradley led with 12 interceptions; Michigan's linebacker John Corker was the sack leader with $28\frac{1}{2}$; and rookie quarterback Bobby Hebert, the most valuable player of the championship game, was the league leader in touchdown passes with 27.

Philadelphia won the Atlantic Division with a 15–3 record; Michigan won the Central Division with 12–6 and the league's top-ranked offense; Oakland's 9–9 record won the Pacific Division; and Chicago, with the league-leading defense and a 12–6 record, was the wild-card team in the play-offs. The USFL expanded from 12 to 18 teams for 1984.

COLLEGE. Nebraska was compared favourably with the greatest teams in college football history as it averaged 52 points in winning all 12 regular-season games, second only to the fabled 1944 Army team's 56-point average. But Miami of Florida won the national championship with a won-lost record of 11–1 by defeating Nebraska 31–30 on Jan. 2, 1984, at the Orange Bowl, Miami's home field. Nebraska had been the only undefeated team in Division I-A of the National Collegiate Athletic Association (NCAA) after Texas lost 10–9 to Georgia earlier in the day at the Cotton Bowl in Dallas.

In the final Associated Press poll the top ten teams were, in order, Miami (11–1), Nebraska (12–1), Auburn (11–1), Georgia (10–1–1), Texas (11–1), Florida (9–2–1), Brigham Young (11–1),

Table III. NFL Final Standings and Play-offs, 1983

AMERICAN CONFERENCE	W	L	T
Eastern Division			
* Miami	12	4	0
Buffalo	8	8	0
New England	8	8	0
New York Jets	7	9	0
Baltimore	7	9	0
Central Division			
* Pittsburgh	10	6	0
Cleveland	9	7	0
Cincinnati	7	9	0
Houston	2	14	0
Western Division			
* Los Angeles Raiders	12	4	0
* Denver	9	7	0
* Seattle	9	7	0
Kansas City	6	10	0
San Diego	6	10	0
NATIONAL CONFERENCE			
Eastern Division			
* Washington	14	2	0
* Dallas	12	4	0
St. Louis	8	7	1
Philadelphia	5	11	0
New York Giants	3	12	1
Central Division			
* Detroit	9	7	0
Chicago	8	8	0
Green Bay	8	8	0
Minnesota	8	8	0
Tampa Bay	2	14	0
Western Division			
* San Francisco	10	6	0
* Los Angeles Rams	9	7	0
New Orleans	8	8	0
Atlanta	7	9	0

*Qualified for play-offs.

Play-offs

Wild-card round
Seattle 31, Denver 7
Los Angeles Rams 24, Dallas 17

American semifinals
Los Angeles Raiders 38, Pittsburgh 10
Seattle 27, Miami 20

National semifinals
Washington 51, Los Angeles Rams 7
San Francisco 24, Detroit 23

American finals
Los Angeles Raiders 30, Seattle 14

National finals
Washington 24, San Francisco 21

Super Bowl
Los Angeles Raiders 38, Washington 9

Michigan (9–3), Ohio State (9–3), and Illinois (10–2). The United Press International rankings were the same except that the positions of Michigan and Ohio State were reversed.

Unranked UCLA decisively upset Big Ten champion Illinois 45–9 at the Rose Bowl on January 2. In other major postseason games Auburn defeated Michigan 9–7 at the Sugar Bowl, and Ohio State beat Pittsburgh 28–23 at the Fiesta Bowl.

The spoils of Nebraska's victories went to Mike Rozier, who won the Heisman Trophy as the country's best college player, and guard Dean Steinkuhler, winner of the Lombardi and Outland awards for the best college lineman. Rozier set a record with 7.81 yd per carry, tied another with 29 touchdowns, and led the country's major football colleges with 2,148 yd rushing, the second-highest total ever. His all-purpose yardage ranked behind only Napoleon McCallum of Navy, who gained 216.8 per game on runs, returns, and pass receptions.

Nebraska and Brigham Young dominated the offensive statistics. Nebraska led in rushing with 401.7 yd per game and trailed only Brigham Young's record-breaking 584.2 yd per game in total offense. Brigham Young also completed a record 70.7% of its passes, led the country with 381.2 passing yards per game, and had the second-best scoring average, 44 points.

Brigham Young quarterback Steve Young, the great-great-great grandson of the school's founder, set records with 395.1 rushing and passing yards per game, 306 pass completions, and a .713 completion percentage. He also led the country in passing efficiency, with 168.5 rating points, and total passing yards, with 3,902. For his entire career Young had the second-best all-time efficiency rating and set records with 7.49 yd per rushing or passing play and a .652 completion percentage.

Other record breakers were Duke's Ben Bennett with 9,614 passing yards for his career, Iowa's Chuck Long with 10.31 yd per pass attempt, and Arizona State junior Luis Zendejas with 112 kicking points and career totals of 295 kicking points and 65 field goals. Individual leaders in other categories included Vanderbilt's Keith Edwards with 97 pass receptions, Boston College's Brian Brennan with 1,168 yd on receptions, and Bowling Green's Martin Bayless with ten interceptions.

Texas had the country's stingiest defense, allowing 212 yd per game, and ranked second in pass defense, fourth in rushing defense, and second in scoring defense. Virginia Tech (9–2) allowed the fewest points, 8.3 per game, and the fewest rushing yards, 69.4 per game, and ranked fourth in rushing offense. Oklahoma State led with 26 interceptions and 53 turnovers.

Conference champions included Nebraska in the Big Eight, Texas in the Southwest, Auburn in the Southeastern, Illinois in the Big Ten, UCLA in the Pacific Ten, Brigham Young in the Western Athletic, Maryland in the Atlantic Coast, Northern Illinois in the Mid-American, and Furman in the Southern.

There was renewed clamour for the big football schools to play a championship tournament after selectors for the major bowl games passed up 10–1 Southern Methodist for its lack of television appeal. But SMU lost at the Sun Bowl to Alabama, which had a 7–4 regular-season record in Ray Perkins's first year succeeding the late coach Paul "Bear" Bryant (*see* OBITUARIES). Bryant died at 69 on January 26, within a month of retiring.

In the tournaments for smaller schools the championship games included: Southern Illinois 43, Western Carolina 7 in NCAA Division 1-AA; North Dakota State 41, Central State (Ohio) 21 in NCAA Division II; Augustana (Ill.) 21, Union (N.Y.) 17 in NCAA Division III; and Carson-Newman (Tenn.) 36, Mesa (Colo.) 28 in Division I of the National Association for Intercollegiate Athletics (NAIA). Northwestern Iowa completed a 14–0 championship season in NAIA Division II by defeating Pacific Lutheran (Wash.) 25–21.

Harvard tied with Pennsylvania for the Ivy League championship and won its 100th game against Yale. Yale's season, at 1–9, was its worst in 111 years of football. Navy beat Army 42–13 in another traditional rivalry, which moved to the Rose Bowl in Pasadena, Calif.

Canadian Football. Substitute quarterback Joe Barnes rallied the Toronto Argonauts to an 18–17 victory against the British Columbia Lions for the Canadian Football League (CFL) championship at Vancouver, B.C., on November 27. Barnes entered the game with Toronto trailing 17–7 shortly before halftime and threw the decisive three-yard touchdown pass to Cedric Minter with 2 minutes 44 seconds to play. Barnes was the game's most valuable offensive player; Toronto defensive back Carl Brazley was the outstanding defensive player. Toronto, which had won just 2 of 16 games in 1981, set an Eastern Division record with 12 regular-season victories en route to its first Grey Cup championship since 1952.

Edmonton failed to win its sixth consecutive Grey Cup, but quarterback Warren Moon set league records with 380 completions, 664 pass attempts, and 5,648 yd passing and led the league in passing efficiency and in touchdown passes, with 31. Moon won the CFL's most outstanding player award over Toronto's Terry Greer, whose 113 pass receptions and 2,003 yd on receptions set CFL records. Kicker Lui Passaglia led the league with 191 points and a record 50.1-yd punting average for the Lions, whose 11–5 record led the Western Division. Winnipeg (9–7), which beat Edmonton (8–8) in the play-offs, produced the most outstanding Canadian player, defensive back Paul Bennett. Hamilton running back Johnny Shepherd was rookie of the year with 1,069 yd rushing, trailing only Ottawa's Skip Walker with 1,431. Ottawa also had the league's most outstanding offensive lineman, guard Rudy Phillips, and most outstanding defensive player, defensive end Greg Marshall.

(KEVIN M. LAMB)

France

A republic of Western Europe, France is bounded by the English Channel, Belgium, Luxembourg, West Germany, Switzerland, Italy, the Mediterranean Sea, Monaco, Spain, Andorra, and the At-

Foreign Aid:
see Economy, World

Foreign Exchange:
see Economy, World

lantic Ocean. Area: 544,000 sq km (210,040 sq mi), including Corsica. Pop. (1983 est.): 54,346,000. Cap. and largest city: Paris (pop., 1982, 2,176,200). Language: French. Religion: predominantly Roman Catholic. President in 1983, François Mitterrand; premier, Pierre Mauroy.

Domestic Affairs. During 1983 mounting economic restraint and the third devaluation of the franc led to acute feelings of discontent in France. These were translated into marked losses for the left in the elections that took place during the year. Municipal elections were held in the spring, in the autumn one-third of the Senate was renewed, and there were also several cantonal by-elections.

The start of the year was marked by industrial unrest, especially in the automotive industry, despite the emphasis on the need for social justice in Pres. François Mitterrand's television broadcast to the French people on January 1. The first round of municipal elections on March 6 indicated a clear swing against the government majority parties (the Socialist Party [PS], the Left Radicals [MRG], the Communist Party [PC], and other left-wing parties), which lost 16 cities of more than 30,000 inhabitants. Of these, the opposition took eight from the Socialist Party and eight from the Communists. According to Ministry of the Interior figures, with a turnout of 78.36%, the opposition held 61.71% of council seats in metropolitan France, as against 38.14% for the majority.

In the second round, despite the loss of 15 more cities, the left-wing majority managed to regain some ground, thanks to increased participation by its voters. Turnout in this second round was 79.7%, with the result that, despite its overall losses, the left managed to hold Marseille and Belfort and to take Châtellerault. Ministry figures for the second round showed a final balance of forces on the mainland of 49.9% for the opposition and 39.54% for the left.

In all, the second round of the elections represented a defeat for the majority and a warning. There had been no actual hardening of the tendency evident in round one, but a continued shift away from the left was evident. As in the first round, this was more obvious in the major cities than in medium-sized towns. The opposition now held 24 of the 36 French cities with more than 100,000 inhabitants (including Paris and Lyon, where it swept to power), representing an increase of 7 cities. The majority, losing Saint-Étienne and Nîmes in the second round after its 7 losses in the first, only controlled 12 of the major cities, though its second-round recovery had limited the extent of the damage. The Communists, under Georges Marchais, continued to suffer spectacular defeats in Languedoc and in their traditional strongholds around Paris.

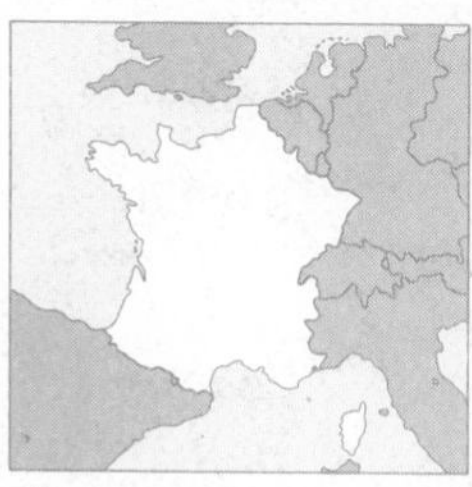

France

Among the leaders of the opposition, Jacques Chirac, reelected for six years as mayor of Paris, confirmed his dominance and that of his party, the Rassemblement pour la République (RPR), which made rather more gains than the Union pour la Démocratie Française (UDF). These results allowed Chirac to stake his claim to the leadership of the opposition against former president Valéry Giscard d'Estaing and former premier Raymond Barre.

Shortly after the second elections, the franc was devalued for the third time in less than two years. The finance ministers of the countries whose currencies were linked in the European Monetary System (EMS) reached agreement on March 21: the French franc was devalued by 2.5%. This was the third EMS revision and the third one in which the franc had been devalued. It resulted in a difference of 8% in favour of the West German currency against the French. Premier Pierre Mauroy immediately stressed that this financial readjustment was only a step toward complete reorganization.

President Mitterrand called on Mauroy to head his third Cabinet, which included the premier, 14 ministers, and a new secretary of state who was to act as spokesman for the government. The Cabinet now consisted of Mauroy (PS), premier; Jacques Delors (PS), economy, finance, and budget; Pierre Bérégovoy (PS), social affairs and national solidarity; Gaston Defferre (PS), interior and decentralization; Charles Fiterman (PC), transport; Robert Badinter (PS), justice; Claude Cheysson (PS), foreign affairs; Charles Hernu (PS), defense; Michel Rocard (PS), agriculture; Laurent Fabius (PS), in-

FRANCE

Education. (1980–81) Primary, pupils 4,621,000, teachers 169,416; secondary, pupils 5,014,000, teachers 280,972; vocational, pupils 799,209, teachers 45,364; higher, students 1,017,775, teaching staff 40,585.

Finance. Monetary unit: franc, with (Sept. 20, 1983) a free rate of Fr 8.06 to U.S. $1 (Fr 12.14 = £1 sterling). Gold and other reserves (June 1983) U.S. $20,780,000,000. Budget (total; 1981 actual): revenue Fr 683.4 billion; expenditure Fr 716.1 billion. Gross domestic product (1982) Fr 3,549,700,000,000. Money supply (April 1983) Fr 854 billion. Cost of living (1975 = 100; June 1983) 226.8.

Foreign Trade. (1982) Imports Fr 758,340,000,000; exports Fr 633,070,000,000. Import sources: EEC 47% (West Germany 17%, Italy 10%, Belgium-Luxembourg 8%, U.K. 6%, The Netherlands 6%); U.S. 8%; Saudi Arabia 6%. Export destinations: EEC 47% (West Germany 14%, Italy 11%, Belgium-Luxembourg 8%, U.K. 7%); U.S. 5%. Main exports: machinery 19%; food 13%; chemicals 13%; motor vehicles 11%; iron and steel 6%. Tourism (1981): visitors 30.5 million; gross receipts U.S. $7,193,000,000.

Transport and Communications. Roads (1982) 802,407 km (including 5,907 km expressways; excluding c. 700,000 km rural roads). Motor vehicles in use (1982): passenger 20.3 million; commercial 2,695,000. Railways: (1981) 34,107 km; traffic (1982) 56,850,000,000 passenger-km, freight 61,199,000,000 net ton-km. Air traffic (1982): 37,846,000,000 passenger-km; freight 2,297,800,000 net ton-km. Navigable inland waterways in regular use (1981) 6,603 km; freight traffic 11,068,000,000 ton-km. Shipping (1982): merchant vessels 100 gross tons and over 1,171; gross tonnage 10,770,880. Telephones (Jan. 1980) 22,212,000. Radio receivers (Dec. 1980) 48 million. Television receivers (Dec. 1980) 19 million.

Agriculture. Production (in 000; metric tons; 1982): wheat 25,342; barley 10,026; oats 1,804; rye 320; corn 9,833; potatoes 6,750; sorghum 259; sugar, raw value c. 4,800; rapeseed 1,171; tomatoes 876; cauliflowers (1981) 481; carrots (1981) 501; apples 3,016; peaches (1981) 480; wine 7,966; tobacco 40; milk 34,500; butter c. 605; cheese c. 1,190; beef and veal c. 1,900; pork c. 1,770; fish catch (1981) c. 768; timber (cu m; 1981) 38,536. Livestock (in 000; Dec. 1981): cattle 23,605; sheep 13,121; pigs 11,859; horses (1980) 317; chickens 186,656.

Industry. Index of production (1975 = 100; 1982) 112. Fuel and power (in 000; 1982): coal (metric tons) 17,054; electricity (kw-hr) 262,813,000; crude oil (metric tons) 1,638; natural gas (cu m) 6,590,000; manufactured gas (cu m; 1980) 4,530,000. Production (in 000; metric tons; 1982): iron ore (30% metal content) 19,392; pig iron 15,131; crude steel 18,415; bauxite 1,671; aluminum 556; lead 163; zinc 268; cement 26,141; cotton yarn 214; cotton fabrics 164; wool yarn 110; man-made fibres 251; sulfuric acid 4,136; petroleum products (1981) 91,328; fertilizers (nutrient content; 1981–82) nitrogenous c. 1,588, phosphate c. 1,300, potash c. 1,726; passenger cars (units) 3,086; commercial vehicles (units) 466. Merchant shipping launched (100 gross tons and over; 1982) 321,000 gross tons.

REBOURS—SIPA PRESS/BLACK STAR

In early May small-business owners and shopkeepers demonstrated in Paris, protesting the government's austerity policies. The protestors clashed with police when they attempted to cross a police line to reach the government's trade and commerce offices.

dustry and research; Alain Savary (PS), education; Edith Cresson (PS), the only woman in the Cabinet, foreign trade and tourism; Roger Quilliot (PS), urban affairs and housing; Michel Crépeau (MRG), commerce and small businesses; Marcel Rigout (PC), professional training; and Max Gallo (PS), secretary of state and government spokesman. A few days later the government was brought to full strength by the addition of 8 delegate ministers, among them Jack Lang (*see* BIOGRAPHIES), delegate minister of culture, who thus did not retain Cabinet rank, and 20 secretaries of state.

This new government imposed a series of austerity measures, including an emergency tax of 1% on all taxable incomes. In addition, there were restraints on budgetary and social expenditure. French tourists going abroad were allowed to take out only Fr 2,000 per adult in any one year (plus Fr 1,000 per child), and there was a campaign to "buy French." On April 1 there was a sharp rise in the cost of public services, with increases of 8% in the price of mainline passenger rail travel, expressway tolls, and gas and electricity charges, as well as varying increases in telephone charges. An agreement with the baking industry fixed the rise in the price of bread at 8% for 1983, and there were to be noticeable increases in the prices of tobacco, cigarettes, alcohol, and gasoline (petrol) as special taxes were levied on these items. On the other hand, the prices of meat and fish were to be more strictly controlled.

This program of increased austerity did not meet with general approval. The unions, especially, expressed their regret that, once more, "the poor were going to pay for the rich." There was only one ray of sunshine in this wintry climate: all workers were to be given the right to retire on full pension at 60. This was hailed as a major achievement by both unions and government, but there remained the question of how to find money to pay for the measure.

In the area of industrial relations, a long and costly conflict in the automobile industry and a strike by medical students, junior hospital doctors, and consultants in the university hospital centres attracted wide support throughout the country. There were signs of militancy among farmers, as well as in the universities during protests over the reform of higher education. Some 20,000 self-employed skilled workers, tradesmen, and owners of small businesses joined a protest march through Paris. Jean Poperen, a member of the PS national secretariat, warned the government of the deterioration in the standing of the left among the general public. In fact, the March municipal elections were followed by 28 cantonal by-elections, in which the majority lost 7 of the 13 cantons that it formerly held. In percentage terms, the loss of votes was considerable.

During the spring parliamentary session 71 bills were passed, as against 52 in 1982, and the government only once had recourse to putting a bill through by decree—for the adoption of its austerity plan. On the whole, however, there was a pause in the government reform program. Both the Chamber of Deputies and the Senate merely strengthened major bills introduced during Mitterrand's term of office. In September the 1984 budget was passed by the Cabinet. It provided for increased taxes on incomes in the middle- and upper-income brackets and an increase in duties on large legacies.

Overall, the elections to the Senate, which involved one-third of the seats in the upper house, confirmed the results of the 1982 cantonal and 1983 municipal elections. The opposition, which already held a majority, was considerably strengthened, emerging with two-thirds of the seats. A few days later there was a minor Cabinet reshuffle as a result of the election of two government ministers to the Senate. Paul Quilès was appointed minister for urban affairs and housing in place of Roger Quilliot, while Jean Gatel was made secretary of state for defense, replacing François Autain.

In October elections were held for trade-union representatives on the management boards of social-security and health-insurance funds. The results were in line with those of other polls. The unions least closely allied to the government gained a majority (53.42% of the vote), while the Confédération Française Démocratique du Travail, which had supported Mitterrand's election, took only 46.55%.

Several municipal elections were annulled because of procedural irregularities: at Dreux, Sarcelles, Antony, Aulnay-sous-Bois, Béziers, and Villeneuve-Saint-Georges, all traditional left-wing strongholds. This provided an opportunity for further gains by the right-wing opposition. In the election at Dreux in September, the National Front, an extreme right-wing party that ran on an openly racist platform, won almost 17% of the vote. (*See* Race Relations.)

The trade balance for September was in the black for the first time, by the sum of Fr 323 million. If this trend continued, the trade deficit would be reduced from Fr 60 billion in 1983 to Fr 15 billion in 1984. However, the number of unemployed remained around two million, and the government was having difficulty controlling inflation. For the first nine months of the year, the inflation rate stood at 7.6%; it was expected to reach 9% for the whole of 1983, as compared with the 8% forecast.

The outlawed Corsican National Liberation Front, which was campaigning for total independence from France, carried out several bomb attacks on mainland France as well as on the island. During the first visit by a French president to the island in five years, Mitterrand repeated his belief that Corsica should remain part of France.

In December the French authorities expelled a number of Iranians, including three diplomats, and accused the Iranian embassy in Paris of coordinating a network of terrorists. The French felt particularly vulnerable because of their support for the Lebanese government. After the December 31 explosions that killed five people in the Marseille railway station and on a passenger train, the Islamic Jihad Organization was among the groups that claimed responsibility for the bombs.

Foreign Affairs. President Mitterrand's foreign policy was still a direct descendant of that pursued by Gen. Charles de Gaulle and his successors, though it included some indication of the president's ambition to play a more visible role in the third world and the Arab countries. Relations with the Maghrib improved, as evidenced by the president's visit to Morocco and Tunisia and the Algerian head of state's visit to France in December 1982—the first since that country gained independence from France. Mitterrand also went to sub-Saharan Africa, visiting Togo, Benin, Gabon, and Cameroon.

Two places demanded the president's particular attention: Chad and Lebanon. In June the war in Chad broke out again and, in accordance with his commitment to the head of the Chad government, Pres. Hissen Habré, Mitterrand sent paratroops and military aid. In an interview with the newspaper *Le Monde*, he maintained that French involvement created the means to counter any renewed offensive, established the climate for a negotiated settlement, and avoided the partition of the country, which might plunge the whole of Africa into an unstable condition.

In Lebanon a cease-fire at the end of September gave rise to hopes of peace, but they were shattered by two terrorist attacks at the end of October. The attacks caused huge loss of life among French and U.S. troops in the multinational force in Beirut and aroused a strong public reaction in France. President Mitterrand paid a lightning visit to Beirut, where he met Pres. Amin Gemayel, and on television he told the French people with solemn conviction that France would remain faithful to its history and its commitments in Lebanon.

The expulsion of 47 Soviet diplomats and residents at the beginning of April on grounds of espionage was an unprecedented move which cleared Mitterrand of any suspicion that his freedom of action might be limited by his alliance with the Communist Party. At the beginning of May the president journeyed to Nepal and to China, where he met the leading figures in the Chinese regime. China was interested in the development of the European Communities (EC) as a stabilizing factor in the West, and the two countries showed equal firmness toward the U.S.S.R., especially in matters of defense. There were discussions concerning the delivery of four French nuclear reactors, as well as major exchanges in the field of technology.

European defense and security were extensively reviewed during talks between President Mitterrand and leaders of various member countries of the EC. Celebrations in Bonn and Paris in January marking the 20th anniversary of the Franco-West German treaty, and later the occasion of the 41st Franco-West German summit meeting, gave Mitterrand the opportunity to stress the importance of the defense of Western Europe and the need for a balance of forces in East and West. The deployment of U.S. medium-range missiles in Europe (though not in France) that began at the end of 1983 was the chief topic of discussion at several meetings of European leaders. In October, during

Forty-seven Soviet diplomats and residents, who were suspected of espionage activities, were expelled from France with their families.

FRANCIS APESTEGUY/LAURENT SOLA—GAMMA/LIAISON

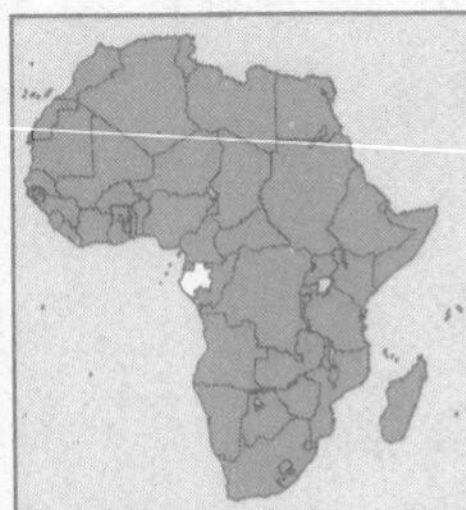
Gabon

The Gambia

an official visit to Belgium, Mitterrand affirmed his continued support for a freeze on nuclear weapons and even for a reduction in such weapons—but not at this "arbitrarily chosen" moment. The current situation was one of "fatal imbalance," with the disequilibrium aggravated by the fact that "pacifism is in the West, while the missiles are in the East." The same theme was taken up at the eighth Franco-British summit in London in October, which brought out a marked similarity in the views of U.K. Prime Minister Margaret Thatcher and President Mitterrand on East-West relations, Soviet policy, and European security.

The members of the EC were no closer to resolving their differences on the financing of the Community budget, though there were several successes in other fields. The agreement reached in May in Brussels on the fixing of agricultural prices for the coming period was followed in October by the successful outcome of a meeting in Luxembourg on a revision of the terms for fruit and vegetables.

During his visit to Lourdes, Pope John Paul II officiated, in the presence of a vast throng, over ceremonies honouring the Virgin Mary and the 125th anniversary of her apparition to Bernadette Soubirous. The pope took advantage of the visit to hold a long talk with President Mitterrand in Tarbes. (JEAN KNECHT)

See also Dependent States.

Gabon

A republic of western equatorial Africa, Gabon is bounded by Equatorial Guinea, Cameroon, the Congo, and the Atlantic Ocean. Area: 267,667 sq km (103,347 sq mi). Pop.: in 1981 estimates varied from 558,000 to 1,409,000; a 1980 official government estimate claimed a population of 1,232,000. Cap. and largest city: Libreville (pop., 1983 est., 350,000). Language: French and Bantu dialects. Religion: traditional tribal beliefs; Christian minority. President in 1983, Omar Bongo; premier, Léon Mébiame.

During his third African tour since taking office, French Pres. François Mitterrand paid a two-day visit to Gabon on Jan. 17–18, 1983, hoping to restore relations that had suffered as a result of the activities of political factions in both countries. In Libreville activists had attempted to antagonize the two heads of state so as to persuade Pres. Omar Bongo to seek a rapprochement with the U.S., while in Paris the maximalist wing of the Socialist Party had openly supported President Bongo's opponents.

Despite the efforts of the two heads of state to defuse the situation, it deteriorated further in February, when a French television program criticized Gabon, and again in October with the publication in Paris of a book (Pierre Péan's *Affaires africaines*) that purported to reveal details of President Bongo's private life.

On the domestic front, strikes by teachers and health workers in March resulted in clashes with the police. Also in March, ministerial changes increased military participation in the government to three. In October the Economic Community of the States of Central Africa, first proposed by President Bongo in 1981, was inaugurated in Libreville. It comprised Burundi, Cameroon, the Central African Republic, Chad, the Congo, Equatorial Guinea, Gabon, São Tomé and Príncipe, Rwanda, and Zaire. (PHILIPPE DECRAENE)

GABON

Education. (1980–81) Primary, pupils 155,081, teachers 3,441; secondary, pupils 22,005, teachers 1,088; vocational, pupils 3,465, teachers 266; teacher training (1979–80), students 2,975, teachers 217; higher, students 3,878, teaching staff 231.

Finance. Monetary unit: CFA franc, with (Sept. 20, 1983) a parity of CFA Fr 50 to the French franc (free rate of CFA Fr 403 = U.S. $1; CFA Fr 607 = £1 sterling). Budget (1982 est.) balanced at CFA Fr 453.5 billion.

Foreign Trade. Imports (1981) CFA Fr 226.8 billion; exports (1980) CFA Fr 459.1 billion. Import sources: France 53%; U.S. 14%; Japan 7%; West Germany 6%. Export destinations (1978): France 25%; U.S. 20%; Argentina 11%; Brazil 8%; Gibraltar 8%; West Germany 6%; Chile 5%. Main exports (1978): crude oil 72%; manganese ore 10%; uranium and thorium ores 8%; timber 8%.

Transport and Communications. Roads (1982) 7,393 km. Motor vehicles in use (1982): passenger 16,040; commercial 10,200. Railways (1981) 224 km. Air traffic (1982): c. 430 million passenger-km; freight c. 28.3 million net ton-km. Telephones (Jan. 1981) 11,600. Radio receivers (Dec. 1980) 96,000. Television receivers (Dec. 1980) 9,000.

Agriculture. Production (in 000; metric tons; 1981): cassava c. 100; corn c. 10; peanuts c. 7; bananas c. 8; plantains c. 63; palm oil c. 2; cocoa c. 4; timber (cu m) c. 2,485. Livestock (in 000; 1981): cattle c. 4; pigs c. 7; sheep c. 100; goats c. 90.

Industry. Production (in 000; metric tons; 1982): crude oil 7,361; natural gas (cu m) 150,000; uranium (metal content: 1981) 1.1; manganese ore (metal content; 1981) 1,015; petroleum products (1981) 1,240; electricity (kw-hr; 1981) 450,000.

French-Canadian Literature:
see Literature

French Guiana:
see Dependent States

French Literature:
see Literature

Friends, Religious Society of:
see Religion

Fuel and Power:
see Energy

Furniture Industry:
see Industrial Review

Furs:
see Industrial Review

Gambia, The

A small republic and member of the Commonwealth, The Gambia extends from the Atlantic Ocean along the lower Gambia River in West Africa and is surrounded by Senegal. Area: 10,690 sq km (4,127 sq mi). Pop. (1983 prelim.): 695,900, including (1978 est.) Malinke 44%; Fulani 17.5%; Wolof 12.3%; Dyola 7%; Soninke 7%; other 12.2%. Cap. and largest city: Banjul (pop., 1983 prelim., 44,500). Language: English (official), Malinke, Fulani, and Wolof. Religion: predominantly Muslim. President in 1983, Sir Dawda Jawara.

During 1983 The Gambia's major preoccupation was to expedite formation of the Senegambia con-

GAMBIA, THE

Education. (1981–82) Primary, pupils 48,949, teachers 2,123; secondary, pupils 10,017, teachers 584; vocational, pupils 405, teachers 62; teacher training, students 291, teachers 38.

Finance. Monetary unit: dalasi, with (Sept. 20, 1983) a free rate of 2.66 dalasis to U.S. $1 (par value of 4 dalasis = £1 sterling). Budget (1982–83 est.): revenue 123 million dalasis; expenditure 131 million dalasis.

Foreign Trade. (1982) Imports 220.5 million dalasis; exports 98,510,000 dalasis. Import sources (1979–80): U.K. 25%; China 16%; France 9%; The Netherlands 8%; West Germany 7%. Export destinations (1979–80): The Netherlands 24%; U.K. 18%; Italy 16%; Belgium-Luxembourg 7%; Switzerland 6%; France 5%. Main exports (1979–80): peanuts and byproducts 67%; fish 8%.

federation, first announced in February 1982. The confederation's Council of Ministers, set up in November 1982, had six Gambian and seven Senegalese members. The merger was taking place slowly, with each move having to be approved by the assemblies of both countries. Protocols relating to telecommunications and transport were agreed on in July.

Senegalese troops had remained in The Gambia to guard strategic positions since the 1981 coup attempt. In August the government released 51 people who had been held on suspicion of involvement in the plot.

The 1982-83 peanut (groundnut) crop was expected to exceed 120,000 metric tons, the largest since 1978–79. Tourism—now the fastest growing sector of the economy—also did well. Following Pres. Sir Dawda Jawara's visit to France in February, there were indications that trade might be redirected toward France and away from Britain. The Gambia and Nigeria entered into an economic, scientific, and technical agreement in June.

(GUY ARNOLD)

Gambling

Casino gambling flourished in Atlantic City, N.J., during 1983, and some analysts predicted that revenues from the East Coast resort would surpass those from Las Vegas, Nev., in 1984 and remain ahead in the future. An indication of the prosperity enjoyed by the casino owners was the planned expansion of many of their facilities. Resorts International, owner of one of the most profitable casinos, broke ground in October for a project that would include a 1,000-room casino hotel, a large exhibit hall, and renovation of the historic Steel Pier. New casino hotels were also to be built by New York developer Donald Trump, Hilton Hotels, Showboat, Inc., and the Golden Nugget.

Two court cases in 1983 involved gambling at Atlantic City. In one, a New Jersey appeals court ruled that Playboy Enterprises, Inc. and its chairman, Hugh Hefner, could not obtain a state casino license because of Hefner's role in a 1960 bribery case and his alleged knowledge of reputed illegal conduct at Playboy gambling halls in the U.K. In the other case a U.S. court of appeals ruled that New Jersey cannot regulate labour unions whose members work in Atlantic City casinos. The state had been trying to prevent the infiltration of organized crime into the leadership of the unions.

Another major court case dealt with gambling in Las Vegas. In October a federal grand jury indicted 15 men, who were described by authorities as leaders of organized crime in the Midwest, for using their influence to obtain loans from Teamsters union pension funds and then using the money to become secret owners of Las Vegas casinos. The men were also charged with skimming—removing large portions of the profits from the casinos before declaring them so that they would not be subject to taxes.

Lotteries continued to attract customers in the states where they were authorized. Especially profitable was the Lotto game in Pennsylvania, where gross sales in October exceeded $4 billion. The profits were distributed to a fund that provided aid to the elderly.

In Britain the aftermath of the previous year's police raids on the Playboy Group, the Knightsbridge Sporting Club, and the Olympic Casino resulted in several changes of ownership, and the number of operating casinos in London fell from 21 to 16. However, in early November John Aspinall's Knightsbridge casino offered 15% of its shares to the public, resulting in a massive oversubscription totaling £500 million. This house alone generated £80 million worth of turnover annually, and a second venture was planned for the spring of 1984, suggesting the beginning of an upturn in the fortunes of casino gambling.

Also as a result of the 1982 police raids, the British Casino Association introduced much stricter controls on "scrip," more commonly known as "house" checks. In 1982 an estimated £1,007 million was staked in Britain's casinos, an increase of

WIDE WORLD

Tom McEvoy, in cowboy hat, won a first prize worth more than $40,000 in the final round of the Dublin International Poker Tournament. He defeated Michael Anderson, right, wearing glasses.

8% over the previous year. The £77 million rise was mainly due to a considerable upsurge in business in July and August, which was in turn caused by an influx of tourists.

There were further closings of licensed betting shops in 1983. The number of such shops in the U.K. had dropped by 25% in the past ten years and the number of permit-holding bookmakers by 16%. The four major bookmakers, Ladbrokes, William Hill, Mecca, and Coral, again increased their share of the betting office population.

(DAVID R. CALHOUN; ROBERT M. POOLE)

See also Equestrian Sports.

Games and Toys

In 1983 the games and toys industry in most parts of the world continued to be influenced by the growth in popularity of video games and home computers. In the U.S. video games, which accounted for 19% of total sales in 1981, rose to 31% of sales of games and toys in 1982. But by mid-1983 the leading U.S. video game and home computer manufacturers, Atari, Texas Instruments, and Mattel, announced large staff reductions because of disappointing sales of those products. Contributing factors were intense and growing competition and disappointingly large retail inventories. Worldwide, however, the expansion of demand for these electronic products continued, and more manufacturers entered the field. Consumer saturation appeared to be a long way off, and there was a growing realization that the first "big toy" for many six- to seven-year-old children during the next few years might be a home computer. This would be followed by software purchases for the basic unit. Much of the impetus stemmed from the desire of parents for their children to be "computer literate."

In July the video game business received a boost with the introduction in game arcades of Dragon's Lair. It was the first game to feature laser videodisc technology, which provided real animation, stereophonic sound, and a pattern of action that was not preset. The game quickly became popular and was followed by Astron Belt and Mach 3.

"Cabbage Patch Kids" were in short supply in the U.S. as Christmas approached. Edward Pennington, a postman from Kansas City, Missouri, flew to London to buy one for his five-year-old daughter and came home with five dolls.

WIDE WORLD

The rapid growth of electronic home entertainment products inevitably continued to cause shrinkage in demand for traditional toys in most of the world's markets. It was estimated that in Europe the decline since 1980 was about 17% in real terms. The sectors most affected were model railway products and car racing sets, radio-controlled toys, and board games. Maintaining their share of the markets in Europe were preschool toys, dolls, and soft toys, and in the U.S. unit sales of preschool items advanced by 20% in the first quarter of 1983.

The sensation of the 1983 Christmas season in the U.S. was, in fact, a soft doll. Coleco's "Cabbage Patch Kids," each slightly different and sold with a birth certificate and adoption papers, proved so popular that stocks ran short. Lines formed at stores rumoured to have received shipments, and there were reports of free-for-alls among distraught parents. Teddy bears and their relatives were other Christmas favourites; demand for the "Care Bears" character animals also outran supply.

In 1983 more leading U.S. and European toy manufacturers moved their production facilities to the Far East and other low-cost areas in order to save on taxes and labour expenses. China, the Philippines, Macao, Haiti, and Mexico were selected as suitable alternatives by some, while others, such as Atari, moved production to the longer established toymaking regions of Hong Kong and Taiwan. Bendy Toys, which had been made in England since the company began to operate shortly after World War II, decided to manufacture in Malaysia. A number of leading Japanese toy producers established plants in Singapore.

This movement of production facilities contributed largely to the increase of toy imports into the U.S. and Europe. More than 25% of the toys currently sold in the U.S. were imported, and in the U.K., which a few years earlier had been a growing area of toy manufacture, imports rose from £120 million in 1979 to £174 million in 1982 while exports declined from £115 million to £87 million. A similar trend was experienced in the other main European toy-producing countries, France and West Germany.

Following the British Toy and Hobby Fair in February, one of the few remaining publicly owned British toy groups, Berwick Timpo, went into receivership. The group's losses for 1982 totaled £2.3 million. In October, Mettoy, the largest remaining manufacturer, also went into receivership. Best known for its Corgi brand die-cast toys, Mettoy lost £3.6 million in 1982.

Meeting in Tokyo during the summer, the International Committee of Toy Industries (ICTI) agreed to take further steps to improve statistical exchanges between member countries. ICTI carried out a review of advertising as it affects children and, having noted the work on this subject by the International Chamber of Commerce (ICC) in Paris, decided to approve and adopt the ICC international guidelines. ICTI also considered in detail current developments in toy safety as part of a continuous program "dedicated to the improvement of existing toy safety standards."

With so much emphasis on electronic products, it was not surprising that few real novelties came into the toy field in 1983. Much of what was new was linked to the characters of films and television programs. *Star Wars* merchandise received a boost from the release of *Return of the Jedi,* the third film in the *Star Wars* series. Trivial Pursuit, a board game based on knowledge of trivia that was first introduced in Canada in 1982, enjoyed strong sales in the U.S. (THEODORE V. THOMAS)

See also Industrial Review: *Advertising.*

Gardening

Despite a weather pattern of drenching spring rains followed by serious summer drought, the 1983 garden season in the U.S. was not substantially hurt. A survey conducted by the American Association of Nurserymen revealed that 44% of the member firms purchased more living plants for spring sales than in previous years. With increased emphasis on a fall as well as a spring planting season, these same firms reported that fewer plants would have to be carried over the winter. Plants ranking high in popularity included impatiens, vinca, petunias, zinnias, and marigolds. The upswing in housing starts brought a slight increase in new landscaping projects, although the major growth area for landscape contractors was in the renovation of existing landscapes.

Industry data showed a continued increase in the sales and breeding of new geraniums. Other popular potted plants included poinsettias, the all-time winner, followed by chrysanthemums, Easter lilies, and azaleas. Hydrangeas were in decline. Of the more exotic pot plants, Reiger begonias, kalanchoes, Persian violets, Cape primroses, and cacti and succulents were gaining favour.

Interior plantscaping had grown into a specialized industry as corporations and institutions sought professional guidance in the landscaping of malls, office complexes, and building lobbies. In response to highly favourable public reaction, many of these interior spaces were kept open on weekends for enjoyment and often for cultural events. Continued interest in home vegetable gardening reflected the stagnant national economy. However, the National Association for Gardening/Gallup Organization did note a drop of four percentage points in the number of households (36 million) that planted vegetable gardens in 1982. Nevertheless, the survey confirmed that vegetable and flower gardening ranked as the number one outdoor leisure activity for Americans. Among all leisure activities gardening ranked sixth, behind TV watching, music, reading, travel, and the movies.

In the continuing battle between home gardeners and insects and plant diseases, there was heightened interest in control without chemical pesticides, either through integrated pest management (IPM), using trap crops, home remedy kitch-

JIM WILSON/THE NEW YORK TIMES

A commercial produce grower set up a greenhouse beside a New York City power plant. Excess heat from the plant is used to grow vegetables hydroponically. Christopher Tontillo (left) and Fred Harned are shown under a heat-distributing blower unit. The gardening concern buys the heat from the utility at less than half the ordinary cost.

en sprays, and introduced predator species, or through wise use of nonpolluting materials such as soap sprays. There was a definite trend toward the planting of native species of wildflowers and shrubs.

In Europe the main gardening event was the International Garden Exhibition in Munich, West Germany, held from May to October. Started soon after World War II, with the object of revitalizing devastated urban areas, these exhibitions now emphasized rehabilitation of former industrial areas. More than ten million visitors attended the Munich event.

Visitors to gardens in Britain increased by 9% in 1982, contrary to the trend for visitors to stately homes. A study of 32 gardens in Scotland helped to clarify the criteria for judging the worth of different types of landscapes and gardens. In The Netherlands the 17th-century garden of the Royal Palace near Apeldoorn was being restored in its historical style and was to be reopened to the public in 1984. In Britain the National Council for the Conservation of Plants and Gardens continued its efforts to find, propagate, and distribute worthwhile garden plants that were in danger of being lost, a situation often aggravated by the industrialization of modern nursery operations. The first step was the establishment of national reference collections of garden plants, usually planted in institutional gardens but sometimes in the care of individual gardeners. About 160 of these collections had already been established.

In the season's trials of new seedlings in the Royal National Rose Society's garden at St. Albans, Hertfordshire, 176 rose varieties were grown. Two gold medals were awarded, both to yellow hybrid tea roses raised by Dicksons of Northern Ireland, but neither had as yet been named. New varieties of fruits coming into garden centres and nurseries included Ben Sarek, a black currant from Scotland, and Invicta, a mildew-resistant gooseberry. Two spineless raspberries,

Glen Prosen and Glen Moy, were released. Beth, a new September pear, was particularly useful for amateur growers. Even newer was Jupiter, an apple seedling from the famous Cox's Orange Pippin that produces a heavier crop than its parent.

Compost shredders were becoming more popular in Europe as motorized models came on the market. Peat and composted bark were also being used more frequently as weed-suppressing mulches. (JOAN LEE FAUST; ELSPETH NAPIER)

See also Agriculture and Food Supplies; Environment; Life Sciences.
[355.C.2–3; 731.B.1]

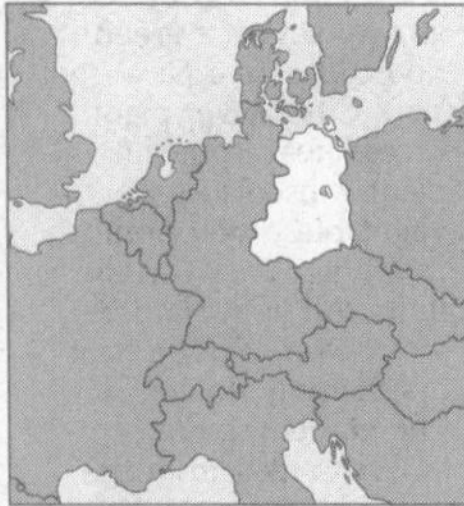
German Democratic Republic

German Democratic Republic

A country of central Europe, Germany was partitioned after World War II into the Federal Republic of Germany (Bundesrepublik Deutschland; West Germany) and the German Democratic Republic (Deutsche Demokratische Republik; East Germany), with a special provisional regime for Berlin. East Germany is bordered by the Baltic Sea, Poland, Czechoslovakia, and West Germany. Area: 108,333 sq km (41,827 sq mi). Pop. (1982 est.): 16,732,500. Cap. and largest city: East Berlin (pop., 1982 est., 1,165,700). Language: German. Religion (1969 est.): Protestant 80%; Roman Catholic 10%. General secretary of the Socialist Unity (Communist) Party and chairman of the Council of State in 1983, Erich Honecker; chairman of the Council of Ministers (premier), Willi Stoph.

Despite heightening tension between the power blocs over nuclear-missile deployment, East and West Germany took pains to protect and cultivate their relationship during 1983. Indeed there was a flurry of activity between the two nations, though to East German leader Erich Honecker the phrase "intra-German relations" was apparently a synonym for West German economic assistance. He was optimistic that West Germany's *Deutschlandpolitik*, aimed at increasing contacts between the people of a divided nation, would prove to be a generous source of income.

Honecker claimed in January that East Germany had achieved strong economic growth in 1982. But this fact may have escaped the people of East Germany, many of whom experienced one of their most frugal years since the period immediately following World War II. There were frequent shortages of basic foods. A frantic export drive was successful, but imports were cut back drastically, and East German life became a good deal grayer. However, Honecker was happy to have West German Chancellor Helmut Kohl make it a little brighter, as long as West Germany acknowledged that there were two German sovereign states, each belonging to different alliances.

In April Honecker canceled his projected visit to West Germany on the grounds that the climate between the two nations had deteriorated since the death earlier that month of a West German citizen who was being questioned at an East German border post—in this and a similar subsequent incident, the cause of death was found to be a heart attack. The East Germans explained that West German press comment on the two episodes amounted to a virulent campaign against East Germany and thus was not conducive to a successful summit. It seemed inconceivable that Honecker would have abandoned the trip without seeking the advice of the Soviet government. In counseling a cancellation the Soviets were more likely to have been influenced by the fact that Honecker's visit was scheduled for September, which was uncomfortably close to the deadline for the deployment of the first U.S. Pershing II nuclear missiles in West Germany.

Soviet Pres. Yury Andropov received Honecker in Moscow in May and used the occasion to warn the West Germans of the grave consequences of allowing deployment of the U.S. missiles on their territory. But in the meantime neither German government sought to make a delicate situation worse. On the contrary, the East Germans concentrated their criticisms on sections of the West German press and on Franz-Josef Strauss, the Christian Social Union premier of the Bavarian state assembly, who was demanding a tougher approach to *Deutschlandpolitik*, rather than on Chancellor Kohl and his government. The East Germans were furious that Strauss had accused them of murdering the first of the two heart-attack victims, basing his verdict on injuries to the man's head. In fact, a West German prosecutor later accepted medical findings that the cause of death was natural.

There was great surprise in June when the West German government underwrote—without attaching political strings—a DM 1 billion bank credit to East Germany. It was one of the largest loans that West German banks had ever granted to East Germany. It was all the more surprising that Strauss had put his considerable weight behind the deal. Strauss's role, though heavily criticized at home, won him a long and cordial meeting with Honecker. Subsequently, East Germany agreed to

"Away with the NATO Missiles Decision!" read an outsized petition signed by demonstrators at an East German "Peace Rally of the Youth of Socialist Countries."

WIDE WORLD

Garment Industry: *see* Fashion and Dress

Gas Industry: *see* Energy

Gemstones: *see* Industrial Review

Genetics: *see* Life Sciences

Geochemistry: *see* Earth Sciences

Geology: *see* Earth Sciences

Geophysics: *see* Earth Sciences

German Literature: *see* Literature

GERMAN DEMOCRATIC REPUBLIC

Education. (1981–82) Primary and secondary, pupils 2,212,715, teachers 170,115; vocational, pupils 448,386, teachers 16,553; teacher training, students 26,106; higher, students 277,938, teaching staff (1979–80) 37,789.

Finance. Monetary unit: Mark of Deutsche Demokratische Republik, with (Sept. 20, 1983) a free rate of M 2.67 to U.S. $1 (M 4.01 = £1 sterling). Budget (1980 est.): revenue M 160,652,000,000; expenditure M 160,283,000,000. Net material product (at 1980 prices; 1981) M 196.1 billion.

Foreign Trade. (1981) Imports M 66,596,000,000; exports M 65,530,000,000. Import sources: U.S.S.R. c. 38%; West Germany c. 8%; Czechoslovakia c. 7%; Poland c. 5%; Hungary c. 5%. Export destinations: U.S.S.R. c. 37%; West Germany c. 9%; Czechoslovakia c. 8%; Poland c. 6%; Hungary c. 5%. Main exports (1975): machinery 37%; transport equipment 12% (ships 5%); chemicals; textiles.

Transport and Communications. Roads (1980) c. 119,000 km (including 1,720 km autobahns in 1981). Motor vehicles in use (1981): passenger 2,811,976; commercial 237,311. Railways: (1981) 14,233 km (including 1,808 km electrified); traffic (1982) 24,785,000,000 passenger-km, freight 53,663,000,000 net ton-km. Air traffic (1980): 2,053,000,000 passenger-km; freight 67 million net ton-km. Navigable inland waterways in regular use (1981) 2,302 km; goods traffic 2,359,000,000 ton-km. Shipping (1982): merchant vessels 100 gross tons and over 419; gross tonnage 1,438,588. Telephones (Jan. 1981) 3,156,700. Radio licenses (Dec. 1980) 6,409,000. Television licenses (Dec. 1980) 5,731,000.

Agriculture. Production (in 000; metric tons; 1982): wheat c. 2,947; barley c. 4,049; rye c. 2,500; cabbages (1981) c. 337; rapeseed c. 312; pork c. 1,320; beef and veal c. 390; fish catch (1981) 241. Livestock (in 000; Dec. 1981): cattle 5,749; sheep 2,169; pigs 12,869; goats 23; poultry 54,392.

Industry. Index of production (1975 = 100; 1982) 138. Production (in 000; metric tons; 1982): cement 11,721; lignite (1981) 267,000; electricity (kw-hr; 1981) 100,720,000; pig iron 2,149; crude steel 7,169; sulfuric acid 920; petroleum products (1981) 19,146; fertilizers (nutrient content; 1981) nitrogenous 967, phosphate 360, potash 3,460; synthetic rubber 155; man-made fibres (1980) 355; plastics and resins (1980) 859; passenger cars (units) 183; commercial vehicles (units) 39.

modify its policy of requiring Western visitors to exchange a minimum sum of money when staying in East Germany.

At least 20 members of the unofficial East German peace movement were expelled to West Germany during the year. Most of them were from the university town of Jena and belonged to an organization that for many years had been a thorn in the flesh of the regime. The government approved peace demonstrations as long as they were held under the official banner, which protested only against NATO's rearmament; the Jena group, however, originally about 60 strong and essentially pacifist, had been campaigning against nuclear weapons in both East and West. The authorities responded for a time with a mixture of harshness and grudging tolerance. Though some members of the group were sent to prison, others were occasionally allowed to unfurl their banners at official peace rallies, though they were usually torn down after a time by party loyalists. The wave of expulsions was the first since 1976.

East Germany celebrated the 500th anniversary of the birth of Martin Luther, the most famous German dissident of all. Honecker, a convinced Marxist, headed the National Luther Committee which prepared Luther Jubilee Year: classic Luther sites were restored at great expense, biographies were published, and exhibitions were staged. Many aspects of Luther's personality were ideally suited to East Germany's understanding of itself as the true heir to German history and culture. Luther's extolling of hard work, obedience to the state, military service in defense of peace—all this was music to the ears of the East German Politburo. The Protestant Church leadership consented to join the state committee only as observers. World religious leaders joined the East German Protestant Church at a service at Luther's birthplace of Eisleben, south of Berlin. (NORMAN CROSSLAND)

Germany, Federal Republic of

A country of central Europe, Germany was partitioned after World War II into the Federal Republic of Germany (Bundesrepublik Deutschland; West Germany) and the German Democratic Republic (Deutsche Demokratische Republik; East Germany), with a special provisional regime for Berlin. West Germany is bordered by Denmark, The Netherlands, Belgium, Luxembourg, France, Switzerland, Austria, Czechoslovakia, East Germany, and the North Sea. Area: 248,687 sq km (96,019 sq mi). Pop. (1983 est.): 61,469,500. Provisional cap.: Bonn (pop., 1982 est., 291,500). Largest city: Hamburg (pop., 1982 est., 1,637,100). (West Berlin, which is an enclave within East Germany, had a population of 1,888,700 in 1982.) Language: German. Religion (1970): Protestant 49%; Roman Catholic 44.6%; Jewish 0.05%. President in 1983, Karl Carstens; chancellor, Helmut Kohl.

Federal elections were held in West Germany on March 6, 1983, some 18 months early, to resolve the situation caused by the breakup in September 1982 of the centre-left coalition of Social Democrats and Free Democrats. Helmut Kohl, the Christian Democrat leader who had succeeded the Social Democrat Helmut Schmidt as federal chancellor after a vote of no confidence in the Bundestag, was decisively confirmed in office. Kohl's main task was to combat the effects of the economic recession. He also had to contend with growing opposition to the deployment of U.S. intermediate-range nuclear missiles in Europe.

Domestic Affairs. After five months in office, Kohl led the Christian Democratic Union (CDU) to a resounding electoral victory. His party and its Bavarian wing, the Christian Social Union (CSU), polled 38.2 and 10.6%, respectively, giving them 48.8% of the total vote, compared with 44.5% at the previous federal election in 1980. Their liberal coalition partner, the Free Democratic Party (FDP), whose popularity had waned since its defection from the Schmidt government, polled 6.9%, while the Green Party, by polling 5.6%, succeeded in winning seats in the Bundestag for the first time. The Social Democratic Party (SPD) received 38.2%, its lowest share since 1961. The result was a 58-seat majority for Kohl's centre-right coalition. (For tabulated results, *see* POLITICAL PARTIES.)

In the campaign Kohl used arguments similar to those that had won former chancellor Konrad Adenauer an absolute majority 26 years earlier. Hard hit by recession, the West Germans voted for the economic upturn promised by Kohl's government. In doing so, they also expressed consent to further

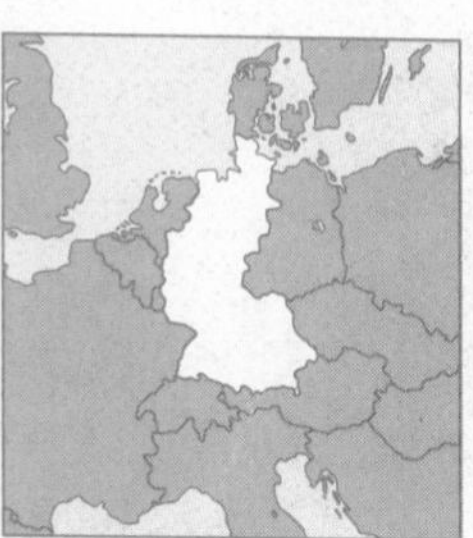
Federal Republic of Germany

belt-tightening and support for the Western alliance and for a no-nonsense attitude toward the U.S.S.R. However, both West Germany and the world had moved on since the 1950s, as events in Bonn clearly demonstrated. The political establishment was shaken by the arrival of the new Green force in the federal parliament—the Green Party won 27 seats—and reacted to it somewhat in the manner of aristocratic pedigree competitors at a superior dog show responding to mongrel intruders.

Some Greens favoured at least a loose collaboration with the sadly depleted Social Democrats, and some left-wing Social Democrats wanted to join the Greens in their fight against missiles. The SPD's candidate for chancellor, Hans-Jochen Vogel (*see* BIOGRAPHIES), had swung the party on a leftish course in the hope of attracting Green voters, though in the closing stages of the campaign it began to appear that he had realized his mistake. He was unclear on the missiles issue, and he never completely clarified the question of the SPD's parliamentary cooperation with the Greens. The architect of Vogel's strategy was Willy Brandt, the SPD chairman, who claimed to have detected a majority of voters to the left of the Christian Democrats.

What seemed to frighten voters most was the spectre of a red-green coalition dominated by Social Democrats like Egon Bahr, for whom *Ostpolitik*—improving relations with the Communist bloc—appeared to take precedence over West Germany's commitment to the Western alliance, so they voted in droves for the safe if unexciting alternative. Kohl's success was overwhelming. Research institutes found that 1.5 million people who in 1980 had voted for the SPD, or perhaps for Schmidt, supported the CDU-CSU in 1983. Even in North Rhine-Westphalia, which included the Ruhr industrial area, the CDU became the strongest party. Moreover, Alois Mertes, the CDU minister of state in the Foreign Ministry, polled more than 69% of direct votes in his constituency of Bitburg, which was earmarked for a nuclear-missile base. The Social Democrats managed to attract

UPI

Helmut Kohl told the West German Bundestag that he accepted reelection as chancellor after leading his party to a decisive victory. The Green Party, led by Petra Kelly (left) and Marieluise Beck-Oberdorf, won representation in the Bundestag for the first time.

support from 37% of the first-time voters, but 32% voted for the CDU-CSU. Some 23% of young voters backed the Greens, and the party also gained support from bourgeois environmentalists and many people who wished a plague on all the "established" parties.

Not since the 1950s had West German voters been faced with such clear options. Thirty years earlier the argument was about rearmament, NATO membership, and Germany's place in the world. Although the issues in 1983 were not quite of such magnitude, there were striking similarities between the political debates and the positions adopted by the main political parties in both elections. Voters were able to choose between a coalition that advocated unswerving loyalty to the Atlantic alliance and a Social Democratic Party that increasingly questioned some fundamental assumptions of West German foreign policy.

As he set about constructing a new government and drafting its program, Kohl discovered that his Bavarian political relatives, the CSU, were much more tiresome than his FDP associates. The CSU, led by Franz-Josef Strauss, premier of the Bavarian state assembly, firmly reminded the chancellor of the role it had played in the CDU's election victory. Although the CSU fielded candidates only within Bavaria, it received a greater share of the vote than the FDP. Before the coalition bargaining started, the CSU made known its "natural and unanimous conviction" that Strauss, as chairman of the second-largest coalition party, had a claim to "cooperate and exercise joint responsibility" in the federal Cabinet. His duties, it was added, should be appropriate to the weight of the party and to Strauss's 35 years of service in federal politics.

Strauss's first choice was to be foreign minister and vice-chancellor, though he would have been glad to accept the Finance Ministry. Neither post was available, and Strauss was not included in the new Cabinet. The retention of the Foreign Ministry by Free Democrat leader Hans-Dietrich Genscher was virtually a condition of the FDP's continued membership in the coalition. Nor could Gerhard Stoltenberg be budged from the Finance Ministry; a Christian Democrat, he had been persuaded to give up the premiership of Schleswig-Holstein in 1982 to go to Bonn to assist Kohl. However, the CSU was given five posts in the new Cabinet instead of four, thus achieving its strongest presence since the chancellorship of Ludwig Erhard in the mid-1960s. The FDP had to be content with three posts.

The new government fulfilled its promise to change the course of policy by prescribing a stiff dose of law and order. It was dispensed by Friedrich Zimmermann, a right-wing CDU member who had become minister of the interior in 1982 in Kohl's most controversial appointment. He set about the task of keeping down the foreign population, which numbered more than 4.6 million; of sharpening the law on demonstrations; and of equipping the state generally with the means to keep a closer watch on its citizens. A scheme was introduced offering a modest financial handshake to tempt certain categories of foreigners from countries that were not members of the European Communities (EC) to return home. Zimmermann also planned to reduce the age limit for the entry of minors from non-EC countries from 16 to 6. His argument was that young children would have a better chance of becoming integrated into West German society than older ones, who arrived without a word of German and, in many cases, without educational qualifications. (*See* RACE RELATIONS.) In December Zimmermann cracked down on the extreme right when he banned the Action Front of National Socialists, one of the most active neo-Nazi groups in the country.

A government bill to tighten the demonstration law provided for the arrest not only of violent demonstrators but also of passive ones who refused to leave a demonstration that had become violent. In Zimmermann's words, "If the police say to a demonstrator, 'Please go away,' and he doesn't do so, he is not a normal citizen." It was intended that the bill should become law early in 1984, after the wave of demonstrations in the fall against nuclear-missile deployment, but the minister hoped that the mere declaration of intent would have a sobering effect. It was also agreed that a new plastic, forgery-proof identity card that could be read by computers should be introduced in 1984. The plan for a new identity card, hatched in 1976 at the height of the terrorist campaign, was ostensibly revived to assist the police in combating crime.

The West Germans were asked to tighten their belts once again to assist the promised economic recovery. The government approved a budget for 1984 in which a saving of DM 6.5 billion ($2.6 billion) was made, most of it in social-welfare spending and public-sector pay. In recent years, state borrowing had been increasing at a rapid rate, the result of falling tax revenues and bigger social-welfare bills in a time of recession. There was little sign of a lasting recovery, certainly not of the kind that would help solve the unemployment problem, the country's biggest domestic dilemma. The unemployment total was expected to reach about 2.3 million by the end of the year. The budget provided for a slight reduction in unemployment benefit for recipients without children and a temporary pay freeze for public-sector employees.

Demonstrations by the peace movement against the deployment of U.S. nuclear missiles reached a climax in the fall. An "action" week in October involved a blockade of several bases. Between Stuttgart and Neu-Ulm some 200,000 people formed a human chain 108 km (67 mi) in length, and in Bonn another chain linked the embassies of the five major nuclear powers—the U.S., the U.S.S.R., the U.K., France, and China. A rally in Bonn, attended by 200,000 people, was addressed by Brandt, who expressed "bitter disappointment" that no political will for agreement had been shown at the intermediate nuclear force (INF) talks between the U.S.S.R. and the U.S. in Geneva. Brandt's participation in the rally was criticized by the government, which claimed that the Social Democrats had finally abandoned a common security policy. On November 23, the day after the Bundestag voted decisively in favour of deployment, the first parts of the Pershing II missiles began to arrive in West Germany, and protests of a more violent nature took place in mid-December. By the end of the year nine of the missiles were reported to be operational.

In December Economics Minister Otto Lambsdorff was charged with having accepted bribes from the Flick holding concern in payment for influencing tax decisions in the company's favour. An opposition move to unseat him was unsuccessful.

In May the scandal of the "Hitler diaries" broke. The magazine *Stern,* which had been publishing the diaries, finally agreed that they were forgeries after scientific tests showed they had been written after World War II. (*See* PUBLISHING: *Sidebar*.)

Foreign Affairs. The Soviet government interfered in the federal election campaign with an unprecedented lack of subtlety. Thanks to the Soviets, the campaign was dubbed the "missiles election" and, apart from choosing the central issue, the Soviet leadership came out unequivocally in favour of a Social Democrat victory. Soviet Pres. Yury Andropov expressed his preference for the Social Democrats during a meeting with Vogel in

GERMANY, FEDERAL REPUBLIC OF

Education. (1982–83) Primary, pupils 4,820,200, teachers 286,500; secondary, pupils 3,597,000, teachers 215,400; vocational, pupils 2,701,300, teachers 84,600; higher, students 1,184,325, teaching staff (1981–82) 129,781; teachers college, students 18,796.

Finance. Monetary unit: Deutsche Mark, with (Sept. 20, 1983) a free rate of DM 2.67 to U.S. $1 (DM 4.01 = £1 sterling). Gold and other reserves (June 1983) U.S. $47,460,000,000. Budget (federal; 1982 actual): revenue DM 222.6 billion; expenditure DM 258.8 billion. Gross national product (1982) DM 1,599,000,000,000. Money supply (June 1983) DM 266.7 billion. Cost of living (1975 = 100; June 1983) 139.9.

Foreign Trade. (1982) Imports DM 376,580,000,000; exports DM 427,770,000,000. Import sources: EEC 48% (The Netherlands 12%, France 11%, Italy 8%, U.K. 7%, Belgium-Luxembourg 7%); U.S. 8%. Export destinations: EEC 48% (France 14%, The Netherlands 8%, Italy 8%, Belgium-Luxembourg 7%, U.K. 7%); U.S. 7%; Switzerland 5%; Austria 5%. Main exports: machinery 27%; motor vehicles 16%; chemicals 12%; iron and steel 6%; textiles and clothing 5%; food 5%. Tourism (1981): visitors 9,309,000; gross receipts U.S. $6,279,000,000.

Transport and Communications. Roads (1982) 485,973 km (including 7,919 km autobahns). Motor vehicles in use (1982): passenger 24,035,900; commercial 1,273,400. Railways: (1981) 31,482 km (including 11,501 km electrified); traffic (1982) c. 36,000,000,000 passenger-km, freight 57,264,000,000 net ton-km. Air traffic (1982): 21,625,000,000 passenger-km; freight 1,687,600,000 net ton-km. Navigable inland waterways in regular use (1981) 4,378 km; freight traffic 50,010,000,000 ton-km. Shipping (1982): merchant vessels 100 gross tons and over 1,782; gross tonnage 7,706,661. Shipping traffic (1982): goods loaded 43,010,000 metric tons, unloaded 88,860,000 metric tons. Telephones (Jan. 1981) 28,554,000. Radio licenses (Dec. 1980) 22,750,000. Television licenses (Dec. 1980) 20,762,000.

Agriculture. Production (in 000; metric tons; 1982): wheat 8,632; barley 9,460; oats 3,113; rye c. 1,700; potatoes 7,821; sugar, raw value c. 3,570; apples 2,775; wine 1,523; cow's milk c. 25,550; butter 548; cheese 836; beef and veal c. 1,410; pork c. 3,080; fish catch (1981) 313. Livestock (in 000; Dec. 1981): cattle 14,992; pigs 22,310; sheep 1,108; horses 364; chickens 77,743.

Industry. Index of production (1975 = 100; 1982) 114. Unemployment (1982) 7.7%. Fuel and power (in 000; metric tons; 1982): coal 89,014; lignite 127,307; crude oil 4,256; coke (1980) 28,500; electricity (kw-hr) 365,000,000; natural gas (cu m) 16,820,000; manufactured gas (cu m) c. 12,600,000. Production (in 000; metric tons; 1982): iron ore (32% metal content) 1,314; pig iron 27,740; crude steel 36,303; aluminum 1,128; copper 394; lead 356; zinc 543; cement 29,920; sulfuric acid 4,426; newsprint 666; cotton yarn 170; woven cotton fabrics 158; wool yarn 47; man-made fibres c. 905; petroleum products (1981) 99,560; fertilizers (1981–82) nitrogenous 1,108, phosphate 559, potash 2,286; synthetic rubber 394; plastics and resins (1980) 6,710; passenger cars (units) 3,776; commercial vehicles (units) 286. Merchant vessels launched (100 gross tons and over; 1982) 682,000 gross tons. New dwelling units completed (1982) 347,100.

PATRICK PIEL—GAMMA/LIAISON

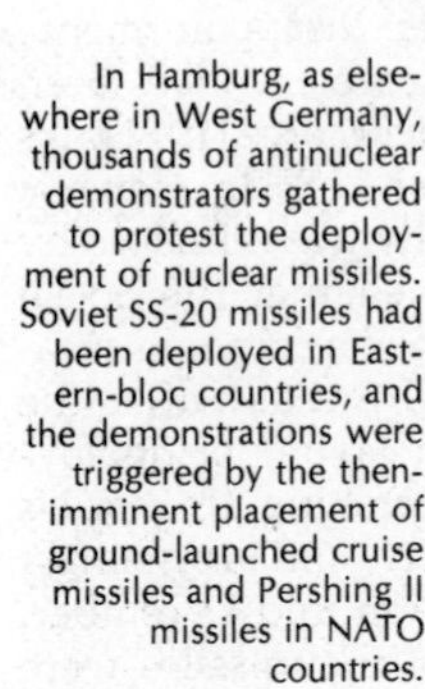
In Hamburg, as elsewhere in West Germany, thousands of antinuclear demonstrators gathered to protest the deployment of nuclear missiles. Soviet SS-20 missiles had been deployed in Eastern-bloc countries, and the demonstrations were triggered by the then-imminent placement of ground-launched cruise missiles and Pershing II missiles in NATO countries.

Moscow on January 11. A week later Soviet Foreign Minister Andrey Gromyko visited Bonn and attempted to whip up anti-U.S. sentiment in the West German electorate. He publicly accused the U.S. of blocking progress in the INF talks, and he dismissed as "unserious" U.S. Pres. Ronald Reagan's proposed zero option, under which NATO would forgo deployment of U.S. missiles if the U.S.S.R. scrapped its missile arsenal directed against Western Europe.

The U.S. was equally anxious to influence West German votes. U.S. Vice-Pres. George Bush was in West Germany at the end of January on the first leg of a Western European tour, designed to drum up support for U.S. policy on missiles and generally to remind the allies of the benefits of NATO membership. This message seemed especially apposite in West Berlin, where Bush made the major speech of his West German trip and where he looked sadly over the Berlin Wall that put détente into perspective. It was clear that the U.S. government wanted Kohl to remain as chancellor. In U.S. eyes, he and his Christian Democrats appeared to be more reliable partners and more enlightened about Soviet intentions.

Kohl visited Andropov at the beginning of July, but their talks brought no shift of position by either side on the missiles issue. However, the chancellor emphasized that, while maintaining closer relations with the U.S., his government wished also to remain on good terms with the Soviet Union and its allies. Subsequently, the chancellor's tone became tougher, and as the INF talks became bogged down, he went so far as to accuse the Soviet Union of threatening to launch a nuclear war limited to Central and Western Europe. He maintained that there was no other explanation for the Soviet Union's attempt to secure a monopoly of land-based medium-range missiles in Europe.

The chancellor was bold enough to raise with Andropov a matter that had been taboo for many years—the question of German reunification. Predictably, it fell on deaf ears. Since the change of government from centre-left to centre-right, it had become fashionable to revive the legal claim that Germany continued to exist within its 1937 frontiers. Heinrich Windelen, the minister of intra-German affairs, declared that public discussion about the German question had been reopened, and he had asked the education ministers of the state parliaments to ensure that the subject was given more attention in schools. During the election campaign, Zimmermann said that the treaties with the Eastern bloc and the intra-German accord of 1972 did not prejudice a peace settlement for Germany as a whole and were not a substitute for such a settlement. Moreover, Zimmermann did not limit the German question to the two German states but maintained that it must include the future of the former German territories beyond the Oder-Neisse line.

The U.S. invasion of Grenada in October was sharply criticized by members of the West German parliament, and government speakers did not hide their dismay at the damage this crisis might cause to East-West relations. Genscher pointed out that the U.S. move also had political and psychological consequences for West Germany. He expressed his government's anger that it had not been consulted beforehand and said that, if it had been consulted, it would have advised against the invasion. He added that the German government's conviction that military solutions should be avoided had been reinforced. (NORMAN CROSSLAND)

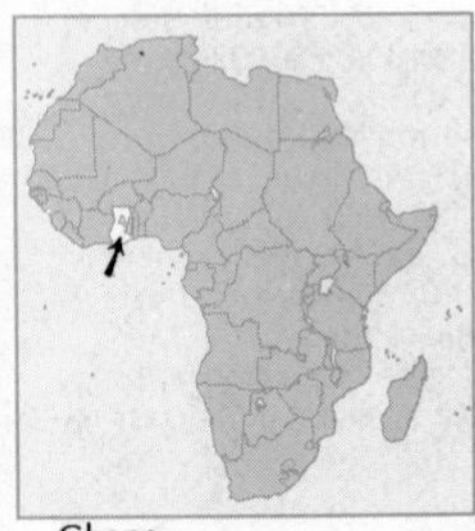
Ghana

Ghana

A republic of West Africa and member of the Commonwealth, Ghana is on the Gulf of Guinea and is bordered by Ivory Coast, Upper Volta, and Togo. Area: 238,533 sq km (92,098 sq mi). Pop. (1982 est.): 12,243,800. Cap. and largest city: Accra (pop., 1982 est., 1,045,400). Language: English (official); local Sudanic dialects (1978 est.) Akan 52.6%; Mole-Dagbani 15.9%; Ewe 11.8%; Ga-Adangme 7.6%; other 12.1%. Religion (1980 est.): Christian 63%; Muslim 16%; animist 21%. Chairman of the Provisional National Defense Council in 1983, Jerry John Rawlings.

Following the Nigerian government's decision to expel all foreigners working in Nigeria illegally, an estimated one million Ghanaian nationals returned home in January 1983. Many traveled overland through Benin and Togo, forcing Ghana to reopen its border with Togo. (All borders had been closed in September 1982 in an attempt to curb smuggling.) The mass return was described by the government as a "national crisis."

In June there was an unsuccessful coup attempt against Jerry John Rawlings, whose support appeared to have fallen dramatically. Leading the revolt was a group of Ghanaian soldiers who had escaped to Togo after attempting to seize power in November 1982.

In December 1982 the government announced a four-year economic recovery program designed to increase state control of the economy. Key measures included making the import-export trade a state monopoly and the exclusion of foreign firms and nationals from the wholesale trade. An austerity budget was introduced in April. A $377 million loan from the International Monetary Fund was agreed on in August, and the cedi was devalued steeply in October. (GUY ARNOLD)

GHANA

Education. (1979–80) Primary, pupils 1,335,463, teachers 48,146; secondary, pupils 626,168, teachers 29,446; vocational, pupils 22,451, teachers (1978–79) 1,101; teacher training (1978–79), students 3,510, teachers 936; higher (1981–82), students 8,229, teaching staff 1,075.

Finance. Monetary unit: cedi, with (Oct. 24, 1983, following devaluation of 91% on Oct 11, 1983) an official rate of 30 cedis to U.S. $1 (44.98 cedis = £1 sterling). Gold and other reserves (June 1983) U.S. $187 million. Budget (1979–80 actual): revenue 2,950,000,000 cedis; expenditure 4,667,000,000 cedis. Gross domestic product (1981) 76,655,000,000 cedis. Money supply (June 1983) 15,461,000,000 cedis. Cost of living (Accra; 1975 = 100; March 1983) 5,891.

Foreign Trade. (1982) Imports 1,939,000,000 cedis; exports 2,402,000,000 cedis. Import sources (1978): U.K. 19%; West Germany 13%; U.S. 11%; Nigeria 10%; Japan 5%; Switzerland 5%. Export destinations: The Netherlands 18%; U.S. 16%; U.K. 16%; U.S.S.R. 10%; West Germany 8%; Japan 6%; Switzerland 6%. Main exports (1981): cocoa and products 38%; gold 15%.

Transport and Communications. Roads (1981) 32,000 km. Motor vehicles in use (1980): passenger c. 66,000; commercial (including buses) c. 48,000. Railways (1980): 953 km; traffic 460 million passenger-km, freight 106 million net ton-km. Air traffic (1982): c. 291 million passenger-km; freight c. 4.8 million net ton-km. Shipping (1982): merchant vessels 100 gross tons and over 130; gross tonnage 256,869. Telephones (Jan. 1980) 68,850. Radio receivers (Dec. 1980) 1.9 million. Television receivers (Dec. 1980) 57,000.

Agriculture. Production (in 000; metric tons; 1982): corn c. 420; cassava c. 1,850; taro c. 1,000; yams c. 500; millet c. 90; sorghum c. 150; tomatoes c. 160; peanuts c. 110; oranges c. 35; cocoa c. 190; palm oil c. 23; meat (1981) c. 116; fish catch (1981) 240; timber (cu m; 1981) c. 9,803. Livestock (in 000; 1981): cattle c. 950; sheep c. 1,700; pigs c. 415; goats c. 2,100; chickens c. 12,000.

Industry. Production (in 000; metric tons; 1981): bauxite 181; petroleum products 878; gold (troy oz) 373; diamonds (metric carats) 836; manganese ore (metal content) c. 112; electricity (kw-hr) 5,053,000.

Golf

A new star emerged in the world of golf in 1983, Hal Sutton. In only his second year as a professional he won one of the four major titles, the Professional Golfers' Association (PGA) championship of the U.S., as well as what might be termed the "fifth major," the Tournament Players' Championship. In addition, Sutton was leading money winner on the U.S. tour with $426,668. All this was accomplished only 12 months after he had been rookie of the year in 1982, winning the Walt Disney World Golf Classic and breaking all records for a first-year professional by earning $237,434.

Although Jerry Pate won the 1976 U.S. Open in his first year, as did Jack Nicklaus in 1962, Sutton's performances bore closer comparison with those of Nicklaus. Sutton finished 11th and first in earnings in two years on the tour. Nicklaus began his career by finishing third, second, and then first in the money list. Pate was tenth in his inaugural year, 27th in his second, and never finished higher than sixth. Even Arnold Palmer took four years on the tour before becoming the year's leading money winner in 1958. Like Palmer, Nicklaus, and Pate, Sutton was a former U.S. amateur champion. Like Nicklaus and Pate he was also a former Walker Cup player, and his amateur background was such that he delayed turning professional until the age of 23—and then only after careful thought.

Tom Watson continued to make his mark, particularly in the British Open championship. His successful defense of the British title at Royal Birkdale equaled the performances of J. H. Taylor, James Braid, and Peter Thomson, all of whom had been champions on five occasions. Watson's five victories were won in nine attempts, and the triumph at Birkdale was one of his most impressive, not because he dominated the field but because he won under pressure. At one time on the final afternoon there were ten players within two strokes of one another, and for a fleeting moment, when Nick Faldo held a one-stroke lead with eight holes to play, there were even visions of a first British victory since 1969. But the challenge to Watson, who was in the last group, began to dwindle as he neared the end of the final round. With two other Americans, Andy Bean and Hale Irwin (who in the third round had missed a one-inch putt as he attempted to tap in one-handed and missed the ball altogether), having set the target at 276, Watson needed one birdie in the last three holes. He got it at the 16th but even so still had to get a par four at the 18th, a very demanding hole from its new tee. Watson's drive and his iron to the middle of the 18th green were two of the finest shots in such circumstances in the history of the game, and he won by a stroke.

A month earlier Watson had had a chance to defend his U.S. Open title at Oakmont Country Club near Pittsburgh, Pa., an already difficult golf course made even more so by some wickedly severe rough. Many players kept their drivers under lock and key for much of the week. With one

Gibraltar:
see Dependent States

Glass Manufacture:
see Industrial Review

Gliding:
see Aerial Sports

round to go, Watson shared the lead with Severiano Ballesteros of Spain; Larry Nelson and Calvin Peete were both two strokes behind. When Watson then shot a 31 for the first nine holes, he was four strokes ahead of the field, but Nelson, who otherwise had a bad year, kept quietly plugging away with neat, orderly golf and, with three holes to play, tied for the lead. A violent thunderstorm then suspended play for the day, and the following morning, with the course still damp and the air heavy with mist, Nelson took the lead for the first time with a long putt for a two at the 16th. It was enough to win the tournament, for though Nelson was to drop a stroke at the 18th, so did Watson, playing behind him, at the 17th. Ballesteros drifted back into a tie for fourth place and missed his best chance yet of winning the U.S. Open.

But in April Ballesteros had won the U.S. Masters at Augusta, Ga., for the second time in commanding style. It was not the dominating performance it had been from the beginning in 1980, for going into the last round he was a stroke behind both Raymond Floyd and Craig Stadler, both former winners, and only a stroke ahead of Watson. This was a formidable array of talent by whom to be surrounded, but Ballesteros surged ahead of them all with an eagle and two birdies in his first four holes. There was no answering counterattack, and Ballesteros, with a final round of 69, won by four strokes over Ben Crenshaw and Tom Kite.

The Spaniard's last shot at Augusta was to hole a chip shot at the 18th for a four, and this uncanny touch around the greens was again in evidence later in the season. In the Italian Open Ballesteros holed a chip for an eagle three to force a tie, though he lost in the play-off to Bernhard Langer of West Germany. But the most famous chip shot of the year was the one Ballesteros holed from short of the 18th green at Wentworth, England, for an eagle three to take Arnold Palmer into extra holes in the first round of the World Match-Play championship. Ballesteros had been two down with two to play, but he won at the third extra hole. Ultimately, however, he failed to become the first man to win this event for a third successive year, being beaten by Greg Norman of Australia, who then went on to defeat Faldo in the final.

Patty Sheehan won the LPGA championship, held at Kings Island, Ohio, by two strokes.

WIDE WORLD

Nick Price, a South African in his first year on the U.S. professional tour, won the World Series of Golf at Akron, Ohio, by four strokes over Nicklaus. He thus atoned for his last-round collapse in the 1982 British Open, when he lost a three-stroke lead in the last six holes.

Although the loss to Norman in the match-play tournament was a disappointment to Faldo, it was in all other respects his best season. For the first time he was the leading money winner on the European circuit, with earnings of £119,416, the first time that £100,000 had been exceeded. He also set a record stroke average of 69.03 and won five tournaments, including a three-way play-off for victory in the French Open. In addition, Faldo spent some time in the U.S., where he played well enough to finish 79th in the money list with earnings of $67,851.

Faldo was also instrumental in helping Europe give the U.S. a close contest in the Ryder Cup match at Palm Beach Gardens, Fla. The U.S. won by 14½–13½ in what was by far the most evenly contested Ryder Cup ever to have taken place in the U.S. There was never more than a point between either side throughout the three days, Europe leading 4½–3½ after the first day, the U.S. drawing level at 8–8 after the second, and the singles being exchanged so evenly on the last afternoon that, with only two games still on the course, the score was 13–13. Moreover, Europe was ahead in one of them and the U.S. in front in the other. Had it stayed that way it would have been a tie, as it had been 14 years earlier at Royal Birkdale when Nicklaus and Tony Jacklin halved the last single. In 1983 the same two men were opposing captains, but history did not repeat itself. Lanny Wadkins, one down and one to play, managed to win the last hole to halve his game with José-Maria Canizares of Spain, while Tom Watson held on to beat Bernard Gallacher of Britain.

There was for a time equal excitement in the amateur Walker Cup at the Royal Liverpool, Hoylake, where the U.S. again defeated Great Britain and Ireland, this time by the comparatively small margin of 13½–10½. Again there was never much of a gap between the sides over the two days. The U.S. held a one-point lead after the first day, but Britain drew level in the second series of foursomes to make it 8–8 with only the singles to come. Briefly, the scales even tipped Britain's way, though not for long. Although at one point all eight British players were either ahead or tied, the U.S. team came back strongly and by the tenth hole had wrested the initiative. Andrew Oldcorn accomplished the unprecedented feat for the U.K. of winning all four of his games in the Ryder and Walker Cup tournaments, but the main British consolation came in the British amateur championship the following week, when Philip Parkin defeated Jim Holtgrieve (U.S.) by five and four in the 36-hole final at Turnberry.

Jay Sigel, the U.S. captain at Hoylake and winner of the British championship at Hillside four years earlier, got no further than the quarterfinals, but in August he joined a select band of golfers by winning the U.S. Amateur championship at the North Shore Country Club in Glenview, Ill., for the second successive year. Ireland won the European amateur team championship at Chantilly, France, defeating Spain in the final, and then went on to take the home internationals as well at Portmarnock.

Ireland also beat England in the final of the European women's golf championship. The women's home internationals at Royal Porthcawl in Wales had to be abandoned because of violent weather, golf being considered impossible in the gales and rain, but earlier Jill Thornhill, at 41 years enjoying something of a second wind at golf, won the British women's amateur championship at Silloth, defeating Regine Lautens of Switzerland in the final.

The U.S. women's amateur championship at Canoe Brook, N.J., was won by Joanne Pacillo, who defeated Sally Quinlan by two and one in the 36-hole final. Professional golf among the women continued to gather momentum. Jo Ann Carner was the leading money winner in the U.S., with $291,404, having triumphed in two tournaments. Jan Stephenson of Australia won the U.S. Women's Open at Tulsa, Okla., by one stroke over Carner and Patty Sheehan. With five consecutive birdies in the last round, Sheehan won the Ladies Professional Golf Association (LPGA) championship at Kings Island, Ohio, by two strokes over Sandra Haynie. Among other winners of LPGA tournaments were Nancy Lopez, Amy Alcott, Kathy Whitworth, Hollis Stacy, and Pat Bradley. Muriel Thomson again topped the list of winners in Britain with earnings of £8,899.

(MICHAEL E. J. WILLIAMS)

Greece

A republic of Europe, Greece occupies the southern part of the Balkan Peninsula. Area: 131,990 sq km (50,962 sq mi), of which the mainland accounts for 107,194 sq km. Pop. (1983 est.): 9,898,000. Cap. and largest city: Athens (pop., 1981, 885,700). Language: Greek. Religion: Orthodox. President in 1983, Konstantinos Karamanlis; prime minister, Andreas Papandreou.

The main problem confronting Greek Prime Minister Andreas Papandreou during 1983 was how to reconcile the legitimate aspirations of his party, the Panhellenic Socialist Movement (Pasok), for rapid socialist reforms with his government's more immediate concern for national security and a stable economy. Pasok's substantial losses to the Greek Communist Party (KKE) in the local elections of October 1982 had revealed growing impatience over its delay in bringing about the promised changes.

The generous increases given to wage earners in 1982 were reflected in higher production costs, which, in turn, robbed Greek products of their competitiveness even in the home markets. A wage freeze in January, combined with deferred indexation benefits and a 15% devaluation, failed to improve the situation. One reason was that the drachma remained pegged to the U.S. dollar, and the rise in the dollar's value dissipated the benefits. Failure to control the huge public-sector deficits starved the private sector of adequate credits and encouraged inflation, which rose above 20% for the fifth consecutive year.

Despite strong incentives, investments were few, and business confidence was eroded by contradictory policies. Thus, while the government relied mainly on private enterprise to bolster the economy, it frightened investors away by setting up worker-participation councils in industry with ill-defined powers. The preliminaries of the five-year (1983–87) plan were introduced in Parliament

GREECE

Education. (1979–80) Primary, pupils 910,576, teachers 33,466; secondary, pupils 613,720, teachers 28,515; vocational (1978–79), pupils 125,039; higher, students 117,407, teaching staff 7,932.

Finance. Monetary unit: drachma, with (Sept. 20, 1983) a free rate of 92.95 drachmas to U.S. $1 (140 drachmas = £1 sterling). Gold and other reserves (June 1983) U.S. $945 million. Budget (1982 actual): revenue 568 billion drachmas; expenditure 731.7 billion drachmas. Gross national product (1982) 2,621,000,000,000 drachmas. Money supply (March 1983) 402.9 billion drachmas. Cost of living (1975 = 100; June 1983) 387.

Foreign Trade. (1982) Imports 665,920,000,000 drachmas; exports 286,280,000,000 drachmas. Import sources: EEC 46% (West Germany 17%, Italy 9%, France 7%, The Netherlands 5%); Saudi Arabia 12%; Libya 7%; Japan 6%. Export destinations: EEC 46% (West Germany 19%, Italy 9%, France 7%, U.K. 5%); U.S. 9%; Saudi Arabia 6%. Main exports (1981): fruit and vegetables 15%; textile yarns and fabrics 11%; petroleum products 9%; clothing 9%; iron and steel 5%; cement 5%; chemicals 5%. Tourism (1981): visitors 5,094,000; gross receipts U.S. $1,881,000,000.

Transport and Communications. Roads (1982) 109,037 km (including 91 km expressways and 68,814 km local roads). Motor vehicles in use (1982): passenger 999,315; commercial 478,104. Railways (1981): 2,479 km; traffic 1,510,000,000 passenger-km, freight 700 million net ton-km. Air traffic (1982): 4,924,000,000 passenger-km; freight 69.4 million net ton-km. Shipping (1982): merchant vessels 100 gross tons and over 3,501; gross tonnage 40,035,204. Telephones (Dec. 1981) 2,943,000. Radio receivers (Dec. 1982) 3.3 million. Television receivers (Dec. 1982) 1.5 million.

Agriculture. Production (in 000; metric tons; 1982): wheat 2,983; barley 853; oats 81; corn 1,448; rice 83; potatoes 888; sugar, raw value (1981) 340; tomatoes 1,918; onions 133; watermelons (1981) c. 710; apples 257; oranges 653; lemons 168; peaches (1981) 449; olives c. 1,590; olive oil 353; wine c. 560; raisins 132; tobacco 115; cotton, lint 115. Livestock (in 000; Dec. 1981): sheep 8,316; cattle (1980) 881; goats 4,623; pigs (1980) 993; horses (1980) 105; asses (1980) 230; chickens 36,296.

Industry. Production (in 000; metric tons; 1982): lignite 27,284; electricity (kw-hr) 21,046,000; petroleum products (1981) 15,795; iron ore (43% metal content) 514; bauxite 2,853; aluminum 137; magnesite (1980) 1,598; cement 13,216; sulfuric acid 1,001; fertilizers (1981–82) nitrogenous c. 309, phosphate c. 159; cotton yarn 114. Merchant vessels launched (100 gross tons and over; 1982) 21,000 gross tons.

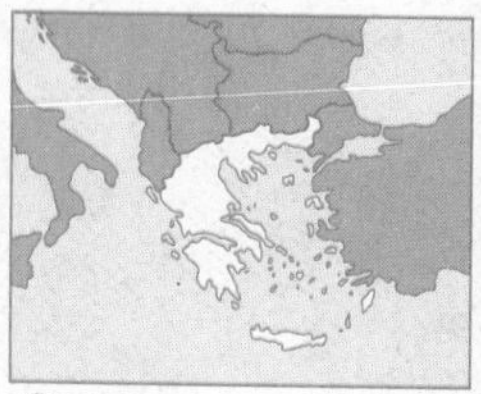
Greece

Great Britain:
see United Kingdom

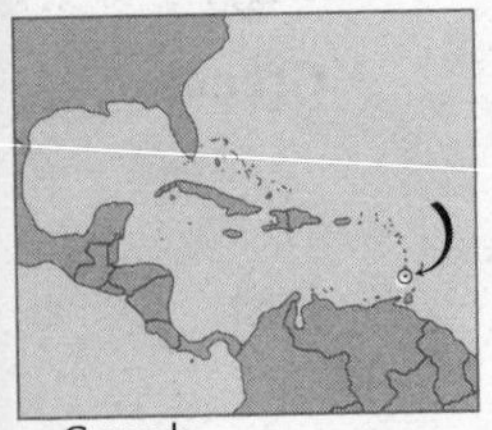

Grenada

in June, but full details were not made available. The absence of investments contributed to a decline of productivity and, together with the bankruptcy of 47,000 small businesses, led to a dramatic increase in unemployment, estimated at over 10% of the work force.

Foreign-exchange revenue from exports, shipping, tourism, and worker remittances dropped sharply. The external deficit was kept within manageable proportions by the decline in imports resulting from recession, the spending of oil reserves, and the inflow of funds from the European Communities (EC). Loans from Western banks took care of the rest. This continuing economic reliance on the West, as well as considerations of national security, forced Papandreou to keep Greece within the Western fold, despite his campaign promises. However, he tried to recoup the political cost of this posture by dissociating his government from the main trends of Western policy. In what it described as a "humanitarian" operation, Greece dispatched five ships to evacuate Palestine Liberation Organization chairman Yasir Arafat (*see* BIOGRAPHIES) and his followers from Tripoli, Lebanon, in December.

The government signed a defense and economic cooperation agreement with the U.S. in September. The five-year agreement authorized the U.S. to operate 4 major and 24 subsidiary military facilities in Greece in exchange for military assistance that would enable Greece to maintain military parity with Turkey.

Relations with NATO remained strained. The Greek government refused to carry on negotiations with Turkey to redefine the boundaries of allied air defense control in the Aegean. Turkey wanted a bigger share of this command, but because this would bring Greek islands under the protection of the Turkish Air Force, Greece was adamantly opposed. The frequently interrupted Greek-Turkish dialogue was resumed in July, focusing this time on cooperation in trade and tourism. The declaration of an independent Turkish Cypriot state on Cyprus in November further strained the relationship between the two countries. (*See* CYPRUS.)

Greek Pres. Konstantinos Karamanlis (right) visited Paris in September, and was received at the Elysée Palace by French Pres. François Mitterrand.

AGIP/PICTORIAL PARADE

In the second half of 1983 Greece assumed the presidency of the EC Council of Ministers. Although it discharged its task with regard to Community affairs quite efficiently, its nonconformist foreign policy caused friction. A Greek proposal for a six-month delay in deploying U.S. medium-range nuclear missiles in Europe angered Greece's NATO partners. It caused a commotion at the Athens meeting of EC foreign ministers in September, coinciding as it did with the Greek decision to block condemnation of the Soviet Union for shooting down a South Korean passenger airliner. A ten-year general economic cooperation agreement was signed between the two countries.

The Greek government's defiant positions on foreign affairs enhanced Papandreou's popularity at home. Above all, it ensured the tolerance and often the cooperation of the KKE. Otherwise, the government's strict austerity measures might have triggered crippling strikes by KKE-controlled unions.

The conservative opposition New Democracy Party was still groping for a credible identity that would dissociate it from the errors of the past. There were doubts that its leader, Evangelos Averoff, could give the party the dynamic and inspired leadership it needed. This triggered a power struggle among ambitious candidates for the succession. The absence of a credible alternative to the government increased concern about the political future of Greece, especially after a mysterious "red alert" of the armed forces on February 27. Though the government promptly dismissed it as an exercise, evidence later emerged that the alert had been ordered following rumours of a possible military coup. The most disturbing aspect of the incident was that Pasok and the KKE took advantage of it to mobilize party cadres and test their ability to thwart such an attempt. The murder of a right-wing newspaper publisher in March and a bomb explosion at a New Democracy meeting in northern Greece added to the apprehension.

The government's main reforms included the passage of a national health bill, as well as legislation to establish equality of the sexes, introduce reforms in university education, and bring about decentralization of administrative powers. All Greek political refugees from the 1946–49 civil war living in Eastern Europe were given permission to return without individual screening.

(MARIO MODIANO)

Greek Orthodox Church:
see Religion

Greenland:
see Dependent States

Grenada

A parliamentary state within the Commonwealth, Grenada, with its dependency, the Southern Grenadines, is the southernmost of the Windward Islands of the Caribbean Sea, 161 km N of Trinidad. Area: 345 sq km (133 sq mi). Pop. (1983 est.): 111,000, including black 84%; mixed 11%; white 1%; and East Indian 3%. Cap.: Saint George's (pop., 1980 est., 7,500). Language: English. Religion (1980): Roman Catholic 64%; Anglican 22%;

Methodist 3%; Seventh-day Adventist 3%. Queen, Elizabeth II; governor-general in 1983, Sir Paul Scoon; prime minister, Maurice Bishop until October 19; head of the Revolutionary Military Council from October 19 to October 25, Gen. Hudson Austin; chairman of the interim advisory council from December 9, Nicholas Braithwaite.

Grenada's four-year-old experiment in socialist-oriented development was dramatically ended in October 1983 by a military coup and a U.S.-led invasion. On October 14 it became known that a serious dispute had broken out within the People's Revolutionary government. Several days of confusion followed, during which Prime Minister Maurice Bishop (*see* OBITUARIES) was deposed by colleagues in his New Jewel Movement, for whom Bishop was not sufficiently radical. Put under house arrest, Bishop was freed by supporters, rearrested, and finally executed on October 19. Power was assumed by a Revolutionary Military Council led by Gen. Hudson Austin. Other ministers shot during the coup were Unison Whiteman (foreign affairs), Jacqueline Creft (education), and Norris Bain (housing). An estimated 60 people died in the coup.

On October 25, less than a week after the coup, approximately 1,200 U.S. Marines, Army Rangers, and Navy Seal commandos invaded the island, supported by a 300-man force of soldiers and police from Antigua and Barbuda, Barbados, Dominica, Jamaica, St. Lucia, and St. Vincent and the Grenadines. Later that day U.S. Army paratroopers also landed on the island. By the end of October the invasion force had been increased to more than 7,000, but fierce resistance from the Grenadian Army, aided by Cuban soldiers and construction workers from the Point Salines airport site, slowed up the U.S. advance. Early in November resistance weakened, and the official troop strength was reduced to 3,000. By December there were only isolated sniper incidents committed by the few Cubans and Grenadian Marxists who remained hidden in the interior jungles. All U.S. combat forces were withdrawn from Grenada by mid-December, leaving only about 300 noncombat advisory personnel, and security was turned over to the Caribbean peacekeeping force.

In the aftermath of the invasion, Austin was arrested and the Revolutionary Military Council disbanded. The Cubans were sent home to the muted protests of Cuban Pres. Fidel Castro, who had distanced himself from the coup and the murder of his friend Bishop. Grenada's governor-general, Sir Paul Scoon, assumed power and appointed a nine-member advisory council that would govern the nation until new elections could be held.

(ROD PRINCE)

See also Defense; United States.

WIDE WORLD

In November Sir Paul Scoon (left), governor-general of Grenada, read off the names of the advisory council that would govern the island until elections could be held. He was guarded by a member of the multinational peacekeeping force.

GRENADA

Education. (1980–81) Primary, pupils 23,065, teachers 704; secondary, pupils 6,120, teachers 284; vocational (1979–80), pupils 384, teachers 28; teacher training (1979–80), students 100, teachers 7; higher (1981–82), students 704, teaching staff 43.

Finance and Trade. Monetary unit: East Caribbean dollar, with (Sept. 20, 1983) a par value of ECar$2.70 to U.S. $1 (free rate of ECar$4.07 = £1 sterling). Budget (total; 1981 est.) balanced at ECar$169 million. Foreign trade (1982): imports ECar$150.9 million; exports ECar$50.1 million. Import sources (1980): U.S. 20%; Trinidad and Tobago 20%; U.K. 18%; Canada 6%; Japan 5%. Export destinations (1980): U.K. 44%; Belgium-Luxembourg 14%; The Netherlands 10%; West Germany 8%; Trinidad and Tobago 8%. Main exports: cocoa 25%; bananas 18%; nutmeg 16%. Tourism (excluding cruise passengers; 1981): visitors 25,000; gross receipts U.S. $21 million.

Guatemala

A republic of Central America, Guatemala is bounded by Mexico, Belize, Honduras, El Salvador, the Caribbean Sea, and the Pacific Ocean. Area: 108,889 sq km (42,042 sq mi). Pop. (1983 est.): 6,394,100. Cap. and largest city: Guatemala City (pop., 1981 prelim., 749,800). Language: Spanish, with some Indian dialects. Religion (1982): Roman Catholic 84%. President in 1983, Gen. Efraín Ríos Montt until August 8; chief of state from August 8, Gen. Oscar Humberto Mejía Victores.

On Aug. 8, 1983, Gen. Oscar Humberto Mejía Victores (*see* BIOGRAPHIES) overthrew the regime of Gen. Efraín Ríos Montt and declared himself chief of state. This was the second military coup in Guatemala within 18 months. The unpopularity of General Ríos Montt, who had seized power in March 1982, was widespread. He was disliked by many Roman Catholics for his evangelical Protestant faith and for his refusal to grant clemency to six guerrillas during the visit of Pope John Paul II. The military was offended by his promotion of young officers in defiance of the Army's traditional hierarchy. Much of the middle class was alienated by his unsuccessful economic policy and his decision on August 1 to introduce the value-added tax, never before levied in Guatemala.

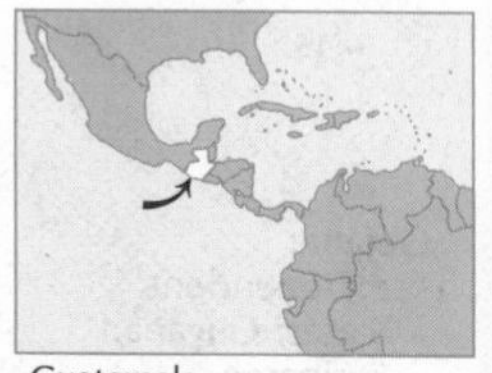

Guatemala

Ríos Montt's initial promises of a return to "authentic" democracy proved empty. Corruption in

GUATEMALA

Education. (1980) Primary, pupils 803,404, teachers 23,770; secondary, pupils 104,588; vocational, pupils 29,768; teacher training, pupils 22,256; secondary, vocational, and teacher training, teachers (all secondary) 9,613; higher (1981–82), students 54,284, teaching staff 4,017.

Finance. Monetary unit: quetzal, at par with the U.S. dollar (free rate, at Sept. 20, 1983, of 1.51 quetzales to £1 sterling). Gold and other reserves (June 1983) U.S. $177 million. Budget (total; 1982 actual): revenue 749 million quetzales; expenditure 1,109,000,000 quetzales. Gross national product (1981) 8,560,000,000 quetzales. Money supply (March 1983) 775 million quetzales. Cost of living (1975 = 100; Feb. 1983) 184.5.

Foreign Trade. (1982) Imports 1,399,000,000 quetzales; exports 1,173,000,000 quetzales. Import sources (1981): U.S. 34%; Japan 8%; Mexico 8%; Venezuela 7%; West Germany 6%; El Salvador 6%; Netherlands Antilles 6%. Export destinations (1981): El Salvador 18%; U.S. 18%; West Germany 8%; Nicaragua 6%; Mexico 5%; Japan 5%; Costa Rica 5%. Main exports: coffee 31%; bananas 10%; chemicals c. 9%; cotton 7%.

Transport and Communications. Roads (1979) 17,278 km. Motor vehicles in use (1980): passenger 166,900; commercial (including buses) 81,500. Railways: (1980) 1,106 km; freight traffic (1976) 117 million net ton-km. Air traffic (1982): 160 million passenger-km; freight 5.5 million net ton-km. Telephones (Jan. 1981) 81,600. Radio licenses (Dec. 1980) 289,000. Television receivers (Dec. 1980) 175,000.

Agriculture. Production (in 000; metric tons; 1982): corn 1,217; sugar, raw value c. 515; tomatoes 90; dry beans 89; bananas c. 655; coffee 162; cotton, lint c. 81; tobacco c. 6. Livestock (in 000; 1981): sheep 734; cattle 1,730; pigs 835; chickens 14,237.

Industry. Production (in 000; metric tons; 1981): cement 568; antimony ore (metal content) c. 51; petroleum products 728; electricity (kw-hr) 1,995,000.

the civil service was reduced slightly, but violations of human rights continued relentlessly. The administration established special military courts that had the power to impose death penalties against alleged guerrillas and terrorists. The number of killings in the countryside escalated, and the campaign known as *frijoles y fusiles* ("beans and guns"), initiated in an attempt to win over the large Indian population to army rule, resulted in widespread fear; many Indians fled over the border into southern Mexico.

The new administration under General Mejía Victores, whose political stance was considered to be to the right of his predecessor, did not bode well for stability. Internal security remained poor, corruption was believed to have increased, kidnappings were common, and the level of political violence rose markedly. Some concessions were made—the state of alarm imposed by Ríos Montt in June was lifted, and the controversial secret courts were abolished—but these had little effect overall. The administration promised to comply with Ríos Montt's election timetable, which was to allow campaigning for a constituent assembly to start on March 23, 1984, in preparation for a vote on July 29. However, these promises were treated with skepticism.

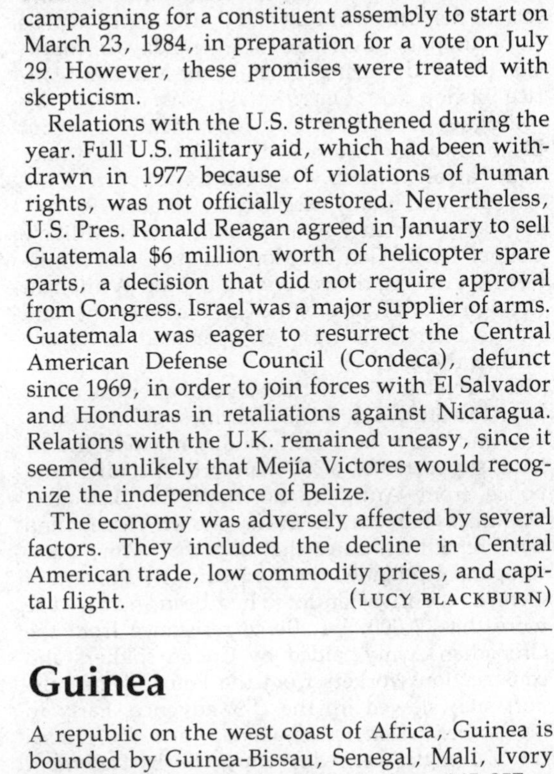

Relations with the U.S. strengthened during the year. Full U.S. military aid, which had been withdrawn in 1977 because of violations of human rights, was not officially restored. Nevertheless, U.S. Pres. Ronald Reagan agreed in January to sell Guatemala $6 million worth of helicopter spare parts, a decision that did not require approval from Congress. Israel was a major supplier of arms. Guatemala was eager to resurrect the Central American Defense Council (Condeca), defunct since 1969, in order to join forces with El Salvador and Honduras in retaliations against Nicaragua. Relations with the U.K. remained uneasy, since it seemed unlikely that Mejía Victores would recognize the independence of Belize.

The economy was adversely affected by several factors. They included the decline in Central American trade, low commodity prices, and capital flight.

(LUCY BLACKBURN)

Guinea

Guinea

A republic on the west coast of Africa, Guinea is bounded by Guinea-Bissau, Senegal, Mali, Ivory Coast, Liberia, and Sierra Leone. Area: 245,857 sq km (94,926 sq mi). Pop. (1982 UN est.): 5,285,000. Cap. and largest city: Conakry (pop., 1980 est., 763,000). Language: French (official), Basari, Fula-

Gen. Oscar Humberto Mejía Victores, newly installed as Guatemala's chief of state, held a press conference shortly after overthrowing the regime of Gen. Efrain Ríos Montt.

UPI

Guiana:
see Dependent States; Guyana; Suriname

GUINEA

Education. (1980–81) Primary, pupils 257,547, teachers 7,165; secondary, pupils 89,900, teachers 3,520; vocational, pupils 2,776; teacher training, students 8,437; vocational and teacher training (1978–79), teachers 607; higher (1978–79), students 20,739, teachers 650.

Finance. Monetary unit: syli, with (Sept. 20, 1983) a free rate of 23.47 sylis to U.S. $1 (35.35 sylis = £1 sterling). Budget (total; 1979 est.) balanced at 11,250,000,000 sylis.

Foreign Trade. (1979) Imports 5,637,000,000 sylis; exports 6,925,000,000 sylis. Import sources: France c. 36%; U.S.S.R. c. 14%; U.S. c. 9%. Export destinations: U.S. c. 24%; France c. 13%; Spain c. 13%; West Germany c. 11%; U.S.S.R. c. 9%; Italy c. 9%; Canada c. 5%. Main exports (1975–76): bauxite c. 57%; alumina c. 31%.

ni, Kissi, Koniagi, Kpelle, Loma, Malinke, and Susu. Religion (1980 est.): Muslim 69%; tribal 30%; Christian 1%. President in 1983, Ahmed Sékou Touré; premier, Louis Lansana Beavogui.

On Dec. 22, 1983, an earthquake (magnitude 6.3 on the Richter scale) occurred near Gaoual in northwestern Guinea, causing at least 300 deaths. A second tremor on December 24 devastated Koumbia near the border with Guinea-Bissau.

The normalization of Guinea's relations with France encountered difficulties. An association of the French families of Guinea's political prisoners, as well as Guinean refugees in France, created an adverse climate of opinion there—as did the publication in Paris in June of a book alleging Pres. Ahmed Sékou Touré's complicity in the assassination of Diallo Telli, former secretary-general of the Organization of African Unity (OAU). Nevertheless, in May a Guinean ministerial delegation negotiated an increase in French aid. In October Touré attended the Franco-African summit. During the year Guinea held talks with Mali on their possible union. (*See* MALI.)

On July 1 a North Korean airliner crashed in central Guinea, killing 23. The victims were North Korean technicians building facilities for the 1984 OAU summit in Conakry. (PHILIPPE DECRAENE)

Guinea-Bissau

Guinea-Bissau

An independent African republic, Guinea-Bissau has an Atlantic coastline on the west and borders Senegal on the north and Guinea on the east and south. Area: 36,125 sq km (13,948 sq mi). Pop. (1983 est.): 827,000, including (1979) Balante 27.2%; Fulani 22.9%; Malinke 12.2%; Mandyako 10.6%; Pepel 10%; other 17.1%. Cap. and largest city: Bissau (pop., 1979, 105,300). Religion (1980 est.): tribal 52%; Muslim 38%; Christian 10%. President of the Council of the Revolution in 1983, João Bernardo Vieira; premier, Victor Saúde Maria.

In August 1983 Pres. João Bernardo Vieira dismissed three ministers from his Cabinet for "irregularities." The Council of the Revolution announced that it was commuting death sentences passed on 38 dissidents in the 1970s, during the regime of former president Luis de Almeida Cabral.

Relations between Guinea-Bissau and Cape Verde, damaged by the 1980 coup that deposed Cabral, were restored in July, despite reports that Cabral was now residing in Cape Verde. President

GUINEA-BISSAU

Education. (1980–81) Primary, pupils 75,143, teachers 3,351; secondary, pupils 4,068, teachers 387; vocational, pupils 569, teachers 54; teacher training, students 557, teachers 62.

Finance and Trade. Monetary unit: Guinea-Bissau peso, with (Sept. 20, 1983) a free rate of 41.84 pesos to U.S. $1 (63.01 pesos = £1 sterling). Budget (1981 est.): revenue 1,137,000,000 pesos; expenditure 1,944,000,000 pesos. Foreign trade (1980): imports 1,859,900,000 pesos; exports 382.3 million pesos. Import sources: Portugal 31%; France 11%; Sweden 8%; The Netherlands 7%; U.S.S.R. 7%; Burma 6%. Export destinations: Portugal 27%; Spain 25%; Switzerland 23%; Cape Verde 6%; The Netherlands 6%. Main exports: fish 33%; peanuts 24%; coconuts 17%.

Agriculture. Production (in 000; metric tons; 1982): rice c. 23; plantains c. 25; peanuts c. 30; palm kernels c. 10; palm oil c. 6; copra c. 5; timber (cu m; 1981) c. 526. Livestock (in 000; 1981): cattle c. 210; pigs c. 120; sheep c. 55; goats c. 130.

Vieira visited The Gambia in December 1982 to dispel tension that had existed between the two states since the leader of the 1981 coup attempt in The Gambia sought refuge in Bissau.

The visit of Portugal's Pres. António Ramalho Eanes toward the end of 1982 signaled a reconciliation between the two countries. Portugal established a $20 million line of credit for Guinea-Bissau and promised technical assistance. There were plans to modernize the port of Bissau, using funds from the Arab countries. Joint Belgian and French enterprises were developing the bauxite and phosphate reserves, while the World Bank offered a $10 million loan for oil exploration. (GUY ARNOLD)

Guyana

Guyana

A republic and member of the Commonwealth, Guyana is situated between Venezuela, Brazil, and Suriname on the Atlantic Ocean. Area: 215,000 sq km (83,000 sq mi). Pop. (1983 est.): 944,000, including (1978) East Indian 50%; African 30%; mixed 10%; Amerindian 5%. Cap. and largest city: Georgetown (pop., 1979 est., 195,000). Language: English (official). Religion (1980 est.): Hindu 34%; Protestant 34%; Muslim 9%; Roman Catholic 8%; other 15%. President in 1983, Forbes Burnham; prime minister, Ptolemy Reid.

GUYANA

Education. (1979–80) Primary, pupils 159,749, teachers 5,831; secondary, pupils 74,965, teachers 4,340; vocational, pupils 3,595, teachers 242; teacher training, pupils 1,052, teachers 106; higher, students 2,491, teaching staff (1978–79) 496.

Finance. Monetary unit: Guyanan dollar, with (Sept. 20, 1983) an official rate of Guy$3 to U.S. $1 (free rate of Guy$4.52 = £1 sterling). Budget (total;1981 est.): revenue Guy$1,010,000,000; expenditure Guy$1,177,000,000.

Foreign Trade. (1982) Imports Guy$850.4 million; exports Guy$724 million. Import sources (1979): U.S. 28%; Trinidad and Tobago 24%; U.K. 20%. Export destinations (1979): U.K. 28%; U.S. 18%; Canada 9%; Trinidad and Tobago 7%; Jamaica 6%. Main exports: sugar 36%; bauxite 34%; rice 8%; alumina 5%.

Agriculture. Production (in 000; metric tons; 1982): rice 303; sugar, raw value 288; plantains c. 21; oranges c. 12. Livestock (in 000; 1981): cattle c. 295; sheep c. 116; goats c. 72; pigs c. 140; chickens c. 13,255.

Industry. Production (in 000; metric tons; 1981): bauxite 1,907; gold (troy oz) 19; diamonds (metric carats) 10; electricity (kw-hr) 440,000.

The principal preoccupation of the government and people of Guyana in 1983 was the continuing stagnation of the economy. The importation of several food items was banned by the government in an attempt to save foreign exchange; other essential items, including medicines, were also in short supply. The result was a sharp rise in prices and an increase in smuggling. Many Guyanese were forced to spend inordinate amounts of time in food lines, while pavement vendors were the target of a police crackdown on smuggled goods. There was a sharp increase in cases of child malnutrition, and an outbreak of beriberi added to the problems of an already underequipped medical service.

In May discontent over the food situation led miners in the Linden and Berbice bauxite plants to start a series of one-day strikes. Management retaliated by cutting the workweek, and the miners struck for six weeks. As a result, bauxite output fell far below target. Production of the other main foreign-exchange earners, rice and sugar, was also below forecast. An attempt to negotiate an International Monetary Fund loan failed in April. In December seven Canadians and an American were arrested in Ohio and Toronto and charged with plotting to overthrow Guyana's government.

(ROD PRINCE)

Gymnastics and Weight Lifting

Gymnastics. In the 22nd World Gymnastics Championships, held Oct. 24–30, 1983, in Budapest, Hung., the Soviet gymnasts established themselves as the best in both the men's and women's divisions. The only surprise occurred when China won the men's team title. Otherwise, the Soviet gymnasts accounted for nine gold medals, five silver, and one bronze.

Romania challenged the Soviet women, but the latter won the team title, two individual titles, and two silver medals. The Romanians were runners-up in the team competition and earned one individual gold medal.

TONY DUFFY/SPORTS ILLUSTRATED

Dmitry Belozerchev, a slight 16-year-old from the Soviet Union, was the youngest competitor ever to win the men's all-around title. He is shown here on the parallel bars in Budapest, Hungary.

For the first time, teenagers won both all-around titles. At 16 Dmitry Belozerchev of the Soviet Union was the youngest competitor ever to win the men's all-around. On the final day of competition he garnered gold medals on the rings, the horizontal bar, and the pommeled horse and placed second in the floor exercises. Other Soviet medal winners included Artour Akopian, first in the vault and third in the all-around; Vladimir Artenov, co-champion on the parallel bars; and Aleksandr Pogotrlov, co-champion on the horizontal bar. For China, Tong Fei was first in the floor exercises, and Lou Yun shared the championship in the parallel bars.

Winner of the women's all-around championship was Natalia Yurchenko, 18, of the Soviet Union. Early in the summer she had won the all-around title in the World University Games in Edmonton, Alta. In the World Championships she edged her teammate Olga Mostepanova by 0.350 points. Yurchenko did not win any individual medals. Mostepanova was first on the balance beam and second in the floor exercises and all-around. Maxi Gnauck of East Germany retained her laurels on the uneven parallel bars. Winner of the floor exercises was Ecaterina Szabo of Romania. The fourth individual titlist was Boriana Stoyanova of Bulgaria in the vault. To its gold medals the U.S.S.R. added two silver and two bronze medals in the individual events. In addition to Szabo's gold medal and the silver in the team competition, Romania won four silver and two bronze medals in the individual events.

Thirty-three perfect scores of ten, an all-time high, were awarded by the judges at the tournament. This resulted from originality and virtuosity in the routines rather than from any easing up in the judging. For the U.S. women, Kathy Johnson placed 11th in the all-around, and the team finished 5th. Peter Vidmar was ninth in the men's all-around, and the team was fourth.

Weight Lifting. The world championship tournament, contested from October 22 to 31 in Moscow, was essentially a dual meet between the Soviet Union and Bulgaria. The Soviet lifters eventually finished first by winning six gold and four silver medals, while Bulgaria won three gold and four silver. Three champions retained their laurels: Soviet superheavyweight Anatoly Pisarenko; Yurik Sarkisian of the Soviet Union in the 60-kg class; and Bulgaria's Blagoi Blagoev at 90 kg, his third straight title.

The only 1980 Olympic champion to win a gold medal was Yurik Vardanyan of the Soviet Union in the 82.5-kg class, his fifth world title. Two other 1982 champions yielded their titles to newcomers. Poland's Stefan Leletko in the 52-kg class finished third as the winner, Neno Terziisky of Bulgaria, set a world record of 260 kg, for one of 21 world marks during the ten days of lifting. Yanko Rusev of Bulgaria, 1980 Olympic champion and 1982 world champion in the 75-kg class, was supplanted by Joachim Kunz of East Germany. In the 56-kg class Oken Mirzoyan of the U.S.S.R. edged Bulgaria's Naim Suleimanov, age 15, by 2.5 kg. In the most notable feat of the tournament, Stefan Topurov of Bulgaria became the first lifter to raise three times his body weight above his head, 180 kg in the 60-kg class.

Capturing the remaining medals in the tournament were: East Germany one gold, two bronze; Poland one silver, three bronze; Hungary one silver and one bronze; Czechoslovakia and Romania each one bronze. No U.S. competitor successfully completed a total lift.

The International Weightlifting Federation meted out two-year suspensions to 11 lifters testing positive to the use of steroids in the Pan American Games. Two of the lifters suspended for a period that would keep them out of the 1984 Olympic Games were 1980 Olympic champion Daniel Nuñez of Cuba and Jeff Michels, the U.S. national heavyweight champion.

(CHARLES ROBERT PAUL, JR.)

[452.B.4.f]

Haiti

The Republic of Haiti occupies the western one-third of the Caribbean island of Hispaniola, which it shares with the Dominican Republic. Area: 27,750 sq km (10,715 sq mi). Pop. (1982 prelim.): 5,053,800, of whom 95% are black. Cap. and largest city: Port-au-Prince (pop., 1982 prelim., 763,200). Language: French (official) and Creole. Religion: Roman Catholic; Voodoo practiced in rural areas. President in 1983, Jean-Claude Duvalier.

During his visit to Haiti in March 1983, Pope John Paul II appealed for peaceful change while addressing a mass attended by 200,000 Haitians.

HAITI

Education. (1979–80) Primary, pupils 580,127, teachers 13,472; secondary, pupils 87,680, teachers 3,637; vocational, pupils 2,880, teachers 245; teacher training, students 687, teachers 136; higher (1981–82), students 4,500, teaching staff 325.

Finance. Monetary unit: gourde, with (Sept. 20, 1983) a par value of 5 gourdes to U.S. $1 (free rate of 7.53 gourdes = £1 sterling). Gold and other reserves (June 1983) U.S. $13 million. Budget (1982 actual): revenue 882 million gourdes; expenditure 1,832,000,000 gourdes. Cost of living (Port-au-Prince; 1975 = 100; March 1983) 180.8.

Foreign Trade. Imports (1981) 2,303,000,000 gourdes; exports (1982) 811 million gourdes. Import sources (1977–78): U.S. 45%; Netherlands Antilles 10%; Japan 9%; Canada 8%; West Germany 5%. Export destinations (1977–78): U.S. 59%; France 13%; Italy 7%; Belgium-Luxembourg 6%. Main exports (1977–78): coffee 39%; bauxite 11%; toys and sports goods 10%; essential oils 6%; electrical equipment 5%.

Transport and Communications. Roads (1981) 3,443 km. Motor vehicles in use (1981): passenger 17,400; commercial 3,100. Railways (1980) c. 250 km. Telephones (Jan. 1980) 34,900. Radio receivers (Dec. 1980) 101,000. Television receivers (Dec. 1980) 16,000.

Agriculture. Production (in 000; metric tons; 1982): rice c. 105; corn c. 180; sorghum c. 110; sweet potatoes (1981) c. 270; cassava (1981) c. 255; sugar, raw value (1981) c. 52; dry beans c. 50; bananas c. 210; plantains c. 310; mangoes c. 335; coffee c. 28; sisal c. 15; timber (cu m; 1981) c. 5,129. Livestock (in 000; 1981): cattle c. 1,200; pigs c. 600; goats c. 1,000; sheep c. 90; horses c. 415.

Industry. Production (in 000; metric tons; 1981): cement 230; bauxite (exports) 556; electricity (kw-hr) 325,000.

His visit was preceded by an announcement that municipal elections were to be held between May and August—the first to take place since 1957, when Pres. Jean-Claude Duvalier's father assumed power. At the same time, legislation was introduced limiting the powers of the new mayors and bringing them under the control of the Interior Ministry and the police. Constitutional changes adopted in August would permit Duvalier to name his own successor.

On May 9, just before the elections, five candidates from the opposition Christian Democratic Party were arrested. Government candidates won in every city except Cap-Haïtien, where an independent became mayor. In October Sylvio Claude, the leader of the Christian Democrats, was rearrested.

The economy suffered from a sharp decline in the number of tourist arrivals and poor agricultural production. The development fund of the Organization of Petroleum Exporting Countries made $1.8 million available to help finance the second stage of the Artibonite Valley project, which involved the construction of access roads, drains, and canals. The European Communities agreed to provide food aid to drought-stricken areas.

(ROBIN CHAPMAN)

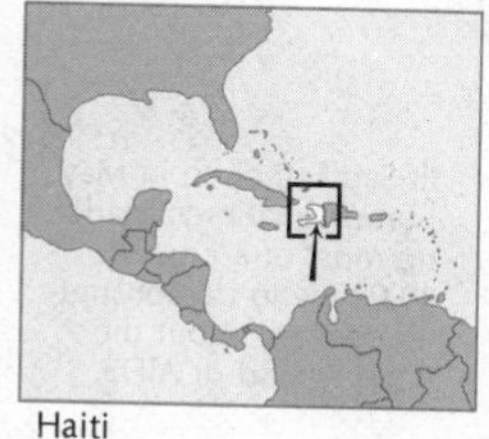
Haiti

Health and Disease

General Developments. Medical news in 1983 was laden with reports on acquired immune deficiency syndrome, or AIDS, a deadly new disease that appeared to afflict mostly homosexuals, intravenous drug users, and hemophiliacs. AIDS victims lose their ability to fight infections and usually succumb to certain forms of cancer or any of a host of rare diseases that almost never afflict people with normal immune function.

From the time AIDS was first described in 1981 until mid-1983, more than 1,600 cases in the U.S. were reported to the Centers for Disease Control in Atlanta, Ga., and outbreaks appeared in Great Britain and other European countries as well. The mortality rate was very high, and the number of known cases continued to grow by four or five per day. By the end of 1983 the theory that AIDS was being spread by an infectious agent that may be carried in blood or semen became well accepted.

These ominous figures and speculations together instilled in many people an "AIDS panic." Patients began to refuse medically necessary blood transfusions. Some people stopped donating blood even though there was no evidence that blood donors were at increased risk of developing the disease. Despite reiterations from medical experts that there was little to suggest that AIDS could be spread other than by intimate contact with blood or semen from victims, morticians refused to embalm the bodies of AIDS victims, nurses and paramedics refused to touch AIDS patients, and some dentists refused to treat persons with AIDS. Homosexuals became pariahs, with landlords turning them out of apartments and employers shunning them. Even the homosexual life-style changed. Homosexual men who regularly had numerous sex partners

Handball:
see Court Games

Harness Racing:
see Equestrian Sports

UPI

In San Francisco in May homosexual men made up most of a crowd of 10,000 who demonstrated concern about the rapid spread of AIDS.

either became celibate or sought out monogamous relationships.

As concern escalated, charges flew that the U.S. government was holding back support for research on the causes of AIDS, perhaps out of an inherent prejudice against homosexuals. Government officials vehemently denied these charges, pointing out that in 1983 alone the U.S. was spending more money on AIDS research than was spent in an eight-year period on toxic shock syndrome and Legionnaires' disease combined. The Department of Health and Human Services (HHS) designated $14.5 million for AIDS research in 1983, to which Congress added $12 million in supplements.

Out of this government-funded AIDS research came at least one promising new lead on the cause of the disease. Medical scientists at the Harvard University School of Public Health, the National Cancer Institute (NCI) in Bethesda, Md., and the Pasteur Institute in Paris suggested a link between AIDS and human T-cell leukemia virus, which was associated with a rare type of human cancer.

In retrospect 1983 might come to be regarded as the year in which the fog obscuring the nature of cancer began to disperse. The relevant research was complex and involved study of so-called oncogenes. These genes can be present in normal cells or may be introduced by a virus; under certain circumstances they promote the unconstrained and disordered cellular growth that produces malignant tumours.

In late 1982 two research teams, one led by Robert Weinberg at the Massachusetts Institute of Technology and the other by Mariano Barbacid of the NCI, published their independent discoveries of the fact that an oncogene found in human bladder cancer cells differs from its normal counterpart by a change in just one of its 4,500 chemical building blocks. This alteration leads to the production of a slightly abnormal cell protein that, in the presence of additional unknown factors, induces the cancerous process. The same aberrant gene was later demonstrated in the normal tissues of a bladder cancer patient, suggesting that inherited genetic material predisposes some people to certain kinds of cancer.

The following spring two groups, one at the Imperial Cancer Research Fund in London and the other comprising workers from the NCI and three U.S. universities, discovered that gene coding for a normal protein of the body known as platelet-derived growth factor (PDGF) is almost identical to an oncogene in a virus that causes cancer in monkeys. Ordinarily PDGF is released by special cells called platelets when blood clots, whereupon it stimulates the growth of new vessels and other cells in damaged tissues. Thus, for the first time a normal body substance was linked with a known carcinogen. Subsequently the London group demonstrated that normal cells infected with the monkey cancer virus—and thus made malignant—produce a substance that, like PDGF, stimulates growth in other, uninfected cells. All cells possess the gene that directs the manufacture of the PDGF found in platelets because all cells possess a full complement of genes, but in most cells the gene is "switched off." The British and U.S. findings and other work, however, raised the possibility that sometimes dormant PDGF genes (and perhaps genes producing other growth-promoting substances) are inappropriately switched on and that this event is one essential factor in the cancerous process. There were already several clues regarding the manner in which chemical, physical, and viral agents might bring about such gene activation.

Figures published during the year showed that the number of smokers in Great Britain had dropped by more than a million since 1980 but that individual consumption had risen among those who still smoked and that these trends were reflected throughout the European Community. More women were smoking, and in the U.K. lung cancer in women increased 4.5% over 1977, while in men the disease was down by 4% from the previous year. Several studies confirmed that smokers gain no benefit from switching to low-tar, low-nicotine cigarettes since they compensate by inhaling more smoke from each cigarette and obstruct ventilation holes around filter tips with their fingers.

In July two American research scientists published a retrospective study of the smoking habits of more than 8,300 people suggesting that smoking was almost wholly responsible for the gap between male and female life expectancies in the U.S. In the early 1980s women outlived men by about 7.5 years, primarily because men developed heart disease earlier. Other experts in the field, although agreeing that smoking was an important factor, felt that the study contained too many defects to yield a reliable conclusion.

In March Barney Clark, the first human recipient of a permanent artificial heart, died at the University of Utah Medical Center, where his operation had been performed the preceding December. Clark, 62, survived for 112 days and enjoyed periods of lucidity accompanied by feelings of comparative well-being, but much of the time he was disoriented or comatose as a result of various complications. He finally died of kidney failure and from the breakdown of other major organ systems, although the mechanical heart remained functioning to the end. In 1982 the U.S. Food and Drug Administration (FDA) had approved a series of seven experimental operations using the new device, but by late 1983 no further such ventures had been undertaken, and the general view among experts was that the technology was not yet up to the task of providing a satisfactory heart replacement.

A new drug, cyclosporine, which was approved by the FDA in the fall of 1983, was expected to greatly increase the number of medical centres offering natural heart, lung, liver, kidney, and other organ transplants. Cyclosporine prevents the rejection of transplanted organs and seemed to be not only more effective but also less toxic than antirejection drugs already in use. Transplant surgeons who had been testing the drug experimentally for several years testified before the U.S. Congress in the spring of 1983, telling how it had transformed their field of medicine. They reported that the success rate for transplants of kidneys taken from cadavers increased from 50% to 80–90% with cyclosporine, while the success rate for liver transplants rose from 35% to 65–70%.

But as a new era of transplants began, medical specialists and patients bemoaned the severe shortage of organs. In 1982 in the U.S., for example, there were about 20,000 potential donors—deceased individuals whose organs were sufficiently healthy to be transplanted—but only 2,500 of them actually donated organs. While lawmakers and government officials wrestled with the problem, desperate parents seeking liver transplants for their critically ill children made public appeals on television and in the press for donors. On several occasions U.S. Pres. Ronald Reagan offered the use of his personal jet, Air Force 1, to transport any livers found for these children.

A new procedure for detecting birth defects prenatally, called chorionic villus biopsy (CVB), attracted widespread interest during the year. Many physicians predicted that it would largely replace amniocentesis in the near future. The procedure, which samples fetal cells from hairlike external projections (villi) of the membrane (chorion) that surrounds the early fetus, is done between the eighth and tenth weeks of pregnancy, at a time when many women first suspect they are pregnant. It is painless for both the woman and the fetus. In contrast to amniocentesis, which is done between 16 and 18 weeks of pregnancy and which yields results only after fetal cells contained in the amniotic fluid have been grown in the laboratory for at least two weeks, results from CVB are available within a few hours. In theory the new technique should provide nearly the same kinds of information as amniocentesis, which could be used to detect prenatally more than 200 genetic diseases, most of which are extremely rare. The main questions about CVB, which concerned its risks and reliability, were to be addressed in a study by the National Institutes of Health (NIH).

In June, after five years of delay, the FDA approved a new biochemical test to aid in the prenatal diagnosis of neural tube defects, considered to be among the most common and most serious of all birth defects. These defects occur about once in every 1,000 births, and they are just as frequent among babies born to younger women as to older mothers. In 19 out of 20 cases there is nothing in a woman's medical history to hint that she is carrying a fetus with a neural tube defect. The problems are caused when the neural tube, the embryonic structure that eventually becomes the brain and spinal cord, fails to close early in embryonic life.

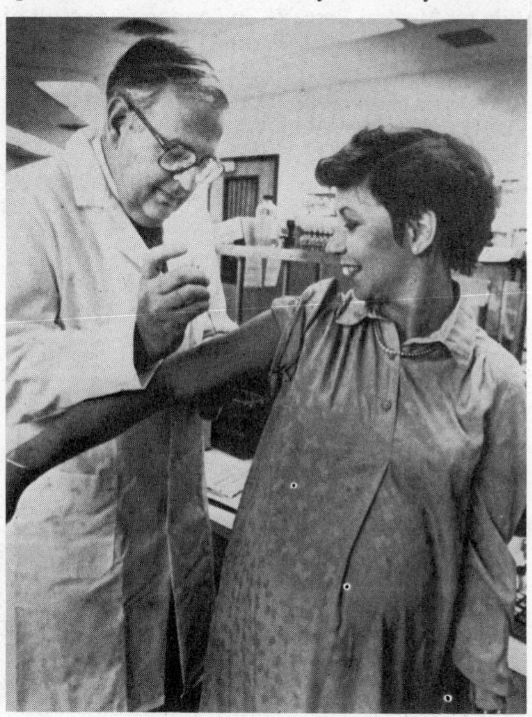
UPI

The tetanus vaccination being given a pregnant mother here by Thomas Gill of Magee-Women's Hospital, Pittsburgh, Pennsylvania, will circulate also in the unborn baby's bloodstream, giving it prenatal immunization. The technique was developed experimentally by Gill and colleagues.

The babies are born either with no brain or only a rudimentary one or with a condition known as spina bifida. Children with spina bifida nearly always are paralyzed below the waist and sometimes are mentally retarded as well.

The new test for neural tube defects formed the first part of a three-stage screening procedure. In the first stage the woman's blood is tested, at 16 to 19 weeks into the pregnancy, for excessive amounts of a fetal blood protein called alpha-fetoprotein (AFP). About 50 out of 1,000 women will have positive tests, and these women are tested again. Afterward, 30 will still show excessive amounts of AFP in their blood, and for the second stage of the procedure they are sent to their physicians for sonograms. Ultrasound imaging will eliminate 25 of these 30 women, and the final 5 women are given amniocentesis to test directly for high AFP concentrations in the amniotic fluid surrounding the fetus. On the average one of these women will be informed that her fetus has a neural tube defect.

International Aspects. In February a scientific group of the World Health Organization (WHO), meeting in Geneva, stated that "for the first time, unique opportunities exist to prevent a frequent cancer by vaccination." The experts were referring to primary liver cancer, one of the ten most common forms of cancer in the world and one of the most prevalent in developing countries. Some 80% of cases were thought to result from infection by hepatitis B virus, which was harboured by at least 200 million of the world's population. Some experts believed that at a conservative estimate a newly developed hepatitis B vaccine could prevent 200,000 liver cancer deaths each year and felt the advance to be a landmark in preventive medicine.

In April tests of a new leprosy vaccine began in Norway. Prepared from whole, dead leprosy bacilli, the vaccine was developed at the National Institute for Medical Research in London as a result of the discovery in 1971 that the nine-banded armadillo can be infected with the disease to provide a source of the necessary bacteria, which could not be grown in the laboratory. Further trials were to take place in Britain and the U.S. The tests had to be carried out in regions where the disease was not endemic, because the efficacy of the vaccine would be judged by skin tests measuring the acquisition of immunity; the "natural" immunity often developed by residents of leprosy-ridden areas would confuse results. If the vaccine proved effective a massive campaign would be mounted to eradicate the infection, which afflicted 12 million people in third world countries.

Progress was also made toward the production of a malaria vaccine. Like leprosy, malaria was rampant in the third world, its spread aided by increasingly drug-resistant malarial parasites and by mosquitoes resistant to pesticides. Figures released by WHO during the year showed that 40% of the world's population was at risk from the disease, with 300 million cases occurring annually. Using bioengineering techniques (inserting gene fragments from a malarial parasite into bacteria), scientists from the Walter and Eliza Hall Institute of Medical Research in Melbourne and the Papua New Guinea Institute of Medical Research at Goroka and Mandang produced a large series of malarial antigens (proteins that stimulate the body's immune system to produce neutralizing antibodies), the most promising of which would be used to prepare vaccines for tests on malaria-infected monkeys. G. N. Godson and colleagues at New York University Medical Center identified and synthesized a molecule present on the surface of the malarial parasite during the brief stage of its life cycle in which it is present as a free particle in the blood of people newly bitten by an infected mosquito. The synthetic antigen was found to react with antibodies present in the blood of malarial patients. If synthetic antigens proved effective, they would greatly simplify the task of producing antimalarial vaccines.

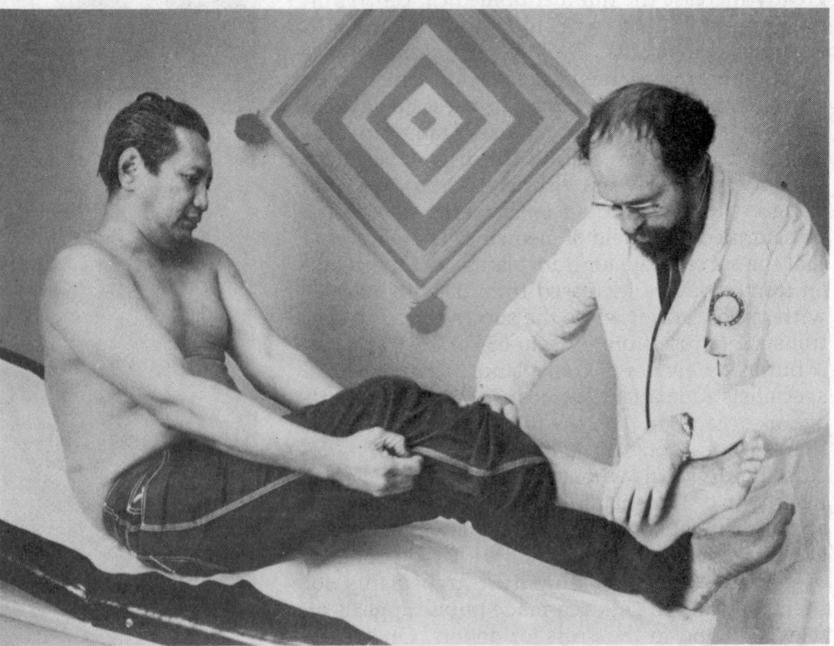

Cases of leprosy have increased fivefold in the U.S. since 1960, largely as a result of increased immigration from Asia, where the disease is still relatively common.

JAMES D. WILSON/NEWSWEEK

Regulation and Legal Matters. Under suspicion for years as a possible cause of birth defects, the controversial morning-sickness drug Bendectin (known as Debendox in the U.K.) was withdrawn by its manufacturer, Merrell Dow, in June after a 12-year-old American girl had been awarded $750,000 compensatory damages by a jury in Washington, D.C. She had been born with finger and arm deformities after her mother had been prescribed Bendectin in early pregnancy. At the time of its withdrawal the drug had been available worldwide for 27 years and had been used during more than 33 million pregnancies. Following the Washington case Merrell Dow vigorously defended the safety of the product but said that the outcome—and the fact that more than 250 further suits had already been filed—made it impossible to continue marketing the drug.

In March McNeil Pharmaceutical asked U.S. doctors to stop prescribing Zomax (zomepirac sodium), and British distributors followed suit. Introduced in 1980, Zomax had been widely prescribed for the relief of arthritic pain but was found to cause severe allergic reactions in some users. Reports of several deaths in the U.S. attributable to the drug prompted the voluntary withdrawal, despite the fact that the FDA recommended only a label change cautioning that the drug should be limited to the relief of severe intractable pain. By the end of the year talks about a possible reintroduction of Zomax were in progress.

In December 1982 an established antiarthritic drug, sodium indomethacin trihydrate, was given a new vigorous promotion by Merck Sharp & Dohme under the trade name Osmosin, only to be withdrawn in both Britain and West Germany in September. Although the active ingredient was contained within a coating designed to release it evenly over the space of 24 hours, the preparation appeared to lodge in the gut in some patients, even producing perforation of the bowel. Other severe side effects were reported, and in August Britain's Committee on Safety of Medicines (CSM) issued a warning concerning these reactions. One British authority on drug safety said, however, that the 15 deaths recorded among the 80,000 patients who had used Osmosin were not excessive for a drug of that kind, and a company spokesman expected that the product would soon again be available in the U.K., after the CSM had heard its case.

The withdrawal of Bendectin, Zomax, and Osmosin by their manufacturers in the absence of any direction from a statutory authority illustrated the nervousness currently felt by the pharmaceutical industry concerning liability for damage done, or allegedly done, by the use of its products.

In March the HHS issued so-called Baby Doe regulations in an attempt to protect the lives of babies born in the U.S. with life-threatening but correctable conditions who might otherwise be allowed to die. These regulations required that hospitals prominently post signs saying "Discriminatory failure to feed and care for handicapped infants in this facility is prohibited by federal law," the law being Section 504 of the Rehabilitation Act, which forbids discrimination against the handicapped. The government set up a 24-hour telephone hot line for persons to report incidences in which infants were denied care as well as "Baby Doe squads" of medical experts to be dispatched immediately to the scene of a suspected violation.

WIDE WORLD

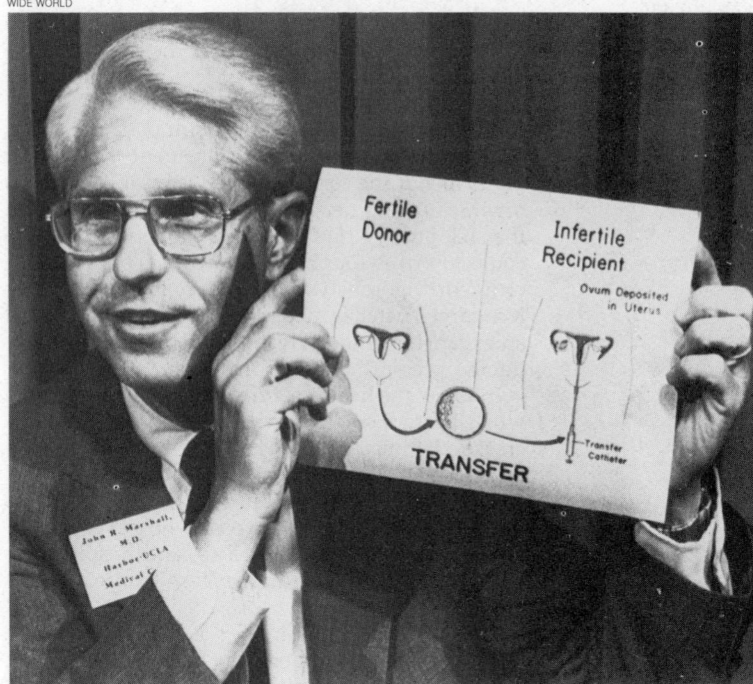

Physicians of the department of obstetrics and gynecology at Harbor-UCLA Medical Center in California claimed the first two impregnations of women as a result of transplanting an embryo directly from one woman to another. John R. Marshall, chairman of the department, holds a drawing illustrating the procedure.

The program met with resistance from medical professionals and hospitals, and the American Academy of Pediatrics filed suit against the government in April. A U.S. district court quickly struck down the Baby Doe regulations, saying that the HHS had failed to consider alternative courses to protect handicapped infants and had issued the final rules without allowing for the required 60-day comment period. The department then issued new proposals, which differed only slightly from the original ones. The hospital signs were to be smaller and to be confined to nurses' quarters, and the law regarding confidentiality of records was to be respected. Furthermore, the regulations were more specific about allowing hospitals discretion in cases in which it was clearly futile to attempt to save the infant's life. By the time the comment period ended in September, the government had received more than 10,000 comments. Representatives of hospitals and physicians still opposed the regulations; child advocacy groups and representatives of the handicapped supported them.

Medical Economics. The eight-month-long industrial dispute over the low pay of ancillary workers in Britain's National Health Service (NHS) hospitals, which was resolved at the end of 1982, left the NHS with the greatest backlog of patients in its history. Waiting lists had grown by 160,000 to 785,000; 147,000 operations had been postponed; and 125,000 outpatient appointments had been canceled. During 1983 the troubled service faced further problems when the government imposed a series of financial cuts and issued directives to regional health authorities ordering significant staff reductions, including doctors and nurses, the first NHS manpower cuts in 30 years. Criticisms of the cuts were voiced not only by the health service unions but also by such bodies as the Royal College of Nursing and the British Medical Association, both organizations claiming that standards of patient care would suffer to the point of danger. Fear was expressed that the government had secret plans to run the service down, leaving a skeleton organization to deal with the chronically ill and the sick poor, while more and more of those who could afford it sought private care. This the government vigorously denied, but Prime Minister Margaret Thatcher made it plain that she favoured an expansion of the private sector as a means of reducing pressure on the NHS.

In Israel the health service came near to collapse when doctors struck, demanding a 100% pay increase. Ultimately the Health Ministry issued mandatory return-to-work instructions to 1,300 of the strikers, threatening prison and a heavy fine for resisters. Back at their posts, however, many doctors went on hunger strikes, and hospital services remained crippled for weeks before a settlement was reached.

In April Canada's minister of health, Monique Begin, proposed a nationwide Canada Health Act to replace existing health legislation under which provincial governments controlled the provision of health care while recovering most of the cost from federal funds. The Canadian Medical Association opposed the idea, and doctors feared that federal control would deprive them of the right to charge over and above government-decreed rates for items of service. In September the Canadian government threatened to cut health-care funding to provinces that put deterrent charges on the use of hospital beds and that permitted their doctors the practice of extra billing. Begin warned doctors that, if extra charges were not stopped, "sooner or later we will be back to pre-Medicare days, with private insurance for those who can afford it." (DONALD W. GOULD; GINA KOLATA)

[421.B.2.d; 423.C.2.k; 424.A.5.b; 424.B.1.a; 424.H; 425.H; 425.I.2.d; 425.I.2.e.i; 425.J]

U.S. Medical Care Price Indexes
(1967 = 100)

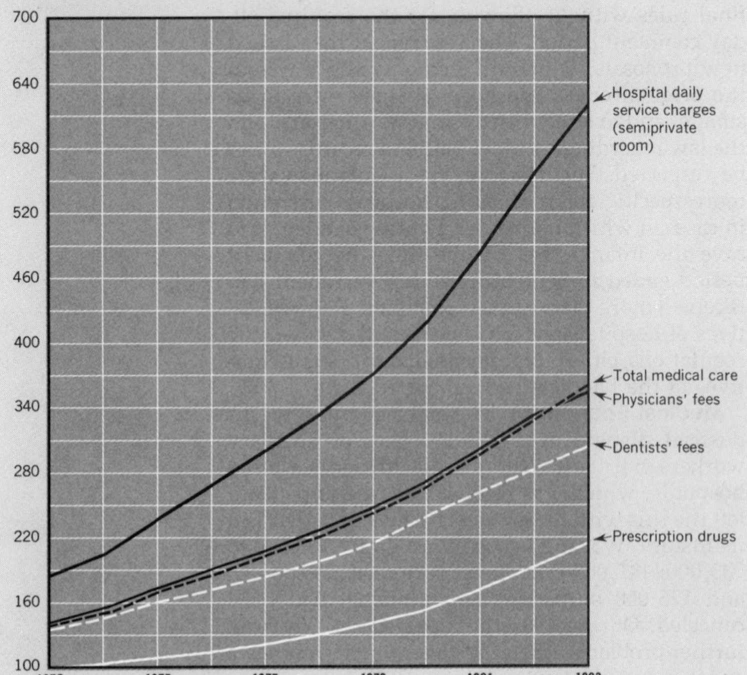

Annual averages, except 1983 data which are for July.
Source: U.S. Department of Labor, Bureau of Labor Statistics, *Monthly Labor Review.*

MENTAL HEALTH

Encouraging progress was made toward understanding the nature of schizophrenia, including the accumulation of further evidence that the disorder has its basis in organic and biochemical abnormalities in the brains of sufferers and is not the response of an anatomically and functionally normal organ to insupportable psychological and emotional pressures.

Tom Crow of the Clinical Research Centre at Northwick Park Hospital in London reported the use of a computed tomographic (CT) scanner to discriminate among structural differences in the brains of certain categories of schizophrenics. The ventricles, fluid-filled cavities in the centre of the brain, were found to be enlarged in patients whose predominant symptoms were a change of mood accompanied by a lack of drive and some loss of control of voluntary movements. Crow suggested that a transient type of the disease, linked with intellectual impairment as well as mood disturbances, is associated with a changed balance of neurotransmitters. These are chemicals (some 40 of which have been identified) mediating the passage of impulses between nerve cells.

It was already known that one such transmitter, dopamine, is unduly active in schizophrenic brains, and in September E. S. Garnett, G. Firnau, and C. Nahmias of the McMaster University Medical Centre, Hamilton, Ont., detailed a method of pinpointing the sites of action of dopamine within the brain. They injected healthy volunteers with radioactively labeled L-dopa, a substance from which the body manufactures dopamine, and three hours later used a positron emission tomographic (PET) scanner to obtain cross-sectional images of the subjects' brains. The scanner was able to identify areas in which radioactive dopamine was concentrated. Such a technique should make it possible to analyze and localize metabolic and biochemical faults associated with schizophrenia and could lead to more specific and effective therapy.

With increasing numbers of people surviving into old age, there was growing interest in senile dementia, a progressive deterioration of the intellect often seen in the elderly. Several lines of research in recent years had made it clear that most cases of senile dementia are pathologically identical to Alzheimer's disease, a label originally applied to a syndrome of mental deterioration found in younger people. In March Mahlon DeLong and colleagues at the Johns Hopkins School of Medicine in Baltimore, Md., reported their examination of the brain of a 74-year-old man who died after suffering from Alzheimer's disease for 14 years. They found a "profound and selective loss" of nerve cells in a small region of the forebrain known as the nucleus basalis of Meynert. The brains of five other Alzheimer patients showed similar changes. The Meynert cells connect with many areas of the cerebral cortex, and in earlier experiments with primates DeLong had shown that the nucleus appears to play an important role in learning and memory. The dead Meynert cells formed "burned-out plaques" containing the degradation products of a particular neurotransmitter, acetylcholine, which the cells normally supply to the cerebral cortex. It was already known that Alzheimer's disease is associated with a lack of two enzymes involved in the synthesis and recycling of acetylcholine, and improvement had been observed in some patients given large doses of choline (the immediate precursor of acetylcholine) or of a drug that protects acetylcholine from destruction. The authors claimed to have shown for the first time that a specific form of dementia is a result of faults in an identifiable nerve pathway and its biochemical machinery.

A new Mental Health Act came into force in the U.K. in September. Among other provisions it redefined the circumstances under which patients might be detained against their will, gave detained patients easier access to tribunals that might order their release, and made a second, independent, expert opinion obligatory before a patient could be subjected to certain forms of treatment (including psychosurgery and prolonged drug therapy) in the absence of informed consent. A 90-strong Mental Health Act Commission, with a large lay element, would monitor the working of the law, investigate complaints, and be empowered to visit and interview patients. Nevertheless, the new law was regarded as an unsatisfactory compromise by some champions of patients' rights, who feared that psychiatrists would still hold too much power over the civil liberties of those under their care.

In March Amnesty International announced that the known number of Soviet citizens confined to psychiatric hospitals for political reasons during the previous eight years had risen to almost 200. A month earlier the Soviet All-Union Society of Psychiatrists and Neuropathologists had resigned from the World Psychiatric Association, apparently to avoid the possibility of being publicly censured for psychiatric abuses and expelled by the WPA's General Assembly, which met in Vienna in July. (DONALD W. GOULD)

[438.D.1.a and e]

DENTISTRY

Two experimental anticancer drugs being tested in Europe and Japan appeared to have potential therapeutic value for several forms of periodontal, or gum, disease, according to Robert J. Genco of the State University of New York at Buffalo School of Dentistry and Masakazu Nakamura, a research fellow at the university. The drugs, Bestatin and Forphenicine, are two of a new class of agents, called immunomodifiers, that enhance the body's natural immunity against disease. Although the two drugs were not approved for clinical experiments in the U.S., they were available as reagents for laboratory studies. Pioneering research at Buffalo and elsewhere demonstrated that, although certain bacteria play a primary role in the development of gum disease, an inappropriate response by the body's immune system against these organisms can also be involved. In test-tube experiments the presence of immunomodifiers increased the tendency of white-blood-cell scavengers called neutrophils to surround offending bacteria. The effect, reported Nakamura, was especially enhanced in neutrophils taken from the blood of youngsters having localized juvenile periodontitis, an oral disease known to be complicated by "lazy" neutrophils that do not turn out quickly enough or in sufficient number to handle the oral bacteria. Further research was needed to determine what factors would make neutrophils more effective against the bacteria.

WIDE WORLD

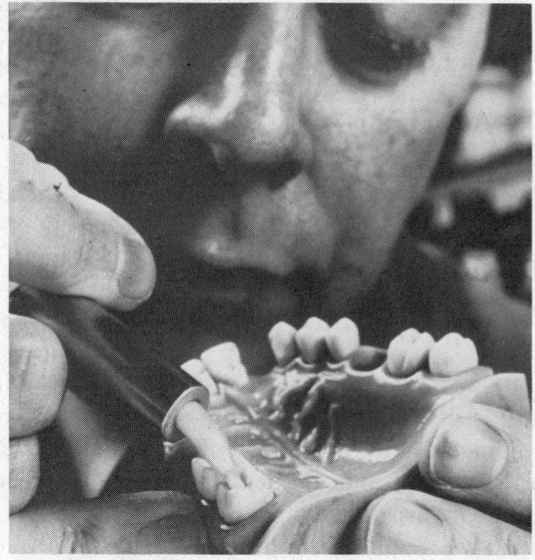

A newly developed resin-bonded ceramic filling, coloured like teeth, may supplant the use of silver fillings in molars.

Morton H. Goldberg of the University of Connecticut School of Dentistry found that impacted wisdom teeth (third molars) were a much more common occurrence in the early 1980s than a generation earlier. Data comparing two consecutive generations revealed a nearly 50% increase in the incidence of impacted third molars. Goldberg attributed this rise in part to such preventive public health services as water fluoridation, which in the process of saving millions of teeth—including first and second permanent molars—from decay made impaction of third molars more likely. Another reason was the increase in oral surgery for impacted wisdom teeth, and therefore in reported incidence, as the postwar "baby-boom" population passed through their susceptible years for third-molar problems. His study found that the vast majority of patients experiencing acute pain or infection at the time of their third-molar extractions were between the ages of 20 and 65. Goldberg felt that "this preponderance of acute symptoms during the productive adult years suggests that extractions of third molars during the late teen years may be a valid means of preventing third molar problems later in life." (LOU JOSEPH)

[422.E.1.a.ii; 10/35.C.1]

See also Demography; Life Sciences; Nobel Prizes; Social Security and Welfare Services.

ETHICS AND EXTREME MEDICAL MEASURES

by Albert R. Jonsen

Self-preservation, wrote the medieval theologian Thomas Aquinas, is the first precept of the natural law. Another thinker of a very different stripe, Thomas Hobbes, declared that man's deepest nature is to repel the supreme evil of death. These thinkers and many others have expressed a truth all of us know: we will take extreme measures to preserve ourselves in being. Yet, "extreme" means many things: we work hard for the sustenance necessary for life; we strive hard to maintain the communities that support life; we fight hard to repulse threats to life. At times, however, "extreme" refers not merely to the intense efforts all humans exert to stay alive but to measures that appear excessive.

In the realm of medical care few interventions could defeat death until recently. Nevertheless, the history of medicine relates many "extreme" measures. The bleeding, burning, purging, and poisoning to which dying patients were subjected seem to us to go beyond the bounds of reason. Furthermore, these actions rarely, if ever, succeeded. Only in the last half-century has medical science produced interventions that, in fact, do succeed in defeating death but at the same time create the impression of being excessive.

The Legacy of Low Technology. One of the glories of modern medicine is the mastery of lethal infection. Pneumonia, tuberculosis, and other life-threatening conditions caused by microorganisms now can usually be cured with powerful drugs. Lewis Thomas, a sage commentator on modern medicine, has named this sort of intervention the true "high technology" of medicine. It is relatively simple to administer, relatively free of risk, and highly effective. The goal of its administration is clear: to remove the infectious agent and restore health.

Medical science also has developed "low technology." Mechanically much more complex, it does not cure disease but staves off death by substituting for some damaged vital function. Usually such intervention is highly effective; it gives time while the body regains its own capacities. This technology for the most part centres on the support of breathing and circulation, the administration of nutrients, and the elimination of wastes. Popularly, we speak of artificial kidneys, artificial lungs, and artificial feeding; more technically, we refer to renal dialysis, ventilators, intravenous alimentation, and related techniques. This sort of technology, despite its manifest advantages, sometimes turns "extreme." A look at several perplexing cases may show how an obvious benefit can become a questionable burden.

Three "Extreme" Cases. In 1981 Clarence Herbert was admitted to a Los Angeles hospital for minor surgery. His operation succeeded, but a few hours afterward his breathing stopped. He was resuscitated and his breathing supported by a respirator. Several days later, after physicians determined that he was in a coma from which recovery was unlikely, Herbert's family decided that the respirator should be removed so that he might die. When this was done, he continued to breathe. In these details Herbert's case resembles that of Karen Ann Quinlan six years earlier. Subsequently, however, the family suggested that artificial feeding be discontinued. It was, and Herbert died one week later. The local district attorney immediately charged the doctors with homicide. Artificial feeding, he contended, was not an extreme or extraordinary measure. In March 1983 the murder charges were dismissed.

In December 1982 Barney Clark's virtually dead heart of flesh was replaced by a plastic pump tethered by hoses to a 350-lb air compressor. This was no temporary measure but was intended to maintain Clark for the rest of his days. He lived 16 weeks, during which time he needed emergency surgery twice and suffered many medical complications. After death, autopsy confirmed that virtually every major organ system in Clark's body had collapsed; the machine alone survived intact.

In San Francisco a 27-year-old woman suffered a stroke in the fifth month of her pregnancy. Her brain activity ceased soon thereafter, but her body was maintained by a variety of mechanical procedures. This support continued for 64 days, until physicians judged that the fetus within her womb could be safely delivered. They had achieved the extreme measure of sustaining two "lives," one a physiologically functioning body of a dead person, the other a developing human organism intricately dependent upon that body. Born small but healthy, the infant was christened "miracle baby" by the press.

In Clarence Herbert's case the measures were nothing more than providing the most basic elements for bodily survival. For the Herbert family and

Albert R. Jonsen is Professor of Ethics in Medicine and Chief of the Division of Medical Ethics at the Institute for Health Policy Studies, School of Medicine, University of California, San Francisco.

the doctors involved this was excessive; for the district attorney it was minimal mandatory service owed by one human to another. In Barney Clark's case the mechanical heart was a novel expedient to thwart death, but it caused extreme suffering. Realistic prospects for success were remote. In the pregnant woman's case medical machinery and attention were concentrated on a legally dead person for the sake of another life. If there is anything common in all of these instances, it is this question: to what lengths should we go to preserve human life? The three instances pose the question most dramatically because they show us people with faces and names. Can we deliberately deny life to Clarence, to Barney, to "miracle baby"?

But draw the curtain over these identifiable fellow humans, and ask the question in the abstract. Shall every such person be so treated? It is conceivable that a time will come when millions of people will be like Clarence and Barney. We nobly speak of life as having inestimable value. Yet we know the protections of life are measured out grudgingly. People are allowed to dwell in life-threatening conditions that could often be alleviated at some cost—in money or inconvenience or by forsaking some progress or profit. Are we forced to employ extreme measures in the dramatic cases because we refuse to pay those costs for the unseen ones?

The Broader Context. The three instances described above no doubt strike many people as extreme. But, lest "extreme" mean merely "unusual," it must be noted that, although such instances may be rare or unprecedented, the technology, skills, and knowledge to perform them now exist and can be perfected. Such instances may soon be commonplace. Again, "extreme" may refer to the significant human investment poured into such events; they do absorb resources that might have been used elsewhere. Yet, what is the measure of expenditure of resources that might allow us to judge one particular effort as inadequate, another as appropriate, and still another as extreme? "Extreme" also has echoes of "unreasonable" but, again, how are the reasonable to be distinguished from the unreasonable? A challenge to scale the most forbidding mountain seems unreasonable to many but eminently reasonable to some. Finally the incidents considered here represent extremity in a literal sense; they are last-ditch attempts to do something in extremis, in the final moment before death destroys life.

These three instances occurred in the United States. It is rare to hear such news from other countries. In other developed nations technology has the potential to create such instances, but that potential does not seem to be activated. Some developed countries have systems of health care in which broader questions of the well-being of the citizens as a whole dominate particular questions about excessive resources for individuals. Great Britain, for example, moved with great care into the relatively simple low technology of renal dialysis. It could not afford to allow a costly treatment that benefits few persons to swamp its health care system. In other countries, such as the Soviet Union and the People's Republic of China, technologies exist but are reserved for those persons who, it is supposed, will most benefit the state. In the less developed nations available health care resources must counter the disastrous effects of widespread starvation and unchecked infection. Preservation of life means taking food and the true high technology of medicine—vaccination and antibiotics—to masses of people. In the U.S. the centre of attention is the individual, for the diseases lethal to communities have, for the most part, been checked.

Thus, the extreme measures seen in American medicine are the product of a society of many extremes—extremely affluent, extremely confident, extremely wasteful, and extremely careless of life in general. This is not to condemn these measures as unethical. Each case must be ethically evaluated on its own terms. In the judgment of many, it is ethical to remove even the minimal measures of artificial feeding from people like Clarence Herbert who will never again recognize and share with their families. Is it unethical to move beyond this clear case to those many human beings whose minds are dim and confused but still may claim our affection and attention? It is ethical to snatch Barney Clark from the jaws of death, but is it unethical to do so without considering the quality of his remaining days and whether the many others with similar needs will be able to afford and obtain similar treatment? It is ethical to sustain the natural life-support system of an almost viable fetus; is it unethical to transform the body of death into a cradle for life?

At present these kinds of questions are being raised by the public. They are also being carefully studied in the nascent discipline of bioethics. Books are being written, conferences held, institutes founded. In the United States the President's Commission for the Study of Ethical Problems in Medicine and Biomedical and Behavioral Research (1978–82) issued a series of thoughtful and comprehensive reports, among them *Deciding to Forgo Life-Sustaining Treatment* and *Access to Health Care*. Still, it is not enough to study, debate, and recommend. Society must be constantly made aware that its extreme technical skills, its extreme scientific prowess, and its extreme wealth can be rightly used only when it is critically aware of the values that infuse its way of life.

Historic Preservation

Operating under the International Convention Concerning the Protection of the World Cultural and Natural Heritage, the World Heritage Committee held its seventh session in Florence, Italy, during Dec. 5–9, 1983, and added 29 monuments and sites to the World Heritage List. This brought the total to 165. Among the historic monuments and sites newly "inscribed" because of their "exceptional universal value" were: the ruins of the Jesuit Church to the Guaraní Indians at São Miguel das Missões (in the southern Brazilian state of Rio Grande do Sul), built about 1780; the ancient city of Nesebur, dating from the Thracian period, and the Rita Monastery (14th–19th centuries), both in Bulgaria; the 18th-century Pilgrimage Church "in der Wiesen" in Steingaden, Bavaria, West Germany; the Place Stanislas, Place de la Carrière, and Place d'Alliance, Nancy, and the Church of Saint-Savin-sur-Gartemps, Vienne, in France; the Agra Ford (1565–73) and the Taj Mahal (1631–48), both in Uttar Pradesh, India; the pre-Columbian-through-19th-century city of Cuzco and the historic sanctuary of Machu Picchu, both in Peru; the historic centre of the town of Angra do Heroísmo (Azores), the Monastery of Batalha (Gothic and Manueline architectural styles), and the Convent of Christ (Tomar), in Portugal; the 9th–18th-century Convent of St. Gall and the Benedictine Convent of St. John (Müstair), famous for its Carolingian frescoes, in Switzerland; and La Fortaleza and San Juan historic site in Puerto Rico.

As of November 1983, 78 nations had deposited an instrument of ratification or acceptance of the 1972 World Heritage Convention. The countries that had adhered to the convention since August 1982 were Antigua and Barbuda, Bangladesh, Cameroon, Colombia, Jamaica, Lebanon, Luxembourg, Madagascar, Mozambique, Turkey, and the Vatican City State.

Based on agreements with the governments of Turkey and Cuba, two international campaigns to safeguard the cultural heritage were launched by the director general of UNESCO in 1983. In Turkey an appeal was made to the international community in May to support the preservation and restoration of selected monuments and sites in Istanbul and Goreme in Cappadocia (central Anatolia). The project in Istanbul would include: the rehabilitation and restoration of the 5th-century land-side city walls and the development of an adjacent greenbelt and archaeological park; the rehabilitation of the seawalls; and the restoration of the historic Suleymaniye quarter.

At Goreme artistic expression and geology had combined to produce unique monuments. Thousands of years of erosion of the subsoil resulted in a landscape characterized by rock outcroppings of extraordinary shapes and valleys surrounded by escarpments. The area had for centuries been used as a refuge for religious communities who hollowed out the outcroppings for use as churches, monasteries, and monastic cells. As a result an important centre of early Christian and Byzantine art was created. These monuments and works of art were now threatened by rain, erosion, and frost. The total cost of the Istanbul and Goreme international campaign was estimated at $109 million.

An appeal for a campaign to preserve and restore the Plaza Vieja in Havana, Cuba, was made by UNESCO's director general in July. Originally built in the mid-16th century, the Plaza Vieja, which is surrounded by structures in Baroque, Neoclassical, and Art Nouveau styles, is an urban square of great historic and artistic value. It was estimated that this project would cost $6.7 million.

The Intergovernmental Committee for Promoting the Return of Cultural Property to its Countries of Origin or its Restitution in Case of Illicit Appropriation convened its third session in Istanbul in May 1983. Questions of return and restitution had frequently resulted in difficult debates; however, the most recent meeting was characterized by a greater willingness to negotiate and to follow the precise mechanisms that the committee had delineated.

Of importance in connection with the training of specialists for the conservation and restoration of cultural property was an international symposium on the conservation of wood, held in Tokyo and Saitama, Japan, in November 1982. The proceedings of this symposium, which was organized by the Tokyo National Research Institute of Cultural Properties, were published in 1983. The participants endorsed a recommendation to establish an international course on wood conservation technology, similar to the UNESCO-sponsored eight-week course in stone conservation conducted in alternate years in Venice by the International Centre for the Study of the Conservation and Res-

IVERSON—GAMMA/LIAISON

The Sphinx of Egypt is eroding, thought by some experts to be occurring because salt levels are rising in its porous limestone skin from pools underground. A protective coating is being applied in hopes of slowing or stopping the shedding.

Hebrew Literature: *see* Literature

Highways: *see* Engineering Projects; Transportation

Hinduism: *see* Religion

toration of Cultural Property. Sponsored by the Norwegian government and UNESCO, the first "International Course on Wood Technology" for young professionals was to take place in June–July 1984 in Trondheim, Norway.

Two world-famous 19th-century monuments, the Eiffel Tower in Paris and the Statue of Liberty in New York Harbor, were undergoing extensive renovation during 1983. Work on the Eiffel Tower, begun in February 1981, was completed during the year, but that on the Statue of Liberty would continue until 1986, when centennial celebrations would mark its first 100 years. Both monuments were tributes to the engineering genius of Alexandre-Gustave Eiffel. (JOHN POPPELIERS)

See also Architecture; Environment; Museums.

Honduras

A republic of Central America, Honduras is bounded by Nicaragua, El Salvador, Guatemala, the Caribbean Sea, and the Pacific Ocean. Area: 112,088 sq km (43,277 sq mi). Pop. (1983 est.): 4,095,000, including 90% mestizo. Cap. and largest city: Tegucigalpa (pop., 1981 est., 502,500). Language: Spanish; some Indian dialects. Religion: Roman Catholic. President in 1983, Roberto Suazo Córdova.

The election of a civilian government in November 1981 did little to quell unrest in Honduras. Throughout 1983 the administration's authority continued to be severely undermined by mounting political tension along the border with Nicaragua, sluggish economic growth, and increasing speculation over the poor health of Pres. Roberto Suazo Córdova. The hard-line leader of the Army, Gen. Gustavo Álvarez Martínez, had consolidated his position in November 1982 when he was made commander in chief of the armed forces, a title formerly held by the president.

Overall security within the region deteriorated. The Nicaraguan Democratic Force rebels, who were based in Honduras and allegedly received backing from the U.S., intensified their raids across the border into Nicaragua. Altogether some 30,000 refugees were believed to have entered the country from El Salvador and Nicaragua. Honduras remained the linchpin of U.S. policy in Central America: in 1983 the U.S. sent additional military advisers there, set up a training base for Salvadoran soldiers at Puerto Castilla, and in August launched Operation Big Pine II, which involved 4,000 U.S. and 6,000 Honduran troops in military maneuvers and was to continue until March 1984. (LUCY BLACKBURN)

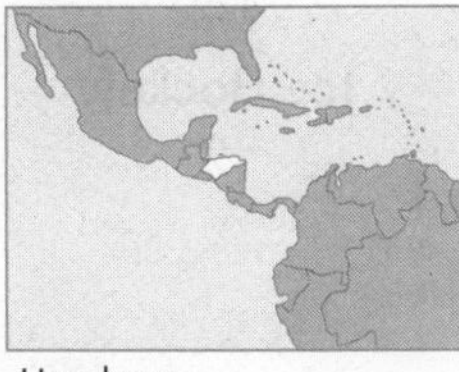
Honduras

HONDURAS

Education. (1983) Primary, pupils 704,612, teachers 19,270; secondary and vocational, pupils 120,912, teachers 3,238; teacher training, students 2,333, teachers 168; higher (universities only), students 27,925, teaching staff 1,606.

Finance. Monetary unit: lempira, with (Sept. 20, 1983) a par value of 2 lempiras to U.S. $1 (free rate of 3.01 lempiras = £1 sterling). Gold and other reserves (June 1983) U.S. $99 million. Budget (1982 actual): revenue 770.1 million lempiras; expenditure 1,149,700,000 lempiras. Gross national product (1982) 5,228,000,000 lempiras. Money supply (Dec. 1982) 716.9 million lempiras. Cost of living (Tegucigalpa; 1975 = 100; Feb. 1983) 203.7.

Foreign Trade. (1981) Imports 1,898,200,000 lempiras; exports 1,520,800,000 lempiras. Import sources: U.S. 41%; Trinidad and Tobago 9%; Japan 7%; Guatemala 6%; Costa Rica 5%. Export destinations: U.S. 52%; West Germany 8%; Japan 6%. Main exports: bananas 27%; coffee 23%; meat 6%; sugar 6%; metal ores 5%.

Transport and Communications. Roads (1982) 9,042 km. Motor vehicles in use (1982): passenger 58,900; commercial 18,200. Railways (1981) 1,768 km. Air traffic (1982): 331 million passenger-km; freight c. 3.1 million net ton-km. Shipping (1982): merchant vessels 100 gross tons and over 172; gross tonnage 234,148. Telephones (Jan. 1980) 27,400. Radio receivers (Dec. 1980) 176,000. Television receivers (Dec. 1980) 49,000.

Agriculture. Production (in 000; metric tons; 1982): corn 509; sorghum 58; sugar, raw value (1981) 220; dry beans c. 42; bananas c. 1,338; plantains c. 170; oranges c. 28; pineapples c. 37; palm oil c. 8; coffee c. 82; cotton, lint c. 7; tobacco c. 8; beef and veal (1981) c. 50; timber (cu m; 1981) c. 5,446. Livestock (in 000; 1981): cattle 2,336; pigs c. 580; horses c. 151; chickens c. 4,900.

Industry. Production (in 000; metric tons; 1981): lead ore (metal content) 14; zinc ore (metal content) 18; cement c. 500; petroleum products 508; electricity (kw-hr) 955,000.

Hungary

A people's republic of central Europe, Hungary is bordered by Czechoslovakia, the U.S.S.R., Romania, Yugoslavia, and Austria. Area: 93,036 sq km (35,921 sq mi). Pop. (1983 est.): 10,685,000, including (1978 est.) Magyar 98.6%; Gypsy 0.3%; German 0.3%; other 0.8%. Cap. and largest city: Budapest (pop., 1983 est., 2,067,000). Language: Hungarian 95.8%. Religion (1980 est.): Roman Catholic 54%; Protestant 21.6%; atheist 7.2%; other 8.5%; none 8.7%. First secretary of the Hungarian Socialist Workers' (Communist) Party in 1983, Janos Kadar; chairman of the Presidential Council (chief of state), Pal Losonczi; president of the Council of Ministers (premier), Gyorgy Lazar.

While Hungary's position within the socialist camp was unusual in many ways, in one respect it was unique: both East and West heaped praises upon it. Soviet Pres. Yury Andropov warmly welcomed First Secretary Janos Kadar to Moscow on July 18, 1983. Andropov had been Soviet ambassador to Hungary during the years 1953–57, a period that covered the 1956 uprising and Kadar's subsequent appointment as head of government. In an official communiqué, the two old friends noted with satisfaction the successful development of relations between the Communist Party of the Soviet Union and the Hungarian Socialist Workers' (Communist) Party (HSWP) and between their two countries. The communiqué added that all the conditions for "further consolidation of fruitful cooperation on the basis of socialist internationalism" existed.

On July 20 Andropov presented Kadar with the Order of Lenin. He described Kadar as a good friend of the Soviet people and talked of the "longstanding and durable ties of international solidarity" that linked Hungary and the Soviet Union. In reply, Kadar expressed his gratitude for "the friendly references to the party and the people of Hungary." He stated that "as a result of the liberation struggle by the Soviet Union," Hungary had "regained independence and embarked on the

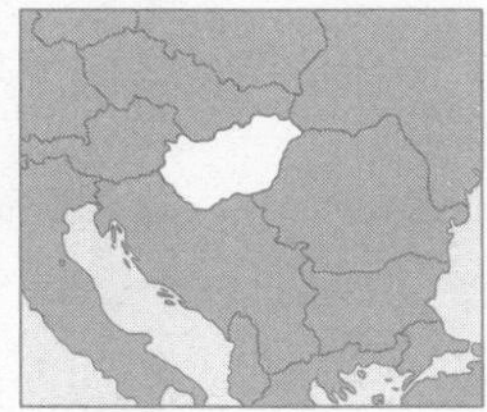
Hungary

Hockey:
see Field Hockey and Lacrosse; Ice Hockey

Holland:
see Netherlands, The

Hong Kong:
see Dependent States

Horse Racing:
see Equestrian Sports; Gambling

Horticulture:
see Gardening

Hospitals:
see Health and Disease

path of independent socialist development." He also asserted that "the extremist circles of the U.S. and NATO" were the main cause of present-day international tensions. During the Hungarian delegation's visit to Moscow, Deputy Premier Jozsef Marjai signed a protocol agreeing to supply the U.S.S.R. with alumina and aluminum for a further five-year period.

Among Western statesmen who visited Budapest were French Premier Pierre Mauroy in July and Sir Geoffrey Howe, the British foreign secretary, and U.S. Vice-Pres. George Bush in September. All three were cordially received. However, Kadar, Premier Gyorgy Lazar, and Peter Varkonyi, who was appointed foreign minister on July 8, all explained to their guests that Hungary could not accept the Western view of the balance of power in nuclear armaments in Europe. While the Western visitors expressed appreciation of the results of the New Economic Mechanism, introduced in 1968, the Hungarian leaders warned them not to misrepresent the nature of the reform. It reduced centralized planning, encouraged initiative at factory level, and improved efficiency, but it was not a return to capitalism and free enterprise.

Andropov appeared convinced that detailed central planning in the huge, diversified Soviet economy was counterproductive. He was interested, therefore, in the Hungarian experience, and in September he sent Mikhail Gorbachev, a Politburo member concerned with agriculture, and Vladimir Dolgikh, head of the entire Soviet energy complex, to Budapest to study it.

In mid-September the prices of consumer goods rose by as much as 23%; sugar and cooking oil went up by 20%, bread by 16%, and margarine by 10%. *Nepszabadsag*, the HSWP daily newspaper, cited the year's poor harvest as the principal cause of shortfalls in agricultural production, but it admitted that the price increases were mainly designed to reduce domestic consumption and encourage exports. Ferenc Havasi, a secretary of the HSWP Central Committee, noted in a speech that slow modernization and inability to compete in foreign markets had contributed to the poor performance of the economy over the January–July period. Hungary's debts to Western banks amounted to nearly $10 billion, the highest debt per capita in Eastern Europe. Nevertheless, it received a $200 million long-term loan from a consortium of Western commercial banks on April 18, as well as a $238 million loan from the World Bank on July 6. (K. M. SMOGORZEWSKI)

U.S. Vice-Pres. George Bush (right) reviewed the honour guard with Hungarian Premier Gyorgy Lazar during an official visit to Budapest in September.

WIDE WORLD

HUNGARY

Education. (1981–82) Primary, pupils 1,213,465, teachers 78,053; secondary, pupils 209,300, teachers 15,966; vocational, students 157,400, teachers 10,700; higher, students 102,564, teaching staff 13,843.

Finance. Monetary unit: forint, with (Sept. 20, 1983) a free rate of 44.71 forints to U.S. $1 (67.33 forints = £1 sterling). Gold and other reserves (June 1983) U.S. $928 million. Budget (1982 actual): revenue 485.8 billion forints; expenditure 498 billion forints. Gross domestic product (1982) 842.9 billion forints. Money supply (March 1983) 166.7 billion forints. Consumer prices (1975 = 100; June 1983) 160.7.

Foreign Trade. (1982) Imports 324,820,000,000 forints; exports 324,490,000,000 forints. Import sources: U.S.S.R. 29%; West Germany 11%; East Germany 7%; Czechoslovakia 5%; Austria 5%. Export destinations: U.S.S.R. 34%; West Germany 7%; East Germany 6%; Czechoslovakia 6%. Main exports: machinery 21%; food 20%; chemicals 10%; motor vehicles 9%; textiles and clothing 6%; crude oil and products 6%.

Transport and Communications. Roads (1981) 87,142 km (including 209 km expressways). Motor vehicles in use (1981): passenger 1,105,400; commercial 129,800. Railways: (1981) 7,829 km; traffic (1982) 11,870,000,000 passenger-km, freight 22,726,000,000 net ton-km. Air traffic (1982): 1,208,000,000 passenger-km; freight c. 9.2 million net ton-km. Inland waterways in regular use (1981) 1,373 km. Telephones (Jan. 1981) 1,261,300. Radio receivers (Dec. 1980) 2.7 million. Television licenses (Dec. 1981) 2,806,000.

Agriculture. Production (in 000; metric tons; 1982): corn c. 7,400; wheat c. 6,200; barley c. 980; rye c. 120; potatoes c. 1,500; sugar, raw value c. 554; cabbages (1981) c. 170; tomatoes c. 365; onions c. 139; sunflower seed 577; rapeseed 77; green peas (1981) c. 197; plums (1981) c. 170; apples c. 1,000; wine c. 600; tobacco c. 21; milk c. 2,740; beef and veal c. 176; pork c. 980. Livestock (in 000; Dec. 1981): cattle 1,945; pigs 8,296; sheep 3,137; horses 112; chickens 63,629.

Industry. Index of production (1975 = 100; 1982) 124. Production (in 000; metric tons; 1982): coal 3,041; lignite 23,041; crude oil 2,026; natural gas (cu m) 6,627,000; petroleum products (1981) 9,792; electricity (kw-hr) 24,416,000; iron ore (24% metal content) 466; pig iron 2,191; crude steel 3,703; bauxite 2,627; aluminum 74; cement 4,369; sulfuric acid 569; fertilizers (1981) nitrogenous 691, phosphate c. 234; cotton yarn 53; man-made fibres 21; commercial vehicles (units) 11.

Ice Hockey

North America. The final matchup in the Stanley Cup tournament for the championship of the National Hockey League was to have been a "dream series" between the league's highest scoring team, the young and fleet Edmonton Oilers, and its best defensive team, the three-time champion New York Islanders. But the hopes of the younger team were dashed in a four-game sweep as the Islanders decisively claimed their fourth consecutive Stanley Cup and a pedestal in NHL history. Only one other team had ever won four cups or more in a row. The Montreal Canadiens took five straight championships from 1956 to 1960 and added another four beginning in 1976.

The Islanders defeated the Washington Capi-

WIDE WORLD

Heroic efforts by Andy Moog, goalie for the Edmonton Oilers, did not prevent this goal by the New York Islanders in the fourth Stanley Cup play-off game, held at Uniondale, New York. Islander Mike Bossy exulted. The Islanders won 4–2 and the victory gave them a four-game sweep and the championship.

tals, the improved New York Rangers, and the Boston Bruins on the way to the finals. Catalyst for the final victory over Edmonton was Billy Smith (*see* BIOGRAPHIES), the contentious and talented goaltender, who worked with his teammates to add the extra fillip of shutting out Wayne Gretzky, the Oilers' record-breaking centre.

A well-reported dispute that broke out between Smith and Gretzky detracted from some fine hockey in which the experienced Islanders under the steady hand of coach Al Arbour consistently foiled the spirited Edmonton attack. After averaging 5.3 goals per game during the season, the Oilers scored only six goals against the Islanders in the four games. Smith won the Conn Smythe Trophy as the play-offs' most valuable player.

Gretzky's scorelessness in the Stanley Cup defeat marred an otherwise astonishing season during which he further demonstrated the magnitude of his talent by setting or tying 18 league records. In just his fourth year in the NHL, "The Great Gretzky" now held 18 of a possible 22 regular-season scoring records. He won the Art Ross Trophy for the third year in a row with 71 goals and 125 assists, 72 points higher than the next closest contender. He also won the Hart Trophy as the regular season's most valuable player, the only player in the league's 66-year history to win four of those trophies in succession.

An improvement in the quality of ice hockey in the United States became evident at the 1983 amateur draft when five U.S.-born players were selected in the first round. Among them was Brian Lawton of Cumberland, R.I., the first U.S. player ever to be chosen number one overall in the draft. Selected by the Minnesota North Stars, the 18-year-old centre gave up a chance to compete for the United States team in the 1984 Winter Olympics and chose instead to sign immediately with the professional team. Pat LaFontaine, a centre from the Detroit suburb of Waterford, Mich., was chosen third in the draft by the Islanders but decided to compete in the Olympics first.

At the close of the 1982–83 season, the NHL governors failed to approve the sale by the Ralston Purina Co. of the St. Louis Blues to Canadian investors who planned to move the team to Saskatchewan. Ralston Purina promptly filed an antitrust suit against the league and prepared to liquidate the team's assets. But the NHL quickly terminated the company's league membership and took control of the players' contracts before they could be auctioned off. The league then found a new group of owners headed by Harry Ornest, a California investor, which bought the team for $12 million and promised to keep it in St. Louis.

Trophy winners for the season included Orval Tessier, Chicago's rookie coach, who led his team to a first-place finish in the Norris Division and won the Adams Award as the league's best coach. Other rookie coaches were Nick Polano, who could make little quick progress with the dismal Detroit Red Wings; Bob Johnson with the respectable Calgary Flames; and Larry Kish, who coached the Hartford Whalers until midseason, when he was relieved by Larry Pleau, the Whalers' director of hockey operations. Pleau then left for health reasons and appointed John Cunniff to coach. At the season's end Emile Francis became the director of operations and replaced Cunniff with Jack ("Tex") Evans.

Pete Peeters of Boston received the Vezina Trophy as best goaltender. Mike Bossy of the Islanders won the Lady Byng Trophy for most gentlemanly player. Rod Langway of Washington was voted the Norris Trophy as best defenseman. Steve Larmer of Chicago, a right wing who led all rookie scorers, was the rookie of the year. Bobby Clarke of Philadelphia won the Selke Trophy as the top defensive forward. The Islanders' Roland Melanson and Billy Smith won the William Jennings Trophy for the goaltending team with the fewest goals scored against it. Lanny McDonald of Calgary won the Bill Masterton Trophy for sportsmanship and dedication to hockey.

In the American Hockey League the Rochester Americans, a Buffalo Sabres affiliate, beat Maine for the championship. In the Central Hockey League the Indianapolis Checkers, a New York Islanders affiliate, won the championship for the second straight season.

(ROBIN CATHY HERMAN)

Hydroelectric Power: *see* Energy; Engineering Projects

Hydrology: *see* Earth Sciences

European and International. Any reasonable chance to compare top North American and European talent during 1983 was thwarted once again by the contracts of players engaged in the Stanley Cup play-offs, necessitating the selection of Canadian and U.S. national teams well below their maximum potential. The International Ice Hockey Federation (IIHF), which celebrated its 75th jubilee, again proposed a world club championship event, perhaps involving a series of games, between the NHL Stanley Cup winners and the European Cup winners. The prospect fired the imagination of many enthusiasts. This and other ideas for increasing transatlantic competition were considered to be inevitable progressions in the sport's best interests, and the IIHF urged its 31 member nations to try to adapt their domestic schedules to permit fuller representation in future world championships.

The 24 participating nations in the 49th world championships were again divided into three sections, the eight in Group A contesting the title on April 16–May 2 in Dortmund, Düsseldorf, and Munich, West Germany. Preliminary round-robin matches in Group A decided which four of the eight teams would play for the medals; they restarted on an equal footing in a second round-robin series. The remaining four teams also played each other once more, these and the previous games determining their final order. The last-place team in Group A, Italy, was relegated to Group B for the 1985 season (there being no world championships during the Olympic year of 1984).

A sixth straight Soviet success took the U.S.S.R.'s total number of world championships to 19, equal to Canada, which last won in 1961. Ironically, it was an 8–2 defeat of Canada in the final match that clinched the verdict, extending the Soviet Union's unbeaten streak to 45 consecutive world championship matches since 1978. However, the Soviets this time finished even on points with the silver medalist, Czechoslovakia, with whom they tied 1–1, and the title was retained only by superior goal difference. Canada took the bronze medal, followed by Sweden, the first four repeating their sequence of the previous season.

Sergey Makarov topped the point scorers with 18 from 9 goals and 9 assists, followed by his Soviet compatriot Vladimir Krutov and Kiri Lala of Czechoslovakia, with 15 and 14, respectively.

The U.S., demoted the previous season, gained quick promotion back to Group A by decisively heading the eight nations in Group B on March 21–31 in Tokyo. Undefeated in its seven matches and conceding just one point in a tied game, the U.S. beat the runners-up from Poland 6–2 to emphasize a clear superiority in this section. Yugoslavia, after gaining promotion the year before, was relegated back to Group C after salvaging only one point, a blow for the 1984 Olympic host nation. Romania, next from last, was also demoted.

The Netherlands won promotion back to Group B with a convincing 100% record in Group C on March 11–20 in Budapest, Hung. Averaging 11 goals a game, the Dutch team finished four points ahead of the next nation, Hungary, which also was promoted.

Twelve nations were nominated for the Olympic competition in 1984 at Sarajevo, Yugos.—the U.S. as defending champions, Yugoslavia as host, seven of the eight Group A nations (the other, East Germany, having declined to compete), and Poland, Austria, and Norway. A separate 1984 tournament was announced, for the Thayer Tutt Trophy, for national teams not qualifying for the Olympics, at a site to be decided. It was agreed that in the future no player could represent a second country without first participating in that country's national championships for three years.

In the seventh world junior (under 21) championship, in January in Leningrad, the U.S.S.R. recaptured the title from the defending champion, Canada, which finished third. With Czechoslovakia second and Sweden fourth, the first four ended in the same order as their national seniors. The other four competing nations, Finland, the U.S., West Germany, and Norway, finished in that sequence. The Soviets won all seven of their games.

Table I. NHL Final Standings, 1983

	Won	Lost	Tied	Goals	Goals against	Pts.
Clarence Campbell Conference						
NORRIS DIVISION						
Chicago	47	23	10	338	268	104
Minnesota	40	24	16	321	290	96
Toronto	28	40	12	293	330	68
St. Louis	25	40	15	285	316	65
Detroit	21	44	15	263	344	57
SMYTHE DIVISION						
Edmonton	47	21	12	424	315	106
Calgary	32	34	14	321	317	78
Vancouver	30	35	15	303	309	75
Winnipeg	33	39	8	311	333	74
Los Angeles	27	41	12	308	365	66
Prince of Wales Conference						
ADAMS DIVISION						
Boston	50	20	10	327	228	110
Montreal	42	24	14	350	286	98
Buffalo	38	29	13	318	285	89
Quebec	34	34	12	343	336	80
Hartford	19	54	7	261	403	45
PATRICK DIVISION						
Philadelphia	49	23	8	326	240	106
N.Y. Islanders	42	26	12	302	226	96
Washington	39	25	16	306	283	94
N.Y. Rangers	35	35	10	306	287	80
New Jersey	17	49	14	230	338	48
Pittsburgh	18	53	9	257	394	45

Table II. World Ice Hockey Championships, 1983

	Won	Lost	Tied	Goals	Goals against	Pts.
GROUP A Championship Section						
U.S.S.R.	2	0	1	13	3	5
Czechoslovakia	2	0	1	10	6	5
Canada	1	2	0	9	14	2
Sweden	0	3	0	2	11	0
GROUP A Relegation Section						
West Germany	5	4	1	31	34	11
East Germany	3	7	0	29	40	6
Finland	2	6	2	30	40	6
Italy	1	8	1	16	56	3
GROUP B						
United States	6	0	1	53	14	13
Poland	5	1	1	43	19	11
Austria	3	0	4	41	27	10
Norway	4	3	0	29	28	8
Japan	2	3	2	23	31	6
Switzerland	1	4	2	25	35	4
Romania	1	5	1	20	48	3
Yugoslavia	0	6	1	18	50	1
GROUP C						
Netherlands, The	7	0	0	78	11	14
Hungary	5	2	0	50	25	10
China	4	2	1	28	23	9
Denmark	4	3	0	24	26	8
France	3	3	1	41	25	7
Bulgaria	1	5	1	20	36	3
Spain	1	5	1	17	55	3
North Korea	1	6	0	15	72	2

Ice Skating:
see Winter Sports

The Canadians, who tied with Czechoslovakia, were denied the silver because they lost to Sweden. Another 13 nations competed in lower groups in the world junior championships.

There was a heartening resurgence for the sport in Great Britain, where, despite inadequate ice time and spectator facilities, a newly formed British League involving Anglo-Scottish participation was well supported. There were good prospects for a rise in playing standards. (HOWARD BASS)

Iceland

Iceland is an island republic in the North Atlantic Ocean, near the Arctic Circle. Area: 103,000 sq km (39,769 sq mi). Pop. (1983 est.): 235,400. Cap. and largest city: Reykjavik (pop., 1983 est., 86,100). Language: Icelandic. Religion: 97% Lutheran. President in 1983, Vigdís Finnbogadóttir; prime ministers, Gunnar Thoroddsen and, from May 26, Steingrímur Hermannsson.

Developments in Iceland during 1983 were dominated by the sharp economic recession that had begun the previous year with a fall of 2% in real gross national product (GNP) and continued in 1983 with an estimated 6% decline. The decrease in both years was due to a shortfall in the fish catch, the mainstay of the economy. The 1982 downturn in production had been accompanied by a continued rise in overall demand, with the result that the current account deficit reached 10% of GNP. However, measures to correct the deficit were not introduced until mid-1983, after parliamentary elections had taken place on April 23.

Prior to the elections the coalition government of the left-wing People's Alliance, the Progressive Party, and a splinter group from the Independence (Conservative) Party had ruled without an effective majority for most of the winter of 1982–83 and had proved unable to come to grips with the major economic issues. The elections produced gains for two new political groups that presented candidates for the first time: the Social Democratic Federation, a splinter group from the Social Democrats, and the Feminists, the first all-woman party to contest an election in Europe. They received 4 and 3 seats, respectively, in the 60-member legislature. The right-of-centre Independence Party received 39% of the vote and 23 seats, a gain of 2 over the 1979 elections. The other three main parties all lost seats. (For tabulated results, *see* POLITICAL PARTIES.)

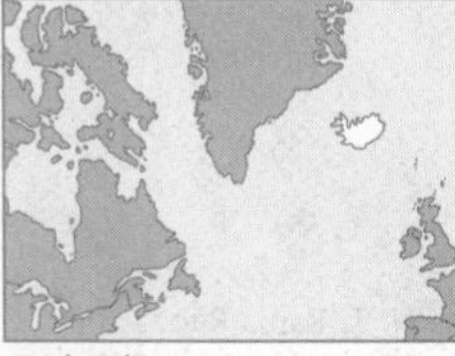
Iceland

After the election the Independence Party and the Progressive Party formed a coalition under the prime ministership of Progressive Party leader Steingrímur Hermannsson (*see* BIOGRAPHIES). The government proceeded immediately to implement a drastic package of economic measures, the principal one being a suspension of the adjustment of wages to price increases. The inflation rate subsided quickly, from 130–150% early in 1983 to an estimated 25% at the end of the year. These measures also meant that real disposable personal income would fall by some 15% between 1982 and 1983 and private consumption by about 10%.

For many years Iceland had been a minor whaling nation. In 1983 the Icelandic government reluctantly bowed to international pressure, and on February 2 Parliament voted 29–28 not to protest the worldwide ban on commercial whaling that was to take effect at the end of 1985.

Since 1980 relations between the Icelandic government and Alusuisse, a Swiss concern that owned an aluminum smelter in Iceland, had become increasingly chilly. The main point at issue was the fact that Alusuisse was purchasing electric power at contractual prices that the government claimed were far too low. Alusuisse was also accused of tax avoidance through questionable bookkeeping practices. The new government took a much friendlier line toward Alusuisse, and in September it reached a provisional agreement with the company for an increase of nearly 50% in the price it was paying for electricity.

On November 6 Thorsteinn Pálsson was elected chairman of the largest political party, the Independence Party, at its semiannual convention. He succeeded Geir Hallgrímsson, who was foreign minister in the new government and had been prime minister during the period 1974–78. Pálsson was a relative newcomer to politics, but he had become very popular within his party in the short time that he had been a member of Parliament.

Gunnar Thoroddsen (*see* OBITUARIES), prime minister in the government that left office in May, died on September 25. (BJÖRN MATTHÍASSON)

ICELAND

Education. (1982–83) Primary, pupils 25,000, teachers (including preprimary and secondary lower level) 2,600; secondary and vocational, pupils 25,900, teachers (1979–80) 1,340; teacher training, pupils (1982–83) 180, teachers (1975–76) 30; higher, students 4,780, teaching staff 280.

Finance. Monetary unit: króna, with (Sept. 20, 1983) a free rate of 28.06 krónur to U.S. $1 (42.26 krónur = £1 sterling). Gold and other reserves (June 1983) U.S. $147 million. Budget (1981 actual): revenue 6,621,000,000 krónur; expenditure 6,382,730,000 krónur. Gross national product (1982) 31,063,000,000 krónur. Money supply (May 1983) 2,690,000,000 krónur. Cost of living (Reykjavik; 1975 = 100; May 1983) 2,162.

Foreign Trade. (1982) Imports 11,647,100,000 krónur; exports 8,486,400,000 krónur. Import sources: West Germany 12%; Denmark 10%; U.S.S.R. 9%; U.K. 9%; U.S. 8%; Sweden 8%; Norway 7%; The Netherlands 7%; Japan 5%. Export destinations: U.S. 26%; U.K. 13%; Portugal 12%; U.S.S.R. 8%; West Germany 7%. Main exports: fish and products 75%; aluminum 10%; textiles and clothing 5%.

Transport and Communications. Roads (1982) 11,631 km. Motor vehicles in use (1982): passenger 94,700; commercial 10,500. There are no railways. Air traffic (1982): 1,405,000,000 passenger-km; freight 23.7 million net ton-km. Shipping (1982): merchant vessels 100 gross tons and over 387; gross tonnage 181,355. Telephones (Dec. 1981) 111,500. Radio licenses (Dec. 1981) 69,700. Television licenses (Dec. 1981) 61,700.

Agriculture. Production (in 000; metric tons; 1981): potatoes 11; hay c. 316; turnips 0.4; milk 116; mutton and lamb 15; fish catch (1982) 766. Livestock (in 000; Dec. 1982): cattle 64; sheep 748; horses 54; poultry 293.

Industry. Production (in 000; 1981): electricity (kw-hr) 3,295,000; cement 115; aluminum (metric tons) 75.

India

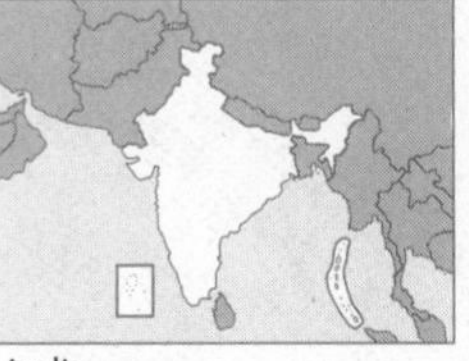
India

A federal republic of southern Asia and a member of the Commonwealth, India is situated on a peninsula extending into the Indian Ocean with the Arabian Sea to the west and the Bay of Bengal to

WIDE WORLD

N. T. Rama Rao, a film star turned politician, led his regional party, Telugu Desam, to an upset victory over Prime Minister Indira Gandhi's Congress (I) party in the southeastern state of Andhra Pradesh.

the east. It is bounded (east to west) by Burma, Bangladesh, China, Bhutan, Nepal, and Pakistan; Sri Lanka lies just off its southern tip in the Indian Ocean. Area: 3,064,063 sq km (1,183,041 sq mi), excluding the Indian-occupied portion of Jammu and Kashmir, which has an area of 100,569 sq km. Pop. (1982 est.): 698 million; Indo-Aryans and Dravidians are dominant, with Mongoloid, Negroid, and Australoid admixtures. Cap.: New Delhi (pop., 1981 prelim., 272,000). Largest cities: Calcutta (metro. pop., 1981 prelim., 9,165,700) and Greater Bombay (metro. pop., 1981 prelim., 8,227,300). Language: Hindi and English (official). Religion (1971): Hindu 83%; Muslim 11%; Christian 3%; Sikh 2%; Buddhist 0.7%. President in 1983, Zail Singh; prime minister, Indira Gandhi.

The year 1983 was marked by a deepening of the political crisis in Punjab, where the Sikhs were demanding autonomy, a bloody election campaign in Assam, and feverish efforts by opposition parties to form alliances in the expectation of a snap parliamentary election.

Domestic Affairs. In the elections for the state assemblies of Andhra Pradesh and Karnataka, which took place in January, the Congress (I) party lost power in both its southern strongholds. The Telugu Desam, a regional party, scored an upset victory in Andhra Pradesh, winning 202 seats out of 294, as against 60 for the Congress (I). A government was formed under the leadership of N. T. Rama Rao (*see* BIOGRAPHIES), an actor, who was new to politics. In Karnataka the alliance of the Janata Party and the Karnataka Kranti Ranga (revolutionary front) formed a government, with the support of other parties, after Janata emerged as the largest single party. A government under Ramakrishna Hegde took office. Elections were also held in January in Tripura, where the Communist Party of India (Marxist) retained power.

Two eastern states, Assam and Meghalaya, went to the polls in February. Opposition parties in Assam boycotted the poll after seeking unsuccessfully to postpone the election. In a very low turnout, the Congress (I) won a huge majority in the 126-member house and formed a government under Hiteswar Saikia. The election was accompanied by violent outbreaks. The worst clashes occurred in Mangaldai and in Nellie, where more than 1,300 persons reportedly lost their lives. Hindu agitators had been campaigning for four years to expel the millions of migrants, mainly Muslims, who had crossed the border from Bangladesh. Suggestions that Muslims had been singled out for punishment in Assam were countered by reports that the victims included adherents of all religions. Later in the year it was announced that, to check further infiltration of aliens, a barbed-wire fence would be erected along the border with Bangladesh. Judicial tribunals were to be set up to detect foreigners.

In Meghalaya the Congress (I) formed a ministry under Williamson Sangma following the defeat of a short-lived non-Congress Cabinet headed by B. B. Lyngdoh. Elections in Jammu and Kashmir resulted in the National Conference winning 47 seats, as against the Congress (I)'s 26. Farooq Abd-

INDIA

Education. (1980–81) Primary, pupils 72,687,840, teachers 1,345,376; secondary and vocational, pupils 29,337,454, teachers 1,731,978; teacher training (1977–78), pupils 14,565; higher, students (1978–79) 4,296,242, teaching staff (1977–78) 244,448.

Finance. Monetary unit: rupee, with (Sept. 20, 1983) a free rate of Rs 10.21 to U.S. $1 (Rs 15.38 = £1 sterling). Gold and other reserves (May 1983) U.S. $5,698,000,000. Budget (1982–83 est.): revenue Rs 175,680,000,000; expenditure Rs 238,710,000,000. Gross national product (1981–82) Rs 1,476,800,000,000. Money supply (Sept. 1982) Rs 241.8 billion. Cost of living (1975 = 100; June 1983) 166.1.

Foreign Trade. (1980–81) Imports Rs 125.6 billion; exports Rs 67.1 billion. Import sources: U.S. 12%; Iran 11%; U.S.S.R. 8%; Iraq 6%; Japan 6%; U.K. 6%; West Germany 6%. Export destinations: U.S.S.R. 18%; U.S. 11%; Japan 9%; U.K. 6%; West Germany 6%. Main exports: food 25%; textile yarns and fabrics 15%; clothing 8%; diamonds 8%; leather 5%; machinery 5%; iron ore 5%.

Transport and Communications. Roads (1979) 1,604,110 km. Motor vehicles in use (1979): passenger 1,035,300; commercial 440,200. Railways: (1980) 60,933 km; traffic (1982) 221,595,000,000 passenger-km, freight 173,107,000,000 net ton-km. Air traffic (1982): 13,259,000,000 passenger-km; freight 446.1 million net ton-km. Shipping (1982): merchant vessels 100 gross tons and over 644; gross tonnage 6,213,489. Telephones (March 1981) 2,785,100. Radio licenses (Dec. 1980) 30 million. Television licenses (Dec. 1980) 1,150,000.

Agriculture. Production (in 000; metric tons; 1982): wheat 37,833; rice c. 68,000; barley 2,012; corn c. 6,500; millet c. 9,000; sorghum c. 10,800; potatoes c. 9,900; cassava (1981) 5,817; sugar, raw value 9,170; sugar, noncentrifugal (1981) c. 7,851; chick-peas 4,567; mangoes (1981) 8,516; bananas c. 4,724; cottonseed 2,620; rapeseed c. 2,363; sesame seed c. 475; linseed 474; peanuts c. 5,700; tea 565; tobacco 525; cotton, lint 1,310; jute (including substitutes) c. 1,220; meat c. 947; fish catch (1981) 2,415. Livestock (in 000; 1982): cattle c. 182,000; sheep c. 41,700; pigs c. 10,500; buffalo c. 62,000; goats c. 72,000; poultry c. 150,000.

Industry. Production (in 000; metric tons; 1982): crude oil 19,726; petroleum products (1981) 27,575; coal (1981) 123,103; lignite (1981) 5,964; natural gas (cu m) 2,566,000; iron ore (63% metal content) 40,787; pig iron 9,838; crude steel 10,853; bauxite 1,847; aluminum 216; gold (troy oz) 71; manganese ore (metal content; 1981) 561; cement 22,493; cotton yarn (1981) 1,015; woven cotton fabrics (m; 1981) 8,120,000; man-made fibres (1981) 199; sulfuric acid (1981) 2,134; caustic soda (1981) 612; electricity (kw-hr; 1981) 125,900,000; passenger cars (units) 63; commercial vehicles (units) 87.

ullah was sworn in as chief minister amid charges by Congress (I) that the poll had been rigged.

N. T. Rama Rao and Farooq Abdullah took the lead in bringing the opposition parties closer together, though the Bharatiya Janata Party and the Lok Dal decided to form a national democratic alliance of their own. Most of the other opposition parties formed a united front and held a conclave in Srinagar in October. The All-India Anna Dravida Munnetra Kazhagam remained aloof from these groupings. The ruling Congress (I) itself was busy setting its house in order. It inducted new chief ministers in three states: Vasantrao Patil in Maharashtra, Virabhadra Singh in Himachal Pradesh, and Chandra Shekhar Singh in Bihar. A plenary session of the party was held in December, the first since 1975.

In Punjab the Akali Dal launched a *morcha* (campaign of defiance of laws) to enforce acceptance of the party's demands. The Sikhs had been granted certain religious concessions, but there was no movement on their central demand for an autonomous Sikh state. Mounting tension was marked by a series of violent incidents against Hindus. Among the leaders of the Sikh activists was Jarnail Singh Bhindranwale (*see* BIOGRAPHIES). Chief Minister Dalbara Singh resigned on October 6, and the state was placed under president's rule. The next day a proclamation declared Punjab and Chandigarh to be "disturbed areas."

One of the rallying points for the opposition parties was the demand that greater autonomy be given to the states. The union (central) government announced the establishment of a commission under Justice R. S. Sarkaria, a former judge of the Supreme Court, to examine whether the division of powers outlined in the constitution needed to be altered. A major stir was created by Seymour Hersh's charge, in his book *The Price of Power: Kissinger in the Nixon White House*, that former prime minister Morarji Desai had worked for the U.S. Central Intelligence Agency; Desai filed suit against the writer. There was satisfaction over the success of the film *Gandhi*, the award of the Nobel Prize in Physics to Indian-born Subrahmanyan Chandrasekhar (*see* NOBEL PRIZES), the victory of India's cricket team in the Prudential World Cup, and the achievement of Sunil Gavaskar, who in December claimed the record for the highest number of centuries scored in test cricket.

The Economy. The agricultural year 1982–83 was marked by widespread drought, which affected 281 of the country's 412 districts. Grain production totaled 128.1 million metric tons, 5 million tons less than in the previous year, but buffer stocks were maintained through better procurement and purchases from abroad. The 1983 monsoon turned out to be encouraging, and the first forecasts were for a 1983–84 grain harvest exceeding 140 million tons. The wholesale price index stood at 317 points on Oct. 22, 1983, a rise of 9.3% over the year. Petroleum production increased from 16.2 million to 21.1 million metric tons, permitting imports to be curtailed. With the balance of payments improving, the government decided not to draw the full third installment of Special Drawing Rights from the World Bank. The Aid-India Consortium pledged assistance amounting to $3.6 billion for 1983–84, 3% less than the 1982–83 commitment.

The 1983–84 union government budget contained proposals for increasing earnings by Rs 6,150,000,000. Including the capital budget, total receipts were placed at Rs 332,810,000,000 and expenditure at Rs 348,360,000,000, leaving a deficit of Rs 15,550,000,000. Some 17% of the central budget was allocated to defense. Provision for development was raised by 21.7% to Rs 254,950,000,000. The Planning Commission published its midterm appraisal of the sixth five-year (1980–85) plan, which estimated that the national income would grow at 5% per year during that period.

Two major power stations were commissioned during the year, a thermal station at Singrauli and the wholly Indian-designed nuclear power station at Kalpakkam. Work was begun on a Rs 2.4 billion hydroelectric project in Jammu and Kashmir. The Rs 2.5 billion refinery at Mathura went into production in May. The launching of the Indian-designed satellite Insat 1-B from the Kennedy Space Center in the U.S. in August represented a major technological milestone. The satellite became fully operational in October. Two Indians were sent to the U.S.S.R. to train as cosmonauts.

Foreign Affairs. The seventh summit conference of the nonaligned movement, which had been scheduled to take place in Baghdad, Iraq, in 1982 but had been postponed because of the Iraq-Iran war, met in New Delhi in March. It was attended by 99 member countries and organizations. The conference adopted a comprehensive declaration and a "New Delhi Message" calling on the major powers to pursue discussions on disarmament and on the North to launch talks with the South on economic and technological cooperation. In response to one of the suggestions made at the conference, 25 heads of state or government met at the UN in September for an informal consideration of the international situation. The shooting down

Sikh demonstrators, with their children dressed as traditional Punjabi warriors, protested near the home of Prime Minister Gandhi. They demanded an autonomous Sikh state and protested killings by police in their community in Punjab.

UPI

of a South Korean commercial plane over Soviet territory cast a shadow over the meeting, but the participants felt that the discussions had helped the North-South dialogue.

Another important conference held in New Delhi was that of Commonwealth heads of government, November 23–29. It was attended by 42 countries and was marked by the visit of Queen Elizabeth II, head of the Commonwealth. Other notable visitors during the year included the presidents of Nigeria and Maldives, the prime ministers of Nepal and Mauritius, Chancellor Helmut Kohl of West Germany, and the heads of the Palestine Liberation Organization, the South West Africa People's Organization, and the African National Congress. During a visit by U.S. Secretary of State George Shultz, it was announced that the U.S. would supply any spare parts for the Tarapur nuclear power plant that India could not secure from other sources. The first consignment of French fuel for the plant was received in May, and an agreement for supply of spare parts was reached with West Germany.

Prime Minister Indira Gandhi visited Yugoslavia, Finland, Denmark, Norway, and Austria in June and Cyprus, Greece, France, and the UN in September. In Belgrade she addressed the UN Conference on Trade and Development and in New York, the UN General Assembly. She also had meetings with U.S. Pres. Ronald Reagan and U.K. Prime Minister Margaret Thatcher. She received the first UN Population Award, along with the Chinese minister for family planning.

At the time of the conference of nonaligned nations, an agreement was signed to establish a joint commission between Pakistan and India. Prime Minister Gandhi's statements on the agitation in Pakistan's Sind Province were described by Pakistan as interference in its internal affairs. Agreements were reached with Bangladesh on the sharing of the waters of the Teesta and with Nepal on the execution of three river valley projects. Two rounds of talks were held with China, the first in Beijing (Peking) in January and the second in New Delhi in November.

Great anxiety was caused by the widespread violence in Sri Lanka in July between Sinhalese and Tamils, since the latter included persons of Indian origin and Indian nationals. Sri Lanka accused India of harbouring and training terrorists. In an effort to promote the restoration of peace and a political solution to the situation, G. Parthasarathi visited Colombo in August and again in November as the prime minister's personal envoy. Sri Lanka's Pres. Julius Jayawardene (*see* BIOGRAPHIES) met the prime minister in New Delhi in November. (H. Y. SHARADA PRASAD)

Indonesia

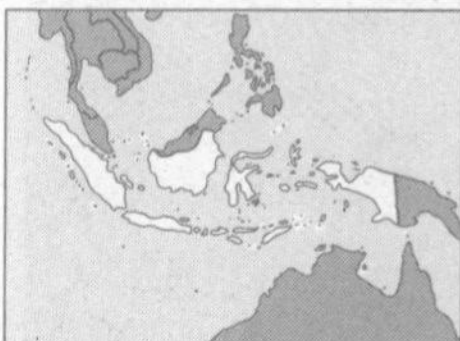
Indonesia

A republic of Southeast Asia, Indonesia consists of the major islands of Sumatra, Java, Kalimantan (Indonesian Borneo), Celebes, and Irian Jaya (West New Guinea) and approximately 3,000 smaller islands and islets. Area: 1,919,443 sq km (741,101 sq mi). Pop. (1982 est.): 151,720,000. Area and population figures include former Portuguese Timor. Cap. and largest city: Jakarta (pop., 1981 est., 6,556,000). Language: Bahasa Indonesia (official); Javanese; Sundanese; Madurese. Religion: mainly Muslim; some Christian, Buddhist, and Hindu. President in 1983, Suharto.

Indonesia ran a gauntlet of events during 1983. President Suharto was elected to an unprecedented fourth five-year term. The world economic recession finally caught up with the nation, causing the devaluation of the rupiah and the implementation of an austerity budget.

In March Suharto was unanimously reelected by Indonesia's 920-member People's Consultative Assembly (MPR) (858 members attended the session). He was unopposed. In a surprise development Suharto selected as his vice-president Gen. Umar Wirahadikusumah, a Sundanese without a political base. "I was startled," Umar said, reflecting the country's opinion. Umar had been among the first of the generals to rally around Suharto in 1965 when an attempted Communist coup failed.

But most attention during the year centred on the economy. Until the last quarter of 1982, Indonesia appeared miraculously unscathed by the world recession. However, in March 1983, facing a glut of oil as a result of the sluggish economy in the industrialized countries, the Organization of Petroleum Exporting Countries (OPEC) dropped the marker price of its oil from $34 a barrel to $29. For Indonesia, a member of OPEC, each $1 drop in

INDONESIA

Education. (1981) Primary, pupils 23,862,488, teachers 713,222; secondary, pupils 5,022,484, teachers 289,979; vocational, pupils 576,791, teachers 2,049; teacher training, pupils 233,633, teachers 17,397; higher (public schools only), students 248,524, teaching staff 22,789.

Finance. Monetary unit: rupiah, with (Sept. 20, 1983) a free rate of 984 rupiah to U.S. $1 (1,482 rupiah = £1 sterling). Gold and other reserves (June 1983) U.S. $2,819,000,000. Budget (1982–83 est.): revenue 13,756,000,000,000 rupiah (excluding foreign aid of 1,851,000,000,000 rupiah); expenditure (total) 15,607,000,000,000 rupiah. Gross national product (1981) 51,580,000,000,000 rupiah. Money supply (Dec. 1982) 7,125,800,000,000 rupiah. Cost of living (1975 = 100; May 1983) 283.2.

Foreign Trade. (1982) Imports U.S. $16,849,000,000; exports U.S. $16,836,000,000. Import sources (1981): Japan 30%; U.S. 14%; Singapore 9%; West Germany 7%; Saudi Arabia 5%. Export destinations (1981): Japan 47%; U.S. 18%; Singapore 10%. Main exports (1981): crude oil 59%; natural gas 15%; petroleum products 5%.

Transport and Communications. Roads (1980) 142,314 km. Motor vehicles in use (1980): passenger 639,500; commercial 473,800. Railways: (1980) 6,877 km; traffic (1982) 6,290,000,000 passenger-km, freight 890 million net ton-km. Air traffic (1982): 8,044,000,000 passenger-km; freight *c.* 190 million net ton-km. Shipping (1982): merchant vessels 100 gross tons and over 1,319; gross tonnage 1,846,824. Telephones (Dec. 1980) 487,000. Radio receivers (Dec. 1980) 6.2 million. Television receivers (Dec. 1980) 1,405,000.

Agriculture. Production (in 000; metric tons; 1982): rice 34,104; corn 3,207; cassava (1981) 13,726; sweet potatoes (1981) 2,079; sugar, raw value 1,629; bananas *c.* 1,800; tea 92; copra *c.* 1,101; soybeans 514; palm oil 874; peanuts 724; coffee 266; tobacco 117; rubber *c.* 990; fish catch (1981) 1,863. Livestock (in 000; 1982): cattle *c.* 6,435; buffalo *c.* 2,506; pigs *c.* 3,296; sheep *c.* 4,196; goats *c.* 7,985; horses *c.* 618; chickens *c.* 114,000.

Industry. Production (in 000; metric tons; 1982): crude oil 65,852; natural gas (cu m) 19,210,000; petroleum products (1981) 24,710; coal 481; bauxite 700; tin concentrates (metal content) 34; cement 5,997; electricity (kw-hr; 1981) 7,750,000.

the export price of oil was the equivalent of a $3 billion loss in revenue. Suharto acted swiftly. In March, the month of his reelection, he devalued the rupiah by 27.5%, scaled down a proposed $10.6 billion in mining contracts, cut back subsidies on domestic oil products, and froze civil service salaries. The economy responded favourably to these measures, but it appeared that more belt-tightening was on the agenda in the foreseeable future.

International support was provided by a group of industrial countries that were underwriting Indonesia's five-year plan. They produced record support pledges for 1984 amounting to $2.2 billion. A World Bank report suggested that Indonesia might need to borrow $15 billion over the next three years to cover the loss of oil revenue. The report said that Indonesia would have to borrow in order to trim its current deficit while maintaining domestic employment.

In world affairs, Indonesia was disappointed by U.S. Pres. Ronald Reagan's announcement in September that he had canceled part of his Asian tour, including a visit to Jakarta. This decision grew out of the assassination of the Philippine opposition leader Benigno S. Aquino, Jr., upon his arrival in August at the heavily guarded Manila airport. The Indonesians said that Reagan's action was understandable, but in November, when the White House announced plans for a visit by Reagan to China first and then to Indonesia, the Indonesians announced their "displeasure." Indonesia, which had no diplomatic relations with China, continued to view that nation as a potentially expansionist power. The Indonesians also believed that, because their country was the most important in Southeast Asia, Reagan should show deference to them over China. (ARNOLD C. BRACKMAN)

Industrial Relations

Most of the important developments in industrial relations in 1983 were linked with the worst economic recession since the 1930s and its accompanying high unemployment, low levels of profitability, and difficulty in balancing public income and expenditure. Labour union demands tended to be moderated by the knowledge that there was little chance of securing appreciable improvements for their members. Indeed, workers' gains from collective bargaining commonly failed to match the rise in prices, and some groups suffered cuts in their existing pay and benefits.

Responses to the pressures differed according to the characteristics of different industrial relations systems. In the decentralized collective bargaining system of the United States, with its low level of unionization, wages and employment conditions adjusted readily, if sometimes painfully, to the economic realities. In some countries that weathered the recession better than most, notably Austria, West Germany, Japan, and Switzerland, the problem of wage determination was less difficult than in others. However, in most of the countries, even though union bargaining power was generally weaker than at any time since World War II, there was a notable tendency for collective bargaining to produce results that were viewed as disturbing by government economic policymakers. This led to a number of governmental interventions aimed at securing restraint. Indexation of wages to prices continued to be limited in most countries where it was practiced; in Italy, where the linkage (the *scala mobile*) was of long standing and had for some time been the subject of tough negotiation among government, unions, and employers' organizations, its modification, by a tripartite agreement in January, was the industrial relations event of the year.

Brazil had a particularly difficult problem. The rigour that the country's economic difficulties demanded, and that was a condition of continued support by the International Monetary Fund, required that wage increases should not be as large as price increases. A decree to ensure this was rejected by Congress, but subsequently a compromise was legislated that softened the loss in purchasing power for low-paid workers.

The need to curtail public expenditure, coupled with a desire by governments to set an example to bargainers in the private sector, led to tough limitations on public service pay and sometimes on other employment conditions. Apart from continuation, in several countries, of restrictions dating from 1982, the pay of West German civil servants was frozen until 1985. Public service pay rises were kept below the rate of price increases in France and were held considerably below that rate in the U.S. In Britain the Treasury made it clear in September that civil servants could look forward to no more than 3% average annual increases in rates of pay and allowances in the forthcoming negotiations. Taking account of the withholding of an increase in 1982, the raise proposed by the Japanese government for public servants in 1983 was modest. In November the Israeli government announced curbs on civil service benefits.

When the government of Quebec in January made substantial (though temporary) cuts in public service pay, a number of strikes occurred, notably one by schoolteachers. The government responded with a strongly phrased law requiring a return to work. British Columbia also took new powers in relation to the public service. In Belgium transport and several other services were virtually at a standstill during a nine-day strike of public servants against what they saw as arbitrary and unduly severe measures taken by the government in relation to their pay and conditions. And in The Netherlands, in November, public servants (whose salaries had already been frozen through 1982) went on strike against a cut of 3½% — later modified to 3% — in their pay proposed by the government, to take effect in January 1984.

Unemployment continued to rise in most countries and was widely expected to increase further, even in nations where an economic recovery seemed to be on the way. A means of countering unemployment that was used frequently during the year was reduction in working time. This aroused considerable controversy. Most trade unions argued that shorter working hours, besides being a form of social advance, would create many new jobs, which would be filled from the ranks of the unemployed. The great majority of employers strongly opposed reduction on the grounds that shorter hours would add to costs and lower competitiveness.

United Kingdom. In Britain the year opened with a strike in support of a demand for higher wages by 29,000 water workers (the first national strike ever called by those workers). The settlement, following a report by a court of inquiry, was high enough to cause some anxiety that it would flow over into other agreements, but this did not happen and the level of wage increases was generally relatively modest during the year.

The government moved ahead cautiously, after publication of a Green Paper in January and a White Paper in July, with a further industrial relations measure—the Trade Union Bill—in October. The bill basically contained three provisions: first, for the governing bodies and certain officers of trade unions to be elected by secret ballot; second, for union funds to be at risk if members concerned were not consulted in a secret ballot before calling a strike or taking any other form of industrial action; and third, that members could vote at least once in ten years on whether their union should continue to maintain a political fund. An additional aspect of the political fund that had been discussed but was left out of the bill was that union members should be required to take positive decisions to contribute to funds rather than, as at present, contributing unless they specifically choose not to do so. On this issue the employment secretary invited the Trades Union Congress (TUC) to make proposals that would be likely to satisfy the government's intentions. If agreement could not be reached by January 1984, it seemed likely that an amendment would be made in the bill. The significance was that trade unions were the major source of income for the British Labour Party.

The British unions and the Labour Party had always regarded themselves virtually as the industrial and political wings of the same labour movement, and the unions exercised an important role in the formulation of party policies. The dismal showing of the Labour Party in the general election in June was thus deeply disturbing to the unions, as was evident at the annual TUC gathering in September. The unions did not seek to dissociate themselves from the Labour Party, but there was a clear realization that it was necessary to reconsider the policies that had so clearly failed to convince the electorate.

In October an important test of recent labour legislation arose when the National Graphical Association (NGA) sought to enforce the reemployment of six workers, dismissed at a printing plant in northwest England in the course of a dispute involving a closed shop issue. At one stage, most of the national press was brought to a halt by a sympathetic action of workers on the newspapers (which subsequently sought writs asking for damages). An injunction was granted requiring the NGA to desist from unlawful industrial action; the union was fined for contempt of court, and substantial union funds were sequestered. The NGA then looked to the TUC for active support, but in December, in a historic decision, the TUC General Council resolved that it could only support lawful action.

United States. During collective bargaining in the U.S. in 1983, union positions were basically defensive. Many unions, faced with declining membership, reduced their staff. Negotiations in some of the airlines were particularly difficult, notably at Eastern, Republic, and Continental; the latter decided to keep flying despite a strike by pilots, flight attendants, and ground personnel. Other negotiations, often difficult and sometimes involving pay cuts, took place in aerospace, the telephone system, the steel industry, the Chrysler Corp., Greyhound Bus Lines, trucking, construction, and West Coast shipyards.

In a departure from its long tradition of refraining from espousing any particular presidential aspirant prior to the nominating conventions, the American Federation of Labor—Congress of Industrial Organizations (AFL-CIO) convention at Hollywood, Fla., in October decided to endorse Walter Mondale as Democratic presidential candidate for the 1984 election. Two major unions gained new presidents during the year. Jackie Presser (*see* BIOGRAPHIES) became head of the Teamsters, and Owen Bieber (*see* BIOGRAPHIES) assumed leadership of the United Auto Workers.

Workers at Caterpillar Tractor Company in Peoria, Illinois, returned to work after a 205-day strike, which damaged the company, split the union, and cost many workers their savings. The settlement was voted two to one by the members of the United Auto Workers against the advice of the union's bargaining committee.

WIDE WORLD

CAMERA PRESS/PHOTO TRENDS

West German workers braved a heavy rain in Bremen to demonstrate in favour of a 35-hour work week.

Australia. It was a memorable year for Australian industrial relations. Fulfilling an electoral promise, in April Prime Minister Bob Hawke—himself a former president of the Australian Council of Trade Unions (ACTU)—called a summit meeting of Commonwealth and state governments, employers, and trade union leaders to review the country's economic problems. The summit generated a considerable measure of agreement between the parties, though as the months went by some employers became critical of the interpretation being placed on the agreement by unions. The wage freeze was discontinued, and a return was made to centralized wage determination by the Commonwealth Conciliation and Arbitration Commission. The commission decided on a system of half-yearly wage adjustments made on price movements but made it clear that wage increases would not automatically keep up with price rises.

Continental Western Europe. After passage of the extensive 1982 legislative program, French industrial relations were relatively quiet in 1983 though by no means free from disputes—in the automobile industry, for instance. There was some grass-roots dissatisfaction with the government's economic austerity measures, and this was probably a reason for the relatively poor showing of the two union centres closest to the government in the October elections for the administrative boards of social security schemes.

Spain introduced a 40-hour week and a minimum annual holiday of four weeks effective from the end of July. A proposal to reduce retirement age to 64, however, was postponed because of its cost. At the end of January employers and unions reached an agreement on pay and certain other issues. In February there was an unprecedented strike by senior civil servants, who had not been included in pay negotiations for the public service generally. In March, at the start of the bullfighting season, there was a two-week strike of picadors and banderilleros about pay and job security.

In Sweden, after some eight years of generally acrimonious debate, the government in November introduced a bill providing for five (regional) wage-earner funds to be set up on the basis of a payroll tax on employers and a new tax on profits. The management of the funds would be, in effect, dominated by the trade unions. Though the underlying principle of the funds was democratization of the ownership of industry, the government also saw the scheme as a means both of providing industry with much-needed investment and new jobs and of encouraging moderation of wage claims on the part of the unions. To the employers, however, the funds appeared to threaten progressive confiscation of their profits, and on October 4, the day of the state opening of the Riksdag (parliament), they mounted an unprecedented protest march in which between 50,000 and 80,000 took part. (R. O. CLARKE)

The views expressed in this article are the author's and should not be attributed to any organization with which he may be connected.

See also Economy, World; Industrial Review.
[521.B.3; 534.C.1.q; 552.D.3 and F.3.b.ii]

Industrial Review

Manufacturing production fell appreciably in 1982 in the advanced industrial countries, and its rate of growth declined in the centrally planned economies; in the less developed areas output continued to rise. Thus, seven years after the deep recession of 1975, world industry was again in a slump, felt most sharply in the advanced nations.

The decline of manufacturing activity was uninterrupted during 1982, reaching its lowest point toward the end of the year; from there, the uneven recovery in the first half of 1983 raised it to the level of the same period a year earlier. At the outset the recovery was largely restricted to North America; in Western Europe and Japan any advance in 1983 was expected to be very moderate. This change from receding to slowly growing activity was expected to have a beneficial effect on the primary producing less developed countries.

Restrictive policies had been in force in almost all countries for some time; in their endeavours to further reduce inflation, most governments had introduced strict limits on all types of public expenditure. Private consumption was adversely affected by reduced disposable income, and the persistent stagnation depressed business investment. All these domestic factors came to a head in 1982, when the volume of world trade in manufactures fell by 2½%, and the outcome was a marked decline in industrial activity.

Among the major industrial centres, the recession was heaviest in North America, where output fell by 8%; production stopped rising in Japan and declined by 2% in Western Europe. In the latter only a few countries could raise their manufacturing output marginally (France, Denmark, Portugal, and Sweden) or maintain it (Belgium and Ireland); in the other 11 nations production fell, in some of them appreciably (by 7% in Switzerland). Manufacturing in some of the less industrialized countries advanced considerably; for example, in Brazil, Mexico, South Korea, and India. Progress in the centrally planned economies was relatively moderate (3% in the U.S.S.R.) except in Poland, where adverse internal political conditions further depressed output.

In the market economies heavy industries were more severely hit by the recession than the light industries that produced chiefly consumer goods. The slump in building and construction and low investment in plant and machinery particularly depressed the base metal and building materials industries, but output of metal products and chemicals also fell. In some of these industries, such as steel, aluminum, and heavy chemicals, pressure from worldwide excess capacity caused a considerable amount of old plant to be taken out of production, much of it permanently. Among the light industries, output was maintained only in the food industry; in all other branches it fell. Industries in the less developed countries all increased production (with the exception of textiles, output of which declined fractionally), and the situation in the centrally planned economies was similar (apart from a fall in chemicals).

Productivity, as measured by output per employee, declined in North America but increased in the major European industries and most of the minor ones. Competitive pressure forced manufacturers to reduce labour costs; while this added to the already high industrial unemployment, it benefited productivity. The benefit was even more obvious if output per hour was taken as a measure of productivity; this increased in all major industrial countries except Japan, where it stabilized on a high level. (G. F. RAY)

Table I. Index Numbers of Production, Employment, and Productivity in Manufacturing Industries

1975 = 100

Area	Relative importance[1] 1975	Relative importance[1] 1982	Production 1981	Production 1982	Employment 1981	Employment 1982	Productivity[2] 1981	Productivity[2] 1982
World[3]	1,000	1,000	124	121	...	...	...	...
Industrial countries	868	845	122	117	...	...	...	...
Less industrialized countries	132	155	136	141	...	...	...	...
North America[4]	315	304	128	117	...	...	...	...
Canada	27	23	119	105	103	96	115	109
United States	288	281	129	118	111	104	116	113
Latin America[5]	74	79	126	128	...	...	...	...
Brazil	27	29	115	129	...	...	...	...
Argentina	15	10	79	76	...	...	...	...
Mexico	12	15	141	151	143	151	99	100
Asia[6]	159	190	142	144	...	...	...	...
India	11	12	136	140	118	...	115	...
Japan	109	127	140	140	101	101	139	139
South Korea	...	...	245	258	...	...	...	...
Europe[7]	416	391	114	112	...	...	...	...
Austria	8	8	123	121	96	92	128	132
Belgium	14	13	113	113	...	...	...	...
Denmark	6	6	119	122	94	93	127	131
Finland	6	6	130	126	103	100	126	126
France	80	74	110	112	93	91	118	123
West Germany	115	111	116	113	99	95	117	119
Greece	3	3	128	121	120	120	107	101
Ireland	1	1	140	140	110	106	127	132
Italy	43	45	128	125	...	...	...	...
Netherlands, The	16	15	116	115	85	82	136	140
Norway	6	5	99	97	...	...	...	...
Portugal	4	5	145	150	...	...	...	...
Spain	24	22	111	109	...	...	...	...
Sweden	17	14	95	96	86	81	110	119
Switzerland	13	12	113	107	94	90	120	119
United Kingdom	50	37	89	88	81	77	110	114
Yugoslavia	11	13	146	145	128	...	...	...
Rest of the world[8]	36	36	...	...	...	...	...	...
Oceania	18	16	107	105	...	...	...	...
South Africa	7	8	136	136	110	109	124	125
Centrally planned economies[9]	...	...	135	139	...	...	...	...

[1]The 1975 weights are those applied by the UN Statistical Office; those for 1982 were estimated on the basis of the changes in manufacturing output since 1975 in the various countries.
[2]This is 100 times the production index divided by the employment index, giving a rough indication of changes in output per person employed.
[3]Excluding Albania, Bulgaria, China, Czechoslovakia, East Germany, Hungary, Mongolia, North Korea, Poland, Romania, the U.S.S.R., and Vietnam.
[4]Canada and the United States.
[5]South and Central America (including Mexico) and the Caribbean islands.
[6]Asian Middle East and East and Southeast Asia, including Japan.
[7]Excluding Albania, Bulgaria, Czechoslovakia, East Germany, Hungary, Poland, Romania, and the U.S.S.R.
[8]Africa and Oceania.
[9]These are not included in the above world total and consist of the European countries listed in note 7 above.

Table II. Pattern of Output, 1979–82

Percent change from previous year

	World[1]				Developed countries				Less developed countries				Centrally planned economies[2]			
	1979	1980	1981	1982	1979	1980	1981	1982	1979	1980	1981	1982	1979	1980	1981	1982
All manufacturing	5	−0.2	0.2	−3	5	−1	0.3	−4	5	5	−0.1	4	4	5	2	3
Heavy industries	5	−0.2	0.6	−4	5	−1	0.8	−5	6	6	−1	4	5	5	2	3
Base metals	5	−5	−0.7	−10	4	−6	−0.6	−13	11	3	−1	6	0.9	3	0.5	1
Metal products	5	0.8	1	−3	5	0.4	2	−4	8	5	−4	4	7	6	4	5
Building materials, etc.	5	−0.2	−3	−5	5	−1	−3	−7	5	6	0.2	1	2	3	1	2
Chemicals	6	−1	0.5	−3	7	−3	0.6	−4	2	7	0.4	4	3	4	−1	−2
Light industries	4	0	−0.3	−0.6	4	−1	−0.5	−2	3	5	1	4	3	5	0	2
Food, drink, tobacco	3	3	2	2	3	1	2	0.1	4	8	3	8	3	2	2	3
Textiles	4	−1	−3	−3	5	−2	−3	−3	2	2	−0.3	−0.2	2	2	−1	0
Clothing, footwear	2	−4	−2	−0.8	1	−5	−4	−1	3	2	5	0.5	5	3	3	0.6
Wood products	4	−3	−4	−5	3	−4	−4	−6	5	6	−3	2	0.3	2	3	4
Paper, printing	5	2	0.5	−0.6	5	1	0.2	−1	7	4	5	4	−2	3	0.5	2

[1]Excluding centrally planned economies. [2]Excluding China.
Source: UN, *Monthly Bulletin of Statistics.*

Table III. Annual Average Rates of Growth of Manufacturing Output, 1968–82

Percent

Area	1968–73	1973–78	1978–81	1982
World[1]: market economies	6.0	2.1	1.6	−2.8
Industrial countries	5.7	1.5	1.4	−4.0
Less industrialized countries	8.7	5.9	3.2	4.0
Centrally planned economies[1]	8.8	7.5	3.7	2.8

[1] For definition *see* Table I.
Source: UN, *Monthly Bulletin of Statistics.*

Table IV. Output per Hour Worked in Manufacturing

1975=100

Country	1977	1978	1979	1980	1981	1982
France	115	121	129	131	132	136
West Germany	110	113	118	116	120	121
Italy	108	111	122	127	130	132
Japan	115	124	132	137	137	137
U.K.	106	107	109	107	113	117
U.S.	108	109	112	115	119	122

Source: National Institute, *Economic Review.*

Table V. Manufacturing Production in the U.S.S.R. and Eastern Europe[1]

1975=100

Country	1979	1980	1981	1982
Bulgaria[2]	128	134	140	147
Czechoslovakia	122	126	129	131
East Germany[2]	121	127	133	138
Hungary	121	118	122	124
Poland	126	126	111	108
U.S.S.R.	121	124	129	133

[1] Romania not available.
[2] All industries.
Source: UN, *Monthly Bulletin of Statistics.*

ADVERTISING

In a $120 million advertising account change in September 1983, the Colgate-Palmolive Co. hired Young & Rubicam to handle one-third of its advertising, including two Colgate product introductions in 1984. Because the two companies are in competition, Young & Rubicam had to give up the Proctor & Gamble account, which represented $62 million in billings in 1982. The switch was one of the largest in recent times.

When seven people died in October 1982 after taking Extra-Strength Tylenol capsules laced with cyanide, the market share of the popular painkiller fell from a commanding 35% to 7%, and it was widely believed that the product would never make a comeback, at least under the Tylenol name. A year later Tylenol had confounded predictions by regaining a 29% market share. Observers credited an open and cooperative stance on the part of the manufacturer, Johnson & Johnson, and an advertising campaign that stressed the reliability of the product and new, tamper-resistant packaging.

More restrictions were placed on advertisements aimed at children in 1983. The guidelines published by the Children's Advertising Review Unit of the Council of Better Business Bureaus broadened the voluntary code to encompass advertisements directed at children in all media, including print and broadcast and cable TV. In October Action for Children's Television filed a complaint with the Federal Communications Commission (FCC) claiming that TV cartoons based on toys and other products, such as "Smurfs" and "Dungeons and Dragons," were, in effect, full-length commercials. TV spokesmen insisted this was not essentially different from the long-standing practice of developing toys based on successful children's shows.

The American Bar Association approved a less restrictive advertising code for lawyers in August. It permitted lawyers to use all media, including direct mail, and eliminated a list of specific "do's and don't's." The code prohibited false, misleading, and deceptive statements but allowed comparative advertising provided the claims could be substantiated. The changes did not affect existing local and state statutes on the subject.

The Federal Trade Commission (FTC) eased rules requiring companies to support advertising claims. Previously, the FTC had insisted that such claims had to be substantiated by laboratory tests. In a decision on two national advertising cases pending since 1973, the standard for claims made for over-the-counter pain relievers was abandoned. The decision stated that if a company did not refer to any drug research, it might be able to rely on other kinds of scientific evidence. However, the amount of proof needed would depend on such factors as the extent to which consumers believe an advertising claim and the consequences they would suffer if the claim proved false. In making the ruling, the FTC maintained that if regulations were too burdensome, consumers could lose more through paying extra costs than they might gain in accurate information.

Each year *Advertising Age* publishes a list of the 100 leading advertisers in the U.S. for the previous year. In 1982 these advertisers accounted for $17.1 billion in expenditures, compared with $14.8 billion in 1981, an increase of 15.5%. The top five advertisers were Proctor & Gamble, Sears, General Motors, R. J. Reynolds Industries, and Philip Morris. As an industry group, the heaviest expenditures came from companies in the leisure and entertainment fields. Proctor & Gamble spent $726.1 million in 1982, compared with $671.8 million in 1981. It was also the largest network television advertiser, spending $390 million in that medium. R. J. Reynolds was ranked number one in newspaper advertising, and Philip Morris was the leading user of magazines.

A survey issued in 1983 by the McCann-Erickson advertising agency indicated that large advertisers were beginning to spend more money on cable TV and independent television stations than on the three major networks.

In July the FCC proposed removing the controls on allowable commercial minutes on television as part of a larger plan to reduce FCC supervision of all TV programming. The changes, if approved, would permit broadcasters to compete freely in programming and commercial practices.

Direct mail and direct response advertising continued to be popular with manufacturers and retailers. These media include coupon advertising in newspapers and magazines as well as commercial spots on television and radio using a toll-free telephone number. So-called marriage mail (two or more advertising pieces wrapped around each other, not enclosed in an envelope) also became more widespread. Direct mail advertising in the U.S. accounted for about $11.6 billion a year. (*See* CONSUMERISM: *Special Report.*)

A federal commission studying public television's financing problems offered a plan that would allow expanded advertising, including the use of brand names and institutional messages. Currently, sponsors on public TV were permitted only verbal and corporate logo identifications at the beginning and end of each program.

On the world scene, the British agency Saatchi and Saatchi handled advertising for the Conservative Party in the campaign leading to its decisive election victory. It had also conducted the Tories' winning campaign of 1979, said to be Britain's first "modern campaign."

A popular British beer billboard featured a celebrity outside the market of Mansfield's bitter beer. The Mansfield Brewing Co. said it had permission from the White House, which did not comment.

WIDE WORLD

The joint venture between the world's two largest agencies, Japan's Dentsu and the U.S. Young & Rubicam, changed its name to DYR from Young & Rubicam/Dentsu, made the Japanese company's Tetsuro Umegaki its chairman, and brought Y & R's Alexander Brody out of semiretirement to be president. The joint operation had offices in New York City, Los Angeles, Tokyo, and Kuala Lumpur, Malaysia.

(EDWARD MARK MAZZE)

AEROSPACE

The slump in the air transport industry entered its fourth consecutive year in 1983, and by the time annual reports for 1982 began to appear, it was clear that the airlines had been going through their worst period ever. Member airlines of the International Air Transport Association at their 39th annual general meeting noted a modest upswing during 1983 but claimed that profits were still far too low to support heavy investment in the new aircraft they needed for the mid-1980s and beyond. (See TRANSPORTATION: *Aviation*.)

Introduction of the new-technology "digital" airliners at last began to help arrest the financial slide of some operators. The Boeing 767, which entered service in September 1982, was followed by the same company's slightly smaller stablemate, the 757, in January 1983 and by Europe's Airbus Industrie A310 in April. Their technical excellence was acclaimed for both the lack of "teething" problems and the substantially better economy stemming from their new fuel-efficient engines. All could use two-man flight crews, the flight engineer becoming unnecessary owing to the introduction of advanced, automated electronic equipment. However, because they are twin-engined aircraft, they were not cleared for long overwater routes, and this limitation would in time begin to affect both the 767 and the A310. Major efforts were under way to investigate the safety implications of using those aircraft on such routes.

The order for seven Airbus A320s by British Caledonian brought the long-awaited new generation 150-seat transport a stage nearer to eventual use. Significantly, it was chosen over the "stopgap" Boeing 737-300 (to fly in March 1984) and the widely used McDonnell Douglas DC-9-Super 80. With forceful French leadership, the A320 might repeat the success of the A300 and fill a gap left vacant by the United States manufacturers.

By and large, the fortunes of the manufacturing industry mirrored those of the air transport sector it served. McDonnell Douglas Corp. completed the last passenger DC-10 on its current order book and was projecting a substantially revised variant for the airlines. Meanwhile, the firm was producing a tanker version of the widebody trijet. Lockheed rolled out its 250th and final L-1011 TriStar—also a widebody trijet—and was then out of the airliner business. Even Boeing's production of new aircraft shrank dramatically, by 38%, the top-of-the-line 747 having slowed to a trickle; the cutback in widebody production reflected the overcapacity in such aircraft, with no fewer than 150 secondhand planes of that type on the market.

UPI

"Digital" airliners include fully computerized control systems such as that being installed on this PW 2037 jet engine by Pratt & Whitney workers at East Hartford, Connecticut.

News in February that Aeroflot had permanently withdrawn its Tu-144 supersonic transport from service came as no surprise to Western observers aware of its severe technical deficiencies. A few weeks earlier the British government had announced that it would no longer support operation of the Anglo-French Concorde supersonic transport, which in January completed its seventh year of service. A technical and potentially money-making success, it had been hampered by lack of routes and by the noise and pollution problems encountered since the project was launched. The handful of British Concordes were reduced to making charter flights around the English coast in order to bolster income from the few scheduled services.

The 1978 Airline Deregulation Act, criticized as being responsible for so much of the U.S. airlines' misery, gave a new lease on life to the regional, or third-level, operators. They largely stepped into the routes that could not profitably be flown by the big operators, using new and largely non-U.S. 30–50-seat airliners such as the de Havilland of Canada DHC-7 and Short 330 and 360; again, U.S. industry failed to meet the challenge. The rest of the small-aircraft market, the general aviation sector, suffered severely. Piper by midsummer had laid off 3,400 people—half its work force—and shut down all production till September, while Cessna sales over the first nine months were down 44% from the corresponding 1982 period. But Beech and Learjet (the latter with a European partner) demonstrated that there was still life in the industry by showing off two remarkable new business aircraft, both using twin turbo-propeller designs, at the 36th National Business Aircraft Association meeting in Dallas, Texas, during October. And at the smallest scale, 10,000 airplanes turned up for the annual meeting of the Experimental Aircraft Association at Oshkosh, Wis.

On the military side, the main focus of attention was the crystallization of the new Western fighter projects, models and mock-ups of which at the Paris Air Show demonstrated the radically new shapes made possible by advanced digital electronics. Most imminent of these aircraft in time was Sweden's JAS39 Gripen (Griffon), given a go-ahead in midsummer. Virtually indistinguishable from one another in size and shape, full-size replicas of Britain's ACA (agile combat aircraft) and France's ACX *(avion de combat expérimental)* hung suspended above their respective company stands. Both would fly in 1986 as technology demonstrators, going into production only if they satisfied stringent performance and financial targets. Meanwhile, Israel's new Lavi (Young Lion) ground-attack aircraft, largely designed around standard U.S. components and technology at low cost, was running into political problems as the U.S. saw in it a real threat to its own aircraft industry's export markets and began to mobilize opposition to it. Eventually, however, thanks partly to powerful pro-Israel supporters in the U.S., objections were overcome and U.S. collaboration was resumed.

Much further off in time were two new U.S. fighter projects, which, however, were already subjects of discussion at Paris; VFMX for the U.S. Navy and ATF (advanced tactical fighter) for the Air Force were to begin service around 1996, a spur to their development being the appearance of new Soviet types of high-performance aircraft including the Tupolev Blackjack A strategic bomber, which began flight tests in 1982, and the MiG-29 Fulcrum and Su-27 Flanker fighters. All were expected to be in service by 1985–87. Reports suggested that a fleet of 800 armed Soviet helicopters was emerging, and this stimulated Western helicopter manufacturers to plan to develop new combat helicopters. (MICHAEL WILSON)

ALCOHOLIC BEVERAGES

Beer. Estimated world beer production in 1982 was 968.5 million hectolitres (hl; 1 hl = 26.4 gal), with the U.S. accounting for 228 million hl, nearly 24% of the world total. The biggest U.S. company, Anheuser-Busch, alone produced more beer (59.1 million U.S. bbl) than the U.K., the world's fourth brewing nation. West Germany and the U.S.S.R. were the second and third largest producers. China, with beer production in 1982 of some 12.3 million hl, forecast an annual growth in output of 20% for the next decade. During the year United Breweries of Denmark, Stella Artois of Belgium, and Sapporo of Japan all signed trade agreements with China to supply brewing technology and expertise.

A survey carried out among the 12 leading hop-growing countries showed a 1982 crop of 68,081 ha (168,160 ac) harvested. The two leading growers remained West Germany and the U.S., 73% of the U.S. crop being grown in the Yakima Valley of Washington. Good crops in 1981 and new methods of hop flavour extraction and preservation resulted in a world surplus of hops, aggravated by exceptionally high yields in 1982. Barley harvests in 1982 were almost universally high in tonnage, but the crop itself was high in nitrogen, and so top-quality malting barley commanded premium prices. In Britain the highest yields in five years were recorded, and France had a record crop of 10.9 million metric tons, though most went for agricultural feed and not to malting. Canada also produced abundant but low-quality harvests. In Australia a disastrous drought resulted in a harvest less than half that of the previous year. The U.S.S.R. emerged as a major consumer, importing an estimated 200,000 metric tons for brewing purposes.

The international Brewex exhibition held in Britain in April 1983 featured the latest innovations in microprocessor brewery control. In June the 19th congress of the European Brewery Convention, also held in Britain, was attended by brewers from Africa, Australasia, North America, and Japan as well as Europe.

(MICHAEL D. RIPLEY)

Spirits. Despite a boom in cocktails and the continued good performance of such white spirits as vodka and rum, 1983 was another difficult year for the spirits industry with sales of light wines biting into the spirits market. Cream liqueurs continued to perform well, further evidence of the trend to lower-strength liqueurs indicated by the success of Suntory's Midori melon liqueur and Grand Metropolitan's Malibu coconut and rum liqueur. Ready-mixed cocktails—a feature of the U.S. market for some years—arrived in the U.K., with first Shakers and then Schenley's U.S. brand leader, Cocktails For Two, being heavily promoted.

Total distilled spirits imported into the U.S. declined from 116.2 million proof gallons in 1981 to 106 million in 1982, while wine imports rose from 114.7 million gal to 122.1 million during the same period. The U.K. market for spirits fell 5.5% in 1982, making a total decline since 1980 of more than 10%.

French grape brandy exports fell by 26.5% in 1982, with West Germany, the biggest market, taking 33% less and the U.K., the second largest importer, 21% less. The only encouraging signs were a 2.3% increase in exports to the U.S. and small increases in sales to Canada and Japan. World sales of cognac fell 7% to 140.7 million bottles, with consumption in France down 8.3% to 110.2 million bottles. The U.S. remained the major export market with 25 million bottles a year; second was the U.K. with 14.8 million bottles.

The Scotch whisky market in the U.K. faced a 4% decline in 1983 following a similar fall in 1982 and one of 7% in 1981. Malt whiskey, however, showed an increase of 14% following the 5.5% fall in 1982. Whiskey imports into the U.S. were down 11% in 1982, with Scotch down 10%, Canadian down 13%, and Irish down 11%. Also in the U.S., gin imports were down 4%, rum was down 20%, and vodka, after years of growth, fell by 11%. The Scotch Whisky Association instigated a major promotional campaign in Japan and the U.S., the two main markets for Scotch.

(ANTONY C. WARNER)

Wine. World production of wine in 1983 was not expected to reach the 1982 record total of 365 million hl, but in many countries the quality was exceptionally good. Italy was the world's largest producer with an estimated 75 million hl, followed by France (70 million hl), a reversal of the previous year's order; total production by European Communities (EC) countries was put at 163 million hl. The Italian wines were generally of good quality, well balanced but with a somewhat lower alcoholic content than in recent years, especially in the south. In France climatic conditions, unfavourable at the start of the harvest, improved markedly, and the quality in general exceeded forecasts; late harvests were particularly favoured, and Alsace produced wines of very high quality. In Bordeaux, where production declined about 10%, quality was also good. The Champagne harvest was exceptional in both quantity (more than 300 million bottles) and quality, restoring producers' confidence after a difficult period. In Spain, the world's third largest wine producer, the 1983 harvest, at 30 million–33 million hl, was well below that of the previous year, but quality was good. The West German harvest was also lower than that of 1982, but quality was generally excellent and was exceptional for some late vintage wines. Austria and Switzerland also produced wines of high quality. Eastern European production was estimated at 50 million hl.

In the U.S. viticulture continued to expand. In 1982 total production was 19.5 million hl, while 1983 production in California alone was estimated at 12.5 million hl, with quality generally good. In Argentina, where stocks had built up, the government introduced measures to curtail output, which was set at 22.5 million hl for 1983. In Chile, with a production of 6 million hl, the wine market was glutted.

South African production maintained its level at about 9 million hl. In Australia, despite the ravages of bad weather during

In mid-November the new Beaujolais became the talk of France—and increasingly so in the rest of Europe and in the U.S. This Paris gendarme was one of the first to sample at a booth manned by a costumed Bourguignon.

WIDE WORLD

Table VI. Estimated Consumption of Beer in Selected Countries
In litres[1] per capita

Country	1980	1981	1982
West Germany	145.7	146.9	147.8
Czechoslovakia	137.8	140.1	146.3
East Germany	139.1	141.4	...
Belgium[2]	131.3	124.2	132.1
Australia[3]	134.2	132.2	128.9
Denmark	121.63	125.13	128.57
Luxembourg	121.0	123.0	124.0
New Zealand	120.9	121.8	121.1
Ireland	121.76	116.4	115.0
Austria	101.9	104.8	108.5
United Kingdom	117.1	111.5	107.3
United States	92.0	93.3	92.0
Hungary	87.0	89.2	87.0
Canada[4]	86.7	84.4	86.48
Venezuela	62.5	83.9	...
Netherlands, The	86.39	89.47	81.96
Switzerland	69.0	70.2	71.9
Bulgaria	60.9	61.8	...
Spain	53.4	55.2	56.9
Finland	57.39	57.24	55.96
Colombia	43.9	45.0	50.0
Romania	43.8	50.0	...
Norway	48.28	44.81	47.07
Sweden	47.2	45.0	46.6
Yugoslavia	44.2	45.0	...

[1] One litre = 1.0567 U.S. quart = 0.8799 imperial quart.
[2] Excluding so-called household beer.
[3] Years ending June 30.
[4] Years ending March 31.

Table VII. Estimated Consumption of Potable Distilled Spirits in Selected Countries
In litres[1] of 100% pure spirit per capita

Country	1980	1981	1982
Luxembourg	9.0	9.5	8.25
Hungary	4.75	4.97	4.8
East Germany	4.7	4.8	...
Poland	6.0	4.3	4.3
Czechoslovakia	3.52	3.6	3.56
Canada[2]	3.37	3.51	3.43
U.S.S.R.	3.3	3.3	3.3
Peru	3.0	3.0	3.0
Spain	2.0	3.0	3.0
United States	3.07	3.04	2.94
Finland	2.79	2.76	2.82
Netherlands, The	2.71	2.52	2.57
West Germany	3.09	2.84	2.51
Sweden	2.75	2.48	2.46
Iceland	2.25	2.23	2.12
Switzerland	2.05	2.11	2.11
Cyprus	2.0	2.1	2.1
Belgium	2.37	2.13	2.04
New Zealand	1.94	2.0	2.0
Yugoslavia	2.2	2.0	...
Romania	2.3	2.0	...
France[3]	2.53	2.0	2.0
Japan	1.83	1.84	1.9
Italy	1.9	1.9	1.9
Ireland	2.04	1.89	1.65

[1] One litre = 1.0567 U.S. quart = 0.8799 imperial quart.
[2] Years ending March 31.
[3] Including aperitifs.

Table VIII. Estimated Consumption of Wine in Selected Countries
In litres[1] per capita

Country	1980	1981	1982
Italy	92.9	92.9	91.4
France	91.0	89.0	86.0
Portugal	68.5	70.8	78.4
Argentina	75.8	73.2	73.8
Spain	64.7	59.0	57.0
Chile	46.9	43.7	54.7
Luxembourg	48.2	42.0	48.3
Switzerland	47.4	48.2	48.2
Greece	44.9	44.9	45.0
Austria[2]	35.8	35.1	35.3
Hungary	35.0	29.7	32.0
Romania	28.9	28.9	...
Yugoslavia	28.2	26.9	...
Uruguay	25.0	25.0	...
West Germany	25.5	24.7	24.8
Bulgaria	22.0	22.0	...
Belgium	20.6	21.0	21.6
Australia[2]	17.3	18.2	19.1
Denmark	14.0	16.09	17.35
Czechoslovakia	15.5	16.0	14.6
Netherlands, The	12.85	12.95	14.15
New Zealand	13.3	14.5	13.2
U.S.S.R.	14.4	13.0	13.0
Cyprus	9.8	10.8	11.8
Sweden	9.54	9.72	10.43

[1] One litre = 1.0567 U.S. quart = 0.8799 imperial quart.
[2] Years ending June 30.

Source: Produktschap voor Gedistilleerde Dranken, *Hoeveel alcoholhoudende dranken worden er in de wereld gedronken?*

the early months of the year, production was not expected to fall below the 4 million hl of 1982.

Suntory of Japan broke new ground with the purchase of a Bordeaux vineyard, Château Lagrange, producing troisième cru Médoc. England's relatively insignificant production continued to increase, and some wine was being exported.

(MARIE-JOSE DESHAYES-CREUILLY)

AUTOMOBILES

The U.S. automobile industry made a strong recovery in 1983 after suffering through four years of heavy losses. The "Big Four" U.S. automakers (General Motors, Ford, Chrysler, and American Motors) reported earning a combined $4.1 billion in the first nine months of 1983. By comparison, in 1980 the Big Four lost a combined $4 billion, a record deficit. The more than $8 billion turnaround in just four years found General Motors (GM), Ford, and Chrysler in the profit column and only American Motors (AMC) still plagued by red ink.

By the time the books were closed on 1983, GM was expected to earn more than $3 billion versus $962.7 million in 1982; Ford expected to be over the $1 billion mark after losing $657.8 million in 1982; Chrysler profited by more than $700 million after earning $170 million in 1982; and AMC would hover around the $150 million loss mark after losing $153.5 million in 1982.

There was good news for investors. GM increased its dividend to $1 a share from the 60 cents that had prevailed since the second quarter of 1980. Ford not only raised its dividend from 30 cents to 45 cents a share, but announced a 3-for-2 stock split, the first since a 5-for-4 in April 1977.

Chrysler had been prohibited from paying a dividend under provisions of the Chrysler Loan Guarantee Act of 1979. The company was barred from a payout until it first paid back the $116 million it was in arrears on preferred stock as well as the remaining $800 million it owed on the $1.2 billion it borrowed from the U.S. government under terms of the federal loan guarantees.

In late 1983 Chrysler repaid the money owed on the preferred stock and all money due on the loans—seven years earlier than required—thus clearing the way for dividend resumption sometime in 1984. Chrysler last paid a ten-cent-per-share dividend in the second quarter of 1979.

Among the reasons for the U.S. automakers' high profits were the return of automobile buyers to the more profitable large and intermediate-size cars (due in turn to lower gas prices) and the higher productivity of the Big Four's slimmed-down corporate operations, which enabled them to make profits on a smaller overall sales volume. Another reason that profits were so high was simply that car sales rose significantly in 1983. In the 1983 model year, which ended September 30, U.S. automakers sold 6.5 million cars, a 17% increase from the 5.5 million sold in the 1982 model year and the largest number since 6.7 million in the 1980 model year. However, this was still far from the record 10 million cars sold in 1973.

Japanese automakers, in their third year of voluntary quotas that limited them to U.S. sales of 1,680,000 cars, reached that ceiling and combined with European producers for total sales of 2.3 million foreign cars in the U.S. in 1983, about 5% above the 2.2 million sold in 1982 but short of the record 2,360,000 sold in 1981. Imports accounted for about 26% of total industry sales in 1983, down from the record 27.8% in 1982. U.S.-made cars and imports combined accounted for sales of 8.8 million cars in 1983, up from 7.6 million a year earlier.

During the model year GM sold 3,876,006 cars, compared with 3,387,607 in 1982, a 14% increase; Ford sold 1,481,382 cars, a 15% increase from the 1,289,983 in 1982; Chrysler sold 819,209 against 658,720, a 24% increase; AMC sold 183,005 versus 99,300, an 84% gain; Volkswagen sold 83,223, a 23% decline from 107,398 a year earlier; while Honda, which began producing its four-door subcompact Accord model in a new plant in Marysville, Ohio, in the spring of 1983, finished the model year with sales of 32,398 units.

Volkswagen's total was the worst since it began manufacturing cars in the U.S. at a former Chrysler plant in New Scranton, Pa., in 1979. Yet VW said that it would remain committed to building cars in the U.S.

As for market share among domestic producers, GM ended the year at 59.8% of the U.S. market, down from 61.1% a year earlier; Ford slipped to 22.9% from 23.3%; Chrysler moved to 12.7% from 11.9%; AMC rose to 2.8% from 1.8%; VW fell to 1.3% from 1.9%; while Honda accounted for 0.05%.

The best-selling cars in the 1983 model year, listed by their order of finish, were the subcompact Ford Escort (323,900 *v.* 321,952 in 1982); intermediate Oldsmobile Cutlass (314,473 *v.* 293,979); intermediate Buick Regal (233,016 *v.* 230,775); full-size Chevrolet Impala/Caprice (226,750 *v.* 205,861); full-size Oldsmobile 88 (218,639 *v.* 254,888); subcompact Chevrolet Cavalier (216,297 *v.* 120,587); subcompact Nissan (Datsun) Sentra (215,800 *v.* 176,470); subcompact Honda Accord (209,567 *v.* 180,646); subcompact Chevrolet Chevette (183,970 *v.* 233,858); subcompact Chevrolet Camaro (175,004 *v.* 148,649); full-size Cadillac DeVille (173,086 *v.* 145,075); mid-size Oldsmobile Cutlass Ciera (169,939 *v.* 79,262); compact Plymouth Reliant (161,757 *v.* 151,279); mid-size Chevrolet Celebrity (155,953 *v.* 67,478); subcompact Toyota Tercel (150,975 *v.* 127,329); and subcompact Toyota Corolla (141,827 *v.* 174,694).

As the sales totals were compiled, the U.S. Environmental Protection Agency released the mileage rankings for the 1984 models for the year beginning Oct. 1, 1983. The EPA rankings placed a new two-passenger car from Honda called the CRX at the top of the pack with a 51-mpg city mileage rating from its 1.3-liter, four-cylinder engine. This marked the first time since 1978 that the Volkswagen Rabbit had not captured the EPA mileage title. It also was the first time since then that a gasoline-engine car and not one powered by diesel fuel had been rated the most fuel-efficient car on the market.

The Nissan Sentra placed second in the ratings with 50 mpg; the Rabbit and Toyota Corolla tied for third at 47 mpg; and the Ford Escort and Mercury Lynx tied for fourth place at 46 mpg. All had four-cylinder diesel engines.

The EPA commented that the fuel economy averages for 1984 represented almost a 100% improvement since it first established its rating system in 1974. The 1984 average was 25.6 mpg, as compared with 13.2 mpg ten years earlier.

Though mileage averages rose, strong demand for large and luxury cars that had relatively low averages and sluggish demand for the smallest economy cars caused both GM and Ford to miss meeting the federal government's Corporate Average Fuel Economy standards for the 1983 model year. CAFE regulations, which went into effect in the 1978 model year, when they required automakers to sell a mix of cars averaging 18 mpg, rose to 26 mpg in 1983. GM and Ford missed the CAFE average by about 2 mpg. But a provision in the law allowed automakers to borrow past credits that they had built up during the last three years in which they exceeded the average; therefore, both GM and Ford avoided having to pay fines. For the 1984 model year the CAFE would rise to 27 mpg, and in 1985, the last year for CAFE increases as the law was originally written, it would move up to 27.5 mpg.

The demand for large cars was unusually strong. The automakers had resorted to special discount loan programs on cars financed through their own financing subsidiaries early in the year in order to encourage sales, but they finished the year with overtime work at the plants making large cars. Yet shortages continued to exist.

Based on this demand, Chrysler scrapped plans to drop full-size cars after the 1983 model run and continued selling the big Plymouth Grand Fury, Dodge Diplomat, and Chrysler Fifth Avenue and New Yorker. Both GM and Ford also mapped plans to continue selling their large cars longer than they had intended.

A good example of changing future product plans was announced by GM. That automaker was to have replaced its intermediate-size and rear-drive Oldsmobile Cutlass Supreme, Buick Regal, and Pontiac Grand Prix models with downsized, front-wheel-drive counterparts after the 1984 model run. But in 1983 GM said that it would keep the rear-drive models that had been selling so well and add the front-wheel-drive versions not as replacements but as companions. The 1985 front-wheel-drive models would be called the Oldsmobile Cutlass Calais, Buick Regal Somerset, and Pontiac Grand AM.

As for new cars, Ford in the spring brought out a pair of compact, front-wheel-drive models called the Ford Tempo and Mercury Topaz to replace the Ford Fairmont and Mercury Zephyr. In the fall it introduced a downsized Mark, called the VII, and a special high-performance Mustang called the SVO, complete with a turbocharged four-cylinder engine.

Early in the year GM brought out the new Corvette, the first total remake of the car since 1968. In the fall GM's Pontiac division unveiled an all new plastic-bodied two-seat sports car called Fiero.

Chrysler brought out a pair of new sports cars called the Dodge Daytona and Chrysler Laser. Both were powered by four-cylinder engines and had turbocharging available. Along with Ford, Chrysler added turbocharged engines to many of its car lines in order to give them added performance.

Chrysler started building its new T-Wagons in the fall but they were not slated to go on sale until the 1984 calendar year. The T-Wagons were mini vans called the Dodge Caravan and Plymouth Voyager. Both featured front-wheel drive, four-cylinder engines that claimed more than 20 mpg in fuel economy in city driving, and had removable seats to handle from one to seven passengers. Chrysler dropped the Dodge Mirada and Chrysler Cordoba.

American Motors added a subcompact hatchback version of its Renault Alliance called the Encore. It was the second vehicle to be produced by American Motors in cooperation with its French partner, Renault. AMC also downsized its Cherokee and Wagoneer Jeep utility vehicles.

International collaboration increased in Europe. By year's end Japanese automakers were engaged in joint ventures in Italy (Nissan-Fiat), the U.K. (Honda-BL—the former British Leyland), and West Germany (Nissan-Volkswagen), in addition to the U.S. (Mitsubishi-Chrysler and Toyota-GM).

Mercedes brought out its first American-model small car, a compact $24,000 luxury sedan called the 190E that was available with either a gas or diesel engine. The 240D model was dropped.

Nissan (Datsun) replaced the 280 ZX sports car with the 300 ZX, which for the first time featured a turbocharged V-6 engine. Nissan also began building pickup trucks in the U.S. for the first time at a plant in Tennessee.

Toyota converted most of its Corolla line to front-wheel drive as well as adding a mini van simply called the Van Wagon. GM and Toyota announced plans to produce jointly a Toyota-designed, GM-built subcompact car in the U.S. using a vacant GM plant in Fremont, Calif. The two planned to build up to 300,000 cars a year starting in 1985. Chrysler and Ford objected, saying that such a venture would be a violation of antitrust laws. GM also said it planned to import small three-cylinder cars from its partner Suzuki of Japan and small four-cylinder-engine cars from its partner Isuzu of Japan starting in 1984–85.

When the automakers introduced new cars in the fall, the average base price was $9,808, a 7.5% increase over the average base starting price a year earlier. The average base price of a GM car was $10,316; at Ford it was $9,716; at Chrysler it was $8,979; and at AMC it was $7,527. Price increases focused on mid- and full-size cars, while prices of most subcompact and compact models either were frozen at 1983 levels or reduced slightly.

During the year American Motors sold its AM General military vehicle subsidiary to LTV Corp. While AM General was AMC's most profitable subsidiary, continued losses in car sales forced the firm to seek cash. Ford Motor Co. announced a lifetime

Another Asian automaker found a U.S. market. The four-wheel-drive Beijing Tiger is the first auto made in the People's Republic of China to be sold in the U.S.

UPI

warranty on service work performed on its cars at its dealerships; the repair was guaranteed for the life of the car. The EPA announced that so many consumers had expressed doubt about the accuracy of its mileage figures that starting in 1984 it would still arrive at a mileage average for each car but would then subtract 10% from that figure to determine the sticker rating for new car windows.

(JAMES L. MATEJA)

BUILDING AND CONSTRUCTION

The construction industry in the U.S. experienced an economic recovery in 1983, ending a four-year decline. On an annual rate basis, the monthly value of new construction put in place in June 1983 was $259,734,000,000, based on preliminary figures released by the Department of Commerce, and it appeared that construction for the entire year would be at about that level. Construction outlays in 1981 had been at an all-time high, and those in 1982 were only slightly lower, but annual comparisons made on a constant dollar basis revealed that the real level of activity had fallen from 1978 through 1982.

The value of publicly financed and owned construction continued to decline in 1983, as it had on a constant (1977) dollar basis since 1978. Thus the recovery in the industry was due entirely to the growth in private construction activity, chiefly residential buildings. In each of the first nine months of 1983, the number of new housing units started was substantially higher than in the corresponding month of 1982. Based on data released by the U.S. Department of Commerce, it was estimated that over 1.7 million new units would be started in 1983, compared with 1,072,000 in 1982. Nonresidential building in 1983 was lower than in 1982, when outlays for nonresidential construction had amounted to a record $65,134,000,000. The estimate for 1983 was for outlays of around $60 billion.

The Department of Commerce composite construction cost index stood at 158.7 in June 1983. It appeared that the index would move up slightly more in 1983 than in 1982. The average effective interest rate for 25-year conventional mortgages continued to fall. On a 75% loan-to-price ratio, it reached 12.99% in May 1983, compared with 17.34% in January 1982.

On a median-priced house, the average monthly payment amounted to $754 in 1982, but by May 1983 it had dropped to $642. An offsetting factor, however, was the continuing rise in the median price of new houses sold. In 1982 the median sales price was $69,300, but by May 1983 it had risen to $75,900. The number of employees in contract construction totaled 4,104,000 in June 1983, about the same as in 1982. Weekly earnings of construction workers averaged $445.36 in June, up slightly from a year earlier.

In Canada economic activity accelerated in the first six months of 1983, and it appeared that recovery would continue throughout the year. As in the U.S., housing starts rose substantially over 1982 levels. Consumer confidence was high, but despite increased consumer spending and investment in housing, indications were that business fixed investment would continue to decline. Nevertheless, gross productivity was expected to rise 2.5% in 1983 and possibly 4% in 1984.

There was little marked improvement in Western Europe, although there were differences among the major countries. Economic activity increased somewhat in Britain. In the second quarter the production index for the construction industry stood at 93 (1975 = 100), compared with 90.8 in 1982. The modest improvement was attributable to increased construction of houses. Housing starts rose sharply in the first quarter of 1983 but declined in the second quarter. Both public and private investment in dwellings rose.

In France 1983 was a year of considerable economic uncertainty. It was expected that business fixed investment would continue to decline and outlays for new housing construction would remain at very low levels. West Germany experienced an upturn in industrial production early in the year, and the economy showed some signs of improvement. However, the outlook for construction and housing was not good. In Italy construction activity remained depressed.

It was expected that construction activity in Japan would be stimulated by an upturn in industrial investment, based on a more favourable outlook for corporate profits. Another factor was the possibility of government policies that would provide housing loans, public works expenditures, and an income tax cut.

(CARTER C. OSTERBIND)

As the demand for housing increased in Japan, manufacturers of prefabricated housing prepared to do battle for the market. This village of model homes set up in Tokyo shows prospective buyers the designs of 12 manufacturers. Computer graphics design modifications and houses of modular cubes are among Japanese prefab innovations.

KAKU KURITA

CHEMICALS

The depressed economic conditions of 1981–82 resulted in poor performances for the chemical industry in the United States and in other countries during 1982. However, the general economic recovery in 1983 had a salutary effect on chemical operations, and by early in the fourth quarter of that year it was clear that the figures for the full year 1983 would be significantly better than those for 1982.

In the U.S., for example, the Federal Reserve Board's index of production for the chemicals and allied products industry, which averaged 215.6 (1967 = 100) for 1981, dropped 9% in 1982 to 196.1. During the first half of 1983, however, the index moved up each month, and in July it stood at 216.9.

Shipments of chemicals and allied products, as tabulated by the U.S. Department of Commerce, fell 4.2% in 1982 to $172.8 billion—from $180,457,000,000 in 1981. The decline was precipitous during the second half of the year; shipments then were $82,420,000,000, compared with $90,380,000,000 during the first half. But shipments of chemicals moved up in the first half of 1983 to $93.6 billion, 3.6% above the figure for the first six months of 1982.

Chemical prices inched up only slightly in 1982 and in the first half of 1983. The U.S. Department of Labor's index of producer prices for chemicals and allied products averaged 287.8 (1967 = 100) in 1981 and 292.3 in 1982. In August 1983 it averaged 294.9.

U.S. trade in chemicals reflected the generally depressed condition of the industry. The value of chemical exports dropped from $21,187,000,000 in 1981 to $19,891,000,000 in 1982, with a big part of the decline taking place during the second half of the year, when exports amounted to only $9.5 billion. U.S. chemical imports in the meantime rose from $9,446,000,000 in 1981 to $9,494,000,000 in 1982. The nation's favourable trade balance in chemicals, as a result, declined from $11,741,000,000 in 1981 to $10,396,000,000 in 1982. Exports in the first six months of 1983 increased from the second half of 1982 and reached $9,725,000,000, although that was still 20% below the figure for the comparable period of 1982. Chemical imports during the first half of 1983 rose to $5.4 billion, and so net chemical exports for the first half of 1983 totaled $4,325,000,000.

Capital spending plans of U.S. chemical companies indicated that the industry was once more growing. Expenditures had dropped from $13.6 billion in 1981 to $13,270,000,000 in 1982, according to a survey by the U.S. Department of Commerce. But during July and August 1983, companies were planning to increase their outlays so that the 1983 total would be $13,760,000,000. One reason for the brighter outlook for spending was that in 1983 the industry was operating at a higher percentage of its capacity. A federal survey showed that capacity utilization in the industry, which had been as low as 64% in 1982, reached 65% at the start of 1983 and rose to 71% by the third quarter.

In Japan the chemical industry struggled through a difficult period in 1982. Chemical sales totaled an estimated $60 billion, and early in 1983 chemical executives in the country were anticipating a sales increase for the year of no more than 1%. The outlook for the major customers for Japan's chemicals, such as the nation's textile, automotive, and construction industries, was not encouraging for chemical suppliers. Considerable overcapacity, moreover, existed for many products, including such key petrochemicals as ethylene.

By mid-1983, however, the prospects for Japanese chemical makers had improved appreciably. Financial reports of chemical companies for fiscal 1982, which ended on March 31, 1982, showed that the two largest chemical companies lost money that year. But indications were that the worst was over. And chemical companies, which had instituted cost-cutting measures—omitting dividends, reducing executive salaries, and cutting capacity for ethylene and major polymers—appeared to be in a good position to benefit from an upturn.

The chemical industry in West Germany embarked on 1982 with high hopes and, indeed, registered a strong first quarter. But the situation deteriorated as the year wore on, and sales for the full year increased only 0.8% from 1981 to approximately $49 billion. Production actually dropped 4.8%, and chemical profits were 25% lower than they had been in 1981.

By late in the second quarter of 1983 it appeared that a solid recovery was under way for West German chemicals. Capacity utilization for the chemical industry, which had been only 70% during the last quarter of 1982, rose to 80% in the first quarter of 1983. Progress was made in solving overcapacity problems in the production of synthetic fibres, thanks to an agreement by Western European countries; talks were held in Brussels about a similar agreement to relieve overcapacity problems on bulk plastics. All in all, West German chemical managers were looking forward to the full year of 1983 with optimism, although their attitude was tempered by the still-fresh memory of 1982, which had also started off well.

In France the chemical industry was facing an uncertain future because of government strategy. In 1982 sales of chemicals in France were approximately $29 billion. Production was only 0.6% higher than it had been in 1981, and the outlook for 1983, according to the French industry association, was for another 0.6% rise.

As part of the government strategy, Rhône-Poulenc, France's largest chemical company, was nationalized in February 1982. The results were not immediately beneficial; the company lost $126 million in 1982 on sales of $5.5 billion. The company, however, said that it was encouraged by the new ownership, which, it believed, would enable it to make and execute long-range growth plans while protecting it from short-range pressures to make profits.

The United Kingdom's chemical industry registered sales of approximately $25.8 billion in 1982. The Chemical Industries Association reported that this figure represented a small increase over 1981 and that the increase was caused by inflation. The U.K. was facing raw material costs that had risen 6.5–7% in 1982 and a relatively strong pound against other major European currencies. Imports were rising faster than exports, and the big chemical companies were experiencing a profit squeeze. Imperial Chemical Industries (ICI), for instance, lost $161 million on plastics and petrochemicals during the first three quarters of 1982.

Stronger economies throughout the world and stronger demand for chemicals helped to improve the U.K.'s chemical operations in 1983. ICI reported first-half earnings of $284 million, as compared with the $220 million that it earned in all of 1982.

(DONALD P. BURKE)

ELECTRICAL

General Electric Co. (GE) was becoming more general and less electric. During the ten years beginning in 1973 the company's production of discrete electrical components fell from 75 to 40% of total output. At the same time GE's involvement in high-technology systems for microelectronic control of sophisticated electrical and mechanical equipment had increased. By 1983 such systems accounted for 28% of the firm's total sales, with a target of 50% within five years.

An area of particular interest to GE was the fully automated factory. By the end of 1983, the company had spent approximately $2 billion in research and development in the advanced technology sector, ranging from computer-aided design to robots. One result was a software system designed to link all aspects of the automated factory from product design through manufacture to warehousing and accounting. GE claimed to have gained a 10% share of the $1.4 billion world market for computer-integrated manufacturing systems in 1982; by 1988 it hoped to become the world's leading supplier, with 20% of the expected $5 billion market.

All the world's major electrical equipment manufacturers were investing heavily in similar advanced technology systems. Late in 1982 Westinghouse Electric Corp. acquired from Condec Corp. a 78% interest in Unimation, the largest U.S. manufacturer of industrial robots, for $107 million. The president and chief executive officer of Allen-Bradley Co., J. T. O'Rourke, forecast that by 1990 50–60% of production plants in the U.S. would have computer-integrated manufacturing systems. Allen-Bradley supplied all the programmable controllers for General Motors' new Buick City plant, which was planned to be 97% automated when it became operational in 1985. Other leaders were GE, Gould, Télémécanique (France), Siemens (West Germany), GEC (U.K.), Asea (Sweden), and the three Japanese companies, Hitachi, Mitsubishi, and Fuji. (*See* Special Report.)

The key mechanical element in all computer-integrated manufacturing systems was the electric motor that powered robot arms and other related movements. Usually the motors and their control systems were supplied as a complete drives package. Developments were largely confined to alternating-current (AC) systems, dominated by Japanese companies.

Electric drive systems was one of the important product groups retained in the previous year's shake-up of AEG, a West German company. Having shed 31,000 workers in 1982 in the course of selling its money-losing subsidiaries, AEG was finally saved from bankruptcy at a creditors' meeting in March 1983. The creditors agreed to write off DM 1.8 billion of the DM 3 billion they were owed. The meeting also heard that a 75% share in AEG's subsidiary Telefunken had been sold to the French state-owned Thomson-Brandt company. In 1982 AEG lost DM 932 million, but it expected to break even in 1983.

Siemens, West Germany's largest electrical manufacturer, reported a 45% rise in net profits in 1981–82; turnover rose 16% to DM 40.1 billion, of which exports represented 55%. But Siemens and other West German companies were worried about future exports; according to the West German trade association, electrical export orders in 1983 had been adversely affected by world financial problems and growing trade protectionism.

In France motor drives and robots made news with the purchase of Compagnie Électro-Mécanique (CEM), a subsidiary of Switzerland's Brown Boveri Group, by the state-owned Compagnie Générale d'Électricité (CGE). In 1982 CGE earned consolidated profits of Fr 550 million on a turnover of Fr 66 billion, and it was looking to the French government for financing to help it double this turnover in the next five years.

The French electrical equipment industry trade association was worried by the government's decision to cut back on its nuclear power construction program. In 1982 export gains helped compensate for the already shrinking home market. In September CGE and Thomson-Brandt, both state-owned, submitted plans for restructuring and streamlining their activities. If these were accepted by the government, they would generate the widest-ranging reorganization of the French electrical industry in 40 years.

In Britain, GEC's profits in 1982–83 rose by 15% to £670 million on a turnover of £5,456 million. By far the largest slice came from its electronics, automation, and telecommunications businesses.

In 1983 the European Commission began investigating the activities of the Swiss-based International Electrical Association (IEA), an export cartel representing the largest European and Japanese heavy electrical equipment manufacturers. The Commission was studying a 1980 U.S. report that accused the IEA of "conspiring to deny overseas markets to U.S. manufacturers."

(T. C. J. COGLE)

FURNITURE

The household furniture industry rebounded in 1983 after almost four years in the economic doldrums. Buoyed by improved housing starts, some easing of consumer credit, and pent-up consumer demand, U.S. retail home furnishings sales rose 9.3% to an estimated $19,360,000,000. According to the National Association of Furniture Manufacturers, 1983 manufacturers' shipments increased 19.1% to $11,580,000,000 as retailers restocked depleted inventories. Wood furniture shipments rose 16.8% to $5,470,000,000, upholstered furniture shipments 19.6% to $3,840,000,000, and summer and casual furniture 13% to $734.7 million. Office furniture shipments, at wholesale value, increased from $3.9 billion to $4.1 billion between 1982 and 1983, according to the Business and Institutional Furniture Manufacturers' Association.

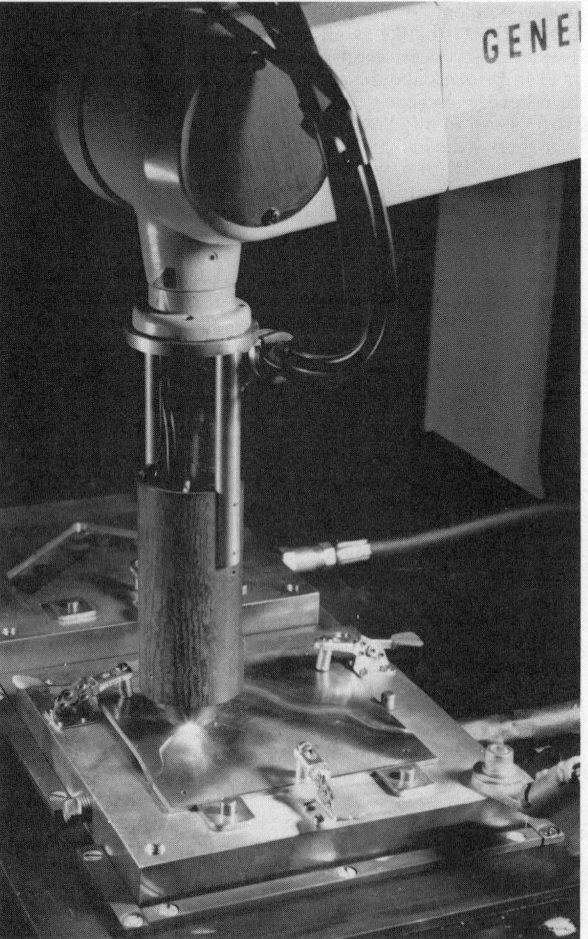

General Electric developed a welding robot that uses advanced vision and control systems to steer itself as it welds along irregularly shaped joints, making necessary adjustments as it proceeds. It was unveiled at a Chicago exposition in April.

AUTHENTICATED NEWS INTERNATIONAL

As a result of business failures, consolidations, and mergers, there were fewer retail home furnishings companies; the National Home Furnishings Association estimated the total in 1983 at 42,000, probably 2,500 to 3,000 fewer than in 1980. However, there had been a marked growth in specialty stores with limited inventories.

Manufacturing had also been affected by losses and mergers. Though the Census Bureau listed almost 6,000 furniture manufacturers, the number of companies with 100 or more workers had fallen from approximately 800 in 1977 to around 550 in 1983. The number of workers had also dropped, from the 278,000 reported in April 1982 to an estimated 260,000. Domestic American dining room, wall system, and occasional table manufacturers continued to face increased competition from foreign imports, especially from Taiwan, Singapore, Hong Kong, and the Philippines. An undetermined number of U.S. manufacturers shifted some of their operations to the Far East.

A growing phenomenon affecting distribution was the appearance of large design centres in major markets (15 since 1977). For many years there had been furniture showroom buildings "open to the trade" in the five major U.S. markets, but new centres were being used to expand markets that had been shrinking because of the growth of specialty stores and the high cost of operating full-service stores. The general public was not welcome unless accompanied by a retailer, interior designer, or contractor. Manufacturers were able to show more products in the centres, and retailers used them as no-cost extensions of their selling floors. In major markets they were having a considerable effect in courting business away from conventional outlets.

There were few dramatic shifts in furniture styles during 1983. Reproductions of Early American and English manor designs prevailed, and French country continued to be popular. The most noticeable new entries were "computerture," furniture designed to accommodate electronics, and knock-down, easy-to-assemble casual furniture, marketed almost exclusively through mail-order catalogs. Cosmetic changes included increased use of high-gloss lacquer finishes, especially the polyesters, a bolder range of colours, innovative hardware designs, and coloured decorative veneers. At the high-fashion end was the "Memphis" look, a trompe l'oeil style inspired by the architects and industrial designers, notably in Europe, who were starting to explore furniture design. Terence Conran's line of affordable furniture from the U.K. proved popular in Japan, and Eiri Iwakura's designs blending Western and Japanese influences were well received there.

(ROBERT A. SPELMAN)

FURS

The international fur business showed a slight improvement in 1983, though it was still hampered by economic problems. Retailers in the U.S., Canada, and Japan made a good showing, but important European markets like West Germany, Italy, France, and the U.K. found it difficult to cope with the strong U.S. dollar. The dollar is the principal monetary unit in the international fur trade, and some European currencies were down as much as 25% against the dollar from the previous year. Indications at year's end were that 1983 retail sales in the U.S. would be about $1.2 billion, at least 10% over 1982.

The developing fur-manufacturing industry of the Far East showed huge gains in 1983. South Korea, Hong Kong, and China had all become major exporters of fur garments to Japan, North America, and Europe, and such imports were expected to account for about 40% of U.S. sales. This caused great concern among U.S. manufacturers, especially since those countries enjoy duty-free status under the Generalized System of Preferences granted to products from less developed areas. The U.S. also ended a 32-year embargo on mink, marten, muskrat, weasel, ermine, fox, and kolinsky from China, although the embargo on the same furs from the Soviet Union remained in force. While the strong dollar sharply reduced U.S. fur exports, particularly of manufactured products, imports almost doubled.

Prices of mink pelts began the year at depressed levels but gained steadily under strong demand. On the other hand, most wild furs declined in price. Again, this was attributed to the strong dollar, since Europe traditionally has been the largest user of North American wild furs. Worldwide production of ranched furs such as mink and fox increased slightly in 1983, but the karakul lamb output continued to decline, reflecting an apathetic market and depressed price levels. Lower prices indicated a smaller wild fur harvest in the season beginning at year's end.

The U.S. Congress changed the Fur Seal Act to end federal administration of the Pribilof Islands off the coast of Alaska. Responsibility for the seal harvest was turned over to the native Aleut community, although it would still be regulated by the act. No substantial change in the harvest was expected. (SANDY PARKER)

GEMSTONES

The year was marked by what might turn out to be the final appearance of the diamond investment phenomenon. In the U.S. overvaluation of stones bought for tax-deductible donations to museums led to the involvement of the Internal Revenue Service. In the U.K. at least one firm attempting to trade in blue sapphires for investment went into liquidation. Many sections of the diamond trade reported a small upturn in activity, especially in small stones, but it was also said that the trade was reluctant to move into high quality goods. Prices were stable by October, and some dealers may have begun to restock. Some cuts, including marquises, were reported to be scarce.

The Pakistan Gem Corporation began to send out material, and the first reports suggested that quality was good and pricing reasonable. Ruby, emerald, and aquamarine were available, and it might be possible to obtain rough as well as cut material. The activities of the Sri Lanka Gem Corporation suffered as a result of the island's political troubles during the year. The practice of altering the colour of corundum (ruby, sapphire) had been rampant in Sri Lanka, and steps were taken to clamp down on it. A desirable colour could be given to poor quality material, which was then sold at high prices, mostly in Thailand. Testing methods by which such stones could be identified were being developed.

Ruby from Kenya was once more available. A new deposit of emerald at Santa Terezinha, Brazil, was producing good quality stones. After some doubt that the De Beers marketing organizations would be able to hold their own, the return of Zaire to the fold and an agreement reached with the Australian producers restored a degree of stability. Prices for coloured stones had risen at least to the level of 18 months earlier, and some of the rarer stones such as tanzanite (which had virtually ceased to be mined) increased in price.

In spite of the general economic climate, jewelry sales at the major auction houses continued to bring high prices. Though in some instances there were fewer items (particularly in some of the Swiss sales, traditionally the chief European showpieces), quality remained high and prices more than kept pace with the trend of the past few years.

(MICHAEL O'DONOGHUE)

GLASS

The glass industry in the developed world continued to be adversely affected by recession, although some flat glass companies, such as Pilkington Brothers of the U.K. and Glaverbel of Belgium (owned by Asahi Glass of Japan), announced improved results. Despite the recession, some important technological achievements were made. The French firm Verrerie de Monteramey developed a light that will stay lit for two hours in the event of a power failure. Corning Glass of the U.S. launched Sunsensor, a line of sunglasses using the unprecedented combination of photochromic and polarizing lenses. Heraus of West Germany developed a quartz telescope mirror for use in space. Of environmental significance was Pilkington's development of a process for making reinforced cement using Cemfil 11 glass fibre as a substitute for asbestos; the new process could utilize the existing machinery.

British Telecom invited tenders for the world's first intercontinental optical fibre undersea cable. A number of agreements were made that would lead to the spread of technological knowledge. Philips's of The Netherlands announced negotiations to set up a factory in the U.S.S.R. making television tubes under license. Mitsubishi Electric Corp. of Japan reached an agreement with the Soviets to produce liquid crystal displays.

In the packaging industry, the difficulties of the last few years continued, with further closings and layoffs. Financial results reflected the fierce competition from other types of packaging and a depressed market. Gerresheimer Glass of West Germany announced the closing of its Oldenburg factory, and the U.S. company Anchor Hocking sold its glass container interests to an affiliate of Wesray. More specialized companies, such as Beatson Clark, manufacturer of pharmaceutical containers in the U.K., fared better. Also in the U.K., glass manufacturers supported the Dairy Trade Federation's campaign to protect the doorstep delivery of milk and, therefore, the sale of milk bottles. Several large firms in the domestic glassware field also experienced financial problems: in Austria the nationalized bank, Creditanstalt-Bankverein,

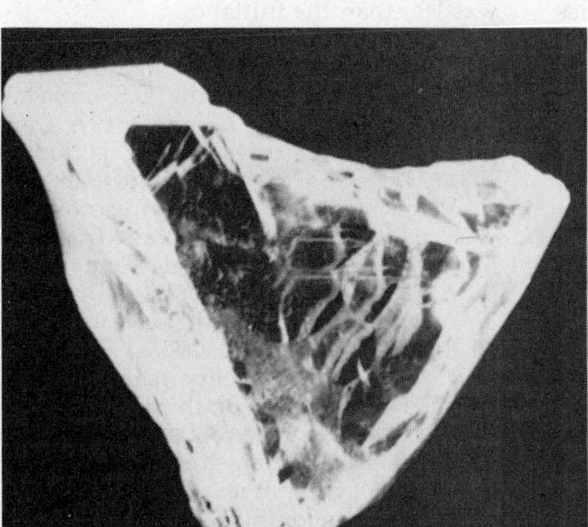

WIDE WORLD

Placed on sale in London in August was the largest heart-shaped diamond in the world, Le Grand Coeur d'Afrique. As a rough stone (left) it weighed 278 carats; out of it was cut the 70.03-carat Grand Coeur (right). Its value is estimated at $7 million.

which held 70% of the shares of Stölzle Oberglas, spent $10 million reorganizing the company.

In the flat glass industry, stability in the European market was again threatened by the announcement of new plants. Luxguard (owned by Guardian Industries of the U.S.) was to invest in a toughened and coated glazing plant in Luxembourg. Guardian also announced that it would build a second float glass unit in Switzerland, while Glaverbel planned to build a float plant in The Netherlands. In the U.K. Pilkington announced a major reorganization, merging its flat and safety glass operations. Pilkington also signed a joint venture with China to employ its float glass technology in a new plant in Shanghai.

At a London conference organized by the Society of Glass Technology and the Society of Chemical Industry, it was predicted that the U.S., with its large deposits of natural soda ash, would emerge as the world's leading low-cost supplier of this material—the most expensive constituent of container and flat glass. The effect of glassmaking on the environment remained a prime concern. There was further progress in the EC on such issues as protection from noise in glassworks, energy conservation, the use of poisonous substances in glass manufacture, air purity, and the use of returnable bottles.

(JOANNA TUDOR)

INSURANCE

Competition in the $500 billion-worldwide private insurance market increased sharply during 1983. A "buyer's market" existed in reinsurance, commercial property-liability insurance, and life and health insurance as many large insurers expanded their operations to include broadened financial services. Global insurance was supplied by approximately 13,000 domestic insurance companies and foreign branch offices, with 80% of the insurers and premiums concentrated in North America and Europe.

Insurers in the U.K., as elsewhere, continued to depend on investments rather than underwriting gains for their financial success. Annual premiums of British insurance companies for general business, more than half of which was from overseas, had risen by 1983 to £11,000 million, almost 15% above a year earlier. Net investment income more than offset underwriting losses of £1,240 million, producing a surplus of £500 million. U.K. long-term (principally life) insurance rose 13.6% to almost £9,500 million.

Despite unfavourable publicity alleging mismanagement by underwriting syndicate managers at Lloyd's, the number of individual underwriting members rose by 1,500, to 21,600. Regulatory improvements resulted in some restructuring of management and, for the first time, Lloyd's statutory returns were changed to conform to other insurance company reports. On its three-year accounting system, Lloyd's 1983 returns for 1980 business resulted in surplus gains of £264 million. Lloyd's paid $27 million of hull coverage under war risk insurance within two weeks after the Soviet Union shot down a Korean Air Lines jet.

Among other developments in the U.K., the House of Lords, the highest appeal court, widened the scope of liability claims by making an award for a defective floor (even though there were no physical damages or injuries) and paying a woman not at the site of an accident for nervous shock resulting from injuries to her family. Claims totaling £14 million were paid for the death of Troy, the 1979 Derby-winning horse, and the kidnapping of Shergar, the 1981 winner.

In the U.S. the American Council of Life Insurance reported $4.5 trillion of life insurance in force by 1983, almost three times that of a decade earlier. The average insured family had $57,000 of life insurance. Assets of U.S. life insurers were at a record $588 billion. Premium income included approximately 40% from life insurance and 30% each from health insurance and annuities. Investment and other income accounted for 30% of total income.

Many large life insurers, banks, stock and real estate brokers, and other financial institutions merged or acquired affiliates in order to provide more comprehensive financial services. New products increased insurance market opportunities. "Universal" life insurance contracts, with flexible premiums, policy amounts, and current interest credits, had been issued for more than $40 billion. Two million persons had Individual Retirement Accounts (IRA's), which deferred taxes on almost $6 billion of assets. More liberal tax laws also expanded the availability of Section 401(K) employee savings plans to profit-making firms. Costs of term and other life insurance continued to fall, and insurers began to use the more current 1980 Commissioners' Standard Ordinary and 1983 Individual Annuity mortality tables.

In the landmark *Norris* case, the U.S. Supreme Court ruled that defined contribution pension plans are discriminatory unless they pay equal retirement benefits to both men and women. Amid considerable controversy, several bills were introduced in Congress that would extend unisex rating to all types of insurance. Health insurance was at the centre of many efforts toward cost control. Because of the explosion of health care costs in the U.S.—from $51 billion in 1967 to $362 billion in 1983—Medicare changed its hospital payments to a prospective fixed-fee system for 467 "diagnostic-related groups" of illnesses. Employers and insurers providing group health care financing increased many deductibles and co-payments for patients. (*See* SOCIAL SECURITY AND WELFARE SERVICES.)

U.S. property and liability insurers reported written premiums of $52 billion for the first half of 1983. Premiums, operating earnings, and investment income were up 4, 69, and 10%, respectively, over the same period a year earlier, and underwriting losses were down 7%. Hurricane Alicia in Texas brought almost $700 million in losses for insurers, the third most costly windstorm in U.S. history. With 24,000 claims pending, asbestos-related liability claims could cost insurers an estimated $10 billion. In efforts to curb motor vehicle accidents, more than half the states had passed stiffer drunk-driving laws, and 40 states now required car restraints for young children.

(DAVID L. BICKELHAUPT)

IRON AND STEEL

World steel activity, as expected, fell sharply in 1982. Crude steel output declined from 708 million metric tons in 1981 to about 645 million tons, a level comparable to that of 1975, the first year of the long and severe recession in steel. There was every sign that 1983 would prove to be no better and almost certainly somewhat worse. The effect of the recession was almost universally felt. In Japan production in 1982 fell below 100 million tons for the first time in ten years and was only slightly higher than in 1972. The largest U.S. steel producer, United States Steel, announced in December 1983 that it would close three plants, accounting for 16% of its production, with the loss of over 15,000 jobs. Even such small traditional producers as Australia and South Africa, which had previously maintained their production levels, suffered heavy declines in steel activity in 1982 and 1983. Only a few of the newer producers, such as Brazil, Taiwan, and Turkey, showed appreciable increases in 1983, together with Poland, which made a recovery from the effects of social and industrial disruption in recent years.

Unquestionably the most dramatic decline in steel production in 1982 occurred in North America, where Canada suffered a 21% fall in comparison with 1981 and the U.S. had a remarkable fall of 38% to 67 million metric tons, only half the peak level of the early 1970s. It was against that background that the complaints filed by a number of U.S. producers against EC companies early in 1982 were ultimately withdrawn in the context of the steel agreement concluded in October 1982 between the U.S. administration and the European Commission, acting on behalf of EC member governments. Under the agreement, to be operative from November 1982 to the end of 1985, exports from EC countries were licensed on the basis of defined percentages of U.S. consumption of ten categories of steel products. EC steel exports to the U.S. were set at an average of about 5% of the total U.S. market. The forecasts of consumption for each product category were revised five times during the 14 months to the end of 1983, as provided by the agreement. Although the forecasts for flat products related to the automobile and consumer goods industries were increased somewhat toward the end of the period, in the case of all categories the final estimate (October 1983) was less than the initial one.

Figures available in the fall of 1983 indicated that for the first eight months of the year steel imports into the U.S. from all sources had declined by about 15% compared with the corresponding period of 1982. However, within that overall perspective, the pattern of supplying countries changed substantially. Imports from the European Coal and Steel Community (ECSC) and from Japan both fell by about 37%, while those from other countries taken together increased by 30%. Thus, the relative shares of total imports into the U.S. changed from about one-third attributable to each of these three groups of suppliers to one quarter each from the ECSC and Japan and one half from other countries.

Toward the end of 1983 a potential threat to the continuance of the agreement arose as

Table IX. World Production of Crude Steel
In 000 metric tons

Country	1978	1979	1980	1981	1982	1983 Year to date	1983 No. of months	1983 Percent change 1983/82
World	717,230	747,520	717,380	707,600	644,700			
U.S.S.R.*	151,440	149,000	147,930	149,000	147,150	63,720	5	+2.4
U.S.	124,310	123,280	101,700	108,790	67,660	55,440	9	+3.2
Japan	102,110	111,750	111,400	101,680	99,550	71,480	9	−5.7
West Germany	41,250	40,040	43,840	41,610	35,880	26,510	9	−7.8
China*	31,780	34,436	37,040	35,600	37,000	‡		
Italy	24,280	24,250	26,520	24,780	24,010	15,870	9	−14.5
France	22,840	23,360	23,180	21,260	18,400	12,710	9	−11.1
United Kingdom	20,370	21,550	11,340	15,570	13,710	11,250	9	+2.8
Poland†	19,250	19,200	19,490	15,720	14,800	6,840	5	+20.3
Czechoslovakia†	15,290	14,800	14,930	15,270	15,000	5,080	4	+1.4
Canada	14,900	16,080	15,900	14,810	11,870	9,330	9	−3.6
Belgium	12,600	13,440	12,320	12,280	9,890	7,380	9	−4.9
Brazil	12,210	13,890	15,310	13,210	13,000	10,590	9	+7.9
Romania†	11,780	12,910	13,180	13,030	13,060	‡		
Spain	11,340	12,250	12,670	12,920	13,150	9,600	9	−1.0
India	10,100	10,130	9,510	10,780	11,000	7,810	9	−3.8
South Africa	7,900	8,880	9,070	8,940	8,200	4,880	9	−25.6
Australia	7,600	8,120	7,590	7,640	6,370	4,090	9	−20.9
East Germany†	6,980	6,960	7,310	7,470	7,170	2,450	4	+3.4
Mexico	6,710	7,010	7,100	7,610	7,070	5,020	9	−7.8
Netherlands, The	5,580	5,810	5,260	5,460	4,350	3,280	9	−4.0
North Korea*	5,080	5,400	5,800	5,500	5,800	‡		
South Korea	4,970	7,610	8,560	10,750	11,760	8,670	9	−0.5
Luxembourg	4,790	4,950	4,620	3,790	3,510	2,370	9	−15.5
Austria	4,340	4,920	4,620	4,660	4,260	3,260	9	−2.5
Sweden	4,330	4,730	4,240	3,770	3,900	2,930	9	+0.5
Hungary†	3,880	3,900	3,770	3,650	3,700	1,590	5	+0.3
Yugoslavia	3,460	3,540	3,630	3,980	3,850	3,140	9	+8.8
Taiwan	3,430	4,250	4,230	3,140	4,150	3,680	9	+22.7
Argentina	2,780	3,200	2,680	2,540	2,910	2,200	9	+2.4
Bulgaria†	2,470	2,390	2,570	2,600	2,590	1,210	5	+9.0
Finland	2,330	2,460	2,510	2,410	2,410	1,750	9	−3.1
Turkey	2,170	2,340	2,540	2,430	2,840	2,580	9	+25.3
Iran†	1,300	1,430	1,200	1,200	1,200	‡		
Greece	940	1,000	940	910	910	510	7	−8.0
Venezuela	800	1,510	1,820	2,030	2,280	1,650	9	−4.1

* Estimated series. †1983 figures estimated. ‡1983 figures not yet available.
Sources: International Iron and Steel Institute; United Nations.

Table X. World Production of Pig Iron and Blast Furnace Ferroalloys
In 000 metric tons

Country	1978	1979	1980	1981	1982
World	498,150	519,770	498,940	492,520	443,370
U.S.S.R.	110,700	109,000	108,000	109,000	106,700
U.S.	79,540	78,900	62,350	66,560	39,120
Japan	78,590	83,830	87,040	80,050	77,660
West Germany*	30,160	35,180	33,670	31,660	27,400
China†	26,000	28,000	30,000	30,000	30,000
France*	18,500	19,410	18,690	16,960	15,050
United Kingdom	11,470	12,930	6,380	9,340	8,330
Italy	11,340	11,330	12,150	12,260	11,540
Poland	11,240	11,100	11,600	9,200	8,200
Canada	10,340	11,080	10,890	9,710	8,000
Belgium	10,130	10,780	9,850	9,770	7,830
Brazil	10,040	11,590	12,680	10,310	9,080
Czechoslovakia	9,940	9,530	9,530	10,000	9,530
India	9,270	8,770	8,510	9,470	9,640
Romania	8,160	8,880	8,900	9,300	8,640
Australia	7,280	7,760	6,960	6,830	5,950
Spain	6,250	6,510	6,380	6,560	5,960
South Africa	5,900	7,020	7,200	7,130	6,760
North Korea†	5,000	5,000	5,400	5,000	5,250
Netherlands, The	4,610	4,810	4,330	4,600	3,610
Luxembourg	3,720	3,800	3,570	2,890	2,590
Mexico	3,510	3,490	3,630	3,770	3,590
Austria	3,080	3,700	3,490	3,480	3,120
South Korea	2,740	5,050	5,580	7,930	8,440
East Germany	2,560	2,390	2,400	2,500	2,150
Sweden	2,360	2,910	2,440	1,780	1,780
Hungary	2,330	2,370	2,370	2,200	2,200
Yugoslavia	2,080	2,370	2,440	2,770	2,730
Finland	1,860	2,040	2,050	1,980	1,940
Turkey	1,710	2,300	2,140	2,050	2,450
Bulgaria	1,490	1,450	1,600	1,510	1,560
Argentina	1,440	1,110	1,040	920	1,020
Norway	550	650	600	620	440

*Including ferroalloys.
†Estimated.
Source: International Iron and Steel Institute.

a result of an antidumping case brought against Belgian and West German suppliers of plates by a U.S. West Coast producer that was not one of the 1982 U.S. petitioners. Early in November 1983 the U.S. International Trade Commission made a unanimous preliminary determination of injury in the case.

With EC production declining a further 8% through the first three quarters of 1983, the EC continued operation of the crisis measures developed progressively over previous years. At the end of June the European Commission ordered eight EC countries to reduce their steelmaking capacity by a further 8.3 million tons, bringing total cuts under a rescue plan to 26.7 million tons since 1980, or about 17% of total capacity. Jobs in the EC steel industry under the plan would fall to 400,000 by 1985, down from a peak of 800,000 in 1974. Failure by an EC country to abide by Commission dictates would mean the withholding of permission to the government to subsidize its steel industry. The system of compulsory quotas on production and deliveries to the EC market was again extended in July 1983, in the first instance for seven months. The product coverage of the system was then further enlarged by the restoration of plates and heavy sections. The arrangements for restraint of imports from non-EC countries, first introduced in 1978 and comprising for the most part voluntary commitments by the governments concerned, were continued in 1983. During the year the Commission imposed antidumping duties on imports of certain products from a number of countries, including Spain, Argentina, Brazil, Canada, and Venezuela.

In the early summer a further decline in demand once more created pressures that the EC's crisis measures proved unable to contain. Effective prices for many products fell sharply below the Commission's guidance price levels, the practical operation of which had in any case been considerably complicated by currency movements. In the closing months of the year efforts focused on the need to restabilize the market on the basis of continuance and strengthening of the crisis measures for 1984.

(TREVOR J. MACDONALD)

MACHINERY AND MACHINE TOOLS

During 1982 the nations that produced the most machine tools included Japan and the United States, each with estimated shipments of approximately $3.7 billion, West Germany with shipments of $3.5 billion, the Soviet Union with shipments of approximately $3 billion, and Italy with shipments of $1.1 billion.

The 1982 shipments of machine tools by U.S. manufacturers can be broken down into shipments of metal-cutting types ($2.9 billion) and metal-forming types ($800 million). The total of $3.7 billion was significantly depressed from the $5.1 billion level of 1981, the result of both a faltering U.S. economy and significant penetration of the U.S. market by manufacturers from other nations, most notably by the Japanese.

Manufacturers from other countries supplied 27% of U.S. needs for machine tools in 1982. The dollar value was approximately $1.2 billion. Japan supplied nearly one half of these imports, which accounted for 44% of the lathes installed in U.S. plants in 1982 and 34% of the gear-cutting and hobbing machines.

U.S. exports of machine tools in 1982 totaled about $600 million, down considerably from the $1 billion level of 1981. Most U.S. shipments in 1982 were to Mexico ($136 million), Canada ($82 million), the U.K. ($60 million), Japan ($51 million), and West Germany ($22 million). The U.S. had negative machine tool trade balances in 1982 with Japan, West Germany, and the U.K.

Users of machinery were becoming increasingly interested in the advantages offered by numerically controlled machine tools, which utilize preprogrammed numerical data to control machine movements and functions. More than 33,000 such machine tools were shipped by U.S. builders from 1979 to 1982. The advent of low-cost microprocessor-based control systems made such machine tools increasingly attractive on a cost/performance basis.

In an effort to increase productivity and limit the need for purchase of new machines with each change in workpiece configuration, factory managers had increasingly sought machines with greater flexibility. These desires had created a market for newly developed machinery installations known as flexible manufacturing systems. These systems typically encompass two or more machine tools operated under common control along with automated material-handling and tool-handling systems such as robots, conveyor lines, pallet shuttles, and tool changers.

Such systems increasingly were being designed and installed in conjunction with factory information systems that gather, analyze, and distribute information about the manufacturing process. Managers hoped that such installations would increase productivity and help shorten the time required to introduce new product designs.

(JOHN B. DEAM)

MICROELECTRONICS

Innovations in microelectronics continued to be made at a rapid pace during 1983. A major new dimension was the computer-aided design of semicustom products, which include gate arrays and standard cells. Gate arrays are symmetric patterns of gates that are implemented by three or four transistors. (A gate is a device that outputs a signal when specified input conditions are met.) In a gate array each transistor and each gate function are the same size. To implement a semicustom design, a percentage of the gates are interconnected by an aluminum pattern. This gives the user a breadboard layout, allowing any necessary changes to be made easily. The number of terminals ranges from 20 to 200. Such a capability can be provided in six to eight weeks. Thus, a user, such as a personal computer manufacturer, can introduce new products in a relatively short time.

Standard cells are a level of complexity higher than that of gate arrays. The gates are connected to form building blocks such as inverters, flip-flops, and counters. In standard cells the sizes of the transistors and gates change depending on their function. All transistors and gates are connected in standard cells, whereas in gate arrays usually 70 to 80% of the gates are connected. The chip area is reduced, resulting in lower costs and also higher performance. Although costs and performance of standard cells are superior to those of gate arrays, the design cost is higher and the delivery time is longer, typically 10 to 12 weeks. The cost of redesign is also much higher for standard cells.

The ideal solution to this trade-off in price and performance is to produce the initial designs in gate arrays. After the system is debugged, the transition would then be made from gate arrays to standard cells for volume production. Advancements in computer-aided designs, which include schematic capture, logic and circuit simulation, automatic placing and routing, design rule checks, and electrical rule checks, have made these features available. The models for the transistors and gates are fed into a computer, and powerful algorithms (sets of well-defined step-by-step rules) perform the design, layout, and checking.

The next generation of standard cells would be equipped with microprocessors, random-access memories (RAM's), and read-only memories (ROM's). The addition of electrically erasable ROM's would allow a user to program the microcode. This would create a new capability much more powerful than that currently in existence. Much of the computer-aided software that allows these new capabilities to be practical was developed at universities such as Stanford, California at Berkeley, and Massachusetts Institute of Technology.

The immediate beneficiary of the new semicustom capabilities would be the computer industry. The capabilities are ideal for portable personal computers that have 32-bit architecture and 16-megabyte main memory. Displays would be made of liquid crystal. Performance would be comparable to top-of-the-line minicomputers in 1984 that cost $250,000–$500,000. Prices of the new portable personal computers could range from $1,000 to $10,000, depending on the peripheral equipment used. Other applications are likely to be in such areas as telecommunications, military equipment, and automobiles. (HANDEL H. JONES)

NUCLEAR INDUSTRY

Statistics released early in the year for 1982 showed that 15 new nuclear reactors began operation, as compared with 17 in 1981. The total number of nuclear units of more than 150 MW in service at the beginning of 1983 was 222, with a total capacity of 159,902 MW (excluding the Soviet-bloc countries, which had about 50 units in operation). They included 111 pressurized water reactors (PWR's), 60 boiling water reactors (BWR's), 16 pressurized heavy-water reactors (PHWR's), and 26 Magnox. Analysis of nuclear unit performance for the previous year put a Canadian PHWR (Candu)-type reactor at the top, followed by two PWR's, one in the United States and the other in Belgium. Overall, PHWR's maintained their higher performance figures with average annual capacity factors (energy produced as a fraction of the maximum possible) of 70.4%, compared with 61.2% for BWR's, 60% for PWR's, and 53% for Magnox. There were seven orders, four in France and three in Japan, for new nuclear units and 20 cancellations, 18 of which were in the United States.

The quiteron is an electronic device that does the work of a conventional transistor but at much lower power-dissipation levels. Because its operation depends on a superconductivity phenomenon instead of semiconductor behaviour, it must be maintained at cryogenic conditions near absolute zero. Here its inventor, Sadeg M. Faris of IBM, holds a wafer with sample quiterons.

COURTESY, IBM

The United States again became a member of the International Atomic Energy Agency (IAEA) after its disagreements with the agency over the IAEA's rejection of Israel's credentials. In making this decision the U.S. declared that the IAEA was critical to U.S. national security.

During the year U.S. Pres. Ronald Reagan signed into law the long-awaited Nuclear Waste Policy Act, for the first time establishing a national policy on the disposal of high-level radioactive waste. The U.S. Congress authorized the Department of Energy to establish "away from reactor" storage facilities for irradiated nuclear fuel, and the department was ordered to study a "monitored retrievable waste storage facility" for radioactive fuel. President Reagan also signed the Nuclear Regulatory Authorization Act, which prevented the government from purchasing civilian nuclear materials for military purposes. The political wrangling over the Clinch River (Tenn.) breeder reactor project apparently ended finally in the fall of 1983, when the U.S. Senate voted to discontinue indefinitely consideration of further funding for the project.

Plans for immediate shutdown of five BWR units and for future shutdowns of other units in order to inspect for stress corrosion cracking were modified by the Nuclear Regulatory Commission during the year to minimize the disruption to electricity supplies that such action would have caused. Under a compromise plan the five units would be inspected over a longer period during already scheduled plant shutdowns.

The Canadian industry announced a new 300-MW Candu design for countries embarking on nuclear power programs. The fourth 600-MW Candu reactor to be commissioned in nine months began operation at Embalse, Argentina, and two 520-MW units, the fifth and sixth at Pickering, Ont., were also commissioned.

Also in Canada a crack in a pressure tube occurred in the Pickering unit 2 reactor in August, putting the unit out of service for the rest of the year. Although the cause of the rupture was still under investigation at the end of the year, it appeared to have been related to the buildup of hydrides in the zircaloy 2 tube and was not evident in the tubes of later units, which have zirconium/niobium alloy tubes. Although a blow to the performance record of the Canadian-designed reactors, the incident served to demonstrate safety features inherent in the design.

Events in Britain centred on the lengthy public inquiry into the proposed PWR unit for Sizewell in Suffolk. The inquiry assumed massive proportions, lasting most of the year. The British industry wanted to gain PWR experience and thereby enable the country to participate in international markets. The Central Electricity Generating Board (CEGB) claimed economic advantages over other British or foreign designs. Most significant among the arguments was the need for Britain to prove that a PWR could meet British requirements. Opponents refuted cost advantages, claiming that, given the additional features required by the CEGB, the economic case was invalid, and the station would take even longer to construct than the standard U.S. plants. Britain announced that it would be collaborating with other European countries on the development of a fast breeder reactor and later announced substantial cuts in its domestic investment in fast breeder reactor development.

The new government in West Germany voted to withdraw the veto over the commissioning of that country's fast breeder reactor, the SNR 300 at Kalkar. The government stressed that energy industries in West Germany would have to provide an increased proportion of the project cost increases. Another advanced reactor project, the THTR 300 high-temperature reactor, was also given government funding after a long delay.

In July more than half of the electricity produced in France was from nuclear plants, a new record for the country. However, the French national utility announced that the PWR program, which had been the most active outside of the Soviet bloc countries, would be slowing down due to the anticipated lack of demand in the next decade. The government decided to order two plants in 1983 instead of the three planned earlier, and similar reductions were expected over the next few years.

China's application to join the IAEA was accepted at the agency's general conference in October. The proposed 900-MW PWR reactor for Guangdong (Kwangtung) in China was the cause of much international marketing activity during the year, involving the French, British, Italian, and U.S. industries, among others. China was seen as one of the biggest potential new markets in the world. The Chinese program included domestic PWR and heavy-water reactor development.

The Soviet bloc countries also cut back on projected new nuclear power capacity, but there remained a substantial program aimed at an installed capacity of about 100,000 MW by 1990. At the beginning of 1983 the Soviet Union had 18,000 MW of nuclear plant in service, and there was a total of just under 5,000 MW in the other Soviet-bloc countries. Delays to the nuclear reactor "production line" at the Atommash facility continued, and the factory only produced one unit, its first, for the South Ukraine station during the year. A new independent safety inspectorate was set up in the U.S.S.R. (RICHARD A. KNOX)

PAINTS AND VARNISHES

The paint industry experienced mixed fortunes in 1983. In the U.S., the U.K., and West Germany some real growth was achieved, compared with the depressed levels of the previous year, but paint makers in France and the Benelux area continued to lose ground. It was the frequently troubled U.K. paint industry that reported the best figures. Output was up 3.5% by volume and 7.2% by value. U.S. and West German production rose about 1.8%, with correspondingly modest gains in income. French paint makers, affected by government policies, saw their markets shrink by more than 3%, but they fared better than their Belgian counterparts, whose losses approached 5% by volume. The Dutch industry's important export market contracted by over 13%. Austrian paint makers experienced a volume loss of 6%, the first such decline in the post-World War II period.

Overcapacity, price cutting, and rising costs combined to keep profitability low in most countries. A period of stable raw material prices came to an end, aggravated by partial failure of the soybean crop in North and South America. Few paint companies were forced out of business, however, and optimists could point to some bright spots. Increases of more than 10% in tonnage of powder coatings were widespread, although low prices for advanced products again caused concern. Coatings for the steel containers widely used for inland and sea transport constituted an interesting market. Over four-fifths of the global container stock was produced in Japan, South Korea, and Taiwan, and four Japanese paint companies supplied most of the coatings.

In the U.K. an official commission recommended moves to reduce the lead content of household paints toward the very low U.S. level of 0.06%. The British industry was unconvinced of the need and resisted the technical and commercial upheaval involved. Meanwhile, efforts continued to find substitutes for the glycol ether family of solvents, reported to be hazardous. The industry also became involved in discussions with the authorities on child-resistant containers and solvent abuse (glue sniffing). In the U.S. 20 paint companies were among the 246 firms involved in a $2.9 million cleanup of hazardous wastes in Zionsville, Ind. (LIONEL BILEFIELD)

PHARMACEUTICALS

Despite continuing efforts by the Reagan administration toward deregulation and a crescendo of rhetoric from U.S. industry leaders deploring the lack of research incentives, there was evidence during the year that legislation to extend patents for drugs and other products might be in trouble. While the Senate was considering such action, the House seemed more intent on a countermeasure to expedite Food and Drug Administration (FDA) clearance of generic competitors for the drugs whose patents had expired after 1962—about 125 drugs including some highly profitable brand-name products. Because the FDA had imposed a semifreeze on processing applications for such drugs, they had been in a sort of administrative limbo, frustrating both generic drug manufacturers and consumerists who hoped that increased generic competition would generate reduced prices.

By early October 1983 there seemed to be a possibility of some sort of compromise, providing patent extension for drug developers and, for generic drug manufacturers, a sliding time scale for drug applications. However, whether the details of such a basically pro-business piece of legislation could be hammered out in a preelection period remained problematical.

The year was an especially significant one for over-the-counter (OTC) drugs. During the first five months, manufacturers were engaged in a frantic attempt to comply with the FDA regulation on tamper-resistant closures and other packaging issued in response to the 1982 deaths of seven persons who took Tylenol capsules tainted with cyanide. This demanded a considerable effort in logistics, machinery and materials procurement, and supplier cooperation. FDA-industry cooperation in this effort was noteworthy.

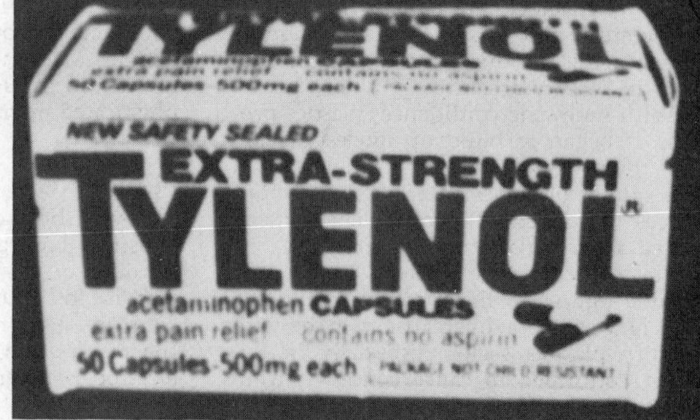

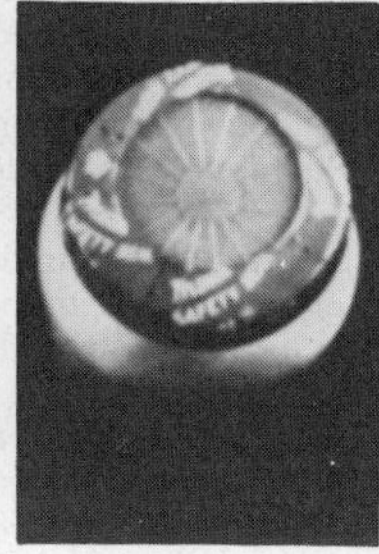
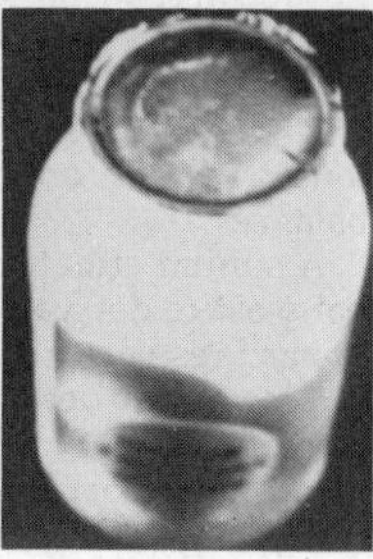

Johnson & Johnson responded to the Tylenol murders with triple-safety-sealed packaging: clockwise from upper left, both ends of the box are glued shut; a yellow label on the bottle warns users to check the safety seals; an inner seal of foil must be punctured to remove the capsules; and a red plastic seal surrounds and closes the outer cap.

WIDE WORLD

The other major development affecting OTC drugs was the issuance of all proposed final monographs as part of the OTC drug review, a ten-year effort by the FDA to ascertain safety and efficacy. The 58 proposed monographs, issued by 17 expert advisory panels, would serve as the regulatory guide for all marketed and future OTC products. Relatively few nonsafe ingredients were discovered (camphorated oil and hexachlorophene were two), but a large number of noneffective or only possibly effective ingredients were identified, and it was these that were bringing about reformulation of many products.

Third world governments were listing drugs essential for human needs and discouraging or banning the sale of others. The Pharmaceuticals Commission of the Ministry of Health in Mozambique twice revised its list of essential drugs down to a total of 343 medicines; only the prescription drugs on this list could be imported. In Bangladesh the first step to the eventual production of only 150 essential drugs was the beginning of a phased withdrawal of 1,700 drugs deemed inessential, wasteful, and unnecessarily harmful, from a total of about 4,000 on the market.

The World Health Organization recommended a change in the composition of the influenza vaccine that had been in use since 1980 for the 1983–84 flu season.

(DONALD A. DAVIS)

PLASTICS

The plastics industry showed definite signs of recovery in 1983. Greater demand from end users in many sectors became evident early in the year, and the third-quarter results of major chemical groups with substantial plastics interests showed sharply higher profits compared with the same period of 1982. U.S. companies did especially well, but even in Europe the picture was encouraging. Imperial Chemical Industries (ICI), for instance, announced that its petrochemical and plastics business broke even during the third quarter for the first time in three years.

With renewing confidence, plastics processors began to build up modest stocks, and there were even signs of tightness in the supply of some materials. In general, prices hardened. Polypropylene experienced a particularly good year, with percentage increases in demand well into double figures in Europe, Japan, and the U.S. Nevertheless, overcapacity in the commodity plastics sector, especially in Europe, continued to cause concern within the industry. It was estimated that Western European capacity for ethylene (the basis of most commodity plastics materials) needed to be reduced by some 3 million metric tons from the current level of about 15 million tons a year in order to achieve a sensible balance.

A similar situation applied to the principal plastics derivatives, but the movement toward restructuring the industry through intercompany deals lost momentum. An exception was in Scandinavia, where the two major manufacturers of commodity plastics, Unifos (polyethylene) and KemaNord (polyvinyl chloride), were bought by Neste of Finland and Norsk Hydro of Norway, respectively. A notable merger in the polypropylene field was between Hercules (U.S.) and Montedison (Italy) to form Himont, with a total capacity exceeding one million metric tons a year. The large West German chemical groups preferred to solve the industry's overcapacity problems by internal action combined with market forces, rather than by concerted agreement or even government edict (a course adopted in France and Japan). Thus, Hoechst revealed that it had cut its European capacity for high-density polyethylene by 38%; for polypropylene by 26%; and for polystyrene by 27%.

Nevertheless, manufacturers were ready to make selective investments in new technology. Linear low-density polyethylene continued to supplant the conventional variety, and British Petroleum announced construction of a 100,000-metric-tons-a-year plant in France, though it emphasized that this would be more than balanced by closures in its existing high-density polyethylene capacity. Once again, polyethylene terephthalate (PET) provided the leading success story, resulting from the rapid growth in its use for large bottles. In 1982, 340 million PET bottles were used in the U.K., representing about 20% of the market for nonreturnable carbonated drink containers, and further major gains were made in 1983.

The engineering plastics market also improved, though the contrast was less dramatic because engineering plastics had suffered less from the recession. The general recovery of the automotive industry, coupled with the still rising usage of plastics in the average car, made an important contribution, as did continuing activity in the electronics and telecommunications sectors. New high-performance materials included ICI's APC1 composite, consisting of PEEK (polyetheretherketone) reinforced with carbon fibre, and the same company's PES (polyethersulfone). A group of new engineering polymers introduced by Bayer of West Germany included polyphosphonate, polyester carbonate, and polyphenylene sulfide. Machinery developments continued to be influenced by increasingly sophisticated microelectronic devices.

(ROBIN C. PENFOLD)

PRINTING

The year brought several breakthroughs. Crosfield Lasergravure, a system of electronic laser engraving of cylinders, went into use in Britain at Sun Printers. In West Germany Dr. Ing-Rudolf Hell announced the resumption of development work on electron-beam engraving in gravure, in cooperation with the European Rotogravure Association. Mitsubishi in Japan introduced a full-size, double-width plastic plate for newspapers that permitted direct platemaking off pasteup or graphic copy without intermediate film; the plate had a life of at least 100,000 impressions and was cheaper than presensitized metal. Also in Japan, Aquaplate offered a new metal-layer offset plate on a paper base. Parallel work at the Department of Scientific and Industrial Research in Australia and Dainippon Printing in Japan resulted in a new system providing extraordinary security for the printing of banknotes and similar documents. Extremely thin plastic film is coated with printable body-heat-sensitive layers that change colour and pattern under heat. While the method was cheap in use, it was said to need expensive equipment. This, the inventors claimed, should discourage all but the richest would-be forgers. Think Laboratories, working with major printers in Japan, developed a method of coppering lightweight aluminum gravure cylinders, as well as a new area-variable method for etching gravure cylinders, using a laser-cut screen with extra-fine lines to produce very thin bridges.

Traditionally, publishers had left technical work to the reproduction houses, printers, and binders, but this reliance on "the trade" was changing. In May Time Inc. signed a $10 million order for electronic prepress equipment. Britain's Crosfield Electronics supplied electronic colour scanners and page composition systems, as well as a new data compression system that would allow simultaneous transmission of colour-separated pages within a fraction of the time previously needed. Transmission would go to Time Inc.'s eight (soon to be more) North American printers and those producing overseas editions of *Time* magazine. Time Inc. then awarded an additional contract for Vista colour layout and graphics stations to Sci-Tex of Israel. The complete systems worked text and other matter into the new setup off Information International Inc. (Triple-I) photocomposition systems. In September *Newsweek* placed an order for similar systems.

Fuji Photo Film introduced a high-speed system to make poster-size "prints" off video images within eight minutes. Interest in the still-expensive inkjet system came mainly from publicity and advertising circles selecting instant large displays of artwork, designs, and news pictures. Japanese manufacturers appeared poised to attack new markets in Europe and North America. Tokyo Kikai Seisakusho reported 250 newspaper press units sold to the U.S. (W. PINCUS JASPERT)

RUBBER

The rubber industry appeared to have weathered the recession rather well, and by late 1983 most firms were increasing production and sales of both raw materials and finished products. Profits of all segments of the industry were up, with some variation depending on the product line. As the year progressed, the demand for original equipment tires was equal to or greater than production. The use of radial tires increased enough so that five U.S. manufacturers planned to install additional radial-tire capacity.

The European rubber industry appeared to be in poorer economic health than that of North America. An example was the sale of Dunlop's four British and West German tire plants to Sumitomo Rubber Industries after substantial losses for several years. In the restructuring of the Dunlop Co. the U.S. was to become the prime tire sales and profit centre for the British firm. The problem of overproduction during the recession adversely affected profits of other European rubber companies. The synthetic rubber industry in Europe was in the doldrums at the end of 1983, with only 44% of name-

Table XI. Natural Rubber Production
In 000 metric tons

Country	1980	1981	1982
Malaysia	1,530	1,510	1,517
Indonesia*	1,020	868	880
Thailand	501	504	552
India	155	151	166
China*	113	128	140
Sri Lanka	133	124	125
Liberia*	78	78	68
Philippines	69	70*	70*
Vietnam*	50	40	40
Nigeria*	47	49	50
Brazil	28	30	33
Others	121	138	114
Total*	3,845	3,690	3,755

*Estimate, or includes estimate.
Source: The Secretariat of The International Rubber Study Group, *Statistical Bulletin,* vol. 37, no.12 (September 1983).

Table XII. Synthetic Rubber Production
In 000 metric tons

Country	1980	1981	1982
U.S.S.R.*	2,040	2,000	1,950
United States	2,215	2,234	1,832
Japan	1,094	1,010	931
France	511	487	480
West Germany	390	397	384
United Kingdom	212	216	245
Brazil	249	223	228
Italy*	250	235	210
Netherlands, The	212	211	203
Canada	253	263	182
East Germany*	150	155	155
Romania	150	148	145*
Mexico	91	105*	115*
China*	90	95	115
Poland	118	111	100
Belgium*	115	108	100
Czechoslovakia	60	63	66
Spain	81	60*	65*
Korea	75	82	64
Taiwan	73	71	58
Argentina	33	30	46*
Australia	46	43	43
South Africa	39	36	32
Others	98	82	106
Total*	8,645	8,465	7,855

*Estimate, or includes estimate.
Source: The Secretariat of The International Rubber Study Group, *Statistical Bulletin,* vol. 37, no. 12 (September 1983).

plate capacity being utilized, compared with 54% in North America.

Akron, Ohio, the location of many company headquarters and general offices but with dwindling production, was becoming the leader in rubber research and development. The University of Akron announced formation of two new groups, the Institute of Polymer Engineering and the Institute of Biomedical Engineering Research. The latter, being developed in cooperation with the Cleveland Clinic and Goodyear Tire & Rubber Co., was to concentrate at first on the development of synthetic cardiovascular replacement parts and, eventually, a fully workable artificial heart. The Institute of Polymer Engineering planned to concentrate on processing problems such as mixing, extrusion, and calendering. These institutes augmented the extensive polymerization and rubber laboratories already established at the university.

The disposal of scrap tires became a major problem in the U.S. because reclaimed rubber was in small demand, and Environmental Protection Agency regulations did not permit open burning. Tires are unstable in a landfill, and their use for other purposes such as breakwaters and artificial reefs accounted for only a small percentage of the worn-out tires. An international symposium on scrap tires heard opposing views on the practicality of pyrolysis of tires to obtain oil, gas, and carbon char (a filler for rubber). The major objection was that it was not economically feasible since the payback of the original investment in the process would be 9.3 years, according to a study by Goodyear. The proponents cited successful tire pyrolysis in Japan and current work at a Struthers, Ohio, plant at a profit. Cost factors could be minor compared with the fire hazard of tire storage areas and the problems of disposal mentioned above. Tire fires are dangerous and are a source of pollution of air, land, and streams, while pyrolysis is a clean process.

The first radial airplane tires were announced by Michelin Tire Corp. and Goodyear, with Michelin in production and Goodyear in the prototype stage. Among the advantages of these tires, compared with those of conventional bias construction, are longer tread life, better traction, and cooler running. Pirelli of Italy developed a radial motorcycle tire in all the common sizes.

Because of competitive forces resulting from the supply-demand situation, rubber materials prices in 1983 did not necessarily reflect costs or inflation. The New York spot price of natural rubber was 43½ cents per pound on Oct. 1, 1982. On Oct. 1, 1983, it was 59¾ cents, a 27% increase. The list price of the most widely used synthetic rubber, SBR (styrene butadiene rubber), showed little change from the 70 cents per pound granted on Oct. 1, 1982. Widespread discounting of this quoted price existed, however, with actual selling prices as low as 44 to 46 cents per pound.

World production of natural rubber in 1982 was estimated at 3,755,000 metric tons, an increase of 65,000 tons over 1981. Production for 1983 was estimated at 3,810,000 tons, an increase of 55,000 tons from 1982. Production of synthetic rubber was estimated at 7,855,000 metric tons in 1982, a decrease of 610,000 tons from 1981.

The U.S. continued to be the largest single user of natural rubber, consuming 585,000 metric tons in 1982. This was, however, a decrease of 50,000 tons from 1981. World consumption of natural rubber latex (dry basis) was estimated at 290,000 tons in 1981. Statistics for 1982 were incomplete, but they suggested lower consumption of natural rubber latex than in 1981. Statistics on world consumption of synthetic latices were incomplete, but U.S. consumption was 77,408 metric tons (dry basis) of the styrene butadiene type, a marked decrease from the 101,856 tons consumed in 1981. World consumption of both natural and synthetic rubber was estimated at 11,650,000 metric tons for 1982, a 510,000-ton decrease from 1981.

Production estimates by country are shown in Table XI for natural rubber and Table XII for synthetic rubber. It is notable that 1982 was the first year since synthetic rubber production was begun that the U.S.S.R. produced more than the U.S.

(JAMES R. BEATTY)

SHIPBUILDING

Although the world shipping industry continued in the throes of the longest depression since the early 1930s, there was a slight improvement in the world shipbuilding order book in 1983. This was due to two major factors: the need to replace aging and inefficient tonnage, and a significant increase in the amount of tonnage going to the shipbreakers' yards. The tonnage on order was 62,786,151 tons deadweight (dw), compared with 61 million tons dw in 1982, with the greater part of the new orders being for bulk cargo carriers and vessels designed to transport chemicals and petroleum products. Very few new crude oil carriers were ordered, and the number of containerships and conventional cargo ships on order showed little change from the past year.

Japanese shipbuilders continued to lead the world in the volume of new orders with 25.7 million tons dw, down slightly more than 1 million tons from 1982. South Korea followed with a greatly increased tonnage of 10 million tons dw; this reflected the South Korean success in obtaining orders, largely at the expense of Japan, although Western European shipbuilders also lost many orders to them. Brazil moved up to third place with just over 3 million tons dw on order, followed by Poland with 2.7 million tons dw. Spain, in third place a year earlier, dropped to fifth place with 2.3 million tons dw. Taiwan also found new orders hard to obtain and suffered a reduction in the order book from 3.1 million tons dw to 1.9 million tons dw.

In terms of vessel types, the total world order book showed that bulk carriers were the most popular, with 40 million tons dw on order, followed by tankers at 12 million tons dw and containerships at 4.5 million tons dw. Orders for dry-cargo ships dropped sharply from just under 9 million tons dw to a modest 5.3 million tons dw. The sector that showed the most improvement in terms of financial value was passenger cruise ships. Orders were placed for six large cruise liners representing an investment in excess of $450 million.

Without exception the major Western European shipbuilding nations continued to support their shipbuilding industries, although in many cases some shipyards were closed in order to reduce the level of future losses. In the U.K. the state-owned British Shipbuilders recorded a loss of £100 million, and heavy losses were sustained by shipyards in West Germany, France, The Netherlands, Belgium, Sweden, and Norway. Harland and Wolff of Belfast, Northern Ireland, also state-owned and suffering losses, signed a cooperation agreement with Ishikawajima-Harima Heavy Industries of Japan, builders of multipurpose cargo ships. The situation in the U.S. shipyards remained serious, but there were signs that more orders would be forthcoming.

The increased level of naval building helped to keep some of the U.S. yards open. This applied elsewhere in the world as well, particularly in the U.K., West Germany, and The Netherlands, where defense requirements and the need for nations to patrol their new exclusive economic zones resulted in more orders for suitable patrol vessels.

After a flurry of orders in 1982, the Chinese shipyards found work harder to obtain but still managed to improve the size of the total order book from 1.5 million tons dw to

1.7 million tons dw, representing about 2% of the world merchant fleet. The Chinese said that it was not their intention to challenge South Korea in the shipbuilding market. This seemed to be a wise decision since world shipbuilding capacity remained at more than 50% above the actual world requirement for new tonnage, a situation that seemed likely to last until at least 1986.

A similar situation existed in regard to world marine engine-building capacity, and the majority of that market was shared between the two main-engine building groups, Burmeister & Wain-MAN (Maschinen Fabrik Augsburg-Nürnberg) and Sulzer Bros. Between them they accounted for nearly 80% of the large marine diesel engines currently on order. The builders emphasized energy-saving main engines that made the greatest use of all waste heat while operating satisfactorily on the very poor quality oil fuel being supplied to the marine market. (W. D. EWART)

TELECOMMUNICATIONS

As deregulation heated up the communications industry in the United States, firms were trying to gain an advantage over their competitors by developing technological expertise. Their marketing efforts for home, office, and factory communications benefited from the year's technological advances in fibre optics, space satellites, voice- and data-handling networks, and cellular telephones, among others.

One of the year's major economic and telecommunications developments was the divestiture of its operating companies by AT&T. Emblematic of the change is the dismantling of the old AT&T sign and its replacement with a new one for the new subsidiary to market telephone equipment and computerized services, American Bell.

WIDE WORLD

A great number and variety of practical fibre-based communications systems were installed during the year. For example, 90 megabit-per-second data flowed in hair-thin strands of glass fibre stretched between Boston and Washington, D.C.; San Francisco and Sacramento, Calif., would soon be similarly linked. And, near Chicago, fibre was used to connect consumers to cable television with the fibre's data-handling capability allowing multiple programs to be handled simultaneously. Similar fibre communications systems were put to work connecting computers.

Communications satellite technology also advanced in 1983, mostly in regard to new applications. New intersatellite communication links were designed to allow improved signal quality and reliability by allowing signals to travel, for example, from Europe to Japan without the need for multiple satellite-to-ground trips.

Companies were looking carefully in 1983 at the private branch exchange—a switching system that can handle voice and data simultaneously. They found that the 64-kilobit-per-second-per-user capabilities of such systems—developed from the older voice-only private branch exchanges—could be combined with computer intelligence to work effectively with existing office communications systems. Moreover, they found that the exchanges could provide local voice and data storage, links to the outside world, and additional features otherwise found only on specially designed communications networks.

The switching technology that is the heart of the private branch exchange was adapted during the year to the cellular telephone system, which would permit high-quality mobile telephones in automobiles and trucks in dozens of U.S. cities. Data communication over cellular telephone channels for car-based personal computers was also studied.

Thus, as the breakup of AT&T continued toward its Jan. 1, 1984, goal, plans were being rushed by the various systems to provide for total voice, data, and video interconnection. The technology of packet-switching—which combines both transmission and switching in one computer-controlled communications network—emerged as the method of choice. Both AT&T and IBM started work on nationwide packet-switching networks to allow subscribers to interconnect with each other, store and transmit data, and use computers at remote sites.

China began updating its national telecommunications system as part of the sixth five-year plan at an estimated total cost of over $2 billion. This would include low-interest loans to cities to upgrade local systems.

Restrictions on transborder data flow (TBDF) created compliance problems for some multinational companies. TBDF regulations had been adopted by 24 countries since Sweden enacted the first such law to protect data privacy. TBDF legislation generally defines practices for collecting, storing, using, and communicating personal data held in public- and private-sector automated records. In Mexico all private-line leasing was being replaced by the state-run network. Brazil controlled and taxed certain classes of data entering and leaving the

Requiescat in Pace

Bell, Mother (AMERICAN TELEPHONE & TELEGRAPH Co.), pioneer telephone operator (b. July 9, 1877, Boston, Mass.—d. Dec. 31, 1983, New York, N.Y.), was an exemplar of U.S. technological expertise, stable business management, and modern capitalism. Born Bell Telephone Co., she was the daughter of Alexander Graham Bell, the speech teacher who invented the telephone a year before her birth.

Her early years were chaotic with family reorganizations and name changes, and in 1900 she formally adopted the name American Telephone and Telegraph Co., which she had used occasionally since 1885. She continued to be identified as a Bell, sometimes as the Bell System, and gradually became known as Mother Bell or, irreverently, Ma Bell. She took over the management of the family business of telephone communications.

In her father's declining years her interests were looked after by Theodore N. Vail, who successfully protected some patents she owned from encroachment by a rival firm. The family business prospered so greatly under her management that in 1918 Congress adopted legislation making her a ward of the Post Office, but this arrangement was abandoned the following year. In 1921 and subsequently she fell under suspicion of being a monopolist, and from that time her every move was monitored by various U.S. government agencies. Despite these distractions she developed what was universally acknowledged as the world's finest telephone system, and she also found time to pursue philanthropic interests, becoming known far and wide for her succour and support of widows and orphans.

Government antagonism and legal battles sapped her strength, and she expired at midnight on New Year's Eve, 1983, leaving eight daughters: AT&T II, Ameritech, Bell Atlantic, Bellsouth, Nynex, Pacific Telesis, Southwestern Bell, and U.S. West.

(BRUCE L. FELKNOR)

Table XIII. Countries Having More than 100,000 Telephones

Telephones in service, 1982

Country	Number of telephones	Percentage increase over 1972	Telephones per 100 population	Country	Number of telephones	Percentage increase over 1972	Telephones per 100 population
Algeria	606,869	187.3	3.3	Korea, South	5,158,357	589.2	13.8
Argentina	3,041,475	66.6	10.7	Kuwait	231,643	240.2	16.0
Australia[1]	7,684,336	96.4	52.5	Lebanon[2]	321,500	67.4	11.2
Austria	3,177,944	105.5	42.1	Luxembourg	228,000	92.1	62.6
Belgium	3,818,626	76.6	38.7	Malaysia	825,289	291.9	6.3
Bolivia	144,300	226.5	2.5	Mexico	5,411,108	215.5	7.4
Brazil	8,536,000	313.4	7.2	Morocco	241,100	40.5	1.1
Bulgaria[1]	1,255,792	165.5	14.1	Netherlands, The	7,769,115	108.8	54.4
Canada	15,741,723	53.0	64.7	New Zealand	1,875,538	46.4	58.8
Chile	595,108	52.7	5.2	Nigeria	708,390	716.4	0.7
Colombia	1,747,689	73.8	6.3	Norway	1,992,090	65.4	48.5
Costa Rica	255,898	278.3	10.9	Pakistan	393,010	86.2	0.5
Cuba	406,355	47.8	4.2	Panama	212,992	98.8	10.7
Cyprus	128,507	170.0	20.0	Peru[1]	487,123	118.7	2.8
Czechoslovakia	3,225,968	52.7	21.0	Philippines	624,101	77.7	1.2
Denmark	3,483,323	94.2	68.0	Poland	3,505,656	77.9	9.7
Dominican Republic	175,054	212.7	3.0	Portugal	1,455,804	79.9	14.8
Ecuador	290,200	146.0	3.2	Puerto Rico	678,447	90.7	22.0
Egypt	521,625	...	1.2	Saudi Arabia	788,576	...	11.2
Finland	2,511,306	94.7	52.2	Singapore	771,400	306.3	31.6
France	26,940,296	182.2	49.8	South Africa	3,208,730	97.6	13.1
East Germany	3,251,950	50.2	19.4	Spain	12,350,058	140.8	32.8
West Germany	30,122,023	97.6	48.8	Sweden	6,889,000	47.2	82.8
Greece	2,956,663	140.4	30.2	Switzerland	4,780,760	48.8	74.9
Hong Kong	1,822,846	163.6	35.0	Syria	471,127	292.5	4.9
Hungary	1,296,682	48.5	12.1	Taiwan	3,820,207	676.0	21.0
Iceland	111,358	48.1	48.0	Thailand	529,106	161.9	1.1
India	2,981,609	120.7	0.5	Tunisia[1]	188,476	146.8	0.3
Indonesia	600,643	161.6	0.4	Turkey[1]	2,104,113	221.5	4.7
Iran	1,041,939	133.0	2.9	U.S.S.R.	23,707,000	115.5	8.8
Ireland	720,000	122.3	20.8	United Kingdom	28,375,982	75.8	50.7
Israel	1,302,000	131.0	32.1	United States	181,893,000	45.9	78.7
Italy	20,444,037	98.1	36.3	Uruguay	294,350	25.1	10.1
Jamaica	124,258	63.8	6.2	Venezuela	1,377,630	210.5	9.4
Japan	60,349,857	102.3	51.0	Yugoslavia	2,303,501	180.6	10.2
Kenya	216,674	154.4	1.3	Zimbabwe[1]	224,452	70.6	3.0

[1]1981.
[2]1979.
Sources: American Telephone and Telegraph Company; *The World's Telephones, 1972; 1982.*

country. France had considered assessing import levies on the intrinsic value of software data. Euronet, the European communications network, now charged more to non-EC users. (HARVEY J. HINDIN)

TEXTILES

For the first time in several years, there appeared to be signs of an upturn in the textile trade. Order levels increased slightly, and in the second half of the year there were signs of growing, if cautious, confidence. Machine builders reported a greater influx of orders, although many countries, particularly in the less developed parts of the world, were unable to proceed with investment plans because of foreign currency shortages.

In Western Europe a number of textile-machine-building companies were totally restructured by what was described as "management buyback." If a faltering company was part of a large group, the procedure was to close it down and sell the assets to its management, which then reorganized a much reduced company on a basis calculated to be profitable. This proved to be an effective means of bringing companies into line with their markets, but it added to the growing number of unemployed, already swollen by automation.

The air-jet loom made considerable advances during the year. Completely automated rotor spinning machines were introduced by most spinning-frame makers. Another development was the emergence of parallel, or wrapped, yarns for such products as carpet pile and upholstery fabrics. A sliver of parallel fibres was drawn to the desired thickness and then wrapped by a very fine strand of synthetic filament yarn that held the mass together. When the pile was cut, the filaments disappeared, and the untwisted fibres they previously surrounded burst open to give a thick, dense pile. This development also had potential for finer yarn count applications such as ultrasoft terry toweling.

(PETER LENNOX-KERR)

Wool. World production of wool in the 1982–83 season (ended June 1983) was 1,630,000 metric tons clean, almost unchanged from 1981–82. Adverse weather reduced output in Australia and the U.S.S.R., the two largest producers, and this, coupled with reductions in Argentina and the U.S., canceled out increases in China and Uruguay. Availability was $2^1/_2$% higher, however.

Demand from the wool textile industries was reduced by recession, and stocks rose as a result of price-support action by wool marketing organizations in Australia, New Zealand, and South Africa. Aggregate statistics available for 11 countries showed that in the third quarter of 1982 usage of virgin wool was 7% lower than in the corresponding quarter of 1981. China developed further as a major wool importer and wool textile manufacturer.

Prices for merino and crossbred wool tended to soften gradually in the early months of the 1982–83 selling season, but 1983 brought recovery. In terms of Australian and New Zealand currency, this was underpinned in March by devaluation and an accompanying increase in floor prices. The 1983–84 season began with very little overall change in floor or market prices, although support buying was again needed. The potential financing burden caused some anxiety, especially since the New Zealand Wool Board reduced its contribution to the International Wool Secretariat, which promotes wool as a fibre as well as playing an associated role in research and monitoring quality standards in manufacture. (H. M. F. MALLETT)

Cotton. World production of cotton in the 1982–83 season was estimated at 75,089,000 bales. Output in South America declined from 4,993,000 bales in 1981–82 to 4,531,000 bales. China's production rose from 13,643,000 bales to 16,531,000, while in the Soviet Union output dropped from 12,975,000 bales to 11,950,000. There was an appreciable decline in the U.S., where production fell from the previous season's record 15,641,000 bales to 12,010,000.

The International Cotton Advisory Committee estimated that by 1983–84 there would be a worldwide decline in cotton production of about 2.6 million bales. This was attributable partly to erratic climatic conditions but also to spectacularly high rises in raw cotton prices that encouraged manufacturers to switch to less expensive synthetic fibres. Nevertheless, there were clear signs of a continuing preference for the natural fibre products in the wealthier countries.

In the U.S. the decline in production was largely the result of adverse weather, but it also reflected the success of the government's program aimed at cutting back output. China's production was expected to fall in the 1983–84 season because of a switch to food crops. Outside China and the U.S., the area planted with cotton continued to increase, about 2.5% overall, while yield was expected to rise by around 4.5%. The largest production gains were expected in the U.S.S.R., India, Pakistan, Australia, Greece, Mexico, Colombia, Argentina, and Peru. (PETER LENNOX-KERR)

Silk. According to the International Silk Association, world production of raw silk in 1981 reached the same level as in 1938 (56,000 tons), which would seem to indicate that silk had surrendered no ground to synthetic fibres. Such a conclusion was misleading, however. Reliable statistics for the years prior to the association's establishment in 1950 were not always available, and production, especially in many Asian countries (with the conspicuous exception of Japan, where painstaking records had been kept for many years), was often underestimated. Considering that the synthetics started as "artificial silk," it was perhaps surprising that they had not made even greater inroads.

Annual production figures do not always tally with consumption, as was illustrated by the current accumulation of some 10,000 tons of government-held silk stocks in Japan. Release of these stocks could one day cause a flood, but meanwhile demand remained steady. The Chinese policy of exporting fabric and garments rather than raw material was meeting enough success to disturb weavers and finishers in the West, whose costs made competition difficult for any but a few of the more sophisticated fabrics.

During 1983 China raised prices only once (in August), to 54.45 yuan for 3A 20/22 denier, but currency fluctuations kept prices on the move in the consuming markets of the West. (PETER W. GADDUM)

Man-Made Fibres. The man-made fibre industry of Western Europe continued to suffer from excess production capacity. One of the first to recognize the situation was ICI Fibres of Britain, which undertook a massive reorganization aimed at retaining almost the same potential volume of production but with less plant and fewer people. At the same time, the spectrum of products was adjusted so the company could aim at particular parts of the trade. Similar actions were taken by Enka in The Netherlands and West Germany, Rhône-Poulenc in France, Bayer and Hoechst in West Germany, and, to a lesser extent, the Italian fibre makers.

During 1983 Monsanto decided to withdraw from acrylic-fibre production in Europe and sold its plants in Northern Ireland and West Germany to the Montefibre group of Italy. Montefibre, however, only wanted the Coleraine facility in Northern Ireland, so the West German plant was resold to Bayer. A significant technical development was the opening of a new viscose rayon plant by Snia Fibre of Italy, despite a major swing away from cellulosic fibres by producers in all developed countries. The Italian company joined forces with the Japanese producer Asahi to pool patents on what appeared to be similar approaches to production of a quality viscose rayon filament yarn.

Du Pont was making a primary carpet backing, Typar III, based on polypropylene. The fastest growing area for this spunbonded fabric was as a geotextile for subsoil stabilization. Spunbonding, a system of cascading still molten fibres onto a conveyor and compressing them into a coherent sheet, seemed to be gaining ground. In the search for asbestos substitutes, the most promising alternative appeared to be a modified acrylic fibre (Dolan) made by Hoechst. (PETER LENNOX-KERR)

TOBACCO

After a century of virtually unchecked growth, world sales of factory-made cigarettes—the most-favoured form of tobacco consumption—faltered in 1983 at around 4,550,000,000,000. Increased smoking in much of Asia and Africa could not offset declines elsewhere, notably in advanced countries hit by sharp increases in tobacco taxes, antismoking campaigns, and economic hard times. Cigar and pipe tobacco consumption also fell, although demand for cut tobacco for hand-rolling into cigarettes remained strong. Nevertheless, the industry began to believe in a return to more buoyant trade. It expected world economic recovery and saw positive demographic trends in low-consumption countries, where smoking was the one small luxury that millions could afford.

World production of leaf tobacco, which rose to an all-time high in 1982 and filled the storage facilities of consuming nations, fell back in 1983 to about 5,320,000,000 kg (11,700,000,000 lb). Price levels disappointed most of the 18 million farmers wholly or largely dependent on this crop. The 56 countries regularly exporting leaf found customers buying less and often drifting to cheaper qualities.

New technology made it possible to use a wider range of tobacco types. Manufacturers who 15 years earlier subjected leaf to minimal processing before it went into smoking products (a philosophy that focused demand on superior grades) could now make pleasing products out of only moderate-quality raw material. They also needed less leaf per unit of finished product. Yet another expansion technique emerged during the year in West Germany: the cells of cut tobacco for cigarettes were inflated, reducing leaf weight per cigarette and lowering tar and nicotine yields in proportion. Use of such techniques and an uncharacteristic boldness in pushing up retail prices helped to restore profitability to the manufacturing sector, which a year earlier was in crisis.

The international export trade in tobacco products, the life raft of manufacturers facing stagnant or falling sales at home, finally responded to the world depression in 1983 by slackening, after years of spirited expansion. Exports were big business for the U.S., Britain, West Germany, the Benelux countries, Switzerland, India, and Bulgaria. Slightly less than 8% of the world's cigarettes were exported in 1983, most into legal trade.

Because tax increases in sophisticated countries were changing tobacco products into luxuries, packaging of mass-market lines was becoming more elegant and elaborate. Hard packs of board, with multicolour printing, embossing, and delicate surface finishes, were replacing simple printed packs. The value of some deluxe cigarette packs now approached that of the tobacco in them. (MICHAEL F. BARFORD)

TOURISM

Tourism got off to a poor start in 1983 but showed signs of improvement in the second half as operators looked for marketing opportunities in a recovering economy. Accordingly, international travel volume grew slightly during the year as a whole. World Tourism Organization (WTO) preliminary estimates revealed a 0.5% growth in international arrivals to 286.5 million, while dollar receipts were valued at some $96.2 billion, representing an increase of 2.1% over the revised 1982 figure. The indications were that domestic travel grew marginally more rapidly than international tourism in 1983.

Negative factors affecting the industry included the continuing recession, French exchange controls, and high unemployment. These were combined with the financial problems of carriers and hoteliers whose occupancy rates had taken a dive in 1982. Positive factors were the strength of the U.S. dollar, which stimulated U.S. travel overseas, lower North Atlantic airfares for the summer season of 1983, sharper competition, and more determined promotional efforts aimed at specific market segments. There was also a tendency for employees to choose longer holidays rather than wage hikes in deference to governments' anti-inflation policies.

In the Americas, U.S. resident travel in the first half of 1983 was unchanged from 1982, but the U.S. National Travel Survey showed that 14% more Americans expected to take vacation trips in the second half of 1983 compared with 1982. Plans for air travel were 50% higher than in the previous year. Canadians made fewer trips within their country and were reported to be traveling to Europe in increasing numbers, despite a Can$80 million budget for domestic tourism promotion. Foreign travel to Mexico performed well in 1983 with arrivals up

Travel agents demonstrated in Paris to protest travel restrictions for French tourists. The restrictions were part of a government austerity program announced to bolster the domestic economy and the currency.

WIDE WORLD (LONDON)

by 25%. Tourists from a number of European markets as well as the U.S. thus reaped the benefits of Mexico's peso devaluation. Not surprisingly, Mexican travel abroad slumped by 45%. Caribbean tourism prospects in 1983 looked brighter as the U.S. moved out of recession. Lower airfares and cuts in hotel rates helped this process. Barbados was typical in expecting a 6% rise in visitor numbers. While tourism in Central America was affected by political events in the subregion, tourism in South America suffered from the financial and monetary crises in a number of countries.

In Europe, Spain reported no change in tourist arrivals over the first nine months of 1983, but overnight stays in hotels rose 3% and receipts 14% in real terms. The West German and U.K. markets for Spain performed well, though arrivals from France and Scandinavia declined. U.S. travelers too were reported to be returning to the "Costas" in increasing numbers. The currency restrictions imposed by France in early 1983 affected outgoing travel, with French tourists down in many destinations. Greece had a mixed season with demand down by 5%. In Italy tourism began badly, and operators demanded a "relaunch" of Italian tourism, pointing out that the country had boomed in the 1982 recession year. U.K. tourism was dominated by the U.S. market. For the first time, two million U.S. residents visited the U.K. in 1983. Austrian tourism continued to mark time, but Switzerland reported better second-half results; 80% of Swiss households reported taking a vacation in 1983 despite the continuing recession. Intourist expected to welcome more than five million foreign tourists to the Soviet Union in 1983, a 12% increase over 1982, and Hungary reported arrivals 15% ahead of the previous season.

In Asia, Thailand reported a 2% decline in visitor arrivals in 1983. Sri Lanka showed signs of recovery after sectarian riots, and tourism stood at only 1% below previous levels at the end of the first half of 1983. China, which joined the WTO in 1983, organized an international travel conference in the spring and reported first-half arrivals 10% above previous levels. Political events continued to overshadow Middle East tourism; however, Syria's new minister showed keen interest in developing package tourism, while in Israel U.S. arrivals were headed for record levels of over 300,000, up 16% from the previous year.

Among modes of transport there was concern about oversupply in the cruise ship industry. Demand for car rental continued sluggish. Air travel demand was boosted by competition, and 10 out of 11 major U.S. airlines reported increases of between 2 and 21% in revenue passenger-miles during the first eight months of 1983. Railways continued to modernize, and France's new TGV high-speed train achieved a two-hour journey time between Paris and Lyon. In Europe fears about safety aspects of bus drivers' hours appeared to affect bookings, but Greyhound Lines in the U.S. sought to boost bus travel by fare cuts, making $10-a-day bus travel once again possible.

The world's largest lodging chain in 1983 was Holiday Inn, with 312,000 rooms. The top non-U.S. chain was the U.K.'s Trusthouse-Forte, with 75,000 rooms. The average U.S. traveler spent $827 per person on overseas trips in 1982, 3% more than in 1981. (PETER SHACKLEFORD)

Table XIV. International Tourist Arrivals and Receipts, 1972–83

	Arrivals		Receipts	
Year	In 000,000	% change	In $000,000,000	% change
1972	182.3	5.9	24.7	18.8
1973	191.3	4.9	31.3	26.7
1974	197.8	3.4	34.1	8.9
1975	215.1	8.7	41.1	20.5
1976	221.6	3.0	44.9	9.2
1977	239.9	8.3	54.4	21.2
1978	258.1	7.6	68.7	26.3
1979	270.0	4.6	82.2	19.7
1980	279.0	3.3	95.3	15.9
1981	287.8	3.2	97.7	2.5
1982	285.1	−0.9	94.2	− 3.6
1983	286.5*	0.5	96.2*	2.1

*Preliminary estimates. International receipts exclude international fares.
Source: World Tourism Organization, *World Tourism Statistics*, 1983.

Table XV. Major Tourism Earners and Spenders in 1982

Major spenders	Expenditure
West Germany	$16,218,000
United States	12,347,000
United Kingdom	6,376,000
France	5,157,000
Japan	4,113,000
Netherlands, The	3,301,000
Canada	3,203,000
Saudi Arabia	2,761,000*
Austria	2,685,000
Venezuela	2,349,000*
Switzerland	2,216,000
Belgium/Luxembourg	2,191,000
Sweden	1,896,000
Australia	1,850,000
Italy	1,737,000
Norway	1,633,000
Mexico	1,547,000*
Argentina	1,471,000*
Denmark	1,331,000
Kuwait	1,123,000
Spain	1,016,000
Major earners	**Receipts**
United States	$11,392,000
Italy	8,338,000
Spain	7,173,000
France	6,991,000
United Kingdom	5,561,000
Austria	5,548,000
West Germany	5,520,000
Switzerland	3,015,000
Canada	2,449,000
Mexico	1,760,000*
Saudi Arabia	1,573,000*
Belgium/Luxembourg	1,578,000
Greece	1,556,000
Netherlands, The	1,543,000
Hong Kong	1,449,000*
Denmark	1,306,000
Australia	1,114,000
Singapore	1,090,000*
Sweden	1,012,000
Thailand	983,000*
Israel	956,000*
Portugal	879,000
Yugoslavia	782,000

*1981 figures.
Source: World Tourism Organization, *World Tourism Statistics*, 1983.

WOOD PRODUCTS

The year began well for U.S. and Canadian wood products firms. Lower interest rates, greater availability of mortgages, and the growing trend toward building additions on existing houses had a major effect on housing construction, always the mainstay of the forest industries. As early as May, new housing starts in the U.S. had increased to an adjusted annual rate of 1,790,000 units, compared with 1.1 million in the previous year. Framing lumber prices had risen 73% since October 1982.

Despite the improved economy, firms were still worried by their commitment to federal timber contracts worth some $4.5 billion—about twice the current market value. In July President Reagan granted a major concession to purchasers: a five-year contract extension free of penalties and interest payments. Companies north of the border were also relieved when a threat by U.S. sawmillers to impose a tariff on imported Canadian lumber failed. The sawmillers had claimed the Canadian industry was subsidized, but provincial and federal subsidies were held to be minimal.

European wood products industries entered 1983 hopeful of recovery after what was reportedly their most difficult year in decades. While the housing market generally remained weak, lumber prices reached their highest point in two years early in 1983. Improvements were patchy. In West Germany, dependent on the prefabricated housing sector, recovery was slow. Throughout Denmark, however, a growing demand for sawn wood reflected the rise in building activity stimulated by lower interest rates and declining inflation. Late in 1982 severe storms blew down thousands of trees, especially in France, leading to increased output from sawmillls early in 1983. Some forestry experts claimed that acid rain was increasing soil acidity, deforming tree roots, and weakening resistance to uprooting. (*See* ENVIRONMENT.)

Elsewhere in the world, 1983 brought the promise of renewed demand for forest products, as the economies of North America, Western Europe, and Japan began to expand. However, Latin-American, African, and Asian nations continued to suffer from indiscriminate logging, lack of reforestation, and poor tree utilization. There were improvements in log exports from Chile, Ivory Coast, and Sabah, Malaysia, but the demand for processed timber increased too slowly for many firms; plywood mill closures, particularly in Japan and Korea, continued well into the year. Increasing markets for medium-density fibreboard led to several new plant installations, three of them in China, bringing total world production capacity to over 3.2 million cu m (113 million cu ft).

Despite the growing impact of telecommunications and electronic media on the demand for newsprint, the paper and board industry began to recover from its poor trading position in 1982. Industry experts forecast U.S. paper and paperboard production of 62.5 million tons, compared with 59.4 million tons in 1982.

Many wood products firms in Europe and North America invested in new technology. Computers were installed to evaluate log lengths and diameters, instruct conveyors to move logs for cutting, and optimize sawing to achieve the best product value. The automated mill, with just one or two operators supervising production, became a reality. (GORDON WILKINSON)

See also Agriculture and Food Supplies; Computers; Consumerism; Economy, World; Energy; Food Processing; Games and Toys; Industrial Relations; Materials Sciences; Mining and Quarrying; Photography; Television and Radio; Transportation.

ROBOTS MAKING ROBOTS? OF COURSE

by Masanori Moritani

The term robot may conjure up the image of a manlike figure, as depicted in the play of the 1920s that gave robots their name, *R.U.R.*, by the Czechoslovak writer Karel Capek. The industrial robot in today's workplace, however, does not look much like a man but instead consists of a long arm extending from a square stand. The stand encases the power source, which, substituting for the various human bodily systems, moves the arm with oil or air pressure or by means of electricity. A separate box analogous to a human head houses the control device.

The industrial robot also differs from a man in that it seldom has legs. Some special robots have four or six legs, but most have none. Walking, especially on two legs, is among the most difficult motions to achieve and is beyond robots at their present level of development.

Some future industrial robots may come closer to resembling human beings in their functions, and conceivably even in shape. A critical element concerning function is software, which includes computer programming and is effectively the language in which instructions are given to the robot. At present more money and more people are used in developing hardware—*i.e.*, robots and control mechanisms—than software, but this situation is expected to be reversed in the future.

Types of Robots. Industrial robots are made in many varieties, which have been classified by the Japan Industrial Robot Manufacturers Association as follows:

Type	Operation	Uses
A. Manual manipulator	"Hand" operated manually (by human)	Handling of heavy materials; working in radiation-contaminated areas and undersea
B. Fixed-sequence robot	Follows moves prescribed in advance	Machine processing, plastic molding, die casting, and assembly
C. Changeable-sequence robot	Moves and sequences are changeable	Same as fixed-sequence robot
D. Playback robot	"Learns" and reproduces the moves taught by human operating the manipulator	Spot welding, arc welding, painting, and machine processing
E. Numerical control robot	Moves by means of numerical information	Same as playback robot
F. Intelligent robot	Capable of recognition and judgment on basis of information detected by sensors	Integrated circuit production, arc welding, inspection and measurement, and assembly

During the past decade Japan has taken the lead in promoting the use of robots for industrial production. The nation's annual production of high-class robots increased from about 100 units in 1972 to 14,000 in 1982. According to the Japan Industrial Robot Manufacturers Association, the number of high-class industrial robots at work in the nation at the end of 1982 was 32,000. This contrasted with 7,000 in the U.S. and 9,000 in Western Europe. Among the major reasons for the wide use of robots in Japan is the fact that there has been little opposition to them by organized labour. This can be accounted for by the traditional guarantee of lifetime employment for workers by many Japanese firms.

Uses and Capabilities. At present industrial robots are used mostly in manufacturing, helping greatly to save human labour from difficult, dangerous, repetitive, and time-consuming tasks. The employment of robots for such purposes as construction, civil engineering, farming, and transportation remains to be developed.

The earliest and still the most popular application of industrial robots in manufacturing is having them place work into production machinery and remove it when completed. This means inserting work (*i.e.*, the product in the course of manufacture) into and removing it from such numerically controlled production equipment as machine tools, casting and forging machines, and molding machinery. The use of robots in welding and painting, particularly in automobile factories, has also increased rapidly.

A major problem for the future is how to employ robots to completely automate the assembly process of a factory in which, say, one-third of the work is mechanical processing and two-thirds is assembling. Robotization to this extent does not seem an immediate prospect.

Actual assembly differs broadly from product to product. Robotization is relatively easy with electronic products because most of the assembly simply requires placing and screwing parts on the flat-shaped chassis. On the other hand, the installation of engines, seats, and tires in or on a car is not an easy task, and so no prompt introduction of industrial robots is expected on automobile assembly lines.

A great step forward is being made by the flexible manufacturing system (FMS). An integrated system including processing machines, industrial robots, monitoring devices, and automatic transport equipment, the FMS permits mass production of a variety of products and can reduce the number of production workers required by about 90%.

Masanori Moritani is senior researcher at the Nomura Research Institute in Tokyo and an authority on robotics. He is the author of Nihon-Chugoku-Kankoku sangyō gijutsu hikaku *("Comparative Technologies of Japan, China, and Korea") and* Gendai Nihon sangyō gijutsu ron *("On Modern Japanese Industrial Technology").*

By 1983 more than 100 factories in Japan were operating under the FMS. For example, for its machine-tool plant in central Japan, Yamazaki Iron Manufactory spent 13 billion yen to set up an advanced FMS to manufacture machine tools in "the factory of the 21st century." Since the introduction of the FMS, the work force has been reduced from 1,500 to 240.

Robots that assemble have also been used in manufacturing small electric and electronic appliances such as video tape recorders, copiers, and electric fans, reducing manpower on production lines by 60 to 80% at many factories. In these plants the few workers that are present are engaged in jobs that are difficult for robots, such as applying rubber rings.

Future Prospects. At present, industrial robots are emerging from the first generation of repeating action into the second generation of recognition and judgment. From the 1990s to the year 2000, they will enter the third generation of learning.

An object of robot development is to imitate man, and so the development of robots seeks to enable them to function at a very high level. However, they must also satisfy the requirements of economy and practicality. Economic feasibility is important for industrial robots, and thus their introduction to new practical uses should be steady rather than rapid.

Based on these requirements, industrial robots are expected to develop in three directions. First, functions will become more sophisticated as a result of their being equipped with sensors that will make them capable of perception and judgment. In regard to sensory perception, emphasis is placed on feeling and sight. In addition to hard materials such as metals, they will be required to hold soft materials such as wood and plastics, and thus their grasp must be soft but sure. These functions require that the "hand" or holding part of the robot's arm have the sense of "touch."

More sophisticated assignments will require a robot to have "eyes." Increasingly, a robot will need to identify objects with its own eyes before performing its task. For such eyes, solid-state image-pickup devices such as a charge-coupled device (CCD) will be used. The CCD, which functions like a television camera, has already been used in robots for arc welding and assembly. In order for a robot to perform complicated tasks such as assembling, it must be programmed with a sophisticated language, and here the development of appropriate software will take on greater importance.

The second direction in the future development of robots is an expanded range of applications. Robots will be used to make large machines—not only small ones. They will be adapted to nonmanufacturing areas such as construction and distribution. They will be used not only in production but also for such jobs as inspection and even maintenance. In shipbuilding, for instance, robots will weld and paint within the hull structure. Such work requires constant movement and accurate performance.

Robots will also be used in maintenance and inspection at nuclear power stations so that humans will not have to perform such potentially hazardous tasks. To meet this latter requirement engineers have developed a robot that has a television camera's eyes, temperature- and radiation-measuring sensors, multijointed arms capable of complicated operations, and five or six feet on which to walk or to sneak into small spaces like a snake.

The third direction of robot development will be in systematizing automatic production facilities by means of the even wider use of robots. For such applications the robots will be combined with the CAD/CAM (computer-aided design/computer-aided manufacturing), which has already been introduced into design and development processes, while the inspection function will be automated into CAT (computer-aided testing). All eventually will be combined into IMS (integrated manufacturing systems).

And then . . . will robots begin making other robots? No, indeed, that has already begun, at the factory of Fujitsu Fanuc, Ltd., at the foot of Mt. Fuji.

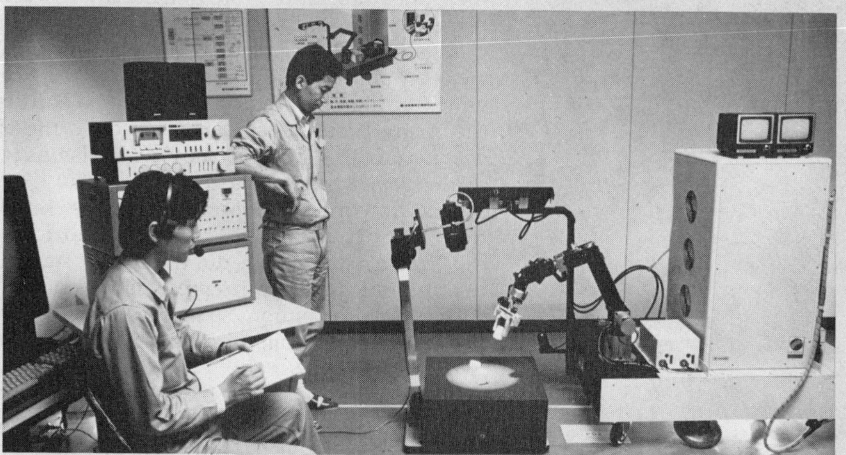

GREG DAVIS

This Japanese robot, which speaks, obeys spoken commands, and can identify shapes of objects, is the prototype of a "smart" robot.

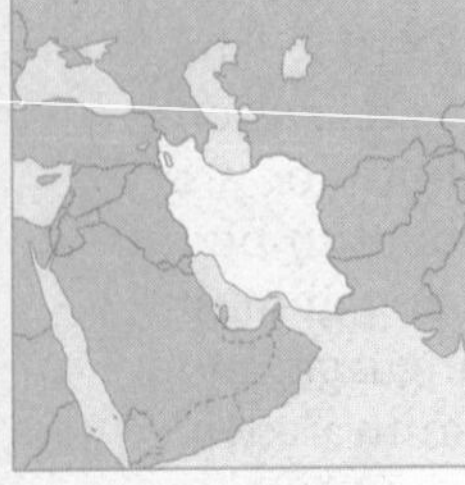

Iran

Iran

An Islamic republic of western Asia, Iran is bounded by the U.S.S.R., Afghanistan, Pakistan, Iraq, and Turkey and the Caspian Sea, the Arabian Sea, and the Persian Gulf. Area: 1,648,000 sq km (636,000 sq mi). Pop. (1983 est.): 42,120,000. Cap. and largest city: Teheran (pop., 1980 est., 6 million). Language: Persian. Religion (1976): Muslim 99%; Christian, Jewish, and Zoroastrian minorities. Supreme *faqih* (spiritual leader) in 1983, Ayatollah Ruhollah Khomeini; president, Sayyed Ali Khamenei; prime minister, Mir Hossein Moussavi.

The intense support for the revolution, carefully sustained since 1979, diminished perceptibly in Iran during 1983. The continuing war against Iraq failed to bring major victories. Offensives were launched in Iraq's Maysan sector in February in what was described as a final solution to the war, a promise repeated in later attacks on the central sector in April and on Kurdistan in July and late October–early November. However, the Iranians failed to break through Iraqi lines.

The Iranian strategy of spreading out Iraq's defensive effort along a broad front proved expensive for the Iraqi government, but it also claimed a high price in Iranian casualties. The number of Iranians killed in action during 1983 was estimated at not less than 50,000. Iran faced growing determination by Iraqi troops once they were pushed back onto their own territory, and the relatively poorly equipped Iranian forces found the going difficult as Iraq increased its deployment of sophisticated weapons and enhanced its air supremacy. Nonetheless, Iranian advances into Iraq, though piecemeal, were sufficient to encourage the leaders in Teheran to believe that victory was feasible.

The Iranian authorities reacted strongly when the French government, in addition to its considerable sales of conventional weapons to Iraq, gave that country five Super Étendard aircraft on free loan in October. Given the potential of these aircraft to hit key Iranian oil installations in the Gulf, Iranian government sources declared that they would implement a blockade of the Gulf or even close the Strait of Hormuz to maritime traffic in retaliation for any disruption of their oil exports. This brought a strong response from the U.S., which specifically pledged that freedom of navigation through the Strait of Hormuz would be maintained. The presence of a large U.S. naval squadron in the adjacent reaches of the Indian Ocean underpinned U.S. policy toward Iran and confirmed the continuing antagonistic relations between those two countries.

The regime's political difficulties led it to retreat to a more limited power base. Leaders of the Tudeh (Communist) Party were arrested in February, their once substantial role in association with the regime now entirely dismantled. Opposition groups made little progress, though guerrilla attacks on public buildings and members of the regime continued sporadically. In Iranian Kurdistan the Army brought temporary peace to the area, despite Kurdish guerrilla activity. Divisions within the government became public in July, when several important conservatives were removed from the Cabinet. The reformers, who followed the "line of the Imam," did not totally succeed in clearing out the Hojjati representatives of conservative Muslim opinion, so there was a continuing struggle in the Majlis (parliament) between the two factions.

The government avoided creating a coordinated policy for the economy. A proposed five-year (1983–88) development plan effectively lapsed, the

IRAN

Education. (1978–79) Primary, pupils 4,403,106, teachers (1977–78) 154,577; secondary, pupils 2,370,341, teachers (1977–78) 91,960; vocational, pupils 256,303, teachers (1976–77) 10,041; teacher training, students 57,832, teachers (1977–78) 2,988; higher, students 175,675, teaching staff (1977–78) 15,453.

Finance. Monetary unit: rial, with (Sept. 20, 1983) a free rate of 87.77 rials to U.S. $1 (132.18 rials = £1 sterling). Budget (1982–83 est.) balanced at 3,393,000,000,000 rials. Gross national product (1980–81) 6,305,000,000,000 rials. Money supply (Feb. 1981) 2,322,870,000,000 rials. Cost of living (1975 = 100; Feb. 1983) 363.8

Foreign Trade. (1982) Imports c. 808 billion rials; exports 1,473,000,000,000 rials. Import sources: West Germany c. 14%; Japan c. 9%; Italy c. 7%; Turkey c. 7%; U.S.S.R. c. 7%; U.K. c. 6%. Export destinations: Italy c. 14%; Japan c. 13%; The Netherlands c. 9%; The Bahamas c. 7%; West Germany c. 6%; India c. 6%; Spain c. 5%; Singapore c. 5%; France c. 5%. Main export: crude oil 96%.

Transport and Communications. Roads (1980) 63,115 km. Motor vehicles in use (1980): passenger 1,079,100; commercial (including buses) 406,000. Railways: (1981) 4,567 km; traffic (1978) 2,981,000,000 passenger-km, freight 4,083,000,000 net ton-km. Air traffic (1982): 1,852,000,000 passenger-km; freight 48.4 million net ton-km. Shipping (1982): merchant vessels 100 gross tons and over 235; gross tonnage 1,312,734. Telephones (Jan. 1981) 1,227,300. Radio receivers (Dec. 1978) 2,288,000. Television receivers (Dec. 1980) 2,085,000.

Agriculture. Production (in 000; metric tons; 1982): wheat c. 6,500; barley c. 1,200; rice c. 1,400; potatoes c. 768; sugar, raw value c. 390; onions c. 253; tomatoes c. 384; watermelons (1981) c. 946; melons (1981) c. 494; dates c. 301; grapes c. 988; apples c. 460; soybeans c. 90; tea c. 22; tobacco c. 24; cotton, lint c. 98. Livestock (in 000; 1982): cattle c. 8,567; sheep c. 34,832; goats c. 13,847; horses c. 350; asses c. 1,800; chickens c. 73,592.

Industry. Production (in 000; metric tons; 1981): cement c. 8,000; coal c. 700; crude oil (1982) 98,491; natural gas (cu m; 1982) 7,100,000; petroleum products 23,630; lead concentrates (metal content) c.10; chromium ore (oxide content) c. 15; electricity (kw-hr) 16,900,000.

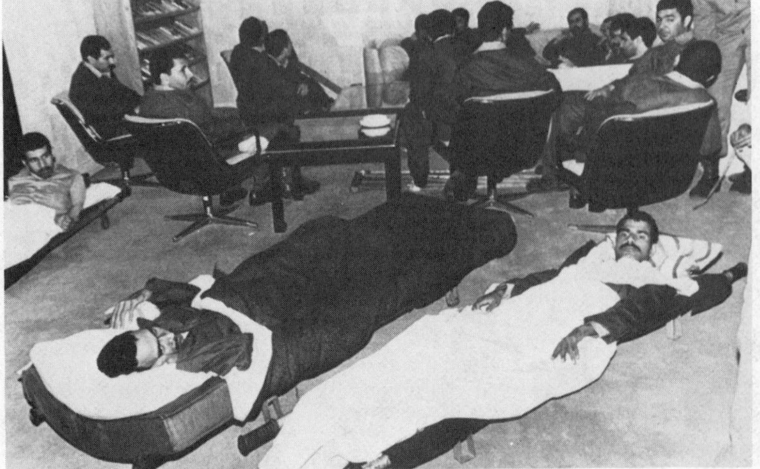

WIDE WORLD

These wounded Iraqi prisoners of war were in a group of 32 that Iran repatriated via Turkey. Thirty-two Iranians were later flown home to complete the first prisoner-of-war exchange between Iraq and Iran to take place on Turkish territory.

victim of shortages of available funds and political commitment. Budget expenditures were forecast at $42.9 billion for 1983–84, and war costs might result in a repeat of the $8 billion deficit recorded for 1982–83. Oil income was expected to rise to $21.8 billion for the year. Although spending on development was set at $15 billion, the prospects of achieving such a level while the war continued seemed poor. Unemployment remained high, and inflation was running at an annual rate of over 20%. Iranian holdings of foreign exchange recovered slightly during the year, to approximately $6 billion, thanks largely to increased oil revenues. Oil production averaged about 2.5 million bbl a day during the first three quarters of 1983. In March Iran's output quota was set at 2.4 million bbl a day by the Organization of Petroleum Exporting Countries.

The government made little headway in economic development. Progress in rehabilitating the large industries was slow, even at the Bandar Khomeini petrochemical plant, where Iran's Japanese partners had come under severe pressures to complete the project. (KEITH S. MCLACHLAN)

Iraq

A republic of southwestern Asia, Iraq is bounded by Turkey, Iran, Kuwait, Saudi Arabia, Jordan, Syria, and the Persian Gulf. Area: 438,317 sq km (169,235 sq mi). Pop. (1983 est.): 14,509,000, including (1978 est.) Arabs 76.9%; Kurds 18.6%; Turkmens 1.5%; Iranians 1.3%; other 1.7%. Cap. and largest city: Baghdad (pop., 1977, 3,205,600). Language: Arabic (official), Kurdish. Religion (1980 est.): Muslim 95.8%; Christian 3.5%; other 0.7%. President in 1983, Saddam Hussein at-Takriti.

An escalation in the Gulf war with Iran dominated Iraqi affairs in 1983. In October Iraq launched a series of devastating missile attacks on Iranian towns and announced that it had mined the approaches to the Iranian port of Bandar Khomeini. The French government agreed to supply Iraq with five Super Étendard aircraft capable of firing Exocet missiles—weapons that had achieved notoriety as a result of their use by Argentina during the Falklands conflict in 1982. There were widespread fears that Iraq would use them to disrupt shipping in the Gulf. Intense pressure from the U.S. and other countries caused the French to delay delivery of the aircraft until October. Diplomats pointed out, however, that the Super Étendard was considered obsolete by the French forces and that the Exocet was by no means the most sophisticated missile held by the Iraqis.

In October Iraq formally denied reports that senior army officers had plotted to kill Pres. Saddam Hussein at-Takriti and that Barzan Ibrahim at-Takriti, head of intelligence and the president's half brother, had been dismissed. However, the Iraq News Agency reported on October 23 that the president's other half brother had been replaced as governor of Salahaddin Province. The Patriotic Union of Kurdistan reported heavy fighting in the province in late September.

Export earnings had fallen dramatically since the start of the war, from $26.3 billion in 1980 to $10.3 billion in 1982. With the war costing over $1 billion a month, by mid-1982 Iraq's foreign currency reserves were substantially depleted. The only working outlet for its crude-oil exports was the pipeline to Turkey. Exports through this pipeline were averaging 800,000 bbl a day in October, with total production at 1.1 million bbl a day. The president announced on October 13 that the Saudi pipeline network might be used to export Iraqi oil through the Red Sea terminal at Yanbu, though this would involve 6–12 months' work to build a connecting pipeline.

An indication of the seriousness of Iraq's financial position was given by Deputy Foreign Minister Esmat Qitani when he was in New York City in early September. He said that aid flows had been halted for some time because of the lower oil revenue of the conservative Arab Gulf states. He also noted that relations with the U.S. had improved, though his government would like to see more U.S. pressure on Iran to halt the fighting. Qitani said the Soviet Union had resumed the sale of weapons and ammunition to Iraq.

By contrast, international banks remained confident in the underlying strength of Iraq's oil-based economy. On March 28 a syndicate of international banks signed a $500 million Euroloan to finance Iraq's foreign trade and development projects. On August 5 Iraq signed a loan agreement with French banks under which $1.6 billion worth of refinancing was provided to cover Iraqi purchases from France. This followed an agreement by the French in May to take 80,000 bbl a day of Iraqi

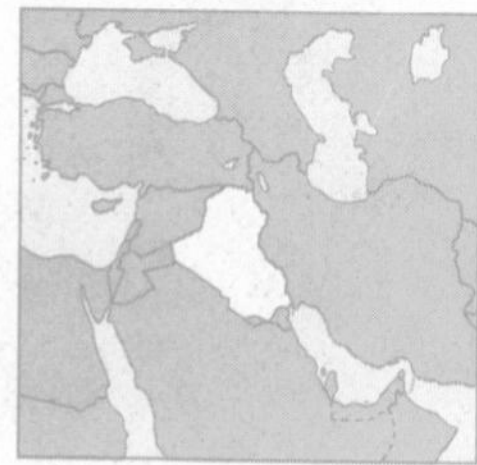
Iraq

IRAQ

Education. (1980–81) Primary, pupils 2,615,910, teachers 94,000; secondary, pupils 954,536, teachers 28,552; vocational, pupils 56,924, teachers 4,148; teacher training, students 21,958, teachers 814; higher, students 102,430, teaching staff 6,515.

Finance. Monetary unit: Iraqi dinar, with (Sept. 20, 1983) a par value of 0.311 dinar to U.S. $1 (free rate of 0.468 dinar = £1 sterling). Budget (total; 1981 est.): revenue 19,435,000,000 dinars; expenditure 19,750,000,000 dinars. Gross domestic product (1977) 5,692,000,000 dinars.

Foreign Trade. (1982) Imports (f.o.b.) c. 5,343,000,000 dinars; exports 3,056,000,000 dinars. Import sources: West Germany c. 16%; Japan c. 14%; Italy c. 9%; U.K. c. 8%; France c. 7%; Romania c. 5%. Export destinations: Brazil c. 22%; Italy c. 13%; Turkey c. 11%; India c. 10%; Spain c. 7%; Japan c. 6%; Syria c. 5%. Main export: crude oil 99%.

Transport and Communications. Roads (1982) 25,265 km. Motor vehicles in use (1982): passenger 229,500; commercial 118,700. Railways: (main; 1978) 1,589 km; traffic (1977–78) 821 million passenger-km, freight 2,497,000,000 net ton-km. Air traffic (1982): 1,470,000,000 passenger-km; freight 54.7 million net ton-km. Shipping (1982): merchant vessels 100 gross tons and over 155; gross tonnage 1,521,491. Telephones (Jan. 1978) 319,600. Radio receivers (Dec. 1980) 2 million. Television receivers (Dec. 1980) 650,000.

Agriculture. Production (in 000; metric tons; 1982): wheat c. 900; barley c. 550; rice c. 250; cucumbers (1981) c. 170; watermelons (1981) c. 683; onions c. 81; tomatoes c. 470; dates c. 400; grapes c. 430; tobacco c. 12; cotton, lint c. 5. Livestock (in 000; 1982): sheep c. 11,900; goats c. 3,800; cattle (1981) c. 2,624; camels (1981) c. 242; asses (1981) c. 462.

Industry. Production (in 000; metric tons; 1981): cement 5,600; crude oil (1982) 45,086; natural gas (cu m; 1982) 680,000; petroleum products 7,180; electricity (kw-hr) 6,290,000.

Information Science and Technology:
see Computers; Industrial Review

Insurance:
see Industrial Review

International Bank for Reconstruction and Development:
see Economy, World

International Law:
see Law

International Monetary Fund:
see Economy, World

Investment:
see Economy, World; Stock Exchanges

oil for one year as partial payment for contracting work. On August 11 an agreement was signed with Japan for a five-year extension on repaying a package of mixed loans valued at $1.8 billion. Japan was working on contracts in Iraq valued at $3 billion.

On August 14 Baghdad radio announced the dismissal of Finance Minister Tamer Razzouki, who was replaced by Hisham Hassan Tawfiq. In a Cabinet change announced earlier in the year, Deputy Premier Tariq Aziz assumed the foreign affairs portfolio previously held by Saadoun Hammadi.

The government's response to its financial difficulties was to introduce stringent economies. Despite an air of normality in Baghdad, by late 1983 there were acute shortages of essential items, including imported foodstuffs. Low output and distribution problems reduced the performance of the agricultural sector. (JOHN WHELAN)

Ireland

Ireland

Separated from Great Britain by the North Channel, the Irish Sea, and St. George's Channel, the Republic of Ireland shares its island with Northern Ireland to the northeast. Area: 70,285 sq km (27,137 sq mi), or 83% of the island. Pop. (1983 est.): 3,534,000. Cap. and largest city: Dublin (pop., 1981, 525,900). Language (1971): mostly English; 28% speak English and Irish or Irish only. Religion: 94% Roman Catholic. President in 1983, Patrick J. Hillery; prime minister, Garret FitzGerald.

Stable government was restored in the Republic of Ireland in 1983, after two successive administrations that had depended on minority groupings of deputies in the Dail (parliament) to remain in power. In the aftermath of the November 1982 election, the coalition administration of Fine Gael and the Labour Party, which commanded a six-seat majority over all other groups, was able to establish itself with a reasonable prospect of surviving a full term. It did so in the most adverse economic circumstances and with a commitment to cut public expenditure and substantially reduce government borrowing.

With unemployment heading toward 200,000 (15.4%) and wage settlements running at excessively high levels, Minister of Finance Alan Dukes faced formidable problems. The budget introduced in February was a tough one, based on an expectation of no growth and containing harsh taxation provisions, as well as cuts in public spending and borrowing. The minister made it clear that five annual budgets would have to be severe if the economic prodigalities of previous years were to be rectified. On April 13 protest marches and strikes against the austerity measures occurred in more than 20 cities and towns. Surprisingly, the budget did not seem to affect the government's rating in the opinion polls.

The government's continuing popularity was due in large measure to the ignominy with which the previous Fianna Fail administration had left office in December 1982, after only nine months in power. Fianna Fail's continuing disarray during the early months of 1983 was occasioned by revelations that the telephones of two journalists had been tapped for political reasons in 1982. An investigation undertaken by the new government in January 1983 led to the resignations of the police commissioner and a deputy commissioner. It also led to a major fight within Fianna Fail when it was revealed that former finance minister Ray McSharry had borrowed a police tape recorder from former justice minister Sean Doherty, who had ordered the tapping of the journalists' phones, in order to record, covertly, a conversation with a colleague. Both men resigned their party posts. A challenge aimed at deposing Charles J. Haughey from the Fianna Fail leadership failed, ensuring his survival through 1983. Many felt that his continued leadership seriously curtailed his party's prospects of recovering credibility.

The three parties in the republic did reach agreement on setting up a "Forum for a New Ireland," in which Northern Irish political parties were invited to participate. Only the Catholic nationalist Social Democratic and Labour Party (SDLP) agreed to attend. Initially the Forum was seen as an attempt by Dublin to give support to the SDLP and its leader, John Hume, in anticipation of the British general election in June. The Forum discussed, for the first time on an all-party basis, a number of serious issues affecting North-South relations. It also invited politicians and experts from the North and from Britain to make submissions. The Forum was scheduled to complete a report in early 1984. By year's end it had become clear that British politicians, particularly in the opposition parties, were prepared to adopt a positive line on the findings of this Dublin initiative.

In November Prime Minister Garret FitzGerald went to London for a meeting with U.K. Prime Minister Margaret Thatcher. Discussion of new proposals on Northern Ireland was carefully played down in order to leave open prospects for an agreed set of proposals coming from the Forum. At the same time, the opportunity to assert the restoration of normal Anglo-Irish relations was not lost. The meeting ended a period of coolness that had followed Ireland's withdrawal from the economic sanctions imposed by the European Communities against Argentina during the South Atlantic conflict in 1982.

WIDE WORLD

Irish Prime Minister Garret FitzGerald visited British Prime Minister Margaret Thatcher in November in the first Anglo-Irish summit meeting in two years.

IRELAND

Education. (1980–81) Primary, pupils 568,364, teachers 20,068; secondary, pupils 287,017, teachers 18,255; vocational, pupils 6,792, teachers 202; higher, students 41,928, teaching staff 3,983.

Finance. Monetary unit: Irish pound (punt), with (Sept. 20, 1983) a free rate of I£0.85 to U.S. $1 (I£1.28 = £1 sterling). Gold and other reserves (June 1983) U.S. $2,105,000,000. Budget (1982 actual): revenue £5,159 million; expenditure £7,186 million. Gross national product (1982) £11,796 million. Money supply (Feb. 1983) £1,794 million. Cost of living (1975 = 100; May 1983) 297.3

Foreign Trade. (1982) Imports £6,812.3 million; exports £5,687.9 million. Import sources: EEC 70% (U.K. 48%, West Germany 8%, France 5%); U.S. 13%. Export destinations: EEC 71% (U.K. 39%, West Germany 9%, France 9%, The Netherlands 5%); U.S. 7%. Main exports: machinery 21%; chemicals 14%; meat 9%; textiles and clothing 7%; dairy products 7%. Tourism (1981): visitors 2,223,000; gross receipts U.S. $537 million.

Transport and Communications. Roads (1978) 92,294 km. Motor vehicles in use (1982): passenger 709,000; commercial 68,100. Railways: (1981) 1,987 km; traffic (1982) 832 million passenger-km, freight 629 million net ton-km. Air traffic (1982): 2,343,000,000 passenger-km; freight 79.4 million net ton-km. Shipping (1982): merchant vessels 100 gross tons and over 165; gross tonnage 239,085. Telephones (Dec. 1981) 721,000. Radio receivers (Dec. 1980) 1.5 million. Television receivers (Dec. 1980) 785,000.

Agriculture. Production (in 000; metric tons; 1982): barley c. 1,450; wheat c. 320; oats c. 90; potatoes c. 1,050; sugar, raw value (1981) c. 196; cabbages (1981) c. 172; cow's milk c. 5,200; butter c. 135; cheese c. 60; beef and veal c. 430; pork c. 130; fish catch (1981) 190. Livestock (in 000; June 1982): cattle 6,688; sheep 3,476; pigs 1,090; horses (1980) c. 77; chickens c. 8,100.

Industry. Production (in 000; metric tons; 1982): coal 60; cement 1,619; petroleum products (1980) 2,011; electricity (kw-hr) 10,938,000; manufactured gas (cu m) c. 203,000; cotton fabrics (sq mi; 1980) 36,000; wool fabrics (sq m; 1980) 2,700; rayon, etc., fabrics (sq m; 1980) 53,300; fertilizers (nutrient content; 1981–82) nitrogenous c. 205, phosphate c. 37.

On September 7 the Irish people went to the polls to vote on the eighth amendment to the constitution. This was a move designed to guard against the possibility that abortion would ever become legal in Ireland; it proposed to insert a clause into the constitution giving the fetus equal rights with the mother. The amendment was the result of a long, bitter, and divisive campaign. The turnout was low, however—only 53.67% of the electorate voted—and the amendment was carried by 66.45% in favour to 32.87% opposed. Support came mainly from the rural areas.

A group of companies prospecting for oil in the Celtic Sea reported promising results during the summer, setting off a speculators' boom that was primarily a Stock Exchange phenomenon. Nevertheless, in the face of the otherwise gloomy economic prospects, the results from drillings in relatively calm and shallow water off the southeast coast injected a minor note of confidence.

Pres. Patrick J. Hillery's term of office ended in September. He had originally indicated that he did not intend to seek a second term but changed his mind when all three political parties pleaded with him to reconsider. He was returned for a further seven years without an electoral contest. George Colley (*see* OBITUARIES), former deputy prime minister under Jack Lynch and a politician of force and integrity, died suddenly in September.

Ireland's unsolved mystery of the year, followed by a world that took little interest in the Forum, the country's economy, or its moral self-examination on abortion, was the kidnapping of the racehorse Shergar in February. Despite increasingly large financial rewards being offered for information, the animal's fate remained unknown, and the search was abandoned in May.

(MAVIS ARNOLD)

See also United Kingdom.

Israel

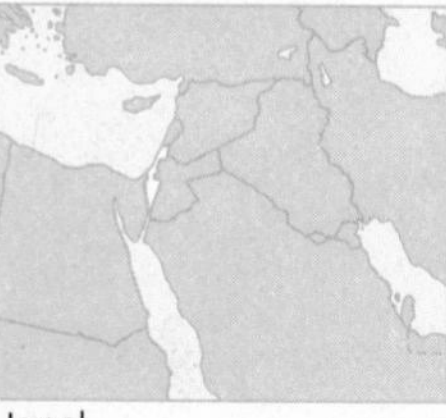
Israel

A republic of the Middle East, Israel is bounded by Lebanon, Syria, Jordan, Egypt, and the Mediterranean Sea. Area (not including territory occupied in the June 1967 war): 20,700 sq km (7,992 sq mi). Pop. (1983 est.): 4,103,700. Cap. and largest city: Jerusalem (pop., 1982 est., 415,000). Language: Hebrew and Arabic. Religion: predominantly Jewish (1983 est., 83%) with Muslim, Christian, and other minorities. Presidents in 1983, Yitzhak Navon and, from May 5, Chaim Herzog; prime ministers, Menachem Begin and, from October 10, Yitzhak Shamir.

For Israel 1983 was a year of traumatic highlights that involved and agitated the entire nation as had seldom happened in the 35 years since it had been established. The year began with a concerned look back at the massacre of some 600 Palestinians and Lebanese in the Sabra and Shatila refugee camps in Beirut, Lebanon, in September 1982, and it ended with an anxious look into an uncertain economic future. At the beginning of the year there was nobody to challenge Prime Minister Menachem Begin in the Knesset (parliament). Yet by late August Begin had announced his intention to resign, and he was replaced by Foreign Minister Yitzhak Shamir (*see* BIOGRAPHIES) in October. At the end of the year Begin had simply and almost inexplicably faded away.

There were the customary political flurries during the first weeks of the year. Defense Minister Ariel Sharon accused the U.S. of "obstructing" moves toward a formal Lebanese-Israeli peace. The Palestinian mayor of Bethlehem, Ilyas Frej, called on the Palestine Liberation Organization (PLO) to recognize Israel. The PLO executive committee, for its part, met in Yemen (Aden) on January 27 and rejected the Reagan plan—U.S. Pres. Ronald Reagan's proposal that the Palestinians of the West Bank and Gaza Strip be granted self-determination in association with Jordan. In a separate resolution, al-Fatah, the largest constituent body of the PLO, called for the "escalation of the armed struggle to all areas under Zionist occupation."

On February 8 the Kahan Commission, the independent committee under Supreme Court Chief Justice Yitzhak Kahan, made public its investigation into the Sabra and Shatila massacres. It cleared the Israeli political and military authorities of any direct responsibility, since no Israeli troops or members of Maj. Saad Haddad's Lebanese Christian forces operating with the Israelis had been involved. However, it found that indirect responsibility, through negligence or lack of forethought, had to rest with Defense Minister Sharon, Chief of Staff Gen. Raphael Eitan, Chief of

Ireland, Northern: see United Kingdom

Iron and Steel Industry: see Industrial Review

Islam: see Religion

Italian Literature: see Literature

Military Intelligence Maj. Gen. Yehoshua Saguy, and Brig. Gen. Amos Yaron, divisional commander in Beirut. They had not foreseen, as they should have done, that the Christian Lebanese forces who were sent to Sabra and Shatila "to flush out remaining terrorists" might exact vengeance on the population in the wake of the assassination of Lebanon's newly elected president, Bashir Gemayel. Begin, too, was censured for showing "absolutely no interest" in the Phalangist operation for two days after he had heard about it. (*See* RELIGION: *Judaism.*)

The Cabinet approved the findings of the commission by a majority of 16 to 1. Sharon resigned as minister of defense, though he remained a member of the Cabinet as minister without portfolio. General Eitan retired prematurely and General Saguy resigned. The report stoked still further the fires of public debate in Israel. Large demonstrations opposed to the war in Lebanon continued, but a substantial popular majority maintained its solid support for the government and for Begin's leadership.

In February Moshe Arens was appointed as successor to Sharon as minister of defense. Arens had been Israel's ambassador in Washington. His appointment was popular in Israel, not least with the Israel Defense Forces (IDF), and in the U.S., where his intelligence and flexibility had impressed observers.

Meanwhile, important developments were taking place in the search for a formal settlement of Israel's relations with Lebanon. Talks were held between a delegation of senior Lebanese officials and a similar Israeli delegation led by David Kimche, director general of the Foreign Ministry. A U.S. delegation participated as observers. At first progress was slow, and the U.S. contribution was seen by the negotiators as not always helpful. However, compromise mixed with persistence finally overcame the opposition to a settlement from the Muslim section of the Beirut government.

On May 17 the agreement between Israel and Lebanon was signed at Khaldah, Lebanon, and Qiryat Shemona, Israel. The peace accords concluded with Egypt in 1979 had settled Israel's southwestern frontier; four years later the agreement with Lebanon laid the foundation for the normalization of the northern border. It set out in detail the terms of such normalization, which was to be achieved within six months of signature. It legalized Lebanon's international boundary with Israel; it ended the state of war between the two countries; and it stipulated the withdrawal of all foreign forces from Lebanese soil. It also set the terms for a security zone in southern Lebanon that would assure Israel of adequate security in an area that had long been used by hostile elements for attacks on and harassment of the Israeli settlements in northern Galilee.

Yitzhak Shamir, who had been foreign minister in the Begin government, became prime minister of Israel in October.

BENAMI NEUMANN—GAMMA/LIAISON

The Israeli Cabinet approved the agreement by a vote of 17 to 2, and the Knesset formally ratified it. The normalization of relations between Israel and Lebanon that the pact signified could remain a reality only on paper, however. Israel stated that its forces would not be withdrawn from southern Lebanon unless both the PLO and Syria withdrew their own troops from Lebanese soil. The normalization of relations was thus made contingent on the acquiescence of the very forces that were most deeply opposed to peace between Lebanon and Israel. Syrian opposition to the treaty was indeed to prove a major obstacle to the pact's execution.

The Lebanese government came under intense pressure from Syrian Pres. Hafez al-Assad not to ratify the agreement with Israel. Despite this, the Lebanese Parliament formally approved the normalization pact on June 14. Public opinion in Israel meanwhile was becoming restless at the seemingly open-ended military commitment in Lebanon. More to the point, the army leadership was pressing for an early withdrawal. The number of troops had already been reduced to 20,000, with further reductions planned, and the budget of the IDF had been severely trimmed because of the government's economic difficulties.

The authorities in Lebanon were warned that Israel planned to withdraw its forces from the Shuf Mountains and from around Beirut. The Lebanese Christians were urged to conclude an agreement with Druze leader Walid Jumblatt (*see* BIOGRAPHIES) before the Israeli withdrawal. The message was conveyed to Pres. Amin Gemayel in early June. He and other Lebanese Christian leaders welcomed the Israeli decision and assured the Israelis that they would make all the necessary arrangements for a takeover of the evacuated districts in the Shuf and elsewhere. The Israelis urged them first to reach a political understanding with the Druze. The Lebanese Christian authorities, for their part, believed that they could first occupy the areas evacuated by the Israelis and then negotiate with the Druze. Late in the day the U.S. became aware of the dangerous illusions harboured in Beirut and pleaded with the Israelis to delay their redeployment.

By then it was too late, however, and the withdrawal was carried out on September 3. The consequences for the villages of the Shuf were tragic. Many Christians and a number of Druze villagers were killed as fighting broke out after the Israelis had left. In Israel the redeployment was the occasion for much soul-searching. All parties rejected Israeli responsibility for the aftermath since they had given advance warning to the Gemayel government. Even so, there were critical voices raised, especially among Israelis who had worked most closely with the Maronite Christian community; they questioned the wisdom of the policy despite the initially strong pressure from the U.S. for an Israeli withdrawal. They acknowledged that domestic pressures in Israel had compelled the IDF to favour redeployment, but they believed that the price paid in Lebanon was too high. The long-standing and deep friendship between Israel and the Maronite Christian community in Lebanon was jeopardized.

Against the background of tragic fighting in the Shuf, Israel's domestic shocks at first came as something of an anticlimax. Prime Minister Begin's impending resignation did not have the impact it would have had earlier in the year, let alone a year previously. The transition to his successor was smooth, almost relaxed, as became the temperament of the new prime minister. Shamir emphatically overcame a brief challenge from Deputy Prime Minister David Levy and then re-formed the old coalition, retaining for himself the Foreign Ministry. Several days after the new Cabinet took office in October, Finance Minister Yoram Aridor resigned over his controversial suggestion to replace the shekel with the U.S. dollar.

Shamir set about mending fences damaged by his predecessor. Relations with European countries were improved, and African connections were established. He gave some encouragement to the U.S.S.R. and to King Hussein of Jordan, and on November 29 he rounded off a visit to Washington by completing an "understanding" with President Reagan of far-reaching proportions in terms of arms, aid, and diplomatic collaboration.

Unlike his predecessor, Shamir had few qualms about the war in Lebanon. The price had been high in Israeli lives and wealth, but he did not see it as an unacceptable cost. The war had broken the PLO terrorist threat not only toward Israel but also toward any Arab nation that sought a peaceful relationship with Israel. The PLO's political credibility was destroyed, in Israel's view, by the final departure of Chairman Yasir Arafat (*see* BIOGRAPHIES) and his PLO fighters from Tripoli, Lebanon, on December 20.

Throughout the year Israeli settlement of the West Bank continued unabated. The nature of the settlements had changed considerably in many instances. Instead of rugged *kibbutzim* (pioneer villages), a new type of urban settlement was flourishing. Urban housing estates were serving Israelis who wanted to live on the West Bank and work in Israel. Large commuter settlements were changing the political and environmental landscape.

Pres. Yitzhak Navon decided not to seek reelection. Chaim Herzog (*see* BIOGRAPHIES), formerly a general in the IDF and Israel's delegate to the UN, was elected president as the Labour Alignment's nominee. In a surprise result on March 22 he won 61 votes against the government nominee's 57.

Israel's economy had suffered irreparable damage not only from the war but from the reckless economic free-for-all introduced by the Begin government on the eve of its reelection in 1981. The foreign debt had risen to \$23.5 billion by June 1983, an increase of \$3 billion in a year. The balance of payments deficit increased to \$5.5 billion, \$800 million more than in 1982. The government received \$2.6 billion in aid from the U.S. to cover part of the shortfall. (JON KIMCHE)

See Middle Eastern Affairs; Feature Article: *At the Core of the Problem of Peace—Israel and the West Bank.*

ISRAEL

Education. (1981–82) Primary, pupils 573,280, teachers 41,888; secondary, pupils 193,516; vocational, pupils 84,919; secondary and vocational, teachers 31,570; higher, students 88,258, teaching staff (1974–75) 13,981.

Finance. Monetary unit: shekel, with (Sept. 20, 1983) a free rate of 61.04 shekels to U.S. \$1 (91.93 shekels = £1 sterling). Gold and other reserves (June 1983) U.S. \$3,945,000,000. Budget (1980–81 actual): revenue 57,139,000,000 shekels; expenditure 81,229,000,000 shekels. Gross national product (1982) 538,952,000,000 shekels. Money supply (Sept. 1982) 23,021,000,000 shekels. Cost of living (1975 = 100; June 1983) 11,212.

Foreign Trade. (1982) Imports 234,606,000,000 shekels; exports 126,717,000,000 shekels. Import sources: U.S. 19%; West Germany 11%; U.K. 8%; Switzerland 6%; Italy 5%. Export destinations: U.S. 21%; U.K. 8%; West Germany 7%; France 6%. Main exports: diamonds 22%; chemicals 14%; machinery 12%; metal manufactures 12%; fruit and vegetables 10%. Tourism (1981): visitors 1,090,000; gross receipts U.S. \$956 million.

Transport and Communications. Roads (1981) *c.* 12,500 km. Motor vehicles in use (1981): passenger 459,200; commercial 96,100. Railways (1981): 827 km; traffic 242 million passenger-km, freight 806 million net ton-km. Air traffic (1982): 4,648,000,000 passenger-km; freight 301.2 million net ton-km. Shipping (1982): merchant vessels 100 gross tons and over 66; gross tonnage 676,295. Telephones (Dec. 1981) 1,325,000. Radio receivers (Dec. 1980) 802,000. Television licenses (Dec. 1980) 581,000.

Agriculture. Production (in 000; metric tons; 1982): wheat *c.* 100; potatoes 226; watermelons (1981) *c.* 82; tomatoes *c.* 340; onions *c.* 54; oranges *c.* 1,050; grapefruit *c.* 500; grapes 85; apples *c.* 130; olives 42; bananas 66; cotton, lint 85; cheese *c.* 60; poultry meat *c.* 202; fish catch (1981) 25. Livestock (in 000; 1981): cattle 265; sheep *c.* 270; goats *c.* 119; pigs *c.* 99; camels *c.* 11; chickens *c.* 24,645.

Industry. Production (in 000; metric tons; 1982): cement 2,172; natural gas (cu m) 160,000; phosphate rock (1981) 2,300; petroleum products (1981) 6,262; sulfuric acid 161; fertilizers (nutrient content; 1981–82) nitrogenous 70, phosphate 38, potash 891; paper (1980) 117; electricity (kw-hr) 13,850,000.

Italy

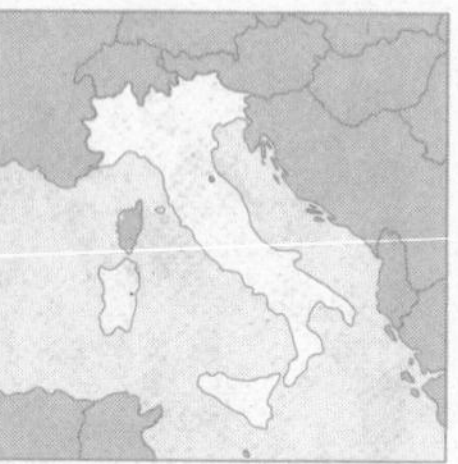
Italy

A republic of southern Europe, Italy occupies the Apennine Peninsula, Sicily, Sardinia, and a number of smaller islands. On the north it borders France, Switzerland, Austria, and Yugoslavia. Area: 301,268 sq km (116,320 sq mi). Pop. (1983 est.): 56,345,000. Cap. and largest city: Rome (pop., 1981 prelim., 2,830,600). Language: Italian. Religion: predominantly Roman Catholic. President in 1983, Alessandro Pertini; premiers, Amintore Fanfani and, from August 4, Bettino Craxi.

The search for a coalition government strong enough to tackle Italy's chronic economic problems continued. Bettino Craxi (*see* BIOGRAPHIES) became the country's first Socialist premier after general elections held in June 1983. At the end of the year Craxi was fighting to push budget cuts of \$25 billion through Parliament and to fulfill the new coalition's commitment to economic rigour and revival. All parties were worried by the decline in gross national product and by the problems of inflation and unemployment. Although the incidence of political terrorism continued to decline, there was a growing awareness of the power and financial strength of organized crime.

Domestic Affairs. Italy's 43rd postwar government, a four-party coalition formed in December 1982 and led by the veteran Christian Democrat Amintore Fanfani, began well. On Jan. 22, 1983, the trade unions accepted a cut of between 15 and 18% in quarterly wage increases linked to the cost of living. This was a well-established system, and the unions had not been expected to give ground. Within a few months, however, Fanfani was in trouble. Craxi, always a restless coalition partner, withdrew the Socialist Party from the coalition after accusing the Christian Democrats of moving the government to the right. Fanfani resigned on April 29 but was reappointed to lead a caretaker government, and general elections were scheduled a year early, on June 26–27.

The main feature of the election campaign was the battle between Craxi and the Christian Democrats' relatively new leader, Ciriaco de Mita. Both claimed to be speaking for modern and modernizing Italy, but both were disappointed by the outcome. (For tabulated results, *see* POLITICAL PARTIES.) The Christian Democrats held their position as the largest party, but their share of the vote for the Chamber of Deputies declined from 38.3% in 1979 to 32.9%. Craxi had to be content with a modest rise of 1.6% to 11.4% of the vote. The small Republican Party increased its support to 5.1% of the vote. The Communist Party considered its results—a slight fall to 29.9% of the vote—a success at a time when a rising number of floating votes and abstentions and a surge toward the smaller parties seemed to be acting against it and the Christian Democrats. Enrico Berlinguer, the Communist leader, urged Craxi to join him in attempting to form a left-wing government, but without success.

The Christian Democrats were in no condition to bid for the premiership of a new coalition, and the Republican Party leader, Giovanni Spadolini, did not press his claim. In spite of his party's limited electoral advance, Craxi was seen as a coming man who ought to be given his chance. Invited by Pres. Alessandro Pertini to try to form a government, Craxi established the same sort of five-party coalition that had provided two of the six governments in the previous Parliament, consisting of Christian Democrats, Socialists, Republicans, Social Democrats, and Liberals. He was sworn in on August 4 and won a vote of confidence in the Chamber of Deputies the following week. In presenting his government to Parliament, he emphasized the fight against inflation, his commitment to development and the creation of jobs, the problems of crime and the administration of justice, and reform of Italy's institutions.

Craxi presented a vigorous program of budget measures to Parliament on September 30. The package included controversial plans to reduce some pensions and family allowances and to save money on health services. The measures, scheduled to go through both chambers by the end of the year, met their first obstacle on October 13 when the Chamber of Deputies rejected a plan to raise money by allowing those who had constructed buildings without obtaining permission to buy immunity. The ensuing uproar highlighted the precarious nature of coalition government.

On January 24 a Rome court sentenced 32 members of the terrorist Red Brigades to life imprisonment for 17 murders (including that of former premier Aldo Moro in 1978), 11 attempted murders, and 4 kidnappings. Of the 63 defendants on trial, 4 were acquitted and another 4 were tried in absentia. The exceptional law that conceded lighter sentences to terrorists who confessed or gave valuable information lapsed on January 29. On July 15 a Padua court gave suspended prison sentences to four police officers for torturing a Red Brigades suspect after the rescue of kidnapped U.S. Brig. Gen. James Dozier in January 1982.

Antonio Negri, a Padua university teacher arrested in 1979 and charged, with 70 others, of offenses related to terrorism, was released from custody when he gained immunity by winning a seat as a Radical Party candidate in the general elections. Parliament voted to lift his immunity on September 21, but Negri avoided rearrest by leaving the country.

On July 29 a car bomb planted by the Mafia killed Palermo's chief investigating magistrate, Rocco Chinnici, two policemen, and a porter. Under pressure as a result of vigorous investigations, the Mafia was apparently anxious to show that it was still to be feared. Shortly before the incident a Palermo court had found 59 of 75 defendants guilty in the first trial brought under new anti-Mafia legislation introduced in 1982. On June 17 Naples magistrates launched the biggest operation of its kind ever mounted in Italy when they issued warrants for the arrest of 856 people allegedly linked to the Camorra, a Naples-based organization of criminal gangs. Among those arrested were local politicians and lawyers, a nun accused of carrying messages for criminals, and a famous television performer.

Italian riot police, carrying shields and batons, broke up a protest by farmers who had halted rail traffic through the Alpine Brenner Pass between Austria and Italy to dramatize their opposition to farm price policies of the European Economic Community.

UPI

ITALY

Education. (1981–82) Primary, pupils 4,335,911, teachers 285,908; secondary, pupils 3,482,521, teachers 276,987; vocational, pupils 1,575,791, teachers 135,614; teacher training, students 241,150, teachers 13,389; higher, students 719,449, teaching staff 48,118.

Finance. Monetary unit: lira, with (Sept. 20, 1983) a free rate of 1,601 lire to U.S. $1 (2,411 lire = £1 sterling). Gold and other reserves (June 1983) U.S. $20,952,000,000. Budget (1982 actual): revenue 155,465,000,000,000 lire; expenditure 214,345,000,000,000 lire. Gross national product (1982) 465,790,000,000,000 lire. Money supply (April 1983) 206,793,000,000,000 lire. Cost of living (1975 = 100; June 1983) 333.2.

Foreign Trade. (1982) Imports 116,212,000,000,000 lire; exports 99,247,000,000,000 lire. Import sources: EEC 42% (West Germany 16%, France 13%); U.S.. 7%; Saudi Arabia 6%. Export destinations: EEC 46% (West Germany 16%, France 15%, U.K. 6%); U.S. 7%. Main exports (1981): machinery 23%; motor vehicles 7%; chemicals 7%; petroleum products 6%; food 6%; clothing 6%; iron and steel 5%; textile yarns and fabrics 5%; metal manufactures 5%. Tourism (1981): visitors 16,330,000; gross receipts U.S. $7,554,000,000.

Transport and Communications. Roads (1981) 297,318 km (including 5,900 km expressways). Motor vehicles in use (1981): passenger c. 18,603,400; commercial c. 1,451,100. Railways: (1980) 19,814 km; traffic (1982) 40,520,000,000 passenger-km, freight 16,498,000,000 net ton-km. Air traffic (1982): 15,143,000,000 passenger-km; freight 582 million net ton-km. Shipping (1982): merchant vessels 100 gross tons and over 1,663: gross tonnage 10,374,966. Telephones (Jan. 1981) 19,269,300. Radio licenses (Dec. 1980) 13,781,000. Television licenses (Dec. 1980) 13,361,000.

Agriculture. Production (in 000; metric tons; 1982): wheat 8,998; corn 6,820; barley 1,020; oats 360; rice 915; potatoes 2,680; sugar, raw value c. 1,290; cabbages (1981) 523; cauliflowers (1981) 508; onions 490; tomatoes 4,075; grapes 11,150; wine c. 7,500; olives 2,500; oranges 1,500; mandarin oranges and tangerines 320; lemons 683; apples 2,200; pears (1981) 1,160; peaches (1981) 1,550; tobacco 133; cheese c. 615; beef and veal c. 860; pork c. 1,100; fish catch (1981) 449. Livestock (in 000; Dec. 1981): cattle 8,904; sheep 9,632; pigs 9,132; goats 1,020; poultry c. 110,200.

Industry. Index of production (1975 = 100; 1982) 125. Unemployment (1982) 9.1%. Fuel and power (in 000; metric tons; 1982): lignite 1,913; crude oil 1,735; natural gas (cu m) 14,490,000; manufactured gas (cu m) 3,335,000; electricity (kw-hr; 1981) 181,755,000. Production (in 000; metric tons; 1982): pig iron 11,671; crude steel 23,933; aluminum (1981) 274; zinc (1981) 182; cement 40,245; cotton yarn (1981) 161; man-made fibres (1981) 543; fertilizers (nutrient content; 1981–82) nitrogenous c. 1,195, phosphate c. 512; sulfuric acid 2,287; plastics and resins (1981) 2,154; petroleum products (1981) 88,438; passenger cars (units; 1981) 1,256; commercial vehicles (units; 1981) 175. Merchant vessels launched (100 gross tons and over; 1982) 280,000 gross tons. New dwelling units completed (1979) 136,700.

The collapse of the Banco Ambrosiano in 1982 and the death of its founder, Roberto Calvi, continued to have repercussions. In London, where Calvi's body had been found hanging from Blackfriars Bridge, a second inquest returned an open verdict in June; the first had decided that he had killed himself. On August 10 the grand master of the banned P2 Masonic lodge, Licio Gelli, who had been associated with Calvi and was wanted on charges of espionage and fraud in Italy, escaped from a Swiss jail.

On May 14, following a serious eruption of Mt. Etna, an attempt—only partly successful—was made to divert the lava into a man-made channel by means of explosive charges. Landslides caused by heavy rain in the far North coincided with fears of drought in the South. Sardinia was swept by fires at the height of summer. In October Pozzuoli, near Naples, was partly evacuated after an earth tremor damaged buildings. A court in Monza on September 26 sentenced five executives to terms of imprisonment for their part in the 1976 Seveso disaster, when highly toxic dioxin was released into the atmosphere after a valve failed.

Italy's last king, Umberto II (*see* OBITUARIES), died in Switzerland on March 18.

Foreign Affairs. Premier Craxi, who had fully supported a previous government's decision to accept U.S. cruise missiles on Italian soil, remained committed to the installation of the weapons at Comiso in Sicily. Craxi's active interest in foreign affairs took him to Paris, London, Bonn, and The Hague in September. His firmly Atlanticist views guaranteed him a warm welcome from U.S. Pres. Ronald Reagan in Washington on October 20, as antimissile demonstrators prepared for a major rally in Rome on October 22.

Italy was deeply interested in helping to bring peace to Lebanon. Craxi invited Lebanese Pres. Amin Gemayel and Druze leader Walid Jumblatt (*see* BIOGRAPHIES) to visit him in Rome. Italy contributed 2,000 troops to the multinational peacekeeping force in Lebanon, although by year's end it appeared to be having doubts about the ability of the force to fulfill its mission.

Relations between Italy and Bulgaria remained strained because of the alleged Bulgarian connection with the 1981 attack on Pope John Paul II. The Italian magistrate who had been investigating the case delivered his findings to the state prosecutor in December. Sergey Antonov, a Bulgarian Airlines employee who had been arrested in Rome in November 1982 for suspected complicity in the attack, was released from jail late in the year for medical reasons and placed under house arrest. On December 17 the pope paid a dramatic private visit to his attacker, Mehmet Ali Agca (*see* BIOGRAPHIES), in Rome's Rebibbia Prison.

The Economy. Carlo Ciampi, governor of the Bank of Italy, gave a sharp warning of economic problems ahead in his annual report on May 31. He stressed that the inflation rate, expected to be 14–15% in 1983, and labour costs were much too high. He expected wages to rise 17.7% by the end of the year. Trade unions criticized the government's 1984 budget measures in September, claiming that employees were once again being asked to bear the heaviest burden.

Italy faced a crisis in its steel industry in July when the European Communities (EC) insisted that it make cuts of 5.8 million metric tons in its steel capacity by 1986. Between 1974 and 1983, while other EC countries were making cuts of up to 65% in the industry's labour force, Italy had reduced the number of its steelworkers by 4.2%.

(CAMPBELL PAGE)

Ivory Coast

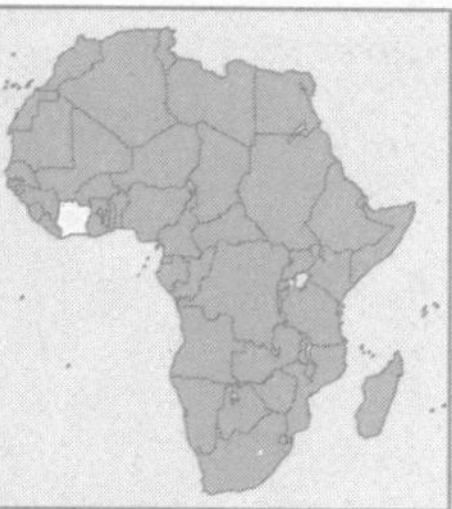

Ivory Coast

A republic on the Gulf of Guinea, the Ivory Coast is bounded by Liberia, Guinea, Mali, Upper Volta, and Ghana. Area: 322,463 sq km (124,504 sq mi). Pop. (1983 est.): 8,890,600, including (1978 est.) Bete 20%; Senufo 14.4%; Baule 12%; Anyi 10.5%; Malinke 7%; other 36.1%. Cap. and largest city: Abidjan (metro pop., 1981 est., 1,686,100). Language: French (official), Akan, Mossi, Dyola, Malinke, and other local dialects. Religion (1980 est.): animist 44%; Christian 32%; Muslim 24%. President in 1983, Félix Houphouët-Boigny.

During 1983 rivalries among Ivory Coast's polit-

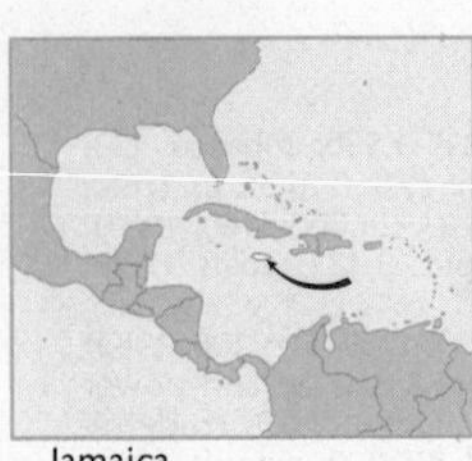
Jamaica

ical elite, arising from continuing uncertainty as to who would eventually succeed Pres. Félix Houphouët-Boigny, contrasted markedly with the equanimity of the president himself. With two main groups in opposition over the succession, one led by Emmanuel Dioullo, mayor of Abidjan, and the other by Henri Konan Bedié, president of the National Assembly, and in an atmosphere of social unrest engendered by strikes of teachers, physicians, and others, President Houphouët-Boigny left in May on an extended visit to Europe, Canada, and the U.S. He returned in October to an enthusiastic welcome by the government and people, giving the impression that challenge to the regime was limited to a few impatient would-be successors and foreign-based opponents.

Developments in neighbouring countries were a matter of concern to Ivory Coast and encouraged it to establish closer ties with France. The takeover in Upper Volta in August by Capt. Thomas Sankara (*see* BIOGRAPHIES) created a sense of encirclement in Abidjan, and in October, at the Franco-African summit at Vittel, France, President Houphouët-Boigny was among the moderates who defended the "legitimacy" of Pres. Hissen Habré of Chad.

In March the National Assembly approved the transfer of the capital from Abidjan to Yamoussoukro, the president's birthplace, situated in the centre of the country. The economy continued to suffer from the effects of the world recession and also from severe drought and brushfires. Production of cocoa and coffee, the main crops, was much reduced. (PHILIPPE DECRAENE)

IVORY COAST

Education. (1979–80) Primary, pupils 954,190, teachers 24,441; secondary, pupils 172,280, teachers (1978–79) 4,026; vocational, pupils (1978–79) 22,437, teachers (1974–75) 620; teacher training, students 2,086, teachers (1970–71) 87; higher (1978–79), students 12,470, teaching staff 580.

Finance. Monetary unit: CFA franc, with (Sept. 20, 1983) a parity of CFA Fr 50 to the French franc (free rate of CFA Fr 403 = U.S. $1; CFA Fr 607 = £1 sterling). Gold and other reserves (June 1983) U.S. $19 million. Budget (1980 actual): revenue CFA Fr 495 billion; expenditure CFA Fr 410 billion. Money supply (March 1983) CFA Fr 486.5 billion. Cost of living (Abidjan; 1975 = 100; June 1983) 270.9.

Foreign Trade. (1982) Imports CFA Fr 718,590,000,000; exports CFA Fr 747,450,000,000. Import sources (1981): France 31%; Venezuela 8%; U.S. 5%; Japan 5%. Export destinations (1981): France 19%; The Netherlands 13%; U.S. 11%; Italy 8%; West Germany 7%. Main exports (1981): cocoa and products 34%; coffee 19%; timber 13%; petroleum products 8%; fruit and vegetables 5%.

Transport and Communications: Roads (1982) 46,580 km. Motor vehicles in use (1982): passenger 166,900; commercial 69,500. Railways (1980): *c.* 680 km; traffic 1,212,000,000 passenger-km, freight 600 million net ton-km. Air traffic (including apportionment of traffic of Air Afrique; 1982): *c.* 316 million passenger-km; freight *c.* 22.6 million net ton-km. Telephones (Dec. 1980) 88,000. Radio receivers (Dec. 1980) 1 million. Television receivers (Dec. 1980) 300,000.

Agriculture. Production (in 000; metric tons; 1982): rice *c.* 500; corn (1981) *c.* 300; millet *c.* 49; yams *c.* 2,000; cassava *c.* 800; peanuts *c.* 60; bananas *c.* 150; plantains (1981) *c.* 830; pineapples *c.* 350; palm kernels *c.* 38; palm oil *c.* 177; coffee *c.* 250; cocoa 390; cotton, lint *c.* 60; rubber *c.* 25; fish catch (1981) 80; timber (cu m; 1981) *c.* 12,032. Livestock (in 000; 1981): cattle *c.* 720; sheep *c.* 1,250; goats *c.* 1,300; pigs *c.* 360; poultry *c.* 13,000.

Industry. Production (in 000; metric tons; 1981): petroleum products 1,137; cement (1979) 1,030; cotton yarn (1979) *c.* 11; electricity (kw-hr) 1,903,000.

Jai Alai:
see Court Games

Jamaica

A parliamentary state within the Commonwealth, Jamaica is an island in the Caribbean Sea about 145 km S of Cuba. Area: 10,991 sq km (4,244 sq mi). Pop. (1982 est.): 2,223,400, predominantly African and Afro-European but including European, Chinese, Afro-Chinese, East Indian, Afro-East Indian, and others. Cap. and largest city: Kingston (metro pop., 1982 est., 684,000). Language: English. Religion: Christian, with Baptists, Church of God, and Anglicans in the majority. Queen, Elizabeth II; governor-general in 1983, Florizel Glasspole; prime minister, Edward Seaga.

Despite receiving strong political support from the U.S., the government of Jamaica faced worsening economic difficulties during 1983. Following a growth rate of 0.2% in 1982, another year of virtually no growth was being forecast in late 1983. In June the government was forced to cut projected spending by 4.6% in an attempt to meet conditions set by the International Monetary Fund for further disbursements of its three-year loan facility.

One attempt to ease the problems—the creation in January of a two-tier exchange rate—caused a lengthy trade dispute with other members of the Caribbean Community (Caricom). The problem was resolved in May by the establishment of a third rate for Caricom members of Jam$2.25 to U.S. $1, compared with the official rate of Jam$1.78 and a commercial rate that stood at Jam$2.91 in October.

On November 27 Seaga called for new elections, on the grounds that his government needed more than its remaining two years to solve the country's economic problems. The elections, held December 15, were boycotted by the opposition, and Seaga's Jamaica Labour Party won all the seats in the House of Representatives.

Jamaica was one of the six Caribbean countries that took part, along with the U.S., in the invasion of Grenada on October 25. (ROD PRINCE)

JAMAICA

Education. (1980–81) Primary, pupils 364,637, teachers 8,676; secondary, pupils 233,723, teachers 9,108; vocational, pupils 8,904, teachers 438; higher, students 8,640, teaching staff 573.

Finance. Monetary unit: Jamaican dollar, with (Sept. 20, 1983) an official par value of Jam$1.78 to U.S. $1 (official free rate of Jam$2.68 = £1 sterling) and a free market rate of Jam$2.65 to U.S. $1 (Jam$3.99 = £1 sterling). Gold and other reserves (June 1983) U.S. $95 million. Budget (1980–81): revenue Jam$1,375,000,000; expenditure Jam$2,375,000,000.

Foreign Trade. (1982) Imports Jam$2,444,500,000; exports Jam$1,265,200,000. Import sources: U.S. 35%; Venezuela 14%; Netherlands Antilles 13%; U.K. 8%. Export destinations: U.S. 34%; U.K. 18%; Canada 12%; Norway 8%; Trinidad and Tobago 7%. Main exports: alumina 45%; bauxite 22%; sugar 6%. Tourism (1981): visitors 406,000; gross receipts U.S. $284 million.

Agriculture. Production (in 000; metric tons; 1982): sugar, raw value *c.* 197; bananas *c.* 100; oranges *c.* 33; grapefruit *c.* 24; sweet potatoes *c.* 25; yams *c.* 160; cassava (1981) *c.* 26; copra *c.* 7. Livestock (in 000; 1981): cattle *c.* 305; goats *c.* 390; pigs *c.* 260; poultry *c.* 4,300.

Industry. Production (in 000; metric tons; 1981): bauxite 11,682; alumina 2,550; cement 160; gypsum 96; petroleum products 944; electricity (kw-hr) 2,325,000.

Japan

A constitutional monarchy in the northwestern Pacific Ocean, Japan is an archipelago composed of four major islands (Hokkaido, Honshu, Kyushu, and Shikoku), the Ryukyus (including Okinawa), and minor adjacent islands. Area: 377,727 sq km (145,843 sq mi). Pop. (1983 est.): 119,420,000. Cap. and largest city: Tokyo (pop., 1983 est., 8,350,000). Language: Japanese. Religion (1980): primarily Shinto and Buddhist; Christian 3%. Emperor, Hirohito; prime minister in 1983, Yasuhiro Nakasone.

Domestic Affairs. After winning the primary within the Liberal-Democratic Party (LDP) on Nov. 24, 1982, Yasuhiro Nakasone was elected by the Diet (parliament) on November 26 to become Japan's 16th postwar prime minister. He promptly formed a Cabinet that reflected the relative strengths of various factions within the LDP. The veteran Shintaro Abe became foreign minister; Noboru Takeshita, finance minister; Masaharu Gotoda, chief Cabinet secretary; and Sadanori Yamanaka, minister of international trade and industry. When Yamanaka resigned for reasons of health in June, Nakasone appointed Sosuke Uno to succeed him. In the party Susumu Nikaido (deputy leader of the most powerful LDP faction) remained as secretary-general. Meanwhile, the LDP retained its solid majority in the (lower) House of Representatives. Party strength as of July 1983 was: LDP 286; Japan Socialist Party (JSP) 100; Clean Government Party (Komeito) 34; Democratic Socialist Party (DSP) 31; Japan Communist Party (JCP) 29; New Liberal Club (NLC) 10; Social Democratic Federation (Shaminren) 3; independents 6; vacancies 12 (total 511).

On April 10, in the first elections held since Nakasone took office, LDP-endorsed candidates won in 11 of 13 gubernatorial contests. These included the victory of incumbent Tokyo Gov. Shunichi Suzuki (also backed by the Komeito, DSP, and NLC). Losses were suffered in Hokkaido and in Fukuoka, where JSP-backed candidates won. In the poll for 44 prefectural assemblies, the LDP won 1,486 out of 2,660 seats at stake. A more important test of the Nakasone government came with elections for the (upper) House of Councillors, held on June 26. Half of the seats (126) were contested, and 50 of those, representing the national constituency (elected at large), were chosen by proportional representation for the first time. The LDP retained a stable majority in the upper house. Party strength in July 1983 was: LDP 137; JSP 44; Komeito 26; JCP 14; DSP 11; NLC-Shaminren alliance 2; other parties 4; independents 11; vacancies 3 (total 252).

These elections appeared to reflect a slow rise in support for Nakasone. An opinion poll conducted by the newspaper *Yomiuri Shimbun* on August 30 showed an approval rating of 42.7% (disapproval 37%). Nakasone enhanced his status by distancing himself from the legal difficulties of former LDP prime minister Kakuei Tanaka (*see* BIOGRAPHIES).

The Nakasone government, the LDP majority, and the various factions within the party all had a large stake in the long-awaited decision in the Lockheed case, which involved procurement of aircraft for All Nippon Airways. On October 12, some seven years after the affair first surfaced, the Tokyo District Court found Tanaka guilty of having accepted 500 million yen in bribes from Lockheed to arrange the purchase of aircraft. The court sentenced him to four years in prison and levied a fine of 500 million yen ($2.1 million), the exact amount of the bribes. The finding sent shock waves through the LDP government and raised a public furor. However, Tanaka immediately appealed to the Tokyo High Court and promised to carry the case to the Supreme Court. It was estimated that the appeals could occupy another decade. Meanwhile, Tanaka refused to resign his Diet seat. Nominally he had left the LDP and continued to serve as an independent, but he remained a power behind the scenes as head of the largest LDP faction.

WIDE WORLD

Yasuhiro Nakasone, here acknowledging applause in the lower house of Japan's Diet, was elected to a second term as prime minister by 266 of 509 votes cast.

The JSP, the largest opposition party, had its own difficulties. On June 30 Ichio Asukata became the second successive Socialist chairman to resign, taking responsibility for the party's poor showing in the upper house elections. The former JSP secretary-general, Masashi Ishibashi, was nominated to be chairman and was approved at the JSP national convention on September 7.

Despite these troubles, the JSP, with other opposition parties, was successful in blocking all Diet action as a protest against Tanaka's refusal to resign from the Diet. Prime Minister Nakasone was forced to dissolve the lower house and to set general elections for December 18. In the poll the LDP failed to retain the 270-seat level required to control Diet committees. Although Nakasone, with the help of independents, retained the prime ministership, he faced continued turmoil in the Diet and a possible challenge to his leadership of the LDP in 1984.

According to final figures released by the Economic Planning Agency (EPA), Japan's gross national product (GNP) for fiscal year 1982 (ended March 1983) totaled 204,567,000,000,000 yen ($818.3 billion). The inflation-adjusted growth rate stood at 3.3%. The Nomura Research Institute pre-

Japan

dicted an increase to 3.5% in fiscal 1983. Consumer prices in metropolitan Tokyo ended fiscal 1982 with the lowest annual increase (2.5%) in 23 years. In March, however, unemployment reached a 30-year high of 2.5% (1,430,000 workers). On March 15 the Nakasone Cabinet cleared a crucial hurdle when the lower house approved a 50,397,600,-000,000 yen general accounts budget for fiscal 1983. One of the few increases was for defense (6.5%), which totaled 2,754,200,000,000 yen (still below 1% of estimated GNP). In June Japan's debt load exceeded 100 trillion yen for the first time.

On March 14 an ad hoc commission on administrative reform gave its final report. Its recommendations included a 4% reduction in government personnel, a ceiling on civil service salaries, and reorganization of public corporations like the Japanese National Railways. Nakasone pledged that the LDP and his government would make joint efforts to carry out the commission's recommendations. However, the prime minister encountered stiff opposition within the LDP and in the bureaucracy. In a 1983 White Paper, the Japan Productivity Centre indicated that Japan's white-collar population now exceeded the blue-collar labour force by about 30%. The drastic shift in the structure of the labour force, which reflected a transition to a service economy and rapid progress in factory and office automation, resulted in white-collar workers occupying 45% of the nation's jobs. This change was affecting existing practices of lifetime employment and business management, welfare plans, and union objectives.

In the fall, as the Tanaka trial was nearing a conclusion, news of another scandal began appearing in the newspapers, this time involving several of the country's well-known pharmaceutical firms. Following a long investigation, police arrested Akira Ejima, chief of the drug division of the National Institute of Health, which tests new drugs. Allegedly, Ejima was bribed to pass confidential information about a new drug developed by the Ono Pharmaceutical Co. to the Teisan Pharmaceutical Co. Others arrested included Mutsuya Ajisaka of the Fujisawa Pharmaceutical Co., who was charged with conspiracy to steal confidential data on another company's products, also by way of the government's testing laboratories. In the U.S. Mitsubishi Electric Corp. and Hitachi, Ltd., two of Japan's largest industrial firms, settled cases in which their employees were accused of stealing industrial secrets from IBM. (*See* COMPUTERS.)

During 1983 Japan suffered several natural disasters. On May 26 an earthquake, which registered 7.7 on the Richter scale and touched off tsunami tidal waves, struck the north of Japan (Akita, Aomori, and Hokkaido). As of May 31 the National Police Agency placed the death toll at 58. Torrential rains swept over southwestern Japan, leaving 82 dead, 28 missing, and 114 injured by July 25. On August 17 Typhoon No. 5 battered central Japan and caused widespread damage around Tokyo.

Japanese demonstrators on board small fishing boats protested the arrival of the nuclear-powered aircraft carrier USS "Enterprise" at the Japanese naval base at Sasebo. Welcoming craft also greeted the "Enterprise."

UPI

Foreign Affairs. Throughout 1983 Japan's foreign policy was inextricably linked with issues of international economic relations. In the fiscal year ended in March, the nation's exports dropped 10% (to $136.6 billion), but imports also fell, by almost 11% (to $127.3 billion). The resulting trade surplus ($9.3 billion) was Japan's third largest on record, according to the Finance Ministry. On March 26 the government ordered a package of import-promotion measures, which included simplification of standards and certification. Foreign countries had been critical of previous standards, which, they claimed, constituted nontariff barriers.

On the export side, on February 12 Japan reached agreement with European Communities delegates on limiting Japanese exports of video tape recorders to the EC to 4.5 million units annually. At the same time, the U.S. was notified of Japan's intention "voluntarily" to maintain the level of automobile exports to the U.S. at 1,680,000 units. In September, however, the Ministry of International Trade and Industry indicated that it proposed to request an increase in the total to 1,960,000 units.

At the seven-nation summit conference of Western industrial democracies, held at Williamsburg, Va., late in May, Nakasone joined other leaders in a pledge to cooperate in lowering inflation, seeking higher employment levels, and establishing more stable currency rates. He stated that Japan was politically bound together with the NATO powers.

Relations with the nation's closest partner, the U.S., were marked by exchanges of views concerning Japan's trade surplus, its security policy, and the level of its defense expenditures. During his first visit to Washington as prime minister, January 17–19, Nakasone stressed that the two nations were "bound by a common destiny." Tokyo and Washington remained divided, however, on U.S. demands for liberalization of Japan's agricultural imports, specifically beef and citrus fruits. In fiscal 1982 Japan's exports to the U.S. declined 8.7% to $35.9 billion, but imports from the U.S. also fell, by 5% to $23.7 billion. Thus, despite Japan's steps

JAPAN

Education. (1982–83) Primary, pupils 11,739,456, teachers 474,018; secondary, vocational, and teacher training, pupils 10,421,973, teachers 526,388; higher, students 2,261,167, teaching staff 130,109.

Finance. Monetary unit: yen, with (Sept. 20, 1983) a free rate of 242 yen to U.S. $1 (365 yen = £1 sterling). Gold and other reserves (June 1983) U.S. $26 billion. Budget (1982–83 est.) balanced at 49,681,000,000,000 yen. Gross national product (1982) 263,939,000,000,000 yen. Money supply (June 1983) 78,810,000,000,000 yen. Cost of living (1975 = 100; June 1983) 150.5.

Foreign Trade. (1982) Imports 32,656,000,000,000 yen; exports 34,433,000,000,000 yen. Import sources: U.S. 18%; Saudi Arabia 16%; Indonesia 9%; United Arab Emirates 6%; Australia 5%. Export destinations: U.S. 26%; Saudi Arabia 5%. Main exports: machinery 34%; motor vehicles 22%; iron and steel 11%; ships 5%; instruments 5%; chemicals 5%.

Transport and Communications. Roads (1982) 1,120,020 km (including 2,993 km expressways). Motor vehicles in use (1982): passenger 25,539,100; commercial 15,538,000. Railways: (1979) 27,493 km; traffic (1982) 314,943,000,000 passenger-km, freight 31,326,000,000 net ton-km. Air traffic (1982): 55,731,000,000 passenger-km; freight 2,342,700,000 net ton-km. Shipping (1982): merchant vessels 100 gross tons and over 10,652; gross tonnage 41,593,612. Telephones (Dec. 1981) 58,677,000. Radio receivers (Dec. 1980) 79.2 million. Television receivers (Dec. 1980) 62,976,000.

Agriculture. Production (in 000; metric tons; 1982): rice 12,838; wheat 742; barley *c.* 393; potatoes 3,650; sweet potatoes *c.* 1,317; sugar, raw value 899; onions 1,230; tomatoes *c.* 1,030; cabbages (1981) *c.* 3,667; cucumbers (1981) *c.* 1,030; aubergines (eggplants) *c.* 620; watermelons *c.* 1,000; apples 927; pears (1981) 522; oranges *c.* 400; mandarin oranges and tangerines 2,847; grapes 338; tea 99; tobacco 136; milk 6,750; eggs 2,112; pork 1,427; fish catch (1981) 10,657; timber (cu m; 1981) 33,172. Livestock (in 000; Feb. 1982): cattle 4,485; sheep 19; pigs 10,040; goats 60; chickens 289,925.

Industry. Index of production (1975 = 100; 1982) 139. Fuel and power (in 000; metric tons; 1982): coal 17,608; crude oil 398; natural gas (cu m) 2,285,000; manufactured gas (cu m) *c.* 8,660,000; electricity (kw-hr;1981) 583,249,000. Production (in 000; metric tons; 1982): iron ore (54% metal content) 361; pig iron 79,207; crude steel 99,548; aluminum 1,153; copper 1,076; petroleum products (1981) 190,080; cement 78,707; cotton yarn 470; woven cotton fabrics (sq m) 2,030,000; man-made fibres 1,759; newsprint 2,580; sulfuric acid 6,531; caustic soda 2,792; plastics and resins 6,005; fertilizers (nutrient content; 1981–82) nitrogenous 1,032, phosphate 580; cameras (35 mm; units) 12,976; wrist and pocket watches (units) 101,079; electronic desk calculators (units) 58,486; radio receivers (units; 1981) 15,196; television receivers (units; 1980) 16,327; video tape recorders (units) 13,134; passenger cars (units) 6,882; commercial vehicles (units) 3,857. Merchant vessels launched (100 gross tons and over; 1982) 8,300,000 gross tons.

to encourage imports, the trade balance with the U.S. came to $12.2 billion in Japan's favour.

Visiting Tokyo in January, U.S. Secretary of State George Shultz assured Japan's leaders that the U.S. would not sacrifice Asia to reach an agreement on arms reduction with the U.S.S.R. On February 8 Nakasone informed the Diet that Japan and the U.S. might conduct joint operations to blockade strategic straits around Japan if that nation were threatened by a "third country." The statement took on new significance after September 1, when a Soviet fighter plane shot down Korean Air Lines (KAL) flight 007 between Sakhalin and Hokkaido. Japanese maritime patrols and U.S. ships joined South Korean vessels in searching the area for remains of the aircraft. On March 8, however, Chief Cabinet Secretary Gotoda informed the Diet that Japan would not export arms to the U.S. during the Nakasone administration, nor would it engage in joint arms production. Gotoda's caution seemed justified later in March, when a port call at Sasebo by the U.S. nuclear-powered carrier "Enterprise" gave rise to an antinuclear demonstration of several thousand protesters—fewer than last year—and there was no violence.

Although U.S. Pres. Ronald Reagan chose to cancel stops in the Philippines, Thailand, and Indonesia, he carried out his plan to visit South Korea and Japan. During November 9–12 he arrived in Tokyo, was welcomed by the emperor, and held talks with government officials, including the prime minister.

Shigeo Nagano, president of the Chamber of Commerce and Industry, led a private 252-member trade delegation to the Soviet Union in February. The Japanese were asked to persuade their government to cooperate in Siberian development projects incorporated in the Soviet five-year (1986–90) plan. Nagano told the press that the Japanese people desired a solution to the dispute over the

MATSUMOTO—SYGMA

Police and fishermen combed the beaches of northern Japan seeking debris washed ashore from the South Korean civilian airliner that had been shot down by the Soviet Union.

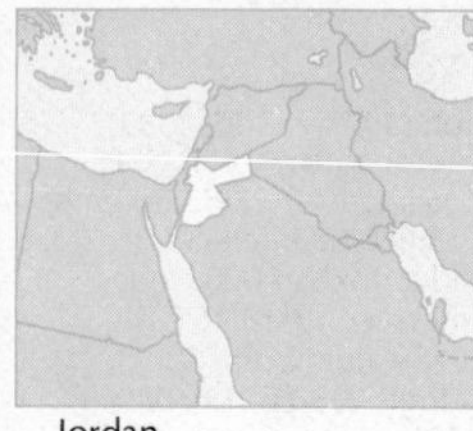

Jordan

Soviet-occupied "northern territories," the southern Kurile Islands off Hokkaido, seized by the U.S.S.R. at the end of World War II. The importance of the area was underlined by the KAL aircraft incident. For the first time since the end of World War II, Japan expelled a Soviet diplomat, on June 19. The first secretary of the embassy in Tokyo, Arkhady Vinogradov, was accused of having been involved in high-technology espionage.

Nakasone's two-day stop in Seoul, January 11–12, was the first official visit to Korea by a Japanese prime minister in 37 years. With South Korean Pres. Chun Doo Hwan, Nakasone concluded an aid agreement providing $4 billion over seven years (official development assistance and Japan Export-Import Bank loans). The agreement was followed on August 17 by a decision of Nippon Steel and other companies to cooperate in establishing a new steel mill in South Korea. The facility was planned to produce up to ten million tons of crude steel per year. Construction was to start in 1985, and the first phase of the project was to be completed in 1988. Relations between Japan and South Korea had been normalized in 1965, but the two countries had not been close. U.S. officials applauded the Japanese effort to aid the hard-pressed South Korean economy.

On a four-day trip to China beginning February 18, LDP Secretary-General Nikaido tried to smooth over differences that had arisen between China and Japan. The Chinese newspaper *People's Daily* had sharply criticized Nakasone for a phrase he had used in Washington earlier in the year, translated as the statement that Japan could become "an unsinkable aircraft carrier" in Asia. The paper warned against "expansion of Japanese defense capabilities." As for the Tokyo-Seoul summit meeting, *People's Daily* concluded that "strengthening of the military alliance between [Japan and South Korea] will cause anxiety in the Far East region." In two talks between Nikaido and the Chinese foreign minister, Wu Xueqian (Wu Hsüeh-ch'ien), both parties expressed apprehension about the possible Soviet transfer of SS-20 missiles to East Asia.

During April 30–May 10, Nakasone visited Indonesia, Thailand, Singapore, the Philippines, Malaysia, and Brunei. He was accompanied on part of the tour by Foreign Minister Abe and Takao Fujinami, the deputy chief Cabinet secretary. On May 9 in Kuala Lumpur, the Japanese leader called for promotion of technology transfers, scientific cooperation, and cultural exchange among Japan and members of the Association of Southeast Asian Nations (ASEAN). On August 15 Abe reported to Nakasone on a 13-day, five-nation trip to Eastern Europe and the Middle East. Abe was the first Western-bloc foreign minister to visit both Iran and Iraq. During his stops in Teheran and Baghdad, he stated that Japan would strive to create an atmosphere conducive to bringing about a peaceful settlement of the prolonged military conflict between those two countries. Japan had long been concerned over the war, both because of its heavy investments in the area and because of its dependence on the Middle East for the bulk of its petroleum imports. (ARDATH W. BURKS)

Japanese Literature: see Literature

Jazz: see Music

Jehovah's Witnesses: see Religion

Jewish Literature: see Literature

Jordan

A constitutional monarchy in southwest Asia, Jordan is bounded by Syria, Iraq, Saudi Arabia, and Israel. Area (including about 5,440 sq km [2,100 sq mi] occupied by Israel in the June 1967 war): 94,946 sq km (36,659 sq mi). Pop. (excluding Israeli-occupied West Bank, 1982 est.): 2,415,700. Cap. and largest city: Amman (pop., 1979 prelim., 648,600). Language: Arabic. Religion (1980 est.): Muslim 93%; Christian 5%; atheist 0.4%; none 1.6%. King, Hussein I; prime minister in 1983, Mudar Badran.

By the fall of 1983 Jordan appeared set to return to the centre of the dispute over the future of the Palestinian people, as U.S. Pres. Ronald Reagan, on October 18, moved to revive the so-called Jordanian option. In 1982 the president had made proposals to Israel for Palestinian self-determination on the West Bank in association with Jordan. King Hussein withdrew from talks on the issue, but U.S. officials were saying in October 1983 that they had "indirect but clear signals" that the king would discuss negotiations on the West Bank's future. (*See* Feature Article: *At the Core of the Problem of Peace—Israel and the West Bank: Two Views.*)

On October 13 it was disclosed, first by Israeli radio and then by Washington, that plans existed for a Jordanian "emergency strike-force," to be trained and equipped by the U.S. to act in defense of the conservative Arab Gulf states. The $225 million earmarked by the U.S. for the force was linked to the supply of U.S. military equipment to Jordan, including advanced F-16 jet fighters, mobile anti-aircraft missiles, and light armoured vehicles.

Palestine Liberation Organization (PLO) chairman Yasir Arafat (*see* BIOGRAPHIES) said on Octo-

For officials of the Palestine Liberation Organization being known as a moderate long has been a kiss of death. In April it was the turn of Issam Sartawi, whose coffin is being carried here in the streets of Amman. He was assassinated in Lisbon.

UPI

ber 13 that he wished to pursue dialogue with Jordan on confederal ties between Jordan and a "liberated West Bank and Gaza Strip." Arafat went on to describe the breakdown in talks between the PLO and Jordan in April as a "misunderstanding." There was speculation that after Arafat's defeat by Syrian-backed PLO dissidents and his evacuation from Tripoli, Lebanon, in December, he might be increasingly disposed toward the Jordanian option. However, Jordan's intention to observe caution in any future dealings with the PLO had been expressed by Crown Prince Hassan, the king's brother and designated successor, during talks held in Brussels in July with the European Communities and the Belgian government. Jordan resumed trade relations with Egypt in December.

Jordan's balance of payments went into deficit in 1982 for the first time in 11 years, mainly because of a drop in Arab aid. The trade deficit totaled $1.4 billion, although after foreign loans and aid payments this was reduced to less than $14 million. Gross domestic product in 1982 totaled 1.4 billion Jordanian dinars, equivalent to $3.8 billion. During that year Jordan had received only $660 million of the $1,250,000,000 a year in aid promised by the Baghdad Arab summit (1978). It was reported in October 1983, however, that Saudi Arabia had paid the final installment for 1982. Jordan remained a sound prospect on the international markets. In January international banks subscribed to a $225 million loan to the government.

The confidence of some foreign banks was shaken in September when the central bank governor, Muhammad Said Nabulsi, issued a statement—later withdrawn—suggesting that foreign banks operating in Jordan would have to surrender 51% of their equity to Jordanians. Localization of the economy was indeed becoming a matter of national policy. The National Consultative Council was attempting to restrict the number of foreign labourers in Jordan. Foreign contractors working on development projects were obliged to use local labour for one-quarter of their labour forces.

During the week ended October 28, two Jordanian diplomats—the ambassador to India and the ambassador to Italy—were injured in shooting incidents, and an employee of the Jordanian embassy in Madrid was killed in December. There were reports throughout the year that Prime Minister Mudar Badran might resign. The palace announced on October 26 that Queen Elizabeth II of the U.K. would make a state visit to Jordan in March 1984. On May 25 the Queen Alya international airport, built at a cost of $300 million, was officially opened. (JOHN WHELAN)

See also Middle Eastern Affairs.

JORDAN

Education. (1980–81) Primary, pupils 454,391, teachers 14,303; secondary (1979–80), pupils 238,763, teachers 11,267; vocational (1979–80), pupils 9,880, teachers 641; higher (1979–80), students 18,905, teaching staff 816.

Finance. Monetary unit: Jordanian dinar, with (Sept. 20, 1983) a free rate of 0.37 dinar to U.S. $1 (0.55 dinar = £1 sterling). Gold and other reserves (June 1983) U.S. $958 million. Budget (1982 actual): revenue 359 million dinars; expenditure 706 million dinars. Gross national product (1982) 1,711,600,000 dinars. Money supply (June 1983) 865,260,000 dinars. Cost of living (1975 = 100; May 1983) 210.

Foreign Trade. (1982) Imports 1,142,500,000 dinars; exports 264,530,000 dinars. Import sources (1981): Saudi Arabia 17%; U.S. 16%; West Germany 11%; Japan 7%; Italy 6%; U.K. 5%. Export destinations (1981): Iraq 38%; Saudi Arabia 12%; Syria 6%; Romania 6%; India 6%. Main exports (1981): phosphates 23%; vegetables 9%; chemicals c. 9%; fruit 6%; beverages 5%; iron and steel 5%; motor vehicles 5%. Tourism (1981): visitors 1,581,000; gross receipts U.S. $504 million.

Transport and Communications. Roads (excluding West Bank; 1982) 5,227 km. Motor vehicles in use (excluding West Bank; 1982): passenger 118,900; commercial 43,600. Railways (1981) c. 618 km. Air traffic (1982): 3,287,000,000 passenger-km; freight c. 131.4 million net ton-km. Telephones (Dec. 1982) 86,100. Radio receivers (Dec. 1980) 536,000. Television receivers (Dec. 1980) 171,000.

Agriculture. Production (in 000; metric tons; 1981): wheat c. 60; barley c. 30; tomatoes 205; aubergines (eggplants) c. 52; watermelons c. 33; olives 19; oranges c. 26; lemons c. 9; grapes c. 18. Livestock (in 000; 1981): cattle c. 37; goats c. 490; sheep c. 1,000; camels c. 13; asses c. 27; chickens c. 26,000.

Industry. Production (in 000; metric tons; 1981): phosphate rock 4,244; petroleum products 2,134; cement 964; electricity (kw-hr) 1,237,000.

Kampuchea

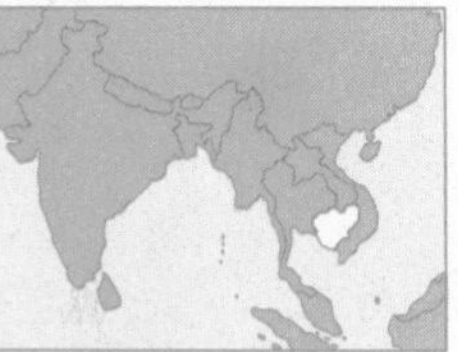
Kampuchea

A republic of Southeast Asia, Kampuchea (formerly Cambodia) occupies the southwest part of the Indochinese Peninsula, on the Gulf of Thailand, bordered by Vietnam, Laos, and Thailand. Area: 181,035 sq km (69,898 sq mi). Pop. (1983 est.): 5,996,000, estimated to comprise Khmer 93%; Vietnamese 4%; and Chinese 3%. Cap.: Phnom Penh (urban area pop., 1981 est., 500,000). Language: Khmer (official) and French. Religion: Buddhist. Secretary-general of the People's Revolutionary (Communist) Party of Kampuchea and president of the Council of State in 1983, Heng Samrin; president of the Council of Ministers (premier), Chan Sy.

The main theme of Kampuchean affairs in 1983 continued to be the unceasing efforts by the Vietnam-backed administration of Pres. Heng Samrin and by the tripartite Democratic Kampuchea resistance coalition to strengthen their respective claims as sole legitimate representative of the nation. It was a tussle involving many countries, waged in the corridors of international diplomacy and on the military battlefields of Kampuchea itself.

The year began with latent strains showing in the UN-recognized Democratic Kampuchea government-in-exile, whose principal partners were Prince Norodom Sihanouk, former premier Son Sann and his supporters in the (anti-Communist) Khmer People's National Liberation Front, and the (Communist) Khmer Rouge. Just when the coalition's backers in the Association of Southeast Asian Nations (ASEAN) wondered whether Sihanouk was serious about his stated intention to resign as president of the coalition, the prince in late January made a high-profile trip through Thailand into western Kampuchea to convene a much-anticipated "Cabinet" meeting with his Khmer allies. He reaffirmed that he would remain president of Democratic Kampuchea and denied rumours that he might reach a separate settlement with the country's Vietnamese occupiers.

Journalism:
see Publishing
Judaism:
see Religion
Judo:
see Combat Sports

WIDE WORLD

Militiawomen carried ammunition and other supplies to Khmer Rouge troops locked in battle with Vietnamese forces near the Thai–Kampuchean border.

Several days after Sihanouk's visit, Vietnamese forces near the Thai-Kampuchean border launched their fiercest attack in years on camps controlled by the Khmer resistance, an act repeated on an even larger scale two months later. Though Vietnam's offensives inflamed regional tensions and drew international criticism, they were designed, as one diplomatic analyst put it, "to demonstrate to the world that Vietnam can wipe out the Khmer resistance at any time."

True to its own carrot-and-stick tradition, however, Vietnam took steps to appear conciliatory. Attempting to placate ASEAN, Vietnam announced in late February that it would begin a "partial withdrawal" of its 170,000 troops in Kampuchea, a move scored by non-Communist Southeast Asian governments as a meaningless rotation. Then, during the summit meeting of the nonaligned movement in New Delhi, India, in March, Vietnamese Foreign Minister Nguyen Co Thach indicated to his Malaysian counterpart, Ghazali bin Shafie, that Hanoi was ready to talk to ASEAN about Kampuchea's political future without insisting, as before, on the participation of its client regime in Phnom Penh. Though Malaysia, Indonesia, and Singapore expressed interest in exploring Thach's proposal, they nonetheless went along with the objections of ASEAN partners Thailand and the Philippines and rejected it.

What ASEAN, chief sponsors of the Democratic Kampuchea coalition, did want was spelled out after the annual conference of the grouping's foreign ministers in June. Vietnamese forces, declared the ministers, should withdraw completely from Kampuchea, paving the way for free elections and for an independent government. ASEAN made a concession to Vietnamese sentiment by dropping its previous demand for negotiations over Kampuchea to be conducted under the auspices of the UN-sponsored International Conference on Kampuchea. However, the foreign ministers were plainly frustrated by the lack of progress toward a settlement. For the first time one of them conceded in public that the tripartite resistance coalition had yet to become a truly effective force. In their own meeting in July, the foreign ministers of Communist Indochina dismissed ASEAN's "absurd demands."

KAMPUCHEA

Education. Primary, pupils (1980–81) 1,328,033, teachers (1979–80) 12,000; secondary, pupils c. 40,000; higher, students c. 1,500.

Finance. Monetary unit: riel, with (end 1982) a reported nominal rate of 4 new riels to U.S. $1 (6.50 riels = £1 sterling). Budget (1974 est.): revenue 23 billion old riels; expenditure 71 billion old riels.

Foreign Trade. (1981) Imports c. U.S. $103 million; exports c. U.S. $43 million. Import sources (1973): U.S. c. 69%; Thailand c. 11%; Singapore c. 5%; Japan c. 5%. Export destinations (1973): Hong Kong c. 23%; Japan c. 22%; Malaysia c. 18%; France c. 12%; Spain c. 10%. Main export (1973): rubber 93%.

Transport and Communications. Roads (1973) 15,029 km. Motor vehicles in use: passenger (1972) 27,200; commercial (including buses; 1973) 11,000. Railways: (1982) c. 620 km; traffic (1973) 54,070,000 passenger-km, freight 9,780,000 net ton-km. Inland waterways (including Mekong River; 1980) c. 1,400 km. Telephones (Dec. 1975) 71,000. Radio receivers (Dec. 1978) 171,000. Television receivers (Dec. 1977) c. 35,000.

Agriculture. Production (in 000; metric tons; 1982): rice c. 1,850; corn c. 100; bananas c. 70; oranges c. 24 ; dry beans (1981) c. 12; rubber c. 12; tobacco c. 5. Livestock (in 000; 1982): cattle c. 1,000; buffalo c. 410; pigs c. 225.

Vietnam's troops in Kampuchea, however, found the going tough once the wet season began in May. Increasingly, there were reports of resistance guerrillas successfully harassing them and recruiting able-bodied Khmers into their ranks. The growing effectiveness of the resistance's efforts at political subversion led to purges within the administration.

Kampuchea continued its economic recovery from the devastation of the years of Khmer Rouge rule (1975–79). In the capital abundant consumer goods were on display in the free markets, while exports of rubber, tobacco, and agricultural produce increased. But with aid from nonsocialist countries virtually drying up by late 1983, the recovery was precarious. One UN study of the food supply in Kampuchea concluded that malnutrition remained a serious problem, especially among children. (THOMAS HON WING POLIN)

Karate:
see Combat Sports

Kashmir:
see India; Pakistan

Kendo:
see Combat Sports

Kenya

Kenya

An African republic and a member of the Commonwealth, Kenya is bordered on the north by Sudan and Ethiopia, east by Somalia, south by Tanzania, and west by Uganda. Area: 580,367 sq km (224,081 sq mi), including 11,230 sq km of inland water. Pop. (1983 est.): 17,850,000, including African 98%, of which Kikuyu 21.2%, Luo 14.5%, Luhya 14.1%, Gusii and Meru 11.5%, Kamba 10.8%, Kalenjin 10.7%; Asian and European 2%. Cap. and largest city: Nairobi (pop., 1981 est., 919,000). Language: Swahili (official) and English. Religion (1980): Protestant 26.5%; Roman Catholic 26.4%; tribal 18.9%; African indigenous 17.6%; Muslim 6%; Orthodox 2.5%; other 2.1%. President in 1983, Daniel arap Moi.

Memories of the attempted coup in August 1982 left the Kenyan government wary of unrest throughout 1983. The trials of those charged with treason and other crimes connected with the coup continued. A number of former members of the disbanded Air Force were sentenced to death and more than 900 others to periods of imprisonment. In February and March, however, Pres. Daniel arap Moi pardoned several hundred former air force personnel charged with mutiny and students charged with sedition. A number of other students and lecturers remained in custody. The University of Nairobi, closed after the coup attempt, was reopened in October.

The prevailing atmosphere of uncertainty was reflected in the currency of a lively rumour to the effect that former vice-president Oginga Odinga, who had been confined to his house in November 1982, had been arrested in connection with the attempted coup. The rumour appeared to be unfounded, although one person found guilty of treason claimed that Odinga had been consulted before the rebellion and had given it his support. Odinga's son was remanded for trial on a treason charge in January but was later released. Odinga himself was freed from house detention in October.

More startling was the president's statement in May that a foreign power was grooming a leading Kenyan politician to take over. Moi named neither the foreign power nor the politician. After considerable speculation in Parliament, however, accusations were leveled against Charles Njonjo, minister of constitutional affairs, while Britain was suspected of being the power in question. Both accusations were denied, but on June 29 Njonjo was suspended from his ministerial post, and the next day he resigned from Parliament. President Moi then ordered a judicial inquiry to determine Njonjo's part in the alleged plot.

In the midst of the crisis, Moi announced on May 17 that the presidential and parliamentary elections scheduled for late 1984 would take place 14 months early. Moi, the only candidate for the presidency, was returned for a five-year term of office on August 29. The parliamentary elections held on September 26 were also a triumph for the president. Although only candidates nominated by the Kenya African National Union (KANU) were accepted for election, there were many contests among KANU members for the available seats. Five of the 25 former ministers lost their seats, as did more than 40% of the other members of Parliament. The result gave Moi a free hand in rearranging his Cabinet. Njonjo did not run for election, but the candidate generally regarded as his substitute, Peter Kinyanjui, was elected with a considerable majority.

As if to counter the political uncertainty, President Moi marked the occasion of the 20th anniversary of Kenya's achieving internal self-government on June 1 by freeing 8,463 prisoners. Included among them were 22 held as a result of the attempted coup. Another 7,000 were freed on the anniversary of independence in December.

Political tensions had the effect of distracting attention from the nation's continuing economic problems. The attempted coup had cost the country $200 million in damage to property, lost income from tourism, and capital outflow. Failure to meet the criteria laid down by the International Monetary Fund as a condition of the $170 million standby loan arranged in January 1982 led to the

CAMERAPIX/KEYSTONE

To honour the 20th anniversary of Kenya's independence, Ethiopia sent a company of its traditional dancers to perform at celebrations in Nairobi.

KENYA

Education. (1982) Primary, pupils 4,184,602, teachers 79,866; secondary, pupils 464,721, teachers 8,611; vocational, pupils 9,199, teachers 343; teacher training, students 13,636, teachers 879; higher (university only), students 8,772, teaching staff 898.

Finance. Monetary unit: Kenyan shilling, with (Sept. 20, 1983) a free rate of KShs 13.37 to U.S. $1 (KShs 20.13 = £1 sterling). Gold and other reserves (June 1983) U.S. $360 million. Budget (1980–81 actual): revenue KShs 13,853,000,000; expenditure KShs 18,329,000,000. Gross national product (1982) KShs 65,770,000,000. Cost of living (Nairobi; 1975 = 100; June 1983) 274.7.

Foreign Trade. (1982) Imports KShs 18,904,000,000; exports KShs 11,391,000,000. Import sources (1981): Saudi Arabia 19%; U.K. 17%; United Arab Emirates 10%; West Germany 8%; Japan 8%; U.S. 7%. Export destinations (1981): West Germany 11%; U.K. 11%; aircraft and ship stores 9%; Uganda 9%; Singapore 7%. Main exports (1981): petroleum products 32%; coffee 20%; tea 11%; fruit and vegetables 6%. Tourism (1981): visitors 373,000; gross receipts U.S. $240 million.

Transport and Communications. Roads (1981) 53,588 km. Motor vehicles in use (1980): passenger 113,600; commercial 23,600. Railways: (1980) 4,531 km; freight traffic (1982) *c.* 2,240,000,000 net ton-km. Air traffic (1982): 942 million passenger-km; freight *c.* 25.2 million ton-km. Telephones (Jan. 1981) 198,300. Radio receivers (Dec. 1980) 540,000. Television receivers (Dec. 1980) 65,000.

Agriculture. Production (in 000; metric tons; 1982): corn 2,300; wheat 250; millet *c.* 130; potatoes 346; sweet potatoes (1981) *c.* 345; cassava (1981) *c.* 640; sugar, raw value (1981) *c.* 440; bananas *c.* 138; coffee 95; tea *c.* 96; sisal *c.* 42; cotton, lint *c.* 10; fish catch (1981) 60. Livestock (in 000; 1981): cattle 11,500; sheep *c.* 4,700; pigs *c.* 80; goats *c.* 4,580; camels 609; chickens *c.* 17,250.

Industry. Production (in 000; metric tons; 1981): cement 1,300; soda ash 158; petroleum products 2,104; electricity (kw-hr) 1,715,000.

suspension of payment of the loan. In an attempt to improve the situation, representatives of donor countries met in Nairobi early in 1983 to try to speed up new aid projects and to turn existing loans into grants. The atmosphere of the meeting was favourable to those proposals, though little extra money was forthcoming. In June, however, the U.S. granted Kenya $30 million, the largest single grant it had made to any African country.

In November Queen Elizabeth II paid a state visit to Kenya. (KENNETH INGHAM)

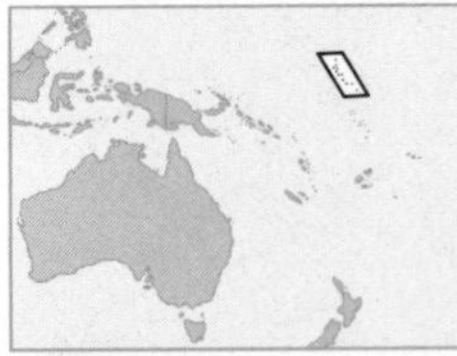
Kiribati

Kiribati

An independent republic in the western Pacific Ocean and member of the Commonwealth, Kiribati comprises the former Gilbert Islands, Banaba (Ocean Island), the Line Islands, and the Phoenix Islands. Area: 712 sq km (275 sq mi). Pop. (1983 est.): 60,000, including (1978) Micronesian 98%; Polynesian 1.4%; non-Pacific islanders 0.6%. Cap.: Bairiki (pop., 1979 est., 1,800) on Tarawa atoll (pop., 1980 est., 22,100). Language: English (official). Religion (1978): Roman Catholic 51%; Congregational 44%; Baha'i 2%. President (*beretitenti*) in 1983, Ieremia Tabai.

In the January 1983 elections, Pres. Ieremia Tabia was returned for his third—and hence necessarily final—term of office. Ten members of the House of Assembly, including two ministers, lost their seats, but the overall shape and policies of the government remained unchanged.

In March the government purchased Fanning and Washington islands, which had been run as private copra plantations. A major development program was launched at another of the Line Islands, Christmas Island, used as a nuclear testing site in the late 1950s and early 1960s and as a British military base. It was cleaned up by Australian troops, and a resettlement scheme was initiated for islanders from the Gilbert Island group 3,200 km (2,000 mi) to the west. The U.S. finally ratified a treaty renouncing its long-standing claims to some of Kiribati's islands.

The government established a shipping registry to generate revenue and employment, but in general economic prospects were not good. Major aid grants were received from the European Communities for an Earth satellite, from Japan for an inter-island vessel, and from Britain for budget expenditure. (BARRIE MACDONALD)

KIRIBATI

Education. (1981) Primary, pupils 13,383, teachers 447; secondary, pupils 1,653, teachers 94; teacher training, students 113, teachers 14; higher (1978), students 741.

Finance and Trade. Monetary unit: Australian dollar, with (Sept. 20, 1983) a free rate of A$1.12 to U.S. $1 (A$1.69 = £1 sterling). Budget (1982 est.): revenue A$15.9 million; expenditure A$15.7 million. Foreign trade (1980): imports A$16,848,000; exports A$2,426,000. Import sources: Australia 57%; Japan 13%; U.S. 7%; U.K. 6%; New Zealand 5%. Export destinations: U.K. 89%; U.S. 6%. Main exports: copra 89%; fish 10%.

Korea

A country of eastern Asia, Korea is bounded by China, the Sea of Japan, the Korea Strait, and the Yellow Sea. It is divided into two parts roughly at the 38th parallel.

For the divided nation of Korea, 1983 was marked by continued, unremitting hostility between the governments in Seoul (South Korea) and Pyongyang (North Korea). Beginning in February 118,000 South Korean and 73,000 U.S. military personnel staged a ten-week military exercise, believed to be one of the largest such war games ever held in the non-Communist world. North Korea responded by placing its 800,000-strong armed forces on a rare "semiwar" alert and warned that the Seoul-U.S. maneuvers could turn into a real war at any moment. U.S. and South Korean commanders in turn accused Pyongyang of building up its armed forces far beyond its defense needs.

Tensions increased during the year. South Korea announced the arrest of several people for engaging in espionage activities on behalf of the Pyongyang regime. In late February a North Korean pilot defected to the South, bringing with him his MiG-19 jet fighter, and two months later a North Korean Army captain crossed the lines. Both men, Seoul authorities asserted, told of detailed preparations by Pyongyang to invade the South. In August South Korean naval forces on two separate occasions attacked and sank North Korean spy vessels.

By far the most explosive incident in North-South relations, however, occurred on October 9. On the morning of the first full day of a planned 19-day, six-nation tour by Pres. Chun Doo Hwan and a score of South Korean ministers and top officials, a bomb went off at the Martyr's Mausoleum in Rangoon, Burma. Twenty-one people died, including 17 South Koreans, and some 50 were injured. Among the dead were four South Korean Cabinet ministers—Deputy Prime Minister Suh Suk Joon, Foreign Minister Lee Bum Suk, Commerce and Industry Minister Kim Dong Whie, and Energy Minister Suh Sang Chul. Chun escaped only because his limousine arrived late, just minutes after the blast. As South Korea's armed forces went on alert, Chun angrily denounced the North Koreans as perpetrators of the carnage and said it was a "carefully premeditated plot" against his own life. Though Pyongyang dismissed these charges, two North Korean Army officers later confessed to carrying out the bombing and were sentenced to death by the Burmese authorities.

Republic of Korea (South Korea). Area: 98,992 sq km (38,221 sq mi). Pop. (1982 est.): 39,331,000. Cap. and largest city: Seoul (pop., 1982 est., 8,961,500). Language: Korean. Religion (1980): Buddhist 40.4%; Christian 27.9%; Confucian 17%; Tonghak (Chondokyo) 3.8%; other 10.9%. President in 1983, Chun Doo Hwan; prime ministers, Kim Sang Hyup and, from October 14, Chin Iee Chong.

The Rangoon bombing and the concern it reawakened in the South about security breaches and North Korean infiltration put a damper on the cautious political liberation that Pres. Chun Doo Hwan had been undertaking. In December 1982 Chun not only had pardoned 47 political prisoners but also had freed the country's leading dissident, Kim Dae Jung (*see* BIOGRAPHIES), and allowed him to go into exile in the U.S. In February the government lifted a ban on political activities that it had imposed on some 250 people three years earlier.

However, among those who continued to be restricted was the prominent politician Kim Young Sam, who was under house arrest. He began a hunger strike on May 18, demanding the abolition of the political ban, restoration of freedom of the press, direct presidential elections, and a rewriting of the present constitution to permit more democracy. By the time he ended his strike on June 9, Kim had focused intense public attention on the issues he raised; though the government did not accede to his demands, an extraordinary ten-day session of the National Assembly was convened to debate them. More significantly, Kim's supporters launched the National Consultation for Democracy, an umbrella group that sought to unite opposition politicians, Christian churches, student activists, and members of the intelligentsia.

In August the government continued on its conciliatory path by granting a special amnesty to more than 1,900 political dissidents and convicted criminals on the occasion of National Liberation Day. Even before the Rangoon bomb attack, however, President Chun had hinted that liberalization would have its limits. Said he: "Dogmatic and blind confrontation between politicians, and between political parties, is a waste of the nation's resources."

The South Korean economy, plagued for four years by recession, made a strong comeback in 1983. Inflation was finally brought under control. The consumer price index rose a mere 2% in the first half of 1983, a notable improvement over the 5% of the previous year and a striking contrast with the 13% of 1981 and 33% of 1980. Gross national product chalked up a remarkable 9.6% growth rate for the first half of the year, outstripping forecasts. Exports were also strong, but nevertheless South Korea's foreign debt of $38 billion remained the largest of any nation in Asia.

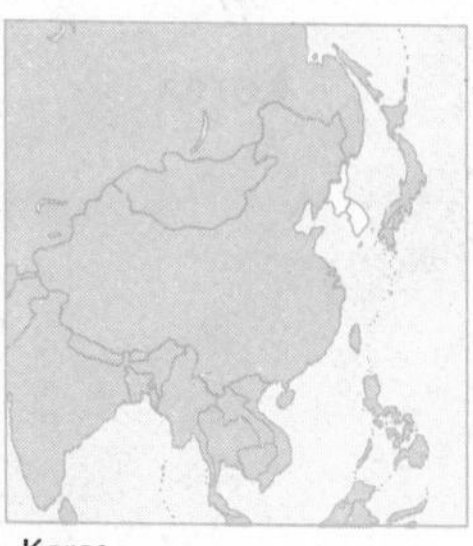

Korea

As in 1982, South Korea's financial circles were hit by a major scandal in the "curb" money market, an underground system of financing used by many companies since credit was relatively hard to secure from most banks. At the centre of the storm was the Myung Sung Group, a conglomerate, whose owner and chairman, Kim Chul Ho, was arrested in August and charged with embezzlement and evasion of taxes. Since the funds involved had come from the "curb" market, the scandal virtually paralyzed the market by scaring away the private money usually available there. Shortly after Kim's arrest, a former transportation minister and several government officials were taken into custody and charged with taking bribes totaling $220,000.

After the Rangoon bombing Chun was forced to remake his Cabinet. The most serious losses on the economic team were Kim Jae Ik, senior presidential adviser and chief architect of Seoul's policy to reduce government control of business, and Deputy Prime Minister Suh, who had been in charge of overall planning and budgeting. In October Chun announced that they would be replaced by economist Sakong Il and Cabinet veteran Shin Byong Hyun, respectively. Lee Bum Suk was replaced as foreign minister by Lee Won Kyung, a former sports minister. Kim Sang Hyup, who had not been in Rangoon, was replaced as prime minister by Chin Iee Chong, chairman of the ruling Democratic Justice Party.

Rivaling the Rangoon bombing in its traumatic effect on South Korea was the shooting down on September 1 of a Korean Air Lines passenger air-

After a massive funeral service for 16 of the 21 victims of the Rangoon, Burma, bombing attack aimed at the South Korean Cabinet, the coffins, draped in the South Korean flag, were taken to Seoul's National Cemetery for burial in mid-October. Burmese authorities announced in November that two North Koreans had confessed to the attack. North Korea denied the allegation.

WIDE WORLD

liner by a Soviet jet fighter. Flight 007, a Boeing 747 with 269 people on board, was en route from Alaska to Seoul when it strayed substantially off its course into Soviet airspace over sensitive military installations on Sakhalin Island, where, in predawn darkness, it was shot down. All on board perished, including more than 100 Koreans. People throughout the world were shocked and angry, nowhere more so than in South Korea, where massive anti-Soviet demonstrations took place nationwide.

The airliner disaster spelled a setback to the Soviet half of Chun's "Nordpolitik," the discreet efforts to improve relations with the U.S.S.R. and China. Another airliner incident, however, helped the Chinese half. In May six Chinese hijacked a Chinese airliner to South Korea. Subsequent negotiations for the return of the plane led to the first-ever visit by a senior Communist Chinese official—the airline chief—to Seoul. The aircraft was returned to China, and the hijackers were sentenced to prison by Korean authorities. Relations also improved with Japan and the U.S., marked by visits to Seoul by Prime Minister Yasuhiro Nakasone in January and Pres. Ronald Reagan in November.

Democratic People's Republic of Korea (North Korea). Area: 121,929 sq km (47,077 sq mi). Pop. (1983 est.): 19,185,000. Cap.: Pyongyang (pop., 1981 est., 1,283,000). Language: Korean. Religion (1980 est.): atheist 68%; animist 16%; Buddhist, Confucian, Tonghak (Chondokyo), and other 16%. General secretary of the Central Committee of the Workers' (Communist) Party of Korea and president in 1983, Marshal Kim Il Sung; chairman of the Council of Ministers (premier), Li Jong Ok.

In North Korea further progress was made in Pres. Kim Il Sung's continuing efforts to pass power on to his son, Kim Chong Il. When three senior members of the ruling Workers' Party Politburo failed to appear for local assembly elections early in the year, analysts speculated that they had fallen from grace for resisting the Kim-Kim succession. It was believed that the younger Kim had moved to consolidate his position in the military establishment; older generals who opposed the succession were removed.

Though Kim Chong Il still lacked a top-level government post, he was a member of the Politburo and of the Supreme People's Assembly. His ascendancy received an important boost in June when he went on a 12-day visit to Beijing (Peking). The trip, observers noted, suggested that China's regime, despite its own expressed distaste for nepotism and personality cults, was prepared to accept Kim Chong Il's rise to the top in Pyongyang. Such recognition would give the Chinese a distinct edge in competition for the affections of North Korea over the Soviets, who remained reluctant to give their blessings to the world's first "Communist dynasty."

Kim Chong Il spearheaded cautious moves to bring his isolated country further into the international mainstream. According to informed sources, large-scale construction work got under way in major cities to improve cultural facilities and to erect high-rise apartments. Tourist facilities were opened, and a golf course for foreign visitors was under construction outside Pyongyang. Thousands of television sets and refrigerators imported from Japan were distributed to party cadres and army generals.

The nation's isolationist economic policy was moderated by a new emphasis on export trade and joint ventures with foreign countries. As a result exports had risen from $1.2 billion in 1980 to about $1.5 billion two years later. Yet North Korea remained troubled by its foreign debt, which at $3.5 billion was considerable for an economy of its size. Foreign currency remained scarce.

(THOMAS HON WING POLIN)

KOREA: Republic

Education. (1981–82) Primary, pupils 5,465,248, teachers 124,572; secondary, pupils 3,672,565, teachers 92,191; vocational, students 879,550, teachers 28,347; higher, students 879,335, teaching staff 26,529.

Finance. Monetary unit: won, with (Sept. 20, 1983) a free rate of 790 won to U.S. $1 (1,189 won = £1 sterling). Gold and other reserves (June 1983) U.S. $2,019,000,000. Budget (total; 1981 actual): revenue 8,604,800,000,000 won; expenditure 8,044,800,000,000 won. Gross national product (1982) 48,268,000,000,000 won. Money supply (June 1983) 5,691,000,000,000 won. Cost of living (1975 = 100; June 1983) 297.9.

Foreign Trade. (1982) Imports 17,780,000,000,000 won; exports 15,910,000,000,000 won. Import sources (1981): Japan 24%; U.S. 23%; Saudi Arabia 14%; Kuwait 6%. Export destinations (1981): U.S. 27%; Japan 16%; Hong Kong 5%; Saudi Arabia 5%. Main exports (1981): clothing 18%; textile yarns and fabrics 12%; electrical machinery and equipment 11%; iron and steel 9%; ships and boats 7%; food 6%; metal manufactures 5%; footwear 5%. Tourism (1981): visitors 1,093,000; gross receipts U.S. $448 million.

Transport and Communications. Roads (1982) 53,936 km (including 1,245 km expressways). Motor vehicles in use (1982): passenger 305,800; commercial 263,900. Railways (1981): 6,045 km; traffic 21,240,000,000 passenger-km, freight (1982) 10,721,000,000 net ton-km. Air traffic (1982): 12,101,000,000 passenger-km; freight 1,068,700,000 net ton-km. Shipping (1982): merchant vessels 100 gross tons and over 1,652; gross tonnage 5,529,398. Telephones (Jan. 1981) 3,386,800. Radio receivers (Dec. 1980) 15 million. Television licenses (Dec. 1980) 6,280,000.

Agriculture. Production (in 000; metric tons; 1982): rice 7,308; barley 749; potatoes 539; sweet potatoes (1981) 1,108; soybeans 233; cabbages (1981) 3,457; watermelons (1981) 291; onions 439; apples 527; oranges 279; tobacco 64; fish catch (1981) 2,366. Livestock (in 000; Dec. 1980): cattle 1,531; pigs 2,140; goats 201; chickens 41,000.

Industry. Production (in 000; metric tons; 1982): coal 18,383; iron ore (56% metal content) 555; pig iron 8,570; crude steel 5,635; cement 17,892; tungsten concentrates (oxide content; 1981) 3.3; zinc concentrates 59; gold (troy oz; 1981) 41; silver (troy oz; 1981) 3,148; sulfuric acid 1,595; fertilizers (nutrient content; 1981–82) nitrogenous c. 666, phosphate c. 324; petroleum products (1981) 24,649; man-made fibres (1981) 646; electricity (kw-hr; 1981) 43,667,000; radio receivers (units; 1981) 5,126; television receivers (units; 1981) 7,697. Merchant vessels launched (100 gross tons and over; 1982) 1,531,000 gross tons.

KOREA: Democratic People's Republic

Education. (1980–81) Primary, pupils c. 2.5 million; secondary and vocational, pupils c. 2.5 million; primary, secondary, and vocational, teachers c. 100,000; higher, students c. 100,000.

Finance and Trade. Monetary unit: won, with (Sept. 20, 1983) a nominal exchange rate of 0.94 won to U.S. $1 (1.42 won = £1 sterling). Budget (1982 est.) balanced at 22,546,000,000 won. Foreign trade (approximate; 1981): imports c. 1.8 billion won; exports c. 1.4 billion won. Import sources: U.S.S.R. c. 22%; Japan c. 18%; China c. 17%. Export destinations: U.S.S.R. c. 26%; China c. 17%; Japan c. 9%; Saudi Arabia c. 9%; India c. 5%. Main exports (1975): lead and ore c. 30%; zinc and ore c. 20%; magnesite c. 15%; rice c. 6%; cement c. 5%; coal c. 5%; fish c. 5%.

Agriculture. Production (in 000; metric tons; 1982): rice c. 4,950; corn c. 2,270; barley c. 380; millet c. 445; potatoes c. 1,520; sweet potatoes (1981) c. 382; soybeans c. 360; fish catch (1981) c. 1,500. Livestock (in 000; 1981): cattle c. 960; pigs c. 2,200; sheep c. 300; goats c. 245; chickens c. 18,050.

Industry. Production (in 000; metric tons; 1981): coal c. 45,000; iron ore (metal content) c. 3,200; pig iron c. 3,000; steel c. 3,500; zinc ore c. 140; magnesite c. 1,900; silver (troy oz) c. 1,550; tungsten concentrates (oxide content) c. 2.2; cement c. 8,000; petroleum products c. 1,840; fertilizers (nutrient content) nitrogenous c. 600, phosphate c. 130; electricity (kw-hr) c. 36,000,000.

Kuwait

An independent constitutional monarchy (emirate), Kuwait is on the northwestern coast of the Persian Gulf between Iraq and Saudi Arabia. Area: 17,818 sq km (6,879 sq mi). Pop. (1983 est.): 1,668,400. Cap.: Kuwait City (pop., 1980 prelim., 60,400). Largest city: Hawalli (pop., 1980 prelim., 152,300). Language: Arabic. Religion (1980): Muslim 91.5% (of which Sunni 85%; Shi'ah 15%); Christian 6.4%; other 2.1%. Emir, Sheikh Jabir al-Ahmad al-Jabir as-Sabah; prime minister in 1983, Crown Prince Sheikh Saad al-Abdullah as-Salim as-Sabah.

The resignation of Finance Minister Abdel Latif al-Hamad on September 14 was the major political event of 1983 in Kuwait. It followed his failure to force through a package of hard-line measures designed to punish delinquent share dealers on the unofficial stock exchange, the Souq al-Manakh, which had collapsed in August 1982. Many prominent Kuwaitis, including some of Cabinet rank, had been involved in the market. One individual's debts reportedly reached more than $10 billion. Al-Hamad's replacement was the powerful oil minister, Sheikh Ali Khalifah as-Sabah, a member of the royal family with a background as a technocrat.

Oil production was running at about 600,000 bbl a day, nearly half of the officially declared ceiling and down from 940,782 bbl a day in 1982. Investment income of about $9 billion in 1983 was thought sufficient to cover any government deficit. A high level of project spending was maintained, but after the stock market collapse, government policy was to reserve contracts for local companies whenever possible.

Kuwait's financial position was solid. At the beginning of 1983 it had official reserves of about $5 billion and other external assets of some $70 billion. However, the intensification of the Iran-Iraq war late in 1983 posed a threat to prosperity. In the past, despite granting assistance to Iraq, Kuwait had sought to mediate in Arab-Islamic quarrels, but the violence of the disputes in the northern Gulf and Lebanon left little room for mediation. Violence came much closer on December 12, when bombs exploded at six sites in Kuwait, including the U.S. and French embassies, killing some 4 persons and injuring about 60. By year's end 18 Muslim fundamentalists had been arrested in connection with the bombings. (JOHN WHELAN)

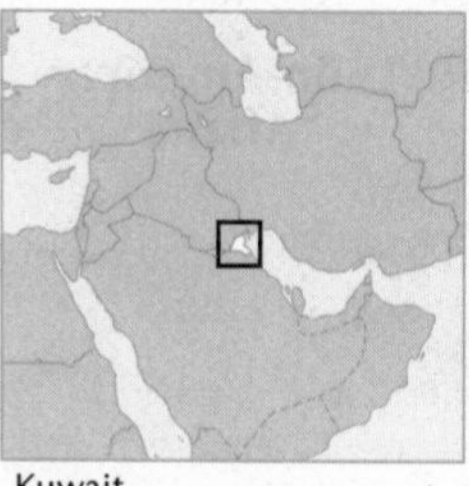
Kuwait

KUWAIT

Education. (1980–81) Primary, pupils 148,983, teachers 8,035; secondary, pupils 181,461, teachers 15,257; vocational, pupils 421, teachers 85; higher (1979–80), students 12,435, teaching staff 1,143.

Finance. Monetary unit: Kuwaiti dinar, with (Sept. 20, 1983) a free rate of 0.29 dinar to U.S. $1 (0.44 dinar = £1 sterling). Gold and other reserves (June 1983) U.S. $4,797,000,000. Budget (total; 1980–81 actual): revenue 6,351,000,000 dinars; expenditure 2,577,000,000 dinars. Gross domestic product (1981–82) 6,764,000,000 dinars. Money supply (June 1983) 1,348,300,000 dinars. Cost of living (1975 = 100; March 1983) 171.

Foreign Trade. (1982) Imports (f.o.b.) c. 2,145,000,000 dinars; exports 2,833,000,000 dinars. Import sources (1980): Japan 21%; U.S. 14%; U.K. 9%; West Germany 9%; Italy 6%. Export destinations (1980): Japan 20%; The Netherlands 11%; Taiwan 9%; South Korea 8%; U.K. 7%; Singapore 7%. Main exports: crude oil 44%; petroleum products 33%.

Transport. Roads (1981) 2,854 km. Motor vehicles in use (1981): passenger 435,300; commercial 146,000. Air traffic (1982): 3,596,000,000 passenger-km; freight 115.6 million net ton-km. Shipping (1982): merchant vessels 100 gross tons and over 217; gross tonnage 2,014,379.

Industry. Production (in 000; metric tons; 1982): crude oil 42,052; natural gas (cu m) c. 3,360,000; petroleum products (1981) 13,886; electricity (kw-hr; 1981) 10,336,000.

Laos

A landlocked people's republic of Southeast Asia, Laos is bounded by China, Vietnam, Kampuchea, Thailand, and Burma. Area: 236,800 sq km (91,400 sq mi). Pop. (1983 est.): 3,993,000. Cap. and largest city: Vientiane (pop., 1981 est., 210,000). Language: Lao (official), French, and English. Religion (1980 est.): Buddhist 58%; tribal 34%; Christian 2%; other 2%; none 4%. President in 1983, Prince Souphanouvong; premier, Kaysone Phomvihan.

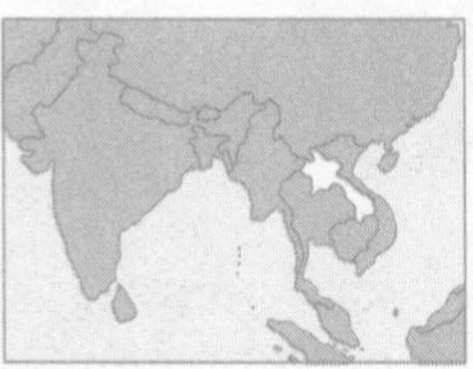
Laos

In 1983 Laos experienced a welcome upturn in its economic life, which in turn helped put a brake on the number of Laotians fleeing their homeland. For the ruling Lao People's Revolutionary (Communist) Party regime, however, problems of internal security remained, as did the government's overwhelming reliance on the support of Vietnam.

Since the Laotian authorities decided to adopt relatively liberal economic policies in 1980, private enterprise, which declined after the Communist takeover in 1975, had made a comeback. By 1983 private shops and restaurants had reopened, and free markets in the streets of Vientiane displayed an array of consumer goods rivaled in Indochina only in Ho Chi Minh City, Vietnam. Though leading customers included Soviet and Vietnamese officials stationed in the city, Laotians also purchased the items with hard currency earned from black-market transactions, smuggling, and remittances from relatives abroad.

Trade expanded, especially with Thailand. A sizable increase was recorded in official Lao exports of timber, electricity, coffee, tin, and agricultural products; for 1982 the figure was $46 million, up from $14.5 million in 1977. In June, taking the advice of the International Monetary Fund, Laos drastically devalued the kip and declared a special exchange rate of 108 kips to the U.S. dollar for private transactions. This rate enabled the government to compete with the black market for dollars spent by foreigners in Laos.

With a middle-ranking government official earning only $5 a month, the temptation of corruption was great. About 70 officials from at least three different ministries were arrested in May and June. The wave of arrests was described by analysts in Thailand as "the latest in a kind of cyclical housecleaning" by the Laotian authorities. Some of those detained were apparently accused of trying to block foreign-aid projects at a time when Laos was trying to improve its relations with capitalist countries. Notable overtures were made to Japan, the U.S., France, and Australia.

Labour Unions:
see Industrial Relations

Lacrosse:
see Field Hockey and Lacrosse

LAOS

Education. (1979–80) Primary, pupils 463,098, teachers 14,983; secondary, pupils 71,600, teachers 3,046; vocational, pupils 1,849, teachers 218; teacher training, students 9,169, teachers 441; higher, students 1,157, teaching staff 118.

Finance. Monetary unit: kip, with (Sept. 20, 1983) an official rate of 10 kip to U.S. $1 (free official rate of 15.06 kip = £1 sterling) and a preferential rate of 35 kip to U.S. $1 (free preferential rate of 53 kip = £1 sterling). Budget (total;1981 est.): revenue 930 million new kip (excluding foreign aid of 1,230,000,000 new kip); expenditure 2,160,000,000 new kip.

Foreign Trade. (1982) Imports c. U.S. $150 million; exports c. U.S. $40 million. Import sources (1974): Thailand 49%; Japan 19%; France 7%; West Germany 7%; U.S. 5%. Export destinations (1974): Thailand 73%; Malaysia 11%; Hong Kong 10%. Main exports (1978): timber 31%; electricity 21%; coffee 12%; tin 9%.

Transport and Communications. Roads (main; 1981) c. 10,200 km. Motor vehicles in use (1974): passenger 14,100; commercial (including buses) 2,500. Air traffic (1982): c. 8 million passenger-km; freight c. 100,000 net ton-km. Inland waterways (total; 1980) c. 4,600 km. Telephones (Dec. 1977) 7,000. Radio receivers (Dec. 1980) 350,000.

Agriculture. Production (in 000; metric tons; 1981): rice 1,155; corn 33; onions c. 32; melons c. 27; oranges c. 20; pineapples c. 32; coffee 5; tobacco 3; cotton, lint 5; timber (cu m) c. 3,631. Livestock (in 000; 1982): cattle 473; buffalo 897; pigs 1,223; chickens (1981) 5,568.

Industry. Production (1981): tin concentrates (metal content) c. 600 metric tons; electricity 1,150 million kw-hr.

The dominant ally, however, remained Vietnam, which stationed about 45,000 troops on its neighbour's territory. Indochinese solidarity was reaffirmed during a late February summit in Vientiane of the leaders of Vietnam, Kampuchea, and Laos. Yet for the Vientiane government security remained a headache. With the support of China, rebel Lao guerrilla groups became more active in 1983. Their biggest exploit of the year was a series of attacks on Vietnamese Army outposts. Even so, the numbers of Laotians fleeing the regime continued to decline; in the first five months of 1983 refugee officials in Thailand recorded 1,355 arrivals, compared with 2,068 during the same period a year earlier. However, the number of refugee Hmong tribesmen, a minority whom the government continued to persecute, rose to 1,785 from 1,234. (THOMAS HON WING POLIN)

Latin-American Affairs

In 1983 Latin America's economic difficulties increased, especially its external indebtedness. The chief political event was the victory of the moderate Radical Civic Union in Argentina in general elections held on October 30. The party's candidate, Raúl Alfonsín (*see* BIOGRAPHIES), took office as president on December 10, bringing to an end a period of military rule that had lasted since a 1976 coup that ousted the previous civilian government. The Alfonsín administration was expected to adopt a more conciliatory stance in sovereignty disputes with the U.K. over the Falkland Islands/ Islas Malvinas and with Chile over the Beagle Channel. A formal declaration of cessation of hostilities with the U.K. was regarded as unlikely, however, unless Britain took the initiative in proposing a resumption of negotiations.

In October contingents from six Caribbean countries—Antigua and Barbuda, Barbados, Dominica, Jamaica, St. Lucia, and St. Vincent and the Grenadines—supported the U.S.-led military intervention in Grenada, which had been undertaken in response to a majority decision by the Organization of Eastern Caribbean States to act to restore order. Antigua, Dominica, St. Lucia, and St. Vincent voted to act; Grenada, Montserrat, and the newly independent St. Christopher and Nevis (St. Kitts-Nevis) did not vote for the proposal. Latin-American reaction to the invasion was negative. At an Organization of American States (OAS) meeting on October 26, a majority of delegates condemned it.

Central America continued to be subjected to political and social disorders. There was a full-scale civil war in El Salvador, widespread guerrilla activity in Guatemala, and incursions into Nicaragua by paramilitary groups based in Honduras and Costa Rica and covertly backed by the U.S. There were several peace initiatives in process during the year. The Contadora Group, which comprised Venezuela, Colombia, Panama, and Mexico, was formed in January when Panama's Pres. Ricardo de la Espriella invited the ministers of the other three governments to meet on Contadora Island, off the Panamanian coast, to try to work toward a negotiated solution to regional difficulties. Pres. Belisario Betancur Cuartas of Colombia organized a meeting in Bogotá between Richard Stone, appointed U.S. special envoy to Central America in April, and Rubén Zamora, deputy leader of the Frente Democrático Revolucionario, the political arm of El Salvador's guerrilla movement.

In March U.S. Pres. Ronald Reagan proposed an emergency $298 million military and economic assistance package for the Central American region, including $110 million in arms aid for El Salvador; $60 million was eventually approved by the U.S. Congress. In a statement to congressional leaders in March, Reagan said that the aim of U.S. policy toward Central America was to spur democracy; to provide economic and military assistance with the hope, in the latter case, of regaining the initiative against guerrillas; to seek peaceful solutions by talks among all parties; and to advance economies in Central America and the Caribbean through the Caribbean Basin Initiative (CBI). On July 19 a 12-member bipartisan commission was established headed by former U.S. secretary of state Henry Kissinger (*see* BIOGRAPHIES). The commission was to make long-term policy recommendations to deal with the area's problems. During the second half of 1983 the Guatemalan government moved to resurrect the Central American Defense Council (Condeca), defunct since 1969, in the hope of setting up a joint defense force with El Salvador and Honduras. The U.S. staged ground-based military maneuvers in Honduras throughout the year, while U.S. naval exercises were held off Nicaragua's coast beginning in August. The U.S. announced plans late in the year to build a major military base in Honduras and to increase covert support for border attacks into Nicaragua. However, as the year ended, the Reagan administration stepped up sharply its pressure on El Salvador to control its right-wing death squads, which were belatedly recognized as effective recruiters for the left.

The CBI became law on August 5, following two years of legislative debate. It was an integrated program of tax and trade measures featuring an agreement that provided duty-free access for a range of Caribbean and Central American products to the U.S. market for 12 years.

The Latin American Integration Association (LAIA), which consisted of Argentina, Bolivia, Brazil, Chile, Colombia, Ecuador, Mexico, Paraguay, Peru, Uruguay, and Venezuela, made little headway during 1983. The aims of the LAIA were to encourage bilateral trade and the opening of new regional markets. During 1982 and 1983 intergovernmental talks took place on a variety of subjects. The results of these talks were submitted to a special conference on evaluation and convergence held in Montevideo, Uruguay, in April. The conference witnessed the signature of 32 agreements, of which 31 were bilateral and one affected four countries. The conference approved the lists of products from the relatively less developed countries (Bolivia, Ecuador, and Paraguay) that would enter all the member countries duty free. In November Costa Rica became the first non-LAIA country to subscribe to a commercial agreement within the LAIA framework by signing partial agreements with Argentina and Mexico.

The presidents of member countries of the Andean Group—Bolivia, Colombia, Ecuador, Peru, and Venezuela—held a summit meeting in Caracas, Venezuela, on July 24 at which an emergency plan to promote intraregional trade was approved. The plan proposed that members should identify products that were manufactured within the Group but which they continued to purchase outside it. The Group planned to grant priority to Bolivia under its Andean Development Corporation and Andean Reserve Fund programs.

In March the Inter-American Development Bank (IDB), which had 43 members, agreed to increase its capital by $15 billion to $35 billion and to channel increased funds into agriculture, water, hydroelectricity, and other long-term development projects in Latin America and the Caribbean. IDB members also agreed to replenish by $703 million the Fund for Special Operations, through which the bank extended loans for 30–40 years at 1–3% interest; and they created a new intermediate financing facility, which was to be a source of loans at interest rates of up to five percentage points below the bank's ordinary capital loans. In August the Inter-American Investment Corporation was set up within the framework of the IDB to provide equity, working capital, and long-term loans for small enterprises in the area. It was to have an initial capital of $200 million.

Brazil and Mexico signed important trade and investment agreements in April. Bilateral trade was to be encouraged by a payments system oper-

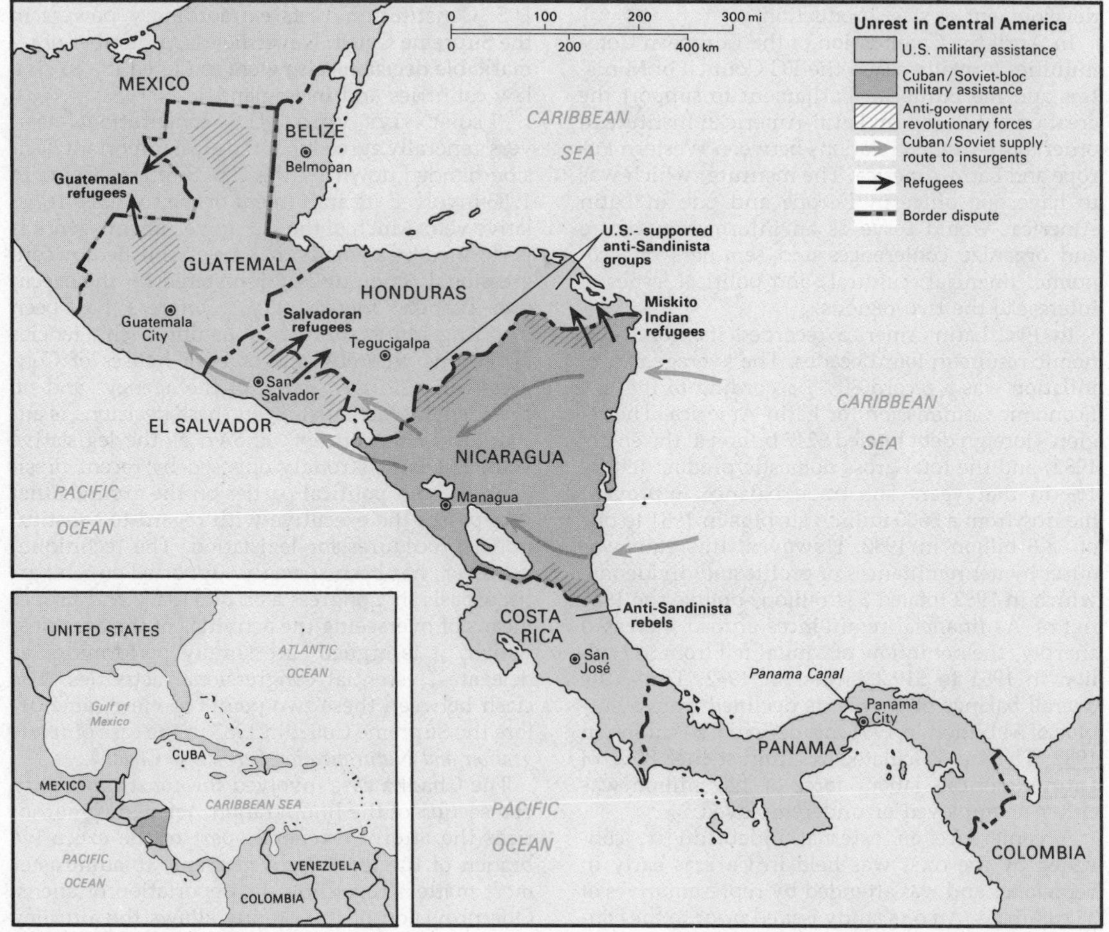

Troubled Central America: from Mexico to Panama the region was beset with guerrilla warfare, counterrevolution, and an unceasing flow of arms and refugees.

UPI

Jeane Kirkpatrick, U.S. ambassador to the UN, and Henry Kissinger, chairman of the President's Commission on Central America, confer with William March, president of Project Hope, a U.S.-based, privately funded organization working to advance international health care. Nicholas Brady, a member of the commission, is at left.

ated by the Brazilian and Mexican central banks. This would permit importers to pay for products from each country in national currencies. Every four months the two central banks would assess the trade flow for the period, and the country that registered a deficit would forward its equivalent in U.S. dollars to the other country's central bank. Brazil agreed to increase imports of Mexican crude oil from 60,000 to 80,000 bbl a day. Agreements were also signed for financial and technical cooperation in the exploitation of coal reserves and the development of steel production.

In April the Commission of the European Communities formally asked the EC Council of Ministers and the European Parliament to support the creation of a European Latin-American Institute in order to strengthen relations between Western Europe and Latin America. The institute, which was to have one office in Europe and one in Latin America, would serve as an information centre and organize conferences and seminars on economic, financial, cultural, and political issues of interest to the two regions.

In 1982 Latin America recorded its worst economic results in four decades. The average rate of inflation was a record 80%, according to the UN Economic Commission for Latin America. The region's foreign debt totaled $247 billion at the end of 1982, and the total gross domestic product fell by 1% in that year. The trade balance improved, moving from a $600 million surplus in 1981 to one of $8.8 billion in 1982. However, this gain was offset by net remittances of profits and dividends, which in 1982 totaled $34 billion, double the 1980 figure. As financial remittances abroad increased sharply, the net inflow of capital fell from $42 billion in 1981 to $19.2 billion in 1982. Thus, the overall balance of payments declined from a surplus of $4 billion in 1981 to a deficit of $4 billion in 1982. The IDB calculated in August that 30% of Latin America's labour force of 120 million was either unemployed or underemployed.

A conference on external indebtedness, convened by the OAS, was held in Caracas early in September and was attended by representatives of 28 countries. An OAS study issued prior to the conference estimated that Latin America and the Caribbean would require $20 billion a year in the period 1984–89, apart from refinancing of existing debts, to overcome the current crisis. In September the U.S. Export-Import Bank approved loan guarantees of up to $1.5 billion for Brazil and $500 million for Mexico. The guarantee for Brazil was the largest single package provided by the bank, a government agency that promotes sales of U.S. products abroad by extending financial incentives to purchasers.

By December all Latin-American countries, apart from Colombia and Paraguay, had been or were engaged in external debt rescheduling or refinancing negotiations. Brazil's foreign payments difficulties caused particular concern to the international financial community; its foreign debt was the largest in the world. (ROBIN CHAPMAN)

See also articles on the various political units.
[971.D.8; 974]

Latin-American Literature:
see Literature

Latter-day Saints:
see Religion

Law

Court Decisions. In 1983, as in past years, the most important judicial decisions handed down by the many courts of the world emanated from the U.S. Supreme Court. This reflected the fact that the common law system prevalent in the English-speaking world attaches more significance to judicial decisions than does the civil law applicable in most other countries, as well as the fact that the U.S. Constitution vests extraordinary powers in the Supreme Court. Nevertheless, a number of remarkable decisions also were rendered in the civil law countries and in England.

"LEGISLATIVE VETO." U.S. constitutional lawyers generally agreed that the most important decision handed down by the U.S. Supreme Court in 1983 involved its annulment of the so-called legislative veto. Much of the U.S. government's work is performed by agencies that are established by congressional action and administered by the executive branch. Increasingly, Congress has been inserting into statutes establishing such agencies provisions whereby one or both houses of Congress can veto any action of the agency, and no presidential participation in these decisions is authorized. This concept, known as the legislative veto, has been strongly opposed by recent presidents of both political parties on the grounds that it bypasses the executive with regard to constitutional procedures for legislation. The technique, however, has been strongly supported on a bipartisan basis in Congress as a necessary and proper means of overseeing the activities of the agencies, which, it is argued, are simply performing, as delegates, essential congressional activities. The clash between these two points of view came before the Supreme Court in 1983 in the case of *Immigration and Naturalization Service* v. *Chadha.*

The Chadha case involved the constitutionality of a section of the Immigration Act, which authorizes the attorney general, part of the executive branch of the federal government, to administer most matters regarding the deportation of aliens. One provision of this statute allows the attorney general to suspend the deportation of an alien otherwise deportable if it can be shown that he or she has good moral character, has been in the U.S. continuously for seven years, and would suffer extreme hardship if deported. This provision, however, was made subject to a legislative veto by either house of Congress. Jagdish Rai Chadha, a native of Kenya, had come to the U.S. lawfully as a student in 1966 but had overstayed his visa. When deportation proceedings were started against him, he admitted his deportability but asked the attorney general to suspend action under the exception provided in the law. The attorney general acceded to this request. The House of Representatives, however, vetoed this action on the ground that Chadha did not meet the hardship requirement. Subsequently, Chadha was ordered deported. He appealed this decision ultimately to the U.S. Supreme Court, contending that any legislative veto is unconstitutional. In a sweeping decision of great importance to the structure of U.S. government, the Supreme Court agreed with his contention.

The court pointed out that, absent the veto provision in the immigration statute, neither the House of Representatives nor the Senate—nor both acting together—could require the attorney general to deport an alien once he, in the exercise of legislatively delegated authority, had determined that the alien was entitled to remain in the U.S. This result could be achieved, if at all, only by new legislation. "Disagreement with the Attorney General's decision on Chadha's deportation . . . no less than Congress' original choice to delegate to the Attorney General the authority to make that decision, involves determinations of policy that Congress can implement in only one way: bicameral passage followed by presentment to the President." This does not mean, of course, that Congress has no power to oversee the activities of its agencies. "Beyond the obvious fact that Congress ultimately controls administrative agencies in the legislation that creates them, other means of control, such as durational limits on authorizations and formal reporting requirements, lie well within Congress' constitutional power."

ABORTION. In 1973 the Supreme Court, in a landmark decision, handed down in *Roe* v. *Wade,* held that the constitutionally guaranteed right of privacy encompasses a woman's right to terminate her pregnancy. A number of states, though paying lip service to this decision, attempted to define the circumstances under which abortions may be performed. States justified these attempts on grounds of their interest in maternal health, whereas others viewed them as efforts to overturn the effect of *Roe* v. *Wade.* These differences of opinion gave rise to three cases reviewed by the Supreme Court in 1983.

In *City of Akron* v. *Akron Center for Reproductive Health, Inc.,* the court found unconstitutional an ordinance passed by the city of Akron, Ohio, that required all abortions after the first trimester to be performed in a hospital; prohibited a physician from performing an abortion on an unmarried minor under age 15 unless the doctor obtained the consent of one of her parents or a court order; required the attending physician to inform the

WIDE WORLD

Former television news anchor Christine Craft won a half-million dollar verdict from her former employers on grounds of fraud involving sexual discrimination. A federal judge later overturned the verdict and ordered a new trial.

patient of the status of her pregnancy, the development of the fetus, the date of possible viability, the physical and emotional complications that might result from an abortion, and the availability of agencies to provide information regarding adoption; prohibited a physician from performing an abortion for 24 hours after the patient signed a consent form; and required disposal of the fetal remains to be done in a humane and sanitary way. The court found that these requirements chilled the exercise of a constitutional right.

In reaffirming *Roe* v. *Wade,* the court restated its position that a state does have a legitimate interest in protecting the potentiality of human life. It asserted, however, that this interest becomes compelling only at viability, the point at which the fetus has the capability of meaningful life outside the body of the mother. When this point is reached, the state may impose any regulation, including an absolute proscription on abortions. Prior to this point, and throughout the pregnancy, the state does have an interest in the mother's health, but it may not, through the guise of health regulation, place a significant burden on the woman's access to abortion.

Using the same analysis, the court held, in *Planned Parenthood Association of Kansas City* v. *Ashcroft,* that a Missouri statute requiring that abortions after 12 weeks of pregnancy be performed in a hospital was unconstitutional. In *Simopoulos* v. *Virgina,* however, it sustained the constitutionality of a Virginia statute that made it unlawful to perform an abortion during the second trimester outside a licensed hospital, because the statute defined "hospital" broadly to include outpatient clinics and other facilities. The court found that this law was not designed to chill access to abortions by encumbering them with the high costs associated with "hospital care."

In Spain the Cabinet adopted a bill to permit abortions in situations where the mother had been

WIDE WORLD

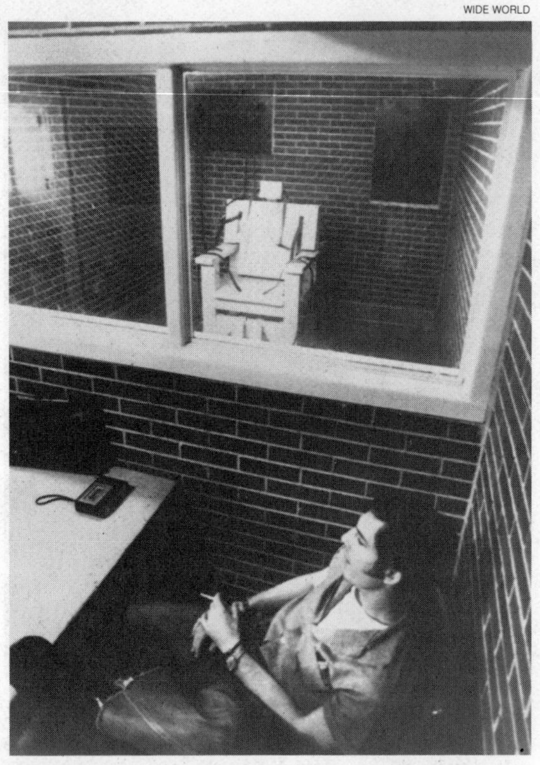

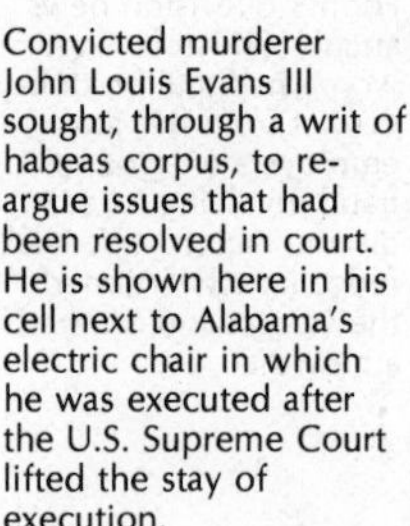

Convicted murderer John Louis Evans III sought, through a writ of habeas corpus, to re-argue issues that had been resolved in court. He is shown here in his cell next to Alabama's electric chair in which he was executed after the U.S. Supreme Court lifted the stay of execution.

raped, delivery would impair her health, or the likelihood that the child would be impaired was clear. In Switzerland, on the other hand, the government issued a counterproposal to a popular initiative which, if accepted, would constitutionally guarantee the protection of life. In the counterproposal, "life" was defined as beginning with conception, and under it no abortion would be permitted. The counterproposal would also affect laws dealing with assisting suicide and the death penalty (which remained as a military penalty that could be imposed in wartime).

Sovereign Immunity. In *Verlinden* v. *Central Bank of Nigeria,* the U.S. Supreme Court sustained the validity of the Foreign Sovereign Immunities Act. This decision was of extreme importance to commercial interests throughout the world. The case involved an action by a Dutch corporation against Nigeria for breach of a letter of credit. The Nigerian government had ordered cement from the Dutch company, and payment was guaranteed by a letter of credit issued by Nigeria's central bank. A New York bank had transmitted the letter from the Nigerian bank to the Dutch corporation, but the New York bank was not liable on it. Subsequently, the Dutch corporation alleged that the Nigerian bank, an instrumentality of the Nigerian government, had breached its agreement, and suit was brought in a federal court in New York. The Nigerian government denied the jurisdiction of this court, but the Dutch corporation countered that jurisdiction was conferred by the Foreign Sovereign Immunities Act of 1976. The Nigerian government replied that Congress had no authority to enact such a statute, which bound it to try a case in a foreign tribunal, but the Supreme Court held that Congress did have this authority.

In *Tracomin S.A.* v. *Sudan Oil Seeds Co. Ltd.*, the English Commercial Court handed down a decision of almost equal importance to the world commercial community, given the propensity of international traders to insert clauses in their contracts calling for arbitration in London. The court held that an English court has jurisdiction to restrain a party to an English arbitration agreement from proceeding in a foreign court. The decision emphasized, however, that this restraint must be exercised with caution. This caveat caused some confusion in commercial circles, making the effect of *Tracomin* somewhat uncertain.

Death Penalty. In the U.S. procedural due process under the Constitution makes it difficult to implement the death penalty because the defendant may appeal and then reappeal the basic decision and death sentence over and over again. In 1983, perhaps for the first time, the U.S. Supreme Court showed impatience with this practice. In *Alabama* v. *Evans,* the defendant, who had been sentenced to death for murder, sought through a writ of habeas corpus to litigate several issues that had been conclusively resolved in prior proceedings and to introduce an issue never before raised. On the basis of these matters, a federal district court had stayed the execution. The State of Alabama moved to vacate this stay order, and the Supreme Court agreed that it should be lifted, permitting the state to proceed with the execution.

In a parallel procedural development, the European Court of Human Rights held, in *Zimmerman and Steiner* v. *Switzerland,* that courts are duty bound to act within a "reasonable time." The case involved an action for compensation for nuisance allegedly caused by the Zürich airport. The Federal Court of Switzerland took more than three and a half years to deliver judgment, and the delay was not attributable to the applicants. Under this circumstance, the European Court held that the applicant was entitled to prevail regardless of the merits of the dispute.

In an important substantive development concerning the death penalty, the Committee of Ministers of the Council of Europe adopted the sixth protocol to the European Convention on Human Rights. This protocol will require all members to abolish the death penalty, with no "derogation or reservation" allowed. Research indicated that, of the Council of Europe members, ten had already abolished the death penalty in all situations, five had abolished it except for certain offenses committed by military personnel in wartime, five retained it for serious offenses (but rarely used it), and one, Turkey, retained it for many offenses and used it regularly. (WILLIAM D. HAWKLAND)

International Law. Breaches of world peace became more widespread and virulent during 1983, with major instances of war, intervention, civil war, and border violations involving complex issues of international law. The time seemed ripe for scholars to revive the study of the international law of war, which had been largely excluded from the teaching of international law in recent decades.

The one classical war—between Iraq and Iran—which continued in a virtual stalemate, gave rise to serious allegations by the International Committee of the Red Cross of ill-treatment of prisoners of war and other violations of the Geneva conventions by both belligerents. More difficult legal problems were raised by intervention. In October the U.S., backed by several Caribbean states, invaded the independent Caribbean island of Grenada, ousted the governing regime (which had just taken power by force and executed the former prime minister), and took over military control of the island. At first it was thought that the invasion was a purely external event, but it later appeared that the governor-general of Grenada had requested the intervention in order to remove the unlawful regime. This led to a prolonged debate among international and constitutional lawyers over the precise legal nature of the action, the constitutional status of the governor-general both before and after the invasion, the implications of the nonintervention provision of Art. 2(4) of the UN Charter, and even over the legal nature of international law itself.

The Israeli intervention in Lebanon officially ended with the signing on May 17 of the agreement on withdrawal of Israeli troops. It was replaced, however, by an exceedingly complex situation reminiscent of Germany during the Thirty Years' War. The country was controlled partly by Israel and Israeli troops and partly by Syria and Syrian troops, with the central area, including Beirut, controlled by the official Lebanese government and the Lebanese Army. Also present were an international peacekeeping force (mainly U.S., British, French, and Italian), invited in by the Lebanese government, and a UN peacekeeping force in the south (UNIFIL), whose mandate was renewed by the Security Council until April 1984, while pockets within the country were dominated by quasi-independent military formations. In such circumstances it became difficult to distinguish intervention from civil war and both from anarchy, and the rules of international law seemed inadequate to deal with the situation.

The significance of border violations lay in their number and frequency, the variety of states concerned, and the evidence they gave of a spreading breakdown in the moral inhibition against unilateral state violence. The violation that attracted the most attention was that by a South Korean civil airliner flying through Soviet airspace in a highly sensitive area over the Kamchatka Peninsula. It was shot down apparently without warning by a Soviet military plane just as it was about to enter Japanese airspace, and all aboard were killed. The U.S.S.R. claimed that the airliner was a U.S. spy plane, but the overreaction was never adequately explained. Civil litigation was started in the U.S. courts, but international claims for violation of the 1944 Chicago Convention on International Civil Aviation were unlikely.

Violation of sea space by Soviet submarines, which had been reported in previous years, continued in 1983. In April a Swedish government report confirmed that in the previous year there had been some 40 violations of Swedish territorial waters by the Soviet Union, one incident involving six submarines. Further sightings took place during the year, and in May the Norwegian Navy fired antisubmarine missiles and depth charges at a suspected submarine in Hardanger Fjord. No wreckage was ever found, however, by either Sweden or Norway.

Border disputes in Africa included an armed conflict between Chad and Nigeria over the borderline through Lake Chad. An agreement was signed to reopen the frontier and appoint a mixed commission to settle the line, but sporadic fighting continued. Mali and Niger agreed to set up a commission to mark out their communal border. Mali and Upper Volta submitted their dispute on delimitation of part of their land frontier to the International Court of Justice (ICJ). The UN secretary-general was accepted as mediator in the border dispute between Guyana and Venezuela. Talks between the U.K., Guatemala, and Belize over recognition of Belize broke down in January, however. The Beagle Channel dispute between Argentina and Chile continued, but the area was quiet except for one incident, when the Argentine Navy intercepted a Brazilian Antarctic research ship as it tried to cross the channel and insisted that it take on an Argentine pilot. The master refused to comply and took a different course.

More positive events included the signing in May of an agreement on the 1,300-km (800-mi) desert border separating Algeria and Mali. The 3,000-km (1,860-mi) border between China and the U.S.S.R. in central Asia was reopened in November for trade exchanges. The Cocos Islands asked the Australian government to organize an "act of self-determination" under UN auspices. Brunei was granted full independence effective from midnight Jan. 1, 1984. The U.K. confirmed that it did not recognize any authorities as constituting the governments of Lithuania, Latvia, or Estonia (since the annexation by the U.S.S.R. in 1940), nor did it recognize de jure their incorporation into the Soviet Union. The unilateral declaration of independence by the Turkish area of Cyprus in November was recognized only by Turkey. Talks between China and the U.K. over the future of Hong Kong when the lease on the New Territories expired in 1997 were held throughout the year, but without any signs of agreement.

REGIONAL AGREEMENTS. The Closer Economic Relations agreement to create a free trade area between New Zealand and Australia was signed in December 1982 and came into force on Jan. 1, 1983. The Benelux countries agreed in October to simplify border formalities so that goods moving among them would need only one document to cover all aspects of interstate trade. Also in October, a treaty was signed in Libreville, Gabon, creating an Economic Community of the States of Central Africa comprising Cameroon, Central African Republic, Congo, Gabon, Burundi, Rwanda, Zaire, Chad, Equatorial Guinea, and São Tomé and Príncipe; Angola refrained from signing because of its economic circumstances. The member states of the Caribbean Community signed a treaty in July setting up an Eastern Caribbean Development Bank. The member states of the Andean Pact resolved to undertake a revision of the pact with a view to greater economic integration, and the Andean Judicial Tribunal became functional following ratification of its constituent treaty by Venezuela. A move in the UN to have Antarctica declared the common heritage of mankind and made available to all states was opposed by the 14 full and 12 associate members of the Antarctic Treaty, which makes participation in Antarctic affairs dependent on the establishment of a research station.

MARITIME AFFAIRS. In the dispute between Libya and Malta over delimitation of the continental shelf, currently before the ICJ, memorials were filed in April, and in October Italy applied to intervene. An agreement was signed in October between Denmark and Sweden settling their continental shelf boundary as the midline between their respective mainlands, disregarding small uninhabited islands. This ended a dispute that arose in the summer when Denmark authorized test borings 15 km (9 mi) off the Swedish coast, claiming rights appurtenant to its midline islands. The 1982 agreement between France and the U.K. on the continental shelf in the English Channel came into force in February 1983. The archives of their arbitration were deposited in Geneva and would remain secret until there was agreement to the contrary.

In the Gulf of Maine case between the U.S. and Canada, the ICJ required replies to be filed by December. The 1979 agreement between Greece and Italy on pollution in the Ionian Sea came into force in February 1983, as did the 1980 treaty on pollution of the Mediterranean. A treaty on protection of the Caribbean Sea was negotiated in March 1983. The U.S. declared a full 200-mi exclusive economic zone to cover not only fisheries but all economic exploitation (including deep-sea mining). The major maritime countries, including the U.S. and the U.K., still refused to sign the UN Convention on the Law of the Sea because of its seabed provisions. (*See* Sidebar.)

GENERAL. Extraterritorial jurisdiction, particularly as exercised by the U.S. courts, continued to cause concern. This was fueled by a revision of the Export Administration Act and a sharpening of U.S. controls over the export of strategic equipment to Eastern Europe. The confirmation, in *Container Corp. of America* v. *Franchise Tax Board*, of the principle of unitary taxation of multinational companies also led to protests by the U.K. government. On the other hand, an attempt was made by the U.K. government, invoking the Protection of Trading Interests Act, to block antitrust proceedings brought in the U.S. by the liquidator of Laker Airways Ltd., a Jersey company, against two major British airlines as well as against U.S. and European companies. A gentlemanly but tough dialogue then ensued at a distance between the courts in the two countries, with the English Court of Appeal ordering Laker to cease its U.S. proceedings and the U.S. District Court appointing an amicus curiae (friend of the court) to advise it on how to enable the proceedings to continue.

There were some unusual incidents involving diplomats during the year. In London, during the first three weeks after the introduction of wheel clamps to immobilize wrongly parked cars, 77 embassy cars were clamped. The diplomatic corps protested that the action violated the Vienna Convention, and embassy cars were exempted from clamping in the future. In Malta the government ordered ambassadors to ensure that their staff refrain from all contact with members of the opposi-

Law of the Sea: What Did It Really Say?

The Convention on the Law of the Sea, promulgated in 1982 by a UN conference and quickly signed by 117 nations (but not by the U.S. and some 20 other, chiefly industrial, states), has two main parts. The first and less controversial defines the rights of countries to the sea and sets forth rules for its use.

Under the convention, each coastal state has sovereign rights over a 12-mi territorial sea and sovereign rights over natural resources and certain economic activities within a 200-mi exclusive economic zone (EEZ). Ships are allowed innocent passage through the territorial sea, and ships and aircraft are allowed transit passage through straits used for international navigation. Coastal states also have sovereign rights regarding exploration and exploitation of the continental shelf (200 mi from shore and in some cases farther).

Provision is made for delimitation of the territorial sea, EEZ, and continental shelf of archipelagic states and for access to the sea for landlocked nations. Other sections cover such matters as freedom of scientific research, rights and duties of states regarding environmental protection and the management of living resources, and the peaceful settlement of disputes.

The second and more controversial part of the convention governs access to seabed resources, notably minerals. Its aim is to manage the seabed as a "common heritage of mankind" while providing a fair return to states and consortia investing in seabed technology, ensuring reasonable prices, and protecting the interests of land-based mineral producers.

To accomplish this, the convention sets up a new layer of international bureaucracy, headed by the International Sea-Bed Authority (ISBA). Its policies are to be set by an Assembly of all signatory states and executed by a Council of 36 states, half chosen on the basis of geography and half on the basis of interest. Rules and procedures for the system are to be drafted by a Preparatory Commission.

The ISBA would contract with states or firms wishing to conduct exploration or mining activities, but it would also conduct its own operations through an agency called the Enterprise, which would have the right to acquire the technology of any other contractor on commercial terms. When a state or firm put up a promising area to the ISBA, the Authority would let a contract for half of it, while the rest would be reserved for the Enterprise or for less developed countries. To protect the rights of consortia that had already begun seabed exploration, a resolution was adopted virtually guaranteeing them contracts. (DAPHNE DAUME)

Law Enforcement:
see Crime and Law Enforcement

Lawn Bowls:
see Bowling

Lawn Tennis:
see Tennis

tion Nationalist Party. The diplomatic corps protested, and the ban was softened to apply only to contacts designed to suggest that the Nationalist Party might be an alternative government. Even more unusual was the consequence of a forced landing by a U.K. RAF Harrier jump jet on the deck of a Spanish cargo vessel. The owners refused to allow the aircraft to be surrendered until salvage terms had been agreed on, but they were ordered to release it by a Spanish maritime court since, as the property of a foreign state, it could not be held while a salvage dispute continued.

(NEVILLE MARCH HUNNINGS)

See also Crime and Law Enforcement; United Nations.

Lebanon

A republic of the Middle East, Lebanon is bounded by Syria, Israel, and the Mediterranean Sea. Area: 10,230 sq km (3,950 sq mi). Pop. (1983 est.): 3,395,000. Cap. and largest city: Beirut (metro. pop., 1975 est., 1,172,000). The populations of both Lebanon and its capital city, Beirut, are thought to have declined since the outbreak of civil war in 1974, but reliable figures are not available. Language: Arabic (official), French, Armenian, and Kurdish. Religion: available estimates show Christians comprising variously from 40 to 55% of the population and Muslims from 45 to 60%; there is a Druze minority. President in 1983, Amin Gemayel; prime minister, Shafiq al-Wazzan.

Pres. Amin Gemayel invited ten political leaders to attend national reconciliation talks, which started in Geneva on Oct. 31, 1983. The talks were held against the backdrop of Lebanon's continued occupation by Israeli and Syrian forces, carnage in Beirut as suicide bombers attacked the international peacekeeping force, and the siege of Palestine Liberation Organization (PLO) chairman Yasir Arafat (*see* BIOGRAPHIES) and 5,000 supporters in the northern city of Tripoli.

The four leading personalities at the Geneva talks were President Gemayel and his father, Pierre Gemayel, leader of the Christian Phalange Party, Druze leader Walid Jumblatt (*see* BIOGRAPHIES), and Nabih Berri, the Shi'ah Muslim leader. Other participants included Suleiman Franjieh, leader of the Maronite Christians in the north, Rashid Karami, leader of the northern Sunni Muslims, and former president Camille Chamoun. Agreement was reached on a definition of Lebanon as "sovereign, free, independent, and united," with boundaries laid down by its constitution. The biggest dilemma facing the talks, however, was the question of what should replace the 1943 National Pact, which ensured a dominant role for Lebanon's Christian communities. With Muslims now a majority of the population, the old system could not be expected to last. Lebanon faced the possibility of disintegration into a number of ministates unless agreement could be reached on a structure for secular government. Both Israel and Syria were still occupying about 40% of the country; external powers were thus of considerable importance to Lebanon's future.

In January President Gemayel called for Arab countries to produce a "Marshall Plan" arrangement to rebuild Lebanon. In a speech on Dec. 31, 1982, he claimed that Israel's invasion in June 1982

UPI

A truck loaded with explosives crashed into an Israeli military headquarters in Tyre on November 4, killing 60 persons.

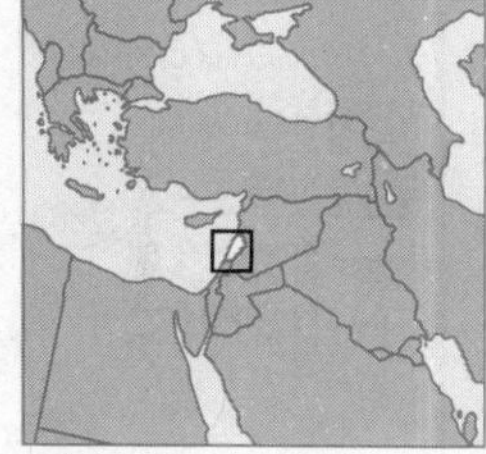

Lebanon

FRANKLIN—SYGMA

French soldiers, part of the international peacekeeping force in Lebanon, removed the 58 killed and dozens wounded by a suicide truck bombing at their Beirut headquarters. Instants before, a similar explosion tore through a U.S. Marines installation nearby.

AN NAHAR—GAMMA/LIAISON

U.S. Marines removed dead and wounded from their devastated quarters at Beirut's International Airport after a truck filled with explosives burst into the compound and exploded. Deaths numbered 241.

The map shows where the larger religious groups are concentrated in Lebanon. Syrian and Israeli occupation of the country has ignited renewed fighting among the groups. In addition to the groups shown, substantial numbers of minorities (Palestinians of various persuasions and such Christian bodies as Greek Orthodox, Melchites, Armenians, and Protestants) also have a stake in Lebanon's future.

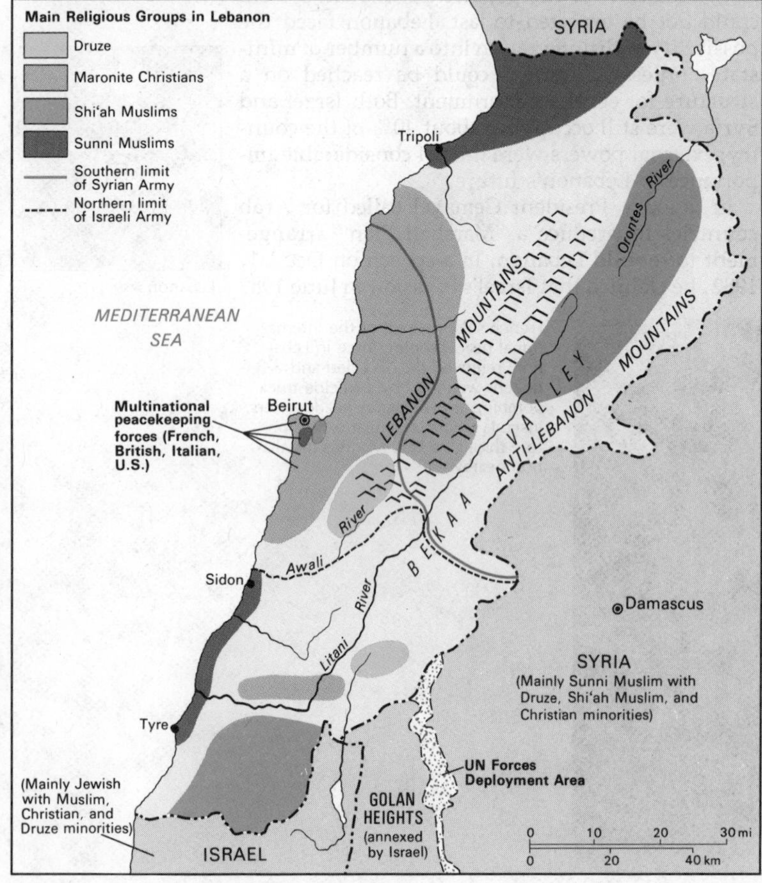

had cost Lebanon $2.5 billion in war damage. Intense efforts were made in the early months of 1983 to secure backing for reconstruction, but the president's efforts were hampered by continuing political fragmentation. In March there were reports that Druze militia forces were massing in the Shuf Mountains. In April Israel was reported to be reinforcing its positions with the aim of holding all the ground south of a line from Damour on the west coast to Khirbet Rouha in the Bekaa Valley. On May 5 Beirut was shelled from villages controlled by Syria, and fighting between Christians and Druze was reported in the Shuf.

On May 17 Israel and Lebanon signed an accord detailing procedures for an Israeli withdrawal from Lebanon and the development of bilateral relations. However, Israel stressed that it would not implement the agreement unless Syria agreed to leave, and this Syria refused to do. Jumblatt emerged as the leading opponent of the accord. He was instrumental in establishing an opposition group called the National Salvation Front, and Lebanon was again plunged into civil war. The U.S. aimed to pressure Syria into leaving Lebanon, but the attempt collapsed on July 7 after a fruitless visit to Damascus by U.S. Secretary of State George Shultz. On July 20 President Gemayel began a visit to the U.S. against a background of mounting violence. On the same day, Israel announced plans for a unilateral withdrawal to the Awali River.

In early August Druze militiamen briefly kidnapped three Cabinet ministers who had attempted to negotiate an end to shelling in the Shuf Mountains. The area had been peaceful in the 1975–76 civil war, but had erupted into violence after the 1982 Israeli invasion. Druze militia were in action again in August shelling the Beirut airport. The situation worsened on August 29–30 after the deaths of two U.S. Marines and four French military personnel during clashes between the Lebanese Army and Druze and Shiʿah militia in Beirut. The French sent Super Étendard aircraft on reconnaissance flights over Druze positions.

On September 3–4 Israel finally carried out its much deferred pullback from the Shuf, and Lebanese forces moved into the mountains. Prominent in the peace moves at this stage was the Saudi Arabian negotiator, Prince Bandar ibn Sultan, but his transfer to the Saudi embassy in Washington on September 26 appeared to end the possibility of Arab mediation. A cease-fire on September 26 was by one reckoning the 179th since the start of the Lebanese civil war in 1975. Also on September 26, Prime Minister Shafiq al-Wazzan submitted his resignation in order to clear the way for a national reconciliation government.

The Geneva talks themselves were overshadowed by the deaths on October 23 of 239 U.S. servicemen (two more died in December) and 58 French soldiers in separate suicide bomb attacks. The attacks symbolized the extent to which bombings had become a way of life in Beirut; more than

LEBANON

Education. (1980–81) Primary, pupils 405,402, teachers 22,646; secondary, pupils 254,444, teachers 21,344; vocational, pupils 31,203, teachers (1979–80) 2,956; teacher training, students 1,663, teachers 392; higher, students (1979–80) 85,087, teaching staff (1972–73) 2,313.

Finance. Monetary unit: Lebanese pound, with (Sept. 20, 1983) a free rate of L£4.90 to U.S. $1 (L£7.38 = £1 sterling). Gold and foreign exchange (June 1983) U.S. $2,311,000,000. Budget (1982 est.) balanced at L£5,945 million.

Foreign Trade. (1982) Imports (f.o.b.) *c.* L£14,658 million; exports *c.* L£2,803 million. Import sources: Italy *c.* 15%; France *c.* 10%; U.S. *c.* 9%; West Germany *c.* 8%; Saudi Arabia *c.* 6%; Switzerland *c.* 6%; Romania *c.* 6%. Export destinations: Saudi Arabia *c.* 33%; Kuwait *c.* 8%; Syria *c.* 8%; Jordan *c.* 6%; United Arab Emirates 5%. Main exports (1977): financial paper 22%; fruit and vegetables 11%; chemicals 10%; machinery 9%; metals 7%; textiles and clothing 6%; cement 5%.

Transport and Communications. Roads (1982) 7,000 km. Motor vehicles in use (1982): passenger 460,400; commercial 21,000. Railways: (1981) 417 km; traffic (1974) 2 million passenger-km, freight 42 million net ton-km. Air traffic (1982): *c.* 968 million passenger-km; freight *c.* 465.2 million net ton-km. Shipping (1982): vessels 100 gross tons and over 240; gross tonnage 368,101. Telephones (Dec. 1978) 231,000. Radio receivers (Dec. 1980) 2 million. Television receivers (Dec. 1980) 750,000.

Agriculture. Production (in 000; metric tons; 1981): potatoes *c.* 147; wheat 28; tomatoes *c.* 76; grapes 150; olives 15; bananas *c.* 20; oranges *c.* 200; lemons 55; apples 65; tobacco 4. Livestock (in 000; 1981): cattle *c.* 60; goats *c.* 445; sheep *c.* 148; chickens *c.* 7,113.

Industry. Production (in 000; metric tons; 1981): cement *c.* 2,390; petroleum products 1,760; electricity (kw-hr) 1,810,000.

50 people died when an explosion ripped through the U.S. embassy in Beirut on April 18. After the attacks there were calls for the peacekeeping force to return home, but the four governments involved—Italy, France, the U.K., and the U.S.—reaffirmed their commitment to remain. A suicide bomb attack on an Israeli military headquarters in Tyre on November 4 killed 60 people. A new cease-fire on December 16 did nothing to stop the wave of terrorist bombings.

Meanwhile, Tripoli was caught in a struggle between PLO factions. PLO dissidents, backed by Syria, overran Arafat's stronghold in the Beddawi refugee camp near Tripoli, forcing him and his followers into the city where they were beseiged for some six weeks. After lengthy negotiations, he and about 4,000 loyalists were evacuated from Tripoli on December 20 by Greek ships flying the UN flag.

In view of the political background, it was surprising that many of Lebanon's public utilities continued to function. Exports, however, were at a low level, estimated in September at only $20 million a month. Inflation was running at 14% in the second half of 1983. A proposal that the crude oil pipeline from Saudi Arabia be shut down threatened to affect the economy severely in 1984.

(JOHN WHELAN)

See also Israel; Middle Eastern Affairs.

Lesotho

Lesotho

A constitutional monarchy of southern Africa and a member of the Commonwealth, Lesotho forms an enclave within the republic of South Africa,

LESOTHO

Education. (1980) Primary, pupils 244,838, teachers (1979) 4,782; secondary, pupils 23,355, teachers (1979) 940; vocational, pupils (1979) 1,140, teachers (1978) 121; higher, students (1978) 1,682, teaching staff (1977) 162.

Finance and Trade. Monetary unit: loti (plural maloti), at par with the South African rand, with (Sept. 20, 1983) a free rate of 1.11 maloti to U.S. $1 (1.67 maloti = £1 sterling). Budget (total; 1982–83 est.): revenue 216 million maloti; expenditure 269 million maloti. Foreign trade (1980): imports 374 million maloti; exports 44.6 million maloti. Import source (1979): South Africa 97%. Export destinations (1979): Switzerland 56%; South Africa 34%. Main exports: diamonds 55%; manufactures 24%; wool 10%; mohair 6%.

Agriculture. Production (in 000; metric tons; 1981): corn *c.* 130; wheat *c.* 25; sorghum 48; dry peas *c.* 5; wool *c.* 2. Livestock (in 000; 1981): cattle *c.* 600; sheep *c.* 1,180; goats *c.* 780.

bordering the Republic of Transkei to the southeast. Area: 30,355 sq km (11,720 sq mi). Pop. (1983 est.): 1,438,000, of which Sotho 99.6%. Cap. and largest city: Maseru (pop., 1980 est., 30,000). Language: English and Southern Sotho (official). Religion (1980): Roman Catholic 43.5%; Lesotho Evangelical Church 29.8%; Anglican 11.5%; other Christian 8%; tribal 6.2%; other 1%. Chief of state in 1983, King Moshoeshoe II; prime minister, Chief Leabua Jonathan.

Events in 1983 were dominated by Lesotho's deteriorating relations with South Africa. In April Chief Leabua Jonathan accused South Africa of armed attacks on his country. During a meeting between the foreign ministers of the two nations, each agreed not to allow his territory to be used as a base for attacks upon the other, but this did not relieve the growing tensions. Clashes took place between the Lesotho security forces and what were described as bandits from South Africa. By September the government was reluctantly obliged to give way to South Africa's demands that certain named members of the African National Congress (ANC), a group in opposition to the government of South Africa, be expelled from Lesotho. In February the Lesotho Liberation Army, an underground opposition group, claimed responsibility for a bomb attack that destroyed a fuel depot in Maseru.

It was a poor year for the economy. The UN Development Program announced a $17 million aid project for the period 1982–86 that emphasized the development of agriculture.

In May Chief Jonathan visited China, North Korea, Yugoslavia, Romania, and Bulgaria. During the year Lesotho broke ties with Taiwan and South Korea.

(GUY ARNOLD)

Liberia

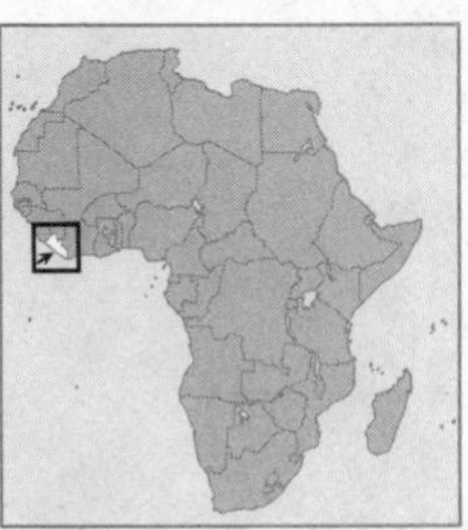

Liberia

A republic on the west coast of Africa, Liberia is bordered by Sierra Leone, Guinea, and Ivory Coast. Area: 99,067 sq km (38,250 sq mi). Pop. (1983 est.): 2,091,000. Cap. and largest city: Monrovia (pop., 1980 est., 243,200). Language: English (official) and tribal dialects. Religion (1980): tribal 43.5%; Christian 35%; Muslim 21.2%; Baha'i 0.3%. Head of state and chairman of the People's Redemption Council in 1983, Gen. Samuel K. Doe.

UPI

Liberian Pres. Samuel K. Doe became the first black African head of state to visit Israel since 1971.

In a bizarre international incident, Liberia closed the border with Sierra Leone for three weeks during February 1983. This resulted from a story in the Sierra Leone press claiming that Gen. Samuel K. Doe, Liberia's head of state, had shot his wife because she had been involved in a plot to poison him.

Doe's much-publicized visit to Israel in August was expected to produce Israeli aid and investment. In October representatives of major Israeli firms visited Liberia to discuss the development of the merchant navy, the road system, and a national airline. The rapprochement with Israel, however, was expected to cost Liberia Arab aid.

In general the economic picture remained gloomy. One encouraging development was a slight upturn early in 1983 in the demand for rubber, Liberia's second-largest foreign-exchange earner. The long-term aim of achieving self-sufficiency in rice production was brought no closer. There was increased unemployment in the iron-ore industry as production was cut back. In an effort to reduce the country's fuel bill, which accounted for 51% of imports, the search for offshore deposits of petroleum continued.

In January all government and public corporation salaries were cut by 16–25%. Doe blamed corruption among officials for the recent decline in foreign investment in Liberia. In the 1983–84 budget, expenditure was reduced to $387 million from the previous year's $420 million, reflecting the continuing economic decline. Doe reshuffled the Cabinet in October. (GUY ARNOLD)

LIBERIA

Education. (1980) Primary, pupils 227,431, teachers 9,099; secondary, pupils 51,666, teachers 1,129; vocational, pupils 2,322, teachers (1976) 63; teacher training, students 635, teachers (1979) 17; higher, students (1979) 3,789, teaching staff (1978) c. 190.

Finance. Monetary unit: Liberian dollar, at par with the U.S. dollar, with a free rate (Sept. 20, 1983) of L$1.51 = £1 sterling. Budget (1980–81 actual): revenue L$219 million; expenditure L$228 million.

Foreign Trade. (1981) Imports L$477,420,000; exports L$531,420,000. Import sources: U.S. 29%; Saudi Arabia 19%; West Germany 10%; The Netherlands 8%; U.K. 5%; Japan 5%. Export destinations: West Germany 25%; U.S. 23%; Italy 13%; France 10%; Belgium-Luxembourg 5%; The Netherlands 5%. Main exports: iron ore 62%; rubber 17%; timber 7%.

Transport and Communications. Roads (1981) 10,087 km. Motor vehicles in use (1980): passenger c. 22,000; commercial c. 20,000. Railways (1981) 490 km. Shipping (1982): merchant vessels 100 gross tons and over 2,189 (mostly owned by U.S. and other foreign interests); gross tonnage 70,718,439. Telephones (Jan. 1980) 7,740. Radio receivers (Dec. 1980) 320,000. Television receivers (Dec. 1980) 21,000.

Agriculture. Production (in 000; metric tons; 1982): rice c. 268; cassava (1981) c. 315; bananas c. 75; palm kernels 8; palm oil c. 30; rubber c. 70; cocoa c. 5; coffee c. 10; timber (cu m; 1981) c. 5,084. Livestock (in 000; 1981): cattle c. 40; sheep c. 210; goats c. 210; pigs c. 107.

Industry. Production (in 000; metric tons; 1981): iron ore (68% metal content) 19,700; petroleum products 605; cement 150; diamonds (metric carats) 336; gold (troy oz) 17; electricity (kw-hr) c. 1,100,000.

Libraries

The effects of recession on libraries all over the world were apparent in 1983. For the past few years the acquisition of materials had been limited or, in some countries, nonexistent. In the industrialized countries the damage was not so great, because rich collections already existed and few libraries actually terminated acquisitions. Even where this happened, it was only for a short period, and some of the losses were made up (although this was not always easy because of the short runs currently being published). Even where purchases were limited, the results differed widely. Surveys undertaken by the Centre for Library and Information Management in England indicated that uneven "cuts" sometimes took place for quite extraneous reasons, such as policy changes vis-à-vis the central government and local administration.

Limitation of resources led to further consideration of the roles of different types of libraries. The aims and objectives of large reference libraries had been under scrutiny in Britain, while industrial libraries everywhere were threatened as companies were forced to retrench. More and more libraries were turning to computerization, for "housekeeping" services in the hope of economizing on staff and—more important in the long term—for information retrieval. There was growing concern over the needs of minority groups, particularly as regards the provision of additional services in order to broaden the appeal of libraries. However, lack of resources led to reductions in hours and in some countries, such as Finland, to a great increase in interlibrary loans. Despite the prevailing austerity, New Zealand opened two new library buildings, at Dunedin and Christchurch.

In many countries libraries were concerned about their mission, not merely as collections of books and other materials but as providers of information in an "information society." In South Korea the National Science Foundation commissioned a study by the Korea Advanced Institute of Science and Technology on the *Long-term Prospect*

WIDE WORLD

William W. Moss, chief archivist of the John F. Kennedy Presidential Library in Boston, released to the press White House recordings of conversations between Kennedy and a number of public figures during the 1962 Cuban missile crisis.

of the Information Society. This study urged an active governmental role in the integration of existing information resources and in raising public awareness of the information society. The Conference of Southeast Asian Librarians met during May–June with the theme "The Library in the Information Revolution," while in Africa the Standing Conference of Eastern, Central, and Southern African Librarians was held in Malawi in August with the theme "Libraries for National Development." Also in August, the International Documentation Federation held its conference in Hong Kong and the International Federation of Library Associations met in Montreal.

Libraries in less developed countries were most seriously affected by cutbacks. This was especially true of countries dependent on hard currency for the purchase of books and periodicals. With the deepening recession, periodical subscriptions all but ceased in some countries (Sierra Leone was an example), except for special-subject libraries considered essential to economic development or to the administration. Educational library services fared badly, since libraries were not seen as essential to the educational process, but recreational and general collections for the public at large suffered most. This was partly because librarians did not respond sufficiently to the conditions within largely illiterate societies. However, the belief that books were unwanted and unread in less developed countries was belied by the experience of countries like Ghana and Singapore, where children particularly ransacked the shelves for available books. (P. HAVARD-WILLIAMS)

In the U.S. a survey contracted by the federal Department of Education and made public in June showed that 307,600 library workers were employed in 1982. Of these, 139,000 were considered librarians, holding 136,000 full-time-equivalent positions in nearly 40,000 libraries (48% in school libraries, 23% in public, 15% in academic, and 14% in special). About 60% of the librarians held master's degrees in library science. In October the U.S. Office of Personnel Management defended its two-year effort to remove the master's degree as a requirement for appointment as a federal librarian. Professional library associations opposed this and related OPM proposals. Meanwhile, the profession itself was reexamining the competencies needed to provide service in the "information age."

According to the 1983 report of the University of Illinois Library Research Center, public library use rose 3% to a record 1,070,000,000 items circulated in 1982. The centre noted that public library circulation had grown more than twice as fast as the U.S. population over the past four decades. Congressional appropriations for public library services ($65 million) and interlibrary cooperation ($15 million) in fiscal year 1984 represented record highs. Although $50 million in emergency job funding became available in 1983 for public library construction, Congress made no provision for public library construction programs or college library resource funding in fiscal 1984. Aid to school libraries was at the 1983 level. Gains in state funding of public libraries included $16 million in Pennsylvania (up 14%), $7.8 million in North Carolina (up 63%), and $6 million earmarked for needy libraries in California.

Censorship pressures on school libraries showed no signs of abating, though the year began with the return of nine banned books to the shelves of the Island Trees, N.Y., high school library following a Supreme Court ruling that students could sue school boards for removing titles. One of the most controversial children's titles of the year was Margot Zemach's *Jake and Honeybunch Go to Heaven,* which some librarians felt perpetuated black stereotyping.

Two national conferences in September reflected major concerns of libraries. At Oberlin (Ohio) College, where convicted book thief James Shinn was apprehended in 1981, librarians addressed means to stop runaway book theft. In Baltimore, Md., participants took stock of the enormous growth of library online services and microcomputer applications at a conference sponsored by a division of the American Library Association. The ALA annual conference in Los Angeles drew 11,005 delegates. (ARTHUR PLOTNIK)

[441.C.2.d; 613.D.1.a; 735.H]

Libya

A socialist country on the north coast of Africa, Libya is bounded by the Mediterranean Sea, Egypt, the Sudan, Tunisia, Algeria, Niger, and Chad. Area: 1,749,000 sq km (675,000 sq mi). Pop.

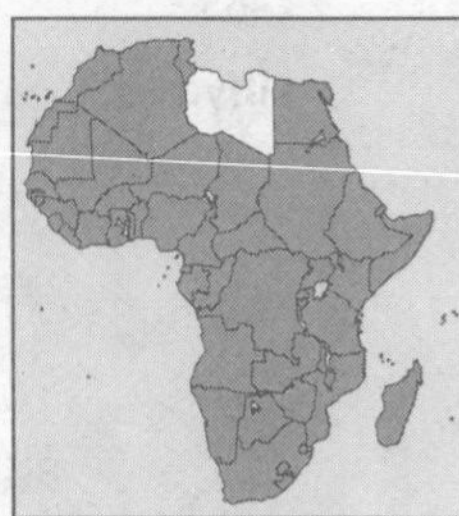

Libya

(1983 est.): 3,498,000. Cap. and largest city: Tripoli (pop., 1981 est., 858,500). Language: Arabic. Religion: predominantly Muslim. Chief of state in 1983, Col. Muammar al-Qaddafi; secretary-general of the General People's Committee (premier), Jadallah Azzuz at-Talhi.

Libya entered 1983 in poor shape economically, with insufficient oil revenue to meet planned current and development expenditure. Though oil output was running at more than double the 1982 low of 500,000 bbl a day, its value was eroded by the fall in crude-oil prices. In 1983 Libya had to manage on revenue estimated at 50–60% of the 1981 level of $23 billion.

Libya's economic tribulations appeared to have an effect on the international posture adopted by the chief of state, Col. Muammar al-Qaddafi (*see* BIOGRAPHIES), during the months up to July. Extraordinarily cordial visits were made to the leaders of Arab states who until 1983 had been singled out by the Libyan leader for severe and unambiguous criticism. In July he visited King Hassan II of Morocco for the first time in 14 years and made concessions on the Western Sahara issue. The previous month he had called on King Hussein of Jordan and visited the Gulf emirates, Saudi Arabia, and Yemen (San'a').

Ostensibly the discussions were aimed at mobilizing all Arabs against Israel. The visits were, however, also very timely with respect to the renewed civil war in Chad and the anticipated confrontation with the U.S. Navy in the Gulf of Sidra, which had become something of an annual event since the 1981 aerial clash. In February the U.S. sent four AWACS (airborne warning and control systems) planes to Egypt when it feared that the Libyans were planning an invasion of Sudan.

The war in Chad involved very few troops on either side, but it attracted world press coverage because of the involvement of Libya, France, and the U.S. The latter, apparently anxious to teach Qaddafi a lesson, sent two AWACS planes to Sudan in early August. It was claimed—prematurely—that they were to assist French troops sent to support the forces of Pres. Hissen Habré of Chad. French and U.S. interest in Chad followed the capture of Faya-Largeau and Abéché by the Libyan-backed forces of Goukouni Oueddei, the country's former president. Libyan air support was crucial in these successes, but though Habré's government claimed that Libyan troops were involved in the fighting, only Libyan-trained Sudanese and Chadian ground troops and a solitary Libyan pilot were captured at that time.

An unwilling Pres. François Mitterrand sent French troops to halt the Goukouni offensive on August 9, at the same time signaling to the U.S. that the AWACS were provocative and unnecessary. The positions taken up by the French forces effectively partitioned Chad, and it was suggested that this maneuver formalized a tacit understanding between Tripoli and Paris, stimulated by the substantial Franco-Libyan trade in oil and weapons. The understanding was complex in that Libyan pilots were being trained in France at the same time that French contingents were facing Goukouni's Libyan-armed troops in northern Chad.

LIBYA

Education. (1980–81) Primary, pupils 674,960, teachers 34,557; secondary, pupils 272,139, teachers 20,699; vocational (1981–82), pupils 16,900, teachers 1,004; teacher training, students 27,800, teachers 2,113; higher, students (1981–82) 25,700, teaching staff (1977–78) 1,340.

Finance. Monetary unit: Libyan dinar, with (Sept. 20, 1983) a par value of 0.296 dinar to U.S. $1 (free rate of 0.446 dinar = £1 sterling). Gold and other reserves (June 1983) U.S. $6,471,000,000. Budget (administrative; 1982 est.) balanced at 1,255,000,000 dinars. Gross domestic product (1981) 8,979,000,000 dinars. Money supply (March 1982) 3,448,400,000 dinars.

Foreign Trade. (1982) Imports (f.o.b.) c. 2,143,000,000 dinars; exports 4,129,300,000 dinars. Import sources (1981): Italy 30%; West Germany 11%; Japan 8%; U.K. 7%; France 6%; U.S. 6%. Export destinations (1981): U.S. 27%; Italy 24%; West Germany 10%; Spain 7%; Turkey 5%; Greece 5%. Main export: crude oil 99.97%.

Transport and Communications. Roads (1977) 14,116 km. Motor vehicles in use (1980): passenger c. 367,400; commercial (including buses) c. 278,900. Air traffic (1982): c. 1,473,000,000 passenger-km; freight c. 5.5 million net ton-km. Shipping (1982): vessels 100 gross tons and over 108; gross tonnage 912,024. Shipping traffic (1980): goods loaded 81.9 million metric tons, unloaded 6.5 million metric tons. Telephones (Dec. 1977) 141,700. Radio licenses (Dec. 1980) 135,000. Television receivers (Dec. 1980) 165,000.

Agriculture. Production (in 000; metric tons; 1982): barley c. 71; wheat c. 140; potatoes (1981) c. 103; watermelons (1981) c. 171; tomatoes c. 235; onions c. 73; oranges c. 40; olives c. 100; dates c. 94. Livestock (in 000; 1981): sheep c. 6,258; goats c. 1,500; cattle c. 185; camels c. 134; asses c. 60.

Industry. Production (in 000; metric tons; 1981): petroleum products c. 5,470; crude oil (1982) c. 55,400; natural gas (cu m) 3,980,000; electricity (kw-hr) 5,600,000.

By early October the relationship was further contorted by the news that 37 French citizens were being harassed and delayed at Tripoli airport. The reason was said to be that the French authorities were detaining a Libyan citizen, Rashid Said Abdullah, prior to his extradition to Italy to face charges of murdering exiled opponents of Qaddafi in Milan in 1980. Throughout its involvement in Chad, Libya's aim was clearly to have the Aozou Strip recognized as sovereign Libyan territory and to have at least the northern part of Chad under the authority of a friendly government.

In March Qaddafi singled out the armed forces for criticism, accusing them of corruption and deviation from the spirit of the revolution. Ostentatious consumerism and abuse of authority merited the criticism, but the admonition was partly the result of numerous attempts on the Libyan leader's life organized by disaffected officers.

On May 25 the former king of Libya, Idris I (*see* OBITUARIES), died in a Cairo hospital.

(J. A. ALLAN)

Liechtenstein

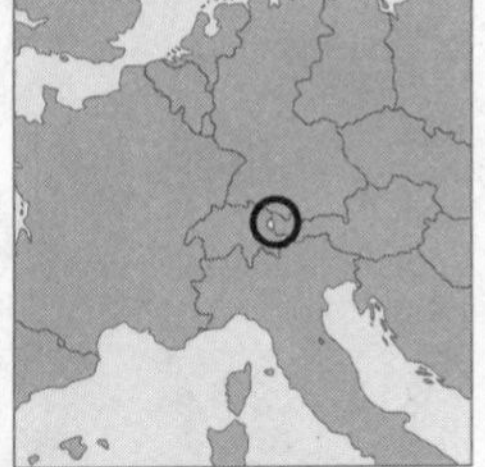

Liechtenstein

A constitutional monarchy between Switzerland and Austria, Liechtenstein is united with Switzerland by a customs and monetary union. Area: 160 sq km (62 sq mi). Pop. (1983 est.): 26,400. Cap. and largest city: Vaduz (pop., 1983 est., 4,900). Language: German. Religion (1982): Roman Catholic 84.7%; Protestant 8.8%. Sovereign prince, Francis Joseph II; chief of government in 1983, Hans Brunhart.

LIECHTENSTEIN

Education. (1982–83) Primary, pupils 1,806, teachers 97; secondary, pupils 1,848, teachers 96; vocational, pupils 78.

Finance and Trade. Monetary unit: Swiss franc, with (Sept. 20, 1983) a free rate of SFr 2.16 to U.S. $1 (SFr 3.25 = £1 sterling). Budget (1982 est.): revenue SFr 243,579,000; expenditure SFr 240,056,000. Foreign trade: imports (1981) SFr 936 million; exports (1982) SFr 894 million. Export destinations: EEC 39%; Switzerland 24%; EFTA (other than Switzerland) 8%. Main exports (1981): machinery and transport equipment 44%; metal manufactures 26%; general manufactures 20%; chemicals 7%. Tourism (1981) 85,300 visitors.

On the occasion of the 45th anniversary of his succession, Prince Francis Joseph II of Liechtenstein, the longest reigning monarch in Europe, announced in July 1983 that he intended to step down in the spring of 1984. Though he would remain the titular head of the principality, he intended to hand over the bulk of his executive authority to Crown Prince Hans Adam, his eldest son by his marriage to Countess Gina von Wilczek. Prince Hans Adam, born in 1945, was married to Countess Marie Kinsky von Wichinitz und Tettau in 1967. The couple had three sons and a daughter.

Since the end of World War II, Liechtenstein had moved away from agriculture toward small-scale industry. By the 1980s it was the most highly industrialized country in Europe in that 55% of the working population was employed in manufacturing industries. There was virtually no unemployment in the country. (K. M. SMOGORZEWSKI)

Life Sciences

Among the smallest and most primitive of living things, the lowly bacteria nevertheless have maintained an incomprehensibly powerful influence on the Earth's biosphere for billions of years. Bacteria are virtuoso biochemists, capable of transforming a wide variety of natural substances into simpler elements and compounds that are vital to higher forms of life. They present for convenient laboratory study many of the same biological processes that take place in more complex organisms, including human beings, and they serve as models for scientists attempting to understand how life first appeared on the Earth. It was hardly surprising, then, that in 1983 bacteria continued to be important tools and subjects of research for life scientists working in many fields, including marine ecology, genetic engineering, cellular function, and evolution (see *Marine Biology, Botany,* and *Molecular Biology,* below).

Bacteria have been found in almost every kind of environment, from ice to hot springs and from the heights and depths of the Earth's surface to the interior of cells. Despite this ubiquity, bacterial life hitherto had been thought to be limited to a maximum environmental temperature of about 100° C (212° F), the boiling point of water under normal atmospheric pressure. During the year, however, John Baross of Oregon State University and Jody Deming of Johns Hopkins Chesapeake Bay Institute in Maryland reported that bacteria sampled from 350° C (660° F) water streaming from sulfide-rich deep-sea hydrothermal vents on the East Pacific Rise indeed could live and thrive at the temperatures and pressures found there. With available laboratory equipment the researchers were able to maintain water in liquid form under a pressure of 265 atmospheres while raising it to 250° C (480° F). Under those conditions vent bacteria added to the water appeared to be much more productive than at 100° C, doubling every 40 minutes, and there seemed no reason why they would not survive even hotter conditions once a new pressure chamber to test them was built.

Baross and Deming believed that their results supported the concept "that microbial growth is limited not by temperature but by the existence of liquid water, assuming that all other conditions necessary for life are provided." If true, it is thus conceivable that bacteria live within the vents themselves and possibly even deeper in the Earth's crust. Their find also rekindled speculations that life may exist in extraterrestrial environments, such as Venus, where conditions formerly appeared too extreme. Furthermore, the existence of such heat-loving bacteria bolstered the controversial hypothesis that life on Earth may have begun with similar organisms in early hydrothermal vent systems via processes fueled by sulfide metabolism and accelerated by hot-seawater chemistry—and perhaps at a time much earlier in the Earth's fiery history than was thought compatable with life. (CHARLES M. CEGIELSKI)

[243.A; 312.A.1–4; 313.D]

ZOOLOGY

The year following the centenary of the death of Charles Darwin in 1882 included a reassessment of some general principles of evolutionary ecology. Among the issues to emerge in professional debate was the role of interspecific competition in community ecology; that is, how influential is competitive interaction among species in determining patterns in ecological communities? During 1983, symposia and publications focused on this issue. A basic and long-held view is that the outcome of direct competition between the species inhabiting a community is the primary cause of the pattern of community structure. This contention, supported by many community ecologists, has been challenged by those who maintain that other factors, such as local environmental events, predation, and climate, are the major forces. According to Daniel Simberloff of Florida State University, who led the attack to assign interspecific competition a more modest role, interspecific competition is less influential than predation, physical environment, or intraspecific competition. This view did not go unchallenged by competitionists and was expected to receive further rebuttal in the coming year.

Debate over the relative importance of competition extended to corollary issues. One of these involved the merits of natural experimentation, in which a community is examined under natural conditions, versus those of field experimentation, in which controlled manipulation is used to reduce variations in experimental conditions between parts of a study or between separate studies. Observations of naturally occurring communities led to the view that competition plays a dominant role in community formation. On the other hand, interpretations of the findings of field experiments generated considerable controversy about the role of competition. Some ecologists suggested that competition is pervasive in its influence on community structure, whereas others considered predation and unpredictable environmental events to play dominant roles.

Whatever the role of competition per se in determining community structure, certain field experiments provided insight into processes of island colonization. Thomas W. Schoener of the University of California at Davis and Amy Schoener of the University of Washington manipulated lizard populations on small Bahamian islands to test hypotheses about what causes species to become extinct. The researchers introduced adult lizards of species characteristic of the region to islands of different sizes. The number of individual lizards used in experimentally colonizing each island was either five or ten so that the effects of number of colonists and island size could be differentiated. The study confirmed expectations that the rate of extinction is more rapid on smaller islands. In contrast to findings reported for birds, mammals, and arthropods, however, the initial size of the experimental colony was not a factor in colonization success for the lizards. From subsequent calculations of demographic and population characteristics of the introduced colonies, it appeared unlikely that the species would go extinct whether the initial size of the colony was five or ten if the island were large enough.

Evidence of the complex interaction between animals and their environments came from Judy L. Meyer, Eric T. Schultz, and Gene S. Helfman of the University of Georgia. In a study of coral reefs and associated fish species in the Virgin Islands, the researchers documented that fish can have a major beneficial effect on the coral. Although coral reefs have long been known to provide food and shelter for various marine fish, Meyer and her associates determined that certain species of fish increased growth rates of the coral. Two species of fish called grunts (genus *Haemulon*) feed in grassbeds at night and return to rest in the coral reefs during the day. By their excretory products the fish increase the amounts of nitrogen and phosphorus in the water surrounding the reef. The researchers found that, because of this high nutrient input, corals in reefs where fish schools rested grew significantly more rapidly than those in reefs where fish were absent.

Red-winged blackbirds served as models for advances in evolutionary ecology during the past year. Frances C. James of Florida State University experimentally transplanted eggs between nests in different geographic regions, demonstrating that a significant portion of the regional difference observed in nestling development is environmental rather than genetic. Making use of morphological differences that exist between birds at different geographic sites, James found that hatchlings from the eggs of reciprocal transplants between regions became measurably less like their parent populations in outward characteristics and more like their foster populations. She concluded that the geographical variations in character observed in adults and presumably maintained by natural selection must therefore vary as a function of environmental as well as genetic components.

Kent L. Fiala and Justin D. Congdon of the University of Michigan used red-winged blackbirds to examine differences in body size between the sexes in relation to energetics. Male red-winged blackbirds are the same size as females upon hatching but are one-third larger by the time they leave the nest. The hatchling sex ratio is approximately 1:1. Using water labeled with hydrogen-3 and oxygen-18 and other techniques to establish an energy budget for nestlings, the investigators confirmed the assumption that larger males represented a greater energetic cost to the parents than females: parents had to provide more food to males to account for the sexual difference in total assimilated energy. Fiala and Congdon concluded that their findings challenge Ronald Fisher's theory that the primary sex ratio in a species is regulated so that fewer of the more costly sex are produced.

Several paleontological discoveries during the

"I foresee an upturn within the next six to eight million years."

year provided evidence relating to evolution of animals in terrestrial environments. William A. Shear of Hampden-Sydney (Va.) College and coworkers reported that several invertebrate fossils found in upstate New York in the late 1970s were estimated to be 365 million years old, the oldest terrestrial animal fossils known from the Western Hemisphere. The fossils include centipedes and arachnids and represent exclusively land-dwelling forms, indicating earlier terrestrial inhabitation of the region than had been confirmed previously. Another noteworthy find was of a fossil marsupial from Bolivia estimated to be more than 70 million years old. Reported by Larry G. Marshall at the University of Arizona, it represented the oldest terrestrial mammal that had been documented from the South American continent. A discovery in Pakistan by Philip D. Gingerich of the University of Michigan and associates confirmed earlier evidence that the ancestors of whales were terrestrial and gradually passed through an aquatic stage in their evolution. Bones of *Pakicetus*, the oldest and most primitive genus of whales, were recovered from freshwater, early Eocene deposits (about 50 million years old) associated with land mammals.

The status of endangered species continued to interest zoologists during 1983, particularly the potential recovery of some species. In March two California condors hatched at the San Diego Zoo, the first ever in captivity. The eggs had been taken from natural nests. The young were being raised to adulthood and would then be released in hopes of augmenting the declining population of the largest bird in North America. Fewer than two dozen California condors were known to exist in the wild.

Another endangered species, the northern elephant seal, was believed to be extinct in the 1800s until a small population was discovered on a Baja California island in 1892. According to Charles F. Cooper and Brent S. Stewart of San Diego State University, elephant seals began breeding on the California Channel Islands in the 1950s. They reported that the elephant seal population in California has doubled every five years since the early 1960s and that approximately 12,000 were born in 1982. The cumulative total of pups for Mexico and California in 1982 was 25,000, indicating a healthy trend toward recovery of this species.

The most critically endangered mammal in the conterminous U.S. recognized in 1983 by the U.S. Fish and Wildlife Service was the woodland caribou. Although there were populations in Alaska, a small population (13–20 animals) also inhabited the Selkirk Mountains in Idaho and Washington. This population was given endangered status by the Department of the Interior and granted full protection from poachers and other human-caused sources of mortality. (J. WHITFIELD GIBBONS)

[339.D; 352.B–C; 354.C.3; 10/34.B.6.d]

Entomology. The Mediterranean fruit-fly crisis that had threatened California horticulture in recent years appeared to be over. From mid-1982 no more medflies had been found, and the $14 billion fruit industry had been saved from quarantine preclusions and from fumigation regulations that at times during the emergency had resulted in consumer resistance and refusals by labour to handle treated consignments. Nevertheless, there would be the legacy of a $4 million-a-year monitoring program and, according to "Operation Medfly" Deputy Director Dick Jackson, the textbooks that had claimed that the medfly could not overwinter north of Santa Barbara would have to be rewritten.

In July 1983 an International Conference on Integrated Plant Protection attracted scientists from more than 30 countries to Budapest, Hung. The main theme to emerge was that chemical pesticides were necessary to maintain the intensive agricultural production on which densely populated areas depended but that it was essential to use compounds that did the least harm to natural enemies of pests and to other beneficial organisms—and only when careful monitoring and prediction showed they were really needed. Only in this way could costs of production and the risk of generating

J.M. LILLEBOE/NATURE MAGAZINE

A giant squid hooked by a fisherman off Bergen, Norway, gave scientists their first chance to study one alive. The low oxygen-carrying ability of its blood suggested that the animal is a poor swimmer and a sluggish predator.

The delicate marine animals known as comb jellies, or ctenophores, became the last animal phylum to find a place in the fossil record when a specimen, below left, was discovered in a 400-million-year-old slate bed in West Germany. An artist's reconstruction appears below.

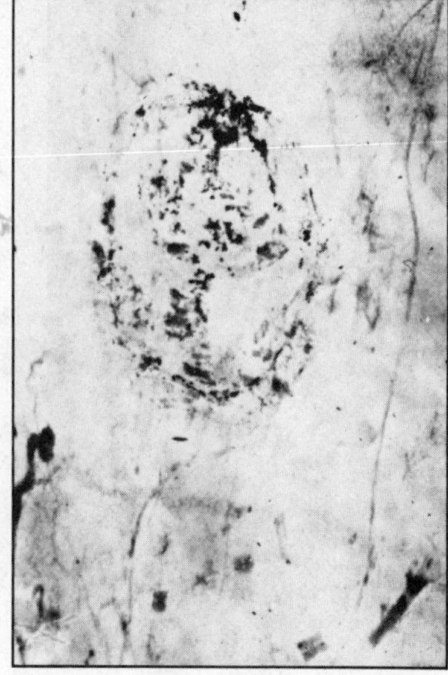

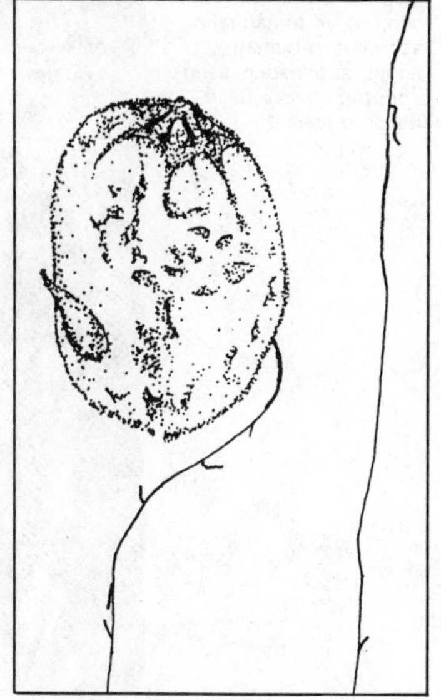

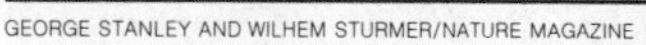

GEORGE STANLEY AND WILHEM STURMER/NATURE MAGAZINE

pesticide-resistant pests be minimized in the long term.

Use of pesticides had already caused apparently irreversible ecological changes. Papers presented by E. Niemczyk and S. Piotrowsky of Poland's Institute of Pomology and Floriculture and by a number of Hungarian scientists, including K. Balazs of the Hungarian Academy of Sciences, indicated that microlepidopterous leaf miners and leaf curlers, insects that had rarely been reported in orchards before widespread use of contact insecticides, had since become regular pests in both insecticide-treated and untreated orchards and gardens in central and northeastern Europe.

One of the most interesting nonchemical methods for insect control is the sterile-male release technique, whereby overwhelming numbers of laboratory-reared, sterile insects are released to mate with wild females and nullify their fertility. But, when successful, this strategy creates an ecological vacuum, readily exploitable by new wild immigrants; hence, geneticists have sought ways to replace pests with races that fill their niches without becoming pests themselves. Ian Maudlin of the Overseas Administration Tsetse Research Laboratory at Bristol, England, found what could be the perfect answer to the problem of sleeping sickness in Africa by demonstrating the possibility of breeding a strain of tsetse fly almost entirely resistant to the disease and thereby incapable of carrying it.

Catherine M. Bristow at the Imperial College of Science and Technology, London, reported that the treehopper *Publilia reticulata,* which commonly lives on ironweeds in the U.S., used ants as babysitters. The female treehoppers protected their young from predators but, when the young were attended by honeydew-collecting ants, which greatly increased the survivability of the treehopper nymphs, the females abandoned their families early and laid new clutches of eggs elsewhere.

Entomologists have long suspected that a powerful cause of speciation among plant-feeding insects has been the tendency of a parent population that is polyphagous (that feeds on more than one kind of food) to split into races, each specially adapted to feeding on a different host. In a remarkable demonstration of this process actually at work, T. K. Wood of the University of Delaware and S. I. Guttman of the University of Miami, Fla., showed that what had been assumed to be one polyphagous species of treehopper, *Enchenopa binotata,* was in fact a complex of six sibling species, each adapted to a different shrub or tree. Mating occurred on the host plant, and eggs hatched at times characteristically different for each species and related to the physiological cycle—usually flowering—of the host. A few cross-matings occurred when different species were caged experimentally together, but under natural conditions each mated at a different time. Wood and Guttman pointed out that such close physiological and behavioural adaptation to a host plant provided a paradigm for sympatric speciation, a still somewhat controversial concept of simultaneous development of sibling species that, although sharing common territory, become in some way reproductively isolated.

(PETER W. MILES)

[312.D; 321.E.2.a.iv; 731.A.5]

Ornithology. The way in which birds choose mates continued to receive scientific attention in 1983. Individual birds do not mate indiscriminately. At one extreme, mating with an individual of the opposite sex but wrong species can at best produce an infertile hybrid; at the other extreme, incestuous couplings can have bad genetic effects. Quails were experimentally shown to avoid both close and distant relations, preferring cousins as mates, though how a quail identified its kin was not known. Such outbreeding in Bewick's swans,

WIDE WORLD

ZOOLOGICAL SOCIETY OF SAN DIEGO

A California condor (far right), born at the San Diego Zoo in March, was the first of this endangered species ever hatched in captivity. To keep the chick from developing an unnatural attachment to human beings, zookeepers used a puppet condor head (right) to feed it.

however, appeared to be achieved by a female selecting a male with very different bill markings from those of her own immediate family. This species of swan displays marked and heritable individual variation in the black and yellow patterns of the bill.

Complementarity of this kind is only one of many factors affecting mate choice. Often in birds it is females who choose among males. They will "wish" to have their offspring fathered by a male with "good" genes, and relative outward physical well-being may well be an effective indicator of genetic health. Some elaborate male feathering has undoubtedly evolved where competition exists among cock birds for female favour. This was neatly proved by Swedish ornithologist Malte Andersson, who showed that cock widowbirds with comparatively long tails secured more mates than shorter tailed ones. Andersson used scissors to halve the tails of some birds and glue to lengthen the tails of others with the pieces taken from the first group. Those with lengthened tails acquired four times as many mates as those with shortened tails. This is a case of classical Darwinian sexual selection, in which members of one sex compete directly among themselves for mating opportunities. Another obvious advantage to the female in selecting the most attractive male is that her male progeny will also be "sexy" and be more likely to secure a mate.

It had been widely assumed that, if gaudy male plumage does not serve to facilitate female choice, then it must function in direct competition between males, as on the communal jousting grounds of such species as black grouse, ruffs, and various species of South American manakins (small, brightly coloured tropical-forest birds). But recently a third possibility was suggested. One of the most striking avian displays is that of the great argus pheasant of the Oriental tropics. The cock sports the longest feathers (more than two metres, or six feet) of any wild bird. Each senior cock takes over, upon the death of its previous occupier, a specially cleared dancing ground in the forest. It was once thought that females, guided by the calling of the cock, visited several males and sized them up visually, each then returning to the one of her choice. The new explanation was that she visits and mates with only one but, being of a solitary and shy species, she has to have her coyness overcome by a visual display so compulsive that it has a hypnotic effect. Thus the most mesmeric male will impregnate the most females and hand down his superior finery to his male offspring.

Most migrant birds travel using their own energy. A few, notably storks, pelicans, and birds of prey (raptors)—all large broad-winged birds—make use of the energy of rising air; they ride on thermals or on wind deflected upward by a slope. This dependency precludes oversea migration and tends to funnel these birds into certain routes. One such route takes many raptors past Elat at the head of the Gulf of Aqaba. More birds of prey pass this one spot than any other in the world en route between winter quarters in Africa and breeding grounds in Europe and Asia. Traveling in this way, hitchhiking across country on rising columns of air, such birds get by on roughly 4% of the energy they would have to expend if they flapped all the way.

THOMAS EISNER

The conspicuous zig-zag line of heavy silk through the web of the golden orb weaver is not a reinforcement but a hazard warning for flying birds that might otherwise inadvertently destroy the web and foul themselves in the process. So concluded Cornell University researchers Thomas Eisner and Stephen Nowicki after studying the role of the so-called stabilimenta woven into the web by some species of spider.

The first case of genuine lie telling by a bird—deceitful mimicry—was observed among female black-headed grosbeaks. If threatened at the nest by an enemy, the female mimics the song of a male grosbeak. Believing a competitor to be present, her mate hurries to the nest and is then in a position to help defend it.

A new species of albatross was discovered. Confined to Amsterdam Island in the French Southern and Antarctic Lands, it was named the Amsterdam albatross. Its population was thought to be 30–50 individuals. This group probably represented all that remained of a once larger population, reduced in the familiar way of isolated island species by the activities of humans and their introduced animals. (JEFFERY BOSWALL)
[313.J; 342.A.6.e.iii; 342.C.2.c.ii]

MARINE BIOLOGY

Continuing expansion of research in marine biology in 1983 was reflected in the launching of two new English-language journals dealing with the immense biota of the Indo-Pacific region; namely, *Asian Marine Biology*, published by the Marine Biological Association of Hong Kong, and the *Chinese Journal of Oceanology and Limnology*.

Internationally there was a notable increase in research efforts concerning the role of microorganisms in marine ecosystems. Hitherto it had been assumed that free-living bacteria, together with their protozoan predators, ensured the cycling of organic matter in the open ocean by attaching to and breaking down the fecal pellets of zooplankton (the animal component of plankton). Observations

REINHARDT M. KRISTENSEN, SMITHSONIAN INSTITUTION

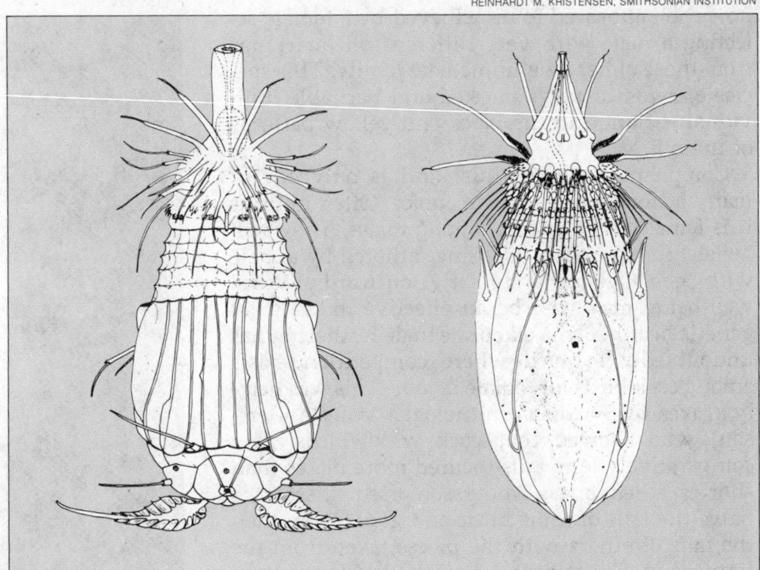

A new phylum of marine animal, Loricifera ("girdle wearer"), was proposed by Reinhardt M. Kristensen of the University of Copenhagen. Kristensen found the larval form of the microscopic animal in 1975 off the coast of Denmark but did not identify an adult form until 1982 in sediments dredged off the Atlantic coast of France.

off California and Mexico demonstrated that zooplankton feces are decomposed initially from inside, possibly by enteric bacteria that metabolize differently from free-living forms.

Dense animal communities associated with hydrothermal vents in the deep ocean are supposedly sustained by free-living chemosynthetic bacteria using reduced inorganic compounds, particularly hydrogen sulfide, as the primary energy source. Yet sulfur-oxidizing bacteria are uncommon in offshore marine sediments in general and in anoxic basins such as the Black Sea and Cariaco Trench where oxidizable inorganic sulfur is abundant. Measured rates of metabolism of free-living bacteria in water emitted from Galápagos Rift vents showed them to be too low to sustain the invertebrate biomass, which probably relies heavily on symbiotic bacteria for nutrient uptake. Bacteria were also implicated in providing the commercially important wood-boring isopod crustacean *Limnoria tripunctata* (gribble) with resistance to creosote. Other species of gribble are checked when creosote is applied to marine timbers, but *L. tripunctata* in low latitudes maintains particularly large populations of enteric bacteria, which appear to metabolize and detoxify the creosote.

Mass mortalities of the green sea urchin *Strongylocentrotus droebachiensis* occurred along the southern coasts of Nova Scotia during the autumns of 1980 and 1981; 440 km (275 mi) of coastline were affected, and annual kills of more than 84,000 metric tons wet weight were estimated. The causal agent was probably biological, a *Labyrinthomysia*-like protozoan being implicated. Because *Strongylocentrotus* feeds on algae, the affected coastline was likely to be extensively colonized by large algal seaweeds such as kelp.

The common herring, *Clupea harengus*, is one of the world's most intensively studied and overfished species, yet little was known of its spawning behaviour in the sea. Diving observations of herring in the Baltic Sea confirmed preliminary hypotheses that spawning is indiscriminate within a shoal and not coordinated between sex pairs. Most eggs were deposited on the alga *Ceramium tenuicorne*.

The southern Australian garfish, *Hyporhamphus melanochir*, had hitherto been considered to be a true herbivore, feeding on eelgrass (*Zostera*), despite the fact that it does not have the long convoluted gut that is necessary for digesting plant tissue and that is characteristic of obligate herbivorous fish. The fish was recently found to feed herbivorously only by day; at night it feeds on swarming amphipod crustaceans, which probably contribute to the balance of its nitrogen budget.

Many marine fish contain bacteria that enable them to luminesce, notably by producing diffuse light over the ventral surface that obscures the fish from predators or prey when viewed from below against daylight above. New methods of luminescence were discovered in a fish from the Philippines, *Gazza minuta*, including the ability to project sporadic beams of light forward and downward from a discrete spot at the posterior margin of each gill cavity. Intraspecific communication may take place by this means, perhaps aiding in schooling.

(ERNEST NAYLOR)

[313.J.3.d; 313.J.3.e.iii; 323.E; 354.B.1–2]

BOTANY

Because the gap between food production and food consumption was rapidly closing and because the greatest promise for increasing food production appeared to lie within the realm of genetic engineering, in the past several years researchers focused attention on the genetic manipulation of plant cells. In 1983 two independent groups of scientists reported the first successful transfer of genes from the bacterium *Agrobacterium tumefaciens*, which causes crown gall disease in plants, into the cells of petunia, carrot, sunflower, and tobacco. One of the transferred genes codes for an enzyme that imparts to the plant cells a resistance to the antibiotic kanamycin (methotrexate), allowing the cells to survive on media containing lethal concentrations of this antibiotic. Another of the transferred genes codes for the enzyme octopine

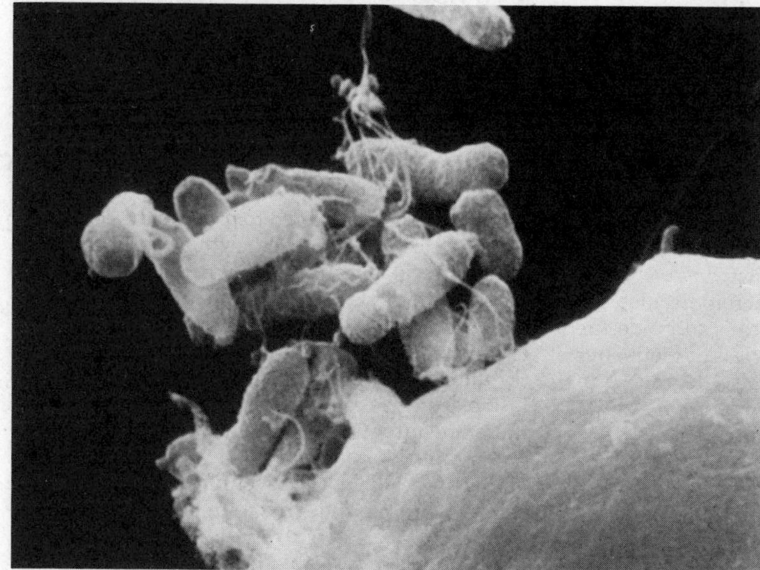

This scanning electron micrograph reveals several rod-shaped bacteria of the species *Agrobacterium tumefaciens* in the process of infecting a carrot cell (foreground). Equipped with a remarkable gene-transfer ability, the bacteria in nature cause crown gall disease in thousands of plant species by inserting some of their own DNA into host plant cells. Scientists were exploring ways to use this characteristic to transfer genes for desirable features from one plant into another.

synthase, which mediates the production of octopine, a compound not normally produced by plant cells. It is noteworthy that not only have mature plants been grown from cells containing the foreign genes but within the cells of those plants the transferred genes remained functional. Thus, the potential existed for improving productivity of crop plants by transplanting into their cells genes that confer resistance to diseases, insects, and herbicides.

Although most of the DNA of photosynthetic eukaryotes (organisms made of nucleated cells) is stored within the nucleus, a small portion resides in two cellular organelles, the mitochondrion and chloroplast. Traditionally, the sequences of nucleotide bases making up these three stores of genetic information had been regarded as distinct and separate. However, investigators at the Plant Breeding Institute in Cambridge, England, recently showed that a sequence of 12,000 bases within the mitochondrial DNA of corn is virtually identical to the sequence of bases in a similar-size portion of chloroplast DNA. The term promiscuous DNA was coined to describe such homologous DNA sequences that occur in more than one organelle. The existence of promiscuous DNA suggests that a mechanism must be present within the cell for copying and moving genes from one organelle to another. If found, such a mechanism could be exploited for the genetic manipulation of plants.

The discovery of promiscuous DNA also has important evolutionary implications. According to the endosymbiont hypothesis, mitochondria and chloroplasts evolved from prokaryotic (nonnucleated) cells that, after invading the forerunners of eukaryotic cells, established a symbiotic relationship with the latter. The fact that some of the proteins used by mitochondria and chloroplasts are coded by nuclear DNA, and not by mitochondrial and chloroplast DNA, suggests that during evolution a reduction in the genetic systems of the endosymbionts must have occurred, with major control and, therefore, genes moving to the nucleus. The finding that mitochondrial and chloroplast DNA contains homologous base sequences provides evidence that movement of genetic material between cell organelles has occurred.

Plant roots have an unerring ability to respond positively to gravity, a phenomenon known as geotropism (gravitropism). The gravitational stimulus is believed to originate in the displacement of amyloplasts (starch-containing organelles) within the cells of the root cap. Amyloplast redistribution is then somehow translated into the downward growth of the root. Although the link between gravity detection and directed growth of the root remained to be elucidated, recently calcium was implicated in the geotropic response. An ion-microscope analysis of the distribution of calcium ions in the root-cap cells of corn, peas, and lettuce revealed that although some calcium is associated with nuclei, the greatest density of calcium is detectable in amyloplasts. A further study showed that when chelating agents—compounds that bind ions like calcium, making them unavailable for cellular processes—were applied to the tips of corn roots, the roots failed to respond to gravity. By contrast, when the chelators were removed and replaced with calcium chloride ($CaCl_2$), a source of calcium ions, geotropic sensitivity was restored.

The leaves of vascular plants may be classified as either microphylls or megaphylls. Microphylls are characterized by a single unbranched vein that extends from the base to the tip of the leaf, whereas megaphylls exhibit a complex, branching pattern of venation. Most plant morphologists contend that the microphyll arose as a superficial outgrowth of the stem, the veins arising de novo as extensions of the vascular cylinder of the stem. The megaphyll, on the other hand, is believed to have been formed as a result of the concrescence of stems; the veins of megaphylls, therefore, are the vascular bundles of once separate stems. During the year an examination of the leaves of two species of *Selaginella*, a genus traditionally accepted as being microphyllous, revealed that the leaves of these plants possess a branching venation pattern. By definition these leaves are megaphylls, suggesting that megaphyllous leaves may have arisen by a pathway other than the accepted one.

(LIVIJA KENT)

[311.B.4.a; 312.A.3; 332.C.2.b–c]

MOLECULAR BIOLOGY

Degradation of Proteins Within Cells. Life is hardly imaginable without proteins, which provide for catalysis, structure, movement, defense, offense, transport, and other purposes as well. It is obvious, therefore, that cells must be able to assemble amino acids into these macromolecules. Indeed, the major function of genes is to guide the assembly of specific proteins. It is less obvious, but no less the case, that cells must also degrade proteins by breaking them down to their constituent amino acids.

The need for protein degradation, or proteolysis, can be appreciated from several perspectives.

1. Accommodation to changing conditions requires adjustment of the levels of specific enzymes, which are proteins. To increase its content of an enzyme the cell makes more of it. Decrease in the level of an enzyme in a nongrowing cell depends upon proteolysis. The rates of synthesis and degradation can be expressed in terms of the half-life, which is the time in which half of a group of protein molecules made together will be replaced. A short half-life denotes rapid synthesis and rapid degradation. Proteins whose levels do not need to be rapidly adjusted exhibit long half-lives measured in days or even months. In contrast, an enzyme catalyzing a reaction whose rate needs to be quickly adjusted will have a short half-life, perhaps only a few minutes.

2. Quality control demands that defective products be culled. Protein synthesis is a complex process, and there are many opportunities for errors. Proteins that are defective—because of a genetic error, because of a random error during assembly, or because of damage sustained after assembly—must be rapidly degraded. Normal hemoglobin, for example, is a very stable protein and has a half-life in excess of 100 days in the mature red cell. Yet when the amino acid valine in hemoglobin has been replaced by the analogue 2-amino-4-chlorobutyrate or when the hemoglobin has been damaged by oxidation, its half-life falls to ten minutes.

3. A constant supply of amino acids is essential for protein synthesis. A cell that is being starved will degrade some proteins in order to synthesize others. This robbing of Peter to pay Paul is essential if the cell is to make the adjustments that will allow it to survive temporary starvation.

4. During the life cycle of a cell, proteins that have served transient needs at early stages must be removed and replaced by other proteins that are essential at later stages. This replacement process again depends upon protein degradation.

What characteristic controls the susceptibility of a protein to degradation? The determining feature seems to be compactness. The susceptible bonds will be less exposed to the enzymes (proteinases) that attack and degrade proteins in a compact protein than in a floppy protein. Other things being equal, one would therefore expect large proteins to have shorter half-lives than small proteins—and they do. Similarly one would expect heat-stable proteins to have longer half-lives than heat-labile proteins—and that is the case.

Substrates (the specific molecules upon which enzymes exert their activity), nonprotein groups attached to the protein, and other substances can exert profound effects on the stability of protein structure and on protein half-lives in the cell, and these effects are exploited to provide the controls so essential to life. Consider tryptophan oxygenase, which initiates the breakdown of the amino acid tryptophan. This enzyme is made more stable by the presence of tryptophan. Hence, should the level of tryptophan rise, the rate of degradation of tryptophan oxygenase would fall. Given a constant rate of synthesis of this enzyme, its level would therefore automatically be elevated and the breakdown rate of tryptophan by it would be increased. Similarly a fall in the level of tryptophan would lead to more rapid degradation of tryptophan oxygenase and a slower breakdown of tryptophan. The result is a desirable homeostasis.

The above discussion has considered intracellular proteolysis, which distinguishes normal from abnormal proteins and which can even discriminate one type of normal protein from another. There is another, more general type of proteolysis that depends upon an organelle (specialized intracellular body) called the lysosome. This organelle contains a variety of enzymes and can degrade nucleic acids, polysaccharides, and phospholipids as well as proteins. Proteins taken into the cell during phagocytosis or pinocytosis (engulfing processes by which the cell takes in particulate matter and fluids, respectively) and proteins that enter after binding to specific receptors on the cell surface are transported to the lysosome, where they are degraded. The lysosome thus functions like a miniature organ of digestion.

There also are circumstances during which massive digestion of cell protein occurs, such as in the tail of a tadpole during metamorphosis into a frog. This self-digestion is called autophagy, and it is also seen in muscle that has become denervated and is consequently atrophying and in liver during starvation. The lysosome is the engine of autophagy.

A. L. Goldberg and co-workers at the Harvard Medical School intensively studied intracellular proteolysis in the bacterium *Escherichia coli.* Having noted that the selective degradation of abnormal proteins within these cells was dependent upon a source of metabolic energy, they set out to isolate the responsible enzyme. They identified eight different endoproteinases in *E. coli,* which they whimsically named *Do, Re, Mi,* etc. Only one, named *La,* showed a requirement for chemical energy supplied by the energy-releasing breakdown (hydrolysis) of adenosine triphosphate (ATP). Moreover, *La* exhibited the properties previously associated with intracellular proteolysis. It was thus active against globin and denatured albumin but not against native hemoglobin or albumin.

The proteinase *La* is much larger than previously encountered proteinases, having a molecular weight of 450,000 daltons. Its proteolytic action is stimulated by ATP and is associated with concomi-

R. L. BRINSTER, UNIVERSITY OF PENNSYLVANIA

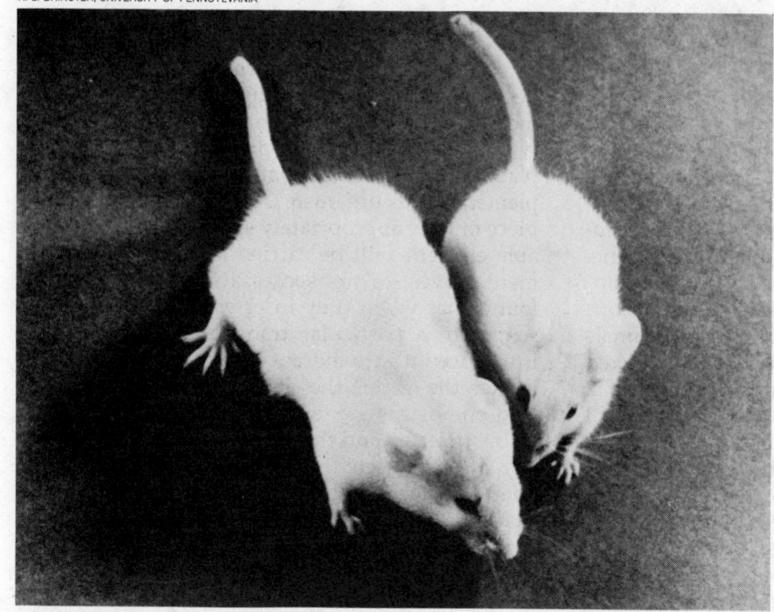

The normal-sized mouse on the right, weighing 29 grams (about an ounce), is dwarfed by its 44-gram littermate whose cells carry several copies of a foreign gene for rat growth hormone. The specially modified genes were injected into fertilized mouse eggs, which were then implanted in foster mother mice and allowed to develop to term. The smaller sibling did not acquire any functioning genes.

tant hydrolysis of ATP. Thus, analogues of ATP, which are not susceptible to hydrolysis, do not stimulate attack on substrate proteins, while only substrate proteins stimulate hydrolysis of ATP.

Occasionally, genetic defects can be localized to a specific gene even though the identity of the protein coded by that gene remains a mystery. This was the case with a specific mutation in *E. coli* that resulted in a defect in cell division, leading to abnormally elongated cells. The affected gene was named the *lon* gene, and mutation of this gene resulted in numerous changes in addition to elongation. Goldberg and co-workers showed that the *lon* gene product is none other than the ATP-dependent proteinase *La*. Among the evidence for this identity was their demonstration that when the *lon* gene was introduced into *E. coli* by means of genetic engineering techniques such that the total number of *lon* genes per cell was increased, *La* production was increased.

The proteinase *La* binds strongly to DNA, and the ATP-dependent proteolytic attack of *La* upon substrate proteins was found to be increased as high as sevenfold by DNA. The hydrolysis of ATP by *La* during its proteolytic attack on substrate proteins was also enhanced by DNA. *La* was the only one of the eight endoproteinases of *E. coli* that responded to DNA. This tight binding of *La* to DNA undoubtedly has great significance in the cell. Thus, in addition to attacking abnormal proteins and enzymes with short half-lives, *La* may attack other proteins that bind to DNA and that act to repress specific genes. By attacking such repressor proteins *La* could affect gene expression itself.

The cells of higher organisms contain semiautonomous organelles called mitochondria, which are responsible for most of the aerobic energy production. It has long been supposed that mitochondria arose from bacteriumlike, nonnucleated (prokaryotic) organisms that invaded the forerunners of nucleated (eukaryotic) cells and established a symbiotic relationship. In that case one might expect that the mitochondrial proteinase system in eukaryotes might resemble the *E. coli* system more than it resembles the corresponding proteinases of the cytosol (the fluid portion of the cytoplasm) surrounding the mitochondria. In fact, the mitochondrial ATP-dependent proteinase is remarkably similar to the *La* proteinase of *E. coli* and clearly different from the ATP-stimulated proteinase found in the cytosol of eukaryotic cells.

Intracellular proteolysis, essential in so many ways to the economy of any cell, may constitute an obstacle to scientists attempting to use recombinant DNA technology to create strains of bacteria that will produce large quantities of human insulin, interferon, growth hormone, and other valuable substances. If these proteins are recognized as aberrant by the proteolytic machinery of the cell, they will be degraded and thus will not accumulate. In that case knowledge of the intimate details of intracellular proteolysis could suggest a way to bypass this obstacle. (IRWIN FRIDOVICH)

Gene Transfer and Transgenic Organisms. One of the mysteries of biology is how a fertilized egg, a single cell, develops into an adult consisting of billions of highly differentiated cells comprising discrete tissues and organs. This differentiation process is ultimately programmed by the genes carried in the chromosomes of each cell. It is the differential expression of these genes during development that causes, for example, a liver cell to be a liver cell and a brain cell to be a brain cell.

Advances in recombinant DNA technology such as cloning and sequencing are giving molecular biologists a better understanding of the way in which genes are organized and expressed. Whereas experiments in the test tube have yielded little detailed information about gene regulation in the living organism during growth, recent experiments using cloned DNA and whole animals have promised great advances. Because some diseases are a result of aberrant gene expression, these advances might eventually lead to an understanding at the molecular level of many heritable diseases, allowing improved diagnoses and treatments.

An advancing area in this regard is gene transfer. One type of gene-transfer experiment proceeds as follows. A cloned gene—say, the gene for rabbit beta-globin (a subunit of hemoglobin)—is introduced by microinjection into the nucleus of a fertilized mouse egg. The egg is then placed in the reproductive tract of a mouse foster mother, where it develops as would a normal embryo. The injected gene sometimes inserts into a mouse chromosome and effectively becomes another mouse gene. If the insertion occurs early enough in development, most of the cells of the animal that develops will carry a copy of the injected gene; such animals have been called transgenic animals. If an injected gene is present in the germ line (gametes) of a transgenic animal, the progeny of that animal will also carry the gene, and its activity and inheritance can be studied. In the past three years a number of cloned genes, including the rabbit beta-globin gene, were transferred successfully by several experimenters to generate transgenic mice.

One major area that may be ideally suited for experiments using gene-transfer technology is that concerned with identifying genetic elements that regulate tissue-specific expression of genes during development—for example, what allows the beta-globin gene to be expressed in cells that make hemoglobin but not in other types of cells. After gene transfer, the different tissues of a transgenic organism would be monitored to determine the tissue-specific level of expression of the transferred gene. Then, in order to find out which parts of the gene carry the instructions for proper tissue-specific regulation, the cloned gene would be altered in the test tube and again injected into embryos to generate more transgenic animals. Monitoring the expression of the transferred gene in different tissues would reveal whether the alteration affected the expression of the gene in a tissue-specific manner. A systematic study involving introduction of alterations into different regions of the gene should eventually provide a clear picture of which parts of the gene regulate its tissue-specific expression during development. Similar studies of a number of genes that are regulated differently during development should identify a series of genetic elements that determine fundamental patterns of developmental regulation.

Gene-transfer experiments of this type, however, do face a number of technical problems. When a cloned, purified gene is injected into an embryo, its fate is uncertain and beyond the control of the experimentalist. First, most of the injected eggs die. In addition, not all surviving animals carry the injected gene. Those that do carry the gene usually do not have a single copy inserted into a chromosome, but many copies. Furthermore, the gene may be inserted in an unstable fashion, so that it does not appear in the progeny of the transgenic animal and therefore cannot be studied further. Finally, the gene may rearrange in the process of transfer and no longer be the same as when it was injected.

Fortunately, for the fruit fly *Drosophila melanogaster* many of these problems were overcome by Gerald Rubin and Allan Spradling of the Carnegie Institution of Washington. Rather than just injecting a gene into *Drosophila* embryos, they first spliced the gene—one that coded for a particular enzyme that fruit flies normally possess—into a vector, or carrier, consisting of a transposable element. Transposable elements are discrete, naturally occurring segments of DNA that can move from place to place in the genome (the total genetic complement of an organism). A foreign or passenger piece of DNA appropriately spliced into a transposable element will be carried along when the element moves, or transposes. Rubin and Spradling found that when they inserted the gene as a passenger in a particular transposable element and introduced it into mutant *Drosophila* embryos that lacked the gene, the gene became incorporated into one or a very few sites in the genome, was stably inserted and therefore passed on to the progeny of the injected fly, and was not rearranged after transfer. Although only about 8% of the injected animals developed into fertile adults, about 39% of those expressed the injected gene. The whole process is efficient enough to allow the systematic study of altered genes proposed above.

These results demonstrated that gene transfer mediated by transposable elements is relatively free from problems of gene rearrangement and instability. Molecular biologists working with *Drosophila* have already begun to use this elegant methodology to investigate the regulatory properties of a number of cloned genes. Transposable elements similar to the one used by Rubin and Spradling (not all are suitable vectors for gene transfer) might be discovered in higher animals and plants and might prove similarly useful for gene-transfer experiments.

Besides advancing knowledge of basic processes of growth and development, gene-transfer experiments have other scientific and practical uses. A dramatic demonstration of this was recently described by Richard Palmiter of the University of Washington, Seattle, and co-workers, who injected a cloned gene for rat growth hormone into fertilized mouse eggs. Twenty-one animals developed from 170 injected eggs, and seven of these contained the transferred gene in their chromosomal DNA. Six of the mice with the transplanted growth-hormone gene grew significantly larger than their normal siblings, two reaching a weight almost twice normal.

Although the injected gene was not regulated in the normal manner, the giant mice offered a model for studies of gigantism, a condition that results from chronic exposure to high levels of the hormone. Additionally, these experiments suggested the possibility for using gene transfer to stimulate the growth of commercially valuable animals. Although many technical problems remained, this approach could also eventually provide a means for correcting genetic diseases. Finally, these experiments suggested the possibility of "genetic farming," wherein transgenic animals would be used to produce high levels of certain polypeptides in their blood sera, much as valuable antibodies are raised. (ARNO GREENLEAF)

[311.B.4.a; 312.A.3; 321.B.3,4,7; 322.B.1.d; 323.A.5; 333.A.2.a–b]

See also Earth Sciences; Environment.

Literature

The 1983 Nobel Prize for Literature was awarded to William Golding (*see* Nobel Prizes). His fellow English authors were pleased with his success but continued to wonder why their favourite, Graham Greene, was so persistently passed over by the Swedish judges. The British novelist and critic Francis King remarked (while reviewing a Swedish book, Ragnar Sohlman's *The Legacy of Alfred Nobel*) that "a prize for world literature is as nonsensical as a prize for the most beautiful animal in the world. . . . If there is an African Homer, writing in Yoruba, how is a committee in Stockholm to recognize his stature?"

Suspicion of literary prizes and their judges was a feature of 1983. It was observed that the most desirable prize in France, the Prix Goncourt, traditionally went to books published by the firms of Grasset, Gallimard, or Le Seuil, and that almost all the ten judges for 1983 were themselves authors published by those three firms. For 18 years the three firms had also been publishers of almost all the winners of two other important French prizes—the Fémina and the Interallié. But, after these complaints had been aired, the 1983 prize went, at last, to a novel from another publisher, Balland. This book, *Les Égarés* ("The Wanderers") by Frédérick Tristan, is a comedy with an appropriate theme: literary prizewinning and the deceptions sometimes involved.

British readers noticed that the main character in *Les Égarés* seemed to be based on G. K. Chesterton (d. 1936), the Roman Catholic poet and detective-story writer. Though popular and wielding some influence with such writers as Franz Kafka and Jorge Luis Borges, Chesterton was not an author much studied by literary men in Britain, nor the sort to win literary prizes. It was noted that Sir Arthur Conan Doyle, the creator of Sherlock

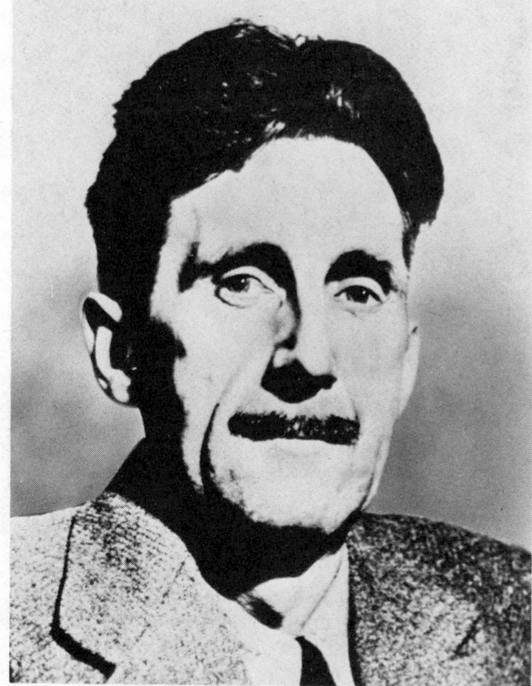

George Orwell

George Orwell: It's His Year

Curiously, the man's pen name and the title of his best known book were casual accidents: Orwell was a river he had known as a youth, and *Nineteen Eighty-Four* simply reversed the last two digits of the year in which he wrote it. That "Orwellian" had taken on a grim resonance by the time 1984 arrived is an irony he might well have bleakly appreciated.

George Orwell (1903–50), born Eric Blair, was a man of his turbulent era, Britain's preeminent social essayist and critic, familiar with rejection, poverty, war, and the disillusionment caused by political rhetoric. He battled totalitarianism and cant passionately, with the clear-eyed conviction that the former inevitably employs the latter.

In *Nineteen Eighty-Four* a middle-level bureaucrat, Winston Smith, is disgusted with his work, rewriting old newspaper stories to make Oceania's official files conform to an ideology largely devoted to endless war as a means of ensuring loyalty. For his sins—retaining a small measure of independence, keeping a diary ("I hate Big Brother"), and entering into a forbidden love affair, all growing into determination to plot against the regime—he is tortured into moral submission.

The book warns of a society in which the tools of mass control are wielded ruthlessly. That vision was the theme during a year of unceasing media attention. The sales of *Nineteen Eighty-Four* soared in dozens of translations, as did those of *Animal Farm* (1945), Orwell's savage barnyard satire of Soviet life.

Orwell was born in India, the son of a colonial civil servant, in a middle-class environment that stressed the importance of appearances. Unhealthy, an outsider at Eton (which he attended on scholarship), and unable to afford the university education required for a decent job, he returned to Burma for five years as a colonial policeman. It was there that he began to reflect and write on the relationship of masters to masses. For the next decade he worked at becoming a novelist, with indifferent success. Only with *Down and Out in Paris and London* (1933), a vivid and uncompromising account of grinding poverty, did he begin to attract attention.

A socialist, Orwell was caught up in the waves of antifascist sentiment sweeping across Europe as Hitler seized power, and he went to Spain in 1936 to fight against Franco's forces. While recovering from a wound in the throat, he became aware that Europe's Communist press had singled out the independent anti-Franco forces for attack. His bitterness, recounted in *Homage to Catalonia* (1938), presaged his unceasing struggle against all forms of totalitarianism. (JAMES L. YUENGER)

WIDE WORLD

William Golding

Holmes, had won similar international popularity without literary prizes or esteem; his fame was commemorated in the international success of an Italian novel, *The Name of the Rose* by Umberto Eco—the story of an Englishman called Baskerville, closely resembling Sherlock Holmes but pursuing his investigations as a monk in 14th-century Italy. After winning the 1982 Premio Strega, *The Name of the Rose* became popular in many countries, especially the U.S.

There was some amusement when U.S. Pres. Ronald Reagan presented a Congressional Gold Medal to a writer not previously admired for literary merit. The only other writer to have been enrolled in this list of distinguished U.S. citizens had been the poet Robert Frost. President Reagan added to this roll of honour the name of Louis L'Amour, the author of 87 cowboy stories that had achieved total sales of 140 million.

ENGLISH

United Kingdom. Public interest in literary prizes was stimulated to such a pitch by journalists and broadcasters that some critics were moved to complain about razzmatazz and ballyhoo, especially in regard to the televised presentation of the Booker McConnell Prize for fiction and the gambling on the winner. More sanguine critics held that the betting and human drama surrounding the judges' serious deliberations added to the hoped-for effect of the competition, attracting readers to ambitious, seriously meant books. J. M. Coetzee, a South African educated in the U.S., was the winner for 1983 with *Life and Times of Michael K*, a sombre, nonrealistic tale of the sufferings of a deformed, slow-witted man (race and nationality unspecified) blundering through a civil war somewhere in Africa. The Booker McConnell Prize had first become exciting in 1972 when the winner, John Berger, announced that he would give part of his prize money to a "black liberation" movement, as compensation for the wrongs committed in the past by the prize-giving firm of Booker McConnell in its capacity as owner of plantations and black slaves. Berger's 1972 victory was remembered by the *Times Educational Supplement* when expressing doubts about Coetzee's in 1983. According to this schoolteachers' journal, "the often relentlessly avant-garde judges" might well be discouraging young readers from attempting to read serious fiction.

Despite grumbles, literary prizes continued to proliferate, usually following something like the Booker McConnell rules, with entrants limited to residents of the U.K., the Commonwealth, and certain former Commonwealth members—such as Ireland, Pakistan, and South Africa. With the new H. H. Wingate Prize, for a book stimulating "awareness of themes of Jewish interest," Israel was added to the list of eligible nations. There was a European connection in the new Kurt Maschler Prize for a children's book with well-matched text and illustrations, won in its second year by Anthony Browne's *Gorilla*. This prize was founded by Kurt Maschler, a patriarch of British publishing who made his name in pre-Hitler Germany by publishing the distinguished children's book *Emil and the Detectives* by Erich Kästner.

Although the Booker McConnell winner was South African and the runner-up, Salman Rushdie (*see* BIOGRAPHIES), was Indian-born, authors and themes from the Commonwealth and ex-Commonwealth did not predominate in literary discussion. However, the veteran Indian writer R. K. Narayan delighted his British readers with a new novel, *A Tiger for Malgudi*, and the admired Indian cricketer Kumar Shri Ranjitsinhji was commemorated by Alan Ross, the poet and literary editor, in his biography *Ranji: Prince of Cricketers*. The Commonwealth Poetry Prize was won by Grace Nichols of Guyana with her memorably titled book *I Is a Long-Memoried Woman*.

Deaths that occurred in 1983 included novelists Richard Llewellyn, Beverley Nichols, and Christina Stead, journalist and novelist Dame Rebecca West, biographer Sir Roger Fulford, and *Poetry London* founder Tambimuttu. (*See* OBITUARIES.)

FICTION. The stories that were most applauded by prize-giving committees in 1983 were not of the traditional British sort, not the thoughtful comedies about down-to-earth "realities" that most readers expect from fiction. This was a year of bizarre and exotic fantasies, rather like children's stories or those dreams of strange places and dark ages that appeal (like Tolkien or science fiction) to young readers of paperbacks. Lisa St. Aubin de Terán was praised in *The Observer* newspaper for making "brilliant use of her extraordinary experiences" in her novel *The Keepers of the House*—since "most 16-year-old English girls don't marry taciturn Venezuelan millionaires and go to live on decaying avocado farms in the Andes with a pet vulture." For this novel the author won the Somerset Maugham award; she also won the John Llewellyn Rhys Prize for another novel, *The Slow Train to Milan* (about baroque expatriate terrorists drifting around Europe), as well as an Eric Gregory award for her poems.

The six novels under consideration for the Booker McConnell Prize were all remote from stories of "real life" as told in newspapers and conversations. Graham Swift's *Waterland* roved in a near-legendary manner over several generations of ghosts and witches in the English Fenland. Anita Mason's *The*

Illusionist was a fanciful tale about Simon Magus, the sorcerer rebuked by St. Peter for attempting to purchase the power of the Holy Spirit with money. *Flying to Nowhere* by the poet John Fuller concerned a holy island off the Welsh coast, with a dreamlike account of an abbot searching for the Soul by cutting up dead bodies. In *Rates of Exchange,* Malcolm Bradbury (a university teacher much concerned with critical theories) invented an imaginary country with an imaginary language for his hero, a British university teacher, to go traveling in. Salman Rushdie in *Shame* invented a country called "Peccavistan" to represent his dreamlike vision of Pakistan. Some of the characters in *Shame* were recognizable as real-life Pakistani statesmen, and the book was held to be politically significant. So was Coetzee's *Life and Times of Michael K,* the eventual winner, since his description of another imaginary country provoked (in a morbid, nightmarish way) gloomy thoughts about the author's native South Africa.

To this list of dreamlike tales the judges might well have added Neil Jordan's *The Dream of a Beast,* a simpler but no less poetic dream in which a man finds himself transformed into some kind of mammal. But there were, of course, several admirable narratives quite apart from the dream-story fashion—stories with feet closer to the ground. One such was *Entry into Jerusalem* by Stanley Middleton, the story of a quiet Midlands artist endangered by an uncharacteristically vulgar picture he has painted; it is about to win him too much fame and fortune for his own good.

David Thomson offered in *Dandiprat's Days* a plausible "diary of a madman," an influential civil servant in his 50s who becomes, whenever he thinks it necessary, a voluntary patient in a psychiatric hospital; the story was a pleasing, even optimistic blend of "realism" and mysticism. There were other serious comedies, bordering on farce, among them Nicholas Salaman's *Dangerous Pursuits,* making mock of the ever-growing surveillance industry and its electronic aids. Even more serious and up-to-date was Peter Prince's *The Good Father,* the story of one of those young men who become committed to the fashion of extreme "feminism," arguing for "women's rights" at every opportunity, and then, rejecting the whole fashion, revert to rather ungentlemanly commitment to their own sex. The versatile John Bowen offered *Squeak,* a surprisingly realistic novel about a bird, a pigeon kept by pigeon-fanciers—a story in the tradition of Henry Williamson's *Tarka the Otter.* Shortly before his death the octogenarian artist Eric Fraser provided fine illustrations for *Squeak.* Closer to "reality" than some of the year's other prizewinners was William Trevor's *Fools of Fortune,* about Anglo-Irish relations, which gained him his second Whitbread Novel Prize.

LETTERS, LIVES. The slow-paced biographers of Britain's patriarchal elders maintained their solemn, steady progress. Alan Bullock at last produced the third volume, *Ernest Bevin: Foreign Secretary,* of his account of that statesman, the trade unionist who became Winston Churchill's minister of labour during World War II and who then supported Clement Attlee as his foreign secretary in the postwar Labour government. Other patriarchs were thought due for reappraisal. Martin Gilbert won a prize for *Finest Hour: Winston S. Churchill 1939–1941.* So did Kenneth Rose for a new biography of King George V, notably for revealing the king's lack of sympathy (perhaps even hardheartedness) toward his deposed kinsman, the tsar of Russia. Robert Skidelsky's *John Maynard Keynes* supplied new material, not previously thought suitable for publication, about the authoritative economist.

William Cobbett and Charles Lamb were among the ever popular writers of the Regency period who were reappraised in pleasing (if not innovative) books that inspired good essays in the reviews. A newcomer to this gallery was John Scott, the subject of Patrick O'Leary's biography *Regency Editor.* Scott (1784–1821) was the Scottish editor of left-wing London journals offering space to such writers as Hazlitt, Lamb, De Quincey, and Keats; he was killed in a London duel by another Scotsman, a representative of the Tory press. O'Leary's experience of London journalism contributed to the success of this useful chapter of literary and political history.

GERALDINE FARLEY

J. M. Coetzee

Margaret Fitzherbert, a daughter of Evelyn Waugh, wrote a biography of her maternal grandfather, Aubrey Herbert, *The Man Who Was Greenmantle.* Born in 1880, Aubrey Herbert took up the causes of nationalist movements struggling against Turkish domination and was offered the throne of Albania. During World War I he was an intelligence officer employed in negotiations with the Turks, and he was used by John Buchan as a model for his fictional hero "Greenmantle." A Tory member of Parliament, he quarreled with his party about their repressive policy in Ireland and their reluctance to negotiate a peace with Germany. His travel diaries and notes about war were much admired. A less melodramatic (but no less exotic) chapter of imperial history was contributed by Sir Rex Niven, at the age of 85; his lively accounts and histories of sober, practical work in West Africa culminated with *Nigerian Kaleidoscope: Memoirs of a Colonial Servant,* taking the reader up to the 1960s and the years of Nigerian independence.

Several dominant figures in the British cultural establishment suffered biographies and criticism. One was Rupert Murdoch, the powerful international newspaper owner, criticized by Michael Leapman in *Bare-Faced Cheek: The Apotheosis of Rupert Murdoch.* Harold Evans, whom Murdoch appointed editor of *The Times* of London and who resigned after a year, told his side of the story, forcefully, in *Good Times, Bad Times.* Then there was a brash but rather fascinating biography, *A Variety of Lives* by Michael Tracey, about Sir Hugh Greene, an unusually "permissive" director general of the British Broadcasting Corporation, a distinguished journalist in the anti-Nazi period, and a brother of Graham Greene.

POETRY. It was widely reported that poetry sales were booming, partly as the result of young people's liking of poetry readings. Michael Horovitz presented many extrovert poets in his eclectic and somewhat rebellious show, "Poetry Olympics," at the Young Vic theatre, accompanied by Horovitz himself playing the kazoo and the psychologist R. D. Laing at the keyboards. Craig Raine, though more a poet of the printed page, recorded that he had been averaging two poetry readings a week and was now promoting through his publisher a scheme for selling poetry cassettes. Slim volumes of poetry were selling 5,000 copies a year, while a so-called cult poet, like the West Indian Linton Kwesi Johnson, might sell 30,000—as many as the most successful serious novels.

The poet most generally admired during the year was probably James Fenton. *The Sunday Times* of London (which had been publishing his weekly drama criticisms) gave him a page for the title poem of his new book, *Children in Exile,* about refugee children from Vietnam and Cambodia (Kampuchea); Fenton had experience of this history from his work as a war correspondent. The *Collected Poems* of Peter Porter were praised for their "bizarre and gaudy mental landscapes"; favourable comment also was given to the more austere *Collected Poems, 1970–1983* of Donald Davie and an exuberant new book, *The River,* by Ted Hughes, with exhilarating accounts of eel, salmon, heron, and cormorant. Porter, an assiduous reviewer, gave high praise to Jenny Joseph, " a suburban mystic posing as surrealist," for her new book, *Beyond Descartes:* "Clear observation, bold aphorisms, and sharp unhappiness are woven together in her poems. The end product feels like joy."

"A strange, rich poem," wrote Conor Cruise O'Brien about Geoffrey Hill's *The Mystery of the Charity of Charles Péguy.* The title refers to Péguy's own poem, *Le Mystère de la Charité de Jeanne d'Arc* (1910). Hill's verses concerned the career of Péguy as a Roman Catholic and nationalist Frenchman, eager to embark on World War I and frustrate the pacifism of his socialist compatriots. O'Brien observed that Hill had not made enough of Péguy's devotion to Joan of Arc—for that poem attracted students of political and religious history as well as the merely "aesthetic" readers of poetry.

(D. A. N. JONES)

United States. FICTION. The mere magnitude of the critical response to Norman Mailer's massive Egyptian fantasy, *Ancient Evenings,* if not its character, would seem to mark the novel as one of the major literary events of the year in the United States. This response ranged from uncertain, somewhat embarrassed enthusiasm to exasperated boredom at the unwieldy result of a decade of composition and apparently enormous, if undigested, research. Employing a central character who survives a number of reincarnations, *Ancient Evenings* provided glimpses of nearly two centuries of Egyptian history, from an imperial high point, the victory of Ramses II at Kadesh, to the reign of the undistinguished Ramses IX. While some passages displayed virtuosity, there was also a frequent resort to falsely imitative archaisms. However, the book's encyclopaedic account of Egyptian sexual practices and occultism was popular, and *Ancient Evenings* spent some weeks on the best-seller lists.

More conventional approaches to the historical novel also appeared during 1983. *Exit Lady Masham* by Louis Auchincloss was a learned, stylish recreation of intrigue at the court of Queen Anne of England in the first decade of the 18th century. Dedicated to historian Barbara Tuchman, *Exit Lady Masham* was the story of Abigail Hill, a poor relation of the formidable Sarah Churchill, duchess of Marlborough. Brought to court by her cousin, Abigail later replaced Sarah as the queen's favourite, coming to exert considerable influence over Anne. Predictably heading the best-seller lists for weeks, James Michener's *Poland* covered 700 years of that country's troubled history, from Genghis Khan to Solidarity.

Satire was lively during the year, ranging from the Juvenalian to the Horatian ends of its spectrum. Gore Vidal's *Duluth* was a vicious, inventive fantasy that employed a variety of fictions, as well as autonomous characters that die in one narrative and reappear in another to create a bizarre soap-opera community located, in Vidal's weirdly transmogrified geography, near "palm-lined Lake Erie." Among his principal satirical targets were recent fashions in literary criticism, which supplied the novel's eccentric narrative method, and American popular culture, which provided the grotesques that people *Duluth.* Thomas Berger's *The Feud* was a well-crafted, macabre comedy set in the late 1930s that described how the grimly widening consequences of a pointless quarrel in a hardware store gradually involve all the members of two working-class families living in small neighbouring Midwestern mill towns.

Philip Roth added a funny, ferocious third novel to his cycle about writer Nathan Zuckerman that began with *The Ghost Writer* and *Zuckerman Unbound.* In *The Anatomy Lesson,* Zuckerman endures literary feuds, writer's block, mid-life crisis, and assorted other tragicomic ills. The deft, shrewd ironies of Cynthia Ozick's second novel, *The Cannibal Galaxy,* brilliantly explored the uncertain impact of progressive education and the anomalous nature of genius. Genial but effective in its satire, Peter De Vries's *Slouching Towards Kalamazoo* was an extravagant account of the arrival of the sexual revolution in a Midwestern small town in the early 1960s. Its plot played on that of Hawthorne's *The Scarlet Letter* as irreverently as did its title on a famous line from Yeats.

Posthumously published works by two writers associated with Chicago appeared during the year. *The Devil's Stocking* by Nelson Algren, author of *The Man with the Golden Arm,* was a generally successful novel based on an account Algren had written for *Esquire* magazine of the murder trial of boxer Rubin "Hurricane" Carter. *Sam Holman* by James T. Farrell, author of the Studs Lonigan trilogy, was a largely lifeless roman à clef dealing with a group of leftist intellectuals in New York in the 1920s and '30s. Another Chicagoan, Harry Mark Petrakis, published his seventh novel, *Days of Vengeance,* a well-executed and moving account of the ironic course of a vendetta that begins with a senseless murder on Crete and ends years later in America.

Mark Helprin's *Winter's Tale,* a richly imaginative fantasy that brilliantly creates two visionary New Yorks, a late 19th-century city inhabited by Dickensian grotesques and an equally gothic megalopolis of a hundred years later that is gripped by a millenarian panic, successfully combined fantastic incident, broad humour, and lush prose with an essential seriousness. Another beautifully crafted and poetic fantasy was *Arcadio,* a final novel by William Goyen, author of *The House of Breath,* who died in August at the age of 68. After hearing an old uncle tell how once long ago he had seen a hermaphrodite bathing in a river, a boy living in East Texas has a vision in which the hermaphrodite appears to him and tells him a strange, tragicomic life story full of impossible marvels that has a flavour of myth.

In *A Gathering of Old Men,* Ernest J. Gaines, author of *The Autobiography of Miss Jane Pittman,* used a large number of narrators, both black and white, to present a multifaceted view of the events of a single long day on a large sugarcane plantation in the bayou country of central Louisiana. Set in the recent past, Gaines's novel was an eloquent fable, beginning with the murder of the brutal racist son of a powerful local white man and climaxing in a violent confrontation between vigilantes and a group of elderly black men who in their solidarity find the courage to resist.

Two of the year's best-selling novels centred on the analyst's couch. Judith Rossner's *August,* which dealt with the relationship of a troubled adolescent and her doctor, a middle-aged woman, was overlong in its clinical detail and uncertain in tone. In Morris West's *The World Is Made of Glass,* the patient is a sexually obsessive Hungarian countess and the analyst is the immortal Carl Jung himself. While providing some fascinating glimpses of the famous, the novel is only partly successful in its use of alternating narration by analyst and patient.

Perhaps the most widely and enthusiastically praised literary debut of 1983 was Joan Chase's accomplished first novel, *During the Reign of the Queen of Persia.* Written in a precise, elegant style and effectively employing the difficult technical device of a collective narrator composed of the four granddaughters of a rural matriarch, Chase's novel masterfully created the world of a prosperous Ohio farm in the early 1950s. Essayist Nora Ephron's first novel, *Heartburn,* was a funny, nasty roman à clef about the breakup of a marriage. Among the year's many fine books dealing with Vietnam was Stephen Wright's first novel, *Meditations in Green,* winner of Scribners' 1983 Maxwell Perkins Prize. Robert Plunket's first novel, *My Search for Warren Harding,* was a brief, hilarious account of the adventures of an academic rogue, a historian scheming to get hold of a trunkful of documents relating to the active sex life of the 29th U.S. president. Other interesting first novels to appear during the year were *Magnetic Field(s)* by Ron Loewinsohn, *Waltz in Marathon* by Charles Dickinson, and *Alice in Bed* by Cathleen Shine.

Bernard Malamud, who won the 1959 National Book Award for his collection of short stories *The Magic Barrel,* chose 25 stories for inclusion in a fine omnibus, *The Stories of Bernard Malamud.* Drawing heavily on his best collections, *The Magic Barrel* and *Idiots First,* these stories impressively displayed Malamud the fabulist. Louis Auchincloss, a fabulist of a very different sort, wittily explored a variety of upper-crust ethical questions, including the morality of corporate takeovers and boardroom theatrics, in a new collection of short stories, *Narcissa and Other Fables.* The critical and popular success in 1982 of Gail Godwin's fine novel *A Mother and Two Daughters* would in any case have been a hard act to follow, but her new collection of short stories, *Mr. Bedford and the Muses,* was uneven in quality. Raymond Carver's third collection of short stories, *Cathedral,* displayed a growing depth and virtuosity. Among the most impressive literary debuts of the year was a volume of short stories, *Shiloh* by Bobbie Ann Mason, that sharply observed lives in a corner of the "new South," small towns in western Kentucky. Other interesting volumes of short stories to appear during 1983 included Frederick Barthelme's first collection, *Moon Deluxe,* Nicholas Delbanco's *About My Table,* Andre Dubus's *The Times Are Never So Bad,* and Elizabeth Tallent's *In Constant Flight.*

HISTORY, BIOGRAPHY, AND BELLES LETTRES. After a decade of neglect, there was a spate of excellent books dealing with the Vietnam war. Journalist Stanley Karnow's *Vietnam: A History,* created in conjunction with a public television documentary, was comprehensive in its treatment, beginning with Vietnam's ancient conflicts with the Chinese and the Khmers and continuing up to the present with portrayals of the grim legacies of the war in both Southeast Asia and the United States. As evenhanded as Karnow's book but more impassioned in its indictments, *Without Honor,* by another journalistic veteran of Vietnam, Arnold Isaacs, was also far narrower in its scope, confining itself to the period between the negotiation of the Paris peace agreements and the final collapse of the Saigon government. Robert Mason's *Chickenhawk* was a well-written memoir of his experiences as a helicopter pilot with the 1st Air Cavalry Division in 1965 and 1966. *Conversations with the Enemy* by Winston Groom and Duncan Spencer was a generally well-done treatment of the case of Robert Garwood, a U.S. Marine accused of collaboration with the enemy during the 14 years he spent

RICKI ROSEN

Cynthia Ozick

as a prisoner of war. *Bloods,* edited by Wallace Terry, was an oral history that collected the combat experience of 20 black Vietnam veterans.

Sometimes brilliantly observed, but offering little insight into what some were calling "the new Vietnam," Joan Didion's *Salvador* was based on a short visit to Central America in 1982. Erring in the opposite direction from Didion's brief, passionless treatment of her subject, Peter Mathiessen's *In the Spirit of Crazy Horse* was a long, ranting, and finally ineffective account of the trial of Leonard Peltier, an Ojibwa-Sioux accused of murder following a 1975 shootout between the militant American Indian Movement and the FBI that left one Indian and two agents dead.

The reassessment of Dwight Eisenhower was given a major impetus with the publication of the first volume of Stephen Ambrose's biography, covering the period to his first election as president. *In the Shadow of FDR: From Harry Truman to Ronald Reagan,* by William Leuchtenburg, was a well-researched and insightful study of the impact of Roosevelt's policies and style on his successors.

Last Stands by Hilary Masters unsentimentally but movingly recalled the last years of the author's father, the poet Edgar Lee Masters. Two biographies of mystery writer Dashiell Hammett appeared during 1983. William F. Nolan's *Hammett: A Life at the Edge* was exhaustively researched if somewhat flat in its treatment. Diane Johnson's *Dashiell Hammett: A Life,* authorized by his literary executor, Lillian Hellman, if occasionally less accurate, was far more effective. *Willa: The Life of Willa Cather* by Phyllis Robinson, while the first biography to discuss Cather's homosexuality and assess its impact on her writing, was in general less satisfactory in its account of her as a writer.

WIDE WORLD

John Updike

Judged solely by the enthusiasm of the critical response, *Hugging the Shore,* a large selection of the essays and reviews of John Updike, was the literary event of the year. The mere volume of Updike's work impressed the professionals; and despite the book's self-deprecatory title ("Writing criticism," Updike observes, "is to writing fiction as hugging the shore is to sailing in the open sea"), the generosity, shrewdness, and elegance of his critical writing impressed them too. *In Search of Our Mothers' Gardens* by Alice Walker, author of the Pulitzer Prize-winning novel *The Color Purple,* collected prose written over the last 20 years. Subtitled "Womanist Prose," these essays dealt thoughtfully and eloquently with the subjects of literature, feminism, and race.

One of the year's interesting literary debuts was a book of travels, *Blue Highways* by William Least Heat Moon, an engaging account of his 21,000-km (13,000-mi) journey down the rural backroads of America. Another traveler, this time on one of the interstates, was John McPhee, whose *In Suspect Terrain* reflects on the complex geology of the country around Interstate 80, which runs through Pennsylvania and Ohio. Paul Theroux, whose previous train trips through Asia and the Americas were memorably described in *The Great Railway Bazaar* and *The Old Patagonian Express,* recorded his recent tour of his adopted home, Britain, in *The Kingdom by the Sea.* Theroux's book was an opinionated and entertaining account of a journey around the coast of Britain and Ulster undertaken in 1982 during the period of the Falklands war.

POETRY. The recent revival of interest in the work of H. D. was reflected in the appearance of her *Collected Poems, 1912–1944,* which included a large number of previously unpublished works. *The Complete Poems, 1927–1979* of the late Elizabeth Bishop, another poet whose posthumous reputation continues to grow, also appeared during 1983. Robert Penn Warren's *Chief Joseph of the Nez Perce* was a long, eloquent narrative poem dealing with the tribe's famous 1877 battle against the U.S. Army. Robert Creeley published both his *Collected Poems, 1945–1975* and a new collection, *Mirrors,* during the year. Gary Snyder's *Axe Handles* was his first collection since the Pulitzer Prize-winning *Turtle Island* in 1974. *Segues: A Correspondence in Poetry* was an interesting experiment conducted by William Stafford and Marvin Bell. Another was Hayden Carruth's *The Sleeping Beauty,* a complex series of lyrics on the theme of the famous fairy tale. Among the other important collections of poetry published during 1983 were *Lake Effect Country* by A. R. Ammons, *First Light* by David Wagoner, and *Opening the Hand* by W. S. Merwin.

(FITZGERALD HIGGINS)

Canada. Although one hears from time to time that the art of the short story is moribund because of difficulties in finding a publisher for such works, quite a few publishers in Canada seemed willing to take a chance on them in 1983. The collections were as varied in style and content as the enigmatic expositions contained in Margaret Atwood's *Bluebeard's Egg* and the zany charm of Sean Virgo's *Through the Eyes of a Cat: Irish Stories,* tales bitten through with melancholy, touched with awe.

Several writers approached the novel form in its more episodic manifestations with their use of a series of linked short stories to explore a place or theme. In Gertrude Story's *The Way to Always Dance,* the heroine's needs to love and be loved and to dance are sometimes brutally opposed. In *A First Class Funeral,* Sonia Birch-Jones observes the ambiguities of childhood and adolescence amid the ambiguities of Wales, themes that Sandra Birdsell treats quite differently in her *Night Travellers,* a many-faceted presentation of the experiences of a small-town family in Manitoba.

Best known for his poetry, A. M. Klein also wrote short stories. His collection *A. M. Klein: Short Stories* demonstrates that his talents as a poet are at home in this longer form. Another poet who did not mind changing forms was Cyril Dabydeen, whose short stories in *The Glass Forehead* approach the concepts of beginnings, originality, and ancestry through the diversity of angles offered by settings in Canada and the Caribbean. Still a third transmogrifier was Elizabeth Brewster, who in *A House Full of Women* uses her poet's eye to great effect in her observations of mothers and daughters and sisters and cousins, both kissing and once-removed.

Novels were also well represented in 1983. Stephen Vizinczey returned with the mordant and witty *An Innocent Millionaire,* a tale in which his characters are enmeshed in events resembling a treasure hunt hybridized with a mutant son of Monopoly—their foibles, itches, bitchery, treachery, and greed deftly laid open like hapless oysters on the half shell. H. R. Percy's *Painted Ladies* also has its painfully funny moments as the author traces the life of a Canadian painter and his temper-tossed affair with his model/mistress. Seal Award winner Janette Turner Hospital escaped the jinx of the second novel in her strongly crafted *The Tiger in the Tiger Pit,* depicting a fierce, proud old man at the centre of his family's disintegration and possible reunification. Morley Callaghan in *A Time for Judas* also contemplates the meaning of loyalty and betrayal as he retells the familiar story of the Crucifixion from the strange angle of Philo of Crete, Pontius Pilate's scribe. Another author who plays effectively with history is Heather Robertson, whose *Willie: A Romance* uses the diaries of MacKenzie King as a springboard into a fantasy tantalizingly close to fact.

Relationships between and among people is a frequent concern of poets, but their style of treatment of this theme varies as widely as Joe Rosenblatt's metaphysical anglings in *Brides of the Stream,* Bronwen Wallace's trenchant observations in *Signs of the Former Tenant,* and the 20-year analysis of mind/matter:left/right in *Richard Sommer: Selected and New Poems.* Another student of the past is Christopher Dewdney in *Predators of the Adoration, Selected Poems, 1972–1982.* More contemporary was Dorothy Livesay in *The Phases of Love,* poems written between 1925 and 1982. Anne Szumigalski delights in *Risks,* a dizzily successful play on words, love, and motorcycles. Also daringly mixing fable, burlesque, and history, Jon Whyte began a projected five-part celebration of the Canadian Rockies with *The Fells of Brightness: Some Fittes and Starts,* while bill bisset experiences dislocation and alienation in his own inimitable way in *Seagull on Yonge Street.* The fourth volume of *The Collected Poems of Raymond Souster* reveals more of his many incarnations as storyteller, magician, child, and humourist. (ELIZABETH WOODS)

FRENCH

France. School textbooks may gloss over the link between Joan of Arc and Gilles de Rais, but the historical association of the saint who is one of France's most potent national symbols and a mass murderer whose crimes made him the original for Bluebeard is a paradox that has fascinated many writers. The meeting of purity and corruption was a dominant theme in the work of Michel Tournier, and in *Gilles et Jeanne* he turned almost inevitably to the story of this heroine and her follower, examining both the sadism of Gilles and the ambiguities in the figure of the warrior-saint. If some recent fiction implied that the Middle Ages were a pleasant retreat from the horrors of modern life, Tournier did well to remind us that they were nothing of the sort.

The French delighted in the analysis of their character by a British academic, Theodore Zeldin, whose *Les Français* sold well in translation. It may have been a sense of security that inspired the mood of premature *fin de siècle* decadence invoked by Tournier and by the usual crop of novels about the Nazi occupation of World War II. These included the year's Prix Renaudot winner, Jean-Marie Rouart's *Avant-Guerre,* which sought to explain the treachery of a Vichy minister; Serge Rezvani's *La Loi humaine,* with its androgynous heroine and references to many cult figures; and Elie Wiesel's *Le Cinquième Fils,* in which an American Jew is faced with the problem of usurping the divine right to judge and punish a war criminal.

Popular taste did not always concur with that of the literary establishment, though it might be guided by it, notably through the system of literary prizes. The 1983 Goncourt went to Frédérick Tristan's *Les Égarés,* a satire on the literary world, remarkable because it came from one of the smaller publishers. The Goncourt short list included Pierre Bourgeade's *Les Serpents,* Henri Coulonges's *A l'approche d'un soir du monde,* Michel Host's *L'Ombre, le fleuve, l'été,* and Yann Queffélec's *Le Charme noir.* In April the third Salon du Livre was the occasion for commentators to confirm, yet again, that the "new novel" was dead, only to discover that some of its principal exponents were enjoying astonishing popular success. Admittedly, Nathalie Sarraute's *Enfance* was a highly readable piece of autobiography, and Philippe Sollers, in *Femmes,* abandoned the impenetrable style of his critical writings in an erotic satire that was one of the year's best-sellers.

What people most wanted to read, however, was history, either in studies like Marie-Christine Pouchelle's *Corps et chirurgie à l'apogée du moyen-âge,* a fascinating investigation of medieval attitudes to health and sickness, or in novels—Bernard Simiot's *Ces Messieurs de Saint-Malo,* Jacques Lacarrière's *Marie d'Égypte,* and a host of others. There were elements of political fantasy in Didier Martin's *Les Petits Maîtres,* set in a penal institution run by children, and of detective fiction in Suzanne Prou's *Le Pré aux narcisses* and Jean Métellus's *Une Eau-forte.* This novel, by a Haitian writer, was a highly suggestive study of the cre-

IMAPRESS/PICTORIAL PARADE

Michel Tournier

ative urge, a theme taken up by François Weyergans in *Le Radeau de la Méduse.* Henri Thomas, in *Le Migrateur,* plundered his notebooks for anecdotes and events that he had transformed in his fictional works, and there was a similar interest in the revelation of the mind of Julien Green through his journals for the years 1978–81, *La Lumière du monde.*

The attention given to well-known literary figures was further evidence of the dictatorship of "good taste" over experimentation. Some might have doubted whether good taste was the main feature of the record by Simone de Beauvoir (*see* Feature Article: *Women's Rights in Today's World;* BIOGRAPHIES) of her relationship with Jean-Paul Sartre, continued in *Lettres au Castor,* but time has a way of pacifying literary controversies. The seventh and eighth volumes of Stéphane Mallarmé's correspondence appeared, as well as the first volume of his complete poetry (it was hard to recall what a marginal and "obscure" poet he had been). The bicentenary of Stendhal's birth was marked by conferences, exhibitions, and studies like René Andrieu's *Stendhal ou le bal masqué.* It was 20 years since the death of Jean Cocteau, and poetry, the guiding spirit of his many-sided talent, was honoured by the publication of René Char's complete works and the Cerisy seminar in September on Yves Bonnefoy.

Other established literary figures like Alain Bosquet, with *Ni Guerre, ni paix,* and Raymond Aron (*see* OBITUARIES), with *Mémoires,* recalled their past, while Françoise Giroud's *Le Bon Plaisir* attracted notice as much because it was a first novel about political power by a former Cabinet minister as for its literary merits. In this conservative climate it was not easy for the reader to identify new talents or new directions. Michel Rio, a linguist, published a remarkable short novel, *Le Perchoir du perroquet,* and there were interesting new works by women writers, including Catherine Rihoit's *Le Triomphe de l'amour,* Florence Delay's *Riche et légère* (Prix Fémina), Suzanne Lilar's *La Confession anonyme* (filmed by André Delvaux under the title *Benvenuta*), and Colette Audry's *La Statue.*

Writers who died during the year included the art historian André Chamson, the right-wing polemicist Alfred Fabre-Luce, the dramatist Paul Géraldy, and the novelist Armand Lanoux, as well as the Belgian strip-cartoonist Hergé, a pioneer in a genre now recognized as a cultural phenomenon of some importance. (*See* OBITUARIES.)

(ROBIN BUSS)

Canada. It was a year of great sadness for Québecois literature, as, in the space of a few months, three of its most illustrious representatives passed away. On July 13, 1983, after a long illness, Gabrielle Roy (*see* OBITUARIES) died in a hospital in Quebec. She was the author of *Bonheur d'occasion,* which had won for her France's Prix Fémina in 1947. Her work (*La Petite Poule d'eau, Alexandre Chenevert, Rue Deschambault,* etc.), marked by great sensitivity, reveals her care for detail and perfection in the description of character and also in the form of the writing.

On September 20 the poet Gatien Lapointe died suddenly. In 1963 he had published *Ode au Saint-Laurent,* without doubt his most beautiful collection of poetry; in it he sings, at one and the same time, of the splendour of the Quebec countryside, the captivating force of life, and love of the word and the text. One month later it was the turn of novelist Yves Thériault to pass away (*see* OBITUARIES). A man of brusque temperament, Thériault wrote dozens of novels, the most celebrated of which, *Agaguk* (1958), was translated into six languages.

Among the outstanding works of 1983, *Le Valet de plume,* which won for its author, Jacques Folch-Ribas, the Prix Molson of 1983, is a kind of novel on art in which a nameless narrator, at once poet, sculptor, and music lover, tells of his life and the lives of his characters. Fashioned with art and refinement, the story risks plunging the reader into a completely strange world.

A very different type of writing was evident in *37½ AA* by Louise Leblanc (Prix Robert Cliche 1983). It is the story of a young girl, Fleur-Ange, who on grounds of expediency lives disguised as a man and works as a mechanic, then falls in love with a rich industrialist from the Antilles. This novel, overflowing with humour, is a sort of parody of the popular romances.

Among essays, *L'Histoire des femmes au Québec depuis quatre siècles,* written by the collective Clio, is a work of great originality and excellent quality. It tries to retrace the collective memory of women, a memory that has never left official traces.

(ROBERT SAINT-AMOUR)

GERMAN

Two of the most debated novels to appear in the German language in 1983 came from East Germany. Both were by women writers; both took as their theme the current threat of nuclear conflict; both related this threat to the patriarchal thought structures that have dominated human culture for the past 2,000 years. Christa Wolf's *Kassandra* approached the subject through the story of the poet-priestess of Troy whose warnings went unheeded; it was a work classical in its tragic dimensions, told by a Cassandra who has learned too late solidarity with her sisters. Irmtraud Morgner's *Amanda* was the romantic counterpiece, a novel overflowing its edges with tales of German "witches" and Greek "sirens," men who turn into ravens, and visitations from the Devil himself, all set in contemporary East Berlin.

A number of other interesting works appeared in East Germany, where despite recent gloomy prognostications, literature was evidently flourishing. The Nazi era and its implications for the present were the subject of Heinrich Ehler's *Hamanns Haus,* in which the daughter of a Jew who survived Hitler encounters latent anti-Semitism and living representatives of the past, and of Helmut Schulz's *Dame in Weiss,* an account of life in the Third Reich viewed not from the angle of the antifascist present but as it was for one who was neither active Nazi nor resistance fighter. Jurij Koch's *Landung der Träume* was a lighthearted account of growing up after World War II on the border between Czechoslovakia and East Germany. Günter Görlich's *Die Chance des Mannes* portrayed a marriage that broke up because of the husband's inability to reconcile his socialist commitment with the demands of human warmth.

The topic of woman and her place in history was also prominent in West Germany. Angelika Mechtel's *Gott und die Liedermacherin* was a militantly feminist work, a montage of stories, myths, and poems linked through the adventures of a female nightclub singer in a militaristic, male-dominated America. Karin Reschke pursued the question to the beginning of the 19th century in her highly praised *Verfolgte des Glücks,* the fictitious diary of Heinrich von Kleist's friend Henriette Vogel. Marie-Thérèse Kerschbaumer's complex novel *Schwestern* presented 20th-century European history in terms of its impact on several pairs of sisters, all more or less exploited by conservative Austrian society. In *Die dreizehnte Fee,* the story of three generations of a Jewish family in Westphalia, Katja Behrens set out to explore the question "How women have become what they are."

Other novels that included a historical dimension were Manfred Bieler's *Der Bar,* set in a small town in Sachsen-Anhalt between 1914 and 1962, and Ernst Herhaus's *Der Wolfsmantel,* which described the fates of a group of people in Austria between 1930 and 1945. Heinrich Goertz's semiautobiographical *Lachen und Heulen* was interesting especially for the light it shed on prominent literary figures of the 1930s. But the most important work of this kind was the final volume of Uwe Johnson's *Jahrestage*; its three time layers—June to August 1968 describing the Soviet invasion of Czechoslovakia, the post-World War II years in East and West Germany, and the more distant past of National Socialism—all illustrated the crushing of man's attempts to gain freedom.

In his *Brief an Lord Liszt,* Martin Walser pursued his preoccupation with internecine conflicts among the executives of large industrial firms. Dieter Wellershoff's *Der Sieger nimmt alles,* a psychological study of the career of a self-made man in the 1950s and 1960s, likewise satirized the struggle for survival in the capitalist world. More hard-hitting was a first novel by Beat Sterchi of Switzerland. *Blösch* described in an almost Joycean range of styles the exploitation of and hostility toward foreign workers in Switzerland, making effective use of symbolism in the slaughterhouse where the central figure works.

A number of novels offered or implied alternatives to the rat race of present-day civilization. Walter Kappacher's exciting if teasing *Der lange Brief* described a popular revolt against the automobile in Detroit and life among the Australian Aborigines, only to unmask both excursions as fictitious and impractical. Frank Werner's *Herzland,* a tale of dropouts in the city jungle, took as its central symbol the image of the predatory carnivores that devour the weak, the old, the unlucky, and the slow. It was in this context too that Sten Nadolny's attractive historical novel *Die Entdeckung der Langsamkeit* had to be viewed. Based on the life of the English explorer John Franklin, it registered an appeal on behalf of the individual's "inner tempo." By contrast, *Aladins Problem* by the indefatigable Ernst Jünger denied all social values other than the cult of the dead; its nihilistic hero, some-

HELGA PARIS © 1982

Christa Wolf

time German aristocrat and officer in the Polish People's Army, finally finds his vocation organizing stylish funerals in Cappadocia.

Among the volumes of short fiction to appear, collections by Jürg Amann (*Die Baumschule,* including his prizewinning "Rondo"), Erich Fried (*Das Unmass aller Dinge*), and Eva Zeller (*Der Tod der Singschwäne*) were outstanding. Lyric poetry was well represented by Michael Krüger's *Aus der Ebene,* Wolf Wondratschek's Mexican sonnets *Die Einsamkeit der Männer,* and especially by Guntram Vesper's *Die Inseln im Weltmeer.* (J. H. REID)

SCANDINAVIAN

Denmark. Kirsten Thorup's *Himmel og Helvede* (1982) had as enthusiastic a reception as any Danish novel in many years. An account of an elderly spinster turned brothel keeper and an immigrant family whose daughter experiences incredible adventures, it provided a compelling picture of a chaotic society. Social evaluation was at the centre of Anders Bodelsen's *Over Regnbuen* (1982), about a family offered a new future in Australia and thereby forced to reassess Denmark. Klaus Rifbjerg's *Hvad sker der i kvarteret* was ostensibly about Copenhagen suburban life in the 1930s, revealing both complacency and dangerous hidden tendencies.

Rifbjerg's *Patience* was concerned with an elderly man and his acceptance of approaching death, together with his determination to live a full life meanwhile. A related theme was that of Dea Trier Mørch's *Aftenstjernen* (1982), a novel about a patient dying of cancer and showing the effect of this on her relationship with her son. Poul Ørum's deeply felt *Ravnen mod aften* (1982) described a man's efforts to overcome the shock and trauma of losing his wife after many years of marriage.

Villy Sørensen returned to the literary scene with a short work entitled *Ragnarok* (1982). This was a retelling in typical Sørensen style of the Nordic myths, filled with the juxtaposed thoughts and ideas in which he had always excelled, and giving his theme significance for the present day. Christian Kampmann ventured into the thriller genre with *Sunshine,* about a hired assassin who changes his mind and tries to avoid the complications he has provided for himself and others. Henrik Nord-brandt, highly esteemed as a poet, also moved into thrillers in *Finckelsteins blodige bazar*, a novel of intrigue and political violence with a Mediterranean background.

Violence, with political overtones, was also at the centre of two novels by Knud B. Thomsen. *Røverne i Skotland* (1982), a picaresque novel set in Scotland in the period following Culloden, depicted a Celtic trio—a Welshman, an Irishman, and a Scot—and their efforts to thwart the English. The theme of *Den irske præst* was related, set in the Ireland of 1920 and again, in a mixture of humour, violence, and tension, showing the confrontation between the Celts and the English.

The 1982 Danish Academy Prize went to Per Højholt. The veteran Hedin Brú, the most important Faroese novelist of his day, was fittingly awarded the Holberg Medal. (W. GLYN JONES)

Norway. A recent tendency to set the action in other countries still applied in Norwegian literature in 1983, reaching a superb climax in Unn Bendeke and Iver Tore Svenning's novel *Selv himmelen brenner*, with its convincing psychological analysis of the character of Adolf Hitler as seen through the eyes of people close to him. Atrocities against Jews in Lithuania during World War II were movingly dealt with in Jahn Otto Johansen's *Min jødiske krig*, the last volume of a documentary trilogy. In Kjartan Fløgstad's best novel to date, *U 3*, he followed the love life and career of a NATO pilot, giving a convincing picture of NATO installations in Norway.

Uncannily topical was Asbjørn Elden's *Rundt neste sving*, describing his life as a young unemployed vagabond in Norway in the 1930s and turning endless humiliations and frustrations into first-rate literature. There was much political dynamite, as well as subtle psychological insight, in Dag Solstad's bitter-humorous account of the disillusionment of a committed Communist, *Gymnaslærer Pedersens berentning om den store politiske vekkelsen som har hjemsøkt vårt land*. Espen Haavardholm's uneven novel *Store fri* had as a main theme the death of the dream of utopian socialism. Uneven also was Tor Edvin Dahl's *Reisen*, focusing on the disappointing realities of Communist China seen through the eyes of a married middle-aged university lecturer and her young lover.

Charm and wisdom were to be found in Elisabeth Tham's *Pannekaker med Marcell*, devoted to the summer meeting of a middle-aged widowed schoolmistress and a girl of five. The main character in Ketil Bjørnstad's *Oda!* was Oda Krohg, the high priestess of free love in the Christiania Bohemian anarchist movement of the 1880s. The documentary novel caught well the spirit of the movement and above all the sadness and suffering of its adherents.

Compassion, humour, irony, and stylistic mastery were much to the fore in Kjell Askildsen's touching short stories *Thomas F's siste nedtegnelser til almenheten*. Kåre Holt's autobiographical *Veien videre: Ny sannferdig beretning om mitt liv some løgner* was a humorous account of numerous meetings with people at home and abroad. Outstanding love poems were central in Stein Mehren's *Timenes Time*, where identity, impermanence, and death were other themes. Collected poems were published by Harald Sverdrup (*Samlede dikt 1948–1982*) and Olav H. Hauge (*Samla verk I-II*).

(TORBJØRN STØVERUD)

Sweden. It was a fine year for poetry. In *Dikter kring noll*, septuagenarian Karl Vennberg demonstrated his habitual formal mastery and even increased his passion and wit. Tomas Tranströmer, with a wide readership abroad, published *Det vilda torget*. This slight volume contained prose poems and verse with a wide emotional register and imagery that was at once luminous and multivalent. Göran Sonnevi published *Dikter utan ordning*, a mixture of sociopolitical texts about oppression and aggression and fine pieces in which the pulse of protest beats in paradoxes. Ylva Eggehorn, whose previous religious poetry had amply demonstrated her talent, showed in *Genombrott* that something had happened—here was pain and the dark night of the soul. Lighter verse was represented by Kristina Lugn's self-ironical *Bekantskap önskas med äldre bildad herre* and Marie Louis Ramnefalk's satirical *Levnadskonster*.

Torgny Lindgren, award-winning novelist in 1982, published *Merab's skönhet*, short stories of exceptional power and quality. The two most memorable novels were written by women: Sara Lidman's *Den underbare mannen*, part four of her cycle about the 19th-century colonization of northern Sweden, written in a marvelously allusive style, with dialect and stream-of-consciousness; and Kerstin Ekman's *En stad av ljus*, a complex and gripping study of a woman living through a crisis. Gerda Antti's novel *Jag reder mig nog* was a slighter, likably humorous account of a woman's predicament, while Björn Håkansson's novel *Kvinnobilden* described the narrator's efforts to replace the traditional female image with an entirely new one. Göran Tunström's *Juloratoriet* was a poetic novel spanning three generations of people somehow trying to keep the spirit of joy—symbolized by Bach's Christmas Oratorio—alive.

Lars Gustafsson's *Sorgemusik för frimurare* showed three individuals attempting, over a span of 20 years, to find meaning in their lives in a Sweden viewed gloomily by the author; the book was enlivened by a thriller-like intrigue. Sven Delblanc's short novel *Jerusalem's natt* was set in AD 70 and showed a confrontation in the Roman camp between Titus, emperor-to-be, and an elderly Christian from the besieged Jerusalem. Clearly, it was concern for contemporary freedom of thought in the face of state oppression that inspired this novel. (KARIN PETHERICK)

ITALIAN

The year started well with the posthumous publication in one volume of Pier Paolo Pasolini's early autobiographical novels *Amado mio* and *Atti impuri*, followed by Elsa Morante's *Aracoeli*. Though all three involved homosexual protagonists, Pasolini's stories were delicate idylls, set in the mythical Friuli of his youth, while Morante's was a bleak tragedy. As Morante's protagonist travels back to the village of his dead mother, he relives his gradual separation from her as a process that leaves him utterly derelict, incapable of accepting himself and adult life and forever searching for a scrap of love and sanity in a world of inescapable ugliness and degradation. Despite or because of Morante's stunning literary style, her success was not entirely uncontroversial, many readers finding that the novel's elaborate language undercut the desperate philosophy that pervaded it. More successful, albeit much less interesting, was Alberto Bevilacqua's *Il curioso delle donne*, a rambling mixture of the narrator's tentative self-analysis with descriptions of his wanderings, spiritual and emotional as well as spatial and temporal, through all degrees of human sophistication and degradation in Rome and Romagna alike.

Among other established novelists, Mario Tobino and Natalia Ginzburg centred their two books on Alessandro Manzoni's life. More convincing than Tobino's *Il Natale del 1833*, which dealt with the deep spiritual crisis undergone by Manzoni at the time of his first wife's death, was Ginzburg's *La famiglia Manzoni*, a sensitive and careful reconstruction of life around Manzoni through the correspondence of his family with friends and relations. The result was not only a book of compelling quality in itself but also one that illuminated, perhaps better than any biography, the intellectual and emotional environment out of which Manzoni's own masterpiece, *I promessi sposi*, arose. Some of Manzoni's fictional characters appeared also in the evocative *La Notte di Toledo* by Ferruccio Ulivi, six short stories set in different times and places but thematically interconnected by the presence throughout the book of a single question about the relationship between freedom and destiny.

Memory novels were still alive and well. Bino Sanminiatelli published *Gli irregolari*, four short stories about one Tuscan family between World Wars I and II; Pier Maria Pasinetti with *Dorsoduro* provided a large fresco of Venetian life in the late 1920s, where comedy and tragedy mingle with daily chatter; Carlo Cassola with *Mio padre* recollected and reappraised the figure of his father and their tormented relationship. Among newcomers there was Adamo Calabrese with his sparkling first novel, *Il libro del Re*. In a language of luxuriant richness and vitality it told the surreal story, set in 16th-century Lombardy, of two equally unhinged and sexually frustrated kings (one French, obsessed with revenge, and the other Italian, a dreamy and down-at-heel intellectual) who fight to the death, while their barber-physician-painter survives them both to enjoy huge quantities of food, drink, and sex. Halfway between novel and essay was *La rovina di Kasch* by Roberto Calasso, a rich and complex work, unfolding in all directions—historical, philosophical, anthropological—but centred on the legend of the fall of Kasch. The mysterious personality of Talleyrand, who reappears throughout the book, provides a semblance of unity to this remarkable, though debatable, view of history and civilization out of which only a faith in style seems ultimately to survive.

Journalists and politicians were as active as ever. Among the most successful were Luciano Doddoli with his harrowing *Lettere di un padre alla figlia che si droga* and Camilla Cederna with *Casa nostra*. The latter comprised penetrating sketches of 18 Italian cities from Turin to Catania, giving an unusually vivid and provocative, though not entirely arbitrary, view of contemporary Italian society. In the thriving field of Mussolini studies, there was, among others, *Mussolini giovane* by Luigi Preti, a collage of the young Duce's public pronouncements which he later thoroughly contradicted in words and deeds alike. At the other end of the political spectrum was *Ragazzo rosso* by Giancarlo Pajetta, an autobiography of the Communist politician from his early youth to the years of the Resistance.

Andrea Zanzotto's collection *Fosfeni* confirmed his position as a major living poet. In *Matinée*, a collection covering events, fashions, and personalities of the last 40 years, Alberto Arbasino was, as usual, irresistibly witty. Finally, the year was saddened by the death of Vittorio Sereni (*see* OBITUARIES), undoubtedly one of the most significant and profound voices of contemporary European poetry. (LINO PERTILE)

SPANISH

Spain. On the heels of a lavish pre-publication campaign, a 50,000-copy first edition of Camilo José Cela's *Mazurka para dos muertos* was sold out in a week, and reputable critics did not hesitate to call it the crowning achievement of that prolific writer's career. Structurally complex, sonorous, and rich in its language, *Mazurka* is a sombre tapestry of mutilated yet hopeful lives and random, violent deaths in the damp Galician hinterlands during the Civil War, woven from a sprawling genealogy of interconnected families, including Cela's own.

Several other veteran novelists were active during 1983. Juan Benet began a "Civil War trilogy" with *Herrumbrosas lanzas*, which marked a shift toward greater clarity in his intricate style while reviving the imaginary setting of "Región" from *Volverás a Región* (1967), which established his high literary reputation. Gonzálo Torrente Ballester's *La princesa durmiente va a la escuela*, confiscated by censors in 1951 and believed lost or destroyed, brings Sleeping Beauty awake in mid-20th-century "Minimuslandia," whose society is the target of ferocious satire. In the convolutions of *El cuento de nunca acabar*, Carmen Martín Gaite turned fiction-making itself into a fiction; and late in 1982 *Conocerás el pozo de la nada*, the last novel of José Luis Castillo Puche's existentialist cycle *Trilogía de la liberación*, received the National Novel Prize. A biographical novel by José Luis Olaizola, *La guerra del general Escobar*, which won the important Planeta Prize, reconstructed the events leading up to the execution in 1940 of a Civil Guard officer who remained faithful to the Republican cause.

In an otherwise inconspicuous year for poetry, Rafael Alberti (Cádiz, 1902) won Spain's highest literary award, the Cervantes Prize, and no one missed the symbolism of this official recognition. A poet of many styles, metres, and voices—from *Marinero en tierra* (1925) to *Versos de cada día* (1982)—Alberti spent nearly 40 years in exile for the socially militant stance of much of his work.

For two decades the many works of the 19th-century writer Benito Pérez Galdós (often called Spain's greatest writer after Cervantes) have enjoyed ever increasing popularity and intense critical scrutiny. In 1983 two of his long-forgotten plays, *La de San Quintín* and *Casandra,* were revived; and the appearance of a previously unknown Galdós novel, *Rosalía* (1872)—discovered in Madrid's National Library by the U.S. Hispanist Alan Smith—was, for many fans and critics, the year's most delightful literary surprise.

(ROGER L. UTT)

Latin America. Major writers of Latin America, including Mario Vargas Llosa, Gabriel García Márquez, Octavio Paz, and José Donoso, published books outside the central focus of their careers in 1983. Recognized younger writers such as Gustavo Sainz, Eduardo Galeano, and Reinaldo Arenas were also active.

Mario Vargas Llosa's novel *La guerra del fin del mundo* (1981), not yet published in English, was still notably visible in the Hispanic world and was a best-seller in France during 1983. This Peruvian novelist's production in 1983, however, was a play, *Katie y el hipótamo.* The Chilean novelist José Donoso also wrote a play which was successfully produced, *Sueños de mala muerte.* Colombian novelist Gabriel García Márquez published a book of conversations in English, *The Fragrance of the Guave.* The Mexican poet Octavio Paz wrote a study of a Colonial poet, *Sor Juana Inés de la Cruz.*

Paz's book on Sor Juana was the literary event of the year in Mexico. It is an insightful portrait of an epoch, an individual, and a body of writing. Several other established Mexican writers published noteworthy novels during 1983. Gustavo Sainz wrote *Fantasmas Aztecas,* based on the excavation of the Aztec Templo Mayor. José Agustín employed more traditional narrative techniques in *Ciudades desiertas,* a straightforward story about a Mexican marital relationship in the foreign ambience of the United States. Joaquín-Armando Chacón's novel *Las amarras terrestres* contrasts a utopian society with contemporary commercialism. *Minas del retorno,* the second novel by Carlos Montemayor, deals with the life of miners in northern Mexico and confirms the author's ability to emphasize individual human concern within a broad social context.

The publication and circulation of literature in Argentina improved with the diminishing of censorship. Julio Cortázar's volume of short stories *Deshoras,* for example, was a best-seller in Argentina, even though recent governments had banned his writing. Cortázar also published the stories *Queremos tanto a Glenda* in late 1982. Osvaldo Soriano published best-selling novels in Argentina, *No habrá más penas ni olvido* and *Cuarteles de invierno.* These works involve Argentina's recent history, dealing with such issues as Peronism and the disappeared persons of the 1970s. The novelist Jorge Asis revealed an interest in similar topics in *La calle de los caballos muertos.*

Some of Colombia's best novelists published in 1983. David Sánchez Juliao was awarded the Plaza y Janés National Novel Prize for *Sigo siendo el rey,* a unique novel based on the music of classic Mexican *rancheras.* The second prize went to the poet Darío Jaramillo Agudelo for *La muerte de Alec,* a fine epistolary novel. Manuel Zapata Olivella, after two decades of silence, published *Changó, el gran putas,* a novel of epic proportions that is the product of extensive anthropological and historical study. Rafael Humberto Moreno Durán, one of Colombia's finest young writers, published his third novel, *Finale capriccioso con Madonna.* Antonio Palomar Avilés wrote his first novel, a short and innovative piece titled *Raspa.* The National Short-Story Contest was won by Oscar Castro García and the fifth National Poetry Prize "Eduardo Cote Lamus" was awarded to Jaime Jaramillo Escobar. The poet Germán Pardo García was named to the Order of Boyacá, the most prestigious award given by the Colombian government.

The most important novel published in Chile was the young Jorge Marchant Lezcano's *La noche que nunca ha gestado el día* (late 1982), a work dealing with decadent night life and social disintegration. Veteran novelists Enrique Lafourcade and Carlos Morand also came forth with works in late 1982. Lafourcade's *Adiós al fuhrer,* a critique of fascism in Hitler's Germany, portrays situations parallel to those in present-day Chile. Morand published a quite traditional novel, *El espejo de los buhos.* Manuel Rojas's posthumous memoirs appeared, *Imágenes de infancia y adolesencia.*

Several noteworthy books were written in other parts of Latin America. *Otra vez el mar* (late 1982) was published by the Cuban novelist in exile Reinaldo Arenas. Eduardo Galeano, in exile from Uruguay, published *Memoria del fuego,* a book that combines essay, history, and fiction. After a hiatus of many years, Emilio Díaz Valcárcel of Peru wrote a novel, *Mi mamá me ama.*

(RAYMOND L. WILLIAMS)

PORTUGUESE

Portugal. Literary experimentation in all fields continued to flourish, but there was a growing awareness of the importance of human experience in the novel and of the need to recapture memories of the past. Many events of the last 48 years had been effectively suppressed by the censor until the April 1974 revolution and, unlikely to appear in history books, were in danger of falling into total oblivion.

To tell what historians were bound to forget was the purpose of José Cardoso Pires in his *Balada de Praia dos Cães,* awarded the National Prize for fiction. His story centres on a group of political conspirators who were in hiding while waiting for a military uprising against the regime of António Salazar. The story, based on fact, is told in an imaginative way and from an investigative viewpoint that reveals Cardoso Pires as not only a master of suspense but also as an author of acute psychological insight. He describes all the tensions that grow in a claustrophobic atmosphere, climaxing with the death of the group's leader. The drama is seen from many angles, and the narrator, like Truman Capote in *In Cold Blood,* is part and parcel of the narrative.

Another impressive literary achievement was José Saramago's *Memorial do Convento,* a tale spun around the 18th-century Mafra monastery and the workers who built it to fulfill a vow made by the king of Portugal. By blending colloquial speech with the learned language of the court, the author imparts to his narrative the quality of an oral tale, to stunning effect.

In *Lúcialima,* Maria Velhe da Costa produced a fascinating novel of rare complexity that was also haunted by the power of memory. Reminiscence is triggered over a 24-hour period by the events of the first day of the April 1974 revolution. The feelings of a wide variety of characters are woven into patterns of time and well-defined situations, charged with symbolic meanings, that make the blind girl, who is the linchpin of the whole narrative, the Tiresias of a wasteland of domestic mysteries. (L. S. REBELO)

Brazil. The uneasy relationship between politics and culture was considered by Silviano Santiago in the essays of his *Vale quanto pesa* and by Nicolau Sevcenko in his study of Euclides da Cunha and Lima Barreto, *Literatura como missão.* Maria Luisa Nunes's *The Craft of an Absolute Winner* is a fine study of the art of Machado de Assis, and David Haberly published *Three Sad Races,* which attempts to show the possible influence of race in the literary processes of six major Brazilian writers. Massaud Moisés published the first volume of his new *História da literatura brasileira.*

Antônio Callado and Millôr Fernandes wrote new plays. Important stage productions included Oduvaldo Viana Filho's biting comedy on problems of Brazil and Latin America, *Dura lex sed lex . . .,* which had been prohibited for more than a decade; *Bella, Ciao,* produced by the Mambembe Group of São Paulo and dealing with the origins of the Brazilian workers' movement; and a musical by Chico Buarque and Edu Lobo based on a poem by the modernist Jorge de Lima. Henriqueta Lisboa wrote a volume of essentially metaphysical poetry, *Pousada no ser,* while Ana Cristina César's *A teus pés* was the most significant collection by a new poet. Gilberto Mendonça Teles's *Saciologia goiana* centres on legends of his native Goiás.

Long and short fiction dominated the literary scene. Amazonian life was among the most popular topics. Benedicto Monteiro's *A terceira margem* presents the sociopolitical and economic existence of the Amazon River people and expresses interest in their language usage. Márcio Souza's *A resistível ascensão do Boto Tucuxi,* set in the Amazon of the 1950s, was a rather off-the-mark satire of the recent political election in the state. Finally, Raimundo Caruso's *Buenos días, Mr. Ludwig* is a satire of multinational exploitation of the Amazon.

The Brazilian woman—as a theme and as author—was also popular in 1983. Fernando Gabeira fictionalized a sordid murder in *Sinais de vida no planeta Minas,* while Paulo Francis's stories in *Filhos do segundo sexo* described present-day sexual politics. Important fiction by women writers expressed concern for existential issues rather than feminist ones. Most notable were works by Edla van Steen, *Coraçoes mordidos,* and by Patrícia Bins, *Jogo de fiar.* Norma Pereira Rego's *Ipanema Dom Divino* evoked the artistic atmosphere of that Rio neighbourhood in the late 1960s.

Novels by Esdras do Nascimento and Márcio Souza and short fiction by Fausto Wolff, João Antônio, and Josué Guimarães returned to a recurrent theme: the almost incredible realities of life in today's Brazil. Stories by Caio Fernando Abreu and Luiz Fernando Veríssimo were of a lighter, more comic nature and were, consequently, runaway best-sellers. (IRWIN STERN)

RUSSIAN

Soviet Literature. Two apparently differing trends interacted during 1983. On the one hand there was an undeniable interest on the writer's part in illuminating contemporary political reality. On the other, there were the probings by writers into the history of their native land, the deep-seated features of the national character, and the main features of Russian classical culture.

The first of the two trends was represented, primarily, by new works in the genres of the political novel or novella. One of these was Aleksandr Chakovsky's *Unfinished Portrait,* dealing with the last part of the life of U.S. Pres. Franklin D. Roosevelt and the experience of Soviet-U.S. cooperation during World War II. Then there were Savva Dangulov's novel *The Tsar's Post,* Daniel Kraminov's *At the Edge of Night,* about the establishment of Soviet diplomacy, and Yuly Semyonov's exciting political detective novel *Condemned to Survive!,* continuing the popular series about the activities of Soviet intelligence agent Isayev-Shtirlik in Nazi Germany. Authors also took a keen interest in political events that had not yet receded into history. M. Domagatsky's novel *South of the River Benhai,* about the war in Vietnam, was one example, while the crimes of Pol Pot constituted the theme of a Kampuchean chronicle, A. Prokhanov's *On Hunter's Island.*

Works about the life of present-day Soviet society also often had a political theme. For example, Y. Chernyakov's story *The Team* was set in the cold war period when, against the background of the mounting arms race, the Soviet Union's nuclear missile shield was created. Belorussian author Vasily Bykov's novella *Sign of Misfortune,* the most noteworthy book of the year about the Great Patriotic War (World War II), was also distinguished by its clear polemicism, as were the novels *Science of Parting* by Veniamin Kaverin and E. Vois-

Vasily Bykov

TASS/SOVFOTO

kunsky's *People from Kronstadt* and the novella *Likhobor* by Vyacheslav Kondratev. The prime inspiration of all these works was the fight for peace, for an end to the arms race, and for the establishment of good-neighbourly relations between peoples and states with differing social systems and political and historical experiences.

Making up the second trend were works that turned to former times and related to various periods in the history of the Russian state and the national culture. Throughout the year new chapters of a widely read novel by Vladimir Chivilikhin, *The Memory*, appeared in the press; they were a kind of summing up of the author's many years of research into historical archives and local history. There was tremendous interest in Bulat Okudjava's novel *Meeting with Bonaparte*, portraying Russian society during the period of the Napoleonic invasion.

The 17th All-Union Pushkin Festival took place during the year, as did the traditional Lermontov, Nekrasov, Tyutchev, Mayakovsky, and Blok poetry celebrations. (SERGEY CHUPRININ)

Expatriate Russian Literature. In 1983 yet another leading Soviet writer was forced to leave the U.S.S.R. and find a new home in the West. Georgy Vladimov, once a highly popular novelist and short-story writer, emigrated to Munich, West Germany, in May. For several years he had suffered harassment by the Soviet authorities following his resignation from the Writers' Union in 1977 and the publication abroad of his novel *Faithful Ruslan.* Soon after his arrival in West Germany, Vladimov became editor of the Russian-language literary magazine *Grani* ("Facets"). At an informal meeting with several British writers, including Stephen Spender, Dan Jacobson, and Richard Adams, Vladimov explained that the Soviet government, through the copyright agency VAAP, kept tight control of all dealings between Soviet authors and their foreign publishers. Once he had become a "nonperson," all his royalties from abroad were stopped, and he was not even told that his Norwegian publisher had invited him to the Frankfurt Book Fair. Yury Galperin, who had emigrated four years before Vladimov and now lived in Switzerland, published in Frankfurt *Most cherez Letu* ("Bridge over Lethe"), a short novel written in 1975, when its author was still in his 20s.

The French historian Michel Heller achieved an unusual literary feat in rescuing from oblivion the last novel of a famous Russian writer, Boris Pilnyak, who was arrested in 1937 and murdered during one of Stalin's purges. The book, *Dvoyniki* ("Doubles"), had been written in 1933 and rejected by several Soviet publishers before being sent to Poland to the author's friend and translator, Wladyslaw Borniewski. It was published in a Polish translation in Warsaw, while the Russian manuscript was most probably destroyed. Having discovered that Pilnyak had lifted parts of the novel from some of his earlier works, Heller pieced the book together from these and from the Polish translation. *Dvoyniki* was brought out by Overseas Publishers Interchange in London, which was also responsible for the first book in Russian on the poet Marina Tsvetayeva. Titled *Marina Tsvetayeva, Myth and Reality*, it was written by Maria Razumovskaya and had earlier appeared in German.

Another important publication was a biography of Lev Shestov (*Zhizn' Lva Shestova*) by the philosopher's daughter, Natalya Baranova Shestova. Based on Shestov's letters and those of his contemporaries, the biography was published by La Presse Libre in Paris. In London Nina Karsov, who specialized in Polish and Russian literature, published the first Russian translation of a work by Friedrich von Hayek, *The Road to Serfdom* (*Doroga Krabstva*).

Among those imprisoned in the U.S.S.R. during the year were Mikhail Meylakh, a philologist and translator who was a foremost expert on modern Russian literature; Sergey Grygoryants, another Russian literature specialist, accused of helping to produce a *samizdat* (clandestinely published) human rights bulletin; and the poet Irina Ratushinskaya. Accused of circulating her uncensored verses and criticizing the U.S.S.R., Ratushinskaya was sentenced to 12 years in prison and internal exile. (GEORGE THEINER)

EASTERN EUROPEAN LITERATURE

Released from prison because of ill health eight months before the end of his 4½-year sentence, the Czechoslovak dramatist Vaclav Havel wrote a one-act play, *Chyba* ("Mistake"), in response to a play written as a tribute to him two years earlier by Samuel Beckett. The Beckett play, *Catastrophe*, and Havel's new piece were performed together at the Stockholm Stadsteater in Sweden in November 1983 during an evening held in support of Havel and his fellow members of the Charter 77 human rights movement.

In a letter published in the *Times Literary Supplement* in London on October 21, Havel and three spokesmen of Charter 77 drew attention to "the consistent and continuous destruction of literary and scientific books in Czechoslovakia, comparable to the destruction of Czech books during the Nazi occupation." The letter went on to say that there were "hundreds of authors, as well as journalists, unable to publish for political reasons," many of them silenced since 1948. The letter cited the case of Jaroslav Savrda, imprisoned for two years in March on charges of "incitement." He had already served a similar sentence in 1978–81 for smuggling into Czechoslovakia literature published in the West. Father Josef Barta died of a heart attack shortly before he was due to start serving a prison term imposed on him and other Franciscans in 1982 for *samizdat* activities.

Jaroslav Seifert's latest collection of verse, *Destnik z Piccadilly* (*Umbrella from Piccadilly*), was published in an English translation by Alan Ross's London Magazine Editions. *The Writing on the Wall*, a volume of short stories and journalistic pieces by 18 banned Czechoslovak writers, was published by Karz-Cohl Inc. in New Jersey. The authors represented included Jiri Grusa, Havel, Eva Kanturkova, Ivan Klima, Alexander Kliment, Pavel Kohout, Eda Kriseova, and Ludvik Vaculik. "What is interesting," wrote A. J. Liehm in his foreword to the book, "is that in its 150 years of modern existence Czech literature has never known such a flowering of talent . . . as in these very years of its persecution."

In August the Polish authorities dissolved the Union of Polish Writers, accusing its leaders of links with "subversive centres"—a reference to the outlawed Solidarity trade union. Two months earlier the leadership of the writers' union had been told that it must purge its ranks of authors whom the authorities considered opposed to their policies and pledge loyalty to "the socialist system." A number of writers were still in prison awaiting trial, having been detained in the first days of martial law in December 1981. Several others who had been abroad, including the poet Anka Kowalska, returned home to Poland. Tadeusz Konwicki's novel, *A Minor Apocalypse,* was published in hardback by Farrar Straus Giroux (New York) and Faber & Faber (London); two of his earlier books, *The Polish Complex* and *A Dreambook for Our Time,* were published in paperback by Penguin in the U.S. Marek Nowakowski's book of short stories, *The Canary and Other Tales of Martial Law,* was published by Harvill Press in London.

In Hungary the Communist Party leader Janos Kadar told the party's Central Committee (in a secret speech leaked to opposition leaders in Budapest) that the activities of the unofficial opposition would no longer be tolerated. While there would be no trials, their lives would be made so unpleasant that they would cease their dissident activity. Early in the year the police raided the homes of six dissident intellectuals, confiscating a large quantity of books and manuscripts. The six—who included Miklos Haraszti and Ferenc Koszeg, editors of the unofficial quarterly *Beszelo;* Gabor Demszky, chief organizer of the AB Publishing House; and Laszlo Rajk, who started the Budapest "Samizdat Boutique"—were detained overnight and released after being accused of unauthorized publication and distribution of unofficial literature. On a later occasion Demszky was accosted and beaten up in the street.

A Yugoslav poet, Gojko Djogo, was sentenced to one year in prison for publishing a book of poems deemed offensive to the memory of Marshal Tito. The book, *Woollen Times,* was published two years earlier but then was banned. Djogo was released in May on grounds of ill health. Vlado Bakotic and Dragan Cancevic, director and editor in chief, respectively, of the Otokar Kersovani publishing house in Opatija, were dismissed from their posts for publishing *The Actual and the Possible* by the Serbian writer Dobrica Cosic. The book contained the text of a speech given by Cosic to the Communist League of Serbia about the potential danger of ethnic Albanian nationalism in Kosovo Province. (GEORGE THEINER)

JEWISH

Hebrew. During 1983 many writers and scholars were occupied with issues concerning Israeli literature. The poet Natan Zach wrote "On Pure and Impure Poetry" and published a collection of essays on Israeli prose. A posthumous volume of Baruch Kurzweil's articles on Israeli fiction also appeared. Yitzhak Oren joined the trend with *haHitpakhut Basifrut haYisra'elit,* and Gershon Shaked and Y. Golan edited an anthology of Israeli stories, *Hayim al Kav haKets.* S. Yizhar, Israel's foremost novelist, contributed a two-volume work, *Likro Sippur,* which argued for a more organic relationship between reader and text.

Major publications of classical writers included letters by Samuel Joseph Agnon to his wife (1924–31), two volumes of Abraham Shlonsky's play translations, a reissue of David Fogel's *Le'ever haDemama,* and a critical edition of Hayyim Bialik's early poetry, with Dan Miron as its chief editor. New prose works were published by D. Tselka, Aharon Megged, A. Semo, Y. Ben-Ner, and Shulamith Hareven. Yoram Kaniuk's novel *haYehudi haAharon* was noteworthy, as were the new and flourishing writers A. Dorit, David Grossman, and Ruth Almog. Poetry works included M. Bejerano's *haHom Vehakor,* M. Geldman's *66–83 Shirim,* and Gavriella Elisha's *Musika Aheret.* Naomi Shahar and Zeli Gurevitch published their first poetry collections.

JUDITH APPELFELD

Aharon Appelfeld

Several significant critical works appeared, including Samuel Werses's study of modern Hebrew criticism, N. Govrin's volume on Shoffman, B. Link's analysis of Ezra Zussman's poetry, and B. Shachevitz's literary biography of Simon Halkin. *Eyn Makom Aher* by Gershon Shaked showed the author moving toward a broader, sociocultural critical perspective.

Ozer Rabin and Nissim Aloni were awarded the Brenner Prize, A. B. Yehoshua the Bialik Prize, and Aharon Appelfeld the Israel Prize. The new journal *Apirion* appeared, edited by Erez Bitoun. (WARREN BARGAD)

Yiddish. Among the most striking poetic works published during the year were Khaym Leyb Fuks's *Towards the Heavens,* a retrospective meditation, and M. M. Shaffir's *By the Mixing-Bowl of My Dreams.* The septuagenarian Abraham Sutzkever provided a mosaic of poems from all his periods in *From Old and New Manuscripts.* Sadness and longing inform Rivke Basman's *Scattered Beads* and Yoyne Fayn's modernistic *Good Guests.* In contrast was Joseph Papiernikow's anthology *The Green Race;* usually occupied with national and social questions, the poet reflects here on the beauty of nature.

Soviet novelists Tevye Gen and Rivke Rubin offered somewhat unconventional novels. Gen's topical *Out Times* delves into human psychology, while Rubin's panoramic *Such a Day* describes the problems facing Soviet intellectuals. Polish Jewry is the theme of *Kalman's Empire* by Yehuda Elberg; his second novel, *A Man Is but a Man,* is set in America and Israel, with the Holocaust in eastern Poland as its background. Joseph Weinberg's *The Grain Child* is a tale of child abandonment in Nazi-occupied Poland, while Hersh Smoliar's *The Last Front, the Last Hope* analyzes postwar attempts to rebuild Jewish culture in that country.

Autumn and the Sun by the Romanian writer Volf Tambur received the League of Writers Prize for fiction. Leib Vilsker, sometime curator of Hebrew manuscripts in Leningrad, published a century-old Yiddish manuscript, "A Story of the Year 1290," in *Sovetish Heymland.* Dov Sadan published two significant titles, *A Word Consists and Insists,* on the relationship between language and literature, and *Between Far and Near*, on Yiddish and Hebrew letters.

Portraits of Yiddish Writers by the late Hersh Remenik provides an evaluation of Soviet Yiddish authors. Zev Wolf Sales's new translation of *The Book of Job* includes valuable exegetical material. A reediting of Ignaz Bernstein's major *Yiddish Proverbs* was the last volume published by teacher-essayist Khaym Bez, who died on Sept. 15, 1983. Meyer Shtiker, a modernist lyric poet of quiet power, died on July 8.

(THOMAS E. BIRD; ELIAS SCHULMAN)

CHINESE

China. A new campaign launched in 1983 signaled a widening purge of liberal intellectuals, writers, and artists blamed for so-called spiritual pollution in China. Cultural and literary figures considered threatening to the Communist regime became the targets of a campaign against certain Western life-styles, ideas, and philosophies as well as pornography and abstract theories of human nature and humanism. Those who questioned the absolute infallibility of socialism, thus threatening the legitimacy of the regime, were removed from their positions, criticized, or forced to engage in self-criticism. Those intellectuals who claimed that alienation was possible in a socialist society were also attacked. Zhou Yang (Chou Yang), chairman of the China Federation of Literary and Art Circles, was pressured to apologize publicly for his views and ideas. Writers who were attempting to deal with the subconscious were severely criticized; they were urged instead to educate and guide people to believe firmly in socialism and the Communist leadership. Literature and art, in the official view, should serve the people and socialism.

As part of the new campaign the Chinese authorities were looking for new heroes in drama and fiction to display at a time when the Chinese, especially youth, were expressing increasing doubts about achieving the goal of Communism or even desiring it. An example was Li Cunbao's (Li Ts'un-pao's) play *Wreathes at the Foot of the Mountain,* which glorified a young soldier who heroically died during China's short but bloody border war with Vietnam in 1979. It became an instant hit on the Chinese stage.

Nevertheless, some Chinese writers continued to pursue their own artistic goals. Zhang Kangkang (Chang K'ang-k'ang), a young woman who portrayed the sufferings, agony, and mental growth of Chinese youths, attracted wide attention. Ignoring the official line, she exposed the dark side of Chinese society and the restraints imposed by the Chinese social system.

Taiwan. A fairly lively literary scene emerged in Taiwan in 1983. A number of notable works on Taiwan's political, social, and economic situation appeared. With a special interest in social change, Taiwan's writers, both native and those from the mainland, continued their emphasis on realistic literature. Even though Ch'en Ying-chen's works on the activities of Taiwan's capitalists were widely read, it was his story *The Mountain Road* that attracted most attention. A powerful revelation of the tragic life of a native Taiwanese woman, it dealt with many complicated themes concerning Taiwan's politics and society.

Among the growing number of young women writers was Hsiao Sa, whose stories present realistic portrayals of various types of women in Taiwan. Her works became especially popular among young readers. (WINSTON L. Y. YANG)

JAPANESE

In sharp contrast to the turbulent political arena, the literary scene in 1983 was subdued. Publishers continued to complain of the decrease in sales and the lack of best-sellers. This had been their standing complaint for several years, but in 1983 their tone became more serious. Literary output had not slackened, but nothing caught the fancy of the reading public.

Nevertheless, several senior novelists made outstanding contributions. Fumio Niwa finished his eight-volume biographical novel *Rennyo,* which proved to be well-documented and yet readable. Rennyo, a Buddhist reformer of the 15th century, is reminiscent of Martin Luther in many respects. Both possessed not only a passionate commitment to faith but also a formidable talent for leadership. Rennyo organized the Jodo-Shinshu sect, still the most popular Buddhist sect in Japan. Niwa was the son of a Jodo priest who gave up the faith to pursue his literary ambitions, and his personal experience as an "apostate" adds psychological depth to his characterization.

Charming autobiographies were published by two senior female novelists, Chiyo Uno and Ineko Sata. In *Thus I Lived,* Uno, born in 1897, provides an amazingly lively evocation of her life. She could be characterized as a liberated woman, but her life-style was free of self-conscious sloganeering. Sata, on the other hand, began her literary career as a proletarian novelist in the early 1930s and remained political. Her autobiography, however, is spontaneous and lively and quite free of leftist cliches.

Awake, New Man by Kenzaburo Oe is an impressive achievement, both for its highly sophisticated literary technique and for the author's frankness in personal confession. The novel concerns the growing up of a mentally retarded boy and the tension and anxiety this causes among the members of his family. It is not a clinical novel, however. Oe manages to put the whole narrative within a symbolic framework, closely allied to the mysticism of William Blake. *Morning Glory* by Yoshikichi Furui, awarded the Tanizaki Prize, is a curious mixture of erotic fantasy and psychic self-scrutiny. Taeko Tomioka's *Undulating Ground* is a more detached analysis of extramarital entanglements from the female point of view.

Among works of literary criticism, Koichi Isoda's *Space in Postwar Japan,* Takeo Okuno's *Structure of Psychological Space,* and Jiro Kawamura's *On Uchida Hyakuken,* an analysis of a subtle humorist, should be mentioned. A posthumous collection of the essays of Hideo Kobayashi was published.

(SHOICHI SAEKI)

See also Art Sales; Libraries; Nobel Prizes; Publishing.

Luxembourg

A constitutional monarchy, the Benelux country of Luxembourg is bounded on the east by West Germany, on the south by France, and on the west and north by Belgium. Area: 2,586 sq km (999 sq mi). Pop. (1983 est.): 365,500. Cap. and largest city: Luxembourg (pop., 1981, 78,900). Language: French, German, Luxembourgian. Religion (1980): Roman Catholic 94.3%; Protestant 1.2%; atheist 1%; none 3.5%. Grand duke, Jean; prime minister in 1983, Pierre Werner.

In July 1981 the European Parliament had decided that in the future its plenary sessions would be held only in Strasbourg, France, eliminating Luxembourg as one of its official meeting places. Prime Minister Pierre Werner of Luxembourg had taken the Parliament to the Court of Justice of the European Communities in order to contest the resolution, but in February 1983 the court upheld the right of members of the Parliament to hold sessions where they chose. The European Parliament had last met in Luxembourg in February 1981. The government of Luxembourg had spent $28 million on accommodations for the Parliament outside the walls of the city of Luxembourg.

Luxembourg's status as Europe's third largest banking centre, after London and Paris, appeared not to have suffered from the Italian government's refusal to stand behind the debt of Banco Ambrosiano Holdings, the Luxembourg subsidiary of the Banco Ambrosiano of Milan, which had crashed in 1982. Banco Ambrosiano had used the Luxembourg company to control its overseas subsidiaries.

It was officially confirmed that in five years' time Grand Duke Jean intended to abdicate in favour of his eldest son, Crown Prince Henri.

(K. M. SMOGORZEWSKI)

LUXEMBOURG

Education. (1981–82) Primary, pupils 27,927, teachers (1978–79) 1,449; secondary, pupils 9,080; vocational, pupils 16,443; secondary and vocational, teachers (1975–76) 1,801; teacher training, students 152; higher (1978–79), students 404, teaching staff 168.

Finance. Monetary unit: Luxembourg franc, at par with the Belgian franc, with (Sept. 20, 1983) a free commercial rate of LFr 53.82 to U.S. $1 (LFr 81.05 = £1 sterling). Budget (1983 est.): revenue LFr 59,263,000,000; expenditure LFr 59,484,000,000. Gross national product (1981) LFr 197.6 billion. Cost of living (1975 = 100; June 1983) 170.

Foreign Trade. (1980) Imports LFr 100,373,000,000; exports LFr 87,013,000,000. Import sources: West Germany 35%; Belgium 34%; France 13%; U.S. 5%. Export destinations: West Germany 29%; Belgium 18%; France 16%; The Netherlands 7%. Main exports: metals 58%; plastics, rubber and products 11%; machinery 8%; textiles 6%.

Transport and Communications. Roads (1982) 5,108 km (including 58 km expressways). Motor vehicles in use (1982): passenger 159,600; commercial 10,400. Railways: (1981) 270 km; traffic (1982) 310 million passenger-km, freight 551 million net ton-km. Air traffic (1982): c. 92 million passenger-km; freight c. 300,000 net ton-km. Telephones (Jan. 1980) 198,900. Radio receivers (Dec. 1980) 186,000. Television receivers (Dec. 1980) 90,000.

Agriculture. Production (in 000; metric tons; 1981): barley 72; wheat 24; oats 33; potatoes 34; wine c. 5. Livestock (in 000; May 1981): cattle 224; pigs 75; poultry 129.

Industry. Production (in 000; metric tons; 1982): iron ore (29% metal content) 430; pig iron 2,589; crude steel 3,509; electricity (kw-hr) 942,000.

Madagascar

Madagascar occupies the island of the same name and minor adjacent islands in the Indian Ocean off the southeast coast of Africa. Area: 587,041 sq km (226,658 sq mi). Pop. (1982 est.): 9.4 million. Cap. and largest city: Antananarivo (pop., 1982 est., 600,000). Language: Malagasy and French (official). Religion: animist 50%; Roman Catholic 25%; Protestant 20%; Muslim 5%. President in 1983, Didier Ratsiraka; premier, Lieut. Col. Désiré Rakotoarijaona.

Following his reelection in November 1982, Pres. Didier Ratsiraka was invested for a second seven-year term on Jan. 2, 1983. The leading governmental party, the Advance Guard of the Malagasy Revolution (Arema), won sweeping victories in provincial elections held during February–July and legislative elections on August 28. Following the latter, seating in the National Assembly was: Arema 117; Madagascar Independence Congress (AKFM) 9; People's Party for National Unity (Vonjy) 6; Movement for Proletarian Power (MFM) 3; Madagascar National Independence Movement (Monima) 2. Monima's veteran leader, Monja Jaona, had been released from eight months' house arrest shortly before the legislative elections. In October the president announced the formation of a new 21-member government, in which Col. Désiré Rakotoarijaona remained as premier.

The trial of those implicated in the plot that the government claimed to have uncovered in January 1982 was held in September 1983. Several of the 13 accused were acquitted, while others received prison sentences of up to five years. At another trial, in October, a military tribunal sentenced for-

MADAGASCAR

Education. (1978) Primary, pupils 1,311,000, teachers 23,937; secondary, pupils (1976) 114,468, teachers (1975) 5,088; vocational, pupils (1980) 9,097, teachers (1973) 879; teacher training (1973), students 993, teachers 63; higher, students (1979) 22,857, teaching staff 557.

Finance. Monetary unit: Malagasy franc, with (Sept. 20, 1983) a free rate of MalFr 428 to U.S. $1 (MalFr 644 = £1 sterling). Budget (1982 est.) balanced at MalFr 275 billion.

Foreign Trade. (1980) Imports MalFr 126,780,000,000; exports MalFr 84,780,000,000. Import sources: France 41%; West Germany 10%; Japan 5%; Iraq 5%. Export destinations: France 20%; U.S. 19%; Japan 10%; West Germany 9%; Spain 8%. Main exports: coffee 51%; cloves 8%; vanilla 5%; petroleum products 5%; meat 5%; fish 5%.

Transport and Communications. Roads (1982) 49,637 km. Motor vehicles in use (1980): passenger c. 56,000; commercial (including buses) c. 49,000. Railways: (1979) 1,036 km; traffic (1980) 274 million passenger-km, freight 201 million net ton-km. Air traffic (1982): c. 506 million passenger-km; freight c. 29.5 million net ton-km. Shipping (1982): merchant vessels 100 gross tons and over 57; gross tonnage 77,102. Telephones (Dec. 1979) 37,000. Radio receivers (Dec. 1980) 1.7 million. Television receivers (Dec. 1980) 45,000.

Agriculture. Production (in 000; metric tons; 1982): rice c. 1,996; corn c. 126; cassava (1981) c. 1,745; sweet potatoes (1981) c. 410; potatoes (1981) c. 258; mangoes c. 175; dry beans c. 51; bananas c. 280; oranges c. 88; pineapples c. 58; peanuts c. 37; sugar, raw value (1981) c. 112; coffee c. 80; cotton 10; tobacco c. 5; sisal c. 20; beef and veal c. 131; fish catch (1981) c. 49. Livestock (in 000; Dec. 1980): cattle c.10,150; sheep c. 620; pigs c. 700; goats c. 1,400; chickens c. 15,000.

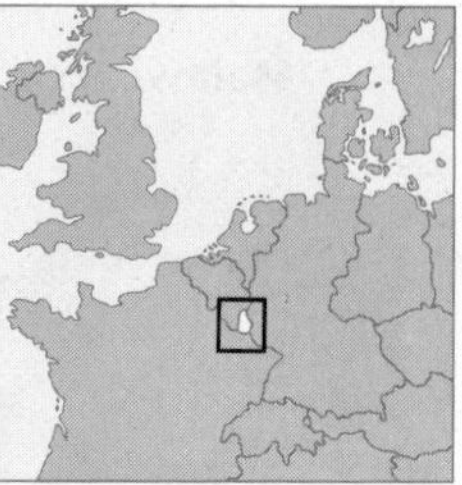

Luxembourg

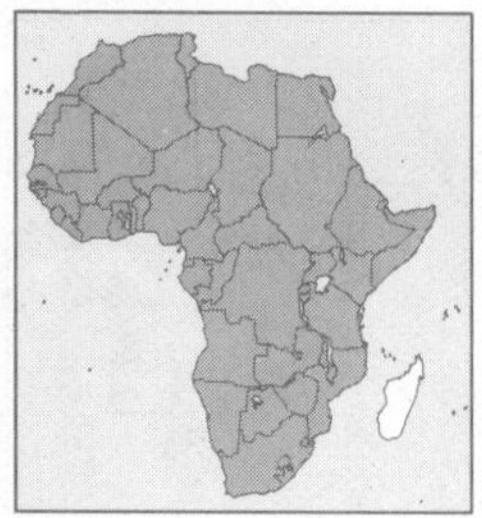

Madagascar

Livestock: see Agriculture and Food Supplies

Lumber: see Industrial Review

Lutheran Churches: see Religion

Macau: see Dependent States

Machinery and Machine Tools: see Industrial Review

mer minister of information Maj. Richard Andriamanolison, detained since 1977, to deportation for life for the attempted assassination of President Ratsiraka.

Substantial French economic aid for Madagascar was agreed on during a visit to Paris by President Ratsiraka. At the summit of nonaligned nations in New Delhi, India, however, Ratsiraka vigorously protested the French presence in Mayotte (Comoros) and France's refusal to negotiate on the sovereignty of the scattered Indian Ocean islands claimed by Madagascar. (PHILIPPE DECRAENE)

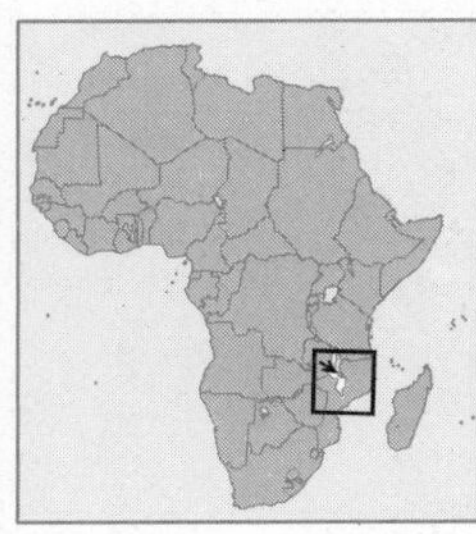
Malawi

Malawi

A republic and member of the Commonwealth in east central Africa, Malawi is bounded by Tanzania, Mozambique, and Zambia. Area: 118,484 sq km (45,747 sq mi). Pop. (1983 est.): 6,612,000. Cap.: Lilongwe (pop., 1981 est., 120,000). Largest city: Blantyre (pop., 1981 est., 230,000). Language (official): English and Chichewa. Religion (1980): Christian 64.5%; tribal 19%; Muslim 16.2%; other 0.3%. President in 1983, Hastings Kamuzu Banda.

Parliamentary elections—only the second to take place since Malawi became independent in 1964—were held on June 29–30, 1983. All candidates were nominated by district and regional committees of the Malawi Congress Party (MCP) and were reviewed by Pres. Hastings Kamuzu Banda himself. Though 21 MP's were returned unopposed, a considerable number lost their seats. In the new Cabinet, Robson Chirwa succeeded the late Dick Matenje as minister without portfolio.

Matenje, secretary-general of the MCP and one of the country's most powerful politicians, was reported killed in an automobile accident in May, along with two other ministers and an MP. The president was believed to have ideas about the succession that had been opposed by Matenje and one of the other dead ministers. This led to conjecture among some critics of the government about the cause of Matenje's death, conjecture that built upon the assassination in Zimbabwe in March of Attati Mpakati, an avowed opponent of the government, and the passing of the death sentence on May 5 upon Orton Chirwa, former minister of justice and attorney general, and his wife on charges of treason. (KENNETH INGHAM)

MALAWI

Education. (1980–81) Primary, pupils 809,862, teachers 12,540; secondary, pupils 18,006, teachers 834; vocational (1979–80), pupils 1,077, teachers 91; teacher training, students 1,754, teachers (1979–80) 108; higher (1979–80), students 2,000, teaching staff 190.

Finance. Monetary unit: kwacha, with (Sept. 20, 1983) a free rate of 1.15 kwacha to U.S. $1 (1.74 kwacha = £1 sterling). Gold and other reserves (June 1983) U.S. $31 million. Budget (1982 actual): revenue 231 million kwacha; expenditure 324 million kwacha.

Foreign Trade. (1982) Imports 325.1 million kwacha; exports 263.2 million kwacha. Import sources (1981): South Africa 32%; U.K. 10%; West Germany 8%; Japan 6%; Zimbabwe 6%; Italy 5%. Export destinations (1981): U.S. 28%; U.K. 17%; Zimbabwe 8%; West Germany 7%; The Netherlands 5%; South Africa 5%. Main exports: tobacco 57%; tea 18%; sugar 14%.

Transport and Communications. Roads (main; 1981) 10,772 km. Motor vehicles in use (1981): passenger 14,100; commercial 13,600. Railways: (1981) 789 km; traffic (1982) 95 million passenger-km, freight 187 million net ton-km. Air traffic (1982): 96 million passenger-km; freight 1.5 million net ton-km. Telephones (Dec. 1979) 29,000. Radio receivers (Dec. 1980) 275,000.

Agriculture. Production (in 000; metric tons; 1982): corn 1,415; cassava c. 90; sorghum c. 140; sugar, raw value (1981) c. 175; peanuts c. 180; tea c. 38; tobacco c. 56; cotton, lint (1981) c. 9. Livestock (in 000; 1981): cattle c. 850; sheep c. 78; goats c. 650; pigs c. 182; poultry c. 8,100.

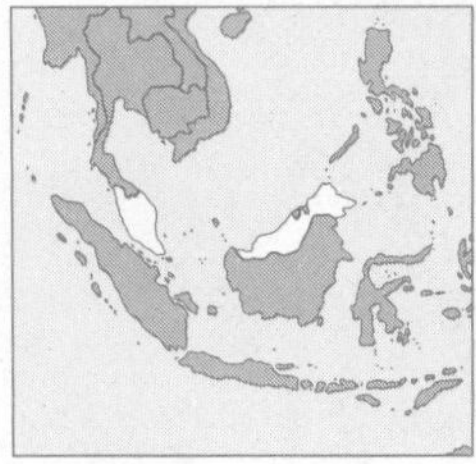
Malaysia

Malaysia

A federation within the Commonwealth comprising the 11 states of the former Federation of Malaya, Sabah, Sarawak, and the federal territory of Kuala Lumpur, Malaysia is a federal constitutional monarchy situated in Southeast Asia at the southern end of the Malay Peninsula (excluding Singapore) and on the northern part of the island of Borneo. Area: 329,747 sq km (127,316 sq mi). Pop. (1983 est.): 14,995,000, including (1980 est.) Malays 47.1%; Chinese 32.7%; Indians 9.6%; Dayaks

Malawi became independent in 1964, and at the end of June 1983 it held its second parliamentary elections. Candidates—including some opposed and some unopposed—were approved by Pres. Hastings Kamuzu Banda.

ALAN COWELL/THE NEW YORK TIMES

Magazines:
see Publishing

3.7%. Cap. and largest city: Kuala Lumpur (pop., 1980, 937,900). Language: Malay (official). Religion: Malays are Muslim; Indians mainly Hindu; Chinese mainly Buddhist, Confucian, and Taoist; indigenous population of Sabah and Sarawak (1980 est.) 47% animist, 38% Muslim, and 15% Christian. Supreme head of state in 1983, with the title of *yang di-pertuan agung,* Tuanku Sultan Haji Ahmad Shah al-Musta'in Billah ibni al-Marhum Sultan Abu Bakar Ri'ayatuddin al-Mu'adzam Shah; prime minister, Datuk Seri Mahathir bin Mohamad.

After a trial lasting 75 days, the Malaysian High Court in March sentenced to death Datuk Mokhtar bin Haji Hashim, federal minister of culture, youth, and sports, for the murder in April 1982 of Datuk Mohamad Taha Abdul Talib, the speaker of the Negri Sembilan state assembly. The death sentence was confirmed by the federal Court of Appeal in July, after which Mokhtar filed for a royal pardon. Meanwhile, in March, Datuk Lee San Choon, federal minister of transport, retired from politics. As a consequence of these and other factors, Prime Minister Datuk Seri Mahathir bin Mohamad announced a minor Cabinet reshuffle in June. The most significant appointment was the elevation of Encik Anwar Ibrahim to the portfolio of culture, youth, and sports.

Deputy Prime Minister Datuk Musa bin Hitam announced the need to trim development projects and find additional revenue halfway through Malaysia's fourth development plan. Escalating costs resulting from inflation and a decrease in export revenue were given as the reasons for the early exhaustion of budget allocations. It was the first time that the government had been obliged to take such measures midway through a development plan.

WIDE WORLD

Datuk Mokhtar bin Haji Hashim, a Malaysian Cabinet minister, was sentenced to death for killing the speaker of the Negri Sembilan state assembly.

MALAYSIA

Education. (1983) Primary, pupils 2,120,050, teachers 81,664; secondary, pupils 1,176,578, teachers 53,176; vocational, pupils 19,916, teachers 1,611; teacher training, students 15,010, teachers 1,526; higher, students 56,521, teaching staff 5,131.

Finance. Monetary unit: ringgit, with (Sept. 20, 1983) a free rate of 2.35 ringgits to U.S. $1 (3.54 ringgits = £1 sterling). Gold and other reserves (June 1983) U.S. $4,153,000,000. Budget (1982 actual): revenue 16,515,000,000 ringgits; expenditure 22,208,000,000 ringgits. Gross national product (1982) 58,232,000,000 ringgits. Money supply (June 1983) 12,575,000,000 ringgits. Cost of living (Peninsular Malaysia; 1975 = 100; April 1983) 148.6.

Foreign Trade. (1982) Imports 29,004,000,000 ringgits; exports 28,139,000,000 ringgits. Import sources: Japan 25%; U.S. 18%; Singapore 14%; Australia 5%. Export destinations: Singapore 25%; Japan 20%; U.S. 12%; The Netherlands 6%. Main exports: crude oil 27%; timber 16%; thermionic valves and tubes 11%; palm oil 9%; rubber 9%; tin 5%.

Transport and Communications. Roads (1981) 31,450 km. Motor vehicles in use (1979): passenger 696,500; commercial 158,700. Railways (1981): 2,681 km; traffic (Peninsular Malaysia only; including Singapore) 1,640,000,000 passenger-km, freight 1,130,000,000 net ton-km. Air traffic (1982): 5,418,000,000 passenger-km; freight 148.7 million net ton-km. Shipping (1982): merchant vessels 100 gross tons and over 329; gross tonnage 1,195,411. Telephones (Jan. 1981) 597,000. Radio receivers (Dec. 1980) 2 million. Television licenses (Dec. 1980) 1,004,000.

Agriculture. Production (in 000; metric tons; 1982): rice 2,062; rubber c. 1,550; copra 206; palm oil 3,511; tea c. 4; bananas c. 470; pineapples 160; pepper (Sarawak only; 1980) 31; tobacco (1981) c. 7; meat (1981) c. 235; fish catch (1981) 796; timber (cu m; 1981) c. 43,541. Livestock (in 000; Dec. 1980): cattle c. 540; buffalo c. 293; pigs c. 1,750; goats c. 365; sheep c. 65; chickens c. 52,000.

Industry. Production (in 000; metric tons; 1981): cement 2,833; tin concentrates (metal content) 60; bauxite 792; iron ore (56% metal content) 532; crude oil 12,391; petroleum products 5,372; electricity (kw-hr) 9,541,000.

In August the government rushed a number of important constitutional amendments through the federal Parliament. Among other things, these amendments restricted the power of the *yang di-pertuan agung* to delay legislation, withdrew his formal right to declare a state of emergency, abolished appeals to the Privy Council in civil cases, and increased the number of federal parliamentary seats from 154 to 176. After a four-month political crisis, the bill was signed, but only after concessions had been made regarding the *yang di-pertuan agung*'s power to delay legislation and declare a state of emergency.

While on a visit to London in March, Prime Minister Mahathir indicated a willingness to revise his government's "buy-British-last" policy in the light of tangible changes in the attitude and policy of the British government, particularly in the areas of trade and education. In early April he withdrew his directive to government departments that had required that all contracts with British firms be scrutinized by the prime minister's office to see whether there was an alternative to purchasing from Britain.

Prime Minister Mahathir and Foreign Minister Ghazali bin Shafie paid a two-day official visit to Brunei in March. Talks centred on foreign relations and defense in the light of Brunei's impending independence. Offers were made to train Brunei officials, and there was an agreement to conduct talks on border arrangements in order to facilitate travel between the two nations.

Controversy arose during the year over large loans made to Hong Kong property firms by a subsidiary of the government-owned Bank Bumiputera, the prime role of which was to assist Malay entrepreneurs. The matter became more than a domestic issue after the murder in Hong Kong in July of Jalil Ibrahim, an official of Bank Bumiputera who had been sent to investigate the circumstances of the loans.

In January an assassination attempt was made on the Soviet ambassador by members of the International Muslim Brotherhood Organization. Its apparent aim was to protest the Soviet occupation of Afghanistan.

It was announced in September that in June Malaysian security forces had occupied Terumbu Layang Layang, an uninhabited coral atoll in the South China Sea off the coast of Sabah. The atoll was part of the Spratly archipelago, the sovereignty of which Malaysia disputed with Vietnam, China, and the Philippines. (MICHAEL LEIFER)

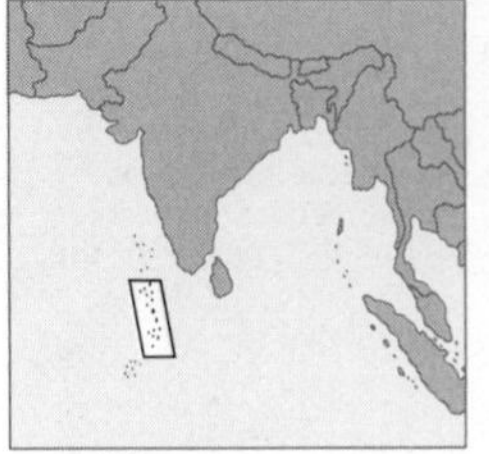

Maldives

Maldives

Maldives, a republic and member of the Commonwealth in the Indian Ocean consisting of about two thousand small islands, lies southwest of the southern tip of India. Area: 298 sq km (115 sq mi). Pop. (1982 est.): 160,200. Cap.: Male (pop., 1978, 29,600). Language: Divehi (official), Arabic, Hindi, and English. Religion: Muslim. President in 1983, Maumoon Abdul Gayoom.

Pres. Maumoon Abdul Gayoom, whose five-year term of office expired on Nov. 11, 1983, was reelected in a public referendum held on September 30. Gayoom had embarked on what was, for the Maldives, a major new economic policy to encourage tourism. At the same time, he was determined that the islands should retain their traditional Muslim character. Currently the president possessed nearly absolute authority. Gayoom had said, however, that he would like to introduce constitutional changes that would lead to greater political freedom.

By joining the Commonwealth in 1982, the Maldives had made possible some assessment of its economic and other problems. Nevertheless, there was still a basic lack of information. There were no

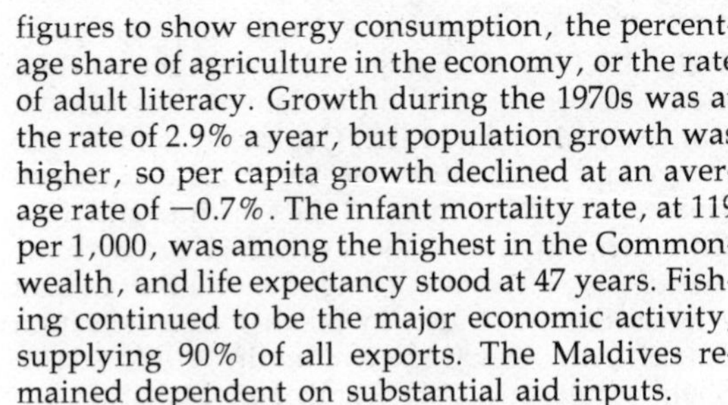

figures to show energy consumption, the percentage share of agriculture in the economy, or the rate of adult literacy. Growth during the 1970s was at the rate of 2.9% a year, but population growth was higher, so per capita growth declined at an average rate of −0.7%. The infant mortality rate, at 119 per 1,000, was among the highest in the Commonwealth, and life expectancy stood at 47 years. Fishing continued to be the major economic activity, supplying 90% of all exports. The Maldives remained dependent on substantial aid inputs. (GUY ARNOLD)

MALDIVES

Education. (1980) Primary, pupils 33,741, teachers 669; secondary, pupils 1,760, teachers 94; vocational, students 23, teachers 9; teacher training, students 86, teachers 8.

Finance and Trade. Monetary unit: rufiyaa, with (Sept. 20, 1983) a free rate of 7.05 rufiyaa to U.S. $1 (10.62 rufiyaa = £1 sterling). Budget (1980 actual): revenue 31 million rufiyaa; expenditure 51 million rufiyaa. Foreign trade (1979): imports 86.6 million rufiyaa; exports 18 million rufiyaa. Main import sources: India c. 25%; West Germany c. 15%; Japan c. 14%; Sri Lanka c. 11%; Burma c. 7%; Pakistan c. 7%. Main export destinations (1978): Japan 56%; Sri Lanka 22%; Singapore 16%. Main exports: fresh fish 64%; dried salt fish 30%. Tourism (1981) 48,000 visitors.

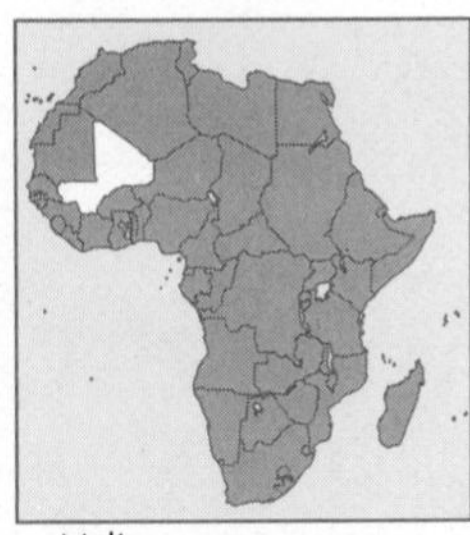

Mali

Mali

A republic of West Africa, Mali is bordered by Algeria, Niger, Upper Volta, Ivory Coast, Guinea, Senegal, and Mauritania. Area: 1,240,192 sq km (478,841 sq mi). Pop. (1982 est.): 7,342,000. Cap. and largest city: Bamako (pop., 1980 est., 440,000). Language: French (official), Bambara, Malinke, Fulani, Soninke, Dogon, Senufo, Berber, and Arabic. Religion: Muslim 65%; Christian 5%; animist 30%. President in 1983, Gen. Moussa Traoré.

In May 1983 an agreement between Mali and Algeria was signed in Algiers on the demarcation of their common frontier. In September, following a visit to Bamako by Upper Volta's head of state, Capt. Thomas Sankara, it was stated that the frontier dispute between Mali and Upper Volta, which during the 1970s had given rise to armed conflict, was to be placed before the International Court of Justice at The Hague. The possible future integration of Mali and Guinea was discussed when Pres. Moussa Traoré visited Conakry in March; a joint secretariat was set up and met in Bamako in August.

Social unrest continued, with opposition to Traoré's regime spearheaded by students. This opposition formed the theme of a film, *Le Vent*, directed by the Malian filmmaker Souleymane Cissé. In October serious drought conditions once again compelled Mali to appeal to the international community for help. (PHILIPPE DECRAENE)

MALI

Education. (1979–80) Primary, pupils 298,831, teachers 7,214; secondary (1978–79), pupils 70,625, teachers 3,004; vocational (1976–77), pupils 2,609, teachers 540; teacher training (1978–79), students 2,511, teachers 121; higher, students 5,281, teaching staff 489.

Finance. Monetary unit: Mali franc, with (Sept. 20, 1983) a par value of MFr 100 to the French franc and a free rate of MFr 806 to U.S. $1 (MFr 1,214 = £1 sterling). Budget (1982 est.) balanced at MFr 88.8 billion.

Foreign Trade. (1982) Imports MFr 218.4 billion; exports MFr 95.8 billion. Import sources (1977): France 38%; Ivory Coast 19%; Senegal 8%; West Germany 7%; China 5%. Export destinations (1977): France 29%; Ivory Coast 14%; U.K. 14%; China 12%; Japan 7%; The Netherlands 6%; West Germany 6%. Main exports (1977): cotton 57%; peanuts and oil 17%; livestock 12%; cereals 5%.

Agriculture. Production (in 000; metric tons; 1982): millet and sorghum c. 950; rice 145; corn (1981) c. 80; peanuts 78; sweet potatoes c. 50; cassava c. 56; cottonseed c. 60; cotton, lint c. 36; beef and veal (1981) c. 69; mutton and goat meat (1981) c. 51; fish catch (1981) c. 100. Livestock (in 000; 1981): cattle 5,134; sheep c. 6,350; goats c. 7,000; camels c. 173; horses c. 139; asses c. 420.

Malta

The Republic of Malta, a member of the Commonwealth, comprises the islands of Malta, Gozo, and Comino in the Mediterranean Sea between Sicily and Tunisia. Area: 320 sq km (124 sq mi), including Malta, Gozo, and Comino. Pop. (1982 est.): 360,200. Cap.: Valletta (pop., 1982 est., 14,000). Largest city: Sliema (pop., 1982 est., 20,000). Language: Maltese and English. Religion: mainly Roman Catholic. President in 1983, Agatha Barbara; prime minister, Dom Mintoff.

The 31 Nationalist Party members who had boycotted Parliament since the December 1981 elections finally took their seats in March 1983 as a result of conciliatory talks between their party and the ruling Malta Labour Party of Prime Minister Dom Mintoff (*see* BIOGRAPHIES). However, hopes of ending the political crisis collapsed in July when the government suspended further talks with the opposition.

Nationalist members walked out of the House of Representatives on numerous occasions to protest partiality in broadcasting. When the General Workers Union directed its members to boycott Nationalist activities on the government-controlled radio and television, the Nationalists instructed their supporters to boycott goods advertised on the broadcasting media. In October, however, the government informed businesses that they would be refused import permits if they did not advertise on these media.

In October an act on the nationalization of certain church property came into force. The archbishop of Malta began judicial proceedings to annul it as unconstitutional. The Roman Catholic Church maintained that the new law restricted the right to the free exercise of religion, discriminated against religious bodies, and provided inadequate compensation for confiscated property.

In September Malta withdrew its objections to the final communiqué of the Madrid conference on European security and cooperation. (*See* SPAIN: *Sidebar*.) (ALBERT GANADO)

MALTA

Education. (1981–82) Primary, pupils 33,405, teachers 1,567; secondary, pupils 21,908, teachers 1,751; vocational, pupils 4,869, teachers 478; higher (universities only), students 1,234, teaching staff 174.

Finance. Monetary unit: Maltese lira (formerly called the Maltese pound), with (Sept. 20, 1983) a free rate of M£0.44 = U.S. $1 (M£0.66 = £1 sterling). Gold and other reserves (June 1983) U.S. $1,033,000,000. Budget (1981 est.): revenue M£205 million; expenditure M£160 million (excludes M£33 million capital expenditure).

Foreign Trade. (1982) Imports M£325.7 million; exports M£173.1 million. Import sources (1981): Italy 27%; U.K. 18%; West Germany 14%; U.S. 7%; Japan 5%. Export destinations (1981): West Germany 31%; U.K. 20%; Belgium-Luxembourg 8%; Libya 8%; Italy 6%; The Netherlands 6%. Main exports (1981): clothing 46%; machinery 9%; instruments 6%; transport equipment 5%; printed matter 5%. Tourism (1981): visitors 706,000; gross receipts U.S. $265 million.

Transport and Communications. Roads (1982) 1,300 km. Motor vehicles in use (1982): passenger 74,800; commercial 17,300. There are no railways. Air traffic (1982): 644 million passenger-km; freight 3.8 million net ton-km. Shipping (1982): merchant vessels 100 gross tons and over 93; gross tonnage 425,563. Shipping traffic (1981): goods loaded 290,000 metric tons, unloaded 1.6 million metric tons. Telephones (Jan. 1981) 82,700. Radio licenses (Dec. 1980) 137,000. Television licenses (Dec. 1980) 76,000.

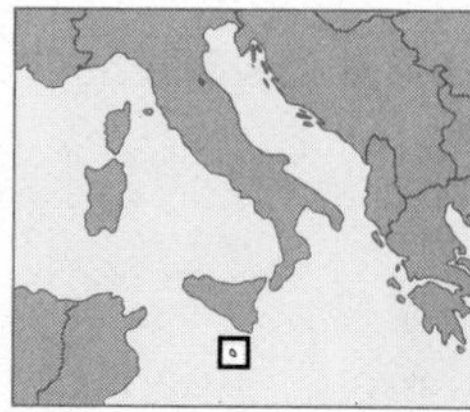
Malta

Materials Sciences

Ceramics. In 1983 Japanese researchers reported the innovative use of grain boundaries and pores to control the properties of ceramic materials. Normally, high-technology ceramics are processed to minimize these features. Shigeru Hayakawa and co-workers at the Matsushita Electric Industrial Co., however, showed that by carefully controlling the structure and composition of the grain boundaries in polycrystalline strontium titanate they could achieve both a voltage-dependent electrical resistance (varistor behaviour) and a high effective electrical capacitance. They also used the effects of the adsorption of water vapour and various gases on the surfaces of open pores to make humidity and gas sensors. For example, they showed that a solid solution of magnesium chromate and titanium dioxide with a carefully controlled size distribution and volume fraction of pores changes

WIDE WORLD

A hijacked Libyan airliner, watched by Maltese soldiers, was held at Malta's Valletta airport for three days by two Libyans who were seeking political asylum.

Manufacturing:
see Economy, World; Industrial Review

Marine Biology:
see Life Sciences

SPECTRA PHYSICS

A carbon dioxide laser is used to harden the surface of a crankshaft lobe in a new industrial application.

resistance by more than a factor of 10,000 over a relative humidity range of 0 to 100%. Such elements were already finding use as cooking controls in microwave ovens. Similarly, controlled-porosity iron oxide sensors appeared promising as very sensitive liquefied petroleum (LP) gas detectors.

Another processing technique that received attention was fabrication of high-temperature ceramics by rapid, self-heating processes. Strongly exothermic reactions, in which high heat is generated as the reactants combine to form very stable compounds, have long been used in the thermite welding process and in various incendiary devices. Recent studies by A. G. Merzhanov and colleagues in the Soviet Union showed that many commercially important refractory ceramics, including the borides, carbides, nitrides, and silicides of many of the metallic elements, could be made simply and quickly by igniting compacted mixtures of the reactant powders.

While the process had many attractive features, it also suffered from a serious drawback: the intensity and speed of the reaction usually prevented 100% conversion of the reactants to the desired end product. In the reactions for making nitrides, for example, molten metal at the combustion front prevents the inward diffusion of gaseous nitrogen that may be required to complete the reaction. Recent studies at Lawrence Livermore National Laboratory in California appeared to point the way to a solution to this problem. They showed that use of a suitable solid source of nitrogen, *e.g.*, sodium azide (NaN_3), leads to both complete conversion and, equally importantly, high purity.

Progress also continued in the development and impending commercialization of ceramics for use in fuel-efficient engines. The Cummins Engine Co. of Columbus, Ind., successfully road-tested an experimental uncooled diesel engine that it had been developing since 1975 for the U.S. Army. The engine featured a plasma-sprayed zirconium dioxide coating on the parts of the combustion chamber and on the intake and exhaust ports to reduce heat losses and to allow higher operating temperatures. The resulting increased thermal efficiency led to a 30–50% increase in fuel economy. Eliminating the cooling system saved weight and, perhaps most importantly, removed a frequent cause of breakdowns.

The Ford Motor Co. also announced near-term ceramic applications for their engines. Probably most imminent was the use of silicon nitride turbocharger rotors. In Japan Hitachi Ltd. successfully tested a new silicon carbide material in the form of cylinders, pistons, and piston pins for diesel engines. Toyota Motor Corp. developed an aluminum alloy reinforced with aluminosilicate ceramic fibre for possible use as a piston material in its diesel engines. NGK Insulators of Japan developed a zirconia composition whose thermal expansion matches that of cast iron well enough that it can be used for components in a hybrid diesel engine; it expected to begin production of ceramic components by 1985. (NORMAN M. TALLAN)
[724.C.5.c]

Metallurgy. Traditionally, new alloys have been developed by modifying the composition of existing alloys. But as metallurgists have begun to exhaust the realm of composition changes, they have turned increasingly to alternative processing strategies combined with alloy-chemistry modifications to achieve desirable properties.

Rapid solidification processes, which quickly transform liquid metal to a solid, have yielded new alloy microstructures. Metallic glasses, for example, are formed by quenching from a liquid or vapour so rapidly that crystallization is bypassed, and the resulting solid is amorphous.

In rapid solidification processes fine droplets or thin sheets of molten metal are chilled at high solidification rates, on the order of tens of thousands to millions of degrees Celsius per second. Certain alloys formed as ribbons, fibres, or flakes are cooled primarily by conduction, the heat being carried away by the cold surface of a rotating drum on which the liquid is cast. Another form, powder, is cooled primarily by convection; the heat is removed from a spray of fine liquid metal droplets by a gas stream. The particulate forms of these alloys can be consolidated by forging, extruding, or rolling into final shape. Typical applications include blades and vanes for gas turbine engines, made from rapidly solidified nickel alloys; aircraft structures, made from forged or extruded aluminum-alloy particles; and transformer materials, made from iron-base metallic glasses.

Another approach to alloy development is mechanical alloying, which can produce finer, more uniform structures than conventional ingot casting. Blends of powders are mixed in a ball mill, a horizontally mounted drum half-filled with steel balls. As the drum turns, the balls collide, trapping powder particles in between and welding some of them with each impact. During early stages of the process the particles are layered composites of the constituent powders. Later, as the particles are further fractured and rewelded, each particle becomes internally more homogeneous and similar in composition to the next. Mechanical alloying has been applied to nickel-, iron-, and aluminum-base alloys.

Improvements in surface-related mechanical properties such as friction, wear, and fatigue traditionally have been achieved by techniques that either alter the stresses at the surface (shot peening), change the chemistry of the alloy surface (nitriding, carburizing, or plating), or change the microstructure of the surface by heating and quenching (induction heating). Although these methods have been successful, new techniques known as ion implantation and laser heating have broadened the range of options.

Ion implantation involves the use of a high-voltage accelerator to drive appropriate ionized atoms into the outermost layer of alloy to alter the local alloy chemistry. Variables that determine the final implanted-layer chemistry include ion species, accelerating voltage, rate of ion bombardment, and total implantation time. Desirable properties of the bulk alloy such as mechanical strength are maintained while surface properties are upgraded.

Laser heating is one of the most accepted of all laser materials-processing techniques. This process subjects the thin surface layer of a metal part to the intense heat of a laser beam such that the layer becomes a single phase. When the laser beam is removed, rapid heat dissipation through the underlying bulk metal causes the single phase to transform to a metastable microstructure which is different from that of the interior. Recent studies demonstrated that laser heating significantly improves the wear resistance of steel surfaces. Current applications include laser-hardened wear tracks for power steering housings and diesel cylinder liners. (THOMAS H. B. SANDERS, JR.)

[125.F; 725.A.5; 725.B]

See also Industrial Review: *Glass; Iron and Steel; Machinery and Machine Tools;* Mining and Quarrying.

Mathematics

The highlight of mathematics research in 1983 was the proof by a young West German mathematician of an important unresolved conjecture about solutions to algebraic equations. This conjecture, first proposed in 1922 by the British number theorist Louis Mordell, suggests a relationship between the number of solutions that equations may have and the geometry of certain surfaces determined by these equations. After 18 months of intense work, 29-year-old Gerd Faltings of Wuppertal University verified Mordell's conjecture in a 40-page proof that builds on and completes half a century of work by Soviet and American mathematicians.

Faltings's proof of Mordell's conjecture is important not just for its own sake but because it is the first major step in more than a century in the struggle to verify Pierre de Fermat's famous claim, scribbled in the margin of a book, to have discovered a "truly marvelous" proof that there were no nontrivial solutions to the Pythagorean-like equation $x^n + y^n = z^n$, in which x, y, z, and n are integers, for values of n greater than 2. For $n = 2$, the

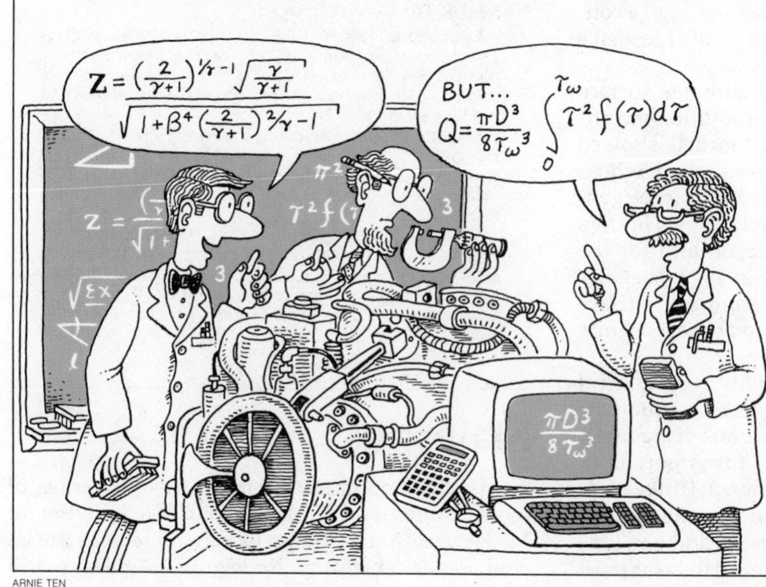

ARNIE TEN

3-4-5 "carpenter's triangle" is a well-known solution: $3^2 + 4^2 = 9 + 16 = 25 = 5^2$. But no similar solutions have ever been found if n is greater than 2.

Mordell's conjecture arose from his study of solutions to algebraic equations, the type of equation studied in high school algebra. One way to classify such equations—indeed, the way it is done in high school algebra classes—is by degree: linear equations such as $2x + 3y = 5$ are of degree 1; quadratic equations such as $x^2 + 3y = 7$ are of degree 2; cubic equations such as $y = (x - 3)^3$ are of degree 3.

Another means of classification is by what geometers call "genus": a counting of the holes in the surface created when one graphs the equation using complex numbers in place of the variables x and y. (Complex numbers are of the form $a + bi$, in which a and b are real numbers and i is the square root of -1.) Since complex numbers are themselves two-dimensional and since each equation expresses a relationship between two or more complex numbers, the "surface" determined in this way will not exist properly in three-dimensional space. Nevertheless, with sufficiently powerful imagination mathematicians can visualize these surfaces of higher dimension and analyze their properties.

The key property of a surface, it turns out, is the number of holes it has. A sphere, for example, has no holes, while the surface of a doughnut has one hole. The number of holes in the surface is its genus. Equations of degrees 1 and 2 produce surfaces of genus 0: they have no holes. Equations of degree 3 usually correspond to surfaces with one hole, although some cubic equations produce no holes, while others produce two holes. Generally, equations of degree higher than 3 yield surfaces with more than one hole.

Neither Fermat's claim nor Mordell's conjecture is primarily about surfaces or complex numbers. Each is concerned, rather, with integer or rational solutions to equations; that is, with values of x and y that satisfy the equation in which x and y are either whole numbers (integers) or fractions (called rational numbers, for "ratio"). But there is a subtle connection between these complex surfaces and the rational solutions to equations, a connection that points to the heart of Mordell's conjecture.

An equation whose associated complex surface has no holes either has no rational solution or infinitely many rational solutions. Mordell showed that the rational solutions to an equation whose complex surface had precisely one hole can be generated from a finite set of basic solutions. He then conjectured, in an enormous leap of faith for the state of mathematical knowledge in 1922, that any equation whose corresponding complex surface had two or more holes could have at most a finite number of rational solutions.

That is what Faltings proved in very general terms, not just for ordinary algebraic equations but for a whole class of generalizations of algebraic equations. Fermat's equation, it turns out, is in this class whenever n is greater than 2. (Integer solutions to $x^n + y^n = z^n$ correspond to rational solutions to $a^n + b^n = 1$, in which $a = x/z$ and $b = y/z$.) So Falting's proof implies that there can be at most finitely many rational solutions to such an equation. The step from here to Fermat's result—that there is no nontrivial rational solution—is still enormous, but it seemed more within grasp in 1983 than ever before. (LYNN ARTHUR STEEN)

Mauritania

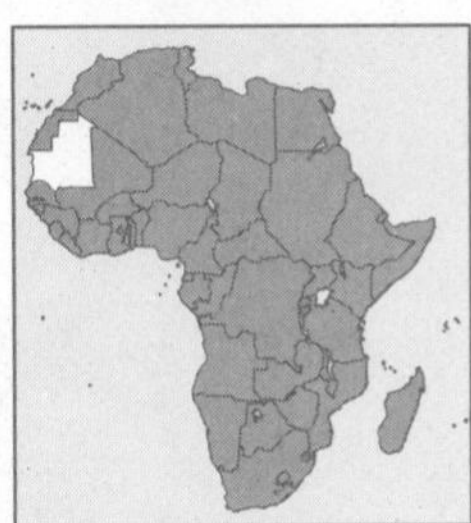
Mauritania

The Islamic Republic of Mauritania is on the Atlantic coast of West Africa, adjoining Western Sahara, Algeria, Mali, and Senegal. Area: 1,030,700 sq km (398,000 sq mi). Pop. (1983 est.): 1,782,000. Cap.: Nouakchott (pop., 1977, 135,000). Language: Arabic, French. Religion: Muslim. President of the Military Committee for National Salvation in 1983, Lieut. Col. Mohamed Khouna Ould Haidalla; premier, Lieut. Col. Maaouya Ould Sidi Ahmed Taya.

In 1983 Mauritania suffered the effects of drought conditions believed to be the worst in the past decade. Cereal crops were expected to cover barely 10% of national requirements. In October Lieut. Col. Mohamed Khouna Ould Haidalla, the head of the military regime, launched an appeal for international aid.

A ministerial reshuffle of a technical character took place in July, followed in September by a more thoroughgoing reorganization of the government designed to promote greater efficiency in dealing with the economic situation. In October a number of persons including political personalities and journalists, arrested in March 1982 on charges of plotting to overthrow the regime, were sentenced to terms of hard labour of up to 12 years.

In May Lieutenant Colonel Haidalla visited Algiers, where he met with Algerian Pres. Chadli Bendjedid and Tunisian Pres. Habib Bourguiba to discuss means of settling the Western Saharan conflict. Prospects for such a settlement improved with a Mauritanian-Libyan reconciliation, effected when Libyan leader Col. Muammar al-Qaddafi visited Mauritania in July. (PHILIPPE DECRAENE)

MAURITANIA

Education. (1980–81) Primary, pupils 90,530, teachers 2,183; secondary, pupils 20,248, teachers 646; vocational, pupils 1,004, teachers (1973–74) c. 117; teacher training, students 850, teachers 51; higher (1977–78), pupils 477, teaching staff 110.

Finance. Monetary unit: ouguiya, with (Sept. 20, 1983) a free rate of 53.95 ouguiya = U.S. $1 (81.25 ouguiya = £1 sterling). Gold and other reserves (June 1983) U.S. $126 million. Budget (1981 est.) balanced at 10.3 million ouguiya.

Foreign Trade. (1982) Imports 14,213,000,000 ouguiya; exports 12,050,000,000 ouguiya. Import sources: France c. 29%; Spain c. 9%; Italy c. 7%; U.S. c. 6%. Export destinations: Italy c. 26%; France c. 21%; Japan c. 20%; Belgium-Luxembourg c. 12%. Main exports: iron ore 60%; fish 40%.

Mauritius

The parliamentary state of Mauritius, a member of the Commonwealth, lies about 800 km east of Madagascar in the Indian Ocean; it includes the island dependencies of Rodrigues, Agalega, and

MAURITIUS

Education. (1982) Primary, pupils 131,594, teachers 6,420; secondary, pupils 76,308, teachers 3,144; vocational, pupils 508, teachers 69; higher, students 436, teaching staff 79.

Finance and Trade. Monetary unit: Mauritian rupee, with (Sept. 20, 1983) a free rate of MauRs 11.41 to U.S. $1 (MauRs 17.19 = £1 sterling). Gold and other reserves (June 1983) U.S. $33 million. Budget (1981–82 actual): revenue MauRs 2,442,000,000; expenditure MauRs 3,680,000,000. Foreign trade (1982): imports MauRs 5,048,200,000; exports MauRs 3,988,700,000. Import sources: Bahrain 15%; France 10%; South Africa 9%; U.K. 9%; Australia 6%; U.S. 5%; China 5%. Export destinations: U.K. 53%; France 22%; U.S. 8%. Main exports (1981): sugar 54%; clothing 27%. Tourism (1981): visitors 122,000; gross receipts U.S. $47 million.

Agriculture. Production (in 000; metric tons; 1982): sugar, raw value 727; bananas c. 7; tea c. 5; tobacco c. 1; milk c. 25. Livestock (in 000; 1981): cattle c. 57; pigs c. 6; sheep c. 4; goats c. 70; chickens c. 1,600.

Cargados Carajos Shoals. Area: 2,040 sq km (787.5 sq mi). Pop. (1983 prelim.): 993,700, including (1980 est.) Indian 69.5%; Creole (mixed French and African) 28%; Chinese 2.4%; other 0.1%. Cap. and largest city: Port Louis (pop., 1983 prelim., 132,200). Language: English (official); French has official standing for certain legislative and judicial purposes, and Creole is the lingua franca. Religion (1980 est.): Hindu 46%; Christian 35%; Muslim 16%; Buddhist 3%. Queen, Elizabeth II; governor-general in 1983, Sir Dayendranath Burrenchobay; prime minister, Aneerood Jugnauth.

The alliance led by the Mauritius Militant Movement, which had won a spectacular victory in June 1982, ran into trouble almost at once, and in March 1983 Finance Minister Paul Berenger and ten of his colleagues resigned. Prime Minister Aneerood Jugnauth then formed a new Mauritius Socialist Movement and joined forces with the Labour Party of Sir Seewoosagur Ramgoolam, the former prime minister, and the right-wing Social Democratic Party. In elections held in August, this new alliance won 41 of 62 directly elected seats.

The government wanted to turn Mauritius into a republic within the Commonwealth, but in December a bill to this effect failed to obtain the 75% majority in the legislature required to change the constitution. The new administration moved to the right in international politics and played down the dispute with the U.K. over the sovereignty of the Chagos Archipelago.

The economy faced a difficult period. Sugar production fell, and international demand declined. Meanwhile, the balance of payments deficit had grown alarmingly. For its size, Mauritius was one of the world's most indebted nations, with debts amounting to £432 million in March.

(GUY ARNOLD)

Mexico

A federal republic of Middle America, Mexico is bounded by the Pacific Ocean, the Gulf of Mexico, the U.S., Belize, and Guatemala. Area: 1,958,201 sq km (756,198 sq mi). Pop. (1982 est.): 73,010,600, including about 55% mestizo and 29% Indian. Cap. and largest city: Mexico City (pop., federal district, 1980 prelim., 9,373,400; metro. area, 1980 prelim., 15 million). Language: Spanish. Religion (1980): Roman Catholic 89.4%; Protestant (including Evangelical) 3.6%; Jewish 0.1%; other 6.9%. President in 1983, Miguel de la Madrid Hurtado.

Pres. Miguel de la Madrid Hurtado faced many problems during his first year in office. (*See* Special Report.) The economic picture was marked by restrictive policies introduced under International Monetary Fund guidelines and complemented by the 1983–88 national development plan. The latter emphasized the directing role of the state and the eventual need to restore growth and raise employment. In 1982 and 1983 real gross domestic product declined. Austerity measures lowered the level of demand and investment, but they significantly improved the external accounts and decelerated the rate of inflation. By the end of 1983 the government had succeeded in rescheduling about one-third of the $60 billion public-sector foreign debt, and an extended repayment scheme for the private sector, which owed some $14 billion, attracted $11.6 billion. Adjustments were made to the exchange rate in September, when it was decided to let the free rate depreciate daily by 0.13 pesos against the U.S. dollar until the end of 1984. This would prevent it from converging with the controlled rate, which had been slipping all year.

A second feature of the new government was its emphasis on reducing corruption at all levels. A controller general was appointed to monitor expenditure and public-sector official expenses, and restrictions were imposed on the hiring of relatives by senior officials. The plainclothes section of the Mexico City police was disbanded in January in order to purge it of individuals considered unfit for police duty.

The dealings of the state oil company, Petróleos Mexicanos (Pemex), came under particular scrutiny. In July the government accused Jorge Díaz Serrano, director general of Pemex during the years 1976–81, of being involved in a $34 million fraud. Díaz Serrano, who denied the charges, was stripped of his senatorial immunity by the Chamber of Deputies. Fraud charges were also filed against a former manager of the Pemex fleet. A top Pemex union official, Héctor García Hernández, was abducted from his home in Texas in September. This followed a complaint by the secretary-general of the union, Sen. Salvador Barragán Camacho, that García had taken 2% of payments made by contractors to the union in 1980–81. García, in turn, accused the senator and the leader of the oil workers' union, Joaquín Hernández Galicia, of having received these funds themselves.

A harder line was shown toward demonstrators. In July, when about 3,000 students were demonstrating against the closing of their teacher-training college and government austerity policies, some 150 students were injured by police in Mexico City. In October police killed two people when they charged and shot into a crowd of left-wing protesters in a small town in Chihuahua.

The ruling Partido Revolucionario Institucional (PRI) suffered defeats in municipal elections in July in the northern states of Durango and Chihuahua. The right-of-centre Partido de Acción Nacional

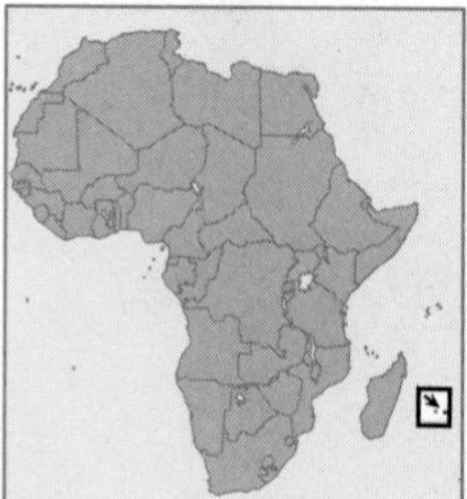
Mauritius

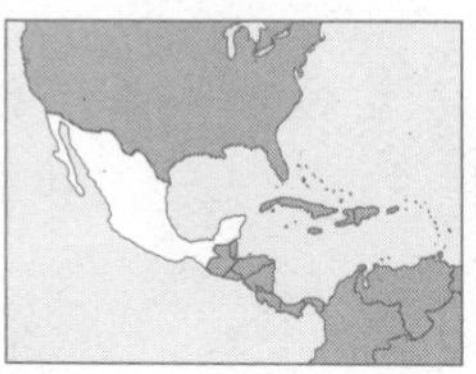
Mexico

Medicine: see Health and Disease

Mental Health: see Health and Disease

Merchant Marine: see Transportation

Metallurgy: see Materials Sciences

Metals: see Industrial Review; Materials Sciences; Mining and Quarrying

Meteorology: see Earth Sciences

Methodist Churches: see Religion

UPI

Some 3,000 students demonstrated in Mexico City in July to protest the closing of their college as part of a government austerity program. They were attacked by riot police shortly after this photo was taken, and some 150 were injured.

(PAN) made significant gains. In the state of Oaxaca, the PRI disbanded the country's only left-wing council, in the town of Juchitán, after two people had been killed at a PRI election rally.

Relations with the U.S. were strained. A bill proposing a crackdown on illegal Mexican immigration was reintroduced in the U.S. Congress. The Mexican legislature strongly condemned the bill, but a counterproposal to limit the number of Mexicans working at U.S. diplomatic facilities in Mexico was overwhelmingly defeated in the Chamber of Deputies. At a summit meeting in La Paz in August, President de la Madrid and U.S. Pres. Ronald Reagan signed only one agreement—on cooperation in joint environmental matters in the border zones. They discussed financial aid, including up to $2 billion in agricultural credit guarantees before the end of the 1984 financial year and advances on Mexican oil purchases. (A $500 million loan guarantee from the U.S. Export-Import Bank and an agreement on scientific and technological cooperation in agriculture and natural resources were signed later.)

Relations with Central America were principally handled through the Contadora Group, established by Mexico, Venezuela, Colombia, and Panama in January 1983. In its document of objectives, the group advocated the principle of nonintervention by foreign countries in the region, respect for human rights, the development of democratic institutions, a reduction of foreign military advisers in the area, and the elimination of arms sales. It also condemned the use of a foreign country as a base to destabilize another. The program was approved by five Central American countries—El Salvador, Guatemala, Costa Rica, Honduras, and Nicaragua—in early October, though misgivings were expressed.

The Mexican government made a forceful protest to Guatemala in February against the incursion into Mexico of armed Guatemalans, who had killed four refugees. Guatemala denied the charge. There were an estimated 25,000–40,000 refugees in Mexico. Guatemala was later granted permission to send personnel across the border to try to encourage the refugees to return to their homeland.

Britain's Queen Elizabeth II visited Mexico in February. (BARBARA WIJNGAARD)

MEXICO

Education. (1981–82) Primary, pupils 14,981,028, teachers 400,417; secondary, pupils 3,767,164, teachers 205,859; vocational, pupils 1,361,410, teachers 82,953; teacher training, students 203,557, teachers 13,127; higher, students 875,600, teaching staff 69,553.

Finance. Monetary unit: peso, with (Sept. 20, 1983) a free rate of 149 pesos to U.S. $1 (224 pesos = £1 sterling) and a controlled market rate of 131 pesos to U.S. $1 (197 pesos = £1 sterling). Gold and other reserves (March 1983) U.S. $2,181,000,000. Budget (total; 1982 est.) balanced at 3,286,000,000,000 pesos. Gross domestic product (1982) 9,255,800,000,000 pesos. Money supply (March 1983) 971.6 billion pesos. Cost of living (1975 = 100; May 1983) 1,011.

Foreign Trade. (1982) Imports 721,210,000,000 pesos; exports 1,231,820,000,000 pesos. Import sources (1981): U.S. 64%; Japan 5%; West Germany 5%. Export destinations (1981): U.S. 55%; Spain 10%; Japan 6%; France 5%. Main exports (1981): crude oil 69%; food 8%. Tourism (1981): visitors 4,031,000; gross receipts U.S. $1,760,000,000.

Transport and Communications. Roads (1982) 214,073 km (including 1,178 km expressways). Motor vehicles in use (1982): passenger 5,221,200; commercial 1,891,400. Railways: (1980) 25,510 km; traffic (1981) 5,240,000,000 passenger-km, freight c. 42,800,000,000 net ton-km. Air traffic (1982): 13,465,000,000 passenger-km; freight c. 118.1 million net ton-km. Shipping (1982): merchant vessels 100 gross tons and over 545; gross tonnage 1,251,630. Telephones (Dec. 1980) 4,992,600. Radio receivers (Dec. 1980) 20.5 million. Television receivers (Dec. 1980) 7.5 million.

Agriculture. Production (in 000; metric tons; 1982): corn 12,215; wheat 4,468; barley 495; sorghum 4,956; rice 600; potatoes c. 914; sugar, raw value c. 2,873; dry beans 1,093; soybeans 672; tomatoes c. 1,450; bananas c. 1,621; oranges c. 1,690; lemons c. 560; cottonseed 273; coffee c. 234; tobacco 67; cotton, lint 185; beef and veal c. 660; pork c. 508; fish catch (1981) 1,565. Livestock (in 000; Dec. 1981): cattle c. 36,200; sheep c. 7,990; pigs c. 13,117; goats c. 7,185; horses (1980) c. 6,502; mules (1980) c. 3,260; asses (1980) c. 3,233; chickens c. 164,000.

Industry. Production (in 000; metric tons; 1982): crude oil 137,071; coal (1981) 8,086; natural gas (cu m) 31,460,000; electricity (kw-hr; 1981) 73,559,000; cement (1981) 17,842; iron ore (63% metal content) 7,653; pig iron 4,664; crude steel 6,944; sulfur (1981) 2,228; petroleum products (1981) 61,047; sulfuric acid (1981) 2,172; fertilizers (nutrient content; 1981–82) nitrogenous 877, phosphate 236; aluminum (1981) 43; copper 65; lead 130; zinc (1981) 125; manganese ore (metal content; 1981) 208; gold (troy oz) 170; silver (troy oz) 42,900; woven cotton fabrics (1981) 71; man-made fibres (1980) 232; radio receivers (units; 1980) 1,029; television receivers (units; 1980) 964; passenger cars (units; 1981) 358; commercial vehicles (units; 1981) 172.

MEXICO BESET: The Great Problems Facing de la Madrid

by George Philip

Pres. Miguel de la Madrid Hurtado of Mexico faced a particularly delicate series of problems when he assumed office on Dec. 1, 1982. It has not been uncommon for Mexican presidents to take office during periods of crisis. What was unusual on this occasion was the complexity of the difficulties and their tendency to act in mutually aggravating ways. Even so, any new president can expect to restore considerable confidence and goodwill during his first two years in office by appearing to offer solutions to problems that—it becomes generally believed—were caused by his predecessor.

The Foreign Debt. Mexico's most immediate problem is its foreign debt. The difficulty does not lie just in its absolute size (impressive though this is) or even in the country's overreliance on oil exports to service it. Mexico's special difficulty, which sets it apart from many Latin-American countries, is an inability to maintain exchange controls except for very short emergency periods. As a result, it is unable to prevent large speculative movements in short-term capital. The economic system must rely on maintaining the confidence of the private sector, but for many in that sector the pastures almost always seem greener across the Rio Grande. Some $30 billion left Mexico in a few months in 1982; much of it, ironically, was deposited in U.S. banks which re-lent the money to Mexico and thus added to the foreign debt. Even if orthodox monetary measures are strictly pursued within Mexico (and certainly if they are not), the country remains vulnerable to financial panic, and the prospect of long, difficult, and repetitive negotiations with foreign banks will hardly help. For these reasons, Mexico will probably experience little or no per capita economic growth during the mid-1980s.

This is a grim prospect for a country where the population is still growing at about 2.5% annually, where half the population is below the age of 16, and where all sectors have become accustomed to rapid economic growth. During the 1970s, when most of the world was in recession, Mexico engineered an unprecedented boom on the basis of large increases in oil production. Despite the inflation, foreign indebtedness, and resulting economic imbalances (culminating in the economic crises of 1982), the elite gave top priority to rapid economic expansion in order to generate employment and take the edge off social discontent. For 40 years economic growth has served as a substitute for the regime's largely rhetorical commitment to reform. With growth unattainable, significant social reform becomes even less likely.

George Philip is lecturer in Latin-American politics at the London School of Economics and Political Science and at the Institute of Latin-American Studies, University of London. He is the author of Oil and Politics in Latin America: Nationalist Movements and State Companies.

Domestic and Foreign Policies. The second set of problems facing Mexico are more specifically political in nature. Successive governments have been promising political reforms—notably more honesty and a greater political role for the opposition—for a decade. It is now likely that serious steps toward this end will have to be taken if the regime is to regain credibility (and it would be dangerous, in a time of economic hardship, to make no attempt to do so).

The political elite has maintained control with the help of the time-honoured techniques of machine politics. These have been effective, in large part, because the ruling Partido Revolucionario Institucional (PRI) has enjoyed a near monopoly of political office and because government members at all levels have rarely been held accountable for corrupt practices. The general rise in living standards has also blunted the demand for political reform. However, these conditions may no longer prevail. In the long run, political reforms will make an increasingly literate, urban, and politically sophisticated people easier to govern, but the transition will not be easy.

President de la Madrid will also have to consider Mexico's foreign policy—or, perhaps more precisely, its relations with its neighbours. The preceding government of Pres. José López Portillo broadly supported the insurgent movements of Central America. This was apparent from his early warmth toward the Sandinista government in Nicaragua and from the Franco-Mexican declaration of August 1981 calling for a negotiated settlement in El Salvador. Yet no Mexican government could feel comfortable if a number of hard-line Marxist states existed in Central America, each seeking to export its revolution. At the same time, there is within Mexico a vocal left-wing constituency for a radical foreign policy—a constituency that may have to be given something if it is not to become seriously alienated. Moreover, no Mexican government would welcome the prospect of escalating conflict in Central America, bringing with it the danger of direct U.S. involvement in the

UPI

Mexico's Pres. Miguel de la Madrid Hurtado, shown here delivering his first state of the union address in September, faced large and difficult problems.

area. But it is doubtful whether Mexico could afford to carry out an active foreign policy independent of the U.S., given current economic conditions.

The Oil Factor. Foreign relations also have a bearing on another dilemma facing Mexican policymakers. This relates to oil. Mexico has the technical capacity to increase its oil production substantially above the current 2,750,000 bbl a day—perhaps to just over 3 million bbl a day. This might markedly improve Mexico's economic prospects. Some powerful U.S. interests are eager to see such an increase because it would put the Organization of Petroleum Exporting Countries (to which Mexico does not belong) under further pressure. However, the failure of OPEC, and the consequent lower oil prices, could seriously damage the long-range prospects of Mexico's own economy. Furthermore, as with Central America, Mexico desperately wants to avoid being labeled as "Uncle Sam's poodle."

Despite the high (and growing) degree of social inequality within Mexico, the political elite has been able to cope with social problems through its ability to isolate and deal with particular sources of pressure. It has been helped, until recently, by world economic trends and the prospect of rapid economic growth based on oil. In the current crisis, however, living standards are falling and are likely to remain depressed for some time. The urban middle class, always a particularly sensitive group, is among the hardest hit.

Furthermore, it is becoming increasingly hard for the Mexican elite to respond to particular pressures without aggravating others. Thus, the reassertion of a radical foreign policy might lead to a financial panic and seriously damage the economy. Any kind of political opening might bring increased pressure on the government to abandon austerity, threatening yet another inflationary boom. It is not yet clear how these various problems can be resolved.

Looking Ahead. It would be misleading to emphasize only Mexico's difficulties. Its system still has enormous strengths. Despite the evidence that Mexicans perceive their political system as corrupt (not without some justification), there is still enormous symbolic value in the idea of the "Revolution," with its emphasis on Mexico's specific identity and links with the past. The PRI may not be particularly representative, but its patronage system serves to redress some local grievances, as well as being a valuable source of political intelligence. Among the elite, adversity is likely to promote unity rather than confrontation. In general, public political relationships in Mexico are nonantagonistic. The rules of the game are well understood, and the system is operated by a very strong presidency. Moreover, every president has a good deal of talent at his disposal; the de la Madrid Cabinet seems particularly strong as regards economic expertise.

Powerful forces outside the system—the Roman Catholic Church, the trade unions, the U.S. government—undoubtedly have objections to particular government policies. At the same time, they do not wish to see the system overthrown or the country polarized. Successive Mexican governments have succeeded in winning over or at least neutralizing the main centres of power outside the state. Public pressure on particular issues—even some opposition electoral activity—is tolerated by the regime. Under certain circumstances it is actively encouraged, but the political elite does not countenance anything that it cannot hope ultimately to control. There can be no doubt that if the political system were ever seriously challenged, the political elite as a whole would be vigorous in its defense.

Middle Eastern Affairs

The Arab-Israeli dispute shifted its emphasis to Lebanon in 1983 after renewed civil strife between Christian and Syrian-backed Muslim militiamen. Tension mounted as a sequence of bomb attacks were perpetrated on U.S. and French members of the international peacekeeping force in Beirut; in their wake there were fears that the United States, covertly supported by Israel, might carry out a reprisal strike that would further escalate the conflict. On September 4 Israel carried out a partial pullback from the Shuf Mountains but did not withdraw completely from Lebanon, despite having made an agreement with the Lebanese government in May to do so, because Syrian forces remained in occupation of some 40% of Lebanon's sovereign territory. Syria's efforts were aimed at supporting Palestinian opponents of the Palestine Liberation Organization (PLO) chairman, Yasir Arafat (*see* BIOGRAPHIES). He and 5,000 of his supporters were besieged from mid-November to late December in the northern Lebanon city of Tripoli by rebel PLO troops and Syrian-controlled units of the Palestine Liberation Army.

At the UN on August 2 the U.S. vetoed a resolution declaring that Israeli settlements in occupied Arab territories were illegal, but U.S. delegate to the UN Charles Lichenstein nevertheless added that his country did want to see a freeze on settlements. U.S. Middle East policy appeared once more to be directed toward persuading King Hussein of Jordan to play a role in the future of the Palestinians who were currently living under Israeli military rule; U.S. Pres. Ronald Reagan had revived the so-called Jordanian option in September 1982. Before the defeat of Arafat, Jordanian Prime Minister Mudar Badran had held talks with PLO leaders. Their aim was to revive the dialogue between the PLO and Jordan that had broken down earlier in the year when the two parties disagreed about President Reagan's proposals.

The Gulf War. Elsewhere in the Middle East, Iran continued to gain ground slowly in the military struggle with Iraq that had started in September 1980. The war appeared to be escalating after France in October agreed to lend Iraq five Super Étendard aircraft equipped to fire Exocet missiles. Threats by Iraq to attack the Iranian oil terminal on Kharg Island were countered by Iranian threats to close the Strait of Hormuz to international shipping. Such a blockade of the shipping lanes, should it be effected, would have serious international implications and, perhaps, lead to intervention in the conflict by Western powers. Responding to Iran's threats, President Reagan said on October 19 that the U.S. would not allow any country to close the Strait of Hormuz, but he stopped short of listing specific U.S. actions should such a crisis arise.

The Crisis in Lebanon. The suicide bomb attacks on October 23 on French and U.S. peacekeeping garrisons left more than 290 people dead. There was little doubt that Shi'ah Muslims were implicated in the attacks. One of the groups claiming responsibility was the Islamic Jihad ("holy war") Organization, a Shi'ah group that also claimed to have carried out the bombing on April 18 of the U.S. embassy in Beirut, an attack that killed more than 60 people. U.S. intelligence sources blamed a Shi'ah splinter group in Lebanon's Bekaa Valley headed by Hussein Mussawi. There was also a sug-

UPI

Druze militia in the Shuf Mountains clashed frequently with the Lebanese Army. These men are training with Soviet-made weapons.

Microbiology: *see* Life Sciences

Microelectronics: *see* Computers; Industrial Review

gestion that Iranians were involved. The bomb attacks briefly diverted attention away from the preparations for national reconciliation talks that began in Geneva a week later.

The violence in Lebanon during 1983, particularly the fighting in the Shuf Mountains between Christian and Druze militia, cast grave doubt on the ability of the country to survive as an independent sovereign state. Fears of a U.S. reprisal in Lebanon grew, particularly after President Reagan's action in authorizing an invasion of Grenada. At the same time, the U.S. showed signs of accepting Syria's role in the crisis, despite the political distance between the two nations. On October 27 foreign ministers from the U.S., the U.K., France, and Italy met in Paris and affirmed their commitment to their peacekeeping role in Lebanon, although Italy later showed signs of wavering. Commenting on the meeting, British Foreign Secretary Geoffrey Howe (*see* BIOGRAPHIES) said on November 11: "It is natural that Syria should have an interest in the future of Lebanon: we hope she will exercise her influence constructively. There will only be stability in Lebanon when all foreign forces are withdrawn."

The national reconciliation talks in Geneva were attended by nine of Lebanon's political leaders, including Pres. Amin Gemayel (a Christian Phalangist), Druze leader Walid Jumblatt (*see* BIOGRAPHIES), and representatives of the country's Sunni and Shi'ah Muslims. U.S. State Department officials conceded that they fully expected any government of Lebanon that might emerge from the Geneva talks to be less to their liking—and Israel's—than the administration of President Gemayel. They stressed that President Reagan was anxious to link the U.S. presence in Lebanon—1,600 U.S. Marines—to the broader pursuit of peace in the Middle East and that Reagan was hoping to see more examples of bilateral settlements similar to the 1978 Camp David accords between Egypt and Israel. It was generally accepted in the U.S. that "turning to Israel for help" in Lebanon would wreck any chance of such accords coming to fruition.

The agreement reached between Israel and Lebanon on May 17 concerning conditions for a withdrawal of Israeli forces could be regarded as a successful step in U.S. diplomacy—although the pact was not fully implemented by Israel. The U.S. was subsequently active in shuttle diplomacy with Syria in an attempt to bring about a corresponding withdrawal of the Syrian forces. However, a Syrian statement issued on July 7 emphasized that Pres. Hafez al-Assad's government considered that the bilateral agreement between Israel and Lebanon undermined Lebanese sovereignty and threatened Syria's security; the pact granted Israel a long-term security role in southern Lebanon. President Assad was also aggrieved at his exclusion from the talks. In his view, U.S. policy was an attempt to remove Arab states one by one from confrontation with Israel.

Arab-Israeli Relations. President Assad's gravest concerns related to the efforts by the U.S. to promote the Jordanian option as a final settlement of the Palestinian question. On Sept. 1, 1982, President Reagan had recommended the establishment of an autonomous entity for the Palestinians on the West Bank and in the Gaza Strip that would be linked with Jordan, thus reviving proposals originally made at Camp David in 1978 and quickly rejected by the Israeli Cabinet.

Jordan's King Hussein and Crown Prince Hassan proved more interested in the U.S. recommendations. Hussein hoped to gain some Arab backing

Syrian-backed Palestinian rebels forced PLO fighters loyal to Yasir Arafat to withdraw from two strongholds outside Tripoli, Lebanon, into the city itself. Here an Arafat supporter fires an AK-47 assault rifle during house-to-house fighting at the Beddawi refugee camp.

WIDE WORLD

UPI

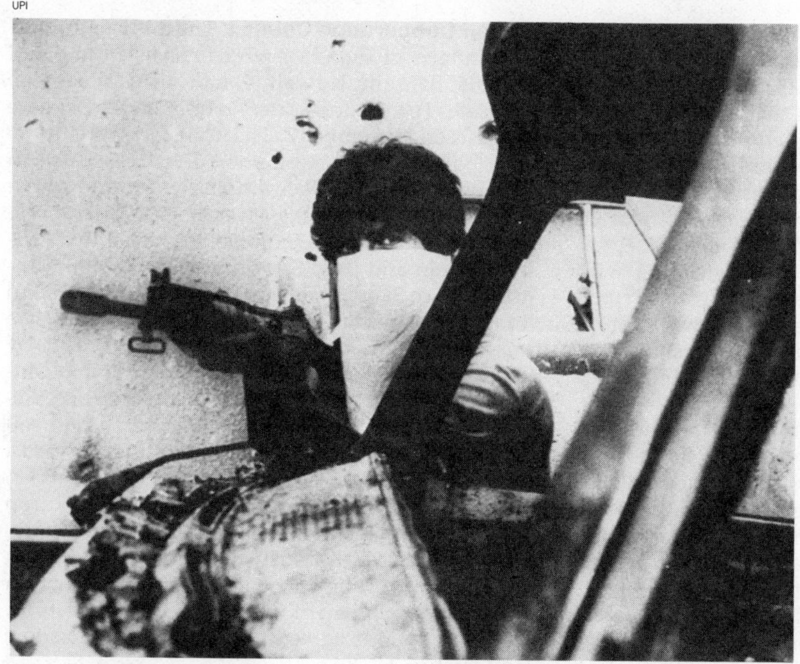

Shi'ah Muslim militia, some masking their features, manned barricades in Beirut's southern suburbs.

for the Reagan plan when he proposed to hold talks with Arafat in March 1983. Israel's Foreign Minister Yitzhak Shamir urged the king to enter into peace negotiations, but at the same time he indicated Israel's inflexibility when he refused to give any assurance about freezing his country's policy of building settlements in occupied Arab lands. A meeting of the European Council (consisting of the heads of government of the European Community nations) on March 22 issued a declaration that urged the PLO to come out in favour of peace negotiations and also condemned Israel for its settlements policy.

Despite his efforts, King Hussein failed to gain the support of the PLO. On March 29 an aide of Arafat stressed that the Palestinians would go along with the king only if he could guarantee the return to them of the West Bank and Gaza. Talks between Hussein and Arafat broke down after three days of negotiation early in April, and on April 10 Jordan announced that it was dropping its efforts to implement the U.S. peace proposal. It was another five months before King Hussein again called for dialogue with Arafat on the Reagan plan. By then the king was warning that, in light of the emerging splits within its ranks, the PLO could forfeit its role as the sole legitimate representative of the Palestinian people.

The Jordanian initiative was frustrated by the disclosure of plans to set up in Jordan an emergency "strike force" that would be equipped to intervene in the Gulf states. The disclosure, on October 13 on Israel Radio, revealed that the plan had been in preparation since the attack on the Grand Mosque in Mecca, Saudi Arabia, in November 1979. The strike force was linked to U.S. proposals to supply Jordan with advanced interceptor aircraft, together with other military equipment. Israel and its supporters in the U.S. were opposed to any moves to give Jordan advanced weapons. The revelations damaged King Hussein's credibility with other Arab states in the Gulf, where heads of state remained opposed to any outside military intervention.

While preoccupied with its campaign to destroy the influence of Arafat, Syria refrained from adopting an overt military posture toward Israel. Its administration claimed that military exercises and moves to mobilize reservists were being undertaken in response to fears of an "imminent" invasion by the U.S. At the same time, President Assad and his government continued to harbour designs to win back the Golan Heights, which Israel had effectively annexed in December 1981.

Pan-Arab moves to bring about an Arab-Israeli settlement were expressed in the final communiqué of the Arab League summit meeting held in Fez, Morocco, in September 1982. Adopted as a response to President Reagan's September 1982 proposals, the Fez plan recognized the PLO as the sole legitimate representative of the Palestinians and called upon the UN Security Council to guarantee the safety of all nations in the region.

Leaders of five radical member groups of the PLO met in Tripoli, Libya, on Jan. 17, 1983, and rejected "all formulae permitting the Jordanian regime to represent the Palestinian people," as well as "all forms of recognition, negotiation, and making peace with the expansionist Zionist state." They were clearly rejecting both the Reagan and Arab League peace plans. The declaration was drawn up in conjunction with Libya and was signed by the Popular Front for the Liberation of Palestine (PFLP), the PFLP-General Command, the Democratic Front for the Liberation of Palestine, the Popular Struggle Front, and Al-Saiqa. All these groups had close relations with Syria. Syria itself was also reported to be on the verge of rejecting the Fez plan, although it had supported the plan at the summit. Having been rejected by Israel, radical Palestinians, and Libya, the Fez proposal made little progress in 1983.

Arab mediation efforts, including those of Saudi Arabia in Lebanon and those of the Gulf Cooperation Council (GCC) to bring about a cease-fire between Arafat's fighters and PLO rebels in November, were subsequently directed more at bilateral issues. A final point that cast gloom over attempts to improve Arab-Israeli relations was the fact that the atmosphere between Egypt and Israel deteriorated markedly. Egypt resisted U.S. pressure to return its ambassador to Israel, withdrawn during the 1982 Israeli invasion of Lebanon. Egyptian Pres. Hosni Mubarak's warm meeting with Arafat after the latter's evacuation from Tripoli and the renewal of trade relations between Egypt and Jordan in December were other signs that Egypt's isolation from the Arab world might be ending.

The PLO in Disarray. The struggle for control of the Palestinian nationalist movement in Lebanon began with dissatisfaction in PLO ranks over Arafat's apparent reluctance to reject the Reagan peace proposal in its entirety. When Arafat appointed two PLO commanders who were viewed as cowardly and incompetent to important leadership posts in Lebanon, hard-line PLO units stationed in Lebanon's Bekaa Valley came out in open rebellion against him. The opposition groups cited Arafat's "autocratic" leadership and the lack of consultation in running the al-Fatah wing of the PLO as additional reasons for trying to remove him. By May 22 about 400 soldiers had rallied to the rebels, and this number grew as top civilian and military PLO leaders took their supporters with them into the ranks of the mutineers. In late June Arafat accused Assad of orchestrating the rebellion within the PLO and was expelled from Syria.

By late July heavy fighting had broken out between loyalists and rebels in the Bekaa Valley. The following months were marked by rebel victories that resulted in their gaining control of the valley and by mass defections from the ranks of al-Fatah, Arafat's own base of support in the PLO, to the rebels' side. Syria gradually gave increasing moral and material support to the rebels, enabling them to roll back the loyalists to two refugee camps near Tripoli by November.

In October Arafat had requested Soviet diplomatic aid as the noose tightened around him. Meeting in Doha, Qatar, on November 7, foreign ministers of the Gulf Cooperation Council affirmed their support for the PLO chairman; but despite this support from moderate Arab leaders, there was little doubt that the Tripoli crisis marked a serious setback for Arafat's leadership. The Nahr al-Bared and Beddawi refugee camps fell to the rebels in a series of bloody attacks in early and mid-November, and the PLA captured Arafat's radio station. With the fall of these camps, Arafat's beleaguered supporters withdrew into Tripoli itself. As civilians fled in fear of an all-out attack on the city, Arafat acceded in principle to Saudi and Syrian proposals that he and his followers be evacuated. The negotiations were protracted, however, and it was not until December 20 that Arafat and 4,000 of his followers (1,000 followers were left behind) sailed from Tripoli on Greek ships flying the United Nations flag. The evacuation was delayed for several days by Israeli shelling of Arafat's positions.

Gulf Cooperation Council. The ministers of foreign affairs of the GCC, which consisted of Saudi Arabia, Bahrain, Kuwait, Oman, the United Arab Emirates (UAE), and Qatar, met in an atmosphere of crisis on November 7. The ministers were, however, able to arrange a short-lived cease-fire in Tripoli between the Palestinians opposed to Arafat and the PLO chairman's supporters.

The GCC summit also discussed the Gulf war between Iran and Iraq. Saudi Arabia's Foreign Minister Prince Saud al-Faisal said he was still hopeful that a UN resolution calling for an immediate cease-fire would be adopted. A proposal made by Bahrain's Foreign Minister Muhammad ibn-Mubarak al-Khalifah recommended that coastal cease-fire zones—including Iran's Kharg Island oil terminal—should be created as a first step toward a truce.

The GCC summit took place against the backdrop of improving relations between a member state, Oman, and the Marxist government in Yemen (Aden; South Yemen), which had supported an insurgency movement in Oman in the early 1970s. The two nations agreed to exchange ambassadors on October 27.

Because of the concentration on political affairs at the summit, the question of economic cooperation was passed over. However, work on planned projects was scheduled to go ahead, coordinated by the GCC's secretariat based in Riyadh, Saudi Arabia. A Gulf Investment Corporation, established by the six members of the GCC, held its first meeting on November 26. The biggest project under study was a proposed oil refinery in Oman. This was to handle the export of Omani and Saudi Arabian crude and would avoid the need for tankers to pass through the Strait of Hormuz. GCC Secretary-General Abdullah Bishara, a Kuwaiti diplomat, reported that 15 other projects were under discussion and might receive backing. These included an integrated gas grid, a coastal highway from Kuwait to Muscat, a Gulf railway, agricultural projects, and a joint freighting organization.

The GCC summit was also thought to have discussed defense cooperation, as joint land exercises between the armies of the six nations took place in the UAE shortly before the summit. Qatar's information minister, Isa al-Kuwari, said on November 1 that "defense cooperation has been the Achilles' heel of the Gulf." He was firmly opposed to allowing this job to be done by outside powers. His stance on this question was understood to be a reference both to the proposed Jordanian strike force and to the U.S. Rapid Deployment Force, which was supported by Oman.

The GCC had been established in 1981 amid hopes that a Gulf Common Market could be established. By 1983 the Riyadh secretariat had a staff of 200, but progress on economic integration was slow. Proposals for a joint 4% customs tariff were resisted by the UAE and Qatar; both countries refused to implement it. Differences born of rivalries dating from colonial times continued to impede the cause of unity. (JOHN WHELAN)

See also Defense; Energy; articles on the various political units.
[978.B]

Migration, International

During 1983 governments of the richer countries imposed increasingly rigorous controls on immigration from the poor countries. On the surface, such measures were in response to rising levels of anti-immigrant tensions, but in practice they had the effect of legitimating much of the racial stereotyping that accompanied continuing high unemployment in the industrial countries.

In France rising anti-immigrant sentiment and two million unemployed combined to create the political atmosphere in which the Socialist government announced a series of anti-immigration measures on August 31. They included new entry controls for Algerian, Moroccan, and Tunisian visitors; new checks on illegal employment; a tightening of rules regarding seasonal workers; and easier deportation of suspected illegal immigrants. Radio advertisements were broadcast offering inducements for immigrant workers to return "home," and the police were given additional powers over immigrants.

In West Germany, unemployment had risen to 8.8% overall and 14.1% for immigrant workers, leading to increased racial tensions and new government measures. In June 1983 the federal minister of labour, Norbert Blüm, announced a series of "humane" measures that would provide relief for the West German labour market and give "development aid" to the countries that had sent workers in the past. Non-European Community foreign workers who lost their jobs through bankruptcies or firm closures, or who had been on short time for more than six months—85,000 out of the 300,000 unemployed "guest workers"—would qualify for a "return premium" of DM 10,500 (*c.* $4,000), plus DM 1,500 (*c.* $560) for each child who arrived in West Germany before June 1983. The plan was designed to encourage rapid acceptance; from the second month of unemployment, the DM 10,500 was reduced by DM 1,500 a month. The entire family had to go at the same time, and permission to return would not be given. The deportation of Turkish political refugees was condemned by various human rights groups and by the UN High Commissioner for Refugees. In August the suicide of a 23-year-old Turk who feared deportation became a focus of political controversy.

The dispute surrounding black immigration continued in Britain, as did discriminatory governmental actions, despite the fall in the number of immigrants from the "New Commonwealth" (*i.e.,* nonwhite Commonwealth and Pakistan) to the lowest figure since 1962. According to official statistics published in June 1983, 30,400 were accepted in 1982, compared with 37,000 in 1979 and 68,000 in 1972. In addition, deportation orders against illegal entrants were up 18%, and orders against those who overstayed were up 30%. On Feb. 15, 1983, Parliament approved new immigration rules regarding the rights of women settled in Britain to bring in husbands and fiancés, which had been defeated in an earlier version in December 1982. The new rules, which were unlikely to satisfy the European Court of Human Rights, still did not give these rights to women settled permanently in Britain who were not British citizens. In the case of women who were British citizens, the burden of proof that the marriage was not a marriage of convenience remained with the couple.

In Australia the link between unemployment and changes in immigration quotas and requirements was clear. In May, with unemployment at 10%, the new Australian Labor Party government's immigration and ethnic affairs minister, Stewart West, announced an immigration ceiling for the coming year of 90,000, compared with 115,000 set at the beginning of 1982–83. There was also a reduction of "wanted" occupations from 75

Illegal aliens from Mexico flooded across the border into California. More than 2,400 were seized on one day. Their fate: a holding tank like this and then return to Mexico.

UPI

Immigration and Naturalization in the United States

Year ended Sept. 30, 1980

Country or region	Total immigrants admitted	Quota immigrants	Nonquota immigrants: Total	Nonquota immigrants: Family—U.S. citizens	Aliens naturalized
Africa	13,981	7,887	6,094	5,398	2,587
Asia	236,097	112,552	123,545	59,029	67,390
China[1]	27,651	18,271	9,380	7,178	12,524
Hong Kong	3,860	2,544	1,316	1,085	. . .
India	22,607	19,585	3,022	2,698	6,552
Iran	10,410	4,717	5,693	5,422	1,591
Iraq	2,658	2,151	507	386	823
Israel	3,517	2,169	1,348	1,204	1,280
Japan	4,225	2,122	2,103	1,747	1,747
Jordan	3,322	2,161	1,161	1,095	1,424
Korea, South	32,320	20,098	12,222	11,042	14,703
Lebanon	4,136	2,858	1,278	1,116	1,221
Philippines	42,316	19,661	22,655	20,834	17,683
Thailand	4,115	1,721	2,394	1,386	1,406
Vietnam	43,483	4,158	39,325	304	1,828
Europe	72,121	36,964	35,157	23,105	35,191
Germany, West	6,595	1,492	5,103	4,593	2,922
Greece	4,699	2,569	2,130	1,932	3,685
Italy	5,467	3,448	2,019	1,855	5,410
Poland	4,725	2,827	1,896	1,399	1,996
Portugal	8,408	7,247	1,161	1,033	3,631
Spain	1,879	719	1,160	978	702
U.S.S.R.	10,543	1,825	8,718	285	1,211
United Kingdom	15,485	9,150	6,335	5,696	7,282
Yugoslavia	2,099	1,335	764	713	2,021
North America	164,772	101,299	63,743	51,939	41,785
Canada	13,609	7,840	5,769	4,978	2,823
Cuba	15,054	7,659	7,395	1,278	12,717
Dominican Republic	17,245	14,244	3,001	2,756	3,392
El Salvador	6,101	4,433	1,668	1,584	988
Haiti	6,540	5,131	1,409	1,293	1,748
Jamaica	18,970	15,673	3,297	3,095	5,840
Mexico	56,680	24,831	31,849	28,556	9,341
Trinidad and Tobago	5,154	4,354	800	734	1,074
Oceania	3,951	2,232	1,719	1,530	637
South America	39,717	28,545	11,172	10,130	10,065
Argentina	2,815	1,924	891	790	1,183
Colombia	11,289	7,853	3,436	3,241	2,940
Ecuador	6,133	4,787	1,346	1,251	1,189
Guyana	8,381	7,481	900	853	1,452
Peru	4,021	2,515	1,506	1,434	1,369
Total[2]	530,639	289,479	241,160	151,131	157,938

Note: Immigrants listed by country of birth, aliens by country of former allegiance.
[1]Taiwan and People's Republic. [2]Includes other countries not listed separately.
Source: *1980 Statistical Yearbook of the Immigration and Naturalization Service.*

to 21, with a bias toward highly skilled jobs. West announced fulfillment of an election pledge to remove the bias toward English-speaking people in immigration procedures. This reflected the changing character of immigration into Australia over the past two decades. Between 1961–62 and 1970–71, 45.9% of immigrants came from the U.K. and Ireland, while in 1980–81 the figure was down to 29.2%. In Canada there was a similar pattern of declining numbers, emphasis on admission of those with close family connections, and a shift from a predominantly European—and largely British—based immigration pattern to one in which Asian immigrants were about equal.

In the U.S. the pattern of increasing Hispanic and Asian migration continued in 1982–83. For a number of years, Hispanic immigrants had been predominantly females of labour-force age who had a high rate of labour-force participation in the U.S. All the studies pointed to increasing immigration from these sources throughout the 1980s. Estimates suggested that legal and illegal immigrants together might account for 30–50% of the country's annual population growth.

In Africa, Nigeria, which for many years had attracted migrants from neighbouring countries, took action in January to expel all illegal immigrants, estimated to number one million. (*See* NIGERIA.) (LOUIS KUSHNICK)

See also Refugees.
[525.A.1.c]

Mining and Quarrying

Judging by the mining company statements of losses, the U.S. mining industry bottomed out in 1982. Improvement in 1983 was perceptible, but it also became evident that the U.S. base metal industry, especially the copper and iron-ore segments, would be noticeably smaller in the future. The reasons were foreign competition and technological changes abetted by socioeconomic factors. Competition from non-U.S. sources was burgeoning for a number of reasons, including richer ores; lower labour costs in less developed countries; environmental restrictions on U.S. production resulting in higher costs; development of new domestic processing industries in other countries; and aggrandizement of mineral production for nationalistic reasons. On the technological side there was miniaturization, as in automobiles and telecommunications, as well as competition from other materials. New technology also advanced the development of mini-processing plants, thereby decentralizing such basic industries as steel.

Not all mined commodities were affected equally. Metals were hardest hit because they are traded internationally, whereas nonmetals, in many cases, depended only on local economic factors.

Mining lagged behind the economic improvement of 1983. For this reason, as in 1982, there were few major developments of new facilities around the world. Exceptions to the general inactivity were intensive exploration for precious metals and the development of new mines and processing facilities.

U.S. oil companies, previously active in acquiring mining operations, in 1983 showed more interest in selling. Cities Service Co., which had been bought by Occidental Petroleum Corp. in 1982, sold its Miami, Ariz., copper operations, capable of producing 70,000 tons per year of copper, to Newmont Mining Co. General Electric, which had acquired Utah International in 1976 for almost $2.2 billion of GE shares, was negotiating to sell it. Although no major acquisitions of U.S. mineral companies were made by outsiders in 1983, as had been the case in preceding years, a deal with Broken Hill Proprietary, an Australian steel company, to buy Utah for $2.4 billion in cash was in the making. Most of Utah's mining assets, including coal and iron ore in Australia and iron ore, copper, and coal mining in North and South America, would be part of the deal.

During the year the labour agreements for steel, aluminum, and copper with the United Steelworkers union expired. Because of the plant closings and layoffs experienced in 1982 and 1983, the strikes that usually accompanied negotiations did not take place to any major extent. Steelworkers accepted a wage cut and postponement of cost of living adjustments (COLA); aluminum workers took a wage freeze and reduced COLA; and copper workers accepted a wage freeze with no increase in COLA payments. Phelps Dodge Corp., the second largest U.S. copper producer, did not sign the contracts, and, although it experienced a strike, it continued operations with some union labourers crossing picket lines.

Industry Developments. A new underground molybdenum mine was brought into production by Molybdenum Corp. of America (Molycorp) at a cost of $250 million. Molycorp had been mining by the open-pit method at Questa, N.M., for 30 years. The new mine started with a capacity of 9,000 tons per day and was to be increased by 1985 to 16,300, when open-pit mining would be phased out. U.S. Borax continued development at its Quartz Hill, Alaska, molybdenum property by taking bulk samples for testing and also by preparing for construction of a refinery in Grays Harbor County, Wash.

A new lead mine, the Bixby, in the Missouri lead belt, began partial production in 1983. The first new lead mine in seven years for St. Joe Minerals Corp., the largest U.S. producer, it was expected to reach a capacity of 3,600 tons per day of ore early in 1984. Begun in April 1980 at a cost of $25 million, the mine is an underground operation from which the ore will be trucked to the company's Viburnum mill; the mill was expanded to 11,000 tons per day in order to treat this new ore. Asarco Inc. was working on a new mine/mill in the same area. The mill was completed, but underground mine development was stopped in 1982. Asarco announced near the end of 1983 that it would restart development of the new West Fork mine. Capacity was planned to be about the same as that of the Bixby.

A new gold mine, Mercur, near Salt Lake City, Utah, produced its first gold in April. Getty Oil Co. invested more than $80 million in this project. The facility was expected to produce up to 80,000 oz per year of gold for 14 years from ore containing about 0.102 oz gold per ton. Placer Development Ltd. of Vancouver, B.C., began operations at the Golden Sunlight gold mine near Butte, Mont., in January at a cost of $50 million. The property was scheduled to yield about 72,000 oz of gold per year for 13 years from an ore having some 0.054 oz per ton.

Considering the depressed uranium market, it was noteworthy that a new uranium mine to exploit a high-grade ore body began operating at the end of September at Key Lake, Sask. The new facility, costing Can$500 million, was expected to have a capacity of nearly 5.5 million kg (12 million lb) per year and to employ 400 to 500 workers. The mine was owned partly by the Canadian Crown Company and the Saskatchewan Mining Development Corporation with a one-third share held by the private-sector West German firm Uranerz Exploration and Mining.

In one of Canada's oldest and largest uranium mining districts at Blind River, Ont., extensive shaft rehabilitation work and new haulage drifts were being prepared to integrate the Stanrock and Can-Met mines of Denison Mines Ltd. for production in 1985. No comparable uranium activities were taking place in the U.S.

A new flash copper smelter and refinery was put into operation on the island of Leyte by the Philippine Associated Smelting and Refining Co. at a cost of $267 million. It was rated to produce 138,000 tons per year of cathode copper. This facility caused considerable furor among Philippine copper producers who were afraid that the benefits of the facility would be less than those derived from selling concentrates to Japan.

The government of Chile, through its mining unit Codelco and its smelting and refining company Enami, planned to increase its annual production of copper metal from about 1.2 million tons per year to 1.7 million tons per year by an expenditure of more than $1 billion on new facilities by the end of 1987. A considerable portion of the new capacity would be gained by treating waste dumps and old residues of oxide treatment facilities with leaching, solvent extraction, and electrowinning (the recovery of metals from solutions by electrolysis).

Technological Developments. Because of the high price of gold, the technology of extracting it from ore was progressing rapidly. Deposits that were not economic at the old fixed price of $35 per ounce prior to 1975 had become profitable. Material containing as little as 0.03 oz per ton was being mined and treated, and, indeed, a deposit that had as much as 0.5 oz per ton was considered a bonanza. Major technological changes included the application of heap leaching to gold and the more widespread use of the recovery system of adsorption of gold on activated carbon. The new systems enabled small miners to return to the mining scene because less capital was required for the heap leaching extraction system.

In heap leaching, which does not require building a mill, ore from the mine is stacked on impervious pads, and sodium cyanide solution is

UPI

A high-pressure spray hose is used by continuous mining vehicles to control coal dust. The hose, developed by Goodyear, is reinforced by a fibre similar to one used for bulletproof vests.

sprinkled over the top. The leach solution is collected on the pads at the bottom, and the gold is removed by adsorption on carbon or precipitated with zinc dust. Extracting the gold from the heaps is accomplished in a matter of months. To be treated, ore must be permeable to the solution and free of elements that consume cyanide.

In the activated carbon system, gold is still leached from the ore with sodium cyanide in a series of tanks. Activated carbon is used to collect the gold from solution. Gold collection may be started during the leaching process by putting carbon in the pulp of ore and solution, or it may take place in a separate series of tanks. Lime solution, air, and sodium cyanide are added to assist the interaction of gold adsorbing on carbon. Carbon is pumped by airlift from the leached pulp to the next tank upstream, whereas the pulp moves from tank to tank downstream until it is discarded. The carbon added at the beginning is approximately 3 by 1 mm (0.12 by 0.39 in) in size. The affinity of carbon and gold has been known for a century, but the success of the carbon-in-pulp process is due to development of a method of stripping the gold from the carbon so that the carbon can be reused. This is achieved by washing the gold and silver cyanide from the activated carbon in the stripping vessels with a hot solution of sodium cyanide and sodium hydroxide. The carbon is reactivated by heating it in a kiln prior to its return to the adsorption circuit. Gold-bearing solution is treated by electrolysis in which the gold is plated on steel wool. After smelting, in which the steel wool and other base metals are fluxed, gold bars are cast for shipment to a refinery.

The advantage of the activated carbon system is its low capital cost because comparatively little equipment and space are required. Also, a wider variety of ores can be processed, including clayey and fouled and/or dilute mill solutions. In addition, less cyanide is required, a purer product is obtained, and the process is simpler to control.

(JOHN V. BEALL)

Indexes of Production, Mining and Mineral Commodities

(1975=100)

	1978	1979	1980	1981	1982	1983 I	1983 II
Mining (total)							
World[1]	112.7	118.6	115.8	113.7	115.1	106.8	. . .
Centrally planned economies[2]	112.0	115.1	116.3	115.5	119.5	125.7	122.0
Developed market economies[3]	112.7	120.3	124.9	128.6	122.7	121.7	117.9
Less developed market economies[4]	113.0	118.9	110.7	104.9	109.3	91.8	. . .
Coal							
World[1]	101.1	106.2	109.3	108.6	111.6	112.5	. . .
Centrally planned economies[2]	105.8	107.6	106.9	102.0	108.4	110.1	109.7
Developed market economies[3]	97.1	104.9	110.4	111.1	111.9	110.2	108.1
Less developed market economies[4]	109.4	110.7	120.3	144.2	140.6	174.8	. . .
Petroleum							
World[1]	116.3	122.3	117.7	115.4	117.8	105.3	. . .
Centrally planned economies[2]	118.2	122.3	125.4	128.1	131.3	139.5	133.8
Developed market economies[3]	127.2	136.1	144.5	153.8	146.3	147.6	134.5
Less developed market economies[4]	113.2	118.8	109.4	103.3	108.1	88.6	. . .
Metals							
World[1]	101.0	103.4	105.1	103.2	98.6	98.0	. . .
Centrally planned economies[2]	103.6	104.9	111.0	98.4	100.0	104.6	105.6
Developed market economies[3]	96.8	100.0	98.4	99.1	88.8	85.8	92.9
Less developed market economies[4]	106.1	108.0	112.2	113.6	114.1	114.1	. . .
Manufacturing (total)	119.1	124.7	126.2	127.0	125.0	126.7	. . .

[1] Excluding Albania, China, North Korea, Vietnam.
[2] Bulgaria, Czechoslovakia, East Germany, Hungary, Poland, Romania, U.S.S.R.
[3] North America, Europe (except centrally planned), Australia, Israel, Japan, New Zealand, South Africa.
[4] Caribbean, Central and South America, Africa (except South Africa), Asian Middle East, East and Southeast Asia (except Israel and Japan).
Source: UN, *Monthly Bulletin of Statistics* (November 1983).

Production. The United Nations overall indexes of mining production for 1982 and the first two quarters of 1983 (*see* TABLE) indicated stagnation or decline in all sectors of the world industry except coal, which showed a marked increase only in the less developed market economies. Results at the end of 1982 were mixed, with energy-related commodities showing only a slight increase and metals showing a slight decrease.

According to data compiled by the U.S. Bureau of Mines, of a group of 86 mineral commodities for which reasonably complete international data were available, output in 1982 declined for 56, rose for 13, and remained about the same for 17. Among metals the losers outnumbered the gainers 31 to 6; half of the gainers were minor metals with only zinc, lead, and gold showing increases among those considered major. Among the nonmetals, losers outnumbered gainers almost four to one (27 and 7, respectively).

The United States mining sector, with an aggregate value at the mine of some $20,029,000,000 in 1982, declined about 21% in absolute terms. These raw mineral commodities increased in value to some $202 billion when processed for end use by other industries, but this total represented a 14.4% decline when measured against 1981 results. The mine value of metals alone in 1982 was approximately $5,610,000,000; this represented a major decline of 37% from $8,843,000,000 in 1981. In quantitative terms only 3 of 21 metals increased their absolute output during the year. The value of nonmetals declined by some 12% in 1982 to a total of $14,419,000,000.

Among metals in the U.S. the only growth was shown by lead (up 14%) and aluminum (secondary; up 7%). Much of the increase in lead production was exported, U.S. consumption decreasing because of environmental considerations and reduced demand for automotive batteries. Recycling of beverage cans generated the increase in secondary aluminum. Losses were greatest in nickel (refined metal from U.S. ores; −71%), mercury (secondary; −64%), tungsten (−59%), bauxite (−54%), iron ore (−52%), and molybdenum (−46%). Metals utilized in the steel industry, including iron ore, nickel, molybdenum, and ferroalloys, as well as aluminum, suffered much reduction in demand, largely because of the poor state of the automobile industry. Environmental concerns and the release of surplus mercury from the U.S. Department of Energy accounted for the loss in secondary mercury production. Tungsten, largely used in making carbide machine tools, was down because of the economic slump.

Among nonmetals the largest gainers were bromine and peat (each up 6%). Large quantities of bromine, used in gasoline additives and in the manufacture of flame retardants, were exported. Peat found increased uses in soil improvement and as potting soil. The biggest losers included ilmenite (−49%) and fluorspar (−36%). Ilmenite, used mostly in titanium pigments, declined because of a mine closure and less demand for it in industry. Fluorspar, used in the aluminum and steel industries, reflected the weakness of those industries in the U.S.

Aluminum. World production of bauxite, the principal ore of aluminum, was estimated to have fallen about 11.6% during 1982, totaling about 75.8 million metric tons. The leading producer continued to be Australia, at an estimated 23 million tons (off about 10% from 1981), followed by Guinea with an estimated 10.2 million tons (about 20% below its 1981 output) and Jamaica, the world's third largest producer, with about 8.3 million tons (more than 3 million tons less than in 1981, a decrease of nearly 30%). Output of alumina (aluminum oxide, the concentrated intermediate stage in the production of aluminum metal) was estimated to have fallen by more than 5%, to approximately 31,460,000 tons, about 21% of which was produced by Australia, followed closely by the U.S. with 17%. World production of aluminum metal fell by nearly 15%, to an estimated 14.2 million tons. The United States, continuing as the major producer, led the decline by producing an estimated 27% less than in 1981. Its 3.6 million tons represented about one-fourth of total world production. The U.S.S.R. produced an estimated 2.1 million tons, Canada 1,190,000 tons, West Germany 780,000 tons, and Japan, with its estimated output falling more than 50%, about 400,000 tons. Weakening demand for aluminum worldwide continued for the third successive year, and accelerating cutbacks in production, begun in 1981, resulted in an underutilization of refining capacity of nearly 25%.

Antimony. Mine output of antimony was estimated to have declined by about 4% during 1982, falling from 59,190 metric tons in 1981 to about 56,603 tons. The major producer continued to be Bolivia at 14,515 tons, down about 5% from 1981. China was second, at 9,979 tons, followed by the U.S.S.R. at 8,981 tons and South Africa at 8,618 tons. The second meeting of the Organización Internacional del Antimonio (OIA)—held at La Paz, Bolivia, in October 1982—was attended by the representatives of the antimony-producing, consuming, and trading countries (excluding China, U.S.S.R., and South Africa). A decision was made at the meeting to cut world production by at least 20% to cope with the reduced demand in the automotive and construction industries.

Cement. World production of cement in 1982 was estimated to have remained virtually unchanged from 1981, reflecting both a continuing trend of cutbacks in the construction industry in developed countries and of expansion in the less developed countries. Total production was about 892 million metric tons, up only 0.01% from the previous year. The U.S.S.R. remained the leading producer, matching its 1981 figure of about 127 million metric tons and representing 14.3% of the total. China was second with 86 million metric tons, up 2.6% from 1981, while Japan produced 85 million metric tons, up only 0.5%. The U.S., with construction stalled by high interest rates and a weakened economy, slid to a seven-year low of 58 million metric tons, down 12.2% from the previous year.

Chromium. World mine production of chromite, the principal ore of chromium, was estimated by the U.S. Bureau of Mines to have fallen slightly (by about 5%) from a 1981 production figure of 9,253,300 metric tons to a total of about 8,799,700 metric tons. The decline was evenly distributed in most of the chromium-producing countries, except South Africa, where output fell almost 10% to some 2,631,000 tons.

Copper. World mined copper output fell during 1982 to an estimated 8,070,000 metric tons, a decline of more than 3% from the previous year. Chile's output of 1,241,000 tons represented a nearly 15% increase, resulting from an effort to compensate for depressed copper prices. Chile thus became the leading copper producer in the world, displacing the U.S., whose 1,135,000 tons was more than 25% below its 1981 production level. Other major producers included the U.S.S.R. with an estimated 1,140,000 tons, Canada 640,000 tons, Zambia 530,000 tons, and Zaire about 500,000 tons. Blister copper production (smelter output) fell by nearly 3% worldwide. More than half of the world's output came from four countries: the U.S.S.R., which led with 1.1 million tons, followed by Chile, Japan, and the U.S., producing about 1 million tons each. World output of refined copper decreased by about 417,000 tons (about 4.3%) to approximately 9,240,000 tons. The 37% decline in Canada's output (largely because of major strikes) to an estimated 298,000 tons and a nearly 16% decline in the U.S. to 1,672,000 tons were major contributors to the decline in copper production worldwide.

Gold. Mine production of gold rose slightly in 1982, gaining about 0.4% and reaching an estimated total of 1,274 metric tons. South Africa's long-time dominance of the world market continued in 1982—representing a 48.7% share of world production, some 659 tons in 1982. Estimates placed the U.S.S.R. second at about 22.7% of world production, approximately the same as in 1981. Canada's production of 62.5 tons, 31% more than in 1981 (and 4.6% of the world total), enabled it to become the world's third most important producer. China ranked fourth at about 4.1% of world production. U.S. production remained static at 43.5 tons; production from newly opened mines was offset by a labour strike lasting four months at the Homestake mine in South Dakota (the largest gold mine in the U.S.) and by severely curtailed copper mine production, a source for secondary gold. A sharp increase in Australian production to 27.4 tons (about 50% more than in 1981) was partially attributable to the opening of new mines in Western Australia. The average gold content of South African ore declined to 6.76 grams per metric ton in 1982 from 6.92 in 1981 and 7.28 in 1980; the overall grade of South African ore had declined by nearly 50% since 1970.

Iron. Production of iron ore worldwide was estimated to have fallen by about 8.4% in 1982, with total output amounting to about 788 million metric tons. This decline was partly the result of a drastic drop in U.S. output. The U.S.S.R. was the world leader, with production of 240 million tons, a slight decline from 1981 and amounting to 30% of the world total. Brazil was the second leading producer, with 98 million tons, also a slight decline from the previous year. Australia's production remained almost constant at 85 million tons. China became the fourth largest producer, with 71 million tons, followed by India, with 42 million tons. In the U.S. output fell by 52% to about 36 million tons, putting it and Canada, also at 36 million tons, in a tie for sixth place among the world's producers. The continued weakness of industrial users of iron and steel in the U.S. led to extensive mine closings, layoffs, and the suspension of operations throughout 1982 and into 1983. World production of pig iron fell by 9.2% to an estimated 454 million tons. The leading producers, both of which suffered slight decreases in production, were the U.S.S.R. at 106 million tons and Japan at 78 million tons.

Lead. World mine output of lead totaled about 3,450,000 metric tons in 1982, up by some 3% from 1981. The U.S. continued as the main producer with 510,000 metric tons, up by about 14% from 1981. Other major producers included Australia with 450,000 tons, Canada 335,000 tons, Peru 210,000 tons, and Mexico 155,000 tons. Output of refined metal totaled some 3,540,000 tons. The main producer was the U.S. with 500,000 tons, only slightly up from 1981. Including 610,000 tons of production from secondary recovery, U.S. output amounted to about 1,110,000 tons. Reported consumption of lead declined by about 8% during the year, reflecting continuing reductions in automotive applications such as batteries and gasoline additives.

Magnesium. World production of magnesium in 1982 was estimated to have dropped about 7.6% from the previous year, to a total of approximately 275,000 metric tons. About 41.3% of this figure, or 113,000 metric tons, was produced (mostly from brines) in the U.S.; this represented a 12.6% decline from 1981. The U.S.S.R. was thought to be the second leading producer with about 78,000 metric tons (principally from magnesite ore), with output matching its 1981 figure. Norway was the third leading producer with its 45,000 metric tons, representing a 6% decline from 1981.

Manganese. World mine production of manganese ore, at about 20,865,000 metric tons, was estimated to have fallen about 11.5% from 1981. Except for the 1% increase in output for the U.S.S.R., the world's decline in output was distributed evenly among the leading producing countries. The Soviet Union's 9.5 million metric tons accounted for more than two-fifths of total production in 1982. Following the Soviet Union were South Africa (about 3,992,000 metric tons) and Brazil (about 1,542,000 metric tons). The Carajas manganese resources in Brazil, estimated at 60 million tons, were to be developed by Vale do Rio Doce Co., and production was expected to start in 1986.

Mercury. World mine production of mercury in 1982 was 189,500 34.5-kg (76-lb) flasks, a decrease of about 8.3% from 1981. The U.S.S.R. remained the world's largest producer, with an estimated production in 1982 of 57,000 flasks, compared with 63,000 flasks in 1981. It was followed by Spain at about 45,000 flasks, the United States with 25,000 flasks, and Algeria with 23,000 flasks. Mercury mine production in the U.S. fell almost 10% from the 1981 level, primarily because of the closing of several mines. By the end of 1982 the bulk of the U.S. output came from Nevada.

Molybdenum. Estimates of world molybdenum output by the U.S. Bureau of Mines indicated a 16.9% decline during 1982 because of a 41% fall in U.S. production, which had accounted for about 60% of the world total in recent years. Most other major producers showed increases. World production was estimated at 90,872 metric tons in 1982, the U.S. output of 37,671 tons representing only 41% of the world total. Chile was the second largest producer, with 19,100 tons, a 30% increase from 1981. Other main producers included Canada, with 16,461 tons, a 16% increase from the previous year, and the U.S.S.R., with 11,022 tons. Mine closings characterized North American operations in 1982 and continued into 1983.

Nickel. World mine production of nickel fell by an estimated 14.6% in 1982, totaling 607,629 metric tons. In the continuing economic recession a decrease in demand and efforts to reduce existing inventories accounted for the decline. Shutdowns of several Inco Ltd. mines as well as the poor market for nickel reduced Canada's production by a staggering 44.6% (88,744 tons, compared with 160,247 in 1981). Historically the world's largest producer, Canada relinquished this status to the U.S.S.R., whose estimated output of 169,643 tons was an increase of 7.5% over 1981. Among other significant producers, Australia mined 82,200 tons, up 10.4% from the previous year, and New Caledonia's production fell by 24.5% to 58,967 tons. The refined nickel output

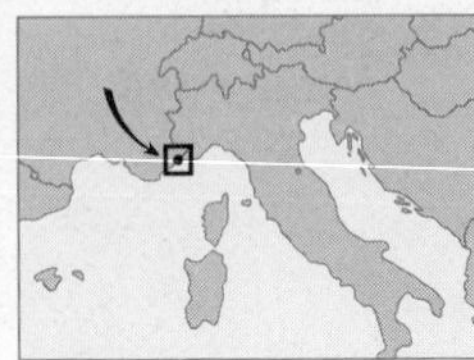
Monaco

of 619,336 tons worldwide amounted to a decline of 11.3%. The U.S.S.R. remained the largest producer with an estimated 189,964 tons. Japan gained second place with 83,733 tons, and Canada slipped to third with 63,412 tons, a 45% decrease in production.

Phosphate Rock. World production of phosphate rock declined 10.4% during 1982. The output of the U.S., the world's major producer, fell by 26.6% to about 38.6 million metric tons. Of the other top producers the U.S.S.R. registered an increase of 4.7% with an estimated 26.6 million tons, and Morocco decreased production by 9.9% with 17.7 million tons. China, the fourth leading producer, increased its output by 4.3% to 12.5 million tons. More than 80% of phosphate rock in 1982 was used for the manufacture of fertilizer. Western Europe and the U.S., where the application of fertilizer is a practice of long standing, have built up large reserves of phosphate in the soil. This factor is thought to be one of the major causes of the decline in phosphate rock demand, together with the reduced level of farm spending on fertilizers because of the current worldwide economic recession.

Platinum-Group Metals. World production of the platinum-group metals (platinum, iridium, palladium, osmium, rhodium, and ruthenium) was estimated to have fallen by 5.8% in 1982 to 6.4 million troy ounces. Virtually all the production was divided between the U.S.S.R., thought to be the leader at about 3.5 million troy ounces, and South Africa with about 2.6 million troy ounces. During 1982 the U.S.S.R. and South Africa together accounted for about 96% of the world production, a 2% increase over 1981. Canadian output was 190,000 troy ounces, a decline of more than 50% from 1981 caused by plant shutdowns.

Silver. World silver production was static in 1982; total production was estimated to be 364 million troy ounces, a decline of 0.2% from 1981. Peru replaced Mexico as chief producer with the U.S.S.R. remaining a close third. Estimated production figures for the top three were: Peru 53.2 million troy ounces, up about 19%; Mexico 49.8 million troy ounces, down about 3%; and the U.S.S.R. 46.9 million troy ounces, up about 1%. Other important producers included Canada with 38.7 million troy ounces, the United States with 35.1 million troy ounces, and Australia with 28.9 million troy ounces. Because of the low silver prices early in the year, Peru's silver export revenue declined by 34% despite the nation's record annual production figure, and Mexico's total production declined despite the opening of the important Real de Angeles mine. In the U.S. a number of mines closed at least temporarily. Overall annual production for the U.S. was down nearly 14%.

Tin. World mine production of tin was about 188,200 metric tons, down by 7% from 1981. The major producing countries included Malaysia with about 51,700 tons, down about 14% from 1981; the U.S.S.R. with approximately 37,000 tons; Indonesia at 34,250 tons; Thailand at 27,850 tons; and Bolivia at 27,000 tons. Smelter production of tin metal fell about 9% to about 178,150 tons worldwide. The leading producer was Malaysia with 61,800 tons, about one-third of the world total; it was followed by Indonesia with 29,850 tons and Thailand with 26,800 tons. The sixth International Tin Agreement entered into force in July 1982 without the participation of the U.S. (the largest consumer) or Bolivia. The Association of Tin Producing Countries was launched in August 1983; its members in late 1983 included Bolivia, Indonesia, Malaysia, Nigeria, Thailand, and Zaire, which together produced about 85% of the world's tin supply. Australia applied for membership starting in early 1984.

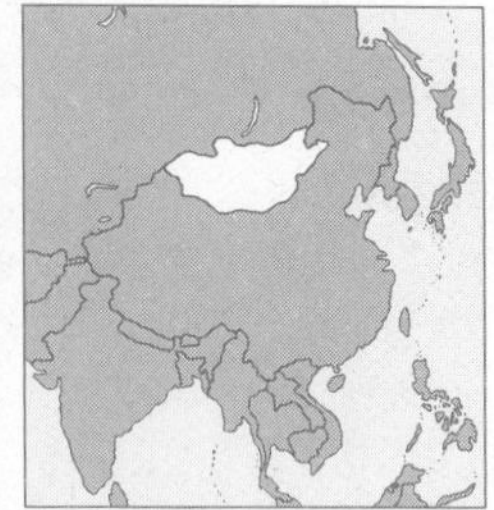
Mongolia

Titanium. World production of titanium sponge metal declined by about 17% during 1982 to a total of 74,842 metric tons, in contrast to 1981, which was a year of strong growth. The drop reflected a lower demand for the metal by the weakened commercial aircraft industry. The U.S.S.R. was the leading sponge producer for which data were available, with about 38,101 tons. U.S. production was estimated at 16,692 tons. Australia continued to lead in ilmenite and rutile production; output of ilmenite in Australia accounted for about one-fourth of the world total.

Tungsten. World mine production of tungsten declined by about 12% during 1982 to a total of 42,728 metric tons. China was believed to be the chief producer at about 11,339 tons. Canada, followed in order by Australia, Bolivia, South Korea, the U.S., Portugal, and Austria produced between 2,993 and 1,179 tons each.

Zinc. According to data from the U.S. Bureau of Mines, mine output of zinc rose by about 4.6% during 1982, reaching a total of about 6,110,000 metric tons. Canadian output of 1,165,000 tons was a gain of about 6%. Another chief producer was the U.S.S.R., estimated to have produced about 1,110,000 tons. Other important producers included Australia, at 620,000 tons showing a small gain of about 2.2%; Peru 535,000 tons, up 7.6%; the U.S. 300,000 tons, off about 4%; Japan 250,000 tons, up 3.3%; and Mexico 245,000 tons, up 8.5%, regaining some of the loss in 1981. Metal production declined by about 5.5% in response to weak demand from all the major consuming nations. In the U.S. production was down 106,000 tons because of mine closings.

See also Earth Sciences; Energy; Industrial Review: *Iron and Steel;* Materials Sciences.
[724.B.1; 724.C.3]

Missiles: see Defense

Molecular Biology: see Life Sciences

Monetary Policy: see Economy, World

Money and Banking: see Economy, World

Monaco

A sovereign principality on the northern Mediterranean coast, Monaco is bounded on land by the French département of Alpes-Maritimes. Area: 1.90 sq km (0.73 sq mi). Pop. (1982): 27,100. Language: French. Religion: predominantly Roman Catholic. Chief of state, Prince Rainier III; minister of state in 1983, Jean Herly.

In his first interview with a daily newspaper since the death of his wife, Princess Grace, in September 1982, Prince Rainier III spoke to *The Times* (London) in June 1983 about the future of the principality. He said that he did not intend to abdicate "tomorrow or even the day after" in favour of his son, Prince Albert; instead, a decision would be taken by father and son together when both felt that Prince Albert was ready.

On February 17 Prince Rainier unveiled a monument commemorating Princess Grace in Villefranche-sur-Mer, France, during the ceremony inaugurating Princess Grace Boulevard. His elder daughter, Princess Caroline, was married for the second time on December 29 to Stefano Casiraghi, son of an Italian industrial family, in a civil ceremony. (K. M. SMOGORZEWSKI)

MONACO

Education. (1980–81) Primary, pupils 1,347; secondary, pupils 1,314; vocational, pupils 751; primary, secondary, and vocational, teachers *c.* 400.

Finance and Trade. Monetary unit: French franc, with (Sept. 20, 1983) a free rate of Fr 8.06 to U.S. $1 (Fr 12.14 = £1 sterling). Budget (1981 est.): revenue Fr 1,259,000,000; expenditure Fr 814 million. Foreign trade included with France. Tourism (1981) 209,000 visitors.

Mongolia

A people's republic of Asia lying between the U.S.S.R. and China, Mongolia occupies the geographic area known as Outer Mongolia. Area: 1,566,500 sq km (604,800 sq mi). Pop. (1983 est.): 1,809,000. Cap. and largest city: Ulan Bator (pop., 1981 est., 435,400). Language: Khalkha Mongolian. Religion: Lamaistic Buddhism. First secretary of the Mongolian People's Revolutionary (Communist) Party in 1983 and chairman of the Presidium of the Great People's Hural, Yumzhagiyen Tsedenbal; chairman of the Council of Ministers (premier), Zhambyn Batmunkh.

On June 3, 1983, the Mongolian government announced that a small number of Chinese residing in Mongolia had been failing to work productively. The authorities had thereupon offered these people a choice: either take an active part in building socialism or return to China.

Reports of the expulsions had first emerged on May 26, when Western travelers on the Trans-Siberian Express noted that 100 Chinese had boarded the train at Ulan Bator. These Chinese claimed that two months earlier the entire Chinese population of Mongolia—estimated at 7,000–8,000—had been ordered to move to remote areas

MONGOLIA

Education. (1980–81) Primary and secondary, pupils 394,400; vocational, pupils 22,100; primary, secondary, and vocational, teachers 13,883; higher, students 23,200, teaching staff 1,100.

Finance. Monetary unit: tugrik, with (Sept. 20, 1983) a nominal exchange rate of 3.36 tugriks to U.S. $1 (5.05 tugriks = £1 sterling). Budget (1983 est.) balanced at 5,146,000,000 tugriks.

Foreign Trade. (1982) Imports *c.* U.S. $1.4 billion; exports *c.* U.S. $550 million. Import source: U.S.S.R. *c.* 90%. Export destination: U.S.S.R. *c.* 80%. Main exports (1980): food 32%; raw materials (except food) 31%; fuels, minerals, and metals 26%.

Transport and Communications. Roads (1980) *c.* 75,000 km (including *c.* 9,000 km main roads). Railways (1982): 1,710 km; traffic 297 million passenger-km, freight 3,449,000,000 net ton-km. Telephones (Dec. 1980) 39,800. Radio receivers (Dec. 1980) 166,000. Television receivers (Dec. 1980) 52,900.

Agriculture. Production (in 000; metric tons; 1982): wheat *c.* 290; oats *c.* 15; barley (1981) *c.* 50; potatoes (1981) *c.* 55; milk (1981) *c.* 253; beef and veal (1981) *c.* 73; mutton and goat meat *c.* 126; wool *c.* 13. Livestock (in 000; Dec. 1980): sheep 14,231; goats 4,567; cattle 2,397; horses 1,985; camels *c.* 591.

Industry. Production (in 000; metric tons; 1982): coal and lignite 4,925; fluorspar 667; cement (1981) 180; electricity (kw-hr) 1,578,000.

of the Gobi Desert or to leave the country by August. In September the expulsions were reportedly still taking place, despite protests from Beijing (Peking). By then some 2,000 Chinese were said to have been sent back to China.

In talks aimed at normalizing Sino-Soviet relations, the Chinese government criticized the presence of Soviet troops in Mongolia.

A treaty of friendship and collaboration was signed on June 17 in Bucharest by Romanian Pres. Nicolae Ceausescu and Chairman Yumzhagiyen Tsedenbal. (K. M. SMOGORZEWSKI)

Morocco

A constitutional monarchy of northwestern Africa, on the Atlantic Ocean and the Mediterranean Sea, Morocco is bordered by Algeria and Western Sahara. Area: 458,730 sq km (177,117 sq mi). Pop. (1982): 20,419,600. Cap.: Rabat (pop., 1982, 518,600). Largest city: Casablanca (pop., 1982, 2,139,200). (Data above refer to Morocco as constituted prior to the purported division of Western Sahara between Morocco and Mauritania and the subsequent Moroccan occupation of the Mauritanian zone in 1979.) Language: Arabic (official), with Berber, French, and Spanish minorities. Religion: Muslim. King, Hassan II; prime ministers in 1983, Maati Bouabid and, from November 30 (interim), Mohammad Karim Lamrani.

For Morocco 1983 was marked by a slowly worsening situation in the Western Sahara, despite improved relations with Algeria and Libya, the major backers of the Popular Front for the Liberation of Saguia el Hamra and Río de Oro (Polisario Front). On February 26 Pres. Chadli Bendjedid of Algeria met Morocco's King Hassan II, and the border between the two countries was opened for the first time since 1976. In July Col. Muammar al-Qaddafi of Libya visited Rabat.

At the Organization of African Unity (OAU) summit in Addis Ababa, Eth., on June 11, Morocco accepted a resolution that named the parties to the conflict as itself and the Front and insisted on negotiations between them and a referendum in the Western Sahara within six months. The Front, which had been militarily quiescent for over a year, launched a large-scale assault against the Moroccan post of Lemseyed on July 10. On September 3 the Front attacked Smara. During the September meeting of the OAU committee handling the Western Sahara dispute, Moroccan delegates refused to meet with Front representatives. King Hassan later claimed, however, that Morocco would accept the result of a referendum.

On January 25 Gen. Ahmed Dlimi (*see* OBITUARIES), the Moroccan commander in the Sahara, was killed, according to official accounts, in an automobile accident. Other reports suggested that the general had been involved in a coup attempt.

A new political party, the Constitutional Union, was created by Prime Minister Maati Bouabid in January. In local elections held in June, amid claims of election rigging, the five royalist parties won a resounding victory. The government postponed national elections, scheduled for later in the year, until early in 1984. In November the king appointed a caretaker government to lead the coun-

MOROCCO

Education. (1982) Primary, pupils 2,418,385, teachers 63,157; secondary, pupils 875,869, teachers 38,252; vocational, pupils 10,300; teacher training, students 24,825, teachers 783; higher, students 98,513, teaching staff (1980–81) 2,558.

Finance. Monetary unit: dirham, with (Sept. 20, 1983) a free rate of 7.88 dirhams to U.S. $1 (11.87 dirhams = £1 sterling). Gold and other reserves (June 1983) U.S. $63 million. Budget (1982 est.): revenue 22,590,000,000 dirhams; expenditure 22,550,000,000 dirhams. Gross national product (1981) 78.1 billion dirhams. Money supply (Dec. 1982) 31,967,000,000 dirhams. Cost of living (1975 = 100; Feb. 1983) 203.7.

Foreign Trade. (1982) Imports 25,983,000,000 dirhams; exports 12,461,000,000 dirhams. Main import sources (1981): France 25%; Saudi Arabia 15%; U.S. 7%; Spain 7%; West Germany 5%. Main export destinations (1981): France 22%; West Germany 7%; Spain 7%; U.S.S.R. 6%; The Netherlands 6%; India 5%; Italy 5%. Main exports (1981): phosphates 31%; phosphoric acid 11%; citrus fruit 9%; vegetables 5%; clothing 5%. Tourism (1981): visitors 1,567,000; gross receipts U.S. $440 million.

Transport and Communications. Roads (1982) 57,533 km. Motor vehicles in use (1982): passenger 480,300; commercial (including buses) 200,900. Railways (1980): 1,756 km; traffic 936 million passenger-km, freight 3,934,000,000 net ton-km. Air traffic (1982): 1,827,000,000 passenger-km; freight *c.* 38.9 million net ton-km. Shipping (1982): merchant vessels 100 gross tons and over 193; gross tonnage 393,979. Telephones (Dec. 1980) 231,000. Radio receivers (Dec. 1980) 3 million. Television licenses (Dec. 1980) 749,000.

Agriculture. Production (in 000; metric tons; 1982): wheat 2,183; barley 2,334; corn 247; potatoes *c.* 539; sugar, raw value *c.* 395; tomatoes *c.* 385; grapes *c.* 210; oranges *c.* 695; mandarin oranges and tangerines *c.* 294; olives *c.* 275; dates *c.* 65; fish catch (1981) 382. Livestock (in 000; 1982): sheep *c.* 14,900; goats *c.* 6,250; cattle (1981) *c.* 3,240; horses (1981) *c.* 310; mules (1981) *c.* 390; asses (1981) *c.* 1,450; camels (1981) *c.* 230; poultry *c.* 24,000.

Industry. Production (in 000; metric tons; 1982): crude oil 50; natural gas (cu m) 80,000; petroleum products (1981) 4,130; coal (1981) 710; electricity (kw-hr) *c.* 5,400,000; cement 3,702; iron ore (55–60% metal content) 230; phosphate rock (1981) 18,562; copper concentrates (metal content) 66; lead concentrates (metal content) 147; manganese ore (metal content; 1981) *c.* 57; zinc concentrates (metal content) 23.

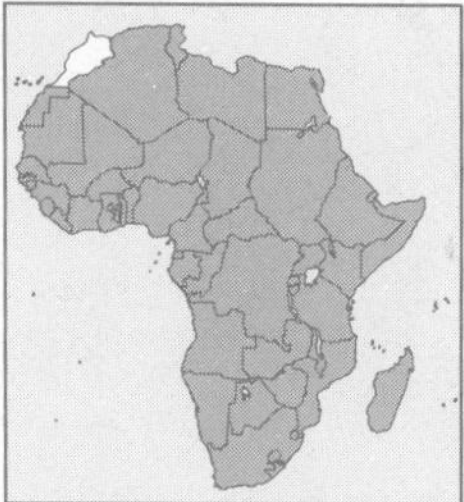

Morocco

Mormons:
see Religion

WIDE WORLD

The visit of Libya's Col. Muammar al-Qaddafi (left) to King Hassan II of Morocco for the first time in 14 years raised hopes that Libya would temper its support of the Polisario guerrilla forces in the Western Sahara.

try through both the Sahara referendum and national elections. The administration was led by Mohammad Karim Lamrani, who had been prime minister in the early 1970s.

The 1983 budget, brought before Parliament in November 1982, anticipated greater austerity, with expenditure up 12% to 53 billion dirhams and foreign debt rising 20% to 5.7 billion dirhams. Phosphate prices fell by $2 to $38 per metric ton in January, and the adverse effect on the trade deficit sapped international confidence. As a result, Morocco turned to the International Monetary Fund for the third time in two years. The IMF agreed to a standby credit of $300 million, but Morocco still had to reschedule some of its foreign debt.

Morocco renewed links with France during Pres. François Mitterrand's visit in January and with the U.S. when Vice-Pres. George Bush visited Rabat in September. (GEORGE JOFFÉ)

Motion Pictures

English-Speaking Cinema. UNITED STATES. Hollywood continued to prove in 1983 that the moviegoing public prefers the well-tried and familiar. The two outstanding box-office successes of the year both recapitulated established formulas. *The Return of the Jedi*, directed by Richard Marquand, was the third episode in the saga that began with *Star Wars* and was planned eventually to extend to another six. At this stage of its evolution, both the story formulas and the special effects had become mechanical, but the fact appeared not to diminish the enthusiasm of the public. *Never Say Never Again*, directed by Irvin Kershner, was actually a remake of an earlier James Bond film, *Thunderball*. Its box-office success, promising to outdo that of all its predecessors, appeared to be largely due to the return of the original creator of the James Bond role, Sean Connery, 13 years after his last appearance in the series.

The attempt to cash in on past success brought the usual rash of sequels, almost invariably worse than their originals. Some typical titles were *Smokey and the Bandit III, The Sting II, The Black Stallion Returns, Psycho II* (a notably unsuccessful revisit to the scene of Hitchcock's horror story), *Superman III, Porky's II*, and *Jaws 3-D. National Lampoon's Vacation* was, exceptionally, a marked improvement over the previous comedies under this rubric, an anarchic road movie about an American family on a nightmarish drive across the continent.

Two notable popular successes of the year were dance musicals that offered sentimental melodrama and choreographic routines of flashy effectiveness. Adrian Lyne's aptly titled *Flashdance* told a tale of a young factory worker's fulfillment of her ambitions to go to ballet school. *Staying Alive*, assembled with artless energy by Sylvester Stallone, exploited to the full the physical and athletic attraction of John Travolta in a story of the dance-mad New York Italian from *Saturday Night Fever* forcing his way to show-dance stardom.

Though comedy was not generally to the fore, one of the year's outstanding pictures was Woody Allen's *Zelig*. Its point of departure was the admirably simple comic notion of the ultimate conformist, a man whose desire to fit in is so overwhelming that he takes on the very form and character of anyone with whom he finds himself. Still more inventive than the idea was the form which Allen gave it—a pastiche, perfect in every detail, of compilation documentary, with almost undetectable re-creations of old news film, and *post facto* opinions on the strange case of Leonard Zelig by such real-life pundits of today as Susan Sontag and Saul Bellow. The only other notable comedy of the year was John Landis's *Trading Places*, the premise of which was the sort of American fairy tale that served Frank Capra 40 years earlier: a petty crook (Eddie Murphy) and a big business tycoon (Dan

Return of the Jedi was the third film in the phenomenally successful *Star Wars* series. Here Mark Hamill, as Luke, and Carrie Fisher, as Princess Leia, prepare to swing to safety from Jabba the Hutt's desert Sail Barge.

WIDE WORLD

Aykroyd) temporarily change places, incidentally exposing some of the most dubious methods of modern commerce.

Some motion pictures, at least, achieved success by striking out in original directions. John Badham's *WarGames* had an ingenious story about a computer-crazy teenaged boy who accidentally connects with the U.S. war computer and sets in motion a chain of events that almost leads to worldwide nuclear destruction. Philip Kaufman's *The Right Stuff* was an ambitious attempt to dramatize the early stages of the U.S. space program and the exploits of the first astronauts. Lawrence Kasdan's *The Big Chill* portrays the bittersweet reunion in 1983 of college classmates from the 1960s. Two directors essayed film biographies of unusual women. Jonathan Kaplan's *Heart like a Wheel* was an energetic account of Shirley Muldowney, the pioneer woman race driver; Martin Ritt's *Cross Creek* proved an oversweet life of Marjorie Rawlings, the best-selling author of *The Yearling*, whose books were based on her experiences in struggling with a lonely life in primitive rural surroundings. In *STAR 80* Bob Fosse effectively tells the story of Dorothy Stratten, a *Playboy* magazine centrefold model, who was pushed to movie stardom by her husband and then murdered by him when their marriage began to fail.

Some notable directors were exploring fresh areas. Robert Altman, having given up his California studio, had moved to New York, where he was experimenting in transferring stage productions to the screen. As in his previous *Come Back to the 5 and Dime, Jimmy Dean, Jimmy Dean*, the film *Streamers* (from a stage success by David Rabe) used the screen to produce a suffocating confinement of the action, which involved the relationships of four young soldiers in the confines of a barracks room. In *The Outsiders* and *Rumble Fish*, Francis Ford Coppola adapted subjects by the novelist Susan Hinton and in these treatments of underprivileged teenagers consciously turned back to both the style and the sentiments of films of the 1930s and '40s. A well-to-do teenager and his sexual coming-of-age was the subject of Paul Brickman's *Risky Business*. Martin Scorsese's *King of Comedy*, though it found little favour with audiences, was a brilliantly executed parable on the social compulsion to succeed. Robert De Niro plays an aspiring stand-up comedian who kidnaps a television star (a haunting, haunted performance by Jerry Lewis) in order to gain the notoriety that (the film seems to say) is a shorter route than talent to the desired goal.

Noteworthy films opening late in the year included James Brooks's strong mother-daughter story *Terms of Endearment*, adapted from the novel by Larry McMurtry. Brian de Palma's *Scarface* was an updated version of the classic 1932 gangster film. In *Silkwood* Mike Nichols recounted the dramatic story of a plutonium-plant worker who may have been killed to ensure her silence about plant conditions. Barbra Streisand turned director as well as star in *Yentl*, a musical film about a Jewish girl who disguised herself as a boy so that she could receive an education in Eastern Europe in the early 20th century.

At the annual awards ceremony of the Academy of Motion Picture Arts and Sciences in Hollywood in April, an Indo-British co-production, *Gandhi*, directed by Sir Richard Attenborough (*see* BIOGRAPHIES), took Oscars for best picture, best actor (Ben Kingsley, in the title role), best director, best original screenplay, best cinematography, best film editing, best art direction, and best costume design. Awards for best original score (John Williams), best sound, best sound effects editing, and best visual effects went to Steven Spielberg's *E.T. The Extra-Terrestrial*. The best actress was Meryl Streep, in *Sophie's Choice*; and best supporting actor and actress were Louis Gossett, Jr., in *An Officer and a Gentleman* and Jessica Lange in *Tootsie*. The award for best screenplay adaptation went to Costa-Gavras and Donald Steward for *Missing*. The best foreign language film was the Spanish *Volver a Empezar*. The veteran actor Mickey Rooney received an honorary award.

GREAT BRITAIN. For the second year in succession, a British film had carried off the lion's share of the Oscars, and optimism ran high in the British industry; there seemed at least a possibility for the renascence of a national cinema. The international success of *Chariots of Fire* and *Gandhi* was a major boost to morale, but a more important factor was the continuing feature-film production program initiated with the establishment of the fourth television channel in 1982. With a planned output of 20 modestly budgeted films per year, added to the less firmly scheduled programs of the other television companies, British production acquired a sense of continuity; and British directors had the opportunity to work without the inhibiting circumstances that mammoth Hollywood-style budgets often impose. Notable new directors to emerge under the patronage of Channel 4 included Michael Darlow, with *Accounts*, a rich, intimate study of the relationship of two young brothers working a farm on the Scottish border; Michael Radford with *Another Time, Another Place*, about a wartime affair between a Scottish farmer's wife and an Italian prisoner of war; Joseph Despins, with a quirky mystery thriller, *The Disappearance of Harry*; Bill Bryden with *Ill Fares the Land*, a recollection of the abandoning of the lonely islands of

Ben Kingsley played the title role in Sir Richard Attenborough's *Gandhi*, which swept the 1983 Academy Awards.

SYGMA

Annual Cinema Attendance[1]

Country	Total in 000	Per capita
Algeria	45,000	2.4
Argentina	65,000	2.4
Australia	36,000	3.0
Austria	18,200	2.4
Bahrain	1,300	3.8
Barbados	1,200	5.2
Belgium	21,700	2.2
Benin	1,100	0.3
Bolivia	31,100	5.7
Brazil	211,700	1.8
Brunei	2,800	14.7
Bulgaria	92,100	27.0
Burma	222,500	8.1
Cameroon	6,500	1.0
Canada	101,100	4.2
Chad	25,400	6.0
Chile	15,800	1.4
China	18,250,000	18.1
Colombia	78,000	2.8
Cuba	88,000	9.1
Czechoslovakia	81,000	5.3
Denmark	15,900	3.1
Dominican Republic	7,700	1.4
Ecuador	38,000	5.6
Egypt	65,200	1.8
El Salvador	15,400	3.4
Finland	9,800	2.0
France	173,700	3.2
Gabon	1,100	2.1
Germany, East	79,500	4.7
Germany, West	135,500	2.2
Ghana	4,000	0.4
Greece	43,000	4.4
Grenada	1,100	12.5
Guatemala	10,100	1.4
Guyana	10,200	12.9
Haiti	6,200	1.3
Hong Kong	58,700	12.0
Hungary	70,000	7.0
Iceland	2,500	11.4
India	2,920,000	4.5
Indonesia	111,300	0.8
Iran	25,000	0.8
Ireland	18,000	5.8
Israel	24,200	6.6
Italy	241,900	4.0
Ivory Coast	7,000	0.9
Japan	149,000	1.3
Jamaica	6,400	3.0
Jordan	15,000	4.9
Kenya	9,200	0.6
Korea, South	65,500	1.7
Kuwait	4,700	4.7
Liberia	1,500	0.8
Libya	11,400	3.8
Luxembourg	1,100	3.2
Macau	2,300	9.3
Madagascar	2,900	0.4
Malaysia	34,000	2.7
Malawi	1,500	0.3
Malta	2,700	7.3
Mauritius	8,000	8.5
Mexico	296,000	4.3
Mongolia	15,300	8.9
Morocco	35,800	2.0
Mozambique	3,200	0.4
Netherlands, The	31,400	2.0
New Zealand	15,000	5.1
Nigeria	22,700	0.3
Norway	17,700	4.4
Pakistan	187,400	2.5
Panama	7,100	4.8
Philippines	318,000	7.5
Poland	98,000	2.7
Portugal	30,800	3.1
Puerto Rico	6,800	2.3
Romania	206,200	9.2
Senegal	3,800	0.7
Singapore	35,800	14.6
Somalia	8,000	2.3
South Africa	31,200	1.2
Spain	173,700	4.6
Sri Lanka	70,700	4.8
Sudan	12,500	0.7
Sweden	22,100	2.6
Switzerland	21,000	3.3
Syria	11,000	1.3
Taiwan	140,000	7.6
Tanzania	3,400	0.2
Thailand	71,000	1.7
Tunisia	8,800	1.5
Turkey	81,400	1.9
Uganda	1,900	0.2
U.S.S.R.	4,244,000	16.0
United Arab Emirates	6,900	10.3
United Kingdom	96,000	1.7
United States	1,100,000	4.8
Upper Volta	4,100	0.6
Venezuela	49,000	3.6
Vietnam	264,000	5.2
Western Samoa	1,100	7.0
Yemen (Aden)	5,600	3.1
Yugoslavia	78,300	3.8
Zaire	1,700	0.1
Zambia	1,600	0.3

[1] Countries having over one million annual attendance.

St. Kilda in the 1930s; and Richard Eyre, with *The Ploughman's Lunch*, an acid study of young intellectuals in the era of the Falklands war. Eyre completed a second film during the year, a comedy "road-movie" from a script by Maggie Brooks, *Loose Connections*. Established directors who made significant new films for Channel 4 included Mike Leigh, with *Meantime*, a horror-comic study of an East-End family degraded by unemployment; Stephen Frears, with *Walter* and *Walter and June*, dramas about a mentally handicapped man; and Desmond Davies with an adaptation of Edna O'Brien's novel *The Country Girls*.

Aside from these television-based feature productions, easily the most original and memorable film of the year was Bill Forsyth's comedy *Local Hero*, which describes, with the same distinctive sense of humour that marked *Gregory's Girl*, the encounter of U.S.-based oil prospectors and a Scottish coastal village. James Ivory, a U.S. director based in Britain, made one of the most successful films that had emerged from his partnership with the producer Ismail Merchant and the writer Ruth Prawer Jhabvala, *Heat and Dust*. Based on Jhabvala's novel, the film compares and contrasts the experiences of two women, today and 60 years earlier, as they submit to the seductions, both spiritual and physical, of India.

Among the notable commercial successes of the year were Lewis Gilbert's attractive adaptation of Willy Russell's stage comedy *Educating Rita*, about the encounter of a disillusioned university teacher (Michael Caine) and a working girl bent on self-education (Julie Walters). There was also the annual British-made James Bond, *Octopussy*, the 13th in the series, with the formula by this time showing signs of wear. Age and use seemed also to have caught up with the once cheerfully anarchic styles of Monty Python comedy, to judge from Terry Jones's purposelessly offensive *Monty Python's The Meaning of Life* (directed by Terry Jones) and a *Treasure Island* spoof, *Yellowbeard*, out of the same school and directed by Mel Damski.

IRELAND. Largely through the encouragement of the Irish Film Board and Radio Telefis Eirann, Irish filmmakers continued to assert an individualistic national style. Robert Wynne-Simmons's *The Outcasts* was the major feature production, an original and haunting film about witchcraft and folklore in 19th-century Ireland. Two successful films, Kieran Hickey's *Attracta* and Pat O'Connor's *One of Ourselves*, were made from stories by William Trevor, who himself adapted them to the screen.

AUSTRALIA. Australian production continued to display remarkable variety of approach. The year's major box-office success was *Phar Lap*, directed by Simon Wincer, which dramatized the career of a famous and popular Australian race horse. Carl Schultz's *Careful, He Might Hear You* was a sensitive melodrama about a small boy between the wars, taken from the security of a modest home with one aunt to the disturbing opulence of the home of another, a rich but neurotic woman. Henry Safran translated Ibsen's *The Wild Duck* to turn-of-the-century Australia.

Several films were concerned with the deprivation of Aboriginal communities. Ned Lander's *The Wrong Side of the Road* was an account of two Aboriginal pop bands and their brushes with white authority. Ken Quinnell's *The City Edge* was a drama that dealt with the plight of urban Aborigines. Alec Morgan's documentary *Lousy Little Sixpence* looked back to the workings of the Aborigines Protection Board between 1909 and 1930, showing how it often served only to turn Aboriginal children, taken from their families, into slave labour.

D. KIRKLAND—SYGMA

Pernilla Allwin (left) and Bertil Guve played the title roles in Ingmar Bergman's *Fanny and Alexander*.

NEW ZEALAND. The most ambitious film of the year was Geoff Murphy's spectacular *Utu* (the title is a Maori word meaning "revenge"). It related the story of a 19th-century Maori who serves as a noncommissioned officer in the British Army until he witnesses the massacre of some of his people, innocent villagers, and thereupon takes up arms against the colonialists.

CANADA. Gilles Carle's adaptation of a well-loved early 20th-century novel, *Marie Chapdelaine*, was one of the most ambitious feature productions so far undertaken in Canada. A new director, Philip Borsos, made *The Grey Fox*, a light and likable film about the real-life bandit Bill Miner, who was sent to prison in the 19th century for stagecoach robbery and released in the 20th century, when the technological changes of 30 years obliged him to change his métier to train robbery.

Western Europe. FRANCE. The older generations of French filmmakers were most in evidence during the year. The great veteran Robert Bresson made a new film, *L'Argent*, an austere anecdote about the effects—escalating into tragedy—of an initially small crime. The leading figures of the *nouvelle vague* of the 1960s all had new films: François Truffaut offered a lightweight thriller, strongly indebted to Alfred Hitchcock, *Vivement Dimanche*; Jean-Luc Godard, a free-wheeling, disillusioned exercise, *Prénom . . . Carmen*; Alain Resnais, a precious, pretty, inconsequential fantasy set in a bizarre palace of eclectic style, *La Vie est un roman*. Chris Marker's *Sans soleil* was an essay on personal memory, embracing Japan, Africa, and

Cape Verde; Alain Robbe-Grillet's *La Belle Captive,* an erotic horror nightmare; and Eric Rohmer's *Pauline à la Plage,* a Musset-like comedy of sex.

France remained hospitable to directors from other countries. Raúl Ruíz made *Les Trois Couronnes du Matelot,* a ghost story told by a mariner, employing rich and imaginative effects. The Turkish director Yilmaz Guney made *Le Mur,* his first film since his escape from jail in his native Turkey, which re-created the grim story of a revolt by children in an Ankara prison in 1976. The distinguished Polish director Andrzej Wajda, who had not worked in his native country since the introduction of martial law, completed his long-awaited French production, *Danton.* Adapted from a play by Stanislawa Przybyszewska that Wajda had previously directed on stage, the film account of the ultimate confrontation of Danton and Robespierre in November 1791 offered gripping drama and rich opportunities for political parable.

ITALY. Outstanding among the films of the year was Ermanno Olmi's *Cammino Cammino,* which suggested a modern equivalent of medieval illuminations of the journey of the Magi in its use of realistic settings and familiar Italian types. Its record of the trek proved both funny and touching. Two other major figures had less success. Federico Fellini's long-awaited *E La Nava Va* was a disappointing, directionless parable about strangely assorted passengers on a great ocean liner. Marco Ferreri's story of *Piera* was a raucous adaptation of the scandalous memoirs of the actress Piera degli Espositi.

The outstanding talent of Soviet cinema, Andrey Tarkovsky, went to Italy to make his first film outside his native country, *Nostalgia.* With the theme of a Soviet musicologist in quest of a 19th-century composer and countryman in Italy, it aimed to explore the sentiments of yearning for native soil. Obscure in meaning but filled with striking set pieces, the film seemed at times to be parodying itself.

WEST GERMANY. It was perhaps only coincidental that since the death of Rainer Werner Fassbinder, the outstanding director of his generation, West German cinema had entered a phase of depression and mediocrity. The most notable productions of an unremarkable year were Rainer Boldt's *Im Zeichen des Kreuzes,* which imagined a future world and a peacetime nuclear accident; and Alexander Kluge's *Das Macht des Gefühle,* a characteristically discursive, philosophical essay on the emotions, with lively dramatized episodes. Two Munich film critics, Hans Stempel and Martin Ripkens, made their debut as feature directors with *Eine Leibe wie Andere Auch,* a film that observed a homosexual couple not as a sensational social problem but as ordinary and ordinarily troubled bourgeois citizens, figures of light social comedy.

SWITZERLAND. Of the country's established directors, Claude Goretta made *Le Mort de Mario Ricci,* which exposed the uglier realities beneath the serene and cozy surface of an ordinary Swiss village, while Alain Tanner went abroad for *Dans la Ville Blanche,* a psychological study of a wandering German in search of emotional identity in Lisbon. A new director, Marcel Schüpfbach, made a striking first feature, *L'Allégement,* a symbolic, aesthetic portrayal of a disturbed girl. Hans-Ulrich Schlumpf's *TransAtlantique* offered an original combination of fiction and documentary in the record of a voyage and of the varied passengers in transit and transition.

SPAIN. The Franco era continued to engage the attention of filmmakers. Manuel Gutiérrez Alea's *Demonios en el jardín* (voted the best Spanish film of the year) viewed a drama of sexual rivalries against the hypocrisy of the period. Roberto Bodegas's *Corazón de Papel* showed how old Civil War loyalties interfered with the sideline of blackmail carried on by the proprietor of a small photographic agency.

SCANDINAVIA. The outstanding film of the year was Ingmar Bergman's period saga of the life of a middle-class family in a small Swedish town, *Fanny and Alexander.* The director himself described it as "a huge tapestry filled with masses of colour and people, houses and forests, mysterious haunts of caves and grottoes, secrets and night skies. Yes, I'm afraid it is rather romantic, but not unbearably so."

Eastern Europe. U.S.S.R. Encouraging signs of a new spirit of social criticism among Soviet filmmakers were evident during the year. Vadim Abdrashitov's *A Train Stopped,* through the story of an inspector investigating a railway accident, went some way toward exposing the habit of the convenient untruth as a factor in official life. Gleb Panfilov's highly decorative adaptation of a Gorky play, *Vassa,* employed an equivocal ending to suggest that some of the worst aspects of 19th-century capitalism might still persist in the Soviet system. Elem Klimov's *Farewell* (originally begun by Klimov's wife, Larissa Shepitko, who was tragically killed during production) adapted a popular novel about the reaction of a community of peasants due to be shifted from their island homes to make way for a vast irrigation scheme.

Other filmmakers dealt with more personal issues. Nikita Mikhalkov's *Without Witnesses* was a tour de force, a duologue between a man and his former wife. The psychological duel in which they engage was played with brilliance by Kirina Kupchenko and Mikhail Ulyanov. Roman Belayan's *Dream Flights,* a comedy about a menopausal man running slightly amok both at his work and in his private life, made some sharp observations about contemporary Soviet values and social restraints. Karel Shakhnazarov's *Jazz Men* was an amusing, ironic, and basically serious story of the struggle of a jazz band in the 1920s against official disapproval of "decadent" music from the West.

HUNGARY. Hungarian cinema retained its lead over other socialist film industries in its range and outspokenness. Zsolt Kezdi-Kovac's *Forbidden Relations* was a sympathetic study of a village couple in a happy and prolific incestuous relationship. Pal Sando's *Daniel Takes a Train* re-created the atmosphere and attitudes of emigrés from the 1956 Hungarian counterrevolution. Miklos Szurdi's *Midnight Rehearsal* was an original, witty, imaginatively produced backstage story that touched on the delicate theme of the mechanics of censorship

BRYSON—SYGMA

In *The Right Stuff,* Sam Shepard plays test pilot Chuck Yeager who, here riding in the desert, first catches sight of the X-1 that he will test and prove.

in socialist societies. Livia Gyarmathy's *Co-existence* was a documentary that dealt with the previously taboo subject of the successive resettlements of people on Hungary's border territories and the resulting social and political problems.

YUGOSLAVIA. Light comedy and detective stories had taken over even from Yugoslavia's old staple of partisan dramas (there was only one film in that genre during the year, *The Igman March*). One of the more notable comedies was Karpo Godina's *Red Boogie,* a humorous treatment of the years when jazz was reckoned a subversive form and thus had the keen attraction of forbidden fruit for the public at large.

Middle East. TURKEY. Erden Kiral's *A Season in Hakkari* dealt with the tribulations and discoveries of a young teacher sent for the winter season to work in a remote, mountainous region of Turkey. On the surface a gentle piece of skillfully dramatized ethnography, the film was interpreted by the Turkish authorities to be critical and so attracted official disapproval.

ISRAEL. Amos Gitai's *Journal de campagne,* a picture of the situation on the West Bank, established the director in the eyes of the Israeli establishment as a dissident filmmaker.

Latin America. Roberto Farías's *Para Frente Brasil* offered an unsparing exposé of a violent totalitarian society through a story of a man who disappears without a trace and the troubles that his family attract when they try to find him. Although ostensibly historical in theme, the film touched official sensibilities; it was banned in Brazil, and its director lost his official post with the government film agency.

The Brazilian director Ruy Guerra made, in Mexico, *Erendira,* a wild, malevolent fantasy about a grande dame who turns her granddaughter into a prostitute in order to extract compensation for the girl's having accidentally burned down the old woman's mansion. In *Alsino and the Condor,* filmed in Mexico, Nicaragua, Cuba, and Costa Rica, the Chilean director Miguel Littin used the story of a child who sprouts wings to develop a rich allegory of Latin-American revolution.

Africa. Two African films made their impact at international film festivals during 1983. From Mali, Souleymané Cissi's *Finye* ("The Wind") exposed social inequalities through the story of a love affair between a poor boy and a rich girl. From Upper Volta, Gaston Kaboré's *Wend Kuuni* ("Gift of God") was the story of a mute boy found wandering in the forest and of his influence upon the tribe that adopts him.

Asia. JAPAN. Two of the year's major box-office successes were literary adaptations. Shohei Imamura's *The Ballad of Narayama* was the second film version of a best-seller. Imamura used the story of a primitive society that exactly inverts the "humanism" of civilization to question some of our own values. Kon Ichikawa's adaptation of another popular Japanese novel, *The Makioka Sisters,* emerged as no more than high-class soap opera. Representing a very different school of filmmaking, Yoshimitzu Morita, in *The Family Game,* took a sharp look at Japanese family life. The most international of Japan's younger directors, Nagisa Oshima, completed an Anglo-Franco-Japanese co-production, *Merry Christmas Mr. Lawrence,* based on Sir Laurens van der Post's novels of English officers in a Japanese prisoner-of-war camp.

CHINA. Perhaps the most striking film to emerge from China since the Cultural Revolution, for the frankness of its social commentary, *Neighbours,* directed by Zhang Dongtian (Chang Tung-t'ien) and Zu Guming (Tsu Ku-ming), was a realistic depiction of daily life in an overcrowded Beijing (Peking) housing complex. It contained sharp comments on the privileges snatched by party functionaries.

INDIA. Mrinal Sen's *The Case Is Closed* used its story of a small everyday incident, the death by carelessness of a 12-year-old houseboy, to condemn, as the greatest of social crimes, indifference to others. In *Market Place* a director of a younger generation, Shyam Benegal, found a rich source of allegory in his picture of a "pleasure house" that has seen far better days. The greatest living Indian film director, Satyajit Ray, was inactive during the year except to assist his son Sandip Ray in his feature film debut as a director of a children's film, *Phatik and the Juggler.* (DAVID ROBINSON)

Nontheatrical Motion Pictures. Nine times in the past 25 years a nontheatrical film has been a runaway winner at film festivals around the world. In 1983 a tenth was added, *Ballet Robotique.* Made for General Motors Corp. for its pavilion at Florida/EPCOT Walt Disney World, the film was created almost as an afterthought. Producer Bob Rogers was impressed with the variety of robots and their actions. "One moves like a chicken. Another like a cat. One paint-spraying robot moves like seaweed, gracefully swaying and curling with the current." Edited to a score by the Royal Philharmonic Orchestra, the film unites high technology and the arts in a space-age fantasy.

Top winner out of 845 entries at the 25th American Film Festival (Emily Award) in 1983 was Jim Brown's *The Weavers: Wasn't That a Time.* The 75-minute documentary traces the rise to fame of the folk-singing group, The Weavers, and its subsequent blacklisting during the era of U.S. Sen. Joseph McCarthy. The film climaxes with a 1980 reunion concert at Carnegie Hall.

One of the few U.S. educational films to win an award in another nation was Encyclopaedia Britannica Educational Corp.'s *Beaver Family*. This nature film of the daily life of the beaver in its natural habitat was awarded a special prize at the Lausanne (Switz.) Children and Teenagers festival.

As in previous years, U.S. student films continued to receive an impressive number of honours worldwide. DeAnaza Community College (Cupertino, Calif.) students David Casci and Chris Perry won 51 awards at 18 foreign and 19 U.S. festivals for their film *Extended Play*. The 13-minute short feature follows a rejected young hero through a strange video amusement centre. The film captured ten first-place prizes at such events as Badalone, Spain; Huy, Belgium; Salerno, Italy; and two in Australia, Melbourne and Victoria.

(THOMAS W. HOPE)

See also Photography; Television and Radio.
[623; 735.G.2]

Motor Sports

Grand Prix Racing. The rules governing international Formula One racing were changed for the 1983 season to eliminate "ground effect" assistance by requiring the cars to have clean underbellies. For tires, special rubber mixes were permitted for qualifying laps that determined starting positions. It was a season without fatal accidents, in which turbocharged $1^1/_2$-litre engines almost always outclassed the normally fed 3-litre engines. The drivers' world championship, open until the last race, went to Nelson Piquet of Brazil.

The season opened in Brazil in March, with Piquet's Brabham turbo winning from Keke Rosberg of Finland, whose Williams later was disqualified for a push-start, and from the McLaren driven by Niki Lauda of Austria. In the U.S. Grand Prix West at Long Beach, Calif., only the first three went the full 245.6 km (1 km = 0.62 mi), John Watson (U.K.) in a McLaren winning from Lauda in a sister car and from René Arnoux (France) in a Ferrari. European racing began at France's Paul Ricard circuit at La Castellet, where the French dominated. Alain Prost (France) won in a Renault, with Piquet's Brabham second and the Renault of Eddie Cheever of the U.S. third. At San Marino, Riccardo Patrese (Italy) crashed his Brabham at the end of the race, and so the crowd saw Patrick Tambay (France) win for Ferrari, ahead of Prost's Renault; Arnoux finished third in the other Ferrari. Monaco was won by Rosberg (Williams), with Piquet's Brabham second and Prost's Renault third. Then the Belgian Grand Prix at Spa saw Prost first and Cheever third in the Renault turbos, sandwiching Tambay's Ferrari.

The Canadian Grand Prix at Montreal was won by Arnoux in the Ferrari, with Cheever second for Renault and the other Ferrari of Tambay third. This followed a surprise at Detroit, where the Tyrrell of Michele Alboreto of Italy had won from Rosberg and Watson. At the British Grand Prix at Silverstone, Prost won for Renault, with Piquet second and Tambay in a Ferrari third. In the German race over the Hockenheimring in August, Arnoux won for Ferrari, with Andrea de Cesaris (Italy) second in an Alfa Romeo 183TB and Patrese's Brabham third. At the Austrian Österreichring, Prost won for Renault, having caught Arnoux's Ferrari near the finish; Piquet finished third in the Brabham. At the Dutch Grand Prix at Zandvoort, Enzo Ferrari's 126C3s were dominant – Arnoux finishing first and Tambay second, beating Watson in the McLaren. At Monza in September in the Italian Grand Prix, Piquet's Brabham made fastest lap at a sizzling 221.113 km/h and won from Arnoux's Ferrari. Cheever's Renault was third, ahead of the other Ferrari.

The drivers' world championship was still open as the teams moved to Brands Hatch, England, for an extra event, dubbed the European Grand Prix. Piquet won from Prost's Renault, while Nigel Mansell (U.K.) got the Lotus-Renault 94T into third place. With the drivers' championship still not decided, the last Grand Prix was held at Kyalami, South Africa, in mid-October. Tambay was quickest in practice and so got his turbo Ferrari on the front of the starting grid. But it was Brabham's day, and Patrese won. De Cesaris in an Alfa Romeo was second of the trio that made the 77 laps of this championship-deciding battle, with Piquet settling for third position, knowing that on points this finish would decide the world championship in his favour. Tambay had retired with a failed engine, and 1982's champion driver, Rosberg, was fifth in the Williams.

Rallies and Other Races. The Monza 1,000-km race was won by the Porsche 956, with Porsche cars occupying the first six places. The "Race of Champions" at Brands Hatch was a victory for Rosberg's Williams, from Danny Sullivan's Tyrrell and Alan Jones in an Arrows A6, before Jones's ultimate retirement from the sport. The Silverstone 1,000-km race was another triumph for the Porsche 956s, and at the equivalent contest at the Nürgburgring in West Germany these turbocharged $2^1/_2$-litre cars won the first four places, ahead of a Lancia LCI of much smaller capacity. It was the same in the classic Le Mans 24-hour marathon in France, the Porsche 956 of Al Holbert (U.S.), Hurley Hayward (U.S.), and Vern Schuppan (Australia) beating that of Jacky Ickx (Belgium) and Derek Bell (U.K.). The 1,000-km events at Spa and Brands Hatch underlined the superiority of the Porsche 956, Derek Warwick winning

Formula One Grand Prix Race Results, 1983

Race	Driver	Car	Average speed
Brazilian	N. Piquet	Brabham BT52	175.300 km/h
U.S. West	J. Watson	McLaren MP4	129.753 km/h
French	A. Prost	Renault RE40	199.866 km/h
San Marino	P. Tambay	Ferrari 126C2	185.460 km/h
Monaco	K. Rosberg	Williams FW08C	129.586 km/h
Belgian	A. Prost	Renault RE40	191.729 km/h
Detroit	M. Alboreto	Tyrrell Oll	130.400 km/h
Canadian	R. Arnoux	Ferrari 126C2	170.661 km/h
British	A. Prost	Renault RE40	224.049 km/h
German	R. Arnoux	Ferrari 126C3	210.319 km/h
Austrian	A. Prost	Renault RE40	223.745 km/h
Dutch	R. Arnoux	Ferrari 126C3	186.1 km/h
Italian	N. Piquet	Brabham BT52	217.548 km/h
European (Brands Hatch)	N. Piquet	Brabham-BMW BT52B	198.214 km/h
South African	R. Patrese	Brabham-BMW BT52B	202.939 km/h

WORLD DRIVERS' CHAMPIONSHIP: Piquet, 59 pt; Prost, 57 pt; Arnoux, 49 pt.
CONSTRUCTORS' WORLD CHAMPIONSHIP: Ferrari, 89 pt; Renault, 79 pt; Brabham-BMW, 72 pt.

Motorboating:
see Water Sports

Motor Industry:
see Industrial Review

WIDE WORLD

Tom Sneva won the Indianapolis 500 in May; it was his first victory, although he had placed second three times.

both races and vanquishing the factory Porsche teams. It was a theme continued in the Fuji 1,000-km race, which Bell and Stefan Bellof took in the Rothmans Porsche 956.

The 1983 rally season was largely a duel between the potent turbocharged four-wheel-drive Audi Quattro and the new Lancia Rally, a mid-engined, front-wheel-drive coupe. The decisive contest took place in the San Remo Rally, where Audi badly needed a win to gain the manufacturers' championship; however, Hannu Mikkola's Quattro burned out, and Lancia took the first three places and the championship. Mikkola, of Finland, won the rally drivers' world championship.

(WILLIAM C. BODDY)

U.S. Racing. Tom Sneva, driving a Texaco March 83C prepared by George Bignotti, finally won the Indianapolis 500-mi race despite a double assault by the Unser family. As he was trying to pass Al Unser, Sr., the bespectacled Sneva, who had finished second in this classic three times (1977, 1978, and 1980), withstood an illegal attempt by 21-year-old Al Unser, Jr., to block his car. Unser, Sr., who subsequently won the Championship Auto Racing Team (CART) crown, was trying for a fourth victory in the race, which pays the winner more than $1 million.

Sneva, whose ultimate margin of victory was 11.1 seconds, had led earlier by as much as 30 seconds. His average speed, 162.117 mph, was not a record (1 mph = 1.61 km/h). The drama began with a caution on the 171st lap. Not among the leaders, Al Unser, Jr., passed illegally during the caution to get between his father and Sneva. For lap after lap he blocked Sneva as Al Unser, Sr., ran in front. Finally on the 191st of 200 laps, Sneva passed the young driver on the main straightaway and, entering the third turn, went by the senior Unser, too. Al Unser, Jr., was penalized two laps.

Rounding out the top five behind Unser, Sr., were Rick Mears, Geoff Brabham, and Kevin Cogan. The Indy 500 remained outside the sanction of CART but counted toward its championship. The latter might have had a different ending had Teo Fabi, the young Italian who won the pole position at Indianapolis with a qualifying time of 207.395 mph (eight qualified over 200 mph), been able to hold his car together in that race. He led the first 47 laps before succumbing to a faulty fuel coupling O-ring. Fabi later won two CART events, including the finale at Phoenix, Ariz., to four for Unser. The final standings were 151 points for Unser, 146 for Fabi, and 133 for Mario Andretti.

In another classic race, contested by U.S. stock cars, Cale Yarborough won the Daytona 500-mi in his backup car, a 1981 Pontiac LeMans, after crashing his new Chevrolet Monte Carlo earlier in the week. The Chevrolet had broken the Daytona International Speedway record by more than 4 mph, clocking 200.503 mph. Yarborough, who allowed a television camera to be mounted in his car, beat two Ford Thunderbirds, driven by Bill Elliott and Buddy Baker, for his third Daytona 500 victory (1968, 1977).

The NASCAR (National Association for Stock Car Auto Racing) season crown was won by Bobby Allison after 20 years of trying. Allison, driving a Buick, clinched the title by finishing ninth at the final race of the season at Riverside, Calif. That foreclosed Darrell Waltrip's attempt at a third straight crown. Both men had six wins, but Allison's were on the major superspeedways while Waltrip's were on the shorter Winston Cup tracks that awarded fewer points. The season was overshadowed by a controversial decision permitting Richard Petty, NASCAR's all-time victory leader, to retain his Miller Charlotte 500 triumph despite the finding that his engine was illegally oversize. Petty was fined $35,000 (a record) and 104 points.

Al Holbert, usually driving a Porsche-March 83G, easily became International Motor Sports Association (IMSA) Camel GT champion in that road racing organization's most successful year to date.

The IMSA-sanctioned 24 Hours of Daytona, the most prestigious endurance event in the U.S., was dominated by Porsche as A. J. Foyt joined French drivers Bob Wollek and Claude Ballot-Lena in the victorious Porsche Twin Turbo. Another Porsche, the GTO 934 piloted by Wayne Baker, Jim Mullen, and Canada's Kees Nierop, won the 12 Hours of Sebring.

The Sports Car Club of America's premier professional road racing series, the Can-Am, was reduced to six events even as its other major series, the Trans-Am, flourished. The Can-Am champion was Canadian Jacques Villeneuve, while David Hobbs of the U.S. in a Camaro edged teammate Willie T. Ribbs for Trans-Am honours. For yet another year the John Buffum-Rod Millen battle for the national rally championship went to Buffum in his four-wheel-drive Audi Quattro.

(ROBERT J. FENDEL)

Motorcycles. After one of the most closely fought struggles in motorcycle road-race history, Freddie Spencer (U.S.), riding a Honda and at 21 years the youngest victor ever, beat Kenny Roberts (U.S.; Yamaha) to take the 500-cc world road-race championship in 1983. The 250-cc championship winner was Carlos Lavado (Venezuela; Yamaha). The 125-cc-class winner, Angel Nieto (Spain; Garelli), became world champion for the 12th time, and Rolf Biland and passenger Kurt Waltisberger (Switz.; LCR) won the sidecar championship. The 50-cc champion was Stefan Dorflinger (Switz.; Kreidler). In the British Grand Prix held at Silverstone in July and marred by a crash resulting in the deaths of Norman Brown (U.K.) and Peter Huber (Switz.), the main event was won by Roberts.

The Tourist Trophy races in the Isle of Man in June resulted in the fastest-ever average speed (184.84 km/h) in a Manx race, recorded by 23-year-old Rob McElnea (U.K.; 997 Suzuki) in the Classic. In the Isle of Man autumn amateur races, the Manx Grand Prix senior race was won by Nick Jefferies (U.K.; Suzuki).

In endurance racing the Bol d'Or 24 hour in France was a surprise win for the Honda France team of Raymond Roche, Guy Bertin, and Dominique Sarron, with a water-cooled 930 V4. The U.S.'s main road-race event, the Daytona 200, in March, was won by Roberts.

In world championship motocross, Hakan Carlqvist (Sweden; Yamaha) won the 500-cc class; Georges Jobe and Erik Geboers (both Belgium; Suzuki), respectively, won the 250 and 125 cc. The U.S. won both the Motocross des Nations (500 cc) and the Trophée des Nations (250 cc) for the third successive year. The world sidecar cross champions were, again, Emil Bollhalders and Karl Beusser (West Germany; Yamaha).

(CYRIL J. AYTON)

See also Water Sports.
[452.B.4.c]

Mountaineering

The 50th anniversary of the formation of the Union Internationale des Associations d'Alpinisme (UIAA) was celebrated in October 1982 at a gathering of representatives of national mountaineering organizations in Kathmandu, Nepal. Discussion of the environmental problems created by mountaineering and trekking expeditions in the Himalayas resulted in the adoption by the UIAA of a set of recommendations specifying rules of conduct for expeditions. The two most important points concerned the use of wood for fuel and the accumulation of litter. The use of wood by expeditions in recent years had accelerated the deforestation that was already rapidly increasing because of the requirements of the expanding native population for fuel, with resultant soil erosion, leaching, and decline in crop yields. Strong recommendations for the use of alternative fuels by expeditions were therefore made.

Litter had become an increasing problem, particularly in Nepal and in Garhwal district, India. Expeditions were therefore urged to undertake organized cleanups or to bury their own litter. The pressure of expeditions caused special problems of nature conservation in the Nanda Devi National Park and the Valley of Flowers National Park in Garhwal. A total ban was therefore imposed on entry to the Nanda Devi Sanctuary, to be enforced by the Indian Forestry Department, and the Indian Mountaineering Federation took action to exclude all foreign expeditions from the Nanda Devi National Park.

The number of expeditions to the highest mountains of the world continued to increase. In 1982 there were 70 expeditions to Nepal, and in the Indian parts of the Himalayas there were 80 Indian and 72 foreign expeditions. The trend was similar in 1983. In China 26 expeditions (from 13 nations) to 11 summits were scheduled for the year.

Mt. Everest was the scene of ever more numerous attempts from both the Nepalese and the Tibetan sides. In late 1982 a Spanish expedition failed on the west ridge. A winter attempt by the French on the same route was also unsuccessful, but a Japanese party climbed the mountain by the normal South Col route—although two members fell to their deaths. In the pre-monsoon period in 1983 a U.S. party also completed this route. Makalu was ascended twice after the monsoon in 1982, first by a Japanese expedition by the north ridge and then by a Polish-Brazilian party. The latter climbed the west face, on which many unsuccessful attempts had previously been made; the summit was reached solo, without oxygen.

Elsewhere in the Everest region the most noteworthy ascent was that of Cho Oyu by a new route, the southwest face, climbed in Alpine style by a party led by Reinhold Messner. Messner thus completed ascents of ten of the world's 14 peaks of 8,000 m (26,000 ft) or more.

(JOHN NEILL)

Mozambique

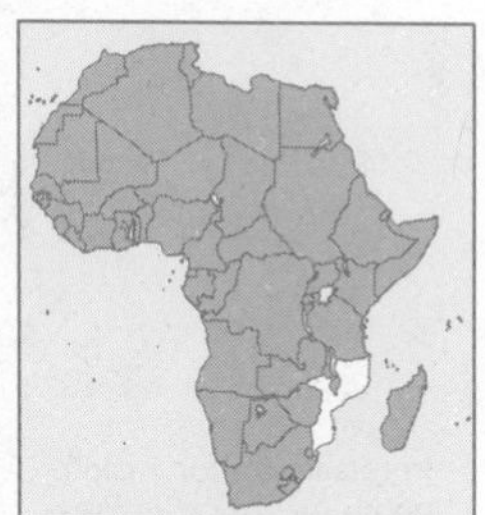
Mozambique

An independent African state, the People's Republic of Mozambique is located on the southeast coast of Africa, bounded by the Indian Ocean, Tanzania, Malawi, Zambia, Zimbabwe, South Africa, and Swaziland. Area: 799,380 sq km (308,642 sq mi). Pop. (1982 est.): 12,615,200. Cap. and largest city: Maputo (pop., 1982 est., 785,500). Language: Portuguese (official); Bantu languages predominate. Religion: traditional beliefs 65%; Christian about 21%; Muslim 10%; with Hindu, Buddhist, and Jewish minorities. President in 1983, Samora Machel.

Like many of its southern African neighbours, Mozambique suffered from drought for the second year in succession in 1983. This contributed to the spread of famine in the southern provinces. The government's agricultural policies, which had been in force since independence, were unable to cope with the problem. At the fourth congress of the governing party, Frelimo, in April, it was decided that a divergence from some of those policies was essential, although stress was still laid upon the country's continuing adherence to African socialism. Greater support was to be given to the peasants and to local industry. Collectivism, which had met with little success, was abandoned, and food rationing was introduced.

The party's Central Committee also recommended a comprehensive program of reforms that included the decentralization of control, the provision of greater opportunities for local initiative, and a reduction in the country's bureaucracy. The decision to reduce the population of Maputo by two-thirds proved impossible to carry out. In the existing state of the agrarian economy the rural areas could not absorb such extra numbers of displaced city people.

Any hope of reconstruction continued to be thwarted by endemic guerrilla warfare. Members of the Mozambican National Resistance were active in every province except Cabo Delgado in the extreme north. Even with the assistance of several thousand Zimbabwean troops, the Army was able to protect the rail link and oil pipeline between Beira and Zimbabwe only with difficulty and not always successfully.

In August, in an attempt to instill greater vigour into the antiguerrilla campaign, Pres. Samora Machel appointed eight new army commanders. The main drive was to be against guerrilla fighters in Zambezia; the most heavily populated and potentially the richest province, Zambezia was, the president declared, the most seriously harassed by opponents of his government. The success of the guerrillas was due in part, he claimed, to the inertia of his own army forces. It was hoped that the new commanders, all men with considerable campaigning experience, would curb the attacks, which had succeeded in destroying the province's communications almost completely. Possibly stimulated to action by the president's criticism, the Army carried out a vigorous sweep through the southern province of Inhambane later in August and claimed to have taken many prisoners.

President Machel frequently referred to the contribution that he believed South Africa was making to the guerrilla campaign, and South Africa was also active on its own behalf. In May and again in October Maputo was raided by South African forces that claimed to be trying to destroy bases from which the African National Congress (ANC) prepared and launched attacks on South Africa. In May South African warplanes bombed and strafed a suburb of Maputo, while in October a small military task force attacked what it claimed was an ANC office in Maputo's diplomatic quarter. In both cases estimates of casualties made by South Africa were much higher than those supplied by Mozambique.

After the May attack President Machel himself took charge of the country's defenses, although Lieut. Gen. Alberto Chipande retained his title of minister of defense. The president explained that the situation in Mozambique demanded centralization of defense leadership at the highest level.

In October Machel visited Portugal, the former colonial power, and France, where he claimed to have received promises of extensive military aid. From there he went to the U.K. in an attempt to arouse interest in the investment that Mozambique badly needed. This trip, plus the dismantling of the collective farms, led to the cutoff of Soviet economic aid in December.

(KENNETH INGHAM)

In retaliation for a car-bomb explosion in Pretoria, the South African Air Force attacked what it claimed were the offices of the African National Congress in a suburb of Maputo, Mozambique. This peasant hut was among the many destroyed.

UPI

MOZAMBIQUE

Education. (1981) Primary, pupils 1,376,865, teachers 18,751; secondary, pupils 135,956, teachers 3,789; higher, students 1,852, teaching staff, 224.

Finance and Trade. Monetary unit: metical, with (Sept. 20, 1983) a free rate of 40.93 meticals to U.S. $1 (61.64 meticals = £1 sterling). Budget (1982 est.): revenue 18.5 billion meticals; expenditure 21.4 billion meticals. Foreign trade (1981): imports 25.8 billion meticals; exports 13.1 billion meticals. Import sources (1977): South Africa 20%; West Germany 15%; Portugal 10%; Iraq 9%; U.K. 7%; Japan 5%. Export destinations (1977): U.S. 27%; Portugal 16%; U.K. 7%; South Africa 7%; The Netherlands 6%; Japan 5%. Main exports: cashew nuts 15%; sugar 12%; tea 9%; cotton 7%.

Transport and Communications. Roads (1975) 39,173 km. Motor vehicles in use (1980): passenger c. 99,400; commercial (including buses) c. 24,700. Railways (1981): 3,933 km; traffic 570 million passenger-km, freight 1,509,000,000 net ton-km. Air traffic (1982): 614 million passenger-km; freight c. 11.1 million net ton-km. Telephones (Jan. 1980) 51,600. Radio licenses (Dec. 1980) 255,000. Television receivers (Dec. 1980) 1,500.

Agriculture. Production (in 000; metric tons; 1982): corn c. 270; sorghum c. 155; cassava c. 2,900; peanuts c. 80; sugar, raw value c. 130; copra c. 50; bananas c. 65; cashew nuts (1981) c. 75; tea c. 18; cotton, lint c. 17; sisal c. 12. Livestock (in 000; 1981): cattle c. 1,420; sheep c. 108; goats c. 340; pigs c. 125; chickens c. 17,500.

Industry. Production (in 000; metric tons; 1981): coal c. 460; petroleum products 392; cement 261; electricity (kw-hr; 1980) 14,000,000.

Museums

A major conflict over the future of the Elgin Marbles, the famous sculptures from the Parthenon in Athens and among the treasures of the British Museum, erupted with a demand by the Greek government for their return. The International Council of Museums (ICOM) passed a resolution interpreted as supporting the Greek claim at its 1983 conference in London, when it called generally for cultural property to be returned to its country of origin. However, the British Museum seemed unlikely to hand over the sculptures. The marbles had been removed by Lord Elgin at the beginning of the 19th century, and in recent years renewed demands were made for their return. Opponents pointed out that, were it not for their removal, they would have deteriorated seriously because of wind erosion and later air pollution in Athens.

Facilities and Administration. In New York City the Metropolitan Museum of Art opened the third and final phase of its Egyptian art installation in June. The ten new galleries, designed by architects Kevin Roche, John Dinkeloo and Associates, housed works of art from the 12th to the mid-18th Dynasty. The whole of the collection of Egyptian art, the largest outside Cairo, was now on display. The museum also opened the Fleischman Gallery, where for the first time in many decades a separate space would be devoted to secular late medieval art. Also in New York the Whitney Museum of American Art opened its third branch space, its second such donation by corporate business; this branch, in the Philip Morris Inc. world headquarters in Manhattan, focused upon a court 13 m (42 ft) high especially designed for monumental sculpture.

In the southern United States the High Museum of Art in Atlanta, Ga., opened a $20 million structure by the much-acclaimed architect Richard Meier. The new Dallas (Texas) Museum of Fine Arts, in anticipation of its 1984 opening, unveiled a sculpture garden and court, while the New Orleans (La.) Museum of Art announced a national design competition for its new building.

In the Middle West, the Art Institute of Chicago, in the midst of a $49 million fund-raising effort, revealed a joint gift of $3.5 million from Marshall Field IV and the Roger McCormick family to be used for an American wing in its planned new South Building. The Toledo (Ohio) Museum of Art reinstalled its Medieval Cloister and opened a new American Art Gallery, which featured a glass ceiling that filters out ultraviolet light rays. The Children's Museum of Indianapolis, Ind., already the largest of its kind, added new facilities to give it more than 27,900 sq m (300,000 sq ft).

On the East Coast the Portland (Maine) Museum of Art opened its new $11.6 million wing, largely financed by Charles Payson. Also in New England the Worcester (Mass.) Art Museum opened the multimillion-dollar Frances L. Hiatt Wing. The National Gallery of Art in Washington, D.C., opened remodeled galleries on the first floor of its original West Building; the additional 3,700 sq m (40,000 sq ft) permitted the museum to double the number of works on public display. A new museum housing a great private collection of medieval European stained glass and sculpture opened in Bryn Athyn, Pa., north of Philadelphia; it was displayed in Glencairn, the castlelike home of its late collector, Raymond Pitcairn.

Plans for London's theatre museum finally moved ahead with formal approval by Minister for the Árts Lord Gowrie (*see* Biographies) and the exchange of contracts for the leasing of the old Covent Garden flower market as the site for the new museum. The museum would open by 1986 and would eventually provide a permanent home for more than 100,000 objects that had been stored at the Victoria and Albert Museum since 1974. A private donation of £250,000 was crucial in enabling the project to go forward. Such a museum was first proposed in 1955. The cost to the government was now estimated at nearly £4 million.

An important new collection for the Kuwait National Museum was officially opened in 1983. The As-Sabah Collection of Islamic Art was lent to the museum by Sheikh Nasser Sabah al-Ahmad as-Sabah and his wife. The collection of 20,000 items had never before been publicly shown. It was formed of items of Islamic art brought together from widely scattered places, and its display was the first attempt by an Islamic country to illustrate the whole range of Islamic art without reference to national origin.

New museums devoted to a vast range of industrial and archaeological subjects as well as local crafts and industries continued to appear. In England the British Commercial Vehicle Museum in Leyland, Lancashire, included exhibits from the horse-drawn era to steam and then internal combustion. Buses, trucks, fire engines, and vans were shown in realistic settings, and special events were staged.

The famous Tudor era warship "Mary Rose," which was raised from the Solent in October 1982, went on display to the public in 1983 in a specially constructed museum at Southsea near Portsmouth. A hull recovered from French waters would be the centrepiece of a new Museum of History at Marseilles; it would be preserved by a remarkable and innovative freeze-drying operation.

THE ILLUSTRATED LONDON NEWS PICTURE LIBRARY

The Ulster Folk and Transport Museum near Belfast was named Museum of the Year by *The Illustrated London News*.

ITSUO INOUE/THE NEW YORK TIMES

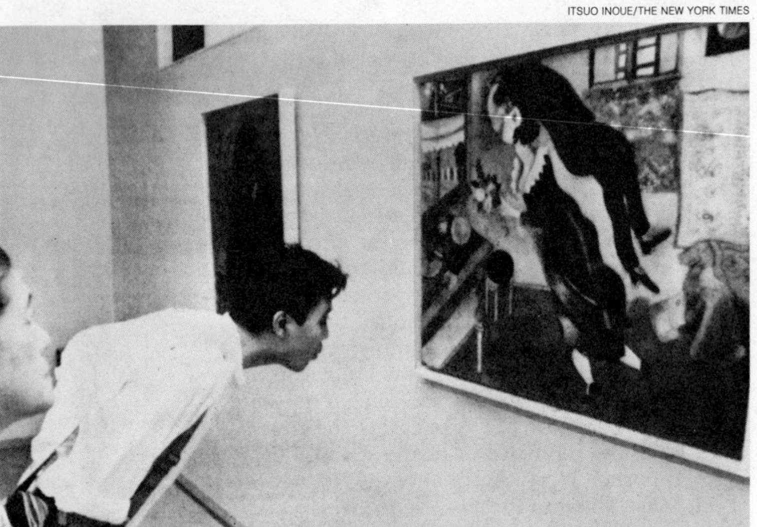

Japan's newest art museum, the Tokyo Metropolitan Teien (Garden) Art Museum, opened in October with a show of 100 works of modern art from the West, loaned by the Guggenheim Museum of New York City.

In April Queen Elizabeth II opened the National Horseracing Museum at Newmarket, England. Situated adjacent to the Jockey Club, the sport's ruling body, the museum's varied collection chronicled the sport of kings over the centuries.

New Acquisitions. The Yale University Art Gallery in New Haven, Conn., received an important gift of 16 paintings from Mr. and Mrs. Paul Mellon, including works by French artists such as Monet, Pissarro, and Degas. The works had been on display at Yale for some time. The Mellons also donated 93 works of art collected over the past 50 years to the National Gallery of Art in Washington. Included among this group were six Monets and ten Boudins. Other institutions in Washington also received large gifts: Armand Hammer donated 1,000 Daumier lithographs to the Corcoran Gallery of Art, with plans to fund a Daumier research centre there; and the Hirshhorn Museum and Sculpture Garden announced that it was to be given 6,000 additional works, with a value of $10 million, from the estate of its late founder, Joseph Hirshhorn.

In Chicago the Art Institute acquired two paintings from the "Haystack" series of Claude Monet; they joined three other paintings from this series already in the collections to form the most comprehensive group in any museum. In California Mr. and Mrs. Joe D. Price presented 300 Japanese scroll paintings and screens, together with $5 million to provide housing for them, to the Los Angeles County Museum of Art.

In London the British Museum acquired one of the most important collections of Palestinian material, consisting of the major part of the finds from the excavations at Tell ed-Duweir, ancient Lachish, found between 1932 and 1938. The National Gallery in London highlighted some recent acquisitions with special exhibitions. One was devoted to the Rubens canvas "Samson and Delilah," purchased for £2.5 million in 1980. Included were preparatory drawings and subsequent engravings.

(JOSHUA B. KIND; SANDRA MILLIKIN)

See also Art Exhibitions; Art Sales.

[613.D.1.b]

Music

Classical. With indications that economic revival might at last be under way and a consequent fresh breeze blowing through some of music's more staid corridors (not to mention those of a recently moribund recording industry), things looked, as 1983 closed, distinctly good. It was a year, too, in which several notable anniversaries fell due: the centenaries of the English composer Sir Arnold Bax (d. 1953) and of the opening of New York City's Metropolitan Opera (see *Opera,* below) and the 80th birthdays of conductor Yevgeny Mravinsky and pianists Claudio Arrau and Rudolf Serkin.

SYMPHONIC MUSIC. Newsworthy events as 1983 progressed included a clutch of guest appearances by Leonard Bernstein as conductor (and pianist) with the Los Angeles Philharmonic that contrasted such well-worn favourites as Copland's *Appalachian Spring* and George Gershwin's *Rhapsody in Blue* with such thoroughgoing rarities as William Schuman's sprightly, if lightweight, *American Festival Overture;* and pianist-turned-conductor Vladimir Ashkenazy's work at Severance Hall with the Cleveland Orchestra (firstfruits of which included an outstanding complete recording, for London Decca, of Prokofiev's ballet *Cinderella*).

Elsewhere, too, things appeared to be on the move. In the U.K. Rudolf Barshai, Marek Janowski, Neeme Järvi, André Previn, Stanislaw Skrowaczewski, and Giuseppe Sinopoli became principal conductors with, respectively, the Bournemouth Symphony, Royal Liverpool Philharmonic, Scottish National, Royal Philharmonic, Hallé (Manchester), and Philharmonia orchestras. Simon Rattle continued to garner generally lavish praise as conductor-in-chief of the City of Birmingham Symphony Orchestra but handed over the artistic directorship of London's South Bank Summer Music Festival to guitarist John Williams; this occurred after a season that (less than happily) included a complete Rattle-led Sibelius symphony cycle in the small-scale surroundings of the capital's Queen Elizabeth Hall.

Biggest disappointment of the year for London concertgoers was the cancellation, owing to illness, of a projected visit by Carlo Maria Giulini and the Los Angeles Philharmonic. Disappointing too was the reappearance, for the first time in decades, at the city's Royal Festival Hall (amid much ballyhoo) of the aging, amazing, but increasingly splashy and unreliable-sounding Vladimir Horowitz. By contrast, welcome riches were yielded up by Sir John Pritchard's first season as principal conductor of the British Broadcasting Corporation (BBC) Symphony Orchestra; by Klaus Tennstedt's continuing efforts (much Mahler included) with a healthy sounding London Philharmonic; and by a vintage BBC-sponsored Sir Henry Wood "Promenade" concert season that included such delights as a powerfully conceived, fearsomely executed account by Czechoslovak maestro Lovro von Matacic and the Philharmonia of Bruckner's Third Symphony.

Attendances at Barbican Hall (home of the London Symphony Orchestra) continued to be disappointing, with performances of varying quality. After squabbles during which the entire venture almost foundered, Suffolk's Aldeburgh Festival, though threatened by financial difficulties, prospered artistically under the joint control of tenor Sir Peter Pears and pianist Murray Perahia, welcoming en route a marvelous talent from yesteryear, pianist Mieczyslaw Horszowski. The London Symphony Orchestra Chorus flew to Moscow to sing Sir William Walton's *Belshazzar's Feast* and, under Yevgeny Svetlanov, Sir Edward Elgar's oratorio (to a text by John Henry Cardinal Newman) *The Dream of Gerontius.* Completion was announced of composer Sir Michael Tippett's most recent work, the choral/orchestral *The Masque of Time.* The first performance was arranged provisionally for the 1983–84 Boston Symphony season.

In continental Europe Herbert von Karajan survived both his 75th birthday and an unprecedented crisis of confidence (when his orchestra, the Berlin Philharmonic, demanded his dismissal after he had hired, without a properly constituted audition, a new first clarinetist, the remarkably gifted Sabine Meyer). Subsequently, Karajan played, as usual, to ecstatic houses at Berlin's Symphony Hall. A Bruckner Eighth Symphony proved especially memorable, as did the rare chance of savouring (in this case under the baton of rising hopeful Riccardo Chailly) Aleksandr Mossolov's ear-bendingly onomatopoeic symphonic poem *The Iron Foundry.* Neville Marriner continued to polish his reputation with the South West German Radio Orchestra, while Leonard Bernstein and James Levine (*see* BIOGRAPHIES) both drew rapturous notices for their work with a lustrous-sounding Vienna Philharmonic, the former floating an exquisite Brahms symphony cycle, the latter (among numerous other delights) an altogether outstanding account of Mahler's "mad" symphony, the nocturnal, mandolin-entwined Seventh.

Highlights in France included a richly moving account (in Paris, under Lorin Maazel) of Benjamin Britten's *War Requiem;* a full-blown festival, also in the French capital, of music by Anton von Webern; and a further season featuring Daniel Barenboim in charge of the Paris Orchestra (a particular pleasure here being the world premiere of a Wagner rarity billed as the "Descente de la Courtille"). In Monte Carlo the U.S.-based conductor Lawrence Foster continued to draw impressive results from a newly rejuvenated Philharmonic, while British music director John Eliot Gardiner started the arduous task of rebuilding from scratch the Lyon Opera Orchestra. Also in Lyon, as part of that city's annual Berlioz Festival, was a memorable reading, from Erich Leinsdorf, of Liszt's *Faust Symphony.*

Notable, too, was the long-hoped-for upturn in programs issued by France's one nationwide classical music broadcasting station, France Musique; these included much fascinating archive material from the likes of conductors Hermann Abendroth, Hans Knappertsbusch, Willem Menzelberg, Fritz Reiner, and Hans Rosbaud and pianists William Kapell and Arturo Benedetti Michelangeli, while an entire series, through the summer and fall, showcased the talents of the late German master pianist Wilhelm Backhaus.

Sad losses to the world of music in 1983 included composers Georges Auric, Werner Egk, Alberto Ginastera, Herbert Howells, Pal Kadosa, Elisabeth Lutyens, Germaine Tailleferre, and Sir William Walton; conductors Sir Adrian Boult and Igor Markevitch; lyricist Ira Gershwin; and singers Dame Isobel Baillie and Edith Coates. (*See* OBITUARIES.)

OPERA. The Metropolitan Opera, New York City, opened its centennial season with Fabrizio Melano's production of Berlioz's *Les Troyens*—first seen at the Met in 1973—with Placido Domingo playing Aeneas for the first time, Tatiana Troyanos as Dido, and Jessye Norman, in her Met debut, as Cassandra. The production, with designs by Peter Wexler and conducted by James Levine, got off to a rather shaky start but after settling down was generally judged to be a worthwhile undertaking that fully exploited the Met's vast resources. Domingo's Aeneas disappointed some critics, but Norman drew high praise for her Cassandra. New York City Opera (David to the

The Met—the Metropolitan Opera House in New York City—gave itself a 100th birthday party in October. Among the great names from opera who celebrated were (from left) Roberta Peters, conductor James Levine, Birgit Nilsson, Leontyne Price, Louis Quilico, Luciano Pavarotti, Paul Plishka (behind Pavarotti), Nicolai Ghiaurov, Robert Merrill, Grace Bumbry, Mignon Dunn, and Marilyn Horne.

DON HOGAN CHARLES/THE NEW YORK TIMES

Met's Goliath), under the artistic direction of retired soprano Beverly Sills, did its best to steal the older house's thunder, its widely praised production, in French (but with projected English subtitles), of Massenet's *Cendrillon* being followed by a newly revised version of Puccini's *Turandot*.

In Europe the Sir Peter Hall/William Dudley production of Wagner's *The Ring of the Nibelung* was finally unveiled at Bayreuth to generally favourable reviews, despite last-minute substitutions to a cast described in rehearsal by conductor Sir Georg Solti as the team of his dreams. A half hour's applause for singers and conductor partly drowned boos for the production and sets.

Critical opinion similarly continued to be divided in Vienna, where Lorin Maazel's tenure as music director at the city's State Opera had not been without incident. Even Maazel's most vociferous critics, however, were mollified (if not battered and dazzled into silence) by a Hal Prince/Timothy O'Brian production, directed by Maazel, of *Turandot*, a glittering, impressive affair in which the young Hungarian soprano Eva Marton (singing the title role) had to descend to the front of the stage by way of row upon row of tinselly steps set at an angle of some 50 degrees.

In the United Kingdom opera continued to thrive despite the chill winds of economic stringency which for 1983–84 were barely tempered by increases of some 7% in Arts Council grants. The Royal Opera House, Covent Garden (London), weighed in with a goodly number of productions, both old and new, including a debut John Copley/Henry Bardon Handel *Semele* (conducted by Sir Charles Mackerras), revivals of Peter Maxwell-Davies's *Taverner* and Stravinsky's *The Nightingale* and *The Rake's Progress*, and Puccini's *Manon Lescaut* with Kiri Te Kanawa (*see* BIOGRAPHIES) in the title role.

It was announced in November that Bernard Haitink was to succeed Sir Colin Davis as the Royal Opera's music director on the expiration of the latter's appointment in 1986. Meanwhile, English National Opera presented new productions of Richard Strauss's *Ariadne auf Naxos* and Wagner's *Rienzi* and *Ring* tetralogy (*Rienzi* receiving its first staging in the U.K. in 70 years, the *Ring* subject to a wholly new interpretation by producer David Pountney), along with revivals that included David Blake's *Toussaint* and Monteverdi's *Orfeo*. A valuable first for English National Opera North, based at Leeds, Yorkshire, was the premiere of Wilfred Joseph's opera *Rebecca* (based on the novel by Daphne du Maurier). Glyndebourne Festival Opera featured, among others, Prokofiev's *The Love of Three Oranges*, Rossini's *La Cenerentola*, and Richard Strauss's *Intermezzo*; while Welsh National Opera went from strength to strength, presenting yet another fresh *Ring* production (this time from producer Göran Järvefelt, with Richard Armstrong conducting), along with Bizet's *Carmen*, Britten's *Peter Grimes*, and Janacek's *From the House of the Dead*.

Subtitles for Cinderella: Beverly Sills's mounting of Massenet's *Cendrillon* for the New York City Opera was sung in the original French but featured English subtitles projected on the proscenium arch.

Take your colors from the rainbow.

MARTHA SWOPE

Opera similarly flourished in Paris, where the Opéra presented (at the Palais Garnier) new stagings of George Chaynes's *Erszebet* (a world premiere, starring Christianne Eda-Pierre), Aribert Reimman's *Lear*, Rossini's *Moses*, and Verdi's *Falstaff* and *Luisa Miller* (*Falstaff* being an especially starry show displaying the combined talents of singers Thomas Allen, Sylvia Sass, and Ingvar Wixell and conductor Seiji Ozawa).

Benjamin Britten's last opera, *Death in Venice*, was revived in both Geneva and Edinburgh, while a notable joint production in Munich between Bavarian Radio and Philips Records brought forth a remarkably fine Wagner *Tristan and Isolde*, featuring Hildegard Behrens, Peter Hofmann, and the Bavarian Radio Orchestra and Chorus under the direction of Leonard Bernstein. Film buffs enjoyed (although in certain instances found banal) Franco Zeffirelli's motion-picture extravaganza of Verdi's *La Traviata* (in which the principal singers were Placido Domingo and Teresa Stratas) and Francesco Rosi's *Carmen* (Bizet), the latter notable for the almost pornographic title role performance by Greek-Puerto Rican soprano Julia Migenes Johnson—a steamily erotic Salomé in Strauss's eponymous opera at Geneva earlier in the year.

ALBUMS. If the previous five years or so had been the age of the audiophile disc, 1983 witnessed the birth, commercially, of what rapidly became regarded as the greatest technological breakthrough since the 1948 advent of the LP record: the digital audio disc (DAD; called Compact Disc, CD, in the U.S.).

On the regular LP front, pressing quality was generally good (except, it seemed, in France and the U.S.). Among other significant developments were the appearance (from DGG) of a mammoth complete edition of Brahms; the launch of no less than two brand new labels, Etcetera and Orfeo; and plans to record complete cycles of Liszt and Rachmaninoff piano music (the former, for London Decca, from Jorge Bolet; the latter, for Hyperion, from Howard Shelley). Also issued were the following valuable albums (the majority of them first issues): from Unicorn-Kanchana and Angel EMI, discs of, respectively, early Britten chamber music and the same composer's orchestral song cycle *Our Hunting Fathers*; from Etcetera, vivid waxings (courtesy Charles Rosen) of Elliott Carter's *Piano Sonata* and *Night Fantasies*; from London Decca, Janacek's *Jenufa,* conducted by Sir Charles Mackerras; and from Philips, Sir Michael Tippett's *Triple Concerto.* (MOZELLE A. MOSHANSKY)

Jazz. Eclecticism dominated jazz in 1983 as it had for a decade or more, but the condition of the music was far from static. Among the brilliant young players who continue to emerge, the most visible was trumpeter Wynton Marsalis. At 21 he led his own quintet, featuring his gifted saxophonist brother, Branford (older by one year); toured a band co-led by Miles Davis alumni Herbie Hancock, Ron Carter, and Tony Williams; and demonstrated his prowess as a classical virtuoso in a recording of trumpet concerti by Haydn, Johann Hummel, and Leopold Mozart. (At 17 he was cited as the outstanding brass player at Tanglewood's Berkshire Music Center.) Marsalis's jazz style was a personal synthesis of the modern jazz tradition, but the trumpeter he most admired was Louis Armstrong.

The Marsalis brothers were born in New Orleans, and so were Terrence Blanchard, recommended by Wynton as his replacement with Art Blakey's Jazz Messengers, and Leroy Jones, another trumpeter barely out of his teens who was beginning to attract attention. It was too soon to speak of a second jazz wave from the city that gave birth to the music, appropriate as this would be as jazz neared its 100th anniversary.

A sign of jazz eclecticism was the proliferation of bands affirming the legacy of the past, such as Dameronia, performing the music of Tadd Dameron; Sphere, celebrating Thelonious Monk (but also playing its own works); the Bechet Legacy, led by former Sidney Bechet pupil Bob Wilber; and Mingus Dynasty, dedicated to the complex task of re-creating the volatile music of Charles Mingus.

Big bands, often associated with nostalgia, showed signs of new creative life. Gil Evans, one of the most accomplished arrangers, was able to maintain a band with stable personnel for the first time in his long career, due to successive, steady Monday-night bookings in two New York clubs. The prominent composer-theorist George Russell, active since the late 1940s, made his first U.S. tour with a big band, comprised of young players from the Boston area. Provocative big-band experiments with unorthodox instrumentation and material were conducted in New York by saxophonist David Murray, trumpeter Olu Dara, and drummer Bob Moses, whose band, Elephant's Memory, also was heard on one of the year's outstanding records. A Count Basie alumni band toured Europe in the fall, while Basie himself, though confined to a wheelchair by arthritis, continued to keep a full schedule. So did fellow veteran Woody Herman, who celebrated his 70th birthday in May. Another big Swing Era name, Artie Shaw, who left music in 1954 with vows never to return, announced in the fall the formation of an orchestra owned and supervised by him and fronted by clarinetist-saxophonist Dick Johnson.

But big-band ranks were thinned by the death of Harry James (*see* OBITUARIES), one of the few Swing Era stars who never gave up bandleading. The trumpeter, who came to prominence with Benny Goodman, launched his first band in 1939.

BRUCE W. TALAMON

Wynton Marsalis, adept at jazz and the classics, is seen as potentially one of the greatest trumpeters.

From 1943 to 1945, it outgrossed all other bands in the wake of hit records featuring the James horn at its most commercial. Nevertheless, James remained committed to good jazz, which he was capable of playing until the end. Another illustrious jazz career ended with the death of Earl Hines (*see* OBITUARIES), justly called the father of mature jazz piano. After his astonishing collaborations with Louis Armstrong in 1927–28, Hines spent 19 years leading big bands, establishing an enviable record as a talent spotter (singers Billy Eckstine and Sarah Vaughan; trumpeter Ray Nance; trombonist Trummy Young; saxophonist-arranger Budd Johnson, and, in his unrecorded 1943 band that served as an incubator of bebop, Dizzy Gillespie and Charlie Parker). Hines's 1948–51 stint with Armstrong's All Stars was followed by years of relative obscurity, but his 1963 New York concerts launched 20 years of renewed acclaim.

Other deaths included that of Muddy Waters (*see* OBITUARIES), one of the leading figures in the world of the blues. A founder of post-World War II urban blues style, he was a superb singer and showman and a master of slide guitar. His artistry was known only to the blues audiences of working-class blacks and a handful of connoisseurs until the Rolling Stones and other British rock stars acknowledged his influence. While he relished the acclaim and tangible rewards that his new status as an international celebrity brought him, Waters did not compromise the integrity of his music.

Five days after his 100th birthday (and some two weeks after the taping, at Washington's Kennedy Center, of a television special celebrating that notable event), pianist-composer Eubie Blake, sole survivor of the golden age of ragtime, died at his Brooklyn home (*see* OBITUARIES). Blake, whose career spanned the entire history of jazz, had become the personification of the music's endurance and vitality, of which the ragtime revival that he helped to spark was symbolic. The current respect for tradition and concomitant absence of a dominant new trend in jazz was read by some as a sign of impending decadence, but it could also be seen as a symptom of maturity. In any event, none of the many styles of jazz went without an audience in 1983. (DAN M. MORGENSTERN)

Popular. It was a year of fashion, style, revivalism, and triumph for all things British, as the record market seemed to be looking to younger and younger record buyers, and artists seemed to become successful for their looks as much as for their music. With the white American pop scene providing little that was new or fresh, British artists succeeded so well in the U.S. that there was talk of a "new British invasion," comparable to the one led by the Beatles in the 1960s. The "new wave" of British music was difficult to summarize simply because it was so varied, involving everything from the transvestite fashion styles of Culture Club to the old-fashioned good looks of Duran Duran or Kajagoogoo, and the more sturdy, masculine rock styles of Scotland's Big Country and Ireland's U2. Musically, these bands had little in common, but in the U.S. they were happily lumped together as the British saviours of the music industry.

If there was one single figure who dominated pop taste during the year, it was the same man who had sporadically managed to stay one jump ahead of pop fashion throughout the 1970s, David Bowie (*see* BIOGRAPHIES). In 1983 Bowie released his most commercial album to date, *Let's Dance*, a strong, melodic mixture of often crooned white funk ballads that led to a crop of hit singles. Bowie toured Britain for the first time in five years during the summer, as part of a world tour. Formerly an exponent of theatrical "glam-rock," he now came on as a cool performer of dance songs, though keeping a strong theatrical element in his show.

The British rock tradition for emphasizing costumes, very much taken to its limits by Bowie during the 1970s, was continued during the year by Boy George, singer and songwriter with Culture Club, who emerged as the outstanding new personality of the year, just as his band as a whole became the new heroes of British club-land, taking over from The Human League. Boy George (George O'Dowd) startled the critics with both his easy, distinctive vocal style and his varied, melodic songs, many influenced by black American styles.

White pop music was often accused—with some justification—of copying black styles, and this was as true as ever with the new crop of British artists. Wham! provided an exuberant if blatant English version of the rhythmic, half-talking "rap" styles that had been developed in the black ghettoes of U.S. cities. Other bands to emerge in Britain included the folksy Dexy's Midnight Runners; the heavy-metal Def Leppard; The Eurythmics, led by singer Annie Lennox; and the Police, featuring singer and bassist Sting (Gordon Sumner), who produced the best-selling album *Synchronicity*.

All of these bands and artists were massively successful in the U.S. during the year. In the 1960s the "British invasion" succeeded because bands went to the U.S. and gave performances throughout the country, gradually winning new followers. In the video age this was no longer necessary. The single most important musical development in the U.S. was the success of MTV, an all-pop music cable television channel that showed the promotional videos made by pop bands to accompany

UPI

British rock star David Bowie (left) toured the U.S. in 1983 as part of his first world tour in five years.

their singles releases. British bands had become skillful and adventurous at making these promo videos and so became very popular on MTV.

Within the U.S. itself black artists continued to set the trends, as white rock bands and performers seemed to go through yet another year of decline (with a few notable exceptions, such as the slick but black-influenced harmony dance duo Hall and Oates, who became the most requested act on MTV, and the heavy-metal group Quiet Riot). Michael Jackson, now arguably the world's greatest superstar and a pop music veteran at 24, seemed to be eclipsing even Stevie Wonder as the musical darling of black America. His new album, *Thriller*, which included such hit singles as "Billie Jean" and "Beat It" and a contribution from Paul McCartney on "This Girl Is Mine," was expected to sell 12 million copies by the end of 1983. Other black American artists who made an impact during the year were Lionel Ritchie, a former member of the Commodores, with his ballad "All Night Long," and Gary Byrd, with his lengthy rap polemic, "The Crown."

U.S. and British veterans continued to flourish, despite all the activity from new bands. In Britain the Rolling Stones released a new album, *Under Cover*, which showed that at 40 Mick Jagger still had the ability to shock. The opening track, "Under Cover of the Night," dealt with the disappearance and execution of political opponents of right-wing South American regimes and was accompanied by a video that was shown on MTV but was banned by the BBC's "Top of the Pops" program. There was a new album from Paul Simon—which turned out, unexpectedly, to be a solo effort, after his reunion tours with his former partner, Art Garfunkel, whose voice was said to have been wiped from the tape. Bob Dylan also reappeared with a new and more gutsy album, *Infidels*, that showed some signs of a return to his earlier form.

African music continued to make a major impact in both Britain and the U.S., thanks largely to the tours by Nigerian guitarist "King" Sunny Ade. With his large band, using traditional instruments like talking drums as well as non-African instruments like the steel guitar, he provided an extraordinary fusion of African and Western styles, dominated by his own guitar work. Two Australian groups, Men at Work and Air Supply, also enjoyed considerable popularity.

It was a quiet year for reggae. The most significant West Indian artist to emerge during the year was Guyana-born Eddy Grant, whose songs "I Don't Want to Dance" and "Electric Avenue" established him as a major performer in Britain and the U.S. (ROBIN DENSELOW)

See also Dance; Motion Pictures; Television and Radio; Theatre.
[624.D-J]

Nauru

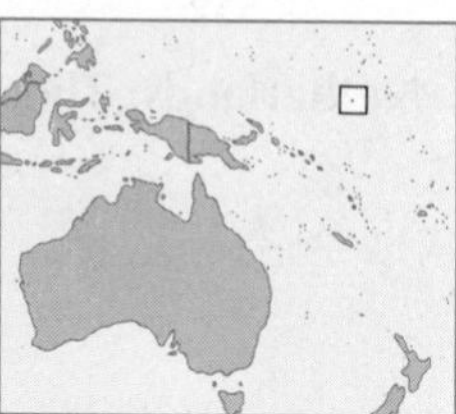
Nauru

An island republic within the Commonwealth, Nauru lies in the Pacific Ocean about 1,900 km east of New Guinea. Area: 21 sq km (8 sq mi). Pop. (1983 est.): 8,000, including (1977) Nauruan 57%; Pacific Islanders 26%; Chinese 9%; European 8%. Capital: Yaren. Language: Nauruan and English. Religion (1980): Protestant 57.6%; Roman Catholic 24%; Confucian and Taoist 8.4%; Buddhist 1.7%; Baha'i 1.7%; none 6.6%. President in 1983, Hammer DeRoburt.

Pres. Hammer DeRoburt resigned on May 16, 1983, but was out of office only four days. Parliament reelected him on May 20 by 11 votes to 4, the unsuccessful candidate being Derog Gioura.

DeRoburt had previously suffered two setbacks. First, his $40 million libel action against the *Pacific Daily News*, published in the U.S. dependency of Guam, failed. Nauru and DeRoburt spent more than $500,000 in legal costs, and the case ran for four years before U.S. federal judge Samuel King, sitting in Honolulu, ruled that a precedent set in 1897 barred U.S. courts from delving into the actions of foreign nations. The newspaper article had connected DeRoburt and the Nauruan government with a loan to separatists in the Marshall Islands. The second reverse was the failure to stop the dumping of nuclear wastes in the Pacific. Nauru joined with Kiribati in opposing this and called for a world ban on the dumping of radioactive material at an international meeting held in London. However, after the U.S., the Soviet Union, and Japan spoke against the Nauru proposal, the London Dumping Convention was adjourned. On the positive side, DeRoburt made progress in his negotiations with Pres. Ferdinand Marcos of the Philippines over the purchase from that nation of an island that could be used as a home or holiday resort for the people of Nauru. (A.R.G. GRIFFITHS)

NAURU

Education. (1980) Primary, pupils 1,704; teachers 102; secondary, pupils 339, teachers 36; vocational, pupils 70, teachers 4; teacher training, students 10, teacher 1.

Finance and Trade. Monetary unit: Australian dollar, with (Sept. 20, 1983) a free rate of A$1.12 to U.S. $1 (A$1.69 = £1 sterling). Budget (1981–82 est.): revenue A$109.5 million; expenditure A$85.6 million. Foreign trade (1978–79): imports A$10.6 million (c. 58% from Australia, c. 30% from The Netherlands in 1973–74); exports A$77.4 million (c. 51% to Australia, c. 41% to New Zealand, c. 5% to Japan in 1976–77). Main export: phosphate c. 100%.

Industry. Production (in 000; 1981): phosphate rock (metric tons) 1,480; electricity (kw-hr) 26,000.

Nepal

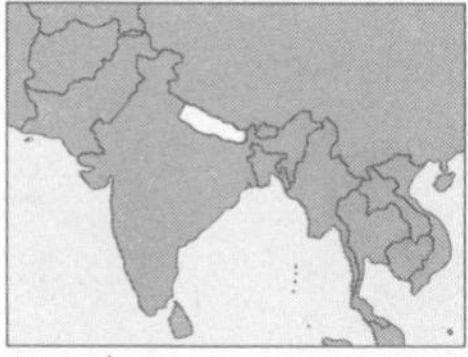
Nepal

A constitutional monarchy of Asia, Nepal is in the Himalayas between India and the Tibetan Autonomous Region of China. Area: 145,391 sq km (56,136 sq mi). Pop. (1982 est.): 15,769,000, including (1978 est.) Nepalese 54.4%; Bihari (including Maithili and Bhojpuri) 18.2%; Tamang 5.8%; Newar 4.5%; Tharu 4.3%; Magar 3.1%; Rai 2.5%; Limbu and Bhutia 2.4%; Gurung 1.9%; other 2.9%. Cap. and largest city: Kathmandu (pop., 1981 prelim., 235,200). Language: Nepali (official), other Indo-Aryan and Tibeto-Burman languages. Religion (1980): Hindu 89.6%; Buddhist 6.1%; Muslim 3%; other 1.3%. King, Birendra Bir Bikram Shah Deva; prime ministers in 1983, Surya Bahadur Thapa and, from July 12, Lokendra Bahadur Chand.

Following charges of official corruption, a motion of no confidence was passed against Prime Minister Surya Bahadur Thapa of Nepal on July 11, 1983. He resigned and was succeeded by Lokendra Bahadur Chand.

Grain production was badly affected by drought, which brought economic problems in its wake. The staple food crop, rice, yielded only 1,830,000 metric tons, 28% below the 1982 figure.

During the year Nepal made concerted efforts to consolidate relations with Pakistan and Bangladesh. Prime Minister Thapa visited both countries in February. In May Pakistan and Nepal launched

NEPAL

Education. (1981–82) Primary, pupils 1,142,900, teachers 29,139; secondary, vocational, and teacher training, pupils 558,996, teachers 17,154; higher, students 38,450, teaching staff 2,918.

Finance. Monetary unit: Nepalese rupee, with (Sept. 20, 1983) a free rate of NRs 14.30 to U.S. $1 (NRs 21.54 = £1 sterling). Gold and other reserves (June 1983) U.S. $171 million. Budget (total; 1981–82 actual): revenue NRs 2,676,000,000 (excludes foreign aid of NRs 993 million); expenditure NRs 5,361,000,000.

Foreign Trade. (1982) Imports NRs 5,263,000,000; exports NRs 1,140,000,000. Import sources: India c. 20%; Japan c. 15%; South Korea c. 7%; China c. 6%. Export destinations: India c. 14%; West Germany c. 12%; U.K. c. 7%. Main exports (excluding India; 1979–80): goat and kid skins 25%; jute 15%; fruit and vegetables 10%; jute fabrics 10%; carpets 7%; curios 6%; timber 5%; rice 5%. Tourism (1981): visitors 162,000; gross receipts U.S. $52 million.

Agriculture. Production (in 000; metric tons; 1982): rice c. 2,300; corn 612; wheat 450; millet c. 122; potatoes 320; jute 39; tobacco 5; buffalo milk c. 485; cow's milk (1981) c. 220. Livestock (in 000; 1982): cattle c. 6,950; buffalo c. 4,250; pigs c. 360; sheep (1981) c. 2,397; goats (1981) c. 2,525; poultry (1981) c. 22,412.

Namibia:
see Dependent States; South Africa

NATO:
see Defense

Navies:
see Defense

a joint commission to promote economic cooperation, while on April 15 Pakistan International Airlines resumed air services to Kathmandu after a lapse of over 12 years. Thapa also visited New Delhi, but relations with India deteriorated over the issues of Indian settlers in Nepal and India's refusal to include Nepal in its discussions about the sharing of river waters with Bangladesh. On May 2 French Pres. François Mitterrand became the first Western head of state to visit the kingdom. In December King Birendra Bir Bikram Shah Deva and Queen Aishwarya made a two-week trip to the U.S. (DILIP GANGULY)

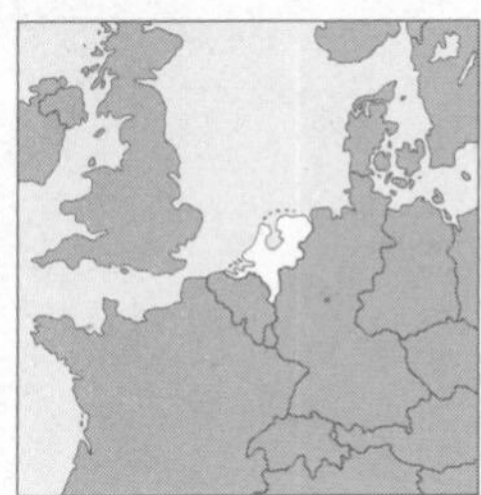
The Netherlands

Netherlands, The

A kingdom of northwest Europe on the North Sea, The Netherlands, a Benelux country, is bounded by Belgium on the south and West Germany on the east. Area: 41,548 sq km (16,042 sq mi). Pop. (1983 est.): 14,339,600. Cap. and largest city: Amsterdam (pop., 1983 est., 687,400). Seat of government: The Hague (pop., 1983 est., 449,300). Language: Dutch. Religion (1971): Roman Catholic 40.4%; no religion 23.6%; Dutch Reformed 23.5%; Reformed Churches 9.4%. Queen, Beatrix; prime minister in 1983, Ruud Lubbers.

Two issues dominated the political climate in The Netherlands during 1983: the high rate of unemployment and the stationing of new U.S. medium-range nuclear missiles in Western Europe. In the spring the government of Prime Minister Ruud Lubbers presented its financial and economic policy. In a three-pronged attack, it aimed to control public-sector expenditure, strengthen the market economy, and redistribute the available labour force in an attempt to ease unemployment. Willem Duisenberg, president of The Netherlands Bank, declared his opposition to the redistribution of labour when he presented the annual report in June; instead, he believed priority should be given to putting employers' profits on the road to recovery.

On September 20 Queen Beatrix presented the queen's speech to Parliament. (She was accompanied by Prince Claus, his first public appearance since the previous year, when he had suffered a depression.) The main concern of the government's economic policy, as outlined in the speech, was to reduce the government deficit, in large measure by cutting back on social services and public-sector salaries. Measures designed to stimulate the economy by subsidizing trade and industry were also announced. The response was predictable. The Christian Democratic Appeal (CDA) and the Liberal Party (VVD)—the two government parties who together held a majority in the lower house—supported the policy; the Socialist Party (PVDA) and the other left-wing parties rejected it. While the employers' associations praised it, the trade unions were outraged.

The public-service unions broke off negotiations with Internal Affairs Minister Koos Rietkerk and announced that public servants would take action. Beginning in the last week of October, public life was severely disrupted by strikes and slowdowns among railway and regional bus staff and postmen and garbage collectors in the large cities. Firemen demonstrated in The Hague, and the police carried out intensive traffic inspections that caused chaos on the roads. The matter was partly settled when the courts ruled that the government and the public servants' unions were obliged to negotiate on conditions of employment.

In March Lubbers paid a visit to the U.S. The central topic in his discussions with Pres. Ronald Reagan was the stationing of U.S. cruise and Pershing II missiles in Western Europe and the related intermediate nuclear force negotiations between the U.S. and the U.S.S.R. The government announced that, should it decide to take them, the 48 cruise missiles earmarked for deployment in The Netherlands would be placed at the Air Force base at Woensdrecht. (The decision was to be made in early 1984.) The announcement gave new impetus to antinuclear activities. Demonstrations all over the country climaxed in a massive peace rally in The Hague on October 29 attended by more than 550,000 people. To assess the consequences of deployment, the chairmen of the three largest parties in the lower house, Bert de Vries (CDA), Joop den Uyl (PVDA), and Ed Nijpels (VVD), visited both Washington and Moscow. During their visits, the differences between the parties became clear: the PVDA opposed deployment, the VVD favoured it, and the CDA remained uncommitted.

NETHERLANDS, THE

Education. (1981–82) Primary, pupils 1,364,176, teachers 66,359; secondary, pupils 820,731, teachers 54,901; vocational, pupils 582,199, teachers 52,000; teacher training, students 7,490, teachers 1,200; higher, students 251,293, teaching staff 26,000.

Finance. Monetary unit: guilder, with (Sept. 20, 1983) a free rate of 2.98 guilders to U.S. $1 (4.49 guilders = £1 sterling). Gold and other reserves (June 1983) U.S. $12,223,000,000. Budget (1982 actual): revenue 126.1 billion guilders; expenditure 147.7 billion guilders. Gross national product (1982) 365.2 billion guilders. Money supply (May 1983) 80,370,000,000 guilders. Cost of living (1975 = 100; June 1983) 154.7.

Foreign Trade. (1982) Imports 171,548,000,000 guilders; exports 176,851,000,000 guilders. Import sources: EEC 54% (West Germany 22%, Belgium-Luxembourg 11%, U.K. 9%, France 7%); U.S. 9%. Export destinations: EEC 72% (West Germany 30%, Belgium-Luxembourg 14%, France 10%, U.K. 9%, Italy 6%). Main exports: food 18%;; petroleum products 16%; chemicals 15%; machinery 12%; natural gas 8%. Tourism (1981): visitors 2,846,000; gross receipts U.S. $1,571,000,000.

Transport and Communications. Roads (1979) 108,528 km (including 1,831 km expressways in 1981). Motor vehicles in use (1982): passenger 4,650,000; commercial 317,400. Railways: (1981) 2,964 km (including 1,799 km electrified); traffic (1982) 9,376,000,000 passenger-km, freight 2,887,000,000 net ton-km. Air traffic (1982): 16,282,000,000 passenger-km; freight 1,086,200,000 net ton-km. Navigable inland waterways (1981) 4,390 km; freight traffic 31,792,000,000 ton-km. Shipping (1982): merchant vessels 100 gross tons and over 1,228; gross tonnage 5,393,104. Shipping traffic (1982): goods loaded 75,704,000 metric tons, unloaded 241,658,000 metric tons. Telephones (Jan. 1981) 7,230,800. Radio licenses (Dec. 1981) 4,483,000. Television licenses (Dec. 1981) 4,294,000.

Agriculture. Production (in 000; metric tons; 1982): wheat 967; barley 247; oats 136; rye 27; potatoes 6,219; tomatoes 455; onions 561; sugar, raw value c. 1,195; cabbages (1981) 289; cucumbers (1981) 375; carrots (1981) 171; apples 470; rapeseed 33; milk 12,750; butter 218; cheese 485; eggs 630; beef and veal c. 420; pork c.1,370; fish catch (1981) 434. Livestock (in 000; May 1982): cattle 5,241; pigs 10,254; sheep 776; chickens 87,073.

Industry. Index of production (1975 = 100; 1982) 110. Production (in 000; metric tons; 1982): crude oil 1,638; natural gas (cu m) 67,870,000; manufactured gas (cu m) 1,044,000; electricity (kw-hr) 60,313,000; pig iron 3,618; crude steel 4,347; aluminum 301; cement 3,103; petroleum products (1981) 45,447; sulfuric acid 1,609; plastics and resins 2,506; fertilizers (nutrient content; 1981–82) nitrogenous 1,463, phosphate 325; newsprint 151. Merchant vessels launched (100 gross tons and over; 1982) 213,000 gross tons. New dwelling units (1982) 127,200.

Alfred Heineken, chairman of the Heineken brewery and reputedly one of the richest men in Europe, was found, unharmed, by police in an Amsterdam warehouse on November 30, 21 days after he had been kidnapped. Twenty-five suspects were subsequently arrested, and 11, most of them members of a single family, were detained.

(DICK BOONSTRA)

See also Dependent States.

New Zealand

New Zealand, a parliamentary state and member of the Commonwealth, is in the South Pacific Ocean, separated from southeastern Australia by the Tasman Sea. The country consists of North and South islands and Stewart, Chatham, and other minor islands. Area: 269,057 sq km (103,883 sq mi). Pop. (1983 est.): 3,203,300. Cap.: Wellington (pop., 1982 est., city proper 134,900; urban area 320,000). Largest city: Manukau (pop., 1982 est., city proper 163,700; urban area included in Auckland). Largest urban area: Auckland (pop., 1982 est., city proper 144,400; urban area 778,200). Language: English (official), Maori. Religion (1981): Church of England 25.6%; Presbyterian 16.5%; Roman Catholic 14.4%; Methodist 4.7%. Queen, Elizabeth II; governor-general in 1983, Sir David Stuart Beattie; prime minister, Robert David Muldoon.

CAMERA PRESS

Prince Charles looked on as Princess Diana received a traditional Maori greeting on a visit to New Zealand.

NEW ZEALAND

Education. (1981) Primary, pupils 493,856, teachers c. 21,300; secondary, pupils 224,926, teachers c. 14,640; vocational, pupils 140,706, teachers 2,506; teacher training, pupils 5,901, teachers 592; higher (universities only), students 31,549, teaching staff 3,043.

Finance. Monetary unit: New Zealand dollar, with (Sept. 20, 1983) a free rate of NZ$1.53 to U.S. $1 (NZ$2.30 = £1 sterling). Gold and other reserves (June 1983) U.S. $874 million. Budget (1981–82 actual): revenue NZ$9,378,000,000; expenditure NZ$10,790,000,000. Gross national product (1981–82) NZ$28,187,000,000. Money supply (May 1983) NZ$3,338,000,000. Cost of living (1975 = 100; 2nd quarter 1983) 285.8.

Foreign Trade. (1981–82) Imports NZ$7,044,800,000; exports NZ$6,733,800,000. Import sources: Australia 20%; U.S. 17%; Japan 17%; U.K. 9%. Export destinations: Australia 15%; U.K. 14%; Japan 13%; U.S. 13%; U.S.S.R. 5%. Main exports: dairy products 17%; wool 14%; lamb and mutton 11%; beef and veal 9%. Tourism (1981): visitors 478,000; gross receipts U.S. $252 million.

Transport and Communications. Roads (1982) 93,137 km. Motor vehicles in use (1982): passenger 1,366,500; commercial 276,300. Railways (1981): 4,433 km; traffic 404 million passenger-km, freight (1982) 3,228,000,000 net ton-km. Air traffic (1982): 5,846,000,000 passenger-km; freight 229.4 million net ton-km. Shipping (1982): merchant vessels 100 gross tons and over 116; gross tonnage 250,208. Telephones (March 1981) 1,799,500. Radio receivers (Dec. 1980) 2,755,000. Television licenses (Dec. 1982) 926,200.

Agriculture. Production (in 000; metric tons; 1982): wheat 320; barley 407; oats 57; corn (1981) c. 177; potatoes (1981) c. 270; dry peas c. 60; tomatoes c. 60; wine 47; apples 228; milk 6,646; butter 247; cheese 111; wool c. 269; sheepskins (1981) c. 103; mutton and lamb 659; beef and veal 540; fish catch (1981) 108; timber (cu m; 1981) 10,309. Livestock (in 000; June 1982): cattle 7,912; sheep 70,301; pigs 406; chickens c. 6,690.

Industry. Production (in 000; metric tons; 1982): coal 2,039; lignite 209; crude oil 658; natural gas (cu m) 2,930,000; manufactured gas (cu m) 32,000; electricity (excluding most industrial production; kw-hr) 23,981,000; cement 781; aluminum 163; petroleum products (1981) 2,592; phosphate fertilizers (1981–82) c. 336; wood pulp 1,048; paper 702.

New Zealand reduced its inflation rate to single figures by mid-1983 for the first time since 1973. Inflation had stood at 17% before the government imposed a wages and prices freeze in June 1982. The freeze slowed the economy, however, and unemployment climbed to 8%. A report by the Organization for Economic Cooperation and Development (OECD), released in midyear, commented that the freeze had held well and produced positive effects, but it was uncertain whether these gains would be maintained. The OECD observed that the economy had become substantially less competitive since the 1970s.

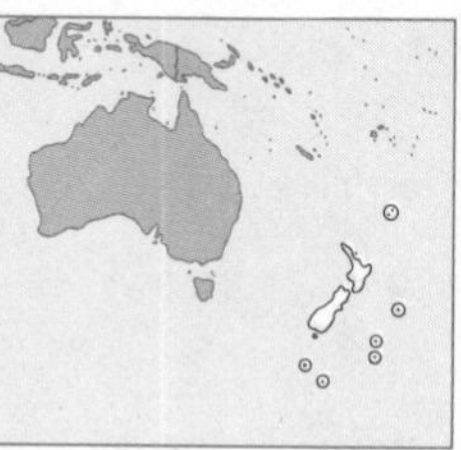

New Zealand

Robert Muldoon, who was finance minister as well as prime minister, presented his budget in July. It provided for a NZ$3,169,000,000 deficit, possibly the highest ever. Muldoon argued that this was inevitable, given that the world economy was just beginning to emerge from recession. Government spending was up 13.1%; most taxes were increased to sustain a cut for low-income families; and there were the usual rises in taxes on liquor and cigarettes. On the world economic scene, Muldoon became a prominent campaigner for a Bretton Woods-type review of the international monetary system.

In March New Zealand entered into a closer formal economic relationship with Australia that gave new incentives to traders on either side of the Tasman Sea. Major strikes disrupted a refinery expansion and a paper mill, but on the whole the unions seemed numbed by the pay freeze and distracted by the need to defend themselves against a government move to legislate against the current compulsory unionism. Unions joined employers and government representatives in talks on how the country could best emerge from the pay freeze. By October a slight improvement in economic conditions was discernible. The rate of decline in output was slowing, and sales were stabilizing.

The National Party (Conservative) government

Netherlands Overseas Territories:
see Dependent States

New Guinea:
see Indonesia; Papua New Guinea

Newspapers:
see Publishing

gained a stronger grip on its parliamentary majority, which had stood at a slender one vote after the election of a speaker at the start of the term. The Labour opposition failed to select two of its sitting members to run in the next general election, causing them to resign from the party. As independents they were a new factor in the House. Labour did not maintain the boost in popularity it received when barrister David Lange succeeded Sir Wallace ("Bill") Rowling as leader in February. In local elections in October, Cath Tizard won Auckland for Labour, the first woman to be proclaimed mayor of a big city in New Zealand.

The native Maori people won a victory in their struggle to have their separate culture recognized and respected, to have some of their lands restored, and to ensure that traditional accesses were kept unpolluted. An industrial planning tribunal ruled that alternative arrangements should be made for siting a waste disposal outlet for a high-technology synthetic fuels plant. In doing so, it was influenced by a provision for the protection of fishing grounds contained in an old treaty signed between British settlers and Maori chiefs.

Visitors during the year included Chinese Premier Zhao Ziyang (Chao Tzu-yang) and other senior ministers, and the prince and princess of Wales and their son, Prince William. South Korean Pres. Chun Doo Hwan canceled a visit when ministerial and other members of his party were killed in a bomb blast at Rangoon, Burma, on the first stage of their tour. (JOHN A. KELLEHER)

See also Dependent States.

Nicaragua

The largest country of Central America, Nicaragua is a republic bounded by Honduras, Costa Rica, the Caribbean Sea, and the Pacific Ocean. Area: 127,662 sq km (49,291 sq mi). Pop. (1983 est.): 2,812,000. Cap. and largest city: Managua (pop., 1979 est., 552,900). Language: Spanish. Religion: Roman Catholic. Coordinator of the three-member Junta of the Government of National Reconstruction in 1983, Daniel Ortega Saavedra.

MICHAEL HONORIN—GAMMA/LIAISON

Nicaragua's Sandinista government troops were aided by Soviet and Cuban supplies and advisers in combat with anti-Sandinista "contras" supplied and advised by the U.S.

The efforts of the Sandinista National Liberation Front government to achieve national reconstruction suffered serious setbacks in 1983 as a result of the increasing number of attacks by U.S.-backed antigovernment forces based in Honduras and Costa Rica. Honduras-based "contras," many of whose leaders were Somocistas (followers of the late dictator Anastasio Somoza), attacked a number of key economic targets in September and October, inflicting significant damage to ports, fuel installations, and other industrial sites. The attacks aggravated an already serious fuel shortage. In response the Sandinista government announced intensified internal security and stricter fuel rationing. The shift from military raids to economic sabotage marked a change in the strategy of the contras, who had failed to erode popular support for the Sandinistas or to make significant military gains on the ground. Rebels in the south led by the former Sandinista hero Edén Pastora Gómez were hampered by financial problems, and efforts to merge the several anti-Sandinista factions were inconclusive.

The U.S. administration, which acknowledged that the Central Intelligence Agency was involved in acts of sabotage, justified the covert aid given to the contras on the grounds that it would halt the export of the Sandinista revolution to other parts of Central America. Although the U.S. House of Representatives voted in July and again in October against the continuation of these covert funds, the Republican-dominated Senate in November rejected the House bill. The Senate voted to continue U.S. aid to the contras but agreed to provide only $19 million of the $50 million sought by the Reagan administration.

Daniel Ortega Saavedra, coordinator of the ruling junta, accused the U.S. of launching an undeclared war on Nicaragua and attempting to destroy the Sandinista revolution. He repeatedly called on the UN Security Council to discuss the crisis in Central America, but the UN's only action was to support the peace efforts of the Contadora group (Colombia, Mexico, Panama, and Venezuela). Nicaragua's diplomatic relations with Honduras and Costa Rica deteriorated in the wake of the rebel raids carried out from their territory.

Support for Nicaragua from Western Europe increased. Bilateral loans were arranged with West Germany and France, and toward the end of 1982 the European Communities, despite opposition from the U.K., included Nicaragua in a multilateral aid package for the Central American region. Nicaragua gained a new respectability within Latin America by winning a two-year term on the UN Security Council that began in January 1983. In October Nicaragua secured an agreement to reschedule $140 million owed to a consortium of foreign banks. Despite U.S. opposition, it also obtained a $30 million loan from the Inter-American Development Bank for its fishing industry. In 1983 the U.S. increased its economic sanctions by suspending 90% of its sugar imports from Nicaragua.

Gross domestic product in 1982 had shown no growth, and there was little prospect of improvement in 1983. The government's major successes

NICARAGUA

Education. (1982) Primary, pupils 509,240, teachers 14,105; secondary, pupils 114,868, teachers (1977–78) 1,731; vocational, pupils 17,982, teachers (1977–78) 1,066; teacher training, students 3,779, teachers (1977–78) 70; higher, students (1980–81) 34,710, teaching staff (1979–80) 1,299.

Finance. Monetary unit: córdoba, with (Sept. 20, 1983) a par value of 10 córdobas to U.S. $1 (free rate of 15.06 córdobas = £1 sterling). Budget (1980 actual): revenue 4,632,000,000 córdobas; expenditure 6,123,000,000 córdobas. Gross domestic product (1979) 13,409,000,000 córdobas. Money supply (Dec. 1982) 6,545,800,000 córdobas.

Foreign Trade. (1982) Imports 7,794,600,000 córdobas; exports 4,097,500,000 córdobas. Import sources (1980): U.S. 27%; Venezuela 17%; Costa Rica 13%; Guatemala 12%; El Salvador 6%. Export destinations: U.S. 39%; West Germany 13%; Costa Rica 9%; France 6%; The Netherlands 5%. Main exports (1980): coffee 42%; beef 14%; cotton 8%; chemicals 7%; fish 7%; sugar 6%.

Transport and Communications. Roads (1981) 16,712 km. Motor vehicles in use (1981): passenger 24,900; commercial 7,900. Railways: (1980) 373 km; traffic (1981) 20 million passenger-km, freight 14 million net ton-km. Air traffic (1982): c. 120 million passenger-km; freight c. 1.2 million net ton-km. Telephones (Jan. 1980) 57,900. Radio receivers (Dec. 1980) 700,000. Television receivers (Dec. 1980) 175,000.

Agriculture. Production (in 000; metric tons; 1982): corn 164; rice (1981) c. 65; sorghum 84; dry beans c. 60; sugar, raw value (1981) c. 193; bananas c. 157; oranges c. 54; cottonseed c. 102; coffee c. 57; cotton, lint c. 62; fish catch (1981) c. 6. Livestock (in 000; 1981): cattle c. 2,301; pigs c. 510; horses c. 270; chickens c. 4,800.

Industry. Production (in 000; metric tons; 1981): cement 100; petroleum products 529; gold (troy oz) c. 70; electricity (kw-hr) 1,110,000.

were in the area of social welfare: polio was eradicated; there was a highly successful literacy campaign; and housing remained a national priority. Minister of the Interior Tomás Borge Martínez (*see* BIOGRAPHIES) reaffirmed in May that the government intended to hold elections in 1985. On December 6, in the most positive U.S. reaction to that time, Secretary of State George Shultz welcomed the promises of elections and amnesty for most guerrillas but warned that the U.S. wanted "reality to be put behind the rhetoric."

(LESLIE CRAWFORD)

Niger

A republic of north central Africa, Niger is bounded by Algeria, Libya, Chad, Nigeria, Benin, Upper Volta, and Mali. Area: 1,189,000 sq km (459,100 sq mi). Pop. (1983 est.): 6,083,000, including (1978 est.) Hausa 52%; Zerma and Songhai 22.6%; Fulani 10%; Kanuri and Manga 9.1%; Tuareg 3%; other 3.3%. Cap. and largest city: Niamey (pop., 1981 est., 343,600). Language: French (official), Mausa, Kanuri, Fulani, and other dialects. Religion: Muslim 85%; animist 14.5%; Christian 0.5%. Chief of state and president of the Supreme Military Council in 1983, Brig. Gen. Seyni Kountché; premiers, Oumarou Mamane from January 24 and, from November 14, Ahmid Algabid.

On Jan. 24, 1983, Pres. Seyni Kountché created the post of premier, to which Oumarou Mamane, formerly minister of youth, sport, and culture, was appointed. While President Kountché was in France for the Franco-African summit in October, Premier Mamane announced that an attempted coup had been put down by the Army. In November, however, all military personnel, apart from the president himself, were removed from the Cabinet and Ahmid Algabid, formerly finance minister, took over as premier.

There was a repetition of the previous year's violent student agitation. At the University of Niamey about 300 students were arrested when the Army intervened early in May; most were released after several days' detention. The government also had to contend with an influx of Niger nationals, variously estimated at from 150,000 to 500,000 in number, during the mass expulsion of illegal immigrants from Nigeria in January.

(PHILIPPE DECRAENE)

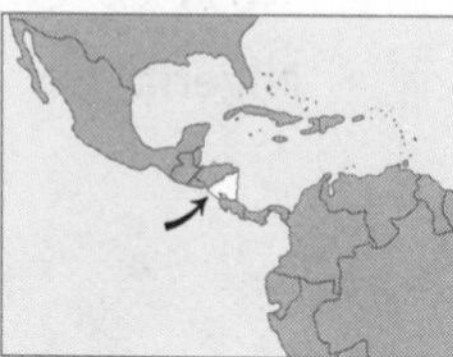
Nicaragua

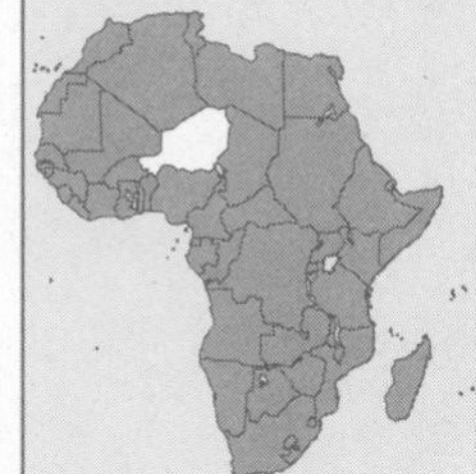
Niger

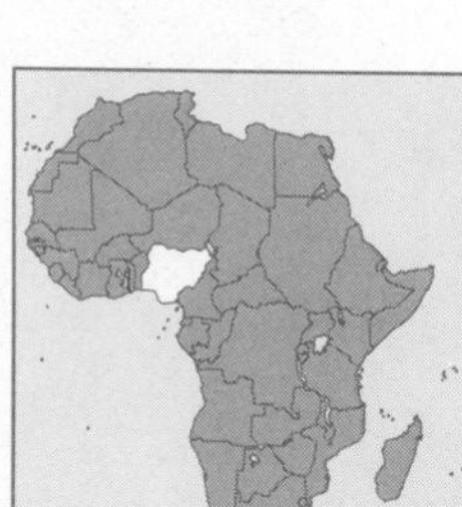
Nigeria

NIGER

Education. (1978–79) Primary, pupils 187,151, teachers 4,762; secondary, pupils (1981–82) 45,846, teachers 866; vocational, pupils 354, teachers 31; teacher training, students 1,259, teachers 64; higher (1980–81), students 1,435, teaching staff 224.

Finance. Monetary unit: CFA franc, with (Sept. 20, 1983) a par value of CFA Fr 50 to the French franc (free rate of CFA Fr 403 = U.S. $1; CFA Fr 607 = £1 sterling). Gold and other reserves (June 1983) U.S. $16 million. Budget (1981–82 est.) balanced at CFA Fr 93.9 billion.

Foreign Trade. (1982) Imports CFA Fr 145 billion; exports CFA Fr 109 billion. Import sources (1981): France 36%; Nigeria 13%; Algeria 7%; Ivory Coast 5%. Export destinations: France 36%; Japan 18%; Nigeria 17%; Libya 15%; Spain 5%. Main exports (1981): uranium 79%; livestock 12%.

Transport and Communications. Roads (main: 1981) 8,547 km. Motor vehicles in use (1980): passenger 25,800; commercial 4,400. There are no railways, but they are planned. Air traffic (1982): 225 million passenger-km; freight c. 22.2 million net ton-km. Inland waterway (Niger River; 1982) c. 300 km. Telephones (Dec. 1978) 8,500. Radio receivers (Dec. 1980) 250,000. Television receivers (Dec. 1980) 5,000.

Agriculture. Production (in 000; metric tons; 1982): millet c. 1,295; sorghum c. 357; rice (1981) c. 38; cassava (1981) c. 225; onions c. 110; peanuts c. 88; goat's milk c. 143. Livestock (in 000; 1981): cattle c. 3,300; sheep c. 2,850; goats c. 7,200; camels c. 365.

Industry. Production (in 000; metric tons; 1981): uranium 4.5; tin concentrates (metal content) 0.05; cement 38; electricity (kw-hr) 60,000.

Nigeria

A republic and a member of the Commonwealth, Nigeria is located in Africa north of the Gulf of Guinea, bounded by Benin, Niger, Chad, and Cameroon. Area: 923,768 sq km (356,669 sq mi). Pop. (1982 est.): 89,117,500, including (1978 est.) Hausa 21.5%; Yoruba 21%; Ibo 18.4%; Fulani 11.1%; other 28%. Cap. and largest city: Lagos (pop., 1982 est., 1,404,000). Language: English (official), Hausa, Yoruba, and Ibo. Religion (1963): Muslim 47%; Christian 34%. President in 1983, Alhaji Shehu Shagari.

General elections held in August 1983 dominated the attention of Nigeria until the last day of the year, when a coup set aside their results. Between August 6 and September 3, presidential elections were followed by elections to the state governorships, the Senate, the House of Representatives, and finally the state assemblies. The key electoral issues were all economic—debt, devaluation, and declining living standards.

The elections resulted in a landslide for the National Party of Nigeria (NPN) and confirmed the national appeal of Pres. Alhaji Shehu Shagari, who was overwhelmingly endorsed for a second term. Shagari's nearest rivals were from the Unity Party of Nigeria and the Nigerian People's Party. The NPN obtained a majority in both the Senate and the House of Representatives. (For tabulated results, *see* POLITICAL PARTIES.)

In the wake of the elections there were many claims and counterclaims of polling irregularities. Violence flared in Ondo and Oyo states and elsewhere over recounts and charges of rigging, resulting in the deaths of more than 70 people. Shagari was inaugurated in October and presented a team of 35 ministers to the Senate, which turned down 6 of them.

Once again the performance of the economy was poor. The budget was conservative; at 10,655,000,000 naira, expenditure was 280 million naira below the 1982 figure. Commenting on the agricultural sector, President Shagari said: "Our ultimate aim is to phase out food imports through self-sufficiency as quickly as possible." It was admitted, however, that the target of regaining self-sufficiency in food by 1985 was unlikely to be met. Nigeria's dependence on oil revenue had increased. While foreign exchange for the 1983 budget was set at 7.2 billion naira, only 400 million naira was expected to come from nonoil exports. In the event, that figure turned out to be optimistic. The government introduced restrictions aimed at reducing imports by one-third.

In February Nigeria announced an oil price cut of $5.50 a barrel. By March the external debt had passed the 10 billion naira mark, and in April the government approached the International Monetary Fund for a $2 billion loan, though it was wary of the IMF's conditions. As the elections ended in September, an IMF team arrived in Lagos to negotiate the loan. Victor Masi, minister of finance, emphasized that he saw no need to devalue the currency.

In January Nigeria announced its decision to expel some two million illegal immigrants, who were given until January 31 to leave the country, though skilled aliens were granted an extension

NIGERIA

Education. (1979–80) Primary, pupils 12,554,222, teachers 309,597; secondary, pupils 1,597,877, teachers 50,952; vocational, pupils 57,492, teachers 2,619; teacher training, students 242,186, teachers 16,440; higher, students 115,166, teaching staff (universities only) 5,748.

Finance. Monetary unit: naira, with (Sept. 20, 1983) a free rate of 0.71 naira to U.S. $1 (1.07 naira = £1 sterling). Gold and other reserves (June 1983) U.S. $1,096,000,000. Federal budget (1982): revenue 8.9 billion naira; expenditure 9,970,000,000 naira. Gross domestic product (1981–82) 43,450,000,000 naira. Money supply (May 1983) 9,919,000,000 naira. Cost of living (1975 = 100; 3rd quarter 1982) 284.6.

Foreign Trade. (1982) Imports (f.o.b.) c. 7,879,000,000 naira; exports 11,018,000,000 naira. Import sources (1979): U.K. 17%; West Germany 16%; Japan 11%; U.S. 10%; France 9%; Italy 6%; The Netherlands 5%. Export destinations: U.S. 44%; The Netherlands 12%; West Germany 8%; France 8%; U.K. 6%. Main export: crude oil 95%.

Transport and Communications. Roads (1980) 107,990 km. Motor vehicles in use (1980): passenger 215,400; commercial 33,100. Railways: (1980) 3,524 km; traffic (1977–78) 1,415,000,000 passenger-km, freight 1,612,000,000 net ton-km. Air traffic (1982): 2,252,000,000 passenger-km; freight 26.9 million net ton-km. Shipping (1982): merchant vessels 100 gross tons and over 147; gross tonnage 463,395. Telephones (Dec. 1979) 186,900. Radio receivers (Dec. 1980) 5.6 million. Television receivers (Dec. 1980) 450,000.

Agriculture. Production (in 000; metric tons; 1982): millet c. 3,300; sorghum c. 3,800; corn c. 1,650; rice c. 1,400; sweet potatoes c. 240; yams c. 15,000; cassava c. 11,000; tomatoes c. 500; peanuts c. 610; palm oil c. 700; cocoa 150; cotton, lint c. 22; rubber c. 45; fish catch (1981) 496. Livestock (in 000; 1982): cattle c. 12,600; sheep c. 12,400; goats c. 25,600; pigs c. 1,220; poultry c. 140,000.

Industry. Production (in 000; metric tons; 1982): crude oil 63,900; natural gas (cu m) c. 1,100,000; cement (1981) c. 1,800; tin concentrates (metal content; 1981) 2.5; petroleum products (1981) 6,565; electricity (kw-hr; 1981) 7,260,000.

STUART FRANKLIN—SYGMA

Expelled by Nigeria, Ghanaians and other unwelcome aliens crowded aboard a ship in the harbour at Lagos.

until February 28. The order affected an estimated one million nationals from Ghana, half a million from Niger, and smaller numbers from Cameroon, Chad, Benin, Togo, Upper Volta, and Ivory Coast. The expulsions were criticized, but they appeared to cause less anger in West Africa than outside the continent. By April aliens were already returning across Nigeria's fluid borders.

Odumegwu Ojukwo, the Biafran leader who had returned to Nigeria in 1982, attempted to make a political comeback by standing as an NPN candidate for the Senate in Onitsha but was unsuccessful. Gen. Yakubu Gowon, military ruler of Nigeria from 1966 until 1975, returned from exile in the U.K. in December 1983.

Meanwhile, the economy worsened, and this, coupled with the perception of President Shagari as personally honest but not tough enough to crack down on corruption, moved nationalist army officers to oust the president on December 31 and suspend the constitution. A federal military government was proclaimed by Maj. Gen. Mohammed Buhari, oil minister in the last military government. The only blood shed was that of a brigadier leading soldiers to arrest the president. Although Buhari was seen as an austere moderate-conservative, the coup appeared to have jeopardized the IMF negotiations. (GUY ARNOLD)

Norway

A constitutional monarchy of northern Europe, Norway is bordered by Sweden, Finland, and the U.S.S.R.; its coastlines are on the Skagerrak, the North Sea, the Norwegian Sea, and the Arctic Ocean. Area: 323,895 sq km (125,057 sq mi), excluding the Svalbard Archipelago, 62,049 sq km, and Jan Mayen Island, 373 sq km. Pop. (1983 est.): 4,125,600. Cap. and largest city: Oslo (pop., 1983 est., 448,000). Language: Norwegian. Religion (1980): Lutheran 87.9%. King, Olav V; prime minister in 1983, Kåre Isaachsen Willoch.

Norway's minority Conservative government was reshuffled in June 1983 to become a majority three-party coalition. The Christian People's and Centre parties, on whose support the government had depended since taking office, were given seats in the new Cabinet in proportion to their parliamentary strength; the former took charge of four portfolios and the latter three. The Conservatives continued to dominate the government, retaining the key posts of finance, defense, and foreign policy.

The smaller parties insisted that the government order an immediate reduction of interest rates in order to stimulate investment and economic activity. In return, they undertook to accept further cuts in personal income taxes in the 1984 budget, despite their belief that cuts in corporate taxes should be given priority during a period of recession.

The recession and the accompanying steady rise in unemployment figures eclipsed most other political issues. The proportion of jobless, though well below the levels of most other Western industrial countries, was high by Norwegian standards and by August had risen to 4.1% of the labour force, from 2.7% a year earlier. It would, moreover, have been even higher had not the government spent heavily on emergency job-creation programs.

In campaigning for the September local government elections, the socialist opposition parties claimed that the government was not spending enough to counter the recession. Curbs on public health and education budgets, causing long hospital waiting lists and overcrowded classrooms, were strongly criticized. They were compared with the government's promise to increase defense spending by 3.5% per year, in real terms, during the four-year life of the Storting (parliament). The small, far-right Progress Party complained that public spending (except on defense) was still too high and that tax cuts had been well below what the Conservatives had promised while in opposition.

The local election results were a severe shock to the Conservative Party. It lost votes to both left and right, and its share of the poll fell to 26.1%,

NORWAY

Education. (1981–82) Primary, pupils 383,599, teachers 30,124; secondary, pupils 282,231, teachers (1980–81) 13,517; vocational and teacher training, pupils 86,393, teachers 14,992; higher, students 71,789, teaching staff 6,695.

Finance. Monetary unit: Norwegian krone, with (Sept. 20, 1983) a free rate of 7.40 kroner to U.S. $1 (11.15 kroner = £1 sterling). Gold and other reserves (June 1983) U.S. $6,565,000,000. Budget (1983 est.): revenue 165,700,000,000 kroner; expenditure 156.2 billion kroner. Gross national product (1982) 350.9 billion kroner. Money supply (March 1983) 58,370,000,000 kroner. Cost of living (1975 = 100; June 1983) 205.

Foreign Trade. (1982) Imports 99,729,000,000 kroner; exports 113,234,000,000 kroner. Import sources: Sweden 17%; West Germany 16%; U.K. 12%; U.S. 9%; Denmark 6%; Japan 6%; Finland 5%. Export destinations: U.K. 37%; West Germany 20%; Sweden 9%; The Netherlands 6%. Main exports: crude oil 28%; natural gas 19%; machinery 7%; chemicals 6%; ships 5%.

Transport and Communications. Roads (1982) 83,371 km (including 71 km expressways). Motor vehicles in use (1982): passenger 1,337,900; commercial 166,500. Railways: (1981) 4,242 km (including 2,443 km electrified); traffic (1982) 2,240,000,000 passenger-km, freight 2,540,000,000 net ton-km. Air traffic (including Norwegian apportionment of international operations of Scandinavian Airlines System; 1982): 4,118,000,000 passenger-km; freight 139.1 million net ton-km. Shipping (1982): merchant vessels 100 gross tons and over 2,409; gross tonnage 21,861,635. Shipping traffic (1982): goods loaded 33,370,000 metric tons, unloaded 18,150,000 metric tons. Telephones (Dec. 1981) 1,992,100. Radio receivers (Dec. 1980) 1,335,000. Television licenses (Dec. 1981) 1,232,900.

Agriculture. Production (in 000; metric tons; 1982): barley 607; oats 501; potatoes 443; apples 44; milk (1981) c. 1,960; cheese 72; beef and veal (1981) c. 76; pork (1981) c. 87; fish catch (1981) 2,680; timber (cu m; 1981) 10,355. Livestock (in 000; June 1981): cattle c. 988; sheep c. 2,155; pigs c. 690; goats c. 75; chickens c. 3,775.

Industry. Fuel and power (in 000; metric tons; 1982): crude oil 24,581; coal (Svalbard mines; Norwegian operated only) 335; natural gas (cu m) 25,380,000; manufactured gas (cu m) 8,000; electricity (kw-hr) 91,871,000. Production (in 000; metric tons; 1982): iron ore (65% metal content) 3,134; pig iron 1,145; crude steel 767; aluminum 646; copper 19; zinc 79; cement 1,705; petroleum products (1981) 7,507; sulfuric acid (1980) 354; fertilizers (nutrient content; 1981–82) nitrogenous 424, phosphate 147; wood pulp (1980) mechanical 901, chemical 583; newsprint 663; other paper (1980) 816. Merchant vessels launched (100 gross tons and over; 1982) 304,000 gross tons. New dwelling units completed (1982) 38,500.

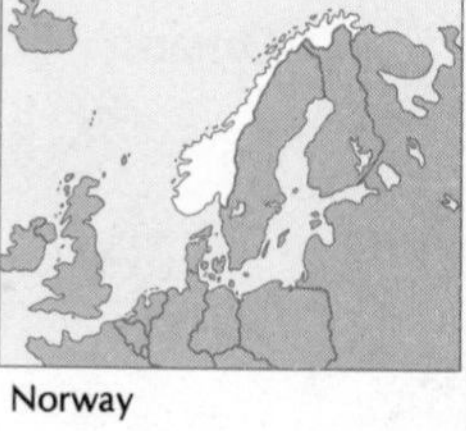
Norway

Nobel Prizes:
see People of the Year

Norwegian Literature:
see Literature

Nuclear Energy:
see Defense; Energy; Industrial Review

Numismatics:
see Philately and Numismatics

from 31.6% in the 1981 general elections and 29.7% in the 1979 local elections. Labour, the largest opposition party, increased its share to 39.3%, from 37.3% in 1981 and 36.1% in 1979. The Progress Party did even better than its most optimistic backers had forecast, gaining 6.3% of the vote, compared with 4.5% in 1981 and 2.5% in 1979.

Meanwhile, some export-oriented sectors of the economy had begun to benefit from the revival in world trade that had started toward the end of 1982; for example, the aluminum and ferroalloy industries both picked up. Despite the fall in oil prices, kroner income from offshore petroleum exports rose because of the strong U.S. dollar and a modest rise in output. Oil-related investment also increased as work began on the giant underwater Statpipe project—a pipeline that was to take gas from the northern North Sea to the European continent via a terminal on the Norwegian mainland and the Ekofisk/Emden line. Other industrial investment fell, however. Private consumption stagnated, and residential construction declined.

The budget for 1984 represented a compromise between the Conservatives and the two smaller parties in the coalition. Business and banking circles feared its inflationary effect—it was the first deficit budget that any Norwegian government had presented in five years. Middle- and upper-income groups were disappointed at the very modest personal income-tax concessions it contained.

The wrecked offshore hotel platform "Alexander L. Kielland," which had lost a leg and capsized in a North Sea storm in March 1980 and had lain upside down in a fjord near Stavanger for nearly three years, was finally uprighted in September at a cost of some 250 million kroner. Of the 123 people killed in the disaster, 36 had never been found; however, a police search of the rig after it was set upright yielded only 6 bodies. (FAY GJESTER)

See also Dependent States.

Oman

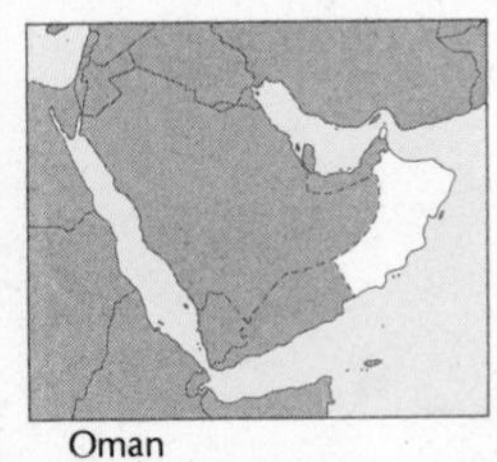

Oman

An independent sultanate, Oman occupies the southeastern part of the Arabian Peninsula and is bounded by the United Arab Emirates, Saudi Arabia, Yemen (Aden), the Gulf of Oman, and the Arabian Sea. A small part of the country lies to the north and is separated from the rest of Oman by the United Arab Emirates. Area: 300,000 sq km (120,000 sq mi). Pop.: in 1982 estimates ranged from 600,000 to 950,000; for planning purposes the government of Oman uses an estimate of 1.5 million; no census has ever been taken. Cap. and largest city: Muscat (pop., 1981 est., 50,000). Language: Arabic. Religion: Muslim (of which Ibadi 75%; Sunni 25%). Sultan and prime minister in 1983, Qabus ibn Sa'id.

Oman's relations with Yemen (Aden; South Yemen) improved in 1983: the two countries announced in October that they had agreed to reestablish diplomatic relations. A high level of military spending was maintained, as well as tight restrictions on immigration and security. Oman's strategic position at the entrance to the Strait of Hormuz, through which one-sixth of the world's oil passed, ensured its continuing importance in the regional conflict between Iran and Iraq.

OMAN

Education. (1980–81) Primary, pupils 91,895, teachers 3,959; secondary, pupils 15,280, teachers 1,733; vocational, pupils 271, teachers (1978–79) 77; teacher training, students 464, teachers 65.

Finance and Trade. Monetary unit: rial Omani, with (Sept. 20, 1983) a par value of 0.345 rial to U.S. $1 (free rate of 0.520 rial = £1 sterling). Gold and other reserves (June 1983) U.S. $1,231,000,000. Budget (1981 actual): revenue 1,076,000,000 rials; expenditure 1,028,000,000 rials. Gross national product (1981) 2,148,600,000 rials.

Foreign Trade. (1982) Imports 927 million rials; exports 1,424,000,000 rials. Import sources: Japan 21%; U.K. 14%; United Arab Emirates 14%; West Germany 8%; U.S. 8%; Bahrain 6%. Export destinations: Japan 39%; Singapore 22%; The Netherlands 8%; U.S. 7%. Main export: crude oil 99%.

Industry. Production (in 000): crude oil (metric tons; 1982) 16,002; electricity (kw-hr; 1981) 965,000.

Sultan Qabus ibn Sa'id visited the U.S. in April and further identified his country with Western policies toward the region. Oman was the only Gulf state with a military-access agreement that permitted its bases to be used by the U.S. in the event of a Gulf emergency. In late 1983 Oman was believed to be negotiating the purchase of advanced U.S. interceptor jets. In July Oman reached agreement with its allies in the Gulf Cooperation Council to jointly appropriate $1.8 billion for defense spending.

Oil production increased to about 400,000 bbl a day, bringing income back to 1981 levels, when production was 320,000 bbl a day and prices were higher. In June international banks agreed upon a $300 million loan to Oman. Foreign-exchange holdings at the start of the year were, however, low, at $1.3 billion. Development spending was controlled through a five-year (1981–85) plan, which was said to be on target. The plan was dependent on Arab aid and credit from international agencies. (JOHN WHELAN)

Pakistan

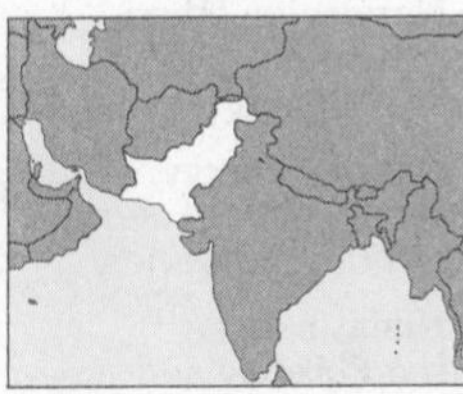

Pakistan

A federal republic, Pakistan is bordered on the south by the Arabian Sea, on the west by Afghanistan and Iran, on the north by China, and on the east by India. Area: 796,095 sq km (307,374 sq mi), excluding the Pakistani-controlled section of Jammu and Kashmir, which has an area of about 78,932 sq km. Pop. (1983 est., excluding some 2.8 million Afghan refugees): 88,220,000. Cap.: Islamabad (pop., 1981 prelim., 201,000). Largest city: Karachi (metro area pop., 1981 prelim., 5,103,000). Language: Urdu (official), English (lingua franca), Punjabi, Sindhi, and Pashto. Religion: Muslim 97% (of which Sunni 70%; Shi'ah 30%); Hindu 1.6%; Christian 1.4%. President in 1983, Gen. Mohammad Zia-ul-Haq.

In open defiance of martial law and Pres. Mohammad Zia-ul-Haq's warning that protests would be dealt with harshly, leaders of banned political parties began a campaign of national civil disobedience in Pakistan on Aug. 14, 1983. Rejecting President Zia's promise that he would hold elections by March 1985, the opposition demanded immediate restoration of the 1973 constitution and a return to a parliamentary form of government, with free elections. Thousands of supporters of the eight-party Movement for the Restoration of Democracy (MRD) gathered in Sind Province. The outpouring was striking for a country ruled by strict martial law, all the more so since Zia had warned on August 12, in an address to the nation, that he would not tolerate civil unrest.

The government admitted that 55 people had died during the disturbances, including police and what it described as saboteurs, and claimed that the unrest was restricted to four districts of Sind. MRD sources, however, suggested that at least 207 people, including 80 soldiers or policemen, had been killed. Dozens of opposition leaders were arrested. This was the first time since he seized power in July 1977 that Zia had faced violent opposition to his military rule.

In his August 12 address, Zia announced that local, provincial, national assembly, and senate elections would be held by March 23, 1985, and that provincial and national governments would be formed under his supervision. He would stay on as president, but from March 1985 his powers would be shared with a prime minister. In October Zia was reported to be considering advancing the date of elections if political conditions were favourable.

Despite domestic troubles, Zia went on several foreign tours. Relations with the U.S. in particular had improved since Zia's trip there in December 1982. U.S. Secretary of State George Shultz, visiting Pakistan in July 1983, said that his talks centred on the "long-term interest of a strong and enduring relationship between the U.S. and Pakistan." Zia went to Nepal on May 24. On February 2 Pakistan ratified an agreement with China on the establishment of joint economic, trade, scientific, and technical cooperation. Arab countries had given Pakistan $1 billion in military aid during the previous three years, while the U.S. proposed to grant $1.5 billion worth of military aid over the coming five years. The Aid-to-Pakistan Consortium met in Paris on April 19 and pledged $1.4 billion in aid, some $50 million more than Pakistan had asked.

Relations with neighbouring India improved on the surface with the setting up of a joint commission on March 10; its first meeting was held in Islamabad in June. In real terms, however, relations remained uneasy and deteriorated after Indian Prime Minister Indira Gandhi said in August that her country supported all movements for democracy anywhere in the world. Though she did not name Pakistan, the obvious reference was to the MRD.

In 1982 Pakistan suffered a balance of payments deficit of $1.6 billion, its worst ever. Despite concessionary rates from Arab countries, oil imports accounted for one-quarter of the total import bill. The sixth five-year plan, launched on July 1, envisaged total expenditure of PakRs 495 billion, including PakRs 200 billion by the private sector and PakRs 295 billion by the state sector. Energy development was allocated PakRs 100 billion, almost three times as much as it had received under the fifth plan. A PakRs 493 million outlay was earmarked for the development of nuclear energy in 1983–84. The bulk of this was to go to a nuclear-fuel reprocessing plant. (DILIP GANGULY)

STEVE McCURRY

Afghan guerrillas blend readily into Pakistan's refugee camps where they find temporary haven from Soviet attacks.

PAKISTAN

Education. (1981–82) Primary, pupils 6,451,000, teachers (1979–80) 147,000; secondary, pupils 2,080,000, teachers, including vocational, (1979–80) 129,035; vocational, pupils 39,000; higher, students 384,181, teaching staff (1979–80) 19,878.

Finance. Monetary unit: Pakistan rupee, with (Sept. 20, 1983) a free rate of PakRs 13.41 to U.S. $1 (PakRs 20.19 = £1 sterling). Gold and other reserves (June 1983) U.S. $1,980,000,000. Budget (1982–83 est.): revenue PakRs 47,206,000,000; expenditure 47,907,000,000. Gross national product (1981–82) PakRs 350,580,000,000. Money supply (June 1983) PakRs 96,495,000,000. Cost of living (1975 = 100; June 1983) 193.

Foreign Trade. (1981–82) Imports PakRs 58,565,000,000; exports PakRs 26,457,000,000. Import sources: Saudi Arabia 15%; Japan 12%; Kuwait 10%; U.S. 9%; United Arab Emirates 7%; U.K. 6%; West Germany 6%. Export destinations: Japan 8%; Saudi Arabia 7%; U.S. 7%; United Arab Emirates 6%; China 6%; U.K. 5%; Hong Kong 5%. Main exports: rice 16%; cotton 11%; cotton fabrics 11%; cotton yarn 8%; petroleum products 8%; carpets 6%; clothing 6%; leather 5%.

Transport and Communications. Roads (1982) 97,488 km. Motor vehicles in use (1980): passenger 283,000; commercial (including buses) 107,900. Railways (1982): 8,823 km; traffic 17,004,000,000 passenger-km, freight 7,206,000,000 net ton-km. Air traffic (1982): 6,425,000,000 passenger-km; freight 230.4 million net ton-km. Shipping (1982): merchant vessels 100 gross tons and over 89; gross tonnage 579,817. Telephones (June 1981) 369,000. Radio receivers (Dec. 1980) 5.5 million. Television receivers (Dec. 1980) 800,000.

Agriculture. Production (in 000; metric tons; 1982): wheat 11,570; corn 950; rice 5,053; millet 265; sorghum 230; potatoes c. 400; sugar, raw value 1,410; sugar, noncentrifugal (1981) 1,810; chick-peas 275; onions c. 435; rapeseed 238; cottonseed 1,582; mangoes c. 552; dates c. 205; oranges c. 520; tobacco 67; cotton, lint 791; beef and buffalo meat c. 354; mutton and goat meat c. 350; fish catch (1981) 318. Livestock (in 000; 1982): cattle 15,131; buffalo 12,046; sheep 30,887; goats 35,638; camels (1981) 867; chickens 76,207.

Industry. Production (in 000; metric tons; 1982): cement 3,698; crude oil 563; coal and lignite 1,819; natural gas (cu m) 9,640,000; petroleum products (1981) 4,175; electricity (kw-hr) 18,059,000; sulfuric acid 61; caustic soda 42; soda ash (1981–82) 107; nitrogenous fertilizers (nutrient content; 1981–82) 715; cotton yarn 425; woven cotton fabrics (sq m) 316,000.

Obituaries: see People of the Year

Oceanography: see Earth Sciences

Oil: see Energy

Opera: see Music

Organization of African Unity: see African Affairs

Organization of American States: see Latin-American Affairs

Ornithology: see Life Sciences

Orthodox Churches: see Religion

Painting: see Art Exhibitions; Art Sales; Museums

Paints and Varnishes: see Industrial Review

Palestine: see Israel; Jordan

Panama

A republic of Central America, Panama is bounded by the Caribbean Sea, Colombia, the Pacific Ocean, and Costa Rica. Area: 77,082 sq km (29,762 sq mi). Pop. (1983 est.): 2,088,600. Cap. and largest city: Panama City (pop., 1980 prelim., 386,400). Language: Spanish. Religion (1980 est.): Roman Catholic 92%; Muslim 4.5%; other 3.5%. President in 1983, Ricardo de la Espriella.

A record level of ships and cargo passing through the Panama Canal in 1982 and the new trans-Isthmian oil pipeline had seemed to presage a more buoyant economy for Panama, but prosperity failed to materialize in 1983. The formal inauguration of the pipeline, connecting Charco Azul on the Pacific Ocean with Chiriqui Grande on the Caribbean, took place on January 19. Panama held 40% of the shares and U.S. companies the remainder. Even before the pipeline opened, canal business had fallen off. To counter the decline, an increase of about 10% in tolls was authorized in October 1982. Other countries, notably Peru, objected strongly and demanded a voice in such decisions.

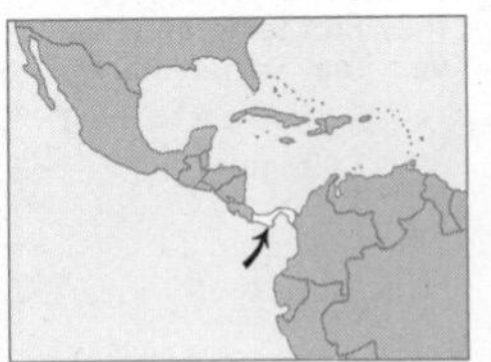

Panama

Pres. Ricardo de la Espriella ascribed rising anti-American sentiment among Panamanian labourers to new wage scales, which appeared to discriminate in favour of those hired after treaties returning control of the canal to Panama were concluded. In October 1982 he and U.S. Pres. Ronald Reagan had signed agreements that gave promise of facilitating U.S. investment and improving the canal bed.

Panamanian officials raised repeated objections to U.S. activities against the Sandinista government in Nicaragua. They viewed the sending of U.S. advisers to El Salvador from bases on the Isthmus as an infringement of Panama's neutrality and urged that surveillance flights by U.S. military planes be confined to canal defense. U.S. naval maneuvers in waters bordering the Isthmus also created tension. At several meetings the so-called Contadora Group, which included Colombia, Mexico, and Venezuela as well as Panama, expressed anxiety that Central America might become involved in a major East-West confrontation.

Foreign ministers from several Latin-American countries seeking peace in Central America honoured the late Panamanian leader Omar Torrijos at this mausoleum in Panama. The ministers pictured are, from left, José Zambrano Velasco (Venezuela), Bernardo Sepúlveda Amor (Mexico), Fidel Chávez Mena (El Salvador), Edgardo Paz Barnica (Honduras), Rodrigo Lloreda Caicedo (Colombia), Miguel d'Escoto Brockman (Nicaragua), and Juan José Amado (Panama).

WIDE WORLD

PANAMA

Education. (1982) Primary, pupils 336,740, teachers 12,853; secondary, pupils 129,203, teachers 6,502; vocational, pupils 44,364, teachers 2,379; teacher training, students 1,224, teachers 43; higher, students 45,361, teaching staff 3,456.

Finance. Monetary unit: balboa, at par with the U.S. dollar, with a free rate (Sept. 20, 1983) of 1.51 balboas to £1 sterling. Gold and other reserves (May 1983) U.S. $83 million. Budget (1982 actual): revenue 1,055,000,000 balboas; expenditure 1,395,000,000 balboas. Gross national product (1980) 3,247,000,000 balboas. Cost of living (Panama City; 1975 = 100; June 1983) 158.5.

Foreign Trade. (1982) Imports 1,569,300,000 balboas; exports 371,510,000 balboas. Import sources (1981): U.S. 35%; Venezuela 8%; Mexico 8%; Saudi Arabia 8%; Japan 6%. Export destinations (1981): U.S. 51%; West Germany 7%; Italy 5%. Main exports: petroleum products 19%; bananas 18%; shrimps 14%; sugar 6%.

Transport and Communications. Roads (1980) 8,612 km. Motor vehicles in use (1979): passenger 97,300; commercial 25,800. Railways (1980) 552 km. Air traffic (1982): c. 400 million passenger-km; freight c. 15 million net ton-km. Shipping (1982): merchant vessels 100 gross tons and over 5,032 (mostly owned by U.S. and other foreign interests); gross tonnage 32,600,278. Panama Canal traffic (1981–82): vessels 14,009; cargo carried 188.4 million metric tons. Telephones (Dec. 1981) 185,300. Radio receivers (Dec. 1980) 285,000. Television receivers (Dec. 1980) 220,000.

Agriculture. Production (in 000; metric tons; 1982): rice c. 150; corn c. 70; sugar, raw value (1981) c. 187; mangoes c. 27; bananas c. 1,100; oranges c. 64; coffee c. 8; fish catch (1981) 132. Livestock (in 000; 1981): cattle c. 1,604; pigs c. 202; horses c. 166; chickens c. 5,195.

Industry. Production (in 000; metric tons; 1981): cement c. 600; petroleum products 1,940; electricity (kw-hr) 2,565,000.

Gen. Rubén Darío Paredes del Río, who disagreed with this attitude toward the U.S., resigned as commander of the National Guard in August. He had indicated his intention to run for president in 1984 but gave up this objective late in the year.

Pope John Paul II visited Panama during his tour of the region in March.

(ALMON R. WRIGHT)

Papua New Guinea

Papua New Guinea is an independent parliamentary state and a member of the Commonwealth. It is situated in the southwest Pacific and comprises the eastern part of the island of New Guinea, the islands of the Bismarck, Trobriand, Woodlark, Louisiade, and D'Entrecasteaux groups, and parts of the Solomon Islands, including Bougainville. It is separated from Australia by the Torres Strait. Area: 462,840 sq km (178,704 sq mi). Pop. (1983 est.): 3,259,000. Cap. and largest city: Port Moresby (pop., 1982 est., 141,000). Language: English, Hiri or Police Motu (a Melanesian pidgin), and Pisin (also called Pidgin English or Neo-Melanesian) are official, although the last is the most widely spoken. Religion (1980): Protestant 63.8%; Roman Catholic 32.8%; tribal 2.5%; other 0.9%. Queen, Elizabeth II; governors-general in 1983, Sir Tore Lokoloko and, from March 1, Sir Kingsford Dibela; prime minister, Michael Somare.

During 1983 Papua New Guinea, hard hit by the world economic recession, successfully lobbied for a reduction in the rate of cuts in Australian aid.

PAPUA NEW GUINEA

Education. (1981) Primary, pupils 300,536, teachers 9,935; secondary, pupils 39,701, teachers 1,625; vocational, pupils 7,984, teachers 499; teacher training, students 1,649, teachers 165; higher (1980), students 2,224, teaching staff 413.

Finance. Monetary unit: kina, with (Sept. 20, 1983) a free rate of 0.87 kina to U.S. $1 (1.31 kinas = £1 sterling). Gold and other reserves (June 1983) U.S. $325 million. Budget (central government; 1980 actual): revenue 339.2 million kinas (excludes grants of 174.6 million kinas); expenditure 496.6 million kinas.

Foreign Trade. (1982) Imports 888 million kinas; exports 524 million kinas. Import sources: Australia 41%; Singapore 15%; Japan 14%; U.S. 9%; New Zealand 5%. Export destinations: Japan 34%; West Germany 27%; Australia 9%; U.K. 6%; Spain 5%. Main exports: copper concentrates 46%; coffee 14%; timber c. 6%; cocoa 6%; coconut products 5%.

Transport. Roads (1976) 19,538 km. Motor vehicles in use (1981): passenger 17,700; commercial 24,400. There are no railways. Air traffic (1982): 527 million passenger-km; freight c. 10 million net ton-km. Shipping (1982): merchant vessels 100 gross tons and over 80; gross tonnage 24,699.

Agriculture. Production (in 000; metric tons; 1982): bananas c. 949; cassava (1981) c. 96; taro c. 250; yams c. 200; palm oil c. 45; cocoa 31; coffee c. 54; copra 135; tea c. 8; rubber c. 4; timber (cu m; 1981) c. 6,088. Livestock (in 000; 1981): cattle c. 132; pigs c. 1,410; goats c. 16; chickens c. 1,400.

Industry. Production (in 000; 1981): copper ore (metal content; metric tons) 165; silver (troy oz) 1,363; gold (troy oz) 540; electricity (kw-hr) 1,237,000.

Strong links were also maintained with New Zealand, whose prime minister, Robert Muldoon, made an official visit to Papua New Guinea in February. Muldoon promised more aid and inspected projects already established, including an experimental sheep farm, a timber industry training centre, and a beekeeping enterprise.

Papua New Guinea's foreign minister, Rabbie Namaliu, met Solomon Islands representatives in March and canvassed the idea of a Melanesian alliance between Papua New Guinea, the Solomon Islands, and Vanuatu to protect regional fishing grounds from illegal foreign trawling. Relations with Indonesia again proved troublesome; Indonesia incorrectly sited major construction on the Papua New Guinea side of the joint border.

(A. R. G. GRIFFITHS)

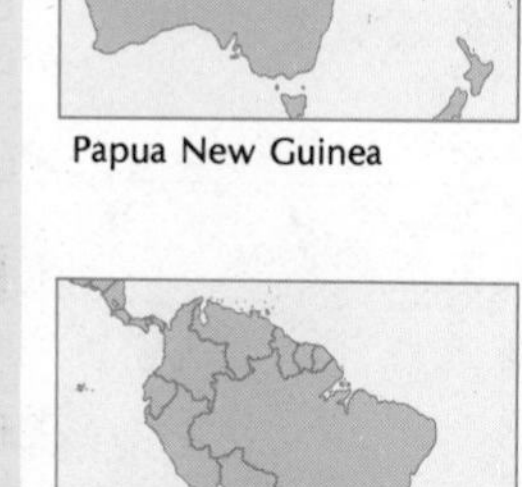

Papua New Guinea

Paraguay

A landlocked republic of South America, Paraguay is bounded by Brazil, Argentina, and Bolivia. Area: 406,752 sq km (157,048 sq mi). Pop. (1982 prelim.): 3,026,200. Cap. and largest city: Asunción (metro. pop., 1982 prelim., 794,200). Language: Spanish (official), though Guaraní is understood by more than 90% of the population. Religion: Roman Catholic (official). President in 1983, Gen. Alfredo Stroessner.

Pres. Alfredo Stroessner was reelected for a seventh term in February 1983. On election day a group of exiled opposition politicians attempted to return to the country but were turned back at the airport. A month before the new term formally began in August, Msgr. Ismael Rolón, archbishop of Asunción, called for the lifting of Paraguay's 25-year-old state-of-siege regulations. The leading opposition party, the Partido Liberal Radical, also called for political liberalization.

Despite the lack of a political alternative, the business class showed impatience with the administration's conservative economic policies, particularly its insistence on maintaining the parity of the guaraní in the face of the exhaustion of foreign currency reserves, a fall in gross domestic product, and rising unemployment. Heavy rains in the first quarter caused the worst flooding in a century.

PARAGUAY

Education. (1981) Primary, pupils 530,083, teachers 19,748; secondary and vocational, pupils 124,481, teachers (1980) 9,830; higher (universities only), students 27,138, teaching staff 2,017.

Finance. Monetary unit: guaraní, with (Sept. 20, 1983) an official rate of 126 guaranis to U.S. $1 (free rate of 190 guaranis = £1 sterling) and a noncommercial rate of 160 guaranis to U.S. $1 (free rate of 241 guaranis = £1 sterling). Gold and other reserves (June 1983) U.S. $679 million. Budget (1981 est.): revenue 64,626,000,000 guaranis; expenditure 70,908,000,000 guaranis. Gross national product (1981) 681.1 billion guaranis. Money supply (June 1982) 60,186,000,000 guaranis. Cost of living (Asunción; 1975 = 100; June 1983) 269.4.

Foreign Trade. (1982) Imports 91,936,000,000 guaranis; exports 47,259,000,000 guaranis. Import sources: Brazil 27%; Argentina 19%; Algeria 13%; U.S. 8%; West Germany 6%; U.K. 6%; Japan 6%. Export destinations: Brazil 25%; Argentina 18%; West Germany 13%; Japan 8%; The Netherlands 5%. Main exports: cotton 37%; soybeans 27%; timber 13%; vegetable oils 6%.

Transport and Communications. Roads (1981) 12,703 km. Motor vehicles in use (1980): passenger 39,000; commercial 33,500. Railways: (main; 1981) 441 km; traffic (1977) 23 million passenger-km, freight (1981) 23 million net ton-km. Air traffic (1982): 479 million passenger-km; freight c. 2.9 million net ton-km. Navigable inland waterways (including Paraguay-Paraná River system; 1982) c. 3,000 km. Telephones (Dec. 1981) 64,300. Radio receivers (Dec. 1980) 190,000. Television receivers (Dec. 1980) 60,000.

Agriculture. Production (in 000; metric tons; 1982): corn c. 620; cassava c. 2,000; sweet potatoes (1981) c. 115; soybeans c. 600; dry beans c. 70; sugar, raw value (1981) c. 80; tomatoes c. 67; oranges c. 227; bananas c. 314; palm kernels c. 15; tobacco 12; cottonseed c. 190; cotton, lint c. 90; beef and veal (1981) c. 98. Livestock (in 000; 1981): cattle c. 5,400; sheep c. 430; pigs c. 1,310; horses c. 330; chickens c. 13,300.

Industry. Production (in 000; metric tons; 1981): cement 161; petroleum products 240; cotton yarn (1980) 75; electricity (kw-hr) 1,014,000.

Paraguay

UPI

"Secure the future," read campaign posters for Gen. Alfredo Stroessner, whose future was secured by his reelection as president of Paraguay, after 29 years in that office.

Paper and Pulp: see Industrial Review

Parachuting: see Aerial Sports

Penology: see Prisons and Penology

Pentecostal Churches: see Religion

President Stroessner named three new Cabinet ministers. Augusto Saldívar replaced Alberto Nogués as foreign minister, while Saúl González, a populist politician disliked by the military, was removed from his post as minister of justice and labour. Gen. Germán Martínez took over as minister of defense from Gen. Marcial Samaniego.

(MICHAEL WOOLLER)

Peru

Peru

A republic on the west coast of South America, Peru is bounded by Ecuador, Colombia, Brazil, Bolivia, Chile, and the Pacific Ocean. Area: 1,285,215 sq km (496,224 sq mi). Pop. (1982 est.): 17,400,600, including 46% Indian; 38% mestizo; 12% white; and 4% other. Cap. and largest city: Lima (metro. area pop., 1981 prelim., 4,600,900). Language: Spanish and Quechua are official; Indians also speak Aymara. Religion (1982): Roman Catholic (92%). President in 1983, Fernando Belaúnde Terry; prime minister, Fernando Schwalb López Aldana.

Prime Minister Fernando Schwalb López Aldana, who took office in December 1982, appointed nine new ministers in a Cabinet reshuffle in January 1983. Subsequently, Interior Minister Fernando Rincón was replaced by Luis Pércovich Roca in April, and in July Patricio Ricketts became minister of labour in place of Alfonso Grados Bertorini.

Municipal elections held in November 1983, heralded as an advance indication of the results of the 1985 presidential election, brought major victories for the left and centre-left opposition parties. Opinion polls suggested that Pres. Fernando Belaúnde Terry's popularity had fallen from 70% of the electorate in November 1980 to 20%. His ruling Acción Popular (AP) party was expected to receive 20% of the votes in the municipal elections, 10% less than the main opposition Alianza Popular Revolucionaria Americana. Nevertheless, AP's congressional dominance was maintained by its renewed alliance with the Partido Popular Cristiano.

These guerrillas of the Sendero Luminoso (Shining Path) movement, imprisoned on an island in Peru, have been accorded the status of political prisoners.

OSCAR MEDRANO/LARAFLET—GAMMA/LIAISON

PERU

Education. (1980) Primary, pupils 3,161,400, teachers (1979) 80,331; secondary and vocational, pupils 1,362,600, teachers (1978) 37,383; higher, students 249,800, teaching staff (1977) 13,468.

Finance. Monetary unit: sol, with (Sept. 20, 1983) a free rate of 2,043 soles to U.S. $1 (3,077 soles = £1 sterling). Gold and other reserves (June 1983) U.S. $1,647,000,000. Budget (total; 1982 actual): revenue 2,484,700,000,000 soles; expenditure 3,037,800,000,000 soles. Gross national product (1981) 8,348,000,000,000 soles. Money supply (June 1983) 1,998,400,000,000 soles. Cost of living (Lima; 1975 = 100; May 1983) 4,117.

Foreign Trade. (1982) Imports 2,512,000,000,000 soles; exports 2,258,000,000,000 soles. Import sources: (1981): U.S. 33%; Japan 9%; West Germany 7%; Brazil 6%. Export destinations (1981): U.S. 33%; Japan 15%. Main exports: crude oil 16%; copper 14%; zinc 8%; petroleum products 7%; silver 6%; fish meal 6%; lead 6%.

Transport and Communications. Roads (1979) 56,642 km. Motor vehicles in use (1980): passenger c. 318,700; commercial (including buses) c. 169,900. Railways (1979): 2,508 km; traffic 494 million passenger-km, freight c. 620 million net ton-km. Air traffic (1982): 1,685,000,000 passenger-km; freight c. 94.3 million net ton-km. Shipping (1982): merchant vessels 100 gross tons and over 696; gross tonnage 836,326. Telephones (Dec. 1980) 475,000. Radio receivers (Dec. 1980) 2,750,000. Television receivers (Dec. 1980) 850,000.

Agriculture. Production (in 000; metric tons; 1982): rice 765; corn 625; wheat (1981) c. 117; barley c. 155; potatoes 1,832; sweet potatoes (1981) c. 151; cassava c. 420; sugar, raw value c. 700; onions c. 153; oranges c. 153; lemons c. 93; coffee c. 90; cotton, lint c. 76; fish catch (1981) 2,751. Livestock (in 000; 1982): cattle c. 3,600; sheep c. 14,500; pigs c. 2,000; goats c. 1,900; horses c. 650; poultry c. 39,000.

Industry. Production (in 000; metric tons; 1981): cement c. 2,500; crude oil (1982) 9,624; natural gas (cu m; 1982) c. 1,340,000; iron ore (60% metal content) 5,660; pig iron (1980) 261; crude steel 350; zinc ore (metal content) 497; tungsten concentrates (metal content) 0.55; copper (1982) 226; lead (1982) 78; gold (troy oz) 800; silver (troy oz) 46,900; fish meal 350; petroleum products 6,812; electricity (kw-hr) 10,100,000.

A severe threat to Peru's democratic stability was posed by the Maoist guerrilla group Sendero Luminoso (Shining Path). In one attack by the group at the end of May, Lima's electricity supply was cut and the Bayer International chemical works was destroyed. When AP party headquarters in Lima was bombed, 2 people were killed and 33 wounded. After this attack, President Belaúnde called publicly for the reinstatement of the death penalty for terrorism. A state of emergency in the five provinces around Ayacucho, southeast of Lima, was extended to the whole country in May but was lifted in September.

In January eight Peruvian journalists were killed by the inhabitants of Uchuraccay, near Ayacucho. A commission led by novelist Mario Vargas Llosa reported that the villagers believed the journalists to be Senderistas. The report criticized the Army for urging villagers to take the law into their own hands when they encountered suspected terrorists, but it cleared the security forces of any blame in the journalists' murder. Regardless of the report, Sendero Luminoso took its own reprisals in the Uchuraccay region, killing about 70 people. An Amnesty International report, while condemning killings perpetrated by the guerrillas, said that counterinsurgency measures by the security forces and civilian antiguerrilla units had led to an unacceptable number of deaths. Amnesty disputed the earlier report's findings that the journalists were attacked without their identities as journalists being known. President Belaúnde strongly rejected Amnesty's accusations.

During the year the government faced strikes by miners, bank workers, paramilitary civil guards, and others. General strikes were organized in March, when three people were killed during demonstrations, and September, when 50 were arrested. The principal concerns of the labour movements were that wages were insufficient to compensate for an inflation rate of over 115% and that by September only 41% of the work force was in full employment. Prime causes for the deterioration were the recession and austerity measures introduced in consultation with the International Monetary Fund.

Industry was also facing a crisis. Manufacturing recorded negative growth of 16.8% in the first half of 1983 compared with the same period in 1982, and the rate of bankruptcies soared. The fish meal industry had to contend with drastically reduced catches because the warm El Niño current drove anchovy shoals away from Peruvian waters. El Niño's presence, and the resulting change in weather patterns, brought floods to the north of the country and drought to the south, devastating crops of cotton, potatoes, sugar, and other foodstuffs.

Poor export returns, therefore, caused Peru to approach the Club of Paris banking group to reschedule $1,040,000,000 of government debts at the end of July, one month after its debt to international banks had been rescheduled. In September the government also renegotiated its debt with the U.S.S.R.

(BEN BOX)

Philately and Numismatics

Stamps. Toward the end of 1983 there was a clear improvement in the market for better-class stamps. Items that slumped badly following the intensive speculative buying of 1981–82 showed strong signs of recovering to normal levels. There was no worldwide "omnibus" series to tempt speculation, and firms offering investment portfolios to nonphilatelists found fewer buyers.

A remarkable number of important single-country collections were auctioned during the year. Among the sales exceeding £100,000 were the Patrick Pearson Ceylon (Harmer's, London), £101,040; the Stuart Rossiter postal history of East Africa (Sotheby's, London), £133,983; the J. A. Naylor collection of Malaya and North Borneo (Harmer's, London), £115,680; and the Charles Robertson Austria and Austrian Italy (Harmer's, London), £142,237. These sales followed the October 1982 record one-country realization of £1,037,830 for the late Sir Joseph Maxwell's collection of the Cape of Good Hope (Sotheby's, London). Two unusual specialized sales were the Hayman Cummings collection of Oxford and Cambridge college stamps (last sold privately by the original owner in 1908 for £250), for which Robson Lowe realized £10,298, and a collection of British and Commonwealth "Specimen" stamps, formerly considered of little value, which Harmer's sold for £124,281.

There were three International Philatelic Federation (FIP)-sponsored international exhibitions. In May TEMBAL, the fourth international thematic (topical) exhibition, was held in Basel, Switz. The major awards were: Grand Prix, Luciano Viti (Italy) for "Venice—Story of a City"; Prix International des Collections Thématiques, Hans Paikert (West Germany) for "League of Nations"; Prix International des Collections Documentaires, Dietrich Oldenburg (West Germany) for "UPU and Its Jubilees." In August BANGKOK 83, an all-classes international, was held in the Thai capital. Major awards were: FIP Grand Prix d'Honneur, John O. Griffiths (U.S.) for classical Australian states 1855–80; Grand Prix International, John Foxbridge (U.S.) for 19th-century Samoa; Grand Prix National, Prakaipet Indhusophon (Thailand) for Siam, pre-stamp to end of Chulalongkorn issues. At BRASILIANA 83, in Rio de Janeiro in August, the major awards were: FIP Grand Prix d'Honneur, Purnendu Gupta (India) for Nepal; Grand Prix International, Feridoun N. Farahbakhsh (Iran) for early Lion stamps Persia; Grand Prix National, Norman S. Hubbard (U.S.) for Brazil 1843. The first competitive international exhibition restricted to philatelic literature, held in Milan, Italy, in November 1982, attracted over 500 entries in four classes.

At the British Philatelic Federation (BPF) congress, held in Bath, four new signatories to the Roll of Distinguished Philatelists were Max Hertsch (Switz.), Alan K. Huggins (Great Britain), Walter E. Tinsley (U.S.), and Deoki N. Jatia (India)—the first Indian to sign the Roll since its inception in 1921. The BPF Congress medal was awarded to George O. I. Hollings of London. The Lichtenstein Medal of the Collectors Club of New York went to George W. Brett (U.S.). In June John B. Marriott, keeper of the Royal Philatelic Collections at Buckingham Palace, was elected president of the Royal Philatelic Society, London.

(KENNETH F. CHAPMAN)

Coins. Several countries issued new coins in 1983, either to reduce the cost of making money or, in a few cases, to raise funds for special causes. The British Royal Mint released a one-pound coin to circulation on April 21, the 57th birthday of Queen Elizabeth II. Officials predicted that the nickel-brass pound, the first such coin in British history, would greatly lessen the need for paper one-pound notes, thus cutting production expenses. Each coin should last for 40 years or more, compared with the 12-month life span of a typical one-pound note. Many British citizens refused to use the pale-yellow coin, however, complaining of its 9.5-gram (0.34-oz) weight, among other things. The 1983-dated specimen depicts Britain's royal coat of arms and Queen Elizabeth. An inscription around the outer edge reads "decus et tutamen," Latin for "an ornament and a safeguard."

In the U.S. a commemorative coin program was being promoted to help finance the 1984 Summer Olympics in Los Angeles, but sales were falling short of the goal set by Congress. Two types of silver dollars and a $10 gold coin, each depicting an Olympic scene, were being offered to collectors. By year's end the Bureau of the Mint had failed to

Petroleum: see Energy

Pharmaceutical Industry: see Industrial Review

A new one-pound coin made of nickel and brass was issued by the British Royal Mint to commemorate the 57th birthday of Queen Elizabeth II. Each coin is expected to stay in service for at least 40 years.

sell even 5% of the 52 million coins it was permitted to make under federal law. Some experts suggested that the coins were too expensive. In late 1983 the government charged $416 for the set of three proof coins, with $70 of the price going to the U.S. and Los Angeles Olympic committees. If all 52 million pieces were sold by the end of 1984—an unlikely prospect judging from 1983 results—the Olympics would receive $600 million. Meanwhile, the National Bank of Yugoslavia issued most of the 18 official government coins minted to raise money for the 1984 Winter Olympics in Sarajevo. The bank was selling the 15 silver and 3 gold coins to collectors throughout the world.

In September 1983 Mexican Pres. Miguel de la Madrid Hurtado proposed legislation to reform the country's monetary system, badly battered by inflation. If it was approved, the government would gradually withdraw all coins from circulation, perhaps starting in early 1984, and produce eight new pieces denominated from 1 to 200 pesos. The proposal would eliminate the 20-centavo and 50-centavo pieces, which cost more to make than their face values. In late 1983 the 50-centavo coin was worth about one-third of a U.S. cent.

Persons owning collectible coins watched their investments edge upward in value during 1983, a turnabout from the declining market during much of the two previous years. Prices for the rarest dates improved most, judging from the results of major auctions. However, some dealers of "bullion coins" filed for bankruptcy during the year, victims of poor business practices and a stagnant market for gold and silver. The International Gold Bullion Exchange of Fort Lauderdale, Fla., once one of the largest retailers of precious metals in the U.S., went out of business in April. Officials were investigating what happened to $40 million or more in orders sent to the firm by thousands of investors who never received the bullion.

Many U.S. collectors searched their pocket change for 1982-dated dimes without mint marks, the country's most publicized error coin of the past decade. Government workers apparently forgot to punch a mint letter into just one of hundreds of dies used to make dimes in 1982, and that die produced 12,000 or more coins. Prices for the errors fluctuated with reports of new finds, but many dealers paid $80 or more for an uncirculated specimen. (ROGER BOYE)

[452.D.2.b; 725.B.4.g]

Philippines

Situated in the western Pacific Ocean off the southeast coast of Asia, the Republic of the Philippines consists of an archipelago of about 7,100 islands. Area: 300,000 sq km (115,800 sq mi). Pop. (1983 est.): 50,926,000. Cap. and largest city: Manila (pop., metro. area, 1980, 5,925,900). Language: Pilipino and English are the official languages. Pilipino, the national language, is based on a local language called Tagalog and is spoken by 55.2% of the population but only by 23.8% as a mother tongue. English is spoken by 44.7% of the population but only by 0.04% as a mother tongue. Other important languages spoken as mother tongues include Cebuano 24.4%; Ilocano 11.1%; Hiligaynon 8%; Bicol 7%. Religion (1970): Roman Catholic 85%; Muslim 4.3%; Aglipayan 3.9%; Protestant 3.1%. President in 1983, Ferdinand E. Marcos; prime minister, Cesar Virata.

The most prominent opposition political leader, Benigno S. Aquino, Jr. (*see* OBITUARIES), was shot to death on Aug. 21, 1983, at Manila International Airport. Aquino was returning from three years of voluntary exile in the United States. In a statement prepared for his return, he said he planned to join those struggling through nonviolence to restore "the rights and freedoms of our people."

Aquino's plane was met by three soldiers who escorted him from it while barring his traveling companions from following. As he was being led away, he was killed by a single shot in the back of the head. After other shots, a second man's body lay nearby. The government identified him as Rolando Galman y Dawang, said he had shot Aquino, and called him a "notorious killer, a gun for hire." No motive was offered.

The suspicious circumstances caused national and international demands for explanations. Pres. Ferdinand Marcos denounced the murder. He said, "The government will apply all its resources and powers toward unearthing every and all aspects, and bring the perpetrators to justice." On August 24 he named an investigating commission headed by the chief justice of the Supreme Court, Enrique Fernando. A former chief justice declined to serve, and the independence and objectivity of the commission were challenged by lawsuits of opposition political leaders. By October 10 the entire commission had resigned because of these challenges and called for a new, independent, nonpolitical commission. On October 22 Marcos swore in a new one, which as the year ended turned up witnesses who denied that Galman had shot Aquino. The inquiry continued.

Hundreds of thousands of Filipinos viewed Aquino's body during an unprecedented period of public mourning, and more than a million persons watched the funeral procession on August 31. In a funeral mass, Jaime Cardinal Sin, leader of the Roman Catholic Church, to which most Filipinos belong, said that Aquino "personified Filipino courage in the face of oppression." The nation, he said, had the "atmosphere of oppression and corruption, the climate of fear and anguish."

Demonstrations to denounce the murder turned into a continuing series of public gatherings that called for Marcos to step down after 17 years as president. In December Marcos, whose health was reportedly poor, accepted a formula approved by his party providing for the succession in case of the president's death or disability. Earlier, his wife, Imelda, had renounced any ambition to succeed her husband.

Some demonstrations were anti-U.S. as well as anti-Marcos. On June 1 Filipino and U.S. negotiators had signed an agreement to extend U.S. use of Clark Air Base and Subic Bay Naval Base for another five years beginning Oct. 1, 1984. The United States agreed to pay $900 million in security assistance for use of the bases for the next five years. Demonstrators charged that the U.S. supported Marcos in order to use the bases, the largest U.S. military installations outside the United States. In this atmosphere, U.S. Pres. Ronald Reagan announced on October 3 that the pressure of congressional business forced him to postpone visits scheduled for November to the Philippines and also to Indonesia and Thailand.

The turmoil complicated already grave economic problems. After a record balance of payments deficit of $1,140,000,000 in 1982, the peso was devalued by 7.3% on June 23. Foreign aid donors responded by promising to try to raise the annual aid total above the $1.2 billion of recent years. However, uncertainty about the Philippines' future after Aquino's assassination caused further financial problems. The payments deficit for July through September was $800 million. The peso was devalued another 21.4% on October 5.

The Communist New People's Army continued to gain strength in remote areas. On September 29 it ambushed a truck near Zamboanga, killing 39 soldiers and 7 civilians. This was the largest government loss in a single Communist attack during more than a decade of low-level guerrilla warfare.

(HENRY S. BRADSHER)

PHILIPPINES

Education. (1980–81) Primary, pupils 8,033,642, teachers 264,241; secondary and vocational, pupils 2,928,525, teachers 85,779; higher (1979–80), students 1,182,103, teaching staff 40,022.

Finance. Monetary unit: peso, with (Sept. 20, 1983) a free rate of 11.01 pesos to U.S. $1 (16.58 pesos = £1 sterling). Gold and other reserves (June 1983) U.S. $1,745,000,000. Budget (1982 actual): revenue 37,710,000,000 pesos; expenditure 40,821,000,000 pesos. Gross national product (1982) 336 billion pesos. Money supply (June 1983) 23,040,000,000 pesos. Cost of living (1975 = 100; June 1983) 230.6.

Foreign Trade. (1982) Imports 70,569,000,000 pesos; exports 42,411,000,000 pesos. Import sources: U.S. 22%; Japan 20%; Saudi Arabia 12%. Export destinations: U.S. 31%; Japan 23%. Main exports: electronic devices 17%; clothing 11%; metal ores 11%; coconut oil 8%; sugar 8%; fruit and vegetables 7%. Tourism (1981): visitors 939,000; gross receipts U.S. $344 million.

Transport and Communications. Roads (1982) 154,421 km. Motor vehicles in use (1980): passenger 465,200; commercial 294,800. Railways: (main; 1980) 1,177 km; traffic (1982) 209 million passenger-km, freight 22 million net ton-km. Air traffic (1982): *c.* 7,369,000,000 passenger-km; freight *c.* 187.1 million net ton-km. Shipping (1982): merchant vessels 100 gross tons and over 882; gross tonnage 2,773,855. Telephones (Jan. 1981) 537,800. Radio receivers (Dec. 1980) 2.1 million. Television receivers (Dec. 1980) 1 million.

Agriculture. Production (in 000; metric tons; 1982): rice 8,346; corn 3,475; sweet potatoes (1981) *c.* 1,100; cassava (1981) *c.* 2,300; sugar, raw value 2,527; bananas *c.* 4,100; pineapples *c.* 871; copra *c.* 2,115; coffee *c.* 160; tobacco *c.* 39; rubber *c.* 70; pork *c.* 454; fish catch (1981) 1,651; timber (cu m; 1981) 34,848. Livestock (in 000; March 1982): cattle *c.* 1,950; buffalo *c.* 2,800; pigs *c.* 7,800; goats *c.* 1,600; horses *c.* 330; chickens *c.* 58,000.

Industry. Production (in 000; metric tons; 1982): coal 552; cement 4,393; chrome ore (oxide content; 1981) *c.* 126; copper concentrates (metal content) 950; gold (troy oz) *c.* 840; silver (troy oz; 1981) 2,023; petroleum products (1981) 9,662; sulfuric acid (1979) 210; cotton yarn (1980) 38; electricity (kw-hr) 17,651,000.

Photography

General photographic activity as reflected in film consumption and volume of photofinishing increased modestly in 1983, but the manufacturers of cameras and accessories continued to experience difficulties in a highly competitive environment. The Disc camera did not fulfill expectations, and sales of 35-mm single-lens-reflex (SLR) cameras remained level or declined slightly. Front-shutter compact 35-mm cameras, however, continued to grow in popularity. Improved economic conditions in the U.S. revived the photographic art market in that country.

Photo Equipment. New 35-mm cameras appeared with novel systems for automatically determining exposure. The Nikon FA, for example, featured automatic multipattern metering (AMP), in which the scene within the viewfinder was divided into five segments and an array of silicon photodiodes read the brightness of each segment. This information was converted into digital light values and fed into a microcomputer, which evaluated the scene in terms of brightness range and contrast. The evaluation was compared with data stored in the computer's memory, information based on a human-eye assessment of some 100,000 photographs that had been analyzed from both technical and esthetic standpoints. Working with this information the microcomputer made a final decision on exposure designed to yield optimum quality. The entire complex procedure required only a fraction of a second to complete. The AMP system was particularly effective in handling backlighted subjects and scenes containing high contrast, which typically mislead automatic metering systems. If not wanted, the AMP could be switched off, leaving the user with conventional Nikon centre-weighted metering.

The FA was a multimode camera, providing a dual-programmed mode that selected higher shutter speeds when used with certain Nikon lenses of 135-mm focal length or longer, as well as shutter-priority, aperture-priority, and manual modes, and through-the-lens flash exposure automation. It included a titanium focal-plane shutter providing a top speed of 1/4,000 sec and electronic flash synchronization at 1/250 sec.

Olympus updated its line of 35-mm SLR cameras with the OM-3 and OM-4, both of which gave a choice of multiple-spot or average metering. A portion of the light from the lens was directed to the floor of the mirror chamber, where a lens system focused it onto a specially designed silicon photo-

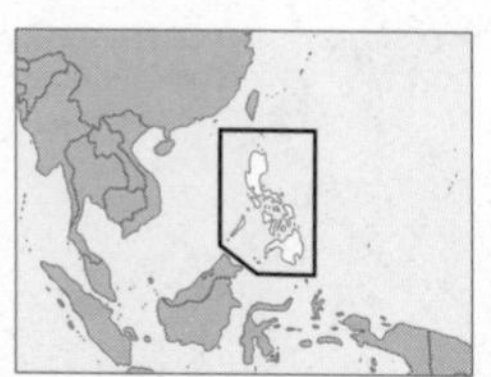
Philippines

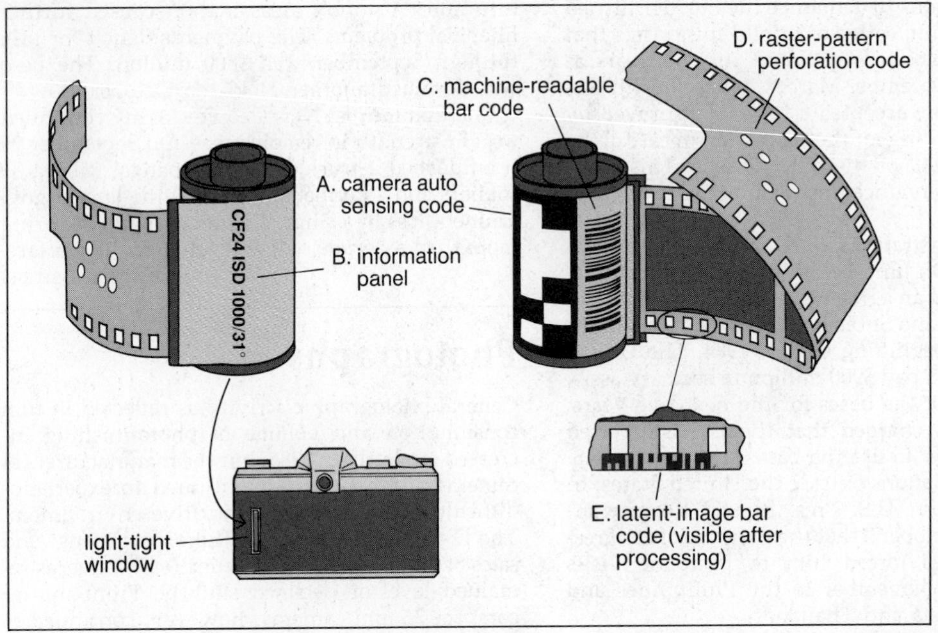

Kodak's new DX film system employs optical, electrical, and mechanical encodings. Electrically conducting patches on the film cartridge (A) tell the camera the film speed and latitude (ability to produce good pictures even when the film is underexposed or overexposed). Lettering on the cartridge (B), which gives film type and number of exposures, is readable through a window on the back of the camera. When the exposed film arrives at the photo lab, it is automatically sorted using the bar code on the cartridge (C). Perforation coding on the film leader (D) provides a darkroom double-check to ensure that the film has been sorted correctly. After film processing, a code on the edge of the film appears (E), identifying the maker and type of film for automatic-printing machinery. Although the film system is presently available, the cameras and processing machinery able to "read" the codings are still in the development stage.

cell. An outer ring of the photocell provided centre-weighted average readings. The centre of the photocell gave spot readings of a small ringed area visible in the centre of the viewfinding screen. As many as eight spot readings could be made of different areas in a scene, while the camera's computer recorded them and calculated a median reading to determine the actual exposure. The exposure reading was displayed on a liquid-crystal display strip below the camera's viewing screen. The OM-4 had an electronically governed shutter that offered a top speed of 1/2,000 sec and automated aperture-preferred or manual exposure modes; the OM-3's mechanically governed shutter did not provide exposure automation.

The popularity of front-shutter compact 35-mm cameras continued to rise, and the number of models proliferated. Designed for the utmost in user convenience, these cameras provided almost total automation in some cases, including automatic exposure programming, automatic film advance, automatic film rewind, and automatic focusing. Some automatically switched to the flash mode at low light levels while others used blinking lights, beepers, or both to convey information and warnings to the user. Minolta's "Talker" carried this concept to an extreme: it featured three prerecorded verbal instructions to guide the camera's operator: "load film," "too dark—use flash," and "check distance."

Eastman Kodak announced a new electronic-plus-mechanical coding system, designated DX, for 35-mm film and cartridges. When used in an appropriately modified camera, DX coding could automatically set the correct ISO (ASA) film-speed index. In addition, the DX system could indicate which frame is being exposed, signal for automatic film rewind, and supply a variety of useful information to automated photofinishing equipment.

Kodak began converting its new VR line of Kodacolor film to DX coding during the year and scheduled all of its 35-mm films for conversion by the end of 1984. Agfa announced plans to adopt the DX system, which had been made freely available to all, but no Japanese manufacturer of film had made that decision as the year came to an end. Nor had any major camera manufacturer produced equipment modified to use DX coding, although it was expected that such models would be forthcoming as DX-coded film became more widely available.

New films introduced during the year included the world's fastest colour transparency film, 3M's Color Slide 1000 Daylight. This 35-mm material yielded acceptable results even when push-processed to allow exposure indexes of ISO 2000 to 4000. Kodak brought forth a line of improved Kodacolor 35-mm colour print films under the VR designation and based upon technology developed in making Disc film: Kodacolor VR 100, VR 200, and VR 400. In terms of grain, sharpness, and colour rendition the new generation proved to be significantly superior to earlier Kodacolor (VR 1000 had been previewed the previous year). Fuji soon followed with improved Fujicolor films designated HR and made available in ISO 100, 200, and 400 emulsions and various formats. Konishiroku, employing a new "cubic crystal" grain structure, announced Sakuracolor SR 100, SR 200, and SR 400 35-mm colour print films. (Konishiroku, which also makes Konica cameras, later decided to market its films in the U.S. under the Konica label.)

After a promising start in 1982 the volume of Disc camera sales proved disappointing. Fuji and Konishiroku, however, introduced their own versions of a disc film, Kodak brought forth new Disc camera models, and a number of other manufacturers entered the field. One reason advanced to explain lagging Disc sales was consumers' disatisfaction with the quality of prints made from the tiny negatives. Late in the year Kodak introduced an improved version of Disc film with finer grain and improved sharpness.

Cultural Trends. The photographic print market recovered somewhat from its low point of the preceding year, although prices generally did not return to their earlier high levels. The closing of major photographic galleries abated. Light Gallery in New York City, which shut down because of financial difficulties in 1982, reopened, and some new galleries appeared. With an improved economy, auction houses reported an increased number of new and active photographic collectors.

Two major photographic cultural institutions opened to the public. The San Diego (Calif.) Museum of Photographic Arts, housed in a section of the historic Casa de Balboa building in Balboa Park, displayed exhibitions of still photography, cinema, and video. In Great Britain a National Museum of Photography, Film, and Television, a branch of the Science Museum in London, was located in Bradford, about 320 km (200 mi) north. The museum emphasized permanent participatory displays as well as exhibitions.

Again it was a good year for retrospective books and exhibitions. Alfred Stieglitz received substantial attention with a major, 171-print exhibition at the National Gallery of Art in Washington, D.C., and a highly acclaimed book, *Alfred Stieglitz: Photographs & Writings*, edited by Sarah Greenough and Juan Hamilton.

Among early photographic processes the calotype had received less attention in the U.S. than the daguerreotype. In a welcome correction of this situation two impressive exhibitions explored the achievements of 19th-century photographers who used the paper-negative technique: "Paper and Light: The Calotype in France and Great Britain 1839–1870" at the Art Institute of Chicago and "Masterpieces of the French Calotype" at the Art Museum, Princeton University.

"Carlton E. Watkins, Photographer of the American West" opened at the Amon Carter Museum in Fort Worth, Texas. Including 111 photographs, many of them not displayed since this 19th-century photographer's lifetime, the exhibition further established Watkins's reputation as a leading topographic photographer of the American West. The portraits of Canadian photographer Yousuf Karsh were displayed in an ambitious retrospective at the International Center of Photography in New York City and also published as one of the season's most lavish picture books. In an unusual but critically acclaimed blend of photography, music, and drama, the life and work of Eadweard Muybridge was the subject of a musical, *The Photographer/Far from the Truth*, at the Brooklyn Academy of Music's Next Wave Festival.

The National Press Photographers Association Magazine Photographer of the Year award went to Jim Brandenburg, a contract photographer for *National Geographic* magazine, for his coverage of China; Newspaper Photographer of the Year was Bill Frakes, staff photographer for the *Miami Herald*. The W. Eugene Smith Grant in Humanistic Photography went to Milton Rogovin to support his ongoing documentation of coal miners. The Pulitzer Prize for spot news photography went to Bill Foley of the Associated Press for pictures of victims and survivors of the massacre at the Sabra camp in Lebanon, and for feature photography to James Dickman of the *Dallas Times Herald* for photographs of life and death in El Salvador.

(ARTHUR GOLDSMITH)

See also Motion Pictures.
[628.D; 735.G.1]

BILL FOLEY—WIDE WORLD

This photograph of a Palestinian woman at a service for victims of the Beirut refugee camp massacre is one of those that won Bill Foley of the Associated Press a Pulitzer Prize for spot news photography.

Physics

In 1983, after years of uncertainty and confusion in the world of particle physics, some order appeared at hand. Whether this state of affairs would continue remained to be seen, but developments during the year, particularly in the discovery of particles long predicted by theory, were encouraging.

Three forces are known to be involved in the realm of nuclear and particle physics: the strong, weak, and electromagnetic interactions. The theories that have been developed for these separate forces are similar in many respects, and it has long been a goal to provide a unified mathematical framework that encompasses all three. In 1979 Steven Weinberg, Abdus Salam, and Sheldon Glashow received the Nobel Prize for Physics for their theory, put forth in the 1960s, that unites the weak and electromagnetic interactions. This so-called electroweak theory not only explains known experimental facts but also gives values for other, as yet unreported, properties. For the theory to remain acceptable, experiments must find these properties in nature to be as predicted.

The theories that describe the basic forces allow each to be understood in terms of the exchange of an intermediate particle, called a vector boson, which mediates the force between a given pair of interacting particles. Massless photons (discrete packets, or quanta, of light energy) carry the electromagnetic interaction between particles having electric charge; *e.g.*, protons and electrons. Other massless vector bosons, called gluons, mediate the strong interaction, which affects quarks and, consequently, all particles composed of quarks; *e.g.*, protons, neutrons, and pi mesons. Similarly the weak interaction, which affects almost all particles and governs many nuclear decay processes, is expected to have its own intermediate particles.

One prominent feature of the electroweak theory is its prediction of three massive intermediate vector bosons—sometimes called weakons—to carry the weak interaction. Two, named the W^+ and W^-, carry one unit of either positive or negative charge and have a calculated rest mass of about 82 GeV (billion electron volts). The third, the Z^0, is electrically neutral and has a rest mass of 94 GeV. It should be noted that the masses of these particles, roughly a hundred times that of the proton, are several times higher than those of any particles previously observed—so heavy that until recently no existing particle accelerators had been capable of producing them. Yet testing this prediction of the electroweak theory was so important to its verification as to mandate building machines and designing experiments capable of exploring the energy range in which the W's and Z^0 could be created.

One approach to achieving the necessary energy is to allow protons with very high kinetic energy to collide with antiprotons of similar energy. Antiprotons are the antimatter equivalent of positively charged protons and thus carry an opposite, negative charge. Protons and antiprotons are both made up of quarks, which are held together by the strong force through the exchange of gluons. Quarks come in several kinds, but all have charges that are fractions of the unit charge on the electron, specifically either $+\frac{2}{3}$ or $-\frac{1}{3}$. A proton comprises three quarks, two with a $+\frac{2}{3}$ charge and one with a $-\frac{1}{3}$ charge. An antiproton is made of three antiquarks, with charges opposite those of their quark counterparts; *i.e.*, $-\frac{2}{3}$ and $+\frac{1}{3}$. Thus, a high-energy proton-antiproton collision can be pictured as a collision between three quarks and three antiquarks.

Once in many thousands of such quark-antiquark collisions, the two particles are predicted to annihilate one another, first becoming pure energy and then rematerializing as a W^+ or a W^- if the charges of the quarks were of the same sign (both positive or both negative) or as a Z^0 if the charges were equal and opposite. Once formed, these massive vector bosons would decay almost immediately by any of several detectable routes. For the W's a particularly distinctive one is their decay into an electron (for a W^-) or a positron (for a W^+) plus a neutrino, which are ejected from the collision site at high energy and in nearly opposite directions. (A positron is an antimatter electron; a neutrino is an uncharged, apparently massless relative of the electron.) The Z^0 should show itself by its decay into energetic, oppositely directed pairs of particles and corresponding antiparticles; *e.g.*, an electron and a positron, or a muon (a heavy relative of the electron) and an antimuon.

Below, the track of a high-energy electron (arrow), captured in the record of a multiparticle spray of debris from a proton-antiproton collision at CERN, gives evidence for the production and decay of the long-sought W particle; centre horizontal lines mark the paths of the incoming beams. At bottom, the tangle of particle tracks emerging from another proton-antiproton collision carries the tell-tale signature of a Z^0 decay—an energetic, oppositely directed electron-positron pair (arrows).

PHOTOGRAPHS, CERN

It can be deduced from the above that the collision energy for each proton-antiproton encounter must be at least six times the energy required for such quark-antiquark annihilations to take place, since each quark carries only $\frac{1}{6}$ of the collision energy. In late 1981 the first experimental facility to achieve the necessary conditions, a modified proton synchrotron, went into operation at the European Laboratory for Particle Physics (CERN) in Geneva. Within it beams of protons and antiprotons, accelerated to 270 GeV each, are kept circulating in opposite directions along a circular path 7 km (4.3 mi) in diameter and are brought together for head-on collisions at a number of intersection points—for a combined collision energy of 540 GeV.

The search for the carriers of the weak interaction proceeded in earnest during an experimental run of several weeks in the fall of 1982 when 540-GeV collisions were allowed to take place within two separate arrays of detectors called UA1 and UA2. At least 200 scientists from more than ten countries took part in the experiments. In January 1983 the team operating the UA2 detector reported four possible W candidates, whereas the team operating the UA1 detector was more positive, describing five decay events that definitely fit the requirements for the W. Four of these were the decay of the W^- and one the decay of the W^+. From its observations the UA1 group calculated the mass of the W boson to be 81 GeV (with an uncertainty of 5 GeV in either direction), in excellent agreement with the theoretical value of 82 GeV. The UA2 team subsequently confirmed its observations and provided a similar mass estimate. By August and with the help of another data-gathering run in the spring, the two teams had amassed 90 candidates for the W.

After the January announcement it was evident that the search would now concentrate on the rarer Z^0, which had escaped detection. It had been calculated that one Z^0 particle should be produced for every ten W's. News of the first sightings of the Z^0 came in June from the UA1 scientists after their analysis of part of the spring run at CERN revealed five decays (later raised to six: four electron-positron and two muon-antimuon) that seemed to fit the requirements. The following month the UA2 team announced four more Z^0 candidates. Mass estimates from the experimental data were about 95 GeV from the UA1 team and 91 GeV from the

UA2 team, with uncertainty ranges of a few GeV.

It is noteworthy that the detection and analysis systems for these experiments were at such a state of sophistication that it seemed difficult to grasp. To observe the first five W particles, for example, the UA1 team had to deal with hundreds of millions of proton-antiproton collisions. In addition, a large group of "semifinalist" events were analyzed in two different ways as a double check on the results. All this was carried out in less than one month. One would expect that even more events had to be examined for Z^0 decays, whereas the announcement came within a matter of weeks.

Of the three particles predicted by the electroweak theory, the Z^0 is perhaps the most important. Although older, nonunifying approaches predict W's, only the unified electroweak theory requires the Z^0 as well. This final discovery fittingly concluded a fascinating year.

More experiments remained to be carried out—and, in particular, many more Z^0 and W candidates observed—for everyone to be convinced that the detected events were not just statistically unlikely mimics of Z^0 and W decays. Strong confirmation would also help support proposals and plans both in Europe and the U.S. for building colossal synchrotons capable of attaining many times the collision energy presently available at CERN. But even by the end of the year the powerful forces of rejuvenation at work in particle physics were already apparent. (S. B. PALMER)

See also Nobel Prizes.
[111.H.1–4,6,7; 723.F.3,7]

Poland

A people's republic of Eastern Europe, Poland is bordered by the Baltic Sea, the U.S.S.R., Czechoslovakia, and East Germany. Area: 312,683 sq km (120,727 sq mi). Pop. (1983 est.): 36,556,000. Cap. and largest city: Warsaw (pop., 1982 est., 1,611,600). Language: Polish. Religion: predominantly Roman Catholic. First secretary of the Polish United Workers' (Communist) Party and chairman of the Council of Ministers (premier) in 1983, Gen. Wojciech Jaruzelski; chairman of the Council of State, Henryk Jablonski.

Martial law, proclaimed on Dec. 13, 1981, and suspended on Dec. 31, 1982, was finally lifted on July 22, 1983. For 19 months Poland had been governed harshly by the Military Council of National Salvation, headed by Gen. Wojciech Jaruzelski. Speaking on Feb. 26, 1983, Jaruzelski criticized members of the Polish United Workers' (Communist) Party (PUWP) for their "irresolute" attitude toward the government. In fact, having lost about 800,000 members—one-third of its component—during 1980–81, the party was in disarray. The PUWP Politburo had decided in July 1981 that something had to be done to repair the party's credibility and had appointed a special commission, chaired by Hieronim Kubiak, to examine "the reasons for successive political crises." The commission published a summary of its report in October 1983. It pointed to many errors and shortcomings in the actions of the party. It also laid to

HIRES/LOCHON/FRANCOLON/MINGAM—GAMMA/LIAISON

In June Pope John Paul II visited Poland. He met with Gen. Wojciech Jaruzelski at Warsaw's Belvedere Palace and delivered a speech calling for dialogue in Poland.

rest some legends; for instance, it was not true that Jaruzelski had opposed Wladyslaw Gomulka's decision to shoot at demonstrators in Gdansk and Gdynia in December 1970.

The composition of the Politburo, made up of 15 full members, 5 deputies, and 3 secretaries, was altered slightly in November when Tadeusz Porebski, a full member, was elected secretary, and Marian Orzechowski, on becoming a deputy member, gave up the post of secretary to which he had been appointed a year earlier. There were also two reshuffles of the Council of Ministers (Cabinet) in March and November. On March 23 Mieczyslaw Moczar, head of the Supreme Chamber of Control, was forced to resign and was replaced by Gen. Tadeusz Hupalowski. The latter's portfolio of regional economy was transferred to Wlodzimierz Oliwa. Stanislaw Ciosek and Jerzy Wozniak were elected ministers of labour and raw materials, respectively, while the replacement of Jerzy Wojtecki as minister of agriculture by Stanislaw Zieba created a small sensation; 69 members of the Sejm (parliament) had voted against Wojtecki's dismissal, and 81 had abstained.

Poland

On November 22 General Jaruzelski handed over his defense portfolio to Gen. Florian Siwicki, a deputy member of the Politburo. On the previous day the Sejm had passed an act creating the National Defense Committee. Jaruzelski was appointed chairman of this new body, which was to supervise the Ministry of Defense. Janusz Obodowski, a vice-premier, gave up the chair of the Planning Commission and was replaced by Manfred Gorywoda, a Politburo secretary responsible for the economy. Obodowski succeeded Zbigniew Madej as Polish member of the executive committee of the Council for Mutual Economic Assistance (Comecon) in Moscow. After these changes, the Council of Ministers comprised the premier, 10 vice-premiers, and 32 ministers.

In an attempt to take over the political role of the Solidarnosc (Solidarity) independent trade-union movement, the government in May launched the Patriotic Movement for National Revival. Jan Dobraczynski, a Catholic writer, was named chairman of its 400-strong council. In January Jaruzelski presided over the foundation of the National Council of Culture, whose members—including Bogdan Suchodolski, its president—were nominated by the government. During the year the

Pipelines:
see Energy; Transportation

Plastics Industry:
see Industrial Review

Poetry:
see Literature

POLAND

Education. (1981–82) Primary, pupils 4,341,800, teachers 224,500; secondary, pupils 392,900, teachers 22,500; vocational, pupils 1,692,000, teachers 82,300; teacher training, students 37,000; higher, students 386,500; teacher training and higher, teaching staff 55,450.

Finance. Monetary unit: zloty, with (Sept. 20, 1983) an official rate of 95.49 zlotys to U.S. $1 (free rate of 143.81 zlotys = £1 sterling). Budget (1981 est.): revenue 1,335,000,000,000 zlotys; expenditure 1,366,000,000,000 zlotys. Net material product (1981) 2,154,700,000,000 zlotys.

Foreign Trade. (1982) Imports 862,040,000,000 zlotys; exports 947,384,000,000 zlotys. Import sources: U.S.S.R. 38%; West Germany 7%; East Germany 7%; Czechoslovakia 6%. Export destinations: U.S.S.R. 30%; East Germany 8%; Czechoslovakia 5%; West Germany 5%. Main exports (1981): machinery 38%; transport equipment 10%; chemicals 9%; coal 6%.

Transport and Communications. Roads (1982) 299,166 km (including 168 km expressways). Motor vehicles in use (1982): passenger 2,881,700; commercial 615,900. Railways: (1981) 24,360 km (including 7,091 km electrified); traffic (1982) 48,954,000,000 passenger-km, freight 112,655,000,000 net ton-km. Air traffic (1982): 778 million passenger-km; freight 6,425,000 net ton-km. Navigable inland waterways in regular use (1981) 2,982 km. Shipping (1982): merchant vessels 100 gross tons and over 816; gross tonnage 3,650,615. Telephones (Dec. 1981) 3,506,000. Radio licenses (Dec. 1981) 8,732,000. Television licenses (Dec. 1981) 8,188,000.

Agriculture. Production (in 000; metric tons; 1982): wheat 4,476; rye 7,245; barley 3,647; oats 2,608; potatoes 31,951; sugar, raw value c. 2,000; rapeseed 482; cabbages (1981) c. 1,600; onions 422; tomatoes 442; carrots (1981) c. 549; cucumbers (1981) c. 400; apples 1,893; tobacco c. 80; butter c. 308; cheese c. 401; hen's eggs 422; beef and veal c. 640; pork c. 1,391; fish catch (1981) 630; timber (cu m; 1981) 20,689. Livestock (in 000; June 1982): cattle 11,912; pigs 18,471; sheep 3,899; horses (1981) c. 1,780; chickens (adult birds) 65,482.

Industry. Index of industrial production (1975 = 100; 1982) 108. Fuel and power (in 000; metric tons; 1982): coal 189,314; brown coal 37,649; coke (1981) 17,918; crude oil c. 300; natural gas (cu m) 5,530,000; manufactured gas (cu m; 1981) 6,833,000; electricity (kw-hr) 117,561,000. Production (in 000; metric tons; 1982): cement 16,034; pig iron 8,523; crude steel 14,479; aluminum (1981) 66; copper (1981) 328; lead (1981) 68; zinc (1981) 167; petroleum products (1981) 12,320; sulfuric acid 2,678; plastics and resins 600; fertilizers (nutrient content; 1981) nitrogenous 1,274, phosphate 866; cotton yarn (1981) 196; wool yarn (1981) 89; man-made fibres 176; cotton fabrics (m) 694,000; woolen fabrics (m) 91,000; passenger cars (units) 229; commercial vehicles (units) 47. Merchant vessels launched (100 gross tons and over; 1982) 302,000 gross tons. New dwelling units completed (1982) 129,000.

government's relations with the various writers' unions were far from easy. The Polish Writers' Union was dissolved in August and a new union was decreed in November; its president, Halina Auderska, and the majority of its governing body were Communists. The same procedure was used to "reform" the Association of Polish Journalists, the Union of Polish Theatrical Artists, and the Polish branch of the International Association of Poets, Playwrights, Editors, Essayists, and Novelists (PEN).

Up to 100,000 people in more than 20 towns took part in demonstrations on May 3 (the 192nd anniversary of the Polish democratic constitution), August 31 (the third anniversary of the birth of Solidarity), and November 11 (the 65th anniversary of the proclamation of Poland's independence). In the view of Lech Walesa (*see* NOBEL PRIZES), whom Vice-Premier Mieczyslaw Rakowski referred to as a former leader of a former union, these and many other manifestations exceeded all expectations. "Solidarity lives," he proclaimed. Another proof of Solidarity's survival was the outcome of the amnesty that was granted by the government on July 21 and expired on October 31. Only 686 Solidarity supporters on the fringes of the opposition reported to police in order to avoid persecution. That meagre result troubled the Polish regime, which extended the amnesty to the end of the year. The awarding of the Nobel Peace Prize to Walesa on October 5 caused even greater concern to Jaruzelski's government.

On the invitation of the Polish government, Pope John Paul II paid his second papal visit to his homeland in June. Millions of enthusiastic people greeted him in Warsaw, Czestochowa, Poznan, Wroclaw, and Cracow. The inclusion of western territories in the papal itinerary contributed significantly to stabilizing the area. The pope also spoke repeatedly of the need for national reconciliation and for responsible dialogue. He met General Jaruzelski twice, in Warsaw and Cracow, and he also met Walesa at a church retreat in the Tatra Mountains. On June 24 *L'Osservatore Romano*, the Vatican daily newspaper, published an article suggesting that Walesa might have to be sacrificed "for the greater good of the whole community." The following day the paper's editor was dismissed.

The Polish national economy remained bleak. Industrial production in 1983 grew by 2–3% over the previous year's output, but the 1982 figure had been 16% below that of 1979. Coal production had improved markedly, however, and in 1982 Poland exported 28.5 million metric tons, more than double the previous year's total. The grain harvest in 1983 amounted to 22 million metric tons, leaving a shortfall of 3 million–3.5 million metric tons that had to be imported. Foodstuffs were still in short supply in the shops, and from November 1 rationing of butter and animal fats was reintroduced.

(K. M. SMOGORZEWSKI)

Police:
see Crime and Law Enforcement

Polo:
see Equestrian Sports; Water Sports

Populations:
see Demography; *see also the individual country articles*

Political Parties

The following table is a general world guide to political parties. All countries that were independent on Dec. 31, 1983, are included; there are a number for which no analysis of political activities can be given. Parties are included in most instances only if represented in parliaments (in the lower house in bicameral legislatures); the figures in the last column indicate the number of seats obtained in the last general election (figures in parentheses are those of the penultimate one). The date of the most recent election follows the name of the country.

The code letters in the affiliation column show the relative political positions of the parties within each country; there is, therefore, no entry in this column for single-party states. There are obvious difficulties involved in labeling parties within the political spectrum of a given country. The key chosen is as follows: F-fascist; ER-extreme right; R-right; CR-centre right; C-centre; L-non-Marxist left; SD-social democratic; S-socialist; EL-extreme left; and K-Communist.

The percentages in the column "Voting strength" indicate proportions of the valid votes cast for the respective parties, or the number of registered voters who went to the polls in single-party states.

[541.D.2]

COUNTRY AND NAME OF PARTY	Affiliation	Voting strength (%)	Parliamentary representation
Afghanistan			
Pro-Soviet government since April 27, 1978	—	—	—
Albania (November 1982)			
Albanian Labour (Communist)	—	99.9	250 (250)
Algeria (March 1982)			
National Liberation Front	—	99.9	281 (261)
Angola (August 1980)			
Movimento Popular de Libertaçao de Angola (MPLA)	—	—	203
Antigua and Barbuda (April 1980)			
Antigua Labour Party	C	59.0	13 (11)
Progressive Labour Movement	L	...	3 (5)
Independents	—	...	1 (1)
Argentina (October 1983)			
Movimiento Justicialista Nacional (Peronist)	CR	40.0	111
Unión Cívica Radical	C	51.0	129
Partido Intransigente	L	2.3	3
Others	—	6.7	11
Australia (March 1983)			
National Country	R	...	17 (20)
Liberal	C	...	33 (54)
Australian Labor	L	...	75 (51)
Austria (April 1983)			
Freiheitliche Partei Österreichs	R	5.0	12 (11)
Österreichische Volkspartei	C	43.2	81 (77)
Sozialistische Partei Österreichs	SD	47.8	90 (95)
Others	—	4.0	0 (0)
Bahamas, The (June 1982)			
Progressive Liberal Party	CR	53	32 (30)
Free National Movement	L	43	8 (2)
Others	—	...	3 ...
Bahrain			
Emirate, no parties	—	—	—
Bangladesh			
On March 24 Gen. Hossain Ershad seized power from the civilian government			
Barbados (June 1981)			
Democratic Labour	C	47.1	10 (7)
Barbados Labour	L	52.2	17 (17)
Belgium (November 1981)			
Vlaams Blok	ER	...	1 (1)
Volksunie	R	...	20 (14)
Front Démocratique Francophone/Rassemblement Wallon	R	...	8 (15)
Parti Libéral — Flemish	CR	...	28 (22)
Parti Libéral — Wallon	CR	...	24 (15)
Parti Social-Chrétien — Flemish	C	...	43 (57)
Parti Social-Chrétien — Wallon	C	...	18 (25)
Parti Socialiste Belge — Flemish	SD	...	26 (26)
Parti Socialiste Belge — Wallon	SD	...	35 (32)
Parti Communiste	K	...	2 (4)
Others	—	...	7 (1)
Belize (November 1979)			
United Democratic Party	R	46.8	5 (6)
People's United Party	C	51.8	13 (12)
Benin (November 1979)			
People's Revolutionary Party	—	—	336
Bhutan			
A monarchy without parties	—	—	—
Bolivia (June 1980)			
Movimiento Nacionalista Revolucionario	R	20.1	44 (43)
Unidad Democrática y Popular	C	38.7	57 (37)
Acción Democrática Nacionalista	L	15.0	...
Five other parties	—	...	...
Botswana (October 1979)			
Botswana Democratic Party	C	...	29 (27)
Botswana People's Party	L	...	1 (2)
Botswana National Front	EL	...	2 (2)
Brazil (November 1982)			
Movimento Democrático Brasileiro	CR	44.1	200
Partido Democrático Social	C	39.4	234
Partido Trabalhista Democrático	S	6.7	24
Partido Trabalhista Brasileiro	S	5.5	13
Partido dos Trabalhadores	EL	4.3	8
Brunei			
Legislative Council	—	...	33
Bulgaria (June 1981)			
Fatherland Front: Bulgarian Communist Party	—	99.9	271
Fatherland Front: Bulgarian Agrarian Union			99
Fatherland Front: No party affiliation			30
Fatherland Front (total)			400 (400)
Burma (October 1981)			
Burma Socialist Program Party	—	99.0	464 (464)
Burundi (October 1974)			
Tutsi ethnic minority government	—	—	—
Cameroon (May 1983)			
Cameroonian National Union	—	99.3	120 (120)
Canada (February 1980)			
Social Credit	R	1.9	0 (6)
Progressive Conservative	CR	33.0	103 (136)
Liberal	C	43.9	147 (114)
New Democratic	L	19.8	32 (26)
Cape Verde (December 1980)			
African Party for the Independence of Guinea-Bissau and Cape Verde	—	93.0	—
Central African Republic			
Military Committee of National Recovery took power on Sept. 1, 1981	—	...	—
Chad			
Military government since 1975	—	—	—
Chile			
Military junta since Sept. 11, 1973	—	—	—
China, People's Republic of (February 1978)			
Communist (Kungchantang) National People's Congress	—	...	3,500
Colombia (March 1982)			
Partido Conservador	R	...	84 (86)
Partido Liberal	C	...	114 (109)
Unión Nacional de Oposición	L	...	1 (4)
Comoros (March 1982)			
Federal Assembly	—	...	38
Congo (July 1979)			
Parti Congolais du Travail	—	—	115
Costa Rica (February 1982)			
Partido de Liberación Nacional	R	55	33 (25)
Partido Cristiano Democrático	C	30	18 (27)
Three left-wing parties	L	15	6 (5)
Cuba (December 1981)			
Partido Comunista Cubano	—	99.0	499 (481)
Cyprus			
Greek Zone: (May 1981):			
Democratic Rally	R	31.89	12
Democratic Party	CR	19.50	8
Socialist Party (EDEK)	S	8.17	3
Communist Party (AKEL)	K	32.79	12
Turkish Zone (June 1981):			
National Unity Party	—	42.6	18 (30)
Socialist Salvation Party	—	28.6	13 (6)
Republican Turkish Party	—	15.1	6 (2)
Democratic People's Party	—	8.1	2 (0)
Turkish Union Party	—	5.5	1 (0)
Czechoslovakia (June 1981)			
National Front	—	99.5	200 (200)
Denmark (December 1981)			
Conservative	R	14.4	26 (22)
Liberal Democratic (Venstre)	CR	11.3	21 (23)
Christian People's	CR	2.3	4 (5)
Progress	C	8.9	16 (20)
Radical Liberal (Radikale Venstre)	C	5.1	9 (10)
Centre Democrats	C	8.3	15 (6)
Social Democrats	SD	32.9	59 (69)
Socialist People's	EL	11.3	20 (11)
Left Socialists	EL	2.6	5 (6)
Others	—	...	4 (2)
Djibouti (May 1982)			
One-party state: National Assembly	—	...	65
Dominica (July 1980)			
Freedom Party	C	...	17 (3)
Labour Party	L	...	2 (16)
Independents	—	...	2 (2)
Dominican Republic (May 1982)			
Partido Reformista	R	37.0	... (42)
Partido Revolucionario	L	48.4	... (49)
Others	—	...	...
Ecuador (April 1979, figures incomplete)			
Partido Conservador	R	...	10
Concentración de Fuerzas Populares	C	...	30
Izquierda Democrática	L	...	14
Unión Democrática Popular	EL	...	3
Egypt (November 1976)			
Arab Socialist Union	—	...	350
El Salvador (March 1982)			
Alianza Republicana Nacionalista	R	29	19
Partido de Conciliación Nacional	CR	13	14
Partido Acción Democrática	C	18	3
Partido Cristiano Democrático	C	40	24
Equatorial Guinea (August 1983)			
National Assembly	—	...	41
Ethiopia			
Military government since 1974	—	—	—
Fiji (July 1982)			
Alliance Party (mainly Fijian)	—	...	28 (36)
National Federation (mainly Indian)	—	...	22 (15)
Others	—	...	2 (1)
Finland (March 1983)			
National Coalition Party (Conservative)	R	22.1	44 (47)
Swedish People's	R	4.6	11 (10)
Centre (including former Liberal) Party	C	17.6	38 (40)
Christian League	C	3.0	3 (9)
Rural Party	C	9.7	17 (7)
Social Democratic	SD	26.7	57 (52)
People's Democratic League (Communist)	K	14.0	27 (35)
Green Party	—	1.5	2 —
Others	—	...	1 (0)
France (June 1981)			
Centre-Right:			
Gaullists (Rassemblement pour la République)	R	...	83 (148)
Giscardians (Union pour la Démocratie Française)	CR	...	64 (137)
Other	—	...	11 (6)
Union of Left:			
Parti Radical	L	...	14 (10)
Parti Socialiste	SD	...	269 (103)
Parti Communiste	K	...	44 (86)
Others	—	...	6 (1)
Gabon (February 1973)			
Parti Démocratique Gabonais	—	...	70
Gambia, The (April 1982)			
People's Progressive Party	C	61.7	27 (28)
Three other parties	—	...	8 (7)
German Democratic Republic (June 1981)			
National Front (Sozialistische Einheitspartei and others)	—	99.2	500 (500)
Germany, Federal Republic of (March 1983)			
Christlich-Demokratische Union	R	38.2	191 (174)
Christlich-Soziale Union	R	10.6	53 (52)
Freie Demokratische Partei	C	6.9	34 (53)
Sozialdemokratische Partei Deutschlands	SD	38.2	193 (218)
The Green (Ecology) Party	—	5.6	27 (0)
Others	—	0.4	0 (0)
Ghana			
Military dictatorship since Dec. 31, 1981	—	—	—
Greece (October 1981)			
Progressive Party	R	1.7	0 (5)
New Democracy Party	CR	35.9	115 (172)
Panhellenic Socialist Movement (Pasok)	SD	48.1	172 (93)
Greek Communist Party	K	10.9	13 (11)
Others	—	2.3	0 (19)
Grenada			
Provisional government since November 1983	—	—	—
Guatemala			
Military government since March 23, 1982			
Guinea (December 1974)			
Parti Démocratique de Guinée	—	100.0	150

COUNTRY AND NAME OF PARTY	Affiliation	Voting strength (%)	Parliamentary representation
Guinea-Bissau			
Governed by the Council of the Revolution since Nov. 14, 1980	—	—	—
Guyana (December 1980)			
People's National Congress	—	...	(37)
People's Progressive Party	—	...	(14)
Others	—	...	(2)
Haiti			
Presidential dictatorship since 1957	—	—	—
Honduras (November 1981)			
Partido Nacional	R	42.0	34 (33)
Partido Liberal	CR	54.0	44 (35)
Partido de Innovación y Unidad	C	2.5	3 (3)
Partido Demócrata Cristiano	C	1.5	1 (0)
Hungary (June 1980)			
Patriotic People's Front	—	97.6	352 (352)
Iceland (April 1983)			
Independence (Conservative)	R	38.7	23 (21)
Progressive (Farmers' Party)	C	19.0	14 (17)
Social Democratic	SD	11.7	6 (10)
Social Democratic Alliance	EL	7.3	4 —
People's Alliance	K	17.3	10 (11)
Feminists	—	5.5	3 —
India (January 1980)			
Congress (I) and allied parties:			
Congress (I)	C	...	351
Dravida Munnetra Kazhagam	R	...	16
Lok Dal (Janata secular)	—	...	41
Three smaller parties	—	...	7
Opposition:			
Janata (People's) Party	C	...	32 (295)
Congress (Urs)	C	...	13 (150)
Communist Party of India (Marxist)	K	...	35 (22)
Communist Party of India (pro-Soviet)	K	...	10 (7)
Anna Dravida Munnetra Kazhagam	R	...	2 (19)
Akali Dal (Sikh Party)	C	...	1 (9)
Six small parties	—	...	11
Independents	—	...	6
Indonesia (May 1982)			
Golkar (Functional Groups)	—	64.3	342
United Development Party	—	27.8	94
Indonesian Democratic Party (merger of five nationalist and Christian parties)	—	7.9	24
Iran (May 1980)			
Islamic Republican Party	R	...	150
Islamic National Party	CR	...	80
Independents	—	...	40
Iraq			
Military and Ba'ath Party governments since 1958	—	...	...
Ireland (November 1982)			
Fianna Fail (Sons of Destiny)	C	...	75 (81)
Fine Gael (United Ireland)	C	...	70 (63)
Irish Labour Party	L	...	16 (15)
Others	—	...	5 (7)
Israel (June 1981)			
Likud	R	37.1	48 (43)
National Religious	CR	4.9	6 (12)
Agudat Israel	C	3.7	4 (4)
Labour Alignment	SD	36.6	47 (32)
Democratic Front (Communist)	K	3.4	4 (5)
Others	—	...	11 (24)
Italy (June 1983)			
Movimento Sociale Italiano	F	6.8	42 (30)
Partito Liberale Italiano	CR	2.9	16 (9)
Democrazia Cristiana	C	32.9	225 (262)
Partito Repubblicano Italiano	C	5.1	29 (16)
Partito Social-Democratico Italiano	L	4.1	23 (20)
Partito Socialista Italiano	SD	11.4	73 (62)
Partito Radicale	EL	2.2	11 (18)
Partito Comunista Italiano	K	29.2	198 (201)
Südtiroler Volkspartei	—	0.5	3 (4)
Others	—	4.2	10 (8)
Ivory Coast (October 1980)			
Parti Démocratique de la Côte d'Ivoire	—	99.9	100
Jamaica (December 1983)			
Jamaica Labour Party	L	...	60 (51)
People's National Party	SD	(Boycotted)	(9)
Japan (December 1983)			
Liberal-Democratic	R	...	250 (284)
Komeito (Clean Government)	CR	...	58 (33)
Democratic-Socialist	SD	...	38 (32)
Socialist	S	...	112 (107)
Communist	K	...	26 (29)
Others	—	...	27 (26)
Jordan			
Royal government, no parties	—	—	60
Kampuchea (May 1981)			
Kampuchean United Front for National Salvation (Vietnamese-backed)	—	99.0	117
Kenya (September 1983)			
Kenya African National Union	—	48.0	158
Kiribati (January 1983)			
House of Assembly, no formal parties	—	...	35
Korea, North (February 1982)			
Korean Workers' (Communist) Party	—	100.0	615 (579)
Korea, South (March 1981)			
Korean National	CR	...	25
Democratic Justice	C	...	151
Democratic Korea	L	...	81
Democratic Socialist	S	...	2
Others	—	...	17
Kuwait (February 1981)			
Princely government with elected Parliament, no parties	—	—	30
Laos, People's Democratic Republic of			
Lao People's Revolutionary Party	—	...	...
Lebanon (April 1972)			
Maronites (Roman Catholics)	—	...	30
Sunni Muslims	—	...	20
Shi'ite Muslims	—	...	19
Greek Orthodox	—	...	11
Druzes (Muslim sect)	—	...	6
Melchites (Greek Catholics)	—	...	6
Armenian Orthodox	—	...	4
Other Christian	—	...	2
Armenian Catholics	—	...	1
Lesotho			
Constitution suspended Jan. 30, 1970	—	—	—
Liberia			
People's Redemption Council since April 1980	—	—	—
Libya			
Military government since Sept. 1, 1969	—	—	—
Liechtenstein (February 1982)			
Vaterländische Union	CR	53.5	8 (8)
Fortschrittliche Bürgerpartei	C	46.5	7 (7)
Luxembourg (June 1979)			
Parti Chrétien Social	CR	34.5	24 (18)
Parti Libéral	C	21.3	15 (14)
Parti Ouvrier Socialiste	SD	24.3	14 (17)
Parti Social Démocratique	S	6.0	2 (5)
Parti Communiste Luxembourgeois	K	5.8	2 (5)
Independents	—	...	2 (0)
Madagascar (August 1983)			
Advance Guard of the Malagasy Revolution (Arema)	C	64.8	117 (112)
Madagascar Independence Congress	L	8.8	9 (16)
Movement for Proletarian Power	L	11.1	3 —
People's Party for National Unity	L	10.6	6 (7)
Madagascar National Independence Movement (Monima)	L	3.7	2 —
Malawi (June 1983)			
Malawi Congress Party	—	...	101 (87)
Malaysia (April 1982)			
National Front (Barisan Nasional)			
United Malays National Organization		70	
Malaysian Chinese Association		24	
Malaysian Indian Congress		4	133 (131)
Gerakan		5	
Sabah and Sarawak		30	
Opposition Parties			
Democratic Action Party		9	
Partai Islam Malaysia		5	21 (23)
Independents		7	
Maldives (February 1975)			
Presidential rule since 1975	—	—	—
Mali			
Military government since Nov. 19, 1968	—	—	—
Malta (December 1981)			
Nationalist Party	R	...	31 (31)
Labour Party	SD	...	34 (34)
Mauritania			
Military government since April 25, 1981	—	—	—
Mauritius (August 1983)			
Independence (Labour) Party			(2)
Parti Mauricien Social-Démocrate	C	...	41 (2)
Mouvement Socialiste Mauricien			—
Mouvement Militant Mauricien	L	...	19 (42)
Parti Socialiste Mauricien	—	—	— (18)
Organization du Peuple Rodriguais	—	...	2 (2)
Mexico (July 1982)			
Partido Revolucionario Institucional	CR	...	296 (296)
Partido Demócrata Mexicano	CR	...	
Partido Acción Nacional	C	...	
Partido Auténtico de la Revolución	L	...	104 (104)
Partido Socialista de los Trabajadores	L	...	
Partido Popular Socialista	S	...	
Partido Comunista Mexicano	K	...	
Monaco (January 1978)			
Union Nationale et Démocratique	—	...	18 (17)
Mongolia (June 1981)			
Mongolian People's Revolutionary Party	—	99.9	354 (354)
Morocco (June 1977)			
Independents (pro-government)	CR	44.7	141 (159)
Popular Movement (rural)	CR	12.4	44 (60)
Istiqlal (Independence)	C	21.6	49 (8)
National Union of Popular Forces	L	14.6	16 (1)
Others	—	...	14 (12)
Mozambique (December 1977)			
Frente da Libertação do Moçambique (Frelimo)	—	...	210
Nauru (November 1977)			
Nauru Party (Dowiyogo)	—	...	9
Opposition Party (DeRoburt)	—	...	8
Independent	—	...	1
Nepal (May 1981)			
140-member Parliament, 112 elected and 28 appointed by the King; no parties	—	—	—
Netherlands, The (September 1982)			
Christian Democratic Appeal	CR	29.3	45 (48)
Liberals (VVD)	C	23.0	36 (26)
Democrats 1966	C	4.3	6 (17)
Labour (Pvd A)	SD	30.4	47 (44)
Others	—	13.0	16 (15)
New Zealand (November 1981)			
National (Conservative)	CR	...	47 (51)
Labour Party	L	...	43 (40)
Social Credit	C	...	2 (1)
Nicaragua			
Provisional government since July 1979	—	...	—
Niger			
Military government since April 1974	—	—	—
Nigeria (August 1983)			
National Party of Nigeria	CR	...	264 (168)
Unity Party of Nigeria	L	...	33 (111)
Nigerian People's Party	L	...	48 (79)
People's Redemption Party	L	...	41 (49)

COUNTRY AND NAME OF PARTY	Affiliation	Voting strength (%)	Parliamentary representation
Norway (September 1981)			
Høyre (Conservative)	R	...	54 (41)
Kristelig Folkeparti	CR	...	15 (22)
Senterpartiet (Agrarian)	C	...	10 (12)
Venstre (Liberal)	C	...	2 (2)
Party of Progress	C	...	4 (0)
Arbeiderpartiet (Labour)	SD	...	66 (76)
Sosialistisk Venstreparti (Socialist Left)	S	...	4 (2)
Oman			
Independent sultanate, no parties	—	—	—
Pakistan			
Military government since July 5, 1977	—	—	—
Panama			
Since July 1982 a civilian president under "indirect" military supervision.			
Papua New Guinea (June 1982)			
Pangu Party	—	34	50 (39)
United Party	—	7.2	9 (38)
People's Progress Party	—	10	14 (18)
National Party	—	10	13 (3)
Independents	—	20.9	4
Paraguay (February 1983)			
Partido Colorado (A. Stroessner)	R	90.0	40
Opposition parties	—	10.0	20
Peru (May 1980)			
Acción Popular	—	...	98
Alianza Popular Revolucionaria Americana	—	...	58
Popular Christian Party	—	...	10
Philippines			
Martial law lifted Jan. 17, 1981	—	—	—
Poland (March 1980)			
Front of National Unity	—	99.0	460 (460)
Communists			261
Peasants			113
Democrats			37
Non-party			49
Portugal (April 1983)			
Democratic and Social Centre	R	12.4	30 (46)
Social Democratic Party	CR	27.0	75 (82)
Socialist Party	SD	36.3	101 (66)
United People's Alliance	K	18.2	44 (41)
Qatar			
Independent emirate, no parties	—	—	—
Romania (March 1980)			
Social Democracy and Unity Front	—	98.5	369 (349)
Rwanda (July 1975)			
National Revolutionary Development Movement	—	—	—
Saint Christopher and Nevis (February 1980)			
People's Action Movement	C	...	3 (0)
Labour Party	L	...	4 (7)
Nevis Reformation Party	—	...	2 (2)
Saint Lucia (May 1982)			
United Workers' Party	C	...	14 (5)
St. Lucia Labour Party	S	...	2 (12)
Progressive Labour Party	EL	...	1 (0)
Saint Vincent and the Grenadines (December 1979)			
St. Vincent Labour Party	—	...	11
New Democratic Party	—	...	2
San Marino (May 1983)			
Communist coalition		...	
Partito Communista			15 (16)
Partito Social Democratico			9 (9)
Partito Socialista Unitario			8 (8)
Christian Democrats		...	26 (26)
São Tomé and Príncipe (1975)			
Movimento Libertaçao	—	—	—
Saudi Arabia			
Royal government, no parties	—	—	—
Senegal (February 1983)			
Parti Socialiste	CR	79.9	111 (83)
Parti Démocratique Sénégalais	L	14.0	8 (17)
Rassemblement National Démocratique	EL	2.6	1 —
Ligue Démocratique	K	1.1	0 —
Seychelles (August 1983)			
People's Progressive Front	—	59.3	23
Sierra Leone (June 1978)			
All People's Congress	CR	...	85 (70)
Singapore (December 1980)			
People's Action Party	CR	75.5	75 (69)
Solomon Islands			
Independent Group	C	...	...
National Democratic Party	L	...	...
Somalia (December 1979)			
Somalian Revolutionary Socialist Party	—	...	171
South Africa (April 1981)			
Herstigte Nasionale Partij	ER	13.8	0 (0)
National Conservative Party	R	...	0 —
National Party	R	56.1	131 (134)
South Africa Party	CR	—	— (3)
New Republic Party	C	7.7	8 (10)
Progressive Federal Party	L	19.1	26 (17)
Spain (October 1982)			
Alianza Popular	R	25.35	105 (9)
Unión Centro-Democrático	C	7.26	11 (168)
Partido Socialista Obrero Español	SD	46.07	201 (121)
Partido Comunista Español	K	3.87	5 (23)
Catalan nationalists	—	3.73	12 (8)
Basque nationalists	—	1.91	8 (7)
Herri Batasuna (Basque radicals)	—	0.97	2 (3)
Others	—	...	6 (14)
Sri Lanka (July 1977)			
United National Party	R	...	140 (19)
Freedom Party	C	...	8 (91)
Tamil United Liberation Front	C	...	18 (12)
Communists and others	—	...	2 (44)
Sudan (December 1981)			
Sudanese Social Union	—	...	151
Suriname			
National Military Council since 1980	—	—	—
Swaziland			
Royal government, no parties	—	—	—
Sweden (September 1982)			
Conservative	R	23.6	86 (73)
Centre	CR	15.6	56 (64)
Liberal	C	5.9	21 (38)
Social Democrats	SD	45.9	166 (154)
Communists	K	5.5	20 (20)
Switzerland (October 1983)			
Christian Democrats (Conservative)	R	...	42 (44)
Republican Movement	R	...	0 (1)
National Campaign	R	...	5 (2)
Evangelical People's	R	...	3 (3)
Swiss People's (ex-Middle Class)	CR	...	23 (23)
Radical Democrats	C	...	54 (51)
League of Independents	C	...	8 (8)
Liberal Democrats	L	...	8 (8)
Social Democrats	SD	...	47 (51)
Progressive Organization (Socialists)	EL	...	3 (3)
Communist Party	K	...	1 (3)
Environmentalist Party	—	...	3 —
Others	—	...	3 (3)
Syria (November 1981)			
National Progressive Front	—	...	195 (159)
Others	—	...	0 (36)
Taiwan (Republic of China)			
Nationalist (Kuomintang)	—	...	773
Tanzania (October 1980)			
Tanganyika African National Union	C	...	111 (218)
Zanzibar Afro-Shirazi (nominated)	L	...	40 (52)
Thailand (April 1983)			
Prachakorn Thai	ER	...	36
Chart Thai (Thai Nation)	R	...	73
Social Action Party	C	...	92
Democratic Party	C	...	56
Siam Democratic Party		...	18
National Democratic Party		...	15
Independents	—	...	24
Four other parties	—	...	10
Togo (December 1979)			
Rassemblement du Peuple Togolais	—	96.0	67
Tonga (May 1981)			
Legislative Assembly (partially elected)	—	—	21
Trinidad and Tobago (November 1981)			
People's National Movement	C	...	26 (24)
Organization for National Reconstruction	—	...	0 —
National Alliance:			
United Labour Front	L	...	8 (10)
Democratic Action Congress	EL	...	2 (2)
Tunisia (November 1981)			
National Front (led by the Parti Socialiste Destourien)	—	94.6	136 (121)
Turkey (November 1983)			
Nationalist Democracy Party	R	23.0	71
Motherland Party	CR	45.0	212
Populist Party	C	30.0	117
Tuvalu (September 1981)			
No political parties	—	...	...
Uganda (December 1980)			
Uganda People's Congress Party	—	...	68
Democratic Party	—	...	48
Union of Soviet Socialist Republics (March 1979)			
Communist Party of the Soviet Union	—	99.99	1,500 (767)
United Arab Emirates			
Federal government of seven emirates	—	—	—
United Kingdom (June 1983)			
Conservative	R	42.4	397 (339)
Alliance			
Liberal	C	25.4	17 (11)
Social Democratic	C		6 —
Labour	L	27.6	209 (268)
Communist	K	...	0 (0)
Scottish National Party	—	1.1	2 (2)
Plaid Cymru (Welsh Nationalists)	—	0.4	2 (2)
Ulster Unionists (three groups)	—	...	15 (10)
Social Democratic and Labour Party	—	...	1 (1)
Sinn Fein (Northern Ireland)	—	...	1 —
United States (November 1982)			
Republican	CR	...	166 (192)
Democratic	C	...	267 (242)
Independent		...	0 (1)
Upper Volta			
National Revolutionary Council since August 1983	—	—	—
Uruguay			
Rule by Council of State from 1973	—	—	—
Vanuatu (New Hebrides) (November 1983)			
Vanuaaku Pati	C	...	24 (26)
Others	—	...	15 (13)
Venezuela (December 1983)			
COPEI (Social Christians)	CR	28.31	... (88)
Acción Democrática	L	44.25	118 (88)
Movimiento al Socialismo	SD	...	... (11)
Partido Comunista Venezolano	K	...	... (7)
Others	—	...	... (7)
Vietnam, Socialist Republic of (April 1981)Communist Party	—	...	...
Yemen, People's Democratic Republic of			
National Liberation Front	—	—	—
Yemen Arab Republic			
Military government since 1974	—	—	—
Yugoslavia (May 1982)			
Communist-controlled Federal Chamber	—	...	220 (220)
Zaire (October 1977)			
Legislative Council of the Mouvement Populaire de la Révolution	—	...	268
Zambia (October 1983)			
United National Independence Party	—	67.0	125
Zimbabwe (February–March 1980)			
Zimbabwe African National Union	—	63.0	57
Zimbabwe African People's Union	—	24.0	20
United African National Council	—	8.0	3
Rhodesian Front (Europeans)	—		20

(K. M. SMOGORZEWSKI)

Portugal

A republic of southwestern Europe, Portugal shares the Iberian Peninsula with Spain. Area: 91,985 sq km (35,516 sq mi), including the Azores (2,247 sq km) and Madeira (794 sq km). Pop. (1982 est.): 10,056,000. Cap. and largest city: Lisbon (pop., 1981 prelim., 812,400). Language: Portuguese. Religion: Roman Catholic. President in 1983, Gen. António dos Santos Ramalho Eanes; premiers, Francisco Pinto Balsemão and, from June 9, Mário Soares.

The breakup of the ruling Democratic Alliance (AD) coalition at the end of 1982 was triggered by Portugal's deepening economic crisis and followed a drop of 4.5% in support for the AD in municipal elections held in December. The leaders of its two major component parties—the Social Democratic Party (PSD) and the Democratic and Social Centre (CSD)—resigned. After the resignation of PSD leader Francisco Pinto Balsemão as premier, the selection of a premier-designate proved complicated. Former premier Mota Pinto, who had served during 1978–79, refused to accept the post.

The eventual compromise candidate, Pereira Crespo, could not persuade several key AD luminaries to join his team of ministers. With the aid of the AD steering committee, Crespo managed, after a considerable delay, to assemble his Cabinet, and on Jan. 18, 1983, the newly constituted Council of State met to endorse the nominations. In the event, the council divided equally for and against the prospective Cabinet, and on January 23 Pres. António Ramalho Eanes announced that he had decided to call fresh general elections and recall Pinto Balsemão to lead a caretaker government. The Assembly was dissolved on February 4, and elections were called for April 25.

The Socialist Party (PSP), which campaigned on a platform of "100 measures in 100 days," proposed to make a loan agreement with the International Monetary Fund (IMF), introduce public-sector austerity, and fight corruption. The Socialists won 101 seats in the 250-seat Assembly, compared with 74 in the previous elections. Both the PSD and the CSD, who had decided to run separately, lost support, as did the Communist Party. (For tabulated results, *see* POLITICAL PARTIES.)

On May 7 the PSP leader, Mário Soares (*see* BIOGRAPHIES), formally invited the PSD to begin negotiations to form a coalition that would command a two-thirds majority in the Assembly. Progress toward an agreement that would survive for four years was slow, and it was not until June 4 that the talks were brought to a successful conclusion. By that time the parties had agreed on the distribution of portfolios, and the PSP had grudgingly accepted the need for reform of the labour laws. There were other contentious decisions: to allow private-sector investment back into the cement, fertilizer, insurance, and banking businesses, all of which had been nationalized in 1974; to adopt a politically neutral approach toward raising agricultural productivity; and to attempt to reach a social pact with industry and labour. Both the PSP and the PSD agreed to implement an economic austerity policy, especially in the public sector, while recognizing that living standards were bound to drop until at least 1985.

WIDE WORLD

Mário Soares, leader of Portugal's Socialist Party, formed a coalition government with the Social Democrats.

Soares's new Cabinet included nine PSP and seven PSD ministers, with Mota Pinto, new leader of the PSD, as minister of defense and vice-premier and one independent, Ernani Lopes, as minister of finance. The government took office on June 9, and the Assembly approved the incoming Cabinet's program 15 days later by 161 votes to 67. In his grim inaugural speech, Soares said that Portugal had been living beyond its means. Many private and state firms were on the verge of bankruptcy, surviving only by means of state handouts. There were severe liquidity problems; a drain on foreign reserves had been fueled by speculation; and inflation had reached record levels. Soares promised strict austerity designed to reverse these trends.

To help the process of economic recovery, the government devalued the escudo by 12% on June 22, raised the prices of energy and subsidized food, and placed a 5% surcharge on company taxation in order to reduce the budget deficit. The Finance Ministry imposed a two-month freeze on state investment and promised a thorough review of public-sector spending. The government also won Assembly approval for a law allowing private investment in banking, insurance, and the cement and fertilizer industries in partial fulfillment of the PSD-PSP four-year political pact.

Portugal was forced to turn to the Bank for International Settlements in March, May, and August to service debts and to pay off $4 billion in short-term loans. The loans were backed by gold; to repay the loan raised in May, the country sold 30 metric tons of gold, while the other two credits were reportedly backed by pledges of 60 metric tons of gold. After completing the sale, Soares stated that no further gold sales were planned in 1983.

Portugal's increasingly difficult financial situation led the government to approach the IMF in August, and on October 7 a standby loan of 445 million Special Drawing Rights and an export compensatory finance facility worth 258 million Special Drawing Rights were announced. The IMF agreement entailed limiting the budget deficit with the aim of encouraging further loans from foreign sources. In its wake, Portugal was soon able to raise $350 million from international banks.

The 1984 budget, which was debated by the Assembly in October, was prepared with the IMF targets in view. The 1984 deficit was to total no more than 6.5% of gross domestic product (GDP). The only real increases in spending were in the education and social-services sectors. The squeeze on all other ministries was designed to slow GDP growth and eventually inflation, which had gained momentum as a result of cuts in subsidies on staples and food.

Soares attended a summit meeting of Europe's five socialist prime ministers in October. The meeting paved the way for an unexpected agreement among the agriculture ministers of the European Economic Community on the EEC's rules for marketing farm products from the Mediterranean.

PORTUGAL

Education. (1979–80) Primary, pupils 1,220,527, teachers 65,124; secondary (1977–78), pupils 409,045, teachers 12,363; vocational, pupils 13,540, teachers 1,905; teacher training, students 1,536, teachers 106; higher, students 81,379, teaching staff 8,637.

Finance. Monetary unit: escudo, with (Sept. 20, 1983) a free rate of 123.90 escudos to U.S. $1 (186.59 escudos = £1 sterling). Gold and other reserves (June 1983) U.S. $1,156,000,000. Budget (1981 est.) balanced at 490 billion escudos. Gross national product (1980) 1,174,900,000,000 escudos. Money supply (Feb. 1983) 612,840,000,000 escudos. Cost of living (1975 = 100; May 1983) 477.5.

Foreign Trade. (1982) Imports 748,530,000,000 escudos; exports 331,760,000,000 escudos. Import sources: EEC 41% (West Germany 12%, France 9%, U.K. 8%, Italy 6%); U.S. 11%; Spain 6%; Saudi Arabia 5%. Export destinations: EEC 57% (U.K. 15%, France 13%, West Germany 13%, The Netherlands 6%, Italy 5%); U.S. 6%. Main exports (1981): clothing 14%; textile yarns and fabrics 13%; machinery 9%; petroleum products 7%; chemicals 6%; cork and manufactures 6%; food 5%; wine 5%; wood pulp 5%. Tourism (1981): visitors 3,021,000; gross receipts U.S. $1,023,000,000.

Transport and Communications. Roads (1980) 51,953 km (including 127 km expressways). Motor vehicles in use (1980): passenger 1,268,970; commercial 186,100. Railways: (1981) 3,611 km; traffic (1982) 5,412,000,000 passenger-km, freight 1,060,000,000 net ton-km. Air traffic (1982): 4,174,000,000 passenger-km; freight 106.7 million net ton-km. Shipping (1982): merchant vessels 100 gross tons and over 356; gross tonnage 1,401,589. Telephones (Jan. 1981) 1,371,700. Radio receivers (Dec. 1980) 1,576,000. Television licenses (Dec. 1980) 1,382,000.

Agriculture. Production (in 000; metric tons; 1982): wheat 445; oats 83; rye *c.* 110; corn 464; rice 143; potatoes 1,100; tomatoes 430; apples 105; oranges 100; wine *c.* 1,000; olives *c.* 350; olive oil 70; cow's milk *c.* 695; meat 455; fish catch (1981) 255; timber (cu m; 1981) 7,655. Livestock (in 000; 1982): sheep *c.* 5,200; cattle *c.* 1,000; goats *c.* 750; pigs (1981) *c.* 3,430; poultry *c.* 17,600.

Industry. Production (in 000; metric tons; 1982): coal 180; petroleum products (1981) 7,818; manufactured gas (cu m) 143,000; electricity (kw-hr) 14,655,000; kaolin (1981) 53; iron ore (50% metal content) 28; crude steel 362; sulfuric acid 492; fertilizers (nutrient content; 1981–82) nitrogenous 181, phosphate 94; plastics and resins (1980) 136; cement 5,885; wood pulp (1980) 642; cork products (1980) 327; cotton yarn 98; woven cotton fabrics 65.

These proposals opened negotiations on the farm dossier, delayed for two years by France's resistance to reform of the EEC common agricultural policy and the increasing difficulties over financing the EEC budget. These delays had caused Soares to hint strongly that, unless progress was made, Portugal would have to consider an alternative to EEC membership. In 1982 the EEC granted Portugal loans worth 80 million European currency units, as well as technical and financial advice to help prepare the country for entry to the Community. In December agreements were signed extending U.S. rights to use an air base in the Azores for seven years in return for increased military and economic aid. (MICHAEL WOOLLER)

See also Dependent States.

Prisons and Penology

The death penalty was again an issue in the U.S. and the U.K. during 1983. The controversy gathered force late in 1982, when Charles Brooks was executed by lethal injection at Huntsville, Texas. Two doctors were present at the execution. Although they did not administer the injection, one was quoted as saying that he had given guidance to those who did. Objections were raised by medical associations in a number of countries where such a practice is regarded as contrary to medical ethics. There was even more contention after the electrocution of John Louis Evans, the seventh American to be put to death since the Supreme Court reinstated the death penalty in 1976 and the first in Alabama in 18 years. Three separate jolts of 1,900 v were applied over a nine-minute period before officials were sure Evans was dead. After the second jolt, his lawyers, upset by the spectacle, appealed to Gov. George C. Wallace for clemency but got no response. More than 1,000 prisoners were under sentence of death in 37 states.

In the U.K., after the reelection of the Conservative government in May 1983 with an increased majority, there was a renewed call by some members of Parliament for reintroduction of the death penalty. As in the U.S., the demand corresponded to popular sentiment. In July, however, when free (nonparty) votes were taken in Parliament on the issue (including capital punishment for the murder of police and prison officers, terrorists, and other special categories of homicide), the restorationists lost by a surprisingly large margin. De facto or de jure, the death penalty for murder therefore remained abolished in all Western European countries. In many other parts of the world, capital punishment continued to be inflicted for a variety of offenses. From China, for example, came reports of numerous executions, carried out as part of a crackdown on common crimes.

The defeat of the effort to reinstate capital punishment in the U.K. gave rise to pressure for stiffer penalties for certain kinds of murderers. Leon Brittan (*see* BIOGRAPHIES), who replaced William Whitelaw as home secretary after the election, undertook to consider the matter. However, prisons in the U.K. were already grossly overcrowded. Hundreds of prisoners remanded to custody pend-

Portuguese Literature:
see Literature

Power:
see Energy; Engineering Projects; Industrial Review

Presbyterian Churches:
see Religion

Prices:
see Economy, World

Printing:
see Industrial Review

WIDE WORLD

Inmates at the Ossining (New York) Correctional Facility demanded attention by the news media as a condition of ending their takeover of a cell block.

ing trial had to be held for long periods in inadequate police cells, with only 15 minutes of exercise a day—and that in manacles. Brittan indicated that the majority of prisoners serving short sentences could expect early release through an extension of parole.

Overcrowding in prisons and poor conditions for both inmates and staff, long prevalent in the U.S. and the U.K., were evident in many other countries as well. In Ireland some convicted prisoners had to report to the police for months before a place could be found for them in jail. In France the amnesty introduced by the incoming Socialist government in 1981 had cut the prison population to its theoretical maximum of 30,000. Since then it had risen to 38,000, of whom 20,000 were awaiting trial; the pretrial period sometimes ran into years. Angry protests and, in one jail, a mass "suicide" attempt (41 prisoners cut their veins) resulted. In June French prison officers went on strike over bad working conditions.

Italy's prisons were even more seriously overcrowded and understaffed. It was estimated that 10,000 additional staff were needed, but the breakdown of orderly prison life, with murders, Mafia influence, and fierce fighting among the inmates, made it almost impossible to recruit personnel. Japan continued to have the least crowded prison system of any developed country, corresponding with its low, though gradually rising, crime rate. The system had no escapes, made a profit, emphasized rehabilitation (contrary to the prevailing trend), and fostered good relations between inmates and staff. Staff training was careful and prolonged, with a high ratio of guards to inmates. (*See* Special Report.)

An inquiry in England by the chief inspector of prisons showed that it was the remand and life-sentence prisoners who were most likely to commit suicide. The suicide rate had risen by one-quarter over the past 25 years. Drugs were rapidly becoming an important factor in jail, and hostage taking of staff was on the increase. Recent legislation had abolished the old indeterminate sentences of Borstal training for young offenders. The 1982 Criminal Justice Act substituted determinate "youth custody" sentences, a provision that might result in more custodial sentences, though of shorter length. The new act also provided for various alternatives to prison, ranging from fines, suspended or deferred sentences, probation, and community service to various schemes for making reparations to the victims of crime, often under the supervision of probation officers. Jail during weekends only, which allowed offenders to remain at work during the week, was being advocated in the U.K. It had already been introduced in Belgium, The Netherlands, West Germany, and some U.S. states.

New Zealand had been one of the first countries to have a state system of compensation for victims of crime. Later, the Criminal Injuries Compensation Board was set up in the U.K. In the U.S. passage of the Victim and Witness Protection Act of 1982, designed to elicit the cooperation of victims and witnesses and to provide them with information, compensation, and understanding, was followed by the establishment of a presidential task force on victims of crime and by state legislation responding to victim and witness needs. Voluntary victim-support systems had also developed rapidly in Western European countries.

Research into the type, growth, and effectiveness of alternatives to prison in Europe, with an eye toward possible adoption in the U.S., was being sponsored by the Council of Europe, supported by Fulbright funds and the German Marshall Fund in the U.S., and carried out by the research department of the French Ministry of Justice. Comparative research was also being undertaken into European sentencing patterns. Measuring the effectiveness of penal methods continued to pose problems, however. Sweden had attempted to set up more sensitive statistics on relapse into further crime by counting the crime-free days after release from imprisonment or upon completion of probation or parole. No one penal method appeared to give better results, although some were more cost-effective.

The reduction of crime depends on a better understanding of criminal behaviour and its extent. On the latter front, a step forward was made in February 1983 with the publication of the first massive *British Crime Survey*. This Home Office report showed that official criminal statistics, which are generally stressed in the media, falsify the real picture. Careful interviewing of 11,000 victims demonstrated that violent crime is underrecorded fivefold and property offenses fourfold. It also showed that, contrary to popular opinion, the elderly are least likely to be attacked. Similar work in the U.S. also indicated that upward or downward tendencies in official statistics do not necessarily convey an accurate picture of crime.

(HUGH J. KLARE)

See also Crime and Law Enforcement; Law.
[521.C.3.a; 543.A.5.a; 10/36.C.5.b]

OVERSTUFFED CELLBLOCKS

by Richard Whittingham

Oscar Wilde, who by 1898 had tasted the bitters of prison life himself, described it with brooding insight in his poem "The Ballad of Reading Gaol":

> The vilest deeds like poison weeds
> Bloom well in prison-air:
> It is only what is good in Man
> That wastes and withers there. . . .

Wilde's observation of a prison, that "cave of black despair" as he called it, is as trenchant today as it was at the turn of the century, when criminal offenders were routinely sent off to the special horrors of such hellholes as Devil's Island. Prison practices like flogging, branding, tattooing, disfigurement, pillorying, and other forms of corporal punishment had all but vanished from the Western world by the 1980s. Still, society was far from solving the problems of what prisons should be like and how those incarcerated in them should be treated.

Those problems are universal. The infamies of prisons around the world range from the gross overcrowding in South African jails to the brutalities carried out in those of many Middle Eastern countries to the filth and squalor of most Southeast Asian prisons. In the West bloody riots and murders have taken place behind prison walls. The violence and sexual atrocities committed by prisoners on other prisoners in many penitentiaries are horrifying.

Crowded Cells. In most Western countries the most immediate problem is overcrowding. It is a problem both for society, which must decide how to handle the proliferation of prisoners, and for the inmates and those who guard and manage the prisons because of the trying and often dangerous conditions that overcrowding creates.

Society's attitude toward prison overcrowding contains a basic ambiguity. On the one hand, people and their governments want the ever increasing number of convicted felons sent to prison to serve appropriate sentences, and they do not want hardened criminals released prematurely. At the same time, they do not want to spend the money to build new prisons or to enlarge existing ones substantially. In various U.S. jurisdictions, for example, prison authorities have been caught between court orders to alleviate "inhumane" overcrowding and an outcry from the public and the law enforcement community against early release. The situation has been compounded by the trend toward determinate sentencing, in which set sentences are prescribed for specific crimes, generally without the chance of parole. At the lower end of the prison system, in the local jails and lockups, delays in the court system result in long periods of incarceration for accused persons unable to make bail.

By 1983 the prison population in the United States had risen to more than 425,000, approximately double what it had been a decade earlier, creating internment problems of major consequence. The rate of increase in the early 1980s was an alarming 12%. In England and Wales, where the prison population was about 45,000 in 1983, then home secretary William Whitelaw suggested that prison overcrowding had become a national emergency. Courts were given powers to impose partly suspended sentences for various offenders and to shorten the sentences of those already in prison.

The governments of the United States and Great Britain, as well as those of many other nations throughout the world, have recognized the problem of overcrowding. The American Correctional Association (ACA), the principal organization of prison officials in the U.S., has revised its lengthy and detailed ledger of standards so as to address the penal problems of the 1980s, especially those associated with overcrowding. Great Britain, along with 19 other European countries, signed the European Convention on Human Rights, which sets forth guidelines for the treatment of prisoners.

It is easier, however, to promulgate such arbitrary rules than to enforce them. The ACA lists as a basic requirement that each prisoner have a cell of his or her own of at least 60 sq ft (5.6 sq m; about 6 by 10 ft or 2 by 3 m). But *Time* magazine reports that "only about a fifth of U.S. inmates have one-man, 60-foot cells." In many British prisons, according to *The Economist* magazine, "such practices as the jamming of three men into a cell intended for only one, and keeping them there 23 hours a day with only a plastic bucket each for a lavatory," have become all too common.

Alternative Answers. Theoretical solutions abound. The most obvious, of course, is to expand existing facilities and build new prisons where necessary. It is also the most expensive. Modern prisons cost an extraordinary amount of money. In the United States, for example, medium- and maximum-security prison complexes built in recent years have cost between $30,000 and $78,000 per cell to con-

---

Richard Whittingham, a free-lance writer, is the author of Martial Justice *and many other books on contemporary affairs.*

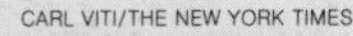
CARL VITI/THE NEW YORK TIMES

To relieve overcrowding in cell blocks, San Quentin prison authorities in California erected army tents within the grounds and established prison camps outside.

struct. It is estimated that the total amount needed to build enough facilities to alleviate prison overcrowding in the U.S. could be as much as $10 billion. In a period of financial stringency, this kind of money is not readily available, nor does it appear that the taxpayers are ready to take on such a financial burden.

To attack the problem now, other alternatives have been proposed. Of the various forms of early release, parole is one of the most familiar and widely used. However, it has fallen into some disfavour with the public, partly because the programs are frequently underfunded (with consequent heavy caseloads and poor training of parole officers) and partly because of the perception that prisoners manipulate the system. Other suggestions include allowing prisoners to spend the last part of their sentences in halfway-house-type facilities, where they can be helped to readjust to society.

A more drastic approach is to reserve prisons for only the most violent, hardened, and dangerous criminals. Where possible, other offenders would be diverted from the criminal justice system entirely; they might be placed, for example, in alcohol or drug rehabilitation programs where this is appropriate. Those convicted of lesser crimes, such as theft, might be given probation, assigned to do community service or charity work, or required to participate in victim-restitution programs. Or they might be sentenced to spend only the nights or weekends in jail or in halfway-house-type facilities or dormitories for the duration of their terms. In Quebec, for instance, prison inmates go out to work in local businesses and factories during the day and return to the prison at night. They earn salaries equivalent to ordinary employees but are required to pay room and board to the prison out of their earnings.

A Growing Crisis. As governments consider whether to solve the overcrowding crisis by letting prisoners out early or settling for probationary sentences in petty crimes, the key question is: which offenders should be allowed to go free in society? Statistics in the United States and Great Britain show that anywhere from a quarter to a third of those inmates who have served time in prison are recidivists, chronic criminals who return to a life of crime after their terms are over. They are obviously not prime candidates for early release. Yet who can really determine who the potential recidivists are, at least until they have been convicted and sent to prison for subsequent crimes?

Many penologists claim that providing alternatives to imprisonment for lesser offenders does not increase the amount of crime, and that the prison experience, if anything, is likely to turn minor offenders into hardened criminals. But every heinous crime committed by an offender on probation or parole or a suspect out on bail understandably raises the level of public fear and the clamour to "lock them up and throw away the key."

Something must be done, however—and soon. Overcrowding is a contributing factor to all the other woes and problems within a prison, and they are many and bizarre. Some prisons are virtually controlled by gangs or tightly knit cadres of the most brutal prisoners. Murder is not uncommon; stabbings are prevalent, as are drug abuse, extortion, and homosexual rape. Some choose suicide as their form of early release. For the most part, life is a matter of the survival of the fittest, often at the basest and most primitive level.

As *The Economist* aptly observed: "Prisons are not hotels for the naughty: they should be forbidding, uncosy places to go. But to make them degrading will only continue to create a degraded class of recidivists among those who emerge (or escape) from them." It is a problem that affects not just the prison population and those directly responsible for administering the prisons. It reaches out with threatening tentacles to all of society.

Publishing

The preliminary financial reports of leading publishers for 1983 generally indicated some recovery from the recession of the preceding years, and there was optimism throughout the industry that the corner had been turned. Newspaper publishers had their own special problems, notably in Britain and France (*see* below). Also in France, press baron Robert Hersant faced possible legislation to limit his holdings, while in the U.S. Australian Rupert Murdoch extended his holdings by acquiring the *Chicago Sun-Times* (*see* below).

Other countries saw familiar clashes between the press and the authorities. In March three leading South African journalists faced a secret trial following their reports of National Intelligence Service involvement in the 1981 coup attempt in Seychelles. In August South African-based foreign correspondents found themselves barred by the neighbouring "front-line" African states, led by Zimbabwe. During the same month Western reporters in Karachi, Pakistan, were attacked by a mob after a fabricated story by the government press agency said that one of them had incited antigovernment demonstrations. In Yugoslavia journalists made an unprecedented public protest against political appointments of editors and other official pressures. Several editors of China's *People's Daily* reportedly were forced out of office in an antiliberal campaign. In Moscow there was unusual criticism of the Soviet media when Konstantin Chernenko of the Central Committee assailed the press and broadcasters for what he called cliché dispatches and commentaries, lack of originality, and insufficient promptness.

The "new world information order" sought by third world countries was again the subject of contention at UNESCO's annual meeting. Threats against press freedom were among the reasons cited by the U.S. for its decision to leave UNESCO at the end of 1984.

Newspapers. In Britain and France economics and the law were entwined to create new forms of old problems for newspaper publishers. It was in France that the troubles hit hardest. The pattern of falling total sales since World War II, in the face of rising prices and competition from television, was common to many other countries, but in France newspaper sales of 15 million in 1946 had declined to 12.4 million in 1970 and plunged even more sharply in the next decade; the 1982 total was 9.3 million, and in 1983 the slide continued. The main Paris dailies fared worst, declining 25% between 1975 and 1981; in 1983 there were 11 such national titles, compared with 28 in 1946, and all were reported to be losing money.

Ironically, given the advent of the Socialist government in 1981, the most evident wounds had been to the left-of-centre papers. The Communist Party's official organ, *L'Humanité*, laid off staff, while the pro-Socialist *Le Matin* instituted salary freezes and staff cuts. Hardest hit was the internationally respected *Le Monde*. Still the second largest national daily, with a circulation of about 400,000, it too had suffered a continuing sales loss, amounting to some 10% in 1982 alone, and the $2.2 million deficit in 1983 seemed likely to continue.

One of the thorns in *Le Monde*'s flesh was the rapid rise of the much smaller (100,000) *Libération*. The increasing objectivity and cultural coverage of this left-wing tabloid helped its middle-ground appeal, and it also received a cash injection from outside business concerns—a contribution that the terms of *Le Monde*'s protective trust expressly forbade.

France's right-wing press was not free of economic problems, but its main new concern was a bill introduced in November that aimed at limiting newspaper ownership. Its provisions would prevent one group or individual from owning more than three national daily newspapers, or both a national and a provincial daily of general or political interest, or more than 15%, in circulation terms, of the publications in any particular category. Although presented as a modernization of the existing 1944 antimonopoly press law, the new measure was widely seen as the Socialist government's bid to curb the regional expansion and national influence of Robert Hersant's publishing empire. The Hersant group already owned three national titles, including the increasingly right-wing *Le Figaro* and *France-Soir*, with 43% of all such sales, and its regional penetration was 14%, with more acquisitions rumoured. On every count the new law would affect Hersant and virtually no one else.

In Britain new legislation and publishing economics became knotted in a potentially destructive way. In general, it was a reasonably stable year. The national newspapers carried on the traditional battles for readers in their various sectors. The *Daily Express*, having slipped below the two million mark, brought in the ex-*Sun* editor, Sir Larry Lamb, to fight the rival *Daily Mail* for the middle ground. Rupert Murdoch was also involved in sur-

FRIEDMAN—BLACK STAR

Katherine Fanning, new editor of the *Christian Science Monitor.*

Profits:
see Economy, World

Protestant Churches:
see Religion

Psychiatry:
see Health and Disease

World Daily Newspapers and Circulation[1]

Location	Daily newspapers	Circulation per 1,000 population
AFRICA		
Algeria	5	29
Angola	4	16
Benin	1	...
Botswana	1	20
Cameroon	1	6
Central African Republic	1	...
Chad	4	...
Congo	5	15
Egypt	7	124
Equatorial Guinea	2	3[2]
Ethiopia	3	1
Gabon	2	11
Gambia	3	5
Ghana	5	...
Guinea	1	2
Guinea-Bissau	1	7
Ivory Coast	1	8
Kenya	3	13
Lesotho	3	32
Liberia	2	6
Libya	3	...
Madagascar	3	2[2]
Malawi	1	2
Mali	1	1
Mauritius	7	69
Morocco	8	12
Mozambique	3	6
Niger	1	1
Nigeria	16	15
Réunion	2	101
Senegal	1	13
Seychelles	1	63
Sierra Leone	1	3
Somalia	2	...
South Africa	25	70[2]
South West Africa/Namibia	3	19
Sudan	4	8[2]
Swaziland	1	17
Tanzania	2	5
Togo	3	5
Tunisia	5	49
Uganda	1	2
Upper Volta	2	2[2]
Zaire	6	1
Zambia	2	30
Zimbabwe	2	20
Total	161	
NORTH AMERICA		
Antigua	2	...
Bahamas, The	3	142
Barbados	2	410
Belize	1	...
Bermuda	1	455
Canada	115	218
Costa Rica	4	121
Cuba	17	133
Dominican Republic	9	52
El Salvador	11	71[2]
Guadeloupe	1	103
Guatemala	6	47[2]
Haiti	4	4
Honduras	6	99
Jamaica	3	137
Martinique	1	105
Mexico	327	130[2]
Netherlands Antilles	7	219[2]
Nicaragua	3	63
Panama	6	95[2]
Puerto Rico	5	178
Trinidad and Tobago	4	143
United States	1,711	276
Virgin Islands (U.S.)	3	170
Total	2,252	
OCEANIA		
American Samoa	3	267[2]
Australia	87	426
Cook Islands	1	250
Fiji	3	106
French Polynesia	4	98
Guam	1	320
New Caledonia	2	164
New Zealand	33	326
Niue	1	60
Papua New Guinea	1	9
Total	136	
ASIA		
Afghanistan	13	4[2]
Bangladesh	30	6
Burma	6	14
China	382	74
Cyprus	15	119[2]
Hong Kong	61	...
India	1,264	...
Indonesia	172	...
Iran	22	25[2]
Iraq	5	19
Israel	26	416
Japan	178	569
Jordan	3	73
Kampuchea	10	...
Korea, North	9	54[2]
Korea, South	34	190
Kuwait	7	267
Laos	3	...
Lebanon	14	49[2]
Macau	9	...
Malaysia	40	133
Mongolia	2	103
Nepal	28	8
Pakistan	107	24
Philippines	22	52
Saudi Arabia	7	...
Singapore	11	264
Sri Lanka	15	52
Syria	5	7
Taiwan	30	163
Thailand	33	53
Turkey	255	...
Vietnam	4	9
Yemen (Aden)	3	6
Yemen (San'a')	2	...
Total	2,827	
EUROPE		
Albania	2	52
Austria	29	780
Belgium	41	315
Bulgaria	12	245
Czechoslovakia	30	283
Denmark	49	356
Finland	63	503
France	84	211
Germany, East	39	515
Germany, West	626	584
Gibraltar	3	200
Greece	110	88[2]
Hungary	29	383
Iceland	5	557
Ireland	7	224
Italy	90	132[2]
Liechtenstein	2	558
Luxembourg	5	352
Malta	4	150
Netherlands, The	80	325
Norway	87	479
Poland	49	287
Portugal	31	74
Romania	33	181
Spain	116	...
Sweden	163	579
Switzerland	98	593
U.S.S.R.	700	312
United Kingdom	110	419
Vatican City	1	...
Yugoslavia	24	97
Total	2,716	
SOUTH AMERICA		
Argentina	167	848[2]
Bolivia	13	45
Brazil	328	44[2]
Chile	37	87
Colombia	35	48[2]
Ecuador	38	49[2]
French Guiana	1	...
Guyana	2	195
Paraguay	5	78
Peru	67	118
Suriname	5	82
Uruguay	23	337
Venezuela	51	120[2]
Total	772	

[1]Only newspapers issued four or more times weekly are included; most recent information.
[2]Partial circulation only.
Sources: UNESCO, *Statistical Yearbook 1982; Editor and Publisher International Year Book* (1983); *Europa Year Book 1983, A World Survey;* various country publications.

prises over editors; he brought in the 34-year-old Andrew Neil, a section editor on *The Economist* with a passion for the new technologies, as editor of *The Sunday Times* and himself became the target of Harold Evans, ex-editor of both *The Sunday Times* and *The Times,* whose memoirs (*Good Times, Bad Times*) accused Murdoch of failing to keep the promises he made to the government when taking over Times Newspapers. Sales of *The Times* began to rise, meanwhile, and losses dropped somewhat, although its rival, *The Guardian,* moved to new records, with a 100,000 lead.

The *Financial Times* (*FT*), smallest and most profitable of the national dailies, suffered the worst problem. In May its management reached an impasse in efforts to negotiate new terms with the machine managers, a group of 24 skilled, highly paid, and mostly nonstaff print workers. The men and their union, the National Graphical Association (NGA), went on strike, and the *FT* remained off the streets for ten weeks, at a cost of £10 million. The resulting settlement was not a total victory for management, and the affair was widely seen as a badly judged bid to achieve much-needed new practices. In late November the NGA was the centre of a wider and more complex dispute, involving a small publisher of free sheets in northwest England, Selim ("Eddie") Shah. The union, in a dispute with him, had sought both a closed-shop agreement and reinstatement of six of its members. In picketing Shah's printing works, the NGA became the first union to defy the new industrial relations legislation, widely denounced by the union movement and the Labour opposition in Parliament. Shah sought court orders against the pickets, and the NGA became liable to fines amounting to £675,000, to be enforced by sequestration of its assets. A sympathy strike, which stopped newspaper publishing in London for several days, in turn brought claims totaling £3 million, as the national newspaper publishers availed themselves of the damages provisions of the new legislation. These developments provoked a crisis in the trade union movement over how far to oppose the law. A threatened national NGA strike, called for December 14, was postponed, but the newspaper industry found itself a testing ground for national legal issues and policies. Furthermore, the dispute involved the craft union with which Britain's major national newspapers must deal if they are ever to bring in the new technology now commonplace in many other countries.

(PETER FIDDICK)

For newspapers in the U.S., the year was marked by rising prosperity and, at the same time, deepening concern about the state of press freedom. The administration of Pres. Ronald Reagan appeared to have launched a campaign to restrict that essential ingredient of the newspaper business, information. The administration was fighting in Congress for limits on the Freedom of Information Act, which guarantees public access to many forms of government data. The White House also indicated its support of proposals calling for fines and jail sentences for journalists who disclosed classified government data.

Perhaps the most dramatic evidence of the administration's restrictive attitude toward the press was its prohibition of newspaper and broadcast coverage during the first two days of the U.S. invasion of Grenada. Unlike nearly every major military operation in the nation's history, the October 25 landing on the Caribbean island took place without a single journalist in attendance. Administration spokesmen said that reporters had been banned out of consideration for their safety, but there was widespread suspicion that U.S. officials merely wanted to avoid unfavourable coverage.

Within days after the Grenada landing the American Society of Newspaper Editors formally protested the U.S. government's "failure to honor the long tradition of on-the-scene coverage of American military operations," and President Reagan's own deputy press secretary for foreign affairs resigned in protest against the reporting restrictions.

On the bright side, average daily newspaper circulation achieved a modern-day high of 62,487,177, according to the 1983 *Editor & Publisher International Yearbook.* That represented a gain of 1.7% over the previous year. Morning circulation rose an impressive 8.6% to 33,174,087, for the first time surpassing evening circulation, which declined by 5.1% to 29,313,090. Eleven new dailies were launched, and 13 old ones ceased publication. Those changes, together with a number of mergers and discontinued editions, brought the total number of daily newspapers to 1,711, a loss of 19. The Bureau of Advertising reported that advertising volume rose 5.4% over the previous year to $18.3 billion, an impressive gain in a U.S. economy that was still recovering from recession.

Perhaps the year's leading newspaper transaction was the sale of the *Chicago Sun-Times* by Field Enterprises to Rupert Murdoch, the Australian publisher, for $90 million. The paper, which had a circulation of 640,000, was the nation's ninth largest daily. It was put on the market earlier in the year after Marshall Field V and his half brother Frederick decided to dissolve Field Enterprises. Many potential buyers were reluctant to bid for the paper, which had for years been overshadowed by its larger competitor, the *Chicago Tribune,* circulation 750,000. Murdoch, however, has made a practice of buying ailing daily newspapers in major cities and trying to restore them to health and prominence. In recent years he had purchased the *New York Post, The Times* and *The Sunday Times* of London, and the *Boston Herald-American,* now known as the *Boston Herald.*

Another major transaction was the sale of the *Oakland* (Calif.) *Tribune* for $22 million to a group headed by Robert Maynard, the paper's editor and one of the nation's most prominent black journalists. Nearly half of the city's population was black, as were many of the *Tribune*'s 175,000 readers. Gannett Co., the largest newspaper chain in the U.S., with 86 dailies, had lost $3 million on the *Tribune* in 1982. Gannett was also under pressure to sell because an antitrust regulation banned the firm from owning both the newspaper and a television station in nearby San Francisco.

In one of the year's most daring ventures, the Dow Jones Co., whose *Wall Street Journal* was the nation's largest daily with a circulation of 1.9 million, launched a European edition. The new paper was being printed in The Netherlands and was on sale at 2,000 newsstands from Scandinavia to Saudi Arabia. About half of the contents of the *Wall Street Journal/Europe* was taken from the U.S. edition, and the other half was produced by a staff of 50 journalists based in Brussels.

In November the Herald Co. announced that its *St. Louis* (Mo.) *Globe-Democrat,* a morning newspaper, would cease publication at the end of the year because of persistent financial losses. On December 23, however, Jeffrey and Debra Gluck, owners of *The Saturday Review,* announced that they had agreed to purchase the newspaper and would continue to publish it as a morning daily.

The Pulitzer Gold Medal for Public Service, the most prestigious of the Pulitzer Prizes, was awarded to the relatively obscure *Jackson* (Miss.) *Clarion-Ledger,* circulation 67,000, for its campaign to improve the state's allegedly inadequate, racially discriminatory public school system. The *Boston Globe* received a Pulitzer for a 56-page special section examining U.S. policy on the use of nuclear weapons. The *Fort Wayne* (Ind.) *News-Sentinel* was cited for its coverage of a 1982 flood that forced many of the city's residents to flee their homes. The *Miami Herald* received a prize for its editorials opposing the continued detention in south Florida of Haitian refugees. Thomas Friedman of the *New York Times* and Loren Jenkins of the *Washington Post* were honoured for their reporting from Lebanon. (DONALD MORRISON)

Magazines. In Britain magazines experienced a steady year with no dramatic downward trend, although circulations were under pressure because of the recession and even the special-interest publications tended to find their readers becoming more selective. The need to keep trying harder, however, was perhaps symbolized by the announcement by *Woman's Own,* one of the "big four" women's weekly magazines, that it would introduce a line of fluorescent inks to grab the reader's eye; the debut came with its cover girl's makeup, but the development was designed more to attract advertisers than for editorial use.

No less symptomatic was the first set of awards from the British Society of Magazine Editors, which included one for "The Relaunch of 1983." There was, indeed, much activity of that sort as publishers sought to reposition themselves in their markets. That award went to Jill Churchill, editor of a magazine distributed principally at supermarket checkouts, the bimonthly *Family Circle.* Selling around 432,000 copies per issue in the second half of 1982, the magazine was forecasting a level comfortably above 500,000 for the same period of 1983 and was billing itself as the world's best-selling woman's magazine. Another award, for the most successful launch, went to the editor of the new *Just Seventeen.* This addition to the not-underpopulated teenage girls' market was notable in that its publishers, the relatively small but growing East Midlands Allied Press group, had reportedly beaten the giant International Publishing Corporation Ltd. combine to that market.

In France *Magazine-hebdo,* a new weekly news-

WIDE WORLD

Publishing fraud of the year was the so-called Hitler diaries, which the West German magazine *Stern* acquired in good faith but later displayed on its front page: "Hitler's Diaries exposed."

magazine proclaimed as "modern and not left-wing," was launched in September. In West Germany the proprietors of *Stern* magazine claimed that the "Hitler diaries" fiasco (*see* Sidebar) had not greatly affected its circulation of some 1.6 million copies weekly. Another West German newsmagazine, Rudolf Augstein's *Der Spiegel*, well known for its investigative crusades, was criticized for aspects of its inquiries into business contributions to political parties—notably alleged payments by the giant Flick conglomerate to Economics Minister Otto Lambsdorff, who in late November was charged with accepting bribes.

An important technical development was the transmission by satellite of pages of *The Economist* of London to Etam, Va., for production of the U.S. edition. (PETER FIDDICK)

Three magazines dominated the news in the U.S. in 1983. *Newsweek* featured the fake Hitler diaries; *Vanity Fair* spent $10 million in quest of an audience; and the *Nation* was involved in a copyright case with Harper & Row.

Newsweek used a cover story to applaud the discovery by *Stern* of the Hitler diaries. While the article raised the possibilities of fraud, it went on for pages indicating the historical significance of the find. When the diaries were revealed as a hoax, *Newsweek* had a second cover story indicating it had helped to reveal the fraud.

Vanity Fair, revived after its death in 1936, proved close to a disaster for Condé Nast. Critics found the first 294-page illustrated issue "splashy," "crude," "a waste," and "without appeal." With the third number and a good deal of the $10 million start-up money gone, the publisher changed format, editor, and approach.

The Nation published part of former president Gerald Ford's memoirs and was promptly challenged by Ford's publisher, Harper & Row. A federal judge ruled in favour of the book publisher,

Faking Out der Führer

One of the more bizarre episodes in recent world publishing history occurred in May 1983, when some of the most renowned publications on both sides of the Atlantic were revealed to have been on the brink of perpetrating a massive hoax on the public. The fact that they were backed in their error by a former regius professor of modern history at the University of Oxford added spice to a 14-day affair that veered wildly between academic mystery and farce, making headlines around the world.

At the heart of the matter were "the Hitler diaries"—not mere jottings, but fully 62 volumes—claimed to have been rescued from a burning German aircraft as World War II ended, later rediscovered, and then made available to the West German weekly magazine *Stern* through one of its own reporters, Gerd Heidemann. *Stern* was said to have paid DM 9 million ($3.7 million) through Heidemann, and it set about trying to resell non-German rights to other major publications, including *Newsweek* in the U.S. and *The Sunday Times* of London. It was through *The Sunday Times* that the story reached the wider public; on April 23 it carried an article by Lord Dacre of Glanton, formerly Hugh Trevor-Roper, Oxford professor and one of the leading authorities on the history of World War II and on Adolf Hitler. Lord Dacre (who was also a director of *The Sunday Times*) declared that he had inspected the diaries and was satisfied with their authenticity.

Others were not. Rival publications, including some who said they had turned down the *Stern* offer, rushed to cast doubt on the documents. Times Newspapers—due to start serialization through *The Sunday Times* on May 8—stood by the claim, but a tide of skepticism and ridicule soon took the world's media to *Stern* itself. The West German government, embarrassed by the sudden surge of interest in the dead Nazi dictator, stepped in to have an independent investigation made. By May 6 it had declared the documents counterfeit. Whatever the text itself might show, the paper, ink, and seals on the volumes were all of postwar manufacture.

By this time *Stern* was on its own. A Paris magazine had pulled out. *Newsweek* contrived to publish quotations from the diaries but treated them as a news story and questioned their authenticity. In London Lord Dacre revealed that his original view of the documents had been based on an insufficiently thorough examination and that he now withdrew it: "I don't want to blame anyone. It is my fault." In Hamburg the debacle reverberated in the publishing house Grüner & Jahr, owners of *Stern*. A well-known dealer in Nazi memorabilia confessed to the forgery, and the reporter, Heidemann, was dismissed and arrested on suspicion of fraud. *Stern*'s two chief editors, Peter Koch and Felix Schmidt, resigned, and the magazine carried fulsome apologies from its publisher and founder, Henri Nannen. (PETER FIDDICK) agreeing that copyright law had been violated. The 117-year-old magazine argued that its use of the memoirs constituted legitimate news gathering relating to a well-known public official, rather than piracy, and its claim was upheld by a federal appeals court in November.

While the U.S. economy was recovering in 1983, magazine publishers did not do so well. After a disastrous 1982—the worst since the recession year of 1975—predictions for 1983 were that advertising revenue would grow only two percentage points from the previous year. One encouraging note was sounded by the Audit Bureau of Circulation, which reported that total subscriptions of its member magazines increased by 39% between 1970 and 1981.

Coda, the poets' and writers' newsletter, reported in mid-1983 that 15 major magazines paid authors an average of from $1,000 to $2,000 per short story. *Cosmopolitan* paid $1,000 for unsolicited manuscripts and $2,500 for pieces by established writers. *Family Circle* might begin as low as $300, while *Seventeen* reported rates "upwards of $600." *Playboy* noted a high of $2,000 but said that the "pay scale goes up for regular contributors."

Computer and video titles were the fastest growing consumer magazines in the U.S. in 1983. *Personal Computing* and *Popular Computing* ranked first and second, and *Video Review* and *Video* were fourth and seventh. Among new contenders in 1983 was *Family Computing,* directed to the general user. A future-oriented quarterly for business executives was launched by the Graduate School of Business Administration of the University of Southern California, *New Management*, edited by James O'Toole.

More magazines became available via computer floppy disks in 1983. Among them were *Microzine,* which featured educational and entertainment programs for children, and *I.B. Magazette*, published for owners of IBM personal computers. Disks, however, remained more expensive to produce than printed magazines.

Among new video magazines in 1983 were *Dimension,* a monthly program guide for Times Mirror Cable television subscribers; *Blip,* a video game magazine for children; *Joystick,* a bimonthly that featured video games played in both the home and arcade; and *Videot,* which covered video games, movies, and rock music.

The combination of magazine format and cable television programming proved to be increasingly successful. Initiated in 1982, *Daytime* was an afternoon service program for women that reached close to eight million homes and frequently drew for its material upon *Good Housekeeping* and *Cosmopolitan.* Among other magazines found on television were *American Baby, Ebony, Essence, Playboy, Reader's Digest, Redbook,* and *Woman's Day.*

After five years of negotiation, a Russian-language version of *Scientific American* appeared in the U.S.S.R. Called *In the World of Science,* it carried translations of all articles found in the U.S. periodical and occasionally added new pieces. The Soviet editor reserved the right to drop social and economic articles as well as consumer advertising. However, the format remained the same, and those familiar with Soviet magazines claimed it to be one of the handsomest available in that country.

(WILLIAM A. KATZ)

WIDE WORLD

Although the American literary establishment tends to look down its nose at Louis L'Amour, the fans of that author's prodigious output of Westerns are numbered in millions and include the U.S. Congress and Pres. Ronald Reagan, who presented L'Amour with a Congressional Gold Medal.

Books. After a period of intense difficulty from 1978 to 1982, the British publishing industry dimly perceived a slight recovery during 1983. Major developed-country markets, particularly Australia, South Africa, Canada, and Western Europe, contributed to better performances by the majority of publishers. There were also occasional glimpses of hope in the strong development of new markets such as China. The third world, however, continued to be undersupplied with books, and crisis conditions in many countries, particularly in Africa, were likely to have a severe impact on educational standards and developmental possibilities into the foreseeable future.

The 1982 improvement in profitability continued in 1983, although real sales increases were small, and a steady decline in volume was a cause of continuing concern to the industry. The rate of inflation in the manufacturing of books continued to fall; book prices remained steady or even fell back slightly. However, demand remained fragile, as governments throughout the world were unwilling to increase educational and institutional book expenditures.

Copyright, piracy, and market infringements remained major international issues. In April the Book Development Council of the British Publishers Association (PA) launched its "Campaign Against Book Piracy" with great success and had financial commitments from concerned publishers totaling close to £500,000 over the following three years. The campaign was so successful that contributions were received from companies and associations outside the U.K. In particular, the Association of American Publishers indicated its willingness to make a substantial contribution to the U.K. campaign. The money raised was to be used to establish antipiracy offices in Hong Kong and Singapore that would assist in a worldwide piracy watch and would provide investigative services to obtain the evidence on which successful court action could be based. In 1983 the focus of piracy shifted back to Taiwan with the discovery that illegal Taiwanese editions were being shipped into Nigeria and Far Eastern markets. One British company estimated its losses to pirates in Nigeria at more than £1 million a year, and it was quite possible that Taiwanese piracy in Nigeria alone cost legitimate publishers £7 million or £8 million a year.

In Greece a Cypriot journalist working in Athens was convicted of libeling and defaming the publisher of Greece's largest selling newspaper. In his book *Take the Nation in Your Hands,* journalist Paul Anastasiades accused publisher Georgios Babolas of being "an agent of influence" for the Soviet Union.

Perhaps the most significant event of 1983 was provided by the 35th Frankfurt (West Germany) Book Fair in October, where 5,890 publishers from nearly 80 countries displayed 300,000 books. For the first time in four years, general optimism was expressed by a majority of exhibitors present. British publishers—once again the largest exhibiting group, with almost 500 stands—were particularly buoyant. Business was considered to be strongest in academic, English-language tuition, and specialist sectors, but all publishers reported favourably. (ANTHONY A. READ)

For U.S. publishers 1983 was the year of the comeback and the computer. After a disastrous 1982, publishers began to enjoy the benefits of the nation's economic recovery. No small part of the publishers' upturn was due to their discovery that people who used computers wanted books that explained the mysteries of the microchip in language that they could understand. The boom in computer-related books and software lines provided a shot in the arm for a sluggish industry.

The depth of the industry's problems at the outset of the year was apparent in final sales figures for 1982. Although total book sales (including texts, professional, reference, mail order, and general trade books) reached the $8 billion mark, the increase was a slight 4.4% over the previous year, and sales of adult hardcover trade books actually declined. The most visible symbols of the recession's impact on publishing were widespread staff cutbacks among publishers and the failure of several firms. The most notable of the latter was the closing of Brentano's, the venerable bookstore chain, which filed for protection under Chapter 11 of the federal bankruptcy code and closed all of its stores. Another major bankruptcy was that of A & W Publishers, a company that published new books and reprints of other company's books and acted as a wholesaler for remainders.

Layoffs and hiring freezes were even more commonplace. Among the hardest hit were the employees of Dell, Delacorte, and Dial Press, three imprints owned by Doubleday, where as many as 100 jobs were eliminated. At Time-Life Books more than 50 editorial workers (one-fourth of the staff) were laid off in the face of economic woes. One of Time-Life's major setbacks was the severe loss incurred after Mexico devalued the peso. Several publishers besides Time-Life lost millions of dollars when Mexico's currency crisis struck, and the future of that country as a book market was seriously in doubt.

By the first half of 1983, the bad news seemed to be fading, however. As the economic recovery gained momentum, sales were pushed upward; by the third quarter, sales of adult hardcovers were up 26.7% over 1982, accompanied by upturns in most other book categories. In this atmosphere of gradually improving conditions, there were other signs of renewed optimism, including new ventures in book publishing. Perhaps most impressive was the announcement by Parker Brothers, the game manufacturer, of its plans to enter the children's book market with $1 million earmarked for initial advertising and promotion.

Another indicator of the return to financial health was the renewed competition for paperback rights to hardcover best-sellers, which led to several large advances paid by paperback houses. In what had been a very soft market for two years, a number of books sold for advances in six and seven figures. One example of the turnabout was Norman Mailer's novel *Ancient Evenings,* which received low bids when offered for paperback initially. But when the book became a best-seller, paperback rights to *Ancient Evenings* were auctioned for half a million dollars. *The Love You Make* (a book about the Beatles) and *The Summer of Katya* (a suspense novel) each went to paperback for more than $750,000. And three books—John Le Carré's *The Little Drummer Girl,* Erma Bombeck's *Motherhood: The Second Oldest Profession,* and Judith Rossner's *August*—were sold for more than $1 million.

The year was also highlighted by litigation, with several cases having broad implications for publishers. In one ongoing action, the Northern California Booksellers Association brought suit against Bantam Books, alleging that the firm discriminates in its discounting policies to retailers. In another publisher-bookseller action, Farrar, Straus & Giroux sued the famous Strand Book Store, accusing the landmark New York City store of selling stolen books. The Association of American Publishers won a major victory when a court ruled in its favour against illegal photocopying by New York University professors and a copying centre near the school. One of the most newsmaking suits involved a controversy begun when South Dakota Gov. William Janklow charged that Peter Matthiessen's book *In the Spirit of Crazy Horse* libeled him. The governor filed suit against the author, the publisher, and, in an unprecedented move, three booksellers. Perhaps the most significant case of the year concerned Harper & Row's suit against *The Nation* magazine in a case that pitted copyright protection against First Amendment principles. (See *Magazines,* above.) In another closely watched case, William Peter Blatty sued the *New York Times,* charging that his book *Legion* had been deliberately kept off the *Times* best-seller list.

In general, however, it was a mixed year for the First Amendment and publishers. Several states moved to enact tougher antiobscenity statutes that booksellers feared would limit their freedom to sell books. Perhaps most disturbing for the publishing industry was a case of censorship by a publisher. Thomas Nelson, a leading religious book publisher, forced its subsidiary, Dodd, Mead, to cancel three books it was publishing because the books contained vulgarities or other words that were deemed offensive by Thomas Nelson's management.

In another notable development, Random House announced in December that it was recalling 58,000 copies of *Poor Little Rich Girl: The Life and Legend of Barbara Hutton* by C. David Heymann. The recall, one of the largest of its kind in publishing history, was made necessary by errors in the book that led to a threatened lawsuit.

On a more optimistic note, there was word that the U.S. Congress was increasing funding for book-related projects. And the U.S. Postal Service announced a temporary reprieve from increases in the book rate. At the same time, B. Dalton Bookseller, the nation's second largest chain of bookstores, announced a $3 million grant to promote literacy. (KENNETH C. DAVIS)

See also Literature.
[441.D; 543.A.4.e]

Qatar

An independent monarchy (emirate) on the west coast of the Persian Gulf, Qatar occupies a desert peninsula east of Bahrain, with Saudi Arabia and the United Arab Emirates bordering it on the south. Area: 11,400 sq km (4,400 sq mi). Pop. (1982 est.): 258,000. Capital: Doha (pop., 1980 est., 190,000). Language: Arabic. Religion: Muslim. Emir and prime minister in 1983, Sheikh Khalifah ibn Hamad ath-Thani.

Qatar suffered the sharpest deterioration in oil revenues of any Gulf state during the year, with total income for 1983 projected at only $2.7 billion, well below the 1982 figure. An oil-production quota of 300,000 bbl a day was established for Qatar at the meeting of the Organization of Petroleum Exporting Countries in London in March, but local production difficulties meant that actual output was some 30% below this ceiling.

QATAR

Education. (1982-83) Primary, pupils 42,592, teachers 3,000; secondary, pupils (1979–80) 13,913, teachers 1,475; vocational, pupils 550, teachers (1979–80) 72; teacher training (1979–80), students 65, teachers 26; higher (1979–80), students 2,025, teaching staff 261.

Finance. Monetary unit: Qatar riyal, with (Sept. 20, 1983) a free rate of 3.64 riyals to U.S. $1 (5.48 riyals = £1 sterling). Gold and other reserves (March 1983) U.S. $379 million. Budget (total; 1981–82 actual): revenue 13,434,000,000 riyals; expenditure 12,619,000,000 riyals.

Foreign Trade. (1982) Imports 7.1 billion riyals; exports 15,477,000,000 riyals. Import sources (1981): Japan 20%; U.K. 16%; U.S. 11%; West Germany 7%; France 6%; Italy 5%. Export destinations (1981): Japan c. 35%; France c. 13%; The Netherlands c. 11%; Italy c. 8%; Spain c. 7%. Main export: crude oil 94%.

Industry. Production (in 000; metric tons; 1982): crude oil 15,988; natural gas (cu m) 4,010,000; petroleum products (1981) 378; nitrogenous fertilizers (1981–82) 264; electricity (kw-hr; 1981) 2,515,000.

Foreign reserves were still high for a country with such a small population, but import bills had also risen. A savage cut in government expenditures—the 1983–84 budget called for a 31% cut in total spending—left many in the merchant elite dissatisfied. Among the canceled or suspended projects were the second phase of the new university and construction of a prestige ministerial complex at West Bay in Doha.

In the long term, Qatar was pinning its hopes on the North Field. The estimated reserves of this field suggested that it was one of the largest outside the Eastern-bloc countries. The high cost of development meant that Qatar had to agree to a joint venture with Western oil companies and ensure long-term sales contracts with buyers from Japan. In June the government took a step forward when it signed a memorandum of understanding with British Petroleum and Compagnie Française des Pétroles-Total.

In November Qatar was host to a summit conference of the Gulf Cooperation Council. (*See* MIDDLE EASTERN AFFAIRS.) (JOHN WHELAN)

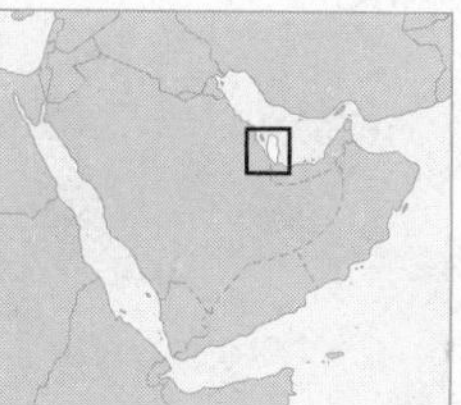
Qatar

Race Relations

During 1983 there was evidence of increasing levels of racial violence and neofascist political activity. (*See* Special Report.) In countries with large immigrant communities, racial prejudice continued to be fed by prevailing conditions of high unemployment and was sometimes reinforced by governmental action.

Great Britain. Race relations in Britain continued to be shaped by structural racism in a variety of institutions. For example, the Commission for Racial Equality reported in December 1982 that widespread racial discrimination was being practiced by local authorities throughout Britain in the housing of black families. The government still had not officially responded to the 1981 interim report of the Rampton Committee of Enquiry into the Education of Children of Ethnic Minorities. The committee had pinpointed patterns of racism, lack of adequate preparation of teachers for teaching in a multiracial society, and use of biased curriculum materials and examinations.

The pattern of higher unemployment rates for blacks continued throughout 1982. The latest figures showed a nonwhite male unemployment rate of 17.2%, compared with 9.9% for white males. For nonwhite women the rate was 15.8%, while that for white women was 8.9%. Unemployment rates for black people under 24 had increased by 150% from February 1979 to February 1982—the latest date for which comprehensive figures were available. Studies of specific areas of black settlement and anecdotal evidence pointed to a worsening of the situation since that time. Studies of the causes of these differential rates of unemployment and of the concentration of black workers in industries and occupations with the lowest pay and status identified discrimination as the major factor. At the same time, enforcement of existing antidiscrimination legislation proved slow and largely ineffective. Out of 200 industrial tribunal cases

Puerto Rico: see Dependent States

Quakers: see Religion

Quarrying: see Mining and Quarrying

WIDE WORLD

Coretta Scott King and her son Martin Luther King III exulted with U.S. Senate majority leader Howard Baker, Jr., as the Senate prepared to adopt legislation, later signed into law by Pres. Ronald Reagan, making the third Monday in January a U.S. national holiday honouring the slain civil rights leader Martin Luther King, Jr.

brought by individuals in 1982, only 30 succeeded. There were also charges of racial bias in the provision of health care and social security benefits.

It was the area of policing that continued to be the most contentious, however. The government's introduction of the tough Police Powers and Criminal Evidence Bill in the 1982 Parliament and its reintroduction following the June 1983 election raised fundamental questions about police powers, police accountability, and police relations with the black community. A number of specific cases reinforced black concerns about lack of police protection and police harassment. Racism among the police was highlighted by a number of studies.

During 1983 racism among police cadets at the Hendon Police College was exposed by lecturer John Fernandes. This reinforced evidence produced by a number of 1982 studies about the racist nature of the police subculture. Fernandes was banned from the college, and senior police officers denied or excused the attitudes he had uncovered. Two studies of police patterns of "stop and search" showed this racism in practice. A Home Office study of London and the provinces and a law centre report on Notting Hill Gate (a London district that had been the scene of frequent confrontations between blacks and police) both found that black people, particularly young people, were two to three times more likely to be stopped and searched than were whites.

Differential arrest, conviction, and custodial sentencing rates led to increasing numbers of blacks in British prisons. In August 1983 the Home Office Prisons Department identified racist behaviour by prison officers in a policy statement warning staff against using "grossly offensive" and "condescending" terms when addressing black prisoners. The fact that such a statement was issued was indicative of growing racial tensions in the prisons.

Continental Western Europe. In France increasing anti-immigrant violence and political activity were accompanied by a series of anti-immigrant government measures. In Dreux in September 1983 the National Front (NF) became the first fascist party to win office in France in 25 years, and it did so in cooperation with the main right-wing opposition party led by Jacques Chirac. The NF slogan was "Two Million Unemployed, Two Million Immigrants, France for the French." Two of the three NF councillors were given posts of responsibility, one for culture and the other for what was ominously called "civil protection." Running on racist platforms, the NF had gained about 10% of the vote in recent municipal elections in the Paris "Red Belt," leading to the defeat of Communist incumbents. The racism of the NF was paralleled in the statements of such "respectable" political figures as the mayor of Toulon, who said he wanted to stop France from becoming "the dustbin of Europe." Even the Socialist Party refused to use posters in the March municipal elections calling on the French electorate to "live in harmony with immigrants."

In West Germany the Christian Democratic-led coalition government gave increased legitimacy to the growing anti-immigrant ideology. Declaring that "Germany is not a country of immigration," the government initiated a number of policies to encourage repatriation of unwanted foreign workers. (*See* MIGRATION, INTERNATIONAL.) Such measures were accompanied by an escalation of racist violence in the streets, incited, in many cases, by neo-Nazis.

South Africa. In a November 1983 referendum, Prime Minister P. W. Botha succeeded in gaining the support of the white Parliament and the white electorate for his new "partial power sharing" constitution, which was designed to incorporate the Coloured and Asian communities into a white-dominated political system. (See SOUTH AFRICA.) The majority black population would continue to be excluded. The African response was marked by the creation of new political organizations, such as the United Democratic Front, and increased militant activity against South Africa's white government.

Relocation of blacks out of the towns and cities to the so-called homelands continued. The situation there was one of massive overcrowding, landlessness, unemployment, and degradation of the land. In Ciskei, South Africa's fourth "independent" black homeland, unemployment ranged between 25 and 35%; studies showed that a Ciskeian would be more than twice as well off financially if, rather than spending a year in the homeland, he spent nine months in a South African jail and worked illegally in South Africa for the other three months.

United States. Two reports, one by the U.S. Commission on Civil Rights and the other by the governor of California's Task Force on Civil Rights, concluded that racial, ethnic, and religious violence was a fact of life in many U.S. communities and that the persistence of racism and anti-Semitism was a root cause of acts of violence and intimidation directed against members of racial and religious minorities. The California study, which identified 450 instances of racism, concluded that "The level of frustration, alienation, and distrust in many minority communities, especially over perceptions of unequal treatment by public officials, is dangerously high." A report by the National Anti-Klan Network identified nearly 500 documented instances of Ku Klux Klan violence and nearly 500 more of "random racist violence"; in contrast, it found fewer than 20 prosecutions against the Klan brought by the U.S. Department of Justice.

The Reagan administration came under considerable criticism during the year for its performance in the civil rights field. On August 27 an estimated 200,000 demonstrators, gathered in the nation's capital to reenact the 1963 March on Washington that had been one of the high points of the 1960s civil rights movement, heard a variety of speakers call for a coalition to defeat Pres. Ronald Reagan in 1984. A letter signed by the heads of 33 state agencies responsible for local oversight for the U.S. Commission on Civil Rights had charged in September 1982 that President Reagan was responsible for a "dangerous deterioration in federal enforcement of civil rights."

The commission itself became a political issue during 1983. A fact-finding and advisory body with no regulatory authority, it had issued several reports and a succession of periodicals criticizing the administration. Members of the commission were appointed by the president with Senate confirmation, but the law made no provision for their removal. Maintaining that they served at the president's pleasure, Reagan attempted to replace three sitting commissioners with nominees of his own choosing, but he encountered stiff opposition in Congress and from civil rights groups. Late in the congressional session a compromise was reached. The six-member commission was reconstituted with eight members, four appointed by the president and four by Congress, who could be removed only for cause. However, an informal understanding between Congress and the White House concerning the actual appointments fell apart, and the commission as finally constituted had a majority of members who reflected the administration viewpoint.

In the electoral arena, racial polarization apparently had contributed to the defeat in November 1982 of Los Angeles's black mayor, Tom Bradley, in his attempt to become governor of California. He lost by 52,295 votes out of 7.5 million cast and, according to a *Los Angeles Times* poll, 500,000 Democrats and independents voted for the white Republican who opposed him. In April 1983 Harold Washington (*see* BIOGRAPHIES) became Chicago's first black mayor in a bitter and racially explosive election. On the brighter side, race appeared to be less of a factor in black-white mayoral contests in Boston and Philadelphia. With the election of W. Wilson Goode in Philadelphia, four of the nation's six largest cities had black mayors. Even more noteworthy was the election of a black, Harvey Gantt, as mayor of Charlotte, N.C., a Southern city with a three-quarters white population. The civil rights leader Jesse Jackson (*see* BIOGRAPHIES) announced his candidacy for president and began a campaign to register black voters throughout the country.

(LOUIS KUSHNICK)

GEORGE JAMES/THE NEW YORK TIMES

U.S. President Reagan's nominees to the U.S. Commission on Civil Rights had distinguished civil rights records but stirred opposition for their views against the use of quotas to redress racial discrimination. They were (from left) Robert A. Destro, Linda Chavez (nominated to be staff director), Morris B. Abram, and John H. Bunzel.

HITLER'S LEGACY: NEOFASCISM

by Paul Wilkinson

Fascist belief and action did not die with Hitler and Mussolini in World War II. Movements that boast their allegiance to fascism and advertise their cause by such means as street violence, racial attacks, terrorism, and the propaganda of racial hatred exist in over 20 countries. They range from the few neofascist mass parties, such as the Italian Social Movement (MSI) and the French National Front, to tiny paramilitary, youth, and terrorist groups. Moreover, although fascism originated in Europe, it is found as far afield as Central and South America, South Africa, and Australia.

How New Is "Neo"? It is not difficult to summarize the crude tenets of fascist ideology: belief in the supremacy of the chosen national group; total subordination of the individual to an absolute state under an absolute leader; suppression of all autonomous secondary institutions; rejection of the values and institutions of parliamentary democracy; total opposition to internationalism and belief in a foreign policy of expansionist war and conquest.

The explicit and defiant commitment of neofascist groups to these ideas is sufficient evidence that they consciously identify with the fascist past. There are other, tangible links. The leader of the Italian Social Movement, Giorgio Almirante, was an undersecretary in Mussolini's Social Republic and, before that, editor of the militant fascist journal *Difesa della Razza* ("Defense of the Race"). Léon Degrelle, a Belgian fascist who founded the Rexist Party and collaborated with the Germans in World War II, organized support for fascist movements in postwar Europe from his sanctuary in Franco Spain. Sir Oswald Mosley tried to stage a comeback in Britain with his Union Movement in the 1950s and influenced a new generation of fascists.

Many of the founders and leaders of neo-Nazi organizations in West Germany are former minor Nazi functionaries. Some of the old Nazis who fled to Spain and Latin America built up links with the new fascist groups. Before his arrest in January 1983, Klaus Barbie (*see* BIOGRAPHIES), known as the "Butcher of Lyon" for his activities during the Nazi occupation of France, recruited Italian fascists as "security guards" for drug smuggling in Bolivia. These direct links with old Nazi personalities are the exception, however. Most new fascist groups express their devotion to the old Nazi cause by symbols—such as use of the swastika insignia or celebrating Hitler's birthday.

In view of all this, what justifies the designation "new" fascists? They include new generations of young followers and leaders and have given new titles to their movements (in West Germany and Italy the postwar constitutions prohibit the formation of "fascist" parties). But by far the most important new feature is that, almost without exception, contemporary fascist movements have broadened their range of ethnic scapegoats, the victims of their race hatred and violence. In addition to preaching anti-Semitism, they now attack a host of other minority groups, including Turks, Arabs, Africans, West Indians, and Asians who migrated to the major cities of Western Europe as "guest workers."

A Present Danger. How dangerous are these new fascist groups to democracy and international peace? It would be foolish to exaggerate their significance as an electoral force. The National Front in Britain was trounced in the 1979 and 1983 general elections and is now split into so many feuding factions that it seems destined to remain an electoral irrelevance. The West German National Democratic Party and other neo-Nazi parties have never succeeded in breaking through the 5% barrier to secure parliamentary representation at the federal level. The MSI made significant gains in the June 1983 Italian general election, but the results were still below its peak of support in 1972.

While there is no new fascist party in Europe with sufficient electoral strength to challenge the powerholders, the ultraright elsewhere has made worrying strides. For example, the Arena party of Maj. Roberto d'Aubuisson became the most powerful group in the ultraright-wing coalition that came to power after the March 1982 elections in El Salvador. In South Africa the extreme right-wing parties combined outpolled the government in a series of crucial spring by-elections in 1983.

Liberal democratic governments can take some comfort from the generally peripheral influence of fascist parties in the major democracies, but the

---

Paul Wilkinson is Professor of International Relations at the University of Aberdeen, Scotland. His books include Terrorism and the Liberal State *and* The New Fascists.

dangers posed by the new fascists cannot be gauged by conventional electoral criteria. Fascists have never believed in waiting for a democratic mandate. Mussolini came to power through the March on Rome. Hitler used a combination of legal electoral stratagems, tactical alliances with conservatives and nationalist groups, and street violence and terror. Countries with a tradition of coups and of fascist movements among top military personnel need to be particularly vigilant. A serious attempt was made in Spain in February 1981 when fascist members of the Civil Guard, acting in concert with certain senior army officers, held the parliament hostage. In Argentina, where the Radicals won a major victory at the polls in late 1983, there is an obvious danger that Peronists and the military may combine to stage another coup. Among the NATO countries, Turkey and Greece, as well as Spain and Portugal, have both a history of coups and senior military officers known to be sympathetic to fascism.

Even where new fascist groups lack any real opportunity of seizing or influencing state power, they still have considerable capacity for endangering lives and property and intimidating minorities and political opponents. Fascist groups have been responsible for some of the worst terrorist attacks in Europe, including the bombing of the Bologna, Italy, railway station in August 1980 that killed 84 and injured over 200. Potentially, fascist terrorists present an even greater threat to innocent life than terrorists of the extreme left, for fascist ideology fully approves of indiscriminate attacks. Moreover, the police and judiciary in most liberal democratic states have been far less effective in apprehending and convicting fascist terrorists than in dealing with groups of the extreme left.

Masked West German youths in military-style uniforms gave the Nazi salute at a rally of ultraright-wing groups to celebrate the 50th anniversary of Hitler's appointment as chancellor of Germany. The meeting was held in Mainz on January 30.

WIDE WORLD

Fascist movements also have a poisoning effect on politics and community relations in multiracial cities. They incite racial hatred and in many cases encourage intimidation of and violent attacks against minority groups. In the first instance, this endangers people, property, and public order as a whole. Furthermore, it provokes members of the victimized minorities and antifascist groups into counterdemonstrations and vigilante activities, bringing the risk of major confrontations on the streets with the police caught in the middle.

Seedbeds of Fascism. Fascist propaganda of racial hatred and violence is spread not only through traditional political rallies and marches but also by exploiting "pop" culture as a means of recruiting disaffected youth. In many Western countries there has also been an upsurge of racist propaganda and fascist activity at the school level. A positive approach to combating this propaganda is urgently needed in many Western countries.

The classic conditions for the growth of fascism are now present in the industrial countries: a lingering economic crisis; the bitterness and frustration of "have-not" groups; massive unemployment; weakening of confidence in and support for liberal democratic values and institutions; deepening middle-class fears that an extreme left government may come to power; the presence of minority groups. Perhaps all that is lacking in many cases is the presence of a demagogic and ruthless leader to exploit these opportunities.

There is another fundamental point that has been missed by many critics of the right. This is that fascist attitudes toward race relations and matters of immigration have been displayed increasingly among left-wing and centrist parties. The fascist mentality is dangerous precisely because it is so contagious in situations of socioeconomic crisis. It was François Mitterrand's Socialist government that introduced the toughest measures seen in France since World War II to root out illegal immigrants and prevent new immigration. At the same time, the Young Conservatives' national organization in Britain issued a report warning against infiltration by people with National Front backgrounds. The diffusion and perpetuation of the fascist mentality, often in covert form within mainstream political parties, is more worrying in the long run than the existence of a handful of tiny extraparliamentary movements. Antifascism, like charity, must begin at home.

Racket Games

Badminton. The world badminton championships took place in Copenhagan in May 1983. China fielded teams in each of the five events and captured titles in the women's singles and women's doubles events. It was the first appearance of China in the world championships since it joined the International Badminton Federation.

In the men's singles Icuk Sugiarto of Indonesia defeated fellow countryman Liem Swie King. In the all-Chinese final of the women's singles Li Lingwei defeated Han Aiping. Steen Fladberg and Jesper Helledie of Denmark won the men's doubles, defeating Mike Tredgett and Martin Dew of the U.K. in the finals. Two teams from China met in the finals of the women's doubles, with Lin Ying and Wu Dixi emerging as champions. In the mixed doubles Thomas Kilstrom of Sweden and Nora Perry of the U.K. defeated the Danish team of Steen Fladberg and Pia Nielsen.

At the 1983 U.S. championships the first black men's singles champion was crowned. Rodney Barton, a college student from California, became the first member of his race to win that title. In the women's singles Cheryl Carton again won the championship. (C. R. ELI)

Squash Rackets. In 1982–83 Jahangir Khan of Pakistan consolidated his position as the world's best player of squash rackets. Khan won the ICI Perspex World Masters held in November 1982 at Leicester, England, where he beat Gamal Awad (Egypt) 9–0, 9–4, 9–3. This was the first event in the world that utilized a completely transparent court, enabling spectators to watch the action from all four sides. Later that month Khan also won the World Open title in Birmingham, England, where he beat Dean Williams (Australia) 9–2, 6–9, 9–1, 9–1 in the final. In April 1983 he won the Davies and Tate British Open title for the second time in Derby, England, defeating Awad 9–2, 9–5, 9–1.

Instituted at the 1983 British Open was an over-35 championship, thereby giving recognition to the growing enthusiasm for competition among that age group. Ahmad Safwat (Egypt) won the inaugural title by beating Jonah Barrington (Ireland) in the final. The British Open veterans championship (over 45) was won by the 1962 British amateur champion, Ken Hiscoe (Australia), while Hasim Khan (Pak.) won his sixth Open vintage (over-55) title in addition to the seven Open titles he won in the 1950s. The women's British Open was won by Vicki Cardwell (Australia) for the fourth time as she defeated England's Lisa Opie 9–10, 9–6, 9–4, 9–5 in the final.

The South African championship was won by Ross Thorne (Australia), who beat Gawain Briars (England) in the final, and the Canadian softball title was taken by Doug Whittaker. Mark Talbott defeated Ned Edwards to win the U.S. Open. In team events Pakistan comfortably won the Asian Men's Teams championship, and Sweden's men defeated England 3–2 in the final of the European championship. England's women again won the European title.

On March 21, 1983, at Chichester, England, in the final of the Patrick International Festival, a new world record was set for the longest match when Jahangir Khan beat Awad 9–10, 9–5, 9–7, 9–2 in a time of 2¾ hours. (ALAN P. H. CHALMERS)

Rackets. John Prenn beat his closest rival, William Boone, in the final of the British Open championship four games to one in April 1983. Earlier, Boone had won when the two met in the finals of the Celestion invitation singles, and he defeated Prenn later in the finals of the U.S. amateur championship in New York City. Boone also won the U.S. doubles title with Tom Pugh. Prenn retained his British amateur title, beating Boone by the narrow margin of 17–15 in the final game. Prenn also won the Canadian title by defeating Randall Crawley in the finals in Montreal.

Boone and Crawley remained the dominant doubles team, retaining the British amateur and Open titles. For years their chief rivals were Charles Hue Williams and Prenn, but in the Open the latter pair lost in the semifinals to the Nicholls brothers, Mark and Paul, who both also reached the semifinals of the Open singles. Norwood Cripps (Eton) regained the professional title.

Real Tennis. Christopher Ronaldson, Hampton Court professional, warded off his first challenge since becoming world champion in 1981. On the Royal Court he beat Wayne Davies, professional at the New York Racquet Club and the first Australian contender for the title, by 7 sets to 4 in March 1983. In the British Open Ronaldson beat another Australian, Graham Hyland, 6–5, 1–6, 3–6, 6–2, 6–5 after the loser had four times held a four-game lead in the final set. Norwood Cripps and the amateur Alan Lovell maintained their unbeaten record in doubles by retaining the British Open title, beating Ronaldson and Michael Dean. Lovell gained the amateur singles title from the former world champion, Howard Angus. Davies won the Australian title, beating Hyland, and also the U.S. title, defeating a third Australian, Lachlan Deuchar. Katrina Allen (Queen's Club) won the women's championship by beating Lesley Ronaldson (Hampton Court) in the finals at Morton Morrell. (ROY MCKELVIE)

Racquetball. In racquetball 1983 could well be termed "the year of Mike Yellen." Yellen unseated five-time national champion Marty Hogan to capture the number one rank in the professional game. Yellen's year-end top-ranked position was accomplished with a string of victories, including the final four tour stops of the season. Among his triumphs were the prestigious Ektelon National title, DP Leach National title, and the Catalina Series championships.

In women's professional competition, Lynn Adams made it two in a row as she maintained her dominance over former champion Heather McKay and the rest of the field. Adams consistently downed all opponents while establishing herself at the top of the Women's Professional Racquetball Association (WPRA) ladder.

On the amateur scene Dan Ferris, 23, of Minnesota stopped New Jersey's Jim Cascio to win the American Amateur Racquetball Association

Radio: see Television and Radio

Railroads: see Transportation

Real Tennis: see Racket Games

Recordings: see Music

Reformed Churches: see Religion

(AARA) national singles title. It was Ferris's first national championship. Cindy Baxter of Pennsylvania captured her first AARA national title, defeating Virginia's Malia Kamahoahoa in the finals.

In competitive doubles play Kamahoahoa gained considerable revenge as she and partner Carol Frenck captured the AARA crown over Mary Halroyd and Gail Lauteria of Florida. The men's team of Stan Wright and Steve Trent (both of California) won their second consecutive crown, stopping former champions Mark Malowitz and Jeff Kwartler (both of Texas) in the finals.

(CHARLES S. LEVE)

Refugees

The worldwide refugee situation remained relatively stable throughout 1983. There were no massive outflows of the kind that marked the late 1970s. Nevertheless, the magnitude and persistence of ongoing refugee problems continued to cause grave concern to the office of the United Nations High Commissioner for Refugees (UNHCR). In the Horn of Africa and Pakistan, especially, large concentrations of refugees continued to require massive international assistance. While the number of Indochinese refugees arriving in the Southeast Asian region fell, resettlement places also became increasingly scarce. There were no dramatic increases in the number of refugees in Central America, but rising political tensions and continuing economic deterioration in the region were a cause of apprehension.

In Africa several positive developments occurred, particularly in the Horn. Most notable was the successful launching in September of a program of voluntary repatriation from Djibouti to Ethiopia, following a series of tripartite meetings between the governments of the two countries concerned and UNHCR. In August, as part of its efforts to facilitate this voluntary repatriation, UNHCR established a special program of assistance to repatriates from Djibouti. Also of major significance was the introduction by Somalia of a policy permitting the creation of local settlements and encouraging self-reliance among the large refugee population there. Large-scale assistance to rural settlements for refugees from Ethiopia and Uganda continued in Sudan.

Many of the African countries burdened by the presence of refugees also were among the poorest in the continent. To ensure adequate assistance both to the refugees and to the countries of refuge, the UN General Assembly adopted a resolution (December 1982) calling for a second International Conference on Assistance to Refugees in Africa (ICARA II), to be held in July 1984. Extensive preparatory work for this conference was undertaken during 1983.

In Pakistan the presence of some three million Afghan refugees still required massive international assistance. Since prospects for a permanent solution continued to be poor, emphasis was placed, whenever possible, on developing self-reliance and income-generating opportunities for the refugees, as well as on projects to offset the extensive environmental damage caused by the presence of such large numbers of refugees and their livestock. UNHCR's assistance program in Pakistan totaled $69 million in 1983—its largest country program.

Arrivals of Indochinese refugees seeking asylum in the Southeast Asian region continued to decline, as did departures from the region for resettlement overseas. A total of 30,228 refugees arrived by boat or overland between Jan. 1 and Sept. 30, 1983, while 52,702 departed, leaving 176,467 in UNHCR camps. In addition, some 200,000 Kampucheans were located in settlements along the Thai-Kampuchean border where they received assistance from other agencies. Since 1976, 861,871 refugees from the region had been resettled with UNHCR assistance. An additional 270,000 were locally resettled in China, while 2,263 Laotian refugees returned to their country under a program of voluntary repatriation coordinated by UNHCR. A special program of assistance to some 400,000 returnees in Kampuchea also continued. The number of those leaving Vietnam under UNHCR's Orderly Departure Program reached 39,475 as of Sept. 30, 1983, and the September total of 2,220 exceeded clandestine departures by small boat for the first time.

There were no major new influxes of refugees in Central America in 1983. Many programs focused increasingly on the promotion of local integration and self-reliance. The development of rural settlements for refugees in Belize, Costa Rica, Nicaragua, and Panama was further consolidated. Within the context of mounting political tensions and economic difficulties, however, it became more difficult to implement such projects. Sizable numbers of Salvadoran and Guatemalan refugees, mainly in Honduras and Mexico, remained entirely dependent on relief assistance.

WIDE WORLD

Thousands of Kampuchean refugees fled into Thailand before occupying Vietnamese troops. Here refugee mothers bathe their children at a new camp near the Thai–Kampuchean border.

A disturbing trend was the widespread deterioration in the situation regarding international protection of refugees and asylum-seekers. World economic recession led to more restrictive attitudes, as well as to increased problems of integration in resettlement countries. Equally troubling was the threat to the physical safety of refugees in southern Africa and elsewhere as a result of armed attacks on refugee camps and settlements.

(UNHCR)

See also Migration, International.

Religion

Throughout 1983 religious leaders around the world cried "peace, peace," but there was no peace. Small wars continued to break out, and the threat of nuclear war hovered over "this fragile Earth, our island home."

In March John Paul II, the most itinerant pope in history, went on a "pilgrimage for peace" in Central America and the Caribbean. His eight-day visit to eight countries dramatized his widely shared yearning for justice and an end to violence but led to no immediate diminution of fighting within the region. After months of negotiations, the leaders of Poland's Communist regime gave the pontiff permission to return to his homeland in June, for the second time during his papacy. Following the visit, the government lifted martial law, but it imposed other restrictions. Clearly, internal peace was not at hand in Poland, where the official atheism of the state met its strongest opposition in the church. (See *Roman Catholic Church,* below.)

Words were the major weapons—indeed, the chief weapons—used by religious leaders in their fight for peace. Probably the most notable example was the decision in May by the National Conference of Catholic Bishops in the U.S. to adopt, by a lopsided vote, a pastoral letter, "The Challenge of Peace," addressed to all the nation's Roman Catholics. The 155-page statement, prepared over two years by a committee under Chicago's Joseph Cardinal Bernadin (*see* BIOGRAPHIES), called for "immediate, bilateral, verifiable agreements to halt the testing, production and deployment of new nuclear weapons." It was regarded as a groundbreaking document by Catholic historians. In the past, the bishops, reflecting the uncritical patriotism of an immigrant church, had generally given their blessing to U.S. war efforts. In contrast, the new statement challenged several major tenets of U.S. defense policy. It acknowledged the right of a nation to defend itself but went on to declare that strategies of deterrence are "justifiable" only when combined with a "resolute determination to pursue arms control and disarmament." It also condemned all nuclear attacks on civilian population centres, questioned the capacity of military leaders to control a "limited nuclear war," and contended that the "deliberate initiation of nuclear war would be an unjustifiable moral risk."

The battle of words was taken up again in August at Vancouver, B.C., where 839 delegates to the sixth General Assembly of the World Council of Churches (WCC), representing Protestant and

RUDI FREY/TIME MAGAZINE

The 500th anniversary of the birth of Martin Luther was celebrated in 1983. A bust of the leader of the Protestant Reformation stands in Eisenach, East Germany, where he once lived.

Orthodox Christians from 100 countries and more than 300 churches, approved a resolution that echoed many of the main points stressed by the U.S. bishops. Although the final vote was nearly unanimous, some churchmen questioned passages that could be interpreted as calls for unilateral disarmament. Spokesmen for churches in the third world went along with the resolution, but not without first registering their fear that delegates from the Northern Hemisphere, in their passion for peace, might fail to take seriously cries for social justice coming from the Southern Hemisphere.

The global preoccupation with peace involved large numbers of Protestant evangelicals, ordinarily conservative on military issues. In May, at Pasadena, Calif., some 1,300 evangelicals from 34 states gathered under the banner "The Church and Peacekeeping in the Nuclear Age." No final document was issued, but speakers at plenary sessions reflected a wide range of views, from pacifists from traditional "peace churches" to advocates of "peace through strength." For some of the sponsors, the fact that the meeting was held at all was a victory, signifying that a growing number of evangelicals, traditionally preoccupied with personal piety and pure doctrine, were eager to be heard in the public debate on nuclear war.

In Western Europe the debate intensified as the U.S. began to deploy Pershing II and cruise missiles there. Some church leaders played highly visible roles in acts of protest, while others took a more moderate line. In the U.K. a nationally televised debate at the General Synod of the Church of England took a stand against "first use" of nuclear weapons but rejected a call for Great Britain to abandon its nuclear arsenal unilaterally. Other world events evoked other kinds of responses from peace-loving churchmen. In Manila, at the funeral of the assassinated opposition leader Benigno S. Aquino, Jr. (*see* OBITUARIES), Jaime Cardinal Sin seized the opportunity to condemn the "oppression" of the Marcos regime.

In some ways, it was easier for religious leaders to preach peace to the world than to achieve it within their own ranks. In the first half of the year, the WCC and the National Council of the Churches of Christ in the U.S.A. (NCC) were preoccupied with efforts to fend off attacks from conservatives. The critics charged that the ecumenical agencies had neglected their pursuit of church unity in favour of social causes, especially "leftist" ones. Fuel was added to the fire when the accusations, including charges that the WCC funded terrorists, reached wide audiences through the CBS television program "Sixty Minutes" and an article in *Reader's Digest* magazine. At the end of the year the NCC was once again embroiled in controversy when it announced a new lectionary (list of readings for Christian worship) that used "inclusive, non-sexist language." In the Garden of Gethsemane, for instance, Jesus addresses his prayer to "God, my Father and Mother." Reception by the various denominations was mixed. Further division in the NCC's ranks was avoided when the governing board delayed indefinitely a decision on the membership application of a denomination serving homosexual men and women. Nevertheless, church unity was at the top of the agenda at the WCC assembly. (*See* Special Report.)

The WCC took a decisive step toward "visible church union" when it called on Protestant, Orthodox, and Roman Catholic churches to participate in a World Conference on Faith and Order in 1987 or 1988. At that event, Christians from around the world would be asked what further steps toward church union they were prepared to take in the light of tentative agreements reached in 1982 at a historic ecumenical gathering in Lima, Peru. The Lima meeting ended with church leaders reporting that they had arrived at "converging" points of view on three doctrinal issues—baptism, the Eucharist, and ministry—that had divided Christians for centuries. Meanwhile, in the U.S., Northern and Southern Presbyterians were reunited after 122 years. (See *Reformed, Presbyterian, and Congregational Churches*, below.)

As Christians around the world participated in celebrations marking the 500th anniversary of the birth of Martin Luther, leader of the Protestant Reformation, the milestone was used as an occasion for burying old enmities between Lutherans and Jews, resulting from some of the reformer's anti-Semitic statements. At a meeting of world Lutheran and Jewish leaders in Stockholm, Jews hailed a statement by the Lutheran delegation that said: "We cannot accept or condone the violent verbal attacks that the Reformer made against the Jews. Lutherans and Jews interpret the Hebrew Bible differently. But we believe that a christological reading of the Scriptures does not lead to anti-Judaism, let alone anti-Semitism."

Signs of ecumenical progress were offset in part, however, by continuing evidence of interreligious conflict. In Iran, Shiʿah Muslim leaders continued to persecute and put to death members of the "heretical" Baha'i faith, prompting Baha'i leaders to level charges of genocide. In Egypt Coptic Christian leaders appealed to world opinion to support them in efforts to free their leader, Shenuda III, from "house arrest." (See *Eastern Non-Chalcedonian Churches*, below.) Similarly, Orthodox Christians struggled to end what they described as "Turkish persecution and harassment against the ecumenical patriarchate of Constantinople."

Following the 1982 war in Lebanon, Christian-Jewish relations showed new signs of strain. While acknowledging Israel's right to secure borders, the WCC condemned Israel's Middle East policies and supported efforts to establish a Palestinian homeland. Middle East tensions also resulted in tensions within the world Jewish community. (See *Judaism*, below; Feature Article: *At the Core of the Problem of Peace—Israel and the West Bank: Two Views*.)

Pope John Paul II also faced tensions when he tried to put his own house in order. In the spring the pontiff stirred up angry objections when he insisted that Agnes Mary Mansour (*see* BIOGRAPHIES), a nun, resign her post as director of the Michigan Department of Social Services, where she was responsible for overseeing state funding of abortions. The Mansour case was seen as part of the pope's continuing worldwide campaign to require priests and members of religious orders to concentrate on traditional religious roles. In the fall he returned to this theme when he told the Jesuits, many involved in the forefront of social change, that they must not confuse "the tasks proper to priests with those that are proper to laypeople." Privately, numerous Catholics in the U.S. expressed concern about what they perceived as a growing rift between the Vatican and American Catholicism. The existence of strained relations was acknowledged in November by Archbishop John Roach who, in his final address as president of the National Council of Catholic Bishops, said, "The tensions of the present moment are best understood as the growing pains in a maturing relationship." (See *Roman Catholic Church*, below.)

Church-state issues continued to play a major role in U.S. religious life. When Pres. Ronald Reagan proclaimed 1983 as the Year of the Bible, 4 ministers and 12 other plaintiffs, backed by the American Civil Liberties Union, filed a suit charging that the proclamation violated the separation of church and state. In a crucial test of the 1973 *Roe v. Wade* abortion decision, the U.S. Supreme Court reaffirmed its earlier stand, declaring that women have a constitutional right to end their pregnancies. In another key opinion, the high court ruled that federal tax exemptions should not be awarded to schools that practice racial discrimination. At issue was a policy against interracial dating at Bob Jones University, a Protestant fundamentalist school in Greenville, S.C.

A California court, meanwhile, took away the tax-exempt status of the Crystal Cathedral, the $18 million showplace of Robert Schuller's television ministry based in Garden Grove, Calif. The state argued that the church had forfeited its right to an exemption when it permitted the lavish building to be used for profit-making concerts. One action drew the support of religious leaders all along the religious spectrum. A statement opposing research that could alter the genes affecting inherited human traits was signed by Catholic bishops, leaders of mainline Protestant denominations, and Jerry Falwell, fundamentalist leader of the Moral Majority.

(ROY LARSON)

PROTESTANT CHURCHES

Anglican Communion. Wide-ranging but relatively unobtrusive ecumenism was the hallmark of 1983 for the Anglican Communion. There was a substantial Anglican presence—and contribution—at the WCC assembly, and fresh rounds of theological talks occurred with representatives of various major traditions. In January, at Woking, England, there was further discussion on the sacraments and ministry with the World Alliance of Reformed Churches. In September the latest meeting of the Anglican-Orthodox Joint Doctrinal Discussions took place at Odessa, U.S.S.R. Also in September, the first session of the second Anglican-Roman Catholic International Commission (ARCIC II) was held in Venice, Italy. Although the churches had only just begun formal consideration of ARCIC I's final report, ARCIC II was already examining the remaining issues that divided the communions.

The year included celebrations for the 150th anniversary of the Oxford Movement, which marked the rise of Anglo-Catholic influence in the Church of England and, through it, in the rest of the communion. The main events took place at Oxford in July and at the second Catholic Renewal Conference at Loughborough, England, in April. The new Spanish-speaking Province of the Southern Cone of South America was inaugurated in April at a ceremony in St. John's Cathedral, Buenos Aires, Arg., after being delayed for almost a year because of the Falklands conflict.

The July meeting of the General Synod of the Church of England took a decision that might lead to a radical revision of marriage discipline throughout the communion. Having agreed earlier that there were some circumstances in which divorced persons might remarry in church, it now approved a procedure for determining which couples should be allowed the privilege. The General Synods of England and Canada considered the issues of nuclear weapons and warfare but, while they condemned these things, neither synod sided with the unilateralists. However, both called for further urgent steps toward disarmament. Five senior Anglicans, led by the Scottish primate, the Most Rev. Alastair Haggart, attended the Eloff Commission inquiry into the affairs of the South African Council of Churches in response to an appeal from the council's general secretary, Bishop Desmond Tutu, for an Anglican gesture of solidarity at the hearings.

Stuart Blanch retired as archbishop of York in August and was succeeded by the bishop of Durham, John Habgood.

(SUSAN YOUNG)

Baptist Churches. Despite rampant criticism of the WCC, and unrest in their own nation, the Baptist Convention of Nicaragua joined the world body at its 1983 assembly. The Nicaraguan Convention had 58 churches and 7,000 members. In another response to Latin-American concerns, the executive committee of the Baptist World Alliance (BWA; 124 member bodies with 31 million members) met in July in Buenos Aires. The committee passed resolutions on evangelism and reaffirmed previous statements calling for peace and opposing the use of torture and illegal detention. Baptist representatives of 14 European nations, meeting in a Peace Forum at Sjövik, Sweden, to endorse the UN declaration of 1986 as International Year of Peace, asked fellow Baptists to "regard the existence of nuclear weapons as contradictory to the will of God."

Illustrating the autonomy and diversity of Baptist churches, 25,000 Baptist fundamentalists from so-called independent Baptist churches (not affiliated with major Baptist bodies) met in Kansas City, Mo. They reiterated five "fundamentals": inerrant scripture; Christ is God in the flesh; Christ died for the sins of mankind; Christ rose bodily; and Christ will return bodily. In a spin-off from this meeting, the General Association of Regular Baptists, a fundamentalist splinter group from the American Baptist Churches in the U.S.A. (formerly Northern Baptists), met in Niagara Falls, N.Y., to denounce the National and World Councils of Churches and to criticize the evangelist Billy Graham in a resolution regarding persecution of Christians behind the iron curtain.

The tensions that for several years had marked the Southern Baptist Convention, the largest Baptist (and largest Protestant) denomination in the U.S., were eased during 1983 by the conciliatory attitude and actions of its president, Jimmy Draper. Draper was reelected to another one-year term, an endorsement that carried the Convention somewhat to the left. The biblical inerrancy controversy, though far from dissipated, had been pushed to the background. The support—untraditional for Baptists—of President Reagan's positive attitude on prayer in the schools, voted affirmatively by the 1982 meeting of the Southern Baptists, was reversed at the 1983 meeting in Pittsburgh, Pa., another sign that the Convention was returning more to the Baptist centre.

The largest black Baptist group in the U.S., the National Baptist Convention, led for many years by Joseph H. Jackson, reelected Theodore J. Jemison to the presidency at its annual meeting in Los Angeles.

(NORMAN R. DE PUY)

Christian Church (Disciples of Christ). Disciples of Christ in the U.S. underlined their "Peace with Justice" program priority by affirming the entry of the Roman Catholic bishops into the nuclear arms debate, urging a halt to military aid to Central America, opposing "covert" action against foreign governments, calling for an end to peacetime draft registration, and urging more openness toward political refugees. Some 83 churches enrolled as "Shalom" congregations, committing themselves to specific study and action concerning peace.

Disciples acted to strengthen their commitment to Christian unity by approving the naming of four representatives of other denominations as full members of the 200-member General Board. They strongly reaffirmed support of the WCC. Some 100 Disciples took part in the WCC assembly.

Chancellor William E. Tucker of Texas Christian University was elected moderator of the 1.2 million-member body for two years. The church's historic Hazel Green Academy, which had provided high school training for the poor of Kentucky's eastern mountains for 103 years, voted to close in view of mounting deficits and declining enrollment. A record one-third of the 122 Disciples ordained over the year were women. Sixteen missionaries were sent out at one commissioning service, the largest number at one time in a decade.

(ROBERT LOUIS FRIEDLY)

Churches of Christ. On July 23, 1983, the World Christian Broadcasting Corporation began transmitting programs in Russian and Mandarin Chinese over KNLS ("new life station"), a $2.5 million, 100,000-w station at Anchor Point, Alaska. Joe R. Barnett, president of Pathway, Inc., produced the first of a planned series of hour-long TV specials aimed at the unchurched. It would be shown on prime time across the U.S. with local sponsorship.

Churches throughout the U.S., Canada, Bermuda, and Europe provided over $1,-750,000 to help Christians in West Africa; $100,000 worth of food, the first of ten such shipments, arrived in Ghana in May. Ministries outside the U.S. with unusual growth included Singapore, the Dominican Republic, and Kenya.

A new edition of *Where the Saints Meet* listed some 13,000 churches of Christ in the U.S. In 1983 the churches operated 103 prison ministries, over 30 nursing homes and retirement communities, and some 75 programs for homeless children. In March congregations in San Antonio, Texas, conducted a citywide campaign in Spanish. Houston, Texas, churches again united to sponsor a Crusade for Christ, held in July.

(M. NORVEL YOUNG)

Church of Christ, Scientist. A renewed commitment to the founding purpose of the *Christian Science Monitor*, "to injure no man, but to bless all mankind" (Mary Baker Eddy, 1908), led to a number of key staff additions and to the expansion of *Monitor* offices in Boston (the church's headquarters), New York City, Chicago, and San Francisco. In June 1983 Katherine W. Fanning, editor and publisher of the *Anchorage* (Alaska) *Daily News*, was named editor of the *Monitor*, the first woman to hold that post in the paper's 75-year history.

Later in June, at the church's annual meeting in Boston, Harvey W. Wood, chairman of the church's board of directors, emphasized that "lives more than words" are needed as "proof of what Christian Science is." He continued: "The airwaves and mental atmosphere are so full, these days, of shrill merchandising of religion and conflicting ideologies. But the Christ . . . accomplished all that he did through his own witnessing. . . ."

James K. ("Kay") Kyser of Chapel Hill, N.C., who many years earlier had left a career as a popular bandleader to devote his full time to the healing ministry of Christian Science, was named president of the Mother Church for 1983–84.

(NATHAN A. TALBOT)

Church of Jesus Christ of Latter-day Saints. Despite the declining health of all but one member of its First Presidency, the church continued to show much vitality, particularly at the local level. At the close of 1983 the only member of the First Presidency able to make consistent public appearances was counselor Gordon B. Hinckley.

Beginning in April, major changes were instituted in the church's welfare system. The entire program was to be financed from voluntary fast offerings. Acquisition of additional welfare farms and facilities was to be financed by churchwide welfare funds. Emphasis was placed on self-reliance and compassionate service. The church shipped food and medical supplies to help disaster victims overseas, but effective local responses to disaster were the focus of greater attention. In Utah thousands of volunteers carried out flood prevention, flood control, and cleanup work in the spring as the area experienced the worst floods and mudslides in its history.

Significant progress was achieved in efforts to make sacred temple ceremonies available to all church members. Temples were completed and dedicated in Atlanta, Ga., Western Samoa, Tonga, and Chile, and construction began on temples in South Africa, Dallas, Texas, Freiberg, East Germany, South Korea, and Chicago. The first stake (diocese) in Fiji was created in June.

Among steps taken to reinforce the church's identity as a Christian religion, a new subtitle was added to the Book of Mormon: "Another Testament of Jesus Christ."

(LEONARD J. ARRINGTON)

Jehovah's Witnesses. During 1983 Jehovah's Witnesses, as a society of ministers, was active in over 200 lands around the globe. A yearly increase of more than 4% brought the total working ministry close to 2.5 million, with another 4 million associated in 45,000 congregations. The theme stressed during 1983 was "Kingdom Unity," strengthening the bond of love that unites the international brotherhood.

This rapid growth made it necessary to enlarge or rebuild many of the facilities used in the 95 branch offices and printing plants. New construction was completed, or nearly so, in 11 countries, and plans were under way for new facilities in 15 others.

The "Kingdom Unity" theme was emphasized at the 104 district conventions held in the U.S. during June and July. The combined peak attendance was 1,124,070, and millions more attended conventions held in other countries. In a verbally adopted "Declaration of Unity," those present expressed their resolve to worship only Jehovah God, to maintain fine conduct wherever they resided, and to guard against deflection from true worship because of wrong influences in the world. Two million copies of a new book entitled *United in Worship of the Only True God* were released.

(FREDERICK W. FRANZ)

Lutheran Churches. In 1983 world Lutheranism celebrated the 500th anniversary of the birth of Martin Luther, the 16th-century German church reformer whose name it bears. The biggest celebrations took place on or near Luther's birth date (November 10), especially in East and West Germany, where most of the sites associated with Luther's life are located, and the U.S. Numerous special events in other countries also marked the anniversary, many of them with prominent ecumenical participation.

In September the official Lutheran-Roman Catholic dialogue group in the U.S. announced their conviction that traditional differences of emphasis on the doctrine of justification need not be considered "church dividing." U.S. Lutherans and Episcopalians marked the first anniversary of an official relationship of "interim sharing of the Eucharist," and representatives of eight major Lutheran and Reformed churches recommended intercommunion and mutual recognition of ministries. Work continued on efforts to unite about two-thirds of U.S. and Canadian Lutherans into one Lutheran denomination in each country by 1988 and 1986, respectively.

World peace and southern Africa continued to rank high on the world Lutheran agenda. The 100th anniversary of Lutheranism in Namibia was marked. Church-state relations continued to cause debate in several countries, notably in Scandinavia (where Lutheranism is at least nominally the church of virtually all the population) and East Germany. Lutheran bishops were prominent in the ecumenical portions of Pope John Paul II's visits to Poland and Austria. In December the pope attended a service in a Lutheran congregation in Rome and spoke briefly about "Christian unity." The historic event marked the Luther anniversary. In the Soviet Union, German-speaking Lutherans were able to hold their first conference in half a century.

Even before the Luther anniversary was behind them, Lutherans were planning for the 1984 assembly of the Lutheran World Federation, to be held in Budapest, Hung. Lutherans were active in the WCC assembly. West German Lutheran theologian and church bureaucrat Heinz Joachim Held (a member of one of the country's regional United Churches) was elected WCC moderator, and East German Lutheran bishop Johannes Hempel succeeded retired Swedish Lutheran archbishop Olof Sundby as one of the seven WCC presidents.

(THOMAS HARTLEY DORRIS)

Methodist Churches. In 1983 the World Methodist Council (WMC) comprised 64 member churches in 90 countries, the latest additions being the Methodist Church of Upper Burma and the African Methodist Church of Zimbabwe. A recently published WMC handbook showed that during the period 1976–81, membership of the Methodist Church worldwide rose from 20,772,825 to 23,696,476—an increase of some 14%. The "Mission to the Eighties" program launched in 1980 by the Evangelism Committee of the WMC continued to report significant patterns of growth. In Indonesia there had been several mass baptisms when more than 2,000 persons at a time had joined the church. In the U.S. the United Methodist Church, now some 9.5 million strong, prepared to celebrate its bicentennial in 1984.

The second International Youth Conference, organized by the Evangelism Committee and the Youth Committee of the WMC and held at Queen's College, Nassau, The Bahamas, in August 1983, brought together 1,200 young people from 44 countries. For the first time the Methodist churches of Europe met in East Germany (at Herrnhut) for their Consultative Conference.

Signs of tension over the church's involvement in political and social issues were evident in many countries. In the U.S. a *Reader's Digest* article, "Do You Know Where Your Church Offerings Go?," and the television program "60 Minutes" both attacked leading Methodists associated with the National Council of the Churches of Christ in the U.S.A. for supposed Communist leanings. (See *Introduction*, above.) In Australia the Uniting Church was charged with being under Marxist influence by the weekly news magazine *The Bulletin*. In Britain the Charity Commissioners put a stop to donations given by the Methodist Church to the WCC's Fund to Combat Racism on the grounds that the latter was a political and not a religious organization.

In South Africa the Methodist Church, in a submission to a parliamentary select committee, expressed its abhorrence of proposed legislation aimed at further restriction of the freedom of blacks. The Methodist Peace Award for 1982 was given to Kenneth Mew of Harare, Zimbabwe, for his work in promoting unity among all races and classes and respect for human rights.

All the ordained pastors of the five conferences in West Malaysia and Sarawak met in Port Dickson, Malaysia, for a time of reflection, fellowship, and study with the theme "Renewed to Serve." African Methodist youth, meeting in Harare, decided to form the African Methodist Youth Council.

(PETER H. BOLT)

Pentecostal Churches. The three largest congregations in the world in 1983 were Pentecostal churches, according to *Christian Life* magazine. They were: the Full Gospel Central Church in Seoul, South Korea (250,000); Jotabeche Pentecostal Methodist Church in Santiago, Chile (90,000); and the Congregação Crista in São Paulo, Brazil (61,250). After several years in the U.S. embassy in Moscow, the two Pentecostal families known as the "Siberian Seven" were allowed to leave the U.S.S.R. in July. The Vashchenkos immigrated to Israel, while the Chmykhalov family was taken to the U.S. by the United Pentecostal Church.

The Pentecostal Holiness Church and the Wesleyan Methodist Church of Brazil completed an affiliation agreement in March that brought together one of the oldest (PHC) and one of the newest (WMC) Pentecostal denominations in the world. A record 20,000 persons attended the 40th General Council of the Assemblies of God in Anaheim, Calif., in August. The sessions were telecast to another million over cable TV. According to the Arbitron ratings, Jimmy Swaggart, an Assembly of God evangelist, produced the most popular religious telecast in the U.S.

The Church of God (Cleveland, Tenn.) began a national weekly telecast. It also announced plans to construct a $2.4 million Pentecostal research centre in Cleveland. At the Pentecostal Church of God General Convention, held in June in Joplin, Mo., the delegates returned Roy Chappell to office as general superintendent and voted to establish permanent headquarters in Joplin.

(VINSON SYNAN)

Reformed, Presbyterian, and Congregational Churches. The WCC assembly was particularly important for the numerous delegates of Reformed, Presbyterian, and Congregational churches who attended it. Ecumenical relations at world level between the Orthodox, Reformed, and Protestant traditions required that each have a sufficient inner unity; the World Alliance of Reformed Churches (WARC), representing one sector within Protestantism, was very much aware of this need. The theme of peace and nuclear disarmament—central to the assembly—was also the subject of a proposal, issued in March 1983 by the Executive Committee of the WARC, that a "Covenant for Peace and Justice" be established under WCC leadership.

Besides ongoing bilateral theological dialogues, a significant encounter took place in March among representatives of the Reformed, Baptist, and Mennonite world organizations. A theological debate was concluded by a religious service of repentance and reconciliation held in the Grossmünster (the chief Reformed church building) in Zürich, Switz., a few yards away from the Limmat River, where 16th-century Anabaptists (spiritual predecessors of the present Baptists and Mennonites) were drowned by the ancestors of the present Reformed.

Not all Reformed, Presbyterian, and Congregational churches were among the 157 members of the WARC. The more doctrinally conservative churches tended to have reservations about what some considered the WARC's theological "liberalism" and ecumenical attitude, although in most cases particular historical conditions also played a role. In Latin America an Association of Reformed and Presbyterian Churches (AIPRAL) included some churches that were members of the WARC and some that were not, thus forming a sort of bridge. After some years of inactivity, AIPRAL held a continental assembly in Bogotá, Colombia, early in 1983.

In the U.S. the Presbyterian Church (U.S.A.) came into being when the general assemblies of the United Presbyterian Church (Northern) and the Presbyterian Church in the United States (Southern), meeting in Atlanta, Ga., in June, both voted for merger. The two wings of American Presbyterianism had been separated since the Civil War. The new 3.1 million-member body was the fourth largest Protestant denomination in the U.S.

Reformed churches in Switzerland and throughout the world were preparing to celebrate, on Jan. 1, 1984, the 500th anniversary of the birth of Huldrych Zwingli, one of the fathers of the Reformation.

(ALDO COMBA)

Religious Society of Friends. The main international event for Quakers in 1983 was the WCC assembly, where the emphasis on issues of social justice and peace was one with which Friends could identify strongly. Friends in Canada and the main two U.S. groups were members of the WCC and sent delegates. British Friends had never felt able to assent formally to the wording of the WCC's basis of membership.

The movement for withholding that part of an individual's tax devoted to defense gained strong support among Quaker groups. In Britain the Society of Friends faced an acute challenge when 37 of its employees at Friends House requested that the

UPI

Lidiya Vashchenko (right), who had been granted an exit visa earlier, greeted her mother, Augustina, and the other members of her Pentecostal Christian family on their arrival in Israel from the U.S.S.R.

society withhold a percentage of their income tax, with the intention of paying it when assurance was given that it would be used for peaceful purposes. London Yearly Meeting, the general assembly of all British Friends, recognized that the employees' request was a genuine conscientious objection that it should support, but some members disapproved so strongly of the Society's apparent intention to break the law that they resigned. The resulting tensions were partly resolved when it was decided to test the law, rather than break it, by withholding a percentage of the employees' tax for October and trying for a court hearing on the matter.

(DAVID FIRTH)

Salvation Army. During 1983 the Salvation Army continued its worldwide ministry of the preaching and practical application of Christian truths. In over 80 countries the Army sought to match its work to the needs of the community. It operated the largest alcoholic rehabilitation program in the U.S. In Sydney, Australia, the problems of the rapidly growing number of unemployed were eased by an extensive feeding program. Two hostel facilities in London were adapted for use as rehabilitation centres for young men under 25. The Salvation Army led the field in the work of tracing missing persons on an international basis; over 8,000 cases were successfully completed during the year.

In June Gen. Jarl Wahlström, the organization's international leader, issued a statement to the UN secretary-general regarding the Salvation Army's stand on world disarmament and peace. A call was made for all governments "to reduce their total weapon capability to the minimum level necessary for present security. . . ."

The 100th birthday of Commissioner Catherine Bramwell-Booth, eldest granddaughter of the Salvation Army's founder and first general, William Booth, was celebrated on July 20.

(ROB GARRAD)

Seventh-day Adventist Church. World membership of the church passed the four million mark. The accelerated growth rate was due, in part, to an evangelistic program entitled "One Thousand Days of Reaping," launched in 1982 and designed to add 1,000 members a day for 1,000 consecutive days. As 1983 drew to a close, the program was on schedule.

The church's oldest and major publishing house, the Review and Herald, moved from Washington, D.C., to an $11 million, five-acre plant in Hagerstown, Md. Net retail sales of $132 million by the church's 50 publishing houses were reported. One of the most popular books was *The Great Controversy* by Ellen G. White, one of the church's founders. It was estimated that five million copies in paperback would be distributed in North America alone during the "1,000 days." Demand for Adventist books was especially high in Poland, where the government authorized establishment of a Seventh-day Adventist printing plant in Warsaw.

"The Voice of Prophecy" began broadcasting by satellite five days a week over 247 stations in North America. A daily program in French was begun on Gabon's powerful Africa 1 radio station. For the first time in more than 25 years, a weekly Adventist program in English was being carried on Radio Luxembourg, which covers much of Western Europe. The newly constructed Kanye, Botswana, hospital was officially opened by Pres. Quett Masire. The Bangkok, Thailand, Hospital added a $2 million wing, and three clinics were established in Zimbabwe. Seventh-day Adventist World Service provided approximately $18 million worth of cash, food, and relief supplies in 48 countries.

(KENNETH H. WOOD)

Unitarian (Universalist) Churches. More than 1,600 persons from a thousand member societies registered for the annual General Assembly of the Unitarian Universalist Association, held June 12–17, 1983, in Vancouver, B.C. Reflecting profound concern over global munitions buildups and military polarization, five of the seven general resolutions approved by the delegates dealt with world peace.

Record giving to the Annual Program Fund in 1982 was exceeded in 1983 by 10.5%. The recently founded Los Lunas

Unitarian Universalist Fellowship in New Mexico was believed to be the first congregation consisting entirely of prisoners to be admitted into membership in a major denomination. International programs of the Unitarian Universalist Service Committee in West Africa, the Caribbean, and India stressed health, economic development, and women's rights. Domestic efforts concentrated on the needs of the aging and of Native Americans and on inequities in the criminal justice system.

Canadian Unitarian Universalists, hosts of the continental General Assembly, observed the 151st anniversary of the first Unitarian services in Canada (Montreal) and the 152nd anniversary of the initial Universalist congregation (London, Ont.). Icelandic churches were founded in Manitoba and Saskatchewan.

In Great Britain the 55th annual General Assembly of Unitarian and Free Christian Churches met in Oxford, April 8–11. The delegates called on her majesty's government to reverse its decision to site cruise missiles in the U.K. and recommended that the General Assembly Council develop a program of peace education. Britain's high unemployment was deplored, and all possible governmental steps toward solution were urged. Closer contacts with ethnic minorities were recommended to constituent congregations. (JOHN NICHOLLS BOOTH)

The United Church of Canada. Disarmament continued to be a major focus for Canada's largest Protestant denomination in 1983. This included opposition to the testing of a U.S. cruise missile in Alberta during the autumn. In initiating a strong protest to the federal government, the United Church was joined by all mainline Protestant denominations.

The Rt. Rev. W. Clarke MacDonald, moderator of the denomination, scheduled a trip to Moscow in September with Christian Initiative for Peace, a coalition of 33 Roman Catholic and Mennonite clergy and laity. The purpose was, in his words, "to indicate to whomever we meet that there is a will to peace on this side of the water." The group carried bags of letters from children and adults to Soviet government officials pleading for disarmament.

The denomination's Working Unit on Social Issues and Justice issued a study stating that "unemployment is a sin against our neighbour . . . and cannot be solved apart from regaining greater economic control." The United Church joined an interdenominational campaign aimed at enlisting public support for native rights. More than 800,000 pamphlets pointing out the inadequate treatment of Indians, Inuit, and Métis people by the federal government were distributed to congregations across Canada.

Preparations were under way for the publication of a six-year study entitled *Confessing Our Faith*, to be presented to the 30th General Council in August 1984. Meanwhile, the moderator called for a conference on seeking a clearer understanding of the nature and work of the Holy Spirit. The draft agenda for the General Council (the denomination's top legislative body) included reports on the ordination of homosexuals, native people, human sexuality, Christian initiation (baptism as the only step required for full church membership), gender-inclusive language, and the lack of a national food policy.

(NORMAN K. VALE)

United Church of Christ. The UCC's calling as a peacemaking church was strongly affirmed at the 14th General Synod, held in Pittsburgh, June 24–28, 1983. The Synod also voted its support of the pastoral letter concerning peace adopted by the Roman Catholic bishops of the U.S. Carol Joyce Brun, assistant to the church's president for the last seven years, was elected secretary of the denomination. She succeeded Joseph H. Evans, who had been secretary since 1967. By action of the Synod, the UCC added youth and young adult ministries as a third major priority of the church, together with peace and family life. Representatives of the Presbyterian Church of the Republic of Korea attended the Synod and signed a covenant of common mission with the UCC officers.

After ten years, the award-winning magazine *A.D.*, published jointly by the UCC and the United Presbyterian Church, ceased publication in midsummer. Plans for a new publication to take its place were being made by the two churches. Everett C. Parker retired after serving as the UCC's chief executive for communications for three decades. Succeeding him as executive director of the church's Office of Communications was Beverly Chain, formerly communications executive with the United Methodist Church Board for Global Ministries. Alford Carleton, one of the shapers of the UCC, died on August 22.

The Executive Council of the UCC set in motion a six-year process that could lead to a new Statement of Faith for the church by 1989. The 15th General Synod, scheduled to meet in Ames, Iowa, in 1985, could commission a body of persons to work on a church-wide basis to give expression to the common faith of the UCC.

(AVERY D. POST)

[827.D; 827.G.H.; 827.J.3]

ROMAN CATHOLIC CHURCH

Pope John Paul II declared a "Holy Year" from March 25, 1983, to Easter Sunday 1984. The number of pilgrims coming to Rome foiled the Communist mayor's plans to turn more streets into pedestrian malls. The Synod of Bishops, which began on September 29, was subordinated to the Holy Year celebrations by its theme of "Reconciliation and Penance in the Mission of the Church." Proposals were made to halt the decline in private confessions, and "general absolution" was not regarded as an acceptable substitute except in danger of death or for vast crowds with no priests in remote mission stations.

More important than the Synod in the long term was the appearance, after 20 years of toil, of the new code of canon law. Compared with the 1917 code it replaced, it was shorter, assigned a much greater role to the laity, reduced the grounds of excommunication to six, and generally reflected the letter if not the spirit of the Second Vatican Council. It continued to exclude the ordination of women. Officially "presented" on January 25, it came into force on November 27, the first Sunday of Advent.

The new code reflected recent decrees

Pope John Paul II signed the decree promulgating a new code of canon law on January 25. The new code replaced an older one dating from 1917.

ARTURO MARI—OSSERVATORE ROMANO

from Vatican departments (congregations). The U.S. bishops in particular felt themselves under attack from the Roman Curia, though they loyally denied it. Investigations began into the state of seminaries in the U.S. and the decline of religious life; a strenuous—and so far unsuccessful—attempt was made to get sisters back into religious garb; girls were not allowed to act as altar servers; and dancing in worship was banned as "profane" and "secularizing." Meeting a group of U.S. bishops on September 5, Pope John Paul said they should withdraw their support "from individuals or groups who in the name of progress, justice or compassion . . . promote the ordination of women to the priesthood." The pope also reiterated his denunciation of homosexuality, premarital sex, artificial birth control, and abortion.

Even the U.S. bishops' pastoral letter on nuclear weapons was subjected to astringent criticism at a private meeting in Rome in January. The bishops were urged to take into account the "geopolitical realities," to distinguish between the moral value of the two competing political systems, and to remember that the "just war" tradition was still valid. They incorporated these points into the final version of the pastoral letter, approved in May. (See *Introduction*, above.) Other hierarchies anticipated or followed the U.S. line. They accepted "deterrence" for the time being but made it clear they thought it was a barely tolerated evil. In Britain criticism by the papal pro-nuncio, Archbishop Bruno Heim, of the unilateralist stance of Msgr. Bruce Kent (*see* BIOGRAPHIES), general secretary of the Campaign for Nuclear Disarmament, aroused controversy and was subsequently declared "unofficial" by the Vatican.

Two visits by the pope brought him face to face with other contemporary problems. The most dramatic moment of his March journey to seven Central American countries came in Managua, Nicaragua, on March 4, when the chanting of revolutionary slogans interrupted his homily and mass in the July 19 Square. Certainly, Pope John Paul found nothing good to say about the avowedly Marxist regime of the Sandinistas and still less about the "popular church" that supports them. He openly rebuked the priest-poet Ernesto Cardenal, the only one of the five priests in the Nicaraguan government who tried to greet him.

The other controversial papal visit was to Poland in June. It made a grim contrast with John Paul's triumphant return home in 1979, when he had given Poles the self-confidence they needed to launch the now suppressed free trade union Solidarity. A long and unscheduled second meeting between the pope and Gen. Wojciech Jaruzelski, the head of the Polish state, gave rise to hopes (or fears) that a deal had been struck, but nothing was divulged. The deputy editor of the Vatican newspaper, Virgilio Levi, was forced to resign after saying that Lech Walesa (*see* NOBEL PRIZES), the leader of Solidarity, had been abandoned. Later events suggested that, if there had been a deal, it soon fell apart. (*See* POLAND.)

Even though other papal visits were less charged, Pope John Paul brought an edge of controversy to them. At Lourdes in August he denounced religious persecution in Communist countries. In Vienna in September he once more evoked his vision of a wider, spiritual Europe, "beyond artificial frontiers," of which the church was the heir and the pope the guardian. His visit marked the 300th anniversary of the defeat of the "Turkish hordes" at the gates of the city. Though John Paul called for another crusade, he insisted that it would be a spiritual one. But détente and dialogue were clearly at an end. The nomination of a Latvian cardinal on February 2—the first Soviet citizen to be granted the title—was seen as a challenge to the Soviet leadership.

Another of the new cardinals, Colombian Alfonso López Trujillo, was expected to play an important role in the Roman Curia. He was known to be hostile to "liberation theology" and favourable to the controversial organization Opus Dei. In September the Jesuits, at last allowed to elect a new superior general, voted for a 54-year-old Dutchman, Peter-Hans Kolvenbach (*see* BIOGRAPHIES). Archbishop Emmanuel Milingo of Lusaka, Zambia, demonstrated his sanity and was rewarded with a post in the Vatican's Office for Tourism and Migration. He vowed to continue the charismatic healing work that had brought him under suspicion of permitting magical practices in Africa.

On the ecumenical front, the 500th anniversary of the birth of Martin Luther was marked by a joint Lutheran-Roman Catholic statement from West Germany on "Luther as a witness to Christ" and by a letter from the pope to the Vatican Secretariat for Christian Unity praising the reformer's "profound religiousness." A second, newly constituted Anglican-Roman Catholic International Commission promised to pay more attention to "Reformation" questions such as "justification." Twenty-five Roman Catholics enjoyed "observer status" at the WCC assembly. (*See* VATICAN CITY STATE.) (PETER HEBBLETHWAITE)
[827.e; 827.G.2; 827.J.2]

THE ORTHODOX CHURCH

Located in many countries of both East and West, the various autocephalous (independent) churches of the Orthodox world faced—as in past years—different challenges and problems. In the Soviet Union the patriarchate of Moscow officially announced that the buildings of the 14th-century monastery of St. Daniel, which had been secularized in the 1920s, were to be placed at the disposal of the church and would serve as its administrative centre. Although it appeared that no monastic community was to be reestablished there, the central location of the ancient monastery would make the headquarters of the Orthodox Church more visible and more accessible to the Soviet capital.

At the same time, government authorities took pitiless measures against representatives of the Orthodox laity who were attempting to spread religious literature. Examples included the arrest and condemnation of Zoia Krakhmalnikova, editor of the privately initiated religious periodical *Nadezhda* ("Hope"), the sentencing to severe prison terms of five Orthodox laymen in Moscow (December 1982), and the repression of a remarkable religious revival—admittedly with nationalistic undertones—in Georgia.

In the Middle East, Orthodox communities in Lebanon, Syria, Israel, and the occupied West Bank continued to find themselves in a situation that precluded any unified political stand on their part and encouraged political neutrality. As the second largest Christian minority in the region (after the Coptic Church of Egypt), Orthodox Christians could not expect a rosy future in monolithic societies dominated by Israel, militant Islam, or defensively Roman Catholic Maronites. As a result, they generally supported a balanced status quo, within an independent Lebanon (several ministers in Amin Gemayel's government were Orthodox) and in the Middle East generally. The visit of the patriarch of Antioch, Ignatius IV Hazim, to Western Europe in May 1983 and his several public pronouncements reflected political independence and the predominance of purely religious and ecumenical concerns.

Prospects for the convening of a pan-Orthodox "Great Council," which has been a major concern of the ecumenical patriarchate of Constantinople (Istanbul) for some years, were hardly enhanced by the preparatory meetings held in Chambésy, Switz., on Sept. 4–8, 1982. The agenda (the date of Easter, marriage discipline, fasting traditions) was seen by many as rather uninspiring. No suggestions for future conciliar debates were made, and the burning issue of Orthodox administrative unity in America and Western Europe was not discussed. However, constructive initiatives in the direction of unity were taken by the autocephalous Orthodox Church in America and the Antiochian Archdiocese of America at their bilateral meeting on Feb. 23, 1983, and also at the Conference of the International Orthodox Youth Association (Syndesmos) in Crete (August 14–19).

Although Orthodox opinion was divided concerning the political aspects of the WCC assembly, the numerous Orthodox participants showed unfailing solidarity on issues involving the Christian faith itself.

The prestigious Templeton Prize for progress in religion was awarded, for the first time, to an Orthodox Christian, the exiled Soviet writer Aleksandr I. Solzhenitsyn. (JOHN MEYENDORFF)

EASTERN NON-CHALCEDONIAN CHURCHES

Following the death of the Armenian catholicos of Cilicia, Khoren I, on Feb. 9, 1983, the auxiliary catholicos Karekin II succeeded him at the headquarters of the church, located in Antelias, Lebanon. The see of Cilicia recognizes the honorary primacy of "the catholicos of all Armenians," whose residence is in Echmiadzin (Soviet Armenia), but competes with him for jurisdiction over the Armenian churches in North America. The new catholicos was a well-known ecumenical personality and, until the WCC assembly, was vice-moderator of the WCC Central Committee.

In Egypt there was no formal change in the status of Patriarch Shenuda III of the Coptic Church, still forced by the government to reside in a remote monastery. A formal exchange of New Year's greetings with Pres. Hosni Mubarak seemed to imply that the president continued to recognize Shenuda as head of the church. However, a Supreme Court decision, challenged by the church, implied that the seat was vacant. Numerous foreign protests, especially by Copts living in America, were voiced in support of Shenuda, a victim of the attempt by the Egyptian government to maintain the highly unstable balance between Muslim extremism and the religious revival within its large Coptic Christian minority.

(JOHN MEYENDORFF)

[827.B; 827.G.1; 827.J.1]

JUDAISM

The apocalyptic events of the military campaign for "Peace in Galilee," which brought the Israeli Army to the gates of Beirut, Lebanon, in the summer of 1982, enveloped the religious life of Judaism during the year. Indeed, no testimony to the vitality of Judaism as a living tradition of ethics and morality proved more decisive. The Jews' reaction to the Christian massacres of Palestinian Arabs in the refugee camps of Sabra and Shatila, in an area under Israeli control, encompassed not only political but also religious concerns. From Reform to Orthodox Judaism, both in the Holy Land and throughout the Diaspora, the moral imperative drew powerful affirmation.

Notably, the commission, headed by Chief Justice Yitzhak Kahan, set up in Israel to investigate the massacres, made a strong case on the basis of Judaism for the view that Israelis bore indirect, if not direct, responsibility. The commission's report explicitly recognized that indirect responsibility is not a precise legal category. Seeking a basis for indirect responsibility, then, the commission referred to Deut. 21:6–7, the case of the neglected corpse, for which the nearest town bears responsibility. The commission further cited a Talmudic authority, Joshua ben Levi (B. Sotah 38b): "The necessity for the offering of the heifer by the nearby town comes from narrowness of spirit. The elders state, 'Our hands have not shed this blood.' But can it enter our minds that the elders of a court of justice might have been murderers! The meaning is that [they must affirm that] the deceased did not come to the village for help and get turned away." What makes this passage striking is its invocation of Judaic theological texts and doctrines in the settlement of political issues. (*See* ISRAEL.)

An important project of Judaism, for a more peaceful time, reached its conclusion. The new English translation of the entire Hebrew Bible, undertaken by the Jewish Publication Society of America, was completed with the publication of The Writings, the third and final part of the whole. Yet a third instance of a vital religious life derived from the 1983 meeting of the Conference on Alternatives in Jewish Education, held Aug. 15–19, 1983, at Brandeis University, Waltham, Mass. The meeting drew 1,700 educators from nearly every U.S. state, as well as Europe and the State of Israel. Projects involving the use of TV, such as a Hebrew version of "Sesame Street," and the use of computers in education for Judaism attracted much attention.

At the same time, trends toward divisiveness were apparent. Some testified to the success of a renewal of Judaic observance and belief. For example, an increasing number of young people from nonobservant homes were choosing to live in accord with Orthodox Judaism. This return to Judaism led to tensions in their relationships with their parents. The movement produced the founding, in the State of Israel, of more than a dozen yeshivas (centres of traditional living and learning) for Americans lacking a formal Jewish background. The new devotees derived, in part, from children of the 1960s alienated by the Vietnam war and those taking a new interest in their own Jewishness in the aftermath of the Israeli-Arab wars.

The perennial issue of the achievement, within Judaism, of full equality between men and women took a new turn. The (Reform) Central Conference of American Rabbis (CCAR), meeting in March 1983, voted that the offspring of a Jewish father and a non-Jewish mother would be regarded, for the purposes of Jewish law as administered by Reform rabbis, as completely Jewish. Traditional Jewish law accords the status of a Jew to the offspring of a Jewish mother and a non-Jewish father, but not the other way around. At the same time, the CCAR stated, "This presumption of the Jewish status of the offspring of any mixed marriage is to be established through appropriate and timely public and formal acts of identification with the Jewish faith and people." The opposition pointed out that the decision would cause new difficulties between Israeli Orthodoxy, in command of matters of personal status for Jews in the State of Israel, and Jews from the Diaspora. That same argument came into play in the debate within Conservative Judaism concerning women rabbis. In the summer the first woman to apply for full membership in the Rabbinical Assembly failed to obtain the required 75% affirmative vote. In October, however, the Jewish Theological Seminary of America voted to admit women to the rabbinical studies program and to ordain them. In the past, the seminary's choices for ordination have always been accepted by the assembly.

Mordecai Menahem Kaplan, founder of the Reconstructionist movement, died Nov. 8, 1983, at the age of 102 (*see* OBITUARIES).

(JACOB NEUSNER)

[826]

BUDDHISM

Buddhism maintained a relatively low profile in Asia during 1982–83. For the most part, the generation of Buddhist leaders trained before World War II had begun to pass, and new leaders had not yet appeared. In traditionally Buddhist nations of South and Southeast Asia, persistent issues

All branches of U.S. Judaism, long hesitant to seek adherents, have begun educational or social activities aimed at creating or reawakening interest among uncommitted Jews. Shown is a dance held for such a purpose by a synagogue in the New York City borough of Queens.

KEITH MEYERS/THE NEW YORK TIMES

remained, such as unrest among ethnic minority groups in Burma, the vocal protests of Muslims in Thailand and Burma, and the discontent of the Hindu Tamils in Sri Lanka. (*See* SRI LANKA). Thailand witnessed the appearance of a new protest movement against the regime by students who adopted such Buddhist symbols as shaved heads and fasting. In Vietnam the regime had begun to harass various religious leaders, Buddhists among them. In Singapore, to combat the erosion of moral values, the Ministry of Education adopted a controversial policy of teaching courses on Buddhism and other world religions in the schools.

Buddhists in China were benefiting from the increasing leniency of the Beijing (Peking) regime toward all religions. The first class of monks—33 strong—was graduated from the Lingyanshan (Ling-yen-shan) Buddhist Seminary in eastern China, and a two-year training program for Buddhist nuns was established at the Chongfu (Ch'ung-fu) Temple in Fujian (Fukien) Province. Chinese Buddhists welcomed a visiting group of U.S. Buddhists for the first time since 1948. It was reported that a new Tibetan Buddhist Institute would soon be established in Lhasa. However, the exiled Dalai Lama had not responded to Beijing's repeated invitations to return to Tibet.

Buddhism continued to make steady but modest gains in the West. In Japan the Soka University, affiliated with the Nichiren Shoshu/Soka Gakkai, announced plans to build a branch on the outskirts of San Diego, Calif. Dom Helder Câmara, Roman Catholic archbishop of Olinda and Recife in Brazil, received the first Niwano Peace Prize from a foundation established by President Niwano of Rissho Koseikai. Ryokei Onishi, chief priest of the Kiyomizu Temple in Kyoto, died early in 1983 at the age of 107. Isaline B. Horner, for many years secretary of the Pali Text Society, London, died in 1982, and Christmas Humphreys, a retired British judge and controversial lay Buddhist leader, died early in 1983. The 14th conference of the World Fellowship of Buddhists opened in December in Jakarta, Indon.

(JOSEPH M. KITAGAWA)

[824]

HINDUISM

In January the government of the state of Uttar Pradesh in India took control of the Vishwanath temple in Varanasi (Benares), one of the holiest sites in that pilgrimage city. The immediate reason was the theft of valuable gold ornaments from the temple. Since some of the high priests were implicated, the government placed the financial management of the temple in the care of a board of trustees, which it appointed. In April the chief minister of the state of Andhra Pradesh put the great temple of Tirupati, sacred to the Lord Venkateswara, under state control.

These events pointed up a problem of increasing concern. The Tirupati and Vishwanath temples, along with many other public Hindu temples in India, enjoy sizable incomes and endowments. Under Hindu and Muslim rulers these temples were government regulated and administered, but under British rule they were, for the most part, managed by the resident priests. With independence in 1947, the state governments began to exercise control over temples because of alleged misuse of revenues. While the Indian constitution imposes no restrictions upon belief and cultic activities, it does allow government regulation of "any economic, financial, political or other secular activity" of religious institutions (Art. 25.2). Some Hindus welcomed the government intervention, while others (especially the priesthood) viewed it as inappropriate for an avowedly secular state and an offense against the deities who are the true owners of the temples.

In other ways, temples and pilgrimage sites figured prominently in Hinduism during 1983. On August 13, 60 persons were killed and scores injured at the Naina Devi temple in Himachal Pradesh state when thousands of pilgrims rushed to view the image of the temple deity during a major festival. At the great pilgrimage shrines of Badrinath and Rishikesh in the Himalayas, a special detail of police was assigned to protect pilgrims from harassment and fraud by temple custodians and guides. In Mathura, traditional birthplace of the Lord Krishna, the Mukharbindu temple was severely damaged in September by monsoon floods. In April a violent dispute between Hindus and Christians in Kerala began over the rehabilitation of an ancient church on the route to an important Hindu pilgrimage shrine. The church, which according to tradition stands on the site of one

Religious violence in northeastern India's Assam state claimed as many as 3,000 lives, and survivors gathered in hurriedly contrived refugee camps wherever they could be established with relative, and fleeting, safety. Assamese Hindus, enraged by illegal immigrants, largely Muslims, from Bangladesh, set upon them with knives, guns, and spears. The victims included Bengali-speaking Muslims and Hindus and even some native Assamese Hindu speakers of Bengali.

BALDEV—SYGMA

built by St. Thomas in the first Christian century, was restored with the assistance of the state government. This led to accusations of inappropriate support of sectarian religion by a secular government and of mischievous interference by the state in the practice of the Hindu religion.

(H. PATRICK SULLIVAN)

[823]

ISLAM

The year was marked by violence as Muslims in many countries experienced fighting and upheaval. Many of these events were continuations from previous years. In the Middle East the war between Iraq and Iran flared anew, and fighting against the occupying Soviet troops continued in Afghanistan. Antigovernment rioting in Pakistan appeared to revolve around fundamentalist issues. In Assam state in India, where the native Assamese tribesmen had resisted the influx of Bengali-speaking Muslim refugees from Bangladesh, there were bloody battles in February between Hindus and Muslims over the issue of eligibility to vote in the state elections. With the government of President Marcos in the Philippines facing riots and demonstrations following the Aquino assassination, a Philippine Muslim spokesman threatened secession by Muslims in Mindanao and the Sulu Archipelago if the Muslim areas continued to be subjected to violence by government troops.

The rise to prominence of activist Islamic fundamentalist organizations had been evident for several years. They espoused many different attitudes and activities; some had claimed responsibility for terrorist acts, but whether or how they were related to any governments in power was unclear. One such group, calling itself the Islamic Jihad Organization, claimed responsibility for an explosion at the U.S. embassy in Beirut in April that killed 63 persons. It seemed to be associated with Shiʿah fundamentalists in Lebanon, with possible links to the government of Iran. Responsibility for the October suicide bombings that killed 240 U.S. and 58 French servicemen attached to peacekeeping forces in Lebanon was claimed by a group calling itself the Islamic Revolutionary Movement. Because the fusion of radical religious beliefs and political action was so close, it was next to impossible to identify the specifically religious dogmatism motivating these groups or to suggest longer term religious trends.

In February the Iranian government brought a number of Baha'i leaders to trial. While the Baha'i faith is not Islamic, it originated in Iran and has a following there. The fundamentalist Shiʿah regime was extremely hostile to the Baha'is and had jailed and executed many of them. A brief problem arose over the beginning of Ramadan. By astronomical calculations, the date was expected to be June 12. However, Islamic law calls for an actual sighting of the moon, and religious authorities in Saudi Arabia announced sighting on June 11. Thus Ramadan started a day earlier than planned. Throughout the month a Muslim takes no food or water during the daylight hours.

The thousandth year of al-Azhar University and Mosque was marked in Cairo in March. Al-Azhar was founded as a Shiʿah missionary training and study centre when the Fatimids became rulers in Egypt, and it is generally acknowledged to be the oldest continuously active university in the world. In August the government of China announced that a number of mosques had become active there. The 1982 census listed the number of Muslims in China at 13 million, although other estimates indicated a higher total.

(REUBEN W. SMITH)

[828]

WORLD CHURCH MEMBERSHIP

Reckoning religious adherence is a precarious exercise. Different religions and even different Christian churches vary widely in their theories and methods of counting and reporting. Some simply depend on government population figures. For others, "numbering the people" is forbidden. Some count only adults and heads of families; others count children, servants, and retainers. Where there is religious liberty, some churches count contributors; others estimate communicants or constituents.

Differing procedures are followed even within the same religion. Quite reliable statistics are available on the mission fields, for renewal movements in Islam, Buddhism, and Hinduism as well as Christianity. Where a religion has been dominant for centuries (*e.g.*, Christianity in Europe, Hinduism in India), whole populations are often counted as adherents, although the decline of religious observance and the rise of antireligious ideologies might call this casual procedure into question. Although Albania is the only officially atheist state, the 20th century has produced a number of governments hostile to all traditional religions. It is difficult to get satisfactory religious estimates for the populations under their control.

The traditional listing of religions used by scholars since the comparative study of religions became an academic discipline makes no provision for several religions or faiths now numerous and/or influential; *e.g.*, Baha'i, Ch'ondokyo, the Unification Church, the religions of the Sikhs and Jains (usually—and erroneously—subsumed under "Hinduism"). Taoism and Confucianism are so blended in many communities that it is becoming common practice to refer to "Chinese folk-religion."

Finally, each year brings reports of major population movements, reflected, for example, in the striking rise of Eastern religions in the religious statistics of western and northern Europe.

The reader is advised to reflect carefully upon the statistics reported and to refer to articles discussing the different countries and religions when pursuing the subject in depth.

(FRANKLIN H. LITTELL)

Estimated Membership of the Principal Religions of the World

Religions	North America[1]	South America	Europe[2]	Asia[3]	Africa	Oceania[4]	World
Total Christian	252,458,670	196,599,780	337,678,150	104,098,695	147,076,000	18,781,550	1,056,692,845
Roman Catholic	138,875,530	185,251,200	178,032,590	57,265,290	56,999,270	5,215,440	621,639,320
Eastern Orthodox	5,648,620	355,250	47,069,040	2,762,810	9,401,840[5]	407,650	65,645,210
Protestant[6]	107,934,520	10,993,330	112,576,520	44,070,595	80,674,890[7]	13,158,460	369,408,315
Jewish	7,611,940	749,580	4,643,810	4,008,850	231,980	73,980	17,320,140
Muslim[8]	1,580,980	406,190	20,190,500	380,068,940	152,943,570	87,000	555,277,180
Zoroastrian	2,750	2,600	14,000	224,370	900	1,000	245,620
Shinto[9]	50,000	—	—	33,000,000	—	—	33,050,000
Taoist	33,250	12,975	13,500	20,500,000	850	2,900	20,563,475
Confucian	99,750	58,925	450,500	162,500,000	2,550	18,390	163,130,115
Buddhist[10]	336,290	241,090	238,300	250,097,200	15,000	23,700	250,951,580
Hindu[11]	309,100	637,400	442,890	459,708,450	1,165,600	326,470	462,589,910
Totals	262,482,730	198,708,540	363,671,650	1,414,206,505	301,436,450	19,314,990	2,559,820,865
Population[12]	389,914,000	259,644,000	761,195,000	2,771,419,000	516,037,000	23,677,000	4,721,886,000

[1]Includes Central America and the West Indies.
[2]Includes the U.S.S.R. and other countries with established Marxist ideology where continuing religious adherence is difficult to estimate.
[3]Includes areas in which persons have traditionally enrolled in several religions, as well as mainland China with a Marxist establishment.
[4]Includes Australia and New Zealand as well as islands of the South Pacific.
[5]Includes Coptic Christians, of restricted status in Egypt and precariously situated under the military junta in Ethiopia.
[6]Protestant statistics vary widely in style of reckoning affiliation. See *World Church Membership.*
[7]Including a great proliferation of new churches, sects, and cults among African Christians.
[8]The chief base of Islam is still ethnic, although missionary work is now carried on in Europe and America. In countries where Islam is established, minority religions are frequently persecuted and accurate statistics are rare.
[9]A Japanese ethnic religion, Shinto declined rapidly after the Japanese emperor surrendered his claim to divinity (1947); a revival of cultic participation in the homeland had chiefly literary significance. Shinto does not survive well outside Japan.
[10]Buddhism has produced several renewal movements in the last century that have gained adherents in Europe and America. Although persecuted in Tibet and sometimes elsewhere in Asia, it has shown greater staying power than other religions of the East. It also transplants better.
[11]Hinduism's strength in India has been enhanced by its connection with the national movement, a phenomenon also observable in the world of Islam. Modern Hinduism has developed several renewal movements that have won adherents in Europe and America.
[12]U.S. Department of Commerce, Bureau of the Census, *World Population: 1983.*

(FRANKLIN H. LITTELL)

THE CHURCH SPEAKS; WHO LISTENS?

by Martin E. Marty

"Who speaks for whom in the field of religion?" The search for answers to this chronic question often leads to puzzles in the minds of those who are members of no religious group. How seriously should they take the public actions and words of various councils that represent churches or synagogues and their members? It becomes an acute question when the members themselves argue over the policies and pronouncements of conferences and councils.

Councils in the News. The main religious news of 1983 forced debate on the issue. Several events pushed the question into prime time and onto the front page. In the United States, many observers named an action by the National Conference of Catholic Bishops as the religious news story of the year. In May the bishops released a carefully worded document on "The Challenge of Peace." This formal letter discussed the issue of nuclear disarmament. (*See* RELIGION: *Introduction*.)

Immediately there was controversy. Polls indicated that most Roman Catholics and the general public were in support of much of the letter. However, many could find details over which to argue. Moreover, since the majority of the bishops came down hard against nuclear weapons, there were vigorous denunciations by some Catholics. Members who were in the armed forces or employed in defense industries often came to be genuinely troubled in conscience. What authority did the bishops have or could they claim to have?

Meanwhile, in the Protestant and Orthodox worlds the news event of the year in North America was the meeting, between July 24 and August 10, of the sixth General Assembly of the World Council of Churches (WCC) in Vancouver, B.C. There are 400 million Christians in more than 300 member churches from 100 countries who make up the council, which was formed in 1948. Delegates came together for joint worship, common action to unite Christians, planning to meet human needs, and debate over social issues. It was the last of these that received most attention in the news.

Martin E. Marty is Fairfax M. Cone distinguished service professor of history of modern Christianity at the University of Chicago and associate editor of The Christian Century.

Of less note but still a front-page story was a meeting of the governing board of the National Council of the Churches of Christ in the U.S.A. (NCC). Its leadership was called upon to face the issue posed by the Universal Fellowship of Metropolitan Community Churches. The UFMCC wanted membership in the council, even though it is constituted on grounds different from those of other council churches. It is made up of homosexuals or people who concentrate on ministry among homosexuals. While there may be wide diversity of opinion about such ministry among members of the NCC's constituent churches, board members seemed to sense how strongly opposed many of them were. Some NCC bodies might well have left the organization if the UFMCC had entered it; but in November the governing board postponed a decision indefinitely, leaving the question of eligibility undetermined.

Serving as background to both the WCC and NCC debates were two January events that drew wide notice. The Institute on Religion and Democracy (IRD), a small neoconservative organization, many of whose members had themselves once been leftist, attacked the National Council in particular for "leftism" and support of Marxist-Leninist causes. NCC leadership vigorously disagreed with such an assessment but found itself on the defensive after the IRD inspired CBS's "60 Minutes" TV program on January 23 to attack the council in a broadcast that could reach almost 23 million households. The leaders of the councils also cried foul, without success, when an IRD-inspired story in the *Reader's Digest* magazine that same month made similar charges.

Bishops as Teachers. Whether or not there were reasons for such accusations—a very weak World Council criticism of the Soviet Union for its actions in Afghanistan gave some plausibility to them—the issue soon came to be: Do these councils represent church members? What do members do if they disagree with councils?

Answers to these questions depend somewhat on the nature of the churches involved. In the Catholic case, the bishops were careful to distinguish in their letter between moral principles, on which all Catholics must agree, and their specific applications. On the issue of nuclear weapons, they acknowledged great freedom for dissent, including dissent by the small minority of bishops who themselves disagreed with the letter. Joseph Cardinal Ratzinger in Rome argued that national bishops' conferences did not have a "mandate to teach." Yet his critics pointed out that bishops' conferences regularly have held teaching authority. What kind? Certainly not like papal infallibility. Nor could they coerce consciences in the civil realm.

In the end, these national bishops' conferences successfully displayed authority to speak and teach to the degree that they could persuade members in the parishes that their teaching squared with what it meant to be a Catholic. There was power in the bishops' letter on peace, but not of the sort that could force a Congress to act, nor was it of the sort that would necessitate a Catholic's choosing whether to remain in the military in the nuclear age or even to remain a Catholic.

Councils as Persuaders. In the case of the WCC and the NCC, a similar answer suggests itself. Perhaps the authority of these councils is weaker, since they represent many loosely attached churches instead of a single communion that promotes deep levels of union. The member bodies of the WCC have all kept their autonomy, as have NCC constituent groups. These are not councils of church *members* but councils of *churches*. The constitutions of the councils do not permit them to take away the authority of the separate churches but only to urge them to move closer to each other and engage in common action.

Much of what the Vancouver assembly promoted in the summer was widely applauded by the members of the constituent churches who heard about them. This sixth assembly was, in many eyes, the most deeply spiritual to date; its worship seemed more profound than before. Evangelicals who previously had been critical of the thought of the council found much to applaud. Mainline church members liked the way it was making progress on basic churchly themes like baptism-Eucharist-ministry. Most North Americans disdained the documents in which the United States was strongly attacked while the Soviet Union got off lightly. The reason for this situation was clear. Delegates from the huge Russian Orthodox Church threatened that they would have to step back from the council if their government found the proposal not to its liking.

So the Protestant-Orthodox case came down to a circumstance much like the Catholic one. The public grows ever more sophisticated about the process by which conferences and councils make their statements. People learn to sift and sort, to learn how and why bishops and assembly delegates speak and act as they do. Some dissenters may protest actions by withholding funds; others may show support by enlarging their financial aid; still others may ignore the whole process. Yet, taken together, these events of 1983 once again demonstrated the power of persuasion and the need to persuade. In the United States they also showed the freedom citizens have to be persuaded or to resist. The conferences and councils, then, have to speak to convinced hearts and minds, which is what they profess to be aiming at in any case.

Roman Catholic bishops of the United States gathered in Chicago to adopt their long-debated challenge to U.S. armaments policy.

JEFF LOWENTHAL/NEWSWEEK

Rodeo

Roy Cooper, a 28-year-old cowboy who has dominated calf roping since 1976, had a sensational year in the Professional Rodeo Cowboys Association (PRCA). By the time the National Finals Rodeo concluded in Oklahoma City, Okla., on December 11, he had won his fifth world championship in calf roping, plus the world all-around championship with record season earnings totaling $153,391. He also became the first rodeo cowboy since 1958 to win three world titles in one year. In September Cooper took the individual steer roping championship at the national finals in Laramie, Wyo., with $30,520 in earnings. His total in individual calf roping amounted to $122,455; the rest of his prize money came in team roping. The last man to win three world titles was Jim Shoulders, who captured the all-around, bareback riding, and bull riding championships a quarter of a century earlier, winning a total of $32,212.

Cooper, his wife Lisa, and their young son, Clint, lived on a ranch outside Durant, Okla. It was also the hometown of another rodeo champion, Betty Gayle Cooper, Roy's older sister, the all-around and calf roping champion in the Women's Professional Rodeo Association (WPRA).

The national finals were held for the 25th year in 1983 with the last go-round televised throughout most of North America. Contestants in seven events competed for a record $806,500 in prize money. Other PRCA champions for 1983 included: Bruce Ford of Kersey, Colo., with $84,126 in bareback riding; Brad Gjermundson of Marshall, N.D., with $97,457 in saddle bronc riding; Joel Edmondson of Columbus, Kan., with $68,747 in steer wrestling; Cody Snyder of Redcliff, Alta., with $73,772 in bull riding; Leo Camarillo of Lockeford, Calif., with $53,161 in team roping; and Marlene Eddleman of Ordway, Colo., with $51,840 in WPRA barrel racing.

One of the highlights of the year was the PRCA Presidential Rodeo held in September at Landover, Md. Virtually every top contender in the country entered the contests. Pres. Ronald Reagan later invited the cowboys and cowgirls to a barbecue on the White House lawn.

In the Canadian Professional Rodeo Association, Tom Eirikson of Longview, Alta., took his third all-around championship. He won more than $15,000 during the year in calf roping, steer wrestling, and saddle bronc riding. In the International Professional Rodeo Association, Dan Dailey was crowned all-around champion. The association's international finals were scheduled to be held in Tulsa, Okla., in January 1984. Champions would be crowned on the basis of their earnings at that single contest. As a consequence, Dailey was not guaranteed a seventh all-around title even though he was the association's top money winner during the regular season, with nearly $45,000 in prize money.

The National Intercollegiate Rodeo Association held its finals in June at Bozeman, Mont. All-around winners included Rocky Steagall of Blue Mountain Community College, Pendleton, Ore., and Anna Crespin of Eastern New Mexico University at Portales. Kelly Foster of Bell City, La., and Scott Selland of Bismarck, N.D., were senior all-around winners in the National High School Rodeo Association. Senior all-around winners in the American Junior Rodeo Association included Gene Baker of Tuscola, Texas, and Jinita Williams of Lovington, N.M. Benny Reynolds of Twin Bridges, Mont., the 1961 PRCA all-around champion, won the National Old-Timers' Rodeo Association all-around title. In the Indian National Finals at Albuquerque, N.M., John Boyd, Jr., a Navajo cowboy from Lower Greasewood, Ariz., captured the all-around buckle. (RANDALL E. WITTE)

Professional rodeo cowboy Roy Cooper won the world all-around championship and record season earnings exceeding $150,000.

COURTESY, PROFESSIONAL RODEO COWBOYS ASSOCIATION

Rhodesia:
see Zimbabwe

Roads:
see Engineering Projects; Transportation

Rockets:
see Defense; Space Exploration

Romania

Romania

A socialist republic on the Balkan Peninsula in southeastern Europe, Romania is bordered by the U.S.S.R., the Black Sea, Bulgaria, Yugoslavia, and Hungary. Area: 237,500 sq km (91,700 sq mi). Pop (1983 est.): 22,649,000, including (1977) Romanian 88.1%; Hungarian 7.9%; German 1.6%. Cap. and largest city: Bucharest (pop., 1981 est., 1,929,400). Religion (1980 est.): Romanian Orthodox 70%; Greek Orthodox 10%; Muslim 1%; atheist 7%; other 3%; none 9%. General secretary of the Romanian Communist Party, president of the republic, and president of the State Council in 1983, Nicolae Ceausescu; chairman of the Council of Ministers (premier), Constantin Dascalescu.

On the occasion of his 65th birthday on Jan. 26, 1983, Pres. Nicolae Ceausescu was awarded the Order of the October Revolution by the U.S.S.R. Significantly, Ceausescu, who had been general secretary of the Romanian Communist Party (RCP) since 1965, did not receive the more prestigious Order of Lenin.

Ceausescu in 1983 continued to mark out Romania as an independent and sovereign state in the political arena. On June 27, on the eve of a meeting of Warsaw Pact leaders, he released the text of an interview that he had granted on May 19 to the Swedish daily newspaper *Aftonbladet*; in it he had criticized the holding of military maneuvers, describing them as "unnecessary displays of force that did not contribute to the policy of détente." It was more necessary, he continued, to promote disarmament, nuclear disarmament first and foremost. In August Ceausescu sent letters to both Soviet leader Yury Andropov and U.S. Pres. Ronald Reagan discussing intermediate-range missiles in Europe. He advised the Soviet leader to "proceed unilaterally to cut down the number of missiles sited in the European zone of the U.S.S.R." Again, when Andropov ordered the Soviet delegation to withdraw from the intermediate-range nuclear force talks in Geneva on November 23, Ceausescu reacted by declaring that the siting of new missiles in East Germany and Czechoslovakia "was pushing the world to the brink of a nuclear catastrophe."

At the plenary meeting of the RCP Central Committee on March 23–24, Ceausescu announced that by the end of 1982 the party had 3,262,125 members, some 100,000 more than at the end of 1981. The share of party members in the total adult population stood at almost 21% and in the total employed population, at 31%. Ceausescu also called for strict economy in the use of energy and raw materials. He explained in detail the importance of exports to the national economy, pointing out that Romania must aim for a trade surplus of $3 billion in 1983 in order to reduce the foreign debt.

The Central Committee unanimously agreed to increase the number of Politburo members from 21 to 23. Manea Manescu was elected a full member; Gen. Constantin Olteanu, the defense minister, was promoted from alternate to full membership; three alternate members, including Emilian Dobrescu, former chairman of the State Planning Committee, were dismissed from the Politburo; and four new alternate members were elected.

ROMANIA

Education. (1981–82) Primary, pupils 3,285,073, teachers 157,709; secondary, pupils 1,020,789, teachers 47,334; vocational, pupils 148,040, teachers 2,060; teacher training (1980–81), students 6,317, teachers 1,134; higher, students 190,903, teaching staff 14,354.

Finance. Monetary unit: leu, with (July 31, 1983) an official rate of 4.47 lei to U.S. $1 (free rate of 6.80 lei = £1 sterling), a noncommercial rate of 13.54 lei to U.S. $1 (free rate of 20.59 lei = £1 sterling), and a commercial rate of 17.62 lei to U.S. $1 (free rate of 26.80 lei = £1 sterling). Gold and other reserves (June 1983) U.S. $675 million. Budget (1982 actual): revenue 277.4 billion lei; expenditure 257.4 billion lei. Gross national product (1981) 641.6 billion lei. Money supply (June 1983) 156,950,000,000 lei.

Foreign Trade. (1982) Imports (f.o.b.) 146 billion lei; exports 135 billion lei. Import sources (1981): U.S.S.R. 18%; U.S. 8%; Iran 7%; West Germany 6%. Export destinations: U.S.S.R. 18%; West Germany 7%; U.S. 5%. Main exports (1980): machinery and transport equipment 26%; petroleum products c. 20%; food 12%; chemicals 10%.

Transport and Communications. Roads (1981) c. 95,000 km (including 96 km expressways). Motor vehicles in use (1980): passenger c. 250,000; commercial c. 130,000. Railways: (1980) 11,110 km; traffic (1981) 24,379,000,000 passenger-km, freight 75,251,000,000 net ton-km. Air traffic (1982): 1,145,000,000 passenger-km; freight 10 million net ton-km. Inland waterways in regular use (1975) 1,628 km. Shipping (1982): merchant vessels 100 gross tons and over 345; gross tonnage 2,203,317. Telephones (Dec. 1980) 1,617,700. Radio licenses (Dec. 1981) 3,218,000. Television receivers (Dec. 1981) 3,813,000.

Agriculture. Production (in 000; metric tons; 1982): wheat 6,460; barley c. 3,000; corn c. 12,600; potatoes c. 5,850; cabbages (1981) c. 1,000; onions c. 300; tomatoes c. 1,400; sugar, raw value c. 690; sunflower seed c. 835; soybeans 431; linseed c. 41; plums (1981) c. 590; apples (1981) c. 395; grapes (1981) c. 1,755; tobacco c. 39; cheese 122; beef and veal c. 325; pork c. 982; timber (cu m; 1981) 20,423. Livestock (in 000; Jan. 1982): cattle c. 6,082; sheep 17,288; pigs 12,444; horses (1981) c. 566; poultry c. 99,000.

Industry. Fuel and power (in 000; metric tons; 1981): coal 8,200; lignite 28,800; coke 2,933; crude oil 11,644; natural gas (cu m) 35,540,000; electricity (kw-hr) 70,138,000. Production (in 000; metric tons; 1981): cement 14,750; bauxite 680; iron ore (26% metal content) 2,304; pig iron 8,857; crude steel 13,025; petroleum products 23,466; sulfuric acid 1,814; caustic soda 767; fertilizers (nutrient content) nitrogenous 1,822, phosphate 717; cotton yarn (1980) 184; cotton fabrics (sq m) 732,000; wool yarn (1980) 74; woolen fabrics (sq m) 128,000; man-made fibres (1980) 199; paper 652. New dwelling units completed (1980) 197,800.

On March 5 Ceausescu addressed some 200 top-level officers of the armed forces. He explained that while it was essential that the Army continue to be able to discharge the highly responsible task of defending Romania's independence and sovereignty, nevertheless defense expenditure for the years 1983–85 would have to be frozen at the 1982 level. The government had to concentrate its energies on completing a number of enterprises of primary importance, in particular the Danube-Black Sea canal.

Many foreign statesmen visited Romania during 1983, among them U.S. Vice-Pres. George Bush on September 18–19. In a joint communiqué, Bush and Ceausescu agreed that their talks had "highlighted the significance of Romanian-U.S. contacts at various levels." Relations had soured earlier when the U.S. criticized Romania for introducing a law requiring anyone who wished to leave the

Roman Catholic Church: *see* Religion

country to pay back the government in hard currency for higher education received. In May Hu Yaobang (Hu Yao-pang), general secretary of the Chinese Communist Party, discussed matters of common interest with the Romanian leader. Ceausescu paid state visits to Turkey in May and to Egypt in October. Two Yugoslav leaders—Mitja Ribicic, president of the Presidium of the League of Communists, and Mika Spiljak, president of the Collective Presidency—visited Bucharest in April and November, respectively, and Greek Prime Minister Andreas Papandreou visited in December. (K. M. SMOGORZEWSKI)

Rowing

East Germany retained its supremacy in world rowing in 1983 by winning 18 of the 32 world championship events. It dominated the junior championships in Vichy, France, and women's competition in Duisburg, West Germany. The Soviet Union collected the five titles in those two tournaments that the East Germans failed to win. In the men's events at Duisburg, East Germany shared the honours with New Zealand and West Germany. In the lightweight events at Duisburg, Spain won two, while Denmark and Italy each triumphed in one.

East Germany topped the men's events with three gold and four silver medals, but the New Zealand rowers stole the limelight by winning the two premier events. They started by defeating East Germany in the coxed fours by 2.40 sec with the Soviet Union only 0.69 sec farther behind. In the eights, the concluding event of the championships, they again defeated East Germany but this time by only 1.55 sec, with Australia third.

In between those races East Germany and West Germany each scored three successes. East Germany was 3.26 sec faster than Norway in double sculls and finished 2.07 sec ahead of the Soviet Union in coxless pairs. The first win for West Germany came in single sculls by 4.42 sec over East Germany, and the latter then scored its third success, in coxed pairs, defeating the Soviet Union by 3.48 sec. The coxless fours ended in the closest verdict of the championships, with West Germany squeezing the Soviet Union out of the gold medal by 0.37 sec. The quadruple sculls produced another exciting finish before West Germany was successful again, this time by 1.90 sec ahead of East Germany. In the women's events East Germany won the coxed fours, double sculls, coxless pairs, and single sculls, while the Soviet Union took the quadruple sculls and eights. New world records were set in three of the men's events and four of the women's contests.

East Germany won 11 events in the junior championships, with the Soviet Union taking the remaining three. In men's events the East Germans won double sculls, coxless pairs, coxed pairs, coxless fours, quadruple sculls, and eights. The Soviet Union won the coxed fours and single sculls. In women's events East Germany won coxed fours, double sculls, coxless pairs, single sculls, and quadruple sculls but could not prevent the Soviet Union from taking the eights.

In recent years the international rowing scene had been troubled by two controversial issues. First was the use of drugs to improve performance; detection of this practice was steadily improving. Formerly the testing was undertaken officially only at world championship and Olympic Games regattas, but by 1983 the governing bodies of many countries were conducting a program of random tests throughout the year. The other major topic of intense discussion concerned the use of

The diamond sculls at the 1983 Henley Royal Regatta was won by Steve Redgrave (foreground) of the Marlow Rowing Club. He defeated Tim Crooks of the Kingston Rowing Club.

JOHN H. SHORE

single sculling boats with sliding riggers and a fixed seat, instead of conventional fixed riggers with a sliding seat. Most of the world finalists in men's single sculls in 1982 and 1983 used the sliding rigger. The debate was ended when the Fédération Internationale des Sociétés d'Aviron, the world governing body for the sport, banned the use of the sliding rigger after Jan. 1, 1984.

In England only two open trophies at the Henley Royal Regatta were won by overseas crews. Harvard University took the Ladies Plate (eights) to the U.S., and the Stewards Cup (coxless fours) was won by Ruderclub Schaffhausen and Ruderclub Thalwil of Switzerland. Oxford won the 129th University Boat Race by $4\frac{1}{2}$ lengths, reducing Cambridge's lead in the series to 68–60.

(KEITH OSBORNE)

Rwanda

A republic in eastern Africa and former traditional kingdom whose origins may be traced back to the 15th century, Rwanda is bordered by Zaire, Uganda, Tanzania, and Burundi. Area: 26,338 sq km (10,169 sq mi). Pop. (1983 est.): 5.5 million, including (1978) Hutu 90%; Tutsi 9%; and Twa 1%. Cap. and largest city: Kigali (pop., 1981 est., 156,650). Language (official): French and Kinyarwanda. Religion (1980): Roman Catholic 56%; Protestant 12%; Muslim 9%; most of the remainder are animist. President in 1983, Maj. Gen. Juvénal Habyarimana.

A massive imbalance between exports, running at $75 million, and imports, at $240 million, caused the Rwandan government to launch an austerity campaign with its 1983 budget. In 1982 coffee exports had fallen 14% below their 1981 level, while sugar production was 24% down. Despite the austerity measures, Pres. Juvénal Habyarimana received 99% of the vote in presidential elections held on December 19.

Plans to construct a giant hydroelectric dam on the Ruzizi River suffered a setback in 1983 when the three countries involved—Burundi, Rwanda, and Zaire—failed to agree on a structure for the development. As a result, the World Bank froze credit worth $45 million.

Rwanda and Uganda continued to dispute responsibility for the estimated 70,000 Rwandan refugees who had been living in border camps since being ordered from their homes in southwest Uganda in October 1982. In September 1983 the Ugandan authorities allowed some 20,000 of the refugees to remain in the country on a temporary basis. There were further reports of violence against Rwandans in Uganda in December.

(GUY ARNOLD)

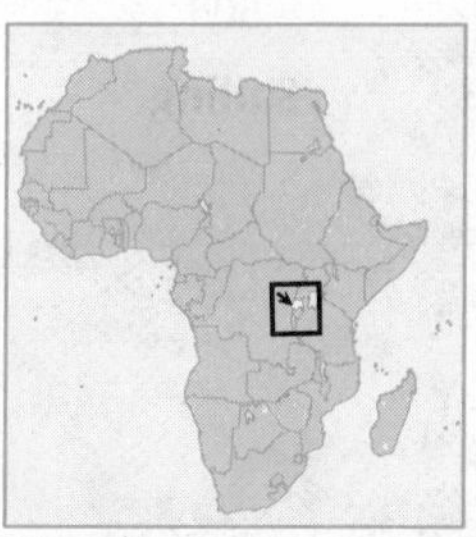

Rwanda

RWANDA

Education. (1980–81) Primary, pupils 704,924, teachers 11,912; secondary, pupils 5,022; vocational, pupils 2,065; teacher training, pupils 3,580; secondary, vocational, and teacher training, teachers 887; higher (1979–80), students 1,266, teaching staff 229.

Finance. Monetary unit: Rwanda franc, with (Sept. 20, 1983) a par value of RwFr 92.84 to U.S. $1 (free rate of RwFr 139.82 = £1 sterling). Gold and other reserves (June 1983) U.S. $111 million. Budget (1982 est.) balanced at RwFr 16.2 billion.

Foreign Trade. (1980) Imports RwFr 22,568,000,000; exports RwFr 7,025,000,000. Import sources: Belgium-Luxembourg 16%; Japan 12%; Kenya 11%; France 10%; China 9%; Iran 9%; West Germany 9%; U.S. 5%. Export destinations: Tanzania 63%; Kenya 13%; Belgium-Luxembourg 9%. Main exports: coffee 59%; tea 19%; tin 8%.

Agriculture. Production (in 000; metric tons; 1982): sorghum c. 180; corn c. 90; potatoes c. 290; sweet potatoes (1981) c. 938; cassava (1981) c. 494; dry beans c. 185; dry peas c. 48; pumpkins c. 70; plantains (1981) c. 2,100; coffee c. 26; tea c. 7. Livestock (in 000; 1981): cattle c. 650; sheep c. 300; goats c. 920; pigs c. 140.

Sailing

Sailing in 1983 was dominated by the America's Cup 12-m racing. This trophy was first won in 1851 by the yacht "America" in a race around the Isle of Wight and had never been lost by the U.S. in 24 subsequent challenges. In 1983 an unprecedented seven clubs from five countries challenged at Newport, R.I., three of them from Australia. The Americans chose their defender from three syndicates. Only one yacht could finally sail against one defender, and therefore a prolonged challenge series was held.

In "Australia II," skippered by John Bertrand and sponsored by Alan Bond, the Australians had an exceptional entry. Designed by Ben Lexcen (*see* BIOGRAPHIES) with a revolutionary wing on the foot of the keel and less body in its aft quarters, it was more maneuverable than its rivals and in light winds displayed outstanding speed. "Australia II"

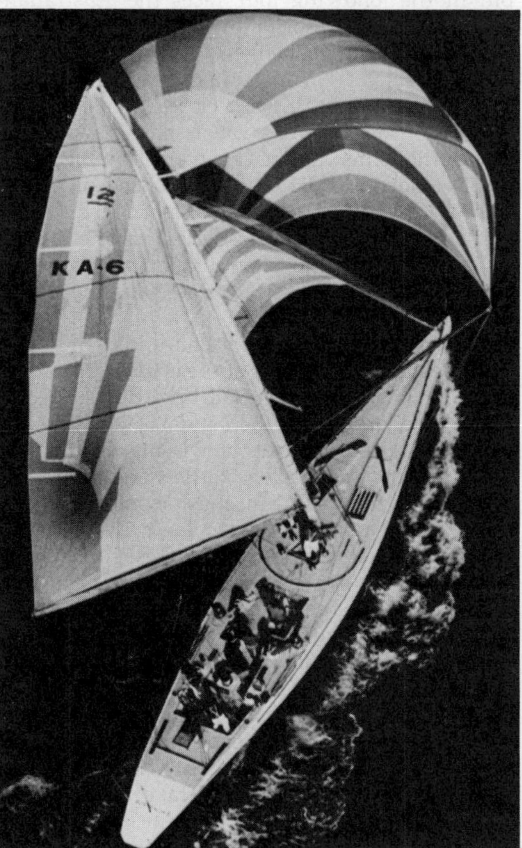

WIDE WORLD

The America's Cup became Australia's cup when the 12-m yacht "Australia II," shown here on a spinnaker run off Newport, R.I., in the sixth race (September 22), bested the U.S. defender, "Liberty," in the seven-race series.

Rubber:
see Industrial Review

Rugby Football:
see Football

Russia:
see Union of Soviet Socialist Republics

Russian Literature:
see Literature

Sabah:
see Malaysia

Radical new keel of "Australia II"

view from the starboard side

view from off the port quarter

view from astern

view from bow

view from off the starboard bow

The controversial and innovative keel of "Australia II" stirred wide interest even before the America's Cup races began. Some U.S. yachtsmen even cried foul, leading the *Washington Post* to describe the contest as between "the New York Whiners versus That Keel." Designer Ben Lexcen aimed to harness principles of fluid mechanics to minimize turbulence at the tip of the keel by thrusting it forward and adding 60-cm wings. This enabled the challenger to sail higher into the wind with less leeway. It seemed to work.

disposed of the challengers from the U.K., Canada, France, and Italy, which was making its first attempt.

Behind "Australia II" the competition was intense, with Australia's second boat and the Canadian, Italian, and British entries all very close in speed. Finally, the British "Victory 83" came out on top and qualified to sail in a seven-match race series against "Australia II" to select the challenger. The British won the first race in a close duel, but in the following four races the Australians stamped their authority over "Victory 83" and won the right to challenge.

Meanwhile, the Americans were sailing their own selection races. It was a close series with little to choose from between yachts and crews. Skippers of the contending yachts were Tom Blackaller on "Defender," John Kolius on "Courageous," and Dennis Conner, who had successfully defended the trophy in the previous series, sailing "Liberty." In the competition Conner used all his match-racing skills and was selected to defend the trophy again.

All the main parts of the yachts and their design must be made by citizens of the challenging country. The Australian keel had been tank-tested in The Netherlands, and the New York Yacht Club challenged the legality of the wing keel, first as to measurement and then as to its national design. Alan Bond and his team satisfied officials as to those requirements, however, and also managed to keep the exact design of their keel secret while sailing in their opponents' territory for some four months prior to the actual defense series.

As the challenge series drew near, the leading question was whether the Australians, with a potentially faster yacht, could beat the match-racing experience of Dennis Conner and the U.S. team. The racing lived up to all expectations as the closest and most exciting ever seen, with the advantage changing at every mistake or piece of ill-fortune. The Americans got the better of the starts and, by skillful use of wind shifts, gained a three-to-one lead in the seven-race series. But, aided by a broken spreader on "Liberty" and their own resolution, the Australians tied the series at three victories apiece. Thus, for the first time in 132 years, the U.S. had to sail a seventh race to decide the winner.

Conner again made the better start in "Liberty," but "Australia II" appeared to gain and, indeed, 20 minutes into the race tacked and crossed ahead. After some tacking and dummy tacking, "Australia II" again crossed "Liberty" but did not tack to cover immediately. The U.S. boat began to edge ahead and rounded the first windward mark 21 seconds ahead of "Australia II." "Liberty" increased its lead to almost a minute at the end of the second windward leg. From that point, sailing downwind, Conner chose the right-hand side, and the Australians immediately jibed over to the left. Conner did not follow immediately, and the Australians picked up more wind and passed the Americans. "Liberty" then began to catch up, but "Australia II" stayed ahead and rounded the last leeward mark 21 seconds ahead. On the final, upwind, leg the Australians covered "Liberty's" every move to find clear air and won the America's Cup by 41 seconds.

World Class Boat Champions

Class	Winner
Cadet	Guillermo Parada (Argentina)
Flying Dutchman	John McKee (United States)
Finn	Paul Van Cleve (United States)
Fireball	Stuart Hamilton (Australia)
505	Terry Kyrwood (Australia)
5.5 metre	Albert Fay (United States)
470	David Barnes (New Zealand)
420	Jason Belben (United Kingdom)
GP14 (equal)	Richard Estaugh (United Kingdom)
	Ian Southworth (United Kingdom)
Hornet	Nick Smithers (United Kingdom)
International 14	Jamie Kidd (Canada)
Mirror	Dave Sherwin (United Kingdom)
OK	Leith Armit (New Zealand)
Soling	Robbie Haines (United States)
Solo	Geoff Carveth (United Kingdom)
Tempest	Sepp Hoess (West Germany)
Tornado	Chris Cairns (Australia)
Wayfarer	Ian Porter (United Kingdom)

It was also Admiral's Cup year with 15 teams challenging in a series of offshore races for that trophy. The West Germans finished first and, though none of their three yachts won a race, they consistently achieved better results than their rivals. The Italians took second and the U.S. third. The Fastnet race, one of the Admiral's Cup events, produced a new course record when Bob Bell's Bermudan Holland-designed maxi "Condor" crossed the finish line 2 days 23 hours 2 minutes and 10 seconds after its start. This was also good enough to gain first place in the overall cup series.

During the Weymouth speed trials three world records were broken. Fred Haywood from Hawaii raised the A-class record from 27 to more than 31 knots; Glen McKinlay and Gordon Way increased the sailboard tandem record to 25.38 knots; and in the B class Andrew Grogono and John Fowler raised the record to 26.59 knots with their Tornado catamaran fitted with foils. (ADRIAN JARDINE)

[452.B.4.a.ii]

Saint Christopher and Nevis

A parliamentary federated state and a member of the Commonwealth, St. Christopher and Nevis is comprised of the islands of St. Christopher (168 sq km) and Nevis (93 sq km) and lies in the northern part of the Leeward group of the Lesser Antilles in the eastern Caribbean Sea. Total area: 261 sq km (101 sq mi). Population (1983 est.): 44,500, including (1970) black 95.4%; mixed 3%; white 1.1%; other 0.5%. Cap.: Basseterre, on St. Christopher (pop., 1980, 14,700). Language: English. Religion (1970): Protestant 76.1%, including Anglican 36.1%, Methodist 32.3%, Moravian 10.3%, other Protestant 7.7%; Roman Catholic 7.7%; other 5.9%. Queen, Elizabeth II; governor-general in 1983, Sir Clement Aurindell; prime minister, Kennedy A. Simmonds.

After 16 years as a British associated state, St. Christopher and Nevis (St. Kitts-Nevis) became fully independent on Sept. 19, 1983. Its federal constitution gave substantial powers to the smaller island of Nevis, including the right of secession. The opposition Labour Party, which had governed the islands for almost 30 years until it lost power in 1980, boycotted the independence celebrations.

The intransigence of the Labour Party was a reminder of the precarious position of the government in the newly independent state. The People's Action Movement of Prime Minister Kennedy A. Simmonds (*see* BIOGRAPHIES) governed in coalition with the Nevis Reformation Party, led by Finance Minister Simeon Daniel. The Labour Party, however, held four of the nine seats in the National Assembly and so in fact had a majority of the seven St. Kitts seats.

Economic problems facing the new state were headed by the need to diversify; the country was still heavily dependent on sugar, a declining and money-losing industry. Food production, light industry, and tourism were earmarked for development. (ROD PRINCE)

GIRAUD—GAMMA/LIAISON

Princess Margaret reviewed the forces of the Caribbean nation of St. Christopher and Nevis in ceremonies marking its independence from the United Kingdom on September 19.

ST. CHRISTOPHER AND NEVIS

Education. (1980–81) Primary, pupils 7,848, teachers 335; secondary, pupils 4,867, teachers 287; vocational, pupils 127, teachers 24; teacher training, students 61, teachers 8.

Finance. Monetary unit: East Caribbean dollar, with (Sept. 20, 1983) a par value of ECar$2,70 to U.S. $1 (free rate of ECar$4.07 = £1 sterling). Budget (1982 est.): revenue ECar$105 million; expenditure ECar$104.6 million.

Foreign Trade. (1981) Imports ECar$128.8 million; exports ECar$65.5 million. Import sources (1976): U.S. 29%; U.K. 18%; Trinidad and Tobago 12%; Canada 7%; Puerto Rico 5%; Japan 5%. Export destinations (1976): U.S. 53%; U.K. 28%; Trinidad and Tobago 10%. Main exports: sugar 58%; television and radio sets and parts 32%. Tourism (1981): 35,500 visitors.

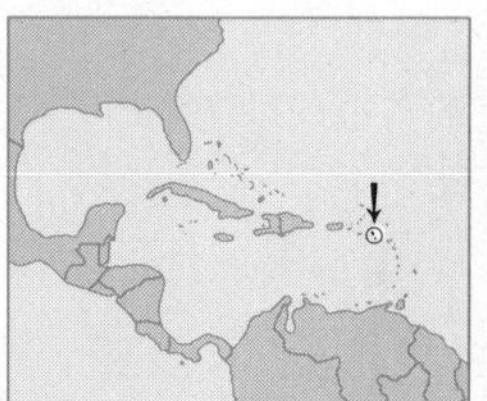

St. Christopher and Nevis

Saint Lucia

A parliamentary state and a member of the Commonwealth, St. Lucia, the second largest of the Windward Islands in the eastern Caribbean, is situated 32 km NE of St. Vincent and 40 km S of Martinique. Area: 622 sq km (240 sq mi). Pop. (1983 est.): 122,000, predominantly of African descent. Cap. and largest city: Castries (pop., 1980 est., 48,800). Language: English (official) and a local French dialect. Religion (1970): Roman Catholic 91%; Anglican 3%; Seventh-day Adventist 2%; other 4%. Queen, Elizabeth II; governor-general in 1983, Sir Allen Lewis; prime minister, John Compton.

ST. LUCIA

Education. (1979–80) Primary, pupils 30,610, teachers 942; secondary, pupils 4,879, teachers 220; vocational, pupils 198, teachers (1978–79) 24; teacher training, students (1978–79) 152, teachers 13.

Finance and Trade. Monetary unit: East Caribbean dollar, with (Sept. 20, 1983) a par value of ECar$2.70 to U.S. $1 (free rate of ECar$4.07 = £1 sterling). Budget (1982–83 est.): revenue ECar$107.3 million; expenditure ECar$120.6 million. Foreign trade (1982): imports ECar$318.3 million; exports ECar$112.3 million. Import sources: U.S. 36%; U.K. 12%; Trinidad and Tobago 11%; Japan 5%. Export destinations: U.S. 28%; U.K. 25%; U.S. Virgin Islands 11%; Jamaica 9%; Trinidad and Tobago 5%. Main exports: bananas 41%; cardboard cartons 14%; clothing 11%; beverages 9%; coconut oil 8%. Tourism: visitors (1981) 85,000; gross receipts (1979) U.S. $34 million.

St. Lucia

By late 1983, after more than a year of the United Workers' Party government headed by Prime Minister John Compton, only minor progress had been made in pulling St. Lucia out of its economic stagnation. Devastated by Hurricane Allen in 1980, the country then suffered two years of political chaos that caused further economic damage. Tourism, manufacturing, and agriculture all remained depressed.

A keen supporter of the U.S. Caribbean Basin Initiative, Compton devoted considerable energy to attacking the left-wing Progressive Labour Party (PLP). Early in the year a law was passed banning the wearing of green fatigues by civilians and the showing of motion pictures in public without police permission; it was claimed that such activities formed part of PLP training for revolution. In July Compton accused Libyan leader Col. Muammar al-Qaddafi of recruiting PLP members for training in Libya in "terrorism and sabotage."

During February Compton was host to Canadian Prime Minister Pierre Trudeau. With the U.S. and other eastern Caribbean countries, St. Lucia participated in the invasion of Grenada in October.

(ROD PRINCE)

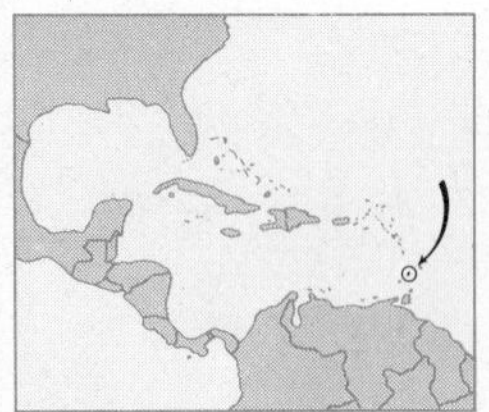

Saint Vincent and the Grenadines

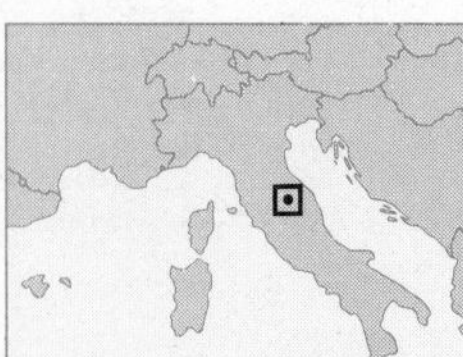

San Marino

Saint Vincent and the Grenadines

A parliamentary state within the Commonwealth, St. Vincent and the Grenadines (islands of the Lesser Antilles in the Caribbean Sea) lies southwest of St. Lucia and west of Barbados. Area (including Grenadines): 388 sq km (150 sq mi). Pop. (1983 est.): 134,000, predominantly of African descent. Cap. and largest city: Kingstown (urban area pop., 1981 est., 32,600). Language: English (official). Religion (1970): Anglican 47%; Methodist 28%; Roman Catholic 13%. Queen, Elizabeth II; governor-general in 1983, Sir Sydney Gun-Munro; prime minister, Milton Cato.

During the first half of 1983 there was a slight increase in tourist arrivals in St. Vincent. A port expansion project, aided by the Caribbean Development Bank, got under way in Kingstown, and a West German company started construction of a brewery, but otherwise the economy remained depressed.

Vincentian banana producers faced another difficult year. While production had recovered from the hurricane damage of 1979 and 1980, a new difficulty had appeared—poor financial returns caused by the declining value of the pound sterling against the U.S. dollar, to which the East Caribbean currency was pegged. The U.K. was virtually the country's sole market for bananas.

In contrast to the opening years of the decade, there was little political challenge in 1983 to the St. Vincent Labour Party government of Prime Minister Milton Cato. A split in the left-wing United People's Movement (UPM) at the end of 1982 led to the formation of an eighth political party, the Movement for National Unity.

St. Vincent was among the eastern Caribbean countries that took part, with the U.S., in the October invasion of Grenada. (ROD PRINCE)

ST. VINCENT

Education. (1980–81) Primary, pupils 24,346, teachers (1979–80) 1,211; secondary, pupils 5,421, teachers (1977–78) 284; vocational, pupils 1,252; teacher training, students 107; vocational and teacher training, teachers (1977–78) 35.

Finance and Trade. Monetary unit: East Caribbean dollar, with (Sept. 20, 1983) a par value of ECar$2.70 to U.S. $1 (free rate of ECar$4.07 = £1 sterling). Budget (1982–83 est.): revenue ECar$79.8 million; expenditure ECar$72.9 million. Foreign trade (1981): imports ECar$157.5 million; exports ECar$65.7 million. Import sources (1979): U.K. 23%; U.S. 20%; Trinidad and Tobago 14%; Canada 12%; Barbados 5%. Export destinations (1979): U.K. 49%; Trinidad and Tobago 22%; Barbados 5%. Main exports: bananas 41%; taro and yams 5%; arrowroot starch 4%.

San Marino

A small republic, San Marino is an enclave in northeastern Italy, 8 km SW of Rimini. Area: 61 sq km (24 sq mi). Pop. (1983 est.): 22,000. Cap. and largest city: San Marino (metro. pop., 1982 est., 4,600). Language: Italian. Religion: Roman Catholic. The country is governed by two *capitani reggenti,* or co-regents, appointed every six months by a Grand and General Council. Executive power rests with three secretaries of state: foreign and political affairs, internal affairs, and economic affairs. In 1983 the positions were filled, respectively, by Giordano Bruno Refi, Alvaro Selva, and Emilio della Balda.

In general elections held on May 29, 1983, the left-wing coalition government in San Marino retained power, winning 32 seats in the 60-seat Grand and General Council. Among the coalition partners, the Communist Party lost one seat, giving it a total of 15, while the San Marino Socialists won 9 seats and the United Socialists 8. The Christian Democrats remained the strongest single party, gaining 42% of the votes cast and 26 seats. The Republicans and the Social Democrats obtained one seat each. On July 6 a new ten-member Cabinet was approved by the Grand and General Council. The three major portfolios remained unchanged: those of foreign affairs and economic affairs were held by Socialists, while the internal affairs portfolio was held by a Communist.

SAN MARINO

Education. (1982–83) Primary, pupils 1,493, teachers 164; secondary, pupils 1,317, teachers 156; vocational, pupils 729; teacher training, pupils 60.

Finance. Monetary unit: Italian lira, with (Sept. 20, 1983) a free rate of 1,601 lire to U.S. $1 (2,411 lire = £1 sterling); local coins are issued. Budget (1981 est.) balanced at 144,103,000,000 lire. Foreign trade included with Italy. Tourism (1980): 3.5 million visitors.

The co-regents Adriano Reffi and Massimo Roberto Rossini, appointed in April for a six-month term, were succeeded in October by Renzo Renzi, a Communist, and Germano de Biagi, a Socialist.

In 1982 the republic's judiciary had proposed to allow Sammarinese women the right to retain their nationality if they decided to marry outside

Salvador, El: *see* El Salvador

Salvation Army: *see* Religion

Samoa: *see* Dependent States; Western Samoa

the republic. However, a referendum held on July 25, 1983, rejected the decision, and it did not become law. In March San Marino attended, with guest status, the seventh conference of the nonaligned movement in New Delhi, India.

(K. M. SMOGORZEWSKI)

São Tomé and Príncipe

São Tomé and Príncipe

An independent African state, the Democratic Republic of São Tomé and Príncipe comprises two main islands and several smaller islets that straddle the Equator in the Gulf of Guinea, off the west coast of Africa. Area: 964 sq km (372 sq mi), of which São Tomé, the larger island, comprises 854 sq km. Pop. (1981 est.): 95,000. Cap. and largest city: São Tomé (pop., 1978 est., 25,000). Language: Portuguese. Religion: mainly Roman Catholic. President in 1983, Manuel Pinto da Costa.

A dispute developed early in 1983 between São Tomé and Príncipe and the former colonial power, Portugal. Minister of Education Joaquim Rafael Branco complained that Portugal had been ineffectual in its assistance—in other words, that Portuguese aid was inadequate. He also threatened that his government would take tough action if opposition groups were allowed to expand their activities in Portugal. The Portuguese government replied that groups in Portugal opposed to the regime of Pres. Manuel Pinto da Costa would be suppressed only if they broke domestic Portuguese laws.

São Tomé and Príncipe concluded a treaty of friendship and cooperation with Cuba that was to run until 1988. Pinto da Costa made official visits to China and also to Paris, where he sought increased aid. In April the trade minister was in Brussels to discuss aid and trade relations with the European Communities.

A European Development Fund (EDF) grant was given jointly to São Tomé and Príncipe and Gabon to finance an oceangoing cargo and passenger vessel to link the two states. Additional aid from the EDF was provided for the cocoa and fisheries industries.

(GUY ARNOLD)

SÃO TOMÉ AND PRÍNCIPE

Education. (1977) Primary, pupils 14,162, teachers 527; secondary, pupils 3,145, teachers 81; vocational, pupils 155, teachers 30.

Finance and Trade. Monetary unit: dobra, with (Sept. 20, 1983) a free rate of 39.38 dobras to U.S. $1 (59.31 dobras = £1 sterling). Budget (1977 est.): revenue 180 million dobras; expenditure 454 million dobras. Foreign trade (1980): imports *c.* 540 million dobras; exports *c.* 590 million dobras. Import sources (1975): Portugal 61%; Angola 13%. Export destinations (1975): The Netherlands 52%; Portugal 33%; West Germany 8%. Main exports (1975): cocoa *c.* 82%; copra *c.* 6%; palm kernels and nuts *c.* 5%.

Saudi Arabia

A monarchy occupying four-fifths of the Arabian Peninsula, Saudi Arabia has an area of 2,240,000 sq km (865,000 sq mi). Pop. (1983 est.): 9,188,000. Cap.: Riyadh (pop., 1981 est., 1,308,000). Largest city: Jeddah (pop., 1983 est., 1.5 million). Language: Arabic. Religion: Muslim, predominantly Sunni; Shi'ah minority in Eastern Province. King and prime minister in 1983, Fahd.

SAUDI ARABIA

Education. (1980–81) Primary, pupils 926,531, teachers 50,511; secondary, pupils 328,328, teachers 24,256; vocational, pupils 5,106, teachers 822; teacher training, students 15,562, teachers 1,710; higher, students 56,252, teaching staff 6,598.

Finance. Monetary unit: riyal, with (Sept. 20, 1983) a free rate of 3.48 riyals to U.S. $1 (5.24 riyals = £1 sterling). Gold and other reserves (May 1983) U.S. $33,792,000,000. Budget (total; 1983–84 est.): revenue 225 billion riyals; expenditure 260 billion riyals. Gross national product (1981–82) 536.9 billion riyals. Money supply (Jan. 1983) 84,920,000,000 riyals. Cost of living (1975 = 100; March 1983) 165.

Foreign Trade. (1982) Imports 139.3 billion riyals; exports 259.9 billion riyals. Import sources (1981): U.S. 21%; Japan 18%; West Germany 10%; Italy 7%; U.K. 6%; France 6%. Export destinations (1981): Japan 17%; U.S. 13%; France 10%; Italy 7%; The Netherlands 6%; Singapore 5%. Main export (1981): crude oil 95%. Tourism (1981): gross receipts U.S. $1,573,000,000.

Transport and Communications. Roads (1981) 55,100 km. Motor vehicles in use (1981): passenger 757,400; commercial 587,800. Railways (1981): *c.* 750 km; traffic 95 million passenger-km, freight 272 million net ton-km. Air traffic (1982): 12,277,000,000 passenger-km; freight *c.* 373.1 million net ton-km. Shipping (1982): merchant vessels 100 gross tons and over 347; gross tonnage 4,301,789. Telephones (Jan. 1981) 442,500. Radio receivers (Dec. 1980) 2.5 million. Television receivers (Dec. 1980) 2.1 million.

Agriculture. Production (in 000; metric tons; 1982): sorghum *c.* 110; wheat *c.* 150; barley *c.* 16; tomatoes *c.* 210; onions (1981) *c.* 95; grapes *c.* 60; dates *c.* 400. Livestock (in 000; 1981): cattle *c.* 410; sheep *c.* 4,201; goats *c.* 2,043; camels *c.* 162; asses *c.* 118; poultry *c.* 5,598.

Industry. Production (in 000; metric tons; 1982): crude oil 324,875; petroleum products (1981) 27,730; natural gas (cu m; 1981) 25,385,000; electricity (kw-hr; 1981) 25,061,000; gypsum (1981) 95; cement (1981) 4,237.

During 1983 Saudi Arabia remained at the centre of efforts to achieve a Middle East peace settlement and a solution to the conflict in Lebanon. Prince Bandar ibn Sultan, who on October 25 presented credentials to U.S. Pres. Ronald Reagan as ambassador to Washington, attempted to act as a mediator in Lebanon during the renewed fighting in the summer months. Earlier in the year King Fahd was at the centre of diplomatic activity that brought Jordan's King Hussein and Iraq's Pres. Saddam Hussein to Riyadh in quick succession. In January Saudi Arabia announced that it would send an ambassador to Libya, thus mending a rift that had opened in October 1980 when Libya bitterly criticized Saudi Arabia for accepting U.S.-supplied airborne warning and control systems surveillance aircraft. In a statement to the Council of Ministers on January 18, King Fahd emphasized the kingdom's mediating role in helping to produce a positive Arab response to President Reagan's 1982 peace proposals, which aimed to bring about Palestinian self-determination in association with Jordan. Meanwhile, Saudi Arabia was a major source of funds to both Iraq and Syria. (*See* MIDDLE EASTERN AFFAIRS.)

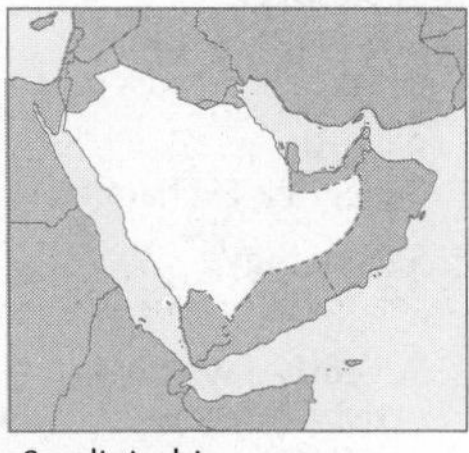
Saudi Arabia

Saudi Arabia's wider international role was evident in its emergence as the dominant force within the Organization of Petroleum Exporting Countries (OPEC) and a deciding voice within the International Monetary Fund (IMF). The OPEC meeting in London in March agreed to give Saudi Arabia

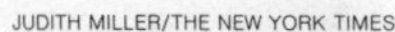

Development projects in Saudi Arabia depend on cheap foreign labour. The prospect of work and wages attracts an abundance of immigrants, like this Pakistani family in Jeddah.

the role of "swing producer," which would allow it to compensate for surpluses or deficits by other oil producers in the cartel. The meeting fixed Saudi oil production at five million barrels a day, although production temporarily exceeded that level in August. Oil Minister Sheikh Ahmad Zaki Yamani (*see* BIOGRAPHIES) reaffirmed that the quota production level would be maintained. He also dismissed speculation that Saudi Arabia was worried about threats posed by the Iran-Iraq war to the Strait of Hormuz, through which one-sixth of the West's oil supply passed. Saudi Arabia was now exporting oil from its terminal at Yanbu on the Red Sea as well as from the Gulf coast.

The effects of reduced oil production appeared to be less serious than had been predicted after the OPEC meeting. Second-quarter figures showed export revenues falling by only 1% to $9,543,000,000, despite a cut of $5 a barrel to $29 a barrel in the OPEC marker price for crude oil. Finance and National Economy Minister Sheikh Muhammad Abalkhail nevertheless introduced financial stringency into the 1983–84 budget. Cuts of up to 30% were made in the spending of some state agencies.

The finance minister emerged during the year as a key figure in King Fahd's government and an influential spokesman for Saudi policy. In a statement before the IMF annual meeting in September, he counseled the IMF to avoid any recourse to commercial borrowing. Saudi Arabia expressed its willingness to lend $3 billion as part of an emergency fund to cover the gap between the IMF's commitments and its available resources. However, the loan hinged on an agreement by the Bank of International Settlements to provide a bridging loan of $3 billion, and this proposal was vetoed by the European nations.

Abalkhail's position as the strongman of the Cabinet was reinforced by the resignation of Sheikh Abdel Aziz al-Quraishi as governor of the Saudi Arabian Monetary Agency (SAMA) in April. Quraishi had been head of the agency, which controlled a portfolio estimated at $150 billion, since 1974. The popular governor's departure was reported to be for private reasons, but it was suggested in Riyadh that Quraishi was angry about lack of consultation by the Finance Ministry over preparation of the annual budget. The departure of Quraishi greatly strengthened Abalkhail's hand, since Quraishi's successor as acting governor was a protégé of Abalkhail, Hamad Saud as-Sayyari. Other sources suggested that Quraishi's removal was part of an overall government strategy designed to replace nationals from the country's Western Province with "pure-blooded" Saudis from the central region of Najd.

Saudi Arabia's internal politics remained stable. The Hajj (pilgrimage to Mecca) in September was marred by relatively few incidents, although there were reports of trouble involving some of the 100,000 Iranian pilgrims visiting the holy cities of Mecca and Medina.

In Cabinet changes made during the year, Information Minister Muhammad Abdu Yamani was replaced on April 24 by Ali Hassan ash-Shaer, former ambassador to Lebanon; Ibrahim ibn Abdullah al-Angari became municipalities and rural affairs minister; and Muhammad al-Ali al-Fayiz became labour and social affairs minister. These were the first Cabinet changes since Fahd succeeded his brother Khalid as king and prime minister in June 1982. On October 22 Abdel-Aziz az-Zamil, regarded as one of the ablest technocrats in the kingdom, was appointed industry and electricity minister. He succeeded Ghazi Abdel-Rahman al-Gosaibi, a distinguished Arabic poet, who was thus free to devote all his time to the health portfolio; he had held both portfolios since mid-1982.

Az-Zamil, as a former managing director of the Saudi Arabian Basic Industries Corporation (SABIC), had been at the centre of Saudi efforts to gain a share of the world market for petrochemicals. SABIC hoped to have all its petrochemical joint ventures on stream by 1985, and Saudi production was expected to reach about 5% of the world output. Fears were expressed in the U.S. that the Saudis would exert unfair pressure in order to dispose of their output. Speaking after a meeting of the U.S.-Saudi joint economic commission on October 26, U.S. Treasury Secretary Donald Regan said: "We do not want to see Saudi Arabia giving subsidies and underselling our producers by unfair means." Regan's comment was interpreted as the first shot in what seemed likely to be a bitter struggle between Saudi Arabia and leaders in the U.S. and Europe over petrochemical exports from the industrial city of Jubail. A number of petrochemical plants were being built there as joint ventures, some with U.S. and Japanese partners. Regan noted that Saudi Arabia was to retain its "most favoured nation" status in the U.S., and that the 4% tariff imposed by the U.S. on petrochemical products was expected to drop to 2% "in a year or so."

Saudi Arabia's relations with its major trading partners in the West strengthened during 1983. West German Chancellor Helmut Kohl paid a three-day visit in early October. The possibility that West Germany might supply advanced Leopard II tanks was raised at talks between the king and the chancellor, but no agreement was reached. After the meeting King Fahd played down the is-

Scandinavian Literature:
see Literature

Schools:
see Education

Scotland:
see United Kingdom

Sculpture:
see Art Exhibitions; Art Sales; Museums

Securities:
see Stock Exchanges

Seismology:
see Earth Sciences

Seventh-day Adventist Church:
see Religion

sue, stressing that friendship between the two countries was not dependent on weapons deliveries. Some Western governments were disturbed, however, by stricter government tendering regulations, aimed at giving local companies a greater share of the rich construction market. A regulation mandating that 30% of a contract be subcontracted to a local company was subject to frequent misinterpretation in 1983. The matter was raised but not clarified at talks between Abalkhail and West Germany's economics minister, Otto Lambsdorff, on June 4. Foreign companies also complained to their governments about frequent retendering of projects by Saudi government agencies.

The long-awaited fourth five-year development plan, to provide a blueprint for the kingdom's development after 1985, was discussed at the first meeting of a committee established to prepare guidelines for it. The meeting on October 1 was chaired by Defense and Aviation Minister Prince Sultan ibn Abdel-Aziz. Commenting on the economic climate over the next few years, Health Minister al-Gosaibi noted that though some government projects needed to be scaled down or delayed, the commitment to spend money on development and modernization was absolute. Among the largest of the current projects being evaluated was Prince Sultan City at Al-Kharg, where substantial savings had been made as a result of the government's determination to put all work out for public tender. The decline in the overall level of construction work showed signs of bottoming out in late 1983, though the level of activity in the mid-1980s seemed likely to be lower than in the boom years after the oil price rises of 1973.

The Council of Ministers' decision to grant a commercial banking license to the Ar-Rajhi Company for Currency Exchange and Commerce was seen as a move of some importance. The Ar-Rajhi family were Saudi Arabia's most influential money exchange dealers, and Sulaiman Abdel-Aziz ar-Rajhi had been described as the richest man in the world. (JOHN WHELAN)

Senegal

A republic of West Africa, Senegal is bounded by Mauritania, Mali, Guinea, and Guinea-Bissau and by the Atlantic Ocean. The independent nation of The Gambia forms an enclave within the country. Area: 196,722 sq km (75,955 sq mi). Pop. (1983 est.): 6,131,000, including Wolof 41%; Serer 14%; Peulh 13%; Tukulor 11%; Dyola 7%; Mandingo 5%; other 9%. Cap. and largest city: Dakar (pop., 1979 est., 978,500). Language: French (official); Wolof, Serer, Fulani, Dyola, Malinke, and other tribal dialects. Religion (1980 est.): Muslim 91%; Christian 6%; animist 3%. President in 1983, Abdou Diouf; premier to April 3, Habib Thiam; interim premier to April 29, Moustapha Niasse.

Elections held on Feb. 27, 1983, consolidated Pres. Abdou Diouf's authority and demonstrated the weakness of the opposition, split by dissension over personalities and programs. The subsequent abolition of the post of premier signaled a return to the presidential rule that existed during 1963–70. In the presidential election, Diouf received 83.5% of the votes, against 14.8% for Abdoulaye Wade, leader of the Senegalese Democratic Party (PDS) and front-runner among the four other candidates. In the legislative election, the ruling Socialist Party was returned with 79.9% of the votes. (For tabulated results, *see* POLITICAL PARTIES.)

On April 3, when President Diouf was sworn in for his first full term of office, Foreign Minister Moustapha Niasse was appointed interim premier pending approval by the National Assembly on April 29 of a constitutional amendment abolishing the premiership. Former premier Habib Thiam became president of the Assembly. The new government excluded the "old guard" of former president Léopold Senghor.

President Diouf's main problems were the separatist movement in Casamance Province, where fighting was reported in December, and the weakness of the economy. A number of austerity measures were introduced in August. While keeping a lower profile in foreign relations than Senghor had done, Diouf was active within the Organization of African Unity in seeking solutions to the Chadian and Western Saharan conflicts. Diouf pressed for further development of the Senegambian confederation as well. (PHILIPPE DECRAENE)

SENEGAL

Education. (1981) Primary, pupils 419,748, teachers (1979–80) 9,842; secondary, pupils 78,695, teachers 3,493; vocational, pupils 7,679, teachers (1978–79) 578; teacher training, students 1,381, teachers 81; higher, students 12,373, teaching staff 638.

Finance and Trade. Monetary unit: CFA franc, with (Sept. 20, 1983) a par value of CFA Fr 50 to the French franc (free rate of CFA Fr 403 = U.S. $1; CFA Fr 607 = £1 sterling). Budget (total; 1981–82 est.) balanced at CFA Fr 220.2 billion. Foreign trade (1982): imports CFA Fr 320.2 billion; exports CFA Fr 156.9 billion. Import sources (1981): France 37%; U.S. 6%. Export destinations (1981): France 25%; Ivory Coast 8%; Mali 7%; Mauritania 7%; U.K. 6%. Main exports (1981): petroleum products 24%; fish and products 22%; phosphates 14%; chemicals 6%; cotton fabrics 5%; peanut oil 5%.

Agriculture. Production (in 000; metric tons; 1982): rice c. 120; millet c. 650; peanuts c. 700; palm kernels c. 5; cotton c. 12; fish catch (1981) 207; timber (cu m; 1981) c. 2,885. Livestock (in 000; 1981): cattle 2,260; sheep c. 2,075; goats c. 1,150; horses c. 255.

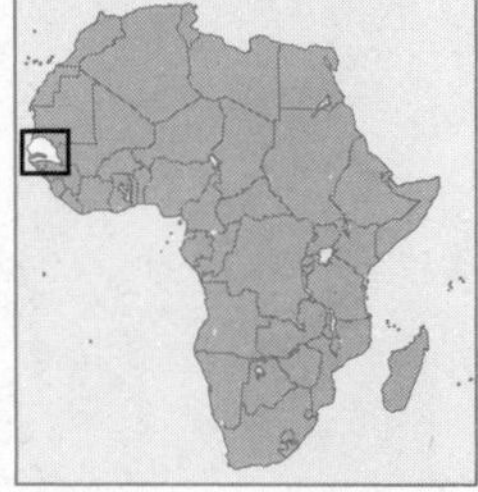
Senegal

Seychelles

A republic and a member of the Commonwealth in the Indian Ocean consisting of 100 islands, Seychelles lies 1,450 km from the coast of East Africa. Area: 444 sq km (171 sq mi), 166 sq km of which includes the islands of Farquhar, Desroches, and Aldabra. Pop. (1983 est.): 64,300, including Creole 94%; French 5%; English 1%. Cap.: Victoria, on Mahé (pop., 1980, 23,900). Language: English and French are official; creole patois is also spoken. Religion: Roman Catholic 90%; Anglican 8%. President in 1983, France-Albert René.

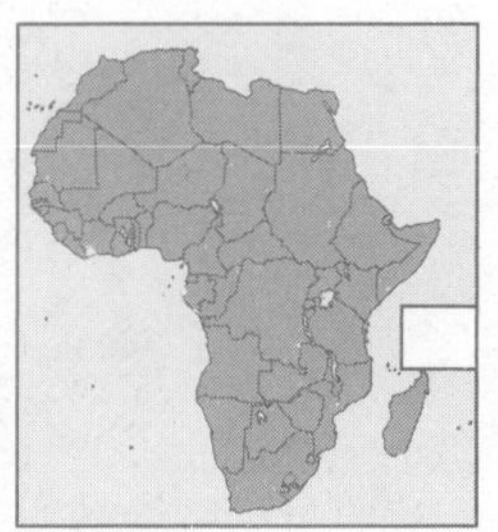
Seychelles

In December 1983 the South African authorities reported that they had uncovered a new plot to overthrow the government of Seychelles: five people were detained. Though the year had been a

SEYCHELLES

Education. (1983) Primary, pupils 14,456, teachers 681; secondary, pupils 2,603, teachers 91; vocational (including teacher training), pupils 974, teachers 148.

Finance and Trade. Monetary unit: Seychelles rupee, with (Sept. 20, 1983) a free rate of SRs 6.88 to U.S. $1 (SRs 10.36 = £1 sterling). Budget (1981 est.): revenue SRs 384 million; expenditure SRs 381 million. Foreign trade (1982): imports SRs 641 million; exports SRs 100 million. Import sources (1980): U.K. 25%; Bahrain 24%; South Africa 10%; Singapore 7%; Japan 5%. Export destinations (excluding ship and aircraft stores; 1980): Pakistan 45%; Réunion 21%; Mauritius 9%; U.K. 8%. Main exports (domestic only; 1981): copra 62%; fish 16%; cinnamon bark 7%. Tourism (1981): visitors 60,000; gross receipts U.S. $45 million.

quiet one until then, the islands continued to witness the effects of two years of political upheaval on their most important industry, tourism. Tourist arrivals in 1982 had fallen to their 1975 level. The economy was further affected by a drop in the price of copra, the main export. On the other hand, Pres. France-Albert René's government had established one of the best social service systems in the world.

The government tried to follow a genuinely nonaligned foreign policy. In 1983 the U.S. provided aid to Seychelles for the first time. The government agreed to allow U.S. and British naval vessels to dock in Seychelles for shore leave. However, René relied upon Tanzanian and North Korean troops and advisers to strengthen the armed forces.

In general elections in August, all candidates belonged to the only party, the People's Progressive Front. In July René pardoned six British and South African mercenaries who had taken part in the 1981 attempted coup. (GUY ARNOLD)

Sierra Leone

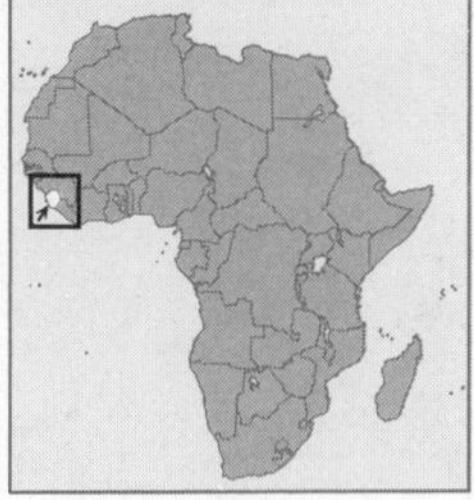

Sierra Leone

A republic within the Commonwealth, Sierra Leone is a West African state on the Atlantic coast between Guinea and Liberia. Area: 71,740 sq km (27,699 sq mi). Pop. (1983 est.): 3,705,000, including (1979) Mende and Temne tribes 60%; other tribes 39.5%; non-African 0.5%. Cap. and largest city: Freetown (pop., 1980 est., 500,000). Language: English (official); tribal dialects. Religion: animist 51.5%; Muslim 39.5%; Christian 9%. President in 1983, Siaka Stevens.

SIERRA LEONE

Education. (1980–81) Primary, pupils 263,724, teachers 8,472; secondary, pupils 60,285, teachers 2,828; vocational, pupils 931, teachers 89; teacher training, students 2,076, teachers 212; higher, students 1,809, teaching staff 270.

Finance and Trade. Monetary unit: leone, with (Sept. 20, 1983) a free value of 2.50 leones to U.S. $1 (3.76 leones = £1 sterling). Budget (1980–81 actual): revenue 221 million leones; expenditure 357 million leones. Foreign trade (1982): imports 368,470,000 leones; exports 136,950,000 leones. Import sources (1980): U.K. *c.* 22%; Japan *c.* 9%; West Germany *c.* 7%; France *c.* 6%; U.S. *c.* 5%. Export destinations (1980): U.K. 41%; U.S. 11%; The Netherlands 8%; Switzerland 7%. Main exports: diamonds 45%; cocoa 13%; coffee 13%.

Agriculture. Production (in 000; metric tons; 1982): rice *c.* 550; cassava *c.* 95; palm kernels *c.* 30; palm oil *c.* 48; coffee *c.* 11; cocoa *c.* 10; fish catch (1981) 49. Livestock (in 000; 1981): cattle *c.* 348; sheep *c.* 268; goats *c.* 150; pigs *c.* 38; chickens *c.* 3,850.

Industry. Production (in 000; metric tons; 1981): bauxite 610; diamonds (metric carats) 305; petroleum products 245; electricity (kw-hr) 235,000.

Ships and Shipping: *see* Industrial Review; Transportation

Presenting the 1983–84 budget to Parliament on June 30, 1983, Finance Minister Salia Jusu-Sheriff reported on the performance of Sierra Leone's economy over the previous financial year. Faced with a decline in all sources of revenue, the government failed to contain the budget deficit within the target of 144 million leones; the actual deficit was expected to be 191 million leones. Both agricultural and mining output declined. Earnings from diamonds, the major export, were estimated at $37.2 million ($54.5 million in 1981–82).

The production slowdown was blamed largely on a lack of foreign exchange with which to buy machinery. Also, diamonds were being smuggled across the border into Liberia, where U.S. dollars were readily available. In an effort to improve the situation, the government exempted agricultural imports from import duties. A two-tier exchange system that had been introduced in December 1982 in the hope of attracting foreign currency was judged unsuccessful and was scrapped.

Gen. Samuel K. Doe, Liberia's head of state, closed the border with Sierra Leone for three weeks in February and March after a story appeared in a Sierra Leone newspaper suggesting that he had shot his wife for being involved in a plot to poison him. (GUY ARNOLD)

Singapore

Singapore, a republic within the Commonwealth, occupies a group of islands, the largest of which is Singapore, at the southern extremity of the Malay Peninsula. Area: 618 sq km (239 sq mi). Pop. (1983 est.): 2,502,000, including (1982 est.) 76.7% Chinese; 14.7% Malays; 6.4% Indians; and 2.2% other. Language: official languages are English, Malay, Mandarin Chinese, and Tamil. Religion: Malays are Muslim; Chinese, mainly Buddhist; Indians, mainly Hindu. President in 1983, Chengara Veetil Devan Nair; prime minister, Lee Kuan Yew.

In March 1983 the ruling People's Action Party in Singapore set up a task force headed by Defense Minister Goh Chok Tong to ensure continuing popular support for the party in the future. Three committees were established dealing with information, branch liaison, and constituency relations. This enterprise was designed as part of a process of political regeneration in preparation for the political succession expected in the 1990s. However, one candidate for succession, trade union leader Lim Chee Onn, was relieved of his post in April and resigned as minister without portfolio in July. He was succeeded as head of the National Trades Union Congress by Ong Teng Cheong, then minister for both communications and labour.

In August J. B. Jeyaretnam, who as a member of the Workers' Party was Singapore's sole opposition member of Parliament, along with Wong Hong Toy, president of the party, pleaded not guilty to charges of making a false declaration and

SINGAPORE

Education. (1982) Primary, pupils 289,092, teachers 9,452; secondary, pupils 176,845, teachers 8,348; vocational, pupils 14,990, teachers 1,199; teacher training, pupils 1,000, teachers 167; higher, students 25,736, teaching staff 2,586.

Finance. Monetary unit: Singapore dollar, with (Sept. 20, 1983) a free rate of Sing$2.14 to U.S. $1 (Sing$3.22 = £1 sterling). Gold and other reserves (May 1983) U.S. $8,826,000,000. Budget (total; 1982–83 est.) balanced at Sing$7,639,000,000. Gross national product (1981) Sing$26,390,000,000. Money supply (May 1983) Sing$8,201,000,000. Cost of living (1975 = 100; June 1983) 135.1.

Foreign Trade. (1982) Imports Sing$60,244,000,000; exports Sing$44,473,000,000. Import sources: Japan 18%; Saudi Arabia 16%; Malaysia 13%; U.S. 13%. Export destinations: Malaysia 18%; U.S. 13%; Japan 11%; Hong Kong 8%. Main exports: petroleum products 32%; machinery 23%; ship and aircraft fuel 7%; food 5%. Tourism (1981): visitors 2,828,000; gross receipts U.S. $1,090,000,000.

Transport and Communications. Roads (1982) 2,529 km. Motor vehicles in use (1982): passenger 194,400; commercial 96,900. Railways (1982): 38 km (for traffic *see* Malaysia). Air traffic (1982): 18,161,000,000 passenger-km; freight 758.6 million net ton-km. Shipping (1982): merchant vessels 100 gross tons and over 849; gross tonnage 7,183,326. Shipping traffic (1982): goods loaded 35,665,000 metric tons, unloaded 59,996,000 metric tons. Telephones (Dec. 1982) 852,000. Radio licenses (Dec. 1982) 608,000. Television licenses (Dec. 1982) 424,100.

Industry. Production (in 000; 1982): electricity (kw-hr) 7,860,000; manufactured gas (cu m) 121,000; petroleum products (metric tons; 1981) c. 32,578. Merchant vessels launched (100 gross tons and over; 1982) 56,000 gross tons.

fraudulently transferring party funds. They were released on bail pending resumption of the case.

Prime Minister Lee Kuan Yew provoked public controversy when, at a national day rally in August, he sought to encourage women graduates to marry their intellectual equals and have children. He claimed that uneducated women in Singapore produced twice as many children as their educated counterparts and that unless the trend was reversed the country would lose its talent pool and its economy would falter. At the end of the month Deputy Prime Minister Goh Keng Swee disclosed that the government intended to provide a computerized matchmaking service to help women university graduates find appropriate marital partners.

Foreign Minister Suppiah Dhanabalan warned in September that the continuing Vietnamese occupation of Kampuchea was making the region a cockpit for the contest between the U.S.S.R. and China. He reiterated Singapore's aim to secure a neutral, nonaligned Kampuchea, which would be achieved by the withdrawal of Vietnamese troops through negotiation. Noting that he was not asking the Vietnamese to withdraw "tomorrow," he added that their forces could be replaced by UN peacekeeping contingents. (MICHAEL LEIFER)

Social Security and Welfare Services

Insofar as social policy was concerned, 1983 was a year of austerity in most Western industrialized nations. Economic problems also affected social security and the social services in other parts of the world, although progress was nevertheless registered in a few less developed nations and, to some extent, in the socialist countries. Despite a recovery in economic activity in major Western countries during the year, unemployment continued to rise. As in previous years, large-scale unemployment meant less tax revenue and more expenditure on benefits.

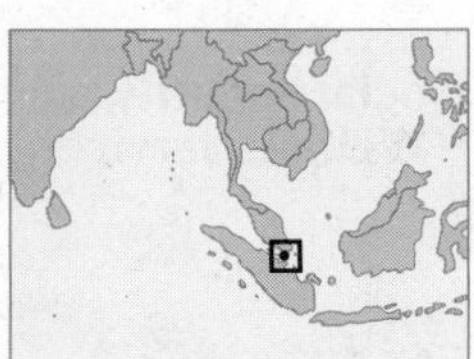
Singapore

International Developments in Social Security. As more and more people became dependent on social security benefits, governments in many countries were trying to reduce the benefits payable and to tighten the qualifying conditions. In West Germany, for instance, the regular adjustment of pensions due to take place in January was postponed by six months, and net pensions were reduced by introducing, in July, a pensioners' sickness insurance contribution, initially set at 1% but scheduled to rise to 5% by 1985. Allowances payable during physical and vocational rehabilitation were also cut, to 70% of normal sickness benefit or 80% for workers with dependents. West Germany also introduced restrictive measures affecting unemployment and sickness insurance and family allowances. For the unemployed, the duration of benefit was reduced from one-half to one-third of the period of insured employment, subject to the same maximum of 52 weeks. Prescription charges were increased, and it was decided that many common medications would no longer be reimbursed, except for children under 16. Family allowances for second and subsequent children, already cut in 1982, were reduced further.

Many countries tightened the conditions for payment of unemployment benefit. In France, for example, employees leaving their last job without just cause now lost benefit for three months, rather than six weeks. The unemployed also lost benefit if they received redundancy payments (severance pay) exceeding the statutory minimum or if they were paid for unused annual leave. Formerly, the regular unemployment benefit was paid for a standard period of one year to workers who had been in employment for at least 3 months out of the last 12, but benefits were now payable for shorter periods to workers whose previous employment lasted less than 12 months. Similar measures were introduced in a number of other Western countries. Given the difficulty of finding a job, the effect was to reduce the incomes of the unemployed and to drive more of them to apply for social assistance (welfare). In some countries the majority of unemployed workers were already dependent on assistance; this was the case in the U.K., where there was even talk of abolishing unemployment insurance altogether.

Nevertheless, certain improvements did take place, even in countries with high unemployment and severe budgetary problems. In April France reduced the pension age for workers who had been in insured employment for 37.5 years from 65 to 60. A combined pension from the basic and complementary schemes, equal to about 70% of previous earnings, was now payable at age 60. When this reform was implemented, an early retirement plan set up in 1977 by employers and workers under the terms of a national agreement was phased out.

Skating:
see Ice Hockey; Winter Sports

Skeet Shooting:
see Target Sports

Skiing:
see Water Sports; Winter Sports

Soccer:
see Football

Finland also embarked on a significant pension reform, to be implemented in stages between 1983 and 1985. The national pension plan in Finland provided a flat-rate basic and a means-tested supplementary pension. The means test was being greatly liberalized, so that the supplementary pension would be reduced only if a person was receiving an occupational pension. While this reform was being phased in, the level of the supplementary pension was being raised. Part of the cost would be recouped by making national pensions taxable. It was estimated that two-thirds of Finland's pensioners would benefit, while about 13% would suffer a reduction in net income.

New social security legislation came into effect in Poland at the beginning of the year. The coverage of the pension system was extended—for example, to persons disabled from infancy—and the level of pensions was raised, with an especially large increase for the disabled and for surviving dependents. The new law provided for a minimum pension equal to 90% of the minimum wage in the socialized sector of the economy. Pensions in general were to be adjusted in line with average earnings as from 1986, with certain adjustments of a more limited nature scheduled to take place between 1983 and 1986. Pensions for farmers were also raised substantially, and various new benefits were introduced for people working in agriculture, including partial disability and maternity benefits. The law also provided for the introduction of means-tested family allowances in 1986; currently, family allowances were payable to farmers only with respect to disabled children.

Higher pensions became payable in the U.S.S.R. as a result of changes in the increments paid to employees who had worked for a long period without interruptions of over a month. The required period was reduced from 35 to 25 years for men and from 30 to 20 years for women, and the amount of the increment was raised from 10 to 20% of the pension.

Bag ladies as they are called, homeless women whose possessions are carried in a shopping bag, are becoming more prevalent in today's economy. Soup kitchens set up by various charitable entities, like this one by the Cathedral of St. John the Divine in New York City, feed homeless women and men, who may number 36,000 in New York City alone.

WIDE WORLD

In less developed countries social security was being adversely affected by the economic crisis. Benefits were being cut as much as or more than in the industrialized countries, simply by not adjusting benefits for inflation. Relatively few new plans were introduced, and existing ones did not expand their coverage to any great extent. However, some noteworthy developments did take place. In February Argentina introduced unemployment benefits payable for six months to workers who had lost their jobs during the previous year and were still unemployed. The plan was introduced on a temporary basis but was, nevertheless, an important innovation. Previously, Argentina, like most less developed countries, had not provided any benefits for the unemployed in general.

Major changes were made in the social security system of Cape Verde at the beginning of the year. The pension age was reduced from 70 to 65 for men and 60 for women, and the minimum period of insured employment required to establish eligibility was reduced from ten to three years. The pension formula was substantially improved, and surviving dependents became entitled to benefits for the first time. To pay for these improvements, a state subsidy was introduced, and contributions from both workers and employers were increased. A new plan was introduced in Gabon with the aim of including categories of the population not previously covered or whose coverage was inadequate. The self-employed and workers employed under contract by the state were covered with respect to old age, invalidity, death, sickness, maternity, occupational risks, and family allowances. The most original feature of the plan was that it also included the indigent, defined as nonemployed persons with an income of less than the national minimum wage, although they were eligible only for family allowances and medical care.

(ROGER A. BEATTIE)

U.S. Developments. One of the most sweeping reforms of the U.S. Social Security system since the program started in 1937 was enacted in 1983. Crafted by a bipartisan blue-ribbon commission and passed overwhelmingly by Congress, the legislation would raise nearly $165 billion for the government's retirement trust funds by 1990 and was designed to keep Social Security solvent well into the next century. If Congress had not acted, the Old-Age and Survivors Insurance Trust Fund would have run short of money in July 1983 and would have faced serious problems throughout the decade.

Among major features of the reform, the age at which a person can retire and still receive full benefits would go up in two stages from the current 65 to 67. Starting in the year 2003, the retirement age would advance two months a year until it reached 66 in 2009; it would then be raised to 67 over six years ending in 2027. Early retirement would still start at age 62, but benefits for those taking it would be cut by 25% beginning in 2009 and by 30% in 2027, compared with the current

20%. The annual cost-of-living increase in benefits would come in January of each year instead of July. For the first time since benefits were paid, some recipients would be taxed on their pensions. Starting in 1984, pensioners would pay federal income tax if their adjusted gross income, plus half of their Social Security benefits, exceeded $25,000 for individuals or $32,000 for couples.

As of Jan. 1, 1984, new federal employees, current and future members of Congress, the president, and other high-ranking federal officials and judges would be included under Social Security. Coverage would also be extended to employees of nonprofit groups. The payroll tax, paid by employees and employers, would be increased to 7% in 1984, 7.05% in 1985, 7.15% in 1986, 7.51% in 1988, and 7.65% in 1990 (the rate in 1983 was 6.7%). Since the maximum taxable earnings base for 1984 was $37,800, the top tax paid by the employee would be $2,532.60, compared with $2,391.90 in 1983; the employer would pay $2,646 in 1984, compared with $2,391.90 in 1983. In 1984 only, employees would get a 0.3% income tax credit to offset the payroll tax boost. Payroll taxes for self-employed individuals would be increased by 33%, but such persons would be given income tax credits to offset the effect of the raise. Starting in 1990, benefits for persons 65 and over would be reduced by $1 for each $3 of outside earnings. Currently, they were reduced by $1 for each $2 of earnings. (*See* Special Report.)

The Social Security Amendments of 1983 also contained an important change in Medicare, aimed at cutting the costs of that program for the elderly and at making hospitals more efficient. In the past, there had been no limit on payments for hospital care under Medicare. As of Oct. 1, 1983, however, fees were established for 467 categories of in-patient treatment; these are the amounts that providers would receive from Medicare for a particular procedure. If a hospital could treat a patient for less, it would keep the difference; if it charged more, it would have to absorb the loss. Although the new payment scheme was expected to cut Medicare costs, it would not save nearly enough money to prevent the bankruptcy that the Congressional Budget Office predicted for the Medicare Hospital Insurance Trust Fund by 1987. However, supporters of the Social Security reform hoped it would set a pattern for a complete overhaul of Medicare.

Complaints increased in 1983 concerning a 1980 law aimed at reducing federal costs for disability benefits by tightening eligibility rules. A growing number of persons charged that they had been unfairly dropped from the disability rolls, and a Senate subcommittee reported that the Social Security Administration had improperly pressured its hearing judges to cut benefits. A stopgap law that allowed persons judged ineligible to collect benefits while they appealed the ruling expired in December, but the Social Security Administration halted the sending of cutoff notices pending a review of the situation.

Two congressional actions represented attempts to deal with the effects of recession. A $3.5 billion Job Training Partnership Act went into effect on October 1, replacing the Comprehensive Educational Training Act. The new program was designed to train disadvantaged youths and adults in marketable skills and to retrain experienced adult workers who had suffered permanent job loss. The long-term unemployed also received help when federal supplemental unemployment benefits were extended through March 31, 1985. Under the extension, expected to cost about $4.6 billion, individuals who had used up all their unemployment benefits would be given 8 to 14 weeks of additional federal assistance. The Center on Budget and Policy Priorities, a private research organization, reported that the proportion of jobless workers receiving unemployment insurance fell to an all-time low of 31.9% in October 1983.

NANCY RICA SCHIFF

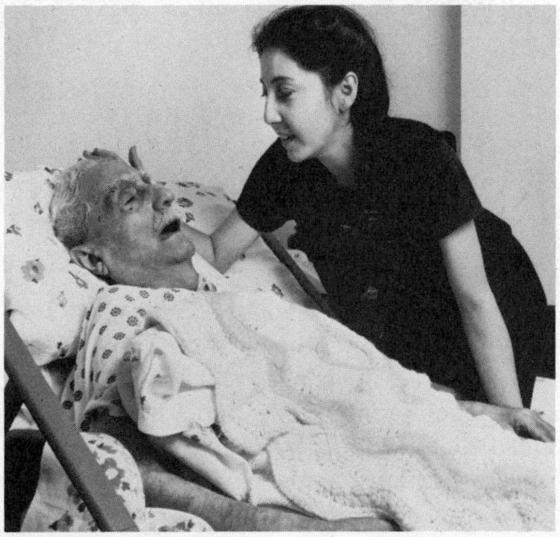

Hospice care for terminally ill patients can enable them to die in dignity and relative comfort at home or in an institutional hospice, which is less costly than a hospital room; but hospice costs are increasing, too.

For the first time since 1978, Congress passed and the president signed an appropriations bill for the Departments of Health and Human Services, Labor, and Education. The measure had been held up in the past by controversies over such issues as abortion and school busing, and funding for the programs covered was included in continuing appropriations. The bill, a major source of money for social programs, provided $96.5 billion for fiscal 1984 and $7.9 billion in advance appropriations for fiscal 1985–86—$9.2 billion more than requested by Pres. Ronald Reagan.

Although Congress appropriated more for social programs than the president wanted, there were indications that the administration had made headway in its efforts to keep a lid on social spending. The Census Bureau reported that 14,615,000 U.S. households, about one in every six, received noncash federal assistance in 1982 under the four main government means-tested programs—Medicaid, food stamps, housing subsidies, and school lunches. This represented a decline of 49,000 households from 1981, even though poverty and unemployment rose during the period. According to the Census Bureau, about 60% of all households living below the poverty level in 1982 ($9,862 for a family of four) received at least one noncash benefit. (DAVID M. MAZIE)

See also Education; Health and Disease; Industrial Review: *Insurance*.
[522.D; 535.B.3.e; 552.D.1]

Soil Conservation: *see* Environment

AROUND THE WORLD, SOCIAL SECURITY GOES BROKE

by A. Lawrence Chickering

Government retirement programs, the most popular and hitherto the most successful components of the modern welfare state, are going broke throughout the Western industrialized world. The current funding problems of social security, especially the pay-as-you-go systems prevalent in Europe and the U.S., promise to become political crises early in the 21st century. By then, the demands and expectations of the postwar "baby boom" generation for undiminished retirement benefits will run afoul of the tax resistance of a shrinking pool of workers.

In most industrial countries, social security programs were established in the late 19th century in response to the social disruptions of rapid industrialization. The programs began to include the majority of salaried people only in the 1930s and '40s and were expanded to cover almost everyone only in the 1950s and '60s, when pay-as-you-go financing replaced actuarial funding. By the 1970s these retirement programs had become their countries' most costly income-transfer programs, funded primarily from payroll deductions that, in the aggregate, were coming to rival the national operating budgets in a number of countries.

Types of Financing. There are two forms of social security financing, both funded mostly by payroll taxes. In an actuarially sound, funded system, payroll taxes are accumulated into a capital fund, which is invested, and the interest is used to pay pensions. In pay-as-you-go systems, payroll taxes are immediately paid out as pensions. In a funded system, future benefits are backed by well-defined assets. Under pay-as-you-go, future benefits depend on an implicit moral claim against future workers.

Funded systems dominated before World War II. During the postwar boom, however, demands for increased benefits, combined with declining median ages, made pay-as-you-go financing politically irresistible, especially to provide pensions for the large numbers of people who came to be covered. Pay-as-you-go systems pay benefits immediately, even to retirees who have contributed little or nothing.

Of the industrialized democracies, only Japan operates its social insurance programs on an actuarial, funded basis, supplemented, however, by a 20% transfer from general revenues. But Japan's policy of investing the fund's capital in public projects, which pay less than market rates, is depleting the fund's capital. Unless the policy is changed, the Japanese will be forced increasingly to resort to current taxes.

Basic systems elsewhere are entirely pay-as-you-go, often supplemented by transfers from general revenues. Switzerland is in the process of converting its supplementary program from voluntary to compulsory, effective in January 1985. British pensioners may opt out of the public supplementary system in favour of approved private funded programs, and 90% elect to do so. France operates a pay-as-you-go supplementary system, while a forced-saving program has added a large capital fund to Sweden's formally pay-as-you-go system. (Sweden, however, suffers the same problem as Japan in management of its capital fund.) There are no public supplementary plans in the U.S., Italy, or West Germany—only private savings and pensions, which operate actuarially.

The Coming Crisis. In most industrialized democracies, pensions are paid subject to an earnings test, which in effect taxes benefits paid above a certain (labour-earned) income level. (There are no earnings tests in France or Switzerland.) Pension amounts pay replacement levels (defined as the percentage of last income earned before receiving benefits) in the 40 to 50% range. In Sweden and Switzerland the figure rises to 60%, and in Italy pensions for private workers amount to 80% of last wages, while the figure for public employees is even higher. In pay-as-you-go systems, all these levels imply a return of contributions plus interest, supplemented by a large transfer from the current working generation. In the U.S. in 1980, average benefits for men included about 80% transfer and 20% return of contribution plus interest; the transfer component was even higher for women.

In the three high-pension countries mentioned above, social security payroll taxes range from 20 to

---

A. Lawrence Chickering is executive director of the Institute for Contemporary Studies in San Francisco. He was a contributor to The World Crisis in Social Security.

BOB NORTH—PICTURE GROUP

Philadelphia senior citizens demanding secure social security reflected identical concerns around the world and pointed to an underlying funding problem that was nearly universal.

25% of earnings, besides added transfers from general revenues in Italy and Switzerland. These high tax levels have already driven substantial numbers of workers into large and growing underground economies, and this explains why further raising of payroll taxes is probably self-defeating. But without benefit reductions or large increases in general revenue transfers, payroll taxes will have to rise to levels exceeding 30% in Italy, Sweden, France, West Germany, and possibly Britain.

The greatest long-term funding problem involves the changing age structures, reflected in the ratio of workers paying taxes to retirees receiving benefits. In Italy only 1.41 workers were paying taxes to support each beneficiary in 1980, compared with 2.19 in West Germany, 3.2 in the U.S., and 6.84 in Sweden. Italy's ratio is expected to drop to 1.32 in the year 2000. The ratio in West Germany will fall to nearly one to one (1.12) in 2030. Despite their problems, the U.S. and Britain will be in relatively good shape, with about two workers paying for each beneficiary in 2035 and 2030, respectively.

The Search for Solutions. Solution of the funding problem means either reducing benefits or raising taxes, or both. Historically, it has been very difficult for politicians in most countries to restrict benefits, even in the shadow of short-term bankruptcy. But the West Germans did it recently, despite an election promise to the contrary.

Long-term solutions, which require time horizons more distant than the next election, are approached even more reluctantly, for they involve imposing current costs on large constituencies in order to solve future problems. Conversion to funded systems, while appealing in principle, is politically impossible, since building a capital fund would require a long period of double contributions to discharge old obligations incurred under the pay-as-you-go system and to build the fund.

Since raising taxes risks economic harm, reducing benefits is the only reasonable solution. How to do it is the political dilemma facing all governments with unfunded systems. Among the alternatives, increasing the retirement age appears to be the least difficult politically. In the U.S., at least, it is the only solution that politicians even seem willing to discuss. In 1983 a law was passed raising the retirement age for full benefits in the U.S. gradually from 65 to 67, with the first increase occurring early in the 21st century. Later retirement both preserves benefit levels and reflects the shorter working lives and longer life expectancies of postindustrial societies. But its political appeal does not apply everywhere. In West Germany the government is thought to be bound contractually to current retirement ages, and the French government fulfilled a campaign pledge by reducing the retirement age to 60 in 1982.

Another means of reducing benefits is to change the formulas by which benefits are indexed to inflation. Current policies on indexing vary widely. France makes its adjustments for inflation by legislation. Britain indexes only to inflation. Other countries index both for inflation and for some part of economic growth as well. In changing indexation, it is important to protect the value of workers' "investment" in future benefits and to guarantee at least a reasonable return. This is necessary to preserve confidence in the programs.

Most students of the problem favour gradually separating social security's two essential functions—funding the earned entitlements function through the payroll tax and the transfer function (*i.e.*, to those in need) from general revenues. In fact, many of the current problems result from the confusion of these two very different purposes; all too often the large costs of the transfer component have been camouflaged by selling the entire program as one of "earned entitlements." If the transfer portion were moved to the general budget, program expenditures would have to compete with other priorities and thus would be subject to more discipline.

Much concern has been expressed about problems of equity, both within and between generations. Within generations, the major debate has been between women as workers and as beneficiaries of working spouses; current policies tend to favour the latter and hurt the former. These problems pale, however, in relation to the long-term funding problem. Policymakers have tended to think the problem can be left for someone else to solve, but the longer they wait, the more painful must be the cure. In the end, the "future" will come when voters begin acting on their fears about that future. There is good reason to believe that this is already starting to happen.

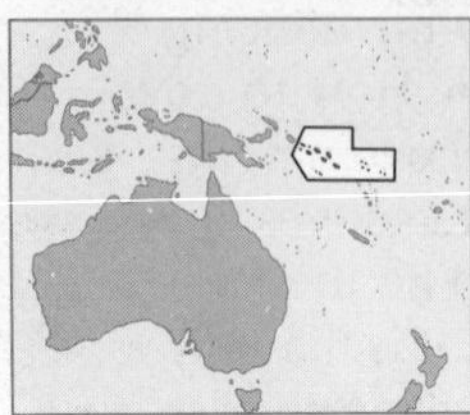
Solomon Islands

Solomon Islands

The Solomon Islands is a parliamentary state and member of the Commonwealth. The nation comprises a 1,450-km (900-mi) chain of islands and atolls in the western Pacific Ocean. Area: 27,556 sq km (10,640 sq mi). Pop. (1982 est.): 244,000 (Melanesian 93.3%; Polynesian 4%; Micronesian 1.4%; other 1.3%). Cap. and largest city: Honiara (pop., 1981 prelim., 21,300). Language: English (official), Pidgin (lingua franca), and some 90 local languages and dialects. Religion (1980): Anglican 33.6%; Roman Catholic 19.1%; South Sea Evangelical 24.6%; other Protestant 15.2%; traditional 7.3%; other 0.2%. Queen, Elizabeth II; governor-general in 1983, Baddeley Devesi; prime minister, Solomon Mamaloni.

The year 1983 was a troubled one for Prime Minister Solomon Mamaloni of the Solomon Islands. In April he dismissed two ministers for misconduct and in June removed a third who had ceased to support the government. An opposition attempt to bring down Mamaloni through a vote of no confidence failed when the motion was withdrawn after a day of acrimonious debate.

When senior officials warned of the implications of the Solomon Islands' high birthrate, Mamaloni criticized population-control programs as "slow genocide" and as contrary to tradition. He claimed that the country needed a larger population to ensure the development of its resources.

The economy continued to suffer from a decline in export earnings. In 1983 the Solomons received $5 million from the International Monetary Fund to alleviate the balance of payments deficit, as well as grants from the Asian Development Bank and the European Communities for specific development purposes. The U.K. remained the major aid donor. (BARRIE MACDONALD)

SOLOMON ISLANDS

Education. (1981–82) Primary, pupils 30,316, teachers 1,199; secondary, pupils 4,262, teachers 239; vocational, pupils 548, teachers 38; teacher training, students (1980–81) 116, teachers (1981–82) 28.

Finance and Trade. Monetary unit: Solomon Islands dollar, with (Sept. 20, 1983) a free value of SI$1.19 to U.S. $1 (SI$1.79 = £1 sterling). Budget (total; 1983 est.): revenue SI$74.5 million; expenditure SI$68.1 million. Foreign trade (1981): imports (f.o.b.) SI$66 million; exports SI$57.6 million. Import sources: Australia 29%; Singapore 23%; Japan 14%; New Zealand 9%; U.K. 7%; Papua New Guinea 5%. Export destinations: Japan 37%; U.S. 22%; U.K. 12%; The Netherlands 12%; West Germany 5%. Main exports (1980): fish 38%; timber 26%; copra 17%; palm oil 11%.

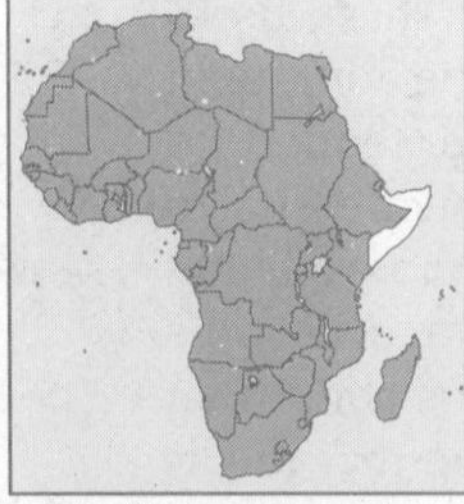
Somalia

Somalia

A republic of northeast Africa, the Somali Democratic Republic, or Somalia, is bounded by the Gulf of Aden, the Indian Ocean, Kenya, Ethiopia, and Djibouti. Area: 638,000 sq km (246,300 sq mi). Pop. (1983 est.): 3,977,000, mainly Hamitic, with Arabic and other admixtures. Cap. and largest city: Mogadishu (pop., 1981 est., 400,000). Language: Somali spoken by a great majority (Arabic also official). Religion: predominantly Muslim. President in 1983, Maj. Gen. Muhammad Siyad Barrah.

The economic situation in Somalia continued to improve during 1983, as Pres. Muhammad Siyad Barrah entered his 15th year of power apparently unshaken by unrest within the country and attacks from without. The unrest was centred on the north. Some groups based in that part of the country had long complained of exclusion from the political process and neglect of their development needs by a government based in the south.

These dissident movements were organized from outside the country by political exiles. The two main groups were the Somali Democratic Salvation Front and the Somali National Movement (SNM). Operating in an uneasy alliance, they launched their attacks from Ethiopia, Somalia's neighbour and traditional enemy. Their greatest impact during the year occurred in January, when SNM fighters attacked the high-security Mandera prison in the extreme north and released, by their own claim, more than 750 people, including 12 important political prisoners. This led to a security clampdown that halted all traffic in the area for 40 days and closed the border with Djibouti. However, in February President Barrah felt able to make a goodwill tour in the north, and there he announced an offer of amnesty for political exiles, over 600 of whom were said to have taken the chance to return to Somalia.

Meanwhile, fighting was renewed in April and again in July near Beledwyen, where Ethiopian troops backing Somali dissidents had crossed the border in 1982 and remained dug in opposite Somali government forces. However, these appeared to be temporary flare-ups, and the stalemate continued.

The economy continued to improve after the low point of the years 1979–81, when it had been severely hit by war, drought, and the huge influx of

SOMALIA

Education. (1981–82) Primary, pupils 418,935, teachers 12,007; secondary (1979–80), pupils 15,338, teachers 925; vocational, pupils 23,810, teachers 2,380; teacher training (1979–80), students 2,156, teachers 130; higher (1977–78), students (1979–80) 2,899, teaching staff (1975–76) 324.

Finance. Monetary unit: Somali shilling, with (Sept. 20, 1983) a free rate of 15.69 Somali shillings to U.S. $1 (23.63 Somali shillings = £1 sterling). Gold and other reserves (June 1983) U.S. $16 million. Budget (1982 est.): revenue 3,130,000,000 Somali shillings; expenditure 2,774,000,000 Somali shillings. Cost of living (Mogadishu; 1975 = 100; March 1983) 568.1.

Foreign Trade. (1982) Imports 2,376,900,000 Somali shillings; exports 1,993,400,000 Somali shillings. Import sources (1980): Italy 35%; U.S. 9%; U.K 8%; France 7%; Saudi Arabia 5%; West Germany 5%. Export destinations (1980): Saudi Arabia 66%; Italy 12%; United Arab Emirates 5%. Main exports: livestock 88%; bananas 7%.

Transport and Communications. Roads (1979) 19,780 km. Motor vehicles in use (1980): passenger 17,200; commercial (including buses) 8,050. There are no railways. Air traffic (1982): 227 million passenger-km; freight c. 4.6 million net ton-km. Shipping (1982): merchant vessels 100 gross tons and over 22; gross tonnage 17,525. Telephones (Dec. 1980) c. 7,000. Radio receivers (Dec. 1980) 87,000.

Agriculture. Production (in 000; metric tons; 1982): sorghum c. 190; corn (1981) c. 120; cassava c. 34; sesame seed c. 28; sugar, raw value (1981) 38; bananas c. 70; goat's milk c. 288. Livestock (in 000; 1981): cattle c. 3,950; sheep c. 10,200; goats c. 16,500; camels c. 5,550.

refugees from the Ogaden region in Ethiopia. The recovery was due in part to a series of good rainy seasons and in part to a government program of financial reorganization and liberalization. In October the World Bank's consultative group for Somalia, representing aid donor countries and agencies, authorized a $1.2 billion package for agricultural development. The major project was the building of an $800 million dam across the Juba River that was to supply irrigation and electricity. This was regarded by Somalia as the keynote of its development program but was a possible cause of tension with Ethiopia, which controlled the upper course of the river.

The estimated 700,000 refugees from the Ogaden remained a major problem. They were still living mainly in camps and were dependent on international aid. The government agreed to make land available to refugees who wished to farm it.

In March a presidential decree banned the sale of qat; the leaves of this plant were the favourite national stimulant. The reasons given for the ban were the harmful social effects of qat and the waste of national currency in importing it from Kenya and Ethiopia. By August it was officially claimed that the quantity being imported had dropped to 3% of its former level.

The seven senior politicians arrested in 1982 on treason charges had not been brought to trial by the year's end. (VIRGINIA R. LULING)

South Africa

The Republic. Occupying the southern tip of Africa, South Africa is bounded by South West Africa/Namibia, Botswana, Zimbabwe, Mozambique, and Swaziland and by the Atlantic and Indian oceans on the west and east. South Africa entirely surrounds Lesotho and partially surrounds the four former black states of Transkei (independent Oct. 26, 1976), Bophuthatswana (independent Dec. 6, 1977), Venda (independent Sept. 13, 1979), and Ciskei (independent Dec. 4, 1981), although the independence of the latter four is not recognized by the international community. Walvis Bay, part of Cape Province since 1910 but administered as part of South West Africa since 1922, was returned to the direct control of Cape Province on Sept. 1, 1977. Area (including Walvis Bay but excluding the four former homelands): 1,123,226 sq km (433,680 sq mi). Pop. (1983 est.): 25,770,000 (excluding the four homelands), including black (Bantu) 67.7%; white 18.3%; Coloured 10.6%; Asian 3.3%. Executive cap.: Pretoria (pop., 1980, 528,400); judicial cap.: Bloemfontein (pop., 1980, 230,700); legislative cap.: Cape Town (pop., 1980, 1.5 million). Largest city: Johannesburg (pop., 1982 estimate, 1,639,000). Language: Afrikaans and English (official); Bantu languages predominate. Religion: mainly Christian. State president in 1983, Marais Viljoen; prime minister, P. W. Botha.

DOMESTIC AFFAIRS. For the greater part of 1983 the national and political life of South Africa centred on the controversial issues surrounding the government's proposed new constitution. The work of the advisory President's Council, it extended the parliamentary franchise, previously exclusively reserved for whites, to the Coloured and Asian (mainly Indian) minorities.

The bill met with strong opposition from the Progressive Federal Party (PFP), which rejected it as a barely veiled entrenchment of apartheid (racial separation), particularly as it made no provision for the political future of the black majority. On the right it was attacked by the Conservative Party, which had broken away from the ruling National Party in 1982 over the issue, as a potential threat to white identity and self-determination. Sections of the Coloured and Indian communities agreed to participate in the new dispensation, while others rejected it.

The new constitution provided for a single Parliament with three separately elected chambers. The chambers were to be a white House of Assembly (178 members, like the existing Parliament), a Coloured House of Representatives (85), and an Asian House of Deputies (45). Each chamber was to be responsible for its community's "own affairs" (education, social welfare, housing, local government, arts, culture, and recreation, except competitive sports). Legislation on "general affairs" (foreign policy, defense, and finance) was to be subject to approval by the three chambers separately, after consideration by joint standing committees.

The government was to be headed by an executive state president chosen by an electoral college drawn from the three chambers, with whites in the majority. The president would appoint a Cabinet of ministers to be in charge of "general affairs," as well as ministers' councils from the three chambers to look after "own affairs." A President's Council consisting of 60 nominated members and containing an overall white majority would act as the final arbitrator.

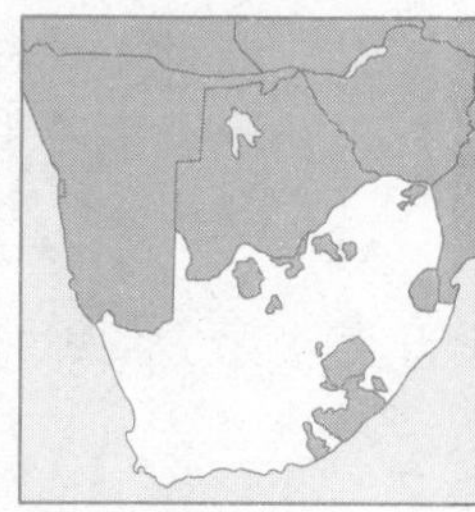
South Africa

After passing through Parliament and before being formally enacted, the proposal was submitted to a referendum of the white electorate. This was preceded by a two-month-long nationwide debate in which every aspect of the new dispensation was exposed to minute scrutiny. An early by-product was a further rift in the National Party's Afrikaner establishment at grass-roots level. There was evidence, too, of a sharp conflict of opinion in English-speaking circles; many English speakers publicly dissociated themselves from the PFP policy of voting against the proposal, notably in the business and financial world where people feared the harm that a "no" majority might do to South African interests abroad.

The final results of the referendum poll on November 2 showed a landslide pro-constitution victory: of the 75.6% of the electorate who voted, 1,360,223 (66.3%) voted yes, while 691,577 (33.7%) voted no. The "no" poll, one-third of the total, was made up of liberals and conservatives of diametrically opposed views.

In a first reaction to the mandate the government had received, Prime Minister P. W. Botha declared that the outcome of the referendum laid the foundation for a new national unity. He said that, subject to further consultation with the Coloured and Indian communities, the new constitution would probably come into effect about the middle of 1984. Indications were that discussions on the political future of the black population were likely to be high on the agenda in the months ahead. After the referendum there was a meeting of the seven-member government committee appointed during the year to investigate the future political and economic development of urban blacks.

An offshoot of the black opposition to the new constitution was the formation of the United Democratic Front (UDF), an alliance of several hundred organizations and individuals, mainly black, which pledged to fight the new order. The UDF and other black organizations rejected, among other things, the official claim that the new Black Local Authorities Act, giving urban black communities a greater measure of local government, was a step toward satisfying black political aspirations. Late in the year, 26 such authorities were established.

Regulations against squatters and "illegal" nonwhites in white areas remained rigidly enforced but they aroused mounting protests that did not go entirely unheeded. The public and private sectors joined in attempts to alleviate the housing shortages, and the Mixed Marriages and Immorality Acts, with their humiliating racial connotations, were submitted to a high-level parliamentary investigation.

The banned African National Congress (ANC) claimed responsibility for a number of terrorist incidents during the year. The worst of these was a bomb explosion in the heart of Pretoria in which 19 people, white and black, were killed and many others injured. The South African security forces reacted at various times by striking at ANC bases in Mozambique and Lesotho and by warning that they would take similar action against any neighbouring country that harboured anyone guilty of committing or planning acts of terrorism against South Africa. Three ANC members were hanged in Pretoria in June, convicted of high treason for involvement in terrorist activities.

In one of the most sensational espionage trials in the country's history, Commodore Dieter Gerhardt and his wife Ruth were convicted in December of spying for the U.S.S.R. It was suggested that Gerhardt, commander of the Simonstown naval dockyard, might have revealed information vital to the security of the West as a whole.

FOREIGN RELATIONS. No tangible progress was made toward an internationally acceptable settlement of the South West Africa/Namibia independence issue in terms of UN resolution 435, which called for UN-supervised elections to clear the way for independence. All attempts at a final agreement continued to be held up, primarily by one obstacle: South Africa's insistence, broadly supported by the U.S., that an agreement for the withdrawal of Cuban forces from Angola was a nonnegotiable precondition for a settlement. Angola rejected the linkage of the Cuban presence with the Namibian question, though it was prepared to consider a Cuban withdrawal on certain conditions, such as the cessation of South African military incursions in southern Angola. (*See* ANGOLA.)

Reporting to the Security Council after an exploratory visit to Cape Town and Namibia in August, UN Secretary-General Javier Pérez de Cuéllar said that resolution 435 could be implemented immediately but for the stand on Cuban withdrawal. The Security Council in October adopted a resolution, with the U.S. abstaining, that dismissed South Africa's demand for the Cuban withdrawal and instructed the secretary-general to go ahead with the implementation of resolution 435. If he should be prevented from doing this, the UN would consider "appropriate measures" under the UN Charter.

In Namibia itself disillusionment and dissatisfaction over the continued lack of progress on independence found expression in the formation of a new 15-party coalition of all races that resolved to end the impasse and to pave the way for an internationally recognized settlement by the efforts of the Namibian people themselves. A lull in the border war with the South West Africa People's Organization (SWAPO) ended in late December when South African troops launched a major assault on SWAPO bases in southern Angola. Angolan forces became involved in the fighting.

Because of the atmosphere of change in South Africa its traditional problems of foreign policy—how to promote a better understanding of the South African situation and how to counter the threats, and sometimes the realities, of isolation in the world community—became at once easier to handle and more exacting. The proposed reforms were received in the world at large with a mixture

SOUTH AFRICA

Education. (1982) Primary, pupils 3,988,191; secondary and vocational, pupils 1,633,092; primary, secondary, and vocational, teachers 182,953; higher, students 251,723, teaching staff 16,673.

Finance. Monetary unit: rand, with (Sept. 20, 1983) a free rate of R 1.11 to U.S. $1 (R 1.67 = £1 sterling). Gold and other reserves (June 1983) U.S. $739 million. Budget (1982 actual): revenue R 16,420,000,000; expenditure R 18,836,000,000. Gross national product (1982) R 76,066,000,000. Money supply (June 1983) R 15,574,000,000. Cost of living (1975 = 100; June 1983) 258.7.

Foreign Trade. (South Africa Customs Union; 1982) Imports R 20,079,000,000; exports R 19,290,000,000. Import sources (23% are unspecified): West Germany 15%; U.S. 15%; U.K. 12%; Japan 10%. Export destinations (45% are unspecified): Japan 9%; U.K. 7%; U.S. 7%; Switzerland 5%. Main exports: gold specie c. 45%; food 9%; nonferrous metals and ores 6%; coal 6%; iron and steel 6%; diamonds 5%; gold coin 5%.

Transport and Communications. Roads (1981) 183,651 km. Motor vehicles in use (1982): passenger 2,557,000; commercial 912,000. Railways: (1981) 20,499 km; freight traffic (including Namibia; 1980–81) 99,173,000,000 net ton-km. Air traffic (1982): 9,287,000,000 passenger-km; freight 338.8 million net ton-km. Shipping (1982): merchant vessels 100 gross tons and over 292; gross tonnage 776,153. Telephones (Dec. 1980) 2,930,000. Radio receivers (Dec. 1980) c. 8 million. Television receivers (Dec. 1980) c. 2 million.

Agriculture. Production (in 000; metric tons; 1982): corn 8,344; wheat 2,296; sorghum 270; potatoes 981; tomatoes c. 390; sugar, raw value 2,210; peanuts 170; sunflower seed 256; oranges c. 630; grapefruit c. 120; pineapples c. 230; apples c. 400; grapes c. 1,300; tobacco 36; cotton, lint 42; wool 53; milk c. 2,500; meat 1,029; fish catch (1981) 612. Livestock (in 000; June 1982): cattle c. 12,200; sheep c. 31,700; pigs c. 1,330; goats c. 5,340; horses c. 225; chickens c. 31,500.

Industry. Index of manufacturing production (1975 = 100; 1981) 136. Fuel and power (in 000; 1981): coal (metric tons) 131,200; manufactured gas (cu m) c. 3,350,000; electricity (kw-hr; 1982) 119,874,000. Production (in 000; metric tons; 1981): cement 8,095; iron ore (60–65% metal content) 28,320; pig iron (1982) 6,797; crude steel (1982) 8,200; copper (1982) 141; chrome ore (oxide content) 1,260; manganese ore (metal content) 2,220; fluorspar 497; uranium 6.1; gold (troy oz; 1982) 21,360; diamonds (metric carats) 9,526; asbestos 236; petroleum products 14,585; fertilizers (nutrient content) nitrogenous c. 447, phosphate c. 510; newsprint 225; man-made fibres (1981) 55.

SIPA PRESS/BLACK STAR

Sabotage directed by guerrillas at the South African armed forces included an automobile bomb which devastated the Air Force headquarters at Pretoria, killing nearly 20 and wounding more than 200.

of sympathy and skepticism. Calls for disinvestment and boycotts were still heard from anti-apartheid quarters, but on the whole South Africa maintained its correct and, for the most part, friendly relations with many Western and some Eastern countries.

South Africa denied the destabilization charges brought against it by some of its immediate neighbours, and despite occasionally strained relations with Lesotho, the two countries continued to discuss plans for a joint irrigation project in the Lesotho Highlands. Farther afield on the continent South Africa claimed to have friendly behind-the-scenes contacts with a number of African nations.

THE ECONOMY. Presenting the 1983 budget near the end of March, Minister of Finance Owen Horwood said that the combined effect of the monetary and fiscal policies applied in the immediate past had vitally contributed to the success of the overall strategy of consolidation and adjustment set as the objective for the coming year. The minister dismissed all thought of a deliberate policy of reflation or stimulation of the economy. Such a move, he believed, would only increase the rate of inflation, weaken the currency, and damage the country's credit rating, thus defeating the entire strategy underlying the budgets of previous years.

Horwood reported that state expenditure was higher than had been anticipated, leaving the final deficit for 1982 before borrowing at R 1.8 billion. Defense expenditure continued to be the largest single item, totaling R 3.1 billion, an increase of almost 16% over the previous year. The second highest allocation, R 2.3 billion, was for the departments and services directly concerned with the black population, including training and education.

In the latter part of the year the inflation rate tended to fall, though it was still much higher than the average for South Africa's major trading partners. It stood at just below 11% in September, as against more than 12% in previous months. Factors inhibiting the economy were an unusually long and severe drought over large parts of the country and a steady decline in the price of gold to a fluctuating level well below the $400 mark from October onward. Summing up the situation in its 1983 annual survey, the Reserve Bank described the economy as being still firmly on the downward trend, marked by falling output and rising unemployment, but indicated that the downturn might soon start to level out, depending largely on the behaviour of gold.

A feature of the economy that was underlined in 1983 was the increasingly important role of the black consumer, despite high unemployment, and the growth of black trade unionism and its bargaining power, both in separate and in mixed unions. For the first time a black union, on its own, successfully negotiated a substantial wage increase in the mining industry.

Bophuthatswana. The republic of Bophuthatswana consists of six discontinuous, landlocked geographic units, one of which borders Botswana on the northwest; it is otherwise entirely surrounded by South Africa. Area: 40,000 sq km (15,444 sq mi). Pop. (1983 est.): 1,395,000, including 99.6% Bantu, of whom Tswana 69.8%; Northern Sotho 7.5%. Cap.: Mmabatho. Largest city: GaRankuwa (pop., 1980 prelim., 48,300). Language (official): Central Tswana, English, Afrikaans. Religion: predominantly Christian (Methodist, Lutheran, Anglican, and Bantu Christian churches). President in 1983, Lucas Mangope.

With its record of political stability and consistent encouragement of free enterprise, Bophuthatswana continued to attract foreign capital investment. This was reflected in the course of regular contacts made by Pres. Lucas Mangope and other official representatives with Western industrial and financial interests. Equally important, it was stressed, was the development of the small business sector and of the area's agricultural resources. New food production schemes were launched during the year, and additional land was made available for purchase by established farmers.

In a case that excited considerable interest the Bophuthatswana Supreme Court ruled that the Terrorism Act which the country had inherited from South Africa was invalid there on the grounds that it was in conflict with Bophuthatswana's Bill of Rights. In a further show of independence Bophuthatswana went ahead with plans for the installation of its own television service, in

BOPHUTHATSWANA

Education. (1979–80) Primary, pupils 343,482, teachers 6,015; secondary, pupils 91,372, teachers 2,501; vocational, students 1,557, teachers 71; teacher training, students 3,298, teachers 151; higher, students 114, teachers 36.

Finance and Trade. Monetary unit: South African rand. Budget (1981–82) balanced at R 421 million. Foreign trade included in South Africa.

CISKEI

Education. (1981) Primary, pupils 180,214, teachers 4,058; secondary, pupils 45,661; vocational, pupils 304; teacher training, students 1,252; secondary, vocational, and teacher training, teachers 1,495; higher (university only), students 2,304.

Finance and Trade. Monetary unit: South African rand. Budget (1980–81): revenue R 119.1 million; expenditure R 137.7 million. Most trade is with South Africa.

TRANSKEI

Education. (1978) Primary, pupils 647,985, teachers 12,627; secondary, pupils 33,636, teachers 1,179; vocational, pupils 908, teachers 59; teacher training, students 3,034, teachers 126; higher, students 503, teaching staff 96.

Finance and Trade. Monetary unit: South African rand. Budget (total; 1981–82 est.) balanced at R 374.6 million. Most trade is with South Africa.

VENDA

Education. (1982) Primary, pupils 157,014, teachers 4,586; secondary, pupils 33,432, teachers 1,062; vocational, pupils c. 796; teacher training, students 704.

Finance and Trade. Monetary unit: South African rand. Budget (1982–83) balanced at R 115.1 million. Most trade is with South Africa.

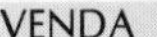

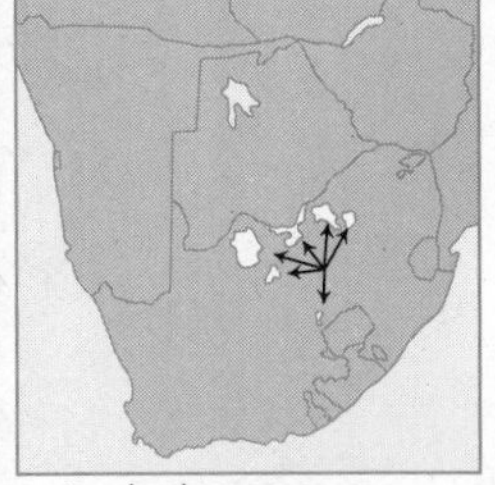

Bophuthatswana

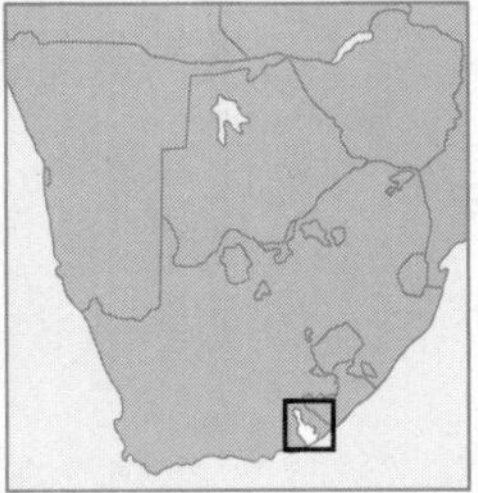

Ciskei

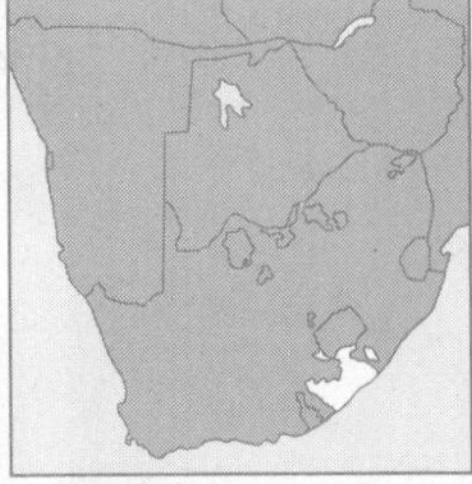

Transkei

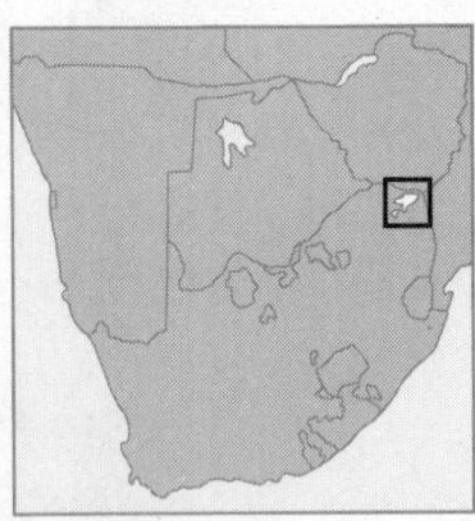

Venda

the face of initial South African objections. Eventually, under pressure from South Africa, it agreed to accept some limitations on the service.

Ciskei. Bordering the Indian Ocean in the south and surrounded on land by South Africa, Ciskei is separated by a narrow corridor of land from Transkei to the east. Area: 5,386 sq km (2,080 sq mi). Pop. (1983 est.) 690,000, including 99.7% Xhosa. Cap.: Bisho (pop., 1970 est., 4,800). Largest city: Mdantsane (pop., 1982 est., 200,000). Language: Xhosa (official); English may be used for official purposes. Religion: predominantly Christian (Methodist, Lutheran, Anglican, and Bantu Christian churches). President in 1983, Lennox Sebe.

Ciskei obtained a material contribution from the South African decentralization program in the shape of incentives to industrial investment. A report drawn up by the Stellenbosch University Institution for Planning and financed by South Africa mapped out a long-term plan of economic growth for Ciskei. Organized efforts were made to stimulate tourism and the flow of foreign capital.

The industrialized area on the border near East London was the scene of considerable labour unrest. Trade unions were active, and a number of their leaders were among more than a hundred detainees, including the secretary-general of the Southern Africa Catholic Bishops' Conference, held by the Ciskei security forces.

Evidence of friction within the administration came to the surface when Charles Sebe, brother of Pres. Lennox Sebe, was dismissed from his post as chief of the combined military and paramilitary security force, along with several senior officials. He was later named as head of a national intelligence service which replaced the combined security force, but which possessed limited powers.

Transkei. Bordering the Indian Ocean and surrounded on land by South Africa, Transkei comprises three discontinuous geographic units, two of which are landlocked. Area: 43,553 sq km (16,816 sq mi). Pop. (1982 est.): 2.4 million, including (1970) Xhosa 95%. Cap. and largest city: Umtata (pop., 1978 est., 30,000). Language: Xhosa (official); English and Sesotho may be used for official purposes. Religion: Christian 65.8%, of which Methodist 25.2%; non-Christian 13.8%; 20.4% unspecified. President in 1983, Kaiser Daliwonga Matanzima; prime minister, George Matanzima.

Alone among the four black homelands that had been granted independence, Transkei associated itself with a "declaration of intent" in which six black national leaders vowed to work for the establishment of "a greater South Africa," free of apartheid. The signatories, besides Pres. Kaiser Matanzima, included Gatsha Buthelezi, chief minister of KwaZulu, whose Inkatha movement had in the past incurred the opposition of Matanzima. During the South African constitutional debate Transkei subscribed to a statement condemning the exclusion of blacks from the proposed constitution. These moves were interpreted as a sign of Transkei's desire to regain a place in a politically integrated multiracial South Africa.

Transkei was one of the areas directly affected by South Africa's program of regional development. At the same time it was openly at odds with the South African government over the proposed repatriation and resettlement of Transkeians, estimated at about 120,000, who were living in South Africa and were in many cases classed as illegal migrant labourers. Transkei was not prepared to accept the policy of large-scale repatriation, as it had no work and no housing for the people concerned.

Venda. The republic of Venda comprises two geographic units in extreme northeastern South Africa separated by a narrow corridor belonging to its eastern neighbour, the Gazankulu homeland. Area: 6,198 sq km (2,393 sq mi). Pop. (1983 est.): 387,000, including (1970) 90% Venda; 6% Shangaan; 3% Northern Sotho. Cap.: Thohoyandou. Largest town: Makerela (pop., 1976 est., 1,972). Language (official): Venda, English, and Afrikaans. Religion: traditional religions predominate; Christian minority. President in 1983. Patrick Mphephu.

Venda was known to have unexploited coal resources, which could, if proved, form the basis of a more diversified economy. Early in 1983 a first step toward their development was taken when the South African Iron and Steel Corp. announced plans to open a pilot coal mine.

Venda benefited to a limited extent from a measure of priority participation in the South African decentralization policy of providing incentives for industrial development. What effect that policy would have in such an area, where 90% of the population depended on subsistence farming, remained to be seen. Meanwhile, Venda looked to the encouragement of tourism as a source of income. (LOUIS HOTZ)

See also Dependent States.

Southeast Asian Affairs

For the nations of Southeast Asia the political and military stalemate over Kampuchea continued in 1983 to be the dominant international issue. Signs of a breakthrough early in the year proved premature, and by year's end the Kampuchean imbroglio seemed as far from resolution as ever. The growing stature on the world stage of the Association of Southeast Asian Nations (ASEAN; comprising Indonesia, Singapore, Malaysia, Thailand, and the Philippines) was confirmed by the group's activities in global forums and the attention given it by the big powers. Other issues that made headlines in 1983 in Southeast Asia were internal security, narcotics, refugees, and economic cooperation.

With a cautious but unmistakable Sino-Soviet thaw already under way in 1982, Indochina watchers were on the lookout for signs that the development might affect events in Vietnam-occupied Kampuchea. Moscow was Vietnam's principal sponsor, while China was the top ally and arms supplier to the Communist Khmer Rouge, the dominant faction in the ASEAN-backed, UN-recognized resistance coalition of Democratic Kampuchea. In late January China gave extensive publicity to the "secret visit" of coalition president Prince Norodom Sihanouk to loyalist troops inside Kampuchea. Chinese Premier Zhao Ziyang (Chao Tzu-yang) even hinted that the internationally respected prince might play a role equal to that of the widely abhorred Khmer Rouge in his country's struggle for "national reconstruction"—presumably after a political settlement involving a withdrawal of Vietnamese troops. The same week Soviet Deputy Foreign Minister Mikhail Kapitsa, on a visit to Bangkok, Thailand, bore a message from Soviet Premier Nikolay Tikhonov pledging Moscow's cooperation in talks "to solve regional problems through political means." After discussions with Kapitsa, his Thai counterpart, Arun Phanuphong, suggested that Vietnam might soon be making "new proposals" to break the Kampuchea deadlock.

Instead, Vietnam went on the warpath and launched two major assaults on refugee camps at the Thai-Kampuchean border. (*See* KAMPUCHEA.) Soon after the second (and fiercer) attack in late March, China began artillery offensives on the Sino-Vietnamese frontier. These skirmishes lasted six days, with Beijing (Peking) claiming to have killed 37 Vietnamese, including supposed "secret agents" and intruders into Chinese territory. More significantly, the new tensions quickly put a brake on the Sino-Soviet thaw—to Vietnam's advantage. China criticized the Soviets for backing the Vietnamese blitzes, and each accused the other of "sabotaging" the thaw.

While those events were cooling Chinese and Soviet enthusiasm to work constructively for a settlement in Kampuchea, another outside power stepped into the breach. Announcing that his government hoped to "facilitate" an Indochinese peace, Australian Foreign Minister William Hayden embarked on a tour of ASEAN countries in late April. The ASEAN governments, however, disagreed with the aim of Canberra's new Labor Party administration to resume aid to Vietnam. Australian-ASEAN differences flared into the open shortly after Australia refused in early October to co-sponsor an ASEAN-drafted UN resolution condemning the 1979 Vietnamese invasion of Kampuchea and calling for the withdrawal of foreign troops and free elections there. Hayden was angered when he read in an Australian newspaper that Singapore Foreign Minister Suppiah Dhanabalan had accused him of "trying to bend over backwards to please Vietnam."

It was left to Australian Prime Minister Robert Hawke (*see* BIOGRAPHIES) to smooth over the most acrimonious ASEAN-Canberra row in years when he visited Bangkok in November. After assuring his Southeast Asian hosts that Australia "had taken no decision in practical terms" to resume development aid to Vietnam, Hawke said that he "could not have been more satisfied" with the results of his trip. Indeed, ASEAN and Australia had good reasons to maintain friendly relations. For Canberra, ASEAN was the keystone of its Asian policy, while for the Southeast Asians, disrupted ties with Australia could jeopardize economic cooperation and development aid.

Another country that saw ASEAN as the key to stability in Southeast Asia was the U.S., despite its lingering nervousness about involvement in the region after the Vietnam war. On a visit to the Philippines and Thailand in June, U.S. Secretary of State George Shultz reaffirmed Washington's support for ASEAN's policy on Kampuchea. However, Shultz turned down an ASEAN request for "nonlethal" military aid to the Khmer resistance, saying only that the U.S. would continue to give diplomatic, political, and moral support. A chance to pursue the issues further was lost when U.S. Pres. Ronald Reagan postponed a trip to Thailand, Indonesia, and the Philippines scheduled for November.

Also interested in good relations with ASEAN was Japanese Prime Minister Yasuhiro Nakasone,

In April Chinese artillery fired on Vietnamese positions in newly intensified fighting along the border between the two countries.

UPI

who made a highly successful 11-day tour in May of the association's five member states and the sultanate of Brunei. He reaffirmed Japan's support for the ASEAN position on Kampuchea, promised more development aid, gave assurances that his country's modest rearmament plans would not threaten Southeast Asia, and promised to consult ASEAN on matters affecting the region. Nakasone had good reason to be pleased with the results of his trip, for Japan had long had an image problem in Southeast Asia, which supplied its economy with vital raw materials. As Philippine Pres. Ferdinand Marcos put it: "The unspoken feeling of most of the countries in Southeast Asia has always been that what Japan failed to get during the war, she has succeeded in obtaining by economic conditions." Nakasone reassured ASEAN leaders on Japan's current defense buildup by making clear that the controversial "1,000-nautical-mile sealanes" the Japanese Navy intended to patrol stopped well short of the nearest Southeast Asian country, the Philippines.

The Soviet Union fared considerably worse in its dealings with the association. Already a bugbear to ASEAN because of its sponsorship of Vietnam's occupation of Kampuchea and its introduction of powerful warships into the ports of Vietnam, Moscow attracted further antagonism by rejecting demands that it remove SS-20 nuclear missiles targeted on Asia. Also taken badly was a warning by Kapitsa that the Soviet Union would join Vietnam in starting to supply arms to insurgents within the ASEAN states unless the association stopped supporting Khmer resistance groups. In Malaysia the threat led to public protests and the burning of the Soviet flag. Moscow-ASEAN ties plummeted further as Soviet personnel were warned or expelled for espionage in several countries in the region.

ASEAN's international stature was underscored during the summit meeting of the 101-nation nonaligned movement in March in New Delhi, India, where the organization (especially Singapore) lobbied its case for Kampuchea vigorously and effectively. As a result, the summit's final declaration urged "a comprehensive political solution which would provide for the withdrawal of all foreign forces, thus ensuring full respect for the sovereignty, independence, and territorial integrity of all states in the Southeast Asian region, including Kampuchea." ASEAN notched up another important diplomatic victory in October when, for the first time in five years, Vietnam declined to press a challenge to the legitimacy of Democratic Kampuchea as the legal representative of the Kampuchean nation.

Internally, non-Communist Southeast Asia continued to be troubled by destabilizing forces. A growing, though as yet containable, threat in ASEAN's Muslim countries was Islamic fundamentalism. Already closely monitored by authorities in Indonesia and Malaysia, it turned a new corner in 1983 when evidence was uncovered that Iran had become involved. Indonesian officials revealed in October that a "strong warning" had been delivered to Iran's chargé d'affaires in Jakarta against the publication and distribution of literature which "printed Ayatollah Khomeini's thinking and incited to revolution." Five men were arrested in Jogjakarta for possessing pamphlets propagating a fundamentalist doctrine that directly challenged the national creed of Indonesia, the world's most populous Muslim country. In Malaysia, too, growing proselytizing by Khomeini-inspired elements put the government on the alert. On the anti-insurgency front, Thailand and Malaysia continued to chalk up successes. Joint border cooperation improved, an important development highlighted by the simultaneous surrender ceremony in November of 470 Thai Muslim separatists, 166 Thai Communist Party members, and 44 Malayan Communist Party guerrillas.

Refugees from Indochina continued to arrive in the ASEAN countries and Hong Kong, though the problem, so acute a few years earlier, appeared to have peaked. (*See* REFUGEES.) There was an upsurge in regional narcotics trafficking, resulting from a third successive bumper crop of opium in the "Golden Triangle" area of Thailand, Burma, and Laos.

As the leading industrialized countries began to climb out of global recession in 1983, so too did the non-Communist economies of Southeast Asia; demand rose for their traditional exports of commodities. In June Malaysia, Indonesia, and Thailand, which together account for the bulk of world tin production, signed a long-debated agreement to form a cartel, the Association of Tin Producing Countries. Private-sector industrial joint ventures were encouraged by an accord signed in October that would open up more markets in the region through preferential tariff treatment.

(THOMAS HON WING POLIN)

See also articles on the various political units.
[976.B]

Space Exploration

Two major events in space exploration took place in 1983. First, on June 13 the U.S. probe Pioneer 10 left the Solar System for a journey through outer space, the first man-made object to do so. Second, after a launch in January, the Infrared Astronomical Satellite (IRAS) detected swarms of large particles around the star Vega. Some astronomers suggested that they were planets. A statement released by the Jet Propulsion Laboratory (JPL) in Pasadena, Calif., said, "The discovery provides the first direct evidence that solid objects of substantial size exist around a star other than the Sun. . . . The material could be a solar system at a different stage of development than our own."

Manned Flight. During the year the U.S. National Aeronautics and Space Administration (NASA) announced that the space shuttle orbiter "Columbia," which had flown five missions, would be grounded until late 1983. The decision was made because of the production of the B-1 bomber at the plant where the space shuttle orbiters are manufactured. During the period of storage at the Kennedy Space Center the "Columbia" was to undergo extensive modifications that were planned earlier. Indicating that manned space-

South West Africa: *see* Dependent States; South Africa

Soviet Literature: *see* Literature

Soviet Union: *see* Union of Soviet Socialist Republics

flight was still extremely popular with the U.S. public, a total of 1,588,000 people called a special toll telephone number to listen in as the astronauts of STS 6 and 7 space shuttle missions communicated with the Mission Control Center at the Johnson Space Center in Houston, Texas.

While the space shuttle made headlines in the U.S., the Soviet Union continued what appeared to be a steady progression toward the ultimate establishment of a large, multimanned space station. A new chapter in this development was written on March 2 when Cosmos 1443 was launched and subsequently docked with the Salyut 7 space station. The docking was accomplished remotely since the space station was not manned. On March 10 the Cosmos 1443 took over the station-keeping functions for the space station.

Cosmos 1443 was described by the Soviets as a space tug, a vehicle that had no planned or existing counterpart in the U.S. space program. Consisting of two compartments, one of which is designed to return to the Earth, the cylindrical spacecraft is 13 m (42.6 ft) long and 4 m (13.1 ft) in diameter. Two solar panels with a span of 16 m (52.5 ft) and a surface area of 16 sq m (430.6 sq ft) provide 3 kw of electric power for its own systems or for the space station to which it is attached. The tug provides an additional 50 cu m (1,765.7 cu ft) of living and work space for the crew of the Salyut 7.

On April 20 a new crew for Salyut 7 was launched in Soyuz T-8. It consisted of Lieut. Col. Vladimir G. Titov, commander; Gennadi M. Strekalov, pilot; and Aleksandr A. Serebrov, scientific researcher. However, their mission was aborted on April 21 and a day later they returned to the Earth without having docked with the space station. Failure in the automatic docking system and a limited supply of propellants for maneuvering the Soyuz T-8 caused mission controllers on the Earth to end the mission.

Soyuz T-9—with cosmonauts Col. Vladimir A. Lyakhov, commander; and Aleksandr P. Aleksandrov, flight engineer—was launched on June 27. The new crew immediately set to work unloading the supplies in the Cosmos 1443. While Lyakhov adapted to weightlessness easily, his companion experienced the familiar symptoms of the "space adaptation syndrome" that has affected many astronauts and cosmonauts—loss of appetite, nausea, and difficulty in sleeping. However, these symptoms disappeared in a few days.

On August 14 the Cosmos 1443 was separated from the space station while the crew monitored the procedure. Among the 350 kg (771.6 lb) of cargo it returned to Earth were materials from more than 45 experiments and a 70-kg (154.3-lb) air regenerator so that engineers on the Earth could inspect its filters. Samples of air and dust from the space station were also included as were exposed photographic films. After performing various experiments aboard Salyut 7, including the attachment to it of a solar cell battery, Lyakhov and Aleksandrov returned to the Earth in November.

The Soviet space program received a temporary setback when a Soviet rocket that was carrying a Soyuz T transport craft with two cosmonauts aboard exploded at the launching pad on September 27. The cosmonauts survived unharmed when emergency escape rockets jettisoned their capsule clear of the blast.

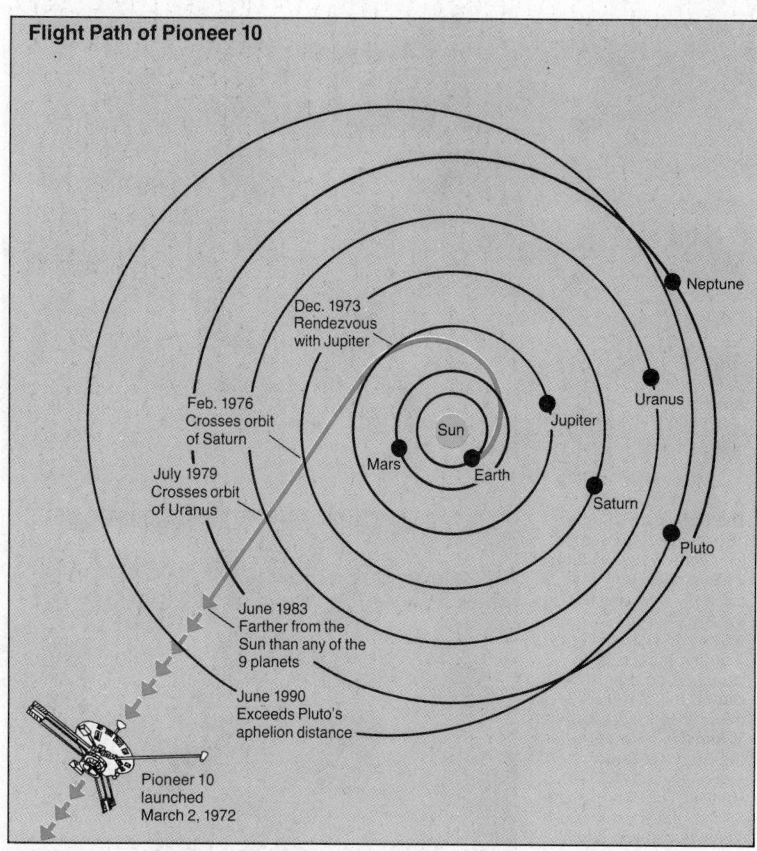

Pioneer 10 was designed to operate just long enough to rendezvous with Jupiter in December 1973, but in June 1983 it became the first human artifact to leave the Solar System. Nearly 11 years after its launching, the still-functioning space probe is farther from the Sun than any of its nine planets. Pluto is normally the outermost planet, but its orbit is so eccentric that it had been closer to the Sun than Neptune for four years and would remain so for nearly a decade after Pioneer 10 exceeded Pluto's maximum possible distance from the Sun in 1990.

In the U.S. the space shuttle continued to demonstrate its versatility and reliability. On April 4 the "Challenger" orbiter lifted off from the Kennedy Space Center in Florida on its first voyage. Its crew consisted of Paul J. Weitz, commander; Col. Karol J. Bobko, pilot; and Donald H. Peterson and F. Story Musgrave, mission specialists. A high point of the mission occurred on April 7 when Musgrave and Peterson left the pressurized compartment of the "Challenger" and entered the open space environment of the cargo bay, thereby testing the space shuttle spacesuits for the first time. The spacesuits performed perfectly. Musgrave and Peterson also supervised the launching of NASA's Tracking and Data Relay Satellite. "Challenger's" mission ended successfully with its landing at Edwards Air Force Base in California on April 9.

The "Challenger" was again launched from the Kennedy Space Center on June 18. On this mission it carried the largest crew ever launched into space at the same time. It included Robert Crippen, commander; Navy Commander Frederick Hauck, pilot; and mission specialists Lieut. Col. John M. Fabian, Norman Thagard, and Sally Ride (*see* BIOGRAPHIES), the first U.S. woman in space.

Primary objectives for the mission were the launching of the Anik C2 Canadian communications satellite and the Indonesian Palaba B communications satellite. They were successfully deployed on June 18 and June 19, respectively.

Thagard, a medical doctor, was included in the

PHOTOGRAPHS, UPI

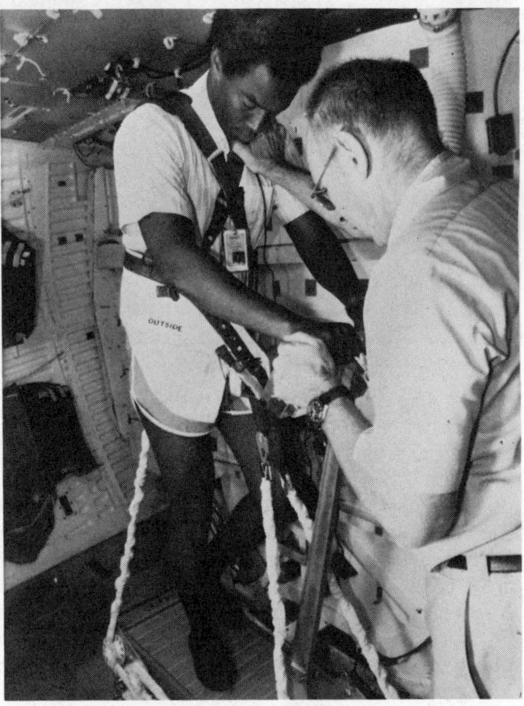

The U.S. space shuttle "Challenger" continued to record firsts. On June 18 Sally Ride (top photo), a mission specialist, became the first U.S. woman in space. (Right) The first night flight, launched on August 30, carried the first black, a mission specialist, Guion S. Bluford, here performing exercises under the eye of space physician William Thornton, at age 54 the oldest astronaut to make a space flight.

crew to conduct medical tests that might lead to clues concerning the causes of the space adaptation syndrome. In doing so, he performed examinations and tests on himself as well as his fellow crew members. The "Challenger" ended its mission by landing at Edwards Air Force Base on June 24.

The "Challenger" accomplished its first night launch on August 30 from Kennedy Space Center. The crew included U.S. Navy Capt. Richard Truly, commander; Commander Daniel Brandenstein, pilot; and mission specialists William Thornton, U.S. Air Force Lieut. Col. Guion Bluford, and Navy Lieut. Comdr. Dale Gardner. Bluford was the first black American to go into space and the second black to orbit the Earth.

The principal tasks for the mission were to launch the Insat 1-B Indian weather-communications satellite and to maneuver a 3,383.8-kg (7,460-lb) payload flight test unit using the orbiter's remote manipulator arm. The Insat 1-B was successfully deployed on August 31. Maneuvers with the payload flight test unit were begun by Gardner on September 1, and after 15 hours of use the remote arm proved it could function as designed.

Thornton, a medical doctor, continued tests and experiments into the causes of the space adaptation syndrome. The highly successful mission ended with a night landing at Edwards Air Force Base on September 5.

Carrying the European-built Spacelab, the space shuttle "Columbia" was launched on November 28 from the Kennedy Space Center. Six astronauts, the most ever carried on one flight, were aboard. The four scientists—Robert Parker, Owen Garriott, Byron Lichtenberg, and Ulf Merbold, a West German—underwent extensive physiological testing during the ten-day mission. Although plagued by malfunctions in its last hours, "Columbia" landed safely on December 8.

Unmanned Satellites. In 1983 the U.S. House of Representatives included in the NASA budget bill provisions that would prohibit the Reagan administration from selling weather and Earth-resources satellites to the private sector. In Europe a multinational organization, Eumetsat, was formed on May 24 to manage a network of European weather satellites. In addition to the 11 member nations of the European Space Agency (ESA), delegates from Austria, Finland, Greece, Norway, Portugal, and Turkey attended the organizing meeting in Paris.

The year 1983 opened with the launch on January 25 of the IRAS, a joint project of the U.S., The Netherlands, and the U.K. The satellite immediately began transmitting a wealth of data that continued to accrue as the spacecraft slowly tumbled end-over-end scanning outer space. By the end of the year NASA administrator James Beggs called the discoveries "nothing short of spectacular." The IRAS ceased operation in late November.

Besides the possible planetary system around the star Vega, early findings included two galaxies that seemed to be colliding, five previously unknown comets—one of which passed the Earth on May 11 at a distance of only 4,670,000 km (2.9 million mi), and what was termed "a monster star" in the Magellanic Clouds.

The IRAS also detected dozens of large and very cold objects outside the Solar System and three bands of dust between Mars and Jupiter. The satellite produced data to indicate that large clouds of carbon particles exist throughout the sky. It also observed a new object, 1983 TB, which may be the parent body for the swarm of meteoroids called Geminids. Additionally, the IRAS continued to report new galaxies that emit infrared radiation not visible through Earth-based telescopes.

The U.S.S.R. launched an advanced scientific satellite for studying cosmic radiation from galactic and extragalactic sources on March 23. Astron was a cooperative project with France, which assisted in development of the satellite's ultraviolet telescope. It was based on the Venera space probe design and was supplied with scientific instruments of the types used on the Salyut manned space station. The primary instrument aboard the spacecraft was an 80-cm (31.5-in)-diameter mirror. Among the valuable new scientific data discovered by Astron, it was found that the star Kappa in the

Major Satellites and Space Probes Launched Oct. 1, 1982–Sept. 30, 1983

Name/country/ launch vehicle/ scientific designation	Launch date, lifetime*	Physical characteristics: Weight in kg†	Shape	Diameter in m†	Length or height in m†	Experiments	Orbital elements: Perigee in km†	Apogee in km†	Period (min)	Inclination to Equator (degrees)
Satcom 5/U.S./Delta/ 1982-105A	10/28/82	1,111 (2,450)	cube with two solar panels and antenna	1.27 (4.17)	1.6 (5.25)	Communications satellite	35,781 (22,233)	35,791 (22,239)	1,436.1	0.1
Progress 16/U.S.S.R./A II/ 1982-107A	10/31/82	7,020 (15,476)	sphere and cone	2.2 (7.22)	7.9 (25.92)	Ferried supplies to Salyut 7 space station	186 (116)	245 (152)	88.75	51.62
STS 5 ("Columbia")/U.S./ Space Shuttle/1982-110A	11/11/82 11/16/82	2,035,976 (4,488,559)	delta with two solid boosters and external tank	24 (78.7)	37 (121.4)	Launched two satellites; crew performed scientific experiments	294 (182)	317 (197)	90.49	28.47
SBS 3/U.S./Space Shuttle/ 1982-110B	11/11/82	580 (1,279)	cylinder	2 (6.6)	6 (19.7)	Business communications satellite	35,788 (22,238)	35,790 (22,239)	1,436.2	0.0
Telsat 6 (Anik C-3)/U.S./ Space Shuttle/1982-110C	11/12/82	2,100 (4,630)	cylinder	1.5 (4.92)	2 (6.6)	Canadian communications satellite	35,777 (22,231)	35,794 (22,241)	1,436.0	0.0
Iskra 3/U.S.S.R./Salyut 7/ 1982-033AD	11/18/82	‡	‡	‡	‡	Amateur radio relay satellite	350 (217)	365 (227)	91.5	51.6
Raduga 11/U.S.S.R./D le/ 1982-113A	11/26/82	2,000 (4,409)	cylinder with two solar panels	2 (6.6)	5 (16.4)	Communications satellite	35,721 (22,196)	35,848 (22,275)	1,436.0	1.0
AMS 5/U.S./Thor/ 1982-118A	12/21/82	751 (1,656)	cylinder	‡	‡	Weather satellite	810 (503)	814 (506)	101.2	98.7
IRAS/U.S./Delta/ 1983-004A	1/25/83	1,073 (2,365)	cylinder	2.0 (6.6)	3.6 (11.81)	Infrared astronomical observatory	889 (552)	913 (567)	103.0	99.1
Sakura-2A/Japan/N-2/ 1983-006A	2/4/83	670 (1,477)	cylinder	2.18 (7.15)	2.05 (6.73)	Communications satellite	35,782 (22,234)	35,794 (22,241)	1,436.2	0.0
Tenma/Japan/Mu-3s/ 1983-011A	2/20/83	‡	‡	‡	‡	Scientific satellite for observation in the X-ray and gamma-ray spectra	488 (303)	503 (313)	94.38	31.5
Cosmos 1443/U.S.S.R./D I/ 1983-013A	3/2/83 8/14/83	20,000 (44,092)	cylinder	4 (13.1)	13 (42.6)	Structural enlargement of Salyut 7 space station	195 (121)	235 (146)	88.7	51.6
Ekran 10 (Stasionar T)/ U.S.S.R./D le/1983-016A	3/12/83	2,000 (4,409)	cylinder with two solar panels	2 (6.6)	5 (16.4)	Communications satellite	35,759 (22,220)	35,809 (22,251)	1,436.0	0.1
Astron/U.S.S.R./D le/ 1983-020A	3/23/83	3,900 (8,598)	cylinder with two solar panels	2.5 (8.2)	3 (9.8)	Astronomical observatory in ultraviolet spectrum	1,950 (1,212)	201,121 (124,971)	5,880.0	51.1
NOAA 8/U.S./Atlas/ 1983-022A	3/28/83	1,712 (3,775)	box	2 (6.6)	4 (13.1)	Meteorological satellite with a search-and-rescue unit	803 (499)	826 (513)	101.2	98.8
STS 6 ("Challenger")/U.S./ Space Shuttle/1983-026A	4/4/83 4/9/83	2,034,666 (4,485,670)	delta with two solid boosters and external tank	24 (78.7)	37 (121.4)	First flight of "Challenger;" launched TDRS 1 communications satellite	285 (177)	291 (181)	90.3	28.5
TDRS 1/U.S./Space Shuttle/1983-026B	4/5/83	1,500 (3,307)	irregular box with two antennas and two solar panels	2 (6.6)	6 (19.7)	Communications satellite	21,839 (13,570)	35,404 (21,999)	1,086.0	2.3
Raduga 12/U.S.S.R./D le/ 1983-028A	4/8/83	2,000 (4,409)	cylinder with pair of solar panels	2 (6.6)	5 (16.4)	Communications satellite	35,780 (22,233)	35,790 (22,239)	1,436.0	1.2
Soyuz T-8/U.S.S.R./A II/ 1983-035A	4/20/83 4/22/83	7,000 (15,432)	sphere and cone with two solar panels	2.2 (7.22)	7.5 (24.61)	Ferried crew of three to Salyut 7 space station	196 (122)	213 (132)	88.6	51.6
GOES 6/U.S./Delta/ 1983-041A	4/28/83	800 (1,764)	cylinder	2 (6.6)	3 (9.8)	Meteorological satellite	33,483 (20,805)	48,400 (30,074)	1,707.4	0.5
Intelsat 5 (F-6)/U.S./Atlas/ 1983-047A	5/19/83	1,870 (4,123)	box with two solar panels	1.8 (5.91)	2 (6.6)	Communications satellite	35,788 (22,238)	35,799 (22,244)	1,436.2	0.0
Exosat/ESA/Delta/ 1983-051A	5/26/83	‡	cube with one solar panel	‡	‡	Study X-rays from deep space	350 (217)	192,000 (119,303)	5,430.0	72.5
Venera 15/U.S.S.R./D le/ 1983-053A	6/2/83	4,000 (8,818)	cylinder with two solar panels	2.3 (7.55)	2.7 (8.86)	Scientific study of Venus	Trajectory to Venus			
Venera 16/U.S.S.R./D le/ 1983-054A	6/7/83	4,000 (8,818)	cylinder with two solar panels	2.3 (7.55)	2.7 (8.86)	Scientific study of Venus	Trajectory to Venus			
ECS 1/ESA/Ariane/ 1983-058A	6/16/83	1,043 (2,299)	hexagon with two solar panels	2.2 (7.22)	2.4 (7.87)	Communications satellite	‡	‡	‡	‡
Amsat P3B (Oscar 10)/ESA/ Ariane/1983-058B	6/16/83	130 (287)	three-pointed star	1.26 (4.13)	0.43 (1.41)	Amateur radio satellite	3,900 (2,423)	35,800 (22,245)	699.6	26.1
STS 7 ("Challenger")/U.S./ Space Shuttle/1983-059A	6/18/83 6/24/83	2,036,592 (4,489,916)	delta with two solid boosters and external tank	24 (78.7)	37 (121.4)	Scientific experiments; launched two communications satellites	298 (185)	298 (185)	95.0	28.0
Anik C-3/Canada/Space Shuttle/1983-059B	6/18/83	925 (2,039)	cylinder	2.2 (7.22)	6.4 (21)	Communications satellite	35,783 (22,235)	35,792 (22,240)	1,436.1	0.1
Palaba B/Indonesia/ Space Shuttle/1983-059C	6/18/83	630 (1,389)	cylinder	2.16 (7.09)	2.73 (8.96)	Communications satellite	35,782 (22,234)	35,791 (22,239)	1,436.1	0.1
Soyuz T-9/U.S.S.R./A II/ 1983-062A	6/27/83	6,850 (15,102)	sphere and cone	2.7 (8.86)	7 (23)	Ferried crew of two to Salyut 7 space station	328 (204)	343 (213)	91.4	51.6
Galaxy 1/U.S./Delta/ 1983-065A	6/28/83	554 (1,222)	cylinder	2.16 (7.09)	6.83 (22.4)	Cable television satellite	35,783 (22,235)	35,788 (22,238)	1,436.1	0.1
NavStar 6/U.S./Atlas F/ 1983-072A	7/14/83	771 (1,700)	polygon with two solar panels	5.33 (17.5)	‡	Military navigation satellite	19,921 (12,378)	20,442 (12,702)	718.0	62.8
China 13/China/ ‡ / 1983-086A	8/19/83	‡	‡	‡	‡	Scientific experiments	160 (99)	266 (165)	88.8	63.3
STS 8 ("Challenger")/U.S./ Space Shuttle/1983-089A	8/30/83 9/5/83	2,037,365 (4,491,622)	delta with two solid boosters and external tank	24 (78.7)	37 (121.4)	Scientific experiments; launch of Insat 1-B satellite	221 (137)	229 (142)	89.0	28.5
Galaxy 2/U.S./Delta/ 1983-098A	9/22/83	559 (1,282)	cylinder	2.16 (7.09)	6.83 (22.4)	Communications satellite	‡	‡	‡	‡

* All dates are in universal time (UT). † English units in parentheses: weight in pounds, dimensions in feet, apogee and perigee in statute miles. ‡ Not available.

(MITCHELL R. SHARPE)

WIDE WORLD

Two Soviet cosmonauts were stranded in orbit for a time in September in a Salyut 7 space station crippled by a propellant leak. They are shown here earlier in the year in training in a mock-up of the craft.

constellation Cancer has approximately 100 times more of the element lead than the Sun.

ESA's European Communications Satellite (ECS 1) was launched on June 16. Two days later it began drifting toward its ultimate location in geostationary orbit. It arrived there on July 7 and was then stabilized. The satellite was the first in a series to be procured by ESA for Eutelsat. Its telephone and television services were to cover an area from Iceland to the Middle East and from Finland to the Azores and parts of North Africa.

Space Probes. Efforts continued throughout the spring to reestablish contact with the Viking 1 lander on Mars. Signals had ceased in November 1982. The problem seemed to lie first in a misdirection in pointing the probe's antenna away from the Earth and later in discharged batteries. In May the decision was made by the JPL to cease further attempts to communicate with the probe.

On June 2 and 7 the U.S.S.R. launched the Venera 15 and Venera 16 probes to Venus. East German scientists participated in developing the instrumentation of the probes. Both spacecraft were instrumented to map the planet by high-resolution imaging radar and study the constituents of its atmosphere. Venera 15 went into orbit around Venus on October 10, and its companion followed on October 14.

One of the most significant events of the year occurred on June 13 when the U.S. probe Pioneer 10 became the first man-made object to leave the known limits of the Solar System. It carried a plaque designed by astronomer Carl Sagan showing the appearance of a man and woman, as well as the Solar System with the planet Earth indicated as the origin of the probe. NASA hoped to continue tracking Pioneer 10 for another decade, when it would be 8,000,000,000 km (5,000,000,000 mi) from the Earth. Electric power for its communications systems was no problem because Pioneer 10 was equipped with a radioisotopic power supply that should last for another 20 years. NASA scientists theorized that its closest approach to another star in the next 850,000 years would be to the star Ross 248, passing it at a distance of 3.27 light-years (1 light-year = 5,878,000,000,000 mi).

(MITCHELL R. SHARPE)

See also Astronomy; Defense; Earth Sciences; Industrial Review: *Aerospace; Telecommunications;* Television and Radio.
[738.C]

Spain

A constitutional monarchy of southwestern Europe, Spain is bounded by Portugal, with which it shares the Iberian Peninsula, and by France. Area: 504,750 sq km (194,885 sq mi), including the Balearic and Canary islands. Pop. (1982 est.): 37,833,900, including the Balearics and Canaries. Cap. and largest city: Madrid (pop., 1982, 3,271,800). Language: Spanish. Religion: Roman Catholic. King, Juan Carlos I; premier in 1983, Felipe González Márquez.

The Partido Socialista Obrero Español (PSOE; Spanish Socialist Labour Party) repeated its success in the 1982 general elections by gaining victories in municipal and regional elections held on May 8, 1983. In the municipal elections the PSOE increased its share of the vote to 43% from 28% in 1979, while the Alianza Popular (AP) won 25% and the Partido Comunista Español (PCE) took 8%. In 200 municipalities the PSOE and PCE agreed to share control of town councils. In the regional elections 13 of the 17 regions went to the polls. The PSOE won an absolute majority in Asturias, Aragón, Extremadura, La Rioja, Madrid, and Valencia and a simple majority in the Canary Islands, Castilla-Leon, Castilla-La Mancha, and Murcia. In Navarra the problems of constructing a solid majority halted the formation of a government. The AP held an overall majority in Cantabria and the balance of power in the Balearics.

On August 10 the Constitutional Court ruled that 14 of 38 articles in the Organic Law on the Harmonization of the Autonomy Process were unconstitutional and that the law was not an organic (basic) one. Opponents of the law maintained that it reinforced central government control. Despite the court's findings, the government announced that it would implement the remaining 24 constitutional articles and speed up the transfer of powers and resources to the regions.

Tension in the Army was high at the start of the year due to the uncertainties surrounding the takeover of power by the first Socialist government in 40 years. The results of a survey taken during the year indicated that six of ten members of the armed services were prepared to intervene to protect Spanish institutions and the unity of the state. The temper of the armed services was not improved by the passage of a bill in the Cortes (parliament) in November that aimed to modernize the Army by shaking out its top-heavy command structure.

The security situation in the Basque region dete-

UPI

A Spanish aristocrat descended from Christopher Columbus, Diego Prado y Colón de Carvajal (centre) was released after being kidnapped and held 73 days for ransom by Basque separatists. He is assisted here by his brother and wife.

riorated. On February 3 the PSOE walked out of the regional government because it claimed that the Basque Nationalist Party was not condemning the violent tactics of the Euzkadi ta Azkatasuna (ETA) terrorist groups. On February 28 ETA moved against the newly formed autonomous Basque police force for the first time, stealing equipment from its barracks. An increase in violence led to the introduction of special security laws for the Basque area on May 20. The legislation was toughened in November. A spate of flag burning occurred in July and August when the central government insisted that the Spanish and Basque flags be flown together. On November 15 the Basque Nationalist Party asked to take control of the police and armed services in the Basque country so that the regional government could be seen to be helping to solve the ETA problem. The appeal was not well received by the PSOE or by the Army, already deeply divided by the murder of officers serving in the area.

The 1983 budget, presented on April 23 and finally passed by August, represented a reinforcement of the previous year's attempts to contain inflation by means of tight money and credit policies. Earlier the employers' associations and trade unions backed the budget's anti-inflationary aspects by agreeing to wage increases of around 11%, below the forecast rate of inflation for 1983. However, the unions were strongly opposed to government plans to restructure heavy industry by eliminating jobs. Relations between the government and the Communist workers' commissions were particularly strained.

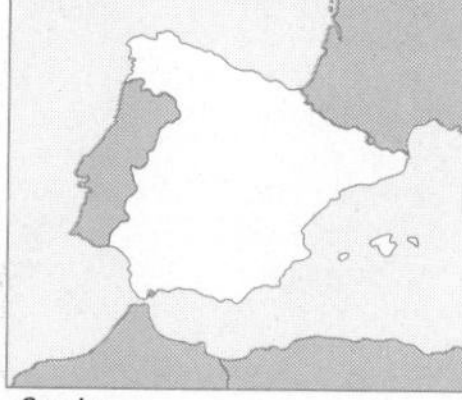

Spain

The government nationalized the Rumasa Group, Spain's largest privately owned holding concern, by decree on February 23. The AP backed an appeal to the Constitutional Court contesting the legality of the decree, but it later cooperated in securing passage of a motion through the Cortes to legalize the expropriation. Later in the year the government estimated that the group's losses totaled $1.7 billion and announced plans to return the business to the private sector.

In April the Supreme Court ruled on the government appeal against the light sentences passed on those involved in the February 1981 coup attempt. Gen. Alfonso Armada's sentence was increased to 30 years, and the maximum 30-year sentences passed on Lieut. Gen. Jaime Milans del Bosch and Lieut. Col. Antonio Tejero Molina were confirmed.

At the summit meeting of the European Communities (EC) in June at Stuttgart, West Germa-

SPAIN

Education. (1980–81) Primary, pupils 6,778,877, teachers 228,307; secondary, pupils 1,091,197, teachers 66,160; vocational, pupils 558,808, teachers 36,556; higher, students 649,098, teachers 40,321.

Finance. Monetary unit: peseta, with (Sept. 20, 1983) a free rate of 151.98 pesetas to U.S. $1 (228.88 pesetas = £1 sterling). Gold and other reserves (June 1983) U.S. $6,347,000,000. Budget (1982 actual): revenue 2,976,000,000,000 pesetas; expenditure 4,107,000,000,000 pesetas. Gross national product (1982) 19,471,000,000,000 pesetas. Money supply (Dec. 1982) 5,158,000,000,000 pesetas. Cost of living (1975 = 100; June 1983) 334.4.

Foreign Trade. (1982) Imports 3,466,000,000,000 pesetas; exports 2,258,000,000,000 pesetas. Import sources: EEC 31% (West Germany 9%, France 8%, U.K. 5%); U.S. 14%; Saudi Arabia 9%; Mexico 6%. Export destinations: EEC 46% (France 16%, West Germany 8%, U.K. 7%, Italy 6%, The Netherlands 5%); U.S. 6%. Main exports (1981): machinery 13%; motor vehicles 9%; fruit and vegetables 9%; iron and steel 9%; chemicals 7%; petroleum products 5%; textiles and clothing 5%. Tourism (1981): visitors 40,129,000; receipts U.S. $6,716,000,000.

Transport and Communications. Roads (including rural paths; 1982) 322,083 km (including 2,057 km expressways). Motor vehicles in use (1982): passenger 8,353,900; commercial 1,461,900. Railways (1981): 15,723 km (including 6,719 km electrified); traffic 15,511,000,000 passenger-km, freight (1982) c. 10,900,000,000 net ton-km. Air traffic (1982): 16,457,000,000 passenger-km; freight 482.2 million net ton-km. Shipping (1982): merchant vessels 100 gross tons and over 2,635; gross tonnage 8,130,693. Telephones (Dec. 1980) 11,844,600. Radio receivers (Dec. 1980) 9.6 million. Television receivers (1980) 9,424,000.

Agriculture. Production (in 000; metric tons; 1982): wheat 4,368; barley 5,280; oats 474; rye 170; corn 2,284; rice 409; potatoes 5,087; sugar, raw value 1,106; tomatoes 2,164; onions 1,061; cabbages (1981) 462; melons (1981) 770; watermelons (1981) 550; apples 913; pears (1981) 520; peaches (1981) 441; oranges 1,693; mandarin oranges and tangerines 837; lemons 428; sunflower seed 656; bananas 460; olives 3,174; olive oil 693; wine 3,901; tobacco c. 39; cotton, lint c. 45; cow's milk 6,080; hen's eggs c. 720; meat 2,624; fish catch (1981) 1,264. Livestock (in 000; 1982): cattle 5,073; pigs 11,712; sheep 17,095; goats 2,531; horses c. 242; chickens 54,158.

Industry. Index of industrial production (1975 = 100; 1982) 113. Fuel and power (in 000; metric tons; 1982): coal 15,585; lignite 23,493; crude oil 1,372; manufactured gas (cu m) c. 1,720,000; electricity (kw-hr) 113,766,000. Production (in 000; metric tons; 1982): cement 29,605; iron ore (50% metal content) 7,622; pig iron 6,081; crude steel 12,743; aluminum 366; copper 168; zinc 183; petroleum products (1981) 48,406; sulfuric acid (1981) 2,880; fertilizers (nutrient content; 1981–82) nitrogenous 890, phosphate 372, potash 721; cotton yarn (1978) 94; wool yarn (1978) 32; man-made fibres (1980) 259; passenger cars (units) 915; commercial vehicles (units) 111. Merchant vessels launched (100 gross tons and over; 1982) 613,000 gross tons.

ny, Pres. François Mitterrand of France again virtually vetoed the entry of Spain and Portugal to the EC by repeating that enlargement of the Communities could only take place after the problems of the common agricultural policy and the budget had been resolved. However, the unexpected breakthrough on Mediterranean farm products achieved by EC agricultural ministers in October removed one potentially serious block to progress.

Spain's participation in NATO remained frozen, although Premier Felipe González Márquez stated in May that he was not unsympathetic to the plan to install new nuclear missiles in Western Europe. Later that month Spain signed a contract with the U.S. for 72 F-18A fighters, while on June 21 González met Pres. Ronald Reagan in Washington for the first time and held cordial talks on the situation in Europe and Spain's efforts to resolve the Central American conflicts. González participated in a summit meeting in October with Europe's other socialist leaders. In November he visited Portugal, where he helped devise a plan for greater cooperation between the two nations in industry, agriculture, and environmental affairs. Portugal rejected a Spanish proposal to establish an Iberian free-trade zone, while the problem of Spanish fishing in Portuguese waters remained unresolved. In August Spain succeeded in negotiating a four-year fishing accord with Morocco, although isolated fishing disputes between the two countries continued. (MICHAEL WOOLLER)

Speleology

Persistent exploration and continued surveying increased the known length of the world's longest cave—the Mammoth Cave-Flint Ridge system in Kentucky—to 379.15 km (235.6 mi). An expedition of Australians and others reached a depth of 520 m (1,706 ft) in Mamo Kanada (formerly known as Hadea Yaneabugair) in the Muller Range of Papua New Guinea, establishing it as the second deepest cave in the Southern Hemisphere. More important, perhaps, they explored it to a length of 52 km (32.3 mi). Other cave expeditions in Southeast Asia included those of France in the Magkalihat and Meratus regions of Indonesian Borneo. Explorers from Belgium, Britain, and France joined Javanese in investigating the previously little-studied caves of Java. In the Gunong Sewa karst area of southern Java, one expedition explored many of the caves in search of a water supply to alleviate the local water shortage.

Cave diving again led to extensions of known caves or connections between them. In the Postojnska Jama system (Yugoslavia), divers penetrated a submerged connection between Crna Jama and Magdalena Jama, bringing the total length of the combined system to 14.6 km (9.07 mi). In Somerset, England, Martin Farr made further progress in the steeply descending Sump 25 of Wookey

Human Rights: Did Helsinki Matter?

The Madrid conference of the 35 governments that had signed the Final Act of the 1975 Helsinki Conference on Security and Cooperation in Europe ended in September 1983. It had first met in November 1980 to review compliance with the Final Act's terms. This was the second such follow-up conference; the first was held in Belgrade, Yugos., in 1977–78.

The conference began at a time of considerable deterioration in East-West relations in the wake of the Soviet occupation of Afghanistan. For a time, it was threatened with collapse, and work was suspended for most of 1982 to allow for an improvement in the political atmosphere. By March 1983 a draft put forward by eight neutral and nonaligned states had narrowed the focus of disagreement to five main areas: Soviet jamming of Western radio broadcasts; the persecution of so-called Helsinki monitoring groups in Eastern Europe; the defense of trade union rights; "human contacts" between East and West; and how to arrange a follow-up conference on disarmament and "confidence-building measures" (various ways of checking military movements in both parts of Europe).

A Spanish compromise formula put forward in June helped to break the deadlock. The deal worked out in Madrid did not guarantee that the Soviet Union and its allies would honour the Helsinki pledges regarding human rights and free contacts between East and West any more than they had done in the past. Before agreement was reached on the final document, proceedings were delayed for two months by Malta, which used the consensus principle to press, unsuccessfully, for a special conference on Mediterranean security problems. The Madrid meeting finally ended on September 9 amid renewed East-West controversy, sparked by the shooting down of a South Korean airliner by the Soviets on September 1.

The main points of the deal enshrined in the final document of the Madrid conference, dated Sept. 6, 1983, were:

(1) The Soviet Union's failure to end its jamming of Western radio broadcasts remained unrectified. (2) All states promised "genuinely" to implement the Helsinki agreement's promises on human rights, but nothing would be done directly to help Helsinki monitoring groups in the Soviet bloc. (3) The right to form and join a trade union was acknowledged, but there was no mention of the right to strike. (4) A special experts' conference would be held in Switzerland in 1986 to discuss family reunification and emigration. (5) A follow-up conference on disarmament and confidence-building measures would open in Stockholm on Jan. 17, 1984. The Soviets agreed to extend the area for prior notification of large military exercises to the Urals, about 965 km (600 mi) inside Soviet territory, instead of the current 240 km (150 mi). Agreements reached at Stockholm would be binding and verifiable, enabling Western governments to ask that observers attend large military maneuvers. (6) Foreign journalists were promised more protection from harassment by governments. Citizens from all the 35 countries were promised easier access to foreign diplomatic missions. (7) A meeting of experts on human rights would be held in Ottawa in 1985 and a review conference in Vienna in November 1986. (K. F. CVIIC)

Hole. The passage was still continuing downward at an underwater depth of 60 m (197 ft) when he had to turn back to ensure adequate decompression time. The long-sought connection between Gaping Gill and Ingleborough Cavern—British exploration sites for nearly 150 years—was discovered at last. Digging at both ends of a boulder choke produced at first only a "hand-shake" connection between the two. This link was enlarged, and on May 28, 1983, Geoffrey Yeadon and Geoffrey Cross came through from Gaping Gill to emerge at Ingleborough Cavern entrance, while Jim Abbott and Julian Griffiths made the reverse journey.

Radiocarbon dating of recent archaeological discoveries in Fraser Cave and Deena-Reena Cave in the Franklin River valley of southwestern Tasmania showed that they had been occupied by humans more than 20,500 years ago. They were thus the most southerly known human habitations in the world, having been occupied at the close of the last ice age. In eastern Tennessee a cave near Knoxville was found to contain Indian drawings made with the fingers on the damp mud of the cave walls. Radiocarbon dating of charcoal from Indian torches there indicated an age of between 400 and 700 years. (T. R. SHAW)

[232.A.5.e]

Sri Lanka

An Asian republic and member of the Commonwealth, Sri Lanka (Ceylon) occupies an island in the Indian Ocean off the southeast coast of peninsular India. Area: 65,610 sq km (25,332 sq mi). Pop. (1982 est.): 15,189,000, including Sinhalese 74%; Tamil 17.5%; Moors 7.1%; other 1.4%. Cap. and largest city: Colombo (pop., 1981 prelim., 585,800). Capital designate: Sri Jayawardenapura. Language: Sinhalese (official), Tamil, English. Religion (1981): Buddhist 69.4%; Hindu 15.5%; Muslim 7.6%; Christian 7.5%. President in 1983, Junius Richard Jayawardene; prime minister, Ranasinghe Premadasa.

Ethnic violence shook Sri Lanka in the last week of July 1983. Clashes between the majority Sinhalese and minority Tamils erupted after 13 government soldiers were slain in an ambush by Tamil guerrillas in the northern town of Jaffna. Rioting soon spread throughout the country and into the capital. The Tamil people, who had originally migrated from India, had first begun their separatist movement in 1965, and from 1975 onward it had assumed violent overtones. The government announced that 387 people, mostly Tamils, had died and 79,000 had been made homeless in the riots.

Relations with India foundered on the Tamil issue, but the downturn was checked after Indian Prime Minister Indira Gandhi rushed her foreign minister to Colombo. Pres. Junius Jayawardene (*see* BIOGRAPHIES) dispatched his brother to New Delhi for talks aimed at dispelling the tensions.

On August 5 Parliament approved a constitutional amendment outlawing any group advocating separatism. The move effectively banned the Tamil United Liberation Front, which held 18 seats in Parliament. Late in the year, however, Jayawardene called an all-party conference in an effort to find a solution to the country's racial problems. By-elections were held during the year to fill 18 parliamentary seats.

Budget proposals presented to Parliament on March 7 were designed to bridge a deficit of Rs 29 billion. The proposals included a two-year embargo on all capital projects, a heavy reduction in energy consumption, and an aggressive export policy. Member nations of the Sri Lanka Aid Consortium, meeting in Paris, commended the government for its success in implementing its development strategy over the previous five years. (DILIP GANGULY)

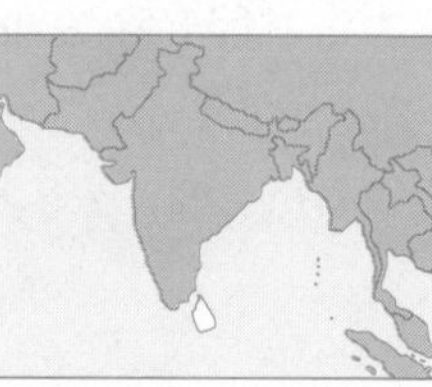

Sri Lanka

SRI LANKA

Education. (1980) Primary, pupils 2,081,391; secondary, pupils 1,258,002; primary and secondary, teachers c. 142,000; vocational (1976), pupils 4,778, teachers 1,239; teacher training, students 9,321, teachers 689; higher (1979), students 36,628, teaching staff 2,017.

Finance. Monetary unit: Sri Lanka rupee, with (Sept. 20, 1983) a free rate of SLRs 24.39 to U.S. $1 (SLRs 36.73 = £1 sterling). Gold and other reserves (June 1983) U.S. $284 million. Budget (1982 actual): revenue SLRs 17,809,000,000; expenditure SLRs 35,485,000,000. Gross national product (1982) SLRs 96,976,000,000. Money supply (May 1983) SLRs 12,490,000,000. Cost of living (Colombo; 1975 = 100; June 1983) 238.3.

Foreign Trade. (1982) Imports SLRs 41,596,000,000; exports SLRs 21,454,000,000. Import sources: Japan 15%; Saudi Arabia 12%; Iran 12%; U.K. 7%; U.S. 6%; Singapore 6%. Export destinations: U.S. 14%; bunkers 9%; U.K. 7%; West Germany 6%; Japan 5%; Iraq 5%. Main exports (1981): tea 33%; clothing 15%; rubber 15%; petroleum products 14%; edible nuts 5%.

Transport and Communications. Roads (1981) 152,423 km. Motor vehicles in use (1981): passenger 126,300; commercial 67,200. Railways: (1981) 1,520 km; traffic (1982) c. 3,110,000,000 passenger-km, freight 218 million net ton-km. Air traffic (1982): 1,947,000,000 passenger-km; freight c. 43 million net ton-km. Telephones (Jan. 1981) 83,500. Radio receivers (Dec. 1980) 1,454,000. Television receivers (Dec. 1980) 35,000.

Agriculture. Production (in 000; metric tons; 1982): rice 2,156; cassava (1981) c. 537; sweet potatoes (1981) c. 136; onions c. 70; mangoes c. 73; lemons c. 51; pineapples c. 49; copra c. 123; tea 190; coffee c. 12; rubber 135; fish catch (1981) 207. Livestock (in 000; June 1981): cattle c. 1,644; buffalo c. 843; sheep c. 29; goats c. 493; pigs c. 71; chickens c. 6,405.

Industry. Production (in 000; metric tons; 1981): cement 706; salt 104; graphite 7.5; petroleum products 1,597; cotton yarn 8.6; electricity (kw-hr; 1982) 2,067,000.

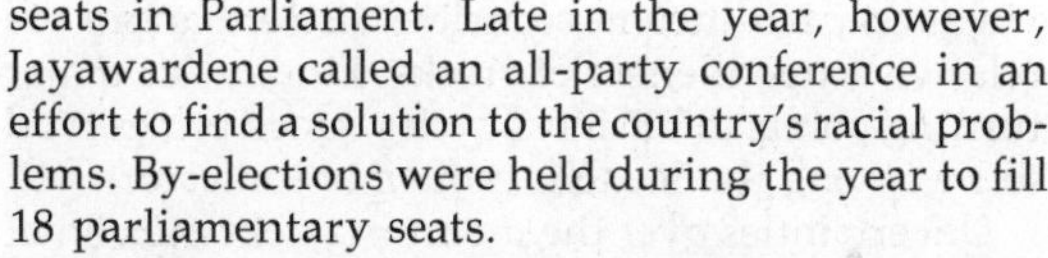

Burned out shops and businesses ransacked by looters were commonplace in Colombo after waves of rioting and general violence in July.

WIDE WORLD

Stock Exchanges

Stock markets throughout the world staged broad-based advances in 1983 (*see* TABLE I), fueled in Western Europe and the Asia Pacific Basin by growing signs that the worldwide recession had ended. In countries where economic activity and stock market prices moved in opposite directions, equity prices were higher, either anticipating future changes in business conditions or influenced by psychological factors.

The economic climate in the industrialized world was more favourable in 1983. The recovery from the steep recession that had engulfed the world economy since late 1979, while slow, clearly was under way. A constant flow of positive economic news—decelerating inflation, declining interest rates, and growing political and economic conservatism—tended to offset bad news of increasing debt, turmoil in international currency markets, and high levels of bankruptcies, unemployment, and labour unrest.

In an unusual number of instances, economic conditions were at odds with the tempo and direction of stock prices, reflecting the transition from high inflation to disinflation. During such a period of adjustment, investors are often willing to pay more for major companies, since they anticipate higher earnings in the future. Moreover, investors tend to buy equity securities well before an economic recovery is actually under way. Lower yields on fixed-income securities also enhanced the relative attractiveness of stocks. Finally, at major turning points in business cycles, stock prices tend to be among the leading economic indicators.

Uncertainties over the mounting debt burden of third world countries and its effects on world trade and the international monetary system left the direction of equity markets in 1984 likely to be determined by the momentum of the recovery and whether high unemployment could be reduced without rekindling inflation and higher interest rates. (ROBERT H. TRIGG)

United States. Trading volume on the nation's major stock options and futures markets achieved record levels in 1983, and stock prices made substantial gains as individual and institutional investors continued the aggressive share-buying activity that began in August 1982. Stock prices surged in the first half, but fears of rising interest rates and an overheated economy slowed the tempo later in the year.

The Dow Jones Industrial Average posted a gain of 20.27% to reach a high of 1,287.20 on November 29 and closed the year at 1,258.64. The National Association of Securities Dealers Automated Quotations (Nasdaq) composite, the broadest measure of over-the-counter activity, advanced 19.87% despite a weak second half. The American Stock Exchange's (Amex's) market value index showed a vigorous 30.95% gain. Wall Street firms underwrote about $97.3 billion of securities in 1983 as contrasted with $63 billion in 1982. A record $12.4 billion of initial public offerings were made by more than 800 corporations.

Squash Rackets: *see* Racket Games

Stamp Collecting: *see* Philately and Numismatics

Steel Industry: *see* Industrial Review

The recovery (real gross national product up 3.3%, personal income up 6.4%, and corporate profits up 13.6%), coupled with a sharp decline in the rate of inflation, raised consumer confidence, although concerns about high unemployment and the risk of increasing interest rates due to large government deficits tempered the widespread market optimism. Small investors returned to the market in full force. A New York Stock Exchange (NYSE) survey found that 42.4 million Americans owned individual stocks or stock mutual funds (18.1% of the total U.S. population); 57% were women; the median age was 34; and the figure was up 10.1 million from 1981.

High interest rates persisted throughout 1983. The yield on 30-year Treasury bonds ranged between 10.29 and 12.16%, closing the year at 11.87%. The low point was reached May 5 and the high on August 8. The prime rate opened the year at 11.5%, fell to 10.5% in February, and bounced back in August to 11%, where it remained for the rest of the year.

Volume on the NYSE was up 31.2% in 1983 with a turnover of 21,589,576,997 shares, compared with 16,458,036,768 in 1982. The index of NYSE stocks rose by 17.46%. The leading sectors of the market in 1983 included trucking, farm machinery, household furnishings and appliances, department stores, retail drugstores, textiles and apparel, leisure time, conglomerates, and coal. The weakest, aside from gold-mining, included copper, oil-well equipment and service, offshore drilling, mobile homes, hospital supplies, air transport, computer services, pollution control, and beverages. The most active issues on the NYSE were: AT&T 388,532,400 shares traded; IBM 222,837,400; Exxon 210,796,100; Chrysler 182,875,000; and General Motors 151,676,300. Bond volume on the NYSE, $7,572,315,000, rose only 5.8% over the 1982 figure of $7,155,443,000.

The Amex established a volume record of 2,081,270,000 shares traded in 1983, 40% above the previous year's figure of 1,485,831,536. Bond sales were $395,190,000, compared with $325,240,000 in 1982. Nasdaq reported turnover volume of 15,908,547,406 shares, an increase of 88.7% over 1982 and more than quadruple the volume traded in 1979. The number of companies with shares traded in this market grew 20% to 3,901, making Nasdaq the third-largest market in the world, after the New York and Tokyo stock exchanges.

Mutual-fund sales (excluding short-term money market and tax-exempt bond funds) climbed to $40 billion in 1983 from $15.7 billion in 1982, a gain of 154.8%. The number of active mutual funds increased by 15% to about 1,000. Long-term municipal bond funds showed especially strong growth, with assets soaring to a record $14.2 billion, up from $6.7 billion a year earlier. For the first time in at least a decade, common stock mutual funds (up 20.2% in 1983) failed to outperform Standard & Poor's Composite Index of 500 stocks (up 22.6%). Money-market funds were hard hit as banks offered competitive accounts, and during the year the money-market fund industry lost 26% of its assets, dropping to $166 billion in December 1983.

The Standard & Poor's 500 performed well above

1982 levels throughout 1983, climbing from 144.27 in January to 166.96 in July, pausing in August, and then rising slowly through October (TABLE II). The 400 stocks represented in the Industrial Average began 1983 at 162.02, rose to 188.32 by July, slipped to 183.16 in August, and then resumed their rise. Public utilities displayed a less vigorous pattern of price movements, starting 1983 at 61.89 and trading irregularly within a fairly narrow range, peaking at 65.06 in July, and, after an August interruption, rising to 66.00 in September. Railroad stocks were at 90.26 in January, 95.45 in March, 110.91 in June, and 121.86 by September. September 1983 marked a 12-month gain of 57.8% in the average price of railroad stocks.

Yields on U.S. government long-term bonds (TABLE III) averaged 10.37% in January 1983, as contrasted with 13.73% during the corresponding month of 1982. Bond yields moved within a very narrow range during the first half of the year, with a high of 10.64% and a low of 10.19%. During the second half these rates rose slightly to 11.10% in July and 11.42% in August before slipping back to 11.26% in September.

The corporate bond market in 1983 was stronger than that of the Treasury securities, but concerns about the corporate creditworthiness of utilities and banks were depressing factors. The total return on bonds (price changes plus interest income) was approximately 8%, consisting of coupon income of about 11% less a price drop of about 3%.

The futures and options markets were particularly strong in 1983 as the variety of contracts proliferated. Equity futures such as the Standard & Poor's 500 and the NYSE composite index were traded on the Chicago Mercantile and New York Futures exchanges; financial futures such as Treasury bonds and Japanese yen were traded on the Chicago Board of Trade and the Chicago Mercantile Exchange; commodity futures such as soybeans, silver, and No. 2 heating oil were traded on the Chicago Board of Trade and the Commodity (Comex) and New York Mercantile exchanges. The Philadelphia Stock Exchange made markets in Canadian dollars, West German Deutsche Marks, Japanese yen, Swiss francs, and British pounds sterling. The U.S. Treasury bond futures contract traded on the Chicago Board of Trade became the most extensively traded contract on any futures exchange. On a typical day it was not uncommon for bond futures contracts with face values of $7 billion–$8 billion to change hands.

Canada. Investors in Canadian stocks had a good year, as share prices closed near record levels and activity surpassed all previous records. The Toronto Stock Exchange's broadly based 300 composite index closed the year at 2,552.35, up 30.3% from the end of 1982 and just slightly below its record set in September. Trading volume of 2,440,000,000 shares was 54.6% ahead of 1982, while the average value of shares traded rose 70.9% to Can$30.20. Both topped records set in 1980. Leaders were forest products issues and shares of consumer products companies. Underperformers were gold-mining stocks, which fell 1.4% as the price of gold continued to decline. Toronto's mining index gained 34.2% in 1983 without any significant increase in the prices of metals. The oil and gas index rose 29.3% against a background of weak international oil markets and the depressive impact of Canada's National Energy Program.

In May the Toronto Stock Exchange moved to a gigantic new trading floor designed to hold three markets—stocks, options, and futures. At the end of the year the prevailing mood was bullish despite the action of the Bank of Canada in setting the bank rate at 10.06%, the highest level all year, in

Table I. Selected Major World Stock Price Indexes*

Country	1983 range† High	1983 range† Low	Year-end close 1982	Year-end close 1983	Percent increase
Australia	775	488	486	775	59
Austria	60	48	52	56	7
Belgium	137	101	103	136	32
Denmark	489	236	252	488	94
France	165	102	104	165	59
West Germany	1,044	728	763	1,033	35
Hong Kong	1,103	690	784	875	12
Italy	215	160	166	191	15
Japan	9,894	7,803	8,017	9,894	23
Mexico	840	280	291	840	189
Netherlands, The	129	84	84	129	54
Norway	223	99	100	222	122
Singapore	1,002	712	732	1,002	37
South Africa	969	705	737	966	31
Spain	129	98	100	116	16
Sweden	1,527	896	903	1,445	60
Switzerland	385	294	288	384	33
United Kingdom	776	598	597	776	30

*Index numbers are rounded and limited to countries for which at least 11 months' data were available on a weekly basis.
†Based on daily closing price.
Sources: *The Economist*, *Financial Times*, *Barron's*, *New York Times*.

Table II. U.S. Stock Market Prices

Month	Railroads (6 stocks) 1983	Railroads (6 stocks) 1982	Industrials (400 stocks) 1983	Industrials (400 stocks) 1982	Public utilities (40 stocks) 1983	Public utilities (40 stocks) 1982	Composite (500 stocks) 1983	Composite (500 stocks) 1982
January	90.26	80.86	162.02	131.08	61.89	51.81	144.27	117.28
February	91.73	75.99	165.15	127.56	61.52	51.39	146.80	114.50
March	95.45	67.73	170.33	122.85	62.13	52.33	151.88	110.84
April	100.90	71.20	176.78	129.19	62.95	54.25	157.71	116.31
May	109.37	71.16	184.10	129.68	64.88	54.88	164.10	116.35
June	110.91	65.49	187.42	122.61	64.14	52.13	166.39	109.70
July	113.04	63.15	188.32	122.49	65.06	51.87	166.96	109.38
August	112.03	64.71	183.16	122.29	64.85	53.34	162.42	109.65
September	121.86	77.20	188.61	137.09	66.00	56.48	167.16	122.43
October	...	86.27	...	148.11	...	59.41	167.65	132.66
November	...	88.27	...	153.90	...	60.08	...	138.10
December	...	85.83	...	156.02	...	59.33	...	139.37

Sources: U.S. Department of Commerce, *Survey of Current Business;* Board of Governors of the Federal Reserve System, *Federal Reserve Bulletin.* Prices are Standard & Poor's monthly averages of daily closing prices, with 1941–43 = 10.

Table III. U.S. Government Long-Term Bond Yields

Month	Yield (%) 1983	Yield (%) 1982	Month	Yield (%) 1983	Yield (%) 1982
January	10.37	13.73	July	11.10	12.97
February	10.60	13.63	August	11.42	12.15
March	10.34	12.98	September	11.26	11.48
April	10.19	12.84	October	...	10.51
May	10.21	12.67	November	...	10.18
June	10.64	13.32	December	...	10.33

Source: U.S. Department of Commerce, *Survey of Current Business.* Yields are for U.S. Treasury bonds that are taxable and due or callable in ten years or more.

Table IV. U.S. Corporate Bond Prices and Yields
Average price in dollars per $100 bond

Month	Average 1983	Average 1982	Yield (%) 1983	Yield (%) 1982	Month	Average 1983	Average 1982	Yield (%) 1983	Yield (%) 1982
January	42.5	30.9	11.79	15.18	July	40.4	32.8	12.15	14.61
February	41.3	31.1	12.01	15.27	August	39.0	35.7	12.51	13.71
March	42.6	32.9	11.73	14.58	September	39.7	38.0	12.37	12.94
April	43.8	33.3	11.51	14.46	October	...	41.7	...	12.12
May	44.4	34.0	11.46	14.26	November	...	44.2	...	11.68
June	42.2	32.1	11.74	14.81	December	...	42.9	...	11.83

Source: U.S. Department of Commerce, *Survey of Current Business.* Average prices are based on Standard & Poor's composite index of A1 + issues. Yields are based on Moody's Aaa domestic corporate bond index.

response to the upward drift in U.S. rates that exerted pressure on the Canadian dollar in the foreign exchange markets. (IRVING PFEFFER)

Western Europe. The trend of stock markets throughout Western Europe was uniformly higher in 1983. Gains in Great Britain and West Germany were modest, while sharply higher stock prices prevailed in France, the Scandinavian nations, Italy, Spain, and the Benelux countries; Switzerland was also strong.

In Britain the *Financial Times* index of 30 industrial issues traded on the London Stock Exchange rose again, and for the year stock prices on average gained 30%. An all-time high was reached on December 22.

Stock prices began 1983 on a strong uptrend and pierced the 700 barrier in May on investor confidence buoyed by lower rates of inflation and sharply lower interest rates. News of Prime Minister Margaret Thatcher's landslide election victory in June and the likelihood that her economic policies would be continued sent the stock market upward, to a level 23% higher than at the 1982 close.

Three weeks of profit taking then cut equity values by almost 7%, but this loss was recovered by mid-August. After three months of trading in a relatively narrow range, reflecting fears that the recovery might not be strong enough, the Bank of England lowered its lending fee to commercial banks to 9%, a level it had not fallen below since 1968. This was followed in November by a government announcement that taxes might have to be raised in the spring 1984 budget owing to higher than expected public spending. These developments tended to reinforce investor expectations of continued economic recovery and raised hopes that a new bout of monetary restraint might be avoided. As a result, stock prices moved higher in the final weeks of the year and finished near record highs.

In West Germany the Commerzbank index of 60 issues traded on the Frankfurt Stock Exchange ended the year 35% higher than at its start.

Stock prices rallied in early February on the belief that inflation would continue to be held in check and that stronger worldwide economic growth would help boost West German exports and lift the nation out of recession. In March Chancellor Helmut Kohl's conservative economic policies were given a vote of confidence as his coalition government emerged victorious in parliamentary elections. The bullish tone added 26% to equity values by the end of April.

After a 6% decline in May, the upward trend resumed, a brief rally continued into late July, and after another decline a much sharper rally ensued. Economic statistics revealed that the economy was recovering more rapidly than expected. On world currency markets the Deutsche Mark traded at its lowest level against the U.S. dollar in more than a decade, not only making West German exports more attractive but also discouraging imports by effectively raising the price of foreign goods. Equity values jumped nearly 11% from the end of August to the end of November. During the final weeks of 1983, stock prices remained in an uptrend, closing the year at their highest level since the end of World War II.

The stock market in France was a star performer in 1983. Despite a French economy in the midst of economic recession and deeply troubled by a combination of persistent high inflation, increasing government deficits, wage and price controls, and high unemployment, the general index of shares traded on the Paris Bourse advanced 59%. This bullish performance was attributable to government programs to encourage stock market investments and austerity measures introduced by Pres. François Mitterrand in March, including tax increases and restrictions on French tourist spending abroad.

In Norway stock prices staged a remarkable recovery after Conservative Prime Minister Kåre Willoch's pledge to fight joblessness and to introduce measures to stimulate the economy. In fact, the year's increase in equity values on the Oslo Stock Exchange was the second largest (+122%) among the major world stock price indexes. From the first trading session in January stock prices surged ahead, and although major economic indicators pointed to a slower recovery than in other

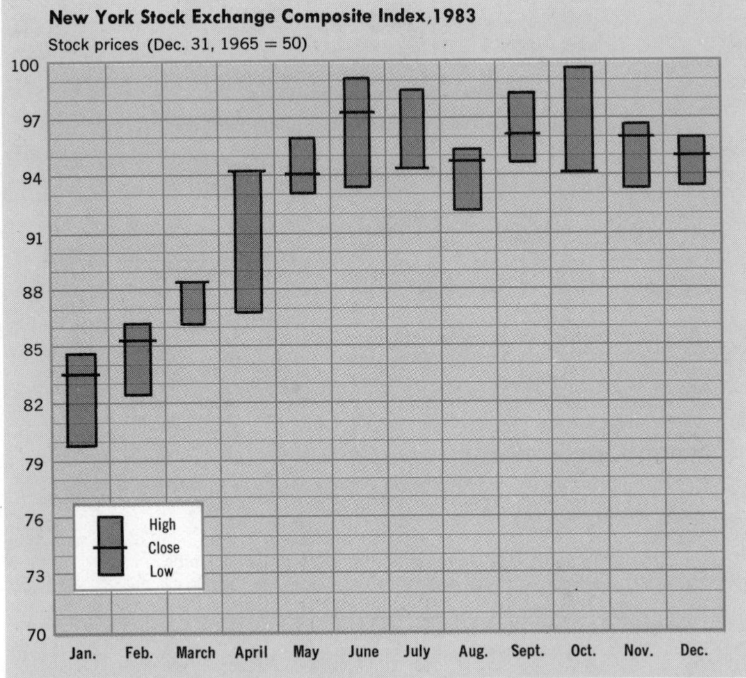

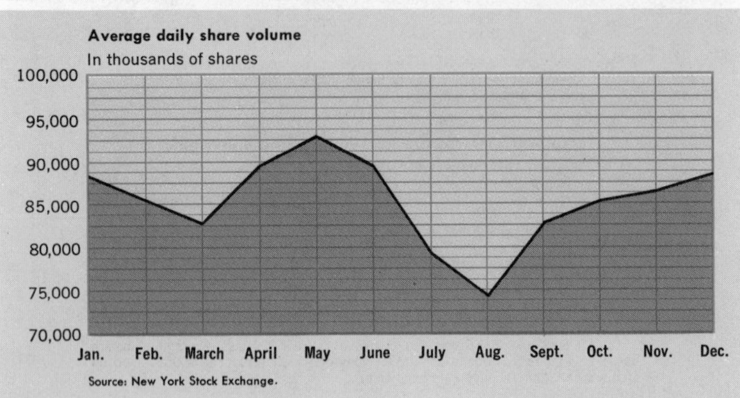

industrialized nations, investors focused on the expected brighter economic outlook for 1984. Stock prices finished the year less than 1% below the 1983 high.

Higher stock prices also prevailed in Denmark and Sweden. For the year, stock prices in Denmark enjoyed the third-largest increase among the major world stock market indexes (+94%), while in Sweden the gain amounted to 60%. Higher prices on the Copenhagen Stock Exchange were fueled by dramatically lower interest rates and proposed tax changes favouring stocks over bonds. Denmark's centre-right minority government lifted restrictions imposed in 1979 on foreign purchases of Danish government bonds. A buying stampede followed, and yields on these securities dropped to 14.3% in May from over 20% at the end of 1982.

The big gain in equity prices on the Stockholm Stock Exchange was a continuation of the bull market that began in October 1980. Since that time there had been a growth of about 275% in the value of equity securities. Contributing factors included the creation of preferential tax treatment for selected types of equity investments, record purchases of Swedish stock by foreign investors, and the 16% devaluation of the krona in October 1982. As 1983 drew to a close, Stockholm's Affarsvarldren index was down 5% from the all-time high recorded on December 21.

In Italy the price index of shares traded on the Milan Stock Exchange finished 1983 with a gain of 15% after a 1982 decline of 15%. Italy's first Socialist premier, Bettino Craxi, was installed in August and, like many of his 43 predecessors, claimed reduced inflation and a halt to the rise in public-sector deficit as his top priorities. The recovery in equity values, which reached its high in March, drifted over the next four months, then staged a run at recovery. An anemic attempt to rally failed in late August and triggered a selling wave. After firming in late November, the market made another attempt to rally but closed with stock prices, on average, 11% below the March highs.

The trend of stock prices in Spain was also up in 1983. Share prices on the Madrid Stock Exchange jumped 16% after declining 34% in 1982. Spain's ruling Socialist Party departed from the belt-tightening programs that many European governments were following and adopted expansionist policies in an effort to reduce unemployment. Despite a nationwide strike against the state-owned railroads in October, stock prices experienced a broad upswing that left equity values 77% higher in November than at the end of September.

Other Countries. In 1983 stock prices in Mexico enjoyed the largest increase of any stock market (+189%). The Bolsa Stock Exchange's index exceeded the March 1979 peak near the end of September. The market continued to move higher during the final quarter of 1983 and closed the year at an all-time high. This performance was achieved despite one of the highest international debt burdens in the free world and an inflation rate of almost 100% annually.

The stock market in Australia also experienced a bull market. After falling 18% in 1982, prices on the Sydney Stock Exchange finished 1983 with a gain of 59%. Fueling the rally was the news that Prime Minister Robert Hawke, who was elected in March, would seek cuts in government spending and would keep union wage increases in 1983 below 4% despite a 10% annual inflation rate.

In Japan the Nikkei Dow Jones average of leading industrial shares jumped 23% in 1983 to its highest level on record. Although industrial output experienced a modest recovery, domestic demand was relatively weak. Thus, the likelihood that Japan's recovery would be led by rising exports in response to economic recovery in countries outside Japan raised fears of an even larger Japanese trade surplus, which could heighten protectionist sentiment throughout the world. Nonetheless, equity prices set a new all-time high on the final trading day of 1983.

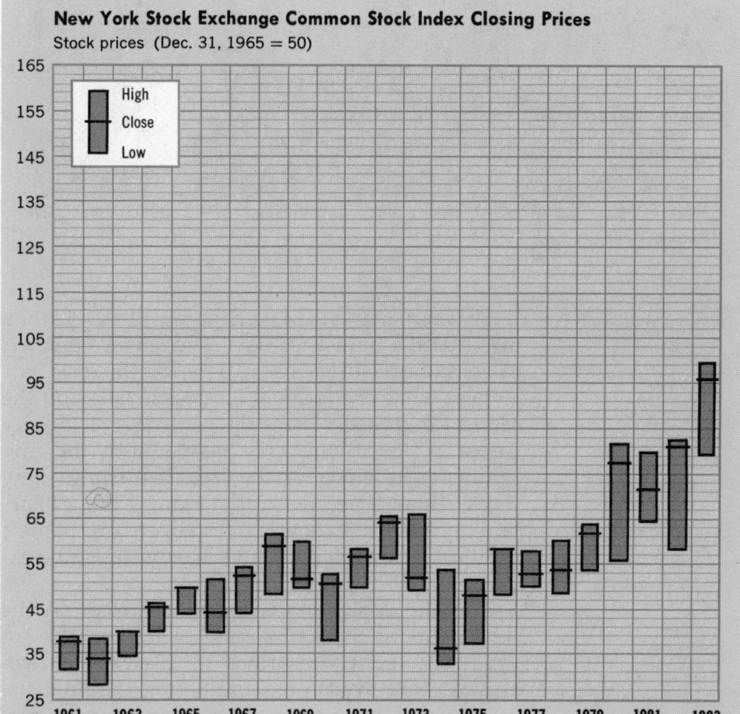

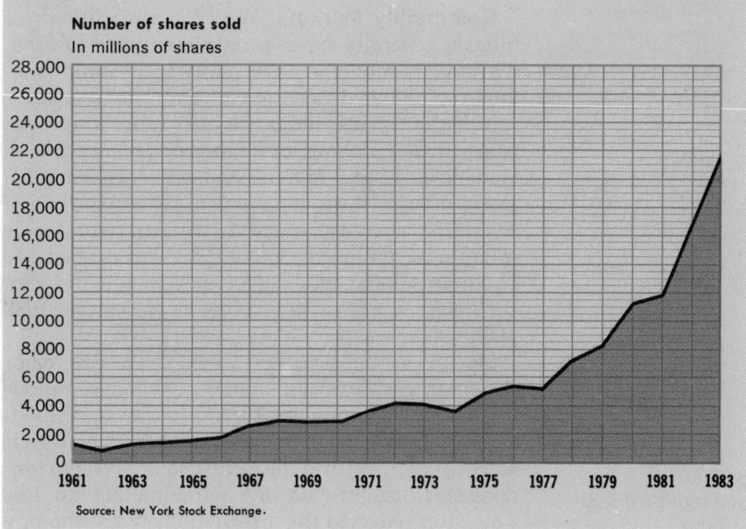

Source: New York Stock Exchange.

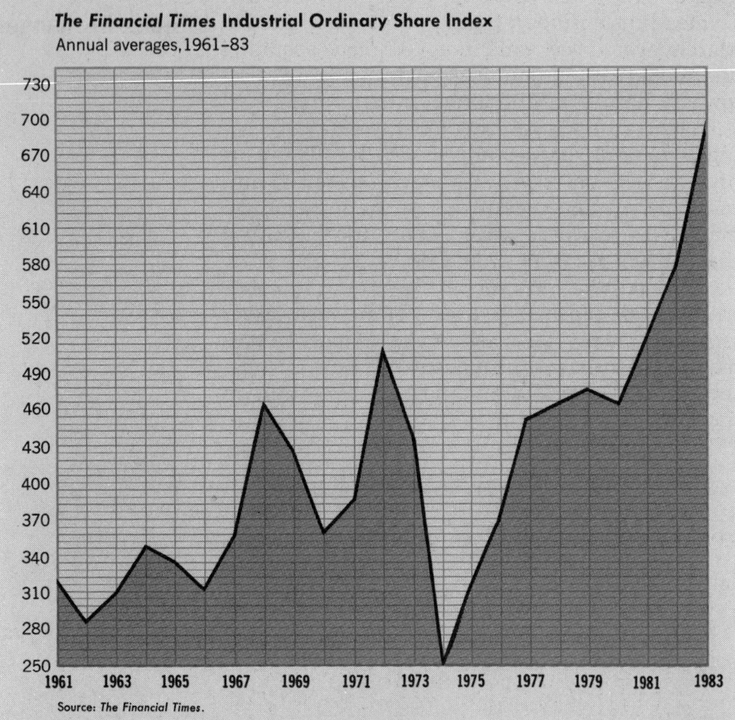

The stock markets in Singapore and Hong Kong also traced a bullish pattern. The *Singapore Straits Times* industrial index rose 37% for the year as a whole, while the index of 33 stocks traded on the Hong Kong Stock Exchange gained 12%. Equity prices in Hong Kong were hampered by the government's takeover of the troubled Hong Lung Bank, an all-time low for the Hong Kong dollar, and uncertainties about the British crown colony's political future after Britain's lease with China expired in 1997.

In South Africa industrial share prices on the Johannesburg Stock Exchange were up 31% in 1983. The country reformed its 22-year-old two-tier currency system by eliminating the financial rand, which had been used exclusively for capital transactions.

Commodity Markets. World commodity price indexes generally experienced sharp gains in 1983, while price movements of many individual commodities followed varying patterns. *The Economist*'s commodity price index, which measures spot prices in U.S. dollars for 29 internationally traded foodstuffs, fibres, metals, and other raw materials, climbed 21% from the end of 1982 to the end of 1983. That increase ended a two-year worldwide collapse in commodity prices that had carried *The Economist*'s dollar index to a four-year low in October 1982, more than 40% below its November 1980 peak.

Sharply higher prices prevailed in the two major sectors of *The Economist*'s index of dollar commodity prices. The average 1983 price level of foodstuffs gained 26%, and industrial raw materials were up 12%. Within the industrial materials component, fibres jumped 16% while metals lost 4%. The latter reflected the disinflationary psychology that had plagued the precious-metals markets, especially gold and silver, since 1980.

The upward movement in foodstuffs was led by cocoa prices, which soared to 3½-year highs, and tea prices, which doubled in the last six months of 1983 alone. Prices of wheat, corn, and soybeans also moved higher, helped by a severe summer drought in the United States. The strength in prices of fibres and raw materials reflected the upturn in global economic activity and the revival of demand for finished goods. At the outset of a business recovery, inventories are typically lean. Thus, any pickup in final demand is quickly translated to restocking inventories, which tends to produce price pressures in raw-materials markets. As a result, the prices of rubber, wool, cotton, and zinc were particularly strong during 1983.

The price of gold, an inflation bellwether, was under downward pressure throughout most of 1983. In late February news of oil price cuts by the Organization of Petroleum Exporting Countries triggered a selling wave in gold in the London market, which caused its price to plunge from nearly $510 per ounce to below $410 near the end of March. The subsequent rebound, which carried gold's price back to about $443, was relatively weak, and by the end of May the decline had resumed. From early June to the end of September, the price of gold generally fluctuated between $400 and $440 per ounce.

The record-setting strength of the U.S. dollar in international currency markets, combined with relatively high U.S. interest rates, tended to push the gold price lower, since a more expensive dollar makes dollar-denominated investments comparatively more attractive, and higher interest rates make it more expensive to finance purchases of gold. In addition, long-term holders of gold became discouraged when signs of economic recovery continued to appear without fueling reflation expectations. In October the yellow metal fell below $400 and, except for a brief period in late November and the first week of December, stayed under that level for the remainder of 1983. The year's final quotation settled at $381.50 an ounce, a net decline of nearly 15% from the 1982 closing price of $448. That also left the price of gold some 55% below its all-time high in January 1980.

As 1983 drew to a close, the outlook for world commodity prices was uncertain. Despite signs of continued worldwide economic recovery, surprising weakness in some key commodities, including those with price structures unsuitable for trading in free markets, suggested that the world could be on the verge of a new cycle of disinflation. On the other hand, the need of some third world countries to refinance their enormous external debts raised the possibility that the worldwide trend toward economic conservatism might be reversed, with a new round of money supply growth and international bank lending leading to a resurgence of inflation that could send commodity prices soaring. The eventual outcome of these forces was likely to determine the overall direction of commodity prices in the years ahead. (ROBERT H. TRIGG)

See also Economy, World.
[534.D.3.g.i]

Strikes:
see Industrial Relations

Sudan

A republic of northeastern Africa, the Sudan is bounded by Egypt, the Red Sea, Ethiopia, Kenya, Uganda, Zaire, the Central African Republic, Chad, and Libya. Area: 2,503,890 sq km (966,757 sq mi). Pop. (1983 prelim.): 22 million, including (1978 est.) Arab 49% and black 51%. Cap. and largest city: Khartoum (metro. pop., 1983 prelim., 1.8 million). Language: Arabic (official), various tribal languages in the south. Religion (1980 est.): Muslim (73%), mainly in the north; animist (18%) and Christian (9%) in the south. President and prime minister in 1983, Gen. Gaafar Nimeiry.

In February 1983 Egypt reported to the U.S. that Libyan troops were massing on the Sudanese border to support an attempted coup in Sudan. The U.S. sent airborne warning and control systems planes to Egypt and ordered an aircraft carrier to Libyan waters. The perceived threat soon passed, though more than 60 people were arrested in Sudan in connection with the attempted coup. The growing rapprochement with Egypt was highlighted in February when Egypt's Pres. Hosni Mubarak flew to Khartoum to inaugurate the Egyptian-Sudanese Higher Council for Integration. In May he attended the first session of the Nile Valley Parliament, which consisted of deputies from both countries.

In April Pres. Gaafar Nimeiry was reelected, unopposed, for a third six-year term. The following month the Army put down a mutiny among troops in Jonglei Province in the south. Ostensibly as part of a decentralization policy but primarily to prevent further unrest, Nimeiry divided the south into three regions, each with its own governor and assembly. Unrest continued to grow, however, and thousands of refugees fled to Ethiopia.

To forestall pressure from Muslim fundamentalists in Khartoum and to win the approval of the Gulf states, Nimeiry enforced the Islamic law against alcoholic drinks in September. He then released 13,000 prisoners as a prelude to the exclusive use of Islamic law to deal with crime. These measures were deeply resented by the Christian population in the south. (KENNETH INGHAM)

SUDAN

Education. (1980–81) Primary, pupils 1,464,227, teachers 43,451; secondary, pupils 362,992, teachers 17,452; vocational, pupils 15,545, teachers 684; teacher training, students 5,657, teachers 695; higher (1979–80), students 26,996, teaching staff 6,497.

Finance. Monetary unit: Sudanese pound, with (Sept. 20, 1983) a par value of Sud£1.30 to U.S. $1 (free rate of Sud£1.96 = £1 sterling). Gold and other reserves (June 1983) U.S. $17 million. Budget (1982–83 est.): revenue Sud£1,340 million; expenditure Sud£1,910 million. Gross national product (1977–78) Sud£2,868 million. Money supply (June 1983) Sud£2,025.7 million.

Foreign Trade. (1982) Imports Sud£1,213,810,000; exports Sud£483,120,000. Import sources (1981): U.K. 13%; Saudi Arabia 11%; West Germany 8%; U.S. Virgin Islands 7%; France 6%; Japan 6%; The Netherlands 5%. Export destinations (1981): Saudi Arabia 21%; Italy 9%; U.S. Virgin Islands 9%; Japan 8%; The Netherlands 7%; China 6%; France 6%; Egypt 5%. Main exports (1981): cotton 24%; peanuts 19%; cereals 11%; sesame 10%; gum arabic 9%; livestock 9%.

Transport and Communications. Roads (1982) *c.* 48,000 km (mainly tracks; including *c.* 3,000 km asphalted). Motor vehicles in use (1980): passenger *c.* 34,600; commercial (including buses) *c.* 38,000. Railways: (1979) 4,786 km; traffic (1979–80): 1,167,000,000 passenger-km; freight 2,620,000,000 net ton-km. Air traffic (1982): *c.* 657 million passenger-km; freight *c.* 6.3 million net ton-km. Navigable inland waterways (1981) *c.* 4,100 km. Telephones (Jan. 1981) 65,000. Radio receivers (Dec. 1980) 1,330,000. Television receivers (Dec. 1980) 105,000.

Agriculture. Production (in 000; metric tons; 1982): wheat *c.* 150; millet *c.* 230; sorghum *c.* 2,100; sesame seed *c.* 220; cottonseed *c.* 300; peanuts *c.* 800; sugar, raw value (1981) *c.* 235; dates *c.* 115; cotton, lint *c.* 160; cow's milk *c.* 978; goat's milk *c.* 405; beef and veal *c.* 220; mutton and goat meat *c.* 140; timber (cu m; 1981) *c.* 35,351. Livestock (in 000; 1982): cattle *c.* 19,234; sheep *c.* 18,547; goats *c.* 13,174; camels (1981) *c.* 2,542; asses (1981) *c.* 693; chickens *c.* 28,021.

Industry. Production (in 000; metric tons; 1981): cement 122; salt 64; petroleum products *c.* 1,077; electricity (kw-hr) *c.* 1,000.

Sudan

HIRES—GAMMA/LIAISON

A massive engineering project is under way in Sudan to divert the White Nile through Jonglei Province to carry water to the arid north. Special excavating equipment designed in West Germany uses a wheel 12.2 metres (40 feet) in diameter and equipped with digging "buckets" to scoop out huge quantities of earth at a single cut.

Sumo:
see Combat Sports

Surfing:
see Water Sports

Suriname

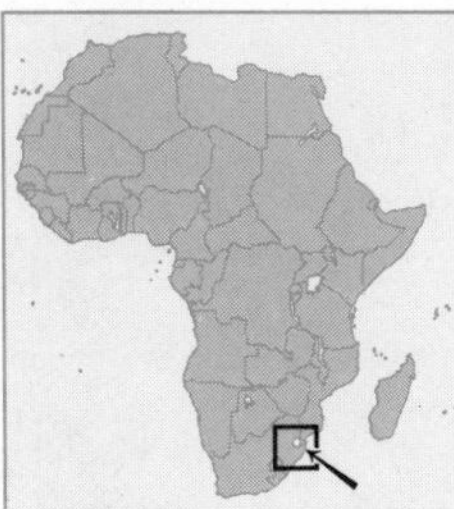
Swaziland

Suriname

A republic of northern South America, Suriname is bounded by Guyana, Brazil, French Guiana, and the Atlantic Ocean. Area (not including a 17,635-sq km area disputed with Guyana): 163,820 sq km (63,251 sq mi). Pop. (1983 est.): 363,000, including (1980 prelim.) Hindustanis 35%; Creoles 32%; Indonesians 15%; Bush Negroes 10%; Amerindians 3%; Chinese 3%; European and other 2%. Cap. and largest city: Paramaribo (pop., 1980 prelim., 67,700). Language: Dutch (official); English and Sranan (a creole) are lingua francas; Hindi, Javanese, Chinese, and various Amerindian languages are used within individual ethnic communities. Religion: predominantly Hindu, Christian, and Muslim. Chairman of the National Military Council in 1983, Dési Bouterse; prime minister from February 26, Errol Alibux.

On Feb. 26, 1983, the National Military Council (NMC), headed by Dési Bouterse, announced that a new civilian Cabinet had been appointed with Errol Alibux as prime minister. The previous Cabinet had resigned following the violent purge of some 15 prominent political opponents of Bouterse in December 1982. Relations between the NMC and The Netherlands were minimal. The Dutch government froze deliveries of aid and military supplies, and Suriname closed its embassy in The Hague. Sgt. Maj. Badressein Sital, leader of the pro-Cuban faction, was sacked from the government in June, and after the U.S. invasion of Grenada, Suriname sent its Cuban advisers home.

Lack of aid and depressed conditions in the bauxite market forced the government to borrow from Western countries. In December some 4,000 bauxite workers went on strike to protest high taxes. (DICK BOONSTRA)

SURINAME

Education. (1980–81) Primary, pupils 75,139, teachers 2,803; secondary, pupils 29,790, teachers 1,854; vocational (1978–79), pupils 4,394, teachers 249; teacher training, students 1,275, teachers 148; higher, students 2,353, teaching staff 155.

Finance. Monetary unit: Suriname guilder, with (Sept. 20, 1983) a par value of 1.785 Suriname guilders to U.S. $1 (free rate of 2.69 Suriname guilders = £1 sterling). Gold and other reserves (June 1983) U.S. $122 million. Budget (1982 actual): revenue 517 million Suriname guilders; expenditure 788 million Suriname guilders.

Foreign Trade. Imports (1982) 913 million Suriname guilders; exports (1981) 846 million Suriname guilders. Import sources (1978): U.S. 31%; The Netherlands 19%; Trinidad and Tobago 15%; Japan 7%; West Germany 5%. Export destinations (1978): U.S. 36%; The Netherlands 17%; Norway 13%; Japan 6%; U.K. 5%. Main exports: alumina 56%; bauxite 13%; aluminum 10%.

Transport and Communications. Roads (1980) 8,779 km. Motor vehicles in use (1980): passenger 26,500; commercial 8,500. Railways (1980) 167 km. Navigable inland waterways (1982) *c.* 1,500 km. Telephones (Jan. 1980) 21,300. Radio receivers (Dec. 1980) 189,000. Television receivers (Dec. 1980) 40,000.

Agriculture. Production (in 000; metric tons; 1982): rice *c.* 280; oranges *c.* 7; grapefruit *c.* 2; bananas *c.* 40; sugar, raw value *c.* 10. Livestock (in 000; 1981): cattle *c.* 45; pigs *c.* 22; goats *c.* 7; chickens *c.* 1,100.

Industry. Production (in 000; metric tons; 1981): bauxite 4,006; alumina 1,248; aluminum 41; cement 71; electricity (kw-hr) 1,670,000 (83% hydroelectric).

Swaziland

A landlocked monarchy of southern Africa and a member of the Commonwealth, Swaziland is bounded by South Africa and Mozambique. Area: 17,364 sq km (6,704 sq mi). Pop. (1982 est.): 585,200. Cap. and largest city: Mbabane (pop., 1982 est., 33,000). Language: English and siSwati (official). Religion (1980): Christian 77%; animist 23%. Regents in 1983, Queen Dzeliwe and, from August 10, Queen Ntombi; prime ministers, Prince Mabandla N. F. Dlamini and, from March 25, Prince Bhekimpi Dlamini.

Events in Swaziland during 1983 were dominated by a power struggle among members of the royal family following the death of King Sobhuza II in August 1982. In March Prince Mabandla Dlamini was replaced as prime minister by Prince Bhekimpi Dlamini. The new prime minister was reported to be a supporter of the proposed land deal whereby South Africa would hand over to Swaziland some 7,800 sq km (3,000 sq mi) of territory and also responsibility for 750,000 black South Africans.

In August Queen Dzeliwe ("the great she-elephant") was replaced as regent in a palace coup by Queen Ntombi, mother of the heir. Queen Dzeliwe's dismissal touched off another crisis, one that divided the royal family into two factions. The teenage heir to the throne, Prince Makhosetive, returned to Swaziland from school in Britain in September to be presented to the people. The regency was to continue for five years, until he reached the age of 21.

In August Queen Dzeliwe was replaced as regent by Queen Ntombi (below), who was named regent until her son became old enough to rule.

WIDE WORLD

During the first months of 1983 the country suffered the worst drought in decades. Presenting the budget on March 1, the minister of finance pointed out that the economy had been adversely affected by world recession and that no growth in revenue could therefore be expected before the middle of the decade. Work began on a new rail link to serve the northeastern part of the country.

(GUY ARNOLD)

SWAZILAND

Education. (1981) Primary, pupils 119,913, teachers 3,586; secondary, pupils 24,826, teachers 1,433; vocational, pupils 538, teachers 65; teacher training, students 624, teachers 159; higher, students 979, teaching staff 108.

Finance and Trade. Monetary unit: lilangeni (plural emalangeni), at par with the South African rand, with (Sept. 20, 1983) a free rate of 1.11 emalangeni to U.S. $1 (1.67 emalangeni = £1 sterling). Budget (1981–82 actual): revenue 175 million emalangeni; expenditure 188 million emalangeni. Foreign trade (1982): imports 570 million emalangeni; exports 332 million emalangeni. Import source (1978): South Africa 90%. Export destinations (1978): U.K. 34%; South Africa 24%. Main exports (1981): sugar 40%; wood pulp 15%; chemicals 12%; citrus and canned fruit 7%; asbestos 6%.

Agriculture. Production (in 000; metric tons; 1981): corn *c.* 95; rice *c.* 5; potatoes *c.* 6; sugar, raw value *c.* 365; pineapples *c.* 28; cotton, lint *c.* 11; timber (cu m; 1981) 2,223. Livestock (in 000; 1981): cattle *c.* 670; sheep *c.* 50; pigs *c.* 22; goats *c.* 264.

Industry. Production (in 000; metric tons; 1981): coal 164; asbestos 35; wood pulp 157; electricity (kw-hr) 310,000.

Sweden

A constitutional monarchy of northern Europe lying on the eastern side of the Scandinavian Peninsula, Sweden has common borders with Finland and Norway. Area: 486,661 sq km (187,901 sq mi). Pop. (1983 est.): 8,330,600. Cap. and largest city: Stockholm (pop., 1982 est., 648,500). Language: Swedish, with some Finnish and Lapp in the north. Religion: predominantly Lutheran. King, Carl XVI Gustaf; prime minister in 1983, Olof Palme.

For Sweden's Social Democrats, governing again after six years in opposition, 1983 was fraught with difficulties. On the one hand, Prime Minister Olof Palme displeased his supporters when he was forced into a policy of wage restraint and continued cutting of public expenditure. On the other, he faced a massive revolt by the Swedish business class against Social Democratic plans to allow trade unionists to buy shares in private industry.

On the international scene, Swedish relations with the U.S.S.R. sank to their lowest level in recent years when, in April, Palme delivered a protest note to Boris Pankin, Moscow's ambassador to Stockholm, concerning violations of Swedish territorial waters by Soviet submarines. This move followed a report by a government commission of inquiry into an incident in 1982, when unidentified foreign submarines had been hunted near the naval base on the island of Muskö. The commission named the U.S.S.R. as the aggressor and released a videotape and still photographs that, it was claimed, showed tracks left on the seabed near the Muskö base by midget submarines.

Sweden temporarily recalled its ambassador to Moscow and accused the Soviet Union of "coordinated and carefully planned submarine maneuvers" deep inside Swedish territory. Palme's protest note added: "The Swedish government request the government of the Soviet Union to give instructions to the Soviet Navy that violations of Swedish territory cease." The Swedish Navy then launched a major but unsuccessful hunt for two suspected Soviet midget submarines off the east coast city of Sundsvall. There were similar scares in other parts of the country.

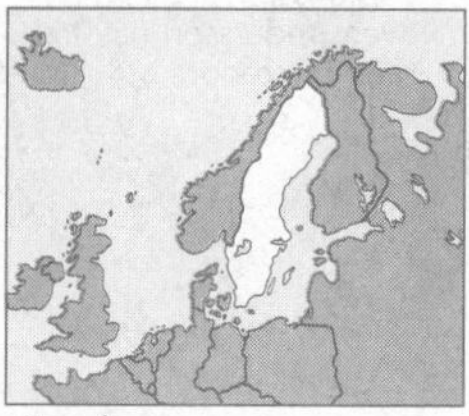

Sweden

The return to power of Palme, the country's only internationally known politician, attracted other visitors to Sweden: Yasir Arafat, leader of the Palestine Liberation Organization; Javier Pérez de Cuéllar, UN secretary-general; George Bush, U.S. vice-president; and Walid Jumblatt, the Lebanese Druze leader. Palme's most spectacular failure on the international scene was in his chosen role of peacemaker: as official UN mediator he brought no lessening of hostilities between Iran and Iraq, and his plan for a nuclear-weapon-free zone in central Europe failed to attract support.

The budget, announced in January and reinforced by further measures in October, aimed to cut public spending and break the recent trend toward annual increases in the central government deficit. Indirect taxes were raised, food subsidies were eliminated, and foreign aid was frozen. This

SWEDEN

Education. (1981–82) Primary, pupils 662,581, teachers 40,747; secondary and vocational, pupils 606,152, teachers 82,393; higher, students 205,431.

Finance. Monetary unit: krona, with (Sept. 20, 1983) a free rate of 7.87 kronor to U.S. $1 (11.85 kronor = £1 sterling). Gold and other reserves (June 1983) U.S. $3,686,000,000. Budget (total; 1982–83 est.): revenue 179,537,000,000 kronor; expenditure 255,301,000,000 kronor. Gross national product (1982) 607,830,000,000 kronor. Money supply (Dec. 1982) 94,150,000,000 kronor. Cost of living (1975 = 100; June 1983) 217.1.

Foreign Trade. (1982) Imports 173,721,000,000 kronor; exports 167,991,000,000 kronor. Import sources: West Germany 17%; U.K. 12%; U.S. 9%; Norway 7%; Denmark 6%; Finland 6%; The Netherlands 5%. Export destinations: Norway 11%; West Germany 10%; U.K. 10%; Denmark 8%; U.S. 7%; Finland 6%; France 6%; The Netherlands 5%. Main exports: machinery 26%; motor vehicles 13%; paper 10%; iron and steel 6%; chemicals 6%; petroleum products 5%.

Transport and Communications. Roads (1982) 129,518 km (including 868 km expressways). Motor vehicles in use (1982): passenger 2,936,000; commercial 193,500. Railways: (1981) 11,956 km (including 7,601 km electrified); traffic (1982) 6,374,000,000 passenger-km, freight 13,628,000,000 net ton-km. Air traffic (including Swedish apportionment of international operations of Scandinavian Airlines System; 1982): 5,573,000,000 passenger-km; freight 189.8 million net ton-km. Shipping (1982): merchant vessels 100 gross tons and over 697; gross tonnage 3,787,567. Telephones (Jan. 1981) 6,621,000. Radio receivers (Dec. 1977) 8.3 million. Television licenses (Dec. 1981) 3,221,000.

Agriculture. Production (in 000; metric tons; 1982): wheat 1,377; barley 2,103; oats 1,559; rye 207; potatoes 1,112; sugar, raw value 385; rapeseed 343; apples *c.* 93; milk 3,654; butter 69; cheese 114; beef and veal *c.* 161; pork *c.* 325; fish catch (1981) 263; timber (cu m; 1981) 49,791. Livestock (in 000; June 1982): cattle 1,941; sheep *c.* 400; pigs 2,716; chickens (1981) *c.* 13,453.

Industry. Index of industrial production (1975 = 100; 1982) 96. Production (in 000; metric tons; 1982): cement 2,302; electricity (kw-hr) 96,522,000 (58% hydroelectric and 37% nuclear in 1981); iron ore (60–65% metal content) 16,140; pig iron 1,794; crude steel 3,899; aluminum 79; petroleum products (1981) 13,721; sulfuric acid (1980) 660; wood pulp (1980) 8,371; newsprint 1,324; other paper (1981) 2,331; passenger cars (units) 269. Merchant vessels launched (100 gross tons and over; 1982) 280,000 gross tons. New dwelling units completed (1982) 45,100.

SVENSKT PRESSFOTO/PICTORIAL PARADE

A Swedish commission of inquiry announced at an April press conference its finding that six Soviet submarines, some of them tracked midget subs, had prowled the waters and floor of the Hårsfjärden, a bay south of Stockholm and west across the Baltic Sea from Soviet Estonia. The commission's chairman, Sven Andersson (centre), read the report.

last measure meant that in 1984, for the first time since 1975, Sweden would fall below its stated goal of giving 1% of gross national product in aid to the third world.

On October 4 a demonstration involving an estimated 75,000–100,000 people, headed by some of the nation's leading industrialists, was held to protest Socialist plans to introduce so-called wage-earner funds in 1984. These funds, financed by a tax on company profits and a levy on workers' wages, would be run by elected committees of trade unionists. Opponents of the funds maintained that they would lead to the "socialization" of industry; Palme said they would buy him wage restraint from the unions and generate capital for the industrial investment needed to create jobs. Legislation establishing the funds was passed by the Riksdag (parliament) on December 21. The official unemployment figure of 4.1% did not take into account the thousands in subsidized jobs and retraining programs and those who had been forced to return to the educational system.

Under attack from the right on the funds issue and from the left for spending cuts and the increased cost of living, Palme appeared to be at the end of his honeymoon with the electorate. Before the end of the year, the Social Democrats had fallen behind in the opinion polls. The party suffered another setback in November when Ove Rainer, the minister of justice, was forced to resign after being accused of tax evasion by the press.

(CHRIS MOSEY)

Swimming

In 1983, the year before the Olympic Games, swimming reached its highest peak since the 1980 Olympics as swimmers from Europe and the United States combined to set world records on 18 occasions. These new marks highlighted a year that featured five major international competitions, events that provided the incentive for outstanding performances.

The World University Games at Edmonton, Alta., July 1–11 attracted 4,294 participants from 95 nations. The games, unfortunately, would best be remembered by the tragic death of Soviet diver Sergey Shalibashvili, who in attempting a reverse 3½ somersault hit his head on the concrete platform and fell 10 m (33 feet) into Kinsmen Aquatic Center diving pool. The U.S.S.R., using the games as a "dress rehearsal" for the 1984 Olympics, sent its best team and won 22 gold medals in 29 swimming events. The Soviet women won 12 of 14 events, and the men 10 of 15. Top competitor was Irina Laritscheva with five gold medals. The United States won one gold medal, that by Bruce Hayes in the 200-m freestyle. World University Games records were broken in 25 of 29 events.

The IX Pan-American Games at Caracas, Venezuela, August 17–22; the XVI European Championships in Rome's Piscina Foro Italico, site of the 1960 Olympics, August 22–27; and the Pan Pacific meet, August 27–28 in Tokyo's Yoyogi Natatorium, site of the 1964 Olympics, provided world swimming powers a chance to lower world records in head-to-head competition. Preceding these meets was the Los Angeles International Invitational at a new Olympic pool, July 14–17, which was advertised as a "shakedown" event prior to the 1984 Olympics.

The first world record of 1983 was not set at any of the five major tournaments but was established during the Soviet Union's winter championship in Moscow's Olympic pool. Vladimir Salnikov lowered the 400-m freestyle record from 3 min 49.57 sec to 3 min 48.32 sec on February 19. Three days later he lowered his 1,500-m freestyle record by almost two seconds, from 14 min 56.35 sec to 14 min 54.76 sec. On July 14 at the Los Angeles meet Salnikov equaled his previous year's achievement of lowering all three distance world marks, winning the 800-m freestyle with a time of 7 min 52.33 sec. His previous record was 7 min 52.83.

United States swimmers made the 1983 national championships at Clovis, Calif., their kickoff for their pre-Olympic effort. Led by Rick Carey from Mount Kisco, N.Y., they achieved six world records. Carey set the pace by erasing the two oldest world records in swimming. On August 3 he lowered the second oldest mark of 1 min 59.19 sec in the 200-m backstroke, set by John Naber in the 1976 Olympics, by clocking 1 min 58.93 sec. On August 6 in the 100-m backstroke preliminary, Carey lowered the oldest swimming mark of 55.49 sec by Naber to 55.44. In the evening final he set a new record of 55.38 sec. Fifteen days later, at the Pan-American Games, Carey again lowered the 100-m backstroke record, to 55.19 sec.

At Clovis on August 6 Steve Lundquist of Jonesboro, Ga., the world record holder for the 100-m breaststroke, clocked 1 min 2.34 sec to lower his world standard, and on August 17 at the Pan-American Games he further lowered the time to 1 min 2.28 sec. On August 6 at Clovis, Matt Gribble of Miami, Fla., followed Lundquist with the third world record when he swam the 100-m butterfly in 53.44 sec. This eclipsed the previous record of 53.81 sec by William Paulus in 1981.

U.S. swimmers dominated the Pan-American Games, winning 25 of 29 events during the six-day competition. The men accounted for three world

World Swimming Records Set in 1983

Event	Name	Country	Time
MEN			
200-m freestyle	Michael Gross	F.R.G.[1]	1 min 48.28 sec
200-m freestyle	Michael Gross	F.R.G.	1 min 47.87 sec
400-m freestyle	Vladimir Salnikov	U.S.S.R.	3 min 48.32 sec
800-m freestyle	Vladimir Salnikov	U.S.S.R.	7 min 52.33 sec
1,500-m freestyle	Vladimir Salnikov	U.S.S.R.	14 min 54.76 sec
100-m backstroke	Rick Carey	U.S.	55.44 sec
100-m backstroke	Rick Carey	U.S.	55.38 sec
100-m backstroke	Rick Carey	U.S.	55.19 sec
200-m backstroke	Rick Carey	U.S.	1 min 58.93 sec
100-m breaststroke	Steve Lundquist	U.S.	1 min 2.34 sec
100-m breaststroke	Steve Lundquist	U.S.	1 min 2.28 sec
100-m butterfly	Matt Gribble	U.S.	53.44 sec
200-m butterfly	Michael Gross	F.R.G.	1 min 57.05 sec
4 × 100-m medley relay	U.S. national team (Rick Carey, Steve Lundquist, Matt Gribble, Rowdy Gaines)	U.S.	3 min 40.42 sec
4 × 200-m freestyle	F.R.G. national team (Thomas Fahrner, Alexander Schwotka, Andreas Schmidt, Michael Gross)	F.R.G.	7 min 20.40 sec
WOMEN			
100-m breaststroke	Ute Geweniger	G.D.R.[2]	1 min 8.51 sec
4 × 100-m medley relay	G.D.R. national team (Ina Kleber, Ute Geweniger, Ines Geissler, Birgit Meinke)	G.D.R.	4 min 5.79 sec
4 × 200-m freestyle relay	G.D.R. national team (Kristin Otto, Astrid Strauss, Cornelia Sirch, Birgit Meineke)	G.D.R.	8 min 2.27 sec

[1]Federal Republic of Germany (West Germany).
[2]German Democratic Republic (East Germany).

records and outclassed teams from Canada and South America. Canada's breaststrokers, Anne Ottenbrite and Kathy Bald, were the only non-U.S. swimmers to win in the women's races, while Brazil's Ricardo Prado, world record holder in the 400-m individual medley, won that event as well as the 200-m medley.

The East German (German Democratic Republic) women strengthened their world domination at the European Championships, setting three world records. Not only did they sweep all the events, placing one-two in 12 individual races and winning the gold medals in the three relays, but two of those victories, in the 4 × 200-m freestyle relay and the 4 × 100-m medley relay, resulted in world records.

Michael Gross of Frankfurt am Main, West Germany (Federal Republic of Germany), opened the European Championships on August 22 by setting a new 200-m freestyle record with a time of 1 min 47.87 sec. Previously, on June 21, at the West German championships in Hanover, Gross had lowered the world record of 1 min 48.93 set by Rowdy Gaines in 1982 to 1 min 48.28 sec.

The Pan Pacific meet in Tokyo resulted in the United States winning 25 out of 29 races. Steve Lundquist was timed in 1 min 2.45 sec to set a new meet 100-m breaststroke record. The other outstanding performance was by Bill Barrett of the U.S., who set a U.S. record of 2 min 2.68 sec for the 200-m individual medley.

Diving. On April 29–30 at The Woodlands, Texas, Greg Louganis of Mission Viejo, Calif. (*see* Biographies), won the springboard and platform gold medals. In women's competition Li Yihua of China won the springboard, and teammate Zhou Jihong the platform.

At the U.S. national championship in Bartlesville, Okla., on August 2–6, Louganis won the 3-m springboard and 10-m platform, the latter his 24th national title. Chris Seufert of Ann Arbor, Mich., won the women's springboard, and Michele Mitchell of Mission Viejo triumphed in the platform.

Louganis repeated his triumphs at the World University Games, winning both the springboard and platform events. Divers from China gained the gold medals in the women's diving, Shi Meigin winning the springboard and Lu Wei the platform. Wendy Wyland of the U.S. was the runner-up in the platform and Megan Neyer in the springboard.

WIDE WORLD

Rick Carey, a 20-year-old from Mount Kisco, New York, set a world record in the 100-metre backstroke during the Pan-American Games, held in Caracas, Venezuela, in August.

UPI

A new world record in the 50-metre freestyle was set by Dara Torres, 16, of Beverly Hills, California, at the U.S. national championships in August. Her time was 25.62 sec.

At the Pan-American Games Louganis again demonstrated his superiority, retaining his 3-m springboard and 10-m platform titles. Kelly McCormick won the springboard, followed by Wyland. The latter won the gold medal in the platform, with Argentina's Veronica Ribot finishing second.

At the Los Angeles International meet Louganis won the springboard but was upset by Bruce Kimball of Ann Arbor and finished second in the platform. Chris Snode of Great Britain placed second in the springboard. Neyer and Wyland finished one-two in the springboard, with the order reversed in the platform.

Synchronized Swimming. The U.S. championships in synchronized swimming, scheduled to be an Olympic event in 1984, took place June 23–28 at New Haven, Conn. Tracie Ruiz of Seattle, Wash., won the solo championship, followed by teammate Candy Costie, and Mary Visniski of Walnut Creek, Calif., won the bronze. Ruiz and Costie paired to win the duet crown over Sarah and Karen Josephson of Columbus, Ohio. The team championship was taken by Walnut Creek. On August 5–7 in Los Angeles, swimmers from 12 nations vied for America Cup II. Ruiz won the solo gold medal, with Sharon Hambrook of Canada and Miwako Motoyoshi of Japan gaining the silver and bronze, respectively. Ruiz and Costie won the duet, followed by Canada and Japan in second and third.

In the Pan-American Games Ruiz completed a sweep of the major titles, winning the solo. Carolyn Waldo and Kelly Kryczka of Canada placed second and third. In the duet competition Ruiz and Costie won the gold medal, outpointing the Canadian pair of Penny and Vicky Vilagos. Mexico's Pilar Ramírez and Claudia Novelo took the bronze medal. (ALBERT SCHOENFIELD)

[452.B.4.a.i]

Switzerland

Switzerland

A federal republic in west central Europe consisting of a confederation of 26 cantons (six of which are demi-cantons), Switzerland is bounded by West Germany, Austria, Liechtenstein, Italy, and France. Area: 41,293 sq km (15,943 sq mi). Pop. (1983 est.): 6,423,100. Cap.: Bern (pop., 1982 est., 145,300). Largest city: Zürich (pop., 1982 est., 366,200). Language (1980): German 65%; French 18.4%; Italian 9.8%; Romansh 1%; other 5.8%. Religion (1980): Roman Catholic 48%; Protestant 44%; other 8%. President in 1983, Pierre Aubert.

The parliamentary elections held on Oct. 23, 1983, in Switzerland reversed the trend established by preceding elections, in which voter participation had dropped from 72.4% in 1947 to 48% in 1979; the turnout rose slightly to 48.9%. In the opinion of some commentators the spread of direct democracy—that is, voting for or against a circumscribed, concrete issue rather than for party representatives or directives—as well as the pronounced regional decentralization of political and governmental activity prevented the elections to the national Parliament from being the crucial event that they are in other countries.

SWITZERLAND

Education. (1981–82) Primary, pupils 469,700, teachers (1970–71) 14,672; secondary, pupils 420,900, teachers (1970–71) 1,758; vocational, pupils 231,100; teacher training, students 9,700; higher, students 77,900, teaching staff (universities only; 1979–80) 5,872.

Finance. Monetary unit: Swiss franc, with (Sept. 20, 1983) a free rate of SFr 2.16 to U.S. $1 (SFr 3.25 = £1 sterling). Gold and other reserves (June 1983) U.S. $16,413,000,000. Budget (1982 actual): revenue SFr 18,857,000,000; expenditure SFr 18,001,000,000. Gross national product (1982) SFr 205.5 billion. Money supply (May 1983) SFr 70,170,000,000. Cost of living (1975 = 100; June 1983) 130.2.

Foreign Trade. (1982) Imports SFr 58,115,000,000; exports SFr 52,687,000,000. Import sources: EEC 66% (West Germany 30%, France 11%, Italy 10%, U.K. 5%); U.S. 7%. Export destinations: EEC 48% (West Germany 18%, France 9%, Italy 8%, U.K. 6%); U.S. 8%. Main exports: machinery 31%; chemicals 21%; precious metals and stones 7%; watches and clocks 7%; instruments, etc. (excluding watches and clocks) 6%; textile yarns and fabrics 5%. Tourism (1981): visitors 11,250,000; gross receipts U.S. $3,035,000,000.

Transport and Communications. Roads (1982) 66,662 km (including 986 km expressways). Motor vehicles in use (1982): passenger 2,473,300; commercial 178,300. Railways: (1980) 5,049 km (including 5,015 km electrified); traffic (1982) 9,023,000,000 passenger-km, freight 6,501,000,000 net ton-km. Air traffic (1982): 11,773,000,000 passenger-km; freight 500.7 million net ton-km. Shipping (1982): merchant vessels 100 gross tons and over 32; gross tonnage 315,161. Telephones (Jan. 1981) 4,612,400. Radio licenses (Dec. 1980) 2,252,900. Television licenses (Dec. 1980) 1,979,500.

Agriculture. Production (in 000; metric tons; 1982): wheat c. 423; barley c. 211; corn (1981) c. 117; potatoes c. 1,050; rapeseed c. 37; apples c. 450; pears (1981) c. 130; sugar, raw value (1981) c. 136; wine c. 170; milk c. 3,650; butter c. 32; cheese c. 125; beef and veal 160; pork 284. Livestock (in 000; April 1982): cattle 1,945; sheep (1981) c. 336; pigs 2,093; chickens (1981) c. 6,146.

Industry. Index of industrial production (1975 = 100; 1982) 109. Production (in 000; metric tons; 1981): cement 4,340; aluminum 82; petroleum products 4,007; man-made fibres (1980) 77; cigarettes (units; 1980) 31,264,000; watches (exports; units; 1980) 28,514; manufactured gas (cu m; 1980) 51,000; electricity (kw-hr; 1982) 50,761,000.

UPI

In September a Bulgarian passenger jetliner entered Swiss airspace without announcement. It was escorted out by two Swiss fighter aircraft (one in foreground).

The October elections did not produce any real change in the political makeup of Parliament. The Socialists and smaller parties to their left lost nine seats, while the centre-right Radicals and smaller parties to their right gained eight. The election of a few environmentalists added the only really new element. (For tabulated results, *see* POLITICAL PARTIES.)

The election was preceded by the resignation, to take effect at the end of the year, of two of the seven members of the federal Council (Cabinet). The Social Democrats nominated a woman, Lilian Uchtenhagen, an economist, to fill one of the seats. However, the Parliament, voting in a secret ballot, rejected her and instead elected Otto Stich, who did not have the party's endorsement. Critics accused Parliament of rejecting Uchtenhagen because she was a woman.

The overall economic situation remained stable but was considered sufficiently stagnant to warrant the launching by the federal government of an ambitious "anticrisis" program. This called for increased investment, much of it for military equipment but some to be spent on renewing railroad rolling stock and building houses and civil protection shelters. The badly suffering watch industry found it difficult to survive Japanese competition.

While gross national product and the balance of payments evolved satisfactorily, the trade balance was less favourable than usual owing to the very strong position of the Swiss franc. The living standard of the Swiss remained one of the highest among industrialized countries. In midyear the Organization for Economic Cooperation and Development noted that the relative recovery in the area covered by its research had begun to make itself felt in Switzerland. As a result of expenditure worth SFr 330 million aimed at economic revival, however, the federal budget deficit was expected to climb to SFr 1,156,000,000. Social services again claimed the highest proportion (21.4%) of federal funds, closely followed by defense (20.7%).

Among issues discussed by Parliament were proposals to develop a nuclear-power policy that would reconcile opposing points of view; to redefine the general concept of military defense; to elaborate a system of price controls as called for by the results of a plebiscite on that issue in 1982; to revise the policy of granting asylum to political refugees; and to introduce an alternative to military service for conscientious objectors.

The final decision on whether Switzerland should apply for full membership in the UN was once again postponed. While everyone seemed to agree that a formal guarantee of the continuation of Switzerland's historic "permanent and armed" neutrality should be made the condition of full adherence to the UN, the actual phrasing of this condition presented problems of logic and diplomacy.

The sacrosanct nature of Switzerland's banking secrecy came under attack from both inside and outside the country. Because the economy was so closely supported by and linked to the traditionally strong banking system, the issue aroused perhaps even more popular discussion than that of adherence to the UN. A certain willingness to review and partially redefine the system of banking secrecy was apparently gaining ground, not only within the government but also among enlightened bankers; only a determined left-wing minority wanted to abolish the system entirely.

(MELANIE STAERK)

Syria

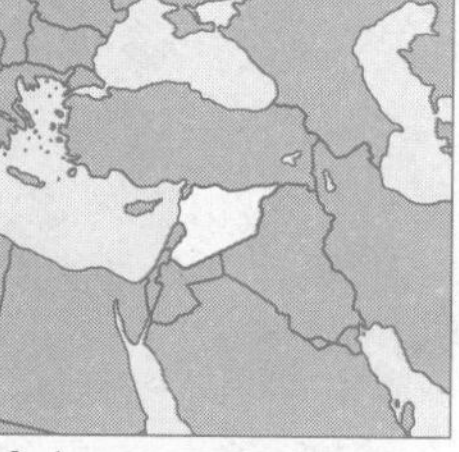

Syria

A republic in southwestern Asia on the Mediterranean Sea, Syria is bordered by Turkey, Iraq, Jordan, Israel, and Lebanon. Area: 185,180 sq km (71,498 sq mi). Pop. (1983 est.): 9,530,000. Cap. and largest city: Damascus (pop., 1982 est., 1,129,000). Language: Arabic (official); also Kurdish, Armenian, Turkish, Kabardian, and Syriac. Religion: predominantly (over 80%) Muslim. President in 1983, Gen. Hafez al-Assad; premier, Abdul Rauf al-Kasm.

Syria moved to the centre of the Middle East political arena in 1983. Pres. Hafez al-Assad demonstrated his objection to being excluded from ne-

WIDE WORLD

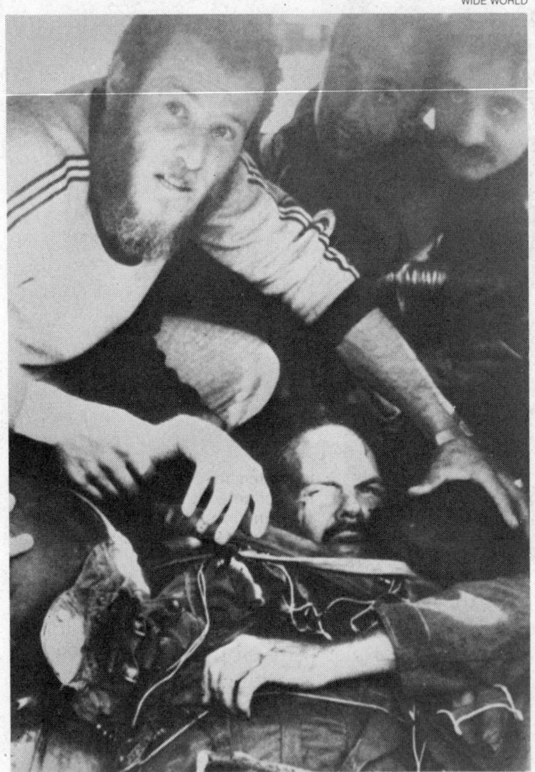

U.S. airman Lieut. Mark Lange lies dying in the back of a car where he was helped by a Lebanese civilian after being shot down by Syrian surface-to-air missiles on December 4.

gotiations about the future of the Palestinians by rejecting the U.S. attempt to revive the so-called Jordanian option, a proposal to grant Palestinians a form of independence under Jordanian guardianship. Assad's hard-line stance was the key to events that later overtook Palestine Liberation Organization (PLO) chairman Yasir Arafat (*see* BIOGRAPHIES). Syria backed the PLO rebels who attacked Arafat's base at Tripoli, Lebanon, in November in a bid to topple him. Arafat and his fighters were evacuated from Tripoli in December.

Before it would agree on a peace settlement in Lebanon, Syria demanded, among other things, withdrawal of Israeli troops from Lebanon and a new U.S. initiative to bring about the return of the Golan Heights, seized from Syria by Israel during the 1967 war. On July 6 U.S. Secretary of State George Shultz had five hours of fruitless talks with Assad on the issue of the withdrawal of foreign troops. A Syrian statement denounced the Israeli-Lebanese withdrawal pact, but it was also clear that Assad objected, once again, to having been excluded from the negotiation process. On November 16 Syria maintained that it would work to help ensure an effective cease-fire in Beirut, but much of the shelling in the capital was reportedly coming from Syrian-controlled areas.

In an editorial on November 9, the *Wall Street Journal* claimed that Saudi Arabia had paid Syria $4 billion "to buy a ceasefire in Lebanon's Shouf Mountains." Saudi Arabian sources denied the report. The newspaper also alleged that Saudi Arabia had given Syria $2 billion with which to buy Soviet-supplied surface-to-air missiles after clashes with Israel in 1982 in which Syria's air-defense system had been destroyed.

Worsening relations with the U.S. were expressed in a statement by U.S. Defense Secretary Caspar Weinberger on November 22, in which he blamed Iranians sponsored by Syria for the deaths of U.S. Marines in the Beirut bomb attack of October 23. On November 15 Weinberger alleged that there were as many as 9,000 Soviet troops in Syria, representing a "serious military presence." Syria appeared to exercise some restraint in failing to retaliate for French air attacks on positions in the Syrian-controlled Bekaa Valley on November 17. However, on December 3 U.S. reconnaissance planes were attacked from Syrian-controlled territory. Two U.S. planes on a retaliatory raid were shot down the following day, and a U.S. airman was captured. U.S. civil rights leader the Rev. Jesse Jackson went to Syria at year's end in an effort to obtain the airman's release.

Syria's relations with Iraq remained poor. It resisted Arab pressure to reopen the Kirkuk–Banias pipeline, which would allow Iraq to export more oil. On November 8 the Kuwaiti National Assembly called for a suspension of aid to Syria because of its role in Lebanon. On November 13 the U.S. Congress voted to cancel previously agreed economic aid to Syria. Syria increased its trade with the Eastern-bloc countries during the year.

President Assad's absence from public view in November was at first attributed to surgery for the removal of his appendix, but on December 29 the defense minister said in an interview that Assad had been suffering from a heart ailment. On November 22 Assad received his ministers, but other matters of state were left in the hands of the foreign minister.

SYRIA

Education. (1980–81) Primary, pupils 1,523,339, teachers 54,519; secondary, pupils 564,793, teachers 30,363; vocational, pupils 25,148, teachers 3,194; teacher training, students 11,147, teachers 1,306; higher, students 110,823, teaching staff (universities only; 1975–76) 1,332.

Finance. Monetary unit: Syrian pound, with (Sept. 20, 1983) an official rate of S£3.925 to U.S. $1 (free rate of S£5.91 = £1 sterling). Gold and other reserves (June 1982) U.S. $157 million. Budget (total; 1982 est.) balanced at S£33,345 million. Gross domestic product (1981) S£63,422 million. Money supply (June 1982) S£25,313 million. Cost of living (Damascus; 1975 = 100; Feb. 1983) 237.

Foreign Trade. (1982) Imports S£15,808 million; exports S£7,954 million. Import sources (1981): Iraq 19%; Italy 10%; Saudi Arabia 8%; West Germany 7%; France 5%. Export destinations (1981): Italy 42%; France 14%; Romania 10%; Greece 8%; U.S.S.R. 5%. Main exports: crude oil 51%; cotton 7%.

Transport and Communications. Roads (1980) 18,844 km. Motor vehicles in use (1980): passenger c. 65,500; commercial c. 69,100. Railways: (1980) 2,017 km; traffic (1981) 443 million passenger-km, freight 704 million net ton-km. Air traffic (1982): 947 million passenger-km; freight 12.9 million net ton-km. Telephones (Dec. 1981) 355,400. Radio receivers (Dec. 1978) 2,022,000. Television receivers (Dec. 1980) 385,000.

Agriculture. Production (in 000; metric tons; 1982): wheat 1,556; barley 661; potatoes (1981) 272; pumpkins (1981) c. 192; cucumbers (1981) c. 285; tomatoes c. 750; onions c. 180; watermelons (1981) c. 923; melons (1981) c. 210; grapes 404; olives c. 460; cottonseed 422; cotton, lint 142. Livestock (in 000; 1981): sheep 10,504; goats 1,060; cattle 817; horses c. 53; asses c. 244; chickens 13,965.

Industry. Production (in 000; metric tons; 1982): cement 2,674; crude oil 8,631; natural gas (cu m) c. 250,000; petroleum products (1981) 5,410; cotton yarn 42; phosphate rock (1981) 1,319; salt (1981) 111; electricity (kw-hr) 5,429,000.

The economy was put under increasing strain by defense spending; nearly 30% of the $9.5 billion budget for 1983 went for defense. A shortfall of more than $600 million was forecast. The foreign debt total of $2.5 billion did not include funds pledged by various Arab states since 1978, when the Arab League summit drew up a support package for the "frontline states" confronting Israel. In 1982 oil production was maintained at the 1981 level, but Western sources predicted a decline in 1983. (JOHN WHELAN)

See also Middle Eastern Affairs.

Table Tennis

In late April Tokyo welcomed athletes from 57 associations to the biennial world table tennis championships. China retained both the Swaythling Cup, the symbol of supremacy in the men's team competition, and the Marcel Corbillon Cup, awarded to the best women's team. Sweden's men's team finished second, ahead of Hungary, England, and Japan. In the women's team standings, Japan was runner-up. North Korea was next, followed by the U.S.S.R. and South Korea.

In individual events, Guo Yuehua (China) defeated Cai Zhenhua (China) in four sets to win the men's singles crown. In the final women's singles match Cao Yanhua (China) triumphed over Yang Young-Ja (South Korea). The Yugoslav pair of Dragutin Surbek and Zoran Kalinic needed five sets to defeat Xie Saike and Jiang Jialiang (China) in the final match of the men's doubles. The women's doubles title went to Shen Jianping and Dai Lili (China), who defeated Geng Lijuan and Huang Junqun (China). The five-set all-China final of the mixed doubles was won by Guo Yuehua and Ni Xialian over Chen Xinhua and Tong Ling.

During the championships the International Table Tennis Federation (ITTF) admitted Bermuda, Brunei, and Papua New Guinea to full membership and the Chinese Taipei Association of Taiwan to "membership in good standing." The total membership of affiliated associations was thus increased to 121. The ITTF also confirmed that Sweden would be the site of the 1985 championships; India was given the option of holding the event in 1987. In addition, the ITTF ruled that as of Jan. 1, 1984, the two surfaces of the racket must have distinguishably different colours, whether the covering material was different or not. This rule would be enforced in all world, open-international, and continental tournaments.

Hong Kong totally dominated the Commonwealth Championships held in Kuala Lumpur, Malaysia, in April. Hong Kong won both team titles, both singles crowns, the mixed doubles, and both the men's and women's doubles. The Indian men's doubles team represented the only association to challenge Hong Kong in a title match.

In early February the European top 12 players tournament got under way in Thornaby, England. After the men's competition Milan Orlowski (Czech.) was ranked number one. Next in order were Desmond Douglas (England), Mikael Appelgren (Sweden), Erik Lindh (Sweden), and Jacques Secretin (France). Olga Nemes (Rom.) was ranked

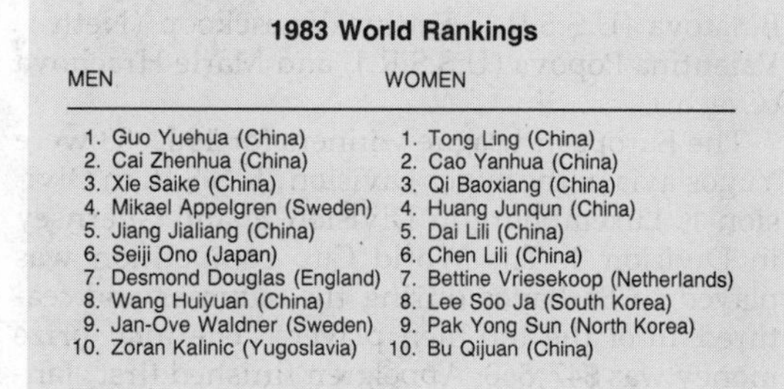

1983 World Rankings

MEN	WOMEN
1. Guo Yuehua (China)	1. Tong Ling (China)
2. Cai Zhenhua (China)	2. Cao Yanhua (China)
3. Xie Saike (China)	3. Qi Baoxiang (China)
4. Mikael Appelgren (Sweden)	4. Huang Junqun (China)
5. Jiang Jialiang (China)	5. Dai Lili (China)
6. Seiji Ono (Japan)	6. Chen Lili (China)
7. Desmond Douglas (England)	7. Bettine Vriesekoop (Netherlands)
8. Wang Huiyuan (China)	8. Lee Soo Ja (South Korea)
9. Jan-Ove Waldner (Sweden)	9. Pak Yong Sun (North Korea)
10. Zoran Kalinic (Yugoslavia)	10. Bu Qijuan (China)

WIDE WORLD

The biennial world table tennis championships were held in Tokyo in April. China retained both the cups for the top-ranked men's and women's teams.

first among the women. She was followed by Flura Bulatova (U.S.S.R.), Bettine Vriesekoop (Neth.), Valentina Popova (U.S.S.R.), and Marie Hrachova (Czech.).

The European League winners for 1982–83 were Yugoslavia in the Super Division, U.S.S.R. in Division 1, Luxembourg in Division 2, and Guernsey in Division 3. The World Cup competition was played in Barbados during the summer and featured 16 of the top men players. The total prize money was $47,560. Appelgren finished first, Jan-Ove Waldner (Sweden) second, Lindh third, Kalinic fourth, and Istvan Jonyer (Yugos.) fifth.

Australia and New Zealand shared the limelight during the Oceania championships held in September 1982. Australia's men players and New Zealand's women players dominated their respective competitions. Players from seven countries competed for the first Asian Cup in Wuxi (Wuhsi), China, in October 1983. Chinese athletes dominated the competition, taking the top three places in both the men's and women's divisions.

(ARTHUR KINGSLEY VINT)

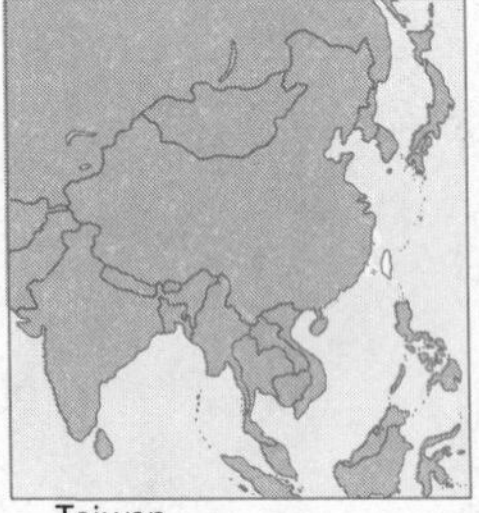

Taiwan

Taiwan

Taiwan, which consists of the islands of Taiwan (also known in the West as Formosa) and Quemoy and other surrounding islands, is the seat of the Republic of China (Nationalist China). It is north of the Philippines, southwest of Japan, and east of Hong Kong. The island of Taiwan has an area of 35,779 sq km (13,814 sq mi); including its 77 outlying islands (14 in the Taiwan group and 63 in the Pescadores group), the area of Taiwan totals 36,002 sq km (13,900 sq mi). Pop. (1983 est.): 18,590,000. Area and pop. exclude the Quemoy and Matsu groups, which are administered as an occupied part of Fujian (Fukien) Province. Their combined area is about 160 sq km; their population at the end of 1980 was 61,000. Cap. and largest city: Taipei (pop., 1983 est., 2,327,600). Language: Mandarin Chinese (official). Religion (1980 est.): Confucian and Taoist 48.5%; Buddhist 43%; Christian 7.4%; other 1.1%. President in 1983, Chiang Ching-kuo; president of the Executive Yuan (premier), Sun Yun-suan.

Throughout 1983 Taiwan persevered in its effort to remain politically and economically viable in the face of pressures to conciliate with the Communist government on the Chinese mainland. Five years after U.S. derecognition of the Nationalist government, Taiwan staunchly continued to reject the efforts of Beijing's (Peking's) leaders to move toward reunification. Although fewer than two dozen states still maintained official diplomatic relations with the island, Taiwan registered important gains in unofficial ties.

Taiwan's success in resisting formal association with the People's Republic of China (PRC) rested on two principal pillars: unhampered commercial dealings with the outside world and continued U.S. support. In the economic arena, Taiwan enjoyed trade relations with nearly 150 states; almost all the major Western countries now maintained semiofficial trade offices in Taipei. Two-way trade in 1982 totaled more than U.S. $40 billion (a modest decrease from 1981), with Taiwan enjoying a record balance of payments surplus in excess of $3 billion. Despite the effect of the global recession on Taiwan's export-oriented economy, the island resumed unexpectedly rapid growth in 1983, with trade for the year likely to surpass $44 billion. Trade with the U.S. alone was expected to exceed $15 billion in 1983, almost three times the amount of U.S. trade with the PRC. Taiwan's per capita income in 1982 reached U.S. $2,342, second only to Japan in Asia.

Taiwan's biggest gains in 1983, however, occurred in the field of commercial aviation. In April China Airlines (the island's flag carrier) and KLM Royal Dutch Airlines began to fly to one another's capitals, thereby providing Taiwan with its first direct commercial air link with Western Europe. During June Pan American World Airways defied warnings from Beijing and resumed direct flights to Taipei, suspended since Pan Am became the first U.S. carrier to fly to the PRC.

Despite the improving atmosphere in U.S.-PRC

UPI

Wang Xiejeng (Wang Hsieh-cheng; second from right) waves after defecting from China to Korea and then to Taiwan in his jet fighter plane. He is shown arm in arm with Wu Henggen (Wu Hung-ken), who defected via South Korea in 1982, as Taiwanese fighter pilots who escorted Wang to Taipei applaud.

TAIWAN

Education. (1981–82) Primary, pupils 2,226,699, teachers 70,055; secondary, pupils 1,269,373, teachers 58,713; vocational, pupils 394,258, teachers 14,442; higher, students 364,162, teaching staff 17,292.

Finance. Monetary unit: new Taiwan dollar, with (Sept. 20, 1983) a free rate of NT$40.15 to U.S. $1 (NT$60.47 = £1 sterling). Budget (total; 1982 actual): revenue NT$467,058,000,000; expenditure NT$481,564,000,000. Gross national product (1982) NT$1,824,244,000,000. Money supply (March 1983) NT$525,230,000,000. Cost of living (1975 = 100; April 1983) 189.2.

Foreign Trade. (1982) Imports NT$736.1 billion; exports NT$864.2 billion. Import sources: Japan 25%; U.S. 24%; Saudi Arabia 10%; Kuwait 7%. Export destinations: U.S. 39%; Japan 11%; Hong Kong 7%. Main exports: machinery 21% (including telecommunications apparatus 9%); clothing 13%; textile yarns and fabrics 8%; food 7%; footwear 7%; toys and sports goods 6%; transport equipment 5%. Tourism (1981): visitors 1,116,000; gross receipts U.S. $1,080,000,000.

Transport and Communications. Roads (1981) 17,522 km. Motor vehicles in use (1982): passenger 592,600; commercial 314,600. Railways: (1981) 3,700 km; traffic (1982) 8,204,000,000 passenger-km, freight 2,175,000,000 net ton-km. Air traffic (1982): 8,198,000,000 passenger-km; freight 1,159,200,000 net ton-km. Shipping (1982): merchant vessels 100 gross tons and over 511; gross tonnage 2,225,377. Telephones (Dec. 1982) 4,356,800. Radio licenses (Dec. 1976) 1,493,100. Television receivers (Dec. 1980) 3,993,000.

Agriculture. Production (in 000; metric tons; 1982): rice 2,483; sweet potatoes 741; cassava 118; sugar, raw value 641; citrus fruit 391; bananas 203; pineapples 145; tea 24; tobacco 26; pork 644; fish catch 923. Livestock (in 000; Dec. 1981): cattle 128; pigs 4,826; goats and sheep 177; chickens 43,899.

Industry. Production (in 000; metric tons; 1982): coal 2,383; crude oil c. 120; natural gas (cu m) 1,232,000; electricity (kw-hr; 1981) 41,381,000; cement 13,432; crude steel 1,712; sulfuric acid 685; plastics and resins (1981) 489; petroleum products (1981) 14,430; cotton yarn 161; man-made fibres 731; paper and board 1,558; radio receivers (units) 6,687; television receivers (units) 4,752.

relations, the Reagan administration reiterated its commitment to close if unofficial ties with Taipei. Over continuing objections from Beijing, the U.S. announced that total military sales to Taiwan for 1983 would amount to $800 million, principally in surface-to-air missiles and spare parts for aircraft and tanks. Some sales of refurbished F-104 fighter aircraft were also announced. But Taipei expressed growing concern about the prospect of U.S. sales of defense-related technology to Beijing, since it feared that an infusion of such technology would diminish Taiwan's qualitative edge over the PRC, especially in combat aircraft.

During July the PRC publicized two separate offers from Deng Xiaoping (Teng Hsiao-p'ing), China's most powerful leader, that promised Taiwan substantial autonomy as an inducement to enter negotiations, including renewed assurances that, following reunification, the island could maintain its present political institutions, armed forces, and capitalist practices. Leading officials on Taiwan denounced Deng's proposals as a ruse and reiterated their opposition to any negotiations with Beijing as long as the PRC continued to espouse Marxism-Leninism.

Deng's overtures reflected mounting concern in Beijing with the succession to Pres. Chiang Ching-kuo, the son of Chiang Kai-shek, now 73 and in declining health. The PRC feared that Chiang's passage from the scene portended the emergence of a leadership much less committed to the principle of a unified Chinese state. But the increasing political participation of the native Taiwanese, who comprise 85% of the island's population, had not led to major shifts in the island's politics. In early December legislative elections, the ruling Kuomintang (Nationalist Party) won 62 out of 71 seats, with several leading nonparty independents defeated in their reelection bid. Although the campaign was conducted without major incident, and with more than 63% voter turnout, the defeat of the regime's moderate critics and the victory of a small number of more vocal Taiwanese political activists renewed concern about the longer term prospects for political stability on the island.

(JONATHAN D. POLLACK)

Tanzania

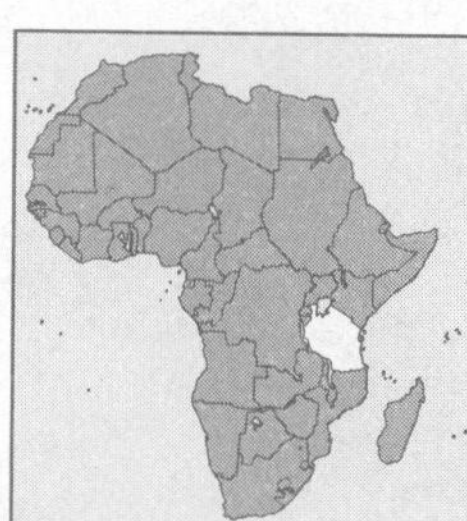

Tanzania

An East African member of the Commonwealth, the republic of Tanzania consists of two parts: Tanganyika, on the Indian Ocean, bordered by Kenya, Uganda, Rwanda, Burundi, Zaire, Zambia, Malawi, and Mozambique; and Zanzibar, just off the coast, including Zanzibar Island, Pemba Island, and small islets. Total area of the united republic: 945,050 sq km (364,886 sq mi). Total pop. (1983 est.): 19,737,000, including 98.9% African and 0.7% Indo-Pakistani. Capital designate: Dodoma. Seat of government and largest city: Dar es Salaam (pop., 1978, 769,400) in Tanganyika. Language: Kiswahili (official) and English. Religion (1980 est.): traditional beliefs 23%; Christian 44%;

TANZANIA

Education. (1980–81) Primary, pupils 3,359,966, teachers 81,153; secondary (1979–80), pupils 68,301, teachers 3,357; vocational (1979–80), pupils 1,097, teachers 126; teacher training (1979–80), pupils 9,567, teachers 685; higher (1979–80), students 4,031, teaching staff 1,068.

Finance. Monetary unit: Tanzanian shilling, with (Sept. 20, 1983) a free rate of TShs 12.25 to U.S. $1 (TShs 18.45 = £1 sterling). Gold and other reserves (June 1983) U.S. $9 million. Budget (1982–83 est.): revenue TShs 10.7 billion; expenditure TShs 14,144,000,000. Gross national product (1981) TShs 43,231,000,000. Money supply (May 1983) TShs 17,838,000,000. Cost of living (1975 = 100; 1st quarter 1983) 366.

Foreign Trade. (1982) Imports TShs 8,808,000,000; exports TShs 4,029,000,000. Import sources (1981): U.K. 14%; Japan 12%; West Germany 10%; Bahrain 7%; The Netherlands 6%; U.S. 6%. Export destinations (1981): West Germany 15%; U.K. 13%; India 7%; Indonesia 6%; Hong Kong 6%; Algeria 5%; The Netherlands 5%. Main exports (1980): coffee 26%; cotton 10%; cloves 9%; fruit and vegetables 9%; textile yarns and fabrics 6%; sisal 6%; petroleum products 5%; diamonds 5%.

Transport and Communications. Roads (1981) 53,613 km. Motor vehicles in use (1981): passenger 43,200; commercial 22,500. Railways (1980) 3,550 km. Air traffic (1982): 210 million passenger-km; freight 1.2 million net ton-km. Telephones (Jan. 1981) 93,200. Radio receivers (Dec. 1980) 500,000. Television receivers (Dec. 1980) 7,000.

Agriculture. Production (in 000; metric tons; 1982): corn c. 800; millet c. 150; sorghum c. 220; rice c. 200; sweet potatoes c. 330; cassava c. 4,700; sugar, raw value (1981) c. 124; dry beans c. 152; mangoes c. 180; bananas c. 800; cashew nuts (1981) c. 72; coffee c. 55; tea c. 16; tobacco c. 16; cotton, lint c. 43; sisal c. 80; meat (1981) 189; fish catch (1981) 226; timber (cu m; 1981) 35,895. Livestock (in 000; 1982): sheep c. 3,937; goats c. 5,906; cattle (1981) 12,701; chickens c. 25,000.

Industry. Production (in 000; metric tons; 1981): cement 400; salt 41; diamonds (metric carats) c. 250; petroleum products 513; electricity (kw-hr) 715,000.

Muslim 33%. President in 1983, Julius Nyerere; prime ministers, Cleopa David Msuya and, from February 24, Edward Moringe Sokoine.

Officials of Tanzania's ruling Revolutionary Party (Chama Cha Mapinduzi) were shown the plans of a Chinese team of town planners for a new city of Zanzibar which would take 20 years to build and would accommodate 300,000 people; the first phase of construction began in 1983. Against the background of Tanzania's shrinking economy and huge foreign debt, the plan appeared an expensive luxury, though it would provide housing for the squatter population and better sanitation for everyone. At a meeting in Arusha in January, the defense ministers of the southern African frontline states, of which Tanzania was one, agreed to step up material as well as political support for nationalist movements in southern Africa. The decision threatened the government with further economic problems.

On January 21 a number of soldiers and civilians were arrested in northwestern Tanzania following rumours of a threatened coup. The charges of treason against them were withdrawn without explanation in June, apparently to avoid a public trial. After their technical release they were immediately detained again under presidential orders.

In February Pres. Julius Nyerere recalled former prime minister Edward Moringe Sokoine, who had retired in 1980 because of ill health, to replace Cleopa David Msuya, who was moved to the Ministry of Finance. Former defense minister Abdallah Twalipo was given special duties relating to state security. The first results of these changes were seen in late March when a campaign was launched that resulted in the arrest of more than 1,200 people accused of economic sabotage; this term embraced smuggling, illegal dealings in currency, and hoarding of scarce goods. The arrested persons were held under the Preventive Detention Act, and some judges and other legal experts claimed that this misused an act passed to deal with political instability. Parliament then passed a new Economic Sabotage Act which set up special tribunals with powers to order detention for up to 15 years and confiscate property. In October some 6,000 persons were reportedly rounded up under a law requiring all able-bodied persons to work.

In May Cleopa Msuya announced that he would have to negotiate with foreign bankers to postpone the repayment of debts. The continuing drought added to the burden of meeting demand for food, and the lack of foreign exchange seriously restricted imports. China agreed to postpone repayment of a $550 million loan for ten years.

It was decided to reopen the border with Kenya at a meeting of the presidents of Tanzania, Kenya, and Uganda in Arusha in November. The dispute over the distribution of the assets of the former East African Community, a disagreement that had led to Tanzania's refusal to reopen the border, was settled after lengthy mediation sponsored by the World Bank. Kenya had inherited the major share of the assets and agreed to make the largest contribution to the settlement. It was hoped that the new accord would lead to the growth of trade within eastern Africa. (KENNETH INGHAM)

Target Sports

Archery. Rick McKinney of Glendale, Ariz., defeated Darrell Pace of Hamilton, Ohio, for the 1983 men's world archery championship in a struggle so close that it was decided by a tie-breaking technicality. Kim Jin-Ho of South Korea easily won the women's title.

The championships were held October 19–22 in Long Beach, Calif. They attracted 200 contestants from 40 nations. Each archer shot a double round, a round consisting of 36 shots at each of four distances. Those distances for men were 30, 50, 70, and 90 m; for women, 30, 50, 60, and 70 m. A perfect double-round score was 2,880.

McKinney and Pace, rivals for a decade, tied for first place at 2,617. Such ties are broken by the number of arrows in the 10, or innermost, ring. McKinney won on that count, 124–116, and thereby gained his second world championship (the first was in 1977). Pace won the title in 1975 and 1979. Pace seemed certain of victory when his final arrow was headed for the gold 10 ring. But it deflected off another arrow and scored 9 instead of 10, and the point he lost cost him the championship.

In the women's competition Kim scored 2,616. Like McKinney's and Pace's scores among the men, it was a record for world-championship competition. The leading U.S. women were Ruth Rowe of Gaithersburg, Md., in sixth place (2,531) and Luonn Ryon of Parker Dam, Calif., in ninth (2,510). The U.S. men retained their team title, while the U.S. women finished third behind South Korea and West Germany.

Natalia Butuzova of the Soviet Union did not defend the women's title because her nation withdrew a week before the competition, citing "existing circumstances." No Soviet athletic teams had competed in the United States since a Soviet military plane shot down a South Korean civilian airliner on September 1.

Pace and Rowe won the Pan-American Games championships in Caracas, Venezuela, while McKinney and Nancy Myrick took the U.S. titles at Long Beach. Actually, non-U.S. competitors, led by Kim, took the first six women's places in the national championships, but only a U.S. citizen can become champion. (FRANK LITSKY)

[452.B.4.h.i]

Shooting. Eighteen nations competed in the shooting events at the Pan-American Games. The U.S. won 31 of 36 gold medals and set five new world records. Thirty nations competed at the 1983 World Moving Target Championships at Edmonton, Alta., where the Soviet Union won six gold medals and the U.S. five. Canada, China, and France each won one. Teams from 23 nations fired at the World Airgun Championships at Innsbruck, Austria. The U.S. rifle and pistol championships were held at Camp Perry, Ohio.

TRAP AND SKEET. Dan Carlisle fired the first perfect International Shooting Union trap score of 200 at the Pan-American Games to win the individual gold medal and set a new world record. The win-

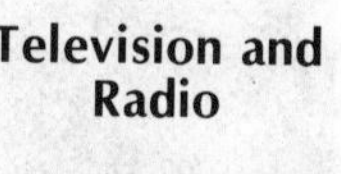

BOB BROWN/SPORTS ILLUSTRATED

Rick McKinney of Glendale, Arizona, won the men's world archery championship with a tie-breaker at Long Beach, California.

ning U.S. team score was a world record 441 out of a possible 450. Carlisle and Matt Dryke each broke 150 skeet targets to lead the U.S. team to another world record score of 442.

At the World Moving Target Championships the U.S. men's trap team won with a score of 413. The Soviet team was second with 399, while the Australians finished third with 397. High individual men's trap score was a 188 fired by John Primrose of Canada. The U.S. men's skeet team won with a 438. Second place went to the Soviet team with 433, while the Czechoslovaks placed third with 431. Dryke had the high individual score with 195.

In the women's events, the U.S. trap team placed first with 357. Spain followed with 339, and China was third with 325. Connie Tomsovic of the U.S. won individual first place with 177. The Chinese skeet team took first place with a score of 405. The U.S. placed second with 374, and Sweden finished third with 357. High individual score was a 290 fired by Svetlana Yakimova of the U.S.S.R.

Rifles. At the Pan-American Games, Lones Wigger of the U.S. won a gold medal for his score of 1,157 in the 300-m free rifle event. His daughter Deena took another for her score of 591 in the women's 50-m English match. The U.S. team won the women's air rifle match with 1,138. Canada placed second with 1,096, and Cuba was third with 1,081. The top individual air rifle score for women was 384, shot by Pat Spurgin of the U.S. In the 50-m English match the U.S. team placed first with 1,776, followed by Canada with 1,768 and Cuba with 1,760.

At the World Moving Target Championships Soviet marksmen won all team events and most top individual awards. Gold medal U.S.S.R. team scores on the running game target were 1,759 for normal runs and 1,179 for mixed runs, both new world records. The 1,211 shot by the Soviet team on the 10-m air rifle range was another record. H. J. Tiefar of West Germany won the individual mixed runs event with 386, while Jean-Luc Tricore of France took the top award in 10-m air rifle with the same score.

The U.S. high-power rifle championship was won by Patrick McCann with an aggregate score of 2,364–113X. David Weaver placed first in both the metallic-sight and any-sight matches to win the small-bore rifle championship with an aggregate of 5,599–494X. Richard Hanson was senior champion with 5,588–443X. Thomas Tamas captured the small-bore junior championship as well as the service rifle title.

Handguns. The free pistol competition at the Pan-American Games was won by the Venezuelan team with a score of 1,640. The U.S. team finished second with 1,631, while Brazil placed third with 1,621. Erich Buljung of the U.S. won the individual gold medal with 558. The U.S. team won the rapid-fire event with 1,766, Cuba following closely with 1,765. Colombia placed third with 1,754. Ecuador's team score of 1,706 took the gold medal for air pistol. The U.S. was second with 1,704, and Venezuela finished third with 1,701. High individual men's score was a 579 shot by C. Hora of Peru. The women's .22 pistol match was won by the U.S. with 1,750, with Venezuela second at 1,696 and Cuba third at 1,694. High individual was K. Dyer of the U.S. The U.S. women's team won the air pistol contest with a score of 1,181. Cuba placed second with 1,094, followed by Venezuela with 1,079. High individual was C. Graham of the U.S., who shot a 379.

The 1983 U.S. pistol champion was M/Sgt. Roger Willis, with a score of 2,652–138X. Thomas Woods placed second with 2,642–143X, followed closely by Ricardo Rodriguez with 2,642–125X.

(ROBERT N. SEARS)

[452.B.4.c]

Television and Radio

Television and radio service was available in some form in all major countries in 1983. Approximately 850 million radio sets were in use, of which about 470 million, or 56%, were in the United States. Television sets numbered about 434 million, of which 172 million, or almost 40%, were in the U.S.

Tariffs: see Economy, World

Taxation: see Economy, World

Telecommunications: see Industrial Review

ORLANDO—GAMMA/LIAISON

U.S. television's seemingly perennial M*A*S*H finally and voluntarily went off the air in February. The character of B. J. Hunnicutt departed from the Korean setting for San Francisco via motorcycle.

The Soviet Union, with 65 million television sets, ranked second, and Japan was third with 29.3 million, according to estimates published in the 1983 *Broadcasting/Cablecasting Yearbook*. Other *Broadcasting* estimates of television sets included West Germany, 21.4 million; United Kingdom, 18.7 million; France, 17.6 million; Brazil, 15.2 million; Italy, 13.5 million; Canada, 11.9 million; Spain, 9.6 million; China, 9 million; Poland, 7.9 million; Mexico, 7.5 million; Australia and Argentina, 5.5 million each; East Germany, 5.2 million; The Netherlands and Sweden, 4.2 million each; Czechoslovakia, 4.1 million; and India, 1.5 million.

Approximately 8,000 television stations were operating or under construction throughout the world. About 2,200 were in the Far East, 2,110 in Western Europe, 1,365 in the U.S., 920 in Eastern Europe, 180 in South America, 105 in Mexico, 100 in Canada, and 50 in Africa. Radio stations numbered about 17,000, most of which transmitted by amplitude modulation (AM), though the proportion of frequency modulation (FM) stations was rising. In the U.S. there were 10,030 radio stations, of which 5,144, or 51%, were FM.

Organization of Services. In the U.S. Pres. Ronald Reagan's policy of deregulation continued to be felt. In June the Federal Communications Commission (FCC) proposed, among other things, to eliminate federal guidelines as to the amount of nonentertainment programming that stations should provide, dispense with its guidelines on time devoted to commercials, and cancel its requirement that broadcasters formally confer with community leaders about local needs that should be addressed in programming. In late December the FCC voted not to require commercial stations to air a set amount of children's programming. While they should consider children's needs, stations could take into account programming available from other sources, such as public TV and cable, and could include "family-oriented" shows in their total.

The most contentious regulatory issue of the year, and of recent years, was the FCC's 1982 proposal to repeal rules that barred television networks from acquiring interests in programs produced by others and from engaging in domestic syndication of any program. Heated debate ensued between networks and producers, and late in the year President Reagan entered the debate on the side of the producers. Congress did not legislate on the issue, and the FCC postponed further action at least until the spring of 1984.

Cable television continued to expand; at midyear the A. C. Nielsen Co., the leading measurer of national TV audiences, put the number of U.S. cable-equipped households at 32.9 million, or 39.3% of all television homes, a gain of 18% in 12 months. But the frantic race for cable franchises was slowing down; the high costs of building new franchises and high interest rates were curbing enthusiasm for new expansion and in some cases causing cutbacks, and advertisers' interest in cable was not up to expectations. The number of major cable program services, which had increased steadily in recent years, contracted. The Entertainment Channel, a "quality" pay-cable service featuring the widely praised offerings of the British Broadcasting Corporation (BBC) and backed by the considerable resources of Rockefeller Center and RCA, closed in March after a loss estimated at $35 million. This followed by a few months CBS's closing of CBS Cable at a loss of $30 million.

Yet there were also significant new cable entries. One of the seemingly most promising was the Disney Channel, a pay-cable service offering "family programming" built around the Walt Disney movies; it began operations on a 16-hour-a-day basis in April. Another was the Nashville Network, a nightly advertiser-supported service featuring country-music artists, which started in March.

Direct broadcast satellites (DBS) beaming multiple channels of programming from satellites in space directly into homes equipped with special small receiving "dish" antennas and thereby bypassing conventional TV stations became a reality in November, when U.S. Satellite Communications Inc. (USCI) began offering five channels of service to a 33-county area around Indianapolis, Ind. USCI's programs included a sports channel, two movie channels, and two variety program channels. Seven other companies were preparing, under FCC authorization, to offer a variety of DBS services throughout the U.S.

The U.S. Corporation for Public Broadcasting (CPB), dependent on both federal and private financing, was again in difficulty as a result of the Reagan administration's insistence on reductions in government spending. CPB's problems were complicated by financial difficulties facing National Public Radio (NPR), its radio programming arm, which in the end accepted an $8.5 million line of credit from CPB that pulled it back from the brink of bankruptcy. The Reagan administration proposed a reduction of CPB's budget for fiscal year 1985 to $85 million, down 35% from the $130 million that had been authorized by Congress, and also proposed to cut another $55 million from the $130 million already authorized for 1986. Congress, however, finally approved conditional increases taking the CPB budget to $145 million for fiscal 1984, $153 million for 1985, and $162 million for 1986.

In the U.K. the government continued to press ahead with its plans for national multichannel cable—the so-called "wiring of Britain." In April the Home Office published a White Paper, *The Development of Cable Systems and Services,* which proposed a new cable authority that would issue licenses to cable system operators and exercise a "light" degree of supervision. Cable systems would be privately financed. British Telecom and Mercury, however, would be allowed to join consortia to bid for such a license. During the summer the Home Office announced that it would issue 12 interim licenses before the cable authority was set up. Thirty-seven companies applied, and the 12 successful bidders were announced at year's end. A bill creating the authority was published, with enactment expected by mid-1984.

Meanwhile, plans went ahead for Britain to have its first DBS. The BBC, which had been allocated two DBS channels in 1982, continued to negotiate with the Unisat (British Telecom, British Aerospace, GEC-Marconi) consortium for a satisfactory lease. The BBC was criticized for moving too rapidly into DBS and for paying too much money. During the summer negotiations came close to breaking down, but it seemed likely that the BBC would not willingly give up its DBS opportunity. In September the government allocated two similar DBS channels to the Independent Broadcasting Authority (IBA), which announced that it would license one or two companies to provide a DBS service if suitable applications were made. Both the BBC and IBA envisioned pay-TV channels, with newly released movies as the prime attraction.

There was widespread concern both inside the BBC and among the public that the introduction of pay-TV services would jeopardize the finances and audiences of the BBC and Independent Television (ITV).

In France and West Germany the governments moved ahead to license pay-TV and continued their collaboration on a project to launch DBS satellites. The French government also confirmed its plans for a new national TV network, Canal Plus, which would transmit films and other entertainment programming on a pay-TV basis. In Luxembourg the Compagnie Luxembourgeoise de Télédiffusion, which had a monopoly of the country's radio and TV services, failed to persuade its shareholders to invest in a DBS service. The stumbling block was the large number of French shareholders who believed that a Luxembourg satellite might compete with the French service. As a result of the impasse, the government of Luxembourg issued an option to a new consortium of U.S., U.K., and other companies to provide a smaller satellite to distribute TV throughout Europe. This turn of events confirmed suspicions that the established broadcasting organizations were losing their grip on their national monopolies.

A new phase in European broadcasting was marked by the successful launch in June of a European Communications Satellite (ECS 1), the first of three that were planned. The satellite was designed to distribute television programs throughout Europe. Nine countries were licensing national organizations to provide the programs, usually on a pay-TV basis. At the end of the year about 1.5 million people were able to receive an ECS channel.

The year in Spain was marked by the introduction of a regional Basque TV service in February and a regional Catalan TV service in September, reflecting a growing sense of independence on the part of those groups and a desire to support local language and culture.

The tempo of change was vividly demonstrated in The Netherlands, where a government White Paper approved pay-TV to be offered by private companies but not by existing broadcasting organizations.

In Australia the election of a Labor government in March put a stop to the previous Liberal-Country Party government's plans for cable TV and satellite pay-TV, which the Australians call "radiated subscription TV" (RSTV). The new minister canceled the plans for cable TV and indicated he was considering a major change in the plans for RSTV. The Australian Broadcasting Commission (ABC), the country's national public broadcasting organization, was supplanted by a newly named Australian Broadcasting Corporation with a new charter and a nine-member board of directors.

WIDE WORLD

Characters in the ABC television special "The Day After" pick their way across the devastation of a Kansas community after a nuclear attack. The show set new viewing records in the U.S. and was widely shown elsewhere in the world. It was received with mixed praise and criticism.

WIDE WORLD

Original footage of Charlie Chaplin that was never made public came to light on British television. Here Chaplin becomes the little blind girl in an outtake from the film *City Lights* (1931).

Programming. In the U.S. the 1983–84 prime-time television season offered the customary mix of drama, action-adventure stories, and situation comedies, but there were some innovative approaches and a few more comedies than in 1982–83. As a group the new shows continued to reflect a declining emphasis on sex and violence, although violence was by no means missing from some of the action-adventure programs. As usual, many of the new shows failed to survive their first few months.

To accommodate the new entries, the networks dropped 18 hours of series programs, including two that commanded respectable or better ratings. These were "Archie Bunker's Place," the latest version of the long-running "All in the Family" hit series, and "M*A*S*H," which was discontinued by its producers. "St. Elsewhere," which had poor ratings but was widely praised by critics, was retained by NBC in the hope that, like other slow starters such as "All in the Family" and "Hill Street Blues," it would in time develop a large following.

CBS, first in the prime-time ratings again in 1982–83, introduced four new one-hour weekly drama series and "AfterMASH," a half-hour comedy series picking up several of the original "M*A*S*H" characters. The new dramas were "Scarecrow and Mrs. King," about a Central Intelligence Agency agent and a divorced housewife who becomes his partner; "Emerald Point, N.A.S.," about a naval base commander and his daughters; "Cutter to Houston," featuring three young physicians recruited to run a hospital in a small Texas town; and "Whiz Kids," about a group of teenagers who use computers to solve mysteries.

ABC, second in the prime-time ratings in 1982–83, offered four new half-hour comedy series and four one-hour weekly dramas. The dramas were "Hardcastle and McCormick," about a former judge who enlists the help of a two-time loser to track down criminals freed on legal technicalities; "Hotel," based on Arthur Hailey's best-selling novel; "Trauma Center," a medical action-adventure series; and "Lottery," fictional accounts of the winners of lotteries. The situation comedies were "Just Our Luck," about a weatherman who acquires the services of a genie; "Oh Madeline," centring on a married couple's midlife crisis; "It's Not Easy," about a divorced couple who live across the street from each other; and "Webster," about a newly married couple bringing up the husband's orphaned godson.

NBC, trailing in the prime-time ratings, brought in three half-hour comedy series and six one-hour dramas. The dramas were "Boone," dealing with the rise of a country-music star in the 1950s; "Manimal," about a young professor who is able to transform himself into an animal and uses that ability to solve crimes; "For Love and Honor," a semiserialized story resembling the hit movie *An Officer and a Gentleman*; "The Rousters," a comedy-adventure whose chief character is the great-grandson and namesake of Wyatt Earp; "Bay City Blues," about a baseball team; and "The Yellow Rose," set on a Western ranch. The new comedies were "We Got It Made," about a pair of young male roommates who have hired a live-in maid; "Mr. Smith," about an orangutan with an IQ of 256 and the ability to talk, who becomes a consultant to the U.S. government; and "Jennifer Slept Here," about an adolescent boy who moves with his family into a California house haunted by the glamorous ghost of a former movie star.

Recent declines in television network audiences appeared to have been stopped in 1983. A *Broadcasting* analysis in midyear showed that the combined three-network ratings in prime time were up 1% from a year earlier and that the number of households tuning in the networks was up 4% from a year earlier. For daytime TV, network ratings were up about 2%. But pay-cable services showed little or no audience increases and in some cases declines.

Only three new entries achieved average ratings high enough to rank among the top 15 programs in the Nielsen ratings through early November. The top 15 were, in order, "Dallas," "AfterMASH" (new), "Simon & Simon," "Dynasty," "The A Team," "60 Minutes," "Magnum, P.I.," "Hotel" (new), "Falcon Crest," "ABC Sunday Night Movie," "Love Boat," "Scarecrow and Mrs. King" (new), "NBC Sunday Night Movie," "Fall Guy," and "Knots Landing."

The most widely watched television program of 1983 or any other year was a special 2½-hour episode bringing CBS's "M*A*S*H" to an end after 11 years at or near the top of the audience ratings. The episode averaged a 60.3 Nielsen rating and a 77 share of audience, representing more than 50 million homes tuned in during its average minute and an estimated more than 125 million people. It easily eclipsed the 53.3 rating set by the former record holder, the "Who Shot J. R.?" episode of the "Dallas" series, in 1980.

Big audiences were also won by several 1983 miniseries. "The Winds of War," an 18-hour dramatization of the Herman Wouk novel about the events leading up to World War II, averaged a 38.6 rating and 53 share of audience during its presentation on ABC across seven nights in February. "The Thorn Birds," a ten-hour adaptation of Colleen McCullough's best-selling novel presented on ABC on four nights in March, did even better, averaging a 41.9 rating and 59 share of audience to become the second-highest-rated miniseries in TV history, exceeded only by "Roots" in 1977.

Considerable publicity and controversy centred on "The Day After," an ABC made-for-television movie depicting the aftermath of a nuclear attack that wiped out Kansas City. Probably no television program had ever generated as much debate in advance. Scheduled at a time of international tension over the planned deployment of new U.S. nuclear weapons in Europe, the program had been denounced by critics as propaganda for a nuclear arms freeze and hailed by others as a proper and salutary depiction of the horrors of nuclear holocaust. Though it did not become the highest-rated TV program of all time, as some had predicted, it did demolish the ratings of other television programs shown that night. It was widely shown elsewhere in the world.

News remained a staple of television programming in 1983, but the networks cut back somewhat the additional hours they had introduced in 1982. They found that the early-morning and late-night news programs they had added, competing with additional news services provided by cable TV networks, could not attract as much viewership or advertising support as they had expected.

Among the growing number of syndicated (nonnetwork) original productions, one of the most successful was "Blood Feud," a two-part drama based on conflicts between the late Robert F. Kennedy and the labour leader James Hoffa. Presented by Operation Prime Time, a consortium of independent stations and network affiliates in 94 cities, it achieved a national average rating of 19.8, surpassing its network competition and ranking first in many major U.S. cities.

TONY AUTH/PHILADELPHIA INQUIRER

The U.S. press was highly critical of the decision to bar correspondents from shared or "pool" coverage of the Grenada invasion.

In the 35th annual Emmy awards, the Academy of Television Arts and Sciences chose "Hill Street Blues" as the outstanding drama for the third consecutive year and named "Cheers" the outstanding comedy series. "The Life and Adventures of Nicholas Nickleby" won the Emmy for limited series; "Motown 25: Yesterday, Today, Forever" for variety, music, or comedy presentations; "Pavarotti in Philadelphia: La Bohème" for classical performing arts programs; "Special Bulletin" for dramatic specials; "The Barbara Walters Specials" for information series; "The Body Human: The Living Code" for information specials; "Ziggy's Gift" for animated programs; and "Big Bird in China" for children's programs.

Emmys for lead actor and actress in a dramatic series were presented to Ed Flanders of "St. Elsewhere" and Tyne Daly of "Cagney and Lacey." Judd Hirsch of "Taxi" and Shelley Long of "Cheers" won for lead actor and actress in comedy series, and Tommy Lee Jones of "The Executioner's Song" and Barbara Stanwyck of "The Thorn Birds" won for lead actor and actress in limited series or specials. Supporting actor and actress Emmys went to James Coco and Doris Roberts, both of "St. Elsewhere," in the drama category and to Christo-

UPI

David Frost (centre) presided over a 2¼-hour morning program on Britain's ITV network titled "Good Morning Britain."

AUTHENTICATED NEWS INTERNATIONAL

U.S. Public Television's Big Bird (Da Niao) and Barkley the Dog from "Sesame Street" got acquainted with Chinese youngsters during a spring visit to Beijing (Peking). Between them is the program's Chinese friend Xiao Foo (played by Ouyang Lien-tze), strolling on the Great Wall.

pher Lloyd and Carol Kane, both of "Taxi," in the comedy, variety, or music category. A special Emmy Governors' Award was presented to Sylvester L. ("Pat") Weaver, former president of NBC and credited with creating that network's long-running "Today" and "Tonight" shows, among other innovations, for "revolutionizing network programming in the late 1940s and early 1950s."

In the tenth annual Emmy awards for daytime programming, the Academy chose "The Young and the Restless" as the outstanding drama series, "$25,000 Pyramid" in the game show category, "This Old House" in talk and service, and "The Merv Griffin Show" in the variety category. "Captain Kangaroo," "The Smurfs," and "Sesame Street" were among the Emmy winners for children's daytime programs.

With sports remaining popular, the costs of broadcast rights continued to rise. *Broadcasting* estimated that networks and stations paid approximately $535.6 million for college and professional football rights for the 1983 season, a gain of about 8.7% over 1982, and approximately $152.7 million for rights to cover major league baseball, an increase of 29%. NBC paid a reported $550 million for approximately half of the major league television package for the years 1984–89, and ABC paid an estimated $575 million for the other half. ABC was preparing for approximately 63 broadcast hours of coverage of the 1984 Winter Olympics in February and 187 hours of the Summer Olympics in July and August.

Music and news remained the basic format in radio, with individual stations specializing in types of music ranging from rock to classical. *Broadcasting*'s annual analysis of programming on the ten highest-rated radio stations in each of the top 50 U.S. markets found that country-and-western music, featured on almost 28% of the stations, had displaced contemporary, or currently popular, music (24%) as the principal fare. All-news and news-and-talk formats were featured on 2.1%, down sharply from about 12% in 1982. Other research indicated that FM stations' share of radio listening had reached 65%.

Public television's audiences continued to grow despite a shortage of funds that forced its program producers to take a more modest approach in many cases. Studies by the A. C. Nielsen Co. found that the Public Broadcasting Service network's weekly cumulative TV audiences averaged 51.9% of all U.S. television households, or about 43 million homes a week, a gain of about 8% from 1982.

The Prix Italia Festival, sponsored by the Italian state broadcasting organization, awarded its prizes in 1983 to productions from a welcome variety of countries; Austria, Finland, France, West Germany, Italy, The Netherlands, and Sweden all received awards. The drama category winner was "The Age of Iron," from Finland, which recaptured the spirit of a bygone age in its retelling of a traditional Finnish saga. "Gustavus III: Farewell to a Player King," from Sweden, was the Prix Italia winner in the music category; an account of the last day in the life of the 18th-century Swedish monarch, the film wove a musical fantasy around the events that led up to the king's assassination. Special prizes were awarded for drama to Austrian Television for "The Village at the Border," which portrayed the day-to-day problems of discrimination against ethnic minorities, and for music to The Netherlands for "The Nightingale," a highly imaginative adaptation of Hans Christian Andersen's fairy tale.

Good comedy was in short supply on British television. Channel 4, the independent network that celebrated its first anniversary in November, began a new comedy series called "Struggle," in which political journalist Peter Jenkins depicted confusion and hypocrisy rife among members of a trendy left-wing local council. On BBC "The Black Adder" was the vehicle for Rowan Atkinson's humour and distinctive facial expressions. The series received an International Emmy in the popular arts category. Jasper Carrott, the ebullient Midlands comedian, returned to the small screen with a live series, "Carrott's Lib," on BBC.

While the BBC continued with its remarkable series of Shakespeare plays, Channel 4 produced an adaptation of "King Lear" on videotape, rather than on film. The production boasted a remarkable cast that included Sir Laurence Olivier and won an International Emmy in the drama category. ITV launched its drama serial "Reilly, Ace of Spies" with great fanfare. Set in tsarist Russia, it was the story of a secret agent whose loyalties were divided between self-preservation and the interests of the British government. Other serials of merit were "Death of an Expert Witness" and "Widows," both from ITV, and "The Citadel," a BBC adaptation of A. J. Cronin's novel.

Television production in other European countries yielded a number of impressive programs. Czechoslovakia showed great care and quality in its animation, as exemplified by "The Seven Ravens," and in its scientific documentaries. Irish Television continued to produce high-quality historical drama with "Caught in a Free State." Spanish, Portuguese, and Italian audience figures all testified to the growing popularity of novellas and drama series in those countries.

(PAUL A. BARRETT; RUFUS W. CRATER; JOHN HOWKINS; LAWRENCE B. TAISHOFF)

Amateur Radio. The number of amateur radio operators continued to increase in 1983. The American Radio Relay League, the leading organization of amateur ("ham") radio operators, estimated that there were 433,921 licensed operators in the U.S. in September 1983, a gain of almost 6% in nine months. Throughout the world licensed amateur radio operators numbered approximately 1.4 million.

Ham operators provided vital services when normal communications links were down, typically summoning aid and coordinating emergency traffic in communities temporarily cut off from the outside world by floods, hurricanes, and other disasters. When U.S. and allied Caribbean forces invaded Grenada, amateur radio operators on the island provided the only independent accounts available to news organizations, which had been excluded from the invasion and were accorded only limited access for several days afterward.

(RUFUS W. CRATER; LAWRENCE B. TAISHOFF)

See also Industrial Review: *Advertising; Telecommunications;* Motion Pictures; Music.
[613.D.4.b; 735.I.4-5]

Tennis

If measured by prize money and spectator attendance, tennis had its most successful year in 1983. The Davis Cup was sponsored for a total of $1,021,000, with $200,000 for the champion nation. Prize money for the U.S. Open championships was $2,001,000, with each singles winner receiving $120,000. At the tournament Martina Navratilova (U.S.) earned $120,000 for the singles, $24,000 for the doubles, and a bonus of $500,000 from a sponsor to gain a total of $644,000 for the tournament, a record. The attendance at the Open was a record 376,676 for 23 sessions, and the Wimbledon attendance was also a record 363,639 for 13 sessions.

All three leading tournaments, the French, Wimbledon, and U.S. championships, accepted an equal number of contestants, 128, for the men's and women's singles. Only the U.S. awarded equal prize money to men and women. At Wimbledon a woman, Virginia Wade, the 1977 champion, became a member of the management committee for the first time.

Administratively, there was a complete break between World Championship Tennis (WCT) and other organizations. WCT initiated a lawsuit in a New York federal court against the Men's International Professional Tennis Council, the Association of Tennis Professionals, and the International Tennis Federation, complaining of their monopolistic actions. WCT staged a diminished 9 events in 1983, down from 22 a year earlier, and announced only three for 1984. Enforcement of the code of discipline resulted in limited suspensions to both Ilie Nastase (Romania) and John McEnroe (U.S.) during the year as punishment for their court misbehaviour.

PICTORIAL PARADE

Yannick Noah of France beat Sweden's Mats Wilander, the titleholder, in the French International tennis championships. It was the first win for France since 1946.

Men's Competition. Björn Borg (Sweden) was again absent from the major events, and three men were dominant—McEnroe, Jimmy Connors (U.S.), and Ivan Lendl (Czech.). Borg announced his permanent retirement, and the only important event in which he played was the Monte Carlo tournament where he lost in an early round.

The Australian championship, contested in Melbourne in December 1982, did not, despite record prize money of $450,000, attract an entry of the highest class. Johan Kriek (South Africa, later U.S.) beat Steve Denton (U.S.) 6–3, 6–3, 6–2 to retain his title. Lendl won the Volvo Grand Prix Masters' championship at Madison Square Garden, New York City, in January, defeating McEnroe in the final 6–4, 6–4, 6–2. McEnroe avenged this loss in the final of the WCT tournament in Dallas, Texas, in early May by beating Lendl 6–2, 4–6, 6–3, 6–7, 7–6.

In the West German championship in Hamburg, Yannick Noah (France) won the final against José Higueras (Spain) 3–6, 7–5, 6–2, 6–0. Jimmy Arias (U.S.) beat Higueras 6–2, 6–7, 6–1, 6–4 in the Italian title final in Rome. The 19-year-old Arias was the most prominent among the young U.S. players. The French championship in Paris featured notable losses in the quarterfinals. Christophe Roger-Vasselin (France) beat Connors 6–4, 6–4, 7–6; Mats Wilander (Sweden) defeated McEnroe 1–6, 6–2, 6–4, 6–0; and Noah triumphed over Lendl 7–6, 6–2, 5–7, 6–0. In the final Noah beat Wilander 6–2, 7–5, 7–6. Noah, aged 23, was the first Frenchman to win the French championship since Marcel Bernard in 1946.

McEnroe won the Wimbledon championship.

Kevin Curren (South Africa) upset Connors in the fourth round. Chris Lewis (New Zealand) subsequently beat Curren to become the first unseeded finalist since Wilhelm Bungert (West Germany) in 1967. In the other semifinal McEnroe beat Lendl 7–6, 6–4, 6–4. He then easily defeated Lewis 6–2, 6–2, 6–2 to win the Wimbledon title for the second time in his fourth successive final.

Connors won the U.S. Open at Flushing Meadow, New York City, for the second year in succession and the fifth time in all. Bill Scanlon (U.S.) beat McEnroe 7–6, 7–6, 4–6, 6–3 in the fourth round, and Arias defeated Noah 7–6, 4–6, 6–3, 1–6, 7–5 in the quarterfinal. Lendl beat Wilander in the same round and then defeated Arias in the semifinal. In the final Connors beat Lendl 6–3, 6–7, 7–5, 6–0 after Lendl double faulted when at set point at 5–4 in the third set.

Major events produced a variety of men's doubles champions. John Alexander and John Fitzgerald (both Australia) won their own title in 1982. Heinz Gunthardt (Switz.) and Balazs Taroczy (Hungary) won the West German championship, while Francisco Gonzalez (U.S.) and Victor Pecci (Paraguay) captured the Italian. The French title went to Anders Jarryd and Hans Simonsson (both Sweden). Peter Fleming (U.S.) and McEnroe were again outstanding. They won the Grand Prix Masters' tournament for the sixth successive year and both the Wimbledon and U.S. Open titles for the third time in five years.

The Davis Cup changed hands in 1983. The U.S., winners in the final against France in November 1982, lost in the first round of the 1983 competition to Argentina 3–2 in Buenos Aires, when both Guillermo Vilas and José-Luis Clerc beat McEnroe. Accordingly, the U.S. played a relegation round to qualify for the World Group for 1984 and in October beat Ireland 4–1 in Dublin. Great Britain also lost in the first round, 4–1 to Australia in Adelaide. In the relegation round at Eastbourne in October, Great Britain beat Chile 4–1.

In the zone competition France, Australia, Sweden, and Argentina qualified for the semifinals. During these tournaments Nastase increased his total of Davis Cup matches to 142, beginning in 1966. This total was 22 short of the record of 164, played by Nicola Pietrangeli of Italy through 1972.

Australia (Pat Cash, Fitzgerald, Mark Edmondson, Paul McNamee) defeated France 4–1 in Sydney in October to reach the final round for the first time since 1977 and for the 40th time in all. Sweden beat Argentina 4–1 in Stockholm at the same time to qualify for its second Davis Cup final. In the final, played in Melbourne in late December, Australia won the cup for the 25th time.

Women's Competition. Martina Navratilova dominated women's tennis to a degree not experienced since Maureen Connolly during 1951–54. She was all but invincible, not only in singles but, with Pam Shriver (U.S.), in doubles as well. During 1983 Navratilova was beaten in only one major event, the French championship. Her rivalry with Chris Evert Lloyd (U.S.) was the main interest of the year. The gap between those two players and all others was wide. Evert Lloyd reached a high note toward the end of 1982, defeating Navratilova 6–3, 3–6, 6–3 in the final of the Australian championship in Melbourne in December. Later that month Navratilova beat Evert Lloyd 4–6, 6–1, 6–2 in the final of the Toyota Championships at the Meadowlands, East Rutherford, N.J. In March 1983 Navratilova won 6–2, 6–0 against Evert Lloyd in the final of the Virginia Slims championship in Madison Square Garden. Neither challenged for the Italian championship in Perugia, where Andrea Temesvari (Hungary) was a young winner at 16, defeating Bonnie Gadusek (U.S.) 6–1, 6–0 in the final. The West German championship, staged in Berlin, was won by Evert Lloyd. She beat Kathy Horvath (U.S.) 6–4, 7–6 in the final. Navratilova did not compete.

Evert Lloyd won the French title in Paris for the fifth time. In the quarterfinal she beat Hana Mandlikova (Czech.). She won the semifinal against Andrea Jaeger (U.S.) and the final 6–1, 6–2 against Mima Jausovec (Yugos.). The tournament was notable for the loss by Navratilova, the defending champion. Horvath beat her 6–4, 0–6, 6–3 in the fourth round. For Evert Lloyd it was the 11th

Martina Navratilova won the U.S. Open women's tennis title for the first time. Here she is shown returning a shot to Pam Shriver on September 9.

UPI

successive year in which she won a Grand Slam (U.S., Wimbledon, French, and Australian championships) singles title, bringing her total of such triumphs to 15.

Navratilova won easily on the grass at Wimbledon. She did not lose a set in seven rounds and in the final beat Jaeger 6–0, 6–3. In the semifinal Jaeger defeated Billie Jean King (U.S.) 6–1, 6–1. King, unique in holding 20 Wimbledon titles, reached the semifinals at the age of 39. At almost 38 Virginia Wade (U.K.) reached the quarterfinals. The most surprising result was in the third round when Kathy Jordan (U.S.) beat an ailing Evert Lloyd 6–1, 7–6. It was the first time since Evert Lloyd began her international career at the age of 16 in 1971 that she failed to get as far as the semifinals of a Grand Slam tournament.

Navratilova won the U.S. title for the first time. She was never extended, defeating Sylvia Hanika (West Germany) 6–0, 6–3 in the quarterfinal, Shriver 6–2, 6–1 in the semifinal, and Evert Lloyd 6–1, 6–3 in the final. Evert Lloyd had defeated Jordan in the fourth round, Mandlikova in the quarterfinal, and Jo Durie (U.K.) 6–4, 6–4 in the semifinal. Durie, also a semifinalist in Paris, had the best record among British players.

In doubles Navratilova and Shriver won every major event in which they competed. They took the Australian 1982 title, the 1982 International Series, the Virginia Slims championship, Wimbledon, and the U.S. Open. In their absence the Italian title was won by Virginia Ruzici (Rom.) and Wade and the West German by Durie and Anne Hobbs (U.K.). Ros Fairbank (South Africa) and Candy Reynolds (U.S.) took the French championship.

The Federation Cup was held in Zürich, Switz., in July. After seven successive U.S. victories, the trophy was won for the second time by Czechoslovakia (Mandlikova, Helena Sukova, Iva Budarova, and Marcela Skuherska), which defeated West Germany 2–1 in the final after beating the U.S. 3–0 in the semifinal.

The U.S. defeated Great Britain 6–1 in Williamsburg, Va., to win the Wightman Cup for the 45th time in 55 contests. Navratilova, with Shriver, Kathy Rinaldi, Paula Smith, and Reynolds, played for the U.S. for the first time. Wade played for Britain for the 19th consecutive year.

(LANCE TINGAY)

Thailand

A constitutional monarchy of Southeast Asia, Thailand is bordered by Burma, Laos, Kampuchea, Malaysia, the Andaman Sea, and the Gulf of Thailand. Area: 513,115 sq km (198,115 sq mi). Pop. (1983 est.): 49,229,600. Cap. and largest city: Bangkok (pop., 1983 est., 5,479,000). Language: Thai. Religion (1970): Buddhist 95.3%; Muslim 3.8%. King, Bhumibol Adulyadej; prime minister in 1983, Gen. Prem Tinsulanond.

For Thailand 1983 proved an eventful and important year in national politics. The highlight was the general election of April, the first since 1979. A key motif was the sustained tussle between the powerful Army and civilian politicians over the traditional role of the military as the dominant force in government.

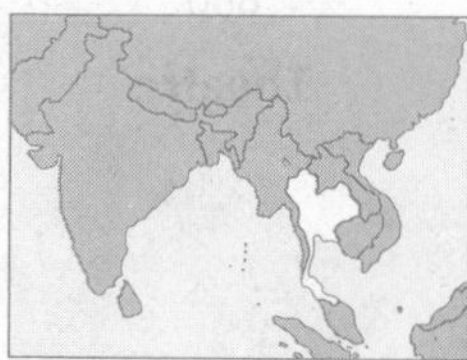
Thailand

THAILAND

Education. (1980–81) Primary, pupils 7,370,846, teachers 304,400; secondary, pupils 1,610,286, teachers 71,446; vocational, pupils 297,114, teachers (1979–80) 12,680; teacher training, students 5,221; higher, students (1979–80) 472,995, teaching staff 25,045.

Finance. Monetary unit: baht, with (Sept. 20, 1983) a free rate of 23 baht to U.S. $1 (34.64 baht = £1 sterling). Gold and other reserves (June 1983) U.S. $1,857,000,000. Budget (1982 actual): revenue 116,056,000,000 baht; expenditure 156,968,000,000 baht. Gross national product (1982) 834,590,000,000 baht. Money supply (Feb. 1983) 84,320,000,000 baht. Cost of living (1975 = 100; June 1983) 196.3.

Foreign Trade. (1982) Imports 196,616,000,000 baht; exports 159,728,000,000 baht. Import sources (1981): Japan 24%; U.S. 13%; Saudi Arabia 13%; Singapore 7%. Export destinations (1981): Japan 14%; U.S. 13%; The Netherlands 12%; Singapore 8%; Hong Kong 5%; Malaysia 5%. Main exports (1981): rice 17%; tapioca 10%; rubber 7%; sugar 7%; tin 6%; corn 5%. Tourism (1981): visitors 2,016,800; gross receipts U.S. $983 million.

Transport and Communications. Roads (1982) 72,152 km. Motor vehicles in use (1981): passenger 451,000; commercial 471,700. Railways (1981): 3,855 km; traffic 9,310,000,000 passenger-km, freight 2,500,000,000 net ton-km. Air traffic (1982): 8,611,000,000 passenger-km; freight c. 320 million net ton-km. Shipping (1982): merchant vessels 100 gross tons and over 197; gross tonnage 441,949. Telephones (Jan. 1981) 496,600. Radio receivers (Dec. 1980) 5,910,000. Television receivers (Dec. 1980) 810,000.

Agriculture. Production (in 000; metric tons; 1982): rice c. 17,500; corn c. 3,004; sweet potatoes c. 350; sorghum 267; cassava (1981) c. 17,900; dry beans c. 250; soybeans 106; peanuts 143; sugar, raw value 2,930; pineapples 1,824; bananas c. 2,028; tobacco c. 90; rubber c. 540; cotton, lint 40; jute and kenaf 248; meat 761; fish catch (1981) 1,650; timber (cu m; 1981) 38,182. Livestock (in 000; 1982): cattle c. 4,500; buffalo c. 6,150; pigs c. 3,700; chickens 63,264.

Industry. Production (in 000; metric tons; 1982): cement 6,609; lignite 1,966; petroleum products (1981) 7,695; tin concentrates (metal content) 26; lead concentrates 50; manganese ore (metal content; 1981) 4; fluorspar 271; gypsum 540; sulfuric acid (1980) 54; electricity (kw-hr; 1981) 15,960,000.

The struggle was set in motion on Dec. 28, 1982, when the commander in chief, Gen. Arthit Kamlang-ek, suggested on national television that Parliament should be quickly reconvened to consider amendments to a new constitution that was to take effect on April 21, 1983. The changes Arthit wanted would retain the old voting system, permit army officials to hold political office, and, most significantly, allow the military-dominated Senate to retain its full voting powers on parliamentary bills. Many politicians condemned the proposals as an attempt by the Army to retain its hold on government and retard the introduction of full democracy.

Under pressure from the military, Parliament was reopened to vote on the proposed constitutional amendments. They were defeated at the final reading by ten votes after massive public protests against them. Stunned by the unexpected defeat, the Army persuaded Prime Minister Prem Tinsulanond to bring the election forward from June 12 to April 18—just three days before the new constitution was to enter into force.

Fears of violence proved largely unfounded as 25 million Thais voted in a turnout that was reportedly the second largest in the kingdom's history. As expected, no political party won an outright majority. Top performers were the right-leaning Chart Thai, the centrist Social Action Party (SAP) and Democratic Party, and the extreme-right-wing Prachakorn Thai Party. (For tabulated results, *see* POLITICAL PARTIES.) On May 7 Prime Minister Prem formed Thailand's 45th government, a coalition including the SAP, the Democrats, and Prachakorn Thai. Though his proposed amendments had been rebuffed, General Arthit moved closer to national leadership by becoming supreme commander of the armed forces in October.

The Army's "hearts-and-minds" campaign, which combined military pressure with a political amnesty, induced more than 5,000 rebel guerrillas to surrender during the year. Disillusioned by factionalism among their leaders, many insurgents chose to accept the government's offer, which included incentives such as a plot of farmland and payment for surrendered firearms. Some military commanders, however, worried that inadequate rehabilitation work on the part of government agencies might send some of the insurgents back into the jungle.

The Thai military was also active on the drug-suppression front. In early August Thai forces cooperated with Burmese troops to launch a major assault against the base of notorious opium warlord Khun Sa in the "Golden Triangle" on the Burmese-Thai-Laotian border. Thai and Malaysian forces began coordinated operations against Communist guerrillas based along their common border in late December.

Like most of its neighbours within the Association of Southeast Asian Nations, Thailand made notable economic progress. Gross domestic product was expected to grow 5.5% in 1983, up from 4.2% the year before. Improvements were expected in the key sectors of agriculture (2.4%), industry (7%), and construction (4%). The recovery was reinforced by active private investment, though trade and current-account deficits were expected to grow substantially. The financial sector, however, was overstretched. Three finance companies collapsed within a week in October, obliging an alliance of large commercial banks and the central bank to step in with huge cash infusions. (THOMAS HON WING POLIN)

Foreign ministers called on Thailand's King Bhumibol Adulyadej at Bangkok in June. From left, they were Shintaro Abe (Japan), Siddhi Savetsila (Thailand), George Shultz (U.S.), the king, Hans-Dietrich Genscher (West Germany), and Bill Hayden (Australia).

WIDE WORLD

Theatre

The U.K. Policy Studies Institute's survey *Facts About the Arts*, published in October 1983, revealed that the total arts funding in Britain had doubled in ten years to £674 million, or £12 per head. Visits to the theatre totaled 40 million with 9 million tickets sold in London alone, 25% of which were bought by foreign visitors. Business sponsorship rose but barely reached the £12 million mark, leaving public funding still the major factor. At the end of the year Arts Minister Lord Gowrie (*see* BIOGRAPHIES) announced an increase in the council grant for 1984–85 to £100 million, but from this gross figure £4 million had to be deducted because it was earmarked to assist four major opera companies and to write off the deficits of the Royal Opera House and the Royal Shakespeare Company (RSC).

Arts Council Chairman Sir William Rees-Mogg welcomed the increase (a gross rise of 4.2% as compared with the council's request for 20%) but complained that the outlying regions had been let down. Widespread concern was voiced by the council, the new National Arts Lobby, and many public and private bodies about the policy of abolishing the Greater London Council and the major metropolitan authorities, whose funding of the arts (about £30 million a year) was unlikely to be replaced by other sources. The council also deplored the midterm cut of 1% forced upon it (reducing the 1983–84 subsidy by about £27 million for the theatre alone).

The deepening crisis was felt in other countries as well, though less in those with socialist or non-monetarist regimes. Financial problems and censorship were discussed at the biennial congresses of the International Theatre Institute in East Berlin and the International Association of Theatre Critics in Mexico.

Great Britain and Ireland. The John Whiting Award was won by playwright Peter Flannery. Sir Roy Shaw was succeeded as Arts Council secretary-general by Luke Rittner of the Association for Business Sponsorship of the Arts (ABSA). The Theatre Museum, which the new government had decided to drop, was reprieved following a public outcry and a private gift of £250,000. The Theatre Royal, Stratford East received £1,000 from an ABSA client for its all-black *Jacko Go Home*, by West Indian Mustapha Matura.

The National Theatre (NT) won one and the RSC two *Plays and Players* (*P&P*) awards. These went to the NT for John Gunter's set for *The Rivals* and to the RSC for David Edgar's *Maydays* as best new play and for Derek Jacobi as best actor in *Cyrano de Bergerac*. Other *P&P* awards were given to Willy Russell's *Blood Brothers* (best musical), Judi Dench in *Pack of Lies* (best actress), Yury Lyubimov from Moscow for his direction of *Crime and Punishment*, Alexandra Mathie and Abigail McKern (most promising newcomers, in *Daisy Pulls It Off* and in *Hay Fever*, respectively), and Jonathan Falla and Sarah Daniels (the most promising new playwrights for, respectively, *Tropicana Martyr's Day* and *Masterpieces*).

With £7 million plus supplementary grants, the NT broke even during the year to March 1983. At the Lyttelton the year began with David Hare's exciting *A Map of the World* and ended with its first pantomime, *Cinderella*. The U.S. musical *Jean Seberg* (director, Peter Hall) at the Olivier was strongly criticized at first but eventually retrieved the NT's reputation. Michael Bogdanov's production of *Lorenzaccio*, *The Rivals* with Beryl Reid and Michael Hordern, and Christopher Hampton's *Tales from Hollywood* did well. Also at the Lyttelton were De Filippo's *Inner Voices* with Sir Ralph Richardson (*see* OBITUARIES) and the U.S. comedy *You Can't Take It with You*. David Mamet's black comedy of warfare among Chicago realtors, *Glengarry Glen Ross* (director, Bill Bryden), received its world premiere at the Cottesloe, where Athol Fugard's *Master Harold . . . and the Boys* was also seen.

The RSC, on a basic £3.6 million plus supplementary grants, claimed a "resounding success" despite a final deficit, with record ticket sales and seven world premieres, two of which, Nicholas Wright's *The Custom of the Country* and Nick Darke's *The Body*, at the Pit, were outstanding. Transfers from Stratford were *Antony and Cleopatra* with Helen Mirren and Michael Gambon, *Peer Gynt* (in David Rudkin's translation), *Much Ado About Nothing*, and *Cyrano de Bergerac* (in Anthony Burgess's translation), all with Jacobi, *King Lear* with Gambon, and *Macbeth* with Bob Peck.

New productions included *Crime and Punishment* (director, Lyubimov) and *Edmund Kean* with Ben Kingsley in Hammersmith; Brian Friel's *The Communication Cord* and Dennis Potter's *Sufficient Carbohydrate* in Hampstead; Ena Lamont Stewart's updated *Men Should Weep* (director, Giles Havergal) in Stratford East; Trevor Rhone's black farce *Smile Orange* at the Tricycle; A. R. Gurney, Jr.'s, *The Dining Room* in Greenwich; Nick Munns's biblical musical *Swan Esther* (director, Frank Dunlop) at the Young Vic; Howard Barker's *Victory*, Howard Brenton's *The Genius*, Snoo Wilson's *The Grass Widow*, Tony Marchant's *Welcome Home*, and Daniels's *Masterpieces* at the Royal Court; Stephen Berkoff's *West* at the Warehouse; and at the Riverside, after the Edinburgh Festival, the (renamed) drama *The Soul of a Jew*, by Yehoshua Sobol and Andrzej Wajda's *Nastasia Filippovna* from Poland.

Other events in the capital were the Actors' Touring Company London season, the second London International Festival of Theatre, an all-black season at the Arts, the repertory season at the Haymarket, Ray Cooney's Theatre of Comedy, and the reopening of Sir John Gielgud's (*see* BIOGRAPHIES) favourite theatre, the Old Vic, with the Tim Rice-Stephen Oliver musical *Blondel*. Andrew Lloyd-Webber's (*see* BIOGRAPHIES) purchase of the Palace contrasted with the closing of the Round House, the ousting of the National Youth Theatre from the Shaw, and the threat posed to many theatres by the midterm cut in the Arts Council grant.

The 25th Dublin Theatre Festival's new plays included Thomas Murphy's comedy of a crazy tycoon, *The Gigli Concert*, at the Abbey; works by Stewart Parker, Aodhan Madden, and Robert Parker; and the Belfast Lyric Players' visiting production of Martin Lynch's *Castles in the Air* (director, Leon Rubin). Other Abbey firsts were Bogdanov's guest-production of *Hamlet* and Bernard Farrell's new version of Molière's *Don Juan*. Harveys' of Bristol Theatre Awards went to director Garry Hynes, playwright J. Graham Reid for *The Hidden Curriculum*, players Clive Geraghty and Marie Kean, and former Festival head Brendan Smith.

France, Italy, Low Countries. The French regional state grants raised output and standards, enabling Jérôme Savary's spectacular fun-show (Béziers) to visit Paris. Under Mira Trailovic the 20th Nancy Festival staged a record program, topped by Jorge Lavelli's *The Tempest* with the Nuria Espert troupe from Barcelona.

Paris productions included the Milan Piccolo's *The Good Person of Sezuan*, winner of the Critics' Best Foreign Production Award; Yevgeny Yevtushenko's rock musical *Juno and Avos* from Moscow; an all-black U.S. company in *Your Arms Too Short to Box with God*; the Brussels Atelier's "Karl Valentin Show" at the Marais Festival; and a rich program at the Autumn Festival.

The new head of the Amandiers in Nanterre, Patrice Chéreau, staged Bernard-Marie Koltès's anticolonialist drama *Fight Between Black Man and Dog*, in which Myriam Boyer won the "discovery of the year" award. Jean-Pierre Vincent launched his regime at the Comédie Française with the world premiere of Jean Audureau's Flaubert-inspired *Felicity* and *The Critique and School for Wives*, starring the "1982 discovery," Nathalie Bécue.

Restored after the 1982 fire, the Théâtre de la Ville put on *The Lower Depths* (director, Lucian Pintilie), *The Art of Comedy* (director, Jean Mercure), *The Master and Marguerite* (director, Andrey Serban), and Jean-Christophe Bailly's symbolic *The Cepheids*, from Avignon. At the Théâtre de l'Est Parisien, Guy Retoré presented *Candida Eréndira*, adapted from Nobel Prize winner Gabriel García Márquez's novel (director, Augusto Boal); Gozzi's *The Green Bird*, which won Benno Besson the best direction award; and Maurice Joly's "duologue in hell," *Machiavelli and Montesquieu*, banned in 1864 and newly adapted by Pierre Franck. At the Chaillot, Antoine Vitez staged Michel Vinaver's *Simple Fare*, inspired by an Andes Mountains plane crash. Jean-Louis Barrault's theatre staged Joyce's *Exiles* with Marthe Keller and

AGIP/PICTORIAL PARADE

Molière's *Le Médecin volant* (*The Flying Doctor*) alternated with his *Amphitryon* at the Comédie Française. Here are Yves Gasc (left) as Gorgibus and Gérard Giroudon as Sganarelle in the former work.

Marguerite Duras's *Savannah Bay*, written for Madeleine Renaud and Bulle Ogier.

New plays at private theatres were *The Rocking Chair* by Jean-Claude Brisville ("best French play of 1983"), Pierette Bruno's musical *Vincent and Margot, Long Live Women* by cartoonist Reiser, and *A Man Called Jesus*, Annie Decaux's and Robert Hossein's "Bible-spectacular." French revivals included *Rameau's Nephew*, in which Michel Bouquet won the best actor award, André Roussin's updated *Mad Love*, and *Cyrano de Bergerac*; those from abroad were *Miss Julie* with Isabel Adjani and Peter Brook's outstanding *The Cherry Orchard*.

The new works by Paul Willems in Brussels were, at the National, *Night with Shadows and Colours*, and at the Rideau, *She Said Sleeping in Lieu of Dying*. The German tour of Pavel Kohout's *The Gambler*, after Dostoyevsky, opened in Antwerp, while Laurent Terzieff took Slavomir Mrozek's *The Ambassador* to the Louvain Atelier. Robert Wilson's "opera" *The CIVIL Wars* with a cast headed by David Bowie (*see* BIOGRAPHIES) began its world tour with Part I in Rotterdam. Seen in Amsterdam were Erik Voss as Harpagon in Molière's *The Miser* and Joop Admiraal as mother and son in the group play *You Are My Mother!*

Lessing's *Minna from Barnhelm*, starring Andrea Jonasson (director, Giorgio Strehler), and Giuseppe Patroni Griffi's versions of *Six Characters in Search of an Author* and *The Miser*, with Paolo Stoppa, were noteworthy in Milan. Anna Proclemer staged and acted in Pirandello's *As Well as Before, Better than Before*, while Giorgio Albertazzi starred in *Richard III* and Vittorio Gassman in *Macbeth*.

Noteworthy were Rossella Falk and Valentina Cortese in Schiller's *Mary Stuart* (director, Franco Zeffirelli); a German production of *Everyman*; and the San Miniato and Parma festivals' presentation of Elie Wiesel's *The Shamgorod Trial* (director, Roberto Guicciardini). Veteran Salvo Randone shared the Armando Curcio Prize with the newcomer Lina Sastri.

Switzerland, West and East Germany, Austria. Of the new plays in Switzerland, Friedrich Dürrenmatt's madhouse *Achterloo*, with Maria Becker as Richelieu and Fritz Schediwy as Napoleon, was the hit of the Zürich season. Benno Besson's compelling *Hamlet*, when staged in Zürich, had Besson's daughter Katharina Talbach as a much-distraught Ophelia. The Théâtre Romand Populaire put on the world premiere of a new eight-hour-long version of Michel Vinaver's political satire *Overboard*.

The West Berlin Theatre Meeting included Stuttgart's version of Schiller's fragment *Demetrius*, Botho Strauss's pseudomythological *Kalldewey, Farce* (director, Luc Bondy), and two of the Zürich successes, *Minna from Barnhelm* and *Ivanov*. The Schaubühne staged Genet's *The Blacks* (director, Peter Stein) and the late Pierre Henri Cami's sketches of Parisian life. The Schiller presented *The Balcony* with Bernhard Minetti, Aleksandr Galin's *Retro* with Martin Held, and Heiner Müller's adaptation of a Mayakovsky drama of 1920.

The refurbished Deutsches Theater in East Berlin celebrated its centenary with Brecht's *Roundheads and Peakheads* and Ibsen's *Ghosts*. A first at the Berliner Ensemble was *Drums in the Night*, with decor by Ezio Toffolutti.

The West German directors' union's monthly *Die Bühne* disclosed that the year's box-office hits had been Dürrenmatt's *The Physicists*, Goethe's *Faust I*, Peter Shaffer's *Amadeus*, and Alan Ayckbourn's *Taking Steps*. Friederike Roth won the best play award and the Gerhardt Hauptmann and Ingeborg Bachmann prizes for *The Ride over the Wartburg*. Despite a money crisis, Stuttgart raised funds to save its summer festival and opened its new Chamber Theatre with a memorable production of *The Persians*. Outstanding in Munich were *To Damascus*, (director, Erwin Axer from Warsaw), *The Master Builder* (director, Peter Zadek), and *Don Juan*, first staged by Ingmar Bergman at Salzburg.

Of special interest were Bernd Karl Tragelehn's *Macbeth* and Peter Palitsch's world premiere of the Brecht fragment *The Real Life of Jacob Hi-You-There* in Düsseldorf, and a hilarious *The Government Inspector* (director, Oleg Tabakov from Moscow) in Cologne. Manfred Wekwerth of the Berliner Ensemble staged Schiller's *Wallenstein Trilogy* at the Burg in Vienna.

Eastern Europe, Scandinavia, Israel. Moscow celebrated the Karl Marx centenary with *Four Times as Large as France* by Aleksey Mishurin, given two separate productions at the Vakhtangov and Malaya Bronnaya, and *Homo Sum* by Aleksandr Sanin at the Yermolova, with Natalya Archangelskaya as Jenny von Westfalen. The veteran Moscow Arts actress Anna Stepanova was impressive in Anatoly Efros's guest production of *The Living Corpse*, while Oleg Tabakov appeared in Galin's *The Eastern Tribune* at the Sovremennik (director, Leonid Heifets).

Despite the departure of such artists as Adam Hanuszkewicz, replaced by Krystyna Skuszanka at the National, and Gustav Holoubek, replaced by Jan Pawel Gawlik (of the Krakow Stary) at the Dramatic (renamed the New), the impetus of Warsaw theatrical life was maintained. A revival of Aleksander Fredro's *Vengeance* (director, Kazimierz Dejmek) at the Polski, Janusz Warminski's production of *Hamlet* with Jerzy Kryszak, and Klaus Mann's *Mefisto* (director, Michal Ratynski) at the Powszechny were highly praised. Yet another "papal" drama, *Job* by Karol Wojtyla (Pope John Paul II), received its world premiere in Krakow.

The newest theatre in Sofia, Bulg., the Bar Havana, opened with *Dance of Shadows*, by Soviet writer Juliu Edlis. Vili Tsankov's tragigrotesque production of *Hamlet*, with Rusi Chanev, and Valery Petrov's children's play *In the Moonlit Room*, featuring Tom Thumb, were staged at the Sofia, and the Kustendil Theatre's *The Living Corpse* (director, Lyubomir Kabakchiev) was presented at the National.

A first play by Iren Kiss about the painter Csontvary, the all-Hungarian *Cats* (director, Tamas Szirtes), and Istvan Horvai's version of *The Seagull*, for which David Borovsky from Moscow had a real pool on the stage of the Vigszinhaz, were the talk of Budapest. Paul Everac's satirical one-acters *The Present* and *The Wardrobe*, with the joint title of *Upstart Tastes*, and O'Neill's *A Moon for the Misbegotten* with Sanda Manu were done at the Bucharest Bulandra.

Vaclav Havel's *Audience and Vernissage*, staged by Ljubomir Draskic as *I, Vaclav Havel*, was the Belgrade Atelje 212 entry at Nancy. Banned from the Novi Sad Festival in 1982, Yovan Radulovic's outspokenly critical *The Dove-Pit* was performed throughout Yugoslavia.

A production in Swedish and English of *The Dance of Death*, the latter for performance in the U.S. by the same cast, headed by Keve Hjelm, was staged by Göran Graffman at the Stockholm Royal Dramatic, which also put on the provocative *Night Is the Mother of Day* (by Lars Norén, author of *Underground Smile*), the City Theatre's entry at Nancy. Stockholm's Jan Håkanson restaged his City Theatre version of *The Father* in Danish (with Jørgen Reenberg) at the Copenhagen Royal, where the world premiere of Ernst Bruun Olsen's updated *The Twilight of the Gods* with Ghita Nørby and Henning Moritzen was also done. Hit of the Oslo season at the National was Toralv Maurstad's *Hamlet*, starring Lasse Lindtner.

The season in Finland included: at the National in Helsinki, *King Lear* with Risto Makela, *The Cherry Orchard* (director, Efros) with Tea Ista, and *Ghosts* with Eeva-Kaarina Volanen and Leif Wager; and in Tampere, *Amadeus* (director, Jack Witikka) and *A Midsummer Night's Dream* (director, Jiri Menzel from Prague), the latter a sellout at the Pyynikki Open-Air Theatre.

MARTHA SWOPE

Broadway's biggest hit, *La Cage aux folles*, was an old-fashioned musical with a major twist: homosexual lovers in a transvestite cabaret. Gene Barry (left) and George Hearn were the stars.

Personal and national dilemmas in Israel were reflected in Sobol's *A Jewish Soul* in Haifa (later seen in Edinburgh and London) and in *The Trojan Women* with Orna Porat at the Habima. A five-handed group play for five actresses (*Through Five Windows*) inaugurated Israel's latest new theatre, the Creative, in Ramat Hasharon.

(OSSIA TRILLING)

United States and Canada. The 1983 theatre year in the United States was a time of facing up to reality and a time of surviving. The prices of producing and seeing Broadway shows continued to soar, with musicals hitting the $5 million mark for investors and up to $45 for ticket buyers. This inevitably created a conservatism on Broadway, with producers seeking what might be called "corporate" theatre, shows so heavily staged and so professionally marketed that they were more like entertainment centres than theatre. Gone were the simply interesting dramas, the diverting comedies, the everyday entertainments typical of a healthy stage. Broadway's biggest hit of the year was a spectacular musical version of the film *La Cage aux folles*. Some might feel that there is nothing conservative in a musical about homosexual lovers that is set among transvestite entertainers. But everything else in this show was traditional in terms of musical theatre, and its central romance, even if a homosexual one, was treated in a traditionally romantic way.

The year's other successful musicals were even more traditional, for they were revivals: Rodgers

MARTHA SWOPE

When *A Chorus Line* became the longest-running show in Broadway history in September, the producers celebrated by combining the casts of the Broadway, national, and international companies on stage at the Shubert Theater in New York City.

and Hart's *On Your Toes* and the Gershwins' *Funny Face* (retitled *My One and Only*). It was, in fact, a year of many musical revivals, others being *Porgy and Bess, Show Boat, Zorba,* and *Mame.* These were not quite as successful, even with such stars as Anthony Quinn, Angela Lansbury, and Donald O'Connor. Thus, while a revival of a once-successful show was less likely than a new one to be an outright failure, neither was its success guaranteed.

Financial conservatism all but eliminated new drama and even comedy on Broadway. The only exception, naturally, was a Neil Simon play, but his charming *Brighton Beach Memoirs* was the only comedy to be presented on Broadway during the entire season. Drama, while even riskier, commercially, than comedy, found its own ways to survive. Three British imports of unusual interest were Peter Nichols's *Passion,* a dramatic comedy about sexual longings in middle-aged married men; David Hare's *Plenty,* a memory play set in England and France that was a triumph for Kate Nelligan (*see* BIOGRAPHIES); and *Quartermaine's Terms,* Simon Gray's Chekhovian study of the British character.

Both the Hare and the Gray plays were presented off-Broadway, as were many dramas seeking to avoid the financial pressures of Broadway. The wisdom of such an approach was underlined by the dismal fate befalling the dramas that did attempt Broadway. Edward Albee's *The Man Who Had Three Arms,* for instance, was a play of serious if unfulfilled ambition, certainly worthy of a hearing. It failed dismally.

For flamboyance of failure, however, nothing surpassed the gala revival of *Private Lives.* Other dramatic revivals proved viable on Broadway, such as Arthur Miller's *A View from the Bridge* and Tennessee Williams's *The Glass Menagerie.* Indeed, *Private Lives* survived for several weeks but only because of the glitter of its stars, Elizabeth Taylor and Richard Burton. However, even the most star-

MARTHA SWOPE

Tommy Tune is a daredevil aviator and Twiggy an English Channel swimmer in George and Ira Gershwin's *My One and Only,* restaged on Broadway by Thommie Walsh and Tommy Tune.

Theology:
see Religion

Timber:
see Industrial Review

Tobacco:
see Industrial Review

Tobogganing:
see Winter Sports

struck of audiences would not accept the inappropriateness of Miss Taylor in the sophisticated Coward play. *Private Lives* had been anticipated as the theatre event of the year, but it was forced to curtail the Broadway engagement and even to cancel most of its national tour.

Meanwhile, other, better trained film stars proved to be the saviours of U.S. drama. They were led by Al Pacino and George C. Scott, both of whom had in recent years chosen to perform in serious plays. Scott was largely responsible for a successful revival of Noel Coward's *Present Laughter*, and Pacino did much the same for David Mamet's *American Buffalo*. Other dedicated stars followed suit, television's Judd Hirsch and Richard Thomas playing in a revival by the Circle Repertory Company of Chekhov's *The Seagull*; Rex Harrison starring in Bernard Shaw's *Heartbreak House* at the Circle in the Square; and Marsha Mason, Jane Alexander, and Anthony Hopkins reviving Harold Pinter's *Old Times* for the Roundabout Theatre. These actors obviously loved drama enough to sacrifice lucrative Hollywood work for it. They were the true heroes of the 1983 stage year, and the key to their heroism was the limited engagement that was possible in institutional theatre. Broadway shows must run a full season in order to recoup production costs, but nonprofit institutions are geared to sustain deficits in order to present short engagements. Financial sacrifices by these actors were thus limited to several months.

The most famous (or infamous) institutional theatre in New York made a splash, if only by opening its doors. The Vivian Beaumont Theater in Lincoln Center had been closed for five of the past six years over a dispute about the redesign of its thrust stage. The reopening was heartening, even though it was used for commercial presentations rather than for its stated purpose of presenting classical theatre. The productions that lighted the Beaumont in 1983 were at least serious-minded—Peter Brook's *La Tragédie de Carmen*, a stark musical-dramatic version of the Bizet opera, and, in the studio theatre below, a polished production of C. P. Taylor's British wartime play, *And a Nightingale Sang. . . .* Brook's *Carmen* was certainly New York's most celebrated theatrical event of 1983, although in terms of significance it was overshadowed by the death of Tennessee Williams (*see* OBITUARIES) earlier in the year. Williams's ranking among the greatest of U.S. playwrights was assured, and his *A Streetcar Named Desire* was considered by many to be the greatest drama ever written by an American.

As for new U.S. drama, in 1983 it seemed consigned to off-Broadway, even though the year's Pulitzer Prize for Drama was won by a Broadway production of *'night, Mother* by Marsha Norman. Most of the U.S. plays, including such stimulating dramas as Tina Howe's *Painting Churches* and Lanford Wilson's *Angels Fall*, were performed in small theatres.

Norman's *'night, Mother* had originated at Harvard University's American Repertory Theatre, but the general trend toward auditioning Broadway plays at regional theatres was easing off. The U.S. government's slashing of funds for the National Endowment for the Arts had put nonprofit theatre in such a crisis that transfers from Broadway seemed their only financial hope. Congress's eventual restoration of most of those funds lessened the crisis and enabled the regional theatres to return to their original purpose of presenting dramas that had little commercial potential. The Seattle (Wash.) Repertory Theatre, for example, programmed Shakespeare through Arthur Miller; the Alley Theatre in Houston, Texas, performed Sheridan and Joe Orton; the Guthrie Theater in Minneapolis, Minn., presented Ibsen and Shaw; while the American Conservatory Theatre in San Francisco ranged from Chekhov to the U.S. dramatist Paul Osborn.

In Canada the Stratford Festival continued to grapple with the weight and responsibilities of its own reputation as the most prestigious of North American theatres. Under the direction of John Hirsch there was an attempt to restate the importance of classical theatre, which Hirsch defined as "a living forum at the very heart of our civilization." For the summer of 1983 he directed *As You Like It* and *Tartuffe* while recalling long-time Stratford artistic director Michael Langham to stage *Love's Labour's Lost* and *Much Ado About Nothing*. In Hirsch, the Stratford Festival found an artistic director to revitalize it without compromise.

At Canada's "other" establishment theatre, the Shaw Festival at Niagara-on-the-Lake, Ont., there was a more discouraging commercialism in program choices: overly familiar Shaw (*Caesar and Cleopatra, Candida*) and such war-horses as *Private Lives* and *Cyrano de Bergerac*. However, the festival also produced one of Shaw's many obscure plays, *The Simpleton of the Unexpected Isles.*

(MARTIN GOTTFRIED)

See also Dance; Music.
[622]

INGE MORATH—MAGNUM

The celebrated Chinese actor Ying Ruocheng played Willy Loman in the Beijing (Peking) production of Arthur Miller's *Death of a Salesman*. Miller (in background here) directed this production.

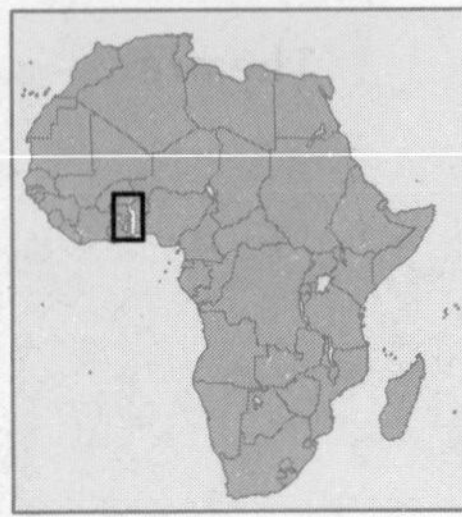
Togo

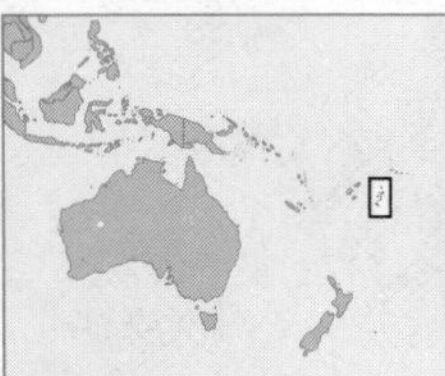
Tonga

Togo

A West African republic on the Bight of Benin, Togo is bordered by Ghana, Upper Volta, and Benin. Area: 56,785 sq km (21,925 sq mi). Pop. (1982 est.): 2,747,000, including (1978 est.) Ewe 46.5%; Kabre 22.4%; Gurma 14.2%; Tem 4.2%. Cap. and largest city: Lomé (pop., 1980 est., 283,000). Language: French (official). Religion (1980 est.): animist 46%; Muslim 17%; Christian 37%. President in 1983, Gen. Gnassingbe Eyadema.

The year began with a huge influx of Togolese and Ghanaian nationals during the mass expulsion of illegal immigrants from Nigeria. The repatriation via Benin and Togo of the hundreds of thousands of Ghanaians was delayed because Togo's border with Ghana had been closed by Ghana since September 1982. Ghana temporarily reopened the frontier in January and again in March 1983, but reclosed it on several occasions, notably after the attempted coup against Ghanaian leader Jerry Rawlings on June 19.

French Pres. François Mitterrand's arrival on January 13 coincided with the 20th anniversary of the assassination of Pres. Sylvanus Olympio. Some hours earlier, Pres. Gnassingbe Eyadema had revealed that plans for his own assassination, in which Olympio's two exiled sons allegedly were implicated, had been thwarted. In February Franco-Togolese relations were further strengthened by the visit of President Mitterrand's special adviser, Régis Debray. In October President Eyadema made his first visit to the U.S.

(PHILIPPE DECRAENE)

TOGO

Education. (1980–81) Primary, pupils 506,356, teachers 9,193; secondary, pupils 128,175, teachers (1979–80) 2,855; vocational, pupils (1979–80) 7,793, teachers (1977–78) 326; teacher training (1979–80), students 300, teachers 22; higher (1979–80), students 3,638, teaching staff 291.

Finance. Monetary unit: CFA franc, with (Sept. 20, 1983) a par value of CFA Fr 50 to the French franc (free rate of CFA Fr 403 to U.S. $1; CFA Fr 607 = £1 sterling). Budget (1982 est.) balanced at CFA Fr 72.3 billion.

Foreign Trade. (1980) Imports CFA Fr 117,769,000,000; exports CFA Fr 56,241,000,000. Import sources: France 32%; U.K. 13%; The Netherlands 9%; West Germany 6%; Japan 6%. Export destinations: The Netherlands 22%; France 17%; Yugoslavia 14%; Belgium-Luxembourg 7%; Ghana 6%. Main exports: phosphates 50%; cocoa 15%; coffee 10%.

Tonga

A monarchy and member of the Commonwealth, Tonga is an island group in the Pacific Ocean east of Fiji. Area: 747 sq km (288 sq mi). Pop. (1983 est.): 104,000, 98% of whom are Tongan. Cap. and largest city: Nukualofa (pop., 1980 est., 19,900). Language: English and Tongan. Religion (1976): Free Wesleyan 47%; Roman Catholic 16%; Free Church of Tonga 14%; Mormon 9%; Church of Tonga 9%; other 5%. King, Taufa'ahau Tupou IV; prime minister in 1983, Prince Fatafehi Tu'ipelehake.

In 1983 King Taufa'ahau Tupou IV maintained political stability in Tonga despite serious economic difficulties. Urban growth in Nukualofa and a decline in outward migration and overseas employment contributed to an increase in social tensions. Even so, remittances from Tongans working overseas still provided about one-half of Tonga's foreign currency earnings, with the balance deriving about equally from tourism and sales of copra. The inflation rate remained at about 7%.

Government activity focused on the need to rehouse families and to restore social services after the two hurricanes of 1982. A loan was secured from the Asian Development Bank for these purposes and for rural development. Most of the funds allocated by the Tongan Development Bank went to small-scale trading, fishing, and agricultural projects.

Interisland air services were furthered by the completion of runways on the islands of Niutoputapu and Niuafoo and of night-landing facilities at the international airport at Fuaamotu on Tongatapu. The project had been initiated in 1976, with aid provided by New Zealand.

(BARRIE MACDONALD)

TONGA

Education. (1979) Primary, pupils 19,744, teachers 818; secondary, pupils 12,563, teachers 666; vocational, pupils 280, teachers 19; teacher training, students 134, teachers 12.

Finance and Trade. Monetary unit: pa'anga, with (Sept. 20, 1983) a free rate of 1.12 pa'anga to U.S. $1 (1.69 pa'anga = £1 sterling). Budget (1981–82 est.): revenue 14,744,000 pa'anga; expenditure 14,736,000 pa'anga. Foreign trade (1982): imports 41,198,000 pa'anga; exports 4,185,000 pa'anga. Import sources: New Zealand 37%; Australia 23%; U.S. 10%; Fiji 7%; Singapore 6%; Japan 6%. Export destinations: Australia 40%; New Zealand 38%. Main exports: coconut oil 31%; vanilla beans 15%; desiccated coconut 7%; watermelons 7%; taro 6%.

Tourism:
see Industrial Review

Toys:
see Games and Toys

Track and Field Sports

Highlights of the year in track and field included 32 new world records and the first separate world championships, in which 1,572 athletes from 157 national federations competed at Helsinki, Fin. More than 442,000 spectators witnessed the meet, held from August 7–14.

Men's International Competition. While the world championships produced the most intense competition of the year, the periods before and after the Helsinki contest produced more outstanding performances. World records fell 14 times in 11 events, with 7 of the new global bests coming before Helsinki, 6 occurring afterward, and 1 during the championships.

Tom Petranoff of the U.S. achieved the first big surprise of 1983 when he threw the javelin 99.72 m (327 ft 2 in) at Los Angeles on May 15. His throw was 30 ft (9.14 m) farther than he had ever thrown and surpassed the former record by 3 m (9 ft 10 in), the second greatest improvement ever.

Shortly thereafter records fell in the other three throwing events. The Soviet Union's Yury Dumchev threw the discus 71.86 m (235 ft 9 in) at Moscow on May 29, while countryman Sergey

(LEFT) UPI; (RIGHT) WIDE WORLD

At far left, Anisoara Cusmir of Romania set a new record for women's long jump with a leap of 7.43 m (24 ft 4$\frac{1}{2}$ in). At left, Udo Beyer of East Germany broke his own world shotput record with a distance of 22.22 m (72 ft 10$\frac{3}{4}$ in).

Litvinov hurled the hammer 84.14 m (276 ft), also at Moscow, on June 20. It was Litvinov's third world record and surpassed his existing standard of 83.98 m (275 ft 6 in).

The fourth throwing record was set when Udo Beyer of East Germany put the shot 22.22 m (72 ft 10$\frac{3}{4}$ in) on June 25 in Los Angeles. Like Litvinov, he bettered his own record.

Another big surprise occurred when Zhu Jianhua (Chu Chien-hua) of China high jumped 2.37 m (7 ft 9$\frac{1}{4}$ in) at Beijing (Peking) on June 11. It was only the second world track and field record made by an athlete from China. The other record-breaking performance had also taken place in the high jump when Ni Chih-chin leaped 2.29 m (7 ft 6 in) in 1970. However, he did not gain official recognition of the record. Zhu placed third in the world championships and then on September 22 at Shanghai raised his record to 2.38 m (7 ft 9$\frac{3}{4}$ in). He thus became the only man to break a record twice in 1983.

Jurgen Hingsen, who set a new decathlon best in 1982 only to lose the record to the man he had previously surpassed, Daley Thompson of the U.K., regained his record on June 4 and 5 at Bernhausen, West Germany. The West German totaled 8,779 points.

When Calvin Smith of the U.S. ran 100 m in 9.93 sec, he broke the oldest of all records. Jim Hines of the U.S. had run the distance in 9.95 sec. in the rarefied air of Mexico City, 2,240 m (7,350 ft) above sea level, in the Olympic Games of 1968. Smith also took advantage of lessened air resistance as he set his record on July 3 at Colorado Springs, Colo., 1,823 m (5,981 ft) above sea level.

There were no more record performances for the remainder of July as the world's best performers prepared for their first world championships. The Olympic Games had been regarded, technically, as a world championship meet, but the international track and field governing body declared the Helsinki tournament to be the first officially recognized worldwide title competition.

Fierce battles for gold, silver, and bronze medals emphasized the competitive aspects of the meet. The emphasis on victory was obvious in the three longest flat races, the 1,500 m, 5,000 m, and 10,000 m. Each developed into a tactical battle with victories obtained in relatively slow time. Perhaps the most anticipated contest of the entire meet was the 1,500-m run. It was won by Steve Cram (*see* BIOGRAPHIES) of the U.K., who outsprinted Steve Scott of the U.S. to win in 3 min 41.59 sec, more than 10 sec slower than the world record.

Most of the prechampionship record breakers did well in Helsinki. Litvinov won the hammer throw and Smith the 200 m. Petranoff placed second as did Hingsen, who lost to Thompson. Zhu finished third in the high jump. Not faring well were Beyer, who was injured and finished sixth, and Dumchev, who failed to finish among the top 12 qualifiers and thus was not in the finals.

The biggest winner was Carl Lewis (*see* BIOGRAPHIES), U.S. sprinter and long jumper. He had a hand in the sole men's world record of the meet, anchoring the U.S. 400-m relay team in a 37.86-sec performance. On the same day, August 10, he won the long jump with 8.55 m (28 ft $\frac{3}{4}$ in), and two days earlier he won the 100 m in 10.07 sec. Only one other athlete had ever taken two track and field gold medals in one day in the Olympic Games or world championships, Paavo Nurmi of Finland winning the 1,500 m and 5,000 m in the 1924 Olympics.

The four members of the record-breaking relay team won ten medals, the first time that each relay runner won at least one other medal. In addition to Lewis, Smith was second in the 100 m and won the 200 m; Emmit King finished third in the 100 m; and Willie Gault placed third in the 110-m hurdles.

Two athletes from the Soviet Union produced the most surprising results of the championships. Neither Gennady Avdeyenko, who won the high jump, nor Sergey Bubka, who was first in the pole vault, had been expected to finish among the first 10 or 15 placers.

Post-Helsinki competition produced six more world marks, including four by athletes who did not live up to expectations in the world championships. Only Zhu and Edwin Moses of the U.S., who for the fourth time set a world best in the 400-m hurdles with a time of 47.02 sec at Koblenz, West Germany, on August 31, were notably successful at Helsinki. Two 1,500-m runners and two French pole vaulters broke records after not performing well in the worldwide meet.

Two of the records fell at Cologne, West Germany, on August 28. Sydney Maree of the U.S., who finished only ninth in the semifinals at Helsinki, showed a return to form by lowering the 1,500-m standard to 3 min 31.24 sec. But he held the record for only a week, as Steve Ovett of the U.K., the former record holder and the fourth-place finisher at Helsinki, regained the mark with 3 min 30.77 sec.

Vaulters Thierry Vigneron and Pierre Quinon tied for 8th and tied for 21st, respectively, at Helsinki. But Quinon vaulted a world record 5.82 m (19 ft 1 in) at Cologne on August 28 and then lost the record when Vigneron vaulted 5.83 m (19 ft 1½ in) at Rome on September 1. Vigneron's record vault was his fourth.

Track and field athletes from the U.S. were affected by rigorous testing for banned drugs that occurred at the Pan American Games in Caracas, Venezuela, during August. After 11 weight lifters from various nations had been stripped of their medals because tests had revealed that they had used such substances as anabolic steroids and testosterone, 11 male U.S. track and field competitors voluntarily withdrew from the tournament before performing in their events. Most were weight throwers, but they also included a sprinter, a long jumper, a triple jumper, and a hurdler. There was no drug testing at U.S. meets.

Indoors, the most attention was attracted by vaulter Billy Olson of the U.S., who increased the best-in-the-world height three times and ultimately became the first man to clear 19 ft (5.79 m) indoors when he reached 5.80 m (19 ft ¼ in). Eamonn Coghlan of Ireland lowered his own mile standard to 3 min 49.78 sec, while Sebastian Coe of the U.K., sidelined much of the outdoor season with illness, earned two records, 1 min 44.91 sec for 800 m and 2 min 18.58 sec for 1,000 m.

Table I. World 1983 Outdoor Records—Men

Event	Competitor, country, date	Performance
100 m	Calvin Smith, U.S., July 3	9.93 sec
1,500 m	Sydney Maree, U.S., August 28	3 min 31.24 sec
	Steve Ovett, U.K., September 4	3.min 30.77 sec
400-m hurdles	Edwin Moses, U.S., August 31	47.02 sec
4 x 100-m relay	United States, August 10	37.86 sec
High jump	Zhu Jianhua, China, June 11	2.37 m (7 ft 9¼ in)
	Zhu Jianhua, China, September 22	2.38 m (7 ft 9¾ in)
Pole vault	Pierre Quinon, France, August 28	5.82 m (19 ft 1 in)
	Thierry Vigneron, France, September 1	5.83 m (19 ft 1½ in)
Shot put	Udo Beyer, East Germany, June 25	22.22 m (72 ft 10¾ in)
Discus	Yury Dumchev, U.S.S.R., May 29	71.86 m (235 ft 9 in)
Hammer	Sergey Litvinov, U.S.S.R., June 20	84.14 m (276 ft)
Javelin	Tom Petranoff, U.S., May 15	99.72 m (327 ft 2 in)
Decathlon	Jurgen Hingsen, West Germany, June 5	8,779 points

Table II. World 1983 Outdoor Records—Women

Event	Competitor, country, date	Performance
100 m	Marlies Gohr, East Germany, June 8	10.81 sec
	Evelyn Ashford, U.S., July 3	10.79 sec
400 m	Jarmila Kratochvilova, Czechoslovakia, August 10	47.99 sec
800 m	Jarmila Kratochvilova, Czechoslovakia, July 26	1 min 53.28 sec
5,000-m walk	Olga Yarutkina, U.S.S.R., August 24	22 min 3.5. sec
10,000 m	Lyudmila Baranova, U.S.S.R., May 28	31 min 35.01 sec
	Raisa Sadreydinova, U.S.S.R., September 7	31 min 27.58 sec
400-m hurdles	Anna Ambraziene, U.S.S.R., June 11	54.02 sec
4 x 100-m relay	East Germany, July 31	41.53 sec
High jump	Ulrike Meyfarth, West Germany, August 21	2.03 m (6 ft 8 in)
	Tamara Bykova, U.S.S.R., August 21	2.03 m (6 ft 8 in)
	Tamara Bykova, U.S.S.R., August 25	2.04 m (6 ft 8¼ in)
Long jump	Anisoara Cusmir, Romania, May 15	7.21 m (23 ft 8 in)
	Anisoara Cusmir, Romania, June 4	7.27 m (23 ft 10¼ in)
	Anisoara Cusmir, Romania, June 4	7.43 m (24 ft 4½ in)
Discus	Galina Savinkova, U.S.S.R., May 21	73.26 m (240 ft 4 in)
Javelin	Tiina Lillak, Finland, June 13	74.76 m (245 ft 3 in)
Heptathlon	Ramona Neubert, East Germany, June 19	6,836 points

Women's International Competition. Most prominent of the 13 women who set 17 world records in 11 events was Jarmila Kratochvilova (*see* BIOGRAPHIES), a powerful sprinter and middle-distance runner from Czechoslovakia. She was the only woman to establish new global standards in two events and was the brightest star of the world championships.

At the beginning of the season Kratochvilova was the second best of all time in the 400 m and third best in the 200-m event. By the end of the year she was the world record holder at 400 m and 800 m, only the second woman ever to hold both of those world marks. She gained the 800-m record on July 26 at Munich, West Germany, running 1 min 53.28 sec. Her second global mark was the only world record set by an individual in the world championships, 47.99 sec in the 400 m.

Eleven other world records preceded the world meet. Romania's Anisoara Cusmir accounted for the first of her three long jump marks when she leaped 7.21 m (23 ft 8 in) at Bucharest, Rom., on May 15. Again at Bucharest, on June 4, she raised her mark to 7.27 m (23 ft 10¼ in) and then to 7.43 m (24 ft 4½ in).

Galina Savinkova of the Soviet Union increased the discus record to 73.26 m (240 ft 4 in) on May 21 at Leselidze, U.S.S.R., and another throwing best took place at Tampere, Fin., on June 13 when Tiina Lillak of Finland threw the javelin 74.76 m (245 ft 3 in). It was her second record in two years. East Germany's veteran sprinter Marlies Gohr was involved in two new world records. She lowered her own 100-m standard to 10.81 sec on June 8 at Berlin, and on July 31, also at Berlin, she anchored the East German 4 x 100-m relay group in a 41.53-sec clocking. With her on the team were Silke Gladisch, Marita Koch, and Ingrid Auerswald. It was the 12th consecutive time the record had been broken by East Germany, and Auerswald and Gohr were on the last six of those teams.

Gohr's time was beaten less than a month later when Evelyn Ashford of the U.S. took advantage of the thin air at Colorado Springs to run the 100 m in 10.79 sec on July 3, in the same meet on the same day that Smith set the men's 100-m record. Ramona Neubert of East Germany, who was to conclude her season without a loss in the heptathlon in three years, raised her total to a world record 6,836 points, at Moscow on June 19. Another record falling prior to the world championships was that for the 400-m hurdles, which Anna Ambraziene of the Soviet Union ran in 54.02 sec on June 11 at Moscow.

Joining Kratochvilova as the most prominent medal winners at Helsinki were Mary Decker of the U.S. and Koch. The latter earned three gold medals and one silver, winning the 200, placing second in the 100, and running on two victorious relay quartets. And she joined Nurmi and Lewis by winning two gold medals, in the 200-m dash and the 4 x 400-m relay, on the same day. Decker scored the two biggest victories in the history of U.S. middle-distance running for women. She won the 3,000-m and 1,500-m runs, turning back strong Soviet entries in both events.

Post-Helsinki action was paced by high jumpers Ulrike Meyfarth of West Germany and Tamara Bykova of the U.S.S.R. Meyfarth, who had won the high jump event in the Olympic Games of 1972, raised the world record to 2.03 m (6 ft 8 in) at London on August 21. Bykova equaled the mark a few minutes later in the same meet and then added another centimetre by jumping 2.04 m (6 ft 8¼ in) at Pisa, Italy, four days later.

There were three records in non-Olympic events, all by Soviets. Lyudmila Baranova set a new 10,000-m mark of 31 min 35.01 sec at Krasnodar, U.S.S.R., on May 28 but lost the record to Raisa Sadreydinova who ran 31 min 27.58 sec on September 7 at Odessa, U.S.S.R. The 5,000-m walk record was lowered to 22 min 3.5 sec by Olga Yarutkina at Dnepropetrovsk, U.S.S.R., on August 24.

Leaders in the indoor competition were Koch, Bykova, and Cusmir, all of whom set at least two all-time indoor bests. Koch ran 60 m in 7.08 sec and 200 m in 22.64 sec and then in 22.39 sec. Bykova increased the high jump mark three times, culminating with a leap of 2.03 m (6 ft 8 in), while Cusmir long jumped 6.92 and 6.94 m (22 ft 8½ in and 22 ft 9¼ in).

U.S. Competition. Carl Lewis's name will not be in the official record books for his 200 m in 19.75 sec and his 8.79 m (28 ft 10¼ in) long jump, both on June 19 in the Athletic Congress championships at Indianapolis, Ind. But both were low-altitude world records, the best marks ever made without the aid of the thin air at high elevations.

In addition to Lewis's 200-m mark and the five world and U.S. bests already reported, there were seven other U.S. records. Doug Padilla ran 3,000 m in 7 min 35.84 sec; Henry Marsh did the 3,000-m steeplechase in 8 min 12.37 sec; and Tyke Peacock first tied the high-jump mark and then increased it to 2.33 m (7 ft 7¾ in). The pole vault standard was equaled by Brad Pursley with 5.75 m (18 ft 10¼ in) and then broken by Jeff Buckingham with 5.76 m (18 ft 10¾ in), while Dave McKenzie added to his hammer record with 74.50 m (244 ft 5 in).

Besides Ashford's world mark in the 100, U.S. women claimed 12 new national records. Discus thrower Leslie Deniz accounted for four of them and had a best mark of 64.94 m (213 ft 1 in). Other multiple record breakers were Louise Ritter, who twice raised the high-jump standard with a best of 2.01 m (6 ft 7 in), and Mary Decker, who ran 800 m in 1 min 57.60 sec and 1,500 m in 3 min 57.12 sec. Sharrieffa Barksdale and Lori McCauley lowered the 400-m hurdle best to 55.78 sec and 55.69 sec, while the 4 x 100-m relay team of Alice Brown, Diane Williams, Chandra Cheeseborough, and Ashford twice reduced the record, to 41.63 sec and then to 41.61 sec.

In team competition Southern Methodist won the men's title and Nebraska the women's in the National Collegiate Athletic Association (NCAA) indoor championships. Outdoors, Southern Methodist was again the NCAA winner, while the University of California at Los Angeles won the women's crown. The Athletic Congress championships were won by Athletics West for the men and Puma Energizers for the women.

Marathon Running and Cross Country. Rob de Castella of Australia, winner of the 1982 Commonwealth Games marathon, won the two most important marathons of 1983. His first victory was at Rotterdam, Neth., on April 4, when he handed world record holder Alberto Salazar his first defeat ever. De Castella won in 2 hr 8 min 37 sec as Salazar finished fifth. Then de Castella won the first official world championships, run at Helsinki on August 14. Greg Meyer won at Boston, and Rod Dixon of New Zealand was the winner at New York City.

Among the women Joan Benoit and Grete Waitz divided honours. Benoit lowered the world record for women to 2 hr 22 min 43 sec in triumphing at Boston, while Waitz won both the world championship and New York events.

Led by first-place finisher Bekele Debele, Ethiopia won the international cross-country meet for the third straight year. Waitz won the women's race at Gateshead, England, with the U.S. taking the team title.

NCAA honours went to Zack Barie and his University of Texas, El Paso, team, and for women to Betty Springs of North Carolina State and the University of Oregon team. Both of the Athletic Congress team titles were won by Athletics West, with Pat Porter repeating his 1982 victory and Springs winning her second national title within a week. (BERT NELSON)

[452.B.3.b]

Transportation

Three anniversaries in 1983 marked significant events in the development of transportation: on June 5, 1783, the Montgolfier brothers launched their first (unmanned) balloon; in May 1883 the Brooklyn Bridge, New York City, was opened; and on Oct. 4, 1958, scheduled jet flights across the Atlantic began, flown by De Havilland Comet IV's. Since 1958, Atlantic crossing time had fallen from over 13 hours to about 3 hours by the supersonic Concorde.

Among developments in 1983, deregulation led to major changes in the U.S. airline industry, and there were plans to sell off to private enterprise British Airways and the U.S. and Japanese public rail companies. At Black Rock Desert, Nev., "Thrust 2," a jet-powered car driven by Richard Noble of the U.K., set a new world land speed record of 633.6 mph (1,020.1 km/h).

(DAVID BAYLISS)

AVIATION

The international air transport industry continued to suffer from economic problems during 1983. International passenger traffic showed only weak growth with the notable exception of North Atlantic routes, on which the relative strength of the U.S. dollar stimulated a summer boom in tourist trips to Europe; this was boosted by the successful

Trade, International: *see* Economy, World

Trade Unions: *see* Industrial Relations

Transkei: *see* South Africa

inauguration by People Express Airlines Inc. of cut-rate ($149) flights between New York City and London's Gatwick Airport. Freight traffic on the other hand showed improved growth in many areas. The year was marked by continuing severe financial problems for some of the major U.S. airlines, related more to the impact of deregulation than to the state of the U.S. economy.

An unprecedented tragedy during the year was the shooting down of a Korean Air Lines Boeing 747 on September 1 by Soviet fighter aircraft. The plane, en route from Anchorage, Alaska, to Seoul, South Korea, had strayed some distance into Soviet airspace. The International Civil Aviation Organization (ICAO) launched an inquiry into the incident; in December the inquiry group reported to the ICAO that human error in operating the navigational equipment was the most likely cause of the plane's going off course. ICAO called a meeting to be held in 1984 to consider amendment of the Chicago Convention of 1944—the legal basis of international civil aviation—with a view to preventing the recurrence of such incidents.

Reviewing the state of the air transport industry in November, Director General Knut Hammarskjöld of the International Air Transport Association (IATA) put the net loss of IATA member airlines in 1982 at $1.4 billion, compared with a loss of $2.1 billion in 1981. The 1981 figure was much worse than preliminary estimates for that year given in IATA's 1982 annual report. On the other hand, compared with its forecasts of a year earlier, the association anticipated improved—though still negative—results up to 1985.

The financing of aircraft fleet replacement remained a serious concern of IATA members and other airlines. Some $1.1 billion worth of equipment orders were canceled or postponed by carriers during 1983, but IATA stressed that the situation could not continue indefinitely. In 1982 IATA estimated that debt amounted to as much as 90% of net assets employed, and it said that continued investment could lead to negative net worth by the end of 1983; in 1983, however, the association reported that debt had fallen to 70% of net assets employed, largely as a result of the slowdown in reequipment.

On October 1 pilots struck Continental Airlines to protest massive pay cuts presented by Continental as one price of survival in the new era of deregulated competition.

WIDE WORLD

"Free! Free! Free!"

© 1983 HERBLOCK—THE WASHINGTON POST

IATA's preliminary figures for 1983 international scheduled traffic of its members, who accounted for the majority of such traffic, indicated an increase of about 2% over 1982, when passengers carried on international services totaled 130 million. It was in freight that IATA saw signs of revival, reflecting an underlying trend of improvement in the world economic situation. The number of international scheduled freight metric ton-kilometres achieved by IATA members in the first half of 1983 was 5% above that of the similar period of 1982, and tentative figures for the whole of 1983 suggested a 4% growth. An annual growth of 6% was forecast for 1984 and 1985.

The world's airlines made considerable progress in minimizing their costs to overcome financial difficulties. Productivity (in available metric ton-kilometres per employee) of the IATA airlines increased from a base figure of 100 in 1978 to 107 in 1981 and 109 in 1982. The cost per available ton-kilometre was held at 40 cents in 1980 and 1981 and reduced to 38 cents in 1982. Only a marginal increase occurred in 1983, and 1984 was expected to be little higher than the 1981 level. Of continuing concern was revenue yield (per revenue ton-kilometre), which in the case of IATA members fell 1.2% in 1982 to 65.6 cents. Attempts by IATA to stem the incidence of unauthorized discounting by its members, many of whom were competing directly with nonmembers, met with only limited success.

In the U.S. continuing price wars and the arrival of "new entrant" scheduled airlines continued to contribute to the instability of the airline industry.

Pan American, in financial difficulties earlier, improved its position considerably in 1983, but Eastern Airlines and Continental Airlines were among the major carriers with financial problems. Continental filed for bankruptcy in September under a part of the legislation that allowed it to continue operating on a reduced scale. By November it was operating 60% of its prebankruptcy system with 65% fewer employees. Eastern concluded a deal with its pilots in November entailing salary reductions of up to 50% for junior pilots.

The 11 major U.S. airlines reported a combined operating loss in the first nine months of 1983 of some $13 million, and a net loss of $236 million. In the July–September peak-season quarter of 1983, however, their combined net profit of $284 million was nearly double the equivalent figure for a year earlier. (DAVID WOOLLEY)

SHIPPING AND PORTS

World shipping continued to pay the price for the disastrous overestimation of world trade prospects in the 1970s that led to huge new building programs, particularly for large tankers. The crisis caused more shipowners to lay up tonnage and in some cases to send comparatively new vessels (10 to 15 years of age) to the breakers' yards. By mid-1983 the total of laid-up tonnage had passed the record 100 million tons deadweight (dw) mark, although by the end of the year it had been reduced slightly to 90 million tons dw represented by 1,721 ships. This reduction was largely in the tanker section, where the laid-up tonnage was 64 million tons dw, 19% of the world tanker fleet. Compared with the previous year's 12 million tons dw of dry-cargo shipping in lay-up, the 1983 total of 26 million tons dw underlined the worsening situation for owners of such ships.

Among the major maritime nations Greece had the largest percentage of its merchant fleet in lay-up, with 29%, followed by Liberia with 22% and Denmark with 21%. Japan, with the second largest merchant fleet in the world, had only 2% in lay-up. With such a large volume of tanker tonnage in lay-up, the immediate need was for more vessels to be broken up, and it was estimated that the tonnage of ships sold for demolition in 1983 would exceed 36 million tons dw, a record figure.

In the overall table of national fleet tonnages, Liberia maintained the lead with 67 million gross registered tons (grt), but after a year in second place Greece, with 37.5 million grt, fell into third behind Japan's 40.7 million grt. The remainder of the top eight fleets included Panama with 34.6 million grt, the U.S.S.R. with 24.5 million grt, the U.S. with 19.3 million grt, Norway with 19.2 million grt, and the U.K. with 19.1 million grt. Significantly, China's fleet registered an increase of from 10 million to 11.5 million grt. The total world merchant fleet actually declined in size in 1983 from 424.7 million grt to 422.6 million grt (694.5 million tons dw).

There was a reduction in the level of port development in 1983 except in China, where work was well advanced on seven new container terminals. Together they were designed to handle 4.3 million metric tons of cargo annually, 2.4 times China's existing container capacity. In Japan the new Odaiba container terminal at the port of Tokyo was nearing completion. At the port of Tacoma, Wash., a new container terminal was under construction, and in New Zealand nearly $40 million was being spent by the Auckland Harbour Board on new cargo-handling facilities for roll-on/roll-off, unit load, and containerships. (W. D. EWART)

FREIGHT AND PIPELINES

The British government introduced regulations to permit the use in the U.K. of 38-metric-ton trucks, but at the year's end the matter remained unsettled, with the Greater London Council seeking to ban them from London while the European Economic Community (EEC) was anxious for the limit to be increased even more so that it would be aligned with the Community standard. While a significant proportion of the world's merchant shipping fleet lay idle or underused, air freight continued to increase and some of the major airports' freight-handling facilities were becoming congested. Innovations in freight technology included the introduction in the U.K. of a 7.5-metric-ton electric truck and the development of a flying "helitruck" with a payload of 23 metric tons, speed of 282 km/h (1 km/h = 1.61 mph), and range of 644 km (1 km = 0.62 mi).

More than 55,000 km of pipeline were built during 1983 for the transportation of crude oil, oil products, and (mainly) gas. Many of the new pipelines were being built in hostile marine and wilderness environments, of which the North Sea was one of the worst. There, the 880-km Norwegian pipeline joining Statfjord to Kårstø was under

UPI

"MS Nieuw Amsterdam" of the Holland America Lines made her maiden voyage into New York Harbor in July. The luxury liner is shown here passing the Statue of Liberty on the trip from Le Havre, France.

World Transportation

Country	Railways: Route length in 000 km	Railways Traffic: Passenger in 000,000 pass.-km	Railways Traffic: Freight in 000,000 net ton-km	Motor transport: Road length in 000 km	Motor transport: Vehicles in use: Passenger in 000	Motor transport: Vehicles in use: Commercial in 000	Merchant shipping (Ships of 100 tons and over): Number of vessels	Merchant shipping: Gross reg. tons in 000	Air traffic: Total km flown in 000,000	Air traffic: Passenger in 000,000 pass.-km	Air traffic: Freight in 000,000 net ton-km
EUROPE											
Austria	6.4	7,246	10,805	106.9	2,312.9	190.3	12	101	23.1	1,235	20.3
Belgium	3.9	6,879	6,773	126.8[1]	3,206.5	284.6	316	2,271	49.8	5,276	492.2
Bulgaria	4.3	*c.* 7,100	18,276	36.0	815.5[1]	*c.* 130.0[1]	193	1,248	*c.* 16.4	*c.* 780	*c.* 9.9
Cyprus	—	—	—	10.8	96.1	26.1	557	2,150	8.8	854	19.9
Czechoslovakia	13.1	18,050[1]	71,583	145.5[1]	2,475.8	298.3	21	185	19.5	1,590	17.1
Denmark	2.9[1]	3,353[1]	1,570	69.4	1,366.9	242.8	1,152	5,214	*c.* 34.8[2]	2,940[2]	128.6[2]
Finland	6.1	3,326	8,000	75.4	1,352.1	161.7	354	2,377	37.1	2,589	66.8
France	34.1	56,850	61,199	802.4	20,300.0	2,695.0	1,171	10,771	268.8	37,846	2,297.8
Germany, East	14.2	24,785	53,663	*c.* 119.0[1]	2,812.0	237.3	419	1,439	34.5[1]	2,053[1]	67.0[1]
Germany, West	31.5	*c.* 36,000	57,264	486.0	24,035.9	1,273.4	1,782	7,707	198.7	21,625	1,687.6
Greece	2.5	1,510	700	109.0	999.3	478.1	3,501	40,035	40.4	4,924	69.4
Hungary	7.8	11,870	22,726	87.1	1,105.4	129.8	21	82	17.6	1,208	*c.* 9.2
Ireland	2.0	832	629	92.3[1]	709.0	68.1	165	239	19.7	2,343	79.4
Italy	19.8[1]	40,520	16,498	297.3	*c.* 18,603.4	*c.* 1,451.1	1,663	10,375	*c.* 129.4	15,143	582.0
Netherlands, The	3.0	9,376	2,887	108.5[1]	4,650.0	317.4	1,228	5,393	112.1	16,282	1,086.2
Norway	4.2	2,240	2,540	83.4	1,337.9	166.5	2,409	21,862	56.1[2]	4,118[2]	139.1[2]
Poland	24.4	48,954	112,655	299.2	2,881.7	615.9	816	3,651	11.8	778	6.4
Portugal	3.6	5,412	1,060	52.0[1]	1,269.0[1]	186.1[1]	356	1,402	*c.* 39.2	4,174	106.7
Romania	11.1[1]	24,379	75,251	*c.* 95.0	*c.* 250.0[1]	*c.* 130.0[1]	345	2,203	17.1	1,145	10.0
Spain	15.7	15,511	*c.* 10,900	322.1	8,353.9	1,461.9	2,635	8,131	160.5	16,457	482.2
Sweden	12.0	6,374	13,628	129.5	2,936.0	193.5	697	3,788	69.1[2]	5,573[2]	189.8[2]
Switzerland	5.0[1]	9,023	6,501	66.7	2,473.3	178.3	32	315	98.3	11,773	500.7
U.S.S.R.	240.4	344,600	3,581,200	1,408.8	*c.* 9,250.0[1]	*c.* 7,910.0[1]	7,713	23,789	. . .	172,206	*c.* 3,007.0
United Kingdom	17.8	27,782[3]	15,880[3]	365.6	15,757.0	1,797.0	2,826	22,505	330.9	43,958	1,225.5
Yugoslavia	9.4	10,822	25,807	133.8	2,568.1	201.7	475	2,532	28.5	2,870	*c.* 59.7
ASIA											
Bangladesh	2.9	5,631	806	5.7[1]	29.4[1]	11.9[1]	223	411	*c.* 13.0	1,308	*c.* 22.8
Burma	4.5[1]	*c.* 3,490	*c.* 670	22.5[1]	43.3[1]	44.7[1]	109	88	*c.* 6.7	*c.* 229	*c.* 1.5
China	50.0	157,500	612,000	897.0	*c.* 60.0[1]	*c.* 870.0	1,108	8,057	*c.* 64.7	6,000	200.0
India	60.9[1]	221,595	173,107	1,604.1[1]	1,035.3[1]	440.2[1]	644	6,213	92.5	13,259	446.1
Indonesia	6.9[1]	6,290	890	142.3[1]	639.5[1]	473.8[1]	1,319	1,847	*c.* 101.2	8,044	*c.* 190.0
Iran	4.6	2,981[1]	4,083[1]	63.1[1]	1,079.1[1]	406.0[1]	235	1,313	14.9	1,852	48.4
Iraq	1.6[1]	821[1]	2,497[1]	25.3	229.5	118.7	155	1,521	13.3	1,470	54.7
Israel	0.8	242	806	*c.* 12.5	459.2	96.1	66	676	*c.* 27.6	4,648	301.2
Japan	27.5[1]	314,943	31,326	1,120.0	25,539.1	15,538.0	10,652	41,594	373.2	55,731	2,342.7
Kampuchea	*c.* 0.6	54[1]	10[1]	15.0[1]	27.2[1]	11.0[1]	3	4	0.8[1]	42[1]	0.4[1]
Korea, South	6.0	21,240	10,721	53.9	305.8	263.9	1,652	5,529	74.0	12,101	1,068.7
Malaysia	2.7	1,640[1,4]	1,130[1,4]	31.4	696.5[1]	158.7[1]	329	1,195	44.3	5,418	148.7
Pakistan	8.8	17,004	7,206	97.5	283.0[1]	107.9[1]	89	580	44.0	6,425	230.4
Philippines	1.2[1]	209	22	154.4	465.2[1]	294.8[1]	882	2,774	*c.* 45.7	*c.* 7,369	*c.* 187.1
Saudi Arabia	*c.* 0.7	95	272	55.1	757.4	587.8	347	4,302	99.4	12,277	*c.* 373.1
Syria	2.0[1]	443	704	18.8[1]	*c.* 65.5[1]	*c.* 69.1[1]	47	43	*c.* 9.6	947	12.9
Taiwan	3.7	8,204	2,175	17.5	592.6	314.6	511	2,225	34.1[1]	8,198	1,159.2
Thailand	3.9	9,310	2,500	72.2	451.0	471.7	197	442	50.8	8,611	*c.* 320.0
Turkey	8.2	6,105	5,943	232.2[1]	714.7	341.7	631	2,128	*c.* 12.2	*c.* 1,177	*c.* 20.0
Vietnam	*c.* 2.5[1]	4,554[1]	779[1]	347.2[1]	*c.* 100.0[1]	*c.* 200.0[1]	106	262	*c.* 0.4	*c.* 23	*c.* 0.1
AFRICA											
Algeria	3.9[1]	1,875[1]	2,529[1]	*c.* 72.1	574.0	248.3	130	1,365	*c.* 29.8	*c.* 2,400	*c.* 16.0
Congo	*c.* 0.8[1]	337[1]	538[1]	8.2[1]	*c.* 20.0[1]	*c.* 14.0[1]	17	8	*c.* 3.0[5]	*c.* 229[5]	*c.* 22.3[5]
Egypt	4.7[1]	10,995[1]	2,472[1]	28.0	461.3	176.6	341	636	*c.* 34.9	3,643	*c.* 56.0
Ethiopia	*c.* 1.0	171[1,6]	148[1,6]	36.4	43.1	13.0	21	29	*c.* 12.6	*c.* 762	*c.* 26.2
Gabon	0.2	. . .	. . .	7.4	16.0	10.2	17	78	*c.* 5.8	*c.* 430	*c.* 28.3
Ghana	1.0[1]	460[1]	106[1]	32.0	*c.* 66.0[1]	*c.* 48.0[1]	130	257	*c.* 3.0	*c.* 291	*c.* 4.8
Ivory Coast	*c.* 0.7[1]	1,212[1,7]	600[1,7]	46.6	166.9	69.5	63	152	*c.* 4.5[5]	*c.* 316[5]	*c.* 22.6[5]
Kenya	4.5[1]	. . .	*c.* 2,240	53.6	113.6[1]	23.6[1]	19	5	11.6	942	*c.* 25.2
Liberia	0.5	—	4,396[1]	10.1	*c.* 22.0[1]	*c.* 20.0[1]	2,189	70,718	*c.* 0.5	*c.* 10	*c.* 0.1
Libya	—	—	—	14.1[1]	*c.* 367.4[1]	*c.* 278.9[1]	108	912	*c.* 14.9	*c.* 1,473	*c.* 5.5
Malawi	0.8	95	187	10.8	14.1	13.6	1	1	3.0	96	1.5
Morocco	1.8[1]	936	3,934	57.5	480.3	200.9	193	394	*c.* 17.7	1,827	*c.* 38.9
Nigeria	3.5[1]	1,415[1]	1,612[1]	108.0[1]	215.4[1]	33.1[1]	147	463	*c.* 22.4	2,252	26.9
Senegal	1.2[1]	180[1]	164[1]	13.9[1]	50.9[1]	27.8[1]	120	40	*c.* 3.0[5]	*c.* 229[5]	*c.* 21.4[5]
Somalia	—	—	—	19.8[1]	17.2[1]	8.0[1]	22	18	3.4	227	*c.* 4.6
South Africa	20.5	. . .	99,173[8]	183.7	2,557.0	912.0	292	776	*c.* 72.1	9,287	338.8
Sudan	4.8[1]	1,167[1]	2,620[1]	*c.* 48.0	*c.* 34.6[1]	*c.* 38.0[1]	18	93	*c.* 8.0	*c.* 657	*c.* 6.3
Tanzania	3.5[1]	. . .	. . .	53.6	43.2	22.5	36	59	4.6	210	1.2
Tunisia	*c.* 2.2	*c.* 930	*c.* 1,560	25.4	141.2	141.4	46	136	15.3	1,531	17.3
Uganda	1.3	. . .	. . .	27.3	10.6	7.7	—	—	*c.* 5.1	*c.* 125	*c.* 29.7
Zaire	5.3[1]	554[1]	1,591[1]	*c.* 160.0[1]	*c.* 93.9[1]	*c.* 84.9[1]	34	92	*c.* 8.3	*c.* 683	*c.* 31.5
Zambia	2.2	320[1]	1,150[1]	37.2	*c.* 103.0[1]	*c.* 66.0[1]	—	—	8.4	557	23.5
Zimbabwe	3.4	. . .	6,259	170.4	224.5	17.3	—	—	8.8	541	9.4
NORTH AND CENTRAL AMERICA											
Canada	67.1[1]	1,610[9]	200,840[9]	882.1[1]	10,255.5[1]	2,902.7[1]	1,299	3,213	*c.* 329.9	35,608	*c.* 848.0
Costa Rica	*c.* 1.0[1]	99[1]	16[1]	28.5	48.2	13.9	27	23	*c.* 8.4	*c.* 578	*c.* 21.5
Cuba	13.7[1]	1,835	2,626	14.8[1]	152.6[1]	*c.* 40.0[1]	414	949	*c.* 15.6	*c.* 1,242	*c.* 14.5
El Salvador	0.6[1]	14	31	12.3	77.3	63.0	7	3	6.4	335	10.4
Guatemala	1.1[1]	. . .	117[1]	17.3[1]	166.9[1]	81.5[1]	10	28	3.5	160	5.5
Honduras	1.8	. . .	. . .	9.0	58.9	18.2	172	234	*c.* 5.8	331	*c.* 3.1
Mexico	25.5[1]	5,240	*c.* 42,800	214.1	5,221.2	1,891.4	545	1,252	*c.* 155.5	13,465	*c.* 118.1
Nicaragua	0.4[1]	20	14	16.7	24.9	7.9	20	21	*c.* 1.8	*c.* 120	*c.* 1.2
Panama	0.6[1]	. . .	. . .	8.6[1]	97.3[1]	25.8[1]	5,032	32,600	*c.* 7.4	*c.* 400	*c.* 15.0
United States	288.1[1]	17,695[1,10]	1,341,717[1,10]	6,365.6[1]	123,461.5	34,451.1	6,133	19,111	4,137.0	408,997	9,845.0
SOUTH AMERICA											
Argentina	34.5	10,152	11,475	207.6[1]	2,866.0[1]	1,244.0[1]	523	2,256	75.9	5,150	175.9
Bolivia	3.9[1]	529	646	38.9[1]	48.3[1]	53.7[1]	2	15	10.5	780	28.3
Brazil	31.1[1]	12,429[1]	86,131[1]	1,399.4	9,565.9	954.8	666	5,678	203.4	16,304	*c.* 670.0
Chile	*c.* 10.1[1]	1,537	1,780	78.0	*c.* 505.0	*c.* 210.0	192	495	26.3	1,794	139.7
Colombia	2.9[1]	312[1]	888[1]	74.7[1]	672.4	110.9	74	314	70.8	4,196	240.8
Ecuador	1.0[1]	69[1]	29[1]	32.2	232.6	23.9	110	354	*c.* 19.4	862	*c.* 39.4
Paraguay	0.4	23[1]	23	12.7	39.0[1]	33.5[1]	31	32	*c.* 7.5	479	*c.* 2.9
Peru	2.5[1]	494[1]	*c.* 620[1]	56.6[1]	*c.* 318.7[1]	*c.* 169.9[1]	696	836	*c.* 27.6	1,685	*c.* 94.3
Uruguay	3.0	339	221	49.8	281.3	43.4	81	202	*c.* 5.5	293	*c.* 1.1
Venezuela	*c.* 0.3	25[1]	18[1]	62.4	1,501.4	763.5	236	911	*c.* 58.1	*c.* 5,031	*c.* 144.6
OCEANIA											
Australia	39.4[1,10]	. . .	32,056[1]	810.9[1]	6,911.0	399.0	558	1,875	*c.* 201.2	24,522	608.7
New Zealand	4.4	404	3,228	93.1	1,366.5	276.3	116	250	*c.* 45.2	5,846	229.4

Note: Data are for 1981 or 1982 unless otherwise indicated, (—) indicates nil or negligible; (. . .) indicates not known; (*c.*) indicates provisional or estimated.
[1]Data given are the most recent available. [2]Including apportionment of traffic of Scandinavian Airlines System. [3]Excluding Northern Ireland. [4]Peninsular Malaysia only; including Singapore traffic. [5]Including apportionment of traffic of Air Afrique. [6]Including Djibouti traffic. [7]Including Upper Volta traffic. [8]Including Namibia traffic. [9]Main railways only. [10]Class 1 railways only.

Sources: UN, *Statistical Yearbook 1981, Monthly Bulletin of Statistics, Annual Bulletin of Transport Statistics for Europe 1981;* Lloyd's Register of Shipping, *Statistical Tables 1982;* International Road Federation, *World Road Statistics 1978–82;* International Civil Aviation Organization, *Civil Aviation Statistics of the World 1982.* (M. C. MacDONALD) construction. In the U.S.S.R. work continued on the 5,600-km Urengai-to-Western Europe gas line. The ban on the provision of U.S.-manufactured equipment for this project, imposed by Pres. Ronald Reagan following the Afghanistan crisis, was lifted to allow U.S. heavy plant manufacturers to compete for contracts that otherwise seemed likely to go to Japan.

Work on the Dampier-Perth pipeline ensured that the Australian average construction rate of 600 km a year was maintained. Another Southern Hemisphere line under construction was the 1,090-km Centro Oeste gas line in Argentina. However, most activity continued to be in the Northern Hemisphere.

ROADS AND TRAFFIC

The world's motorized vehicle fleet (passenger cars, trucks, vans, buses, and motorized tricycles and bicycles) reached about 520 million at the end of 1983. Behind the total lay some striking contrasts; for example, General Motors Corp. produced as many cars in one week as were owned in the whole of China. Despite low levels of vehicle ownership in many less developed countries, growth was substantial. In India, for example, automobile traffic had grown 12-fold in the past 30 years and truck traffic 14-fold, yet the main road system had been expanded by a factor of only four and only 30% of India's villages were connected to the all-weather road network.

The 209,000-km Pan-American highway system was now 99% complete; the Darien Gap at the border of Panama and Colombia was the main stretch still to be completed. The longest underwater road tunnel in Europe (2.86 km), between the island of Vardø and the mainland of Norway, was completed at a cost of $22 million, and in the Arabian Gulf the 2.4-km bridge between mainland Kuwait and Bubiyan Island was opened; it had cost $47 million. In France a $370 million, 36-km section of the Calais–Dijon toll road was opened in November 1982, while in the U.K. the 10-km Black Country motorway was being financed by a commercial developer. As traffic loading increased, the maintenance costs of the trunk highway networks in the developed nations were rising rapidly. An additional five-cent gasoline tax was introduced in the U.S., four cents of which (total yield, $4 billion) was for highway maintenance.

One of the most important road safety measures was the wearing of seat belts. In the U.K. after January 1983 front-seat occupants were required by law to wear seat belts. The marked reduction in the number and degree of traffic injuries reported by many hospitals reflected the experience of other countries such as Australia and Sweden. The U.S. Supreme Court in June ruled that the National Highway Traffic Safety Administration had acted improperly in 1981 when it repealed a regulation requiring either air bags or automatic seat belts to be installed in all U.S. cars in the 1984 model year.

INTERCITY RAIL

The completion of the Train à Grande Vitesse (TGV) Sud-Est in France consolidated the French railway's position at the top of the world speed table, with a journey speed of 216 km/h between Paris and Mâcon. The success of the TGV service to Lyon was such that a new line was to be built to Nantes, Rennes, and Bordeaux (the TGV-Atlantique) at an estimated cost of $1.5 billion.

In Japan the Shinkansen line was extended to 1,835 km with the commissioning of the Joetsu line, and the national railway's 7-km magnetic levitation (maglev) test track opened at Miyazaki. Manned vehicles reached 216 km/h on this track and unmanned 517 km/h. Also in Japan the pilot tunnel for the 60-km undersea Seikan railway tunnel between Hokkaido and Honshu was joined. The West German railways' maglev development program took a step forward with the opening of a 20-km guideway at Elmsland on which 200-seat trains were to be tested.

WIDE WORLD

The bullet hole in the windshield of Robert Whitted's truck was made by one of three shots fired into his vehicle in a violent episode during the U.S. truck strike in February. The driver was cut by flying glass.

WIDE WORLD

Greyhound Lines continued to operate some buses during a nationwide strike by Greyhound employees. The strike was settled in December.

UPI

West Germany's electromagnetic Transrapid 60, the largest such train in the world, was tested in Munich in March. It was expected to travel at 300 kilometres per hour (186 miles per hour) by the end of 1983 and 400 kilometres per hour eventually.

In the U.K. and Belgium financial support for the railways was being cut. In the U.S. the government-financed Conrail was to be sold to the private sector, and similar plans were afoot in Japan for the national system. In India railway traffic had increased more than threefold over the past 30 years, from 70,000,000,000 passenger-km in 1953 to 230,000,000,000 in 1983. This had led to an acute shortage of capacity, as train lengths were increased to up to 22 coaches to handle the traffic. One means of increasing capacity was the use of double decker coaches, which were becoming increasingly popular in France, West Germany, Canada, Australia, Italy, and Scandinavia.

The largest passenger trains were dwarfed by the freight giants. In South Africa the Ermelo-Richards Bay Line was converted from 3 kv to 25 kv to enable it to haul 44 million metric tons of coal a year. To do this, 200-car trains carried 20,800 tons of coal each. Even those trains were surpassed by the 25,000-ton, 210-car, diesel-hauled iron-ore trains on the Pilbarra railway in Australia.

In Egypt turbine-powered locomotives were hauling passenger trains at speeds of up to 160 km/h between Cairo and Alexandria. The first 400-km stretch of the 3,145-km Baikal-to-Amur railway in the U.S.S.R. was opened. When complete, it would provide the second through rail link across the U.S.S.R. to the Pacific (the Trans-Siberian being the first). More generally, electrification programs were being pursued on many of the more developed railway systems.

In November Baltimore, Maryland, opened a 13-kilometre (8-mile) subway system that was seven years in the building. First-day commuters found automated ticket dispensers.

WIDE WORLD

URBAN MASS TRANSIT

The opening of subway (metro) systems in Baltimore, Md., Lille (France), Caracas (Venezuela), and Miami, Fla., brought the number of cities with full metros to 75. Such systems were under construction in 17 additional cities, and almost half the existing systems were undergoing some form of extension. Among the extensions recently opened were those in West Berlin, Bucharest (Romania), Vienna, and Madrid. A new section of the Chicago subway was designed to link the world's busiest airport (O'Hare) to the world's sixth longest metro system. The year marked the 50th anniversary of the formation of London Transport Executive and also brought the announcement that it was to be replaced by a new regional transport authority.

Interest continued to mount in urban light railways because of their relatively low cost. In Turin, Italy, the first 4.7 km of a 54-km system were opened, and a demonstration track for the new Vancouver, B.C., light railway was operating successfully. In West Germany Stuttgart was converting its narrow-gauge streetcar line (tramway) to modern standard-gauge light railway, and in The Netherlands the Utrecht-Nieuwegein streetcar line was reequipped with new passenger cars and rails. Developments in unconventional guided systems were still on a modest scale, with "people movers" being opened at London's Gatwick Airport and over a 4.2–km route in Yukarigaoka, Japan. The maglev people mover at the Birmingham (England) Airport/National Exhibition complex entered its test phase.

Innovation in the bus industry centred on increases in vehicle capacity. In Paris 174-passenger articulated buses were introduced into service, and 225-passenger vehicles became available. In Nancy, France, the trolley made its return with the introduction of 48 articulated hybrid trolley/diesel buses, and in Johannesburg, South Africa, a return of the trolley bus was also under consideration. In Adelaide, South Australia, construction of a guided bus route continued. One of the most promising areas of technological development in bus engineering was that of vehicles powered by a combination of diesel fuel and electric batteries. The EEC was financing a demonstration of the application of this form of bus technology in the U.K.

(DAVID BAYLISS)

See also Energy; Engineering Projects; Environment; Industrial Review: *Aerospace; Automobiles.*
[725.C.3; 734; 737.A.3]

Trinidad and Tobago

A republic and a member of the Commonwealth, Trinidad and Tobago consists of two islands off the coast of Venezuela, north of the Orinoco River delta. Area: 5,128 sq km (1,980 sq mi). Pop. (1982 est.): 1,185,000, including (1979 est.) Negro 43%; East Indian 40%; mixed 14%; other 3%. Cap. and largest city: Port-of-Spain (pop., 1979 est., 120,000). Language: English (official), Hindi, French, Spanish. Religion (1980 est.): Christian 64%; Hindu 25%; Muslim 6%; other 5%. President in 1983, Sir Ellis Clarke; prime minister, George Chambers.

Increasing financial difficulties throughout 1983 led the government of Trinidad and Tobago to impose stringent import controls, including strict rationing of foreign exchange for imports, in October. Announcing the measures, Prime Minister George Chambers stated that the country's foreign-exchange reserves had fallen by one-fifth, to TT$5.5 billion, since the beginning of the year.

Embarking on a major campaign to reduce the losses of public enterprises, the government announced cuts in subsidies, a wage squeeze, and large-scale layoffs. Sugar, transport, oil, and public utilities were among the industries most affected. The opposition made considerable gains in local elections held in July.

Relations with Jamaica and Barbados, soured by the trade war within the Caribbean Community early in the year, worsened dramatically in October after the invasion of Grenada. Trinidad and Tobago opposed this move, while the other two countries played a leading part in it. A visit from Venezuela's foreign minister in May marked the beginning of a thaw in relations with that country.

(ROD PRINCE)

TRINIDAD AND TOBAGO

Education. (1979–80) Primary, pupils 166,763, teachers 6,443; secondary, pupils 82,482, teachers (1975–76) 1,631; vocational, pupils 4,092, teachers (1975–76) 114; higher, students 1,878, teaching staff (1975–76) c. 500.

Finance and Trade. Monetary unit: Trinidad and Tobago dollar, with (Sept. 20, 1983) a par value of TT$2.409 to U.S. $1 (free rate of TT$3.63 = £1 sterling). Gold and other reserves (June 1983) U.S. $2,503,000,000. Budget (total; 1981 est.) balanced at TT$6,679,600,000. Foreign trade (1982): imports TT$8,873,100,000; exports TT$7,372,400,000. Import sources (1981): U.S. 26%; Saudi Arabia 26%; Indonesia 10%; U.K. 9%; Japan 6%. Export destinations (1981): U.S. 59%; Italy 6%; The Netherlands 5%. Main exports (1981): petroleum products 47%; crude oil 43%.

Transport and Communications. Roads (1982) c. 6,400 km. Motor vehicles in use (1982): passenger 180,900; commercial 45,600. There are no railways in operation. Air traffic (1982): 1,540,000,000 passenger-km; freight c. 5.5 million net ton-km. Telephones (Dec. 1979) 77,800. Radio receivers (Dec. 1980) 300,000. Television receivers (Dec. 1980) 210,000.

Agriculture. Production (in 000; metric tons; 1982): sugar, raw value c. 79; rice c. 26; tomatoes c. 10; grapefruit c. 4; copra c. 8; coffee c. 2; cocoa c. 3. Livestock (in 000; 1981): cattle c. 78; pigs c. 60; goats c. 47; poultry c. 7,500.

Industry. Production (in 000; metric tons; 1982): crude oil 9,104; natural gas (cu m) 2,550,000; petroleum products (1981) 8,830; cement (1981) 140; nitrogenous fertilizers (nutrient content; 1981–82) 23; electricity (kw-hr; 1981) 2,050,000.

Tunisia

A republic of North Africa lying on the Mediterranean Sea, Tunisia is bounded by Algeria and Libya. Area: 154,530 sq km (52,664 sq mi). Pop. (1983 est.): 6,893,000. Cap. and largest city: Tunis (pop., 1975, city proper 550,400; 1982 est., governorate 1,179,600). Language: Arabic (official). Religion: Muslim; Jewish and Christian minorities. President in 1983, Habib Bourguiba; prime minister, Mohammed Mzali.

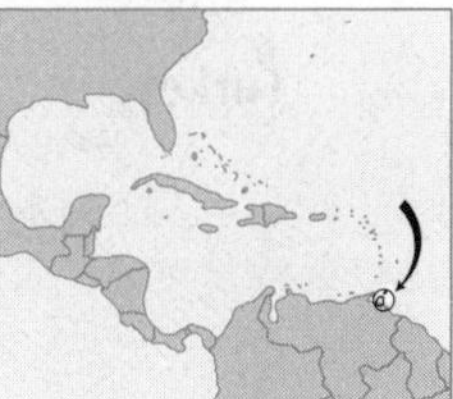

Trinidad and Tobago

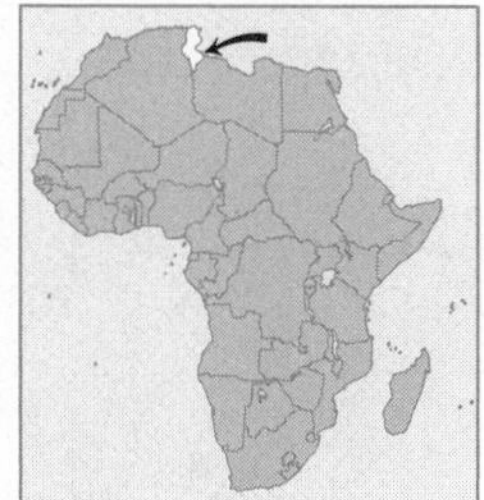

Tunisia

For Tunisia 1983 began with arrests of members of dissident groups, but toward the year's end there was an extension of the liberalization moves initiated in recent years by Pres. Habib Bourguiba (who in August celebrated his 80th birthday). During January some 40 dissidents were arrested, including secondary-school teachers and Islamic fundamentalists. In July, 12 alleged members of an unauthorized organization, the Popular Revolutionary Movement, who had been arrested in the fall of 1982, received sentences of from two years in prison to ten years at hard labour. A month later 30 Muslim extremists allegedly belonging to the Islamic Liberation Party were sentenced to from two to eight years in prison.

In the first of several governmental changes in 1983, President Bourguiba in June dismissed the minister for planning and finance, Mansour Moalla, splitting the portfolio between two new ministers, Ismail Khelil (planning) and Sala Ben M'Barka (finance). In October Abdel Aziz Lasram was replaced as minister of economy by Rashid Sfar, previously minister of health. These changes were seen as reinforcing the authority of Prime Minister Mohammed Mzali. Further changes in November reflected an extension of liberalization and multipartyism. For the first time women were included in the government: Fethia Mzali, the prime minister's wife, became minister for family and women's affairs, and Souad Yaacoubi became state secretary at the Ministry of Health. Later in November Mohammed Saya, regarded as an opponent of liberalization, was replaced as minister for supply by Sadok Ben Jemaa. Two socialist opposition parties were officially recognized.

Foreign relations centred largely on moves toward unity in northern Africa. In March Algerian Pres. Chadli Bendjedid visited Tunis, and he and Bourguiba signed a 20-year treaty of peace and friendship. In April, to mark the 25th anniversary of the Maghrib Unity Congress, Moroccan, Algerian, and Tunisian party leaders met in Tangier, Morocco. President Bourguiba met with the presidents of Algeria and Mauritania in Algiers in June,

WIDE WORLD

Yasir Arafat (centre) called this meeting of the PLO executive council in Gammarth, Tunisia, in July, vainly seeking support to settle the rebellion against him by al-Fatah guerrillas in Lebanon.

TUNISIA

Education. (1980–81) Primary, pupils 1,045,011, teachers 26,989; secondary, pupils 210,895; vocational, pupils 80,190; secondary and vocational, teachers 12,629; teacher training, students 4,101, teachers 148; higher, students 31,887, teaching staff (1979–80) 3,647.

Finance. Monetary unit: Tunisian dinar, with (Sept. 20, 1983) a free rate of 0.71 dinar to U.S. $1 (1.07 dinars = £1 sterling). Gold and other reserves (June 1983) U.S. $356 million. Budget (1980 actual): revenue 1,121,000,000 dinars; expenditure 802 million dinars (excludes 333 million dinars capital expenditure). Gross domestic product (1981) 3,992,000,000 dinars. Money supply (June 1983) 1,405,000,000 dinars. Cost of living (Tunis; 1975 = 100; June 1983) 187.3.

Foreign Trade. (1982) Imports 2,022,720,000 dinars; exports 1,153,900,000 dinars. Import sources: France 26%; Italy 15%; West Germany 11%; U.S. 7%; Spain 5%. Export destinations: U.S. 23%; France 19%; Italy 17%; West Germany 10%. Main exports (1981): crude oil 51%; clothing 13%; phosphates and products 10%; food 5%; chemicals (except phosphatic) 5%. Tourism (1981): visitors 2,151,000; gross receipts U.S. $581 million.

Transport and Communications. Roads (1982) 25,352 km. Motor vehicles in use (1982): passenger 141,200; commercial 141,400. Railways: (1981) c. 2,208 km; traffic (1982) c. 930 million passenger-km, freight c. 1,560,000,000 net ton-km. Air traffic (1982): 1,531,000,000 passenger-km; freight 17.3 million net ton-km. Telephones (Dec. 1981) 201,504. Radio receivers (Dec. 1980) 1 million. Television receivers (Dec. 1980) 300,000.

Agriculture. Production (in 000; metric tons; 1982): wheat c. 1,000; barley c. 300; potatoes c. 130; tomatoes c. 380; watermelons (1981) c. 206; grapes c. 100; dates c. 52; olives c. 385; oranges 93. Livestock (in 000; 1981): sheep c. 4,967; cattle c. 950; goats c. 987; camels c. 170; poultry c. 19,000.

Industry. Production (in 000; metric tons; 1982): crude oil c. 5,100; natural gas (cu m) c. 430,000; cement 1,810; iron ore (53% metal content) 274; pig iron 97; crude steel 106; phosphate rock (1981) 4,924; phosphate fertilizers (1981) c. 474; petroleum products (1981) 1,521; sulfuric acid (1980) 1,634; electricity (kw-hr) c. 3,090,000.

and in August Col. Muammar al-Qaddafi of Libya visited Tunis. Wider international relations were marked by the visit of U.S. Vice-Pres. George Bush in September and that of French Pres. François Mitterrand in October.

Tunisia's economy was adversely affected by lower prices for crude oil, its chief source of hard currency, reduced tourist income, and failures of the agricultural sector. Almost half the grain for domestic consumption had to be imported. An announcement at year's end that the price of bread would rise 110% on Jan. 1, 1984, was followed by reports of rioting in Tunis and other cities.

(PHILIPPE DECRAENE)

Turkey

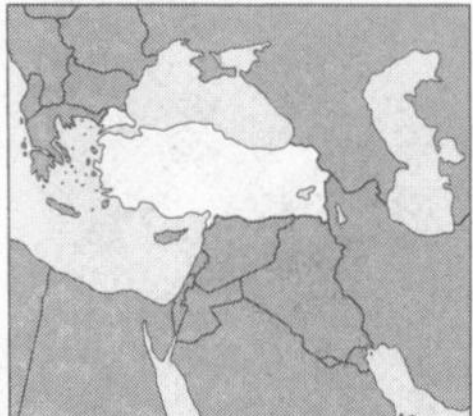
Turkey

A republic of southeastern Europe and Asia Minor, Turkey is bounded by the Aegean Sea, the Black Sea, the U.S.S.R., Iran, Iraq, Syria, the Mediterranean Sea, Greece, and Bulgaria. Area: 779,452 sq km (300,948 sq mi), including 23,698 sq km in Europe. Pop. (1983 est.): 47,279,000. Cap.: Ankara (pop., 1980, 1,887,700). Largest city: Istanbul (pop., 1980, 2,772,700). Language: Turkish (official); Kurdish and Arabic minorities. Religion: predominantly Muslim. President in 1983, Gen. Kenan Evren; prime ministers, Bulent Ulusu until November 24 and, from December 13, Turgut Ozal.

The commanders of the armed forces who made up the National Security Council (NSC) and who had ruled Turkey since Sept. 12, 1980, formally transferred power to an elected Parliament in 1983. Political activity resumed with the promulgation of a law on political parties on April 24 and a new electoral law on June 13. All party founders and parliamentary candidates had to be approved by the NSC, and former parties and politicians were banned.

The registration of new parties began on May 16. The Grand Turkey Party (GTP), regarded as a reincarnation of Suleyman Demirel's centre-right Justice Party (JP), which had been ousted from power by the military coup, was dissolved on May 31. Its two main founders, together with Demirel and 13 other prominent politicians of the JP and its former centre-left rival, the Republican People's Party (RPP), were detained until September 30. The Right Path Party, standing in for the GTP and JP, and the Social Democratic Party, standing in for the RPP, were prevented by NSC vetoes from completing the requisite panel of 30 founding members

TURKEY

Education. (1980–81) Primary, pupils 5,691,066, teachers 215,073; secondary, pupils 1,681,669, teachers 77,196; vocational, pupils 503,205, teachers 33,840; teacher training, students 15,785, teachers 1,012; higher, students 271,138, teaching staff 15,502.

Finance. Monetary unit: Turkish lira, with (Sept. 20, 1983) a free rate of 242.65 liras to U.S. $1 (365.43 liras = £1 sterling). Gold and other reserves (June 1983) U.S. $1,294,000,000. Budget (1981–82 est.): revenue 1,503,944,000,000 liras; expenditure 1,540,965,000,000 liras. Gross national product (1982) 8,736,000,000,000 liras. Money supply (Dec. 1982) 1,342,700,000,000 liras. Cost of living (1975 = 100; March 1983) 1,577.

Foreign Trade. (1982) Imports 1,461,420,000,000 liras; exports 937,310,000,000 liras. Import sources: Iraq 16%; West Germany 11%; Libya 10%; U.S. 9%; Iran 9%; Saudi Arabia 6%; U.K. 5%; Italy 5%. Export destinations: Iran 14%; West Germany 12%; Iraq 10%; Saudi Arabia 6%; Italy 6%; Switzerland 6%. Main exports (1981): fruit and vegetables 23%; textile yarns and fabrics 12%; tobacco 8%; cotton 8%; clothing 7%; livestock 5%. Tourism (1981): visitors 1,405,000; gross receipts U.S. $381 million.

Transport and Communications. Roads (1979) 232,162 km (including 189 km expressways). Motor vehicles in use (1981): passenger 714,700; commercial 341,700. Railways (1981): 8,193 km; traffic 6,105,000,000 passenger-km, freight 5,943,000,000 net ton-km. Air traffic (1982): c. 1,177,000,000 passenger-km; freight c. 20 million net ton-km. Shipping (1982): merchant vessels 100 gross tons and over 631; gross tonnage 2,127,921. Telephones (Dec. 1981) 1,301,600. Radio licenses (Dec. 1981) 4,291,000. Television licenses (Dec. 1981) 4,566,000.

Agriculture. Production (in 000; metric tons; 1982): wheat c. 17,650; barley c. 6,000; corn c. 1,400; rye c. 480; oats c. 330; rice (1981) 290; potatoes c. 2,990; tomatoes c. 3,824; onions c. 1,151; sugar, raw value c. 1,740; sunflower seed c. 620; cottonseed c. 753; chick-peas c. 290; dry beans c. 172; cabbages (1981) c. 588; pumpkins (1981) c. 361; watermelons (1981) c. 4,457; cucumbers (1981) c. 511; oranges c. 746; lemons c. 314; apples c. 1,257; grapes c. 3,741; raisins c. 313; olives c. 1,250; tea c. 70; tobacco c. 180; cotton, lint c. 455. Livestock (in 000; Dec. 1981): cattle 15,981; sheep 49,598; buffalo 1,002; goats 18,926; horses (1980) 794; asses (1980) 1,345; chickens 55,928.

Industry. Fuel and power (in 000; metric tons; 1982): lignite 13,500; coal (1981) c. 4,100; crude oil 2,405; electricity (kw-hr) 26,492,000. Production (in 000; metric tons; 1982): cement 15,718; iron ore (55–60% metal content) 2,596; pig iron 227; crude steel 2,101; petroleum products (1981) 13,184; sulfuric acid 550; fertilizers (nutrient content; 1981–82) nitrogenous c. 695, phosphate c. 545; bauxite 454; chrome ore (oxide content; 1981) 205; cotton yarn c. 142; man-made fibres (1980) 103.

UPI

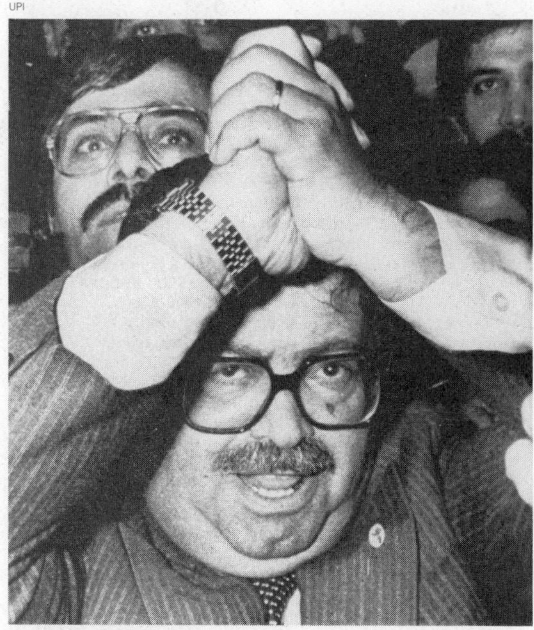

In Turkey's first general election since the military's takeover in 1980, Turgut Ozal of the Motherland Party won decisively and became prime minister.

in time for the start of the electoral campaign on August 25, though they were later allowed to register.

Three parties contested parliamentary elections on November 6. They were the Nationalist Democracy Party (NDP), led by retired general Turgut Sunalp, which was believed to enjoy the backing of the NSC; the centre-left Populist Party, led by Necdet Calp; and the Motherland Party, formed by Turgut Ozal. The campaign was contested under martial law, which was extended after the elections, and was notable only for a last-minute intervention by Gen. Kenan Evren, chairman of the NSC, who implicitly supported Sunalp and criticized Ozal.

Nevertheless, the Motherland Party finished first in the election, winning 45% of the total vote and an absolute majority in the new single-chamber Parliament. The Populist Party gained 30% and the NDP 23%. All independent candidates were unsuccessful. (For tabulated results, *see* POLITICAL PARTIES.) Opponents of the regime urged voters to spoil their ballots, but fewer than 5% of them took that course. When the new Parliament met on November 24, Bulent Ulusu resigned as prime minister and Ozal was named as his successor two weeks later. Ozal's civilian Cabinet was approved by Evren and took office on December 13. In late December Ozal presented an economic package that included measures to encourage trade and a 50% increase in the prices of cigarettes and spirits.

The elections were the culmination of a process that included the enactment of new laws on higher education, labour relations, public assembly, martial law and states of emergency, and broadcasting and the press. Other measures included the subordination of the police to the chief of the general staff and the transfer of the prison service from the Ministry of Justice to that of the Interior.

On November 14 members of the executive of the dissolved Peace Association were given prison sentences ranging from five to eight years. By May 31 military courts had handed down over 33,000 sentences; included were 173 death sentences.

Both the European Parliament and the Council of Europe passed resolutions critical of Turkey's election arrangements. Relations with Europe were further strained by Turkey's immediate recognition of the Turkish Cypriot assembly's unilateral declaration of independence in November.

The effect of the Iran-Iraq war on Kurdish areas bordering on Turkey was a major preoccupation. After three Turkish soldiers were killed by raiders from Iraq in May, a Turkish incursion across the border was undertaken with Iraqi permission. Turkish targets abroad came under attack from Armenian terrorists: the Turkish ambassador to Yugoslavia was killed in March, and there were bombings in Paris, Brussels, and Lisbon.

More than 1,300 people died in an earthquake that devastated parts of the provinces of Erzurum and Kars in eastern Turkey on the night of October 29–30. (ANDREW MANGO)

Tuvalu

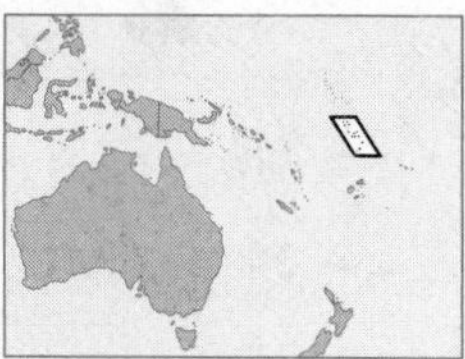

Tuvalu

A constitutional monarchy within the Commonwealth comprising nine main islands and their associated islets and reefs, Tuvalu is located in the western Pacific Ocean just south of the Equator and west of the International Date Line. Area: 26 sq km (10 sq mi). Pop. (1982 est.): 9,000, mostly Polynesians. Cap.: Funafuti (pop., 1979, 2,100). Queen, Elizabeth II; governor-general in 1983, Penitala Fiatau Teo; prime minister, Tomasi Puapua.

Events in Tuvalu in 1983 highlighted the problems caused by isolation, dependence on aid, and geographic fragmentation. The feeder service for the South Pacific Forum shipping line, which operated between Suva, in Fiji, and Tuvalu, had hardly come into service before its future was called into question. Australia refused to continue giving aid to what seemed to be a permanently nonviable enterprise. Moreover, at a time when Tuvalu's only ship was due for replacement and dependence on its seaplane service was greatest, a termination of British aid for this latter service led to its abandonment. Peace Corps volunteers had to be withdrawn from outer islands because the government could no longer provide for emergency evacuation.

After protracted negotiations, fees for the use of Tuvalu's 200-mi exclusive economic zone were

TUVALU

Education. (1982) Primary, pupils 1,269, teachers (1979) 44; secondary, pupils 275, teachers (1979) 10.

Finance and Trade. Monetary unit: Australian dollar, with (Sept. 20, 1983) a free rate of A$1.12 to U.S. $1 (A$1.69 = £1 sterling). Budget (1983 est.) balanced at A$3.5 million (including U.K. aid of A$950,000). Foreign trade (1981): imports A$2,587,100 (52% from Fiji, 32% from Australia, 5% from U.K.); exports A$36,000. Main export: copra 80%.

Tunnels:
see Engineering Projects

agreed on with South Korea. The U.S. Senate finally ratified a treaty under which the U.S. dropped 50-year-old sovereignty claims to some of Tuvalu's islands, while Tuvalu agreed to consult the U.S. on defense and fisheries.

During a visit to London, Prime Minister Tomasi Puapua was sworn in as a privy councillor.

(BARRIE MACDONALD)

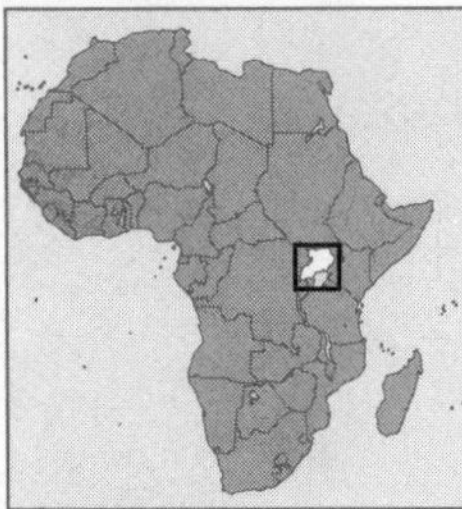
Uganda

Uganda

A republic and a member of the Commonwealth, Uganda is bounded by Sudan, Zaire, Rwanda, Tanzania, and Kenya. Area: 241,139 sq km (93,104 sq mi), including 44,081 sq km of inland water. Pop. (1983 est.): 13,819,000, virtually all of whom are African. Cap. and largest city: Kampala (pop., 1980 prelim., 458,000). Language: English (official), Swahili, and Luganda. Religion: Christian 63%; Muslim 6%; traditional beliefs. President in 1983, Milton Obote; prime minister, Erifasi Otema Allimadi.

When Pres. Milton Obote, in his role as finance minister, introduced Uganda's budget for 1983–84, he claimed that the long-standing black market had been brought under control and that there were no more shortages of everyday commodities. He added that there was still much to be done to recover the position the country had enjoyed before former president Idi Amin's tyrannical rule. Uganda was fortunate in escaping the drought that devastated many African countries. However, though coffee exports met quota levels, there were serious shortfalls of cotton, tea, tobacco, and cocoa.

As an incentive to farmers, Obote's budget offered considerably higher prices for export crops, while it was hoped that aid from Britain would help to rehabilitate the cotton industry. A $5 million credit extended by the U.S.S.R. was to be used to reestablish a textile mill, originally built with Soviet help in 1960, as well as to found a school for agricultural technicians. The government learned in September that its economic policies had been endorsed by the World Bank, which would continue to make substantial loans.

When he opened the new session of Parliament in March, the president announced that the foundations had been laid for a stable future. His claim was not wholly unjustified, and his insistence on his desire to achieve a reconciliation with the government's opponents was intended to carry conviction. In October, for example, he ordered the release of 2,100 prisoners to mark the 21st anniversary of independence. Five days later he urged former presidents Yusufu Lule and Godfrey Binaisa, together with all other Ugandans in exile, to return and promised them an opportunity to express their opinions freely.

However, some in Uganda believed that Obote could not control the excesses of the Army, and this view was borne out to some extent by reports of brutal acts against civilians by men in army uniform. While some of those crimes were not necessarily attributable to the Army, guerrilla activities in the far northwestern part of the country, as well as in a limited area just north of Kampala,

UGANDA

Education. (State aided; 1979) Primary, pupils 1,223,850, teachers 36,442; secondary, pupils 66,730, teachers 3,108; vocational, pupils 3,926, teachers 274; teacher training, students 7,273, teachers 393; higher, students 6,192, teaching staff 677.

Finance and Trade. Monetary unit: Uganda shilling, with (Sept. 20, 1983) a free rate for traditional exports, essential imports, and official loans of UShs 176 to U.S. $1 (UShs 265 = £1 sterling) and a free rate for other transactions of UShs 268 to U.S. $1 (UShs 404 = £1 sterling). Budget (1982–83 est.): revenue UShs 56.4 billion; expenditure UShs 59.7 billion. Foreign trade (1980): imports UShs 2,175,000,000; exports UShs 2,558,000,000. Import sources (1979): Kenya c. 30%; U.K. 23%; India 13%; West Germany 11%; Italy 8%. Export destinations (1979): U.K. 17%; U.S. 15%; France c. 14%; Spain c. 14%; The Netherlands 14%; Japan 10%. Main export: coffee 99%.

Transport and Communications. Roads (1982) 27,325 km. Motor vehicles in use (1982): passenger 10,600; commercial 7,700. Railways (1982) 1,286 km. Air traffic (1982): c. 125 million passenger-km; freight c. 29.7 million net ton-km. Telephones (Dec. 1980) 47,000. Radio receivers (Dec. 1980) 275,000. Television receivers (Dec. 1980) 72,000.

Agriculture. Production (in 000; metric tons; 1982): millet 528; sorghum c. 400; corn (1981) 342; sweet potatoes (1981) c. 680; cassava c. 1,440; peanuts c. 90; dry beans 361; bananas c. 372; plantains (1981) c. 3,550; coffee 155; cotton, lint c. 18; meat (1981) c. 142; fish catch (1981) 167; timber (cu m; 1981) c. 5,967. Livestock (in 000; 1981): cattle c. 5,000; sheep c. 1,075; goats c. 2,160; pigs c. 250; chickens c. 13,300.

Industry. Production (in 000; metric tons; 1981): cement 40; tungsten concentrates (oxide content) c. 0.02; electricity (kw-hr) 657,000.

sometimes encouraged military reprisals that took little account of who the victims were. As a result, thousands of refugees continued to pour over the northern border into Sudan. An estimated 100,000 people who had sought refuge from guerrillas in ill-equipped camps north of Kampala found themselves harassed by both guerrillas and government troops.

Rwanda was pressing the Ugandan government to readmit thousands of Rwandan refugees who had crossed the border into Rwanda after being ordered to leave their homes in Uganda in October 1982. Both countries denied responsibility for the refugees, but in September Uganda decided to relocate, if only on a temporary basis, some 20,000 refugees who had not crossed the border but were crowded into inadequate camps in southwestern Uganda. There were reports of violent attacks on the Rwandan refugees in October and again in December.

An attempt to implement the law passed in 1982 to make restitution to Asians dispossessed and driven into exile by Idi Amin met with a less than enthusiastic response. The conditions attached to the restoration of property, and more particularly the extremely vague promises of compensation announced by the president in February, were thought to be both inadequate and discriminatory in comparison with the terms offered to dispossessed Europeans. The government denied this charge, but the British government agreed to seek clarification of the terms of compensation on behalf of the Asians. Britain's involvement seemed likely to increase when the High Court in London accepted the British government's responsibility for negotiating on the Asians' behalf.

(KENNETH INGHAM)

Unemployment:
see Economy, World; Social Security and Welfare Services

Union of Soviet Socialist Republics

The Union of Soviet Socialist Republics is a federal state covering parts of eastern Europe and northern and central Asia. Area: 22,402,200 sq km (8,649,500 sq mi). Pop. (1983 est.): 271.2 million, including (1979) Russians 52%; Ukrainians 16%; Uzbeks 5%; Belorussians 4%; Kazakhs 3%. Cap. and largest city: Moscow (pop., 1983 est., 8,396,000). Language: officially Russian, but many others are spoken. Religion: about 40 religions are represented in the U.S.S.R., the major ones being Christianity and Islam. General secretary of the Communist Party of the Soviet Union in 1983 and, from June 16, chairman of the Presidium of the Supreme Soviet (president), Yury Vladimirovich Andropov; acting president to June 16, Vasily V. Kuznetsov; chairman of the Council of Ministers (premier), Nikolay A. Tikhonov.

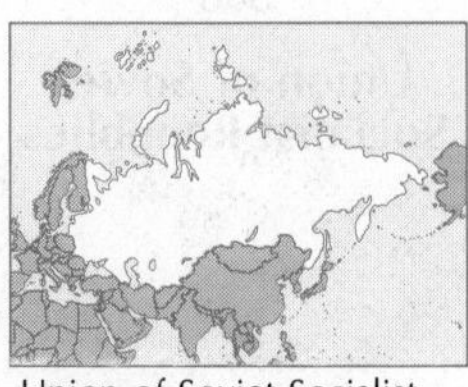

Union of Soviet Socialist Republics

Domestic Affairs. When Yury Andropov succeeded Leonid Brezhnev as general secretary of the Communist Party of the Soviet Union (CPSU) in November 1982, he was hailed as a "liberal" by many Western commentators. Great expectations were aroused about the possibility of fundamental changes in Soviet domestic and foreign policy. These hopes, however, were largely dissipated during 1983. Andropov's need to secure his own power base, his ill health, and foreign-policy disasters such as the shooting down of a South Korean airliner and the bitterness of Soviet-U.S. relations all contributed to this.

It emerged clearly that Brezhnev had supported Konstantin Chernenko as his successor right up until his death, and that it had required the powerful intervention of Defense Minister Marshal Dmitry Ustinov and the military before Andropov secured the prize. In the continuing power struggle in the Politburo with the Chernenko faction, Andropov recorded significant gains during the year. In May he was confirmed as chairman of the Defense Council; he thus gained the office after less than six months, whereas the announcement that Brezhnev was chairman had not come until he had been CPSU leader for 11 years. In June Andropov was strong enough to be elected chairman of the Presidium of the Supreme Soviet (president). Within seven months, therefore, he had accumulated the three major offices held by Brezhnev before his death.

However, at the June Central Committee (CC) meeting no one was promoted to full membership in the Politburo despite the fact that Arvid Pelshe (*see* OBITUARIES) had died in May. Pelshe's position as chairman of the party control commission went to Mikhail Solomentsev, premier of the Russian Federation and a candidate (nonvoting) member of the Politburo. The only promotion to candidate membership in the Politburo was that of Vitaly Vorotnikov, first secretary of the CPSU in Krasnodar territory. Grigory Romanov, first secretary in Leningrad oblast, moved to Moscow to become a CC secretary, a significant promotion. Romanov was therefore in a key position in the party hierarchy. Besides Romanov, only Andropov, Chernenko , and Mikhail Gorbachev, CC secretary for agriculture, were members of both the secretariat and the Politburo. Experience had revealed that someone on both those bodies was in a position to launch a powerful challenge for succession when the occasion arose.

The CC meeting held in late December and the session of the Supreme Soviet that followed it were most notable for Andropov's absence. An illness that some sources identified as kidney disease had kept the Soviet leader out of public sight since mid-August. It seemed that Andropov nevertheless maintained control over political appointments. Solomentsev and Vorotnikov were both promoted to full CC membership; Viktor Chebrikov, a career officer in the State Security Committee (KGB), was made a candidate member; and Yegor Ligachev, head of the CC's department for organizational work, was named a secretary of the CC.

Nikolay Podgorny (*see* OBITUARIES), former chairman of the Presidium of the Supreme Soviet, died in January. Two candidate members of the Politburo also died during the year: Tikhon Kiselev, first secretary of the party in Belorussia, and Sharaf Rashidov (*see* OBITUARIES), party leader in Uzbekistan. The June plenum also dealt severely with two of its members. Gen. Nikolay Shchelokov, former minister of internal affairs and a close associate of Brezhnev, and Sergey Medunov, former party chief in Krasnodar territory, were both expelled from the CC. They were accused of inefficiency and corruption.

Whereas Gorbachev and Romanov added to their stature in the party apparatus, Foreign Minister Andrey Gromyko increased his role in government. He became a first deputy premier with the role of coordinating foreign policy. There was now clearly a ruling triumvirate within the Politburo made up of Andropov, Ustinov, and Gromyko. Consequently, the military showed a higher profile in Moscow.

The decision to shoot down a South Korean commercial airliner on September 1 was taken by the military; Andropov apparently was informed "lat-

After worldwide furor over the shooting down of Korean Air Lines flight 007 by Soviet fighters, U.S.S.R. Chief of Staff Marshal Nikolay Ogarkov held an unprecedented press conference to put forward the Soviet position.

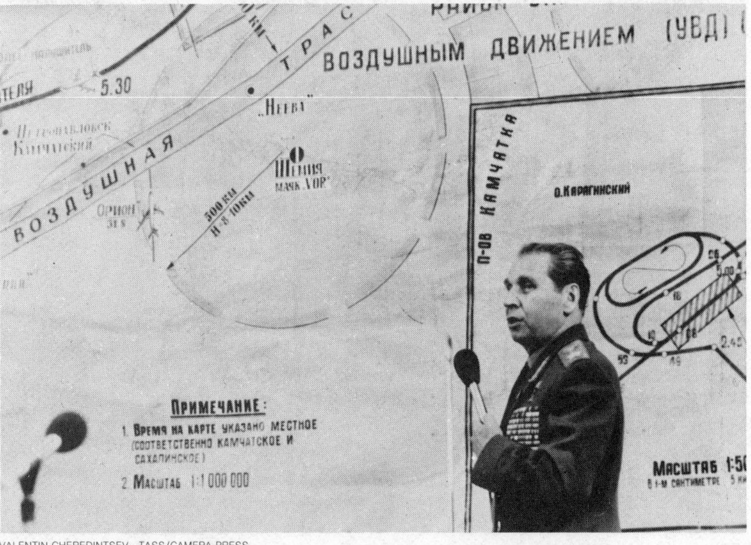

VALENTIN CHEREDINTSEV—TASS/CAMERA PRESS

er." A Boeing 747, the jet had been carrying 240 passengers and 29 crew members. A Soviet fighter downed the passenger plane with a heat-seeking missile after it flew over a strategically sensitive portion of the Kamchatka Peninsula—well off its scheduled course. The military seized the opportunity to play the major role, both domestically and internationally, in explaining this action. Andropov kept a low profile, not addressing the problem directly until almost a month had passed.

Andropov's absence from the ceremony marking the anniversary of the Bolshevik Revolution on November 5—he was the first Soviet leader to miss this event—was what first fueled serious rumours about his health. Ustinov delivered the main speech and accused the U.S. of launching an unprecedented arms race and of various "provocations," a clear reference to the Korean disaster.

The campaign against inefficiency and corruption continued throughout the year. Several key ministries, such as those for heavy- and transport-machine building and for electrical equipment, received new heads. In Azerbaijan it was revealed that 259 officials had been removed in 1982 for corruption and taking bribes. The director of the Sokolniki Sports Palace in Moscow was given a 12-year prison sentence for embezzlement. The death penalty was given to several criminals.

In August the Soviet press announced severe penalties for absenteeism and alcoholism. Police in Moscow began a crackdown on the former; they entered shops, motion-picture theatres, and bathhouses and checked everyone's papers and workbooks. In this way they discovered many people who should have been at work, but the culprits protested that they had to take time off as that was the only way for them to purchase basic necessities. In an attempt to solve the problem, shops received extra deliveries in late afternoon and stayed open longer. The campaign had its drawbacks, however; con men in Moscow began posing as militiamen and imposing fines on the spot.

Dissent and opposition were dealt with harshly throughout the year. The departure of Georgy Vladimov, a writer, for West Germany was a significant success for the KGB security force. Before he left the country, he had been the last important dissident author who had not been expelled, imprisoned, exiled, or silenced by political police pressure. In January he wrote to Andropov saying that he could no longer stand the harassment by the KGB and asking for permission to leave. His case was taken up by some Western leaders, and he left in May. He had been under pressure since 1977, when he had become head of the unofficial Moscow chapter of Amnesty International. In August he was stripped of his Soviet citizenship.

In Lithuania Alfonsas Svarinskas, a priest and leading member of the Catholic Committee for the Defense of Believers' Rights, was sentenced in May to seven years in prison and five years of internal exile for "slandering the Soviet state and social system." Together with the impending trial of another priest, this event dispelled the optimism that had surrounded the return in July 1982 of Bishop Vincentas Sladkevicius after 25 years of exile to his see at Kaisiadorys and the consecration of a new bishop, Antanas Vaicius, to the see of Telsiai, vacant since 1975. With some lay Catholics also facing trial, there were indications that an open struggle between Catholics and the state might be beginning. Lithuania's four bishops visited the Vatican in May for discussions with Pope John Paul II. The visit was the first permitted by the state since 1938, and it followed the creation of the Soviet Union's first cardinal, Bishop Julijans Vaivods of Riga, on February 2.

By the end of September there were an estimated 171 Baptist prisoners, and the number seemed likely to rise as further arrests were made. Some of the sentences were severe. In September 70 Pentecostals in the Siberian village of Chuguyevka began a protest fast in an attempt to gain permission to emigrate to the West. They were almost all Soviet Germans. The last of the "Siberian Seven," a family of Pentecostals who had taken refuge in the U.S. embassy in Moscow, left the U.S.S.R. in July. Vadim Shcheglov, an Orthodox Christian, arrived in Vienna with his family in June; a leading member of the Christian Committee for the Defense of Believers' Rights, he maintained that repression of all dissent and opposition had increased sharply.

A day in two Soviet markets: upper photo shows a state-operated meat market where a queue of customers find sausage but no fresh meat. At bottom, on the same day, a private market has plenty of beef, no crowds, and prices about triple the official level.

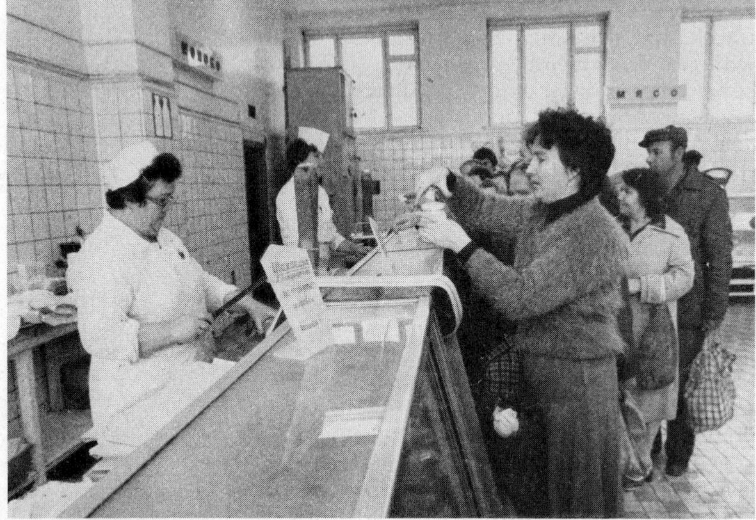

PHOTOGRAPHS, UPI

On the other hand, the country's oldest monastery, the Danilovsky, situated near Moscow, was to become the administrative centre of the Orthodox Church. It had been seized by the state in 1917 and had been closed to the public for many years.

Jewish emigration slowed to an average of about 120 per month. Josef Begun, a Jewish rights activist, was sentenced in October to the maximum sentence of seven years in prison and five years of internal exile for "anti-Soviet agitation and propaganda." This was because he had taught Hebrew and had tried to have such teaching legalized in the U.S.S.R. Valery Senderov, one of the leaders of the unofficial free interprofessional association of workers (SMOT), was sentenced in February to seven years in a labour camp and five years of internal exile. Senderov had revealed the discrimination that was practiced against Jews in Soviet education and the professions. Menachem Nidel became the first officially ordained rabbi to serve in Latvia in 20 years when he took up his duties in June.

In February the All-Union Scientific Medical Society of Neuropathologists and Psychiatrists withdrew from the World Psychiatric Association. This was the result of Western criticisms of Soviet use of psychiatry to silence dissenters. Had the Soviets not resigned, they would almost certainly have been expelled, although on July 10 the association asked the Soviet group to rejoin.

Vladimir Danchev, a Radio Moscow commentator, referred to the Soviet Army in Afghanistan as "invaders" in English-language broadcasts on five occasions in May. He refused to retract his statements and was returned to his home town of Tashkent, Uzbekistan, and confined to a psychiatric hospital. He was returned to work in mid-December, but it was considered unlikely that he would be announcing for the English-language service. During a Russian-language broadcast on Radio Moscow, sloppy editorial work led to passages from a speech by a high military figure being incorporated into a speech by Andropov. After this error an instruction was issued that all news items were to be recorded in advance.

Alcoholism continued to be the scourge of Soviet society, as more and more young people were becoming addicted. In addition, the divorce rate in European Russia stood at about 50%. Every fourth adult in the U.S.S.R. lived alone. A woman's position in society was often difficult, and the inadequate supply of consumer goods added to the working mother's problems. Not surprisingly, women were slowly beginning to protest against the burdens placed upon them.

The Economy. Performance was better than in 1982. Stricter discipline resulted in industrial growth of 4.1% during the first nine months of 1983 compared with the same period in 1982. This brought the annual plan target of 3.2% growth well within reach. It was also claimed that labour productivity rose by 3.5%, again higher than the 2.9% planned for the whole year. However, output of coal, oil-industry equipment, refrigerators, and freezers failed to meet the targets for the first nine months of the year. As had been the trend since 1980, no information was provided on the harvest, and it seemed unlikely that the harvest would meet planned goals in 1983. An estimated 20 million–30 million metric tons of grain were expected to be imported during the year 1983–84. In August the U.S.S.R. signed a new five-year grain agreement with the U.S. by which the Soviets were obliged to import a minimum of nine million metric tons annually. The deal was worth an estimated $2 billion a year to the U.S.

There was much speculation about economic reform, but only a modest experiment emerged. Some of the key industrial ministries and the associations subordinate to them were involved in a

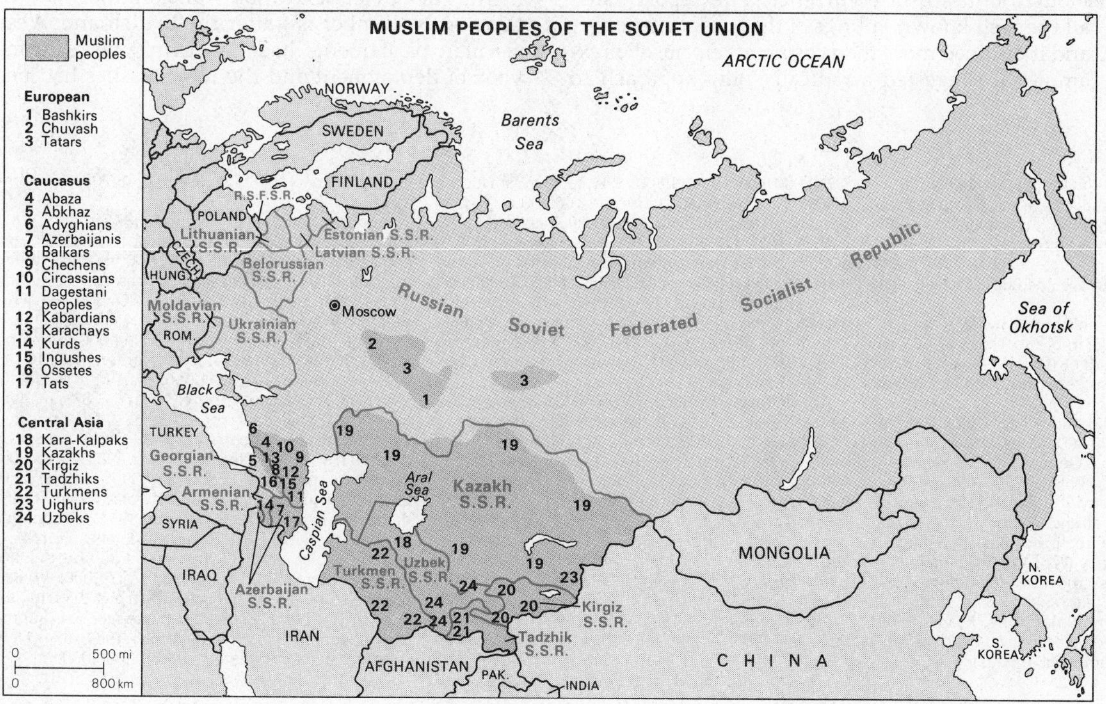

World attention to the condition of religious minorities in the Soviet Union in 1983 centred mainly on Jews and certain Christian sects. Less familiar in the West are the number and diversity of Muslim peoples, located mainly in Soviet Central Asia, who make up about 17% of the population.

limited decentralization of decision-making authority. If it proved satisfactory, it was to be extended to other sectors of industry. Hungarian industrial practice appeared to be especially relevant here, though it was worth pointing out that the Hungarian economy had performed poorly in recent years. Andropov was said to be impressed by the Hungarian way of doing things, and Soviet economists had been advised to examine practices in other socialist states in an effort to improve Soviet performance. Some Soviet farms were beginning to benefit from Hungarian managerial expertise.

The major problem facing agricultural planners was not production but packing and transport. The minister of fruit and vegetables was dismissed as part of a campaign aimed at improving supplies. However, industry held the key to the problem; the road network was quite inadequate, and there was a shortage of refrigerator cars on the railways. One of the reasons for this situation was the irrational transportation of goods. The most absurd example, according to the central press, was the transport of reinforced-concrete blocks hundreds of kilometres when factories making them were almost as common as bakeries. In 1970 the average delivery journey for such a block was 500 km (310 mi), but by 1982 it had risen to 842 km. The Ministry of Transport estimated that 40 days a year were totally wasted as a result of the railways' carrying freight that need not have been moved in the first place. The agricultural reforms announced by Brezhnev in May 1982 had made little impact, partly because CC Secretary for Agriculture Gorbachev was only a lukewarm supporter of them. He appeared to favour a system that gave greater emphasis to local initiative on the farms.

A confidential report on the state of the Soviet economy, written by specialists in Novosibirsk, was leaked to the Western press in August, a previously unheard-of occurrence. The report listed all the well-known failings of the Soviet economy, and it outlined more than cosmetic reforms. For example, it suggested a radically new approach to the running of industry, thus striking at the entrenched interests and privileges of the economic bureaucracy.

Environmental pollution was becoming an increasingly serious problem. Legislation was adequate, but inspection and the fines imposed for violation were insufficient. Irrigation had led to disaster in Kazakhstan; so much water had been drained from the Aral Sea that the average depth had dropped 10 m (33 ft) from its former depth of 20–25 m (66–82 ft). The sea had receded 60 km (37 mi) from the old shore. A salt desert had resulted, killing plant and animal life and bringing to an end the fishing industry that had at one time produced an annual catch of 50,000 metric tons. The Kara-Bogaz-Gol Gulf, also in Kazakhstan, was in danger of suffering the same fate.

Foreign Policy. The year was dominated by relations with the U.S. The main goal of Soviet foreign policy was to delay or prevent the deployment of the U.S. Pershing II and cruise nuclear missiles in Western Europe in December. Two approaches were followed: the intermediate nuclear force (INF) talks between the U.S.S.R. and the U.S. in Geneva provided the main platform for discussion; and peace campaigns in Western Europe, especially in West Germany, were encouraged in the hope that popular pressure and protest would undermine the resolve of Western governments to deploy the weapons. A number of Soviet-U.S. confrontations, culminating in that over the shooting down of the South Korean airliner, exacerbated East-West tension and reduced the impact of Soviet proposals. Moscow found it difficult to agree on what concessions should be offered in Geneva. When Andropov eventually presented them in the form of an interview with *Pravda* on October 26, they turned out to be less radical than Soviet sources had led NATO to expect. The price of a deal was the same as before—no NATO deployment. The Soviet delegation walked out of the INF talks on November 23, after the British and West German parliaments had taken final votes in favour of deployment and the first missiles had be-

U.S.S.R.

Education. (1982) Primary, pupils 34.8 million; secondary, pupils 9.5 million; primary and secondary, teachers 2.6 million; vocational, pupils 3,713,000; teacher training, students 449,000; vocational and teacher training, teachers (1979–80) 231,300; higher, students 5,284,000, teaching staff (1978–79) 345,000.

Finance. Monetary unit: ruble, with (Sept. 20, 1983) a free rate of 0.77 ruble to U.S. $1 (1.15 rubles = £1 sterling). Budget (state; 1983 est.): revenue 354.1 billion rubles; expenditure 353.9 billion rubles.

Foreign Trade. (1982) Imports 56,411,000,000 rubles; exports 63,165,000,000 rubles. Import sources: Eastern Europe 43% (East Germany 10%, Czechoslovakia 8%, Bulgaria 8%, Poland 7%, Hungary 7%); Japan 5%; West Germany 5%; Finland 5%; Yugoslavia 5%. Export destinations: Eastern Europe 42% (East Germany 10%, Czechoslovakia 8%, Bulgaria 8%, Poland 8%, Hungary 6%); West Germany 6%; Cuba 5%. Main exports: crude oil and products 40%; machinery 9%; natural gas 9%.

Transport and Communications. Roads (1981) 1,408,800 km. Motor vehicles in use (1980): passenger c. 9,250,000; commercial (including buses) c. 7,910,000. Railways (1981): 240,400 km (including 97,600 km industrial); traffic 344,600,000,000 passenger-km, freight 3,581,200,000,000 net ton-km. Air traffic (1982): 172,206,000,000 passenger-km; freight c. 3,007,000,000 net ton-km. Navigable inland waterways (1981) 140,000 km; freight traffic 255,600,000,000 ton-km. Shipping (1982): merchant vessels 100 gross tons and over 7,713; gross tonnage 23,788,668. Telephones (Dec. 1980) 23,707,000. Radio receivers (Dec. 1980) 130 million. Television receivers (Dec. 1979) 80 million.

Agriculture. Production (in 000; metric tons; 1982): wheat c. 87,000; barley c. 41,000; oats c. 14,000; rye c. 10,000; corn c. 12,000; rice c. 2,500; millet c. 2,000; potatoes 78,000; sugar, raw value c. 6,800; tomatoes c. 7,300; watermelons (1981) c. 2,800; apples c. 7,400; sunflower seed c. 5,300; cottonseed c. 5,660; linseed c. 210; soybeans c. 460; dry peas c. 5,200; wine c. 3,500; tea c. 145; tobacco c. 280; cotton, lint c. 2,890; flax fibres c. 300; wool 270; hen's eggs 3,971; milk c. 89,600; butter c. 1,405; cheese c. 1,525; meat c. 15,337; fish catch (1981) 9,546; timber (cu m; 1981) c. 356,600. Livestock (in 000; Jan. 1982): cattle 115,919; pigs 73,302; sheep 142,358; goats 6,123; horses c. 5,700; chickens 1,006,000.

Industry. Index of production (1975 = 100; 1982) 132. Fuel and power (in 000; metric tons; 1982): coal and lignite 718,000; crude oil 613,000; natural gas (cu m) 501,000,000; manufactured gas (cu m; 1981) 36,560,000; electricity (kw-hr) 1,366,000,000. Production (in 000; metric tons; 1982): cement 124,000; iron ore (60% metal content) 244,000; pig iron (1981) 108,000; steel 147,000; aluminum (1981) c. 1,950; copper (1981) c. 1,060; lead (1981) c. 630; zinc (1981) c. 870; magnesite (1981) c. 2,075; manganese ore (metal content; 1981) c. 2,930; tungsten concentrates (metal content; 1981) c. 8.8; gold (troy oz; 1981) c. 8,400; silver (troy oz; 1981) c. 46,500; petroleum products (1981) 445,590; sulfuric acid 23,800; caustic soda (1981) 2,800; plastics and resins 4,100; fertilizers (nutrient content; 1981) nitrogenous 10,581, phosphate 6,343, potash 8,449; paper (excluding paperboard) 5,400; man-made fibres (1980) 1,176; cotton fabrics (sq m; 1981) 7,171,000; woolen fabrics (sq m; 1981) 768,000; rayon and acetate fabrics (sq m; 1981) 1,806,000; passenger cars (units) 1,307; commercial vehicles (units; 1981) 874. New dwelling units completed (1980) 2,050,000.

gun to arrive. When the strategic arms reduction talks went into recess in December, the Soviets refused to agree to a date for their resumption.

One reason for the lack of incisive leadership in Moscow was Andropov's poor health, but the other, more significant, reason was the influence of the military in making decisions. The tensions of the superpower relationship required a crisp and rapid response from the Kremlin, and this was lacking.

A particular case in point was the Soviet handling of the Korean airliner disaster. It was inept and laboured. It became clear that the Soviets shot down the airliner because they mistook it for a U.S. spy plane. Since this mistake could not be admitted, the Soviets accused the U.S. of using a civilian airliner to gather military intelligence over Kamchatka Peninsula and Sakhalin Island. Gromyko, usually a masterful performer in the UN and elsewhere, had seldom been seen to less advantage. Chief of the General Staff Nikolay Ogarkov presided at an unprecedented international press conference to explain Soviet behaviour. In doing so he revealed information about Soviet bases in the Far East that had previously been regarded as secret. The prominent role of the military during the crisis increased speculation about the role of the military in policy formation. The administration of U.S. Pres. Ronald Reagan emerged as clear victor in the confrontation, conducted as it was in the full glare of world publicity.

Elsewhere, Moscow could derive some satisfaction from an improvement in relations with China. Two border posts in Central Asia that had been closed for 20 years were reopened. Thus China appeared to be adopting a more evenhanded approach to the two superpowers. However, Soviet-Japanese relations remained cool owing to Soviet intransigence in the dispute over the northern islands and the stationing of SS-20 missiles in the eastern parts of the Soviet Union. The situation was further complicated by the fact that the Japanese government regarded as reliable the allegations of widespread Soviet spying in Japan made by a KGB officer who had defected in 1979.

In the Middle East relations with Egypt, Syria, and Iraq improved, while those with Iran deteriorated. Soviet-Egyptian trade increased, but Egypt was still faced with the problem of rescheduling its $10 billion military aid debt to the U.S.S.R. Syria received valuable military aid, including SA-5 antiaircraft missile batteries. It was thought that their deployment could bring the U.S.S.R. and Syria air superiority in the Middle East. Iraq also received military supplies. Relations with Iran reached a low ebb. The Tudeh (Communist) Party was banned by the Iranian authorities on May 4, and its leaders were arrested and accused of spying for the Soviet Union. Tudeh leader Nureddin Kianuri publicly confessed to having been a Soviet spy since 1945 and to having passed top-secret military and political documents to a KGB officer at the Soviet embassy in Teheran.

During the year Soviet diplomats were expelled from many countries, accused of spying. France topped the list with 47 expulsions.

(MARTIN MCCAULEY)

United Arab Emirates

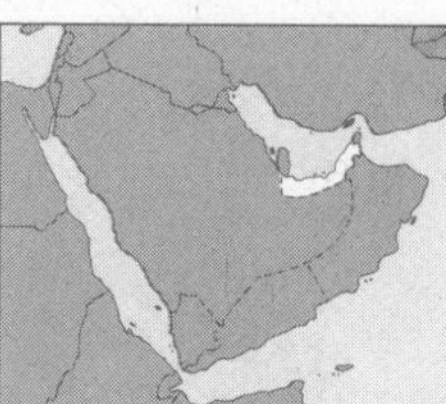
United Arab Emirates

Consisting of Abu Dhabi, Ajman, Dubai, Fujairah, Ras al-Khaimah, Sharjah, and Umm al-Qaiwain, the United Arab Emirates is a federation of seven largely autonomous emirates located on the eastern Arabian Peninsula. Area: 77,700 sq km (30,000 sq mi). Pop. (1982 est.): 1,121,800, including Arab 42%; South Asian 50% (predominantly Iranian, Indian, and Pakistani); others 8% (mostly Europeans and East Asians). Cap.: Abu Dhabi (pop., 1980 prelim., 243,000). Language: Arabic. Religion: Muslim. President in 1983, Sheikh Zaid ibn Sultan an-Nahayan; prime minister, Sheikh Rashid ibn Said al-Maktum.

Six new ministers were sworn in and two ministers dismissed in a Cabinet reshuffle in 1983—the first major changes in the federal government of the United Arab Emirates (U.A.E.) since 1980. Said Salman was dismissed as minister of education and replaced by a civil servant, Faraj Fadhil al-Mazroui. Saif Ali al-Jarwan became trade and economy minister. The federal budget, finally approved on August 15 by the president, Sheikh Zaid, provided for a $1.5 billion deficit, with spending totaling $5,010,000,000. Oil revenue from the three producing emirates of Abu Dhabi, Dubai, and Sharjah was running at about $9 billion a year. A small oil find in Ras al-Khaimah was expected to come into production during 1984.

The ill health of the federal prime minister, Sheikh Rashid, ruler of Dubai, continued to hamper the administration of that emirate. Sheikh Maktum, the heir apparent, and his brothers Muhammad and Hamdan seemed likely to assume a more dominant role: Muhammad began to take charge of the emirate's petroleum policy.

There was a further tightening of the legislation controlling foreign companies operating in the U.A.E. Tariffs were to be raised to 4% in line with measures adopted by the Gulf Cooperation Council (GCC). The U.A.E. was the site of joint military maneuvers by the GCC allies in late 1983.

(JOHN WHELAN)

See also Middle Eastern Affairs.

UNITED ARAB EMIRATES

Education. (1980–81) Primary, pupils 88,617, teachers 5,424; secondary, pupils 31,940, teachers (1979–80) 2,499; vocational, pupils 422, teachers (1979–80) 83; higher, students 2,519, teaching staff 344.

Finance. Monetary unit: dirham, with (Sept. 20, 1983) a free rate of 3.67 dirhams to U.S. $1 (5.53 dirhams = £1 sterling). Gold and other reserves (Sept. 1982) U.S. $3,187,000,000. Budget (central total; 1981 actual): revenue 22,460,100,000 dirhams; expenditure 18,666,000,000 dirhams. Gross domestic product (1982) 108.9 billion dirhams.

Foreign Trade. (1982) Imports 34,577,000,000 dirhams; exports 61,808,000,000 dirhams. Import sources (1981): Japan 18%; U.S. 14%; U.K. 11%; Bahrain 7%; West Germany 6%; France 5%. Export destinations (1981): Japan 36%; France 10%; U.S. 7%; The Netherlands 6%. Main exports (1981): crude oil 84%; natural gas 6%.

Industry. Production (in 000; metric tons; 1982): crude oil 59,439; petroleum products (1981) 1,969; natural gas (cu m) c. 7,100,000; cement (1981) c. 2,200; aluminum (1981) 106; electricity (kw-hr; 1981) 6,050,000.

Unions:
see Industrial Relations

Unitarian (Universalist) Churches:
see Religion

United Church of Canada:
see Religion

United Church of Christ:
see Religion

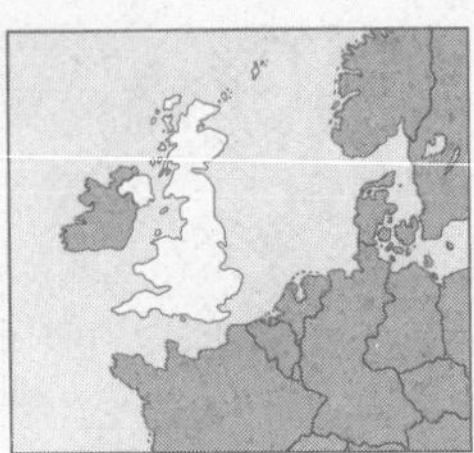

United Kingdom

United Kingdom

A constitutional monarchy in northwestern Europe and member of the Commonwealth, the United Kingdom comprises the island of Great Britain (England, Scotland, and Wales) and Northern Ireland, together with many small islands. Area: 244,035 sq km (94,222 sq mi), including 3,084 sq km of inland water but excluding the crown dependencies of the Channel Islands and Isle of Man. Pop. (1983 est.): 56,124,000. Cap. and largest city: London (Greater London pop., 1982 est., 6,765,100). Language: English; some Welsh and Gaelic also are used. Religion: mainly Protestant, with Roman Catholic, Muslim, and Jewish minorities, in that order. Queen, Elizabeth II; prime minister in 1983, Margaret Thatcher.

Domestic Affairs. The first clear hint that 1983 might be an election year for Britain came when Prime Minister Margaret Thatcher (*see* BIOGRAPHIES) made a surprise visit to the Falkland Islands in January to mark the 150th anniversary of British rule. Since the islands had been recaptured from the Argentine forces by a British task force the previous June, the so-called Falklands factor—the public memory of this bold and dashing victory—had been generally viewed as Thatcher's chief asset when appealing to the voters for reelection. This she was not obliged to do until May 1984, but her highly publicized visit to Port Stanley reinforced the expectation that she would either call for the election in the autumn of 1983 or, as she was urged by influential voices within her Conservative Party, make a dash for it in the spring.

If election year it was to be, two issues would dominate the contest at the polls. One was the economy, especially the number of unemployed, and the other was nuclear weapons. The economic prospect as the year began was unusually uncertain because so much depended upon the course of the U.S. recovery and the performance of the world economy generally. Unemployment stood at more than three million (some 13% of the registered work force), and nobody pretended that that total could be significantly reduced within the lifetime of the current Parliament. Inflation, on the other hand, was down to an annual rate of 5% from 12% in the first quarter of the previous year; this, plainly, would be the government's chief electoral claim to economic success. Real wages were rising again and had been for some months, and the question was whether this would count for more with voters—the vast majority of whom remained in employment—than the unprecedented number of unemployed.

The budget, presented to the House of Commons on March 15 by Chancellor of the Exchequer Sir Geoffrey Howe (*see* BIOGRAPHIES), was characteristically unexciting. Nobody could accuse him of a giveaway election budget; nevertheless, within the limited room for maneuver provided by a slow-growing economy, Sir Geoffrey concentrated his economic reliefs this time not on the corporate sector but on the individual taxpayer. He did not reduce the basic rate of income tax, which remained at 30%, but he increased tax allowances by 14%, which was 8.5% more than was required to compensate for price inflation. Excise duties on beer, spirits, wine, and tobacco were kept strictly in line with inflation. The overall effect of the budget was mildly reflationary, and professional commentators noted that a once arch-monetarist government had become exceedingly vague about its monetary policies.

STUART FRANKLIN—SYGMA

Margaret Thatcher and the Conservative Party won a resounding victory in British parliamentary elections in June. Here she acknowledges the cheers of supporters at Tory Party headquarters.

As important from an electoral point of view as the performance of the real economy was the state of people's expectations. The Thatcher government had set out to diminish them, along with the rate of inflation, and in early 1983 it looked as though it might have succeeded. The Conservative central office was encouraged to discover from its opinion surveys that people were inclined to blame the high level of unemployment chiefly on the condition of the world economy and also on the profligacy of previous governments rather than on the policies of the Conservative regime. Trade-union militancy, another measure of expectation, was at its lowest ebb in years. Some 28,000 water workers began a month-long strike at the end of January, and at its peak more than seven million people were having to boil their drinking water. The miners, however, always a cause of anxiety to Conservative governments at election time, firmly rejected a call to strike in protest at the closure of money-losing mines.

Election or no election, nuclear weapons were bound to be a subject of intensifying controversy during the year. At the end of the year the first group of U.S. cruise missiles was due to be installed at the U.S. Air Force base at Greenham Common near Newbury, Berkshire, where a women's peace camp had been established at the end of 1981. The missiles were to be deployed in Britain as part of the decision made by NATO in December 1979 to augment its intermediate-range nuclear forces (INF) while at the same time seeking to negotiate a reduction in the equivalent weaponry of the U.S.S.R. Since the decision was first announced, a wave of nuclear anxiety had spread across northern Europe, and in Britain the Campaign for Nuclear Disarmament (CND), which espoused a policy of unilateral nuclear disarmament by Britain, was at its strongest since its heyday in the early 1960s. (*See* DEFENSE: *Special Report.*)

It was taken as another hint of an imminent election when in January Thatcher appointed Michael Heseltine, one of the government's most vigorous and able publicists, as secretary of state for defense in place of John Nott, who was retiring from politics. From that moment the propaganda war with CND and its general secretary, Msgr. Bruce Kent (*see* BIOGRAPHIES), began. At Easter, while some 70,000 demonstrated at Greenham Common, Heseltine visited the Berlin Wall, where he denounced the campaigners for unilateral nuclear disarmament as "naive and reckless."

When Heseltine took over, the state of public opinion, according to a variety of polls, was that somewhat over one-half were opposed to the siting of cruise missiles in Britain while somewhat fewer than one-quarter were in favour of unilateral nuclear disarmament. For this reason the visit in February to London and other European capitals by U.S. Vice-Pres. George Bush was welcome to the government. It was followed a few weeks later by an important development in the U.S. negotiating position at the Geneva INF arms-limitation talks. While continuing to prefer the "zero option" (no cruise or Pershing II missiles in return for no Soviet SS-20s and other intermediate-range missiles in Europe), Pres. Ronald Reagan declared his willingness to negotiate an interim agreement that would limit equally the numbers of missiles deployed on both sides. The British government hoped that this would mute criticism that the U.S. was insufficiently committed to arms control.

Another important event was the debate on nuclear weapons at the General Synod of the Church of England. It was a sign of the times that this sedate assembly of clergy and laymen should find itself at the centre of national attention, its proceedings continuously televised. A working-party report had endorsed the policy of unilateral nuclear disarmament by Britain on moral and theological grounds. But the archbishop of Canterbury, Robert Runcie, argued that in the world as it was nuclear deterrence was morally justifiable, and the Synod accepted this view and rejected the working party's report. It did, however, voice its objection to NATO's strategy, which depended upon the threat of first use of tactical nuclear weapons.

Election fever reached a new pitch following a sensational by-election in Bermondsey, south London, on February 24. A once impregnable Labour stronghold fell heavily to the Liberal Party-Social Democratic Party (SDP) Alliance. This was due in part to a long history of corruption and internal division within the Bermondsey Labour Party and dissatisfaction with Michael Foot's national party leadership but chiefly to the controversial character of Labour's candidate, Peter Tatchell. Foot had been obliged to endorse Tatchell's candidacy in spite of having earlier declared that he would never do so after Tatchell had written an article that raised doubts about the degree of his commitment to parliamentary democracy.

At a second by-election a month later in Darlington, County Durham, Labour, with a more traditional candidate this time, held the seat in a narrow victory over the Conservative candidate; a weak Alliance candidate finished in third place. Although this victory gave some boost to Labour's morale, its more significant meaning was that the Conservatives, when not tactically squeezed as in Bermondsey, could give Labour a close contest even in a northern area of high unemployment. This reinforced the argument of ministers who were now pressing for a June election.

Thatcher delayed until the local government elections on May 5 and then four days later called the general election for June 9. The opinion polls

KEITH BUTLER/JACOB SUTTON/SPOONER—GAMMA/LIAISON

Demonstrators against the stationing of NATO cruise missiles formed a human chain 23 kilometres (14 miles) long, connecting the U.S. air base at Greenham Common with the nuclear weapons research facility at Aldermaston and an armaments factory at Burghfield.

LONDON EXPRESS/PICTORIAL PARADE

New leadership was chosen by the British Labour Party after its worst defeat in a generation. Neil Kinnock (right), a leftist from Wales and a fiery orator, was elected leader and rightist Roy Hattersley won the contest for the deputy leadership.

were united in giving the government a substantial lead over Labour, ranging from 8 to 19 percentage points, and the outcome was never in serious doubt. (*See* Sidebar; for tabulated results, *see* POLITICAL PARTIES.) Thatcher thus became the first Conservative prime minister to lead a party to a second full term since Lord Salisbury in 1900.

The chief casualty of the postelection Cabinet reshuffle was Francis Pym, who had been appointed foreign secretary only a year earlier. That Pym was not in favour with the prime minister had become apparent during the election campaign, when she had publicly interrupted and contradicted him at a press conference. Nigel Lawson (*see* BIOGRAPHIES), an intellectual monetarist, became chancellor of the Exchequer, while Sir Geoffrey Howe, who had occupied that post throughout the first term, took over from Pym at the Foreign Office. Leon Brittan (*see* BIOGRAPHIES) became home secretary. Thus the last remnants of the old guard were removed, and all key Cabinet posts were in the hands of the prime minister's own men.

The new Parliament was promised legislation to democratize the trade unions, curb the power of local authorities to raise taxes, and denationalize the telecommunications industry. In addition, the controversial Police and Criminal Evidence Bill was to be brought back in amended form. However, the election was followed by a lull in political activity that was further encouraged by one of the most glorious British summers in living memory. The only momentary excitement occurred in July, when the House of Commons debated capital punishment and, contrary to hopes or fears that the new Conservative intake might tip the balance, once again firmly opposed it.

When the political season reopened in the autumn, the notion that the government, by its landslide victory in June, had established an unassailable authority began to recede quickly. The Labour Party began to take on a new look with a new young leader, Neil Kinnock (*see* BIOGRAPHIES). The leadership of the SDP had passed from Roy Jenkins to David Owen, who, like Kinnock, was in his 40s. The prime minister, at 57, began to look like a member of an older generation that before long would have to give way to a new one. Moreover, the jubilation of the election had barely ended before her luck showed signs of running out and, with it, in the opinion of some, her good judgment, too. First, a minor eye irritation she contracted at a Buckingham Palace garden party led to a partially detached retina that required an alarming eye operation. Then, after only two weeks of holiday and recuperation, she set off on a strenuous tour of Canada and the U.S. during which the shrill tone of some of her utterances, especially when directed at the Soviets, caused some consternation at home.

Meanwhile, ministers had been disgruntled by the brusque way they had been rushed into a round of emergency spending cuts in mid-July and were further dismayed by an inept handling of cuts in the National Health Service that fueled public suspicions that the government, its election pledges notwithstanding, intended to dismantle or fundamentally reduce the free health service.

On top of these troubles broke the "Parkinson affair." Cecil Parkinson, newly appointed secretary of state for trade and industry, was obliged to make a public statement in early October after it became known that Sara Keays, his former secretary, was expecting his child: he admitted that he

UNITED KINGDOM

Education. (1979–80) Primary, pupils 5,133,710, teachers 270,346; secondary, pupils 5,116,354; vocational, pupils 243,743; secondary and vocational, teachers 333,515; higher, students 799,462, teaching staff (universities only; 1981–82) 42,840.

Finance. Monetary unit: pound sterling, with (Sept. 20, 1983) a free rate of £0.66 to U.S. $1 (U.S. $1.51 = £1 sterling). Gold and other reserves (June 1983) U.S. $12.3 billion. Budget (1983–84 est.): revenue £125,900 million; expenditure £134,100 million. Gross national product (1982) £275,760 million. Money supply (June 1983) £40,123 million. Cost of living (1975 = 100; June 1983) 248.2.

Foreign Trade. (1982) Imports £56,940 million; exports £55,538 million. Import sources: EEC 44% (West Germany 13%, The Netherlands 8%, France 7%, Belgium-Luxembourg 5%, Italy 5%); U.S. 12%; Japan 5%. Export destinations: EEC 42% (West Germany 10%, The Netherlands 8%, France 8%, Ireland 5%); U.S. 13%. Main exports: machinery 23%; crude oil 15%; chemicals 11%; motor vehicles 6%. Tourism (1981): visitors 11,486,000.

Transport and Communications. Roads (1981) 365,567 km (including 2,944 km expressways). Motor vehicles in use (1981): passenger 15,757,000; commercial 1,797,000. Railways: (1981) 17,788 km; traffic (excluding Northern Ireland; 1982) 27,782,000,000 passenger-km, freight 15,880,000,000 net ton-km. Air traffic (1982): 43,958,000,000 passenger-km; freight 1,225,500,000 net ton-km. Shipping (1982): merchant vessels 100 gross tons and over 2,826; gross tonnage 22,505,265. Shipping traffic (1982): goods loaded *c.* 126 million metric tons, unloaded *c.* 120 million metric tons. Telephones (March 1981) 27,793,000. Radio receivers (Dec. 1980) 53 million. Television receivers (Dec. 1980) 22.6 million.

Agriculture. Production (in 000; metric tons; 1982): wheat 10,258; barley 10,884; oats 587; potatoes 6,818; sugar, raw value 1,340; cabbages (1981) *c.* 883; cauliflowers 265; green peas *c.* 700; carrots (1981) *c.* 620; apples 320; dry peas *c.* 93; tomatoes 121; onions 236; rapeseed 567; hen's eggs 750; cow's milk 16,720; butter 214; cheese 244; wool 40; beef and veal 994; mutton and lamb 284; pork 927; fish catch (1981) 848. Livestock (in 000; June 1982): cattle 13,275; sheep 33,049; pigs 8,082; poultry 132,649.

Industry. Index of production (1975 = 100; 1982) 104. Fuel and power (in 000; metric tons; 1982): coal 124,657; crude oil 103,414; natural gas (cu m) 38,280,000; electricity (kw-hr) 272,121,000. Production (in 000; metric tons; 1982): cement 12,960; iron ore (26% metal content) 514; pig iron 8,503; crude steel 13,697; petroleum products 70,747; sulfuric acid 2,587; plastics and resins 1,966; fertilizers (nutrient content; 1981–82) nitrogenous 1,270, phosphate 346, potash 281; man-made fibres 334; cotton fabrics (m) 258,000; woolen fabrics (sq m) 100,300; newsprint 85; television receivers (units) 1,812; passenger cars (units) 888; commercial vehicles (units) 269. Merchant vessels launched (100 gross tons and over; 1982) 525,000 gross tons. New dwelling units completed (1982) 176,800.

had proposed marriage to Keays but had then decided to remain with his wife. The prime minister's office insisted that the matter was entirely a private one and that there was no question of his resignation. However, on the eve of Thatcher's keynote address to the Conservative Party conference on October 14, Keays gave *The Times* her own full version of the story, pointing out the child was conceived in a "long-standing, loving relationship" and that marriage had been discussed on a number of occasions between 1979 and election day, June 9, 1983. Faced with such embarrassing and damaging disclosure, Parkinson had no alternative but to resign from the Cabinet; he was replaced as trade and industry secretary by Norman Tebbit. While nobody doubted that the prime minister had acted honourably and courageously in support of a friend, many Conservatives were left wondering about the wisdom and prudence with which she had handled the matter.

Nevertheless, the government remained firmly in control. By the end of an intensely political year Kinnock was still in the process of establishing himself as leader of a party that had suffered a historic defeat of calamitous proportions. He brought to the task much enthusiasm but no ministerial experience. By the end of the year the economy was recovering, although forecasters challenged the chancellor's bullish prognostications in his autumn statement to Parliament. The cruise missiles arrived at Greenham amid scenes of protest, and 16 of them were operational by December 31. More serious disorders took place outside a small printing plant in Warrington, Cheshire, where litigation by the employer against the National Graphical Association trade union put the industrial relations laws, passed during the Thatcher government's first term, to their first serious test. (*See* Industrial Relations.)

Foreign Affairs. While political considerations dominated the domestic year, the chief preoccupation in foreign affairs was with nuclear weapons

How Labour Lost the Labour Vote

According to an old saying, "Oppositions don't win elections, governments lose them." The British general election of 1983 was an exception to this rule. The opposition lost the election first of all because it was split between the Labour Party and the Alliance, in which the breakaway Social Democratic Party (SDP), contesting its first general election, had joined with the Liberal Party. It lost because most of the policies of the Labour Party, which had swung well to the left of its customary posture, were unacceptable to majorities of the people and because the support of the Alliance was spread too thinly and evenly across all classes, age groups, and parts of the country.

The Conservative Party strategy aimed at holding and consolidating its power. Its manifesto contained few new or radical proposals. It dwelt upon the achievements of four years of Conservative government, especially in supposedly reviving national pride and purpose through the successful campaign to win back the Falkland Islands from Argentina in 1982. It offered no remedy for unemployment beyond a continuation of firm public-expenditure control, responsible monetary policies, and economic liberalization. Labour, on the contrary, promised a massive reflation of £11,000 million, which, it claimed, would reduce unemployment by 2.5 million during the five-year term of Parliament. The Alliance proposed a more modest reflationary package of £3,000 million, which was designed to reduce unemployment by one million over a period of two years.

The Conservative tactic was to neutralize the unemployment issue by stressing its success at bringing down the inflation rate and by contrasting its defense policies with Labour's commitment to unilateral nuclear disarmament. Rather than risk reopening contentious ideological issues within the party, the Labour leadership decided to publish as its manifesto the voluminous policy document published a few weeks previously. This had endeavoured to paper over the huge division within the leadership between the unilateral disarmers and the multilateralists.

The campaign soon exposed this major difference within Labour's ranks, as Denis Healey, deputy leader, explained that the U.K.'s Polaris nuclear submarine force would be made part of arms-reduction negotiations, while party leader Michael Foot held firm to the manifesto's commitment to "carry through in the lifetime of the next Parliament our non-nuclear defence policy." Matters were made worse when James Callaghan, former party leader and prime minister, roundly repudiated Labour's unilateralist policies. Labour's campaign never recovered from these disasters.

The Alliance lost ground in the early phase of the campaign, and the polls reported that SDP leader Roy Jenkins was a liability compared with Liberal leader David Steel. The Alliance scored some helpful publicity by staging a mid-campaign "summit" at Steel's Scottish home. The secret purpose of this gathering, it later transpired, was to downgrade the role of Jenkins in favour of a more prominent one for Steel. Whether this contributed to an increase in support for the Alliance in the remaining days of the campaign was doubtful, but some polls reported that the Alliance, whose gains were made chiefly at the expense of Labour, had moved into second place.

The result of the June 9 election gave the Conservatives 397 seats, Labour 209, and the Alliance 23, of which the Liberals won 17 and the SDP 6. An analysis of the results showed that Labour had failed, for the first time, to command a majority among skilled workers and had won the support of only two out of five trade-union members. It held only three seats south of a line from the Severn to the Wash, excluding London constituencies. The Alliance, although only some two points behind Labour in its share of the popular vote, did poorly in terms of seats as a result of the electoral system and the even spread of its support across the country.

and the strains within the Atlantic alliance that were resulting from the implementation of NATO's decision of 1979. Underlying the show of Western solidarity was increasing concern about the intentions and conduct of the Reagan administration. Thatcher, who before the election had rejected ministerial and official urgings to repair Britain's poor bilateral relations with the U.S.S.R., modified her tone when speaking to the Conservative Party conference in October and stressed the importance of dialogue. Later it was announced that she would be visiting Hungary in 1984, her first visit as prime minister to a Soviet-bloc country apart from two hours once spent at the airport in Moscow.

Thatcher's visit to Washington in September resulted as usual in a celebration of Britain's supposed "special relationship" with the U.S. Yet during the next month, when the U.S. invaded Grenada, the U.K. refused to participate, and the prime minister subsequently condemned the intervention. Her behaviour caused resentment in the U.S. and bewildered many of her supporters at home. Where was the "resolute approach" that she had demonstrated during the recapture of the Falklands? What had happened to the staunchly anti-Communist "Iron Lady?" The explanation, it appeared, was the consistency of the prime minister's convictions: she had fought the war in the Falklands to uphold sovereignty and deny the fruits of aggression; those principles she now applied to the U.S. intervention in Grenada.

Northern Ireland. The general election campaign in Northern Ireland highlighted divisions between and within the Protestant and Roman Catholic communities. Among the Protestant parties the Official Unionist Party (OUP) made significant gains. Sinn Fein, political wing of the Provisional Irish Republican Army (IRA), won its first seat in Parliament when Gerry Adams defeated the Social Democratic and Labour Party (SDLP) candidate in West Belfast. In its manifesto Sinn Fein defended the Provisional IRA's campaign of violence and dismissed the Forum for a New Ireland, a Dublin-backed initiative, as an attempt to bolster the fortunes of the SDLP.

In September the Northern Ireland Office was severely criticized after 38 inmates broke out of the top-security Maze Prison in Belfast. It was reportedly the biggest breakout in the U.K.'s prison history. The efforts of James Prior, secretary of state for Northern Ireland, to devolve power to the province suffered a setback in November; the OUP withdrew from the Northern Ireland Assembly in the wake of a sectarian attack on a Pentecostal church hall in Darkley, County Armagh, that resulted in the deaths of three church elders. The Unionist parties subsequently called for a tougher security policy in the province.

A pre-Christmas bombing campaign in London culminated in a car-bomb explosion outside Harrods department store in Knightsbridge on December 17. Six people, including three police officers, were killed. The Provisional IRA accepted responsibility for the attack, though it claimed not to have "authorized" it. (PETER JENKINS)

See also Commonwealth of Nations; Dependent States; Ireland.

United Nations

"For 1983 my message is simple," UN Secretary-General Javier Pérez de Cuéllar said at the end of 1982. "No alternative [to the UN exists] that could conceivably work" because only in the UN can all nations "take part in managing the present and planning the future." Member states had to make the UN an "effective instrument" for maintaining international peace and security. Too often, he continued, the UN "has been kept on the sidelines" or has been used "in sterile ways as yet another forum for fighting." He urged states to devise ways of "refocusing" the UN on its "original goal" of controlling and resolving conflict and achieving disarmament. The secretary-general also indicted the tendency of states "to follow the path of parochialism and isolationism," which, he warned, could lead only to decline or disaster.

By September, when Pérez de Cuéllar issued his annual report to the 38th General Assembly (September 20–December 20), he found developments "far from encouraging." He warned states against superimposing East-West tensions on regional conflicts and stressed the danger of nuclear war.

Africa. One illustration of what the secretary-general had in mind was certainly the former territory of South West Africa/Namibia. Since 1978 the UN had been trying to secure independence for Namibia, which South Africa administered under a League of Nations mandate that the General Assembly and the International Court of Justice had declared null and void. As Pérez de Cuéllar pointed out during the year on visits to Africa (in February and again in August) and at a UN-sponsored Conference in Support of the Struggle of the Namibian People for Independence (Paris, April 25–29), virtually the only obstacle remaining to the UN plan for Namibian independence was South Africa's precondition that Cuba withdraw its troops from Angola. The secretary-general considered Namibia a "bilateral problem" between the UN and South Africa with no links to the Cuban question. On December 1, by a vote of 117 in favour, none opposed, and 28 abstentions, the General Assembly endorsed the secretary-general's position and asked the Security Council to impose comprehensive sanctions against South Africa.

Opposing the majority view, South Africa insisted that the Cubans were "Soviet surrogates" and a major obstacle to attaining a peaceful Namibia. South Africa had said that it would not accept any deadline for Namibian independence until the Cubans withdrew and stopped supporting the forces of the South West Africa People's Organization (SWAPO), which, they alleged, were increasingly being integrated into the Angolan Army. (The United States supported the South African position.) On December 15 South Africa offered to disengage its forces from Angola for 30 days beginning Jan. 31, 1984, but Angola and SWAPO rejected the proposal, calling it one-sided. Then, on December 23, South Africa began what was reported to be the largest military strike against Angola since 1981, allegedly to preempt a guerrilla attack.

UN organs were also troubled by South Africa's pressure on Lesotho to either return to South Africa certain refugees who, it claimed, threatened its own security or to expel them to a third country. Lesotho had refused, and on June 29 the Security Council commended Lesotho for steadfastly opposing apartheid (racial separation) and for giving generously to the refugees. The UN was organizing financial aid for Lesotho, but that country, anticipating a new wave of refugees from South Africa, asked for additional help.

In March, May, and August, Chad complained of "repeated acts of aggression" by Libya. Libya, meanwhile, periodically charged that U.S. forces were engaging in "provocative military actions" against it, at sea and on land, by dispatching Rapid Deployment Forces and equipment to the Middle East and Africa. The U.S. contended that its naval maneuvers were all taking place in international waters and that it had merely altered the dates of scheduled training exercises.

On August 3 the Security Council considered Chad's complaints that Libya was carrying out indiscriminate bombings in Chad and moving its army into Chad's territory. Libya insisted that the fighting in Chad arose from civil war and maintained that it wanted only peace and prosperity for Chad and to reconcile opposing forces there. In mid-August France interposed its own forces between the Libyan and Chadian armies.

Middle East. In the Middle East during 1983 states acted outside the UN more often than they did inside it. In Lebanon, for instance, a multinational force composed of British, French, Italian, and U.S. troops attempted—unsuccessfully for the most part—to keep order among the warring factions. Meanwhile, the UN Interim Force in Lebanon (UNIFIL), originally dispatched in 1978, found itself largely on the sidelines.

Jorge Illueca of Panama was elected president of the UN General Assembly in September. Behind him as he addresses the body is UN Secretary-General Javier Pérez de Cuéllar.

UPI

Similarly, because of Israeli distrust of the UN, negotiations between Israel and Lebanon had been conducted largely by the U.S. As a result of U.S. efforts, Israel and Lebanon signed an agreement on May 17 terminating the state of war between them. The secretary-general then implied that the Security Council should change the role of UNIFIL, but on October 18 the Council merely extended the UNIFIL mandate for six more months.

Syria denounced the Lebanese-Israeli accord and strengthened its forces confronting Israel. Its military actions, however, were conducted mainly in support of rebels who mutinied against Yasir Arafat's leadership of the Palestine Liberation Organization (PLO). By year's end, Arafat was cornered in Tripoli, and on December 3 the Security Council authorized the chartering of ships to evacuate Arafat and his men under the UN flag—a condition that Arafat insisted upon. The Israeli mission to the UN said on December 21 that using the UN flag amounted to "aiding and abetting a group of international outlaws" bent on destroying a UN member state. Israeli bombardments of Tripoli in fact delayed Arafat's departure by one day, but the evacuation was completed successfully on December 21. Pérez de Cuéllar defended the use of UN flags as a humanitarian action.

On August 29 the secretary-general said that, although conditions under which Lebanon could fully regain its sovereignty were not in sight, preoccupation with events there should not overshadow the need to consider other major Middle East problems. He referred to the increasing number of Israeli settlements on the West Bank of the Jordan River, the difficulty of getting Israel to withdraw from occupied territories, mutual recognition and long-term security of all states in the area, and the future of Jerusalem. Various UN organs discussed these issues in 1983 but, as Pérez de Cuéllar said at the International Conference on the Question of Palestine (Geneva, August 29–September 7), the Palestine issues had taken up more time and attention in the UN than any other problem and, after 36 years, the organization was no nearer resolving them than it had been in 1947. (*See* Feature Article: *At the Core of the Problem of Peace.*)

The secretary-general said on December 21 that, in his opinion, a UN peacekeeping force would be more effective in Lebanon than the present multinational body; it would have broader support within the international community and more likelihood of being accepted by the local people.

The stalemate continued in the war between Iran and Iraq, now three years old. The Security Council and the General Assembly both expressed their concern, but they made no progress during the year in reconciling the parties.

Cyprus. On May 13, at a resumed 37th session, the General Assembly overwhelmingly approved a resolution calling for the withdrawal of all occupation troops from Cyprus and urging the Greek and Turkish communities to agree on some mutually acceptable solution to the island's government. Turkey insisted that its troops (the subject of the resolution) were in Cyprus, as they had been since they invaded in 1974, to protect the Turkish community and not to occupy the island.

On July 4 the secretary-general met in Geneva with Turkish-Cypriot leaders to discuss the possibilities of resuming negotiations between them and the Greek Cypriots. All efforts to get the intercommunal talks going again came to naught, however, when Turkish Cypriots proclaimed an independent state, the Turkish Republic of Northern Cyprus, on November 15. On November 18 the Security Council condemned the Turkish-Cypriot action, 13–1–1. It called on all states not to recognize the breakaway state and demanded that local authorities retract their declaration of independence. On December 15 the Council unanimously decided, on the secretary-general's recommendation, to keep the UN Force in Cyprus in place for six more months.

Afghanistan. UN officials met several times with interested parties during the year (January–February, April, and June) to discuss how best to get Soviet troops out of Afghanistan (which they had invaded in December 1979), arrange international guarantees against future intervention, and provide for returning refugees. The secretary-general said in late September that considerable work had been done, but the pace of negotiations was slow. On November 23, for the fourth consecutive year, the Assembly (116–20, with 17 abstentions) called upon "foreign [Soviet] troops" to withdraw from Afghanistan.

Central America and the Caribbean. In March, May, and September, Nicaragua alleged in the Security Council that the U.S. was supporting aggression against it from Honduras. In return, the U.S. charged Nicaragua with aggression against its neighbours. On May 19 the Council unanimously urged the Contadora Group (Colombia, Mexico, Panama, and Venezuela) to pursue its peace efforts. The Council also reaffirmed the right of Nicaragua and all other countries in the area to live in peace, free from outside interference. On November 11, without a vote, the Assembly adopted a resolution on Nicaragua. U.S. Ambassador Jeane J. Kirkpatrick said that she was pleased with it. Portions of it, however, were clearly directed against U.S. support for guerrilla groups combating Nicaragua's Sandinista government.

On March 28 Grenadian officials told the press that the U.S. was planning to destabilize Grenada economically, was refusing requests to talk, and was planning a military attack. On October 25, in response to requests from the Organization of Eastern Caribbean States, the U.S. did invade Grenada. The U.S. justified its intervention primarily on the grounds that American students at the island's medical school were in danger after the assassination on October 19 of Prime Minister Maurice Bishop and other Grenadian leaders. On October 28 the U.S. vetoed a Security Council resolution that would have deeply deplored the invasion as a "flagrant violation of international law." The Assembly adopted (108–9, with 27 abstentions) a resolution couched in similar terms on November 2. It asked for "the immediate withdrawal of the foreign [U.S.] troops from Grenada," but the next day U.S. President Ronald Reagan dismissed the vote by saying, "It didn't upset my breakfast at all." The last U.S. combat troops withdrew from Grenada on December 15, leaving behind 300 men for what U.S. authorities described as "routine police duties."

UN-U.S. Relations. On September 1 the U.S.S.R. shot down a South Korean civilian airliner that had strayed into its airspace, killing all 269 persons aboard. (A preliminary report by the International Civil Aviation Organization, issued in mid-December, rejected the Soviet contention that the jet was on an intelligence mission and accused the U.S.S.R. of failing to make sufficiently exhaustive efforts to identify the aircraft.) Soviet Foreign Minister Andrey Gromyko had planned to attend the General Assembly in New York City, but in light of the airliner incident, the governors of New York and New Jersey refused landing rights at any civilian airport in the New York metropolitan area to the Soviet plane he had intended to use. The U.S. offered to allow Gromyko to land at a convenient military airfield, but on September 17 the Soviet Union canceled Gromyko's trip. The Soviets claimed the U.S. had violated the 1947 Headquarters Agreement, which guarantees access to the UN by persons coming on official business.

In defending the U.S. actions, Charles M. Lichenstein, alternate U.S. delegate to the UN, said the agreement did not specify that the U.S. had to allow delegations to arrive in New York in any particular place or manner. When the Soviets questioned whether the UN should remain in a country that failed to fulfill its obligations, Lichenstein responded that if any UN members believed the UN should move from the U.S., the U.S. would "put no impediment" in their way; members of the U.S. delegation to the UN would "be down at the dockside waving you a fond farewell as you sail into the sunset." When asked if this statement represented official U.S. policy, President Reagan endorsed a suggestion by Kirkpatrick that the UN might profitably meet six months a year in Moscow and six months in New York so that delegates

The fate of Korean Air Lines flight 007 occupied the UN Security Council in September as television screens and an audio channel recorded what the U.S. identified as the voice of the Soviet pilot as he was firing on the passenger craft. Listeners in the foreground were (from left) Soviet Ambassador Oleg Troyanovsky, U.K. Ambassador John Thomson, and U.S. Ambassador Jeane Kirkpatrick.

UPI

could compare conditions in the two countries. Later, however, he added that the U.S. very much wanted the UN to remain.

On December 28 the U.S. notified the secretary-general of the UN Educational, Scientific and Cultural Organization (UNESCO) that it would withdraw from the agency on the last day of 1984. The U.S. statement said that UNESCO "has extraneously politicized virtually every subject it deals with, has exhibited hostility toward the basic institutions of a free society . . . and has demonstrated unrestrained budgetary expansionism."

Organizational Matters. Meeting in Kingston, Jamaica (March 15–April 8 and in mid-September), the Preparatory Commission for the International Sea-Bed Authority and the International Tribunal for the Law of the Sea completed its organizational work and elected Joseph Warioba (Tanzania) as chairman. The U.S., which had not signed the UN Convention on the Law of the Sea, had announced on Dec. 30, 1982, that it would withhold its share of funds (estimated at between $500,000 and $700,000) for the work of the commission. (*See* LAW: *Sidebar*.)

UN membership rose to 158 on September 23 when the Assembly admitted Saint Christopher and Nevis, as recommended by the Security Council. On October 31 the Assembly elected five nonpermanent members of the Security Council: Egypt, India, Peru, the Ukrainian S.S.R., and Upper Volta. They would replace Guyana, Jordan, Poland, Togo, and Zaire, whose terms expired on December 31. (RICHARD N. SWIFT)

[552.B.2]

United States

The United States of America is a federal republic composed of 50 states, 49 of which are in North America and one of which consists of the Hawaiian Islands. Area: 9,363,123 sq km (3,615,122 sq mi), including 202,711 sq km of inland water but excluding the 156,192 sq km of the Great Lakes that lie within U.S boundaries. Pop. (1983 est.): 234,249,000, including 83.2% white and 11.7% black. Language: English. Religion (1981 est.): Protestant 73.5 million; Roman Catholic 50.4 million; Jewish 5.9 million; Orthodox 3.8 million. Cap.: Washington, D.C. (pop., 1982 est., 631,000). Largest city: New York (pop., 1982 est., 7,096,600). President in 1983, Ronald Reagan.

The economic difficulties that preoccupied the administration of Pres. Ronald Reagan (*see* BIOGRAPHIES) during its first two years took a back seat in 1983 to a series of foreign crises. The main trouble spots included El Salvador, Nicaragua, Lebanon, and Grenada. U.S. relations with the Soviet Union continued to deteriorate, while apprehension mounted in Western Europe over the deployment there of intermediate-range Pershing II and cruise missiles. Concern grew in the United States that the country might be drawn into a full-scale war in the Middle East.

Foreign Affairs. President Reagan set the tone of his hard-line approach to the Soviet Union in an address before a convention of Protestant evangelicals in Orlando, Fla., on March 8. Calling Soviet Communism "the focus of evil in the modern world," Reagan cautioned that a nuclear weapons freeze would encourage Moscow's "unparalleled" military buildup and eliminate any incentive for Soviet leaders to negotiate arms reductions. The Soviet government news agency TASS on March 9 termed the president's speech "provocative" and said that his remarks showed that his administration "can think only in terms of confrontation and bellicose, lunatic anticommunism."

The war of words between the U.S. and the Soviet Union escalated after a South Korean commercial airliner en route from Alaska to Seoul was shot down September 1 after flying off course over strategically sensitive Soviet territory. All 269 on board died when the plane, a Boeing 747, crashed in the Sea of Japan after being hit by a heat-seeking missile fired by a Soviet jet fighter. Among the dead were 61 Americans, including Rep. Larry P. McDonald (Dem., Ga.), head of the ultra-right-wing John Birch Society.

The airliner tragedy generated a storm of protest in the United States and other countries. In a nationally televised speech on September 5, Reagan denounced the Soviet Union for what he called the "Korean Air Line massacre." He said that the attack on the plane had pitted "the Soviet Union against the world and the moral precepts which guide human relations among people everywhere. . . ." The president, however, avoided suggesting any major retaliatory steps. Congress responded to the incident by unanimously adopting a strongly worded resolution condemning "this cold-blooded barbarous attack" as "one of the most infamous and reprehensible acts in history."

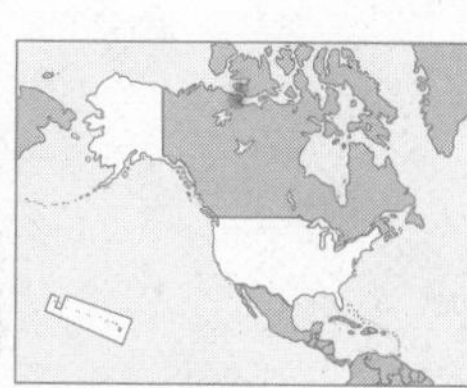
United States

Outrage over the airliner tragedy also led to the cancellation of Soviet Foreign Minister Andrey Gromyko's plans to attend the opening of the 38th UN General Assembly when Governors Mario Cuomo of New York and Thomas Kean of New Jersey ordered the Port Authority of New York and New Jersey not to permit Gromyko's plane to land at either Kennedy or Newark International airports. Special authorization was required because landing rights for the Soviet airline Aeroflot had been withdrawn by Reagan in 1981 following the imposition of martial law in Poland. (*See* UNITED NATIONS.)

But the main cause of U.S.-Soviet conflict in 1983 was the long-planned deployment, starting in December, of 572 Pershing II and cruise missiles in Western Europe. (*See* DEFENSE: *Special Report*.) During the year a series of proposals and counterproposals were launched by the U.S. and the Soviet Union, all of them having the twin purposes of advancing the Soviet-U.S. talks on intermediate-range nuclear missiles, then being held in Geneva, and influencing public opinion in the NATO countries where the missiles were to be installed. In a nationally televised speech on March 30, Reagan offered to reduce the number of U.S. intermediate-range missiles in Europe in return for comparable Soviet reductions in Europe and Asia. This was a departure from the administration's previous insistence on the so-called zero option, which called for the total elimination of Soviet intermediate-

UPI

The Soviet airline Aeroflot, denied landing rights in the U.S. after martial law was declared in Poland, closed its U.S. offices after the South Korean airliner incident, on order of President Reagan. Employees at the Washington, D.C., office here remove a Lenin mural among other objects.

range missiles in Europe and Asia in exchange for cancellation of the planned NATO deployment. Under the new plan both sides would have the same number of warheads, although the president did not specify the number of nuclear warheads to be permitted, apparently leaving the limit open to negotiation.

In an April 2 news conference Soviet Foreign Minister Gromyko dismissed Reagan's proposal as "unacceptable" and "absurd." The Soviet Union found it "impossible to close our eyes to" independent French and British nuclear forces, which were not part of Reagan's plan, Gromyko said. He also complained that the president's offer did not take into account hundreds of nuclear-capable aircraft based in Western Europe and on aircraft carriers.

Addressing the UN General Assembly on September 26, Reagan offered further concessions in an attempt to reach an agreement in Geneva. Under the new proposal, the U.S. would still insist on equal numbers of Soviet and U.S. medium-range missiles, but the U.S. would abandon its insistence on stationing all of its missiles on European soil. Reagan implied the U.S. was also now willing to consider setting ceilings on the number of medium-range bombers capable of carrying nuclear weapons. Finally, the U.S. was willing to reduce the number of Pershing II missiles, rather than just reducing cruise missiles. (The Pershing II missiles were to be based in West Germany, where their proximity to the Soviet Union presumably posed a greater danger to that country than the 464 cruise missiles to be deployed in other NATO countries of Western Europe.)

The Soviet response to Reagan's UN speech was even harsher. The United States, Communist Party General Secretary Yury Andropov charged, did "not even try to conceal" that it was dragging out the medium-range missile talks in Geneva (which had resumed May 17) in the hope of deploying its missiles without political opposition in Western Europe. The Soviet leader charged the Reagan administration with pursuing a "militarist course" that was in contradiction with its professed arms reduction efforts.

A month later, on October 26, Andropov said that the Soviet Union was ready to make further reductions in its intermediate-range missiles stationed in Europe. But he added that the scheduled deployment of U.S. medium-range missiles in Europe would signal the end of U.S.-Soviet negotiations in Geneva on reducing those systems. Making good on this threat, the Soviet Union withdrew from the talks on November 23, nine days after the first U.S. cruise missiles arrived at Britain's Greenham Common air base. Reagan responded by saying, "I think they'll come back because they must be aware . . . that there cannot and must not be a nuclear confrontation in the world by the only two nations that truly have the great destructive nuclear capability."

In spite of their deep differences on nuclear arms reduction, the United States and the Soviet Union on August 25 signed a five-year agreement that required the U.S.S.R. to increase its yearly grain purchases in return for a guarantee that the United States would not unilaterally embargo shipments. At a news conference after the signing ceremony in Moscow, U.S. Secretary of Agriculture John Block (*see* BIOGRAPHIES) praised the accord as "an early building block in the effort to build a more stable and constructive relationship" between the countries. He estimated that the long-term pact could be worth more than $10 billion to U.S. farmers.

The nation was shocked on October 23 by the news that an undetermined number of U.S. Marines and sailors, members of a multinational peacekeeping force in Lebanon, had been killed in a suicide terrorist attack shortly after dawn that morning. The attack came when a truck loaded with powerful explosives crashed into the Marine compound at the Beirut airport and detonated, demolishing a headquarters building where U.S. troops were sleeping.

The size of the death toll emerged gradually over the next few days. As the number of missing was reduced and as some of the injured died, it was determined that a total of 241 American troops had lost their lives. The number of Marine dead far surpassed that incurred in any single action of the Vietnam war, and only one day of that war had created more U.S. fatalities.

President Reagan was outraged by the "vicious, cowardly, and ruthless" attack but stressed that the United States should be "more determined than ever" that the forces responsible for the bombing "cannot take over that vital and strategic area of the Earth." Reagan and other U.S. officials subsequently reiterated U.S. determination to remain in Lebanon.

Responsibility for the bomb attack remained unclear, with conjecture focusing primarily on fundamentalist Shiʿah Muslim groups with connections to Iran and Syria. Reagan, speaking on October 24 to a group of broadcast editors at the White House, said that the United States had found "strong circumstantial evidence linking the perpetrators of this latest atrocity to others that have occurred against us in the recent past, including the bombing of our embassy in Beirut last April."

The explosion at the Marine base, together with the similar destruction of the Beirut embassy six months earlier, raised questions about the security measures that had been taken. The U.S. Department of Defense appointed a commission of inquiry headed by retired Adm. Robert L. J. Long to examine all the circumstances surrounding the Marine base tragedy. The report proved to be highly critical of the entire Marine chain of command. However, on December 27, shortly before the report was made public, President Reagan called a news conference at which he accepted full blame for lack of security at the base and said the Marine commanders had "suffered enough" and should not be punished. A House subcommittee report issued a few days earlier also blamed the Marine chain of command for "very serious errors in judgment."

Eight more U.S. Marines were killed and two were wounded on December 4 in a massive barrage on their Beirut compound hours after U.S. air strikes on Syrian positions in which two U.S. jets were shot down. The navigator of one of the planes, Navy Lieut. Robert O. Goodman, Jr., was captured by Syrian forces. Syria announced that he would not be released until the U.S. withdrew its forces from Lebanon. At the end of the year the Rev. Jesse Jackson (*see* BIOGRAPHIES), a prominent civil rights leader and contender for the Democratic presidential nomination, went to Syria in an effort to secure Goodman's release.

More trouble erupted in the Middle East on December 12 when bomb-laden trucks exploded at the U.S. embassy and several other locations in the capital of Kuwait. Damage to the buildings was extensive, and several people (none of them Americans) were killed. As with the attack on the Marine compound in Beirut, fundamentalist Muslims were believed to be responsible.

On October 25, only two days after the Beirut bomb disaster, U.S. Marines, Army Rangers, and Navy personnel along with a detachment from six Caribbean nations invaded the Caribbean island of Grenada. Reagan said that the United States was acting in response to a request on October 23 from the Organization of Eastern Caribbean States to help reestablish law and order in Grenada, where the government of Prime Minister Maurice Bishop (*see* OBITUARIES) had been overturned by hardline Marxist members of his ruling New Jewel Movement the previous week. Reagan added that his administration also was concerned with ensuring the safety of the 1,100 U.S. citizens residing in Grenada.

World leaders criticized the attack, as did many Democratic Party members of Congress. Questions were raised about the legality of the invasion under international law, and members of Congress complained that they had not been consulted in advance. The question of the applicability of the War Powers Resolution also was raised.

Administration officials declared their hope that peace would be restored to Grenada quickly and said that U.S. forces would be withdrawn as soon as possible. However, as fighting went on the fact emerged that the number of Cubans on Grenada exceeded the original estimate, and they put up a stronger opposition than had been expected. Most major pockets of Cuban and Grenadian resistance were wiped out by October 26.

The United States announced on November 2 that hostilities in Grenada were over and began removing its forces from the island. Except for a small peacekeeping force of about 300, all U.S. troops were evacuated by mid-December. The first Cuban prisoners were returned to Cuba on November 2. Bernard Coard and Gen. Hudson Austin, who had been responsible for ousting and later killing Bishop, were arrested October 29 and October 30, respectively.

The Grenada invasion could be seen as a logical outgrowth of Reagan administration policy toward Central America and the Caribbean. In an address to the National Association of Manufacturers on March 10, the president said: "Soviet military theorists want to destroy our capacity to

UPI

A mournful salute greeted the body of U.S. Marine Staff Sgt. Alexander M. Ortega of Rochester, N.Y., on its return to the U.S. He was slain in Lebanon in August.

resupply Western Europe in case of an emergency. They want to tie down our forces on our own southern border and so limit our capacity to act in more distant places, such as Europe, the Persian Gulf, the Indian Ocean, the Sea of Japan."

Reagan's speech to the manufacturers came a month after some 1,600 U.S. military personnel and 4,000 Honduran troops carried out the largest war games ever held in Central America. U.S. soldiers played a noncombat role in the games, which administration officials had described as a training exercise for Honduran forces. However, neighbouring Nicaragua had repeatedly charged that the games would be used to train the Honduran troops for an actual invasion aimed at overthrowing Nicaragua's leftist Sandinista regime. On May 27 the United States announced that it would send at least 100 military advisers to Honduras in order to train some 2,400 troops from El Salvador in counterinsurgency warfare. In an effort to blunt persistent public criticism of his policy toward the region, Reagan announced on July 18 that he was establishing a National Bipartisan Commission on Central America, to be headed by former secretary of state Henry Kissinger (*see* BIOGRAPHIES). The commission was to offer long-term recommendations for U.S. policy in Central America. The panel visited Panama, Costa Rica, El Salvador, Guatemala, Honduras, and Nicaragua in October.

Reagan, meanwhile, denied in a nationally televised news conference on July 26 that his administration was drifting toward deeper involvement in Central America. He listed four elements of U.S. policy that he said reinforced each other "in a carefully balanced manner." He said that the United States supported "democracy, reform and human freedom"; economic development; "dialogue and negotiations among and within the countries of the region," and "a security shield for the region's threatened nations in order to protect these other goals." Reagan's remarks were prompted by criticism of a second set of military maneuvers scheduled to begin in Honduras in August.

Domestic Affairs. Facing the prospect of making up shortages in Social Security funds in July and acting on the recommendation of a bipartisan presidential commission, Congress in March approved one of the most extensive overhauls of the program since it began in 1937. (*See* SOCIAL SECURITY AND WELFARE SERVICES.) The rescue plan, pushed through both the House of Representatives and the Senate in just over a month, raised the retirement age from 65 to 67 by the year 2027, delayed for six months the annual cost-of-living increases for the system's 36 million recipients, and increased payroll taxes for employees and employers. Intended to raise $165 billion over seven years, the measure also taxed, for the first time, benefits of high-income recipients and brought new federal employees, members of Congress, the president, the vice-president, and federal judges under Social Security.

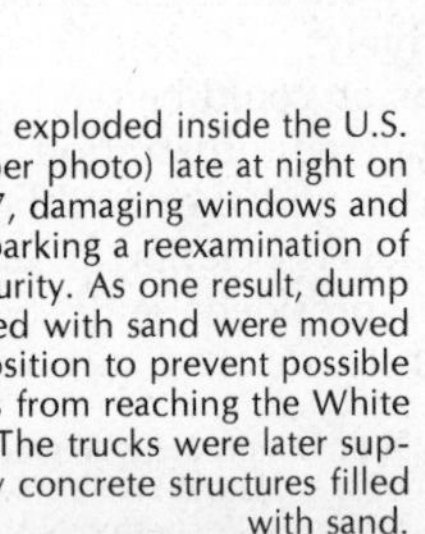

A bomb was exploded inside the U.S. Capitol (upper photo) late at night on November 7, damaging windows and walls and sparking a reexamination of capital security. As one result, dump trucks loaded with sand were moved into position to prevent possible truck bombs from reaching the White House. The trucks were later supplanted by concrete structures filled with sand.

PHOTOGRAPHS, WIDE WORLD

Production of the ten-warhead MX intercontinental missile was approved by Congress, though by a narrow margin in the House and only after President Reagan adopted a seemingly more flexible stance in the strategic arms reduction talks (START) with the Soviet Union. Although he initially assumed that the MX would be deployed in a so-called dense pack of heavily armoured underground silos, Reagan dropped that approach when he accepted the April 11 recommendation of a bipartisan advisory group headed by former White House adviser Brent Scowcroft. The Scowcroft panel called for deploying 100 MX's in existing missile silos while developing a new, smaller missile with only one warhead—generally referred to as "Midgetman"—that could be deployed on mobile launchers.

In late August the first Marines were killed by hostile fire in Lebanon, and Congress reasserted its authority on the issue. After lengthy negotiations between the administration and House Democratic leaders, Congress on September 29 cleared legislation invoking the 1973 War Powers Resolution for the first time and authorizing the Marines to stay in Lebanon for up to 18 months. Reagan signed the bill but expressed reservations about its constitutionality. The 18-month period was due to expire in April 1985.

A time bomb exploded outside the Senate chamber in the Capitol on the night of November 7. No one was killed or injured, but the damage was considerable. A group calling itself the Armed Resistance Unit claimed responsibility for the action, which it had undertaken as an expression of support for the struggle against U.S. military "aggression" in Lebanon and Grenada. Subsequently, new security regulations involving admittance to the Capitol and access to certain areas within it were put into force. Late in the year measures were also taken to improve the security of the White House and the Department of State, especially in regard to terrorist bomb attacks.

Abandoning earlier opposition, President Reagan signed into law on November 2 a bill making the third Monday in January, starting in 1986, a legal public holiday honouring the Rev. Martin Luther King, Jr., the late civil rights leader. This marked a major victory for civil rights groups, which had urged the government to establish a holiday honouring King since his assassination in 1968. It also marked a major defeat for Sen. Jesse Helms (Rep., N.C.), who led the sometimes virulent opposition to the measure in the Senate.

After a six-month battle with Reagan, Congress on November 16 cleared a bill reconstituting the U.S. Civil Rights Commission and extending it for six years. The legislation replaced the old six-member presidentially appointed commission with a panel of eight members—four appointed by the president and four by Congress—who could be removed only for cause. Reagan had started the controversy on May 25, when he announced that he was replacing with his own nominees three sitting members of the commission, which had repeatedly attacked the administration's civil rights policies. The bill was passed after a compromise was reached with Congress that civil rights advocates believed would keep the commission evenly divided. However, it was later claimed that there had been no binding agreement, and pro-Reagan congressional appointments weighted the commission, as finally constituted, in favour of the administration.

WIDE WORLD

The 52nd governor of Kentucky was the first woman to hold that position. Elected in November, she is Martha Layne Collins, who had been lieutenant governor.

Another personnel dispute between Congress and the White House was resolved in May when the Senate unanimously confirmed William Ruckelshaus (*see* BIOGRAPHIES) to succeed Anne Burford as administrator of the Environmental Protection Agency (EPA). Burford resigned under fire on March 9 amid at least six congressional inquiries into charges of unethical conduct, political manipulation, and "sweetheart deals" between the EPA and some of the industries that it was regulating.

A constitutional confrontation between Congress and Reagan was eased when the House on August 3 effectively dropped its Dec. 16, 1982,

UPI

Her Majesty Queen Elizabeth II and U.S. Pres. Ronald Reagan stand at attention as national anthems are played during the queen's visit to the U.S. in March. They are shown here at Santa Barbara, Calif.

PHOTOS, (LEFT) UPI, (RIGHT) WIDE WORLD

And then there were eight. The seven contenders for the Democratic presidential nomination appeared together in New York City on October 6. Then the Rev. Jesse Jackson (right) enlivened the contest with his declaration. The New York seven, from left: former senator George McGovern, Sen. Alan Cranston, Sen. Ernest Hollings, former governor Reubin Askew, Sen. John Glenn, Sen. Gary Hart, and former vice-president Walter Mondale.

contempt of Congress citation against Burford for refusing, on Reagan's orders, to provide materials sought by a House subcommittee. The Department of Justice had filed a civil lawsuit to prevent the House from seeking prosecution of Burford on the contempt charge. Indeed, the only EPA official to be prosecuted as a result of the extensive congressional and Justice Department probes was Rita Lavelle, former head of the "superfund" program for the cleanup of toxic waste dumps. A U.S. District Court jury in Washington, D.C., found her guilty in December of four criminal charges involving lies to Congress about conflicts of interest in her management of the superfund.

Secretary of the Interior James Watt (*see* BIOGRAPHIES) resigned on October 9. He thereby avoided an almost certain no-confidence vote in the Senate, where his support had eroded steadily in the wake of his remark in September that his appointees to a federal coal-leasing commission were "balanced" because they included "a black . . . a woman, two Jews and a cripple." Although opposition to Watt's policies had been mounting, it was his penchant for attempts at humour that turned out to be politically damaging remarks that led to his downfall. Watt's successor as interior secretary was William Clark, formerly President Reagan's national security adviser. At year's end another personnel problem for the administration loomed when it was revealed that Charles Wick, director of the U.S. Information Agency, had secretly recorded telephone conversations.

Reagan on January 12 dismissed Eugene Rostow as director of the Arms Control and Disarmament Agency and named Kenneth Adelman, deputy representative to the United Nations, as his replacement. The Senate approved Adelman's nomination but only after a three-month wrangle over administration arms-control policy. Liberal arms-control advocates had made Adelman's nomination a symbol of what they insisted was the administration's subordination of arms-control efforts to a nuclear buildup.

Paul Volcker was easily confirmed by the Senate to serve a second four-year term as chairman of the Federal Reserve Board. While Volcker's supporters gave him substantial credit for bringing inflation under control, his critics blamed him and the Fed's tight monetary policy for the longest and deepest recession since the Great Depression of the 1930s. Early in the year Reagan's Cabinet gained two woman members. Elizabeth Hanford Dole (*see* BIOGRAPHIES) was nominated on January 5 as secretary of transportation, succeeding Drew Lewis. A week later the president named former representative Margaret Heckler of Massachusetts to replace Richard Schweicker as secretary of health and human services.

Election results in 1983 showed blacks and women continuing to make political gains at the local and state levels. Rep. Harold Washington (*see* BIOGRAPHIES), a Democrat, was elected mayor of Chicago April 12 by a slim margin over former state legislator Bernard Epton after a bitterly contested campaign. The election of Washington as Chicago's first black mayor followed a campaign in which race, often injected by fellow Democrats and stressed by the news media, came to overshadow the other issues.

In contrast with Chicago, the race issue was muted by politicians and journalists in W. Wilson Goode's successful campaign to win election as Philadelphia's first black mayor on November 8. An analysis of exit polls indicated that Goode had won about 27% of the white vote. In balloting elsewhere Harvey Gantt and James Sharp, Jr., became the first elected black mayors of Charlotte, N.C., and Flint, Mich., respectively. But Melvin King, the first black candidate to reach the mayoral runoff in Boston in the city's history, was easily defeated on November 15 by Raymond Flynn.

The most impressive victory by a woman candidate was that of Martha Layne Collins, a Democrat, elected as Kentucky's first female governor. Kathy Whitmire, a Democrat, won a second term as mayor of Houston, Texas; Dianne Feinstein, also a Democrat, was returned for a second term as mayor by San Francisco voters; and Donna Owens was an upset winner in the mayoral race in Toledo, Ohio. Mississippi voters elected Bill Allain (Dem.) as governor, thus rejecting charges of homosexuality leveled against him late in the campaign. And Daniel Evans (Rep.) of Washington state retained the Senate seat to which he was appointed on September 8 after the death of Democrat Henry Jackson (*see* OBITUARIES).

Meanwhile, both major parties were preparing for the 1984 presidential race. By the year's end the Democratic field comprised eight announced candidates: Senators Alan Cranston (Calif.), Gary Hart (Colo.), Ernest Hollings (S.C.), and John Glenn (Ohio); former vice-president Walter Mondale; former senator George McGovern (S.D.); former governor Reubin Askew (Fla.); and the Rev. Jesse Jackson. Although President Reagan did not formally declare his candidacy for reelection, he did consent in October to the formation of a reelection committee. Sen. Paul Laxalt (Nev.), the Republican Party's national chairman, said he had "no doubt" that "Ronald Reagan's going to be a candidate for reelection."

One of the issues in the 1984 presidential campaign could be the state of American public education. The question came to the fore April 26 with the publication of a report by the 18-member National Commission on Excellence in Education. The commission warned that "a rising tide of mediocrity" was afflicting the nation's schools and declared that an estimated 23 million adults were functionally illiterate. In an apparent reaction to the panel's report, Reagan called for a return to "the basics" in education during speeches in June in Knoxville, Tenn., and Albuquerque, N.M. The president deplored the abandonment of compulsory courses in such subjects as English, mathematics, and science. He also reasserted, as he had in the past, his budget position on education—that more federal aid was not the solution to the problem. (*See* EDUCATION.)

In a decision with far-reaching implications for individuals and businesses throughout the nation, U.S. District Court Judge Harold Greene issued a nine-page order on August 5 in Washington, D.C., giving final approval to the plan under which American Telephone & Telegraph Co. would divest itself of its 22 wholly owned local telephone companies. The breakup would take effect as of Jan. 1, 1984.

Greene's order clarified several minor points, including provisions on the power of the divested units to conduct business outside their regional territories. The 22 units were to be organized into seven separate companies, each serving a specific region of the country. Greene empowered each divested unit to sell Yellow Pages advertising and telephone equipment outside its region.

In a decision handed down on June 15, the U.S. Supreme Court curbed the power of state and local governments to limit access to legal abortions. The court thus strongly reaffirmed its landmark 1973 ruling in *Roe* v. *Wade*, which gave women an unrestricted right to abortions during the first three months of pregnancy. On the last day of its term, July 6, the court ruled 5 to 4 that a federal appeals court had properly refused to grant a stay of execution to a prisoner in Texas whose constitutional challenge to his murder conviction technically was still pending. The action in *Barefoot* v. *Estelle* would make it more difficult for inmates facing execution to draw out the appeals process.

In still another major decision, the court on June 23 invalidated the legislative veto, the delegation by Congress of authority to the executive branch and the subsequent blocking by Congress of executive orders made on the basis of that authority. Congress responded by searching for substitutes that could be upheld by the courts. (*See* LAW.)

The National Weather Service announced on September 20 that August 1983 was "the hottest August on record, even topping record Dust Bowl years." Rainfall was one half or less of the average in many parts of the United States. The Weather Service said that the combination of heat and drought had "claimed at least 220 lives and withered $10 billion worth of crops." A few months later, much of the country experienced its coldest recorded December, with new records set throughout the plains states and as far south as Texas. (RICHARD L. WORSNOP)

See also Dependent States.

UNITED STATES

Education. (1983) Primary and preprimary, pupils 30,780,000, teachers 1,359,000; secondary and vocational, pupils 13,495,000, teachers 1,035,000; higher (including teacher-training colleges), students 12.4 million, teaching staff 870,000.

Finance. Monetary unit: U.S. dollar, with (Sept. 20, 1983) a free rate of U.S. $1.51 to £1 sterling. Gold and other reserves (June 1983) $32.6 billion. Federal budget (1983–84 est.): revenue $659.7 billion; expenditure $848.5 billion. Gross national product (1982) $3,073,000,000,000. Money supply (March 1983) $461.3 billion. Cost of living: (1975 = 100; June 1983) 184.9.

Foreign Trade. (1982) Imports $254.9 billion; exports $212.3 billion. Import sources: Canada 18%; Japan 16%; Mexico 6%; U.K. 5%; West Germany 5%. Export destinations: Canada 16%; Japan 10%; Mexico 6%; U.K. 5%. Main exports: machinery 28%; chemicals 9%; cereals 7%; motor vehicles 7%; aircraft 6%. Tourism (1981): visitors 23.1 million; gross receipts U.S. $12.2 billion.

Transport and Communications. Roads (1980) 6,365,578 km (including 520,340 km expressways). Motor vehicles in use (1981): passenger 123,461,500; commercial 34,451,100. Railways (1980): 288,072 km; traffic (Class I railways only) 17,695,000,000 passenger-km, freight 1,341,717,000,000 net ton-km. Air traffic (1982): 408,997,000,000 passenger-km (including domestic services 326,010,000,000 passenger-km); freight 9,845,000,000 net ton-km (including domestic services 5,797,000,000 net ton-km). Inland waterways (1981) 41,099 km; freight traffic (1980) 594,100,000,000 ton-km. Shipping (1982): merchant vessels 100 gross tons and over 6,133; gross tonnage 19,111,092. Shipping traffic (1982): goods loaded 363,653,000 metric tons, unloaded 341,502,000 metric tons. Telephones (Jan. 1981) 191.6 million. Radio receivers (Dec. 1980) 478 million. Television receivers (Dec. 1980) 142 million.

Agriculture. Production (in 000; metric tons; 1982): corn 213,302; wheat 76,443; barley 11,374; oats 8,955; rye 506; rice 6,995; sorghum 21,364; sugar, raw value 5,092; potatoes 15,842; soybeans 61,970; dry beans 1,123; cabbages (1981) 1,494; onions 1,875; tomatoes 7,862; apples 3,724; oranges 6,931; grapefruit 2,625; peaches (1981) 1,430; grapes 5,838; peanuts 1,560; sunflower seed 2,661; linseed 296; cottonseed 4,334; cotton, lint 2,617; tobacco 896; butter 595; cheese 2,311; hen's eggs c. 4,100; beef and veal c. 10,360; pork c. 6,450; fish catch (1981) 3,767; timber (cu m; 1981) 411,292. Livestock (in 000; Jan. 1982): cattle 115,690; sheep c. 12,936; pigs 58,688; horses c. 9,928; chickens c. 392,110.

Industry. Index of production (1975 = 100; 1982) 118; mining 112; manufacturing 118; electricity, gas, and water 116. Unemployment (1982) 9.7%. Fuel and power (in 000; metric tons; 1982): coal 708,920; lignite 47,160; crude oil 426,706; natural gas (cu m) 497,170,000; manufactured gas (cu m; 1981) c. 19,100,000; electricity (kw-hr) 2,241,211,000. Production (in 000; metric tons; 1982): iron ore (63% metal content) 37,080; pig iron 39,132; crude steel 66,654; cement (shipments) 58,010; newsprint 4,574; other paper (1981) 55,500; petroleum products (1981) 660,587; sulfuric acid 29,305; caustic soda 9,758; plastics and resins (1980) 12,418; man-made fibres (1981) 3,872; synthetic rubber 1,632; fertilizers (including Puerto Rico; nutrient content; 1981–82) nitrogenous 10,513, phosphate 7,085, potash 1,662; passenger cars (units) 5,049; commercial vehicles (units) 1,905. Merchant vessels launched (100 gross tons and over; 1982) 282,000 gross tons. New dwelling units started (1982) 1,070,000.

FOREIGN CAPITAL IN THE U.S. ECONOMY

by Jon Schriber

An American following the headlines in the financial press could easily become convinced that the U.S. is being invaded in force by foreign capital. Within the space of a few months, the Bank of Montreal agreed to purchase Harris Bankcorp of Chicago for $547 million, and the Toronto Sun Publishing Corp., owner of a chain of Canadian tabloids, paid $100 million for the *Houston* (Texas) *Post,* the 17th-largest newspaper in the U.S. In New York, subway ads admonished riders that "with the change in the season" it was time to get used to a "change in name." That was the way Britain's huge National Westminster Bank told the locals that it now owned New York's National Bank of North America.

Tidal Wave or Ripple? On the surface it appeared that the U.S. was the subject of a corporate buying spree by foreigners with deep pockets. Such a spree was feared after the 1973–74 oil price shock, when analysts surmised that billions of petrodollars might look for a permanent home in the U.S., but it failed to develop. A real acquisition frenzy did occur in 1981, fueled by another jump in oil prices and the attractions of the booming American real estate market. But the statistics for 1983 show that, in reality, this was a flurry rather than a deluge. In 1981 foreigners pumped a massive $23 billion into U.S. plants, equipment, and real estate—not counting bank assets. In 1982 the figure fell to $10 billion, and the 1983 total would probably be about the same.

What caused the retrenchment by foreign investors? One reason was the effect of turmoil in the oil market on worldwide capital flows. Much of the investment growth in 1981 was fueled by oil money. One deal alone—the Kuwaiti purchase of Santa Fe International—contributed $2.5 billion. Falling oil prices dried up this source. The onset of recession also contributed to the decline. The weakened state of the world economy reduced a major source of capital investment for foreign corporations—reinvested earnings of U.S. affiliates. From a high of $6.2 billion in 1980, this sum shriveled to near zero in 1982. Finally, and perhaps most significantly, the strong dollar tended to make foreign purchases in the U.S. more expensive.

The experience of Canadian investors makes a good case study. Starting in the mid-1970s, Canadians began gambling huge sums of money, largely borrowed from their own banks, to secure assets in the U.S. This turned into a full-blown gold rush as Canadian oil and gas companies and real estate developers swarmed over the border to buy natural resource companies and land. The invasion peaked in 1981 and then collapsed.

What happened was that the acquisition-hungry Canadians became victims of inflation. Initially, inflation had been one of the attractions. Soaring prices bloated the values of assets and made it advantageous to hold debt. But the situation backfired as inflated prices were matched by towering interest rates. Many of the acquisitions were suddenly rendered uneconomic, and overextended Canadians had trouble paying for new loans at such high rates. To make matters worse, the U.S. real estate market collapsed, leaving Canadian developers who had stakes in the U.S. with highly vulnerable loans outstanding. The final blow was the unanticipated slide in oil and metal prices.

This meant big losses for some companies. Hiram Walker Resources Ltd., for instance, wrote down its 1981 purchase of $600 million in U.S. oil and gas properties by about $140 million. The Bank of Montreal and Toronto Sun acquisitions notwithstanding, such losses put a damper on the takeover binge.

Dimensions of Foreign Ownership. Despite these setbacks, the flow of foreign capital from Canada and other countries continues, and alien capital invested in the U.S. is growing in both size and influence. The true dimensions of foreign investment in the U.S. are difficult to gauge, but a recent study by the U.S. Commerce Department's Bureau of Economic Analysis, the most comprehensive yet made, indicates that a significant measure of control over the U.S. economy is in the hands of foreigners. This benchmark survey, based on 1980 census data, finds that foreign-owned U.S. businesses other than banks had assets of $292 billion in 1980, or about 9% of total U.S. assets. According to David Belli, an economist with the Bureau of Economic Analysis,

---

Jon Schriber is a financial journalist, producer for the Financial News Network, and a former reporter for Forbes.

the percentage has continued to grow, probably to 12 or 13% in 1982.

The breakdown of these foreign-owned assets by industry category shows manufacturing accounting for $82 billion (nearly one-third in chemicals), followed by wholesale trade, $50 billion; petroleum, $44 billion; insurance, $36 billion; and finance (except banking), $32 billion. By country of origin, the U.K. led the list in 1980, with $57 billion, trailed by Canada with $48 billion, but Canada passed the U.K. in 1982. Third and fourth were The Netherlands ($36 billion) and West Germany ($31 billion). (*See* CHART.) Fully one-fourth of these holdings were in the Southeast. Among states, California had the largest amount of property, plant, and equipment investment, followed in order by Texas, Alaska, Louisiana, and New York. Affiliates of foreign businesses owned 1% of the nation's privately held real estate acreage; the greatest concentration was in Maine, with its vast tracts of timberland.

The same trends appeared to be continuing. At the Union Bank of Switzerland's New York office, Richard Capone, vice-president in charge of corporate banking, reported that the bank's European clients were still interested in the kinds of manufacturing properties and real estate deals that had attracted them during the past few years. "Many people still are interested in buying shopping centres, condos, land in residential areas, the kinds of things Europeans can comprehend," Capone said. From his own personal experience, a client interested in manufacturing would now often consider starting a facility from scratch. "Some of our Swiss clients have gotten burned taking over existing companies and having their management style clash with the style American workers are used to."

Foreign investments in the United States, in billions of dollars.

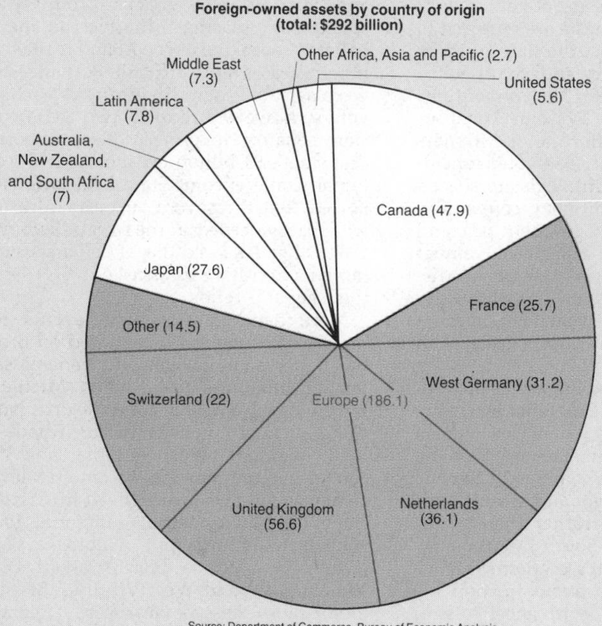

Asian investors may also have difficulty adapting their business methods to the American scene. As a result, they usually stick to the type of enterprises they know. Antony Lee, president of TCS (Transcontinental Services), which acts as an agency for investors seeking opportunities in the U.S., says many Hong Kong investors "acquire a controlling interest in small American companies in fields like the garment business, jewelry, leather goods, and import-export." Lee's Hong Kong clientele has been growing as the approaching expiration of Britain's lease in 1997 raises the possibility that the colony will revert to Chinese ownership. Fearing the worst, Hong Kong entrepreneurs are seeking a safe haven for their money in the U.S.

Europeans also view the U.S. as a safe place to put their capital. "In the past 18 months there has been a tremendous interest in the U.K. to invest in the United States," according to John Trott, managing director of Kleinwort Benson International Investment in London. "The reasons why have lost a little of their force lately but not enough to stop the trend."

Future Outlook. The disappearance of one of the reasons why, a relatively undervalued dollar, has helped to cool the enthusiasm of Europeans for further investments in the U.S. Just as important is the fact that the European economy, which had lagged behind the U.S., showed signs of recovery in 1983. This could create attractive investment opportunities for European capital at home.

Taking into account the strong dollar, recovery abroad, and the greater caution being exercised by some foreign investors, Belli saw 1983 as "shaping up to be a blah year" for direct foreign investments in the U.S. He expected them to be a shade stronger in 1984. On the bullish side, he cited continued growth of the U.S. economy and increasing confidence in it. Another plus was that interest rates were down. Finally, political and economic insecurity in other parts of the world would continue to make U.S. investments increasingly attractive.

Does this worry him? Does he think the growth of foreign ownership poses a threat to U.S. control of its own economic destiny? The answer is no. "You can't make too much of foreign ownership," he says. "When you are talking about two companies like, say, Exxon and Royal Dutch Shell, you are talking about two companies that are more alike than different." The implication is that each will be motivated first and foremost by business considerations rather than the special interests of its home country.

Despite the headlines, there seems little danger that the U.S. economy will fall under outside control.

UNITED STATES STATISTICAL SUPPLEMENT

DEVELOPMENTS IN THE STATES IN 1983

The effects of the national economic recession dominated state government activity across the United States during 1983, with the vast majority of states being forced to raise taxes and trim services to avoid budgetary red ink. By the end of the year, the economy's recovery had eased fiscal problems markedly in many states. At the same time, some states became embroiled in a new problem over taxation of multinational corporations.

As the federal government pulled back on enforcement of some consumer protection and safety regulations, many states moved in to fill the void. Trends toward stiffer state laws on faulty automobiles, drunken driving, and use of child safety seats accelerated during the year. States also edged closer to a showdown with the federal government over the calling of a constitutional convention to balance the federal budget. Although the incidence of serious crime declined again, states continued to struggle with record overcrowding of prisons. Full-scale resumption of capital punishment nationwide was widely anticipated, and additional jurisdictions adopted lethal injections as an alternative method of administering the death penalty.

All states except Kentucky held regular legislative sessions during 1983. Fifteen (including Kentucky) staged special sessions, often to deal with budget problems.

Party Strengths. Voters made few significant changes in political party lineups during the few state elections in 1983, leaving Democrats in control of both chambers of 34 state legislatures and Republicans enjoying a majority in both houses in only 11. All states were dominantly Democratic except Alaska, Arizona, Colorado, Idaho, Indiana, Kansas, New Hampshire, South Dakota, Utah, Vermont, and Wyoming (where Republicans had control in both houses); Montana, New York, North Dakota, and Pennsylvania (where Republicans organized the upper house and Democrats the lower chamber); and Nebraska (a nonpartisan, one-house legislature). Even that listing slightly exaggerated Republican strength since Democrats controlled the Alaskan Senate through a coalition arrangement.

Democrats captured the governorship from the Republicans in Louisiana, establishing the prospective gubernatorial lineup for 1984 at 35 Democrats and 15 Republicans. One state campaign, for governor of Mississippi, was conspicuously dirty. Republicans accused Democratic candidate Bill Allain, the state attorney general, of having sex with male transvestite prostitutes, producing sworn affidavits to that effect from three prostitutes and from three Jackson, Miss., policemen who said that Allain regularly cruised that city's tenderloin strip. Allain denied the charges and won the election with more than 56% of the vote. The male prostitutes later recanted.

Government Structures and Powers. Preoccupation with fiscal problems caused 1983 to be a quiet year in regard to structural changes in state governments. South Carolina established a new court of appeals, and Alaska created an Office of Management and Budget. Kentucky adopted a new election schedule to eliminate a "lame duck" interim legislative session. Virginia gave preliminary approval to a state balanced-budget and tax-growth-limitation amendment.

As usual, many rulings affecting governmental powers came from the courts. The U.S. Supreme Court, for example, ruled that while congressional districts must be apportioned to have populations as nearly equal as possible, state legislatures can allot a representative to each geographic county. The high court also approved the Nebraska legislature's use of a chaplain to give an opening prayer before each session. The New Jersey Supreme Court invalidated that state's legislative oversight act as a violation of the doctrine of separation of powers. In September the Supreme Court in California canceled a voter-demanded initiative election, scheduled to be held in December, that was designed to overturn Democratic-drawn apportionment boundaries.

Government Relations. Progress on the "new federalism" program of the administration of Pres. Ronald Reagan came to a halt during 1983, with virtually no new responsibilities or funding sources finding their way from federal to state control. Some businessmen encouraging economic deregulation on the federal level found themselves with an unanticipated backlash as numerous states moved to fill the resulting regulatory voids. State and Federal Associates, a Washington, D.C., consulting firm, noted that the trend, which was prompting corporations to post additional lobbyists in state capitals throughout the nation, was causing businessmen 50 potential regulatory headaches rather than one.

Missouri became the 32nd state to call formally for a constitutional convention to write a federal balanced-budget amendment; only 34 such requests are required to mandate such a body. But the state attorney general ruled that Maryland could withdraw its 1975 demand for the convention, an opinion challenged by some constitutional scholars. California petitioners planned an initiative for 1984 voter consideration that would require legislators to either submit a constitutional convention request or face a cutoff in their pay and benefits. The balanced-budget movement received a setback, however, when a Missouri court invalidated on a technicality that state's 1980 constitutional amendment restricting the growth of taxes and spending.

Legislators in the New England states approved the nation's first regional interstate banking system. New York Gov. Mario Cuomo resolved an interstate problem by allowing Indian-rights activist Dennis Banks to serve out his riot and assault term in a New York prison rather than be returned as requested to South Dakota.

Finances. The nation's economic recovery arrived too late to avoid turmoil for states during the year, with most raising taxes and cutting services to meet the financial problems caused by high unemployment and reduced revenue collections. The fiscal situation improved markedly in many states by the year's end, with tax increases and rosier economic conditions turning deficit projections almost overnight into anticipated surpluses. But the recovery was lopsided, with industrial and oil-producing states failing to share fully in it, and conditions remained grim in several states.

Some analysts blamed the roller-coaster state fiscal scene in part on cutbacks in federal aid under the Reagan administration, a development that reduced a previously steady source of revenue and forced states to depend increasingly on more volatile sales and state income taxes. "At the very moment when states can least afford it, the federal government has withdrawn or reduced its support in nearly every area of the state-federal partnership," complained *State Legislatures* magazine.

A survey by the Tax Foundation revealed that 39 states raised taxes by more than $7 billion during the year, the largest dollar increase in history. That brought total state tax increases over the past three years to more than $16 billion—a 10% jump. Legislatures also used other devices to balance their books, refusing to allow $3 billion in "temporary" taxes to expire on schedule and accelerating revenue collections for a onetime gain. Indexing provisions to protect income-tax payers from inflationary "bracket creep" were suspended or postponed in Colorado, Maine, Minnesota, Oregon, South Carolina, and Wisconsin. Pennsylvania and California were forced early in the year to delay income-tax refund checks; California temporarily sent out IOU's instead, but the state's fiscal situation had recovered sufficiently by the end of the year to allow a forecast of a $2 billion surplus.

Ohio legislators increased taxes by $1.2 billion, the largest increase in the country, and tax-limitation groups promptly responded by placing initiatives on the fall ballot to repeal the tax boost and to make future increases more difficult. Both measures were defeated soundly. Incensed Michigan voters, however, recalled two Democratic state senators to protest their support of that state's $1 billion tax increase. The National Conference of State Legislatures reported that the severe austerity measures were badly needed; at the start of fiscal year 1984, 11 states faced illegal deficits, and 15 more had positive balances of 1% or less in their general funds.

More than half of the new revenue-raising measures were concentrated on broad-based personal income and general sales taxes. Illinois, Indiana, Kansas, Michigan, Minnesota, Nebraska, New Mexico, North Dakota, Ohio, Pennsylvania, Rhode Island, Vermont, West Virginia, and Wisconsin boosted personal income-tax levies. General sales taxes were hiked in Arizona, Colorado, Idaho, Illinois, Indiana, Iowa, Minnesota, Mississippi, Nebraska, New Jersey, New Mexico, North Dakota, Utah, Washington, and West Virginia. Boosting motor-fuel excise levies were Colorado, Connecticut, Florida, Idaho, Illinois, Kansas, Michigan, Minnesota, Montana, Nevada, North Dakota, Ohio, Oregon, Rhode Island, Vermont, Washington, and Wisconsin. Corporate income taxes were increased in Connecticut, Idaho, Illinois, Maine, Nebraska, New Hampshire, New Mexico, North Dakota, Ohio, Rhode Island, Utah, and West Virginia. Alcohol excise taxes rose in Alaska, Connecticut, Florida, Nevada, New York, North Dakota, and South Carolina. Tobacco and cigarette duties were increased in Arkansas, Connecticut, Kansas, Maine, Massachusetts, Missouri, Montana, Nevada, New Hampshire, New Jersey, New York, North Dakota, Pennsylvania, Rhode Island, Utah, Vermont, and Wisconsin. Kansas approved a new severance tax on oil and minerals, and West Virginia became the eighth state to put a minimum tax provision on its state income levy.

Figures compiled in 1983 showed that state revenue from all sources totaled $330.9 billion during the 1982 fiscal year, an increase of 6.5% over the preceding 12 months. General revenue (excluding state liquor and state insurance trust revenue) was $275.2 billion, up 6.6%. Total state expenditures rose 6.4% to $310.3 billion, creating a technical surplus of $20.6 billion for the year. General expenditures, not including outlays of the liquor stores and insurance trust systems, amounted to $269.5 billion, up 6.2% for the year. Of the general revenue, 59.1% came from state taxes and licenses; 15.7% came from charges and miscellaneous revenue, including educational tuition; and 25.2% came from intergovernmental revenue (mostly from the federal government).

The largest state outlay was $103 billion for education, of which $34.3 billion went to state colleges and universities and $60.7 billion to local public schools. Other major outlays included $55.3 billion for public welfare, $25.1 billion for highways, and $22.3 billion for health and public hospitals.

Ethics. New York state Sen. Joseph Pisani was indicted in December on tax and fraud charges stemming from the embezzlement of $83,000 from state, campaign fund, and private law firm accounts. A former New York state senator, Vander Beatty, was found guilty in December of vote forgery; authorities said he masterminded a scheme to "create irregularities" in courthouse voter registration records and force a new congressional election in 1981. An Alabama circuit judge, Wilson Hayes, was suspended in September after he allegedly pressured a black father of seven to undergo a vasectomy in a divorce case. Texas Attorney General Jim Mattox was indicted in September for commercial bribery; he was accused of threatening to ruin a Houston law firm's municipal bond business unless one of the firm's lawyers stopped questioning Mattox's sister in a civil case. North Carolina Lieut. Gov. Jimmy Green was indicted in June on bribery charges, but a federal jury took only two hours in October to acquit him on all counts.

Former Tennessee House majority leader Tommy Burnett received an 18-month sentence in June after pleading guilty to failure to file a tax return. Two top Oklahoma legislators, House Speaker Dan Draper and Majority Leader Joe Fitzgibbon, were suspended from office in August after being found guilty on federal vote fraud charges. South Dakota Gov. William Janklow filed libel charges against a book publisher, three South Dakota bookstores, and *Newsweek* magazine over a book's account of allegations that Janklow had raped a 15-year-old Indian girl in 1967 while serving as a legal-aid attorney on an Indian reservation.

Arizona, Massachusetts, and New York tightened ethical codes for state officials during the year. Illinois became the 50th state to enact a freedom-of-information statute covering state and local government records. The Ohio Supreme Court stripped the state bar association of authority to discipline its own members, substituting government ethical investigations financed by a $50-per-capita annual assessment on the state's 30,000 attorneys. Montana became the first state to limit political action committee contributions; each could now donate only $600 to a House candidate and $1,000 a Senate aspirant.

Education. In a ruling that set an important precedent, a federal judge in May declared that Florida could withhold diplomas from high-school seniors who failed minimum competency tests. A dozen other states had similar laws on their books, but their legal validity had been under question prior to the Florida ruling. Another judicial decision contained an important clarification of permissible state action in aiding private and parochial schools. The U.S. Supreme Court ruled constitutional a Minnesota law allowing all taxpayers to take income-tax deductions for tuition and school expenses, even though opponents noted that only private and parochial schools charged tuition.

Wyoming moved to equalize per-pupil spending among wealthy and poor school districts. West Virginia lowered the compulsory school age from seven to six and approved the use of paddling as a disciplinary tool.

Health and Welfare. Encouraged by federal-assistance budget cuts, states took steps during 1983 to reduce welfare expenses. Eighteen states, plus the District of Columbia and Puerto Rico, started a computerized antifraud project to detect discrepancies in welfare payments, wages, unemployment records, and medical payments. The Reagan administration decided in March that Medicaid rules were not violated by state laws requiring adult children to support their financially destitute parents. Indiana and Virginia already had such laws on their books, and Idaho approved a new support law following the administration directive.

A Roman Catholic nun, Agnes Mary Mansour (*see* BIOGRAPHIES), was ordered by the Vatican to resign as head of Michigan's welfare department after she refused to oppose the use of Medicaid funds for voluntary abortions. Mansour decided instead to quit the Sisters of Mercy but said she was donating her entire $58,000 state salary to the order.

Development and Infrastructure. State efforts to lure new business development accelerated during 1983, with competition for high-technology businesses particularly intense. Louisiana and Montana approved new state venture-capital corporations, bringing to ten the states supplying seed money to new and expanding companies that showed promise of providing states with added jobs and tax revenues. Other state efforts included direct investment of taxpayer funds, state pension-fund investment in securities, and tax credits for promising firms. Connecticut, Hawaii, Iowa, Massachusetts, Michigan, New Mexico, and South Carolina were among the states that strengthened their high-tech promotion activities during the year—by providing training programs, advice from special high-tech councils, and research assistance. A survey at the end of the year found that 33 states were spending approximately $250 million annually to attract high-technology industry.

National concern over the country's deteriorating infrastructure was underscored in June when an interstate highway bridge in Connecticut collapsed, killing three. The Federal Highway Administration ordered states to inspect 200 similarly designed bridges nationwide, and the incident resulted in renewed resolve in many states to tackle dangerous and run-down bridges. One cent of a five-cent federal gasoline-tax increase in April was earmarked for state construction and repair use, but the added revenue required matching state funds, which many hard-pressed state treasuries could not immediately supply.

Drugs. A nationwide legislative effort against drunk drivers continued during the year, with 47 of the 50 states considering tougher highway safety bills, driving-while-intoxicated legislation, and/or a higher drinking age. Alaska, Arkansas, Connecticut, Georgia, Hawaii, Idaho, Louisiana, Maryland, Minnesota, Mississippi, New Hampshire, North Carolina, Ohio, Oklahoma, Pennsylvania, South Carolina, Texas, Utah, Virginia, and West Virginia stiffened requirements and increased penalties for driving while intoxicated, some for the second time in three years. In February the U.S. Supreme Court upheld a South Dakota law that allowed a driver's refusal to take a blood alcohol test to be used as evidence against him; 19 other jurisdictions had similar laws.

In another legislative attack on the same problem Alaska, Connecticut, Delaware, Maryland, New Jersey, North Carolina, Oklahoma, Virginia, West Virginia, and Wisconsin raised the legal drinking age; Vermont's governor vetoed a similar bill, however. At the year's end only Hawaii, Louisiana, and Vermont still permitted 18-year-olds to drink hard liquor, and 16 states mandated the age of 21 before hard liquor could be legally consumed.

Arizona became the first state to impose a luxury tax on seized illegal drugs in an attempt to siphon off dealer profits. Pennsylvania considered turning over sales of alcoholic beverages, now a state monopoly, to private storekeepers in the interests of efficiency.

Law and Justice. Concern over the abuse of the very young and very old was reflected in much legislative action during the year. Alaska and Massachusetts approved laws requiring citizens to report known incidents of mistreatment of the elderly. Alaska, Florida, Georgia, Massachusetts, Minnesota, New Hampshire, and Vermont toughened laws governing the exploitation of minors for use in pornography. Utah became the first state to establish a registry of missing children to check fingerprints of disappeared young people against adoption agency records. No state voted a mandatory fingerprinting statute, however; such laws were widespread earlier in the century but were all repealed during the 1960s and 1970s owing to privacy concerns.

Hawaii, Minnesota, New York, and Rhode Island approved laws enhancing the rights of crime victims. Reacting to highly publicized incidents of recent years, Rhode Island also required persons witnessing a rape to notify the police. Utah's legislature overrode a gubernatorial veto and banned transmission, of sexually explicit material over cable television.

Arizona shifted the burden of proving insanity to a criminal defendant. South Dakota provided for a new verdict of guilty but mentally ill that required convicts to serve a full term in an institution even if their mental illness was cured. Pro-gun lobbyists convinced the Arizona, North Dakota, South Dakota, and Washington legislatures to preempt all authority concerning firearm law, forbidding local governments from restricting gun purchase, possession, and use.

With the U.S. Supreme Court allowing more executions during the year, states continued to wrestle with possible public reaction to capital punishment on a large scale, even though opinion polls showed increasing approval for the death penalty. The New York governor again vetoed a capital punishment law, but Massachusetts became the 38th state to relegalize execution. Arkansas, Illinois, Massachusetts, Montana, and New Jersey provided for execution by lethal injection, bringing to ten the jurisdictions utilizing a technique thought to be less painful and more humane.

Environment. A survey by the National Governors Association (NGA) determined that natural resources problems—energy, water, and toxic waste—were the most vexing issues facing state governments during the 1980s. "Water is the problem of the future," said one NGA staff member. "Water quality in the eastern U.S., water supply in the west."

Arkansas, Florida, Idaho, Louisiana, Minnesota, and Tennessee approved new or more stringent hazardous-waste cleanup laws during the year. Texas adopted a comprehensive statewide water plan. Massachusetts attempted a novel requirement that made mortgage lenders responsible for any toxic-waste cleanup but backed down when large financiers threatened to abandon the state. Six more states, for a total of nine, overrode industry opposition and adopted "right to know" laws requiring state notification of potentially hazardous contents of trucks, pipelines, boxcars, and other means of transport. Virginia became the first state to limit discharge of mercury compounds into freshwater rivers and streams.

Maine voters rejected a proposal to halt the state's six-day moose-hunting season. Nine more states, for a total of 20, during 1983 authorized a checkoff for donation of state income-tax refunds to help finance wildlife conservation projects. Colorado, the first state to enact the "chickadee checkoff," had raised $3 million in voluntary donations since 1978.

Energy. The tax-exempt bond market was rocked in July when the Washington Public Power Supply System officially defaulted on $2,250,000,000 in bonds for two nuclear power plants. The system, which became known as "Whoops" as a result of the episode, was originally backed by 88 public utilities in Washington, Oregon, Idaho, Montana, and Nevada, most of which subsequently refused to pay their share of costs for the final two facilities of an ambitious five-plant nuclear array. Construction on the two was stopped in 1982 owing to declining energy consumption and escalating nuclear plant costs. By the end of 1983 the default had ensnarled the system—and virtually every organization and individual connected with it—in a maze of litigation.

Connecticut became the first state to limit the cost to electricity consumers for nuclear plant construction, setting a ceiling of $3.5 billion on the amount chargeable to ratepayers for the Millstone 3 facility then being built. The U.S. Department of Energy (DOE) angered state officials by eliminating energy-efficiency standards for six household appliances. A 1975 federal law said that state energy standards could not be more stringent than federal regulations, and as a consequence DOE officials insisted that states could not enact their own standards even if federal rules were revoked.

Another clash over federal deregulation efforts occurred during the spring when the U.S. Department of Transportation overrode 13 state laws prohibiting tandem, or twin-trailer, trucks. Nationwide approval of the energy-saving trucks was mandated in the 1982 federal tax law that brought states an extra one cent per gallon in federal motor-fuel revenues. Georgia and Vermont filed suit to halt the trucks, which state officials maintained caused an increase in accidents and in damage to roads; the suits were denied.

Reduced demand for oil and other energy had an unfavourable effect on producing-state revenues. Alaska, which in 1982 had awarded every citizen a $1,000 bonus as a share of the state's oil wealth, doled out only $385 per head in 1983.

Equal Rights. Three more states—Maine, Rhode Island, and West Virginia—in 1983 approved a proposed constitutional amendment that would give the District of Columbia full voting rights in the U.S. Congress. Although 13 states had approved the amendment, experts doubted that the required 38 state signatures could be obtained before the deadline of Aug. 22, 1985.

Idaho became the 13th state to legislate a prohibition of harassment on account of race, religion, or national origin. Vermont gave preliminary approval to a state equal-rights constitutional amendment. North Carolina, site of ten federal slavery convictions in the past three years, approved its own involuntary servitude law aimed at protecting migrant farm workers. A federal judge in Washington, D.C., ruled in March that nine states had failed to integrate their college systems as required under law; he indicated that a cutoff of U.S. funds could follow for Arkansas, Georgia, Florida, Kentucky, North Carolina, Oklahoma, Pennsylvania, Texas, and Virginia if progress was not made.

A judicial determination in September ruled that female state workers in Washington had been underpaid for comparable work, a judgment that was estimated to be worth from $225 million to $1 billion in salary increases plus back pay to 1979. Women's rights advocates noted that secretaries had been paid $500 per month less than truck drivers, two jobs they judged to be of "comparable worth." State officials had attempted to forestall the verdict earlier in the year by requiring comparable pay for all employees, but the legislature had appropriated only $1.5 million to correct the inequities.

Louisiana received national publicity over two laws. The state Supreme Court, in a 4–3 decision, ruled that the state legislature was within its rights in requiring that "scientific creationism," the biblical version of creation, be taught in public schools as well as evolution theory. A federal court had struck down a similar Arkansas law in 1982. The legislature also repealed a 1970 "black blood" statute requiring anyone with $\frac{1}{32}$ of black ancestry to be designated officially as black. A state court had upheld the law earlier in the year.

Prisons. Although the nation's crime rate dropped slightly for the third consecutive year, the population of state prisons continued to rise during 1983, further exacerbating the severe overcrowding problems in many states. Texas began using tents to house the overflow, while Arizona employed Vietnam-style huts, Hawaii built wooden bungalows, and Illinois appropriated floor space in prison chapels and gymnasiums. Some 31 states were under some type of court order to relieve overcrowded conditions during the year. Florida, South Carolina, Tennessee, and Texas passed inmate release laws, bringing to 21 the number of states utilizing early-release or work-release programs when crowding reached a specified point.

States had $2 billion worth of new prison facilities under construction contract in mid-1983, but several jurisdictions were prompted to innovate. New York used Urban Development Corporation funds to build utilitarian inmate dormitories; if the prison population should drop later, the buildings could be easily converted to housing for the elderly. New York also became the first state to require judges to consider monetary restitution as an alternative to prison sentences. Minnesota considered the introduction of an elaborate computerized system to "put sentencing into the computer age."

Execution of death-row inmates increased markedly during 1983 as the U.S. Supreme Court began showing impatience with lengthy appeals. Alabama, Mississippi, Florida, Louisiana, and Georgia overcame legal roadblocks and put to death convicted murderers during the year, bringing to 11 the number executed since the high court allowed resumption of capital punishment in 1976. At the year's end there were still more than 1,250 convicts on death rows nationwide.

Consumer Protection. Sixteen additional states approved "lemon laws" during 1983 that required automobile manufacturers to replace chronically defective cars. Connecticut, California, and Kentucky had started the lemon law trend in 1982, but several of the new versions were attacked by consumer groups as overly liberal toward automakers. Nebraska's law, for example, prohibited a claim until a car had been out of service for 40 days, and Florida's version permitted a charge of 20 cents a mile on a car before it was replaced.

Another 22 states, plus the District of Columbia, ordered the use of safety seats for children, bringing the number of jurisdictions with child restraint laws to 43. Rhode Island became the first state to mandate the use of automobile seat belts by adults, and New York became the first to ban the use by drivers of headphones in both ears. Eleven more states approved bans on custom-installed dark glass or one-way windows in autos; 17 states now restricted or prohibited dark glass installed outside the auto factory. Reversing a trend of the 1970s, several states considered junking their no-fault auto insurance laws, and New Jersey repealed its no-fault statute. Of 23 states with no-fault laws, critics said, only those of New York, Michigan, and Florida worked properly by allowing lawsuits solely after serious injury or death.

(DAVID C. BECKWITH)

AREA AND POPULATION

Area and Population of the States

State	AREA in sq mi		POPULATION (000)		
	Total	Inland water[1]	1980 census	1982 estimate	Percent change 1980–82
Alabama	51,705	938	3,894	3,943	1.3
Alaska	591,004	20,171	402	438	8.9
Arizona	114,000	492	2,718	2,860	5.2
Arkansas	53,187	1,109	2,286	2,291	0.2
California	158,706	2,407	23,668	24,724	4.5
Colorado	104,091	496	2,890	3,045	5.3
Connecticut	5,018	147	3,108	3,153	1.5
Delaware	2,044	112	594	602	1.3
Dist. of Columbia	69	6	638	631	−1.1
Florida	58,664	4,511	9,746	10,416	6.9
Georgia	58,910	854	5,463	5,639	3.2
Hawaii	6,471	46	965	994	3.0
Idaho	83,564	1,153	944	965	2.3
Illinois	56,345	700	11,427	11,448	0.2
Indiana	36,185	253	5,490	5,471	−0.4
Iowa	56,275	310	2,914	2,905	−0.3
Kansas	82,277	499	2,364	2,408	1.9
Kentucky	40,409	740	3,661	3,667	0.2
Louisiana	47,752	3,230	4,206	4,362	3.7
Maine	33,265	2,270	1,125	1,133	0.8
Maryland	10,460	623	4,217	4,265	1.1
Massachusetts	8,284	460	5,737	5,781	0.8
Michigan	58,527	1,573	9,262	9,109	−1.7
Minnesota	84,402	4,854	4,076	4,133	1.4
Mississippi	47,689	457	2,521	2,551	1.2
Missouri	69,697	752	4,917	4,951	0.7
Montana	147,046	1,657	787	801	1.8
Nebraska	77,355	711	1,570	1,586	1.0
Nevada	110,561	667	800	881	10.0
New Hampshire	9,279	286	921	951	3.3
New Jersey	7,787	319	7,365	7,438	1.0
New Mexico	121,593	258	1,303	1,359	4.3
New York	49,108	1,731	17,558	17,659	0.6
North Carolina	52,669	3,826	5,882	6,019	2.3
North Dakota	70,702	1,403	653	670	2.6
Ohio	41,330	325	10,798	10,791	−0.1
Oklahoma	69,956	1,301	3,025	3,177	5.0
Oregon	97,073	889	2,633	2,649	0.6
Pennsylvania	45,308	420	11,864	11,865	[2]
Rhode Island	1,212	158	947	958	1.2
South Carolina	31,113	909	3,122	3,203	2.6
South Dakota	77,116	1,164	691	691	[2]
Tennessee	42,144	989	4,591	4,651	1.3
Texas	266,807	4,790	14,229	15,280	7.4
Utah	84,899	2,826	1,461	1,554	6.3
Vermont	9,614	341	511	516	0.9
Virginia	40,767	1,063	5,347	5,491	2.7
Washington	68,139	1,627	4,132	4,245	2.7
West Virginia	24,231	112	1,950	1,948	−0.1
Wisconsin	56,153	1,727	4,706	4,765	1.3
Wyoming	97,809	820	470	502	6.8
TOTAL U.S.	3,618,770	79,481	226,546[3]	231,534[3]	2.2

[1] Excludes the Great Lakes and coastal waters.
[2] Represents zero or rounds to zero.
[3] State figures do not add to total given because of rounding.
Source: U.S. Department of Commerce, Bureau of the Census, *Current Population Reports.*

Largest Metropolitan Areas[1]

Name	Population		Percent change 1970–80	Land area in sq mi[3]	Density per sq mi 1980
	1970 census[2]	1980 census			
New York-Newark-Jersey City SCSA	17,035,270	16,121,297	−5.4	4,824	3,342
New York City	9,973,716	9,120,346	−8.6	1,382	6,599
Nassau-Suffolk	2,555,868	2,605,813	2.0	1,198	2,175
Newark	2,057,468	1,965,969	−4.4	1,005	1,956
New Brunswick-Perth Amboy-Sayreville	583,813	595,893	2.1	316	1,886
Jersey City	607,839	556,972	−8.4	46	12,108
Long Branch-Asbury Park	461,849	503,173	8.9	472	1,066
Paterson-Clifton-Passaic	460,782	447,585	−2.9	187	2,394
Stamford	206,340	198,854	−3.6	128	1,554
Norwalk	127,595	126,692	−0.7	89	1,424
Los Angeles-Long Beach-Anaheim SCSA	9,980,859	11,497,568	15.2	34,009	338
Los Angeles-Long Beach	7,041,980	7,477,503	6.2	4,070	1,837
Anaheim-Santa Ana-Garden Grove	1,421,233	1,932,709	36.0	798	2,422
Riverside-San Bernardino-Ontario	1,139,149	1,558,182	36.8	27,279	57
Oxnard-Simi Valley-Ventura	378,497	529,174	39.8	1,862	284
Chicago-Gary-Kenosha SCSA	7,726,039	7,869,542	1.9	4,916	1,601
Chicago	6,974,755	7,103,624	1.8	3,724	1,908
Gary-Hammond-East Chicago	633,367	642,781	1.5	919	699
Kenosha	117,917	123,137	4.4	273	451
Philadelphia-Wilmington-Trenton SCSA	5,627,719	5,547,902	−1.4	4,851	1,144
Philadelphia	4,824,110	4,716,818	−2.2	3,532	1,336
Wilmington	499,493	523,221	4.8	1,093	478
Trenton	304,116	307,863	1.2	227	1,356
San Francisco-Oakland-San Jose SCSA	4,630,576	5,179,784	11.9	6,957	745
San Francisco-Oakland	3,109,249	3,250,630	4.5	2,482	1,310
San Jose	1,065,313	1,295,071	21.6	1,293	1,002
Vallejo-Fairfield-Napa	251,129	334,402	33.2	1,579	212
Santa Rosa	204,885	299,681	46.3	1,604	187
Detroit-Ann Arbor SCSA	4,669,154	4,618,161	−1.1	4,649	993
Detroit	4,435,051	4,353,413	−1.8	3,939	1,105
Ann Arbor	234,103	264,748	13.1	710	373
Boston-Lawrence-Lowell SCSA	3,526,349	3,448,122	−2.2	1,861	1,853
Boston	2,899,101	2,763,357	−4.7	1,238	2,232
Lawrence-Haverhill	258,564	281,981	9.1	307	919
Lowell	218,268	233,410	6.9	178	1,311
Brockton	150,416	169,374	12.6	139	1,219
Houston-Galveston SCSA	2,169,128	3,101,293	43.0	7,151	434
Houston	1,999,316	2,905,353	45.3	6,752	430
Galveston-Texas City	169,812	195,940	15.4	399	491
Washington, D.C.	2,910,111	3,060,922	5.2	2,810	1,089
Dallas-Fort Worth	2,377,623	2,974,805	25.1	8,326	357
Cleveland-Akron-Lorain SCSA	2,999,811	2,834,062	−5.5	2,919	971
Cleveland	2,063,729	1,898,825	−8.0	1,520	1,249
Akron	679,239	660,328	−2.8	905	730
Lorain-Elyria	256,843	274,909	7.0	495	555
Miami-Fort Lauderdale SCSA	1,887,892	2,643,981	40.0	3,167	835
Miami	1,267,792	1,625,781	28.2	1,955	832
Fort Lauderdale-Hollywood	620,100	1,018,200	64.2	1,211	841
St. Louis	2,410,884	2,356,460	−2.3	4,968	474
Pittsburgh	2,401,362	2,263,894	−5.7	3,054	741
Baltimore	2,071,016	2,174,023	5.0	2,247	968
Minneapolis-St. Paul	1,965,391	2,113,533	7.5	4,609	459
Seattle-Tacoma SCSA	1,836,949	2,093,112	13.9	5,902	355
Seattle-Everett	1,424,605	1,607,469	12.8	4,226	380
Tacoma	412,344	485,643	17.8	1,675	290
Atlanta	1,595,517	2,029,710	27.2	4,342	468
San Diego	1,357,854	1,861,846	37.1	4,212	442
Cincinnati-Hamilton SCSA	1,613,414	1,660,278	2.9	2,609	636
Cincinnati	1,387,207	1,401,491	1.0	2,139	655
Hamilton-Middletown	226,207	258,787	14.4	470	551

[1] Standard Metropolitan Statistical Area, SMSA, unless otherwise indicated; SCSA is a Standard Consolidated Statistical Area and combines two or more contiguous SMSA's.
[2] Revised.
[3] SMSA figures may not add to SCSA figures because of rounding.
Source: U.S. Dept. of Commerce, Bureau of the Census, *1980 Census of Population, Characteristics of the Population, Number of Inhabitants.*

Population Change

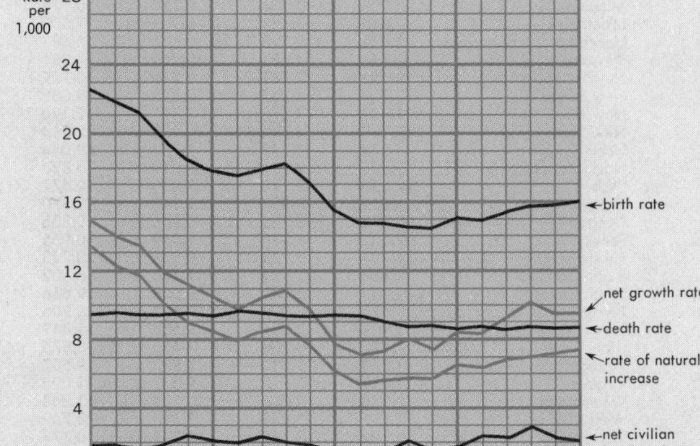

Source: U.S. Department of Commerce, Bureau of the Census, *Current Population Reports.*

Marriage and Divorce Rates

Rate per 1,000 population

16, 14, 12, 10, 8, 6, 4, 2, 0

1957, 1962, 1967, 1972, 1977, 1982

marriage rate

divorce rate*

*Includes annulments.

Source: U.S. Department of Health and Human Services, Public Health Service, *Monthly Vital Statistics Report.*

Church Membership

Religious body	Total clergy	Inclusive membership
Baptist bodies		
American Baptist Association	...	225,000
American Baptist Churches in the U.S.A.	6,951	1,621,795
Baptist General Conference	1,146	129,928
Baptist Missionary Association of America	3,500	226,953
Conservative Baptist Association of America	...	225,000
Free Will Baptists	2,890	243,658
General Baptists (General Association of)	1,373	75,028
National Baptist Convention of America	28,574	2,668,799
National Baptist Convention, U.S.A., Inc.	27,500	5,500,000
National Primitive Baptist Convention	636	250,000
Primitive Baptists	...	72,000
Progressive National Baptist Convention	863	521,692
Regular Baptist Churches, General Assn. of	2,045	300,839
Southern Baptist Convention	61,600	13,991,709
United Free Will Baptist Church	915	100,000
Buddhist Churches of America	115	100,000
Christian and Missionary Alliance	1,819	204,713
Christian Congregation	1,443	100,694
Church of God (Anderson, Ind.)	3,186	184,685
Church of the Brethren	1,913	168,844
Church of the Nazarene	8,043	498,491
Churches of Christ—Christian Churches		
Christian Church (Disciples of Christ)	6,608	1,156,458
Christian Churches and Churches of Christ	8,074	1,063,254
Churches of Christ	...	1,605,000
Community Churches, National Council of	...	190,000
Congregational Christian Churches, Natl. Assn. of	776	106,460
Eastern churches		
American Carpatho-Russian Orth. Greek Catholic Ch.	68	100,000
Antiochian Orthodox Christian Archdiocese of N. Am.	132	152,000
Armenian Apostolic Church of America	34	125,000
Armenian Church of America, Diocese of the (including Diocese of California)	61	450,000
Bulgarian Eastern Orthodox Church	11	86,000
Coptic Orthodox Church	27	100,000
Greek Orthodox Archdiocese of N. and S. America	655	1,950,000
Orthodox Church in America	531	1,000,000
Russian Orth. Ch. in the U.S.A., Patriarchal Parishes of	60	51,500
Russian Orthodox Church Outside Russia	168	55,000
Serbian Eastern Orth. Ch. for the U.S.A. and Canada	73	97,123
Ukrainian Orthodox Church in the U.S.A.	131	87,745
Episcopal Church	12,974	2,794,139
Evangelical Covenant Church of America	847	81,324
Evangelical Free Church of America	1,180	110,555
Friends United Meeting	557	59,338
Independent Fundamental Churches of America	1,366	120,446
Jehovah's Witnesses	none	619,188
Jews	3,500	5,725,000
Latter Day Saints (Mormons)		
Church of Jesus Christ of Latter-day Saints	26,686	3,521,000
Reorganized Church of Jesus Christ of L.D.S.	16,553	201,460
Lutherans		
American Lutheran Church	7,246	2,346,710
Evangelical Lutheran Churches, Association of	665	110,934
Lutheran Church in America	8,216	2,925,655
Lutheran Church—Missouri Synod	7,559	2,630,823
Wisconsin Evangelical Lutheran Synod	1,349	412,259
Mennonite Church	2,400	101,501
Methodists		
African Methodist Episcopal Church	6,550	2,210,000
African Methodist Episcopal Zion Church	6,269	1,134,179
Christian Methodist Episcopal Church	2,877	786,707
Free Methodist Church of North America	1,733	70,657
United Methodist Church	36,676	9,457,012
Wesleyan Church	2,384	105,221
Moravian Church in America	246	54,710
North American Old Roman Catholic Church	150	62,383
Old Order Amish Church	...	82,460
Pentecostals		
Apostolic Overcoming Holy Church of God	350	75,000
Assemblies of God	24,498	1,879,182
Church of God	2,737	75,890
Church of God (Cleveland, Tenn.)	10,985	463,992
Church of God in Christ	10,425	3,709,661
Church of God in Christ, International	1,600	200,000
Church of God of Prophecy	5,546	74,084
Full Gospel Fellowship of Ch. and Min., Intl.	809	65,000
International Church of the Foursquare Gospel	2,690	89,215
Pentecostal Church of God	1,542	91,008
Pentecostal Holiness Church	2,889	86,103
United Pentecostal Church, International	6,659	465,000
Plymouth Brethren	500	98,000
Polish National Catholic Church of America	141	282,411
Presbyterians		
Cumberland Presbyterian Church	739	97,813
Presbyterian Church in America	1,415	149,548
Presbyterian Church in the U.S.	6,077	814,931
United Presbyterian Church in the U.S.A.	15,093	2,342,441
Reformed bodies		
Christian Reformed Church in North America	1,014	223,976
Reformed Church in America	1,602	346,293
Roman Catholic Church	57,870	52,088,774
Salvation Army	5,119	419,475
Seventh-day Adventist Church	4,541	606,310
Triumph the Church and Kingdom of God in Christ	1,375	54,307
Unitarian Universalist Association	949	131,844
United Church of Christ	10,029	1,716,723

Table includes churches reporting a membership of 50,000 or more and represents the latest information available.
Source: National Council of Churches, *Yearbook of American and Canadian Churches*, 1984.

(CONSTANT H. JACQUET)

THE ECONOMY

Gross National Product and National Income

in billions of dollars

Item	1970[1]	1981[1]	1982[1]	1983[2]
GROSS NATIONAL PRODUCT	982.4	2,954.1	3,073.0	3,272.0
By type of expenditure				
Personal consumption expenditures	618.8	1,857.2	1,991.9	2,147.0
Durable goods	84.9	236.1	244.5	277.7
Nondurable goods	264.7	733.9	761.0	799.6
Services	269.1	887.1	986.4	1,069.7
Gross private domestic investment	140.8	474.9	414.5	450.1
Fixed investment	137.0	456.5	439.1	464.6
Changes in business inventories	3.8	18.5	−24.5	−14.5
Net exports of goods and services	3.9	26.3	17.4	−8.5
Exports	62.5	368.8	347.6	327.1
Imports	58.5	342.5	330.2	335.6
Government purchases of goods and services	218.9	595.7	649.2	683.4
Federal	95.6	229.2	258.7	273.7
State and local	123.2	366.5	390.5	409.7
By major type of product				
Goods output	456.2	1,291.8	1,208.9	1,346.8
Durable goods	170.8	528.0	500.8	536.8
Nondurable goods	285.4	763.9	780.1	810.0
Services	424.6	1,374.2	1,511.1	1,623.4
Structures	101.6	288.0	281.0	301.9
NATIONAL INCOME	798.4	2,373.0	2,450.4	2,612.8
By type of income				
Compensation of employees	609.2	1,769.2	1,865.7	1,968.7
Proprietors' income	65.1	120.2	109.0	127.2
Rental income of persons	18.6	41.4	49.9	54.8
Corporate profits	67.9	192.3	164.8	218.2
Net interest	37.5	249.9	261.1	243.8
By industry division[3]				
Agriculture, forestry, and fisheries	24.5	74.8	68.4	68.6
Mining and construction	51.6	153.8	146.5	144.9
Manufacturing	215.4	580.2	548.9	581.6
Nondurable goods	88.1	234.8	232.2	337.7
Durable goods	127.3	345.4	316.7	243.8
Transportation	30.3	85.8	83.0	83.8
Communications and public utilities	32.5	106.4	116.9	120.6
Wholesale and retail trade	122.2	351.9	362.1	383.0
Finance, insurance, and real estate	92.6	338.4	369.8	392.7
Services	103.3	348.8	386.0	417.1
Government and government enterprises	127.4	336.7	363.5	386.3

[1] Revised. [2] Second quarter, seasonally adjusted at annual rates.
[3] Without capital consumption adjustment.
Source: U.S. Department of Commerce, Bureau of Economic Analysis, *Survey of Current Business.*

Personal Income Per Capita

State	1960[1]	1970[1]	1980[1]	1982
Alabama	$1,515	$2,903	$ 7,477	$ 8,649
Alaska	2,755	4,726	12,916	16,257
Arizona	2,012	3,688	8,832	10,173
Arkansas	1,370	2,773	7,166	8,479
California	2,729	4,510	10,920	12,567
Colorado	2,272	3,887	10,042	12,302
Connecticut	2,868	4,913	11,536	13,748
Delaware	2,756	4,505	10,066	11,731
District of Columbia	2,830	4,775	12,296	14,550
Florida	1,974	3,779	9,201	10,978
Georgia	1,658	3,323	8,061	9,583
Hawaii	2,305	4,674	10,222	11,652
Idaho	1,842	3,315	8,044	9,029
Illinois	2,639	4,515	10,471	12,100
Indiana	2,169	3,735	8,896	10,021
Iowa	2,010	3,792	9,336	10,791
Kansas	2,125	3,777	9,942	11,765
Kentucky	1,593	3,096	7,648	8,934
Louisiana	1,653	3,041	8,525	10,231
Maine	1,867	3,303	7,672	9,042
Maryland	2,339	4,322	10,385	12,238
Massachusetts	2,464	4,349	10,089	12,088
Michigan	2,339	4,044	9,872	10,956
Minnesota	2,093	3,893	9,688	11,175
Mississippi	1,208	2,556	6,680	7,778
Missouri	2,103	3,706	8,720	10,170
Montana	2,016	3,428	8,361	9,580
Nebraska	2,078	3,748	9,137	10,683
Nevada	2,784	4,691	10,761	11,981
New Hampshire	2,151	3,781	9,010	10,729
New Jersey	2,704	4,737	10,976	13,089
New Mexico	1,821	3,072	7,891	9,190
New York	2,718	4,695	10,283	12,314
North Carolina	1,592	3,220	7,753	9,044
North Dakota	1,780	3,216	8,759	10,876
Ohio	2,332	3,971	9,430	10,677
Oklahoma	1,859	3,337	9,187	11,370
Oregon	2,218	3,711	9,356	10,335
Pennsylvania	2,242	3,928	9,389	10,955
Rhode Island	2,187	3,924	9,174	10,723
South Carolina	1,404	2,975	7,298	8,502
South Dakota	1,824	3,140	8,028	9,666
Tennessee	1,575	3,097	7,662	8,906
Texas	1,904	3,536	9,538	11,419
Utah	1,972	3,220	7,656	8,875
Vermont	1,879	3,530	7,832	9,507
Virginia	1,889	3,712	9,357	11,095
Washington	2,372	4,046	10,198	11,560
West Virginia	1,597	3,043	7,665	8,769
Wisconsin	2,192	3,774	10,227	10,774
Wyoming	2,248	3,686	12,217	12,372
United States	2,216	3,945	9,503	11,107

[1] Revised.
Source: U.S. Department of Commerce, Bureau of Economic Analysis, *Survey of Current Business.*

Average Employee Earnings

September figures

Industry	HOURLY 1982	HOURLY 1983[1]	WEEKLY 1982	WEEKLY 1983[1]
MANUFACTURING				
Durable goods				
Lumber and wood products	$7.65	$7.84	$296.06	$318.30
Furniture and fixtures	6.40	6.73	241.28	271.22
Stone, clay, and glass products	9.03	9.42	365.72	398.47
Primary metal industries	11.54	11.31	438.52	468.23
Fabricated metal products	8.90	9.22	345.32	381.71
Machinery, except electrical	9.41	9.71	367.93	399.08
Electric and electronic equipment	8.37	8.74	325.59	359.21
Transportation equipment	11.24	11.81	443.98	505.47
Instruments and related products	8.24	8.61	328.78	351.29
Nondurable goods				
Food and kindred products	7.91	8.13	315.61	329.27
Tobacco manufactures	9.55	9.86	379.14	379.61
Textile mill products	5.86	6.23	223.85	257.92
Apparel and other textile products	5.23	5.39	183.57	198.35
Paper and allied products	9.63	10.09	402.53	437.91
Printing and publishing	8.91	9.25	331.45	351.50
Chemicals and allied products	10.19	10.67	419.83	448.14
Petroleum and coal products	12.61	13.35	572.49	591.41
Rubber and misc. plastics products	7.78	8.08	308.09	338.55
Leather and leather products	5.41	5.57	192.06	209.43
NONMANUFACTURING				
Metal mining	12.53	12.69	448.57	503.79
Coal mining	13.02	13.93	499.97	564.17
Oil and gas extraction	10.52	10.68	458.67	469.92
Construction	11.74	12.00	433.21	454.80
Local and interurban passenger transit	7.33	7.62	246.29	258.32
Electric, gas, and sanitary services	10.91	11.64	450.58	481.90
Wholesale trade	8.10	8.48	311.04	328.18
Retail trade	5.50	5.77	165.55	171.95
Hotels and other lodging places[2]	5.07	5.29	154.64	163.46
Banking	5.92	6.26	215.49	225.99

[1] Preliminary. [2] Excludes tips. Source: U.S. Dept. of Labor, Bureau of Labor Statistics, *Employment and Earnings.*

Unemployment Trends

quarterly averages, seasonally adjusted

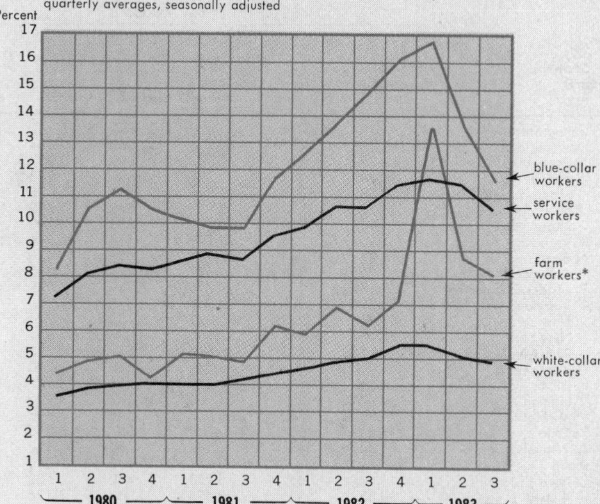

*A change in the occupational classification system in 1983 increased the farm worker category to include forestry and fishing occupations; therefore, 1983 data are not exactly comparable with previous years.
Source: U.S. Department of Labor, Bureau of Labor Statistics, *Monthly Labor Review* and *Employment and Earnings.*

Value of Agricultural Products, with Fisheries, 1982

in thousands of dollars

State	PRINCIPAL CROPS: Corn (grain)	Hay	Soybeans	Wheat	Tobacco	Cotton (lint)	Potatoes	LIVESTOCK AND PRODUCTS: Cattle, calves	Hogs, pigs	Sheep, lambs	Milk	Eggs[1]	Chickens[1]	FISHERIES[2]
Alabama	69,795	74,100	285,155	80,520	[3]	127,402	17,649	323,313	95,030	...	84,680	178,738	6,630	47,348
Alaska	...	...	...	...	...	...	...	1,100	781	13	2,963	873	87	575,569
Arizona	10,800	88,111	...	44,231	...	372,401	9,393	304,132	35,124	7,394	168,710	4,797	40	...
Arkansas	6,027	71,280	622,440	216,216	...	148,061	...	268,015	105,995	...	118,224	214,376	13,891	7,390
California	137,280	685,212	...	309,013	...	913,536	186,546	1,007,303	28,841	41,095	1,948,316	363,290	5,886	241,188
Colorado	287,014	245,287	...	289,464	...	...	58,470	925,606	61,275	30,439	147,355	31,350	625	...
Connecticut	...	18,988	...	...	17,138	...	1,988	14,081	1,367	188	94,135	77,513	1,059	9,618
Delaware	42,697	3,792	36,288	5,865	...	...	7,517	2,750	6,211	...	18,765	8,962	708	2,267
Florida	37,216	42,675	85,053	...	35,840	4,892	60,434	308,222	51,043	...	345,876	122,471	2,823	168,008
Georgia	173,188	72,000	375,233	148,962	189,478	61,051	...	212,159	241,025	...	203,328	303,464	13,859	22,344
Hawaii	...	...	...	...	...	...	...	28,991	8,474	...	29,650	14,542	169	14,426
Idaho	19,110	304,551	...	344,898	...	...	368,549	399,921	18,444	22,067	289,285	11,106	148	28
Illinois	3,583,562	213,285	2,073,494	205,875	...	...	2,390	477,744	1,202,883	5,789	358,695	55,970	1,183	1,410
Indiana	1,793,616	157,185	989,280	143,964	39,977	...	6,166	282,380	776,076	2,916	317,424	208,320	5,069	53
Iowa	3,580,088	433,650	1,747,406	9,450	...	...	1,448	1,564,159	2,655,235	13,236	567,732	77,084	2,455	1,266
Kansas	378,594	324,702	247,065	1,547,700	...	...	...	1,563,446	338,741	5,773	190,382	18,827	662	55
Kentucky	363,262	217,408	297,472	84,240	1,031,397	...	...	394,539	152,216	891	319,140	21,941	590	...
Louisiana	8,424	38,600	433,355	60,800	[3]	238,867	1,188	154,337	18,181	158	142,464	26,430	1,408	239,883
Maine	...	27,392	...	...	...	...	92,750	18,479	1,959	506	108,115	93,308	2,602	100,900
Maryland	162,426	50,007	64,598	18,666	65,490	...	1,509	40,997	46,455	523	221,340	42,770	1,497	51,438
Massachusetts	...	25,784	...	...	4,080	...	3,311	8,876	7,855	242	89,369	21,980	391	204,223
Michigan	676,236	269,309	172,484	78,720	...	...	45,658	228,848	144,416	2,927	715,984	64,813	1,836	8,118
Minnesota	1,579,175	574,348	942,840	448,818	...	...	54,921	705,302	805,945	10,742	1,342,262	100,320	2,767	2,831
Mississippi	15,903	78,750	519,480	119,700	...	508,570	...	230,623	54,612	...	128,880	86,233	4,227	39,877
Missouri	481,468	382,005	985,871	219,878	11,285	63,504	...	898,831	601,809	3,390	386,365	61,395	3,338	310
Montana	3,290	268,013	...	640,420	...	...	14,430	520,661	29,937	16,788	45,353	8,617	206	...
Nebraska	1,887,333	363,165	442,980	329,875	...	...	12,859	1,947,992	678,738	6,121	180,880	28,180	547	39
Nevada	...	97,832	...	6,237	...	426	12,285	100,572	1,669	3,615	29,925	78	2	...
New Hampshire	...	16,849	...	...	...	...	...	8,612	1,333	286	53,434	10,167	219	3,776
New Jersey	25,704	30,012	22,525	6,101	...	...	10,475	11,636	4,063	214	69,667	14,950	486	45,007
New Mexico	27,225	103,108	...	43,725	...	26,544	6,174	223,057	7,280	9,179	126,422	15,100	196	...
New York	161,184	401,508	[3]	17,945	...	...	62,883	175,098	20,646	1,436	1,533,827	85,979	2,206	45,392
North Carolina	370,418	41,832	294,000	64,800	1,235,555	28,800	16,282	131,061	372,945	151	247,842	169,341	8,987	63,824
North Dakota	76,024	243,078	38,761	1,122,920	...	...	70,725	429,095	37,588	5,629	125,625	3,145	162	157
Ohio	1,045,044	340,100	752,155	173,250	52,277	...	13,718	327,893	363,666	8,120	625,170	117,088	4,319	2,674
Oklahoma	16,200	182,620	26,600	785,565	...	59,280	...	1,244,303	41,943	2,811	169,974	48,161	982	...
Oregon	14,280	221,042	...	254,775	...	...	79,060	280,281	20,417	13,282	184,222	29,346	492	57,493
Pennsylvania	296,335	423,500	16,000	26,266	20,280	...	31,669	305,055	96,202	2,877	1,319,194	208,993	16,269	79
Rhode Island	...	1,974	...	...	...	...	2,628	835	1,171	...	6,891	5,026	128	55,401
South Carolina	67,320	34,122	227,920	57,420	218,583	44,268	...	73,454	71,376	...	89,062	78,246	2,358	23,731
South Dakota	395,076	379,940	135,083	341,423	...	...	5,425	973,137	286,704	27,819	229,589	13,019	305	478
Tennessee	143,585	105,120	348,975	100,980	299,782	97,655	2,185	299,590	170,182	216	316,801	46,367	1,085	...
Texas	353,115	365,586	121,992	489,600	...	678,528	29,449	3,515,171	103,462	53,008	555,698	178,998	4,983	186,197
Utah	5,918	135,552	...	32,875	...	...	5,220	150,512	5,234	16,172	151,757	18,291	198	...
Vermont	...	70,226	...	...	...	...	593	37,395	3,750	402	333,373	6,123	95	...
Virginia	143,693	124,937	104,272	42,883	218,286	94	12,922	260,510	109,016	5,482	286,201	53,650	1,968	68,768
Washington	82,650	218,120	...	555,520	...	...	187,440	348,016	9,477	2,296	440,125	60,253	1,221	90,071
West Virginia	14,835	54,684	...	1,069	5,447	...	...	56,887	13,125	3,215	48,302	8,342	358	21
Wisconsin	850,230	907,902	71,610	17,348	21,796	...	89,171	627,977	264,829	3,761	3,071,006	37,988	1,239	3,129
Wyoming	12,091	119,991	...	28,041	...	...	3,853	298,153	5,432	20,038	17,947	372	10	...
TOTAL U.S.	19,397,431	9,649,234	12,480,387	9,516,018	3,466,691	3,373,879	1,589,333	22,711,107	10,180,178	351,209	18,597,726	3,456,693	122,971	2,384,887

[1] Gross income, Dec. 1, 1981–Nov. 30, 1982. [2] Preliminary. [3] Estimates discontinued.
Sources: U.S. Department of Agriculture, Statistical Reporting Service, Crop Reporting Board, *Crop Values, Meat Animals, Milk, Poultry*; U.S. Department of Commerce, National Oceanic and Atmospheric Administration, National Marine Fisheries Service, *Fisheries of the United States, 1982.*

Income by Industrial Source, 1982

State and region	SOURCES OF PERSONAL INCOME: Total personal income[1]	Farm income	Private nonfarm income	Government income: Federal	Government income: State, local	SOURCES OF LABOUR AND PROPRIETORS' INCOME % OF TOTAL EARNINGS: Total earnings[2]	Farms	Mining	Construction	Mfg.	Wholesale, retail trade	Finance, insurance, real estate	Transportation, communications, public util.	Service	Govt.	Other
United States	$2,571,592	$33,474	$1,483,890	$102,879	$206,467	$1,826,710	%1.8	%2.0	%5.3	%24.4	%16.3	%6.2	%7.9	%18.7	%16.9	%0.4
New England	148,868	477	89,816	3,868	10,254	104,416	0.5	0.1	4.5	31.3	15.4	7.0	6.1	21.2	13.5	0.4
Connecticut	43,351	116	26,887	802	2,533	30,338	0.4	0.2	4.5	35.5	15.2	8.7	5.6	18.7	11.0	0.3
Maine	10,249	56	5,589	608	798	7,052	0.8	0.1	5.0	29.3	15.5	4.3	6.3	17.8	20.0	1.0
Massachusetts	69,882	134	42,941	1,707	5,098	49,881	0.3	0.1	3.9	28.9	15.5	6.9	6.5	23.9	13.6	0.4
New Hampshire	10,202	26	5,959	249	639	6,872	0.4	0.1	8.1	32.8	16.2	5.3	5.7	18.2	12.9	0.3
Rhode Island	10,278	10	5,691	386	790	6,876	0.1	0.1	4.0	31.3	15.1	5.9	5.0	20.9	17.1	0.5
Vermont	4,907	135	2,749	117	396	3,396	4.0	0.4	5.4	30.2	15.0	4.5	6.1	18.9	15.1	0.5
Mideast	513,248	1,944	299,393	21,551	41,570	364,458	0.5	0.5	4.2	23.9	15.3	7.9	8.3	21.6	17.3	0.3
Delaware	7,065	116	4,622	227	582	5,547	2.1	[3]	[3]	38.5	12.9	4.6	5.6	15.1	14.6	[3]
District of Columbia	9,186	—	7,874	6,449	1,089	15,412	—	[3]	[3]	2.6	5.9	4.8	5.6	29.6	48.9	[3]
Maryland	52,195	323	24,510	4,396	4,263	33,493	1.0	0.2	5.8	15.3	17.0	5.6	7.1	21.9	25.9	0.4
New Jersey	97,361	209	54,283	2,434	7,199	64,124	0.3	0.1	4.4	27.8	17.3	5.4	9.1	20.2	15.0	0.3
New York	217,457	543	131,635	4,376	19,854	156,408	0.3	0.2	3.6	21.7	15.4	11.3	8.9	22.8	15.5	0.3
Pennsylvania	129,985	753	76,470	3,670	8,583	89,475	0.8	1.7	4.8	31.1	14.9	5.4	7.8	19.5	13.7	0.2
Great Lakes	459,698	4,888	275,347	9,342	35,440	325,018	1.5	0.8	4.4	33.7	15.7	5.5	7.2	17.1	13.8	0.2
Illinois	138,519	1,434	81,740	3,214	10,195	96,583	1.5	1.1	4.8	26.6	17.4	7.7	8.2	18.6	13.9	0.2
Indiana	54,819	550	33,688	1,187	3,905	39,329	1.4	0.9	5.1	38.1	14.9	4.6	7.4	14.3	12.9	0.2
Michigan	99,802	749	60,075	1,599	8,660	71,082	1.1	0.5	3.7	38.3	14.4	4.3	6.0	17.1	14.4	0.2
Ohio	115,217	667	70,274	2,587	8,310	81,838	0.8	1.2	4.4	35.6	15.6	4.7	7.1	17.1	13.3	0.2
Wisconsin	51,341	1,488	29,571	755	4,370	36,185	4.1	0.1	4.0	34.2	15.3	5.1	6.5	16.2	14.2	0.3
Plains	187,104	7,021	103,487	5,643	15,045	131,196	5.4	1.2	5.2	22.5	17.8	5.8	9.0	17.0	15.8	0.3
Iowa	31,347	1,652	15,923	482	2,582	20,639	8.0	0.2	5.0	25.1	17.8	5.9	7.2	15.7	14.8	0.4
Kansas	28,325	1,186	14,494	1,062	2,156	18,898	6.3	3.1	5.3	21.1	16.8	5.3	9.2	15.7	17.0	0.3
Minnesota	46,184	1,464	27,473	810	4,104	33,851	4.3	1.0	4.9	25.3	18.0	6.1	7.9	17.6	14.5	0.3
Missouri	50,346	486	30,711	1,915	3,545	36,657	1.3	0.6	5.2	25.2	17.9	5.8	10.5	18.5	14.9	0.3
Nebraska	16,939	963	8,595	651	1,560	11,769	8.2	0.4	4.8	15.5	18.1	6.9	10.8	16.0	18.8	0.4
North Dakota	7,287	549	3,558	387	581	5,075	10.8	5.8	8.2	5.8	18.8	4.6	10.3	16.3	19.1	0.4
South Dakota	6,675	720	2,732	337	516	4,306	16.7	1.4	4.4	10.7	17.6	5.0	7.7	16.2	19.8	0.4
Southeast	520,232	7,910	284,861	28,618	42,105	363,494	2.2	2.6	5.9	22.5	16.5	5.2	8.3	16.8	19.5	0.5
Alabama	34,101	617	18,327	2,205	2,905	24,054	2.6	2.2	5.1	26.7	14.8	4.5	7.9	14.7	21.2	0.4
Arkansas	19,430	774	10,181	649	1,455	13,059	5.9	1.3	5.2	26.5	16.1	4.7	8.5	15.2	16.1	0.5
Florida	114,347	1,302	56,383	4,067	8,040	69,791	1.9	0.4	7.5	13.4	19.5	7.4	8.8	22.9	17.3	0.9
Georgia	54,035	777	32,479	3,209	4,711	41,175	1.9	0.4	5.2	22.4	19.1	5.7	10.3	15.5	19.2	0.3
Kentucky	32,762	1,065	18,047	1,513	2,446	23,071	4.6	7.9	5.1	24.0	14.6	4.1	7.8	14.4	17.2	0.4
Louisiana	44,633	376	27,289	1,302	4,049	33,016	1.1	9.4	9.1	16.2	16.2	4.6	10.1	16.8	16.2	0.4
Mississippi	19,840	515	10,499	1,017	1,768	13,799	3.7	2.5	6.4	25.3	15.4	4.4	7.4	14.1	20.2	0.5
North Carolina	54,431	1,331	32,169	2,664	4,811	40,974	3.2	0.2	4.6	32.3	15.6	4.3	7.2	13.8	18.2	0.3
South Carolina	27,231	282	15,349	1,967	2,518	20,115	1.4	0.2	5.9	32.1	14.0	4.4	6.8	12.7	22.3	0.4
Tennessee	41,420	570	24,659	1,900	3,248	30,377	1.9	0.8	4.9	29.2	16.8	5.0	7.3	17.1	16.9	0.2
Virginia	60,923	306	29,517	7,747	4,651	42,220	0.7	1.7	4.8	19.0	14.6	4.6	7.5	17.5	29.4	0.3
West Virginia	17,078	–5	9,962	379	1,504	11,840	[4]	18.1	4.6	21.0	13.9	3.3	9.3	13.8	15.9	0.2
Southwest	252,206	2,610	153,132	10,455	19,812	186,009	1.4	8.1	7.4	18.3	18.0	5.6	8.0	16.5	16.3	0.4
Arizona	29,100	345	15,610	1,298	2,648	19,900	1.7	2.8	7.4	18.4	17.0	6.1	7.0	19.1	19.8	0.7
New Mexico	12,492	189	6,413	951	1,520	9,073	2.1	8.9	7.3	7.2	15.2	4.1	9.0	18.6	27.2	0.3
Oklahoma	36,119	705	20,333	1,701	2,800	25,540	2.8	13.3	5.4	16.6	16.7	4.9	7.9	14.6	17.6	0.3
Texas	174,493	1,371	110,776	6,505	12,843	131,496	1.0	7.8	7.8	19.3	18.5	5.8	8.1	16.4	14.7	0.4
Rocky Mountain	73,837	1,264	42,711	3,892	6,549	54,416	2.3	7.0	7.1	15.2	16.8	5.5	9.2	17.2	19.2	0.4
Colorado	37,453	461	22,671	1,983	3,133	28,248	1.6	5.9	6.8	16.8	17.1	6.5	8.6	18.3	18.1	0.4
Idaho	8,716	458	4,372	367	749	5,947	7.7	1.8	6.9	17.1	16.7	4.6	8.1	17.4	18.8	0.8
Montana	7,673	217	3,825	370	740	5,152	4.2	5.6	7.1	9.0	18.3	4.9	12.0	16.2	21.5	0.5
Utah	13,788	101	8,043	946	1,275	10,366	1.0	5.8	6.4	17.8	16.3	4.9	9.3	16.8	21.4	0.2
Wyoming	6,207	27	3,800	225	651	4,704	0.6	24.2	11.1	4.7	14.5	3.3	10.8	11.8	18.6	0.3
Far West[5]	397,703	7,104	225,411	16,798	33,570	282,882	2.5	0.7	5.2	22.1	16.4	6.3	7.4	20.8	17.8	0.7
California	310,704	5,390	177,731	12,911	25,685	221,716	2.4	0.8	5.0	22.4	16.3	6.5	7.3	21.2	17.4	0.7
Nevada	10,552	52	6,390	427	921	7,790	0.7	2.1	7.4	5.3	14.4	4.5	8.4	39.7	17.3	0.3
Oregon	27,373	526	15,014	804	2,611	18,955	2.8	0.2	4.7	23.6	18.5	5.7	8.4	17.4	18.0	0.7
Washington	49,074	1,137	26,276	2,655	4,353	34,421	3.3	0.2	6.3	23.4	16.6	5.5	7.4	16.0	20.4	0.9
Alaska	7,118	4	4,317	863	1,102	6,286	0.1	7.9	13.3	5.5	11.9	3.2	12.0	14.2	31.3	0.7
Hawaii	11,579	252	5,415	1,848	1,021	8,536	3.0	[4]	5.7	5.0	15.6	6.5	9.3	20.9	33.6	0.4

Dollar figures in millions. Percentages may not add to 100.0 because of rounding.
[1] Includes dividends, interest, rent, and transfer payments. [2] Excludes dividends, interest, rent, and transfer payments. [3] Figures not available. [4] Less than 0.05%.
[5] Totals for Far West do not include Alaska and Hawaii.
Source: U.S. Department of Commerce, Bureau of Economic Analysis, *Survey of Current Business*.

Farms and Farm Income

State	Number of farms 1983[1,2]	Land in farms 1983 in 000 acres[1,2]	CASH RECEIPTS, 1982, IN $000 — Farm marketings: Total[3]	Crops[3]	Livestock and products
Alabama	54,000	12,100	2,212,073	994,658	1,217,415
Alaska	450	1,540[4]	16,489	10,081	6,408
Arizona	7,000	38,900	1,576,128	893,707	682,421
Arkansas	56,000	16,200	3,147,480	1,521,708	1,625,772
California	78,000	33,700	14,069,097	9,688,375	4,380,722
Colorado	25,300	35,700	2,887,325	876,356	2,010,969
Connecticut	4,500	500	309,092	116,920	192,172
Delaware	3,400	650	404,101	116,897	287,204
Florida	41,000	12,800	4,246,680	3,304,344	942,336
Georgia	55,000	15,000	3,156,082	1,496,177	1,659,905
Hawaii	4,400	1,960	484,136	406,277	77,859
Idaho	24,400	15,100	2,027,500	1,213,682	813,818
Illinois	101,000	28,700	6,844,605	4,472,111	2,372,494
Indiana	87,000	16,800	4,315,514	2,552,377	1,763,137
Iowa	115,000	33,700	9,385,444	3,372,376	6,013,068
Kansas	75,000	48,500	5,182,945	1,859,005	3,323,940
Kentucky	103,000	14,500	2,883,553	1,610,058	1,273,495
Louisiana	36,500	10,100	1,724,448	1,218,091	506,357
Maine	8,100	1,560	408,214	159,223	248,991
Maryland	18,000	2,700	1,059,219	344,617	714,602
Massachusetts	5,300	600	341,076	206,150	134,926
Michigan	65,000	11,500	2,713,467	1,538,429	1,175,038
Minnesota	103,000	30,400	6,035,501	2,494,887	3,540,614
Mississippi	51,000	14,300	2,232,802	1,289,640	943,162
Missouri	117,000	31,400	3,489,729	1,434,236	2,055,493
Montana	24,000	62,100	1,476,228	823,614	652,614
Nebraska	63,000	47,600	6,099,567	1,868,161	4,231,406
Nevada	2,700	8,900	234,644	68,504	166,140
New Hampshire	3,200	540	104,047	29,001	75,046
New Jersey	9,500	1,030	515,215	388,775	126,440
New Mexico	13,500	47,000	922,489	295,341	627,148
New York	50,000	9,500	2,564,416	697,121	1,867,295
North Carolina	85,000	10,800	4,076,310	2,483,661	1,592,649
North Dakota	37,500	41,700	2,221,687	1,617,163	604,524
Ohio	92,000	16,100	3,520,796	1,969,493	1,551,303
Oklahoma	71,000	34,000	2,869,415	778,401	2,091,014
Oregon	37,000	18,200	1,746,050	1,094,207	651,843
Pennsylvania	59,000	8,700	2,985,826	820,262	2,165,564
Rhode Island	800	80	32,688	18,678	14,010
South Carolina	31,000	5,900	1,129,709	734,770	394,939
South Dakota	36,500	44,500	2,380,247	744,514	1,635,733
Tennessee	95,000	13,400	2,058,188	1,172,937	885,251
Texas	184,000	138,300	8,763,153	3,332,441	5,430,712
Utah	12,800	12,300	539,285	127,786	411,499
Vermont	7,500	1,700	407,505	33,684	373,821
Virginia	58,000	9,800	1,672,182	666,753	1,005,429
Washington	38,000	16,300	2,865,594	1,872,493	993,101
West Virginia	21,200	4,300	224,579	54,122	170,457
Wisconsin	90,000	18,200	5,105,804	1,002,052	4,103,752
Wyoming	9,200	35,300	527,273	112,722	414,551
TOTAL U.S.	2,369,750	1,035,160	136,195,597	65,997,038	70,198,559

[1] Preliminary. [2] Places with annual sales of agricultural products of $1,000 or more. [3] Excludes Commodity Credit Corporation loans.
[4] Exclusive of grazing land leased from the U.S. Government, Alaska farmland totals about 70,000 acres.
Sources: U.S. Department of Agriculture, Statistical Reporting Service, *Crop Production,* and Economic Research Service, *Economic Indicators of the Farm Sector.*

Principal Minerals, Production and Value

State	Principal nonfuel minerals, in order of value, 1981	Value ($000)	% of U.S. total prod.	Crude Petroleum, 1982: Production (000 bbl)	Crude Petroleum, 1982: Value ($000)	Natural Gas, 1982: Production[1] (000,000 cu ft)	Natural Gas, 1982: Value ($000)	Coal, 1982: Production (000 ST)	Coal, 1982: Value ($000)
Alabama	Cement, stone, lime, clays	$312,657	1.24	20,014	$646,852	75,003	$258,298	26,226	$1,133,750
Alaska	Sand and gravel, stone, gold, tin	127,541	.51	618,910	12,440,091	264,364	166,549	833	...
Arizona	Copper, molybdenum, cement, silver	2,565,840	10.19	335	10,596	99	256	12,364	...
Arkansas	Bromine, cement, stone, sand and gravel	281,548	1.12	18,849	567,732	124,611	265,030	138	5,510
California	Cement, boron minerals, sand and gravel, stone	1,975,016	7.85	401,472	9,828,035	383,977	1,184,904	—	—
Colorado	Molybdenum, cement, sand and gravel, silver	965,766	3.84	30,545	964,306	209,892	664,323	18,307	411,541
Connecticut	Stone, sand and gravel, feldspar, lime	62,691	.25	—	—	—	—	—	—
Delaware	Magnesium compounds, sand and gravel	2,800	.01	—	—	—	—	—	—
Florida	Phosphate rock, stone, cement, clays	1,725,589	6.85	25,626	810,550	22,515	55,420	—	—
Georgia	Clays, stone, cement, sand and gravel	804,455	3.20	—	—	—	—	—	—
Hawaii	Stone, cement, sand and gravel, lime	58,727	.23	—	—	—	—	—	—
Idaho	Silver, phosphate rock, zinc, lead	430,748	1.71	—	—	—	—	—	—
Illinois	Stone, sand and gravel, cement, lime	428,316	1.70	27,710	878,130	1,162	3,043	60,259	1,737,870
Indiana	Stone, cement, sand and gravel, lime	258,832	1.03	5,563	176,125	233	360	31,722	783,216
Iowa	Cement, stone, sand and gravel, gypsum	232,311	.92	—	—	—	—	564	12,301
Kansas	Cement, salt, stone, helium	249,060	.99	70,525	2,171,465	429,597	647,137	1,401	37,281
Kentucky	Stone, lime, cement, sand and gravel	207,759	.83	7,349	232,449	51,924	78,830	147,930	4,502,989
Louisiana	Sulfur, salt, sand and gravel, cement	573,959	2.28	458,395	14,911,589	6,171,627	16,033,702	—	—
Maine	Cement, sand and gravel, stone, gem stones	38,369	.15	—	—	—	—	—	—
Maryland	Stone, cement, sand and gravel, clays	178,655	.71	—	—	36	28	3,764	122,142
Massachusetts	Stone, sand and gravel, lime, clays	97,037	.39	—	—	—	—	—	—
Michigan	Iron ore, cement, magnesium compounds, salt	1,438,355	5.71	31,462	995,143	153,051	488,233	—	—
Minnesota	Iron ore, sand and gravel, stone, lime	2,151,871	8.55	—	—	—	—	—	—
Mississippi	Cement, sand and gravel, clays, stone	91,791	.36	33,047	960,015	167,231	653,873	—	—
Missouri	Lead, cement, stone, lime	870,326	3.46	202	6,313	—	—	5,336	137,028
Montana	Copper, cement, silver, gold	305,071	1.21	30,921	965,972	56,517	121,251	27,882	378,359
Nebraska	Cement, sand and gravel, stone, lime	73,995	.29	6,872	212,826	2,280	4,536	—	—
Nevada	Gold, barite, silver, diatomite	503,649	2.00	613	19,389	—	—	—	—
New Hampshire	Sand and gravel, stone, clays, gem stones	25,510	.10	—	—	—	—	—	—
New Jersey	Stone, sand and gravel, zinc, titanium concentrate	142,012	.56	—	—	—	—	—	—
New Mexico	Copper, potassium salts, gold, cement	694,677	2.76	71,024	2,261,404	991,178	2,443,891	19,940	382,649
New York	Stone, cement, salt, sand and gravel	491,971	1.95	834	26,379	15,877	59,500	—	—
North Carolina	Phosphate rock, stone, sand and gravel, cement	376,530	1.50	—	—	—	—	—	—
North Dakota	Sand and gravel, salt, lime, clays	22,445	.09	47,271	1,507,472	53,818	123,781	17,848	163,131
Ohio	Stone, lime, sand and gravel, salt	554,190	2.20	14,571	450,244	138,391	375,588	36,337	1,167,508
Oklahoma	Cement, stone, sand and gravel, iodine	236,612	.94	158,621	5,082,217	1,934,412	5,300,088	4,770	155,216
Oregon	Stone, sand and gravel, cement, nickel	146,847	.58	—	—	3	10	—	—
Pennsylvania	Cement, stone, lime, sand and gravel	633,056	2.51	4,282	135,440	121,111	339,110	78,279	2,638,785
Rhode Island	Sand and gravel, stone, gem stones	5,279	.02	—	—	—	—	—	—
South Carolina	Cement, stone, clays, sand and gravel	205,476	.82	—	—	—	—	—	—
South Dakota	Gold, stone, cement, sand and gravel	193,374	.77	1,158	36,628	2,331	7,181	—	—
Tennessee	Zinc, stone, pyrites, cement	417,618	1.66	1,132	35,805	2,976	8,928	7,287	214,894
Texas	Cement, sulfur, stone, sand and gravel	1,658,203	6.59	925,296	29,433,666	6,468,817	14,047,213	34,818	352,706
Utah	Copper, gold, molybdenum, potassium salts	783,232	3.11	23,453	714,847	94,255	288,761	17,029	500,993
Vermont	Stone, asbestos, sand and gravel, talc	51,019	.20	—	—	—	—	—	—
Virginia	Stone, cement, lime, sand and gravel	282,533	1.12	49	1,550	6,880	25,363	39,068	1,350,581
Washington	Cement, sand and gravel, stone, lime	212,478	.84	—	—	—	—	4,161	...
West Virginia	Sand and gravel, stone, cement, salt	96,447	.38	3,227	102,070	150,850	482,720	127,889	4,824,350
Wisconsin	Sand and gravel, stone, iron ore, lime	156,333	.62	—	—	—	—	—	—
Wyoming	Sodium carbonate, clays, iron ore, cement	770,338	3.06	118,300	3,467,373	424,657	1,368,858	108,360	1,381,590
TOTAL U.S.		$25,173,000	100.00	3,157,215	$90,043,772	18,519,675	$45,496,765	832,524	$22,686,279

Total values based on U.S. average values. [1]Excludes nonhydrocarbon gases.
Sources: U.S. Department of the Interior, *Minerals Yearbook*; Department of Energy, various petroleum, gas, and coal reports.

Services

Kind of service	Number of services 1980	Number of services 1981	Number of employees[1] 1980	Number of employees[1] 1981
Hotels and other lodging places	41,418	41,264	1,085,973	1,097,920
Hotels, tourist courts, and motels	32,102	31,963	1,034,352	1,045,451
Rooming and boarding houses	1,914	1,856	13,425	12,573
Camps and trailering parks	3,575	3,511	16,600	16,704
Sporting and recreational camps	1,949	1,870	10,147	9,727
Personal services	152,322	152,734	953,081	953,112
Laundry, cleaning, garment services	40,237	39,720	358,812	352,747
Photographic studios, portrait	6,171	6,308	41,376	43,639
Beauty shops	65,669	65,184	285,439	279,640
Barber shops	8,864	8,379	25,853	24,387
Shoe repair and hat cleaning shops	2,515	2,541	6,937	7,249
Funeral service and crematories	13,974	13,808	70,652	72,477
Miscellaneous personal services	14,028	15,173	161,214	167,220
Business services	161,446	174,413	2,955,907	3,092,626
Advertising	10,645	11,301	139,726	144,710
Credit reporting and collection	5,579	5,479	64,826	65,103
Mailing, reproduction, stenographic	14,554	15,156	135,509	138,679
Building services	23,376	24,129	496,916	496,039
Employment agencies	7,991	8,462	109,085	117,105
Temporary help supply services	5,178	5,393	416,071	401,361
Computer and data processing services	13,610	15,052	303,317	323,964
Research and development laboratories	2,300	2,510	99,317	103,318
Management and public relations	27,225	29,051	324,582	357,261
Detective and protective services	6,752	7,126	337,619	331,294
Equipment rental and leasing	12,149	12,708	114,534	122,428
Photofinishing laboratories	2,672	2,835	75,353	76,580
Auto repair, services, and garages	99,514	102,160	559,891	555,352
Automobile rentals, without drivers	8,694	8,695	100,832	103,036
Automobile parking	7,013	6,885	35,309	35,369
Automotive repair shops	75,082	76,961	358,779	352,400
Automotive services, except repair	7,914	8,117	62,323	59,315
Car washes	4,960	4,861	42,498	40,006
Miscellaneous repair services	48,021	48,974	318,982	322,897
Radio and television repair	7,156	6,837	36,759	34,578
Motion pictures	14,941	15,010	207,755	205,657
Motion picture production	4,139	4,724	82,867	83,250
Motion picture distribution	1,157	1,090	15,172	15,867
Motion picture theatres	9,467	9,160	109,192	106,406

Kind of service	Number of services 1980	Number of services 1981	Number of employees[1] 1980	Number of employees[1] 1981
Amusement and recreation services	45,499	46,798	706,288	714,903
Producers, orchestras, entertainers	5,893	5,901	96,081	97,607
Bowling and billiard establishments	7,180	6,959	114,486	112,971
Racing, including track operation	1,529	1,500	40,981	40,206
Public golf courses	2,436	2,390	17,881	18,551
Amusement parks	502	543	44,527	42,783
Membership sports, recreation clubs	9,517	9,346	172,041	173,662
Health services	310,843	327,445	5,258,027	5,538,149
Physicians' offices	147,247	155,854	741,855	781,985
Dentists' offices	85,691	88,544	350,827	369,669
Osteopathic physicians' offices	5,527	5,809	24,011	24,994
Chiropractors' offices	8,861	10,151	22,131	25,562
Optometrists' offices	12,498	12,876	37,836	39,318
Nursing and personal care facilities	12,801	13,123	1,002,037	1,033,092
Hospitals	5,261	5,294	2,672,700	2,805,292
Medical and dental laboratories	10,849	11,176	98,148	102,264
Outpatient care facilities	8,611	8,966	164,734	180,605
Legal services	97,335	102,926	503,474	545,157
Educational services	23,323	23,756	1,245,564	1,303,522
Elementary and secondary schools	11,332	11,268	302,747	311,986
Colleges and universities	2,433	2,443	819,625	864,746
Libraries and information centres	1,315	1,301	12,893	12,352
Correspondence and vocational schools	2,753	2,758	46,656	48,964
Social services	60,561	61,438	1,023,841	1,048,899
Residential care	9,948	10,136	214,443	226,454
Museums, botanical, zoological gardens	1,496	1,478	28,231	28,857
Membership organizations	130,668	129,315	1,214,158	1,227,559
Business associations	11,097	10,965	78,575	80,075
Professional organizations	4,524	4,435	39,778	40,422
Labour organizations	20,753	20,229	171,815	163,570
Civic and social organizations	30,541	30,151	279,466	282,003
Political organizations	1,147	912	6,287	4,441
Religious organizations	55,998	55,940	573,087	590,345
Miscellaneous services	85,540	100,257	925,470	1,004,093
Engineering, architectural services	37,456	39,779	523,539	546,692
Noncommercial research organizations	2,023	1,971	73,576	75,516
Accounting, auditing and bookkeeping	40,774	43,115	301,940	321,988
TOTAL[2]	1,278,185	1,333,297	17,195,327	17,814,081

[1]Mid-March pay period. [2]Includes other services not shown separately.
Source: U.S. Department of Commerce, Bureau of the Census, *County Business Patterns 1980* and *1981*.

Principal Manufactures, 1981

monetary figures in millions of dollars

Industry	Employees (000)	Cost of labour[1]	Cost of materials	Value of shipments	Value added by mfg.
Food and kindred products	1,511	$24,696	$191,595	$272,140	$80,795
Meat products	317	4,861	55,744	65,909	10,159
Dairy products	147	2,463	29,125	36,942	7,908
Preserved fruits and vegetables	228	3,088	17,226	27,720	10,598
Grain mill products	109	2,095	22,012	31,915	9,852
Beverages	199	3,940	21,305	36,075	14,855
Tobacco products	61	1,219	6,691	13,130	6,430
Textile mill products	785	9,574	31,061	50,262	19,463
Apparel and other textile products	1,251	11,805	24,657	49,823	25,640
Lumber and wood products	649	8,991	29,473	46,807	17,321
Furniture and fixtures	460	5,983	11,426	23,865	12,669
Paper and allied products	636	12,644	48,313	80,234	32,367
Printing and publishing	1,270	20,609	28,131	77,261	49,352
Chemicals and allied products	892	19,723	102,329	180,459	80,032
Industrial chemicals	114	2,707	8,843	17,945	9,274
Plastics materials and synthetics	147	3,354	20,793	30,697	10,211
Drugs	170	3,715	7,550	22,316	14,879
Soap, cleaners, and toilet goods	122	2,320	10,914	24,599	13,881
Paints, allied products	60	1,167	5,351	9,144	3,867
Agricultural chemicals	56	1,156	10,376	16,336	6,217
Petroleum and coal products	152	4,076	197,898	224,131	26,740
Rubber, misc. plastics products	691	11,047	27,750	53,173	26,006
Leather and leather products	228	2,363	5,344	10,468	5,230
Stone, clay, and glass products	590	10,575	23,549	48,004	24,854
Primary metal industries	1,063	25,322	94,307	141,942	49,551
Blast furnace, basic steel products	477	13,364	46,229	70,125	24,663
Iron, steel foundries	208	4,031	6,090	12,947	6,901
Primary nonferrous metals	58	1,554	11,963	15,217	3,944
Nonferrous drawing and rolling	181	3,813	22,149	30,685	8,898
Nonferrous foundries	84	1,482	2,515	5,256	2,742
Fabricated metal products	1,568	28,531	62,601	123,662	61,558
Ordnance and accessories	80	1,617	1,508	4,506	3,083
Machinery, except electrical	2,380	$48,643	$92,277	$201,539	$111,394
Engines and turbines	126	3,087	7,948	15,281	7,382
Farm and garden machinery	143	2,932	8,733	15,954	7,053
Construction and related mach.	361	8,116	19,229	39,029	20,749
Metalworking machinery	342	7,006	8,140	22,344	14,466
Special industry machinery	195	3,748	5,871	13,266	7,460
Refrigeration and service mach.	192	3,466	8,965	17,131	8,291
General industrial machinery	334	6,707	11,319	25,691	14,643
Office, computing machines	388	8,235	17,143	37,839	21,174
Electric and electronic equipment	1,959	35,989	62,412	140,194	79,720
Electric distributing equip.	117	2,031	3,600	8,344	4,827
Electrical industrial apparatus	210	3,819	6,766	15,056	8,559
Household appliances	148	2,344	7,344	13,108	5,926
Electric lighting, wiring equip.	175	2,770	5,509	12,075	6,649
Radio, TV receiving equipment	79	1,323	5,162	8,782	3,728
Communication equipment	574	12,223	16,149	40,322	24,984
Electronic components, access.	504	8,664	12,159	30,421	18,537
Transportation equipment	1,749	42,336	123,699	205,222	82,938
Motor vehicles and equipment	696	17,028	81,827	116,981	34,841
Aircraft and parts	581	14,770	26,106	52,482	28,144
Ship, boat building, repairing	220	4,329	5,913	13,249	7,361
Railroad equipment	49	1,094	2,953	5,420	2,302
Guided missiles, space vehicles	152	4,228	4,034	12,355	8,211
Instruments and related products	612	11,565	17,284	48,291	31,494
Measuring, controlling devices	227	4,210	4,472	13,511	9,180
Medical instruments and supplies	137	2,183	3,586	9,206	5,699
Photographic equipment and supplies	114	2,888	5,902	16,927	11,199
Miscellaneous manufacturing industries	413	5,630	13,172	26,940	13,954
All establishments, including administrative and auxiliary	20,264	379,214	1,193,970	2,017,543	873,507

[1] Payroll only. Source: U.S. Department of Commerce, *1981 Annual Survey of Manufactures, Statistics for Industry Groups and Industries.*

Business Activity

Category of activity	WHOLESALING 1965	1970	1975	1980	RETAILING 1965	1970	1975	1980	SERVICES 1965	1970	1975	1980
Number of businesses (in 000)												
Sole proprietorships	265	274	336	330	1,554	1,689	1,765	2,066	2,208	2,507	3,034	3,843
Active partnerships	32	30	31	32	202	170	162	168	169	176	199	263
Active corporations	147	166	220	281	288	351	395	515	188	281	436	671
Business receipts (in $000,000)												
Sole proprietorships	17,934	21,556	33,339	42,654	77,760	89,315	112,453	153,815	29,789	40,869	55,997	87,965
Active partnerships	10,879	11,325	16,009	28,426	23,244	23,546	29,133	37,307	12,442	18,791	30,167	58,627
Active corporations	171,414	234,885	501,988	1,104,360	183,925	274,808	449,269	813,019	36,547	66,460	125,747	266,089
Net profit (less loss; in $000,000)												
Sole proprietorships	1,483	1,806	2,861	3,127	5,019	5,767	6,725	5,688	11,008	15,063	18,385	26,433
Active partnerships	548	557	820	913	1,654	1,603	1,836	1,558	4,402	6,189	7,224	12,424
Active corporations	3,288	4,441	13,929	26,716	4,052	5,217	8,552	11,548	1,505	1,199	3,397	8,194

Data refer to accounting periods ending between July 1 of year shown and June 30 of following year.
Sources: U.S. Department of the Treasury, Internal Revenue Service, *Statistics of Income: Business Income Tax Returns, Corporation Income Tax Returns, Partnership Returns*, and *Sole Proprietorship Returns.*

Retail Sales

in millions of dollars

Kind of business	1970	1975	1980	1982
Durable goods[1]	109,195	182,966	292,811	320,868
Automotive dealers	62,576	106,616	158,276	182,390
Motor vehicles, misc. automotive dealers	56,939	96,762	140,662	161,481
Auto, home supply stores	5,637	9,854	17,614	20,909
Furniture, home furnishings, equipment stores	17,688	26,921	44,939	46,513
Furniture, home furnishings stores	10,578	16,187	26,344	26,673
Household appliance, radio, TV stores	6,029	8,316	14,648	15,817
Building materials, hardware, garden supply, mobile home dealers	17,561	27,033	50,443	48,975
Building materials, supply stores	11,244	17,938	35,148	34,181
Hardware stores	3,178	5,057	8,535	8,363
Nondurable goods[1]	259,208	405,180	670,005	754,811
Apparel, accessory stores	20,194	31,315	46,188	51,991
Men's and boys' clothing, furnishings stores	4,371	6,355	7,813	8,110
Women's clothing, specialty stores	7,748	12,374	17,184	19,288
Family clothing stores	3,763	6,647	9,796	10,830
Shoe stores	3,630	4,633	8,307	9,854
Drug and proprietary stores	13,839	19,872	30,613	35,849
Eating and drinking places	31,065	51,067	90,367	107,357
Food stores	88,675	138,371	222,687	252,802
Grocery stores	81,516	129,182	207,775	236,489
Bakeries	1,608	1,892	3,502	3,860
Gasoline service stations	29,181	47,547	97,434	104,633
General merchandise group stores	50,251	78,043	115,733	131,282
Department stores and misc. general merchandise stores	43,646	70,018	107,553	122,547
Variety stores	6,605	8,025	8,180	8,735
Liquor stores	8,312	11,809	17,507	19,031
TOTAL	368,403	588,146	962,816	1,075,679

[1] Includes some kinds of business not shown separately.
Source: U.S. Department of Commerce, Bureau of the Census, *Revised Monthly Retail Sales and Inventories.*

Sales of Merchant Wholesalers

in millions of dollars

Kind of business	1970	1975	1980	1982
Durable goods[1]	127,214	229,527	438,439	457,713
Motor vehicles, automotive equipment	21,401	39,681	81,629	87,662
Electrical goods	14,963	22,747	46,436	54,574
Furniture, home furnishings	5,524	8,265	15,580	15,995
Hardware, plumbing, heating equipment	10,489	15,200	27,623	26,844
Lumber, construction supplies	11,550	17,261	33,245	...
Machinery, equipment, supplies	33,836	69,153	129,048	135,267
Scrap, waste materials	6,151	8,736	16,327	...
Nondurable goods[1]	160,096	329,945	605,447	686,639
Groceries and related products	54,405	95,754	149,889	179,845
Beer, wine, distilled alcoholic beverages	13,103	19,370	31,697	36,091
Drugs, chemicals, allied products	5,633	8,750	13,051	...
Tobacco, tobacco products	6,330	9,067	10,998	...
Dry goods, apparel	10,206	14,702	25,790	...
Paper, paper products	7,416	11,215	21,643	22,776
Farm products	24,842	83,264	120,224	...
Other nondurable goods	19,550	34,584	58,941	81,723
TOTAL	287,310	559,472	1,043,886	1,144,352

[1] Includes some kinds of business not shown separately.
Source: U.S. Dept. of Commerce, Bureau of the Census, Current Business Reports, *Revised Monthly Wholesale Trade.*

Commercial Banks[1]

December 31, 1982

State	Number of banks	Total assets or liabilities $000,000	SELECTED ASSETS ($000,000) Loans	Investments[2]	Reserves, cash, and bank balances	SELECTED LIABILITIES ($000,000) Deposits Total[3]	Demand	Time, savings	Capital accounts
Ala.	294	20,427	9,159	6,208	2,588	16,632	4,366	12,104	1,692
Alaska	14	3,374	1,610	926	500	2,670	943	1,727	308
Ariz.	30	16,657	10,135	2,845	2,340	13,437	3,664	9,735	1,038
Ark.	260	13,619	3,170	3,806	1,109	11,317	2,653	8,664	1,126
Calif.	360	275,446	172,246	22,624	39,875	218,788	40,548	124,728	12,620
Colo.	373	20,285	11,426	3,295	2,873	16,419	5,433	10,749	1,508
Conn.	53	15,551	8,762	2,614	2,758	12,576	4,451	7,807	933
Del.	27	7,759	4,723	1,472	971	5,285	840	4,127	914
D.C.	17	10,577	5,086	1,752	2,590	8,553	2,273	4,266	639
Fla.	477	59,845	26,983	15,638	9,148	49,623	14,256	34,904	4,109
Ga.	416	30,363	14,448	7,024	4,281	23,430	7,690	15,377	2,249
Hawaii	10	6,702	3,907	1,144	1,045	6,020	1,405	4,040	411
Idaho	27	5,884	3,433	1,208	752	4,815	972	3,843	400
Ill.	1,250	158,088	91,807	28,375	22,799	124,168	22,724	69,113	9,409
Ind.	400	36,529	17,930	9,700	4,583	30,102	6,053	23,793	2,663
Iowa	643	25,488	11,975	8,162	2,235	21,523	3,864	17,609	2,064
Kan.	620	19,619	9,443	5,971	1,622	16,549	3,713	12,836	1,645
Ky.	342	23,576	11,144	6,534	2,292	18,998	4,749	14,150	1,894
La.	278	30,894	15,245	8,635	3,371	25,921	7,316	18,556	2,492
Maine	35	3,890	1,990	1,071	427	3,215	786	2,429	283
Md.	91	20,179	9,612	4,471	3,419	15,667	4,538	10,327	1,328
Mass.	136	44,688	22,235	7,606	9,036	33,054	8,779	16,782	1,618
Mich.	374	58,949	30,068	11,777	11,674	48,204	8,943	37,077	3,854
Minn.	759	38,821	21,116	8,548	4,990	30,028	6,785	21,220	2,724
Miss.	167	13,695	6,567	4,279	1,377	11,571	2,610	8,922	1,033
Mo.	732	41,483	19,304	10,270	5,337	31,947	8,945	22,530	2,950
Mont.	166	6,207	3,449	1,572	644	5,291	1,098	4,193	497
Neb.	461	13,965	7,012	3,470	1,402	11,429	2,857	8,572	1,153
Nev.	13	4,584	2,323	756	1,057	3,933	1,196	2,738	349
N.H.	71	3,986	2,351	821	457	3,459	694	2,766	294
N.J.	148	42,228	20,906	10,573	6,164	35,045	10,189	24,368	2,728
N.M.	92	7,766	3,857	1,898	922	6,629	1,559	5,070	574
N.Y.	205	520,011	301,196	50,564	94,554	368,847	64,582	127,044	26,055
N.C.	69	32,452	15,541	7,453	4,854	24,446	5,886	15,961	2,034
N.D.	176	5,784	2,902	1,795	483	5,040	927	4,113	478
Ohio	355	63,381	30,236	15,212	9,861	48,472	10,715	36,840	4,859
Okla.	509	29,636	15,752	7,300	2,899	25,158	6,231	18,809	2,246
Ore.	88	14,215	8,060	2,225	1,868	11,528	2,545	8,948	995
Pa.	340	105,812	51,843	25,076	17,257	80,203	16,461	56,883	7,260
R.I.	15	8,416	4,712	1,088	1,548	6,559	1,181	4,693	474
S.C.	78	10,267	4,361	3,058	1,288	8,301	2,641	5,659	760
S.D.	152	8,783	5,905	1,748	542	6,703	859	5,844	767
Tenn.	346	28,292	14,056	6,685	3,737	23,012	5,331	17,562	2,025
Texas	1,598	163,424	87,291	32,619	24,753	131,092	34,552	85,742	11,239
Utah	61	8,230	4,373	1,256	1,515	6,768	1,666	4,864	589
Vt.	27	2,870	1,872	528	205	2,547	457	2,090	210
Va.	202	30,212	16,654	6,386	3,920	24,717	5,827	18,517	2,054
Wash.	100	26,334	16,395	3,296	2,926	21,632	4,897	14,725	1,617
W.Va.	241	11,951	5,223	4,187	943	9,943	1,857	8,086	1,033
Wis.	624	30,450	16,221	7,850	3,028	24,732	5,337	19,003	2,321
Wyo.	111	4,108	2,123	1,076	393	3,588	852	2,736	368
TOTAL	14,433	2,185,752	1,188,218	384,447	331,212	1,699,586	369,696	1,023,241	134,883

[1] Excludes noninsured banks.
[2] Excludes federal funds sold and securities purchased.
[3] Includes deposits in foreign offices not shown separately.
Source: Federal Deposit Insurance Corporation, *1982 Bank Operating Statistics.*

Life Insurance, 1982

Number of policies in 000s; value in $000,000

State	Total: Number of policies	Total: Value	Ordinary: Number of policies	Ordinary: Value	Group: Number of certificates	Group: Value	Industrial: Number of policies	Industrial: Value	Credit[1]: Number of policies	Credit[1]: Value
Ala.	11,855	$70,526	2,430	$35,934	1,882	$28,781	6,097	$2,431	1,446	$3,380
Alaska	670	9,979	151	4,313	344	5,401	9	3	166	262
Ariz.	3,972	48,522	1,348	26,879	1,514	19,278	161	119	949	2,246
Ark.	2,643	30,796	1,044	16,876	796	12,439	339	186	464	1,295
Calif.	29,645	458,021	10,715	233,517	12,399	212,409	1,556	1,142	4,975	10,953
Colo.	4,838	70,048	1,821	36,952	1,897	30,488	220	153	900	2,455
Conn.	5,740	78,044	2,275	35,906	2,405	40,087	211	194	849	1,857
Del.	1,442	16,311	486	6,253	425	9,056	180	127	351	875
D.C.	2,549	33,292	413	6,408	1,342	26,156	521	315	273	413
Fla.	16,338	169,426	6,093	94,858	4,095	65,441	2,994	2,020	3,156	7,107
Ga.	12,410	112,075	4,065	57,645	2,810	47,692	3,214	2,008	2,321	4,730
Hawaii	1,833	23,713	623	12,810	848	9,963	4	2	358	938
Idaho	1,371	15,854	506	8,841	550	6,105	21	14	294	894
Ill.	21,114	246,667	8,957	122,154	7,047	116,108	2,411	1,767	2,699	6,638
Ind.	9,776	104,461	4,091	51,695	2,847	47,947	1,288	872	1,550	3,947
Iowa	4,855	59,643	2,541	34,234	1,461	23,265	182	119	671	2,025
Kan.	4,159	50,163	1,944	29,098	1,293	19,120	257	165	665	1,780
Ky.	6,119	55,270	2,404	27,374	1,539	24,705	1,130	630	1,046	2,561
La.	10,068	84,746	2,476	45,901	2,175	32,445	3,618	2,204	1,799	4,196
Maine	1,762	16,744	701	8,469	676	7,499	57	47	328	729
Md.	7,795	88,573	2,997	43,092	2,212	41,934	1,527	921	1,059	2,626
Mass.	8,472	109,999	3,749	51,057	2,854	55,769	551	425	1,318	2,748
Mich.	16,291	187,679	5,308	70,677	6,210	109,778	1,515	1,036	3,258	6,188
Minn.	6,596	89,494	2,497	41,897	2,969	44,795	192	139	938	2,663
Miss.	3,891	36,635	1,057	18,991	1,057	14,972	606	356	1,171	2,316
Mo.	8,698	95,592	3,728	46,462	2,777	45,424	966	632	1,227	3,074
Mont.	1,130	13,244	436	7,695	446	4,903	20	12	228	634
Neb.	2,768	34,891	1,398	21,156	811	12,405	97	62	462	1,268
Nev.	1,499	17,329	310	7,055	533	7,560	8	6	648	2,708
N.H.	1,601	18,138	691	9,274	530	8,009	71	61	309	794
N.J.	11,712	168,121	5,137	76,689	4,064	86,672	1,158	1,049	1,353	3,711
N.M.	1,750	22,486	644	11,170	616	10,142	71	46	419	1,128
N.Y.	25,197	341,700	10,496	155,506	8,568	173,949	1,455	1,177	4,678	11,068
N.C.	12,491	105,054	4,491	53,559	2,843	45,256	2,709	1,447	2,448	4,792
N.D.	1,058	14,557	465	8,379	378	5,346	3	3	212	829
Ohio	19,069	214,764	8,018	105,587	5,900	100,095	2,532	1,778	2,619	7,304
Okla.	5,109	60,808	1,803	32,956	1,429	23,902	316	194	1,561	3,756
Ore.	3,138	45,431	1,153	21,848	1,363	22,038	66	45	556	1,500
Pa.	22,668	223,936	9,692	108,996	6,144	103,791	3,516	2,477	3,316	8,672
R.I.	1,938	19,185	759	9,689	758	8,837	122	91	299	568
S.C.	7,659	54,634	2,682	27,974	1,714	22,852	2,096	1,263	1,167	2,545
S.D.	996	12,661	519	7,976	298	4,108	4	3	175	574
Tenn.	9,318	86,316	2,912	41,154	2,836	40,132	1,967	1,105	1,603	3,925
Texas	25,170	314,767	9,100	167,524	7,894	131,761	2,891	1,846	5,285	13,636
Utah	2,148	26,359	674	15,078	966	9,998	72	40	436	1,243
Vt.	766	8,510	356	4,591	239	3,529	26	22	145	368
Va.	10,532	111,201	3,567	52,164	2,945	53,103	2,144	1,310	1,876	4,624
Wash.	5,328	75,064	1,917	37,840	2,349	35,067	129	81	933	2,076
W.Va.	3,249	28,706	1,111	12,649	916	14,187	500	330	722	1,540
Wis.	7,692	87,047	3,320	46,383	3,062	37,779	372	288	938	2,597
Wyo.	672	9,477	276	5,203	253	3,883	4	3	139	388
TOTAL	389,560	$4,476,659	146,347	$2,216,388	124,279	$2,066,361	52,176	$32,766	66,758	$161,144

[1] Life insurance on loans of ten years' or less duration.
Source: American Council of Life Insurance, *Life Insurance Fact Book, 1983.*

Savings and Loan Associations

Dec. 31, 1982[1]

State	Number of assns.	Total assets ($000,000)	Per capita assets
Alabama	38	$5,229	$1,326
Alaska	5	408	932
Arizona	10	8,730	3,052
Arkansas	48	5,180	2,261
California	171	152,907	6,185
Colorado	43	9,687	3,181
Connecticut	38	7,609	2,413
Delaware	15	262	435
District of Columbia	8	3,598	5,702
Florida	116	55,673	5,345
Georgia	71	11,822	2,096
Guam	2	75	667
Hawaii	8	4,676	4,704
Idaho	9	1,179	1,222
Illinois	295	48,394	4,227
Indiana	131	10,760	1,967
Iowa	60	7,692	2,648
Kansas	71	8,206	3,408
Kentucky	79	6,381	1,740
Louisiana	119	10,217	2,342
Maine	17	678	598
Maryland	159	12,693	2,976
Massachusetts	133	8,014	1,386
Michigan	53	23,506	2,581
Minnesota	40	11,005	2,663
Mississippi	51	3,005	1,178
Missouri	96	16,765	3,386
Montana	12	1,124	1,403
Nebraska	27	5,872	3,702
Nevada	7	2,696	3,060
New Hampshire	13	1,272	1,338
New Jersey	170	31,005	4,169
New Mexico	28	3,096	2,278
New York	89	23,808	1,348
North Carolina	157	13,200	2,193
North Dakota	7	2,688	4,012
Ohio	325	43,037	3,988
Oklahoma	55	7,168	2,256
Oregon	22	7,704	2,908
Pennsylvania	288	26,422	2,227
Puerto Rico	11	2,983	904
Rhode Island	4	879	917
South Carolina	45	7,056	2,203
South Dakota	18	1,190	1,722
Tennessee	81	7,933	1,706
Texas	288	44,515	2,913
Utah	15	5,019	3,230
Vermont	5	273	528
Virginia	75	12,969	2,362
Washington	45	11,240	2,648
West Virginia	25	1,835	942
Wisconsin	88	13,108	2,751
Wyoming	12	1,067	2,126
TOTAL U.S.	3,833	$706,045	$3,034

[1] Preliminary. Components do not add to totals because of differences in reporting dates and accounting systems.
Source: U.S. League of Savings Institutions, *'83 Savings and Loan Sourcebook.*

GOVERNMENT AND POLITICS

The National Executive

December 21, 1983

Department, bureau, or office	Executive official and official title
PRESIDENT OF THE UNITED STATES	Ronald Reagan
Vice-President	George Bush
EXECUTIVE OFFICE OF THE PRESIDENT	
Assistant to the President	James A. Baker III, chief of staff
	Richard G. Darman
	Michael K. Deaver
	Craig L. Fuller
	John S. Herrington
	Edward V. Hickey, Jr.
	Robert C. McFarlane (acting)
	M. B. Oglesby, Jr.
	John F. W. Rogers
	Edward J. Rollins
	Larry M. Speakes
	John A. Svahn
	Lee Verstandig
	Faith Ryan Whittlesey
Press Secretary to the President	James Scott Brady
Counsel to the President	Fred F. Fielding
Counselor to the President	Edwin Meese III
Special Assistant to the President	Richard Smith Beal
Office of Management and Budget	David A. Stockman, director
Council of Economic Advisers	Martin S. Feldstein, chairman
National Security Council	[1]
Central Intelligence Agency	William J. Casey, director
Office of Policy Development	Roger B. Porter, director
Office of the United States Trade Representative	William E. Brock, trade representative
Council on Environmental Quality	A. Alan Hill, chairman
Office of Science and Technology Policy	George A. Keyworth II, director
Office of Administration	John F. W. Rogers, director
DEPARTMENT OF STATE	George P. Shultz, secretary
	Kenneth W. Dam, deputy secretary
Foreign Service	Alfred L. Atherton, Jr., director general
Permanent Mission to the Organization of American States	J. William Middendorf II, permanent representative
Mission to the United Nations	Jeane J. Kirkpatrick, representative
African Affairs	Chester A. Crocker, asst. secretary
East Asian and Pacific Affairs	Paul D. Wolfowitz, asst. secretary
European Affairs	Richard Burt, asst. secretary
Inter-American Affairs	Langhorne A. Motley, asst. secretary
Near Eastern and South Asian Affairs	Nicholas A. Veliotes, asst. secretary
Oceans and International Environmental and Scientific Affairs	James L. Malone, asst. secretary
Consular Affairs	Joan M. Clark, asst. secretary
International Narcotics Matters	Dominick L. DiCarlo, asst. secretary
DEPARTMENT OF THE TREASURY	Donald T. Regan, secretary
	R. T. McNamar, deputy secretary
Office of the Comptroller of the Currency	C. T. Conover, comptroller
Internal Revenue Service	Roscoe L. Egger, Jr., commissioner
Bureau of Government Financial Operations	W. E. Douglas, commissioner
Bureau of the Public Debt	W. M. Gregg, commissioner
Bureau of Alcohol, Tobacco and Firearms	Stephen E. Higgins, director
U.S. Customs Service	William von Raab, commissioner
U.S. Secret Service	John R. Simpson, director
Office of the Treasurer	Katherine D. Ortega, treasurer
U.S. Savings Bonds Division	Katherine D. Ortega, national director
Bureau of the Mint	Donna Pope, director
Bureau of Engraving and Printing	Robert J. Leuver, director
DEPARTMENT OF DEFENSE	Caspar W. Weinberger, secretary
	W. Paul Thayer, deputy secretary
Joint Chiefs of Staff	Gen. John W. Vessey, USA, chairman
Chief of Staff, Air Force	Gen. Charles A. Gabriel, USAF
Chief of Staff, Army	Gen. John A. Wickham, Jr., USA
Chief of Naval Operations	Adm. James D. Watkins, USN
Commandant of the Marine Corps	Gen. P. X. Kelley, USMC
Department of the Air Force	Verne Orr, secretary
Department of the Army	John O. Marsh, Jr., secretary
Department of the Navy	John F. Lehman, Jr., secretary
DEPARTMENT OF JUSTICE	
Attorney General	William French Smith
Solicitor General	Rex E. Lee
Antitrust Division	William F. Baxter, asst. attorney general
Civil Rights Division	William Bradford Reynolds, asst. attorney general
Criminal Division	Stephen S. Trott, asst. attorney general
Federal Bureau of Investigation	William H. Webster, director
Bureau of Prisons	Norman A. Carlson, director
Immigration and Naturalization Service	Alan C. Nelson, commissioner
Drug Enforcement Administration	Francis M. Mullen, Jr., administrator (acting)
U.S. Marshals Service	William E. Hall, director
DEPARTMENT OF THE INTERIOR	William P. Clark, secretary
	Ann Dore McLaughlin, under secretary (designate)
Territorial and International Affairs	Richard Montoya, asst. secretary
Fish and Wildlife and Parks	G. Ray Arnett, asst. secretary
National Park Service	Russell E. Dickenson, director
U.S. Fish and Wildlife Service	Robert A. Jantzen, director
Land and Minerals Management	Garrey E. Carruthers, asst. secretary
Bureau of Land Management	Robert F. Burford, director
Minerals Management Service	William D. Bettenberg, director
Office of Surface Mining Reclamation and Enforcement	James R. Harris, director
Water and Science	Robert N. Broadbent, asst. secretary
Bureau of Reclamation	Robert A. Olson, commissioner (acting)

Department, bureau, or office	Executive official and official title
U.S. Geological Survey	Dallas L. Peck, director
Bureau of Mines	Robert C. Horton, director
Indian Affairs	Kenneth L. Smith, asst. secretary
DEPARTMENT OF AGRICULTURE	John R. Block, secretary
	Richard E. Lyng, deputy secretary
International Affairs and Commodity Programs	Daniel G. Amstutz, under secretary
Small Community and Rural Development	Frank W. Naylor, Jr., under secretary
Farmers Home Administration	Charles W. Shuman, administrator
Rural Electrification Administration	Harold V. Hunter, administrator
Federal Crop Insurance Corporation	Merritt Sprague, manager
Marketing and Inspection Services	C. W. McMillan, asst. secretary
Food and Consumer Services	Mary C. Jarratt, asst. secretary
Natural Resources and Environment	John B. Crowell, Jr., asst. secretary
Forest Service	R. Max Peterson, chief
Soil Conservation Service	Peter C. Myers, chief
Economics	William G. Lesher, asst. secretary
Office of Energy	Earle E. Gavett, director
World Agricultural Outlook Board	James R. Donald, chairperson
Science and Education	Orville G. Bentley, asst. secretary
DEPARTMENT OF COMMERCE	Malcolm Baldrige, secretary
	Clarence J. Brown, deputy secretary
International Trade Administration	Lionel Olmer, under secretary
Economic Development Administration	Carlos C. Campbell, asst. secretary
Minority Business Development Agency	Victor M. Rivera, director
National Bureau of Standards	Ernest Ambler, director
National Oceanic and Atmospheric Administration	John V. Byrne, administrator
National Technical Information Service	Joseph F. Caponio, director
Patent and Trademark Office	Gerald J. Mossinghoff, commissioner
Bureau of the Census	Bruce Chapman, director
Bureau of Economic Analysis	George Jaszi, director
Bureau of Industrial Economics	Kenneth M. Brown, director (acting)
National Telecommunications and Information Administration	David J. Markey, administrator
United States Travel and Tourism Administration	Peter McCoy, under secretary
DEPARTMENT OF LABOR	Raymond J. Donovan, secretary
	Ford Barney Ford, under secretary
Women's Bureau	Lenora Cole-Alexander, director
Occupational Safety and Health	Thorne G. Auchter, asst. secretary
Veterans Employment	William C. Plowden, Jr., asst. secretary
Employment and Training	Albert Angrisani, asst. secretary
Mine Safety and Health	David A. Zegeer, asst. secretary
DEPARTMENT OF HEALTH AND HUMAN SERVICES	Margaret M. Heckler, secretary
	vacancy (under secretary)
Office of Human Development Services	Dorcas R. Hardy, asst. secretary
Public Health Service	Edward N. Brandt, Jr., asst. secretary
Alcohol, Drug Abuse, and Mental Health Administration	William E. Mayer, administrator
Centers for Disease Control	James O. Mason, director
Food and Drug Administration	Mark Novitch, commissioner (acting)
Health Resources and Services Administration	Robert Graham, administrator
National Institutes of Health	James B. Wyngaarden, director
Health Care Financing Administration	Carolyne K. Davis, administrator
Social Security Administration	Martha McSteen, commissioner (acting)
Office of Child Support Enforcement	Martha McSteen, director (acting)
Office of Community Services	Harvey R. Veith, director
DEPARTMENT OF HOUSING AND URBAN DEVELOPMENT	Samuel R. Pierce, Jr., secretary
	Philip Abrams, under secretary
Community Planning and Development	Stephen J. Bollinger, asst. secretary
Federal Housing Commissioner	Maurice Lee Barksdale, asst. secretary
Fair Housing and Equal Opportunity	Antonio Monroig, asst. secretary
Policy Development and Research	E. S. Savas, asst. secretary
DEPARTMENT OF TRANSPORTATION	Elizabeth Hanford Dole, secretary
	James H. Burnley IV, deputy secretary
United States Coast Guard	Adm. James S. Gracey, USCG, commandant
Federal Aviation Administration	J. Lynn Helms, administrator
Federal Highway Administration	R. A. Barnhart, administrator
Federal Railroad Administration	John Riley, administrator
National Highway Traffic Safety Administration	Diane K. Steed, administrator
Urban Mass Transportation Administration	Ralph Leslie Stanley, administrator
Maritime Administration	Harold E. Shear, administrator
Saint Lawrence Seaway Development Corporation	James L. Emery, administrator
Research and Special Programs Administration	Howard Dugoff, administrator
DEPARTMENT OF ENERGY	Donald P. Hodel, secretary
	William Patrick Collins, under secretary
Federal Energy Regulatory Commission	Anthony G. Sousa, chairman (acting)
General Counsel	Theodore J. Garrish
Nuclear Energy	Shelby T. Brewer, asst. secretary
DEPARTMENT OF EDUCATION	Terrell H. Bell, secretary
	Gary L. Jones, under secretary
Office of Bilingual Education	Jesse M. Soriano, director
Educational Research and Improvement	Donald J. Senese, asst. secretary
Special Education and Rehabilitative Services	Madeline C. Will, asst. secretary (acting)

[1] Council comprised of the President of the United States and certain other members.

Senate January 1984

State, name, and party	Term expires
Ala.—Heflin, Howell (D)	1985
Denton, Jeremiah (R)	1987
Alaska—Stevens, Ted (R)	1985
Murkowski, Frank H. (R)	1987
Ariz.—Goldwater, Barry M. (R)	1987
DeConcini, Dennis (D)	1989
Ark.—Bumpers, Dale (D)	1987
Pryor, David (D)	1985
Calif.—Cranston, Alan (D)	1987
Wilson, Pete (R)	1989
Colo.—Hart, Gary W. (D)	1987
Armstrong, William L. (R)	1985
Conn.—Weicker, Lowell P., Jr. (R)	1989
Dodd, Christopher J. (D)	1987
Del.—Roth, William V., Jr. (R)	1989
Biden, Joseph R., Jr. (D)	1985
Fla.—Chiles, Lawton M. (D)	1989
Hawkins, Paula (R)	1987
Ga.—Nunn, Samuel A. (D)	1985
Mattingly, Mack (R)	1987
Hawaii—Inouye, Daniel K. (D)	1987
Matsunaga, Spark M. (D)	1989
Idaho—McClure, James A. (R)	1985
Symms, Steven D. (R)	1987
Ill.—Percy, Charles H. (R)	1985
Dixon, Alan J. (D)	1987
Ind.—Lugar, Richard G. (R)	1989
Quayle, Dan (R)	1987
Iowa—Jepsen, Roger W. (R)	1985
Grassley, Charles E. (R)	1987
Kan.—Dole, Robert J. (R)	1987
Kassebaum, Nancy Landon (R)	1985
Ky.—Huddleston, Walter (D)	1985
Ford, Wendell H. (D)	1987
La.—Long, Russell B. (D)	1987
Johnston, J. Bennett, Jr. (D)	1985
Maine—Cohen, William S. (R)	1985
Mitchell, George J. (D)	1989
Md.—Mathias, Charles, Jr. (R)	1987
Sarbanes, Paul S. (D)	1989
Mass.—Kennedy, Edward M. (D)	1989
Tsongas, Paul E. (D)	1985
Mich.—Riegle, Donald W., Jr. (D)	1989
Levin, Carl (D)	1985
Minn.—Durenberger, David (R)	1989
Boschwitz, Rudy (R)	1985
Miss.—Stennis, John C. (D)	1989
Cochran, Thad (R)	1985
Mo.—Eagleton, Thomas F. (D)	1987
Danforth, John C. (R)	1989
Mont.—Melcher, John (D)	1989
Baucus, Max (D)	1985
Neb.—Zorinsky, Edward (D)	1989
Exon, J. James (D)	1985
Nev.—Laxalt, Paul (R)	1987
Hecht, Chic (R)	1989
N.H.—Humphrey, Gordon J. (R)	1985
Rudman, Warren (R)	1987
N.J.—Bradley, Bill (D)	1985
Lautenberg, Frank R. (D)	1989
N.M.—Domenici, Pete V. (R)	1985
Bingaman, Jeff (D)	1989
N.Y.—Moynihan, Daniel P. (D)	1989
D'Amato, Alfonse M. (R)	1987
N.C.—Helms, Jesse A. (R)	1985
East, John P. (R)	1987
N.D.—Burdick, Quentin N. (D)	1989
Andrews, Mark (R)	1987
Ohio—Glenn, John H., Jr. (D)	1987
Metzenbaum, Howard M. (D)	1989
Okla.—Boren, David L. (D)	1985
Nickles, Don (R)	1987
Ore.—Hatfield, Mark O. (R)	1985
Packwood, Robert W. (R)	1987
Pa.—Heinz, H. John, III (R)	1989
Specter, Arlen (R)	1987
R.I.—Pell, Claiborne (D)	1985
Chafee, John H. (R)	1989
S.C.—Thurmond, Strom (R)	1985
Hollings, Ernest F. (D)	1987
S.D.—Pressler, Larry (R)	1985
Abdnor, James (R)	1987
Tenn.—Baker, Howard H., Jr. (R)	1985
Sasser, James R. (D)	1989
Texas—Tower, John G. (R)	1985
Bentsen, Lloyd M. (D)	1989
Utah—Garn, Jake (R)	1987
Hatch, Orrin G. (R)	1989
Vt.—Stafford, Robert T. (R)	1989
Leahy, Patrick J. (D)	1987
Va.—Warner, John W. (R)	1985
Trible, Paul S., Jr. (R)	1989
Wash.—Gorton, Slade (R)	1989
Evans, Daniel J. (R)	1989
W.Va.—Randolph, Jennings (D)	1985
Byrd, Robert C. (D)	1989
Wis.—Proxmire, William (D)	1989
Kasten, Robert W., Jr. (R)	1987
Wyo.—Wallop, Malcolm (R)	1989
Simpson, Alan K. (R)	1985

Supreme Court

Chief Justice Warren Earl Burger (appointed 1969)

Associate Justices (year appointed)

William J. Brennan, Jr.	(1956)	Lewis F. Powell, Jr.	(1972)
Byron R. White	(1962)	William H. Rehnquist	(1972)
Thurgood Marshall	(1967)	John Paul Stevens	(1975)
Harry A. Blackmun	(1970)	Sandra Day O'Connor	(1981)

House of Representatives membership at the opening of the second session of the 98th Congress in January 1984

State, district, name, party

Ala.—1. Edwards, Jack (R)
2. Dickinson, William L. (R)
3. Nichols, William (D)
4. Bevill, Tom (D)
5. Flippo, Ronnie G. (D)
6. Erdreich, Ben (D)
7. Shelby, Richard C. (D)
Alaska—Young, Don (R)
Ariz.—1. McCain, John (R)
2. Udall, Morris K. (D)
3. Stump, Bob (R)
4. Rudd, Eldon D. (R)
5. McNulty, Jim (D)
Ark.—1. Alexander, Bill (D)
2. Bethune, Ed (R)
3. Hammerschmidt, J. P. (R)
4. Anthony, Beryl F. (D)
Calif.—1. Bosco, Douglas H. (D)
2. Chappie, Eugene A. (R)
3. Matsui, Robert T. (D)
4. Fazio, Vic (D)
5. Burton, Sala (D)
6. Boxer, Barbara (D)
7. Miller, George, III (D)
8. Dellums, Ronald V. (D)
9. Stark, Fortney H. (D)
10. Edwards, Don (D)
11. Lantos, Tom (D)
12. Zschau, Ed (R)
13. Mineta, Norman Y. (D)
14. Shumway, Norman D. (R)
15. Coelho, Tony (D)
16. Panetta, Leon E. (D)
17. Pashayan, Charles, Jr. (R)
18. Lehman, Richard (D)
19. Lagomarsino, Robert J. (R)
20. Thomas, William M. (R)
21. Fiedler, Bobbi (R)
22. Moorhead, Carlos J. (R)
23. Beilenson, Anthony C. (D)
24. Waxman, Henry A. (D)
25. Roybal, Edward R. (D)
26. Berman, Howard L. (D)
27. Levine, Mel (D)
28. Dixon, Julian C. (D)
29. Hawkins, Augustus F. (D)
30. Martinez, Matthew G. (D)
31. Dymally, Mervyn M. (D)
32. Anderson, Glenn M. (D)
33. Dreier, David (R)
34. Torres, Esteban (D)
35. Lewis, Jerry (R)
36. Brown, George E., Jr. (D)
37. McCandless, Al (R)
38. Patterson, Jerry M. (D)
39. Dannemeyer, W. E. (R)
40. Badham, Robert E. (R)
41. Lowery, Bill (R)
42. Lungren, Daniel E. (R)
43. Packard, Ron (R)
44. Bates, Jim (D)
45. Hunter, Duncan L. (R)
Colo.—1. Schroeder, Patricia (D)
2. Wirth, Timothy E. (D)
3. Kogovsek, Ray (D)
4. Brown, Hank (R)
5. Kramer, Ken (R)
6. Schaefer, Dan (R)
Conn.—1. Kennelly, Barbara B. (D)
2. Gejdenson, Samuel (D)
3. Morrison, Bruce A. (D)
4. McKinney, Stewart B. (R)
5. Ratchford, William R. (D)
6. Johnson, Nancy L. (R)
Del.—Carper, Thomas R. (D)
Fla.—1. Hutto, Earl D. (D)
2. Fuqua, Don (D)
3. Bennett, Charles E. (D)
4. Chappell, William, Jr. (D)
5. McCollum, Bill (R)
6. MacKay, Kenneth H. (D)
7. Gibbons, Sam (D)
8. Young, C. William (R)
9. Bilirakis, Michael (R)
10. Ireland, Andrew P. (D)
11. Nelson, Bill (D)
12. Lewis, Tom (R)
13. Mack, Connie, III (R)
14. Mica, Daniel A. (D)
15. Shaw, E. Clay, Jr. (R)
16. Smith, Larry (D)
17. Lehman, William (D)
18. Pepper, Claude (D)
19. Fascell, Dante B. (D)
Ga.—1. Thomas, Lindsay (D)
2. Hatcher, Charles F. (D)
3. Ray, Richard (D)
4. Levitas, Elliott H. (D)
5. Fowler, Wyche, Jr. (D)
6. Gingrich, Newt (R)

State, district, name, party

7. Darden, George (D)
8. Rowland, J. Roy (D)
9. Jenkins, Edgar L. (D)
10. Barnard, Doug (D)
Hawaii—1. Heftel, Cecil (D)
2. Akaka, Daniel (D)
Idaho—1. Craig, Larry (R)
2. Hansen, George V. (R)
Ill.—1. Hayes, Charles A. (D)
2. Savage, Gus (D)
3. Russo, Martin A. (D)
4. O'Brien, George M. (R)
5. Lipinski, William O. (D)
6. Hyde, Henry J. (R)
7. Collins, Cardiss (D)
8. Rostenkowski, Dan (D)
9. Yates, Sidney R. (D)
10. Porter, John E. (R)
11. Annunzio, Frank (D)
12. Crane, Philip M. (R)
13. Erlenborn, John N. (R)
14. Corcoran, Tom (R)
15. Madigan, Edward R. (R)
16. Martin, Lynn M. (R)
17. Evans, Lane (D)
18. Michel, Robert H. (R)
19. Crane, Daniel B. (R)
20. Durbin, Richard J. (D)
21. Price, Melvin (D)
22. Simon, Paul (D)
Ind.—1. Hall Katie (D)
2. Sharp, Philip R. (D)
3. Hiler, John P. (R)
4. Coats, Daniel R. (R)
5. Hillis, Elwood H. (R)
6. Burton, Dan (R)
7. Myers, John (R)
8. McCloskey, Francis X. (D)
9. Hamilton, L. H. (D)
10. Jacobs, Andrew, Jr. (D)
Iowa—1. Leach, James (R)
2. Tauke, Tom (R)
3. Evans, Cooper (R)
4. Smith, Neal (D)
5. Harkin, Tom (D)
6. Bedell, Berkley (D)
Kan.—1. Roberts, Pat (R)
2. Slattery, Jim (D)
3. Winn, Larry, Jr. (R)
4. Glickman, Dan (D)
5. Whittaker, Robert (R)
Ky.—1. Hubbard, Carroll, Jr. (D)
2. Natcher, William H. (D)
3. Mazzoli, Romano L. (D)
4. Snyder, Gene (R)
5. Rogers, Harold (R)
6. Hopkins, Larry J. (R)
7. Perkins, Carl D. (D)
La.—1. Livingston, Bob (R)
2. Boggs, Lindy (D)
3. Tauzin, William J. (D)
4. Roemer, Buddy (D)
5. Huckaby, Jerry (D)
6. Moore, W. Henson, III (R)
7. Breaux, John B. (D)
8. Long, Gillis W. (D)
Maine—1. McKernan, John R., Jr. (R)
2. Snowe, Olympia J. (R)
Md.—1. Dyson, Roy (D)
2. Long, Clarence D. (D)
3. Mikulski, Barbara A. (D)
4. Holt, Marjorie S. (R)
5. Hoyer, Steny H. (D)
6. Byron, Beverly (D)
7. Mitchell, Parren J. (D)
8. Barnes, Michael D. (D)
Mass.—1. Conte, Silvio O. (R)
2. Boland, Edward P. (D)
3. Early, Joseph D. (D)
4. Frank, Barney (D)
5. Shannon, James M. (D)
6. Mavroules, Nicholas (D)
7. Markey, Edward J. (D)
8. O'Neill, Thomas P., Jr. (D)
9. Moakley, Joe (D)
10. Studds, Gerry E. (D)
11. Donnelly, Brian J. (D)
Mich.—1. Conyers, John, Jr. (D)
2. Pursell, Carl D. (R)
3. Wolpe, Howard (D)
4. Siljander, Mark D. (R)
5. Sawyer, Harold S. (R)
6. Carr, Bob (D)
7. Kildee, Dale E. (D)
8. Traxler, Bob (D)
9. Vander Jagt, Guy (R)
10. Albosta, Donald J. (D)
11. Davis, Robert W. (R)
12. Bonior, David E. (D)
13. Crockett, George W. (D)
14. Hertel, Dennis M. (D)
15. Ford, William D. (D)
16. Dingell, John D. (D)
17. Levin, Sander (D)
18. Broomfield, William S. (R)
Minn.—1. Penny, Timothy J. (D)
2. Weber, Vin (R)
3. Frenzel, William (R)
4. Vento, Bruce F. (D)
5. Sabo, Martin Olav (D)
6. Sikorski, Gerry (D)
7. Stangeland, Arlan (R)

State, district, name, party

8. Oberstar, James L. (D)
Miss.—1. Whitten, Jamie L. (D)
2. Franklin, Webb (R)
3. Montgomery, G. V. (D)
4. Dowdy, Wayne (D)
5. Lott, Trent (R)
Mo.—1. Clay, William (D)
2. Young, Robert A. (D)
3. Gephardt, Richard A. (D)
4. Skelton, Ike (D)
5. Wheat, Alan (D)
6. Coleman, E. Thomas (R)
7. Taylor, Gene (R)
8. Emerson, William (R)
9. Volkmer, Harold L. (D)
Mont.—1. Williams, Pat (D)
2. Marlenee, Ron (R)
Neb.—1. Bereuter, D. K. (R)
2. Daub, Harold (R)
3. Smith, Virginia (R)
Nev.—1. Reid, Harry (D)
2. Vucanovich, Barbara (R)
N.H.—1. D'Amours, Norman (D)
2. Gregg, Judd (R)
N.J.—1. Florio, James J. (D)
2. Hughes, William J. (D)
3. Howard, James J. (D)
4. Smith, Christopher (R)
5. Roukema, Marge (R)
6. Dwyer, Bernard J. (D)
7. Rinaldo, Matthew J. (R)
8. Roe, Robert A. (D)
9. Torricelli, Robert G. (D)
10. Rodino, Peter W., Jr. (D)
11. Minish, Joseph G. (D)
12. Courter, James A. (R)
13. Forsythe, Edwin B. (R)
14. Guarini, Frank J. (D)
N.M.—1. Lujan, Manuel, Jr. (R)
2. Skeen, Joseph (R)
3. Richardson, Bill (D)
N.Y.—1. Carney, William (C-R)
2. Downey, Thomas J. (D)
3. Mrazek, Robert J. (D)
4. Lent, Norman F. (R)
5. McGrath, Raymond J. (R)
6. Addabbo, Joseph P. (D)
7. Ackerman, Gary L. (D)
8. Scheuer, James H. (D)
9. Ferraro, Geraldine (D)
10. Schumer, Charles E. (D)
11. Towns, Edolphus (D)
12. Owens, Major R. (D)
13. Solarz, Stephen J. (D)
14. Molinari, Guy V. (R)
15. Green, S. William (R)
16. Rangel, Charles B. (D)
17. Weiss, Theodore S. (D)
18. Garcia, Robert (D)
19. Biaggi, Mario (D)
20. Ottinger, Richard L. (D)
21. Fish, Hamilton, Jr. (R)
22. Gilman, B. A. (R)
23. Stratton, Samuel S. (D)
24. Solomon, Gerald (R)
25. Boehlert, Sherwood L. (R)
26. Martin, David O'B.(R)
27. Wortley, George (R)
28. McHugh, Matthew F. (D)
29. Horton, Frank J. (R)
30. Conable, B. B., Jr. (R)
31. Kemp, Jack F. (R)
32. LaFalce, John J. (D)
33. Nowak, Henry J. (D)
34. Lundine, Stanley N. (D)
N.C.—1. Jones, Walter B. (D)
2. Valentine, Tim, Jr. (D)
3. Whitley, Charles (D)
4. Andrews, Ike F. (D)
5. Neal, Stephen L. (D)
6. Britt, C. Robin (D)
7. Rose, C. G., III (D)
8. Hefner, Bill (D)
9. Martin, James G. (R)
10. Broyhill, James T. (R)
11. Clarke, James McC. (D)
N.D.—Dorgan, Byron L. (D)
Ohio—1. Luken, Thomas A. (D)
2. Gradison, Bill (R)
3. Hall, Tony P. (D)
4. Oxley, Michael G. (R)
5. Latta, Delbert L. (R)
6. McEwen, Robert (R)
7. DeWine, Michael (R)
8. Kindness, Thomas N. (R)
9. Kaptur, Marcy (D)
10. Miller, Clarence E. (R)
11. Eckart, Dennis E. (D)
12. Kasich, John R. (R)
13. Pease, Donald J. (D)
14. Seiberling, John F., Jr. (D)
15. Wylie, Chalmers P. (R)
16. Regula, Ralph S. (R)
17. Williams, Lyle (R)
18. Applegate, Douglas (D)
19. Feighan, Edward F. (D)
20. Oakar, Mary Rose (D)
21. Stokes, Louis (D)
Okla.—1. Jones, James R. (D)
2. Synar, Mike (D)
3. Watkins, Wes (D)
4. McCurdy, Dave (D)

State, district, name, party

5. Edwards, Mickey (R)
6. English, Glenn (D)
Ore.—1. AuCoin, Les (D)
2. Smith, Bob (R)
3. Wyden, Ron (D)
4. Weaver, James (D)
5. Smith, Denny (R)
Pa.—1. Foglietta, Thomas (D)
2. Gray, William H., III (D)
3. Borski, Robert A. (D)
4. Kolter, Joseph P. (D)
5. Schulze, Richard T. (R)
6. Yatron, Gus (D)
7. Edgar, Robert W. (D)
8. Kostmayer, Peter H. (D)
9. Shuster, E. G. (R)
10. McDade, Joseph M. (R)
11. Harrison, Frank (D)
12. Murtha, John P. (D)
13. Coughlin, R. L. (R)
14. Coyne, William J. (D)
15. Ritter, Donald L. (R)
16. Walker, Robert S. (R)
17. Gekas, George W. (R)
18. Walgren, Doug (D)
19. Goodling, William F. (R)
20. Gaydos, Joseph (D)
21. Ridge, Thomas J. (R)
22. Murphy, Austin J. (D)
23. Clinger, William F., Jr. (R)
R.I.—1. St. Germain, Fernand (D)
2. Schneider, Claudine (R)
S.C.—1. Hartnett, Thomas F. (R)
2. Spence, Floyd D. (R)
3. Derrick, Butler C., Jr. (D)
4. Campbell, Carroll A., Jr. (R)
5. Spratt, John (D)
6. Tallon, Robert M., Jr. (D)
S.D. Daschle, Thomas A. (D)
Tenn.—1. Quillen, James H. (R)
2. Duncan, John J. (R)
3. Lloyd Bouquard, Marilyn (D)
4. Cooper, Jim (D)
5. Boner, Bill (D)
6. Gore, Albert, Jr. (D)
7. Sundquist, Don (R)
8. Jones, Edward (D)
9. Ford, Harold E. (D)
Texas—1. Hall, Sam B. (D)
2. Wilson, Charles (D)
3. Bartlett, Steve (R)
4. Hall, Ralph M. (D)
5. Bryant, John (D)
6. Gramm, Phil (R)
7. Archer, William R. (R)
8. Fields, Jack (R)
9. Brooks, Jack (D)
10. Pickle, J. J. (D)
11. Leath, J. Marvin (D)
12. Wright, James C., Jr. (D)
13. Hightower, Jack (D)
14. Patman, William N. (D)
15. de la Garza, E. (D)
16. Coleman, Ronald (D)
17. Stenholm, Charles W. (D)
18. Leland, Mickey (D)
19. Hance, Kent (D)
20. Gonzalez, Henry B. (D)
21. Loeffler, Tom (R)
22. Paul, Ron (R)
23. Kazen, Abraham, Jr. (D)
24. Frost, Martin (D)
25. Andrews, Mike (D)
26. Vandergriff, Tom (D)
27. Ortiz, Solomon P. (D)
Utah—1. Hansen, James V. (R)
2. Marriott, Dan (R)
3. Nielson, Howard C. (R)
Vt.—Jeffords, James M. (R)
Va.—1. Bateman, Herbert H. (R)
2. Whitehurst, G. W. (R)
3. Bliley, Thomas J. (R)
4. Sisisky, Norman (D)
5. Daniel, Dan (D)
6. Olin, James R. (D)
7. Robinson, J. Kenneth (R)
8. Parris, Stanford E. (R)
9. Boucher, Frederick C. (D)
10. Wolf, Frank R. (R)
Wash.—1. Pritchard, Joel (R)
2. Swift, Al (D)
3. Bonker, Don (D)
4. Morrison, Sid (R)
5. Foley, Thomas S. (D)
6. Dicks, Norman D. (D)
7. Lowry, Mike (D)
8. Chandler, Rodney (R)
W.Va.—1. Mollohan, Alan B. (D)
2. Staggers, Harley O., Jr. (D)
3. Wise, Bob (D)
4. Rahall, Nick J. (D)
Wis.—1. Aspin, Leslie (D)
2. Kastenmeier, Robert W. (D)
3. Gunderson, Steven (R)
4. (vacancy) [1]
5. Moody, Jim (D)
6. Petri, Thomas E. (R)
7. Obey, David R. (D)
8. Roth, Tobias A. (R)
9. Sensenbrenner, F. J. (R)
Wyo.—Cheney, Richard (R)

[1]Rep. Clement J. Zablocki died Dec. 3, 1983.

The Federal Administrative Budget

in millions of dollars; fiscal years ending Sept. 30

Source and function	1982 actual	1983 estimate	1984 estimate
BUDGET RECEIPTS	$617,800	$597,500	$659,700
Individual income taxes	297,700	285,200	295,600
Corporation income taxes	49,200	35,300	51,800
Excise taxes	36,300	37,300	40,400
Social insurance taxes and contributions	201,500	210,300	242,900
Estate and gift taxes	8,000	6,100	5,900
Customs duties	8,900	8,800	9,100
Miscellaneous receipts	16,200	14,500	14,000
BUDGET EXPENDITURES	728,400	805,200	848,500
National defense	187,400	214,800	245,300
Department of Defense military functions	182,900	208,900	238,600
Atomic energy defense activities	4,300	5,500	6,400
Defense-related activities	300	400	300
International affairs	10,000	11,900	13,200
Conduct of foreign affairs	1,600	1,700	2,000
Foreign economic and financial assistance	3,900	4,300	4,500
Foreign information and exchange activities	600	700	800
International financial programs	900	1,300	1,400
International security assistance	3,100	4,000	4,600
General science, space, and technology	7,100	7,800	8,200
Agriculture	14,900	21,100	12,100
Farm income stabilization	13,300	19,400	10,500
Agricultural research and services	1,600	1,700	1,700
Natural resources and environment	12,900	12,100	9,800
Water resources	4,000	4,000	3,300
Conservation and land management	2,700	2,700	2,200
Recreational resources	1,500	1,700	1,500
Pollution control and abatement	5,000	4,300	4,100
Other natural resources	1,500	1,600	1,400
Energy	4,700	4,500	3,300
Commerce and housing credit	3,900	1,900	400
Mortgage credit and thrift insurance	1,200	−600	−1,400
Payment to the Postal Service	700	800	400
Other advancement and regulation	1,900	1,800	1,400
Transportation	20,600	21,900	25,100
Air transportation	3,600	4,200	4,800
Water transportation	2,700	3,100	3,000
Ground transportation	14,300	14,600	17,200
Other transportation	100	100	100
Community and regional development	7,200	7,400	7,000
Community development	4,600	4,500	4,400
Area and regional development	2,700	2,800	2,400
Disaster relief and insurance	−100	100	100

Source and function	1982 actual	1983 estimate	1984 estimate
Education, training, employment, and social services	$26,300	$26,700	$25,300
Elementary, secondary, and vocational education	6,800	6,500	6,400
Higher education	6,500	6,700	6,100
Research and general education aids	1,000	1,100	1,000
Training and employment	5,500	5,200	4,700
Social services	6,000	6,500	6,400
Other labour services	600	600	700
Health	74,000	82,400	90,600
Health care services	68,400	76,500	84,900
Health research	3,900	4,200	4,300
Education and training of health care work force	700	600	400
Consumer and occupational health and safety	1,000	1,100	1,100
Income security	248,300	282,500	282,400
General retirement and disability insurance	161,800	176,200	185,700
Federal employee retirement and disability	19,400	20,900	22,200
Unemployment compensation	23,800	36,900	28,800
Public assistance and other income supplements	43,400	48,500	45,800
Veterans benefits and services	24,000	24,400	25,700
Income security for veterans	13,700	14,200	14,600
Veterans education, training, and rehabilitation	1,900	1,600	1,300
Hospital and medical care for veterans	7,500	8,300	8,900
Other veterans benefits and services	800	200	900
Administration of justice	4,700	5,300	5,500
Federal law enforcement activities	2,500	3,000	3,300
Federal litigative and judicial activities	1,500	1,700	1,600
Federal correctional activities	400	400	500
Criminal justice assistance	300	200	200
General government	4,700	5,800	6,000
Legislative functions	1,200	1,300	1,300
Central fiscal operations	2,700	3,300	3,500
General property and records management	300	600	400
Other general government	700	800	1,000
General purpose fiscal assistance	6,400	6,400	7,000
Interest	100,800	105,300	120,000
Allowances for contingencies, civilian agency pay raises, and management reforms and savings	—	—	900
Undistributed offsetting receipts	−29,400	−36,700	−39,700
Employer share, employee retirement	−7,000	−8,200	−9,900
Interest received by trust funds	−16,100	−16,300	−16,900
Rents and royalties on the Outer Continental Shelf	−6,200	−11,800	−11,900
Federal surplus property disposition	—	−400	−1,000

Source: Executive Office of the President, Office of Management and Budget, *The United States Budget in Brief: Fiscal Year 1984*.

State Government Revenue, Expenditure, and Debt

1982 in thousands of dollars

	GENERAL REVENUE						GENERAL EXPENDITURE[1]					DEBT		
		State taxes												
State	Total	Total	General sales	Income[2]	Intergov-ernmental	Charges & misc.	Total	Education	Highways	Public welfare	Hospitals	Total	Issued 1982[3]	Retired 1982[3]
Ala.	4,158,745	2,195,831	629,453	480,969	1,178,508	784,406	3,044,499	1,109,302	336,432	532,044	293,527	1,958,569	742,420	81,512
Alaska	5,582,926	2,539,193	—	1,488	367,144	2,676,589	2,041,684	409,972	225,964	167,767	15,106	3,700,774	1,396,952	95,055
Ariz.	2,888,380	1,856,009	800,921	438,985	524,000	508,371	1,773,827	665,973	254,191	175,385	108,010	240,258	96,935	4,488
Ark.	2,238,436	1,263,746	419,378	353,733	700,848	273,842	1,491,953	436,427	216,816	357,679	110,062	554,540	77,780	11,132
Calif.	34,420,723	21,818,694	7,720,805	7,467,709	8,804,999	3,797,030	17,867,132	4,598,817	1,049,690	4,833,890	1,080,382	10,330,999	1,829,128	452,919
Colo.	3,174,292	1,690,034	612,900	548,944	835,420	648,838	2,014,967	738,862	267,390	305,944	178,457	741,305	56,608	27,031
Conn.	3,846,307	2,339,524	1,004,164	137,726	848,432	658,351	2,737,847	461,132	256,956	726,805	260,111	4,620,575	543,161	435,640
Del.	1,065,586	594,816	—	286,069	219,324	251,446	790,568	217,627	93,899	98,100	39,762	1,359,539	354,830	69,426
Fla.	8,337,735	5,555,936	2,783,889	—	1,925,500	856,299	5,245,272	1,104,533	844,029	1,135,095	368,872	2,993,388	292,675	115,001
Ga.	5,376,281	3,281,065	1,088,279	1,182,783	1,562,884	532,332	3,741,502	876,326	769,708	910,492	268,046	1,645,941	379,327	111,597
Hawaii	1,843,279	1,066,225	576,927	283,000	385,826	391,228	1,798,062	644,041	94,098	285,946	82,471	2,109,692	338,714	103,559
Idaho	1,009,106	578,613	146,206	220,073	273,298	157,195	666,851	188,740	96,443	115,125	23,741	427,178	73,997	20,593
Ill.	11,878,859	7,429,268	2,333,153	2,222,143	2,982,031	1,467,560	8,305,781	1,684,775	903,508	3,017,237	472,723	7,470,299	842,108	319,649
Ind.	5,099,096	3,063,657	1,510,453	748,769	1,145,675	889,764	3,102,932	1,238,644	397,110	532,248	213,368	1,024,784	7,200	45,965
Iowa	3,270,832	1,996,971	523,397	720,883	778,956	494,905	2,186,444	648,183	315,992	563,473	242,404	458,042	30,000	14,438
Kan.	2,428,389	1,442,737	470,762	459,822	593,005	392,647	1,691,889	479,551	240,616	435,336	173,035	397,481	—	22,638
Ky.	4,251,541	2,491,052	682,432	600,823	1,104,216	656,273	3,117,421	741,188	569,422	724,136	166,711	2,659,592	802,275	1,173,630
La.	5,784,891	3,127,229	926,912	220,134	1,200,100	1,457,562	4,172,970	959,650	465,549	851,195	430,797	4,146,609	705,478	120,835
Maine	1,361,185	730,979	248,943	209,585	422,505	207,701	1,009,982	196,413	142,179	317,996	34,713	860,782	84,685	58,603
Md.	5,591,135	3,193,087	797,397	1,354,613	1,301,191	1,096,857	3,708,320	827,202	424,176	895,661	348,377	4,212,457	419,420	218,370
Mass.	7,882,932	4,803,664	917,362	2,324,052	2,093,341	985,927	5,455,220	671,610	356,414	2,028,429	356,553	6,420,794	751,655	383,116
Mich.	11,440,971	6,307,161	1,843,651	2,126,630	3,227,867	1,905,943	7,681,663	1,986,332	418,540	2,862,546	690,552	3,859,420	565,494	203,881
Minn.	6,094,728	3,799,371	875,008	1,549,121	1,444,213	851,144	3,368,552	971,116	388,454	783,665	295,925	2,659,518	484,236	230,560
Miss.	2,723,626	1,462,293	767,072	168,471	874,946	386,387	1,776,556	452,067	277,537	440,200	141,091	748,192	2,750	49,604
Mo.	4,002,908	2,313,057	839,003	760,711	1,151,889	537,962	2,799,007	641,758	349,541	780,754	255,896	1,836,490	373,106	147,642
Mont.	1,088,341	529,144	—	143,804	292,061	267,136	700,263	154,417	132,691	134,667	27,495	399,215	93,495	18,559
Neb.	1,560,764	860,527	288,517	226,560	407,237	293,000	1,093,606	327,336	187,997	217,074	95,875	295,479	53,835	4,696
Nev.	1,102,274	745,460	375,973	—	230,684	126,130	653,150	161,617	110,989	100,999	23,781	648,313	111,179	17,437
N.H.	789,273	325,515	—	15,076	251,853	211,905	682,050	147,420	116,241	153,852	38,246	1,270,612	204,423	52,320
N.J.	9,253,811	5,577,236	1,379,206	1,305,567	2,138,528	1,538,047	5,184,491	931,705	541,248	1,117,926	435,499	8,795,893	1,429,282	259,782
N.M.	2,773,047	1,226,543	533,809	14,263	476,633	1,069,871	1,442,540	390,048	275,448	215,130	100,703	823,500	137,062	77,383
N.Y.	26,512,744	15,438,003	3,196,779	8,034,066	8,390,965	2,683,776	13,682,815	2,516,412	1,052,247	2,475,449	1,910,267	25,813,504	1,791,150	1,014,439
N.C.	6,123,494	3,790,035	779,512	1,449,370	1,536,436	797,023	3,740,232	1,151,085	513,919	672,045	341,898	1,591,067	350,883	88,134
N.D.	1,142,455	532,631	146,935	35,342	269,401	340,423	763,157	192,769	110,204	94,915	53,540	324,836	125,720	15,711
Ohio	10,170,249	5,819,461	1,819,381	1,243,618	2,541,012	1,809,776	6,854,710	1,691,775	623,195	1,989,249	671,547	4,999,271	240,847	207,739
Okla.	4,237,497	2,712,960	481,996	641,428	794,874	729,663	2,536,041	814,353	283,480	685,659	226,649	1,171,937	31,500	37,145
Ore.	3,356,364	1,552,313	—	968,264	927,496	876,555	2,430,444	486,995	271,376	461,765	162,130	6,220,641	306,835	183,948
Pa.	12,973,482	8,185,625	2,229,436	1,985,270	3,339,170	1,448,687	8,338,784	1,448,340	1,119,123	2,973,936	732,772	6,244,149	382,700	426,913
R.I.	1,421,454	674,792	199,809	215,156	393,168	353,494	1,166,326	232,347	56,255	329,780	102,814	1,987,036	389,039	100,690
S.C.	3,343,611	1,959,205	646,544	641,838	824,236	560,170	2,191,683	729,433	163,692	462,339	199,188	3,077,471	610,285	125,457
S.D.	793,458	328,785	178,687	—	252,321	212,352	634,274	135,437	123,249	109,046	24,562	708,707	38,095	23,846
Tenn.	3,952,564	2,146,242	1,117,859	44,469	1,264,630	541,692	2,745,340	770,751	387,907	655,220	214,550	1,587,121	57,070	130,104
Texas	14,691,385	9,099,849	3,480,790	—	2,776,697	2,814,839	8,937,069	2,651,712	1,932,729	1,622,657	812,489	2,587,117	100,000	132,010
Utah	1,862,191	950,869	387,624	331,145	564,007	347,315	1,230,976	472,880	158,800	209,121	80,235	722,510	152,780	17,183
Vt.	738,119	332,308	48,440	112,520	256,437	149,374	609,377	154,008	70,219	128,795	22,141	673,362	45,970	42,849
Va.	5,771,565	3,235,829	670,512	1,446,187	1,371,167	1,164,569	4,024,570	1,083,385	610,237	721,250	469,000	2,614,239	606,312	144,026
Wash.	5,620,729	3,528,362	1,892,066	—	1,355,331	737,036	3,765,335	1,189,735	528,948	843,318	170,997	2,492,091	476,530	68,097
W.Va.	2,467,841	1,468,886	781,223	305,964	680,247	318,708	1,676,531	298,899	436,707	271,400	90,380	1,804,135	63,550	106,393
Wis.	6,296,324	3,934,495	961,068	1,680,372	1,552,840	808,989	3,440,598	1,084,912	367,546	926,058	190,631	2,647,931	293,343	160,063
Wyo.	1,365,940	762,533	228,018	—	332,244	271,163	631,923	132,883	173,919	63,987	26,088	532,745	93,270	11,025
TOTAL	275,161,865	162,657,820	50,342,651	45,707,515	69,165,793	43,338,252	170,747,186	42,300,895	20,103,020	41,512,785	13,874,169	147,470,100	19,436,079	7,981,833

Fiscal year ending June 30, 1982, except Alabama and Michigan, September 30; New York, March 31; and Texas, August 31. [1]Direct only, intergovernmental excluded. [2]Includes individual only. [3]Long term only. Source: U.S. Department of Commerce, Bureau of the Census, *State Government Finances in 1982*.

EDUCATION

Public Elementary and Secondary Schools

Fall 1982 estimates

State	ENROLLMENT[1] Elementary	Secondary	INSTRUCTIONAL STAFF Total[2]	Principals and supervisors	Teachers, elementary	Teachers, secondary	TEACHERS' AVERAGE ANNUAL SALARIES Elementary	Secondary	STUDENT-TEACHER RATIO Elementary	Secondary	Expenditure per pupil
Alabama	386,828	337,209	41,173	1,773	19,951	19,449	$17,400	$18,000	19.4	17.3	$1,546
Alaska	48,669	38,014	6,547	286	3,102	2,528	33,784	34,154	15.7	15.0	6,620
Arizona	382,000	164,000	31,818	800	19,909	8,947	18,637	19,318	19.2	18.3	2,603
Arkansas	235,773	201,248	26,228	1,331	11,541	11,964	14,789	15,548	20.4	16.8	2,093
California	2,712,572	1,246,203	195,719	12,152	104,640	65,757	23,240	24,538	25.9	19.0	2,490
Colorado	310,000	234,800	32,613	1,653	15,022	13,978	20,267	21,453	20.6	16.8	2,986
Connecticut	337,300	168,100	36,608	2,380	19,090	12,608	20,700	20,800	17.7	13.3	3,746
Delaware	47,751	44,894	6,139	390	2,488	2,856	20,062	21,166	19.2	15.7	4,008
District of Columbia	48,772	38,809	5,776	312	2,897	2,012	26,068	26,021	16.8	19.3	3,767
Florida	794,530	681,470	94,762	4,668	46,504	35,537	18,720	18,124	17.1	19.2	3,009
Georgia	649,800	396,100	59,633	2,617	34,740	22,276	17,111	17,847	18.7	17.8	2,369
Hawaii	86,925	74,949	9,658	352	4,987	3,137	25,335	24,024	17.4	23.9	3,213
Idaho	118,243	86,777	11,350	625	5,350	4,775	16,892	18,255	22.1	18.2	2,110
Illinois	1,288,218	586,981	116,062	6,304	67,805	36,444	21,747	24,242	19.0	16.1	3,201
Indiana	530,563	474,596	57,624	3,770	25,533	25,519	19,657	20,483	20.8	18.6	2,672
Iowa	263,300	233,000	33,883	1,307	14,615	16,398	17,978	19,361	18.0	14.2	3,147
Kansas	245,500	160,310	29,808	1,628	14,500	11,780	18,213	18,385	16.9	13.6	3,094
Kentucky	432,667	219,333	36,400	2,150	21,000	11,200	17,850	19,150	20.6	19.6	2,193
Louisiana	550,000	224,000	46,436	1,982	23,783	18,716	18,810	19,690	23.1	12.0	2,529
Maine	146,848	65,138	13,624	1,224	7,778	4,499	15,288	16,604	18.9	14.5	2,651
Maryland	342,576	356,560	43,943	3,188	18,073	19,673	21,780	23,142	19.0	18.1	3,486
Massachusetts	613,974	311,186	63,446	3,446	22,000	30,000	18,781	19,165	27.9	10.4	2,958
Michigan	917,337	844,569	89,736	6,700	40,099	37,107	23,732	24,217	22.9	22.8	3,648
Minnesota	358,302	360,360	45,951	2,117	19,404	21,239	21,450	23,068	18.5	17.0	3,157
Mississippi	253,600	207,400	28,027	1,657	13,664	11,178	14,049	14,571	18.6	18.6	2,076
Missouri	554,792	251,608	55,257	3,000	24,000	24,257	17,268	18,192	23.1	10.4	2,587
Montana	107,017	44,971	10,015	398	4,972	3,934	18,786	20,314	21.5	11.4	2,981
Nebraska	149,811	114,667	18,096	968	8,119	8,130	16,650	18,173	18.5	14.1	2,605
Nevada	81,640	69,460	8,443	402	3,917	3,525	20,585	21,306	20.8	19.7	2,311
New Hampshire	93,539	67,759	11,852	713	5,321	4,784	15,250	15,471	17.6	14.2	2,341
New Jersey	728,910	428,090	87,791	6,000	41,776	31,515	21,244	22,175	17.4	13.6	4,190
New Mexico	149,900	119,211	16,340	910	6,930	7,320	20,290	21,000	21.6	16.3	2,904
New York	1,308,600	1,384,500	184,000	12,000	73,800	89,300	24,300	25,700	17.7	15.5	4,302
North Carolina	770,863	333,357	64,076	3,666	34,208	22,251	17,847	17,754	22.5	15.0	2,680
North Dakota	80,647	35,922	8,407	434	4,719	2,780	17,680	19,110	17.1	12.9	3,055
Ohio	1,117,300	733,500	110,980	5,930	53,380	41,630	19,850	21,020	20.9	17.6	2,807
Oklahoma	332,832	248,000	37,731	2,151	17,900	16,000	17,660	18,600	18.6	15.5	2,792
Oregon	275,329	172,120	29,300	2,100	15,000	9,500	21,872	23,136	18.4	18.1	3,643
Pennsylvania	880,100	900,900	116,500	5,300	47,242	55,458	20,500	21,300	18.6	16.2	3,290
Rhode Island	69,201	68,337	10,152	543	4,664	4,094	24,070	22,154	14.8	16.7	3,792
South Carolina	421,100	183,500	37,000	2,060	20,130	11,950	15,890	17,040	20.9	15.4	2,016
South Dakota	85,718	37,907	8,984	470	5,278	2,696	15,386	15,988	16.2	14.1	2,386
Tennessee	590,423	237,434	45,393	2,610	24,481	14,752	17,369	17,517	24.1	16.1	2,124
Texas	1,906,000	1,076,000	185,700	9,300	92,800	74,000	19,000	20,100	20.5	14.5	2,299
Utah	221,521	147,817	17,467	1,036	9,085	5,804	19,078	20,615	24.4	25.5	2,128
Vermont	48,261	43,336	8,301	850	2,987	3,604	14,877	15,778	16.2	12.0	2,940
Virginia	600,386	375,331	65,000	3,662	33,674	23,218	18,020	19,655	17.8	16.2	2,740
Washington	381,414	357,157	40,098	2,860	18,381	16,116	22,977	23,923	20.8	22.2	2,887
West Virginia	224,769	150,357	24,763	1,564	12,713	9,288	17,290	17,479	17.7	16.2	2,480
Wisconsin	445,000	339,800	54,400	2,200	28,800	23,400	20,480	21,470	15.5	14.5	3,421
Wyoming	59,120	42,403	8,122	472	3,959	3,338	22,740	24,293	14.9	12.7	3,467
TOTAL U.S.	23,786,241	15,719,450	2,427,132	136,411	1,176,711	961,861	$20,042	$21,100	20.2	16.3	$2,917

[1] Kindergartens included in elementary schools; junior high schools, in secondary schools. [2] Includes librarians, guidance, health and psychological personnel, and related educational workers.

Source: National Education Association Research, *Estimates of School Statistics, 1982–83* (Copyright 1983. All rights reserved. Used by permission.).

Universities and Colleges

state statistics

State	NUMBER OF INSTITUTIONS 1981–1982 Total	Public	Enrollment[1] fall, 1980	EARNED DEGREES CONFERRED 1979–1980 Bachelor's and first professional	Master's except first professional	Doctor's
Alabama	59	37	164,306	17,199	5,527	249
Alaska	15	12	21,296	419	184	0
Arizona	28	19	202,716	10,535	3,890	417
Arkansas	35	19	77,607	7,336	1,782	110
California	272	136	1,790,993	91,613	31,133	3,981
Colorado	45	27	162,916	14,928	4,953	618
Connecticut	47	24	159,632	13,957	5,639	499
Delaware	8	5	32,939	3,276	468	70
District of Columbia	19	1	86,675	8,907	5,488	487
Florida	81	37	411,891	30,428	8,299	1,536
Georgia	78	34	184,159	18,182	6,820	549
Hawaii	12	9	47,181	3,339	1,009	103
Idaho	9	6	43,018	2,987	660	55
Illinois	158	63	644,245	48,719	16,298	1,872
Indiana	74	28	247,253	25,737	8,313	1,036
Iowa	60	21	140,449	15,186	2,584	532
Kansas	52	29	136,605	12,349	3,126	388
Kentucky	57	21	143,066	12,821	5,210	271
Louisiana	32	20	160,058	16,170	4,190	314
Maine	29	12	43,264	4,958	599	21
Maryland	56	32	225,526	16,656	5,126	529
Massachusetts	118	32	418,415	41,765	14,653	1,839
Michigan	91	44	520,131	40,294	15,056	1,334
Minnesota	70	30	206,691	20,135	3,222	503
Mississippi	41	25	102,364	9,180	2,845	226
Missouri	89	28	234,421	24,137	7,555	637
Montana	16	9	35,177	3,954	638	56
Nebraska	31	16	89,488	8,329	1,689	221
Nevada	7	6	40,455	1,459	425	21
New Hampshire	26	11	46,794	5,926	880	58
New Jersey	61	31	321,610	25,928	7,965	645
New Mexico	19	16	58,283	4,882	1,713	166
New York	294	86	992,237	91,388	32,845	3,375
North Carolina	127	74	287,537	25,157	5,252	757
North Dakota	17	11	34,069	3,813	474	83
Ohio	136	59	489,145	44,263	13,007	1,488
Oklahoma	44	29	160,295	13,701	3,485	377
Oregon	45	21	157,458	11,481	3,203	346
Pennsylvania	202	61	507,716	58,694	13,060	1,669
Rhode Island	13	3	66,869	7,119	1,472	203
South Carolina	60	33	132,476	12,329	3,268	191
South Dakota	20	8	32,761	4,072	604	37
Tennessee	79	24	204,581	19,217	4,848	543
Texas	156	98	701,391	57,464	16,750	1,660
Utah	14	9	93,987	9,678	2,333	453
Vermont	21	6	30,628	4,145	1,164	32
Virginia	69	39	280,504	23,088	5,282	550
Washington	50	33	303,603	17,150	4,281	512
West Virginia	28	16	81,973	7,774	2,167	145
Wisconsin	64	30	269,086	22,741	5,323	760
Wyoming	9	8	21,147	1,392	295	76
TOTAL U.S.	3,243	1,488	12,047,087	996,357	297,052	32,600

Excludes service academies. [1] Excludes non–degree-credit students.

Source: U.S. Department of Health, Education and Welfare, National Center for Education Statistics, *Digest of Education Statistics* and *Education Directory*.

Universities and Colleges, 1983–84[1]

Selected four-year schools

Institution	Location	Year founded	Total students[2]	Total faculty[3]	Bound library volumes
ALABAMA					
Alabama A. & M. U.	Normal	1875	4,142	305	236,300
Alabama State U.	Montgomery	1874	4,034	179	195,100
Auburn U.	Auburn	1856	18,401	1,094	1,164,200
Birmingham-Southern	Birmingham	1856	1,587	131	143,400
Jacksonville State U.	Jacksonville	1883	6,522	529	345,000
Troy State U.	Troy	1887	8,531	392	200,200
Tuskegee Institute	Tuskegee Institute	1881	3,440	347	230,000
U. of Alabama	University	1831	15,497	919	1,473,100
U. of South Alabama	Mobile	1963	9,380	439	60,600
ALASKA					
U. of Alaska	Fairbanks	1917	4,622	395	502,900
ARIZONA					
Arizona State U.	Tempe	1885	39,919	1,477	2,000,000
Northern Arizona U.	Flagstaff	1899	11,501	521	764,700
U. of Arizona	Tucson	1885	33,006	1,444[4]	1,624,400
ARKANSAS					
Arkansas State U.	State University	1909	8,368	357	641,500
U. of Arkansas	Fayetteville	1871	14,461	850	1,041,200
U. of A. at Little Rock	Little Rock	1927	10,065	569	310,000
U. of Central Arkansas	Conway	1907	5,739	299	294,000
CALIFORNIA					
California Inst. of Tech.	Pasadena	1891	1,750	282	364,900
Cal. Polytech. State U.	San Luis Obispo	1901	15,624	958	555,000
Cal. State Polytech. U.	Pomona	1938	16,558	974	375,000
Cal. State U., Chico	Chico	1887	14,057	770	500,000
Cal. State U., Dominguez Hills	Dominguez Hills	1960	8,300	430	288,300
Cal. State U., Fresno	Fresno	1911	16,170	930	686,000
Cal. State U., Fullerton	Fullerton	1957	22,997	1,279	581,200
Cal. State U., Hayward	Hayward	1957	11,624	598	655,900
Cal. State U., Long Beach	Long Beach	1949	31,492	1,449	845,600
Cal. State U., Los Angeles	Los Angeles	1947	20,740	812	829,800
Cal. State U., Northridge	Northridge	1958	28,111	1,502	750,000
Cal. State U., Sacramento	Sacramento	1947	21,636	1,295	75,000
Golden Gate U.	San Francisco	1901	11,451	675	200,000
Humboldt State U.	Arcata	1913	6,430	500	300,000
Loyola Marymount U.	Los Angeles	1911	5,146	314	248,000
Occidental	Los Angeles	1887	1,650	149	350,000
San Francisco State U.	San Francisco	1899	23,874	1,695	554,400
San Jose State U.	San Jose	1857	25,338	1,570	700,000
Sonoma State U.	Rohnert Park	1960	5,508	421	287,000
Stanford U.	Stanford	1885	13,784	1,964	4,889,400
U. of C., Berkeley	Berkeley	1868	30,400	3,100	5,750,000
U. of C., Davis	Davis	1905	19,323	1,288	1,755,000
U. of C., Irvine	Irvine	1960	10,200	580	930,000
U. of C., Los Angeles	Los Angeles	1919	33,435	3,000	4,230,000
U. of C., Riverside	Riverside	1868	4,600	389	980,000
U. of C., San Diego	La Jolla	1912	13,245	2,581	1,583,800
U. of C., Santa Barbara	Santa Barbara	1944	16,000	740	1,500,000
U. of C., Santa Cruz	Santa Cruz	1965	6,721	462	709,500
U. of the Pacific	Stockton	1851	3,940	291[4]	350,000
U. of San Francisco	San Francisco	1855	5,339	542	420,000
U. of Santa Clara	Santa Clara	1851	7,401	441	544,100
U. of Southern California	Los Angeles	1880	27,647	2,700	2,035,700
COLORADO					
Colorado	Colorado Springs	1874	1,897	220	500,000
Colorado School of Mines	Golden	1874	3,000	200	250,300
Colorado State U.	Fort Collins	1870	18,295	1,111	1,500,000
Metropolitan State	Denver	1963	16,408	698	453,800
U. S. Air Force Academy	USAF Academy	1954	4,544	530	500,000
U. of Colorado	Boulder	1876	23,241	1,162	1,750,000
U. of Denver	Denver	1864	8,391	591	1,005,900
U. of Northern Colorado	Greeley	1889	9,784	495	514,800
U. of Southern Colorado	Pueblo	1933	5,105	268	166,000
CONNECTICUT					
Central Connecticut State	New Britain	1849	13,209	624	352,200
Southern Connecticut State	New Haven	1893	11,368	616	396,400
Trinity	Hartford	1823	1,804	160	655,000
U. S. Coast Guard Acad.	New London	1876	930	113	127,000
U. of Bridgeport	Bridgeport	1927	7,000	539	300,000
U. of Connecticut	Storrs	1881	21,874	1,562	1,476,700
U. of Hartford	West Hartford	1877	9,320	630	280,000
Wesleyan U.	Middletown	1831	2,651	285	976,000
Western Connecticut State	Danbury	1903	6,047	963	174,000
Yale U.	New Haven	1701	10,310	1,346	7,880,000
DELAWARE					
Delaware State	Dover	1891	2,113	154	128,300
U. of Delaware	Newark	1833	18,233	929	1,400,000
DISTRICT OF COLUMBIA					
American U.	Washington	1893	11,237	591	548,200
Catholic U. of America	Washington	1887	6,847	850	1,136,000
George Washington U.	Washington	1821	16,232	1,665	1,270,000
Georgetown U.	Washington	1789	12,020	1,375	1,344,000
Howard U.	Washington	1867	11,748	1,922	1,012,500
FLORIDA					
Florida A. & M. U.	Tallahassee	1887	5,015	355	369,000
Florida State U.	Tallahassee	1857	22,424	1,379	1,509,100
Rollins	Winter Park	1885	4,227	112	174,700
U. of Central Florida	Orlando	1963	15,629	550	583,900
U. of Florida	Gainesville	1853	35,365	3,205	2,300,000
U. of Miami	Coral Gables	1925	13,221	. . .	1,343,400
U. of South Florida	Tampa	1960	25,000	1,265	787,321
GEORGIA					
Atlanta U.	Atlanta	1865	1,065	143	366,700
Augusta	Augusta	1925	4,252	150	320,600
Emory U.	Atlanta	1836	7,864	1,270	1,790,000
Georgia	Milledgeville	1889	3,422	170	135,000
Georgia Inst. of Tech.	Atlanta	1885	10,884	537	1,569,000
Georgia Southern	Statesboro	1906	7,018	400	337,500
Georgia State U.	Atlanta	1913	21,335	921	721,500
Mercer U.	Macon	1833	5,000	150	240,000

Institution	Location	Year founded	Total students[2]	Total faculty[3]	Bound library volumes
Morehouse[5]	Atlanta	1867	1,980	125	500,000
Oglethorpe U.	Atlanta	1835	1,050	55	66,000
Spelman[6]	Atlanta	1881	1,366	117	60,000
U. of Georgia	Athens	1785	25,679	1,587	2,141,600
HAWAII					
Brigham Young U.-Hawaii	Laie	1955	1,868	133	123,000
U. of Hawaii	Honolulu	1907	20,880	1,635	1,914,800
IDAHO					
Boise State U.	Boise	1932	9,401	378	265,000
Idaho State U.	Pocatello	1901	11,634	402	350,000
U. of Idaho	Moscow	1889	8,998	700	1,015,000
ILLINOIS					
Augustana	Rock Island	1860	2,335	144	260,000
Bradley U.	Peoria	1897	5,604	307[4]	341,800
Chicago State U.	Chicago	1869	7,504	383	266,400
Concordia Teachers	River Forest	1864	1,320	144	133,000
De Paul U.	Chicago	1898	12,867	763	573,800
Eastern Illinois U.	Charleston	1895	10,481	444	498,400
Illinois Inst. of Tech.	Chicago	1892	5,680	521	360,000
Illinois State U.	Normal	1857	19,817	1,082	912,400
Knox	Galesburg	1837	1,050	85	206,200
Lake Forest	Lake Forest	1857	1,166	99	200,000
Loyola U. of Chicago	Chicago	1870	16,474	1,170	847,800
Northeastern Ill. U.	Chicago	1867	10,404	398	410,600
Northern Illinois U.	De Kalb	1895	24,524	1,204	1,107,000
Northwestern U.	Evanston	1851	10,471	1,059	2,235,000
Southern Illinois U.	Carbondale	1869	23,383	1,498	1,837,500
SIU at Edwardsville	Edwardsville	1965	11,342	687	705,000
U. of Chicago	Chicago	1891	8,992	1,130	4,688,400
U. of Illinois	Urbana	1867	34,632	2,389	6,511,900
U. of I. at Chicago Circle	Chicago	1965	19,821	167	1,246,500
Western Illinois U.	Macomb	1899	11,937	765	600,000
Wheaton	Wheaton	1860	2,475	172	250,000
INDIANA					
Ball State U.	Muncie	1918	18,359	984	1,205,100
Butler U.	Indianapolis	1855	3,800	250	300,000
De Pauw U.	Greencastle	1837	2,394	208	400,000
Indiana State U.	Terre Haute	1865	12,091	717	903,800
Indiana U.	Bloomington	1820	33,109	1,495	4,105,700
Purdue U.	West Lafayette	1869	31,856	3,817	1,538,100
U. of Evansville	Evansville	1854	4,491	229	197,000
U. of Notre Dame du Lac	Notre Dame	1842	9,294	775	1,500,000
Valparaiso U.	Valparaiso	1859	4,190	305	240,000
IOWA					
Coe	Cedar Rapids	1851	1,371	89	125,000
Drake U.	Des Moines	1881	6,008	293[4]	500,000
Grinnell	Grinnell	1846	1,131	111	260,000
Iowa State U.	Ames	1858	24,906	2,116	1,450,000
U. of Iowa	Iowa City	1847	29,599	1,601	2,356,100
U. of Northern Iowa	Cedar Falls	1876	11,204	683	583,800
KANSAS					
Emporia State U.	Emporia	1863	5,358	244	651,100
Kansas State U.	Manhattan	1863	19,497	1,544	950,000
U. of Kansas	Lawrence	1866	24,219	1,331[4]	2,251,900
Wichita State U.	Wichita	1895	17,242	540	710,800
KENTUCKY					
Berea	Berea	1855	1,563	150	271,000
Eastern Kentucky U.	Richmond	1906	14,081	725	500,000
Kentucky State U.	Frankfort	1886	2,431	130	234,000
Murray State U.	Murray	1922	7,587	421	381,500
U. of Kentucky	Lexington	1865	42,258	1,953	1,854,100
U. of Louisville	Louisville	1798	19,744	1,355	932,100
Western Kentucky U.	Bowling Green	1907	12,666	613	866,000
LOUISIANA					
Grambling State U.	Grambling	1901	3,928	234	218,992
Louisiana State U.	Baton Rouge	1860	29,863	1,385	1,965,300
Louisiana Tech. U.	Ruston	1894	11,172	435	855,700
Northeast Louisiana U.	Monroe	1931	11,300	476	717,800
Northwestern State U.	Natchitoches	1884	6,272	282	268,000
Southern U.	Baton Rouge	1880	9,512	430	325,400
Tulane U.	New Orleans	1834	10,397	499	1,478,000
U. of Southwestern La.	Lafayette	1898	15,493	640	499,800
MAINE					
Bates	Lewiston	1864	1,414	109[4]	416,000
Bowdoin	Brunswick	1794	1,371	106[4]	635,000
Colby	Waterville	1813	1,750	141	380,000
U. of Maine, Farmington	Farmington	1864	1,986	105	91,500
U. of Maine, Orono	Orono	1865	11,507	687	590,000
U. of Southern Maine	Portland	1878	8,172	350	433,600
MARYLAND					
Goucher[6]	Towson	1885	1,041	130	205,900
Johns Hopkins U.	Baltimore	1876	8,358	795	1,832,000
Morgan State U.	Baltimore	1867	4,554	341	350,000
Towson State U.	Baltimore	1866	15,528	965	372,000
U.S. Naval Academy	Annapolis	1845	4,556	600	500,000
U. of Maryland	College Park	1807	37,864	1,942	2,000,000
MASSACHUSETTS					
Amherst	Amherst	1821	1,534	171	604,800
Boston	Chestnut Hill	1863	14,069	677	1,000,000
Boston U.	Boston	1869	28,707	2,513	1,000,000
Brandeis U.	Waltham	1948	3,461	457	730,800
Clark U.	Worcester	1887	2,570	228	421,100
Harvard U.	Cambridge	1636	19,322	5,170	10,261,000
Holy Cross	Worcester	1843	2,548	214	400,000
Mass. Inst. of Tech.	Cambridge	1861	9,475	1,931	1,900,000
Mt. Holyoke[6]	South Hadley	1837	1,926	195	486,700
Northeastern U.	Boston	1898	43,184	3,049	1,123,600
Radcliffe[6]	Cambridge	1879	2,479	. . .	20,000
Salem State	Salem	1854	8,742	278	201,400
Simmons[6]	Boston	1899	3,049	191	200,000

Institution	Location	Year founded	Total students[2]	Total faculty[3]	Bound library volumes
Smith	Northampton	1871	2,699	284	888,900
Tufts U.	Medford	1852	5,712	. . .	548,000
U. of Lowell	Lowell	1894	15,579	766	318,000
U. of Massachusetts	Amherst	1863	24,903	1,201	1,878,000
Wellesley[6]	Wellesley	1870	2,096	292	600,000
Wheaton[6]	Norton	1834	1,222	125	245,000
Williams	Williamstown	1793	2,052	185	500,000
MICHIGAN					
Albion	Albion	1835	1,726	123	235,000
Central Michigan U.	Mt. Pleasant	1892	16,400	770	673,600
Eastern Michigan U.	Ypsilanti	1849	19,156	780	633,300
Ferris State	Big Rapids	1884	10,767	565	215,000
Hope	Holland	1866	2,519	180	190,000
Michigan State U.	East Lansing	1855	41,765	2,511	2,900,000
Michigan Tech. U.	Houghton	1885	7,414	400	570,400
Northern Michigan U.	Marquette	1899	9,376	376	368,200
U. of Detroit	Detroit	1877	6,310	450	467,000
U. of Michigan	Ann Arbor	1817	34,432	2,746	4,255,200
Wayne State U.	Detroit	1868	33,524	2,310	1,839,400
Western Michigan U.	Kalamazoo	1903	20,296	958	838,800
MINNESOTA					
Carleton	Northfield	1866	3,734	150	354,500
Concordia	Moorhead	1891	2,505	187	265,000
Gustavus Adolphus	St. Peter	1862	2,180	195	196,000
Hamline U.	St. Paul	1854	1,378	121	270,000
Macalester	St. Paul	1874	1,682	175	310,000
Mankato State U.	Mankato	1867	12,565	595	560,000
Moorhead State U.	Moorhead	1885	6,227	343	280,000
St. Catherine[6]	St. Paul	1905	2,284	184	224,700
St. Cloud State U.	St. Cloud	1869	11,698	581	483,900
St. John's U.[5]	Collegeville	1857	2,011	159	400,000
St. Olaf	Northfield	1874	2,934	307	324,300
St. Thomas	St. Paul	1885	4,236	194	205,200
U. of Minnesota	Minneapolis	1851	58,903	6,481	3,250,000
Winona State U.	Winona	1858	5,408	253	180,500
MISSISSIPPI					
Alcorn State U.	Lorman	1871	2,418	162	138,000
Jackson State U.	Jackson	1877	6,503	344	370,000
Mississippi	Clinton	1826	2,592	155	260,000
Mississippi U. for Women	Columbus	1884	2,307	160	341,400
Mississippi State U.	Mississippi State	1878	12,361	824	992,000
U. of Mississippi	University	1848	9,236	431	565,500
U. of Southern Mississippi	Hattiesburg	1910	12,394	644	750,000
MISSOURI					
Central Missouri State U.	Warrensburg	1871	9,600	445	313,600
Northeast Missouri State U.	Kirksville	1867	6,990	300	255,300
St. Louis U.	St. Louis	1818	7,932	1,180	790,000
Southeast Missouri State U.	Cape Girardeau	1873	9,093	433	250,000
Southwest Missouri State U.	Springfield	1906	14,573	642	397,000
U. of Missouri-Columbia	Columbia	1839	24,059	834	2,200,000
U. of Missouri-Kansas City	Kansas City	1929	11,419	1,092	562,800
U. of Missouri-Rolla	Rolla	1870	7,061	706	369,600
U. of Missouri-St. Louis	St. Louis	1963	12,390	519	383,100
Washington U.	St. Louis	1853	10,839	2,515	2,000,000
MONTANA					
Montana State U.	Bozeman	1893	11,447	871	445,700
U. of Montana	Missoula	1893	9,101	487	700,000
NEBRASKA					
Creighton U.	Omaha	1878	6,301	986	499,800
U. of Nebraska	Lincoln	1869	24,789	1,319	2,000,000
U. of Nebraska at Omaha	Omaha	1908	15,978	478	500,000
NEVADA					
U. of Nevada-Las Vegas	Las Vegas	1951	9,122	339	439,100
U. of Nevada-Reno	Reno	1864	8,937	376	730,000
NEW HAMPSHIRE					
Dartmouth	Hanover	1769	4,700	430	1,000,000
U. of New Hampshire	Durham	1866	12,105	643	818,900
NEW JERSEY					
Glassboro State	Glassboro	1923	9,558	500	376,800
Jersey City State	Jersey City	1927	7,003	359[4]	315,000
Kean Col. of N. J.	Union	1855	12,990	641	265,000
Montclair State	Upper Montclair	1908	15,000	500	600,000
Princeton U.	Princeton	1746	6,127	671	3,519,000
Rider	Lawrenceville	1865	5,251	294	313,400
Rutgers State U.	New Brunswick	1766	50,003	2,500	2,000,000
Seton Hall U.	South Orange	1856	9,902	568	300,000
Stevens Inst. of Tech.	Hoboken	1870	3,100	140	103,500
Trenton State	Trenton	1855	11,000	395	400,000
Upsala	East Orange	1893	1,383	71	175,400
William Patterson	Wayne	1855	11,997	393	270,700
NEW MEXICO					
New Mexico State U.	Las Cruces	1888	12,926	674	700,000
U. of New Mexico	Albuquerque	1889	23,701	1,366	1,086,500
NEW YORK					
Adelphi U.	Garden City	1896	11,500	4,000	333,200
Alfred U.	Alfred	1836	2,448	187	266,400
Canisius	Buffalo	1870	4,522	301	230,000
City U. of New York					
Bernard M. Baruch	New York	1919	13,915	865	290,000
Brooklyn	Brooklyn	1930	15,252	1,400	629,000
City	New York	1847	13,161	708	1,000,000
Herbert H. Lehman	Bronx	1931	10,112	457	420,100
Hunter	New York	1870	17,840	1,122	512,700
Queens	Flushing	1937	17,400	1,250	550,000
Staten Island	Staten Island	1955	10,502	343	165,000
York	Jamaica	1966	5,359	166[4]	156,000
Colgate U.	Hamilton	1819	2,610	246	372,000
Columbia U.	New York	1754	16,165	1,388	5,300,000
Barnard[6]	New York	1889	2,240	200	150,000
Teachers	New York	1887	4,058	135	450,000
Cornell U.	Ithaca	1865	17,158	1,553	5,000,000

Institution	Location	Year founded	Total students[2]	Total faculty[3]	Bound library volumes
Elmira	Elmira	1855	2,475	160	230,900
Fordham U.	Bronx	1841	13,000	864	1,384,300
Hamilton	Clinton	1812	1,656	135	353,800
Hofstra U.	Hempstead	1935	11,110	620	900,000
Ithaca	Ithaca	1892	5,252	415	280,500
Long Island U.	Greenvale	1926	23,300	1,400	600,000
Manhattan	Bronx	1853	4,928	375	234,200
Marymount[6]	Tarrytown	1907	1,189	136	107,000
New School for Soc. Res.	New York	1919	26,530	1,690	193,200
New York U.	New York	1831	31,759	3,792	3,009,300
Niagara U.	Niagara University	1856	3,596	241	235,700
Polytechnic Inst. of N.Y.	Brooklyn	1854	3,199	395	265,000
Pratt Inst.	Brooklyn	1887	3,699	494	185,100
Rensselaer Polytech. Inst.	Troy	1824	5,945	650	500,000
Rochester Inst. of Tech.	Rochester	1829	15,162	1,165	215,100
St. Bonaventure U.	St. Bonaventure	1856	2,733	185	200,000
St. John's U.	Jamaica	1870	18,490	754	924,800
St. Lawrence U.	Canton	1856	2,421	177	312,000
State U. of N.Y. at Albany	Albany	1844	11,454	872	1,062,500
SUNY at Buffalo	Buffalo	1846	26,406	1,957	2,181,200
SUNY at Stony Brook	Stony Brook	1957	14,666	877	1,182,900
State U. Colleges					
Brockport	Brockport	1836	7,234	468	421,200
Buffalo	Buffalo	1867	21,759	556	408,400
Cortland	Cortland	1868	6,217	370	235,000
Fredonia	Fredonia	1867	5,161	267	341,400
Geneseo	Geneseo	1867	5,314	284	372,600
New Paltz	New Paltz	1828	7,433	420	334,900
Oneonta	Oneonta	1889	6,124	350	500,000
Oswego	Oswego	1861	7,615	722	400,000
Plattsburgh	Plattsburgh	1889	6,155	375	230,800
Potsdam	Potsdam	1816	4,780	252	327,600
Syracuse U.	Syracuse	1870	21,288	978[4]	2,065,900
U.S. Merchant Marine Acad.	Kings Point	1943	1,100	80	100,000
U.S. Military Academy	West Point	1802	4,400	548	500,000
U. of Rochester	Rochester	1850	8,320	1,024	1,900,000
Vassar	Poughkeepsie	1861	2,358	240	572,300
Wagner	Staten Island	1883	2,311	168	300,000
Yeshiva U.	New York	1886	4,384	2,486	850,000
NORTH CAROLINA					
Appalachian State U.	Boone	1899	10,051	584	425,000
Catawba	Salisbury	1851	885	74	174,000
Davidson	Davidson	1837	1,371	107	290,000
Duke U.	Durham	1838	9,527	744	3,264,800
East Carolina U.	Greenville	1907	13,358	854	702,000
Lenoir-Rhyne	Hickory	1891	1,407	93	116,300
N. Carolina A. & T. St. U.	Greensboro	1891	5,615	328	317,800
N. Carolina State U.	Raleigh	1887	18,850	1,340	1,092,700
U. of N.C. at Chapel Hill	Chapel Hill	1789	21,757	2,093	2,952,900
U. of N.C. at Greensboro	Greensboro	1891	9,924	627	1,500,000
Wake Forest U.	Winston-Salem	1834	4,829	1,065	818,700
Western Carolina U.	Cullowhee	1889	6,026	382	338,800
NORTH DAKOTA					
North Dakota State U.	Fargo	1890	9,476	423[4]	368,900
U. of North Dakota	Grand Forks	1883	10,905	501	425,000
OHIO					
Antioch	Yellow Springs	1852	4,000	500	240,000
Bowling Green State U.	Bowling Green	1910	16,866	831	769,000
Case Western Reserve U.	Cleveland	1826	8,698	1,556	1,431,600
Cleveland State U.	Cleveland	1964	18,942	796	525,700
Denison U.	Granville	1831	2,138	191	260,000
John Carroll U.	Cleveland	1886	3,221	223	360,000
Kent State U.	Kent	1910	19,687	998	1,500,000
Kenyon	Gambier	1824	1,450	116	275,800
Marietta	Marietta	1835	1,256	105	250,000
Miami U.	Oxford	1809	14,870	810	1,080,000
Oberlin	Oberlin	1833	2,941	466	790,000
Ohio State U.	Columbus	1870	53,747	3,262	3,779,800
Ohio U.	Athens	1804	14,400	863	1,200,000
U. of Akron	Akron	1870	27,022	960	1,328,600
U. of Cincinnati	Cincinnati	1819	31,382	2,705	1,300,000
U. of Dayton	Dayton	1850	7,158	656	800,000
U. of Toledo	Toledo	1872	21,386	1,194	711,300
Wooster	Wooster	1866	1,642	140	309,900
Xavier U.	Cincinnati	1831	3,985	360	300,000
Youngstown State U.	Youngstown	1908	15,584	834	473,000
OKLAHOMA					
Central State U.	Edmond	1890	12,309	492	604,700
Oklahoma State U.	Stillwater	1890	23,053	1,580	1,300,000
U. of Oklahoma	Norman	1890	21,532	908	2,045,500
U. of Tulsa	Tulsa	1894	5,769	425	879,800
OREGON					
Lewis and Clark	Portland	1867	2,301	181	192,700
Oregon State U.	Corvallis	1868	16,119	1,335	949,100
Portland State U.	Portland	1955	14,449	728	669,600
Reed	Portland	1909	1,128	107	300,000
U. of Oregon	Eugene	1872	15,405	1,299	1,590,000
PENNSYLVANIA					
Allegheny	Meadville	1815	1,955	159	298,900
Bryn Mawr	Bryn Mawr	1885	1,832	171	793,600
Bucknell U.	Lewisburg	1846	3,325	251	41,000
Carnegie-Mellon U.	Pittsburgh	1900	5,998	475	633,800
Dickinson	Carlisle	1773	1,789	122	312,000
Drexel U.	Philadelphia	1891	12,470	484	480,000
Duquesne U.	Pittsburgh	1878	6,628	503	450,700
Edinboro State	Edinboro	1857	5,913	339	353,900
Franklin and Marshall	Lancaster	1787	2,600	166	210,000
Gettysburg	Gettysburg	1832	1,938	178	280,000
Indiana U. of Pa.	Indiana	1875	12,503	676	530,000
Juniata	Huntingdon	1876	1,273	97	205,000
Lafayette	Easton	1826	2,383	185	380,000
La Salle	Philadelphia	1863	6,045	405	300,000
Lehigh U.	Bethlehem	1865	6,355	405	810,000
Moravian	Bethlehem	1742	1,809	114	173,000
Muhlenberg	Allentown	1848	2,309	133	172,800
Pennsylvania State U.	University Park	1855	35,757	1,594	1,691,700

Universities and Colleges (continued)

Selected four-year schools

Institution	Location	Year founded	Total students[2]	Total faculty[3]	Bound library volumes
St. Joseph's	Philadelphia	1851	6,281	371	198,000
Slippery Rock State	Slippery Rock	1889	6,159	337	430,100
Susquehanna U.	Selinsgrove	1858	1,843	92	126,200
Swarthmore	Swarthmore	1864	1,270	188	609,500
Temple U.	Philadelphia	1884	31,474	2,686	1,600,000
U. of Pennsylvania	Philadelphia	1740	22,895	6,298	3,054,000
U. of Pittsburgh	Pittsburgh	1787	29,358	2,682	2,472,500
Ursinus	Collegeville	1869	2,031	157	120,000
Villanova U.	Villanova	1842	8,290	445	500,000
West Chester State	West Chester	1812	9,539	525	420,000
PUERTO RICO					
Inter American U.	San Juan	1912	24,296	1,169	213,800
U. of Puerto Rico	Rio Piedras	1903	20,996	1,288	2,250,000
RHODE ISLAND					
Brown U.	Providence	1764	6,974	490	1,810,000
Rhode Island	Providence	1854	9,178	376	275,000
U. of Rhode Island	Kingston	1892	10,231	1,090	1,000,000
SOUTH CAROLINA					
The Citadel[5]	Charleston	1842	3,435	197	367,000
Clemson U.	Clemson	1889	12,459	713[4]	1,259,000
Furman U.	Greenville	1826	3,033	165	280,000
U. of South Carolina	Columbia	1801	24,093	1,127	2,003,300
SOUTH DAKOTA					
South Dakota State U.	Brookings	1881	7,028	401[4]	200,000
U. of South Dakota	Vermillion	1882	6,001	382	345,400
TENNESSEE					
Fisk U.	Nashville	1867	1,100	91	189,200
Memphis State U.	Memphis	1912	22,183	953	850,000
Middle Tennessee State U.	Murfreesboro	1911	11,369	909	700,000
Tennessee State U.	Nashville	1912	8,131	518	48,700
Tennessee Tech. U.	Cookeville	1915	7,827	717	292,300
U. of Tennessee	Knoxville	1794	45,402	3,392	1,436,000
Vanderbilt U.	Nashville	1873	9,035	1,946	1,517,000
TEXAS					
Austin	Sherman	1849	1,190	114	179,000
Baylor U.	Waco	1845	10,666	524[4]	979,500
East Texas State U.	Commerce	1889	8,752	365	527,700
Hardin-Simmons U.	Abilene	1891	1,927	128	168,600
Lamar U.	Beaumont	1923	14,700	627	650,000
North Texas State U.	Denton	1890	20,368	935	1,412,400
Prairie View A. & M.	Prairie View	1876	4,800	292	195,000
Rice U.	Houston	1891	3,836	410	1,000,000
Sam Houston State U.	Huntsville	1879	10,580	331[4]	659,200
Southern Methodist U.	Dallas	1911	9,332	637	1,987,800
Southwest Texas State U.	San Marcos	1899	18,317	1,120	700,400
Stephen F. Austin State U.	Nacogdoches	1923	12,275	435	254,000
Texas A. & I. U.	Kingsville	1925	5,521	219[4]	420,300
Texas A. & M. U.	College Station	1876	38,846	1,642	1,400,000
Texas Christian U.	Fort Worth	1873	6,878	389	1,072,700
Texas Southern U.	Houston	1947	9,001	470	400,000
Texas Tech. U.	Lubbock	1923	23,129	1,386	2,500,000
U. of Houston	Houston	1927	31,114	2,328	1,240,000
U. of Texas at Arlington	Arlington	1895	23,157	940	750,000
U. of Texas at Austin	Austin	1881	47,631	1,911[4]	5,057,600
U. of Texas at El Paso	El Paso	1913	15,750	663	482,800
West Texas State U.	Canyon	1909	6,823	361	270,100
UTAH					
Brigham Young U.	Provo	1875	27,715	1,604	1,625,300
U. of Utah	Salt Lake City	1850	23,373	1,373	1,500,000
Utah State U.	Logan	1888	11,849	170	982,000
Weber State	Ogden	1889	11,048	425	382,000
VERMONT					
Bennington	Bennington	1925	649	68[4]	80,000
Middlebury	Middlebury	1800	1,938	179	457,000
U. of Vermont	Burlington	1791	10,907	865	1,050,000
VIRGINIA					
James Madison U.	Harrisonburg	1908	9,242	548	310,000
Old Dominion U.	Norfolk	1930	15,200	646	638,100
U. of Richmond	Richmond	1830	4,411	295	289,100
U. of Virginia	Charlottesville	1819	17,118	1,681	2,466,800
Virginia Commonwealth U.	Richmond	1838	19,000	2,269	550,000
Virginia Military Inst.[5]	Lexington	1839	1,309	118	268,300
Va. Polytech. Inst. & State U.	Blacksburg	1872	21,756	2,053	1,391,700
Washington & Lee U.[5]	Lexington	1749	1,719	166	302,600
William & Mary	Williamsburg	1693	4,732	537	764,400
WASHINGTON					
Central Washington U.	Ellensburg	1891	7,121	321	100,000
Eastern Washington U.	Cheney	1890	8,492	712	355,200
Gonzaga U.	Spokane	1887	3,488	271	310,000
U. of Washington	Seattle	1861	34,308	6,611	4,000,000
Washington State U.	Pullman	1890	16,403	1,031	1,346,600
Western Washington U.	Bellingham	1893	9,617	450	400,000
Whitman	Walla Walla	1859	1,171	89	287,380
WEST VIRGINIA					
Bethany	Bethany	1840	886	75	144,000
Marshall U.	Huntington	1837	11,767	506	356,400
West Virginia U.	Morgantown	1867	20,624	2,321	1,030,500
WISCONSIN					
Beloit	Beloit	1846	1,064	91	189,800
Lawrence U.	Appleton	1847	1,066	109	250,000
Marquette U.	Milwaukee	1881	12,000	873	681,000
Ripon	Ripon	1851	900	85	124,000
St. Norbert	De Pere	1898	1,720	127	140,000
U. of W.-Eau Claire	Eau Claire	1916	11,072	559	444,700
U. of W.-Green Bay	Green Bay	1965	5,173	175	263,300
U. of W.-La Crosse	La Crosse	1909	9,000	450	500,000
U. of W.-Madison	Madison	1848	43,075	2,136	4,500,000
U. of W.-Milwaukee	Milwaukee	1956	26,468	1,222	1,365,000
U. of W.-Oshkosh	Oshkosh	1871	11,129	544	671,500
U. of W.-Platteville	Platteville	1866	4,713	354	195,000
U. of W.-River Falls	River Falls	1874	5,368	260	212,700
U. of W.-Stevens Point	Stevens Point	1894	8,906	413	522,000
U. of W.-Stout	Menomonie	1893	7,470	343[4]	177,000
U. of W.-Superior	Superior	1896	2,220	136	220,000
U. of W.-Whitewater	Whitewater	1868	10,493	388	297,600
WYOMING					
U. of Wyoming	Laramie	1886	10,248	962	775,000

[1] Latest data available; coeducational unless otherwise indicated. [2] Total includes part-time students. [3] Total includes both part-time and full-time faculties. [4] Total includes full-time equivalent only. [5] Men's school. [6] Women's school.

LIVING CONDITIONS

Health Personnel and Facilities

State	Physicians Dec. 31, 1981[1]	Dentists 1982	Registered Nurses 1982[2]	Hospital facilities 1982: Hospitals	Hospital facilities 1982: Beds	Nursing homes 1980: Facilities	Nursing homes 1980: Beds
Alabama	5,229	1,489	11,651	146	25,904	210	20,651
Alaska	513	285	1,241	25	1,718	9	1,029
Arizona	5,846	1,384	9,015	80	12,125	120	9,309
Arkansas	3,060	838	5,453	97	13,635	196	19,238
California	60,633	15,221	73,417	593	111,541	4,134	163,482
Colorado	6,164	1,929	9,882	97	15,127	161	17,310
Connecticut	8,433	2,333	10,485	65	18,171	320	21,244
Delaware	1,060	279	2,068	14	3,975	32	2,530
District of Columbia	3,559	636	5,774	17	8,752	49	3,180
Florida	21,425	4,878	34,401	253	59,644	355	36,122
Georgia	8,395	2,388	15,415	191	33,016	326	30,041
Hawaii	2,138	717	2,287	27	4,108	243	2,805
Idaho	1,150	496	2,135	52	4,047	57	4,355
Illinois	22,440	6,404	43,164	281	71,211	761	88,383
Indiana	7,601	2,386	15,706	133	31,898	458	44,511
Iowa	3,957	1,519	9,839	139	20,481	489	34,641
Kansas	3,981	1,162	7,964	166	18,512	357	25,208
Kentucky	5,282	1,741	10,077	118	18,794	310	26,265
Louisiana	7,040	1,808	10,412	157	26,010	201	21,672
Maine	1,940	504	3,741	47	6,588	424	11,317
Maryland	12,088	2,701	15,079	85	24,881	187	20,726
Massachusetts	16,957	4,013	27,478	178	41,444	800	52,254
Michigan	15,758	5,129	28,351	233	48,328	3,038	80,082
Minnesota	8,372	2,575	13,722	182	29,349	409	41,931
Mississippi	2,893	872	5,934	118	17,457	156	12,253
Missouri	8,613	2,413	17,124	169	34,249	867	46,691
Montana	1,143	484	2,430	67	5,242	86	5,652
Nebraska	2,491	1,002	6,230	110	11,841	262	18,990
Nevada	1,292	407	2,385	25	3,563	31	2,022
New Hampshire	1,768	508	3,123	34	4,695	87	6,672
New Jersey	15,430	4,824	22,348	131	42,362	471	37,825
New Mexico	2,249	590	3,136	57	6,310	72	3,075
New York	50,634	12,928	68,173	344	125,884	828	103,952
North Carolina	9,662	2,451	17,596	159	32,548	940	32,173
North Dakota	958	320	2,620	59	6,039	86	6,450
Ohio	18,976	5,394	37,925	237	62,683	960	76,280
Oklahoma	4,194	1,397	8,199	142	17,697	348	27,101
Oregon	5,335	1,819	7,942	83	11,901	196	17,382
Pennsylvania	24,447	6,743	48,106	310	82,941	550	75,907
Rhode Island	2,138	533	3,459	21	5,924	110	8,653
South Carolina	4,527	1,242	7,358	91	17,133	194	11,990
South Dakota	853	331	2,402	68	5,674	138	8,647
Tennessee	7,692	2,226	14,335	164	31,751	249	21,692
Texas	23,666	6,712	40,603	561	84,599	997	101,328
Utah	2,622	979	3,909	42	5,279	74	5,052
Vermont	1,241	275	1,604	19	2,907	172	4,706
Virginia	10,021	2,876	15,639	137	31,550	436	27,377
Washington	8,256	2,890	11,108	121	15,689	543	39,153
West Virginia	2,861	797	5,978	76	12,906	120	6,423
Wisconsin	8,122	2,879	14,653	163	28,967	427	49,847
Wyoming	618	255	1,228	31	2,733	19	1,759
TOTAL U.S.	455,723	126,963	744,304	6,915	1,359,783	23,065	1,537,338

[1] Non-federal only. [2] Hospital nurses only. Sources: Eiler, Mary Ann, *Physician Characteristics and Distribution in the U.S.*, 1982 Edition, Division of Survey and Data Resources, American Medical Association, Chicago, 1983; American Dental Association, *1982 Distribution of Dentists in the United States by State and Region;* American Hospital Association, *Hospital Statistics, 1983 Edition;* U.S. Department of Health and Human Services, National Center for Health Statistics.

Crime Rates per 100,000 Population

State or metropolitan area	VIOLENT CRIME										PROPERTY CRIME							
	Total		Murder		Rape		Robbery		Assault		Total		Burglary		Larceny		Auto theft	
	1977	1982	1977	1982	1977	1982	1977	1982	1977	1982	1977	1982	1977	1982	1977	1982	1977	1982
Alabama	414.4	447.7	14.2	10.6	25.2	26.0	96.8	112.0	278.3	299.1	3,298.2	4,185.8	1,135.5	1,256.2	1,881.9	2,656.4	280.7	273.3
Alaska	443.2	623.7	10.8	**18.5**	**51.6**	**85.4**	96.8	133.8	284.0	386.1	5,454.8	5,588.8	1,331.7	1,188.1	3,369.8	3,806.4	753.3	594.3
Arizona	494.2	517.0	9.5	8.3	34.2	38.5	138.2	158.6	312.3	311.6	**7,253.0**	6,614.0	2,346.1	1,883.3	**4,467.4**	4,360.9	439.5	369.8
Arkansas	322.9	324.7	8.8	8.2	27.6	27.1	83.2	78.8	203.4	210.6	3,018.1	3,546.9	972.6	1,071.5	1,862.1	2,289.4	183.4	186.0
California	706.0	814.7	11.5	11.2	49.4	50.7	287.0	372.1	358.0	380.7	6,302.7	6,470.7	2,139.4	2,020.2	3,499.8	3,785.1	663.5	665.5
Colorado	511.9	504.2	6.3	6.0	42.0	44.5	170.7	150.6	292.9	303.1	6,315.6	6,575.7	1,935.2	1,749.1	3,903.2	**4,429.3**	477.1	397.3
Connecticut	282.3	399.5	4.2	5.2	16.8	21.9	129.5	208.5	131.8	163.9	4,559.8	5,028.0	1,346.0	1,410.8	2,620.7	3,065.0	593.2	552.2
Delaware	382.1	559.8	6.0	5.3	24.9	30.9	157.0	122.4	194.2	401.2	5,828.0	5,825.1	1,682.6	1,444.9	3,678.4	3,968.6	467.0	411.6
Florida	686.8	896.8	10.2	13.5	39.6	53.6	187.9	297.6	449.1	532.0	6,051.8	6,568.4	1,859.9	2,034.7	3,840.5	4,103.9	351.4	429.8
Georgia	439.8	478.2	11.7	12.6	31.1	39.8	140.5	154.6	256.5	271.2	3,819.2	4,736.6	1,351.1	1,497.9	2,170.2	2,926.9	297.9	311.7
Hawaii	224.8	255.7	7.2	3.1	25.5	34.4	128.0	156.9	64.1	61.3	6,321.3	6,328.6	1,911.5	1,657.6	3,920.4	4,250.3	489.4	420.6
Idaho	236.9	259.2	5.5	2.5	19.4	16.6	39.6	30.3	172.5	209.8	3,888.0	3,824.0	1,050.8	1,031.9	2,599.6	2,617.2	237.6	174.9
Illinois	452.0	453.8	9.9	8.8	21.8	21.1	211.3	204.9	209.0	219.0	4,442.1	4,363.3	1,085.0	1,097.9	2,828.5	2,789.2	528.6	476.3
Indiana	310.6	300.6	7.4	6.5	26.5	27.8	123.2	109.0	153.5	157.2	3,962.3	4,128.9	1,086.2	1,088.8	2,498.7	2,713.5	377.4	326.6
Iowa	144.0	172.7	2.3	2.3	10.6	12.5	41.2	36.2	89.8	121.8	3,717.5	3,963.8	812.5	947.8	2,685.1	2,842.3	219.9	173.7
Kansas	309.8	335.9	6.6	5.7	22.0	24.8	100.7	87.0	180.5	218.4	4,254.0	4,616.1	1,270.4	1,344.8	2,739.3	3,048.8	244.3	222.5
Kentucky	233.6	315.0	10.1	9.7	19.1	20.0	81.1	97.3	123.3	188.0	2,779.8	3,253.4	872.2	1,029.1	1,662.1	1,991.3	245.4	233.1
Louisiana	524.8	669.1	15.5	16.0	30.9	39.9	142.9	212.6	335.5	400.6	3,973.1	4,642.1	1,165.5	1,424.8	2,469.9	2,881.7	337.7	335.6
Maine	224.7	163.0	2.4	2.1	13.5	13.4	38.7	30.5	170.0	117.0	3,850.7	3,696.7	1,253.1	1,047.0	2,350.7	2,459.2	246.9	190.6
Maryland	693.8	850.0	8.0	10.1	34.8	37.4	292.1	360.5	358.9	441.9	5,006.2	5,162.3	1,400.0	1,419.6	3,177.7	3,350.6	428.5	392.1
Massachusetts	425.3	571.4	3.1	3.8	20.8	25.3	169.9	213.8	231.6	328.5	4,983.7	4,932.4	1,532.2	1,422.1	2,311.3	2,541.7	**1,140.1**	**968.6**
Michigan	584.7	656.6	9.3	9.1	38.9	46.6	261.9	271.1	274.6	329.7	5,227.3	6,128.0	1,522.7	1,813.1	3,159.0	3,623.1	545.5	691.7
Minnesota	193.8	219.3	2.7	2.3	19.5	22.7	85.9	101.3	85.8	92.9	4,037.0	4,235.4	1,134.7	1,182.1	2,559.3	2,815.8	343.1	237.6
Mississippi	288.7	294.6	14.3	14.0	19.6	26.5	65.7	73.0	189.1	181.1	2,299.9	3,278.0	915.6	1,183.8	1,239.9	1,940.6	144.4	153.6
Missouri	460.4	506.5	9.6	9.7	28.3	25.9	189.0	193.0	233.5	278.0	4,120.8	4,441.3	1,318.3	1,391.3	2,424.2	2,714.3	378.4	335.8
Montana	218.0	224.8	5.4	3.9	16.7	14.9	39.2	33.1	156.8	173.0	3,887.3	4,108.4	804.9	843.8	2,773.2	3,006.1	309.2	258.4
Nebraska	199.4	229.6	3.9	2.0	18.1	20.7	64.7	61.9	112.7	145.0	3,325.2	3,721.2	760.0	811.3	2,316.1	2,732.1	249.1	177.9
Nevada	743.0	805.4	**15.8**	13.6	49.1	61.5	323.1	419.6	355.0	310.7	7,225.0	**7,095.6**	**2,453.1**	**2,412.7**	4,212.6	4,117.9	559.2	564.9
New Hampshire	113.1	124.8	3.2	2.2	10.7	16.2	23.2	33.9	76.0	72.6	3,679.0	3,704.4	1,041.7	945.0	2,343.9	2,535.8	293.4	223.7
New Jersey	392.0	607.4	5.6	6.5	21.0	28.9	180.4	307.6	185.1	264.4	4,721.8	5,068.8	1,435.8	1,430.7	2,774.5	3,011.3	511.5	626.8
New Mexico	500.9	734.5	8.8	11.6	39.1	48.3	109.6	126.2	343.4	**548.4**	4,686.7	5,873.1	1,418.7	1,628.8	3,008.6	3,929.5	259.5	314.9
New York	**831.8**	**990.1**	10.7	11.4	29.4	29.2	**472.6**	**610.7**	319.1	338.7	5,255.8	5,478.1	1,728.0	1,671.9	2,782.0	3,025.3	745.8	780.8
North Carolina	407.1	446.3	10.6	9.1	17.0	22.0	61.3	85.9	318.3	329.5	3,384.0	4,096.9	1,154.1	1,309.0	2,037.8	2,603.4	192.1	184.5
North Dakota	67.1	61.8	0.9	0.7	9.0	9.9	13.3	12.7	43.8	38.5	2,433.8	2,586.3	446.1	458.8	1,843.0	1,987.2	144.7	140.3
Ohio	406.7	436.7	7.8	6.3	27.3	29.9	190.5	183.6	181.1	217.0	4,313.2	4,498.8	1,216.0	1,309.6	2,696.8	2,807.5	400.4	381.7
Oklahoma	316.6	443.9	8.6	10.8	29.2	37.1	73.8	132.8	205.0	263.2	3,843.0	4,778.5	1,288.2	1,603.9	2,228.1	2,685.7	326.8	488.9
Oregon	455.8	473.0	4.9	5.1	39.9	39.9	124.1	167.3	286.9	260.6	5,531.4	6,094.5	1,636.4	1,789.7	3,506.1	4,003.8	388.9	301.0
Pennsylvania	282.8	360.4	5.6	5.7	19.0	20.6	130.3	175.4	128.0	158.7	2,834.7	3,092.3	877.5	900.7	1,624.1	1,859.4	333.2	332.2
Rhode Island	301.6	401.8	3.6	3.7	10.5	19.4	86.5	114.7	201.0	264.0	5,125.0	4,962.3	1,489.5	1,400.2	2,844.1	2,826.4	791.4	735.7
South Carolina	636.2	720.0	11.9	10.9	33.0	38.8	105.9	122.4	**485.3**	547.9	4,201.1	4,641.2	1,613.6	1,490.9	2,342.4	2,872.6	245.1	277.7
South Dakota	189.1	99.0	2.0	2.7	13.5	11.4	17.9	17.1	155.7	67.7	2,422.4	2,545.9	570.5	562.2	1,704.4	1,865.3	147.5	118.4
Tennessee	389.5	421.1	10.1	9.7	29.7	35.5	145.8	175.7	203.9	200.2	3,350.2	3,992.5	1,259.7	1,288.6	1,776.5	2,371.9	314.0	332.0
Texas	407.7	577.1	13.3	16.1	33.8	44.6	152.4	220.0	208.2	296.3	4,989.4	5,725.1	1,603.1	1,871.5	2,988.7	3,283.6	397.6	570.1
Utah	240.0	285.7	3.5	3.4	20.3	23.7	68.8	86.5	147.3	172.1	4,510.6	5,048.3	1,171.6	1,106.9	3,004.6	3,689.9	334.5	251.5
Vermont	149.5	126.9	1.4	2.3	15.9	34.9	30.8	23.1	101.2	66.7	3,814.5	4,564.9	1,348.2	1,178.3	2,201.0	3,131.8	265.2	254.8
Virginia	290.0	309.1	9.0	7.4	23.3	24.9	92.1	122.2	165.7	154.6	3,734.0	3,946.7	986.2	973.5	2,521.2	2,789.1	226.7	184.1
Washington	374.9	406.4	4.3	4.4	39.6	45.9	106.2	117.9	224.8	238.3	5,352.8	5,875.8	1,605.6	1,680.1	3,386.9	3,914.9	360.3	280.8
West Virginia	152.3	174.8	6.0	5.2	13.2	15.5	42.2	49.8	90.9	104.3	2,102.4	2,336.4	597.4	717.9	1,341.7	1,435.4	163.3	183.1
Wisconsin	131.5	190.5	2.8	3.1	12.9	14.3	52.2	71.2	63.7	101.9	3,681.9	4,248.6	846.9	977.2	2,614.2	3,088.7	220.7	182.7
Wyoming	240.9	304.2	5.4	9.2	21.9	27.1	39.7	34.3	173.9	233.7	3,865.8	4,499.8	811.6	882.9	2,772.2	3,367.1	282.0	249.8
Atlanta	590.6	719.4	11.3	12.6	45.8	54.2	240.8	276.0	292.6	376.6	5,083.3	6,226.8	1,698.9	1,966.1	2,928.6	3,777.5	455.8	483.2
Baltimore	971.9	1,173.3	10.2	13.3	41.0	39.8	417.6	510.6	**503.1**	**609.6**	5,461.2	5,694.6	1,518.7	1,556.8	3,415.2	3,716.9	527.4	420.9
Boston	515.6	680.2	3.6	5.3	22.6	24.2	238.5	306.3	251.0	344.4	5,192.4	5,351.1	1,489.3	1,387.8	2,271.2	2,632.2	**1,431.9**	1,331.1
Chicago	560.5	536.7	13.7	11.7	24.6	23.5	289.4	285.4	232.7	216.1	5,124.3	4,746.6	1,190.8	1,117.5	3,196.5	2,950.7	737.1	678.4
Dallas	564.6	718.0	15.2	15.9	42.0	63.4	208.2	290.7	299.2	348.0	6,715.0	**7,329.6**	2,084.5	2,228.4	4,167.0	**4,571.7**	463.5	529.5
Detroit	825.6	890.5	14.1	14.3	47.5	49.8	454.3	475.6	309.7	350.8	5,848.1	7,284.9	1,661.3	2,249.9	3,296.7	3,792.3	890.1	1,242.7
Houston	468.9	763.1	**18.0**	**28.2**	45.9	56.7	268.4	462.3	136.6	215.9	5,557.9	6,849.7	1,736.8	**2,465.3**	3,133.1	3,046.3	687.9	**1,338.1**
Los Angeles	1,004.1	1,270.0	16.0	18.1	**64.9**	**67.7**	429.0	651.8	494.2	532.3	6,009.0	6,902.2	2,199.9	2,301.2	2,899.8	3,496.8	909.4	1,104.2
Minneapolis	309.2	359.8	3.6	3.3	28.3	33.7	148.8	183.3	128.5	139.5	5,082.5	5,537.6	1,477.1	1,622.2	3,129.3	3,584.1	476.1	331.3
New York	**1,339.3**	**1,633.1**	17.1	19.1	42.8	41.5	**810.2**	**1,077.6**	469.2	494.9	6,103.4	6,863.6	2,112.7	2,128.3	2,897.7	3,464.0	1,092.9	1,271.3
Philadelphia	430.3	627.8	8.9	10.1	27.2	31.5	212.2	320.3	182.0	265.9	3,606.0	4,309.3	1,118.0	1,245.9	2,003.7	2,483.6	484.3	579.9
Pittsburgh	319.0	385.2	4.8	4.5	20.9	21.3	155.2	221.5	138.2	137.8	2,649.6	2,841.4	825.6	879.7	1,396.2	1,519.5	427.8	442.2
St. Louis	663.9	691.2	13.0	14.8	38.9	31.2	311.5	276.4	300.5	368.8	5,142.5	5,296.9	1,610.8	1,668.5	2,941.2	3,145.3	590.6	483.0
San Francisco	768.8	875.4	11.9	10.0	51.9	51.1	378.6	443.5	326.5	370.9	**7,170.2**	6,899.9	**2,255.1**	1,881.2	**4,170.0**	4,490.8	745.1	527.8
Washington, D.C.	604.5	804.5	10.3	10.8	36.1	42.2	352.9	479.0	205.2	272.5	5,223.3	5,520.0	1,387.1	1,404.9	3,439.5	3,683.9	396.7	431.2

Boldface: highest rate among states or listed metropolitan areas. Source: U.S. Department of Justice, Federal Bureau of Investigation, *Uniform Crime Reports.*

TRANSPORTATION AND TRADE

Transportation

State	Road and street mi[1] 1983	Motor vehicles in 000s, 1982[2]			Railroad mileage 1981[3]	Airports 1983[4]	Pipeline mileage 1981[5]
		Total	Auto-mobiles	Trucks and buses			
Ala.	87,483	3,039	2,195	845	4,322	138	19,664
Alaska	9,885	319	200	119	550[6]	508	1,212
Ariz.	76,290	2,216	1,583	633	1,865	168	16,817
Ark.	76,649	1,481	965	516	2,720	152	18,387
Calif.	173,888	17,130	13,421	3,709	6,530	566	80,837
Colo.	75,433	2,502	1,843	658	3,413	222	23,488
Conn.	19,479	2,258	2,099	159	452	54	6,798
Del.	5,269	415	334	81	257	21	1,339
D.C.	1,102	231	213	19	56	2	1,162
Fla.	93,797	8,335	6,754	1,581	3,421	374	12,651
Ga.	104,253	3,916	2,995	921	4,747	242	25,147
Hawaii	4,172	586	528	58	...	36	587
Idaho	68,395	873	529	343	2,386	179	4,435
Ill.	134,405	7,242	5,855	1,387	10,143	737	53,501
Ind.	91,654	3,884	2,874	1,009	5,644	429	28,762
Iowa	112,188	2,346	1,668	678	4,887	244	18,042
Kan.	132,207	2,061	1,393	668	7,201	355	37,318
Ky.	68,674	2,615	1,810	806	3,569	102	20,110
La.	56,932	2,800	2,010	790	3,310	178	42,256
Maine	21,953	743	541	202	46	105	389
Md.	27,133	2,893	2,421	472	1,125	105	8,764
Mass.	33,800	3,750	3,297	453	1,286	77	16,915
Mich.	117,425	6,250	5,006	1,245	4,080	379	44,486
Minn.	131,214	3,278	2,338	940	6,207	414	17,232
Miss.	70,789	1,593	1,215	378	2,823	164	18,101
Mo.	118,610	3,412	2,540	871	6,855	343	21,404
Mont.	71,432	758	451	307	3,803	179	8,538
Neb.	91,901	1,215	805	410	4,778	318	14,149
Nev.	43,850	710	513	197	1,491	101	3,658
N.H.	14,467	774	661	113	496	42	1,162
N.J.	33,692	4,917	4,390	528	1,525	119	23,106
N.M.	53,752	1,193	780	413	2,076	147	25,373
N.Y.	109,825	8,235	7,202	1,033	4,531	356	41,681
N.C.	92,921	4,583	3,446	1,138	2,845	237	12,090
N.D.	86,041	653	381	272	4,935	439	2,950
Ohio	111,150	7,636	6,325	1,311	7,140	515	52,981
Okla.	109,875	2,780	1,788	992	3,850	283	38,578
Ore.	133,734	2,075	1,467	607	2,944	258	10,070
Pa.	115,964	6,725	5,618	1,107	6,961	487	52,527
R.I.	6,275	586	507	79	93	12	2,425
S.C.	63,015	1,975	1,519	456	2,558	126	9,973
S.D.	73,249	615	377	239	2,120	159	2,622
Tenn.	83,757	3,381	2,766	615	3,035	127	16,502
Texas	272,427	11,388	7,993	3,395	13,050	1,200	120,880
Utah	44,147	1,038	712	326	1,656	79	8,504
Vt.	13,942	351	270	81	142	48	404
Va.	64,905	3,705	3,153	552	3,451	204	11,345
Wash.	83,324	3,237	2,296	940	4,297	287	11,883
W.Va.	34,568	1,142	793	349	3,534	59	22,331
Wis.	108,059	3,162	2,560	602	4,165	392	22,197
Wyo.	36,945	508	299	209	1,988	94	8,457
TOTAL	3,866,296	159,510	123,698	35,812	174,359	12,562	1,064,170

[1] Includes federally controlled roads. [2] Detail does not add to total because of rounding; excludes vehicles owned by military. [3] Class I only; class II and III not available. [4] Public and private. [5] Gas utility industry miles only. [6] 1980 data; includes class I and II. Sources: Assn. of American Railroads; Dept. of Transportation, FAA, FHWA, Dept. of Energy.

Communications Facilities

State	Post Offices Oct. 15, 1982	TELEPHONES Dec. 31, 1981 Total	Residential	BROADCAST STATIONS Commercial Radio, 1980 AM	FM	Comm. TV 1982	Public TV 1982	NEWSPAPERS 1982 Daily Number[1]	Daily Circulation[2]	Weekly Number	Weekly Circulation	Sunday Number[1]	Sunday Circulation[2]
Alabama	611	2,640,727	2,013,822	143	77	17	9	27	734,026	104	477,696	20	693,931
Alaska	186	325,000	208,000	22	12	7	4	8	129,869	13	23,486	2	104,897
Arizona	210	2,194,558	1,630,688	62	32	13	2	19	656,016	48	283,777	10	620,604
Arkansas	618	1,461,555	1,114,927	93	54	8	4	32	486,807	112	333,082	17	489,586
California	1,109	21,163,281	14,994,878	235	208	57	13	120	6,027,511	429	5,928,745	55	5,649,132
Colorado	406	2,560,912	1,823,533	72	53	12	3	28	953,878	114	452,172	10	1,000,230
Connecticut	242	2,702,082	1,999,582	39	25	5	4	25	900,869	60	666,853	10	747,832
Delaware	55	540,123	391,222	10	7	—	1	3	153,992	12	61,241	2	154,294
District of Columbia	1	1,094,898	511,118	8	9	5	2	3	1,343,231	...	...	1	971,957
Florida	459	8,679,284	6,504,473	200	118	33	10	50	2,675,954	157	1,812,712	33	2,862,492
Georgia	628	4,339,135	3,214,403	187	93	20	10	37	1,031,969	201	1,372,658	15	1,028,084
Hawaii	76	721,926	470,475	26	8	10	2	7	253,210	1	112,459	3	410,187
Idaho	256	717,652	529,417	44	23	8	3	14	214,421	55	131,525	7	193,205
Illinois	1,258	10,275,846	7,700,284	128	132	23	6	75	2,755,940	685	4,108,700	24	2,731,161
Indiana	749	4,117,473	3,140,906	86	95	20	7	76	1,603,256	181	684,714	18	1,202,489
Iowa	949	2,297,443	1,736,326	77	75	14	8	40	843,069	335	748,473	9	722,459
Kansas	686	2,008,332	1,521,149	60	47	12	2	47	572,205	213	458,387	18	498,774
Kentucky	1,200	2,337,658	1,775,985	123	88	10	15	25	736,570	141	629,307	11	613,379
Louisiana	526	3,091,845	2,327,514	95	65	18	6	25	798,571	97	837,044	16	842,050
Maine	490	815,587	629,480	38	33	7	5	9	288,392	39	221,305	2	216,778
Maryland	425	3,648,571	2,708,286	50	38	7	4	16	779,298	61	656,113	5	662,123
Massachusetts	422	4,654,749	3,384,834	67	39	12	3	45	2,003,853	180	1,720,825	10	1,555,669
Michigan	853	7,253,301	5,526,140	131	122	25	8	52	2,491,888	257	1,813,342	15	2,447,080
Minnesota	852	3,256,597	2,394,889	94	73	13	6	26	931,373	339	1,337,573	11	994,064
Mississippi	454	1,612,513	1,246,448	107	75	11	8	24	410,276	92	300,275	12	332,974
Missouri	957	3,878,677	2,901,274	112	80	22	4	48	1,499,732	260	1,507,415	19	1,393,909
Montana	359	630,733	461,943	46	25	13	—	11	200,510	73	178,961	8	201,905
Nebraska	541	1,344,341	998,285	49	37	14	9	19	478,764	190	487,367	7	422,985
Nevada	88	756,148	516,269	22	13	7	1	8	239,450	16	67,817	5	250,050
New Hampshire	239	727,611	545,041	28	15	1	5	9	202,662	39	387,425	3	101,473
New Jersey	519	6,797,352	5,026,272	39	36	1	4	26	1,711,322	190	1,978,105	17	1,736,835
New Mexico	326	896,584	625,661	57	29	10	3	20	285,756	25	194,262	14	263,728
New York	1,623	12,749,979	9,370,000	161	120	32	12	76	8,204,999	415	2,951,988	34	5,821,428
North Carolina	772	4,325,419	3,261,481	215	89	19	9	55	1,380,831	121	600,018	25	1,171,171
North Dakota	435	541,479	396,208	28	10	12	4	10	193,293	89	180,562	5	146,415
Ohio	1,069	8,085,385	6,179,172	124	130	29	13	92	3,013,323	270	1,976,032	29	2,600,251
Oklahoma	614	2,550,326	1,869,598	67	53	14	3	53	848,475	201	424,910	43	876,678
Oregon	345	2,034,403	1,421,853	80	37	12	5	20	647,383	89	405,523	8	629,191
Pennsylvania	1,773	9,894,620	7,509,655	179	125	29	7	98	3,538,186	219	1,789,084	21	2,914,870
Rhode Island	55	730,133	551,639	15	7	3	1	7	315,344	17	117,156	2	252,857
South Carolina	387	2,131,681	1,590,516	108	56	13	10	17	600,408	69	267,080	8	521,895
South Dakota	402	529,264	390,112	33	19	11	8	12	169,515	144	231,487	4	123,193
Tennessee	563	3,247,787	2,480,683	164	81	19	6	31	1,070,631	126	523,704	16	1,031,739
Texas	1,484	11,690,638	8,367,781	290	199	59	11	116	3,598,953	504	1,822,109	97	4,127,555
Utah	207	1,094,279	822,818	35	22	4	2	6	287,456	54	261,652	6	375,071
Vermont	282	377,716	278,625	19	12	3	4	8	119,350	28	94,587	3	80,914
Virginia	884	3,956,259	2,923,675	138	74	15	9	38	1,167,159	94	544,533	15	874,314
Washington	460	3,341,681	2,335,422	96	49	14	5	28	1,160,023	128	946,233	18	1,161,408
West Virginia	1,005	1,137,637	869,808	63	34	9	3	25	467,987	73	303,120	10	402,522
Wisconsin	774	3,501,055	2,622,358	102	94	19	8	35	1,205,363	229	771,908	11	956,924
Wyoming	165	429,361	296,592	31	10	6	—	10	103,858	37	109,540	4	76,052
TOTAL U.S.	30,049	181,891,596	134,111,520	4,498	3,057	757	291	1,711	62,487,177	7,626	44,295,042	768	56,260,764

[1]Data as of Feb. 1, 1983. [2]Data for 6 months ending Sept. 30.

Sources: U.S. Postal Service; Federal Communications Commission; American Telephone and Telegraph Co.; *International Television Almanac, 1983;* The Editor & Publisher Co., Inc., *International Year Book, 1983* (Copyright 1983. All rights reserved. Used by permission.); National Newspaper Association, *National Directory of Weekly Newspapers, 1983.*

Major Trading Partners, by Value

in millions of dollars

Country	EXPORTS 1977	EXPORTS 1982	IMPORTS 1977	IMPORTS 1982
North America	34,466	52,056	41,310	70,013
Canada	25,788	33,720	29,598	46,477
Mexico	4,822	11,817	4,694	15,566
South America	9,285	15,256	10,417	14,454
Argentina	731	1,294	392	1,128
Brazil	2,490	3,423	2,241	4,285
Chile	520	925	273	666
Colombia	782	1,903	820	801
Peru	500	1,117	513	1,099
Venezuela	3,172	5,206	5,111	4,768
Europe	37,304	63,664	28,877	53,413
Belgium and Luxembourg	3,138	5,229	1,453	2,396
France	3,503	7,110	3,048	5,545
Germany, West	5,989	9,291	7,252	11,975
Italy	2,790	4,616	3,042	5,301
Netherlands, The	4,812	8,604	1,497	2,494
Spain	1,875	3,456	973	1,505
Sweden	1,101	1,689	998	1,992
Switzerland	1,749	2,707	1,190	2,340
United Kingdom	5,951	10,645	5,146	13,095
U.S.S.R.	1,628	2,587	457	228
Asia	32,418	64,822	50,210	85,170
China	172	2,912	205	2,284
Hong Kong	1,292	2,493	2,897	5,540
India	779	1,598	776	1,404
Indonesia	763	2,025	3,475	4,224
Israel	1,447	2,271	572	1,164
Japan	10,529	20,966	18,555	37,744
Korea, South	2,371	5,529	2,883	5,637
Malaysia	561	1,736	1,318	1,885
Philippines	876	1,854	1,110	1,806
Saudi Arabia	3,575	9,026	6,448	7,443
Singapore	1,172	3,213	883	2,195
Taiwan	1,798	4,367	3,669	8,892
Oceania	2,876	5,700	1,729	3,130
Australia	2,356	4,535	1,186	2,287
Africa	4,563	10,271	17,826	17,770
Algeria	527	909	3,089	2,673
Nigeria	958	1,295	6,461	7,045
South Africa	1,054	2,368	1,261	1,967
TOTAL	121,293	212,275	150,390	243,952

Sources: U.S. Department of Commerce, International Trade Administration, *Overseas Business Reports; Highlights of U.S. Export and Import Trade.*

Major Commodities Traded

in millions of dollars

Item	1979	1980	1981	1982
TOTAL EXPORTS[1]	182,025	220,786	233,739	212,275
Agricultural commodities				
Grains and preparations	14,450	18,079	19,457	14,747
Soybeans	5,708	5,883	6,200	6,240
Raw cotton other than linters	2,198	2,864	2,260	1,955
Nonagricultural commodities				
Ores and metal scrap	3,325	4,518	2,718	2,174
Coal	3,394	4,621	5,909	6,072
Chemicals	17,308	20,740	21,187	19,890
Machinery	45,914	57,263	64,426	59,324
Agricultural machinery, tractors, parts	1,685	3,442	3,716	2,388
Electronic computers, parts	5,671	7,763	8,741	5,349
Transport equipment	24,577	27,366	31,310	27,824
Civilian aircraft	6,177	8,256	8,613	4,848
Paper and manufactures	1,967	2,831	2,961	2,653
Metalworking machinery	1,391	1,756	2,158	1,611
Iron and steel mill products	2,227	2,998	2,801	2,101
Textiles other than clothing	3,189	3,632	3,619	2,784
Firearms of war and ammunition	1,854	2,006	2,165	3,270
TOTAL IMPORTS[1]	209,458	244,871	261,305	243,952
Agricultural commodities				
Meat and preparations	2,539	2,346	1,996	2,075
Fish	2,639	2,612	2,962	3,143
Coffee	3,820	3,872	2,622	2,730
Sugar	974	1,988	2,142	863
Nonagricultural commodities				
Ores and metal scrap	3,249	3,696	3,838	2,684
Petroleum, crude	49,361	65,112	61,940	45,862
Petroleum products	9,753	12,525	13,637	13,534
Natural gas	2,765	3,940	5,719	5,934
Chemicals	7,479	8,594	9,446	9,494
Machinery	28,530	32,297	38,546	39,457
Transport equipment	25,148	28,260	31,081	33,863
Automobiles, new	14,812	16,775	17,541	19,757
Iron and steel mill products	6,764	6,686	10,347	9,184
Nonferrous metals	4,678	5,183	5,370	5,320
Textiles other than clothing	2,216	2,493	3,046	2,808
Gold bullion	1,462	2,715	2,118	1,827

[1]Totals include Virgin Islands.

Sources: U.S. Department of Commerce, International Trade Administration, *Overseas Business Reports;* Bureau of the Census, *Highlights of U.S. Export and Import Trade.*

Upper Volta

A republic of West Africa, Upper Volta is bordered by Mali, Niger, Benin, Togo, Ghana, and Ivory Coast. Area: 274,200 sq km (105,900 sq mi). Pop. (1983 est.): 6,569,000. Cap. and largest city: Ouagadougou (pop., 1980 est., 235,000). Language: French (official). Religion: animist 49.8%; Muslim 16.6%; Roman Catholic 8.3%. Heads of state in 1983, Maj. Jean-Baptiste Ouedraogo and, from August 4, Capt. Thomas Sankara; premier from January 10 to May 17, Captain Sankara.

On Aug. 4, 1983, Upper Volta experienced its second coup in two years when Capt. Thomas Sankara (*see* BIOGRAPHIES), premier from January 10 until May 17, ousted head of state Maj. Jean-Baptiste Ouedraogo. Sankara had been arrested on May 17, along with other radical members of the ruling People's Salvation Council (CSP). He was released on May 30 after the dissolution of the CSP by Major Ouedraogo, who announced a return to civilian rule within six months and then formed a new government excluding Sankara's supporters.

Two months later Sankara mounted his successful coup, supported by a unit of paratroopers. A National Revolutionary Council was set up under his presidency, and on August 24 a predominantly civilian government was named. The political situation remained tense. On October 28 Sankara alleged the existence of a plot to overthrow "our young revolution." In December it was announced that two former presidents, Sangoulé Lamizana and Saye Zerbo, and perhaps 36 former ministers were to be tried on charges of corruption.

(PHILIPPE DECRAENE)

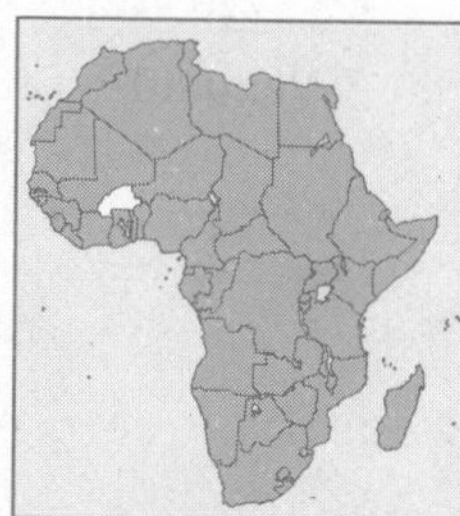

Upper Volta

UPPER VOLTA

Education. (1980–81) Primary, pupils 201,595, teachers 3,700; secondary, pupils 23,420, teachers (1979–80) 580; vocational, pupils 3,871, teachers (1979–80) 580; teacher training, students 248, teachers (1979–80) 28; higher (1979–80), students 3,173, teaching staff 166.

Finance. Monetary unit: CFA franc, with (Sept. 20, 1983) a par value of CFA Fr 50 to the French franc (free rate of CFA Fr 403 = U.S. $1; CFA Fr 607 = £1 sterling). Budget (1982 est.) balanced at CFA Fr 47.6 billion.

Foreign Trade. (1981) Imports CFA Fr 91,440,000,000; exports CFA Fr 19,920,000,000. Import sources: France 33%; Ivory Coast 22%; U.S. 11%. Export destinations: Ivory Coast 31%; France 12%; West Germany 6%; China 5%; Japan 5%. Main exports: cotton 41%; livestock 17%; oilseeds and nuts 16%.

Uruguay

A republic of South America, Uruguay is on the Atlantic Ocean and is bounded by Brazil and Argentina. Area: 176,215 sq km (68,037 sq mi). Pop. (1983 est.): 2,954,000, including white 90%; mestizo 10%. Cap. and largest city: Montevideo (pop., 1983 est., 1,255,000). Language: Spanish. Religion (1980): Roman Catholic 59.5%; atheist 3.4%; Protestant 2%; Jewish 1.7%; other Christian 1.7%; none 31.7%. President in 1983, Gen. Gregorio Conrado Álvarez Armelino.

Following the legalization of three political parties in Uruguay in 1982, discussions on a new constitution began in May 1983 between the parties and the military government. Party representatives withdrew on July 4, however, because they did not accept the government's proposals to write considerable power for the military into the constitution. Despite the breakdown of talks, the government confirmed that elections would be held in November 1984.

Uruguay

URUGUAY

Education. (1980) Primary, pupils 331,247, teachers 14,768; secondary, pupils 125,438, teachers (1976) c. 13,980; vocational (1978), pupils 45,663, teachers (1976) c. 4,200; teacher training, students (1979) 4,765, teachers (1973) 341; higher, students 36,298, teaching staff 3,847.

Finance. Monetary unit: new peso, with (Sept. 20, 1983) a free rate of 35.87 new pesos to U.S. $1 (54.02 new pesos = £1 sterling). Gold and other reserves (June 1983) U.S. $222 million. Budget (1981 actual): revenue 29,061,000,000 new pesos; expenditure 30,512,000,000 new pesos. Gross domestic product (1981) 126,469,000,000 new pesos. Cost of living (Montevideo; 1975 = 100; June 1983) 2,164.

Foreign Trade. (1982) Imports U.S. $1,051,900,000; exports U.S. $1,022,900,000. Import sources: U.S. 12%; Nigeria 12%; Brazil 12%; Venezuela 9%; Iran 8%; Mexico 8%; Argentina 8%; West Germany 6%. Export destinations: Brazil 14%; Argentina 11%; West Germany 9%; U.S.S.R. 8%; U.S. 7%; Iran 5%; Egypt 5%. Main exports (1981): wool 20%; beef and veal 18%; clothing 9%; rice 9%; fish 5%; leather 5%.

Transport and Communications. Roads (1981) 49,813 km. Motor vehicles in use (1981): passenger 281,300; commercial 43,400. Railways (1981): 3,004 km; traffic 339 million passenger-km, freight 221 million net ton-km. Air traffic (1982): 293 million passenger-km; freight c. 1.1 million net ton-km. Shipping (1982): merchant vessels 100 gross tons and over 81; gross tonnage 201,677. Telephones (Jan. 1981) 287,100. Radio receivers (Dec. 1980) 1,630,000. Television receivers (Dec. 1980) 363,000.

Agriculture. Production (in 000; metric tons; 1982): wheat 316; corn (1981) 196; rice 419; sorghum 123; potatoes (1981) c. 130; sweet potatoes c. 60; sugar, raw value (1981) c. 79; linseed 11; sunflower seed 46; apples c. 22; oranges 69; grapes c. 110; wool c. 46; beef and veal c. 390; fish catch (1981) 145. Livestock (in 000; 1982): cattle c. 10,872; sheep (1981) c. 20,429; pigs c. 430; horses c. 530; chickens (1981) c. 8,000.

Industry. Production (in 000; metric tons; 1981): crude steel 10; cement c. 690; petroleum products 1,691; electricity (kw-hr) 3,603,000.

Uruguayan students joined a national day of protest demanding freedom in education, an end to military rule, and amnesty for political prisoners.

WIDE WORLD

For the first time in nine years, the government permitted a May Day march by the labour unions. More than 100,000 turned out in Montevideo to call for freedom, amnesty, and the right to strike. On August 25, in response to a call by the political parties, the civilian population stayed indoors, emerging from their homes at the scheduled time to bang on pots and pans and sound car horns in protest against the government's austerity policy and its refusal to continue the dialogue with the parties.

A second national day of protest took place on September 25. Two days earlier, a leading politician, Eladio Fernández Menéndez, had been arrested for handing out leaflets promoting the protest. The arrest was widely taken as a signal of the military's negative reaction to the prospect of reopening discussions with the politicians.

(MICHAEL WOOLLER)

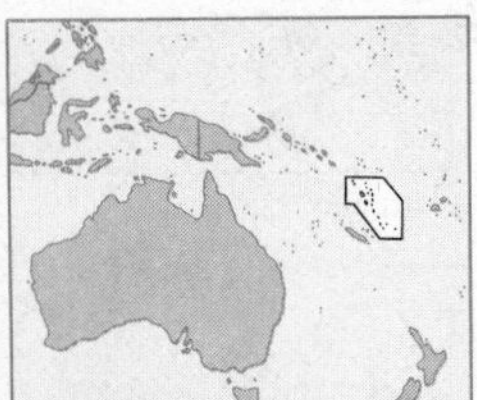
Vanuatu

Vatican City State

Vanuatu

The republic of Vanuatu, a member of the Commonwealth, comprises 12 main islands, the largest of which are Espíritu Santo, Malekula, Efate, Ambrym, Aoba, and Tanna, and some 60 smaller ones in the southwest Pacific Ocean, forming a chain some 800 km in length. Area: 12,190 sq km (4,707 sq mi). Pop. (1983 est.): 128,000, predominantly Melanesian. Cap. and largest city: Vila, on Efate Island (pop., 1979, 14,600). Language: Bislama, a Melanesian pidgin (national); French and English (official). Religion (1979): Presbyterian 36.7%; Roman Catholic 15%; Anglican 15%; other Christian 10%; other 23.3%. President in 1983, George Sokomanu; prime minister, the Rev. Walter Lini.

In elections held in Vanuatu on Nov. 2, 1983, Prime Minister Walter Lini's Vanuaaku Party was returned to office with a reduced majority. The electoral success was achieved despite divisions within the party during the year. Parliament approved legislation that made adultery a criminal offense and also restricted overseas ownership of locally produced newspapers. The publisher-editor of the only independent newspaper was asked to leave the country after she had criticized the prime minister's handling of an overseas loan.

Financial aid from France was devoted to the preservation of the French-language system, while a soft loan was used to establish a major cocoa development. British aid went toward social services and development projects. Vanuatu clashed with France over the latter's nuclear testing at Mururoa Atoll and over ownership of Matthew and Hunter islands, both uninhabited, which were of importance in the demarcation of a 200-mi exclusive economic zone.

(BARRIE MACDONALD)

VANUATU

Education. (1982) Primary, pupils 23,595, teachers 1,063; secondary, pupils 2,067, teachers 126; vocational, pupils 293, teachers 31; teacher training, students 58, teachers 9.

Finance. Monetary unit: vatu, with (Sept. 20, 1983) a free rate of 101 vatu = U.S. $1 (152 vatu = £1 sterling). Budget (1982 est.): revenue 2,415,000,000 vatu; expenditure 2,472,000,000 vatu.

Foreign Trade. (1981) Imports 5,123,000,000 vatu; exports 2,882,000,000 vatu. Import sources: Australia c. 39%; Fiji c. 17%; Japan c. 13%; France c. 10%; New Zealand c. 8%; Spain c. 6%. Export destinations (domestic exports only): Belgium-Luxembourg 34%; France 27%; The Netherlands 25%; New Caledonia 6%. Main exports: copra 38%; frozen fish 29%; beef and veal 6%.

Agriculture. Production (in 000; metric tons; 1981): bananas c. 1; copra c. 46; cocoa c. 1; fish catch 2.7. Livestock (in 000; 1981): cattle c. 95; pigs c. 68; chickens c. 154.

Universities:
see Education

Urban Mass Transit:
see Transportation

U.S.S.R.:
see Union of Soviet Socialist Republics

Vatican City State

This independent sovereignty is surrounded by but is not part of Rome. As a state with territorial limits, it is properly distinguished from the Holy See, which constitutes the worldwide administrative and legislative body for the Roman Catholic Church. The area of Vatican City is 44 ha (108.8 ac). Pop. (1982 est.): 736. As sovereign pontiff, John Paul II is the chief of state. Vatican City is administered by a pontifical commission of five cardinals headed by the secretary of state, in 1983 Agostino Cardinal Casaroli.

On Jan. 5, 1983, Pope John Paul II named 18 new cardinals: from Africa, Archbishops Bernard Yago of Abidjan, Ivory Coast, and Alexandre do Nascimento of Lubango, Angola; from North America,

Joseph L. Bernardin, archbishop of Chicago, was elevated to the Sacred College of Cardinals on February 2. He received a cardinal's ring from Pope John Paul II in ceremonies in St. Peter's Basilica at the Vatican.

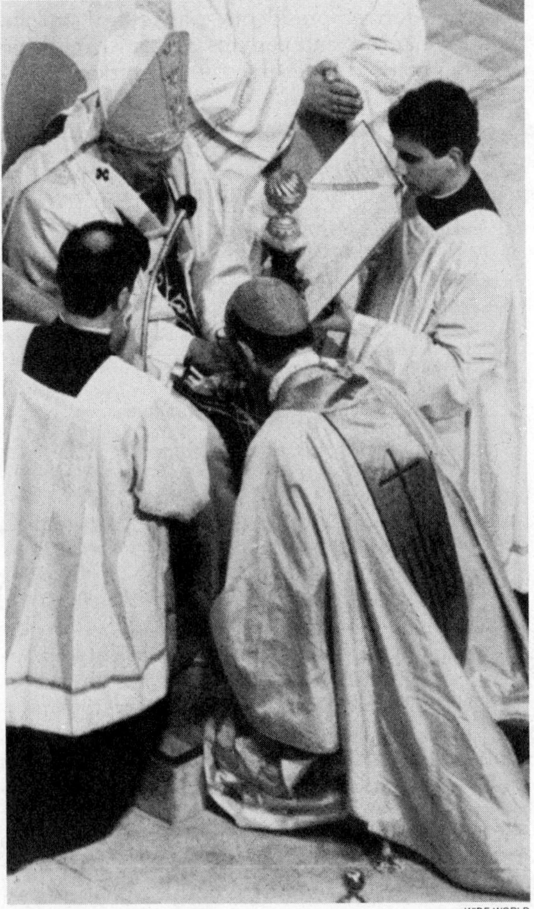
WIDE WORLD

Archbishop Joseph Bernardin of Chicago (*see* BIOGRAPHIES); from South America, Archbishops Alfonso López Trujillo of Medellín, Colombia, and José Lebrun Moratinos of Caracas, Venezuela; from Asia, Antoine Khoraiche, Maronite patriarch of Antioch, Lebanon, and Archbishop Michael Kitbunchu of Bangkok, Thailand; from Europe, Archbishops Franjo Kuharic of Zagreb, Yugos., Godfried Danneels of Malines-Brussels, Belgium, Carlo Maria Martini of Milan, Italy, Jean-Marie Lustiger of Paris, Jozef Glemp of Gniezno and Warsaw, Bishop Joachim Meisner of Berlin, East Germany, and Archbishop Julijans Vaivods of Riga, Latvian S.S.R. (the first Soviet citizen to be appointed to the Sacred College); and from Oceania, Archbishop Thomas Williams of Wellington, N.Z. The other new cardinals were two Curia prelates, Archbishops Aurelio Sabattani and Giuseppe Casoria, and the French Jesuit scholar Henri de Lubac.

In November the U.S. Congress repealed an 1867 ban on diplomatic relations with the Vatican. Several presidents had had personal representatives there but restoring more formal ties foundered on the question of church-state relations. In December the administration was considering naming an ambassador. (MAX BERGERRE)

See also Religion: *Roman Catholic Church.*

Venezuela

A republic of northern South America, Venezuela is bounded by Colombia, Brazil, Guyana, and the Caribbean Sea. Area: 912,050 sq km (352,144 sq mi). Pop. (1983 est.): 15,117,000, including mestizo 69%; white 20%; Negro 9%; Indian 2%. Cap. and largest city: Caracas (metro. area pop., 1981 est., 3,041,000). Language: Spanish. Religion: predominantly Roman Catholic. President in 1983, Luis Herrera Campins.

Presidential and congressional elections were held in Venezuela on Dec. 4, 1983. Jaime Lusinchi, the presidential candidate of the main opposition party, the social democratic Acción Democrática, won election easily, becoming the first candidate to receive more than 50% of the vote since 1947. His chief opponent, former president Rafael Caldera of the ruling Social Christian Party, (COPEI), obtained somewhat over 30%. Acción Democrática also gained a majority (118 seats) in the Congress. Lusinchi, who would take office in February 1984, announced that he would introduce austerity measures to cope with Venezuela's serious economic problems.

The government was forced to take action at the beginning of 1983 to halt massive capital flight, which, together with reduced earnings from oil exports, had caused a cash crisis and a decline in the money supply. Loss of confidence among private investors and fears of devaluation had pushed sales of foreign currency to a record $150 million a day when the exchange markets were closed on February 20. The government subsequently introduced a three-tier exchange rate system, a 60-day price freeze, and import controls. A preferential exchange rate of 4.30 bolivares to U.S. $1 was retained for essential imports, government transactions, the oil industry, and public-sector debt repayments; a second rate of 6 bolivares to $1 was created for most other trade payments; and a free-floating rate was introduced for tourism, private-sector remittances, and other transactions.

VENEZUELA

Education. (1979–80) Primary, pupils 2,456,815, teachers 88,493; secondary, pupils 751,356; vocational, pupils 40,264; teacher training, pupils 29,040; secondary, vocational, and teacher training, teachers 45,888; higher, students 299,773, teaching staff 27,025.

Finance. Monetary unit: bolívar, with (Sept. 20, 1983) a main official rate of 4.30 bolivares to U.S. $1 (free rate of 6.48 bolivares = £1 sterling). Gold and other reserves (June 1983) U.S. $6,439,000,000. Budget (total; 1981 actual): revenue 97,429,000,000 bolivares; expenditure 82,885,000,000 bolivares. Gross national product (1982) 292.7 billion bolivares. Money supply (April 1983) 53,543,000,000 bolivares. Cost of living (Caracas; 1975 = 100; June 1983) 228.2.

Foreign Trade. (1982) Imports 53,584,000,000 bolivares; exports 70,583,000,000 bolivares. Import sources (1981): U.S. 48%; Japan 8%; West Germany 6%; Canada 5%. Export destinations (1981): U.S. 25%; Netherlands Antilles 21%; Canada 9%; Italy 7%; Brazil 5%. Main exports: crude oil 63%; petroleum products 32%.

Transport and Communications. Roads (1981) 62,449 km. Motor vehicles in use (1981): passenger 1,501,400; commercial 763,500. Railways: (1981) *c.* 268 km; traffic (1979) 25 million passenger-km, freight 18 million net ton-km. Air traffic (1982): *c.* 5,031,000,000 passenger-km; freight (1981) *c.* 144.6 million net ton-km. Shipping (1982): merchant vessels 100 gross tons and over 236; gross tonnage 910,841. Telephones (Dec. 1979) 789,000. Radio receivers (Dec. 1980) 5,350,000. Television receivers (Dec. 1980) 1,710,000.

Agriculture. Production (in 000; metric tons; 1982): corn 501; rice 670; sorghum 337; potatoes *c.* 216; cassava *c.* 360; sugar, raw value *c.* 367; tomatoes *c.* 135; sesame seed 53; bananas *c.* 926; oranges *c.* 370; coffee *c.* 59; cocoa *c.* 15; tobacco *c.* 17; cotton, lint *c.* 16; beef and veal *c.* 302; fish catch (1981) 181. Livestock (in 000; 1982): cattle 11,500; pigs *c.* 2,600; sheep *c.* 351; goats *c.* 1,395; horses *c.* 486; asses *c.* 450; poultry *c.* 44,000.

Industry. Production (in 000; metric tons; 1982): crude oil 99,649; natural gas (cu m; 1981) 16,640,000; petroleum products (1981) 43,071; iron ore (64% metal content) 11,680; crude steel 2,036; cement (1981) *c.* 4,900; gold (troy oz; 1981) 18; diamonds (metric carats; 1981) *c.* 500; electricity (kw-hr; 1981) 37,542,000.

Venezuela

The business sector subsequently suffered delays in obtaining authorization from the government for foreign currency for imports. There was also much debate about whether preferential-rate dollars should be made available for private-sector debt servicing. Because over 95% of export revenue was earned by the public sector, the exchange market was heavily dependent upon the central bank for provision of foreign currency, and there were periods in which the commercial banks had their supplies severely rationed or suspended. The situation led to much criticism of the government's policies; the central bank, however, was able to accumulate reserves of over $10.7 billion by October, up from $8.7 billion in February.

On March 24 the government imposed a partial moratorium on principal repayments of public-sector debt, with the effect that virtually no capital was repaid during the year. Total public-sector debt was estimated at $25.1 billion, of which the government wished to reschedule about $17.4 billion due for repayment in 1983 and 1984. In negotiations with international banks, however, the government continually stalled, its aim apparent-

Venda:
see South Africa

WIDE WORLD

Jaime Lusinchi, elected president of Venezuela on December 4, was congratulated by supporters in Caracas after his victory.

ly being to postpone the rescheduling until after the December elections. The creditor banks were insistent that Venezuela implement an economic adjustment program approved by the International Monetary Fund (IMF) before reaching an agreement on rescheduling details, but the government resisted, declaring that it did not need IMF finance in 1983. This was also seen as an election maneuver, since an IMF austerity program would not win votes for COPEI.

Oil production in the period January–August reached 1.8 million bbl a day, an increase of 4.2% over the same period in 1982 and slightly above Venezuela's production quota of 1.7 million bbl a day set by the Organization of Petroleum Exporting Countries (OPEC). The slump in the world oil market and reduced income from oil exports forced the state oil company, Petróleos de Venezuela (PDVSA), to slash its investment budget by 40%. Revenue from oil exports in 1983 was expected to decline to $13.8 billion from $15.6 billion in 1982, though a reduction in imports could, nevertheless, bring about a trade surplus of about $5.7 billion. Unemployment was officially expected to rise to 12% from 8% in 1982, although the labour unions put the figure at nearer 20%.

(SARAH CAMERON)

Veterinary Science

The state of animal health worldwide was reviewed at the 22nd congress of the World Veterinary Association (WVA) in August 1983. For the first time the meeting was held in the Southern Hemisphere; Perth, Western Australia, was host to some 2,000 veterinary scientists from throughout the world.

The congress heard that rinderpest (cattle plague) was sweeping across the central part of the African continent. Eradicated from the Western countries, rinderpest is a viral disease that remains one of the most serious threats to world food production. It may kill nine out of ten animals in a herd. R. B. Griffiths of the UN Food and Agriculture Organization (FAO) said that the plague was spreading to areas that had been disease-free for many years. The breakdown in control of the disease had several different causes. Resulting partly from political instability and consequent deterioration in the operation of control schemes in some countries, it was caused elsewhere by sheer lack of veterinary resources. In Africa 1% of the world's veterinary population had to cope with controlling disease in 10% of the world population of domestic livestock. The FAO allocated up to $3 million toward an emergency program to prevent the spread of rinderpest.

Throughout the world generally, the increase in the international movement of animals and animal products brought with it a greater risk of spreading diseases. Some countries did not take adequate precautions to prevent infections from being transmitted or were unprepared to recognize and deal with unusual diseases. This led to such recent incidents as the spread of African swine fever first to Malta, where the whole pig population had to be slaughtered, and then to Brazil and the Dominican Republic.

One of the organizations actively engaged in efforts to control animal disease was the International Office of Epizootics (OIE). With 103 member countries, the OIE collated and disseminated information about disease outbreaks. At the WVA congress it was announced that improvements in the method of recording, storing, and accessing information by the OIE should result in better understanding of the way animal diseases spread and in greater efficiency in preventive and control programs.

One of the most puzzling animal diseases is scrapie, which affects the central nervous system of sheep. It is caused by one of the "slow viruses," elusive organisms that apparently can lie dormant within a host for years before causing illness. Slow viruses are responsible for kuru, a related disease that occurs in humans in New Guinea. During the year workers at the University of California stated their belief that they were close to establishing the nature of those two ailments. A pure protein organism called a prion, said to be without genes yet capable of reproducing itself, was isolated. When injected into sheep, prions cause scrapie. It was hoped that further work on the structure of prions would help to identify the cause of various diseases of humans that involve an immunological factor, such as rheumatoid arthritis and certain types of cancer.

Equine influenza is a troublesome cause of poor performance in racehorses. Vaccines exist but have been of variable benefit. International efforts to improve their efficacy took a step forward at a meeting in Newmarket, England, sponsored jointly by the WHO and Britain's Animal Health Trust, where it was decided to launch collaborative studies to establish new methods of standardizing the vaccines.

(EDWARD BODEN)

[353.C]

Vietnam

The Socialist Republic of Vietnam is a southeast Asian state bounded on the north by China, on the west by Laos and Kampuchea, and on the south and east by the South China Sea. Area: 329,465 sq km (127,207 sq mi). Pop. (1983 est.): 57,036,000. Capital: Hanoi (pop., 1980 est., 2,543,800). Largest city: Ho Chi Minh City (pop., 1980 est., 3,486,100). Language: Vietnamese, French, English. Religion: Buddhist, animist, Confucian, Christian (Roman Catholic), Hoa Hao and Cao Dai religious sects. Secretary-general of the Communist Party in 1983, Le Duan; chairman of the National Assembly, Nguyen Huu Tho; chairman of the State Council (president), Truong Chinh; chairman of the Council of Ministers (premier), Pham Van Dong.

By Vietnam's own tumultuous standards, 1983 was a relatively placid year, but by those of most other nations, it was an eventful one. At home, politics took a back seat to the continuing, increasingly desperate struggle for a better livelihood. Abroad, Vietnam's military occupation of Kampuchea remained the key factor in its relations with other countries.

Attracting the most attention was a midyear decision by Vietnamese leaders to reverse some of the comparatively liberal economic policies that had permitted limited private enterprise for two years. Though those policies had led to increased output and a notable rise in living standards, Hanoi was worried that the drift toward an underground free market was turning into a tidal wave. One unofficial estimate had it that as much as 70% of goods in circulation were beyond the control of the state-run economy. Even worse, as Vietnam's leaders saw it, the transformation of the country into a giant black market was led by the mistrusted Hoa (ethnic Chinese) minority. "Too many capitalists have emerged," warned the Communist Party newspaper, *Nhan Dan.* It went on to attack those who "want to suppress Communist ideals by spreading, especially among youth, an egotistical and irresponsible mode of living, by trying to divide national unity, the north from the south, the party from the masses. We cannot allow such a situation to continue, especially in the cities [where most Hoa live]."

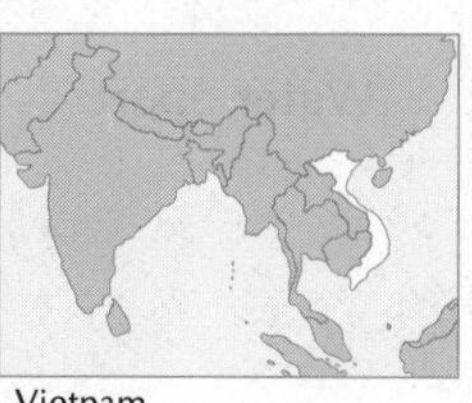
Vietnam

The authorities took stringent measures. A June plenum of the all-powerful Communist Party Central Committee stressed the need for tighter centralized control over economic policy and criticized laxity and sluggishness in socializing industry and agriculture. Taxation on free-market businesses rose sharply, to as much as 10% on sales and 60% on profits. Many privately run restaurants were closed, and street vendors came under pressure to quit. Severe restrictions were imposed on the flow of family parcels and cash remittances to the south, where the black market was most vigorous.

Parallel to the crackdown on backdoor capitalism was an attempt to revive the state-sponsored "New Economic Zones." The land-development scheme, under the stewardship of the popular chief economic planner, Vo Van Kiet, was being implemented with greater sensitivity than during the widely unpopular campaign suspended in the late 1970s. The move, analysts felt, would help relieve pressures caused by a large unproductive urban population.

One bright spot was a record 16 million-ton grain crop in 1982, with a 17 million-ton harvest within sight by late 1983. All year long, however, average Vietnamese were plagued by skyrocketing inflation and shortages of food and other goods at government outlets. Shortly after midyear the value of the dong had plunged to 135 to the U.S. dollar, compared with about 60 a year before. (The official rate was about 9.90 dong to $1.) A government clerk was paid 150–200 dong a month, and

UPI

More than 270,000 Vietnamese became refugees in China. Here some of the 650 who settled into agricultural work at the Quyang (Ch'ü-yang) state farm carry their hoes into pineapple fields.

VIETNAM

Education. (1979–80) Primary, pupils 7,923,495, teachers 217,493; secondary, pupils 3,703,199, teachers 156,164; vocational (1980–81), pupils 131,000, teachers 12,160; teacher training, pupils 42,510, teachers 4,454; higher (1980–81), students 148,600, teaching staff 16,400.

Finance. Monetary unit: dong, with (Sept. 20, 1983) a free rate of 9.90 dong to U.S. $1 (14.90 dong = £1 sterling). Budget (1979 est.) balanced at 10.5 billion dong.

Foreign Trade. (1982) Imports c. U.S. $1.9 billion; exports c. U.S. $550 million. Import sources: U.S.S.R. c. 58%; India c. 6%; Japan c. 5%. Export destinations: U.S.S.R. c. 52%; Hong Kong c. 13%; Japan c. 6%; Czechoslovakia 5%. Main exports (1974): clothing c. 10%; fish c. 10%; rubber (1980) c. 10%; coal c. 5%; beverages c. 5%.

Transport and Communications. Roads (1980) 347,243 km. Motor vehicles in use (1976): passenger c. 100,000; commercial (including buses) c. 200,000. Railways (1980): c. 2,500 km; traffic 4,554,000,000 passenger-km, freight 779 million net ton-km. Navigable waterways (1981) c. 6,000 km. Shipping (1982): merchant vessels 100 gross tons and over 106; gross tonnage 261,847. Telephones (South only; Dec. 1973) 47,000. Radio receivers (Dec. 1980) c. 5 million. Television receivers (Dec. 1980) c. 2 million.

Agriculture. Production (in 000; metric tons; 1982): rice c. 13,780; sweet potatoes (1981) c. 2,400; cassava (1981) c. 3,400; bananas c. 1,000; tea (1981) c. 23; coffee (1981) c. 7; tobacco c. 30; jute c. 36; rubber c. 50; pork c. 440; fish catch (1981) c. 1,013; timber (cu m; 1981) c. 66,010. Livestock (in 000; 1981): cattle 1,765; buffalo 2,378; pigs 10,500; chickens c. 49,200; ducks c. 30,000.

Industry. Production (in 000; metric tons; 1981): coal c. 5,900; cement c. 650; salt c. 500; chromite 15; zinc ore 6; phosphate rock c. 550; fertilizers (nutrient content) nitrogenous c. 40, phosphate 28; crude steel c. 110; cotton fabrics (m; 1979) 287,000; electricity (kw-hr) c. 4,000,000.

while rice, Vietnam's staple food, cost half a dong per kilogram at state stores, shortages led to a 15-dong price tag on the black market.

Exacerbating Vietnam's economic problems was the cost of keeping a 170,000-strong army of occupation in neighbouring Kampuchea. In early February Vietnamese forces in western Kampuchea launched an attack against encampments of Khmer guerrillas resisting Hanoi's occupation of their country. (*See* KAMPUCHEA.) At one point, Vietnamese troops in hot pursuit of the guerrillas crossed briefly into Thailand, sparking fierce artillery duels with the Thais and protests at the UN.

Much more serious, however, was a fiercer, multifront assault by Vietnam against the Khmer resistance at the end of March. Repeated crossings by Vietnamese troops into Thai territory provoked heated air and ground counterattacks from Thai forces and bursts of diplomatic outrage from Bangkok. Other countries joined in the condemnation when it became apparent that Vietnam's operation had taken a significant toll on Khmer civilian refugees encamped near the Thai-Kampuchean border. Total casualties numbered in the hundreds, and 50,000 refugees poured into Thailand. By mid-April the situation had become even more ominous as artillery battles erupted on Vietnam's border with its archenemy, China, marking the highest tide of Sino-Vietnamese hostility in two years. Though the action cooled before long, the events triggered by Vietnam's assault on the guerrillas increased regional tensions, especially between Hanoi and the countries of the Association of Southeast Asian Nations (ASEAN).

Aware of this fact, Vietnam in early May announced it would effect a partial withdrawal of its forces from Kampuchea. Some 1,500 soldiers went home that month, and more would follow later. ASEAN and Khmer resistance leaders, however, were skeptical and tended to see the exercise more as a rotation of troops than a real pullback. Though the regional "shuttle diplomacy" of Australian Foreign Minister William Hayden in July and August underscored his country's new active role in Asian affairs, it did little to break down the suspicion and hostility dividing the parties to the Kampuchean dispute.

The Soviet Union remained by far Hanoi's most important ally, contributing an estimated U.S. $3 million a day to prop up Vietnam's shaky economy and underwrite its military effort in Kampuchea. China was still enemy number one. Though Hanoi made some veiled overtures to Beijing (Peking) early in the year, by July *Nhan Dan* was saying, "China's tactics and strategy toward our country . . . have not changed in the least. Instead, [the Chinese] are showing increased hostility toward our people." Relations with the U.S. changed little. Though Hanoi continued to indicate its desire for normalized ties with Washington, the implacably anti-Soviet stance of Pres. Ronald Reagan's administration made progress virtually impossible, barring major changes in Hanoi's policies.

(THOMAS HON WING POLIN)

See also Southeast Asian Affairs.

Virgin Islands:
see Dependent States

Vital Statistics:
see Demography

Volleyball:
see Court Games

Wages and Hours:
see Economy, World; Industrial Relations

Wales:
see United Kingdom

Warsaw Treaty Organization:
see Defense

Water Resources:
see Earth Sciences; Environment

Water Sports

Motorboating. Change marked the 1983 season in power boat racing. Heightened competition in American Power Boat Association (APBA) events brought new boats, drivers, and locations to the sport.

Outboard-powered craft were added to the inboard-dominated ranks of unlimited hydroplanes. The two outboard boats made stunning debuts at the world championships in Houston, Texas, placing second and third. The world title went to Milner Irvin of Coral Gables, Fla., in "Miss Renault," a new inboard entry.

Fierce competition among the unlimiteds resulted in a varied roster of winners. Five different rigs posted victories in the season's ten races. The 1982 champion, Lee "Chip" Hanauer of Seattle, Wash., repeated his winning performance aboard "Atlas Van Lines," claiming the 1983 APBA Gold Cup trophy and the U.S. championship.

Equipment innovation also affected offshore racing, with the midseason introduction of two 50-ft (15-m) "superboats," "Popeye's Pepsi Challenger" and "MerCruiser Special." Capable of reaching speeds of more than 195 km/h (120 mph) under nearly 11,000 horsepower, both these giant catamarans achieved respectable 1983 performances, winning one race apiece. George Morales of Fort Lauderdale, Fla., drove the "MerCruiser Special" to victory in the Michelob Light World Championships in Key West, Fla., earning himself the APBA national championship in Offshore Class I. Tony Garcia of Atherton, Calif., aboard "Arneson Special," repeated his 1982 victory to capture the World Class I title at Key West. Other U.S. champions included: Class II—Henry Ryan, Detroit; Class III—Bob Sheer, Fort Lauderdale; Class IV—Pete Aitkin, South Norwalk, Conn.; Class V-B—Jeff Kalibat, Island Park, N.Y.; Class V-A—Walter Beasley, Boynton Beach, Fla. In the Offshore Time Trial contests Ted Toleman of the U.K. successfully defended his place in the world record books, posting a speed of 194.731 km/h (120.951 mph).

The season in Formula One outboard racing was one of high-speed excitement, as the tunnel-hulled boats roared through their inaugural U.S. Grand Prix circuit. Drivers from throughout the world competed in four U.S. cities, drawing record crowds at each site. The series was part of a ten-race world tour. (HILARY S. ROSE)

River Sports. The 1983 U.S. national white-water racing championships were held in early August on the Wisconsin River in Wausau, Wis. Bruce Swomley of Chester, Vt., won the men's kayaking, and Linda Harrison of Northampton, Mass., was the women's champion. David Hearn of Bethesda, Md., won the C-1 class (single canoe) and, together with partner Alan Blanchard of Unionville, Conn., also won the C-2 (tandem canoe).

The world championships in white-water racing took place in the mountain resort town of Merano, Italy, in June. Previous champion Richard Fox of the U.K. won the men's kayak event, and Elizabeth Sharman, also of the U.K., won the women's. In C-1 competition Jon Lugbill of the U.S. was first, followed within one second by fellow American David Hearn. U.S. paddlers Fritz Haller and Lecky Haller won the C-2 class. The winners of all the wild-water (downriver) races were Italian, French, and German competitors.

The U.S. national flat-water championships took place August 3–7 at Indianapolis, Ind. Terry White won the men's 500-m and 1,000-m kayak races. Greg Barton won the 10,000-m race. In C-1 racing Rob Plankenhorn won the 500-m, 1,000-m, and 10,000-m events. Cathy Marino won the women's 500-m kayaking, and Ann Turner won the 5,000-m race.

The flat-water world championships were held in late July in Tampere, Fin. Previous champion Vladimir Parfenovich of the Soviet Union was first in the men's 500-m kayak competition. Other Soviet and Eastern European paddlers won the first three places in almost all the other events.

In recreational river running, river flows in the southwestern U.S. during 1983 were the highest on record since the construction of the region's major dams. For the first time National Park Service officials temporarily closed parts of the Grand Canyon and Cataract Canyon on the Colorado River to rafting and kayaking. (ERIC LEAPER)

Water Skiing. Sammy Duvall of the U.S. successfully defended his overall crown in the 18th biennial world water ski championships at Göteborg, Sweden, while Ana María Carrasco of Venezuela won overall honours among the women contenders. U.S. skiers captured six out of eight individual gold medals and won the team title for the 18th time.

The U.S. won all three men's events. Bob LaPoint took the slalom title, tying the record he held jointly with his brother Kris by running three buoys on a 10.75-m line. Cory Pickos again won the tricks with a record-tying run of 9,940 points. Duvall won the jumping, but he was well off the world record of 61.5 m set earlier in the year by Glen Thurlow of Australia.

Cindy Todd of the U.S. won gold medals in slalom and jumping. Natalia Ponomareva of the Soviet Union was best among the women in the tricks. The U.S. team led the 28 nations participating with a total of 8,549.99 points. Great Britain finished second with 7,814.08, and Australia was third with 7,622.72.

Carl Roberge, who finished third overall in the world meet behind Duvall and Mike Hazelwood of Great Britain, won the U.S. national overall title for the third year in a row, with victories in slalom and jumping and a second-place finish in tricks behind Pickos. Carl's sister Karin won the women's tricks and overall. Deena Brush was best in women's slalom and jumping. (THOMAS C. HARDMAN)

Surfing. The International Surfing Association's ninth world amateur surfing championships took place in 1983 in Australia. Tommy Curren of the U.S. captured the men's title, Robert Wolff and Ross Marshall of Australia placing second and third. Australia's Jenny Gilly won the women's competition. The 1984 world amateur championships were to held in the U.S.

Competing in the International Professional Surfing (IPS) tour, Mark Richards of Australia gar-

WIDE WORLD

Soviet and Soviet-bloc canoeists placed one-two-three-four in the men's 1,000-metre event during the flat-water world championships held in Tampere, Finland, in July.

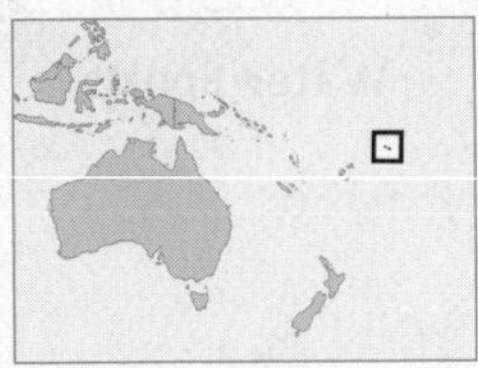
Western Samoa

nered his fourth consecutive title in 1982. Cheyne Horan and Tom Carroll followed in the next two spots to give Australia a clean sweep.

The end of the 1982 season marked the final year for the IPS, which had been suspended as the world controlling body of professional surfing. It was replaced in 1983 by the Association of Surfing Professionals. Sponsored by Ocean Pacific Sportswear, the ASP claimed a world circuit prize money total of at least $600,000. This figure was a 50% gain over that of the previous year.

(JACK C. FLANAGAN)

Water Polo. International water polo competition in 1983 was dominated by the national team from the Soviet Union, which won the two major events in the pre-Olympic year. The first of these was the third Fédération Internationale de Natation Amateur (FINA) Cup, held in May at the 1984 Olympic pool in Los Angeles. Seven of the top eight teams from the 1982 world championships took part, and Italy rounded out the field of eight. The competition was extremely close, but on the final day the Soviets defeated the second-place West German team 6–5 to finish with a record of five wins, one tie, and one loss, thus winning the gold medal. A surprisingly strong team from Italy placed third, followed by the United States, Spain, The Netherlands, Hungary, and Cuba. In August in Rome the same Soviet team was undefeated in winning the European championships. Hungary, recovering after a disappointing seventh at the FINA Cup, finished second, with Spain taking the bronze. Other teams, in order, were Yugoslavia, West Germany, The Netherlands, Italy, and Romania.

In other international competition the U.S. defeated Cuba 8–6 to win the Pan-American Games in Caracas, Venezuela. The Soviets showed that they would be tough in the years to come by winning the world university games in Edmonton, Alta. The U.S. placed second, while Cuba was third and Romania fourth. The world junior championships were held in Barcelona, and the host Spanish team won the gold medal by defeating Cuba 9–6 on the last day of the tournament. Yugoslavia was second.

(WILLIAM ENSIGN FRADY)

Western Samoa

A constitutional monarchy and member of the Commonwealth, Western Samoa is an island group in the South Pacific Ocean, about 2,600 km E of New Zealand and 3,500 km S of Hawaii. Area: 2,831 sq km (1,093 sq mi), with two major islands, Savai'i (1,708 sq km) and Upolu (including several islets, 1,123 sq km). Pop. (1982 est.): 158,000. Cap. and largest city: Apia (pop., 1981 est., 33,800). Language: Samoan and English. Religion (1976): Congregational 50%; Roman Catholic 22%; Methodist 16%; other 12%. Head of state (*O le Ao o le Malo*) in 1983, Malietoa Tanumafili II; prime minister, Tofilau Eti.

In response to the 1982 Privy Council ruling that all Western Samoans born between 1928 and 1949 were entitled to New Zealand citizenship, Western Samoa and New Zealand agreed on an alteration to their treaty of friendship: Western Samoans agreed to relinquish citizenship rights granted by the ruling, and in return New Zealand allowed Western Samoans resident in New Zealand at the time of the decision to become citizens on application and allowed the same right to those subsequently granted permanent residence. Opposition to these proposals faded after Prime Minister Tupuola Efi resigned in December 1982. He had wanted more generous migration opportunities.

By-elections and shifting allegiances returned the Human Rights Protection Party to power in January 1983. A tough budget was presented in February by Tofilau Eti, the new prime minister. A 10% devaluation of the tala in February, fol-

The U.S. water polo team won a gold medal in the Pan-American Games at Caracas, Venezuela, in August. Here U.S. goalie Craig Wilson deflects a shot by Cuba.

WIDE WORLD

WESTERN SAMOA

Education. (1982) Primary, pupils 40,475, teachers 1,460; secondary, pupils 11,839, teachers 495; vocational, pupils 211, teachers 38; teacher training, students 243, teachers 17; higher, students 85, teaching staff 6.

Finance and Trade. Monetary unit: tala, with (Sept. 20, 1983) a free rate of 1.63 tala to U.S. $1 (2.45 tala = £1 sterling). Budget (1982 est.): revenue 22.7 million tala; expenditure 23.2 million tala. Foreign trade (1982): imports 60.1 million tala; exports 15.1 million tala. Import sources (1981): New Zealand 24%; U.S. 23%; Australia 16%; Singapore 10%; Japan 9%. Export destinations (1981): New Zealand 33%; American Samoa 14%; West Germany 13%; The Netherlands 13%; U.S. 12%. Main exports (1981): copra 37%; taro and taamu 18%; cocoa 14%; canned coconut cream 5%.

lowed by an additional 6% in March, raised import prices and created a scarcity of consumer goods. Despite increased taxes and duties, a chronic shortage of foreign exchange necessitated a special application to the International Monetary Fund for $12 million. The UN listed Western Samoa as one of the world's "least developed countries." (BARRIE MACDONALD)

Winter Sports

Every major sport on snow and ice benefited in 1983 from a continuing worldwide increase in participation at both championship and recreational levels. Courses and arenas multiplied substantially, and equipment became more sophisticated and varied to cater to the expanding demand.

New, mechanically refrigerated bobsled and luge tobogganing runs were among the specially created facilities at Sarajevo, Yugos., site of the 1984 Olympic Winter Games. Generally satisfactory pre-Olympic competitions in all events were held at Sarajevo well in time to make any adaptations considered necessary. Progress was also already evident at the sites around Calgary, Alta., chosen for the 1988 Winter Olympics.

Skiing. The senior competition results confirmed a significant improvement in the performances of U.S. athletes. U.S. skiers were more prominent than ever before in both Alpine and Nordic disciplines, successfully challenging traditional European dominance.

ALPINE RACING. The 17th annual Alpine World Cup series comprised 32 single and 5 combined events for men and 26 single and 4 combined events for women, spread over four months at 34 sites in 11 countries. In a season sometimes ravaged by adverse weather conditions and saved by hasty rescheduling, the grueling tour was particularly successful for U.S. and Swiss competitors and notable for spectacular comebacks by two men who had dominated the sport in the late 1970s.

Phil Mahre of the U.S. (*see* BIOGRAPHIES) clinched the men's overall title for a third successive year, followed by Ingemar Stenmark, the veteran Swede, and Andreas Wenzel of Liechtenstein. Mahre topped the giant slalom standings, while Stenmark gained his eighth slalom crown, this time because he won more individual races than his fellow countryman Stig Strand, who scored the same number of points. Stenmark's giant slalom victory at Gällivare, Sweden, extended his World Cup career record number of race wins to 72.

Another veteran, Franz Klammer of Austria, gained his fifth downhill title, a record, having last won in 1978. He beat Conradin Cathomen of Switzerland by three points. After ten years on the circuit, Klammer said that he would continue through 1984 and perhaps after that.

Tamara McKinney, fighting back after breaking a wrist the previous season, became the first skier from the U.S. to win the women's overall title. Hanni Wenzel, sister of Andreas, was runner-up, only a point ahead of Erika Hess of Switzerland. McKinney comfortably headed the giant slalom ratings, as she had in 1981. Hess narrowly beat her in the slalom, and the leading downhiller was another Swiss, Doris De Agostini.

Switzerland regained the concurrently decided Nations Alpine Cup. Austria, the defending champion, was runner-up, while the U.S. finished third for the seventh time.

Georg Ager of Austria became the international professional tour overall champion. Dave Stapleton of the U.S. placed second with Reidar Wahl of Norway and Hans Hinterseer of Austria sharing third. Toril Forland of Norway gained the women's crown for a fourth year and the third in succession. Viki Fleckenstein of the U.S. and Jocelyne Perrilat of France tied for second place.

NORDIC EVENTS. The fourth Nordic World Cup series, for cross-country racing, was contested over 14 weeks at 13 sites in 13 countries. The men's title was won by Aleksandr Zavjalov of the U.S.S.R., who in the final event defeated Gunde Svan of Sweden and defending champion Bill Koch of the U.S. after Koch had held the lead for much of the season. Svan and Koch finished second and third, respectively. Marja Liisa Hamalainen of Finland gained the women's title, also in the last event, after Brit Pettersen of Norway, the runner-up for a second year, had earlier built a seemingly insurmountable advantage. Kvetaslava Jeriova of Czechoslovakia finished third.

The Nordic World Cup jump title, decided at 18 hills in 11 countries, was captured by Matti Nykaenen of Finland. He and Horst Bulau, the Canadian runner-up, dominated the season with exciting duels. Third was Armin Kogler of Austria. The Nordic Nations Cup was captured by the U.S.S.R., with Norway second and Sweden third.

In the world biathlon championships, combining cross-country skiing with rifle shooting, at Anterselva, Italy, on February 20–27, Frank Ulrich of East Germany retained the 20-km title to increase his record number of individual world victories to six. His compatriot Frank-Peter Roetsch was runner-up, only 17 seconds behind, and a West German, Peter Angerer, finished third. The 10 km was also successfully defended, by Erik Kvalfoss of Norway. Angerer placed second, and Alfred Eder of Austria finished third. Although no Soviet competitor gained a medal in either of the individual events, the U.S.S.R. won the 4 × 7-km relay against 17 opposing nations. East Germany, the defending champion, was runner-up, and Norway finished third.

Weather:
see Earth Sciences

Weight Lifting:
see Gymnastics and Weight Lifting

Welfare:
see Social Security and Welfare Services

Wine:
see Industrial Review

UPI

Phil Mahre of the U.S. won the Alpine World Cup men's overall title for the third successive year in March.

Recreational Nordic skiing attracted a greater proportion of winter holidaymakers than in previous years. More coaching was available, and the specialized equipment was easier to obtain at resorts throughout Scandinavia, Switzerland, Austria, and North America.

OTHER EVENTS. The world ski-flying championship, in March at Harrachov, Czech., was won by Klaus Ostwald of East Germany. Pavel Ploc placed second for the host country, and Nykaenen was third.

The men's world cup for freestyle skiing, involving a grand prix circuit of eight events in Europe and North America, was won by Peter Judge of Canada. The women's title went to Connie Kissling of Switzerland. In speed-skiing competitions at Velocity Park, Silverton, Colo., on April 23, Franz Weber of Austria set a new world men's speed record of 208.292 km/h (129.303 mph), and Kirsten Culver of the U.S. achieved a women's best speed of 194.384 km/h (120.785 mph).

Ice Skating. New rinks in every continent provided additional indoor ice for the continuing worldwide growth of participation in recreational skating, a development no doubt influenced by increased television coverage of major competitions to wider audiences. Ice dancing continued to increase in popularity, but fewer were prepared to take up pair skating, perhaps partly because of the greater risk element.

FIGURE SKATING. Twenty-three countries were represented by 123 skaters in the 73rd world championships, in Helsinki, Fin., on March 7–12. Scott Hamilton comfortably gained a third straight men's victory for the U.S., leading at every stage except in the compulsory figures, when Jean-Christophe Simond of France set the pace for a third successive season. In the final free skating Hamilton landed six triple jumps, four of them different, in a nearly flawless performance that was rich also in well-centred spins, clever combinations, and superb linking footwork. Norbert Schramm of West Germany was runner-up for a second year. Brian Orser of Canada, though second to the champion in the long free skating, could manage only the bronze because he was eighth in the figures. Brian Boitano of the U.S. and Thomas Hlavik of Austria landed the difficult triple axel jump, which has been achieved only twice in previous championships.

Rosalynn Sumners became the seventh U.S. skater to take the women's crown after her compatriot Elaine Zayak, defending the title, had to drop out during the figures because of a badly swollen right ankle. The women's competition, unlike the men's, was generally disappointing, and Sumners, a petite blonde from Edmonds, Wash., became the new queen of the ice a month before her 19th birthday without appearing seriously extended. Claudia Leistner, the West German runner-up, fell while attempting a triple lutz, and Elena Vodorezova, hoping to become the first Soviet victor, had to settle for the bronze medal after crashing during a triple salchow.

The pairs final produced a pulsating finish between the top three, ending in a title switch. Oleg Vasiliev and Elena Valova, the new Soviet champions from Leningrad, narrowly defeated the East German defending champions, Tassilo Thierbach and Sabine Baess. The issue was probably clinched by the Soviet skaters' side-by-side triple toe loop jumps. A close third were the always menacing Canadians, Paul Martini and Barbara Underhill.

The ice dance contest provided a performance of unprecedented ability by Christopher Dean and Jayne Torvill (*see* BIOGRAPHIES). Impressively gaining their third consecutive win, the elegant British couple were in a class by themselves, a fact endorsed by their record-shattering marks. In the three compulsory dances, for which a maximum 6 had never been gained, they earned many 5.9 marks. For their set pattern dance they received six

6s for presentation and another for composition. An incredible climax followed in the free skating, when each of the nine judges gave them 5.9 for technical merit before a historic moment when, for artistic presentation, each awarded them a 6. Never before in any figure-skating event had a complete set of perfect marks been signaled.

The champions' rendition was a remarkable transposition to music from the stage musical *Barnum,* subtly miming circus juggling, clowning, acrobatics, and even tightrope balancing in a program of technical finesse perhaps never to be surpassed. This event attracted major interest, not only because of its prime performers, but also on account of a tremendous struggle for second place. Andrey Bukin and Natalia Bestemianova, Soviet runners-up for a second time, finished even on points with the U.S. skaters Michael Seibert and Judy Blumberg, who lost by a "tie-breaker" because they had a lower score than the Soviet pair in the free dance.

Thanks to commercial sponsorships, a notable trend in international figure skating was the growth of annual nonchampionship competitions in which leading skaters took part. These tournaments afforded the skaters more top-level experience than their predecessors were able to gain and enabled many more people to watch the stars in "live" action as well as on television.

Speed Skating. Rolf Falk-Larssen, third the previous year, won the overall men's world championship for the host country in Oslo, Norway, on February 12–13. Tomas Gustafson of Sweden placed second, and Aleksandr Baranov of the U.S.S.R. finished third. In the individual events Falk-Larssen was fastest in the 500 m, 1,500 m, and 5,000 m, while Gustafson proved best in the 10,000 m.

Andrea Schöne of East Germany, runner-up in 1982, became the new women's world champion at Karl-Marx-Stadt, East Germany, on February 19–20. Her compatriot Karin Enke finished second, and Valentina Lalenkova of the U.S.S.R. was third. Schöne finished first in the 1,500 m, 3,000 m, and 5,000 m, and the Soviet skater Natalia Glebova clocked the lowest time in the 500 m.

In the separate world sprint championships, in Helsinki on February 26–27, Akira Kuroiwa of Japan gained the men's title, ahead of Pavel Pegov of the U.S.S.R. and Hilbert van der Duim of The Netherlands. The women's championship was won by Enke, followed by Natalia Petruseva of the U.S.S.R. and Christa Rothenburger from East Germany.

Three new men's world records were set, all at Medeo, U.S.S.R., and two of them by Pegov. He lowered the 500 m to 36.57 sec—skating at an average speed exceeding 48 km/h (30 mph)—and the 1,000 m to 1 min 12.58 sec. Another Soviet skater, Igor Zhelezovsky, clocked 1 min 54.26 sec for the 1,500 m. Four new women's world records were also established. At Medeo, Rothenburger sprinted 500 m in 39.69 sec, and Petruseva clocked 1,000 m in 1 min 19.31 sec and 1,500 m in 2 min 4.04 sec. At Heerenveen, Neth., Schöne reduced the 5,000 m to 7 min 40.97 sec.

In the third world short-track (indoor) championships in Tokyo on April 8–10, the men's and women's titles were gained, respectively, by Louis Grenier and Sylvie Daigle of Canada. With outdoor speed circuits existing in very few countries, the relatively new short-track contests proved a boon to skaters from nations that provided only indoor facilities. The technique required for the short straightaways and sharp bends meant that racers tended to specialize in either outdoor or short-track style because adapting between the two was not very practicable.

TREVOR JONES/SPORTS ILLUSTRATED

Christopher Dean and Jayne Torvill, both of Nottingham, England, won wide acclaim during 1983 for the virtual perfection of their ice dancing. They were expected to be formidable competitors in the 1984 Winter Olympic Games.

Growing Winter Sport

On a winter day in snow-covered areas of North America, a visitor should not be surprised to hear shouted commands and see teams of dogs pulling sleds across the countryside. These dogs most likely are not performing their duty of an earlier age, providing basic transportation for the inhabitants. Instead, they and their drivers are competing against one another in the fast-growing sport of sled-dog racing.

From Maine, New Hampshire, and Labrador to Alaska and the Yukon, sled-dog racing is gaining in popularity. In 1983 the International Sled Dog Racing Association had approximately 3,000 members, a sixfold increase since 1978, and sanctioned more than 60 annual events. They ranged from races of about 16 km (10 mi) to the grueling 1,830-km (1,137-mi) Iditarod International Sled Dog Race in Alaska, which can take at least two weeks to complete. Many of the events were for professionals and offered varying amounts of prize money.

A modern racing dogsled consists of an ash or hickory frame reinforced with aluminum and lashed together with leather; its runners are sheathed with steel, aluminum, or plastic. It weighs about 14 kg (30 lb). The number of dogs in a team generally ranges from 5 to 14, depending on the event. Often a single dog leads a number of pairs. Most sled dogs can run over a considerable distance at an average speed of about 32 km/h (20 mph).

Most sled dogs originally were Siberian huskies and Alaskan Malamutes, both bred in the far north for that purpose. As racing competition became more intense, they were crossbred with greyhounds and various other types of dogs in an effort to achieve greater speed. The dominant variety today is the Alaskan husky, an unofficial and still evolving breed that is most often a mixture of Siberian husky, Alaskan Malamute, greyhound, Irish setter, and Labrador retriever.

(DAVID R. CALHOUN)

Bobsledding. Swiss crews won both bobsledding events in the 50th world championships at Lake Placid, N.Y., on February 19–27. Ralph Pichler and Urs Lüthold outpaced their compatriots and defending champions, Erich Schaerer and brakeman Max Ruegg, to take the two-man title. In third place were Wolfgang Hoppe and Dietmar Schauerhammer of East Germany. One of the winning sled's runs was 59.74 sec, the fastest ever for a two-man crew on the 16-curve, 1,548-m (5,108-ft) Mt. Van Hoevenberg course.

Ekkehard Fasser steered his four-man bob to victory and set a track record of 58.99 sec. Klaus Kopp's West German crew had an aggregate time for their four runs only half a second slower than Fasser. An East German sled driven by Detlev Richter finished third.

Tobogganing. Miroslav Zajonc of Canada gained the men's title in the world luge championships, at Lake Placid on February 5–6. Sergey Danilin of the U.S.S.R. was runner-up for a second successive year. Paul Hildgartner of Italy, winner of third place, had been Olympic silver medalist on the same track in 1980. The men's two-seater title was won by Jorg Hoffman and Joachim Pietzsch of East Germany. Hans Jorg Raffl and Norbert Huber from Italy were runners-up, and third place went to Hans Stanggasinger and Anton Wembacher of West Germany.

Swiss riders continued to monopolize the medals in both the classic races for skeleton tobogganists on the Cresta Run at St. Moritz, Switz. Franco Gansser won the 74th Grand National along the full course, followed by his brother, Reto, and Marcel Melcher. Reto Gansser avenged that defeat by winning the 60th Curzon Cup, over the shorter distance. Second was Nico Baracchi, who had won both events the year before, and Franco Gansser was third. Yet another Swiss, Urs Nater, set a new record on February 20 of 42.75 sec from the inter-

Sled-dog racing has been gaining in popularity in recent years. In the Iditarod International Sled Dog Race, run from Anchorage, Alaska, to Nome in March, Rick Malley of Wasilla, Alaska, won by covering the 1,830-kilometre (1,137-mile) distance in 12 days 14 hours 10 minutes 4 seconds. The purse was $100,000, of which he received $24,000.

WIDE WORLD

mediate Junction station. The Run was open for 66 days of the winter, when 2,406 descents were made from Top and another 5,497 from Junction.

Curling. Canada played host to all three major international meetings during 1983. In the 25th men's world championship for the Air Canada Silver Broom at Regina, Sask., on April 10–17, Canada increased its record number of wins to 15. Ed Werenich skipped the winning rink from Toronto's Avonlea Club, defeating Keith Wendorf of West Germany 7–4 in the final before a sellout crowd of 6,537. It was the second year in a row that an Ontario team had taken the title. Supported by Paul Savage, John Kawaja, and Neil Harrison, Werenich beat Stefan Hasselborg of Sweden 8–5 in the semifinal, while the West Germans defeated Eigil Ramsfjell of Norway 4–3.

In the fifth women's world championship, at Moose Jaw, Sask., on April 3–10, Erika Mueller's Swiss rink from Bern scored a comfortable 18–3 victory over Eva Vanvik's team from Norway. Mueller was backed by Barbara Meyer, Barbara Meier, and Christine Wirz. Switzerland defeated Sweden 12–10 in the semifinal, while Norway upset Canada 6–3. The total attendance for the week was a record 24,395.

The ninth men's world junior championship, at Medicine Hat, Alta., on March 13–20, was won by a Canadian rink from Mississauga, Ont., skipped by John Base with Bruce Webster, Dave McAnerney, and Jim Donahoe. They beat Pål Trulsen's Norwegian team 7–2 in the final after defeating Mike Hay's Scottish four 7–5 in the semifinal; in the other semifinal Trulsen outscored the U.S. team skipped by Al Edwards 6–4.

(HOWARD BASS)

See also Ice Hockey.

[452.B.4.g–h]

Yemen, People's Democratic Republic of

A people's republic in the southern coastal region of the Arabian Peninsula, Yemen (Aden; South Yemen) is bordered by Yemen (San'a'), Saudi Arabia, and Oman. Area: 338,100 sq km (130,541 sq mi). Pop. (1983 est.): 2,086,000. Cap. and largest city: Aden (pop., 1981 est., 365,000). Language: Arabic. Religion: predominantly Muslim. Chairman of the Presidium of the Supreme People's Council and prime minister in 1983, Ali Nasir Muhammad Husani.

On Oct. 27, 1983, it was announced that South Yemen was to establish diplomatic relations with Oman for the first time since the Marxist government supported a rebellion against Sultan Qabus ibn Sa'id of Oman in the early 1970s. The improvement in relations between the two countries, first announced in October 1982, had been jeopardized for a time by Yemeni criticism of joint U.S.-Omani military exercises later that year.

On October 14 South Yemen marked the 20th anniversary of its independence with a gesture of friendship toward its former colonial master, the U.K. An oil concession was to be awarded to British Petroleum as part of an attempt to improve bilateral relations. It was reported in July that ambassadors had been exchanged with Saudi Arabia for the first time since 1977.

During the year further progress was made on unification talks with Yemen (San'a'; North Yemen). In mid-1982 South Yemen had withdrawn assistance—both moral and material—from the National Democratic Front rebels in North Yemen. South Yemen continued to receive economic and military assistance from the U.S.S.R.

(JOHN WHELAN)

YEMEN, PEOPLE'S DEMOCRATIC REPUBLIC OF

Education. (1977–78) Primary, pupils 212,795; secondary, pupils 64,388; primary and secondary, teachers 10,078; vocational, pupils 1,223, teachers (1976–77) 68; teacher training, students 1,070, teachers 57; higher, students 2,517, teaching staff 246.

Finance and Trade. Monetary unit: Yemen dinar, with (Sept. 20, 1983) a par value of 0.345 dinar to U.S. $1 (free rate of 0.52 dinar = £1 sterling). Budget (1980–81 actual): revenue 86,020,000 dinars; expenditure 96,020,000 dinars. Foreign trade (1980): imports 527.4 million dinars; exports 269 million dinars. Import sources: United Arab Emirates c. 28%; Egypt c. 16%; Kuwait c. 9%; Libya c. 7%; Japan c. 6%; U.S.S.R. c. 5%. Export destinations: United Arab Emirates c. 22%; Italy c. 11%; India c. 7%. Main export: petroleum products 95%.

Agriculture. Production (in 000; metric tons; 1982): millet and sorghum c. 60; wheat (1981) c. 15; watermelons c. 60; dates c. 43; cotton, lint c. 4; fish catch (1981) c. 75. Livestock (in 000; 1981): cattle c. 120; sheep c. 987; goats c. 1,350; asses c. 171; camels c. 100; chickens c. 1,594.

Industry. Production (in 000; metric tons; 1981): petroleum products 2,043; salt c. 75; electricity (kw-hr) c. 260,000.

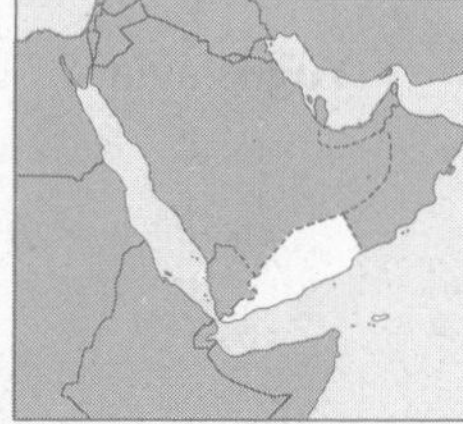
People's Democratic Republic of Yemen

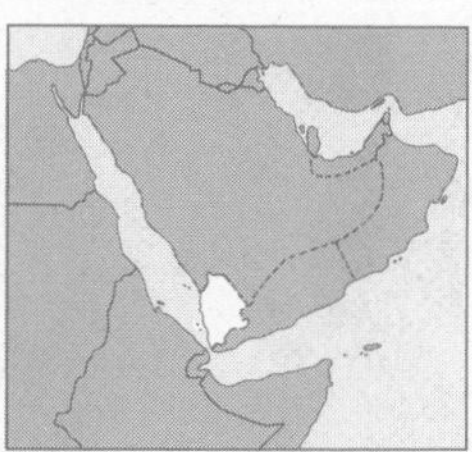
Yemen Arab Republic

Yemen Arab Republic

A republic situated in the southwestern coastal region of the Arabian Peninsula, Yemen (San'a'; North Yemen) is bounded by Yemen (Aden), Saudi Arabia, and the Red Sea. Area: 200,000 sq km (77,200 sq mi). Pop. (1982 est.): 7,340,800. Cap. and largest city: San'a' (pop., 1981, 277,800). Language: Arabic (official) and English. Religion: Muslim. President in 1983, Col. Ali Abdullah Saleh; premier, Abdel Karim al-Iriani and, from November 13, Abdel Aziz Abdel Ghani.

On May 22, 1983, Pres. Ali Abdullah Saleh was returned unopposed for a second term of office under North Yemen's Egyptian-style constitution. On May 18 the president said that he would not stand for reelection, but the People's Constituent Assembly reelected the soldier-president by acclamation.

The economy worsened in 1983 as aid from Saudi Arabia was reduced. Remittances from Yemeni expatriates working in the Gulf states, amounting to some $1.2 billion a year, were the mainstay of the nation's wealth. Foreign reserves had fallen to $428 million by April. In July Citibank of the U.S. announced plans to close its branch in San'a'.

Political talks on unification with Yemen (Aden; South Yemen) progressed during a meeting of the joint Yemeni Supreme Council on August 15. President Saleh and his South Yemeni counterpart held talks with Palestine Liberation Organization leader Yasir Arafat (*see* BIOGRAPHIES), who had sol-

Wood Products:
see Industrial Review

World Bank:
see Economy, World

Wrestling:
see Combat Sports

Yachting:
see Sailing

Yiddish Literature:
see Literature

YEMEN ARAB REPUBLIC

Education. (1980–81) Primary, pupils 412,573, teachers 10,576; secondary, pupils 28,852, teachers (1975–76) c. 1,172; vocational (1975–76), pupils 1,148, teachers 60; teacher training, students 1,558, teachers (1975–76) 113; higher, students (1977–78) 4,058, teaching staff (1973–74) 58.

Finance and Trade. Monetary unit: rial, with (Sept. 20, 1983) a par value of 4.56 rials to U.S. $1 (free rate of 6.87 rials = £1 sterling). Budget (1981 actual): revenue 3,282,-600,000 rials; expenditure 6,219,900,000 rials. Foreign trade (1981): imports 8,022,000,000 rials; exports 217 million rials. Import sources: Saudi Arabia 20%; Japan 16%; France 8%; Italy 5%; West Germany 5%. Export destinations: Yemen (Aden) 23%; Pakistan 19%; France 14%; United Arab Emirates 9%; Saudi Arabia 8%; West Germany 5%. Main exports (1980): machinery 21%; bakery products 18%; sugar 10%; fruit and vegetables 8%; textile yarns and fabrics 6%.

Agriculture. Production (in 000; metric tons; 1982): barley 53; corn c. 50; wheat (1981) c. 70; sorghum 583; potatoes (1981) c. 138; grapes (1981) c. 64; dates c. 90; coffee c. 4; tobacco c. 6; cotton, lint c. 2. Livestock (in 000; 1981): cattle c. 950; sheep c. 3,159; goats c. 7,500; asses c. 745; camels c. 115.

diers based in both countries. The council meeting resulted in agreement on closer coordination in foreign affairs and domestic policy. A joint ministerial committee was to be established, and travel between the two Yemens was to be made easier.

(JOHN WHELAN)

Yugoslavia

Yugoslavia

A federal socialist republic, Yugoslavia is bordered by Italy, Austria, Hungary, Romania, Bulgaria, Greece, Albania, and the Adriatic Sea. Area: 255,804 sq km (98,766 sq mi). Pop. (1983 est.): 22,826,000, including (1981) Serbs 36.3%; Croats 19.7%; Bosnian Muslim 8.9%; Slovenes 7.8%; Albanians 7.7%; Macedonians 6%; Montenegrins 2.6%; other 11%. Cap. and largest city: Belgrade (metro. pop., 1981 prelim., 1,470,100). Language: Serbo-Croatian, Slovenian, Macedonian, and Albanian. Religion (1953): Orthodox 41%; Roman Catholic 32%; Muslim 12%. Presidents of the Presidium of the League of Communists in 1983, Mitja Ribicic and, from June 30, Dragoslav Markovic; presidents of the Collective Presidency, Petar Stambolic and, from May 13, Mika Spiljak; president of the Federal Executive Council (premier), Milka Planinc.

Yugoslavia maintained its independent position between East and West, though it placed greater emphasis on its position in Europe during 1983. Soviet Premier Nikolay Tikhonov was the most senior visitor from the Soviet bloc. During his visit in March a long-term agreement on economic co-operation to 1990 was signed. Yugoslavia's trade with the U.S.S.R., its most important trading partner, was worth $7 billion in 1983. Two European presidents, Italy's Alessandro Pertini and West Germany's Carl Karstens, visited in September, as did U.S. Vice-Pres. George Bush, who reaffirmed the West's support for Yugoslavia's nonaligned foreign policy. French Pres. François Mitterrand paid a visit in December. Premier Milka Planinc traveled to Greece, Iraq, and the U.K. in October and November. In Greece she caused controversy by calling for Greek acceptance of the Slav Macedonian minority in Greece as a "historical reality."

In September Albania objected to the holding of two-day military maneuvers in Macedonia, the Yugoslav republic that borders on Albania, Bulgaria, and Greece. Albania also protested against prison sentences passed on Albanians in Yugoslavia's Kosovo Province; they were accused of advocating separatism of the province from Yugoslavia. On October 14 two explosions occurred in Pristina, Kosovo's capital. The government announced that in the first half of the year 116 members of nationalist and separatist groups in Kosovo had been apprehended. In Bosnia and Hercegovina 13 prominent Muslim intellectuals were sentenced on August 20 to a total of 90 years in prison. They had been accused of advocating the setting up of a purely Muslim state in the republic.

Serbian nationalism was fueled by the Muslim resurgence in Bosnia and the continuing Albanian agitation for Kosovo to be upgraded to a republic. In August more than 100,000 people attended the (unpublicized) funeral of Aleksandr Rankovic (*see* OBITUARIES), former head of secret police, who had been associated with tough anti-Albanian and anti-Muslim measures in the post-1945 period.

Slovenia emerged as one of the fiercest critics of

YUGOSLAVIA

Education. (1980–81) Primary, pupils 1,431,582, teachers 59,391; secondary, pupils 1,835,636; vocational, pupils 587,895; teacher training, pupils 2,633; secondary, vocational, and teacher training, teachers 131,348; higher (1979–80), students 448,755, teaching staff 24,171.

Finance. Monetary unit: dinar, with (Sept. 20, 1983) a free rate of 103.57 dinars to U.S. $1 (155.98 dinars = £1 sterling). Gold and other reserves (June 1983) U.S. $692 million. Budget (federal; 1982 est.) balanced at 203.9 billion dinars. Gross material product (1980) 1,553,000,000 dinars. Money supply (April 1983) 749 billion dinars. Cost of living (1975 = 100; June 1983) 566.8.

Foreign Trade. (1982) Imports 690.6 billion dinars; exports 535.9 billion dinars. Import sources (1981): U.S.S.R. 19%; West Germany 15%; Italy 8%; U.S. 6%; France 5%. Export destinations (1981): U.S.S.R. 33%; Italy 9%; West Germany 8%; Iraq 5%; Czechoslovakia 5%. Main exports (1981): machinery 19%; chemicals 12%; transport equipment 9%; food 8%; clothing 6%; footwear 6%; textile yarn and fabrics 5%. Tourism (1981): visitors 6,616,000; gross receipts U.S. $1,350,000,000.

Transport and Communications. Roads (1981) 133,827 km (including 430 km expressways). Motor vehicles in use (1981): passenger 2,568,100; commercial 201,700. Railways: (1981) 9,393 km; traffic (1982) 10,822,000,000 passenger-km, freight 25,807,000,000 net ton-km. Air traffic (1982): 2,870,000,000 passenger-km; freight c. 59.7 million net ton-km. Shipping (1982): merchant vessels 100 gross tons and over 475; gross tonnage 2,531,506. Telephones (Jan. 1981) 2,133,200. Radio licenses (Dec. 1980) 4,635,000. Television licenses (Dec. 1980) 4.3 million.

Agriculture. Production (in 000; metric tons; 1982): wheat 5,218; barley 669; oats 269; corn 11,137; potatoes c. 2,774; sunflower seed 202; sugar, raw value c. 800; onions c. 319; tomatoes c. 465; cabbages (1981) c. 767; chillies and peppers (1981) c. 381; watermelons (1981) c. 661; plums (1981) 809; apples c. 667; wine c. 850; tobacco c. 63; beef and veal c. 350; pork c. 745; timber (cu m; 1981) 14,094. Livestock (in 000; Jan. 1982): cattle 5,160; sheep c. 7,398; pigs c. 8,431; horses (1981) 580; chickens c. 67,838.

Industry. Fuel and power (in 000; metric tons; 1982): coal c. 390; lignite c. 53,400; crude oil 4,320; natural gas (cu m) 2,290,000; manufactured gas (cu m; 1980) 760,000; electricity (kw-hr; 1981) 60,390,000. Production (in 000; metric tons; 1982): cement 9,727; iron ore (35% metal content) c. 4,800; pig iron 2,877; crude steel c. 1,960; magnesite (1980) 262; bauxite (1981) 3,252; aluminum 246; copper 127; lead 80; zinc 86; petroleum products (1981) 13,971; sulfuric acid 1,183; plastics and resins (1981) 481; cotton yarn (1981) 118; wool yarn (1981) 51; man-made fibres (1980) 140; wood pulp (1980) 628; newsprint 29; other paper (1980) 1,052; television receivers (units; 1980) 505; passenger cars (units; 1981) 175; commercial vehicles (units; 1981) 73. Merchant vessels launched (100 gross tons and over; 1982) 407,000 gross tons.

Belgrade centralism in 1983. It objected strongly to a proposal to introduce a common basic educational program for schools on the grounds that it underplayed the position of Slovene and some other national cultures.

Despite a good harvest the country continued to be plagued by shortages, including those of various foodstuffs, because of the need to export grain for hard currency. During the year Yugoslavia paid $6 billion toward servicing and repaying its $20 billion hard-currency debt. A $5.2 billion international aid package was arranged but only on condition that the Yugoslav national bank take on the role of ultimate guarantor of the country's financial obligations. This was agreed to after a stormy special session of the federal Assembly.

Throughout the year a sliding devaluation of the dinar continued; the U.S. dollar, which had been worth 19.6 dinars in 1979, was worth 109 dinars in October. The annual inflation rate was over 40%. Unemployment for the country as a whole stood at 15% in midyear; in Kosovo it was 44%. Real incomes dropped by about 5%, the fifth successive decline in as many years. Industrial production stagnated, though exports to the non-Communist world increased by 17% in current dollar terms.

The trade and cooperation agreement between Yugoslavia and the European Economic Community (EEC), signed three years earlier, came into force in February. It provided concessions for industrial and agricultural exports to the EEC; social and legal benefits for Yugoslav workers in EEC countries; and financial aid for Yugoslavia from the EEC through the European Investment Bank.

Vladimir Bakaric, one of the most prominent leaders from the Tito era, died after a long illness on January 16 (*see* OBITUARIES). (K. F. CVIIC)

Zaire

A republic of equatorial Africa, Zaire is bounded by the Central African Republic, Sudan, Uganda, Rwanda, Burundi, Tanzania, Zambia, Angola, Congo, and the Atlantic Ocean. Area: 2,344,885 sq km (905,365 sq mi). Pop. (1983 est.): 30,730,000, including Luba 18%; Kongo 16%; Mongo 13%; Bantu tribes 10%; other 43%. Cap. and largest city: Kinshasa (pop., 1980 est., 3 million). Language: French, Swahili, Lingala, Kikongo, Tshiluba. Religion: animist approximately 50%; Christian 43%. President in 1983, Mobutu Sese Seko; prime minister, Kengo wa Dondo.

After Yitzhak Shamir, Israel's foreign minister, visited Zaire at the end of 1982, there was considerable speculation as to whether Pres. Mobutu Sese Seko had discussed with him the possibility that Israel might help to solve Zaire's petroleum shortage by providing access to the clandestine oil supplies that sustained Israel and South Africa. This would be of the greatest importance to a country that began 1983 with a foreign debt of $5.2 billion and a record budget deficit and whose oil-producing neighbours would only deliver supplies in return for cash payment. In January Ariel Sharon, then Israel's defense minister, also visited Kinshasa and agreed that his country would take responsibility for restructuring a division of the Zairian Army as part of a five-year program to assist in building up the country's defenses.

This involvement with Israel, which was contrary to Organization of African Unity (OAU) policy, caused concern among both Zaire's neighbours and its potential Arab oil suppliers. Nevertheless, in spite of difficulties over the repayment of its debts, Zaire appeared to find no difficulty in enlisting the aid of individuals and corporations prepared to do business or to give aid. In February a South Korean corporation signed a $300 million contract to build a plywood factory, a hotel, and twelve 100-bed hospitals. At the same time, the World Bank's International Development Association agreed to provide funds for a rural development project in the northeast that would increase food-crop and livestock production. The hope was that 120,000 farming families and 7,500 livestock producers would benefit from the scheme. In April the African Development Bank agreed to lend $110 million over the period 1983–85, of which 40% would be devoted to agricultural development.

On a less optimistic note, eight Japanese firms forming the Zaire Mining Development Co. said in June that they would pull out of their copper-mining venture because of the slump in copper prices and the increase in transportation costs due to the political uncertainty in neighbouring countries. They planned to sell their majority shares in the firm to the government but promised to provide a $20 million loan and to continue to buy the copper concentrate produced by the mines.

In March Parliament adopted a finance bill aimed at centralizing control of the country's finances and restricting the powers of administrators to transfer funds from one project to another without government approval. Mobutu reshuffled his Cabinet and appointed new people to the finance and planning ministries in the hope of forming a dynamic and homogeneous team that would assist the president in carrying out the government's new policies. Mobutu announced a further Cabinet shake-up in November, at which time the financial and planning ministers exchanged portfolios and the foreign affairs and several other ministers were replaced.

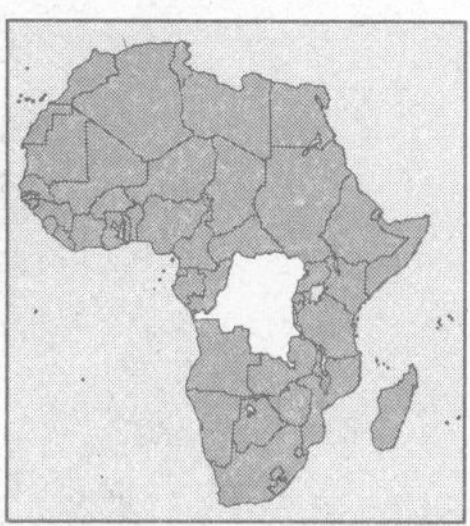
Zaire

Political exiles from Zaire continued to organize opposition to the government. Nguza Karl-I-Bond, former prime minister, formed a shadow cabinet among his fellow exiles in Brussels in January to bring an end, by force if necessary, to the rule of Mobutu. Not surprisingly he was among the first to reject the offer of a political amnesty made by the president in May. He declared that he and his associates had no intention of returning to Zaire because to do so would be a denial of all their principles. The Congolese Socialist Party, which had no links with Nguza, also turned down the offer, saying that its members would only return to their country when its national institutions had been reorganized and free elections agreed upon. It also called for an end to judicial proceedings against exiles and for financial assistance for those who had suffered under the existing regime.

These criticisms received some support on March 1 when Amnesty International published a

MICHAEL T. KAUFMAN

Zaire's currency was devalued by 80% in September; even modest transactions resulted in great stacks of paper money changing hands.

report accusing the government of arresting several hundred opponents of President Mobutu during the previous five years. Few of them had been tried, and some had been detained without trial for more than a year. Amnesty also claimed to have corroborated numerous reports of torture. These accusations were denied by Zaire's ambassador to France, who said that Amnesty's information came from the false reports of political refugees.

In July the government dispatched troops to assist the government of Chad in its struggle against rebel forces backed by Libya, and some weeks later Mobutu himself flew to Chad to demonstrate his support for Pres. Hissen Habré. Zaire's military involvement did not win the approval of all the members of the OAU, but it was praised by the U.S. When Mobutu visited the U.S. in August, his discussions there centred mainly on the situation in Chad, but he also had talks with the president of the World Bank and with private bankers about measures to deal with Zaire's economic problems. He was therefore concerned by news that Belgian foreign policy was to take a new course that might result in less aid and technical assistance for his nation. His suggestion that Zaire might retaliate by withdrawing its copper from the Belgian market aroused concern among the Belgian firms engaged in importing large quantities of Zairian copper.

(KENNETH INGHAM)

ZAIRE

Education. (1978–79) Primary, pupils 3,919,395, teachers (1972–73) 80,481; secondary, pupils 611,349; vocational, pupils (1977–78) 70,342; teacher training, students 138,170; secondary, vocational, and teacher training, teachers (1973–74) 14,483; higher, students 28,430, teaching staff 2,782.

Finance. Monetary unit: zaire, with (Sept. 20, 1983; following an 80% devaluation on Sept. 12, 1983) a free rate of 29.60 zaires to U.S. $1 (44.60 zaires = £1 sterling). Gold and other reserves (June 1983) U.S. $196 million. Budget (1981 actual): revenue 4.8 billion zaires; expenditure 7.6 billion zaires. Gross national product (1981) 23,090,000,000 zaires. Money supply (Feb. 1983) 7,766,100,000 zaires. Cost of living (Kinshasa; 1975 = 100; March 1983) 3,311.

Foreign Trade. (1982) Imports 2,750,500,000 zaires; exports 3,265,900,000 zaires. Import sources: Belgium-Luxembourg c. 22%; France c. 13%; U.S. c. 10%; West Germany c. 10%; Japan c. 6%; Italy c. 5%. Export destinations: U.S. c. 36%; Belgium-Luxembourg c. 31%; France c. 6%: West Germany c. 5%. Main exports: copper 40%; coffee 19%; diamonds 12%; cobalt 7%.

Transport and Communications. Roads (1980) c. 160,000 km. Motor vehicles in use (1980): passenger c. 93,900; commercial (including buses) c. 84,900. Railways: (1980) 5,254 km; traffic (1979) 554 million passenger-km, freight 1,591,000,000 net ton-km. Air traffic (1982): c. 683 million passenger-km; freight c. 31.5 million net ton-km. Shipping (1982): merchant vessels 100 gross tons and over 34; gross tonnage 92,044. Inland waterways (including Zaire River; 1982) c. 15,000 km. Telephones (Dec. 1980) 27,000. Radio receivers (Dec. 1980) 150,000. Television receivers (Dec. 1980) 8,000.

Agriculture. Production (in 000; metric tons; 1982): rice c. 255; corn c. 527; sweet potatoes (1981) c. 309; cassava (1981) c. 13,000; peanuts c. 358; palm kernels c. 65; palm oil c. 160; mangoes c. 137; pineapples c. 153; bananas c. 313; oranges c. 141; coffee c. 85; rubber c. 23; cotton, lint c. 10; meat (1981) c. 182; fish catch (1981) c. 102; timber (cu m; 1981) c. 10,566. Livestock (in 000; 1981): cattle c. 1,230; sheep c. 753; goats c. 2,833; pigs c. 737; poultry c. 15,500.

Industry. Production (in 000; metric tons; 1981): copper ore (metal content) 495; zinc ore (metal content; 1982) 83; manganese ore (metal content) 10; cobalt ore (metal content) 14; gold (troy oz) 70; silver (troy oz; 1980) 2,733; diamonds (metric carats; 1980) 10,235; crude oil (1982) 1,050; coal 140; petroleum products 341; sulfuric acid (1979) 135; cement c. 400; electricity (kw-hr) 4,560,000.

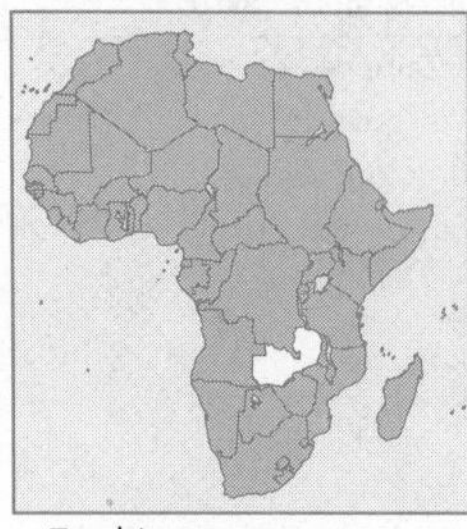

Zambia

Zambia

A republic and a member of the Commonwealth, Zambia is bounded by Tanzania, Malawi, Mozambique, Zimbabwe, South West Africa/Namibia, Angola, and Zaire. Area: 752,614 sq km (290,586 sq mi). Pop. (1983 est.): 6,346,000, about 99% of whom are Africans. Cap. and largest city: Lusaka (pop., 1980 prelim., 538,500). Language: English and Bantu. Religion: predominantly animist, with Roman Catholic (21%), Protestant, Hindu, and Muslim minorities. President in 1983, Kenneth Kaunda; prime minister, Nalumino Mundia.

The harsh budget presented early in 1983 reflected the general view that Zambia's economy was in a shambles. The highest increases in duties on beer, spirits, tobacco, and gasoline since independence were among the measures proposed, together with a 4% tax on the export value of minerals to

ZAMBIA

Education. (1981) Primary, pupils 1,068,314, teachers 23,100; secondary, pupils 98,862, teachers 4,650; vocational, pupils 5,487, teachers (1980) 515; teacher training, students 4,485, teachers 406; higher, students 3,603, teaching staff 334.

Finance. Monetary unit: kwacha, with (Sept. 20, 1983) a free rate of 1.22 kwacha to U.S. $1 (1.83 kwacha = £1 sterling). Gold and other reserves (June 1983) U.S. $76 million. Budget (1982 est.): revenue 1,038,000,000 kwacha; expenditure 1,501,000,000 kwacha. Gross national product (1981) 3,069,000,000 kwacha. Cost of living (1975 = 100; Dec. 1982) 271.2.

Foreign Trade. (1982) Imports 927.3 million kwacha; exports 985.2 million kwacha. Import sources (1979): U.K. 26%; Saudi Arabia 15%; South Africa 11%; U.S. 9%; West Germany 8%. Export destinations (1979): Japan 18%; U.K. 13%; France 12%; U.S. 10%; West Germany 9%; Italy 8%; India 6%. Main export: copper 89%.

Transport and Communications. Roads (1982) 37,232 km. Motor vehicles in use (1980): passenger c. 103,000; commercial (including buses) c. 66,000. Railways (1981) 2,188 km. Air traffic (1982): 557 million passenger-km; freight 23.5 million net ton-km. Telephones (Dec. 1980) 61,000. Radio receivers (Dec. 1980) 135,000. Television receivers (Dec. 1980) 60,000.

Agriculture. Production (in 000; metric tons; 1982): corn 810; cassava (1981) c. 178; millet c. 80; sorghum c. 40; sugar, raw value (1981) c. 102; tobacco 3. Livestock (in 000; 1981): cattle 2,225; sheep c. 50; goats c. 320; pigs 235; poultry c. 12,500.

Industry. Production (in 000; metric tons; 1981): copper ore (metal content) 701; lead ore (metal content; 1982) 17; zinc ore (metal content; 1982) 45; coal 506; petroleum products 747; cement 262; electricity (kw-hr) 9,100,000.

make up for the absence of any other revenue from the mines. In January the government removed price controls from most goods, and prices rose sharply. This measure was followed by the devaluation of the currency by 20%.

In April the International Monetary Fund promised a standby credit aimed at restoring financial stability, and in May some creditors agreed to reschedule Zambia's debts. One condition attached to the loan was that wage increases should be restricted to a maximum of 10%, which led to disputes between the government and the unions.

At the ninth general conference of the United National Independence Party in August, Pres. Kenneth Kaunda proposed a five-year program for national recovery. Two months later he was elected to a fifth term of office; and in one-party parliamentary elections, seven ministers of state lost their seats. (KENNETH INGHAM)

Zimbabwe

A republic in eastern Africa and member of the Commonwealth, Zimbabwe is bounded by Zambia, Mozambique, South Africa, and Botswana. Area: 390,759 sq km (150,873 sq mi). Pop. (1982 prelim.): 7,539,000, of whom 96% are African and 4% white. Cap. and largest city: Harare (pop., 1982 prelim., 656,000). Language: English (official) and various Bantu languages (1978 est., Shona 69%, Ndebele 15%). Religion: predominantly traditional tribal beliefs; Christian minority. President in 1983, the Rev. Canaan Banana; prime minister, Robert Mugabe.

The economy of Zimbabwe, already gravely affected by an acute shortage of fuel, suffered a further setback in January 1983 when Mozambican rebels sabotaged the pipeline from Beira, Mozambique, that supplied the major part of Zimbabwe's petroleum. Suggestions that a contract might be made for the supply of oil by South Africa were vigorously rejected. Instead, in February the price of gasoline was raised 40% as one of a number of price increases. Corruption was again the focus of government attention in August after further indications of the misuse of public funds were brought to its notice. Plans were discussed for the introduction of legislation to impose heavy penalties on those found guilty of corruption.

With a foreign debt that had quadrupled since independence to $1.5 billion and the prospect of a decline in the gross national product, Finance Minister Bernard Chidzero introduced a budget of considerable severity in July. Anyone earning above the stipulated minimum for industrial and commercial workers, which had not been raised for 18 months in spite of a 17% inflation rate, would now be subject to income tax. Food subsidies were to be halved, and sales taxes on all purchases were to be increased. The finance minister admitted that his budget provided for only the basic maintenance of existing services with minimal growth in a very few cases.

For most of the year relations with the U.K., Zimbabwe's main source of aid and technical assistance, were strained by rumours of human-rights violations, including the torture of senior white air force officers awaiting trial on charges of having been involved in the sabotage of fighter aircraft in 1982. A visit to Harare in January by Cranley Onslow, British minister of state for foreign relations, and his inadvertent reference to "Rhodesia" rather than to Zimbabwe, did little to improve the situation. Prime Minister Robert Mugabe countered by criticizing the Western powers for their failure to condemn South African policies wholeheartedly and by blaming the U.S. in particular for introducing the question of the withdrawal of Cuban troops from Angola into the discussions about the future of South West Africa/Namibia. British attitudes were not softened by the immediate rearrest of the six air force officers when in August they were found not guilty of sabotage. (Three of the officers were released shortly afterward, and the remaining three in December.) Mugabe accused the U.K. of interfering in Zimbabwe's internal affairs, and it was only after discussions with British Prime Minister Margaret Thatcher during the Commonwealth conference in November that he was prepared to admit that the relations between their two countries were once again amicable.

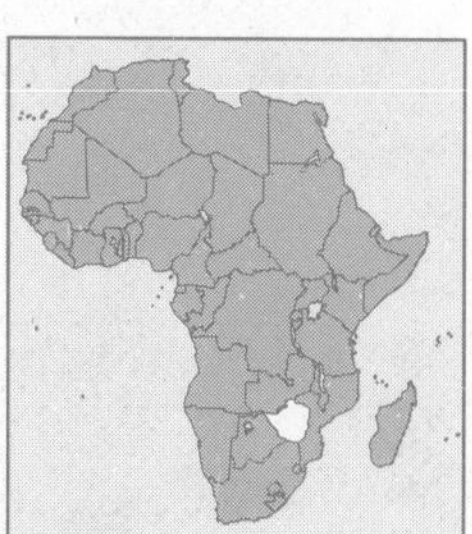
Zimbabwe

Relations with the U.S. were strained when Zimbabwe's representative on the UN Security Council abstained on a motion to condemn the U.S.S.R. for shooting down a South Korean commercial airliner in September. Though Mugabe explained that the action was taken at the request of a number of other African countries, the U.S. nevertheless cut its aid to Zimbabwe in December.

In March the Army ordered a search of Bulawayo to seek out dissidents. Joshua Nkomo, leader of the opposition Patriotic Front party, the Zimba-

UPI

Joshua Nkomo (left), leader of Zimbabwe's opposition party, fled to London in March for his personal safety. He returned to Zimbabwe in August and reclaimed his seat in Parliament.

bwe African People's Union (ZAPU [PF]), fled to Botswana and then to the U.K. Simultaneously, numerous charges of excessive brutality were leveled against army operations in the western province of Matabeleland. The editor of the Harare newspaper, *The Herald*, and a senior government official both claimed that foreign correspondents had grossly distorted events in the province, but former Rhodesian prime minister Garfield Todd, speaking in the Senate, said that a conflict of terror was taking place in Matabeleland and that Zimbabwe's reputation was suffering as a consequence. On March 15 Sen. Mark Patridge proposed a motion of grave concern about the situation, and at the end of the month the Roman Catholic bishops of Zimbabwe firmly censured army brutality in the province.

Mugabe's view was that government troops were facing people determined to destroy the country's development plans and to damage government property and that a force of guerrillas based in neighbouring Botswana was spearheading the attack. He said that the government, if given concrete evidence of excesses by the Army in Matabeleland, would investigate the charges as objectively as possible. The government, however, was quick to reject the accusations leveled by the bishops, claiming them to be utterly one-sided and based upon the fabricated reports of a hostile foreign press. Mugabe himself described the church leaders' statement as "the sermonizing of sanctimonious prelates" and added that the government's conscience regarding the deployment of troops in Matabeleland was clear.

Late in March six former members of the military wing of ZAPU (PF) were found not guilty of plotting to overthrow the government, and in April they were acquitted on charges of illegally possessing firearms. A seventh was found guilty on the latter charge. But the six were at once served with further detention orders, although no charges were preferred against them. They were later ordered to be held indefinitely without trial.

To mark the celebration of three years of independence in April, the prime minister spoke out vigorously against corruption. He also announced plans for the government to take control of a number of important industries. This marked a change from his former pragmatic approach to Zimbabwe's economic problems. In May he visited Hungary, Czechoslovakia, and East Germany, and during his return journey he paid a private visit to the U.K. He also visited the U.K. in July and took the opportunity to discuss with Thatcher the situation in Namibia and in Zimbabwe itself.

In August, on the occasion of the 20th anniversary of the founding of the ruling Patriotic Front party, the Zimbabwe African National Union (ZANU [PF]), Mugabe renewed his pledge to create a one-party state. A week later Nkomo returned to Harare. An attempt had been made in his absence to deprive him of his seat in Parliament on the grounds that he had absented himself from the house for more than 21 consecutive days, but the Assembly failed on two occasions to muster sufficient members to pass the motion. His reception from ZANU (PF) members when he reclaimed his seat on August 17 was far from friendly, however, and accusations of treachery were leveled against him. In Bulawayo Nkomo received a more friendly welcome. He took the opportunity to express the hope that discussion rather than force would be used to resolve the country's problems.

In November attention was switched from Nkomo to Bishop Abel Muzorewa, former prime minister, who was arrested when he was about to fly to the U.S. via South Africa. The bishop's supporters denied the suggestion that he had had any plans to hold discussions with the South African government, and Muzorewa went on a hunger strike for a brief period in protest against an order

ZIMBABWE

Education. (1982) Primary, pupils 1,934,614, teachers (1981) 36,734; secondary, pupils 224,609, teachers (1981) 6,112; vocational (1981), pupils 640, teachers 36; higher (university only), students (1981) 2,525, teaching staff (1979) 483.

Finance. Monetary unit: Zimbabwe dollar, with (Sept. 20, 1983) a free rate of Z$1.06 to U.S. $1 (Z$1.59 = £1 sterling). Gold and other reserves (June 1983) U.S. $74 million. Budget (1982–83 est.): revenue Z$1,948,000,000; expenditure Z$2,129,000,000. Gross national product (1981) Z$4,418,000,000. Cost of living (1975 = 100; May 1983) 239.7

Foreign Trade. (1982) Imports Z$1,244,070,000; exports Z$968.4 million. Import sources (1981): South Africa 27%; U.K. 10%; U.S. 7%; West Germany 7%; Japan 6%. Export destinations (1981): South Africa 22%; West Germany 8%; U.S. 8%; U.K. 7%; Italy 5%. Main exports (1981): tobacco 23%; food 13%; ferrochrome 8%; gold 8%; asbestos 8%; cotton 6%; settlers' possessions 6%; nickel 5%.

Transport and Communications. Roads (1982) 170,400 km. Motor vehicles in use (1982): passenger 224,500; commercial 17,300. Railways (1982): 3,394 km; freight traffic 6,259,000,000 net ton-km. Air traffic (1982): 541 million passenger-km; freight 9.4 million net ton-km. Telephones (June 1982) 242,300. Radio licenses (June 1982) 274,300. Television licenses (June 1982) 82,600.

Agriculture. Production (in 000; metric tons; 1982): corn *c.* 1,800; millet *c.* 190; wheat (1981) *c.* 190; sugar, raw value *c.* 430; peanuts *c.* 115; tobacco *c.* 90; cotton, lint *c.* 51; beef and veal (1981) *c.* 109. Livestock (in 000; 1981): cattle 5,261; sheep *c.* 370; goats *c.* 990; pigs *c.* 150.

Industry. Production (in 000; metric tons; 1982): coal 2,769; cement 576; asbestos 194; chrome ore 207; iron ore (metal content) 536; copper ore (metal content) 25; nickel ore (metal content) 13; gold (troy oz) 430; electricity (kw-hr) 4,196,000.

Zoology:
see Life Sciences

WILLIAM CAMPBELL

To Zimbabwe's problems of often violent intertribal hostility, economic hardships, and a wave of robbery and murder was added a gasoline shortage. Motorists in Harare lined up when gas was available.

providing for his indefinite detention. A week later one of Muzorewa's sons was also arrested but was released after a day's detention. Another critic, the Rev. Ndabaningi Sithole, was warned not to conspire against the government, and *The Herald* claimed that he was engaged in subversive activity. Simultaneously, the High Court ordered the release of Dumiso Dabengwa, one of Nkomo's senior aides, who had been among those detained without trial since April. (KENNETH INGHAM)

Zoos and Botanical Gardens

Zoos. Debate as to the future of the nearly extinct Californian condor continued in 1983. The debate illustrated the problem facing all conservationists when dealing with species in danger of extinction—whether or not to interfere. In March there was a dramatic step forward for those favouring intervention when four condor chicks were successfully hatched at the San Diego (Calif.) Wild Animal Park. The chicks, all from eggs taken from the wild, were being reared artificially, fed through puppet heads resembling adult condors.

The total population of Californian condors in the wild was under 20 individuals, all confined to relatively small areas and subject to the effects of advancing urbanization and agriculture. The Condor Research Center's program, for which $25 million was budgeted, included trying to protect the birds in the wild and breeding in captivity. Opponents of interference argued that the money could be better spent elsewhere and that unnecessary damage would result from the proposed intrusions, such as taking eggs, radio-tagging birds, and removing some adults into captivity.

Interference in reproduction also had its opponents, though manipulative techniques were being used successfully in many zoos and allied research centres. On June 14 the Cincinnati (Ohio) Wildlife Research Federation announced the birth of a female African eland, the result of the first successful nonsurgical embryo transfer in an exotic species and the first in any species of antelope. Other noteworthy breedings and rearings included an echidna (*Tachyglossus aculeatus*) at Philadelphia; the 23rd Asian elephant birth at Washington Park Zoo, Portland, Ore.; white (not albino) leopard cubs at San Leandro, Calif.; an ornate hawk eagle (*Spizaetus ornatus*) at Oklahoma City; the hand rearing of a Chilean flamingo (*Phoenicopterus ruber chilensis*) at Slimbridge, Gloucestershire; 70 offspring, double the normal number, from a gaboon viper (*Bitis gabonica*) at Madrid; and second-generation Puerto Rican crested toads (*Bufo lemur*) at Buffalo, N.Y., for eventual release into the wild in Puerto Rico.

Twelve blackbuck, donated by the Western Plains Zoo, Australia, and Copenhagen (Denmark) Zoo, were sent to Karachi, Pakistan. They would be released into the Cholistan Desert, part of the Lal Suhara National Park near Bahawalpur, an area once famous for these antelopes.

The number of new zoos and aquariums opening throughout the world had fallen markedly since the surge of the 1950s and '60s. Many that had survived were changing their exhibits to provide a more naturalistic environment. One of the most ambitious new exhibits was the "Penguin

Five white Bengal tiger cubs were born in the Cincinnati (Ohio) Zoo in August. They are shown at the age of eight weeks as they received their first physical examination.

WIDE WORLD

Encounter" display, opened in May at Sea World in California. It featured a simulated polar ice shelf requiring 5,500 kg (12,000 lb) of crushed ice each day. This provided the natural substrate for six species of penguins, as well as skuas, sheathbills, giant petrels, blue-eyed shags, and kelp gulls. A moving sidewalk transported visitors past 30.5-m (100-ft) viewing windows. Outdoors, an area of simulated volcanic rock with a pool of filtered seawater harboured Humboldt's penguins, ruddy-headed geese, and Patagonian crested ducks. An area of rocky cliffs and pools housed Arctic and subarctic birds.

The justification for keeping certain wild animals in zoos was questioned in October when a 17-year-old African elephant at London Zoo had to be given a lethal injection after attempts to transport it to Whipsnade Park Zoo had failed. Pole Pole, brought to London from Kenya in 1968, had adapted poorly to confinement, and it had been hoped that the more open Whipsnade environment would suit it better. (P. J. OLNEY)

Botanical Gardens. While the worldwide economic recession resulted in some cutbacks in the development of botanical gardens, there was evidence that this trend was less serious than many had thought. The gardens under greatest threat were those where the arguments for their continued support either had been poorly presented or were not fully understood by funding agencies—for example, in less developed countries where the necessary subsidies were given low priority. Unfortunately, some of the established botanical gardens had been slow to recognize that their own security was dependent on the validity of the services they gave to the botanical and allied sciences and to mankind generally. Increasing pressure on natural ecosystems throughout the world necessitated urgent research, and the support botanical gardens could give to this end would increase their stature and importance.

The Botanic Gardens Conservation Body, whose aims were to provide listings of threatened and endangered plants, encourage the exchange of ideas and information, and act as a focus for the conservation activities of botanical gardens throughout the world, now had 127 members representing 33 countries. Already it had been found that a great number of seriously threatened plants were held by member gardens, and in some instances plants known to be extinct in the wild had been found in cultivation. Regional groups of botanical gardens also met regularly, particularly in the U.S. and Europe, to discuss strategy in this and other areas of their work.

Of the emerging botanical gardens that were orienting their activities toward local conservation problems, the Jardín Botánico Viera y Clavijo, Tafira Alta, Canary Islands, had established nature reserves for threatened plants of the region and was receiving government support. The garden had produced 10,000 seedlings of the endangered Canarian dragon tree (*Dracaena draco*); these were being distributed to schools that would cultivate them for two years and then replant selected sites. In Mexico the Jardín Botánico F.C.O. Javier Clavijero in Jalapa, Vera Cruz, was actively pursuing a policy related to problems of agricultural development and land clearance in natural vegetation areas. The Waimea Arboretum in Hawaii was cultivating a collection of indigenous species that were threatened by tourism and urban development. Similar work was being undertaken at the National Botanic Garden in Zimbabwe. New botanical gardens in Malaysia included developments in Kuala Lumpur and Sabah. Planning of projected gardens was under way in India, Bangladesh, South Korea, and Chile.

The introduction of wild collected plants to maximize the scientific value of living plant collections was receiving increasing emphasis, particularly in Australia, South Africa, the U.S., and in the major European botanical gardens. Interchange of this material would go some way toward creating a network of gardens that could supply material for research, thus reducing the need to denude wild plant populations.

During 1983 work was started on a new tropical display greenhouse complex at the Royal Botanic Gardens, Kew, England, to replace older structures that were no longer economical to maintain. The complex would incorporate the latest labour- and energy-saving technology. Scheduled for completion in 1986, it would be the largest greenhouse at Kew, with a floor area of 4,490 sq m (48,330 sq ft). (REGINALD IAN BEYER)

See also Environment; Gardening.
[355.C.6]

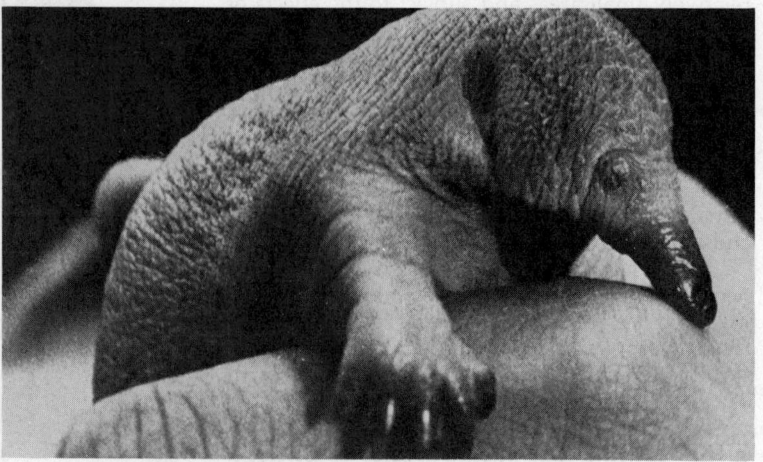

An infant anteater climbs a hand at the Philadelphia Zoo, where this spiny echidna was born in May. Here it is a day old, four inches long, weighs five ounces, and still has skin covering its eyes.

WIDE WORLD

CONTRIBUTORS

Names of contributors to the Britannica Book of the Year *with the articles written by them. The arrangement is alphabetical by last name.*

AARSDAL, STENER. Journalist, *Børsen* (Denmark's Business Daily), Copenhagen.
Denmark

ADAMS, ANDREW M. Free-lance Foreign Correspondent; Editor and Publisher, *Sumo World* magazine. Author of *Ninja: The Invisible Assassins; Born to Die: The Cherry Blossom Squadrons.* Co-author of *Sumo History and Yokozuna Profiles; Japan Sports Guide.*
Combat Sports: *Judo; Karate; Kendo; Sumo*

AGRELLA, JOSEPH C. Correspondent, *Blood-Horse* magazine; former Turf Editor, *Chicago Sun-Times.* Co-author of *Ten Commandments for Professional Handicapping; American Race Horses.*
Equestrian Sports: *Thoroughbred Racing and Steeplechasing (in part)*

ALLABY, MICHAEL. Free-lance Writer and Lecturer. Author of *Who Will Eat?; Inventing Tomorrow; World Food Resources; A Year in the Life of a Field.* Co-author of *A Blueprint for Survival; Home Farm.* Editor of *The Survival Handbook; Dictionary of the Environment.*
Environment *(in part)*

ALLAN, J. A. Senior Lecturer in Geography, School of Oriental and African Studies, University of London.
Libya

ALSTON, REX. Broadcaster and Journalist; retired BBC Commentator. Author of *Taking the Air; Over to Rex Alston; Test Commentary; Watching Cricket.*
Cricket

ANDERSON, PETER J. Assistant Director, Institute of Polar Studies, Ohio State University, Columbus.
Antarctica

ARCHIBALD, JOHN J. Feature Writer, *St. Louis Post-Dispatch;* Adjunct Professor, Lindenwood Colleges, St. Charles, Mo. Author of *Bowling for Boys and Girls.*
Bowling: *Tenpin Bowling (in part)*

ARNOLD, GUY. Free-lance Writer. Author of *Modern Nigeria; Kenyatta and the Politics of Kenya; Aid in Africa; The Unions; Modern Kenya.*
Botswana; Burundi; Cape Verde; Equatorial Guinea; Gambia, The; Ghana; Guinea-Bissau; Lesotho; Liberia; Maldives; Mauritius; Nigeria; Rwanda; São Tomé and Príncipe; Seychelles; Sierra Leone; Swaziland

ARNOLD, MAVIS. Free-lance Journalist, Dublin.
Ireland

ARRINGTON, LEONARD J. Formerly Church Historian, Church of Jesus Christ of Latter-day Saints. Author of *Great Basin Kingdom; An Economic History of the Latter-day Saints; Building the City of God: Community and Cooperation Among the Mormons; The Mormon Experience: A History of the Latter-day Saints.*
Religion: *Church of Jesus Christ of Latter-day Saints*

AVINERI, SHLOMO. Professor of Political Science, Hebrew University of Jerusalem; Director General, Israeli Ministry of Foreign Affairs, 1976–77. Author of *Hegel's Theory of the Modern State; The Making of Modern Zionism.*
Feature Article: *At the Core of the Problem of Peace—Israel and the West Bank: Two Views (in part)*

AYTON, CYRIL J. Editor, *Motorcycle Sport,* London.
Motor Sports: *Motorcycles*

BAIR, DEIRDRE. Associate Professor of English, University of Pennsylvania; currently at work on a critical biography of Simone de Beauvoir. Author of *Samuel Beckett: A Biography.*
Feature Article: *Women's Rights in Today's World*

BAKER, CARL G. Medical Director, Ludwig Institute for Cancer Research, Zurich; Director, National Cancer Institute, Bethesda, Md., 1969–72.
Revised *Macropædia* **article:** *Cancer (in part)*

BAPTIST, INES T. Administrative Assistant, Encyclopædia Britannica, Special Projects.
Belize

BARFORD, MICHAEL F. Editor and Director, *World Tobacco,* London.
Industrial Review: *Tobacco*

BARGAD, WARREN. Milton D. Ratner Professor of Hebrew Literature and Dean, Spertus College of Judaica, Chicago. Author of *Ideas in Fiction: The Works of Hayim Hazaz; Anthology of Israeli Poetry.*
Literature: *Hebrew*

BARRETT, PAUL A. Managing Editor, *TV World* magazine, London.
Television and Radio *(in part)*

BASS, HOWARD. Journalist and Broadcaster. Editor, *Winter Sports,* 1948–69. Winter Sports Correspondent, *Daily Telegraph* and *Sunday Telegraph,* London; *The Standard,* London; *Toronto Star,* Toronto; *Canadian Skater,* Ottawa; *Skating,* U.S.; *Ski Racing,* U.S.; *Ski,* London. Author of *The Magic of Skiing; International Encyclopaedia of Winter Sports; Let's Go Skating.*
Biographies *(in part);* **Ice Hockey:** *European and International;* **Winter Sports**

BAYLISS, DAVID. Chief Transport Planner, Greater London Council. Co-author of *Developing Patterns of Urbanization; Uses of Economics.* Advisory Editor of *Models in Urban and Regional Planning.*
Transportation *(in part)*

BEALL, JOHN V. Sales Manager, Davy McKee Corp. Author of sections 1 and 34, *Mining Engineering Handbook.* Frequent Contributor to *Mining Engineering.*
Mining and Quarrying *(in part)*

BEATTIE, ROGER A. Member of Secretariat, International Social Security Association, Geneva.
Social Security and Welfare Services *(in part)*

BEATTY, JAMES R. Retired Research Fellow, B. F. Goodrich Research and Development Center, Brecksville, Ohio. Co-author of *Concepts in Compounding; Physical Testing of Elastomers and Polymers in Applied Polymer Science; Physical Properties of Rubber Compounds in the Mechanics of Pneumatic Tires.*
Industrial Review: *Rubber*

BECKWITH, DAVID C. National Economic Correspondent, *Time* magazine, Washington, D.C.
United States Statistical Supplement: *Developments in the States in 1983.*

BERENSON, LOUIS S. President, Berenson Pari-Mutuel, Inc., doing business as Berensons' Hartford Jai-Alai and Berensons' Belmont Greyhound Track.
Court Games: *Jai-Alai*

BERGERRE, MAX. Vatican Affairs Correspondent, *La Vie Catholique,* Paris.
Vatican City State

BERKOVITCH, ISRAEL. Free-lance Writer and Consultant. Author of *Coal on the Switchback; Coal: Energy and Chemical Storehouse.* Editor of *World Energy: Looking Ahead to 2020.*
Energy: *Coal*

BERMAN, BRENDA E. Assistant Editor, *Encyclopædia Britannica.*
Feature Article: *Women's Rights in Today's World (table)*

BEYER, REGINALD IAN. Deputy Curator, Royal Botanic Gardens, Kew, England. Author of *Conservation of Threatened Plants.*
Zoos and Botanical Gardens: *Botanical Gardens*

BICKELHAUPT, DAVID L. Professor of Insurance and Finance, College of Administrative Science, Ohio State University, Columbus. Author of *General Insurance* (11th ed.); *Transition to Multiple-Line Insurance Companies;* co-author of *International Insurance.*
Industrial Review: *Insurance*

BILEFIELD, LIONEL. Technical Journalist.
Industrial Review: *Paints and Varnishes*

BIRD, THOMAS E. Assistant Director, Yiddish Program, Queens College, City University of New York. Contributor to *Lexicon of Modern Yiddish Literature.*
Literature: *Yiddish (in part)*

BLACKBURN, LUCY. Economist, Group Economics Department, Lloyds Bank PLC, London. Contributor to *EEC and the Third World: A Survey.*
Biographies *(in part);* **Chile; Guatemala; Honduras**

BODDY, WILLIAM C. Editor, *Motor Sport.* Full Member, Guild of Motoring Writers. Author of *The History of Brooklands Motor Course; The World's Land Speed Record; Continental Sports Cars; The Bugatti Story; History of Montlhéry; The VW Beetle.*
Motor Sports: *Grand Prix Racing; Rallies and Other Races*

BODEN, EDWARD. Editor, *The Veterinary Record;* Executive Editor, *Research in Veterinary Science.*
Veterinary Science

BOLT, PETER H. Secretary, British Committee, World Methodist Council. Author

of *A Way of Loving.*
Religion: *Methodist Churches*

BOLTZ, C. L. Free-lance Industrial Writer, London.
Energy: *Electricity*

BOONSTRA, DICK. Assistant Professor, Department of Political Science, Free University, Amsterdam.
Netherlands, The; Suriname

BOOTH, JOHN NICHOLLS. Lecturer and Writer; Co-founder, Japan Free Religious Association; Senior Pastor of a number of U.S. churches. Author of *The Quest for Preaching Power; Introducing Unitarian Universalism.*
Religion: *Unitarian (Universalist) Churches*

BOSWALL, JEFFERY. Producer of Sound and Television Programs, BBC Natural History Unit, Bristol, England.
Life Sciences: *Ornithology*

BOTHELL, JOAN N. Free-lance Writer and Editor; former Staff Writer, Encyclopædia Britannica.
Biographies *(in part)*

BOX, BEN. Free-lance Writer and Researcher on Latin America and Iberia.
Argentina; Biographies *(in part)*; **Colombia; Peru**

BOYE, ROGER. Coin Columnist, *Chicago Tribune.*
Philately and Numismatics: *Coins*

BRACKMAN, ARNOLD C. Asian Affairs Specialist. Author of *Indonesian Communism: A History; Southeast Asia's Second Front: The Power Struggle in the Malay Archipelago; The Communist Collapse in Indonesia; The Last Emperor.*
Brunei; Indonesia

BRADSHER, HENRY S. Foreign Affairs Writer.
Philippines

BRAIDWOOD, ROBERT J. Professor Emeritus of Old World Prehistory, the Oriental Institute and the Department of Anthropology, University of Chicago. Author of *Prehistoric Men; Archeologists and What They Do.*
Archaeology: *Eastern Hemisphere*

BRAZEE, RUTLAGE J. Geophysical Consultant.
Earth Sciences: *Geophysics*

BRECHER, KENNETH. Professor of Astronomy and Physics, Boston University. Co-author and co-editor of *Astronomy of the Ancients; High Energy Astrophysics and Its Relation to Elementary Particle Physics.*
Astronomy

BRUNO, HAL. Director of Political Coverage, ABC News, Washington, D.C.
Biographies *(in part)*

BURDIN, JOEL L. Professor of Educational Administration, Ohio University, Athens, Ohio. Co-author of *A Reader's Guide to the Comprehensive Models for Preparing Elementary Teachers; Elementary School Curriculum and Instruction.*
Education *(in part)*

BURKE, DONALD P. Executive Editor, *Chemical Week,* New York City.
Industrial Review: *Chemicals*

BURKS, ARDATH W. Emeritus Professor of Asian Studies, Rutgers University, New Brunswick, N.J. Author of *The Government of Japan; East Asia: China, Korea, Japan; Japan: Portrait of a Postindustrial Power.*
Japan

BUSS, ROBIN. Lecturer in French, Woolwich College of Further Education, London. Author of *Vigny's Chatterton.*
Biographies *(in part)*; **Literature:** *French (in part)*

BUTLER, FRANK. Former Sports Editor, *News of the World,* London. Author of *A History of Boxing in Britain.*
Combat Sports: *Boxing*

CALHOUN, DAVID R. Editor, Encyclopædia Britannica, Yearbooks.
Gambling *(in part)*; **Winter Sports** *(sidebar)*

CAMERON, SARAH. Economist, Group Economics Department, Lloyds Bank PLC, London.
Dominican Republic; Ecuador; Venezuela

CARTER, ROBERT W. Free-lance Journalist, London. Author of numerous newspaper and magazine articles.
Equestrian Sports: *Thoroughbred Racing and Steeplechasing (in part)*

CASSIDY, RICHARD J. Senior Public Relations Officer, British Gas Corporation. Author of *Gas: Natural Energy.*
Energy: *Natural Gas*

CEGIELSKI, CHARLES M. Associate Editor, Encyclopædia Britannica, Yearbooks.
Life Sciences: *Introduction*

CHALMERS, ALAN P. H. Present post, The Lodge, Brantridge Forest, West Sussex, England.
Racket Games: *Squash Rackets*

CHAPMAN, KENNETH F. Former Editor, *Stamp Collecting* and *Philatelic Magazine*; Philatelic Correspondent, *The Times,* London. Author of *Good Stamp Collecting; Commonwealth Stamp Collecting.*
Philately and Numismatics: *Stamps*

CHAPMAN, ROBIN. Senior Economist, Group Economics Department, Lloyds Bank PLC, London.
Haiti; Latin-American Affairs

CHAPPELL, DUNCAN. Professor and Chairman, Department of Criminology, Simon Fraser University, Vancouver, B.C. Co-author of *The Police and the Public in Australia and New Zealand.* Co-editor of *The Australian Criminal Justice System* (1st and 2nd ed.); *Forcible Rape: the Crime, the Victim and the Offender.*
Crime and Law Enforcement

CHICKERING, A. LAWRENCE. Executive Director, Institute for Contemporary Studies, San Francisco, Calif. Co-author of *The World Crisis in Social Security.*
Social Security and Welfare Services: *Special Report*

CHUPRININ, SERGEY. Journalist, Novosti Press Agency, Moscow.
Literature: *Russian (in part)*

CLARKE, R. O. Writer on Industrial Relations, Paris.
Industrial Relations

COGLE, T. C. J. Editor, *Electrical Review,* London.
Industrial Review: *Electrical*

COMBA, ALDO. Executive Secretary, Department of Cooperation and Witness, World Alliance of Reformed Churches; former President, Federation of Protestant Churches in Italy. Author of *Le Parabole di Gesù.*
Religion: *Reformed, Presbyterian, and Congregational Churches*

COPPOCK, CHARLES DENNIS. Vice-President, English Lacrosse Union. Author of "Men's Lacrosse" in *The Oxford Companion to Sports and Games.*
Field Hockey and Lacrosse: *Lacrosse (in part)*

COSTIN, STANLEY H. British Correspondent, *Herrenjournal International* and *Men's Wear, Australasia.* Council of Management Member, British Men's Fashion Association Ltd. Former President, Men's Fashion Writers International.
Fashion and Dress *(in part)*

CRATER, RUFUS W. Senior Editorial Consultant, *Broadcasting,* New York City.
Television and Radio *(in part)*

CRAWFORD, LESLIE. Economist, Group Economics Department, Lloyds Bank PLC, London.
Biographies *(in part)*; **Brazil; El Salvador; Nicaragua**

CROSS, COLIN J. Editor, *The Polo Times;* U.K. Chairman, European Polo Academy.
Equestrian Sports: *Polo*

CROSSLAND, NORMAN. Former Bonn Correspondent, *The Economist,* London.
Biographies *(in part)*; **German Democratic Republic; Germany, Federal Republic of**

CVIIC, K. F. Leader Writer and East European Specialist, *The Economist,* London.
Spain *(sidebar)*; **Yugoslavia**

DAUME, DAPHNE. Editor, Encyclopædia Britannica, Yearbooks.
Law (sidebar)

DAVID, TUDOR. Managing Editor, *Education,* London.
Education *(in part)*

DAVIS, DONALD A. Editor, *Drug & Cosmetic Industry* and *Cosmetic Insider's Report,* New York City. Contributor to *The Science and Technology of Aerosol Packaging; Advances in Cosmetic Technology.*
Industrial Review: *Pharmaceuticals*

DAVIS, KENNETH C. Free-lance Writer. Author of *Two-Bit Culture.*
Publishing: *Books (in part)*

DEAM, JOHN B. Technical Director, National Machine Tool Builders Association, McLean, Va. Author of *The Synthesis of Common Digital Subsystems.*
Industrial Review: *Machinery and Machine Tools*

DECRAENE, PHILIPPE. Member of editorial staff, *Le Monde,* Paris. Professor, Institute of Political Studies, Paris. Author of *Tableau des Partis Politiques Africains; Lettres de l'Afrique Atlantique; L'expérience socialiste Somalienne; Le Mali; Vieille Afrique, Jeunes Nations.*
Benin; Biographies *(in part)*; **Cameroon; Central African Republic; Chad; Comoros; Congo; Dependent States** *(in part)*; **Djibouti; Gabon; Guinea; Ivory Coast; Madagascar; Mali; Mauritania; Niger; Senegal; Togo; Tunisia; Upper Volta**

de la BARRE, KENNETH. Director, Katimavik, Montreal.
Arctic Regions

DENSELOW, ROBIN. Rock Music Critic, *The Guardian,* London; Current Affairs Producer, BBC Television. Co-author of *The Electric Muse.*
Biographies *(in part)*; **Music:** *Popular*

DE PUY, NORMAN R. Minister, First Baptist Church, Newton Centre, Mass.; Columnist, *American Baptist* magazine. Author of *The Bible Alive; Help in Understanding Theology.*
Religion: *Baptist Churches*

DESHAYES-CREUILLY, MARIE-JOSE. Head of Documentation Service, International Vine and Wine Office, Paris.
Industrial Review: *Alcoholic Beverages (in part)*

DIRNBACHER, ELFRIEDE. Austrian Civil Servant.
Austria

DORRIS, THOMAS HARTLEY. Editor, Ecumenical Press Service, Geneva. Author of several periodical articles on religion, education, and medicine.
Religion: *Lutheran Churches*

EIU. The Economist Intelligence Unit, London.
Economy, World

ELI, C. R. Former Executive Director, U.S. Badminton Association.
Racket Games: *Badminton*

ELKINGTON, JOHN. Environmental Consultant to national and international organizations; Associate Editor, *Biotechnology Review* magazine. Author of *Pollution 1990; The Ecology of Tomorrow's World; Seven Bridges to Cross.*
Environment: *Special Report*

ENGELS, JAN R. Editor, *Vooruitgang* (Bimonthly of the Centre Paul Hymans, liberal study and documentation centre), Brussels.
Belgium

EWART, W. D. Editorial Consultant, *Fairplay International Shipping Weekly*, London. Author of *Marine Engines; Atomic Submarines; Hydrofoils and Hovercraft.*
Industrial Review: *Shipbuilding;* **Transportation** *(in part)*

FARR, D. M. L. Professor of History and Director, Paterson Centre for International Programs, Carleton University, Ottawa. Co-author of *The Canadian Experience.*
Canada

FAUST, JOAN LEE. Garden Editor, *New York Times.*
Gardening *(in part)*

FELKNOR, BRUCE L. Director of Yearbooks, Encyclopædia Britannica.
Industrial Review *(sidebar)*

FENDELL, ROBERT J. Auto Editor, *Science & Mechanics.* Author of *The New Era Car Book and Auto Survival Guide; How to Make Your Car Last Forever.* Co-author of *Encyclopedia of Motor Racing Greats.*
Motor Sports: *U.S. Racing*

FERRIER, R. W. Group Historian,British Petroleum Company PLC, London.
Energy: *Petroleum*

FIDDICK, PETER. Specialist Writer, *The Guardian*, London.
Publishing: *Newspapers (in part); Magazines (in part); sidebar*

FIELDS, DONALD. Helsinki Correspondent, BBC, *The Guardian*, and *The Sunday Times*, London.
Finland

FIRTH, DAVID. Editor, *The Friend*, London; formerly Editor, *Quaker Monthly*, London.
Religion: *Religious Society of Friends*

FISHER, DAVID. Civil Engineer, Freeman Fox & Partners, London; formerly Executive Editor, *Engineering*, London.
Engineering Projects: *Bridges*

FLANAGAN, JACK C. Travel Counselor.
Water Sports: *Surfing*

FRADY, WILLIAM ENSIGN, III. Editor, *Water Polo Scoreboard*, Newport Beach, Calif.
Water Sports: *Water Polo*

FRANKLIN, HAROLD. Editor, *English Bridge Quarterly.* Bridge Correspondent, *Yorkshire Post; Yorkshire Evening Post.* Author of *Best of Bridge on the Air.*
Contract Bridge

FRANZ, FREDERICK W. President, Watch Tower Bible and Tract Society of Pennsylvania.
Religion: *Jehovah's Witnesses*

FRIDOVICH, IRWIN. James B. Duke Professor of Biochemistry, Duke University Medical Center, Durham, N.C.
Life Sciences: *Molecular Biology (in part)*

FRIEDLY, ROBERT LOUIS. Vice President for Communication, Christian Church (Disciples of Christ), Indianapolis, Ind.
Religion: *Christian Church (Disciples of Christ)*

FRISKIN, SYDNEY E. Hockey Correspondent, *The Times*, London.
Field Hockey and Lacrosse: *Field Hockey*

FROST, DAVID. Rugby Union Correspondent, *The Guardian*, London.
Football: *Rugby*

GADDUM, PETER W. Chairman, H. T. Gaddum and Company Ltd., Silk Merchants, Macclesfield, Cheshire, England. Honorary President, International Silk Association, Lyons. Author of *Silk—How and Where It Is Produced.*
Industrial Review: *Textiles (in part)*

GANADO, ALBERT. Lawyer, Malta.
Malta

GANGULY, DILIP. Special Correspondent, South Asian Bureau, Agence France Presse, New Delhi, India.
Afghanistan; Bangladesh; Bhutan; Biographies *(in part);* **Burma; Nepal; Pakistan; Sri Lanka**

GARRAD, ROB. Director of Information Services, International Headquarters, Salvation Army.
Religion: *Salvation Army*

GIBBONS, J. WHITFIELD. Research Ecologist, Savannah River Ecology Laboratory, Aiken, South Carolina.
Life Sciences: *Zoology*

GIBNEY, FRANK B., JR. Tokyo Correspondent, *Newsweek* magazine.
Biographies *(in part)*

GILLESPIE, HUGH M. Director of Communications, International Road Federation, Washington, D.C.
Engineering Projects: *Roads*

GJESTER, FAY. Oslo Correspondent, *Financial Times*, London.
Norway

GOLDSMITH, ARTHUR. Editorial Director, *Popular Photography*, New York City. Author of *The Photography Game; The Nude in Photography; The Camera and Its Images.* Co-author of *The Eye of Eisenstaedt.*
Photography

GOLOMBEK, HARRY. British Chess Champion, 1947, 1949, and 1955. Chess Correspondent, *The Times*, London. Author of *Penguin Handbook of the Game of Chess; A History of Chess; The Encyclopedia of Chess.*
Chess

GOODWIN, NOËL. Associate Editor, *Dance & Dancers;* U.K. Dance Correspondent, *International Herald Tribune*, Paris, and *Ballet News*, New York City. Author of *A Ballet for Scotland;* editor of Royal Ballet and Royal Opera yearbooks for 1978, 1979, 1980. Contributor to the *Encyclopædia Britannica* (15th ed.).
Dance *(in part)*

GOODWIN, ROBERT E. Formerly Executive Director, Billiard Congress of America; Managing Director, Billiard and Bowling Institute of America.
Billiard Games

GOTTFRIED, MARTIN. Drama Critic, New York City. Author of *A Theater Divided; Opening Nights; Broadway Musicals; Jed Harris, The Curse of Genius.*
Theatre *(in part)*

GOULD, DONALD W. Medical Writer and Broadcaster, U.K.
Health and Disease: *Overview (in part); Mental Health*

GREENLEAF, ARNO. Assistant Professor, Department of Biochemistry, Duke University Medical Center, Durham, N.C.
Life Sciences: *Molecular Biology (in part)*

GRIFFITHS, A. R. G. Senior Lecturer in History, Flinders University of South Australia. Author of *Contemporary Australia.*
Australia; Australia: *Special Report;* **Biographies** *(in part);* **Nauru; Papua New Guinea**

GROSSMAN, JOEL W. Archaeologist.
Archaeology: *Western Hemisphere*

GRUMET, ROBERT S. Fellow, Newberry Library Center for the History of the American Indian, Chicago. Author of *Native Americans of the Northwest Coast.*
Anthropology

HALLGREN, RICHARD F. Acting Assistant Administrator for Weather Services, National Oceanic and Atmospheric Administration. Author of numerous scientific periodical articles.
Earth Sciences: *Meteorology*

HARDMAN, THOMAS C. Consulting Editor, *The Water Skier*, American Water Ski Association. Co-author of *Let's Go Water Skiing.*
Water Sports: *Water Skiing*

HASEGAWA, RYUSAKU. Editor, TBS-Britannica Co., Ltd., Tokyo.
Baseball *(in part)*

HAVARD-WILLIAMS, P. Professor, Department of Library and Information Studies, Loughborough University, Leicestershire, England.
Libraries *(in part)*

HAWKLAND, WILLIAM D. Chancellor and Professor of Law, Louisiana State University, Baton Rouge. Author of *Sales and Bulk Sales Under the Uniform Commercial Code; Cases on Bills and Notes; Transactional Guide of the Uniform Commercial Code; Cases on Sales and Security.*
Law: *Court Decisions*

HAWLEY, H. B. Specialist, Human Nutrition and Food Science, Switzerland.
Food Processing

HEBBLETHWAITE, PETER. Vatican Affairs Writer, *National Catholic Reporter*, Kansas City, Mo. Author of *The Council Fathers and Atheism; Christian-Marxist Dialogue and Beyond; The Year of Three Popes; Introducing John Paul II.*
Biographies *(in part)*; **Religion:** *Roman Catholic Church*

HENDERSHOTT, MYRL C. Professor of Oceanography, Scripps Institution of Oceanography, La Jolla, Calif.
Earth Sciences: *Oceanography*

HENRIKSSON, ANDERS. Historian, formerly of McMaster University, Hamilton, Ont., and the University of Alberta, Edmonton.
Education *(sidebar)*

HERMAN, ROBIN CATHY. Free-lance Journalist.
Ice Hockey: *North American*

HESS, MARVIN G. Executive Vice-President, National Wrestling Coaches Association, Salt Lake City, Utah.
Combat Sports: *Wrestling*

HIGGINS, FITZGERALD. Editor and Reviewer.
Literature: *United States*

HINDIN, HARVEY J. Senior Editor, *Electronics* magazine, New York City. Author of numerous articles on electronics and mathematics.
Industrial Review: *Telecommunications*

HOPE, THOMAS W. President, Hope Reports, Inc., Rochester, N.Y. Author of *Hope Reports AV-USA; Hope Reports Industrial AV Business; Hope Reports Quarterly; Communicating in the Global Village.*
Motion Pictures *(in part)*

HOTZ, LOUIS. Former Editorial Writer, *Johannesburg* (S.Af.) *Star.* Co-author and contributor to *The Jews in South Africa.*
South Africa

HOWKINS, JOHN. Editor, *InterMedia*, International Institute of Communications, London. Author of *Understanding Television; Mass Communications in China.*
Television and Radio *(in part)*

HUNNINGS, NEVILLE MARCH. Editorial Director, European Law Centre Ltd., London. Editor, *Common Market Law Reports; European Commercial Cases.* Author of *Film Censors and the Law.* Co-editor of *Legal Problems of an Enlarged European Community.*
Law: *International Law*

INGHAM, KENNETH. Professor of History, University of Bristol, England. Author of *Reformers in India; A History of East Africa.*
Angola; Kenya; Malawi; Mozambique; Sudan; Tanzania; Uganda; Zaire; Zambia; Zimbabwe

JACQUET, CONSTANT H. Staff Associate for Information Services, Office of Research, Evaluation and Planning, National Council of Churches. Editor of *Yearbook of American and Canadian Churches.*
United States Statistical Supplement: *Church Membership table*

JARDINE, ADRIAN. Company Director. Member, Guild of Yachting Writers.
Sailing

JASPERT, W. PINCUS. Technical and Editorial Consultant. European Editor, North American Publishing Company, Philadelphia. Member, Inter-Comprint Planning Committee; Member, Society of Photographic Engineers and Scientists; Life Member, *Eurographic Press.* Author of *State of the Art.* Editor of *Encyclopaedia of Type Faces.*
Industrial Review: *Printing*

JENKINS, PETER. Policy Editor and Political Columnist, *The Guardian,* London.
United Kingdom

JOFFÉ, GEORGE. Journalist and Writer on North African Affairs.
Algeria; Morocco

JONES, C. M. Consultant, *World Bowls* and *Tennis.* Member, British Society of Sports Psychology; Associate Member, British Association of National Coaches. Player-Captain, Great Britain's Britannia Cup tennis team (1979–81). Author of *Winning Bowls; How to Become a Champion;* numerous books on tennis. Co-author of *Tackle Bowls My Way; Bryant on Bowls.*
Bowling: *Lawn Bowls*

JONES, D. A. N. Novelist and Critic. Author of *Parade in Pairs; Never Had It so Good.*
Biographies *(in part)*; **Literature:** *Introduction; United Kingdom*

JONES, HANDEL H. Vice-President for Strategic and International Management, Commercial Electronics Operations, Dallas, Texas.
Industrial Review: *Microelectronics*

JONES, W. GLYN. Professor of Scandinavian Studies, University of Newcastle upon Tyne, England. Author of *Johannes Jørgensens modneår; Johannes Jørgensen; William Heinesen; Færo og kosmos; Danish: A Grammar and Exercises.*
Literature: *Danish*

JONSEN, ALBERT R. Professor of Ethics in Medicine and Chief, Division of Medical Ethics, Institute for Health Policy Studies, University of California School of Medicine, San Francisco.
Health and Disease: *Special Report*

JOSEPH, LOU. Senior Science Writer, Hill and Knowlton, Chicago. Author of *A Doctor Discusses Allergy: Facts and Fiction; Natural Childbirth; Diabetes; Childrens' Colds.*
Health and Disease: *Dentistry*

KALDOR, MARY. Senior Fellow, Science Policy Research Unit, University of Sussex, England. Author of *The Arms Trade with the Third World; The Disintegrating West; The Baroque Arsenal.*
Feature Article: *Flourishing, Worldwide, Deadly—The Open Market in Arms*

KARASEK, FRANCIS W. Professor of Chemistry, University of Waterloo, Ont.
Revised *Macropædia* **article:** *Instrumentation*

KATZ, WILLIAM A. Professor, School of Library Science, State University of New York, Albany. Author of *Magazines for Libraries* (4th ed.); *Magazine Selection.*
Publishing: *Magazines (in part)*

KELLEHER, JOHN A. Group Relations Editor, INL (newspapers), Wellington, N.Z.
New Zealand

KENNEDY, RICHARD M. Agricultural Economist, International Economics Division of the Economic Research Service, U.S. Department of Agriculture.
Agriculture and Food Supplies

KENT, LIVIJA. Associate Professor, Botany Department, University of Massachusetts.
Life Sciences: *Botany*

KHINDARIA, BRIJESH. Financial Correspondent, *International Herald Tribune,* Geneva, specializing in the effect on international business of regulation by government agencies.
Economy, World: *Special Report*

KILIAN, MICHAEL D. Washington Columnist, *Chicago Tribune.* Captain, U.S. Air Force Civil Air Patrol. Author of *Who Runs Chicago?; The Valkyrie Project; Who Runs Washington?; Northern Exposure.*
Aerial Sports

KILLHEFFER, JOHN V. Associate Editor, *Encyclopædia Britannica.*
Nobel Prizes *(in part)*

KIMCHE, JON. Formerly Editor, *Afro-Asian Affairs,* London. Author of *There Could Have Been Peace: The Untold Story of Why We Failed With Palestine and Again with Israel; Seven Fallen Pillars; Second Arab Awakening; Spying for Peace; Unfought War.*
Biographies *(in part)*; **Israel**

KIND, JOSHUA B. Professor of Art History, Northern Illinois University, De Kalb. Author of *Rouault; Naive Art in Illinois 1830–1976; Geometry as Abstract Art: The Third Generation.*
Museums *(in part)*

KITAGAWA, JOSEPH M. Professor of History of Religions, Divinity School, University of Chicago. Author of *Religions of the East; Religion in Japanese History.*
Religion: *Buddhism*

KLARE, HUGH J. Chairman, Gloucestershire Probation Training Committee, England. Secretary, Howard League for Penal Reform 1950–71. Author of *People in Prison.* Regular Contributor to *Justice of the Peace.*
Prisons and Penology

KNECHT, JEAN. Formerly Assistant Foreign Editor, *Le Monde,* Paris; formerly Permanent Correspondent in Washington and Vice-President of the Association de la Presse Diplomatique Française.
France

KNOX, RICHARD A. Senior Public Affairs Officer, Atomic Energy of Canada Limited, CANDU Operations; formerly Editor, *Nuclear Engineering International,* London. Author of *Experiments in Astronomy for Amateurs; Foundations of Astronomy.*
Industrial Review: *Nuclear Industry*

KOLATA, GINA. Writer, *Science* magazine, Washington, D.C. Co-author of *The High Blood Pressure Book; Combatting the Number One Killer.*
Health and Disease: *Overview (in part)*

KOPPER, PHILIP. Author and Free-lance Journalist, Washington, D.C.
Biographies *(in part)*; **Nobel Prizes** *(in part)*

KRIEGSMAN, SALI ANN. Consultant in Dance, Smithsonian Institution, Washington, D.C. Author of *Modern Dance in*

America: The Bennington Years.
Dance (*in part*)

KUSHNICK, LOUIS. Lecturer, Department of American Studies, University of Manchester, England. Editor, *Sage Race Relations Abstracts.*
Migration, International; Race Relations

LABERIS, WILLIAM E. Senior Editor, Computer Industry, *Computerworld.*
Computers

LAMB, KEVIN M. Sports Writer, *Chicago Sun-Times.*
Biographies (*in part*); **Football:** *U.S. Football; Canadian Football*

LARSON, ROY. Religion Editor, *Chicago Sun-Times.*
Religion: *Introduction*

LEAPER, ERIC. Executive Director, National Organization for River Sports, Colorado Springs, Colo.
Water Sports: *River Sports*

LEGUM, COLIN. Associate Editor (1947–81), *The Observer*; Editor, *Middle East Contemporary Survey* and *Africa Contemporary Record*, London; Editor, *Third World Reports.* Author of *Must We Lose Africa?; Congo Disaster; Pan-Africanism: A Political Guide; South Africa: Crisis for the West.*
African Affairs

LEIFER, MICHAEL. Reader in International Relations, London School of Economics and Political Science. Author of *Dilemmas of Statehood in Southeast Asia.*
Malaysia; Singapore

LENNOX-KERR, PETER. Editor, *High Performance Textiles*; European Editor, *Textile World.* Author of *The World Fibres Book.* Editor of *Nonwovens '71*; Publisher of *OE-Report*, New Mills, England.
Industrial Review: *Textiles (in part)*

LEVE, CHARLES S. Associate Publisher and Editor, *National Racquetball* magazine; Director of Associate Membership, International Racquet Sports Association. Author of *Inside Racquetball*; co-author of *Winning Racquetball.*
Racket Games: *Racquetball*

LIM SIANG JIN. Research Officer, International Organization of Consumers Unions, Regional Office for Asia and the Pacific, Penang, Malaysia.
Consumerism (*in part*)

LITSKY, FRANK. Sports Writer, *New York Times.*
Target Sports: *Archery*

LITTELL, FRANKLIN H. Professor of Religion, Temple University, Philadelphia, Pa. Co-editor of *Weltkirchenlexikon*; Author of *Macmillan Atlas History of Christianity.*
Religion: *World Church Membership*

LOGAN, ROBERT G. Sportswriter, *Chicago Tribune.* Author of *The Bulls and Chicago—A Stormy Affair.*
Basketball (*in part*)

LULING, VIRGINIA R. Social Anthropologist.
Somalia

LUNDE, ANDERS S. Consultant; Adjunct Professor, Department of Biostatistics, University of North Carolina. Author of *The Person-Number Systems of Sweden, Norway, Denmark and Israel.*
Demography

McCAULEY, MARTIN. Lecturer in Russian and Soviet Institutions, School of Slavonic and East European Studies, University of London. Author of *Khrushchev and the Development of Soviet Agriculture: The Virgin Land Programme 1953–1964; Marxism-Leninism in the German Democratic Republic; The Soviet Union Since 1917.* Editor of *The Russian Revolution and the Soviet State 1917–1921; Communist Power in Europe 1944–1949; The Soviet Union Since Brezhnev.*
Union of Soviet Socialist Republics

MACDONALD, BARRIE. Reader in History, Massey University, Palmerston North, N.Z. Author *Cinderellas of the Empire: Towards a History of Kiribati and Tuvalu* and of several articles on the history and politics of Pacific islands.
Dependent States (*in part*); **Fiji; Kiribati; Solomon Islands; Tonga; Tuvalu; Vanuatu; Western Samoa**

MacDONALD, M. C. Director, World Economics Ltd., London.
Agriculture and Food Supplies: *grain table*; **Transportation:** *table*; statistical sections of articles on the various countries

MACDONALD, TREVOR J. Manager, International Affairs, British Steel Corporation.
Industrial Review: *Iron and Steel*

MACGREGOR-MORRIS, PAMELA. Equestrian Correspondent, *Horse and Hound*, London. Author of books on equestrian topics.
Equestrian Sports: *Show Jumping*

McKELVIE, ROY. Sports writer; Rackets and Real Tennis Correspondent, *The Times*, London.
Racket Games: *Rackets; Real Tennis*

McLACHLAN, KEITH S. Senior Lecturer, School of Oriental and African Studies, University of London.
Iran

MALLETT, H. M. F. Editor, *Wool Record Weekly Market Report*, Bradford, England.
Industrial Review: *Textiles (in part)*

MANGO, ANDREW. Orientalist and Broadcaster.
Turkey

MARTY, MARTIN E. Fairfax M. Cone Distinguished Service Professor of the History of Modern Christianity, University of Chicago; Associate Editor, *The Christian Century.* Author of *Righteous Empire; A Nation of Behavers.*
Religion: *Special Report*

MATEJA, JAMES L. Auto Editor and Financial Reporter, *Chicago Tribune.*
Industrial Review: *Automobiles*

MATTHÍASSON, BJÖRN. Economist, Central Bank of Iceland.
Biographies (*in part*); **Iceland**

MAZIE, DAVID M. Associate of Carl T. Rowan, syndicated columnist. Free-lance Writer.
Social Security and Welfare Services (*in part*)

MAZZE, EDWARD MARK. Dean and Professor of Marketing, School of Business Administration, Temple University, Philadelphia. Author of *Personal Selling: Choice Against Chance; Introduction to Marketing: Readings in the Discipline.*
Consumerism (*in part*); **Industrial Review:** *Advertising*

MERMEL, T. W. Consultant; formerly Chairman, Committee on World Register of Dams, International Commission on Large Dams. Author of *Register of Dams in the United States.*
Engineering Projects: *Dams; Dams table*

MERRY, FIONA B. Economist, Group Economics Department, Lloyds Bank PLC, London. Contributor to *EEC and the Third World: A Survey (vol. 2 and 3).*
Costa Rica; Cuba

MEYENDORFF, JOHN. Professor of Church History and Patristics, St. Vladimir's Orthodox Theological Seminary; Professor of History, Fordham University, New York City. Author of *Christ in Eastern Christian Thought; Byzantine Theology; Byzantium and the Rise of Russia.*
Religion: *The Orthodox Church; Eastern Non-Chalcedonian Churches*

MILES, PETER W. Dean of Agricultural Science, University of Adelaide, Australia.
Life Sciences: *Entomology*

MILLIKIN, SANDRA. Architectural Historian.
Architecture; Art Exhibitions; Biographies (*in part*); **Museums** (*in part*)

MITCHELL, K. K. Lecturer, Department of Physical Education, University of Leeds, England. Director, English Basket Ball Association.
Basketball (*in part*)

MODIANO, MARIO. Athens Correspondent, *The Times*, London.
Greece

MONACO, ALBERT M., JR. Executive Director, United States Volleyball Association, Colorado Springs, Colo.
Court Games: *Volleyball*

MOORE, JOHN E. Hydrologist, Reston, Va.
Earth Sciences: *Hydrology*

MORGENSTERN, DAN M. Director, Institute of Jazz Studies, Rutgers, The State University of New Jersey. Author of *Jazz People.*
Music: *Jazz*

MORITANI, MASANORI. Senior Researcher, Nomura Research Institutue, Tokyo. Author of *Nihon-Chugoku-Kankoku sangyo gijutso hikaku* ("Comparative Technologies of Japan, China, and Korea"); *Gendai Nihon sangyo gijutsu ron* ("On Modern Japanese Industrial Technology").
Industrial Review: *Special Report*

MORRIS, JACQUI M. Editor, *Oryx* magazine.
Environment (*in part*)

MORRISON, DONALD. Senior Editor, *Time* magazine.
Consumerism: *Special Report*; **Publishing:** *Newspapers (in part)*

MORTIMER, MOLLY. Commonwealth Correspondent, *The Spectator*, London. Author of *Trusteeship in Practice; Kenya.*
Commonwealth of Nations

MOSEY, CHRIS. Associate Editor, *Sweden Now*, Stockholm; Swedish Correspondent, *The Observer, Daily Mail*, and *The Times.* Contributor to *The Boat People.*
Sweden

MOSHANSKY, MOZELLE A. Music Journalist and Writer.
Biographies (*in part*); **Music:** *Classical*

MUCK, TERRY CHARLES. Editor, *Leadership* magazine, Carol Stream, Ill.
Court Games: *Handball*

NAPIER, ELSPETH. Editor of publications of the Royal Horticultural Society.
Gardening *(in part)*

NAYLOR, ERNEST. Lloyd Roberts Professor of Zoology, University College of North Wales, Bangor. Author of *British Marine Isopods.* Co-editor, *Estuarine, Coastal and Shelf Science; Cyclic Phenomena in Marine Plants and Animals.*
Life Sciences: *Marine Biology*

NEILL, JOHN. Consultant, Submerged Combustion Ltd. Author of Climbers' Club Guides; *Cwm Silyn and Tremadoc, Snowdon South;* Alpine Club Guide: *Selected Climbs in the Pennine Alps.*
Mountaineering

NELSON, BERT. Editor, *Track and Field News.* Author of *Little Red Book; The Decathlon Book; Olympic Track and Field; Of People and Things; Little Green Book.*
Track and Field Sports

NETSCHERT, BRUCE C. Vice-President, National Economic Research Associates, Inc., Washington, D.C. Author of *The Future Supply of Oil and Gas.* Co-author of *Energy in the American Economy: 1850–1975.*
Energy: *World Summary*

NEUSNER, JACOB. University Professor, Brown University, Providence, R.I. Author of *Judaism, The Evidence of the Mishnah.*
Religion: *Judaism*

NEWBURN, RAY L., JR. Leader, International Halley Watch and Cometary Science Team, Earth and Space Sciences Division, Jet Propulsion Laboratory, California Institute of Technology, Pasadena.
Revised *Macropædia* **article:** *Solar System (in part)*

NOBLETT, GEOFFREY J. Tunneling Division Manager, Tarmac National Construction, Wolverhampton, England.
Engineering Projects: *Tunnels*

NOEL, H. S. Consulting Editor, *World Fishing*, England.
Fisheries

NORMAN, GERALDINE. Saleroom Correspondent, *The Times*, London. Author of *The Sale of Works of Art; Nineteenth Century Painters and Painting: A Dictionary.*
Art Sales

OATES, DAVID A. Assistant Copy Editor, *Encyclopædia Britannica.*
Biographies *(in part)*

OBERMAN, BONNIE. Free-lance Writer and Editor.
Biographies *(in part)*

O'DONOGHUE, MICHAEL. Curator, Science Reference Library, London. Editor, *Gems, Gemmological Newsletter*, and *Synthetic Crystals Newsletter.* Author of *Encyclopedia of Minerals and Gemstones; Synthetic Gem Materials; Beginner's Guide to Minerals.*
Industrial Review: *Gemstones*

O'DWYER, THOMAS. News Director, MEMO (Middle East Media Operations), Nicosia, Cyprus.
Cyprus

O'KEEFFE, MARGARET-LOUISE. Retired Press Officer, All England Women's Lacrosse Association.
Field Hockey and Lacrosse: *Lacrosse (in part)*

OLNEY, P. J. Curator of Birds and Reptiles, Zoological Society of London. Editor, *International Zoo Yearbook.* Co-editor of *Birds of the Western Palearctic.*
Zoos and Botanical Gardens: *Zoos*

ORTON, GLENN S. Technical Staff Member, Earth and Space Sciences Division, Jet Propulsion Laboratory, California Institute of Technology, Pasadena.
Revised *Macropædia* **article:** *Solar System (in part)*

OSBORNE, KEITH. Editor, *Rowing, 1961–63;* Honorary Editor, *British Rowing Almanack,* 1961– . Author of *Boat Racing in Britain, 1715–1975.*
Rowing

OSTERBIND, CARTER C. Associate, Gerontology Center, and Professor Emeritus of Economics, University of Florida. Editor of *Income in Retirement; Migration, Mobility, and Aging;* and others.
Industrial Review: *Building and Construction*

PAGE, CAMPBELL. Southern European Correspondent, *The Guardian*, London.
Biographies *(in part);* **Italy**

PALMER, JOHN. Former European Editor, *The Guardian*, London.
European Unity

PALMER, S. B. Reader, Department of Applied Physics, University of Hull, England.
Physics

PARKER, SANDY. Publisher of weekly international newsletter on fur industry.
Industrial Review: *Furs*

PAUL, CHARLES ROBERT, JR. Director of Communications, U.S. Olympic Committee, Colorado Springs, Colo. Author of *The Olympic Games.*
Gymnastics and Weight Lifting

PENFOLD, ROBIN C. Free-lance Writer specializing in industrial topics. Editor, *Shell Polymers.* Author of *A Journalist's Guide to Plastics.*
Industrial Review: *Plastics*

PERTILE, LINO. Reader in Italian, University of Sussex, England.
Literature: *Italian*

PETHERICK, KARIN. Reader in Swedish, University of London.
Literature: *Swedish*

PFEFFER, IRVING. Attorney. Chairman, Pacific American Group, Inc. Author of *The Financing of Small Business; Perspectives on Insurance.*
Stock Exchanges *(in part)*

PHILIP, GEORGE. Lecturer in Latin-American Politics, London School of Economics and Political Science and Institute of Latin-American Studies, University of London. Author of *Oil and Politics in Latin America: Nationalist Movements and State Companies.*
Mexico: *Special Report*

PIERI, DAVID C. Technical Staff Member, Planetology Group Supervisor, and Viking Lander Monitor Mission Project Scientist, Earth and Space Sciences Division, Jet Propulsion Laboratory, California Institute of Technology, Pasadena.
Revised *Macropædia* **article:** *Solar System (in part)*

PINFOLD, GEOFFREY M. Director, NCL Consulting Engineers, London. Author of *Reinforced Concrete Chimneys and Towers.*
Engineering Projects: *Buildings*

PLOTNIK, ARTHUR. Editor, *American Libraries* magazine, American Library Association. Author of *The Elements of Editing; Library Life—American Style.*
Libraries *(in part)*

POLIN, THOMAS HON WING. Assistant Managing Editor, *Asiaweek* magazine, Hong Kong.
Biographies *(in part);* **Kampuchea; Korea; Laos; Southeast Asian Affairs; Thailand; Vietnam**

POLLACK, JONATHAN D. Staff Member, Political Science Department, Rand Corporation, Santa Monica, Calif. Author of *Security, Strategy, and the Logic of Chinese Foreign Policy; The Sino-Soviet Rivalry and Chinese Security Debate.*
China; Taiwan

POOLE, ROBERT M. Director, R & A Racing, Bookmakers, London.
Gambling *(in part)*

POPPELIERS, JOHN. Chief, Section for Operations and Training, Cultural Heritage Division, UNESCO, Paris.
Historic Preservation

POST, AVERY D. President, United Church of Christ, New York City.
Religion: *United Church of Christ*

PRASAD, H. Y. SHARADA. Information Adviser to the Prime Minister, New Delhi, India.
India

PRINCE, ROD. Caribbean Editor, Latin American Newsletters Ltd.
Antigua and Barbuda; Bahamas, The; Barbados; Biographies *(in part);* **Dependent States** *(in part);* **Dominica; Grenada; Guyana; Jamaica; Saint Christopher and Nevis; Saint Lucia; Saint Vincent and the Grenadines; Trinidad and Tobago**

RANGER, ROBIN. Associate Professor, Defense and Strategic Studies Program, School of International Relations, University of Southern California; Department of National Defence Fellow in Strategic Studies, 1978–79; NATO Fellow, 1980–81. Author of *Arms and Politics, 1958–1978; Arms Control in a Changing Political Context.*
Defense; Defense: *Special Report*

RAY, G. F. Senior Research Fellow, National Institute of Economic and Social Research, London; Visiting Professor, University of Surrey, Guildford, England.
Industrial Review: *Introduction*

READ, ANTHONY A. Director, Book Development Council, London.
Publishing: *Books (in part)*

REBELO, L. S. Reader, Department of Portuguese Studies, King's College, University of London.
Literature: *Portuguese (in part)*

REID, J. H. Senior Lecturer in German, University of Nottingham, England. Co-editor of *Renaissance and Modern Studies.* Author of *Heinrich Böll: Withdrawal and Re-emergence;* Co-author of *Critical Strategies: German Fiction in the Twentieth Century.*
Literature: *German*

RIPLEY, MICHAEL D. Senior Public Relations Officer, Brewers' Society, U.K.; formerly Editor, *Brewing Review.*

Industrial Review: *Alcoholic Beverages (in part)*

ROBERTS, JOHN. Senior Staff Writer, *Middle East Economic Digest*, London.
Biographies *(in part)*

ROBINSON, DAVID. Film Critic, *The Times*, London. Author of *Buster Keaton; The Great Funnies—A History of Screen Comedy; A History of World Cinema; Chaplin.*
Biographies *(in part)*; **Motion Pictures** *(in part)*

RODERICK, JOHN. Special Correspondent, Associated Press, Tokyo, and an expert on Chinese affairs.
Biographies *(in part)*

ROGALY, JOE. Executive Director, *Financial Times*, London. Author of *Grunwick; Parliament for the People.*
Feature Article: *Structural Unemployment: The Reality Behind the Myth*

ROSE, HILARY S. Publications Editor, American Power Boat Association.
Water Sports: *Motorboating*

SAEKI, SHOICHI. Professor of Literature, Chuo University, Tokyo. Author of *In Search of Japanese Ego.*
Literature: *Japanese*

SAINT-AMOUR, ROBERT. Professor, Department of Literary Studies, University of Quebec at Montreal.
Literature: *French (in part)*

SANDERS, THOMAS H. B., JR. Associate Professor of Metallurgy, Purdue University, West Lafayette, Ind.
Materials Sciences: *Metallurgy*

SARAHETE, YRJÖ. General Secretary, Fédération Internationale des Quilleurs, Helsinki.
Bowling: *Tenpin Bowling (in part)*

SARMIENTO, SERGIO. Editor-in-Chief, Spanish-language publications, Encyclopædia Britannica Publishers, Inc.
Baseball *(in part)*; **Football:** *Association Football (in part)*

SCARPELLI, DANTE G. Magerstadt Professor and Chairman, Department of Pathology, Northwestern University, Chicago.
Revised *Macropædia* **article:** **Cancer** *(in part)*

SCHNEIDER, STEPHEN H. Head, Visitors program, and Deputy Director, Advanced Study Program, National Center for Atmospheric Research, Boulder, Colo. Primary author of *The Coevolution of Climate and Life.*
Earth Sciences: *Special Report*

SCHNITZER, SHMUEL. Co-founder and Editor, *Ma'ariv* evening daily newspaper, Tel Aviv, Israel.
Feature Article: *At the Core of the Problem of Peace—Israel and the West Bank: Two Views (in part)*

SCHOENFIELD, ALBERT. Formerly Publisher, *Swimming World*; Vice-Chairman, U.S. Olympic Swimming Committee. U.S. Representative to FINA Technical Committee. Member of 1984 Los Angeles Olympic Organizing Swimming Commission. Contributor to *The Technique of Water Polo; The History of Swimming; Competitive Swimming as I See It; International Swimming and Water Polo* magazine.
Swimming

SCHÖPFLIN, GEORGE. Lecturer in East European Political Institutions, London School of Economics and School of Slavonic and East European Studies, University of London.
Czechoslovakia

SCHRIBER, JON. Producer, Wall Street Bureau, Financial News Network; formerly Reporter, *Forbes* magazine.
United States: *Special Report*

SCHULMAN, ELIAS. Adjunct Professor, Queens College, City University of New York. Author of *Israel Tsinberg, His Life and Works; A History of Yiddish Literature in America; Soviet-Yiddish Literature; Portraits and Studies.*
Literature: *Yiddish (in part)*

SEARS, ROBERT N. Editor, National Rifle Association, Washington, D.C.
Target Sports: *Shooting*

SHACKLEFORD, PETER. Chief of Studies, World Tourism Organization, Madrid.
Industrial Review: *Tourism*

SHARPE, MITCHELL R. Science Writer; Historian, Alabama Space and Rocket Center, Huntsville. Author of *Living in Space: The Environment of the Astronaut; "It Is I, Seagull": Valentina Tereshkova, First Woman in Space; Satellites and Probes, the Development of Unmanned Spaceflight.*
Space Exploration

SHAW, T. R. Advisory Editor, *International Journal of Speleology*. Author of *History of Cave Science.*
Speleology

SHEPHERD, MELINDA. Copy Editor, *Encyclopædia Britannica.*
Biographies *(in part)*

SIMPSON, NOEL. Managing Director, Sydney Bloodstock Proprietary Ltd., Sydney, Australia.
Equestrian Sports: *Harness Racing*

SMITH, REUBEN W. Dean, Graduate School, and Professor of History, University of the Pacific, Stockton, Calif. Editor of *Venture of Islam* by M. G. S. Hodgson.
Religion: *Islam*

SMOGORZEWSKI, K. M. Writer on contemporary history. Founder and Editor, *Free Europe*, London. Author of *The United States and Great Britain; Poland's Access to the Sea.*
Albania; Andorra; Biographies *(in part)*; **Bulgaria; Hungary; Liechtenstein; Luxembourg; Monaco; Mongolia; Poland; Political Parties; Romania; San Marino**

SPELMAN, ROBERT A. President, Home Furnishings Services, Washington, D.C.
Industrial Review: *Furniture*

STAERK, MELANIE. Member, Swiss Press Association. Former Member, Swiss National Commission for UNESCO.
Switzerland

STEEN, LYNN ARTHUR. Professor of Mathematics, St. Olaf College, Northfield, Minn. Author of *Mathematics Tomorrow; Mathematics Today; Counterexamples in Topology; Annotated Bibliography of Expository Writing in the Mathematical Sciences.*
Mathematics

STERN, IRWIN. Assistant Professor of Portuguese, Columbia University, New York City. Author of *Júlio Dinis e o romance português (1860–1870)*; Co-editor of *Modern Iberian Literature: A Library of Literary Criticism.*
Literature: *Portuguese (in part)*

STØVERUD, TORBJØRN. Honorary Research Fellow, University College, London.
Literature: *Norwegian*

STRAUSS, MICHAEL. Ski, Sports and Feature Writer, *New York Times*. Author of *Ski Areas, U.S.A.*
Combat Sports: *Fencing*

SULLIVAN, H. PATRICK. Dean of the College and Professor of Religion, Vassar College, Poughkeepsie, N.Y.
Religion: *Hinduism*

SWEETINBURGH, THELMA. Fashion Writer, Paris.
Fashion and Dress *(in part)*

SWIFT, RICHARD N. Professor of Politics, New York University, New York City. Author of *International Law: Current and Classic; World Affairs and the College Curriculum.*
United Nations

SYNAN, VINSON. Assistant General Superintendent, Pentecostal Holiness Church. Author of *The Holiness-Pentecostal Movement; The Old Time Power.*
Religion: *Pentecostal Churches*

TAISHOFF, LAWRENCE B. President, Broadcasting Publications, Inc., and Publisher, *Broadcasting* magazine and other publications.
Television and Radio *(in part)*

TALBOT, NATHAN A. Manager, Committees on Publication, The First Church of Christ, Scientist, Boston.
Religion: *Church of Christ, Scientist*

TALLAN, NORMAN M. Chief, Metals and Ceramics Division, Materials Laboratory, Wright-Patterson Air Force Base, Dayton, Ohio. Editor of *Electrical Conductivity in Ceramics and Glass.*
Materials Sciences: *Ceramics*

THEINER, GEORGE. Assistant Editor, *Index on Censorship*, London. Co-author of *The Kill Dog*; editor of *New Writing in Czechoslovakia*; translator of *Poetry of Miroslav Holub.*
Literature: *Eastern European; Russian (in part)*

THOMAS, HARFORD. Retired City and Financial Editor, *The Guardian*, London.
Biographies *(in part)*

THOMAS, THEODORE V. Free-lance Journalist and Press Consultant. Editor (1961–79), *British Toys and Hobbies.*
Games and Toys

TINGAY, LANCE. Formerly Lawn Tennis Correspondent, *Daily Telegraph*, London. Author of *100 Years of Wimbledon; Tennis, A Pictorial History; Tennis Facts and Feats.*
Tennis

TRIGG, ROBERT H. Assistant Vice-President, Economic Research, New York Stock Exchange.
Stock Exchanges *(in part)*

TRILLING, OSSIA. Vice-President, International Association of Theatre Critics (1956–77). Co-editor and Contributor, *International Theatre.* Contributor, BBC, the *Financial Times*, London.
Biographies *(in part)*; **Theatre** *(in part)*

TUDOR, JOANNA. Information Officer, Glass Manufacturers Federation, London.
Industrial Review: *Glass*

UNHCR. The Office of the United Nations High Commissioner for Refugees.
Refugees

UTT, ROGER L. Assistant Professor of Spanish, Department of Romance Languages and Literatures, University of Chicago.
Literature: *Spanish (in part)*

VALE, NORMAN K. Retired Director of News Services, The United Church of Canada.
Religion: *United Church of Canada*

VERDI, ROBERT WILLIAM. Sportswriter, *Chicago Tribune.*
Baseball *(in part)*

VINT, ARTHUR KINGSLEY. Counselor, International Table Tennis Federation, Hastings, East Sussex, England.
Table Tennis

WARD, PETER. Owner and Operator, Ward News Service, Ottawa; Parliamentary Reporter and Commentator.
Canada: *Special Report*

WARNER, ANTONY C. Editor, *Drinks Marketing,* London.
Industrial Review: *Alcoholic Beverages (in part)*

WATSON, LOUISE. Assistant Editor, Encyclopædia Britannica, London.
Biographies *(in part)*; **Dependent States** *(in part)*

WAY, DIANE LOIS. Historical Researcher, Ontario Historical Studies Series.
Biographies *(in part)*

WHELAN, JOHN. Deputy Editor and Special Reports Publisher, *Middle East Economic Digest,* London; Managing Editor, *Arab Banking and Finance;* Associate Editor, MEED Books.
Bahrain; Biographies *(in part)*; **Egypt; Iraq; Jordan; Kuwait; Lebanon; Middle Eastern Affairs; Oman; Qatar; Saudi Arabia; Syria; United Arab Emirates; Yemen, People's Democratic Republic of; Yemen Arab Republic**

WHITTINGHAM, RICHARD. Free-lance Writer and Editor. Author of *Martial Justice* and many other books on contemporary affairs.
Prisons and Penology: *Special Report*

WIJNGAARD, BARBARA. Economist, Group Economics Department, Lloyds Bank PLC, London.
Mexico

WILKINSON, GORDON. Information Consultant and Free-lance Science Writer; Science Consultant, *Laboratory News;* formerly Chemistry Consultant, *New Scientist,* London. Author of *Industrial Timber Preservation; The Village School.*
Chemistry; Industrial Review: *Wood Products*

WILKINSON, JOHN R. Sports Writer, East Midland Provincial Newspapers Ltd., U.K.
Cycling

WILKINSON, PAUL. Professor of International Relations, University of Aberdeen, Scotland. Author of *Political Terrorism; Terrorism and the Liberal State; The New Fascists.*
Race Relations: *Special Report*

WILLIAMS, MICHAEL E. J. Golf Correspondent, *Daily Telegraph,* London.
Golf

WILLIAMS, RAYMOND L. Assistant Professor of Spanish, Washington University, St. Louis, Mo. Author of *La novela colombiana contemporánea; Aproximaciones a Gustavo Álvarez Gardeazabal; Una década de la novela colombiana.*
Literature: *Spanish (in part)*

WILLIAMSON, TREVOR. Chief Sports Subeditor, *Daily Telegraph,* London.
Football: *Association Football (in part)*

WILSON, MICHAEL. Consultant Editor, Jane's Publishing Co. Ltd.
Industrial Review: *Aerospace*

WITTE, RANDALL E. Associate Editor, *The Western Horseman* magazine, Colorado Springs, Colo.
Rodeo

WOOD, KENNETH H. Retired Editor, *Adventist Review;* President, Ellen G. White Estate, Inc., and Chairman of the Board of Trustees. Author of *Meditations for Moderns; Relevant Religion;* co-author of *His Initials Were F.D.N.*
Religion: *Seventh-day Adventist Church*

WOODS, ELIZABETH. Writer. Author of *The Yellow Volkswagen; Gone; Men; The Amateur.*
Literature: *English (in part)*

WOOLLER, MICHAEL. Economist, Group Economics Department, Lloyds Bank PLC, London.
Biographies *(in part)*; **Bolivia; Paraguay; Portugal; Spain; Uruguay**

WOOLLEY, DAVID. Air Transport Editor, *Interavia,* London.
Transportation *(in part)*

WORSNOP, RICHARD L. Associate Editor, Editorial Research Reports, Washington, D.C.
United States

WRIGHT, ALMON R. Retired Senior Historian, U.S. Department of State.
Panama

WYLLIE, PETER JOHN. Chairman, Division of Geological and Planetary Sciences, California Institute of Technology. Author of *The Dynamic Earth; The Way the Earth Works.*
Earth Sciences: *Geology and Geochemistry*

YANG, WINSTON L. Y. Professor of Chinese Studies, Department of Asian Studies, Seton Hall University, South Orange, N.J. Author of *Modern Chinese Fiction; Teng Hsiao-p'ing: A Political Biography* (forthcoming).
Biographies *(in part)*; **Literature:** *Chinese*

YOUNG, M. NORVEL. Chancellor, Pepperdine University, Malibu, California; Chairman of the Board, 20th Century Christian Publishing Company. Author of *Preachers of Today; History of Colleges Connected with Churches of Christ; The Church Is Building.*
Religion: *Churches of Christ*

YOUNG, SUSAN. News Editor, *Church Times,* London.
Religion: *Anglican Communion*

YUENGER, JAMES L. Director of News and Information, University of Chicago.
Biographies *(in part)*; **Literature** *(sidebar)*

Index

The black type entries are article headings in the *Book of the Year*. These black type entries do not show page notations because they are to be found in their alphabetical position in the body of the book. They show the dates of the issues of the *Book of the Year* in which the articles appear. For example "Archaeology 84, 83, 82" indicates that the article "Archaeology" is to be found in the 1984, 1983, and 1982 *Book of the Year*.

The light type headings that are indented under black type article headings refer to material elsewhere in the text related to the subject under which they are listed. The light type headings that are not indented refer to information in the text not given a special article. Biographies and obituaries are listed as cross references to the sections "Biographies" and "Obituaries" within the article "*People of the Year.*" References to illustrations are preceded by the abbreviation "il."

All headings, whether consisting of a single word or more, are treated for the purpose of alphabetization as single complete headings. Names beginning with "Mc" and "Mac" are alphabetized as "Mac"; "St." is treated as "Saint."

A

B

C

D

E

G

H

I

J

K

L

R

S

U

V

W

X

Y

Z

Now there's a way to identify all your fine books with flair and style. As part of our continuing service to you, Britannica Home Library Service, Inc. is proud to be able to offer you the fine quality item shown on the next page.

Booklovers will love the heavy-duty personalized **Ex Libris** embosser. Now you can personalize all your fine books with the mark of distinction, just the way all the fine libraries of the world do.

To order this item, please type or print your name, address and zip code on a plain sheet of paper. (Note special instructions for ordering the embosser). Please send a check or money order only (your money will be refunded in full if you are not delighted) for the full amount of purchase, including postage and handling, to:

Britannica Home Library Service, Inc.
Attn: Yearbook Department
Post Office Box 6137
Chicago, Illinois 60680

(Please make remittance payable to: Britannica Home Library Service, Inc.)